P9-BIX-590

精选英汉汉英词典

Concise English-Chinese Chinese-English Dictionary

英语文本顾问 A.P. Cowie, A. Evison

英汉词典 朱 原 王良碧 任永长编译

汉英词典 吴景荣 梅 平 任小萍 编

商 务 印 书 馆
The Commercial Press

牛 津 大 学 出 版 社
Oxford University Press

Oxford University Press, Hong Kong
Oxford New York Toronto
Kuala Lumpur Singapore Hong Kong Tokyo
Delhi Bombay Calcutta Madras Karachi
Nairobi Dar es Salaam Cape Town
Melbourne Auckland Madrid

and associated companies in
Berlin Ibadan

Oxford is a trade mark of Oxford University Press

English text of the English-Chinese section originally published as
Oxford Keys English Dictionary by Oxford University Press © Oxford University Press 1980

First published 1986
Eighth impression 1993

©牛津大学出版社与商务印书馆1986
Oxford University Press and The Commercial Press 1986

All rights reserved. No part of this publication may be reproduced, stored in a retrieval system, or transmitted, in any form or by any means, without the prior permission in writing of Oxford University Press. Within Hong Kong, exceptions are allowed in respect of any fair dealing for the purpose of research of private study, or criticism of review, as permitted under the Copyright Ordinance currently in force. Enquiries concerning reproduction outside these terms and in other countries should be sent to Oxford University Press at the address below

版权所有，本书任何部分若未经版权持
有人允许，不得用任何方式抄袭或翻印

This book is sold subject to the condition that it shall not, by way of trade or otherwise, be lent, re-sold, hired out or otherwise circulated without the publisher's prior consent in any form of binding or cover other than that in which it is published and without a similar condition including this condition being imposed on the subsequent purchaser

ISBN 0 19 584048 8（胶面精装版 Flexi-cover）

Printed in Hong Kong
Published by Oxford University Press, Warwick House, Quarry Bay, Hong Kong, and The Commercial Press, 36 Wang Fu Jing Street, Beijing. Distributed outside China by Oxford University Press, Hong Kong.

本词典由香港鲗鱼涌和域大厦牛津大学出版社暨北京王府井大街36号商务印书馆出版。
香港牛津大学出版社并为中国以外总发行。

前　言

本词典包括英汉词典和汉英词典两部分，是一本供中、初等程度读者使用的语文工具书，主要供汉语读者学习和使用英语，同时照顾英语读者学习和使用汉语。求解、作文、翻译(英译汉、汉译英)三者兼顾。本词典力求内容简明扼要，编排紧凑醒目，装帧小巧，便于携带。

英汉词典系根据《牛津精选英语词典》*Oxford Keys English Dictionary*，增补新词新义和缩略语，编译而成，共收词条本词一万八千条，连同习语、短语动词、复合词、派生词，共收词汇约二万三千个。每个词条，除提供正确的拼写、发音和释义外，在语法、用法、搭配等方面作必要的说明，同时以醒目的字体列出有关的习语、短语动词、派生词和复合词，并作简明的释义和举例。汉语释义附汉语拼音并注明有关的繁体字。

汉英词典收汉语常用单字条目和多字条目共约二万余个，按汉语拼音顺序排列。简化汉字注出其繁体字。除结构形式和成语词组外，一般注明语法词类。有些条目还加注修辞色彩等用法说明。义项中附必需的例句或例语。词典正文前有汉字新式部首与汉语拼音对照的检字表。

编　者

1985.1.

目录 CONTENTS

英汉词典

English-Chinese Dictionary

用法说明

本　词

1. 本词排黑正体，如 **acid, dance.**

2. 分音节用中黑点表示，如 **con·vey, ac·cu·mulate.**

3. 同形异义词作为不同词目出现时，在左上角用数码标出，如 **crash¹, crash².**

复合词和派生词

复合词和派生词用黑正体排在词条的末尾，如:

crash¹ /kræʃ/ *n* [C]…………………… **~-course**

cour·age /'kʌrɪdʒ/ *n* [U] ………………… **~ous** /kə'reɪdʒəs/ *adj*

习语和短语动词

习语和短语动词用黑斜体标出，以简明的释义和必要的例证阐明其用法，如:

come round **(a)** 绕〔繞〕道而来〔來〕 ràodào ér lái. **(b)** 过〔過〕访 guòfǎng. **(c)** 重又来到 chóngyòu láidào: *My birthday will soon ~ round.* 我的生日很快就又来到。**(d)** 改变〔變〕主意 gǎibiàn zhǔyì，回心转〔轉〕意 huíxīn zhuǎnyì.

名　词

1. 有单数和复数形式的可数名词用 [C] (countable) 表示，没有复数形式的不可数名词用 [U] (uncountable) 表示，可用作可数名词也可用作不可数名词的用 [C,U] 表示，如:

grape /greɪp/ *n* [C]

linen /'lɪnɪn/ *n* [U]

collision /kə'lɪʒn/ *n* [C,U]

2. 名词的不规则复数变化用方括号加以注明，如:

man' /mæn/ *n* [C] [*pl* men/men/]

形 容 词

单音节形容词和大部分双音节形容词的比较级和最高级的词尾变化用方括号加以注明，如：

gentle /ˈdʒentl/ *adj* [-r, -st]

green' /griːn/ *adj* [-er, -est]

happy /ˈhæpɪ/ *adj* [-ier, -iest]

hot /hot/ *adj* [-ter, -test]

动 词

1．动词不规则变化用方括号加以注明，如：

know /nəʊ/ *vt*/*i* [*pt* knew/njuː/; *pp* ~n/nəʊn/]

2．末尾只有一个辅音字母的动词，构成过去式、过去分词及现在分词时，需双写辅音字母，用方括号加以注明，如：

pin² /pɪn/ *vt* [-nn-]

释 义

本词、习语、短语动词、复合词及派生词的汉语释义都注以汉语拼音，并加声调符号(ˉ阴平，ˊ阳平，ˇ上声，ˋ去声，不加调号者表示轻声)，其中的简化汉字用六角括号注明其繁体字(在每一词条中第一次出现时注出，再次出现不注，常用的简化偏旁不注)，如：

cruel /kruːəl/ *adj* [-er, -est] 残〔殘〕忍的 cánrěnde，残酷的 cánkùde…

若干符号用法

1．词性改变号□　用于本词词性改变的开始。

2．代字号～　用于代表词条的本词。

3．方括号[ ]　用于注出学科、语法、用法、文体和修辞色彩等的说明。

4．圆括号( )　用于注出有关拼写、内容或意义的补充说明、代换部分、可省略部分。

5．箭头号⇒　表示“参见”。

6．提醒号⚠　表示“禁忌语”。

略 语 表

adj = adjective 形容词

adv = adverb 副词

aux verb = auxiliary verb 助动词

[C] = countable noun 可数名词

conj = conjunction 连接词

eg = for example 例如

ie = in other words 即,就是

n = noun 名词

[P] = proprietary name 专利商标名

pl = plural 复数

pp = past participle 过去分词

prep = preposition 介词

pres part = present participle 现在分词

pron = pronoun 代词

pt = past tense 过去时

rel pron = relative pronoun 关系代词

sb = somebody 某人

sing = singular 单数

sth = something 某事

[U] = uncountable noun 不可数名词

vi = verb intransitive 不及物动词

vt = verb transitive 及物动词

发 音 简 表

元音和双元音 Vowels and diphthongs

音标	例词	读音	音标	例词	读 音
iː	see	/siː/	ɜː	fur	/fɜː(r)/
ɪ	sit	/sɪt/	ə	ago	/ə'gəʊ/
e	ten	/ten/	eɪ	page	/peɪdʒ/
æ	hat	/hæt/	əʊ	home	/həʊm/
ɑː	arm	/ɑːm/	aɪ	five	/faɪv/
ɒ	got	/gɒt/	aʊ	now	/naʊ/
ɔː	saw	/sɔː/	ɔɪ	join	/dʒɔɪn/
ʊ	put	/pʊt/	ɪə	near	/nɪə(r)/
uː	too	/tuː/	eə	hair	/heə(r)/
ʌ	cup	/kʌp/	ʊə	pure	/pjʊə(r)/

辅音 Consonants

音标	例词	读音	音标	例词	读 音
p	pen	/pen/	s	so	/səʊ/
b	bad	/bæd/	z	zoo	/zuː/
t	tea	/tiː/	ʃ	she	/ʃiː/
d	did	/dɪd/	ʒ	vision	/'vɪʒn/
k	cat	/kæt/	h	how	/haʊ/
g	got	/got/	m	man	/mæn/
tʃ	chin	/tʃɪn/	n	no	/nəʊ/
dʒ	june	/dʒuːn/	ŋ	sing	/sɪŋ/
f	fall	/fɔːl/	l	leg	/leg/
v	voice	/vɔɪs/	r	red	/red/
θ	thin	/θɪn/	j	yes	/jes/
ð	then	/ðen/	w	wet	/wet/

/'/ 主重音符号，如 about /ə'baʊt/.

/ˌ/ 次重音符号，如 academic /ˌækə'demɪk/.

(r) 表示后面紧接元音时，发 r 音，否则省略。

/-/ 表示省略了的相同的音标。

A a

A¹, a /eɪ/ [*pl* A's, a's /eɪz/] 英语的第一个〔個〕字母 yīngyǔde dìyīgè zìmǔ.

a² /ə 强式: eɪ/, **an** /ən 强式: æn/ *indefinite article* [*an* 用于以元音开头的词前] **1** 一 yī; 一个 yī gè (但不特指某一个). **2** [表示数量、群等时使用] *a lot of money* 很多钱. **3** 每 měi; 每一 měi yī: *60 miles an hour* 每小时六十英里.

A.1. 最高等 zuì gāoděng, 最优〔優〕zuì yōu.

A.A. = Automobile Association 汽车〔車〕协〔協〕会〔會〕qìchē xiéhuì.

A.A.A. =Amateur Athletics Association 业〔業〕余〔餘〕体〔體〕育协〔協〕会〔會〕yèyú tǐyù xiéhuì.

aback /ə'bæk/ *adv* 向后〔後〕 *be taken* ~ 受惊〔驚〕shòu jīng, 吃惊 chījīng.

aba·cus /'æbəkəs/ *n* [C] [*pl* ~es] 算盘 suànpán.

aban·don /ə'bændən/ *vt* **1** 离〔離〕弃〔棄〕líqì; 遗弃 yíqì. **2** 放弃 fàngqì: ~ *an idea* 放弃一种想法. **~ed** *adj* 被遗弃的 bèi yíqì de: *an ~ed car* 丢弃的汽车. **~ment** *n* [U]

abashed /ə'bæʃt/ *adj* [正式用语] 窘迫的 jiǒngpòde; 羞愧的 xiūkuìde.

abate /ə'beɪt/ *vt/i* 减少 jiǎnshǎo; 减轻〔輕〕jiǎnqīng: *The wind ~d.* 风减弱了. **~ment** *n* [U]: *noise ~ment* 减轻噪音.

ab·at·toir /'æbətwɑ:(r)/ *n* [C] 屠宰场〔場〕túzǎichǎng.

ab·bess /'æbes/ *n* [C] 女修道院院长〔長〕nǚxiūdàoyuàn yuànzhǎng.

ab·bey /'æbɪ/ *n* [C] [*pl* ~s] 修道院 xiūdàoyuàn.

ab·bot /'æbət/ *n* [C] 修道院院长 xiūdàoyuàn yuànzhǎng; 寺庙〔廟〕住持 sìmiào zhùchí.

ab·brevi·ate /ə'bri:vɪeɪt/ *vt* 简〔簡〕略 jiǎnlüè; 缩写〔寫〕suōxiě. **ab·brevi'ation** *n* [C] 缩略 suōlüè; 缩略语 suōlüèyǔ.

ABC 字母表 zìmǔbiǎo; 字母顺序 zìmǔ shùnxù.

ab·di·cate /'æbdɪkeɪt/ *vt/i* 让〔讓〕位 ràngwèi. **ab·di'ca·tion** *n* [U]

ab·do·men /'æbdəmən/ *n* [C] 腹 fù, 腹部 fùbù. **ab·domi·nal** /æb'dɒmɪnl/ *adj*

ab·duct /æb'dʌkt/ *vt* 绑架 bǎngjià ⇨ kidnap. **ab'duction** /-ʃn/ *n* [C, U]

abet /ə'bet/ *vt* [-tt-] 怂〔慫〕恿 sǒngyǒng; 支持 zhīchí. *aid and ~ sb* [法律] 支持某人作恶〔惡〕zhīchí mǒurén zuò'è.

ab·hor /əb'hɔ:(r)/ *vt* [-rr-] [正式用语]憎恨 zènghèn; 厌〔厭〕恶〔惡〕yànwù. **~rence** /əb'hɒrəns/ *n* [U] **~rent** *adj*

abide /ə'baɪd/ *vt/i* ~ *by* 信守 xìnshǒu. *cannot* ~ 不能忍受 bù néng rěnshòu.

abil·ity /ə'bɪlətɪ/ *n* [*pl* -ies] [C, U] 才干〔幹〕cáigàn; 能力 nénglì.

ab·ject /'æbdʒekt/ *adj* [正式用语] 情况可怜〔憐〕的 qíngkuàng kělián de: *living in ~ poverty* 生活赤贫.

ablaze /ə'bleɪz/ *adj, adv* [正式用语] **1** 着火 zháohuǒ; 燃烧 ránshāo. **2** [喻]闪〔閃〕耀 shǎnyào: *Her eyes ~ with excitement.* 她的两眼闪耀着激动的神色.

able /'eɪbl/ *adj* **1** 能够的 nénggòude. *be ~ to do sth* 能 néng (有能力、有办法、有机会)做某事 zuò mǒushì. ⇨ can². **2** [-r, -st] 聪〔聰〕明的 cōngmíngde; 能干〔幹〕的nénggànde. **,~-'bodied** *adj* 健壮〔壯〕的 jiànzhuàngde. **ably** *adv*

ab·nor·mal /,æb'nɔ:ml/ *adj* 变〔變〕态〔態〕的 biàntàide; 反常的 fǎnchángde. **~ity** /-'mælətɪ/ *n* [C, U] [*pl* -ies]

aboard /ə'bɔ:d/ *adv, prep* 在船上 zài chuán shàng, 在飞机〔機〕上 zài fēijī shàng, [美国]在火车〔車〕上 zài huǒchē shàng.

abode /ə'bəʊd/ *n* 住所 zhùsuǒ. *of* (或 *with*) *no fixed* ~ 无〔無〕固定住所 wú gùdìng zhùsuǒ.

abol·ish /ə'bɒlɪʃ/ *vt* 废〔廢〕除 fèichú: ~ *taxes* 废除赋税. **abol·ition** /,æbə'lɪʃən/ *n* [U]

A-bomb /'eɪ bɒm/ *n* ⇨ atomic bomb.

abom·in·able /ə'bɒmɪnəbl/ *adj* **1** 可恶〔惡〕的 kěwùde, 讨厌〔厭〕的 tǎoyànde. **2** [非正式用语]极〔極〕坏〔壞〕的 jíhuàide: ~ *weather* 糟糕透了的天气. **abom·in·ably** *adv*

abo·rig·inal /,æbə'rɪdʒənl/ *n* [C], *adj* 土著 tǔzhù; 土生动〔動〕植物 tǔshēng dòng zhí wù; 某地区〔區〕土生土长〔長〕的 mǒu dìqū tǔshēngtǔzhǎng de.

abort /ə'bɔ:t/ *vt/i* **1** 夭折 yāozhé; 取消 qǔxiāo: ~ *a space flight* 取消一次空间飞行. **2** 流产〔產〕liúchǎn, 堕胎 duòtāi. **~ive** *adj* 失败的 shībàide: *an ~ive revolution* 一次失败的革命.

abor·tion /ə'bɔ:ʃn/ *n* [C, U] [法律]流产[産](事例) liúchǎn.

abound /ə'baʊnd/ *vi* 多 duō; 富于 fùyú.

about¹ /ə'baʊt/ *adv of degree* (时刻、大小、数量等)大约 dàyuē; 差不多 chàbùduō: *~ enough* 差不多够了 (很够了的委婉说法); *~ ten o'clock* 大约十点钟. ⇨ exactly, just²(2).

about² /ə'baʊt/ *adv, prep* **1** (表示方位、动向)到处[處] dàochù: *walking ~ (the town)* (在城里)到处走走; *papers lying ~ (the room)* (房间里)到处是报纸. **2** [与 be 连用]附近 fùjìn: *There was no one ~.* 附近没有人. **3** 关[關]于 guānyú: *Tell me all ~ it.* 关于这方面的情况请全都告诉我. ***How*** (或 ***What***) ~ (用于提出建议) ... 怎么[麼]样[樣]? ... zěnmeyàng? **4** ***be ~ to start, etc*** 就要... jiùyào; 即将[將]... jíjiāng. **5** ***bring sth ~*** ⇨ bring(5).

above¹ /ə'bʌv/ *adv* **1** 在上面 zài shàngmiàn; 高于 gāoyú. **2** (用于书籍等)上文 shàngwén; 前文 qiánwén.

above² /ə'bʌv/ *prep* **1** 在...上面 zài...shàngmiàn, 高于 gāoyú: *fly ~ the clouds* 在云层上面飞行. **2** (数量、价格、重量等)大于 dàyú. **3** ***~ all*** 首先 shǒuxiān, 尤其重要的 yóuqí zhòngyào de. ***over and ~*** 除...之外 chú...zhīwài.

ab·ra·sion /ə'breɪʒn/ *n* **1** [U] 磨损 mósǔn; 擦伤[傷] cāshāng. **2** [C] 擦伤处[處] cāshāng chù.

ab·ras·ive /ə'breɪsɪv/ *n* [C, U] 磨料 móliào. □ *adj* **1** 有磨研[研] 作用的 yǒu móyán zuòyòng de. **2** [喻] 粗暴的 cūbàode: *his ~ manner* 他的粗暴态度.

abreast /ə'brest/ *adv* 并排 bìngpái; 并肩 bìngjiān. ***be*** (或 ***keep***) ***~ of*** (或 ***with***) 同...并进[進] tóng...bìngjìn: *be ~ of the news* 不断了解最新消息.

abridge /ə'brɪdʒ/ *vt* (书等)删节[節] shānjié. **abridg(e)·ment** *n* [C, U]

abroad /ə'brɔ:d/ *adv* 在国[國]外 zài guówài; 去国外 qù guówài: *travel ~* 到国外旅行.

abrupt /ə'brʌpt/ *adj* **1** 突然的 tūránde, 不意的 bùyìde: *an ~ stop* 突然停止. **2** 粗暴的 cūbàode; 不友好的 bù yǒuhǎode. **~ly** *adv* **~ness** *n* [U]

ab·scess /'æbses/ *n* [C] 脓[膿]肿[腫] nóngzhǒng.

ab·scond /əb'skɒnd/ *vi* 潜[潛]逃 qiántáo.

ab·sence /'æbsəns/ *n* **1** [C, U] 不在 búzài; 缺席 quēxí: *~ from school* 缺课. **2** [U] 缺乏 quēfá; 没有 méiyǒu: *in the ~ of information* 缺乏资料.

ab·sent¹ /'æbsənt/ *adj* 不在的 búzàide; 缺席的 quēxíde. ***~ from*** 没有参[參]加... méiyǒu cānjiā.... **~-'minded** *adj* 心不在焉的 xīn bú zài yān de.

ab·sent² /əb'sent/ *vt* 缺席 quēxí. ***~ oneself from*** [正式用语]未出席 wèi chūxí.

ab·sen·tee /ˌæbsən'ti:/ *n* [C] 缺席者 quēxízhě.

ab·so·lute /'æbsəlu:t/ *adj* **1** 完全的 wánquánde: *~ trust* 充分的信任. **2** 独[獨]裁的 dúcáide: *an ~ ruler* 独裁的统治者. **3** 确[確]实[實]的 quèshíde: *~ proof* 确凿的证据. **~ly** *adv* **(a)** /'æbsəlu:tlɪ/ 完全地 wánquánde: *He's ~ly right.* 他完全正确. **(b)** /ˌæbsə'lu:tlɪ/ [非正式用语]当[當]然 dāngrán.

ab·solve/əb'zɒlv/ *vt* 免除 miǎnchú, 赦免 shèmiǎn. ***~ from*** 免除... miǎnchú....

ab·sorb /əb'sɔ:b/ *vt* **1** 吸收 xīshōu. **2** 吸引 xīyǐn: *~ed in his work* 全神贯注于工作. **~ent** *adj* 能吸收的 néng xīshōu de: *~ent paper* 吸水纸 xīshuǐzhǐ.

ab·sorp·tion /əb'sɔ:pʃn/ *n* [U] 吸收 xīshōu.

ab·stain /əb'steɪn/ *vi* 节[節]制 jiézhì; 戒除 jièchú. ***~ (from)*** 戒除... jièchú...; 避开[開]... bìkāi....

ab·sten·tion /əb'stenʃn/ *n* [C, U] 节[節]制 jiézhì; 弃[棄]权[權] qìquán.

ab·sti·nence /'æbstɪnəns/ *n* [U] 戒除 jièchú; 戒酒 jièjiǔ.

ab·stract /'æbstrækt/ *adj* 抽象的 chōuxiàngde. **~'art** 抽象派艺[藝]术[術] chōuxiàngpài yìshù. □ *n* [C] (书籍、演说等的)摘要 zhāiyào.

ab·surd /əb'sɜ:d/ *adj* 荒谬的 huāngmiùde; 可笑的 kěxiàode. **~ity** *n* [C, U] [*pl* -ies]. **~ly** *adv*

abun·dance /ə'bʌndəns/ *n* [U] 丰[豐]富 fēngfù: *an ~ of food* 丰富的食物. **abun·dant** /-ənt/ *adj* 丰富的 fēngfùde.

abuse¹ /ə'bju:s/ *n* **1** [C, U] 滥[濫]用 lànyòng; 妄用 wàngyòng: *an ~ of power* 滥用权力. **2** [C] 恶[惡]习[習] èxí; 陋习 lòuxí. **3** [U] 辱

骂〔駡〕rǔmà; 咒骂 zhòumà.

abuse² /ə'bjuːz/ *vt* **1** 滥〔濫〕用 lànyòng; 妄用 wàngyòng: ~ *one's authority* 滥用职权. **2** 辱骂〔駡〕rǔmà. **abus·ive** /ə'bjuːsɪv/ *adj* 辱骂的 rǔmàde.

abys·mal /ə'bɪzməl/ *adj* 很坏〔壞〕的 hěnhuàde: *an* ~ *failure* 彻底的失败. ~**ly** *adv*

abyss /ə'bɪs/ *n* [C] [*pl* ~es] **1** 深渊〔淵〕 shēnyuān. **2**〔喻〕最深 zuìshēn

A/C, Acc. = account.

a.c. = alternating current.

aca·demic /ˌækə'demɪk/ *adj* **1** 学〔學〕校的 xuéxiàode; 研〔硏〕究的 yánjiūde; 教学的 jiàoxuéde. 学术〔術〕的 xuéshùde. **2** 学究的 xuéjiūde. □ *n* [C] 职〔職〕业〔業〕学者 zhíyè xuézhě. ~**ally** *adv*

ac·cel·er·ate /ək'seləreɪt/ *vt/i* **1** 加速 jiāsù. **2** 变〔變〕快 biànkuài. **ac·cel·e'ration** *n* [U]. **ac·cel·er·ator** *n* [C] **1** 变速器 biànsùqì. **2**〔物理〕粒子加速器 lìzǐ jiāsùqì.

ac·cent¹ /'æksənt/ *n* [C] **1** 重音 zhòngyīn. **2** 重音符号〔號〕 zhòngyīn fúhào. **3** 个〔個〕人口音 gèrén kǒuyīn.

ac·cent² /æk'sent/ *vt* 重读〔讀〕 zhòngdú.

ac·cen·tu·ate /ək'sentʃʊeɪt/ *vt* 强调 qiángdiào.

ac·cept /ək'sept/ *vt/i* **1** 接受 jiēshòu **2** 同意 tóngyì; 承认〔認〕 chéngrèn: ~ *a responsibility* 同意承担某事的责任. ~**able** /-əbl/ *adj* ~**ance** /-əns/ *n* [U]

ac·cess /'ækses/ *n* [U] **1** 通路 tōnglù. **2** ~ *to* 接近或使用的机〔機〕会〔會〕 jiējìn huò shǐyòng de jīhuì ~ *to good books* 读到好书. ~**ible** /ək'sesəbl/ *adj*

ac·ces·sion /æk'seʃn/ *n* [U] 就职〔職〕 jiùzhí; 到达〔達〕某种〔種〕状态〔態〕 dàodá mǒuzhǒng zhuàngtài.

ac·cess·ory /ək'sesərɪ/ *n* [C] [*pl* -ies] **1** 同谋者 tóngmóuzhě; 从〔從〕犯 cóngfàn. **2** 附件 fùjiàn; 辅〔輔〕助设备〔備〕 fǔzhù shèbèi.

ac·ci·dent /'æksɪdənt/ *n* **1** [C] 事故 shìgù; 偶然的事 ǒuránde shì. **2** [U] *by accident* 偶然 ǒurán: *I met her by* ~. 我偶然遇见了她. ~**al** /-'dentl/ *adj* ~**ally** /-təlɪ/ *adv*

ac·claim /ə'kleɪm/ *vt* 欢〔歡〕呼 huānhū. □ *n* [U] 欢呼 huānhū; 赞同 zàntóng.

ac·cli·mat·ize /ə'klaɪmətaɪz/ *vt/i* 适〔適〕应〔應〕气〔氣〕候或环〔環〕境 shìyìng qìhòu huò huánjìng.

ac·col·ade /'ækəleɪd/ *n* [C]〔喻〕赞扬 zànyáng; 赞同 zàntóng.

ac·com·mo·date /ə'kɒmədeɪt/ *vt* **1** 提供住宿 tígòng zhùsù **2** 使适〔適〕应〔應〕 shǐ shìyìng: ~ *oneself to a new plan* 适应新的计划. **ac·com·mo'da·tion** *n* 〔英国英语〕提供家具或不提供家具的房间〔間〕 tígòng jiājù huò bù tígòng jiājù de fángjiān. **ac·'com·mo·dating** 乐〔樂〕于助人的 lèyú zhùrén de.

ac·com·pani·ment /ə'kʌmpənɪmənt/ *n* [C] **1** 伴随物 bànsuíwù **2**〔音乐〕伴奏 bànzòu; 伴唱 bànchàng.

ac·com·pan·ist /ə'kʌmpənɪst/ *n* [C] 伴奏者 bànzòuzhě; 伴唱者 bànchàngzhě.

ac·com·pany /ə'kʌmpənɪ/ *vt* [*pt, pp* -ied] **1** 陪伴 péibàn: *accompanied by his wife* 由他的妻子陪伴. **2**〔音乐〕伴奏 bànzòu; 伴唱 bànchàng.

ac·com·plice /ə'kʌmplɪs/ *n* [C] 帮凶 bāngxiōng, 共犯 gòngfàn.

ac·com·plish /ə'kʌmplɪʃ/ *vt* 完成 wánchéng, 实〔實〕现 shíxiàn. ~**ed** *adj* 熟练的 shúliànde; 训练有素的 xùnliàn yǒusù de. ~**ment** *n* 〔正式用语〕**(a)** [U] 完成 wánchéng. **(b)** [C] 成就 chéngjiù; 技艺〔藝〕 jìyì.

ac·cord /ə'kɔːd/ *n* [U] 一致 yízhì; 符合 fúhé. *of one's own* ~ 自发〔發〕地 zìfāde; 自愿地 zìyuànde.

ac·cord·ing /ə'kɔːdɪŋ/ *prep* 按照 ànzhào. ~ *to* **1** 遵照…所说 zūnzhào…suǒ shuō. **2** 随着…的不同而不同 suízhe…de bù tóng ér bùtóng: *punished* ~ *to the crime* 按照罪行判刑. **3** 按…次序 àn…cìxù: *books arranged* ~ *to subject* 按主题和内容来布置、安排的书籍. ~**ly** 因此 yīncǐ; 所以 suǒyǐ.

ac·cord·ion /ə'kɔːdɪən/ *n* [C] 手风〔風〕琴 shǒufēngqín.

ac·cost /ə'kɒst/ *vt* 向…打招呼 xiàng…dǎ zhāohu.

ac·count¹ /ə'kaʊnt/ *n* **1** [C] 账〔賬〕目 zhàngmù; 账〔賬〕户 zhànghù. *open an* ~ 开〔開〕立账户 kāilì zhànghù. ⇨ current¹(2), deposit¹(3), joint¹ 和 save¹. **2** [C] 计算 jìsuàn. **3** [C] 报告 bàogào; 叙述 xùshù: *give an* ~ *of the meeting* 报道会议的情况. **4** [U] *take sth into* ~; *take* ~ *of sth* 考虑〔慮〕到某事物 kǎolǜ dào mǒu shìwù 计及某事物 jìjí mǒu shìwù. **5** [U] *on* ~ *of* 因为〔爲〕 yīnwéi. *on no* ~ 决不 juébù.

ac·count² /ə'kaʊnt/ *vt/i* 说明 shuōmíng ~ ***for*** **(a)** 说明 shuōmíng; 解释 jiěshì. **(b)** 说明钱〔錢〕的开〔開〕支 shuōmíng qiánde kāizhī. ~**able** /-əbl/ *adj* ~***able for*** 对〔對〕...应〔應〕负责任 duì...yīng fù zérèn.

ac·count·ancy /ə'kaʊntənsɪ/ *n* [U] 会〔會〕计工作 kuàijì gōngzuò.

ac·count·ant /ə'kaʊntənt/ *n* [C] [英国英语]会计员 kuàijìyuán.

ac·crue /ə'kru:/ *vi* 自然产〔產〕生 zìrán chǎnshēng; 增长〔長〕zēngzhǎng: *interest ~s on your loan* 你的贷款产生利息.

ac·cu·mu·late /ə'kju:mjʊleɪt/ *vt/i* 积〔積〕累 jīlěi; 积聚 jījù. **ac·cu·mu'la·tion** *n* [C, U]

ac·cu·racy /'ækjərəsɪ/ *n* [U] 准确〔確〕性 zhǔnquèxìng; 精密性 jīngmìxìng.

ac·cu·rate /'ækjərət/ *adj* 准确〔確〕的 zhǔnquède; 精密的 jīngmìde. ~**ly** *adv*

ac·cu·sa·tion /ˌækjʊ'zeɪʃn/ *n* [C] 控告 kònggào; 谴责 qiǎnzé.

ac·cuse /ə'kju:z/ *vt* 控告 kònggào **the accused** 被告 bèigào. **accuser** 原告 yuángào.

ac·cus·tom /ə'kʌstəm/ *vt* 使习〔習〕惯于 shǐ xíguàn yú. ***be ~ed to*** 习惯于 xíguàn yú. ~**ed** *adj* 惯常的 guànchángde: *in his ~ed seat* 在他惯常的座席上.

ace /eɪs/ *n* [C] **1** 骰子或扑〔撲〕克牌上的幺点〔點〕tóuzi huò pūkèpái shàng de yāodiǎn. **2** [非正式用语]专〔專〕家 zhuānjiā.

ache /eɪk/ *vi, n* [C] 使疼痛 shǐ téngtòng; 疼痛 téngtòng: *My back was aching.* 我的背正疼着. ~ ***for*** 渴望 kěwàng.

achieve /ə'tʃi:v/ *vt* **1** 完成 wánchéng. **2** 达〔達〕到 dádào: ~ *success* 获〔獲〕得成功. **achiev·able** /-əbl/ *adj* ~**ment** /-mənt/ *n* [C, U]

acid /'æsɪd/ *adj* **1** 酸的 suānde. **2** [喻]尖刻的 jiānkède; 讽〔諷〕刺的 fěngcìde: ~ *comments* 尖刻的评论. □ *n* [C, U] [化学]酸 suān. '~ **test** (喻)严〔嚴〕峻的考验〔驗〕yánjùnde kǎoyàn.

ac·knowl·edge /ək'nɒlɪdʒ/ *vt* **1** 承认〔認〕chéngrèn: *I ~ my mistake.* 我承认错误. **2** 表示收到信件等 biǎoshì shōudào xìnjiàn děng. **3** 表示感谢 biǎoshì gǎnxiè. **ac·know·ledg(e)·ement** *n* [C, U]

acne /'æknɪ/ *n* [U] 粉刺 fěncì.

acorn /'eɪkɔ:n/ *n* [C] 橡子 xiàngzi, 橡果 xiàngguǒ.

acous·tic /ə'ku:stɪk/ *adj* 听〔聽〕觉〔覺〕的 tīngjuéde; 声〔聲〕音的 shēngyīnde. **acous·tics** *n* [U] **(a)** [与单数动词连用]声学〔學〕shēngxué. **(b)** [与复数动词连用]音响〔響〕效果 yīnxiǎng xiàoguǒ.

ac·quaint /ə'kweɪnt/ *vt* **1** 使认〔認〕识〔識〕shǐ rènshi; 使熟悉 shǐ shúxī. ~ ***sb (oneself) with*** 熟悉 ... shúxī.... **2** ***be ~ed (with sb)*** 见过〔過〕某人 jiànguò mǒurén; 认〔認〕识〔識〕某人 rènshi mǒurén. ~**ance** /-əns/ *n* **(a)** [U] 熟悉 shúxī. ***make sb's ~ance*** 熟悉某人 shúxī mǒurén. **(b)** [C] 结识〔識〕某人. jiéshí mǒurén.

ac·quire /ə'kwaɪə(r)/ *vt* 获〔獲〕得 huòdé, 取得 qǔdé.

ac·qui·si·tion /ˌækwɪ'zɪʃn/ *n* **1** [U] [正式用语]获〔獲〕得 huòdé. **2** [C] 获得物 huòdéwù. **ac·quis·itive** /ə'kwɪzətɪv/ *adj* 渴望获得的 kěwàng huòdé de.

ac·quit /ə'kwɪt/ *vt* [-tt-] 宣告无〔無〕罪 xuāngào wúzuì ~ ***sb (of*** 或 ***on sth)*** 宣告某人无〔無〕罪 xuāngào mǒurén wúzuì. ~**tal** *n* [C, U]

acre /'eɪkə(r)/ *n* [C] 英亩〔畝〕yīngmǔ. ~**age** /'eɪkərɪdʒ/ *n* [U] 英亩数〔數〕yīngmǔshù.

ac·rid /'ækrɪd/ *adj* 辣的 làde.

ac·ri·moni·ous /ˌækrɪ'məʊnɪəs/ *adj* [正式用语]尖刻的 jiānkède; 讥〔譏〕讽〔諷〕的 jīfěngde. **ac·ri·mony** /'ækrɪmənɪ/ *n* [U]

ac·ro·bat /'ækrəbæt/ *n* [C] 杂〔雜〕技演员 zájì yǎnyuán. ~**ic** /-'bætɪk/ *adj* ~**ics** *n pl*

ac·ro·nym /'ækrənɪm/ *n* [C] 首字母缩写〔寫〕词 shǒuzìmǔ suōxiěcí.

across /ə'krɒs/ *adv, prep* (⇨ come, get, put, run 等动词词条) **1** 横过〔過〕héngguò; 越过 yuèguò: *walk ~ the street* 横过街道. **2** 在...那一边〔邊〕zài...nà yī biān: *My house is just ~ the street.* 我家就在街的那一边. **3** 交叉地 jiāochāde: *He sat with his arms ~ his chest.* 他坐着,两手交叉在胸前.

act¹ /ækt/ *n* [C] **1** 行为〔爲〕xíngwéi. **2** 行动〔動〕xíngdòng: *caught in the ~* 当场捉住. **3** 法令 fǎlìng; 条〔條〕例 tiáolì: *an ~ of Parliament* 议院的一项法案. **4** [戏剧]幕 mù. **5** 简〔簡〕短的演出 jiǎnduǎnde yǎnchū: *a circus ~* 马戏演出. ***put on an ~*** 装〔裝〕腔作势〔勢〕zhuāngqiāng-zuòshì; 炫耀自己 xuányào zìjǐ. ˌ**A~ of 'God** 不可抗拒力 (如水灾等) bùkě kàngjù lì.

act² /ækt/ *vt/i* **1** 做 zuò, 干〔幹〕gàn, 作 zuò: *We must ~ at once.* 我们必须立刻行动. **2** 表演 biǎoyǎn, 扮演 bànyǎn. **~ing** *adj* 代 dài: *the ~ manager* 代经理.

act·ing /'æktɪŋ/ *n* [U] 表演艺〔藝〕术〔術〕biǎoyǎn yìshù.

ac·tion /'ækʃn/ *n* **1** [U] 行动〔動〕xíngdòng; 动作 dòngzuò. ***put (sth) out of ~*** 使停止工作或活动 shǐ tíngzhǐ gōngzuò huò huódòng. **2** [C] 作为〔爲〕zuòwéi; 行为 xíngwéi. **3** [C, U] 战〔戰〕斗〔鬥〕zhàndòu: *killed in ~* 阵〔陣〕亡, *go into ~* 投入战斗.

ac·ti·vate /'æktɪveɪt/ *vt* 使活动〔動〕shǐ huódòng; 触〔觸〕发〔發〕chùfā: *~ a bomb* 触发炸弹.

ac·tive /'æktɪv/ *adj* 积〔積〕极〔極〕的 jījíde; 活跃的 huóyuède; 活动〔動〕的 huódòngde. **~ly** *adv*

ac·tiv·ist /'æktɪvɪst/ *n* [C] 积〔積〕极〔極〕分子 jījífènzǐ.

ac·tiv·ity /æk'tɪvətɪ/ *n* [*pl* -ies] **1** [U] 活动〔動〕性 huódòngxìng. **2** [C] 活动 huódòng.

ac·tor /'æktə(r)/ *n* [C] 演员 yǎnyuán.

ac·tress /'æktrɪs/ *n* [C] 女演员 nǚ yǎnyuán.

ac·tual /'æktʃʊəl/ *adj* 实〔實〕际〔際〕的 shíjìde; 真实的 zhēnshíde. **~ly** /'æktʃʊlɪ/ *adv* **(a)** 实际地 shíjìde: *A ~ly he's a thief.* 实际上他是个贼. **(b)** 居然 jūrán: *He ~ly won the race!* 他居然赛赢了!

acu·men /ə'kju:men/ *n* [U] 敏锐 mǐnruì; 聪〔聰〕明 cōngming: *business ~* 高明的经营本领,生意眼.

acu·punc·ture /'ækjʊpʌŋktʃə(r)/ *n* [U] [医学]针刺 zhēncì, 针术〔術〕zhēnshù.

acute /ə'kju:t/ *adj* **1** 厉〔厲〕害的 lìhaide; 敏锐的 mǐnruìde. **2** (疾病)急性的 jíxìngde. ⇨ chronic. **3** (声音)尖削的 jiānxiāode, 刺耳的 cì'ěrde. **~ accent** 重音符号〔號〕zhòngyīn fúhào. **~ angle** 尖角 jiānjiǎo. **~ly** *adv* **~ness** *n* [U]

A.D. 公元 gōngyuán.

ad /æd/ *n* [C] [非正式用语] (advertisement 的缩略语)广〔廣〕告 guǎnggào.

Adam's apple /'ædəmz æpl/ *n* 喉结 hóujié; 喉核 hóuhé.

ada·mant /'ædəmənt/ *adj* 思想坚〔堅〕定的 sīxiǎng jiāndìng de.

adapt /ə'dæpt/ *vt* 使适〔適〕应〔應〕shǐ shìyìng; 改编 gǎibiān. **~able** /-əbl/ *adj* **~ation** /ædæp'teɪʃn/ *n* [C, U] 适应 shìyìng; 适合 shìhé. **~er**, **~or** /-tə(r)/, **(a)** 改编者 gǎibiānzhě. **(b)** 三通插头〔頭〕sāntōng chātóu.

A.D.C. 副官 fùguān, 侍从〔從〕武官 shìcóng wǔguān.

add /æd/ *vt/i* **1** 加 jiā, 增加 zēngjiā. ***~ sth up*** 加起来〔來〕jiā qǐlái. ***~ up (to)*** **(a)** 合计达〔達〕héjì dá: *The figures ~ up to 365.* 这些数字合计为 365. **(b)** [非正式用语]意味着 yìwèi zhe. **(c)** [非正式用语]可信的 kěxìnde: *It just doesn't ~ up.* 这简直不可相信. **2** 补〔補〕充说 bǔchōngshuō.

ad·der /'ædə(r)/ *n* [C] 蝮蛇 fùshé.

ad·dict /ə'dɪkt/ *vt* 使沉迷 shǐ chénmí; 使嗜好 shǐ shìhào. ***be ~ed to*** 嗜好… shìhào. □ *n* /'ædɪkt/ 癖嗜者 pìshìzhě, 有瘾的人 yǒu yǐn de rén: *a 'drug ~* 吸毒者.

ad·diction /ə'dɪkʃn/ *n* [C, U] **~ive** /ə'dɪktɪv/ *adj* 上瘾的 shàngyǐnde.

ad·di·tion /ə'dɪʃn/ *n* **1** [U] 加 jiā; 加法 jiāfǎ. **2** [C] 附加物 fùjiāwù; 附加的人 fùjiāde rén. ***in ~ (to)*** 除…以外 chú… yǐwài. **~al** /ə'dɪʃənl/ *adj* 附加的 fùjiāde; 额外的 éwàide: *~al costs* 附加费用.

ad·di·tive /'ædɪtɪv/ *n* [C] 添加物 tiānjiāwù, 添加剂〔劑〕tiānjiājì: *food ~s* 食品添加剂. *petrol ~s* 汽油添加剂.

ad·dress /ə'dres/ *n* [C] **1** 通讯处〔處〕tōngxùnchù; 住址 zhùzhǐ. **2** 致词 zhìcí. □ *vt* /ə'dres/ **1** 向…致词 xiàng … zhìcí. **2** 在信封上写〔寫〕姓名,住址 zài xìnfēn shàng xiě xìngmíng, zhùzhǐ. **3** ***~ sth to*** 向…传〔傳〕话 xiàng … chuánhuà; 向…发〔發〕泄不满 xiàng … fāxiè bùmǎn.

adept /'ædept/ *adj* 擅长〔長〕的 shànchángde; 熟练的 shúliànde: *~ in photography* 擅长摄影.

ad·equate /'ædɪkwət/ *adj* 可胜〔勝〕任的 kě shèngrèn de; 充份的 chōngfènde. **~ly** *adv*

ad·here /əd'hɪə(r)/ *vi* [正式用语] **1** 粘着 zhānzhe; 坚〔堅〕持 jiānchí. **2** 忠于 zhōngyú. **ad·her·ence** /-rəns/ *n* [U] 坚持 jiānchí; 忠诚 zhōngchéng. **ad·her·ent** /-rənt/ *n* [C] 追随者 zhuīsuízhě; 依附者 yīfùzhě.

ad·hesive /əd'hi:sɪv/ *adj* 粘着的 zhānzhede; 有粘性的 yǒu niánxìng de. □ *n* [C, U] 胶〔膠〕jiāo; 粘剂〔劑〕zhānjì. **ad·hesion** /əd'hi:ʒn/ *n* [U]

ad·jac·ent /ə'dʒeɪsnt/ *adj* 邻〔鄰〕接的 línjiēde; 邻近的 línjìnde.

ad·jec·tive /ˈædʒɪktɪv/ *n* [C] [语法]形容词 xíngróngcí. **ad·jec·tival** /ˌædʒɪkˈtaɪvl/ *adj*

ad·journ /əˈdʒɜːn/ *vt/i* 休会[會] xiūhuì; 延期 yánqī. ~**ment** *n* [C, U]

ad·ju·di·cate /əˈdʒuːdɪkeɪt/ *vt/i* [正式用语]判决 pànjué, 宣判 xuānpàn: ~ *on* (或 *upon*) *a disagreement* 判决一起争执. **ad·ju·di·ˈca·ˈion** *n* [C, U] **ad·ju·di·ca·tor** /-tə(r)/ *n* [C]

ad·just /əˈdʒʌst/ *vt* 校准 jiàozhǔn; 调整 tiáozhěng. ~**able** /-əbəl/ *adj* ~**ment** *n* [C]

ad lib /ˌæd ˈlɪb/ *adv* [非正式用语]即兴[興]地 jíxìngde. □ *vi* [-bb-] [非正式用语]即兴演唱 jíxìng yǎnchàng; 即兴演奏 jíxìng yǎnzòu; 即兴讲话 jíxìng jiǎnghuà. □ *adj*: 即兴的 jíxìngde: ~ *remarks* 即兴讲话.

ad·min·is·ter /ədˈmɪnɪstə(r)/ *vt/i* **1** 支配 zhīpèi; 管理 guǎnlǐ: ~ *a country* 管理国家. **2** 给予 gěiyǔ: ~ *justice* 审判, 执法. ~ *help to people* 给人民以救助.

ad·min·is·tra·tion /ədˌmɪnɪˈstreɪʃn/ *n* [U] **1** 管理 guǎnlǐ; 经[經]营[營] jīngyíng; 行政 xíngzhèng; 政府 zhèngfǔ. **2** 给予 gěiyǔ, 施予shīyǔ. **ad·min·is·tra·tive** /ədˈmɪnɪstrətɪv/ *adj* **adˈmin·is·tra·tor** *n* [C]

ad·mir·able /ˈædmərəbl/ *adj* 极[極]好的 jíhǎode. **ad·mir·ably** *adv*

ad·miral /ˈædmərəl/ *n* [C] 海军[軍]上将[將] hǎijūn shàngjiàng; 舰[艦]队[隊]司令 jiànduì sīlìng.

ad·mir·ation /ˌædməˈreɪʃn/ *n* [U] 赞赏 zànshǎng; 钦佩 qīnpèi.

ad·mire /ədˈmaɪə(r)/ *vt* 赞赏 zànshǎng; 钦佩 qīnpèi. **ad·mirer** 赞赏者 zànshǎngzhě. **ad·mir·ing** *adj*

ad·mis·sion /ədˈmɪʃn/ *n* **1** [U] 准入 zǔn rù; 接纳 jiēnà; 入场[場]费 rùchǎngfèi: *A~ free* 免费入场. **2** [C] 承认[認] chéngrèn: *make an ~ of guilt* 供认犯罪.

ad·mit /ədˈmɪt/ *vt/i* [-tt-] **1** 允许进入 yǔnxǔ jìnrù: *The secretary ~ted me* (*into the office*). 秘书把我让进办公室. **2** 承认[認] chéngrèn: *I ~ my mistake* (或 *I ~ that I was mistaken.*) 我承认自己错了. ~ *to* 承认 chéngrèn. ~**tance** *n* [U] 准许进入 zhǔnxǔ jìnrù. ~**ted·ly** /ədˈmɪtɪdlɪ/ *adv* 公认地 gōngrènde.

ado /əˈduː/ *n* [U] 忙乱[亂] mángluàn; 麻烦 máfan. *Without more ~, he agreed.* 没有多费唇舌他就同意了.

ado·lescence /ˌædəˈlesns/ *n* [U] 青春 qīngchūn; 青春期 qīngchūnqī. **ado·lescent** /ˌædəˈlesnt/ *adj, n* [C] 青少年 qīngshàonián.

adopt /əˈdɒpt/ *vt* **1** 收养[養](子女) shōuyǎng. ⇨ foster. **2** 采[採]用 cǎiyòng. **adoption** /əˈdɒpʃn/ *n* [U] ~**ive** *adj* 收养的 shōuyǎngde: *his ~ive parents* 他的养父母.

ador·able /əˈdɔːrəbl/ *adj* 可爱[愛]的 kě'àide: *an ~ child* 一个可爱的孩子, *an ~ puppy* 一条可爱的小狗.

ador·ation /ˌædəˈreɪʃn/ *n* [U] 崇拜 chóngbài; 喜爱[愛] xǐ'ài.

adore /əˈdɔː(r)/ *vt* **1** 崇拜 chóngbài; 崇敬 chóngjìng; 深爱[愛] shēn'ài **2** [非正式用语]非常喜爱 fēicháng xǐ'ài: *She ~s being tickled.* 她非常喜爱人家胳肢她.

ador·ing /əˈdɔːrɪŋ/ *adj* 喜爱[愛]的 xǐ'àide; 爱慕的 àimùde: ~ *parents* 爱慕的双亲.

adorn /əˈdɔːn/ *vt* 装[裝]饰 zhuāngshì. ~**ment** *n* [U]

adrift /əˈdrɪft/ *adv, adj* 漂流地(的) piāoliúde; 漂泊地(的) piāobóde.

adu·la·tion /ˌædjʊˈleɪʃn/ *n* [U] 谄媚 xiǎnmèi, 奉承 fèngcheng.

adult /ˈædʌlt/ *adj* 成熟的 chéngshúde; 成年的 chéngniánde. □ *n* [C] **1** 成人 chéngrén; 成熟的动[動]物 chéngshúde dòngwù. **2** [法律]成年人 chéngniánrén.

adul·tery /əˈdʌltərɪ/ *n* [U] 通奸 tōngjiān, 私通 sītōng. **adul·terer** *n* [C] **adul·ter·ess** *n* [C] **adul·ter·ous** *adj*

adv. = advertisement.

ad·vance¹ /ədˈvɑːns/ *n* [C U] **1** 前进[進] qiánjìn; 进展 jìnzhǎn. *in ~ (of)* 事先 shìxiān. **2** [用作定语]事先 shìxiān: *have ~ notice* 得到事先通知.

ad·vance² /ədˈvɑːns/ *v/i* **1** 前进[進] qiánjìn, 推进 tuījìn. **2** 进步 jìnbù; 提高 tígāo. ~**ment** *n* [U] **ad·vanced** *adj* 高级的 gāojíde; 程度高的 chéngdùgāo le. ⇨ elementary.

ad·van·tage /ədˈvɑːnɪdʒ/ *n* **1** [C] 有利条[條]件 yǒulì tiáojiàn, 优[優]势[勢] yōushì. **2** [U] 利益 lìyì. *take ~ of sb* 欺骗[騙]某人 qīpiàn mǒurén. *tak* (*full*) *~ of sth* (充分)利用... ˈyòng.... ~**ous** /ˌædvənˈteɪdʒəs/ *dj* 有利的 yǒulìde; 有用的 yǒuyòngde.

advent /ˈædvənt/ *n* **1** 降临[臨]

jiànglín; 出现 chūxiàn: *the ~ of atomic power* 原子动力的出现.

ad·ven·ture /əd'ventʃə(r)/ *n* **1** [C] 冒险〔險〕màoxiǎn. **2** [U] 奇遇 qíyù; 历〔歷〕险 lìxiǎn. **ad·ven·turer (a)** 冒险家 màoxiǎnjiā. **(b)** 投机〔機〕者 tóujīzhě. **ad·ven·tur·ous** *adj* **(a)** 冒险的 màoxiǎnde. 准备〔備〕冒险的 zhǔnbèi màoxiǎn de. **(b)** 惊〔驚〕险的 jīngxiǎnde.

ad·verb /'ædvɜ:b/ *n* [C] [语法] 副词 fùcí. **~ial** /æd'vɜ:bɪəl/ *adj, n* [C]

ad·ver·sary /'ædvəsərɪ/ *n* [C] [*pl* -ies] 敌〔敵〕人 dírén; 对〔對〕手 duìshǒu.

ad·verse /'ædvɜ:s/ *adj* 不利的 búlìde; 逆 nì: *~ conditions* 不利条件. **~ly** *adv* **ad·ver·sity** /əd'vɜ:sətɪ/ *n* [C, U][*pl* -ies] 逆境 nìjìng; 不幸 búxìng: *cheerful in adversity* 在逆境中仍胸怀开朗.

ad·vert /'ædvɜ:t/ *n* [C] [非正式用语]广〔廣〕告 (advertisement 的缩略语) guǎnggào.

ad·ver·tise /'ædvətaɪz/ *vt/i* 做广〔廣〕告 zuò guǎnggào. **~ment** /əd'vɜ:tɪsmənt/ *n* **(a)** [U] 广告 guǎnggào. **(b)** [C] 公告 gōnggào.

ad·vice /əd'vaɪs/ *n* [U] 劝〔勸〕告 quàngào, 忠告 zhōnggào. ***(give sb) a piece*** (或 ***a word***) ***of ~*** (向某人) 提出劝告 tíchū quàngào.

ad·vise /əd'vaɪz/ *vt/i* **1** 劝〔勸〕告 quàngào; 建议〔議〕jiànyì. **2** 通知 tōngzhī: *Please ~ us when you are coming.* 你来的时候,请通知我们. **ill-advised** ⇨ ill. **well-advised** ⇨ well. **ad·viser** 提出忠告的人 tíchū zhōnggào de rén. **ad·vis·able** /-əbl/ *adj* 贤〔賢〕明的 xiánmíngde; 可取的 kěqǔde. **ad·vis·ory** *adj* 劝告的 quàngàode; 顾〔顧〕问〔問〕的 gùwènde.

ad·vo·cate /'ædvəkət/ *n* [C] 倡导〔導〕者 chàngdǎozhě; 辩护〔護〕人 biànhùrén: *an ~ of peace* 和平鼓吹者. □ *vt* /'ædvəkeɪt/ 提倡 tíchàng; 支持 zhīchí.

aer·ial /'eərɪəl/ *adj* 空气〔氣〕的 kōngqìde; 空中的 kōngzhōngde: *an ~ photograph* 从空中拍摄的照片. □ *n* [C] (无线电)天线 tiānxiàn.

aero·bat·ics /ˌeərə'bætɪks/ *n* [U] 特技飞〔飛〕行 tèjì fēixíng; 航空表演 hángkōng biǎoyǎn.

aero·drome /'eərədrəʊm/ *n* [C] 小飞〔飛〕机〔機〕场〔場〕[通常用语] xiǎo fēijīchǎng.

aero·dy·nam·ics /ˌeərəʊdaɪ'næmɪks/ *n* [U] 空气〔氣〕动〔動〕力学〔學〕kōngqì dònglì xué.

aero·plane /'eərəpleɪn/ *n* [C] 飞〔飛〕机〔機〕fēijī.

aero·sol /'eərəsɒl/ *n* [C] 按钮式喷雾〔霧〕器 ànniǔshì pēnwùqì.

aero·space /'eərəʊspeɪs/ *n* [U] 航空和宇宙航行空间〔間〕hángkōng hé yǔzhòu hángxíng kōngjiān.

afar /ə'fɑ:(r)/ *adv* 遥远〔遠〕地 yáoyuǎnde. ***from ~*** 从〔從〕远处〔處〕cóng yuǎnchù.

af·fable /'æfəbl/ *adj* 亲〔親〕切的 qīnqiède, 和蔼的 hé'ǎide. **af·fably** *adv*

af·fair /ə'feə(r)/ *n* [C] **1** 事务〔務〕shìwù: *his business ~s* 他的业务. **2** 两性关〔關〕系〔係〕liǎngxìng guānxì: *have an ~ with her* 同她有两性关系. **3** 事情 shìqing; 事件 shìjiàn: *The fire was a terrible ~.* 这次火灾是一次可怕的事件.

af·fect /ə'fekt/ *vt* 影响〔響〕yǐngxiǎng: *The cold climate ~ed his health.* 寒冷的气候影响了他的健康. **~ed** *adj* 假装〔裝〕的 jiǎzhuāngde; 做作的 zuòzuòde: *~ed speech* 矫揉造作的讲话. **~a·tion** /ˌæfek'teɪʃn/ *n* [C, U] 装模作样〔樣〕zhuāngmózuòyàng, 造作 zàozuò.

af·fec·tion /ə'fekʃn/ *n* [U] 友好 yǒuhǎo; 爱〔愛〕情 àiqíng. **~ate** *adj* 亲〔親〕爱〔愛〕的 qīn'àide, **~ately** *adv*

af·fi·da·vit /ˌæfɪ'deɪvɪt/ *n* [C] [法律]宣誓书〔書〕xuānshìshū.

af·fili·ate /ə'fɪlɪeɪt/ *vt/i* 使加入 shǐ jiārù; 接受为〔爲〕分支机〔機〕构〔構〕jiēshòu wéi fēnzhī jīgòu; 接受为会〔會〕员 jiēshòu wéi huìyuán: *groups ~d to the University* 附属于大学的团体. **af·fili'ation** *n* [C, U]

af·fin·ity /ə'fɪnətɪ/ *n* [*pl* -ies] **1** [C] 密切的关〔關〕系〔係〕mìqiède guānxì; 姻亲〔親〕关系 yīnqīn guānxì. **2** [C] 吸引力 xīyǐnlì: *She feels a strong ~ to* (或 *for*) *him.* 她觉得他极有吸引力.

af·firm /ə'fɜ:m/ *vt/i* 断〔斷〕定 duàndìng; 肯定 kěndìng. **~ation** /ˌæfə'meɪʃn/ [C, U] **~ative** *adj, n* (回答)肯定的 kěndìngde: *an affirmative answer* 肯定的回答.

af·fix[1] /ə'fɪks/ *vt* 附加 fùjiā; 贴上 tiēshàng; 盖印 gàiyìn: *~ a stamp to a document* 在文件上盖上戳子.

af·fix[2] /'æfɪks/ *n* [C] 词缀 cízhuì.

af·flict /ə'flɪkt/ *vt* 使痛苦 shǐ tòngkǔ; 使苦恼 shǐ kǔnǎo: *~ed with rheumatism* 受风湿病折磨. **af'flic·tion** /-ʃn/ *n* [C, U] 痛苦 tòngkǔ,

苦恼 kǔnǎo.

af·fluence /'æfluəns/ *n* [U] 富裕 fùyù. **af·fluent** *adj* 富裕的 fùyùde.

af·ford /ə'fɔːd/ *vt* **1**[和 *can, could* 连用]…得起… déqǐ: *We can't ~ a holiday.* 我们抽不出时间(花不起钱)度假. **2**[和 *can, could* 连用]冒险〔險〕mào xiǎn: *I can't ~ to neglect my work.* 我的工作可疏忽不得. **3** 供给 gōngjǐ; 给予 gěiyǔ.

af·front /ə'frʌnt/ *vt, n* [C] 冒犯 màofàn; 当〔當〕众〔衆〕侮辱 dāngzhòng wǔrǔ.

afield /ə'fiːld/ *adv* **far** ~ 远离家乡〔鄉〕yuǎnlí jiāxiāng.

afloat /ə'fləʊt/ *adj* **1** 漂浮的 piāofúde. **2** 在船上 zài chuán shàng.

afoot /ə'fʊt/ *adj* 在进〔進〕行中 zài jìnxíngzhōng: *a scheme ~ to improve the roads* 正在计划改善道路.

aforesaid /ə'fɔːsed/ *adj* [法律]上述的 shàngshùde.

afraid /ə'freɪd/ *adj* **1** 害怕 hàipà: *be ~ of the dark* 害怕黑暗, *be ~ of hurting him* 害怕把他弄伤. **2** *be ~* (表示歉意)恐怕 kǒngpà: *I'm ~ we shall be late.* 我恐怕我们要迟〔遲〕到了.

afresh /ə'freʃ/ *adv* 再 zài; 重新 chóngxīn.

aft /ɑːft/ *adv* 在船尾 zài chuánwěi; 向船尾 xiàng chuánwěi.

after /'ɑːftə(r)/ *adv, conj* …之后〔後〕… zhīhòu: *He died three days ~.* 三天之后他死了. *He died three days ~ I had left.* 我离开三天之后他死了. □ *prep* **1**…在…之后 zài … zhīhòu: *~ dinner* 饭后. **2** (顺序)在…之后 zài … zhīhòu: *'Against' comes ~ 'again' in a dictionary.* 词典里 against 排在 again 的后面. **3** (地点)在…的后面 zài … de hòumiàn: *Shut the door ~ you.* 随手关门. **4** 由于 yóuyú: *I shall never speak to him again ~ what he said.* 他既然这样说, 我就再不同他说话了. **5** 尽〔儘〕管 jǐnguǎn: *He failed ~ all his efforts.* 尽管他作了一切努力,还是失败了. **6** 反复〔復〕fǎnfù: *day ~ day* 日复一日. **7** 仿〔倣〕照 fǎngzhào: *a painting ~ Rembrandt* 一幅模仿仑布兰特的画. **8** 追寻 zhuīxún: *The police are ~ my brother.* 警察在追寻我的兄弟.

after- /ɑːftə(r)/ *prefix* 后〔後〕来 hòulái; 随后 suíhòu. **'~-effect** 副作用 fùzuòyòng; 后效 hòuxiào. **'~-math** [喻]后果 hòuguǒ: *the ~math of war* 战争的后果. **'~-thought** 事后的想法 shìhòude xiǎngfǎ.

after·noon /ˌɑːftə'nuːn/ *n* [C] 下午 xiàwǔ.

after·wards /'ɑːftəwədz/ *adv* 后〔後〕来〔來〕hòulái; 以后 yǐhòu.

again /ə'gen/ *adv* **1** 再 zài: *If you fail the first time, try ~.* 如果第一次失败了,再试一次. ***now and ~*** 常常 chángcháng, 不时〔時〕地 bùshíde. **ˌtime and (ˌtime) ~** 再三再四 zàisān zàisì; 反复〔復〕fǎnfù. **2** 重又 chóngyòu: *to be home ~* 又回到了家. **3** ***as many*** (或 ***much***) **~** **(a)** 同等数〔數〕量 tóngděng shùliàng. **(b)** 加倍 jiābèi.

against /ə'genst/ *prep* **1** 反对〔對〕fǎnduì: *vote ~ a proposal* 投票反对一项提议, *write ~ a proposal* 写文章反对一项提议. **2** 碰 pèng, 撞 zhuàng: *The rain was beating ~ the windows.* 雨打着窗子. **3** 对比 duìbǐ; 以…为〔爲〕背景 yǐ … wéi bèijǐng: *The trees were black ~ the sky.* 衬着天空,树是黑黝黝的. **4** 防备〔備〕fángbèi: *have an injection ~ smallpox* 注射预防天花药剂. **5** 接触〔觸〕jiēchù: *Place the ladder ~ the tree.* 把梯子靠在树上.

age¹ /eɪdʒ/ *n* **1** [C] 年龄 niánlíng. ***be*** (或 ***come***) ***of ~*** 成年 chéngnián. ***under ~*** 未成年 wèi chéngnián. **2** [U] 老年 lǎonián. **3** [C] 时〔時〕代 shídài: *the Stone A~* 石器时代, *the atomic ~* 原子时代. **4** [*pl*] [非正式用语]长〔長〕时间〔間〕cháng shíjiān: *waiting for ~s* 等候很久. **'~-group** 同一年龄的人们 tóng yí niánlíng de rénmen. **'~limit** (能做某种事情的)年龄限制 niánlíng xiànzhì. **ˌ~-'old** *adj* 古老的 gǔlǎode; 久远〔遠〕的 jiǔyuǎnde: *~-old customs* 古老的习惯.

age² /eɪdʒ/ *vt/i* [*pres part* ~ing 或 aging, *pp* ~d /eɪdʒd/] 使变〔變〕老 shǐ biànlǎo; 变老 biànlǎo: *He's ag(e)ing fast.* 他老得很快. **aged** *adj* **(a)** /'eɪdʒd/ = …岁〔歲〕的 … suìde: *a boy ~ ten* 一个十岁的男孩. **(b)** /eɪdʒɪd/ *adj* 老的 lǎode, 年老的 niánlǎode. **ag(e)ing** *n* [U] 变老 biànlǎo, 变陈 biànchén.

agency /'eɪdʒənsɪ/ *n* [*pl* -ies] [C] 代理商 dàilǐshāng; 机〔機〕构〔構〕jīgòu, 社 shè: *a travel ~* 旅行社.

agenda /ə'dʒendə/ *n* [C] [*pl* ~s] 待办〔辦〕事项表 dàibàn shìxiàngbiǎo; 议事日程 yìshìrìchéng.

agent /'eɪdʒənt/ *n* [C] **1** 代理人 dàilǐrén: *a 'house-~* 房产经纪人. **2** [科学]动〔動〕力 dònglì; 动因

dòngyīn: *Rain and frost are ~s that wear away rocks*. 雨和霜是侵蚀岩石的自然力.

ag·gra·vate /ˈægrəveɪt/ *vt* **1** 使恶〔惡〕化 shǐ è huà; 使加剧〔劇〕shǐ jiājù: ~ *an illness* 使病情恶化. **2** [非正式用语]使气〔氣〕恼 shǐ qìnǎo: *an aggravating delay* 令人讨厌的耽搁. **ag·gra'va·tion** *n* [C, U]

ag·gre·gate /ˈægrɪgət/ *n* [C] 共计 gòngjì, 合计 héjì.

ag·gres·sion /əˈgreʃn/ *n* [C, U] 侵略 qīnlüè; 进〔進〕犯 jìnfàn. **ag·gres·sor** /əˈgresə(r)/ *n* [C] 侵略者 qīnlüèzhě.

ag·gress·ive /əˈgresɪv/ *adj* **1** 侵略的 qīnlüède. **2** 有闯〔闖〕劲〔勁〕的 yǒu chuǎngjìn de. **~ly** *adv* **~ness** *n* [U]

aghast /əˈgɑːst/ *adj* 吃惊〔驚〕的 chījīngde; 吓〔嚇〕呆的 xiàdaide.

agile /ˈædʒaɪl/ *adj* 敏捷的 mǐnjiéde, 活泼〔潑〕的 huópode. **~ly** *adv* **agil·ity** /əˈdʒɪlətɪ/ *n* [U]

ag·ing /ˈeɪdʒɪŋ/ *n* ⇨ ageing.

agi·tate /ˈædʒɪteɪt/ *vt/i* **1** 摇动〔動〕(液体) yáodòng; 搅〔攪〕动 jiǎodòng. **2** 鼓动 gǔdòng; 激动 jīdòng. **3** ~ *for* 鼓吹… gǔchuī …. **agi'ta·tion** *n* **(a)** [U] 摇动(液体) yáodòng; 搅动 jiǎodòng. **(b)** [U] 焦虑〔慮〕jiāolǜ: *in a state of* ~ 内心焦虑. **(c)** [U] 社会〔會〕或政治动荡〔盪〕shèhuì huò zhèngzhì dòngdàng. **'agi·ta·tor** *n* [C] 鼓动家 gǔdòngjiā.

aglow /əˈgləʊ/ *adj* 发〔發〕光彩的 fā guāngcǎi de: ~ *with pleasure* 喜形于色.

A.G.M = Annual General Meeting 年度大会 niándù dàhuì

ag·nos·tic /ægˈnɒstɪk/ *adj, n* [C] 不可知论〔論〕的 bùkězhīlùnde; 不可知论者 bùkězhīlùnzhě.

ago /əˈgəʊ/ *adv* [和过去时连用]以前 yǐqián: *The train left a few minutes* ~. 火车在几分钟以前开走了.

agog /əˈgɒg/ *adj* 渴望的 kěwàngde; 焦急的 jiāojíde: ~ *for news* 渴望得到消息.

ag·ony /ˈægənɪ/ *n* [*sing*, 或 *pl* -ies] 极〔極〕度痛苦 jídù tòngkǔ. **ag·on·ized** /ˈægənaɪzd/ *adj* 表示痛苦的 biǎoshì tòngkǔ de. **ag·on·iz·ing** /ˈægənaɪzɪŋ/ *adj* 引起痛苦的 yǐnqǐ tòngkǔ de.

agrar·ian /əˈgreərɪən/ *adj* 耕地的 gēngdìde; 农〔農〕民的 nóngmínde.

agree /əˈgriː/ *vt/i* **1** 同意 tóngyì; 应〔應〕允 yīngyǔn. **2** 意见一致 yìjiàn yízhì: *We ~d that we should start early*. 我们一致认为要早些出发. **3** 符合 fúhé: *This bill does not ~ with your original estimate*. 帐单同你原来的估计不符. **4** 适〔適〕宜 shìyí: *The climate doesn't ~ with me*. 这天气对我不适宜. **5** 批准 pīzhǔn: *The manager has ~d your expenses*. 经理批准了你的费用. **~-able** /-əbl/ *adj* **(a)** 令人愉快的 lìngrén yúkuàide. **(b)** 乐〔樂〕于同意的 lèyú tóngyì de: *Are you ~ to the proposal?* 你同意这个提议吗? **~ably** *adv* 愉快地 yúkuàide. **~-ment** *n* **(a)** *be in ~* 一致 yízhì, 同意 tóngyì. **(b)** [C] 协〔協〕议〔議〕xiéyì, 协定 xiédìng: *come to* (或 *reach*) *an ~* 达成协议, *sign an ~* 签订协议.

ag·ri·cul·ture /ˈægrɪkʌltʃə(r)/ *n* [U] 农〔農〕业〔業〕nóngyè. **ag·ri'cul·tural** *adj* 农业的 nóngyède.

aground /əˈgraʊnd/ *adv, adj* 搁〔擱〕浅〔淺〕gēqiǎn.

A. H. 伊斯兰〔蘭〕教纪元 yīsīlánjiào jìyuán.

ahead /əˈhed/ *adv* 向前 xiàngqián; 在前 zàiqián. ***go ~*** **(a)** 前进 qiánjìn. **(b)** [非正式用语]继〔繼〕续〔續〕下去 jìxù xiàqù. ***look ~*** 考虑〔慮〕未来的需要 kǎolǜ wèiláide xūyào.

aid /eɪd/ *vt* [通常用语]帮〔幫〕助 bāngzhù, 援助 yuánzhù. □ *n* **1** [U] 帮助 bāngzhù: *He came to my ~*. 他帮助了我. ***What's it in ~ of*** 那是干什么用的? nà shì gàn shén me yòng de? **2** [C] 辅〔輔〕助装〔裝〕置 fǔzhù zhuāngzhì: *a 'hearing-~*. 助听器.

ail /eɪl/ *vt/i* **1** 苦恼 kǔnǎo: *What ~s you?* 什么事使你苦恼? **2** 生病 shēngbìng: *The child was ~ing*. 这孩子生病了. **~ment** *n* [C] 病痛 bìngtòng.

aim /eɪm/ *n* **1** [U] 瞄准〔準〕miáozhǔn. **2** [C] 目标〔標〕mùbiāo; 目的 mùdì. □ *vt/i* **1** 瞄准 miáozhǔn. **2** 对〔對〕着…打去 duìzhe… dǎqù: *She ~ed a book at his head*. 她用一本书向他的头打去. *My remarks were not ~ed at you*. 我的话不是对你的. **3** 打算 dǎsuàn: *Harry ~s at becoming a doctor*. 哈里打算做一个医生. **~less** *adj* 无〔無〕目的的 wú mùdì de. **~less·ly** *adv* 无目的地 wú mùdì de.

ain't /eɪnt/ [俚语] = are not, is not, am not, have not, has not: *I ~ going*. 我不去. *We ~ got any*. 我们没有.

air[1] /eə(r)/ *n* **1** [U] 空气〔氣〕kōngqì; 大气 dàqì. ***in the ~*** **(a)** 未

定的 wèidìngde: *My plans are still in the* ~. 我的计划还没有定. (b) 流传〔傳〕的 liúchuánde. ***clear the*** ~ 〔喻〕消除误会〔會〕 xiāochú wùhuì. ⇨ also hot. **2** ***by*** ~ 乘飞〔飛〕机〔機〕 chéng fēijī; 用飞机 yòng fēijī. **3** [U] ***on the*** ~ 广〔廣〕播 guǎngbō. ***go off the*** ~ 停止广播 tíngzhǐ guǎngbō. **4** [C] 样〔様〕子 yàngzi; 气派 qìpài: *an* ~ *of importance* 煞有介事的神气. ***give oneself*** (或 ***put on***) ~***s*** 装〔裝〕腔作势〔勢〕 zhuāngqiāng-zuòshì; 摆〔擺〕架子 bǎijiàzi. '~**base** *n* 空军〔軍〕基地 kōngjūn jīdì. '~**crew** *n* 空勤人员 kōngqín rényuán. '~-**traffic** *n* 空中交通 kōngzhōng jiāotōng. ~-**traffic control** 空中交通管制. kōngzhōng jiāotōng guǎnzhì ⇨ ground control. '~**borne** *adj* (a) 空运〔運〕的 kōngyùnde. (b) 在飞行中的 zài fēixíng zhōng de. ,~-**con'ditioned** *adj* 有空调设备〔備〕的 yǒu kōngtiáo shèbèi de. '~-**conditioner** *n* [C] '~**craft** [与单数或复数动词连用]飞机 fēijī. '~-**craft car·rier** 航空母舰〔艦〕hángkōngmǔjiàn. '~**field** 飞机场〔場〕 fēijīchǎng. '~**force** 空军〔軍〕 kōngjūn. '~**hostess** 客机上的女服务〔務〕员 kèjī shàngde nǚfúwùyuán, 空中小姐 kōngzhōng xiǎojiě. '~-**lift** 空中补〔補〕给线〔線〕 kōngzhōng bǔjǐxiàn. '~**line** 客机定期航线 kèjī dìngqī hángxiàn. '~**mail** 航空邮〔郵〕件 hángkōng yóujiàn. '~**plane** 〔美语〕 = aeroplane. '~**port** 飞机场 fēijīchǎng. '~**raid** 空袭〔襲〕 kōngxí. '~**ship** 飞艇 fēitǐng. '~**strip** 飞机跑道 fēijī pǎodào. '~ **terminal** (航空运输的)市内终点〔點〕站 shìnèi zhōngdiǎnzhàn. '~**tight** *adj* 密封的 mìfēngde. '~**way** 航空线 hángkōngxiàn.

air² /eə(r)/ *vt* **1** 晾晒〔曬〕 liàngshài. **2** 通空气〔氣〕 tōngkōngqì; 通风〔風〕 tōngfēng. **3** 发〔發〕表意见 fābiǎo yìjiàn: ~ *one's views* 表示见解.

air·ing /'eərɪŋ/ *n* 通风〔風〕tōngfēng. ***give sth an*** ~ (a) 使通风 shǐ tōngfēng. (b) 讨论〔論〕 tǎolùn. '~-**cupboard** 晾干〔乾〕橱 liànggānchú.

air·less /'eəlɪs/ *adj* 新鲜空气〔氣〕不足的 xīnxiān kōngqì bùzú de.

airy /'eərɪ/ *adj* [-ier, -iest] **1** 通气的 tōngqìde; 通风〔風〕的 tōngfēngde. **2** 空气的 kōngqìde; 空气似的 kōngqì sì de.

aisle /aɪl/ *n* [C] (大厅中席位中间的)通道 tōngdào.

ajar /ə'dʒɑ:(r)/ *adj* (门)微开〔開〕的 wēi kāi de.

akin /ə'kɪn/ *adj* 〔书面语〕类〔類〕似的 lèisìde.

alarm /ə'lɑ:m/ *n* **1** [C] 警报〔報〕 jǐngbào: *give* (或 *raise*) *the* ~ 发警报, '*fire*-~ 火警. **2** [U] 惊〔驚〕慌 jīnghuāng. □ *vt* 使忧〔憂〕虑〔慮〕 shǐ yōulǜ: ~*ed at the news*. 这消息使他忧虑不安. ~ **clock** 闹钟〔鐘〕 nàozhōng. ~**ing** *adj* 使人惊恐的 shǐ rén jīngkǒng de.

alas /ə'læs/ *int* 哎哟! āiyō! 哎呀! āiyā!

al·ba·tross /'ælbətrɒs/ *n* [C] 信天翁 xìntiānwēng.

al·bino /,æl'bi:nəʊ/ *n* [C] [*pl* ~s] 白化病患者 báihuàbìng huànzhě.

al·bum /'ælbəm/ *n* [C] **1** 相片册 xiàngpiàncè; 集邮〔郵〕册 jíyóucè. **2** 放唱时〔時〕间〔間〕长〔長〕的唱片 fàngchàng shíjiān cháng de chàngpiàn.

al·co·hol /'ælkəhɒl/ *n* [U] 酒精 jiǔjīng; 酒 jiǔ. ~**ic** /-'hɒlɪk/ *adj* 酒精的 jiǔjīngde; 含酒精的 hán jiǔjīng de. □ *n* [C] 酒鬼 jiǔguǐ. ~**ism** *n* [C] 酒瘾 jiǔyǐn.

al·cove /'ælkəʊv/ *n* [C] 壁龛〔龕〕 bìkān.

ale /eɪl/ *n* [C, U] 淡色啤酒 dànsè píjiǔ.

alert /ə'lɜ:t/ *adj* 警惕的 jǐngtìde, 提防的 tífángde. □ *n* 警报〔報〕 jǐngbào. ***on the*** ~ 警惕 jǐngtì. □ *vt* 使警觉〔覺〕 shǐ jǐngjué.

alga /'ælgə/ *n* [C] [*pl* algae /'ældʒi:/] 藻类〔類〕 zǎolèi; 海藻 hǎizǎo.

al·gebra /'ældʒɪbrə/ *n* [U] 代数〔數〕 dàishù.

alias /'eɪlɪəs/ *n* [C] [*pl* ~es] 别名 biémíng, 化名 huàmíng. □ *adv* also called. 别名叫 biémíng jiào; 化名叫 huàmíng jiào.

alibi /'ælɪbaɪ/ *n* [C] [*pl* ~s] **1** [法律]不在犯罪现场〔場〕 bú zài fànzuì xiànchǎng. **2** [非正式用语] 藉口 jièkǒu, 托词 tuōcí.

alien /'eɪlɪən/ *n* [C] 外侨〔僑〕 wàiqiáo. □ *adj* **1** 外国〔國〕的 wàiguóde. **2** 不相容的 bù xiāngróng de: *Cruelty is quite* ~ *to her*. 残〔殘〕忍绝非她的天性.

alien·ate /'eɪlɪəneɪt/ *vt* 离〔離〕间〔間〕 líjiān, 使疏远〔遠〕 shǐ shūyuǎn.

alight¹ /ə'laɪt/ *adj* 燃着的 ránzhede, 点〔點〕亮的 diǎnliàngde.

alight² /ə'laɪt/ *vi* **1** (从马背、火车等高处)下来〔來〕 xiàlái. **2** (鸟)飞〔飛〕落 fēiluò.

align /ə'laɪn/ *vt/i* **1** 成一直线〔線〕 chéng yì zhíxiàn. **2** 与〔與〕...一致 yǔ ... yízhì 与...结盟 yǔ ... jiéméng: *They ~ed themselves with the socialists.* 他们与社会主义者结成同盟. **~ment** *n* [C, U]

alike /ə'laɪk/ *adj* 同样〔樣〕的 tóngyàngde; 相似的 xiāngsìde. □ *adv* 同样地 tóngyàngde; 相似地 xiāngsìde.

ali·men·tary /ˌælɪ'mentərɪ/ *adj* 食物的 shíwùde; 消化的 xiāohuàde. **the ~ canal** 消化道 xiāohuàdào.

ali·mony /'ælɪmənɪ/ *n* [U] 离〔離〕婚后〔後〕付给妻子的生活费 líhūn hòu fùgěi qīzi de shēnghuófèi.

alive /ə'laɪv/ *adj* **1** 活的 huóde. **2** 存在的 cúnzàide: *interest kept ~ by the newspapers* 报纸使公众继续保持的兴趣. **~ to** 注意到 zhùyìdào. **~ with** 充满着...的 chōngmǎn zhe ... de.

al·kali /'ælkəlaɪ/ *n* [C] [*pl* ~s] 〔化学〕碱 jiǎn.

all[1] /ɔːl/ *adj* **1** 〔与复数名词连用〕全部的 quánbùde, 所有的 suǒyǒude: *~ the horses* 所有的马. **2** 一切的 yíqiède, 整个〔個〕的 zhěnggède: *A~ hope is lost* 一切希望都已破灭. *~ the way* 从远道, 自始至终,一路上. **3** 任何 rènhé: *beyond ~ doubt* 毫无疑问.

all[2] /ɔːl/ *adv* **1** 完全地 wánquánde: *dressed ~ in black* 穿一身黑色服装. **2** 更加 gèngjiā: *You'll be ~ the better for a holiday.* 度一次假会对你更有好处. **3** *~ along* **(a)** 整个 zhěnggè. **(b)** 〔非正式用语〕始终 shǐzhōng; 一直 yìzhí: *I knew that ~ along!* 我对那件事一直是了解的! *~ for* 〔非正式用语〕极〔極〕为〔爲〕赞成 jíwéi zànchéng. *~ the same* = nevertheless. *~ the same to* 无〔無〕所谓 wúsuǒwèi: *It's ~ the same to me if you go now.* 你现在就走,我无所谓. *~ in* **(a)** 〔非正式用语〕精疲力尽〔盡〕 jīngpí-lìjìn. **(b)** 包括一切的 bāokuò yíqiè de: *an ~-in price* 全价. *~ out* 〔非正式用语〕全力以赴 quánlìyǐfù: *an ~-out effort* 最大限度的努力. *~ right* (亦作 *alright*) **(a)** 安然无〔無〕恙 ānrán wúyàng. **(b)** 赞同 zàntóng. *~ there* 〔非正式用语〕机〔機〕智的 jīzhìde. *~ told* 总〔總〕共 zǒnggòng: *20 men, ~ told.* 总共二十人.

all[3] /ɔːl/ *pron* **1** 全部 quánbù; 大家 dàjiā; 全体〔體〕 quántǐ: *They were ~ broken.* 它们全被打破了. *~ of* 所有 suǒyǒu, 全部 quánbù: *Take ~ of them* (或 *it*). 全拿去. **2** *at ~* 根本 gēnběn. *not at ~* 根本不 gēnběnbù, 一点〔點〕不 yìdiǎnbù; 不谢 búxiè: *not at ~ suitable* 一点也不合适. *once (and) for ~* 只此一次,下不为〔爲〕例 zhǐ cǐ yícì xiàbùwéilì. *in ~* ⇨ in. *~ in ~* 总〔總〕的来〔來〕说 zǒngde lái shuō.

Allah /'ælə/ *n* 安拉,真主(伊斯兰教的主神) ānlā, zhēnzhǔ.

al·lege /ə'ledʒ/ *vt* 断〔斷〕言 duànyán, 宣称〔稱〕 xuānchēng: *He ~s that he saw the thief.* 他声称看见了那个小偷. **al·le·ga·tion** /ˌælɪ'geɪʃən/ *n* [C]

al·le·giance /ə'liːdʒns/ *n* [U] 忠诚 zhōngchéng.

al·le·gory /'ælɪgərɪ/ *n* [C] [*pl* -ies] 寓言 yùyán; 讽〔諷〕喻 fěngyù: '*The Pilgrim's Progress' is an ~.* 《天路历程》是一部讽喻性作品.

al·lergy /'ælədʒɪ/ *n* [C] [*pl* -ies] (医)过〔過〕敏症 guòmǐnzhèng. **al·ler·gic** /ə'lɜːdʒɪk/ *adj*

al·levi·ate /ə'liːvɪeɪt/ *vt* 减轻〔輕〕(痛苦等) jiǎnqīng. **al·levi'ation** *n* [U]

al·ley /'ælɪ/ *n* [C] [*pl* ~s] **1** 小巷 xiǎoxiàng. **2** 滚球戏〔戲〕等的球场〔場〕 gǔnqiúxì děng de qiúchǎng.

al·li·ance /ə'laɪəns/ *n* [C, U] 联〔聯〕盟 liánméng; 同盟 tóngméng; 联合 liánhé: *enter into an ~* 与...联合.

al·lied /ə'laɪd/ ⇨ ally.

al·li·ga·tor /'ælɪgeɪtə(r)/ *n* [C] 短吻鳄 duǎnwěn'è.

al·lo·cate /'æləkeɪt/ *vt* 分配 fēnpèi; 配给 pèijǐ. **al·lo'ca·tion** *n* [C, U]

al·lot /ə'lɒt/ *vt* [-tt-] 分配 fēnpèi; 拨〔撥〕给 bōgěi. **~ment** *n* [C] **(a)** 部分 bùfen; 份额 fèn'é. **(b)** 小块〔塊〕菜地 xiǎokuài càidì.

al·low /ə'laʊ/ *vt/i* **1** 允许 yǔnxǔ. **2** 允给(钱,时间等) yǔngěi. *~ for* 考虑〔慮〕到 kǎolǜdào; 体〔體〕谅 tǐliàng: *~ for delays because of traffic* 考虑到交通上的耽搁. **~able** /-əbl/ *adj* **~ance** *n* [C] 津贴 jīntiē. *make ~ance(s) for* 考虑到 kǎolǜdào; 体谅 tǐliàng.

al·loy /'ælɔɪ/ *n* [C, U] 合金 héjīn.

al·lude /ə'luːd/ *vi* 提到 tídào. 暗指 ànzhǐ.

al·lu·sion /ə'luːʒn/ *n* [C] 〔正式用语〕提及 tíjí; 暗指 ànzhǐ: *books full of ~s to his work.* 多处提到他的作品的那些书.

ally[1] /'ælaɪ/ *n* [C] [*pl* -ies] **1** 同盟者 tóngméngzhě; 盟国〔國〕 méngguó. 2 伙伴 huǒbàn; 助手 zhùshǒu.

ally² /ə'laɪ/ *vt* [*pt, pp* -ied] **1 ~** ***(oneself) with*** (或 ***to***) 结盟 jiéméng; 联〔聯〕姻 liányīn. **2 *allied to*** (指事物)有关〔關〕系〔係〕 yǒu guānxì; 同属〔屬〕一系 tóngshǔ yíxì: *English is allied to German.* 英语和德语同源.

al·ma·nac /'ɔːlmənæk/ *n* [C] 历〔曆〕书〔書〕 lìshū.

Al·mighty /ˌɔːl'maɪtɪ/ *n* 上帝 shàngdì.

almond /'ɑːmənd/ *n* [C] 杏核 xìnghé, 杏仁 xìngrén.

al·most /'ɔːlməʊst/ *adv* 几〔幾〕乎 jīhū; 差不多 chàbùduō: *~ five years old* 快五岁.

alms /ɑːmz/ *n* [U] 施舍 shīshě, 救济〔濟〕物 jiùjìwù.

aloft /ə'lɒft/ *adv* 在高处〔處〕 zài gāochù; 在桅杆〔桿〕高处 zài wéigān gāochù.

alone /ə'ləʊn/ *adj, adv*⇨lonely. **1** 孤独〔獨〕的 gūdúde; 孤独地 gūdúde: *living ~* 孤独地生活. **2 *let ~*** 更不用说 gèn búyòng shuō: *He cannot afford his fares let ~ cigarettes.* 他伙食费都付不起, 更不用说花钱买香烟了. ***let*** (或 ***leave***) ***sb*** (或 ***sth***) ~. 别管某人(某事) bié guǎn mǒurén.

along /ə'lɒŋ/ *adv* **1** 向前 xiàngqián: *Come ~!* 来吧! **2** (非正式请求) *Come ~ to my office.* 到我办公室来吧. ***get ~***⇨get.□ *prep* 沿着 yánzhe: *We walked ~ the road.* 我们在路上走. **~ *with*** 一道 yídào, 一起 yìqǐ.

along·side /əˌlɒŋ'saɪd/ *adv, prep* 在旁 zài páng; 靠近 kàojìn.

aloof /ə'luːf/ *adv* 离〔離〕开〔開〕 líkāi; 隔开 gékāi. □ *adj* 孤零的 gūlīngde; 冷淡的 lěngdànde. **~ness** *n* [U]

aloud /ə'laʊd/ *adv* 高声〔聲〕地 gāoshéngde, 大声地 dàshēngde: *He called ~ for help.* 他大声呼救.

alp /ælp/ *n* [C] 高山 gāoshān; 高峰 gāofēng; **the Alps** 阿尔〔爾〕卑斯山脉 Ā'ěrbēisīshānmài. **~ine** *adj*

al·pha·bet /'ælfəbet/ *n* [C] 字母表 zìmǔbiǎo. **~i·cal** /-'betɪkl/ *adj* 按字母表顺序 àn zìmǔbiǎo shùnxù. **~i·cally** *adv*

al·ready /ˌɔːl'redɪ/ *adv* 早已 zǎoyǐ: *I've ~ been there* (*I've been there ~.*) 我早已到过那里.

al·right /ɔːl'raɪt/ *adv* = all right.

Al·sa·tian /æl'seɪʃn/ *n* [C] 艾尔萨星狗(一种大狼狗, 在美国又叫德国牧羊狗) āi'ěrsàxīnggǒu.

also /'ɔːlsəʊ/ *adv* 也 yě: *Tom has been to Canada. Harry has ~ been there.* 汤姆去过加拿大. 亨利也去过. ***not only ... but ~*** 不但...而且 búdàn...érqiě: *He not only read it but ~ remembered it.* 他不但读了, 而且记住了.

al·tar /'ɔːltə(r)/ *n* [C] **1** 祭坛〔壇〕 jìtán. **2** (基督教堂)圣〔聖〕坛〔壇〕 shèngtán.

al·ter /'ɔːltə(r)/ *vt/i* 改变〔變〕 gǎibiàn; 改做 gǎizuò: *These clothes must be ~ed.* 这些衣裳必须改做. **~ation** /ˌɔːltə'reɪʃn/ *n* [C, U] 改变 gǎibiàn; 变更 biàngēn: *make alterations* 改变.

al·ter·nate¹ /ɔːl'tɜːnət/ *adj* 交替的 jiāotìde; 轮〔輪〕流的 lúnliúde: *Tom and Harry do the work on ~ days.* 汤姆和亨利隔日轮流工作. **~ly** *adv*

al·ter·nate² /'ɔːltəneɪt/ *vt/i* 交替 jiāotì: *He ~s between happiness and sadness.* 他时而高兴时而伤心. ˌ**alternating 'current** 交流电〔電〕 jiāoliúdiàn. ⇨ direct current.

al·ter·na·tive /ɔːl'tɜːnətɪv/ *adj* 可供选〔選〕择〔擇〕的 kě gòng xuǎnzé de; 可供替代的 kě gòng tìdài de: *There are ~ answers to your question.* 你的问题有不同的答案. □ *n* [C] **1** 两者选一 liǎngzhě xuǎn yī. **2** 两种〔種〕或多种可能性之一 liǎngzhǒng huò duōzhǒng kěnéngxìng zhīyī. **~ly** *adv* 作为〔爲〕一种选择 zuòwéi yìzhǒng xuǎnzé.

al·though /ɔːl'ðəʊ/ *conj* ⇨ though.

al·tim·eter /'æltɪmiːtə(r)/ *n* [C] 测〔測〕高计 cègāojì, 高度表 gāodùbiǎo

al·ti·tude /'æltɪtjuːd/ *n* [C] 高度(尤指海拔) gāodù.

alto /'æltəʊ/ *n* [C] [*pl* ~s] **1** 高男高音 gāo nángāoyīn. **2** 中音乐〔樂〕器 zhōngyīn yuèqì.

al·to·gether /ˌɔːltə'geðə(r)/ *adv* **1** 完全 wánquán: *I don't ~ agree.* 我不完全同意. **2** 整个〔個〕说来〔來〕 zhěnggè shuōlái: *A~, it was a bad journey.* 整个说来, 这是一次糟糕的旅行.

al·tru·ism /'æltruːɪzəm/ *n* [U] 利他主义〔義〕 lìtāzhǔyì. **al·tru·ist** *n* [C] **al·tru·is·tic** /-'ɪstɪk/ *adj*

alu·min·ium /ˌæljʊ'mɪnɪəm/ [美语=**alu·mi·num** /ə'luːmɪnəm/] *n* [U] 铝 lǚ (化学符号 Al)

al·ways /'ɔːlweɪz/ *adv* **1** 总〔總〕是 zǒngshì: *It ~ rains in April.* 四月里总是下雨. **2** 永远〔遠〕 yǒngyuǎn: *I'll ~ love her.* 我永远爱她.

am /æm/ ⇨ be.

a.m. 上午 shàngwǔ

amal·ga·mate /ə'mælgəmeɪt/ *vt/i* 混合 hùnhé; 合并 hébìng. **amal-ga'ma·tion** *n* [C, U]

amass /ə'mæs/ *vt* 积〔積〕聚 jījù: ~ *a fortune* 积聚财富.

ama·teur /'æmətə(r)/ *n* [C] **1** 业〔業〕余〔餘〕爱〔愛〕好者 yèyú àihàozhě; 业余活动〔動〕者 yèyú huódòngzhě. ~**ish** *adj* 不够熟练的 búgòu shúliàn de.

amaze /ə'meɪz/ *vt* 使惊〔驚〕奇 shǐ jīngqí: ~*d at the news* 对这消息感到惊奇. **amaz·ing** *adj* 令人惊异〔異〕的 lìngrén jīngyì de. ~**ment** *n* [U]

ama·zon /'æməzən/ *n*[C] 魁梧而活泼的女子 kuíwǔ ér huópo de nǚzǐ.

am·bas·sa·dor /æm'bæsədə(r)/ *n* [C] **1** 大使 dàshǐ. **2** 授权〔權〕代表 shòuquán dàibiǎo.

am·ber /'æmbə(r)/ *n* [U] 琥珀 hǔpò; 淡黄色 dànhuángsè.

am·bi·dex·trous /,æmbɪ'dekstrəs/ *adj* 左右两手都善于使用的 zuǒ yòu liǎng shǒu dōu shànyú shǐyòng de.

am·bi·guity /,æmbɪ'gju:ətɪ/ *n* [*pl* -ies] **1** [U] 含糊 hánhu, 模棱两可 móléng liǎngkě. **2** [C] 有多种〔種〕意义〔義〕的词句 yǒu duōzhǒng yìyì de cíjù.

am·bigu·ous /æm'bɪgjʊəs/ *adj* 含糊的 hánhude.

am·bi·tion /æm'bɪʃn/ *n* **1** [U] 雄心 xióngxīn; 野心 yěxīn. **2** [C] 抱负 bàofù: *achieve one's* ~*(s)* 实现自己的抱负. **am·bi·tious** *adj*

amble /'æmbl/ *vi* 骑〔騎〕马〔馬〕缓行 qímǎ huǎnxíng; 漫步 mànbù. □ *n* [C]

am·bu·lance /'æmbjʊləns/ *n* [C] 救护〔護〕车〔車〕jiùhùchē.

am·bush /'æmbʊʃ/ *n* [C,U] 伏击〔擊〕fújī. □ *vt* 伏击 fújī.

amen /,eɪ'men ɑ:'men/ *int* "阿门〔門〕"(基督教祈祷结束时用语, 意为"诚心所愿") āmén.

amen·able /ə'mi:nəbl/ *adj* 能听〔聽〕教诲的 néng tīng jiàohuì de: *be* ~ *to advice* 听得进忠告.

amend /ə'mend/ *vt/i* **1** 改进〔進〕gǎijìn. **2** 修正 xiūzhèng. ~**ment** *n*[C] 改变〔變〕gǎibiàn; 改正 gǎizhèng.

amends /ə'mendz/ *n pl* ***make*** ~ ***(for sth)*** 赔偿〔償〕péicháng; 赔罪 péizuì; 道歉 dàoqiàn.

amen·ity /ə'mi:nətɪ/ *n* [*pl* -ies] **1** [*pl*] 使人愉快的事物 shǐ rén yúkuài de shìwù. **2** [U] 愉快 yúkuài, 舒适〔適〕shūshì.

am·ethyst /'æmɪθɪst/ *n* [C] 紫晶 zǐjīng; 水碧 shuǐbì.

ami·able /'eɪmɪəbl/ *adj* [正式用语] 亲〔親〕切的 qīnqiède; 和蔼的 hé'ǎide: *an* ~ *man* 一个平易近人的人. **ami·ably** *adv*

amic·able /'æmɪkəbl/ *adj* 温柔的 wēnróude; 友善的 yǒushànde: *reach an* ~ *agreement* 达成友好的协议. **amic·ably** *adv*

amid /ə'mɪd/, **amidst** /ə'mɪdst/ *prep* 在…当〔當〕中 zài…dāngzhōng.

amiss /ə'mɪs/ *adj, adv* 有差错的 yǒu chācuò de; 错误地 cuòwùde; 偏 piān; 歪 wāi: *not much* ~ 没有多大毛病. ***take sth*** ~ 因某事而见怪 yīn mǒushì ér jiànguài: *Please don't take my comments* ~. 我的话请别见怪.

am·me·ter /'æmɪtə(r)/ *n* [C] 安培计 ānpéijì; 电〔電〕表 diànbiǎo.

am·mo·nia /ə'məʊnɪə/ *n* [U] 氨 ān, 阿摩尼亚〔亞〕āmóníyà, 氨水 ānshuǐ.

am·mu·ni·tion /,æmjʊ'nɪʃn/ *n* [U] 军〔軍〕火 jūnhuǒ; 弹〔彈〕药 dànyào.

am·nesia /æm'ni:zɪə/ *n* [U] (医) 健忘症〔癥〕jiànwàngzhèng.

am·nesty /'æmnəstɪ/ *n* [C] [*pl* -ies] 大赦 dàshè.

amoeba /ə'mi:bə/ *n* [C] [*pl* ~s 或 ~e /-bi:/] 阿米巴变〔變〕形虫〔蟲〕āmǐbā biànxíngchóng. **amoe-bic** *adj* 变形虫的 biànxíngchóngde.

amok, amuck /ə'mɒk/ *adv* ***run*** ~ 胡作非为〔爲〕húzuò-fēiwéi.

among /ə'mʌŋ/, **amongst** /ə'mʌŋst/ *prep* **1** 在…中间〔間〕zài…zhōngjiān: *hiding* ~ *the bushes* 藏在灌木丛中. **2** 在一群之中 zài yìqún zhī zhōng: *decide* ~ *yourselves* 你们自己决定. **3** …之一… zhī yī: ~ *the best in the world* 世界上最好的之一.

am·or·ous /'æmərəs/ *adj* 色情的 sèqíngde; 多情的 duōqíngde. ~**ly** *adv*

amount /ə'maʊnt/ *vi* ~ ***to*** 等于 děngyú. □ *n* [C] **1** 总〔總〕数〔數〕zǒngshù: *He could pay only half that* ~. 他只付得出总数的一半. **2** [C] 数量 shùliàng: *a large* ~ *of money* 一大笔款子.

amp /æmp/ *n* [C] (ampere 的缩略)

am·pere /'æmpeə(r)/ *n* [C] 安培 ānpéi.

am·phib·ian /æm'fɪbɪən/ *n* [C] **1** 两栖〔棲〕动〔動〕物 liǎngqī dòngwù. **2** 水陆两用飞〔飛〕机〔機〕和车〔車〕辆〔輛〕shuǐ lù liǎngyòng fēijī hé chēliàng. **am·phibi·ous** *adj*

amphi·theatre [美语 = **-ter**]

/'æmfɪθɪətə(r)/ *n* [C] 有梯式座位的建筑物 yǒu tīshì zuòwèi de jiànzhùwù.

ample /'æmpl/ *adj* [-r, -st] 宽敞的 kuānchangde: *an ~ garage* 宽敞的汽车间. **2** 丰〔豐〕富的 fēngfùde; 充分的 chōngfènde: *~ resources* 丰富的资源. **am·ply** /'æmplɪ/ *adv*

am·plify /'æmplɪfaɪ/ *vt* [*pt, pp* -ied] **1** 详述 xiángshù; 引申 yǐnshēn. **2** 增强 zēngqiáng; 放大 fàngdà. **am·pli·fi·ca·tion** /ˌæmplɪfɪ'keɪʃn/ *n* [U] **am·pli·fier** *n* [C] 放大器 fàngdàqì; 扩〔擴〕大器 kuòdàqì.

am·pu·tate /'æmpjʊteɪt/ *vt* 截肢 jiézhī. **am·pu'ta·tion** *n* [C, U]

amuck /ə'mʌk/ *adv* ⇨ amok.

amu·let /'æmjʊlət/ *n* [C] 护〔護〕身符 hùshēnfú; 驱〔驅〕邪物 qūxiéwù.

amuse /ə'mju:z/ *vt* **1** 使娱乐〔樂〕shǐ yúlè: *keep the baby ~d* 让婴儿高兴. **2** 逗…笑 dòu…xiào. **~ment** *n* **(a)** [U] 娱乐 yúlè; 消遣 xiāoqiǎn. **(b)** [C] 娱乐活动〔動〕 yúlè huódòng. **amus·ing** /ə'mju:zɪŋ/ *adj*

an/ən强式: æn/⇨ a.

anach·ron·ism /ə'nækrənɪzəm/ *n* [C] **1** 弄错时〔時〕代 nòngcuò shídài: *In the sentence 'Julius Caesar looked at his watch' there is an ~.* 'Julius Caesar looked at his watch' 这个句子把时代弄错了. **2** 与〔與〕时〔時〕代不合的人或事物 yǔ shídài bù hé de rén huò shìwù.

ana·conda /ˌænə'kɒndə/ *n* [C] [*pl* ~s] (南美等地的)蟒蛇 mǎngshé.

anae·mia [美语=**anemia**] /ə'ni:mɪə/ *n* [U]贫血症pínxuèzhèng.**anae·mic** *adj*

an·aes·thesia [美语= **an·es**]/'ænɪs'θi:zɪə/ *n* [U] 麻木 mámù; 麻醉 mázuì. **an·aes·thetic** /-'θetɪk/ *n* [C] 麻醉剂〔劑〕mázuìjì. ⇨ general, local. **an·aes·the·tize** /ə'ni:sθətaɪz/ *vt* **an·aes·the·tist** /ə'ni:sθətɪst/ *n* [C]

ana·gram /'ænəgræm/ *n* [C] 变〔變〕换单〔單〕词中字母位置而构〔構〕成的另一个〔個〕单词(如 plum — lump) biànhuàn dāncí zhōng zìmǔ wèizhì ér gòuchéng de lìng yí gè dāncí.

anal·ogy /ə'nælədʒɪ/ *n* [*pl* -ies] **1** [C] 类〔類〕似 lèisì: *an ~ between the heart and a pump* 心脏同抽水机的相类似. **2** [U] 类推 lèituī. **anal·og·ous** /ə'næləgəs/ *adj* 类似的 lèisìde.

ana·lyse [美语 = **-lyze**] /'ænəlaɪz/ *vt* **1** 分析 fēnxī. **2** 研究 yánjiū: *~ the facts* 对论据进行研究.

analy·sis /ə'næləsɪs/ *n* [*pl* -ses /-si:z/] **1** [C,U] 分析 fēnxī. **2** = psychoanalysis. **ana·lyst** /'ænəlɪst/ *n* [C] **(a)** 分析者 fēnxīzhě; 化验员 huàyànyuán. **(b)** = psychoanalyst. **ana'ly·tic** *adj*

ana·lyze ⇨ analyse.

an·archy /'ænəkɪ/ *n* [U] 无〔無〕政府状〔狀〕态〔態〕 wúzhèngfǔ zhuàngtài; 混乱 hùnluàn. **an·arch·ist** *n* [C] 无政府主义〔義〕者 wúzhèngfǔzhǔyìzhě.

anat·omy /ə'nætəmɪ/ *n* [U] 解剖 jiěpōu; 解剖学〔學〕 jiěpōuxué. **ana·tomi·cal** /ˌænə'tɒmɪkl/ *adj*

an·ces·tor /'ænsestə(r)/ *n* [C] 祖先 zǔxiān. **an·ces·tral** /æn'sestrəl/ *adj* 祖传〔傳〕的 zǔchuánde; 祖先的 zǔxiānde: **an·ces·try** /'ænsestrɪ/ *n* [C] [*pl* -ies] 世系 shìxì; 家世 jiāshì.

an·chor /'æŋkə(r)/ *n*[C] **1** 锚 máo **2** 危难〔難〕时〔時〕可依靠的人或物 wēinàn shí kě yīkào de rén huò wù. □ *vt/i* 用锚泊船 yòng máo bóchuán. **~age** *n* [C] 锚地 máodì.

an·chovy /'æntʃəʊvɪ/ *n* [C][*pl* -ies] 鳀 tí.

ancient /'eɪnʃənt/ *adj* **1** 古代的 gǔdàide; 古老的 gǔlǎode. **2** 旧〔舊〕式的 jiùshìde; 旧的 jiùde: *an ~ hat* 一顶旧式的帽子.

an·cil·lary /æn'sɪlərɪ/ *adj* **1** 支援的 zhīyuánde; 帮助的 bāngzhùde: *~ workers* 帮工. **2** 辅〔輔〕助的 fǔzhùde: *~ industries* 辅助性行业.

and /ənd 强式: ænd/ *conj* **1** 和 hé, 与〔與〕yǔ: *a table ~ four chairs* 一张桌子和四把椅子. **2** 那末 nàmò; 于是 yúshì: *Work hard ~ you will pass.* 只要努力,你就会通过. **3** 又 yòu; 加 jiā: *for hours ~ hours* —连好多钟头. **4** [非正式用语] = to: *Try ~ come early.* 设法早点来.

an·ec·dote /'ænɪkdəʊt/ *n* [C] 轶〔軼〕事 yìshì; 趣闻〔聞〕qùwén.

anemia, anemic, ⇨ anaemia, anaemic.

anem·one /ə'nemənɪ/ *n* [C] 银莲〔蓮〕花 yínliánhuā.

an·es·thesia ⇨ anaesthesia.

anew /ə'nju:/ *adv* 再 zài; 重新 chóngxīn: *begin ~* 重新开始.

angel /'eɪndʒəl/ *n* **1** 天使 tiānshǐ; 安琪儿〔兒〕ānqí'ér. **2** 天真可爱〔愛〕的人 tiānzhēn kě'ài de rén. **~ic** /æn'dʒelɪk/ *adj* 天使般的 tiānshǐbānde.

anger /'æŋgə(r)/ *n* [U] 愤怒 fènnù: *filled with ~* 怒火中烧. □ *vt* 激怒 jīnù, 使怒 shǐnù: *He is easily*

~*ed.* 他爱发脾气.

angle[1] /'æŋgl/ *n* **1** 角 jiǎo: *an acute* ~锐角; *obtuse* ~ 钝角. **2** [喻]观[觀]点[點] guāndiǎn, 看[看]法 kànfǎ: *What* ~ *are you using in the story?* 你的这番话是什么意思?

angle[2] /'æŋgl/ *vi* **1** 钓鱼 diào yú. **2** [喻] 使用花招得到某物 shǐyòng huāzhāo dédào mǒuwù: ~ *for an invitation* 使用花招弄到一张请帖. **angler** *n* [C] **angling** *n* [U]

Ang·li·can /'æŋglɪkən/ *n* [C], *adj* 英国[國]国教的 yīngguó guójiàode.

ang·li·cize /'æŋglɪsaɪz/ *vt* 使英语化 shǐ yīngyǔhuà. ~ *a French word* 把一个法语单词英语化.

Anglo- /ˌæŋgləʊ/ *prefix* 英国 [國] yīngguó; 英国的 yīngguóde. ~-'*French* 英法; ~-'*Saxon* 盎格鲁撒格逊人.

angry /'æŋgrɪ/ *adj* [-ier, -iest] **1** 愤怒的 fènnùde. **2** 肿[腫]痛发[發]炎的 zhǒngtòng fāyán de. **3** 暴风[風]雨的 bàofēngyǔde;风浪大的 fēnlàng dà de. **angri·ly** *adv*

an·guish /'æŋgwɪʃ/ *n* [U] 思想感情上极[極]度痛苦 sīxiǎng gǎnqíng shàng jídù tòngkǔ. ~**ed** *adj*

angu·lar /'æŋgjʊlə(r)/ *adj* **1** 有角的 yǒujiǎode. **2** 骨瘦如柴的 gǔshòurúcháide.

ani·mal /'ænɪml/ *n* [C] **1** 动[動]物 dòngwù: *Men, birds, flies, fish are all* ~*s.* 人、鸟、苍蝇和鱼都是动物. **2** 人以外的动物 rén yǐ wài de dòngwù. **3** [用作定语]肉体[體]的 ròutǐde; 动物的 dòngwùde.

ani·mate[1] /'ænɪmət/ *adj* 有生命的 yǒu shēngmìng de; 有生气[氣]的 yǒu shēngqì de.

ani·mate[2] /'ænɪmeɪt/ *vt* 使有生命 shǐ yǒu shēngmìng; 使活泼[潑] shǐ huópo. ˌ~**d car'toon** 动[動]画[畫]片 dònghuàpiàn. **ani'ma·tion** *n* [U] **(a)** 生气[氣]shēngqì. 活泼 huópo. **(b)** 动画片制[製]作 dònghuàpiàn zhìzuò.

ani·mos·ity /ˌænɪ'mɒsətɪ/ *n* [C, U] [*pl* -ies] 仇恨 chóuhèn; 憎恨 zēnghèn.

ankle /'æŋkl/ *n* [C] 踝 huái.

an·nex[1], **an·nexe** /'ænəks/ *n* [C] 附属[屬]建筑物 fùshǔ jiànzhùwù.

an·nex[2] /ə'neks/ *vt* 兼并 jiānbìng.

an·ni·hi·late /ə'naɪəleɪt/ *vt* 消灭[滅] xiāomiè; 歼[殲]灭 jiānmiè. **an·ni·hi'la·tion** *n* [U]

an·ni·ver·sary /ˌænɪ'vɜːsərɪ/ *n* [C] [*pl* -ies] 周年纪念 zhōunián jìniàn.

an·no·tate /'ænəteɪt/ *vt* 注释[釋] zhùshì. **an·no'ta·tion** *n* [C, U]

an·nounce /ə'naʊns/ *vt* **1** 宣布 xuānbù: *He* ~*d his engagement.* 他宣布已经[經]订婚了. **2** 报[報]告某人来[來]到 bàogào mǒurén láidào: *He* ~*d Mrs Brown.* 他报告布朗夫人来到. ~**ment** *n* [C] **an·nouncer** 电[電]台或电视台的播音员 diàntái huò diànshìtái de bōyīnyuán.

an·noy /ə'nɔɪ/ *vt* 使烦恼 shǐ fánnǎo; 使生气[氣] shǐ shēngqì. ~**ance** *n* [C,U]

an·nual /'ænjʊəl/ *adj* **1** 每年的 měiniánde. **2** 一年生的 yì nián shēng de. □ *n* [C] **1** 年刊 niánkān. **2** 一年生植物 yì nián shēng zhíwù. ~**ly** *adv*

an·nu·ity /ə'njuːətɪ/ *n* [C] [*pl* -ies] 年金 niánjīn.

an·nul /ə'nʌl/ *vt* [-ll-] 取消 qǔxiāo, 注销 zhùxiāo. ~**ment** *n* [C, U]

an·ode /'ænəʊd/ *n* [C] (电)阳[陽]极[極] yángjí.

anoint /ə'nɔɪnt/ *vt* 涂[塗]油于(一种宗教仪式) túyóu yú. ~**ment** *n* [C, U]

anom·aly /ə'nɒməlɪ/ *n* [C] [*pl* -ies] 异[異]常 yìcháng, 反常 fǎncháng, 异态[態] yìtài: *A bird that cannot fly is an* ~. 不能飞的鸟是一种异态.

anon /ə'nɒn/ *adv* [旧词]立刻 lìkè.

anon·ym·ity /ˌænə'nɪmətɪ/ *n* [U] 匿名 nìmíng; 无[無]名 wúmíng.

anony·mous /ə'nɒnɪməs/ *adj* 匿名的 nìmíngde; 无[無]名的 wúmíngde; 不知名的 bù zhī míng de.

an·or·ak /'ænəræk/ *n* [C]带[帶]风[風]帽的厚茄克 dài fēngmào de hòu jiākè.

an·other /ə'nʌðə(r)/ *pron, adj* **1** 再一 zàiyī: ~ *cup of coffee?* 再来一杯咖啡好吗? **2** 类[類]似的 lèisìde: ~*Napoleon* 又一个拿破仑. **3** 别的 biéde: *Do that* ~ *time.* 别的时间做那件事.

answer /'ɑːnsə(r)/ *n* [C] **1** 答复[復] dáfù: *an* ~ *to your letter* 对你的来信的答复. **2** 答案 dá'àn: *The* ~ *to* 3× 17 *is* 51. 3×17 的答案是 51. □ *vt/i* **1** 答复 dáfù: *Have you* ~*ed his letter?* 你回复他的来信了吗? ~ *the door* 听[聽]到敲门[門]就去开 tīngdào qiāomén jiù qù kāi. **2** ~ *back* 向某人回嘴 xiàng mǒurén huízuǐ; 与[與]某人顶嘴 yǔ mǒurén dǐngzuǐ. ~ *for* **(a)** 对[對]…负责 duì…fùzé. **(b)** 为[爲]…受罚 wèi…shòufá. ~**able** /-əbl/ *adj* **(a)** 能够回答的 nénggòu huídá de. **(b)** 负责的 fùzéde: ~-

able for one's actions 对其行为负责.

ant /ænt/ *n* [C] 蚂〔螞〕蚁〔蟻〕máyǐ. '~**-hill** 蚁冢 yǐzhǒng.

an·tag·on·ism /æn'tægənɪzəm/ *n* [C, U] 反对〔對〕fǎnduì; 不喜欢〔歡〕bù xǐhuān: *feel ~ for* (或 *toward*) *a person* 不喜欢某人. **an·tag·on·ist** *n* [C] 反对〔對〕者〔通常用语〕fǎnduìzhě. **an·tag·on'is·tic** *adj*

an·tag·on·ize /æn'tægənaɪz/ *vt* 引起…的反抗 yǐnqǐ...de fǎnkàng; 招怨 zhāoyuàn.

ant·arc·tic /æn'tɑ:ktɪk/ *adj, n* 南极〔極〕的 nánjíde; 南极 nánjí.

ante·ced·ent /ˌæntɪ'si:dnt/ *adj* 先行的 xiānxíngde. □ *n* [*pl*] 祖先 zǔxiān; 履历〔歷〕lǚlì.

ante·date /ˌæntɪ'deɪt/ *vt* **1** 在信、文件上写〔寫〕上比实〔實〕际〔際〕早的日期 zài xìn, wénjiàn shàng xiě shàng bǐ shíjì zǎo de rìqī. **2** 先于 xiānyú: *This ~s Columbus by several centuries.* 这比哥伦布早了几个世纪.

ante·di·luvian /ˌæntɪdɪ'lu:vɪən/ *adj* 古老的 gǔlǎode; 老式的 lǎoshìde.

ante·lope /'æntɪləʊp/ *n* [C] 羚羊 língyáng.

ante me·ridi·em /æntɪ mə'rɪdɪəm/ *adj* (略作 **am**) 午前 wǔqián, 上午 shangwǔ; *7.30 am.* 上午七点三十分 ⇨ *pm.*

ante·natal /ˌæntɪ'neɪtl/ *adj* 产〔產〕前的 chǎnqiánde. ~ *clinic* 产前检查诊所, ~ *care* 产前护理.

an·tenna /æn'tenə/ *n* [C] [*pl* ~e /-ni:/] **1** 昆虫〔蟲〕触〔觸〕角 kūnchóng chùjiǎo. **2** 天线〔線〕tiānxiàn.

an·them /'ænθəm/ *n* [C] 赞美诗 zànměishī, 圣〔聖〕歌 shènggē. ⇨ national.

an·thol·ogy /æn'θɒlədʒɪ/ *n* [C] [*pl* -ies] 诗集 shījí.

an·thro·poid /'ænθrəpɔɪd/ *adj* 似人的 sìrénde. □ *n* [C] 类〔類〕似人的动〔動〕物, 如大猩猩 lèisì rén de dòngwù, rú dàxīngxīng.

an·thro·pol·ogy /ˌænθrə'pɒlədʒɪ/ *n* [U] 人类〔類〕学〔學〕rénlèixué. ˌ**an·thro'pol·ogist** *n* [C]

anti- /ˌæntɪ/ *prefix* 反对〔對〕fǎnduì: *antiseptic* 抗菌剂

anti-air·craft /ˌæntɪ 'eəkrɑ:ft/ *adj* 防空的 fángkōngde: ~ *guns* 高射炮.

anti·biotic /ˌæntɪbaɪ'ɒtɪk/ *n* [C], *adj* 抗生素 kàngshēngsù; 抗菌的 kàngjūnde.

anti·body /'æntɪbɒdɪ/ *n* [C] [*pl* -ies] 抗体〔體〕kàngtǐ.

an·tics /'æntɪks/ *n pl* 滑稽动〔動〕作 huájì dòngzuò; 古怪行为〔爲〕gǔguài xíngwéi.

an·tici·pate /æn'tɪsɪpeɪt/ *vt* **1** 占先 zhànxiān; 抢〔搶〕先 qiǎngxiān. **2** 预先处〔處〕理 yùxiān chǔlǐ: ~ *an attack* 防范敌人的进攻. **3** 预期 yùqī; 预料 yùliào: *We ~ trouble.* 我们预料会发生麻烦. **an·tici'pa·tion** *n* [U]

anti-cli·max /ˌæntɪ 'klaɪmæks/ *n* [C] 虎头〔頭〕蛇尾 hǔtóu-shéwěi.

anti-clock·wise /ˌæntɪ 'klɒkwaɪz/ *adv* 反时〔時〕钟〔鐘〕方向地 fǎn shízhōng fāngxiàng de.

anti·cyc·lone /ˌæntɪ'saɪkləʊn/ *n* [C] 高气〔氣〕压〔壓〕区〔區〕gāo qìyā qū. ⇨ depression(4).

anti·dote /'æntɪdəʊt/ *n* [C] 解毒药 jiědúyào.

anti·freeze /'æntɪfri:z/ *n* [U] 抗冻〔凍〕剂〔劑〕kàngdòngjì.

anti·quated /'æntɪkweɪtɪd/ *adj* 过〔過〕时〔時〕的 guòshíde; 老式的 lǎoshìde.

an·tique /æn'ti:k/ *adj* 古代的 gǔdàide. □ *n* [C] 古玩 gǔwán; 古物 gǔwù.

an·tiquity /æn'tɪkwətɪ/ *n* [*pl* -ies] **1** [U] 古代 gǔdài. **2** [*pl*] 古代建筑 gǔdài jiànzhù; 古迹 gǔjì.

anti·sep·tic /ˌæntɪ'septɪk/ *n* [C] *adj* 防腐的 fángfǔde; 防腐剂〔劑〕fángfǔjì.

anti·so·cial /ˌæntɪ'səʊʃl/ *adj* **1** 反社会〔會〕的 fǎn shèhuì de: *It is ~ to leave litter.* 到处乱扔脏物是违反公德的. **2** 厌〔厭〕恶〔惡〕社交的 yànwù shèjiāo de.

an·tith·esis /æn'tɪθəsɪs/ *n* [*pl* -ses /-si:z/] [C,U] 对〔對〕立 duìlì; 对立面 duìlìmiàn.

ant·ler /'æntlə(r)/ *n* [C] 鹿角 lùjiǎo.

an·to·nym /'æntənɪm/ *n* [C] 反义〔義〕词 fǎnyìcí: *Hot is the ~ of cold.* hot 是 cold 的反义词. ⇨ synonym.

anus /'eɪnəs/ *n* [C] [*pl* ~es] [解剖] 肛门〔門〕gāngmén.

an·vil /'ænvɪl/ *n* [C] 铁〔鐵〕砧 tiězhēn.

anxiety /æŋ'zaɪətɪ/ *n* [*pl* -ies] **1** [C,U] 忧〔憂〕虑〔慮〕yōulǜ. **2** [U] 渴望 kěwàng: ~ *to please* 急于讨好.

anxious /'æŋkʃəs/ *adj* **1** 忧〔憂〕虑的 yōulǜde. **2** 引起忧虑的 yǐnqǐ yōulǜ de: *an ~ time* 焦虑的时刻. **3** ~ *to* (或 *for* 或 *that*) 渴望 kěwàng; 急要 jíyào: *He's very ~ to* *please.* 他迫不及待地要去讨好. ~**ly** *adv*

any¹ /ˈenɪ/ *adj* **1** 一个〔個〕yígè; 一些 yìxiē: *Have you ~ milk?* 你有牛奶吗? *They haven't ~ children.* 他们没有孩子. [注: 用于否定句和疑问句] **2** 任何的 rènhéde: *Come ~ day.* 随便那一天,来吧. **3** [非正式用语]一yī; 一个yígè: *It hasn't ~ handle.* 连个把手都没有. **4** *in* ˈ~ *case; at* ˈ~ *rate* 不管怎样〔樣〕bùguǎn zěnyàng.

any² /ˈenɪ/ *adv* 丝毫 sīháo; 任何程度 rènhé chéngdù: *Is he feeling ~ better?* 他好些了吗?

any³ /ˈenɪ/ *pron* = some².

any·body /ˈenɪbɒdɪ/ *n, pron* **1** 任何人 rènhé rén: *Is ~ there?* 那里有人吗? *A~ will tell you.* 任何人都会告诉你.

any·how /ˈenɪhaʊ/ *adv* **1** 不论〔論〕用何种〔種〕方法 búlùn yòng hézhǒng fāngfǎ. **2** 无〔無〕论如何 wúlùnrúhé: *It's too late now, ~.* 无论如何,现在是太晚了.

any·one /ˈenɪwʌn/ *n, pron* = anybody.

any·thing /ˈenɪθɪŋ/ *n, pron* 任何事物 rènhé shìwù. 无论〔論〕什〔甚〕么〔麽〕wúlùn shénme: *Has ~ unusual happened?* 出了什么事吗? *(as) easy, etc as ~* [非正式用语]很容易 hěn róngyì.

any·way /ˈenɪweɪ/ *adj* = anyhow.

any·where /ˈenɪweə(r)/ *adv* 任何地方 rènhé dìfang: *I'm not going ~.* 我哪里也不去. *Put it down ~.* 放在哪里都行.

aorta /eɪˈɔːtə/ *n* [C] [*pl* ~s] 主动〔動〕脉 zhǔdòngmài.

apart /əˈpɑːt/ *adv* **1** 相隔 xiānggé; 相距 xiāngjù: *The houses are 500 metres ~.* 这些房子相隔 500 米. **2** 分离〔離〕fēnlí; 分开〔開〕fēnkāi: *with his feet ~* 他两脚分开. **3** 拆开 chāikāi: *It fell ~.* 土崩瓦解. *~ from* 除去 chúqù: *five boys ~ from me.* 除了我,还有五个男孩子.

apart·ment /əˈpɑːtmənt/ *n* **1** [C] 房间〔間〕fángjiān. **2** [*pl*] 一套房子 yítào fángzi

apa·thy /ˈæpəθɪ/ *n* [U] 冷淡 lěngdàn. 缺乏感情 quēfá gǎnqíng. **apa·thetic** /ˌæpəˈθetɪk/ *adj*

ape /eɪp/ *n* [C] **1** 无〔無〕尾猿 wúwěiyuán; 类〔類〕人猿 lèirényuán. **2** 模仿者 mófǎngzhě. □ *vt* 模仿 mófǎng; 学〔學〕...的样〔樣〕xué...deyàng.

aperi·tif /əˈperətɪf/ *n* [C] 开〔開〕胃酒 kāiwèijiǔ.

ap·er·ture /ˈæpətʃə(r)/ *n* [C] 孔 kǒng; 眼 yǎng: *the ~ of a camera* 照相机的光圈.

apex /ˈeɪpeks/ *n* [C] [*pl* ~es 或 apices /ˈeɪpɪsiːz/] 顶点〔點〕dǐngdiǎn: *the ~ of a triangle* 三角形的顶点.

apiece /əˈpiːs/ *adv* 每个〔個〕měigè; 各 gè: *Give them a pound ~.* 给他们每人一英镑.

aplomb /əˈplɒm/ *n* [U] 自信 zìxìn; 自恃 zìshì.

apolo·getic /əˌpɒləˈdʒetɪk/ *adj* 表示歉意的 biǎoshì qiànyì de. ~**ally** *adv*

apolo·gize /əˈpɒlədʒaɪz/ *vi* 道歉 dàoqiàn: *~ to her for being rude* 为自己的唐突向她表示歉意

apol·ogy /əˈpɒlədʒɪ/ *n* [C] [*pl* -ies] 道歉 dàoqiàn: *make one's ~* 表示道歉. *an ~ for* 聊以充数〔數〕的东〔東〕西 liáoyǐ chōngshù de dōngxi.

apostle /əˈpɒsl/ *n* [C] **1** (基督教)使徒 shǐtú. **2** 改革家 gǎigéjiā.

apos·trophe /əˈpɒstrəfɪ/ *n* [C] 撇号〔號〕piěhào; 省字号 shěngzìhào.

ap·pal /əˈpɔːl/ *vt* [-ll-] 使丧胆〔膽〕shǐ sàngdǎn; 使吃惊〔驚〕shǐ chījīng. *~led at the news* 闻讯大为吃惊. ~**ling** *adj*

ap·par·atus /ˌæpəˈreɪtəs/ *n* [C] [*pl* ~es] 仪〔儀〕器 yíqì; 设备〔備〕shèbèi.

ap·par·ent /əˈpærənt/ *adj* **1** 明显〔顯〕的 míngxiǎnde: *His loyalty was ~.* 他的忠诚是显而易见的. **2** 表面上的 biǎomiàn shàng de: *the ~ cause* 表面的原因. ~**ly** *adv*

ap·par·ition /ˌæpəˈrɪʃn/ *n* [C] 幻象 huànxiàng; 鬼怪等的出现 guǐguài děng de chūxiàn.

ap·peal /əˈpiːl/ *vi* **1** 呼吁〔籲〕hūyù; 要求 yāoqiú: *~ to him for mercy* 求他开恩. **2** [法律]上诉 shàngsù. **3** 请求重作决定 qǐngqiú chóng zuò juédìng. **4** 吸引 xīyǐn; 引起爱〔愛〕好 yǐnqǐ àihào: *She ~s to me.* 我为她所吸引. □ *n* **1** [C] 恳〔懇〕求 kěnqiú; 呼吁 hūyù. **2** [C] 上诉 shàngsù, 请求重作决定 qǐngqiú chóngzuò juédìng. **3** [U] 吸引力 xīyǐnlì: *ˈsex-~* 性感. ~**ing** *adj* **(a)** 恳求的 kěnqiú. **(b)** 吸引人的 xīyǐnrénde, 有感染力的 yǒu gǎnrǎnlì de.

ap·pear /əˈpɪə(r)/ *vi* **1** 出现 chūxiàn; 显〔顯〕露 xiǎnlù. **2** 来〔來〕到 láidào. **3 (a)** 演员登台〔臺〕yǎnyuán dēngtái. **(b)** 出版 chūbǎn. **(c)** [法律]出庭 chūtíng: *~ before a court* 到庭 **4** 看来 kànlái: *She ~s sad.* 她看来心里难过. **~ance** *n* [C] **(a)** 出现 chūxiàn. **(b)** 外貌 wàimào, 外表 wàibiǎo. **(c)** 衣着风[風]度 yīzhāo fēngdù. *an untidy ~* 衣冠不整.

ap·pend /ə'pend/ *vt* [正式用语]附加 fùjiā; 附注[註] fùzhù. **~age** *n* [C] 附属[屬]物 fùshǔwù; 附加物 fùjiāwù.

ap·pen·di·ci·tis /ə,pendə'saɪtɪs/ *n* [U] 阑[闌]尾炎 lánwěiyán.

ap·pen·dix /ə'pendɪks/ *n* [C] [*pl* ~es 或 -dices /dɪsi:z/] **1** 附录[錄] fùlù. **2** 阑尾 lánwěi.

ap·pe·tite /'æpɪtaɪt/ *n* [C,U] 食欲 shíyù.

ap·pe·tizer /'æpɪtaɪzə(r)/ *n* [C] 开[開]胃品 kāiwèipǐn. **ap·pe·tiz·ing** *adj* 开胃的 kāiwèide.

ap·plaud /ə'plɔ:d/ *vt/i* **1** 鼓掌欢[歡]迎 gǔzhǎng huānyíng; 鼓掌赞成 gǔzhǎng zànchéng. **2** 赞成 zànchéng: *I ~ your decision.* 我赞成你的决定. **ap·plause** /ə'plɔ:z/ *n* [U]

apple /'æpl/ *n* [C] 苹[蘋]果 píngguǒ. ⇨ Adam's apple.

ap·pli·ance /ə'plaɪəns/ *n* [C] 用具 yòngjù; 设备[備] shèbèi; 装[裝]置 zhuāngzhì.

ap·pli·cable /'æplɪkəbl/ *adj* 合用的 héyòngde; 合适[適]的 héshìde.

ap·pli·cant /'æplɪkənt/ *n* [C] 申请人 shēnqǐngrén; 请求者 qǐngqiúzhě.

ap·pli·ca·tion/,æplɪ'keɪʃn/ *n* **1**[C, U] 请求 qǐngqiú; 申请表 shēnqǐngbiǎo: *on ~* 申请(即给); *~ form* 申请表. **2** [U] 涂[塗] tú, 敷 fū. [C] 涂敷物 túfūwù: *an ~ for burns* 烧伤涂敷物. **3** [U]应[應]用 yìngyòng: *the ~ of a new process to industry*—种新的方法在工业上的应用. **4**[U][正式用语]努力 nǔlì: *put ~ into your studies* 你要专心学习.

ap·ply /ə'plaɪ/ *vt/i* [*pt, pp* -ied] **1** 要求 yāoqiú; 申请 shēnqǐng: *~ for a visa* 申请签证. **2 (a)** 涂[塗] tú; 敷 fū: *~ cream to a cut* 在伤口上涂凡士林. **(b)** 施行 shīxíng, 实[實]施shíshī. *~ economic sanctions*施行经济制裁. **3** 与[與]…有关[關] yǔ…yǒuguān; 适[適]用 shìyòng: *It does not ~ to you.* 那与你无关. **4 ~ oneself (to sth)** 专[專]心致志于 zhuānxīn zhìzhì yú. **applied** *adj* 应[應]用的 yìngyòngde; *applied science* 应用科学

ap·point/ə'pɔɪnt/ *vt* **1**约定 yuēdìng: *the time ~ed* 约定的时间. **2** 任命 rènmìng. **~ment** *n* **(a)** [C, U] 约会 yuēhuì: *make an ~* 定一个约会. **(b)** [C] 职[職]位 zhíwèi: *He got the ~ment as manager.* 他得到了经理的职位.

ap·praise /ə'preɪz/ *vt* [非正式用语]估价[價] gūjià, 评价 píngjià, 鉴[鑒]定 jiàndìng. **ap·praisal** /ə'preɪzl/ *n* [C, U]

ap·preci·able /ə'pri:ʃəbl/ *adj* 可以看到的 kěyǐ kàndào de, 可见的 kějiànde; 明显[顯]的 míngxiǎnde: *~ difference* 明显的差异; *~ growth* 明显的增长. **ap·preci·ably** *adv*

ap·preci·ate /ə'pri:ʃɪeɪt/ *vt/i* **1** 欣赏 xīnshǎng: *~ a holiday* 领略假日的乐趣. **2** 重视 zhòngshì; 感激 gǎnjī: *We ~ your help.* 我们感激你的帮助. **3**(土地等)涨[漲]价[價] zhàngjià. **ap·preci'ation** *n* **(a)** [C,U] 鉴[鑑]别 jiànbié. **(b)** [U] 珍惜 zhēnxī; 赏识[識] shǎngshí: *in appreciation of your help* 感谢你的帮助. **(c)**[U] 涨[漲] 价[價] zhàngjià. **ap·preci·ative**/ə'pri:ʃətɪv/ *adj* 感激的 gǎnjīde.

ap·pre·hend /,æprɪ'hend/ *vt* **1** [法律]逮捕 dàibǔ, 拘捕 jūbǔ. **2** 理解 lǐjiě, 明白 míngbai.

ap·pre·hen·sion /,æprɪ'henʃn/ *n* [U] **1** 理解 lǐjiě: *an ~ of the problems* 对问题的理解. **2** [也用复] 忧[憂]虑 yōulǜ; 恐怕 kǒngpà: *feel ~ for her safety* 担心她的安全. **3** [法律]逮捕 dàibǔ. **ap·pre·hen·sive** /,æprɪ'hensɪv/ *adj* 担[擔]心的 dānxīnde, 忧虑的 yōulǜde.

ap·pren·tice /ə'prentɪs/ *n* [C] 学[學]徒 xuétú, 徒工 túgōng. □ *vt* 使当[當]学徒 shǐ dāng xuétú: *a boy ~d to a builder* 给建筑工人当学徒的男孩子. **~ship** *n* 学徒期 xuétúqī.

ap·proach /ə'prəʊtʃ/ *vt/i* **1** 接近 jiējìn; 走近 zǒujìn. **2** [喻]同…一样[樣]好 tóng…yíyàng hǎo: *Few writers ~ Shakespeare.* 没有那个作家可以同莎士比亚相比拟. **3** 向…提出请求 xiàng… tíchū qǐngqiú; 向…接洽 xiàng…jiēqià: *~ the manager for an increase in salary* 请求经理给增加工资. □ *n* **1**[U] 接近 jiējìn. **2**[C] 方法 fāngfǎ, 途径[徑] tújìng. **~able** /-əbl/ *adj* **(a)** 可接近的 kě jiējìn de. **(b)** 谈得拢[攏]的 tándelǒngde.

ap·pro·pri·ate[1] /ə'prəʊprɪət/ *adj* 合适[適]的 héshìde; 正确的 zhèngquède. **~ly** *adv*

ap·pro·pri·ate[2] /ə'prəʊprɪeɪt/ *vt* **1** 拨[撥]作专[專]用 bō zuò zhuānyòng. **2** 私占 sīzhàn: *~ ideas* 剽窃别人的见解. **ap·pro·pri'ation** *n*

[C, U]

ap·pro·val /ə'pru:vl/ *n* [U] 允许 yǔnxǔ; 批准 pīzhǔn; 赞同 zàntóng: *Your plans have my* ～. 我赞同你的计划. *on* ～ 送货上门〔門〕(中意就买,不中意就退) sòng huò shàng mén.

ap·prove /ə'pru:v/ *vt/i* **1** 赞同 zàntóng: ～ *of a marriage* 赞同一项婚事. **2** 同意 tóngyì: *The minutes of the meeting were* ～*d.* 大家同意会议记录是正确的. **ap·prov·ing·ly** *adv*

approx. = approximately.

ap·proxi·mate[1] /ə'prɒksɪmət/ *adj* 近似的 jìnsìde; 约略的 yuēlüède. ～**ly** *adv*

ap·proxi·mate[2] /ə'prɒksɪmeɪt/ *vt/i* 接近 jiējìn; 近似 jìnsì. **ap·proxi'ma·tion** *n* [C] 近似值 jìnsìzhí.

Apr. =April.

apri·cot /'eɪprɪkɒt/ *n* **1** [C] 杏树〔樹〕xìngshù; 杏 xìng. **2** [U] 杏黄色 xìnghuángsè.

April /'eɪprəl/ *n* 四月 sìyuè.

apron /'eɪprən/ *n* [C] 围〔圍〕裙 wéiqún.

apt /æpt/ *adj* [-er, -est] **1** 伶俐的 línglìde; 聪〔聰〕明的 cōngmingde. **2** 合适〔適〕的 héshìde; 妥当〔當〕的 tuǒdangde: *an* ～ *remark* 一番得体的话. **3** 易于 yìyú; 倾向于 qīngxiàngyú: ～ *to break* 易断. ～**ly** *adv* 适合地 shìhéde. ～**ness** *n* [U]

ap·ti·tude /'æptɪtju:d/ *n* [C, U] 才能 cáinéng, 能力 nénglì: *an* ～ *for languages* 语言的才能.

aqua·lung /'ækwəlʌŋ/ *n* [C] (*P*) 水中呼吸器 shuǐzhōng hūxīqì.

aqua·mar·ine /ˌækwəmə'ri:n/ *n* [C, U] 水蓝〔藍〕宝〔寶〕石 shuǐlán bǎoshí; 蓝绿色 lánlǜsè.

aquar·ium /ə'kweərɪəm/ *n* [C] [*pl* ～s, -ria /-rɪə/] 水族馆 shuǐzúguǎn; 养〔養〕鱼池 yǎngyúchí.

aquatic /ə'kwætɪk/ *adj* **1** 水产〔產〕的 shuǐchǎnde; 水生的 shuǐshēngde. **2** [运动]水上的 shuǐshàngde; 水中的 shuǐzhōngde.

aque·duct /'ækwɪdʌkt/ *n* [C] 渡槽 dùcáo.

Ara·bic /'ærəbɪk/ *adj* 阿拉伯的 ālābóde. □ *n* [U] 阿拉伯语 ālābóyǔ. **A～ numeral** 阿拉伯数〔數〕字 ālābó shùzì.

ar·able /'ærəbl/ *adj* (土地)可耕的 kěgēngde.

ar·bit·rary /'ɑ:bɪtrərɪ/ *adj* **1** 任性的 rènxìngde. **2** 专〔專〕断〔斷〕的 zhuānduànde: *an* ～ *ruler* 专断的统治者.

ar·bi·trate /'ɑ:bɪtreɪt/ *vt/i* 仲裁 zhòngcái; 公断〔斷〕gōngduàn. **ar·bi'tra·tion** *n* [U] 仲裁 zhòngcái; 公断 gōngduàn. **'ar·bi·tra·tor** *n* [C] 仲裁人 zhòngcáirén; 公断人 gōngduànrén.

arc /ɑ:k/ *n* [C] 弧 hú. ～ **lamp (light)** 弧光灯〔燈〕húguāngdēng.

ar·cade /ɑ:'keɪd/ *n* [C] 上有顶棚旁有商店的街道 shàng yǒu dǐngpéng páng yǒu shāngdiàn de jiēdào.

arch /ɑ:tʃ/ *n* [C] 拱 gǒng; 桥〔橋〕洞 qiáodòng. □ *vt/i* 拱起 gǒngqǐ; 弯〔彎〕成弓形 wān chéng gōngxíng: *The cat* ～*ed its back.* 猫弓起了背.

ar·chae·ol·ogy [美语 **ar·che·ol-**] /ˌɑ:kɪ'ɒlədʒɪ/ *n* [U] 考古学〔學〕kǎogǔxué **ar·chaeo·logi·cal** *adj* /ɑ:kɪə'lɒdʒɪkl/ **ar·chae'ol·ogist** *n* [C]

ar·chaic /ˌɑ:'keɪɪk/ *adj* (语言,词汇等)已废〔廢〕的 yǐfèide.

arch·angel /ˌɑ:k'eɪndʒl/ *n* [C] 大天使 dàtiānshǐ.

arch·bishop /ˌɑ:tʃ'bɪʃəp/ *n* [C] 大主教 dàzhǔjiào.

archer /'ɑ:tʃə(r)/ *n* [C] 弓箭手 gōngjiànshǒu. **arch·ery** *n* [U] 弓箭术〔術〕gōngjiànshù, 射术 shèshù.

archi·pel·ago /ˌɑ:kɪ'peləgəʊ/ *n* [C] [*pl* ～s, ～es] 群岛 qúndǎo; 多岛的海域 duōdǎo de hǎiyù.

archi·tect /'ɑ:kɪtekt/ *n* [C] 建筑〔築〕师〔師〕jiànzhùshī; 设计师 shèjìshī. ～**ural** /ˌɑ:kɪ'tekʃərəl/ *adj* 建筑的 jiànzhùde; 建筑学〔學〕的 jiànzhùxuéde. ～**ure** /'ɑ:kɪtektʃə(r)/ *n* [U] 建筑学 jiànzhùxué; 建筑风〔風〕格 jiànzhù fēnggé.

ar·chives /'ɑ:kaɪvz/ *n pl* 档〔檔〕案室 dǎng'ànshì.

arch·way /'ɑ:tʃweɪ/ *n* ⇨ arch.

arc·tic /'ɑ:ktɪk/ *adj, n* 北极〔極〕的 běijíde.

ar·dent /'ɑ:dnt/ *adj* 热〔熱〕情的 rèqíngde; 热心的 rèxīnde. ～**ly** *adv*

ar·du·ous /'ɑ:djʊəs/ *adj* 艰〔艱〕巨的 jiānjùde, 艰苦的 jiānkǔde. ～**ly** *adv*

are /ə(r) 强式: ɑ:(r)/ ⇨ be.

area /'eərɪə/ *n* [C] **1** 面积〔積〕miànjī: *the* ～ *of the page* 版面的面积. **2** 地区〔區〕dìqū; 区域 qūyù: *desert* ～*s* 沙漠地区. **3** [喻]范〔範〕围〔圍〕fànwéi; 领域 lǐngyù: ～*s of disagreement* 有分歧的领域.

arena /ə'ri:nə/ *n* [C] [*pl* ～s] **1** 竞〔競〕技场〔場〕jìngjìchǎng. **2** [喻]比赛场所 bǐsài chǎngsuǒ: *the* *political* ~ 政治舞台.

aren't /ɑ:nt/ = *are not.*

ar·gue /'ɑ:gju:/ *vt/i* **1** 不同意 bùtóngyì; 争论〔論〕zhēnglùn: *arguing over* (或 *about*) *it* 辩论某事 **2** ~ *for* 为〔爲〕赞成…而辩论 wèi zànchéng … ér biànlùn. ~ **against** 为反对〔對〕…而辩论 wèi fǎnduì …ér biànlùn. ~ **that** 辩论说 biànlùn shuō. **3** 辩论 biànlùn: *The lawyers* ~*d the case.* 律师们辩论案件. **ar·gu·able** /-əbl/ *adj* 可争辨的 kě zhēngbiàn de **ar·gu·ably** *adv*

ar·gu·ment /'ɑ:gjʊmənt/ *n* **1** [C] 不同意 bù tóngyì. **2** [C, U] 争论〔論〕zhēnglùn. ~**a·tive** /ˌɑ:gjʊ'mentətɪv/ *adj* 爱〔愛〕争论的. ài zhēnglùn de.

aria /'ɑ:rɪə/ *n* [C] [*pl* ~s] 咏叹〔嘆〕调 yǒngtàndiào.

arid /'ærɪd/ *adj* 干〔幹〕旱的 gānhànde; 贫瘠的 pínjíde.

arise /ə'raɪz/ *vi* [*pt* arose /ə'rəʊz/, *pp* arisen /ə'rɪzn/] **1** 出现 chūxiàn; 发〔發〕生 fāshēng: *A difficulty has* ~*n.* 发生了困难. **2** [旧用法]起身 qǐshēn. 起来〔來〕qǐlái.

ar·is·toc·racy /ˌærɪ'stɒkrəsɪ/ *n* [C,U] [*pl* -ies] 贵族(总称) guìzú.

ar·is·to·crat /'ærɪstəkræt/ *n* [C] 贵族 guìzú. ~**ic** /-'krætɪk/ *adj*

arith·me·tic /ə'rɪθmətɪk/ *n* [U] 算术〔術〕suànshù; 计算 jìsuàn. ~**al** /-'metɪkl/ *adj* 算术的 suànshùde; 计算的 jìsuànde.

ark /ɑ:k/ *n* (圣经)方舟 fāngchōu.

arm¹ /ɑ:m/ *n* [C] **1** 臂 bì. *keep sb at* ~*'s length* [喻]避免同某人接近 bìmiǎn tóng mǒurén jiējìn. *with open* ~*'s* 热〔熱〕烈地(欢迎) rèliède. **2** 袖子 xiùzi. **3** 臂状〔狀〕物 bìzhuàngwù: *the* ~*s of a chair* 椅子的把手. **4** 武器 wǔqì: *a 'fire*~ 火器. '~**chair** 扶手椅 fúshǒuyǐ. '~**pit** 腋窝 yèwō.

arm² /ɑ:m/ *vt/i* 武装〔裝〕wǔzhuāng; 装备〔備〕zhuāngbèi. **the** ~**ed forces** 军〔軍〕事力量 jūnshì lìliàng.

ar·mada /ɑ:'mɑ:də/ *n* [C] [*pl* ~s] 舰〔艦〕队〔隊〕jiànduì.

ar·ma·dillo /ˌɑ:mə'dɪləʊ/ *n* [C] [*pl* ~s] 犰狳 qiúyú.

ar·ma·ment /'ɑ:məmənt/ *n* **1** [常用复] 兵器 bīngqì; 大炮 dàpào. **2** [U] 武装〔裝〕wǔzhuāng.

ar·mis·tice /'ɑ:mɪstɪs/ *n* [C] 停战〔戰〕tíngzhàn; 休战 xiūzhàn.

ar·mour [美语 =**ar·mor**]/'ɑ:mə(r)/ *n* [U] **1** 盔甲 kuījiǎ: *a suit of* ~ 一套盔甲. **2** 装〔裝〕甲 zhuāngjiǎ. **3** (总称)装甲部队〔隊〕zhuāngjiǎbùduì. ~**ed** *adj* **ar·mourer** 武器制〔製〕造者 wǔqì zhìzàozhě. **ar·moury** 军〔軍〕械库〔庫〕jūnjièkù.

arms /ɑ:mz/ *n pl* **1** 武器 wǔqì. *lay down (one's)* ~ 停止战〔戰〕斗〔鬥〕tíngzhǐ zhàndòu. *take up* ~ *(against)* 准〔準〕备〔備〕战斗 zhǔnbèi zhàndòu. *(be) up in* ~ *(about* 或 *over)* [喻]强烈反对〔對〕qiángliè fǎnduì. **2** 纹章 wénzhāng; 徽章 huīzhāng. '~**-race** 军〔軍〕备〔備〕竞〔競〕赛 jūnbèi jìngsài.

army /'ɑ:mɪ/ *n* [C] [*pl* -ies] **1 the** ~ 陆〔陸〕军〔軍〕lùjūn. **2** 群 qún; 大队〔隊〕dàduì: *an*~ *of workmen* 一群工人.

aroma /ə'rəʊmə/ *n* [C] 芳香 fángxiāng. ~**tic** /ˌærə'mætɪk/ *adj*

arose /ə'rəʊz/ *pt* of arise.

around /ə'raʊnd/ *adv, prep* **1** 在…周〔週〕围〔圍〕zài…zhōuwéi. **2** 大约 dàyuē; 附近 fùjìn: *He lives* ~ *London.* 他住在伦敦的附近. *It's* ~ *six o'clock.* 大约六点钟.

arouse /ə'raʊz/ *vt* **1** 唤醒 huànxǐng; 引起 yǐnqǐ: ~ *suspicion* 引起怀疑. **2** 唤起 huànqǐ.

arr. = arrive.

ar·range /ə'reɪndʒ/ *vt/i* **1** 整理 zhěnglǐ; 排列 páiliè: ~ *flowers* 整理花束. **2** 筹〔籌〕备〔備〕chóubèi: ~ *a meeting* 筹备一个会议. **3** 商定 shāngdìng: ~ *a loan* 商定一笔贷款. **4** 改编 gǎibiān: ~ *a piece for the violin* 改编成一首小提琴曲. ~**ment** *n* **(a)** [U] 整理 zhěnglǐ; 排列 páiliè. **(b)** [*pl*] 准〔準〕备 zhǔnbèi; 安排 ānpái. **(c)** [U] 商定 shāngdìng: *to come to an* ~*ment over expenses.* 商定各项开支. **(d)** [C] 改编 gǎibiān: *an* ~ *for the piano* 一首改编的钢琴曲.

ar·ray /ə'reɪ/ *n* [C] 阵〔陣〕式 zhènshì.

ar·rears /ə'rɪəz/ *n pl* **1** 欠款 qiànkuǎn: ~ *of rent* 欠租. **be in** ~ **(with)** 拖欠 tūqiàn. **2** 待做的工作 dài zuò de gōngzuò.

ar·rest /ə'rest/ *vt* **1** 逮捕 dèibǔ. **2** 抑制 yìzhì; 阻止 zǔzhǐ: *Poor food* ~*s natural growth.* 低劣的食品妨碍了自然生长. **3** 吸引 xīyǐn. □ *n* [C] 逮捕 dèibǔ; 阻止 zǔzhǐ. *(be* 或 *place) under* ~ 被逮捕 bèi dèibǔ.

ar·ri·val /ə'raɪvl/ *n* **1** [U] 到达〔達〕dàodá, 抵达 dǐdá. **2** [C] 来〔來〕者 láizhě; 来物 láiwù: *The new* ~ (= baby) *is a boy.* 生下的是个男孩子.

ar·rive /ə'raɪv/ *vi* **1** 到达〔達〕dàodá, 抵达 dǐdá: ~ *home* 到家. **2** (时间)到来 dàolái: *The day* ~*d.* 这一天来到了. **3** ~ *at* 达成 dáchéng; 得到 dédào; 作出(决定等) zuòchū. **4**〔现代用法〕成功 chénggōng.

ar·ro·gant /'ærəgənt/ *adj* 傲慢的 àomànde, 自负的 zìfùde. ~**ly** *adv* **ar·ro·gance** *n* [U]

ar·row /'ærəʊ/ *n* [C] **1** 箭 jiàn. **2** 箭头〔頭〕标〔標〕志 jiàntóu biāozhì.

ar·senal /'ɑːsənl/ *n* [C] 火药库〔庫〕huǒyàokù; 军〔軍〕火库 jūnhuǒkù.

ar·senic /'ɑːsnɪk/ *n* [U] 砒霜 pīshuāng.

ar·son /'ɑːsn/ *n* [U] 放火 fànghuǒ, 纵〔縱〕火 zònghuǒ.

art /ɑːt/ *n* **1** [U] 美术〔術〕měishù; 艺〔藝〕术 yìshù. **2** [C] 文艺 wényì. **3** [C, U] 诡计 guǐjì, 花招 huāzhāo. ~**ful** *adj* 巧妙的 qiǎomiàode; 狡猾的 jiǎohuáde. ~**fully** *adv*

ar·te·fact ⇨ artifact.

ar·ter·ial /ɑː'tɪərɪəl/ *adj* **1** 动〔動〕脉的 dòngmàide; 动脉似的 dòngmài sì de. **2** ~ *roads* 〔喻〕(交通)干线〔綫〕gànxiàn; 主要道路 zhǔyào dàolù.

ar·tery /'ɑːtərɪ/ *n* [C] [*pl* -ies] **1** 动〔動〕脉 dòngmài. **2** 主要道路或河流 zhǔyào dàolù huò héliú.

ar·thri·tis /ɑː'θraɪtɪs/ *n* [U] 关〔關〕节〔節〕炎 guānjiéyán. **ar·thri·tic** /ɑː'θrɪtɪk/ *adj*

ar·ti·choke /'ɑːtɪtʃəʊk/ *n* [C] **1 globe** ~ 朝鲜蓟 cháoxiǎnjì. **2 Jerusalem** ~ 菊芋 júyú.

ar·ticle /'ɑːtɪkl/ *n* [C] **1** 物品 wùpǐn; ~*s of clothing* 服装. **2** 文章 wénzhāng. **3**〔法律〕条〔條〕款 tiáokuǎn. **4**〔语法〕冠词 guàncí: *definite* ~ 定冠词; *indefinite* ~ 不定冠词.

ar·ticu·late[1] /ɑː'tɪkjʊlət/ *adj* **1** 发〔發〕音清晰的 fāyīn qīngxī de. **2** 说话表达〔達〕力强的 shuōhuà biǎodálì qiángde. ~**ly** *adv*

ar·ticu·late[2] /ɑː'tɪkjʊleɪt/ *vt/i* **1** 清晰地发〔發〕音 qīngxīde fāyīn; 清楚地说话 qīngchude shuōhuà. **2** (用关节)连结 liánjiē. ~**d lorry** *n* 铰接式卡车〔車〕jiǎojiēshì kǎchē. **ar·ticu'la·tion** *n* [U] **(a)** 发〔發〕音 fāyīn. **(b)** 关〔關〕节〔節〕的咬合 guānjiéde yǎohé.

ar·ti·fact, ar·te·fact /'ɑːtɪfækt/ *n* [C] 人工制〔製〕品 réngōng zhìpǐn.

ar·ti·fi·cial /ˌɑːtɪ'fɪʃl/ *adj* **1** 人工的 réngōngde; 不真的 bù zhēn de. **2** 矫〔矯〕揉做作的 jiǎoróuzuòzuòde: ~ *laughter* 做作的笑(声). ~**ly** *adv*

ar·til·lery /ɑː'tɪlərɪ/ *n* [U] 大炮 dàpào; 炮兵 pàobīng.

ar·ti·san /ˌɑːtɪ'zæn/ *n* [C] 手艺〔藝〕人 shǒuyìrén; 技工 jìgōng.

art·ist /'ɑːtɪst/ *n* [C] **1** 艺〔藝〕术〔術〕家 yìshùjiā; 美术家 měishùjiā. **2** 能手 néngshǒu. ~**ic** /ɑː'tɪstɪk/ *adj* **(a)** 有艺术性的 yǒu yìshùxìng de. **(b)** 艺术的 yìshùde; 艺术家的 yìshùjiāde. ~**ally** *adv* **art·istry** /'ɑːtɪstrɪ/ *n* [U] 艺术技巧 yìshù jìqiǎo.

art·iste /ɑː'tiːst/ *n* [C] 艺〔藝〕人 yìrén; 能手 néngshǒu.

arty /'ɑːtɪ/ *adj* 〔非正式用语〕冒充艺〔藝〕术〔術〕的 màochōng yìshù de

as[1] /əz 强式: æz/ *adv* **as... as** 如…一样〔樣〕rú...yíyàng; 如…一般 rú...yìbān: ~ *tall* ~ 一样高.

as[2] /əz 强式: æz/ *conj* **1** 当〔當〕dāng, 在…的时〔時〕候 zài... de shíhòu: *I saw him* ~ *he was getting off the bus.* 他下公共汽车的时候我看见了他. **2** 由于 yóuyú; 既然 jìrán: *A* ~ *he wasn't ready, we went without him.* 由于他没有准备好, 他没有同我们一起去. **3**〔表示比较〕: *twice* ~ *large* ~ 两倍大. **4** *much* ~ 虽〔雖〕然 suírán. **5** 按照 ànzhào; 如同 rútóng: *Leave it* ~ *it is.* 保持原状, 不要动它. **6** 像 xiàng, 如 rú: *dressed* ~ *a woman* 妇女般打扮. **7**〔避免重复〕: *He is tall,* ~ *are his brothers.* 他长得很高, 他的一些兄弟也一样. **8** 作为〔爲〕zuòwéi: *respected* ~ *a judge* 作为法官, 受到尊敬. **9** *such* ~ 例如 lìrú. **10** ~ *for* 至于 zhìyú; 就…方面说 jiù... fāngmiàn shuō. **11** *so* ~ *to* **(a)** 为了 wèile. **(b)** 以致于 yǐ zhìyú: *behave so* ~ *to annoy your neighbours* 弄得你的四邻不安. **12** ~ *(so) long* ~ **(a)** 只要 zhǐyào: *You can go, so long* ~ *you get back soon.* 只要你很快就回来, 你可以走. **(b)** 当〔當〕dāng, 在…的时〔時〕候 zài...de shíhòu. *You shall never enter* ~ *long* ~ *I live in it.* 只要我还有一口气, 你就不要想进得来. **13** ~ *much* 也 yě: *I thought* ~ *much.* 我也这样想. ~ *well* 也 yě. ~ *yet* 至今 zhìjīn, 迄今 qìjīn.

as·bes·tos /æs'bestɒs/ *n* [U] 石棉 shímián; 石绒 shíróng.

as·cend /ə'send/ *vt/i* **1**〔正式用语〕登(山等) dēng; 上升 shàngshēng. **2** ~ *the throne* 登位(为帝或皇后) dēngwèi. ~**ancy** (亦作 **-ency**)/-ənsɪ/

n [U] 优〔優〕势〔勢〕 yōushì; 权〔權〕势 quánshì.

as·cen·sion /ə'senʃn/ *n* [C] 上升 shàngshēng; 升腾 shēngténg. **the A～** 耶稣升天节〔節〕 yēsū shēngtiānjié.

as·cent /ə'sent/ *n* [C] 上升 shàngshēng; 上坡 shàngpō.

as·cer·tain /ˌæsə'teɪn/ *vt* 查明 chámíng; 探查 tànchá.

as·cribe /ə'skraɪb/ *vt* [正式用语]归〔歸〕因于 guī yīn yú, 把…归于 bǎ...guīyú: ～ *failure to bad luck* 把失败归因于运气不好.

A.S.E.A.N. = Association of South-East Asian Nations 东〔東〕南亚〔亞〕国〔國〕家联〔聯〕盟 Dōngnányà guójiā liánméng.

asep·tic /ˌeɪ'septɪk/ *adj* 无〔無〕病菌的 wú bìngjūn de, 防腐的 fángfǔde.

asex·ual /ˌeɪ'sekʃʊəl/ *adj* **1** 无〔無〕性的 wúxìngde. **2** 无性欲的 wú xìngyù de.

ash¹ /æʃ/ *n* [C] 桉树〔樹〕 ānshù; 桉树木 ānshùmù.

ash² /æʃ/ *n* [U or *pl*] **1** 灰 huī, 灰烬〔燼〕 huījìn. **2** [*pl*] 骨灰 gǔhuī. **'～-tray** 烟灰碟 yānhuīdié. **A～ Wednesday** 圣〔聖〕灰星期三(四旬节的第一天) shènghuī xīngqīsān.

ashamed /ə'ʃeɪmd/ *adj* 羞愧的 xiūkuìde; 害臊的 hàisàode. **～ly** /ə'ʃeɪmɪdlɪ/ *adv*

ashore /ə'ʃɔ:(r)/ *adv* 上岸 shàng'àn; 在岸上 zài ànshàng.

Asian /'eɪʃn/ *n* [C], *adj* 亚〔亞〕洲人 yàzhōurén; 亚洲的 yàzhōude.

aside /ə'saɪd/ *adv* 在旁边〔邊〕 zài pángbiān; 向旁边 xiàng pángbiān: *He laid the book* ～. 他把书放到一边. □ *n* [C] 旁白 pángbái.

ask /ɑ:sk/ *vt/i* [*pt, pp* ～ed] **1** 问〔問〕wèn, 询问 xúnwèn. ～ *(him) how to get there* 问(他)到那里怎么走法. **2** 邀请 yāoqǐng; 请 qǐng: ～ *him in* 请他进来. ～ ***for it*** (或 ***trouble***) 自找麻烦 zìzhǎo máfan. **3** 索价〔價〕 suǒjià, 要价 yàojià: *What are they* ～*ing for the house?* 这所房子他们要价多少?

askance /ə'skɑ:ns/ *adv* ***look ～ at*** 斜视(表示怀疑) xiéshì.

askew /ə'skju:/ *adv, adj* 歪斜 wāixié; 歪斜的 wāixiéde.

asleep /ə'sli:p/ *adj* **1** 睡着了的 shuìzháolede: *He fell* ～. 他睡着了. ***fast*** ～ 熟睡 shúshuì. **2** (四肢)发〔發〕麻 fāmá.

asp /æsp/ *n* [C] 一种〔種〕北非洲的小毒蛇 yìzhǒng běi fēizhōu de xiǎo dúshé.

as·para·gus /ə'spærəgəs/ *n* [U] 芦〔蘆〕笋 lúsǔn; 石刁柏 shídiāobǎi.

as·pect /'æspekt/ *n* [C] **1** 样〔樣〕子 yàngzi, 外貌 wàimào. **2** 方向 fāngxiàng; 方位 fāngwèi: *a house with a southern* ～ 朝南的房子. **3** 方面 fāngmiàn: *study every* ～ *of the question* 研究问题的各个方面.

as·per·sion /ə'spɜ:ʃn/ *n* ***cast ～s on sb*** 对某人进〔進〕行诽谤 duì mǒurén jìnxíng fěibàng.

as·phalt /'æsfælt/ *n* [U] 沥〔瀝〕青 lìqīng. □ *vt* 铺沥青(路面) pū lìqīng.

as·phyxia /əs'fɪksɪə/ *n* [U] 窒息 zhìxī.

as·phyxi·ate /əs'fɪksɪeɪt/ *vt* 使窒息 shǐ zhìxī; 掐死 qiāsǐ. **as·phyxi·'ation** *n* [U]

as·pir·ate /'æspərət/ *n* [C] "*h*" 音 "*h*" yīn. □ /'æspəreɪt/ *vt* 发〔發〕"*h*"音 fā "*h*" yīn.

as·pir·ation /ˌæspə'reɪʃn/ *n* [C, U] 抱负 bàofù; 渴望 kěwàng.

as·pire /ə'spaɪə(r)/ *vi* 渴望 kěwàng: ～ *to become an author* 渴望写出一本书.

as·pirin /'æsprɪn/ *n* (*P*) [U] 阿斯匹林 āsīpīlín [C] 阿斯匹林药片 āsīpīlín yàopiàn

ass /æs/ *n* [C] **1** 驴〔驢〕 lǘ **2** [喻] 傻瓜 shǎguā.

as·sail /ə'seɪl/ *vt* 攻击〔擊〕 gōngjī. **～ant** *n* [C] 攻击者 gōngjīzhě.

as·sas·sin /ə'sæsɪn/ *n* [C] 凶手 xiōngshǒu, 刺客 cìkè. **～ate** *vt* 暗杀〔殺〕 ànshā, 行刺 xíngcì. **～ation** /-'neɪʃn/ *n* [C,U] 暗杀 ànshā.

as·sault /ə'sɔ:lt/ *n* [C] 袭〔襲〕击〔擊〕 xíjī; 突击 tūjī. □ *vt* 袭击 xíjī.

as·semble /ə'sembl/ *vt/i* **1** 聚集 jùjí, 聚合 jùhé: *A crowd* ～*ed.* 聚集起一群人. **2** 装〔裝〕配 zhuāngpèi.

as·sem·bly /ə'semblɪ/ *n* [*pl* -ies] **1** [C] 集会〔會〕 jíhuì; 集合 jíhé. *school* ～ 学生集会. **2** [U] 装〔裝〕配 zhuāngpèi. **'～line** 装配线〔綫〕 zhuāngpeixiàn.

as·sent /ə'sent/ *n* [C] (官方的)同意 tóngyì. □ *vi* [正式用语]同意 tóngyì.

as·sert /ə'sɜ:t/ *vt* **1** 维护〔護〕wéihù; 辩护 biànhù: ～ *one's rights* 维护自己的权利. **2** 宣称〔稱〕 xuānchēn, 断〔斷〕言 duànyán: ～ *one's innocence* 认定自己无罪. **as'sertion** /-ʃn/ *n* **(a)** [U] 维护〔護〕 wéihù. **(b)** [C] 主张〔張〕 zhǔzhāng. 断〔斷〕言 duànyán. **～ive** *adj* 断言

的 duànyánde; 过〔過〕分自信的 guòfèn zìxìn de.

as·sess /ə'ses/ *vt* **1** 估值 gūzhí; 确定 quèdìng. **2**〔喻〕评价〔價〕píngjià: ~ *a speech* 对一次演说作评价. **~ment** *n* [C,U] **~sor** *n* [C] 估税员 gūshuìyuán.

as·set /'æset/ *n* [C] **1**〔常用复〕财产〔產〕cáichǎn; 资产 zīchǎn. ⇨ liability. **2** 宝〔寶〕贵的性质或技能 bǎoguìde xìngzhì huò jìnéng.

as·sign /ə'saɪn/ *vt* **1** 分配 fēnpèi; 指派 zhǐpài: ~ *work to be done* 分配要做的工作. **2** 确定时〔時〕间〔間〕或地点〔點〕quèdìng shíjiān huò dìdiǎn. **3** 指派 zhǐpài; 选〔選〕派 xuǎnpài: *A~ your best man.* 指派你们最好的人. **~ment** *n* [C,U]

as·simi·late /ə'sɪməleɪt/ *vt/i* 吸受 xīshōu; 同化 tónghuà; 归〔歸〕化 guīhuà. **as·simi'la·tion** *n* [U]

as·sist /ə'sɪst/ *vt/i*〔正式用语〕帮助 bāngzhù, 援助 yuánzhù. **~ance** *n* [U] 帮助 bāngzhù. **~ant** *n* [C] 帮助者 bāngzhùzhě: *a 'shop-~ant* 商店店员.

as·so·ci·ate /ə'səʊʃɪət/ *n* [C] **1** 伙〔夥〕伴 huǒbàn; 同事 tóngshì; 同伙 tóng huǒ. **2** 同伴 tóngbàn. □ /ə'səʊʃɪeɪt/ *vt/i* **1** 发〔發〕生联〔聯〕系〔繫〕fāshēng liánxì. **2** 参〔參〕加 cānjiā; 结交 jiējiāo.

as·so·ci·ation /əˌsəʊsɪ'eɪʃn/ *n* **1** [U] 联〔聯〕结 liánjiē; 联合 liánhé. *in ~* **(with)** 与〔與〕...联合、结交 yǔ...liánhé, jiējiāo **2**[C] 协〔協〕会〔會〕xiéhuì; 社团〔團〕shètuán: *the 'Automobile A~* 汽车协会. ~ **'football** (略作 *soccer*) 英国〔國〕式足球 yīngguóshì zúqiú.

as·sorted /ə'sɔːtɪd/ *adj* 各式各样〔樣〕的 gèshìgèyàngde, 什锦的 shíjǐnde.

as·sort·ment /ə'sɔːtmənt/ *n* [C] 各式物品的配合 gèshì wùpǐn de pèihé.

asst. =assistant.

as·sume /ə'sjuːm/ *vt* **1** 假定 jiǎdìng: ~ *his innocence* 假定他是无罪的. **2** 承担〔擔〕chéngdān; 担任 dānrèn: ~ *office* 就职〔職〕jiùzhí. **3** 装〔裝〕出 zhuāngchū; 使用 shǐyòng: ~ *a new name* 使用新名字.

as·sump·tion /ə'sʌmpʃn/ *n* [C] **1** 假定之事 jiǎdìng zhī shì. **2** 承担〔擔〕chéngdān; 担任 dānrèn.

as·sur·ance /ə'ʃʊərəns/ *n* **1** [U](常作 *self-~*) 自信 zìxìn; 把握 bǎwò. **2** [C] 承诺 chéngnuò; 保证〔證〕bǎozhèng: *give an ~* 作出保证. **3** [U] 保险〔險〕bǎoxiǎn: *life ~* 人寿保险.

as·sure /ə'ʃʊə(r)/ *vt* **1** 断〔斷〕言 duànyán. **2** 使确〔確〕信 shǐ quèxìn. **3** 保险〔險〕(特指保人寿险) bǎoxiǎn. **as·sured** *adj* 自信的 zìxìnde; 有信心的 yǒu xìnxīn de.

as·ter·isk /'æstərɪsk/ *n* [C] 星形符号 xīngxíng fúhào.

astern /ə'stɜːn/ *adv* 在船尾部 zài chuán wěibù.

as·ter·oid /'æstərɔɪd/ *n* [C] 小行星 xiǎo xíngxīng.

asthma /'æsmə/ *n* [U] 气〔氣〕喘病 qìchuǎnbìng. **~tic** /ˌæs'mætɪk/ *adj*

as·ton·ish /ə'stɒnɪʃ/ *vt* 使惊〔驚〕讶 shǐ jīngyà, 吃惊 chījīng. **~ing** *adj* 惊讶的 jīngyàde. **~ment** *n* [U]

astound /ə'staʊnd/ *vt* 使震惊 shǐ zhènjīng.

as·tral /'æstrəl/ *adj* 星的 xīngde; 星状〔狀〕的 xīngzhuàngde.

astray /ə'streɪ/ *adv, adj* 在歧途上(的) zài qítú shàng; 迷途(的) mítú: *led ~* 引入歧途.

astride /ə'straɪd/ *adv, adj, prep* 跨着 kuàzhe.

as·trol·ogy /ə'strɒlədʒɪ/ *n* [U] 占星术〔術〕zhānxīngshù. **as·trol·oger** *n* [C]

as·tro·naut /'æstrənɔːt/ *n* [C] 宇宙航行员 yǔzhòu hángxíng yuán.

as·tron·omy /ə'strɒnəmɪ/ *n* [U] 天文学〔學〕tiānwénxué. **as·tron·omer** *n* [C] **as·tro·nomi·cal** /ˌæstrə'nɒmɪkl/ *adj* **(a)** 天文学的 tiānwénxuéde. **(b)** 极〔極〕巨大的 jí jùdà de: *an astronomical amount.* 天文数字.

as·tute /ə'stjuːt/ *adj* 机〔機〕敏的 jīmǐnde; 狡猾的 jiǎohuáde: *an ~ businessman* 机敏的商人. **~ly** *adv* **~ness** *n* [U]

asy·lum /ə'saɪləm/ *n* **1** [C, U] 避难〔難〕所 bìnànsuǒ; 收容所 shōuróngsuǒ. **2**〔正式用语〕疯〔瘋〕人院 fēngrényuàn, 精神病院 jīngshénbìngyuàn. **3** 避难 pìnàn: *political ~* 政治避难.

at /ət 强式: æt/ *prep* **1 (a)** 在...里〔裡〕面或附近 zài lǐmiàn huò fùjìn: ~ *the station* 在火车站. **(b)** 向着 xiàngzhe, 朝着 cháozhe: *look ~ him* 看着他; *guess ~ the meaning.* 猜想含意. **2 (a)** (表示时间): ~ *2 o'clock* (在)两点钟(的时候). ⇨ in². ⇨ on². **(b)** (表示年龄): ~ *(the age of) 15* 十五岁(的时候). **(c)** (表示次序): *~first* 起初. **3 (a)** (表示所做的事) ~ *work* 在工作. **(b)**〔用于形容词的

后面]: *good* ~ *translation* 善于翻译. **(c)** (表示状态): ~ *war* 从事战争. **4** (表示速度、价钱等): ~ *full speed* 全速地; *sell them* ~ *25p* 以25便士卖出. **5** 被 bèi: *shocked* ~ *the news* 被这些消息所震惊.

ate /et/ *pt* of eat.

athe·ism /'eɪθɪɪzəm/ *n* [U] 无[無]神论[論] wúshénlùn. **athe·ist** *n* [C] **athe'is·tic** *adj*

ath·lete /'æθli:t/ *n* [C] 体[體]育家 tǐyùjiā. 运[運]动[動]员 yùndòngyuán. **ath·letic** /æθ'letɪk/ *adj* **(a)** 体育的 tǐyùde, 运动的 yùndòng de. **(b)** 体格健壮的 tǐgéjiànzhuàngde. **ath·let·ics** *n pl* 竞[競]技 jìngjì, 运动 yùndòng, 体育 tǐyù.

at·las /'ætləs/ *n* [C] 地图集 dìtújí.

at·mos·phere /'ætməsfɪə(r)/ *n* **1** *the* ~ 大气[氣] dàqì. **2** [C] 空气 kōngqì. **3** [C] 气氛 qìfēn: *an* ~ *of peace in the country* 升平景象. **at·mos·pheric** /-'ferɪk/ *adj* 大气的 dàqìde.

atoll /'ætɒl/ *n* [C] 环[環]礁 huánjiāo.

atom /'ætəm/ *n* [C] **1** 原子 yuánzǐ. **2** [喻]微粒 wēilì. **~ic** /ə'tɒmɪk/ *adj* 原子的 yuánzǐde. **,~ic 'bomb** 原子弹[彈] yuánzǐdàn.

atro·cious /ə'trəʊʃəs/ *adj* **1** 残[殘]忍的 cánrěnde; 万[萬]恶[惡]的 wàn'ède: *an* ~ *crime* 万恶的罪行. **2** [非正式用语]坏[壞]透了的 huài tòu le de: ~ *weather* 坏透了的天气。**~ly** *adv*

atroc·ity /ə'trɒsətɪ/ *n* [*pl* -ies] [U] 恶[惡]毒 èdú; [C] 残[殘]忍 cánrěn, 残暴 cánbào.

at·tach /ə'tætʃ/ *vt/i* **1** 系[繫]上 jìshàng; 附上 fùshàng; 加上 jiāshàng. **2** *be* ~*ed to* 依恋[戀] yīliàn. **3** 认[認]为[爲]...有 rènwéi...yǒu: ~ *importance to* 重视. **~ment** *n* **(a)** [U] 附着 fùzhuó. **(b)** [C] 附着物 fùzhuówù; 附件 fùjiàn. **(c)** [C] 爱[愛]慕 àimù: *an* ~*ment for her* 对她的爱慕.

at·taché /ə'tæʃeɪ/ *n* [C] 大使馆馆员 dàshǐguǎn guǎnyuán. *the naval* ~ 海军武官.

at·tack /ə'tæk/ *n* **1** [C] 攻击 gōngjī, 进[進]攻. jìngōng: *make an* ~ *on* 向...发起进攻. **2** [C] 非难 fēinàn, 抨击 pēngjī. **3** [C] 疾病的发[發]作 jíbìngde fāzuò: *a 'heart* ~ 心脏病发作. □ *vt* 攻击 gōngjī, 进[進]攻 jìngōng. **~er** *n* [C]

at·tain /ə'teɪn/ *vt/i* [正式用语]取得 qǔdé, 得到 dédào: ~ *one's hopes* 实现希望; ~ *one's success* 取得成功. **~ment, (a)** [U] 达[達]到 dádào, 得到 dédào. **(b)** [C] [常用复]造诣 zàoyì.

at·tempt /ə'tempt/ *vt* 尝[嘗]试 chángshì; 企图[圖] qǐtú. □ *n* [C] 企图 qǐtú; 尝试 chángshì: *an* ~ *to escape* 企图逃跑.

at·tend /ə'tend/ *vt/i* **1** 专[專]心 zhuānxīn; 注意 zhùyì: ~ *to your work* 专心你的工作. **2** 护[護]理 hùlǐ; 照顾 zhàogù. *Which doctor is* ~*ing you?* 那一位医生在给你治病? **3** 出席 chūxí, 到场[場] dàochǎng: ~ *a meeting* 出席会议. **~ance** *n* **(a)** [C, U] 到场 dàochǎng, 出席 chūxí. **(b)** [C] 出席人数[數] chūxí rénshù: *a large* ~*ance* 出席人数众多. **~ant** *n* [C] 服务[務]员 fúwùyuán, 仆[僕]人 púrén, 随从[從] suícóng.

at·ten·tion /ə'tenʃn/ *n* **1** [U] 注意 zhùyì: *pay* (或: *attract*) ~ 注意. **2** 照料 zhàoliào; 关[關]心 guānxīn: *My old car needs some* ~. 我的旧汽车需要修理一下. **3** [U] [军事]立正 lìzhèng.

at·tent·ive /ə'tentɪv/ *adj* 注意的 zhùyìde, 专[專]心的 zhuānxīnde. **~ly** *adv*

at·test /ə'test/ *vt/i* **1** 证[證]明 zhèngmíng: *His wealth* ~*s his ability.* 他的财富证明了他的才干. **2** 宣誓 xuānshì.

at·tic /'ætɪk/ *n* [C] 顶楼[樓] dǐnglóu; 阁[閣]楼[樓] gélóu.

at·ti·tude /'ætɪtju:d/ *n* [C] **1** 态[態]度 tàidù; 看法 kànfǎ. **2** 姿势[勢] zīshì; 姿态 zītài: *in a threatening* ~ 威胁的姿态.

at·tor·ney /ə'tɜ:nɪ/ *n* [C] [*pl* ~s] 律师[師] lǜshī.

at·tract /ə'trækt/ *vt* **1** 吸引 xīnyǐn: *A magnet* ~*s steel.* 磁石吸引钢. **2** 引起兴[興]趣、注意等 yǐnqǐ xìngqù zhùyì děng; 招引 zhāoyǐn: *Lights* ~ *moths.* 光亮招引蛾子. **3** 诱惑 yòuhuò; 有吸引力 yǒu xīnyǐnlì: **at'traction** /-ʃn/ *n* **(a)** [U] 吸引 xīyǐn; 吸引力 xīyǐnlì. **(b)** [C] 吸引人的事物 xīyǐn rén de shìwù: *the attractions of a big city* 大城市吸引人的地方. **~ive** *adj* 有吸引力的 yǒu xī yǐnlì de, 讨人喜欢[歡]的 tǎo rén xǐhuān de.

at·tribute /ə'trɪbju:t/ *vt* 归[歸]因于 guīyīnyú: ~ *his success to hard work.* 他的成功是因为勤奋. □ /'ætrɪbju:t/ *n* [C] **1** 属[屬]性 shǔxìng; 性质[質] xìngzhì. **2** 象征[徵] xiàngzhēng; 标[標]志 biāozhì.

auber·gine /'əʊbəʒi:n/ *n* [C] 茄子 qiézi.
auburn /'ɔ:bən/ *adj* 赭色的 zhěsède.
auc·tion /'ɔ:kʃn/ *n* [C, U] 拍卖〔賣〕pāimài. □ *vt* 拍卖 pāimài. **~eer** /-'nɪə(r)/ *n* [C] 拍卖人 pāimàirén.
aud·acious /ɔ:'deɪʃəs/ *adj* 大胆〔膽〕的 dàdǎnde; 鲁莽的 lǔmǎngde. **~ly** *adv*
aud·ac·ity /ɔ:'dæsətɪ/ *n* [U] 大胆〔膽〕dàdǎn; 鲁莽 lǔmǎng; 无〔無〕礼〔禮〕wúlǐ.
aud·ible /'ɔ:dəbl/ *adj* 听〔聽〕得见的 tīng dé jiàn de. **aud·ibly** *adv*
audi·ence /'ɔ:dɪəns/ *n* [C] **1** (聚集在一起的)听〔聽〕众〔衆〕tīngzhòng. **2** (分散的)听众 tīngzhòng; 读〔讀〕者 dúzhě: *The programme has a large ~.* 这个节目听众很多. **3** 接见 jiējiàn: *The Pope granted an ~.* 教皇答应接见.
audio- /,ɔ:dɪəʊ/ (*prefix*) 听〔聽〕觉〔覺〕的 tīngjuéde **~-'typ·ist** *n* 听音打字员 tīngyīn dǎzìyuán **~-'visual** *adj* 听觉视觉的 tīngjué shìjuéde: *~ visual teaching aid.* 直观教具 zhí guān jiàojù
audit /'ɔ:dɪt/ *n* [C] 审〔審〕计 shěnjì; 查账〔賬〕cházhàng. □ *vt* 查账 cházhàng. **~or** *n* [C] 查账人 cházhàngrén.
aud·ition /ɔ:'dɪʃn/ *n* [C] 试听〔聽〕shìtīng; 试演 shìyǎn. □ *vt* 试听 shìtīng; 试演 shìyǎn.
audi·tor·ium /,ɔ:dɪ'tɔ:rɪəm/ *n* [C] [*pl* ~s] 会〔會〕堂 huìtáng, 礼〔禮〕堂 lǐtáng.
Aug. = August.
aug·ment /ɔ:g'ment/ *vt/i* [正式用语] 增大 zēngdà; 增加 zēngjiā.
august /ɔ:'gʌst/ *adj* 尊严〔嚴〕的 zūnyánde.
August /'ɔ:gəst/ *n* 八月 bāyuè.
aunt /ɑ:nt/ *n* [C] 姑母 gūmǔ; 姨母 yímǔ; 伯母 bómǔ; 叔母 shūmǔ; 舅母 jiùmǔ. **~ie** *n* [非正式用语] *aunt* 的昵称 *aunt* de nìchēng.
au pair /,əʊ'peə(r)/ *adj* (英国)国外来的姑娘帮助料理家务〔務〕换取食宿的 guó wài lái de gūniang bāngzhù liàolǐ jiāwù huànqǔ shí sù de
aus·pices /'ɔ:spɪsɪz/ *n pl* 赞助 zànzhù. ***under the ~ of*** 在…的赞助下 zài ... de zànzhùxià
aus·pi·cious /ɔ:'spɪʃəs/ *adj* 吉祥的 jíxiángde; 繁荣〔榮〕的 fánróngde. **~ly** *adv*
aus·tere /ɔ:'stɪə(r)/ *adj* **1** 严〔嚴〕峻的 yánjùnde; 严格的 yángéde. **2** 简〔簡〕朴〔樸〕的 jiǎnpǔde. **~ly** *adv* **aus·ter·ity** /ɔ:'sterətɪ/ *n* [U]
auth·en·tic /ɔ:'θentɪk/ *adj* 真实〔實〕的 zhēnshíde; 可靠的 kěkàode. **~ally** *adv* **~ate** *vt* 证〔證〕实〔實〕zhèngshí; 鉴〔鑒〕定 jiàndìng. **~a·tion** /ɔ:,θentɪ'keɪʃn/ *n* [U] 证明 zhèngmíng. **~ity** /,ɔ:θen'tɪsətɪ/ *n* [U] 可靠性 kěkàoxìng; 真实性 zhēnshíxìng.
author /'ɔ:θə(r) / *n* [C] **1** 作者 zuòzhě; 作家 zuòjiā. **2** 创〔創〕始人 chuàngshǐrén. **~ess** *n* [C] 女作者 nǚ zuòzhě; 女作家 nǚ zuòjiā. **~-ship** *n* [U] 书〔書〕籍作者(为谁) shūjí zuòzhě.
auth·ori·tat·ive /ɔ:'θɒrɪtətɪv/ *adj* **1** 有权〔權〕威的 yǒu quánwēi de. **2** 命令的 mìnglìngde: *in an ~ manner* 以命令的方式. **3** 可靠的 kěkàode: *an ~ report* 可靠的报告. **~ly** *adv*
auth·or·ity /ɔ:'θɒrətɪ/ *n* [*pl* -ies] **1** [U] 权力 quánlì; 威信 wēixìn. **2** [C] 当〔當〕局 dāngjú. **3** [C] 权〔權〕威 quánwēi; 专〔專〕家 zhuānjiā; 权威著作 quánwēi zhùzuò.
auth·or·ize /'ɔ:θəraɪz/ *vt* 授权〔權〕shòuquán. **,A~d 'Version** (略作 **AV**) 钦定本英译圣经〔經〕(1611 年初版) qīndìngběn yīngyì shèngjīng. **auth·or·i'zation** *n* [U]
auto·bi·ogra·phy /,ɔ:təbaɪ'ɒgrəfɪ/ *n* [*pl* -ies] **1** [C] 自传〔傳〕zìzhuàn. **2** [U] 自传写〔寫〕作 zìzhuàn xiězuò; 自传文学〔學〕zìzhuàn wénxué. **auto·bio·graphic(al)** /'-græfɪk(əl)/ *adj*
auto·crat /'ɔ:təkræt/ *n* [C] **1** 专〔專〕制君主 zhuānzhì jūnzhǔ. **2** 独〔獨〕裁者 dúcáizhě. **~ic** /,ɔ:tə'krætɪk/ *adj*
auto·graph /'ɔ:təgrɑ:f/ *n* [C] 手迹 shǒujì: 亲〔親〕笔〔筆〕签〔簽〕名 qīnbǐ qiānmíng. □ *vt* 签署 qiānshǔ.
auto·mate /'ɔ:təmeɪt/ *vt* 自动〔動〕化 zìdònghuà.
auto·matic /,ɔ:tə'mætɪk/ *adj* **1** 自动〔動〕的 zìdòngde. **2** 无〔無〕意识〔識〕的 wú yìshí de. □ *n* [C] 小型自动武器 xiǎoxíng zìdòng wǔqì. **~ally** *adv* **~'pilot** *n* (略作 'autopilot) (航空)自动驾〔駕〕驶〔駛〕仪〔儀〕zìdòng jiàshǐyí.
auto·ma·tion /,ɔ:tə'meɪʃn/ *n* [U] 自动〔動〕化 zìdònghuà; 自动操作 zìdòng cāozuò.
auto·mo·bile /'ɔ:təməbi:l/ *n* [C] 汽车〔車〕qìchē.
auton·omous /ɔ:'tɒnəməs/ *adj* 自治的 zìzhìde; 自主的 zìzhǔde. **auton·omy** /ɔ:'tɒnəmɪ/ *n* [C, U] 自治 zìzhì; 自治权〔權〕zìzhìquán.
au·topsy /'ɔ:tɒpsɪ/ *n* [C] [*pl* -ies]

(医学)尸体〔體〕检〔檢〕验〔驗〕shītǐ jiǎnyàn.

autumn /'ɔ:təm/ *n* [C] 秋季 qiūjì; 秋天 qiūtiān. ~**al** /ˌɔ:'tʌmnəl/ *adj* 秋季的 qiūjìde.

aux·ili·ary /ɔ:g'zɪlɪərɪ/ *adj* 辅〔輔〕助的 fǔzhùde; 协〔協〕助的 xiézhùde.

avail /ə'veɪl/ *vt*/*i* 有益于 yǒuyìyú, 有用 yǒuyòng. ~ ***oneself of*** [正式用语]利用 lìyòng. □ *n* 用处〔處〕yòngchù; 利益 lìyì. ***of no (little)*** ~ 无〔無〕用 wúyòng. ***to no*** ~ 完全无〔無〕用 wánquán wúyòng.

avail·able /ə'veɪləbl/ *adj* 可获〔獲〕得的 kě huòdé de; 可用的 kěyòng de: *There are no tickets* ~. 没有票了. **avail·a'bil·ity** *n* [U]

ava·lanche /'ævəlɑ:nʃ/ *n* [C] **1** 雪崩 xuěbēng. **2** 大量涌来 dàliàng yǒnglái: *an* ~ *of letters* 大量信件涌来.

av·ar·ice /'ævərɪs/ *n* [U] [通常用字]贪心 tānxīn. **av·a'r·icious** *adj* [正式用语]贪心的 tānxīnde, 贪婪的 tánlánde.

Ave. = avenue.

avenge /ə'vendʒ/ *vt* 替…报〔報〕仇 tì...bàochóu: ~ *an insult* 雪耻

av·enue /'ævənju:/ *n* [C] **1** 林荫〔蔭〕道 línyīndào. **2** [喻]方法 fāngfǎ; 途径 tújìng: ~*s to success* 成功之路.

av·er·age /'ævərɪdʒ/ *n* [C] **1** 平均数〔數〕píngjūnshù. **2** 一般水准〔準〕yìbān shuǐzhǔn. □ *adj* **1** 平均的 píngjūnde. *The* ~ *age of the boys is fifteen.* 男孩子的平均年龄是十五岁. **2** 一般的 yìbānde, 平常的 píngchángde. □ *vt*/*i* **1** 平均 píngjūn. **2** 平均做 píngjūnzuò; 平均分配 píngjūn fēnpèi: ~ *200 miles a day* 平均一天 200 英里.

aver·sion /ə'vɜ:ʃn/ *n* **1** [C, U] 嫌恶〔惡〕xiánwù. **2** [C] 讨厌〔厭〕的人或事物 tǎoyànde rén huò shìwù.

avert /ə'vɜ:t/ *vt* [正式用语] **1** 避开〔開〕bìkāi. **2** 防止 fángzhǐ: ~ *disaster* 防止灾难.

avi·ary /'eɪvɪərɪ/ *n* [C] [*pl* -ies] 鸟〔鳥〕舍 niǎoshè.

avi·ation /ˌeɪvɪ'eɪʃn/ *n* [U] 航空 hángkōng; 航空学〔學〕hángkōngxué; 航空术〔術〕hángkōngshù.

avid /'ævɪd/ *adj* [正式用语]渴望的 kěwàngde ~**ly** *adv*

avo·cado /ˌævə'kɑ:dəʊ/ *n* [C] [*pl* ~s] 鳄梨 èlí.

avoid /ə'vɔɪd/ *vt* 避免 bìmiǎn; 逃避 táobì: ~ *danger* 避免危险. ~**able** *adj* 可避免的 kě bìmiǎn de. ~**ance** *n* [U]

avoir·du·pois /'ævədə'pɔɪz/ *n* [U] 英国常衡制 yīngguó chánghéngzhì.

await /ə'weɪt/ *vt* 等待 děngdài, 等候 děnghòu.

awake[1] /ə'weɪk/ *vi* [*pt, pp* awoke /ə'wəʊk/] = wake.

awake[2] /ə'weɪk/ *adj* 醒着的 xǐngzhede; 醒来的 xǐngláide. ~ ***to*** 注意到 zhùyìdào; 意识〔識〕到 yìshìdào.

awaken /ə'weɪkən/ *vt* = wake.

awaken·ing /ə'weɪknɪŋ/ *n* [C] 觉〔覺〕悟 juéwù; 明白 míngbai.

award /ə'wɔ:d/ *vt* 授予 shòuyǔ; 判给 pàngěi: ~ *first prize* 授予一等奖. □ *n* [C] **1** 判决 pànjué. **2** 奖〔獎〕jiǎng, 奖品 jiǎngpǐn.

aware /ə'weə(r)/ *adj* 知道的 zhīdàode 意识〔識〕的 yìshìde. ~ ***of (that)*** 意识到 yìshìdào; 认〔認〕识到 rènshìdào. ~**ness** *n* [U]

away /ə'weɪ/ *adv* **1** 在远〔遠〕处〔處〕zài yuǎnchù; 到远处 dào yuǎnchù: *The sea is two miles* ~. 海有两英里远. **2** 继〔繼〕续〔續〕不断〔斷〕地 jìxù búduàn de: *He was working* ~. 他在继续不断地工作. **3** (表示消失,减少): *The water has boiled* ~. 水被煮掉了. **4** ***right*** (或 ***straight***) ~ 立刻 lìkè, 马〔馬〕上 mǎshàng.

awe /ɔ:/ *n* [U] 敬畏 jìngwèi. '~-**inspiring** *adj* 令人畏惧〔懼〕的 lìngrén wèijù de. '~·**some** *adj* 可畏的 kěwèide.

aw·ful /'ɔ:fl/ *adj* **1** 可怕的 kěpàde: *an* ~ *death* 死得可怕. **2** [非正式用语]糟糕的 zāogāode; 极〔極〕度的 jídùde. ~**ly** *adv* 非常 fēicháng: ~ *hot* 非常热.

awhile /ə'waɪl/ *adv* 片刻 piànkè.

awk·ward /'ɔ:kwəd/ *adj* **1** 难使用的 nán shǐyòng de 不方便的 bù fāngbiàn de. ***an*** ~***customer*** 难〔難〕对〔對〕付的家伙 nánduìfù de jiāhuo. **2** 笨拙的bènchuóde; 不灵〔靈〕活的 bù líng huó de. **3** 尴〔尷〕尬的 gāngàde; 为〔爲〕难的 wéinánde: *an* ~ *silence* 尴尬的沉默. ~**ly** *adv* ~**ness** *n* [U]

awoke ⇨ awake.

axe /æks/ *n* [C] [*pl* ~s /'æksɪz/] 斧 fǔ. ,***have an*** '~ ***to grind*** 别有用心 bié yǒu yòngxīn; 另有企图〔圖〕lìng yǒu qǐtú. □ *vt* 削减 xiāojiǎn; 解雇 jiěgù.

ax·iom /'æksɪəm/ *n* [C] 公理 gōnglǐ. ~'**matic** *adj* 不言自喻的 bù yán zì yù de.

axis /'æksɪs/ *n* [C] [*pl* axes /'æksi:z/] **1** 轴〔軸〕zhóu: *the earth's ~* 地轴. **2** 轴心 zhóuxīn.

axle /'æksl/ *n* [C] 轮〔輪〕轴〔軸〕lúnzhóu.

ay, aye /aɪ/ *int, adv* 〔苏格兰地方语〕是 shì. ☐ *n* 赞成票 zànchéngpiào.

B b

B, b /bi:/ (*pl* B's, b's /bi:z/) 英语的第二个字母 yīngyǔde dìergè zìmǔ.

b = born 出生 chūshēng.

B.A. = Bachelor of Art 文学〔學〕士 wénxuéshì.

babble /'bæbl/ *vt/i* 孩子般喋喋不休 háizibān diédié bù xiū. ☐ *n* [U] 说无〔無〕意义〔義〕的话 shuō wú yìyì de huà. 说话模糊不清 shuōhuà móhú bùqīng.

babe /beɪb/ *n* [C] 〔书面语〕婴儿〔兒〕yīng'ér.

ba·boon /bə'bu:n/ *n* [C] 狒狒 fèifèi.

baby /'beɪbɪ/ *n* [C] [*pl* -bies] **1** 婴儿〔兒〕yīng'ér. **2** 〔俚语〕爱〔愛〕人 àirén. **'~·ish** 幼儿〔兒〕般的 yòu'ér bān de; 孩子气〔氣〕的 háiziqìde. **'~-sit·ter** 临〔臨〕时〔時〕保姆 línshí bǎomǔ. **~sit** *vi* [-tt-]

bach·elor /'bætʃələ(r)/ *n* [C] **1** 单〔單〕身汉〔漢〕dānshēnhàn. ⇨ spinster. **2** 学〔學〕士 xuéshì. *B~ of Arts (Science)* 文(理)学士 wénxuéshì.

back¹ /bæk/ *adv* **1** 向后〔後〕xiàng hòu; 在后面 zài hòumiàn: *Stand ~, please!* 请往后站 qǐng wǎng hòu zhàn. *go ~ on one's word* 食言 shíyán; 违〔違〕约 wéiyuē. **2** 返回 fǎnhuí: *Throw the ball ~ to me.* 把球扔回给我. **3** 回答 huídá; 作为〔爲〕报〔報〕复〔復〕zuòwéi bàofù: *hit her ~* 向她反击. ***have*** (或 ***get***) ***one's 'own ~*** (***on sb***) 〔非正式用语〕报复某人 bàofù mǒurén. **4** 以往 yǐwǎng, 过〔過〕去 guòqù: *a few years ~* 几年以前.

back² /bæk/ *n* [C] **1** 背 bèi. ***do (say) sth behind sb's ~*** 搞小动〔動〕作(背着某人说闲话) gǎo xiǎo dòngzuò. ***get off sb's ~*** 不再嘲笑某人 bùzài cháoxiào mǒurén. ***put one's ~ into sth*** 发〔發〕奋〔奮〕做某事 fāfèn zuò mǒushì, 埋头〔頭〕做某事 máitóu zuò mǒushì. ***put*** (或 ***get***) ***sb's ~ up*** 使某人生气〔氣〕shǐ mǒurén shēngqì. ***turn one's ~ on sb*** 不顾〔顧〕búgù, 不理睬 bù lǐcǎi. **2** 动〔動〕物的背脊 dòngwùde bèijǐ. **3** 椅背 yǐbèi. **4** 后〔後〕面 hòumiàn: *the ~ of the house* 房子后面. **'~ache** 背痛 bèitòng. **'~bite** *vt/i* 背后说人坏〔壞〕话 bèihuò shuō rén huàihuà. **'~bone,** **(a)** 脊椎骨 jǐzhuīgǔ. **(b)** 〔喻〕刚强 gāngqiáng, 坚〔堅〕毅 jiānyì. **'~-breaking** *adj* 累死人的 lèisǐrénde. **,~'date** *vt* 回溯 huísù. **,~'fire** *n* [U] 逆火 nìhuǒ. ☐ *vi* **(a)** 发〔發〕生逆火的响〔響〕声〔聲〕fāshēngnìhuǒde xiǎngshēng. **(b)** 〔喻〕失败 shībài: *His plan ~fired.* 他的计划失败了. **'~ground (a)** 背景 bèijǐng; 后〔後〕景 hòujǐng. **(b)** 有关〔關〕情况 yǒuguān qíngkuàng, 背景 bèijǐng: *the political ~ground* 政治背景. **(c)** 个人经〔經〕历〔歷〕gèrén jīnglì. **'~hand** (网球等)反手击〔擊〕球 fǎnshǒu jīqiú. **,~hand-ed,** *adj* 〔喻〕讽〔諷〕刺挖苦的 fěngcìwākǔde. **'~ing** *n* **(a)** 支援 zhīyuán, 支持 zhīchí. **(b)** 衬垫〔墊〕物 chèndiànwù. **'~lash** 〔喻〕强烈的反应〔應〕qiángliède fǎnyìng. **'~log** 积〔積〕压〔壓〕的工作 jīyāde gōngzuò. **'~num·ber** 过〔過〕期报〔報〕纸等 guòqī bàozhǐ děng. **,~'side** 〔非正式用语〕屁股 pìgǔ. **,~'stage** 后台 huòtái. **'~stroke** 仰泳 yǎngyǒng. **'~water (a)** 死水 sǐshuǐ. 滞水 zhìshuǐ **(b)** 〔喻〕死气〔氣〕沉沉的地方 sǐqì chéngchéng de dìfang.

back³ /bæk/ *vt/i* **1** 倒退 dàotuì; 使退后〔後〕shǐ tuìhòu: *~ a car* (汽车)倒车. **2** 支持 zhīchí, 援助 yuánzhù. ***~ sb up*** 支持某人 zhīchímǒurén, 为〔爲〕某人撑腰 wèimǒurén chēngyāo. **3** 下赌注于 xiàdǔzhù yú. **4** ***~ down (from)*** 放弃〔棄〕要求 fàngqì yāoqiú. ***~ out (of)*** 收回(诺言等) shōuhuí. **5** 加于背面 jiāyú bèimiàn: *~ed with iron* 背面包上铁. **6** 位于…的背后 wèiyú…de bèihòu: *Their house ~s on to our garden.* 他们的房子在我们花园的背后. **~er (a)** (赛马)下赌注的人 xià dǔzhù de rén. **(b)** 支持者 zhīchízhě.

back·gam·mon /bæk'gæmən/ *n* [U] 十五子游戏〔戲〕shíwǔzǐ yóuxì.

back·ward /'bækwəd/ *adj* **1** 向后

〔後〕的 xiànghòude. **2** 落后的 luòhòude: *a ~ child* 成长迟缓的孩子. **3** 迟〔遲〕疑的 chíyíde, 畏缩的 wèisuōde. **back·ward(s)** *adv* **(a)** 向后地 xiànghòude: *He looked ~s.* 他朝后看. **(b)** 倒 dào; 反 fǎn: *say the alphabet ~(s)* 倒背字母表. ***know sth ~s*** 极〔極〕其熟悉某事 jíqí shúxī mǒushì.

bacon /'beɪkən/ *n* [U] 咸〔鹹〕肉 xiánròu.

bac·terium /bæk'tɪərɪəm/ *n* [C] [*pl* -ria /-rɪə/] 细菌 xìjūn. **bac·terial** /-rɪəl/ *adj* 细菌的 xìjūnde.

bad[1] /bæd/ *adj* [worse, worst] **1** 坏〔壞〕的 huàide; 不道德的 bú dàodéde. **2** 使人不愉快的 shǐ rén bù yúkuài de: *~ news* 不好的消息. **3** 严〔嚴〕重的 yánzhòngde; 厉〔厲〕害的 lìhaide: *a ~ mistake* 严重的错误. **4** 低劣的 dīliède. ***be in a ,~'way*** 病情严重 bìngqíng yánzhòng. ***not (so) ~*** [非正式用语]不坏 búhuài, 不错 búcuò. **5** 变〔變〕坏的 biànhuàide, 腐坏的 fǔhuàide: *~ eggs* 坏了的蛋. ***go ~*** 坏了 huàile, 不能吃了 bù néng chī le. **6** *~ for* 有害于 yǒuhàiyú; 不适〔適〕于 búshìyú: *Smoking is ~ for the health.* 吸烟对健康有害. **7** 有病的 yǒubìngde: *a ~ finger* 疼痛的手指. **8** [非正式用语]不幸 búxìng: *It's too ~ she's ill.* 太不幸, 她病了. **9** [非正式用语]抱歉 bàoqiàn: *I feel so ~ about that.* 对此我很为抱歉. **~ debt** 坏账〔賬〕huàizhàng, 倒账 dǎozhàng. **~ly** *adv* [worse, worst] **(a)** 很坏 hěnhuài; 恶〔惡〕劣 èliè: *~ly made* 做得很坏. **(b)** 大大地 dàdàde: *~ly defeated* 大败. **(c)** 非常地 fēichángde: *want it ~ly* 非常需要它. **(d)** *~ly off* 穷的 qióngde. **~ness** *n* [U]

bad[2] /bæd/ *n* [U] 坏 huài.

bade /bæd/ ⇨ bid.

badge /bædʒ/ *n* [C] 徽章 huīzhāng; 证〔證〕章 zhèngzhāng; 标〔標〕记 biāojì.

badger[1] /'bædʒə(r)/ *n* [C] 獾 huān.

badger[2] /'bædʒə(r)/ *vt* 烦扰〔擾〕fánrǎo, 使困扰 shǐ kùnrǎo.

bad·min·ton /'bædmɪntən/ *n* [U] 羽毛球 yǔmáoqiú.

baffle[1] /'bæfl/ *vt* 阻碍〔礙〕zǔ'ài; 使困惑 shǐ kùnhuò.

baffle[2] /'bæfl/ *n* [C] 挡〔擋〕板 dǎngbǎn.

bag[1] /bæg/ *n* [C] **1** 袋 dài, 包 bāo: *a 'hand~* 手提包 shǒutíbāo. ***let the cat out of the ~*** 透露秘密 tòulù mìmì. **2** *~s of* [俚语]许多 xǔduō: *~s of money* 许多钱

bag[2] /bæg/ *vt/i* [-gg-] **1** 装〔裝〕进〔進〕袋 zhuāngjìn dài. **2** 捕杀〔殺〕pǔshā: *~ a deer* 打到一只鹿. **3** 肥大地垂挂 féidàde chuíguà: *trousers that ~ at the knees* 肥大地垂挂在膝上的裤子.

bag·gage /'bægɪdʒ/ *n* [U] 行李 xíngli.

baggy /'bægɪ/ *adj* [-ier, -iest] 松〔鬆〕垂的 sōngchuíde: *~ trousers* 松垂的裤子.

bag·pipes /'bægpaɪps/ *n pl* 风〔風〕笛 fēngdí.

bail[1] /beɪl/ *n* [U] 保证〔證〕金 bǎozhèngjīn: *release on ~* 交保证金释放. □ *vt ~ sb out* 交保证金释放某人 jiāo bǎozhèngjīn shìfàng mǒurén.

bail[2] /beɪl/ *n* [C] (板球)柱门〔門〕上的横木 zhùmén shàng de héngmù.

bail[3] /beɪl/ *vt/i* 将〔將〕船内的水舀出 jiāng chuán nèi de shuǐ yǎochū. ***~ out*** ⇨ bale[2].

bail·iff /'beɪlɪf/ *n* [C] **1** 法警 fǎjǐng. **2** 地主代理人 dìzhǔ dàilǐrén.

bait /beɪt/ *n* [U] **1** 饵 ěr. **2** [喻]诱惑物 xiùhuòwù. □ *vt/i* **1** 装〔裝〕饵 zhuāng'ěr. **2** 辱骂〔罵〕rǔmà; 欺侮 qīwǔ.

bake /beɪk/ *vt/i* **1** 烤 kǎo, 烘 hōng, 焙 bèi. **2** 烧硬 shāoyìng, 烤硬 kǎoyìng. **'baking-powder** 焙粉(化学发松剂) bèifěn. **baker** 面〔麵〕包师〔師〕傅 miànbāo shīfù. **~ry** 面包房 miànbāofáng.

bal·ance[1] /'bæləns/ *n* **1** [C] 秤 chèng; 天平 tiānpíng. ***be*** (或 ***hang***) ***in the ~*** [喻]悬〔懸〕而未决 xuán ér wèi jué. **2** [U] 平衡 pínghéng: *keep (lose) one's ~* 保持(失却)平衡. **3** [U] 艺〔藝〕术〔術〕作品的和谐、协〔協〕调 yìshù zuòpǐn de héxié, xiétiáo. **4** 账目上的余〔餘〕额 zhàngmù shàng de yú'é. **5** 结欠 jiéqiàn. **'~-sheet** 资产〔產〕负债表 zīchǎn fùzhàibiǎo.

bal·ance[2] /'bæləns/ *vt/i* **1** 平衡 pínghéng, 均衡 jūnhéng. **2** 结算 jiésuàn, 相抵 xiāngdǐ. **3** 对〔對〕比 duìbǐ, 比较〔較〕bǐjiào.

bal·cony /'bælkənɪ/ *n* [C] [*pl* -ies] **1** 阳〔陽〕台〔臺〕yángtái. **2** (剧院)楼〔樓〕厅〔廳〕lóutīng.

bald /bɔːld/ *adj* [-er, -est] **1** 秃头〔頭〕的 tūtóude; 秃的 tūde; 无〔無〕毛的 wú máo de. **2** [喻]单〔單〕调的 dāndiàode; 简〔簡〕单的 jiǎndānde: *a ~ statement* 枯燥无味的陈述. **~ly** *adv* **~ness** *n* [U]

bale[1] /beɪl/ *n* [C] 包 bāo, 捆 kǔn. □ *vt* 打包 dǎbāo, 打捆 dǎkǔn.

bale[2]/beɪl/ *vt* ~ *out (of)* 飞〔飛〕机〔機〕出事时〔時〕跳伞 fēijī chūshì shí tiàosǎn.

ball[1] /bɔːl/ *n* [C] **1** 球 qiú; 球戏〔戲〕qiúxì: *cricket* ~ 板球. *be on the* ~ 提高警惕 tígāo jǐngtì. **2** 球状物 qiúzhuàngwù: *a* ~ *of wool* 一团毛线. **3** 球形突出部分 qiúxíng tūchū bùfen: *the* ~ *of the thumb* (姆指)球. **'~-point** 圆珠笔〔筆〕yuánzhūbǐ.

ball[2] /bɔːl/ *n* [C] 舞会〔會〕wǔhuì. **'~room** 舞厅〔廳〕wǔtīng.

bal·lad /'bæləd/ *n* [C] 民歌 míngē, 歌谣 gēyáo.

bal·last /'bæləst/ *n* [U] **1** 压〔壓〕舱〔艙〕物 yācāngwù. **2**(气球)沙囊 shānáng. □ *vt* 使稳定 shǐ wěndìng; 在…上放重物 zài...shàng fàng zhòngwù.

bal·ler·ina /ˌbælə'riːnə/ *n* [C] 芭蕾舞女演员 bāléiwǔ nǚ yǎnyuán.

bal·let /'bæleɪ/ *n* [C,U] **1** 芭蕾舞 bāléiwǔ. **2** 芭蕾舞演员 bāléiwǔ yǎnyuán.

bal·lis·tic /bə'lɪstɪk/ *adj* 弹〔彈〕道〔導〕(学)的 dàndàode. **bal·is·tics** *n* [U] 〔与单数动词连用〕弹道学 dàndàoxué.

bal·loon /bə'luːn/ *n* [C] 气〔氣〕球 qìqiú. □ *vi* 膨胀〔脹〕如气球 péngzhàng rú qìqiú. **~ist** 气球驾〔駕〕驶〔駛〕员 qìqiú jiàshǐyuán.

bal·lot/'bælət/ *n* **1** [C] 无〔無〕记名投票用纸 wú jìmíng tóupiào yòngzhǐ. **2** 票数〔數〕piàoshù. □ *vi* 投票 tóupiào. **'~-box** 票箱 piàoxiāng.

balm /bɑːm/ *n* [U] **1** 止痛香油 zhǐtòng xiāngyóu. **2** 〔喻〕安慰物 ānwèiwù. **balmy** *adj* [-ier, -iest] **(a)** 温和的 wēnhéde. **(b)** 疗〔療〕伤〔傷〕的 liáoshāngde.

balsa /'bɔːlsə/*n* [C,U] 热〔熱〕带美洲之一种轻〔輕〕质〔質〕木材 rèdài měizhōu zhī yìzhǒng qīngzhì mùcái.

bal·us·trade /ˌbælə'streɪd/ *n* [C]栏〔欄〕杆 lángān.

bam·boo /ˌbæm'buː/ *n* [U] 竹 zhú.

ban /bæn/ *vt* [-nn-] 禁止 jìnzhǐ. □ *n* [C] 禁令 jìnlìng.

ba·nal /bə'nɑːl/ *adj* 枯燥无〔無〕味的 kūzào wúwèide; 平庸的 píngyōngde: ~ *remarks* 枯燥无味的话, 陈词滥调.

ba·nana /bə'nɑːnə/ *n* [C] 香蕉 xiāngjiāo.

band /bænd/ *n* [C] **1** 带〔帶〕子 dàizi *a rubber* ~ 橡皮筋. **2** 条〔條〕饰 tiáoshì; 镶边〔邊〕xiāngbiān: *a white plate with a red* ~ *round the edge* 边上有一圈红色花边的白盘子. **3** (一)群 qún; (一)伙〔夥〕huǒ: *a* ~ *of robbers* 一伙强盗. **4** 乐〔樂〕队〔隊〕yuèduì, 乐团〔團〕yuètuán. **5** 〔无线电〕波段 pōduàn. □ *vt/i* **1** 加带于 jiā dài yú; 用带绑札〔紮〕yòng dài bǎngzhā. **2** 结伙 jiéhuǒ; 结合 jiéhé: ~ *together* 结合起来. **'~stand** 室外音乐〔樂〕台〔臺〕shìwài yīnyuètái. **'~wagon,** *jump on the* ~ 赶〔趕〕浪头〔頭〕gǎn làngtou.

ban·dage /'bændɪdʒ/ *n* [C] 绷带〔帶〕bēngdài. □ *vt* 上绷带shàng bēngdài.

ban·dit /'bændɪt/ *n* [C] 土匪 tǔfěi, 匪徒 fěitú.

bandy[1] /'bændɪ/ *adj* 膝外屈的 xī wài qū de.

bandy[2] /'bændɪ/ *vt* 来回掷〔擲〕球 láihuí zhìqiú; 争吵 zhēngchǎo; 互殴〔毆〕hù'ōu.

bang /bæŋ/ *n* [C] 猛击 měngjī; 砰砰的声〔聲〕音 pēngpēngde shēngyīn. □ *vt/i* 猛敲 měngqiāo; 砰然作声 pēngrán zuòshēng: ~ *at the door* 砰砰地用力敲门. *The door* ~*-ed shut.* 门砰地关上.

banger /'bæŋə(r)/ *n* **1** [C] 〔俚语〕香肠〔腸〕xiāngcháng. **2** 鞭炮 biānpào. **3** 破旧的汽车 pòjiùde qìchē.

bangle /'bæŋgl/ *n* [C] 手镯 shǒuzhuó; 脚镯 jiǎozhuó.

ban·ish /'bænɪʃ/ *vt* **1** 驱〔驅〕逐出境 qūzhú chūjìng, 放逐 fàngzhú. **2** 消除 xiāochú. **~ment** *n* [U]

ban·is·ter /'bænɪstə(r)/ *n* [C] 栏〔欄〕杆小柱 lángān xiǎozhù; 楼〔樓〕梯扶手 lóutī fúshǒu.

banjo /bæn'dʒəʊ/ *n* [C] [*pl* ~s 或 ~es] 班卓琴 bānzhuóqín.

bank[1] /bæŋk/ *n* [C] **1** 河岸 hé'àn, 河边〔邊〕hébiān. **2** 堤 tí; 斜坡 xiépō. **3 ('sand~)** 沙洲 shāzhōu, 浅〔淺〕滩〔灘〕qiǎntān. □ *vt/i* **1** 筑〔築〕堤 zhùdī; 堆积〔積〕duījī. ~ *up* **(a)** 筑堤 zhùdí; 堆积 duījī. **(b)** 封(炉,炉火) fēng. **2** 汽车或飞〔飛〕机〔機〕转〔轉〕弯〔彎〕时〔時〕倾斜行进〔進〕qìchē huò fēijī zhuǎnwān shí qīngxié xíngjìn.

bank[2] /bæŋk/ *n* [C] **1** 银行 yínháng. **2** 库 kù: *a 'blood-*~ 血库. □ *vt/i* **1** 把钱〔錢〕存入银行 bǎ qián cúnrù yínháng. **2** ~ *on* 指望 zhǐwàng; 信赖 xìnlài. **ˌ~'holiday** 星期日以外的银行休息日 xīngqīrì yǐwàide yínháng xiūxirì. **'~note** 钞票 chāopiào. **~er** 银行家 yínhángjiā. **~ing** 银行业〔業〕yínhángyè.

bank·rupt /'bæŋkrʌpt/ *adj*, *n* [C] [法律]破产〔產〕了的 pòchǎnlede; 破产者 pòchǎnzhě. □ *vt* 使破产 shǐ pòchǎn. **bank·rupcy** /'bæŋkrəpsɪ/ *n* [C, U]

ban·ner /'bænə(r)/ *n* [C] 旗 qí: *the~ of freedom* [喻]自由的旗帜.

banns /bænz/ *n pl* 教堂里〔裡〕的结婚预告 jiàotáng lǐde jiéhūn yùgào: *put up the ~* 公告某人即将与某人结婚.

ban·quet /'bæŋkwɪt/ *n* [C] 宴会〔會〕yànhuì. □ *vt/i* 举〔舉〕行,参〔參〕加宴会 jǔxíng, cānjiā yànhuì.

ban·tam /'bæntəm/ *n* [C] 矮脚鸡〔鷄〕ǎijiǎojī.

ban·ter /'bæntə(r)/ *vt/i* 开〔開〕玩笑 kāiwánxiào; 戏〔戲〕弄 xìnòng. □ *n* [U] 玩笑话 wánxiàohua.

bap·tism /'bæptɪzəm/ *n* 1 [C, U] 洗礼〔禮〕xǐlǐ. 2 *~ of fire* 第一次经〔經〕历〔歷〕战〔戰〕争 dìyīcì jīnglì zhànzhēng, 炮火的洗礼 pàohuǒde xǐlǐ. **bap·tize** /bæp'taɪz/ *vt* 给…施洗礼 gěi...shī xǐlǐ.

bar[1] /bɑ:(r)/ *n* [C] **1** 棍 gùn, 棒 bàng, 杆 gǎn. **2** 门〔門〕窗等的闩〔閂〕mén chuāng děng de shuān: *prison ~s* (牢房)铁窗. **3** 酒吧间〔間〕jiǔbājiān; 餐柜〔櫃〕cānguì. **4** [喻]障碍〔礙〕zhàng'ài; 障碍物 zhàng'àiwù: *Poor health is a ~ to success.* 不健康是成功的障碍. **5** 光、色等的带〔帶〕、条〔條〕guāng, sè děng de dài, tiáo. **6** [音乐]小节〔節〕xiǎojié; 节线〔綫〕jiéxiàn. **7** 河口的沙洲 hékǒude shāzhōu. **8** 法庭上的围〔圍〕栏〔欄〕fǎtíng shàng de wéilán. **the B~** 律师〔師〕的职〔職〕业〔業〕lǜshīde zhíyè. *be called to the ~* 成为〔爲〕律师 chéngwéi lǜshī '**~maid** 酒吧间〔間〕女招待员 jiǔbājiān nǚ zhāodàiyuán. '**~man** 酒吧间男招待员 jiǔbājiān nán zhāodàiyuán. '**~ten·der** 酒吧间招待员 jiǔbājiān zhāodàiyuán.

bar[2] /bɑ:(r)/ *vt* [-rr-] **1** 闩门 shuānmén. **2** 阻挡〔擋〕zǔdǎng: *~ the way* 挡路 dǎnglù. **3** 排斥 páichì; 不准 bùzhǔn: *~ from a competition* 不准参加比赛.

bar[3] /bɑ:(r)/, **bar·ring** /'bɑ:rɪŋ/ *prep* [非正式用语]除…chú.... *~none* 无〔無〕例外 wú lìwài. *~* **chart,~graph** *n* (亦作 **histogram**) 条〔條〕线〔綫〕图〔圖〕(一种统计表) tiáoxiàntú

barb /bɑ:b/ *n* [C] 倒钩 dàogōu, 倒刺 dàocì. **~ed** *adj* 装〔裝〕倒钩 zhuāng dàogōu: *~ed wire* 带刺铁丝网.

bar·bar·ian /bɑ:'beərɪən/ *adj*, *n* [C] 野蛮〔蠻〕的 yěmánde; 野蛮人 yěmánrén. **bar·baric** /bɑ:'bærɪk/ *adj* **(a)** 野蛮人的 yěmánrénde; 野蛮人似的 yěmánrénsìde. **(b)** 粗野的 cūyěde. **bar·bar·ity** /bɑ:'bærətɪ/ *n* [C, U] [*pl* -ies] 野蛮 yěmán, 残〔殘〕暴 cánbào.

bar·be·cue /'bɑ:bɪkju:/ *n* [C] **1** 烤肉架 kǎoròujià. **2** 烤肉野餐 kǎoròu yěcān. □ *vt* 烧烤 shāokǎo.

bar·ber /'bɑ:bə(r)/ *n* [C] 理发〔髮〕员 lǐfàyuán.

bar·bitu·rate /bɑ:'bɪtjʊrət/ *n* [C, U] [化学]巴比土酸盐〔鹽〕bābǐtǔ suānyán.

bard /bɑ:d/ *n* [C] [书面语]诗人 shīrén.

bare /beə(r)/ *adj* [-r, -st] **1** 裸露的 luǒlùde. *lay ~* 揭露 jiēlù, 暴露 bàolù. **2** 最起码〔碼〕的 zuì qǐmǎde: *the ~ necessities* 最起码的必需品. □ *vt* 揭露 jiēlù, 揭开〔開〕jiēkāi. '**~faced** 露骨的 lùgǔde; 公开〔開〕的 gōngkāide; 蛮〔蠻〕横的 mánhèngde: *a ~faced lie* 公然的谎话. '**~foot** *adv* 赤脚的 chìjiǎode. **~ly** *adv* 仅〔僅〕仅 jǐn jǐn; 勉强 miǎnqiáng. **~ness** *n* [U]

bar·gain /'bɑ:gɪn/ *n* [C] **1** 契约 qìyuē; 合同 hétong; 交易 jiāoyì. *into the ~* 另外 lìngwài; 另加 lìngjiā. **2** 劳〔勞〕资协〔協〕议〔議〕láozī xiéyì. **3** 便宜货 piányìhuò, 廉价〔價〕品 liánjiàpǐn. □ *vt/i* **1** 讲〔講〕价〔價〕钱〔錢〕jiǎngjiàqián. **2** *get more than you ~ for* [非正式用语] 没有想到结果如此之坏〔壞〕méiyǒu xiǎngdào jiéguǒ rúcǐ zhī huài.

barge[1] /bɑ:dʒ/ *n* [C] 驳〔駁〕船 bóchuán.

barge[2] /bɑ:dʒ/ *vi* [非正式用语] **1** *~ into* 闯〔闖〕入 chuǎngrù. **2** *~ in* (或 *into*) 粗暴地干扰〔擾〕cūbàode gānrǎo: *~ into a conversation* 打断别人的谈话.

bari·tone /'bærɪtəʊn/ *n* [C] 男中音 nánzhōngyīn.

bark[1] /bɑ:k/ *n* [U] 树〔樹〕皮 shùpí.

bark[2] /bɑ:k/ *n* [C, U] 犬吠 quǎnfèi. □ *vt/i* **1** 狗叫 gǒujiào. **2** 咆哮地说话 páoxiàode shuōhuà.

bar·ley /'bɑ:lɪ/ *n* [U] 大麦〔麥〕dàmài.

barn /bɑ:n/ *n* [C] 谷〔穀〕仓〔倉〕gǔcāng.

bar·nacle/ 'bɑ:nəkl/ *n* [C] 藤壶(附在岩石、船底上的甲壳动物) ténghú.

ba·rom·eter /bəˈrɒmɪtə(r)/ *n* [C] 气〔氣〕压〔壓〕计 qìyājì; 晴雨表 qíngyǔbiǎo. **baro·met·ric** /ˌbærəˈmetrɪk/ *adj*

bar·on /ˈbærən/ *n* [C] **1** 男爵 nánjué. **2** [美语]工业〔業〕巨子 gōngyè jùzǐ,大王 dàwáng. ~**ess** *n* [C] 男爵夫人 nánjué fūrén; 有男爵爵位的女人 yǒu nánjué juéwèi de nǚrén. ~**et** *n* [C] 从〔從〕男爵 cóngnánjué.

bar·rack /ˈbærək/ *vt/i* 嘲弄 cháonòng; 叫嚣 jiàoxiāo.

bar·racks /ˈbærəks/ *n pl* 营〔營〕房 yíngfáng.

bar·rage /ˈbærɑːʒ/ *n* [C] **1** 坝〔壩〕bà, 堰 yàn. ⇨ dam. **2** [军事]弹幕射击〔擊〕. dànmù shèjī.

bar·rel /ˈbærəl/ *n*[C] **1** 圆桶 yuántǒng; 一圆桶的量 yì yuántǒng de liàng. **2** 枪〔槍〕管 qiāngguǎn; 炮筒 pàotǒng. □ *vt* [-ll-] 把…装〔裝〕桶 bǎ...zhuāngtǒng. ˈ~-**organ** 手摇风〔風〕琴 shǒuyáofēngqín.

bar·ren /ˈbærən/ *adj* **1** 贫瘠的 pínjíde,不毛的 bùmáode; 不结果实〔實〕的bù jié guǒshí de, 不会生育的 búhuì shēngyù de. **2** [喻]无〔無〕益的 wúyìde; 无价〔價〕值的 wújiàzhí de; 无兴〔興〕趣的 wúxìngqùde: *a* ~ *discussion* 枯燥乏味的讨论.

bar·ri·cade /ˌbærɪˈkeɪd/ *n* [C] 路障 lùzhàng; 阻塞 zǔsè. □ *vt* 设路障 shèlùzhàng.

bar·rier /ˈbærɪə(r)/ *n* [C] **1** 障碍〔礙〕物 zhàng'àiwù; 栅栏〔欄〕 zhàlan **2** 界线〔綫〕 jièxiàn: *the* ˈ*sound*-~ 音障. **3** [喻]阻碍 zǔ'ài: *a* ~ *to progress* 对进步的障碍.

bar·ris·ter /ˈbærɪstə(r)/ *n* [C] 律师〔師〕[美语不用] lǜshī. ⇨ counsel (2).

bar·row /ˈbærəʊ/ *n* **1** = wheelbarrow. **2** 手推车〔車〕 shǒutuīchē.

Bart. = Baronet 从〔從〕男爵 cóngnánjué.

bar·ter /ˈbɑːtə(r)/ *vt/i* 货物交换 huòwù jiāohuàn. □ *n* [U] 交换货物 jiāohuàn huòwù; 易货贸易 yìhuò màoyì.

base[1] /beɪs/ *n* [C] **1** 基础〔礎〕jīchǔ, 根基 gēnjī. **2** 基地 jīdì, 根据〔據〕地 gēnjùdì. **3** [数学]底 dǐ; 基点〔點〕jīdiǎn. ~**less** *adj* 无〔無〕原无故的 wúyuánwúgùde: ~*less fears* 无原无故的恐惧.

base[2] /beɪs/ *vt* 设基地于 shè jīdì yú ~ **on** (或 **upon**) 把…基地设于 bǎ...jīdì shè yú

base[3] /beɪs/ *adj* 低劣的 dīliède. ~ **metal** 贱〔賤〕金属〔屬〕 jiàn jīnshǔ.

base·ball /ˈbeɪsbɔːl/ *n* [U] 棒球 bàngqiú.

base·ment /ˈbeɪsmənt/ *n* [C] 底层〔層〕dǐcéng, 地下室 dìxiàshì.

bash /bæʃ/ *vt* [非正式用语] 猛击 měngjī, 猛撞 měngzhuàng. □ *n* [C] 猛击 měngjī.

bash·ful /ˈbæʃfl/ *adj* [通常用语] 害羞的 hàixiūde; 忸怩的 niǔníde. ~**ly** *adv*

basic /ˈbeɪsɪk/ *adj* 基础〔礎〕的 jīchǔde, 基本的 jīběnde: ~ *vocabulary* 基本词汇. ~**ally**/-klɪ/ *adv* 基本地 jīběnde.

basil /ˈbæzl/ *n* [U] (植物)罗勒 luólè.

basin /ˈbeɪsn/ *n* [C] **1** 盆 pén; 一盆的容量 yìpénde róngliàng. ⇨ wash-basin. **2** 碗(盛粥等用) wǎn. **3** 水洼 shuǐwā; 水池 shuǐchí. **4** 流域 liúyù.

basis /ˈbeɪsɪs/ *n* [C] [*pl* bases /-siːz/] **1**混合物之最主要成分 hùnhéwù zhī zuìzhǔyào chéngfen. **2**[喻]基础〔礎〕jīchǔ: *arguments with a firm* ~ 有事实为基础的论说.

bask /bɑːsk/ *vi* **1** 取暖 qǔnuǎn: ~-*ing in the sun* 晒太阳(取暖). **2** [喻]感到舒服 gǎndào shūfu; 得乐〔樂〕趣 dé lèqù.

bas·ket /ˈbɑːskɪt/ *n* [C] 篮〔籃〕子 lánzi; 筐 kuāng: *a* ˈ*shopping* ~ 购物篮子.

bas·ket·ball /ˈbɑːskɪtbɔːl/ *n* [U] 篮〔籃〕球 lánqiú.

bass[1] /bæs/ *n* [C] [*pl*] 欧〔歐〕洲产〔產〕的鲈〔鱸〕鱼 ōuzhōu chǎn de lúyú.

bass[2] /beɪs/ *adj* 声〔聲〕音低沉的 shēngyīn dīchén de. □ *n* [C] 低音部 dīyīnbù.

bas·soon /bəˈsuːn/ *n* [C] 巴松管 bāsōngguǎn, 大管 dàguǎn, 低音管 dīyīnguǎn.

bas·tard /ˈbɑːstəd/ *n* [C] **1** 私生子 sīshēngzǐ. **2** ⚠ [粗俗语]杂〔雜〕种〔種〕(用于骂人) zázhǒng **3** ⚠ 不幸的人 búxìngde rén: *Poor* ~! 可怜的倒楣鬼! □ *adj* **1** 私生的 sīshēngde. **2** 假的 jiǎde.

baste /beɪst/ *vt* **1** 把油脂涂〔塗〕在烤肉上 bǎ yóuzhǐ tú zài kǎoròu shàng. **2** 用长针脚疏缝 yòng chángzhēnjiǎo shūfèng.

bas·tion /ˈbæstɪən/ *n* [C] **1** 棱堡 léngbǎo. **2** 堡垒 bǎolěi: *a* ~ *of free speech* 言论自由的堡垒.

bat[1] /bæt/ *n* [C] 蝙蝠 biānfú. *as blind as a* ~ 半瞎的 bànxiāde.

bat[2] /bæt/ *n* [C] 球棒 qiúbàng; 球

拍 qiúpāi. ***do sth off one's own*** ~ [喻]独[獨]立地做某事 dúlìde zuò mǒushì. □ *vt/i* [-tt-] 用球棒、球拍打球 yòngqiúbàng qiúpāi dǎqiú. **'bats·man** (板球)击球手 jīqiúshǒu.

bat³ /bæt/ *vt* [-tt-] 眨眼睛 zhǎ yǎnjīng ***not ~ an 'eyelid*** 处[處]之泰然 chù zhī tàirán.

batch /bætʃ/ *n* [C] 一批(人或物) yìpī.

bath /bɑ:θ/ *n* [*pl* ~s /bɑ:ðz/] **1** [C] 洗澡 xǐzǎo, 浴 yù. **2** [C] 洗缸 xǐgāng. **3** [*pl*] 公共浴室 gōnggòng yùshì, 澡堂 zǎotáng. **4** = bathtub. □ *vt/i* **1** 为[爲]...洗澡 wèi...xǐzǎo. **2** 洗澡 xǐzǎo. **'~-room** 浴室 yùshì **'~tub** 浴缸 yùgāng; 澡盆 zǎopén.

bathe /beɪð/ *vt/i* **1** 浸到水中 jìn dào shuǐzhōng. **2** 下海游泳 xià hǎi yóuyǒng. ⇨ also sunbathe. □ *n* 游泳 yóuyǒng. **bather** 洗澡的人 xǐzǎode rén. **bath·ing** *n* [U] 海中游泳 hǎizhōng yóuyǒng. **'bathing-costume** 女游泳衣 nǚ yóuyǒngyī.

bat·man /'bætmən/ *n* [C] [*pl* -men] (英国军事)勤务[務]兵 qínwùbīng.

baton /'bætən/ *n* [C] **1** 警棍 jǐnggùn. **2** (乐队指挥用) 指挥棒 zhǐhuībàng.

bat·tal·ion /bə'tælɪən/ *n* [C] 营[營] yíng.

bat·ten /'bætn/ *n* [C] **1** 板条[條] bǎntiáo. **2** 船上压[壓]条[條] chuán shàng yā tiáo; 板条 bǎntiáo. □ *vt* ***~ down*** 用压条压牢 yòng yātiáo yāláo.

bat·ter¹ /'bætə(r)/ *vt/i* 连[連]续[續]猛击[擊] liánxù měngjī; 打烂[爛] dǎlàn: *~ the door down* 把门击破. **'~ing ram** [军事]攻城槌 gōngchéngchuí.

bat·ter² /'bætə(r)/ *n* [U] 面[麵]粉, 鸡[鷄]蛋, 牛奶等调成的糊状[狀]物(用以做蛋糕) miànfěn, jīdàn, niúnǎi děng tiáochéng de húzhuàngwù.

bat·tery /'bætərɪ/ *n* [C] [*pl* -ies] **1** 电[電]池(组) diànchí. **2** 炮兵连[連] pàobīnglián. **3** (一)组 zǔ, (一)套 tào: *a ~ of lenses* 透镜组; *a ~ of tests* 一组测试. **4** 生蛋箱组 shēngdànxiāng zǔ: *~ hens* 生蛋母鸡.

battle /'bætl/ *n* **1** [C] 战[戰]役 zhànyì; 战斗[鬥] zhàndòu. **2** [C] [喻]斗争 dòuzhēng. □ *vi* 斗争 dòuzhēng; 战斗 zhàndòu: *battling against poverty* 向贫穷开战. **'~-field** 战场[場] zhànchǎng, 疆场 jiāngchǎng. **'~ship** 军[軍]舰[艦] jūnjiàn.

battle·ments /'bætlmənts/ *n pl* 城垛 chéngduǒ.

bauble /'bɔ:bl/ *n* [C] 小装[裝]饰品 xiǎo zhuāngshìpǐn.

bawl /bɔ:l/ *vt/i* 大喊 dàhǎn, 大叫 dàjiào: *~ for help* 大声求助.

bay¹ /beɪ/ *n* [C](亦作 *'~laurel*) 月桂树[樹] yuèguìshù.

bay² /beɪ/ *n* [C] 海湾[灣] hǎiwān; 湾 wān.

bay³ /beɪ/ *n* [C] **1** 柱间[間]部位 zhùjiān bùwèi. **2** 房间向外凸出部份 fángjiān xiàng wài tūchū bùfen; 壁凹 bì'āo. **3** 大学[學]中生病学生宿舍 dàxué zhōng shēngbìng xuéshēng sùshè: *the 'sick-~* 病房.

bay·onet /'beɪənɪt/ *n* [C] (枪上的)刺刀 cìdāo. □ *vt* 用刺刀刺杀[殺] yòng cìdāo cìshā.

ba·zaar /bə'zɑ:(r)/ *n* [C] **1** 廉价[價]商店 liánjià shāngdiàn. **2** 义卖[賣] yìmài. **3** (东方国家)市场[場] shìchǎng.

ba·zoo·ka /bə'zu:kə/ *n* [C] [*pl* ~s] 火箭筒 huǒjiàntǒng.

B.B.C. = British Broadcasting Corporation 英国[國]广[廣]播公司 yīngguó guǎngbō gōngsī.

B.C. 公元前 gōngyuán qián.

B.D. = Bachelor of Oivinity 神学[學]士 shénxuéshì.

be¹ /bi:/ *vi* [*pres tense* **am, is** *pl* **are;** *pt* **was, were;** *pres part* **being;** *pp* **been**] **1** (表示存在、等同、地点、时间): *There is a house.* 这是一所房子. *Tim is big.* 蒂姆个子高. *The books are on the table.* 书放在桌子上. *Today is Monday.* 今天是星期一 **2** (表示变化): *He wants to ~ a fireman.* 他想成为一名消防队员. **3** [特别是 *pp* **been**]: 去 qù, 到 dào: *He has been to Paris.* 他到过巴黎. ***for the time ~ing*** 暂[暫]时[時] zànshí, 眼下 yǎnxià. **the ... to-'be** 未来[來]的 wèiláide: *the ˌbride to-'be* 未来的新娘.

be² /bi:/ *aux* **1** [同现在分词连用, 构成各种进行时态]: *They are* (或 *were*) *reading.* 他们正在阅读. **2** [同过去分词连用构成被动式]: *He was killed.* 他被弄死了. **3** [同动词不定式连用] **(a)** 必须 bì xū: *You are to be congratulated.* 你该受到庆贺. **(b)** 打算 dǎsuàn: *They are to be married.* 他们打算结婚.

beach /bi:tʃ/ *n* [C] 海滩[灘] hǎitān; 湖滩 hútān; 河滩 hétān. □ *vt* 使(船)冲向岸滩 shǐ chōngxiàng àntān. **'~head** 滩头〔頭〕阵〔陣〕地 tāntóu zhèndì. **'~wear** 海滩装〔裝〕hǎitānzhuāng.

bea·con /'bi:kən/ *n* [C] 灯〔燈〕塔 dēngtǎ.

bead /bi:d/ *n* [C] **1** 念珠 niànzhū. **2** [*pl*] 珠子项链〔鏈〕zhūzi xiàngliàn. **3** 水珠 shuǐzhū: *~s of sweat* 汗珠.

beady /'bi:dɪ/ *adj* (眼睛)小而亮的 xiǎo ér liàng de.

beak /bi:k/ *n* [C] 鸟喙 niǎohuì.

beaker /'bi:kə(r)/ *n* [C] **1** 烧杯 shāobēi. **2** 大酒杯 dà jiǔbēi.

beam /bi:m/ *n* [C] **1** 梁 liáng; 桁条〔條〕héngtiáo. **2 (a)** 光束 guāngsù; 光柱 guāngzhù. **(b)** 飞〔飛〕机〔機〕导〔導〕航无〔無〕线〔綫〕电〔電〕射束 fēijī dǎoháng wúxiàndiàn shèsù. □ *vt/i* **1** 发〔發〕光 fāguāng; 发热〔熱〕fārè. **2** [喻]微笑 wēixiào. **3** 定向发出(无线电节目等) dìngxiàng fāchū.

bean /bi:n/ *n* [C] 豆 dòu: *'soya-~s* 大豆, *'coffee-~s* 咖啡豆. ***full of ~s*** 精神旺盛 jīngshén wàngshèng 兴〔興〕高彩烈 xìnggāo-cǎiliè. ***spill the ~s*** 说漏嘴 shuō lòuzuǐ, 不慎泄密 búshèn xièmì.

bear¹ /beə(r)/ *n* [C] **1** 熊 xióng. **2** 粗鲁的人 cūlǔde rén.

bear² /beə(r)/ *vt/i* [*pt* bore /bɔ:(r)/, *pp* borne /bɔ:n/] **1** 携带〔帶〕xiédài; 负荷 fùhé. **2** 有 yǒu; 显〔顯〕示 xiǎnshì: *~ the marks of blows* 有伤痕. **3** 怀〔懷〕有 huáiyǒu: *the love she bore him* 她对他的爱. **4** 承受 chéngshòu; 经〔經〕得起 jīngdeqǐ: *The ice is too thin to ~ your weight.* 这冰太薄承受不住你的重量. **5** 忍受 rěnshòu: *I can't ~ that man.* 那个人使我受不了. **6** 生育 shēngyù, 养〔養〕: yǎng *~ a child* 生孩子 (注:比较 *born*: *He was born in 1932.* 他生于1932年.) **7** 转〔轉〕: *~ (to the) right* 向右转. **8** *~* ***(sth or sb) out*** 证〔證〕实〔實〕zhèngshí. *~* ***up (against*** 或 ***under sth)*** 不失望 bù shīwàng, 不气〔氣〕馁 bú qìněi. *~* ***with (sb)*** 宽容 kuānróng; 耐心等待 nàixīn děngdài.

bear·able /'beərəbl/ *adj* 可以忍受的 kěyǐ rěnshòu de.

beard /bɪəd/ *n* [C] (下巴上的) 胡〔鬍〕须〔鬚〕húxū. **~ed** *adj* 有胡须的 yǒu húxū de.

bearer /'beərə(r)/ *n* [C] **1** 带〔帶〕信人 dài xìn rén. **2** 抬棺材的人 tái guāncai de rén. **3** 持票(支票、票据)人 chí piào rén.

bear·ing /'beərɪŋ/ *n* **1** [U] 举〔舉〕止 jǔzhǐ; 姿态〔態〕zītài. **2** [C, U] 关〔關〕系 guānxì; 联〔聯〕系 liánxì: *That has no ~ on the subject.* 那同本题没有关系. **3** [C] 方位 fāngwèi; 方向 fāngxiàng: *a 'compass ~* 罗〔羅〕盘〔盤〕方位. ***find one's ~s*** [喻]方向明 fāngxiàng míng, 信心足 xìnxīn zú. ***lose one's ~s*** [喻]迷失方向 míshī fāngxiàng, 不知所措 bù zhī suǒ cuò.

beast /bi:st/ *n* [C] **1** 四足兽〔獸〕sìzúshòu. **2** 凶暴而残〔殘〕忍的人 xiōngbào ér cánrěn de rén. **~ly** *adj* [非正式用语]令人厌〔厭〕恶〔惡〕的 lìngrén yànwù de: *What ~ly weather!* 讨厌的天气!

beat¹ /bi:t/ *n* [C] **1** (接连地)打 dǎ, 敲 qiāo; 敲打声〔聲〕qiāodǎshēng: *the ~ of a drum* 鼓声. **2** 节〔節〕拍 jiépāi, 拍子 pāizi. **3** 巡逻〔邏〕路线〔綫〕xúnluó lùxiàn.

beat² /bi:t/ *vt/i* [*pt* ~, *pp* ~en /'bi:tn/] **1** (接连地)打 dǎ, 击〔擊〕jī. *~* ***a retreat*** [喻]匆匆撤退 cōngcōng chètuì, 打退堂鼓 dǎ tuìtánggǔ. **2** 日晒〔曬〕rìshài, 雨打 yǔdǎ. **3** 搅〔攪〕拌 jiǎobàn: *~ eggs* 打鸡蛋. **4** 敲变〔變〕形 qiāo biànxíng: *~ something flat* 敲平. **5** 胜 shèng, 打败 dǎbài: *He ~ me at chess.* 下国际象棋,他赢了我. **6** (心脏等) 跳动〔動〕tiàodòng: *His heart was still ~ing.* 他的心脏还在跳动. *~* ***time*** (音乐)打拍子 dǎ pāizi. **7** *~* ***about the bush*** 旁敲侧击〔擊〕pángqiāo-cèjī. ***dead ~*** 疲倦极〔極〕了 píjuàn jíle. ***~it*** [俚语]走 zǒu, 滚 gǔn. **8** *~* ***down (on)*** (太阳)火辣辣地照射 huǒ làlà de zhàoshè: *The sun was ~ing down on our heads.* 太阳火辣辣地晒在我们头上. *~* ***sb*** (或 ***sth) off*** 击退 jītuì, 打退 dǎtuì. *~* ***sb up*** 打伤〔傷〕某人 dǎshāng mǒurén. **~en** *adj* 锤薄的 chuíbóde; 敲平的 qiāopíngde. ***go off the ~en track*** 不落俗套 bú luò sútào, 不走老路 bù zǒu lǎolù. ***keep to the ~en track*** 循规蹈矩 xúnguī-dǎojù. **~er** *n* [C] 拍打器 pāidǎqì; 搅拌器 jiǎobànqì. **~ing** *n* [C] 挨打 āidǎ; 失败 shībài, 溃败 kuìbài.

beau·ti·cian /bju:'tɪʃn/ *n* [C] 美容师〔師〕měiróngshī.

beau·ti·ful /'bju:tɪfl/ *adj* 美的 měide; 美好的 měihǎode, 优〔優〕美的 yōuměide. **~ly** *adv* **beau·tify** /'bju:tɪfaɪ/ *vt* [*pt, pp* -ied] 使美丽 shǐ měilì, 美化 měihuà; 化装〔裝〕huàzhuāng.

beauty /'bju:tɪ/ *n* [*pl* -ies] **1** [U] 美丽〔麗〕měilì, 美 měi. **2** [C] 美

人 měirén; 美好的事物 měihǎode shìwù. ~-**parlour** (或 **salon**) 美容院 měiróngyuàn.

bea·ver /ˈbi:və(r)/ *n* **1** [C] 河狸 hélí. **2** [U] 河狸皮毛 hélí pímáo.

be·came pt of become.

be·cause /bɪˈkɒz/ *conj* **1** 因为〔爲〕yīnwéi: *I did it ~ they asked me.* 我做了,因为他们要我做. **2** ~ *of* 因为 yīnwéi: *B~ of his bad leg, he couldn't walk fast.* 他因为腿坏了,走不快.

beckon /ˈbekən/ *vt/i* (用手势)招唤 zhāohuàn.

be·come /bɪˈkʌm/ *vt/i* [*pt* **became** /bɪˈkeɪm/; *pp* ~] **1** 成为〔爲〕chéngwéi; 变〔變〕得 biàndé: *He became a doctor.* 他成为一名医生. **2** ~ *of* (命运等)降临〔臨〕jiànglín; 使遭〔遭〕遇 shǐ zāoyù: *What's ~ of John?* 约翰情况怎样? **3** 适〔適〕合 shìhé; 同…相称〔稱〕tóng …xiāng chèn: *That hat ~s you.* 那顶帽子适合你戴. **be·com·ing** *adj* 好看的 hǎokànde; 引人注意的 yǐnrén zhùyì de; 相配的 xiāngpèide.

bed[1] /bed/ *n* [C] **1** 床 chuáng, 床铺 chuángpù: *go to ~* 睡觉去. **2** 底座 dǐzuò: *The machine stands on a ~ of concrete.* 机器安装在水泥底座上. **3** (海)底 dǐ; (河)床 chuáng; (湖)底 dǐ. **4** (花)坛〔壇〕tán. ˈ~-**clothes** *n pl* 床上用品 chuáng shàng yòngpǐn. ˈ~**pan** (病人在床上使用的)便盆 biànpén. ˈ~**ridden** *adj* 卧病的 wòbìngde, 久病不起的 jiǔbìngbùqǐde. ˈ~**room** 卧室 wòshì. ˌ~ˈ**sitting-room** [非正式用语 = ˌ~ˈ**sitter**, ˈ~-**sit**] 卧室兼起居室 wòshì jiān qǐjūshì. ˈ~**spread** 床罩 chuángzhào. ˈ~**stead** 床架 chuángjià.

bed[2] /bed/ *vt/i* [-dd-] **1** 栽 zāi, 种〔種〕zhòng: ~ *out plants* 栽种幼苗. **2** ~ *down* (为牲畜睡觉)铺草 pūcǎo, 睡觉〔覺〕shuìjiào.

bed·ding /ˈbedɪŋ/ *n* [U] **1** = bed-clothes. **2** (家畜用)垫〔墊〕草 diàncǎo.

be·dev·il /bɪˈdevl/ *vt* [-ll-] 使混乱〔亂〕shǐ hùnluàn; 折磨 zhémó: *Plans ~led by accidents.* 被事故打乱了的计划.

bed·lam /ˈbedləm/ *n* [C] 骚〔騷〕乱〔亂〕的情景 sāoluànde qíngjǐng.

be·drag·gled /bɪˈdrægld/ *adj* 拖湿〔濕〕tuōshī; 拖脏〔髒〕tuōzāng.

bee /bi:/ *n* [C] 蜜蜂 mìfēng. ***make a*** ˈ~-***line for*** 径〔徑〕直朝某地而去 jìngzhí cháo mǒudì ér qù. ˈ**hive** 蜂房 fēngfáng, 蜂箱 fēngxiāng.

beech /bi:tʃ/ *n* [C] 山毛榉〔櫸〕shānmáojǔ; [U] 山毛榉木料 shānmáojǔ mùliào.

beef /bi:f/ *n* [U] 牛肉 niúròu. □ *vi* [俚语]抱怨 bàoyuàn, 发〔發〕牢骚〔騷〕fā láosāo. ˈ~**steak** 牛排 niúpái. **beefy** *adj* 肌肉发〔發〕达〔達〕的 jīròu fādá de, 粗壮〔壯〕的 cūzhuàngde.

been ⇨ be[1].

beer /bɪə(r)/ *n* [U] 啤酒 píjiǔ. **beery** *adj* 啤酒似的 píjiǔ shì de; (人)带〔帶〕有啤酒味的 dàiyǒu píjiǔwèi de.

beet /bi:t/ *n* [C] 甜菜 tiáncài, 糖萝〔蘿〕卜〔蔔〕tángluóbo. ˈ~**root** 甜菜根 tiáncàigēn.

beetle /ˈbi:tl/ *n* [C] 甲虫〔蟲〕jiǎchóng.

be·fall /bɪˈfɔ:l/ *vt/i* [*pt* befell /bɪˈfel/; *pp* ~en] [书面语]临〔臨〕到…头〔頭〕上 líndào … tóu shàng, 发〔發〕生于 fāshēngyú.

be·fit /bɪˈfɪt/ *vt* [-tt-] 适〔適〕合 shìhé, 适〔適〕宜 shìyí. ~**ting** *adj* 适宜的 shìyíde.

be·fore /bɪˈfɔ:(r)/ *adv* (表示时间)以前 yǐqián: *I've seen that film ~.* 我以前看过那部电影 □ *conj* (时间)在…之前 zài … zhīqián: *Do it ~ you go.* 走以前就做. □ *prep* **1** (时间)在…之前 zài … zhīqián: *the day ~ yesterday* 前天. ~ ***long*** 不久 bù jiǔ. **2** (表示次序)在…之前 zài … zhīqián: *B comes ~ C.* B 在 C 之前

be·fore·hand /bɪˈfɔ:hænd/ *adv* 预先 yù xiān; 事先 shì xiān.

be·friend /bɪˈfrend/ *vt* 以朋友态〔態〕度对〔對〕待 yǐ péngyou tàidù duìdài

beg /beg/ *vt/i* (-gg-) **1** 乞讨(食物、钱〔錢〕等) qǐ tǎo, 靠乞讨生活 kào qǐ tǎo shēnghuó. **2** 请求 qǐng qiú, 恳〔懇〕求 kěn qiú. ***go ~ging*** (商品) 销路极〔極〕坏〔壞〕xiāo lù jí huài

be·gan ⇨ begin.

beg·gar /ˈbegə(r)/ *n* [C] 乞丐 qǐgài ~**ly** *adj* 赤贫的 chìpínde, 可鄙的 kě bǐ de

be·gin /bɪˈgɪn/ *vt/i* (*pt* began /bɪˈgæn/; *pp* begun /bɪˈgʌn/) (-nn-) 开〔開〕始 kāishǐ ***to ~ with*** 首先 shǒuxiān, 第一 dìyī. ~**ner** 初学〔學〕者 chūxuézhě, 生手 shēngshǒu. ~**ning** 开端 kāi duān, 开始 kāishǐ.

be·grudge /bɪˈgrʌdʒ/ *vt* 妒忌 dùjì: *We don't ~ your going to Italy.* 我们不妒忌你去意大利.

be·gun ⇨ begin.

be·half /bɪ'hɑːf/ *n* (用于 on ~ of, in ~ of 等习语中)利益 lìyì, 方面 fāngmiàn,支持 zhīchí. ***on ~ of*** 代表…dàibiǎo…为〔爲〕了…wèile…: *speak on his* ~ 代表他说话.

be·have /bɪ'heɪv/ *vi* **1** 举〔舉〕动〔動〕 jǔdòng; 表现 biǎoxiàn: *make your boy ~ (himself)* 让你的男孩子规矩一些. **2** 运〔運〕转〔轉〕 yùnzhuǎn, 开〔開〕动〔動〕 kāidòng.

be·hav·iour (美语 = **-ior**) /bɪ'heɪvɪə(r)/ *n* [U] 举〔舉〕止 jǔzhǐ, 行为〔爲〕 xíngwéi, (对人的) 态〔態〕度 tàidù.

be·head /bɪ'hed/ *vt* 斩〔斬〕首 zhǎnshǒu, 砍头〔頭〕 kǎntóu.

be·hind¹ /bɪ'haɪnd/ *adv, prep* **1** 在…的后〔後〕面 zài … de hòumiàn: *hide ~ the tree* 藏在树后面. **2** 不如 bù rú, 落后于 luò hòu yú: *~ other boys in his class* 不如他班上其他男孩子. **3** 留于身后 liú yú shēn hòu: *the storm left ruin ~ it.* 暴风雨过后留下一片疮痍满目. **4** 积〔積〕欠 jīqiàn: *~ with the rent* 积欠租金.

be·hind² /bɪ'haɪnd/ *n* [C] [非正式用语]屁股 pìgu.

be·hind·hand /bɪ'haɪndhænd/ *adj* 落后〔後〕的 luòhòude, 耽误了的 dānwùlede: *be ~ with the rent* 欠租.

beige /beɪʒ/ *n* [U] 灰棕色 huīzōngsè. □ *adj* 灰棕色的 huīzōngsède.

be·ing /'biːɪŋ/ *n* **1** [U] 存在 cúnzài, 生存 shēngcún. ***come into ~*** 形成 xíngchéng, 产〔產〕生 chǎnshēng. **2** [C] 人 rén.

be·lated /bɪ'leɪtd/ *adj* 来迟〔遲〕的 *a ~ apology* 为时已晚的道歉.

belch /beltʃ/ *vt/i* **1** 冒(烟、气) mào. **2** 打嗝 dǎgé; 打噎 dǎyē. □ *n* [C] 打嗝(声) dǎgé; 喷射 pēnshè.

bel·fry /'belfrɪ/ *n* [C] [*pl* -ies](教堂的)钟〔鐘〕楼〔樓〕 zhōnglóu, 钟塔 zhōngtǎ.

be·lief /bɪ'liːf/ *n* **1** [U] 信任 xìnrèn: *~ in his honesty* 信任他的诚实. **2** [C] 信仰 xìnyǎng: *religous ~s* 宗教信仰.

be·lieve /bɪ'liːv/ *vt/i* **1** 相信 xiāngxìn. **2** ~ ***in*** **(a)** 信任 xìnrèn, 信赖 xìnlài: *I ~ in that man.* 我信任那个人. **(b)** 相信 xiāngxìn: *~ in God* 相信上帝. **(c)** 相信…的益处〔處〕、价〔價〕值 xiāngxìn … de yìchù, jiàzhí: *He ~s in getting plenty of exercise.* 他相信多做运动必有益. **be·liever** *n* [C]

be·little /bɪ'lɪtl/ *vt* 轻〔輕〕视 qīngshì, 小看 xiǎokàn: *Don't ~ his work.* 别轻视他的工作.

bell /bel/ *n* [C] 钟〔鐘〕 zhōng, 铃 líng. ***ring a ~*** [非正式用语]使回忆 shǐ huíyì. **'~-push** 电〔電〕铃按钮 diànlíng ànniǔ.

bel·liger·ent /bɪ'lɪdʒərənt/ *adj, n* [C] 交战〔戰〕中的 jiāozhàn zhōng de; 好战的 hàozhànde.

bel·low /'beləʊ/ *vt/i* 吼叫 hǒujiào, 大声〔聲〕叫喊 dàshēng jiàohǎn.

bel·lows /'beləʊz/ *n pl* (亦作 *a pair of ~*)(手用)风〔風〕箱 fēng xiāng.

belly /'belɪ/ *n* [C] [*pl* -ies] **1** [非正式用语]=abdomen. **2** 胃 wèi: *have a ~ache* 胃痛. **3** 物件的凸部 wùjiànde tūbù. **'~-ache** [非正式用语]抱怨 bàoyuàn. **~ful** [非正式用语]饱量的 bǎoliàngde, 过〔過〕多的 guò duō de: *I've had a ~ful of your noise.* 我受不了你的吵闹.

be·long /bɪ'lɒŋ/ *vi* **1** ~ ***to*** **(a)** 属〔屬〕于 shǔyú: *These ~ to me.* 这些是我的. **(b)** 是…的一员 shì … de yìyuán: *~ to a club* 俱乐部的一个成员. **2** 应〔應〕该在 yīnggāi zài: *Does it ~ here?* 应该把它放在这里吗? **~ings** *n pl* 个〔個〕人所有物 gèrén suǒyǒuwù; 财物 cáiwù.

be·loved /bɪ'lʌvd/ *pp, adj* 被热〔熱〕爱〔愛〕的 bèirèài de □ *n* /bɪ'lʌvɪd/ [C] 被热爱的人 bèi rèài de rén.

be·low /bɪ'ləʊ/ *adv* **1** 在…下面 zài … xiàmian: *We saw the ocean ~* 我们看见下面的海洋. *~ sixty (years of age)* 不到六十岁; ~ £20 二十英镑以下. **2** 在下文 zài xiàwén. **3** 在…的下游 zài … de xiàyóu: *a few yards ~ the bridge* 桥的下游几码处. ***hit ~ the belt*** 用不正当〔當〕手段打人 yòng bú zhèngdāng shǒuduàn dǎrén. 暗箭伤〔傷〕人 ànjiàn shāng rén.

belt /belt/ *n* [C] **1** 腰带〔帶〕 yāodài. **2** 机〔機〕器皮带〔帶〕 jīqì pídài: *a 'fan-~* 风扇皮带. **3** 地带 dìdài; 区〔區〕 qū. ⇨ green ~. □ *vt* **1** 用带缚住 yòng dài fùzhù. **2** [非正式用语]用拳头〔頭〕打 yòng quántou dǎ. **3** [非正式用语] 快速移动〔動〕kuàisù yídòng: *~ing along the road* 在路上快速行驶. **~ing** *n* 用皮带抽打 yòng pídài chōudǎ: *give him a good ~ing* 用皮带狠狠抽他一顿.

be·moan /bɪ'məʊn/ *vt* 悲叹〔嘆〕 bēitàn: *~ his fate* 悲叹他的苦命.

bench /bentʃ/ *n* [C] **1** 长〔長〕凳 chángdèng. **2** (木工等的) 工作台〔臺〕 gōngzuòtái. **3 the B~** 法官席 fǎguānxí; 法官 (总称) fǎguān; 法院 fǎyuàn.

bend /bend/ *n* [C] **1** 弯〔彎〕wān; 弯曲处〔處〕wānqūchù: *a ~ in the road* 马路上拐弯的地方. ***round the ~*** 〔俚语〕疯〔瘋〕狂的 fēngkuángde, 发〔發〕疯的 fāfēngde. **2** ***the ~s*** 〔非正式用语〕潜水员病（潜水员过快地浮到水面引起的疼痛）qiánshuǐyuánbìng. □ *vt/i* [*pt, pp* bent /bent/] **1** 使弯曲 shǐ wānqū: *~ the wire back* 把金属线弯回来. **2** 弯曲 wānqū; 弯腰 wānyāo: *~ down and touch your toes* 弯下腰来，用手碰到脚尖. **3** ***be bent on*** 专〔專〕心致志于 zhuānxīn zhìzhìyú: *~ on learning English* 专心学习英语.

be·neath /bɪ'ni:θ/ *prep, adv* **1** 在下面 zài xiàmiàn. **2** 不值得 bù zhídé: *~ contempt* 卑鄙到极点 bēibǐ dào jídiǎn.

ben·edic·tion /ˌbenɪ'dɪkʃn/ *n* [C] 祝福 zhù fú,（牧师施予的）祝福 zhùfú.

ben·efac·tion /ˌbenɪ'fækʃn/ *n* **1** [U] 做好事 zuò hǎoshì. **2** [C] 善行 shànxíng; 捐助物 juānzhùwù. **ben·efac·tor** /'benɪfæktə(r)/ *n* [C] 捐助人 juānzhùrén, 恩人 ēnrén. **ben·efac·tress** *n* [C] 女捐助人 nǚ juānzhùrén 女恩人 nǚ ēnrén.

ben·efi·cial /ˌbenɪ'fɪʃl/ *adj* 有益的 yǒuyìde; 有利的 yǒulìde.

ben·efici·ary /ˌbenɪ'fɪʃərɪ/ *n* [C] [*pl* -ies] （遗嘱等的）受益人 shòuyìrén.

bene·fit /'benɪfɪt/ *n* **1** [U] 利益 lìyì, 好处〔處〕hǎochù; 帮〔幫〕助 bāngzhù. ***give sb the ~ of the doubt*** 在证〔證〕据〔據〕不足的情况下，假定某人是无〔無〕罪的 zài zhèngjù bùzú de qíngkuàng xià jiǎdìng mǒu rén shì wúzuìde, 对某人的嫌疑作善意的解〔解〕释 duì mǒurén de xiányí zuò shànyìde jiěshì. **2** [C] 恩惠 ēnhuì; 受益 shòuyì: *the ~s of education* 教育的效益. **3** [C] 津贴 jīntiē: *unemployment ~* 失业津贴. □ *vt/i* 有益于 yǒuyìyú.

ben·ev·ol·ence /bɪ'nevələns/ *n* [U] 仁慈 réncí. **ben·ev·ol·ent** *adj* 仁慈的 réncíde; 慈善的 císhànde.

be·nign /bɪ'naɪn/ *adj* **1** 慈祥的 cíxiángde 宽厚的 kuānhòude. **2**（指病）不危险〔險〕的 bùwēixiǎnde, 良性的 liángxìngde. ⇨ malignant (2).

bent[1] /bent/ *n* [C] 爱〔愛〕好 àihào, 癖好 pǐhào: *a ~ for music* 爱好音乐.

bent[2] *pt, pp* of bend[2].

be·queath /bɪ'kwi:ð/ *vt* 死后遗赠 sǐ hòu yízèng.

be·quest /bɪ'kwest/ *n* **1** [U] 遗赠 yízèng. **2** [C] 遗产〔產〕yíchǎn, 遗物 yíwù.

be·rate /bɪ'reɪt/ *vt* 严〔嚴〕责 yánzé; 骂〔罵〕mà.

be·reave /bɪ'ri:v/ *vt* [*pt, pp* bereft /bɪ'reft/ 或 bereaved] **1** 使失去 shǐ shīqù: *bereft of reason* 丧失理性，发疯. **2** 使失去亲〔親〕人 shǐ shīqù qīnrén: *the ~d husband* 丧失妻子的人. **~ment** *n* [C, U]

be·reft *pt, pp* of bereave.

be·ret /'bereɪ/ *n* [C] 贝雷帽（兵士带的扁平帽子）bèiléimào.

berry /'berɪ/ *n* [C] [*pl* -ies] **1** 浆果 jiāngguǒ: *'straw~* 草莓. **2** 咖啡豆 kāfēidòu.

ber·serk /bə'sɜ:k/ *adj* 狂暴的 kuángbàode. ***go ~*** 发〔發〕狂 fākuáng.

berth /bɜ:θ/ *n* [C] **1**（火车、船上的）卧铺〔舖〕wòpù. **2** 停泊地 tíngbódì, 锚位 máowèi. ***give sb a wide ~*** 远〔遠〕离〔離〕（躲开）某人 yuǎnlí mǒu rén. □ *vt/i* 使停泊 shǐ tíngbó.

be·set /bɪ'set/ *vt* [*pt, pp* ~] [-tt-] 包围〔圍〕bāowéi: *~ with difficulties.* 困难重重 kùnnan chóngchóng.

be·side /bɪ'saɪd/ *prep* **1** 在…旁边〔邊〕zài … pángbiān: *Sit ~ me.* 坐到我旁边来. **2** ***~ the point*** 离〔離〕题 lítí; 不中肯 bù zhòngkěn. **3** ***~ oneself*** 若狂 ruòkuáng; 发〔發〕狂 fākuáng.

be·sides /bɪ'saɪdz/ *adv* 而且 érqiě; 还〔還〕有 háiyǒu. □ *prep* 除…之外 chú … zhīwài.

be·siege /bɪ'si:dʒ/ *vt* **1** 包围〔圍〕bāowéi; 围攻 wéigōng. **2** ***~ with*** 拥〔擁〕在…周围 yōngzài … zhōuwéi.

be·spoke /bɪ'spəʊk/ *adj*（衣裳等）定做的 dìngzuòde.

best /best/ *adj* 最好的 zuìhǎode: *the ~* (= quickest) *way to Paris* 去巴黎最好（快）的走法. ⇨ good, better. □ *adv* 最好地 zuìhǎode: *He works ~ in the morning.* 他早晨工作得最好. ⇨ well, better. □ *pron* 最好的人 zuìhǎode rén; 最好的事物 zuìhǎode shìwù: *the ~ of friends* 最好的朋友. ***All the ~!***（分别时用语）一切顺利! yíqiè shùnlì! ***at its ~*** 处〔處〕在最好状〔狀〕态〔態〕chǔzài zuìhǎo zhuàngtài. ***do one's ~*** 尽〔盡〕最大努力 jìn zuìdà nǔlì. ***make the ~ of a bad***

job 尽力把损失减少到最小 jìnlì bǎ sǔnshī jiǎnshǎo dào zuìxiǎo. ,~-'**man** 男傧〔儐〕相 nán bīnxiàng. ,~'-**seller** 畅销书〔書〕chàngxiāoshū.

bes·tial /'bestɪəl/ *adj* 残〔殘〕忍的 cánrěnde, 野蛮〔蠻〕的 yěmánde. ~**ity** /-'ælətɪ/ *n* [U]

be·stow /bɪ'stəʊ/ *vt* 赠予 zèngyǔ; 给予 jǐyǔ: ~ *an honour on him* 给他以荣誉.

bet /bet/ *vt/i* [*pt, pp* ~ 或 ~ted] [-tt-] **1** (用钱)打赌 dǎdǔ. **2** [非正式用语]敢断〔斷〕定 gǎn duàndìng: *I ~ I win.* 我敢断定我会赢. □ *n* [C] 打赌 dǎdǔ; 赌注 dǔzhù: *make a ~* 打赌 dǎdǔ; *win (lose) a ~* 打赌赢(输)了 dǎdǔ yíngle. ~**ter**, ~ **tor**打赌者 dǎdǔzhě.

be·tray /bɪ'treɪ/ *vt* **1** 背叛 bèipàn, 出卖〔賣〕chūmài. **2** 泄漏(秘密等) xièlòu. **3** 暴露 bàolù; 表现 biǎoxiàn: *His face ~ed his guilt.* 他的表情显示他是有罪的. ~**al** *n* **(a)** [U] 背叛 bèipàn, 出卖 chūmài. **(b)** [C] 背叛的事例 bèipànde shìlì. ~**er** 背叛者 bèipànzhě.

be·trothed /bɪ'trəʊðd/ *adj, n* [U] [书面语]订了婚的 dìng le hūn de; 订婚者 dìnghūnzhě. **be·trothal** /-ðəl/ *n* 订婚 dìnghūn.

bet·ter /'betə(r)/ *adj* **1** 较〔較〕好的 jiàohǎode; 更好的 gènghǎode: *He's a ~ man than his brother.* 他是一个比他的兄弟更好的人. **2** (健康状况)好转〔轉〕的 hǎozhuǎngde: *He feels ~ today.* 他今天好些了. ⇨ good, best. □ *adv* **1** 更好地 gènghǎode: *You play tennis ~ than I do.* 你网球打得比我好. *be ~ off* 较富裕 jiào fùyù. *know ~ (than)* 很明白 (而不致于) hěn míngbai: *You know ~ than to go out with wet hair.* 你该明白, 不能湿着头发往外走的. **2** *had ~* 最好还〔還〕是 zuìhǎo háishì, 还是…的好 háishì … de hǎo: *You'd ~ not say that.* 你最好不说那话. ⇨ best, well. □ *n get the ~ of sb* 打败 dǎ bài; 智胜〔勝〕zhìshèng. □ *vt* 改善 gǎishàn, 超过〔過〕chāoguò: *She hopes to ~ herself* 她希望收入多一些.

be·tween /bɪ'twi:n/ *adv* (时间或位置的)中间〔間〕zhōngjiān; 当〔當〕中 dāngzhōng. *few and far ~* 稀少 xīshǎo; 罕见 hǎnjiàn. □ *prep* **1** (地点, 时间) 在…中间 zài … zhōngjiān: ~ *London and Oxford* 伦敦和牛津之间; ~ *the two world wars* 两次世界大战之间. **2** (距离、数量等)中间 zhōngjiān: ~ *five and six miles* 5英里到6英里之间. **3** 来回 lái huí: *This liner sails ~ Southampton and New York.* 这艘班轮来往于南安普敦与纽约之间. **4** 分 (两者之间) fēn: *Divide the money ~ you.* 你们两人分这笔钱.

bevel /'bevl/ *n* [C] 斜面 xiémiàn. □ *vt* [-ll- 美语 = -l-] 斜截 xiéjié.

bev·er·age /'bevərɪdʒ/ *n* [C] 饮料 (汽水、茶、酒等) yǐnliào.

bevy /'bevɪ/ *n* [C] [*pl* -ies] (妇女、鸟等)群 qún.

be·ware /bɪ'weə(r)/ *vt/i* 谨防 jǐnfáng, 当〔當〕心 dāngxīn: *B~ of the dog!* 当心狗!

be·wil·der /bɪ'wɪldə(r)/ *vt* 迷惑 míhuò, 弄糊涂〔塗〕nòng hútu; 为〔爲〕难〔難〕wéinán: *She was ~ed by the crowds.* 她被大群的人愣住了. ~**ing** *adj*

be·witch /bɪ'wɪtʃ/ *vt* **1** 施魔力于 shī mólì yú. **2** 使着迷 shǐ zháomí, 使心醉 shǐ xīnzuì. ~**ing** *adj*

be·yond[1] /bɪ'jɒnd/ *adv* 在远〔遠〕处〔處〕zài yuǎnchù; 更远地 gèngyuǎnde: *India and the lands ~* 印度和过去更远的一些地方. □ *prep* **1** 在, 向…的那边〔邊〕zài, xiàng … de nàbiān: *The house is ~ the bridge.* 房子在桥的那边. **2** 超出 chāochū: ~ *repair* 修不了; ~ *expectations* 出乎所料 chūhū suǒ liào: *It's quite ~ me.* 这我完全不懂. ~ *a joke* 玩笑开〔開〕得过〔過〕火 wánxiào kāi dé guòhuǒ.

bi- /,baɪ/ *prefix* **1** (一定时期内)两次 liǎngcì: *bi-monthly* 一月两次地. **2** 存续〔續〕二… cúnxù èr…; 每两…发〔發〕生一次 měi liǎng … fāshēng yícì. *bicentennial* 二百年的, 每二百年发生一次的. **3** 两的 liǎngde, 双的 shuāngde: *bilingual* 双语的 shuāngyǔde.

bias /'baɪəs/ *n* **1** [C][*pl* ~es] 偏见 piānjiàn; 嗜好 shìhuò: *He has a strong ~ against the plan.* 他非常反对这项计划. **2** [U] (统计)偏性piānxìng, 偏倚 piānyǐ. □ *vt*[*pt, pp* ~(s)ed] 以偏见影响〔響〕yǐ piānjiàn yǐngxiǎng.

bib /bɪb/ *n* [C] **1** (小孩的)围〔圍〕涎 wéixián. **2** 裙的上部 qúndeshàngbù.

Bible /'baɪbl/ *n* (基督教)圣〔聖〕经〔經〕shèngjīng. **bib·li·cal** /'bɪblɪkl/ *adj*

bib·li·ography /,bɪblɪ'ɒgrəfɪ/ *n* [C] [*pl* -ies] 书〔書〕目 shūmù; 文献〔獻〕目录〔録〕wénxiàn mùlù.

bib·li·ogra·pher 书籍(文献)目录的编者或研究者 shūjí, mùlùde biānzhě huò yánjiūzhě.

bi·cen·ten·ary /ˌbaɪˌsen'ti:nərɪ/ *n* [C] [*pl* -ies] 二百年纪念 èrbǎinián jìniàn.

bi·cen·ten·nial /ˌbaɪˌsen'tenɪəl/ *adj* 二百年纪念的 èrbǎinián jìniàn de: ~ *celebrations* 二百年纪念(活动) èrbǎinián jìniàn. □ *n* [C] 二百周年 èrbǎi zhōunián.

bi·ceps /'baɪseps/ *n* [C] [复数不变]二头[頭]肌 èrtóujī.

bicker /'bɪkə(r)/ *vi* 口角 kǒujiǎo, 争吵 zhēngchǎo.

bi·cycle /'baɪsɪkl/ *n* [C] 自行车 zìxíngchē, 单[單]车 dānchē. □ *vi* (常作 *cycle*) 骑[騎]自行车 qí zìxíngchē.

bid[1] /bɪd/ *n* [C] **1** (拍卖中的)出价[價] chūjià, 喊价 hǎnjià. **2** ***make a ~ for*** 以给些东[東]西的办[辦]法企图[圖]获[獲]得… yǐ gěi xiē dōngxi de bànfǎ qìtú huòdé …. □ *vt/i* [*pt, pp* ~] [-dd-] 出价 chūjià, 喊价 hǎnjià. **~ding** *n* [U] 拍卖[賣]时[時]的出价 pāimài shí de chūjià.

bid[2] /bɪd/ *vt/i* [*pt* bade /bæd/, *pp* ~den /'bɪdn/ 或 ~] [旧词] **1** 命令 mìnglìng; 吩咐 fēnfù. **2** 说 shuō: ~ *him good morning* 祝他早安.

bi·en·nial /baɪ'enɪəl/ *adj* 延续[續]两年的 yánxù liǎngnián de; 两年一次的 liǎngnián yícì de.

bier /bɪə(r)/ *n* [C] 棺材架 guāncaijià.

bi·focal /ˌbaɪ'fəʊkl/ *adj* (眼镜)双焦点[點]的 shuāng jiāodiǎn de. **bi·focals** *n pl* 双焦点眼镜 shuāng jiāodiǎn yǎnjìng.

big /bɪg/ *adj* [-ger, -gest] (opposite = *little*; ⇨ *large, small*) 大的 dàde, 重大的 zhòngdàde: ~ *feet* 大脚; *a ~ day* 重大的日子. **'~head** [非正式用语]自高自大的人 zìgāo zìdà de rén. **'~wig** [俚语]重要人物 zhòngyào rénwù; 名人 míngrén.

big·amy /'bɪgəmɪ/ *n* [U] 重婚罪 chónghūnzuì. **'big·am·ist** 重婚罪犯 chónghūn zuìfàn. **big·am·ous** *adj*

bigot /'bɪgət/ *n* [C] 执[執]拗的人 zhíniùde rén; 抱偏见的人 bào piānjiàn de rén. **~ed** *adj* 执拗的 zhíniùde; 心胸狭窄的 xīnxiōng xiázhǎi de.

bike /baɪk/ *n, vi* [bicycle, cycle 的非正式缩略语]自行车[車] zìxíngchē.

bi·kini /bɪ'ki:nɪ/ *n* [C] [*pl* ~s] 三点[點]式女游泳衣 sāndiǎnshì nǚ yóuyǒngyī.

bi·lat·eral/ˌbaɪ'lætərəl/ *adj* 双[雙]边[邊]的 shuāngbiānde: *a ~ agreement* 双边协定.

bile /baɪl/ *n* [U] 胆[膽]汁 dǎnzhī.

bilge /bɪldʒ/ *n* [U] **1** 船底 chuándǐ; (亦作 '*~-water*) 船底污水 chuándǐ wūshuǐ. **2** [俚语] 废[廢]话 fèihuà.

bi·lin·gual /ˌbaɪ'lɪŋgwəl/ *adj* **1** 说两种[種]语言的 shuō liǎngzhǒng yǔyán de. **2** 用两种语言写[寫]成的 yòng liǎngzhǒng yǔyán xiě chéng de.

bil·ious /'bɪlɪəs/ *adj* 恶[惡]心的 ěxīnde.

bill[1] /bɪl/ *n* [C] 鸟[鳥]嘴 niǎozuǐ.

bill[2] /bɪl/ *n* [C] **1** 账[賬]单[單] zhàngdān. **2** 招贴 zhāotiē; 广[廣]告 guǎnggào; 传[傳]单 chuándān. **3** [法律] 议[議]案 yì'àn; 法案 fǎ'àn. **4** [美语]钞票 chāopiào, 纸币[幣] zhǐbì. **5** 证[證]明书[書] zhèngmíngshū. □ *vt* **1** 宣布…扮演… xuānbù … bànyǎn …. **2** ~ ***sb for sth*** 为[爲]…向某人送账单 wèi … xiàng mǒuren sòng zhàngdān; 向某人收…钱[錢] xiàng mǒurén shōu … qián.

bil·let /'bɪlɪt/ *n* [C] (军营以外的)部队[隊]宿舍 bùduì sùshè. □ *vt* 安顿[頓]士兵在军营以外的地方住宿 āndùn shìbīng zài jūnyíng yǐwài de dìfang zhùsù.

bil·liards /'bɪlɪədz/ *n* [U] 台球游戏[戲] táiqiú yóuxì; 弹[彈]子游戏 dànzǐ yóuxì.

bil·lion /'bɪlɪən/ *n* [C] **1** [英国英语]万[萬]亿[億] wànyì. **2** [美语]十亿 shíyì.

bil·low /'bɪləʊ/ *n* [C] [喻]雾[霧]烟[煙]等波浪般滚滚向前的东[東]西 wù yān děng pōlàng bān gǔngǔn xiàngqián de dōngxi. □ *vi* 波浪般滚动[動] pōlàng bān gǔndòng. **bill·owy** *adj*

billy-goat /'bɪlɪ gəʊt/ *n* [C] 公山羊 gōng shānyáng.

bin /bɪn/ *n* [C] (贮藏食物、煤等的)箱子 xiāngzi: *a 'dust~* 垃圾箱 lājīxiāng.

bi·nary /'baɪnərɪ/ *adj* 二 èr, 双[雙] shuāng, 复[複] fù: *the ~ scale (system)* 二进制标[標]度 èrjìnzhì biāodù.

bind /baɪnd/ *vt/i* [*pt, pp* bound /baʊnd/] **1** 捆 kǔn, 绑 bǎng. **2** [喻]使结合 shǐ jiéhé: *bound by friendship* 由于友谊而结合. **3** 包扎[紮] bāo zhā; 裹围[圍] guǒwéi:

~ *up a wound* 包扎伤口. **4** 装〔裝〕订 zhuāngdīng: *a book bound in leather* 皮面精装的书. **5** 使受诺言、法律等约束 shǐ shòu nuòyán fǎlǜ děng yuēsù: ~ *him to secrecy* 使他答应保守秘密. **~er** 包扎者 bāozhāzhě; 装订工 zhuāngdīnggōng; 绳〔繩〕索 shéngsuǒ, 带〔帶〕子 dàizi. **~ery** 装订厂 zhuāngdīngchǎng. **~ing** 书籍封面 shūjí fēngmiàn.

bingo /'bɪŋgəʊ/ *n* [U] 一种〔種〕用纸牌搭成方块〔塊〕的赌博 yìzhǒng yòng zhǐpái dāchéng fāng kuài de dǔbó.

bin·ocu·lars /bɪ'nɒkjʊləz/ *n pl* (亦作 *a pair of* ~) (双筒)望远〔遠〕镜 wàngyuǎnjìng.

bio·chem·is·try /ˌbaɪəʊ'kemɪstrɪ/ *n* [U] 生物化学〔學〕shēngwù huàxué. **bio·chem·ist** *n* [C]

bio·de·grad·able/ˌbaɪəʊdi'greɪdəbl/ *adj* 生物可降解的 shēngwù kějiàngjiě de.

bi·ogra·phy /baɪ'ɒgrəfɪ/ *n* **1** [C] 传〔傳〕记 zhuànjì. **2** [U] 传记文学〔學〕zhuànjì wénxué. **bi·ogra·pher** *n* [C] 传记作家 zhuànjì zuòjiā. **bio·graphic(al),** /baɪəʊ'græfɪk(l)/ *adj*

bi·ol·ogy /baɪ'ɒlədʒɪ/ *n* [U] 生物学〔學〕 shēngwùxué; 生态〔態〕学 shēngtàixué. **bi·ol·ogist** *n* [U] 生物学家 shēngwùxuéjiā; 生物学者 shēngwùxuézhě. **bio·logi·cal** /ˌbaɪə'lɒdʒɪkl/ *adj* **bio·logi·cal'clock** *n* 生物钟〔鐘〕shēngwùzhōng. **biologi·cal'warfare** *n* 生物战〔戰〕shēngwùzhàn.

bi·on·ic /baɪ'ɒnɪk/ *adj* 仿生的 fǎngshēngde.

bi·on·ics /baɪ'ɒnɪks/ *n* 〔与单数动词连用〕仿生学〔學〕fǎngshēngxué.

bio·phys·ics /ˌbaɪəʊ'fɪzɪks/ *n* 〔与单数动词连用〕生物物理学〔學〕shēngwù wùlǐxué.

bio·sphere /'baɪəsfɪər/ *n* [C] 生命层〔層〕,生物圈(地球表面有生物生存部分) shēngmìngcéng, shēngwùquān.

bi·plane /'baɪpleɪn/ *n* [C] 双〔雙〕翼飞〔飛〕机〔機〕shuāngyì fēijī.

birch /bɜːtʃ/ *n* **1** [C] 桦〔樺〕huá; 白桦 báihuá. **2** [U] 桦木 huámù.

bird /bɜːd/ *n* [C] **1** 鸟〔鳥〕niǎo, 禽 qín. *kill two ~s with one stone* 一箭双〔雙〕雕〔鵰〕yíjiàn shuāngdiāo. **2** 〔俚语〕年轻〔輕〕姑娘 niánqīng gūniang.

biro /'baɪərəʊ/ *n* [C] [*pl* ~s] 圆珠笔〔筆〕yuánzhūbǐ.

birth /bɜːθ/ *n* **1** [C, U] 分娩 fēnmiǎn, 出生 chūshēng. *give ~ to* 分娩 fēnmiǎn. **2** [U] 出身 chūshēn; 血统 xuětǒng: *Russian by ~* 俄罗斯血统. '**~-control** 节〔節〕制生育 jiézhì shēngyù. '**~day** 生日 shēngrì. '**~rate** *n* 出生率(每年的千分比) chūshēnglǜ.

bis·cuit /'bɪskɪt/ *n* [C] 饼干〔乾〕bǐnggān.

bi·sect /ˌbaɪ'sekt/ *vt* 把…分为〔爲〕二 bǎ … fēn wéi èr.

bi·sex·ual /ˌbaɪ'sekʃʊəl/ *adj* 受到两性吸引的 shòudào liǎngxìng xīyǐn de. □ *n* [C] 受到两性吸引的人 shòudào liǎngxìng xīyǐn de rén. **bi·sex·ual·ity** /baɪˌseksjʊ'ælɪtɪ/ *n* [U]

bishop /'bɪʃəp/ *n* [C] **1** (基督教)主教 zhǔjiào. **2** (国际象棋中的)象 xiàng. **~ric** 主教职〔職〕位或管区〔區〕zhǔjiào zhíwèi huò guǎnqū.

bi·son /'baɪsn/ *n* [C] [*pl* 不变]欧〔歐〕洲野牛 ōuzhōu yěniú; 美洲水牛 měizhōu shuǐniú.

bit[1] /bɪt/ *n* [C] **1** 马〔馬〕嚼子 Mǎjiáozi. **2** 钻〔鑽〕头〔頭〕zuàntóu.

bit[2] /bɪt/ *n* [C] 一点〔點〕yìdiǎn; 一些 yìxiē; 小片 xiǎopiàn: *He ate every ~ of* (= all) *his dinner.* 他把饭吃得精光. *~ by ~* 一点一点地 yìdiǎn yìdiǎn de, 慢慢地 mànmànde, 渐〔漸〕渐地 jiànjiànde. *do one's ~* 尽〔盡〕自己的一份力量 jìn zìjǐde yífèn lìliàng. *not a ~* 一点也不 yìdiǎn yě bù, 毫不 háo bù.

bit[3] /bɪt/ *n* [C] (二进制数)位(有时译作"彼特") wèi.

bit /biːt/ *pt* of bite[2]

bitch/bɪtʃ/ *n* **1** 母狗 mǔgǒu. **2** 〔非正式用语〕坏〔壞〕女人 huàinǚrén.

bite[1] /baɪt/ *n* **1** [C] 咬 yǎo; 叮 dīng. **2** [C] 咬伤〔傷〕yǎoshāng. **3** [C] 咬下的一块〔塊〕yǎo xià de yíkuài. **4** [C] 鱼上钩 yú shànggōu.

bite[2] /baɪt/ *vt/i* [*pt* bit /bɪt/, *pp* bitten /'bɪtn/], **1** 咬 yǎo. *~ off more than one can chew* 贪多嚼不烂〔爛〕tān duō jiáo bù làn. **2** 刺 cì; 鱼上钩 yú shànggōu. **3** (被寒风等)刺痛 cìtòng: *His fingers were 'frost-bitten.* 他的手指被冻伤. **4** 紧〔緊〕握 jǐnwò, 抓紧 zhuājǐn: *The tyres did not ~ on the icy road.* 轮胎在结冰的路面上打滑. **bit·ing** *adj* 尖厉〔厲〕刺人的 jiānlì cìrén de: *a biting wind* 刺骨的风.

bit·ten /'bɪtn/ *pp* of bite[2].

bit·ter /'bɪtə(r)/ *adj* **1** 有苦味的 yǒu kǔwèi de. **2** 辛酸的 xīnsuānde; 痛苦的 tòngkǔde: ~ *disappointments* 令人难过的失望. **3** 怀〔懷〕恨的 huáihènde; 抱怨的 bàoyuànde: ~ *enemies* 死敌. **4** 严〔嚴〕寒的 yánhánde, 刺骨的 cìgǔde: *a ~ wind* 刺骨寒风. □ *n* [C, U] 苦啤酒 kǔpíjiǔ: *a pint of ~* 一品脱苦啤酒. **~ly** *adv*: *~ly cold* 苦寒, *~ly disappointed* 极为失望 jí wéi shīwàng. **~ness** *n* [U]

bitu·men /'bɪtʃʊmən/*n* [U] 沥〔瀝〕青 lìqīng.

biv·ouac /'bɪvʊæk/ *n* [C], *vi* [*pt, pp* ~ked] 露营〔營〕lùyíng.

bi·zarre /bɪ'zɑ:(r)/ *adj* 异〔異〕乎寻常的 yìhū xúncháng de, 稀奇古怪的 xīqí gǔguài de.

blab /blæb/ *vt/i* [-bb-] [俚语]泄露(秘密) xièlù.

black /blæk/ *adj* [-er, -est] **1** 黑的 hēide, 漆黑的 qīhēide. **2** 极〔極〕度的 jídùde: ~ *despair* 绝望; ~ *moods* 抑郁的心情. **3** 黑人的 hēirénde. □ *n* **1** [U] 黑色 hēisè. **2** [C] 黑人 hēirén. □ *vt* **1** 使黑 shǐ hēi, 弄黑 nònghēi. **2** 宣布不干〔幹〕工作, 不处〔處〕理物资 xuānbù bú gàn gōngzuò, bú chùlǐ wùzī: *The strikers ~ed the cargo.* 罢工工人宣布拒绝装卸货物. **'~berry** 黑莓 hēiméi. **'~bird** 乌〔烏〕鸫〔鶇〕wūdōng. **'~board** 黑板 hēibǎn. **~'box** *n* [非正式用语]黑盒子(飞机上的飞行情况记录装置) hēihézi. **'~cur·rant** 黑醋栗 hēicùlì. **,~'eye** 被打得发〔發〕青的眼圈 bèi dǎdé fāqīng de yǎnquān. **'~head** 黑头〔頭〕粉刺 hēitóu fěncì. **~'hole** *n* (天文)黑洞 hēidòng. **,~'ice** 马〔馬〕路上察觉〔覺〕不出的冰 mǎlù shàng chájué bùchū de bīng. **'~leg** *n* [C] 罢工中擅自上工的人 bàgōng zhōng shànzì shànggōng de rén. □ *vt/i* [-gg-] 罢工中擅自上工 bàgōng zhōng shànzì shànggōng. **'~list** *n* [C] 黑名单〔單〕hēi míngdān. □ *vt* 把某人列入黑名单 bǎ mǒurén lièrù hēi míngdān. **,~'magic** 妖术〔術〕yāoshù; 巫术 wūshù. **'~mail** *vt, n* [U] 敲诈 qiāozhà, 勒索 lēsuǒ. **'~mailer** 敲诈勒索者 qiāozhà lēsuǒ zhě. **,~'market** 黑市 hēishì. **'~out** *n* [C] **(a)** (战时)灯〔燈〕火管制 dēnghuǒ guǎnzhì. **(b)** 临〔臨〕时记忆〔憶〕缺失 línshí jìyì quēshī; 临时眩晕 línshí xuànyūn. **(c)** (因供电问题引起的) 灯火熄灭〔滅〕dēnghuǒ xīmiè. □ *vt/i* 灯火熄灭 dēnghuǒ xīmiè; 施行灯火管制 shīxíng dēnghuǒ guǎnzhì; 临时记忆缺失 línshí jìyì quēshī. **,~'sheep** 败家子 bàijiāzǐ. **'~smith** 铁匠 tiějiàng.

blacken /'blækən/ *vt/i* **1** 使变〔變〕黑 shǐ biànhēi. **2** 诽谤 fěibàng.

blad·der /'blædə(r)/ *n* [C] **1** 膀胱 pángguāng. **2** 囊状〔狀〕物 nángzhuàngwù.

blade /bleɪd/ *n* [C] **1** 刀刃 dāorèn, 刀口 dāokǒu. **2** 桨〔槳〕片 jiǎngpiàn, 螺旋桨桨片 luóxuánjiǎng jiǎngpiàn. **3** 草片 cǎopiàn.

blame /bleɪm/ *vt* 责备〔備〕zébèi; 找…的差错 zhǎo ... de chācuò. □ *n* [U] 责任 zérèn. **~less** *adj* 无〔無〕可责难〔難〕的 wúkě zénàn de, 无过〔過〕错的 wú guòcuò de. **~worthy** /'bleɪmwɜ:ðɪ/ *adj* 该受责备的 gāi shòu zébèi de.

blanc·mange /blə'mɒnʒ/ *n* [U] 牛奶冻 niúnǎidòng.

bland /blænd/ *adj* **1** 温和的 wēnhéde, 和蔼的 hé'ǎide. **2** 刺激性少的 cìjīxìng shǎo de. **~ly** *adv* **~ness** *n* [U]

blank /blæŋk/ *adj* **1** (纸)没有写〔寫〕字的 méiyǒu xiězì de, 白的 báide. **2** (表格等)空白的 kòngbáide. **3** 失色的 shīsède; 没有表情的 méiyǒu biǎoqíng de: *a ~ look* 茫然若失的样子: *My mind went ~.* 我心情空虚. □ *n* [C] **1** 空白 kòngbái. **2** 空虚 kōngxū. **3** 空弹〔彈〕kōngdàn. ***draw a ~*** 终于失败 zhōngyú shībài. **~ cheque** 开〔開〕支票人已签〔簽〕字, 由收款人自填款数〔數〕的支票 kāi zhīpiào rén yǐ qiānzì yóu shōukuǎnrén zì tián kuǎnshù de zhīpiào. **~ verse** 无〔無〕韵诗 wúyùnshī. **~ly** *adv*

blan·ket /'blæŋkɪt/ *n* [C] **1** 床单〔單〕chuángdān. **2** 〔喻〕厚的覆盖物 hòude fùgàiwù: *a ~ of snow* 一层雪 □ *vt* 覆盖 fùgài: *houses ~ed with snow* 盖着雪的屋子.

blare /bleə(r)/ *n* [U] (喇叭的)嘟嘟声〔聲〕dūdū shēng. □ *vt/i* (喇叭)嘟嘟响〔響〕dūdūxiǎng.

blas·pheme /blæs'fi:m/ *vt/i* 亵渎 xièdú. **blas·phemer** 渎神者 dúshénzhě. **blas·phem·ous** /'blæsfəməs/ *adj* **blas·phemy** /'blæsfəmɪ/ *n* [C, U]

blast /blɑ:st/ *n* [C] **1** 一阵〔陣〕(风) yízhèn. **2** 爆炸气〔氣〕浪 bàozhà qìlàng. **3** 管乐〔樂〕器的声〔聲〕音 guǎnyuèqìde shēngyīn. ***at full ~*** 全力地 quánlìde. □ *vt* **1** (用炸药)炸 zhà. **2** 摧毁 cuīhuǐ, 毁灭〔滅〕huǐmiè: *His hopes were ~ed.* 他的希望破灭了. **3** *~ off* (宇宙飞船等)发〔發〕射 fāshè. **'~-furnace** 鼓风炉〔爐〕gǔfēnglú; 高

炉 gāolú.

bla·tant /'bleɪtnt/ *adj* 厚颜的 hòuyánde; 炫耀的 xuànyàode, 显〔顯〕眼的 xiǎnyǎnde: ~ *rudeness to one's parents* 用不知羞耻的粗暴态度对待父母. ~**ly** *adv*

blaze[1] /bleɪz/ *n* [C] **1** 火焰 huǒyàn; 火 huǒ. **2** 光辉〔輝〕 guānghuī, 光彩 guāngcǎi: *The tulips made a ~ of colour.* 郁金香光彩夺目. **3** 爆发〔發〕 bàofā: *in a ~ of anger* 大发雷霆.

blaze[2] /bleɪz/ *vt/i* **1** 熊熊燃烧 xióngxióng ránshāo. **2** 闪〔閃〕耀 shǎnyào, 发〔發〕光彩 fā guāngcǎi: *Her eyes ~d.* 她的眼睛放射着光芒. **3** (感情) 激发 jīfā: *blazing with anger* 发怒 fānù. **blaz·ing** *adj*

blazer /'bleɪzə(r)/ *n* [C] 运〔運〕动〔動〕茄克 yùndòng jiākè.

bldg(s). = building(s)

bleach /bli:tʃ/ *n* [U] 漂白剂〔劑〕 piǎobáijì. □ *vt/i* 漂白 piǎobái. bones ~ed by the sun 白骨 báigǔ.

bleak /bli:k/ *adj* [-er, -est] **1** (天气)阴〔陰〕冷的 yīnlěngde; 光秃秃的 guāngtūtūde, 无〔無〕遮盖的 wú zhēgài de. **2** [喻]凄凉的 qīliángde; 暗淡的 àndànde: *The future looks ~* 前途看来是暗淡的. ~**ly** *adv*

bleary /ˌblɪə'ri:/ *adj* (眼睛)疲倦疼痛的 píjuàn téngtòng de.

bleat /bli:t/ *vt/i, n* [C, U] (羊)叫 jiào.

bleed /bli:d/ *vt/i* [*pt, pp* bled /bled/] **1** 流血 liúxuě, 出血 chūxuě. **2** 悲痛 bēitòng, 同情 tóngqíng: *Our hearts ~ for them.* 我们同情他们.

blem·ish /ˈblemɪʃ/ *n* [C, U] 瑕疵 xiácī, 污点〔點〕 wūdiǎn. □ *vt* 损害…的完美 sǔnhài ... de wánměi; 玷污 diànwū.

blend /blend/ *vt/i* 混合 hǔnhé. 把…混成一体〔體〕 bǎ ... hǔnchéng yìtǐ. □ *n* [C] 混成品 hǔnchéngpǐn; 混合物 hǔnhéwù.

bless /bles/ *vt* [*pt, pp* ~ed /blest/] **1** 求上帝赐福于 qiú shàngdì cìfú yú. **2** 祝福 zhùfú. **3** 使神圣〔聖〕化 shǐ shénshènghuà: *bread ~ed at the altar* 奉献于祭坛的面包. ~-**ed** /'blesɪd/ *adj* **(a)** 神圣的 shénshèngde. **(b)** 幸运〔運〕的 xìngyùnde. 幸福的 xìngfúde.

bless·ing /'blesɪŋ/ *n* [C] **1** 上帝的赐福 shàngdìde cìfú. 感恩祷〔禱〕告 gǎn'ēn dǎogào. **2** 幸事 xìngshì, 喜事 xǐshì: *His help was a ~.* 幸好有他的帮助.

blew /blu:/ *pt* of blow[2].

blight /blaɪt/ *n* **1**[U] 植物凋枯病. zhíwù diāogūbìng. **2** [C] 挫折 cuōzhé, 打击〔擊〕 dǎjī. □ *vt* 挫折 cuōzhé, 损毁 sǔnhuǐ.

blind[1] /blaɪnd/ *adj* **1** 瞎的 xiāde, 盲的 mángde. **2** 不能识〔識〕别的 bùnéng shíbié de: ~ *to the faults of her children* 看不出她的孩子的毛病和缺点. *turn a ~ eye to* 装〔裝〕作看不见 zhuāngzuò kànbújiàn. **3** 轻〔輕〕率的 qīngshuàide: ~ *haste* 莽撞. **4** 无〔無〕目的的 wú mùdì de: *governed by ~ forces* 被盲目的势力所支配. ~ '**alley** **(a)** 死巷 sǐxiàng, 死胡同 sǐhútòng. **(b)** [喻]没有发〔發〕展前途的职〔職〕业 méiyǒu fāzhǎn qiántú de zhíyè. ˌ~ '**drunk** 醉得厉害的 zuìde lìhài de. '~ **spot** [喻] 不明了〔瞭〕、有偏见或不关〔關〕心的事物 bù míngliǎo, yǒu piānjiàn huò bùguānxīn de shìwù. ~**ly** *adv* ~**ness** *n* [U]

blind[2] /blaɪnd/ *vt* **1** 使失明 shǐ shīmíng. **2** [喻]使失去判断〔斷〕力 shǐ shīqù pànduànlì: ~*ed by love* 被爱情迷住了心窍.

blind[3] /blaɪnd/ *n* [C] **1** 窗帘 chuānglián. **2** [喻]障眼物 zhàngyǎnwù.

blind·fold /'blaɪndfəʊld/ *vt* 蒙住…的眼睛 méngzhù ... de yǎnjīng. □ *n* [C] 障眼的蒙布或带〔帶〕子 zhàngyǎnde méngbù huò dàizi. □ *adj* 眼睛被蒙住的 yǎnjīng bèi méngzhù de.

blink /blɪŋk/ *vt/i* 眨眼睛 zhǎ yǎnjīng. □ *n* [C] 眨眼睛 zhǎ yǎnjīng; 一瞥 yìpiě.

blink·ers /'blɪŋkəz/ *n pl* (马的)眼罩 yǎnzhào.

bliss /blɪs/ *n* [U] 巨大的幸福 jùdàde xìngfú, 福 fú. '~**ful** *adj* '~**fully** *adv*

blis·ter /'blɪstə(r)/ *n* [C] **1** 水疱 shuǐpào, 疱 pào. **2** (植物的)疱状〔狀〕突起 pàozhuàng tūqǐ. □ *vt/i* 使…起疱 shǐ ... qǐpào.

B. Litt = Bachelor of Letters 文科学〔學〕士 wénkē xuéshì.

blitz /blɪts/ *n* [C] 闪〔閃〕电〔電〕战〔戰〕 shǎndiànzhàn; 猛烈的空袭〔襲〕 měngliède kōngxí. □ *vt* 用闪电战攻击〔擊〕 yòng shǎndiànzhàn gōngjī.

bliz·zard /'blɪzəd/ *n* [C] 暴风〔風〕雪 bàofēngxué.

bloated /'bləʊtɪd/ *adj* **1** 肿〔腫〕胀〔脹〕的 zhǒngzhàngde: *his ~ stomach* 他的撑得鼓鼓的胃. **2** [喻] 得意忘形 déyìwàngxíng: ~ *with pride* 因荣誉而得意忘形.

blob /blɒb/ *n* [C] 一滴 yìdī, 一小团〔團〕yì xiǎo tuán.

bloc /blɒk/ *n* [C] 集团〔團〕jítuán.

block¹ /blɒk/ *n* [C] **1** 大块〔塊〕木料 dàkuài mùliào 大块石头〔頭〕dàkuài shítóu. **2** 一排房屋 yìpái fángwū, 街区〔區〕(四条街道当中的地区) jiēqū. *a ~ of flats* 一排公寓房子; 公寓大楼. **3** 事物的聚集 shìwùde jùjí: *a ~ of seats* 剧院内的座位划区; *a ~ of shares* 大宗股票. **4** 障碍〔礙〕物 zhàngàiwù, 阻碍 zǔ'ài: *a ~ in the pipe* 管子内的阻塞物. ⇨ road-block. ,~ 'letters 大写〔寫〕字母 dàxiě zìmǔ.

block² /blɒk/ *vt* **1** 阻碍 zǔ'ài, 阻塞 zǔsè: *roads ~ed by snow* 被雪阻塞的马路. **2** 破坏〔壞〕pòhuài: *~ the enemy's plans* 破坏敌人的计划.

block·ade /blɒ'keɪd/ *n* [C] 封锁 fēngsuǒ. □ *vt* 封锁 fēngsuǒ.

block·age /'blɒkɪdʒ/ *n* [C] **1** 封锁状〔狀〕态〔態〕fēngsuǒ zhuàngtài. **2** 阻塞物 zǔsèwù.

bloke /bləʊk/ *n* [C] [俚语] 人 rén, 家伙(指男子) jiāhuo.

blond /blɒnd/ *n* [C] (男人)白肤〔膚〕金发〔髮〕的 báifū jīnfà de.

blonde /blɒnd/ *n* [C], *adj* (女人) 白肤〔膚〕金发〔髮〕的 báifū jīnfà de.

blood /blʌd/ *n* [U] **1** 血 xuè, 血液 xuèyè. **2** 气〔氣〕质〔質〕qìzhì; 脾气 píqì. ***make one's ~ boil*** 使发〔發〕怒 shǐ fānù. ***(kill sb) in cold ~*** 蓄意 xùyì. **3** 家世 jiāshì, 家族 jiāzú, 血统 xuètǒng: *of the same ~* 同一家族的. '**~ bank** ⇨ bank²(2). '**~-bath** 血洗 xuèxǐ, 大规模屠杀〔殺〕dàguīmó túshā. '**~-curdling** *adj* 令人毛骨悚然的 lìngrén máogǔ sǒngrán de. '**~-donor** 献〔獻〕血人 xiànxuèrén, 供血者 gòngxuèzhě. '**~-group** (或 **-type**) 血型 xuèxíng. '**~hound** 一种〔種〕大警犬 yìzhǒng dàjǐngquǎn. '**~pressure** 血压〔壓〕xuèyā. '**~-shed** 流血 liúxuè; 杀〔殺〕戮 shālù. '**~shot** *adj* (眼睛)充血的 chōngxuède. '**~-sports** *n pl* 可能流血的运〔運〕动〔動〕(如打猎、斗牛等) kěnéng liúxuè de yùndòng. '**~-stream** 血流 xuèliú. '**~thirsty** *adj* [-ier, -iest] 嗜血的 shìxuède, 残〔殘〕忍好杀〔殺〕的 cánrěn hàoshā de. '**~-vessel** 血管 xuèguǎn. **~-less** *adj* 不流血的 bù liúxuè de: *a ~less victory* 不流血的胜利. **~-less·ly** *adv*

bloody /'blʌdɪ/ *adj* **1** 出血的 chūxuède, 流血的 liúxuède. **2** 流血很多的 liúxuè hěnduō de, 伤〔傷〕亡很大的 shāngwáng hěndà de: *a ~ battle* 伤亡很重的战争. **3** [粗俗语](表示强调): *a ~ fool!* 大笨蛋! 大傻瓜! *a ~ genius!* 特大天才! □ *adv* [粗俗俚语](表示强调): *too ~ quick* 特快. ,**~-'minded** [俚语]故意刁难〔難〕的 gùyì diāonàn de, 不易亲〔親〕近的 bùyì qīnjìn de

bloom /blu:m/ *n* **1** [C] 花 huā. **2** 兴〔興〕旺时〔時〕期 xīngwàng shíqī: *in the full ~ of youth* 青春时期. □ *vi* **1** 开〔開〕花 kāihuā. **2** [喻]在青春时期 zài qīngchūn shíqī: 焕发〔發〕青春 huànfā qīngchūn.

blos·som /'blɒsəm/ *n* [C] 花 huā; 果树〔樹〕花 guǒshùhuā. □ *vi* **1** 开〔開〕花 kāihuā. **2** 发〔發〕展 fāzhǎn; 成长〔長〕chéngzhǎng: *He ~ed out as a good athlete.* 他成长为一个优秀的运动员.

blot /blɒt/ *n* [C] **1** 墨水渍 mòshuǐzì. **2** 污点〔點〕wūdiǎn; 缺点 quēdiǎn: *a ~ on his character* 他性格上的一个缺点. □ *vt* [-tt-] **1** 涂〔塗〕污 túwū. **2** (用吸墨水纸)吸干〔乾〕墨水 xīgān mòshuǐ. **3** *~ out* 遮暗 zhē'àn; 把…弄模糊 bǎ … nòng móhū: *The mist ~ted out the view.* 雾遮住了视线. **~ter** 吸墨水纸滚台 xīmòshuǐzhǐ gǔntái. '**~ting-paper** 吸墨水纸 xīmòshuǐzhǐ.

blotch /blɒtʃ/ *n* [C] 皮肤〔膚〕上的斑 pífū shàng de bān.

blouse /blaʊz/ *n* [C] 妇〔婦〕女穿的宽大短外套 fùnǚ chuān de kuāndà duǎn wàitào.

blow¹ /bləʊ/ *n* [C] **1** 打 dǎ; 打击〔擊〕dǎjī. ***come to ~s*** 动〔動〕手互殴〔毆〕dòngshǒu hù ōu. **2** 精神上的打击 jīngshén shàng de dǎjī; 灾〔災〕祸 zāihuò: *His wife's death was a great ~.* 他的妻子的死对他是一次大的打击.

blow² /bləʊ/ *vt/i* [*pt* blew /blu:/; *pp* ~n /bləʊn/] **1** (风)吹 chuī. **2** (风)吹动〔動〕chuīdòng: *The wind blew my hat off.* 风吹落了我的帽子. **3** 吹气〔氣〕于 chuī qì yú; 充气于 chōng qì yú: *~ one's nose* 擤鼻子. *~ a whistle* 吹哨子. **4** 吹响〔響〕乐〔樂〕器、号〔號〕角等 chuīxiǎng yuèqì, hàojiǎo děng. **5** 烧〔燒〕断〔斷〕保险〔險〕丝 shāoduàn bǎoxiǎnsī. **6** [俚语]挥〔揮〕霍 huīhuò. **7** ~ ***(sth) out*** 吹熄 chuīxī: *~ out a candle* 吹熄腊烛. ***~ one's brains out*** 以枪〔槍〕弹〔彈〕射入头〔頭〕部自杀〔殺〕yǐ qiāngdàn shèrù tóubù zìshā. ~

over 平息 píngxī: *The storm will soon ~ over.* 暴风雨很快就会平息. ~ **up** (a) 爆炸 bàozhà: *The gunpowder blew up.* 黑色火药爆炸. (b) 发〔發〕脾气〔氣〕fāpíqì. ~ *sth* **up** (a) 把…炸掉 bǎ … zhàdiào, (b) 充气 chōngqì: ~ *up a tyre* 给轮胎打气. (c) 放大 fàngdà: ~ *up a photograph* 放大照片. '~-**lamp** (或 ~ **torch**) 喷灯〔燈〕pēndēng. '~**out** (a) 突然漏气〔氣〕tūrén lòuqì. (b) 保险〔險〕丝烧〔燒〕断〔斷〕bǎoxiǎnsī shāoduàn. '~-**up** 放大了的照片 fàngdà le de zhàopiān.

blow[2] /bləʊ/ *n* [C] 吹 chuī; 吹风〔風〕chuīfēng: *Give your nose a good ~.* 好好擤一下你的鼻子.

blower /'bləʊə(r)/ *n* [C] **1** 风〔風〕箱 fēngxiāng; 吹风机〔機〕chuīfēngjī. **2** 吹制玻璃等的工人 chuīzhì bōlí děng de gōngrén: *a 'glass-~* 玻璃器皿吹制工人.

blown /bləʊn/ *pp* of blow[2].

blub·ber /'blʌbə(r)/ *n* [U] 鲸脂 jīngzhī.

bludgeon /'blʌdʒən/ *n* [C] 短棒 duǎnbàng. □ *vt* **1** 用棒打击〔擊〕yòngbàng dǎjī. **2** [喻] 强迫某人做某事 qiángpò mǒurén zuò mǒushì.

blue[1] /blu:/ *adj* [-r, -st] 蓝〔藍〕色的 lánsède, 青的 qīngde, 蔚蓝的 wèilánde. *once in a ~ moon* 千载〔載〕难〔難〕逢地 qiānzǎi nánféng de.

blue[2] /blu:/ *n* **1** 蓝〔藍〕色 lánsè. 青色 qīngsè. **2** *out of the ~* 蓦〔驀〕然地 mòránde. 出乎意料地 chūhūyìliàode. **3 the** ~**s** (a) 一种〔種〕伤〔傷〕感的美国〔國〕南方音乐〔樂〕yìzhǒng shānggǎnde měiguó nánfāng yīnyuè. (b) [非正式用语]忧〔憂〕伤〔傷〕yōushāng. ,~'**blooded** *adj* 贵族出身的 guìzú chūshēn de. '~**bottle** 青蝇〔蠅〕qīngyíng. ,~-'**collar** *adj* 体〔體〕力劳〔勞〕动〔動〕的 tǐlìláodòngde. ,~ '**film** 色情电〔電〕影 sèqíng diànyǐng. '~**print** (a) 蓝图〔圖〕lántú. (b) [喻]行动〔動〕计划〔劃〕xíngdòng jìhuà. '~-**stock·ing** 女学〔學〕者 nǚxuézhě; 女才子 nǚcáizǐ. **blu·ish** /'blu:ɪʃ/ *adj* 带〔帶〕蓝色的 dàilánsède.

bluff[1] /blʌf/ *n* [C] 断〔斷〕崖 duànyá, 绝壁 juébì. □ *adj* **1** 陡峭的 dǒuqiàode, 绝壁的 juébìde. **2** 直率的 zhíshuàide. ~**ness** *n* [U]

bluff[2] /blʌf/ *vt/i* 虚张〔張〕声〔聲〕势〔勢〕地诈骗〔騙〕xūzhāngshēngshìde zhàpiàn. □ *n* [U] 虚张声势的诈骗 xūzhāng shēngshìde zhàpiàn. *call sb's ~* 诱使某人摊〔攤〕牌 yòushǐ mǒurén tānpái.

blun·der /'blʌndə(r)/ *vt/i* **1** 瞎闯〔闖〕xiāchuǎng. **2** 犯愚蠢的错误 fàn yúchǔnde cuòwù. □ *n* [C] 因疏忽所犯的错误 yīn shūhū suǒ fàn de cuòwù.

blunt /blʌnt/ *adj* [-er, -est] **1** 钝的 dùnde. **2** 生硬的 shēngyìngde; 直率的 zhíshuàide. □ *vt* 使钝 shǐdùn, 把…弄迟钝 bǎ … nòng chídùn. ~**ly** *adv* 直爽地 zhíshuǎngde. ~**ness** *n* [U]

blur /blɜ:(r)/ *n* [C] 模糊不清的东〔東〕西 móhu bùqīng de dōngxī; 模糊一片 móhu yípiàn: *If you see only a ~, you need glasses.* 如果你只看到模糊一片, 你就需要戴眼镜了. □ *vt/i* [-rr-] 使模糊 shǐ móhu, 变〔變〕模糊 biàn móhu: *Tears ~red her eyes.* 泪水模糊了她的眼睛.

blurb /blɜ:b/ *n* [C] 书〔書〕籍护〔護〕封上的内容简〔簡〕介 shūjí hùfēng shàng de nèiróng jiǎnjiè.

blurt /blɜ:t/ *vt* 脱口说出 tuōkǒu shuōchū. ~ *sth* **out** 脱口漏出秘密 tuōkǒu lòuchū mìmì.

blush /blʌʃ/ *vi* **1** 脸〔臉〕红 liǎn hóng. **2** 羞愧 xiūkuì. □ *n* [C] (因羞愧)脸红 liǎnhóng.

blus·ter /'blʌstə(r)/ *vt/i* **1** (大风)狂吹 kuángchuī, 怒号〔號〕nùháo. **2** 恫吓〔嚇〕dònghè; 大叫大嚷 dàjiào dàrǎng. □ *n* [U] **1** 狂风声〔聲〕kuángfēng shēng. **2** 大吵大嚷 dàchǎo dàrǎng **blus·tery** *adj* 狂风〔風〕大作的 kuángfēng dàzuò de.

B.M.A. = British Medical Association 英国〔國〕医〔醫〕学〔學〕会〔會〕yīngguó yīxuéhuì.

boa /'bəʊə/ *n* [C] (亦作 '~-**constrictor**) 蟒蛇 mǎngshé, 王蛇 wángshé.

boar /bɔ:(r)/ *n* [C] **1** 母猪 mǔzhū. **2** 野猪 yězhū.

board[1] /bɔ:d/ *n* [C] **1** 长木板 cháng mùbǎn. **2** 有专〔專〕门〔門〕用途的木板 yǒu zhuānmén yòngtú de mùbǎn: *a 'notice~* 公告牌. **3** *go by the ~* 失败 shībài, 落空 luòkōng; 被丢弃〔棄〕bèi diūqì. *be* (或 *go*) *on ~* 在船上 zài chuán shàng; 在飞〔飛〕机〔機〕上; zài fēijī shàng. *above ~* 诚实〔實〕的 chéngshíde; 合法的 héfǎde. **4** 理事会〔會〕lǐshìhuì: *the B~ of Directors* 董事会 dǒngshìhuì. **5** [U] 伙食 huǒshí: ~ *and lodging* 食宿 shísù.

board[2] /bɔ:d/ *vt/i* **1** 用板盖 yòng

bǎn gài; 加板 jiā bǎn: ~ *up a window* 用木板盖住窗户. **2** 供应〔應〕伙食 gòngyìng huǒshí. **3** 登上船、火车〔車〕、公共汽车等 dēng shàng chuán, huǒchē, gōnggòngqìchē děng. ~**er** **(a)** 搭伙者 dāhuǒzhě. ⇨ 2 above. **(b)** 寄宿学〔學〕校的男女学生 jìsù xuéxiào de nán nǚ xuéshēng. ~**ing** **(a)** 木板建造物 mùbǎn jiànzàowù. **(b)** 供膳 gòngshàn; 寄膳 jìshàn. '~**ing-card** 登机〔機〕卡 dēngjīkǎ; 登船卡 dēngchuánkǎ. '~**ing-house** 供膳宿之私人住房 gòng shànsù zhī sīrén zhùfáng. '~**ing school** 供膳食的学校 gòng shànshí de xuéxiào.

boast /bəʊst/ *n* [C] 自夸〔誇〕zì kuā, 自豪 zì háo. □ *vt/i* **1** 自夸 zìkuā. **2** 自豪地拥〔擁〕有 zìháode yōngyǒu: *Our school ~s a fine swimming-pool.* 我们学校很可自豪地拥有一个漂亮的游泳池. '~**ful** /-fʊl/ *adj* 爱〔愛〕自夸的 ài zìkuā de. '~**fully** *adv*

boat /bəʊt/ *n* [C] 小船 xiǎo chuán; 艇 tǐng: '*rowing-~* 划艇. ***be (all) in the same ~*** 同舟共济〔濟〕tóngzhōu gòngjì. □ *vi* 乘船游玩 chéngchuán yóuwán. '~-**house** 船坞 chuánwū. '~-**train** 与〔與〕船联〔聯〕运〔運〕的火车〔車〕yǔ chuán liányùn de huǒchē.

boat·swain /'bəʊsən/ *n* [C] 水手长〔長〕shuǐshǒuzhǎng.

bob[1] /bɒb/ *vi* [-bb-] 上下跳动〔動〕shàng xià tiàodòng: *A cork ~bing on the water.* 浮子在水上上下浮动. □ *n* [C] 上下快速活动 shàng xià kuàisù huódòng; 妇〔婦〕女屈膝礼〔禮〕fùnǚ qūxīlǐ.

bob[2] /bɒb/ *vt* [-bb-] (给妇女)剪短发〔髮〕jiǎn duǎnfà.

bob·bin /'bɒbɪn/ *n* [C] 筒管 tǒng guǎn; 筒子 tǒngzi.

bob·sleigh, bob·sled /'bɒbsleɪ, -sled/ *n* [C] 连〔連〕橇 liánqiào. □ *vi* 乘连橇 chéng liánqiào.

bode /bəʊd/ *vt/i* 预兆 yùzhào, 预示 yùshì. ~ ***well for*** 主吉 zhǔjí. ~ ***ill for*** 主凶 zhǔxiōng.

bod·ice /'bɒdɪs/ *n* [C] (妇女穿的)紧〔緊〕手围〔圍〕腰 jǐnshǒu wéiyāo.

bod·ily /'bɒdəlɪ/ *adj* 身体〔體〕的 shēntǐde; 肉体的 ròutǐde. □ *adv* **1** 全部地 quánbùde, 整体地 zhěngtǐde: *transported ~* 整体运〔運〕输〔輸〕zhěngtǐ yùnshū. **2** 亲〔親〕自 qīnzì.

body /'bɒdɪ/ *n* [C] [*pl* -ies] **1** 身体〔體〕shēntǐ, 躯〔軀〕体 qūtǐ. **2** 尸〔屍〕体 shītǐ. **3** 躯干〔幹〕(无头和四肢) qūgàn. **4** (车,船)身 shēn: *the ~ of a car* 汽车的车身. **5** 团〔團〕体 tuántǐ: ***in a ~*** 全体 quántǐ; 一块〔塊〕儿〔兒〕yīkuài'ér. **6** 团 tuán; 片 piàn: *A lake is a ~ of water.* 一个湖就是一潭水. '~-**guard** 警卫〔衛〕员 jǐngwèiyuán, 保镖 bǎobiāo. '~**work** 汽车车身 qìchē chēshēn.

bog /bɒg/ *n* [C] 泥塘 nítáng; 沼泽〔澤〕zhǎozé. □ *vt/i* [-gg-] ~ ***down*** 使陷入泥沼 shǐ xiànrù nízhǎo: *The car was ~ged down in the mud.* 汽车陷入烂泥. ~**gy** *adj* [-ier, -iest] 多沼泽的 duō zhǎozé de.

bo·gey /'bəʊgɪ/ = bogy.

boggle /'bɒgl/ *vi* 畏缩不前 wèisuō bù qián, 犹〔猶〕豫 yóuyù: *The mind ~s (at the idea).* 心存犹豫.

bo·gus /'bəʊgəs/ *adj* 伪〔僞〕的 wěide, 伪造的 wěizàode.

bogy, bo·gey /'bəʊgɪ/ *n* [C] [*pl* -ies, ~s] 妖怪 yāoguài; 令人害怕的人或物 lìng rén hàipà de érn huò wù.

boil[1] /bɔɪl/ *n* [C] 疖〔癤〕jiē.

boil[2] /bɔɪl/ *n* [U] 沸点〔點〕fèidiǎn. ***be on the ~*** 沸腾〔騰〕着 fèiténgzhe; 滚着 gǔnzhe.

boil[3] /bɔɪl/ *vt/i* **1** 沸腾 fèiténg: *When water ~s it changes into steam.* 水沸腾时就变成蒸汽. *The kettle is ~ing.* 水壶(的水)正开着. **2** (海水) 翻腾〔騰〕fānténg; (感情) 激动〔動〕jīdòng. **3** 煮沸 zhǔ fèi; 在沸水中煮 zài fèishuǐ zhōng zhǔ: *~ an egg* 煮鸡蛋. **4** ~ ***away*** (或 ***dry***) 汽化 qìhuà; 煮干〔乾〕zhǔ gān. ~ ***down to*** 归〔歸〕结起来是 guījié qǐlái shì, 问〔問〕题是 wèntí shì: *All this ~s down to is another delay for us.* 总之, 问题是我们又要耽搁一次. ~ ***over*** 沸溢 fèiyì. '~**ing-point** **(a)** 沸点 fèidiǎn. **(b)** 〔喻〕气〔氣〕愤的极〔極〕点 qìfènde jídiǎn.

boiler /'bɔɪlə(r)/ *n* [C] 煮器(壶、锅等的泛称) zhǔqì; 锅炉〔爐〕guōlú. '~-**suit** 连衫裤工作服 liánshānkù gōngzuòfú.

bois·ter·ous /'bɔɪstərəs/ *adj* 吵吵闹闹的 chǎochǎonàonào de; 兴〔興〕高采〔彩〕烈的 xìnggāocǎiliè de.

bold /bəʊld/ *adj* [-er, -est] **1** 大胆〔膽〕的 dàdǎnde; 勇敢的 yǒnggǎnde. **2** 无〔無〕耻的 wúchǐde. 无礼〔禮〕的 wúlǐde. **3** 醒目的 xǐngmùde; 清楚的 qīngchǔde: *a ~ outline* 清楚的轮廓. ~**ly** *adv* ~**ness** *n* [U]

bol·lard /'bɒləd/ *n* [C] **1** 系〔繫〕

缆〔纜〕柱 xìlǎnzhù. **2** (行人安全岛顶端的)护〔護〕柱 hùzhù.

bol·ster[1] /'bəʊlstə(r)/ *n* [C] 长〔長〕枕 chángzhěn.

bol·ster[2] /'bəʊlstə(r)/ *vt* 费力支持 fèilì zhīchí.

bolt[1] /bəʊlt/ *n* [C] **1** 插销 chāxiāo. **2** 螺栓 luóshuān. **3** 闪〔閃〕电〔電〕shǎndiàn. ⇨ thunderbolt. □ *vt/i* 栓紧〔緊〕shuānjǐn.

bolt[2] /bəʊlt/ *vt/i* **1** 马〔馬〕脱韁逃跑 mǎ tuōjiāng táopǎo. **2** 囫囵〔圇〕吞下 húlún tūnxià. □ *n*[C] 快跑 kuàipǎo; 逃走 táozǒu: *make a ~ for it* 赶快逃走.

bolt[3] /bəʊlt/ *adv* (只用于) *~ upright* 笔〔筆〕笔直直 bǐbǐzhízhí.

bomb /bɒm/ *n* [C] 炸弹〔彈〕zhàdàn. □ *vt/i* 轰炸 hōngzhà, 投弹于 tóudàn yú. **~er** **(a)** 轰炸机〔機〕hōngzhàjī. **(b)** 投弹手 tóudànshǒu. **'~shell** 令人大为〔爲〕震惊〔驚〕的意外事件 lìngrén dàwéi zhènjīng de yìwài shìjiàn: *His death was a real ~shell to us.* 他的死对我们来说真是一个出乎意外的事件.

bom·bard /bɒm'bɑ:d/ *vt* **1** 炮击〔擊〕pàojī. **2** [喻]发〔發〕出连〔連〕珠炮似的问〔問〕题 fāchū liánzhūpào sì de wèntí. **~ment** *n*[C, U]

bond /bɒnd/ *n* [C] **1** 契约 qìyuē. **2** [常作喻] 结合 jiéhé; 连〔連〕接 liánjiē: *the ~(s) of affection* 感情上的联系. **3** 债券 zhàijuàn.

bond·age /'bɒndɪdʒ/ *n* [U] 奴役 núyì; 束缚 shùfú.

bone /bəʊn/ *n* [C] 骨骼 gǔgé. ***feel in one's ~s that*** 确〔確〕有把握 què yǒu bǎwò. ***have a '~ to pick with sb*** 与〔與〕某人有争执〔執〕或怨恨 yǔ mǒurén yǒu zhēngzhí huò yuànhèn. ***make no ,~s a'bout doing sth*** 毫不犹〔猶〕豫地做某事 háo bù yóuyù de zuò mǒushì. □ *vt* 剔去…的骨 tīqù ... de gǔ. **,~'dry** *adj* 干〔乾〕透了 gāntòule. **,~-'idle** *adj* 极〔極〕懒的 jílǎnde.

bon·fire /'bɒnfaɪə(r)/ *n* [C] 大篝火 dàgōuhuǒ.

bon·net /'bɒnɪt/ *n* [C] **1** (无边有带的)女帽 nǚmào. **2** [英国英语] 汽车〔車〕引擎盖子 [美语称 *hood*] qìchē yǐnqíng gàizi.

bonny /'bɒnɪ/ *adj* [-ier, -iest] 健康的 jiànkāngde; 强壮〔壯〕的 qiángzhuàngde.

bo·nus /'bəʊnəs/ *n* [C] [*pl* ~es] 奖〔獎〕金 jiǎngjīn; 额外津贴 éwài jīntiē.

bony /'bəʊnɪ/ *adj* [-ier, -iest] **1** 多骨的 duōgǔde: *a ~ fish* 骨刺多的鱼. **2** 骨头〔頭〕突出的 gútóu tūchū de: *~ fingers* 皮包骨头的手指.

boo /bu:/ *int* 呸 (表示嫌恶) pēi. □ *vt/i* 讥〔譏〕笑 jīxiào, 发〔發〕出呸的声〔聲〕音 fāchū pēide shēngyīn.

booby /'bu:bɪ/ *n* [C] 笨蛋 bèndàn, 呆子 dāizi. **'~ prize** 殿军〔軍〕奖〔獎〕diànjūn jiǎng. **'~-trap** 陷阱 xiànjǐng.

book[1] /bʊk/ *n* [C] **1** 书〔書〕shū, 书籍 shūjí. **2** 篇 piān, 卷 juàn. **3** 一捆 yìkǔn; 一束 yíshù. **4** [*pl*] 商业〔業〕帐〔賬〕册 shāngyè zhàngcè. ***be in sb's good ~s*** 得到某人的好感 dédào mǒurén de hǎogǎn. **'~-case** 书橱 shūchú, 书柜〔櫃〕shūguì. **'~keeper** 簿记员 bùjìyuán, 记帐人 jìzhàngrén. **'~-keep·ing** 簿记 bùjì. **'~maker**(赛马等)登记赌注的人 dēngjì dǔzhù de rén. **'~-mark(er)** 书签〔簽〕shūqiān. **'~-stall** 书摊〔攤〕shūtān; 书亭 shūtíng. **'~ token** (定额的)书籍预约证〔證〕shūjí yùyuēzhèng. **'~-worm** **(a)** 蠹鱼 dùyú. **(b)** 书呆子 shūdāizi; 极〔極〕爱〔愛〕读〔讀〕书的人 jí ài dúshū de rén.

book[2] /bʊk/ *vt* **1** 登记入册 dēngjì rùcè. **2** (警察) 登记 (违章者) dēngjì: *be ~ed for speeding* 因超速行驶被警察登记. **3** 预定车〔車〕票等 yùdìng chēpiàoděng. **~able** /-əbl/ *adj* 可预约的 kě yùyuēde, 可预订的 kě yùdìngde. **'~ing clerk** 售票员 shòupiàoyuán. **'~ing office** 售票处〔處〕shòupiàochù.

bookie /'bʊkɪ/ *n* [C] [非正式用语] =bookmaker.

book·let /'bʊklət/ *n* [C] 小册子 xiǎocèzi; 薄本书〔書〕bóběnshū.

boom[1] /bu:m/ *n* [C] **1** 帆的下桁 fānde xiàhéng. **2** 水栅 shuǐzhà 横江铁〔鐵〕索 héngjiāng tiěsuǒ.

boom[2] /bu:m/ *vt/i* **1** (大炮等) 发〔發〕出隆隆声〔聲〕fāchū lónglóng shēng. **2** *~ out* 用低沉的声音说 yòng dīchénde shēngyīn shuō. □ *n* [C] (炮等的) 隆隆声 lónglóngshēng.

boom[3] /bu:m/ *n* [C] (商业等的) 景气〔氣〕jǐngqì, 繁荣〔榮〕fánróng. □ *vi* 兴〔興〕旺 xīngwàng; 迅速发〔發〕展 xùnsù fāzhǎn: *Sales are ~ing.* 销路正旺.

boom·er·ang /'bu:məræŋ/ *n* [C] 飞〔飛〕镖(澳大利亚土著的武器,用曲形坚木制成,投出后可飞回原处) fēibiāo.

boor /bʊə(r)/ *n* [C] 态〔態〕度粗鲁的人 tàidù cūlǔ de rén. **~ish** *adj*

boost /buːst/ *vt* 增加(价值) zēngjiā; 吹捧 chuīpěng: *~ sales* 增加销售额. □ *n* [C] 升 shēng, 提高 tígāo; 增加 zēngjiā; 吹捧 chuīpěng.

boo·ster /ˈbuːstə(r)/ *n* [C] **1** (火箭的)助推器 zhùtuīqì. **2** 外加注射剂〔劑〕量 wàijiā zhùshè jìliàng.

boot /buːt/ *n* [C] **1** 靴 xuē. ***give sb the ~*** [俚语]解雇〔僱〕jiěgù. ***put the ~ in*** [俚语]踢某人 tī mǒurén. **2** [英国英语] 汽车的行李箱(美语称 *trunk*) qìchēde xínglixiāng. □ *vt* 踢人 tīrén; 解雇 jiěgù.

booth /buːð/ *n* [C] **1** 有篷的售货摊〔攤〕yǒu péng de shòuhuòtān. **2** 隔开〔開〕的小间〔間〕gékāide xiǎojiān: *telephone ~* 电话间; *polling ~* 投票站.

booze /buːz/ *n* [U] **1** [非正式用语]酒 jiǔ. **2** 酒宴 jiǔyàn. □ *vi* 痛饮 tòngyǐn; *go boozing* 痛饮一番. **boozer** *n* [C] [英国英语俚语] **(a)** 痛饮者 tòngyǐnzhě. **(b)** 酒店 jiǔdiàn.

bor·der /ˈbɔːdə(r)/ *n* [C] **1** 边〔邊〕biān, 边沿 biānyán. **2** 边界 biānjiè, 国〔國〕界 guójiè. **3** 花园〔園〕中的花坛〔壇〕huāyuán zhōng de huātán. □ *vt/i* **1** 接界 jiējiè. **2** ***~ on*** (或***upon***) **(a)** 接近 jiējìn; 邻接 línjiē. **(b)** 近似 jìnsì: *The proposal ~s on the absurd.* 这提议近乎可笑. **ˈ~line** 边界线〔線〕biānjièxiàn. ***a ˌ~line ˈcase*** 难〔難〕以确〔確〕定的两可情况 nányǐ quèdìng de liǎngke qíngkuàng.

bore[1] /bɔː(r)/ *vt/i* 钻〔鑽〕孔 zuānkǒng, 挖洞 wādòng. □ *n* [C] **1** (亦作 *ˈ~-hole*) 孔 kǒng, 洞 dòng. **2** 枪〔槍〕炮等的内径〔徑〕、口径〔徑〕qiāng pào děng de nèijìng, kǒujìng.

bore[2] /bɔː(r)/ *vt* 厌〔厭〕烦 yànfán. □ *n* [C] 惹人厌烦的人 rěrén yànfán de rén. **bor·ing** *adj* **~dom** *n* [U] 厌烦 yànfán, 无〔無〕趣 wúqù.

bore[3] /bɔː(r)/ *pt* of bear[2].

born /bɔːn/ *pp* of bear[2] **1** ***be ~*** 出生 chūshēng; 出世 chūshì. **2** 生来 shēnglái, 命中注定 mìngzhōngzhùdìng: *He was ~ a poet.* 他是个天生的诗人.

borne /bɔːn/ *pp* of bear[2] except of birth; ⇨ bear[2] (6).

bor·ough /ˈbʌrə/ *n* [C] [英国英语] 有权〔權〕派议〔議〕员到议会并实〔實〕行自治的城市 yǒuquán pài yìyuán dào yìhuì bìng shíxíng zìzhì de chéngshì.

bor·row /ˈbɒrəʊ/ *vt/i* 借 jiè. ⇨ lend. **~er** 借东〔東〕西的人 jiè dōngxi de rén; 借用者 jièyòngzhě.

bor·stal /ˈbɔːstl/ *n* [C] 青少年犯教养〔養〕感化院 qīngshàoniánfàn jiàoyǎng gǎnhuà yuàn.

bosom /ˈbʊzəm/ *n* [C] **1** [旧词]胸 xiōng. **2** 内心 nèixīn; 胸怀〔懷〕xiōnghuái: *a ~ friend* 知心朋友.

boss /bɒs/ *n* [C] [俚语]工头〔頭〕gōngtóu; 老板〔闆〕lǎobǎn. □ *vt* 指挥〔揮〕zhǐhuī. **bossy** *adj* [-ier, -iest] 专〔專〕横的 zhuānghéngde; 爱〔愛〕指手划〔劃〕脚的 àizhǐshǒu huàjiǎode.

boss-eyed /ˈbɒs æɪd/ *adj* [俚语]一只〔隻〕眼睛的 yìzhī yǎnjīng de; 斜视眼的 xiéshìyǎnde.

bot= bought.

bot·any /ˈbɒtənɪ/ *n* [U] 植物学〔學〕zhíwùxué. **botan·ical** /bəˈtænɪkl/ *adj* **bot·an·ist** *n* [C] 植物学家 zhíwùxuéjiā.

botch /bɒtʃ/ *vt* 拙劣地修补〔補〕zhuōliède xiūbǔ. □ *n* [C] 粗劣的工作 cūliède gōngzuò.

both /bəʊθ/ *adj, pron* 两 liǎng, 双〔雙〕shuāng; 两者 liǎngzhě. *~ books* 两本书. *B~ are good.* 两者都好.

bother /ˈbɒðə(r)/ *vt/i* **1** 烦扰〔擾〕fánrǎo; 打扰 dǎrǎo: *Don't ~ me when I'm working.* 我工作时, 别来打扰. **2** 麻烦 máfán: *Don't ~ to stand up.* 别麻烦, 不用站起来. □ *n* [U] 麻烦 máfán. **ˈ~some** *adj* 麻烦的 máfánde.

bottle /ˈbɒtl/ *n* [C] 瓶 píng, 一瓶(的量) yìpíng. □ *vt* **1** 装〔裝〕瓶 zhuāngpíng. **2** ***~ up*** [喻] 抑制 yìzhì. **ˌ~-ˈgreen** *adj* 深绿色 shēnlǜsè. **ˈ~-neck** **(a)** 交通容易阻塞的狭口 jiāotōng róngyì zǔsè de xiákǒu. **(b)** 妨碍〔礙〕生产流程的环〔環〕节〔節〕fáng'ài shēngchǎn liúchéng de huánjié.

bot·tom /ˈbɒtəm/ *n* [C] **1** 底 dǐ, 底部 dǐbù. **2** 最后〔後〕部 zuìhòubù, 最里〔裏〕面 zuìlǐmiàn: *at the ~ of the garden* 在花园的最后部. **3** (海等的)底 dǐ. **4** [非正式用语] 屁股 pìgu. ***get to the ~ of sth*** 弄清真相 nòngqīng zhēnxiàng, 盘根究底 pángēnjiūdǐ. **~less** *adj* 很深 hěnshēn.

bough /baʊ/ *n* [C] 大树〔樹〕枝 dàshùzhī.

bought /bɔːt/ *pt, pp* of buy.

boul·der /ˈbəʊldə(r)/ *n* [C] 巨砾〔礫〕jùlì.

bounce /baʊns/ *vt/i* **1** (球等)反跳 fǎntiào; 弹〔彈〕起 tánqǐ: *The ball ~ed over the wall.* 球弹跳着越过

了墙. 2 跳上跳下 tiàoshàng tiàoxià 乱〔亂〕冲〔衝〕luànchōng: ~ *on a bed* 在床上蹦跳. *He ~d into the room.* 他冲进了房间. 3〔非正式用语〕支票因银行无〔無〕存款被拒付而退回. zhīpiào yīn yínháng wú zúnkuǎn bèi jùfù ér tuìhuí. □ *n* [C] 球的弹跳 qiú de tántiào.

bounc·ing /'baʊnsɪŋ/ *adj* 大而强壮〔壯〕的 dà ér qiángzhuàng de; 健康的 jiànkāngde.

bound[1] /baʊnd/ *vt* 跳跃 tiàoyuè;跳跃前进〔進〕tiàoyuè qiánjìng. □*n* [C] 跳跃 tiàoyuè.

bound[2] /baʊnd/ *pp* of bind. ~ *to* 一定的 yídìngde; 必定的 bìdìngde: ~ *to win* 必胜. ~ *up in* 忙于 mángyú.

bound·ary /'baʊndrɪ/ *n* [C] [*pl* -ies] 边〔邊〕界 biānjiè,分界线〔線〕fēnjièxiàn.

bound·less /'baʊndlɪs/ *adj* 无〔無〕限的 wúxiànde. ~**ly** *adv*

bounds /baʊndz/ *n pl* 界限 jièxiàn; 范〔範〕围〔圍〕fànwéi. *out of* ~ 不许进〔進〕入的范围 bùxǔ jìnrù de fànwéi.

boun·ti·ful /'baʊntɪfl/ *adj* 丰〔豐〕富的 fēngfùde: *a* ~ *harvest* 丰收.

bounty /'baʊntɪ/ *n* [*pl* -ies] 1 [U] 慷慨 kāngkǎi. 2 [C] 捐赠品 juānzèngpǐn; 施舍品 shīshěpǐn. 3 [C] 奖〔獎〕品 jiǎngpǐn.

bou·quet /bʊ'keɪ/ *n* [C] 1 花束 huāsù. 2 酒香 jiǔxiāng.

bour·geois /'bʊəʒwɑ:/ *n* [C] *adj* 店主 diànzhǔ; 商人 shāngrén; 资产〔產〕阶级分子 zīchǎnjiējífènzǐ. ~**ie** /'bʊəʒwɑ:'zi:/ *n* [U] **the** ~**ie** 资产阶级 zīchǎnjiējí.

bout /baʊt/ *n* [C] 一回 yìhuí;一场〔場〕yìchǎng; 一阵〔陣〕yízhèn: *a 'wrestling* ~摔交的一个回合; *a* ~ *of influenza* 一次流行性感冒.

bou·tique /bu:'ti:k/ *n* [C] 出售服装〔裝〕的小铺 chūshòu fúzhuāng de xiǎopù.

bow[1] /bəʊ/ *n* [C] 1 弓 gōng. 2 琴弓 qíngōng. 3 弓形 gōngxíng; 虹 hóng. 4 蝴蝶结 húdiéjié. □ *vt* 用弓拉琴 yòng gōng lāqín. ,~'**legged** *adj* 弓形腿 gōngxíngtuǐ. ,~'**tie** 蝴蝶结领结 húdiéjié lǐngjié.

bow[2] /baʊ/ *vt/i* 1 鞠躬 jūgōng; 点〔點〕头〔頭〕diǎntóu: ~ *to the king* 向国王鞠躬致敬. 2 弯〔彎〕曲 wānqū: *The branches ~ed down with snow.* 树枝被雪压弯. 3 屈服 qūfú, 服从〔從〕fúcóng: *I* ~ *to your authority.* 我服从你的权力. □ *n* [C] 鞠躬 jūgōng, 点头 diǎntóu.

bow[3] /baʊ/ *n* [C]〔常用复〕船头〔頭〕chuángtóu.

bowel /'baʊəl/ *n* 1 [C]〔常用复〕肠〔腸〕cháng. 2 [*pl*] 内部 nèibù: *the ~s of the earth* 地球内部.

bowl[1] /bəʊl/ *n* [C] 1 碗 wǎn. 2 一碗的量 yìwǎnde liàng. 3 碗状〔狀〕物 wǎnzhuàngwù.

bowl[2] /bəʊl/ *n* 1 [C] 滚木球 gǔnmùqiú. 2 [*pl*] 滚木球戏〔戲〕gǔnmùqiúxì. □ *vt/i* 1 在板球戏中投球给击〔擊〕球手 zài bǎnqiúxì zhōng tóuqiú gěi jīqiúshǒu. 2 ~ *(sb) over* (a) 击倒某人 jīdǎo mǒurén. (b) 使大吃一惊〔驚〕shǐ dà chī yìjīng: *~ed over by the news* 被这消息弄得不知所措. 3 玩滚木球戏 wán gǔnmùqiúxì.

bowler[1] /'bəʊlə(r)/ *n* [C] 1 板球戏〔戲〕中的投球手 bǎnqiúxì zhōng de tóuqiúshǒu. 2 玩滚木球戏者 wán gǔnmùqiúxì zhě.

bowler[2] /'bəʊlə(r)/ *n* [C] (亦作 ,~ *'hat*) (通常为黑色的) 圆顶硬礼〔禮〕帽 yuándǐng yìnglǐmào.

bow win·dow /,bəʊ 'wɪndəʊ/ *n* [C] 凸肚窗 tūdùchuāng.

box[1] /bɒks/ *n* [C] 1 盒子 hézi: *a* ~ *of matches* 一盒火柴. 2 (剧院的) 包厢 bāoxiāng. 3 法庭上的专〔專〕席 fǎtíng shàng de zhuānxí: *a 'jury*-~ 陪审〔審〕席. □ *vt* 装〔裝〕盒 zhuānghé. '~-**number** 报〔報〕纸广〔廣〕告中使用的邮〔郵〕政信箱号码〔碼〕bàozhǐ guǎngbō zhōng shǐyòng de yóuzhèng xìnxiāng hàomǎ. '~-**office** 电〔電〕影院等的订票处〔處〕diànyǐngyuàn děng de dìngpiàochù.

box[2] /bɒks/ *vt/i* 拳击〔擊〕quánjī. □ *n* [C] 打耳光 dǎ ěrguāng.

boxer /'bɒksə(r)/ *n* [C] 1 拳击家 quánjījiā, 拳击员 quánjīyuán. 2 一种戏〔戲〕牛犬 yìzhǒng xìniúquǎn.

box·ing /'bɒksɪŋ/ *n* [U] 拳击 quánjī: ~ *glove* 拳击手套; ~ *match* 拳赛.

Box·ing Day /'bɒksɪŋ deɪ/ *n* 节〔節〕礼〔禮〕日 (圣诞节的次日如为星期日, 改为十二月二十七日) jiélǐrì.

boy /bɔɪ/ *n* [C] 男孩子 nánháizi. '~**friend** 女孩子的男朋友 nǚháizide nánpéngyǒu. '~**hood** 男孩子的孩童时〔時〕代 nánháizide háitóng shídài. ~**ish** *adj* 男孩似的 náihái sìde; 孩子气〔氣〕的 háiziqìde.

boy·cott /'bɔɪkɒt/ *vt* 联〔聯〕合抵制 liánhé dǐzhì. □ *n* [C] 抵制 dǐzhì.

Bp.= Bishop.

bra /brɑ:/ *n* [C]〔非正式用语〕brassiere 的缩写〔寫〕.

brace[1] /breɪs/ *n* [C] 1 用以夹住或

支撑的东西 yòngyǐjiāzhù huò zhīchēng de dōngxi. **2** 拉条〔條〕lātiáo; 撑臂 chēngbì. **3** [英国英语] [*pl*] 背带〔帶〕bēidài. **4** [常用复]牙科矫〔矯〕形钢〔鋼〕丝套 yákē jiǎoxíng gāngsītào.

brace² /breɪs/ *vt/i* **1** 支住 zhīzhù; 撑牢 chēngláo. **2** 奋〔奮〕起 fènqǐ; 振作 zhènzuò.

brace·let /ˈbreɪslɪt/ *n* [C] 手镯 shǒuzhuó.

brac·ing /ˈbreɪsɪŋ/ *adj* 振奋〔奮〕精神的 zhènfèn jīngshen de: ~ *sea air* 令人精神爽快的海上空气.

bracken /ˈbrækən/ *n* [U] 欧〔歐〕洲蕨 ōuzhōujué.

bracket /ˈbrækɪt/ *n* [C] **1** 托架 tuōjià. **2** 括号〔號〕kuòhào. **3** 等级 děngjí: *an* ˈ*income* ~ 收入等级. □ *vt* 套以括号〔號〕tào yǐ kuòhào; 放在一起 fàngzài yìqǐ.

brack·ish /ˈbrækɪʃ/ *adj* (水)微咸〔鹹〕wēixián.

brag /bræg/ *vi* [-gg-] 夸〔誇〕口 kuākǒu; 吹牛皮 chuīniúpí.

brag·gart /ˈbrægət/ *n* [C] 吹牛皮的人 chuīniúpíde rén.

Brah·min /ˈbrɑːmɪn/ *n* 印度婆罗〔羅〕门〔門〕种姓的成员 yìndù póluó mén zhǒngxìng de chéngyuán.

braid /breɪd/ *n* **1** [C] 发〔髮〕辫 fàbiàn. **2** [U] 编带〔帶〕biāndài, 缏 biàn. □ *vt* 编成缏 biān chéng biàn.

braille /breɪl/ *n* [U] 布莱叶〔葉〕盲文 bùláiyè mángwén.

brain /breɪn/ *n* [C] **1** [*sing*] 脑 nǎo. **2** 脑力 nǎolì; 智力 zhìlì: *have a good* ~ 智力好. *have sth on the* ~ 一心想着某事 yìxīn xiǎngzhě mǒushì. **3** [C] 智囊 zhìnáng. □ *vt* 猛击〔擊〕头〔頭〕部致死 měngjī tóubù zhìsǐ. ˈ**~-child** 新颖的主意 xīnyǐngde zhǔyi. ˈ**~ drain** 智囊流失 zhìnáng liúshī, 人才外流 réncái wàiliú. ˈ**~-storm** 脑猝病 nǎocùbìng. ˈ**~-wave** [非正式用语]灵〔靈〕机〔機〕língjī. **~-less** *adj* 笨拙的 bènzhuóde; 没有头〔頭〕脑的 méiyǒu tóunǎo de. **brainy** *adj* [-ier, -iest] 聪〔聰〕明的 cōngmingde, 多智的 duōzhìde.

braise /breɪz/ *vt* (用文火)燉肉 dùn ròu.

brake /breɪk/ *n* [C] 刹车〔車〕shāchē, 制动〔動〕器 zhìdòngqì. □ *vt/i* 刹车 shāchē.

bramble /ˈbræmbl/ *n* [C,U] 荆棘 jīngjí; 黑莓灌木丛〔叢〕hēiméi guànmùcóng.

bran /bræn/ *n* [U] 麸〔麩〕fū; 糠 kāng.

branch /brɑːntʃ/ *n* [C] **1** 树〔樹〕枝 shùzhī. **2** 支线〔線〕zhīxiàn; 支路 zhīlù. **3** 家族的支系 jiāzúde zhīxì; 分支机〔機〕构〔構〕fēnzhī jīgòu: *a* ~ *office* 分局; 分店. □ *vi* 分支 fēnzhī, 分岔 fēnchà. ~ ***out*** 扩〔擴〕充出新的业〔業〕务〔務〕kuòchōng chū xīnde yèwù.

brand /brænd/ *n* [C] **1** 商标〔標〕shāngbiāo, 牌子 páizi; 某种〔種〕牌子的货物 mǒuzhǒng páizide huòwù. **2** (亦作ˈ~*ing-iron*) 打印用烙铁〔鐵〕dǎyìnyònglàotie; 烙印 làoyìn. □ *vt* **1** (在牲口等身上)打烙印 dǎ làoyìn. **2** 污辱 wūrǔ; 给以恶〔惡〕名 gěi yǐ èmíng: ~*ed as a thief* 被指为窃贼. ˌ**~-ˈnew** *adj* 全新的 quánxīnde.

bran·dish /ˈbrændɪʃ/ *vt* 挥〔揮〕舞 huīwǔ: ~*ing a pistol* (*sword*) 挥舞手枪(大刀).

brandy /ˈbrændɪ/ *n* [C,U] [*pl* -ies] 白兰〔蘭〕地(酒) báilándì.

brash /bræʃ/ *adj* [非正式用语] 自信的 zìxìnde; 脸〔臉〕皮厚的 liǎnpí hòude.

brass /brɑːs/ *n* **1** [U] 黄铜 huángtóng. **2** [U] 或 [*pl*] 黄铜器 huángtóngqì, 黄铜制品 huángtóng zhìpǐn. **3 the** ~铜管乐〔樂〕器 tóngguǎn yuèqì. **4** [U] [英国俚语]钱〔錢〕qián. ˌ**top** ˈ~ [非正式用语] 高级官员 gāojí guānyuán. ˌ~ ˈ**band** 铜管乐队〔隊〕tóngguǎn yuèduì.

brass·iere, brass·iere /ˈbræsɪə(r)/ *n* [C] (缩作 **bra**) 奶罩 nǎizhào.

brat /bræt/ *n* [C] 讨人嫌的小孩 tǎo rén xián de xiǎohái.

bra·vado /brəˈvɑːdəʊ/ *n* [*pl* ~es, ~s] [C,U] 虚张〔張〕声〔聲〕势〔勢〕xūzhāng shēngshì.

brave /breɪv/ *adj* [-r, -st] **1** 勇敢的 yǒnggǎnde. **2** 需要勇气〔氣〕的 xūyào yǒngqì de: *a* ~ *act* 英勇的行为. □ *vt* 冒…危险〔險〕mào…wēixiǎn; 敢于 gǎnyú. ~ *great dangers* 危险面前不低头. **~ly** *adv* **~ry** /ˈbreɪvərɪ/*n* [U] 勇敢 yǒnggǎn, 大胆〔膽〕dàdǎn.

bravo /ˌbrɑːˈvəʊ/ *int, n* [C] [*pl* ~-es, ~s] 好啊! hǎo'ā! 妙啊! miào'ā!

brawl /brɔːl/ *n* [C] 吵架 chǎojià. □ *vi* 争吵 zhēngchǎo.

bray /breɪ/ *n* [C] 驴〔驢〕叫声〔聲〕lǘ jiào shēng. □ *vt* 驴叫 lǘ jiào.

brazen /ˈbreɪzn/ *adj* **1** 黄铜制的 huángtóng zhì de; 黄铜般的 huángtóng bān de. **2** 无〔無〕耻的 wúchǐde: *a* ~ *woman* 厚颜无耻的女人.

braz·ier /'breɪzɪə(r)/ *n* [C] 火盆 huǒpén, 火钵 huǒbō.

breach /bri:tʃ/ *n* [C] **1** 违〔違〕犯 wéifàn, 违背 wéibèi: *a ~ of the peace* 扰乱治安;骚乱. **2** 缺口 quēkǒu, 裂口 lièkǒu. □ *vt* 突破 tūpò, 使有缺口 shǐ yǒu quēkǒu.

bread /bred/ *n* [U] **1** 面〔麵〕包 miànbāo: *a loaf (slice) of ~* 一块(片)面包. **2** [俚语]钱〔錢〕qián. ***on the ~line*** 很穷 hěnqióng. **'~-winner** 养〔養〕家活口的人 yǎngjiā huókǒu de rén.

breadth /'bretθ/ *n* ⇨ broad[1] (2) 宽度 kuāndù; 广〔廣〕度 guǎngdù.

break[1] /breɪk/ *n* **1** [C] 破裂 pòliè; 破裂处〔處〕pòlièchù. **2** [U] *~ of day* (= *day~*) 破晓〔曉〕pòxiǎo, 黎明 límíng. **3** (工作中间的)休息时〔時〕间〔間〕xiūxi shíjiān: *~ for lunch* (工作中间的)吃饭时间. **4** (= *~out*) 越狱〔獄〕yuèyù. ***make a ~ for it*** 逃跑 táopǎo. **5** [非正式用语]好运气 hǎo yùnqì.

break[2] /breɪk/ *vt/i* [*pt* broke /brəʊk/, *pp* broken /'brəʊkən/] **1** 打破 dǎpò; 断〔斷〕duàn: *The boy fell and broke his leg.* 男孩子跌倒下来,摔断了腿. **2** 折断〔斷〕zhéduàn: *He broke a branch from the tree.* 他从树上折下一根树枝. **3** 破坏〔壞〕pòhuài; 破除 pòchú. **4** *~ even* 不亏〔虧〕不赢 bù kuī bù yíng. **5** [与各种主语连用] *The storm broke.* 暴风雨突然来了. *The fine weather broke.* 好天气结束了. ⇨ daybreak. **6** [与各种宾语连用] *~ new ground* [喻]开辟〔闢〕新天地; *~ a person's heart* 令某人伤心; *~ the news* 透露消息; *~ a (world, etc) record* 打破纪录. **7** 训练 xùnliàn; 驯服 xùnfú: *~ a horse (in)* 驯马. **8** 制服 zhìfú: *~ a person's spirit* 挫某人的锐气. *~ resistance* 粉碎抵抗. **9** 违〔違〕反 wéifǎn; 违背 wéibèi: *~ the law* 犯法; *~ one's word (a promise)* 食言. **10** 中止 zhōngzhǐ, 打断 dǎduàn: *~ (the) silence* 打破沉默; *~ one's journey* 中断旅行. **11** *~ away (from)* (a) 突然走开〔開〕tūrán zǒukāi. (b) 放弃〔棄〕fàngqì; 革除 géchú. *~ down* (a) 破裂 pòliè; 失败 shībài: *Talks have broken down.* 谈判已经破裂. (b) 坏〔壞〕huài: *The car broke down.* 汽车坏了. (c) (精神)垮下来 kuǎ xiàlái. *~ down sth* (a) 破坏 pòhuài: *~ down resistance* 粉碎抵抗. (b) 分析 fēnxī; 分类〔類〕fēnlèi: *~ down expenditure* 把开支分成细类. *~ in* 破门〔門〕而入 pò mén ér rù, 闯〔闖〕入 chuǎngrù. **'~-in** *n* 闯入 chuǎngrù. *~ in on (*或 *upon)* 打断 dǎduàn. *~ into* (a) 破门而入 pò mén ér rù. (b) 突然…起来〔來〕tūrán … qǐlái: *~ into song* 突然唱起歌来; *~ into a run* 突然跑了起来. *~ off* (a) 停止说话 tíngzhǐ shuōhuà. (b) 停止 tíngzhǐ. *~ off (sth)* (a) 折断 zhéduàn: *The mast broke off.* 桅杆折断了. (b) 突然结束 tūrán jiésù: *~ off diplomatic relations* 突然中断外交关系. *~ out* 暴发〔發〕bàofā; 突然发生 tūrán fāshēng. ⇨ outbreak. *~ out (of)* 逃出 táochū. **'~·out** *n*. *~ out in* 突然被…覆盖 tūrán bèi … fùgài: *~ out in spots* 突然布满了斑点. *~ through* 突破 tūpò, 冲垮 chōngkuǎ. ⇨ breakthrough. *~ up* (a) 打碎 dǎsuì; 破碎 pòsuì. (b) [喻]精神上垮了 jīngshen shàng kuǎle. (c) 学〔學〕校期终放假 xuéxiào qīzhōng fàngjià. (d) 关〔關〕系结束 guānxì jiésù. *~ sth up* (a) 打碎 dǎsuì, 打破 dǎpò. (b) 分解 fēnjiě; 分开 fēnkāi: *~ up a piece of work* 把一项工作分解开来. (c) 打断 dǎduàn; 结束 jiésù: *The police broke up a meeting.* 警察驱散了一次集会. *~ up an alliance.* 联盟关系中止. **'~-up** *n* 停止 tíngzhǐ, 完结 wánjié.

break·able /'breɪkəbl/ *adj* 易碎的 yìsuìde.

break·age /'breɪkɪdʒ/ *n* [C] **1** 破损 pòsǔn, 损毁 sǔnhuǐ. **2** 破损物 pòsǔnwù.

break·down /'breɪkdaʊn/ *n* [C] **1** (机械的)损坏〔壞〕sǔnhuài, 故障 gùzhàng. **2** 身体〔體〕垮下来 shēntǐ kuǎ xiàlái; 会〔會〕谈破裂 huìtán pòliè: *a ,nervous '~* 精神崩溃. **3** 统计的分类〔類〕tǒngjìde fēnlèi: *a ~ of expenses* 开支的分类.

breaker /'breɪkə(r)/ *n* [C] **1** 碎浪 suìlàng; 激浪 jīlàng. **2** 打破者 dǎpòzhě, 开〔開〕拓者 kāituòzhě; 破碎装〔裝〕置 pòsuì zhuāngzhì. **'ice-~** 破冰船 pòbīngchuán.

break·fast /'brekfəst/ *n* [C] 早餐 zǎocān. □ *vi* 吃早饭 chī zǎofàn.

break·through /'breɪkθru:/ *n* [C] **1** 军〔軍〕事突破 jūnshì tūpò. **2** 科技等方面的重大发〔發〕明、发现 kējì děng fāngmiàn de zhòngdà fāmíng, fāxiàn.

break·water /'breɪkwɔ:tə(r)/ *n* [C] 防浪堤 fánglàngtí.

breast /brest/ *n* [C] **1** 乳房 rǔfáng **2** 胸 xiōng. ***make a clean ~ of sth*** 坦白 tǎnbái, 和盘托出 hépán tuōchū.

breath /breθ/ *n* **1** [U] 呼吸之空

气〔氣〕hūxī zhī kōngqì; 气息 qìxī. **2** [C] 一次呼吸 yícì hūxī. ***out of*** ~ 上气不接下气 shàngqì bùjiē xiàqì. ***take sb's ~ away*** 使某人大吃一惊 shǐ mǒurén dàchī yìjīng. ***under one's*** ~ 耳语 ěryǔ. **3** [C] 微风〔風〕wēifēng. **~less** *adj* **(a)** 上气不接下气 shàngqì bùjiē xiàqì. **(b)** 无〔無〕风的 wúfēngde. **~lessly** *adv* **'~taking** *adj* 惊〔驚〕人的 jīngrénde, 惊险〔險〕的 jīngxiǎnde.

breath·alys·er /'breθəlaɪzə(r)/ *n* [C] 测醉器(分析某人呼气,测定其酒醉程度) cèzuìqì.

breathe /bri:ð/ *vt/i* **1** 呼吸 hūxī. **2** 低语 dīyǔ. 耳语 ěryǔ. **breather** 短暂〔暫〕的休息 duǎnzhǎnde xiūxi.

bred /bred/ *pt, pp* of breed.

breech /bri:tʃ/ *n* [C] 枪〔槍〕炮的后〔後〕膛 qiāngpàode hòutáng.

breed /bri:d/ *vt/i* (*pt, pp* bred /bred/) **1** 繁殖 fánzhí. 育种〔種〕yùzhǒng: ~ *horses(cattle)* 繁殖马匹(家畜). **2** (动物)生育 shēngyù. **3** 教养〔養〕jiàoyǎng; 养育 yǎngyù: *a well-bred boy* 有教养的男孩子. **4** 引起 yǐnqǐ, 惹起 rěqǐ. *Dirt ~s disease.* 脏东西会引起疾病. □ *n*[C] **1** 品种〔種〕pǐngzhǒng. **2** 种类〔類〕zhǒnglèi. 类型 lèixíng: *a new ~ of manager* 新型的经理. **~er** 饲养〔養〕员 sìyǎngyuán. **~ing** *n* [U] **(a)** 饲养 sìyǎng: *the ~ing of horses* 养马. **(b)** 教养 jiàoyǎng: *a man of good ~ing* 有教养的人.

breeze /bri:z/ *n* [C, U] 微风〔風〕wēifēng. □ *vi* ~ ***in*** [非正式用语] 忽然来到 hūrán láidào; ~ ***out*** [非正式用语] 飘〔飄〕然而去 piāorán ér qù. **breez·ily** *adv* **breezy** *adj* **(a)** 惠风和畅的 huìfēng héchàngde. **(b)** 活泼〔潑〕的 huópōde.

breth·ren /'breðrən/ *n pl* [旧词] 兄弟 xiōngdì.

brev·ity /'brevətɪ/ *n* [U] (生命等的)短暂〔暫〕duǎnzhǎn,短促 duǎncù.

brew /bru:/ *vt/i* **1** 酿〔釀〕造(啤酒等) niàngzào; 沏(茶等) qī. **2**[喻] 形成 xíngchéng; 酝酿 yùnniàng: *A storm is ~ing.* 一场暴风雨正在形成. □ *n* [C] 酿出的饮料 niàngchūde yǐnliào. **~er** *n* [C] **~ery** 啤酒厂〔廠〕píjiǔchǎng.

bribe /braɪb/ *n* [C] 贿赂 huìlù; 行贿物 xínghuìwù. □ *vt* 行贿 xínghuì. **~ry** 行贿 xínghuì; 受贿 shòuhuì.

bric-a-brac /'brɪk ə bræk/ *n* [U] 古玩 gǔwán; 小摆〔擺〕设 xiǎobǎishè.

brick /brɪk/ *n* [C,U] 砖〔磚〕zhān. □ *vt* ~ ***up*** (或 ***in***) 砌砖填补〔補〕qìzhuān tiánbǔ. **'~layer** 砌砖工人 qìzhuān gōngrén. **'~work** 砖结构 zhuānjiégòu.

bri·dal /'braɪdl/ *adj* 新娘的 xīnniángde; 婚礼〔禮〕的 hūnlǐde.

bride /'braɪd/ *n* [C] 新娘 xīnniáng. **'~groom** /-gru:m/ *n* [C] 新郎 xīnláng.

brides·maid /'braɪdzmeɪd/ *n* [C] 女傧〔儐〕相 nǚbīnxiàng. ⇨ best man.

bridge[1] /brɪdʒ/ *n* [C] **1** 桥〔橋〕qiáo, 桥梁 qiáoliáng. **2** (船上的)驾〔駕〕驶〔駛〕台 jiàshǐtái. 桥楼〔樓〕qiáolóu. **3** 鼻梁 bíliáng. **4** (提琴等的)桥马〔馬〕qiáomǎ. □ *vt* 架桥于 jiàqiáoyú: ~ *a canal* 在运河上架桥. **'~head** (军事)桥头〔頭〕堡 qiáotóubǎo.

bridge[2] /brɪdʒ/ *n* [U] 桥〔橋〕牌戏〔戲〕qiáopáixì.

bridle /'braɪdl/ *n* [C] 马〔馬〕勒 mǎlē. 马笼〔籠〕头〔頭〕mǎlóngtóu. □ *vt/i* **1** 给马上笼头 gěi mǎ shàng lóngtóu. **2** [喻]抑制 yìzhì, 约束 yuēsù: ~ *your passions* 压住你强烈的情感.

brief[1] /bri:f/ *adj* [-er, -est] 短暂〔暫〕的 duǎnzhǎnde. ***in*** ~简〔簡〕言之 jiǎnyánzhī. **~ly**

brief[2] /bri:f/ *n* **1** [C] 诉讼要点〔點〕, 摘录〔錄〕sùsòng yàodiǎn, zhāilù. **2** 事先提供的背景材料, 指示等 shìxiān tígòng de bèijǐng cáiliào, zhǐshì děng. □ *vt* **1** 向辩护〔護〕律师作指示 xiàng biànhù lǜshī zuò zhǐshì; 聘请律师 pìnqǐng lǜshī. **2** 事先提供背景材料 shìxiān tígòng bèijǐng cáiliào. **'~case** 公事皮包 gōngshì píbāo.

briefs /bri:fs/ *n pl* (亦作 *a pair of* ~)三角裤 sānjiǎokù.

Brig.= Brigadier.

brig·ade /brɪ'geɪd/ *n* [C] **1**(军事)旅 lǚ **2** (执行一定任务的)队〔隊〕duì: *the 'fire-~* 消防队.

briga·dier /ˌbrɪgə'dɪə(r)/ *n* [C]旅长〔長〕lǚzhǎng.

bright /braɪt/ *adj* [-er, -est] **1** 明亮的 míngliàngde,光辉〔輝〕的 guānghuīde. **2** 欢〔歡〕乐〔樂〕的 huānlède. **3** 聪〔聰〕明的 cōngmingde. **~en** *vt/i* 使发〔發〕亮 shǐ fāliàng. **~ly** *adv* **~ness** *n* [C]

bril·liant /'brɪlɪənt/ *adj* **1** 光辉〔輝〕的 guānghuīde, 辉煌的 huīhuángde. **2** 英明的 yīngmíngde. **~ly** *adv* **bril·liance** *n* [U]

brim /brɪm/ *n* [C] **1** 杯边〔邊〕bēibiān. **2** 帽边 màobian. □ *vi* [-mm-] ~ ***over*** 满溢 mǎnyì.

brine /braɪn/*n* [U] 盐〔鹽〕水 yánshuǐ; 咸〔鹹〕水 xiánshuǐ.

bring /brɪŋ/ *vt* [*pt, pp* brought /brɔːt/] **1** 带〔帶〕来〔來〕 dàilái; 拿来 nálái: ~ *me my coat* 把我的上衣拿来. **2** 使来到 shǐ láidào: *Spring* ~*s warm weather.* 春天带来温暖的天气. **3** ~*sb* (*oneself*) *to do sth* 说服 shuōfú, 劝〔勸〕使 quànshǐ: *I can't* ~ *myself to tell him.* 我鼓不起勇气来告诉他. **4** [法律]提出 tíchū: ~ *a case against her* 对她提出控诉. **5** ~ *about* 带来 dàilái, 造成 zàochéng. ~ *back* (a) 归〔歸〕还〔還〕guīhuán: ~ *back a book* 归还一本书. (b) 使回忆 shǐhuíyì. (c) 重新采〔採〕用 chóngxīn cǎiyòng: ~ *back hanging* 重新采用绞刑. ~ *down* (a) 使落下 shǐ luòxià; 使倒下 shǐ dǎoxià: ~ *down prices* 使物价跌落;~ *down the government* 推翻政府. (b) 打死 dǎsǐ; 打伤〔傷〕 dǎshāng: *He brought down the antelope.* 他打死了羚羊. ~ *forward* (a) 提出 tíchū. (b) 提前 tíqián: *The meeting has been brought forward.* 会议提前了. ⇨postpone ~ *in* (a) 产〔產〕生 chǎnshēng. (b) 引进〔進〕yǐnjìng; 采〔採〕用 cǎiyòng: ~ *in a new fashion* 引进新的式样; ~ *in a new legislation* 提出新的立法. ~ *off* 使成功 shǐ chénggōng. ~ *on* 引起 yǐnqǐ, 导〔導〕致 dǎozhì: *The rain brought on his cold.* 这场雨导致了他的感冒. ~ *out* (a)使显〔顯〕出 shǐ xiǎnchū: ~ *out the meaning* 使意义明白表现出来. (b) 使性质〔質〕表现出来 shǐ xìngzhì biǎoxiàn chūlái: *Danger* ~*s out the best in him.* 危险面前显出了他的高贵品质. (c) 使罢〔罷〕工 shǐ bàgōng: *Union leaders brought out the workers.* 工会领袖发动工人罢工. ~ *round* (a) 使复〔復〕苏〔蘇〕 shǐfùsū. (b) 说服 shuōfú. ~ *to* = bring round(a). ~ *up* (a)养〔養〕育 yǎngyù; 教育 jiàoyù: ~ *up children* 养育孩子; ~ *animals* 饲养动物. (b) 呕〔嘔〕出 ǒuchū. (c) 促使注意 cùshǐ zhùyì.

brink /brɪŋk/ *n* [C] **1** 悬〔懸〕崖等的边〔邊〕沿 xuányá děng de biānyán. **2** [喻]边缘 biānyuán: *on the* ~ *of war* 战争边缘.

brisk /brɪsk/ *adj* [-er,-est] 活泼〔潑〕的 huópode, 轻〔輕〕快的 qīngkuàide: *walk at a* ~ *pace* 轻快地散步. ~**ly** *adv*

bristle /'brɪsl/ *n* [C] 动〔動〕物的短而硬的毛 dòngwùde duǎn ér yìng de máo. 刷子的毛 shuāzide máo ☐ *vi* **1** (毛发等)直立 zhílì. **2** [喻]发〔發〕怒 fānù. **3** ~ *with* 从〔叢〕生 cóngshēng, 重重 chóngchóng: *bristling with guns* 枪械林立.

Brit·ish /'brɪtɪʃ/ *adj* 英国〔國〕的 yīngguóde; 英国人的 yīngguórénde: *the B*~ 英国人.

brittle /'brɪtl/ *adj* 易碎的 yìsuìde, 脆弱的 cuìruòde.

broad[1] /brɔːd/ *adj* [-er, -est] **1** 宽的 kuānde, 广〔廣〕阔〔闊〕的 guǎngkuòde. **2** 宽 kuān: *a river fifty feet* ~ 一条宽五十五英尺的河. **3** 充足的 chōngzúde: *in* ~ *daylight* 光天化日之下. **4** 大概的 dàgàide, 概略的 gàilüède: *a* ~ *distinction* 大概的区别. **5** 宽宏大量的 kuānhóng dàliàng de. **6** 方言性的 fāngyán xìngde; 口音重的 kǒuyīn zhòng de. ,~-'**minded** *adj* 能容纳不同意见的 néng róngnà bùtóng yìjiàn de ~-**ly** *adv* 广义〔義〕地 kuǎngyìde; 一般地 yìbānde: ~*ly speaking* 广义地说.

broad[2] /brɔːd/ *n* [C] 宽的部分kuānde bùfen: *the* ~ *of the back* 背部的宽处.

broad·cast /'brɔːdkaːst/ *vt/i* [*pt, pp* ~]广〔廣〕播 guǎngbō. ☐ *n* [C] 广播 guǎngbō; 播音 bōyīn.

broad·side /'brɔːdsaɪd/ *n* [C] **1** 舷炮的齐〔齊〕射 xiánpàode qíshè. **2** [喻]连〔連〕珠炮似的攻讦或谴责 liánzhūpào sì de gōngjié huò qiǎnzé.

broc·coli /'brɒkəlɪ/ *n* [C,U] [*pl*] 硬花球花椰菜 yìnghuāqiúhuāyēcài 花茎〔莖〕甘蓝〔藍〕 huājìng gānlán.

bro·chure /'brəʊʃə(r)/ n [C] 有插图〔圖〕的小册子 yǒu chātú de xiǎocèzi.

brogue[1] /brəʊg/ *n* [C] 粗革厚底皮鞋 cūgé hòudǐ píxié.

brogue[2] /brəʊg/ *n* [C] 爱〔愛〕尔〔爾〕兰〔蘭〕人说英语的土腔 àiěrlánrén shuō yīngyǔ de tǔqiāng.

broil /brɔɪl/ *vt/i* 烤 kǎo; 烧 shāo; 炙 zhì.

broke /brəʊk/ *adj* ***stony*** (或 ***flat***) ~ [俚语]一个〔個〕钱〔錢〕也没有 yígè qián yě méiyǒu.

bro·ken /'brəʊkən/ *pp* of break: *a* ~ *home* 破裂的家庭(夫妻离婚, 子女无人照顾) ~ (= imperfect) *English* 不标准的英语; ~-'*hearted* 心碎的,悲伤过度的.

bro·ker /'brəʊkə(r)/ *n* [C] (通常作'*stock*-~) 股票经〔經〕纪人 gǔpiào jīngjìrén; 掮客 qiánkè.

brolly /'brɒlɪ/ *n* [C] [*pl* -ies] [非正式用语]伞 sǎn.

bron·chial /'brɒŋkɪəl/ *adj* 支气〔氣〕

管 zhīqìguǎn.

bron·chi·tis /brɒŋ'kaɪtɪs/ *n* [C] 支气[氣]管炎 zhīqìguǎnyán.

bronze /brɒnz/ *n* **1** [U] 青铜 qīngtóng. **2** [U] 青铜色 qīngtóngsè. **3** [C] 青铜器 qīngtóngqì. 青铜艺[藝]术[術]品 qīngtóng yìshùpǐn. □ *vt/i* 上青铜色于 shàng qīngtóngsè yú; 成为[爲]青铜色 chéngwéi qīngtóngsè.

brooch /brəʊtʃ/ *n* [C] 胸针 xiōngzhēn; 饰针 shìzhēn.

brood /bru:d/ *n* [C] **1** 同窝幼鸟 tóngwō yòuniǎo. **2** [非正式用语] 一个[個]家庭的孩子 yígè jiātíng de háizi. □ *vi* **1** 孵幼雏[雛] fū yòuchú. **2** ~ *over* (或 *on*) (喻)沉思 chénsī, 忧[憂]思 yōusī. **broody** *adj* **(a)** (母鸡等) 要孵小鸡的 yào fū xiǎojī de. **(b)** [喻]思虑[慮]的 sīlǜde.

brook /brʊk/ *n* [C] 小河 xiǎohé, 溪 xī.

broom /bru:m/ *n* [C] 扫[掃]帚 sàozhou.

Bros. =Brothers.

broth /brɒθ/ *n* [U] 肉汤 ròutāng.

brothel /'brɒθl/ *n* [C] 妓院 jìyuàn.

brother /'brʌðə(r)/ *n* [C] **1** 兄弟 xiōngdì. **2** 同胞 tóngbāo; 同事 tóngshì. '~**hood** **(a)** [U] 兄弟般的关[關]系[係] xiōngdì bān de guānxì. **(b)** [C]兄弟会[會]xiōngdìhuì; 同道会 tóngdàohuì; 同道tóngdào. '~**-in-law** *n* [C] [*pl* ~s-in-law] 大伯 dàbó; 小叔 xiǎoshū; 内兄 nèixiōng; 内弟 nèidì; 姐夫 jiěfu; 妹夫 mèifu. '~**ly** *adj*

brought /brɔ:t/ *pt*, *pp* of bring.

brow /braʊ/ *n* **1** (常用复；亦作'eye-~) 眉méi, 眉毛 méimao. **2** 额 é. **3** 坡顶 pōdǐng.

brow·beat /'braʊbi:t/ *vt* [*pt*~, *pp* ~en /-bi:tn/] 欺侮 qīwǔ.

brown /braʊn/ *n* [C,U] *adj* [-er, -est] 褐色 hèsè, 棕色 zōngsè. □ *vt/i* (使)变[變]成褐色或棕色 biànchéng hèsè huò zōngsè.

browse /braʊz/ *vi* **1** 放牧 fàngmù. **2** 浏[瀏]览[覽] liúlǎn. □ *n* [C] 放牧 fàngmù; 浏览 liúlǎn.

bruise /bru:z/ *n* [C] 青肿[腫] qīngzhǒng; 伤[傷]痕 shānghén. □ *vt/i* **1** 使青肿 shǐ qīngzhǒng; 碰伤 pèngshāng. **2** 受伤 shòushāng.

bru·nette /bru:'net/ *n* [C] 浅[淺]黑型的白种[種]女人 qiǎnhēi xíng de báizhǒng nǚrén.

brunt /brʌnt/ *n* [C] 主要部分 zhǔyào bùfen: *bear the* ~ *of an attack* 首当其冲.

brush[1] /brʌʃ/ *n* [C] **1** 刷子 shuāzi, 毛刷 máoshuā. **2** 刷 shuā. **3** [U] 灌木丛[叢] guànmùcóng. **4** 小接触[觸] xiǎo jiēchù: *a* ~ *with the enemy* 与敌人的一场小接触.

brush[2] /brʌʃ/ *vt/i* **1** 刷 shuā. **2** ~ *sth aside* (或 *away*)[喻]不顾[顧]困难 búgù kùnnan. ~ *up(on)* 复[復]习[習] fùxí: ~ *up(on) your French* 复习你的法语. **3** 擦过[過] cāguò, 掠过 lüèguò.

brusque /bru:sk/ *adj* 粗鲁的 cūlǔde, 鲁莽的 lǔmǎngde. ~**ly** *adj* ~**ness** *n* [U]

Brus·sels sprout /ˌbrʌslz 'spraʊt/ *n* [C] 球芽甘蓝[藍] qiúyá gānlán.

bru·tal /'bru:tl/ *adj* 野蛮[蠻]的 yěmánde, 残[殘]忍的 cánrěnde. ~**ly** *adv* ~**ity** /bru:'tælətɪ/, [C,U] [*pl* -ies] 暴行 bàoxíng, 残[殘]忍 cánrěn.

brute /bru:t/ *n* [C] **1** 兽 shòu; 畜牲 chùshēng. **2** 残[殘]忍的人 cánrěnde rén. □ *adj* 没有思想的 méiyǒu sīxiǎng de, 身体[體]的 shēntǐde. ~ *strength* 蛮[蠻]力 mánlì; 暴力 bàolì. **brut·ish** *adj* 野兽[獸]的 yěshòude, 野蛮[蠻]的 yěmánde.

B.Sc. =Bachelor of Science.

bubble /'bʌbl/ *n* [C] **1** 空气[氣]中的气泡 kōngqì zhōng de qìpào. **2** 液体[體]中的气泡 yètǐ zhōng de qìpào; 泡沫 pàomò. □ *vi* 冒泡 màopào. '~**-gum** 泡泡糖 pàopàotáng. **bub·bly** /'bu:blɪ/ *adj* 泡多的 pàoduōde; 冒泡的 màopàode.

buck[1] /bʌk/ *n* [C] 雄鹿 xiónglù; 公羊 gōngyáng; 牡兔 mǔtù. ⇨doe.

buck[2] /bʌk/ *vt/i* **1** (马)猛然弯[彎]背跃[躍]起 měngrán wānbèi yuèqǐ; 弯背跃起将[將]骑[騎]者摔落地上 wānbèi yuèqǐ jiāng qízhě shuāi luò dì shàng. **2**[非正式用语]使精神振奋[奮] shǐ jīngshén zhèngfèn: *The good news* ~*ed us all up.* 这个好消息使我们大家欢欣鼓舞.

buck[3] /bʌk/ *n* [C] [俚语]美元 měiyuán. *pass the* ~ *(to sb)* [俚语] 向某人推卸责任 xiàngmǒurén tuīxiè zérèn.

bucket /'bʌkɪt/ *n* [C] **1**水桶 shuǐtǒng; 提桶 tītǒng. **2**(亦作 '~**ful**) 一桶之量 yìtǒng zhī liàng

buckle /'bʌkl/ *n* [C] 扣子 kòuzi; 带[帶]扣 dàikòu. □ *vt/i* **1** 把…扣住 bǎ … kòuzhù; 把…扣紧[緊] bǎ … kòujǐn. **2** 由于压[壓]力或热[熱]力而弯[彎]曲 yóuyú yālì huò rèlì ér wānqū.

bud /bʌd/ *n* [C] 芽 yá. *nip sth in the* ~ 把 … 消灭[滅]于萌芽状

〔狀〕态〔態〕bǎ ... xiāomiè yú méngyá zhuàngtài. □ *vi* [-dd-] 发〔發〕芽 fāyá, 萌芽 méngyá: ~-**ding** *adj* 开〔開〕始发〔發〕展的 kāishǐ fāzhǎn de: *a ~ poet* 崭露头角的诗人.

Bud·dhism /'bʊdɪzəm/ *n* 佛教 fójiào, 释〔釋〕教 shìjiào. **Bud·dhist** /'bʊdɪst/ *n* [C], *adj* 佛教徒 fójiàotú; 佛教的 fójiàode.

budge /bʌdʒ/ *vt/i* [非正式用语](使)移动〔動〕yídòng: *I can't ~ this stone.* 我推不动这块石头.

bud·geri·gar /'bʌdʒərɪgɑ:(r)/ *n* [C] 小长尾鹦〔鸚〕鹉〔鵡〕xiǎo chángwěi yīngwǔ.

budget /'bʌdʒɪt/ *n* [C] 预算 yùsuàn. □ *vi* ~ *for* 为〔爲〕...编预算 wèi ... biān yùsuàn.

buff /bʌf/ *n* [U] **1** 坚〔堅〕韧〔韌〕而柔软〔軟〕的皮革 jiānrèn ér róuruǎn de pígé. **2** 暗黄色 ànhuángsè. □ *vt* 擦亮(金属)cāliàng.

buf·falo /'bʌfələʊ/ *n* [C] [*pl* ~s] **1** 水牛 shuǐniú. **2** 北美野牛 běiměi yěniú.

buf·fer /'bʌfə(r)/ *n* [C] 缓冲〔衝〕器 huǎnchōngqì.

buf·fet[1] /'bʊfeɪ/ *n* [C] **1** (火车内)餐室 cānshì. **2** (旅馆内) 冷食桌 lěngshízhuō.

buf·fet[2] /'bʌfɪt/ *n* [C] (用手) 打 dǎ. □ *vt/i* 打击〔擊〕dǎjī: *~ed by the wind* 被风摧残.

buf·foon /bə'fu:n/ *n* [C] 小丑 xiǎochǒu.

bug /bʌg/ *n* [C] **1** 臭虫〔蟲〕chòuchóng. **2** [非正式用语] 病毒传〔傳〕染 bìngdú chuánrǎn. **3** [俚语] (电子计算机等的)缺陷 quēxiàn. **4** 窃〔竊〕听〔聽〕器. □ *vt* [-gg-] [非正式用语]窃听 qiètīng.

bug·bear /'bʌgbeə(r)/ *n* [C] 吓〔嚇〕人的事 xiàrénde shì. 令人厌〔厭〕恶〔惡〕的事 lìngrén yànwùde shì.

bugle /'bju:gl/ *n* [C] 军〔軍〕号〔號〕jūnhào. **bugler** 司号兵 sīhàobīng.

build[1] /bɪld/ *vt/i* [*pt,pp* built/bɪlt/] **1** 建筑 jiànzhù, 造 zào: *~ a house* 建筑房屋. **2** 依赖 yīlài; 指望 zhǐwàng: *~ hopes on* 寄希望于. **3** ~ *up* 增加 zēngjiā: *Traffic is ~ing up.* 交通量正在增加. ~ *up sb* (*sth*) (a) 夸赞 kuāzàn; 吹捧 chuīpěng. (b) 扩〔擴〕大 kuòdà: *~ up a business* 扩大经营一个店铺. (c) 盖起、布满建筑物 gàiqǐ, bùmǎn jiànzhùwù. **'~-up** (a) 增加 zēngjiā; 集结 jíjié: *a ~-up of forces.* 军队的集结. (b) 增加 zēngjiā: *a ~-up of traffic* 交通阻塞. (c) 吹捧 chuīpěng. **~er** 建筑师 jiànzhùshī.

build[2] /bɪld/ *n* [U] 体〔體〕格 tǐgé: *a man of powerful ~* 一个体格强健的人.

build·ing /'bɪldɪŋ/ *n* **1** [C] 建筑〔築〕物 jiànzhùwù. **2** [U] 建筑术〔術〕jiànzhùshù.

bulb /bʌlb/ *n* [C] **1** 鳞茎〔莖〕línjìng, 球茎 qiújìng. **2** 球状〔狀〕物 qiúzhuàngwù: *an electric light ~* 电灯泡. **~ous** /'bʌlbəs/ *adj* 鳞茎状的 línjìngzhuàngde.

bulge /bʌldʒ/ *n* [C] 膨胀〔脹〕péngzhàng; 肿〔腫〕胀 zhǒngzhàng. □ *vt/i* (使)膨胀 péngzhàng.

bulk /bʌlk/ *n* [U] 容量 róngliàng; 体〔體〕积 tǐjī; 大块〔塊〕dàkài. *in ~* 大批 dàpī, 大量 dàliàng: *buy in ~* 大量购买. *the ~ of* 大多数〔數〕dàduōshù. **bulky** *adj* [-ier, -iest] 体〔體〕积大的 tǐjī dà de; 笨大的 bèndàde.

bull /bʊl/ *n* [C] **1** 公牛 gōngniú *a ~ in a 'china shop* 鲁莽而爱〔愛〕闯〔闖〕祸的人 lǔmǎng ér ài zhuǎnghuò de rén. *take the ~ by the 'horns* 大无〔無〕畏 dà wúwèi, 不避艰〔艱〕险〔險〕búbì jiānxiǎn. **2** 雄性的鲸、象等大动〔動〕物 xióngxìngde jīng, xiàng děng dà dòngwù. **'~dog** 叭喇狗 bālǎgǒu. **'~doze** *vt* (a) 用推土机〔機〕推土 yòng tuītǔjī tuītǔ. (b) 强迫某人做某事 qiángpò mǒurén zuò mǒushì. **~-dozer** 推土机 tuītǔjī. **'~'s-eye** 靶的中心 bǎde zhōngxīn.

bul·let /'bʊlɪt/ *n* [C]枪〔槍〕弹〔彈〕qiāngdàn; 子弹 zǐdàn. **'~-proof** *adj* 防弹的 fángdànde.

bull·etin /'bʊlətɪn/ *n* [C] 公报〔報〕gōngbào.

bul·lion /'bʊlɪən/ *n* [U] 条〔條〕金 tiáojīn; 条银 tiáoyín; 块〔塊〕金 kuàijīn; 块银 kuàiyín.

bul·lock /'bʊlək/ *n* [C] 阉〔閹〕公牛 yāngōngniú.

bully /'bʊlɪ/ *n* [C] [*pl* -ies]恶〔惡〕霸 èbà; 暴徒 bàotú. □ *vt* [*pt,pp* -ied] 欺侮 qīwǔ.

bul·rush /'bʊlrʌʃ/ *n* [C] 芦〔蘆〕苇〔葦〕lúwěi.

bul·wark /'bʊlwək/ *n* [C] **1** 堡垒〔壘〕bǎolěi, 防御〔禦〕工事 fángyù gōngshì. **2** [喻]屏藩 píngfān, 保障 bǎozhàng.

bum[1] /bʌm/ *n* [C] [非正式用语] 屁股 pìgu.

bum[2] /bʌm/ *n* [C] [俚语]游民 yóumín, 乞丐 qǐgài, 懒汉〔漢〕lǎnhàn.

bumble·bee /'bʌmbl bi:/ *n* [C]

大蜂 dàfēng.

bump /bʌmp/ *vt/i* **1** 撞 zhuàng, 撞击〔擊〕zhuàngjī. **2** 颠簸地行驶〔駛〕diānbǒde xíngshǐ: *The bus ~ed along the rough road.* 公共汽车在凹凸不平的路上颠簸前进. **3** *~ sb off* 〔俚语〕谋杀〔殺〕móushā. □ *adv* 猛烈地 měngliède. □ *n* [C] **1** 撞 zhuàng, 撞击 zhuàngjī; 碰撞声〔聲〕pèngzhuàngshēng. **2**（撞伤）肿〔腫〕块〔塊〕zhǒngkuài. **3** 路面上的凹凸不平 lùmiàn shàng de āotūbùpíng. **bumpy** *adj* [-ier, -iest] 凹凸不平的 āotūbùpíngde.

bum·per[1] /ˈbʌmpə(r)/ *n* [C] 汽车〔車〕上的保险〔險〕杆〔桿〕qìchē shàng de bǎoxiǎngān.

bum·per[2] /ˈbʌmpə(r)/ *adj* 大的 dàde; 丰〔豐〕富的 fēngfùde: *a ~ harvest* 丰收.

bump·kin /ˈbʌmpkɪn/ *n* [C] 乡〔鄉〕下佬 xiāngxiàlǎo; 乡下人 xiāngxiàrén.

bun /bʌn/ *n* [C] **1** 小圆(甜)面〔麵〕包 xiǎoyuán miànbāo. **2** 颈〔頸〕后〔後〕的发〔髮〕髻 jǐnghòude fàjì.

bunch /bʌntʃ/ *n* [C] 束 sù; 串 chuàn; 球 qiú: *a ~ of grapes* 一串葡萄; *a ~ of flowers* 一束花. □ *vt/i ~ up* 串成一串 chuànchéng yíchuàn; 捆成一束 kǔnchéng yísù.

bundle /ˈbʌndl/ *n* [C] 捆 kǔn; 包 bāo. □ *vt/i* **1** *~ up* 打成捆 dǎchéng kǔn; 打成包 dǎchéng bāo. **2** 匆忙地放进 cōngmángde fàngjìn: *They ~d him into a taxi.* 他们匆匆忙忙地把他推进一辆出租汽车.

bung /bʌŋ/ *n* [C] 桶塞 tǒngsāi. □ *vt* 塞上桶塞 sāishàng tǒngsāi. *~-ed up* 被污物堵塞 bèi wūwù dǔsè.

bun·ga·low /ˈbʌŋgələʊ/ *n* [C] 平房 píngfáng.

bungle /ˈbʌŋgl/ *vt/i* 搞坏〔壞〕gǎohuài; 粗制〔製〕滥〔濫〕造 cūzhì lànzào.

bun·ion /ˈbʌnɪən/ *n* [C] 姆指肿〔腫〕胀 mǔzhǐ zhǒngzhàng.

bunk[1] /bʌŋk/ *n* [C] 车〔車〕、船上的床位 chē chuán shàng de chuángwèi.

bunk[2] /bʌŋk/ *n* 逃 táo. *do a ~*〔俚语〕逃走 táozǒu.

bunker /ˈbʌŋkə(r)/ *n* [C] **1** 煤舱〔艙〕méicāng. **2** 高尔〔爾〕夫球场〔場〕上的沙窪 gāoěrfū qiúchǎng shàng de shāwā. **3**（军事）地堡 dìbǎo.

bunny /ˈbʌnɪ/ *n* [C] [*pl* -ies] 小兔子(儿童语) xiǎotùzi.

buoy /bɔɪ/ *n* [C] **1** 浮标〔標〕fúbiāo. **2** =lifebuoy. □ *vi* **1** 用浮标标出 yòng fúbiāo biāochū. **2** *~ up* **(a)** 浮起 fúqǐ. **(b)**〔喻〕鼓励〔勵〕gǔlì.

buoy·ant /ˈbɔɪənt/ *adj* **1** 有浮力的 yǒu fúlì de. **2**〔喻〕愉快的 yúkuàide; 轻〔輕〕松〔鬆〕的 qīngsōngde. **3**〔喻〕(股票市场等)保持高价〔價〕的 bǎochí gāojià de. **~ly** *adv* **buoy·ancy** *n* [U]

bur·den /ˈbɜːdn/ *n* [C] **1** 负担〔擔〕fùdān; 担子 dànzi. **2** 重负 zhòngfù: *the ~ of taxation* 捐税的重负. □ *vt* 使负担 shǐ fùdān, 使负重担 shǐfù zhòngdàn. **~some** *adj* 难以负担的 nányǐ fùdānde.

bureau /ˈbjʊərəʊ/ *n* [C] [*pl* ~x /-rəʊz/] **1** 有抽屉的写〔寫〕字桌 yǒu chōuti de xiězìzhuō. **2** 局 jú; 司 sī; 处〔處〕chù; 所 suǒ: *the ˌInforˈmation B~* 情报局.

bureau·cracy /bjʊəˈrɒkrəsɪ/ *n* [U] 官僚（总称）guānliáo. **bureau·crat** /ˈbjʊərəkræt/ *n* [C] 官僚 guānliáo. **bureauˈcratic** *adj* 官僚主义〔義〕的 guānliáozhǔyìde.

bur·glar /ˈbɜːglə(r)/ *n* [C] 夜贼 yèzéi. *ˈ~-proof adj* 防夜贼的 fáng yèzéi de. **bur·glary** *n* [C,U] [*pl* -ies] 夜窃〔竊〕yèqiè. **burgle** /ˈbɜːgl/ *vt/i* 夜晚偷盗 yèwǎn tōudào.

bur·ial /ˈberɪəl/ *n* [C, U] 葬 zàng; 埋藏 máicáng.

burly /ˈbɜːlɪ/ *adj* [-ier, -iest] 强壮的 qiángzhuàngde, 壮实〔實〕的 zhuàngshide.

burn[1] /bɜːn/ *n* [C] 烧〔燒〕伤〔傷〕shāoshāng, 灼伤 zhuóshāng; 烙印 luòyìng. **~er** 燃烧器 ránshāoqì; 炉〔爐〕子 lúzi: *an ˈoil~er* 煤油炉. **~ing** *adj* **(a)** 炽〔熾〕烈的 zhìliède; 热〔熱〕切的 rèqiède: *a ~ing thirst* 热切的渴望, 灼热的干渴; *~ desire* 炽烈的愿望. **(b)** 引起争论〔論〕的 yǐnqǐ zhēnglùn de: *a ~ing question* 引起争论的问题.

burn[2] /bɜːn/ *vt/i* [*pt, pp* ~t /bɜːnt/ 或 ~ed /bɜːnd/] **1** 烧〔燒〕shāo; 点〔點〕(烛, 灯等) diǎn: *~ coal in a fire* 在炉子里烧煤. **2** 烧坏〔壞〕shāo huài; 烧毁 shāohuǐ; 烧伤〔傷〕shāoshāng; 烫〔燙〕伤 tàngshāng; 灼伤 zhuóshāng: *~ old papers* 烧毁旧文件 **3**〔喻〕激动〔動〕jīdòng; 激怒 jīnù: *~ with anger* 怒火中烧. **4** *~ away* **(a)** 继〔繼〕续〔續〕燃烧 jìxù ránshāo. **(b)** 烧掉 shāodiào. *~ down* 被烧毁 bèi shāohuǐ; 将〔將〕…烧毁 jiāng … shāohuǐ: *The house ~t down.* 房子烧毁了. *~ out* **(a)** 烧光 shāoguāng, 烧完 shāowán. **(b)**（火箭）燃尽〔盡〕

燃料 ránjìn ránliào. (c) 烧毁shāohuǐ: *~t-out factories* 被烧毁的工厂.

bur·nish /'bɜːnɪʃ/ *vt/i* 擦亮 cāliàng.

burp /bɜːp/ *n* [C] *vi* [俚语]打嗝 dǎgér.

bur·row /'bʌrəʊ/ *n* [C] 兔等的地洞 tù děng de dìdòng. □ *vt/i* 打(地洞) dǎ, 掘(穴) jué.

bur·sar /'bɜːsə(r)/ *n* [C] 大学[學]等的财务[務]人员 dàxué děng de cáiwù rényuán.

burst[1] /bɜːst/ *n* [C] **1** 爆炸 bàozhà. **2** 短暂[暫]而猛烈的努力 duǎnzhǎn ér měngliè de nǔlì: *a ~ of energy* 一股猛劲. **3** 爆发[發] bàofā: *a ~ of gunfire* 一阵炮火射击.

burst[2] /bɜːst/ *vt/i* [*pt, pp*~] **1** 使炸弹[彈]等爆炸 shǐ zhàdàn děng bàozhà. **2** 溃决 kuìjué; 胀破 zhàngpò; 绽开[開] zhànkāi. ***be ~ing to*** 急切要 jíqiè yào. **3** 满盈 mǎnyíng: *~ing with impatience* 不耐烦, 急不可耐. **4** 突然进入 tūrán jìnrù; 急速离[離]去 jísù líqù: *~ out of the room* 突然迈出房间. **5** ***~ in (on*** 或 ***upon)*** 打断[斷] dǎduàn; 突然来[來]到 tūrán láidào. ***~ into*** 突然发[發]作 tūrán fāzuò: *~ into flames* 一下子烧了起来; *~ into tears* 突然哭了起来; *~ into song* 突然唱起歌来. ***~ out laughing*** 突然笑起来 tūrán xiào qǐlái, ***~ out crying*** 突然哭起来 tūrán kū qǐlái.

bury /'berɪ/ *vt* [*pt, pp* -ied] **1** 埋葬 máizàng, 葬 zàng. **2** 埋藏 máicáng; 掩藏 yǎncáng: *buried treasure* 被埋藏的宝物. *She buried* (= hid) *her face in her hands.* 她两手捂着脸. ***~ oneself in*** 专[專]心致志于 zhuānxīn zhìzhì yú.

bus /bʌs/ *n* [*pl*~es] 公共汽车[車] gōnggòngqìchē. □ *vt/i* [-ss-] 乘公共汽车去 chéng gōnggòngqìchē qù. **'~ stop** 公共汽车站 gōnggòngqìchēzhàn.

bush /bʊʃ/ *n* **1** [C] 灌木 guànmù; 多枝矮树[樹] duōzhī ǎishù. **2** [U] 澳大利亚[亞]未开[開]垦的土地 àodàlìyǎ wèi kāikěn de tǔdì. **'bushy** *adj* [-ier, -iest] **(a)** 被灌木遮盖的 bèi guànmù zhēgài de. **(b)** 浓[濃]密的 nóngmìde. *~y eyebrows* 浓眉.

busier, busiest ⇨ busy.

busi·ly /'bɪzɪlɪ/ *adv* 繁忙地 fánmángde.

busi·ness /'bɪznɪs/ *n* **1** [U] 买卖[賣] mǎimài; 商业[業] shāngyè, 贸易 màoyì. **2** [C] 商店 shāngdiàn, 商业企业 shāngyè qǐyè. **3** [U] 任务[務] rènwù; 职[職]责 zhízé: *It is a teacher's ~ to help his pupils.* 教师的职责是帮助自己的学生. ***get down to ~*** 着手干[幹]正事 zhuóshǒu gàn zhèngshì. ***mind one's own ~*** 各人自扫[掃]门[門]前雪,莫管他人瓦上霜 gèrén zìsǎo ménqiánxiě mòguǎn tārén wǎ shàng shuāng. **'~-like** *adj* 有效率的 yǒu xiàolǜ de; 有条[條]理的 yǒu tiáolǐ de. **'~man** 商人 shāngrén.

bust[1] /bʌst/ *n* [C] **1** 半身雕塑像 bànshēn diāosùxiàng. **2** 妇[婦]女的胸部 fùnǚde xiōngbù.

bust[2] /bʌst/ *vt/i* [俚语] ***~ sth*** 打破 dǎpò, 击[擊]破 jīpò. ***go ~*** 失败 shībài; 破产[產] pòchǎn: *The business went ~.* 这家商店破产了.

bustle /'bʌsl/ *vt/i* 使活跃[躍]、忙碌 shǐ huóyuè, mánglù. □ *n* [U] 熙嚷 xī rǎng; 喧闹 xuānnào.

busy /'bɪzɪ/ *adj* [-ier, -iest] **1** 繁忙的 fánmángde, 忙碌的 mánglùde. **2** 没空的 méikòngde: *a ~ day* 忙碌的一天. **3** 电[電]话占线[綫] diànhuà zhànxiàn. □ *vt* 使忙碌 shǐ mánglù.

but[1] /bʌt/ *adv* 只 zhǐ, 仅仅 jǐnjǐn: *We can ~ try.* 我们只能试试看.

but[2] /bət 强式: bʌt/ *conj* 但 dàn: *Tom was not there ~ his brother was.* 汤姆不在那里,但是他的兄弟在那里.

but[3] /bət 强式: bʌt/ *prep* 除了 chúle. *No-one knew ~ John.* 除了约翰谁也不知道. **'~ for** 要不是 yàobúshì: *B~ for your help we should not have finished.* 要不是你的帮助,我们就完不成了.

butcher /'bʊtʃə(r)/ *n* [C] **1** 屠夫 túfū; 屠宰, 卖[賣]肉的人 túzǎi, màiròu de rén. **2** 残[殘]杀[殺]者 cánshāzhě. □ *vt* **1** 屠宰 túzǎi. **2** 屠杀 túshā. **butchery** *n* 屠宰场[場] túzǎichǎng; 肉店 ròudiàn; 屠杀[殺] túshā.

but·ler /'bʌtlə(r)/ *n* [C] 管家 guǎnjiā.

butt[1] /bʌt/ *n* [C] **1** 大桶 dàtǒng. **2** 枪[槍]托 qiāngtuō. **3** 香烟未点[點]燃的一端 xiāngyān wèi diǎnrán de yìduān.

butt[2] /bʌt/ *n* [C] 嘲笑的对[對]象 cháoxiàode duìxiàng.

butt[3] /bʌt/ *vt/i* **1** 用头[頭]顶撞 yòng tóu dǐngzhuàng. **2** ***~ in*** [非正式用语] 插嘴 chāzuǐ; 打断[斷]说话 dǎduàn shuōhuà.

but·ter /'bʌtə(r)/ *n* [U] 黄油 huángyóu. □ *vt* **1** 涂[塗]黄油 tú huángyóu; 用黄油煎煮 yòng huángyóu jiānzhǔ. **2** ***~ sb up*** 奉承 fèngcheng, 阿谀 ēyú. **'~cup** 毛茛属

〔属〕植物 máogēnshǔ zhíwù. '~-scotch [U] 黄油硬糖 huángyóu yìngtáng.

but·ter·fly /'bʌtəflaɪ/ *n* [C] [*pl* -ies] 蝴蝶 húdié.

but·tock /'bʌtək/ *n* [C] 半边〔邊〕屁股 bànbian pìgu.

but·ton /'bʌtn/ *n* [C] **1** 钮扣 niǔkòu. **2** 按钮 àn'niǔ: *press* (或 *push*) *the* ~ 揿按钮 qìn àn'niǔ. □ *vt/i* 扣钮扣 kòu niǔkòu. '~**hole** *n* [C] **(a)** 钮孔 niǔkǒng, 钮眼 niǔyǎn. **(b)** 戴在外衣翻领上的花 dài zài wàiyī fānlǐng shàng de huā. □ *vt* 拉住某人以引起他注意 lāzhù mǒurén yǐ yǐnqǐ tā zhùyì.

but·tress /'bʌtrɪs/ *n* [C] **1** 扶垛 fúduò, 扶壁 fúbì. **2** [喻] 支持物 zhīchíwù, 支柱 zhīzhù. □ *vt* 加强 jiāqiáng; 支持 zhīchí.

buxom /'bʌksəm/ *adj* (妇女)丰〔豐〕满的 fēngmǎnde, 健康的 jiànkāngde.

buy /baɪ/ *vt/i* [*pt, pp* bought /bɔ:t/] 买 mǎi, 购买 gòumǎi. □ *n* [非正式用语]买〔買〕卖 mǎimài; 买得的货物 mǎidéde huòwù: *a good* ~ 一桩合算的买卖. ~**er** 买者 mǎizhě.

buzz /bʌz/ *vt/i* **1** (蜜蜂) 嗡嗡叫 wēngwēngjiào. **2** 匆忙行走 cōngmáng xíngzǒu. ~ *off* [俚语] 离〔離〕开〔開〕 líkāi. **3** 耳鸣 ěrmíng. **4** [非正式用语]威胁性地飞〔飛〕近另一飞机〔機〕 wēixié xìng de fēijìn lìng yī fēijī. □ *n* [C] **1** 嘁嘁喳喳声〔聲〕 qīqīchāchā shēng. **2** 蜜蜂等的嗡嗡声 mìfēng děng de wēngwēngshēng. ~**er** 蜂音器 fēngyīnqì, 蜂音电〔電〕铃 fēngyīn diànlíng.

buz·zard /'bʌzəd/ *n* [C] 鹰〔鷹〕 yīng.

by[1] /baɪ/ *adv* **1** 靠近 kàojìn, 在…近旁 zài…jìnpáng: *A large crowd stood* ~. 一大群人站在旁边. **2** 经〔經〕过〔過〕 jīngguò: *He hurried* ~ *without a word.* 他匆匆走过, 一句话没有说. ,~ *and* '*large* 大体〔體〕上 dàtǐshàng; 总〔總〕的说 zǒngdeshuō.

by[2] /baɪ/ *prep* **1** 靠近 kàojìn, 在…旁边〔邊〕 zài… pángbian. *sit* ~ *me* 坐在我旁边. ~ *oneself* 单〔單〕独 dāndú; 独力 dúlì; 自行 zìxíng. *stand* ~ *sb* 支持某人 zhīchí mǒurén. **2** 沿 yán; 由 yóu; 经〔經〕 jīng: *We came* ~ *the fields, not* ~ *the roads.* 我们从田野上穿行过来, 没有走大路. **3** 经〔經〕过〔過〕 jīngguò: *He walked* ~ *me.* 他从我身旁走过. **4** 在 zài: *The enemy attacked* ~ *night.* 敌人在夜间进攻. **5** 不迟〔遲〕于 bù chíyú: *Can you finish the work* ~ *tomorrow?* 你能在明天以前完成这项工作吗? **6** 按 àn; 根据〔據〕 gēnjù: *rent a house* ~ *the year* 按年租房子; *sell cloth* ~ *the metre* 按米卖布. **7** 用 yòng; 靠 kào; 通过 tōngguò: *live* ~ *teaching* 靠教书生活; *killed* ~ *lightning* 被雷打死. **8** 表示方法 biǎoshì fāngfǎ: *travel* ~ *land* 陆路旅行; *travel* ~ *sea* 海上旅行; *travel* ~ *air* 乘飞机旅行; ~ *car* 乘汽车; ~ *boat* 乘船. **9** 按照 ànzhào, 根据 gēnjù: *B~ my watch it is 2 o'clock.* 按照我的手表, 是两点钟. **10** 到…程度 dào… chéngdù: *The bullet missed me* ~ *two inches.* 子弹没有打中我, 偏了二英寸.

B.V.M.=The Blessed Virgin Mary. 圣〔聖〕母玛〔瑪〕利亚〔亞〕 shèngmǔ mǎlìyà.

by-elec·tion /'baɪ ɪlekʃn/ *n* [C] 补〔補〕缺选〔選〕举〔舉〕 bǔqiē xuǎnjǔ. ⇨ general election.

by·gone /'baɪgɒn/ *adj* 过〔過〕去的 guòqùde, 以往的 yǐwǎngde: *in* ~ *days* 在往日. □ *n* [*pl*] *Let* ~*s be* ~*s.* 既往不咎 jì wǎng bù jiū, 让〔讓〕过去的事过去了吧 ràng guòqùde shì guòqù le ba.

by-law, bye-law /'baɪlɔ:/ *n* [C] 地方当〔當〕局订立的规章 dìfāng dāngjú dìnglì de guīzhāng.

by-pass /'baɪpɑ:s/ *n* [C] 迂回的旁道 yūhuíde pángdào; 旁路 pánglù. □ *vt* **1** 加设旁道 jiā hè pángdào. **2** 回避 huíbì, 躲开〔開〕 duǒkāi: ~ *a problem* 回避问题; ~ *a blockage* 绕过封锁.

by-prod·uct /'baɪprɒdʌkt/ *n* [C] 副产〔產〕品 fùchǎnpǐng.

by·stander /'baɪstændə(r)/ *n* [C] 旁观〔觀〕者 pángguānzhě.

C c

C, c /si:/ [*pl* C's, c's /si:z/] **1** 英语的第三个〔個〕字母 yīngyǔde dìsān-gè zìmǔ. **2** 罗〔羅〕马〔馬〕 数〔數〕字的 100 luómǎ shùzì de 100.

C=Centigrade.

c= **1** cent(s). **2** century. **3** about. **4** cubic. **5** centimetre.

ca 大约 dàyuē.

C.A.= Charted Accountant (英国)会〔會〕计师〔師〕(持有皇家特许状) kuàijìshī.

cab /kæb/ *n* [C] **1** 出租汽车〔車〕 chūzū qìchē, 计程汽车 jìchéng qìchē. **2** (机车等的)司机〔機〕室 sījī shì.

cab·aret /'kæbəreɪ/ *n* [C] (餐馆等中的)歌舞表演 gēwǔ biǎoyǎn.

cab·bage /'kæbɪdʒ/ *n* [C, U] 甘蓝〔藍〕 gānlán, 卷心菜 juǎnxīncài, 洋白菜 yángbáicài.

cabin /'kæbɪn/ *n* [C] **1** 船舱〔艙〕 chuáncāng, 飞〔飛〕机〔機〕舱 fēijīcāng, 船的房舱 chuánde fángcāng **2** 小木屋 xiǎo mùwū; (铁路的)信号〔號〕室 xìnhàoshì. '~ **cruiser** 有舱位的汽艇 yǒu cāngwèi de qìtǐng.

cabi·net /'kæbɪnɪt/ *n* [C] **1** 柜〔櫃〕橱 guìchú. *a* '*filing* ~ 文件柜. **2** 内阁〔閣〕 nèigé.

cable /'keɪbl/ *n* **1** [C, U] 缆〔纜〕 lǎn; 索 suǒ. **2** 电〔電〕缆 diànlǎn; 电报〔報〕 diànbào. □ *vt/i* 拍电报 pāi diànbào. '~-**car** 电缆车〔車〕 diànlǎnché, ~ **railway** 缆车铁〔鐵〕道 lǎnchē tiědào.

cackle /'kækl/ *n* **1** [C] 母鸡〔鷄〕咯咯叫声〔聲〕 mǔjī gēgē jiàoshēng. **2** [C]废〔廢〕话 fèihuà; 咯咯的笑声 gēgē de xiàoshēng. □ *vi* **1** (母鸡)咯咯地叫 gēgēde jiào. **2** 大声地谈话或笑 dàshēngde tánhuà huò xiào.

cac·tus /'kæktəs/ *n* [C] [*pl* ~es, cacti /'kæktaɪ/] 仙人掌 xiānrénzhǎng.

ca·det /kə'det/ *n* [C] 警校学〔學〕生 jǐngxiào xuésheng; 军〔軍〕校学生 jūnxiào xuésheng.

cadge /kædʒ/ *vt/i* [非正式用语]乞求 qǐqiú, 乞讨 qǐtǎo, 借 jiè: ~ *£5 from a friend* 向朋友借 5 英镑钱.

caf·é /'kæfeɪ/ *n* [C] 咖啡馆 kāfēiguǎn; 餐馆 cānguǎn; 酒吧 jiǔbā.

cafe·teria /ˌkæfɪ'tɪərɪə/ *n* [C] 自助食堂 zìzhù shítáng; 自助餐馆zìzhù cānguǎn.

cage /keɪdʒ/ *n* [C] 笼〔籠〕子 lóngzi. □ *vt* 关〔關〕入笼子 guānrù lóngzi.

cagey /'keɪdʒɪ/ *adj* 保守秘密的 bǎoshǒu mìmì de.

cairn /keən/ *n* [C] 石标〔標〕 shíbiāo. (用作纪念或路标等的)圆锥形石堆 yuánzhuīxíng shíduī.

ca·jole /kə'dʒəʊl/ *vt* 哄骗〔騙〕 hǒngpiàn, 勾引 gōuyǐn, 引诱 yǐnyòu: *He ~d me into (out of) going.* 他用甜言蜜语哄骗我去(不去).

cake /keɪk/ *n* **1** [C, U] 饼〔餅〕 bǐng, 糕 gāo, 蛋糕 dàngāo. **2** [C] 饼状〔狀〕食物 bǐngzhuàng shíwù: '*fish-~s* 鱼饼. **3** [C] 块〔塊〕, 饼状物 kuài, bǐng zhuàng wù: *a ~ of soap* 一块肥皂. *a piece of ~* 轻〔輕〕松〔鬆〕易做的事 qīngsōng yìzuò de shì. □ *vt/i* 粘上泥土等 zhānshàng nítǔ děng.

ca·lam·ity /kə'læmətɪ/ *n* [C] [*pl* -ies] 灾〔災〕难〔難〕 zāinàn, 灾祸 zāihuò, 祸患 huòhuàn.

cal·cium /'kælsɪəm/ *n* [U] 钙(化学符号 Ca) gài.

cal·cu·lable /'kælkjʊləbl/ *adj* 能计算的 néng jìsuàn de.

cal·cu·late /'kælkjʊleɪt/ *vt/i* **1** 计算 jìsuàn, 核算 hésuàn: ~ *the cost* 计算成本. **2** 计划〔劃〕 jìhuà, 打算 dǎsuàn: *~d to attract attention* 有意吸引注意. **3** 以为〔爲〕yǐwéi, 认〔認〕为 rènwéi. **cal·cu·lat·ing** *adj* 阴〔陰〕谋的 yīnmóude; 有策略的 yǒu cèlüè de. ˌ**cal·cu·'la·tion** *n* [C, U] **cal·cu·la·tor** *n* [C] 计算机〔機〕jìsuànjī.

cal·en·dar /'kælɪndə(r)/ *n* [C] **1** 历〔曆〕书〔書〕 lìshū; 日历 rìlì; 周历 zhōulì; 月历 yuèlì. **2** 历法 lìfǎ: *the Muslim* ~ 伊斯兰教历.

calf[1] /kɑ:f/ *n* **1** [C] [*pl* calves /kɑ:vz/] 小牛 xiǎoniú, 犊 dú; 小海豹 xiǎohǎibào; 小鲸 xiǎojīng. **2** [U] (亦作 '~ *skin*) 小牛皮 xiǎoniúpí.

calf[2] /kɑ:f/ *n* [C] [*pl* calves /kɑ:vz/] 腓 féi.

cal·ibre [美语 = **-ber**] /'kælɪbə(r)/ *n* **1** [C] 口径〔徑〕 kǒujìng. **2** [U] 才干〔幹〕cáigàn, 才能cáinéng: *soldiers of high* ~ 很有才干的军人.

cali·pers *n pl* ⇨ callipers.

call[1] /kɔ:l/ *n* [C] **1** 喊 hǎn, 叫 jiào: *a ~ for help* 喊救. **2** 鸟〔鳥〕的特殊鸣〔鳴〕声〔聲〕. niǎode tèshū míngshēng. **3** 拜访 bàifǎng; 小停 xiǎotíng. **4** 信息 xìnxī; 召唤 zhāohuàn; 邀请 yāoqǐng: '*telephone ~s* 电话. *a close* ~ 幸免 xìngmiǎn, 绝处〔處〕逢生 juéchùféngshēng. '~-**box** 公用电〔電〕话亭 gōngyòngdiànhuàtíng.

call[2] /kɔ:l/ *vt/i* **1** 叫 jiào, 喊 hǎn. **2** 访问〔問〕 fǎngwèn, 拜访 bàifǎng: *I ~ed on Mr Green.* 我拜访格林先生. ~ **for** 邀约 yāoyuē; 拿取 náqǔ. **3** 叫做 jiàozuò, 称〔稱〕呼 chēnghū: *He's ~ed John.* 他名叫约翰. **4** 认〔認〕为〔爲〕 rènwéi: *I ~ that a shame.* 我认为那是一种耻辱. **5** 请来〔來〕 qǐnglái, 传〔傳〕唤 chuánhuàn: *Please ~ a doctor.* 请去请一位医生. **6** ~ ***a meeting (election)***

宣布举〔舉〕行会〔會〕议〔議〕(选举) xuānbù jǔxíng huìyì. ~ ***a strike*** 下令举行罢〔罷〕工 xiàlìng jǔxíng bàgōng. **7** ~ ***by*** 〔非正式用语〕拜访 bàifǎng, 顺道拜访 shùndào bàifǎng. ~ ***for*** 要求 yāoqiú, 需要 xūyào: *The problem ~ed for quick action.* 这问题需要紧急行动. ~ ***(sth) off*** **(a)** 叫走 jiàozǒu; 把…叫开〔開〕去 bǎ ... jiào kāiqù: ~ *your dog off* 把你的狗赶走. **(b)** 停止 tíngzhǐ, 取消 qǔxiāo: *The strike was ~ed off.* 罢工被取消. ~ ***on*** 访问〔問〕fǎngwèn, 拜访 bàifǎng. ~ ***on*** (或 ***upon***) 恳〔懇〕请 kěnqǐng; 邀约 yāoyuē: ~ *on the enemy to surrender* 向敌人劝降 xiàng dírén quànxiáng. ~ ***out*** **(a)** 出动〔動〕chūdòng: ~ *out the fire brigade* 出动消防队. **(b)** 命令 (工人) 罢工 mìnglìng bàgōng. ~ ***sb (sth) up*** **(a)** 打电〔電〕话给 dǎ diànhuà gěi **(b)** 征〔徵〕召 zhēngzhāo. '~-**up** *n* [C]

cal·ler /ˈkɔːlə(r)/ *n* [C] 访问〔問〕者 fǎngwènzhě. 打电〔電〕话者 dǎ diànhuà zhě.

cal·ligra·phy /kəˈlɪgrəfɪ/ *n* [U] 书〔書〕法 shūfǎ.

cal·ling /ˈkɔːlɪŋ/ *n* [C] 职〔職〕业〔業〕zhíyè, 行业 hángyè.

cal·li·pers /ˈkælɪpəz/ *n pl* **1** 卡钳 kǎqián, 测径器 cèjìngqì. **2** 支具(装于残废人腿部) zhījiù.

cal·lous /ˈkæləs/ *adj* **1** 硬结 yìngjié; 起老茧〔繭〕的 qǐ lǎojiǎng de. **2** [喻]无〔無〕感觉〔覺〕的 wú gǎnjué de; 无情的 wúqíngde.

cal·low /ˈkæləʊ/ *adj* 年幼的 niányòude, 无〔無〕经〔經〕验〔驗〕的 wú jīngyàn de.

cal·lus /ˈkæləs/ *n* [C] [*pl* ~es] 胼胝 piánzhī.

calm /kɑːm/ *adj* [-er, -est] **1** (天气)无〔無〕风〔風〕的 wúfēngde, (海洋)风平浪静的 fēngpíng làngjìng de. **2** 镇静的 zhènjìngde; 沉着的 chénzháode: *keep* ~ 保持镇静. □ *n* [C] 平静 píngjìng. □ *vt/i* 使平静 shǐ píngjìng; 使镇静 shǐ zhènjìng: ~ *him down* 使他镇静下来. ~**ly** *adv* ~**ness** *n* [U]

cal·orie /ˈkælərɪ/ *n* [C] 卡(热量单位) kǎ.

calve /kæv/ *vi* 生(小牛等) shēng.

calves /kævz/ *pl* of calf.

ca·lyp·so /kəˈlɪpsəʊ/ *n* [C] [*pl* ~-s] 一种〔種〕西印度群岛小调 yìzhǒng xīyìndùqúndǎo xiǎodiào, 加力骚〔騷〕jiālìsāo.

cam·ber /ˈkæmbə(r)/ *n* [C] (道路等) 中间〔間〕的轻〔輕〕微凸起 zhōngjiānde qīngwēi tūqǐ.

came /keɪm/ *pt* of come.

camel /ˈkæml/ *n* [C] 骆〔駱〕驼〔駝〕luòtuo.

cameo /ˈkæmɪəʊ/ *n* [C] [*pl* ~s] 浮雕宝〔寶〕石 fúdiāo bǎoshí.

cam·era /ˈkæmərə/ *n* [C] 照相机〔機〕zhàoxiàngjī, 摄〔攝〕像机 shèxiàngjī, 摄影机 shèyǐngjī.

cam·ou·flage /ˈkæməflɑːʒ/ *n* [U] 伪〔僞〕装〔裝〕wěizhuāng. □ *vt* 伪装 wěizhuāng; 掩饰 yǎnshì.

camp /kæmp/ *n* [C] **1** 营〔營〕yíng; 野营 yěyíng. **2** (亦作 *'holiday-~*) 家庭假日野营 jiātíng jiàrì yěyíng. **3** 阵〔陣〕营 zhènyíng: *join the enemy* ~ 投入敌人的阵营. □ *vi* 设营 shèyíng, 宿营 sùyíng; 露宿 lùsù. ***go ~ing*** 进〔進〕行野营 jìnxíng yěyíng. ~**er** 野营者 yěyíngzhě, 露营者 lùyíngzhě.

cam·paign /kæmˈpeɪn/ *n* [C] **1** 战〔戰〕役 zhànyì. **2** 运〔運〕动〔動〕yùndòng: *an 'advertising* ~ 一系列广告活动. □ *vi* 参〔參〕加运动 cānjiā yùndòng. ~**er** 参加运动的人 cānjiā yùndòng de rén.

cam·pus /ˈkæmpəs/ *n* [C] [*pl* ~-es] 校园〔園〕xiàoyuán.

can[1] /kæn/ *n* [C] 装〔裝〕液体〔體〕等用的金属〔屬〕罐 zhuāng yètǐ děng yòng de jīnshǔguàn; 罐头〔頭〕guàntóu. *an 'oil-~* 油罐; *a ~ of beer* 一罐头啤酒. ⇨ tin. □ *vt* [-nn-] 装罐头 zhuāng guàntou. ~**nery** 罐头食品厂〔廠〕guàntoushípǐngchǎng.

can[2] /kən 强式: kæn/ *aux verb* [否定式 **cannot, can't**; 过去式 **could**, 否定式 **couldn't**] **1** (表示能力)能 néng, 会〔會〕huì: *C ~ you lift this box?* 你能举起这箱子吗? *She ~ speak French.* 她会说法语. **2** (表示可能性)能够 nénggòu: *I ~ hear you.* 我听得见你(说的话). **3** [非正式用语](表示允诺)可以 kěyǐ: *You ~ go home now.* 你现在可以回去了. *C~* (或 *could*) *I see you for a moment?* 我可以见一见你吗? **4** (表示现在的可能性) 可能 kěnéng: *That can't* (或 *couldn't*) *be true.* 那不可能是真的.

ca·nal /kəˈnæl/ *n* [C] **1** 运〔運〕河 yùnhé, 沟〔溝〕渠 gōuqú, 水道 shuǐdào. **2** 动〔動〕植物体〔體〕内的管道 dòng zhí wù tǐ nèi de guǎndào: *the alimentary* ~ 消化道.

ca·nary /kəˈneərɪ/ *n* [C] [*pl* -ies] 金丝雀 jīnsīquè.

can·cel /ˈkænsl/ *vt/i* [-ll-, 美语 = -l-] **1** 删去 shānqù; 注销 zhùxiāo; 作废〔廢〕zuòfèi. **2** 取消qǔxiāo: *The meeting was ~led.* 会议被取消. ~ **out** 消去帐〔帳〕目 xiāoqù zhàngmù; 势〔勢〕均力敌〔敵〕shìjūn-lìdí: *The two arguments ~ out.* 争论双方势均力敌. **~la·tion** /-'leɪʃn/ *n* [C, U]

can·cer /'kænsə(r)/ *n* [C, U] 癌症 áizhèng: *lung* ~肺癌. **~ous** *adj* 癌的 áide; 象癌的 xiàng ái de.

can·did /'kændɪd/ *adj* 正直的 zhèngzhíde; 坦率的 tǎnshuàide: *a ~ discussion* 坦率的讨论. **~ly** *adv*

can·di·date /'kændɪdət/ *n* [C] **1** 候选〔選〕人 hòuxuǎnrén. **2** 应〔應〕试人 yìngshìrén.

candle /'kændl/ *n* [C] 腊〔臘〕烛〔燭〕làzhú. **'~stick** 烛台 zhútái.

can·dour [美语=-dor] /'kændə(r)/ *n* [U] 坦白 tǎnbái, 爽直 shuǎngzhí.

candy /'kændɪ/ *n* [U] [亦作 ,*sugar-'~*] 冰糖 bīngtáng [C] [-ies] 糖果 tángguǒ. □ *vt/i* [-ied] 蜜饯〔餞〕mìjiàn.

cane /keɪn/ *n* [C] **1** 竹等的茎〔莖〕zhú děng de jìng: *sugar-~* 甘蔗; *a walking-~* 手杖. **2** [C] 藤鞭 téngbiān. □ *vt* 用藤鞭打 yòng téngbiān dǎ.

ca·nine /'keɪnaɪn/ *adj* 犬的 quǎnde; 似犬的 sì quǎn de.

can·is·ter /'kænɪstə(r)/ *n* [C] **1** 金属〔屬〕罐 jīnshǔguàn. **2** (榴) 霰弹〔彈〕筒 sǎndàntǒng: *a 'tear-gas ~* 滤毒罐.

can·ker /'kæŋkə(r)/ *n* [U] **1** 植物溃疡〔瘍〕zhíwù kuìyáng. **2** 溃疡 kuìyáng. **~ous** *adj* 溃疡的 kuìyángde; 溃疡似的 kuìyáng sì de.

can·na·bis /'kænəbɪs/ *n* [U] 麻醉剂〔劑〕mázuìjì; 毒品 dúpǐng. ⇨ hemp. **can·nery** ⇨ can[1].

can·ni·bal /'kænɪbl/ *n* [C] 吃人肉的人 chī rénròu de rén, 吃同类〔類〕肉的动〔動〕物 chī tónglèiròu de dòngwù. **~ism** *n* [U] 同类相食 tónglèi xiāngshí. **~is·tic** /-'lɪstɪk/ *adj*

can·non /'kænən/ *n* **1** [C] [复数常不变换字形]大炮 dàpào; 加农〔農〕炮 jiānóngpào. **2** [C] 飞〔飛〕机〔機〕上的机〔機〕关〔關〕炮 fēijī shàng de jīguānpào.

can·not /'kænət/ ⇨ can[2].

ca·noe /kə'nu:/ *n* [C] 独〔獨〕木舟 dúmùzhōu; 轻〔輕〕舟 qīngzhōu. □ *vt* 用独木舟载〔載〕运〔運〕yòng dúmùzhōu zǎiyùn. **~ist** 划独木舟者 huá dúmùzhōu zhě.

canon /'kænən/ *n* [C] **1** (基督教或天主教)教规 jiàoguī; 宗教法规 zōngjiào fǎguī. **2** 准〔準〕则 zhǔnzé, 标〔標〕准 biāozhǔn, 原则 yuánzé: *the ~s of good taste* 高尚趣味的准则. **3** 牧师〔師〕mùshī, 神父 shénfù, 教士 jiàoshì. **~i·cal** /kə'nɒnɪkəl/ *adj* 依照〔照〕教规的 yīzhào jiàoguī de; 正规的 zhèngguīde. **~ize** /'kænənaɪz/ *vt* 使某人成为〔爲〕圣〔聖〕徒 shǐ mǒurén chéngwéi shèngtú.

ca·ñon ⇨ canyon.

can·opy /'kænəpɪ/ *n* [C] [*pl* -ies] **1** 床、王座等的罩篷(通常为布料) chuáng wángzuò děng de zhào péng; 华〔華〕盖 huágài. **2** 飞〔飛〕机〔機〕座舱〔艙〕罩 fēijī zuòcāng zhào.

cant /kænt/ *n* [U] 假话 jiǎhuà; 伪〔僞〕善的话 wěishànde huà.

can't /kɑ:nt/ = cannot.

can·tank·er·ous /kæn'tæŋkərəs/ *adj* 脾气〔氣〕坏〔壞〕的 píqì huàide; 爱〔愛〕争吵的 ài zhēngchǎo de.

can·teen /kæn'ti:n/ *n* [C] **1** 食堂 shítáng; 食品小卖〔賣〕部 shípǐng xiǎomàibù. **2** 餐具箱 cāngjiùxiāng. **3** 水壶 shuǐhú.

can·ter /'kæntə(r)/ *n* [C] (马的) 慢跑 mànpǎo. □ *vt/i* 使慢跑 shǐ mànpǎo.

can·ti·lever /'kæntɪli:və(r)/ *n* [C] (建筑)悬〔懸〕臂 xuánbì; 悬臂梁 xuánbìliáng.

can·vas /'kænvəs/ *n* [*pl* ~ses] **1** [U] 粗帆布 cū fānbù. **2** [C] 油画〔畫〕布 yóuhuàbù.

can·vass /'kænvəs/ *vt/i* 兜揽〔攬〕生意 dōulǎn shēngyì; 游说拉选〔選〕票 yóushuì lā xuǎnpiào. □ *n* [C, U] 拉选票 lā xuǎnpiào.

can·yon, cañon /'kænjən/ *n* [C] 峡〔峽〕谷 xiágǔ.

cap /kæp/ *n* [C] **1** 便帽 biànmào; 制服帽 zhìfúmào. **2** 盖 gài; 套 tào. □ *vt* [-pp-] **1** 给…戴帽 gěi … dài mào. **2** 胜〔勝〕过〔過〕shèngguò, 凌驾〔駕〕língjià. ~ *a story* 说一个〔個〕更好的 shuōyīge gènghǎode. **3** 挑选〔選〕运〔運〕动〔動〕员进〔進〕全国〔國〕性运动队〔隊〕tiāoxuǎn yùndòngyuán jìn quánguóxìng yùndòngduì.

ca·pa·bil·ity /,keɪpə'bɪlətɪ/ *n* [*pl* -ies] **1** [U] 能力 nénglì; 才能 cáinéng: *nuclear ~* 核能力. **2** [*pl*] 潜〔潛〕在能力 qiánzài nénglì.

ca·pable /'keɪpəbl/ *adj* **1** 有才能的 yǒu cáinéng de; 有能力的 yǒu nénglì de:有技能的 yǒu jìnéng de: *a ~ man* 能干的人. **2** ~ *of* (a) 有能力的 yǒu nénglì de, 有本领的 yǒu běnlǐng de; 做得出 (坏事) 的 zuò de chū de: *He's ~ of any crime.*

他什么罪恶的事都做得出. **(b)** 能…的 néng … de; 可以…的 kěyǐ … de: *The situation is ~ of improvement.* 境况是可以改善的. **ca·pably** *adv*

ca·pac·ity /kə'pæsətɪ/ *n* [*pl* -ies] **1** [U] 容量 róngliàng; 容积〔積〕róngjī; 理解力 lǐjiělì: *a tank with a ~ of two litres* 两升容量的桶. **2** [C] position: 地位 dìwèi; 身份 shēnfèn; 资格 zīgé: *in my ~ as manager* 我作为经理的身份.

cape[1] /keɪp/ *n* [C] 披肩 pījiān; 斗篷 dǒupéng.

cape[2] /keɪp/ *n* [C] 海角 hǎijiǎo; 岬 jiǎ.

cap·il·lary /kə'pɪlərɪ/ *n* [C] [*pl* -ies] 毛细管 máoxìguǎn.

capi·tal /'kæpɪtl/ *n* [C] [常作定语] **1** 首都 shǒudū. **2** 大写〔寫〕字母 dàxiě zìmǔ. **3** [U] 资本 zīběn. □ *adj* 可处〔處〕死刑的 kě chù sǐxíng de. ~ *offence* 死罪. ,~ **'letter** 大写字母 dàxiě zìmǔ.

capi·tal·ism /'kæpɪtəlɪzəm/ *n* [U] 资本主义〔義〕. zīběnzhǔyì ⇨ socialism. **capi·tal·ist (a)** 资本主义者 zīběnzhǔyìzhě. **(b)** 资本家 zīběnjiā.

capi·tal·ize /'kæpɪtəlaɪz/ *vt/i* **1** 资本主义〔義〕化 zīběnzhǔyìhuà. **2** [喻]利用 lìyòng: ~ *on the enemy's mistakes* 利用敌人的错误.

ca·pitu·late /kə'pɪtʃʊleɪt/ *vt* (有条件)投降 tóuxiáng. **ca·pitu'la·tion** *n* [U]

cap·size /kæp'saɪz/ *vt/i* 使(船等)倾覆 shǐ qīngfù.

cap·stan /'kæpstən/ *n* [C] 绞盘 jiǎopán; 起锚机〔機〕qǐmáojī.

cap·sule /'kæpsju:l/ *n* [C] **1** 荚 jiá. **2** 装〔裝〕一剂〔劑〕药的小囊 zhuāng yíjì yào de xiǎonáng. **3** 宇宙密闭〔閉〕小舱〔艙〕yǔzhòu mìbì xiǎocāng.

capt. = captain.

cap·tain /'kæptɪn/ *n* [C] **1** 队〔隊〕长〔長〕duìzhǎng. **2** 连长 liánzhǎng. **3** 舰长 jiànzhǎng. □ *vt* 做…的首领 zuò … de shǒulǐng; 指挥〔揮〕zhǐhuī.

cap·tion /'kæpʃn/ *n* [C] 报〔報〕纸文章的标〔標〕题 bàozhǐ wénzhāng de biāotí; 照片说明 zhàopiàn shuōmíng.

cap·ti·vate /'kæptɪveɪt/ *vt* 迷住 mízhù, 强烈感染 qiángliè gǎnrǎn: *~d by her beauty* 被她的美貌迷住.

cap·tive /'kæptɪv/ *n* [C], *adj* 被俘虏〔虜〕的 bèi fúlǔ de; 被拴住的 bèi shuānzhù de. **cap'tiv·ity** *n* [U] 俘虏 fúlǔ, 监禁 jiānjìn, 束缚 shùfú.

cap·tor /'kæptə(r)/ *n* [C] 捕捉者 bǔzhuōzhě; 夺〔奪〕得者 duódézhě.

cap·ture /'kæptʃə(r)/ *vt* 捕获〔獲〕bǔhuò, 俘虏〔虜〕fúlǔ; 夺〔奪〕得 duódé. □ *n* **1** [U] 捕获 bǔhuò, 夺得 duódé. **2** [C] 战〔戰〕利品 zhànlìpǐn, 缴获品 jiǎohuòpǐn.

car /kɑ:(r)/ *n* [C] **1** = motor-car. **2** 火车〔車〕车厢 huǒchē chēxiāng: *the 'dining-~* 餐车. '~ **park** 停车场〔場〕tíngchēchǎng.

cara·mel /'kærəmel/ *n* **1** [U] 酱〔醬〕色 jiàngsè. **2** [C] 一种〔種〕小糖果 yìzhǒng xiǎotángguǒ.

carat /'kærət/ *n* [C] **1** 克拉(宝石重量单位) kèlā. **2** 开〔開〕(金的纯度单位) kāi.

cara·van /'kærəvæn/ *n* [C] **1** 商队〔隊〕, 旅行队(穿过沙漠的) shāngduì, lǚxíngduì. **2** 大篷车〔車〕dàpéngchē. **3** 供住家用的汽车〔車〕拖车 gòng zhùjiā yòng de qìchē tuōchē.

carbo·hy·drate /ˌkɑ:bəʊ'haɪdreɪt/ *n* **1** [C,U] 碳水化合物 tànshuǐ huàhéwù. **2** [*pl*] 淀粉类〔類〕食物 diànfěnlèi shíwù.

car·bon /'kɑ:bən/ *n* **1** [U] 碳(化学符号C) tàn. **2** [C, U] [亦作 '~-*paper*] 复〔復〕写〔寫〕纸 fùxiězhǐ. **3** [C] 复写的副本 fùxiěde fùběn.

car·buncle /'kɑ:bʌŋkl/ *n* [C] 痈〔癰〕yōng.

car·bu·ret·tor [亦作 **-retor, -retter**] /ˌkɑ:bjʊ'retə(r)/ *n* [C] (汽车)汽化器 qìhuàqì.

car·cass, car·case /'kɑ:kəs/ *n* [C] 动物尸体〔體〕dòngwù shītǐ.

car·cino·gen /'kɑ:sɪnədʒen/ *n* [C] 致癌物 zhì ái wù, 诱癌剂〔劑〕yòu ái jì. **carcino'genic** *adj*

card /kɑ:d/ *n* [C] **1** 卡片 kǎpiàn, 卡 kǎ: *a 'Christmas ~* 圣〔聖〕诞卡. ⇨ also postcard. **2** [常作 '*playing*-~] 纸牌 zhǐpái. *on the ~s* 可能的 kěnéngde; 有可能实〔實〕现的 yǒu kěnéng shíxiàn de: *War is on the ~s.* 战争可能爆发. *put one's ~s on the table* 摊〔攤〕牌 tānpái; 公布自己的打算 gōngbù zìjǐde dǎsuàn.

card·board /'kɑ:dbɔ:d/ *n* [U] 硬纸板 yìngzhǐbǎn.

car·diac /'kɑ:dɪæk/ *adj* 心脏〔臟〕的 xīnzàngde.

car·di·gan /'kɑ:dɪgən/ *n* [C] 羊毛衫 yángmáoshān; 羊毛背心 yángmáo bèixīn.

car·di·nal[1] /'kɑ:dɪnl/ *adj* 主要的 zhǔyàode; 基本的 jīběnde. ~**number** 基数〔數〕jīshù.

car·di·nal[2] /'kɑ:dɪnl/ *n* **1** [C] 红衣主教 hóngyīzhǔjiào, 枢〔樞〕机〔機〕主教 shūjīzhǔjiào. **2** [U] 深红色 shēnhóngsè.

care[1] /keə(r)/ *n* **1** [U] 小心 xiǎoxīn, 谨慎 jǐnshèn; 注意 zhùyì: *take ~ over your work* 你在工作上要用心. *take ~ of* [非正式用语] 照管 zhàoguǎn, 负责处〔處〕理 fùzé chǔlǐ. **2** [U] 照管 zhàoguǎn: *The child was left in its sister's ~.* 孩子留给他（她）的姐姐照管. **3** [常用复数] 心事 xīnshì, 牵累 qiānlěi: *the ~s of a large family* 大家庭的牵累. '~**free** *adj* 无忧〔憂〕无虑〔慮〕的 wúyōu wúlǜ de. '~**taker** (空屋等的)看管人 kānguǎnrén. ~**ful** *adj* **(a)** (人)细心的 xìxīnde, 仔细的 zǐxìde. **(b)** 细致的 xìzhìde: *a ~ful piece of work* 精心细致的工作. ~**fully** *adv* ~**ful·ness** *n* [U] ~**less** *adj* **(a)** (人)粗心的 cūxīnde, 粗枝大叶的 cūzhīdàyède. **(b)** 由于粗心而引起的 yóuyú cūxīn ér yǐnqǐ de: *a ~less mistake* 由于粗心造成的错误. **(c)** 不介意的 bú jièyìde, 不在乎的 búzàihude: *~less of his reputation* 不顾及他的名声. ~**less·ly** *adv* ~**less·ness** *n* [U]

care[2] /keə(r)/ *vi* **1** 关〔關〕心 guānxīn; 担〔擔〕心 dānxīn: *He failed but I don't think he ~s.* 他失败了, 但我认为他并不在乎. **2** 喜爱〔愛〕xǐ'ài: *Would you ~ to go for a walk?* 出去散散步, 好吗? **3** ~ **for** **(a)** 喜欢〔歡〕xǐhuan; 想望 xiǎngwàng: *Would you ~ for a drink?* 你想喝酒吗? **(b)** 照管 zhàoguǎn: *~ for children* 照管孩子们.

ca·reer /kə'rɪə(r)/ *n* **1** [C] 生涯 shēngyá, 经〔經〕历〔歷〕jīnglì. **2** [C] 事业〔業〕shìyè; 职〔職〕业 zhíyè. □ *vi* 飞〔飛〕跑 fēipǎo: *~ down the street* 在街上飞跑.

ca·ress /kə'res/ *n* [C] 爱〔愛〕抚〔撫〕àifǔ. □ *vt* 抚爱 fǔ'ài; 抚摸 fǔmō.

cargo /'kɑ:gəʊ/ *n* [C, U] [*pl* ~es] 货物（船或飞机上的）huòwù.

cari·ca·ture /ˌkærɪkə'tʃʊə(r)/ *n* [C] 漫画〔畫〕mànhuà, 讽〔諷〕刺画 fěncìhuà. □ *vt* 用漫画表现 yòng mànhuà biǎoxiàn; 使丑化 shǐ chǒuhuà.

car·nage /'kɑ:nɪdʒ/ *n* [U] 大屠杀〔殺〕dàtúshā; 残〔殘〕杀 cánshā.

car·nal /'kɑ:nl/ *adj* 肉体〔體〕的 ròutǐde; 性欲的 xìngyùde, 色情的 sèqíngde: ~ *pleasures* 声色之娱.

car·na·tion /kɑ:'neɪʃn/ *n* [C] 麝香石竹 shèxiāng shízhú.

car·ni·val /'kɑ:nɪvl/ *n* [C, U] 狂欢〔歡〕节〔節〕kuánghuānjié.

car·ni·vore /'kɑ:nɪvɔ:(r)/ *n* [C] 食肉动〔動〕物 shíròu dòngwù. **car·ni·vor·ous** /kɑ:'nɪvərəs/ *adj*

carol /'kærəl/ *n* [C] 颂歌 sònggē; 欢〔歡〕乐〔樂〕之歌 huānlè zhī gē. □ *vt* [-ll-] 愉快地唱歌 yúkuàide chànggē.

carp[1] /kɑ:p/ *n* [C] [*pl* ~] 鲤科的鱼 lǐkēde yú; 鲤鱼 lǐyú.

carp[2] /kɑ:p/ *vt* 找岔子 zhǎo chàzi, 挑剔 tiāoti.

car·pen·ter /'kɑ:pɪntə(r)/ *n* [C] 木工 mùgōng, 木匠 mùjiang. **car·pen·try** 木工业〔業〕mùgōngyè.

car·pet /'kɑ:pɪt/ *n* [C] 地毯 dìtǎn. □ *vt* 铺地毯于 pū dìtǎn yú.

car·riage /'kærɪdʒ/ *n* **1** [C] 四轮〔輪〕马〔馬〕车〔車〕sìlún mǎchē. **2** [C] (火车)客车厢 kèchēxiāng. **3** [U] 运〔運〕输〔輸〕(费) yùnshū. **4** [U] 仪〔儀〕态〔態〕yítài, 走路姿态 zǒulù zītài. '~**way** 车行道 chēxíngdào. ⇨ dual.

car·rier /'kærɪə(r)/ *n* [C] **1** 运〔運〕货人 yùnhuòrén; 运货公司 yùnhuò gōngsī. **2** 带〔帶〕菌者 dàijūnzhě. **3** 运输〔輸〕军〔軍〕队〔隊〕之交通工具 yùnshū jūnduì zhī jiāotōnggōngjù: *an 'aircraft-~* 航空母舰.

car·rot /'kærət/ *n* [C] 胡萝〔蘿〕卜〔蔔〕húluóbo.

carry /'kærɪ/ *vt/i* [*pt*, *pp* -ied] **1** 传〔傳〕送 chuánsòng; 运〔運〕送 yùnsòng; 携带〔帶〕xiédài: ~ *a box* 带着一只箱子. **2** 带有 dàiyǒu: ~ *an umbrella* 带有一把伞. **3** 支撑 zhīcheng; 支持 zhīchí: *These pillars ~ the weight of the roof.* 这些柱子支撑屋顶的重量. **4** 使获〔獲〕得赞同（或通过）shǐ huòdé zàntóng; 获得…的赞同（或通过）huòdé ... de zàntóng: *The motion was carried.* 动议被通过. **5** 保持一定的姿势〔勢〕bǎochí yídìngde zīshì: *He carries himself like a soldier.* 他的举止行动象个军人. **6** (火箭、声音等)达〔達〕到、传〔傳〕到(某种距离) dádào, chuándào: *Their voices carried many miles.* 它们的声音传到许多英里远. **7** *be carried away* 失去自制力 shīqù zìzhìlì. ~ *off* 获得（奖品等）huòdé. ~ *on* **(a)** 经〔經〕营〔營〕jīngyíng; 经理 jīnglǐ: ~ *on a business* 经营商业. **(b)** 大声谈说 dàshēng tánshuō, 吵吵闹〔鬧〕闹 chǎochǎo nàonào; 举止愚蠢幼稚 jǔzhǐ yúchǔn yòuzhì. ~ *on (with)* **(a)** 继〔繼〕续〔續〕

jìxù. *C~ on (with your work).* 继续你的工作. **(b)** 调情 diàoqíng. ~ ***out*** 实〔實〕现 shíxiàn, 进行到底 jìnxíng dàodǐ; 执〔執〕行 zhíxíng: ~ *out a plan* 执行计划, ~ ***through*** **(a)** 维持 wéichí, 使渡过难〔難〕关〔關〕shǐ dùguò nánguān: *Their courage will ~ them through.* 他们的勇气会使他们渡过难关的. **(b)** 完成 wánchéng.

cart /kɑ:t/ *n* [C] 马〔馬〕车〔車〕mǎchē. ***put the ~ before the horse*** 本末倒置 běnmò dàozhì. □ *vt* **1** 用车运〔運〕送 yòng chē yùnsòng. **2** [非正式用语] 携带 xiédài: ~ *parcels around* 提着小包到处走. '~**-horse** 担〔擔〕负沉重工作的壮〔壯〕马 dānfù chénzhòng gōngzuò de zhuàngmǎ.

car·ti·lage /'kɑ:tɪlɪdʒ/ *n* [C, U] 软〔軟〕骨 ruǎngǔ.

car·ton /'kɑ:tn/ *n* [C] 纸板箱 zhǐbǎnxiāng; 塑料箱 sùliàoxiāng.

car·toon /kɑ:'tu:n/ *n* [C] **1** 漫画〔畫〕mànhuà. **2** [亦作 *animated* ~] 卡通 kǎtōng; 动〔動〕画片 dònghuàpiàn. ~**ist** 漫画家 mànhuàjiā; 动画片画家 dòng huàpiàn huàjiā.

car·tridge /'kɑ:trɪdʒ/ *n* [C] **1** 子弹〔彈〕zǐdàn. **2** 唱机〔機〕的唱头〔頭〕chàngjīde chàngtóu. **3** 音乐〔樂〕匣 (一种较普通匣式录音带宽两倍的匣式录音带) yīnyuèxiá.

carve /'kɑ:v/ *vt/i* **1** 雕刻 diāokè, 刻 kè, 做雕刻工作 zuò diāokè gōngzuò: ~ *a statue* 雕刻一个像. **2** 切(熟肉等) qiē. **carver (a)** 切肉刀 qiēròudāo. **(b)** 雕刻家 diāokèjiā; 切肉人 qiēròurén. **carving** 雕刻品 diāokèpǐn.

cas·cade /kæ'skeɪd/ *n* [C] 小瀑布 xiǎo pùbù; 瀑布 pùbù. □ *vi* 瀑布似地落下 pùbù sì de luòxià.

case[1] /keɪs/ *n* [C] **1** 情况 qíngkuàng, 状〔狀〕况 zhuàngkuàng: *I can't make an exception in your ~.* 我不能把你的情况看作例外. *It's a ~ of cheating.* 这是一次欺骗. ***(just) in ~*** 假使 jiǎshǐ, 万〔萬〕一 wànyī: *In ~ I forget, please remind me.* 如果我忘记了, 请提醒我. ***in 'any ~*** 无〔無〕论〔論〕如何 wúlùn rúhé. ***in 'that ~*** 假如这样的话 jiǎrú zhèyàng de huà. **2** 患者 huànzhě. **3** [法律] 诉讼 sùsòng, 案件 ànjiàn. ***make out a ~ for (against)*** 提出论证〔證〕tíchū lùnzhèng. **4** [语法] 格 gé. ,~-'**history** 病历〔歷〕bìnglì.

case[2] /keɪs/ *n* [C] 箱子 xiāngzi; 袋子 dàizi; 套子 tàozi: *a 'pillow-~* 枕头套. ⇨ suitcase, bookcase. □ *vt* 装〔裝〕箱 zhuāngxiāng; 装盒 zhuānghé.

case·ment /'keɪsmənt/ *n* [C] 象门〔門〕一样〔樣〕的窗 xiàng mén yíyàng de chuāng.

cash /kæʃ/ *n* [U] **1** 现金 xiànjīn, 现款 xiànkuǎn. **2** 钱〔錢〕qián, 款子 kuǎnzi: *be short of ~* 缺钱. □ *vt/i* **1** 兑现 duìxiàn, 兑付 duìfù: ~ *a cheque* 兑付支票. **2** ~ ***in on*** 以…获〔獲〕利 yǐ … huòlì; 营〔營〕利 yínglì. '~ **crop** 商品作物 shāngpǐn zuòwù. ~ **register** 现金收入记录〔録〕机〔機〕xiànjīn shōurù jìlùjī.

ca·shew /'kæʃu:/ *n* [C] ('~*-nut*) 槚如树〔樹〕坚〔堅〕果 jiǎrúshù jiānguǒ

cash·ier /kæ'ʃɪə(r)/ *n* [C] 出纳员 chūnàyuán.

cash·mere /'kæʃmɪə(r)/ *n* [U] 开〔開〕士米 (一种细毛料) kāishìmǐ; 山羊绒 shānyángróng.

ca·sino /kə'si:nəʊ/ *n* [C] [*pl* ~s] 娱乐〔樂〕场〔場〕yúlèchǎng; 赌场 dǔchǎng.

cask /kɑ:sk/ *n* [C] **1** 木桶 mùtǒng. **2** 一桶的量 yìtǒngde liàng.

cas·ket /'kɑ:skɪt/ *n* [C] **1** 精美的小盒子 jīngměide xiǎohézi; 首饰盒 shǒushìhé. **2** [美语] = coffin.

cas·sava /kə'sɑ:və/ *n* [C, U] 木薯 mùshǔ.

cas·ser·ole /'kæsərəʊl/ *n* [C] **1** (烧菜用的)有盖焙盘〔盤〕yǒugài bèipán; 蒸锅 zhēnguō. **2** 用焙盘烧〔燒〕制〔製〕的食品 yòng bèipán shāozhì de shípǐn.

cas·sette /kə'set/ *n* [C] [美语 = *cartridge*] 磁带〔帶〕盒 cídàihé; 照相软〔軟〕片盒 zhàoxiàng ruǎnpiàn hé.

cas·sock /'kæsək/ *n* [C] 教士穿的长〔長〕袍 jiàoshì chuān de chángpáo.

cast[1] /kɑ:st/ *n* [C] **1** 投 tóu; 掷〔擲〕zhì; 抛 pāo; 撒 sǎ. **2** 铸〔鑄〕件 zhùjiàn; 模压〔壓〕品 múyāpǐn: *a plaster ~* 石膏绷带. **3** 铸型 zhùxíng; 模子 múzi. **4** 演员表 yǎnyuánbiǎo; 班底 bāndǐ. **5** (眼睛)轻〔輕〕微歪斜 qīngwēi wāixié.

cast[2] /kɑ:st/ *vt/i* [*pt, pp* ~] **1** 投 tóu; 掷〔擲〕zhì; 扔 rēng; 撒 sǎ: ~ *a net* 撒网. ~ ***one's eye over sth*** 向…瞧了瞧 xiàng … qiáole qiáo. **2** 浇〔澆〕于模中 jiāoyú mú zhōng; 铸〔鑄〕造 zhùzào: *a figure ~ in bronze* 铜像. **3** 选〔選〕…扮演角色 xuǎn … bànyǎn juésè. **4** ~ ***sb (sth) aside*** 抛弃 pāoqì; 废〔廢〕除 fèichú. ~ ***off*** **(a)** 解缆〔纜〕放船 jiělǎn fàngchuán. **(b)** [喻] 抛弃

pāoqì. '~ **iron** *n* [U] 铸铁〔鐵〕zhùtiě. ,~-'**iron** *adj* **(a)** 铁铸的 tiězhùde. **(b)** 〔喻〕坚〔堅〕强的 jiānqiángde; 不懈的 búxiède: *a ~-iron excuse* 无转弯余地的推托. ,~-**ing** '**vote** 决定性投票 juédìngxìng tóupiào.

cas·ta·nets /ˌkæstə'nets/ *n pl* 响〔響〕板(硬木或象牙的两片板,系于手指上,互击作响, 配合音乐歌舞) xiǎngbǎn.

cast·away /'kɑ:stəweɪ/ *n* [C] 乘船遇难〔難〕的人 chéngchuán yùnàn de rén.

caste /kɑ:st/ *n* [C] 印度的社会等级 yìndùde shèhuì děngjí.

cas·ti·gate /'kæstɪgeɪt/ *vt* 惩〔懲〕罚 chěngfá; 申斥 shēnchì. 严〔嚴〕厉〔厲〕批评 yánlì pīpíng. **cas·ti·'ga·tion** *n* [C, U]

cast·ing /'kɑ:stɪŋ/*n* [C] 铸〔鑄〕件 zhùjiàn. ⇨ cast[2](2).

castle /'kɑ:sl/ *n* [C] **1** 城堡 chéngbǎo. **2** (国际象棋)车〔車〕jū.

cas·tor, cas·ter /'kɑ:stə(r)/ *n* [C] **1** (椅子等的)小脚轮〔輪〕xiǎo jiǎolún. **2** 盛调味品的小瓶 chéng tiáowèipǐn de xiǎopíng. '~ **sugar** 细白砂糖 xì báishātáng.

cas·tor oil /ˌkɑ:stər 'ɔɪl/ *n* [U] 蓖麻油 bìmáyóu.

cas·trate /kæ'streɪt/ *vt* 阉〔閹〕割 yāngē. **cas'tra·tion** *n* [C, U]

cas·ual /'kæʒʊəl/ *adj* **1** 偶然 ǒurán, 碰巧的 pèngqiǎode: *a ~ meeting* 偶然的相会, 巧遇. **2** 随便的 suíbiànde; 漫不经〔經〕心的 mànbùjīngxīnde: *~ clothes* 便服. **3** 临〔臨〕时〔時〕的 línshíde: *~ labourers* 零工, 短工, 临时工. **~ly** *adv*

casu·alty /'kæʒʊəltɪ/ *n* [C] [*pl* -ies] 伤〔傷〕亡人员 shāngwáng rényuán.

cat /kæt/ *n* [C] **1** 猫 māo. **2** 猫科动〔動〕物 māokē dòngwù. '~**burglar** 翻墙〔牆〕入室的窃〔竊〕贼 fānqiángrùshì de qièzéi. '~-**nap** 小睡 xiǎoshuì; 假寐 jiǎmèi.

cata·combs /'kætəku:mz/ *n pl* 地下墓穴 dìxià mùxué; 陵寝 língqǐn.

cata·logue [美语= **-log**] /'kætəlɒg/ *n* [C] (人, 地名等)目录〔録〕mùlù. □ *vt* 把…编入目录 bǎ … biānrù mùlù.

cata·lyst /'kætəlɪst/ *n* [C] **1** 〔化学〕催化剂〔劑〕cuīhuàjì. **2** 造成变〔變〕化的人或事 zàochéng biànhuà de rén huò shì.

cat·a·pult /'kætəpʌlt/ *n* [C] **1** 弹〔彈〕弓 dàngōng. **2** 古代的石弩 gǔdàide shínǔ. □ *vt* 用弹弓射 yòng dàngōng shè.

cata·ract /'kætərækt/ *n* [C] **1** 大瀑布 dà pùbù. **2** 白内障 bái nèizhàng.

ca·tarrh /kə'tɑ:(r)/ *n* [U] 卡他 kǎtā; 粘膜炎 niánmóyán.

ca·tas·trophe /kə'tæstrəfɪ/ *n* [C] 大灾〔災〕难〔難〕dàzāinàn, 大祸 dàhuò. **cata·strophic** /ˌkætə'strɒfɪk/ *adj*

catch[1] /kætʃ/ *n* [C] **1** 抓 zhuā; 接球 jiēqiú. **2** 捕获〔獲〕物 pǔhuòwù; 捕获量 pǔhuòliàng: *a good ~ of fish* 捕获很多的鱼. **3** 欺骗〔騙〕qīpiàn; 诡计 guǐjì: *There's a ~ in it somewhere.* 这里面有蹊跷. **4** 窗钩 chuānggōu. 门〔門〕扣 ménkòu.

catch[2] /kætʃ/ *vt/i* [*pt, pp* caught /kɔ:t/] **1** 接住 jiēzhù; 抓住 zhuāzhù: *~ a ball* 接住球. **2** 逮住 dǎizhù; 捕获〔獲〕pǔhuò: *~ a thief* 逮住小偷. **3** 撞见(某人)做某事(恶事) zhuàngjiàn zuò mǒushì. *~ sb out* 发〔發〕觉〔覺〕某人的错误 fājué mǒurénde cuòwù. **4** 赶〔趕〕上 gǎnshàng: *~ a train* 赶上火车. **5** *~ on* **(a)** 理解 lǐjiě. **(b)** 变〔變〕得流行 biàndé liúxíng. *~ sb up* (*up with sb*) 赶上 gǎnshàng. **6** 绊住 bànzhù; 挂住 guàzhù: *I caught my fingers in the door.* 我的手指夹在门缝里. **7** 懂得 dǒngdé; 了解 liǎojiě; 听〔聽〕到(声音) tīngdào. *~ sb's eye* 吸引注意 xīyǐng zhùyì. *~ sight of* ⇨ sight (2). **8** 感染到 gǎnrǎndào: *~ a cold* 感冒, 伤风. *~ fire* 着火 zháohuǒ. '~**word** 标〔標〕语 biāoyǔ; 口号〔號〕kǒuhào.

catch·ing /'kætʃɪŋ/ *adj* 传〔傳〕染性的 chuánrǎnxìngde.

catchy /'kætʃɪ/ *adj* [-ier, -iest] (曲调等)易记的 yìjìde.

cat·egori·cal /ˌkætɪ'gɒrɪkl/ *adj* 无〔無〕条〔條〕件的 wútiáojiànde; 绝对〔對〕的 juéduìde. **~ly** *adv*

cat·egor·ize /'kætɪgəraɪz/ *vt* 分类〔類〕fēnlèi.

cat·egory /'kætɪgərɪ/ *n* [C] [*pl* -ies] 种〔種〕类 zhǒnglèi, 类目 lèimù.

ca·ter /'keɪtə(r)/ *vi* **1** 供应〔應〕伙食 gōngyìng huǒshí. **2** 提供娱乐〔樂〕节〔節〕目 tígòng yúlè jiémù: *TV programmes ~ for all tastes.* 电视节目适应各种兴趣. **~er** 包办伙食者 bāobàn huǒshí zhě.

cat·er·pil·lar /'kætəpɪlə(r)/ *n* [C] **1** 毛虫〔蟲〕máochóng. **2** 履带〔帶〕lǚdài.

cat·gut /'kætgʌt/ *n* [U] (用作小提琴弦、网球拍等) 肠〔腸〕线〔線〕chángxiàn.

ca·the·dral /kə'θi:drəl/ *n* [C] 总〔總〕教堂 zǒngjiàotáng, 大教堂

dàjiàotáng.

cath·ode /'kæθəʊd/ *n* [C] 阴〔陰〕极〔極〕yīnjí. ,~'**ray tube** *n* [C] 阴极射线〔綫〕管 yīnjí shèxiànguǎn.

cath·olic /'kæθəlɪk/ *adj* **1** 普遍的 pǔbiànde; 广〔廣〕泛的 guǎngfànde: *a man with ~ tastes* 有广泛兴趣的人. **2** **C~** = Roman Catholic. □ *n* **C~** = Roman Catholic.

Ca·tholi·cism /kə'θɒləsɪzəm/ *n* [U] 天主教教义〔義〕tiānzhǔjiào jiàoyì.

catty /'kætɪ/ *adj* [-ier, -iest] 狡猾的 jiǎohuáde; 恶〔惡〕毒的 èdúde.

cattle /'kætl/ *n pl* 牲口 shēngkou, 家畜 jiāxù.

caught /kɔ:t/ *pt, pp* of catch[2].

caul·dron /'kɔ:ldrən/ *n* [C] 大锅 dàguō.

cauli·flower /'kɒlɪflaʊə(r)/ *n* [C, U] 菜花 càihuā.

cause /kɔ:z/ *n* **1** [C, U] 原因 yuányīn: 起因 qǐyīn: *the ~ of the fire* 起火的原因. **2** [U] 理由 lǐyóu: *~ for complaint* 抱怨的理由. **3** [C] 事业〔業〕shìyè; 目标〔標〕mùbiāo: *fight in the ~ of justice* 为正义而战. □ *vt* 使产〔產〕生 shǐ chǎnshēng; 使发〔發〕生 shǐ fāshēng: *What ~d his death?* 他怎么死的?

cause·way /'kɔ:zweɪ/ *n* [C] 堤道 tídào; 高于路面的人行道 gāoyú lùmiàn de rénxíngdào.

caus·tic /'kɔ:stɪk/ *adj* **1** 腐蚀性的 fǔshíxìngde, 苛性的 kēxìngde: *~ soda* 苛性钠. **2** [喻]讽〔諷〕刺的 fěngcìde; 刻薄的 kèbóde. **~·ally** /-klɪ/ *adv*

cau·tion /'kɔ:ʃn/ *n* **1** [U] 小心 xiǎoxīn, 谨慎 jǐnshèn. **2** [C] 告诫 gàojiè, 警告 jǐnggào: *give him a ~* 告诫他. □ *vt* 警告 jǐnggào. **~·ary** /'-rɪ/ *adj* 忠告的 zhōnggàode, 警告的 jǐnggàode.

cau·tious /'kɔ:ʃəs/ *adj* 小心的 xiǎoxīnde, 谨慎的 jǐnshènde. **~ly** *adv*

cav·al·cade /,kævl'keɪd/ *n* [C] 车〔車〕队〔隊〕chēduì; 马〔馬〕帮 mǎbāng.

cav·alry /'kævlrɪ/ *n* [*sing or pl*, -ies] 骑〔騎〕兵 qíbīng.

cave /keɪv/ *n* [C] 山洞 shāndòng 窑洞 yáodòng, 地窖 dìjiào. □ *vt/i ~ 'in* 塌方 tāfāng, 坍陷 tāxiàn: *The roof ~d in.* 屋顶坍陷.

cav·ern /'kævən/ *n* [C] [书面语] 大山洞 dàshāndòng, 大洞穴 dàdòngxué.

caviar, cavi·are /'kævɪɑ:(r)/ *n* [U] 鱼子酱〔醬〕yúzǐjiàng.

cav·ity /'kævətɪ/ *n* [C] [*pl* -ies] 洞 dòng: *a ~ in a tooth* 牙齿的龋洞.

cay·enne /keɪ'en/ *n* [U] [亦作~ *pepper*] 辣椒 làjiāo.

c.c.= cubic centimetre(s) 立方厘米 lìfāng límǐ.

Cent. =**1** Centigrade. **2** century.

C.E.= Church of England 英国〔國〕国教 yīngguó guójiào.

cease /si:s/ *vt/i* [通常用语] 停止 tíngzhǐ: *C~ fire!* 停火! **~less** *adj* 不停的 bùtíngde; 不绝的 bùjuéde. **~less·ly** *adv*

cedar /'si:də(r)/ *n* **1** [C] 雪松 xuěsōng. **2** [U] 雪松木 xuěsōngmù.

ceil·ing /'si:lɪŋ/ *n* [C] **1** 天花板 tiānhuābǎn; 顶篷 dǐngpéng. **2** 最高限度 zuìgāo xiàndù: *price (wage) ~* 物价(工资)最高限度.

cel·ebrate /'selɪbreɪt/ *vt* **1** 庆〔慶〕祝 qìngzhù: *~ a birthday* 庆祝生日. **2** 歌颂 gēsòng, 赞美 zànměi.

cele·brated *adj* 著名的 zhùmíngde, 有名的 yǒumíngde. **cel·e'bra·tion** *n* [C, U]

ce·leb·rity /sɪ'lebrətɪ/ *n* [*pl* -ies] **1** [U] 著名 zhùmíng, 名声〔聲〕míngshēng. **2** [C] 著名人士 zhùmíng rénshì: *television celebrities* 电视名人.

cel·ery /'selərɪ/ *n* [U] 芹菜 qíncài.

ce·les·tial /sɪ'lestɪəl/ *adj* 天的 tiānde; 天空的 tiānkōngde: *Stars are ~ bodies.* 星是天体.

celi·bate /'selɪbət/ *adj, n* [C] 独〔獨〕身的 dúshēnde; 独身者 dúshēnzhě. **celi·bacy** *n* [U] 独身生活 dúshēn shēnghuó; 独身 dúshēn.

cell /sel/ *n* [C] **1** 小房间〔間〕xiǎo fángjiān; 单〔單〕人牢房 dānrén láofáng; (修道院中的)密室 mìshì. **2** 电〔電〕池 diànchí. **3** 细胞 xìbāo. **4** (秘密组织的) 小组 xiǎozǔ: *terrorist ~s* 恐怖分子小组.

cel·lar /'selə(r)/ *n* [C] 地窖 dìjiào; 酒窖 jiǔjiào.

cel·list /'tʃelɪst/ *n* [C] 大提琴手 dàtíqínshǒu.

cello /'tʃeləʊ/ *n* [C] [*pl* ~s] 大提琴 dàtíqín.

cel·lu·lar /'seljʊlə(r)/ *adj* 由细胞组成的 yóu xìbāo zǔchéng de.

Cel·sius /'selsɪəs/ *n* = centigrade.

ce·ment /sɪ'ment/ *n* [U] **1** 水泥 shuǐní. ⇨ concrete. **2** 结合剂〔劑〕jiéhéjì, 黏固剂 niángùjì. □ *vt* 黏结 niánjiē; 胶〔膠〕合 jiāohé.

cem·etery /'semətrɪ/ *n* [C] [*pl*

-ies] 墓地mùdì.

ceno·taph /'senətɑ:f/ *n* [C] (为葬于别处的死者所立的)纪念碑 jìniànbēi.

cen·sor /'sensə(r)/ *n* [C] 审〔審〕查官 shěncháguān, 审查员 shěncháyuán. □ *vt* 审查 shěnchá, 检〔檢〕查 jiǎnchá. '~**ship** 审查(制度) shěnchá, 审查职〔職〕位 shěnchá zhíwèi.

cen·sure /'senʃə(r)/ *vt* [正式用语] 指责 zhǐzé, 非难〔難〕 fēinàn. □ *n* [C, U] 非难 fēinàn, 指责 zhǐzé.

cen·sus /'sensəs/ *n* [C] [*pl* ~es] 人口调查 rénkǒu diàochá.

cent /sent/ *n* [C] 分(货币单位) fēn. *per* ~, 百分率 bǎifēnlǜ, 百分之… bǎifēnzhī …: *a 10 per ~ increase* 增加百分之十.

cen·taur /'sentɔ:(r)/ *n* [C] [希腊神话]半人半马〔馬〕怪物 bànrén bànmǎ guàiwù.

cen·ten·ar·ian /ˌsentɪ'neərɪən/ *n* [C], *adj* 百岁〔歲〕老人的 bǎisuì lǎorénde.

cen·ten·ary /ˌsen'ti:nərɪ/ *adj*, *n* [C] [*pl* -ies] 百年的 bǎiniánde; 百年纪念 bǎinián jìniàn.

cen·ten·nial /sen'tenɪəl/ *adj*, *n* = centenary. ~**ly** *adv*

cen·ter /'sentə(r)/ *n* [美语] = centre.

cen·ti·grade /'sentɪgreɪd/ *adj* 摄氏温度计的 shèshì wēndùjì de.

cen·ti·metre [美语= **-meter**] /'sentɪmi:tə(r)/ *n* [C] 公分 gōngfēn, 厘米 límǐ.

cen·ti·pede /'sentɪpi:d/ *n* [C] 蜈蚣 wúgōng.

cen·tral /'sentrəl/ *adj* **1** 中央的 zhōngyāngde; 中心的 zhōngxīnde. **2** 最重要的 zuìzhòngyàode. 主要的 zhǔyàode. ˌ~ '**heating** 中央暖气〔氣〕系统 zhōngyāng nuǎnqì xìtǒng. ˌ~'**processing unit** (略作 CPU)中央处〔處〕理部件 zhōngyāng chùlǐ bùjiàn. ~**ly** *adv*

cen·tral·ize /'sentrəlaɪz/ *vt/i* **1** 集中到中央 jízhōng dào zhōngyāng. **2** 由中央政府管理 yóu zhōngyāngzhèngfǔ guǎnlǐ. **cen·trali'z·ation** *n* [U]

centre [美语= **cen·ter**] /'sentə(r)/ *n* [C] **1** 中心 zhōngxīn; 中央 zhōngyāng. **2** 中心区〔區〕 zhōngxīnqū; 核心 héxīn: *a* '*shopping* ~ 商业中心,商业区. *the* ~ *of attraction* 惹人注意的中心人物(或事物). □ *vt/i* 置于中心 zhì yú zhōngxīn. ~ *on* 集中 jízhōng: ~ *one's attention on an idea* 集中注意于一种主意.

cen·trifu·gal /sen'trɪfjʊgl/ *adj* 离〔離〕心的 líxīnde: ~ *force* 离心力.

cen·tury /'sentʃərɪ/ *n* [C] [*pl* -ies] **1** 一百年 yìbǎinián, 世纪 shìjì. **2** 板球的一百分 bǎnqiúde yìbǎifēn.

ce·ramic /sɪ'ræmɪk/ *adj* 陶器的 táoqìde; 陶瓷的 táocíde. **ce·ramics** **(a)** [与单数动词连用]陶瓷艺〔藝〕术〔術〕 táocí yìshù. **(b)** [与复数动词连用]陶瓷制〔製〕品 táocí zhìpǐn.

cer·eal /'sɪərɪəl/ *n* [C] [常用复]谷〔穀〕类〔類〕粮食 gǔlèi liángshi.

cer·emo·nial /ˌserɪ'məʊnɪəl/ *adj* 礼〔禮〕仪〔儀〕的 lǐyíde: *a* ~ *carriage* 彩车. □ *n* [C, U] 礼仪 lǐyí; 仪式 yíshì. ~**ly** *adv*

cer·emo·ni·ous /ˌserɪ'məʊnɪəs/ *adj* 过〔過〕分讲究礼〔禮〕仪〔儀〕的 guòfèn jiǎngjiu lǐyí de; 仪式隆重的 yíshì lóngzhòng de. ~**ly** *adv*

cer·emony /'serɪmənɪ/ *n* [C] [*pl* -ies] **1** [C] 典礼〔禮〕 diǎnlǐ, 仪〔儀〕式 yíshì. **2** [U] 礼节〔節〕 lǐjié, 礼仪 lǐyí.

cer·tain /'sɜ:tn/ *adj* **1** 确定的 quèdìngde; 无〔無〕疑的 wúyíde. **2** 一定的 yídìngde, 必然的 bìránde. *make* ~弄确实〔實〕 nòngquèshí, 弄清楚 nòngqīngchǔ. *I'll make* ~ *he comes.* 我要弄确实,他一定来. **3** 可靠的 kěkàode: *a* ~ *cure* 可靠的治疗. **4** 某 mǒu, 某种〔種〕 mǒuzhǒng; 某一 mǒuyī: *on* ~ *conditions* 在某些条件下. **5** 一些 yìxiē, 一定 yídìng: *There was a* ~ *coldness in her attitude.* 她的态度有些冷淡. ~**ly** *adv* **(a)** 无疑 wúyí: *He will* ~*ly die.* 他一定会死的. **(b)** (回答疑问) 好的 hǎode, 当然可以 dāng rán kěyǐ.

cer·tain·ty /'sɜ:təntɪ/ *n* **1** [C] [*pl* -ies] 必然的事 bìránde shì. **2** [U] 必然 bìrán, 确实〔實〕quèshí, 肯定 kěndìng.

cer·tifi·cate /sə'tɪfɪkət/ *n* [C] 证〔證〕书〔書〕 zhèngshū. 执〔執〕照 zhí zhào: *a* '*birth* ~出生证书.

cer·tify /'sɜ:tɪfaɪ/ *vt/i* [*pt*, *pp* -ied] (发给证书)证〔證〕明 zhèngmíng: ~ *him dead* (*insane*) 证明他死亡(精神失常).

cess·pit /'sespɪt/,**cess·pool** /'sespu:l/ *n* [C] 污水坑 wūshuǐkēng; 粪坑 fènkēng.

chafe /tʃeɪf/ *vt/i* **1** 擦热〔熱〕皮肤〔膚〕 cārè pífū; 擦痛皮肤 cātòng pífū. **2** 发〔發〕怒 fānù, 焦躁 jiāozào: ~ *at the delay* 因拖延而焦躁. □ *n* [C] 皮肤擦伤处 pífū cāshāngchù.

chaff /tʃɑ:f/ *n* [U] **1** 谷〔穀〕壳

〔殼〕gǔqiào. **2** 秣 mò, 切细的稻草(作饲料) qiēxìde dàocǎo.

chag·rin /'ʃægrɪn/ *n* [U] 懊恼 àonǎo; 悔恨 huǐhèn.

chain /tʃeɪn/ *n* [C] **1** 链〔鏈〕liàn, 链条〔條〕liàntiáo. **2** 一连〔連〕串 yìliánchuàn; 一系列 yíxìliè: *a ~ of mountains* 山脉, 山系. □ *vt* 用链条拴住 yòng liàntiáo shuānzhù: *He was ~ed to the wall.* 他被用链条拴在墙上. **'~ reaction** 连锁反应〔應〕liánsuǒ fǎnyìng. **'~-smoker** 一根接一根的吸烟〔煙〕者 yìgēn jiē yìgēn de xīyānzhě. **'~-store** 连锁商店 liánsuǒ shāngdiàn.

chair /tʃeə(r)/ *n* [C] **1** 椅子 yǐzi. **2** 会〔會〕议〔議〕主席职〔職〕位 huìyì zhǔxí zhíwèi; 会议主席席位 huìyì zhǔxí xíwèi. **3** 大学〔學〕教授的职〔職〕位 dàxuéjiàoshòu de zhíwèi. □ *vt* **1** (把比赛获胜者)用椅子抬着走 yòng yǐzi táizhe zǒu. **2** 任(会议)主席 rèn zhǔxí; 主持(会议)zhǔchí. **'~man** 主席(会议) zhǔxí.

chalet /'ʃæleɪ/ *n* [C] **1** 瑞士山上的小木屋 ruìshì shānshàng de xiǎomùwū. **2** 木屋式别墅 mùwūshì biéshù.

chalk /tʃɔːk/ *n* **1** [U] 白垩〔堊〕bái'è. **2** [C, U] 粉笔〔筆〕fěnbǐ. □ *vt* 用粉笔写、画 yòng fěnbǐ xiě, huà. **chalky** *adj* 白垩的 bái'è-de; 象白垩的 xiàng bái'è de.

chal·lenge /'tʃælɪndʒ/ *n* [C] 邀请比赛 yāoqǐng bǐsài; 挑战〔戰〕tiǎozhàn. □ *vt* 挑战 tiǎozhàn, 要求提出事实〔實〕(以证明一项声明) yāoqiú tíchū shìshí; 提出异〔異〕议〔議〕tíchū yìyì. *~ a person's right to do something* 对某人做某事的权利提出异议. **chal·lenger** 挑战者 tiǎozhànzhě; 诘难〔難〕者 jiénànzhě; 质〔質〕问〔問〕者 zhìwènzhě.

cham·ber /'tʃeɪmbe(r)/ *n* **1** [旧用法]房间〔間〕fángjiān. **2** 议〔議〕院 yìyuàn. 立法机〔機〕关〔關〕的会〔會〕议〔議〕厅〔廳〕lìfǎjīguānde huìyìtīng. **3** 贸易团〔團〕体〔體〕màoyì tuántǐ: *a C~ of Commerce* 商会. **4** (枪的)弹〔彈〕膛 dàntáng; 药〔藥〕室 yàoshì. **'~maid** (旅馆)卧室女服务〔務〕员. wòshì nǚ fúwùyuán, 女招待 nǚzhāodài. **'~ music** 室内乐〔樂〕shìnèiyuè.

cha·meleon /kə'miːlɪən/ *n* [C] 变〔變〕色蜥蜴 biànsè xīyì, 变色龙〔龍〕biànsèlóng.

cham·ois /'ʃæmwaː/ *n* **1** [C] 欧〔歐〕洲和高加索地区〔區〕的小羚羊 ōuzhōu hé gāojiāsuǒ dìqū de xiǎo língyáng. **2** 羚羊皮 língyángpí.

champ /tʃæmp/ *vt/i* **1** 马〔馬〕大声〔聲〕地嚼或咬 mǎ dàshēngde jiáo huò yǎo. **2** [喻]不耐烦 búnàifán, 焦急 jiāojí.

cham·pagne /ʃæm'peɪn/ *n* [C, U] 香槟〔檳〕酒 xiāngbīnjiǔ.

cham·pion /'tʃæmpɪən/ *n* [C] **1** 战〔戰〕士 zhànshì; 拥〔擁〕护〔護〕者 yōnghùzhě. **2** 冠军〔軍〕guànjūn, □ *vt* 支持 zhīchí; 拥护 yōnghù, 保卫〔衛〕bǎowèi. **~ship (a)** [U] 拥护 yōnghù, 支持 zhīchí. **(b)** [C] 冠军赛 guànjūnsài; 锦标〔標〕赛 jǐnbiāosài.

chance[1] /tʃaːns/ *n* **1** [U] 机〔機〕会〔會〕jīhuì; 幸运〔運〕xìngyùn, 运气〔氣〕yùnqì. *by ~* 意外地 yìwàide. **2** [C, U] 可能性 kěnéngxìng: *no ~ of winning* 没有胜的可能. **3** [C] 机遇 jīyù, 机会 jīhuì: *the ~ of a lifetime* 一生中难得的机会. □ *adj* 偶然的 ǒuránde. **chancy** *adj* [-ier, -iest] [非正式用语]危险〔險〕的 wēixiǎnde.

chance[2] /tʃaːns/ *vt/i* **1** 碰巧 pèngqiǎo, 偶然发〔發〕生 ǒurán fāshēng: *I ~d to be there.* 我碰巧在那里. **2** 冒…的险 mào…de xiǎn.

chan·cel /'tʃaːnsl/ *n* [C] (教堂东端的)圣〔聖〕坛〔壇〕shèngtán.

chan·cel·lor /'tʃaːnsələ(r)/ *n* [C] **1** 大臣 dàchén; 司法官 sīfǎguān: *the C~ of the Exchequer* 财政大臣. **2** (某些大学的)名誉〔譽〕校长 míngyù xiàozhǎng. **3** (德国等) 总〔總〕理 zǒnglǐ.

chan·de·lier /ˌʃændə'lɪə(r)/ *n* [C] 枝形吊灯〔燈〕架 zhīxíng diàodēngjià; 枝形吊灯 zhīxíng diàodēng.

change[1] /tʃeɪndʒ/ *n* **1** [C] 改变〔變〕gǎibiàn; 替换物 tìhuànwù: *a ~ of clothes* 换洗的衣服. **2** [U] 零钱〔錢〕língqián, 找头〔頭〕zhǎotou. **3** [C, U] 替代 tìdài. *for a ~* 为了变换花样 wèile biànhuàn huāyàng.

change[2] /tʃeɪndʒ/ *vt/i* **1** 更换地方 gēnghuàn dìfang: *~ address* 更换地址. **2** 替换 tìhuàn; 替代 tìdài; 更换 gēnghuàn: *to ~ clothes* 换衣服. **3** 兑换 duìhuàn, 互换 hùhuàn, 交换 jiāohuàn: *~ a traveller's cheque* 兑换旅行支票. **4** 改变〔變〕gǎibiàn, 变化 biànhuà. *~ one's mind* 改变主意 gǎibiàn zhǔyi. **~-able** /-əbl/ *adj* 可变的 kěbiànde; 易变的 yìbiànde.

chan·nel /'tʃænl/ *n* [C] **1** 海峡〔峽〕hǎixiá: *The English C~* 英吉利海峡. **2** 水道 shuǐdào; 河床 héchuáng; 航道 hángdào. **3** [喻] 路线〔線〕lùxiàn, 途径〔徑〕tújìng;

系统 xìtǒng. ***through the usual ~s*** 通过正常途径 tōngguò zhèngcháng tújìng. **4** (广播)波段 pōduàn; (电视) 频道 píndào. □ *vt* [-ll-, 美语亦作 -l-] **1** 形成水道 xíngchéng shuǐdào. **2** 引导 yǐndǎo: *~ water into fields* 引水入田; *~ one's efforts into hard work* 引导某人努力工作.

chant /tʃɑːnt/ *n* [C] **1** 圣〔聖〕歌 shènggē, 赞美诗 zànměishī. **2** 单〔單〕调的歌 dāndiàode gē. □ *vt/i* 唱单调的歌 chàng dāndiàode gē. 唱圣歌 chàngshènggē: *~ing football crowds* 单调地唱着的足球观众.

chaos /ˈkeɪɒs/ *n* [U] 混乱〔亂〕 hùnluàn; 纷乱 fēnluàn. **cha·otic** /keɪˈɒtɪk/ *adj* 混乱的 hùnluànde, 无〔無〕秩序的 wú zhìxù de, **cha·oti·cally** *adv*

chap[1] /tʃæp/ *n* [C] 〔非正式用语〕家伙 jiāhuo; 小伙子 xiǎohuǒzi.

chap[2] /tʃæp/ *vt/i* [-pp-] (使皮肤)粗糙 cūzào, 皲〔皸〕裂 jūnliè. □ *n* [C] 龟〔龜〕裂 guīliè, 皲裂 jūnliè.

chapel /ˈtʃæpl/ *n* [C] **1** 学〔學〕校等的小教堂 xuéxiào děng de xiǎojiàotáng. **2** 教堂内的私人祈祷〔禱〕处〔處〕 jiàotáng nèi de sīrén qídǎochù.

chap·lain /ˈtʃæplɪn/ *n* [C] 军〔軍〕队〔隊〕、学〔學〕校内之牧师〔師〕 jūnduì, xuéxiào nèi zhī mùshī.

chap·ter /ˈtʃæptə(r)/ *n* [C] **1** (书的)章 zhāng; 回 huí. **2** 牧师〔師〕会〔會〕 mùshīhuì.

char[1] /tʃɑː(r)/ *vt/i* [-rr-] 使烧〔燒〕焦 shǐ shāojiāo, 使烧黑 shǐ shāohēi.

char[2] /tʃɑː(r)/ *vi* [-rr-] 打杂〔雜〕 dǎzá, 做家庭杂务〔務〕 zuò jiātíng záwù. □ *n* [C] = charwoman. **'~woman** 替人打扫〔掃〕清洁〔潔〕的女工 tìrén dǎsǎo qīngjié de nǚgōng.

char·ac·ter /ˈkærəktə(r)/ *n* **1** [U] (个人等的)天性 tiānxìng, 性格 xìnggé, 特性 tèxìng. ***out of ~*** (同自己的个性)不适〔適〕合 bú shìhé, 不相称〔稱〕 bù xiāngchèn. **2** [U] 道德的力量 dàodéde lìliàng, 品性 pǐnxìng: *a man of ~* 品格高尚的人. **3** [U] (事物等的)特点〔點〕 tèdiǎn; 特征〔徵〕 tèzhēng: *the ~ of the desert* 沙漠的特征. **4** [C] 社会〔會〕知名人士 shèhuì zhīmíng rénshì; 小说中的人物 xiǎoshuō zhong de rénwù; 戏〔戲〕剧〔劇〕的角色 xìjùde juésè. **5** [C] 文字 wénzì; 字母 zìmǔ: *Chinese ~s* 汉字. **~less** *adj* 平常的 píngchángde; 无〔無〕特点〔點〕的 wú tèdiǎn de.

char·ac·ter·is·tic /ˌkærəktəˈrɪstɪk/ *adj* 特有的 tèyǒude, 表示特征〔徵〕的 biǎoshì tèzhēng de: *his ~ angry reply* 他特有的怒气冲冲的回答. □ *n* [C] 特性 tèxìng, 特点〔點〕 tèdiǎn. **~ally** /-keɪ/ *adv*

char·ac·ter·ize /ˈkærəktəraɪz/ *vt* 表示…的特征〔徵〕 biǎoshì ... de tèzhēng.

cha·rade /ʃəˈrɑːd/ *n* [C] **1** 一种〔種〕猜字游戏〔戲〕 yìzhǒng cāizì yóuxì. **2** 无〔無〕意义〔義〕的行为〔爲〕 wú yìyì de xíngwéi.

char·coal /ˈtʃɑːkəʊl/ *n* [U] 炭 tàn, 木炭 mùtàn; 炭笔〔筆〕 tànbǐ.

charge[1] /tʃɑːdʒ/ *n* [C] **1** 控告 kònggào, 指控 zhǐkòng. **2** 冲〔衝〕锋 chōngfēng; 突然猛攻 tūrán měnggōng. **3** 费用 fèiyòng, 价〔價〕钱〔錢〕 jiàqián. **4** 造成爆炸的炸药量 zàochéng bàozhà de zhàyào liàng; 电〔電〕荷 diànhé. **5** [C, U] 主管 zhǔguǎn, 掌管 zhǎngguǎn: *Mary was in ~ of the baby.* 玛丽看管婴儿. ***take ~ of*** 负责 fùzé; 掌管 zhǎngguǎn.

charge[2] /tʃɑːdʒ/ *vt/i* **1** 控告 kònggào, 指控 zhǐkòng: *He was ~d with murder.* 他被控告有谋杀罪. **2** 冲〔衝〕锋 chōngfēng. **3** 要求支付(多少钱) yāoqiú zhīfù, 要价〔價〕 yàojià. **4** (为火炮)装〔裝〕炸药 zhuāng zhàyào. 充电〔電〕 chōngdiàn. **5 ~ with** 给以责任 gěi yǐ zérèn, 交付使命 jiāofù shǐmìng.

charge d'affaires /ˌʃɑːʒeɪ dæˈfeə(r)/ *n* [C] [*pl* charges d'affaires] 代办〔辦〕 dàibàn.

char·iot /ˈtʃærɪət/ *n* [C] 古代双〔雙〕轮〔輪〕马〔馬〕拉战〔戰〕车〔車〕 gǔdài shuānglún mǎlā zhànchē. **~eer** /ˌtʃærɪəˈtɪə(r)/ *n* [C] 驾〔駕〕驶〔駛〕战车者 jiàshǐ zhànchē zhě.

chari·table /ˈtʃærɪtəbl/ *adj* 慈善的 císhànde, 宽厚的 kuānhòude. **chari·tably** /-əblɪ/ *adv*

char·ity /ˈtʃærətɪ/ *n* [*pl* -ies] **1** [U] 赈〔賑〕济〔濟〕款, 物 zhènjì kuǎn, wù. **2** [C] 慈善团〔團〕体〔體〕 císhàn tuántǐ. **3** [U] 博爱〔愛〕 bó'ài.

char·la·tan /ˈʃɑːlətən/ *n* [C] 冒充内行者 màochōng nèiháng zhě.

charm /tʃɑːm/ *n* **1** [U] 吸引力 xīyǐnlì, 诱力 yòulì. **2** [C] 可爱〔愛〕之处〔處〕 kě'ài zhī chù. **3** [C] 有魔力的东西 yǒu mólì de dōngxi: *a lucky ~* 吉祥物. □ *vt/i* **1** 吸引 xīyǐn. 迷人 mírén; 使陶醉 shǐ táozuì. **2** 对…行魔法 duì ... xíng mófǎ. **~ing** *adj* 可

爱〔愛〕的 kě'àide, 媚人的 mèirénde.

chart /tʃɑ:t/ *n* [C] **1** 海图〔圖〕hǎitú, 航线〔線〕图 hángxiàntú. **2** 图 tú, 图表 túbiǎo: *a 'weather* ~ 天气图. □ *vt* 制〔製〕...的海图 zhì ... de hǎitú.

char·ter /'tʃɑ:tə(r)/ *n* [C] **1** 君主或政府颁发〔發〕的特许状〔狀〕, 凭〔憑〕照〔照〕jūnzhǔ huò zhèngfǔ bānfā de tèxǔzhuàng, píngzhào. **2** (飞机,船等)租赁 zūlìn: *a '~ flight* 包租的班机. **3** 宪〔憲〕章 xiànzhāng: □ *vt* **1** 特许 tèxǔ, 发执〔執〕照〔照〕给 fā zhízhào gěi. **2** 租,包(船,飞机等) zū, bāo.

char·woman /'tʃɑ:wʊmən/ *n* ⇨ char².

chase /tʃeɪs/ *vt/i* 追逐 zhuīzhú; 追击〔擊〕zhuījī; 追赶〔趕〕zhuīgǎn; 追猎〔獵〕zhuīliè. □ *n* [C] 追逐 zhuīzhú; 追赶 zhuīgǎn; 追击 zhuījī.

chasm /'kæzəm/ *n* [C] **1** (地壳)陷窟 xiànkū; 断〔斷〕层〔層〕duàncéng; 裂口 lièkǒu. **2** [喻](感情,兴趣等)巨大分歧 jùdà fēnqí, 巨大差别 jùdà chābié.

chas·sis /'ʃæsɪ/ *n* [C] [*pl* ~] **1** 汽车〔車〕等的底盘〔盤〕qìchē děng de dǐpán. **2** [飞机]起落装〔裝〕置 qǐluò zhuāngzhì.

chaste /tʃeɪst/ *adj* **1** 有道德的 yǒu dàodé de; 善良的 shànliángde. **2** (特指)贞洁〔潔〕的 zhēnjiéde. **3** (文风等)简〔簡〕洁朴〔樸〕实〔實〕的 jiǎnjié pǔshí de.

chas·ten /'tʃeɪsn/ *vt* 惩〔懲〕戒 chéngjiè; 遏止 èzhǐ.

chas·tise /tʃæ'staɪz/ *vt* 严〔嚴〕惩〔懲〕yánchěng. **~ment** *n* [U] 惩罚 chéngfá.

chas·tity /'tʃæstətɪ/ *n* [U] 贞洁〔潔〕zhēnjié; 纯洁 chúnjié; 高雅 gāoyǎ.

chat /tʃæt/ *n* [C] 闲〔閒〕谈 xiántán, 聊天 liáotiān. □ *vt/i* [-tt-] 闲谈 xiántán, 聊天 liáotiān. **~ty** *adj* [-ier, -iest] 爱〔愛〕闲聊的 ài xiánliáode.

châ·teau /'ʃætəʊ/ *n* [C] [*pl* ~x /-təʊz/] 法国封建城堡 fǎguó fēngjiàn chéngbǎo.

chat·ter /'tʃætə(r)/ *vi* **1** 喋喋不休 diédié bùxiū, 饶〔饒〕舌 ráoshé. **2** □ *n* [C] **1** 喋喋不休 diédié bùxiū; (牙齿)打战〔戰〕dǎzhàn. **2** 迅速而不清晰的声〔聲〕音 xùnsù ér bùqīngxī de shēngyīn. **'~box** 唠〔嘮〕唠叨叨的人 láoláodaodaode rén.

chauf·feur /'ʃəʊfə(r)/ *n* [C] 受雇的私人汽车〔車〕司机〔機〕shòugùde sīrén qìchē sījī.

chau·vin·ism /'ʃəʊvɪnɪzəm/ *n* [U] 大国主义〔義〕dàguózhǔyì; 本性别第一主义 běnxìngbié dìyī zhǔyì. **'chau·vin·ist** 大国主义者 dàguózhǔyìzhě; 本性别第一主义者 běnxìngbié dìyī zhǔyìzhě: *a male* ~ 大男子主义者. **chau·vi'n·is·tic** *adj*

cheap /tʃi:p/ *adj* [-er, -est] **1** 便宜的 piányìde, 廉价〔價〕的 liánjiàde. **2** 低劣的 dīliède, 劣质〔質〕的 lièzhìde: ~ *and nasty* 质量低劣的. **3** 肤〔膚〕浅〔淺〕的 fūqiǎnde; 虚伪〔僞〕的 xūwěide: ~ *emotion* 虚伪的感情. **~ly** *adv* **~ness** *n* [U] **~en** *vt/i* 降低价〔價〕钱〔錢〕jiàngdī jiàqian, 减价 jiǎnjià, 跌价 diējià.

cheat /tʃi:t/ *vt/i* 欺诈 qīzhà; 欺骗〔騙〕行为〔爲〕qīpiàn xíngwéi: ~ *a person out of his money* 骗取某人的钱; ~ *in an examination* 考试作弊. □ *n* [C] 骗子 piànzi; 欺诈 qīzhà.

check¹ /tʃek/ *n* [U] **1** 控制 kòngzhì; 阻碍〔礙〕的人或物 zǔ'àide rén huò wù: *a* ~ *on his progress* 对他的进步的阻碍. **2** 检〔檢〕查 jiǎnchá, 核查 héchá. **3** 寄存物的凭〔憑〕证〔證〕jìcúnwùde píngzhèng. **'~up** 体〔體〕格检查 tǐgé jiǎnchá.

check² /tʃek/ *vt/i* **1** 检〔檢〕查 jiǎnchá, 核对〔對〕héduì: ~ *a student's answer* 检查学生的答案. **2** 控制 kòngzhì; 制止 zhìzhǐ; 妨碍〔礙〕fáng'ài: *He couldn't* ~ *his anger.* 他怒不可遏. **3** (国际象棋用语)将〔將〕jiāng. **4** ~ *in* 在旅馆等登记 zài lǚguǎn děng dēngjì. ~ *out* 付帐〔帳〕后〔後〕离〔離〕开〔開〕fùzhànghòu líkāi. **'~-out** (超级市场等)付款处〔處〕fùkuǎnchù.

check³ /tʃek/ *n* [U] 方格图〔圖〕案 fānggé tú'àn.

check·mate /'tʃekmeɪt/ *vt* **1** (国际象棋中) 将〔將〕死 (对方的王) jiāngsǐ. **2** [喻]阻止并击〔擊〕败(某人,或他的计划) zǔzhǐ bìng jībài. □ *n* [C] **1** 彻底打败 chèdǐ dǎbài. **2** 将死(对方的王) jiāngsǐ.

cheek /tʃi:k/ *n* [C] **1** 面颊〔頰〕miànjiá, 脸〔臉〕蛋儿 liǎndànr. **2** [U] 厚脸皮 hòu liǎnpí; 没礼〔禮〕貌 méi lǐmào. □ *vt* 对...无〔無〕礼〔禮〕duì ... wúlǐ, 对...顶撞 duì ... dǐngzhuàng. **cheeky** *adj* [-ier, -iest] 无〔無〕礼〔禮〕的 wúlǐde. **~ily** *adv*

cheer¹ /tʃɪə(r)/ *n* **1** [U] 振奋〔奮〕zhènfèn; 高兴〔興〕gāoxìng. **2** [C]

喝采 hècǎi, 欢〔歡〕呼 huānhū. ~-ful *adj* **(a)** 使人高兴的 shǐrén gāoxìngde, 使人愉快的 shǐrén yúkuàide: *a ~ day* 愉快的一天. **(b)** 高兴的 gāoxìngde; 乐〔樂〕意的 lèyìde. **~fully** *adv* **~less** *adj* 不舒服的 bùshūfude; 阴〔陰〕暗的 yīn'ànde.

cheer² /tʃɪə(r)/ *vt/i* **1** 使高兴〔興〕shǐ gāoxìng, 振奋〔奮〕zhènfèn: *The good news ~ed me (up).* 好消息使我高兴起来. **2** 高兴 gāoxìng. **3** 喝采 hècǎi; 欢〔歡〕呼 huānhū. **~ing** *n* [U] *adj*

cheerio /ˌtʃɪərɪ'əʊ/ *int* 〔非正式用语〕再见 zàijiàn.

cheery /'tʃɪərɪ/ *adj* [-ier, -iest] 活泼〔潑〕的 huópode; 喜气〔氣〕洋洋的 xǐqì yángyáng de. **cheer·ily** *adv*

cheese /tʃi:z/ *n* [C, U] 乳酪 rǔlào; 干酪 gānlào. **'~-cloth** 粗布 cūbù; 干酪包布 gānlào bāobù.

chee·tah /'tʃi:tə/ *n* [C] 猎〔獵〕豹 lièbào.

chef /ʃef/ *n* [C] [*pl* ~s] 男厨师〔師〕长〔長〕nán chúshīzhǎng.

chemi·cal /'kemɪkl/ *adj* 化学〔學〕的 huàxuéde; 用化学方法得到的 yòng huàxué fāngfǎ dédào de. □ *n* [C] 化学制品 huàxué zhìpǐn. **~ly** /-klɪ/ *adv*

chem·ist /'kemɪst/ *n* [C] **1** 化学〔學〕家 huàxuéjiā, 化学师〔師〕huàxuéshī. **2** 药剂师 yàojìshī; 药剂商 yàojìshāng; 化妆品商 huàzhuāngpǐnshāng.

chem·is·try /'kemɪstrɪ/ *n* [U] they combine. 化学〔學〕huàxué.

cheque /tʃek/ *n* [C] [美语 =**check**] 支票 zhīpiào. **'~-book** 支票簿 zhīpiàobù.

cher·ish /'tʃerɪʃ/ *vt* **1** 爱〔愛〕护〔護〕àihù. **2** 抱有(希望) bàoyǒu, 怀〔懷〕有(情感) huáiyǒu: *~ the memory of* 怀念.

cherry /'tʃerɪ/ *n* [C] [*pl* -ies] 樱桃 yīngtao; 樱桃树〔樹〕yīngtaoshù. □ *adj* 鲜红色 xiānhóngsè.

cherub /'tʃerəb/ *n* [C] **1** [*pl* ~s] 美丽〔麗〕可爱〔愛〕的小孩子 měilì kě'ài de xiǎoháizi. 绘〔繪〕画〔畫〕中有翅膀的孩子 huìhuà zhōng yǒu chìbǎng de háizi. **2** [*pl* ~im /-bɪm/] 天使 tiānshǐ.

chess /tʃes/ *n* [U] 国〔國〕际〔際〕象棋 guójì xiàngqí.

chest /tʃest/ *n* [C] **1** 箱子 xiāngzi, 柜〔櫃〕子 guìzi. **2** 胸腔 xiōngqiāng. **,~ of 'drawers** 衣柜 yīguì; 五斗橱 wǔdǒuchú.

chest·nut /'tʃesnʌt/ *n* **1** [C, U] 栗树〔樹〕lìshù. **2** 栗色 lìsè. □ *adj* 红褐色的 hónghèsède.

chew /tʃu:/ *vt/i* 嚼 jiáo, 咀嚼 jǔjué. □ *n* [C] 咀嚼 jǔjué, 嚼物 jiáowù. **'~ing-gum** 橡皮糖 xiàngpítáng, 口香糖 kǒuxiāngtáng.

chic /ʃi:k/ *n* [U] 漂亮 piàoliang, 时〔時〕式 shíshì. □ *adj* 时式的 shíshìde.

chick /tʃɪk/ *n* [C] 小鸡〔鷄〕xiǎojī; 小鸟〔鳥〕xiǎoniǎo.

chicken /'tʃɪkɪn/ *n* [C] **1** 小鸡〔鷄〕xiǎojī; 小鸟〔鳥〕xiǎoniǎo. ***(Don't) count your ~s before they are hatched*** (别)蛋还没有孵就数鸡 dàn hái méiyǒu fū jiù shǔ jī, (别)过〔過〕早乐〔樂〕观〔觀〕guò zǎo lèguān. **2** [U] 鸡肉 jīròu. □ *adj* 〔非正式用语〕胆〔膽〕怯的 dǎnqiède, 软〔軟〕弱的 ruǎnruòde. **'~pox** 水痘 shuǐdòu.

chic·ory /'tʃɪkərɪ/ *n* [U] **1** 菊苣(蔬菜) jújù. **2** 菊苣粉(与咖啡同用) jújùfěn.

chief /tʃi:f/ *n* [C] **1** 领袖 lǐngxiù, 首领 shǒulǐng. **2** 部门〔門〕主任 bùmén zhǔrèn. □ *adj* **1** 主要的 zhǔyàode, 首要的 shǒuyàode. **2** 首席的 shǒuxíde. **-in-'chief** 最高的 zuìgāode: *the Commander-in-~* 统帅, 总司令. **~ly** *adv* 大半 dàbàn, 主要 zhǔyào.

chief·tain /'tʃi:ftən/ *n* [C] 首领 shǒulǐng, 酋长〔長〕qiúzhǎng.

child /tʃaɪld/ *n* [C] [*pl* children /'tʃɪldrən/] **1** 儿〔兒〕童 értóng, 小孩 xiǎohái. **2** 儿子 érzi, 女儿 nǚ'ér. **'~hood** 幼年 yòunián, 童年 tóngnián; 童年时〔時〕代 tóngnián shídài. **'~ish** *adj* 幼稚的 yòuzhìde, 傻气〔氣〕的 shǎqìde. **~less** *adj* 无〔無〕子女的 wú zǐnǚ de. **'~like** *adj* 孩子般天真的 háizibān tiānzhēn de.

chill /tʃɪl/ *n* **1** [只用 *sing*] 寒冷 hánlěng, 冷飕〔颼〕飕 lěng sōusōu. **2** [只用单][喻]扫〔掃〕兴〔興〕sǎoxìng, 寒心 hánxīn: *The bad news cast a ~ over the meeting.* 这个坏消息使到会的人感到沮丧. **3** [C] 寒慄 hánlì, 寒战〔戰〕hánzhàn, 感冒 gǎnmào, 风〔風〕寒 fēnghán. □ *adj* 冷飕飕的 lěngsōusōude. □ *vt/i* 使寒冷 shǐ hánlěng, 变〔變〕冷 biànlěng. 感到寒冷 gǎndào hánlěng. **chilly** *adj* [-ier, -iest] **(a)** 寒冷的 hánlěngde, 感到寒冷的 gǎndào hánlěngde. **(b)** [喻]不友善的 bù yǒushàn de, 冷淡的 lěngdànde.

chilli /'tʃɪlɪ/ *n* [C, U] 干〔乾〕辣椒 gān làjiāo.

chime /tʃaɪm/ *n* [C] 编钟〔鐘〕

biānzhōng, 一套编钟的谐和的钟声〔聲〕 yítào biānzhōng de xiéhéde zhōngshēng. □ *vt/i* (乐钟, 时钟)鸣〔鳴〕响〔響〕 míngxiǎng.

chim·ney /'tʃɪmnɪ/ *n* [C] [*pl* ~s] 烟〔煙〕囱 yāncōng, 烟突 yāntū. '~**pot** 烟囱管帽 yāncōng guǎnmào. '~**stack** 丛〔叢〕烟囱(有几个顶管的烟囱) cóngyāncōng. '~-**sweep(er)** 扫烟囱工人 sǎo yāncōng gōngrén.

chim·pan·zee /ˌtʃɪmpæn'zi:/ *n* [C] 黑猩猩 hēixīngxīng.

chin /'tʃɪn/ *n* [C] 颏 kē, 下巴 xiàba.

china /'tʃaɪnə/ *n* [U] **1** 瓷 cí. **2** 瓷器 cíqì.

chink[1] /tʃɪŋk/ *n* [C] 裂缝 lièfèng, 裂口 lièkǒu.

chink[2] /tʃɪŋk/ *n* [C] *vt/i* (金属, 玻璃等)丁〔叮〕当〔當〕声〔聲〕 dīngdāngshēng; 使作丁当声 shǐzuò dīng dāngshēng, 作丁当声 zuò dīng dāngshēng;

chip /tʃɪp/*n* [C] **1** 片屑 piànxiè, 碎片 suìpiàn, 切屑 qiēxiè. *have a ~ on one's shoulder* 好斗〔鬥〕 hàodòu,气〔氣〕势〔勢〕汹汹 qìshì xiōngxiōng. **2** (土豆等)薄片 bópiàn: *fish and ~s* 油炸的鱼和土豆片. **3** (瓷器)碎裂的缺口 suìliède quēkǒu. **4** (电子学)集成电〔電〕路块〔塊〕 jíchéng diànlùkuài. □ *vt/i* [-pp-] **1** 削 xiāo, 铲〔鏟〕 chǎn. **2** 形成缺口 xíngchéng quēkǒu. **3** ~ '*in* [非正式用语] **(a)** 插嘴 chāzuǐ, 打断〔斷〕别人的话 dǎduàn biérénde huà. **(b)** 捐助 juānzhù.

chi·rop·ody /kɪ'rɒpədɪ/ *n* [U] 足病的治疗〔療〕 zúbìngde zhìliáo. **chi·'rop·odist** *n* [C]

chirp/tʃɜ:p/ *n* [C] *vt/i* 小鸟〔鳥〕啾啾喳喳叫声〔聲〕 xiǎoniǎo, qīqīchāchā jiàoshēng, 啾啾喳喳地叫 qīqīchāchāde jiào 啾啾喳喳说出 qīqīchāchā shuōchū.

chirpy /'tʃɜ:pɪ/ *adj* [-ier,-iest] 快活的 kuàihuode, 活泼〔潑〕的 huópōde.

chisel /'tʃɪzl/ *n* [C] 凿子 záozi,錾〔鏨〕子 zànzi. □*vt* [-ll-] 凿 záo, 雕 diāo.

chit /tʃɪt/ *n* [C] 欠条〔條〕 qiàntiáo, 欠款单〔單〕据〔據〕 qiànkuǎn dānjù.

chiv·alry /'ʃɪvlrɪ/ *n* [U] **1** 中世纪的骑〔騎〕士制度 zhōngshìjìde qíshì zhìdù. **2** 帮助弱者和妇〔婦〕女的慈爱〔愛〕精神 bāngzhù ruòzhě hé fùnǚ de cí'ài jīngshen. **chiv·al·rous** *adj*

chloro·form /'klɒrəfɔ:m/ *n* [U] 氯仿 lùfǎng. □ *vt* 用氯仿进行麻醉 yòng lùfǎng jìnxíng mázuì.

choc·olate /'tʃɒklət/ *n* **1** [U] 巧克力 qiǎokèlì, 朱古力 zhūgǔlì. **2** [C] 巧克力饮料 qiǎokèlì yǐnliào, 巧克力糖 qiǎokèlìtáng. □ *adj* 赭色的 zhěsède.

choice /'tʃɔɪs/ *n* **1** [C] 选〔選〕择〔擇〕 xuǎnzé. **2** [U] 选择的机〔機〕会〔會〕 xuǎnzéde jīhuì:*I had no ~ but to leave.* 我没有选择的余地, 只得离开. **3** [C] 选择的种〔種〕类〔類〕 xuǎnzéde zhǒnglèi: *a large ~ of bags* 很多种类的提包可供选择. **4** [C] 被选中的人或物 bèi xuǎnzhòng de rén huò wù: *This is my ~.* 这是我选中的. □ *adj* 精选的 jīngxuǎnde, 上等的 shàngděngde: *~ fruit* 上等水果.

choir /'kwaɪə(r)/ *n* [C] **1** (教会的)歌唱队〔隊〕 gēchàngduì, 唱诗班 chàngshībān. **2** 歌唱队的席位 gēchàngduìde xíwèi.

choke[1] /tʃəʊk/ *vt/i* **1** 闷〔悶〕塞 mēnsāi, 压〔壓〕抑 yāyì, 抑制 yìzhì. **2** 闷死 mènsǐ, 掐死 qiāsǐ. **3** 堵塞 dǔsè, 阻塞 zǔsè: *a drain ~d (up) with dirt* 被脏物堵塞的水沟.

choke[2] /tʃəʊk/ *n* [C] (机械)阻气〔氣〕门〔門〕 zǔqìmén.

chol·era /'kɒlərə/ *n* [U] 霍乱〔亂〕 huòluàn.

cho·les·ter·ol /kə'lestərɒl/ *n* [U] (生化)胆〔膽〕固醇 dǎngùchún.

choose /tʃu:z/ *vt/i* [*pt* chose /tʃəʊz/, *pp* chosen /'tʃəʊzn/] **1** 选〔選〕择〔擇〕 xuǎnzé; 挑选 tiāoxuǎn. **2** 选定 xuǎndìng; 决定 juédìng: *He ~s to become a doctor.* 他决定当医生.

chop[1] /tʃɒp/ *n* [C] **1** 砍 kǎn; 劈 pī; 剁 duò. **2** 一块〔塊〕排骨 yíkuài páigǔ.

chop[2] /tʃɒp/ *vt/i* [-pp-] 劈 pī; 砍 kǎn; 剁 duò.

chop·per /'tʃɒpə(r)/ *n* [C] **1** 斧头〔頭〕 fǔtóu; 屠刀 túdāo; 砍刀 kǎndāo. **2** [非正式用语]直升飞〔飛〕机〔機〕 zhíshēngfēijī.

choppy /'tʃɒpɪ/ *adj* [-ier, -iest] **1** (海)波涛〔濤〕汹涌的 pōtāo xiōngyǒng de. **2** (风)方向常变〔變〕的 fāngxiàng chángbiàn de.

chop·sticks /'tʃɒpstɪks/ *n pl* 筷子 kuàizi.

choral /'kɔ:rəl/ *adj* 合唱队〔隊〕的 héchàngduìde, 合唱的 héchàngde.

chord /kɔ:d/ *n* [C] **1** [数学]弦 xián. **2** [音乐]和弦 héxián, 和音 héyīn.

chore /tʃɔ:(r)/ *n* [C] **1** 日常工作 rìcháng gōngzuò. **2** 琐碎烦人的杂〔雜〕务〔務〕 suǒsuì fánrén de záwù.

chor·eogra·phy /ˌkɒrɪ'ɒgrəfɪ/ *n* [U] 舞蹈设计 wǔdǎo shèjì. **chore'ogra·pher** *n* [C]
chor·is·ter /'kɒrɪstə(r)/ *n* [C] 唱诗班歌手 chàngshībān gēshǒu.
chorus /'kɔ:rəs/ *n* [C] [*pl* ~es] **1** 合唱 héchàng. **2** (歌的)合唱句 héchàngjù, 合唱部分 héchàng bùfen. **3** 齐〔齊〕声 qíshēng: *a ~ of approval* 齐声赞同. □ *vt* 合唱 héchàng; 齐声地说 qíshēngde shuō.
chose, chosen ⇨ choose.
Christ /kraɪst/ *n* 基督 jīdū.
christen /'krɪsn/ *vt* 为〔爲〕…施洗礼〔禮〕 wèi ... shī xǐlǐ; 洗礼时〔時〕命名 xǐlǐshí mìngmíng. **'~ing** *n* [C]
Christen·dom /'krɪsndəm/ *n* 全体基督教徒 quántǐ jīdūjiàotú; 基督教世界 jīdūjiào shìjiè.
Chris·tian /'krɪstʃən/ *adj* 基督的 jīdūde; 基督教的 jīdūjiàode. □ *n* 基督教徒 jīdūjiàotú. **'~ name** 教名 jiàomíng.
Chris·ti·an·ity /ˌkrɪstɪ'ænətɪ/ *n* [U] 基督教 jīdūjiào.
Christ·mas /'krɪsməs/ *n* [C] [*pl* ~es] [亦作 ˌ~'*Day*] 圣〔聖〕诞节〔節〕 shèngdànjié.
chrome /krəʊm/ *n* [U] 铬黄 gèhuáng.
chro·mium /'krəʊmɪəm/ *n* [U] 铬(化学符号 **Cr**) gè.
chro·mo·some /'krəʊməsəʊm/ *n* [C] 染色体 rǎnsètǐ.
chronic /'krɒnɪk/ *adj* (疾病)慢性的 mànxìngde. ⇨ acute(2). **~ally** /-kəlɪ/ *adv*
chron·icle /'krɒnɪkl/ *n* [C] 年代纪 niándàijì; 编年史 biānniánshǐ. □ *vt* 把…载入编年史 bǎ ... zǎirù biānniánshǐ.
chrono·logi·cal /ˌkrɒnə'lɒdʒɪkl/ *adj* 按时〔時〕间〔間〕顺序的 àn shíjiān shùnxù de. **~ly** *adv*
chron·ol·ogy /krə'nɒlədʒɪ/ *n* [*pl* -ies] **1** [U] 年代学〔學〕 niándàixué. **2** [C] 年表 niánbiǎo.
chron·ometer /krə'nɒmɪtə(r)/ *n* [C] 精密记时〔時〕计 jīngmì jìshíjì.
chrysa·lis /'krɪsəlɪs/ *n* [C] [*pl* ~-es] 蛹 yǒng.
chry·san·the·mum /krɪ'sænθəməm/ *n* [C] [*pl* ~s] 菊花 júhuā.
chubby /'tʃʌbɪ/ *adj* [-ier, -iest] 圆的 yuánde; 丰〔豐〕满的 fēngmǎnde.
chuck[1] /tʃʌk/ *vt* [非正式用语] **1** 扔 rēng, 抛 pāo. **2** 丢弃 diūqì, 放弃 fàngqì: ~ *in one's job* 抛弃其职业.
chuck[2] /tʃʌk/ *n* [C] **1** 车〔車〕床的夹〔夾〕盘〔盤〕 chēchuángde jiāpán. **2** 夹头〔頭〕 jiātóu.
chuckle /'tʃʌkl/ *n* [C] 暗自笑 ànzìxiào, 轻〔輕〕声〔聲〕笑 qīngshēngxiào. □ *vt* 抿着嘴轻声地笑 mǐnzhe zuǐ qīngshēngde xiào.
chum /tʃʌm/ *n* [C] [过时用法](特指男孩之间)好朋友 hǎo péngyǒu. **~my** *adj* [-ier, -iest] 亲〔親〕密的 qīnmìde, 友好的 yǒuhǎode.
chump /tʃʌmp/ *n* [C] **1** 厚肉块〔塊〕 hòu ròukuài, 厚木块 hòu mù kuài. **2** [俚语]笨蛋 bèndàn.
chunk /tʃʌŋk/ *n* [C] 厚块〔塊〕 hòukuài. **chunky** *adj* [-ier, -iest] 矮胖的 ǎipàngde.
church /tʃɜ:tʃ/ *n* [C] 基督教教堂 jīdūjiào jiàotáng. ***enter the C~*** 做牧师〔師〕 zuò mùshī. **'~yard** 教堂的墓地 jiàotángde mùdì.
churn /tʃɜ:n/ *n* [C] **1** (炼制黄油用的)搅〔攪〕乳器 jiǎorǔqì. **2** 大的盛奶罐 dàde chéngnǎiguàn. □ *vt/i* **1** 在搅乳器中炼制黄油 zài jiǎorǔqì zhōng liànzhì huángyóu. **2** 剧〔劇〕烈搅拌 jùliè jiǎobàn.
chute /ʃu:t/ *n* [C] **1** 滑运〔運〕道 huáyùndào. **2** 瀑布 pùbù.
chut·ney /'tʃʌtnɪ/ *n* [U] 水果辣椒等混合制〔製〕成的辣酱〔醬〕shuǐguǒ làjiāo děng hùnhé zhìchéng de làjiàng.
C.I.A.=Central Intelligence Agency (美国)中央情报〔報〕局 zhōngyāng qíngbàojú.
C.I.D.=Criminal Investigation Department 伦〔倫〕敦警察厅〔廳〕刑事调查部 lúndūn jǐngchátīng xíngshìdiàochá bù.
cider /'saɪdə(r)/ *n* [U] 苹〔蘋〕果汁 píngguǒzhī; 苹果酒 píngguǒjiǔ.
c.i.f.= cost, insurance and freight 到岸价〔價〕格. dào àn jiàgé
cigar /sɪ'gɑ:(r)/ *n* [C] 雪茄烟〔煙〕 xuějiāyān.
ciga·rette /ˌsɪgə'ret/ *n* [C] 香烟〔煙〕 xiāngyān, 纸烟 zhǐyān, 卷〔捲〕烟 juǎnyān.
C.-in-C.=Commander-in-Chief.
cin·der /'sɪndə(r)/ *n* [C] 炉〔爐〕渣 lúzhā, 煤渣 méizhā.
cin·ema /'sɪnəmə/ *n* **1** [C] 电〔電〕影院 diànyǐngyuàn. **2** [U] 电影 diànyǐng, 电影工业〔業〕 diànyǐng gōngyè.
cin·na·mon /'sɪnəmən/ *n* [U] **1** 肉桂 ròuguì; **2** 肉桂色 ròuguìsè, 黄褐色 huánghèsè.
cipher, cypher /'saɪfə(r)/ *n* [C] **1** 零(即 0) líng. **2** [喻]不重要的人 bú zhòngyào de rén; 无〔無〕价〔價〕值的东〔東〕西 wú jiàzhí de

dōngxi. 3 密码〔碼〕mìmǎ.

circa /'sɜ:kə/ *prep* 〔拉丁语〕(略作 **c, ca**) 约在某时〔時〕yuē zài mǒushí. *born* ~ *150* BC 约生于公元前150年.

circle /'sɜ:kl/ *n* [C] **1** 圆 yuán, 圆周 yuánzhōu. **2** 圆形物 yuánxíngwù, 环〔環〕huán, 圈 quān. **3** 楼〔樓〕厅〔廳〕(剧场的二楼厅座) lóutīng. **4** 圈子 quānzi, 集团〔團〕jítuán, 界 jiè: *a* ~ *of friends* 交游的朋友. □ *vt/i* 环绕〔繞〕huánrǎo, 盘〔盤〕旋 pánxuán.

cir·cuit /'sɜ:kɪt/ *n* [C] **1** 周游 zhōuyóu, 巡行 xúnxíng. **2** 电〔電〕路 diànlù. ⇨ short-circuit. **3** 协〔協〕会〔會〕xiéhuì: *the tennis* ~ 网球联赛. **~ous** /sɜ:'kju:ɪtəs/ *adj* 迂迴的 yúhuíde, 绕〔繞〕行的 ràoxíngde: *a* ~*ous route* 迂迴路线.

cir·cu·lar /'sɜ:kjʊlə(r)/ *adj* 圆形的 yuánxíngde, 环〔環〕绕〔繞〕的 huánràode. □ *n* [C] 通知 tōngzhī, 通告 tōnggào, 通函 tōnghán.

cir·cu·late /'sɜ:kjʊleɪt/ *vt/i* **1** 循环〔環〕xúnhuán, 流通 liútōng. **2** 使循环 shǐ xúnhuán, 使流通 shǐ liútōng. **cir·cu'la·tion** *n* **(a)** [U] 循环 xúnhuán. **(b)** [U] 流通 liútōng: *put coins into* ~ 发行硬币. **(c)** [C] 报〔報〕纸发〔發〕行量 bàozhǐ fāxíngliàng.

cir·cum·cise /'sɜ:kəmsaɪz/ *vt* 割除包皮 gēchú bāopí. **cir·cum·ci·sion** /-'sɪʒn/ *n* [C, U]

cir·cum·fer·ence /sɜ:'kʌmfərəns/ *n* [C] **1** 圆周 yuánzhōu. **2** 周围长度 zhōuwéi chángdù: *the earth's* ~ 地球的周围长度.

cir·cum·flex /'sɜ:kəmfleks/ *n* [C] 元音字母上的声〔聲〕调符号〔號〕(如法语中的 ʌ) yuányīn zìmǔ shàng de shēngdiào fúhào.

cir·cum·navi·gate /ˌsɜ:kəm'nævɪgeɪt/ *vt* 环〔環〕航 huánháng; 环球航行 huánqiú hángxíng. **cir·cum·navi'ga·tion** *n* [C, U]

cir·cum·stance /'sɜ:kəmstəns/ *n* [C] **1** [常用复]情况 qíngkuàng, 形势〔勢〕xíngshì 环〔環〕境 huánjìng. ***in*** (或 ***under***) ***the*** ~***s*** 在此种〔種〕情况下 zài cǐzhǒng qíngkuàng xià. **2** 事件 shìjiàn, 事实〔實〕shìshí: *His death is an unfortunate* ~. 他的死是一件不幸的事.

cir·cum·stan·tial /ˌsɜ:kəm'stænʃl/ *adj* **1** 详细的 xiángxìde; 详尽〔盡〕的 xiángjìnde. **2** (指证据)根据〔據〕情况的 gēnjù qíngkuàngde, 间〔間〕接的 jiànjiēde.

cir·cus /'sɜ:kəs/ *n* [C] [*pl* ~es] **1** 马〔馬〕戏〔戲〕表演 mǎxì biǎoyǎn. **2** (尤用于专有名词)几〔幾〕条〔條〕街道交叉处〔處〕的广〔廣〕场〔場〕jǐtiáo jiēdào jiāochā chù de guǎngchǎng: *Piccadilly C*~ (伦敦)皮卡迪利广场.

cis·tern /'sɪstən/ *n* [C] 水箱 shuǐxiāng, 水槽 shuǐcáo.

cite /saɪt/ *vt* **1** 引用 yǐnyòng, 举〔舉〕例 jǔlì. **2** [法律]传〔傳〕讯 chuánxùn. **ci·ta·tion** /saɪ'teɪʃn/ *n* [C, U]

citi·zen /'sɪtɪzn/ *n* [C] **1** 市民 shìmín, 城市居民 chéngshì jūmín. **2** 公民 gōngmín. **'~ship** 公民或市民身份 gōngmín huò shìmín shēnfen; 公民的权〔權〕利和义〔義〕务〔務〕gōngmínde quánlì hé yìwù.

cit·ric /'sɪtrɪk/ *adj* 柠〔檸〕檬的 níngméngde: ~ *acid* 柠檬酸 níngméngsuān.

cit·rous /'sɪtrəs/ *adj* 柑桔〔橘〕属〔屬〕的 gānjúshǔde.

cit·rus /'sɪtrəs/ *n* [C] [*pl* ~es] 柑桔〔橘〕属〔屬〕植物 gānjúshǔzhíwù. □ *adj* 柑桔属植物的 gānjúshǔ zhíwù de: *'~ fruit* 柑桔属水果.

city /'sɪtɪ/ *n* [C] [*pl* -ies] **1** 都市 dūshì, 城市 chéngshì; 享有特别自治权之城市 xiǎngyǒu tèbié zìzhì quán zhī chéngshì. **2 the C** ~ 英国〔國〕伦敦之金融中心 yīngguó lúndūn zhī jīnróng zhōngxīn. **3** 全市居民 quánshì jūmín.

civic /'sɪvɪk/ *adj* 城市的 chéngshìde, 市民的 shìmínde, 公民的 gōngmínde.

civil /'sɪvl/ *adj* **1** 人类〔類〕社会〔會〕的 rénlèi shèhuìde; 公民的 gōngmínde: ~ *rights* 公民权. **2** 民用的 mínyòngde, 平民的 píngmínde. ⇨ military. **3** 文明的 wénmínde, 有礼〔禮〕貌的 yǒu lǐmào de, 客气〔氣〕的 kèqìde. **ˌ~ engi'neering** 土木工程 tǔmùgōngchéng. **ˌ~ 'rights** 公民权〔權〕gōngmínquán. **ˌ~ 'servant** 文官 wénguān. **the ˌC~ 'Service** 政府部门〔門〕zhèngfǔ bùmén. **~ly** *adv* 客气地 kèqìde. **~ity** /sɪ'vɪlətɪ/ *n* **(a)** [U] 客气 kèqì, 礼貌 lǐmào. **(b)** [*pl*] 礼仪〔儀〕lǐyí, 客套〔套〕kètào.

ci·vil·ian /sɪ'vɪlɪən/ *n* [C],*adj* 平民 píngmín, 老百姓 lǎobǎixìng, 平民的 píngmínde, 民用的 mínyòngde, 民间〔間〕的 mínjiānde.

civi·li·za·tion /ˌsɪvəlaɪ'zeɪʃn/ *n* **1** [U] 开〔開〕化 kāihuà, 教化 jiàohuà. **2** [C] 文明 wénmíng, 文化 wénhuà: *Greek* ~希腊文化. **3** [U] 文明世界 wénmíngshìjiè, 文明国〔國〕家(总称) wénmíng guójiā.

civi·lize /'sɪvəlaɪz/ *vt* **1** 使文明 shǐ wénmíng. **2** 教育 jiàoyù.

claim¹ /kleɪm/ *n* **1** [C](根据权利而提出的)要求 yāoqiú: *a ~ for more pay* 要求增加工资. **2** [C] 有所根据而索取的款项 yǒu suǒ gēnjù ér suǒqǔ de kuǎnxiàng. **3** [U] 要求权 yāoqiúquán. **4** [C] 要求之物 yāoqiúzhī wù. 分给金矿〔礦〕矿工的一份土地 fēngěi jīnkuàng kuànggōng de yífèn tǔdì.

claim² /kleɪm/ *vt/i* **1** 要求承认〔認〕yāoqiú chéngrèn: *~ to be the owner* 要求承认是所有者. **2** 宣称〔稱〕 xuānchēng, 声〔聲〕言 shēngyán: *He ~s to be English* 他宣称是英国人. **3** (事物)值得 zhídé: *matters that ~ attention* 值得注意的事. **~ant** *n* [C] 根据〔據〕权〔權〕利提出法律上的要求的人 gēnjù quánlì tíchū fǎlǜ shàng de yāoqiú de rén.

clair·voy·ance /kleə'vɔɪəns/ *n* [U] 洞察力 dòngchálì. **clair·voy·ant** 有洞察力的人 yǒu dòngchálì de rén.

clam /klæm/ *n* [C] 蛤 gé.

clam·ber /'klæmbə(r)/ *vi* 攀登 pāndēng, 爬 pá. ☐ *n* [C] 艰〔艱〕难〔難〕的攀登 jiānnánde pāndēng.

clammy /'klæmɪ/ *adj* [ier, -iest] 滑腻的 huánìde, 粘糊糊的 niánhūhūde.

clam·our [美语 = **clam·or**] /'klæmə(r)/ *n* [C, U] 喧闹 xuānnào, 吵嚷 chǎorǎng. ☐ *vt/i* ~ *for* 吵吵闹闹地要求 chǎochǎonàonàode yāoqiú.

clamp /klæmp/ *n* [C] 螺丝钳 luósīqián. ☐ *vt/i* **1** 用螺丝钳夹〔夾〕 yòng luósīqián jiā. **2** *~ down (on)* [非正式用语]取缔 qǔdì, 压〔壓〕制 yāzhì: *~ down on drunken drivers* 取缔酒后开车. **'~-down** *n* [C]

clan /klæn/ *n* [C] 氏族 shìzú, 苏〔蘇〕格兰〔蘭〕高地人的氏族 sūgélángāodì rén de shìzú.

clan·des·tine /klæn'destɪn/ *adj* 秘密的 mìmìde, 私下的 sīxiàde: *~ organizations* 秘密组织.

clang /klæŋ/ *vt/i n* [C] 发〔發〕铿〔鏗〕锵〔鏘〕声〔聲〕 fā kēngqiāngshēng; 铿锵声 kēngqiāngshēng.

clap /klæp/ *vt/i* [-pp-] **1** 拍手喝采〔彩〕 pāishǒu hècǎi. **2** 用手轻〔輕〕拍 yòng shǒu qīngpāi: *~ somebody on the back* 拍拍某人的背. **3** 猛推 měngtuī: *~ed in prison* 投入牢狱. *~ eyes on sb* [非正式用语] 看见 kànjiàn, 见到 jiàndào. ☐ *n* **1** 霹雳〔靂〕声〔聲〕 pīlìshēng. **2** 拍手喝采声 pāishǒu hècǎi shēng.

claret /'klærət/ *n* [U] **1** 法国〔國〕波尔〔爾〕多产〔產〕的红酒 fǎguó pō'ěrduō chǎn de hóngjiǔ. **2** 紫红色 zǐhóngsè. ☐ *adj* 紫红色的 zǐhóngsède.

clar·ify /'klærɪfaɪ/ *vt/i* [*pt, pp* -ied] **1** 澄清 chéngqīng. **2** 使液体〔體〕清洁〔潔〕 shǐ yètǐ qīngjié. **clari·fi·ca·tion** /ˌklærɪfɪ'keɪʃn/ *n* [U] 澄清 chéngqīng, 清洁 qīngjié.

clari·net /ˌklærɪ'net/ *n* [C] 单〔單〕簧管 dānhuángguǎn. **~tist** 单簧管演奏者 dānhuángguǎn yǎnzòuzhě.

clar·ity /'klærətɪ/ *n* [U] 清澈 qīngchè, 明晰 míngxī.

clash /klæʃ/ *vt/i* **1** 金属〔屬〕碰撞声〔聲〕 jīnshǔ pèngzhuàng shēng. **2** 互碰 hùpèng, 互撞 hùzhuàng. **3** 时〔時〕间〔間〕冲〔衝〕突 shíjiān chōngtū. **4** 意见抵触〔觸〕yìjiàn dǐchù. ☐ *n* [C] **1** 碰撞声 pèngzhuàngshēng. **2** 抵触 dǐchù, 冲突 chōngtū.

clasp /klɑːsp/ *n* [C] **1** 扣子 kòuzi, 扣紧〔緊〕物(如书夹子等) kòujǐnwù. **2** 紧握 jǐnwò, 拥〔擁〕抱 yōngbào. ☐ *vt/i* **1** 拥抱 yōngbào. **2** 扣住 kòuzhù.

class /klɑːs/ *n* [C] **1** 等级 děngjí; 种〔種〕类〔類〕 zhǒnglèi. **2** [U] 阶级 jiējí. **3** 年级 niánjí. **4** 优〔優〕等(考试成绩) yōuděng. **5** [非正式用语]优秀 yōuxiù, 风〔風〕度:fēngdù. *a top ~ tennis player* 最优网球选手. ☐ *vt* 归〔歸〕入某等级 guīrù mǒu děngjí. **'~room** 教室 jiàoshì.

clas·sic /'klæsɪk/ *adj* **1** 第一流的 dìyīliúde, 最优〔優〕秀的 zuìyōuxiùde. **2** 传〔傳〕统的 chuántǒngde, 有悠久历〔歷〕史的 yǒu yōujiǔ lìshǐ de. ☐ *n* [C] **1** 文豪 wénháo; 艺〔藝〕术〔術〕大师〔師〕 yìshù dàshī; 名著 míngzhù. **2** 古罗〔羅〕马〔馬〕、希腊〔臘〕作家 gǔ luómǎ xīlà zuòjiā. **3** [*pl*] **the ~s** 古希腊, 罗马的语文和文学〔學〕经〔經〕典 gǔ xīlà, luómǎ de yǔwén hé wénxué jīngdiǎn. **4** 大学的古典作家, 作品课程 dàxuéde gǔdiǎn zuòjiā, zuòpǐn kèchéng.

clas·si·cal /'klæsɪkl/ *adj* **1** (文学, 艺术等)第一流的 dìyīliúde, 经〔經〕典的 jīngdiǎnde. **2** 古典的 gǔdiǎnde; 有定评的 yǒu dìngpíngde: *~ music* 古典音乐. **~ly** *adv*

clas·sify /'klæsɪfaɪ/ *vt* [*pt, pp* -ied] 把…分类〔類〕 bǎ … fēnlèi, 把…分等级 bǎ … fēn děngjí. **clas·si·fi·ca·tion** /ˌklæsɪfɪ'keɪʃn/ *n* [C, U] **clas·si·fied** *adj* **(a)** 分成类的 fēnchéng lèi de. **(b)** 机〔機〕密的

jīmìde, 保密的 bǎomìde.

clat·ter /'klætə(r)/ *n* [U] 卡嗒声〔聲〕(物体坠落) kādāshēng. □ *vt/i* 发出卡嗒声 fāchū kādāshēng; 使生卡嗒声 shǐ shēng kādāshēng.

clause /klɔːz/ *n* [C] **1**〔语法〕子句 zǐjù, 从〔從〕句 cóngjù. **2**〔法律〕条〔條〕款 tiáokuǎn.

claus·tro·pho·bia /ˌklɔːstrə'fəʊbɪə/ *n* [U] 幽闭〔閉〕恐怖 yōubì kǒngbù.

claw /klɔː/ *n* [C] **1** 爪 zhǎo, 脚爪 jiǎozhǎo. **2** 蟹等的钳, 螯 xiè děng de qián, áo. **3** 爪形器具 zhǎoxíng qìjù. □ *vt* 用爪抓 yòng zhǎo zhuā, 搔 sāo.

clay /kleɪ/ *n* [U] 粘土 niántǔ; 泥土 nítǔ.

clean[1] /kliːn/ *adj* [-er, -est] **1** 清洁〔潔〕的 qīngjiéde, 干〔乾〕净的 gānjìngde. **2** 没有用过〔過〕的 méiyǒu yòngguò de: *a ~ sheet of paper* 一张没有用过的纸. **3** 纯洁的 chúnjiéde, 清白的 qīngbáide: *a ~ joke* 文雅的玩笑. **4** 匀称〔稱〕的 yúnchende, 规则的 guīzéde: *a ~ cut* 干净利落的切削. □ *adv* 彻底地 chèdǐde, 完全地 wánquánde: *I ~ forgot it.* 我把它完全忘了. ***come ~*** 全盘〔盤〕招供 quánpáng zhāogòng. □ *n* [U] 打扫〔掃〕dǎsǎo, 清洁 qīngjié. ˌ**~-'cut** *adj* 轮〔輪〕廓鲜明的 lúnkuò xiānmíng de, ˌ**~-'shaven** *adj* 脸〔臉〕刮得光光的 liǎn guā dé guāngguāngde.

clean[2] /kliːn/ *vt/i* **1** 干〔乾〕净 gānjìng, 使干净 shǐ gānjìng. **2** *~ sb out* 使…失去钱〔錢〕财 shǐ … shīqù qiáncái. *~ sth out* 打扫〔掃〕干净 dǎsǎo gānjìng, 打扫内部 dǎsǎo nèibù. *~ up* 收拾整洁〔潔〕shōushi zhěngjié, 打扫干净 dǎsǎo gānjìng. *~ sth up* **(a)** 清除不法现象 qīngchú bùfǎ xiànxiàng: *The police must ~ up the city.* 警察必须清除这个城市的不法现象. **(b)**〔非正式用语〕赚钱〔錢〕zhuànqián, 获〔獲〕利 huòlì **~er** *n* [C] 清洁工 qīngjiégōng; 清洁器 qīngjiéqì. *a 'vacuum-~* 真空吸尘器.

clean·ly[1] /'klenlɪ/ *adj* [-ier, -iest] 爱〔愛〕清洁〔潔〕的 ài qīngjié de. **clean·li·ness** *n* [U]

clean·ly[2] /'kliːnlɪ/ *adv* 干〔乾〕干净净地 gāngānjìngjìngde, 利落地 lìluode, 整整齐〔齊〕齐地 zhěngzhěngqíqíde: *cut it ~ into two pieces* 整整齐齐地切成两块.

cleanse /klenz/ *vt* 使纯洁〔潔〕shǐ chúnjié, 净化 jìnghuà.

clear[1] /klɪə(r)/ *adj* [-er, -est] **1** 清澈的 qīngchède, 透明的 tòumíngde: *~ glass* 透明的玻璃. **2** 无〔無〕罪的 wúzuìde, 清白的 qīngbáide: *a ~ conscience* 清白的良心. **3** 响〔響〕亮的 xiǎngliàngde, 清晰可闻〔聞〕的 qīngxī kěwén de. **4** 清楚的 qīngchude. ***make oneself ~*** 讲清楚 jiǎngqīngchu. **5** 无障碍〔礙〕的 wú zhàngài de, 无阻的 wúzǔde. **6** 明确〔確〕的 míngquède: *I am not ~ as to what to do.* 我不明确要做什么. □ *n* [U] ***in the ~*** 无嫌疑 wú xiányí, 无罪 wúzuì. ˌ**~-'headed** 头〔頭〕脑清楚的 tóunǎo qīngchu de.

clear[2] /klɪə(r)/ *adv* **1** 清楚地 qīngchude, 清晰地 qīngxīde: *I can hear you loud and ~.* 我能听清楚你响亮的声音. **2** 十分地 shífēnde, 完全地 wánquánde: *The prisoner got ~ away.* 这囚徒逃得无影无踪. **3** 不接触〔觸〕bù jiēchù: *He jumped ~ of the bar.* 他干净利落地跳过了横杆. ***keep*** (或 ***stand***) ***~*** 避开〔開〕bìkāi. **~ness** *n* [U] 清楚 qīngchu, 明显〔顯〕míngxiǎn; 晴朗 qínglǎng, 清晰 qīngxī.

clear[3] /klɪə(r)/ *vt/i* **1** 清除 qīngchú, 扫〔掃〕清 sǎoqīng. **2** 越过〔過〕而未触〔觸〕及 yuèguò ér wèi chùjí: *~ a wall* 不碰而越过一座墙. **3** 变〔變〕得晴朗 biàn dé qínglǎng: *The sky soon ~ed.* 天空立刻晴朗起来. **4** ***~ away*** 把…除掉 bǎ … chúdiào; 消失 xiāoshī. ***~ off*** (不受欢迎的人)走开〔開〕zǒukāi: *C~ off!* 走开! ***~ out*** **(a)** 出空 chūkōng. **(b)** 离〔離〕开 líkāi, 走开 zǒukāi. ***~ up*** 变晴 biànqíng. ***clear sth up*** **(a)** 收拾 shōushi, 清理 qīnglǐ. **(b)** 消除疑虑〔慮〕等 xiāochú yílǜ děng.

clear·ance /'klɪərəns/ *n* [C] **1** 清除 qīngchú, 清理 qīnglǐ, 出清 chūqīng. **2** [C, U] 净空 jìngkòng: *~ under a bridge* 桥下的净空. **3** [U] 许可(船只离港等) xǔkě.

clear·ing /'klɪərɪŋ/ *n* [C] 林中空地 línzhōng kòngdì.

clear·ly /'klɪəlɪ/ *adv* **1** 清楚地 qīngchude, 明白地 míngbaide. **2** (用于回答)肯定 kěngdìng, 无〔無〕疑 wúyí.

cleave /kliːv/ *vt/i* [*pt* clove /kləʊv/, cleft /kleft/; *pp* cleft or cloven /'kləʊvn/] 劈 pī, 劈开〔開〕pīkāi.

clef /klef/ *n* [C] 音乐〔樂〕谱号〔號〕yīnyuè pǔhào.

cleft /kleft/ ⇨ cleave.

clem·ency /'klemənsɪ/ *n* [U] **1** 仁慈 réncí. **2** 气〔氣〕候温暖 qìhòu wēnnuǎn, 温和 wēnhé. **clem·ent** *adj*

clench /klentʃ/ *vt* 紧〔緊〕握 jǐnwò; 咬紧 yǎojǐn: *a ~ed fist* 攥紧的拳头 zuànjǐnde quántou.

clergy /'klɜ:dʒɪ/ *n pl* 正式委任的牧师〔師〕zhèngshì wěirèn de mùshī, 教士 jiàoshì. '~**man** 牧师 mùshī, 教士 jiàoshì.

cleri·cal /'klerɪkl/ *adj* **1** 牧师的 mùshīde, 教士的 jiàoshìde. **2** 办〔辦〕事员的 bànshìyuánde; 办公室的 bàngōngshìde.

clerk /klɑ:k/ *n* [C] 职〔職〕员 zhíyuán; 办〔辦〕事员 bànshìyuán; 秘书〔書〕mìshū.

clever /'klevə(r)/ *adj* [-er, -est] **1** 聪〔聰〕明的 cōngmingde, 伶俐的 línglìde. **2** 精巧的 jīngqiǎode, 机〔機〕敏的 jīmǐnde. ~**ly** *adv* ~**ness** *n* [U]

cliché /'kli:ʃeɪ/ *n* [C] 陈〔陳〕腐思想 chénfǔ sīxiǎng; 陈词滥〔濫〕调 chéncí làndiào.

click /klɪk/ *vi, n* [C] 卡嗒一声〔聲〕(上锁等的声音) kādā yì shēng.

cli·ent /'klaɪənt/ *n* [C] **1** 律师〔師〕等的当〔當〕事人 lǜshī děng de dāngshìrén, 委托人 wěituōrén. **2** 商店顾〔顧〕客 shāngdiàn gùkè.

cli·en·tele /ˌkli:ən'tel/ *n* 〔集合名词〕顾〔顧〕客 gùkè.

cliff /klɪf/ *n* [C] 悬〔懸〕崖 xuányá, 峭壁(尤指海边的) qiàobì.

cli·mac·tic /ˌklaɪ'mæktɪk/ *adj* 顶点〔點〕的 dǐngdiǎnde, 极〔極〕点的 jídiǎnde.

cli·mate /'klaɪmɪt/ *n* [C] **1** 气〔氣〕候 qìhòu. **2** 社会〔會〕趋〔趨〕势〔勢〕shèhuì qūshì: *the political ~* 政治气候. **cli·matic** /ˌklaɪ'mætɪk/ *adj*

cli·max /'klaɪmæks/ *n* [C] [*pl* ~es] 顶点〔點〕dǐngdiǎn, 小说等的高潮 xiǎoshuō děng de gāocháo. □ *vt/i* 达〔達〕到高潮 dádào gāocháo.

climb /klaɪm/ *vt/i* **1** 攀登 pāndēng, 爬 pá. **2** 飞〔飛〕机〔機〕爬升 fēijī páshēng. **3** (社会地位方面)向上爬 xiàngshàng pá, 钻〔鑽〕营〔營〕zuānyíng. □ *n* [C] 攀登 pāndēng; 爬升 páshēng; 山坡 shānpō. ~**er** **(a)** 爬山的人 pá shānde rén. **(b)** 攀缘植物 pānyuán zhíwù.

clinch /klɪntʃ/ *vt/i* **1** 确〔確〕定 quèdìng, 决定(论据,交易等) juédìng. **2** 拥〔擁〕抱 yōngbào. □ *n* [C] 拥抱 yōngbào.

cling /klɪŋ/ *vi* [*pt, pp* clung /klʌŋ/] 抱紧〔緊〕bàojǐn; 坚守 jiānshǒu.

clinic /'klɪnɪk/ *n* [C] 诊所 zhěnsuǒ, 门〔門〕诊所 ménzhěnsuǒ: *an ˌante-'natal ~* 产前检查诊所. ~**al** *adj* **(a)** 临〔臨〕床的 línchuángde; 临诊的 línzhěnde. **(b)** [喻]冷静的 lěngjìngde, 不偏不倚的 bùpiānbùyǐde: *a ~al statement of the facts* 对有关事实的冷静的陈述.

clink /klɪŋk/ *vt/i n* [C] 丁当作响〔響〕dīngdāng zuòxiǎng; 使作丁当声〔聲〕shǐ zuò dīngdāngshēng, 丁当声 dīngdāngshēng.

clip[1] /klɪp/ *n* [C] 回形针 huíxíngzhēn; 夹〔夾〕子 jiāzi. □ *vt* [-pp-] 夹住 jiāzhù, 钳牢 qiánláo.

clip[2] /klɪp/ *vt* [-pp-] **1** 剪短 jiǎnduǎn; 剪整齐〔齊〕jiǎn zhěngqí. **2** [俚]猛击〔擊〕měngjī, 痛打 tòngdǎ. □ *n* [C] **1** 剪 jiǎn, 剪短 jiǎnduǎn, 修剪 xūjiǎn. **2** 猛打 měngdǎ. ~**pers** *n pl* (亦作 *a pair of ~pers*) 大剪刀 dàjiǎndāo; 轧〔軋〕刀 zhádāo. ~**ping** (特指)剪报〔報〕jiǎnbào.

clique /kli:k/ *n* [C] 派系 pàixì, 小集团〔團〕xiǎojítuán.

cloak /kləʊk/ *n* [C] **1** 斗篷 dǒupeng; 大氅 dàchǎng. **2** [喻]遮盖物 zhēgàiwù: *a ~ of secrecy* 一层笼罩着的神秘气氛. □ *vt* 掩盖 yǎngài, 包藏 bāocáng. '~**room** 衣帽间〔間〕yīmàojiān.

clock /klɒk/ *n* [C] 时〔時〕钟〔鐘〕shízhōng. □ *vt/i* 为〔爲〕运〔運〕动〔動〕员揿秒表〔錶〕wèi yùndòngyuán qìn miǎobiǎo: *He ~ed 10 seconds for the race.* 他跑了10秒. ~ **in (out)** 记上班(下班)时〔時〕间〔間〕jì shàngbān shíjiān. '~**wise** *adv* 顺时针方向地 shùn shízhēn fāngxiàng de.

clod /klɒd/ *n* [C] 土块〔塊〕tǔkuài, 泥块 níkuài.

clog[1] /klɒg/ *n* [C] 木底鞋 mùdǐxié.

clog[2] /klɒg/ *vt/i* [-gg-] 阻塞 zǔsè, 填塞 tiánsè.

clois·ter /'klɔɪstə(r)/ *n* [C] **1** 迴廊 huíláng, 走廊 zǒuláng. **2** 修道院 xiūdàoyuàn; 修道院生活 xiūdàoyuàn shēnghuó. □ *vt* 居于修道院中 jūyú xiūdàoyuàn zhōng. ~**ed** 隐居的 yǐnjūde; 有迴廊的 yǒu huílángde.

close[1] /kləʊs/ *adj* [-r, -st] **1** (时间或空间)接近的 jiējìnde. **2** 严〔嚴〕密的 yánmìde, 严格的 yángéde: *under ~ arrest* 严密拘禁; *on ~r examination* 在进一步严密检查之下. ***keep a ~ watch on*** 严密的监〔監〕视 yánmìde jiānshì. **3** 亲〔親〕密的 qīnmìde: *a ~ friend* 亲密的朋友. **4** 势〔勢〕均力敌〔敵〕的 shìjūnlìdíde: *a ~ race* 不相上下的竞赛. **5** 湿〔濕〕热〔熱〕的 shīrède. □ *adv* 紧〔緊〕密地 jǐnmìde: *stand ~ against* *the wall* 挨着墙站立. ˌ~-'**fitting** *adj* 紧身的 jǐnshēnde, 贴切的 tiēqiède. '~-**up** 特写〔寫〕镜头〔頭〕 tèxiě jìngtóu. ~**ly** *adv* 紧密地 jǐnmìde. ~**ness** *n* [U]

close² /kləʊs/ *n* [C] **1** 大教堂周围的场〔場〕地 dàjiàotáng zhōuwéide chǎngdì. **2** = cul-de-sac.

close³ /kləʊz/ *vt/i* **1** 关〔關〕 guān, 闭〔閉〕 bì, 合起 héqǐ: ~ *the door* 关门. ~ *one's eyes to* 无〔無〕视 wúshì. ⇨ shut. **2** 不开〔開〕放 bù kāifàng: *This road is ~d.* 这条路不开放. **3** 终止 zhōngzhǐ, 停止 tíngzhǐ: ~ *a discussion* 停止讨论. **4** 靠紧〔緊〕 kàojǐn, 靠拢〔攏〕 kàolǒng. **5** ~ *down* **(a)** (工厂, 企业等)关闭 guānbì, 停业〔業〕 tíngyè. **(b)** (电台)停止广〔廣〕播 tíngzhǐ guǎngbō. '~-**down** *n* ~ *in* 渐〔漸〕短 jiànduǎn: *The days are closing in.* 白天正在短起来. ~ *in on* (或 *upon*) **(a)** 笼〔籠〕罩 lǒngzhào: *Darkness ~d in on us.* 黑暗来临. **(b)** 包围〔圍〕 bāowéi, 迫近 pòjìn. ~-**circuit tele'vision** *n* 闭路电〔電〕视〔視〕 bìlù diànshì. ˌ~**d 'shop** 只〔衹〕雇〔僱〕佣工会〔會〕会员的工厂〔廠〕或行业〔業〕 zhǐ gùyōng gōnghuì huìyuán de gōngchǎng huò hángyè.

close⁴ /kləʊz/ *n* [U] **1** (时间)终止 zhōngzhǐ: *at ~ of day* 黄昏. **2** 结束(活动等) jiésù.

closet /'klɒzɪt/ *n* [C] 〔主要是美语〕小储藏室 xiǎo chǔcángshì. ⇨ cupboard.

clo·sure /'kləʊʒə(r)/ *n* [C] 关〔關〕闭〔閉〕 guānbì: *the ~ of a factory* 工厂的关闭.

clot /klɒt/ *n* [C] **1** 血等的凝块〔塊〕 xuě děng de níngkuài; 泥块 níkuài. **2** [俚语]傻子 shǎzi, 蠢人 chǔnrén. □ *vt/i* [-tt-] (血等)凝块 níngkuài.

cloth /klɒθ/ *n* [*pl* ~s /klɒθs/] **1** [U] (棉花, 羊毛等的)布, 织〔織〕物 bù, zhīwù. **2** [C] 布块 bùkuài: *a table ~* 桌布.

clothe /kləʊð/ *vt* 穿衣 chuānyī, 供给…衣穿 gōngjǐ … yī chuān.

clothes /kləʊðz/ *n pl* 衣服 yīfu, 服装〔裝〕 fúzhuāng. '**bed**~ 床单〔單〕, 毯, 被褥等 chuángdān, tǎn, bèi, rù, děng.

cloth·ing /'kləʊðɪŋ/ *n* [U] 〔集合名词〕衣服 yīfu.

cloud /klaʊd/ *n* **1** [C, U] 云〔雲〕 yún. **2** [C] 云状〔狀〕物 yúnzhuàngwù. **3** [C] 引起悲伤〔傷〕, 恐惧〔懼〕之物 yǐn qǐ bēishāng kǒngjù zhī wù: *the ~s of war* 战云. **4** *under a ~* 受嫌疑 shòu xiányí. □ *vt/i* 变〔變〕得不清楚 biàndé bù qīngchu; 使不清楚 shǐ bù qīngchu: *Her eyes ~ed over with tears.* 她两眼蒙上了泪水. **cloudy** *adj* [-ier, -iest] **(a)** 有云的 yǒu yún de, 阴〔陰〕的 yīn de. **(b)** (特指液体)不清 bù qīng.

clove¹ /kləʊv/ *pt* of cleave

clove² /kləʊv/ *n* [C] 丁香 dīngxiāng.

clove³ /kləʊv/ *n* [C] 小鳞茎〔莖〕 xiǎo línjìng: *a ~ of garlic* 一瓣蒜.

clo·ver /'kləʊvə(r)/ *n* [U] 三叶〔葉〕草 sānyècǎo.

clown /klaʊn/ *n* [C] **1** (马戏等)小丑 xiǎochǒu, 丑角 chǒujué. **2** 行动〔動〕象小丑的人 xíngdòng xiàng xiǎochǒu de rén. □ *vt* 做出小丑似的行为〔爲〕 zuòchū xiǎochǒu sì de xíngwéi.

club /klʌb/ *n* [C] **1** 棍棒 gùnbàng. **2** 高尔〔爾〕夫球球棒 gāo'ěrfūqiú qiúbàng. **3** (纸牌)梅花 méihua. **4** 俱乐〔樂〕部 jùlèbù; 会〔會〕 huì; 社 shè. **6** 俱乐部的会所 jùlèbùde huìsuǒ. □ *vt/i* [-bb-] 用棍棒打 yòng gùnbàng dǎ. ~ *together* 联〔聯〕合行动〔動〕 liánhé xíngdòng: *They ~bed together to buy a house.* 他们联合起来买一所房子.

cluck /klʌk/ *vi, n* [C] 咯咯叫 gēgē jiào; 咯咯声〔聲〕 gēgēshēng.

clue /klu:/ *n* [C] 线〔綫〕索 xiànsuǒ. ~**less** *adj* 〔非正式用语〕愚蠢的 yúchǔnde, 迟钝的 chídùnde.

clump¹ /klʌmp/ *n* [C] (树, 灌木)丛〔叢〕 cóng.

clump² /klʌmp/ *vi* 用沉重的脚步行走 yòng chénzhòngde jiǎobù xíngzǒu: ~ *about the room* 用沉重的脚步在房间里来回行走.

clumsy /'klʌmzɪ/ *adj* [-ier, -iest] **1** 笨拙的 bènzhuóde. **2** 愚笨的 yúbènde, 不灵〔靈〕活的 bùlínghuóde: *a ~ remark* 笨拙的话. **clumsily** *adv* **clum·si·ness** *n* [U]

clung /klʌŋ/ *pt, pp* of cling.

clus·ter /'klʌstə(r)/ *n* [C] 一串 yíchuàn; 一簇 yícù; 一组 yìzǔ. □ *vi* 群集 qúnjí, 丛〔叢〕生 cóngshēng.

clutch /klʌtʃ/ *vt/i* 抓住 zhuāzhù, 攫住 juézhù. □ *n* [C] **1** 抓 zhuā, 攫 jué. **2** [*pl*] 控制 kòngzhì: *He's in her ~es.* 他被她控制. **3** 离〔離〕合器 líhéqì.

clut·ter /'klʌtə(r)/ *vt* 弄乱〔亂〕 nòngluàn. □ *n* [U] 零乱 língluàn, 杂〔雜〕乱 záluàn.

cm=centimetre.
C.O.=**1** commanding officer 指挥〔揮〕官 zhǐhuīguān. **2** conscientious objector to military service (因道德等原因)抗拒服兵役者 kàngjù fú bīngyì zhě.
Co.=**1** company. **2** county.
c/o=care of 由…转〔轉〕交 yóu…zhuǎnjiāo.
coach[1] /kəʊtʃ/ *n* [C] **1** 长途公共汽车〔車〕chángtú gōnggònggìchē. **2**〔美语 = *car*〕铁路客车〔車〕tiělù kèchē. **3** 公共马〔馬〕车 gōnggòng mǎchē.
coach[2] /kəʊtʃ/ *n* [C] **1** 教师〔師〕jiàoshī, 私人教师 sīrén jiàoshī. **2** 体〔體〕育教练 tǐyù jiàoliàn. □ *vt/i* 辅导 fǔdǎo, 训练 xùnliàn.
co·agu·late /ˌkəʊˈægjʊleɪt/ *vt/i* 使凝结 shǐ níngjié, 凝结 níngjié. **co·agu'lation** *n* [U]
coal /kəʊl/ *n* [C, U] 煤 méi. **'~face** 采〔採〕煤工作面 cǎiméi gōngzuòmiàn. **~field** 煤田 méitián, 产〔產〕煤区〔區〕chǎnméiqū. **'~-gas** 煤气〔氣〕méiqì. **'~mine** 煤矿〔礦〕méikuàng. **'~miner** 煤矿工人 méikuàng gōngrén.
co·alesce /ˌkəʊəˈles/ *vi* 接合 jiēhé, 结合 jiéhé.
co·ali·tion /ˌkəʊəˈlɪʃn/ *n* **1** [U] 结合 jiéhé, 联〔聯〕合 liánhé. **2** [C] (政党等)联盟 liánméng.
coarse /kɔːs/ *adj* [*-r, -st*] **1** 粗的 cūde, 粗糙的 cūcāode. **2** (语言等)粗俗的 cūsúde, 粗鲁的 cūlǔde. **~ly** *adv* **~ness** *n* [U]
coarsen /ˈkɔːsn/ *vt/i* 使粗 shǐ cū, 变〔變〕粗 biàn cū.
coast[1] /kəʊst/ *n* [C] 海岸 hǎi'àn, 海滨〔濱〕hǎibīn. **'~guard** 海岸警卫〔衛〕队〔隊〕hǎi'àn jǐngwèiduì. **'~line** 海岸线〔線〕hǎi'ànxiàn. **~al** *adj*
coast[2] /kəʊst/ *vt/i* **1** 沿海岸航行 yán hǎi'àn hángxíng. **2** 顺坡滑行 shùn pō huáxíng.
coat /kəʊt/ *n* [C] **1** 外套 wàitào, 上衣 shàngyī. **2** 动物皮毛 dòngwù pímáo, 植物表皮 zhíwù biǎopí. **3** 涂〔塗〕层〔層〕túcéng, 膜 mó. □ *vt* 涂以油漆等 tú yǐ yóuqī děng. **,~ of 'arms** 盾形纹章 dùnxíng wénzhāng. **'~-hanger** 衣架 yījià.
coat·ing /ˈkəʊtɪŋ/ *n* [C] 涂层〔層〕túcéng.
coax /kəʊks/ *vt/i* **1** 劝〔勸〕诱 quànyòu: *I ~ed her into coming with me.* 我说服了她同我一起来. **2** 哄出 hǒngchū, 诱出 yòuchū.
cob /kɒb/ *n* [C] **1** 矮脚马〔馬〕ǎijiǎomǎ. **2** (亦作 *'corn-~*) 玉米棒子 yùmǐ bàngzi: *corn on the ~* 未剥下之玉米. **3** 雄鹄〔鵠〕xiónghú.
cobble[1] /ˈkɒbl/ *n* [C] (亦作 *'~-stone*) (铺路等用的)大鹅〔鵝〕卵石 dà éluǎnshí, 圆石块〔塊〕yuánshíkuài. □ *vt* 用鹅卵石铺路 yòng éluǎnshí pūlù.
cobble[2] /ˈkɒbl/ *vt* 〔过时用法〕修(鞋) xiū, 补 bǔ. **cobbler** *n* [C] 〔过时用法〕= shoe-repairer. 修鞋匠 xiūxiéjiàng.
co·bra /ˈkəʊbrə/ *n* [C] 眼镜蛇 yǎnjìngshé.
cob·web /ˈkɒbweb/ *n* [C] 蜘蛛网 zhīzhuwǎng.
co·caine /kəʊˈkeɪn/ *n* [U] 可卡因 kěkǎyīn.
cock[1] /kɒk/ *n* [C] 雄禽 xióngqín; 公鸡〔鷄〕gōngjī.
cock[2] /kɒk/ *n* [C] **1** 开〔開〕关〔關〕kāiguān; 龙〔龍〕头〔頭〕lóngtóu; 旋塞 xuánsāi. **2** (枪的)击〔擊〕铁〔鐵〕jītiě.
cock[3] /kɒk/ *vt* **1** 使翘起 shǐqiàoqǐ, 竖〔豎〕起 shùqǐ: *The horse ~ed its ears.* 马竖起了耳朵. **2** 扳起枪的击铁 bānqǐ qiāngde jītiě.
cocka·too /ˌkɒkəˈtuː/ *n* [C] 白鹦〔鸚〕báiyīng.
cock·erel /ˈkɒkərəl/ *n* [C] 小公鸡〔鷄〕xiǎo gōngjī.
cock-eyed /ˈkɒkaɪd/ *adj* 〔俚语〕**1** 斜的 xiéde, 歪的 wāide. **2** 荒谬的 huāngmiùde.
cockle /ˈkɒkl/ *n* [C] 鸟〔鳥〕蛤 niǎogě (亦作 *'~-shell*) 鸟蛤壳〔殼〕niǎogěqiào.
cock·ney /ˈkɒknɪ/ *adj, n* [C] 伦敦佬 lúndūnlǎo.
cock·pit /ˈkɒkpɪt/ *n* [C] 小型飞〔飛〕机〔機〕的座舱〔艙〕xiǎoxíng fēijī de zuòcāng.
cock·roach /ˈkɒkrəʊtʃ/ *n* [C] 蟑螂 zhāngláng.
cocks·comb /ˈkɒkskəʊm/ *n* [C] 鸡〔鷄〕冠 jīguān.
cock·tail /ˈkɒkteɪl/ *n* [C] **1** 鸡〔鷄〕尾酒 jīwěijiǔ. **2** 水果, 贝类〔類〕开胃品 shuǐguǒ, bèilèi kāiwèipǐn: *fruit ~* (开胃)什锦水果.
co·coa /ˈkəʊkəʊ/ *n* [U] 可可粉 kōukōufěn; 可可茶 kōukōuchá.
coco·nut /ˈkəʊkənʌt/ *n* [C, U] 椰子果 yēziguǒ.
co·coon /kəˈkuːn/ *n* [C] 茧〔繭〕jiǎn.
C.O.D.=cash to be paid on delivery 货到付款 huò dào fùkuǎn.
cod /kɒd/ *n* [C] [*pl* ~] (亦作 *'~fish*) 鳕 xuě.
coddle /ˈkɒdl/ *vt* **1** 小心照料

xiǎoxīn zhàoliào. 2 嫩煮(鸡蛋等) nènzhǔ.

code /kəʊd/ *n* [C] 1 规则 guīzé, 准则 zhǔnzé: *a ~ of behaviour* 行为准则. 2 代号〔號〕dàihào, 密码 mìmǎ. ***break a ~*** 破译〔譯〕(密码) pòyì. □ *vt* (亦作 **en~** /en'kəʊd/) 把…译成密码. bǎ … yìchéng mìmǎ.

co-ed /ˌkəʊ 'ed/ *n* [C] 〔非正式用语〕男女同校的学〔學〕校 (的学生) nán nǚ tóng xiào de xuéxiào.

co-edu·ca·tion /ˌkəʊ ˌedʒʊ'keɪʃn/ *n* [U] 男女同校 nán nǚ tóng xiào. **~al** *adj*

co·erce /ˌkəʊ'ɜːs/ *vt* 强迫 qiángpò, 胁〔脅〕迫 xiépò, 迫使 pòshǐ. **co·ercion** /keʊ'ɜːʃn/ *n* [U] 强迫 qiángpò, 强制 qiángzhì. **co·ercive** /keʊ'ɜːsɪv/ *adj* 强迫的 qiángpòde, 强制的 qiángzhìde.

co·exist /ˌkəʊɪg'zɪst/ *vi* 共存 gòngcún. **~ence** *n* [U] 和平共处〔處〕hépíng gòngchù.

C. of E.=Church of England 英国〔國〕国教 yīngguó guójiào.

cof·fee /'kɒfɪ/ *n* 1 [U] 咖啡树〔樹〕kāfēishù, 咖啡豆 kāfēidòu; [C, U] 咖啡 kāfēi; 咖啡茶 kāfēichá. 2 咖啡色 kāfēisè.

cof·fer /'kɒfə(r)/ *n* [C] (盛金钱的)保险〔險〕箱 bǎoxiǎnxiāng.

cof·fin /'kɒfɪn/ *n* [C] 棺材 guāncai, 棺木 guānmù.

cog /kɒg/ *n* [C] 齿〔齒〕轮〔輪〕的轮牙 chǐlúnde lúnyá.

cognac /'kɒnjæk/ *n* [U] 法国〔國〕白兰〔蘭〕地酒 fǎguó báilándìjiǔ.

co·habit /ˌkəʊ'hæbɪt/ *vi* 男女姘居 nánnǚ pīnjū. **~a·tion** /ˌkəʊhæbɪ'teɪʃn/ *n* [U]

co·here /ˌkəʊ'hɪə(r)/ *vi* 1 黏着 niánzhe, 黏合 niánhé. 2 (论据等)连〔連〕贯 liánguàn, 前后〔後〕一致 qiánhòu yízhì.

co·her·ent /ˌkəʊ'hɪərənt/ *adj* 1 黏着的 niánzhede, 连结的 liánjiēde. 2 (话语, 论据等) 连〔連〕贯的 liánguànde, 紧〔緊〕凑的 jǐncòude, 清楚的 qīngchude. **~ly** *adv*

co·he·sion /ˌkəʊ'hiːʒn/ *n* [U] 内聚性 nèijùxìng, 内聚力 nèijùlì. **co·he·sive** /-sɪv/ *adj*

coil /kɔɪl/ *vt/i* 盘〔盤〕绕〔繞〕pánrǎo, 缠绕 chánrǎo. □ *n* [C] 1 一卷 yìjuǎn, 一圈 yìquān; 盘绕物 pánrǎowù. 2 线〔線〕圈 xiànquān.

coin /kɔɪn/ *n* [C, U] 铸〔鑄〕币〔幣〕zhùbì, 硬币 yìngbì. □ *vt* 1 铸造(硬币) zhùzào. 2 创〔創〕造 chuàngzào; 杜撰(新字, 词) dùzhuàn. **~age** /'kɔɪnɪdʒ/ *n* (a) [U] 铸造硬币 zhùzào yìngbì. (b) [C] 币制 bìzhì: *a decimal ~* 十进币制. (c) [C] 新造的词语 xīnzàode cíyǔ.

co·incide /ˌkəʊɪn'saɪd/ *vi* 1 恰好相合 qiàhǎo xiānghé. 2 时〔時〕间〔間〕巧合 shíjiān qiǎohé. 3 意见一致 yìjiàn yízhì.

co·inci·dence /ˌkəʊ'ɪnsɪdəns/ *n* [U] 符合 fúhé, 巧合 qiǎohé; [C] 巧合的事例 qiǎohéde shìlì: *Our meeting was a pure ~.* 我们的见面纯然是一种巧合. **co·inci·den·tal** /ˌkəʊˌɪnsɪ'dentl/ *adj* 巧合的 qiǎohéde.

coke /kəʊk/ *n* [U] 焦 jiāo, 焦炭 jiāotàn. □ *vt* 使成焦炭 shǐ chéng jiāotàn.

col·an·der, cul·len·der /'kʌləndə(r)/ *n* [C] 滤〔濾〕器 lǜqì, 滤锅 lǜguō.

cold¹ /kəʊld/ *adj* [-er, -est] 1 冷 lěng, 寒冷 hánlěng. ***have ~ feet*** 害怕 hàipà; 临〔臨〕时〔時〕畏缩 línshí wèisuō. ***throw ~ water on sth*** 对…泼〔潑〕冷水 duì … pō lěngshuǐ. 2 〔喻〕冷淡的 lěngdànde, 不热〔熱〕情的 bú rèqíngde: *a ~ welcome* 冷淡的接待. **~-'blooded** *adj* (a) 冷血的 lěngxuěde. (b) 〔喻〕无〔無〕情的 wúqíngde. **ˌ~-'hearted** *adj* 冷心肠〔腸〕的 lěngxīnchángde, 冷淡的 lěngdànde. ***give sb the ~-shoulder*** 冷淡对〔對〕待某人 lěngdàn duìdài mǒurén. **ˌ~ 'war** 冷战〔戰〕lěngzhàn. **~ness** *n* [U]

cold² /kəʊld/ *n* 1 [U] 寒冷 hánlěng. ***(be left) out in the ~*** 〔喻〕不理睬某人 bù lǐcǎi mǒurén. 2 [C, U] 伤〔傷〕风〔風〕shāngfēng, 感冒 gǎnmào: *catch (a) ~* 患伤风.

col·lab·or·ate /kə'læbəreɪt/ *vi* 1 协〔協〕作 xiézuò, 合作 hézuò. 2 *~ with* (特指同敌人)勾结 gōujié. **col·lab·or'ation** *n* [U] **col·lab·or·ator** 协作者 xiézuòzhě, 勾结者 gōujiézhě, 投敌〔敵〕者 tóudízhě.

col·lage /'kɒlɑːʒ/ *n* [C] 抽象派的拼贴画〔畫〕chōuxiàngpàide pīntiēhuà.

col·lapse /kə'læps/ *vt/i* 1 倒坍 dǎotān: *The building ~d in the earthquake.* 该建筑物在地震中倒坍. 2 (精神, 健康等)垮下来〔來〕kuǎxiàlái. 3 (椅子等)折叠起来 zhédiéqǐlái. □ *n* [C] 倒坍 dǎotān, 崩溃 bēngkuì, 衰弱 shuāiruò. **col·laps·ible, -able** /-əbl/ *adj* 可折叠的 kě zhédié de.

col·lar /'kɒlə(r)/ *n* [C] **1** 领子 lǐngzi. **2** (狗等的)围〔圍〕脖 wéibó, 颈〔頸〕圈 jǐngquān. □ *vt* 扭住…的领口 niǔzhù ... de lǐngkǒu. '~**bone** 锁骨 suǒgǔ.

col·league /'kɒli:g/ *n* [C] 同事 tóngshì, 同僚 tóngliáo.

col·lect /kə'lekt/ *vt/i* **1** 收集 shōují, 采〔採〕集 cǎijí. **2** 搜集 sōují. **3** 聚集 jùjí: *a crowd ~ed* 聚集起一群人. **4** 接 jiē: *~ a child from school* 从学校接回小孩. **5** 集中(思想等) jízhōng: *~ one's thoughts* 集中思想. ~**ed** *adj* 镇静的 zhènjìngde, 安静的 ānjìngde. **col'lec·tion** *n* **(a)** [U,C] 收集 shōují, 采〔採〕集 cǎijí. **(b)** 收集物 shōujíwù, 收藏品 shōucángpǐn. **(c)** [C] 捐款 juānkuǎn, 募捐 mùjuān. ~**ive** *adj* 集体的 jítǐde. ~**ive noun** [语法] 集合名词 jíhé míngcí. ~**or** *n* [C] 收集人 shōujírén, 收藏家 shōucángjiā; 募款人 mùkuǎnrén.

col·lege /'kɒlɪdʒ/ *n* [C] **1** (独立的)学〔學〕院 xuéyuàn; 综合大学中的学院 zōnghé dàxué zhōng de xuéyuàn. **2** 学会〔會〕 xuéhuì, 社团〔團〕 shètuán: *the C~ of Surgeons* 外科医生学会.

col·lide /kə'laɪd/ *vi* **1** 猛冲〔衝〕 měngchōng. **2** 冲突 chōngtū, 抵触〔觸〕 dǐchù: *The two politicians ~d over the new law.* 这两位政治家在新法律问题上发生意见冲突.

col·lier /'kɒlɪə(r)/ *n* [C] **1** 煤矿〔礦〕工人 méikuàng gōngrén. **2** 运〔運〕煤船 yùn méichuán.

col·liery /'kɒlɪərɪ/ *n* [C] [*pl* -ies] 煤矿〔礦〕 méikuàng.

col·li·sion /kə'lɪʒn/ *n* [C, U] **1** 碰 pèng, 撞 zhuàng. **2** 冲突 chōngtū, 抵触〔觸〕 dǐchù.

col·loquial /kə'ləʊkwɪəl/ *adj* 口语的 kǒuyǔde; 会〔會〕话的 huìhuàde. ~**ly** *adv* ~**ism** 口语 kǒuyǔ; 口语词 kǒuyǔcí.

col·lu·sion /kə'lu:ʒn/ *n* [U] 共谋 gòngmóu, 勾结 gōujié: *be in ~ with* 与…勾结.

co·lon[1] /'kəʊlən/ *n* [C] 结肠〔腸〕 jiécháng.

co·lon[2] /'kəʊlən/ *n* [C] 冒号〔號〕 (:) màohào.

co·lonel /'kɜ:nl/ *n* [C] 陆〔陸〕军〔軍〕上校 lùjūn shàngxiào.

co·lo·nial /kə'ləʊnɪəl/ *adj* 殖民地的 zhímíndìde; 关〔關〕于殖民的 guānyú zhímín de. □ *n* [C] 殖民地居民 zhímíndì jūmín. ~**ism** 殖民主义〔義〕 zhímínzhǔyì. ~**ist** 殖民主义者 zhímínzhǔyìzhě.

col·on·ist /'kɒlənɪst/ *n* [C] 殖民地开〔開〕拓者 zhímíndì kāituòzhě.

col·on·ize /'kɒlənaɪz/ *vt* 开拓殖民地 kāituò zhímíndì. **col·on·iz'ation** *n* [U]

col·on·nade /ˌkɒlə'neɪd/ *n* [C] 一列柱子 yíliè zhùzi.

col·ony /'kɒlənɪ/ *n* [C] [*pl* -ies] **1** 殖民地 zhímíndì; 殖民队〔隊〕 zhímínduì. **2** 侨〔僑〕民 qiáomín.

color [美语] = colour.

co·los·sal /kə'lɒsl/ *adj* 庞〔龐〕大的 pángdàde.

co·los·sus /kə'lɒsəs/ *n* [C] [*pl* -si /-saɪ/, ~es] **1** 巨像 jùxiàng. **2** 巨人 jùrén.

col·our[1] [美语 = **color**] /'kʌlə(r)/ *n* **1** [C, U] 颜色 yánsè, 色彩 sècǎi, 彩色 cǎisè: *Red, blue and yellow are ~s.* 红,蓝和黄都是颜色. **2** [U] 红晕〔暈〕 hóngyùn, 血色 xuěsè, 脸〔臉〕色 liǎnsè. *be* (*feel* 或 *look*) *off* ~ [非正式用语] 脸〔臉〕色不好 liǎnsè bù hǎo. **3** [*pl*] 颜料 yánliào. **4** [U] (细节描写的)色彩 sècǎi. **5** [*pl*] (船)旗 qí. *with flying ~s* 成功地 chénggōngde; 出色地 chūsède. **6** 有色人种〔種〕 yǒusè rénzhǒng. '~**-bar** 对〔對〕有色人种的歧视 duì yǒusè rénzhǒng de qíshì, 种族隔离〔離〕 zhǒngzú gélí. '~**-blind** *adj* ~**ful** *adj* 多采的 duōcǎide; 引人的 yǐnrénde.

colo·ur[2] [美语 = **color**] /'kʌlə(r)/ *vt/i* **1** 给…着色 gěi ... zháosè, 染色 rǎnsè. **2** 变〔變〕红 biàn hóng. **3** 歪曲 wāiqū, 渲染 xuànrǎn: *News is often ~ed.* 新闻常常是被歪曲报导的. ~**ed** *adj* **(a)** 有某种〔種〕颜色的 yǒu mǒuzhǒng yánsè de: *'cream-~ed* 奶油色的. **(b)** 有色人种的 yǒusèrénzhǒngde. ~**ing** 面色 miànsè, 脸〔臉〕色 liǎnsè.

colt /kəʊlt/ *n* [C] 小公马〔馬〕 xiǎo gōngmǎ. ⇨ filly. '~**ish** *adj* 小马似的 xiǎo mǎ sì de; 活泼〔潑〕的 huópode.

col·umn /'kɒləm/ *n* [C] **1** 柱 zhù. **2** 柱状〔狀〕物 zhùzhuàngwù. **3** 书〔書〕, 报〔報〕等上的栏〔欄〕 shū, bào děng shàng de lán. **4** 纵列 zòngliè.

coma /'kəʊmə/ *n* [C] 昏迷 hūnmí.

comb /kəʊm/ *n* [C] **1** 梳 shū. **2** 精梳机〔機〕 jīngshūjī. **3** = honeycomb. □ *vt/i* **1** 梳 shū. **2** 彻底搜查 chèdǐ sōuchá. **3** *~ out* [喻] 除掉不需要的物或人 chúdiào bù xūyào de wù huò rén.

com·bat /'kɒmbæt/ *n* [C], *vt/i* 战〔戰〕斗〔鬥〕 zhàndòu, 搏斗 bódòu.

com·bat·ant /'kɒmbətənt/ *adj* 战〔戰〕斗〔鬥〕的 zhàndòude. □ *n* [C] 战斗者 zhàndòuzhě.

com·bi·na·tion /ˌkɒmbɪ'neɪʃn/ *n* **1** [U] 联〔聯〕合 liánhé, 结合 jiéhé, 合并 hébìng: *work in ~ with* 同…一起工作. **2** [C] 团〔團〕体〔體〕tuántǐ; 组合物 zǔhéwù. **3** 保险〔險〕柜〔櫃〕的暗码〔碼〕bǎoxiǎnguìde ànmǎ.

com·bine¹ /kəm'baɪn/ *vt/i* 联〔聯〕合 liánhé, 连〔連〕结 liánjié.

com·bine² /'kɒmbaɪn/ *n* [C] 集团〔團〕jítuán; 联〔聯〕合企业〔業〕liánhé qǐyè. **'~-harvester** 联合收割机〔機〕liánhéshōugējī, 康拜因 kāngbàiyīn.

com·bust·ible /kəm'bʌstəbl/ *adj, n* [C] 易燃的 yìránde, 可燃的 kěránde; 易燃物 yìránwù, 可燃物 kěránwù.

com·bus·tion /kəm'bʌstʃən/ *n* [U] 燃烧〔燒〕ránshāo.

come /kʌm/ *vi* [*pt* came /keɪm/; pp~] **1** 来〔來〕lái, 来到 láidào. **2** 达〔達〕到 dádào, 共计 gòngjì: *Your bill ~s to £20.* 你共计应付 20 英镑. **~ *to an agreement*** 同意 tóngyì. **~ *to light*** 暴露 bàolù, 显〔顯〕露 xiǎnlù. **3 ~ *to sb*** 被想到 bèi xiǎngdào: *The idea came to him in his bath.* 他在浴缸里想出了这个主意. **4** 开〔開〕始 kāishǐ: *~ to realize something* 开始认识某事. **5** 出现 chūxiàn; 位于 wèiyú: *May ~s between April and June.* 五月在四月和六月之间. **6** 成为〔爲〕chéngwéi, 变〔變〕得 biàndé: *The handle has ~ loose.* 把手松了. **~ *true*** 实〔實〕现 shíxiàn. **7** 未来 wèilái: *in years to ~* 在今后的岁月里. **8 ~ *about*** 发〔發〕生 fāshēng. **~ *across (sb, sth)*** 偶然碰见 ǒurán pèngjiàn **~ *along*** **(a)** (用于祈使句)快点〔點〕kuàidian, 赶快 gǎnkuài. **(b)** 进展 jìnzhǎn; 进步 jìnbù: *The garden is coming along nicely.* 这花园越来越象样了. **(c)** 来到 láidào, 出现 chūxiàn. **~ *apart*** 破碎 pòsuì, 瓦解 wǎjiě. **~ *back*** 回来 huílái. **~ *back (to one)*** 回忆 huíyì. **'~back** *n* 复〔復〕原 fùyuán, 复辟 fùbì. **~ *before sb*** 由…处〔處〕理 yóu … chǔlǐ. ~ *before a judge* 由法官审判. **~ *between*** 妨碍 fáng'ài. **~ *by sth*** 得到 dédào, 获〔獲〕得 huòdé. **~ *down*** **(a)** 倒塌 dǎotā, 倒下 dǎoxià. **(b)** 下降 xiàjiàng, 降落 jiàngluò. **~ *down in the world*** 没落 mòluò, 潦倒 liáodǎo. **'~-down** *n* **~*down in favour of sb(sth)*** 决定支持某人(某物) juédìng zhīchí mǒurén. **~ *down to*** **(a)** 下垂 xiàchuí, 垂及 chuíjí. **(b)** 可归〔歸〕结为〔爲〕kěguījiéwéi: *Your choices ~ down to these.* 你们的选择可归结为这几点. **(c)** (传统等)流传〔傳〕liúchuán. **~ *in*** **(a)** (潮水)升涨〔漲〕shēngzhǎng. **(b)** 流行起来〔來〕liúxíng qǐlái. **(c)** (钱)被收入 bèi shōurù, 到手 dào shǒu. **~ *into*** 继〔繼〕承 jìchéng. **~ *of*** 是…的结果 shì … de jiēguǒ: *Nothing will ~ of it.* 这不会有什么结果的. **~ *of age*** ⇨ age¹ (1). **~ *off (sth)*** 分离〔離〕fēnlí, 脱落 tuōluò: *A button has ~ off my coat.* 我的外衣掉了一颗纽扣. **~ *off*** **(a)** 发〔發〕生 fāshēng, 举〔舉〕行 jǔxíng. *Did your holiday ever ~ off?* 你度假了吗? **(b)** (计划等)实〔實〕现 shíxiàn, 成功 chénggōng: *The experiment did not ~ off.* 试验没有成功. **~ *on*** **(a)** 跟随 gēnsuí. **(b)** (挑战语)来吧! láibā! **(c)** 发展 fāzhǎn, 进步 jìnbù, 改进 gǎijìn: *Your singing is coming on.* 你唱歌有进步. **(d)** (雨、夜、病等)开〔開〕始 kāishǐ. **~ *out*** **(a)** 出现 chūxiàn, 显〔顯〕现 xiǎnxiàn. **(b)** 传〔傳〕出 chuánchū; 出版 chūbǎn. *When will your book ~ out?* 你的书什么时候出版? **(c)** (工人)罢〔罷〕工 bàgōng. **(d)** 表露 biǎolù. **(e)** (污点)被去掉 bèi qùdiào. **~ *out in*** 被部分地覆盖 bèi bùfende fùgài. **~ *over sb*** (感觉等)支配 zhīpèi, 攫住 juézhù: *What has ~ over you?* 你为什么变成这样? **~ *round*** **(a)** 绕〔繞〕道而来〔來〕ràodào ér lái. **(b)** 过〔過〕访 guòfǎng. **(c)** 重又来到 chóng yòu láidào: *My birthday will soon ~ round.* 我的生日很快就又来到. **(d)** 改变〔變〕主意 gǎibiàn zhǔyi, 回心转〔轉〕意 huíxīn zhuǎnyì. **(e)** 苏〔蘇〕醒 sūxǐng. **~ *through*** **(a)** 经〔經〕历〔歷〕…而活着 jīnglì … ér huózhe. **(b)** 来到(通过电话, 无线电等) láidào. **~ '*to*** = come round(e). **~ *under sth*** **(a)** 编入…(某一项目等) biānrù …. **(b)** 受到(影响等) shòudào: *~ under her influence* 受到她的影响. **~ *up*** **(a)** (种子)出土 chūtǔ. **(b)** 被提出 bèi tíchū: *The question hasn't ~ up yet.* 问题还未被提出. **~ *up against*** 碰到(困难, 反对) pèngdào. **~ *up (to)*** 达〔達〕到 dádào: *The water came up to my waist.* 水齐我的腰. **~ *up with*** 产〔產〕生 chǎnshēng; 找到 zhǎodào: *~ up with a solution* 找到解决的办法. **~ *upon*** 突然袭〔襲〕击

〔擊〕 tūrán xíjī; 突然来到 tūrán láidào.

com·edian /kə'mi:dɪən/ *n* [C] **1** 喜剧〔劇〕演员 xǐjù yǎnyuán. **2** 丑角式人物 chǒujuéshì rénwù.

com·edienne /kə,mi:dɪ'en/ *n* [C] 女喜剧〔劇〕演员 nǚ xǐjù yǎnyuán.

com·edy /'kɒmədɪ/ *n* [*pl* -ies] **1** [U] 喜剧〔劇〕 xǐjù. **2** [C] 一出〔齣〕喜剧 yìchū xǐjù. **3** [C, U] 喜剧性事件 xǐjùxìng shìjiàn, 有趣的事 yǒu qù de shì.

comet /'kɒmɪt/ *n* [C] 彗星 huìxīng.

com·fort /'kʌmfət/ *n* **1** [U] 舒适〔適〕 shūshì, 安逸 ānyì. **2** [U] 安慰 ānwèi: *words of* ~ 安慰的话. **3** [C] 给予安慰的人或物 gěi yǔ ānwèide rén huò wù. □ *vt* 安慰 ānwèi. **~able** /'kʌmftəbl/ *adj* **(a)** 舒适的 shūshìde: *a* ~ *chair*(*bed*) 舒适的椅子(床). **(b)** 享有舒适的 xiǎngyǒu shūshì de: *a* ~ *life* 舒适的生活. **(c)** 感到舒适的 gǎndào shūshì de. **~ably** *adv* 舒适地 shūshìde.

comic /'kɒmɪk/ *adj* **1** 滑稽的 huájī de, 使人发〔發〕笑的 shǐ rén fāxiào de. **2** 喜剧〔劇〕的 xǐjùde. □ *n* [C] **1** 连环〔環〕漫画〔畫〕杂〔雜〕志〔誌〕 liánhuán mànhuà zázhì. **2** 喜剧演员 xǐjù yǎnyuán. ~ **strip** 连环漫画 liánhuán mànhuà. **~-al** *adj*

com·ing /'kʌmɪŋ/ *n* [C] 来〔來〕到 láidào, 到来 dàolái: *the* ~ *of winter* 冬天的到来. □ *adj* 未来的 wèiláide: *the* ~ *months* 未来的几个月.

comma /'kɒmə/ *n* [C] 逗点〔點〕 dòudiǎn. ⇨ inverted commas.

com·mand¹ /kə'mɑ:nd/ *n* **1** [C] 命令 mìnglìng. **2** [U] 指挥〔揮〕 zhǐhuī, 统帅 tǒngshuài: *Who's in* ~ *here?* 这里由谁指挥? **3** [C] 部队〔隊〕 bùduì; 军〔軍〕区〔區〕 jūnqū: *Bomber C*~ 英国皇家空军战略轰炸机部队. **4** [U] 掌握 zhǎngwò, 运〔運〕用能力 yùnyòng nénglì: ~ *of the English language* 对英语的掌握和运用能力.

com·mand² /kə'mɑ:nd/ *vt*/*i* **1** 命令 mìnglìng. **2** 指挥〔揮〕 zhǐhuī, 统帅 tǒngshuài: ~ *an army* 指挥一个集团军. **3** 支配 zhīpèi, 使用 shǐyòng: *He* ~*s great sums of money*. 他可以支配大笔款子. **4** 应〔應〕得 yīngdé, 博得 bódé: ~ *respect* 不得不受人尊敬. **5** 俯视 fǔshì. **~ing** *adj*

com·man·dant /,kɒmən'dænt/ *n* [C] 司令 sīlìng, 指挥〔揮〕官 zhǐhuīguān.

com·man·deer /,kɒmən'dɪə(r)/ *vt* 征〔徵〕用 zhēngyòng.

com·man·der /kə'mɑ:ndə(r)/ *n* [C] 指挥〔揮〕官 zhǐhuīguān, 司令 sīlìng.

com·mand·ment / kə'mɑ:ndmənt/ *n* [C] 戒律 jièlǜ.

com·mando /kə'mɑ:ndəʊ/ *n* [C] [*pl* ~s or ~es] 突击〔擊〕队 tūjīduì, 突击队员 tūjīduì yuán.

com·mem·or·ate /kə'meməreɪt/ *vt* 纪念 jìniàn. **com·mem·or·ation** /-'reɪʃn/ *n* **(a)** [U]纪念 jìniàn. **(b)** [C] 纪念会 jìniànhuì. 纪念仪〔儀〕式 jìniànyíshì. **com·mem·or·ative** /kə'memərətɪv/ *adj*

com·mence /kə'mens/ *vt*/*i* [正式用语]开〔開〕始 kāishǐ. **~ment** 开始 kāishǐ, 开端 kāiduān.

com·mend /kə'mend/ *vt* [正式用语] **1** 称〔稱〕赞 chēngzàn, 表扬〔揚〕 biǎoyáng: ~ *his brave actions* 称赞他的勇敢行为. **2** ~ *sth to* 委托保管 wěituō bǎoguǎn. **~able** /-əbl/ *adj* 值得称赞的 zhídé chēngzàn de, 值得表扬的 zhídé biǎoyáng de.

com·men·sur·ate /kə'menʃʊrət/ *adj* 同量的 tóngliàngde 同大的 tóngdàde; 相称〔稱〕的 xiāngchènde, 相当〔當〕的 xiāngdāngde: *pay* ~ *with the work done*. 按劳付酬.

com·ment /'kɒment/ *n* [C, U] 评论〔論〕 pínglùn, 批评 pīpíng. □ *vi* 评论 pínglùn.

com·men·tary /'kɒməntrɪ/ *n* [C] [*pl* -ies] **1** 集注 jízhù; 集释 jíshì. **2** 评论 pínglùn: *a* ~ *on a football match* 对一场足球赛的评论.

com·men·tate /'kɒmənteɪt/ *vi* [与 on 连用] 评论〔論〕 pínglùn. **com·men·ta·tor** 评论员 pínglùnyuán.

com·merce /'kɒmɜ:s/ *n* [U] **1** 贸易 màoyì, 国〔國〕际〔際〕贸易 guójì màoyì. **2** 易货贸易 yìhuò màoyì.

com·mer·cial /kə'mɜ:ʃl/ *adj* 贸易的 màoyìde, 商业〔業〕的 shāngyède. □ *n* [C] 电〔電〕视或无〔無〕线电广〔廣〕告 diànshì huò wúxiàndiàn guǎnggào. ~ **'radio** 依靠广告收入的无线电台〔臺〕 yīkào guǎnggào shōurù de wúxiàndiàntái. ~ **'television** 依靠广告的电视台 yīkào guǎnggào de diànshìtái. ~ **'traveller** 旅行推销员 lǚxíng tuīxiāoyuán. ~ **vehicle** 货车〔車〕 huòchē, 商用汽车 shāngyòng qìchē. **~ly** *adv*

com·miser·ate /kə'mɪzəreɪt/ *vt*/*i* 表示同情 biǎoshì tóngqíng, 表示怜〔憐〕悯〔憫〕 biǎoshì liánmǐn: ~

with him after he had lost the fight 对他拳击失败表示同情. **com·mise'ration** *n* [C, U]

com·mis·sion /kə'mɪʃn/ *n* **1** [C, U] 委任 wěirèn; 委托 wěituō. **2** [U] 佣金 yōngjīn; 回扣 huíkòu. **3** [C] 军〔軍〕事任职〔職〕令 jūnshì rènzhílìng. **4** [C] 考察团〔團〕kǎochátuán, 调查团 diàochátuán; 委员会 wěiyuánhuì. □ *vt* 委任 wěirèn; 委托 wěituō; 任命 rènmìng.

com·mis·sion·aire /kə,mɪʃə'neə(r)/ *n* [C] (剧院, 旅馆等)穿制服的守门〔門〕人 chuān zhìfú de shǒuménrén.

com·mis·sioner /kə'mɪʃənə(r)/ *n* [C] **1** 专〔專〕员 zhuānyuán, 委员 wěiyuán. **2** 政府高级代表 zhèngfǔ gāojí dàibiǎo; 高级专员 gāojí zhuānyuán: *the British High C~ in Accra* 英国驻阿克拉高级专员.

com·mit /kə'mɪt/ *vt* [-tt-] **1** 犯(罪行等) fàn, 干〔幹〕(坏事) gàn. **2** 把…交托给 bǎ…jiāotuōgěi: *~ a patient to a mental hospital* 把病人交给精神病院. **3 ~ *oneself* (*to*)** 承诺 chéngnuò; 答应〔應〕负责 dāyìng fùzé: *He has ~ted himself to supporting his brother's children.* 他答应抚养他兄弟的孩子. **~ment** *n* [C] 所承诺之事 suǒ chéngnuò zhī shì.

com·mit·tee /kə'mɪtɪ/ *n* [C] 委员会 wěiyuánhuì.

com·mod·ity /kə'mɒdətɪ/ *n* [C] [*pl* -ies] 日用品 rìyòngpǐn; 商品 shāngpǐn.

com·mon[1] /'kɒmən/ *adj* [-er, -est] **1** 公共的 gōnggòngde, 共有的 gòngyǒude. **2** 普通的 pǔtōngde, 一般的 yìbānde. **3** 粗俗的(人) cūsúde, 低劣的 dīliède. ,~ **'ground** [喻] 共同立论〔論〕基础 gòngtóng lìlùn jīchǔ. '~ **'knowledge** 常识〔識〕chángshí. ,~ **'law**(英国)不成文法 bùchéngwénfǎ;习〔習〕惯法 xíguànfǎ. '~**place** *adj* 普通的 pǔtōngde, 平凡的 píngfánde. '~**-room** 公共休息室 gōnggòng xiūxishì. ,~**'sense** (由经验而来的) 常识 chángshí. **~ly** *adv* **(a)** 通常地 tōngchángde. **(b)** 粗鄙地 cūbǐde.

com·mon[2] /'kɒmən/ *n* **1** [C] 公用草地 gōngyòng cǎodì. **2 *in* ~** 共用 gòngyòng, 公有 gōngyǒu. ***have in* ~ (*with*)** 与〔與〕…共有 yǔ…gòngyǒu.

com·moner /'kɒmənə(r)/ *n* [C] 平民 píngmín.

Com·mons /'kɒmənz/ *n pl* **the ~** (通常作 *the House of* '~) (英国)下议〔議〕院 xiàyìyuàn.

com·mon·wealth /'kɒmənwelθ/ *n* [C] **1** 全体〔體〕国〔國〕民 quántǐ guómín. **2** 联邦 liánbāng. **3 the C~** 英联邦 yīngliánbāng.

com·mo·tion /kə'məʊʃn/ *n* [C,U] 混乱〔亂〕hùnluàn, 动〔動〕乱 dòngluàn, 骚〔騷〕乱 sāoluàn.

com·mu·nal /'kɒmjʊnl/ *adj* **1** 公社的 gōngshède. **2** 公共的 gōnggòngde.

com·mune[1] /'kɒmju:n/ *n* [C] **1** (法国等) 最小行政区〔區〕zuìxiǎo xíngzhèngqū. **2** 公社 gōngshè.

com·mune[2] /kə'mju:n/ *vi* 亲〔親〕密地交谈 qīnmìde jiāotán.

com·muni·cate /kə'mju:nɪkeɪt/ *vt/i* **1** 传〔傳〕达〔達〕chuándá; 传送(消息等) chuánsòng; 传染(疾病) chuánrǎn. **2** 互通(消息等) hùtōng: *~ by telephone* 同某人通电话. **3** (房间等)互通 hùtōng.

com·muni'cation *n* **(a)** [U] 通讯 tōngxùn, 通信 tōngxìn; 交往 jiāowǎng, 交流 jiāoliú. **(b)** [C] 传〔傳〕达〔達〕的消息 chuándáde xiāoxi; 信 xìn. **(c)** [C,U] 通讯系统 tōngxùn xìtǒng; 交通 jiāotōng; 交通设备〔備〕jiāotōng shèbèi. **~ sattellite** *n* 通讯卫〔衛〕星 tōngxùn wèixīng. **com·muni·cat·ive** /kə'mju:nɪkətɪv/ *adj* 爱〔愛〕说话的 ài shuōhuà de.

com·mu·nion /kə'mju:nɪən/ *n* [U] (思想, 感情等)交流 jiāoliú. **Holy ~** (基督教)圣〔聖〕餐 shèngcān.

com·muniqué /kə'mju:nɪkeɪ/ *n* [C] 公报〔報〕gōngbào.

com·mu·nism /'kɒmjʊnɪzəm/ *n* [U] 共产〔產〕主义〔義〕gòngchǎnzhǔyì. **com·mu·nist** *n* [C] 共产主义者 gòngchǎnzhǔyìzhě. □ *adj* 共产主义的 gòngchǎnzhǔyìde.

com·mun·ity /kə'mju:nətɪ/ *n* [C] [*pl* -ies] **1** [C] **the ~** 社会 shèhuì; 社区〔區〕shèqū. **2**[C] 团〔團〕体〔體〕tuántǐ, 社团 shètuán. **3** [U] 共有 gòngyǒu; 共同性 gòngtóngxìng; 一致 yízhì: *~ of interests* 利益一致.

com·mute /kə'mju:t/ *vt/i* **1** 交换 jiāohuàn, 兑换 duìhuàn. **2** 减轻〔輕〕(刑罚等) jiǎnqīng. **3** 经〔經〕常往来〔來〕jīngcháng wǎnglái. **com·muter** 长〔長〕期车〔車〕票使用者 chángqī chēpiào shǐyòngzhě.

com·pact[1] /kəm'pækt/ *adj* 紧〔緊〕密的 jǐnmìde; 紧凑的 jǐncòude. **~ly** *adv* **~ness** *n* [U]

com·pact[2] /'kɒmpækt/ *n* [C] 连〔連〕镜小粉盒 liánjìng xiǎo fěnhé.

com·pan·ion /kəm'pænɪən/ *n* [C]

同伴 tóngbàn. ~**ship** 伴侣关〔關〕系 bànlǚ guānxì.

com·pany /'kʌmpənɪ/ *n* [*pl* -ies] **1** [U] 伴随 bànsuí, 陪伴 péibàn: *Old people are bored without* ~ 老年人无伴会感到厌烦. **2** [U] 人群 rénqún; 客人 kèren. **3** [U] 同伴 tóngbàn, 伙〔夥〕伴 huǒbàn: *That boy keeps very bad* ~. 那个男孩子同坏人交往. **4** [C] 公司 gōngsī. **5** [C] 一群一起工作的人 yìqún yìqǐ gōngzuò de rén: *a theatrical* ~ 剧团. **6** [C] (步兵)连〔連〕lián.

com·par·able /'kɒmprəbl/ *adj* 可比较〔較〕的 kě bǐjiào de.

com·para·tive /kəm'pærətɪv/ *adj* **1** 比较〔較〕的 bǐjiàode, 比较上的 bǐjiào shàng de. **2** 比较而言的 bǐjiào ér yán de: *living in* ~ *comfort* 比较舒适的生活. **3** [语法]比较级的 bǐjiàojíde. □ *n* [C] 比较级 (*better* 是 *good* 的比较级) bǐjiàojí. ~**ly** *adv*

com·pare /kəm'peə(r)/ *vt/i* **1** 比较〔較〕bǐjiào, 对〔對〕照 duìzhào. **2** 喻为〔爲〕yùwéi, 比拟〔擬〕bǐnǐ. **3** ~ *with* 可比 kěbǐ.

com·pari·son /kəm'pærɪsn/ *n* **1** [U] *by* ~ *(with), in* ~ *(with)* 比较〔較〕起来〔來〕bǐjiào qǐlái. **2** [C] 比较 bǐjiào, 对〔對〕照 duìzhào. **3** [U] 同等价〔價〕值 tóngděng jiàzhí: *There is no* ~ *between them.* 两者不可同日而语.

com·part·ment /kəm'pɑ:tmənt/ *n* [C] 分隔间〔間〕fēngéjiān; 火车〔車〕车厢的分隔间 huǒchē chēxiāng de fēngéjiān.

com·pass /'kʌmpəs/ *n* [C] [*pl* ~es] **1** 指南针 zhǐnánzhēn: **2** [*pl*] (亦作 *a pair of* ~*es*) 圆规 yuánguī. **3** 界限 jièxiàn, 范〔範〕围〔圍〕fànwéi: *outside the* ~ *of her voice* 超出她的音域.

com·pas·sion /kəm'pæʃn/ *n* [U] 怜〔憐〕悯〔憫〕liánmǐn, 同情 tóngqíng. ~**ate** /-ʃənət/ *adj* 表示怜悯 biǎoshì liánmǐn, 表示同情 biǎoshì tóngqíng.

com·pat·ible /kəm'pætəbl/ *adj* 可和谐共存的(思想,人,原则等) kě héxié gòngcún de, 相容 xiāng róng. **com·pat·ibly** *adv*

com·pa·triot /kəm'pætrɪət/ *n* [C] 同胞 tóngbāo.

com·pel /kɒm'pel/ *vt* [-ll-] 强迫 qiǎngpò, 迫使 pòshǐ.

com·pen·sate /'kɒmpenseɪt/ *vt/i* 赔偿 péicháng, 补〔補〕偿 bǔcháng. **com·pen'sa·tion** *n* [C, U] 赔偿 péicháng; 赔偿物 péichángwù; 赔偿费 péichángfèi.

com·père /'kɒmpeə(r)/ *n* [C] 表演节〔節〕目主持人 biǎoyǎn jiémù zhǔchírén. □ *vt* 主持(演出) zhǔchí.

com·pete /kəm'pi:t/ *vi* 比赛 bǐsài: *to* ~ *against* (或 *with*) *others* 与别人比赛.

com·pet·ence /'kɒmpɪtəns/ *n* **1** [U] 能力 nénglì, 胜〔勝〕任 shèngrèn. **2** 权〔權〕能 quánnéng, 权限 quánxiàn. **com·pet·ent** *adj* 能胜任的 néng shèngrèn de; 有权能的 yǒu quánnéng de. **com·pet·ent·ly** *adv*

com·pe·ti·tion /ˌkɒmpə'tɪʃn/ *n* **1** [U] 比赛 bǐsài, 竞〔競〕争 jìngzhēng. **2** [C] 比赛会〔會〕bǐsài huì. **com·peti·tive** /kɒm'petətɪv/ *adj*

com·peti·tor /kəm'petɪtə(r)/ *n* [C] 竞〔競〕争者 jìngzhēngzhě, 比赛者 bǐsàizhě, 敌〔敵〕手 díshǒu.

com·pi·la·tion /ˌkɒmpɪ'leɪʃn/ *n* [U] 编辑〔輯〕biānjì, 汇〔匯〕编 huìbiān. [C] 编辑物 biānjìwù.

com·pile /kəm'paɪl/ *vt* 编辑〔輯〕biānjì, 编写〔寫〕biānxiě. **com·piler** 编辑者 biānjìzhě, 编写者 biānxiězhě.

com·pla·cence /kəm'pleɪsns/ *n* [U] 自满 zìmǎn. **com·pla·cency** *n* [U] **com·placent** *adj*

com·plain /kəm'pleɪn/ *vi* 不满意 bùmǎnyì, 埋怨 mányuàn, 抱怨 bàoyuàn, 诉苦 sùkǔ: ~ *about the food* 对食物表示不满.

com·plaint /kəm'pleɪnt/ *n* **1** [C] 抱怨 bàoyuàn, 叫屈 jiàoqū. **2** 疾病 jíbìng.

com·ple·ment /'kɒmplɪmənt/ *n* [C] **1** 补〔補〕足物 bǔzúwù; 补充物 bǔchōngwù: *Wine is the perfect* ~ *to a meal.* 吃饭有酒,再好不过. **2** (船上的)定员 dìngyuán: *a ship's* ~ *of men* 船上的编制员额. **3** [语法]补〔補〕足语. bǔzúyǔ. □ *vt* 补足 bǔzú, 补充 bǔchōng. ~**ary** /'mentrɪ/ *adj*

com·plete[1] /kəm'pli:t/ *adj* **1** 完全的 wánquánde, 全部的 quánbùde. **2** 完成的 wánchéngde, 结束了的 jiésùlede. **3** 彻底的 chèdǐde, 完完全全的 wánwánquánquán de: *a* ~ *surprise* 十足的意外 ~**ly** *adv* 完全地 wánquánde, 彻底地 chèdǐde. ~**ness** *n* [U]

com·plete[2] /kəm'pli:t/ *vt* 完成 wánchéng, 结束 jiésù: ~ *a course in English* 读完英语课程; ~ *a painting* 完成一幅绘画. **com·ple·tion** *n* [U]

com·plex[1] /'kɒmpleks/ *adj* 复〔復〕

杂〔雜〕的 fùzáde. ~**ity** /kəm'pleksɪtɪ/ *n* [C,U]

com·plex² /'kɒmpleks/ *n* [C] **1** 复〔復〕合体〔體〕fùhétǐ: *a building* ~ 综合大楼. **2** 变〔變〕态〔態〕心理 biàntài xīnlǐ.

com·plexion /kəm'plekʃn/ *n* [C] **1** 肤〔膚〕色 fūsè: *a dark (fair)* ~ 黑色（淡色）肤色. **2** 情况 qíngkuàng, 局面 júmiàn.

com·pli·ance /kəm'plaɪəns/ *n* [U] 顺从〔從〕shùncóng, 依从 yīcóng: *in* ~ *with the rules* 按照规则. **com·pli·ant** *adj* 依从的 yīcóngde, 屈从的 qūcōngde.

com·pli·cate /'kɒmplɪkeɪt/ *vt* 使复〔復〕杂〔雜〕shǐ fùzá; 使麻烦 shǐ máfan. **com·pli·cated** *adj* 结构〔構〕复杂的 jiégòu fùzá de; 困难〔難〕的 kùnnande. ˌ**com·pli'ca·tion** *n* [C]

com·plic·ity /kəm'plɪsətɪ/ *n* [U] 同谋关〔關〕系 tóngmóu guānxì, 共犯关系 gòngfàn guānxì: *prove his* ~ *in the crime* 证明他是共犯.

com·pli·ment /'kɒmplɪmənt/ *n* [C] **1** 敬意 jìngyì; 赞扬〔揚〕zànyáng. **2** [*pl*] 问〔問〕候 wènhòu, 致意 zhìyì. □ *vt* /'kɒmplɪment/ 恭维 gōngwei, 称〔稱〕赞 chēngzàn. ~**ary** /-'mentrɪ/ *adj* **(a)** 恭维的 gōngweide, 表示钦羡的 biǎoshìqīnxiàn de. **(b)** 赠送的 zèngsòngde: ~*ary tickets* 招待券.

com·ply /kəm'plaɪ/ *vt* [*pt, pp* -ied] 照做 zhàozuò, 遵守 zūnshǒu.

com·po·nent /kəm'pəʊnənt/ *adj* 组成的 zǔchéngde, 合成的 héchéngde. □ *n* [C] 组成部分 zǔchéng bùfēn, 成分 chéngfen: *car* ~*s* 汽车部件.

com·pose /kəm'pəʊz/ *vt/i* **1** 组成 zǔchéng, 构〔構〕成 gòuchéng. **2** 创〔創〕作(音乐等) chuàngzuò: ~ *a poem* 写诗; ~ *a symphony* 谱写交响乐. **3** (印刷)拼版 pīnbǎn, 排字 páizì. **4** 使安定 shǐ āndìng, 使平静 shǐ píngjìng, 把思想理出头〔頭〕绪 bǎ sīxiǎng lǐchū tóuxù: ~ *one's thoughts* 理清思路. **composed** *adj* 镇静的 zhènjìngde. **com·poser** *n* [C] 作曲家 zuòqǔjiā.

com·pos·ite /'kɒmpəzɪt/ *adj* 合成的 héchéngde, 复〔復〕合的 fùhé de, 混成的 hǔnchéngde.

com·po·si·tion /ˌkɒmpə'zɪʃn/ *n* **1** [U] 写〔寫〕作 xiězuò; 作曲 zuò qǔ. **2** [C] 作品 zuòpǐn, 乐〔樂〕曲 yuèqǔ. **3** [C] 作文 zuòwén. **4** [U] 构〔構〕成 gòuchéng, 成分 chéngfen.

com·posi·tor /kəm'pɒzɪtə(r)/ *n* [C] 排字工人 páizì gōngrén.

com·post /'kɒmpɒst/ *n* [U] 堆肥 duīféi; 混合肥料 hǔnhé féiliào.

com·po·sure /kəm'pəʊʒə(r)/ *n* [U] 沉着 chénzhuo, 镇静 zhènjìng: *lose (regain) one's* ~ 失去(恢复)镇静.

com·pound¹ /'kɒmpaʊnd/ *n, adj* **1** [C] 混合物 hǔnhéwù; 化合物 huàhéwù. **2** [语法]复〔復〕合词 fùhécí. ˌ~'**interest** 复〔複〕利 fùlì.

com·pound² /kəm'paʊnd/ *vt/i* [正式用语] **1** 使混合 shǐ hǔnhé; 使化合 shǐ huàhé: ~ *several chemicals* 化合几种化学制品. **2** 使复〔複〕杂〔雜〕shǐ fùzá.

com·pound³ /'kɒmpaʊnd/ *n* [C] 院子 yuànzi.

com·pre·hend /ˌkɒmprɪ'hend/ *vt* [正式用语] **1** 了解 liǎojiě, 领会〔會〕lǐnghuì. **2** 包括 bāokuò, 包含 bāohán.

com·pre·hen·sion /ˌkɒmprɪ'henʃn/ *n* **1** [U] 理解 lǐjiě; 理解力 lǐjiělì. **2** [C, U] 理解练〔練〕习〔習〕lǐjiě liànxí. **com·pre·hen·sible** /-'hensəbl/ *adj* 能理解的 néng lǐjiě de. **com·pre·hen·sive** *adj* 包罗〔羅〕广〔廣〕泛的 bāoluó guǎngfàn de: *a* ~ *description* 综合性的描述. ˌ**com·pre'hen·sive (school)** 综合学〔學〕校 zōnghé xuéxiào. **com·pre·hen·sive·ly** *adv*

com·press¹ /kəm'pres/ *vt* **1** 压〔壓〕缩 yāsuō. **2** 使语言精炼 shǐ yǔyán jīngliàn.

com·press² /'kɒmpres/ *n* [C] (止血等用) 敷布 fūbù, 压布 yābù. ~**ion** /kəm'preʃən/ *n* [U] 压缩 yāsuō, 浓〔濃〕缩 nóngsuō.

com·prise /kəm'praɪz/ *vt* 包含 bāohán, 包括 bāokuò.

com·pro·mise /'kɒmprəmaɪz/ *n* [C,U] 妥协〔協〕tuǒxié, 折衷 zhézhōng. □ *vt/i* **1** 妥协 tuǒxié. **2** 使遭受损害 shǐ zāoshòu sǔnhài, 危及 wēijí.

com·pul·sion /kəm'pʌlʃn/ *n* **1** [U] 强制 qiángzhì, 强迫 qiǎngpò. **2** [C] 冲〔衝〕动〔動〕chōngdòng. **com·pul·sive** *adj* 强烈愿〔願〕望的 qiángliè yuànwàng de, 冲动的 chōngdòngde: *a compulsive desire to kill* 杀戮的强烈愿望.

com·pul·sory /kəm'pʌlsərɪ/ *adj* 义〔義〕务〔務〕的 yìwùde, 强制的 qiángzhìde. **com·pul·sor·ily** /-sərəlɪ/ *adv*

com·punc·tion /kəm'pʌŋkʃn/ *n* [U] 内疚 nèijiù; 疑虑〔慮〕yílǜ: *kill him without* ~ 毫无顾忌地杀

死他.

com·pu·ter /kəm'pju:tə(r)/ *n* [C] 电〔電〕子计算机〔機〕 diànzǐjìsuànjī ~**ize** /-raɪz/ *vt* 用电子计算机储存(信息) yòng diànzǐjìsuànjī chǔcún.

com·rade /'kɒmreɪd/ *n* [C] **1** 可靠的伙伴 kěkàode huǒbàn, 忠实〔實〕的朋友 zhōngshíde péngyou. **2** 同志 tóngzhì. ~**ship** *n* [U]

con /kɒn/ *vt* [-nn-] [非正式用语] 欺骗〔騙〕 qīpiàn, 诈骗 zàpiàn. □ *n* [C] 诡计 guǐjì, 骗局 piànjú.

con·cave /'kɒŋkeɪv/ *adj* 凹的 āode.

con·ceal /kən'si:l/ *vt* 隐藏 yǐncáng, 隐蔽 yǐnbì. ~**ment** *n* [U]

con·cede /kən'si:d/ *vt* 承认〔認〕 chéngrèn, 给与〔與〕 gěiyǔ.

con·ceit /kən'si:t/ *n* [U] 自负 zìfù, 自高自大 zìgāozìdà, 骄〔驕〕傲 jiāo'ào. ~**ed** *adj* ~**ed·ly** *adv*

con·ceive /kən'si:v/ *vt/i* **1** 想出(主意) xiǎngchū. **2** 怀〔懷〕孕 huáiyùn. **con·ceiv·able** /-əbl/ *adj* 可以相信的 kěyǐ xiāngxìn de. **con·ceiv·ably** *adv*

con·cen·trate /'kɒnsntreɪt/ *vt/i* **1** 集中 jízhōng. 使集中于一点〔點〕 shǐ jízhōng yú yìdiǎn. **2** 集中注意力于 jízhōng zhùyìlì yú, 全神贯注于 quánshén guànzhù yú: ~ *on one's work* 全神贯注于工作. **3** 浓〔濃〕缩 nóngsuō, 提浓 tínóng. □ *n* [C] 浓缩物 nóngsuōwù.

con·cen·tra·tion /ˌkɒnsn'treɪʃn/ *n* **1** [C] 集中物 jízhōngwù, 集结物 jíjiéwù: *troop* ~*s* 军队在数处的集结. **2** [U] 专〔專〕心 zhuānxīn, 集中注意 jízhōng zhùyì: *lose one's* ~ 注意力不集中. ~ **camp** 集中营〔營〕 jízhōngyíng.

con·cen·tric /kən'sentrɪk/ *adj* (圆)同心的 tóngxīnde.

con·cept /'kɒnsept/ *n* [C] 概念 gàiniàn, 思想 sīxiǎng.

con·cep·tion /kən'sepʃn/ *n* **1** [U] 概念的形成 gàiniànde xíngchéng; [C] 概念 gàiniàn; 想法 xiǎngfǎ. **2** 怀〔懷〕孕 huáiyùn.

con·cern[1] /kən'sɜ:n/ *vt* **1** 影响〔響〕 yǐnxiǎng, 对…有重要性 duì...yǒu zhòngyàoxìng; 涉及 shèjí. *So* (或 *As*) *far as I'm* ~*ed* 就我来说. **2** 忙于 mángyú; 关〔關〕心 guānxīn. **3** 担〔擔〕心 dānxīn, 记挂〔掛〕 jìguà: ~*ed for* (或 *about*) *her safety* 担心她的安全. ~**ing** *prep* = about[2](3).

con·cern[2] /kən'sɜ:n/ *n* **1** [C] 所关〔關〕切的事. suǒ guānqiè de shì. **2** [C] 商行 shāngháng, 企业〔業〕 qǐyè: *a profitable* ~ 赚钱的企业. **3** [U] 关心 guānxīn, 担〔擔〕心 dānxīn, 忧〔憂〕虑〔慮〕 yōulǜ: *a cause for* ~ 忧虑的原因.

con·cert /'kɒnsət/ *n* **1** [C] 音乐〔樂〕会〔會〕 yīnyuèhuì. **2** [U] 一致 yízhì, 和谐 héxié.

con·certed /kən'sɜ:tɪd/ *adj* 商定的 shāngdìngde, 一致的 yízhìde: *make a* ~ *effort.* 齐心协力.

con·cer·tina /ˌkɒnsə'ti:nə/ *n* [C] [*pl* ~s] 六角手风〔風〕琴 liùjiǎo shǒufēngqín.

con·certo /kən'tʃeətəʊ/ *n* [C] [*pl* ~s] 协〔協〕奏曲 xiézòuqǔ.

con·ces·sion /kən'seʃn/ *n* [U] 让〔讓〕步 ràngbù, [C] 让与〔與〕物 ràngyǔwù : *make* ~*s to the enemy* 对敌人让步.

con·cili·ate /kən'sɪlɪeɪt/ *vt* 安抚〔撫〕 ānfǔ, 劝〔勸〕慰 quànwèi. **con·ˌcili'ation** *n* [U] **con·cili·atory** /kən'sɪlɪətərɪ/ *adj* 抚慰的 fǔwèide.

con·cise /kən'saɪs/ *adj* 简〔簡〕明的 jiǎnmíngde; 简要的 jiǎnyàode: *a* ~ *report* 简要的报告. ~**ly** *adv* ~**ness** *n* [U]

con·clude /kən'klu:d/ *vt/i* **1** 结束 jiésù. **2** 安排 ānpái; 缔结 dìjié: ~ *an agreement* 缔结协定. **3** 作结论〔論〕 zuò jiélùn: *The jury* ~*d that the man was not guilty.* 陪审团作出结论此人无罪. **con·clu·sion** /kən'klu:ʒn/ *n* [C] **(a)** 结束 jiésù, 终了 zhōngliǎo. **(b)** 决定 juédìng; 解决 jiějué.

con·clus·ive / kən'klu:sɪv/ *adj* (证据等)令人信服的 lìngrén xìnfú de. ~**ly** *adv*

con·coct /kən'kɒkt/ *vt* **1** 调合 tiáohé, 混合 hùnhé. **2** 编造(故事等) biānzào. **con'coction** *n* [U] 混合 hùnhé; [C] 混合物 hùnhéwù; 调制〔製〕物 tiáozhìwù.

con·cord /'kɒŋkɔ:d/ *n* [C,U] 和谐 héxié, 一致 yízhì.

con·course /'kɒŋkɔ:s/ *n* [C] **1** 集合 jíhé, 汇〔匯〕合 huìhé. **2** 群集场〔場〕所 qúnjí chǎngsuǒ.

con·crete /'kɒŋkri:t/ *adj* **1** 有形的 yǒuxíngde. **2** 具体〔體〕的 jùtǐde, 明确〔確〕的 míngquède: ~ *evidence* 确凿的证据. □ *n* [U] 混凝土 hùnníngtǔ. □ *vt* 浇〔澆〕混凝土于 jiāo hùnníngtǔ yú.

con·cur /kən'kɜ:(r)/ *vi* [-rr-] [正式用语] **1** 同意 tóngyì, 赞成 zànchéng. **2** 同时〔時〕发〔發〕生 tóngshí fāshēng. ~**rence** /kən'kʌrəns/ *n* [U] 同意 tóngyì, 一致 yízhì. ~**rent** *adj* ~**rent·ly** *adv* 同时 tóngshí; 兼任 jiānrèn.

con·cuss /kən'kʌs/ *vt* 震动〔動〕 zhèndòng. **con'cussion** *n* [C, U]

con·demn /kən'dem/ *vt* **1** 谴责 qiǎnzé. **2**［法律］宣判有罪 xuānpàn yǒuzuì, 判刑 pànxíng: *~ed to death* 宣判死刑. **3** 迫使(做不愿做的事) pòshǐ. **4** 宣告(建筑物)不宜使用 xuāngào búyí shǐyòng. **~a·tion** /ˌkɒndəm'neɪʃn/ *n* [U]

con·den·sa·tion /ˌkɒnden'seɪʃn/ *n* **1** [U] 凝结 níngjié, 冷凝 lěngníng. **2** [C, U] 水蒸气〔氣〕凝结成的水滴 shuǐzhēngqì níngjié chéng de shuǐdī.

con·dense /kən'dens/ *vt/i* **1** (液体)浓〔濃〕缩 nóngsuō: *~d milk* 炼乳. **2** (使)冷凝 lěngníng, (使)凝结 níngjié. **3** 精简〔簡〕 jīngjiǎn, 压缩 yāsuō: *~ a speech* 压缩讲话.

con·den·ser /kən'densə(r)/ *n* [C] **1** 冷凝器 lěngníngqì. **2** 电〔電〕容器 diànróngqì.

con·de·scend /ˌkɒndɪ'send/ *vi* **1** 俯就 fǔjiù, 屈尊 qūzūn, 俯允 fǔyǔn: *The manager ~ed to talk to the workers.* 经理放下架子同工人们谈话. **2** 高人一等地 gāorén yìděng de. **~ing** *adj* **con·di·ment** /'kɒndɪmənt/ *n* [C,U]［正式用语］= seasoning.

con·di·tion¹ /kən'dɪʃn/ *n* **1** [C] 条〔條〕件 tiáojiàn. *on ~ that* 如果 rúguǒ; 在…条件下 zài…tiáojiàn xià. **2** [U] 状〔狀〕况 zhuàngkuàng, 状态〔態〕 zhuàngtài: *a car in good ~* 完好的汽车. **3** [*pl*] 环〔環〕境 huánjìng, 情形 qíngxíng.

con·di·tion² /kən'dɪʃn/ *vt* **1** 决定 juédìng, 支配 zhīpèi. **2** 训练 xùnliàn; 使适〔適〕应〔應〕 shǐ shìyìng: *a dog ~ed to obey* 听从命令的狗.

con·di·tional /kən'dɪʃənl/ *adj* 附有条〔條〕件的 fù yǒu tiáojiàn de, 视…而定的 shì…ér dìng de. **~ clause**［语法］条件子句 tiáojiàn zǐjù. **~ly** *adv*

con·dol·ence /kən'dəʊləns/ *n* [C]［常作 *pl*］吊唁 diàoyàn, 吊慰 diàowèi, 慰问〔問〕 wèiwèn.

con·done /kən'dəʊn/ *vt* 宽恕 kuānshù, 原谅 yuánliàng.

con·duc·ive /kən'dju:sɪv/ *adj* 有益于…的 yǒuyìyú… de, 有助于…的 yǒu zhùyú…de: *~ to health* 有益于健康.

con·duct¹ /'kɒndʌkt/ *n* [U] **1** 行为〔爲〕 xíngwéi, 举〔舉〕动〔動〕 jǔdòng, 品行 pǐnxíng. **2** 处〔處〕理方法 chǔlǐ fāngfǎ.

con·duct² /'kən'dʌkt/ *vt/i* **1** 引导〔導〕 yǐndǎo, 陪伴 péibàn, 指导 zhǐdǎo: *~ tourists round a city* 陪同游客游览城市. **2** 经〔經〕营〔營〕 jīngyíng, 处〔處〕理 chǔlǐ. **3** 指挥〔揮〕(乐队) zhǐhuī. **4** 行为〔爲〕 xíngwéi, 表现 biǎoxiàn. **5** 传〔傳〕导 chuándǎo, 输〔輸〕送 shūsòng. **con'duction** /-ʃn/ *n* [U] 传导 chuándǎo. **~ive** *adj* 能传导的 néng chuándǎo de. **~or** *n* [C] **(a)** 乐〔樂〕队〔隊〕指挥 yuèduì zhǐhuī. **(b)** 公共汽车〔車〕售票员 gōnggòngqìchē shòupiàoyuán. **(c)** 导体〔體〕 dǎotǐ. **~ress** *n* [C] 公共汽车女售票员 gōnggòngqìchē nǚ shòupiàoyuán.

cone /kəʊn/ *n* [C] **1** 圆锥体〔體〕 yuánzhuītǐ. **2** 圆锥形的东〔東〕西 yuánzhuīxíngde dōngxi: *an ice-cream ~* 蛋卷冰淇淋. **3** (松树的)球果 qiúguǒ.

con·fec·tion /kən'fekʃn/ *n*［正式用语］[C] 糖果 tángguǒ, 点〔點〕心 diǎnxīn. **~er** 制〔製〕造, 销售糖果点心的人 zhìzào, xiāoshòu tángguǒ diǎnxīn de rén. **~ery** *n* **(a)** [U] 糖果点心 tángguǒ diǎnxīn. **(b)** [C] [*pl* -ies] 糖果点心店 tángguǒdiǎnxīndiàn.

con·fed·er·acy /kən'fedərəsɪ/ *n* [C] [*pl* -ies] 邦联〔聯〕 bānglián, 同盟 tóngméng, 联盟 liánméng.

con·fed·er·ate¹ /kən'fedərət/ *adj* 联〔聯〕合的 liánhéde, 同盟的 tóngméngde. □ *n* [C] **1** 同盟者 tóngméngzhě, 联盟者 liánméngzhě; 同盟国〔國〕 tóngméngguó. **2** 同谋 tóngmóu, 同伙〔夥〕 tónghuǒ.

con·fed·er·ate² /kən'fedəreɪt/ *vt/i* (使)结成同盟 jiéchéng tóngméng, (使)结党〔黨〕 jiédǎng. **con·fed·e'ration** *n* [C] 同盟 tóngméng, 联盟 liánméng, 邦联 bānglián.

con·fer /kən'fɜ:(r)/ *vt/i* [-rr-] **1** *~ sth on* (或 *upon*) 授予(学位,称号等) shòuyǔ **2** 协〔協〕商 xiéshāng.

con·fer·ence /'kɒnfərəns/ *n* [C,U] 会〔會〕议〔議〕 huìyì, 大会 dàhuì; 讨论〔論〕 tǎolùn.

con·fess /kən'fes/ *vt/i* **1** 承认〔認〕 chéngrèn, 坦白 tǎnbái. **2** (罗马天主教)向神父忏〔懺〕悔 xiàng shénfù chànhuǐ.

con·fes·sion /kən'feʃn/ *n* [C, U] **1** 招供 zhāogòng, 交代 jiāodài, 坦白 tǎnbái. **2** 自白书〔書〕 zìbáishū, 供状〔狀〕 gòngzhuàng. **~al** /-ʃənl/ *n* [C] 忏〔懺〕悔室(神父听取忏悔处) chànhuǐshì.

con·fetti /kən'fetɪ/ *n* [U] (婚礼中投掷的)五彩纸屑 wǔcǎi zhǐxiè.

con·fi·dant /ˌkɒnfɪ'dænt/ *n* [C] 知心人 zhīxīnrén.

con·fide /kən'faɪd/ *vt/i* **1** 吐露秘密 tǔlù mìmì. **2** ~ *in* 信任 xìnrèn.

con·fi·dence /'kɒnfɪdəns/ *n* **1** [U] 信任 xìnrèn. *in strict* ~ 严〔嚴〕格保守秘密 yángé bǎoshǒu mìmì. **2** [C] 秘密 mìmì, 私房话 sīfánghuà. **3** [U] 信心 xìnxīn, 自信 zìxìn. **con·fi·dent** *adj* 确〔確〕信的 quèxìnde, 有把握的 yǒu bǎwò de. **con·fi·dent·ly** *adv*

con·fi·den·tial /ˌkɒnfɪ'denʃl/ *adj* **1** 机〔機〕密的 jīmìde, 秘密的 mìmìde. **2** 信任的 xìnrènde, 心腹的 xīnfùde.

con·fine /kən'faɪn/ *vt* **1** 限制 xiànzhì, 控制 kòngzhì: *We ~d the illness to one village.* 我们把这种病控制在一个村子里. **2** 禁闭〔閉〕jìnbì. *~d to bed with a cold* 因感冒而卧床. **con·fined** *adj* (空间)有限的 yǒuxiànde; 狭〔狹〕窄的 xiázhǎide. **~ment** *n* **(a)** [U] 监〔監〕禁 jiānjìn, 禁闭〔閉〕jìnbì. **(b)** [C, U] 分娩 fēnmiǎn.

con·fines /'kɒnfaɪnz/ *n pl* 界限 jièxiàn, 边〔邊〕界 biānjiè.

con·firm /kən'fɜːm/ *vt* **1** (权力)使更巩〔鞏〕固 shǐ gèng gǒnggù; (意见)使更有力 shǐgèngyǒulì; (信念)使更坚〔堅〕定 shǐ gèng jiāndìng. **2** 认〔認〕可(任命等) rènkě. **3** (基督教)施坚信礼〔禮〕(使成为教徒) shī jiānxìnlǐ. **~ed** *adj* 确〔確〕定的 quèdìngde. **~a·tion** /ˌkɒnfə'meɪʃən/ *n* [C,U]

con·fis·cate /'kɒnfɪskeɪt/ *vt* 没收(私人财产) mòshōu. **con·fis'ca·tion** *n* [C,U]

con·flict /'kɒnflɪkt/ *n* [C] **1** 战〔戰〕斗〔鬥〕zhàndòu; 斗争 dòuzhēng. **2** (意见) 分歧 fēnqí. □ /kən'flɪkt/ *vi* 抵触〔觸〕dǐchù, 冲〔衝〕突 chōngtū.

con·form /kən'fɔːm/ *vt/i* 符合 fúhé, 遵从〔從〕zūncóng: ~ *to the law* 遵守法律. **~ist** *n* [C] 遵奉者. **~ity** *n* [U] **(a)** 遵从〔從〕社会〔會〕习〔習〕俗的 zūncóng shèhuì xísú de. **(b)** 一致 yízhì, 符合 fúhé.

con·found /kən'faʊnd/ *vt* **1** 使困惑 shǐ kùnhuò, 使迷惑 shǐ míhuò. **2** 混淆 hùnxiáo, 混乱〔亂〕hùnluàn.

con·front /kən'frʌnt/ *vt* 使面对〔對〕shǐ miànduì, 面临〔臨〕miànlín. **~a·tion** /ˌkɒnfrʌn'teɪʃən/ *n* [C,U] 对抗 duìkàng: *the ~ between the police and the demonstrators* 警察同示威者的对抗.

con·fuse /kən'fjuːz/ *vt* **1** 使混乱〔亂〕shǐ hùnluàn, 混淆 hùnxiáo, 混同 hùntóng. **2** 弄错 nòngcuò. **con·fu·sion** *n* [U]

con·geal /kən'dʒiːl/ *vt/i* (使)冻结 dòngjié, (使)凝结 níngjié.

con·gen·ial /kən'dʒiːnɪəl/ *adj* **1** 性情相近的 xìngqíng xiāngjìn de. **2** 相宜的 xiāngyíde. 惬意的 qièyìde. **~ly** *adv*

con·geni·tal /kən'dʒenɪtl/ *adj* (疾病等)先天的 xiāntiānde.

con·gested /kən'dʒestɪd/ *adj* 拥〔擁〕挤〔擠〕的 yōngjǐde. **con·ges·tion** *n* [U]

con·glom·er·ate[1] /kən'glɒmərət/ *adj, n* [C] 成团〔團〕的 chéngtuánde.

con·glom·er·ate[2] /kən'glɒməreɪt/ *vt/i* (使) 成团 chéngtuán. **con·glome'ration** *n* [C, U]

con·gratu·late /kən'grætʃʊleɪt/ *vt* 祝贺 zhùhè, 庆贺 qìnghè: ~ *him on his victory* 祝贺他的胜利. **con·gratu'la·tions** *n* [C] 祝贺词 zhùhècí.

con·gre·gate /'kɒŋgrɪgeɪt/ *vt/i* (使)集合 jíhé. **con·gre'ga·tion** *n* [U] 集合 jíhé, [C] 集会〔會〕jíhuì; 教徒集会 jiàotú jíhuì. **con·gre'ga·tional** *adj*

con·gress /'kɒŋgres/ *n* **1** [C] 代表会〔會〕议〔議〕dàibiǎohuìyì. **2** C~ (美国等)议会 yìhuì. **'~man (woman)** 男(女)议员 nányìyuán. **~ion·al** /kən'greʃənl/ *adj*

con·gru·ent /'kɒŋgruənt/ *adj* **1** 适〔適〕合的 shìhéde; 一致的 yízhìde. **2** 全等的 quánděngde, 迭合的 diéhéde: ~ *triangles* 全等的三角形.

con·gru·ous /'kɒŋgruəs/ *adj* 适〔適〕合的 shìhéde, 协〔協〕调的(后接 to) xiétiáode.

coni·cal /'kɒnɪk/ *adj* 圆锥形的 yuánzhuīxíngde.

coni·fer /'kɒnɪfə(r)/ *n* [C, U] 针叶〔葉〕树〔樹〕zhēnyèshù. **~ous** /kə'nɪfərəs/ *adj*

con·jec·ture /kən'dʒektʃə(r)/ *vt/i* [正式用语]猜想 cāixiǎng, 猜测 cāicè, 推测 tuīcè. □ *n* [C, U] [正式用语]推测 tuīcè, 假设 jiǎshè. **con·jec·tural** *adj*

con·ju·gal /'kɒndʒʊgl/ *adj* [正式用语]婚姻的 hūnyīnde, 夫妇〔婦〕关〔關〕系的 fūfù guānxì de, 夫妇的 fūfùde.

con·ju·gate /'kɒndʒʊgeɪt/ *vt* [语法] **1** 列举〔舉〕动〔動〕词的变〔變〕化形式 lièjǔ dòngcíde biànhuà xíngshì. **2** (动词)有各种〔種〕变形 yǒu gèzhǒng biànxíng. **con·ju'ga·tion** *n* **(a)** [C, U] 动词的各种变形 dòngcíde gèzhǒng biànxíng. **(b)**

[C]变化形式相似的一组动词 biànhuà xíngshì xiāngsì de yìzǔ dòngcí.

con·junc·tion /kən'dʒʌŋkʃn/ *n* **1** [C] [语法] 连[連]词 liáncí. **2** [U] 联[聯]合 liánhé, 接合 jiēhé, 连接 liánjiē. *in* ~ *with* 与[與]...协[協]力 yǔ...xiélì. 与...连同 yǔ ...liántóng. **3** [C] (事件等) 同时[時]发[發]生 tóngshí fāshēng.

con·jure /'kʌndʒə(r)/ *vt/i* **1** 用戏[戲]法变[變]出 yòng xìfǎ biànchū, 用魔术[術]影响[響] yòng móshù yǐngxiǎng. **2** ~ *up* **(a)** 用魔法召来[來] yòng mófǎ zhāolái. **(b)** 用魔法召鬼 yòng mófǎ zhāoguǐ. **con·jurer**, **con·juror** 施魔法者 shī mófǎ zhě.

con·nect /kə'nekt/ *vt/i* **1** 连[連]结 liánjiē, 连接 liánjiē: ~ *the two wires together* 把这两条电线连接起来. **2** 联[聯]想 liánxiǎng.

con·nec·tion /kə'nekʃn/ *n* **1** [C, U] 连[連]接 liánjiē, 连结 liánjié; 连结点[點] liánjiédiǎn, 连结物 liánjiéwù. **2** [C] (火车, 飞机等) 联运[運] liányùn. **3** (贸易上的) 往来[來]关[關]系 wǎnglái guānxì. **4** *in* ~ *with* 关于 guānyú.

con·nexion /kə'nekʃən/ = connection

con·nive /kə'naɪv/ *vi* ~ *at* 默许 mòxǔ, 纵[縱]容 zòngróng. **conniv·ance** *n* [U]

con·nois·seur /ˌkɒnə'sɜː(r)/ *n* [C] 鉴[鑒]赏家 jiànshǎngjiā. 鉴定家 jiàndìngjiā; 行家 hángjiā, 内行 nèiháng.

con·no·ta·tion /ˌkɒnə'teɪʃn/ *n* [C] 言外之意 yánwàizhīyì: *Slang words usually have obscene* ~*s.* 俚语常有下流的含义.

con·quer /'kɒŋkə(r)/ *vt* **1** 征服 zhēngfú, 战[戰]胜[勝] zhànshèng. **2** 攻克 gōngkè: ~ *a city* 攻克一座城市 ~**or** 征服者 zhēngfúzhě, 占领者 zhànlǐngzhě.

con·quest /'kɒŋkwəst/ *n* **1** [U] 征服 zhēngfú. **2** [C] 征服地 zhēngfúdì. 掠取物 lüèqǔwù.

Cons. =Conservative 保守党[黨]人 bǎoshǒudǎngrén

con·science /'kɒnʃəns/ *n* [C, U] **1** 是非感 shìfēigǎn, 良心 liángxīn. **2** 犯罪感 fànzuìgǎn. ***have sth (sb) on one's*** ~ 因某事(某人)而感到内疚 yīn mǒushì ér gǎndào nèijiù.

con·scien·tious /ˌkɒnʃɪ'enʃəs/ *adj* **1** 认[認]真的 rènzhēnde. **2** 诚心诚意的 chéngxīnchéngyìde. ~**ly** *adv* ~**ness** *n* [C]

con·scious /'kɒnʃəs/ *adj* **1** 清醒的 qīngxǐngde, 知道的 zhīdàode. **2** 故意的 gùyìde: *He spoke with* ~ *superiority.* 他说话时带着有意识的优越感. ~ *of* 意识[識]到的 yìshì dào de: *He was* ~ *of his mistakes.* 他意识到了自已的错误. ~**ly** *adv* ~**ness** *n* [U] 意识 yìshì, 自觉[覺] zìjué, 觉悟 juéwù 知觉 zhījué: *regain* ~*ness after an accident* 事故之后恢复了知觉.

con·script /kən'skrɪpt/ *vt* 征[徵]募 zhēngmù, 征兵 zhēngbīng, 征召 zhēngzhāo. ⇨ draft(2). □ *n* /'kɒnskrɪpt/ [C] 应[應]征士兵 yìngzhēng shìbīng. **con'scrip·tion** /-ʃn/ *n* [U]

con·se·crate /'kɒnsɪkreɪt/ *vt* 奉为[爲]神圣[聖] fèngwéi shénshèng, 使成为神圣 shǐ chéngwéi shénshèng: ~ *a church* 主持教堂的奉献礼. **con·se'cra·tion** *n* [C,U] 献祭 xiànjì, 奉献 fèngxiàn.

con·secu·tive /kən'sekjʊtɪv/ *adj* 连[連]续[續]的 liánxùde, 连贯的 liánguànde, 顺序的 shùnxùde. ~**ly** *adv*

con·sen·sus /kən'sensəs/ *n* [C] [*pl* ~es] 一致 yízhì, 合意 héyì.

con·sent /kən'sent/ *vi* 同意 tóngyì, 赞成 zànchéng: ~ *to a marriage* 答应结婚. □ *n* [U] 同意 tóngyì, 赞成 zànchéng, 允许 yǔnxǔ.

con·se·quence /'kɒnsɪkwəns/ *n* **1** [C] 结果 jiéguǒ, 后[後]果 hòuguǒ: *the* ~*s of his action* 他的行为的后果. **2** [U]重要(性) zhòngyào, 重大 zhòngdà: *a man of* ~ 要人.

con·se·quent /'kɒnsɪkwənt/ *adj* [正式用语]随之发[發]生的 suízhī fāshēng de. ~**ly** *adv* 因而 yīn'ér, 所以 suǒyǐ.

con·se·quen·tial /ˌkɒnsɪ'kwenʃl/ *adj* [正式用语] **1** = consequent. **2** 自高自大的 zìgāozìdàde. ~**ly** *adv*

con·ser·va·tion /ˌkɒnsə'veɪʃn/ *n* [U] 保存 bǎocún, 保护[護] bǎohù.

con·serva·tive /kən'sɜːvətɪv/ *adj* **1** 保守的 bǎoshǒude, 守旧[舊]的 shǒujiùdè. **2 the C~ Party** 英国[國]保守党[黨] yīngguó bǎoshǒudǎng. □ *n* [C] **1** 保守主义[義]者 bǎoshǒuzhǔyìzhě. **2 C~** 英国保守党人 yīngguó bǎoshǒudǎngrén; 英国保守党的支持者 yīngguó bǎoshǒudǎngde zhīchízhě. ~**ly** *adv* **con·serva·tism** *n* [U]

con·serva·tory /kən'sɜːvətrɪ/ *n* [C] [*pl* -ies] **1** (培养植物的)暖房 nuǎnfáng, 温室 wēnshì. **2** 公立艺[藝]术[術]学[學]校 gōnglì yìshù xuéxiào.

con·serve /kən'sɜːv/ *vt* 保存 bǎocún, 保藏 bǎocáng. □ *n* [常作 *pl*] 果酱[醬] guǒjiàng; 蜜饯[餞] mìjiàn.

con·sider /kən'sɪdə(r)/ *vt* **1** 想 xiǎng, 考虑[慮] kǎolǜ. **2** 顾[顧]及 gùjí, 体[體]谅 tǐliàng: ~ *the feelings of others* 体谅别人的感情. **3** 认[認]为[爲] rènwéi, 以为 yǐwéi: ~ *him a fool* 认为他是傻瓜.

con·sider·able /kən'sɪdərəbl/ *adj* 相当[當]大的 xiāngdāng dà de; 重要的 zhòngyàode.

con·sider·ate /kən'sɪdərət/ *adj* 体谅别人的 tǐliàng biérén de, 考虑[慮]周到的 kǎolǜ zhōudào de. ~**ly** *adv* **con·side'r·ation** *n* [C, U]

con·sider·ing /kən'sɪdərɪŋ/ *prep* 考虑[慮]到 kǎolǜdào; 就…而论[論] jiù…ér lùn: *He's very well ~ his age.* 考虑到他的年龄,他的身体是很好的.

con·sign /kən'saɪn/ *vt* **1** 运[運]送(货物) yùnsòng. **2** 交付 jiāofù, 把…委托给 bǎ…wěi tuōgěi: ~ *the boy to his brother's care* 把男孩子托付给他的兄弟照顾. ~**ment** *n* [U] 交付 jiāofù, 托付 tuōfù; [C] 托付物 tuōfùwù.

con·sist /kən'sɪst/ *vi* **1** ~ *of* 由…组成 yóu…zǔchéng, 由…构[構]成 yóu…gòuchéng. **2** ~ *in* 存在于 cúnzàiyú, 以…为[爲]主要成分 yǐ…wéi zhǔyào chéngfen.

con·sist·ency /kən'sɪstənsɪ/ *n* [*pl* -ies] **1** [U] 一致性 yízhìxìng; 连[連]贯性 liánguànxìng. **2** [C, U] 浓[濃]度 nóngdù, 稠度 chóudù, 密度 mìdù. **con·sist·ent** *adj* **(a)** 始终如一的 shǐzhōngrúyīde. **(b)** 与[與]…一致 yǔ…yízhì. **con·sist·ent·ly** *adv*

con·so·la·tion /ˌkɒnsə'leɪʃn/ *n* **1** [U] 安慰 ānwèi, 慰藉 wèijiè. **2** [C] 安慰的人或物 ānwèide rén huò wù.

con·sole[1] /kən'səʊl/ *vt* 安慰 ānwèi, 慰问[問] wèiwèn.

con·sole[2] /'kɒnsəʊl/ *n* [C] 控制盘[盤] kòngzhìpán.

con·soli·date /kən'sɒlɪdeɪt/ *vt/i* **1** 巩[鞏]固 gǒnggù; 加强 jiāqiáng. **2** 把…合为[爲]一体[體] bǎ…héwéi yìtǐ. **con·soli'da·tion** *n* [C,U]

con·sommé /kən'sɒmeɪ/ *n* [U] [法语]清燉肉汤[湯] qīngdùn ròutāng.

con·son·ant /'kɒnsənənt/ *n* [C] 辅[輔]音 fǔyīn.

con·sort[1] /'kɒnsɔːt/ *n* [C] 帝王的夫或妻 dìwángde fū huò qī; 配偶 pèi'ǒu.

con·sort[2] /kən'sɔːt/ *vi* ~ *with* 陪伴 péibàn.

con·sort·ium /kən'sɔːtɪəm/ *n* [C] [*pl* -tia /-tɪə/] 国[國]际[際]财团[團] guójì cáituán.

con·spicu·ous /kən'spɪkjʊəs/ *adj* 明显[顯]的 míngxiǎnde, 引人注目的 yǐnrénzhùmùde. ~**ly** *adv*

con·spir·acy /kən'spɪrəsɪ/ *n* [*pl* -ies] **1** [U] 阴[陰]谋 yīnmóu, 密谋 mìmóu. **2** [C] 同谋 tóngmóu, 共谋 gòngmóu. **con·spira·tor** /kən'spɪrətə(r)/ *n* [C] 阴谋家 yīnmóujiā, 共谋者 gòngmóuzhě.

con·spire /kən'spaɪə(r)/ *vt/i* **1** 密商 mìshāng, 阴[陰]谋 yīnmóu, 密谋 mìmóu: ~ *to kill the king* 密谋弄死国王. **2** 协[協]力 xiélì, 联[聯]合 liánhé.

con·stable /'kʌnstəbl/ *n* [C] [过时用法]警察 jǐngchá. **chief** ~ (英国)警察局长[長] jǐngchá júzhǎng. **con·stabu·lary** /kən'stæbjʊlərɪ/ *n* [C] [*pl* -ies] 警察 jǐngchá, 保安队[隊] bǎo'ānduì.

con·stant /'kɒnstənt/ *adj* **1** 经[經]常的 jīngchángde, 经久的 jīngjiǔde, 不变[變]的 búbiànde, 不断[斷]的 búduànde: ~ *noise* 不断的噪音. **2** [正式用语]坚[堅]定的 jiāndìngde, 坚贞的 jiānzhēnde: *a ~ friend* 忠实的朋友. ~**ly** *adv* 不断地 búduànde. **con·stancy** *n* [U]

con·stel·la·tion /ˌkɒnstə'leɪʃn/ *n* [C] 星座 xīngzuò.

con·ster·na·tion /ˌkɒnstə'neɪʃn/ *n* [U] 惊[驚]恐 jīngkǒng, 惊愕 jīng'è.

con·sti·pa·tion /ˌkɒnstɪ'peɪʃn/ *n* [U] 便秘 biànmì. **con·sti·pate** /'kɒnstɪpeɪt/ *vt* 使便秘 shǐ biànmì.

con·stitu·ency /kən'stɪtʃʊənsɪ/ *n* [C] [*pl* -ies] 选[選]区[區] xuǎnqū; 全体[體]选民 quántǐ xuǎnmín.

con·stitu·ent /kən'stɪtʃʊənt/ *adj* **1** 有选[選]举[舉]权[權]的 yǒuxuǎnjǔquánde: *a ~ assembly* 立宪会议, 国民代表大会. **2** 组成的 zǔchéngde. □ *n* [C] **1** 选民 xuǎnmín; 选举人 xuǎnjǔrén. **2** 成分 chéngfen, 要素 yàosù.

con·sti·tute /'kɒnstɪtjuːt/ *vt* **1** 设立 shèlì, 制定 zhìdìng. **2** 组成 zǔchéng, 构[構]成 gòuchéng.

con·sti·tu·tion /ˌkɒnstɪ'tjuːʃn/ *n* [C] **1** 宪[憲]法 xiànfǎ. **2** (人的)体[體]格 tǐgé, 体质[質] tǐzhì, 素质 sùzhì. **3** (事物的)构[構]造 gòuzào, 组成(方式) zǔchéng. ~-

al *adj* 宪法的 xiànfǎde, 体格的 tǐgéde.

con·strain /kən'streɪn/ *vt* 强迫 qiǎngpò, 强使 qiǎngshǐ: *I felt ~ed to obey.* 我觉得非遵命不可. **con·straint** /kən'streɪnt/ *n* [U]

con·strict /kən'strɪkt/ *vt* 缩小 suōxiǎo, 压缩 yāsuō. **con'stric·tion** /-ʃn/ *n* **(a)** [U] 压缩 yāsuō, 收缩 shōusuō. **(b)** [C] 压迫感 yāpògǎn.

con·stric·tor /kən'strɪktə(r)/ *n* [C] **1** 缩肌 suōjī. **2** ⇨ boa.

con·struct /kən'strʌkt/ *vt* 建造 jiànzào, 建筑 jiànzhù. **~or** 建造者 jiànzàozhě.

con·struc·tion /kən'strʌkʃn/ *n* **1** [U] 建设 jiànshè, 建造 jiànzào, 建筑 jiànzhù. **2** [C]结构〔構〕jiégòu, 建筑物 jiànzhùwù. **3** [C] 意义〔義〕yìyì; 解释 jiěshì: *Do not put a wrong ~ on his action.* 对他的行为不要有错误的理解. **~al** *adj* 构造上的 gòuzàoshàngde; 建筑物的 jiànzhùwùde.

con·struc·tive /kən'strʌktɪv/ *adj* 建设性的 jiànshèxìngde, 建设的 jiànshède, 积〔積〕极〔極〕的 jījíde. **~ly** *adv*

con·sul /'kɒnsl/ *n* [C] 领事 lǐngshì. **~ar** /'kɒnsjʊlə(r)/ *adj* 领事职〔職〕权〔權〕的 lǐngshì zhíquánde; 领事(馆)的 lǐngshìde. **~ate** /'kɒnsjʊlət/ *n* [C] 领事馆 lǐngshìguǎn, 领事职权 lǐngshì zhíquán.

con·sult /kən'sʌlt/ *vt/i* 协〔協〕商 xiéshāng, 磋商 cuōshāng, 商量 shāngliang. **~ant** *n* [C] 顾〔顧〕问〔問〕gùwèn. **~a·tion** /-'teɪʃn/ *n* [C,U]

con·sume /kən'sjuːm/ *vt/i* [正式用语] **1** 吃光 chīguāng, 喝光 hēguāng. **2** 消耗 xiāohào, 用尽〔盡〕yòngjìn: *My car ~s a lot of petrol.* 我的汽车很费汽油. **3** 烧〔燒〕毁 shāohuǐ, 毁灭〔滅〕huǐmiè. **con·sum·ing** *adj* 热〔熱〕切的 rèqiède: *a ~ ambition* 热切的野心.

con·sumer /kən'sjuːmə(r)/ *n* [C] 消费者 xiāofèizhě, 用户 yònghù. ⇨ producer(1).

con·sum·mate /'kɒnsəmeɪt/ *vt* **1** [正式用语]使完善. shǐ wánshàn. **2** 使完成 shǐ wánchéng; 完婚 wánhūn, 圆房 yuánfáng. **con·sum'ma·tion** *n* [C,U]

con·sump·tion /kən'sʌmpʃn/ *n* [U] **1** 消费（量） xiāofèi, 消耗 xiāohào. **2** 结核病 jiéhébìng; 肺结核 fèijiéhé. **con·sump·tive** *n* [C], *adj* 结核病人 jiéhébìngrén.

con·tact /'kɒntækt/ *n* **1** [U] 接触〔觸〕jiēchù, 联〔聯〕络 liánluò. *come into ~ with* 接触到... jiēchùdào.... **2** [C] 会〔會〕晤的人 huìwùde rén. *business ~s* (有来往的)商业界人士 shāngyèjiè rénshì. **3** [C] (电)接点〔點〕jiēdiǎn; 触〔觸〕点 chùdiǎn. □ *vt* 接触 jiēchù.

con·ta·gion /kən'teɪdʒən/ *n* **1** [U] 传〔傳〕染 chuánrǎn. **2** [C] 能接触〔觸〕传染的疾病 néng jiēchù chuánrǎn de jíbìng. **3** [喻](思想, 谣言等)传播 chuánbō, 蔓延 mànyán. **con·ta·gi·ous** *adj*

con·tain /kən'teɪn/ *vt* **1** 容纳 róngnà, 包含 bāohán: *This bottle ~s two litres of milk.* 这个瓶盛两升牛奶. **2** 控制 kòngzhì, 抑制 yìzhì.

con·tainer /kən'teɪnə(r)/ *n* [C] **1** 容器 róngqì. **2** 集装〔裝〕箱 jízhuāngxiāng.

con·tami·nate /kən'tæmɪneɪt/ *vt* 弄脏〔髒〕nòngzāng, 污染 wūrǎn, 传〔傳〕染 chuánrǎn: *~d food* 被污染的食物. **con·tami'na·tion** *n* **(a)** [U] 污染 wūrǎn. **(b)** [C]污染物 wūrǎnwù.

con·tem·plate /'kɒntempleɪt/ *vt* **1** 注视 zhùshì, 沉思 chénsī. **2** 期望 qīwàng, 打算 dǎsuàn. **con·tem'pla·tion** *n* [U] 注视 zhùshì, 沉思 chénsī. **con·tem·pla·tive** /kən'templətɪv/ *adj* [正式用语]沉思的 chénsīde.

con·tem·por·ary /kən'temprərɪ/ *adj* **1** 同时〔時〕代的 tóngshídàide **2** 当〔當〕代的 dāngdàide □ *n* [C] [*pl* -ies] 同龄〔齡〕人 tónglíngrén, 同时代的人 tóngshídàide rén.

con·tempt /kən'tempt/ *n* [U] **1** 轻〔輕〕蔑 qīngmiè, 轻视 qīngshì. **2** 不顾〔顧〕búgù, 不尊敬 bù zūnjìng: *in ~ of the rules* 置规定于不顾. **~ible** *adj* 可轻视的 kě qīng shì de; 卑鄙的 bēibǐde. **~u·ous** /-tʃʊəs/ *adj* 轻视的 qīngshìde, 傲慢的 àomànde.

con·tend /kən'tend/ *vt/i* **1** 斗〔鬥〕争 dòuzhēng, 竞〔競〕争 jìngzhēng. **2** 争论〔論〕zhēnglùn; 主张 zhǔzhāng. **~er** 竞争者 jìngzhēngzhě, 对〔對〕手 duìshǒu.

con·tent[1] /kən'tent/ *adj* 满意的 mǎnyìde; 甘愿〔願〕的 gānyuànde: *~ to stay at home* 满足于呆在家里. □ *n* [U] 满意 mǎnyì, 满足mǎnzú. □ *vt* 使满意 shǐ mǎnyì. **~ed** *adj* 心满意足的 xīnmǎnyìzúde, 满意的 mǎnyìde. **~ed·ly** *adv* **~ment** *n* [U] 满意 mǎnyì.

con·tent[2] /'kɒntent/ *n* **1** [*pl*] 内容 nèiróng; 容纳物 róngnàwù: *the ~s of her bag* 她提包里装的东西. **2** [*pl*] (书籍)目录[錄]mùlù. **3** [C] (书籍)内容 nèiróng.

con·ten·tion /kən'tenʃn/ *n* **1** [U] 争论〔論〕zhēnglùn. **2** [C] 论点〔點〕lùndiǎn. **con·ten·tious** *adj* 好争论的 hào zhēnglùn de. 引起争论的 yǐnqǐ zhēnglùn de.

con·test[1] /'kɒntest/ *n* [C] 争夺〔奪〕zhēngduó 竞〔競〕争 jìngzhēng, 比赛 bǐsài. **~ant** /kən'testənt/, 竞争者 jìngzhēngzhě, 争夺者 zhēngduózhě.

con·test[2] /kən'test/ *vt/i* **1** 争论〔論〕zhēnglùn, 争议〔議〕zhēngyì. **2** = contend(1).

con·text /'kɒntekst/ *n* [C, U] **1** 上下文 shàngxiàwén, 前后〔後〕关〔關〕系 qiánhòu guānxì. **2** (事情的)来〔來〕龙〔龍〕去脉 láilóngqùmài. **~ual** /kən'tekstʃʊəl/ *adj* 上下文的 shàngxiàwénde.

con·ti·nent /'kɒntɪnənt/ *n* [C] **1** 大陆〔陸〕dàlù, 大洲 dàzhōu. **2** the C~ 欧〔歐〕洲大陆 ōuzhōu dàlù. **~al** /-'nentl/ *adj* **(a)** 大陆的 dàlùde, 大陆性的 dàlùxìngde. **(b)** 欧洲大陆的 ōuzhōu dàlù de.

con·tin·gency /kən'tɪndʒənsɪ/ *n* [C] [*pl* -ies] 偶然 ǒurán; 偶然事件 ǒurán shìjiàn: *prepared for every ~* 以防万一.

con·tin·gent /kən'tɪndʒənt/ *n* [C] **1** 分遣部队〔隊〕fēnqiǎn bùduì; 分遣舰队 fēnqiǎn jiànduì. **2** 构〔構〕成一个大集团的一批人 gòuchéng yígè dà jítuán de yìpīrén.

con·tin·ual /kən'tɪnjʊəl/ *adj* 频繁的 pínfánde, 不断〔斷〕的 búduàn de. **~ly** *adv* 不断地 búduànde, 一再地 yízàide.

con·tinue /kən'tɪnju:/ *vt/i* **1** 继〔繼〕续〔續〕jìxù, 延伸 yánshēn. **2** 恢复〔復〕huīfù. **con·ˌtinu'ation** *n* [C, U]

con·ti·nu·ity /ˌkɒntɪ'nju:ətɪ/ *n* [U] 继〔繼〕续〔續〕性 jìxùxìng.

con·tinu·ous /kən'tɪnjʊəs/ *adj* 继续的 jìxùde, 连〔連〕续的 liánxùde: *a ~ line (supply) of food* 源源不断的食品(供应). **~ly** *adv* **con·tinu·um** /kən'tɪnjʊəm/ *n* [*pl* -nums 或 -ua] **1** 连〔連〕续〔續〕统一体〔體〕liánxù tǒngyītǐ. **2** 连续统 liánxùtǒng, 闭〔閉〕连集 bìliánjí.

con·tort /kən'tɔ:t/ *vt* 扭弯〔彎〕niǔwān, 弄歪 nòngwāi. **con'tor·tion** /-ʃn/*n* [C, U]

con·tour /'kɒntʊə(r)/ *n* [C] 轮〔輪〕廓 lúnkuò, 外形 wàixíng. □ *vt* 画〔畫〕…的外形 huà...de wàixíng. '**~line** (地图的)等高线 děnggāoxiàn.

contra·band /'kɒntrəbænd/ *n* [U] 走私 zǒusī; 走私货 zǒusīhuò.

contra·cep·tion /ˌkɒntrə'sepʃn/ *n* [U] 避孕法 bìyùnfǎ. **contra·cep·tive** *n* [C] 避孕药 bìyùnyào. 避孕器具 bìyùnqìjiù. □ *adj* 避孕的 bìyùnde.

con·tract[1] /'kɒntrækt/ *n* [C,U] 合同 hétong; 契约 qìyuē. **~ual** /kən'træktʃʊəl/ *adj* 契约性的 qìyuēxìngde; 契约的 qìyuēde.

con·tract[2] /kən'trækt/ *vt/i* **1** 缔结 dìjié, 订约 dìngyuē. **2** 负(债) fù. **3** 得病 débìng. **~or** 订约人 dìngyuērén.

con·tract[3] /kən'trækt/ *vt/i* 缩小 suōxiǎo: *Metal ~s when it cools.* 金属遇冷时收缩. **con'trac·tion** /-ʃn/ *n* **(a)** [U] 收缩 shōusuō, 缩短 suōduǎn. **(b)** [C] 收缩物 shōusuōwù, 缩写〔寫〕式 suōxiěshì.

con·tra·dict /ˌkɒntrə'dɪkt/ *vt* **1** 反驳〔駁〕fǎnbó, 否认〔認〕fǒurèn, 驳斥 bóchì: *Don't ~ your mother.* 不要同你母亲顶嘴. **2** 同…矛盾 tóng...máodùn, 同…抵触〔觸〕tóng...dǐchù. **con·tra·dic·tion** /-ʃn/ *n* [C,U] **~ory** *adj* 矛盾的 máodùnde, 对〔對〕立的 duìlìde.

con·tralto /kən'træltəʊ/ *n* [C] [*pl* ~s] 女低音 nǚdīyīn.

con·trap·tion /kən'træpʃn/ *n* [C] [非正式用语]新发〔發〕明的玩意儿〔兒〕xīnfāmíng de wányì'ér; 奇特的装〔裝〕置 qítède zhuāngzhì.

con·trary[1] /'kɒntrərɪ/ *adj* **1** ~ to 相反的 xiāngfǎnde, 相对〔對〕的 xiāngduìde, 对抗的 duìkàngde: *~ to what you believe* 同你认为的相反. **2** (风,天气)不利的 búlìde. **3** [非正式用语]顽固的 wángùde, 不讲〔講〕理的 bù jiǎnglǐ de. **con·trari·ness** /'kɒntrərɪnɪs/ *n* [C] 固执〔執〕gùzhí, 倔强 juéjiàng.

con·trary[2] /'kɒntrərɪ/ *n* [C] [*pl* -ies] 反面 fǎnmiàn, 对〔對〕立面 duìlìmiàn. *on the ~* 正相反 zhèngxiāngfǎn. *to the ~* 意思相反的(地) yìsī xiāngfǎn de.

con·trast /kən'trɑ:st/ *vt/i* **1** 使对〔對〕比 shǐ duìbǐ, 使对照 shǐ duìzhào. **2** 形成对照 xíngchéng duìzhào: *His paintings ~ favourably with yours.* 他作的画比你好. □ /'kɒntrɑ:st/ *n* [C] 明显〔顯〕的差别 míngxiǎnde chābié.

con·tra·vene /ˌkɒntrə'vi:n/ *vt* 违〔違〕反 wéifǎn, 触〔觸〕犯 chùfàn. **con·tra·ven·tion** /kɒntrə'venʃn/

n [C,U]

con·trib·ute /kən'trɪbju:t/ *vt/i* **1** 贡献〔獻〕gòngxiàn, 捐助 juānzhù. **2** 促成 cùchéng: ~ *to his success* 促成他的成功. **3** 投稿 tóugǎo. **,con·tri'bu·tion** *n* [C, U] **con·tribu·tor** 捐助者 juānzhùzhě; 投稿者 tóugǎozhě. **con·tribu·tory** *adj*

con·trive /kən'traɪv/ *vt/i* 设计 shèjì; 发〔發〕明 fāmíng; 造成 zàochéng; 设法 shèfǎ: *He ~d to escape punishment.* 他设法逃避处罚. **con·triv·ance** *n* **(a)** [U] 发明 fāmíng; 设计 shèjì. **(b)** [C] 发明物 fāmíngwù.

con·trol /kən'trəʊl/ *n* **1** [U] 控制 kòngzhì, 支配 zhīpèi, 抑制 yìzhì. ***be*** (或 ***get***) ***out of*** ~ 失去控制 shīqù kòngzhì, 不受控制 búshòu kòngzhì **2** [C] 控制器 kòngzhìqì; 统制 tǒngzhì, 管理 guǎnlǐ: *~s on pollution* 污染控制装置. ⇨ birth-control. **3** [C] (鉴定实验结果)对〔對〕照标〔標〕准〔準〕duìzhào biāozhǔn. **4** [常作 *pl*] 操纵〔縱〕装〔裝〕置 cāozòng zhuāngzhì. □ *vt* [-ll-] **1** 控制 kòngzhì, 支配 zhīpèi. **2** 管理 guǎnlǐ. **3** 抑制 yìzhì. ~ *one's temper* 控制自己的脾气. **~ler** *n* [C] 管理员 guǎnlǐyuán, **~ tower** *n* 机〔機〕场〔場〕指挥〔揮〕塔台〔臺〕jīchǎng zhǐhuī tǎtái.

con·tro·versy /'kɒntrəvɜ:sɪ, kən'trɒvəsɪ/ *n* [C,U] [*pl* -ies] 论〔論〕战〔戰〕lùnzhàn. **con·tro·ver·sial** /,kɒntrə'vɜ:ʃl/ *adj* 引起争论的 yǐnqǐ zhēnglùn de.

con·va·lesce /,kɒnvə'les/ *vi* 痊愈 quányù. 恢复〔復〕健康 huīfù jiànkāng. **con·va·lescence** *n* [U] 恢复健康 huīfù jiànkāng; 恢复期 huīfùqī. **con·va·lescent** *n* [C], *adj* 恢复健康的人 huīfù jiànkāng de rén. 恢复健康的 huīfù jiànkāng de.

con·vene /kən'vi:n/ *vt/i* **1** 召集 zhāojí, 召唤 zhāohuàn. **2** 集合 jíhé. **con·vener** 召集人 zhāojírén.

con·veni·ence /kən'vi:nɪəns/ *n* **1** [U] 便利 biànlì, 方便 fāngbiàn. **2** [C] 便利的设施 biànlìde shèshī.

con·veni·ent /kən'vi:nɪənt/ *adj* 便利的 biànlìde, 方便的 fāngbiànde, 近便的 jìnbiànde: *a ~ place to stay* 停留的近便地方. **~ly** *adv*

con·vent /'kɒnvənt/ *n* [C] **1** 女修道会 nǚ xūdàohuì. ⇨ monastery. **2** 女修道院 nǚ xūdàoyuàn.

con·ven·tion /kən'venʃn/ *n* **1** [C] 会议〔議〕huìyì; 大会 dàhuì; 全国〔國〕性大会 quánguóxìng dàhuì. **2** [C] 协〔協〕定 xiédìng, 公约 gōngyuē. **3** [C] 惯例 guànlì, 常规 chángguī; 习〔習〕俗 xísú: *the ~s of writing letters* 写信的格式. **~al** *adj* 惯例的 guànlìde, 常规的 chángguīde, 传〔傳〕统的 chuántǒngde. **~ly** *adv*

con·verge /kən'vɜ:dʒ/ *vt/i* 会〔會〕聚 huìjù, 集中 jízhōng. **con·vergence** *n* [U]

con·ver·sa·tion /,kɒnvə'seɪʃn/ *n* [U,C] 会〔會〕话 huìhuà, 谈话 tánhuà. **~al** *adj* 会话的 huìhuàde, 谈话的 tánhuàde.

con·verse[1] /kən'vɜ:s/ *vi* [正式用语] 谈话 tánhuà.

con·verse[2] /'kɒnvɜ:s/ *n* [U 与 *the* 连用] *adj* 反题 fǎntí; 相反的 xiāng fǎnde, 逆的 nìde. **~ly** *adv*

con·ver·sion /kən'vɜ:ʃn/ *n* **1** [U] 变〔變〕换 biànhuàn, 转〔轉〕变 zhuǎnbiàn. **2** [C] (宗教、政党等) 皈依 guīyī, 改变 gǎibiàn; 兑换 duìhuàn.

con·vert[1] /'kɒnvɜ:t/ *n* [C] 皈依宗教者 guīyī zōngjiào zhě. 改变〔變〕宗教者 gǎibiàn zōngjiào zhě.

con·vert[2] /kən'vɜ:t/ *vt* **1** 转〔轉〕变〔變〕zhuǎnbiàn, 变换 biànhuàn; 兑换 duìhuàn: *to ~ pounds into francs* 把英镑兑换成法郎. **2** 使改变信仰 shǐ gǎibiàn xìnyǎng. **~-ible** /-əbl/ *adj* 可改变的 kě gǎibiàn de. 可变换的 kě biànhuàn de

con·vex /'kɒnveks/ *adj* 凸的 tūde, 凸面的 tūmiànde.

con·vey /kən'veɪ/ *vt* **1** 运〔運〕送 yùnsòng, 搬运 bānyùn. **2** 转〔轉〕达〔達〕, 传〔傳〕达(思想, 感情等) zhuǎndá; chuándá. **~er-belt** 传送带〔帶〕chuánsòngdài. **~ance** *n* [C, U] **(a)** 运输〔輸〕yùnshū, 搬运 bānyùn; 传达(思想等) chuándá. **(b)** 运输工具 yùnshū gōngjù.

con·vict[1] /'kɒnvɪkt/ *n* [C] 罪犯 zuìfàn.

con·vict[2] /kən'vɪkt/ *vt* 证〔證〕明…有罪 zhèngmíng…yǒu zuì; 宣判…有罪 xuānpàn…yǒu zuì.

con·vic·tion /kən'vɪkʃn/ *n* **1** [C, U] 定罪 dìngzuì; 证〔證〕明有罪 zhèngmíng yǒu zuì. **2** [C, U] 深信 shēnxìn, 确〔確〕信 quèxìn.

con·vince /kən'vɪns/ *vt* 使信服 shǐ xìnfú, 使确〔確〕信 shǐ quìxìn: *I ~d him that I was right.* 我使他确信我是对的. **con·vinc·ing** *adj* 有说服力的 yǒu shuōfúlì de; 使人深信的. shǐ rén shēnxìn de. **con·vin·cing·ly** *adv*

con·vo·ca·tion /ˌkɒnvəˈkeɪʃn/ *n* **1** [U] 召集 zhāojí. **2** [C] 集会〔會〕jíhuì; 宗教集会 zōngjiàojíhuì.

con·voy /ˈkɒnvɔɪ/ *n* **1** [U] 护〔護〕送 hùsòng; 护航 hùháng. *sail under* ~ 有保护的航行. **2** [C] 护航舰〔艦〕hùhángjiàn; 护航队〔隊〕hùhángduì. **3** [C] 被护航的船 bèi hùháng de chuán. □ *vt* 护航 hùháng.

con·vulse /kənˈvʌls/ *vt* 使剧〔劇〕烈震动〔動〕shǐ jùliè zhèndòng; 摇动 yáodòng. **conˈvul·sion** *n* [C] **con·vuls·ive** *adj*

coo /kuː/ *vt/i*, *n* [C] (鸽)咕咕叫 gūgūjiào.

cook /kʊk/ *vt/i* **1** 烹调 pēngtiáo; 烧〔燒〕shāo, 煮 zhǔ. **2** 被煮 bèi zhǔ, 被烧 bèi shāo. **3** 伪〔偽〕造 wěizào; 窜〔竄〕改 cuàngǎi: ~ *the accounts* (*books*) 伪造帐册. □ *n* [C] 厨师〔師〕chúshī. **~er** *n* [C] 炊具 chuījù. **~ery** *n* [U] 烹调艺〔藝〕术〔術〕pēngtiáo yìshù **~ing** *n* [U]

cool[1] /kuːl/ *adj* [-er, -est] **1** 凉的 liángde, 凉快的 liángkuàide. **2** 沉着的 chénzhuóde, 冷静的 lěngjìngde. **ˌcool-ˈheaded** *adj* 头〔頭〕脑冷静的 tóunǎo lěngjìng de. *play it* ~ 抑制住感情 yìzhìzhù gǎnqíng, 不表态〔態〕bù biǎotài. **3** 厚颜的 hòuyánde, 无〔無〕耻的 wúchǐde. **4** 冷淡的 lěngdànde. □*n* [U, 与 *the* 连用] 凉 liáng; 凉快的地方 liángkuaide dìfang; 凉快的空气〔氣〕liángkuaide kōngqì. **~ly** *adv* **~ness** *n* [U]

cool[2] /kuːl/ *vt/i* 使冷却 shǐ lěngquè; 变〔變〕凉 biànliáng. ~ *down* (或 *off*). 〔喻〕平静下来〔來〕píngjìng xiàlái.

coop /kuːp/ *n* [C] 笼〔籠〕lóng; 鸡〔鷄〕笼 jīlóng. □ *vt* ~ *up* 禁闭〔閉〕jìnbì.

Co-op=Co-operative Society 合作社 hézuòshè.

co-op·er·ate /kəʊˈɒpəreɪt/ *vt* 协〔協〕作 xiézuò, 合作 hézuò. **co-op·eˈr·ation** *n* [U] **co-op·er·ative** *adj* 愿〔願〕意合作的 yuànyì hézuò de. □ *n* [C] 合作社 hézuòshè.

co-opt /kəʊˈɒpt/ *vt* (由原有成员)增选〔選〕某人为〔爲〕成员 zēngxuǎn mǒurén wéi chéngyuán.

co-or·di·nate[1] /ˌkəʊˈɔːdɪnət/ *adj* 同等的 tóngděngde. □ *n* [C] 同等的人或事物 tóngděngderén huò shìwù.

co-or·di·nate[2] /ˌkəʊˈɔːdɪneɪt/ *vt* 使协〔協〕调 shǐ xiétiáo. **ˌco-or-diˈna·tion** *n* [C,U]

coot /kuːt/ *n* [C] 大鹬〔鷸〕dàfán.

cop /kɒp/ *n* [C] [俚语] = policeman.

cope /kəʊp/ *vi* 对〔對〕付 duìfu, 妥善处〔處〕理 tuǒshàn chǔlǐ. *She couldn't* ~ *with all her work.* 她不能妥善处理自己的全部工作.

copi·ous /ˈkəʊpɪəs/ *adj* [正式用语] 丰〔豐〕富的 fēngfùde, 富饶〔饒〕的 fùráode: *a* ~ *supply* 丰富的供应. **~ly** *adv*

cop·per[1] /ˈkɒpə(r)/ *n* **1** [U] 铜(化学符号 Cu) tóng. **2** [C] 铜币〔幣〕tóngbì. **3** [C] 金属〔屬〕锅 jīnshǔguō. ⇨ boiler. **4** [U] 铜色 tóngsè. □ *adj* 铜色的 tóngsède. **ˈ~-plate** *n* [U] 铜板 tóngbǎn; 铜版 tóngbǎn.

cop·per[2] /ˈkɒpə(r)/ *n* [C] [俚语] = policeman.

copse /kɒps/ *n* [C] 小灌木林 xiǎo guànmùlín; 矮树〔樹〕林 ǎishùlín.

copu·late /ˈkɒpjʊleɪt/ *vi* 交配 jiāopèi, 交媾 jiāogòu. **copuˈla·tion** *n* [C, U]

copy[1] /ˈkɒpɪ/ *n* [C] [*pl* -ies] **1** 抄本 chāoběn, 副本 fùběn, 复〔複〕制〔製〕品 fùzhìpǐn; (电影)拷贝 kǎobèi. **2** 一本 yìběn, 一册 yícè, 一份 yífèn.

copy[2] /ˈkɒpɪ/ *vt/i* [*pt*, *pp* -ied] **1** 抄写〔寫〕chāoxiě; 复〔複〕制 fùzhì. **2** 模仿 mófǎng. **3** 抄袭〔襲〕chāoxí.

copy·right /ˈkɒpɪraɪt/ *n* [U] 版权〔權〕bǎnquán. □ *vt* 保护〔護〕版权 bǎohù bǎnquán.

coral /ˈkɒrəl/ *n* [U] 珊瑚 shānhú. □ *adj* 珊瑚的 shānhúde.

cord /kɔːd/ *n* **1** [C, U] 粗线 cūxiàn; 细绳〔繩〕xìshéng; 索 suǒ. **2** [C] 人体〔體〕的带〔帶〕状〔狀〕部分 réntǐde dàizhuàng bùfen: *the vocal* ~*s* 声带.

cor·dial /ˈkɔːdɪəl/ *adj* 热〔熱〕诚的 rèchéngde; 衷心的 zhōngxīnde; 亲〔親〕切的 qīnqiède. **~ly** *adv*

cor·don /ˈkɔːdn/ *n* [C] 警戒线 jǐngjièxiàn; 警卫〔衛〕圈 jǐngwèiquān. □ *vt* ~ *off* 用警戒线围〔圍〕住 yòng jǐngjièxiàn wéizhù: *The army* ~*ed off the area.* 军队警戒了这个地区.

cor·du·roy /ˈkɔːdərɔɪ/ *n* [U] 灯芯〔蕊〕绒 dēngxīnróng.

core /kɔː(r)/ *n* [C] **1** 果实〔實〕的心 guǒshíde xīn. **2** 核心 héxīn; 精髓 jīngsuí. *to the* ~ 彻〔徹〕底 chèdǐ. □ *vt* 挖去…的果心 wāqù …de guǒxīn.

cork /kɔːk/ *n* **1** [U] 软〔軟〕木

ruǎnmù. 2 [C] 软木塞 ruǎnmùsāi. □ *vt* 塞住 sāizhù. '~**screw** 瓶塞钻〔鑽〕píngsāi zuàn.

corn[1] /kɔːn/ *n* 1 [U] 谷〔穀〕物 gǔwù; 五谷 wǔgǔ. 2 [C] 谷粒 gǔlì. '~-**cob** 玉米穗轴〔軸〕yùmǐ suìzhóu. '~**flour** 玉米粉 yùmǐfěn.

corn[2] /kɔːn/ *n* [C] 鸡〔鷄〕眼 jīyǎn, 钉胼 dīngpián.

cor·nea /'kɔːnɪə/ *n* [C] [*pl* ~s] 角膜 jiǎomó.

cor·ner /'kɔːnə(r)/ *n* [C] 1 角 jiǎo; 犄角 jījiao. *a tight* ~ 困境 kùnjìng; 绝路 juélù. 2 冷僻地方 lěngpìdìfang; 角落 jiǎoluò. 3 地区〔區〕dìqū: *from all ~s of the world* 从世界各地. □ *vt/i* 1 逼入困境 bīrù kùnjìng 使走投无〔無〕路 shǐ zǒutóu wúlù. 2 转〔轉〕弯〔彎〕zhuǎn wān.

cor·net /'kɔːnɪt/ *n* [C] 1 (乐器) 短号〔號〕duǎnhào. 2 (盛冰淇淋等的) 锥形鸡〔鷄〕蛋卷 zhuīxíng jīdànjuǎn.

cor·nice /'kɔːnɪs/ *n* [C] (建筑)上楣(柱) shàngméi; 檐口 yánkǒu.

cor·on·ary /'kɒrənrɪ/ *adj* 冠状〔狀〕动〔動〕脉〔脈〕guānzhuàng dòngmài. □ *n* [C] [*pl* -ies] (亦作~ **thrombosis**) 冠状动脉血栓形成 guānzhuàng dòngmài xuèshuān xíngchéng.

cor·on·ation /ˌkɒrə'neɪʃn/ *n* [C] 加冕典礼〔禮〕jiāmiǎn diǎnlǐ.

cor·oner /'kɒrənə(r)/ *n* [C] 验〔驗〕尸官 yànshīguān.

cor·onet /'kɒrənet/ *n* [C] (贵族戴的)小冠冕 xiǎo guānmiǎn.

Corp.,Cpl =Corporal.

cor·poral[1] /'kɔːpərəl/ *adj* 肉体〔體〕的 ròutǐde, 身体的 shēntǐde: ~ *punishment* 肉刑 ròuxíng; 体罚 tǐfá.

cor·poral[2] /'kɔːpərəl/ *n* [C] (军队) 下士 xiàshì.

cor·por·ate /'kɔːpərət/ *adj* 1 社团〔團〕的 shètuánde; 法人的 fǎrénde. 2 共同的 gòngtóngde, 全体〔體〕的 quántǐde: ~ *responsibility* 共同的责任.

cor·por·ation /ˌkɔːpə'reɪʃn/ *n* [C] 1 市镇自治机〔機〕关〔關〕shì zhèn zìzhì jīguān 2 法人 fǎrén, 公司 gōngsī; 社团〔團〕shètuán.

corps /kɔː(r)/ *n* [C] [*pl* ~ /kɔːz/] 1 技术〔術〕兵种〔種〕jìshù bīngzhǒng; 特殊兵种 tèshū bīngzhǒng: *the Medical C*~ 医疗队. 2 军〔軍〕团〔團〕jūntuán; 军 jūn.

corpse /kɔːps/ *n* [C] 尸体〔體〕shītǐ, 死尸 sǐshī.

cor·puscle /'kɔːpʌsl/ *n* [C] 血球 xuèqiú.

cor·ral /kə'rɑːl/ *n* [C] 畜栏〔欄〕xùlán. □ *vt* [-ll-] 把…关〔關〕进〔進〕畜栏 bǎ...guānjìn xùlán.

cor·rect[1] /kə'rekt/ *adj* 1 正确〔確〕的 zhèngquède: *the ~ answer* 正确的答案. 2 恰当〔當〕的 qiàdàngde; 端正的 duānzhèngde. ~**ly** *adv* ~**ness** *n* [U]

cor·rect[2] /kə'rekt/ *vt* 1 改正 gǎizhèng; 纠正 jiūzhèng, 修正 xiūzhèng. 2 责备〔備〕zébèi, 惩〔懲〕罚 chěngfá. **cor'rec·tion** /-ʃn/ *n* (a) [U] 改正 gǎizhèng, 纠正 jiūzhèng, 修改 xiūgǎi. (b) [C] 修改之处〔處〕xiūgǎi zhī chù, 改正的东〔東〕西 gǎizhèngde dōngxi: *C~s are written in red ink* 修改之处用红墨水书写. ~**ive** *n, adj*

cor·re·late /'kɒrəleɪt/ *vt/i* (使)相互关〔關〕联〔聯〕xiānghù guānlián: *try to ~ two sets of facts* 设法把两组事实联系起来. **cor·re'la·tion** *n* [C] 互相关系 hùxiāng guānxì.

cor·re·spond /ˌkɒrɪ'spɒnd/ *vi* 1 符合 fúhé, 一致 yízhì. 2 ~ *to* 相当〔當〕于 xiāngdāngyú; 相等 xiāng děng; 相似 xiāngsì; 相称〔稱〕xiāngchèn. 3 通信 tōngxìn. ~**ing** *adj* 相等的 xiāngděngde; 相称的 xiāngchènde; 相当的 xiāngdāngde. ~**ing·ly** *adv*

cor·re·spon·dence /ˌkɒrɪ'spɒndəns/ *n* 1 [C, U] 符合 fúhé, 一致 yízhì. 2 [U] 通信 tōngxìn, 信件 xìnjiàn. **cor·re·spon·dent** *n* [C] (a) 通信者 tōngxìnzhě. (b) (新闻)通讯员 tōngxùnyuán; 记者 jìzhě.

cor·ri·dor /'kɒrɪdɔː(r)/ *n* [C] 走廊 zǒuláng; 通路 tōnglù; 回〔迴〕廊 huíláng.

cor·rob·or·ate /kə'rɒbəreɪt/ *vt* 巩固(信仰) gǒnggù; 证〔證〕实〔實〕zhèngshí.

cor·rode /kə'rəʊd/ *vt/i* 腐蚀 fǔshí; 侵蚀 qīnshí.

cor·rosion /kə'rəʊʒn/ *n* [U] 1 腐蚀 fǔshí; 侵蚀 qīnshí. 2 锈 xiù, 铁〔鐵〕锈 tiěxiù: *There's a lot of ~ on my car.* 我的汽车上有不少的锈. **cor·ros·ive** /kə'rəʊsɪv/ *n* [C], *adj* 腐蚀剂〔劑〕fǔshíjì. 腐蚀的 fǔshíde.

cor·ru·gate /'kɒrəgeɪt/ *vt/i* 弄皱〔皺〕nòngzhòu; 起皱 qǐzhòu.

cor·rupt /kə'rʌpt/ *adj* 腐败的 fǔbàide; 贪污的 tānwūde. □ *vt/i* (使)腐败 fǔbài, 贿赂 huìlù. **cor·rup·tion** /-ʃn/ *n* [U] *adj*

cor·set /'kɔːsɪt/ *n* [C] 妇〔婦〕女紧〔緊〕身胸衣 fùnǚ jǐnshēn xiōngyī.

cor·tege, cor·tège /kɔː'teɪʒ/ *n*

[C] (送葬人的)行列 hángliè; 随从〔從〕们〔們〕 suícóngmén.

cosh /kɒʃ/ *vt, n* [C] [英国俚语] 内装〔裝〕金属〔屬〕的橡皮棒 nèizhuāng jīnshǔ de xiàngpíbàng; 用棍棒打 yòng gùnbàng dǎ.

cos·metic /kɒz'metɪk/ *adj, n* [C] 化妆〔粧〕品 huàzhuāngpǐn; 化妆用的 huàzhuāng yòng de.

cos·mic /'kɒzmɪk/ *adj* 宇宙的 yǔzhòude.

cos·mo·naut /'kɒzmənɔ:t/ *n* [C] = astronaut.

cos·mo·poli·tan /ˌkɒzmə'pɒlɪtən/ *adj* **1** 全世界的 quánshìjiède. **2** 世界主义〔義〕的 shìjièzhǔyìde. □ *n* [C] 世界主义者 shìjièzhǔyìzhě.

cos·mos /'kɒzmɒs/ *n* **the** ~ 宇宙 yǔzhòu.

cost[1] /kɒst/ *n* **1** [C, U] 费用 fèiyòng; 成本 chéngběn. **2** 代价〔價〕dàijià: *the ~ of victory* 胜利的代价. ***to one's*** ~ 吃了苦头〔頭〕之后〔後〕才…chī le kǔtou zhīhòu cái …. ***at all ~s*** 不惜任何代价 bùxī rènhé dàijià. **3** [*pl*] [法律]诉讼费 sùsòngfèi.

cost[2] /kɒst/ *vi* [*pt, pp* ~] **1** 价〔價〕值为〔爲〕 jiàzhí wéi: *Shoes ~ £20 a pair.* 鞋每双二十英镑. **2** 花费 huāfèi, 使失去 shǐ shīqù: *~ many lives* 使许多人丧失了生命 □ *vt* [*pt pp* ~ed] 估定商品价格 gūdìng shāngpǐn jiàgé.

cost·ly /'kɒstlɪ/ *adj* [-ier, -iest] 价〔價〕值高的 jiàzhí gāo de, 昂贵的 ángguìde.

cos·tume /'kɒstju:m/ *n* **1** [U] 服装〔裝〕式样〔樣〕 fúzhuāng shìyàng. **2** [C] 化装服 huàzhuāngfú; 戏〔戲〕服 xìfú.

cosy[1] /'kəʊzɪ/ *adj* [-ier, -iest] 温暖而舒适〔適〕的 wēnnuǎn ér shūshì de, 安逸的 ānyìde. **cosily** *adv* **cosi·ness** *n* [U]

cosy[2] /'kəʊzɪ/ *n* [C] 茶壶上保暖的棉罩 cháhú shàng bǎonuǎn de miánzhào.

cot /kɒt/ *n* [C] 儿〔兒〕童床 értóngchuáng.

cot·tage /'kɒtɪdʒ/ *n* [C] 村舍 cūnshè, 小屋 xiǎowū.

cot·ton /'kɒtn/ *n* [U] **1** 棉花 miánhua; 棉 mián. **2** 棉线 miánxiàn; 棉布 miánbù. ˌ~-'**wool** 原棉 yuánmián; 脱脂棉 tuōzhīmián; 棉花 miánhua.

couch[1] /kaʊtʃ/ *n* [C] 长〔長〕沙发〔發〕 cháng shāfā.

couch[2] /kaʊtʃ/ *vt* 表达〔達〕biǎodá: *A reply ~ed in formal terms* 正式措词的答复.

cou·gar /'ku:gə(r)/ *n* [C] (*=puma*) 美洲狮 měizhōushī.

cough /kɒf/ *n* [C] **1** 咳嗽 késou, 咳嗽声〔聲〕 késoushēng. **2** 咳嗽病 késoubìng. □ *vt/i* 咳嗽 késou.

could /kʊd 弱式: kəd/ *aux verb*; *pt* of *can*.

coun·cil /'kaʊnsl/ *n* [C] 政务〔務〕会〔會〕 zhèngwùhuì; 会议〔議〕huìyì; 委员会 wěiyuánhuì; 理事会 lǐshìhuì. '~-**house** 市议〔議〕会所有的房产〔產〕 shìyìhuì suǒyǒude fángchǎn. ~**lor** [美语 =-**cilor**] *n* [C] 地方议会议员 dìfāng yìhuì yìyuán.

coun·sel /'kaʊnsl/ *n* **1** [U] 忠告 zhōnggào, 劝〔勸〕告 quàngào; 商议〔議〕 shāngyì, 评议 píngyì. **2** [C] [*pl* ~] 律师〔師〕lǜshī. □ *vt* [-ll-, 美语亦作 -l-] [正式用语]忠告 zhōnggào; 劝〔勸〕告 quàngào. ~**lor** [美语 =-**selor**] *n* [C] 顾〔顧〕问〔問〕 gùwèn.

count[1] /kaʊnt/ *n* [C] **1** 点〔點〕diǎn, 数〔數〕 shǔ; 得数 déshù: *There were 50, at the last ~* 最后一次点数是 50. ***make a ~ of*** 点…的数. **2** [法律]被控告事项 bèi kònggào shìxiàng: *guilty on all ~s* 被控各项均为有罪.

count[2] /kaʊnt/ *vt/i* **1** 点〔點〕diǎn, 数〔數〕 shǔ: *Has John learned to ~ yet at school?* 约翰在学校里学数数了吗? **2** 计数 jìshù. **3** 计算在内 jìsuàn zàinèi: *ten people, ~ing John* 约翰计算在内, 十个人. **4** 认〔認〕为〔爲〕 rènwéi, 看作 kànzuò: *~ oneself lucky* 认为自己幸运. **5** 重要 zhòngyào; 有考虑〔慮〕价〔價〕值 yǒu kǎolǜ jiàzhí: *Every minute ~s.* 每一分钟都重要. **6** ~ **(sth) against sb** 认为…是不利于…的 rènwéi… shì búlìyú…de. ~ **on** (或 **upon**) 依靠 yīkào, 期待 qīdài, 指望 zhǐwàng. ~***out*** **(a)** 点…的数 diǎn… de shù. **(b)** 把…不计在内 bǎ…bújì zài nèi: *C~ me out, I'm not going.* 不算我, 我不去. ~ ***up*** 把…加起来〔來〕 bǎ…jiā qǐlái. ˌ~**down** *n* (用)倒数方式(计算发射导弹前的秒数) dàoshù fāngshì.

count[3] /kaʊnt/ *n* [C] (法国, 意大利等)伯爵 bójué.

count·able /'kaʊntəbl/ *adj* 可数的 kěshǔde, 可计算的 kě jìsuàn de.

coun·ten·ance[1] /'kaʊntɪnəns/ *n* [正式用语] **1** [C] 面目 miànmù; 面部表情 miànbùbiǎoqíng, 面容 miànróng, 脸〔臉〕色 liǎnsè. **2** [U] 赞助 zànzhù, 支持 zhīchí; 鼓励〔勵〕 gǔlì.

coun·ten·ance[2] /'kaʊntɪnəns/ *vt*

[正式用语]赞成 zànchéng, 支持 zhīchí, 鼓励[勵] gǔlì: *I cannot ~ violence.* 我不能鼓励暴力.

coun·ter[1] /'kaʊntə(r)/ *n* [C] 柜[櫃]台[臺] guìtái.

coun·ter[2] /'kaʊntə(r)/ *n* [C] **1** 游戏[戲]等记分用的筹[籌]码[碼] yóuxì děng jìfēn yòng de chóumǎ. **2** 计数[數]器 jìshùqì.

coun·ter[3] /'kaʊntə(r)/ *adv* ~ *to* 相反地 xiāngfǎnde, 违[違]反 wéifǎn, 与[與]…背道而驰[馳] yǔ… bèidào ér chí.

coun·ter[4] /'kaʊntə(r)/ *vt*/*i* 反对[對] fǎnduì; 反击[擊] fǎnjī: ~ *his arguments* 反对他的说法.

coun·ter- /ˌkaʊntə(r)-/ *prefix* **1** 反 fǎn, 逆 nì: ˌ~-*pro'ductive.* 有碍[礙]于进展的. **2** 回报[報]huíbào: '~-*attack* 反攻,反击. **3** 对[對]应[應] duìyìng: '~ *part*配对物或人; 对应物或人.

coun·ter·act /ˌkaːʊntə'rækt/ *vt* 抵抗 dǐkàng, 抵制 dǐzhì; 阻碍[礙] zǔ'ài, 抵销 dǐxiāo: ~ *a poison* 抵消毒物的作用.

coun·ter·bal·ance/'kaʊntəbæləns/ *n* [C] 平衡 pínghéng; 抗衡 kànghéng; 平衡力 pínghénglì. □ *vt* /ˌkaʊntə'bæləns/ 使平衡 shǐ pínghéng; 抵销 dǐxiāo.

coun·ter·feit /'kaʊntəfɪt/ *n* [C], *adj* 伪[僞]造的 wěizàode, 假冒的 jiǎmàode, 仿造的 fǎngzàode: ~ *banknotes* 假钞票. □ *vt* 伪造 wěizào, 仿造 fǎngzào.

coun·ter·foil /'kaʊntəfɔɪl/ *n* [C] (支票,收据等的)存根 cúngēn.

coun·ter·mand /ˌkaʊntə'maːnd/ *vt* 取消, 撤回(命令等) qǔxiāo, chèhuí.

coun·ter·part /'kaʊntəpaːt/ *n* [C] 对[對]应[應]物或人 duìyìng wù huò rén, 配对人或物 pèiduì rén huò wù.

coun·ter·sign /'kaʊntəsaɪn/ *vt* 连[連]署 liánshǔ, 会[會]签[簽] huìqiān, 副署 fùshǔ.

count·ess /'kaʊntɪs/ *n* [C] 伯爵夫人 bójué fūrén.

count·less /'kaʊntlɪs/ *adj* 无[無]数[數]的 wúshùde; 数不清的 shǔbùqīngde.

coun·try /'kʌntrɪ/ *n* [*pl* -ies] **1** [C] 国[國]家 guójiā. **2** [C] 家乡[鄉] jiāxiāng, 故乡 gùxiāng; 祖国 zǔguó; 国籍所属[屬]的国家 guójí suǒshǔ de guójiā. **3 the** ~ 国民 guómín; 选[選]民 xuǎnmín. ***go to the*** ~ 举[舉]行大选 jǔxíng dàxuǎn. **4 the** ~ 土地 tǔdì. **5** 农[農]村 nóngcūn. **6** [用作定语]乡下的 xiāngxiade, 农村的 nóngcūnde.

coun·try·man /'kʌntrɪmən/, **coun·try·woman** /'kʌntrɪwʊmən/ *n* [C] [*pl* -men, -women] **1** 农[農]村人 nóngcūnrén, 农民 nóngmín. **2** 同胞 tóngbāo.

coun·try·side /'kʌntrɪsaɪd/ *n* [U] 农[農]村 nóngcūn, 乡[鄉]村 xiāngcūn.

county /'kaʊntɪ/ *n* [*pl* -ies] [C] 郡jùn; 县[縣] xiàn.

coup /kuː/ *n* [C] [*pl* ~s /kuːz/] **1** 突然行动[動] tūrán xíngdòng; 军[軍]事政变[變] jūnshì zhèngbiàn. **2** (亦作 ~ **d'etat**) 政变 zhèngbiàn.

couple[1] /'kʌpl/ *n* [C] **1** 一对[對] yīduì, 一双[雙] yīshuāng. **2** 夫妇[婦] fūfù.

couple[2] /'kʌpl/ *vt*/*i* **1** 使连[連]接 shǐ liánjiē, 使接合 shǐ jiēhé: ~ *two railway carriages* 把两节火车客车挂在一起. **2** (动物)交尾 jiāowěi; 连结 liánjiē, 接合 jiēhé.

coup·let /'kʌplɪt/ *n* [C] 两[兩]行诗 liǎnghángshī; 对[對]联[聯] duìlián, 对句 duìjù

coup·ling /'kʌplɪŋ/ *n* [C] 连[連]接器 liánjiēqì. (火车)车[車]钩 chēgōu, 挂[掛]钩 guàgōu.

cou·pon /'kuːpɒn/ *n* [C] 证[證]明持券人有某种[種]权[權]利的卡片,票,证 zhèngmíng chíquànrén yǒu mǒuzhǒng quánlì de kǎpiàn, piào, zhèng.

cour·age /'kʌrɪdʒ/ *n* [U] 勇气[氣] yǒngqì, 胆[膽]量 dǎnliàng. ~**ous** /kə'reɪdʒəs/ *adj* 英勇的 yīngyǒngde, 有胆量的 yǒu dǎnliàng de. ~**ous·ly** *adv*

cour·gette /kʊə'ʒet/ *n* [C] [美语 =*zucchini*] 葫芦[蘆]科蔬菜 húlukē shūcài.

cour·ier /'kʊrɪə(r)/ *n* [C] **1** 被雇用照料旅行事务[務]并陪伴旅客的服务员 bèi gùyòng zhàoliào lǚxíng shìwù bìng péibàn lǚkè de fúwùyuán. **2** 信使 xìnshǐ; 送急件的人 sòng jíjiàn de rén.

course[1] /kɔːs/ *n* **1** [C] 进行方向 jìnxíng fāngxiàng, 路线 lùxiàn: *the ~ of a river* 河流所经区域. ~ *of a rocket* 导弹的轨道. ***(as) a matter of*** ~ 当[當]然之事 dāngrán zhī shì, 自然之事 zìrán zhī shì. ***of*** ~ 当然 dāngrán, 自然 zìrán. **2** [C] 跑道 pǎodào. **3** [C] 课程 kèchéng, 学[學]程 xuéchéng. **4** [C] 一道菜 yīdàocài. ***in due*** ~ 及时[時]地 jíshíde, 在适[適]当[當]的时候 zài shìdāngde shíhòu.

in the ~ of 在…的期间〔間〕 zài …de qījiān, 在…的过程中 zài… de guòchéng zhōng.

course² /kɔːs/ *vt/i* 1 运〔運〕行 yùnxíng; 流淌 liútǎng. 2 (猎犬)追猎〔獵〕 zhuīliè.

court¹ /kɔːt/ *n* 1 [C] 法院 fǎyuàn, 法庭 fǎtíng. 2 **the** ~ 宫廷 gōngtíng, 朝廷 cháotíng. 3 [C] 球场〔場〕 qiúchǎng: *a tennis* ~ 网球场. '~**yard** 庭院 tíngyuàn, 院子 yuànzi.

court² /kɔːt/ *vt/i* 1 讨好 tǎohǎo, 奉承 fèngcheng; 求爱〔愛〕 qiú'ài: *He ~ed Mary for two years.* 他向玛丽求爱有两年时间. 2 招致 zhāozhì, 招惹 zhāorě: ~ *disaster* 招致灾难.

cour·teous /'kɜːtɪəs/ *adj* 有礼〔禮〕貌的 yǒu lǐmào de; 殷勤的 yīnqínde. ~**ly** *adv*

cour·tesy /'kɜːtəsɪ/ *n* [*pl* -ies] 1 [C, U] 礼〔禮〕貌 lǐmào; 谦恭 qiāngōng. 2 *by* ~ *of* 蒙…的好意 méng… de hǎoyì; 蒙…的允许 méng … de yǔnxǔ.

court·ier /'kɔːtɪə(r)/ *n* [C] 廷臣 tíngchén, 朝臣 cháochén.

court-mar·tial /ˌkɔːt'mɑːʃl/ *n* [C] [*pl* ~s-martial] 军〔軍〕事法庭 jūnshì fǎtíng, 军事审〔審〕判 jūnshì shěnpàn. □ *vt* [-ll-] 军事审判(某人) jūnshì shěnpàn.

court·ship /'kɔːtʃɪp/ *n* [C, U] 求爱〔愛〕 qiú'ài, 求婚 qiúhūn; 求爱期间〔間〕 qiú'ài qījiān.

cousin /'kʌzn/ *n* [C]: 堂, 表兄弟 táng biǎo xiōngdì; 堂, 表姐妹 táng biǎo jiěmèi. (*first*) ~ 堂, 表兄弟或姐妹; *second* ~ 父母的堂, 表兄弟或姐妹所生的孩子.

cove /kəʊv/ *n* [C] 小海湾〔灣〕 xiǎo hǎiwān.

cover¹ /'kʌvə(r)/ *n* 1 [C] 盖子 gàizi; 套子 tàozi: *a chair* ~ 椅套. 2 [C] (书, 杂志)封面 fēngmiàn; 封底 fēngdǐ. 3 [C] 封皮 fēngpí, 包皮 bāopí. *under separate* ~另邮〔郵〕寄达〔達〕 lìngyóu jìdá. 4 [U] 庇护〔護〕所 pìhùsuǒ; 隐蔽处〔處〕 yǐnbìchù. *take* ~ 隐蔽 yǐnbì, 躲避 duǒbì. 5 [U] *under* ~ *of* 在…掩护下 zài…yǎnhùxià; 趁着 chènzhe: *under* ~ *of friendship* (*darkness*) 在友谊(黑暗)的掩护下. 6 [U] 掩护陆〔陸〕海军〔軍〕作战〔戰〕的空军能力 yǎnhù lù hǎi jūn zuòzhàn de kōngjūn nénglì. 7 安全保险〔險〕 ānquán bǎoxiǎn.

cover² /'kʌvə(r)/ *vt* 1 遮盖zhēgài, 遮掩 zhēyǎn: ~ *a chair* (*one's face*) 把椅子(某人的脸)遮起来. ~ *up* 遮盖 zhēgài, 掩饰 yǎnshì. 2 *be ~ed with* (a) 被落满 bèi luòmǎn, 被盖满 bèi gàimǎn: *hills ~ed with snow* 满山是雪. (b) 天然生有(毛, 皮等) tiānrán shēng yǒu. 3 行过〔過〕路程 xíngguò lùchéng. 4 枪〔槍〕口对〔對〕准〔準〕某人 qiāngkǒu duìzhǔn mǒurén. 5 (钱)够用 gòuyòng, 支付 zhīfù: *write a cheque to* ~ *expenses* 签一张支票清偿费用. 6 包括 bāokuò, 包含 bāohán: *His researches ~ed a wide field.* 他的研究包括很广的范围. 7 (记者)采访(某一事件) cǎifǎng. ~**age** *n* [U] 采访新闻〔聞〕 cǎifǎng xīnwēn. ⇨ cover²(7).

cov·ert¹ /'kʌvət/ *adj* 隐蔽的 yǐnbìde, 暗地里的 àndìlǐde, 偷偷摸摸的 tōutōumōmōde. ~**ly** *adv*

cov·ert² /'kʌvət/ *n* [C] 小兽〔獸〕等的隐蔽处〔處〕 xiǎoshòu děng de yǐnbìchù.

cow¹ /kaʊ/ *n* [C] 1 母牛 mǔniú, 奶牛 nǎiniú. 2 (象, 鲸, 犀牛等) 母兽〔獸〕 mǔshòu. '~**boy** (美国西部)牛仔 niúzǎi. '~**hand**, '~**herd** 牧牛人 mùniúrén. '~**hide** 牛皮 niúpí.

cow² /kaʊ/ *vt* 吓〔嚇〕唬 xiàhu, 威胁〔脅〕 wēixié.

cow·ard /'kaʊəd/ *n* [C] 1 胆〔膽〕小者 dǎnxiǎozhě. 2 懦夫 nuòfū. ~**ly** *adj* (a) 懦怯的 nuòqiède. (b) 胆小的 dǎnxiǎode. **cow·ardice** /-dɪs/ *n* [U]

cower /'kaʊə(r)/ *vi* 畏缩 wèisuō, 抖缩 dǒusuō.

cowl /kaʊl/ *n* [C] 1 带〔帶〕头〔頭〕巾的僧衣 dài tóujīn de sēngyī, 僧衣的头巾 sēngyīde tóujīn. 2 烟囱帽 yāncōngmào.

cox /kɒks/ *n* [C] [非正式用语] coxswain 的缩略. □ *vt/i* 做赛船的舵手 zuò sàichuánde duòshǒu.

cox·swain /'kɒksn/ *n* [C] 赛船的舵手 sàichuánde duòshǒu.

coy /kɔɪ/ *adj* [-er, -est] (女子)怕羞的 pàxiūde; 装〔裝〕着怕羞的 zhuāngzhe pàxiūde. ~**ly** *adv*

coy·ote /'kɔɪəʊt/ *n* [C] 美国西北部的小狼 měiguó xīpěibù de xiǎoláng.

cp.=compare.

Cr.=creditor.

crab / kræb/ *n* [C] 蟹 xiè; 蟹肉 xièròu.

crack¹ /kræk/ *n* [C] 1 裂缝 lièfèng. 2 破裂声〔聲〕 pòlièshēng; 爆裂声 bāolièshēng. *the* ~ *of a whip* 抽鞭子的噼啪声. *the* ~ *of a rifle* 枪声. 3 (砰的)一击〔擊〕 yījī: *a* ~ *on the head* 迎头一击. □ *adj* 第一流的 dìyīliúde: *He's a* ~

shot. 他是一名神枪手.

crack² /kræk/ *vt/i* **1** 使破裂 shǐ pòliè, 裂开〔開〕 lièkāi: ~ *a plate* 把盘子碰裂. **2** (使) 噼啪作响〔響〕 pīpā zuòxiǎng. **3** 声〔聲〕音变〔變〕哑〔啞〕 shēngyīn biàn yǎ; 男孩声音变粗 nánhái shēngyīn biàn cū. **4** 解开〔開〕(难题,密码) jiěkāi. **5** ~ ***down on*** (***sb***, ***sth***) 处〔處〕罚 chǔfá. ~ ***up*** 衰退 shuāituì; 垮掉 kuǎdiào. ~ ***a joke*** 说笑话 shuō xiàohuà. ***get*** ~***ing***动〔動〕工 dònggōng.

cracker /ˈkrækə(r)/ *n* [C] **1** 薄脆饼干〔乾〕 bócuì bǐnggān. **2** 鞭炮 biānpào, 爆竹 bàozhú. ⇨ nut-crackers

crackers /ˈkrækəz/ *adj* [俚语]发〔發〕疯〔瘋〕的 fāfēngde.

crackle /ˈkrækl/ *vi* 噼啪作响〔響〕 pīpā zuòxiǎng. □ *n* [U] 噼啪声〔聲〕 pīpāshēng, 爆裂声 bàolièshēng.

crack·pot /ˈkrækpɒt/ *adj*, *n* [C] 古怪的 gǔguàide; 发〔發〕疯〔瘋〕的 fāfēngde: *a*~ *idea* 古怪的主意.

cradle /ˈkreɪdl/ *n* [C] **1** 摇篮 yáolán. **2** [喻]策源地 cèyuán dì, 发〔發〕源地 fāyuándì: *the* ~ *of Western culture* 西方文化的发源地. **3** 支船架 zhīchuánjià, 水架 shuǐjià. □ *vt* 把…放在摇篮里 bǎ… fàngzài yáolán lǐ. 放在摇篮里似地兜着 fàngzài yáolán lǐ sì de dōuzhe.

craft /krɑːft/ *n* **1** [C] 工艺〔藝〕 gōngyì; 手艺 shǒuyì; 手工业〔業〕 shǒugōngyè. **2** [C] [*pl* ~] 船 chuán, 小船 xiǎochuán. **3** [U] 技巧 jìqiǎo; 诡计 guǐjì, 手腕 shǒuwàn. **crafts·man** *n* [C] [*pl* -men] 手艺人 shǒuyìrén, 工匠 gōngjiàng; 名匠 míngjiàng. **crafty** *adj* [-ier, -iest] 巧妙的 qiǎomiàode, 灵〔靈〕巧的 língqiǎode, 狡猾的 jiǎohuáde. ~**ily** *adv* ~**i·ness** *n* [U]

crag /kræg/ *n* [C] 岩 yán, 峭壁 qiàobì, 危岩 wēiyán. ~**gy** *adj* [-ier, -iest] 峻〔峻〕峭的 jùnqiàode.

cram /kræm/ *vt/i* [-mm-] **1** ~ ***into*** (或 ***with***) 塞进 sāijìn, 塞满 sāimǎn: ~ *clothes into a suitcase* 把衣服塞进箱子. **2** 为〔爲〕考试而死记硬背 wèi kǎoshì ér sǐjìyìngbèi.

cramp¹ /kræmp/ *n* [U] (肌肉)痉〔痙〕挛〔攣〕 jìngluán, 抽筋 chōujīn.

cramp² /kræmp/ *vt* **1** 束缚 sùfú: *a* ~*ed room* 狭窄的房间. **2** 使抽筋 shǐ chōujīn. **3** 以铁〔鐵〕箍扣紧〔緊〕 yǐ tiěgū kòujǐn.

cramp³ /kræmp/ *n* [C] 铁〔鐵〕箍 tiěgū.

cram·pon /ˈkræmpɒn/ *n* [C] (登冰山用的)鞋底铁〔鐵〕钉 xiédǐ tiědīng.

cran·berry /ˈkrænbərɪ/ *n* [C] [*pl* -ies] 蔓越桔〔橘〕(酸果蔓的果实) mànyuèjú.

crane¹ /kreɪn/ *n* [C] **1** 鹤〔鶴〕 hè. **2** 起重机〔機〕 qǐzhòngjī, 吊车〔車〕 diàochē.

crane² /kreɪn/ *vt/i* 伸(颈) shēn.

cran·ium /ˈkreɪnɪəm/ *n* [C] [解剖]头〔頭〕盖〔蓋〕 tóugài, 脑〔腦〕壳〔殼〕 nǎoké; 头盖骨 tóugàigǔ. **cran·ial** *adj*

crank¹ /kræŋk/ *n* [C] 曲柄 qūbǐng. □ *vt* 转〔轉〕动〔動〕曲柄 zhuàndòng qūbǐng, ˈ~**shaft** 曲轴〔軸〕 qūzhóu.

crank² /kræŋk/ *n* [C] 怪人 guàirén, 脾气〔氣〕古怪的人 píqì gǔguài de rén. **cranky** *adj* [-ier, -iest] 古怪的 gǔguàide, 脾气坏〔壞〕的 píqì huài de.

crash¹ /kræʃ/ *n* [C] **1** 坠〔墜〕地撞击〔擊〕声〔聲〕zhuìdì zhuàngjīshēng. 突然坠落 tūrán zhuìluò. **2** 事故 shìgù: *a plane* ~飞机坠毁; *car* ~ 汽车撞车. **3** 倒闭〔閉〕 dǎobì, 垮台 kuǎtái. □ *adv* 砰地一声〔聲〕 pēngde yīshēng. ˈ~**-course** (或 **-programme**) 速成课程 sùchéng kèchéng. ˈ~**-helmet** (摩托车驾驶者用的)防撞头〔頭〕盔 fáng zhuàng tóukuī. ˌ~-ˈ**land** *vt/i* (飞机失控而) 猛撞降落 měngzhuàng jiàngluò. ˌ~-ˈ**landing** *n* [C, U]

crash² /kræʃ/ *vt/i* **1** (发出猛烈声音地) 坠〔墜〕毁 zhuìhuǐ, 碰撞 pèngzhuàng. **2** 使碰撞 shǐ pèngzhuàng: ~ *a car* 撞车. **3** 冲〔衝〕过〔過〕 chōngguò; 撞过 zhuàngguò. **4** (公司等)倒闭〔閉〕 dǎobì.

crass /kræs/ *adj* (愚蠢,无知等)极〔極〕度的 jídùde, 非常的 fēichángde.

crate /kreɪt/ *n* [C] 板条〔條〕箱 bǎntiáoxiāng; 柳条箱 liǔtiáoxiāng. □ *vt* 用板条箱装〔裝〕 yòng bǎntiáoxiāng zhuāng.

cra·ter /ˈkreɪtə(r)/ *n* [C] **1** 火山口 huǒshānkǒu. **2** 弹〔彈〕坑 dànkēng.

cra·vat /krəˈvæt/ *n* [C] 旧〔舊〕式领带〔帶〕 jiùshì lǐngdài.

crave /kreɪv/ *vt/i* 恳〔懇〕求 kěnqiú; 渴望 kěwàng. **crav·ing** *n* [C] 渴望 kěwàng, 热〔熱〕望 rèwàng.

crawl /krɔːl/ *vi* **1** 爬行 páxíng, 匍匐前进 púfú qiánjìn. **2** 缓慢地行进 huǎnmànde xíngjìn: *Traffic* ~*s into London every morning*. 每天早晨车

辆缓慢地开进伦敦. **3** 爬满 pámǎn, 充斥着爬虫 chōngchìzhe páchóng: *~ing with ants* 爬满蚂蚁. **4** (似乎感到皮肤上有爬虫而) 起鸡〔鷄〕皮疙瘩 qǐ jīpí gēda. ⇨creep(5). □ *n* **1** [U] 爬行 páxíng, 爬 pá, 蠕动〔動〕rúdòng. **2 the ~** 自由泳 zìyóuyǒng, 爬泳 páyǒng.

cray·fish /ˈkreɪfɪʃ/ *n* [C] 蝲蛄 làgǔ; (产于淡水中的一种) 小龙〔龍〕虾 xiǎo lóngxiā.

crayon /ˈkreɪən/ *n* [C] 粉笔〔筆〕fěnbǐ; 蜡〔蠟〕笔 làbǐ; 颜色笔 yánsèbǐ. □ *vt* 用粉笔等画〔畫〕yòng fěnbǐ děng huà.

craze /kreɪz/ *vt* 使发狂 shǐ fākuáng, 使疯〔瘋〕狂 shǐ fēngkuáng. □ *n* [C] 狂热〔熱〕kuángrè, 躁狂 zàokuáng. ⇨ rage(3).

crazy /ˈkreɪzɪ/ *adj* [-ier, -iest] **1** 狂热的 kuángrède; 热衷于 rèzhōngyú: *~ about football* 热衷于足球. **2** 疯〔瘋〕狂的 fēngkuángde, 糊涂的 hútude. **craz·ily** *adv* **crazi·ness** *n* [U]

creak /kri:k/ *n* [C], *vi* 吱吱嘎嘎地响〔響〕zhīzhīgāgāde xiǎng. **creaky** *adj* [-ier, -iest] 吱吱响的 zhīzhīxiǎngde.

cream /kri:m/ *n* [U] **1** 乳脂 rǔzhī, 奶油 nǎiyóu. **2** 奶油状〔狀〕物 nǎiyóuzhuàng wù: *'furniture ~* 家具蜡. **3** 精华〔華〕jīnghuá, 最精采的部分 zuìjīngcǎide bùfen: *the ~ of society* 社会中坚. **4** 奶油色 nǎiyóusè, 米色 mǐsè. □ *adj* 奶油色的 nǎiyóusède, 米色的 mǐsède. □ *vt* **1** 使牛奶结成奶油 shǐ niúnǎi jiéchéng nǎiyóu; 加奶油于 jiā nǎiyóu yú. **2** 取出最好部分 qǔchū zuìhǎo bùfen. **creamy** *adj* [-ier, -iest] 奶油似的 nǎiyóu sì de; 含奶油的 hán nǎiyóu de.

crease /kri:s/ *n* [C] **1** (衣服, 纸等的) 折缝 zhéfèng, 皱〔皺〕痕 zhòuhén. **2** (板球) 球员位置的白线 qiúyuán wèizhì de báixiàn. □ *vt/i* (使) 起折痕 qǐ zhéhén.

cre·ate /krɪˈeɪt/ *vt* **1** 创〔創〕造 chuàngzào, 创作 chuàngzuò. **2** 产生 chǎnshēng; 造成 zàochéng; 引起 yǐnqǐ: *~ problems* 引起问题.

cre·ation /krɪˈeɪʃn/ *n* **1** [U] 创〔創〕造 chuàngzào; 创作 chuàngzuò. **2** [U] 创作物 chuàngzuòwù; 创造物 chuàngzàowù. **the C~** 天地万〔萬〕物 tiāndì wànwù; 宇宙 yǔzhòu.

cre·ative /krɪˈeɪtɪv/ *adj* 有创〔創〕造力的 yǒu chuàngzàolì de, 有创造性的 yǒu chuàngzàoxìng de, 创作的 chuàngzuòde. **~ly** *adv*

cre·ator /krɪˈeɪtə(r)/ *n* [C] 创〔創〕造者 chuàngzàozhě, 创作者 chuàngzuòzhě. **the C~** 上帝 shàngdì; 造物主 zàowùzhǔ.

crea·ture /ˈkri:tʃə(r)/ *n* [C] 动〔動〕物 dòngwù, 人 rén.

crèche /ˈkreɪʃ/ *n* [C] [法语] 日托托儿〔兒〕所 rìtuō tuō'érsuǒ.

cre·den·tials /krɪˈdenʃlz/ *n pl* 信任状〔狀〕xìnrènzhuàng; 证〔證〕书〔書〕zhèngshū.

cred·ible /ˈkredəbl/ *adj* 可信任的 kě xìnrèn de, 可靠的 kěkàode. **cred·ibly** *adv* 可信地 kěxìnde. **credi·ˈbil·ity** *n* [U]

credit[1] /ˈkredɪt/ *n* **1** [U] 信任 xìnrèn, 信誉〔譽〕xìnyù. **2** [U] 存款 cúnkuǎn, 债权〔權〕zhàiquán. **3** [C] (银行) 信用贷款 xìnyòng dàikuǎn. **4** (簿记) 贷方 dàifāng. **5** *get* (或 *take*) *~* (*for sth*) 把某事的功劳〔勞〕归〔歸〕于自己 bǎ mǒushìde gōngláo guī yú zìjǐ. **6** *be a ~ to sb* (*sth*) 为〔爲〕某人 (某事) 增光 wèi mǒurén zēngguāng. **7** [U] 相信 xiāngxìn: *give ~ to his story* 相信他的话. **ˈ~ card** 信用卡 xìnyòngkǎ; 记帐〔帳〕卡 jìzhàngkǎ. **ˈ~-worthy** 值得提供信贷的 zhídé tígòng xìndài de.

credit[2] /ˈkredɪt/ *vt* **1** 相信 xiāngxìn. **2** 把…记入贷方 bǎ...jìrù dàifāng. **~able** /-əbl/ *adj* 可信的 kěxìnde; 带〔帶〕来〔來〕荣〔榮〕誉〔譽〕的 dàilái róngyùde. **~ably** *adv*

credi·tor /ˈkredɪtə(r)/ *n* [C] 债权〔權〕人 zhàiquánrén.

cre·du·lity /krəˈdju:lətɪ/ *n* [U] 轻〔輕〕信 qīngxìn, 易信 yìxìn. **ˈcredu·lous** *adj*

creed /kri:d/ *n* [C] 信条〔條〕xìntiáo, 教义〔義〕jiàoyì.

creek /kri:k/ *n* [C] **1** [英国英语] 小湾〔灣〕xiǎowān, 小港 xiǎogǎng. **2** (北美) 小河 xiǎohé.

creep /kri:p/ *vi* [*pt*, *pp* crept /krept/] **1** 爬行 páxíng, 匍匐而行 púfú ér xíng. **2** 缓慢移行 huǎnmàn yíxíng; 悄悄移行 qiāoqiāo yíxíng. **3** (时间, 年纪等) 悄悄过〔過〕去 qiāoqiāo guòqù. **4** (植物) 蔓延 mànyán. **5** (因为似乎有爬虫在身上爬) 起鸡〔鷄〕皮疙瘩 qǐ jī pí gēda. ⇨ crawl(4).

creeper /ˈkri:pə(r)/ *n* [C] 匍匐植物 púfú zhíwù.

creepy /ˈkri:pɪ/ *adj* [-ier, -iest] 令人毛骨悚然的 lìngrén máogǔ sǒngrán de.

cre·mate /krɪˈmeɪt/ *vt* 焚尸〔屍〕fénshī. **creˈma·tion** *n* [C, U] 焚化

fénhuà; 火葬 huǒzàng.

cre·ma·tor·ium /ˌkremə'tɔːrɪəm/ *n* [C] [*pl* ~s] 焚尸〔屍〕炉〔爐〕 fénshīlú; 火化场〔場〕 huǒhuàchǎng.

crêpe, crepe /kreɪp/ *n* [U] 绉〔縐〕布 zhòubù; 绉纸 zhòuzhǐ: ~ *paper* 绉纸; ~ *rubber* 绉橡胶.

crept /krept/ *pt*, *pp* of creep.

cres·cendo /krɪ'ʃendəʊ/ *n* [C], *adj* [*pl* ~s] **1** (音乐)渐〔漸〕强 jiànqiáng. **2** [喻]向高潮渐进 xiàng gāocháo jiànjìn.

cres·cent /'kresnt/ *n* [C] **1** 月牙 yuèyá, 新月 xīnyuè. 新月状〔狀〕物 xīnyuèzhuàng wù. **2** 新月形排房 xīnyuèxíng páifáng.

cress /kres/ *n* [U] 水芹 shuǐqín.

crest /krest/ *n* [C] **1** 鸟〔鳥〕禽等的冠 niǎo qín děng de guān. **2** 盔上的羽毛饰 kuī shàng de yǔmáoshì. **3** 盾上的纹章 dùn shàng de wénzhāng. **4** 山顶 shāndǐng; 浪峰 làngfēng. □ *vt* 达〔達〕到山顶,浪峰 dádào shāndǐng, làngfēng. '~**-fallen** [喻]垂头〔頭〕丧气〔氣〕的 chuí tóu sàng qì de.

cre·tin /'kretɪn/ *n* [C] **1** 白痴〔癡〕báichī. **2** [非正式用语]笨人 bènrén.

cre·vasse /krɪ'væs/ *n* [C] 冰上裂缝 bīng shàng lièfèng.

crev·ice /'krevɪs/ *n* [C] (岩石,墙等)裂缝 lièfèng.

crew /kruː/ *n* [C] **1** 全体〔體〕船员 quántǐ chuányuán, 全体空勤人员 quántǐ kōngqín rényuán. **2** 同事们〔們〕 tóngshìmen, 一起工作的人们 yìqǐ gōngzuò de rénmen, 一帮人 yìbāngrén: *a camera* ~ 摄影组. □ *vi* 以船员身份操作 yǐ chuányuán shēnfen cāozuò.

crib[1] /krɪb/ *n* [C] **1** 食槽 shícáo. **2** 婴儿〔兒〕小床 yīng'ér xiǎochuáng.

crib[2] /krɪb/ *n* [C] **1** 剽窃〔竊〕piāoqiè, 抄袭〔襲〕 chāoxí. **2** 学〔學〕生作弊用的外文对〔對〕照本 xuésheng zuòbì yòng de wàiwén duìzhàoběn. □ *vt/i* [-bb-] **1** 用外文对照本 yòng wàiwén duìzhàoběn. **2** 剽窃 piāoqiè, 抄袭 chāoxí.

cricket[1] /'krɪkɪt/ *n* [C] 蟋蟀 xīshuài.

cricket[2] /'krɪkɪt/ *n* [U] 板球 bǎnqiú. ~**er** 板球选〔選〕手 bǎnqiú xuǎnshǒu.

cried /kraɪd/ *pt*, *pp* of cry[2].

cries /kraɪz/ *pres·tense* of cry[2]; *pl* of cry[1].

crime /kraɪm/ *n* [C, U] 罪 zuì, 罪行 zuìxíng, 罪过〔過〕 zuìguò.

crimi·nal /'krɪmɪnl/ *adj* 犯罪的 fànzuìde, 刑事上的 xíngshì shàng de; 犯了罪的 fànle zuì de. □ *n* [C] 罪犯 zuìfàn, 犯人 fànrén. ~**ly** *adv*

crim·son /'krɪmzn/ *adj*, *n* [U] 深红 shēnhóng, 绯红 fēihóng.

cringe /krɪndʒ/ *vi* **1** 畏缩 wèisuō. **2** 卑恭屈膝 bēigōng-qūqī.

crinkle /'krɪŋkl/ *n* [C] 皱〔皺〕折 zhòuzhé. □ *vt/i* (使)起皱 qǐzhòu.

cripple /'krɪpl/ *n* [C] 残〔殘〕废〔廢〕人 cánfèirén; 跛子 bǒzi. □ *vt* 使跛 shǐbǒ, 使残废 shǐ cánfei.

cri·sis /'kraɪsɪs/ *n* [C] [*pl* crises /siːz/] **1** 转〔轉〕折点〔點〕zhuǎnzhédiǎn, 危急存亡关〔關〕头〔頭〕 wēijí cúnwáng guāntóu. **2** 危机〔機〕 wēijī.

crisp /krɪsp/ *adj* [-er, -est] **1** 脆的 cuìde, 易碎的 yìsuìde. **2** 霜冻〔凍〕的 shuāngdòngde; 冷的 lěngde. **3** 干〔乾〕脆的 gāncuìde, 干净利落的 gānjìnglìluòde: *his* ~ *way of speaking* 他说话干净利落. □ *n* [C] [常作复]油炸马〔馬〕铃薯片(袋装) yóuzhá mǎlíngshǔpiàn. □ *vt/i* (使)发〔發〕脆 fācuì. ~**ly** *adv* ~**ness** *n* [C]

criss·cross /'krɪskrɒs/ *adj* 十字形的 shízìxíngde; 交叉的 jiāochāde. □ *vt/i* 画〔畫〕十字押于 huà shízìyā yú.

cri·terion /kraɪ'tɪərɪən/ *n* [C] [*pl* -ria /-rɪə/] 判断〔斷〕的标〔標〕准〔準〕 pànduànde biāozhǔn.

critic /'krɪtɪk/ *n* [C] **1** 批评家 pīpíngjiā; 评论〔論〕家 pínglùnjiā; 文艺〔藝〕评论家 wényì pínglùnjiā. **2** 爱〔愛〕挑剔的人 ài tiāotìde rén. '~**al** *adj* **(a)** 危急的 wēijíde, 紧〔緊〕要的 jǐnyàode. **(b)** 批评(性)的 pīpíngde, 评论〔論〕性的 pínglùnxìngde. **(c)** 苛求的 kēqiúde. ~**ally** *adv* 危急地 wēijíde, 岌岌可危地 jíjíkěwēide.

criti·cism /'krɪtɪsɪzəm/ *n* **1** [U] 批评 pīpíng, 批评性意见 pīpíngxìng yìjiàn. **2** [C] 文艺〔藝〕批评 wényì pīpíng. **3** [C] 非难〔難〕fēinàn.

criti·cize /'krɪtɪsaɪz/ *vt/i* 批评 pīpíng; 评论〔論〕 pínglùn; 非难〔難〕 fēinàn.

croak /krəʊk/ *n* [C] (蛙等)呱呱叫声〔聲〕 guāguājiàoshēng. □ *vt/i* **1** 呱呱地叫 guāguāde jiào. **2** 用嘶哑〔啞〕的声音说 yòng sīyǎde shēngyīn shuō.

crock /krɒk/ *n* [C] **1** 瓦罐 wǎguàn; 瓦壶 wǎhú. **2** 破旧〔舊〕的

汽车〔車〕pòjiùde qìchē.

crock·ery /'krɒkərɪ/ *n* [U] 陶器 táoqì; 瓦器 wǎqì.

croco·dile /'krɒkədaɪl/ *n* [C] **1** 鳄鱼 èyú. **2** [非正式用语]两人一排的学〔學〕生行列 liǎngrén yìpái de xuéshēng hángliè. **'~ tears** 鳄鱼的眼泪〔淚〕èyúde yǎnlèi,假慈悲 jiǎ cíbēi

cro·cus /'krəʊkəs/ *n* [C] [*pl* ~es] 藏红花 zànghónghuā.

crook /krʊk/ *n* [C] **1** 牧羊人用的弯〔彎〕柄杖 mùyángrén yòng de wānbǐngzhàng. **2** [非正式用语] 骗〔騙〕子 piànzi, 流氓 liúmáng. □ *vt/i* (使)弯曲 wānqū.

crooked /'krʊkɪd/ *adj* **1** 弯〔彎〕曲的 wānqūde, 扭曲的 niǔqūde. **2** 欺诈的 qīzhàde, 不正当〔當〕的 búzhèngdāngde. **~ly** *adv*

crop[1] /krɒp/ *n* [C] **1** (农作物等) 一熟 yīshú; 收成 shōuchéng. **2** [*pl*] 作物 zuòwù, 庄稼 zhuāngjia. **3** 一批 yīpī, 一群 yīqún: *a new ~ of problems* 一大堆新问题.

crop[2] /krɒp/ *vt/i* [-pp-] **1** (牲畜)咬掉草等的顶端 yǎodiào cǎo děng de dǐngduān; 吃青草 chī qīngcǎo. **2** 剪短 (头发、马尾等) jiǎnduǎn. **3** ~ *up* 突然发〔發〕生, 出现 tūrán fāshēng, chūxiàn: *A new problem has ~ped up.* 突然发生了新的问题.

cro·quet /'krəʊkeɪ/ *n* [U] 槌球游戏〔戲〕chuíqiú yóuxì.

cross[1] /krɒs/ *adj* **1** [非正式用语] 脾气〔氣〕坏〔壞〕的 píqì huài de; 易怒的 yìnùde. **2** (风)逆的 nìde.

cross[2] /krɒs/ *n* [C] **1** 十字形记号〔號〕shízìxíng jìhào. **2 the C~** 耶稣被钉死的十字架 yēsū bèi dìngsǐ de shízìjià. **3** [喻] 苦难〔難〕kǔnàn, 磨难 mónàn. **4** (动植物的)异〔異〕种〔種〕交配 yìzhǒng jiāopèi, 杂〔雜〕交 zájiāo; 杂种 zázhǒng.

cross[3] /krɒs/ *vt/i* **1** 横穿 héngchuān, 横过〔過〕héngguò, 横渡 héngdù. ~ ***one's mind*** 想出(主意) xiǎngchū. **2** 画〔畫〕横线穿过〔過〕huà héngxiàn chuānguò: *~ out a word* 勾掉一个字. **3** 交叉 jiāochā. ***keep one's fingers ~ed*** [喻]两指交叉以求好运〔運〕或减轻〔輕〕罪过 liǎngzhǐ jiāochā yǐ qiú hǎo yùn huò jiǎnqīng zuìguò. **4** ~ ***oneself*** 在自己身上画〔畫〕十字 zài zìjǐ shēn shàng huà shízì. **5** 反对〔對〕fǎnduì, 阻挠〔撓〕zǔnáo. **6** 使杂〔雜〕交 shǐ zájiāo.

cross·bow /'krɒsbəʊ/ *n* [C] 十字弓 shízìgōng, 弩 nǔ.

cross·bred /'krɒsbred/ *adj* 杂〔雜〕交的 zájiāode, 杂种〔種〕的 zázhǒngde.

cross·breed /'krɒsbri:d/ *n* [C] 杂〔雜〕种〔種〕zázhǒng.

cross-check /krɒs'tʃek/ *vt/i* (从不同角度或以不同资料) 反复〔復〕核对〔對〕fǎnfù héduì. □ *n* [C] 反复核对 fǎnfù héduì.

cross·country /ˌkrɒs'kʌntrɪ/ *adj*, *adv* 横穿全国〔國〕的 héngchuān quánguó de; 越野的 yuèyěde: *a ~ race* 越野赛跑.

cross-current /'krɒs 'kʌrənt/ *n* [C] **1** 逆流 nìliú. **2** (政治等)相反的趋〔趨〕势〔勢〕xiāngfǎnde qūshì.

cross-exam·ine /ˌkrɒs ɪg'zæmɪn/ *vt* 盘〔盤〕问〔問〕pánwèn. **cross-exami'nation** *n* [C]

cross·eyed /'krɒsaɪd/ *adj* 内斜视 nèixiéshì, 斗〔鬥〕鸡〔鷄〕眼 dòujīyǎn.

cross-fer·ti·lize /ˌkrɒs 'fɜ:təlaɪz/ *vt* **1** 异〔異〕体〔體〕受精 yìtǐ shòujīng. **2** [喻] 使相互取长补短 shǐ xiānghù qǔcháng bǔduǎn **cross-fer·ti·li·za·tion** /ˌkrɒsˌfɜ:təlaɪ'zeɪʃn/ *n* [U]

cross·fire /'krɒsfaɪə(r)/ *n* [U] 交叉火力 jiāochā huǒlì.

cross·ing /'krɒsɪŋ/ *n* [C] **1** 横渡 héngdù; 横穿 héngchuān: *a stormy ~ of the Atlantic* 暴风雨中横渡大西洋. **2** 交叉 jiāochā; 交叉点〔點〕jiāochādiǎn; 十字路口 shízì lùkǒu. ⇨ level crossing.

cross-legged /ˌkrɒs 'legd/ *adv* 盘〔盤〕着腿的 pánzhetuǐ de, 跷〔蹺〕着二郎腿的 qiàozhe èrlángtuǐ de.

cross-pur·poses /ˌkrɒs'pɜ:pəsɪz/ *n pl* ***be at*** ~ 互相误解 hùxiāng wùjiě, 有矛盾 yǒu máodùn.

cross-ref·er·ence /ˌkrɒs 'refrəns/ *n* [C] 相互参〔參〕照 xiānghù cānzhào, 互见条〔條〕目 hùjiàn tiáomù.

cross·roads /'krɒsrəʊdz/ *n* [*pl* 用 *sing verb*] 十字路 shízìlù, 十字路口 shízìlùkǒu.

cross-sec·tion /ˌkrɒs 'sekʃn/ *n* [C] **1** 横断〔斷〕面 héngduànmiàn, 截面 jiémiàn; 断面图〔圖〕duànmiàntú. **2** [喻]样〔樣〕品 yàngpǐn, 典型 diǎnxíng: *a ~ of society* 社会的缩影.

cross·word /'krɒswɜ:d/ *n* [C] (亦作 *'~ puzzle*) 一种〔種〕纵〔縱〕横填字字谜 yìzhǒng zònghéng tiánzì zìmí.

crotch /krɒtʃ/ *n* [C] **1** 树〔樹〕的丫叉 shùde yāchà. **2** 人体〔體〕两

腿分叉处〔處〕réntǐ liǎngtuǐ fēnchàchù

crouch /kraʊtʃ/ *vi* 蹲伏 dūnfú: *The tiger ~ed ready to attack.* 老虎猫着身子准备攻击. □ *n* [C] 蹲伏(姿势) dūnfú.

crou·pier /'kru:pɪeɪ/ *n* [C] 赌场〔場〕收付赌钱〔錢〕的人 dǔchǎng shōufù dǔqián de rén.

crow[1] /krəʊ/ *n* [C] 鸦〔鴉〕yā, 乌〔烏〕鸦 wūyā. *as the '~ flies* 笔〔筆〕直地 bǐzhíde: *It's ten miles away, as the ~ flies.* 直线距离 10 英里. **'~'s feet** *n pl* 眼睛外角的皱〔皺〕纹 yǎnjīng wàijiǎo de zhòuwén. **'~'s-nest** 桅上了〔瞭〕望台 wéi shàng liáowàngtái.

crow[2] /krəʊ/ *vi* **1** (公鸡)啼 tí. **2** 得意洋洋 déyì yángyáng. □ *n* [C] 鸡〔鷄〕啼 jītí.

crow·bar /'krəʊbɑ:(r)/ *n* [C] 撬棍 qiàogùn.

crowd /kraʊd/ *n* [C] **1** 人群 rénqún. **2** [非正式用语]一伙〔夥〕yīhuǒ, 一帮 yībāng: *the golf ~* 打高尔夫球的一帮人. □ *vt/i* **1** 群聚 qúnjiū, 拥〔擁〕挤〔擠〕yōngjǐ. **2** 拥过〔過〕yōngguò; 挤满 jǐmǎn. **~ed** *adj* 拥挤的 yōngjǐde, 密集的 mìjíde.

crown[1] /kraʊn/ *n* [C] **1** 王冠 wángguān; 冕 miǎn; 王权〔權〕wángquán. **2** 顶部 dǐngbù, 帽顶 màodǐng.

crown[2] /kraʊn/ *vt* **1** 为〔爲〕...加冠 wèi...jiāguān; 为...加冕 wèi...jiāmiǎn. **2** 褒奖〔獎〕bāojiǎng; 赏赐 shǎngcì: *~ed with success* 获得圆满成功. **3** 顶上有 dǐngshàng yǒu: *a hill ~ed with trees* 顶上长着树木的小山. **4** 圆满完成 yuánmǎn wánchéng. *to ~ (it) all* 更使人高兴〔興〕的是 gèn shǐ rén gāoxìng de shì; 更糟糕的是 gèn zāogāo de shì. **~ing** *adj* 登峰造极〔極〕的 dēngfēngzàojíde.

cru·cial /'kru:ʃl/ *adj* 决定性的 juédìngxìngde, 紧〔緊〕要关〔關〕头〔頭〕的 jǐnyào guāntóu de. **~ly** *adv*

cru·ci·fix /'kru:sɪfɪks/ *n* [C] 耶稣钉在十字架上的图〔圖〕像 yēsū dīng zài shízìjià shàng de túxiàng. **~ion** /ˌkru:sɪ'fɪkʃn/ *n* [C, U] 在十字架上钉死的刑罚 zài shízìjià shàng dīngsǐ de xíngfá.

cru·cify /'kru:sɪfaɪ/ *vt* [*pt, pp* -ied] 钉死在十字架上 dīngsǐ zài shízìjià shàng.

crude /kru:d/ *adj* [-r, -st] **1** 天然的 tiānránde, 未加工的 wèi jiāgōng de: *~ oil* 原油,石油. **2** 粗鲁的 cūlǔde, 粗鄙的 cūbǐde. **3** 粗制〔製〕的 cūzhìde, 粗糙的 cūcāode: *~ methods* 不完善的方法. **~ly** *adv*

crud·ity /'kru:dɪtɪ/ *n* [U] 粗鲁 cūlǔ; [C] [*pl* -ies] 粗鲁的言行 cūlǔde yánxíng.

cruel /kru:əl/ *adj* [-er, -est] **1** 残〔殘〕忍的 cánrěnde, 残酷的 cánkùde. **2** 残暴的 cánbàode, 无〔無〕情的 wúqíngde: *a ~ attack* 残暴的攻击. **~ly** *adv.* **~ty** *n* [C, U] [*pl* -ies].

cruet /'kru:ɪt/ *n* [C] (餐桌上的)调味品瓶 tiáowèipǐnpíng.

cruise/ kru:z/ *vi* **1** 巡航 xúnháng: 巡游 xúnyóu. **2** (汽车、飞机等)以最节〔節〕省燃料的速度行进 yǐ zuì jiéshěng ránliào de sùdù xíngjìn. □ *n* [C] 乘船巡游 chéngchuán xúnyóu. **cruiser** *n* [C] 巡洋舰〔艦〕xúnyángjiàn.

crumb /krʌm/ *n* [C] **1** 面〔麵〕包屑 miànbāoxiè; 糕饼屑 gāobǐngxiè. **2** [喻]一点〔點〕点 yīdiǎndiǎn, 少许 shǎoxǔn: *not a ~ of proof* 一点证据也没有.

crumble /'krʌmbl/ *vt/i* **1** 弄碎 nòngsuì; 破碎 pòsuì. 碎裂 suìliè **2** [喻]灭〔滅〕亡 mièwáng, 消失 xiāoshī. **crum·bly** *adj* [-ier, -iest] 易碎的 yìsuìde, 易摧毁的 yì cuīhuǐ de.

crumple /'krʌmpl/ *vt/i* **1** 把...弄皱〔皺〕bǎ...nòngzhòu. **2** 满是皱痕 mǎnshì zhòuhén. **3** *~ up* 压碎 yāsuì; 崩溃 bēngkuì; 弄皱 nòngzhòu.

crunch /krʌntʃ/ *vt/i* **1** 嘎嘎吱吱地咬嚼 gāgā zhīzhī de yǎojiáo. **2** 嘎嘎吱吱地压碎 gāgā zhīzhī de yāsuì. □ *n* [C] **1** 嘎嘎吱吱的咬嚼 gāgā zhīzhī de yǎojiáo; 嘎嘎吱吱的声〔聲〕音 gāgā zhīzhī de shēngyīn. **2 the ~** [非正式用语]摊〔攤〕牌 tānpái; 危机〔機〕wēijī: *when the ~ comes* 危机发生的时候.

cru·sade /kru:'seɪd/ *n* [C] **1** 十字军〔軍〕东〔東〕侵 shízìjūn dōng qīn. **2** 讨伐 tǎofá, 改革运〔運〕动〔動〕gǎigé yùndòng: *a ~ for human rights* 民权运动. □ *vi* 参〔參〕加某种〔種〕运动 cānjiā mǒuzhǒng yùndòng. **cru·sader** *n* [C]

crush[1] /krʌʃ/ *n* [U] 拥〔擁〕挤〔擠〕的人群 yōngjǐde rénqún.

crush[2] /krʌʃ/ *vt/i* **1** 压碎 yāsuì, 压坏〔壞〕yāhuài. **2** 弄皱〔皺〕nòngzhòu; 揉皱 róuzhòu. **3** 压垮 yākuǎ, 制服 zhìfú. **4** 挤入 jǐrù: *Crowds ~ed into the theatre.* 人群

挤进剧场. ~**ing** *adj* 压倒的 yādǎode, 决定性的 juédìngxìngde: *a ~ing defeat* 彻〔徹〕底的失败. ~**-ing·ly** *adv*

crust /krʌst/ *n* **1** [C, U] 面〔麵〕包,饼等的皮 miànbāo bǐng děng de pí. **2** [C, U] 硬外皮 yìng wàipí, 外壳〔殼〕wàiqiào.

crus·ta·cean ˌkrʌ'steɪʃn/ *n* [C] 甲壳〔殼〕纲〔綱〕动〔動〕物 jiǎqiàogāng dòngwù.

crusty /'krʌstɪ/ *adj* [-ier, -iest] **1** 有硬皮的 yǒu yìngpí de; 有外壳〔殼〕的 yǒu wàiqiào de; 象硬皮一样〔樣〕硬的 xiàng yìngpí yíyàng yìng de. **2** 易发〔發〕脾气〔氣〕的 yì fā píqì de.

crutch /krʌtʃ/ *n* [C] **1** (跛子用的)拐杖 guǎizhàng. **2** [喻]支持 zhīchí. **3** = crotch(2).

crux /krʌks/ *n* [C] [*pl* ~es] 难〔難〕题 nántí, 症〔癥〕结 zhēngjié.

cry[1] /kraɪ/ *n* [C] [*pl* cries] **1** 叫喊 jiàohǎng, 喊 hǎng: *a ~ of pain* 喊痛; *a ~ for help* 呼救. ***a far ~ from*** 大不相同 dàbù xiāngtóng. **2** 一阵〔陣〕哭 yìzhèngkū; 哭声〔聲〕kūshēng.

cry[2] /kraɪ/ *vt/i* [*pt, pp* cried] **1** (人,动物)叫喊 jiàohǎn; 叫 jiào. **2** (人)哭 kū. **3** 高声〔聲〕喊叫 gāoshēng hǎnjiào. ~ ***off*** 取消(约会等) qǔxiāo.

crypt /krɪpt/ *n* [C] 地窖 dìjiào; 教堂的地下室 jiàotángde dìxiàshì.

cryp·tic /'krɪptɪk/ *adj* 秘密的 mìmìde; 隐蔽的 yǐnbìde; 隐义〔義〕的 yǐnyìde.

crys·tal /'krɪstl/ *n* **1** [U] 水晶 shuǐjīng; [C] 水晶饰品 shuǐjīng shìpǐn. **2** [U] 质〔質〕量最好的玻璃器皿 zhìliàng zuìhǎo de bōli qìmǐn. **3** [C] 结晶体〔體〕 jiéjīng tǐ: *salt ~s* 盐结晶体. ~**line** *adj* 水晶的 shuǐjīngde; 水晶似的 shuǐjīngsìde; 清澈透明的 qīngchètòumíngde. ~**lize** *vt/i* **(a)** (使)结晶 jiéjīng. **(b)** 给水果等裹上糖的结晶 gěi shuǐguǒ děng guǒshàng tángde jiéjīng. **(c)** [喻]使定形 shǐ dìngxíng; 使具体化 shǐ jùtǐhuà.

cub. =cubic.

cub /kʌb/ *n* [C] 幼狐 yòuhú; 幼兽〔獸〕yòushòu.

cubby-hole /'kʌbɪ həʊl/ *n* [C] 围〔圍〕起来〔來〕的小天地 wéi qǐlái de xiǎotiāndì.

cube /kju:b/ *n* [C] **1** 立方体〔體〕lìfāngtǐ. **2** [数学]立方 lìfāng. □ *vt* 自乘三次 zìchéng sāncì: *3 ~d is 27.* 3 的立方是 27. **cu·bic** /'ju:bɪk/ *adj* 立方形的 lìfāngxíngde, 立方体的 lìfāngtǐde: *one ~ metre* 1 立方米.

cu·bicle /'kju:bɪkl/ *n* [C] 大房间〔間〕中用帷幕等隔开〔開〕的小室 dà fángjiān zhōng yòng wéimù děng gékāi de xiǎoshì.

cuckoo /'kʊku:/ *n* [C] 杜鹃〔鵑〕dùjuān; 布谷〔穀〕鸟〔鳥〕bùgǔniǎo.

cu·cum·ber /'kju:kʌmbə(r)/ *n* [C, U] 黄瓜 huángguā.

cud /kʌd/ *n* [U] 反刍〔芻〕的食物 fǎnchúde shíwù. ***chew the ~*** [喻]深思 shēnsī; 细想 xìxiǎng.

cuddle /'kʌdl/ *vt/i* **1** 拥〔擁〕抱 yōngbào, 怀〔懷〕抱 huáibào. **2** 贴身而睡 tiēshēn ér shuì, 蜷曲着身子 juǎnqū zhe shēnzi: *The dog ~d close to the fire.* 狗在火旁蜷曲地躺着. □ *n* [C] 拥抱 yōngbào, 搂〔摟〕抱 lǒubào. **cud·dly** *adj* 引人搂抱的 yǐnrén lǒubào de.

cud·gel /'kʌdʒəl/ *vt, n* [C] [-ll-] 用短粗的棍棒打 yòng duǎncūde gùnbàng dǎ; 短粗的棍棒 duǎncūde gùnbàng.

cue[1] /kju:/ *n* [C] **1** [戏剧]尾白 wěibái; 提示 tíshì. **2** 暗示 ànshì.

cue[2] /kju:/ *n* [C] (台球戏中的)弹〔彈〕子棒 dànzǐbàng.

cuff[1] /kʌf/ *n* [C] 袖口 xiùkǒu; 护〔護〕腕 hùwàn. ***off the ~*** 即兴〔興〕地 jìxìngde; 非正式地 fēizhèngshìde. '**~-link** (衬衫袖口的)链〔鏈〕扣 liànkòu.

cuff[2] /kʌf/ *vt, n* [C] 掌击〔擊〕zhǎngjī; 打一巴掌 dǎ yī bāzhang.

cui·sine /kwɪ'zi:n/ *n* [U] [法语] 烹饪 pēngrèn, 烹饪法 pēngrènfǎ.

cul-de-sac /'kʌl də sæk/ *n* [C] 死胡同 sǐhútòng, 死巷 sǐxiàng.

cul·len·der /'kʌləndə(r)/ *n* [C] = colander.

cul·mi·nate /'kʌlmɪneɪt/ *vt* ~ ***in*** 达〔達〕到顶点〔點〕 dádào dǐngdiǎn; 告终 gàozhōng. **cul·mi'na·tion** *n* [C] 顶点 dǐngdiǎn, 极〔極〕点 jídiǎn.

cul·prit /'kʌlprɪt/ *n* [C] 犯人 fànrén, 罪犯 zuìfàn.

cult /kʌlt/ *n* [C] **1** 宗教崇拜 zōngjiào chóngbài, 迷信 míxìn **2** 崇拜 chóngbài, 狂热〔熱〕kuángrè.

cul·ti·vate /'kʌltɪveɪt/ *vt* **1** 耕作(土地) gēnzuò, 培植(作物) péizhí. **2** 培养〔養〕péiyǎng, 磨炼〔煉〕móliàn. **cul·ti·vated** *adj* 有教养的 yǒu jiàoyǎng de, 有修养的 yǒu xiūyǎng de, 举〔舉〕止文雅的 jǔzhǐ wényǎ de. ˌ**cul·ti'va·tion** *n* [C]

cul·ture /'kʌltʃə(r)/ *n* **1** [U] 人类

〔類〕能力的高度发〔發〕展 rénlèi nénglì de gāodù fāzhǎn; 身,心修养〔養〕 shēn xīn xiūyǎng; 教养 jiàoyǎng; 陶冶 táoyě. **2** [C] 文化 wénhuà, 精神文明 jīngshén wénmíng: *Chinese* ~ 中国文化. **3** [U] 栽培 zāipéi, 养殖 yǎngzhí. **4** [C] 培养 péiyǎng. **cul·tural** *adj* 文化的 wénhuàde; 文化上的 wénhuà shàng de. **cul·tured** *adj* 有修养的 yǒu xiūyǎng de, 有教养的 yǒu jiàoyǎng de.

cul·vert /'kʌlvət/ *n* [C] 排水沟〔溝〕páishuǐgōu; 阴〔陰〕沟 yīngōu.

cum·ber·some /'kʌmbəsəm/ *adj* 笨重的 bènzhòngde, 不便携〔攜〕带〔帶〕的 búbiàn xiédài de.

cumu·lat·ive /'kju:mjʊlətɪv/ *adj* 累积〔積〕的 lěijīde, 累加的 lěijiāde.

cun·ning /'kʌnɪŋ/ *adj* 狡猾的 jiǎohuáde, 精巧的 jīngqiǎode. □ *n* [U] 狡猾 jiǎohuá, 精巧 jīngqiǎo. ~**ly** *adv*

cup[1] /kʌp/ *n* [C] **1** 杯 bēi; 一杯 yībēi; 一杯的量 yībēide liàng. ***not my ~ of tea*** [非正式用语]不是我所喜爱〔愛〕的 búshì wǒ suǒ xǐài de. **2** 奖〔獎〕杯 jiǎngbēi, 优〔優〕胜〔勝〕杯 yōushèngbēi. '~**ful** *n* [C] 一满杯 yīmǎnbēi, 半品脱的量 bànpǐntuōde liàng.

cup[2] /kʌp/ *vt* [-pp-] 作杯状〔狀〕zuò bēizhuàng: ~ *one's hands* 两手作成杯的样子.

cup·board /'kʌbəd/ *n* [C] 碗橱 wǎnchú, 食橱 shíchú.

cur /kɜ:(r)/ *n* [C] **1** 恶〔惡〕狗 ègǒu, 劣种〔種〕狗 lièzhǒnggǒu. **2** 卑怯的家伙 bǐqiède jiāhuo; 坏〔壞〕人 huàirén.

cur·able /'kjʊərəbl/ *adj* 可以医〔醫〕好的 kěyǐ yīhǎo de.

curate /'kjʊərət/ *n* [C] 副牧师〔師〕fùmùshī.

cura·tive /'kjʊərətɪv/ *adj* 治病的 zhìbìngde, 有疗〔療〕效的 yǒu liáoxiào de: *the ~ power of a medicine* 药物的疗效.

cu·ra·tor /kjʊ'reɪtə(r)/ *n* [C] (博物馆,画廊等的) 馆长〔長〕 guǎnzhǎng.

curb /kɜ:b/ *n* [C] **1** 勒马〔馬〕的皮带〔帶〕lēmǎde pídài. **2** [喻]控制 kòngzhì, 抑制 yìzhì, 约束 yuēsù: *a ~ on price increases* 控制物价上涨. **3** = kerb. □ *vt* **1** 勒住马 lēzhù mǎ. **2** 控制 kòngzhì, 约束 yuēsù.

curd /kɜ:d/ *n* **1** [C] [常用 *pl*] 凝乳 níngrǔ. **2** [U] 凝乳样〔樣〕的东〔東〕西 níngrǔyàngde dōngxi: ,*lemon-*'~ 柠檬乳糕.

curdle /'kɜ:dl/ *vt/i* (使)凝结 níngjié.

cure /kjʊə(r)/ *vt/i* **1** 治愈〔癒〕zhìyù; 纠正(弊病) jiūzhèng. **2** 加工处〔處〕理(肉,鱼等) jiāgōng chǔlǐ. □ *n* [C] 治愈 zhìyù, 痊愈 quányù; 疗〔療〕法 liáofǎ, 药〔藥〕 yào; 对策 duìcè.

cur·few /'kɜ:fju:/ *n* [C] 戒严〔嚴〕jièyán, 宵禁 xiāojìn.

curi·os·ity /ˌkjʊərɪ'ɒsətɪ/ *n* [*pl* -ies] **1** [U] 好奇 hàoqí, 好奇心 hàoqíxīn. **2** [C] 奇异〔異〕的东〔東〕西 qíyìde dōngxi, 珍品 zhēnpǐn, 奇特性 qítèxìng.

curi·ous /'kjʊərɪəs/ *adj* **1** 好奇的 hàoqíde, 爱〔愛〕打听〔聽〕的 ài dǎtīng de. **2** 爱管闲〔閑〕事的 ài guǎn xiánshì de. **3** 稀奇古怪的 xīqígǔguàide, 不寻〔尋〕常的 bùxúnchángde.

curl /kɜ:l/ *n* [C] 卷毛 juǎnmáo; 卷发〔髮〕juǎnfà. □ *vt/i* (使)卷曲 juǎnqū.

curly /'kɜ:lɪ/ *adj* [-ier, -iest] 卷曲的 juǎnqūde, 卷缩的 juǎnsuō de 有卷毛的 yǒu juǎnmáo de, 有卷发的 yǒu juǎnfà de.

cur·rant /'kʌrənt/ *n* [C] **1** 无〔無〕核小葡萄干〔乾〕wúhé xiǎo pútaogān. **2** 红醋栗 hóngcùlì; 红醋栗树〔樹〕hóngcùlìshù.

cur·rency /'kʌrənsɪ/ *n* [*pl* -ies] **1** [U] 通用 tōngyòng, 流通 liútōng. **2** [C, U] 通货 tōnghuò, 货币〔幣〕huòbì.

cur·rent[1] /'kʌrənt/ *adj* **1** 通用的 tōngyòngde, 流行的 liúxíngde. **2** 当〔當〕前的 dāngqiánde, 现今的 xiànjīnde, 现行的 xiànxíngde: ~ *news* (或 *affairs*) 时事. '~ **account** 活期存款 huóqī cúnkuǎn. ,~ **af'fairs** 时事 shíshì. ~**ly** *adv*

cur·rent[2] /'kʌrənt/ *n* [C] **1** 流 liú; 水流 shuǐliú; 气〔氣〕流 qìliú; 电〔電〕流 diànliú. **2** 趋〔趨〕势〔勢〕qūshì, 倾向 qīngxiàng, 潮流 cháoliú.

cur·ricu·lum /kə'rɪkjʊləm/ *n* [C] [*pl* ~s 或 -la /-lə/] 学〔學〕校的课程 xuéxiàode kèchéng. ~ '**vitae** /'vi:taɪ/ [拉丁语]简〔簡〕短的履历〔歷〕书〔書〕jiǎnduǎnde lǚlìshū.

curry[1] /'kʌrɪ/ *n* [C, U] [*pl* -ies] 咖喱 gālí; 咖喱食品 gālí shípǐn. □ *vt* [*pt, pp* -ied] 加咖喱 jiā gālí.

curry[2] /'kʌrɪ/ *vt* [*pt, pp* -ied] ~ ***favour (with sb)*** 求宠〔寵〕qiúchǒng, 献〔獻〕媚 xiànmèi, 拍马〔馬〕屁 pāimǎpì.

curse[1] /kɜːs/ *n* [C] **1** 咒骂〔駡〕 zhòumà, 诅咒 zǔzhòu. **2** 祸因 huòyīn, 祸根 huògēn: *Alcohol was his* ~. 酒是他的祸根. **3** 骂人话 màrén huà, 恶〔惡〕语 èyǔ.

curse[2] /kɜːs/ *vt/i* **1** 咒骂〔駡〕 zhòumà, 咒诅 zhòuzǔ. **2** *be ~d with* 被…所苦 bèi…suǒ kǔ. 因…遭殃 yīn…zāoyāng. **cursed** /-t, '-ɪd/ *adj* **(a)** 可恨的 kěhènde. **(b)** [非正式用语]该死的 gāisǐde, 万〔萬〕恶〔惡〕的 wàn'è de.

curt /kɜːt/ *adj* 草率的 cǎoshuàide, 简〔簡〕短的 jiǎnduǎnde. **~ly** *adv* **~ness** *n* [U]

cur·tail /kɜː'teɪl/ *vt* 截短 jiéduǎn, 缩短 suōduǎn, 削减 xiāojiǎn. **~ment** *n* [C, U] 缩短 suōduǎn, 缩减 suōjiǎn, 减少 jiǎnshǎo.

cur·tain /'kɜːtn/ *n* [C] **1** 帘 lián; 窗帘 chuānglián. **2** 幕 mù. **3** 遮蔽 zhēbì, 保护〔護〕 bǎohù: *a* ~ *of mist* 一层薄雾. □ *vt* 装〔裝〕上帘子 zhuāngshàng liánzi; 用帘子遮住 yòng liánzi zhēzhù.

curt·sey, curtsy /'kɜːtsɪ/ *n* [C] [*pl* ~s, -ies] 西方女子的屈膝礼〔禮〕 xīfāng nǚzǐ de qūqīlǐ. □ *vi* [*pt, pp* ~ed, -ied] 行屈膝礼 xíng qūqīlǐ.

curve /kɜːv/ *n* [C] 曲线 qūxiàn. □ *vt/i* 弄弯〔彎〕 nòng wān; 使成曲线 shǐ chéng qūxiàn; 成曲线 chéng qūxiàn.

cushion /'kʊʃn/ *n* [C] **1** 垫〔墊〕子 diànzi; 坐垫 zuòdiàn; 靠垫 kàodiàn. **2** 垫状〔狀〕物 diànzhuàngwù: *a* ~ *of air* 气垫. □ *vt* **1** 装〔裝〕垫子 zhuāng diànzi. **2** 使减少震动〔動〕 shǐ jiǎnshǎo zhèndòng, 缓和冲〔衝〕击〔擊〕huǎnhé chōngjī.

cus·tard /'kʌstəd/ *n* [C, U] 牛奶蛋糊 niúnǎi dànhú.

cus·tod·ian /kə'stəʊdɪən/ *n* [C] **1** 保管人 bǎoguǎnrén; 监〔監〕护〔護〕人 jiānhùrén. **2** 公共建筑〔築〕的看守人 gōnggòngjiànzhùde kānshǒurén

cus·tody /'kʌstədɪ/ *n* [U] **1** 保管 bǎoguǎn; 保护〔護〕 bǎohù; 监〔監〕护 jiānhù: *give her* ~ *of the child* 由她监护孩子. **2** 监〔監〕禁 jiānjìn; 拘留 jūliú. **(*be*) *in*** ~ 被拘留 bèi jūliú; 被监禁 bèi jiānjìn.

cus·tom /'kʌstəm/ *n* **1** [U] 习〔習〕俗 xísú, 惯例 guànlì. **2** [C] 习惯 xíguàn. **3** [U] (顾客的)光顾〔顧〕 guānggù. **4** [*pl*] (*the C~s*) 海关〔關〕 hǎiguān. **~-built** 定做的 dìngzuòde, 定制〔製〕的 dìngzhìde. **~ary** *adj* 通常的 tōngchángde, 惯例的 guànlìde, 常例的 chánglìde.

cus·tomer /'kʌstəmə(r)/ *n* [C] 顾〔顧〕客 gùkè.

cut[1] /kʌt/ *n* [C] **1** 切 qiē; 割 gē; 剪 jiǎn; 砍 kǎn; 削 xiāo; 截 jié. **2** 削减 xiāojiǎn, 缩短 suōduǎn, 删节〔節〕 shānjié: *a* ~ *in taxes* 减税. **3** 切下的部分 qiēxiàde bùfen: *a* ~ *of beef* 一块牛肉. **4** 剪裁式样〔樣〕 jiǎncái shìyàng; 发〔髮〕式 fàshì.

cut[2] /kʌt/ *vt/i* [*pt, pp* ~] [-tt-] **1** 割 gē; 切 qiē; 剪 jiǎn; 砍 kǎn; 削 xiāo. **2 (a)** (切,削,剪等工具)使用 shǐyòng. **(b)** 能被割开〔開〕, 切开 néng bèi gēkāi, qiēkāi. **3** 离〔離〕开〔開〕 líkāi: ~ *a class* 旷课. **4** (线条)相交 xiāngjiāo. **5** ~ **(*off*) *a corner*** 抄近路 chāojìnlù, 不绕〔繞〕角走 bú rào jiǎo zǒu. ~ ***corners*** [喻]走捷径〔徑〕 zǒu jiéjìng. ~ ***one's losses*** 赶紧〔緊〕脱手以免多受损失 gǎnjǐn tuōshǒu yǐmiǎn duō shòu sǔnshī. **6** ~ ***sb dead*** 装〔裝〕作未看见某人 zhuāngzuò wèi kànjiàn mǒurén. ~ ***sth open*** 打开〔開〕口子 dǎkāi kǒuzi. ~ ***sth short*** 缩短 suōduǎn, 截短 jiéduǎn. **7** ,~ ***and 'dried*** 早已准〔準〕备〔備〕好的 zǎoyǐ zhǔnbèi hǎo de; 陈〔陳〕套的 chéntàode. **8** ~ ***across sth*** 抄近路通过〔過〕 chāo jìnlù tōngguò; 对〔對〕直通过 duìzhí tōngguò. ~ ***sth back*** **(a)** 修剪枝叶〔葉〕 xiūjiǎn zhīyè; 截短 jiéduǎn. **(b)** 削减 xiāojiǎn; 减缩 jiǎnsuō: ~ *back the number of workers* 减缩工人的数额. **'cut·back** *n* [C] ~ ***sth (sb) down*** **(a)** 砍倒 kǎndǎo. **(b)** 砍死 kǎnsǐ; 砍伤〔傷〕 kǎnshāng. **(c)** 削减 xiāojiǎn, 减少 jiǎnshǎo, 缩短 suōduǎn. **(d)** 说服某人降低价〔價〕格 shuōfú mǒurén jiàngdī jiàgé. ~ ***down on*** 减少对〔對〕…的消费 jiǎnshǎo duì…de xiāofèi. ~ ***in*** 插嘴 chāzuǐ. ~ ***sb (sth) off (from)*** **(a)** 切掉 qiēdiào; 割掉 gēdiào; 剪掉 jiǎndiào; 删去 shānqù; 砍掉 kǎndiào. **(b)** 切断〔斷〕 qiēduàn: ~ *off the gas* 切断煤气供应. **(c)** 使隔绝 shǐ géjué, 孤立 gūlì, 断绝 duànjué: *towns* ~ *off by floods* 被洪水围困的市镇. ~ ***out*** 停止起作用 tíngzhǐ qǐ zuòyòng, 停止运〔運〕转〔轉〕 tíngzhǐ yùnzhuǎn. ~ ***sth out*** **(a)** 切去 qiēqù, 剪下 jiǎnxià, 割掉 gēdiào. **(b)** 切成 qiēchéng; 剪成 jiǎnchéng. **(c)** [非正式用语]省去 shěngqù, 略去 lüèqù, 删去 shānqù. **(d)** [非正式用语]停止 tíngzhǐ, 中

止 zhōngzhǐ: ~ *out cigarettes* 戒烟. **(*not*) *be* ~ *out for*** 天生(不)是…的料子 tiānshēng shì... de liàozi; (没)有…的能力 yǒu...de nénglì. **~ *sth* (*sb*) *up*** **(a)** 切碎 qiēsuì. **(b)** [非正式用语] 使丧气〔氣〕shǐ sàngqì, 使心烦意乱〔亂〕shǐ xīnfányìluàn. ,~'**price** 削价〔價〕xiāojià, 减价 jiǎnjià. ,~-'**rate** *adj* 减价的 jiǎnjiàde, 削价的 xiāojiàde.

cute /kju:t/ *adj* [-r, -st] [非正式用语]漂亮的 piàoliangde, 逗人喜爱〔愛〕的 dòurén xǐ'ài de.

cu·ticle /'kju:tɪkl/ *n* [C] 指甲根部的表皮 zhǐjiā gēnbù de biǎopí.

cut·lass /'kʌtləs/ *n* [C]水手用的短剑〔劍〕, 弯〔彎〕刀 shuǐshǒu yòng de duǎnjiàn, wāndāo.

cut·lery /'kʌtlərɪ/ *n* [U] 刀叉餐具 dāo chā cānjù.

cut·let /'kʌtlɪt/ *n* [C] 肉片 ròupiàn; 鱼片 yúpiàn; 炸肉排 zháròupái.

cut·ter /'kʌtə(r)/ *n* [C] **1** 从事切, 割, 剪, 削的人 cóngshì qiē, gē, jiǎn, xiāo de rén. 切, 割机〔機〕器 qiē gē jīqì. **2** 独〔獨〕桅帆船 dúwéi fānchuán.

cut-throat /'kʌtθrəʊt/ *n* [C] 凶手 xiōngshǒu, 谋杀〔殺〕者 móushāzhě. □ *adj* 杀人的 shārénde; 残〔殘〕酷的 cánkùde: ~ *competition between shops* 商店与商店之间你死我活的竞争.

cut·ting[1] /'kʌtɪŋ/ *adj* **1** 锋利的 fēnglìde. **2** 尖刻的 jiānkède, 刻薄的 kèbóde: ~ *remarks about the singer's performance* 对歌唱家的表演的刻薄评语.

cut·ting[2]/'kʌtɪŋ/ *n* [C] **1** 开〔開〕凿〔鑿〕出来〔來〕的公路, 铁〔鐵〕路 kāizáo chūlái de gōnglù, tiělù. **2** 剪报〔報〕jiǎnbào. **3** 供扦插用的插枝, 插条〔條〕gòng qiānchā yòng de chāzhī, chātiáo.

cuttle·fish /'kʌtlfɪʃ/ *n* [C] 乌贼鱼 wūzéiyú, 墨鱼 mòyú.

cy·an·ide /'saɪənaɪd/ *n* [U] 氰化物 qínghuàwù.

cy·ber·net·ics /ˌsaɪbə'netɪks/ *n* [U] 控制论〔論〕kòngzhìlùn **cy·ber·net·ic** *adj*

cycle /'saɪkl/ *n* [C] **1** 循环〔環〕xúnhuán; 周期 zhōuqī; 周转〔轉〕zhōuzhuǎn: *the ~ of the seasons* 四季循环. **2** 自行车〔車〕zìxíngchē (bicycle 的缩略). □ *vi* 乘自行车 chéng zìxíngchē. **cyc·lic(al)** *adj* 循环的 xúnhuánde, 周期的 zhōuqīde, 轮〔輪〕转的 lúnzhuànde. **cyc·list** 骑自行车的人 qí zìxíngchē de rén.

cyc·lone /'saɪkləʊn/ *n* [C] 旋风〔風〕xuànfēng; 气〔氣〕旋 qìxuàn. **cyc·lonic** /saɪ'klɒnɪk/ *adj*

cyclo·tron /'saɪklətron/ *n* [C] (原子能)回旋加速器 huíxuán jiāsùqì.

cyg·net /'sɪgnɪt/ *n* [C] 小天鹅〔鵝〕xiǎo tiān'é.

cyl·in·der /'sɪlɪndə(r)/ *n* [C] **1** 圆桶 yuántǒng. **2** 汽缸 qìgāng. **cy·lin·dri·cal** /sɪ'lɪndrɪkl/ *adj* 圆柱体〔體〕的 yuánzhùtǐde; 圆桶形的 yuántǒngxíngde.

cym·bal /'sɪmbl/*n* [C] [音樂]铙〔鐃〕钹 náobó; 钗 chǎ.

cynic /'sɪnɪk/ *n* [C] 好挖苦人的人 hào wākǔ rén de rén; 愤世嫉俗者 fènshìjísúzhě. **~ism** /'sɪnɪsɪzəm/ *n* [U] 挖苦话 wākǔhuà; 冷言冷语 lěngyánlěngyǔ. **~al** *adj* 冷嘲热〔熱〕讽〔諷〕的 lěngcháorèfěngde. **~ally** *adv*

cy·pher /'saɪfə(r)/*n* [C] = cipher.

cy·press /'saɪprəs/ *n* [C] 柏属〔屬〕植物 bǎishǔ zhíwù.

cyst /sɪst/ *n* [C] [生物]胞 bāo; 囊 náng.

czar /zɑ:(r)/ *n* (亦作 **tsar**) 俄国〔國〕沙皇 éguó shāhuáng. **~ina** /zɑ:'ri:nə/ *n* 俄国沙皇皇后 éguó shāhuáng huánghòu; 女沙皇 nǚshāhuáng.

D d

D, d /di:/ [*pl* D's, d's /di:z/] **1** 英语的第四个字母 yīngyǔde dìsìgè zìmǔ. **2** 罗〔馬〕数〔數〕字的 500 luómǎ shùzìde 500.

d. =**1** daughter. **2** died. **3** penny. **4** pence.

dab /dæb/ *vt/i* [-bb-] 轻〔輕〕拍 qīngpāi; 轻敲 qīngqiāo; 轻搽 qīngchá. □ *n* [C] **1** (轻搽, 轻敷用的)湿〔濕〕而软〔軟〕的小块 (颜料等) shī ér ruǎn de xiǎokuài. **2** 轻拍 qīngpāi; 轻打 qīngdǎ.

dabble /'dæbl/ *vt/i* **1** 溅〔濺〕湿〔濕〕jiànshī; 弄湿 nòngshī. **2** 涉猎〔獵〕shèliè; 把…作为〔爲〕业〔業〕余〔餘〕爱〔愛〕好 bǎ ... zuòwéi yèyú àihào.

dachs·hund /'dækshʊnd/ *n* [C] 德国〔國〕种〔種〕的小猎〔獵〕狗 déguózhǒngde xiǎoliègǒu.

dad /dæd/ *n* [C] [非正式用语] = father.

daddy /'dædɪ/ *n* [C] [*pl* -ies] 儿〔兒〕语: 爸爸 éryǔ: bàba.

daf·fo·dil /'dæfədɪl/ *n* [C] 黄水仙 huángshuǐxiān.

daft /dɑ:ft/ *adj* [-er, -est] [非正式用语]傻的 shǎde, 愚笨的 yúbènde. ~**ly** *adv*

dag·ger /'dægə(r)/ *n* [C] 短剑〔劍〕duǎnjiàn, 匕首 bǐshǒu. ***look ~s at*** 怒目而视 nùmùérshì.

daily /'deɪlɪ/ *adj, adv* 每天的 měitiānde, 每天地 měitiānde. □ *n* [C] [*pl* -ies] 日报〔報〕rìbào.

dainty /'deɪntɪ/ *adj* [-ier, -iest] **1** 秀丽〔麗〕的 xiùlìde; 优〔優〕雅的 yōuyǎde. **2** 精致〔緻〕的 jīngzhìde, 精巧的 jīngqiǎode: *a ~ flower* 娟秀的花. **dain·tily** *adv* **dainti·ness** *n* [U]

dairy /'deərɪ/ *n* [C] [*pl* -ies] **1** 牛奶及乳品店 niúnǎi jí rǔpǐn diàn. **2** 牛奶房 niúnǎifáng, 牛奶场 niúnǎichǎng; 制〔製〕酪场〔場〕zhìlàochǎng. '~**cattle**奶牛nǎiniú.

dais /'deɪɪs/ *n* [C] [*pl*~es/-sɪz/] (宴会大厅一端的) 台〔臺〕tái; 高台 gāotái.

daisy /'deɪzɪ/*n* [C] [*pl* -ies] 雏〔雛〕菊 chújú. '~**wheel** *n* 菊花轮〔輪〕(打印机) júhuālún.

dale /deɪl/ *n*[C] =valley.

dam /dæm/ *n* [C] 水坝〔壩〕shuǐbà; 水堤 shuǐdī; 水闸〔閘〕shuǐzhá. □ *vt* [-mm-] **1** 筑〔築〕水坝蓄水 zhùshuǐbà xùshuǐ. **2** [喻] 控制 kòngzhì; 抑制 yìzhì; 阻拦〔攔〕zǔlán: *~ the flood of criticism* 阻止了洪水般的批评.

dam·age / 'dæmɪdʒ/ *n* **1** [U] 损坏〔壞〕sǔnhuài; 损失 sǔnshī; 毁坏 huǐhuài; 破坏 pòhuài: *The fire caused great ~*. 火灾造成巨大损失. **2** [*pl*] [法律]损失赔偿〔償〕金 sǔnshī péichángjīn. □ *vt* 损坏 sǔnhuài 毁坏 huǐhuài

dame /deɪm/*n* [C] 夫人 fūrén; 贵夫人 guìfūrén.

damn /dæm/ *vt* **1** (上帝) 罚…入地狱 fá … rù dìyù; 诅咒 zǔzhòu. **2** 谴责 qiǎnzé; 指责 zhǐzé. □ *n* ***not (be) worth a ~*** 毫无〔無〕价〔價〕值 háowú jiàzhí; 根本不值得 gēnběn bùzhídé. ~**able** /'dæmnəbl/ *adj* **(a)** 活该的 huógāide; 该死的 gāisǐde. **(b)** [非正式用语] 糟糕透了的 zāogāo tòule de. ~**a·tion** /dæm'neɪʃn/ *n* [U] 罚入地狱 fárù dìyù; 毁灭〔滅〕huǐmiè. □ *int* 该死 gāisǐ; 混帐〔帳〕hùnzhàng. ~**ed** *adj* **(a)** ***the ~ed*** 打入地狱的 dǎrù dìyù de. **(b)** [非正式用语]该死的 gāisǐde. □ *adv* [非正式用语]非常 fēicháng; 要命地 yàomìngde: *~ed lucky* 运气太好了.

damp[1] /dæmp/ *adj* [-er, -est] 潮湿〔濕〕的 cháoshīde, 有湿气〔氣〕的 yǒu shīqì de: *a ~ room* 潮湿的房间. □ *n* [U] 潮湿 cháoshī, 湿气 shīqì. ~**ness** *n* [U]

damp[2] /dæmp/ *vt/i* **1** 使潮湿 shǐ cháoshī; 变〔變〕潮湿 biàn cháoshī. **2** (亦作 **'dampen**) 使沮丧 shǐ jǔsàng, 使败兴〔興〕shǐ bàixìng: *~ his enthusiasm* 给他的热情泼冷水. **3** ***~ down*** 减弱火势〔勢〕jiǎnruò huǒshì.

dampen /'dæmpən/ *vt/i* = damp[2] (2).

damper /'dæmpə(r)/ *n* [C] **1** 风〔風〕挡〔擋〕fēngdǎng; 气〔氣〕流调节〔節〕器 qìliú tiáojiéqì. **2** 令人扫〔掃〕兴〔興〕的人或事 lìngrén sǎoxìng de rén huò shì: *put a ~ on the party* 使聚会大为扫兴.

dam·son /'dæmzn/ *n* [C] 布拉斯李 bùlāsīlǐ; 布拉斯李树〔樹〕bùlāsīlǐ shù.

dance /dɑ:ns/ *n* [C] **1** 舞蹈 wǔdǎo, 跳舞 tiàowǔ; 舞曲 wǔqǔ. **2** 舞会〔會〕wǔhuì. □ *vt/i* **1** 跳舞 tiàowǔ. **2** 表演某一舞蹈 biǎoyǎn mǒuyī wǔdǎo. **3** 手舞足蹈 shǒuwǔzúdǎo; 跳跃〔躍〕tiàoyuè. **dancer** 跳舞者 tiàowǔzhě, 舞蹈演员 wǔdǎo yǎnyuán. **danc·ing** *adj, n* [U]

dan·de·lion /'dændɪlaɪən/ *n* [C] 蒲公英 púgōngyīng.

dan·druff /'dændrʌf/ *n* [U] 头〔頭〕垢 tóugòu, 头皮屑 tóupíxiè.

dan·ger /'deɪndʒə(r)/ *n* **1** [U] 危险〔險〕wēixiǎn. ***in ~*** 在危险中 zài wēixiǎn zhōng. ***out of ~*** 脱离〔離〕危险 tuōlí wēixiǎn. **2** [C] 危险的事物 wēixiǎnde shìwù; 危险人物 wēixiǎn rénwù. '~**ous** /'deɪndʒərəs/ *adj* 危险的 wēixiǎnde. ~**ously** *adv*

dangle /'dæŋgl/ *vt/i* 摇晃地悬〔懸〕挂〔掛〕着 yáohuàngde xuánguà zhe.

dank /dæŋk/ *adj* [-er, -est] 湿〔濕〕冷的 shīlěngde; 阴〔陰〕湿的 yīnshīde.

dare[1] /deə(r)/ *aux* [第三人称单数是 dare, 不是 dares] 敢 gǎn, 竟敢 jìnggǎn: *How ~ he say rude things about me!* 他怎么敢说这种对我无礼的话!

dare[2] /deə(r)/ *vt/i* **1** 敢 gǎn: *I ~n't do that.* 我不敢那样做. **2** 估计…没胆〔膽〕量 (激将) gūjì … méi dǎnliàng: *I ~ you (to say that again)*! 我估计你没胆量(再说一遍)! □*n*[只用于] ***do sth for a ~*** 逞能而为 chěngnéng érwéi. **'~-devil** 胆大妄为的人 dǎndà wàngwéi de rén.

dar·ing /'deərɪŋ/ *n* [U]大胆〔膽〕dàdǎn, 鲁莽 lǔmǎng. □ *adj* 大胆的 dàdǎnde, 鲁莽的 lǔmǎngde. **~-ly** *adv*

dark[1] /dɑːk/ *adj* [-er, -est] **1** 黑暗的 hēi'ànde, 暗的 ànde: *a ~ colour* 暗色; *a ~ room* 黑暗的房间. **2** (指颜色)深色的 shēnsède, 暗色的 ànsède. **3** (指肤色) 黑色的 hēisède, 浅〔淺〕黑的 qiǎnhēide. **4**〔喻〕隐藏的 yǐncángde, 秘密的 mìmìde: *a ~ secret* 严守的秘密. ***a ~ horse*** 〔喻〕黑马〔馬〕hēimǎ, 竞〔競〕争中出人意料的胜〔勝〕利者 jìngzhēng zhōng chūrényìliàode shènglìzhě. **5** 没有希望的 méi yǒu xīwàng de; 无〔無〕精打采的 wújīngdǎcǎide: *the ~ days of war* 战争中悲观失望的时期. **~ly** *adv* **~ness** *n* [U]

dark[2] /dɑːk/ *n* [U] **1** 黑暗 hēi'àn, 黄昏 huánghūn. **2**〔喻〕无〔無〕知 wúzhī: *be in the ~* 不知道. *keep him in the ~* 不让他知道.

dar·ling /'dɑːlɪŋ/ *n* [C] 心爱〔愛〕的人 xīn'àide rén; 宠〔寵〕物 chǒngwù.

darn /dɑːn/ *vt/i* 织〔織〕补〔補〕zhībǔ. □ *n* [C] 织补处〔處〕zhībǔchù.

dart[1] /dɑːt/ *n* [C] **1** 突进 tūjìn. **2** 标〔標〕枪〔槍〕biāoqiāng.

dart[2] /dɑːt/ *vt/i* (使)突进 tūjìn, (使)急冲〔衝〕jíchōng.

dash[1] /dæʃ/ *n* **1** [C] 撞击〔擊〕zhuàngjī; 猛冲〔衝〕měngchōng. **2** [C] 液体〔體〕的撞击声〔聲〕yètǐde zhuàngjīshēng: *the ~ of waves on the rocks* 波浪撞击岩石的声音. **3** [C] 少量的搀〔攙〕和物 shǎoliàngde chānhéwù: *a ~ of pepper* 加一点胡椒. **4** [C] 破折号〔號〕pòzhéhào. **5** 短跑 duǎnpǎo; 猛冲 měngchōng. **6** [U] 锐气 ruìqì, 闯〔闖〕劲〔勁〕chuǎngjìn: *a man with great ~* 很有闯劲的人. **'~board** 车〔車〕辆〔輛〕的挡〔擋〕泥板 chēliàngde dǎngníbǎn.

dash[2] /dæʃ/ *vt/i* **1** 猛冲〔衝〕měngchōng; 猛砸 měngzá; 击〔擊〕碎 jīsuì: *~ a glass against the wall* 把玻璃杯摔到墙上. **2** ***~ sb's hopes*** 使某人希望破灭〔滅〕shǐ mǒurén xīwàng pòmiè. **~ing** *adj* 闯劲很大的 chuǎngjìn hěndà de; 精神抖擞〔擻〕的 jīngshén dǒusǒu de.

data /'deɪtə/ *n pl* **1** 事实〔實〕资料 shìshí zīliào; 已知材料 yǐzhī cáiliào. **2** 供电〔電〕子计算机〔機〕程序用的资料 gōng diànzǐjìsuànjī chéngxù yòng de zīliào. **'~bank** 资料库 zīliàokù. **,~'processing** 数〔數〕据〔據〕处〔處〕理 shùjù chǔlǐ.

date[1] /deɪt/ *n* [C] **1** 日期 rìqī, 日子 rìzi. **2** ***(be* 或 *go) out of ~*** 过〔過〕时〔時〕的 guòshíde, 陈〔陳〕旧〔舊〕的 chénjiùde. ***to ~*** 到此刻为〔爲〕止 dào cǐkè wéizhǐ. ***(be* 或 *bring) up to ~*** 现代的 xiàndàide; 新式的 xīnshìde, 时新的 shíxīnde. **3**〔非正式用语〕约会〔會〕yuēhuì. **4**〔非正式用语〕约会的异〔異〕性对〔對〕象 yuēhuìde yìxìng duìxiàng.

date[2] /deɪt/ *vt/i* **1** 注明…的日期 zhùmíng … de rìqī. **2** ***~ from* (或 *back to*)** 自…时〔時〕代至今 zì … shídài zhì jīn. 属〔屬〕于…时代 shǔyú … shídài. **3** 过〔過〕时 guòshí. **4** 和…约会〔會〕hé … yuēhuì. **dated** *adj* 过时的 guòshíde.

date[3] /deɪt/ *n* [C] 海枣〔棗〕hǎizǎo; 枣椰子 zǎoyēzi.

daub/dɔːb/ *vt/i* **1** 涂〔塗〕抹 túmǒ. **2** 乱〔亂〕画〔畫〕luànhuà. **3** 弄脏〔髒〕nòngzāng. □ *n* [C, U] 涂料(泥灰,油脂等) túliào.

daugh·ter /'dɔːtə(r)/ *n* [C] 女儿〔兒〕nǚ'ér **'~-in-law** [*pl* ~s-in-law] 儿媳 érxí.

daunt /dɔːnt/ *vt* 威吓〔嚇〕wēixià. 使胆〔膽〕怯 shǐ dǎnquè **~less** *adj* 大胆的 dàdǎnde, 无〔無〕所畏惧〔懼〕的 wúsuǒ wèijù de, 吓不倒的 xià bù dǎo de.

dawdle /'dɔːdl/ *vt/i* 游荡〔蕩〕yóudàng, 胡混 húhùn.

dawn /dɔːn/ *n* [C] **1** 黎明 límíng, 破晓〔曉〕pòxiǎo. **2**〔喻〕开〔開〕始 kāishǐ; 发〔發〕生 fāshēng: *the ~ of civilisation* 文明的发端. □ *vi* **1** 破晓 pòxiǎo. **2** ***~ on*** 渐〔漸〕被理解 jiàn bèi lǐjiě: *It ~ed on her that she was wrong.* 她逐渐明白她是错了.

day /deɪ/ *n* **1** [U] 白天 báitiān, 白昼〔晝〕báizhòu. **2** [C] 一天 yìtiān, 一日 yírì, 一昼夜 yízhòuyè. ***~ in, ~ out*** 天天 tiāntiān, 一天又一天 yìtiān yòu yìtiān; 连〔連〕续〔續〕不断〔斷〕地 liánxù búduàn de. ***one ~*** (过去) 某一天 mǒuyìtiān; (将来)有一天 yǒu yìtiān. ***the other ~*** (过去) 某一天 mǒuyìtiān. **3** [C] 工作日 gōngzuòrì. ***call it a ~*** 收工 shōugōng. **4** [C] 〔常用 *pl*〕日子 rìzi, 时代 shídài. ***make sb's ~*** 使某人快活

shǐ mǒurén kuàihuo. *the present* ～现代 xiàndài. **5** ***his*** **(*her*, *etc*)** ～(他,她等的)一生 yìshēng; 鼎盛时期 dǐngshèng shíqī. '**～break** 黎明 límíng, 破晓〔曉〕pòxiǎo. '**～-dream** *vi*, *n* [C] 白日做梦 báirìzuòmèng 白日梦 báirìmèng, 幻想 huànxiǎng. '**～light** *n* [U] **(a)** 日光 rìguāng; 白昼 báizhòu. **(b)** 黎明 límíng.

daze /deɪz/ *vt* 使茫然 shǐ mángrán; 使发〔發〕昏 shǐ fāhūn. □*n* ***in a ～*** 迷乱〔亂〕míluàn, 茫然 mángrán.

dazzle /'dæzl/ *vt* 眩眼 xuànyǎn, 耀眼 yàoyǎn.

d.c.= direct current.

D.C.L.= Doctor Divinity 民法学〔學〕博士 mínfǎxué bóshì.

D.D.= Doctor of Divinity 神学〔學〕博士 shénxué bóshì.

D.D.T.= *dichloro-diphenyl-trichloroethane* insecticide 滴滴涕 dīdītì.

de·ac·ti·vate /di:'æktɪˌveɪt/ *vt* 使去活化 shǐ qù huóhuà, 使(炸弹)不能爆炸 shǐ bùnéng bàozhà: *～ a bomb* 使炸弹不能爆炸. **de·ac·ti·va·tion** /di:ˌæktɪ'veɪʃn/ *n* [U]

dead /ded/*adj*, *n* [U] **1** 死的 sǐde; 死者 sǐzhě. **2** 无〔無〕动〔動〕静的 wú dòngjìng de: *The town is ～ after 10 o'clock.* 这个市镇十点钟以后就一片静寂. **3** (语言, 习惯等)废〔廢〕弃〔棄〕了的 fèiqìlede. **4** (手等)被冻得麻木 bèi dòng de mámù. **5** 完全的 wánquánde; 突然的 tūránde: *a ～ stop* 突然停住. **6** 失灵的 shīlíngde: 不能用的 bùnéng yòng de: *The telephone went ～.* 这电话坏了. **7** (声音)闷〔悶〕住的 mēnzhùde. **8** (颜色)灰暗的 huī'ànde. □*adv* 完全地 wánquánde, 绝对〔對〕地 juéduìde: *～ certain* 完全肯定; *～ accurate* 绝对正确. **～ centre** (机械)死点〔點〕sǐdiǎn; 静点 jìngdiǎn. ˌ**～'end** (街道)一头〔頭〕不通的 yìtóu bùtōng de, 死胡同 sǐhútong. '**～line** 最后〔後〕限期 zuìhòu xiànqī. **～ loss** 失败 shībài.

deaden /'dedn/ *vt* 闷抑(声音等) mēnyì; 使缓和 shǐ huǎnhé; 使失去光泽〔澤〕shǐ shīqù guāngzé.

dead·lock /'dedlɒk/*n* [C, U] 僵持 jiāngchí; 僵局 jiāngjú.

dead·ly /'dedlɪ/ *adj* [-ier, -iest] **1** 致命的 zhìmìngde 切中要害的 qièzhòng yàohài de: *a ～ poison* 致命的毒药. **2** 殊死的 shūsǐde, 不共戴天的 búgòngdàitiānde: *～ enemies* 不共戴天的敌人. □ *adv* 死一般的 sǐ yībān de.

deaf /def/ *adj* [-er, -est] **1** 聋〔聾〕的 lóngde. **2** 不听〔聽〕bùtīng. ***turn a ～ ear to*** 拒不倾听 jùbù qīngtīng. '**～-aid** 助听器 zhùtīngqì. ˌ**～'mute** 聋哑〔啞〕人 lóngyǎrén. **～ness** *n* [U]

deafen /'defn/ *vt* 震耳欲聋 zhèn ěr yù lóng.

deal[1] /di:l/ *n* [U] ***a good*** (或***great***) ～ 大量 dàliàng: *a good ～ of money* 大量金钱. □ *adv* 很 hěn; 常常 chángcháng: *I see him a great ～.* 我常常看见他.

deal[2] /di:l/ *n* [C] **1** 发〔發〕纸牌 fā zhǐpái, 轮〔輪〕到发纸牌 lúndào fā zhǐpái. **2** 买〔買〕卖〔賣〕mǎimài, 交易 jiāoyì.

deal[3] /di:l/ *vt*/*i* [*pt*, *pp* ～t /delt/] **1** 分配 fēnpèi, 分给 fēngěi: *～ cards* 发牌. **2** ～ ***in sth*** 经〔經〕营〔營〕jīngyíng: *shops ～ing in cheap goods* 经营廉价货品的商店. **3** 给予 gěiyǔ: *～ him a blow on the nose* 朝他的鼻子用力一击. **4** ～ ***with*** **(a)** 与〔與〕…有关〔關〕系, 有来〔來〕往 yǔ … yǒu guānxì, yǒu láiwǎng. **(b)** 处〔處〕理 chǔlǐ: *～ with an emergency* 处理紧急情况. **(c)** 有关 yǒuguān: *a book ～ing with Africa* 一本有关非洲的书. **～er** *n* [C] **(a)** 发纸牌的人 fā zhǐpái de rén. **(b)** 商人 shāngrén. **～ing** *n* **(a)** [U] 分配 fēnpèi, 分给 fēngěi; 对〔對〕待 duìdài, 处理 chǔlǐ. **(b)** [*pl*] 买〔買〕卖〔賣〕mǎimài, 交易 jiāoyì.

dealt /delt/ *pt*, *pp* of deal[3].

dean /di:n/ *n* [C] **1** (基督教)教长〔長〕jiàozhǎng. **2** (大学)系主任 xìzhǔrèn.

dear /dɪə(r)/ *adj* [-er, -est] **1** 亲〔親〕爱〔愛〕的 qīn'àide, 可爱的 kě'ài de. **2** 亲爱的(信件开头的套语) qīn'àide: *D～ Madam* 亲爱的女士, *D～ Sir* 亲爱的先生. **3** 昂贵的(价格) ángguìde, 索价〔價〕高的 suǒjià gāo de. **4** 可贵的 kěguìde. □ *adv* 高价地 gāojiàde. □ *n* [C] **1** 可爱的人 kě'àide rén, 亲爱的人 qīn'àide rén. **2** (对人的称呼)亲爱的 qīn'àide: "*Yes, ～.*" "好,亲爱的." □ *int* 呵! 哎呀! (表示惊讶, 伤感等) *Oh ～!* 呵,哎呀! *D～ me!* 哎呀, 我的天啊! **～ly** *adv* **(a)** 极〔極〕jí, 非常 fēicháng. **(b)** 高价地 gāojiàde.

dearth /dɜ:θ/ *n* [U] 缺乏 quēfá, 供应〔應〕不足 gōngyìng bùzú.

death /deθ/ *n* [C, U] **1** 死 sǐ, 死亡 sǐwáng. ***sick*** (或 ***bored***) ***to ～ of*** 对〔對〕…极〔極〕厌〔厭〕倦

duì ... jí yànjuàn. 对…腻得要命 duì ... nìde yàomìng. 2 ***put to*** ~ 处[處]死 chùsǐ. 3 死亡状[狀]态[態] sǐwáng zhuàngtài. 4 [喻]消灭[滅] xiāomiè, 毁灭 huǐmiè. '~-**duties** 遗产[產]税 yíchǎnshuì. '~-**trap** 非常危险[險]的场[場]所或境地 fēicháng wēixiǎn de chǎngsuǒ huò jìngdì. '~-**warrant** 死刑执[執]行令 sǐxíng zhíxínglìng. ~-**ly** *adj, adv* 死一般的 sǐ yìbān de, 死样[樣]地 sǐyàngde.

de·base /dɪ'beɪs/ *vt* 降低价[價]格 jiàngdī jiàgé. ~**ment** *n* [U]

de·bate /dɪ'beɪt/ *n*[C, U] 争论[論] zhēnglùn, 辩论 biànlùn; 讨论 tǎolùn. □ *vt/i* 辩论 biànlùn, 争论 zhēnglùn; 讨论 tǎolùn. **de·bat·able** /-əbl/ *adj* 争论中的 zhēnglùn zhōng de, 成问[問]题的 chéng wèntí de, 可争论的 kě zhēnglùnde.

de·bauch /dɪ'bɔːtʃ/ *vt* 使道德败坏[壞] shǐ dàodé bàihuài; 使堕落 shǐ duòluò. □ *n* [C] 酗酒 xùjiǔ; 放荡[蕩] fàngdàng; 荒淫 huāngyín. ~**ery** *n* [C, U] [*pl* -ies] 放纵[縱]行为[爲] fàngzòng xíngwéi.

de·bili·tate /dɪ'bɪlɪteɪt/ *vt* 使(人)衰弱 shǐ shuāiruò. **de·bil·ity** /dɪ'bɪlətɪ/ *n* [U] 衰弱 shuāiruò, 虚弱 xūruò.

debit /'debɪt/ *n* [C] (会计) 借方 jièfāng. □ *vt* 将[將]…记入借方 jiāng ... jìrù jièfāng.

de·bris /'deɪbriː/ *n* [U] 碎片 suìpiàn, 瓦砾[礫]堆 wǎlìduī.

debt /det/ *n* [C, U] 债 zhài, 债务[務] zhàiwù, 欠款 qiànkuǎn. ~-**or** 债务人 zhàiwùrén, 欠债人 qiànzhàirén.

de·bug /diː'bʌg/ *vt* [-gg-] [非正式用语] 1 (自动化) 移去(程序等中的)错误 yíqù cuòwù. 2 寻出并拆除暗藏的窃[竊]听[聽]器 xúnchū bìng chāichú àncángde qiètīngqì.

debut, début /'deɪbjuː/ *n* [C] (演员,音乐家)首次演出 shǒucì yǎnchū.

Dec=December.

dec·ade /'dekeɪd/ *n* [C] 十年 shínián.

deca·dence /'dekədəns/ *n* [U] 堕落 duòluò, 颓废[廢] tuífèi, 衰微 shuāiwēi. **deca·dent** *adj*

de·cant /dɪ'kænt/ *vt* 移注 yízhù, 倾注 qīngzhù. ~**er** 倾析器 qīngxìqì.

de·capi·tate /dɪ'kæpɪteɪt/ *vt* 杀[殺]头[頭] shātóu, 斩[斬]首 zhǎnshǒu.

de·cay /dɪ'keɪ/ *vi* 腐朽 fǔxiǔ, 腐烂[爛] fǔlàn; 衰退 shuāituì, 衰微 shuāiwēi. □ *n* [U] 腐朽 fǔxiǔ, 腐烂 fǔlàn, 衰微 shuāiwēi: *tooth* ~龋齿, 蛀牙, 虫[蟲]牙.

de·cease /dɪ'siːs/ *vi* 亡故 wánggù. □ *n* [法律]死亡 sǐwáng. **the ~d** 死者 sǐzhě.

de·ceit /dɪ'siːt/ *n* 1 [U] 欺骗[騙] qīpiàn. 欺诈 qīzhà. 2 [C] 虚假 xūjiǎ, 欺骗行为[爲] qīpiàn xíngwéi. ~**ful** *adj* (a) 惯于欺骗的 guànyú qīpiàn de. (b) 欺骗的 qīpiànde. ~**fully** /-fəlɪ/ *adv* ~ **fulness** *n* [U]

de·ceive /dɪ'siːv/ *vt* 欺骗[騙] qīpiàn, 诓骗 kuāngpiàn. **de·ceiver** *n* [C]

de·celer·ate /diː'seləreɪt/ *vt, vi* (使)减速 jiǎnsù **de·celer·ation** /diːˌselə'reɪʃn/ *n* [U] 减速 jiǎnsù: *a car with good deceleration* 减速性能好的汽车.

De·cem·ber /dɪ'sembə(r)/ *n* 十二月 shí'èryuè.

de·cent /'diːsnt/ *adj* 1 正当[當]的 zhèngdàngde; 合适[適]的 héshìde; 尊重人的 zūnzhòng rén de: *wear ~ clothes to the party* 穿像样的衣服去参加这次聚会. 2 文雅的 wényǎde, 受人尊重的 shòurén zūnzhòng de: ~ *language* (*behaviour*) 文雅的谈吐(举止). 3 [非正式用语]尚可的 shàngkěde. ~**ly** *adv* 高雅地 gāoyǎde; 合适地 héshìde. **de·cency** *n* [U]

de·cep·tion /dɪ'sepʃn/ *n* 1 [U] 欺骗[騙] qīpiàn, 诓骗 kuāngpiàn, 蒙蔽 méngbì. 2 [C] 诡计 guǐjì, 骗术[術] piànshù.

de·cep·tive /dɪ'septɪv/ *adj* 骗[騙]人的 piànrénde: 靠不住的 kàobúzhùde: *a ~ appearance* 骗人的外表. ~**ly** *adv*

deci·bel /'desɪbel/ *n* [C] 分贝(测量音强的单位) fēnbèi.

de·cide /dɪ'saɪd/ *vt/i* 1 解决 jiějué; 裁决 cáijué; 判决 pànjué. 2 决定 juédìng, 决意 juéyì: *I ~d to leave.* 我决意离开. 3 使决意 shǐ juéyì: *His behaviour ~d me to leave.* 他的所作所为使我决意离开. **de·cided** *adj* (a) 明显[顯]的 míngxiǎnde; 明确[確]的 míngquède. (b) (人)坚[堅]决的 jiānjuéde, 果断[斷]的 guǒduànde. ~**d·ly** *adv* 明确地 míngquède.

de·cidu·ous /dɪ'sɪdjʊəs/ *adj* (树木)每年落叶[葉]的 měi nián luòyè de.

deci·mal /'desɪml/ *adj* 十进[進]法的 shíjìnfǎde; 小数[數]的 xiǎoshùde. ~ **point** 小数点〔點〕xiǎoshùdiǎn. ~**ize** /-aɪz/ *vt* 使成为〔爲〕十进制 shǐ chéngwéi shíjìnzhì; 使成为小数 shǐ chéngwéi xiǎoshù. ~**iz·ation** /ˌdesɪməlaɪ'zeɪʃn/ *n* [U]

deci·mate /'desɪmeɪt/ *vt* 大批杀〔殺〕死或毁坏〔壞〕dàpī shāsǐ huò huǐhuài.

de·cipher /dɪ'saɪfə(r)/ *vt* 译〔譯〕解(密码等) yìjiě.

de·ci·sion /dɪ'sɪʒn/ *n* **1** [U] 决定 juédìng; 判决 pànjué; [C] 问〔問〕题的解决 wèntíde jiějué: *reach* (或 *come*) *to a* ~ 决定下来. **2** [U] 果断〔斷〕guǒduàn; 坚〔堅〕定 jiāndìng: *a man of* ~ 果断的人. **de·cis·ive** /dɪ'saɪsɪv/ *adj* **(a)** 决定性的 juédìngxìngde. **(b)** 果断〔斷〕的guǒduànde;明确〔確〕的 míngquède. **de·cis·ive·ly** *adv*

deck[1] /dek/ *n* [C] **1** 甲板 jiǎbǎn, 舱〔艙〕面 cāngmiàn; 公共汽车〔車〕的一层车厢 gōnggòngqìchēde yīcéng chexiāng. **2** 一副纸牌 yīfù zhǐpái. '~-**chair** 折迭〔叠〕式帆布椅 zhédiéshì fānbùyǐ.

deck[2] /dek/ *vt* 装〔裝〕饰 zhuāngshì, 打扮 dǎbàn.

dec·lar·ation /ˌdeklə'reɪʃn/ *n* [C] 宣布 xuānbù; 宣言 xuānyán; 宣告 xuāngào; 声〔聲〕明 shēngmíng: *a* ~ *of war* 宣战.

de·clare /dɪ'kleə(r)/ *vt/i* **1** 宣告 xuāngào, 宣布 xuānbù; 声〔聲〕明 shēngmíng. ~ ***war(on*** 或 ***against)*** 对〔對〕...宣战〔戰〕duì ... xuānzhàn. **2** 断〔斷〕言 duànyán; 宣称〔稱〕xuānchēn. **3** (向海关官员)申报〔報〕应〔應〕纳税物品 shēnpào yīng nàshuì wùpǐn: *Have you anything to* ~? 你有什么要申报的吗?

de·cline[1] /dɪ'klaɪn/ *n* [C] 下降 xiàjiàng, 衰退 shuāituì, 减弱 jiǎnruò: *a* ~ *in strength* 力量衰退; *a* ~ *in exports* 出口下降.

de·cline[2] /dɪ'klaɪn/ *vt/i* **1** 拒绝 jùjué; 谢绝 xièjué. **2** 减少 jiǎnshǎo; 衰退 shuāituì: *His strength is declining.* 他的体力在衰弱下去.

de·clutch /ˌdiː'klʌtʃ/*vi* 分开〔開〕汽车〔車〕的离〔離〕合器 fēnkāi qìchēde líhéqì.

de·code /ˌdiː'kəʊd/ *vt* 译〔譯〕电〔電〕报〔報〕yì diànbào.

de·com·pose /ˌdiːkəm'pəʊz/ *vt/i* **1** 分解 fēnjiě. **2** (使)腐败 fǔbài, (使)腐烂〔爛〕fǔlàn. **de·com·po·si·tion** /-pə'zɪʃn/ *n* [U]

de·con·tami·nate /ˌdiːkən'tæmɪˌneɪt/ *vt* 清除...的污染 qīngchú... de wūrǎn **de·con·tami·na·tion** /ˌdiːkənˌtæmɪ'neɪʃn/ *n* [U]

de·cor /'deɪkɔː(r)/ *n* [C] 装〔裝〕饰 zhuāngshì; 布置 bùzhì.

dec·or·ate /'dekəreɪt/ *vt* **1** 装〔裝〕饰 zhuāngshì, 装璜 zhuānghuáng. **2** 油漆,纸糊(房间) yóuqī,zhǐhú. **3** 授勋〔勳〕章给... shòu xūnzhāng gěi ...: ~*d for bravery* 因英勇而被授勋. **dec·or·ator** *n* [C] (室内)装饰家zhuāngshìjiā; 制〔製〕景人员 zhìjǐng rényuán. **dec·o'ra·tion** *n* **(a)** [U] 装饰 zhuāngshì, 装璜 zhuānghuáng. **(b)** [C] 装饰品 zhuāngshìpǐn: *Christmas* ~*s* 圣诞节装饰品. **(c)** [C] 勋章 xūnzhāng; 奖〔獎〕章 jiǎngzhāng. **dec·or·ative** /'dekərətɪv/ *adj* 可作装饰的 kě zuò zhuāngshì de.

de·coy /'diːkɔɪ/ *n* [C] **1** (诱擒鸟兽用的)引诱物, 囮子 yǐnyòuwù, ézi. **2** [喻] 诱人入圈套的东〔東〕西 yòurén rù quāntào de dōngxi. □ *vt* /dɪ'kɔɪ/ 诱骗 yòupiàn.

de·crease /di'kriːs/ *vt/i* (使) 减小 jiǎnxiǎo, (使)减少 jiǎnshǎo: *sales are decreasing* 销量减少. □*n* /'diːkriːs/ [U] 减小 jiǎnxiǎo, 减少 jiǎnshǎo; [C] 减少量 jiǎnshǎoliàng; 减小额 jiǎnxiǎo'é: *a small* ~ *in sales* 销售稍有减少.

de·cree /dɪ'kriː/*n* [C] **1** 法令 fǎlìng; 政令 zhènglìng: *by royal* ~ 诏书,敕令. **2** [法律]判决 pànjué. □*vt/i* 颁布〔佈〕法令 bānbù fǎlìng; 下令 xiàlìng.

de·crepit /dɪ'krepɪt/ *adj* 老弱的 lǎoruòde, 衰老的 shuāilǎode.

dedi·cate /'dedɪkeɪt/ *vt* **1** 奉献〔獻〕fèngxiàn, 供献 gòngxiàn. **2** 供奉(上帝) gòngfèng. **3** 题献(著作) tíxiàn. **dedi'ca·tion** *n* **(a)** [U]供献 gòngxiàn, 奉献 fèngxiàn. **(b)** [C] 献题xiàntí; 献词 xiàncí.

de·duce /dɪ'djuːs/ *vt* 演绎〔繹〕yǎnyì; 推演 tuīyǎn; 推论〔論〕tuīlùn.

de·duct /dɪ'dʌkt/ *vt* 扣除 kòuchú, 减去 jiǎnqù: ~ *£10 from his wages* 从他工资中扣掉10英镑.

de·duc·tion /dɪ'dʌkʃn/*n* **1** [U] 扣除 kòuchú; [C] 扣除量 kòuchúliàng; 回扣 huíkòu. **2** [U] 演绎 yǎnyì [C] 推论 tuīlùn.

deed /diːd/ *n* [C] **1** 行为〔爲〕xíngwéi, 行动〔動〕xíngdòng. **2** [法律]契约 qìyuē.

deep[1] /diːp/ *adj* [-er, -est] **1** 深的 shēnde: *a* ~ *river* 水深的河; *a hole two feet* ~ 两英尺深的洞. **2** [喻]深刻的 shēnkède: *a* ~ *thinker*

思想深刻的思想家. 3 (声音) 深沉的 shēnchénde. 4 (颜色) 深色的 shēnsède, 浓〔濃〕色的 nóngsède. 5 深厚的 shēnhòude; 深切的 shēnqiède: ~ *hatred* 深仇大恨. 6 [喻] 深奥的 shēn'àode. 7 沉睡的 chénshuìde. **~ly** *adv* 深入地 shēnrùde; 深刻地 shēnkède; 深厚地 shēnhòude: *~ly hurt by your remarks* 被你的话深深地伤害. **~ness** *n* [U]

deep² /di:p/ *adv* 深 shēn. ,**~-'freeze** *vt* 以极〔極〕低温度快速冷藏 yǐ jídī wēndù kuàisù lěngcáng. □ *n* [C] 以极低温度快速冷藏的冷藏箱 yǐ jídī wēndù kuàisù lěngcáng de lěngcángxiāng. ,**~-'rooted** [喻] 根深蒂固的 gēnshēndìgùde: *~-rooted hatred* 深仇大恨. ,**~-'seated** 由来〔來〕已久的 yóulái yǐjiǔ de; 根深蒂固的 gēnshēndìgùde.

deepen /'di:pən/ *vt/i* 加深 jiāshēn, 深化 shēnhuà, 深入 shēnrù.

deer /dɪə(r)/ *n* [C] [*pl* ~] 鹿 lù

de·face /dɪ'feɪs/ *vt* 损伤〔傷〕...的外貌 sǔnshāng ... de wàimào; 损毁 sǔnhuǐ: ~ *public buildings* 损坏公共建筑. **~ment** *n* [C, U]

de·fame /dɪ'feɪm/*vt* 破坏〔壞〕名誉〔譽〕pòhuài míngyù, 诽谤 fěibàng. **defa·ma·tion** /,defə'meɪʃn/ *n* [U]

de·fault /dɪ'fɔ:lt/ *vi* 拖欠 tuōqiàn, 不履行 bù lǚxíng; 不出庭 bù chūtíng. □ *n* [C] 拖欠 tuōqiàn, 不履行 bù lǚxíng; 违〔違〕约 wéiyuē; 不出庭 bù chūtíng. **~er** 拖欠者 tuōqiànzhě; 缺席者 quēxízhě; 违约者 wéiyuēzhě.

de·feat /dɪ'fi:t/ *vt* 1 打败 dǎbài, 战〔戰〕胜〔勝〕zhànshèng, 击〔擊〕败 jībài. 2 废〔廢〕弃〔棄〕fèiqì: *Our hopes were ~ed.* 我们的希望破灭了. □*n* [C] [U] 击败 jībài, 失败 shībài.

de·fect¹/'di:fekt/ *n* [C] 欠缺 qiànquē, 缺点〔點〕quēdiǎn, 不足之处〔處〕bùzúzhīchù. **~ive** /dɪ'fektɪv/ *adj*

de·fect² /dɪ'fekt/ *vi* 背叛 bèipàn; 逃跑 táopǎo, 开〔開〕小差 kāi xiǎochāi. **de'fection** /-ʃn/ *n* [C, U] **~or** 背叛者 bèipànzhě; 逃兵 táobīng.

de·fence [美语 = **-fense**] /dɪ'fens/*n* 1 [U] 防卫〔衛〕fángwèi, 保卫 bǎowèi, 防护〔護〕fánghù. 2 [C] 防务〔務〕fángwù, 防御〔禦〕物 fángyùwù. 3 [C, U] [法律] 辩护 biànhù, 答〔答〕辩 dábiàn, 被告律师 bèigào lǜshī. **~less** *adj* 无〔無〕防御的 wú fángyù de, 没有保护的 méiyǒu bǎohù de.

de·fend /dɪ'fend/ *vt* 1 保卫〔衛〕bǎowèi, 防御〔禦〕fángyù. 2 为〔為〕...辩护〔護〕wèi ... biànhù 为...答〔答〕辩 wèi ... dábiàn: ~ *a claim* 为一项索赔而辩护. **~ant** *n* [C] [法律]被告 bèigào. **~er** *n* [C]防御者 fángyùzhě; 保护人 bǎohùrén. **de·fens·ible**/dɪ'fensəbl/ *adj* 能防御的 néng fángyù de; 能辩护的 néng biànhù de. **de·fens·ive** / dɪ'fensɪv / *adj* 防御的 fángyùde, 守势〔勢〕的 shǒushìde. □ *n* **on the** ~ 采取守势 cǎiqǔ shǒushì, 进行防御 jìnxíng fángyù. **de·fens·ive·ly** *adv*

de·fer¹ /dɪ'fɜ:(r)/ *vt* [-rr-] 推迟〔遲〕tuīchí, 延期 yánqī: ~ *a decision* 暂缓作出决定.

de·fer² /dɪ'fɜ:(r)/ *vi* [-rr-] 听〔聽〕从〔從〕tīngcóng; 遵从 zūncóng: *I shall ~ to your advice.* 我将听从你的劝告. **~ence** /'defərəns/ *n* [U] 听从 tīngcóng, 依从 yīcóng; 尊重 zūnzhòng.

de·fiance /dɪ'faɪəns/ *n* [U] 蔑视 mièshì; 违〔違〕抗 wéikàng, 不服从〔從〕bùfúcóng. **in ~ of** 蔑视 mièshì: *in ~ of my orders* 蔑视我的命令. **de·fiant** *adj*挑战〔戰〕的 tiǎozhànde; 违抗的 wéikàngde.

de·fi·ciency /dɪ'fɪʃnsɪ/ *n* [*pl* -ies] 1 [C, U] 缺乏 quēfá, 缺少 quēshǎo, 不足 bùzú: *a ~ of vitamins* 缺乏维生素. 2 [C] 不足之数〔數〕bùzú zhī shù. **de·ficient** *adj*

defi·cit /'defɪsɪt/ *n* [C] 空额 kòng'é, 赤字 chìzì. ⇨ surplus.

de·file /dɪ'faɪl/ *vt* 弄脏〔髒〕nòngzāng, 污损 wūsǔn.

de·fine/dɪ'faɪn/ *vt* 1 解释〔釋〕jiěshì; 给...下定义〔義〕gěi... xià dìngyì. 2 明确〔確〕表示míngquè biǎoshì: ~ *one's position on an issue* 明确表示自己对一个问题的立场. **de·fin·able** /-əbl/ *adj* 可限定的 kě xiàndìng de; 可下定义的 kě xià dìngyì de.

defi·nite / 'defɪnət / *adj* 确〔確〕切的 quèqiède, 明确的 míngquède. ,**~'article** 定冠词 dìngguàncí. **~ly** *adv* (a) 确切地 quèqiède; 明确地 míngquède. (b) [非正式用语] 肯定地kěndìngde: *He ~ly agreed to come.* 他同意来.

defi·ni·tion /,defɪ'nɪʃn/ *n* 1 [U] 解说 jiěshuō; [C] 定义〔義〕dìngyì: *a ~ of a word* 词的定义. 2 [U] 清晰度 qīngxīdù: *the ~ of a photograph* 照片的清晰度.

de·fini·tive /dɪ'fɪnətɪv/ *adj* 决定的 juédìngde, 最后〔後〕的 zuìhòude, 权〔權〕威性的 quánwēixìngde.

de·flate /dɪ'fleɪt/ *vt* 1 使(轮胎等)

瘪下去 shī biē xiàqù. 2〔喻〕降低重要性 jiàngdī zhòngyàoxìng. 3 /diː'fleɪt/ 紧〔緊〕缩通货 jǐnsuō tōnghuò. **de'fla·tion** *n*[C, U] 放气〔氣〕 fàngqì; 紧缩通货 jǐnsuō tōnghuò.

de·flect /dɪ'flekt/ *vt/i* (使)偏斜 piānxié: *The bullet was ~ed by a wall and missed him.* 子弹碰到墙上,偏了,没有打中他. **de'flection** /-ʃn/ *n* [C, U]

de·form /dɪ'fɔːm/ *vt* 损坏〔壞〕…形象 sǔnhuài ... xíngxiàng; 使不成形 shǐ bù chéngxíng. **~ed** *adj* 丑〔醜〕的 chǒude, 变〔變〕了形的 biànle xíng de, 破相的 pòxiàngde. **~ity** *n* [C, U]

de·fraud /dɪ'frɔːd/ *vt* 欺骗〔騙〕qīpiàn, 欺诈 qīzhà: *~ him of £100* 骗了他100英镑.

de·frost /ˌdiː'frɒst/ *vt* 除去…的冰霜 chúqù ... de bīngshuāng; 使不结冰 shǐ bù jiébīng.

deft /deft/ *adj* 灵〔靈〕巧的 língqiǎode, 熟练的 shúliànde. **~ly** *adv*

de·funct /dɪ'fʌŋkt/ *adj* 已死的 yǐsǐde, 已消灭〔滅〕的 yǐ xiāomiède.

de·fuse /ˌdiː'fjuːz/ *vt* 去掉炸弹〔彈〕等的信管 qùdiào zhàdàn děng de xìnguǎn.

defy /dɪ'faɪ/ *vt* [*pt, pp* -ied] 1 公然反抗 gōngrán fǎnkàng; 蔑视 mièshì. 2 拒绝服从〔從〕jùjué fúcóng: *~ the law* 拒不遵守法律.

deg.=degree.

de·gen·er·ate /dɪ'dʒenərət/ *adj, n* [C] 堕落的 duòluòde; 颓废〔廢〕的 tuífèide. □ /dɪ'dʒenəreɪt/ *vi* 堕落 duòluò; 退化 tuìhuà.

de·grade /dɪ'greɪd/ *vt* 1 降级 jiàngjí, 贬黜 biǎnchù. 2 堕落 duòluò: *His dishonesty ~d him.* 他欺诈蒙骗自甘堕落. **degra·da·tion** /ˌdegrə'deɪʃn/ *n* [U] 降级 jiàngjí; 贬黜 biǎnchù; 堕落 duòluò.

de·gree /dɪ'griː/ *n* [C] 1 (角的)度数〔數〕 dùshù. 2 (温度的)度数 dùshù. 3 程度 chéngdù. *by ~s* 逐渐〔漸〕地 zhújiànde. 4 学〔學〕位 xuéwèi; 学衔 xuéxián. **first ~** 非常 fēicháng, 极〔極〕度 jídù: *first ~ burns* 严重烧伤.

de·hy·drate /ˌdiːhaɪ'dreɪt/ *vt* 使脱水 shǐ tuōshuǐ.

de-ice /ˌdiː'aɪs/ *vt* 防止…结冰 fángzhǐ ... jiébīng.

deign /deɪn/ *vi* 屈尊 qūzūn, 垂顾〔顧〕chuígù: *She didn't ~ to speak to me.* 她不屑于同我说话.

de·ity /'deɪətɪ/ *n* [*pl* -ies] 1 [U] 神性 shénxìng. 2 [C] 神 shén.

de·ject /dɪ'dʒekt/ *vt* 使气〔氣〕馁 shǐ qìněi; 使沮丧 shǐ jǔsàng. **de'jection** /-ʃn/ *n* [U] 沮丧 jǔsàng, 气馁 qìněi.

de·lay /dɪ'leɪ/ *vt/i* 1 延缓 yánhuǎn, 耽搁〔擱〕dānge. 2 推迟〔遲〕tuīchí, 延期 yánqī. □*n* 1 [U] 延缓 yánhuǎn, 耽搁 dānge, 延迟 yánchí. 2 [C] 延迟的事例 yánchíde shìlì; 延迟的时〔時〕间〔間〕 yánchíde shíjiān.

de·lec·table /dɪ'lektəbl/ *adj* 使人愉快的 shǐ rén yúkuài de; 美味的 měiwèide: *~ chocolates* 美味的巧克力.

del·egate[1] /'delɪgət/ *n* [C] 代表 dàibiǎo.

del·egate[2] /'delɪgeɪt/ *vt* 委派…为〔爲〕代表 wěipài ... wéi dàibiǎo; 授权〔權〕 shòuquán. **del·e'ga·tion** *n* (a) [U] 委派 wěipài, 派遣 pàiqiǎn. (b) [C] 代表团〔團〕 dàibiǎotuán.

de·lete /dɪ'liːt/ *vt* 删除(文字) shānchú; 擦去(字迹)cāqù. **de'le·tion** *n* [U] 删除 shānchú, 擦去 cāqù; [C] 删除部分 shānchú bùfen.

de·lib·er·ate[1] /dɪ'lɪbərət/ *adj* 1 故意的 gùyìde, 蓄意的 xùyìde, 存心的 cúnxīnde: *a ~ insult* 故意的侮辱. 2 从〔從〕容的 cóngróngde; 谨慎的 jǐnshènde. **~ly** *adv*

de·lib·er·ate[2] /dɪ'lɪbəreɪt/ *vt/i* [正式用语]仔细考虑〔慮〕 zǐxì kǎolǜ; 商议〔議〕 shāngyì.

de·lib·er·ation /dɪˌlɪbə'reɪʃn/ *n* [正式用语] 1 [C, U] 仔细讨论〔論〕zǐxì tǎolùn; 审〔審〕议〔議〕 shěnyì. 2 [U] 谨慎 jǐnshèn, 审慎 shěnshèn.

deli·cacy /'delɪkəsɪ/ *n* [*pl* -ies] 1 [U] 精美 jīngměi, 细致 xìzhì, 纤〔纖〕弱 xiānruò, 优〔優〕美 yōuměi, 浅〔淺〕淡 qiǎndàn, 美味 měiwèi, 灵〔靈〕敏 língmǐn, 精密 jīngmì, 体〔體〕贴 tǐtiē. 2 [C] 精美的食品 jīngměide shípǐn.

deli·cate /'delɪkət/ *adj* 1 细软〔軟〕的 xìruǎnde, 纤〔纖〕细的 xiānxìde, 柔嫩的 róunènde: *the ~ wings of a butterfly* 蝴蝶柔嫩的双翅. 2 精美的 jīngměide, 雅致的 yǎzhìde: *~ workmanship* 精美的工艺. 3 娇〔嬌〕嫩的 jiāonènde, 脆弱的 cuìruòde, 病弱的 bìngruòde: *in ~ health* 身体瘦弱. 4 难〔難〕办〔辦〕的 nánbànde: *a ~ operation* 精细的手术. 5 (颜色)浅〔淺〕淡的 qiǎndànde; 柔和的 róuhéde. 6 (感官,仪器)灵〔靈〕敏的 língmǐnde. 7 微妙的 wēimiàode: *a ~*

situation 微妙的局势. 8 (食物) 美味的 měiwèide. ~**ly** *adv*

deli·ca·tes·sen /ˌdelıkə'tesn/ *n* [C, U] 熟食 shúshí; 熟食店 shúshídiàn.

de·li·cious /dı'lıʃəs/ *adj* 美味的 měiwèide, 可口的 kěkǒude.

de·light[1] /dı'laıt/ *n* **1** [U] 高兴〔興〕gāoxìng, 快乐〔樂〕kuàilè: *take ~ in his victory* 为他的胜利而高兴. **2** [C] 乐事 lèshì. ~**ful** *adj* 令人快乐的 lìngrén kuàilè de, 令人高兴的 lìngrén gāoxìng de. ~**fully** *adv*

de·light[2] /dı'laıt/ *vt/i* **1** 使高兴〔興〕shǐ gāoxìng; 使快乐 shǐ kuàilè. **2** *be ~ed* 感到高兴 gǎndào gāoxìng. **3** 喜爱〔愛〕xǐ'ài; 取乐〔樂〕qǔlè: *He ~s in working hard.* 他以努力工作为乐.

de·lin·quency /dı'lıŋkwənsı/ *n* [*pl* -ies] [C, U] 过〔過〕失 guòshī; 为〔爲〕非作歹 wéifēi zuòdǎi; 失职〔職〕shīzhí. **de·lin·quent** *n* [C], *adj* (人)做坏〔壞〕事的 zuò huàishì de; 失职的 shīzhíde.

de·liri·ous /dı'lırıəs/ *adj* **1** 神志昏迷的 shénzhì hūnmí de. **2** 发〔發〕狂的 fākuáng de; 极〔極〕度兴〔興〕奋〔奮〕的 jídù xìngfèn de. ~**ly** *adv*

de·lir·ium /dı'lırıəm/ *n* [U] **1** 神志昏迷 shénzhì hūnmí; 说胡话 shuō húhuà. **2** [喻]极度兴奋 jídù xìngfèn.

de·liver /dı'lıvə(r)/ *vt* **1** 投递〔遞〕(信件、货物等) tóudì: *~ milk* 送牛奶; *~ newspapers* 送报纸. **2** *~ from* [正式用语]解救 jiějiù, 拯救 chěngjiù. **3** 发〔發〕表 fābiǎo, 表达〔達〕biǎodá: *to ~ a lecture* 发表演说. **4** (产妇) 接生 jiēshēng. **5** 移交 yíjiāo, 引渡 yǐndù. **6** 施加 shījiā: *to ~ a blow* 给以一击. ~**er** 救助者 jiùzhùzhě. ~**ance** *n* [U] 解救 jiějiù; 拯救 chěngjiù.

de·liv·ery/dı'lıvərı/ *n* [*pl* -ies] **1** [C, U] 投递〔遞〕(信件, 货物等) tóudì. **2** [C] 分娩 fēnmiǎn: *The mother had an easy ~.* 母亲顺利分娩. **3** [U] 演讲的腔调 yǎnjiǎngde qiāngdiào.

delta /'deltə/ *n* [C][*pl* ~s] (河流的) 三角洲 sānjiǎozhōu.

de·lude/dı'lu:d /*vt* 欺骗〔騙〕qīpiàn, 哄骗 hǒngpiàn.

del·uge /'delju:dʒ/ *n* [C] **1** 洪水 hóngshuǐ; 暴雨 bàoyǔ. **2** 洪水般的泛滥〔濫〕hóngshuǐ bān de fànlàn: *a ~ of letters* 信件纷至沓来. □ *vt* 使泛滥 shǐ fànlàn; 使满溢 shǐ mǎnyì.

de·lu·sion /dı'lu:ʒn/ *n* [U] 欺骗〔騙〕qīpiàn; [C]误会〔會〕wùhuì; 误认〔認〕wùrèn.

de luxe /dı'lʌks/ *adj* 豪华〔華〕的 háohuáde; 高级的 gāojíde.

delve/delv/ *vt/i* ~ **(into)** 探究 tànjiū, 钻〔鑽〕研 zuānyán.

de·mand[1] /dı'ma:nd/ *n* **1** [C] 要求 yāoqiú; 要求的事物 yāoqiúde shìwù: *a ~ for more pay* 要求增加工资. *on ~* 在要求时〔時〕. **2** [U] 需要 xūyào, 需求 xūqiú: *Our goods are in great ~.* 我们的货物需求量很大.

de·mand[2] /dı'ma:nd/ *vt* **1** 要求 yāoqiú. **2** 需要 xūyào: *work ~ing great care* 需要很细心的工作.

de·mar·cate /'di:ma:keıt/ *vt* 给…划〔劃〕界 gěi ... huàjiè. **de-mar'ca·tion** *n* [U]

de·mean·our〔美语= -or〕/dı'mi:nə(r)/ *n* [U] 行为〔爲〕xíngwéi, 举〔舉〕止 jǔzhǐ.

de·mented /dı'mentıd/ *adj* 发〔發〕狂的 fākuángde. ~**ly** *adv*

deme·rara /ˌdemə'reərə/ *n* [U] (亦作~ *sugar*) 红糖 hóngtáng.

de·mili·tar·ized /ˌdi:'mılıtəraızd/ *adj* 非军〔軍〕事化的 fēi jūnshìhuà de.

de·mist /ˌdi:'mıst/ *vt* 除去 (汽车挡风玻璃等上的) 雾〔霧〕chúqù wù.

democ·racy /dı'mɒkrəsı/ *n* [*pl* -ies] **1** [C] 民主国〔國〕mínzhǔguó; [U] 民主政体〔體〕mínzhǔ zhèngtǐ; 民主政治 mínzhǔ zhèngzhì. **2** [U] 民主 mínzhǔ; [C] 民主社会 mínzhǔ shèhuì.

demo·crat /'deməkræt/ *n* [C] **1** 民主主义〔義〕者 mínzhǔzhǔyìzhě. **2** D~[美语] 民主党〔黨〕人 mínzhǔdǎngrén. ~**ic** /-'krætık/ *adj* 民主的 mínzhǔde, 主张〔張〕民主的 zhǔzhāng mínzhǔ de. ~**i·cally** *adv*

de·mol·ish /dı'mɒlıʃ/ *vt* **1** 拆毁 (旧建筑) chāihuǐ. **2** 推翻论〔論〕据〔據〕tuīfān lùnjù. **demo·li·tion** /ˌdemə'lıʃn/ *n* [C, U]

de·mon, dae·mon /'di:mən/ *n* [C] **1** 精灵〔靈〕jīnglíng; 恶〔惡〕魔 èmó. **2** [非正式用语]凶猛或精力过〔過〕人的人 xiōngměng huò jīnglì guòrén de rén.

dem·on·strate /'demənstreıt/ *vt/i* **1** 论〔論〕证〔證〕lùnzhèng, 证明 zhèngmíng. **2** 示威 shìwēi.

dem·on·stra·tion /ˌdemən'streıʃn/ *n* [C, U] **1** 论〔論〕证 lùnzhèng, 证明 zhèngmíng. **2** 示威 shìwēi.

de·mon·stra·tive /dɪ'mɒnstrətɪv/ *adj* **(a)** 感情外露的 gǎnqíng wàilù de. **(b)** [语法]指示的 zhǐshìde: ~ *pronoun* 指示代名词. **dem·on·stra·tor** *n* [C] **(a)** 示威者 shìwēizhě. **(b)** 示范〔範〕者 shìfànzhě.

de·moral·ize /dɪ'mɒrəlaɪz/ *vt* 使士气〔氣〕低落 shǐ shìqì dīluò: *troops ~d by a surprise attack* 部队被突然袭击弄得士气低落.

de·mote /ˌdi:'məʊt/ *vt* 使降级 shǐ jiàngjí. **de'mo·tion** *n* [U]

de·mure /dɪ'mjʊə(r)/ *adj* **1** 娴〔嫻〕静的 xiánjìngde; 严〔嚴〕肃〔肅〕的 yánsùde. **2** 拘谨的 jūjǐnde: *a ~ smile* 拘谨的一笑. **~ly** *adv*

den /den/ *n* [C] **1** 兽〔獸〕穴 shòuxuè, 窝 wō. **2** 秘密处〔處〕所 mìmì chùsuǒ. **3** [非正式用语] 私人的工作室 sīrénde gōngzuòshì.

de·nial /dɪ'naɪəl/ *n* **1** [C, U] 拒绝 jùjué; 拒绝一项请求 jùjué yíxiàng qǐngqiú. **2** [C] 否认〔認〕fǒurèn, 否定 fǒudìng.

denim /'denɪm/ *n* **1** [U] 斜纹粗棉布 xiéwén cūmiánbù. **2** [*pl*] [非正式用语] 斜纹粗棉布制〔製〕成的工作服 xiéwén cūmiánbù zhìchéng de gōngzuòfú.

de·nomi·na·tion /dɪˌnɒmɪ'neɪʃn/ *n* [C] **1** 命名 mìngmíng, 取名 qǔmíng. **2** (度量衡, 货币等的) 单〔單〕位 dānwèi. **~al** *adj* 教派的 jiàopàide.

de·nomi·na·tor /dɪ'nɒmɪneɪtə(r)/ *n* [C] 分母 fēnmǔ.

de·note /dɪ'nəʊt/ *vt* [正式用语] **1** 是…的符号〔號〕shì ... de fúhào. 是…的名称〔稱〕shì ... de míngchēng. **2** 指示 zhǐshì, 表示 biǎoshì: *Tears usually ~ sadness.* 哭泣通常表示悲伤.

de·nounce /dɪ'naʊns/ *vt* 谴责 qiǎnzé, 斥责 chìzé: ~ *the government's actions* 谴责政府的所作所为.

dense /dens/ *adj* [-r, -st] **1** (液体,蒸气等)浓〔濃〕密的 nóngmìde: *a ~ fog* 浓雾. **2** 密集的 mìjíde. **3** [非正式用语]愚笨的 yúbènde. **~ly** *adv*

den·sity /'densətɪ/ *n* [*pl* -ies] **1** [U] 稠密度 chóumìdù. **2** [C, U] [物理]密度 mìdù.

dent /dent/ *n* [C] 凹部 āobù; 凹痕 āohén. □ *vt/i* 使出现凹痕 shǐ chūxiàn āohén.

den·tal /'dentl/ *adj* 牙齿〔齒〕的 yáchǐde.

den·tist /'dentɪst/ *n* [C] 牙医〔醫〕yáyī. **~ry** *n* [U] 牙科 yákē.

de·nunci·ation /dɪˌnʌnsɪ'eɪʃn/ *n* [C, U] 谴责 qiǎnzé, 斥责 chìzé.

deny /dɪ'naɪ/ *vt* [*pt, pp* -ied] **1** 否认〔認〕fǒurèn, 否定 fǒudìng. **2** 拒绝一项要求 jùjué yíxiàng yāoqiú.

de·odor·ant /ˌdi:'əʊdərənt/ *n* [C] 除臭剂〔劑〕chúchòujì.

dep. =depart.

de·part /dɪ'pɑ:t/ *vi* 离〔離〕开〔開〕líkāi, 启〔啓〕程 qǐchéng.

de·part·ment /dɪ'pɑ:tmənt/ *n* [C] (行政,企业,大学等的)部,司,局,处〔處〕,科,系 bù, sī, jú, chù, kē, xì. ~ **store** 百货商店 bǎihuò shāngdiàn.

de·par·ture /dɪ'pɑ:tʃə(r)/ *n* [C, U] 离〔離〕开〔開〕líkāi, 启〔啟〕程 qǐchéng.

de·pend /dɪ'pend/ *vi* ~ *on* **1** 依靠 yīkào, 靠 kào. **2** 相信 xiāngxìn, 信任 xìnrèn. **~able** *adj* 可以依靠的 kěyǐ yīkào de; 可靠的 kěkàode.

de·pend·ant (亦作 -ent) /dɪ'pendənt/ *n* [C] 被赡养〔養〕者 bèi shànyǎng zhě. ⇨ dependent *adj*.

de·pend·ence /dɪ'pendəns/ *n* [U] **1** 依靠 yīkào, 依赖 yīlài. **2** 信赖 xìnlài, 信任 xìnrèn.

de·pend·ent /dɪ'pendənt/ *n* [C] = dependant. □ *adj* 依靠的 yīkàode, 依赖的 yīlàide.

de·pict /dɪ'pɪkt/ *vt* 描绘〔繪〕miáohuì, 描写〔寫〕miáoxiě.

de·plete /dɪ'pli:t/ *vt* 耗尽〔盡〕hàojìn, 用尽 yòngjìn: *Our food supplies are badly ~d.* 我们的食物已消耗殆尽. **de·ple·tion** *n* [U]

de·plore /dɪ'plɔ:(r)/ *vt* 哀悼 āidào; 非难〔難〕fēinàn: *We ~ the death of three men.* 我们对这三个人的去世表示哀悼. **de·plor·able** *adj* /-rəble/

de·port /dɪ'pɔ:t/ *vt* 驱〔驅〕逐出境 qūzhú chūjìng. **~ation** /ˌdi:pɔ:'teɪʃn/ *n* [U]

de·pose /dɪ'pəʊz/ *vt/i* 废〔廢〕黜 fèichù.

de·posit[1] /dɪ'pɒzɪt/ *n* [C] **1** 存款 cúnkuǎn; 定金 dìngjīn. **2** 沉淀〔澱〕chéndiàn; 沉淀物 chéndiànwù. **3** 沉积〔積〕chénjī; 矿〔礦〕藏 kuàngcáng ~ **account** 须预先通知方可取的银行存款 xū yùxiān tōngzhī fāngkě qǔ de yínháng cúnkuǎn.

de·posit[2] /dɪ'pɒzɪt/ *vt* **1** 放 fàng, 置 zhì. **2** 存放 cúnfàng, 贮存 zhùcún. **3** 付定金 fù dìngjīn. **4** 沉淀〔澱〕chéndiàn, 淤积〔積〕yūjī.

de·pot /'depəʊ/ *n* [C] **1** 仓〔倉〕库 cāngkù. **2** [美语]车〔車〕站 chēzhàn.

de·prave /dɪ'preɪv/ *vt* 使腐败 shǐ fǔbài, 使堕落 shǐ duòluò. **de·prav·ity** /dɪ'prævətɪ/ *n* [U]

de·pre·ci·ate /dɪ'pri:ʃɪeɪt/ *vt/i* 降低…的价〔價〕值 jiàngdī …de jiàzhí, 贬值 biǎnzhí. **de·preci'ation** *n* [U]

de·press /dɪ'pres/ *vt* **1** 降低 jiàngdī, 压〔壓〕下 yāxià. **2** 使沮丧 shǐ jǔsàng, 使消沉 shǐ xiāochén. **3** 使萧〔蕭〕条〔條〕 shǐ xiāotiáo: *a ~ed market for coffee* 咖啡市场萧条.

de·pres·sion /dɪ'preʃn/ *n* **1** [U] 沮丧 jǔsàng, 消沉xiāochén. **2** [C] 凹陷 āoxiàn, 凹地 āodì. **3** [C] 萧〔蕭〕条〔條〕时〔時〕期 xiāotiáo shíqī. **4** [C] 〔气象〕低气〔氣〕压〔壓〕 dīqìyā.

de·prive /dɪ'praɪv/ *vt* 剥夺〔奪〕 bōduó, 使丧失 shǐ sàngshī: *children ~d of love* 失去了爱的儿童; *children ~d of food* 忍饥挨饿的孩子们. **depri·va·tion** /ˌdeprɪ'veɪʃn/ *n* [C,U]

dept. =department.

depth /depθ/ *n* **1** [C, U] 深 shēn, 深度 shēndù, 厚度 hòudù. **2** [C] 深奥 shēn'ào, 深沉 shēnchén. 深厚 shēnhòu. *in ~* 详细地 xiángxìde; 彻底地 chèdǐde.

depu·ta·tion /ˌdepjʊ'teɪʃn/ *n* [C] 委派代表 wěipài dàibiǎo; 代表团〔團〕 dàibiǎotuán.

depu·tize /'depjʊtaɪz/ *vi* 担〔擔〕任代表 dānrèn dàibiǎo: *~ for* 担任…的代表.

deputy /'depjʊtɪ/ *n* [C] [*pl* -ies] 代表 dàibiǎo, 代理人 dàilǐrén.

de·rail /dɪ'reɪl/ *vt* 使(火车)出轨〔軌〕 shǐ chūguǐ. **~ment** *n* [C,U]

de·range /dɪ'reɪndʒ/ *vt* 扰〔擾〕乱〔亂〕秩序 rǎoluàn zhìxù, 捣乱 dǎoluàn: *mentally ~d* 精神错乱, 发疯

der·el·ict /'derəlɪkt/ *adj* 被抛弃〔棄〕的 bèi pāoqìde. **der·el'iction** /-ʃn/ *n* [C, U] 玩忽职〔職〕守 wánhū zhíshǒu.

deri·va·tion /ˌderɪ'veɪʃn/ *n* **1** [U] 引出 yǐnchū; 起源 qǐyuán. **2** [C] 词源 cíyuán. **de·riva·tive** /dɪ'rɪvətɪv/ *adj, n* [C] 衍生的 yǎnshēngde, 派生的 pàishēngde; 派生词 pàishēngcí.

de·rive/dɪ'raɪv/ *vt/i* **1** 得到 dédào, 取得 qǔdé: *to ~ pleasure from something* 从某事得到乐趣. **2** *~ (from)* 起源于 qǐyuán yú: *words ~d from Latin* 起源于拉丁语的词.

de·roga·tory /dɪ'rɒgətrɪ/ *adj* 贬抑的 biǎnyìde, 毁损的 huǐsǔnde.

der·rick /'derɪk/*n* [C] **1** (亦作 *'~-crane*) 人字起重机〔機〕 rénzì qǐzhòngjī; (船用) 起重摇臂吊杆 qǐzhòng yáobì diàogān. **2** (油井) 井架 jǐngjià.

de·sali·na·tion /di:ˌsælɪ'neɪʃn/ *n* [U] (海水)去盐〔鹽〕 qùyán. **~ plant** *n* 海水去盐设备〔備〕 hǎishuǐ qùyán shèbèi **de·sali·nate** /di:'sælɪˌneɪt/ *vt.*

de·scend /dɪ'send/*vt/i* **1** [正式用语]下降 xiàjiàng; 下来〔來〕 xiàlái. **2** *be ~ed from* 传〔傳〕下 chuánxià, 遗传 yíchuán. **3** *~ on* 袭〔襲〕击〔擊〕 xíjī. **de'scend·ant** *n* [C] 后〔後〕裔 hòuyì, 后代 hòudài, 子孙〔孫〕 zǐsūn.

de·scent /dɪ'sent/ *n* **1** [C,U] 下降 xiàjiàng, 降下 jiàngxià. **2** [C] 斜坡 xiépō; 下坡 xiàpō. **3** [U] 血统 xuètǒng; 遗传〔傳〕 yíchuán: *of French ~* 法国血统.

de·scribe /dɪ'skraɪb/ *vt* **1** 描述 miáoshù, 描绘〔繪〕 miáohuì, 形容 xíngróng. **2** 画〔畫〕 huà: *~ a circle* 画一个圆圈.

de·scrip·tion /dɪ'skrɪpʃn/ *n* [C, U] 描写〔寫〕 miáoxiě, 描述 miáoshù, 叙述 xùshù. **de·scrip·tive** *adj*

des·ecrate /'desəkreɪt/ *vt* 亵渎〔瀆〕 xièdú, 污辱 wūrǔ. **ˌdes·e'cra·tion** *n* [U]

de·seg·re·gate /ˌdi:'segrɪgeɪt/ *vt* 取消种〔種〕族隔离〔離〕 qǔxiāo zhǒngzú gélí.

de·sert[1] /dɪ'zɜ:t/ *vt/i* **1** 丢弃〔棄〕 diūqì; 离〔離〕开〔開〕 líkāi. **2** 背弃 bèiqì, 置…于不顾〔顧〕 zhì … yú búgù: *~ one's family* 置家庭于不顾. **3** 开〔開〕小差 kāi xiǎochā. **~er** 逃兵 táobīng. **~ion** /dɪ'zɜ:ʃn/ *n* [C, U]

des·ert[2] /'dezət/ *n* [C, U] 沙漠 shāmò; 不毛之地 bùmáozhīdì. □ *adj* **1** 沙漠的 shāmòde, 不毛的 bùmáode. **2** 无〔無〕人居住的 wúrén jūzhù de; 荒无人烟的 huāng wú rényān de: *a ~ island* 荒无人烟的岛屿.

de·serts /dɪ'zɜ:ts/ *n pl* 应〔應〕得的赏罚 yīngdéde shǎngfá. *get one's just ~* 得到应得的赏罚.

de·serve /dɪ'zɜ:v/ *vt/i* 应〔應〕得 yīngdé, 应受 yīngshòu:值得 zhídé: *He ~d to win.* 他的获胜是应该的.

de·sign /dɪ'zaɪn/ *n* **1** [C] 设计 shèjì, 构〔構〕思 gòusī. **2** [U] 设计制〔製〕图〔圖〕术〔術〕 shèjì zhìtú shù. **3** [U](图画, 建筑,机器等的)设计 shèjì; 配置 pèizhì; 布局 bùjú. **4** [C]图样〔樣〕 túyàng, 图案

tú'àn. 5 计划〔劃〕jìhuà, 图谋 túmóu. □ *vt/i* 1 设计 shèjì, 构思 gòusī. 2 打算 dǎsuàn: *This room was ~ed for the children.* 这个房间是打算给孩子们用的. ~**er** *n* [C]

de·sir·able /dɪˈzaɪərəbl/ *adj* 值得弄到手的 zhídé nòngdào shǒu de; 吸引人的 xīyǐn rén de. 称〔稱〕心的 chènxīnde.

de·sire /dɪˈzaɪə(r)/ *n* 1 [C, U] 愿〔願〕望 yuànwàng, 心愿 xīnyuàn. 2 [C] 想望的事物 xiǎngwàngde shìwù. □ *vt* 〔正式用语〕想望 xiǎngwàng, 希望 xīwàng.

de·sist /dɪˈzɪst/ *vi* ~ (*from*) 〔正式用语〕停止 tíngzhǐ.

desk /desk/ *n* [C] 写〔寫〕字台〔臺〕xiězìtái, 办〔辦〕公桌 bàngōngzhuō.

deso·late /ˈdesələt/ *adj* 1 荒芜〔蕪〕的 huāngwúde, 无〔無〕人居住的 wúrén jūzhù de. 2 孤寂的 gūjìde, 凄凉的 qīliángde. □ *vt* /ˈdesəleɪt/ 使荒芜 shǐ huāngwú, 使荒凉 shǐ huāngliáng. **desola·tion** /-ˈleɪʃn/ *n* [U]

des·pair /dɪˈspeə(r)/ *n* [U] 绝望 juéwàng. □ *vi* 绝望 juéwàng, 丧失信心 sàngshī xìnxīn. ~**ing·ly** *adv*

des·patch /dɪˈspætʃ/ *n, v* = dispatch.

des·per·ate /ˈdespərət/ *adj* 1 绝望的 juéwàngde, 不顾〔顧〕一切的 búgù yíqiè de. 2 危急的 wēijíde: *a ~ situation* 危急的形势. ~**ly** *adv* **des·pe·ra·tion** /-ˈreɪʃn/ *n* [U]

des·pic·able /dɪˈspɪkəbl/ *adj* 可鄙的 kěbǐde, 卑鄙的 bēibǐde. **des·pic·ably** *adv*

des·pise /dɪˈspaɪz/ *vt* 鄙视 bǐshì, 看不起 kànbùqǐ.

des·pite /dɪˈspaɪt/ *prep* 尽〔盡〕管 jǐnguǎn: *We lost ~ our efforts.* 尽管作了努力,我们输了.

de·spon·dency /dɪˈspɒndənsɪ/ *n* [U] 失望 shīwàng, 沮丧 jǔsàng. **de·spon·dent** *adj*

des·pot /ˈdespɒt/ *n* [C] 专〔專〕制统治者 zhuānzhì tǒngzhìzhě; 暴君 bàojūn. ~**ic** /dɪsˈpɒtɪk/ *adj*

des·sert /dɪˈzɜːt/ *n* [C] 甜食(正餐的最后一道菜) tiánshí. ~**spoon** 点〔點〕心匙 diǎnxīnchí; 中匙 zhōngchí.

des·ti·na·tion /ˌdestɪˈneɪʃn/ *n* [C] 目的地 mùdìdì.

des·tine /ˈdestɪn/ *vt* 预定 yùdìng; 注定 zhùdìng, 命定 mìngdìng: *They were ~d never to meet again.* 他们注定再也见不了面.

des·tiny /ˈdestɪnɪ/ *n* [*pl* -ies] [C] 命运〔運〕mìngyùn.

des·ti·tute /ˈdestɪtjuːt/ *adj* 赤贫的 chìpínde. **des·tiˈtu·tion** *n* [U]

de·stroy /dɪˈstrɔɪ/ *vt* 破坏〔壞〕pòhuài, 毁坏 huǐhuài, 摧毁 cuīhuǐ. ~**er** *n* [C] (a) 破坏者 pòhuàizhě; 起破坏作用的东西 qǐ pòhuài zuòyòng de dōngxi. (b) 驱〔驅〕逐舰〔艦〕qūzhújiàn.

de·struc·tion /dɪˈstrʌkʃn/ *n* [U] 破坏 pòhuài, 毁灭〔滅〕huǐmiè.

de·struc·tive /dɪˈstrʌktɪv/ *adj* 破坏〔壞〕的 pòhuàide; 破坏性的 pòhuàixìngde.

de·tach /dɪˈtætʃ/ *vt* 分开〔開〕fēnkāi, 拆开 chāikāi. ~**ed** *adj* (a) 超然的 chāoránde; 公正的 gōngzhèngde. (b) (建筑物)独〔獨〕立的 dúlìde. ~**ment** *n* (a)[U] 超然 chāorán, 公正 gōngzhèng. (b) [C] 分遣队〔隊〕fēnqiǎnduì, 支队 zhīduì.

de·tail[1] /ˈdiːteɪl/ *n* 1 [C] 细节〔節〕xìjié, 详情 xiángqíng. 2 [C] = detachment(b).

de·tail[2] /ˈdiːteɪl/ *vt* 1 详细叙述 xiángxì xùshù, 细说 xìshuō. 2 派遣 pàiqiǎn.

de·tain /dɪˈteɪn/ *vt* 扣留 kòuliú 拘留 jūliú.

de·tainee /ˌdiːteɪˈniː/ *n* [C] 被拘留者 bèi jūliú zhě.

de·tect /dɪˈtekt/ *vt* 发〔發〕现 fāxiàn, 发觉〔覺〕fājué; 侦察 zhēnchá. ~**or** 探测器 tàncèqì. **deˈtec·tion** /-ʃn/ *n* [U] 侦察 zhēnchá; 发现 fāxiàn, 发觉 fājué. ~**ive** *n* [C] 侦查员 zhēncháyuán.

de·ten·tion /dɪˈtenʃn/ *n* [U] 拘留 jūliú, 关〔關〕押 guānyā.

de·ter /dɪˈtɜː(r)/ *vt* [-rr-] ~ (*from*) 阻止 zǔzhǐ, 使不敢 shǐ bùgǎn, 吓〔嚇〕住 xiàzhù. *~red by the rain from going out* 因为下雨没有出去.

de·ter·gent /dɪˈtɜːdʒənt/ *n* [C, U] *adj* 去垢剂〔劑〕qùgòujì, 清洁〔潔〕剂 qīngjiéjì.

de·terio·rate /dɪˈtɪərɪəreɪt/ *vt/i* 恶〔惡〕化 èhuà, 败坏〔壞〕bàihuài: *His health ~d.* 他的健康状况恶化. **de·terioˈra·tion** *n* [U]

de·ter·mi·na·tion /dɪˌtɜːmɪˈneɪʃn/ *n* [U] 1 决定 juédìng; 确〔確〕定 quèdìng. 2 决心 juéxīn.

de·ter·mine /dɪˈtɜːmɪn/ *vt/i* 1 决定 juédìng; 确〔確〕定 quèdìng: *~ one's position* 决定某人的立场. 2 测定 cèdìng.

de·ter·rent /dɪˈterənt/ *n* [C] *adj* 制止的 zhìzhǐde; 威慑〔懾〕的 wēishède; 制止物 zhìzhǐwù.

de·test /dɪˈtest/ *vt* 痛恨 tònghèn,

憎恶〔惡〕zèngwù
de·throne /dɪ'θrəʊn/ *vt* 废〔廢〕黜 fèichù.
det·on·ate /'detəneɪt/ *vt/i* (使)爆炸 bàozhà. ˌ**det·o'n·ation** *n* [C, U]**det·on·ator** *n* [C] 起爆剂〔劑〕qǐbàojì; 雷管 léiguǎn.
de·tour /'di:tʊə(r)/ *n* [C] 弯〔彎〕路 wānlù; 迂回 yūhuí.
de·tract /dɪ'trækt/ *vi* ~ (*from*)贬低 biǎndī; 减损(价值,名誉等) jiǎnsǔn: *Nothing ~s from the value of his work.* 不论什么都无损于他的功绩.
det·ri·ment /'detrɪmənt/ *n* [U] 损害 sǔnhài, 损伤〔傷〕sǔnshāng. **~al** /-'mentl/ *adj* 有害的yǒuhàide, 有损的 yǒusǔnde.
de·value /ˌdi:'vælju:/ *vt* 使货币〔幣〕贬值 shǐ huòbì biǎnzhí. **de-valu'ation** *n* [C]
dev·as·tate /'devəsteɪt/ *vt* 破坏〔壞〕pòhuài, 蹂躏 róulìn. **dev·a-sta·tion** *n* [U]
de·velop /dɪ'veləp/ *vt/i* **1** (使)成长〔長〕chéngzhǎng; 发〔發〕展 fāzhǎn. **2** (摄影)显〔顯〕影 xiǎnyǐng, 冲洗 chōngxǐ. **3** 开〔開〕发利用 kāifā lìyòng. **~ment** *n* **(a)**[U] 发〔發〕展 fāzhǎn; 成长 chéngzhǎng; 显影 xiǎnyǐng; 开发利用 kāifā lìyòng. **(b)** [C] 发展的新阶〔階〕段 fāzhǎnde xīnjiēduàn; 进〔進〕展 jìnzhǎn.
de·vi·ate /'di:vɪeɪt/ *vi* ~ (*from*) 偏离〔離〕piānlí, 背离 bèilí. **de-vi'ation** *n* [C, U]
de·vice /dɪ'vaɪs/ *n* [C] **1** 设计 shèjì; 计划〔劃〕jìhuà. **2** 手段 shǒuduàn; 方法 fāngfǎ. **3** (装饰性)图〔圖〕案 tú'àn, 纹章 wénzhāng.
devil /'devl/ *n* [C] **1** 恶〔惡〕魔 èmó, 魔鬼 móguǐ. **the D~** 魔王 mówáng, 撒旦 sādàn. **2** 可怜〔憐〕的人 kěliánde rén, 不幸的人 búxìngde rén: *Oh, you poor ~!* 呵, 你这不幸的人!
de·vi·ous /'di:vɪəs/ *adj* 狡猾的 jiǎohuáde, 不正当〔當〕的 bú zhèngdāng de. 歪门〔門〕斜道的 wāimén xiédào de.
de·vise /dɪ'vaɪz/ *vt* 设计 shèjì, 想出 xiǎngchū.
de·void /dɪ'vɔɪd/ *adj* ~ *of* 缺乏 quēfá, 没有 méiyǒu: *A man ~ of love.* 没有爱情的人.
de·vote /dɪ'vəʊt/ *vt* 把…奉献〔獻〕给… bǎ … fèngxiàn gěi …. **de-voted** *adj* 热〔熱〕心的 rèxīnde; 忠诚的 zhōngchéngde. 虔诚的 qiánchéngde. **devo·tee** /ˌdevəʊ'ti:/ *n* [C] 热心的人 rèxīnde rén. 信徒 xìntú. **de'vo·tion** *n* **(a)** [U] 忠诚 zhōngchéng, 献身 xiànshēn. **(b)** [*pl*]祈祷〔禱〕qídǎo.
de·vour /dɪ'vaʊə(r)/ *vt* **1** 狼吞虎咽地吃 lángtūnhǔyànde chī **2** 〔喻〕挥〔揮〕霍 huīhuò; 耗尽〔盡〕hàojìn; 吸引 xīyǐn, 毁灭〔滅〕huǐmiè: *forests ~ed by fire* 大火毁灭了的森林.
de·vout /dɪ'vaʊt/ *adj* **1** 虔诚的 qiánchéngde, 虔敬的 qiánjìngde. **2** 诚恳〔懇〕的 chéngkěnde, 衷心的 zhōngxīnde. **~ly** *adv*
dew /dju:/ *n* [U] 露水 lùshuǐ, 露 lù. **dewy** *adj* [-ier, -iest]
dex·ter·ity /ˌdek'sterətɪ/ *n* [U] (手)灵〔靈〕巧的 língqiǎode; 敏捷的 mǐnjiéde. **'dex·ter·ous, 'dex-trous** *adj*
dia·betes /ˌdaɪə'bi:tɪz/ *n* [U] 糖尿病 tángniàobìng. **dia·betic** /ˌdaɪə'betɪk/ *adj*, *n* [C] 糖尿病的 tángniàobìngde; 糖尿病人 tángniàobìngrén.
dia·bolic /ˌdaɪə'bɒlɪk/ (亦作~al) *adj* **1** 恶〔惡〕魔的 èmóde, 恶魔似的 èmó sì de. **2** 凶〔兇〕暴的 xiōngbàode, 残暴的 cánbàode. **~ally** *adv*
di·ag·nose /ˌdaɪəg'nəʊz/ *vt* 诊断〔斷〕(疾病) zhěnduàn. **di·ag·nosis** /-'nəʊsɪs/ *n* [*pl* -noses] **(a)** [U] 诊断法 zhěnduànfǎ. **(b)** [C] 诊断 zhěnduàn, 诊断书〔書〕zhěnduànshū. **di·ag·nos·tic** /-'nɒstɪk/ *adj*
di·ag·onal /daɪ'ægənl/ *n* [C], *adj* 对〔對〕角线〔線〕duìjiǎoxiàn. **~ly** *adv*
dia·gram /'daɪəgræm/ *n* [C] 图〔圖〕解 tújiě. ˌ**~'matic** /ˌdaɪəgrə'mætɪk/ *adj*
dial /'daɪəl/ *n* [C] **1** 表〔錶〕面 biǎobiàn, 钟〔鐘〕面 zhōngmiàn 罗〔羅〕盘〔盤〕面板 luó pán miànbǎn. **2** (电话)拨〔撥〕号〔號〕盘〔盤〕bōhàopán □ *vt*[-ll-] 打电〔電〕话 dǎ diànhuà, 拨电话号码〔碼〕bō diànhuà hàomǎ: ~ *a friend's number* 拨一个朋友的电话号码.
dia·lect /'daɪəlekt/ *n* [C, U] 方言 fāngyán; 俚语 lǐyǔ.
dia·logue〔美语亦作 **dia·log**〕/'daɪəlɒg/ *n* **1** [U] 对〔對〕话 duìhuà. 对话体〔體〕作品 duìhuàtǐ zuòpǐn. **2** [C] 交换意见 jiāohuàn yìjiàn.
di·am·eter /daɪ'æmɪtə(r)/ *n* [C] (圆的)直径〔徑〕zhíjìng.
dia·metri·cally /ˌdaɪə'metrɪklɪ/ *adv* 完全地 wánquán de; 全然地 quánránde: ~ *opposed* 完全相反.
dia·mond /'daɪəmənd/ *n* [C] **1** 金刚〔剛〕石 jīngāngshí, 钻〔鑽〕石 zuànshí. **2** 菱形 língxíng. **3** (纸

牌)方块〔塊〕牌 fāngkuàipái.

dia·phragm /'daɪəfræm/ *n* [C] **1** (解剖)膈 gé. **2** 膜片 mópiàn; 振动〔動〕膜 zhèndòngmó.

di·ar·rhoea (also **-rrhea**) /ˌdaɪə'rɪə/ *n* [U] 腹泻〔瀉〕fùxiè, 泻肚 xièdù.

diary /'daɪərɪ/ *n* [C] [*pl* -ies] 日记 rìjì; 日记簿 rìjìbù. **dia·rist** *n* 记日记的人 jì rìjì de rén.

dice /daɪs/ *n pl* 骰子 tóuzi. □ *vt* 将〔將〕…(食物) 切成小方块〔塊〕jiāng…qiē chéng xiǎofāngkuài.

dic·tate /dɪk'teɪt/ *vt/i* **1** (使)听〔聽〕写〔寫〕tīngxiě. **2** 命令 mìnglìng; 支配 zhīpèi.

dic·ta·tion /dɪk'teɪʃn/ *n* **1** [U] 听〔聽〕写〔寫〕tīngxiě. **2** [C] 听写的一段文字 tīngxiěde yíduàn wénzì.

dic·ta·tor /ˌdɪk'teɪtə(r)/ *n* [C] 独〔獨〕裁者 dúcáizhě; 支配者 zhīpèizhě. **~ial** /ˌdɪktə'tɔːrɪəl/ *adj* **~-ship** *n* [C, U] 独裁政府 dúcái zhèngfǔ; 独裁国〔國〕家 dúcái guójiā; 专〔專〕政 zhuānzhèng.

dic·tion /'dɪkʃn/ *n* [U] 措词 cuòcí; 用词风〔風〕格 yòngcí fēnggé.

dic·tion·ary /'dɪkʃənrɪ/ *n* [C] [*pl* -ies] 词典 cídiǎn, 字典 zìdiǎn.

did/dɪd/ ⇨ do.

die[1] /daɪ/ *n* [C] 印模 yìnmó; 冲模 chòngmó; 钢〔鋼〕型 gāngxíng.

die[2] /daɪ/*vi* [*pt, pp* ~d; *pres part* dying] **1** 死 sǐ, 死亡 sǐwáng. **2** 渴望 kěwàng; 切望 qièwàng: *dying for a drink* 渴得要死. **3** ~ ***away*** 消沉的 xiāochénde, 颓丧〔喪〕的 tuísàngde. ~ ***down*** 渐熄 jiànxī; 渐渐消失 jiànjiàn xiāoshī: *The flames gradually ~d down.* 火焰渐渐熄灭. ~ ***out*** 死光 sǐ guāng, 绝种〔種〕juézhǒng, 灭〔滅〕绝 mièjué.

die·sel /'diːzl/ *n* **1** '~ **(engine)** *n* 内燃机〔機〕nèiránjī **2** ~ oil (或 **fuel)** *n* 柴油 cháiyóu

diet /'daɪət/ *n*[C] **1** 饮食 yǐnshí, 食物 shíwù. **2** 规定的饮食(如为了减肥)guīdìngde yǐnshí. □ *vi* 吃规定的饮食 chī guīdìngde yǐnshí; 忌食 jìshí. **~ary** *adj*

diff. =**1** difference. **2** different.

dif·fer /'dɪfə(r)/ *vi* **1** ~ **(*from*)** 不相同 bù xiāngtóng. **2** 意见不一致 yìjiàn bù yízhì.

dif·ference /'dɪfrəns/ *n* [C, U] **1** 差别 chābié, 差异〔異〕chāyì. **2** 数〔數〕量, 程度, 方式方法上的差别 shùliàng chéngdù fāngshì fāngfǎ shàng de chābié. **3** ***make a (no)*** ~ 有些(没有)关〔關〕系 yǒu xiē guānxi. **4** 争论〔論〕zhēnglùn; 不一致 bù yízhì. **dif·ferent** *adj* **(a)** 不同的 bùtóngde. 相异〔異〕的 xiāngyìde. **(b)** 分别的 fēnbiéde 各别的 gèbiéde: *at ~ times* 在不同的时代.

dif·fer·en·ti·ate /ˌdɪfə'renʃɪeɪt/ *vt* 区〔區〕别 qūbié, 区分 qūfēn.

dif·fi·cult /'dɪfɪkəlt/ *adj* **1** 困难〔難〕的 kùnnande, 难的 nánde. **2** (人)难对〔對〕付的 nán duìfu de. **dif·fi·culty** *n* [*pl* -ies] **(a)** [U] 困难 kùnnan. **(b)** [C] 困境 kùnjìng; 疑难之处〔處〕yínánzhīchù.

dif·fi·dence /'dɪfɪdəns/ *n* [U] 缺乏信心 quēfá xìnxīn; 胆〔膽〕怯 dǎnquè; 羞怯 xiūqiè. **dif·fi·dent** *adj*

dif·fuse /dɪ'fjuːz/ *vt/i* (使)散开〔開〕sànkāi; (使)扩〔擴〕散 kuòsàn; (使)传〔傳〕播 chuánbō. □ /dɪ'fjuːs/ *adj* **1** 扩散的 kuòsànde, 散开的 sànkāide: ~ *light* 漫射光. **2** 冗长〔長〕的 yǒngchángde. **dif-fu·sion** /dɪ'fjuːʒn/ *n* [U]

dig[1]/dɪg/ *n* [C] 〔非正式用语〕**1** 推 tuī; 刺 cì: *a ~ in the ribs* 对肋骨部位的一杵. **2** 挖苦 wākǔ; 讽〔諷〕刺话 fěngcìhuà. **3** 考古挖掘的地点〔點〕kǎogǔ wājué de dìdiǎn. **4** [*pl*] 〔英国英语非正式用语〕住宿处〔處〕zhùsùchù.

dig[2] /dɪg/ *vt/i* [*pt, pp* dug /dʌg/] [-gg-] **1** 掘取 juéqǔ, 采掘 cǎijué, 挖(洞) wā. **2** 〔俚语〕喜欢〔歡〕xǐhuan 理解 lǐjiě: *I don't ~ modern jazz.* 我不喜欢现代爵士乐. **3** ~ ***sb (sth) out (of sth)*** 掘出 juéchū 挖掉 wādiào ~ ***sth up*** 挖出 wāchū, 掘掉 juédiào.

di·gest[1] /'daɪdʒest/ *n* [C] 摘要 zhāiyào, 文摘 wénzhāi.

di·gest[2] /daɪ'dʒest/ *vt/i* **1** 消化(食物) xiāohuà. **2** 领会〔會〕lǐnghuì, 透彻〔徹〕了解 tòuchè liáojiě, 融会贯通 rónghuìguàntōng: ~ *the facts in a book* 将书中的资料理出一个头绪. **di·ges·tion** /dɪ'dʒestʃn/ *n* [U] 消化 xiāohuà; 消化力 xiāohuàlì; 消化作用 xiāohuà zuòyòng. **~ive** *adj* 消化的 xiāohuàde.

digit /'dɪdʒɪt/ *n* [C] **1** 数〔數〕字 (0 到 9 中的任何一个数字) shùzì; 位数 wèishù: *The number 57306 has five ~s.* 57306 是五位数. **2** 手指 shǒuzhǐ, 脚趾 jiǎozhǐ. **~al** *adj* 数字的 shùzìde; 计数的 jìshùde: *a ~al clock* 数字钟.

dig·ni·fied /'dɪgnɪfaɪd/ *adj* 高贵的 gāoguìde; 尊贵的 zūnguìde.

dig·ni·tary /'dɪgnɪtərɪ/ *n* [C] [*pl* -ies] 职〔職〕位高的人 zhíwèi gāo de rén.

dig·nity /'dɪgnətɪ/ *n* [*pl* -ies] **1**[U]

高贵 gāoguì; 尊贵 zūnguì. **2** [C] 高位 gāowèi, 显〔顯〕贵 xiǎnguì.

di·gress /daɪ'gres/ *vi* 离〔離〕题 lítí. **~ion** /daɪ'greʃn/ *n* [U]

dike, dyke /daɪk/ *n* [C] **1** 排水道 páishuǐdào, 沟 gōu, 渠 qú. **2** 堤 dī, 堤防 dīfáng; 堰 yàn.

dil·api·dated /dɪ'læpɪdeɪtɪd/ *adj* 破旧〔舊〕的 pòjiùde, 坍坏〔壞〕的 tānhuàide.

di·late /daɪ'leɪt/*vt/i* (使)扩〔擴〕大 kuòdà, (使)张〔張〕大 zhāngdà: *Her eyes ~d with fear*.她害怕得张大着眼睛. **dila·tion** /-ʃn/ *n* [U]

di·lemma /dɪ'lemə/ *n* [C][*pl* ~s] 进〔進〕退两难〔難〕的境地 jìntuì liǎng nán de jìngdì, 困境 kùnjìng.

dili·gence/ 'dɪlɪdʒəns/ *n* [U] 勤奋〔奮〕qínfèn, 用功 yònggōng, 勤勉 qínmiǎn: *work with ~* 工作勤奋. **dili·gent** *adj*

di·lute /daɪ'lju:t/ *vt* 使变〔變〕淡 shǐ biàndàn, 冲淡 chōngdàn, 稀释〔釋〕xīshì. □ *adj* 稀释的 xīshìde, 淡的 dànde.

dim /dɪm/ *adj* [-mer, -mest] **1** 暗的 ànde, 暗淡的 àndànde, 不明亮的 bù míngliàng de: *a ~ light* 暗淡的光线. **2** (眼睛, 目力)看不清楚的 kàn bù qīngchu de; 模糊的 móhude **3** 〔非正式用语〕迟〔遲〕钝的 chídùnde. □ *vt/i* [-mm-] (使)变〔變〕模糊 biàn móhu. (使)变暗淡 biàn àndàn. **~ly** *adv*

dime /daɪm/ *n* [C](美国, 加拿大)一角钱〔錢〕硬币〔幣〕 yìjiǎoqián yìngbì.

di·men·sion /dɪ'menʃn/ *n* **1** [C] 尺寸 chǐcùn, 尺度 chǐdù. **2** [*pl*] 大小 dàxiǎo. **-~al** *suffix*: 度的 dùde: *two-~al* 平面的.

dim·in·ish /dɪ'mɪnɪʃ/ *vt/i* 减小 jiǎnxiǎo, 减少 jiǎnshǎo, 缩小 suōxiǎo: *Our chances of success are ~ing*. 我们成功的机会正在减少.

dim·inu·tive /dɪ'mɪnjʊtɪv/ *adj* 微小的 wēixiǎode. □ *n* [C] 指小词(如 *kitchenette* 是 kitchen 的指小词) zhǐxiǎocí

dimple /'dɪmpl/ *n* [C] 酒窝 jiǔwō, 笑窝 xiàowō, 笑靥〔靨〕xiàoyè.

din /dɪn/ *n* [U] 喧闹声〔聲〕xuānnàoshēng; 嘈杂〔雜〕声 cāozáoshēng. □ *vt/i* [-nn-] 以闹声吵人 yǐ nàoshēng chǎorén; 喧闹 xuānnào.

dine /daɪn/ *vt/i* 吃饭 chīfàn, 进〔進〕餐 jìncān. **'dining-car** (火车)餐车〔車〕cānchē.

din·ghy /'dɪŋgɪ/ *n* [C][*pl* -ies,~s] 小艇 xiǎotǐng; 橡皮筏 xiàngpífá.

dingy /'dɪndʒɪ/ *adj* [-ier, -iest] 肮〔髒〕的 zāngde; 褴〔襤〕褛〔褸〕的 lánlǚde, 邋遢的 lātāde. **dingi·ness** *n* [U]

din·ner /'dɪnə(r)/ *n* [C] 正餐 zhèngcān. **'~-jacket** 男式晚礼〔禮〕服 nánshì wǎnlǐfú.

dino·saur /'daɪnəsɔ:(r)/ *n* [C] 恐龙〔龍〕kǒnglóng.

dio·cese /'daɪəsɪs/ *n* [C] [*pl* ~s /-si:zɪz/] 主教管区〔區〕 zhǔjiào guǎnqū.

Dip. = Diploma.

Dip,Ed. = Diploma in Education 文凭〔憑〕wénpíng.

dip¹ /dɪp/ *n* [C] **1** 蘸湿〔濕〕zhànshī, 浸渍 jìnzì. **2** 斜坡 xiépō. **3** 短时〔時〕的游泳 duǎnshíde yóuyǒng.

dip² /dɪp/ *vt/i* [-pp-] **1** 沾 zhān,蘸 zhàn; 浸 qìn. **2** 把…下降后〔後〕再升起 bǎ...xiàjiàng hòu zài shēngqǐ: *to ~ the headlights of a car*. 使汽车前灯变暗. **3 ~ into ~** *into one's purse* (或 *pocket*) 花钱 huāqián; **~ *into a book*** 随便浏览.

diph·theria /dɪf'θɪərɪə/ *n* [U] 白喉 báihóu.

diph·thong /'dɪfθɒŋ/ *n* [C] 双〔雙〕元音 shuāngyuányīn, 复〔復〕合元音 fùhé yuányīn.

di·ploma /dɪ'pləʊmə/ *n*[C] [*pl* ~s] 毕〔畢〕业〔業〕证〔證〕书〔書〕 bìyè zhèngshū, 文凭〔憑〕wénpíng.

di·plo·macy /dɪ'pləʊməsɪ/ *n* [U] **1** 外交 wàijiāo. **2** 外交手腕 wàijiāo shǒuwàn, 交际〔際〕手腕 jiāojì shǒuwàn.

diplo·mat /'dɪpləmæt/ *n* [C] 外交家 wàijiāojiā 外交人员 wàijiāo rényuán, 外交官 wàijiāoguān. **~·ic** /-'mætɪk/ *adj* 外交的 wàijiāode, 外交上的 wàijiāo shàng de, 外交手腕的 wàijiāo shǒuwàn de. **~·i·cally** *adv*

dire /'daɪə(r)/*adj* **1** 可怕的 kěpàde; 悲惨〔慘〕的 bēicǎnde. **2** 极〔極〕端的 jíduānde, 迫切的 pòqiède: *in ~ need* 极需帮助.

di·rect¹ /dɪ'rekt/ *adj* **1** 笔〔筆〕直的 bǐzhíde, 笔直前进〔進〕的 bǐzh[í] qiánjìn de. **2** 直系的 zhíxìde, 直接的 zhíjiēde: *a ~ result* 直接的结果. **3** 直率的 zhíshuàide, 直截了当〔當〕的 zhíjiéliǎodàngde, 坦白的 tǎnbáide: *a ~ way of speakin[g]* 说话直截了当. **4** 正好的 zhèngh[ǎode]: *the ~ opposite* 正好相反. □ *adv* 径直地 jìngzhíde, 直接地 zhí[jiēde]. **'~ current** 直流电〔電〕zhíliúdiàn. **'~ speech** 〔语法〕直接引语 zhíjiē yǐnyǔ. **~ness** *n* [U] **~ly** *adv* **(a)** 直接地 zhíjiēde, 径[直]

地 jìngzhíde. **(b)** 即刻 jìkè.

di·rect² /dɪ'rekt/ *vt/i* **1** 指引 zhǐyǐn; 指点〔點〕zhǐdiǎn: *Could you ~ me to the station?* 请问到车站怎么走? **2** 指导 zhǐdǎo; 管理 guǎnlǐ; 支配 zhīpèi. **3** 对准〔準〕目标〔標〕duìzhǔn mùbiāo: *~ criticism at an opponent* 向敌手展开批判.

di·rec·tion /dɪ'rekʃn/ *n* **1** [C] 方向 fāngxiàng, 方位 fāngwèi. **2** [C] 〔常用 *pl*〕说明 shuōmíng, 指引 zhǐyǐn. **3** [U] 指导 zhǐdǎo, 管理 guǎnlǐ; 指挥〔揮〕zhǐhuī. **di·rec·tive** *n* [C] 命令 mìnglìng; 指示 zhǐshì.

di·rec·tor /dɪ'rektə(r)/ *n* [C] **1** 董事 dǒngshì; 处〔處〕长〔長〕chùzhǎng; 署长 shǔzhǎng; 总〔總〕监〔監〕zǒngjiān. **2** 导〔導〕演 dǎoyǎn; 指挥〔揮〕zhǐhuī. **~ship** 董事,导演等的职〔職〕位 dǒngshì, dǎoyǎn děng de zhíwèi.

di·rec·tory /dɪ'rektərɪ/ *n* [C] [*pl* -ies] 名录〔錄〕(姓名地址录,电话号码簿等) mínglù: *a telephone ~* 电话号码簿.

dirt /dɜ:t/ *n* [U] **1** 脏〔髒〕物 zāngwù, 污垢 wūgòu. **2** 松〔鬆〕土 sōngtǔ, 泥土 nítǔ: *a ~ road* 土路. **dirty** *adj* [-ier, -iest] **(a)** 脏的 zāngde. **(b)** 淫猥的 yínwěide, 黄色的 huángsède: *a ~y joke* 下流的笑话. **(c)** [非正式用语]卑鄙的 bēibǐde: *a ~ trick* 卑鄙的伎俩. □ *vt/i* [*pt, pp* -ied] 弄脏 nòngzāng, 变〔變〕脏 biànzāng. **dirt·ily** *adv*

dis·abil·ity /ˌdɪsə'bɪlətɪ/ *n*[*pl* -ies] **1** [U] 无〔無〕能 wúnéng; 无力 wúlì. **2** 残〔殘〕废〔廢〕cánfèi.

dis·able /dɪs'eɪbl/ *vt* 使无〔無〕能力 shǐ wú nénglì, 使伤〔傷〕残 shǐ shāngcán. **~ment** *n* [U]

dis·ad·van·tage /ˌdɪsəd'vɑ:ntɪdʒ/ *n* **1** [C] 不利条〔條〕件 búlì tiáojiàn. **2** [U] 损失 sǔnshī; 损伤〔傷〕sǔnshāng. **~ous** /ˌdɪsˌædvən'teɪdʒəs/ *adj*

dis·agree/ˌdɪsə'gri:/ *vt* ~ **(with) 1** 不同意 bù tóngyì. **2** 有害 yǒuhài, 不适〔適〕合 bú shìhé. **~able**/-əbl/ *adj* 讨厌〔厭〕的 tǎoyànde, 不合意的 bù héyì de. **~ably** *adv* **~ment** *n* [C, U] 意见不一致 yìjiàn bù yízhì, 分歧 fēnqí.

dis·ap·pear /ˌdɪsə'pɪə(r)/ *vi* 不见 bújiàn, 消失 xiāoshī. **~ance** *n* [C, U]

dis·ap·point /ˌdɪsə'pɔɪnt/ *vt* 失望 shīwàng, 使希望落空 shǐ xīwàng luòkōng. **~ed** *adj* 失望的 shīwàngde. **~ing** *adj* **~ment** *n* [C, U] 失望 shīwàng, 扫〔掃〕兴〔興〕sǎoxìng. 令人扫兴的事物 lìngrén sǎoxìng de shìwù.

dis·ap·prove /ˌdɪsə'pru:v/ *vt/i* ~ **(of)** 不赞成 bú zànchéng; 不同意 bù tóngyì. **dis·ap·proval** *n* [U]

dis·arm /dɪs'ɑ:m/ *vt/i* **1** 缴…的械 jiǎo ... de xiè, 解除武装〔裝〕jiěchú wǔzhuāng. **2** 裁军〔軍〕cáijūn. **3** 消除(怒气,怀疑等) xiāochú: *~-ed by his kindness* 他的好言善语使人怒气消失. **~a·ment** *n* [U] 裁军 cáijūn.

dis·array /ˌdɪsə'reɪ/ *n* [U], *vt* 弄乱〔亂〕nòngluàn, 扰〔擾〕乱 rǎoluàn.

dis·as·ter /dɪ'zɑ:stə(r)/ *n* [C, U] 灾〔災〕难〔難〕zāinàn, 祸患 huòhuàn. **dis·as·trous** /dɪ'zɑ:strəs/ *adj*

dis·band /dɪs'bænd/ *vt/i* 解散 jiěsàn, 遣散 qiǎnsàn.

dis·be·lieve /ˌdɪsbɪ'li:v/ *vt/i* 不相信 bù xiāngxìng, 怀〔懷〕疑 huáiyí. **dis·be·lief** /ˌdɪsbɪ'li:f/ *n* [U]

disc, (also **disk**) /dɪsk/ *n* [C] **1** 圆盘〔盤〕yuánpán; 圆面 yuánmiàn; 圆板 yuánbǎn. **2** 椎间〔間〕盘〔盤〕zhuījiānpán: *a slipped ~* 脱出的椎间盘. **'~ jockey** 无〔無〕线〔綫〕电〔電〕唱片音乐〔樂〕节〔節〕目广〔廣〕播员 wúxiàndiàn chàngpiàn yīnyuè jiémù guǎngbōyuán.

dis·card /dɪ'skɑ:d/ *vt* 〔正式用语〕抛弃〔棄〕pāoqì, 遗弃 yíqì.

dis·cern /dɪ'sɜ:n/ *vt* 〔正式用语〕看出 kànchū, 辨出 biànchū. **~ing** *adj* 有眼力的 yǒu yǎnlì de.

dis·charge /dɪs'tʃɑ:dʒ/ *vt/i* **1** 卸(船上的)货 xièhuò. **2** 排出(液体,气体等)páichū. **3** 开〔開〕(炮等) kāi. **4** 释〔釋〕放 shìfàng; 允许离〔離〕开 yǔnxǔ líkāi. **5** 偿〔償〕付(债款) chángfù; 履行(义务) lǚxíng. □ *n* [C] **1** 卸货 xièhuò; 发〔發〕射 fāshè; 排出 páichū, 放出 fàngchū. **2** 流出物 liúchūwù, 排泄物 páixièwù.

dis·ciple /dɪ'saɪpl/ *n* [C] 信徒 xìntú, 门〔門〕徒 méntú, 追随者 zhuīsuízhě.

dis·ci·pline¹ /'dɪsɪplɪn/ *n* **1** [U] 训练 xùliàn. **2** [U] 纪律 jìlǜ, 风〔風〕纪 fēngjì. **3** [C] 戒律 jièlǜ. **4** [U] 惩〔懲〕罚 chěngfá, 处〔處〕罚 chǔfá. **5** [C] 学〔學〕科 xuékē.

dis·ci·pline² /'dɪsɪplɪn/ *vt* 训练 xùnliàn, 训导〔導〕xùndǎo; 惩〔懲〕罚 chěngfá.

dis·claim/dɪs'kleɪm / *vt* 否认〔認〕fǒurèn 不承认 bù chéngrèn: *~ responsibility for* 不承认负有…责任.

dis·close /dɪs'kləʊz/ *vt* 透露 tòulù, 泄露 xièlù: ~ *one's identity* 泄露某人的身份. **dis·clos·ure**/-ʒə(r)/ *n* [C, U]

dis·co /'dɪskəʊ/ *n* [C]=discotheque.

dis·colour [美语=**-color**] /dɪs'kʌlə(r)/ *vt/i* (使) 变[變]色 biànsè, (使)变污 biànwū. ~**ation** /dɪˌkʌlə'reɪʃən/ *n* [C, U]

dis·com·fort /dɪs'kʌmfət/ *n* [C, U] 不舒服 bù shūfu; 使不舒服的原因 shǐ bù shūfude yuányīn; 困苦 kùnkǔ: *the ~s of travelling* 旅途的困难.

dis·con·cert /ˌdɪskən'sɜːt/ *vt* 使不安 shǐ bù ān, 使仓[倉]惶失措 shǐ cānghuáng shīcuò: *I was ~ed to learn that he didn't like me.* 听说他不喜欢我,我就仓惶失措起来.

dis·con·nect /ˌdɪskə'nekt/ *vt* 拆开[開] chāikāi, 断[斷]开 duànkāi, 分离[離] fēnlí. ~**ed** *adj* (说话, 写作)不连[連]贯的 bù liánguàn de, 凌乱[亂]的 língluànde, 无[無]条[條]理的 wú tiáolǐ de.

dis·con·so·late /dɪs'kɒnsələt/ *adj* 忧[憂]郁[鬱]的 yōuyùde, 不愉快的 bù yúkuài de.

dis·con·tent /ˌdɪskən'tent/ *n* [C, U] 不满意 bù mǎnyì. 不满的原因 bù mǎn de yuányīn. ~**ed** *adj* 不满意的 bù mǎnyì de.

dis·con·tinue /ˌdɪskən'tɪnjuː/ *vt/i* [正式用语]停止 tíngzhǐ, 中止 zhōngzhǐ, 中断[斷] zhōngduàn.

dis·cord /'dɪskɔːd/ *n* **1** [C, U]不和 bùhé, 争吵 zhēngchǎo. **2** [C, U] (声音)不谐和 bù xiéhé. ~**ant** *adj*

dis·co·theque /'dɪskətek/ *n* [C] 唱片舞会[會] chàngpiàn wǔhuì.

dis·count[1] /'dɪskaʊnt/ *n* [C] (价格)折扣 zhékòu.

dis·count[2] /dɪs'kaʊnt/ *vt* 不全信 bù quánxìn; 看轻[輕] kànqīng.

dis·cour·age /dɪ'skʌrɪdʒ/ *vt* **1** 使泄气[氣] shǐ xièqì, 使失掉信心 shǐ shīdiào xìnxīn; 沮丧 jǔsàng: *He isn't ~d by his failure.* 他不因失败而丧失信心. **2** 阻拦[攔] zǔlán. ~**ment** *n* [C, U]

dis·course /'dɪskɔːs/ *n* [C] 演说 yǎnshuō, 讲话 jiǎnghuà.

dis·cour·teous /dɪs'kɜːtɪəs/ *adj* 不客气的 bù kèqi de, 不礼[禮]貌的 bù lǐmào de.

dis·cour·tesy /dɪs'kɛːtəsɪ/ *n* [C, U] 粗暴 cūbào, 失礼 shīlǐ.

dis·cover /dɪ'skʌvə(r)/ *vt* 发[發]现 fāxiàn. ~**er** 发现人 fāxiànrén. **dis·covery** *n* [*pl* -ies][C, U] 发现 fāxiàn, 被发现的事物 bèi fāxiàn de shìwù.

dis·credit[1] /dɪs'kredɪt/ *vt* 不信 búxìn, 怀[懷]疑 huáiyí.

dis·credit[2] /dɪs'kredɪt/ *n* [U] 丧失信誉[譽] sàngshī xìnyù, 丧失名声[聲] sàngshī míngshēng.

dis·creet /dɪ'skriːt/ *adj* 谨慎的 jǐnshènde, 思虑[慮]周全的 sīlǜzhōuquánde: *a ~ inquiry* 考虑周到的调查. ~**ly** *adv*

dis·crep·ancy /dɪ'skrepənsɪ/ *n* [C, U] [*pl* -ies] 不一致 bù yízhì, 差异[異] chāyì, 不符 bùfú.

dis·cre·tion /dɪ'skreʃn/ *n* [U] **1** 谨慎 jǐnshèn. **2** 处[處]理权[權] chǔlǐquán.

dis·crimi·nate /dɪ'skrɪmɪneɪt/ *vt/i* **1** 区[區]别 qūbié, 区分 qūfēn, 辨别 biànbié: ~ *good books from bad ones* 辨别书的好坏. **2** ~ (*against*)歧视 qíshì. **dis·crimi·nating** *adj* 有辨别力的 yǒu biànbiélì de. **dis·crimi·'na·tion** *n* [U]

dis·cus /'dɪskəs/ *n* [C] [*pl*~es][体育]铁[鐵]饼 tiěbǐng.

dis·cuss /dɪ'skʌs/ *vt* 讨论 tǎolùn, 商讨 shāngtǎo. ~**ion** /dɪ'skʌʃn/ *n* [C, U]

dis·dain /dɪs'deɪn/ *vt* [正式用语] 蔑视 mièshì, 轻[輕]视 qīngshì. □ *n* [U] 蔑视 mièshì, 轻视 qīngshì. ~**ful** *adj*

dis·ease /dɪ'ziːz/ *n* [C, U] 疾病 jíbìng, 病 bìng. **dis·eased** *adj* 生病的 shēngbìngde, 有病的 yǒu bìng de.

dis·em·bark /ˌdɪsɪm'bɑːk/ *vt/i* (使)上岸shàng'àn, (使)登岸 dēng'àn. ~**a·tion** /ˌdɪsembɑː'keɪʃn/*n* [C, U]

dis·en·gage /ˌdɪsɪn'geɪdʒ/ *vt/i* 解除 jiěchú; (使)脱离[離] tuōlí.

dis·en·tangle /ˌdɪsɪn'tæŋgl/ *vt/i* 解开[開] jiěkāi; 清理 qīnglǐ.

dis·fig·ure /dɪs'fɪgə(r)/ *vt* 损毁容貌 sǔnhuǐ róngmào, 破…的相 pò …de xiàng, 破坏[壞]外形 pòhuài wàixíng: *His face was ~d in the accident.* 这次事故损毁了他的面容. ~**ment** *n* [C, U]

dis·grace /dɪs'greɪs/ *n* [U] 耻辱 chǐrǔ, 丢脸[臉]diūliǎn. [C]使人丢脸的事 shǐ rén diūliǎn de shì 使人丢脸的人 shǐ rén diūliǎn de rén. □ *vt* 使丢脸 shǐ diūliǎn, 使蒙受耻辱 shǐ méngshòu chǐrǔ. ~**ful** *adj*

dis·gruntled /dɪs'grʌntld/ *adj* 不满意的 bù mǎnyì de; 不高兴[興]的 bù gāoxìng de.

dis·guise /dɪs'gaɪz/ *vt* **1** 把…

装〔裝〕起来 bǎ...jiǎzhuāng qǐlái, 把...假扮起来 bǎ...jiǎbàn qǐlái. 2 掩饰 yǎnshì, 隐蔽 yǐnbì: ~ *one's anger* 按捺住怒火. □ *n* [C, U] 伪〔僞〕装衣 wěizhuāngyī; 用作伪装的动〔動〕作 yòng zuò wěizhuāng de dòngzuò.

dis·gust /dɪs'gʌst/ *n* [U] 厌〔厭〕恶〔惡〕yànwù, 讨厌 tǎoyàn. □ *vt* 使厌恶 shǐ yànwù. **~ing** *adj* 厌恶的 yànwùde, 讨厌的 tǎoyànde.

dish /dɪʃ/ *n* [C] **1** 盘〔盤〕pán, 碟 dié. **2 the ~es** 全部餐具 quánbù cānjù. **3** 盘中的食物 pán zhōng de shíwù, 菜肴 càiyáo. □ *vt* ~ **(up)** **1** 上菜 shàngcài. **2** 阐〔闡〕述论〔論〕点〔點〕chǎnshù lùndiǎn. ~ ***sth out*** 分饭菜 fēn fàn cài. 分发〔發〕fēnfā. **'~cloth** 洗碟布 xǐdiébù.

dis·hearten /dɪs'hɑ:tn/ *vt* 使沮丧 shǐ jǔsàng, 使失去勇气〔氣〕shǐ shīqù yǒngqì.

di·shev·elled [美语=**-eled**] /dɪ'ʃevld/ *adj* (衣服, 头发)散乱〔亂〕的 sǎnluànde 不整洁〔潔〕的 bù zhěngjié de.

dis·hon·est /dɪs'ɒnɪst/ *adj* 不诚实〔實〕的 bù chéngshí de, 不老实的 bù lǎoshi de. **dis·hon·esty** *n* [C, U]

dis·hon·our [美语 = **-honor**] /dɪs'ɒnə(r)/ *n* [C] **1** 耻辱 chǐrǔ, 不光彩 bù guāngcǎi, 不名誉〔譽〕bù míngyù. **2** 带〔帶〕来〔來〕耻辱的人或事 dài lái chǐrǔ de rén huò shì. □ *vt* **1** 使受耻辱 shǐ shòu chǐrǔ, 使丢脸〔臉〕shǐ diūliǎn, 使不光彩 shǐ bù guāngcǎi. **2** (票据)拒付 jùfù: ~ *a cheque, etc* 拒付支票等. **~able** /-rəbl/ *adj*

dis·il·lu·sion /ˌdɪsɪ'lu:ʒn/ *vt* 使醒悟 shǐ xǐngwù; 使幻想破灭〔滅〕shǐ huànxiǎng pòmiè. **~ment** *n* [C] 醒悟 xǐngwù, 幻想破灭 huànxiǎng pòmiè.

dis·in·fect /ˌdɪsɪn'fekt/ *vt* 给...消毒 gěi ... xiāodú, 杀〔殺〕死 ... 的细菌 shāsǐ...de xìjūn. **~ant** *adj*, *n* [C, U] 消毒剂〔劑〕xiāodújì.

dis·in·herit /ˌdɪsɪn'herɪt/ *vt* 剥夺〔奪〕...的继〔繼〕承权〔權〕bōduó... de jìchéngquán.

dis·in·te·grate /dɪs'ɪntɪgreɪt/ *vt/i* 使瓦解 shǐ wǎjiě, 使崩溃 shǐ bēngkuì. **dis·in·te'gra·tion** *n* [U]

dis·in·ter /ˌdɪsɪn'tɜ:(r)/ *vt* [-rr-] 从〔從〕坟墓中掘出(尸体) cóng fénmù zhōng juéchū. **~ment** *n* [C, U]

dis·in·ter·ested /dɪs'ɪntrəstɪd/ *adj* 无〔無〕私的 wúsīde. 无偏见的 wú piānjiàn de: *a ~ judgement* 公正的判决.

dis·jointed /dɪs'dʒɔɪntɪd/ *adj* 不连〔連〕贯的 bù liánguàn de, 没有条〔條〕理的 méiyǒu tiáolǐ de. **~ly** *adv*

disk /dɪsk/ *n* ⇨ disc.

dis·like /dɪs'laɪk/ *vt* 不喜欢〔歡〕bù xǐhuān, 不爱〔愛〕bú ài, 厌〔厭〕恶〔惡〕yànwù. □ *n* [C]: 厌恶 yànwù: *feel ~ for somebody* 厌恶某人.

dis·lo·cate /'dɪsləkeɪt/ *vt* **1** 使(骨骼)脱位 shǐ tuōwèi, 使离〔離〕开〔開〕原位 shǐ líkāi yuánwèi. **2** 使紊乱〔亂〕shǐ wěnluàn. **dis·lo'ca·tion** *n* [C, U]

dis·lodge /dɪs'lɒdʒ/ *vt* 驱〔驅〕逐出 qūzhúchū; 取出 qǔchū: ~ *a tooth* 取出牙齿; ~ *enemy soldiers* 把敌兵赶走.

dis·loyal /dɪs'lɔɪəl/ *adj* 不忠诚的 bù zhōngchéng de. **~ly** *adv* **~ty** *n* [C, U]

dis·mal /'dɪzməl/ *adj* 忧〔憂〕愁的 yōuchóude, 阴〔陰〕沉的 yīnchénde. **~ly** *adv*

dis·mantle /dɪs'mæntl/ *vt* 拆除 chāichú; 拆散 chāisàn; 拆卸 chāixiè.

dis·may /dɪs'meɪ/ *n* [U] 灰心丧气〔氣〕huīxīn sàngqì. 惊〔驚〕愕 jīng'è. □ *vt* 使灰心 shǐ huīxīn, 使沮丧 shǐ jǔsàng.

dis·mem·ber /dɪs'membə(r)/ *vt* **1** 肢解 zhījiě. **2** 瓜分(国家) guāfēn.

dis·miss /dɪs'mɪs/ *vt* **1** 解雇 jiěgù; 开〔開〕除 kāichú; 免职〔職〕miǎnzhí. **2** 解散 jiěsàn: ~ *a class* 下课. **3** 不考虑〔慮〕bù kǎolǜ, 消除 xiāochú: ~ *all thoughts of revenge* 消除报复的念头. **~al** *n* [C, U]

dis·mount /ˌdɪs'maʊnt/ *vt/i* (使)下马〔馬〕xiàmǎ; (使)下车〔車〕xiàchē.

dis·obedi·ence /ˌdɪsə'bi:dɪəns/ *n* [U] 不服从〔從〕bù fúcóng, 不顺从 bú shùncóng. **dis·obedi·ent** *adj*

dis·obey /ˌdɪsə'beɪ/ *vt* 不服从〔從〕bù fúcóng, 不顺从 bú shùncóng.

dis·order /dɪs'ɔ:də(r)/ *n* **1** [U] 混乱〔亂〕hùnluàn; 杂〔雜〕乱 záluàn. **2** [C] 骚〔騷〕乱 sāoluàn, 骚动〔動〕sāodòng. **3** [C, U] (身,心)失调 shītiáo. □ *vt* 使混乱 shǐ hùnluàn, 使失调 shǐ shītiáo, 扰〔擾〕乱 rǎoluàn. **~ly** *adj*

dis·or·gan·ize /ˌdɪs'ɔ:gənaɪz/ *vt* 打乱〔亂〕dǎluàn.

dis·own /dɪs'əʊn/ *vt* 否认〔認〕知道 ... fǒurèn zhīdào ...; 否认与〔與〕...有关〔關〕fǒurèn yǔ ... yǒuguān.

dis·par·ate /'dɪspərət/ *adj* 完全不相同的 wánquán bù xiāngtóng de, 不能比拟〔擬〕的 bùnéng bǐnǐ de. **dis·par·ity** /di:'spærətɪ/ *n* [C,U] [*pl* -ies] 不同 bùtóng, 悬〔懸〕殊 xuánshū.

dis·pas·sion·ate /dɪ'spæʃənət/ *adj* 不动〔動〕感情的 búdòng gǎnqíng de' 冷静的 lěngjìngde. **~ly** *adv*

dis·patch des·patch /dɪ'spætʃ/ *vt* **1** 派遣 pàiqiǎn, 发〔發〕送 fāsòng: *to ~ letters* 送信. **2** 迅速办〔辦〕理 xùnsù bànlǐ, 了结 liǎojié. **3** 杀〔殺〕死 shāsǐ, 处〔處〕决 chǔjué. □ *n* **(a)** [U] 派遣 pàiqiǎn, 发〔發〕送 fāsòng. **(b)** [C] 公文 gōngwén; 急件 jíjiàn; 电讯 diànxùn.

dis·pel /dɪ'spel/ *vt* [-ll-] 驱〔驅〕散 qūsàn, 消除 xiāochú: *~ rumours* 消除谣言, *~ doubts* 解除疑虑.

dis·pen·sa·tion /ˌdɪspen'seɪʃn/ *n* **1** [U] 分配 fēnpèi, 分发〔發〕fēnfā. **2** [C, U] 特许 tèxǔ.

dis·pense /dɪ'spens/ *vt/i* **1** 分配 fēnpèi, 分发 fēnfā. **2** 配药 pèiyào; 配方 pèifāng; 发药 fāyào. **3** *~ with* 省掉 shěngdiào, 免除 miǎnchú: *Let's ~ with formalities.* 咱们就把俗套免了吧. **dis·pens·ary** *n* [C] [*pl* -ies] 药房 yàofáng.

dis·perse /dɪ'spɜ:s/ *vt/i* 使散开〔開〕shǐ sànkāi, 使疏开 shǐ shūkāi, 使分散 shǐ fēnsàn. **dis·per·sal** *n* [U]

dis·pirited /dɪ'spɪrɪtɪd/ *adj* 没精打采的 méijīngdǎcǎide, 垂头〔頭〕丧气的 chuídóusàngqìde.

dis·place /dɪs'pleɪs/ *vt* **1** 转〔轉〕移 zhuǎnyí, 移置 yízhì. **2** 取代 qǔdài, 撤换 chèhuàn. **~ment** *n* [U] **(a)** 转移 zhuǎnyí, 移置 yízhì, 取代 qǔdài, 撤换 chèhuàn. **(b)** 排水量 páishuǐliàng.

dis·play /dɪ'spleɪ/ *vt* 展览〔覽〕zhǎnlǎn, 陈〔陳〕列 chénliè. □ *n* [C, U] 展览 zhǎnlǎn, 陈列 chénliè.

dis·please /dɪs'pli:z/ *vt* 使不愉快 shǐ bù yúkuài, 使不高兴〔興〕shǐ bù gāoxìng, 冒犯 màofàn, 使生气〔氣〕shǐ shēngqì. **dis·pleasure** /dɪs'pleʒə(r)/ *n* [U] 生气 shēngqì, 不愉快 bù yúkuài.

dis·pos·able /dɪ'spəʊzəbl/ *adj* **1** 可任意处〔處〕置的 kě rènyì chùzhì de: *~ nappies* 用毕扔掉的尿布. **2** 可自由使用的 kě zìyóu shǐyòng de: *~ income* 可自由使用的收入.

dis·pose /dɪ'spəʊz/ *vt/i* *~ of* 处〔處〕理 chùlǐ, 处置 chùzhì; 除去 chúqù. **dis·posal** *n* [U] **(a)** 处理 chùlǐ, 处置 chùzhì. **(b)** *at one's ~* 由某人作主 yóu mǒurěn zuòzhǔ, 由某人支配 yóu mǒurén zhīpèi.

dis·po·si·tion /ˌdɪspə'zɪʃn/ *n* [C] **1** 性情 xìngqíng, 气〔氣〕质〔質〕qìzhì: *a cheerful ~* 开朗的性格. **2** 布置 bùzhì, 部署 bùshǔ,配置 pèizhì: *the ~ of troops* 军队的部署.

dis·pos·sess /ˌdɪspə'zes/ *vt* 剥夺 bōduó.

dis·pro·por·tion·ate /ˌdɪsprə'pɔ:ʃənət/ *adj* 不相称〔稱〕的 bù xiāngchèn de, 不匀称的 bù yúnchèn de. **~ly** *adv*

dis·prove /ˌdɪs'pru:v/ *vt* 证〔證〕明为〔爲〕错误 zhèngmíng wéi cuòwù, 证明为伪〔僞〕zhèngmíng wéi wěi.

dis·pute /dɪ'spju:t/ *vt/i* **1** 争论〔論〕zhēnglùn, 争执〔執〕zhēngzhí. **2** 对〔對〕... 提出质〔質〕疑 duì ... tíchū zhìyí: *to ~ a decision* 对一项决定提出质疑. □ /'di:spju:t/ *n* [C] 争论 zhēnglùn, 辩论 biànlùn. ***in ~*** 正在争论中 zhèngzài zhēnglùn zhōng. **dis·put·able** /-əbl/ *adj* 可争论的 kě zhēnglùn de;可质疑的 kě zhìyí de.

dis·qual·ify /dɪs'kwɒlɪfaɪ/ *vt* [*pt, pp* -ied] 使不合格 shǐ bù hégé: *disqualified from driving* 失去开车的资格. **dis·quali·fi·ca·tion** /-fɪ'keɪʃn/ *n* [C, U]

dis·quiet /dɪs'kwaɪət/ *vt* [正式用语]打搅〔攪〕dǎjiǎo, 使忧〔憂〕虑〔慮〕shǐ yōulǜ. □ *n* [U]不安 bù'ān, 焦虑 jiāolǜ. **~ing** *adj*

dis·re·gard /ˌdɪsrɪ'gɑ:d/ *vt* 不理 bùlǐ,不顾〔顧〕búgù, 漠视 mòshì: *Don't ~ my instructions*. 要注意我的指令. □ *n* [U] 漠视 mòshì, 忽视 hūshì.

dis·re·pair /ˌdɪsrɪ'peə(r)/*n* [U] 破损 pòsǔn; 失修 shīxiū.

dis·repu·table /dɪs'repjʊtəbl/ *adj* 声〔聲〕名狼藉的 shēngmíng lángjí de.

dis·re·pute /ˌdɪsrɪ'pju:t/ *n* [U] *fall into ~* 声〔聲〕名狼藉 shēngmínglángjí

dis·re·spect /ˌdɪsrɪ'spekt/ *n* [U] 无〔無〕礼〔禮〕wúlǐ, 失敬 shījìng. **~ful** *adj* **~fully** *adv*

dis·rupt /ˌdɪs'rʌpt/ *vt* 使分裂 sh[illegible] fēnliè, 瓦解 wǒjiě;使混乱〔亂〕sh[illegible] hùnluàn, 破坏〔壞〕pòhuài: *~ traff[illegible]* 引起交通混乱; *~ negotiations* 破[illegible]谈判. **~ion** /dɪs'rʌpʃən/ *n* [U] **~ive** *adj*

dis·sat·isfy /dɪ'sætɪsfaɪ/*vt* [*pt,* [illegible] -ied] 使不满 shǐ bùmǎn. **dis·sa[illegible]is·fac·tion** /-'fækʃn/ *n* [U]

dis·sect /dɪ'sekt/ *vt* 解剖 jiěpā[illegible]

分割 fēngē. **dis·section** /-ˈsekʃn/ *n* [C, U]

dis·semi·nate /dɪˈsemɪneɪt/ *vt* 散布 sànbù, 传〔傳〕播 chuánbō. **dis-semi'na·tion** *n* [U]

dis·sent /dɪˈsent/ *vi* **1** ~ (*from*) 不同意 bù tóngyì, 持不同意见 chí bùtóng yìjiàn. **2** 拒不信奉宗教教义〔義〕 jù bú xìnfèng zōngjiào jiàoyì. □ *n* [U] 不同意 bù tóngyì, 异〔異〕义〔義〕 yìyì. ~**er** 持不同意见者 chí bùtóng yìjiàn zhě. **dis·sen·sion** /-ʃn/ *n* [C, U] 意见分歧 yìjiànfēnqí, 激烈争吵 jīliè zhengchao.

dis·ser·ta·tion /ˌdɪsəˈteɪʃn/ *n* [C] 长〔長〕篇论〔論〕文 chángpiān lùnwén; 专〔專〕题演讲 zhuāntí yǎnjiǎng.

dis·si·dent /ˈdɪsɪdənt/ *adj* 持异〔異〕义〔義〕的 chí yìyì de. □ *n* [C] 持不同意见者 chí bùtóng yìjiàn zhě; 持不同政见者 chí bùtóng zhèngjiàn zhě.

dis·simi·lar /dɪˈsɪmɪlə(r)/ *adj* 不同的 bùtóngde, 不一样〔樣〕的 bù yíyàng de. **dis·simi·larity** /-ˈlærɪtɪ /*n* [C, U] [*pl* -ies]

dis·so·ciate /dɪˈsəʊʃɪeɪt/ *vt* 使分离〔離〕 shǐ fēnlí, 使无〔無〕关〔關〕系 shǐ wú guānxī. **dis·soci'a·tion** *n* [U]

dis·solve /dɪˈzɒlv/ *vt/i* **1** 使液化 shǐ yèhuà; 使融化 shǐ rónghuà. **2** 液化 yèhuà, 融化 rónghuà. **3** 使解散 shǐ jiěsàn, 使终结 shǐ zhōngjié: ~ *a marriage* 离婚; ~ *a parliament* 解散议会. **dis·so'l·ution** *n* [C, U]

dis·suade /dɪˈsweɪd/ *vt* 劝〔勸〕阻 quànzǔ. **dis·sua·sion** /-ʒn/ *n* [U]

dis·tance /ˈdɪstəns/ *n* [C, U] 距离〔離〕 jùlí. *in the* ~ 远〔遠〕处〔處〕 yuǎnchù.

dis·tant /ˈdɪstənt/ *adj* **1** 远〔遠〕隔的 yuǎngéde, 远处〔處〕的 yuǎnchùde, 久远的 jiǔyuǎnde. **2** 不密切的 bú mìqiè de. 关〔關〕系不亲近的 guānxī bù qīnjìn de; 不亲〔親〕密的 bù qīnmì de. **3** 冷淡的 lěngdànde. ~**ly** *adv* 不近地 bùjìnde: ~*ly related* 关系不近.

dis·taste /dɪsˈteɪst/ *n* [U] 不喜欢〔歡〕bù xǐhuān, 讨厌 tǎoyàn. ~**ful** *adj* 讨厌的 tǎoyànde, 不合口味的 bù hé kǒuwèi de. ~**fully** *adv*

dis·tend /dɪˈstend/ *vt/i* (使)扩〔擴〕张〔張〕 kuòzhāng; (使) 膨胀〔脹〕 péngzhàng.

dis·til[美语=-till] /dɪˈstɪl/*vt/i* [-ll-] **1**蒸馏 zhēngliú. **2** 用蒸馏法制〔製〕造威士忌酒等 yòng zhēngliúfǎ zhìzào wēishìjìjiǔ děng. ~'**la·tion** /-eɪʃn/*n* [C, U] ~**lery** 蒸馏室 zhēngliúshì, 酒厂〔廠〕 jiǔchǎng.

dis·tinct / dɪˈstɪŋkt/ *adj* **1** 清楚的 qīngchude, 清晰的 qīngxīde. **2** 不同的 bùtóngde, 独〔獨〕特的 dútède. ~**ly** *adv*

dis·tinc·tion /dɪˈstɪŋkʃn/ *n* **1** [U] 区〔區〕分 qūfēn, 区别 qūbié. **2** [C] 差别 chābié: *see a* ~ *between* 看出两者的差别. **3** [U] 卓著 zhuózhù, 卓越 zhuóyuè. **4** [C] 荣〔榮〕誉〔譽〕róngyù, 荣誉称〔稱〕号〔號〕 róngyù chēnghào. **dis·tinc·tive** *adj* 表示有别的 biǎoshì yǒu bié de, 有特色的 yǒu tèsè de. ~**ly** *adv*

dis·tin·guish /dɪˈstɪŋgwɪʃ/ *vt/i* **1** 区〔區〕别 qūbié, 分别 fēnbié, 辨别 biànbié. **2** 识〔識〕别 shíbié. **3** 区分 qūfēn: *Speech* ~*es men from animals.* 能否说话是人和动物的区分点. **4**使显〔顯〕赫 shǐ xiǎnhè, 使扬名 shǐ yángmíng. ~**able** /-əbl/ *adj* ~**ed** *adj* 著名的 zhùmíngde.

dis·tort /dɪˈstɔːt/ *vt* **1** 弄歪 nòngwāi. **2** 歪曲 wāiqū; 曲解 qūjiě: ~ *the facts* 歪曲事实. **dis'tortion** /-ʃən/ *n* [C, U]

dis·tract /dɪˈstrækt/ *vt* 分散(注意力等) fēnsàn. **dis'traction** /-ʃn/ *n* **(a)** [U] 精神涣散 jīngshén huànsàn. **(b)** [C] 消遣 xiāoqiǎn; 娱乐〔樂〕 yúlè.

dis·traught /dɪˈstrɔːt/ *adj* 极〔極〕其激动〔動〕的 jíqí jīdòng de, 狂乱〔亂〕的 kuángluànde.

dis·tress /dɪˈstres/ *n* [U] **1** 悲痛 bēitòng, 忧〔憂〕伤〔傷〕 yōushāng; 痛苦 tòngkǔ; 贫苦 pínkǔ. **2** 危难〔難〕 wēinàn: *a* ~ *signal* 求救信号. □ *vt* 使痛苦 shǐ tòngkǔ, 使悲痛 shǐ bēitòng. ~**ing** *adj* 令人痛苦的 lìngrén tòngkǔde, 令人悲痛的 lìngrén bēitòngde.

dis·trib·ute /dɪˈstrɪbjuːt/ *vt* **1** 分发〔發〕 fēnfā; 分配 fēnpèi; 发行 fāxíng: ~ *leaflets* (*books*) 发行单张印刷品(书籍). **2**散布 sànbù, 分布 fēnbù. **dis·tribu·tion** /ˌdɪstrɪˈbjuːʃn/ *n* [C, U] **dis·tri·bu·tor** *n* [C] **(a)** 分发者 fēnfāzhě, 散布者 sànbùzhě; 销售者 xiāoshòuzhě. **(b)** 分配器 fēnpèiqì.

dis·trict /ˈdɪstrɪkt/ *n* [C] 区〔區〕(县以下单位) qū.

dis·trust /dɪsˈtrʌst/ *n* [U] 不信任 bú xìnrèn, 疑惑 yíhuò. □ *vt* 不信任 bú xìnrèn, 怀〔懷〕疑 huáiyí. ~**ful** *adj* ~**fully** *adv*

dis·turb /dɪˈstɜːb/ *vt* 打扰〔擾〕 dǎrǎo, 扰乱〔亂〕 rǎoluàn. ~**ance**

n [C, U] 打扰 dǎrǎo; 骚〔騷〕动〔動〕sāodòng. 骚乱 sāoluàn.

dis·use /dɪsˈjuːs/ *n* [U] 废〔廢〕弃〔棄〕fèiqì, 搁〔擱〕置不用 gēzhì búyòng: *fall into* ～ 废而不用. **dis·used** /dɪsˈjuːzd/ *adj* 废弃的 fèiqìde, 不用的 búyòngde.

ditch /dɪtʃ/ *n* [C] 排水沟〔溝〕páishuǐgōu; 沟 gōu; 沟渠 gōuqú. □ *vt/i* **1** (使)坠〔墜〕入沟中 zhuì rù gōuzhōng. **2** [喻]抛弃〔棄〕pāoqì. **3** [非正式用语] (飞机) 坠入海中 zhuì rù hǎi zhōng.

dither /ˈdɪðə(r)/ *vi* [非正式用语]踌〔躊〕躇 chóuchú, 犹〔猶〕豫 yóuyù.

ditto /ˈdɪtəʊ/ *n* [C] [*pl* ～s] 同上 tóngshàng, 同前 tóngqián.

ditty /ˈdɪtɪ/ *n* [C] [*pl* -ies] 小调 xiǎodiào, 小曲 xiǎoqǔ.

di·van /dɪˈvæn/ *n* [C] 无〔無〕靠背的长〔長〕沙发〔發〕wú kàobèi de cháng shāfā.

dive /daɪv/ *vi* **1** 跳水 tiàoshuǐ, 潜〔潛〕水 qiǎnshuǐ. **2** 突然下降 tūrán xiàojiàng, 俯冲〔衝〕fǔchōng. **3** 猛冲 měngchōng: ～ *through a window* 从窗户窜过. □ *n* [C] 跳水 tiàoshuǐ; 潜水 qiǎnshuǐ. **diver** 跳水者 tiàoshuǐzhě; 潜水员 qiǎnshuǐyuán.

di·verge /daɪˈvɜːdʒ/ *vi* 岔开〔開〕chàkāi; 分歧 fēnqí; 背驰〔馳〕bèichí.

di·verse /daɪˈvɜːs/ *adj* 多种〔種〕多样〔樣〕的 duōzhǒng duōyàng de. ～**ly** *adv* **di·ver·sity** *n* [U] 差异〔異〕chāyì, 多样性 duōyàngxìng.

di·ver·sify /ˌdaɪˈvɜːsɪfaɪ/ *vt* [*pt*, *pp* -ied] 使多样化 shǐ duōyànghuà.

di·ver·sion /daɪˈvɜːʃn/ *n* **1** [C, U] 转〔轉〕向 zhuǎn xiàng: *the* ～ *of a stream* 河流的改道. **2** [C] 消遣 xiāoqiǎn, 娱乐〔樂〕yúlè. **3** 改道 gǎidào, 迂回 yúhuí: *traffic* ～*s* 交通改道. ～**ary** *adj*

di·vert /ˌdaɪˈvɜːt/ *vt* 转〔轉〕向 zhuǎnxiàng: ～ *a stream* 改变河道; ～ *his attention* 转移他的注意.

di·vide /dɪˈvaɪd/ *vt/i* **1** 分 fēn, 划〔劃〕分 huàfēn. **2** (数学)除(尽) chú. **3** (使)意见分歧 yìjiàn fēnqí. □ *n* [C] 分水岭〔嶺〕fēnshuǐlǐng, 分界线〔線〕fēnjièxiàn. ～**rs** *n pl* 两脚规 liǎngjiǎoguī; 分线〔線〕规 fēnxiànguī.

divi·dend /ˈdɪvɪdənd/ *n* [C] 红利 hónglì; 股息 gǔxī.

di·vine[1] /dɪˈvaɪn/ *adj* **1** 神的 shénde, 神样〔樣〕的 shényàngde. **2** [非正式用语]极〔極〕好的 jíhǎode. ～**ly** *adv*

di·vine[2] /dɪˈvaɪn/ *vt/i* 占卜 zhānbǔ. **di·viner** *n* [C] 占卜者 zhānbǔzhě.

di·vin·ity /dɪˈvɪnətɪ/ *n* **1** [U] 神性 shénxìng. **2** [U]神学〔學〕shénxué.

di·vis·ible /dɪˈvɪzəbl/ *adj* 可除尽〔盡〕的 kě chújìn de.

div·ision /dɪˈvɪʒn/ *n* **1** [U] 分开〔開〕fēnkāi, 分割 fēngē. **2** [C] 分成的一部分 fēnchéngde yíbùfēn. **3** [C] [军事]师〔師〕shī. **4** [C] 分割线〔線〕fēngēxiàn, 分界线 fēnjièxiàn. **5** [C]意见分歧 yìjiàn fēnqí.

di·vorce /dɪˈvɔːs/ *n* **1** [C, U] 离〔離〕婚 líhūn. **2** [C] 分离 fēnlí, 脱离 tuōlí. □ *vt* **1** 离婚 líhūn. **2** [喻]使分离 shǐ fēnlí, 使脱离 shǐ tuōlí. **di·vor·cee** /dɪˌvɔːˈsiː/ 离了婚的人 lí le hūn de rén.

di·vulge /daɪˈvʌldʒ/ *vt* 泄露(秘密) xièlù.

dizzy /ˈdɪzɪ/ *adj* [-ier, -iest] **1** 眩晕〔暈〕的 xuànyùnde; 被弄糊涂了的 bèi nòng hútu le de. **2** 使人头〔頭〕晕的 shǐ rén tóu yūn de. **diz·zily** *adv* **diz·zi·ness** *n* [U]

D.J. = **1** dinner jacket 晚礼〔禮〕服 wǎnlǐfú. **2** disc jockey 无〔無〕线〔线〕电〔電〕唱片音乐〔樂〕节〔節〕目广〔廣〕播员 wúxiàndiàn chàngpiàn yīnyuè jiémù guǎngbōyuán.

D. Lit. = Doctor of Literature 文学〔學〕博士 wénxué bóshì.

D. M. = **1** Doctor of Medicine 医〔醫〕学〔學〕博士 yīxué bóshì. **2** 联〔聯〕邦德国〔國〕马〔馬〕克 liánbāng déguó mǎkè.

do[1] /də 强式: du/*aux verb*[*3rd pers pres tense* does; *pt* did/dɪd/; *pp* done /dʌn/] **1** [与主要动词连用] **(a)** [构成否定句]: *He didn't go.* 他没有去. **(b)**[构成疑问句]: *Does he want it?* 他要那个吗? **(c)** [构成强语势]: *That's exactly what he 'did say.* 那正是他说的. **2** **(a)** [用于比较]: *She runs faster than I do.* 她跑得比我快. **(b)** [用于疑问短语]: *He lives in London, doesn't he?* 他住在伦敦, 是吗? **(c)** [用于回答]: *Who broke the window?* 谁打坏了窗子? I did! 是我!

do[2] /duː/ *vt/i* **1** 做 zuò, 干 gàn: *What are you* ～*ing now?* 现在你在做什么? **2** **(a)** 产〔產〕生 chǎnshēng, 制〔製〕造 zhìzào: *I have done six copies.* 我复制了六份. **(b)** 尽〔盡〕(力) jìnlì; 忙于 mángyú: *She's* ～*ing her knitting.* 她正在编织. **(c)** 实〔實〕行 shíxíng, 履行 lǚxíng *D*～ *your duty.* 尽你的责任. **(d)** 学〔學〕习〔習〕xuéxí, 研究 yánjiū

Are you ~ing science at school? 你在学校里学科学吗；**(e)** 解决 jiějué，求…答案 qiú…dá'àn: *I can't ~ this sum.* 我不会做这算术题. **(f)** 处[處]理 chùlǐ，照料 zhàoliào: *I have a lot of correspondence to ~.* 我有很多信件要处理. **3** [用过去分词]完成 wánchéng，结束 jiéshù: *It's done.* 做完了. **4** ~ **(for)** 行 xíng，对[對]…有效 duì…yǒuxiào: *These shoes won't do for mountain-climbing.* 这些鞋用来爬山不行. **5 (a)** 进[進]展 jìnzhǎn: *He's ~ing well at school.* 他在学校学得不错. **(b)** (健康)进步 jìnbù. ***How ~ you ~?*** 你好！(打招呼) nǐhǎo! **6** 旅行(一定距离) lǚxíng，行进[進](一定速度) xíngjìn. **7** 烹调 pēngtiáo: *How would you like your steak done?* 您的牛排要煎嫩一点还是老一点? **8** ***have to ~ with*** 与[與]…有关[關]系 yǔ…yǒu guānxì，与…有来往 yǔ…yǒu láiwǎng. **9** ~ ***away with*** **(a)** 废[廢]除 fèichú，去掉 qùdiào. **(b)** 弄死 nòngsǐ. ~ ***for*** [非正式用语] **(a)** 设法弄到 shèfǎ nòngdào: *How will you ~ for water in the desert?* 在沙漠里你们水的问题怎样解决； **(b)** 毁掉 huǐdiào，干掉 gàndiào: *The country's done for.* 这个国家毁灭了. ~ ***sb in*** [俚语]杀[殺]死某人 shāsǐ mǒurén. ~ ***sth out*** 扫[掃]除 sǎochú，打扫 dǎsǎo. ~ ***sth up*** **(a)** 修复[復] xiūfù，修理 xiūlǐ. **(b)** 捆好 kǔnhǎo，包起 bāoqǐ. ~ ***with*** [与 *can, could* 连用]需要 xūyào: *You could ~ with a good night's sleep.* 你需要好好睡上一夜. ~ ***without*** 没有…也行 méiyǒu… yě xíng.

do. =ditto 同上 tóngshàng，同前 tóngqián.

doc·ile /'dəʊsaɪl/ *adj* 容易驯服的 róngyì xùnfú de，容易管教的 róngyì guǎnjiào de，驯良的 xùnliáng de.

dock¹ /dɒk/ *n* [C] 船坞 chuánwù，码[碼]头[頭] mǎtóu. **~er** 船坞工人 chuánwù gōngrén；码头工人 mǎtóu gōngrén. **'~yard** 造船所 zàochuánsuǒ. 修船厂[廠] xiūchuánchǎng.

dock² /dɒk/ *vt/i* **1** 引入船坞 yǐnrù chuánwù，引入码头 yǐnrù mǎtóu. **2** 使(宇宙飞行器)在空间[間]对[對]接 shǐ zài kōngjiān duìjiē.

dock³ /dɒk/ *n* [C] 刑事法庭的被告席 xíngshì fǎtíng de bèigàoxí.

dock⁴ /dɒk/ *vt* 削减薪金，供应[應]等 xiāojiǎn xīnjīn，gōngyìng děng.

doc·tor /'dɒktə(r)/ *n* [C] **1** 博士 bóshì. **2** 医[醫]生 yīshēng. ⇨ physician, surgeon. □ *vt* **1** [非正式用语]医治 yīzhì: ~ *a cold* 医治感冒；~ *a child* 为孩子看病. **2** (对食品等)掺[摻]杂[雜] chānzá. **3** [喻]窜[竄]改(帐目，证据) cuàngǎi. **~ate** /'dɒktərət/ *n* [C] 博士学位 bóshì xuéwèi；博士衔 bóshì xián.

doc·tri·naire /ˌdɒktrɪ'neə(r)/ *adj* 空谈理论[論]的 kōngtán lǐlùn de，教条[條]主义[義]的 jiàotiáozhǔyìde.

doc·trine /'dɒktrɪn/ *n* [C, U] 教条[條] jiàotiáo，教义[義] jiàoyì，主义 zhǔyì.

docu·ment /'dɒkjʊmənt/ *n* [C] 文献[獻] wénxiàn，文件 wénjiàn. □ *vt* 用文件证[證]明 yòng wénjiàn zhèngmíng；为[爲]… 提供文件 wèi … tígòng wénjiàn. **~a·tion** /ˌdɒkjʊmen'teɪʃn/ *n* [U] 文件 wénjiàn，文献 wénxiàn. **~ary** /ˌdɒkjʊ'mentrɪ/ *adj* 有文件的 yǒu wénjiàn de；文件的 wénjiànde. □ *n* [C] [*pl* -ies] (亦作~*ary film*) 纪录[錄]影片 jìlù yǐngpiàn.

dodge /dɒdʒ/ *n* [C] **1** 闪[閃]开 shǎnkāi，躲闪 duǒshǎn. **2** [非正式用语]诡计 guǐjì，蒙骗[騙] méngpiàn. □ *vt/i* **1** 躲闪 duǒshǎn，闪开 shǎnkāi. **2** 推托 tuītuō. **dodger** 油滑的人 yóuhuáde rén. **dodgy** *adj* [-ier,-iest] [非正式用语]冒险[險]的 màoxiǎnde.

doe /dəʊ/ *n* [C] 雌鹿 cílù，雌兔 cítù.

does /dʌz/, **doesn't** /'dʌznt/ ⇨do.

dog¹ /dɒg/ *n* [C] 狗 gǒu；雄狗 xiónggǒu. ⇨ bitch. ***go to the ~s*** 毁灭[滅] huǐmiè；堕落 duòluò. ***let sleeping ~s 'lie*** 勿惹事生非 wù rěshì shēngfēi. ***lead a ~'s life*** 过[過]困苦的生活 guò kùnkǔde shēnghuó. **'~-collar** [非正式用语]牧师[師]的领子 mùshīde lǐngzi. **'~-eared** (书)翻旧[舊]了的 fān jiù le de. ***be in the '~house*** [俚]失宠[寵] shīchǒng，受耻辱 shòu chǐrǔ. **'dogs·body** 工作疲劳[勞]而乏味的人 gōngzuò píláo ér fáwèi de rén.

dog² /dɒg/ *vt* [-gg-] **1** 尾随 wěisuí，跟踪 gēnzōng. **2** [喻] 跟随 gēnsuí: *~ged by misfortune* 灾难缠身.

dog·ged /'dɒgɪd/ *adj* 顽强的 wánqiángde，顽固的 wángùde. **~ly** *adv* **~ness** *n* [U]

dogma /'dɒgmə/ *n* [*pl* ~s] [C, U] 教理 jiàolǐ；教条[條] jiàotiáo；教义[義] jiàoyì. **~tic** /dɒg'mætɪk/ *adj* **(a)** 教条的 jiàotiáode；

教义的 jiàoyìde. **(b)** 教条主义的 jiàotiáozhǔyìde. ~**tism** *n* [U] 教条主义 jiàotiáozhǔyì.

dol·drums /'dɒldrəmz/ *n pl in the* ~[喻]消沉的 xiāochénde, 不高兴[興]的 bù gāoxìng de.

dole /dəʊl/ *vt* 少量发[發]放(救济品,救济金) shǎoliàng fāfàng. □ *n* [C] **1** 少量的施舍物 shǎoliàngde shīshěwù. **2** [非正式用语]周失业[業]救济金 zhōu shīyè jiùjìjīn. ~**ful** *adj* 消沉的 xiāochénde ~**fully** *adv*

doll /dɒl/ *n* [C] 玩偶 wán'ǒu, 洋娃娃 yángwáwa. □ *vt/i* ~ *oneself up* [非正式用语] 打扮得漂漂亮亮 dǎbànde piàopiàoliàngliàng.

dol·lar /'dɒlə(r)/ *n* [C] 元[圓] (货币单位) yuán.

dol·phin /'dɒlfɪn/ *n* [C] 海豚 hǎitún.

do·main /dəʊ'meɪn/ *n* [C] [正式用语] **1** 领域 lǐngyù; 领土 lǐngtǔ; 领地 lǐngdì. **2** [喻]范[範]围[圍] fànwéi, 领域 lǐngyù.

dome /dəʊm/ *n* [C] 圆屋顶 yuánwūdǐng, 圆顶形之物 yuándǐngxíng zhī wù.

do·mes·tic /də'mestɪk/ *adj* **1** 家的 jiāde, 家庭的 jiātíngde, 家里[裏]的 jiālǐde. **2** 本国[國]的 běnguóde: ~ *news* 国内新闻. **3** 驯[馴]养[養]的(非野生的) xúnyǎngde. ⇨ wild. □ *n* [C] 佣人 yōngren. ~**ate** *vt* **(a)** 使能做家务[務] shǐ néng zuò jiāwù. **(b)** 驯化(动物) xúnhuà.

domi·nant /'dɒmɪnənt/ *adj* 支配的 zhīpèide, 统治的 tǒngzhìde;俯视的 fǔshìde. **domi·nance** *n* [U]

domi·nate /'dɒmɪneɪt/ *vt/i* **1** 支配 zhīpèi, 统治 tǒngzhì. **2** 俯瞰 fǔkàn, 俯视 fǔshì: *The hill* ~*s the city.* 这山俯视着城市. **domi'na·tion** *n* [U]

domi·neer /ˌdɒmɪ'nɪə(r)/ *vi* 盛气[氣]凌人 shèngqìlíngrén, 作威作福 zuòwēi-zuòfú. ~**ing** *adj*

do·min·ion /də'mɪnɪən/ *n* **1** [U] 统治 tǒngzhì, 支配 zhīpèi, 管辖[轄] guǎnxiá. **2** [C] 领土 lǐngtǔ, 版图[圖] bǎntú, 疆土 jiāngtǔ. **3** [C] (英联邦)自治领 zìzhìlǐng.

dom·ino /'dɒmɪnəʊ/*n* [C] [*pl* ~es or ~s] **1** 西洋骨牌 xīyáng gǔpái. **2** [*pl*] 西洋骨牌游戏[戲] xīyáng gǔpái yóuxì.

do·nate /dəʊ'neɪt/ *vt* 捐赠 juānzèng, 捐献[獻] juānxiàn. **do'na·tion** *n* [C, U]

done /dʌn/ ⇨ do.

don·key /'dɒŋkɪ/ *n* [C] [*pl* ~s] 驴[驢] lǘ.

do·nor /'dəʊnə(r)/ *n* [C] 捐献[獻]者 juānxiànzhě,赠与[與]者 zèngyǔzhě: *a blood-*~ 输血人.

don't /dəʊnt/= *do not.* ⇨ do.

doom /du:m/ *n* [U] 毁灭[滅] huǐmiè; 死亡 sǐwáng; 厄运[運] èyùn. □ *vt* 注定 zhùdìng, 判定 bàndìng, 命定 mìngdìng; **Dooms·day** *n* 世界末日 shìjiè mòrì.

door /dɔ:(r)/ *n* [C] **1** 门[門] mén. **2** 通道 tōngdào. **3** 机[機]会[會] jīhuì; 可能 kěnéng: *the* ~ *to success.* 成功的机会. *next* ~ 在隔壁 zài gébì; 到隔壁 dào gébì. *out of* ~*s* 在户外 zài hùwài, 在室外 zài shìwài. '~**step** 门前石阶[階] ménqián shíjiē. '~**way** 门口 ménkǒu.

dope /dəʊp/ *n* [U] [非正式用语] 毒品 dúpǐn, 麻醉品 mázuìpǐn. □*vt* 给…毒品服 gěi…dúpǐn fú. **dopey, dopy** *adj* [俚] **(a)** 半睡的 bànshuìde. **(b)**处[處]于麻醉状[狀]态[態]的 chùyú mázuì zhuàngtài de. **(c)** 迟[遲]钝的 chídùnde.

dor·mant /'dɔ:mənt/ *adj* 休眠的 xiūmiánde, 暂[暫]死的 zhǎnsǐde: *a* ~ *volcano* 暂死的火山,休眠的火山.

dor·mi·tory /'dɔ:mɪtrɪ/ *n* [C] [*pl* -ies] 集体[體]寝室 jítǐ qǐnshì, 宿舍 sùshè.

dor·mouse /'dɔ:maʊs/ *n* [C] [*pl* dormice/'dɔ:maɪs/] 睡鼠 shuìshǔ.

dos·age /'dəʊsɪdʒ/ *n* [C]剂[劑]量 jìliàng.

dose /dəʊs/ *n* [C] (药的)一剂[劑] yíjì, 一服 yìfú. □ *vt* 给…服药 gěi … fúyào.

doss /dɒs/ *vi* [英国俚语] ~ *down* 在简[簡]陋的床上睡 zài jiǎnlòude chuáng shàng shuì. '~**-house** 廉价[價]小旅店 liánjià xiǎolǚdiàn.

dos·sier /'dɒsɪeɪ/ *n* [C] 一宗档[檔]案材料 yìzōng dǎng'àn cáiliào.

dot /dɒt/ *n* [C] 小圆点[點] xiǎoyuándiǎn, 小点 xiǎodiǎn. *on the* ~[非正式用语]准时[時]地 zhǔnshíde. □ *vt* [-tt-] 加上小点 jiā shàng xiǎodiǎn. ~*ted about* 散布 sànbù.

do·tage /'dəʊtɪdʒ/ *n* [U] 老年昏愦 lǎonián hūnkuì: *old men in their* ~ 昏愦的老年人.

dote /dəʊt/ *vi* ~ **(on)** 过[過]分喜爱[愛] guòfèn xǐ'ài: ~ *on a child* 溺爱孩子.

double[1] /'dʌbl/ *adj* **1** 加倍的 jiābèide, 两倍的 liǎngbèide. **2** 双〔雙〕的 shuāngde, 双重的 shuāngchóngde: *a ~ chin* 双下巴. **3** 双人的 shuāngrénde: *a ~ bed* 双人床. ,**~-'bass** 低音提琴 dīyīntíqín. ,**~-'breasted** *adj* (外套)对〔對〕襟的 duìjīnde. ,**~-'cross** *vt* [非正式用语]欺骗〔騙〕qīpiàn, 出卖〔賣〕chūmài. □ *n* 出卖 chūmài. ,**~-'dealer** 两面派人物 liǎngmianpài rénwù. ,**~-'dealing** *n*, *adj* ,**~-'decker** 双层〔層〕公共汽车〔車〕shuāngcéng gōnggòngqìchē.

double² /'dʌbl/ *adv* **1** 双倍 shuāngbeì: *cost ~* 双倍价钱. **2** 双双地 shuāngshuāngde. *see ~* (醉眼)把一物看成两物 bǎ yíwù kànchéng liǎngwù.

double³ /'dʌbl/ *n* [C] **1** 两倍 liǎngbèi. **2** 极〔極〕其相似的人或物 jí qí xiángsì de rén huò wù. **3** [*pl*] (网球,乒乓球等)双〔雙〕打 shāngdǎ.

double⁴ /'dʌbl/ *vt/i* **1** 使加倍 shǐ jiābèi, 成倍 chéngbèi. **2** 把…对〔對〕折 bǎ … duìzhé. **3** *~(back)* 往回走 wǎng huí zǒu. *~ up* (因大笑或痛)弯〔彎〕身 wānshēn.

doubly /'dʌblɪ/ *adv* 双〔雙〕倍地 shuāngbèide: *be ~ careful* 要加倍小心.

doubt /daʊt/ *n* [C, U] 怀〔懷〕疑 huáiyí, 疑惑 yíhuò, 疑问〔問〕yíwèn. *no ~* 十有八九 shí yǒu bājiǔ, 多半 duōbàn. □ *vt/i* 怀疑 huáiyí, 不信仰 bú xìngyǎng. **~ful** *adj* **~less** *adv* 无〔無〕疑 wúyí.

dough /dəʊ/ *n* [U] **1** 揉好的生面〔麵〕róuhǎode shēngmiàn. **2** [俚语]钱〔錢〕qián. '**~nut** 炸面饼圈 zhámiànbǐngquān.

douse, dowse /daʊs/ *vt* 把…浸到水中 bǎ … jìn dào shuǐ zhōng; 把水浇〔澆〕在上面 bǎ shuǐ jiāo zài shàngmiàn.

dove /dʌv/ *n* [C] **1** 鸽〔鴿〕gē. **2** [非正式用语]从〔從〕事和平运〔運〕动〔動〕的人 cóngshì hépíng yùndòng de rén. ⇨ hawk(2). '**~-cote** 鸽棚 gēpéng, 鸽房 gēfáng.

dove·tail /'dʌvteɪl/ *n* [C] 鸠〔鳩〕尾榫 jiūwěisǔn. 楔形榫 xiēxíngsǔn. □ *vt/i* **1** 用鸠尾榫接合 yòng jiūwěisǔn jiēhé. **2** [喻]和…吻合 hé …wěnhé.

down¹ /daʊn/ *n* [U] **1** 绒毛 róngmáo, 羽绒 yǔróng. **2** (植物)茸毛 róngmáo.

down² /daʊn/ *adv* **1 (a)** 降下 jiàngxià: *The sun went ~* 日落. **(b)** 倒下 dǎoxià: *knocked ~ by a bus* 被公共汽车撞倒. **2** 往较〔較〕次要的地方 wǎng jiǎocìyàode dìfāng: *We went ~ to Brighton* (eg from London). 他(从伦敦)去布赖顿. **3** 下降 xiàjiàng, 减少 jiǎnshǎo: *The temperature has gone ~.* 温度降低. **4** 写〔寫〕下 xiěxià: *write something ~* 把某事记下来. *D~ with* 打倒 dǎdǎo. *get ~ to sth* 认〔認〕真处〔處〕理 rènzhēn chùlǐ, 专〔專〕心做 zhuānxīn zuò. ,**~-to-'earth** 实〔實〕事求是的 shíshì-qiúshìde, 切实的 qièshíde.

down³ /daʊn/ *prep* **1** 往下 wǎngxià, 向下 xiàngxià: *run ~ a hill* 跑下山. **2** 在(河流)下游 zài xiàyóu: *farther ~ the river* 在河的下游远处. **3** 沿着 yánzhe: *walking ~ the street* 沿着街道走.

down⁴ /daʊn/ *vt* [非正式用语]喝下 hēxià, 吞下 tūnxià: *~ a beer* 喝啤酒,把这杯啤酒干了.

down·cast /'daʊnkɑ:st/ *adj* **1** (人)垂头〔頭〕丧气〔氣〕的 chuítóu sàngqì de, 消沉的 xiāochénde. **2** (眼睛)往下看 wǎng xià kàn.

down·fall /'daʊnfɔ:l/ *n* [C] **1** (雨,雪等)暴降 bàojiàng. **2** [喻]垮台 kuǎtái, 毁灭〔滅〕huǐmiè: *His ~ was drink.* 酗酒是他垮台的原因.

down·grade /,daʊn'greɪd/ *vt* 降低等级 jiàngdī děngjí, 降低级别 jiàngdī jíbié.

down·hearted /,daʊn'hɑ:tɪd/ *adj* 消沉的 xiāochénde, 沮丧的 jǔsàngde.

down·hill /daʊn'hɪl/ *adv* 趋〔趨〕向衰退 qūxiàng shuāituì. *go ~* [喻]恶〔惡〕化 èhuà; 衰退 shuāituì.

down·pour /'daʊnpɔ:(r)/ *n* [C] 倾盆大雨 qīngpén dàyǔ.

down·right /'daʊnraɪt/ *adj* **1** 爽直的 shuǎngzhíde, **2** 彻〔徹〕头〔頭〕彻尾的 chètóuchèwěide; 明显〔顯〕的 míngxiǎnde: *a ~ lie* 明显的谎话. □ *adv* 彻底地 chèdǐde.

downs /daʊnz/ *n pl* 丘陵 qiūlíng, 开〔開〕阔〔闊〕的高地 kāikuòde gāodì.

down·stairs /,daʊn'steəz/ *adv* 往楼〔樓〕下 wǎng lóuxià; 在楼下 zài lóuxià.

down·stream /daʊn'stri:m/ *adv* 顺流地 shùnliúde.

down·town /'daʊntaʊn/ *adj*, *adv* 在城市的商业〔業〕区〔區〕zài chéngshìde shāngyèqū 往城市的商业区 wǎng chéngshìde shāngyèqū.

down·trod·den /,daʊn'trɒdn/ *adj* 受压〔壓〕制的 shòu yāzhìde: *~ workers* 受压制的工人.

down·ward /'daʊnwəd/ *adj* 向下

的 xiàng xià de.
down·wards /'daʊnwədz/ *adv* 向下地 xiàng xià de.
dowry /'daʊərɪ/ *n* [C] [*pl* -ies] 嫁妆〔妝〕jiàzhuang.**dowse** /daʊs/*vt* ⇨ douse.
doze /dəʊz/ *vi* 打盹儿〔兒〕dǎdǔnr, 打瞌睡 dǎ kēshuì. □ *n* [C] 小睡 xiǎoshuì, 打盹儿 dǎ dǔn'r.
dozen /'dʌzn/ *n* [*pl* ~] 一打 yìdá 十二个〔個〕shíèrgè.
drab /dræb/ *adj* [喻]单〔單〕调的 dāndiàode, 没有兴〔興〕趣的 méiyǒu xìngqù de. ~**ness** *n* [U]
draft /drɑːft/ *n* [C] **1** 草稿 cǎogǎo, 草案 cǎo'àn, 草图〔圖〕cǎotú: *a ~ of a letter* 信稿. **2** 汇票 huìpiào. **3** 征〔徵〕兵 zhēngbīng. □ *vt* **1** 起草 qǐcǎo; 设计 shèjì. **2** 征兵 zhēngbīng **drafts·man** *n* [C] 起草人 qǐcǎorén.
drafty /'drɑːftɪ/ *adj* [美语]= draughty.
drag /dræg/ *vt*/*i* [-gg-] **1** 拖 tuō, 拉 lā, 拽 zhuài. **2** 吃力而慢吞吞地前进〔進〕chīlì ér màntūntūnde qiánjìn. **3** 用拖网捉 yòng tuōwǎng zhuō; 打捞〔撈〕dǎlāo. **4** 拖沓 tuōtā; 厌〔厭〕烦 yànfán. □ *n* **1** [C] 被拖的东〔東〕西 bèi tuō de dōngxi; 大耙 dàpá; 拖网 tuōwǎng. **2** [C] 累赘 léizhuì, 讨厌的人或事物 tǎoyànde rén huò shìwù.
dragon /'drægən/ *n* [C] **1** 龙〔龍〕lóng. **2** 严〔嚴〕厉的老妇〔婦〕人 yánlìde lǎofùrén.
drain[1]/dreɪn/ *n* [C]**1**排水管 páishuǐguǎn; 排水沟〔溝〕páishuǐgōu; 阴〔陰〕沟 yīngōu, 排水设备〔備〕páishuǐ shèbèi. **2** 消耗 xiāohào, 负担〔擔〕fùdān. ⇨ brain drain. '~**pipe** 排水管 páishuǐguǎn.
drain[2] /dreɪn/ *vt*/*i* **1** ~ *away* (或 *off*) 排去(液体) páiqù, (水等)流掉 liúdiào. **2** (土地等)排水 páishuǐ, 使干〔乾〕shǐ gān. **3** [喻](使)耗尽〔盡〕hàojìn: ~ *the energy from a battery* 耗尽电池的能源. '~**ing-board** 滴水板 dīshuǐbǎn. ~**age** *n* [U] **(a)** 排水 páishuǐ, 放水 fàngshuǐ. **(b)** 污水 wūshuǐ, 排放出的水 páifàng chū de shuǐ.
drake /dreɪk/ *n* [C] 雄鸭〔鴨〕xióngyā.
dram. pers. 剧〔劇〕中人物 jù zhōng rénwù.
drama /'drɑːmə/ *n* **1** [U] 戏〔戲〕剧〔劇〕xìjù; [C] 剧本 jùběn. **2** [C, U] 戏剧性事件 xìjùxìng shìjiàn. ~**tic** /drə'mætɪk/ *adj* **(a)** 戏剧的 xìjùde. **(b)** 戏剧性的 xìjùxìngde. ~**ti·cally** *adv* ~**t·ics** **(a)** 演剧活动〔動〕yǎnjù huódòng, 戏剧作品 xìjù zuòpǐn. **(b)** [非正式用语]戏剧性的行为〔爲〕xìjùxìng de xíngwéi. ~**tist** /'dræmətɪst/ *n* [C] 剧作家 jùzuòjiā. ~**tize** /'dræmətaɪz/ *vt* **(a)** 把(小说等)改编为戏剧 bǎ gǎibiānwéi xìjù. **(b)** [非正式用语]为造成刺激而扩〔擴〕张〔張〕wèi zàochéng cìjī ér kuòzhāng.
drank /dræŋk/ *pt* of drink.
drape /dreɪp/ *vt* **1** (成褶地)悬〔懸〕挂〔掛〕xuánguà. **2** ~ *with* 披盖〔蓋〕pīgài; 装〔裝〕饰 zhuāngshì.
dra·per /'dreɪpə(r)/ *n* [英国英语](出售衣服, 桌布等的)布商 bùshāng. **dra·pery** 服装〔裝〕fúzhuāng; 布 bù; 织〔織〕物 zhīwù.
dras·tic /'dræstɪk/ *adj* 猛烈的 měngliède, 激烈的 jīliède. ~**ally** *adv*
draught [美语=**draft**]/drɑːft/ *n* **1** [C, U] 穿堂风〔風〕chuāntángfēng; 气〔氣〕流 qìliú. **2** [U] (船的)吃水(深度) chīshuǐ. **3** [U] (从容器)汲出(液体) jíchū: ~ *beer* 桶装啤酒,散装啤酒,生啤酒. **4** 一饮 yìyǐn. **5** [*pl*] [美语 =*checkers*] 西洋跳棋 xīyáng tiàoqí. □ *vt* = draft. **draughts·man** **(a)**= draftsman. **(b)** 西洋跳棋子 xīyáng tiàoqízǐ.
draughty *adj* [-ier, -iest] 通风〔風〕的 tōngfēngde; 有穿堂风的 yǒu chuāntángfēngde.
draw[1] /drɔː/ *n* [C] **1** 拉 lā, 拖 tuō; 吸 xī; 抽签〔簽〕chōuqiān; 平局 píngjú: *The game ended in a ~*. 比赛结果不分胜负. **2** 有吸引力的人或事物 yǒu xīyǐnlì de rén huò shìwù. ⇨ draw[2](4).
draw[2] /drɔː/ *vt*/*i* [*pt* drew /druː/;*pp* ~n / drɔːn/] **1** 拖 tuō, 拉 lā. **2** 拔(出) bá: ~ *a cork* 拔瓶塞;~ *a gun* 拔出枪来. **3** 汲取 jíqǔ, 引出 yǐnchū, 提取 tíqǔ, 领取 lǐngqǔ:~ *water from a well* 从井中汲水; ~ *one's salary* 领工资. ~ **a blank** 落空 luòkōng, 白费力气〔氣〕báifèi lìqì, 一无〔無〕所得 yì wú suǒ dé. **4** 引起 yǐnqǐ, 招来 zhāolái: ~ *a crowd* 招来一大群人. **5** 吸(入) xī: ~ *a deep breath* 长长吸进一口气. **6** 移动〔動〕yídòng: *The ships drew near.* 船驶近了. **7** 划〔劃〕huà, 画〔畫〕huà, 绘〔繪〕制〔製〕huìzhì: ~ *a picture* 画图. ~ ***the line*** **(*at*)** 不许 bùxǔ, 禁止 jìnzhǐ: ~ *the line at robbery* 以不抢劫为限. **8** 打成平局 dǎchéng píngjú, 不分胜〔勝〕负 bù fēn shèngfù. **9** [常用过去分词]扭歪 niǔwāi: *a*

face ~n with pain 疼得脸扭歪起来，因为疼痛而扭歪的脸. **10** ~ ***back*** 拉开〔開〕lākāi. ~ ***in*** (白昼)变〔變〕短 biànduǎn. ~ ***out*** **(a)** (白昼)变长〔長〕biàncháng. **(b)** 逗引(某人)说话 dòuyǐn shuōhuà. **(c)** 变长 biàncháng; 拉长 lācháng, 拖长 tuōcháng: *a long-~-out discussion.* 拖拖沓沓的讨论. ~ ***up*** **(a)** 写〔寫〕出 xiěchū,草拟〔擬〕cǎonǐ. **(b)** 逼近 bījìn: *His car drew up outside.* 他的汽车来到外面 **(c)** ~ ***oneself up*** 笔〔筆〕直地站立 bǐzhíde zhànlì.

draw·back /'drɔːbæk/ *n* [C] 障碍 zhàng'ài, 不利 búlì.

drawer /drɔː(r)/ *n* [C] 抽屉 chōutì. ⇨ chest of drawers.

draw·ing /'drɔːɪŋ/ *n* [U] 绘〔繪〕图〔圖〕huìtú, [C] 图画〔畫〕túhuà, 图样〔樣〕túyàng; 素描 sùmiáo, 速写〔寫〕sùxiě. '~-**pin** 图钉 túdīng.

draw·ing-room /'drɔːɪŋ rʊm/ *n* [C] 客厅〔廳〕kètīng, 休憩室 xiūqìshì.

drawl /drɔːl/ *vt/i* 慢吞吞地说 màntūntūnde shuō. □ *n* [U] 说话慢吞吞的样〔樣〕子 shuōhuà màntūntūnde yàngzi.

drawn /drɔːn/ *pp* of draw².

dread /dred/ *n* [U] 〔或与 *a* 连用〕恐怖 kǒngbù, 害怕 hàipà; 担〔擔〕忧〔憂〕dānyōu. □ *vt/i* 惧〔懼〕怕 jùpà, 担心 dānxīn. ~**ful** *adj* **(a)** 令人担心的 lìngrén dānxīn de, 令人担忧的 lìngrén dānyōu de. **(b)** 〔非正式用语〕糟透的 zāotòude. ~**fully** *adv* 〔非正式用语〕极〔極〕端的 jíduānde.

dream /driːm/ *n* [C] **1** 梦〔夢〕mèng. **2** 梦想 mèngxiǎng, 空想 kōngxiǎng: *~s of wealth* 梦想发财. **3** 美妙的事物 měimiàode shìwù. □ *vt/i* [*pt, pp* ~ed or ~t /drempt/] **1** 做梦 zuòmèng, 梦见 mèngjiàn, 梦到 mèngdào. **2** ~ ***sth up*** 〔非正式用语〕凭〔憑〕空想出(计划等) píngkōng xiǎngchū. ~-**er** **(a)** 做梦的人 zuòmèngde rén. **(b)** 空想家 kōngxiǎngjiā. **dreamy** /'driːmɪ/ *adj* [-ier, -iest]. **(a)** 神情恍惚的 shénqíng huǎnghū de, 似睡非睡的 sìshuìfēishuì de. **(b)** 〔非正式用语〕美妙的 měimiàode. ~-**ily** *adv* ~**like** *adj*

dreary /'drɪərɪ/ *adj* [-ier,-iest] 沉闷〔悶〕的 chénmènde, 阴〔陰〕沉的 yīnchénde. **drear·ily** *adv*

dredge /dredʒ/ *n* [C] 挖泥机〔機〕wāníjī, 疏浚机 shūjùnjī. □ *vt/i* 疏浚(河道) shūjùn. **dredger** 挖泥船 wāníchuán,疏浚船 shūjùnchuán.

dregs /dregz/ *n pl* **1** 残〔殘〕渣 cánzhā, 渣滓 zhāzi, 糟粕 zāopò. **2** 〔喻〕废〔廢〕料 fèiliào, 渣滓 zhāzi. *the ~ of society* 社会渣滓.

drench /drentʃ/ *vt* 使淋透 shǐ líntòu, 使湿〔濕〕透 shǐ shītòu: *We were ~ed in the rain.* 我们被雨淋透。

dress[1] /dres/ *n* **1** [C] 女服 nǚfú. **2** [U] 服装〔裝〕fúzhuāng. ⇨ evening dress. '~ **rehearsal** (戏剧)彩排 cǎipái.

dress[2] /dres/ *vt/i* **1** 穿(衣) chuān. ~ ***up*** 穿上盛装 chuān shàng shèngzhuāng. **2** 穿上晚礼〔禮〕服 chuāng shàng wǎnlǐfú: ~ *for dinner* 穿晚礼服赴宴. **3** 准〔準〕备〔備〕zhǔnbèi; 调制〔製〕tiáozhì: *to ~ a salad* 拌色拉. ⇨ dressing(3). **4** 敷裹伤〔傷〕口 fūguǒ shāngkǒu. **5** 装〔裝〕饰 zhuāngshì: *to ~ a shop-window* 布置商店橱窗.

dresser /'dresə(r)/ *n* [C] 食具柜〔櫃〕shíjùguì.

dress·ing /'dresɪŋ/ *n* **1** [U] 穿衣 chuānyī; 化装〔裝〕huàzhuāng; 装饰 zhuāngshì, 修饰 xiūshì. **2** [C, U] (医用)敷料 fūliào. **3** [C, U] 调味品 tiáowèipǐn, 调味油 tiáowèiyóu. '~-**gown** 晨衣 chényī. '~-**table** 梳妆〔妝〕台〔臺〕shūzhuāngtái.

drew /druː/ *pt* of draw².

dribble /'drɪbl/ *vt/i* **1** (使)液体点〔點〕滴流淌 yètǐ diǎndī liútǎng. **2** (足球)短传〔傳〕duǎnchuán.

dried /draɪd/ *pt, pp* of dry.

drier /'draɪə(r)/ *adj* ⇨ dry. □ *n* ⇨ dryer.

drift /drɪft/ *n* **1** [U] 漂流 piāoliú. **2** [C] 漂流物 piāoliúwù. 吹积〔積〕物 chuījīwù: *~s of snow* 吹积成的雪堆 **3** [U] 大概意思 dàgài yìsī, 要旨 yàozhǐ: *the ~ of his arguments* 他的话的主要内容. **4** [U] 趋〔趨〕势〔勢〕qūshì, 倾向 qīngxiàng, 动〔動〕向 dòngxiàng. □ *vt/i* **1** 漂流 piāoliú. **2** 〔喻〕流浪 liúlàng. ~**er** 流浪者 liúlàngzhě.

drill[1] /drɪl/ *n* [C] 钻〔鑽〕zuàn, 钻头〔頭〕zuàntóu. □ *vt/i* 钻孔 zuànkǒng.

drill[2] /drɪl/ *n* [C, U] **1** 操练 cāoliàn, 训练 xùnliàn. **2** 练习〔習〕liànxí. **3** 规定的步骤〔驟〕guīdìngde bùzòu. □ *vt/i* 操练 cāoliàn, 训练 xùnliàn.

drily /'draɪlɪ/ *adv* ⇨ dry.

drink /drɪŋk/ *vt/i* [*pt* drank /dræŋk/; *pp* drunk/ drʌŋk/] **1** 饮 yǐn,喝 hē. **2** 饮酒 yǐnjiǔ, 喝酒 hējiǔ. **3** 大量

吸取液体 dàliàng xīqǔ yètǐ: *My car ~s petrol.* 我的汽车汽油耗量很大. □ *n* [C, U] **1** 饮料 yǐnliào. **2** 酒 jiǔ. **~able** /-əbl/ *adj* **~er** 酒徒 jiǔtú.

drip /drɪp/ *vt/i* [-pp-] (使)滴下 dī xià. ,**~ing 'wet** 全部湿〔濕〕透 quánbù shītòu. □ *n* [C] 水滴 shuǐdī; 滴水声〔聲〕dīshuǐshēng. ,**~-'dry** *adj* 用快速晾干〔乾〕料子做的 yòng kuàisù liànggān liàozi zuò de. **'~-feed** *n* [医学]输〔輸〕液 shūyè.

drip·ping /'drɪpɪŋ/ *n* [U] 烤肉上滴下的油 kǎoròu shàng dī xià de yóu.

drive[1] /draɪv/ *n* **1** [C] 驾〔駕〕车〔車〕旅行 jiàchē lǚxíng. **2** [C] 私宅内的汽车道 sīzhá nèi de qìchēdào. **3** [C] (球赛)抽球 chōuqiú, 扣球 kòuqiú; 击〔擊〕球 jīqiú. **4**[U] 精力 jīnglì, 魄力 pòlì. **5** [C] 运〔運〕动〔動〕yùndòng, 努力 nǔlì: *the 'export ~* 增加出口运动.

drive[2] /draɪv/ *vt/i* [*pt* drove /drəʊv/; *pp* ~n /'drɪvn/] **1** 赶〔趕〕(牲口) gǎn, 驱〔驅〕qū. **2** 开〔開〕机〔機〕动车〔車〕kāi jīdòngchē. **3** 用车送(人) yòng chē sòng: *He drove me home.* 他用车送我回家. **4** 推动 tuīdòng, 发〔發〕动 fādòng. **5** (风)吹动, 刮动(某物) chuīdòng, guādòng. **6** 击〔擊〕jī. **7** 迫使(某人)处〔處〕于某种状〔狀〕态〔態〕pòshǐ chùyú mǒuchǒng zhuàngtài: *You'll ~ me mad.* 你要把我弄得发疯的. **~ *a hard bargain*** (在交易中)拚命地讨价〔價〕还〔還〕价 pīnmìngde tǎojià huánjià. **8 *be driving at*** 意指 yìzhǐ, 意欲 yìyù. **~r** *n* [C] 司机 sījī, 赶牲口的人 gǎn shēngkou de rén.

driven /'drɪvn/ *pp* of drive[2].

drizzle /'drɪzl/ *vt* 下蒙蒙细雨 xià méngméng xìyǔ. □ *n* [U] 蒙蒙细雨 méngméng xìyǔ.

drone /drəʊn/ *n* **1** [C] 雄蜂 xióngfēng. **2** [U] 低沉的嗡嗡声〔聲〕dīchénde wēngwēngshēng. **3** [C] 单〔單〕调而沉闷〔悶〕的话 dāndiào ér chénmèn de huà. □ *vt/i* 发〔發〕出嗡嗡声 fāchū wēngwēngshēng; 用单调沉闷的声调说话 yòng dāndiào chénmèn de shēngdiào shuōhuà.

droop /dru:p/ *vt/i* **1** 下垂 xiàchuí, 低垂 dīchuí. **2** 使头〔頭〕下垂 shǐ tóu xiàchuí, 低头 dītóu. □ *n* [C] 低垂 dīchuí.

drop[1] /drɒp/ *n* **1** [C] 滴 dī. **2** [*pl*] (药)滴剂〔劑〕dījì. **3** 落下 luòxià, 下降 xiàjiàng: *a ~ in temperature* 温度下降.

drop[2] /drɒp/ *vt/i* [-pp-] **1** (使)滴下 dīxià, (使)落下 luòxià. **2** 减弱 jiǎnruò, 降低 jiàngdī: *The wind ~ped.* 风减弱了. **3** 不经〔經〕意地说或写〔寫〕出 bù jīngyì de shuō huò xiěchū: *~ her a short note* 给她写了一封短信. **4** 中断〔斷〕来〔來〕往 zhōngduàn láiwǎng: *~ one's girlfriend* 断了同女朋友的关系. **5** 丢弃〔棄〕diūqì: *~ a bad habit* 改了坏习惯. **6** 不再讨论 bú zài tǎolùn: *~ the subject* 不再讨论这个问题. **7 ~ *back/behind*** 落后〔後〕luòhòu, 落在…之后 luò zài…zhīhòu. **~ *in (on sb)***; **~ *by*** 随便访问某人 suíbiàn fǎngwèn mǒurén. **~ *off*** **(a)** 睡着 shuìzháo. **(b)** 逐渐〔漸〕减少 zhújiàn jiǎnshǎo: *Sales have ~ped off.* 销售逐渐减少. **~ *out*** 退出 tuìchū, 离〔離〕队〔隊〕líduì. **'drop-out** 退学〔學〕学生 tuìxué xuéshēng.

drought /draʊt/ *n* [C, U] 干〔乾〕旱 gānhàn.

drove[1] /drəʊv/ *pt* of drive[2].

drove[2] /drəʊv/ *n* [C] 被驱〔驅〕赶〔趕〕的畜群 bèi qūgǎn de chùqún. **drover** 赶牲口的人 gǎn shēngkou de rén.

drown /draʊn/ *vt/i* **1** 淹死 yānsǐ, 溺死 nìsǐ. **2** (高声音)遮掩(低声音) zhēyǎn. **~ing** *adj*, *n* [C, U]

drowse /draʊz/ *vt/i* 打瞌睡 dǎ kēshuì, 瞌睡 kēshuì. □ *n* **drowsy** *adj* [-ier, -iest] **drows·ily** *adv*

drudge /drʌdʒ/ *n* [C] 做苦工的人 zuò kǔgōng de rén. □ *vi* 做苦工 zuò kǔgōng. **~ry** /'drʌdʒərɪ/ 苦工 kǔgōng, 重活 zhònghuó, 单〔單〕调乏味的工作 dāndiào fáwèi de gōngzuò.

drug /drʌg/ *n* [C] **1** 药 yào, 药物 yàowù. **2** 麻醉药 mázuìyào, 成瘾性毒品 chéngyǐnxìng dúpǐn: *a '~ addict* 吸毒成瘾的人. □ *vt* [-gg-] **1** 掺〔摻〕毒药于(食物,饮料) chān dúyào yú. **2** 使服毒品 shǐ fú dúpǐn. **'~store** [美语] 杂〔雜〕货店 záhuòdiàn.

drum /drʌm/ *n* [C] **1** 鼓 gǔ, 鼓声〔聲〕gǔshēng. **2** 鼓状〔狀〕物 gǔzhuàngwù, 圆桶 yuántǒng: *an oil-~* 油桶. ⇨ eardrum. □ *vt/i* [-mm-] **1** 打鼓 dǎgǔ. **2** 咚咚地敲 dōngdōngde qiāo. **3 ~ *sth into sb*** 反复〔復〕向某人灌输〔輸〕某事物 fǎnfù xiàng mǒurén guànshū mǒushìwù. **~mer** 鼓手 gǔshǒu. **'~stick** 鼓槌 gǔchuí.

drunk /drʌŋk/ *adj* [*pp* of drink] 酒醉的 jiǔzuìde. □ *n* [C] 醉汉

〔漢〕 zuìhàn, 酒鬼 jiǔguǐ. ~**en** *adj* ~**en·ness** *n*

dry /draɪ/ *adj* [-ier, -iest] **1** 干〔乾〕的 gānde, 干燥的 gānzàode. **2** 干涸的 gānhéde, 干枯的 gānkūde: *a* ~ *well* 干涸的井. **3** (酒) 不甜的 bùtiánde. **4** 枯燥乏味的 kūzào fáwèide: *a* ~ *speech* 枯燥乏味的讲话. □ *vt/i* [*pt, pp* dried] **1** (使)干 gān. **2** ~ *up* 〔喻〕用完 yòngwán, 耗尽〔盡〕 hàojìn. ~**er, drier** *n* [C] 干燥器 gānzàoqì. ˌ~-'**clean** *vt* 干洗 gānxǐ. ˌ~-'**cleaners** 干洗剂〔劑〕 gānxǐjì; 干洗商 gānxǐshāng. ˌ~-'**cleaning** 干洗gānxǐ. ˌ~'**dock** 干船坞 gānchuánwū. ˌ~ '**rot** 干朽 gānxiǔ, 干枯 gānkū. **drily** /'draɪlɪ/ *adv* ~**ness** *n* [U]

D.Sc. = Doctor of Science 理科博士 lǐkē bóshì.

dual /'dju:əl/ *adj* 双〔雙〕的 shuāngde, 二重的 èrchóngde; 二体〔體〕的 èrtǐde. ˌ~ '**carriageway** 双车〔車〕道 shuāngchēdào.

dub /dʌb/ *vt* [-bb-] **1** 以剑〔劍〕拍肩封…为爵士 yǐ jiàn pāijiān fēng …wéi juéshì. **2** 给…起绰号〔號〕 gěi…qǐ chuòhào. **3** (电影, 广播等)配音 pèiyīn.

du·bi·ous /'dju:bɪəs/ *adj* 半信半疑的 bànxìn bànyí de. ~**ly** *adv*

duch·ess /'dʌtʃɪs/ *n* [C] 公爵夫人 gōngjué fūrén. 女公爵 nǚ gōngjué.

duchy /'dʌtʃɪ/ *n* [C] [*pl* -ies] (亦作 *dukedom*) 公爵领地 gōngjué lǐngdì.

duck[1] /dʌk/ *n* **1** [C] 鸭〔鴨〕 yā; 雌鸭 cíyā. ⇨ drake; [U] 鸭肉 yāròu. **2** (板球)零分 língfēn; 鸭蛋 yādàn.

duck[2] /dʌk/ *vt/i* **1** 突然低下(头或身子) tūrán dīxià; 躲闪〔閃〕 duǒshǎn. **2** 把(人)暂〔暫〕按入水中 bǎ zhàn ànrù shuǐ zhōng. □ *n* [C] 躲闪 duǒshǎn; 潜水 qiánshuǐ.

duck·ling /'dʌklɪŋ/ *n* [C] 小鸭〔鴨〕 xiǎoyā, 幼鸭 yòuyā.

duct /dʌkt/ *n* [C] **1** (身体内的)管 guǎn. **2** 气〔氣〕道 qìdào.

dud /dʌd/ *n* [C], *adj* 〔俚语〕不中用的 bu zhōngyòng de, 假的 jiǎde: *a* ~ *cheque* 假支票.

due[1] /dju:/ *adj* **1** 应〔應〕支付的 yīng zhīfù de: *The gas bill is* ~. 该付煤气费了. **2** 正当〔當〕的 zhèngdàngde, 适〔適〕当的 shìdàngde; 应〔應〕有的 yīnyǒude. **3** 预定应到的 yùdìng yīngdào de, 预期的 yùqīde: *The train is* ~ *(in) at 1:30.* 列车一点半钟到站. **4** ~ *to* 由于 yóuyú: *His success is* ~ *to hard work.* 他由于努力而获得成功. □ *adv* (罗盘指针)正(南, 北等) zhèng: ~ *east* 正东.

due[2] /dju:/ *n* **1** [只用 *pl*] 应〔應〕得之物 yīngdé zhī wù, 应得权〔權〕益 yīngdé quányì: *give the man his* ~ 给此人应得之权益. **2** [*pl*] 俱乐〔樂〕部会〔會〕员会费 jùlèbù huìyuán huìfèi.

duel /'dju:əl/ *n* [C] **1** 决斗〔鬥〕 juédòu, **2** 双〔雙〕方的斗争 shuāngfāngde dòuzhēng. □ *vi* [-ll-, 美语亦作 -l-] 决斗 juédòu. ~**list** *n* [C] 决斗者 juédòuzhě, 斗争者 dòuzhēngzhe.

duet /dju:'et/ *n*[C] 二重唱 èrchóngchàng; 二重奏 èrchóngzòu.

duffle (亦作 **duffel**) /'dʌfl/ *n* [U] 粗厚的呢料 cūhòude níliào. *a* ~-*coat* 粗呢上衣.

dug /dʌg/ *pt, pp* of dig.

dug-out /'dʌgaʊt/ *n* [C] **1** 地下掩蔽部 dìxià yǎnbìbù. **2** 独〔獨〕木舟 dúmùzhōu.

duke /dju:k/ *n* [C] 公爵 gōngjué, 欧〔歐〕洲公国〔國〕君主 ōuzhōu gōngguó jūnzhǔ. ~**dom** **(a)** 公爵爵位 gōngjué juéwèi. **(b)** (= *duchy*) 公国公爵领地 gōngguó gōngjué lǐngdì.

dull /dʌl/ *adj* (-er, -est) **1** 阴〔陰〕暗的 yīn'ànde. **2** 迟〔遲〕钝的 chídùnde. **3** 沉闷〔悶〕的 chénmènde. **4** 钝的 dùnde: *a* ~ *knife* 一把钝刀. □ *vt/i* (使)变〔變〕钝 biàndùn.

duly /'dju:lɪ/ *adv* 适〔適〕当〔當〕地 shìdàngde; 按时〔時〕地 ànshíde.

dumb /dʌm/ *adj* [-er, -est] **1** 哑〔啞〕的 yǎde, 不能说话的 bùnéng shuōhuà de. **2** 暂〔暫〕不说话的 zhàn bù shuōhuà de; 沉默的 chénmòde. 无〔無〕言的 wúyánde: *struck* ~ *by the news* 被这个消息惊得说不出话来. **3** [非正式用语]愚笨的 yúbènde, 蠢的 chǔnde. ~**ly** *adv* ~**ness** *n* [U]

dumb·found (美语亦作 **dumfound**) /dʌm'faʊnd/ *vt* 惊〔驚〕讶 jīngyà, 惊得发〔發〕呆 jīngde fādāi.

dummy /'dʌmɪ/ *n* [C] [*pl* -ies] 模仿物 mófǎngwù, 样〔樣〕本 yàngběn: *a tailor's* ~ (服装店试样用)人体模型; *a baby's* ~ 奶嘴. ˌ~ '**run** 演习〔習〕 yǎnxí, 排演 páiyǎn.

dump /dʌmp/ *n* [C] **1** 堆垃圾的地方 duī lājī de dìfang. 垃圾堆 lājīduī. **2** 军〔軍〕需品堆集处〔處〕 jūnxūpǐn duījíchù. **3** [俚]丑〔醜〕陋的处〔處〕所 chǒulòude chùsuǒ. *down in the* ~*s* 不高兴〔興〕的 bù gāoxìng de, 心灰意懒的 xīnhuīyìlǎn de, 沮丧的 jǔsàngde. □ *vt* 1 倒垃圾 dào lājī, 随便抛弃〔棄〕 suíbiàn pāoqì. 2 [商业] 倾销 qīngxiāo. '~**truck** *n* [C] (亦作 '~·**er**) 自动〔動〕卸货卡车〔車〕zìdòng xièhuò kǎchē.

dump·ling /'dʌmplɪŋ/ *n* [C] 苹〔蘋〕果布丁 píngguǒ bùdīng, 汤〔湯〕团〔團〕 tāngtuán.

dumpy /'dʌmpɪ/ *adj* [-ier, -iest] 矮而胖的 ǎi ér pàng de.

dunce /dʌns/ *n* [C] 笨人 bènrén, 笨学〔學〕生 bèn xuésheng.

dune /dju:n/ *n* [C] (风吹积成的) 沙丘 shāqiū.

dung /dʌŋ/ *n* [U] (牲畜的)粪 fèn, 粪肥 fènféi.

dunga·rees /ˌdʌŋgə'ri:z/ *n pl* 粗布工作服 cūbù gōngzuòfú.

dun·geon /'dʌndʒən/ *n* [C] 土牢 tǔláo, 地牢 dìláo.

dupe /dju:p/ *vt* 欺骗〔騙〕 qīpiàn, 诈骗 zhàpiàn. □ *n* [C] 受骗者shòupiànzhě.

dupl. =duplicate 副本 fùběn, 抄件 chāojiàn.

du·pli·cate[1] /'dju:plɪkət/ *adj* 1 完全一样〔樣〕的 wánquán yíyàngde. 复〔複〕制〔製〕的 fùzhìde. 2 成对〔對〕的 chéngduìde. □ *n* [C] 复制品 fùzhìpǐn, 副本 fùběn. *in* ~ 正副两份 zhèngfù liǎngfèn.

du·pli·cate[2] /'dju:plɪkeɪt/ *vt* 复〔複〕写〔寫〕 fùxiě, 复制〔製〕 fùzhì. **du·pli'ca·tion** *n* [C, U] **du·pli·ca·tor** 复印机〔機〕 fùyìnjī.

dur·able /'djʊərəbl/ *adj* 耐用的 nàiyòngde. □ *n pl* 耐用品nàiyòngpǐn.

dur·ation /djʊ'reɪʃn/ *n* [U] 持续〔續〕时〔時〕间〔間〕 chíxù shíjiān.

dur·ess (亦作 **-esse**) /djʊ'res/ *n* [U] 威胁〔脅〕 wēixié, 强迫 qiǎngpò: *act under* ~ 在被胁迫情况下的行为.

dur·ing /'djʊərɪŋ/ *prep* 1 在…期间〔間〕 zài…qījiān: *Don't smoke* ~ *the concert.* 音乐会上不要吸烟. 2 在…的时〔時〕候 (在…期间的某个时候) zài ... de shíhòu: *He died* ~ *the night.* 他夜里死了.

dusk /dʌsk/ *n* [U] 黄昏 huánghūn, 薄暮 bómù.

dusky /'dʌskɪ/ *adj* [-ier, -iest] 暗淡的 àndànde, 暗黑的 ànhēide.

dust /dʌst/ *n* [U] 灰尘〔塵〕 huīchén, 尘土 chéntǔ, 尘埃 chén'āi. *bite the* ~ [非正式用语]倒地死了 dǎo dì sǐ le. 受伤〔傷〕倒地 shòu shāng dǎo dì. □ *vt* 1 去掉尘土 qùdiào chéntǔ, 掸〔撣〕掉尘土 dǎndiào chéntǔ. 2 撒粉状〔狀〕物于 ... sǎ fěnzhuàngwù yú... ~-**er** 揩布 kāibù, 抹布 mǒbù; 撢子 dǎnzi; 除尘器 chúchénqì. **dusty** *adj* [-ier, -iest] '~**bin** 垃圾箱 lājīxiāng. '~-**bowl** 干〔乾〕旱不毛之地区〔區〕 gānhàn bù máo zhī dìqū. '~-**jacket** 书〔書〕的护〔護〕封 shūde hùfēng. '~**man** 倒垃圾工 dàolājīgōng. '~**pan** 畚箕 běnjī.

duty /'dju:tɪ/ *n* [*pl*-ies] 1 [C, U] 责任 zérèn, 本分 běnfèn, 义〔義〕务〔務〕 yìwù. *on* ~ 值班 zhíbān, 上班 shàngbān; *off* ~ 下班 xiàbān. 2 [C, U] (*'customs duties'*) 关〔關〕税 guānshuì. ,~-'**free** (货物)免税的 miǎnshuìde. **duti·ful** *adj* 恭敬的 gōngjìngde, 孝敬的 xiàojìngde. **duti·fully** *adv*

duvet /'dju:veɪ/ *n* [C] 褥垫〔墊〕 rùdiàn.

dwarf /dwɔ:f/ *n* [C] [*pl* ~s] 矮人 ǎirén, 矮小的动〔動〕植物 ǎixiǎode dòng zhíwù. □ *vt* 使显〔顯〕得矮小 shǐ xiǎnde ǎixiǎo: *houses* ~-*ed by the surrounding mountains* 因周围的高山而显得矮小的屋子.

dwell /dwel/ *vi* [*pt* dwelt /dwelt/] 1 居住 jūzhù. 2 ~ *on* 细思 xìsī; 详述 xiángshù; 详论〔論〕 xiánglùn. ~**er** 居住者 jūzhùzhě, 居民 jūmín: *'city-~ers* 城市居民. ~**ing** 住处〔處〕 zhùchù, 住宅 zhùzhái, 寓所 yùsuǒ.

dwindle /'dwɪndl/ *vt* 缩小 suōxiǎo, 减少 jiǎnshǎo.

dye /daɪ/ *vt/i* [第三人称单数现在式 ~s; 过去式, 过去分词~d, 现在分词 ~ing] 染色 rǎnsè 使…染色 shǐ ... rǎnsè. □ *n* [C, U] 染料 rǎnliào, 染色 rǎnsè. **dyer** 染工 rǎngōng, 染色技师〔師〕 rǎnsè jìshī.

dy·ing ⇨ die[2].

dyke *n* = dike.

dy·namic /daɪ'næmɪk/ *adj* 1 动〔動〕力的 dònglìde. ⇨ static. 2 精力充沛的 jīnglì chōngpèi de, 精悍的 jīnghànde. □ *n* [*pl*] [使用 *sing verb*] 力学〔學〕 lìxué; 动力学 dònglìxué. ~**ally** *adv*

dyna·mite /'daɪnəmaɪt/ *n* [U] 炸药 zhàyào. □ *vt* 用炸药爆炸 yòng zhàyào bàozhà.

dy·namo /'daɪnəməʊ/ *n* [C][*pl* ~s] 发〔發〕电〔電〕机〔機〕 fādiànjī.

dyn·asty /'dɪnəstɪ/ *n* [C] [*pl* -ies] 朝代 cháodài; 王朝 wángcháo.

E e

E, e /iː/ [*pl* E's, e's/iːz/] 英语的第五个字母 yīngyǔde dìwǔgè zìmǔ.
E.=East.
E.and O.E.—errors and omissions excepted 无〔無〕错误与〔與〕省略 wú cuòwù yǔ shěnglüè.
each /iːtʃ/*adj* 每一 měiyī, 各 gè, 各自的 gèzìde: *on ~ side of him* 他的两边. □ *pron* **1** 每个〔個〕měigè, 各 gè, 各自 gèzì: *~ of the boys* 每个男孩. **2** 分别地 fēnbiéde, 每个地 měigède: *He gave the boys 50p ~.* 他给孩子们每人五十便士.
eager /'iːgə(r)/ *adj* 渴望的 kěwàngde, 热〔熱〕切的 rèqiède. **~ly** *adv* **~ness** *n* [U]
eagle /'iːgl/ *n* [C] 鹰〔鷹〕yīng.
ear¹ /ɪə(r)/ *n* [C] **1** 耳朵 ěrduo. ***be all ~s*** 专〔專〕心倾听〔聽〕zhuānxīn qīngtīng. **2** 听觉〔覺〕tīngjué: *a good ~ for music* 对音乐有很好的欣赏力. **(*play sth*) *by ~*** (a) 凭〔憑〕听觉记忆〔憶〕演奏(不凭乐谱) píng tīngjué jìyì yǎnzòu. (b)〔喻〕干〔幹〕事无〔無〕计划〔劃〕gànshì wú jìhuà. **'~ache** 耳中疼痛 ěr zhōng téngtòng. **'~-drum** 耳鼓 ěrgǔ; 鼓膜 gǔmó. **'~-mark** *vi* 〔喻〕留作专〔專〕用 liúzuò zhuānyòng: *~ mark money for research.* 拨出研究用专款. **'~-ring** 耳环〔環〕ěrhuán. **'~shot** 听觉所及的距离〔離〕tīngjué suǒ jí de jùlí.
ear² /ɪə(r)/ *n* [C] 穗 suì.
earl /ɜːl/ *n* [C] (英国)伯爵 bójué.
early /'ɜːlɪ/ [-ier, -iest] *adj, adv* **1** 早的 zǎode: *~ morning* 清晨. **2** 较〔較〕先的 jiàoxiānde, 较先地 jiàoxiānde: *arrive too ~* 到得太早. ***earlier on*** 在更早一些时〔時〕候 zài gèn zǎo yìxiē shíhòu. **,~-'warning** *adj* (雷达)预警的 yùjǐngde, 远〔遠〕程警戒的 yuǎnchéng jǐngjiède.
earn /ɜːn/ *vt* **1** 赚得 zhuàndé, 挣得 zhèngdé: *~ a salary* 挣工资. **2** 赢得 yíngdé, 博得 bódé: *~ our praise* 赢得我们的赞扬. **~ings** *n pl* 挣得的钱〔錢〕zhéngdéde qián.
ear·nest /'ɜːnɪst/ *adj* 认〔認〕真的 rènzhēnde, 坚〔堅〕决的 jiānjuéde. □ *n* ***in ~*** 坚决地 jiānjuéde, 认真地 rènzhēnde. **~ly** *adv* **~ness** *n* [U]
earth /ɜːθ/ *n* **1** 世界 shìjiè, 地球 dìqiú. **2** [U] 大地 dàdì, 地面 dìmiàn. **3** [U] 土 tǔ, 泥 ní. **4** [C] 狐等的洞穴 hú děng de dòngxuè. **5** [C, U] 〔电〕接地 jiēdì. □*vt* (电)把…接地 bǎ … jiēdì. **~-quake** /'ɜːθkweɪk/ *n* [C] 地震 dìzhèn. **'~worm** 蚯蚓 qiūyǐn. **~ly** *adj* (a) 尘〔塵〕世的 chénshìde, 世俗的 shìsúde. (b)〔非正式用语〕可能的 kěnéngde, 想得出的 xiǎngdechūde: *no ~ly use* 完全没有用. **earthy** *adj* [-ier, -iest] (a) 泥土的 nítǔde; 泥土似的 nítǔsìde. (b)〔喻〕粗糙的 cūcāode; 强壮〔壯〕的 qiángzhuàngde.
earthen·ware /'ɜːθnweə(r)/*n* [U] 陶器 táoqì.
ear·wig /'ɪəwɪg/ *n* [C] 蠼螋 qúsōu.
ease /iːz/ *vt/i* **1** 减轻〔輕〕(痛苦,不舒服,焦虑) jiǎnqīng. **2** 放松〔鬆〕fàngsōng; 减低速度 jiǎndī sùdù: *~ off a bit* (= slow down) 慢一点. **3** 小心移置 xiǎoxīn yízhì: *~ the injured man out of the car* 小心翼翼地把受伤的人移出汽车. □ *n* [U] 舒适〔適〕shūshì, 悠闲〔閑〕yōuxián, 自在 zìzài. ***do sth with ~*** 容易 róngyì, 不费劲〔勁〕bū fèijìn.
easel /'iːzl/ *n* [C] 画〔畫〕架 huàjià.
easily /'iːzəlɪ/ *adv* **1** 容易地 róngyìde, 不费力地 bú fèilì de. **2** 毫无〔無〕疑问〔問〕地 háowú yíwèn de: *~ the best* 毫无疑问地最好.
east /'iːst/ *n* **1 *the ~*** 东〔東〕方 dōngfāng, 东 dōng. **2** 东部地区〔區〕dōngbù dìqū. **3 *an ~ wind*** 东风〔風〕dōngfēng. □ *adv* 向东方 xiàng dōngfāng. ⇨ the Far, Middle East. ***the E~*** 亚〔亞〕洲 yàzhōu. **~er·ly** *adj, adv* 向东方的 xiàng dōngfāng de; 东的 dōngde; 从〔從〕东方来的 cóng dōngfāng lái de; 向东方 xiàngdōngfāng; 从东方 cóng dōngfāng. **~-ern** *adj* 东方的 dōngfāngde; 东的 dōngde. **~ward** *adj* 朝东的 cháo dōng de. **~ward(s)** *adv*
Easter /'iːstə(r)/ *n* 耶稣复〔復〕活节〔節〕yēsūfùhuójié.
easy /'iːzɪ/ [-ier, -iest] *adj* **1** 容易的 róngyìde. **2** 舒适〔適〕的 shūshìde, 安心的 ānxīnde, 自在的 zìzàide. □ *adv* 容易地 róngyìde, 不费力地 bú fèilì de. ***take it (things) ~*** 不紧〔緊〕张〔張〕bù jǐnzhāng,

从[從]容 cóngróng. ***go ~ on*** [非正式用语]有节[節]制地消费 yǒu jiézhì de xiāofèi: *Go ~ on the beer.* 少喝点啤酒. ,**~'going** 悠闲[閑]的 yōuxiánde; 舒适的 shūshìde; 懒散的 lǎnsǎnde; 随和的 suíhéde.

eat /i:t/ *vt/i* [*pt* ate /eɪt/; *pp* ~en /'i:tn/] **1** 吃 chī; 喝 hē. **2** 腐蚀 fǔshí; 蛀 zhù: *Acid has ~en into the metal.* 酸腐蚀了金属. ***~ one's words*** 收回前言 shōuhuí qiányán, 认[認]错道歉 rèncuò dàoqiàn. **~-able** *adj* 可吃的 kěchīde.

eaves /i:vz/ *n pl* 屋檐 wūyán. **'~drop** *vi* [-pp-] 偷听[聽] tōutīng, 窃[竊]听 qiètīng.

ebb /eb/ *vi* **1** 退潮 tuìcháo, 落潮 luòcháo. **2** [喻]衰退 shuāituì, 衰落 shuāiluò, 减少 jiǎnshǎo: *His strength was ~ing.* 他的体力正在衰退. □ *n* [C] **1** 落潮 luòcháo, 退潮 tuìcháo. **2** [喻]低潮 dīcháo, 衰败 shuāibài.

eb·ony /'ebənɪ/ *n* [U] 乌[烏]木 wūmù, 黑檀 hēitán. □ *adj* 乌木制[製]的 wūmù zhì de. 乌木色的 wūmùsède, 漆黑的 qīhēide.

ec·cen·tric /ɪk'sentrɪk/ *adj* **1** (人)古怪的 gǔguàide; 不正常的 bú zhèngcháng de; 偏执[執]的 piānzhíde. **2** (圆)不同心的 bù tóngxīn de. *n* [C] 古怪的人 gǔguàide rén. **~ity** /-'trɪsətɪ/ *n* [*pl* -ies] [C,U]

echo /'ekəʊ/ *n* [*pl* ~es] [C, U] 回声 huíshēng, 反响[響] fǎnxiǎng. □ *vt/i* **1** 发[發]出回声 fāchū huíshēng; 起反响 qǐ fǎnxiǎng: *His voice ~ed round the empty room.* 他的声音在这间空屋子里发出回声. **2** 重复[複] chóngfù. **'~sounder** *n* 回声[聲]测深仪[儀] huíshēng cèshēngyí.

éclair /eɪkleə(r)/ *n* [C] 巧克力包奶油的小蛋糕 qiǎokèlì bāo nǎiyǒu de xiǎodàngāo.

eclipse /ɪ'klɪps/ *n* [C] [天文]食 shí, □*vt* 使食 shǐ shí, 掩蔽(天体的光) yǎnbì.

ecol·ogy /i:'kɒlədʒɪ/ *n* [U] 生态[態]学[學] shēngtàixué. □ **eco·logi·cal** /-'lɒdʒɪkl/ *adj*

econ·omic /,i:kə'nɒmɪk/ *adj* **1** 经[經]济[濟]学[學]的 jīngjìxuéde. **2** 经济的 jīngjìde: *~ level of production* 生产的经济水平. **3** [非正式用语]便宜的 piányìde. **~al** *adj* 节[節]约的 jiéyuēde. **~ally** *adv*

econ·omics /,i:kə'nɒmɪks/ *n* [U] 经[經]济[濟]学[學] jīngjìxué.

econom·ist /i:'kɒnəmɪst/ *n* [C] 经济学家 jīngjìxuéjiā.

econ·om·ize /i:'kɒnəmaɪz/ *vt/i* 节[節]约 jiéyuē, 节省 jiéshěng.

econ·omy /i:'kɒnəmɪ/ *n* [*pl* -ies] **1** [C, U] 节[節]约 jiéyuē, 节省jiéshěng. **2** [C, U] 经[經]济[濟] jīngjì.

ec·stasy /'ekstəsɪ/ *n* [C, U] [*pl* -ies] 狂喜 kuángxǐ; 心醉神迷 xīnzuì-shénmí. **ec·static** /ɪk'stætɪk/ *adj*

eddy /'edɪ/ *n* [C] [*pl* -ies] (空气,水,烟等)旋涡 xuànwō, 涡流 wōliú. □ *vi* [*pt, pp* -ied] (使)旋转[轉] xuánzhuàn; (使)起旋涡 qǐ xuánwō.

edge /edʒ/ *n* [C] **1** 刀口 dāokǒu, 锋 fēng. ***be on ~*** 紧[緊]张[張]不安 jǐnzhāng bù ān. **2** 边[邊] biān, 边缘 biānyuán, 边界 biānjiè: *the ~ of a table* 桌子边上. □ *vt/i* **1** 给…加上边 gěi…jiā shàng biān. **2** (使)徐徐移动[動]xúxú yídòng: *He ~d along the cliff.* 他在悬崖上慢慢移动. **edg·ing** *n* [C] 边缘 biānyuán. **edgy** *adj* [-ier, -iest] 紧张的 jǐnzhāngde; 不安的 bù'ānde.

ed·ible /'edɪbl/ *adj* 可以食用的 kěyǐ shíyòng de.

edit /'edɪt/ *vt* **1** 编辑[輯](他人作品) biānjì. **2** 编辑(报纸, 书等) biānjì. **3** 剪辑 jiǎnjì.

edi·tion /ɪ'dɪʃn/ *n* [C] **1** 版本 bǎnběn: *a paperback ~* 纸面平装版. **2** 版次 bǎncì.

edi·tor /'edɪtə(r)/ *n* 编辑[輯]biānjì **~·ial** /-'tɔ:rɪəl/ *adj* 编辑的 biānjìde, 编者的 biānzhěde. □ *n* [C] 社论[論] shèlùn.

edu·cate /'edʒʊkeɪt/ *vt* 教育 jiàoyù, 培养[養] péiyǎng.

edu·ca·tion /,edʒʊ'keɪʃən/ *n* [U] **1** 教育 jiàoyù. **2** 修养[養] xiūyǎng, 教养 jiàoyǎng. **~al** *adj*

eel /i:l/ *n* [C] 鳝[鱔] shàn; 鳗[鰻] mán.

E.E.C. = European Economic Community 欧[歐]洲经济[濟]共同体[體] ōuzhōu jīngjì gòngtóngtǐ.

eerie, eery /'ɪərɪ/ *adj* [-ier, -iest] 引起恐惧[懼]的 yǐnqǐ kǒngjù de; 奇怪的 qíguàide.

ef·fect /ɪ'fekt/ *n* **1** [C, U] 结果 jiéguǒ, 效果 xiàoguǒ. ***take ~*** **(a)** 见效 jiànxiào. **(b)** 生效 shēngxiào: *The law takes ~ today.* 此一法律今日生效. **2** 印象 yìnxiàng: *sound ~s* 音响效果. **3** *pl* 财产[產] cáichǎn, 所有物 suǒyǒuwù. □ *vt* 产生 chǎngshēng, 引起yǐnqǐ, 使 shǐ. **~ive** **(a)** 有效果的 yǒu xiàoguǒ de, 生效的 shēngxiàode. **(b)** 实〔實〕在的 shízàide; 实际〔際〕的 shíjìde: *our ~ive profit* 我们的实际利润. **~ive·ly** *adv* **~ive·ness** *n* [U] **~ual** *adj* 〔正式用语〕有效的 yǒuxiàode: *an ~ual remedy* 有效的治疗.

ef·femi·nate /ɪ'femɪnət/ *adj* 女人气〔氣〕的 nǚrénqìde, 无〔無〕大丈夫气概的 wú dàzhàngfuqìgài de.

ef·fer·vesce /ˌefə'ves/ *vi* **1** 冒气〔氣〕泡 mào qìpào. **2** 〔喻〕(人)兴〔興〕高采烈的 xìnggāo cǎiliè de. **ef·fer·vescent** *adj*

ef·fi·cient /ɪ'fɪʃnt/ *adj* **1** 能胜〔勝〕任的 néng shèngrèn de. **2** 效率高的 xiàolǜ gāo de. **~ly** *adv* **ef·fi·ciency** *n* /-nsɪ/ [U]

ef·figy /'efɪdʒɪ/ *n* [C] [*pl* -ies] (被憎恨的人的)肖像 xiāoxiàng, 雕像 diāoxiàng, 模拟〔擬〕像 mónǐxiàng.

ef·fort /'efət/ *n* **1** [C, U] 努力 nǔlì, 尽〔盡〕力 jìnlì. **2** 努力尝〔嘗〕试 nǔlì chángshì, 企图〔圖〕qìtú: *make an ~ to escape* 企图逃跑. **3** 成就 chéngjiù, 成果 chéngguǒ. **~-less** 不努力的 bù nǔlì de, 不费力的 bú fèilì de.

ef·front·ery /ɪ'frʌntərɪ/ *n*[*pl* -ies][C, U] 厚颜 hòuyán, 无〔無〕耻 wúchǐ.

E.F.T.A.＝European Free Trade Association 欧〔歐〕洲自由贸易联〔聯〕盟 ōuzhōu zìyóu màoyì liánméng.

e.g. 例如 lìrú.

egg¹ /eg/ *n* **1** [C] 蛋 dàn. [U] 蛋的碎片,碎块〔塊〕dànde suìpiàn, suìkuài. **2** 卵 luǎn, 卵细胞 luǎn xìbāo. **~-cup** (吃煮鸡蛋用的)蛋杯 dànbēi. **'~-head** 知识〔識〕分子 zhīshifènzǐ.

egg² /eg/ *vt* **~ sb on** 怂〔慫〕恿某人 sǒngyǒng mǒurén.

egg·plant /'egplɑːnt/ *n* [C] 茄子 qiézi.

ego /'egəʊ/ *n* [C] 自我 zìwǒ,自己 zìjǐ; 个〔個〕人思考和感觉〔覺〕的能力 gèrén sīkǎo hé gǎnjué de nénglì.

ego·cen·tric /ˌegəʊ'sentrik/ *adj* 利己的 lìjǐde, 自我中心的 zìwǒ zhōngxīn de.

ego·ism /'egəʊɪzəm/ *n* **1** [U] 自我主义〔義〕zìwǒzhǔyì, 利己主义 lìjǐzhǔyì. **2** 自私自利 zìsī zìlì. **ego·ist** *n* [C] 自我主义者 zìwǒzhǔyìzhě.

ego·tism /'egətɪzm/ *n* [U] 自我中心 zìwǒzhōngxīn, 利己主义〔義〕lìjǐzhǔyì. **ego·tist** *n* [C] 自私自利者 zìsī zìlì zhě.

eider·down /'aɪdədaʊn/ *n* [C] 鸭〔鴨〕绒 yāróng; 鸭绒被 yāróngbèi; 鸭绒垫〔墊〕yāróngdiàn.

eight /eɪt/ *adj, n* [C] 八 bā, 八个〔個〕bāgè. **eighth** /eɪtθ/ *adj, n* [C] (略作 8th) 八分之一 bāfēn zhī yī, 八分之一的 bāfēn zhī yī de, 第八 dìbā. 第八个 dìbāgè.

eight·een /ˌeɪ'tiːn/ *adj, n* [C] 十八 shíbā, 十八个〔個〕shíbāgè. **eight-eenth** *adj, n* [C] (缩略形式 18th) 十八分之一 shíbāfēn zhī yī, 十八分之一的 shíbāfēn zhī yī de, 第十八 dì shíbā, 第十八个 dì shíbāgè.

eighty /'eɪtɪ/ *adj, n* [C] 八十 bāshí, 八十个〔個〕bāshígè. **eight·ieth** *adj, n* [C](缩略形式 80th)八十分之一 bāshífēn zhī yī, 八十分之一的 bāshífēn zhī yī de; 第八十 dì bāshí, 第八十个 dì bāshígè.

either /'aɪðə(r)/ *adj, pron* **1** (两者中)任一的 rènyīde, 两者之一 liǎngzhě zhī yī: *take ~ half* 任选一半. **2** (两者中)任一方的 rènyìfāngde. *a chair at ~ end of the table* 桌子两头的(两把)椅子. □ *adv conj* **1** [与 not 连用]也 yě: *I don't like the red one, and I don't like the pink one, ~.* 我不喜爱这红的,也不喜爱这粉红的。⇨neith. **2** 或者 huòzhě, 要末 yàomò: *He is ~ mad or drunk.* 他要末是疯了,要末是喝醉了.

eject /ɪ'dʒekt/ *vt/i* **1** 驱〔驅〕逐 qūzhú, 逐出 zhúchū. **2** 排出(液体等) páichū. **ejec·tion** /-ʃn/ *n* [C, U] **~or-seat** (飞机)弹〔彈〕射座椅 dánshè zuòyǐ.

eke /iːk/ *vt* **~out** 使(供应)能持久 shǐ néng chíjiǔ, 竭力维持 jiélì wéichí.

elab·or·ate /ɪ'læbərət/ *adj* 复〔複〕杂〔雜〕的 fùzáde, 详尽〔盡〕的 xiángjìnde. □ *vt* /ɪ'læbəreɪt/ 作详细说明 zuò xiángxì shuōmíng. **elab·or·ation** /-'reɪʃn/ *n* [C, U]

elapse /ɪ'læps/ *vi* (时间)流逝 liúshì.

elas·tic /ɪ'læstɪk/ *adj* 弹〔彈〕性的 tánxìngde, 有伸缩性的 yǒu shēnsuōxìng de: *an ~ band* 松〔鬆〕紧〔緊〕带〔帶〕sōngjǐndài. □ *n* [U] 橡皮圈 xiàngpíquān. **~ity** /ˌelæ'stɪsətɪ/ *n* [U]

elated /ɪ'leɪtɪd/ *adj* 欢〔歡〕欣鼓舞的 huānxīngǔwǔde, 兴〔興〕高采烈的 xìnggāo-cǎiliède.

el·bow /'elbəʊ/ *n* [C] 肘 zhǒu, 衣服的肘部 yīfude zhǒubù. □ *vt* 用肘推 yòng zhǒu tuī, 挤〔擠〕jǐ. **'~ grease**[非正式用语]苦差使 kǔchāishi, 重活 zhònghuó. **'~-room** 活动〔動〕余〔餘〕地 huódòng yúdì.

E.L.B.S. = English Language Book Society 英语图〔圖〕书〔書〕协〔協〕会〔會〕yīngyǔ túshū xiéhuì.

el·der¹ /'eldə(r)/ *adj* 年长〔長〕的 niánzhǎngde: *my* ～ *brother* 我的哥哥. ⇨ old. □ *n pl* **1** 长〔長〕者 zhǎngzhě, 前辈〔輩〕qiánbèi. **2** (教会的)长〔長〕老 zhǎnglǎo. **3** 二人中之较〔較〕年长者 èr rén zhōng zhī jiào niánzhǎng zhě. **～ly** *adj* 年纪相当〔當〕大的 niánjì xiāngdāngdà de. **el·dest** *adj* 排行第一的 páiháng dìyī de, 最年长的 zuì niánzhǎng de.

el·der² /eldə(r)/ *n* [C] 〔植物〕接骨木 jiēgǔmù.

elect /ɪ'lekt/ *vt* **1** 选〔選〕举〔舉〕xuǎnjǔ. **2** 选择〔擇〕xuǎnzé: *They* ～*ed to stay*. 他们决定留下来. □ *adj* 选出而未上任的 xuǎnchū ér wèi shàngrèn de: *president*-～ 当选(尚未上任)总统. **～or** *n* [C] 有选举权〔權〕的人 yǒu xuǎnjǔquán de rén. **～oral** *adj*. **～or·ate** /-rət/ 全体〔體〕选民 quántǐ xuǎnmín.

elec·tion /ɪ'lekʃn/ *n* [C, U] 选〔選〕举〔舉〕xuǎnjǔ.

elec·tric /ɪ'lektrɪk/ *adj* 电〔電〕的 diànde, 导〔導〕电的 dǎodiànde, 发〔發〕电的 fādiànde: *an* ～ *fire* 电火花; *an* ～ *generator* 发电机. **～al** *adj*

elec·tri·cian /ɪˌlek'triʃn/ *n* [C] 电〔電〕学〔學〕家 diànxuéjiā; 电工 diàngōng.

elec·tric·ity /ɪˌlek'trisəti/ *n* **1** [U] 电〔電〕流 diànliú, 电能 diànnéng. **2** 电 diàn, 电学〔學〕diànxué.

elec·trify /ɪ'lektrɪfaɪ/ *vt* [*pt pp* -ied] **1** 使充电〔電〕shǐ chōngdiàn; 使起电 shǐ qǐdiàn: *an electrified fence* 通了电的栅栏. **2** 使激动〔動〕shǐ jīdòng; 使震惊〔驚〕shǐ zhènjīng: ～ *the audience with one's performance* 他的表演使观众大为惊异.

elec·tro·cardio·gram /ɪˌlektrəʊ'kɑːdɪəʊgræm/ *n* [C] 心电〔電〕图〔圖〕xīndiàntú. **elec·tro·cardio·graph** /-grɑːf/ *n* [C] 心电图描记器 xīndiàntú miáojìqì

elec·tro·cute /ɪ'lektrəkjuːt/ *vt* 用电〔電〕刑处〔處〕死 yòng diànxíng chùsǐ. **elec·tro'cu·tion** *n* [C, U]

elec·trode /ɪ'lektrəʊd/ *n* [C] 电〔電〕极〔極〕diànjí. ⇨ anode cathode.

elec·tro·en·cepha·lo·gram /ɪˌlektrəʊen'sefələgræm/ *n* [C] 脑〔腦〕电〔電〕图〔圖〕nǎodiàntú. **elec·tro·en·cepha·lo·graph** /-grɑːf/ *n* [C] 脑电图记录〔録〕器 nǎodiàntú jìlùqì

elec·tro·ly·sis /ɪˌlek'trɒləsɪs/ *n* [U] 电〔電〕解 diànjiě

elec·tro·lyze /ɪ'lektrəʊˌlaɪz/ *vt* 电解 diànjiě

elec·tro·mag·net /ɪˌlektrəʊ'mægnɪt/ *n* [C] 电〔電〕磁铁〔鐵〕diàncítiě. **elec·tro·mag·netic** /ɪˌlektrəʊˌmæg'netɪk/ *adj* 电磁的 diàncíde ～*ic radiation* 电磁辐〔輻〕射 diàncí fúshè **～ism** *n* [U]

elec·tron /ɪ'lektrɒn/ *n* [C] 电〔電〕子 diànzǐ. **elec·tronic** *adj* **(a)** 电子的 diànzǐde. **(b)** 用电子操纵〔縱〕的 yòng diànzǐ cāozòng de: ～*ic music* 电子音乐. ～ **data processing** *n* [U] (略作 **EDP**) 电子数〔數〕据〔據〕处〔處〕理 diànzǐ shùjù chùlǐ. ～ **gun** *n* [C] 电子枪〔槍〕diànzǐqiāng. **elec·tronics** *n* [与单数动词连用] 电子学〔學〕diànzǐxué.

elec·tro·plate /ɪ'lektrəʊpleɪt/ *vt* 电〔電〕镀 diàndù

el·egant /'elɪgənt/ *adj* 雅致的 yǎzhìde, 优〔優〕美的 yōuměide. **～ly** *adv* **el·egance** *n* [U]

el·ement /'elɪmənt/ *n* [C] **1** (科学)元素 yuánsù. **2** *in one's* ～ 处〔處〕于适〔適〕宜环〔環〕境之中 chùyú shìyí huánjìng zhı zhōng. *out of one's* ～处于不适宜环境之中 chùyú bú shìyí huánjìng zhī zhōng. **3** **the** ～**s** 大自然的力量(风, 雨等) dàzìránde lìliàng. **4** *pl* 原理 yuánlǐ; 基础〔礎〕jīchǔ. **5** 要素 yàosù, 特征〔徵〕tèzhēng: *Hard work is an important* ～ *in his life*. 他一生中的一个重要特征是努力工作. **6** 提示 tíshì; 迹象 jìxiàng; 少量 shǎoliàng: *There is an* ～ *of truth in his statement*. 他的陈述有些许真实. **7** 电〔電〕阻线〔線〕diànzǔxiàn. **～al** /-'mentl/ 大自然的力量的 dàzìránde lìliàng de.

ele·men·tary /ˌelɪ'mentərɪ/ *adj* 基本的 jīběnde, 初级的 chūjíde, 基础〔礎〕的 jīchǔde.

el·eph·ant /'elɪfənt/ *n* [C] 象 xiàng, 大象 dàxiàng. ⇨ white elephant.

el·ev·ate /'eliveɪt/ *vt* **1** 升高 shēnggāo, 抬起 táiqǐ. **2** 〔喻〕提高(思想等) tígāo.

el·ev·ation /ˌelɪ'veɪʃn/ *n* **1** [C, U] 提高 tígāo, 提升 tíshēng. **2** [C] 高度 gāodù, 海拔 hǎibá. **3** [C] (建筑物) 正视图〔圖〕zhèngshìtú ⇨ plan (1)

el·ev·ator /'elɪveɪtə(r)/ *n* [C] **1** 起卸机〔機〕qǐxièjī. **2** 〔美语〕电〔電

梯 diàntī.

eleven /ɪ'levn/ *adj n* [C] 十一 shíyī, 十一个〔個〕 shíyīgè. **eleventh** /ɪ'levnθ/ *adj n* [C] (略作 11th) 十一分之一 shíyīfēnzhīyī, 第十一 dìshíyī, 第十一个 dìshíyīgè.

elicit /ɪ'lɪsɪt/ *vt* 引出 yǐnchū, 诱出 yòuchū.

eligible/'elɪʤəbl/ *adj* ~ **(*for*)** 合格的hégéde;适〔適〕宜的 shìyíde, 符合要求的 fǔhé yāoqiú de. **el·igi'bil·ity** *n* [U]

elim·in·ate /ɪ'lɪmineit/ *vt* 消灭〔滅〕xiāomiè, 消除 xiāochú. ~ *mistake* 消灭错误; ~ *a possibility* 消除一种可能性. **e,lim·i'na·tion** *n* [U]

élite /eɪ'li:t/*n* [C] 社会〔會〕精华〔華〕shèhuì jīnghuá; 高贵者 gāoguìzhě.

elk /elk/ 麋 mí.

el·lipse /ɪ'lɪps/ *n* 椭圆 tuǒyuán. **el·lip·tic(al)** *adj*

elm /elm/ *n* [C] 榆 yú. [U] 榆木 yúmù.

elon·gate /'i:lɒŋgeit/ *vt/i* (使)伸长〔長〕 shēncháng, (使)拉长 lācháng, (使)延长 yáncháng.

elope /ɪ'ləʊp/ *vi* 逃走 táozǒu, 私奔 sībēn.

elo·quence /'eləkwəns/ *n* [U] 雄辩 xióngbiàn, 口才 kǒucái. **elo·quent** *adj*

else /els/ *adv* **1** 另外 lìngwài, 其他 qítā: *somebody* ~ 别人. **2** 否则 fǒuzé: *Run or* ~ *you'll be late.* 快跑, 否则你就晚了. **~where** /-'weə(r)/ *adv*. 在别处〔處〕 zài biéchù, 向别处 xiàng biéchù.

elude /ɪ'lu:d/ *vt* [正式用语]逃避 táobì, 躲避 duǒbì. **elu·sive** /ɪ'lu:sɪv/ *adj* 难〔難〕以捉摸的 nányǐ zhuōmó de, 难以理解的 nányǐ lǐjiě de, 难以记忆〔憶〕的 nányǐ jìyì de.

em·aci·ate /ɪ'meɪʃɪeɪt/ *vt* [正式用语]使消瘦 shǐ xiāoshòu: *children* ~*d by illness* 被疾病折磨得消瘦了的孩子们. **emaci'ation** *n* [U]

eman·ci·pate /ɪ'mænsɪpeɪt/ *vt* 解放 jiěfàng. **emanci'pa·tion** *n* [U]

em·balm /ɪm'bɑ:m/ *vt* 使(尸体)不腐 shǐ bùfǔ.

em·bank·ment /ɪm'bæŋkmənt/ *n* 堤岸 dī'àn; 路堤 lùdī.

em·bargo /ɪm'bɑ:gəʊ/ *n* [C] [*pl* -es] 禁止贸易令 jìnzhǐ màoyì lìng. □ [*pt pp* ~ed] 禁止贸易 jìnzhǐ màoyì.

em·bark /ɪm'bɑ:k/ **1** *vt/i* 上船 shàngchuán. **2** ~ ***on*** (或 ***upon***) 从〔從〕事 cóngshì; 开〔開〕始 kāishǐ. **~ation** /-'keɪʃən/ *n* [C, U]

em·bar·rass /ɪm'bærəs/ *vt* 使为〔爲〕难〔難〕 shǐ wéinán, 使尴〔尷〕尬 shǐ gāngà; 使难为情 shǐ nánwéiqíng: *feel* ~*ed about speaking in public* 在公共场合讲话感到难为情.

em·bassy /'embəsɪ/ *n* [C] [*pl* -ies] 大使馆 dàshǐguǎn.

em·bel·lish /ɪm'belɪʃ/ *vt* **1** 装〔裝〕饰 zhuāngshì: ~ *a dress with flowers* 用花装饰衣裳. **2** 添加细节〔節〕 tiānjiā xìjié: ~ *a story with comments* 在小说中增加议论. **~ment** *n* [C, U]

em·ber /'embə(r)/ *n* [C] [常用 *pl*] 余〔餘〕烬〔燼〕 yújìn.

em·bezzle /ɪm'bezl/ *vt* 盗用 dàoyòng, 贪污 tānwū. **~ment** *n* [C, U]

em·blem /'embləm/ *n* [C] 象征〔徵〕 xiàngzhēng, 标〔標〕志 biāozhì: *A dove is the* ~ *of peace.* 鸽子是和平的象征.

em·body /ɪm'bɒdɪ/ *vt* [*pt pp* -ied] [正式用语]体〔體〕现 tǐxiàn, 使具体化 shǐ jùtǐhuà. **em·bodi·ment** *n* [C] *He is the embodiment of goodness* 他是仁慈的化身.

em·boss /ɪm'bɒs/ *vt* 在…上浮雕图〔圖〕案 zài...shàng fúdiāo tú'àn.

em·brace /ɪm'breɪs/ *vt/i* **1** 拥〔擁〕抱 yōngbào. **2** [正式用语]利用 lìyòng, 抓住 zhuāzhù: ~ *an opportunity* 抓住机会. **3** 包含 bāohán, 包括 bāokuò: *A book embracing many subjects* 一本包括许多专题的书. □ *n* [C] 拥抱 yōngbào.

em·broider /ɪmbrɔɪdə(r)/ *vt/i* 绣〔繡〕花 xiùhuā, 刺绣 cìxiù. **em·broid·ery** *n* [U]

em·bryo /'embrɪəʊ/ *n* [C] [*pl* ~s] **1** 胚胎 pēitāi, 胚 pēi. **2** [喻]萌芽时〔時〕期 méngyá shíqī. **~nic** /ˌembri'ɒnɪk/ *adj*

emend /ɪ'mend/ *vt* 订正 dìngzhèng, 校勘 jiàokān, 修正 xiūzhèng, 校订 jiàodìng: ~ *a text* 校订正文.

em·er·ald /'emərəld/ *n* **1** [C] 绿宝〔寶〕石 lǜbǎoshí. **2** [U] 艳〔艷〕绿色 yànlǜsè.

emerge /ɪ'mɜ:ʤ/ *vi* **1** 出现 chūxiàn, 浮现 fúxiàn. **2** 暴露 bàolù. **emerg·ence** /-ʤəns/ *n* [U] 出现 chūxiàn. **emerg·ent** /-ʤənt/ *adj* 新出现的 xīn chūxiàn de, 发〔發〕展的 fāzhǎnde: *emergent nations* 新兴〔興〕国〔國〕家 xīnxīng guójiā.

emerg·ency /ɪ'mɜ:ʤənsɪ/ *n* [*pl* -ies] [C] 紧〔緊〕急情况 jǐnjí qíngkuàng, 突发〔發〕事件 tūfā shìjiàn.

em·ery /'emərɪ/ *n* [U] 金刚〔剛〕砂 jīngāngshā, 宝〔寶〕砂 bǎoshā.

emi·grant /'emɪgrənt/ *n* [C] 移民 yímín, 移居外国〔國〕的人 yíjū wàiguó de rén.

emi·grate /'emɪgreɪt/ *vi* 移居国〔國〕外 yíjū guówài. **emi'gra·tion** *n* [C, U]

emi·nent /'emɪnənt/ *adj* [正式用语]著名的 zhùmínde, 卓越的 zhuōyuède. **~ly** *adv* 高度地 gāodùde: *~ly qualified* 优异的. **emi·nence** *n* [U]

emir /e'mɪə(r)/ *n* [C] 阿拉伯王子 ālābó wángzǐ; 阿拉伯总〔總〕督 ālābó zǒngdū. **~ate** /'emərət/ *n* [C] 阿拉伯王子或总督的地位, 土地 ālābó wángzǐ huò zǒngdū de dìwèi, tǔdì.

emis·sion /ɪ'mɪʃn/ *n* **1** [U] 散发〔發〕sànfā, 发射 fāshè: *the ~ of gas* 气体的散发; *the ~ of light* 光的放射. **2** [C] 发射物 fāshèwù, 发出物 fāchūwù.

emit /ɪ'mɪt/ *vt* [-tt-] 散发〔發〕sànfā, 发射 fāshè: *~ light* 放射出光亮; *~ a cry* 发出喊叫.

emo·tion /ɪ'məʊʃn/ *n* **1** [U] 激动〔動〕jīdòng. **2** [C] 情绪 qíngxù; 情感 qínggǎn. **~al** *adj* **(a)** 激起情感的 jīqǐ qínggǎn de. 激动人心的 jīdòng rénxīnde: *an ~al speech* 激动人心的演说. **(b)** 易激动的 yì jīdòng de, 易动感情的 yì dòng gǎnqíng de. **~ally** *adv*

emot·ive /ɪ'məʊtɪv/ *adj* 激动情感的 jīdòng qínggǎn de.

em·peror /'empərə(r)/ *n* [C] 皇帝 huángdì.

em·pha·sis /'emfəsɪs/ *n* [C, U] [*pl* ~es] **1** 强语气〔氣〕qiángyǔqì; 强音qiángyīn. **2** 强调 qiángdiào.

em·pha·size /'emfəsaɪz/ *vt* 强调 qiángdiào, 加强…的语气 jiāqiáng …de yǔqì.

em·phatic /ɪm'fætɪk/ *adj* 强调的 qiángdiàode, 加强语气的 jiāqiáng yǔqì de.

em·pire /'empaɪə(r)/ *n* [C] 帝国〔國〕dìguó.

em·piri·cal /ɪm'pɪrɪkəl/ *adj* 经〔經〕验〔驗〕主义〔義〕的 jīngyànzhǔyìde.

em·ploy /ɪm'plɔɪ/ *vt* **1** 雇用 gùyòng. **2** [正式用语]使用 shǐyòng, 用 yòng: *~ new weapons in a war* 在战争中使用新式武器. **~er** 雇主 gùzhǔ. ˌ**~'ee** 雇工 gùgōng, 受雇者 shòugùzhě, 雇员 gùyuán. **~ment** *n* [U] **(a)** 雇用 gùyòng, 使用 shǐyòng. **(b)** 职〔職〕业〔業〕zhíyè.

em·press /'emprɪs/ *n* [C] 女皇 nǚhuáng; 皇后 huánghòu.

empty /'emptɪ/ *adj* [-ier, -iest] **1** 空的 kōngde. **2** 无〔無〕用的 wúyòngde: *~ promises* 无信用的许诺. □ *n* [C] [*pl* -ies]空桶 kōngtǒng; 空瓶 kōngpíng, 空箱 kōngxiāng.□ *vt/vi* [*pt, pp* -ied] (使)成为〔爲〕空的 chéngwéi kōngde. ˌ**~-'handed** *adj* 空手的 kōngshǒude, 一无〔無〕所获〔獲〕的 yìwúsuǒhuòde: *The thieves left ~-handed* 小偷什么也没有偷到. **emp·ti·ness** *n* [U]

emu /'i:mju:/ *n* [C] 鸸〔鴯〕鹋〔鶓〕érmiáo.

emu·late /'emjʊleɪt/ 同…竞〔競〕争 tóng…jìngzhēng, 努力 nǔlì; 超过〔過〕chāoguò. **emu'la·tion** *n* [U]

emul·sion /ɪ'mʌlʃn/ *n* [C, U] 乳浊〔濁〕液 rǔzhúyè.

en·able /ɪ'neɪbl/ *vt* 使能够 shǐ nénggòu: *His discovery ~d men to fly.* 他的发现使人类的飞行成为可能.

en·amel /ɪ'næml/ *n* [U] **1** 釉药 yòuyào, 珐琅 fǎláng, 搪瓷 tángcí. **2** 珐琅质〔質〕fǎlángzhì. □ *vt* [-ll- 美语亦作 -l-] 涂〔塗〕瓷釉于 … tú cíyòu yú ….

en·chant /ɪn'tʃɑ:nt/ *vt* **1** 使喜悦 shǐ xǐyuè, 使心醉 shǐ xīnzuì. **2** 施魔法于 shī mófǎ yú. **~ing** *adj* 迷人的 mírénde, 醉人的 zuìrénde. **~ment** *n* [C, U]

en·circle /ɪn'sɜ:kl/ *vt* 包围〔圍〕bāowéi, 环〔環〕绕〔繞〕huánrǎo.

encl. = enclosed 函内封入 hánnèi fēngrù.

en·close /ɪn'kləʊz/ *vt* **1** 把…围〔圍〕起来〔來〕bǎ…wéi qǐlái. **2** 把…封入(信封) bǎ … fēngrù. **en·clos·ure** /-ʒə(r)/ *n* [C, U]

en·core /'ɒŋkɔ:(r)/ *int* 再来〔來〕一个〔個〕! zài lái yígè! □ *n* [C] 重演 chóngyǎn; 重唱 chóngchàng.

en·coun·ter /ɪn'kaʊntə(r)/ *vt* 遇到 yùdào; 意外地遇到(朋友) yìwàide yùdào. □ *n* [C] 遭遇(敌人) zāoyù.

en·cour·age /ɪn'kʌrɪdʒ/ *vt* 鼓励〔勵〕gǔlì, 支持 zhīchí. **~ment** *n* [C, U]

en·croach /ɪn'krəʊtʃ/ *vi* 侵犯 qīnfàn, 侵占 qīnzhàn: *~ on his land* 侵占他的土地; *~ on his rights* 侵犯他的权利. **~ment** *n* [C, U]

en·cy·clo·pedia (also **-paedia**) /ɪnˌsaɪklə'pi:dɪə/ *n* [C] [*pl* ~s] 百科全书〔書〕bǎikēquánshū.

end /end/ *n* [C] **1** 末尾 mòwěi, 末端 mòduān, 尽〔盡〕头〔頭〕jìntóu: *make ~s 'meet* 量入为〔爲〕出 liàng rù wéi chū. *at a ˌloose '~* 不

知做什么好 bù zhī zuò shénme hǎo, 无〔無〕事可做 wúshì kě zuò. ***on*** **'～ (a)** 直立 zhílì, 竖〔竪〕着 shùzhe. **(b)** 连〔連〕续〔續〕地 liánxùde: *for hours on* ～ 连续几个小时. ***put an*** ～ ***to*** 停止 tíngzhǐ, 结束 jiésù. **2** 残〔殘〕余〔餘〕cányú: *a cigarette* ～ 香烟头. **3** 结束 jiésù. ***in the*** ～ 最后〔後〕zuìhòu, 终于 zhōngyú. **4** 死亡 sǐwáng. **5** 目的 mùdì, 目标〔標〕mùbiāo: *achieve one's* ～*(s)* 实现其目的. □ *vt/i* (使)结束 jiésù. ～ ***up*** 告终 gàozhōng, 结束 jiésù: *He* ～*ed up in Spain.* 他结果到了西班牙. **～ing** 词尾 cíwěi, 结尾 jiéwěi. 结局 jiéjú **～less** *adj* 无〔無〕止境的 wú zhǐjìng de, 无穷的 wúqióngde, 没完的 méiwánde. **～less·ly** *adv*

en·dan·ger /ɪn'deɪndʒə(r)/ *vt* 危及 wēijí, 危害 wēihài.

en·dear /ɪn'dɪə(r)/ *vt* 使受喜欢〔歡〕shǐ shòu xǐhuan. **～ment** *n* [C, U] 亲〔親〕爱〔愛〕的表示 qīn'ài de biǎoshì.

en·deav·our [美语 = **-vor**] /ɪn'devə(r)/ *n* [C][正式用语]努力 nǔlì: *make an* ～ *to win* 努力争取胜利. □ *vi* 努力 nǔlì, 力图〔圖〕lìtú.

en·demic /en'demɪk/ *n* [C] 地方性流行病 dìfāngxìng liúxíngbìng. *adj* (疾病)流行于某地方的 liúxíngyú mǒu dìfang de. ⇨ epidemic.

en·dorse /ɪn'dɔːs/ *vt* **1** 背签〔簽〕(支票) bèiqiān. **2** 赞同 zàntóng, 支持 zhīchí. **3** (驾驶员执照)被写〔寫〕上违〔違〕章记录〔録〕bèi xiěshàng wéizhāng jìlù. **～ment** *n* [C, U]

en·dow /ɪn'daʊ/ *vt* **1** 捐款 juānkuǎn, 资助 zīzhù. **2** ***be*** ～***ed with*** 有...的天赋 yǒu ... de tiānfù. **～ment** *n* [C, U]

en·dur·ance /ɪn'djʊərəns/ *n* [U] 忍耐力 rěnnàilì; 忍耐 rěnnài.

en·dure /ɪn'djʊə(r)/ *vt/i* **1** 忍耐 rěnnài, 忍受 rěnshòu. **2** 持久 chíjiǔ, 持续〔續〕chíxù: *fame that will* ～ *for ever* 永世长存的好名声. **en·dur·ing** *adj* 持久的 chíjiǔde, 不朽的 bùxiǔde.

en·emy /'enəmɪ/ *n* [C] [*pl* -ies] **1** 敌〔敵〕人 dírén. **2 the** ～ 敌军〔軍〕díjūn, 敌国〔國〕díguó.

en·er·getic /ˌenə'dʒetɪk/ *adj* 精力旺盛的 jīnglìwàngshèngde, 精力充沛的 jīnglìchōngpèide. **～ally** *adv*

en·ergy /'enədʒɪ/ *n* [*pl* -ies] **1** [U] 活力 huólì, 劲〔勁〕jìn. **2** [*pl*] (人的)精力 jīnglì, 能力 nénglì. **3** [U] 能 néng, 能量 néngliàng: *electrical* ～ 电能.

en·fold /ɪn'fəʊld/ *vt* 拥〔擁〕抱 yōngbào, 包 bāo.

en·force /ɪn'fɔːs/ *vt* **1** 强迫服从〔從〕qiángpò fúcóng, 实〔實〕施 shíshī: ～ *the law* 实施法律. **2** 加强 jiāqiáng; 坚〔堅〕持 jiānchí: ～ *an argument* 加强叙述一种论点. **～ment** *n* [U]

Eng. = **1** Engineer(ing). **2** England. **3** English.

en·gage /ɪn'geɪdʒ/ *vt/i* **1** 雇用 gùyòng, 聘 pìn: ～ *a servant* 雇用一名仆人. **2** ～ ***in*** (使)从事 cóngshì, (使)参〔參〕加 cānjiā. **3** 订婚 dìnghūn: *Tim and Susan are* ～*d.* 蒂姆同苏姗订了婚. **4** [正式用语] 吸引 xīyǐn: ～ *his attention* 吸引他的注意力. **5** 接合 jiēhé, 啮〔嚙〕合 nièhé. **en·gag·ing** *adj* 吸引人的 xīyǐnrénde, 迷人的 mírénde. **～ment** *n* [C] **(a)** 订婚 dìnghūn. **(b)** 约会〔會〕yuēhuì. **(c)** 交战〔戰〕jiāozhàn.

en·gine /'endʒɪn/ *n* [C] **1** 发〔發〕动〔動〕机〔機〕fādòngjī, 引擎 yǐnqíng. **2** 火车〔車〕头〔頭〕huǒchētóu. **'～-driver** 火车司机 huǒchē sījī.

en·gin·eer /ˌendʒɪ'nɪə(r)/ *n* [C] **1** 工程师〔師〕gōngchéngshī: *a civil* ～ 土木工程师; *an electrical* ～ 电气工程师. **2** 技工 jìgōng; 技师 jìshī. □ *vt/i* **1** 设计 shèjì; 建造 jiànzào; 指导〔導〕zhǐdǎo, 管理 guǎnlǐ. **2** [正式用语] 策划〔劃〕cèhuà: ～ *his defeat* 策划使他失败. **～ing** 工程 gōngchéng, 工程学〔學〕gōngchéngxué.

Eng·lish /'ɪŋglɪʃ/ *n* 英语 yīngyǔ. **the** ～ 英国〔國〕人 yīngguórén. □ *adj* 英国的 yīngguóde, 英语的 yīngyǔde. **E～ man** 英国人 yīngguórén. **E～ woman** 英国妇〔婦〕女 yīngguó fùnǚ.

en·grave /ɪn'greɪv/ *vt* **1** 刻上 kèshàng, 雕上 diāoshàng. **2** [喻]铭记 míngjì, 铭刻(于心) míngkè. **en·grav·ing** *n* [C, U]

en·gross /ɪn'grəʊs/ *vt* 占用(全部时间) zhànyòng, 吸引(注意力) xīyǐn: ～*ed in his book* 埋头读书.

en·gulf /ɪn'gʌlf/ *vt* 吞没 tūnmò: *The village was* ～*ed by the flood.* 村庄被洪水吞没.

enigma /ɪ'nɪgmə/ *n* [C] [*pl* ～s] 神秘的事物 shénmìde shìwù, 谜 mí. **～tic** /ˌenɪg'mætɪk/ *adj*

en·joy /ɪn'dʒɔɪ/ *vt* **1** 欣赏 xīnshǎng, 喜爱〔愛〕xǐ'ài. **2** 享受 xiǎngshòu, 享有 xiǎngyǒu: ～ *good* *health* 身体健康. **3 ~ *oneself*** 生活快乐〔樂〕 shēnghuó kuàilè. **~able** /-əbl/ *adj* **~ment** *n* [C, U]

en·large /ɪn'lɑːdʒ/ *vt/i* **1** 扩〔擴〕大 kuòdà, 放大 fàngdà: ~ *a photograph* 放大照片. **2 ~ *on*** (或 ***upon***) [正式用语]详述 xiángshù. **~ment** *n* [C, U]

en·lighten /ɪn'laɪtn/ *vt* 启〔啓〕发〔發〕 qǐfā, 开〔開〕导〔導〕 kāidǎo. **~ment** *n* [U]

en·list /ɪn'lɪst/ *vt/i* **1** 征〔徵〕募 zhēngmù, (使)服兵役 fú bīngyì. **2** [正式用语]谋取 móuqǔ, 罗〔羅〕致 luózhì: ~ *help* 谋取帮助. **~ment** *n* [C, U]

enor·mity /ɪ'nɔːmətɪ/ *n* [*pl* -ies] [正式用语] **1** [C, U] 穷〔窮〕凶极〔極〕恶〔惡〕 qióngxiōng jí'è, 无〔無〕法无天 wúfǎ wútiān. **2** [U] 庞〔龐〕大 pángdà, 巨大 jùdà.

enor·mous /ɪ'nɔːməs/ *adj* 庞〔龐〕大的 pángdàde, 巨大的 jùdàde. **~ly** *adv* 极大地 jídàde, 巨大地 jùdàde.

enough /ɪ'nʌf/ *adj, n, adv* 足够的 zúgòude, 充足的 chōngzúde; 足够 zúgòu, 充分 chōngfèn; 足够地 zúgòude 充分地 chōngfènde: ~ *money to buy a ticket* 够买一张票的钱; *run fast* ~ *to win* 跑得很快,能赢. *sure* ~ 果真 guǒzhēn.

en·quire, en·quiry ⇨ inquire, inquiry.

en·rich /ɪn'rɪtʃ/ *vt* 使丰〔豐〕富 shǐ fēngfù, 加料于 jiāliào yú, 增进〔進〕 zēngjìn: *soil ~ed with fertilizer* 施用了肥料的土壤. **~ment** *n* [C, U]

en·roll, en·rol /ɪn'rəʊl/ *vt/i* 招收 zhāoshōu, (使)入伍 rùwǔ, (使)入会〔會〕 rùhuì; (使) 入学〔學〕 rùxué, 注册 zhùcè. **~ment** *n* [C, U]

en·semble /ɑːn'sɑːmbl/ *n* [C] **1** 全体〔體〕 quántǐ, 总〔總〕体 zǒngtǐ. **2** 演唱组 yǎnchàngzǔ, 演奏组 yǎnzòuzǔ.

en·sign /'ensən/ *n* [C] **1** 军〔軍〕舰〔艦〕旗 jūnjiànqí. **2** 海军少尉 hǎijūn shàowèi.

en·slave /ɪn'sleɪv/ *vt* 奴役 núyì. **~ment** *n* [U]

en·sue /ɪn'sjuː/ *vi* 跟着发〔發〕生 gēnzhe fāshēng, 结果产〔產〕生 jiéguǒ chǎnshēng, 结果是 jiéguǒ shì: *in the ensuing battle* 在接着发生的战争中.

en·sure [美语 = **in·sure**] /ɪn'ʃʊə(r)/ *vt/i* **1** 保证〔證〕 bǎozhèng, 担〔擔〕保 dānbǎo. **2** 保护〔護〕 bǎohù. ~ *oneself against disappointment* 使自己免遭失望.

en·tail /ɪn'teɪl/ *vt* 使必需 shǐ bìxū: *Your plan ~s a lot of work.* 你的计划需要大量的工作.

en·tangle /ɪn'tæŋgl/ *vt* 缠〔纏〕住 chánzhù, 套住 tàozhù. **~ment** *n* [C, U]

en·ter /'entə(r)/ *vt/i* **1** 进〔進〕 jìn, 入 rù. **2** 加入 jiārù, 参〔參〕加 cānjiā: ~ *university* 进入大学. **3 ~ *into sth*** 开〔開〕始从〔從〕事 kāishǐ cóngshì: ~ *into a contract* 着手订约; ~ *into a discussion* 开始讨论. **4 ~*on*** (或 ***upon***) 开始 kāishǐ, 着手 zhāoshǒu. **5** 登录〔錄〕入册 dēnglù rùcè.

en·ter·prise /'entəpraɪz/ *n* **1** [C] (需要勇气的)艰〔艱〕巨的事业〔業〕 jiānjù de shìyè. **2** [U] 事业心 shìyèxīn, 进〔進〕取心 jìnqǔxīn. **3** [U] 商业企业 shāngyè qǐyè: *private* ~私人企业. **en·ter·pris·ing** *adj* 有进〔進〕取心的 yǒu jìnqǔxīn de, 有事业心的 yǒu shìyèxīn de.

en·ter·tain /ˌentə'teɪn/ *vt* **1** 招待 zhāodài, 款待 kuǎndài. **2** 使娱乐〔樂〕 shǐ yúlè, 使有兴〔興〕趣 shǐ yǒu xìngqǔ. **3** 怀〔懷〕有 huáiyǒu; 持有 chíyǒu, 准〔準〕备〔備〕考虑〔慮〕 zhǔnbèi kǎolǜ: ~ *ideas* 怀有主意; ~ *doubts* 心存疑虑. **~ing** *adj* 娱乐的 yúlède, 有趣的 yǒuqùde. **~er** 表演者 biǎoyǎnzhě. **~ment** *n* **(a)** [U] 招待 zhāodài, 款待 kuǎndài; 娱乐 yúlè. **(b)** [C] 表演 biǎoyǎn, 文娱节〔節〕目 wényù jiémù.

en·thral [美语亦作 **en·thrall**] /ɪn'θrɔːl/ *vt* [-ll-] 迷住 mízhù.

en·throne /ɪn'θrəʊn/ *vt* 使(国王)登位 shǐ dēngwèi.

en·thusi·asm /ɪn'θjuːzɪæzəm/ *n* [U] 热〔熱〕情 rèqíng, 热心 rèxīn; 积〔積〕极〔極〕性 jījíxìng. **en·thusi·ast** *n* [C] 热心人 rèxīnrén, 热情者 rèqíngzhě. **en·thusi·'astic** *adj* 热心的 rèxīnde, 热情的 rèqíngde. **en·thusi·asti·cally** /-klɪ/ *adv*

en·tice /ɪn'taɪs/ *vt* 诱惑 yòuhuò, 怂〔慫〕恿 sǒngyǒng: ~ *a girl away from home* 怂恿一个姑娘离家出逃. **~ment** *n* [C, U]

en·tire /ɪn'taɪə(r)/ *adj* 全部的 quánbùde, 完全的 wánquánde, 完整的 wánzhěngde. **~ly** *adv* **~ty** /-rətɪ/ *n* [U]

en·title /ɪn'taɪtl/ *vt* **1** 给(书)题名 gěi tímíng. **2** 给予…权〔權〕利 gěiyǔ ... quánlì. **~ment** *n* [U]

en·tity /'entətɪ/ *n* [*pl* -ies] [C, U] 存在 cúnzài, 实〔實〕体〔體〕 shítǐ.

en·trails /'entreɪlz/ *n pl* 肠〔腸〕 cháng.

en·trance¹ /'entrəns/ *n* **1** [C] 入口 rùkǒu, 门〔門〕口 ménkǒu. **2** [C, U] 进〔進〕入 jìnrù. **3** [C, U] 入场〔場〕 rùchǎng, 入学〔學〕 rùxué, 入港 rùgǎng.

en·trance² /ɪn'trɑːns/ *vt* 使入迷 shǐ rùmí, 使快乐〔樂〕 shǐ kuàilè: *~d with the music* 被音乐迷住了.

en·trant /'entrənt/ *n* [C] 刚〔剛〕就业〔業〕者 gāng jiùyè zhě; 参〔參〕加竞〔競〕赛者 cānjiā jìngsài zhě.

en·treat /ɪn'triːt/ *vt* 恳〔懇〕求 kěnqiú, 央求 yāngqiú. **en·treaty** *n* [C, U] [*pl* -ies] 恳求 kěnqiú.

en·trench /ɪn'trentʃ/ *vt* **1** 筑壕防守 zhùháo fángshǒu. **2** 牢固树〔樹〕立 láogù shùlì: *well ~ed beliefs* 牢固树立的信仰.

entre·pre·neur /ˌɑːntrəprə'nɜː(r)/ *n* [C] 企业〔業〕家 qǐyèjiā, 演出承包人 yǎnchū chéngbāorén.

en·trust /ɪn'trʌst/ *vt* [正式用语] 委托 wěituō, 托管 tuōguǎn.

en·try /'entrɪ/ *n* [C] [*pl* -ies] **1** 进〔進〕入 jìnrù: *Britain's ~ into the war.* 英国进入战争. **2** 入口 rùkǒu, 门〔門〕口 ménkǒu. **3** 条〔條〕目 tiáomù, 项目 xiàngmù, 词条 cítiáo: *dictionary entries* 词典词条.

enu·mer·ate /ɪ'njuːməreɪt/ *vt* 数〔數〕 shǔ, 点〔點〕 diǎn. **enu·me'r·ation** *n* [C, U]

enun·ci·ate /ɪ'nʌnsɪeɪt/ *vt/i* 发〔發〕音 fāyīn. **enun·ci'ation** *n* [U]

en·velop /en'veləp/ *vt* 包 bāo; 裹 guǒ; 封 fēng: *~ed in fog* 被雾遮蔽. **~ment** *n* [U]

en·vel·ope /'envələʊp/ *n* [C] 信封 xìnfēng.

en·vi·able /'envɪəbl/ *adj* 引起妒忌的 yǐnqǐ dùjì de.

en·vi·ous /'envɪəs/ *adj* 妒忌的 dùjìde. **~ly** *adv*

en·vi·ron·ment /ɪn'vaɪərənmənt/ *n* [C] 环〔環〕境 huánjìng.

en·vis·age /ɪn'vɪzɪdʒ/ *vt* 想象 xiǎngxiàng; 期望 qīwàng; 设想 shèxiǎng: *He had not ~d seeing her again.* 他没有期望再见到她.

en·voy /'envɔɪ/ *n* [C] **1** 使节〔節〕 shǐjié, 代表 dàibiǎo, 使者 shǐzhě. **2** (外交)公使 gōngshǐ.

envy /'envɪ/ *n* [U] **1** 妒忌 dùjì; 羡慕 xiànmù. **2** 妒忌的对〔對〕象 dùjìde duìxiàng; 羡慕的对象 xiànmùde duìxiàng: *His new house was the ~ of all his friends.* 所有他的朋友都羡慕他的新居. □ *vt* [*pt, pp* -ied] 妒忌 dùjì; 羡慕 xiànmù: *I don't ~ him his job.* 我不羡慕他的工作.

en·zyme /'enzaɪm/ *n* [C] 酶 méi.

ep·aulet (亦作 **ep·aul·ette**) /'epəlet/ *n* [C] 肩章 jiānzhāng.

ephem·er·al /ɪ'femərəl/ *adj* 短暂〔暫〕的 duǎnzànde.

epic /'epɪk/ *n* [C], *adj* **1** 史诗的 shǐshīde. **2** 宏大的 hóngdàde, 规模大的 guīmódàde, 场〔場〕面大的(影片) chǎngmiàndàde.

epi·demic /ˌepɪ'demɪk/ *n* [C] (疾病) 流行性的 liúxíngxìngde, 传〔傳〕染的 chuánrǎnde. ⇨ endemic.

epi·lepsy /'epɪlepsɪ/ *n* [U] 癫痫〔癇〕 diānxián, 羊痫疯〔瘋〕 yángxiánfēng. **epi'lep·tic** *adj, n* [C]

epi·logue[美语 = **-log**] /'epɪlɒg/ *n* [C] (书或剧本)结尾部分 jiéwěi bùfen, 尾声〔聲〕 wěishēng; 跋 bá.

epi·sode /'epɪsəʊd/ *n* [C] 一系列事件中的一个〔個〕事件 yíxìliè shìjiàn zhōng de yígè shìjiàn.

epi·taph /'epɪtɑːf/ *n* [C] 墓志铭 mùzhìmíng.

epi·thet /'epɪθet/ *n* [C] 表示性质〔質〕, 特征〔徵〕的形容词 biǎoshì xìngzhì, tèzhēng de xíngróngcí, 称〔稱〕号〔號〕 chēnghào.

epit·ome /ɪ'pɪtəmɪ/ *n* [C] 概括 gàikuò, 缩影 suōyǐng, 集中体〔體〕现 jízhōng tǐxiàn: *His wife is the ~ of beauty.* 他的妻子是美的集中体现. **epit·om·ize** /-aɪz/ *vt* 为〔爲〕…的缩影 wéi … de suōyǐng; 集中体现 jízhōng tǐxiàn.

ep·och /'iːpɒk/ *n* [C] 新纪元 xīnjìyuán, 新时〔時〕代 xīnshídài.

equal /'iːkwəl/ *adj* 相等的 xiāngděngde, 相同的 xiāngtóngde. □ *n* [C] 相等的事物 xiāngděngde shìwù, 匹敌〔敵〕者 pǐdízhě. □ *vt* [-ll- 美语亦作 -l-] 相等于 xiāngděngyú. **~ly** *adv* **~ity** /'kwɒlətɪ/ *n* [U] **~ize** /'iːkwəlaɪz/ *vt* 使相等 shǐ xiāngděng; 使平等 shǐ píngděng.

equate /ɪ'kweɪt/ *vt* 使相等 shǐ xiāngděng; 同等对〔對〕待 tóngděng duìdài.

equa·tion /ɪ'kweɪʒn/ *n* [C] 方程式 fāngchéngshì; 等式 děngshì.

equa·tor /ɪ'kweɪtə(r)/ *n* (常作 **the E~**) 赤道 chìdào. **~ial** /ˌekwə'tɔːrɪəl/ *adj*

eques·trian /ɪ'kwestrɪən/ *adj* 骑〔騎〕马〔馬〕的 qímǎde, 马术〔術〕的 mǎshùde.

equi·lib·rium /ˌi:kwɪ'lɪbrɪəm/ *n* [U] 平衡 pínghéng, 均衡 jūnhéng: *lose one's* ~ 失去平衡.
equi·nox /'i:kwɪnɒks/ *n* [C] (天文)昼〔晝〕夜平分时〔時〕zhòuyè píngfēnshí.
equip/ɪ'kwɪp/*vt* [-pp-]装〔裝〕备〔備〕zhuāngbèi, 配备 pèibèi. **~ment** **(a)** 装备 zhuāngbèi, 设备 shèbèi. **(b)** 装备品 zhuāngbèipǐn.
equi·table /'ekwɪtəbl/ *adj* 公正的 gōngzhèngde, 公平的 gōngpíngde: *an* ~ *judgement* 公正的判决. **equi·tably** *adv*
equity /'ekwətɪ/ *n* **1** [U] 公平 gōngpíng, 公道 gōngdào. **2** [*pl* -ies] 无〔無〕固定利息之股票 wú gùdìng lìxī zhī gǔpiào.
equiv·al·ent /ɪ'kwɪvələnt/ *adj, n* [C] 相等的 xiāngděngde; 相同的 xiāngtóngde.
equivo·cal /ɪ'kwɪvəkl/ *adj* 暧〔曖〕昧的 àimèide, 可疑的 kěyíde, 不明确〔確〕的 bù míngquè de: *an* ~ *answer* 不明确的回答.
E.R. = Elizabeth Regina (Queen Elizabeth II) 伊丽莎白二世女王 yīlìshābái èrshì nǚwáng.
era /'ɪərə/ n [C] 时〔時〕代 shídài, 年代 niándài: *the Roman* ~ 罗马时代.
eradi·cate /ɪ'rædɪkeɪt/ *vt* 根除 gēnchú, 消除 xiāochú: ~ *a disease* 消除疾病. **eradi'ca·tion** *n* [U]
erase /ɪ'reɪz/ *vt* 擦掉 cādiào, 抹掉 mǒdiào. **era·ser** 擦除器 cāchúqì; 橡皮 xiàngpí; 黑板擦 hēibǎncā.
erect /ɪ'rekt/ *vt* **1** 建立 jiànlì, 树〔樹〕立 shùlì: ~ *a tent* 搭帐篷, ~ *a statue* 立塑像.**2**使竖〔豎〕立 shǐ shùlì. □ *adj* 直立的 zhílìde, 竖直的 shùzhíde: *stand* ~ 直立. **erec·tion** /-ʃn/ *n* **(a)** [U] 直立 zhílì; 建立 jiànlì, 建造 jiànzào. **(b)** [C] 建筑物 jiànzhù wù. **~ly** *adv* 直立地 zhílìde. **~ness** *n* [U]
erode /ɪ'rəʊd/ *vt* 腐蚀 fǔshí, 侵蚀 qīnshí. **ero·sion** /-ʒn/ *n* [U]
erotic /ɪ'rɒtɪk/ *adj* 引起性爱〔愛〕的 yǐnqǐ xìng'ài de, 性爱的 xìng'àide.
err /ɜ:(r)/ *vi* 犯错误 fàncuòwù, 弄错 nòngcuò.
er·rand /'erənd/ *n* [C] **1** 差使(取物等) chāishi. **2** 差事 chāishì.
er·ratic /ɪ'rætɪk/ *adj* **1** (人)古怪的 gǔguàide, 反复〔復〕无〔無〕常的 fǎnfù wúcháng de. **2** 不稳定的 bù wěndìng de; 无规律的 wú guīlǜ de. **~ally** *adv*
er·ror /'erə(r)/ *n* **1** [C] 错误 cuòwù. **2** [U] 弄错 nòngcuò: *do it in* ~ 做错一事.
eru·dite /'eru:daɪt/ *adj* 〔正式用语〕有学〔學〕问〔問〕的 yǒu xuéwen de, 博学的 bóxuéde.
erupt /ɪ'rʌpt/ *vi* 喷发〔發〕pēnfā, 喷出 pēnchū, 爆发 bàofā: *The volcano* ~*ed.* 火山爆发. **erup·tion** /-ʃn/ *n* [C]
es·ca·late /'eskəleɪt/ *vt/i* 升级 shēngjí, 逐步发〔發〕展 zhúbù fāzhǎn. **es·ca'la·tion** *n* [U]
es·ca·la·tor /'eskəleɪtə(r)/ *n* [C] 自动〔動〕楼〔樓〕梯 zìdòng lóutī.
es·ca·pade /'eskəpeɪd/ *n* [C] 越轨〔軌〕行为〔爲〕yuèguǐ xíngwéi.
es·cape /ɪ'skeɪp/ *vt/i* **1** 逃跑 táopǎo, 逃脱 táotuō, 逃亡 táowáng; 漏出 lòuchū, 流出 liúchū. **2** 逃避 táobì, 避免 bìmiǎn: ~ *punishment* 逃避惩罚. **3** 被忘记 bèi wàngjì: *His name* ~*s me.* 我忘记了他的名字. □ *n* **1** [C, U] 逃跑 táopǎo, 逃脱 táotuō. **2** [C] 逸出 yìchū, 漏出 lòuchū. **es·cap·ism** *n* [U] 逃避现实〔實〕táobì xiànshí. **es·cap·ist** 逃避现实的人 táobì xiànshí de rén.
es·carp·ment /ɪ'skɑ:pmənt/ *n* [C] 急斜面 jíxiémiàn; 悬〔懸〕崖 xuányá.
es·cort[1] /'eskɔ:t/ *n* [C] **1** 护〔護〕卫〔衛〕者 hùwèizhě, 护送者 hùsòngzhě. **2** 护航舰〔艦〕hùhángjiàn, 护航机〔機〕hùhángjī.
es·cort[2] /ɪ'skɔ:t/ *vt* 护〔護〕送 hùsòng; 护卫〔衛〕hùwèi.
eso·teric /ˌesəʊ'terɪk/ *adj* 奥秘的 àomìde, 深奥的 shēn'àode.
es·pec·ially /ɪ'speʃəlɪ/ *adv* 特别 tèbié, 尤其 yóuqí, 主要 zhǔyào.
espion·age /'espɪənɑ:ʒ/ *n* [U] 间〔間〕谍活动〔動〕jiàndié huódòng.
Es·quire /ɪ'skwaɪə(r)/ *n* [C] (略作 *Esq.*) 先生(正式函件中的称谓) xiānsheng.
es·say /'eseɪ/ *n* [C] 文章 wénzhāng; 小品文 xiǎopǐnwén; 随笔 suíbǐ. **~ist** 小品文作家 xiǎopǐnwén zuòjiā; 随笔作家 suíbǐ zuòjiā.
es·sence /'esns/ *n* **1** [U] 本质〔質〕běnzhì, 实〔實〕质 shízhì. **2** [C, U] 香精 xiāngjīng; 香料 xiāngliào.
es·sen·tial /ɪ'senʃl/ *adj* 本质〔質〕的 běnzhìde, 基本的 jīběnde; 必要的 bìyàode, 必不可少的 bìbùkěshǎode: *an* ~ *piece of machinery* 机器的主要部件. *Food is* ~ *to life.* 食物对于生命是必不可少的. □ *n* [C] 本质 běnzhì, 要素 yàosù. **~ly** *adv* 基本上 jīběnshàng, 本

质上 běnzhìshàng: *He is ~ly good.* 他本质上是好的.

es·tab·lish /ɪ'stæblɪʃ/ *vt* **1** 建立 jiànlì, 确〔確〕立 quèlì: *a well-~ed business* 信誉卓著的企业. **2** 委任 wěirèn, 安置 ānzhì, 使定居 shǐ dìngjū. **3** 证〔證〕实〔實〕 zhèngshí, 使被接受 shǐ bèi jiēshòu: ~ *the facts* 证明事实; ~ *a claim* 证实一项对某物的权利. **~ment** *n* **(a)** [U] 建立 jiànlì, 设立 shèlì. **(b)** [C] 建立的机〔機〕构〔構〕jiànlìde jīgòu, 公司 gōngsī, 企业〔業〕qǐyè.

es·tate /ɪ'steɪt/ *n* **1** [C] 房地产〔產〕fángdìchǎn. ⇨ housing, industrial. **2** [U] 〔法律〕财产 cáichǎn, 产业〔業〕chǎnyè. ⇨ real estate. ~ **agent** 房地产经〔經〕纪人 fángdìchǎn jīngjìrén. ~ **car** 客货两用轿〔轎〕车〔車〕kè huò liǎngyòng jiàochē.

es·teem /ɪ'sti:m/ *n* 〔正式用语〕[U] 尊重 zūnzhòng, 尊敬 zūnjìng: *hold him in great* ~ 非常尊重他. □ *vt*〔正式用语〕尊敬 zūnjìng, 尊重 zūnzhòng.

es·ti·mate[1] /'estɪmət/ *n* [C] 估计 gūjì, 估量 gūliàng, 估价〔價〕gūjià.

es·ti·mate[2] /'estɪmeɪt/ *vt/i* 评价〔價〕píngjià, 估计 gūjì, 估量 gūliàng. **es·ti'ma·tion** *n* [U] 评价 píngjià, 估计 gūjì.

es·tu·ary /'estʃʊərɪ/ *n* [C] [*pl* -ies] 河口湾〔灣〕hékǒuwān, 江口湾 jiāngkǒuwān.

et cet·era /ɪt 'setərə/ 〔拉丁文〕(略作 etc.) 等等 děngděng.

etch /etʃ/ *vt/i* 蚀刻 shíkè. **~ing** *n* [U] 蚀刻法 shíkèfǎ, [C] 蚀刻画〔畫〕shíkè huà.

eter·nal /ɪ'tɜ:nl/ *adj* **1** 永久的 yǒngjiǔde, 永存的 yǒngcúnde, 不朽的 bùxiǔde. **2**〔非正式用语〕不停的 bùtíngde. ~ *arguments* 无休止的争辩. **~ly** *adv*

eter·nity /ɪ'tɜ:nətɪ/ *n* [*pl* -ies] [U] 永恒 yǒnghéng, 无〔無〕穷〔窮〕wúqióng; 来〔來〕生 láishēng.

ether /'i:θə(r)/ *n* [U] 醚 mí; 乙醚 yǐmí.

ethic /'eθɪk/ *n* 伦〔倫〕理 lúnlǐ: *the Christian* ~ 基督教伦理. **~al** *adj* **(a)** 伦理学〔學〕的 lúnlǐxuéde. **(b)** 合乎道德的 héhū dàodéde. **~ally** *adv* **eth·ics** *n* [U] **(a)** 伦理学 lúnlǐxué. **(b)** *pl* 美德 měidé.

eth·nic /'eθnɪk/ *adj* 种〔種〕族的 zhǒngzúde, 人种学〔學〕的 rénzhǒngxuéde. **~ally** *adv*

eti·quette /'etɪket/ *n* [U] 礼〔禮〕节〔節〕lǐjié, 礼仪〔儀〕lǐyí.

ety·mol·ogy /ˌetɪ'mɒlədʒɪ/ *n* **1** [U] 词源学〔學〕cíyuánxué. **2** [C] 词源 cíyuán.

euca·lyptus /ˌju:kə'lɪptəs/ *n* [C] [*pl* ~es] 桉树〔樹〕ānshù.

eu·phem·ism /'ju:fəmɪzəm/ *n* [C, U] 委婉法 wěiwǎnfǎ, 婉言法 wǎnyánfǎ. **eu·phe'm·is·tic** *adj* 委婉的 wěiwǎnde, 婉言的 wǎnyánde.

eu·phoria /ju:'fɔ:rɪə/ *n* [U] 异〔異〕常欣快 yìcháng xīnkuài. **euphoric** /ju:'fɒrɪk/ *adj*

eu·tha·nasia /ˌju:θə'neɪzɪə/ *n* [U] 无〔無〕痛苦致死术〔術〕(为结束不治之症患者的痛苦) wú tòngkǔ zhìsǐ shù.

evacu·ate /ɪ'vækjʊeɪt/ *vt* **1** 撤离〔離〕chèlí, 疏散 shūsàn. **2** 排清(肠子等) páiqīng. **evacu·'ation** *n* [C, U]

evade /ɪ'veɪd/ *vt* **1** 躲避 duǒbì, 逃避 táobì. **2** 回避 huíbì, 规避 guībì: ~ *income tax* 逃避所得税, ~ *a question* 回避问题. **evas·ion** /-ʒn/ *n* [C, U] **evas·ive** /-sɪv/ *adj*

evalu·ate /ɪ'væljʊeɪt/ *vt* 估…的价〔價〕gū ... de jià, 定…的值 dìng ... de zhí. **evalu'ation** *n* [C, U]

evan·gelic /ˌi:væn'dʒelɪk/, **~al** /-kl/ *adj* 福音的 fúyīnde, 合乎福音的 héhū fúyīn de.

evan·gel·ist /ɪ'vændʒəlɪst/ *n* [C] **1** 福音作者之一 fúyīn zuòzhě zhī yī. **2** 福音传〔傳〕道者 fúyīn chuándào zhě. **~ic** /-'lɪstɪk/ *adj*

evap·or·ate /ɪ'væpəreɪt/ *vt/i* **1** 使蒸发〔發〕shǐ zhēngfā. **2** 使脱水 shǐ tuōshuǐ: ~*d milk* 炼〔煉〕乳. **3** 消失 xiāoshī, 失踪 shīzōng. **evap·o'r·ation** *n* [U]

eve /i:v/ *n* [C] (节日)前夕 qiánxī, 前夜 qián'yè: *on the ~ of war* 战争的前夕.

even[1] /'i:vn/ *adj* **1** 平的 píngde; 平滑的 pínghuáde; 平坦的 píngtǎnde: *an ~ surface* 平坦的表面. **2** 一致的 yízhìde, 同样〔樣〕的 tóngyàngde. ***break*** ~〔非正式用语〕不盈不亏〔虧〕bùyíng bùkuī. **3** 双〔雙〕数〔數〕的 shuāngshùde. **4** 均等的 jūnděngde, 对〔對〕等的 duìděngde: *The two teams are very* ~. 这两个队旗鼓相当. **5** 心平气〔氣〕和的 xīnpíng qìhé de. □ *vt* ~ **(up)** 使平坦 shǐ píngtǎn; 使相等 shǐ xiāngděng. **~ly** *adv* **~ness** *n* [U]

even[2] /'i:vn/ *adv* **1** 甚至…(也) shènzhì ..., 连〔連〕…都 lián ... dōu: *He never ~ opened the letter.*

他甚至没有把信拆开（因此他肯定没有看信）. **2** ~ *if* (或 *though*) 即使 jìshǐ, 纵〔縱〕使 zòngshǐ: *She won't ask*, ~ *though she needs help*. 即使她需要帮助,她也不会求人的. **3** 甚至(比…)还 shènzhì hái: *You know* ~ *less than I do*. 你甚至比我知道得还少. **4** ~ *now* 即使情况如此 jìshǐ qíngkuàng rúcǐ, 即使现在 jìshǐ xiànzài, ~ *then* 即使情况那样〔樣〕jìshǐ qíngkuàng nàyàng, 即使那时〔時〕jìshǐ nàshí: *E~ now he won't believe me*. 即使现在他也不相信我.

even·ing /ˈiːvnɪŋ/ *n* [C] 晚上 wǎnshàng, 傍晚 bàngwǎn, 黄昏 huánghūn. ~ *dress* 夜礼〔禮〕服 yèlǐfú.

event /ɪˈvent/ *n* [C] **1** 事件 shìjiàn, 事变〔變〕shìbiàn; 大事 dàshì. **2** *in the* ~ *of* 倘若 tǎngruò, 万〔萬〕一 wànyī. *in that* ~ 如果那样〔樣〕rúguǒ nàyàng. **3** (运动会等)比赛项目 bǐsài xiàngmù. ~**ful** *adj*

event·ual /ɪˈventʃʊəl/ *adj* 最后的 zuìhòude, 结果的 jiéguǒde. ~**ly** /-tʃʊəlɪ/ *adv* 最后〔後〕zuìhòu, 终于 zhōngyú: *He fell ill and* ~*ly died*. 他得了病,最后去世了. ~**ity** /-ˈæləti/ *n* [C] [*pl* -ies] 可能发〔發〕生的事 kěnéng fāshēng de shì.

ever /evə(r)/ *adv* **1** 在任何时〔時〕候 zài rènhé shíhòu: *Nothing* ~ *happens here*. 这里平静无事. *Have you* ~ *been in an aeroplane?* 你乘过飞机吗? **2** 不断〔斷〕地 búduànde: *for* ~ (*and* ~) 永远. **3** 究竟 jiūjìng, 到底 dàodǐ: *What* ~ *do you mean?* 你到底是什么意思?

ever·green /ˈevəgriːn/ *n* [C], *adj* 常绿的 chánglǜde. ⇨ deciduous.

ever·last·ing /ˌevəˈlɑːstɪŋ/ *adj* 永久的 yǒngjiǔde, 永恒的 yǒnghéngde.

every /ˈevrɪ/ *adj* **1** 所有的 suǒyǒude, 全部的 quánbùde: ~ *book* (= all the books) *on that shelf* 那个书架上的所有的书. **2** 每一的 měiyīde, 每个〔個〕的 měigède: ~ *day* 每天. **3** 一切可能的 yíqiè kěnéng de; 充分的 chōngfènde: *You have* ~ *reason to be satisfied*. 你有充分的理由感到满足. **4** 每隔…的 měigé … de, 每…中的 měi … zhōng de: ~ *ten minutes* 每隔十分钟. ~**body,** ~**one** *pron* 每个人 měigèrén. ~**day** *adj* 日常的 rìchángde, 普通的 pǔtōngde. ~**thing** *pron* 每件事 měijiànshì, 事事 shìshì. ~**where** *adv* 到处〔處〕dàochù.

evict /ɪˈvɪkt/ *vt* 驱〔驅〕逐 qūzhú. **evic·tion** /-ʃn/ *n* [C, U]

evi·dence /ˈevɪdəns/ *n* **1** [U] 证〔證〕明 zhèngmíng, 证据〔據〕zhèngjù: ~ *of his guilt* 他犯罪的证据, ~ *of his innocence* 他无罪的证据. **2** 证明 zhèngmíng, 证据 zhèngjù; 证词 zhèngcí: *give* ~ 提供证据,作证.

evi·dent /ˈevɪdənt/ *adj* 明白的 míngbaide, 显〔顯〕然的 xiǎnránde, 明显的 míngxiǎnde. ~**ly** *adv*

evil /ˈiːvl/ *adj* 坏〔壞〕的 huàide, 邪恶〔惡〕的 xié'ède, 有害的 yǒuhàide. □ *n* [C, U] -**ly** *adv*

evoca·tive /ɪˈvɒkətɪv/ *adj* 引起…的 yǐnqǐ … de, 唤起…的 huànqǐ … de: ~ *words* 勾起往日之情的言语.

evoke /ɪˈvəʊk/ *vt* 引起 yǐnqǐ, 唤起 huànqǐ: *stories that* ~ *happy memories* 唤起愉快的记忆的故事.

evol·ution /ˌiːvəˈluːʃn/ *n* **1** [U] 演变〔變〕yǎnbiàn, 进〔進〕展 jìnzhǎn, 发〔發〕展 fāzhǎn, 渐〔漸〕进 jiànjìn. **2** [U] 进化 jìnhuà.

evolve /ɪˈvɒlv/ *vt/i* (使)发〔發〕展 fāzhǎn.

ewe /juː/ *n* [C] 母羊 mǔyáng. ⇨ ram(1).

exact[1] /ɪgˈzækt/ *adj* **1** 正确〔確〕的 zhèngquède; 确切的 quèqiède: *the* ~ *size of the room* 房间的确切面积. **2** 精确的 jīngquède: *the* ~ *time* 精确的时间. ~**ly** *adv* **(a)** 精确地 jīngquède; 完全地 wánquánde: ~*ly right* 完全正确. **(b)** (用于回答)确实〔實〕如此 quèshí rúcǐ, 一点〔點〕不错 yìdiǎn búcuò. ~**ness** *n* [U]

exact[2] /ɪgˈzækt/ *vt* 强求 qiángqiú, 坚〔堅〕持 jiānchí: ~ *obedience* 强求服从. ~**ing** *adj* 苛求的 kēqiúde, 严〔嚴〕格的 yángéde.

exag·ger·ate /ɪgˈzædʒəreɪt/ *vt/i* 夸〔誇〕大 kuādà, 夸张〔張〕kuāzhāng. **exag·ge'r·ation** *n* [C, U]

exam /ɪgˈzæm/ *n* 考试 kǎoshì. (examination 的缩略)

exam·in·ation /ɪgˌzæmɪˈneɪʃn/ *n* [C, U] **1** [U] 检〔檢〕查 jiǎnchá. **2** [C] 考试 kǎoshì. **3** 诊查 zhěnchá: *a medical* ~ 体格检查. **4** 审〔審〕问〔問〕shěnwèn.

exam·ine /ɪgˈzæmɪn/ *vt* **1** 检〔檢〕查 jiǎnchá. **2** 审〔審〕查 shěnchá, 查问 cháwèn. **exam·iner** 检查人 jiǎncharén, 主考人 zhǔkǎorén.

example /ɪgˈzɑːmpl/ *n* [C] **1** 例子 lìzi, 例证〔證〕lìzhèng. *for* ~ 例如 lìrú, 举〔舉〕例来〔來〕说 jǔlì láishuō: *Many people, Peter for* ~, *went home*. 许多人,例如彼得,回

家了. **2** 样〔樣〕本 yàngběn, 范〔範〕例 fànlì: *an ~ of his work.* 他的作品的样本. **3** 榜样 bǎngyàng, 模样 móyàng: *follow my ~* 模仿我的样子. ***make an ~ of sb.*** 拿…开〔開〕刀 ná...kāidāo.

exas·per·ate /ɪg'zɑ:spəreɪt/ *vt* 激怒 jīnù, 使恼〔惱〕火 shǐ nǎohuǒ. **exas·pe'ration** *n* [U]

ex·ca·vate /'ekskəveɪt/ *vt* 挖掘 wājué, 挖出 wāchū. **ex·ca'vation** *n* [C, U] **ex·ca·va·tor** 发〔發〕掘者 fājuézhě; 挖土机〔機〕 wātǔjī; 电〔電〕铲〔鏟〕 diànchǎn.

ex·ceed /ɪk'si:d/ *vt* **1** 比…大 bǐ ... dà, 大于 dàyú. **2** 超出(规定) chāochū: *~ a speed limit* 超出规定的最高速度. **~ing·ly** *adv* 极〔極〕端地 jíduānde, 非常 fēicháng.

ex·cel /ɪk'sel/ *vt/i* [-ll-] 杰〔傑〕出 jiéchū, 胜〔勝〕过〔過〕 shèngguò, 优〔優〕于 yōuyú: *He ~s at sport.* 他擅长体育运动.

ex·cel·lence /'eksələns/ *n* [U] 优〔優〕秀 yōuxiù, 卓越 zhuōyuè.

Ex·cel·lency /'eksələnsɪ/ *n* [C] [*pl* -ies] 阁〔閣〕下 géxià.

ex·cel·lent /'eksələnt/ *adj* 优〔優〕秀的 yōuxiùde, 杰〔傑〕出的 jiéchūde. **~ly** *adv*

ex·cept /ɪk'sept/ *prep* **1** 除…之外 chú ... zhīwài: *Everybody was late ~ me.* 除了我,全都迟到了. **2** *~ that* 除了 chúle: *I would go ~ that it's late.* 要是不晚,我会去的. □ *vt* 除去 chúqù, 除掉 chúdiào.

ex·cep·tion /ɪk'sepʃn/ *n* **1** [C] 除外 chúwài. **2** [C] 例外 lìwài. **3** *take ~ to* 反对〔對〕 fǎnduì. **~al** /-ʃənl/ *adj* 异〔異〕常的 yìchángde, 优〔優〕越的 yōuyuède. **~ally** *adv*

ex·cerpt /'eksɜ:pt/ *n* [C] 摘录〔録〕 zhāilù, 节〔節〕录 jiélù.

ex·cess /ɪk'ses/ *n* **1** [U] 超越 chāoyuè, 超过〔過〕 chāoguò; 超过量 chāoguòliàng. ***in ~ of*** 超过 chāoguò. **2** [*pl*] 暴行 bàoxíng. □ *adj* /'ekses/ 额外的 éwàide, 附加的 fùjiāde: *~ baggage* 超重行李. **~ive** *adj* 过多的 guòduōde, 过份的 guòfènde. **~ly** *adv*

ex·change /ɪks'tʃeɪndʒ/ *vt/i* 交换 jiāohuàn, 兑换 duìhuàn: *~ pounds for dollars* 以英镑兑换美元. □ *n* **1** [C, U] 交换 jiāohuàn, 互换 hùhuàn; 交易 jiāoyì. **2** [U] 兑换 duìhuàn, 兑换率 duìhuànlǜ. **~able** /-əbl/ *adj*

ex·chequer /ɪks'tʃekə(r)/ *n* [C] **1** *the E~* (英国)财政部 cáizhèngbù: *Chancellor of the ~* 英国财政大臣 **2** 金库 jīnkù.

ex·cise /'eksaɪz/ *n* [U] 国〔國〕内货物税 guónèi huòwùshuì.

ex·cite /ɪk'saɪt/ *vt* **1** 刺激 cìjī, 使激动〔動〕 shǐ jīdòng: *~d by the news* 被这个消息所激动. **2** 引起 yǐnqǐ, 激发〔發〕 jīfā: *~ envy* 引起忌妒, *~ a riot* 激起骚动. **ex·cit·able** /-əbl/ *adj* 易激动〔動〕的 yì jīdòng de, 易兴〔興〕奋〔奮〕的 yì xìngfèn de. **~ment** *n* [C, U]

ex·claim /ɪk'skleɪm/ *vt/i* 呼叫 hūjiào, 呼喊 hūhǎn, 惊〔驚〕叫 jīngjiào. **,ex·cla·mation** /,ekskləˈmeɪʃn/ *n* [C, U] **excla'mation mark** 惊叹〔嘆〕号〔號〕 jīngtànhào.

ex·clude /ɪk'sklu:d/ *vt* **1** 把某人排除在外 bǎ mǒurén páichú zàiwài. **2** 排除(可能性等) páichú: *~ the possibility of failure* 排除了失败的可能性. **ex·clu·sion** /-ʒn/ *n* [U] **ex·clus·ive** /-sɪv/ *adj* **(a)** 孤傲的 gū'àode, 孤僻的 gūpìde. **(b)** (团体) 不愿〔願〕吸收新会〔會〕员的 bú yuàn xīshōu xīnhuìyuán de. **(c)** (商店) 索价〔價〕高昂的 suǒjià gāo'áng de. **ex·clus·ive·ly** *adv*

ex·com·muni·cate /,ekskə'mju:nɪkeɪt/ *vt* 开〔開〕除…的教籍 kāichú ... de jiàojí, 逐出教门〔門〕 zhúchū jiàomén. **ex·com·muni'cation** *n* [C, U]

ex·cre·ment /'ekskrəmənt/ *n* [U] 粪便 fènbiàn.

ex·crete /ɪk'skri:t/ *vt* 排泄 páixiè.

ex·cru·ciat·ing /ɪk'skru:ʃɪeɪtɪŋ/ *adj* 极〔極〕痛苦的 jí tòngkǔ de, 难〔難〕忍受的 nán rěnshòu de. **~ly** *adv*

ex·cur·sion /ɪk'skɜ:ʃn/ *n* [C] 远足 yuǎnzú, 短途旅行 duǎntú lǚxíng.

ex·cuse[1] /ɪk'skju:s/ *n* [C] 借口 jièkǒu; 理由 lǐyóu.

ex·cuse[2] /ɪk'skju:z/ *vt* **1** 原谅 yuánliàng. **2** 给…免去 gěi ...miǎnqù. **3** 为…辩解 wèi ... biànjiě: *Nothing can ~ such rudeness.* 无法为这种粗鲁行为辩解. **4** ***E~ me*** 对〔對〕不起(客套话) duìbùqǐ. **ex·cus·able** /-əbl/ *adj*

ex·ecute /'eksɪkju:t/ *vt* **1** 实〔實〕行 shíxíng; 贯彻 guànchè. **2** 实施 shíshī, 使生效 shǐ shēngxiào: *~ a will* 执行遗嘱. **3** 处〔處〕死 chùsǐ, 执〔執〕行死刑 zhíxíng sǐxíng. **4** 演奏 yǎnzòu: *~ a piece of music* 演奏一首乐曲. **ex·e'cu·tion** *n* **(a)** [U] 演奏技巧 yǎnzòu jìqiǎo. **(b)** [C, U] 死刑 sǐxíng. **ex·ecu·tioner**

刽[劊]子手 guìzishǒu, 死刑执行人 sǐxíng zhíxíngrén.

ex·ecu·tive /ɪg'zekjʊtɪv/ *adj* **1** 执[執]行的 zhíxíngde, 实[實]行的 shíxíngde: ~ *duties* 管理职责。**2** 行政的 xíngzhèngde: *the* ~ *head of state* 国家的行政首脑. □ *n* [C] **1 the E~** 政府的行政部门 zhèngfǔde xíngzhèng bùmén. **2** 行政人员 xíngzhèng rényuán.

ex·ecu·tor /ɪg'zekjʊtə(r)/ *n* [C] 指定的遗嘱执行人 zhǐdìngde yízhǔ zhíxíngrén.

ex·emp·lify /ɪg'zemplɪfaɪ/ *vt* [*pt, pp* -ied] 举[舉]例说明 jǔlì shuōmíng, 作为[爲]...的例证[證] zuòwéi ... de lìzhèng. **ex·emp·lifi·ca·tion** /-fɪ'keɪʃn/ *n* [C,U]

ex·empt /ɪg'zempt/ *vt* 免除 miǎnchú, 豁免 huòmiǎn. □ *adj* 被免除的 bèi miǎnchú de, 被豁免的 bèi huòmiǎn de. *goods* ~ *of tax* 免税货物. **exemp·tion** /-ʃn/ *n* [C, U]

ex·er·cise /'eksəsaɪz/ *n* **1** [U] 行使 xíngshǐ, 运[運]用 yùnyòng, 实[實]行 shíxíng, 运动[動] yùndòng: *Walking is good* ~ 散步是一种好的运动. *the* ~ *of patience* 耐性的发挥. **2** [C] 训练[練] xùnliàn. □ *vt/i* **1** 锻炼[煉] duànliàn, 训练 xùnliàn: ~ *oneself* 锻炼自己, ~ *a horse* 训练马. **2** 利用 lìyòng, 行使 xíngshǐ: ~ *a right* 行使权力.

exert /ɪg'zɜːt/ *vt* **1** 发[發]挥[揮] fāhuī; 行使 xíngshǐ: ~ *all one's energy* 发挥其全部精力. **2** 尽[盡]力 jìnlì. **exer·tion** /-ʃn/ *n* [C, U]

ex·hale /eks'heɪl/ *vt/i* **1** 呼气[氣] hūqì. **2** 散发[發]气体[體] sànfā qìtǐ. **ex·ha·la·tion** /,ekshə'leɪʃn/ *n* [C, U]

ex·haust[1] /ɪg'zɔːst/ *n* [C, U] 排气[氣] páiqì: *the* ~*-pipe on a motor-car* 汽车排气管.

ex·haust[2] /ɪg'zɔːst/ *vt* 抽完 chōuwán, 汲光 jíguāng. **ex·haus·tion** /-tʃən/ *n* [U] **~ive** *adj* 彻[徹]底的 chèdǐde.

ex·hi·bit /ɪg'zɪbɪt/ *n* [C] **1** 展览[覽] zhǎnlǎn, 陈列 chénliè, 展出 zhǎnchū. **2** [法律] 正式提交证[證]据[據] zhèngshì tíjiāo zhèngjù. □ *vt* **1** 展出 zhǎnchū, 陈列 chénliè, 铺陈 pūchén. **2** 显[顯]示 xiǎnshì, 呈现 chéngxiàn.

ex·hi·bi·tion /,eksɪ'bɪʃn/ *n* [C] **1** 展览[覽]会[會] zhǎnlǎnhuì; 陈列品 chénlièpǐn, 展览品 zhǎnlǎnpǐn. **2** 显[顯]示 xiǎnshì; 展览 zhǎnlǎn; 表演 biǎoyǎn: *an* ~ *of good behaviour* 品行端正的表现. **~ism** *n* [U] 出风[風]头[頭] chūfēngtou; 风头主义[義] fēngtóuzhǔyì. **~ist** 好出风头的人 hào chū fēngtou de rén.

ex·hil·ar·ate /ɪg'zɪləreɪt/ *vt* 使振奋[奮] shǐ zhènfèn; 使高兴[興] shǐ gāoxìng. **ex·hil·a'ration** *n* [U]

ex·hort /ɪg'zɔːt/ *vt* 劝[勸]告 quàngào, 规劝 guīquàn: ~ *him to try harder* 劝他努力. **~ation** /-'teɪʃn/ *n* [C, U]

ex·ile /'eksaɪl/ *n* [C, U] 流放 liúfàng, 放逐 fàngzhú; 离[離]乡[鄉]背井 líxiāng bèijǐng, 离开[開]本国[國] líkāi běnguó. □ *vt* 流放 liúfàng, 放逐 fàngzhú.

ex·ist /ɪg'zɪst/ *vi* 存在 cúnzài, 生存 shēngcún. **~ence** *n* **(a)** [U] 存在 cúnzài: *the number of places now in* ~*ence* 目前仍存在的寓所的数目. **(b)** 生活 shēnghuó, 生活方式 shēnghuó fāngshì: *lead a comfortable* ~*ence* 过幸福生活. **~ent** *adj* 存在的 cúnzàide, 实[實]在的 shízàide.

exit /'eksɪt/ *n* [C] **1** 演员退场[場] yǎnyuán tuìchǎng. **2** 出口 chūkǒu, 太平门[門] tàipíngmén.

ex·on·er·ate /ɪg'zɒnəreɪt/ *vt* 免除 miǎnchú, 使免罪 shǐ miǎnzuì. **ex·on·e'ration** *n* [U]

ex·or·bi·tant /ɪg'zɔːbɪtənt/ *adj* 过[過]高的 guògāode, 价[價]格高昂的 jiàgé gāo'áng de. **~ly** *adv*

ex·or·cize, -cise /'eksɔːsaɪz/ *vt* 驱[驅]除(妖魔等) qūchú.

ex·otic /ɪg'zɒtɪk/ *adj* **1** [植物]外国[國]种[種]的 wàiguózhǒngde, 外国传[傳]入的 wàiguó chuánrù de. **2** 奇异[異]的 qíyìde, 吸引人的 xīyǐn rén de.

ex·pand /ɪk'spænd/ *vt/i* **1** (使)扩[擴]大 kuòdà, (使)膨胀[脹] péngzhàng, (使)扩张 kuòzhāng: *Metal* ~*s when heated.* 金属受热就膨胀. ⇨ contract[3]. **2** 展开[開] zhǎnkāi, 张开 zhāngkāi

ex·panse /ɪk'spæns/*n* [C] 广[廣]阔[闊]地区[區] guǎngkuò dìqū: *the wide* ~ *of the sea* 浩瀚的大海.

ex·pan·sion /ɪk'spænʃn/ *n* [C, U] 扩[擴]张[張] kuòzhāng, 扩大 kuòdà, 膨胀[脹] péngzhàng.

ex·pan·sive /ɪk'spænsɪv/ *adj* **1** 使扩[擴]张[張]的 shǐ kuòzhāng de, 扩张性的 kuòzhāngxìngde, 膨胀的 péngzhàngde. **2** (人)爱[愛]说的 àishuōde; 豪爽的 háoshuǎngde, 开〔開〕朗的 kāilǎngde.

ex·patri·ate /eks'pætrɪət/ *adj, n* [C] （人）移居国〔國〕外的 yíjū guówài de.

ex·pect /ɪk'spekt/ *vt* **1** 预期 yùqī, 期望 qīwàng. **2** *be ~ing* 怀〔懷〕孕 huáiyùn. **~ancy** *n* [U] 期待 qīdài, 期望 qīwàng. **~ant** *adj* 怀孕的 huáiyùnde. **~a·tion** /-'teɪʃn/ *n* [常用 *pl*] 期待的事物 qīdàide shìwù, 前程 qiánchéng, 前景 qiánjǐng.

ex·pedi·ent /ɪk'spi:dɪənt/ *adj* 得计的 déjìde, 有用的 yǒuyòngde, 有利的 yǒulìde: *It was ~ to wait until he arrived.* 最好等到他来到. □ *n* [C]紧〔緊〕急的办〔辦〕法 jǐnjíde bànfǎ, 权〔權〕宜之计 quányízhījì. **ex·ped·iency** *n* [U]

ex·pedi·tion /ˌekspɪ'dɪʃn/ *n* [C] 远〔遠〕征 yuǎnzhēng; 远征队〔隊〕 yuǎnzhēngduì; 探险〔險〕 tànxiǎn; 探险队 tànxiǎnduì; 考察 kǎochá, 考察队 kǎocháduì: *an ~ to the North Pole* 赴北极的考察. **~ary** /-ʃənərɪ/ *adj*

ex·pel /ɪk'spel/ *vt* [-ll-] 驱〔驅〕逐 qūzhú, 赶出 gǎnchū; 排出 páichū; 开〔開〕除 kāichú: *~ air from the lungs* 从肺里排出空气; *~ a pupil from school* 学校开除一名小学生.

ex·pend /ɪk'spend/ *vt* 消费 xiāofèi, 花费 huāfèi, 用尽〔盡〕 yòngjìn: *~ energy* 花费能源.

ex·pendi·ture /ɪk'spendɪtʃə(r)/ *n* **1** [U] 花费 huāfèi, 消费 xiāofèi, 支出 zhīchū, 使用 shǐyòng. **2** [C, U] 消费量 xiāofèiliàng, 支出额 zhīchū'é.

ex·pense /ɪk'spens/ *n* **1** [U] 消费 xiāofèi, 花费 huāfèi, 支出 zhīchū. **2** [常用 *pl*] 开〔開〕支 kāizhī, 经〔經〕费 jīngfèi.

ex·pens·ive /ɪk'spensɪv/ *adj* 花费的 huāfèide, 昂贵的 ángguìde, 花钱〔錢〕多的 huāqiánduōde: *~ clothes* 昂贵的服装. **~ly** *adv*

ex·peri·ence /ɪk'spɪərɪəns/ *n* **1** [U] 体〔體〕验〔驗〕 tǐ'yàn; 经〔經〕验 jīngyàn: *learn by ~* 从经验中学习. **2** [C] 经历〔歷〕 jīnglì, 阅〔閱〕历 yuèlì: *an unpleasant ~* 不愉快的经历. □ *vt* 体验 tǐyàn, 经历 jīnglì, 感受 gǎnshòu. **ex·peri·enced** *adj*

ex·peri·ment /ɪk'sperɪmənt/ *n* [C, U] 实〔實〕验〔驗〕 shíyàn, 试验 shìyàn: *test by ~* 用实验来检查. □ *vi* 实验 shíyàn, 试验 shìyàn. **~a·tion** /-'teɪʃn/ *n* [U] **~al** /-'mentl/ *adj* 实验的 shíyànde, 根据〔據〕实验的 gēnjù shíyàn de.

ex·pert /'ekspɜ:t/ *n* [C] 专〔專〕家 zhuānjiā, 能手 néngshǒu. □ *adj* 有经〔經〕验〔驗〕的 yǒu jīngyàn de, 熟练〔練〕的 shúliànde, **~ly** *adv*

ex·pert·ise /ˌekspɜ:'ti:z/ *n* [U] 专〔專〕门〔門〕知识〔識〕 zhuānmén zhīshi, 专门技能 zhuānmén jìnéng.

ex·pire /ɪk'spaɪə(r)/ *vi* 满期 mǎnqī, 到期 dàoqī: *The contract has ~d.* 合同满期. *My passport has ~d.* 我的护照满期了. **ex·piry** *n* [U] 满期 mǎnqī.

ex·plain /ɪk'spleɪn/ *vt* **1** 解释〔釋〕 jiěshì, 阐〔闡〕明 chǎnmíng, 说明 shuōmíng. **2** 说明…的理由 shuōmíng ... de lǐyóu, 为〔爲〕…辩解 wèi... biànjiě: *~ one's behaviour* 为其行为辩解. **ex·pla·na·tion**/ˌekspləˈneɪʃn/ *n* **(a)** [U] 解释 jiěshì, 说明 shuōmíng. **(b)** [C] 解释的语言, 事实〔實〕等jiěshìde yǔyán shìshí děng. **ex·plana·tory** /ɪk'splænətrɪ/ *adj* 解释的 jiěshìde, 说明的 shuōmíngde.

ex·pli·cit /ɪk'splɪsɪt/ *adj* 清楚的 qīngchude, 明确〔確〕的 míngquède: *~ instructions* 明确的指示. **~ly** *adv* **~ness** *n* [U]

ex·plode /ɪk'spləʊd/ *vt/i* **1** (使)爆炸 bàozhà, (使) 爆发〔發〕 bàofā: *The bomb ~d.* 炸弹爆炸了. **2** (人)感情发〔發〕作 gǎnqíng fāzuò.

ex·ploit[1] /'eksplɔɪt/ *n* [C] 英雄行为〔爲〕 yīngxióng xíngwéi, 辉〔輝〕煌功绩 huīhuáng gōngjì.

ex·ploit[2] /ɪk'splɔɪt/ *vt* **1** 开〔開〕拓 kāituò, 开发〔發〕 kāifā, 开采〔採〕 kāicǎi: *~ a gold-mine* 开采金矿. **2** 剥削 bōxuē: *~ poor workers* 剥削穷苦工人. **~a·tion** /-'teɪʃn/ *n* [U]

ex·plore /ɪk'splɔ:(r)/ *vt* **1** 考察 kǎochá, 勘察 kānchá. **2** 探索 tànsuǒ, 探究 tànjiū. **ex·plorer** 探索者 tànsuǒzhě, 勘察者 kāncházhě. **ex·plo'ra·tion** /ˌekspləˈreɪʃn/ *n* [C, U]. **ex·plora·tory** /ɪks'plɒrətrɪ/ *adj*

ex·plo·sion /ɪk'spləʊʒn/ *n* [C] **1** 爆炸 bàozhà; 爆发〔發〕 bàofā: *a bomb ~* 炸弹爆炸. **2** 感情爆发 gǎnqíng bàofā. **3** 激增 jīzēng, 剧〔劇〕变〔變〕 jùbiàn: *the population ~* 人口激增.

ex·plos·ive /ɪk'spləʊsɪv/ *n* [C], *adj* 爆炸的 bàozhàde, 爆炸性的 bàozhàxìngde, 爆发〔發〕(性)的 bàofāde. **~ly** *adv*

ex·port /ɪk'spɔ:t/ *vt/i* 出口 chūkǒu, 输〔輸〕出 shūchū. □ /'ekspɔ:t/ *n* **1** [U] 出口 chūkǒu, 出口企业〔業〕

chūkǒuqǐyè. **2** [C] 出口品 chūkǒupǐn. **~er** 出口商 chūkǒushāng, 输出者 shūchūzhě.

ex·pose /ɪk'spəʊz/ *vt* **1** 使暴露 shǐ bàolù. **2** 揭发〔發〕 jiēfā, 揭露 jiēlù: *~ a plot* 揭发阴谋. **3** 使曝光 shǐ bàoguāng. **ex·po·sure** /-ʒə(r)/ *n* [C, U]

ex·pound /ɪk'spaʊnd/ *vt* 〔正式用语〕详述 xiángshù, 陈述 chénshù: *~ a theory* 详述一种理论.

ex·press¹ /ɪk'spres/ *adj* 快的 kuàide, 特快的 tèkuàide: *an ~ train* 特快列车. □ *adv* 快速递〔遞〕送 kuàisù dìsòng: *send a letter ~* 发一封快信. □ *n* [C] 特快列车 tèkuài lièchē.

ex·press² /ɪk'spres/ *vt* 表示 biǎoshì, 表白 biǎobái: *~ one's disapproval* 表示其不赞成. □ *adj* 明白的 míngbaide, 明确〔確〕的 míngquède: *his ~ wish* 他的明确的愿望. **~ly** *adv* 明确地 míngquède.

ex·pres·sion /ɪk'spreʃn/ *n* **1** [U] 表示 biǎoshì, 表达〔達〕 biǎodá. **2** [C] 表达方式 biǎodáfāngshì, 词句 cíjù, 措词 cuòcí: *an ~ of thanks* 表示感谢的话. **3** 表情 biǎoqíng, 腔调 qiāngdiào. **~less** *adj* 没有表情的 méiyǒu biǎoqíng de, 呆板的 áibǎnde.

ex·press·ive /ɪk'spresɪv/ *adj* 富于表情的 fùyúbiǎoqíng de. **~ly** *adv*

ex·pul·sion /ɪk'spʌlʃn/ *n* [C, U] 驱〔驅〕除 qūchú, 开〔開〕除 kāichú.

ex·quis·ite /ek'skwɪzɪt/ *adj* 优〔優〕美的 yōuměide 精巧的 jīngqiǎode. **~ly** *adv*

ex·tend /ɪk'stend/ *vt/i* **1** 伸出 shēnchū, 延长〔長〕 yáncháng: *~ the runway* 延长机场跑道. **2** 伸展 shēnzhǎn. **3** 给予 gěiyǔ, 提供 tígòng: *~ an invitation* 发出邀请. **4** 扩〔擴〕大 kuòdà, 延伸 yánshēn: *The park ~s to the river.* 公园延伸到河边.

ex·ten·sion /ɪk'stenʃn/ *n* **1** [U] 扩〔擴〕大 kuòdà, 伸展 shēnzhǎn, 延伸 yánshēn. **2** [C] 附加部分 fùjiābùfēn, 增设部分 zēngshèbùfēn. **3** [C] 电〔電〕话分机〔機〕 diànhuà fēnjī.

ex·ten·sive /ɪk'stensɪv/ *adj* 广〔廣〕大的 guǎngdàde; 广泛的 guǎngfànde. **~ly** *adv*

ex·tent /ɪk'stent/ *n* [U] **1** 广〔廣〕度 guǎngdù; 长〔長〕度 chángdù, 范〔範〕围〔圍〕 fànwéi: *the ~ of the damage* 破坏的范围; *the ~ of his knowledge* 他的知识的广度. **2** 程度 chéngdù: *to some ~* 多少, 有些.

ex·ter·ior /ek'stɪərɪə(r)/ *adj* 外部的 wàibùde, 外面的 wàimiànde; 外来〔來〕的 wàiláide. ⇨ interior (1). □ *n* [C] 外部 wàibù, 外表 wàibiǎo.

ex·ter·mi·nate /ɪk'stɜːmɪneɪt/ *vt* 灭〔滅〕绝 mièjué, 根除 gēnchú. **ex·ter·mi'na·tion** *n* [C, U]

ex·ter·nal /ek'stɜːnl/ *adj* 外面的 wàimiànde, 外部的 wàibùde: *an ~ examination* 校外主持的考试. **~ly** *adv*

ex·tinct /ɪk'stɪŋkt/ *adj* **1** 消灭〔滅〕了的 xiāomièlede: 熄灭了的 xīmièlede: *an ~ volcano* 死火山. **2** (感情)熄灭了的 xīmièlede. **3** 灭绝的 mièjuéde, 绝种〔種〕的 juézhǒngde: *an ~ animal* 绝了种的动物. **ex·tinction** /-ʃn/ *n* [U] 消灭 xiāomiè, 熄灭 xīmiè, 灭绝 mièjué.

ex·tin·guish /ɪk'stɪŋgwɪʃ/ *vt* **1** 熄灭〔滅〕(火) xīmiè, 扑〔撲〕灭 pūmiè. **2** 熄灭(希望等) xīmiè. **~er** 灭火器 mièhuǒqì; 熄灯〔燈〕器 xīdēngqì.

ex·tort /ɪk'stɔːt/ *vt* 强取 qiángqǔ, 勒索 lèsuǒ. **ex·tor·tion** /-ʃn/ *n* [C, U] **ex·tor·tion·ate** /-ʃənət/ *adj* 过〔過〕份的 guòfènde, 昂贵的 ángguìde.

ex·tra /'ekstrə/ *adj* 额外的 éwàide, 附加的 fùjiāde. □ *adv* **1** 非常 fēicháng, 特别地 tèbiéde 格外 géwài: *~ fine* 特别好. **2** 另外 lìngwài, 另加 lìngjiā: *postage ~* 外加邮资. □ *n* [C] **1** 额外的东〔東〕西 éwàide dōngxī. **2** (群众场面的)临〔臨〕时〔時〕演员 línshí yǎnyuán. **3** 报〔報〕纸号〔號〕外 bàozhǐ hàowài.

ex·tract /ɪk'strækt/ *vt* **1** 拔出 báchū. 用力取出 yònglì qǔchū: *~ a tooth* 拔牙. **2** [喻]榨取 zhàqǔ: *~ money from a person* 向某人榨取金钱. **3** 榨取(果汁等) zhàqǔ. **4** 摘录〔録〕 zhāilù. □ *n* /'ekstrækt/ [C, U] **1** 抽出物 chōuchūwù. **2** 摘录 zhāilù, 选〔選〕录 xuǎnlù. **ex·trac·tion** /-ʃn/ *n* [C, U] **(a)** 抽出 chōuchū; 拔出 báchū; 榨出 zhàchū. **(b)** 血统 xuètǒng, 出身 chūshēn: *of French extraction* 法国血统的.

extra·ordi·nary /ɪk'strɔːdnrɪ/ *adj* 非常的 fēichángde, 特别的 tèbiéde, 非凡的 fēifánde, 令人惊〔驚〕讶的 lìngrén jīngyà de: *~ behaviour* 惊人的行为. **ex·tra·ordi·nar·ily** /-rəlɪ/ *adv*

extra·sen·sory /ˌekstrə'sensərɪ/ *adj* 超感觉〔覺〕的 chāo gǎnjué de

~ **perception** *n* [U] (略作 **ESP**) 超感知觉 chāogǎn zhījué

ex·trava·gant /ɪk'strævəgənt/ *adj* **1** 奢侈的 shēchìde, 浪费的 làngfèide. **2** 过〔過〕分的 guòfènde, 过度的 guòdùde. ~**ly** *adv* **ex·trava·gance** /-gəns/ *n* **(a)** [C,U] 奢侈 shēchǐ, 浪费 làngfèi; 过〔過〕分 guòfèn; 奢侈品 shēchǐpǐn **(b)** [C] 放肆的言行 fàngsìde yánxíng.

ex·treme /ɪk'stri:m/ *n* [C] **1** 极〔極〕端 jíduān, 极度 jídù: *~s of temperature* 热和冷. **2** [*pl*] 相反的性质〔質〕 xiāngfǎnde xìngzhì. *Love and hate are ~s.* 爱和恨是两个极端. □ *adj* **1** 尽〔盡〕头〔頭〕的 jìntóude, 末端的 mòduānde: *the ~ edge* 边界. **2** 极度的 jídùde. **3** (人)走极端的 zǒu jíduān de. ~**ly** *adv* **ex·trem·ist** /-ɪst/ *n* [C] 极端分子 jíduānfènzi. □ *adj* 极端主义〔義〕的 jíduānzhǔyìde. **ex·trem·ity** /ɪk'stremətɪ/ *n* [C] [*pl* -ies] [正式用语] **(a)** 尽头 jìntóu, 终极 zhōngjí. **(b)** [*pl*] 极端措施 jíduān cuòshī, 激烈手段 jīliè shǒuduàn. **(c)** [*pl*] 人的手和脚 rénde shǒu hé jiǎo.

ex·tro·vert /'ekstrəvɜ:t/ *n* [C] **1** 性格外向的人 xìnggé wàixiàng de rén. **2** [非正式用语]活泼〔潑〕愉快的人 huópo yúkuài de rén. ⇨ introvert.

ex·uber·ant /ɪg'zju:bərənt/ *adj* **1** 茂盛的 màoshèngde, 繁茂的 fánmàode: ~ *plants* 茂盛的草木. **2** 精力充沛的 jīnglì chōngpèi de: ~ *children* 充满活力的儿童. **ex·uber·ance** *n* [U]

ex·ude /ɪg'zju:d/ *vt/i* [正式用语] (汗)流出 liúchū, 渗〔滲〕出 shènchū; [喻]流露 liúlù.

eye /aɪ/ *n* **1** 眼睛 yǎnjīng. ***have an ~ for*** 善于鉴〔鑑〕赏 shànyú jiànshǎng. ***keep an ~ on*** 密切注视 mìqiè zhùshì. ***make ~s at*** 向某人送秋波 xiàng mǒurén sòng qiūpō. ***open sb's ~s to*** 使某人看清 shǐ mǒurén kànqīng. ***see ~ to ~ (with)*** 看法完全一致 kànfǎ wánquán yízhì. ***up to one's eyes in*** 埋头〔頭〕于 máitóuyú. **2** 眼状〔狀〕物 yǎnzhuàngwù: *the ~ of a needle* 针眼. □ *vt* 看 kàn, 注视 zhùshì. '~**ball** 眼球 yǎnqiú. '~**brow** 眉毛 méimao. '~**lash** 睫毛 jiémáo. '~**lid** 眼睑〔瞼〕yǎnjiǎn. '~**sight** 视力 shìlì, 目力 mùlì. '~**sore** 刺眼的东〔東〕西 cìyǎnde dōngxi.

F f

F, f /ef/ [*pl* F's, f's /efs/] 英语的第六个〔個〕字母 yīngyǔde dìliùgè zìmǔ.

fable /'feɪbl/ *n* **1** [C] 寓言 yùyán. **2** [U] 神话 shénhuà. **fabled** *adj* 传〔傳〕说的 chuánshuōde, 虚构〔構〕的 xūgòude: *his ~d wealth* 他的虚构的财富.

fab·ric /'fæbrɪk/ *n* [C, U] **1** 织〔織〕物 zhīwù, 布 bù. **2** 构〔構〕造 gòuzào, 结构 jiégòu: *the ~ of a building* 建筑物的构造, *the ~ of a society* 社会的结构.

fab·ri·cate /'fæbrɪkeɪt/ *vt* **1** 装〔裝〕配 zhuāngpèi, 制〔製〕造 zhìzào. **2** 捏造 niēzào, 伪〔僞〕造 wěizào: *~ a story* 捏造故事; *~ an excuse* 制造借口. **fab·ri'ca·tion** *n* [C, U]

fabu·lous /'fæbjʊləs/ *adj* **1** 传〔傳〕说中的 chuánshuō zhōng de, 神话中的 shénhuà zhōng de: *~ monsters* 神话中的怪物. **2** 难〔難〕以相信的 nányǐ xiāngxìn de 惊〔驚〕人的 jīngrénde: *~ wealth* 惊人的财富. **3** [非正式用语]极〔極〕好的 jíhǎode. ~**ly** *adv* 极〔極〕度地 jídùde, 极端地 jíduānde: *~ly rich* 极富.

fa·cade /fə'sa:d/ *n* [C] **1** 建筑物的正面 jiànzhùwùde zhèngmiàn. **2** [喻]门〔門〕面 ménmiàn, 假象 jiǎnxiàng: *a ~ of honesty* 诚实的外表.

face /feɪs/ *n* [C] **1** 脸〔臉〕liǎn, 面孔 miànkǒng. ***~ to ~*** 面对〔對〕面 miàn duì miàn, 当〔當〕面 dāngmiàn. ***in one's ~*** 公开〔開〕地 gōngkāide. ***to one's ~*** 坦白地 tǎnbáide, 当面地 dāng miàn de: *criticise him to his ~* 坦率地批评他. ***show one's ~*** 露面 lùmiàn,出现 chūxiàn, 到场〔場〕dàochǎng. **2** 表情 biǎoqíng. ***keep a straight ~*** 板着面孔 bǎnzhe miànkǒng, 一本正经〔經〕yìběnzhèngjīng. ***lose ~*** 丢面子 diū miànzi. ***pull a ~*** (或 ***~s***) 做怪相 zuò guàixiàng, 做鬼脸 zuò guǐliǎn. ***save (one's) ~*** 保全面子 bǎoquán miànzi. **3** 表面 biǎomiàn, 正面 zhèngmiàn. □ *vt/i* **1** 面向 miànxiàng, 朝向 cháoxiàng. 2 正视 zhèngshì, 有信心地面对〔對〕yǒuxìnxīnde miànduì, 蔑视 mièshì: ~ *danger* 蔑视危险. ~ ***up to (sth)*** 勇敢地对付 yǒnggǎnde duìfu. 3 承认〔認〕…的存在 chéngrèn ... de cúnzài: ~ *the facts* 承认事实. 4 呈现于…之前 chéngxiànyú ... zhī qián: *the problem facing us* 呈现在我们面前的问题. '~**-cloth** 洗脸毛巾 xǐliǎn máojīn. '~ **value (a)** 票面价〔價〕值 piàomiàn jiàzhí. **(b)**〔喻〕表面价值 biǎomiàn jiàzhí. ~**less** *adj*〔喻〕不露面的 bú lùmiàn de.

facet /'fæsɪt/ *n* [C] **1** 刻面 kèmiàn. **2** (问题等的) 一个〔個〕方面 yígè fāngmiàn.

fa·cetious /fə'si:ʃəs/ *adj* 幽默的 yōumòde, 爱〔愛〕开〔開〕玩笑的 ài kāiwánxiào de. ~**ly** *adv*

fa·cial /'feɪʃl/ *adj* 面部的 miànbùde, 面部用的 miànbù yòng de.

facile /'fæsaɪl/ *adj* 草草写〔寫〕成的 cǎocǎo xiěchéng de, 随口说出的 suí kǒu shuōchū de.

fa·cili·tate /fə'sɪlɪteɪt/ *vt* 使便利 shǐ biànlì: ~ *his escape* 便利了他的逃跑.

fa·cil·ity /fə'sɪlətɪ/ *n* [*pl* -ies] **1** [U] 灵〔靈〕巧 língqiǎo, 熟练 shúliàn: *a ~ for learning languages* 学习语言的才能. **2** [*pl*] 设备〔備〕shèbèi, 工具 gōngjù: *'sports facilities* 体育设备,运动器材.

fac·sim·ile /fæk'sɪməlɪ/ *n* [C] 摹真本 mózhēnběn.

fact /fækt/ *n* **1** [C] 事实〔實〕shìshí. **2** [C] 实情 shíqíng, 真相 zhēnxiàng. **3** [U] 实际〔際〕shíjì. ***in*** ~ 事实上 shìshíshàng.

fac·tion /'fækʃn/ *n* **1** [C] 宗派 zōngpài, 派系 pàixì, 小集团〔團〕xiǎo jítuán. **2** [U] 派系斗〔鬥〕争 pàixì dòuzhēng.

fac·tor /'fæktə(r)/ *n* [C] 因素 yīnsù, 要素 yàosù: *His age was a ~ in his success.* 他的年龄是他成功的要素.

fac·tory /'fæktərɪ/ *n* [C] [*pl* -ies] 工厂〔廠〕gōngchǎng, 制〔製〕造厂 zhìzàochǎng.

fac·tual /'fæktʃʊəl/ *adj* 事实〔實〕的 shìshíde.

fac·ulty /'fækltɪ/ *n* [C] [*pl* -ies] **1** 才能 cáinéng, 本领 běnlǐng, 能力 nénglì: *mental faculties* 智力. **2** (大学的) 系科 xìkē, 学〔學〕院 xuéyuàn, 系, 科, 学院的全体〔體〕教员 xì, kē, xuéyuàn de quántǐ jiàoyuán.

fade /feɪd/ *vt/i* **1** (使) 褪色 tuìsè: *Colours ~ in the sunlight.* 颜色在阳光下褪色. **2** 逐渐消失 zhújiàn xiāoshī, 淡忘 dànwàng. **3** ~ ***in (to)*** (电影,广播) 使淡入 shǐ dànrù, 使渐〔漸〕强 shǐ jiànqiáng. ~ ***out*** (电影, 广播) 使淡出 shǐ dànchū, 使渐弱 shǐ jiànruò: ~ *a scene out* 使画面淡出.

fag /fæg/ *n* **1** [只用 *pl*] 累人的工作 lèiréndе gōngzuò. **2** [C] [俚语] 香烟 xiāngyān. □ *vt/i* [-gg-] **1** 做累人的工作 zuò lèrénde gōngzuò. **2** ~ ***sb out*** (工作) 使人疲劳 shǐrén píláo.

fag·got [美语亦作 **fagot**] /'fægət/ *n* [C] **1** 柴把 cháibǎ, 柴捆 cháikǔn. **2** 待炸的肉丸子 dài zhá de ròuwánzi.

Fahr·en·heit /'færənhaɪt/ *n* 华〔華〕氏温度计 huáshì wēndùjì.

fail[1] /feɪl/ *n* (只用于) ***without*** ~ 一定 yídìng, 必定 bìdìng, 无〔無〕误 wúwù.

fail[2] /feɪl/ *vt/i* **1** 失败 shībài. **2** 不及格 bù jígé. **3** 不足 bùzú, 歉收 qiànshōu, 缺乏 quēfá: *The rice crop ~ed because of draught.* 水稻因干旱而歉收. **4** (健康, 视力等) 衰弱 shuāiruò, 衰退 shuāituì. **5** 忘记 wàngjì: ~ *to keep an appointment* 忘记一次约会. **6** 破产〔產〕pòchǎn: *The company ~ed.* 公司破产. ~**ing** *n* [C] 缺点〔點〕quēdiǎn. □ *prep* 如果没有… rúguǒ méiyǒu…: ~*ing an answer* 如得不到答复. ~**ure** /-jə(r)/ *n* **(a)** [C, U] 失败 shībài; 失败者 shībàizhě; 失败的尝〔嘗〕试 shībàide chángshì. **(b)** [C, U] 疏忽 shūhū, 没做到 méi zuòdào: *His ~ure to arrive was very sad.* 他没有来,太糟了. **(c)** (机器) 断〔斷〕裂 duànliè: *engine ~ure* 发动机断裂.

faint /feɪnt/ *adj* [-er, -est] **1** 微弱的 wēiruòde, 不清楚的 bù qīngchu de: *a ~ outline* 不清楚的轮廓. **2** (记忆中的事物) 模糊的 móhude. **3** (人) 将〔將〕要昏晕〔暈〕的 jiāngyào hūnyùn de. □ *vi* 昏晕 hūnyùn. □ *n* [C] 昏厥 hūnjué. ,~'**hearted** *adj* 懦怯的 nuòquède, 优〔優〕柔寡断〔斷〕的 yōuróu guǎduàn de. ~**ly** *adv*

fair[1] /feə(r)/ *adj* [-er, -est] **1** 公正的 gōngzhèngde, 公平的 gōngpíngde; 诚实〔實〕的 chéngshíde: *a ~ decision* 公正的决定. **2** 一般的 yìbānde, 尚好的 shànghǎode: *a ~ chance of success* 相当的成功机会. **3** (天气) 晴 qíng. **4** (肤色) 白皙的 báixīde, (头发) 金色的 jīnsède. **5** 干〔乾〕净的 gānjìngde, 清楚的 qīngchude: *a ~ copy* 清楚

的抄件. □ *adv* 公平地 gōngpíngde, 公正地 gōngzhèngde. ,~ 'play [喻]公平对[對]待 gōngpíng duìdài, 光明磊落 guāngmíng lěiluò ~ly *adv* (a) 正当[當]地 zhèngdāngde, 公正地 gōngzhèngde: *be ~ly treated in prison* 在狱中受到正当对待. (b) 还[還]算 háisuàn, 相当 xiāngdāng: *a ~ly easy book* 一本相当容易的书. ~ness *n* [U]

fair² /feə(r)/ *n* [C] **1** 集市 jíshì. **2** 流动[動]表演团[團] liúdòng biǎoyǎntuán. **3** 商品展览[覽]会[會] shāngpǐn zhǎnlǎnhuì. '~**ground** 流动表演场[場]地 liúdòng biǎoyǎn chǎngdì.

fairy /'feərɪ/ *n* [C] [*pl* -ies] 仙女 xiānnǚ; 小妖精 xiǎoyāojing. '~-**tale** (a) 神话 shénhuà; 童话 tónghuà. (b) 谎言 huǎngyán.

faith /feɪθ/ *n* **1** [U] 信任 xìnrèn. *have ~ in me* 信任我. **2** [C] 信仰 xìnyǎng; 宗教 zōngjiào. **3** (*do sth*) *in bad* ~ 欺诈地 qīzhàde;(*do sth*) *in good* ~诚实[實]地 chéngshíde. ~**ful** *adj* (a) 忠实的 zhōngshíde, 守信的 shǒuxìnde. (b) 如实的 rúshíde: *a ~ful description* 如实的描述. (c) **the** ~ [*pl*] 虔诚的教徒 qiánchéngde jiàotú. ~**fully** *adv* **Yours ~fully** 你的忠实的(正式函件署名前的客套语) nǐde zhōngshíde. ~**less** *adj* 不忠实的 bù zhōngshí de, 奸诈的 jiānzhàde.

fake /feɪk/ *n* [C] **1** 假货 jiǎhuò, 伪[僞]品 wěipǐn. **2** 骗[騙]子 piànzi, 伪造者 wěizàozhě. □ *vt* 伪造 wěizào, 捏造 niēzào.

fal·con /'fɔːlkən/ *n* [C] 猎[獵]鹰[鷹] lièyīng. ~**ry** *n* [U] 鹰猎 yīngliè, 猎鹰训练[練]术[術] lièyīng xùnliànshù.

fall¹ /fɔːl/ *n* [C] **1** 落下 luòxià; 跌倒 diēdǎo; 垂下 chuíxià. **2** 降雨量 jiàngyǔliàng; 落差 luòchā. **3** [*pl*] 瀑布 pùbù. **4** [美语]秋季 qiūjì.

fall² /fɔːl/ *vi* [*pt* fell /fel/; *pp* ~en /'fɔːlən/] **1** 落下 luòxià, 降落 jiàngluò; 跌落 diēluò: *fall off a ladder* 从梯子上跌下. ~ **short of** 不足 bùzú, 达[達]不到 dá bú dào. **2** 倒下 dǎoxià, 倒坍 dǎotān, 垮台 kuǎtái: *The old house fell down.* 这所老屋子倒坍了. **3** 垂下 chuíxià: *Her hair fell over her shoulders.* 她的头发垂到双肩. **4** 成为[爲] chéngwéi: *He fell asleep.* 他睡着了. ~ **in love (with)** 与[與]…相爱[愛] yǔ…xiāng ài. **5** 阵[陣]亡 zhènwáng; 战[戰]败 zhànbài; (城市等)失陷 shīxiàn. **6** ~ **on** 落在 luòzài, 落到 luòdào: *His eye fell on* (= He suddenly saw) *a curious object.* 他忽然看见一个奇怪的东西. **7** (土地)下斜 xiàxié. **8** (日期)适[適]逢 shìféng: *Our holiday ~s in June this year.* 我们的假日在今年六月. ~ **back** 后[後]退 hòutuì, 退却 tuìquè. ~ **back on** 求助于 qiúzhùyú, 要求…支持 yāoqiú…zhīchí. ~ **behind** 落后 luòhòu, 跟不上 gēn bú shàng. ~ **behind with** 拖欠未付(租金等) tuōqiàn wèifù. ~ **for** [非正式用语]听信(谎话) tīngxìn; 迷恋[戀] míliàn; 爱[愛]上 àishàng: *He ~s for all the pretty girls.* 所有好看的姑娘他都爱. ~ **in** 倒坍 dǎotān: *The roof fell in* 房顶倒坍. ~ **off** 减少 jiǎnshǎo, 缩小 suōxiǎo: *Attendance has ~en off.* 出席人数减少. ~ **out (with)** 争吵 zhēngchǎo, 吵架 chǎojià. ~ **through** 失败 shībài: *The business deal fell through.* 交易失败.

fal·lacy /'fæləsɪ/ *n* [*pl* -ies] [C, U] 谬论[論] miùlùn, 谬见 miùjiàn.

fallen *pp* of fall².

fal·lible /'fæləbl/ *adj* 易犯错误的 yìfàn cuòwù de: 错误难[難]免的 cuòwù nánmiǎn de. **fal·li'bil·ity** *n* [U]

fall-out /'fɔːl aʊt/ *n* [U] 放射性尘[塵]埃 fàngshèxìng chén'āi.

fal·low /'fæləʊ/ *adj*, *n* [U] 休闲[閑]的 xiūxiánde, 休闲地 xiūxiándì.

false /fɔːls/ *adj* **1** 错误的 cuòwùde, 不正确[確]的 bú zhèngquè de. **2** 欺诈的 qīzhà de, 不忠诚的 bù zhōngchéngde: *a ~ friend* 不可靠的朋友. **3** 假的 jiǎde; 人工的 réngōngde, 人造的 rénzàode: ~-*teeth* 假牙 ~**ly** *adv* ~**hood** *n* [C, U] 谎言 huǎngyán, 说谎 shuōhuǎng.

fal·setto /fɔːl'setəʊ/ *n* [C] [*pl* ~s] (音乐)男子假声[聲] nánzǐ jiǎshēng.

fals·ify /'fɔːlsɪfaɪ/ *vt* [*pt,pp* -ied] 窜[竄]改 cuàngǎi, 伪[僞]造 wěizào: ~ *documents* 窜改文件. **falsi·fi·'ca·tion** /-fɪ'keɪʃn/ *n* [C, U]

fal·ter /'fɔːltə(r)/ *vt/i* **1** 蹒跚 pánshān, 踉跄[蹌] liàngqiàng. **2** (声音)发[發]抖 fādǒu; 支吾 zhīwu. ~**ing·ly** *adv*

fame /feɪm/ *n* [U] 名声[聲] míngshēng, 声誉[譽] shēngyù. **famed** *adj* 有名的 yǒumíngde.

fam·il·iar /fə'mɪliːə(r)/ *adj* **1** ~

with 熟悉的 shúxīde, 通晓〔曉〕的 tōngxiǎode. **2** ~ *to* 为…所熟悉的 wèi...suǒ shúxī de. **3** 常见的 chángjiànde; 听〔聽〕惯的 tīngguànde: *Tourists are a ~ sight in London.* 游客在伦敦是常见的. **4** 亲〔親〕密的 qīnmìde; 个〔個〕人的 gèrénde: *on ~ terms with* 与…有交情, 与…亲密. **5** 无〔無〕拘束的 wújūsùde, 随便的 suíbiànde: *too ~ with a girl* 对女孩子太随便. **~ly** *adv* **~ity** /-'ærətɪ/ *n* [*pl* -ies] [C, U]

fam·il·iar·ize /fə'mɪlɪəraɪz/ *vt* 使熟悉 shǐ shúxī: *~ oneself with the rules* 使自己熟悉规则.

fam·ily /'fæməlɪ/ *n* [*pl* -ies] **1** [C] 家庭 jiātíng, 家 jiā. **2** 孩子 háizi, 子女 zǐnǚ: *He has a large ~.* 他有很多子女. **3** [C] 家族 jiāzú, 氏族 shìzú. **4** [C] (动植物)科 kē, 语族 yǔzú: *the cat ~* 猫科. ,**~ 'planning** 计划〔劃〕生育 jìhuà shēngyù. ,**~ 'tree** 家系 jiāxì; 家谱 jiāpǔ.

fam·ine /'fæmɪn/ *n* [C, U] 饥荒 jīhuāng.

fam·ish /'fæmɪʃ/ *vt/i* **be ~ed** (使)挨饿 āi'è.

fa·mous /'feɪməs/ *adj* 著名的 zhùmíngde, 有名的 yǒumíngde. **~ly** *adv* 极好 jíhǎo: *He's progressing ~ly.* 他进展得极好.

fan[1] /fæn/ *n* [C] **1** 风〔風〕扇 fēngshàn, 扇子 shànzi; 鼓风机〔機〕gǔfēngjī. **2** 扇形物 (孔雀尾等) shànxíngwù. **'~ belt** 鼓风机皮带〔帶〕gǔfēngjī pídài. □ *vt/i* [-nn-] **1** 扇风 shānfēng. **2** 展开〔開〕成扇形 zhǎnkāi chēng shànxíng: *Troops ~ned out across the field.* 部队在田野上成扇形展开.

fan[2] /fæn/ *n* [C] [非正式用语]狂热〔熱〕爱〔愛〕好者 kuángrè àihàozhě: *football ~s* 足球迷. **'~ mail** 狂热者寄出的信 (如影迷寄给电影明星的信) kuángrèzhě jìchū de xìn.

fa·natic /fə'nætɪk/ *n* [C] 狂热者 kuángrèzhě: *a religious ~* 宗教狂. □ *adj* (亦作 **~al**) 狂热的 kuángrède. **~ally** *adv*

fan·ci·ful /'fænsɪfl/ *adj* [正式用语] **1** (人)爱〔愛〕空想的 ài kōngxiǎng de. **2** 不真实〔實〕的 bù zhēnshí de; 奇异〔異〕的 qíyìde: *~ ideas* 奇异的想法. **~ly** *adv*

fancy[1] /'fænsɪ/ *adj* **1** (小东西)颜色鲜艳〔艷〕的 yánsè xiānyàn de. **2** 奇特的 qítède, 异〔異〕样〔樣〕的 yìyàngde: *~ dress* (化装舞会上的)化装服饰 huàzhuāng fúshì.

fancy[2] /'fænsɪ/ *n* [*pl* -ies] **1** [U] 想象力 xiǎngxiànglì; 幻想力 huànxiǎnglì. **2** [C] 设想 shèxiǎng, 想象 xiǎngxiàng: *I have a ~ she'll be late.* 我想她大概要晚来. **3** [C] 爱〔愛〕好 (*for*) àihào, 喜爱 xǐ'ài. **take a ~ to** 爱好上… àihàoshàng.... □ *vt* [*pt, pp* -ied] **1** 想象 xiǎngxiàng, 设想 shèxiǎng. **2** (根据印象)认〔認〕为〔爲〕 rènwéi, 想 xiǎng: *I ~ he won't come.* 我想他不会来了. **3** 喜爱 xǐ'ài, 想要 xiǎngyào: *Do you ~ some food?* 你想吃点什么吗? **4**(表示惊讶): *F~ that!* 真想不到!

fan·fare /'fænfeə(r)/ *n* [C] 嘹亮的喇叭声〔聲〕liáoliàngde lǎbāshēng.

fang /fæŋ/ *n* [C] **1** (狗等的)尖牙 jiānyá. **2** 蛇的毒牙 shéde dúyá.

fan·tas·tic /fæn'tæstɪk/ *adj* **1** 奇异〔異〕的 qíyìde. **2** (思想)荒谬的 huāngmiùde. **3** [非正式用语]极〔極〕好的 jíhǎode: *a ~ party* 极好的聚会. **~ally** *adv*

fan·tasy /'fæntəsɪ/ *n* [*pl* -ies] [C, U] 幻想 huànxiǎng; 幻想作品 huànxiǎng zuòpǐn. 怪念头〔頭〕guàiniàntou: *Space travel is no longer a ~.* 空间旅行不再是幻想.

far[1] /fɑ:(r)/ *adj* (⇨ farther, farthest, further, furthest) 遥远〔遠〕的 yáoyuǎnde; 久远的 jiǔyuǎnde: *a ~ country* 遥远的国家. **the ,~ 'East** 远东〔東〕yuǎndōng.

far[2] /fɑ:(r)/ *adv* (⇨ farther, farthest, further, furthest) **1** 遥远〔遠〕地 yáoyuǎnde: *How ~ can you run?* 你能跑多远? *It isn't very ~ to London.* 伦敦不是太远. **~ from (a)** 完全不 wánquánbù, 远非 yuǎnfēi: *~ from satisfactory* 完全不满意. **(b)** 而不 érbù: *F~ from happy, I'm very sad.* 我非常悲痛,一点也不高兴. **go ~ (a)** (人)成功 chénggōng, 大有前途 dàyǒuqiántú. **(b)** (钱) 购〔購〕买〔買〕力高 gòumǎilì gāo. **so ~** 迄今为〔爲〕止 qìjīn wéizhǐ. **as** (或 **so**) **~ as** (表示范围,程度)就… jiù...: *as ~ as I know* 就我所知. **2** (强调程度,性质)大大… dàdà, …得多 …de duō: *He was too ~ behind.* 他落后得太多. **'~away** *adj* **(a)** 遥远的 yáoyuǎnde. **(b)** (表情) 恍惚的 huǎnghūde. ,**~-'fetched** *adj* 牵强的 qiānqiángde. ,**~-'reaching** *adj* 意义〔義〕深远的 yìyìshēnyuǎnde: *a ~-reaching decision* 有深远意义的决定. ,**~-'sighted** *adj* [喻]有远见的 yǒu yuǎnjiàn de.

farce /fɑ:s/ *n* **1** [C] 笑剧〔劇〕xiàojù, 滑稽戏〔戲〕huájīxì; [U] 滑稽戏剧 huájī xìjù. **2** [C] 一系列可

笑的事物 yíxìliè kěxiàode shìwù. **far·ci·cal** *adj*

fare /feə(r)/ *n* [C] 车[車]费 chēfèi, 船费 chuánfèi: *bus ~s* 公共汽车费.

fare·well /ˌfeə'wel/ *int, adj, n* [C] [书面语]再见 zàijiàn.

farm /fɑ:m/ *n* [C] **1** 农[農]场[場] nóngchǎng, 农庄[莊] nóngzhuāng. **2** 农舍 nóngshè. □ *vt/i* 耕种[種] gēngzhòng; 饲养[養] sìyǎng. '~-**yard** 农场建筑物范[範]围[圍]内的空地 nóngchǎng jiànzhùwù fànwéi nèi de kōngdì. **farmer** *n* [C] 农场主 nóngchǎngzhǔ.

far·ther /'fɑ:ðə(r)/ *adv* 更远地 gènyuǎnde: *They went ~ into the forest.* 他们更深入地走进森林.

far·thest /'fɑ:ðɪst/ *adv, adj* 最远 zuìyuǎn, 最远的 zuìyuǎnde: *Which village in England is ~ from London?* 英国那个村庄距离伦敦最远?

fas·ci·nate /'fæsɪneɪt/ *vt* 使神魂颠倒 shǐ shénhúndiāndǎo, 迷住 mízhù. **fas·ci·nat·ing** *adj* **fas·ci·'na·tion** *n* [C,U]

Fas·cism /'fæʃɪzəm/ *n* [U] 法西斯主义[義] fǎxīsīzhǔyì. **Fas·cist** *adj*

fashion /'fæʃn/ *n* **1** [*sing*] 方式 fāngshì, 样[樣]子 yàngzi: *behaving in a strange ~* 行为古怪. **2** [C, U] (服装等)流行式样 liúxíng shìyàng: *the latest ~ in hats* 帽子的最新款式. *in ~* 时[時]新的 shíxīnde, 时髦的 shímáode. *come into ~* 合于时尚 héyú shíshàng. *go out of ~* 不合时尚 bù hé shíshàng. □ *vt* 形成 xíngchéng, 把…塑造成 bǎ…sùzào chéng. ~**able** *adj* **(a)** 时髦的 shímáode, 流行的 liúxíngde. **(b)** 为[爲]很多的人所使用、光顾[顧]的 wéi hěnduōde rén suǒ shǐyòng, guānggù de: *a ~able restaurant* 高级饭馆. ~**ably** *adv*

fast¹ /fɑ:st/ *adj* **1** 牢固的 láogùde, 紧[緊]的 jǐnde: *make the boat ~* 把船拴牢; *stick ~* 粘牢. **2** 不褪色的 bú tuìsè de. □ *adv* 牢固地 láogùde, 紧紧地 jǐnjǐnde. *~ asleep* ⇨ asleep(1).

fast² /fɑ:st/ *adj* [-er, -est] **1** 快的 kuàide, 迅速的 xùnsùde: *~ cars* 开得快的汽车. **2** (钟表) 偏快的 piānkuàide. □ *adv* 快地 kuàide, 迅速地 xùnsùde.

fast³ /fɑ:st/ *vi* 禁食 jìnshí, 斋[齋]戒 zhāijiè. □ *n* [C] 斋戒 zhāijiè, 斋戒期 zhāijièqī.

fas·ten /'fɑ:sn/ *vt/i* **1** 扎[紮]牢 zhāláo; 扣紧[緊] kòujǐn; 闩[閂]牢 shuānláo. **2** 变[變]紧[緊] biànjǐn. 变牢固 biàn láogù. **3** [正式用语] 集中(注意力等)于 jízhōng yú: *~ on an idea* 集中于一个想法. ~**er** /'fɑ:snə(r)/ 扣件 kòujiàn, 钮扣 niǔkòu, 钩扣 gōukòu: *a 'zip-~er* 拉链. ~**ing** 扣件 kòujiàn, 闩[閂] shuān.

fas·tid·ious /fə'stɪdɪəs/ *adj* 难[難]讨好的 nán tǎohǎo de, 爱[愛]挑剔的 ài tiāotì de. ~**ly** *adv*.

fat¹ /fæt/ *adj* [-ter, -test] **1** 肥的 féide, 胖的 pàngde. **2** 厚的 hòude, 丰[豐]满的 fēngmǎnde: *a ~ wallet* 鼓鼓的皮夹子. **3** (土地)肥沃的 féiwòde, 富的 fùde. '~-**head** 笨人 bènrén, 傻子 shǎzi. ~**ness** *n* [U] ~**ty** *adj* [-ier, -iest] 含脂肪的 hán zhīfáng de, 脂肪似的 zhīfáng shìde.

fat² /fæt/ *n* [C, U] 脂肪 zhīfáng.

fa·tal /'feɪtl/ *adj* **1** 致命的 zhìmìngde, 毁灭[滅]性的 huǐmièxìngde: *a ~ accident* 惨祸, 人命事故. **2** 命运[運]的 mìngyùnde, 决定命运的 juédìng mìngyùn de, 注定的 zhùdìngde: *the ~ day* 决定命运的一天. ~**ly** *adv*

fa·tal·ity /fə'tælətɪ/ *n* [*pl* -ies] **1** [C] 不幸 búxìng, 灾[災]祸 zāihuò, 灾难[難] zāinàn. **2** [C] 因事故死亡 yīn shìgù sǐwáng.

fate /feɪt/ *n* **1** [U] 命运[運] mìngyùn, 天数[數] tiānshù. **2** [C] 未来[來]的吉凶 wèiláide jíxiōng; 结局 jiéjú. ~**ful** /-fl/ *adj* 命中决定的 mìng zhōng juédìng de, 重要的 zhòngyào de. ~**fully** /-fəlɪ/ *adv*

fa·ther /'fɑ:ðə(r)/ *n* [C] **1** 父亲[親] fùqin, 爸爸 bàba. **2** [常用 *pl*] 祖先 zǔxiān. **3** 创[創]始人 chuàngshǐrén, 奠基人 diànjīrén: *the ~ of the revolution* 革命之父. **4** 神父 shénfù, 教士 jiàoshì. **Our (Heavenly) F~** 上帝 shàngdì. **the Holy F~** 罗[羅]马[馬]教皇 luómǎ jiàohuáng. □ *vt* 当…的父亲 dāng…de fùqin. '~-**in-law** *n* [C] [*pl* ~s-in-law] 岳父 yuèfù; 公公(丈夫的父亲) gōnggong. '~**land** *n* [C] 祖国[國] zǔguó. ~**ly** *adj* 父亲的 fùqinde, 慈父般的 cífù bān de.

fathom /'fæðəm/ *n* [C] 㖊[噚](测量水深的单位,约合 1.8 米)xún. □ *vt* **1** 测…的深度 cè…de shēndù. **2** 充分了解 chōngfèn liǎojiě. ~**less** *adj* 高深莫测的 gāoshēn mòcède.

fa·tigue /fə'ti:g/ *n* **1** [U] 疲劳[勞] píláo, 劳累 láolèi. **2** [U] (金属材料)疲劳 píláo. **3** [C] [军事]杂

〔雜〕役 záyì. □ *vt* 使疲劳 shǐ píláo.

fat·ten /ˈfætn/ *vt/i* 养〔養〕肥 yǎngféi. 使肥沃 shǐ féiwò, 长〔長〕肥 zhǎngféi; 致富 zhìfù.

fatu·ous /ˈfætʃʊəs/ *adj* 愚昧的 yúmèide, 蠢的 chǔnde: ~ *remarks* 蠢话. ~**ly** *adv*

fau·cet /ˈfɔːsɪt/ *n* [C] 〔美语〕= tap[1].

fault /fɔːlt/ *n* **1** [C] 缺点 quēdiǎn, 毛病 máobing: *an electrical ~ in the engine* 发动机中电路的毛病. *at* ~ 出毛病 chū máobing, 生故障 shēng gùzhàng. *find ~ with* 埋怨 mányuàn, 挑剔 tiāoti. **2** [U] 过〔過〕错 guòcuò, (错误的)责任 zérèn: *It's your ~.* 是你的过错. **3** [C] 〔地质〕断〔斷〕层〔層〕duàncéng. □ *vt* 找…缺点〔點〕zhǎo … quēdiǎn: *I cannot ~ his performance.* 我挑不出他的毛病. **faulty** *adj* [-ier, -iest]

fauna /ˈfɔːnə/ *n* [U] 动〔動〕物群(同一地区或同一时代) dòngwùqún.

fa·vour [美语 = **favor**] /ˈfeɪvə(r)/ *n* **1** [U] 好感 hǎogǎn, 喜爱〔愛〕xǐ'ài: *look upon a scheme with ~* 赞成一项方案. **2** [U] 赞成 zànchéng, 支持 zhīchí. *in ~ of* **(a)** 赞成 zànchéng, 支持 zhīchí. **(b)** 以…为〔爲〕收款人yǐ…wéi shōukuǎnrén. *cheques paid in ~ of a club* 开给一个俱乐部的支票. *in sb's ~* 对某人有利 duì mǒurén yǒulì. **3** [C] *do sb a ~* 为某人帮个〔個〕忙 wèi mǒurén bāng gè máng. □ *vt* **1** 支持 zhīchí. **2** 偏爱 piān'ài, 偏袒 piāntǎn. ~**able** /-rəbl/ *adj* 赞成的 zànchéngde, 起促进〔進〕作用的 qǐ cùjìn zuòyòng de. ~**ably** *adv*

fa·vour·ite [美语 = **-vor-**] /ˈfeɪvərɪt/ *n* [C] **1** 宠〔寵〕儿〔兒〕chǒng'ér, 宠物 chǒngwù. **2** *the ~* 有希望获〔獲〕胜〔勝〕的马〔馬〕yǒu xīwàng huòshèng de mǎ. □ *adj* 宠爱〔愛〕的 chǒng'ài de, 受宠的 shòuchǒngde.

fawn[1] /fɔːn/ *n* **1** [C] 幼鹿 yòulù. **2** [U] 浅〔淺〕黄褐色 qiǎnhuánghèsè. □ *adj* 浅黄褐色的 qiǎnhuánghèsède.

fawn[2] /fɔːn/ *vi* **1** (狗)摇尾乞怜〔憐〕yáowěiqǐlián. **2** ~ *on sb* 奉承 fèngcheng, 讨好 tǎohǎo.

F.B.I. =Federal Bureau of Investigation (美国)联〔聯〕邦调查局 liánbāng diàochájú.

fear /fɪə(r)/ *n* **1** [C, U] 恐惧〔懼〕kǒngjù, 害怕 hàipà. **2** [U] 忧〔憂〕虑〔慮〕(*of*) yōulǜ, 担〔擔〕心 dānxīn: *in ~ of his life* 担心他有生命危险. **3** [U] 可能性 kěnéngxìng: *There's no ~ of me going.* 没有我去的可能性. 我不会去的. *No ~!* 〔非正式用语〕当〔當〕然不! dāngránbù! □ *vt/i* **1** 害怕 (of) hàipà, 惧怕 jùpà. **2** ~ *for* 担心 dānxīn, 担忧 dānyōu: ~ *for one's life* 担心他有生命危险. **3** 担心 dānxīn: ~ *the worst* 担心最坏的情况已经(将要)发生. ~**ful** *adj* **(a)** 吓〔嚇〕人的 xiàrénde, 可怕的 kěpàde. **(b)** 〔非正式用语〕极〔極〕大的 jídàde: *a ~ful mess* 非常混乱. **(c)** 受惊〔驚〕的 shòujīngde. ~**fully** *adv* ~**less** *adj* 不怕的 búpàde, 无〔無〕畏的 wúwèide. ~**less·ly** *adv*

feas·ible /ˈfiːzəbl/ *adj* **1** 可行的 kěxíngde, 可做的 kězuòde. **2** 〔非正式用语〕可信的 kěxìnde. **feasiˈbility** *n* [U]

feast /fiːst/ *n* [C] **1** 宗教节〔節〕日 zōngjiào jiérì. **2** 筵席 yánxí, 宴会〔會〕yànhuì. □ *vt/i* **1** 宴请 yànqǐng, 参〔參〕加宴会 cānjiā yànhuì. **2** 使享受 shǐ xiǎngshòu: ~ *one's eyes on* 饱看.

feat /fiːt/ *n* [C] 功绩 gōngjì.

feather /ˈfeðə(r)/ *n* [C] 羽毛 yǔmáo. *a ~ in one's cap* 引以为〔爲〕荣〔榮〕的事物 yǐn yǐ wéiróng de shìwù. □ *vt* 用羽毛装〔裝〕饰 yòng yǔmáo zhuāngshì. ~ *one's nest* 营〔營〕私 yíngsī, 自肥 zìféi. **feath·ery** *adj* 轻〔輕〕而软〔軟〕的 qīng ér ruǎn de.

fea·ture /ˈfiːtʃə(r)/ *n* [C] **1** 脸〔臉〕的一部分(眼,口,鼻等) liǎnde yíbùfen. **2** [*pl*] 面貌 miànmào. **3** 特征〔徵〕tèzhēng: *a major ~ of the place* 该地方的主要特征. **4** (报纸)特写〔寫〕tèxiě. **5** 故事片 gùshìpiàn, 艺〔藝〕术〔術〕片 yìshùpiàn. □ *vt* 以…为〔爲〕特色 yǐ…wéi tèsè, 是…的特色 shì…de tèsè: *A film featuring Ted Jones* 特德·琼斯主演的影片. ~**less** *adj* 平凡的 píngfánde; 不吸引人的 bù xīyǐn rén de.

Feb. =February.

Feb·ru·ary /ˈfebrʊərɪ/ *n* 二月 èryuè.

fed /fed/ *pt,pp* of feed.

Fed.= **1** Federal. **2** Federated. **3** Federation.

fed·eral /ˈfedərəl/ *adj* **1** 联〔聯〕邦制的 liánbāngzhìde, 以联邦制为基础的 yǐ liánbāngzhì wéi jīchǔ de. **2** 关〔關〕于联邦政府的 guānyú liánbāng zhèngfǔ de.

fed·er·ate /ˈfedəreɪt/ *vt/i* (使)结成同盟 jiéchéng tóngméng.

fed·er·ation /ˌfedəˈreɪʃn/ *n* **1** [C]

联〔聯〕邦 liánbāng. **2** [C] 同盟 tóngméng. **3** [U] 联盟 liánméng.

fee /fi:/ *n* **1** [C] 费(学费,手续费等) fèi. **2** 报〔報〕名费 bàomíngfèi; 会〔會〕费 huìfèi.

feeble /'fi:bl/ *adj* [-r, -st] 虚弱的 xūruòde, 无〔無〕力的 wúlìde. ˌ**~-'minded** *adj* 低能的 dīnéngde, 笨的 bènde. **feebly** *adv*

feed /fi:d/ *n* **1** [C] (动物和婴儿)一餐 yīcān: *The dog has two ~s a day.* 这狗一天吃两顿. **2** [U] 饲料 sìliào. **3** [C] (机器)进〔進〕料管 jìnliàoguǎn, 进料槽 jìnliàocáo; [U] 供给的原料 gōngjǐde yuánliào. ☐ *vt/i* [*pt, pp* fed/fed/] **1** 喂 wèi, 饲 sì. *be* ˌ*fed* '*up* (*with*) [俚语]生气〔氣〕shēngqì, 厌〔厭〕烦 yànfán. **2** (动物)吃 chī. **3** *~ on* 以…为〔爲〕食物 yǐ...wéi shíwù. **4** 供给 gōngjǐ, 供料 gòngliào: *~ power (oil) into a machine* 为机器供电(油). '**~ing-bottle** 婴儿〔兒〕奶瓶 yīng'ér nǎipíng.

feed·back /'fi:dbæk/ *n* [U] 反应〔應〕fǎnyìng, 用户反应 yònghù fǎnyìng: *~ from our customers has been very positive (negative)* 用户对我们产品的反应很好(不好).

feel /fi:l/ *vt/i* [*pt, pp* felt /felt/] **1** 触〔觸〕chù, 摸 mō. **2** 摸索 mōsuǒ. **3** 感知 gǎnzhī, 觉〔覺〕得 juédé, 感觉 gǎnjué: *~ cold* 感觉冷. **4** 觉得(非由接触) juédé: *She felt concern for them.* 她很关心他们. **5** 有某种〔種〕感觉〔覺〕yǒu mǒuzhǒng gǎnjué, 身受 shēnshòu: *~ happy* 感到快乐. **6** *~ for* 同情 tóngqíng. **7** 给人某种印象 gěi rén mǒuzhǒng yìnxiàng: *This suit doesn't ~ right.* 这身衣服好象不太合适. **8** *~ like* 想要 xiǎngyào: *~ like (eating) a meal* 想要吃饭. **9** 感觉难〔難〕受, 痛苦 gǎnjué nánshòu, tòngkǔ: *~ the heat* 感到热. **10** 以为〔爲〕yǐwéi, 认〔認〕为 rènwéi: *He felt he would succeed.* 他认为他会成功. **11** 理解 lǐjiě, 领会〔會〕lǐnghuì: *~ the force of an argument* 领会到论据的力量. ☐ *n* [只用 *pl*] **1** 感受 gǎnshòu. **2** 感觉 gǎnjué, 触觉 chùjué.

feeler /'fi:lə(r)/ *n* [C] **1** 触〔觸〕角 chùjiǎo, 触须〔鬚〕chùxū. **2** 试探性建议〔議〕shìtànxìng jiànyì.

feel·ing /'fi:lɪŋ/ *n* **1** [U] 知觉〔覺〕zhījué. **2** [C] 触〔觸〕觉 chùjué, 感觉 gǎnjué; 情绪 qíngxù. **3** [常用单] 一般人的意见 yìbānrénde yìjiàn: *Public ~ was hostile to the proposal.* 舆论反对这个建议. **4** [*pl*] 情绪 qíngxù. **5** [U] 同情 tóngqíng, 体〔體〕谅 tǐliàng.

feet /fi:t/ *n pl* of foot.

feint /feɪnt/ *n* [C] 假象 jiǎxiàng, 伪〔僞〕装〔裝〕wěizhuāng. ☐ *vi* 装作 zhuāngzuò.

fe·line /'fi:laɪn/ *adj* 猫的 māode, 猫一样〔樣〕的 māo yíyàng de.

fell[1] /fel/ *pt* of fall.

fell[2] /fel/ *n* [C] 荒野 huāngyě, 沼泽〔澤〕地 zhǎozédì.

fell[3] /fel/ *vt* 击〔擊〕倒 jīdǎo, 砍倒 kǎndǎo.

fel·low /'feləʊ/ *n* [C] **1** [过时的非正式用语] 家伙 jiāhuo; 小伙子 xiǎohuǒzi. **2** [常用 *pl*] 伙伴 huǒbàn: '*school ~s* 同学. **3** [用作定语] 同伴 tóngbàn: '*~-'prisoners* 同监犯人. **4** 学〔學〕术〔術〕团〔團〕体〔體〕的成员 xuéshùtuántǐde chéngyuán. **~ship** *n* **(a)** [U] 交情 jiāoqing, 友谊 yǒuyí. **(b)** [C] 团体 tuántǐ; 协〔協〕会〔會〕xiéhuì.

fel·ony /'felənɪ/ *n* [C, U] [*pl* -ies] [法律] 重罪 zhòngzuì. **felon** *n* [C] 重罪犯 zhòngzuìfàn.

felt[1] /felt/ *pt, pp* of feel.

felt[2] /felt/ *n* [U] 毡 zhān.

fe·male /'fi:meɪl/ *adj* **1** 雌的 cíde. **2** (植物)雌性的 cíxìngde. **3** 女性的 nǚxìngde, 妇〔婦〕女的 fùnǚde. **4** (机械) 阴〔陰〕的 yīnde, 内的 nèide. ☐ *n* [C] 雌性动〔動〕物 cíxìng dòngwù.

femi·nine /'femənɪn/ *adj* **1** 女性的 nǚxìngde, 妇〔婦〕女的 fùnǚde. **2** [语法] 阴〔陰〕性的 yīnxìngde. **femi'nin·ity** 女人气〔氣〕nǚrénqì. **fem·in·ism** 女权〔權〕运〔運〕动〔動〕nǚquán yùndòng; 男女平等主义〔義〕nánnǚpíngděngzhǔyì. ⇨ lib. **fem·in·ist** 男女平等主义者 nánnǚpíngděngzhǔyìzhě.

fen /fen/ *n* [C] 沼泽〔澤〕zhǎozé.

fence[1] /fens/ *n* [C] 篱〔籬〕笆 líba; 栅栏〔欄〕zhàlan. *sit on the ~* 骑〔騎〕墙〔牆〕qíqiáng, 观〔觀〕望不作决定 guānwàng búzuò juédìng. ☐ *vt* 把…用篱笆围〔圍〕起来〔來〕bǎ...yòng líba wéi qǐlái. **fenc·ing** *n* [U] 筑栅栏的材料 zhù zhàlan de cáiliào.

fence[2] /fens/ *vt* **1** 击〔擊〕剑〔劍〕jījiàn. **2** [喻] 搪塞 tángsāi; 模棱两可 móléngliǎngkě. **fencer** 击剑者 jījiànzhě. **fenc·ing** *n* [U] 击剑术〔術〕jījiànshù.

fend /fend/ *vt/i* **1** *~ off* 挡〔擋〕开〔開〕dǎngkāi: *~ off a blow* 挡开一击; *~ off an attack* 挡开攻击. **2** *~ for oneself* 照料自己 zhàoliào zìjǐ.

fer·ment[1] /'fɜ:ment/ *n* **1** [C] 酵素

xiàosù; 酶 méi. **2** *in a* ~ [喻]骚〔騷〕动〔動〕sāodòng; 激动 jīdòng.

fer·ment² /fə'ment/ *vt/i* **1** (使)发〔發〕酵 fāxiào. **2** [喻](使)激动〔動〕jīdòng; (使)骚〔騷〕动 sāodòng. **~a·tion** /-'teɪʃn/ *n* [U]

fern /fɜ:n/ *n* [C,U] (植物) 蕨类〔類〕juélèi.

fer·ocious /fə'rəʊʃəs/ *adj* 凶猛的 xiōngměngde, 凶残〔殘〕的 xiōngcánde, 凶恶〔惡〕的 xiōng'ède. **~ly** *adv*

fer·oc·ity /fə'rɒsətɪ/ *n* [正式用语] [U] 凶猛 xiōngměng, 凶恶〔惡〕xiōng'è: *the ~ of his attack* 他进攻凶猛; [C] [*pl* -ies] 暴行 bàoxíng.

fer·ret /'ferɪt/ *n* [C] 白鼬 báiyòu, 雪貂 xuědiāo. □ *vt/i* **1** 用雪貂狩猎 yòng xuědiāo shòuliè. **2** 搜出 sōuchū; 查获〔獲〕cháhuò; 搜索 sōusuǒ: *~ing about for a lost book* 到处查找一本失去的书.

ferry /'ferɪ/ *n* [C] [*pl* -ies] 渡口 dùkǒu, 渡船 dùchuán. □ *vt/i* 摆〔擺〕渡 bǎidù. **'~-boat** 渡船 dùchuán. **'~man** 渡船工人 dùchuán gōngrén.

fer·tile /'fɜ:taɪl/ *adj* **1** 肥沃的 féiwòde, 富饶〔饒〕的 fùráode, 多产〔產〕的 duōchǎnde. **2** 创〔創〕造力丰〔豐〕富的 chuàngzàolì fēngfù de, 想象力丰富的 xiǎng xiànglì fēngfù de. **3** 能结果实〔實〕的 néng jiē guǒshí de. ⇨ sterile. **fer·til·ity** /fə'tɪlətɪ/ *n* [U]

fer·til·ize /'fɜ:təlaɪz/ *vt* 使肥沃 shǐ féiwò, 使丰富 shǐ fēngfù. **fer·til·izer** *n* [C,U] 肥料 féiliào.

fer·vent /'fɜ:vənt/ *adj* 热〔熱〕情的 rèqíngde, 热烈的 rèliède: *~ desire* 热烈的希望; *~ belief* 热情的信仰; *~ support* 热烈的支持. **~ly** *adv*

fer·vour [美语 = **-vor**] /'fɜ:və(r)/ *n* [U] 炽〔熾〕热〔熱〕zhìrè, 热情 rèqíng; 热烈 rèliè.

fes·ter /'festə(r)/ *vi* **1** 脓〔膿〕疮〔瘡〕nóngchuāng. **2** [喻] (怨恨等) 郁〔鬱〕积〔積〕yùjī; 恶〔惡〕化 èhuà.

fes·ti·val /'festɪvl/ *n* [C] **1** 节〔節〕日 jiérì. **2** 表演会〔會〕期 biǎoyǎn huìqī; 音乐〔樂〕节 yīnyuèjié; 戏〔戲〕剧〔劇〕节 xìjùjié. □ *adj* 节日的 jiérìde.

fes·tive /'festɪv/ *adj* 欢〔歡〕乐〔樂〕的 huānlede.

fes·tiv·ity /fe'stɪvətɪ/ *n* [*pl* -ies] **1** [U] 欢〔歡〕庆〔慶〕huānqìng, 欢乐〔樂〕huānlè. **2** [*pl*] 庆祝活动〔動〕qìngzhù huódòng.

fetch /fetʃ/ *vt/i* **1** (去)取 qǔ. (来) 拿去 náqù, 请来〔來〕qǐnglái: *~ a doctor* 去请一位医生. **2** (货物)售得(价钱) shòudé: *My car ~ed £200.* 我的汽车卖了 200 英镑.

fête /feɪt/ *n* [C] 节〔節〕日 jiérì; 盛宴 shèngyàn. □ *vt* 款待 kuǎndài, 盛宴招待 shèngyàn zhāodài.

fetid /'fetɪd/ *adj* 腐臭的 fǔchòude.

fet·ish /'fetɪʃ/ *n* [C] [*pl* ~es] 偶像 ǒuxiàng, 迷信物 míxìnwù.

fet·ter /'fetə(r)/ *n* [C] **1** 脚镣 jiǎoliào. **2** [喻][常用 *pl*] 羁〔羈〕绊 jībàn, 束缚 sùfú: *the ~s of government controls* 政府控制的束缚. □ *vt* **1** 为…上脚镣 wèi…shàng jiǎoliào. **2** [喻]束缚 sùfú, 拘束 jūsù.

feud /fju:d/ *n* [C] 长〔長〕期不和 chángqī bùhé. □ *vt* 长期争吵 chángqī zhēngchǎo.

feu·dal /'fju:dl/ *adj* 封建的 fēngjiànde, 封建制度的 fēngjiànzhìdù de. **~ism** *n* [U] 封建主义 fēngjiànzhǔyì.

fe·ver /'fi:və(r)/ *n* **1** [U] 发〔發〕烧〔燒〕fāshāo, 热〔熱〕度 rèdù. **2** [U] 热病 rèbìng. **3** [*sing* 与 *a* 连用] 狂热 kuángrè, 兴〔興〕奋〔奮〕xìngfèn: *in a ~ of impatience* 急不可耐. **~ish** *adj* 有热病症〔癥〕状〔狀〕的 yǒu rèbìng zhèngzhuàng de, 热病的 rèbìngde. **~ish·ly** *adv*

few /fju:/ *adj* [-er, -est] *pron* [与 *many* 相对; ⇨ little, much] **1** [与 *pl noun* 连用] 很少 hěnshǎo: *F~ men came home from the war.* 这场战争很少人生还. **2** [与 *a* 连用]少数〔數〕的 shǎoshùde, 不多的 bùduōde: *A ~ of us survived.* 我们中有少数几个人幸存.

fi·ancé /fɪ'ɑ:nseɪ/ *n* [C] 未婚夫 wèihūnfū. **~e** *n* [C] 未婚妻 wèihūnqī.

fi·asco /fɪ'æskəʊ/ *n* [C] [*pl* ~s] 惨〔慘〕败 cǎnbài, 大败 dàbài.

fib /fɪb/ *n* [C] [非正式用语]小小的谎话 xiǎoxiǎode huǎnghuà. □ *vi* [-bb-] 撒小谎 sā xiǎohuǎng. **~ber** *n* [C]

fibre [美语 = **fiber**] /'faɪbə(r)/ *n* **1** [C] 纤〔纖〕维 xiānwéi. **2** [U] 纤维组织〔织〕xiānwéi zǔzhī. **3** [U] 结构〔構〕jiégòu; 质〔質〕地 zhìdì. **4** [U] [喻]性格 xìnggé; 品质 pǐnzhì: *moral ~* 品格. **'~-glass** 玻璃纤维 bōli xiānwéi. **fi·brous** /-brəs/ *adj* 纤维构〔構〕成的 xiānwéi gòuchéng de. 纤维状〔狀〕的 xiānwéizhuàngde.

fickle /'fɪkl/ *adj* (感情等)易变〔變〕的 yìbiànde, 无〔無〕常的 wúchángde.

fic·tion /'fɪkʃn/ *n* **1** [C] 虚构[構] xūgòu. 杜撰 dùzhuàn. **2** [U] 小说 xiǎoshuō.

fic·ti·tious /fɪk'tɪʃəs/ *adj* 虚构[構]的 xūgòude, 杜撰的 dùzhuànde.

fiddle /'fɪdl/ *n* [C] **1** 小提琴 xiǎotíqín. **2** 欺骗[騙]行为[爲] qīpiàn xíngwéi. □ *vt* **1** 用提琴演奏(曲调) yòng tíqín yǎnzòu. **2** 无[無]意识[識]地拨[撥]弄 wú yìshí de bōnòng. **3** [俚语]造假帐[帳] zào jiǎzhàng; 欺骗 qīpiàn. **fid·dler** *n* [C](a)小提琴手 xiǎotíqínshǒu. **(b)** 弄虚作假者 nòngxūzuòjiǎzhě, 造假帐者 zào jiǎzhàng zhě. **fid·dling** *adj* [非正式用语]微不足道的 wēi bù zú dào de. 无[無]足轻[輕]重的 wúzú qīngzhòng de: *fiddling amounts of money* 微不足道的一点钱.

fi·del·ity /fɪ'delətɪ/ *n* [U] **1** 忠诚 zhōngchéng, 忠实[實] zhōngshí. **2** 精确[確] jīngquè, 逼真 bīzhēn: *the ~ of a report* 报告的精确性. ⇨ high-fidelity.

fidget /'fɪdʒɪt/ *vt/i* **1**(使)坐立不安 zuò lì bù ān, (使)烦燥 fánzào. □ *n* [C] **2** 烦燥不安的人 fánzào bù ān de rén. **fidgety** *adj*

field¹ /fiːld/ *n* [C] **1** 田野 tiányě, 田地 tiándì. **2** 场[場]地 chǎngdì, 空地 kōngdì: *a 'football ~* 足球场. **3** 矿[礦]田 kuàngtián: *a coal ~* 煤田 **4** 战[戰]场 zhànchǎng. **5**(学术等)界 jiè, 领域 lǐngyù. **6** (物理)场 chǎng: *a magnetic ~* 磁场. ,**~ marshal** 最高级陆[陸]军将[將]官 zuì gāojí lùjūn jiàngguān. '**~ study** 对[對]第一手材料的有计划[劃]的研究 duì dìyīshǒu cáiliào de yǒu jìhuà de yánjiū.

field² /fiːld/ *vt/i* **1** (板球)截(球) jié; 守(球) shǒu. **2**(使)(足球队等)上场[場] shàngchǎng: *~ a strong team* 派一个强队上场 **~er** (板球等)外场员 wàichǎngyuán; 守队[隊]队员 shǒuduì duìyuán.

fiend /fiːnd/ *n* [C] **1** 魔鬼 móguǐ; 魔王 mówáng. **2** 非常坏[壞]的人 fēicháng huàide rén. **~ish** *adj*

fierce /fɪəs/ *adj* [-r, -st] **1** 凶猛的 xiōngměngde, 残[殘]忍的 cánrěnde; 愤怒的 fènnùde. **2** 狂热[熱]的 kuángrède; 强烈的 qiángliède. **~ly** *adv* **~ness** *n* [U]

fiery /'faɪərɪ/ *adj* [-ier, -iest] **1** 火焰的 huǒyànde, 燃烧[燒]着的 ránshāo zhe de, 火一般的 huǒ yìbān de, 火热[熱]的 huǒrède. **2**(人)易怒的 yìnùde, 脾气[氣]暴躁的 píqì bàozào de. **fier·ily** *adv*

fif·teen /,fɪ'fti:n/ *adj, n* [C] 十五 shíwǔ, 十五个[個] shíwǔgè. **fif·teenth** *adj, n* [C] (略作 15*th*) 十五分之一 shíwǔfēn zhī yī; 十五分之一的 shíwǔfēn zhī yī de; 第十五 dìshíwǔ, 第十五个 dìshíwǔgè.

fifth /fɪfθ/ *adj, n* [C] (略作 5*th*) 五分之一 wǔfēn zhī yī; 五分之一的 wǔfēn zhī yī de; 第五 dìwǔ, 第五个[個] dìwǔgè.

fifty /'fɪftɪ/ *adj, n* [C] 五十 wǔshí, 五十个[個] wǔshígè. **fif·ti·eth** /-əθ/ *adj, n* [C] (略作 50*th*) 五十分之一 wǔshífēn zhī yī; 五十分之一的 wǔshífēn zhī yī de; 第五十 dìwǔshí, 第五十个 dìwǔshígè.

fig /fɪg/ *n* [C] 无[無]花果 wúhuāguǒ, 无花果树[樹] wúhuāguǒshù.

fig. = figure.

fight /faɪt/ *vt/i* [*pt,pp* fought /fɔ:t/] 打架 dǎjià, 搏斗[鬥] bódòu, 打仗 dǎzhàng. **~ *it out*** 决一雌雄 juéyìcíxióng. □ *n* **1** [C] 战[戰]斗 zhàndòu, 搏斗 bódòu. **2** [U] 战斗力 zhàndòulì, 战斗的愿[願]望 zhàndòude yuànwàng. **~er (a)** 战士 zhànshì, 兵士 bīngshì. **(b)** 战斗机 zhàndòujī.

fig·ment /'fɪgmənt/ *n* [C] 想象的事 xiǎngxiàngde shì, 虚构[構]的事 xūgòude shì: *a ~ of his imagination* 他想象中的事物.

fig·urat·ive /'fɪgjərətɪv/ *adj* (词语)比喻的 bǐyùde. **~ly** *adv*

fig·ure /'fɪgə(r)/ *n* [C] **1** 数[數]字 shùzì. **2** [*pl*] 算术[術] suànshù, 计算 jìsuàn. **3** 图[圖]形 túxíng; 图表 túbiǎo. **4** 人像 rénxiàng; 画[畫]像 huàxiàng; 雕像 diāoxiàng; 鸟[鳥]兽[獸]像 niǎoshòuxiàng. **5** 人形 rénxíng, 体[體]态[態] tǐtài: *She has a good ~.* 她体态优美. **6** 人物 rénwù, 地位 dìwèi, 身份 shēnfen: *famous ~s in history* 历史上的著名人物. □ *vt/i* **1** 相信 xiāngxìn, 估计 gūjì: *I ~ he's dead.* 我相信他是死了. **2** 露头[頭]角 lù tóujiǎo, 扮演角色 bànyǎn juésè: *~ in history* 在历史上崭露头角. **3 ~ *sth out*** 计算出 jìsuànchū, 解决 jiějué. **~ *sb out*** 理解 lǐjiě, 推断[斷]出 tuīduànchū. '**~-head** 挂[掛]名首脑 guàmíng shǒunǎo. ,**~ of 'speech** 修辞格 xiūcígé.

fila·ment /'fɪləmənt/ *n* [C] 细丝 xìsī; 灯[燈]丝 dēngsī.

file¹ /faɪl/ *n* [C] 锉 cuò, 锉刀 cuòdāo. □ *vt* 锉 cuò; 锉平 cuòpíng; 锉光 cuòguāng. **fil·ings** *n pl* 锉屑 cuòxiè.

file² /faɪl/ *n* [C] **1** 文件夹 wénjiànjiā, 公文箱 gōngwénxiāng; 卷宗 juànzōng. **2** 档〔檔〕案 dàng'àn. □ *vt* 把…归〔歸〕档 bǎ...guīdàng.

file³ /faɪl/ *n* [C] 纵〔縱〕列 zòngliè. ***the rank and*** ~ **(a)** 普通士兵 pǔtōng shìbīng. **(b)** 〔喻〕普通人 pǔtōngrén. □ *vi* 成纵队〔隊〕前进〔進〕 chéng zòngduì qiánjìn: ~ *out of the room* 从房里鱼贯而出.

fill /fɪl/ *vt/i* **1** 装〔裝〕满 zhuāngmǎn, 注满 zhùmǎn, 充满 chōngmǎn. **2** 担〔擔〕任职〔職〕务〔務〕 dānrèn zhíwù, 派人担任 pàirén dānrèn: ~ *a vacancy* 补上空缺. **3** ~ ***in*** 填充 tiánchōng, 填写〔寫〕 tiánxiě; 填满 tiánmǎn: ~ *in a form* 填写表格. ~ ***out*** **(a)** 变〔變〕大 biàndà, 使长〔長〕大 shǐ zhǎngdà. **(b)** 〔美语〕= fill in. ~ ***up*** 填补〔補〕 tiánbǔ, 装满 zhuāngmǎn. □ *n* [U] 饱 bǎo; 充分 chōngfèn: *eat one's* ~ 吃饱 chībǎo. ~**ing** 填补物 tiánbǔwù.

fil·let /ˈfɪlɪt/ *n* [C] 肉片 ròupiàn, 鱼片 yúpiàn. □ *vt* (把鱼,肉)切成片 qiē chéng piàn.

filly /ˈfɪlɪ/ *n* [C] [*pl* -ies] 小母马〔馬〕 xiǎo mǔmǎ.

film /fɪlm/ *n* **1** [C] 薄膜 bómó, 膜 mó, 薄层〔層〕 bócéng: *a* ~ *of oil* 一层油; *a* ~ *of ice* 一层薄冰. **2** [C,U] 胶〔膠〕卷 jiāojuǎn, 软〔軟〕片 ruǎnpiàn. **3** [C] 影片 yǐngpiàn, 电〔電〕影 diànyǐng. □ *vt/i* 拍电影 pāi diànyǐng. ˈ~ **star** 电影明星 diànyǐng míngxīng. ˈ~ **strip** 幻灯〔燈〕卷片 huàndēng juǎnpiàn. **filmy** *adj* [-ier, -iest] 薄膜似的 bómó sìde.

fil·ter /ˈfɪltə(r)/ *n* [C] **1** 滤〔濾〕器 lǜqì; 滤纸 lǜzhǐ. **2** 滤光器 lǜguāngqì; 滤色器 lǜsèqì. **3** (无线电)滤波器 lǜbōqì. □ *vt/i* **1** 滤过〔過〕 lǜguò. 〔喻〕透过 tòuguò, 渗〔滲〕入 shènrù. ˈ~ **tip** 香烟〔煙〕过滤嘴 xiāngyān guòlǜzuǐ. ˌ~-ˈ**tipped** *adj*

filth /fɪlθ/ *n* [U] **1** 污秽〔穢〕 wūhuì, 污物 wūwù. **2** 淫猥 yínwěi: *sex films and other* ~ 色情片等低级下流的东西.

filthy *adj* [-ier, -iest]

fin /fɪn/ *n* [C] **1** 鳍 qí. **2** 鳍状〔狀〕的东〔東〕西 qízhuàngde dōngxi. *tail-*~ (飞机)直尾翅 zhíwěichì.

fi·nal /ˈfaɪnl/ *adj* **1** 最后〔後〕的 zuìhòude, 最终的 zuìzhōngde. **2** 确〔確〕定性的 quèdìngxìngde, 决定性的 juédìngxìngde: *a* ~ *decision* 最后的决定. □ *n* [C] 〔常用 *pl*〕期终考试 qīzhōng kǎoshì; 最后考试 zuìhòu kǎoshì; 决赛 juésài: *the Cup F*~ 足球杯决赛. ~**ly** *adv* **(a)** 最后地 zuìhòude, 最终地 zuìzhōngde. **(b)** 决定性地 juédìngxìngde, 只此一次 zhǐcǐyícì: *It's* ~*ly agreed.* 完全达成一致. ~**ize** *vt* 把(计划等)最后定下来〔來〕 bǎ zuìhòu dìng xiàlái.

fi·nance /ˈfaɪnæns/ *n* **1** [U] 财政 cáizhèng; 金融 jīnróng: *an expert in* ~ 财政专家. **2** [*pl*] (政府或企业的)财源 cáiyuán; 资金 zījīn. □ *vt* 为…提供资金 wèi...tígòng zījīn. **fiˈnan·cial** /-ʃl/ *adj* **fi·nan·cially** *adv* **fin·an·cier** /fɪˈnænsɪə(r)/ *n* [C] 金融专〔專〕家 jīnróng zhuānjiā, 财政专家 cáizhèng zhuānjiā.

finch /fɪntʃ/ *n* [C] 雀科鸣〔鳴〕禽 quèkē míngqín.

find /faɪnd/ *vt* [*pt,pp* found/faʊnd/] **1** 找到 zhǎodào, 寻得 xúndé. **2** 发〔發〕现 fāxiàn: ~ *a solution* 发现解决办法. ~ ***fault (with)*** ⇨ fault (1). **3** 自然地到达〔達〕 zìránde dàodá: *Rivers* ~ *their way to the sea.* 条条江河归大海. **4** 感到 gǎndào, 认〔認〕为〔爲〕 rènwéi: *I* ~ *it difficult to understand him.* 我觉得了解他是困难的. **5** (常用 ~ ***out***) 打听〔聽〕 dǎtīng, 了解 liáojiě, 获〔獲〕知 huòzhī: ~ *out when a train leaves* 打听火车开的时间. **6** 供给 gōngjǐ, 供应〔應〕 gōngyìng, 提供 tígòng: ~ *the money for something* 为某事筹款. **7** 〔法律〕判决 pànjué, 裁决 cáijué: ~ *him innocent* 判他无罪. □ *n* [C] 发现 fāxiàn, 被发现的东西 bèi fāxiàn de dōngxi. ~**ing** 〔常用 *pl*〕 **(a)** 发现 fāxiàn; 发现物 fāxiànwù. **(b)** 裁决 cáijué, 判决 pànjué.

fine¹ /faɪn/ *adj* [-r, -st] **1** (天气)晴朗的 qínglǎngde. **2** 体〔體〕格健全的 tǐgé jiànquán de. **3** 可爱〔愛〕的 kě'àide, 美好的 měihǎo de: *a* ~ *meal* 一顿美餐; *a* ~ *view* 美丽的景色. **4** 纤〔纖〕细的 xiānxìde, 精巧的 jīngqiǎode. **5** 微小的 wēixiǎode: ~ *powder* 细微的粉末. **6** 细的 xìde, 尖的 jiānde: *a* ~ *needle* 尖的针. **7** (金属)纯的 chúnde. **8** 不容易理解的 bù róngyì lǐjiě de; 细微的 xìwēide: *a* ~ *distinction* 细微的区别. **9** (感觉等)灵〔靈〕敏的 língmǐnde, 精细的 jīngxìde: *a* ~ *taste* 精明的鉴赏力. ***cut it*** ~ 时〔時〕间〔間〕抠〔摳〕得很紧〔緊〕 shíjiān kōu de hěnjǐn. □ *adv* 很好 hěnhǎo, 妙 miào. ~ **art; the ~ arts** 诗歌, 音乐〔樂〕, 绘〔繪〕画〔畫〕等 shīgē, yīnyuè, huìhuà děng. **~ly** *adv* **(a)** 美好地 měihǎode, 华〔華〕丽〔麗〕地 huálìde. **(b)** 细小地 xìxiǎode: *~ly cut meat* 切得很细的肉.

fine² /faɪn/ *n* [C] 罚款 fákuǎn, 罚金 fájīn. □ *vt* 处〔處〕以罚金 chùyǐ fájīn.

fin·ery /ˈfaɪnərɪ/ *n* [U] 华丽〔麗〕的服饰 huálìde fúshì, 优〔優〕美的外表 yōuměide wàibiǎo.

fi·nesse /fɪˈnes/ *n* [U] 手腕 shǒuwàn; 策略 cèlüè.

fin·ger /ˈfɪŋgə(r)/ *n* [C]手指 shǒuzhǐ. *keep one's ~s crossed* 〔喻〕祈求好运〔運〕qíqiú hǎoyùn. *lay a ~ on* 触〔觸〕chù, 碰 pèng. *not lift a ~* 不作举〔舉〕手之劳〔勞〕búzuò jǔshǒu zhī láo. □ *vt* 用手指碰 yòng shǒuzhǐ pèng, 拨〔撥〕弄 bōnòng. **ˈ~nail** 指甲 zhǐjia. **ˈ~print** 指纹印 zhǐwényìn. **ˈ~-tip** 指尖 zhǐjiān. *have sth at one's ~tips* 熟知某事物 shúzhī mǒushìwù.

fin·ish /ˈfɪnɪʃ/ *vt/i* **1** 完成 wánchéng, 结束 jiésù. **2** 使完美 shǐ wánměi. *~ off* 结束 jiésù, 干〔幹〕掉 gàndiào, 杀〔殺〕死 shāsǐ. □ *n* [只用 *sing*] **1** 结束 jiésù, 最后〔後〕阶段 zuìhòu jiēduàn. **2** 完美 wánměi, 举〔舉〕止优〔優〕雅 jǔzhǐ yōuyǎ: *woodwork with a good ~* 漆得精美的木器. **3** 表面抛光 biǎomiàn pāoguāng.

fi·nite /ˈfaɪnaɪt/ *adj* **1** 有限的 yǒuxiànde: *~ resources* 有限的资源. **2** 〔语法〕限定的 xiàndìngde: *'Is' and 'was' are ~ forms of 'be'.* "Is" 和 "was" 是 "be" 的限定形式.

fiord, fjord /ˈfɪɔːd/ *n* [C] 峡〔峽〕湾〔灣〕xiáwān.

fir /fɜː(r)/ *n* [C] 冷杉 lěngshān; [U] 冷杉木 lěngshānmù. **ˈ~-cone** ⇨ cone(3).

fire¹ /ˈfaɪə(r)/ *n* **1** [U] 火 huǒ. *Animals dislike ~.* 动物不喜欢火. *on ~* 着火 zháohuǒ, 失火 shīhuǒ. *catch ~* 着火 zháohuǒ, 开〔開〕始燃烧〔燒〕kāishǐ ránshāo. *set sth on ~; set ~ to sth* 使燃烧 shǐ ránshāo. **2** [C] 失火 shīhuǒ, 火灾〔災〕huǒzāi: *forest ~s* 森林火灾. **3** [C] 炉〔爐〕火 lúhuǒ. **4** [U] 炮火 pàohuǒ. *open ~* 开〔開〕火 kāihuǒ; *cease ~* 停火 tínghuǒ. *under ~* **(a)** 遭炮击〔擊〕zāo pàojī. **(b)** 〔喻〕受批评 shòu pīpíng. **5** [U] 热〔熱〕情 rèqíng, 激情 jīqíng. **ˈ~ alarm** 火警 huǒjǐng; 报〔報〕火机〔機〕bàohuǒjī. **ˈ~arm** 火器 huǒqì; 步枪〔槍〕bùqiāng; 手枪 shǒuqiāng. **ˈ~ brigade** 消防队〔隊〕xiāofángduì. **ˈ~ drill** 消防演习〔習〕xiāofáng yǎnxí. **ˈ~-engine** 消防车〔車〕xiāofángchē. **ˈ~-escape** 安全梯 ānquántī. **ˈ~-extinguisher** 灭〔滅〕火器 mièhuǒqì. **ˈ~guard** 火炉栏〔欄〕huǒlúlán. **ˈ~man** 救火员 jiùhuǒyuán. 消防队员 xiāofángduìyuán. **ˈ~place** 壁炉 bìlú. **ˈ~proof** *adj* 防火的 fánghuǒde, 耐火的 nàihuǒde. **ˈ~ station** 消防站 xiāofángzhàn. **ˈ~work** 焰火 yànhuǒ.

fire² /ˈfaɪə(r)/ *vt/i* **1** 使燃烧〔燒〕shǐ ránshāo. **2** 烧制〔製〕shāozhì; 烘制 hōngzhì: *~ pottery in a kiln* 在窑里烧陶器. **3** 给(炉子)加燃料 gěi jiā ránliào. **4** 激起 jīqǐ, 激动〔動〕jīdòng: *~ his imagination* 激起他的想象. **5** 射击〔擊〕shèjī. **6** 〔非正式用语〕开〔開〕除(雇员) kāichú. **ˈfir·ing-line** 火线〔線〕huǒxiàn. **ˈfiring-squad** 执〔執〕行军〔軍〕事法庭判决的行刑队〔隊〕zhíxíng jūnshì fǎtíng pànjué de xíngxíngduì.

firm¹ /fɜːm/ *adj* [-er, -est] **1** 结实〔實〕的 jiēshide, 坚〔堅〕硬的 jiānyìngde. **2** 坚定的 jiāndìngde. **3** 稳定的 wěndìngde, 沉着的 chénzhuóde: *walk with ~ steps* 走路步子坚稳. □ *vt/i* 使坚定 shǐ jiāndìng; 使牢固 shǐ láogù. 变〔變〕坚定 biàn jiāndìng; 变牢固 biàn láogù. □ *adv* = firmly. **~ly** *adv* 坚定地 jiāndìngde, 稳固地 wěngùde. **~ness** *n* [U]

firm² /fɜːm/ *n* [C]商号〔號〕shānghào, 商行 shāngháng.

first¹ /fɜːst/ *adj* (略作 *1st*) 第一 dìyī, 第一个〔個〕dìyīgè. *~ thing* 立即 lìjí. **~ˈaid** (对病人的)急救 jíjiù. **~ˈclass** *n* [U] 头〔頭〕等舱〔艙〕tóuděngcāng, 头等车〔車〕tóuděngchē. □ **ˈ~-class** *adj, adv* 头等的 tóuděngde; 乘头等车 chéng tóuděngchē. **~ ˈfloor** 〔英国英语〕二(层) 楼〔樓〕èrcénglóu; 〔美语〕底层 dǐcéng, 一楼 yīlóu. **~-ˈhand** *adj, adv* (资料等)第一手的 dìyīshǒude, 直接的 zhíjiēde; 直接地 zhíjiēde. **ˈ~ name** 西方人名的第一个〔個〕字 xīfāng rénmíng de dìyīgè zì. **~ ˈperson** 〔语法〕第一人称〔稱〕dìyīrénchēng. **~-ˈrate** *adj* 第一流的 dìyīliúde. **~ly** *adv* 首先 shǒuxiān, 第一 dìyī.

first² /fɜːst/ *adv* **1** 第一 dìyī; 最初 zuìchū, 最先 zuìxiān. **2** 第一次 dìyīcì: *when I ~ saw London* 当

我初访伦敦的时候. '~**born** *adj*, *n* [C] 最先出生的 zuìxiān chūshēng de; 长〔長〕子 zhǎngzǐ; 长女 zhǎngnǚ.

first³ /fɜ:st/ *n* **1** *at* ~ 最初 zuìchū, 当〔當〕初 dāngchū. **2** [C] (比赛) 冠军〔軍〕 guànjūn, 第一名 dìyīmíng.

firth /fɜ:θ/ *n* [C] (苏格兰)河口湾〔灣〕 hékǒuwān.

fish /fɪʃ/ *n*[*pl* ~ 或 ~es] **1** [C] 鱼 yú. **2** [U] 鱼肉 yúròu. '~**monger** 鱼贩子 yúfànzi. □ *vt*/*i* **1** 捕鱼 pǔyú; 钓鱼 diàoyú. **2** [喻]捞〔撈〕取 lāoqǔ; 摸索出 mōsuǒchū: ~ *for compliments* 转弯抹角引出(对方的)恭维. **3** 拉出 lāchū, 掏出 tāochū: ~ *a coin from one's pocket* 从口袋里掏出一个硬币. ~**ing** 捕鱼 pǔyú; 钓鱼 diàoyú: ~*ing-line* 钓丝; ~*ing-rod* 钓杆. ~**er·man** *n* [C] [*pl* -men] 渔民 yúmín, 渔夫 yúfū. ⇨ angler. ~**ery** *n* [C] [*pl* -ies] 渔场〔場〕 yúchǎng. **fishy** *adj* [-ier, -iest] **(a)** (味道等) 象鱼的 xiàng yú de. **(b)** [非正式用语]可疑的 kěyíde: *a* ~*y story* 可疑的说法.

fis·sion /'fɪʃn/ *n* [C, U] (原子)裂变〔變〕 lièbiàn.

fist /fɪst/ *n* [C] 拳 quán, 拳头〔頭〕 quántou.

fit¹ /fɪt/ *adj* [-ter, -test] **1** 适〔適〕合的 shìhéde, 适宜的 shìyíde, 恰当〔當〕的 qiàdāngde: ~ *to eat* 适宜食用. **2** 适当的 shìdāngde, 正当的 zhèngdāngde: *Do as you think* ~. 你认为怎样合适就怎样办. **3** 齐〔齊〕备〔備〕的 qíbèide, 就要…的 jiùyào…de: *laughing* ~ *to burst* 笑不可支. **4** 强健的 qiángjiànde, 健康的 jiànkāngde. ~**ness** *n* [U] **(a)** 适当 shìdāng, 合宜 héyí. **(b)** 健康 jiànkāng.

fit² /fɪt/ *n* [C] **1** (病的) 发〔發〕作 fāzuò. **2** 歇斯底里发作 xiēsīdǐlǐ fāzuò; 痉〔痙〕挛〔攣〕jīngluán. *have a* ~ [非正式用语] 大为〔爲〕惊〔驚〕讶 dàwéi jīngyà, 大发〔發〕脾气〔氣〕 dàfāpíqì. **3** (感情)突发 tūfā: *a* ~ *of enthusiasm* 突然产生热情. ~**ful** *adj* 间〔間〕歇的 jiānxiēde, 不规则的 bù guīzé de. ~**fully** *adv*

fit³ /fɪt/ *vt*/*i* [-tt-] **1** (使)适〔適〕合 shìhé, 合身 héshēn: *These shoes don't* ~. 这双鞋不合脚. **2** (衣服) 试穿 shìchuān: *have a new coat* ~*ted.* 试穿一件新上衣. **3** 安装〔裝〕 ānzhuāng, 装置 zhuāngzhì: ~ *a new window* 安装新窗户. **4** 使符合 shǐ fúhé, 使适应 shǐ shìyìng: *make the punishment* ~ *the crime* 按罪量刑. **5** ~ *in* (*with*) 相合 xiānghé, 合得来〔來〕 hédelái: *I don't* ~ *in with his friends.* 我同他的朋友们合不来. ~ *sb* (*sth*) *out* 装备〔備〕 zhuāngbèi, 配备 pèibèi: ~ *out a ship* 装备一条船. □ *n* 合身 héshēn, 适合 shìhé: *a tight* ~ 贴身. ~**ment** *n* [C] 家具 jiājù, 设备 shèbèi. ~**ter** *n* [C] **(a)** 剪裁并试样〔樣〕的服装工人 jiǎncái bìng shìyàng de fúzhuāng gōngrén. **(b)**装备工 zhuāngbèigōng.

fit·ting /'fɪtɪŋ/ *adj* 适〔適〕合的 shìhéde, 恰当〔當〕的 qiàdāngde. □ *n* [C] **1** 试衣 shìyī, 试穿 shìchuān. **2** 建筑物中的装置 jiànzhùwù zhōng de zhuāngzhì. **3** 家具 jiājù, 陈设 chénshè.

five /faɪv/ *adj*, *n* [C] 五 wǔ 五个〔個〕 wǔgè ⇨ fifth. ~**pence** /'faɪfpəns/ *n* [C] [*pl* ~ pieces]五便士 wǔbiànshì; 五便士硬币〔幣〕 wǔbiànshì yìngbì. **fiver** /-ə(r)/ [非正式用语]五镑钞票 wǔbàng chāopiào.

fix¹ /fɪks/ *n* [C] [*pl* ~es] **1** 窘境 jiǒngjìng, 困境 kùnjìng: *be in a* ~ 处于窘境. **2** 方位 fāngwèi. **3** [俚语]吸毒者的毒品注射 xīdúzhě de dúpǐn zhùshè.

fix² /fɪks/ *vt*/*i* **1** 使固定 shǐ gùdìng, 安装〔裝〕 ānzhuāng, 安置 ānzhì. **2** ~ *on* 盯住 dīngzhù, 凝视 níngshì; 吸引(注意) xīyǐn. **3** 确〔確〕定 quèdìng, 决定 juédìng: ~ *a date for a meeting* 确定开会日期. **4** (摄影)定(影) dìng. **5** ~ *sb up* (*with*) 安排 ānpái, 安顿〔頓〕 āndùn; 解决 jiějué. **6** [非正式用语] 整理 zhěnglǐ: ~ *one's hair* 梳头. **7** [非正式用语] 修理 xiūlǐ. ~**ation** /-'eɪʃn/ *n* [C] 着迷 zháomí; 执〔執〕着 zhízhuó. ~**a·tive** /-'ətɪv/ *n* [C] 固定剂〔劑〕 gùdìngjì. 固着剂 gùzhuójì. ~**ture** /-'tʃə(r)/ *n* [C] **(a)** 附属〔屬〕装〔裝〕置(壁橱等) fùshǔ zhuāngzhì. **(b)** 运〔運〕动〔動〕项目 yuàndòng xiàngmù; 运动项目举〔舉〕行日 yùndòng xiàngmù jǔxíngrì. **(c)** [非正式用语] 不会〔會〕离〔離〕开〔開〕或移动的人 bú huì líkāi huò yídòng de rén.

fizz /fɪz/ *vi* 嘶嘶作响 sīsī zuò xiǎng. □ *n* [U] 嘶嘶声〔聲〕 sīsīshēng. ~**zy** *adj* [-ier, -iest]

fizzle /'fɪzl/ *vi* 嘶嘶地响〔響〕 sīsīde xiǎng. ~ *out* 归〔歸〕于失败 guī yú shībài; 以失败告终 yǐ shībài gàozhōng: *The rebellion soon*

~*d out.* 叛乱很快以失败告终.
fjord /'fi:ɔ:d/ ⇨ fiord.
flabby /'flæbɪ/ *adj* [-ier, -iest] **1** (肌肉)不结实[實]的 bù jiēshide, 松[鬆]弛的 sōngchíde. **2** [喻]软[軟]弱的 ruǎnruòde: *a* ~ *character* 软弱的性格. **flab·bi·ness** *n* [U]
flag¹ /flæg/ *n* [C] 旗 qí. □ *vt* [-gg-] 打旗号[號](使车辆停下) dǎ qíhào: ~ *down a car* 打旗号使汽车停下. '~**pole** 旗杆 qígān. '~**ship** 旗舰[艦] qíjiàn.
flag² /flæg/ *vi* [-gg-] **1** (植物等)萎垂 wěichuí, 凋萎 diāowěi. **2** [喻]衰退 shuāituì, 低落 dīluò.
flagon /'flægən/ *n* [C] 大肚酒瓶 dàdù jiǔpíng.
fla·grant /'fleɪgrənt/ *adj* 明目张[張]胆[膽]的 míngmùzhāngdǎnde, 公然的 gōngránde: ~ *disobedience* 公然抗拒. ~**ly** *adv*
flair /fleə(r)/ *n* [C] [常用 *sing*] 资质[質] zīzhì: *a* ~ *for languages* 学语言的本领.
flake /fleɪk/ *n* [C] 薄片 báopiàn: '*snow-*~*s* 雪片. □ *vi* 撒落 sǎluò, 散落 sànluò. **flaky** *adj* [-ier, -iest]
flam·boy·ant /flæm'bɔɪənt/ *adj* **1** 艳[艷]丽[麗]的 yànlìde, 火红色的 huǒhóngsède. **2** (人)炫耀的 xuànyàode. ~**ly** *adv* **flam·boy·ance** /-əns/ *n* [U]
flame /fleɪm/ *n* **1** [C, U] 火焰 huǒyàn, 火舌 huǒshé. **2** [C] [非正式用语]情人 qíngrén: *an old* ~ 旧情人,过去的情人. □ *vi* **1** 发[發]出火焰 fāchū huǒyàn, 燃烧[燒] ránshāo. **2** 呈火红色 chéng huǒhóngsè. **flam·ing** *adj*
fla·mingo /flə'mɪŋgəʊ/ *n* [C] [*pl* ~s, ~es] 火烈鸟[鳥] huǒlièniǎo.
flam·mable /'flæməbl/ *adj* (= *inflammable*) 易燃的 yìránde.
flan /flæn/ *n* [C] 果酱[醬]饼 guǒjiàngbǐng.
flange /flændʒ/ *n* [C] 凸缘 tūyuán.
flank /flæŋk/ *n* [C] **1** 胁 xié, 胁腹 xiéfù. **2** [军事]侧翼 cèyì. □ *vt* **1** 位于…的侧翼 wèiyú...de cèyì. **2** 包抄…的侧翼 bāochāo...de cèyì.
flan·nel /'flænl/ *n* **1** [U] 法兰[蘭]绒 fǎlánróng. **2** [*pl*] 法兰绒裤子 fǎlánróng kùzi. **3** [C] (洗脸用)法兰绒布块[塊] fǎlánróng bùkuài.
flap /flæp/ *n* [C] **1** 拍打 pāidǎ, 拍击 pāijī, 拍打声[聲] pāidǎshēng. **2** 垂下物 chuíxiàwù; 袋盖 dàigài; 信封口盖 xìnfēng kǒu gài. **3** (飞机)襟翼 jīnyì. **4** *be in (get into) a* ~ [俚语]慌乱[亂] huāngluàn, 神经[經]紧[緊]张[張] shénjīng jǐnzhāng. □ *vt/i* [-pp-] **1** (使)上下左右拍动 shàngxià zuǒyòu pāidòng. 挥[揮]动[動] huīdòng; 拍动 pāidòng; 摆[擺]动 bǎidòng: ~ *one's arms* 挥动手臂; ~ *its wings* 拍动翅膀. **2** 拍打 pāidǎ: ~ *the flies away* 拍掉苍蝇. **3** [俚语]神经紧张 shénjīng jǐnzhāng.
flare¹ /fleə(r)/ *vi* **1** 熊熊地燃烧[燒] xióngxióngde ránshāo. **2** ~ ***up*** **(a)** 突然燃烧 tūrán ránshāo. **(b)** [喻](暴烈行为等)突然爆发[發] tūrán bàofā. '~**-up** *n* □ *n* **1** [U] 摇曳的火焰 yáoyède huǒyàn, 闪烁[爍]的火光 shǎnshuòde huǒguāng. **2** [C] 闪光信号[號]装[裝]置 shǎnguāng xìnhào zhuāngzhì.
flare² /fleə(r)/ *vt/i* (衣裙等)张[張]开[開] zhāngkāi. □ *n* [C] (衣裙等)张开 zhāngkāi.
flash /flæʃ/ *n* [C] **1** 闪[閃]光 shǎnguāng. **2** [喻](思想等)闪现 shǎnxiàn. ***in a*** ~ 刹那 shànà, 转[轉]瞬间[間] zhuǎnshùnjiān. **3** (亦作 '**news**~) (新闻)简[簡]讯 jiǎnxùn. **4** [非正式用语] [用作定语]浮华[華] fúhuá, 华而不实[實] huáérbùshí. ⇨ flashy. □ *vt/i* **1** (使)闪光 shǎnguāng, 闪耀 shǎnyào, 闪烁[爍] shǎnshuò. **2** 闪现 shǎnxiàn, 掠过[過]心头[頭] lüèguò xīntóu. **3** 突然发[發]出 tūrán fāchū: ~ *news* (by TV) (电视)发出新闻. **4** 闪过 shǎnguò: *The train* ~*ed past us.* 火车从我们身旁闪过. '~**back** (电影等)倒叙部分 dàoxù bùfen. '~**bulb** 闪光灯[燈]泡 shǎnguāng dēngpào. ⇨ flashlight(a). '~**light** *n* **(a)** 闪光灯 shǎnguāngdēng. **(b)** 手电[電]筒 shǒudiàntǒng. **flashy** *adj* [-ier, -iest] 华[華]而不实[實]的 huá ér bù shí de, 浮华的 fúhuáde: ~*y clothes* 奇装异服. ~**ily** *adv*
flask /flɑ:sk/ *n* [C] **1** 细颈[頸]瓶 xìjǐngpíng. **2** (亦作 '**hip-**~) (可装在口袋里的)扁形酒瓶 biǎnxíng jiǔpíng. **3** = vacuum flask.
flat¹ /flæt/ *n* [C] [英国英语](在同一层楼上的)一套[套]房间[間] yí tào fángjiān.
flat² /flæt/ *adj* [-ter, -test] **1** 平的 píngde, 平坦的 píngtǎnde, 扁平的 biǎnpíngde. **2** 平展的 píngzhǎnde, 平伸的 píngshēnde: ~ *on his back* 平躺着. **3** 浅[淺]的 qiǎnde. **4** 枯燥的 kūzàode, 单[單]调的 dāndiàode. **5** [音乐]降音的 jiàngyīnde, 降半音的 jiàng bànyīn de. ⇨ sharp(8). **6** 绝对[對]的 juéduìde, 直接了当[當]的 zhí-

jiē liǎodàng de: *a ~ refusal* 断然拒绝. **7** (电池)没有电〔電〕的 méiyǒu diànde. **8** (轮胎)没有气〔氣〕了的 méiyǒu qì le de. □ *adv* **1** 平坦地 píngtǎnde, 平直地 píngzhíde, 以降调 yǐ jiàngdiào: *sing ~* 用降调演唱. **2** *~ broke* 〔非正式用语〕一个〔個〕钱〔錢〕也没有. yígèqián yě méiyǒu. **3** *~ out* **(a)** 〔非正式用语〕用尽〔盡〕全力 yòng jìn quánlì: *work ~ out* 竭力工作. **(b)** 疲惫〔憊〕的 píbèide. □ *n* [C] **1** 平坦部分 píngtǎn bùfen. **2** 平地 píngdì, 沼泽〔澤〕地 zhǎozédì: *mud ~s* 泥泞的沼泽地. **3** [音乐]降半音 jiàngbànyīn; 降号 jiànghào. **4** 没有气了的轮胎 méi yǒu qì le de lúntāi. **,~-'footed** *adj* **(a)** 扁平脚的 biǎnpíng jiǎo de. **~ly** *adv* **~ness** *n* [U]

flat·ten /'flætn/ *vt/i* 把…弄平 bǎ…nòngpíng.

flat·ter /'flætə(r)/ *vt* **1** 阿谀 ēyú, 奉承 fèngcheng. **2** 使高兴〔興〕 shǐ gāoxìng. **3** (肖像, 画等) 胜〔勝〕过〔過〕(真人,真物) shèngguò. **~er** 阿谀奉承的人 ēyú fèngcheng de rén, 拍马〔馬〕屁的人 pāimǎpìde rén **flat·tery** 捧场〔場〕 pěngchǎng, 阿谀 ēyú.

flaunt /flɔ:nt/ *vt* 夸〔誇〕耀 kuāyào, 夸示 kuāshì: *~ one's wealth (body)* 炫耀财富(体格).

flau·tist /'flɔ:tɪst/ *n* [C] 笛手 díshǒu.

fla·vour [美语 = **-vor**] /'fleɪvə(r)/ *n* **1** [U] 味 wèi. **2** [C] 风〔風〕味 fēngwèi, 情味 qíngwèi, 风〔風〕韵 fēngyùn. **3** [C] 特点〔點〕 tèdiǎn. □ *vt* 给…调味 gěi…tiáowèi; 给…增添风趣 gěi…zēngtiān fēngqù. **~ing** 调味品 tiáowèipǐn.

flaw /flɔ:/ *n* [C] 瑕疵 xiácī. 缺点〔點〕 quēdiǎn **~less** *adj* 无〔無〕缺点的 wú quēdiǎn de, 完美的 wánměide. **~lessly** *adv*

flax /flæks/ *n* [U] 亚〔亞〕麻 yǎmá. **~en** *adj* (头发)亚麻色的 yǎmásède, 淡黄色的 dànhuángsède.

flea /flɪ/ *n* [C] 蚤 zǎo.

fleck /flek/ *n* [C] **1** 斑点〔點〕 bāndiǎn, 雀斑 quèbān. **2** (尘土等)微粒 wēilì. □ *vt* 使有斑点 shǐ yǒu bāndiǎn.

fled /fled/ *pt, pp* of flee.

flee /fli:/ *vt/i* [*pt, pp* fled /fled/] 逃 táo, 逃走 táozǒu.

fleece /fli:s/ *n* [C, U] (未剪下的)羊毛 yáng máo. □ *vt* 诈取 zhàqǔ. **fleecy** *adj* [-ier, -iest] 羊毛似的 yángmáo shì de.

fleet /fli:t/ *n* [C] **1** 舰〔艦〕队〔隊〕jiànduì, 一国〔國〕拥〔擁〕有的全部军〔軍〕舰 yìguó yōngyǒu de quánbù jūnjiàn. **2** 船队〔隊〕 chuánduì; 机〔機〕群 jīqún. 汽车〔車〕队 qìchēduì.

fleet·ing /'fli:tɪŋ/ *adj* 飞〔飛〕逝的 fēishìde, 短暂〔暫〕的 duǎnzhǎnde: *a ~ glimpse of her* 对她瞟了一眼.

flesh /fleʃ/ *n* [U] **1** 肉 ròu. ***one's own ~ and blood*** 亲〔親〕骨肉 qīngǔròu, 亲属〔屬〕 qīnshǔ. ***in the ~*** 以肉体形式 yǐ ròutǐ xíngshì. **2** 肉体〔體〕(与精神, 灵魂相对而言) ròutǐ. **3** 果肉 guǒròu. **fleshy** *adj* [-ier, -iest] 肥胖的 féipàngde.

flew /flu:/ *pt* of fly[2].

flex[1] /fleks/ *n* [C, U] [*pl* -es] (电)花线〔線〕 huāxiàn; 皮线 píxiàn.

flex[2] /fleks/ *vt* 屈曲 qūqū.

flex·ible /'fleksəbl/ *adj* **1** 易弯〔彎〕曲的 yì wānqū de, 柔软〔軟〕的 róuruǎnde. **2** [喻] 灵〔靈〕活的 línghuóde, 能适〔適〕应〔應〕的 néng shìyìng de: *The plan is ~.* 这个计划是灵活的. **flexi'bil·ity** *n* [U]

flick /flɪk/ *n* [C] **1** 轻〔輕〕打 qīngdǎ, 轻弹〔彈〕 qīngtán. **2** 抖 dǒu: *with a ~ of the wrist* 手腕一抖. □ *vt* 轻打 qīngdǎ, 轻拍 qīngpāi, 轻弹 qīngtán. *~ through* 快速地翻页 kuàisùde fānyè.

flicker /'flɪkə(r)/ *vi* **1** 闪〔閃〕烁〔爍〕 shǎnshuò; 摇曳 yáoyè. **2** [喻](希望等)闪现 shǎnxiàn □ *n* [C] 闪烁 shǎnshuò, 忽隐忽现 hū yǐn hū xiàn.

flier /'flaɪə(r)/ ⇨ flyer.

flight[1] /flaɪt/ *n* **1** [U] 飞〔飛〕行 fēixíng, 飞翔 fēixiáng: *Man still dreams of ~.* 人类还在梦想飞翔. **2** [C] (飞机)航程 hángchéng. **3** [C] 空军〔軍〕小队〔隊〕 kōngjūn xiǎoduì. **4** [U] 飞驰〔馳〕 fēichí: *the ~ of an arrow* 箭在空中飞驰. **5** [C] 一群飞鸟〔鳥〕 yìqún fēiniǎo. **6** [C] 一段楼〔樓〕梯 yíduàn lóutī. **'~ deck** *n* **1** 驾〔駕〕驶〔駛〕舱〔艙〕 jiàshǐcāng. **2** 飞行甲板 fēixíng jiǎbǎn. **'~ path** *n*[C](飞机)飞行经〔經〕路 fēixíng jīnglù. **'~ recorder** 飞行记录〔錄〕器 fēixíng jìlùqì ⇨ black box. **~less** *adj* (鸟)不能飞的 bùnéng fēi de.

flight[2] /flaɪt/ *n* [C, U] 逃跑 táopǎo.

flimsy /'flɪmzɪ/ *adj* [-ier, -iest] **1** 轻〔輕〕而薄的 qīng ér bó de; 容易损坏〔壞〕的 róngyì sǔnhuài de. **2** [喻] 脆弱的 cuìruòde: *a ~*

excuse 站不住脚的借口. **flims·ily** *adv*

flinch /flɪntʃ/ *vi* 退缩 tuìsuō; 畏缩 wèisuō.

fling /flɪŋ/ *vt/i* [*pt, pp* flung /flʌŋ/] **1** 掷[擲] zhì, 抛 pāo, 扔 rēng. **2** 猛烈移动[動] měngliè yídòng, 忿怒地移动 fènnùde yídòng. **3** [喻](毅地)投入 tóurù: ~ *oneself into a job* 投入工作. □ *n* [C] **1** 抛 pāo, 掷 zhì, 扔 rēng. **2** 奔放的苏格兰[蘭]舞蹈 bēnfàngde sūgélán wǔdǎo. **3** *have a* ~ 恣意行乐[樂] zìyì xínglè.

flint /flɪnt/ *n* **1** [C, U] 燧石 suìshí, 打火石 dǎhuǒshí. **2** [C] (打火机)电[電]石 diànshí.

flip /flɪp/ *vt/i* [-pp-] 用手指轻[輕]弹[彈] yòng shǒuzhǐ qīngtán. □ *n* [C] 弹 tán; 抛 pāo; 轻击[擊] qīngjī.

flip·pant /ˈflɪpənt/ *adj* 无[無]礼[禮]的 wúlǐde, 不客气[氣]的 bú kèqì de. **ˈflip·pancy** *n* [U] 轻[輕]率 qīngshuài; 无礼 wúlǐ; [C] 无礼的言语 wúlǐde yányǔ.

flip·per /ˈflɪpə(r)/ *n* [C] **1** (某些海中动物的)鳍状[狀]肢 qízhuàngzhī. **2** 橡皮脚掌(游泳用) xiàngpí jiǎozhǎng, 足蹼 zúpǔ.

flirt /flɜːt/ *vi* **1** 调情 tiáoqíng, 卖[賣]俏 màiqiào: ~ *with a girl* 同一个姑娘调情. **2** [非正式用语]不认[認]真地考虑[慮] bú rènzhēn de kǎolǜ. □ *n* [C] 调情者 tiáoqíngzhě. **~ation** /-ˈteɪʃn/ *n* [C, U] **~atious** /-ˈteɪʃəs/ *adj* 爱[愛]调情的 ài tiáoqíngde, 轻[輕]佻的 qīngtiāode.

flit /flɪt/ *vi* [-tt-] 掠过[過] lüèguò; 飞[飛]过 fēiguò.

float[1] /fləʊt/ *n* [C] **1** (钓鱼用的)浮子 fúzi, 浮标[標] fúbiāo. **2** (游行中的)彩车[車] cǎichē.

float[2] /fləʊt/ *vt/i* **1** 漂浮 piāofú, 浮 fú: *ships ~ing on the sea* 浮在海上的船. **2** 使浮 shǐfú, 使漂浮 shǐ piāofú. **3** 筹[籌]资开[開]办[辦] chóuzī kāibàn: ~ *a company* 筹资开办一家公司. **4** 使(币值)浮动[動] shǐ fúdòng. **~ing** *adj* 不固定的 bú gùdìng de, 浮动的 fúdòngde, 变[變]化的 biànhuàde. **ˈ~ing dock** 浮坞 fúwù.

flock /flɒk/ *n* [C] **1** (鸟, 兽等)群 qún. **2** 一群人 yìqúnrén. **3** 基督教会[會]的会众[衆] jīdūjiàohuì de huìzhòng. □ *vi* 聚集 jùjí, 群集 qúnjí; 成群地去 chéngqúnde qù: *Crowds ~ed to the cinema.* 人们成群地去到电影院.

flog /flɒg/ *vt* [-gg-] **1** 鞭打 biāndǎ, 抽打 chōudǎ. ~ *a dead horse* 白费力气[氣] báifèi lìqì. **2** [俚语]卖 mài: *I'm ~ging my car.* 我正在卖汽车. **~ging** *n* [C, U] 鞭打 biāndǎ.

flood /flʌd/ *n* [C] **1** 洪水 hóngshuǐ, 水灾[災] shuǐzāi: *villages destroyed by* ~ 被洪水破坏的村庄. **2** 大量发[發]出 dàliàng fāchū: *a ~ of tears* 泪流满面; *a ~ of letters* 信件雪片飞来. **3** 泛滥[濫] fànlàn. □ *vt/i* **1** 淹没 yānmò. **2** 泛滥 fànlàn. **ˈ~light** 泛光灯[燈]照明 fànguāngdēng zhàomíng. □ *vt* [*pt, pp* -lit] 用泛光灯照明 yong fànguāngdēng zhàomíng. **ˈ~ tide** 涨[漲]潮 zhàngcháo. ⇨ ebb.

floor /flɔː(r)/ *n* [C] **1** 地面 dìmiàn, 地板 dìbǎn. **2** 楼[樓]层[層] lóucéng: *I live on the fourth* ~. 我住在五楼. **3** *take the* ~ 在辩论[論]中发[發]言 zài biànlùn zhōng fāyán. □ *vt* **1** 在…上铺地板 zài...shàng pū dìbǎn; 在…上铺地面 zài...shàng pū dìmiàn. **2** 击[擊]败 jībài, 把…打倒在地 bǎ ...dǎdǎo zàidì: *The champion was ~ed in the first round.* 冠军在第一个回合中被击倒. **3** 使困惑 shǐ kùnhuò; 难[難]倒 nándǎo. **ˈ~board** 做地板用的木板 zuò dìbǎn yòng de mùbǎn. **ˈ~ show** 夜总[總]会[會]的节[節]目表演 yèzǒnghuìde jiémù biǎoyǎn.

flop /flɒp/ *vt/i* [-pp-] **1** 笨拙地移动[動]或倒下 bènzhuóde yídòng huò dǎoxià, 无[無]奈地移动或躺下 wúnàide yídòng huò tǎngxià: ~ *exhausted into a chair* 精疲力尽噗地一下坐到椅上. **2** [非正式用语](书, 电影)失败 shībài. □ *n* [C] **1** 拍击 pāijī; 拍击声[聲] pāijīshēng; 重坠[墜]声 zhòngzhuìshēng; 重坠 zhòngzhuì. **2** [非正式用语](书, 电影等)失败 shībài. **~py** *adj* [-ier, -iest] **(a)** 松[鬆]软[軟]地下垂的 sōngruǎnde xiàchuíde, 耷拉着的 dālazhede: *a ~py hat* 耷拉着的帽子. **~py ˈdisc** 软[軟]磁盘[盤] ruǎn cípán. **(b)** [非正式用语]松软的 sōngruǎnde.

flora /ˈflɔːrə/ *n* [U] 某一地区[區]或某一时[時]期的植物群 mǒuyì dìqū huò mǒuyì shíqī de zhíwùqún.

floral /ˈflɔːrəl/ *adj* 花的 huāde.

flor·ist /ˈflɒrɪst/ *n* [C] 花商 huāshāng.

flo·tilla /fləˈtɪlə/ *n* [C] [*pl* ~s] 小舰[艦]队[隊] xiǎo jiànduì.

floun·der /ˈflaʊndə(r)/ *vi* **1** 挣扎

zhēngzhá, （肢体）乱〔亂〕动〔動〕luàndòng. **2**〔喻〕错乱地做事 cuòluànde zuòshì.

flour /'flaʊə(r)/ *n* [U] 面〔麵〕粉 miànfěn.

flour·ish /'flʌrɪʃ/ *vt/i* **1** 繁荣〔榮〕fánróng, 兴〔興〕旺 xīngwàng, 兴盛 xīngshèng. **2** 挥〔揮〕舞 huīwǔ: *He ran in, ~ing a sword.* 他挥着剑跑了进来. □ *n* [C] **1** 挥舞 huīwǔ. **2** 高昂的乐〔樂〕段 gāoángde yuèduàn.

flout /flaʊt/ *vt* 藐视 miǎoshì, 轻〔輕〕视 qīngshì: ~ *authority* 藐视权威.

flow /fləʊ/ *vi* [*pt, pp* ~ed] **1** 流 liú, 流通 liútōng; 涌出 yǒngchū. **2**（头发等）飘〔飄〕垂 piāochuí; 飘拂 piāofú. **3** ~ ***from*** 是…的结果 shì...de jiéguǒ. □ *n* [只用 *sing*] 流通 liútōng; 流通量 liútōngliàng. '~ **chart** 流程图〔圖〕liúchéngtú, 生产〔產〕过〔過〕程图解 shēngchǎn guòchéng tújiě.

flower /'flaʊə(r)/ *n* [C] **1** 花 huā, 花卉 huāhuì. **2**〔喻〕精华〔華〕jīnghuá: *the ~ of the nation's men* 一个国家最优秀的男子. □ *vi* 开〔開〕花 kāihuā. '~**bed** 花坛〔壇〕huātán. '~**pot** 花盆 huāpén. **flow·ery** *adj* [-ier, -iest] **(a)** 多花的 duōhuāde. **(b)** 〔喻〕词藻华〔華〕丽〔麗〕的 cízǎo huálì de: *~y speech* (*writing*) 词藻华丽的演说（文章）.

flown /fləʊn/ *pp* of fly[2].

flu /flu:/ *n* [U] 流行性感冒（influenza 的非正式缩写）liúxíng xìng gǎnmào.

fluc·tu·ate /'flʌktʃʊeɪt/ *vi* （物价等）涨〔漲〕落 zhàngluò, 起落 qǐluò, 波动〔動〕 pōdòng. **fluc·tu·ation** *n* [C, U]

flu·ent /'flu:ənt/ *adj* **1**（人）说话流利的 shuōhuà liúlì de: *speak ~ English* 英语说得流利. **2**（演说等）流畅〔暢〕的 liúchàngde. ~**ly** *adv* **flu·ency** /-ənsɪ/ *n* [U]

fluff /flʌf/ *n* [U] （织物上的）绒毛 róngmáo. □ *vt* 抖开〔開〕dǒukāi, 抖松〔鬆〕dǒusōng: ~ *up a pillow* 抖松枕头. **fluffy** *adj* [-ier, -iest] 绒毛的 róngmáode; 绒毛状〔狀〕的 róngmáozhuàngde; 有绒毛的 yǒu róngmáode: *a ~y cat* 毛绒绒的猫.

fluid /'flu:ɪd/ *adj* **1** 流动〔動〕的 liúdòngde. **2**（思想等）不固定的 bú gùdìng de, 易变〔變〕的 yìbiànde. □ *n* [C, U] 流体〔體〕liútǐ, 液 yè.

flung /flʌŋ/ *pt, pp* of fling.

flu·or·escent /flʊə'resnt/ *adj* 荧〔熒〕光的 yíngguāngdə, 发〔發〕荧光的 fā yíngguāng de: ~ *lamp* (*lighting*) 日光灯〔燈〕rìguāngdēng. **flu·or·escence** /-sns/ *n* [U]

flurry /'flʌrɪ/ *n* [C] [*pl* -ies] **1** 阵〔陣〕风〔風〕zhènfēng, 一阵雪 yízhèn xuě. **2**〔喻〕慌张〔張〕huāngzhāng, 仓〔倉〕皇〔惶〕cānghuáng: *a ~ of activity* 一阵慌慌张张的行动. □ *vt* 使慌张 shǐ huāngzhāng.

flush[1] /flʌʃ/ *adj* **1** 齐〔齊〕平的 qípíngde. **2**〔俚语〕富有的 fùyǒude.

flush[2] /flʌʃ/ *n* [C] 奔流 bēnliú; （脸）红晕〔暈〕hóngyùn, 兴〔興〕奋〔奮〕xìngfèn, 激动〔動〕jīdòng: *the ~ of victory* 胜利的兴奋和激动. □ *vt/i* **1**（脸）发〔發〕红 fāhóng. **2** 使脸〔臉〕发红 shǐ liǎn fāhóng. **3**〔喻〕得意 déyì. **4** 冲洗 chōngxǐ. **5** 泛滥〔濫〕fànlàn.

flus·ter / 'flʌstə(r)/ *vt* 使慌张〔張〕shǐ huāngzhāng, 使慌乱〔亂〕shǐ huāngluàn. □ *n* [U] 慌张 huāngzhāng. **flute** /flu:t/ *n* [C] 长〔長〕笛 chángdí.

flut·ter /'flʌtə(r)/ *vt/i* **1** （鸟）振翼 zhènyì, 拍翅pāichì. **2**颤动〔動〕chàndòng, 使颤动 shǐ chàndòng: ~ *one's eyelids*眼跳. **3**（心脏）不规则跳动 bù guīzé tiàodòng. □ *n* **1**〔常用 *sing*〕振翼 zhènyì, 飘〔飄〕扬 piāoyáng. **2** 不安 bù'ān, 焦急 jiāojí.

flux /flʌks/ *n* [U] 流 liú, 流动〔動〕liúdòng.

fly[1] /flaɪ/ *n* [C] [*pl* flies] 苍〔蒼〕蝇〔蠅〕cāngying, 蝇 yíng.

fly[2] /flaɪ/ *vt/i* [*pt* flew/flu:/; *pp* flown /fləʊn/] **1** 飞〔飛〕fēi, 飞翔 fēixiáng, 乘飞机〔機〕旅行 chéng fēijī lǚxíng. **2**空运〔運〕kōngyùn. **3** 飞跑 fēipǎo, 疾驰〔馳〕jíchí, 飞奔 fēibēn. ~ ***into a rage*** 勃然大怒 bórán dànù. **4** 使（旗）飘〔飄〕扬 shǐ piāoyáng. **5** 逃走 táozǒu, 逃跑 táopǎo. ˌ~**ing 'saucer** 飞碟 fēidié, 不明飞行物 bùmíng fēixíngwù. '~**ing-squad**（警察局处理危急犯罪的）机〔機〕动〔動〕小组 jīdòng xiǎozǔ. ˌ~**ing 'visit** 匆促的访问〔問〕cōngcùde fǎngwèn.

fly[3] /flaɪ/ *n* [C] [*pl* flies]〔常用复〕裤子上拉链〔鏈〕的遮盖 kùzi shàng lāliànde zhēgài.

flyer, flier /'flaɪə(r) / *n* [C] 飞〔飛〕行员 fēixíngyuán.

fly·over /'flaɪəʊvə(r)/ *n* [C] 〔美语 =*overpass*〕公路上的陆〔陸〕桥〔橋〕gōnglù shàng de lùqiáo, 立交桥 lìjiāoqiáo.

foal /fəʊl/ *n* [C] 小马〔馬〕xiǎomǎ, 驹〔駒〕jū.

foam /fəʊm/ *n* [U] 泡沫 pàomò. □ *vi* 起泡沫 qǐ pàomò, 发〔發〕出泡沫 fāchū pàomò. ˌ~-'**rubber** 海棉橡皮 hǎimián xiàngpí, 泡沫橡皮 pàomò xiàngpí. **foamy** *adj* [-ier, -iest]

f.o.b.=free on board. 船上交货 chuán shàng jiāohuò.

fo·cus /'fəʊkəs/ *n* [C] [*pl* ~es or foci /'fəʊsaɪ/] **1** 焦点〔點〕jiāodiǎn: *out of* ~ 焦距未对准, 模糊; *in* ~ 对准焦点, 清晰. **2** (兴趣等的) 集中点〔點〕jízhōng diǎn, 中心 zhōngxīn: *the* ~ *of attention*. 注意的中心. □ *vt/i* [-s- 或 -ss-] **1** (使)聚焦 jùjiāo. **2** 集中 jízhōng: ~ *one's attention on* 集中注意力于; ~ *one's efforts on* 集中力量于. **fo·cal** *adj*

fod·der /'fɒdə(r)/ *n* [U] 粗饲料 cūcìliào, 草料 cǎoliào.

foe /fəʊ/ *n* [C] (诗)敌〔敵〕人 dírén.

foe·tus, fe·tus /'fiːtəs/ *n* [C] [*pl* ~es] 发〔發〕育完全了的胎儿 fāyù wánquán le de tāi'ér; 发育完全了的胚胎 fāyù wánquán le de pēitāi.

fog /fɒg/ *n* **1** [U] 雾〔霧〕wù. **2** [C] 雾期 wùqī. **3** [C, U] (影象的)模糊 móhu. □ *vt* [-gg-] **1** 以雾笼〔籠〕罩 yǐ wù lǒngzhào. **2** 困惑 kùnhuò, 迷惑 míhuò. **3** 使(照像底片) 形成雾翳 shǐ xíng chéng wùyì. '~**bound** *adj* 因雾而不能航行的 yīn wù ér bùnéng hángxíng de. '~**horn** 雾角(警告浓雾的号角) wùjiǎo. '~**lamp** 雾灯〔燈〕(汽车在雾天使用的灯) wùdēng. ~**gy** *adj* [-ier, -iest] 雾蒙蒙的 wùméngméngde.

foil[1] /fɔɪl/ *n* **1** [U] 金属〔屬〕薄片 jīnshǔ bópiàn, 箔 bó. **2** [C] 陪衬物 péichènwù.

foil[2] /fɔɪl/ *n* [C] (练剑术用的)钝头〔頭〕剑〔劍〕dùntóujiàn.

foil[3] /fɔɪl/ *vt* 挫败 cuōbài.

fold[1] /fəʊld/ *vt/i* **1** 折迭〔疊〕zhédié, 对〔對〕折 duìzhé. **2** 折起来〔來〕zhéqǐlái, 可被折迭 kěbèi zhédié: *Paper* ~*s easily.* 纸折起来容易. ~ *up* (企业) 倒闭〔閉〕dǎobì. **3** ~ *one's arms* 交臂(无行动) jiāobì. □ *n* [C] 褶痕 zhěhén, 褶页 zhěyè. ~**er** *n* [C] 文件夹〔夾〕wénjiànjiā.

fold[2] /fəʊld/ *n* [C] **1** 羊栏〔欄〕yánglán. **2** [喻]教会〔會〕团〔團〕体〔體〕jiàohuì tuántǐ.

fo·li·age /'fəʊlɪɪdʒ/ *n* [U] 树〔樹〕或植物的叶〔葉〕子的总〔總〕称〔稱〕shù huò zhíwù de yèzi de zǒngchēng.

folk /fəʊk/ *n* **1** 人们〔們〕rénmen. **2** [*pl*] [非正式用语] 家属〔屬〕jiāshǔ, 亲〔親〕属 qīnshǔ: *the* ~*s at home* 家乡的亲人. **3** 民间〔間〕音乐〔樂〕mínjiānyīnyuè. '~-**dance** 民间舞 mínjiānwǔ. 民间舞的音乐 mínjiānwǔde yīnyuè. '~**lore** 民俗 mínsú; 民俗学〔學〕mínsúxué. '~ **music** 民间音乐 mínjiānyīnyuè. '~ **song** 民歌 míngē.

fol·low /'fɒləʊ/ *vt/i* **1** 跟随 gēnsuí, (次序)接着 jiēzhe. *as* ~*s* 如下 rúxià. **2** 沿着 (路等) yánzhe. **3** 领会〔會〕lǐnghuì, 懂 dǒng: *I don't* ~ *your meaning*. 我不懂你的意思. **4** 从〔從〕事(商业等) cóngshì, 经〔經〕营〔營〕jīngyíng. **5** 听〔聽〕从〔從〕tīngcóng, 遵循 zūnxún: ~ *her advice* 听从她的忠告. ~ *suit* ⇨ suit[1]. **6** 作为〔爲〕…的必然结果 zuòwéi…de bìrán jiéguǒ, 因…而起 yīn…érqǐ: *It* ~*s from what you say that* 根据你所说的…, 则…是必然的结果. **7** ~ *sth up* 追逐 zhuīzhú. '~-**up** *n* [C] ~**er** (a) 拥〔擁〕护〔護〕者 yōnghùzhě. (b) 追随者 zhuīsuízhě. ~**ing** *adj* (a) 接着的 jiēzhede, 其次的 qícìde. (b) *the* ~*ing* [用作代名词]下述的 xiàshùde, 下列的 xiàliède. □ *n* [C] 一群追随者 yìqún zhuīsuízhě.

folly /'fɒlɪ/ *n* [*pl* -ies] **1** [U] 愚蠢 yúchǔn, 笨拙 bènzhuó. **2** [C] 笨事 bènshì, 傻话 shǎhuà.

fond /fɒnd/ *adj* **1** *be* ~ *of* 喜欢〔歡〕的 xǐhuande, 喜爱〔愛〕的 xǐ'àide. **2** 多情的 duōqíngde, 慈爱的 cí'àide: *a* ~ *embrace* 慈爱的拥抱. ~**ly** *adv* (a) 亲〔親〕爱地 qīn'àide. (b) 天真地 tiānzhēnde, 乐〔樂〕观〔觀〕地 lèguānde: ~*ly believe him* 天真地相信他. ~**ness** *n* [U]

fondle /'fɒndl/ *vt* 爱〔愛〕抚〔撫〕àifǔ, 抚弄 fǔnòng.

font /fɒnt/ *n* [C] 洗礼〔禮〕盘〔盤〕xǐlǐpán.

food /fuːd/ *n* **1** [U] 食物 shíwù. **2** ~ *for thought* 思考的材料 sīkǎode cáiliào. '~**stuff** 粮食 liángshi, 食料 shíliào.

fool /fuːl/ *n* [C] **1** 傻子 shǎzi, 笨人 bènrén. *make a* ~ *of sb* 愚弄某人 yúnòng mǒurén. *play the* ~ 干〔幹〕傻事 gàn shǎshì. □ *adj* [非正式用语]愚蠢的 yúchǔnde. □ *vt/i* **1** 装〔裝〕傻 zhuangshǎ; 游荡〔蕩〕yóudàng: *Stop* ~*ing around*. 别闲荡. **2** 欺骗〔騙〕qīpiàn. ~**ery** *n* [C, U] 愚蠢的行为〔爲〕yúchǔnde xíngwéi. ~**hardy** /-hɑːdɪ/ *adj* 蛮〔蠻〕干

〔幹〕的 mángànde, 莽撞的 mǎngzhuàngde. ~**ish** *adj* 愚蠢的 yúchǔnde. ~**ish·ly** *adv* ~**ish·ness** *n* [U] ~**proof** *adj* 十分安全的 shífēn ānquán de: *a* ~*proof plan* 万全之策.

foot /fʊt/ *n* [*pl* feet /fi:t/] **1** 脚 jiǎo, 足 zú. ***on*** ~ 步行 bùxíng. ***be rushed off one's feet*** 极〔極〕其忙碌 jíqí mánglù. ***put one's*** ~ ***down*** 〔非正式用语〕抗议〔議〕kàngyì; 坚〔堅〕决 jiānjué. ***put one's*** ~ ***in it*** 〔非正式用语〕说错话 shuō cuòhuà, 做错事 zuò cuòshì. ***put one's feet up*** 〔非正式用语〕休息 xiūxi. **2** 步 bù, 脚步 jiǎobù. **3** 最下部 zuìxiàbù, 底部 dǐbù: *the* ~ *of the column* 柱子的底部. **4** 英尺(=12 英寸) yīngchǐ, 呎 chǐ. □ *vt* ~ ***the bill*** 付帐 fùzhàng, 付钱〔錢〕fùqián. '~**ball** *n* [C] 足球 zúqiú; [U] 足球比赛 zúqiú bǐsài. '~**ball pools** 足球比赛结果赌博 zúqiú bǐsài jiéguǒ dǔbó. '~**hills** 山麓的丘陵地带〔帶〕shānlùde qiūlíng dìdài. '~**hold** (a) 立足处〔處〕(攀登) lìzúchù. (b) 〔喻〕立足点〔點〕lìzúdiǎn, 据〔據〕点 jùdiǎn. '~**note** 脚注 jiǎozhù. '~**path** 人行道 rénxíngdào, 小路 xiǎolù. '~**print** 足迹 zújì, 脚印 jiǎoyìn. '~**step** 脚步 jiǎobù. ***follow in sb's*** ~***steps*** 效法某人 xiàofǎ mǒurén. '~**wear** 鞋类〔類〕xiélèi.

foot·ing /'fʊtɪŋ/ *n* [C] **1** 立足点〔點〕lìzúdiǎn. **2** 〔只用 *sing*〕社会〔會〕地位 shèhuì dìwèi, 社会关〔關〕系 shèhuì guānxì.

for /fə(r) 强读: fɔ:(r)/ *prep* **1** (表示目标,去向)往 wǎng, 向 xiàng: *set out* ~ *home* 动身回家. **2** (表示目的)为〔爲〕了 wèile: *destined* ~ *something great* 注定要做伟大的事. **3** (表示最后的所有权)…的 …de: *Here's a letter* ~ *you.* 这是你的信. **4** (表示准备): *prepare* ~ *an examination* 准备考试. **5 (a)** (表示目的)为 wèi: *go* ~ *a walk* 出去散步. **(b)** (表示用途)供 gòng, 适〔適〕合于 shìhéyú: *What's this tool* ~? 这个器械是干什么用的? **6** 作为 zuòwéi, 当〔當〕作 dāngzuò: *They left him* ~ *dead.* 他们把他扔下,以为他已经死了. ***take sb (sth)*** ~ 误认〔認〕为 wù rènwéi. **7** (表示爱好,能力等)对〔對〕于 duìyú: *a taste* ~ *art* 对艺术的爱好; *a good ear* ~ *music* 审辨音乐的好耳力. **8** (表示适合) 对于 duìyú: *good* ~ *your health* 有益于你的健康. **9** 考虑〔慮〕到 kǎolǜdào, 就…而言 jiù…ér yán: *She's tall* ~ *her age.* 考虑到她的年龄,她的身材是高的. **10** 代表 dàibiǎo: *B* ~ *Benjamin B* 代表 *Benjamin.* **11** 赞成 zànchéng: *Are you* ~ *or against the proposal?* 你赞成还是反对这项建议? **12** 关〔關〕心 guānxīn, 挂〔掛〕念 guàniàn: *anxious* ~ *his safety* 关心他的安全. **13** 由于 yóuyú, 因为 yīnwéi: ~ *this reason* 因为这个原因. **14** 换 huàn: *I paid 60p* ~ *the book.* 我花 60 便士买这本书. **15** (表示空间,时间)达〔達〕dá, 计 jì: *go away* ~ *a few days* 走开几天的时间. *walk* (~) *three miles* 走了三英里. ~ ***good*** ⇨ good²(2).

for·age /'fɒrɪdʒ/ *n* [U] 饲料 sìliào, 草料 cǎoliào. □ *vi* 搜索 (*for*) (粮秣等) sōusuǒ.

for·bad, for·bade /fə'bæd/ *pt* of forbid.

for·bear 〔美语 = **forebear**〕/'fɔ:beə(r)/ *n* [C] 祖先 zǔxiān.

for·bid /fə'bɪd/ *vt* [*pt* forbade 或 forbad /fə'bæd/; *pp* ~den /fə'bɪdn/ 或 ~] 禁止 jìnzhǐ, 不许 bùxǔ. ~**ding** *adj* 严〔嚴〕峻的 yánjùnde, 险〔險〕恶〔惡〕的 xiǎn'ède.

force /fɔ:s/ *n* **1** [U] 力量 lìliàng 力 lì. **2** [C] 引起重大变〔變〕革的人或物 yǐnqǐ zhòngdà biàngé de rén huò wù: *the* ~*s of nature* 自然力. **3** [C] 武装〔裝〕组织〔織〕wǔzhuāng zǔzhī, 部队〔隊〕bùduì, 兵力 bīnglì: *the po'lice* ~ 警察. **4** [C, U] 改变或阻止运〔運〕动〔動〕的力 gǎibiàn huò zǔzhǐ yùndòng de lì: *the* ~ *of gravity* 重力. **5** 效力 xiàolì: *That law is no longer in* ~. 那项法律不再有效. □ *vt* **1** 强迫 qiǎngpò, 迫使 pòshǐ: ~ *him to talk* 强迫他说. **2** 强行 qiángxíng, 强加 qiángjiā: ~ (*open*) *a door* 用力打开门. **3** 强作 qiángzuò: ~ *a smile* 强作笑颜. **4** 促使(植物)早熟 cùshǐ zǎoshú. ~**ful** *adj* 有说服力的 yǒu shuōfúlì de. ~**fully** *adv* **forc·ible** *adj* 强迫的 qiǎngpòde. **forc·ibly** *adv*

for·ceps /'fɔ:seps/ *n* [*pl*] (亦作 *a pair of* ~) (医用)镊〔鑷〕子 nièzi, (医用)钳子 qiánzi.

ford /fɔ:d/ *n* [C] 津 jīn, 可涉水而过〔過〕的地方 kě shèshuǐ ér guò de dìfang. □ *vt* 徒涉 túshè.

fore /fɔ:(r)/ *adj* 前部的 qiánbùde: *the* ~ *legs of a horse* 马的前腿. □ *n* ***to the*** ~ 在显〔顯〕著的地位 zài xiǎnzhùde dìwèi.

fore·arm /'fɔ:rɑ:m/ *n* [C] 前臂 qiánbì.

fore·bear *n* = forbear.

fore·cast /'fɔ:kɑ:st/ *vt* [*pt, pp* ~ or ~ed] 预报 yùbào, 预测 yùcè: *~ a disaster* 预测灾祸. □ *n* [C] 预告 yùgào, 预报〔報〕 yùbào: *the weather ~* 天气预报.

fore·court /'fɔ:kɔ:t/ *n* [C] 前院 qiányuàn.

fore·fathers /'fɔ:fɑ:ðəz/ *n pl* = ancestors.

fore·fin·ger /'fɔ:fɪŋgə(r)/ *n* [C] 食指 shízhǐ.

fore·front /'fɔ:frʌnt/ *n* **(in)** *the* ~ 最前线〔線〕 zuì qiánxiàn, 最前方 zuì qiánfāng: *in the ~ of world politics* 世界政治的最前线.

forego = forgo.

fore·gone /'fɔ:gɒn/ *adj*: 预知的 yùzhīde, 预先决定的 yùxiān juédìng de, 无〔無〕可避免的 wúkě bìmiǎn de: *a ~ conclusion* 预料的必然结果.

fore·ground /'fɔ:graʊnd/ *n* [C] **1** 前景 qiánjǐng. **2** [喻]最突出的地位 zhì tūchū de dìwèi.

fore·hand /'fɔ:hænd/ *adj n* [C] (网球等)正手打 zhèngshǒudǎ.

fore·head /'fɒrɪd, 'fɔ:hed/ *n* [C] 额 é.

foreign /'fɒrən/ *adj* **1** 外国〔國〕的 wàiguóde, 在外国的 zài wàiguó de. **2** ~ *to* 无〔無〕关〔關〕的 wúguānde, 不相干的 bù xiānggān de: *~ to her character* 不是她的性格. **3** 外来〔來〕的 wàiláide, 异〔異〕质〔質〕的 yìzhìde: *a ~ body in the eye* 眼睛里的异物. ~**er** 外国人 wàiguórén.

fore·man /'fɔ:mən/ *n* [C] [*pl* -men /-mən/] **1** 工头〔頭〕 gōngtóu, 领班 lǐngbān. **2** 陪审〔審〕长〔長〕 péishěnzhǎng.

fore·most /'fɔ:məʊst/ *adj* 最重要的 zuì zhòngyào de, 第一流的 dìyīliúde. □ *adv* ˌ*first and* '~ 首先 shǒuxiān.

for·en·sic /fə'rensɪk/ *adj* 法庭的 fǎtíngde. ~ *medicine* 法医学.

fore·run·ner /'fɔ:rʌnə(r)/ *n* [C] 前征〔徵〕 qiánzhēng, 先驱〔驅〕 xiānqū: *a ~ of the modern motor-car* 现代汽车的先驱.

fore·see /fɔ:'si:/ *vt* [*pt* foresaw /fɔ:'sɔ:/, *pp* ~n /fɔ:'si:n/] 预见 yùjiàn, 预知 yùzhī. ~**able** *adj* 可以预见到的 kěyǐ yùjiàn dào de.

fore·shore /'fɔ:ʃɔ:(r)/ *n* [C] 岸坡 ànpō, 海滩〔灘〕 hǎitān.

fore·sight /'fɔ:saɪt/ *n* [U] 预见的能力 yùjiànde nénglì, 远〔遠〕虑〔慮〕 yuǎnlǜ.

for·est /'fɒrɪst/ *n* [C, U] 森林 sēnlín, 森林地带〔帶〕 sēnlín dìdài. ~**er** 林务〔務〕员 línwùyuán. ~**ry** *n* [U] 林业〔業〕 línyè, 林学〔學〕 línxué.

fore·stall /fɔ:'stɔ:l/ *vt* 抢〔搶〕先行动〔動〕 qiǎngxiān xíngdòng.

fore·tell /fɔ:'tel/ *vt* [*pt,pp* foretold /-'təʊld/] 预言 yùyán; 预告 yùgào.

fore·thought /'fɔ:θɔ:t/ *n* [U] 预先计划〔劃〕 yùxiān jìhuà, 预谋 yùmóu.

for·ever /fə'revə(r)/ *adv* 永远〔遠〕 yǒngyuǎn, 常常 chángcháng.

fore·word /'fɔ:wɜ:d/ *n* [C] 序 xù, 前言 qiányán.

for·feit /'fɔ:fɪt/ *vt* 没收 mòshōu, 丧失 sàngshī. □ *n* [C] 没收物 mòshōuwù, 丧失物 sàngshīwù.

for·gave *pt* of forgive.

forge[1] /fɔ:dʒ/ *n* [C] 锻工车〔車〕间〔間〕 duàngōng chējiān, 铁〔鐵〕工厂〔廠〕 tiěgōngchǎng, 铁匠店 tiějiàngdiàn. □ *vt* **1** 锻造 duànzào, 打铁 dǎtiě. **2** [喻]经〔經〕锻炼而形成 jīng duànliàn ér xíngchéng: *a friendship ~d by poverty* 贫困之交. **3** 伪〔僞〕造 wěizào. **forger** 伪造者 wěizàozhě. ~**ry** /-ərɪ/ *n* [*pl* -ies] **(a)** [U] 伪造 wěizào. **(b)** [C] 伪造品 wěizàopǐn, 赝品 yànpǐn.

forge[2] /fɔ:dʒ/ *vi* ~ **ahead** 稳步前进〔進〕 wěnbù qiánjìn.

for·get /fə'get/ *vt/i* [*pt* forgot /fə'gɒt/; *pp* forgotten /fə'gɒtn/] **1** 忘记 wàngjì. **2** 忘记做某事 wàngjì zuò mǒushì: *Don't ~ to post the letters.* 别忘记寄这些信. **3** 不以…为〔爲〕意 bùyǐ...wéi yì, 不再思念 búzài sīniàn: *~ a quarrel* 忘掉争执. ~**ful** *adj* 健忘的 jiànwàngde.

for·give /fə'gɪv/ *vt/i* [*pt* forgave /fə'geɪv/; *pp* ~n /fə'gɪvn/] 原谅 yuánliàng, 宽恕 kuānshù. **for·giv·able** *adj* 可原谅的 kě yuánliàng de. **for·giv·ing** *adj* 宽大的 kuāndàde, 仁慈的 réncíde. ~**ness** *n* [U]

for·go /fɔ:'gəʊ/ *vt* [*pt* forwent /fɔ:'went/; *pp* forgone /fɔ:'gɒn/] 放弃 fàngqì, 摒绝 bìngjué: *~ a party in order to study* 为学习而放弃一次聚会.

for·got, for·got·ten ⇨ forget.

fork /fɔ:k/ *n* [C] **1** 叉 chā. **2** 耙 pá. **3** (路, 树干等) 分叉 fēnchà, 叉路 chàlù; 叉枝 chàzhī. □ *vt/i* **1** 叉 chā, 叉起 chāqǐ. **2** (路等) 分叉 fēnchà. **3** (人)转〔轉〕向(左或右) zhuǎnxiàng. **4** ~ *out* [非正式用语] 支付 zhīfù. ˌ~-**lift** '**truck** 叉车 chāchē. ~**ed** *adj* 有

叉的 yǒuchàde.

for·lorn /fə'lɔːn/ *adj* [书面语]悲惨[慘]的 bēicǎnde, 可怜[憐]的 kěliánde. ~**ly** *adv*

form[1] /fɔːm/ *n* **1** [C, U] 形状[狀] xíngzhuàng, 外貌 wàimào. **2** [C, U] 体[體]制 tǐzhì; 种[種]类[類] zhǒnglèi, 类型 lèixíng: ~*s of government* 政体. **3** [语法] [C, U] 词形 cíxíng; 形式 xíngshì. **4** [C, U] 礼[禮]貌 lǐmào: *accepted ~s of behaviour* 公认的礼仪. **5** [C] 表格 biǎogé: *appli'cation ~s* 申请表. **6** [U] 竞[競]技状[狀]态[態] jìngjì zhuàngtài: *be on (off) ~* 竞技状态良好(不好). **7** [U] 精神 jīngshén, 心境 xīnjìng: *in good (great) ~* 心情愉快 (极为愉快). **8** [C] 长[長]板凳 cháng bǎndèng. **9** [C] [英国英语]年级 niánjí.

form[2] /fɔːm/ *vt/i* **1** 使形成 shǐ xíngchéng, 制[製]作 zhìzuò. **2** 培养[養] péiyǎng, 养成 yǎngchéng: ~ *good habits* 培养良好习惯. **3** 组成 zǔchéng, 建立 jiànlì: *They ~ed a committee.* 他们组成一个委员会. **4** 作为[爲](…的材料) zuòwéi, 为…的一部分 wéi…de yíbùfen: *This ~s part of a course.* 这构成了一门教程的一部分. **5** 形成 xíngchéng: *An idea ~ed in his mind.* 他心生一计.

for·mal /'fɔːml/ *adj* **1** 正式的 zhèngshìde, 合于习[習]俗的 héyú xísúde: *a ~ dinner party* 正式宴会. **2** 正规的 zhèngguīde. ⇨ informal. **3** 整齐[齊]的 zhěngqíde. **4** 形式的 xíngshìde, 外表的 wàibiǎode: ~ *similarity* 形式上的相似. ~**ity** /fɔː'mælətɪ/ *n* [*pl* ies] **(a)** [U] 拘泥形式 jūní xíngshì. **(b)** [C] 手续[續] shǒuxù: *a legal ~ity* 法律手续. ~**ly** *adv*

for·ma·tion /fɔː'meɪʃn/ *n* [C, U] **1** 形成 xíngchéng. **2** 构[構]造 gòuzào. 排列 páiliè.

for·ma·tive /'fɔːmətɪv/ *adj* 形成的 xíngchéngde, 构[構]成的 gòuchéngde: *a boy's ~ years* 男孩子形成性格的时期.

for·mer /'fɔːmə(r)/ *adj* **1** 以前的 yǐqiánde, 从[從]前的 cóngqiánde: *the ~ President* 前任总统. **2** [用作代名词] 前者 qiánzhě. ~**ly** *adv* 从前 cóngqián, 以前 yǐqián.

for·mi·dable /'fɔːmɪdəbl/ *adj* **1** 可怕的 kěpàde. **2** 难[難]以对[對]付的 nányǐ duìfu de. ~ *obstacles* 难以克服的障碍. **for·mi·dably** *adv*

for·mula /'fɔːmjʊlə/ *n* [C] [*pl* ~s, ~e /-liː/] **1** 俗套话 (如 How do you do?) sútàohuà. **2** 公式 gōngshì, 程式 chéngshì: *chemical ~* 化学式.

for·mu·late /'fɔːmjʊleɪt/ *vt* 精确[確]地表达[達] jīngquède biǎodá: ~ *a request* 明确提出一项要求. **for·mu·la·tion** *n* [C, U]

for·sake /fə'seɪk/ *vt* [*pt* forsook /fə'sʊk/; *pp* ~n /fə'seɪkən/] 抛弃[棄] pāoqì, 遗弃 yíqì.

fort /fɔːt/ *n* [C] 堡垒 bǎolěi, 要塞 yàosài.

forte /'fɔːteɪ/ *n* [C] 长[長]处[處] chángchù, 特长 tècháng: *Singing is not my ~.* 唱歌不是我的特长.

forth /fɔːθ/ *adv* 向前方 xiàng qiánfāng, 向前 xiàngqián. **and 'so ~** 等等 děngděng. **,back and '~** 前后[後] qiánhòu, 来[來]回 láihuí.

forth·com·ing /fɔːθ'kʌmɪŋ/ *adj* **1** 即将出现的 jìjiāng chūxiàn de. **2** 现有的 xiànyǒude, 唾手可得的 tuòshǒu kědé de, 现成的 xiànchéngde: *When he asked for a loan, the money was not ~.* 当他要借一笔贷款时, 没有现成的钱. **3** [非正式用语] 愿[願]意帮助的 yuànyì bāngzhù de.

for·ti·eth /'fɔːtɪəθ/ *adj, n* [C] (略作 40*th*) 第四十 dìsìshí, 第四十个[個] dìsìshígè, 四十分之一 sìshífēn zhī yī, 四十分之一的 sìshífēn zhī yī de.

for·tify /'fɔːtɪfaɪ/ *vt* [*pt, pp* -ied] 设防于 shèfángyú, 增强 zēngqiáng. **for·ti·fi·ca·tion** /-fɪ'keɪʃn/ *n* [C, U]

fort·night /'fɔːtnaɪt/ *n* [C] 两星期 liǎngxīngqī. ~**ly** *adj, adv* 每两周的 měi liǎngzhōu de, 每两周地 měi liǎngzhōu de.

for·tress /'fɔːtrs/ *n* [C] 要塞 yàosài, 堡垒 bǎolěi.

for·tu·nate /'fɔːtʃənət/ *adj* 幸运[運]的 xìngyùnde, 吉利的 jílìde. ~**ly** *adv*

for·tune /'fɔːtʃuːn/ *n* **1** [C, U] 命运[運] mìngyùn, 运气[氣] yùnqì, 好运 hǎoyùn, 坏[壞]运 huàiyùn. **tell sb's ~** 为某人算命, 为某人看相 wèi mǒurén suànmìng, wèi mǒurén kànxiàng. **2** [C, U] 繁荣[榮] fánróng, 大量资财 dàliàng zīcái. **make a ~** 发[發]财 fācái. **'~ teller** 给人算命的人 gěi rén suànmìng de rén.

forty /'fɔːtɪ/ *adj, n* [C] 四十 sìshí, 四十个[個] sìshígè.

fo·rum /'fɔːrəm/ *n* [C] [*pl* ~s] 论[論]坛[壇] lùntán.

for·ward /'fɔːwəd/ *adj* **1** 向前的

xiàngqiánde; 在前部的 zài qiánbù de, 向前进〔進〕行的 xiàngqián jìnxíng de: ~ *march* 前进; ~ *planning* 预先的谋划. 2(庄稼,儿童等)早熟的 zǎoshúde. 3 急切的 jíqiède, 热〔熱〕心的 rèxīnde: *a ~ young girl* 孟浪的少女. □ *n* [C] (足球等)前锋 qiánfēng. □ *vt* 1 促进 cùjìn, 促使 cùshǐ: *~ his career* 促进他的事业. 2 发〔發〕送 fāsòng, 寄发 jìfā. 3 转〔轉〕交 zhuǎnjiāo, 转送 zhuǎnsòng.

for·ward(s) /ˈfɔːwəd(z)/ *adv* 1 向前 xiàngqián, 前进〔進〕 qiánjìn. 2 至未来〔來〕 zhì wèilái, 至将〔將〕来 zhì jiānglái.

fos·sil /ˈfɒsl/ *n* [C] 化石 huàshí. **~ize** /-aɪz/ *vt/i* (使)成化石 chéng huàshí.

fos·ter /ˈfɒstə(r)/ *vt* 1 养〔養〕育 yǎngyù, 抚〔撫〕育 fǔyù. 2 领养 lǐngyǎng: *~-brother* 奶兄弟; *~-child* 养子,养女; *~-parent* 养父,养母. ⇨ adopt(1).

fought /fɔːt/ *pt, pp* of fight.

foul /faʊl/ *adj* [-er, -est] 1 恶〔惡〕臭的 èchòude, 难〔難〕闻〔聞〕的 nánwénde, 腐败的 fǔbàide. 2 邪恶的 xié'ède, 可恶的 kě'ède: *a ~ murder* 罪恶的谋杀. 3 暴风〔風〕雨的 bàofēngyǔde. ***fall ~ of*** 同…发生纠缠〔纏〕 tóng…fāshēng jiūchán. □ *n* [C] (体育)犯规 fànguī. □ *vt/i* 1 弄脏〔髒〕 nòngzāng, 玷污 diànwū: *~ a stream with chemicals* 化学物品污染了一条小河. 2 (使)缠结 chánjié: *Weeds ~ed the propeller.* 水草同螺旋桨缠在一起. 3 〔体育〕犯规 fànguī. **~ ˈplay** (a) 〔体育〕犯规 fànguī. (b) 凶暴罪 xiōngbàozuì, 行凶罪 xíngxiōngzuì. **~ly** /ˈfaʊlɪ/ *adv*

found[1] /faʊnd/ *pt, pp* of find.

found[2] /faʊnd/ *vt* 1 建立 jiànlì, 设立 shèlì. 2 使…有根据〔據〕 shǐ…yǒu gēnjù: *beliefs ~ed on facts* 根据事实建立的信念. **~er** *n* [C] 创〔創〕建者 chuàngjiànzhě.

foun·da·tion /faʊnˈdeɪʃn/ *n* 1 [U] (城市,学校等)创〔創〕建 chuàngjiàn, 建立 jiànlì. 2 [C] 创建物(如学校,医院等) chuàngjiànwù. 3 [C] (慈善等)基金 jījīn. 4 [C] 〔常作 *pl*〕 地基 dìjī, 房基 fángjī. 5 [C, U] 基础〔礎〕 jīchǔ.

foun·der /ˈfaʊndə(r)/ *vt/i* (使)(船)沉没 chénmò.

foun·dry /ˈfaʊndrɪ/ *n* [C] [*pl* -ies] 铸〔鑄〕工车〔車〕间〔間〕 zhùgōng chējiān, 铸工厂〔廠〕 zhùgōngchǎng.

foun·tain /ˈfaʊntɪn/ *n* [C] 1 泉水, quánshuǐ, 人造喷泉 rénzào pēnquán. 2 〔喻〕源泉 yuánquán, 根源 gēnyuán: *the ~ of knowledge* 知识的源泉. **ˈ~-pen** 自来〔來〕水笔〔筆〕 zìláishuǐbǐ.

four /fɔː(r)/ *adj, n* [C] 四 sì, 四个 sìgè. ***on all ~s*** 爬 pá, 匍匐 púfú. **ˈ~th** *adj, n* [C](略作 4*th*)四分之一 sìfēn zhī yī, 四分之一的 sìfēn zhī yī de, 第四 dìsì, 第四个〔個〕 dìsìgè. **ˈ~th·ly** *adv* 第四(列举时用) dìsì.

four·teen /ˌfɔːˈtiːn/ *adj, n* [C] 十四 shísì, 十四个〔個〕 shísìgè. **four·teenth** *adj, n* [C] (略作 14*th*) 十四分之一 shísìfēn zhī yī, 十四分之一的 shísìfēn zhī yī de, 第十四 dì shísì, 第十四个 dì shísì gè.

fowl /faʊl/ *n* [C] 1 较〔較〕大的鸟〔鳥〕 jiàodàde niǎo: *ˈwild~* 野禽. 2 鸡〔鷄〕 jī. 3 [U] 禽肉 qín ròu.

fox /fɒks/ *n* [C] 狐 hú. ⇨ vixen. □ *vt* 迷惑 míhuò, 欺骗〔騙〕 qīpiàn.

foyer /ˈfɔɪeɪ/ *n* [C] 门〔門〕厅〔廳〕 méntīng; 休息室 xiūxishì.

Fr. = 1 Father. 2 French.

frac·tion /ˈfrækʃn/ *n* [C] 1 碎片 suìpiàn, 片断〔斷〕 piànduàn: *a ~ of a second* 瞬间. 2 [数学]分数〔數〕 fēnshù **~al** *adj*

frac·ture /ˈfræktʃə(r)/ *n* [C, U] 断〔斷〕裂 duànliè, 折断 zhéduàn, 骨折 gǔzhé. □ *vt/i* (使)断裂 duànliè, (使)折断 zhéduàn.

frag·ile /ˈfrædʒaɪl/ *adj* 脆的 cuìde, 易断〔斷〕的 yìduànde. **fra·gil·ity** /frəˈdʒɪlətɪ/ *n* [U]

frag·ment /ˈfrægmənt/ *n* [C] 碎片 suìpiàn, 碎块〔塊〕 suìkuài, 片断〔斷〕 piànduàn. □ *vi* /frægˈment/ 裂成碎片 lièchéng suìpiàn **~ary** *adj* 不完全的 bù wánquán de. **~a·tion** /-ˈteɪʃn/ *n* [U]

fra·grance /ˈfreɪgrəns/ *n* [U] 香味 xiāngwèi, 香气〔氣〕 xiāngqì. **fra·grant** *adj*

frail /freɪl/ *adj* [-er, -est] 虚弱的 xūruòde, 脆弱的 cuìruòde. **~ty** *n* (a) [U] 虚弱 xūruò, 脆弱 cuìruò. (b) [C] [*pl* -ies] 过〔過〕失 guòshī, 弱点〔點〕 ruòdiǎn.

frame /freɪm/ *n* [C] 1 构〔構〕架 gòujià, 骨架 gǔjià, 结构 jiégòu. 2 框架 kuàngjià, 框 kuàng. 3 眼镜架 yǎnjìngjià. 4 (人或动物)身躯〔軀〕 shēnqū. 5 ***~ of mind*** 精神状〔狀〕态〔態〕 jīngshén zhuàngtài, 心情 xīnqíng. 6 画〔畫〕面 huàmiàn, 镜头〔頭〕 jìngtóu. □ *vt/i* 1 构造 gòuzào, 建造 jiànzào, 拟〔擬〕定 nǐdìng: ~

a plan 拟定计划. **2** 给…装〔裝〕框架 gěi ...zhuāng kuàngjià. **3**〔俚语〕诬陷 wūxiàn, 陷害 xiànhài. '**~work** 构架 gòujià, 框架 kuàngjià.

fran·chise /'fræntʃaɪz/ *n* [U]〔与 *the* 连用〕公民权〔權〕gōngmínquán, 选〔選〕举〔舉〕权 xuǎnjǔquán; 特权 tèquán, 特许 tèxǔ.

Franco- /ˌfræŋkəʊ/ *prefix* 表示"法国〔國〕" biǎoshì "fǎguó": '~-*German* 法德.

frank¹ /fræŋk/ *adj* [-er, -est] 坦率的 tǎnshuàide, 坦白的 tǎnbáide. **~ly** *adv* **~ness** *n* [U]

frank² /fræŋk/ *vt* 用自动〔動〕邮〔郵〕资盖印机〔機〕盖印于 (邮件) yòng zìdòng yóuzīgàiyìnjī gàiyìn yú.

frank·furter /'fræŋkfɜːtə(r)/ *n* [C] 猪牛肉混合香肠〔腸〕zhū niú ròu hùnhé xiāngcháng.

fran·tic /'fræntɪk/ *adj* (因快乐, 痛苦, 焦虑等) 激动〔動〕得发〔發〕狂 jīdòngde fākuáng. **~ally** *adv*

fra·ter·nal /frə'tɜːnl/ *adj* 兄弟般的 xiōngdìbānde, 兄弟的 xiōngdìde. **~ly** *adv*

fra·ter·nity /frə'tɜːnətɪ/ *n* [*pl* -ies] **1** [U] 友爱〔愛〕yǒu'ài, 博爱 bó'ài; 兄弟关〔關〕系 xiōngdì guānxī. **2** [C] 趣味相投的人 qùwèi xiāngtóu de rén. **3**〔美语〕大学〔學〕生联〔聯〕谊会〔會〕dàxuéshēng liányìhuì.

frat·er·nize /'frætənaɪz/ *vi* 亲〔親〕善 (*with*) qīnshàn, 友好 yǒuhǎo. **frat·er·ni'z·ation** *n* [U]

fraud /frɔːd/ *n* **1** [C, U] 诈骗〔騙〕zhàpiàn, 欺诈行为〔爲〕qīzhà xíngwéi. **2** [C] 骗子 piànzi, 假货 jiǎhuò. **~u·lent** /-jʊlənt/ *adj* 欺骗性的 qīpiànxìngde, 骗来〔來〕的 piànláide.

fraught /frɔːt/ *adj* **1** 牵涉…的 qiānshè...de, 预示…的 yùshì...de: ~ *with danger* 充满危险的; ~ *with meaning* 意味深长的.

fray /freɪ/ *vt/i* **1** 磨损 mósǔn, 磨破 mópò. **2**〔喻〕忍受不住 rěnshòu bú zhù: ~*ed temper* 因忍受不住而烦燥的心情.

freak /friːk/ *n* [C] **1** 怪诞的想法或行为〔爲〕guàidànde xiǎngfǎ huò xíngwéi. **2** 畸形的人或动〔動〕植物 jīxíngde rén huò dòngzhíwù. **~ish** *adj* 怪诞的 guàidànde, 畸形的 jīxíngde. **freaky** *adj* [-ier, -iest] = freakish.

freckle /'frekl/ *n* [C] 雀斑 quèbān, (皮肤)斑点〔點〕bāndiǎn. □ *vt/i* (使)生雀斑 shēng quèbān, (使)生斑点 shēng bāndiǎn.

free /friː/ *adj* [-r, -st] **1** (人)自由的 zìyóude, 无〔無〕约束的 wú yuēsùde. **2** 不在狱中的 bú zài yùzhōng de. **3** 行动〔動〕自由的 xíngdòng zìyóu de. **4** ***have a ~ hand*** 有放手处〔處〕理的权〔權〕力 yǒu fàngshǒu chǔlǐ de quánlì. ***give sb a ~ hand*** 给某人以放手处理的权力 gěi mǒurén yǐ fàngshǒu chǔlǐ de quánlì. **5** ~ ***from*** 没有…的 méi yǒu...de: ~ *from blame* 无可指责. ~ ***of*** (a) 离〔離〕开〔開〕líkāi: ~ *of her* 离开她. (b) 无〔無〕…的 wú...de: ~ *of charge* 不收费. **6** 免费的 miǎnfèide. **7** 空闲〔閑〕的 kòngxiánde, 空余〔餘〕的 kòngyúde. **8** 无阻的 wúzǔde: *a ~ flow of water* 畅通的水流. **9** 无约束的 wú yuēsù de: ~ *in conversation* 随便说话. □ *vt* [*pt, pp* ~d] 使自由 shǐ zìyóu, 解放 jiěfàng, 使摆〔擺〕脱 shǐ bǎituō. ˌ**~-and-'easy** *adj* 不拘礼〔禮〕仪〔儀〕的 bù jū lǐyí de, 自由的 zìyóude. **~dom** 自由 zìyóu. '**~-for-all** 可自由发〔發〕表见解的争论〔論〕kě zìyóu fābiǎo jiànjiě de zhēnglùn. '**~-hand** *adj* 徒手画〔畫〕的 túshǒu huà de. '**~hold** [法律]地产〔產〕的完全保有 dìchǎnde wánquán bǎoyǒu, 完全保有的地产 wánquán bǎoyǒu de dìchǎn. ⇨ leasehold. '**~lance** /-lɑːns/ *n* [C] 自由职〔職〕业〔業〕者 zìyóuzhíyèzhě. □ *vi* 做自由职业 zuò zìyóuzhíyè. ˌ~ '**speech** 言论〔論〕自由 yánlùn zìyóu. ˌ**~-'trade** 自由贸易 zìyóu màoyì. ˌ~ '**verse** (无格律的)自由诗 zìyóushī. '**~way**〔美语〕快车〔車〕道 kuàichē dào. ˌ~ '**will** 自愿〔願〕的 zìyuàn de, 自由意志 zìyóu yìzhì. **~ly** *adv* 自由地 zìyóude, 无拘束地 wú jūsù de; 免费地 miǎnfèide.

free·mason /'friːmeɪsn/ *n* [C] 共济〔濟〕会〔會〕成员 gòngjìhuì chéngyuán. '**~ry** *n* [U]

freeze /friːz/ *vt/i* [*pt* froze /frəʊz/, *pp* frozen /'frəʊzn/] **1** 冷至结冰 lěngzhì jiébīng, 酷寒 kùhán. **2** 冻〔凍〕结 dòngjié, 冻僵 dòngjiāng. **3** 感到极〔極〕冷 gǎndào jílěng. **4** 使冷 shǐ lěng: *frozen food* 冷冻食物. ⇨ deep-freeze. **5** 冻结物价〔價〕, 工资 dòngjié wùjià, gōngzī. **6** 无〔無〕变〔變〕动〔動〕wú biàndòng. □ *n* [C] **1** 严〔嚴〕寒期 yánhánqī. **2** 工资, 物价等冻结 gōngzī, wùjià děng dòngjié. **freezer** 冰箱 bīngxiāng. '**~-dry** *vt* [*pt, pp* ~-dried] 冻〔凍

干〔乾〕dònggān. 'freezing-point 冰点〔點〕bīngdiǎn.
freight /'freɪt/ *n* [C] 货运〔運〕huòyùn; (运输的)货物 huòwù; 运费 yùnfèi. □ *vt* 运输(货物) yùnshū. ~**er** 货船 huòchuán, 运输机〔機〕yùnshūjī.
French /frentʃ/ *adj, n* 法国〔國〕人的 fǎguóréndе; 法国的 fǎguóde; 法语的 fǎyǔde; 法国人 fǎguórén; 法语 fǎyǔ. ~**man** 法国人 fǎguórén. ,~'**window** 落地长〔長〕窗 luòdì chángchuāng.
frenzy /'frenzɪ/ *n* [U] 疯〔瘋〕狂的激动〔動〕fēngkuángde jīdòng. **fren·zied** *adj*
fre·quency /'fri:kwənsɪ/ *n* [*pl* -ies] **1** [U] 频繁 pínfán. **2** [C] 频率 pínlǜ. '~**band** *n* 频(率)带〔帶〕píndài. ~ **modu'lation** *n* (略作 FM) 调频 tiáopín.
fre·quent[1] /'fri:kwent/ *adj* 时〔時〕常发〔發〕生的 shícháng fāshēng de. ~**ly** *adv*
fre·quent[2] /frɪ'kwent/ *vt* 常到(某地) chángdào, 常去 chángqù.
fresco /'freskəu/ *n* [C] [*pl* ~s, ~es] 壁画〔畫〕bìhuà.
fresh /freʃ/ *adj* [-er, -est] **1** 新的 xīnde, 新近的 xīnjìnde: ~ *flowers* 刚开的花; ~ *paint* 新刷的漆. **2** (食物)新鲜的 xīnxiānde, 鲜的(非腌制, 罐装或冷冻的) xiānde. **3** 新奇的 xīnqíde, 不同的 bùtóngde: ~ *news* 新消息. **4** (气候)凉爽的 liángshuǎngde, 清新的 qīngxīnde. ~**en** *vt/i* **(a)** (使)显〔顯〕得新鲜 xiǎnde xīnxiān. **(b)** (风)变〔變〕强 biàn qiáng '~**man** 一年级大学〔學〕生 yīniánjí dàxuéshēng. '~-**water** 淡水 dànshuǐ. ~**ly** *adv* [与 *pp* 连用] 新近地 xīnjìnde. ~**ness** *n* [U]
fret[1] /fret/ *vt/i* [-tt-] **1** (使)烦恼〔惱〕fánnǎo, (使)烦燥 fánzào. **2** 侵蚀 qīnshí, 磨损 mósǔn. □ *n* [U] 烦恼 fánnǎo, 烦燥 fánzào. ~**ful** *adj* 烦恼的 fánnǎode, 烦燥的 fánzàode. ~**fully** *adv*
fret[2] /fret/ *vt* [-tt-] 用回纹装〔裝〕饰 yòng huíwén zhuāngshì. '~**saw** 线〔綫〕锯 xiànjù. '~**work** *n* [U] 浮雕细工 fúdiāo xìgōng 雕花 diāohuā.
fret[3] /fret/ *n* [C] (吉他等弦乐器上的)品 pǐn, 柱 zhù, 桥〔橋〕qiáo.
friar /'fraɪə(r)/ *n* [C] 男修道士 nánxiūdàoshì.
fric·tion /'frɪkʃn/ *n* **1** [U] 摩擦 mócā. **2** [C, U] 不和 bùhé, 倾轧〔軋〕qīngyà.
Fri.=Friday.
Fri·day /'fraɪdɪ/ *n* 星期五 xīngqīwǔ. ,**Good 'F**~ (基督教)耶稣受难〔難〕日 yēsū shòunànrì.
fridge /frɪdʒ/ *n* [C] (=) refrigerator
fried /fraɪd/ *pt, pp* of fry.
friend /frend/ *n* [C] **1** 朋友 péngyou, 友人 yǒurén. **2** 赞助者 zànzhùzhě, 支持者 zhīchízhě. ~**ly** *adj* [-ier, -iest] 友好的 yǒuhǎode, 友谊的 yǒuyìde. ~**li·ness** *n* [U] ~**ship** *n* [U] 友谊 yǒuyí [C, U] 友爱〔愛〕yǒuài, 友情 yǒuqíng.
frieze /fri:z/ *n* [C] 墙〔牆〕等的横饰带〔帶〕qiáng děng de héngshìdài.
frig·ate /'frɪgət/ *n* [C] 快速护〔護〕航舰〔艦〕kuàisù hùhángjiàn; 巡航舰 xúnhángjiàn.
fright /fraɪt/ *n* [C, U] 惊〔驚〕恐 jīngkǒng, 惊吓〔嚇〕jīngxià.
frighten /'fraɪtn/ *vt* 使惊〔驚〕恐 shǐ jīngkǒng, 吓〔嚇〕唬 xiàhu. ~**ed** *adj* ~**ing** *adj*
fright·ful /'fraɪtfl/ *adj* **1** 可怕的 kěpàde, 吓〔嚇〕人的 xiàrénde. **2** [非正式用语]讨厌〔厭〕的tǎoyànde. ~**ly** *adv* **(a)** 讨厌地 tǎoyànde. **(b)** [非正式用语]非常地 fēichángde: ~*ly hot* 特热.
frigid /'frɪdʒɪd/ *adj* **1** 寒冷的 hánlěngde: *a* ~ *climate* 寒冷的天气. **2** 冷淡的 lěngdànde. **3** (妇女)性冷感的 xìnglěnggǎnde. ~**ly** *adv*. ~**ity** /frɪ'dʒɪtɪ/ *n* [U]
frill /frɪl/ *n* [C] **1** (服装)褶边〔邊〕zhěbiān, 饰边 shìbiān. **2** [*pl*] 虚饰 xūshì, 矫〔矯〕饰 jiāoshì, 装〔裝〕腔作势〔勢〕zhuāngqiāngzuòshì. **frilly** *adj*
fringe /frɪndʒ/ *n* [C] **1** 缘饰 yuánshì, 毛边〔邊〕máobiān, 蓬边 péngbiān. **2** 边缘 biānyuán. **3** (妇女发式)前刘〔劉〕海 qián liúhǎi. □ *vt* 装〔裝〕上缘饰 zhuāngshàng yuánshì.
frisk /frɪsk/ *vt/i* **1** 欢〔歡〕跃〔躍〕huānyuè, 跳跳蹦蹦 tiàotiào bèngbèng. **2** 搜身 sōushēn. **frisky** *adj* [-ier, -iest] 活泼〔潑〕的 huópode.
frit·ter[1] /'frɪtə(r)/ *vt* 浪费 làngfèi: ~ *away one's money* 浪费金钱.
frit·ter[2] /'frɪtə(r)/ *n* [C] (果馅, 肉馅)油煎饼 yóujiānbǐng.
friv·ol·ous /'frɪvələs/ *adj* 轻〔輕〕薄的 qīngbóde, 轻浮的 qīngfúde. ~**ly** *adv*
friv·ol·ity /frɪ'vɒlətɪ/ *n* [*pl* -ies] **1** [U] 轻〔輕〕薄 qīngbó, 轻浮 qīngfú. **2** [C] 轻薄的举〔舉〕动

〔動〕或言语 qīngbóde jǔdòng huò yányǔ.

fro /frəʊ/ *adv* 〔只用于〕 ˌ*to and* ˈ~ 来〔來〕回地 láihuíde, 往返地 wǎngfǎnde.

frock /frɒk/ *n* [C] 女上衣 nǚshàng yī.

frog /frɒg/ *n* [C] 青蛙 qīngwā. ˈ~**man** 蛙人(穿戴蛙式潜水设备的人) wārén.

frolic /ˈfrɒlɪk/ *vi* [*pt*, *pp* ~ked] 嬉戏〔戲〕 xīxì. 打打闹闹 dǎdǎnàonào. *lambs ~king in the fields* 在地里跳跳蹦蹦的羊羔. □ *n* [C] 欢〔歡〕乐〔樂〕 huānlè, 嬉戏 xīxì.

from /frəm 强式 frɒm/ *prep* **1** (表示起点) 从〔從〕 cóng: *jump (down) ~ a wall* 从墙上跳下. **2** (表示时间的开始): *~ the first of May* 从五月一日开始. **3** (表示距离)离〔離〕 lí, 距 jù: *ten miles ~ the coast* 距海岸 10 英里. **4** (表示施予者)来〔來〕自 láizì: *a letter ~ my brother* 我兄弟的来信. **5** (表示限度)从 cóng: *~ ten to fifteen boys* 10 到 15 个男孩子. **6** (表示来源) 来自 láizì; 用 yòng: *quotations ~ Shakespeare* 引自莎士比亚作品的文句; *made ~ grapes* 用葡萄制作的. **7** (表示分离,除去等)从 cóng: *released ~ prison*出狱. **8** (表示变化)由 yóu, 从 cóng: *~ bad to worse* 愈来愈糟. **9** (表示原因)由于 yóuyú, 因为〔爲〕 yīnwéi: *suffer ~ starvation* 忍饥挨饿. **10** (表示区别) 与〔與〕 yǔ: *know an Englishman ~ an American* 分清英国人与美国人.

front /frʌnt/ *n* **1** 〔与 *the* 连用〕 正面 zhèngmiàn, 前面 qiánmiàn: *the ~ of a building* 建筑物的正面. *in ~ adv*: 在前面 zài qiánmiàn: *go in ~* 在前面走. *in ~ of prep*: 在…的前面 zài ... de qiánmiàn: *in ~ of the house* 在屋子的前面. **2** [C] 前线〔綫〕qiánxiàn, 前方 qiánfāng; 战〔戰〕线 zhànxiàn. **3** [C] 海滨〔濱〕人行道 hǎibīn rénxíngdào. **4** [U] 外表 wàibiǎo, 装〔裝〕腔作势〔勢〕 zhuāngqiāng zuòshì: *put on a brave ~* 装作勇敢的样子. **5** 〔气象〕锋 fēng. □ *vt/i* 面对〔對〕 miànduì, 朝 cháo: *doors that ~ on to the street* 朝街的门. ⇨ seafront. ~ **door** 大门〔門〕 dàmén, 正门 zhèngmén. ~**age** /-ɪdʒ/ *n* [C] 土地或建筑物之正面长〔長〕度 tǔdì huò jiànzhùwù zhī zhèngmiàn chángdù. ~**al** *adj* 正面的 zhèngmiànde, 在正面 zài zhèngmiàn. 至正面 zhì zhèngmiàn.

fron·tier /ˈfrʌntɪə(r)/ *n* [C] **1** 国〔國〕界 guójiè, 边〔邊〕界 biānjiè. **2** 〔喻〕尖端 jiānduān, 新领域 xīnlǐngyù: *the ~s of science* 科学尖端.

frost /frɒst/ *n* **1** [C, U] 冰点〔點〕以下的气〔氣〕候 bīngdiǎn yǐxià de qìhòu. 严〔嚴〕寒 yánhán. **2** [U] 霜 shuāng. □ *vt/i* **1** 结霜于 jié shuāng yú, 起霜 qǐshuāng. **2** 使(玻璃)具有无〔無〕光泽〔澤〕的表面 shǐjùyǒu wúguāngzé de biǎomiàn. **3** (在糕饼上)撒糖粒 sǎ tánglì. ˈ~**-bite** 冻〔凍〕伤〔傷〕 dòngshāng, 霜害 shuānghài. ˈ~**-bitten** *adj* 冻伤的 dòngshāngde, 受霜害的 shòu shuānghài de. ˈ~**-bound** *adj* (土地)冻硬的 dòngyìngde. **frosty** *adj* [-ier, -iest] **(a)** 霜冻的 shuāngdòngde. **(b)** 〔喻〕冷若冰霜的 lěng ruò bīngshuāng de, 冷淡的 lěngdànde: *a ~y welcome* 冷淡的接待.

F.R.S. = Fellow of the Royal Society (英国) 皇家学〔學〕会〔會〕会员 huángjiā xuéhuì huìyuán.

froth /frɒθ/ *n* [U] 泡沫 pàomò. □ *vi* 起泡沫 qǐ pàomò. **frothy** *adj* [-ier, -iest] 泡沫的 pàomòde, 泡沫状〔狀〕的 pàomòzhuàngde, 有泡沫的 yǒu pàomò de.

frown /fraʊn/ *vi* 皱〔皺〕眉(表示不满等) zhòu méi. ~ *on* (或 *upon*) 不赞成 bú zànchén. □ *n* [C] 皱眉 zhòuméi.

froze, frozen ⇨ freeze.

fru·gal /ˈfruːgl/ *adj* 俭〔儉〕朴〔樸〕的 jiǎnpǔde, 花钱〔錢〕少的 huāqián shǎo de: *a ~ supper* 一顿节约的晚饭.

fruit /fruːt/ *n* **1** [U] 水果 shuǐguǒ. **2** [C] 果实〔實〕 guǒshí. **3** 〔喻〕〔常用 *pl*〕收获〔穫〕shōuhuò, 报〔報〕酬 bàochóu; 果实 guǒshí. □ *vi* (树等)结果 jiéguǒ. ~**erer** 水果商 shuǐguǒshāng. ~**ful** *adj* **(a)** 果实结得多的 guǒshí jié de duō de. **(b)** 〔喻〕多产的 duōchǎnde, 收效大的 shōuxiào dà de. ~**fulness** *n* [U] ~**less** *adj* **(a)** 不结果的 bù jiéguǒ de. **(b)** 〔喻〕无效益的 wú xiàoyì de. ~**less·ly** *adv* **fruity** *adj* [-ier, -iest] **(a)** 水果的 shuǐguǒde, 水果味的 shuǐguǒwèi de. **(b)** 〔非正式用语〕圆润〔潤〕的 yuánrùnde: *a ~y voice* 圆润的声音.

fru·ition /fruːˈɪʃn/ *n* [U] 实〔實〕现 shíxiàn, 完成 wánchéng: *His plans all came to ~.* 他的计划全都实现.

frus·trate /frʌˈstreɪt/ *vt* 挫败 cuòbài, 阻挠〔撓〕 zǔráo. **frus·tra**

tion *n* [C, U]
fry /fraɪ/ *vt/i* [*3rd pers sing pres tense* fries; *pt, pp* fried] 油煎 yóujiān, 油炸 yóuzhá, 油炒 yóuchǎo. **'~-ing-pan** 煎锅 jiānguō.
ft.=**1** foot. **2** feet.
fudge /fʌdʒ/ *n* [U] 一种〔種〕牛奶软〔軟〕糖 yìzhǒng niúnǎiruǎntáng.
fuel /'fju:əl/ *n* [C, U] **1** 燃料 ránliào. **2**〔喻〕刺激感情之物 cìjī gǎnqíng zhīwù. □ *vt/i* [-ll-,美语亦作 -l-] 供给燃料 gōngjǐ ránliào.
fugi·tive /'fju:dʒətɪv/ *n* [C] 逃犯 táofàn. □ *adj* 逃亡的 táowángde, 逃犯的 taotande.
ful·crum /'fʌlkrəm/ *n* [C] [*pl* ~s] (横杆)支点〔點〕zhīdiǎn.
ful·fil [美语亦作 **-fill**] /fʊl'fɪl/ *vt* [-ll-] 完成 wánchéng, 履行 lǚxíng. **~ment** *n* [U]
full /fʊl/ *adj* [-er, -est] **1** 满的 *(of)* mǎnde, 充满的 chōngmǎnde: *a ~ bottle* 装满的瓶. **2** *~ of* 有很多的 yǒu hěnduō de, 富于(思想等)的 fùyú de. **3** 丰〔豐〕满的 fēngmǎnde, 又胖又圆的 yòupàng yòuyuán de: *She has a ~ figure.* 她身材丰满. **4** (衣服)有宽褶的 yǒu kuānzhě de. **5** *in ~* 完全地 wánquánde, 无〔無〕省略地 wú shěnlüè de. *at ~ speed* 以最高速度 yǐ zuìgāo sùdù. *to the ~* 充分地 chōngfènde, 彻〔徹〕底地 chèdǐde: *enjoy life to the ~* 充分享受. **6** 完全的 wánquánde, 详尽〔盡〕的 xiángjìnde: *a ~ account of his life* 他的一生的详尽记录. **,~-'length** *adj* **(a)** (象)全身的 quánshēnde. **(b)** 标〔標〕准〔準〕长〔長〕的 biāozhǔn cháng de, 一般长的 yìbān cháng de. **,~'stop** (标点符号)句点〔點〕jùdiǎn. ***come to a ~ stop*** 完全停止 wánquán tíngzhǐ. **,~-'scale** *adj* (图样等)实〔實〕比的 shíbǐde. **'~-time** *adj, adv* 全部工作时〔時〕间〔間〕的(地) quánbù gōngzuò shíjiān de. **fully** *adv* **(a)** 完全地 wánquánde, 充分地 chōngfènde. **(b)** 至少 zhìshǎo: *~y two hours* 至少两小时. **,fully-'grown** *adj* 成熟的 chéngshúde. **~-ness** *n* [U]
fumble /'fʌmbl/ *vt/i* 笨手笨脚地做 bènshǒu bènjiǎo de zuò, 乱〔亂〕摸 luànmō.
fume /fju:m/ *n* [C] [常用 *pl*] (气味浓烈的)烟, 汽 yān, qì. □ *vt/i* **1** 熏 xūn; 冒烟 màoyān; 冒汽 màoqì. **2**〔喻〕发〔發〕怒 fānù.
fun /fʌn/ *n* [U] **1** 玩笑 wánxiào. 乐〔樂〕趣 lèqù. ***make ~ of*** 取笑 qǔxiào. ***for*** (或 ***in***) *~* 开〔開〕玩笑地 kāiwánxiàode. **2** 有趣的人或事 yǒuqùde rén huò shì. **'~ fair** = fair²(2).
func·tion /'fʌŋkʃn/ *n* [C] **1** 职〔職〕责 zhízé, 作用 zuòyòng, 功能 gōngnéng. **2** 正式社会〔會〕集会 zhèngshì shèhuì jíhuì. □ *vi* 起作用 qǐzuòyòng, 运〔運〕行 yùnxíng: *The lift doesn't ~.* 电梯坏了. **~al** *adj* **(a)** 实〔實〕用的 shíyòngde. **(b)** 有功能的 yǒu gōngnéng de.
fund /fʌnd/ *n* [C] **1** (非物质的东西的)蕴藏 yùncáng. *a ~ of amusing stories* 大量有趣的故事. **2** 专〔專〕款 zhuankuan, 基金 jījin. **3** [*pl*] 财源 cáiyuán. □ *vt* 提供一笔钱以备取息 tígòng yìbǐqián yǐbèi qǔxī.
fun·da·men·tal /,fʌndə'mentl/ *adj* 基础〔礎〕的 jīchǔde, 作为〔爲〕起点〔點〕的 zuòwéi qǐdiǎnde. 十分重要的 shífēn zhòngyàode □ *n* [C] [常用 *pl*] 基本原则 jīběn yuánzé, 基本原理 jīběn yuánlǐ. **~ly** *adv*
fu·neral /'fju:nərəl/ *n* [C] 丧葬 sàngzàng, 葬礼〔禮〕zànglǐ.
fun·gus /'fʌŋgəs/ *n* [C, U] [*pl* -gi /-gaɪ/] 真菌 zhēnjūn.
funnel /'fʌnl/ *n* [C] **1** 漏斗 lòudǒu. **2** (轮船等的)烟囱 yāncong. □ *vt/i* [-ll-] (使)汇〔匯〕集 huìjí.
funny /'fʌnɪ/ *adj* [-ier, -iest] **1** 可笑的 kěxiàode, 有趣的 yǒuqùde. **2** 奇特的 qítède. **'~-bone** 肘部尺骨端 zhǒubù chǐgǔduān. **fun·nily** *adv*
fur /fɜ:(r)/ *n* **1** [U] (兽类)软〔軟〕毛 ruǎnmáo. **2** [C] 毛皮 máopí, 毛皮衣 máopíyī. **~ry** *adj* [-ier, -iest] 毛皮的 máopíde, 象毛皮的 xiàng máopíde; 穿毛皮的 chuān máopí de.
furi·ous /'fjʊərɪəs/ *adj* 狂怒的 kuángnùde. **~ly** *adv*
fur·long /'fɜ:lɒŋ/ *n* [C] 弗隆(=201 米) fúlóng.
fur·nace /'fɜ:nɪs/ *n* [C] **1** 炉〔爐〕子 lúzi. **2** 熔炉 rónglú.
fur·nish /'fɜ:nɪʃ/ *vt* 供应〔應〕gōngyìng, 用家具装〔裝〕备〔備〕房子 yòng jiājù zhuāngbèi fángzi. **~ings** *n pl* 家具 jiājù, 设备 shèbèi, 陈设 chénshè.
fur·ni·ture /'fɜ:nɪtʃə(r)/ *n* [U] 家具 jiaju.
fur·rier /'fʌrɪə(r)/ *n* [C] 皮货商 píhuòshāng; 毛皮加工制〔製〕作者 máopí jiāgōng zhìzuòzhě.
fur·row /'fʌrəʊ/ *n* [C] **1** 犁沟〔溝〕lígōu. **2** (面部)皱〔皺〕纹 zhòuwén. □ *vt* 犁田 lítián, 使起

皱纹 shìqǐ zhòuwén.

furry /'fɜːrɪ/ ⇨ fur.

fur·ther /'fɜːðə(r)/ *adv, adj* **1** (常用作 *farther* 的意义): 更远[遠]的 gènyuǎnde; 更远地 gènyuǎnde: *It's not safe to go any* ~. 走得更远是不安全的. **2** (不是 *farther* 的意义) 更多的 gènduōde, 进[進]一步的 jìnyíbùde: ~ *information* 更多的情报. **3** (= furthermore) 而且 érqiě, 此外 cǐwài. □ *vt* 促进 cùjìn, 增进 zēngjìn: ~ *the cause of peace* 促进和平事业. **~ance** *n* [U] [非正式用语]促进 cùjìn, 推动[動] tuīdòng. **~more** *adv* 而且 érqiě, 此外 cǐwài. **~most** *adj* 最远的 zuìyuǎnde.

fur·thest /'fɜːðɪst/ *adj, adv* 最远的 zuìyuǎnde, 最远地 zuìyuǎnde.

fur·tive /'fɜːtɪv/ *adj* 偷偷摸摸的 tōutōumōmōde, 鬼鬼祟祟的 guǐguǐsuìsuìde. **~ly** *adv* **~ness** *n* [U]

fury /'fjʊərɪ/ *n* [*pl* -ies] **1** [U] 狂怒 kuángnù, 暴怒 bàonù. **2** [C] 愤怒的暴发[發] fènnùde bàofā.

fuse[1] /fjuːz/ *n* [C] **1** 导[導]火线[綫] dǎohuǒxiàn, 导爆线 dǎobàoxiàn. **2** [美语 = *fuze*] 信管 xìnguǎn, 引信 yǐnxìn.

fuse[2] /fjuːz/ *vt/i* **1** 熔 róng, 熔化 rónghuà, 熔合 rónghé. **2** 因保险[險]丝烧[燒]断[斷]而电[電]路中断 yīn bǎoxiǎnsī shāoduàn ér diànlù zhōngduàn. □ *n* [C] 保险丝 bǎoxiǎnsī.

fu·sel·age /'fjuːzəlɑːʒ/ *n* [C] 飞[飛]机[機]机身 fēijī jīshēn.

fu·sion /'fjuːʒn/ *n* [C, U] 熔合 rónghé, 熔接 róngjiē.

fuss /fʌs/ *n* [U] [与 *a, an* 连用]大惊[驚]小怪 dàjīng xiǎoguài, ***make a ~ of*** 大惊小怪 dàjīng xiǎoguài. 忙乱[亂] mángluàn. □ *vt/i* 忙乱 mángluàn. 使烦燥 shǐ fánzào. **~ily** /-ɪlɪ/ *adv* **fussy** *adj* [-ier, -iest] **(a)** 大惊小怪的 dàjīng xiǎoguài de, 忙乱的 mángluànde. **(b)** 过[過]分注意琐事的 guòfèn zhùyì suǒshì de. **(c)** (服装) 过分装[裝]饰的 guòfèn zhuāngshì de, (文章) 过分华[華]丽[麗]的 guòfèn huálì de.

fu·tile /'fjuːtaɪl/ *adj* 无[無]效的 wúxiàode, 无用的 wúyòngde: *a ~ attempt* 枉费心机的企图. **fu·til·ity** /fjuː'tɪlətɪ/ *n* [C, U]

fu·ture /'fjuːtʃə(r)/ *adj* 将[將]来[來]的 jiāngláide, 未来的wèiláide. □ *n* [C] 将来 jiānglái, 未来 wèilái. ***in ~*** 在将来 zàijiānglái.

fuzz /fʌz/ *n* [U] 茸毛 róngmáo, 绒毛 róngmáo.

fuzzy /'fʌzɪ/ *adj* [-ier, -iest] **1** 模糊的 móhude: *The outline is very ~*. 轮廓不清楚. **2** 有绒毛的 yǒu róngmáo de.

G g

G, g /dʒiː/ [*pl* G's, g's /dʒiːz/] 英语的第七个字母 yīngyǔde dìqīgè zìmǔ.

g.=gram(s).

gab·ar·dine /ˌgæbə'diːn/ *n* [U] 华[華]达[達]呢 huádání.

gabble /'gæbl/ *vt/i* 急促而不清楚地说话 jícù ér bù qīngchu de shuōhuà. □ *n* [U] 急促不清的话 jícù bùqīng de huà.

gab·er·dine /ˌgæbə'diːn/ *n* = gabardine.

gable /'geɪbl/ *n* [C] 山墙[牆] shānqiáng.

gadget /'gædʒɪt/ *n* [C] [非正式用语]小机[機]件 xiǎojījiàn, 小装[裝]置 xiǎozhuāngzhì. **~ry** *n* [U] (总称)小机件 xiǎojījiàn.

gag /gæg/ *n* [C] **1** 塞口物 sāikǒuwù. **2** 笑话 xiàohuà, 插科打诨 chākē dǎhùn. □ *vt/i* [-gg-] 塞住…的嘴 sāizhù ... de zuǐ.

gaggle /'gægl/ *n* [C] (鹅)群 qún.

gai·ety /'geɪətɪ/ *n* [*pl* -ies] **1** [U] 高兴[興] gāoxìng, 快乐[樂] kuàilè. **2** [*pl*] 欢[歡]乐 huānlè, 娱乐 yúlè.

gaily /'geɪlɪ/ *adv* 快乐[樂]地 kuàilède, 娱乐地 yúlède.

gain[1] /geɪn/ *n* [C, U] 增加 zēngjiā, 增进[進] zēngjìn. **~ful** *adj* 有收益的 yǒu shōuyìde: *~ful employment* 有报酬的雇佣. **~fully** *adv*

gain[2] /geɪn/ *vt/i* **1** 获[獲]得 huòdé. ~ ***time*** (用拖延的办法)赢得时[時]间[間] yíngdé shíjiān. **2** 增进[進] zēngjìn, 获利 huòlì. **3** (钟,表)走快 zǒukuài. **4** ~ ***on*** (或 ***upon***) 逼近 bījìn, 超过[過] chāoguò. **5** (经过努力)到达[達] dàodá.

gal.=gallon(s)

gala /'gɑːlə/ *n* [C] 盛会[會] shènghuì, 节[節]日 jiérì, 庆[慶]祝 qìngzhù.

ga·lac·tic /gə'læktɪk/ *adj* 银河的 yínhéde.

gal·axy /ˈgæləksɪ/ *n* [C] [*pl* -ies] **1**[天文]星系 xīngxì. **2** 一群人 yìqúnrén: *a ~ of beautiful women* 一群美丽的妇女.

gale /geɪl/ *n* [C] **1** 大风〔風〕dàfēng. **2** 一阵〔陣〕喧闹 yízhèn xuānnào.

gal·lant /ˈgælənt/ *adj* **1** 勇敢的 yǒnggǎnde. **2** 对妇女献〔獻〕殷勤的 duì fùnǚ xiàn yīnqín de. **~ly** *adv* **~ry** *n* [U] **(a)** 勇敢 yǒnggǎn, 豪侠〔俠〕háoxiá. **(b)** (对女子的)殷勤 yīnqín.

gal·leon /ˈgælɪən/ *n* [C] (15—17世纪)西班牙帆船 xībānyá fānchuán.

gal·lery /ˈgælərɪ/ *n* [C] [*pl* -ies] **1** 画〔畫〕廊 huàláng, 美术〔術〕品陈〔陳〕列室 měishùpǐn chénlièshì. **2** (剧场)顶层〔層〕楼〔樓〕座 dǐngcéng lóuzuò. **3** (教堂等)楼座 lóuzuò. **4** (矿井)横坑道 héngkēngdào.

gal·ley /ˈgælɪ/ *n* [C] [*pl* ~s] **1** 单〔單〕层〔層〕甲板大帆船 dāncéng jiǎbǎn dàfānchuán. **2** 船上厨房 chuán shàng chúfáng.

gal·lon /ˈgælən/ *n* [C] 加仑(液量单位, = 4 升) jiālún.

gal·lop /ˈgæləp/ *n* [C] (马等)飞跑 fēipǎo. □ *vt/i* **1** (使)飞跑 fēipǎo. **2** 急速行动〔動〕 jísù xíngdòng.

gal·lows /ˈgæləʊz/ *n pl* [常与 *sing verb* 连用]绞刑架 jiǎoxíngjià, 绞台 jiǎotái.

ga·lore /gəˈlɔ:(r)/ *adv* 许多 xǔduō, 大量 dàliàng, 丰〔豐〕盛 fēngshèng: *whisky ~* 大量供应的威士忌酒.

gamble /ˈgæmbl/ *vt/i* **1** 赌博 dǔbó, 投机〔機〕tóujī, 冒险〔險〕màoxiǎn. **2** *~ sth away* 赌输〔輸〕dǔshū. □ *n* [C] 投机 tóujī. **gam·bler** 赌徒 dǔtú, 赌博者 dǔbózhě. **gamb·ling** *n* [U]

game[1] /geɪm/ *adj* **1** 勇敢的 yǒnggǎnde, 雄纠纠的 xióngjiūjiūde. **2** 愿〔願〕意…的 yuànyì … de.

game[2] /geɪm/ *n* **1** [C] 游戏〔戲〕yóuxì, 运〔運〕动〔動〕yùndòng. *play the ~* **(a)** 遵守比赛规则 zūnshǒu bǐsài guīzé. **(b)** [喻]诚实〔實〕chéngshí, 光明正大 guāngmíng zhèngdà. **2** [C] 游戏器具 yóuxì qìjù. 比赛用具 bǐsài yòngjù. **3** 比赛 bǐsài, 竞〔競〕赛 jìngsài: *a ~ of football* 足球赛. **4** [*pl*] 运动会〔會〕yùndònghuì. **5** [C] 计策 jìcè, 花招 huāzhāo. ˌ*give the* ˈ*~ away* 泄〔洩〕露秘密 xièlù mìmì, 暴露意图〔圖〕bàolù yìtú. **6** [U] 猎〔獵〕物 lièwù, 野味 yěwèi. ˈ**big ~** 大的猎物(狮子、象等) dàde lièwù. ˈ**fair ~ (a)** 合法的猎物 héfǎde lièwù. **(b)** [喻]可据〔據〕理加以批评, 攻击〔擊〕的对〔對〕象 kě jùlǐ jiāyǐ pīpíng, gōngjī de duìxiàng. ˈ**~keeper** 猎场〔場〕看守人 lièchǎng kānshǒurén.

gam·mon /ˈgæmən/ *n* [U] 熏猪腿 xūnzhūtuǐ, 腌腿 yāntuǐ.

gan·der /ˈgændə(r)/ *n* [C] 雄鹅〔鵝〕xióng'é.

gang /gæŋ/ *n* [C] **1** (劳动者的)一组 yìzǔ, 一队〔隊〕yíduì. *a ~ of workmen* 一组工人. **2** (罪犯等)一帮 yìbāng, 一群 yìqún. ⇨ gangster. □ *vi ~ up(on)* 合伙 héhuǒ.

gan·gling /ˈgæŋglɪŋ/ *adj* (人)细长〔長〕的 xìchángde, 瘦长难〔難〕看的 shòucháng nánkàn de.

gan·grene /ˈgæŋgri:n/ *n* [U] (医学)坏〔壞〕疽 huàijū. **gan·gren·ous** /ˈgæŋgrɪnəs/ *adj*

gang·ster /ˈgæŋstə(r)/ *n* [C] (一帮中的一个)匪徒 fěitú.

gang·way /ˈgæŋweɪ/ *n* [C] **1** (船)跳板 tiàobǎn. **2** (座位中间的)通道 tōngdào.

gaol, jail /dʒeɪl/ *n* [C] 监〔監〕狱 jiānyù. □ *vt* 监禁 jiānjìn. **~er, jailer, jailor** *n* [C] 监狱看守 jiānyù kānshǒu.

gap /gæp/ *n* [C] **1** 裂口 lièkǒu, 缺口 quēkǒu. **2** 距离〔離〕jùlí: *a ~ of two miles* 两英里的距离; *a ~ of ten minutes* 十分钟的间隔. **3** 隘口 àikǒu, 山峡 shānxiá. **4** (知识等的)空白 kòngbái, 脱漏 tuōlòu. *~s in one's knowledge* 知识上的空白.

gape /geɪp/ *vi* **1** 张〔張〕口 zhāngkǒu. **2** 张开〔開〕zhāngkāi, 裂开 lièkāi: *a gaping hole* 裂口. □ *n* [C] 目瞪口呆 mùdèng kǒudāi.

garage /ˈgærɑ:ʒ/ *n* [C] **1** 汽车〔車〕房 qìchēfáng. **2** 汽车修理站(并供应汽油) qìchē xiūlǐzhàn. □ *vt* 把汽车送入汽车房或修理站 bǎ qìchē sòngrù qìchēfáng huò xiūlǐzhàn.

gar·bage /ˈgɑ:bɪdʒ/ *n* [U] [美语]垃圾 lājī, 污物 wūwù. ˈ**~-can** *n* [美语] = dustbin.

garble /ˈgɑ:bl/ *vt* 歪曲 wāiqū, 窜〔竄〕改 cuàngǎi: *a ~d report* 歪曲事实的报告.

gar·den /ˈgɑ:dn/ *n* **1** [C, U] 花园〔園〕huāyuán, 菜园 càiyuán. **2** [常用 *pl*]公园 gōngyuán. □ *vi* 从〔從〕事园艺〔藝〕cóngshì yuányì. **~er** 园林工人 yuánlín gōngrén.

gargle /ˈgɑ:gl/ *vt/i* 漱喉 shùhóu;

漱口 shùkǒu. □ *n* [C] **1** 漱口剂〔劑〕shùkǒujì. **2** 漱口 shùkǒu, 漱喉 shùhóu.

gar·goyle /'gɑːgɔɪl/ *n* [C] (建筑) 滴水嘴(常作怪兽状) dīshuǐzuǐ.

gar·ish /'geərɪʃ/ *adj* 颜色俗不可耐的 yánsè súbùkěnàide. **~ly** *adv*

gar·land /'gɑːlənd/ *n* [C] 花环〔環〕huāhuán, 花冠 huāguān. □ *vt* 用花环装饰 yòng huāhuán zhuāngshì.

gar·lic /'gɑːlɪk/ *n* [U] 大蒜 dàsuàn.

gar·ment /'gɑːmənt/ *n* [C](一件) 衣服(长袍,外套) yīfu.

gar·nish /'gɑːnɪʃ/ *vt* 装〔裝〕饰 zhuāngshì, 加配菜于 jiā pèicài yú. □ *n* [C] 装饰品 zhuāngshìpǐn, 配菜 pèicài.

gar·ret /'gærət/ *n* [C] 屋顶层〔層〕wūdǐngcéng, 阁楼〔樓〕gélóu.

gar·ri·son /'gærɪsn/ *n* [C] 卫〔衛〕戍部队〔隊〕wèishù bùduì. 警卫部队 jǐngwèi bùduì. □ *vt* 卫戍 wèishù, 守卫(城市) shǒuwèi.

gar·ter /'gɑːtə(r)/ *n* [C] 吊袜〔襪〕带〔帶〕diàowàdài.

gas /gæs/ *n* [C] [*pl* ~es] **1** 气〔氣〕体〔體〕qìtǐ. **2** [U] 可燃气 kěránqì, 煤气 méiqì, 沼气 zhǎoqì. **3** [美语] = petrol. □ *vt/i* [-ss-] **1** 用毒气杀伤人 yòng dúqì shāshāng rén. **2** [非正式用语]空谈 kōngtán, 瞎扯 xiāchě. **'~-main** 煤气总〔總〕管 méiqì zǒngguǎn. **'~-mask** 防毒面具 fángdú miànjù. **'~-station** [美语] = petrol station. **~eous** *adj* 气体的 qìtǐde, 气态〔態〕的 qìtàide.

gash /gæʃ/ *n* [C] 深而长〔長〕的切口 shēn ér cháng de qiēkǒu, 深而长的伤〔傷〕口 shēn ér cháng de shāngkǒu. □ *vt* 划〔劃〕开 huákāi, 划深长切口 huá shēncháng qiēkǒu.

gas·ket /'gæskɪt/ *n* [C] 垫〔墊〕圈 diànquān, 垫片 diànpiàn.

gaso·line (亦作 **-lene**) /'gæsəliːn/ *n* [U] [美语] = petrol.

gasp /gɑːsp/ *vt/i* **1** 喘气〔氣〕chuǎnqì, 透不过〔過〕气 tòu bú guò qì. **2** 气喘吁吁地说 qìchuǎn xūxū de shuō: ~ *a reply* 气喘吁吁地回答. □ *n* [C] 气喘 qìchuǎn.

gassy /'gæsɪ/ *adj* 气的 qìde, 气体〔體〕样〔樣〕的 qìtǐ yàng de. 充满气体的 chōngmǎn qìtǐ de.

gas·tric /'gæstrɪk/ *adj* 胃的 wèide: ~ *ulcers* 胃溃疡.

gate /geɪt/ *n* [C] **1** 门〔門〕mén, 大门 dàmén, 篱〔籬〕笆门 líbamén. **2** (运动会等) 观〔觀〕众〔衆〕人数〔數〕guānzhòng rénshù; 门票收入 ménpiào shōurù. **'~crash** *vt* 擅自进〔進〕入 shànzì jìnrù, 无〔無〕票入场〔場〕wúpiào rùchǎng. **'~crasher** *n* [C] **'~way** **(a)** 门〔門〕口 ménkǒu, 入口 rùkǒu. **(b)** [喻]途径〔徑〕tújìng, 手段 shǒuduàn: *the* ~ *to success* 成功的途径.

gâ·teau /'gætəʊ/ *n* [C] [*pl* ~x /-təʊz/] 糕饼 gāobǐng.

gather /'gæðə(r)/ *vt/i* **1** (使)聚集 jùjí, (使)集拢〔攏〕jílǒng. **2** 采集 cǎijí, 收集 shōují. **3** 积〔積〕聚 jījù, 积累 jīlěi: ~ *information* 积累资料. **4** 猜想 cāixiǎng, 推测 tuīcè: *I* ~ *you have resigned.* 我猜想你已辞职. **5** 增加 zēngjiā: ~ *speed* 增加速度. **~ing** *n* [C] 集会〔會〕jíhuì.

gauche /gəʊʃ/ *adj* 不善交际〔際〕的 búshàn jiāojì de; 粗鲁的 cūlǔde.

gaudy /'gɔːdɪ/ *adj* [-ier, -iest] 炫丽〔麗〕的 xuànlìde. **gaud·ily** *adv*

gauge [美语亦作 **gage**] /geɪdʒ/ *n* [C] **1** 标〔標〕准〔準〕尺寸 biāozhǔn chǐcùn. **2** (铁道)轨〔軌〕距 guǐjù. **3** (雨量)器 qì; (电线等)直径〔徑〕zhíjìng. □ *vt* **1** 测量 cèliáng, 测定 cèdìng. **2** [喻]估计 gūjì, 评价〔價〕(人物) píngjià.

gaunt /gɔːnt/ *adj* **1** (人)憔悴的 qiáocuìde, 瘦弱的 shòuruòde. **2** (地方)荒凉的 huāngliángde. **~ness** *n* [U]

gauze /gɔːz/ *n* [U] 薄纱 bóshā, 罗〔羅〕luó, 网〔網〕纱 wǎngshā; 纱布 shābù.

gave /geɪv/ *pt* of give[1].

gay /geɪ/ *adj* [-er, -est] **1** 快乐〔樂〕的 kuàilède, 愉快的 yúkuàide. **2** 表示快乐的 biǎoshì kuàilè de, 鲜艳〔艷〕的 xiānyànde: ~ *colours* 鲜艳的颜色. **3** [非正式用语] 同性恋〔戀〕的 tóngxìngliànde. **~ness** *n* [U] ⇨ gaily.

gaze /geɪz/ *n* [只用 *sing*] 注视 zhùshì, 凝视 níngshì. □ *vi* 注视 zhùshì, 凝视 níngshì.

ga·zelle /gə'zel/ *n* [C] 小羚羊 xiǎolíngyáng, 瞪羚 dènglíng.

ga·zette /gə'zet/ *n* [C] **1** (政府等)公报〔報〕gōngbào. **2** (报纸名)…报 …bào.

G.B. = Great Britain.

G.C.E. = General Certificate of Education (英国)一般教育证〔證〕书〔書〕yìbān jiàoyù zhèngshū.

gear /gɪə(r)/ *n* **1** [C] 齿〔齒〕轮〔輪〕chǐlún. **2** [C] 轮, 杠杆〔桿〕等装〔裝〕置 lún, gànggǎn děng zhuāngzhì: *the 'landing-~ of a* *aircraft* 飞机的起落架. **3** [U] 设备〔備〕 shèbèi, 用具 yòngjù: '*hunting-*~ 打猎用具. □ *vt/i* (使)相适〔適〕合 xiāng shìhé: *purchases* ~*ed to needs* 适合需要的采购物 '~**-box** 齿轮箱 chǐlúnxiāng. '~**-lever,** ~**-shift,** ~**-stick** 变〔變〕速装置 biànsù zhuāngzhì.

geese /gi:s/ *n pl* of goose.

gela·tine /ˌʤelə'ti:n/ (亦作 **gela·tin** /-tɪn/) *n* [U] 明胶〔膠〕míngjiāo, 动〔動〕物胶 dòngwùjiāo.

geld·ing /geldɪŋ/ *n* [C] 阉〔閹〕割的公马〔馬〕 yāngēde gōngmǎ.

gel·ig·nite /'ʤelɪgnaɪt/ *n* [U] 葛里炸药 gělǐzhàyào.

gem /ʤem/ *n* [C] **1** 宝〔寶〕石 bǎoshí. **2** 珍宝 zhēnbǎo, 珍贵的物品 zhēnguìde wùpǐn.

Gen. =General.

gen·der /'ʤendə(r)/ *n* [C] 〔语法〕性 xìng.

gene /ʤi:n/ *n* [C] 〔生物〕基因 jīyīn.

gen·eal·ogy /ˌʤi:nɪ'æləʤɪ/ *n* [*pl* -ies] **1** [U] 家系学〔學〕 jiāxìxué, 系谱学 xìpǔxué. **2** [C] 系谱图〔圖〕 xìpǔtú, 系统图 xìtǒngtú. **genea·logi·cal** /ˌʤi:nɪə'lɒʤɪkl/ *adj*

gen·eral /'ʤenrəl/ *adj* **1** 普遍的 pǔbiànde, 全面的 quánmiànde, 一般的 yìbānde: *of* ~ *interest* 普遍有兴趣的. *in* ~ 一般地 yìbānde, 大体〔體〕上 dàtǐshàng. **2** 总〔總〕的 zǒngde, 概括的 gàikuòde: *a* ~ *idea* 总的想法. **3** (职衔)总 zǒng: ˌ*postmaster-*'~ 邮政总长. □ *n* [C] 将〔將〕军〔軍〕 jiāngjūn. ˌ~ **anaes'thetic** 全身麻醉 quánshēn mázuì. ˌ~ **e'lection** 普选〔選〕 pǔxuǎn. ⇨ by-election. ˌ~ **'knowledge** 一般知识〔識〕 yìbān zhīshī, 各方面的知识 gèfāngmiànde zhīshī. ˌ~ **prac'titioner** [英国英语] 普通医生 (非专科医生) pǔtōng yīshēng. ˌ~ **'strike** 总罢〔罷〕工 zǒngbàgōng. ~**ity** /ˌʤenə'rælətɪ/ *n* [*pl* -ies] **(a)** [C] 通则 tōngzé, 概论〔論〕 gàilùn. **(b)** [U] 一般性 yìbānxìng, 普遍性 pǔbiànxìng. ~**iz·ation** /-aɪ'zeɪʃn/ *n* [C, U] 概括 gàikuò. ~**ize** *vt/i* 概括 gàikuò, 归〔歸〕纳 guīnà. ~**ly** *adv* **(a)** 一般地 yìbānde, 通常地 tōngchángde: *I* ~*ly get up at six.* 我通常六点钟起床. **(b)** 广〔廣〕泛地 guǎngfànde, 普遍地 pǔbiànde: *The plan was* ~*ly welcomed.* 这计划受到普遍的欢迎. **(c)** 一般地 yìbānde, 概括地 gàikuòde: ~*ly speaking* 一般地说.

gen·er·ate /'ʤenəreɪt/ *vt* 使产〔產〕生 shǐ chǎnshēng, 使发〔發〕生 shǐ fāshēng: ~ *electricity* 发电.

gen·er·at·ive /'ʤenərətɪv/ *adj* 有生产〔產〕力的 yǒu shēngchǎnlì de.

gen·er·ator *n* [C] 发电〔電〕机〔機〕 fādiànjī, 发生器 fāshēngqì.

gen·er·ation /ˌʤenə'reɪʃn/ *n* **1** [U] 发〔發〕生 fāshēng, 产〔產〕生 chǎnshēng: *the* ~ *of electricity* 发电. **2** [C] 代 dài, 一代 yídài, 辈〔輩〕 bèi, 世代 shìdài. **3** [C] 一代人 yídàirén.

gen·eric /ʤɪ'nerɪk/ *adj* 一般的 yìbānde, 普通的 pǔtōngde. ~**ally** *adv*

gen·er·os·ity /ˌʤenə'rɒsətɪ/ *n* [*pl* -ies] [U] 宽宏大量 kuānhóngdàliàng, 慷慨 kāngkǎi; 宽宏大量的行为〔爲〕 kuānhóngdàliàngde xíngwéi, 慷慨的行为 kāngkǎide xíngwéi.

gen·er·ous /'ʤenərəs/ *adj* **1** 慷慨的 kāngkǎide: *He's* ~ *with his money.* 他用钱慷慨. **2** 丰〔豐〕盛的 fēngshèngde, 丰富的 fēngfùde. ~**ly** *adv*

gen·etic /ʤɪ'netɪk/ *adj* 发〔發〕生的 fāshēngde, 遗传〔傳〕学〔學〕的 yíchuánxuéde. ~**'code** *n* 遗传〔傳〕密码〔碼〕 yíchuán mìmǎ. ~ **engi'neering** 遗传工程 yíchuán gōngchéng. **gen·etics** *n* [U] 〔与 *sing verb* 连用〕遗传学 yíchuánxué.

ge·nial /'ʤi:nɪəl/ *adj* **1** 和蔼的 hé'ǎide, 亲〔親〕切的 qīnqiède, 友好的 yǒuhǎode. **2** 温和的 wēnhéde: *a* ~ *climate* 温和的天气. ~**ly** *adv*

geni·tal /'ʤenɪtl/ *adj* 生殖器的 shēngzhíqìde. **geni·tals** *n pl* 生殖器 shēngzhíqì, 外阴〔陰〕部 wàiyīnbù.

gen·ius /'ʤi:nɪəs/ *n* [C] [*pl* ~es] **1** [U] 天才 tiāncái. **2** [C] 天才人物 tiāncái rénwù. **3** 才华〔華〕cáihuá, 天资 tiānzī; 天赋 tiānfù: *have a* ~ *for languages* 在语言上有天赋.

geno·cide /'ʤenəsaɪd/ *n* [U] 种〔種〕族灭〔滅〕绝 zhǒngzú mièjué, 灭绝种族的屠杀〔殺〕mièjué zhǒngzú de túshā.

gent /ʤent/ *n* [C] (gentleman 的非正式的缩略)〔谑〕绅士 shēnshì; 假绅士 jiǎ shēnshì; 人 rén, 家伙 jiāhuo. **gents** 〔非正式英国英语〕男公共厕所 nán gōnggòngcèsuǒ.

gen·tile /'ʤentaɪl/ *n* [C], *adj* 非犹〔猶〕太人 fēi yóutài rén, 非犹太人的 fēi yóutàirén de.

gentle /'ʤentl/ *adj* [-r, -st] 文雅的

wényǎde, 有礼〔禮〕貌的 yǒu lǐmào de. ~**ness** *n* [U]

gentle·man /'ʤentlmən/ *n* [C] [*pl* -men /-mən/] **1** 有教养〔養〕的人 yǒu jiàoyǎng de rén, 有礼〔禮〕貌的人 yǒu lǐmào de rén. **2** [过时用法]绅士 shēnshì, 有钱〔錢〕有社会〔會〕地位的人 yǒuqián yǒu shèhuì dìwèi de rén. **3** (尊称)先生 xiānsheng, 阁〔閣〕下 géxià. ~**ly** *adj* 绅士风〔風〕度的 shēnshì fēngdù de.

gen·tly /'ʤentlɪ/ *adv* 文雅地 wényǎde, 有礼〔禮〕貌地 yǒu lǐmàode.

genu·ine /'ʤenjʊɪn/ *adj* 真正的 zhēnzhèngde, 名副其实〔實〕的 míngfùqíshíde. ~**ly** *adv* ~**ness** *n* [U]

ge·nus /'ʤi:nəs/ *n* [C] [*pl* genera /'ʤenərə/] (生物)属〔屬〕shǔ.

ge·ogra·phy /ʤɪ'ɒgrəfɪ/ *n* [U] **1** 地理学〔學〕dìlǐxué. **2** 位置 wèizhì; 地形 dìxíng: *the ~ of the house* 这所屋子的位置. **ge·ographer** *n* [C] 地理学家 dìlǐxuéjiā. **geo'graphi·cal** *adj*

ge·ol·ogy /ʤɪ'ɒləʤɪ/ *n* [U] **1** 地质〔質〕学〔學〕dìzhìxué. **2** (某地的)地质 dìzhì. **geo'logi·cal** *adj* **ge·ologist** *n* [C] 地质学家 dìzhìxuéjiā.

ge·ometry /ʤɪ'ɒmətrɪ/ *n* [U] 几〔幾〕何学〔學〕jǐhéxué. **geo'metric(al)** *adj*

ger·anium /ʤə'reɪnɪəm/ *n* [C] [*pl* ~s] 天竺葵 tiānzhúkuí.

geri·atrics /ˌʤerɪ'ætrɪks/ *n* [U] 老年病学〔學〕lǎoniánbìngxué. **geri·atric** *adj*

germ /ʤɜ:m/ *n* [C] **1** 幼芽 yòuyá; 胚芽 pēiyá. **2** [喻]起源 qǐyuán, 萌芽 méngyá. **3** 微生物 wēishēngwù; 病菌 bìngjūn.

Ger·man /'ʤɜ:mən/ *adj, n* [C] 德国〔國〕人的 déguórénde; 德语的 déyǔde; 德语 déyǔ; 德国人 déguórén.

ger·mi·nate /'ʤɜ:mɪneɪt/ *vt/i* (使)发〔發〕芽 fāyá; (使)发生 fāshēng. **ger·mi'na·tion** *n* [U]

ger·und /'ʤerənd/ *n* [C] [语法] 动〔動〕名词 dòngmíngcí.

ges·ticu·late /ʤɪ'stɪkjʊleɪt/ *vi* 打手势〔勢〕dǎ shǒushì, (说话时)做手势 zuò shǒushì. **ges·ticu'la·tion** *n* [C, U]

ges·ture /'ʤestʃə(r)/ *n* [C] **1** 姿势〔勢〕zīshì; 手势 shǒushì. **2** 姿态〔態〕zītài; 表示 biǎoshì. □ *vi* 打手势〔勢〕dǎ shǒushì; (说话时)做手势 zuò shǒushì.

get /get/ *vt/i* [*pt* got /gɒt/; *pp* got] **1** 使得 shǐdé; 变〔變〕得 biàndé, 成为〔爲〕chéngwéi: ~ *wet* 变潮, ~ *the children ready* 让孩子们准备好. **2** (使)成为某种〔種〕状〔狀〕态〔態〕chéngwéi mǒuzhǒng zhuàngtài: *It's time we got started.* 我们该动身了. ~ *that car going* 把那辆汽车修好. **3** (开始)…起来〔來〕… qǐlái; 逐渐〔漸〕…起来 zhújiàn … qǐlái: ~ *to know someone* 逐渐了解某人. **4** 使…做 shǐ … zuò: ~ *him to understand* 使他理解. **5** 收到 shōudào: *I've got your telegram.* 我收到了你的电报. ~ ***the sack*** ⇨ sack². ~ ***one's own way*** ⇨ way(4). **6** 感染上(疾病) gǎnrǎnshàng: ~ *measles* 得了麻疹. **7** 受到(刑罚) shòudào: ~ *six months* 判刑六个月. **8** [非正式用语]了解 liáojiě: *I don't ~ you.* 我不了解你. **9** 使迷惑 shǐ míhuò; 难〔難〕住 nánzhu: *That's got him!* 那可难住他了! **10** ***has*** (或 ***have, had***) ***got*** 有 yǒu: *What ugly teeth he's got!* 他的牙齿多难看! **11** ***has*** (或 ***have, had***) ***got to*** 必须 bìxū, 不得不 bùdébù. ⇨ have²(5). **12** (使)到 dào, (使)离〔離〕开〔開〕líkāi: *G~ to bed!* 上床睡觉! *We must ~ him to a hospital.* 我们必须把他送医院. ~ *off a bus* 下公共汽车; ~ *off a train* 下火车. ~ ***somewhere*** (使)有结果 yǒu jiéguǒ. ~ ***anywhere*** (使)有任何结果 yǒu rènhé jiéguǒ. ~ ***nowhere*** (使)无〔無〕结果 wújiéguǒ. **13** ~ ***(sth) across (to sb)*** [非正式用语] 使某事为〔爲〕…所理解 shǐ mǒushì wéi…suǒ lǐjiě. ~ ***along*** 过〔過〕活 guòhuó, 生活 shēnghuó; 进〔進〕展 jìnzhǎn. ~ ***at sb (sth)*** 到达〔達〕dàodá; 得到 dédào; 接近 jiējìn. ~ ***at sb*** (a) 贿赂 huìlù, 腐蚀 fǔshí. (b) 批评 pīpíng. ***be ~ting at*** [非正式用语]意指 yìzhǐ 暗示 ànshì: *What are you ~ting at?* 你的意思是什么? ~ ***away*** 离开 líkāi; 逃脱 táotuō: *Two prisoners got away.* 两名犯人逃走. '~***away*** *n* ~ ***away with sth*** 侥〔僥〕幸做成 jiǎoxìng zuòchéng: ~ *away with cheating* 干了欺骗的勾当(未被发现和处罚). ~ ***back*** 回来 huílai. ~ ***one's 'own back (on sb)*** 报〔報〕仇 bàochóu; 报复 bàofù. ~ ***by*** 侥幸躲过 jiǎoxìng duǒguò; 勉强生活 miǎnqiáng shēnghuó: *Sh*… *can't ~ by without him.* 没有他,… 就活不下去. ~ ***sb down*** [非正式用语]使沮丧 shǐ jǔsàng, 使抑… shǐ yìyù. ~ ***sth down*** (a) 吞… tūnxià, 咽下 yànxià: ~ *the medici*…

down 把药咽下. **(b)** 写〔寫〕下 xiěxià. ~ ***down to sth*** 开始认真对〔對〕待 kāishǐ rènzhēn duìdài. ~ ***in*** 到达 dàodá: *The train got in late.* 火车到晚了. ~ ***sb in*** 请…来做… qǐng … lái zuò: ~ *someone in to repair the TV* 请人来修电视机. ~ ***sth in*** 得到供应〔應〕 dédào gòngyǐng: ~ *coal in for the winter* 得到过冬用的煤. ~ ***into*** **(a)** 穿上 chuānshàng: ~ *into one's shoes* 穿上鞋. **(b)** 陷入 xiànrù, 染上(习惯) rǎnshàng: ~ *into trouble* 遭到麻烦; ~ *into bad habits* 染上坏习惯. **(c)** 对… 有兴〔興〕趣 duì … yǒu xìngqù: ~ *into a book* 对一本书有了兴趣. ~ ***off*** 开始 kāishǐ. ~ ***sb off*** 使某人逃脱处〔處〕分 shǐ mǒurén táotuō chǔfèn. ~ ***off with sth*** 因…而逃脱更严〔嚴〕厉〔厲〕的处分 yīn … ér táotuō gèn yánlì de chǔfèn: *He got off with a fine.* 他被罚款了事. ~ ***on*** 使前进〔進〕 shǐ qiánjìn, 使进步 shǐ jìnbù. ~ ***on one's nerves*** ⇨ nerve(2). ~ ***on to sb*** 联〔聯〕系(电话等) liánxì. ~ ***on (with sb)*** 与…相处 yǔ … xiāngchù. ~ ***on (with sth)*** 继〔繼〕续〔續〕jìxù. ~ ***out*** 公布〔佈〕gōngbù: *The news will soon ~ out.* 这消息很快就公布. ~ ***out of (sth*** 或 ***doing sth)*** 〔喻〕避免 bìmiǎn. ~ ***over sth*** **(a)** (从疾病等)恢复〔復〕过〔過〕来 huīfù guòlái. **(b)** 克服 kèfú: ~ *over shyness* 克服害臊. ~ ***round sb*** 说服某人做某事 shuōfú mǒurén zuò mǒushì. ~ ***round sth*** 规避(法律) guībì. ~ ***round to doing sth*** 终于处理某事 zhōngyú chùlǐ mǒushì. ~ ***through*** 打通电话 dǎ tōng diànhuà: *I rang you but couldn't ~ through.* 我打电话给你但没有打通. ~ ***through (sth)*** 通过(考试等) tōngguò. ~ ***up*** **(a)** 起身 qǐshēn: *When do you ~ up?* 你什么时候起床? **(b)** 起立 qǐlì. ~ ***up to sth*** **(a)** 达到 dádào: ~ *up to page ten* 看(学)到第十页. **(b)** 玩弄(花招, 诡计等) wánnòng: *What will they ~ up to next?* 他们下一步有什么花招?

ey·ser /ˈgiːzə(r)/ *n* [C] **1** 天然喷泉 tiānrán pēnquán. **2** (浴室等)热〔熱〕水锅炉〔爐〕 rèshuǐ guōlú.

hast·ly /ˈgɑːstlɪ/ *adj* [-ier, -iest] **1** 苍〔蒼〕白的 cāngbáide. **2** 可怕的 kěpàde, 恐怖的 kǒngbùde: *a ~ accident* 可怕的事故. **3** [非正式用语]令人不快的 lìngrén búkuài de: *a ~ dinner* 很糟糕的一顿饭.

her·kin /ˈgɜːkɪn/ *n* [C] 小黄瓜 xiǎohuángguā.

ghetto /ˈgetəʊ/ *n* [C] [*pl* ~s] 少数民族居住区〔區〕(美国) shǎoshù-mínzú jūzhùqū.

ghost /gəʊst/ *n* [C] 鬼魂 guǐhún, 幽灵〔靈〕 yōulíng. ***give up the ~*** 死 sǐ. ***not the ~ of a chance*** 一点〔點〕机〔機〕会〔會〕也没有 yìdiǎn jīhuì yě méiyǒu. **the Holy G~** (宗教)圣〔聖〕灵 shènglíng. **~ly** *adj* 鬼的 guǐde, 鬼一样〔樣〕的 guǐ yíyàng de.

G.H.Q. = General Headquarters 总〔總〕司令部 zǒngsīlìngbù.

gi·ant /ˈdʒaɪənt/ *n* [C] 巨人 jùrén, 巨物 jùwù. **~ess** *n* [C] 女巨人 nǚ jùrén.

gib·ber·ish /ˈdʒɪbərɪʃ/ *n* [U] 无〔無〕意义〔義〕的谈话 wú yìyì de tánhuà.

gib·bon /ˈgɪbən/ *n* [C] 长〔長〕臂猿 chángbìyuán.

gib·lets /ˈdʒɪblɪts/ *n pl* (鸡鸭等)内脏〔臟〕 nèizàng.

giddy /ˈgɪdɪ/ *adj* [-ier, -iest] **1** 眼花缭乱〔亂〕的 yǎnhuāliáoluànde; 头〔頭〕晕〔暈〕的 tóuyūnde. **2** 轻〔輕〕浮的 qīngfúde, 轻佻的 qīngtiāode: *a ~ young girl* 轻佻的少女. **gid·di·ness** *n* [U]

gift /gɪft/ *n* [C] **1** 赠品 zèngpǐn, 礼〔禮〕物 lǐwù. **2** 天赋 tiānfù, 才能 cáinéng: *a ~ for languages* 语言的天赋. **~ed** *adj* 有天赋的 yǒu tiānfù de.

gi·gan·tic /dʒaɪˈgæntɪk/ *adj* 巨大的 jùdàde, 庞〔龐〕大的 pángdàde.

giggle /ˈgɪgl/ *vi* 咯咯地笑 gēgēde xiào, 傻〔儍〕笑 shǎxiào. □ *n* [C] 傻笑 shǎxiào.

gild /gɪld/ *vt* 镀金 dùjīn, 包金 bāojīn. **~ing** *n* [U] 镀金材料 dùjīn cáiliào.

gill[1] /gɪl/ *n* [C] [常用 *pl*] 腮 sāi.

gill[2] /dʒɪl/ *n* [C] 及耳(流量单位, = .142 升) jí'ěr.

gilt /gɪlt/ *n* [U] = gilding.

gim·mick /ˈgɪmɪk/ *n* [C] 骗〔騙〕人的花招 piànrénde huāzhāo, 鬼把戏〔戲〕 guǐbǎxì.

gin /dʒɪn/ *n* [U] 杜松子酒 dùsōngzǐjiǔ, 荷兰〔蘭〕酒 hélánjiǔ.

gin·ger /ˈdʒɪndʒə(r)/ *n* [U] **1** 生姜 shēngjiāng, 姜 jiāng. **2** 姜黄色〔作定语〕 jiānghuángsè: ~ *hair* 姜黄色头发. □ *vt* ~ ***up*** 使有活力 shǐ yǒu huólì. **,~ 'ale** (或 **'beer**) 姜汁啤酒 jiāngzhī píjiǔ.

gin·ger·ly /ˈdʒɪndʒəlɪ/ *adv* 小心谨慎地 xiǎoxīn jǐnshèn de. □ *adj* 谨慎的 jǐnshènde.

ging·ham /ˈgɪŋəm/ *n* [U] 方格花

布 fānggé huābù.

gipsy, gypsy /ˈdʒɪpsɪ/ *n* [C] [*pl* -ies] 吉普赛人 jípǔsàirén.

gi·raffe /dʒɪˈrɑːf/ *n* [C] 长〔長〕颈〔頸〕鹿 chángjǐnglù.

girder /ˈgɜːdə(r)/ *n* [C] (建筑) 大梁 dàliáng.

girdle /ˈgɜːdl/ *n* [C] **1** 腰带〔帶〕yāodài. **2** = corset. **3** 围〔圍〕绕〔繞〕物 wéiràowù. □ *vt* 围绕 wéirào, 束 sù: *a lake ~d with trees* 树木环绕的湖泊.

girl /gɜːl/ *n* [C] 女孩子 nǚháizi, 姑娘 gūniang; 女儿〔兒〕nǚ'ér, **ˈ~-friend** 女朋友 nǚ péngyou. **~ish** *adj* 少女的 shàonǚde, 少女似的 shàonǚ sìde.

giro /ˈdʒaɪərəʊ/ *n* [U] 邮〔郵〕汇〔匯〕yóuhuì, 汇款 huìkuǎn.

girth /gɜːθ/ *n* [C] **1** (马) 肚带〔帶〕dùdài. **2** (圆柱体) 围〔圍〕长〔長〕wéicháng.

gist /dʒɪst/ *n* **the ~** 要旨 yàozhǐ: *Tell me the ~ of what he said.* 告诉我他说话的要点.

give[1] /gɪv/ *vt/i* [*pt* gave /geɪv/; *pp* **~n** /ˈgɪvn/] **1** 给 gěi, 送给 sònggěi: *~ him a cheque* 给他一张支票; *~ him birthday a present* 送给他生日礼物. **2** 付给 fùgěi, 报〔報〕偿〔償〕bàocháng: *I gave him £400 for his old car.* 我用 400 英镑买了他的旧汽车. **3** 允许 yǔnxǔ, 同意 tóngyì: *~ him a week to decide.* 允许他用一周的时间作出决定. **4** 供给 gōngjǐ, 供应〔應〕gōngyìng. **5** *~ a groan* 呻吟; *~ her a ring* 给她打电话. **6** (用于固定短语) ***give or take*** 增减…而无〔無〕大变〔變〕化 zēngjiǎn … ér wú dàbiànhuà. **~ *way*** **(a)** 撤退 chètuì, 后〔後〕退 hòutuì. **(b)** 坍陷 tānxiàn, 不能支撑 bùnéng zhīchēng: *The rope gave way.* 绳子断了. **~ *way (to sth)*** **(a)** 给…让〔讓〕路 gěi … rànglù: *~ way to traffic from the right* 给右边来的车让路. **(b)** 为〔爲〕…所代替 wéi … suǒ dàitì: *Sorrow gave way to smiles.* 欢笑代替了忧伤. **~ *way (to sb)*** 让步 ràngbù, 屈服 qūfú: *Don't ~ way to them.* 别向他们让步. **7** 传〔傳〕达〔達〕chuándá, 传送 chuánsòng: *~ an account of one's journey* 叙述旅途情况. **8** 塌下 tāxià, 弯〔彎〕下 wānxià; 支撑不住 zhīchēng búzhù: *His knees seemed to ~ under the weight.* 在重压下, 他的两膝似乎支撑不住了. **9** **~n** **(a)** 假设的 jiǎshède: *G~n good health, I hope to go.* 假使身体健康, 我希望去. **(b)** 约定的 yuēdìngde, 同意的 tóngyìde: *at a ~n time* 在约定的时间. **10** 作为主人 zuòwéi zhǔrén: *~ a party* 主办一次聚会. **11** **~ *sth away*** **(a)** 赠送 zèngsòng. **(b)** 泄露 xièlù: *His accent gave him away.* 他的口音露出了他的身份. **ˈ~-away** *n* [C] **ˌ~ *the* ˈ*game away*** ⇨ game[2](5). **~ *sth back (to sb)***; **~ *sb back sth*** 还〔還〕huán, 归〔歸〕还 guīhuán. **~ *in (to sb)*** 屈服 qūfú, 投降 tóuxiáng. **~ *sth off*** 发〔發〕出 (烟, 气等) fāchū. **~ *out*** 用完 yòngwán, 耗尽〔盡〕hàojìn: *His strength gave out.* 他精疲力尽. *Our supplies gave out.* 我们的给养耗用完. **~ *sth out*** 分发〔發〕fēnfā: *~ out prizes (leaflets)* 分发奖品 (小册子). **~ *up*** 放弃〔棄〕(寻求答案等) fàngqì: *I ~ up, you'll have to tell me.* 我不想了, 你得告诉我. **~ *sb up*** **(a)** 表示对…不抱希望 biǎoshì duì … búbào xīwàng: *The doctors have ~n him up.* 医生认为他已经治不好了. **(b)** [非正式用语] 不与〔與〕某人来〔來〕往 bù yǔ mǒurén láiwǎng. **(c)** 把…送交 bǎ … sòngjiāo. **~ *oneself up*** 自首 zìshǒu. **~ *sth up*** 放弃 fàngqì, 戒 (烟等) jiè: *~ up one's seat in a bus* 在公共汽车里让出座位; *~ up smoking* 戒烟.

give[2] /gɪv/ *n* [U] **1** 弹〔彈〕性 tánxìng: *A stone floor has no ~ in it.* 石头地面没有弹性. **2** [喻] (人) 适〔適〕应〔應〕性 shìyìngxìng: ***~ and take*** 妥协〔協〕tuǒxié, 互相让〔讓〕步 hùxiāng ràngbù.

given /ˈgɪvn/ *pp* of give[1]. **ˈ~ name** = first name.

gla·cial /ˈgleɪsɪəl/ *adj* 冰的 bīngde, 冰河期的 bīnghéqīde.

gla·cier /ˈglæsɪə(r)/ *n* [C] 冰川 bīngchuān, 冰河 bīnghé.

glad /glæd/ *adj* [-der, -dest] **1** 高兴〔興〕的 gāoxìngde, 乐〔樂〕意的 lèyìde. **2** 令人愉快的 lìngrén yúkuài de: *~ news* 好消息. **~den** *vt* 使高兴 shǐ gāoxìng, 使快乐 shǐ kuàilè. **~ly** *adv* 乐意地 lèyìde, 情愿〔願〕地 qíngyuànde: *will ~ly help you.* 我乐意帮助你. **~ness** *n* [U]

glade /gleɪd/ *n* [C] 林间〔間〕空地 línjiān kōngdì.

gladi·ator /ˈglædɪeɪtə(r)/ *n* [C] (古罗马) 斗〔鬥〕士 dòushì, 斗剑〔劍〕士 dòujiànshì.

glam·our [美语亦作**glamor**] /ˈglæmə(r)/ *n* [U] **1** 魅力 mèilì. **2** 迷人的女性美 mírénde nǚxìngměi. **~ous** *adj* **~ize** /-raɪz/ *vt* 使有魅力 shǐ yǒu mèilì. 美化 měihuà

Don't ~ *war.* 不要美化战争.

glance /'glɑːns/ *vt/i* **1** 扫[掃]视 sǎoshì, 给…一瞥 gěi … yìpiē. **2** ~ *off* (武器或打击)擦过[過] cāguò. □ *n* [C] 一瞥 yīpiē, 扫视 sǎoshì. *at a* ~ 一眼 yìyǎn, 一下子 yíxiàzi.

gland /glænd/ *n* [C] 腺 xiàn. ~-**u·lar** /-jʊlə(r)/ *adj*

glare /gleə(r)/ *n* **1** [U] 眩目地照射 xuánmùde zhàoshè, 闪[閃]耀 shǎnyào. **2** [C] 瞪视 dèngshì, 怒视 nùshì. □ *vt/i* **1** 闪耀 shǎnyào. **2** 怒视 nùshì, 瞪视 dèngshì. **glar·ing** *adj* **(a)** 耀眼的 yàoyǎnde, 刺目的 cìmùde. **(b)** 愤怒的 fènnùde. **(c)** 显[顯]眼的 xiǎnyǎnde: *a glaring mistake* 显著的错误.

glass /glɑːs/ *n* **1** [U] 玻璃 bōli. **2** [C] 玻璃制[製]品 bōli zhìpǐn. **3** [*pl*] 眼镜 yǎnjìng. **4** [*pl*] 望远[遠]镜 wàngyuǎnjìng. **5** 一杯(容量) yìbēi: *a* ~ *of beer* 一杯啤酒. □ *vt* 给…装[裝]上玻璃 gěi … zhuāng shàng bōli. '~**house** = greenhouse. '~**ware** 玻璃制品 bōli zhìpǐn, 料器 liàoqì. **glassy** *adj* [-ier, -iest] 象玻璃的 xiàng bōli de: *a* ~*y stare* 呆滞的目光.

glaze /gleɪz/ *vt/i* **1** 装[裝]玻璃于 zhuāng bōli yú: ~ *a house* (*window*) 给房屋(窗户)装玻璃. **2** 上釉于 shàng yòu yú, 上光于 shàng guāng yú: ~ *pottery* 给陶瓷器上釉. **3** (眼)变[變]呆滞[滯] biàn dāizhì. □ *n* [C, U] 釉彩 yòucǎi, 釉面 yòumiàn. **glaz·ier** *n* [C] 装玻璃工人 zhuāngbōli gōngrén.

gleam /gliːm/ *n* [C] **1** 微光 wēiguāng, 闪[閃]光 shǎnguāng. **2** [喻]短暂[暫]而微弱的闪现 duǎnzàn ér wēiruò de shǎnxiàn: *a* ~ *of hope* 一线希望. □ *vi* 闪烁[爍] shǎnshuò.

glean /gliːn/ *vt/i* 搜集 sōují.

glee /gliː/ *n* [U] 高兴[興] gāoxìng, 快乐[樂] kuàilè. ~**ful** *adj* ~**fully** *adv*

glen /glen/ *n* [C] [苏格兰语] 峡[峽]谷 xiágǔ.

glib /glɪb/ *adj* [-ber, -best] 圆滑的 yuánhuáde, 流利的 liúlìde: *a* ~ *answer* 圆滑的回答. ~**ly** *adv* ~**ness** *n* [U]

glide /glaɪd/ *vi* **1** 滑动[動] huádòng, 滑行 huáxíng. **2** (飞机)滑翔 huáxiáng. □ *n* [C] 滑动 huádòng, 滑行 huáxíng. **glider** 滑翔机 huáxiángjī. **glid·ing** *n* [U] 滑翔运[運]动 huáxiáng yùndòng.

glim·mer /'glɪmə(r)/ *vi* 发[發]微光 fā wēiguāng. □ *n* [C] **1** 微光 wēiguāng. **2** [喻]少许 shǎoxǔ, 微量 wēiliàng: *a* ~ *of hope* 一线希望.

glimpse /glɪmps/ *n* [C] **1** 一瞥 yīpiē, 一看 yíkàn: *catch a* ~ *of the secret papers* 瞥见了秘密文件. **2** 匆匆一看 (*at*) cōngcōng yíkàn. □ *vt* 瞥见 piējiàn.

glint /glɪnt/ *vi* 闪[閃]烁[爍] shǎnshuò, 发[發]微光 fā wēiguāng. □ *n* [C] 闪光 shǎnguāng, 闪烁 shǎnshuò.

glis·ten /'glɪsn/ *vi* 反光 fǎnguāng, 闪耀 shǎnyào.

glit·ter /'glɪtə(r)/ *vi* 闪[閃]闪发[發]光 shǎnshǎn fāguāng: ~*ing jewels* 闪闪发光的宝石. □ *n* [U] 闪光 shǎnguāng. ~**ing** *adj* 光辉[輝]灿[燦]烂[爛]的 guānghuī cànlàn de; 吸引人的 xīyǐnrénde.

gloat /gləʊt/ *vi* ~ **(over)** 洋洋得意地注视 yángyángdéyìde zhùshì: ~ *over one's victory* 因胜利而洋洋得意. ~**ing·ly** *adv*

glo·bal /'gləʊbl/ *adj* **1** 全世界的 quánshìjiède, 全球的 quánqiúde: ~ *war* 全球战争. **2** 综合的 zōnghéde, 概括的 gàikuòde.

globe /gləʊb/ *n* [C] **1** 球体[體] qiútǐ. **2** [与 *the* 连用] 地球 dìqiú.

gloom /gluːm/ *n* [C] **1** 黑暗 hēi'àn, 阴[陰]暗 yīn'àn. **2** 忧[憂]愁 yōuchóu, 忧郁 yōuyù. **gloomy** *adj* [-ier, -iest] **(a)** 黑暗的 hēi'ànde. **(b)** 忧[憂]闷[悶]的 yōumènde. ~**ily** *adv*

glor·ify /'glɔːrɪfaɪ/ *vt* [*pt*, *pp* -ied] **1** 崇拜(上帝) chóngbài. **2** 颂扬 sòngyáng, 赞美 zànměi. **3** 美化 měihuà: *His cottage is only a glorified barn.* 他的小别墅不过是一个美化的谷仓. **glori·fi·ca·tion** /-fɪ'keɪʃn/ *n* [U]

glori·ous /'glɔːrɪəs/ *adj* **1** 辉[輝]煌的 huīhuángde. 壮[壯]丽[麗]的 zhuànglìde. **2** 光荣[榮]的 guāngróngde: *a* ~ *victory* 光荣的胜利. ~**ly** *adv*

glory /'glɔːrɪ/ *n* [U] **1** 光荣[榮] guāngróng. 荣誉[譽] róngyù. **2** (对上帝的) 赞美 zànměi, 崇拜 chóngbài. **3** 壮[壯]观[觀] zhuàngguān, 壮丽[麗] zhuànglì: *the* ~ *of a sunset* 落日的壮观. □ *vi* [*pt*, *pp* -ied] ~ *in* 自豪 zìháo, 得意 déyì.

gloss[1] /glɒs/ *n* **1** [U] 光泽[澤] guāngzé; 光滑 guānghuá. **2** [喻] 虚饰 xūshì, 假象 jiǎxiàng □ *vt* ~ **over** **1** 给以光滑的表面 gěiyǐ guānghuáde biǎomiàn. **2** 掩饰 yǎnshì, 遮掩 zhēyǎn. '~ **paint** 清漆 qīngqī, 有光涂〔塗〕料 yǒuguāngtúliào. **glossy** *adj* [-ier, -iest] 光滑的 guānghuáde, 光泽的 guāngzéde.

gloss² /glɒs/ *n* [C] 注释〔釋〕zhùshì. □*vt* 注释 zhùshì.

gl ss·ary /'glɒsərɪ/ *n* [C] [*pl* -ies] **1** 词汇表 cíhuìbiǎo. **2** 术语汇〔彙〕编 shùyǔ huìbiān.

glove /glʌv/ *n* [C]手套 shǒutào.

glow /gləʊ/ *vi* **1** 发〔發〕白热〔熱〕光 fā báirèguāng: *The hot metal ~ed red.* 炽热的金属烧得通红. **2** [喻] (因运动等)脸〔臉〕发红发热 liǎn fāhóng fārè. **3** 鲜艳〔艷〕夺〔奪〕目 xiānyànduómù. □ *n* [*sing*] 光辉〔輝〕guānghuī: *the ~ of sunset* 落日的光辉. '**~-worm** 萤〔螢〕火虫 yínghuǒchóng. **~ing** *adj* **(a)** 发白热光的 fā báirèguāng de. **(b)** 热情的 rèqíngde: *describe in ~ing terms* 用热情的言语描述. **~ingly** *adv*

glu·cose /'glu:kəʊs/ *n* [U] 葡萄糖 pútáotáng.

glue /glu:/ *n* [U] 胶〔膠〕jiāo, 胶水 jiāoshuǐ. □ *vt* [*pt, pp* ~d; gluing] **1** 粘贴 zhāntiē, 胶合 jiāohé. **2** 紧〔緊〕贴 jǐntiē: *eyes ~d to a keyhole* 眼睛贴着钥匙孔看.

glum /glʌm/ *adj* [-mer, -mest] 忧〔憂〕郁的 yōuyùde, 阴〔陰〕郁的 yīnyùde. **~ly** *adv*

glut /glʌt/ *vt* [-tt-] **1** 使充斥 shǐ chōngchì: *~ the market with butter* 使黄油充斥市场. **2** 使过〔過〕量 shǐ guòliàng. □ *n* [C] 过量供应〔應〕guòliàng gōngyìng.

glut·ton /'glʌtn/ *n* [C] 贪食者 tānshízhě, 好食者 hàoshízhě. **~ous** *adj* 贪吃的 tānchīde. **gluttony** *n* [U] 贪食 tānshí, 暴食 bàoshí.

G.M.T.=Greenwich Mean Time 格林威治时〔時〕间 gélínwēizhì shíjiān.

gnarled /nɑ:ld/ *adj* (树干等)扭曲 niǔqū.

gnash /næʃ/ *vt/i* 咬(牙) yǎo.

gnat /næt/ *n* [C] 咬人的小昆虫〔蟲〕yǎoréndе xiǎokūnchóng.

gnaw /nɔ:/ *vt/i*. **1** 咬 yǎo; 啃 kěn; 啮〔嚙〕niè. **2** 折磨 zhémó: *~ed by hunger* 挨饿.

gnome /nəʊm/ *n* [C] (故事中的)地下小妖魔 dìxià xiǎoyāomó.

G.N.P.=Gross Nationl Product 国〔國〕民生产总〔總〕值 guómín shēngchǎn zǒngzhí.

go¹ /gəʊ/ *vi* [*3rd pers, pres tense* goes; *pt* went; *pp* gone] **1** 去 qù, 离〔離〕去 líqù: *~ shopping* 去购物, *~ for a walk* 去散步, *~ to the cinema* 去看电影, *~ home* 回家. **2** **(a)** 放置 fàngzhì: *The piano ~es in the corner.* 钢琴放在角落上. **(b)** 被容得下 bèi róngdéxià: *My clothes won't ~ into this suitcase.* 这箱子放不下我的衣裳. **3** 达〔達〕到 dádào, 通到 tōngdào: *This road ~es to London.* 这条路通到伦敦. **~ (very) far (a)** 经〔經〕用 jīngyòng, 持久 chíjiǔ: *A pound doesn't ~ far now.* 眼下一英镑买不了多少东西. **(b)**(人)成功 chénggōng. **~ too far** 过〔過〕火 guòhuǒ. **4** **(a)** 进〔進〕入或从〔從〕某种〔種〕状〔狀〕态〔態〕jìnrù huò cóng mǒuzhǒng zhuàngtài: *~ from bad to worse* 愈来愈坏, *~ to sleep* 入睡, 睡着. **(b)** 参〔參〕加 cānjiā: *~ to school* 上学. **5** 变〔變〕成 biànchéng. **~ bad** ⇨ bad¹ (5). **6** 行动〔動〕xíngdòng, 运〔運〕转〔轉〕yùnzhuǎng: *This clock doesn't ~.* 这钟不走了. **7** 处〔處〕于某种状态 chùyú mǒuzhǒng zhuàngtài: *~ hungry* 挨饿. **8** (表示进展): *How's everything ~ing* (= progressing)? 情况(进展得)怎样? **~ slow** 怠工 dàigōng. **9** **~ (to sb) for** 出售 chūshòu, 作价〔價〕zuòjià. **10** 消失 xiāoshī, 衰退 shuāituì: *My sight is ~ing.* 我的视力正在衰退. **let oneself ~**放松〔鬆〕fàngsōng, 言谈,行动自由 yántán, xíngdòng zìyóu. **11** **~ it alone** 独〔獨〕自干〔幹〕dúzì gàn. **12** 有某种表达法, 曲调 yǒu mǒuzhǒng biǎodáfǎ, qǔdiào: *How does the song ~?* 这首歌怎么唱来着? **13** 开〔開〕始行动 kāishǐ xíngdòng: *One, two, three, ~!* 一,二,三,开始! **14** **be ~ing to do sth (a)** 准〔準〕备〔備〕做 zhǔnbèi zuò; 计划〔劃〕做 jìhuà zuò: *We're ~ing to spend our holidays in Wales next year.* 我们打算明年在威尔士度假. **(b)** 很可能的 hěn kěnéngde: *It's ~ing to rain.* 可能要下雨了. **(c)** 将〔將〕要 jiāngyào: *I'm ~ing to be twenty next month.* 我下个月就是二十岁了. **15** **~ about** 走动 zǒudòng, 流传〔傳〕liúchuán. **~ about sth** 从〔從〕事 cóngshì, 着手干 zháoshǒugàn: *~ about a job* 着手一件工作. **~ after sb (sth)** 追求 zhuīqiú, 追逐 zhuīzhú. **~ against sb (a)** 反对某人 fǎnduì mǒurén. **(b)** 不利于 búlìyú: *The war is ~ing against them.* 他们战争中失利. **~ ahead** 干吧 gànba; 说吧 shuōba; 走吧 zǒubà. '**~ahead** *n* 许可 xǔkě: *get the ~-ahead* 得到许可. **~ along** 进

jìnxíng. ~ ***along with sb*** **(a)** 陪…一起去 péi … yìqǐ qù. **(b)** 赞同 zàntóng: *The manager ~es along with your idea.* 经理赞同你的意见. ~ ***at sb (sth)*** **(a)** 进攻 jìngōng. **(b)** 努力对〔對〕付 nǔlì duìfu. ~ ***away*** 离开 líkāi. ~ ***back*** **(a)** 回去 huíqù. **(b)** 追溯 zhuīsù, 回溯 huísù: *Our family ~es back 300 years.* 我们的家系可追溯到三百年以前. ~ ***back on*** 违〔違〕约 wéiyuē, 违背 wéibèi: ~ *back on your word* 你食言. ~ ***by*** 走过 zǒuguò, 过去 guòqù: *as time ~es by* 随着时间的推移. ~ ***by*** (或 ***under***) ***the name of*** 称〔稱〕作 chēngzuò, 叫做 jiàozuò. ~ ***down*** **(a)** (船等) 下沉 xiàchén. **(b)** (太阳,月亮等)落下 luòxià. **(c)** (食物)吞下 tūnxià, 咽下 yànxià. **(d)** (海,风等) 平静下来 píngjìng xiàlái. **(e)**(价格)下降 xiàjiàng. ~ ***down (in sth)*** 被载〔載〕于 bèi zǎiyú, 被记录〔錄〕bèi jìlù: *His name will ~ down in history.* 他将青史留名. ~ ***down with sb*** 被赞许 bèi zànxǔ: *His suggestion went down very well.* 他的建议大受赞许. ~ ***down with sth*** 感染(疾病) gǎnrǎn. ~ ***for sb*** **(a)** 去请(人) qùqǐng, 去找(人) qùzhǎo. **(b)** 袭〔襲〕击〔擊〕xíjī. ~ ***in*** **(a)** 进入 jìnrù. **(b)** (太阳,月亮等)被云〔雲〕遮掩 bèi yún zhēyǎn. ~ ***in for sth*** **(a)** 参〔參〕加(竞争等) cānjiā. **(b)** 酷爱〔愛〕kù'ài: ~ *in for golf* 喜欢高尔夫球. ~ ***into sth*** **(a)** 进入 jìnrù: ~ *into the Army* 参军. **(b)** 从事 cóngshì: ~ *into (the) details* 详述. **(c)** (使自己)进入(某种状态) jìnrù: ~ *into fits of laughter* 发出阵阵笑声. ~ ***off*** **(a)** 爆炸 bàozhà, 发射 fāshè. **(b)** = go bad. ⇨ bad[1](5). **(c)** 进行 jìnxíng: *The concert went off well.* 音乐会开得很好. ~ ***off sb (sth)*** 失去兴〔興〕趣 shīqù xìngqù. ~ ***on*** **(a)** (时间)过去 guòqù. **(b)** 举〔舉〕止 jǔzhǐ, 表现 (不好) biǎoxiàn. **(c)** 发生 fāshēng: *What's ~ing on here?* 这里出了什么事? ~ ***on about sth*** 喋喋不休 diédié bùxiū. ~ ***on (at sb)*** 不停地责怪 bùtíngde zéguài. ~ ***on to sth*** (或 ***to do sth***) 转〔轉〕入 zhuǎnrù. ~ ***on (with sth*** 或 ***doing sth)*** 继 jì. ~ ***out*** **(a)** 离家外出. **(b)** 参〔參〕加社交活动 cānjiā shèjiāo huódòng: *We don't ~ out much nowadays.* 近来我们不大参加社交活动. **(c)** 熄灭 〔滅〕xīmiè: *The fire went out.* 火灭了. **(d)** (衣服式样等) 过时 guòshí. ~ ***out with sb*** 〔非正式用语〕经〔經〕常同…一起出去 jīngcháng tóng … yìqǐ chūqù. ~ ***over sth*** 仔细检〔檢〕查 zǐxì jiǎnchá. ~ ***round*** **(a)** 足够分配 zúgòu fēnpèi: *There aren't enough apples to ~ round.* 苹果不够分配. **(b)** 绕〔繞〕道走 ràodàozǒu. ~ ***round (to a place)*** 非正式去: *We're ~ing round to see Bob.* 我们顺便去看鲍勃. ~ ***round the bend*** 〔非正式用语〕生气〔氣〕shēngqì, 发〔發〕怒 fānù. ~ ***through*** (生意)成交 chéngjiāo: *The deal did not ~ through.* 这笔生意没有成交. ~ ***through sth*** **(a)** 仔细讨论〔論〕zǐxì tǎolùn. **(b)** 搜查 sōuchá: ~ *through his pockets* 搜查他的口袋. **(c)** 经〔經〕受 jīngshòu. **(d)** 用光(钱) yòngguāng. ~ ***through with sth*** 完成 wánchéng. ~ ***to*** (或 ***towards***) ***sth*** 捐赠 juānzèng: *This money will ~ towards the new hospital.* 这钱要捐给新建的医院. ~ ***under*** **(a)** 沉没 chénmò. **(b)** 〔喻〕失败 shībài. ~ ***up*** **(a)** 上升 shàngshēng. **(b)** 被建立 bèi jiànlì. **(c)** 被炸毁 bèi zhàhuǐ, 被烧〔燒〕毁 bèi shāohuǐ. ~ ***up sth*** 攀登 pāndēng. ~ ***with sb (sth)*** **(a)** 陪伴…去 péibàn … qù. **(b)** 与〔與〕…相配 yǔ … xiāngpèi: *These curtains ~ well with your rugs.* 这些窗帘同你的地毯配得很好. ~ ***without (sth)*** 在缺少…的情况下勉强对〔對〕付 zài quēshǎo … de qíngkuàngxià miǎnqiáng duìfu: ~ *without food for four days* 挨了四天的饿. ~ ***without saying*** 不言而喻 bùyán ér yù; 理所当〔當〕然 lǐsuǒ dāngrán.

go[2] /gəʊ/ *n* [C] [*pl* goes /gəʊz/] 〔非正式用语〕精力 jīnglì: *He's full of ~.* 他精力充沛. ***be on the ~*** 忙碌 mánglù. ***have a ~ (at sth)*** 企图〔圖〕做某事 qǐtú zuò mǒushì.

go-between /ˈgəʊbɪtwiːn/ *n* [C] 中间〔間〕人 zhōngjiānrén; 媒人 méirén.

goad /gəʊd/ *n* [C] **1** (赶家畜用的)刺棒 cìbàng. **2** 〔喻〕刺痛物 cìtòngwù, 驱〔驅〕使 qūshǐ. □ *vt* 激励〔勵〕jīlì, 刺激 cìjī.

goal /gəʊl/ *n* [C] **1** (足球) 球门〔門〕qiúmén; 得分 défēn. **2** 〔喻〕目的 mùdì, 目标〔標〕mùbiāo. **ˈ~keeper** (足球) 守门员 shǒuményuán.

goat /gəʊt/ *n* [C] 山羊 shānyáng. ⇨ kid[1](1). ***get one's ~*** 惹怒某人 rěnù mǒurén.

gobble[1] /ˈgɒbl/ *vt/i* ~ ***(up)*** 狼吞虎咽〔嚥〕lángtūn-hǔyàn.

gobble² /'gɒbl/ *vi, n* [C] 发〔發〕火鸡〔鷄〕叫声〔聲〕fā huǒjī jiàoshēng. 火鸡叫声 huǒjī jiàoshēng.

gob·let/ 'gɒblɪt/ *n* [C] 高脚无〔無〕把手酒杯 gāojiǎo wú bǎshǒu jiǔbēi.

gob·lin /'gɒblɪn/ *n* [C] 妖怪 yāoguài.

god /gɒd/ *n* [C] **1** 神 shén; 神像 shénxiàng. **2 G~** (宗教) 上帝 shàngdì. **3** 神化的人 shénhuàde rén. **~ess** *n* [C] 女神 nǚshén. **'~child** 教子 jiàozǐ; 教女 jiàonǚ. **'~daughter** 教女 jiàonǚ. **'~son** 教子 jiàozǐ. **'~father** 教父. jiàofù. **'~mother** 教母 jiàomǔ. **'~parent** 教父或教母 jiàofù huò jiàomǔ. **'~fearing** *adj* 虔诚的 qiánchéngde. **'~for·saken** *adj* (地方) 凄凉的 qīliángde. **'~send** 来〔來〕得正好的 láide zhènghǎo de; 天赐 tiāncì. **~less** *adj* 邪恶〔惡〕的 xié'ède; 不信神的 bú xìnshén de. **~like** *adj* 上帝般的 shàngdìbānde, 如神的 rúshénde. **~ly** *adj* [-ier, -iest] 虔诚的 qiánchéngde. **~li·ness** *n* [U]

goggle /'gɒgl/ *vi* 瞪视 dèngshì, 凝视 níngshì.

goggles /'gɒglz/ *n pl* 风〔風〕镜 fēngjìng, 护〔護〕目镜 hùmùjìng.

go·ing /'gəʊɪŋ/ *n* **1** [U] 工作或行驶〔駛〕的速度 gōngzuò huò xíngshǐ de sùdù: *50 miles an hour is good* ~. 每小时五十英里是相当好的速度. **2** *,comings and '~s* [书面语][喻]来〔來〕来去去 láiláiqùqù. □ *adj* ***the ~ rate*** 时〔時〕价〔價〕shíjià. ***a ~ concern*** 兴〔興〕隆昌盛的企业〔業〕xīnglóngchāngshèngde qǐyè.

go-kart /'gəʊ kɑːt/ *n* [C] 微型竞〔競〕赛汽车〔車〕wēixíng jìngsài qìchē.

gold /gəʊld/ *n* [U] **1** 黄金 huángjīn, 金 jīn. **2** 财富 cáifù, 钱〔錢〕财 qiáncái. **3** [喻]宝〔寶〕贵的东〔東〕西 bǎoguìde dōngxi, 高贵的品质〔質〕gāoguìde pǐnzhì: *a heart of* ~高贵的心. **4** [亦作定语] 金黄色 jīnhuángsè, 黄色 huángsè. **'~finch** 金翅雀 jīnchìquè. **'~fish** 金鱼 jīnyú. **,~-'leaf** 金叶〔葉〕jīnyè. **'~mine (a)** 金矿〔鑛〕jīnkuàng. **(b)** [喻]财源 cáiyuán. **'~smith** 金首饰工 jīnshǒushìgōng. **~en** *adj* **(a)** 黄金的 huángjīnde, 黄金般的 huángjīnbānde, 金黄色的 jīnhuángsède. **(b)** 贵重的 guìzhòngde, 极〔極〕好的 jíhǎode. **the ,~en 'rule** 金科玉律 jīnkēyùlǜ.

golf /gɒlf/ *n* [U] 高尔夫球戏〔戲〕gāo'ěrfūqiúxì. **'golf-clubs** 高尔夫球棍 gāo'ěrfū qiúgùn. **'golf-course** 高尔夫球场〔場〕gāo'ěrfū qiúchǎng.

gon·dola /'gɒndələ/ *n* [C] 威尼斯一种〔種〕狭〔狹〕长的平底船 wēinísī yìzhǒng xiáchángde píngdǐchuán. **gon·do·lier** /,gɒndə'lɪə(r)/ *n* [C] 平底船船夫 píngdǐchuán chuánfū.

gone /gɒn/ *pp* of go¹.

gong /gɒŋ/ *n* [C] 锣〔鑼〕luó. □ *vt* 敲锣 qiāoluó.

good¹ /gʊd/ *adj* [better, best] **1** 好的 hǎode: *a ~ cook* 好厨师. **2** 有益的 yǒuyìde: *Milk is ~ for children.* 牛奶对儿童有益. **3** 有效的 yǒuxiàode, 能干〔幹〕的 nénggànde: *~ at mathematics* 擅长数学. **4** 使人愉快的 shǐrényúkuài de, 悦人的 yuèrénde: *~ news* 好消息. ***be a ~ thing*** ...是件好事情 ...shì jiàn hǎoshìqing. ***have a ~ time*** 过〔過〕得愉快 guòde yúkuài. **5** 好心的 hǎoxīnde, 慈心的 cíxīnde: *He was ~ enough to help us.*他心好,帮助我们. **6** 大大的 dàdàde, 十足的 shízúde: *a ~ scolding* 一顿痛骂. **8** 强健的 qiángjiànde: *~ eyesight* 视力很好. **9** 可靠的 kěkàode, 安全的 ānquánde: *a car with ~ brakes* 一辆刹车可靠的汽车. ***~ for*** **(a)** 有支付...能力的 yǒu zhīfù ... nénglì de: *My credit is ~ for £500.* 我的信用可以周转500英镑. **(b)** 有效的 yǒuxiàode: *tickets ~ for three months.* 有效期为三个月的票证. **10** 有教养〔養〕的 yǒu jiàoyǎng de, 诚实〔實〕的 chéngshíde. **11** 有品德的 yǒu pǐndé de: *a ~ girl* 品德好的姑娘. **12** (用于打招呼和告别): *G~ morning* 早晨好; *G~ afternoon* 下午好. **13** 相当〔當〕多的 xiāngdāngduōde: *a ~ deal of money* 很多钱. **14** 不少于 bù shǎoyú: *for a ~ hour* 整整一小时. ***make ~*** 发〔發〕达〔達〕fādá. **'~-for-nothing** *adj, n* [C] 无〔無〕用的(人) wúyòngde. **,~-'looking** *adj* 美丽〔麗〕的 měilìde, 漂亮的 piàoliangde. **,~-'natured** *adj* 和蔼的 hé'ǎide. **,~-'sense** 机〔機〕智 jīzhì. **,~-'tempered** *adj* 脾气〔氣〕好的 píqì hǎo de.

good² /gʊd/ *n* [U] **1** 好事 hǎoshì. **2** ***for ~ (and all)*** 永久地 yǒngjiǔde. 一劳〔勞〕永逸地 yìláo yǒngyì de. **3** 好人 hǎorén. **4** [*pl*] 动〔動〕产〔產〕dòngchǎn, 货物 huòwù: *metal ~s* 五金货品. **5** [*pl*] 货运〔運〕huòyùn: *a '~s train* (铁路)货运列车.

good·bye /,gʊd'baɪ/ *int, n* [C] 再见! zàijiàn! 告别 gàobié.

good·ness /'gʊdnɪs/ *n* [U] **1** 优〔優〕良 yōuliáng, 善良 shànliáng. **2** 精华〔華〕jīnghuá: *the ~ of fruit juice* 果汁的精华. **3** [在感叹句中代替 God]: *For ~' sake!* 看在老天爷面上! *Thank ~!* 谢天谢地!

goods /gʊdz/ *n pl* ⇨ good².

good·will /,gʊd'wɪl/ *n* [U] **1** 亲〔親〕善 qīnshàn, 友好 yǒuhǎo. **2** (商店企业等)信誉〔譽〕xìnyù.

goose /guːs/ *n* [*pl* geese /giːs/] **1** [C] ⇨ gander. 鹅〔鵝〕é; 母鹅 mǔ'é. **2** [U] 鹅肉 éròu.

goose·berry /'gʊzbərɪ/ *n* [C] [*pl* -ies] [植物]醋栗 cùlì, 醋栗果实〔實〕cùlì guǒshí.

gore /gɔː(r)/ *vt* (牛,羊用角)抵伤〔傷〕dǐshāng; 划〔劃〕破 huápò.

gorge/gɔːdʒ/ *n* [C] **1** 山峡〔峽〕shānxiá, 峡谷 xiágǔ. **2** 咽喉 yānhóu. □ *vt/i* 暴食 bàoshí, 狼吞虎咽〔嚥〕lángtūn-hǔyàn.

gorg·eous /'gɔːdʒəs/ *adj* **1** 华〔華〕丽〔麗〕的 huálìde. 灿〔燦〕烂〔爛〕的 cànlànde. **2** [非正式用语] 宜人的 yírénde, 可喜的 kěxǐde: *a ~ present* 令人喜爱的礼物. **~ly** *adv*

gor·illa /gə'rɪlə/ *n* [C] [*pl* ~s] 大猩猩 dàxīngxīng.

gorse /gɔːs/ *n* [U] (植物)荆豆 jīngdòu.

gory /'gɔːrɪ/ *adj* [-ier, -iest] 血淋淋的 xuělínlínde, 沾满血的 zhānmǎnxuěde.

gosh /gɒʃ/ *int* [俚语] 天哪! 哎呀! tiānna! āiyā!

gos·ling /'gɒzlɪŋ/ *n* [C] 小鹅〔鵝〕xiǎo'é.

gos·pel /'gɒspl/ *n* **1 the G~**(基督教)《新约》四福音书〔書〕之一《xīnyuē》sìfúyīnshū zhī yī. **2** [C] 信条〔條〕xìntiáo, 准〔準〕则 zhǔnzé.

gos·sip /'gɒsɪp/ *n* **1** [C, U] 流言蜚语 liúyán fēiyǔ. **2** [U] 报〔報〕纸上社会〔會〕新闻〔聞〕的漫谈 bàozhǐ shàng shèhuì xīnwén de màntán: *a ~ column* 社会漫谈栏. **3** [C] 爱〔愛〕传〔傳〕流言蜚语的人 ài chuán liúyán fēiyǔ de rén. □ *vi* [-pp-] 闲〔閑〕聊 xiánliáo, 传播流言蜚语 chuánbō liúyán fēiyǔ.

got *pt, pp* of get. ⇨ also have²³.

gouge /gaʊdʒ/ *n* [C] 半圆凿〔鑿〕bànyuánzáo. □ *vt* **1** (用半圆凿)凿 záo. **2** 挖出 wāchū: *~ his eyes out* 把他的眼珠挖出.

gou·lash /'guːlæʃ/ *n* [C, U] 菜燉牛肉 càidùn niúròu.

gourd /gʊəd/ *n* [C] **1** 葫芦〔蘆〕húlu 葫芦属〔屬〕植物 húlushǔ zhíwù. **2** 葫芦制成的容器 húlu zhìchéng de róngqì.

gour·met /'gʊəmeɪ/ *n* [C] 食物品尝〔嚐〕家 shíwù pǐnchángjiā.

gov(t). = government.

Gov. = Governor.

gov·ern /'gʌvn/ *vt/i* **1** 统治 tǒngzhì; 管理 guǎnlǐ. **2** 控制 kòngzhì, 抑制 yìzhì: *~ one's temper* 捺住性子. **3** 影响〔響〕yǐngxiǎng, 支配 zhīpèi: *~ed by the opinions of others* 受别人意见的影响.

gov·ern·ess /'gʌvənɪs/ *n* [C] 家庭女教师〔師〕jiātíng nǚjiàoshī.

gov·ern·ment /'gʌvənmənt/ *n* **1** [U] 政治 zhèngzhì, 政体〔體〕zhèngtǐ: *democratic ~* 民主政治. **2** [C] 政府 zhèngfǔ, 内阁〔閣〕nèigé. **~al** /-'mentl/ *adj*

gov·ernor /'gʌvənə(r)/ *n* [C] **1** 地方长〔長〕官 dìfāng zhǎngguān, (英国)殖民地总〔總〕督 zhímíndì zǒngdū; (美国)州长 zhōuzhǎng. **2** 学〔學〕校等主管人员 xuéxiào děng zhǔguǎn rényuán, 管理者 guǎnlǐzhě, 理事 lǐshì.

gown /gaʊn/ *n* [C] **1** 长〔長〕服 chángfú: *a 'dressing-~* 晨衣. **2** 妇〔婦〕女的正式服装〔裝〕fùnǚde zhèngshì fúzhuāng. **3** 教授, 法官等的礼〔禮〕服 jiàoshòu fǎguān děng de lǐfú.

G.P. = General Practitioner 普通医〔醫〕生(通治各科疾病) pǔtōng yīshēng.

G.P.O. = General Post Office 邮〔郵〕政总〔總〕局 yóuzhèng zǒngjú.

grab /græb/ *vt/i* [-bb-] 攫取 juéqǔ, 抓取 zhuāqǔ: □ *n* [C] **1** 攫取 juéqǔ, 掠夺〔奪〕lüèduó: *make a ~ for* 抓取. **2** 抓扬〔揚〕机〔機〕zhuāyángjī, 挖掘机 wājuéjī.

grace /greɪs/ *n* **1** [U] 优〔優〕美 yōuměi, 优雅 yōuyǎ, 雅致〔緻〕yǎzhì. **2** [U] 善意 shànyì, 恩惠 ēnhuì. *give sb a week's, etc ~* 给予某人一周等的宽限 gěiyǔ mǒurén yìzhōu děng de kuānxiàn. **3** *do sth with a good ~* 欣然做某事 xīnrán zuò mǒushì. *do sth with a bad ~* 勉强做某事 miǎnqiáng zuò mǒushì. **4** (宗教)饭前饭后〔後〕的感恩祷〔禱〕告 fànqián fànhòu de gǎn'ēn dǎogào. **5** [U] (宗教)上帝的恩典 shàngdìde ēndiǎn. □ *vt* 使优美 shǐ yōuměi, 给…增光 gěi ... zēngguāng: *a dinner ~d by the presence of the Queen* 因女王之光临而增光的宴会. **~ful** *adj* 优美的 yōuměide, 雅致的 yǎzhì-

de. ~**fully** *adv*
gra·cious /'greɪʃəs/ *adj* 亲〔親〕切的 qīnqiède, 和善的 héshànde, 仁慈的 réncíde. ~**ly** *adv* ~**ness** *n* [U]
grade /greɪd/ *n* [C] **1** 等级 děngjí, 级别 jíbié: *a high ~ of intelligence* 智力很高. **2** 学校给的分数, 等级 xuéxiào gěi de fēnshù, děngjí. ***make the~*** [非正式用语] 达〔達〕到好的标〔標〕准〔準〕dádào hǎode biāozhǔn. **3** [美语] = gradient. □ *vt* 给…分等 gěi … fēnděng.
gradi·ent /'greɪdɪənt/ *n* [C] 坡度 pōdù, 斜度 xiédù.
grad·ual /'grædʒʊəl/ *adj* **1** 逐渐〔漸〕的 zhújiànde. **2** 不陡的 bùdǒude. ~**ly** /-dʒʊlɪ/ *adv* 慢慢地 mànmànde.
grad·uate[1] /'grædʒʊət/ *n* [C] [英国英语] 大学〔學〕毕〔畢〕业〔業〕生 dàxué bìyèshēng.
grad·uate[2] /grædʊeɪt/ *vt/i* **1** 刻度数〔數〕于 kè dùshù yú. **2** 给…分等 gěi … fēnděng. **3** 毕〔畢〕业〔業〕bìyè, 大学〔學〕毕业 dàxué bìyè, 获〔獲〕学位 huò xuéwèi. **gradu'ation** *n* [C, U] **(a)** 毕业 bìyè, 获学位 huò xuéwèi. **(b)** 毕业典礼〔禮〕bìyè diǎnlǐ, 授学位典礼 shòu xuéwèi diǎnlǐ. **(c)** 刻度 kèdù: *graduations on a thermometer* 温度计上的刻度.
graf·fiti /grə'fi:tɪ/ *n pl* 墙〔牆〕壁等处〔處〕的乱〔亂〕涂〔塗〕qiángbì děng chù de luàntú.
graft /grɑ:ft/ *n* [C] **1** 接穗 jiēsuì. **2** [医学] 移植物 yízhíwù, 移植片 yízhípiàn. □ *vt/i* 移植 yízhí.
grain /greɪn/ *n* **1** [U] 谷〔穀〕物 gǔwù, 谷类〔類〕gǔlèi. **2** [C] 谷粒 gǔlì. **3** [C] 粒子 lìzǐ, 细粒 xìlì: *~s of sand* 沙粒. **4** [喻] 少数 shǎoshù: *not a ~ of truth* 完全是谎言. **5** [C] 木纹 mùwén. ***be*** (或 ***go***) ***against the ~*** [喻] 格格不入 gégébúrù.
gram /græm/ ⇨ gramme.
gram·mar /'græmə(r)/ *n* [U] 语法 yǔfǎ. ~**ian** /grə'meərɪən/ *n* [C] 语法家 yǔfǎjiā.
gram·mati·cal /grə'mætɪkl/ *adj* 语法的 yǔfǎde, 合于语法的 héyúyǔfǎde.
gramme /græm/ (亦作 **gram**) *n* [C] 克(重量单位) kè.
gramo·phone /'græməfəʊn/ *n* [C] [过时用法] = record-player.
gran·ary /'grænərɪ/ *n* [C] [*pl* -ies] 谷〔穀〕仓〔倉〕gǔcāng. 粮仓 liángcāng.
grand /grænd/ *adj* [-er, -est] **1** 最重大的 zuì zhòngdà de, 重大的 zhòngdàde: *the ~ finale.* (音乐会等)终场演奏, 终曲, 终局. **2** 豪华〔華〕的 háohuáde, 华丽〔麗〕的 huálìde: *living in ~ style* 生活豪华. **3** 傲慢的 àomànde, 骄〔驕〕傲的 jiāo'àode: *a ~ manner* 骄傲的态度; *a ~ air* 骄气. **4** [非正式用语] 美妙的 měimiàode, 惬〔愜〕意的 qièyìde: *We had a ~ time.* 我们过得很愉快. **5** 全部的 quánbùde, 总〔總〕的 zǒngde: *the ~ total* 总计. □ *n* [C] [非正式用语] **1** 大钢〔鋼〕琴 dàgāngqín. **2** 一千英镑或美元 yìqiān yīngbàng huò měiyuán. ,~**pi'ano** 大钢琴 dàgāngqín. '~**stand** 大看台〔臺〕dàkàntái. ~**ly** *adv*
grand- *prefix* 祖…zǔ…, 外祖… wàizǔ …, 孙〔孫〕…sūn… ,外孙 …wàisūn …, '~·**child** 孙子, 孙女 sūnzi, sūnnǚ, 外孙, 外孙女 wàisūn, wàisūnnǚ; '~·**daughter** 孙女, 外孙女 sūnnǚ, wàisūnnǚ. '~·**son** 孙子,外孙 sūnzi, wàisūn. '~·**father** 祖父 zǔfù; '~·**mother** 祖母 zǔmǔ.
gran·deur /'grændʒə(r)/ *n* [U] 壮〔壯〕观〔觀〕zhuàngguān; 宏伟〔偉〕hóngwěi.
gran·di·ose /'grændɪəʊs/ *adj* 宏伟〔偉〕的 hóngwěide, 宏大的 hóngdàde.
gran·ite/'grænɪt /*n* [U] 花岗〔崗〕石 huāgāngshí.
grant /grɑ:nt/ *vt* **1** 同意给予 tóngyì gěiyǔ, 授予 shòuyǔ: *~ a favour* 答应一项帮助. **2** 承认〔認〕chéngrèn: *He's nice, I'll ~ you that.* 他讨人喜欢, 我(将)向你承认这一点. ***take sth for ~ed*** 认为〔爲〕…理所当〔當〕然 rènwéi … lǐsuǒdāngrán. □ *n* [C] 拨〔撥〕款 bōkuǎn, 补〔補〕助款 bǔzhùkuǎn.
granu·lar /'grænjʊlə(r)/ *adj* 颗粒状〔狀〕的 kēlìzhuàngde, 细粒的 xìlìde.
granu·late /'grænjʊleɪt/ *vt/i* (使)成颗粒 chéngkēlì. ,~**d 'sugar** 沙糖 shātáng.
gran·ule /'grænju:l/ *n* [C] 细粒 xìlì.
grape /greɪp/ *n* [C] 葡萄 pútáo '~**vine** *n* [C] **(a)** 葡萄藤 pútáoténg. **(b)** 小道消息 xiǎodào xiāoxī.
grape·fruit /'greɪpfru:t/ *n* [C] [*pl* ~或 ~s] 葡萄柚 pútáoyòu.
graph /græf/ *n* [C] 曲线〔綫〕图〔圖〕qūxiàntú, 图表 túbiǎo. '~**paper** 方格纸 fānggézhǐ, 座标〔標

纸 zuòbiāozhǐ.

graphic /'græfɪk/ *adj* **1** 图〔圖〕示的 túshìde, 图解的 tújiěde. **2** 生动〔動〕的 shēngdòngde, 鲜明的 xiānmíngde. □ *n* [*pl*] 书〔書〕画〔畫〕刻印作品 shūhuà kèyìng zuòpǐn. **~ally** /-klɪ/*adv* **(a)** 用书写〔寫〕或图表 yòng shūxiě huò túbiǎo. **(b)** 生动地 shēngdòngde, 鲜明地 xiānmíngde: *~ally described* 生动地描写的.

graph·ite /'græfaɪt/ *n* [U] 〔化学〕石墨 shímò.

grapple /'græpl/ *vi* **1** 格斗〔鬥〕gédòu, 扭打 niǔdǎ. **2**〔喻〕尽〔盡〕力解决(问题) jìnlì jiějué.

grasp /grɑ:sp/ *vt/i* **1** 抓住 zhuāzhù, 抓紧〔緊〕zhuājǐn. **2** 领会〔會〕lǐnghuì, 掌握 zhǎngwò. **3** ~ *at* 抓住 zhuāzhù, 攫取 juéqǔ: ~ *at an opportunity* 抓住机会. □ *n* [C] [常用 *sing*] 抓 zhuā, 掌握 zhǎngwò, 了解 liáojiě.

grass /grɑ:s/ *n* **1** [U] 草 cǎo,青草 qīngcǎo. **2** [C] [*pl* ~es] 禾本科植物 héběnkē zhíwù. **3** [U] 草地 cǎodì; 牧场〔場〕mùchǎng: *put cattle out to* ~把牲口放到草地上. ,**~-'roots** *n pl* [常用作定语]基层〔層〕jīcéng, 基层群众〔衆〕jīcéng qúnzhòng. **grassy** *adj* [-ier, -iest] 生满草的 shēngmǎn cǎo de, 多草的 duōcǎode.

grass·hopper /'grɑ:shɒpə(r)/ *n* [C] 蚱蜢 zhàmɑ.

grate[1] /greɪt/ *n* [C] 火炉〔爐〕huǒlú: 炉格 lúgé, 炉篦 lúbì.

grate[2] /greɪt/ *vt/i* **1** 擦碎 cāsuì, 磨碎 mósuì: ~ *cheese* 磨碎干酪. **2** 擦响〔響〕cāxiǎng. **3** ~ **(on)**〔喻〕使人烦燥 shǐ rén fánzào: *His voice ~s on my nerves.* 他的声音使我神经不安. **grater** 擦子 cāzi. **grat·ing** *adj*

grate·ful /'greɪtfl/ *adj* 感激的 gǎnjide, 感谢的 gǎnxiède. **~ly** *adv*

grat·ify /'grætɪfaɪ/ *vt* [*pt, pp* -ied] **1** 使满意 shǐ mǎnyì. **2** 使满足 shǐ mǎnzú: ~ *one's curiosity* 满足自己的好奇心. **~ing** *adj* 令人愉快的 lìng rén yúkuài de. **grati·fi·ca·tion** /-fɪ'keɪʃn/ *n* [C, U]

grat·ing /'greɪtɪŋ/ *n* [C] (门, 窗等)格 gé, 栅 shān.

grati·tude /'grætɪtju:d/ *n* [U] 感激 gǎnji 感恩 gǎn'ēn.

gra·tu·itous /grə'tju:ɪtəs/ *adj* **1** 免费的 miǎnfèide. **2** 无〔無〕故的 wúgùde, 无理的 wúlǐde: *a* ~ *insult* 无故的侮辱. **~ly** *adv*

gra·tu·ity /grə'tju:ətɪ/ *n* [C] [*pl* -ies] **1** 退职〔職〕金 tuìzhíjīn. **2** 小帐〔帳〕xiǎozhàng. 小费 xiǎofèi.

grave[1] /greɪv/ *adj* [-r, -st] 严〔嚴〕重的 yánzhòngde: *a* ~ *situation* 严重的局势. **~ly** *adv*

grave[2] /greɪv/ *n* [C] 墓 mù, 坟墓 fénmù. '**~stone** 墓碑 mùbēi. '**~-yard** 墓地 mùdì.

gravel /'grævl/ *n* [U] 砾〔礫〕lì, 砾石 lìshí. □ *vt* [-ll-, 美语亦作 -l-] 铺以砾石 pūyǐ lìshí.

gravi·tate /'grævɪteɪt/ *vi* 受吸引 shòu xīyǐn, 倾向 qīngxiàng. **gravi·ta·tion** /-'teɪʃn/ *n* [U] **(a)** 引力作用 yǐnlì zuòyòng, 倾向 qīngxiàng, 吸引力 xīyǐnlì **(b)** 地心吸力 dìxīn xīlì.

grav·ity /'grævətɪ/ *n* [U] **1** 地球引力 dìqiú yǐnlì. **2** 重量 zhòngliàng: *centre of* ~ 重心. **3** 严〔嚴〕重性 yánzhòngxìng, 重要性 zhòngyàoxìng: *the* ~ *of the situation* 形势的严重性.

gravy /'greɪvɪ/ *n* [U] 肉汁 ròuzhī. '**~-boat** 盛调味汁的船形器皿 chéng tiáowèizhī de chuánxíng qìmǐn.

gray /greɪ/ *adj, n* ⇨grey.

graze[1] /greɪz/ *vt/i* **1** (牲畜) 吃草 chīcǎo. **2** 放牧 fàngmù.

graze[2] /greɪz/ *vt/i* 擦过〔過〕cāguò, 擦去…的皮 cāqù ... depí. □ *n* [C] 擦破处〔處〕cāpòchù.

grease /gri:s/ *n* [U] **1** 动〔動〕物脂肪 dòngwù zhīfáng, 熔化的动物脂肪 rónghuàde dòngwù zhīfáng. **2** 油脂状〔狀〕物 yóuzhī zhuàngwù. □ *vt* 涂〔塗〕油脂于 tú yóuzhī yú. ~ ***sb's palm*** 向…行贿 xiàng ... xínghuì. **greasy** *adj* [-ier, -iest] 油污的 yǒuwūde, 涂有油脂的 tú yǒu yóuzhīde. **greas·ily** *adv*

great /greɪt/ *adj* [-er, -est] **1** (体积,数量,程度) 超过〔過〕一般标〔標〕准〔準〕的 chāoguò yibān biāozhǔn de: 巨大的 jùdàde, 非常的 fēichángde: *a* ~ *friend* 亲密的朋友, *a* ~ *work of art* 艺术精品. **2** 伟〔偉〕大的 wěidàde: ~ *men* 伟人. **3** 重要的 zhòngyàode, 重大的 zhòngdàde: *a* ~ *occasion* 盛大的场合. **4**〔非正式用语〕(表示强调)多么〔麽〕duōme: *Look at that* ~ *big yacht!* 瞧那好大的游艇! **5** (表示巨大数量): *a* ~ *deal* 大量, *a* ~ *number* 很多. **6**〔非正式用语〕绝妙的 juémiàode, 美妙的 meimiaode: *a* ~ *party* 美妙的聚会. **G~ 'Britain** 大不列颠 dàbúlièdiān. **the G~ War** 第一次世界大战〔戰〕dìyīcì shìjiè dàzhàn. **~ly**

adv 大大地 dàdàde, 非常 fēicháng. ~**ness** *n* [U]

great- /greɪt/ *prefix* 曾 zēng, ˌ~-'*grandfather* 曾祖父 zēngzǔfù; 外曾祖父 wàizēngzǔfù.

greed /gri:d/ *n* [U] 贪心 tānxīn, 贪婪 tānlán. **greedy** *adj* [-ier, -iest] 贪吃的 tānchīde, 贪婪的 tānlánde. ~**ily** *adv*

Greek /gri:k/ *n* 希腊[臘]人 xīlàrén; 希腊语 xīlàyǔ. *be ~ to sb* 完全不懂 wánquán bùdǒng. □ *adj* 希腊人的 xīlàrénde; 希腊语的 xīlàyǔde.

green¹ /gri:n/ *adj* [-er, -est] **1** 绿的 lǜde, 青的 qīngde. **2** (水果)未熟的 wèishúde, (木材)未干〔乾〕的 wèigānde. **3 (a)** 没有经〔經〕验〔驗〕的 méiyǒu jīngyàn de. **(b)** 易受骗〔騙〕的 yì shòupiàn de. **4** (脸色)发〔發〕青的 fāqīngde, 苍〔蒼〕白的 cāngbáide. ~ *with envy* 非常妒忌 fēicháng dùjì. '~ **belt** 绿化地带〔帶〕 lǜhuà dìdài. ~**fingers** [非正式用语]园〔園〕艺〔藝〕技能 yuányì jìnéng. '~**gage** /-geɪdʒ/ 青梅子 qīngméizi, 青李子 qīnglǐzi. '~**grocer** 蔬菜水果商 shūcài shuǐguǒ shāng. '~**house** 温室 wēnshì, 玻璃暖房 bōli nuǎnfáng.

green² /gri:n/ *n* **1** [C, U] 绿色 lǜsè, 青色 qīngsè. **2** [*pl*] 蔬菜 shūcài. **3** 草地 cǎodì, 草坪 cǎopíng. **(a)** 公有草地 gōngyǒu cǎodì: *the village ~* 村中公有草地. **(b)** (滚球戏)场〔場〕地 chǎngdì. **(c)** 高尔〔爾〕夫球场球洞四周的草地 gāo'ěrfū qiúchǎng qiúdòng sìzhōu de cǎodì.

greenery /'gri:nərɪ/ *n* [U] 草木 cǎomù, 绿叶〔葉〕 lǜyè.

greet/gri:t/ *vt* **1** 迎接 yíngjiē, 欢〔歡〕迎 huānyíng. **2** [正式用语] (被眼,耳)察觉〔覺〕 chájué; 呈现 chéngxiàn. ~**ing** 问〔問〕候 wènhòu; 贺辞〔辭〕 hècí, 欢迎辞 huānyíngcí: '*Good morning*' *and* '*Dear Sir*' *are ~ings*. "早安"和"敬启者"是问候和致敬用语.

greg·ari·ous /grɪ'geərɪəs/ *adj* **1** 群居的 qúnjūde. **2** 爱群居的 ài qúnjū de, 合群的 héqúnde.

gre·nade /grɪ'neɪd/ *n* [C] 手榴弹〔彈〕 shǒuliúdàn.

grew /gru:/ *pt* of grow.

grey (亦作 **gray**) *adj* [-er, -est] 灰色的 huīsède, 灰白的 huībáide. □ *n* 灰色 huīsè. □ *vt/i* (使)成灰色 chéng huīsè. '~**matter** **(a)** 脑〔腦〕 nǎo. **(b)** 智力 zhìlì.

grey·hound /'greɪhʊnd/ *n* [C] 一种身体细长而善跑的狗 yìzhǒng shēntǐ xìcháng ér shànpǎo de gǒu.

grid /grɪd/ *n* [C] **1** 高压〔壓〕输〔輸〕电〔電〕线〔線〕路网〔網〕 gāoyā shūdiàn xiànlùwǎng. **2** 地图〔圖〕的坐标〔標〕方格 dìtúde zuòbiāo fānggé. **3** 格子 gézi, 格栅 géshān: *a 'cattle ~* 牲口栅栏.

grief /gri:f/ *n* **1** [C] 悲伤〔傷〕 bēishāng, 悲痛 bēitòng. **2** *bring sb to ~* 使某人遭受不幸 shǐ mǒurén zāoshòu búxìng. *come to ~* 遭到不幸 zāodào búxìng.

griev·ance /'gri:vns/ *n* [C] 冤情 yuānqíng, 牢骚〔騷〕 láosāo, 苦情 kǔqíng.

grieve /gri:v/ *vt/i* (使)悲痛 bēitòng, (使)伤〔傷〕心 shāngxīn.

grill /grɪl/ *n* [C] **1** = grating; grille. **2** 炙烤的肉类〔類〕食品 zhìkǎode ròulèi shípǐn. □ *vt/i* **1** 炙 zhì, 烤 kǎo. **2** [喻] 加酷热〔熱〕于 jiā kùrè yú. **3** 对〔對〕...严〔嚴〕加盘〔盤〕问〔問〕 duì ... yánjiā pánwèn.

grille /grɪl/ *n* [C] 铁〔鐵〕栅 tiězhà, 邮〔郵〕局柜〔櫃〕台〔臺〕上的铁栅 yóujú guìtái shàngde tiězhà.

grim /grɪm/ *adj* [-mer, -mest] 严〔嚴〕厉〔厲〕的 yánlìde, 严格的 yángéde: *a ~ struggle* 严酷的斗争, *a ~smile* 狞笑. ~**ly** *adv* ~**ness** *n* [U]

gri·mace /grɪ'meɪs/ *n* [C] 怪脸〔臉〕 guàiliǎn, 怪相 guàixiàng. □ *vi* 做怪脸 zuò guàiliǎn, 做怪相 zuò guàixiàng.

grime /graɪm/ *n* [U] 尘〔塵〕垢(积于表面的) chéngòu. □ *vt* 使肮〔骯〕脏〔髒〕 shǐ āngzāng, 使积〔積〕垢 shǐ jīgòu. **grimy** *adj* [-ier, -est]

grin /grin/ *vt/i* [-nn-] **1** 露齿〔齒〕而笑 lùchǐ'érxiào. *~ and bear it* 逆来〔來〕顺受 nìlái-shùnshòu. **2** 咧嘴一笑地表示 liězuǐ yíxiào de biǎoshì: *~ approval* 咧嘴一笑表示赞同. □ *n* [C] 露齿的笑 lùchǐde xiào.

grind /graɪnd/ *vt/i* [*pt, pp* ground /graʊnd/] **1** 磨碎 mósuì, 碾碎 niǎnsuì: *~ corn into flour* 磨谷成粉. **2** [喻]折磨 zhémó, 压〔壓〕榨 yāzhà: *people ground (down) by poverty* 被贫困折磨的人们. **3** 磨光 móguāng, 磨快 mókuài: *~ a knife* 磨小刀. **4** 咬(牙) yǎo: *~ one's teeth* 磨牙, 咬牙切齿. **5** *~ to a halt* (车)嘎然而止 gārán'érzhǐ. □ *n* **1** [C] 磨 mó; 磨擦声 mócāshēng. **2** [U] [非正式用语]苦差使 kǔchāshi. ~**er** *n* [C] 磨床 móchuáng; 磨工 mógōng. ~**stone** *n*

[C] 磨石 mòshí.

grip /grɪp/ *vt/i* [-pp-] **1** 紧〔緊〕握 jǐnwò, 抓紧 zhuājǐn. **2** 吸引(注意) xīyǐn. □ *n* [C] **1** 紧握 jǐnwò, 紧夹〔夾〕jǐnjiā; 握力 wòlì; 握法 wòfǎ; 掌握 zhǎngwò, 理解 lǐjiě: *have a good ~ of a problem* 对某一问题有很好的理解. ***come*** (或 ***get***) ***to ~s with*** 努力解决(问题) nǔlìjiějué. **2** (机器) 柄 bǐng, 夹〔夾〕jiā. **3** 手提包 shǒutíbāo, 旅行包 lǚxíngbāo.

gris·ly /'grɪzlɪ/ *adj* 可怕的 kěpàde: *n ~ murder* 可怕的谋杀.

gristle /'grɪsl/ *n* [U] 软〔軟〕骨 ruǎngǔ.

grit /grɪt/ *n* [U] **1** 粗砂 cūshā, 砂砾〔礫〕shālì. **2** 刚〔剛〕毅 gāngyì, 勇气〔氣〕yǒngqì, 坚〔堅〕忍 jiānrěn. □ *vt* [-tt-] 铺〔鋪〕砂砾于 pū shālì yú: *~ the roads in winter* 冬天在公路上铺砂砾. ***~ one's teeth*** 咬牙 yǎoyá, 〔喻〕咬牙表示坚决 yǎoyá biǎoshì jiānjué. **~ty** *adj* [-ier, -iest]

groan /grəʊn/ *vt/i* **1** 呻吟 shēnyín. **2** 承受重压〔壓〕发〔發〕出的声音 chéngshòu zhòngyā fāchū de shēngyīn. **3** 呻吟着表示 shényínzhe biǎoshì, 呻吟着说 shēnyínzhe shuō. □ *n* [C] 呻吟 shēnyín, 呻吟声〔聲〕shēnyínshēng.

grocer /'grəʊsə(r) /*n* [C] 杂〔雜〕货商 záhuòshāng, 食品商 shípǐnshāng.

grocery *n* [*pl* -ies] **(a)** [U] 食品杂货业〔業〕shípǐn záhuò yè. **(b)** [*pl*] 食品 shípǐn, 杂货 záhuò.

groggy /'grɒgɪ/ *adj* [-ier, -iest] 不稳的 bùwěnde, 身体〔體〕虚弱的 shēntǐ xūruòde.

groin /grɔɪn/ *n* [C] **1** 腹股沟〔溝〕fùgǔgōu. **2** (建筑)交叉拱 jiāochāgǒng.

groom /gru:m/ *n* [C] **1** 马〔馬〕夫 mǎfū. **2** = bridegroom. □ *vt* **1** 饲养〔養〕(马) sìyǎng. **2** [用 *pp*] 使整洁〔潔〕shǐ zhěngjié, 修饰 xiūshì: *well ~ed* 很整洁 hěnzhěngjié. **3** [非正式用语]推荐(某人) tuījiàn.

groove /gru:v/ *n* [C] **1** 槽 cáo, 沟〔溝〕gōu. **2** 常规 chángguī, 习〔習〕惯 xíguàn. ***get into*** (或 ***be stuck in***) ***a ~*** 成习惯 chéng xíguàn. □ *vt* 作槽于 zuò cáo yú: *a ~d shelf* 有槽的架子.

grope /grəʊp/ *vt/i* 暗中摸索 ànzhōng mōsuǒ.

gross[1] /grəʊs/ *n* [C] [*pl* ~] (商业用语)罗〔羅〕luó(=144).

gross[2] /grəʊs/ *adj* **1** 粗俗的 cūsúde, 粗野的 cūyěde, 粗的 cūde. **2** 显〔顯〕著的 xiǎnzhùde: *~ injustice* 显著的不公. **3** (草木) 茂密的 màomìde. **4** (人)过〔過〕胖的 guòpàngde. **5** (与*net* "净" 相反) 总〔總〕的 zǒngde, 毛的 máode: *his ~ income* 他的总收入. □ *vt* 计得(毛收入) jìdé: *~ five million pounds* 毛收入五百万英镑. **~ly** *adv* **~ness** *n* [U]

gro·tesque /grəʊ'tesk/ *adj* **1** 奇形怪状〔狀〕的 qíxíng-guàizhuàngde, 奇异〔異〕的 qíyìde. **2** (艺术) 风〔風〕格奇异的 fēnggé qíyì de. □ *n*[C] 奇形怪状的人, 动物, 图〔圖〕形 qíxíng-guàizhuàng de rén, dòngwù, túxíng. **~ly** *adv*

grotto /'grɒtəʊ/ *n* [*pl* ~es 或 ~s] 洞 dòng, 穴 xuè.

ground[1] /graʊnd/ *n* **1** [*sing* 与 *the* 连用] 地面 dìmiàn. ***get off the ~*** **(a)** (飞机) 起飞〔飛〕qǐfēi. **(b)** 〔喻〕开〔開〕始 kāishǐ. **2** [U] 地面上的区〔區〕域, 距离〔離〕dìmiàn shàng de qūyù, jùlí. ***cover*** (***much, etc***) ***~*** **(a)** 旅行 (很长路程) lǚxíng. **(b)** 〔喻〕(演说, 调查等) 范〔範〕围〔圍〕很广〔廣〕fànwéi hěnguǎng. ***gain ~*** 发〔發〕展 fāzhǎn, 进〔進〕展 jìnzhǎn. ***give*** (或 ***lose***) ***~*** 退却 tuìquè, 失利 shīlì. ***hold*** (或 ***stand, keep***) ***one's ~*** 坚〔堅〕守阵地 jiānshǒu zhèndì, 坚持立场〔場〕jiānchí lìchǎng. ***common ~*** 共同点〔點〕gòngtóngdiǎn. **3** [U] 泥土 nítǔ. **4** [C] 场地 chǎngdì: *a 'football ~* 足球场 **5** [*pl*] 场地 chǎngdì, 庭园〔園〕tíngyuán: *The Palace ~s* 皇宫庭园. **6** [*pl*] 渣滓 zhāzi, 沉积〔積〕物 chénjīwù: *'coffee-~s* 咖啡渣. **7** (*pl* 或 [U]) 根据〔據〕gēnjù, 理由 lǐyóu: *~s for divorce* 离婚的理由. **~con'trol** *n* (航空) 地面控制(站, 设备) dìmiàn kòngzhì. **,~'floor** 楼房的底层〔層〕lóufángde dǐcéng. **'~-sheet** 铺〔鋪〕在地上的防潮布 pū zài dìshàng de fángcháobù. **'~-work** [常作喻]基础〔礎〕工作 jīchǔ gōngzuò. **~less** *adj* 无〔無〕理由的 wúlǐyóude, 无根据的 wúgēnjùde: *a ~less accusation* 无根据的控告.

ground[2] /graʊnd/ *vt/i* **1** (使) 船搁〔擱〕浅〔淺〕chuán gēqiǎn. **2** 使(飞机)停飞〔飛〕shǐ tíngfēi. **3** 给…基础〔礎〕训练 gěi … jīchǔ xùnliàn. **~ing** 基础训练〔練〕jīchǔ xùnliàn.

ground[3] /graʊnd/ *pt, pp* of grind.

group /gru:p/ *n* [C] 群 qún, 批 pī. □ *vt/i* 把…分组 bǎ … fēnzǔ.

grouse[1] /graʊs/ *n* [C] [*pl* ~] 松鸡〔鷄〕sōngjī.
grouse[2] /graʊs/ *vi* [非正式用语]埋怨 mányuàn, 发〔發〕牢骚〔騷〕fā láosāo. □ *n* [C] 牢骚 láosāo.
grove /grəʊv/ *n* [C] 树〔樹〕丛〔叢〕shùcōng, 小树林 xiǎoshùlín.
grovel /'grɒvl/ *vi* [-ll-; 美语亦作 -l-] **1** 匍匐作乞怜〔憐〕状〔狀〕púfú zuò qǐliánzhuàng. **2** [喻] 卑躬屈节〔節〕bēigōng-qūjié. ~**ler** 卑躬屈节的人 bēigōng-qūjiéde rén.
grow /grəʊ/ *vt/i* [*pt* grew /gru:/; *pp* ~n /grəʊn/] **1** 发〔發〕展 fāzhǎn, 增长〔長〕zēngzhǎng. ~ *out of* **(a)** 大得与〔與〕…不相称〔稱〕dàde yǔ … bù xiāngchèn. **(b)** 长大得不宜… zhǎngdàde bùyí: ~ *out of playing with toys.* 长大了，不玩玩具了. **(c)** 来〔來〕自 láizì, 产〔產〕生自 chǎnshēngzì: *His troubles grew out of his bad temper.* 他的麻烦来自脾气暴躁. ~ *up* **(a)** (人,动物)成熟 chéngshú, 成年 chéngnián. **(b)** 发展 fāzhǎn: *A warm friendship grew up between them.* 他们之间发展起了亲密的友谊. **2** 变〔變〕得 biàndé, 成为〔爲〕chéngwéi: ~ *older* 变老. **3** 种〔種〕植 zhòngzhí: ~ *roses* 种植玫瑰. **4** ~ *on* 引起…的爱好 yǐnqǐ…de àihào: *The new house will* ~ *on you.* 这所新屋子将引起你的爱好. '~**n-up** 成人 chéngrén.
growl /graʊl/ *vt/i* **1** (动物) 嗥叫 háojiào, (雷)轰〔轟〕鸣〔鳴〕hōngmíng: *The dog* ~*ed at the burglars* 那狗向小偷汪汪直叫. **2** 咆哮着说 páoxiàozhe shuō. □ *n* [C]咆哮声〔聲〕páoxiàoshēng, 轰鸣声 hōngmíngshēng: *a* ~ *of anger* 愤怒的咆哮.
grown /grəʊn/ *pp* of grow.
growth /grəʊθ/ *n* **1** [U] 生长〔長〕shēngzhǎng; 发〔發〕展 fāzhǎn. **2** [U] 种〔種〕植 zhòngzhí, 栽培 zāipéi. **3** [C] 生长物 shēngzhǎngwù: *a new* ~ *of beard* 新长出的胡须. **4** [C] [医学]瘤 liú.
grub[1] /grʌb/ *n* **1** [C] (动物) 蛴〔蠐〕螬 qícáo. **2** [U] [俚语] 食物 shíwù.
grub[2] /grʌb/ *vt/i* [-bb-] ~ **(*about*)** 掘地(掘出某物) juédì.
grubby /'grʌbɪ/ *adj* [-ier, -iest] 污秽〔穢〕的 wūhuìde.
grudge /grʌdʒ/ *vt* 吝惜 lìnxī, 不愿〔願〕给 búyuàngěi: *I* ~ *paying for water.* 我不愿付水钱. □ *n* [C] 恶〔惡〕意 èyì, 怨恨 yuànhèn, 忌妒 jìdù. **grudg·ingly** *adv*
grue·some /'gru:səm/ *adj* 可怕的 kěpàde; 讨厌〔厭〕的 tǎoyànde, ~**ly** *adv*
gruff /grʌf/ *adj* 粗暴的 cūbàode, 不友好的 bùyǒuhǎode. ~**ly** *adv*
grumble /'grʌmbl/ *vi* **1** 埋怨 mányuàn. 发〔發〕牢骚〔騷〕fāláosāo. **2** 咕哝〔噥〕gūnong; 隆隆响〔響〕lónglóngxiǎng. □ *n* [C] 埋怨 mányuàn.
grumpy /'grʌmpɪ/ *adj* [-ier, -iest] 脾气〔氣〕坏〔壞〕的 píqi huài de. **grump·ily** *adv* **grumpi·ness** *n* [U]
grunt /grʌnt/ *vt/i* **1** (猪等) 作呼噜声〔聲〕zuò hūlū shēng. **2** (人) 发〔發〕哼哼声 fā hēnghēng shēng. □*n* [C] (猪等)呼噜声 hūlū shēng, 哼哼声 hēnghēng shēng.
guar·an·tee /ˌgærən'ti:/ *n* [C] **1** 保证〔證〕bǎozhèng. **2** 担〔擔〕保 dānbǎo. **3** (法律 = **guarantor**) 保证人 bǎozhèngrén. **4** 担保物 dānbǎowù. □ *vt* **1** 保证 bǎozhèng, 担保 dānbǎo. **2** [非正式用语] 管保 guǎnbǎo, 包 bāo: ~ *satisfaction* 管保满意.
guar·an·tor /ˌgærən'tɔ:(r)/ *n* ⇨ guarantee(3).
guard /gɑ:d/ *n* **1** [U] 警惕 jǐngtì, 警戒 jǐngjiè: *on* ~警惕, 警戒. **2** [C] 卫〔衛〕兵 wèibīng, 哨兵 shàobīng. **3** [英国英语] 列车〔車〕员 lièchēyuán. **4** [C] 警卫员 jǐngwèiyuán: *the* ~ *of honour* 仪仗队. **5** (监狱)看守 kānshǒu. **6** (用于复合词)防护〔護〕器 fánghùqì. *a 'mud*~ 挡泥板 (自行车). □ *vt/i* **1** 保护 bǎohù. **2** 看守 kānshǒu, 监〔監〕视 jiānshì. **3** 防止 fángzhǐ, 防范〔範〕fángfàn: ~ *against disease* 防病. ~**ed** *adj* 小心谨慎的 xiǎoxīn jǐnshèn de.
guard·ian /'gɑ:dɪən/ *n* [C] 保护〔護〕人 bǎohùrén, 监〔監〕护人 jiānhùrén. ~**ship** 监护人的职责 jiānhùrénde zhízé.
guer·rilla, guer·illa /gə'rɪlə/ *n* [C] [*pl* ~s] 游击〔擊〕队〔隊〕员 yóujīduìyuán. ~ '**war** 游击战〔戰〕yóujīzhàn.
guess /ges/ *vt/i* 猜想 cāixiǎng, 推测 tuīcè. □ *n* [C] 猜测 cāicè, 推测 tuīcè. '~**work** 猜测 cāicè, 推测 tuīcè.
guest /gest/ *n* [C] 客人 kèren, 宾〔賓〕客 bīnkè. '~**house** 宾馆〔館〕bīnguǎn, 高等寄宿舍 gāoděng jìsùshè.
guid·ance /'gaɪdns/ *n* [U] **1** 指导〔導〕zhǐdǎo, 指引 zhǐyǐn. **2** 忠告 zhōnggào.
guide /gaɪd/ *n* [C] **1** 领路人

lǐnglùrén, 响〔響〕导〔導〕xiǎngdǎo: *a tourist* ～导游. **2** 影响行为〔爲〕之物 yǐngxiǎng xíng wéi zhī wù; 指南 zhǐnán: *Experience is my* ～. 经验是我行为的指南. **3** (亦作 '～-**book**) 指南 zhǐnán. **4** 手册 shǒucè, 入门〔門〕书〔書〕rùménshū: *a* ～ *to growing roses* 种植玫瑰的入门书. □ *vt* 为…领路 wèi ... lǐnglù, 指引 zhǐyǐn. ˌ～**d** '**missile** 导弹〔彈〕dǎodàn.

guild /gɪld/ *n* [C] 行会〔會〕hánghuì, 同业〔業〕公会 tóngyè gōnghuì.

guile /gaɪl/ *n* [U] 诡计 guǐjì.

guillo·tine /ˌgɪlə'tiːn/ *n* [C] **1** 断〔斷〕头〔頭〕台〔臺〕duàntóutái. **2** (切纸用)闸〔閘〕刀 zhádāo. □ *vt* 在断头台上斩〔斬〕首 zài duàntóutái shàng zhǎnshǒu; 切开〔開〕qiēkāi

guilt /gɪlt/ *n* [U] 内疚 nèijiù; 罪责 zuìzé. ～**ily** *adv* **guilty** *adj* [-ier, -iest] **(a)** 有罪的 yǒuzuìde. **(b)** 内疚的 nèijiùde, 自觉〔覺〕有罪的 zìjué yǒuzuì de.

guinea /'gɪnɪ/ *n* [C] (略作 **gns**) [过时用法] 二十一先令 èrshíyī xiānlìng.

guinea-pig /'gɪnɪ pɪg/ *n* [C] **1** [动物]豚鼠 túnshǔ. **2** 供试验〔驗〕用的人 gòng shìyàn yòng de rén.

guitar /gɪ'tɑː(r)/ *n* [C] [音乐] 六弦琴 liùxiánqín, 吉他 jítā. ～**ist** *n* [C]

gulf /gʌlf/ *n* **1** 海湾〔灣〕hǎiwān: *the G*～ *of Mexico* 墨西哥湾. **2** 深坑 shēnkēng, 深渊〔淵〕shēnyuān. **3** [喻] 深刻的分歧 shēnkède fēnqí.

gull[1] /gʌl/ *n* [C] 鸥〔鷗〕ōu.

gull[2] /gʌl/ *vt* 欺骗〔騙〕qīpiàn: ～ *a fool out of his money* 骗傻子的钱. ～**ible** *adj* 容易受骗的 róngyì shòupiàn de.

gul·let /'gʌlɪt/ *n* [C] 咽喉 yānhóu.

gulp /gʌlp/ *vt/i* **1** 吞食 tūnshí. **2** 忍住 rěnzhù, 抑制 yìzhì: ～ *back tears* 忍住不流泪. □ *n* [C] 吞食 tūnshí, 一口吞咽〔嚥〕量 yìkǒu tūn yànliàng.

gum[1] /gʌm/ *n* [C] 牙床 yáchuáng, 齿〔齒〕龈 chǐyín.

gum[2] /gʌm/ *n* **1** [U] 树〔樹〕胶〔膠〕shùjiāo. **2** [U] 口香糖 kǒuxiāngtáng, 橡皮糖 xiàngpítáng: '*chewing*-～ 口香糖. **3** *up a* ～-*tree* [俚语]骑〔騎〕虎难〔難〕下 qíhǔnánxià. □ *vt* [-mm-] 黏合 niánhé, 涂〔塗〕树胶 tú shùjiāo. '～ **boots** 胶靴 jiāoxuē. ～**my** *adj* [-ier, -iest] 黏性的 niánxìngde.

gun /gʌn/ *n* [C] 炮 pào; 枪〔槍〕qiāng. *go great* ～*s* 获〔獲〕得很大成功 huòdé hěndà chénggōng. *stick to one's* ～*s* 固执〔執〕己见 gùzhí jǐjiàn. □ *vt* ～ *sb* (*down*) 向…开〔開〕枪 xiàng ... kāiqiāng. '～**boat** 炮艇 pàotǐng. '～-**carriage** 炮架 pàojià. '～**dog** 猎〔獵〕犬 lièquǎn. '～**man** 持枪歹徒 chíqiāng dǎitú. '～**powder** 炸药 zhàyào. '～-**running** 军〔軍〕火走私 jūnhuǒ zǒusī. '～**smith** 军器工人 jūnqì gōngrén. ～**ner** *n* [C] **(a)** 陆军炮兵 lùjūn pàobīng. **(b)** 海军炮兵长〔長〕官 hǎijūn pàobīng zhǎngguān. ～**nery** 炮术〔術〕pàoshù.

gurgle /'gɜːgl/ *n* [C, U] (流水) 汩汩声〔聲〕gǔgǔshēng. □ *vi* 汩汩地流 gǔgǔde liú.

gush /gʌʃ/ *vi* **1** 涌〔湧〕出 yǒngchū, 喷出 pēnchū: *blood* ～*ing from a wound* 伤口涌出的血. **2** 滔滔不绝地说 tāotāobùjuéde shuō. □ *n* [C] 迸发〔發〕bèngfā. ～**ing** *adj*

gust /gʌst/ *n* [C] **1** 阵〔陣〕风〔風〕zhènfēng. **2** [喻] (感情的) 迸发〔發〕bèngfā. **gusty** *adj* [-ier, -iest] 起大风的 qǐ dàfēng de.

gut /gʌt/ *n* [C] **1** [*pl*] 内脏〔臟〕nèizàng. *hate sb's* ～*s* [俚语] 恨之入骨 hèn zhī rù gǔ. **2** [*pl*] [非正式用语]勇气〔氣〕yǒngqì, 毅力 yìlì. **3** [U] 肠〔腸〕线〔線〕chángxiàn. ⇨ catgut. **4** [*pl*] [非正式用语]主要部分 zhǔyào bùfen: *the* ～*s of an engine* 引擎的主要部分. □ *vt* [-tt-] **1** 取出 (鱼等) 内脏 qǔchū nèizàng. **2** 损毁内部装〔裝〕置 sǔnhuǐ nèibù zhuāngzhì: *a house* ～*ted by fire* 被烧毁了内部装置的房子.

gut·ter /'gʌtə(r)/ *n* [C] **1** 檐槽 yáncáo. **2** [喻] 贫民区〔區〕pínmínqū: *born in the* ～ 出生在贫民区.

guy[1] /gaɪ/ *n* [C] 牵索 qiānsuǒ; 稳索 wěnsuǒ.

guy[2] /gaɪ/ *n* [C] **1** 衣着古怪的人 yīzhāo gǔguài de rén. **2** [俚语]人 rén, 家伙 jiāhuo.

guzzle /'gʌzl/ *vt/i* [非正式用语]大吃大喝 dàchīdàhē.

gym /dʒɪm/ *n* [C] [俚语]体〔體〕育馆〔館〕tǐyùguǎn; 体操 tǐcāo. '～-**shoes** = plimsolls.

gym·khana /dʒɪm'kɑːnə/ *n* [C] [*pl* ～s] 运〔運〕动〔動〕会〔會〕yùndònghuì.

gym·nasium /dʒɪm'neɪzɪəm/ *n* [C] [*pl* ～s]体〔體〕育馆 tǐyùguǎn.

gym·nast /'dʒɪmnæst/ *n* [C]体〔體〕操家 tǐcāojiā.

gym·nas·tic /dʒɪmˈnæstɪk/ *adj* 体〔體〕操的 tǐcāode, 体育的 tǐyùde. **gym·nastics** *n pl* 体操 tǐcāo; 体育 tǐyù.

gynae·col·ogy 〔美语＝ **gyne-**〕/gaɪnɪˈkɒlədʒɪ/ *n* [C] 妇〔婦〕科学〔學〕fùkēxué. **gynae·colo·gist** *n* [C] 妇科医〔醫〕生 fùkē yīshēng.

gypsy /ˈdʒɪpsɪ/ *n* [C] = gipsy.

gyro·com·pass/ˈdʒaɪrəʊkʌmpəs/ *n* [C] (略作 ***gyro***) 陀螺罗〔羅〕盘〔盤〕tuóluó luópán

gyro·scope /ˈdʒaɪrəskəʊp/ *n* [C] (略作 **gyro**) 陀螺仪〔儀〕tuóluóyí **gyro·scopic** /ˌdʒaɪrəˈskɒpɪk/ *adj*

gyro·sta·bi·lizer /ˌdʒaɪrəʊˈsteɪbɪlaɪzə(r)/ *n* [C] 陀螺安定器 tuóluó āndìngqì 回转〔轉〕稳定器 huízhuǎn wěndìngqì.

H h

H, h /eɪtʃ/ [*pl* H's, h's /ˈeɪtʃɪz/] 英语的第八个〔個〕字母 yīngyǔde dìbāgè zìmǔ.

ha·= hectare(s)

hab·er·dasher /ˈhæbədæʃə(r)/ *n* [C] 零星服饰针线〔綫〕商 língxīng fúshì zhēnxiàn shāng. **hab·er·dash·ery** *n* [U] 零星服饰针线业〔業〕língxīng fúshì zhēnxiàn yè; 零星服饰针线 língxīng fúshì zhēnxiàn.

habit /ˈhæbɪt/ *n* **1** [C, U] 习〔習〕惯 xíguàn, 习性 xíxìng. ***fall*** (或 ***get***) ***into bad ~s*** 沾染坏〔壞〕习性 zhānrǎn huài xíxìng. ***get out of a ~*** 戒除习性 jièchú xíxìng. **2** [C] 表示宗教级别的衣着 biǎoshì zōngjiào jíbié de yīzhuó.

hab·it·able /ˈhæbɪtəbl/ *adj* 可居住的 kě jūzhù de.

ha·bit·ual /həˈbɪtʃʊəl/ *adj* **1** 惯常的 guànchángde, 通常的 tōngchángde. **2** 习〔習〕惯的 xíguànde: *an ~ liar* 惯于说谎的人. **~ly** /-tʃʊəlɪ/ *adv* 习惯地 xíguànde.

h.c.= hot water and cold water.

hack[1] /hæk/ *vt/i* 劈 pī, 砍 kǎn. **ˈ~-saw** 钢〔鋼〕锯 gāngjù, 弓锯 gōngjù.

hack[2] /hæk/ *n* [C] **1** 出租的马〔馬〕匹 chūzūde mǎpǐ. **2** 雇佣文人 gùyōng wénrén.

hack·neyed /ˈhækni:d/ *adj* 陈腐的 chénfǔde.

had /hæd/ *pt, pp* of have.

had·dock /ˈhædək/ *n* [C] [*pl* ~] 黑线〔綫〕鳕 hēixiànxuě.

hæm·or·rhage /ˈhemərɪdʒ/ *n* = hemorrhage.

hag /hæg/ *n* [C] 女巫 nǚwū, 丑〔醜〕老妇〔婦〕chǒulǎofù.

hag·gard /ˈhægəd/ *adj* 憔悴的 qiáocuìde, 枯槁的 gūgǎode.

hag·gis /ˈhægɪs/ *n* [C, U] (苏格兰食品)一种羊肉杂〔雜〕碎布丁 yìzhǒng yángròu zásuì bùdīng.

haggle /ˈhægl/ *vi* ~ (***over*** 或 ***about***) 讨价〔價〕还〔還〕价 tǎojià huánjià.

hail[1] /heɪl/ *n* **1** [U] 冰雹 bīngbáo, 雹子 báozi. **2** (冰雹般)一阵〔陣〕yízhèn: *a ~ of blows* 一阵打击. □ *vt/i* **1** 下冰雹 xià bīngbáo. **2** (冰雹般)落下 luòxià **ˈ~stone** 冰雹 bīngbáo, 雹子 báozi. **ˈ~-storm** 雹暴 báobào.

hail[2] /heɪl/ *vt/i* 致敬 zhìjìng, 向…打招呼 xiàng...dǎ zhāohu.

hair /heə(r)/ *n* **1** [U] 头〔頭〕发〔髮〕tóufa; 毛 máo. ***let one's ˈ~ down*** 〔喻〕轻〔輕〕松〔鬆〕随便下来〔來〕qīngsōng suíbiàn xiàlái. ***make one's ˈ~ stand on end*** 使某人毛骨悚然 shǐ mǒurén máogǔ sǒngrán. **2** [C] 一根头发 yìgēn tóufa; 一根毛 yìgēn máo. ***split ~s*** 作繁琐的区〔區〕分 zuò fánsuǒde qūfēn. **ˈ~('s) -breadth** 一发之差 yífà zhīchā, 极细微的距离〔離〕jí xìwēide jùlí. **ˈ~-do** [非正式用语]女发式 nǚfàshì. **ˈ~dresser** 理发(女发)师〔師〕lǐfàshī. ⇨ barber. **ˈ~line (a)** 头部生发部分的轮〔輪〕廓 tóubù shēngfà bùfen de lúnkuò. **(b)** 细缝 xìfèng: *a ~line fracture* 细微的裂缝. **ˈ~pin** 发夹〔夾〕fàjiā, 发卡 fàqiǎ. **ˌ~pin ˈbend** (道路)急转〔轉〕弯〔彎〕jízhuǎnwān. **ˈ~-raising** *adj* 恐怖的 kǒngbùde. **hairy** *adj* [-ier, -iest] 毛的 máode, 毛状〔狀〕的 máozhuàngde, 长〔長〕毛的 zhǎng máo de.

hale /heɪl/ *adj* 〔只用于〕 ~ ***and hearty*** 矍铄〔鑠〕juéshuò, 健壮〔壯〕jiànzhuàng.

half /hɑ:f/ *n* [*pl* halves /hɑ:vz/] *adj, adv* **1** 一半 yíbàn, 一半的 yíbànde. ***go halves (with sb)*** (与某人)平分 píngfēn. **2** 部分地 bùfende, 一半地 yíbànde: ~ *cooked* 半熟. **~-ˈdead** [非正式用语]筋疲力竭的. jīnpílìjiéde, **ˌ~-ˈbaked** *adj* [非正式用语]肤〔膚〕浅〔淺〕的

fūqiǎnde: *a ~-baked idea* 肤浅的想法. **'~-breed** 混血的 hùnxuěde, 杂[雜]种[種]的 zázhǒngde. **'~-caste** 混血儿[兒] hùnxuě'ér. **,~-'hearted** *adj* 不认[認]真的 bú rènzhēn de, 半心半意的 bànxīn bànyì de. **,~-'mast,** *at ~-mast* (表示哀悼)半旗 bànqí **,~-'way** *adv* 半途 bàntú. **,~-'witted** *adj* 低能的 dīnéngde, 笨的 bènde. **'~-wit** *n* [C]

hall /hɔːl/ *n* [C] **1** 礼[禮]堂 lǐtáng, 会[會]堂 huìtáng, 大厅[廳] dàtīng. **2** 食堂 shítáng. **3** 大学[學]生宿舍 dàxuéshēng sùshè: *a ~ of residence* 大学宿舍. **4**(英国)地主庄园 dìzhǔ zhuāngyuán. **5** 门[門]厅 méntīng. **'~-mark** *n* [C] **(a)** 金银纯度标[標]记 jīnyín chúndù biāojì. **(b)** 质[質]量标记 zhìliàng biāojì. □ *vt* 加金银纯度标记于 jiā jīnyín chúndù biāojì yú.

hal·le·lu·jah /ˌhælɪ'luːjə/ *n* [C], *int* 哈利路亚[亞](犹太教和基督教欢呼语,意为"赞美神") hālìlùyǎ.

hallo /hə'ləʊ/ *int, n* [C] 喂! wèi! 你好! (打招呼) nǐhǎo!

Hal·low·e'en /ˌhæləʊ'iːn/ 十月三十一日(万圣节前夕) shíyuè sānshíyīrì.

hal·luci·na·tion /həˌluːsɪ'neɪʃn/ *n* [C, U] 幻觉[覺] huànjué, 幻觉中的事物 huànjué zhōng de shìwù.

halo /'heɪləʊ/ *n* [C] [*pl* ~es, 或 ~s] **1** (日,月)晕[暈] yūn. **2**(绘于神象头上的)光环[環] guānghuán.

halt¹ /hɔːlt/ *n* [C] **1** *call a ~ (to)* **(a)** (途中)暂[暫]停 zhàntíng. **(b)** [喻]命令停止 mìnglìng tíngzhǐ. **2** 停止 tíngzhǐ. □ *vt/i* **1** (使)停止前进[進] tíngzhǐ qiánjìn. **2** 终止 zhōngzhǐ.

halt² /hɔːlt/ *vi* 犹[猶]豫 yóuyù, 踌[躊]躇 chóuchú: *a ~ing voice* 犹豫的声音. **~ing·ly** *adv*

hal·ter /'hɔːltə(r)/ *n* [C] (马)笼[籠]头[頭] lóngtóu; 缰绳[繩] jiāngshéng.

halve /hɑːv/ *vt* **1** 把…等分为[為]两半 bǎ…děngfēn wéi liǎngbàn. **2** 减少一半 jiǎnshǎo yíbàn: *~ your speed* 把你的速度减半.

halves /hɑːv/*n pl* of half.

ham /hæm/ *n* **1** [C U] 火腿 huǒtuǐ. **2** [C][俚语]拙劣的演员zhuóliède yǎnyuán. **3** [C] 业[業]余[餘]无[無]线[線]电[電]爱[愛]好者 yèyú wúxiàndiàn àihàozhě. □ *vt/i* [-mm-] [非正式用语]过[過]火地表演某一角色 guòhuǒde biǎoyǎn mǒuyì juésè. **,~-'fisted** *adj* 笨手笨脚地 bènshǒubènjiǎode.

ham·burger /'hæmbɜːgə(r)/ *n* [C] **1** 牛肉饼 niúròubǐng. **2** 面[麵]包片夹[夾]牛肉饼 miànbāopiān jiā niúròubǐng, 汉[漢]堡包 hànbǎobāo.

ham·let /'hæmlɪt/ *n* [C] 小村庄 xiǎocūnzhuāng.

ham·mer /'hæmə(r)/ *n* [C] **1** 锤 chuí, 榔头[頭] lángtou. **2** (钢琴)音锤 yīnchuí; (枪支)击[擊]铁[鐵] jītiě. □ *vt/i* **1** 锤击 chuíjī, 锤打 chuídǎ. **2** [喻]致力于 zhìlìyú, 埋头于 máitóuyú: *~ away at a problem* 苦苦研究一个问题. **3** [喻]强迫 qiǎngpò: *~ an idea into his head* 迫使他接受一种观念. **4** [非正式用语]使惨[慘]败 shǐ cǎnbài.

ham·mock /'hæmək/ *n* [C] 吊床 diàochuáng.

ham·per¹ /'hæmpə(r)/ *n* [C] (装送食品用)有盖篮[籃]子 yǒu gài lánzi.

ham·per² /'hæmpə(r)/ *vt* 阻碍 zǔ'ài, 妨碍 fáng'ài, 牵制 qiānzhì: *~ed by his broken leg* 被他的断腿牵制.

ham·ster /'hæmstə(r)/ *n* [C] 仓[倉]鼠 cāngshǔ.

hand¹ /hænd/ *n* [C] **1** 手 shǒu, *at* (或 *to*)*~* 在手边[邊] zài shǒubiān, 在手头[頭] zài shǒutóu, 在附近 zài fùjìn. *by ~* **(a)** 用手 yòng shǒu, 用手工制[製]作 yòng shǒugōng zhìzuò. **(b)** 专[專]人(递送) zhuānrén: *deliver a letter by ~* 由专人递送一封信. *in ~* **(a)** 可以动[動]用的 kěyǐ dòngyòng de: *have money in ~* 有可动用的钱. **(b)** 在处[處]理中 zài chùlǐ zhōng: *The work is in ~.* 这项工作正在处理中. *~ in ~* **(a)** 手拉手 shǒu lā shǒu. **(b)** 合作 hézuò. *in the ~s of* 由…照管 yóu…zhàoguǎn. *off one's ~s* 已不由某人负责 yǐ bù yóu mǒurén fùzé. *on one's ~s* 由某人负责 yóu mǒurén fùzé. *on ~* 手头[頭]现有 shǒutóu xiànyǒu. *out of ~* 失去控制 shīqù kòngzhì. *give* (或 *lend*) *a ~* 帮助 bāngzhù. *have* (或 *give*)*sb a free ~* ⇨ free(4). *have one's ~s full* 工作很忙 gōngzuò hěnmáng. *have* (或 *get*) *the upper ~* 取得优[優]势[勢] qǔdé yōushì, 占上风[風] zhàn shàngfēng. *live from ~ to mouth* 做一天吃一天 zuò yìtiān chī yìtiān. *wash one's ~s of* 不再管某事 búzài guǎn mǒushì. **2**

[*pl*] 掌握 zhǎngwò, 责任 zérèn. *change* ~*s* 易主 yìzhǔ. **3** *play into sb's* ~*s* 干对〔對〕某人有利的事 gàn duì mǒurén yǒulìde shì. **4** *try one's* ~ *at* 试做 shì zuò. **5** *an old* ~ *at* 在…方面是老手 zài...fāngmiàn shì lǎoshǒu. **6** 人手(工人) rénshǒu, 雇员(船工等) gùyuán. **7** (钟,表)指针 zhǐzhēn: *the hour* ~ 时针. **8** *on the ˌone* ~ *... the 'other* ~ |一方面…另一方面… yìfāngmiàn...lìngyìfāngmiàn .... **9** [只用 *sing*]手迹 shǒujì, 字迹 zìjì: *a legible* ~ 清楚的字迹. **10** (牌戏)一手牌 yìshǒupái, 手中牌 shǒuzhōngpái. **11** [C] (马等的量度)一手之宽 yìshǒu zhī kuān. **12** [非正式用语]鼓掌 gǔzhǎng: *give him a big* ~ 向他鼓掌. **'~bag** 女用手提包 nǚyòng shǒutíbāo. **'~brake** 手闸〔閘〕 shǒuzhá. **'~cuffs** *n* [C] 手梏 shǒugù. ☐ *vt* 使戴上手梏 shǐ dàishàng shǒugù. **~ful** **(a)** 一把 yìbǎ. **(b)** 一小撮 yìxiǎocuō, 少数〔數〕 shǎoshù: *a ~ful of people* 少数人. **(c)** [非正式用语]难〔難〕控制的人或动〔動〕物 nán kòngzhì de rén huò dòngwù. **ˌ~-'picked** *adj* 精选〔選〕的 jīngxuǎnde. **'~writing** 手书〔書〕 shǒushū, 手迹 shǒujì, 字迹 zìjì.

hand² /hænd/ *vt* 传〔傳〕递〔遞〕 chuándì, 交 jiāo, 给 gěi, 用手帮助 yòng shǒu bāngzhù: *H~ me that knife please.* 请把那把小刀递给我. ~ *sth down* (*to sb*) (作为传统)传〔傳〕下 chuánxià. ~ *sth on* (*to sb*) 传给 chuángěi. ~ *sth out* 分发〔發〕 fēnfā. ~ *sth over* (*to sb*) 移交 yíjiāo, 交出 jiāochū. **'~out** **(a)** (免费分发的)传〔傳〕单〔單〕, 广〔廣〕告单等 chuándān, guǎnggàodān děng. **(b)** 施舍物 shīshěwù, 救济〔濟〕品 jiùjìpǐn. ~ *sb over* 把某人送交当〔當〕局 bǎ mǒurén sòngjiāo dāngjú.

handi·cap /'hændɪkæp/ *n* [C] **1** 给予优〔優〕者的不利条〔條〕件以使竞〔競〕赛机〔機〕会相等 gěiyǔ yōuzhěde búlì tiáojiàn yǐ shǐ jìngsài jīhuì xiāngděng, 让〔讓〕分竞赛 ràngfēn jìngsài. **2** 障碍 zhàng'ài, 不利条件 búlì tiáojiàn. **3** 残〔殘〕废〔廢〕 cánfèi. ☐ *vt* [-pp-] 妨碍 fáng'ài.

handi·craft /'hændɪkrɑ:ft/ *n* [C] 手工业〔業〕 shǒugōngyè, 手艺〔藝〕 shǒuyì.

handi·work /'hændɪwɜ:k/ *n* **1** [C, U] 手工 shǒugōng, 手工制〔製〕品 shǒugōng zhìpǐn. **2** [C] 所做事物 suǒzuò shìwù: *This is your* ~. 这是你的所为.

hand·ker·chief /'hæŋkətʃɪf/ *n* [C] 手帕 shǒupà.

handle /'hændl/ *n* [C] 把手 bǎshǒu, 柄 bǐng. *fly off the* ~ [非正式用语]勃然大怒 bórán dànù. ☐ *vt* **1** 摸 mō, 触〔觸〕 chù, 弄 nòng: *Wash your hands before you* ~ *food.* 先洗手再弄食物. **2** 处〔處〕理 chùlǐ, 管理 guǎnlǐ: ~ *a situation* 对付局势. **3** 对待 duìdài: *roughly* ~*d* 粗暴对待. **'~bar** [常用 *pl*] (自行车等)把手 bǎshǒu. **handler** 管理者 guǎnlǐzhě, 训练者 xùnliànzhě.

hand·some /'hænsəm/ *adj* **1** 漂亮的 piàoliangde, 清秀的 qīngxiùde. **2** 慷慨的 kāngkǎide, 大方的 dàfangde. **~ly** *adv* 慷慨地 kāngkǎide, 大方地 dàfangde: *~ly paid* 收到优厚的报酬.

handy /'hændɪ/ *adj* [-ier, -iest] **1** (人)手灵〔靈〕巧的 shǒu língqiǎo de. **2** (物品)使用方便的 shǐyòng fāngbiàn de, *come in* ~ 迟早有用 chízǎo yǒuyòng. **3** 手边〔邊〕的 shǒubiānde, 近便的 jìnbiànde: *Always keep a first-aid kit* ~. 手边经常有一个急救箱. **~man** 善于做零碎修理活的人 shànyúzuò língsuì xiūlǐhuó de rén. **hand·ily** *adv*

hang¹ /hæŋ/ *n get the* ~ *of sth* 得知某事物的诀窍〔竅〕 dézhī mǒushìwù de juéqiào.

hang² /hæŋ/ *vt/i* [*pt, pp* hung /hʌŋ/ 或下列第二义项, ~ed] **1** 挂〔掛〕 guà, 悬〔懸〕挂 xuánguà. **2** [*pt, pp* ~ed] 吊死 diàosǐ, 绞死 jiǎosǐ. **3** 贴 tiē, 糊 hú: ~ *wallpaper* 糊墙纸. **4** 把肉等挂起来(晾晒)至可以食用 bǎ ròu děng guà qǐlái zhì kěyǐ shíyòng. **5** ~ *about* (或*round, around*) 闲〔閑〕荡〔蕩〕 xiándàng. ~ *back* 畏缩 wèisuō, 犹〔猶〕豫 yóuyù. ~ *on* **(a)** 紧〔緊〕握 jǐnwò. **(b)** [非正式用语] 等待 děngdài. ~ *up* 挂断〔斷〕电〔電〕话 guàduàn diànhuà. *be hung up* [非正式用语] 陷入困境 xiànrù kùnjìng. **~man** 执〔執〕行绞刑者 zhíxíng jiǎoxíngzhě. **'~over** 宿醉 sùzuì. **'~-up** (感情上的)大难〔難〕题 dànántí.

han·gar /'hæŋə(r)/ *n* [C] 飞〔飛〕机〔機〕库 fēijīkù.

hang·er /'hæŋə(r)/ *n* [C] 挂〔掛〕钩 guàgōu: *a 'coat-*~ 衣架. **ˌ~-'on**, [*pl* ~s-on] 为〔為〕讨便宜而与〔與〕人交好者 wèi tǎo piányì ér yǔ rén jiāohǎo zhě, 食客 shíkè.

han·ker /'hæŋkə(r)/ *vi* ~ *for* (或 *after*) 渴望 kěwàng. ~**ing** *n* [C]

hanky /'hæŋkɪ/ *n* [C] [*pl*-ies] [非正式用语] = handkerchief.

hap·haz·ard /hæp'hæzəd/ *adj,adv* 杂[雜]乱[亂]的 záluànde, 任意的 rènyìde, 杂乱地 záluànde; 任意地 rènyìde.

hap·pen /'hæpən/ *vi* **1** 发[發]生 fāshēng: *What ~s now?* 现在发生了什么事? **2** 偶然 ǒurán: *I ~ed to meet him.* 我偶然遇见他. **3** ~ *on sth* 偶然发现 ǒurán fāxiàn. ~**ing** (a) [常用 *pl*]事件 shìjiàn. (b) [俚语]即兴[興]表演 jíxìng biǎoyǎn.

happy /'hæpɪ/ *adj* [-ier, -iest] **1** 幸福的 xìngfúde,幸运[運]的 xìngyùnde. **2** 愉快的 yúkuàide: *I shall be ~ to accept your invitation.* 我们欣然接受你的邀请. **3** 恰当[當]的 qiàdàngde, 巧妙的 qiǎomiàode. ,~-**go-'lucky** *adj* 无[無]忧[憂]无虑[慮]的 wúyōuwúlǜde. **hap·pily** *adv* **hap·pi·ness** *n* [U]

har·angue /hə'ræŋ/ *n* [C] 长[長]篇的训斥性演说 chángpiānde xùnchìxìng yǎnshuō. □ *vt/i* (向…)作冗长的训斥性演说 zuò rǒngchángde xùnchìxìng yǎnshuō.

har·ass /'hærəs/ *vt* **1** 使烦恼[惱] shǐ fánnǎo, 折磨 zhémó: *~ed by problems* 被一些问题折磨. **2** 骚[騷]扰[擾] sāorǎo: ~ *the enemy forces* 骚扰敌军. ~-**ment** *n* [U]

harbour [美语= -**bor**] /'hɑ:bə(r)/ *n* [C] **1** 港 gǎng, 港湾[灣] gǎngwān, 港口 gǎngkǒu. **2** [喻]安全处[處]所 ānquán chùsuǒ, 避难[難]所 bìnànsuǒ. □ *vt/i* **1** 隐匿 yǐnnì, 包庇 bāobì. **2** 怀[懷]有 huáiyǒu: ~ *evil thoughts* 不怀好意.

hard¹ /hɑ:d/ *adj* [-er, -est] **1** 坚[堅]硬的 jiānyìngde, 坚固的 jiāngùde: *as ~ as rock* 坚如磐石. **2** 困难[難]的 kùnnande: *a ~ exam* 困难的考试. **3** 难忍的 nánrěnde, 艰[艱]难的 jiānnánde. *learn sth the ~ way* 经[經]过[過]艰难困苦而学[學]到 jīngguò jiānnánkùnkǔ ér xuédào. **4** 严[嚴]厉的 yánlìde, 严酷的 yánkùde: *a ~ life* 严酷的生活; *a ~ winter* 严冬. **5** (身体)结实[實]的 jiēshide. **6** 辛苦的 xīnkǔde, 费力的 fèilìde: *a ~ worker* 辛苦的工人. **7** 发[發]硬音的 fā yìngyīn de: *The letter 'g' is ~ in 'gun' and soft in 'gin'.* 字母 *g* 在 *gun* 中发硬音,在 *gin* 中发软音. **8** ~ *and fast* (*rules, etc*) (规则等)严格的 yángéde. ~ *of hearing* 有些聋[聾] yǒuxiē lóng. '~**back** 硬皮书[書] yìngpíshū. '~**board** 硬质[質]纤[纖]维板 yìngzhì xiānwéibǎn. ,~'**cash** 现金 xiànjīn. ,~'**currency** 硬通货 yìngtōnghuò. ,~'**drugs** 毒品 dúpǐn. ,~'**facts** 可靠的论[論]据[據] kěkàode lùnjù. ,~-'**headed** *adj* 精明而讲实[實]际[際]的 jīngmíng ér jiǎng shíjì de. ,~-'**hearted** *adj* 冷酷的 lěngkùde, 缺乏同情心的 quēfá tóngqíngxīn de. ,~'**luck** 倒霉 dǎoméi, 不走运[運] bù zǒuyùn. ,~'**shoulder** 汽车[車]道边[邊]的硬路面 qìchēdào biān de yìnglùmiàn. '~**ware** (a) 金属[屬]日用器皿 jīnshǔ rìyòng qìmǐn. (b) (电子计算机)硬件 yìngjiàn. ⇨ software. '~**wood** 坚硬的木材 jiānyìngde mùcái.

hard² /hɑ:d/ *adv* **1** 努力地 nǔlìde, 尽[盡]力地 jìnlìde: *try* ~ 努力干. **2** 重重地 zhòngzhòngde, 猛烈地 měngliède: *raining* ~ 下大雨. **3** 困难[難]地 kùnnande: *my* '~-*earned money* 我的血汗钱. *be* ~ *up* (钱)短缺 duǎnquē. **4** 使成坚硬地 shǐ chéng jiānyìng de: '~-*boiled eggs* 煮得老的鸡蛋. **5** 接近地 jiējìnde, 立即地 lìjìde: *follow* ~ *after someone* 紧跟某人.

harden /'hɑ:dn/ *vt/i* (使)变[變]硬 biànyìng. (使)变强壮[壯] biàn qiángzhuàng.

hard·ly /'hɑ:dlɪ/ *adv* **1** 刚[剛]刚 gānggāng,简[簡]直不 jiǎnzhíbù: *I can ~ walk.* 我简直走不动了. **2**决不 juébù: *You can ~ expect me to lend you money again.* 你别想我再借给你钱. **3** 几[幾]乎没有 jīhū méiyǒu, 几乎不 jīhū bù: ~ *ever* 很少.

hard·ship /'hɑ:dʃɪp/ *n* **1** [C, U] 苦难[難] kǔnàn, 困苦 kùnkǔ.

hardy /'hɑ:dɪ/ *adj* [-ier, -iest] 耐劳[勞]的 nàiláode, 能吃苦的 néng chīkǔ de. **hardi·ness** *n* [U]

hare /heə(r)/ *n* [C] 野兔 yětù. □ *vi* 飞[飛]跑 fēipǎo. ,~-'**brained** *adj* 轻[輕]率的 qīngshuàide, 粗忽的 cūhūde.

hark /hɑ:k/ *vi* **1** [非正式用语]听[聽] tīng. **2** ~ *back* (*to*) 回到原题 huídào yuántí.

harm /hɑ:m/ *n* [U] 损害 sǔnhài, 伤[傷]害 shānghài. *out of ~'s way* 在安全的地方 zài ānquánde dìfang. □ *vt* 损害 sǔnhài, 损伤 sǔnshāng. ~**ful** *adj* 有害的 (*to*) yǒuhàide. ~**less** *adj* (a) 无[無]害的 (*to*) wúhàide. (b) 无恶[惡]意的 wúèyìde, 无辜的 wúgūde.

har·mon·ica /hɑ:'mɒnɪkə/ *n* [C]

[*pl* ~s] 口琴 kǒuqín.

har·mon·ize /ˈhɑːmənaɪz/ *vt/i* **1** (使)协〔協〕调 xiétiáo. **2** 用和声〔聲〕唱或演奏 yòng héshēng chàng huò yǎnzòu.

har·mony /ˈhɑːmənɪ/ *n* [*pl* -ies] **1** [U] 一致 yí zhì, 融洽 róngqià. **2** [C, U] 协〔協〕调 xiétiáo, 融和 rónghé: ~ *of colour* 色彩的协调. **3** [C, U] 和声〔聲〕 héshēng; 和声学〔學〕 héshēngxué: **har·moni·ous** /hɑːˈməʊnɪəs/ *adj*

har·ness /ˈhɑːnɪs/ *n* [U] **1**挽〔輓〕具 wǎnjù; 马〔馬〕具 mǎjù. **2** 降落伞等的背带〔帶〕 jiàngluòsǎn děng de bēidài. □ *vt* **1** 上挽具 shàng wǎnjù. **2** 治理(河流等) zhìlǐ, 利用 lìyòng.

harp /hɑːp/ *n* [C] 竖〔豎〕琴 shùqín. □ *vi* **1** 弹〔彈〕竖琴 tán shùqín. **2** ~ *on sth* 〔喻〕唠〔嘮〕唠叨叨地说 lāolāodāodāode shuō. **~ist** 竖琴师〔師〕 shùqínshī.

har·poon /ˌhɑːˈpuːn/ *n* [C] 鱼叉 yúchā, 标〔標〕枪〔槍〕 biāoqiāng. □ *vt* 用鱼叉叉 yòng yúchā chā.

harp·si·chord /ˈhɑːpsɪkɔːd/ *n* [C] 拨〔撥〕弦古钢〔鋼〕琴 bōxián gǔgāngqín.

har·row /ˈhærəʊ/ *n* [C] 耙 pá. □ *vt* 耙地 pádì. **2** 〔喻〕折磨 zhémó, 使痛苦 shǐ tòngkǔ: *a ~ing journey* 折磨人的旅行.

harsh /hɑːʃ/ *adj* [-er, -est] **1** 粗糙的 cūcāode. **2** 严〔嚴〕厉〔厲〕的 yánlìde: *a ~ punishment* 严厉的处罚. **~ly** *adv* **~ness** *n* [U]

har·vest /ˈhɑːvɪst/ *n* [C] **1** 收获〔獲〕 shōuhuò, 收成 shōucheng: *a good wheat ~* 小麦丰收. **2** 〔喻〕成果 chéngguǒ, 结果 jiéguǒ: *reap the ~ of one's work* 取得工作的成果. □ *vt* 收割 shōugē, 收获 shōuhuò.

has /hæz/ ⇨ have¹.

hash /hæʃ/ *vt* 切细(肉等) qiēxì. □ *n* **1** [U] 回锅肉丁 huíguō ròudīng. **2** *make a ~ of sth* 〔喻〕把…弄糟 bǎ…nòngzāo.

hash·ish, hash·eesh /ˈhæʃiːʃ/ *n* [U] = cannabis.

hasn't /ˈhæznt/ = *has not*. ⇨ have¹.

hasp /hæsp/ *n* [C] (门, 窗等)搭扣 dākòu.

haste /heɪst/ *n* [U] 急速 jísù, 仓〔倉〕促 cāngcù.

hasten /ˈheɪsn/ *vt/i* **1** 急忙 jímáng, 赶〔趕〕快 gǎnkuài. **2** 急忙说 jímáng shuō: *I ~ to add that your child is safe.* 我急忙补充说你的孩子安然无恙.

hasty /ˈheɪstɪ/ *adj* [-ier, -iest] 急速的 jísùde, 匆促的 cōngcùde, 仓〔倉〕促的 cāngcùde: *a ~ decision* 仓促的决定. **hast·ily** *adv*

hat /hæt/ *n* [C] 帽子 màozi. *take one's ~ off to* 〔喻〕向…(脱帽)致敬 xiàng…zhìjìng.

hatch¹ /hætʃ/ *n* [C] **1** 地板上的开〔開〕口 dìbǎn shàng de kāikǒu; 舱〔艙〕口 cāngkǒu, 舱口盖 cāngkǒugài. **2** 两室间〔間〕墙〔牆〕上的开口 liǎngshì jiān qiáng shàng de kāikǒu.

hatch² /hætʃ/ *vt/i* **1** 孵出 fūchū, 孵fū: *The chickens are ~ing.* 小鸡正在孵化. **2** 策划〔劃〕 cèhuà, 计划 jìhuà.

hatchet /ˈhætʃɪt/ *n* [C] 短柄小斧 duǎnbǐng xiǎofǔ. *bury the ~* 和解 héjiě, 休战〔戰〕 xiūzhàn.

hatch·way /ˈhætʃweɪ/ *n* ⇨ hatch¹.

hate /heɪt/ *vt* **1** 恨 hèn, 憎恨zènghèn, 讨厌〔厭〕 tǎoyàn. **2** 抱歉 bàoqiàn,遗憾yíhàn: *I ~ to trouble you.* 真抱歉，麻烦你了. □ *n* [U] 憎恶〔惡〕 zèng'è, 憎恨 zènghèn. **~ful** *adj* 可恨的 kěhènde, 讨厌的 tǎoyànde. **~fully** *adv*

hatred /ˈheɪtrɪd/ *n* [U] 仇恨 chóuhèn, 憎恨 zènghèn.

haughty /ˈhɔːtɪ/ *adj* [-ier, -iest] 傲慢的 àomànde, 骄〔驕〕傲的 jiāo'àode. **haught·ily** *adv* **haugh·ti·ness** *n* [U]

haul /hɔːl/ *vt/i* 用力拉 yònglì lā, 拖 tuō. □ *n* [C] **1** 拖 tuō, 拉 lā. **2** 拖运〔運〕的距离〔離〕 tuōyùnde jùlí. **3** 捕获〔獲〕量 pǔhuòliàng. 一网〔網〕打上的鱼量 yìwǎng dǎ shàng de yúliàng. **~age** *n* [U] 拖运 tuōyùn. **~ier** *n* [C] 货物承运(陆运)人 huòwù chéngyùnrén.

haunch /hɔːntʃ/ *n* [C] (人的)腿臀部 tuǐtúnbù.

haunt /hɔːnt/ *vt* **1** 常去 chángqù, 常到 chángdào. **2** (鬼魂)常出没于 chángchūmò yú. **3** (思想等)萦〔縈〕绕〔繞〕 yíngrǎo; 缠〔纏〕住 chánzhù: *~ed by fear* 提心吊胆. □ *n* [C] 常去的地方 chángqùde dìfang.

have¹ /常式 həv; 强式 hæv/ *aux verb* [*3rd person sing* **has**; *pt, pp* **had**] **1** 〔构成完成时态〕已经〔經〕 yǐjīng, 曾经 céngjīng: *I ~* (或 *I've*) *finished.* 我完成了. *He has* (或 *He's*) *gone.* 他走了. **2** (表示假设): *Had I* (= If I had) *known* 如果我知道. ⇨ if(1).

have² /hæv/ *vt* 〔在否定句和疑问句中可以用 do 也可以不用 do, 在非正式文体中常被

have got 所代替] **1** (代替动词 be): *I ~ no doubt* (=There is no doubt in my mind) *that* 我确信…. **2** 有 yǒu, 据[據]有 jùyǒu: *He's (got) a house.* 他有一所房子. *Has she (got)* (或 *Does she ~*) *blue eyes?* 她的眼睛是蓝的吗? *How many children ~ they?* 他们有几个孩子? **3** [非正式用语][常与 *got* 连用]怀[懷]有 huáiyǒu: *H~ you (got) any idea where he lives?* 你知道他住在哪里吗? **4** 允许 yǔnxǔ: *I won't '~ such conduct.* 我不容许这种行为. **5** (表示必须,不得不): *You ~n't (got) to go to school today.* 你今天不必上学. **6** 遭受 zāoshòu: *~ a cold* 患感冒. **7** [不同 *got* 连用]生 shēng: *~ a baby* 生孩子.

have³ *verb* [在否定句和疑问句中常与 "*do*" 连用] **1** 吃 chī, 喝 hē, 得到 dédào: *What shall we ~ for dinner?* 我们正餐吃什么? **2** 进[進]行 jìnxíng: *~ a swim* 游泳; *~ a walk* 散步. **3** 经[經]历[歷] jīnglì: *~ a good holiday* 假日过得愉快. ***let sb '~ it*** [俚语]让[讓]某人吃顿苦头[頭] ràng mǒurén chī dùn kǔtou. 射某人 shè mǒurén. **4** 使 shǐ, 要 yào: *~ your shoes repaired* 让人把你的鞋修一修. ⇨ get(2). **5** 遭受 zāoshòu: *He had his house burgled.* 他家遭到夜窃. **6** 欺骗[騙] qīpiàn: *You've been had.* 你被骗了. **7** 说 shuō: *Rumour has it* (= There is a rumour) *that* 有谣言说…. **8** ***~ sth back*** 收回某物 shōuhuí mǒuwù. ***~ sb on*** [非正式用语]使受骗 shǐ shòupiàn. ⇨ 6 above. ***~ sth on*** (a) 穿着 chuānzhe; 戴着 dàizhe. (b) 手头[頭]有事 shǒutóu yǒu shì: *I've a lot on this week.* 本周我很忙. ***~ sth out*** 使被取出 shǐ bèi qǔchū: *~ a tooth out* 拔牙. ***~ it out with sb*** 通过[過]争论[論]解决争端 tōngguò zhēnglùn jiějué zhēngduān. ***~ sb up*** 控告某人 kònggào mǒurén: *He was had up for murder.* 他被控告谋杀.

ha·ven /'heɪvn/ *n* [C] [喻]安全处[處]所 ānquán chùsuǒ, 避难[難]所 bìnànsuǒ.

hav·er·sack /'hævəsæk/ *n* [C] 帆布背包 fānbù bēibāo.

havoc /'hævək/ *n* [U] 大灾难[難] dàzāinàn, 浩劫 hàojié.

hawk /hɔːk/ *n* [C] **1** 鹰[鷹] yīng, 隼 sǔn. **2** 主战[戰]份子 zhǔzhàn fènzi. ⇨ dove(2).

hay /heɪ/ *n* [U] 干[幹]草(饲料) gāncǎo. **'~ fever** [医学]枯草热[熱] kūcǎorè, 花粉热 huāfěnrè. **'~stack** 干草堆 gāncǎoduī. **'~wire** [非正式用语]乱[亂]七八糟 luànqībāzāo: *go ~ wire* 杂乱不堪.

haz·ard /'hæzəd/ *n* [C] 危险[險] wēixiǎn, 危害 wēihài. □ *vt* **1** 使遭危险 shǐ zāo wēixiǎn. **2** 冒险作出 màoxiǎn zuòchū: *~ a guess* 无把握地猜测. **~ous** *adj* 危险的 wēixiǎnde, 冒险的 màoxiǎnde.

haze /heɪz/ *n* [U] **1** 薄雾[霧] bówù, 霾 mái. **2** [喻](使)困惑 kùnhuò, (使)糊涂[塗] hútu.

hazel /'heɪzl/ *n* **1** [C] 榛 zhēn. **2** [U] 淡褐色(尤指眼睛) dànhèsè. □ *adj* 淡褐色的 dànhèsède.

hazy /'heɪzɪ/ *adj* [-ier, -iest] **1** 雾蒙蒙的 wùméngméngde. **2** [喻]模糊的 móhude; 困惑的 kùnhuòde: *a ~ memory of* 对[對]…的模糊的记忆. **haz·ily** *adv* **hazi·ness** *n* [U]

H-bomb /'eɪtʃ bɒm/ *n* [C] 氢[氫]弹[彈] qīngdàn.

H.E. =His Excellency 阁下 gèxià.

he /hiː/ *pron* **1** 他 tā: *Where's your brother?* 你的兄弟在哪里? *H~'s in Paris.* 他在巴黎. **2** [前缀]雄性的 xióngxìngde: *a '~-goat* 公山羊.

head¹ /hed/ *n* [C] **1** 头[頭] tóu. **2** (硬币的有头像的)正面 zhèngmiàn. ⇨ tail(3). ***be unable to make ,~ or 'tail of sth*** 对[對]某事摸不着头[頭]脑[腦] duì mǒushì mōbùzháo tóunǎo. **3** 人 rén. *It costs £10 a ~.* 每客十英镑. **4** [*pl* ~] (牲口)头数[數] tóushù: *50 ~ of cattle* 五十头牲口. **5** 才智 cáizhì, 想象力 xiǎngxiànglì: *an idea out of his own ~* 他自己想出来的主意. **6** 天资 tiānzī, 天才 tiāncái: *a good ~ for business* 经营的天才. **7** 头状[狀]物 tóuzhuàngwù: *the ~ of a pin* 针头; *the ~ of a hammer* 锤头. **8** 顶端 dǐngduān: *at the ~ of the page* 这一页的顶端. **9** 上端 shàngduān: *the ~ of a bed* 床的上端(放枕头的一端). **10** 首长[長] shǒuzhǎng: *~s of government* 政府首脑. **11** 前端 qiánduān, 前面 qiánmiàn: *at the ~ of the queue* 队的前端. **12** 压[壓]力 yālì: *a good ~ of steam* 大的蒸气压力. **13** ***bite sb's ~ off*** 痛骂[罵]某人 tòngmà mǒurén, 对某人大发[發]脾气 duì mǒurén dàfā píqì. ***come to a ~*** [喻]达[達]到危急的关[關]头[頭] dádào wēijíde guāntóu. ***go to one's ~*** (a)

喝醉 hēzuì. **(b)** 兴〔興〕奋〔奮〕xìngfèn. ˌ~ **over 'heels (a)** 头朝下 tóucháoxià: *fall ~ over heels* 头朝下跸倒. **(b)**〔喻〕深深地 shēnshēnde: *~ over heels in love* 坠入情海. ***keep one's ~*** 保持镇静 bǎochí zhènjìng. ***laugh one's ~ off*** 狂笑 kuángxiào. ***scream one's ~ off*** 大叫 dàjiào. ***lose one's ~*** 惊〔驚〕慌失措 jīnghuāngshīcuò. ***put our*** (或 ***your, etc***) ***~s together*** 商量 shāngliang. '**~ache** *n* [C, U] **(a)** 头痛 tóutòng. **(b)**〔非正式用语〕使人头痛的事 shìrén tóutòng de shì. '**~lamp** (汽车等的)前灯〔燈〕qiándēng. '**~light** = headlamp. '**~line** (报纸)标〔標〕题 biāotí. ˌ**~'master** 校长 xiàozhǎng. **~'mistress** 女校长 nǚxiàozhǎng. '**~-on** *adj, adv* (碰撞)迎头的 yíngtóude, 正面的 zhèngmiànde, 迎头地 yíngtóude; 正面地 zhèngmiànde. '**~phones** 耳机〔機〕ěrjī. ˌ**~'quarters** *n* [*sing* 或 *pl*] 总〔總〕部 zǒngbù. '**~-rest** (理发椅等的)头靠 tóukào. '**~room,** = clearance(2). '**~stone** 墓碑 mùbēi. '**~way** 前进〔進〕qiánjìn, 进展 jìnzhǎn: *make ~way* 取得进展.

head² /hed/ *vt/i* **1** 居于前列 jūyú qiánliè, 作为〔爲〕…的首脑 zuòwéi…de shǒunǎo, 率领 shuàilǐng: *~ a list* 居名单之首; *~ a company* 领导一家公司. **2** 用头顶(球) yòng tóu dǐng. **3** *~ **sth(sb) off*** 赶到〔趕〕…前面, 使其回转〔轉〕gǎn dào…qiánmiàn, shǐ qí huízhuǎn. **4** 朝…前进 cháo…qiánjìn: *~ south* 朝南(走).

head·ing /'hedɪŋ/ *n* [C] 标〔標〕题 biāotí.

head·long /'hedlɒŋ/ *adv, adj* **1** 头〔頭〕向前的 tóu xiàngqián de; 头向前地 tóu xiàngqiánde: *fall ~* 头着地跸下. **2** 轻〔輕〕率地 qīngshuàide: *rush ~ into a decision* 轻率作出决定.

head·strong /'hedstrɒŋ/ *adj* 任性的 rènxìngde, 顽固的 wángùde.

heady /'hedɪ/ *adj* [-ier, -iest] **1**(酒)易醉的 yìzuìde. **2**〔喻〕(成就等)令人兴〔興〕奋〔奮〕的 lìngrén xìngfèn de.

heal /hi:l/ *vt/i* **1** 治愈(尤指伤口) zhìyù. **2**〔喻〕和解 héjiě: *~ a quarrel* 平息一场争吵.

health /helθ/ *n* [U] **1** 健康状〔狀〕况 jiànkāng zhuàngkuàng. **2** 健康 jiànkāng.

healthy /helθɪ/ *adj* [-ier, -iest] **1** 健康的 jiànkāngde. **2** 有益于健康的 yǒuyì yú jiànkāng de: *a ~ climate* 有益于健康的气候. **3** 表示健康的 biǎoshì jiànkāng de: *a ~ appetite* 健康的胃口. **~ily** *adj*

heap /hi:p/ *n* [C] **1** 堆 duī, 一堆 yìduī. **2**〔非正式用语〕许多 xǔduō, 大量 dàliàng: *~s of books* 许多书, *~s of time* 大量的时间. □ *vt* **1** 堆积〔積〕duījī. **2** 装〔裝〕载〔載〕zhuāngzǎi: *~ a plate with food* 把盘子盛上食品.

hear /hɪə(r)/ *vt/i* [*pt, pp* ~d /hɜ:d/] **1** 听〔聽〕tīng, 听见 tīngjiàn. **2** 听说 tīngshuō, 得知 dézhī: *I ~ he's leaving.* 我听说他要离开. *~ **from sb*** 接到某人的信 jiēdào mǒurénde xìn; 听到某人的消息 tīngdào mǒurén de xiāoxī. *~ **of sb(sth)*** 知道 zhīdào, 听说过 tīngshuōguò: *I've never heard of you.* 我从未听说过你. **3** 倾听 qīngtīng 注意听取 zhùyì tīngqǔ: *You'd better ~ what they have to say.* 你最好听听他们怎么说. *~ **sb out*** 听某人把话说完 tīng mǒurén bǎ huà shuōwán. ***not ~ of sth*** 不同意 bù tóngyì, 不允许 bù yǔnxǔ. **4** (法官审案时用语) ˌ**H~! 'H~!** 说得对〔對〕! 说得对! shuōdeduì! shuōdeduì!

hear·ing /'hɪərɪŋ/ *n* **1** [U] 听〔聽〕力 tīnglì. ***be hard of ~*** 耳聋〔聾〕ěrlóng. **2** [U] 听力所及的距离〔離〕tīnglì suǒjí de jùlí: *He's out of ~.* 他在(我们互相)叫得应的距离以外. **3** [C] (尤其辩护时)被听到的机会 bèi tīngdào de jīhuì. **4** [C] 〔法律〕审〔審〕讯 shěnxùn. '**~-aid** 助听器 zhùtīngqì.

hear·say /'hɪəseɪ/ *n* [U] 谣言 yáoyán, 传〔傳〕闻〔聞〕chuánwén.

hearse /hɜ:s/ *n* [C] 柩车〔車〕jiùchē.

heart /hɑ:t/ *n* [C] **1** 心脏〔臟〕xīnzàng, 心 xīn. **2** 感情 gǎnqíng, 爱〔愛〕心 àixīn; 内心 nèixīn, 心地 xīndì. ***from*** (***the bottom of***) ***one's ~*** 衷心地 zhōngxīnde. ***break a person's ~*** 使某人非常伤〔傷〕心 shǐ mǒurén fēicháng shāngxīn. (***learn*** 或 ***know sth***) ***by ~*** 记住 jìzhù, 背下 bèixià. ***lose ~*** 丧失信心 sàngshī xìnxīn. ***take ~*** (***from***)鼓起勇气〔氣〕gǔqǐ yǒngqì. ***take sth to ~*** 为〔爲〕某事耿耿于怀〔懷〕wèi mǒushì gěnggěng yú huái. **3** 中心 zhōngxīn. **4** 心状物 xīnzhuàngwù, (纸牌上的)桃 táo. '**~ache** 痛心 tòngxīn, 伤心 shāngxīn. '**~ attack** 心脏病发〔發〕作 xīnzàngbìng fāzuò. **~'-**

beat 心搏 xīnbó, 心跳 xīntiào. '~**break** 极〔極〕度伤心jídù shāngxīn. '~**broken** 极度伤心的 jídù shāngxīn de. '~**felt** *adj* 衷心的 zhōngxīnde. ~**less** *adj* 残〔殘〕忍的 cánrěnde. ~**less·ly** *adv*

hearten /'hɑ:tn/ *vt* 鼓励〔勵〕 gǔlì. 激励 jīlì.

hearth /hɑ:θ/ *n* [C] **1** 壁炉〔爐〕 bìlú; 壁炉地面 bìlú dìmiàn. **2** 〔喻〕家庭 jiātíng.

heart·ily /'hɑ:tɪlɪ/ *adv* **1** 衷心地 zhōngxīnde; 精神饱满地 jīngshén bǎomǎn de; 胃口很好地 wèikǒu hěnhǎo de. **2** 非常地 fēichángde: ~ *sick of it* 非常讨厌….

hearty /'hɑ:tɪ/ *adj* [-ier, -iest] **1** 衷心的 zhongxinde, 热〔熱〕忱的 rèchénde: *a* ~ *welcome* 衷心的欢迎. **2** 健壮〔壯〕的 jiànzhuàngde. **3** 丰〔豐〕盛的 fēngshèngde, 胃口好的 wèikǒu hǎo de.

heat[1] /hi:t/ *n* **1** [U] 热〔熱〕 rè, 热度 rèdù. **2** [U] 〔喻〕热烈 rèliè, 激烈 jīliè. **3** [C] 竞〔競〕赛中之一次 jìngsài zhōng zhī yícì. **4** [U] *be on* ~ (母兽)发〔發〕情 fāqíng. '~**wave** 〔气象〕热浪 rèlàng.

heat[2] /hi:t/ *vt/i* **1** 加热〔熱〕于 jiārèyú, 变〔變〕热 biànrè. **2** 〔喻〕激动〔動〕 jīdòng. ~**ed** *adj* 忿怒的 fènnùde, 热烈的 rèliède: *a* ~*ed argument* 热烈的争论. ~**er** 加热器 jiārèqì, 发热器 fārèqì.

heath /hi:θ/ *n* **1** [C] 石南丛〔叢〕生的荒地 shínán cóngshēng de huāngdì. **2** [C, U] 石南属〔屬〕植物 shínánshǔ zhíwù.

hea·then /'hi:ðn/ *n* **1** [C] 异〔異〕教徒(基督教徒, 犹太教徒, 伊斯兰教徒以外的人) yìjiàotú. **2** [C] 野蛮〔蠻〕人 yěmánrén.

heather /'heðə(r)/ *n* [U] 石南属〔屬〕植物 shínánshǔ zhíwù.

heave /hi:v/ *vt/i* [*pt*, *pp* ~d 或 hove /həʊv/] **1** 用力举〔舉〕起 yònglì jǔqǐ. **2** 说出 shuōchū, 发〔發〕出 fāchū: ~ *a sigh* 长叹一声. **3** 掷〔擲〕zhì, 扔 rēng. **4** ~ *to* 停船 tíngchuán. □ *n* [C] 举 jǔ; 拉 lā; 扔 rēng.

heaven /'hevn/ *n* [C] **1** 天国〔國〕 tiānguó, 天堂 tiāntáng. **2** (常作 H~)上帝 shàngdì. **3** (表示感叹) *Good H~s!* 天哪! **4** 极〔極〕乐〔樂〕之地 jílè zhī dì. **5** 〔常用 *pl*〕天空 tiānkōng. ~**ly** *adj* **(a)** 天空的 tiānkōngde; 天国的 tiānguóde. **(b)** 〔非正式用语〕非常可爱〔愛〕的 fēicháng kě'ài de. ,~**ly** '**body** 天体〔體〕 tiāntǐ.

heavy /'hevɪ/ *adj* [-ier, -iest] **1** 重的 zhòngde. **2** 大的 dàde, 多的 duōde, 大量的 dàliàngde. ~ *rain* 大雨; *a* ~ *smoker* 吸烟多的人. ~ *going* 难〔難〕办〔辦〕的(任务) nánbànde, 令人厌〔厭〕倦的(旅行) lìngrén yànjuàn de. **3** 迟钝 chídùn, 呆滞〔滯〕 āizhì: ~ *with wine* 因饮酒而呆滞. **4** 沉闷〔悶〕的 chénmènde, 冗长〔長〕乏味的 rǒngcháng fáwèi de. **5** (身体情况)懒散的 lǎnsǎnde, 不活跃〔躍〕的 bù huóyuè de. □ *adv* 沉重地 chénzhòngde, 大量地 dàliàngde. **heav·ily** *adv* *Guilt hung* ~ *on him.* 他深深地感到内疚. **heavi·ness** *n* [U]

He·brew /'hi:bru:/ *n* [C] **1** 希伯来〔來〕语 xībóláiyǔ. **2** 犹〔猶〕太语 yóutàiyǔ. □ *adj* 希伯来语的 xībóláiyǔde; 希伯来人的 xībóláirénde.

heckle /'hekl/ *vt* 当〔當〕众〔衆〕诘问〔問〕 dāngzhòng jiéwèn. **heckler** *n* [C] 诘问者 jiéwènzhě.

hec·tare /'hektɑ:(r)/ *n* 公顷(一万平方米) gōngqǐng.

hec·tic /'hektɪk/ *adj* 闹哄哄的 nàohōnghōng de, 兴〔興〕奋〔奮〕的 xìngfènde: *Lead a* ~ *life* 生活闹哄哄的.

he'd /hi:d/ = *he had*; *he would*.

hedge /hedʒ/ *n* [C] **1** 树〔樹〕篱〔籬〕 shùlí. **2** 〔喻〕障碍〔礙〕 zhàng'ài, 障碍物 zhàng'àiwù: *a* ~ *against inflation* 反通货膨胀的手段. □ *vt/i* **1** 用树篱围〔圍〕住 yòng shùlí wéizhù, 设障碍于 shè zhàng'ài yú. **2** 躲闪〔閃〕 duǒshǎn, 推诿 tuīwěi. '~**row** 栽成树篱的一排灌木 zāichéng shùlí de yìpái guànmù.

hedge·hog /'hedʒhɒg/ *n* [C] 刺猬 cìwei.

heed /hi:d/ *vt* 注意 zhùyì, 留意 liúyì. □ *n* [U] 注意 zhùyì: *take* ~ *of* 注意, 留心.

heel[1] /hi:l/ *n* [C] **1** 脚后〔後〕跟 jiǎohòugēn, 踵 zhǒng; 袜〔襪〕后跟 wàhòugēn, 鞋后跟 xiéhòugēn. *at* (或 *on*, *upon*) *sb's* ~(*s*) 紧〔緊〕跟某人后〔後〕面 jǐngēn mǒurén hòumiàn. *down at* ~ 衣着褴〔襤〕褛〔褸〕的 yīzhuó lánlǚ de. *head over* ~*s* ⇨ head[1](13). *come to* ~ **(a)** (狗)紧跟主人 jǐngēn zhǔrén. **(b)** 〔喻〕顺从〔從〕 shùncóng. *take to one's* ~*s* 逃走 táozǒu, 逃之夭夭 táozhīyāoyāo. *turn on one's* ~ 急转〔轉〕身 jízhuǎnshēn. **2** 〔俚语〕下流人 xiàliúrén, 卑鄙的家伙 bēibǐde jiāhuo. □ *vt* 给…钉后掌 gěi…dīng hòuzhǎng. ,**well-**'~**ed** *adj* 〔俚语〕有钱〔錢〕的 yǒuqiánde; 富的 fùde.

heel² /hi:l/ *vt/i* ~ *over* (使)(船)倾侧 qīngcè.

hef·ty /'heftɪ/ *adj* [-ier, -iest] 大的 dàde, 重的 zhòngde.

heifer /'hefə(r)/ *n* [C] 小母牛 xiǎomǔniú.

height /haɪt/ *n* [C] **1** 高度 gāodù, 高 gāo. **2** 高地 gāodì, 高处〔處〕gāochù. **3** 顶点〔點〕dǐngdiǎn, 最高程度 zuìgāo chéngdù. *the ~ of a storm* 暴风雨的最猛烈阶段. **4** 海拔 hǎibá. **~en** *vt/i* 加高 jiāgāo, 提高 tígāo, 增大 zēngdà: *my fears ~ened.* 我更加害怕.

heir /eə(r)/ *n* [C] 继〔繼〕承人 jìchéngrén. **~ess** *n* [C] 女继承人 nǚjìchéngrén. **~loom** *n* [C] 传〔傳〕家宝〔寶〕chuánjiābǎo, 祖传物 zǔchuánwù.

held /held/ *pt, pp* of hold³.

heli·cop·ter /'helɪkɒptə(r)/ *n* [C] 直升飞〔飛〕机〔機〕zhíshēngfēijī.

he·lium /'hi:lɪəm/ *n* [C] 氦 hài.

hell /hel/ *n* [C] **1** 地狱 dìyù, 阴〔陰〕间〔間〕yīnjiān. **2** 苦境 kǔjìng, 极大的困苦 jídàde kùnkǔ. **3** [非正式用语](表示咒骂和加强语气): *What the ~ do you want?* 你到底要什么? *for the ~ of it* 只是为〔為〕了捣乱〔亂〕zhǐshì wèile dǎoluàn. *like ~* 拼命地 pīngmìngde: *run like ~* 拼命跑. **~ish** *adj* 可怕的 kěpàde, 凶恶〔惡〕的 xiōng'ède.

he'll /hi:l/ = *he will*; *he shall*.

hello /he'ləʊ/ *int* = hallo.

helm /helm/ *n* [C] 舵 duò; 舵柄 duòbǐng; 舵轮〔輪〕duòlún. *at the ~* 掌握(权力)zhǎngwò. **helmsman** 舵手 duòshǒu.

hel·met /'helmɪt/ *n* [C] 头〔頭〕盔 tóukuī, 安全帽 ānquánmào.

help /help/ *vt/i* **1** 帮助 bāngzhù, 援助 yuánzhù. *~ 'out* 帮助(解脱困境) bāngzhu. **2** 进〔進〕食 jìnshí: *H~ yourself to coffee.* 你随意取咖啡喝吧. **3** 避免 bìmiǎn;阻止 zǔzhǐ: *She couldn't ~ crying.* 她不禁失声痛哭. □ *n* **1** [U] 帮助 bāngzhù, 救助 jiùzhù. **2** 帮助者 bāngzhùzhě, 帮手 bāngshǒu, 助手 zhùshǒu; 帮助的东西 bāngzhùde dōngxi. **3** [U] 治疗〔療〕zhìliáo, 挽救的办〔辦〕法 wǎnjiùde bànfǎ: *There's no ~ for it.* 没有办法. **4** [C] 女佣人 nǚyòngrén. ⇨ home help. **~er** 帮手 bāngshǒu, 助手 zhùshǒu. **~ful** *adj* 有帮助的 yǒu bāngzhù de, 有用的 yǒuyòngde. **~fulness** *n* [U] **~less** *adj* **(a)** 未受到帮助的 wèi shòudào bāngzhù de. **(b)** 依赖他人的 yīlài tārénde. **~less·ly** *adv* **~ing** 一份食物 yīfèn shíwù.

hem /hem/ *n* [C] (衣服等)折边〔邊〕zhébiān. □ *vt* [-mm-] **1** 给…缝边 gěi…féngbiān, 给…镶边 gěi…xiāngbiān. **2** ~ *in* 包围〔圍〕bāowéi; 禁闭〔閉〕jìnbì. **'~line** (衣服)下摆 xiàbǎi.

hemi·sphere /'hemɪsfɪə(r)/ *n* [C] **1** 半球 bànqiú. **2** (地球的)半球 bànqiú.

hem·or·rhage (also **hæm-**) /'hemərɪdʒ/ *n* [C, U] [医学]出血 chūxuě.

hemp /hemp/ *n* [U] **1** 大麻 dàmá. **2** (亦作 *Indian* ~) 由大麻制成的麻醉剂〔劑〕yóu dàmá zhìchéngde mázuìjì.

hen /hen/ *n* [C] **1** 母鸡〔鷄〕mǔjī. ⇨ cock¹. **2** 母禽 mǔqín. **'~-pecked** *adj* [非正式用语]怕老婆的 pà lǎopo de.

hence /hens/ *adv* **1** 从〔從〕此地 cóng cǐdì; 从此时〔時〕cóng cǐshí. **2** 因此 yīncǐ, 由此 yóucǐ. **,~'forth**, **,~'forward** 今后〔後〕jīnhòu.

hench·man /'hentʃmən/ *n* [C] [*pl* -men] 亲〔親〕信 qīnxìn, 仆〔僕〕从〔從〕púcóng.

henna /'henə/ *n* [U] [植物]散沫花 sànmòhuā.

her /hə(r) 强式: hɜ:(r)/ *personal pron* [she 的宾格]: *Give ~ the book.* 给她这本书. □ *adj* 她的 tāde: *That's '~ hat.* 那是她的帽子. **hers** *possessive pron* 她的 tāde: *Is that ~s?* 那是她的吗?

her·ald /'herəld/ *n* [C] **1** 传〔傳〕令官 chuánlìngguān. **2** 先驱〔驅〕xiānqū; 预兆 yùzhào. □ *vt* 预示…的来〔來〕到 yùshì…de láidào.

her·aldry /'herəldrɪ/ *n* [U] 纹章学〔學〕wénzhāngxué.

herb /hɜ:b/ *n* [C] **1** 草本植物 cǎoběn zhíwù. **2** 药草 yàocǎo; 香草 xiāngcǎo. **~al** *adj* 药草的 yàocǎode. **~al·ist** 种〔種〕草药的人 zhòng cǎoyào de rén; 卖〔賣〕草药的人 mài cǎoyào de rén.

her·ba·ceous /hɜ:'beɪʃəs/ *adj* 草本的 cǎoběnde.

herd /hɜ:d/ *n* [C] **1** 兽〔獸〕群 shòuqún, 牲口群 shēngkouqún. **2** [用于复合词]牧人 mùrén: *a 'cow~* 牧牛人. □ *vt/i* 把…赶〔趕〕到一起 bǎ…gǎndào yìqǐ, 成群 chéngqún. **herds·man** 牧人 mùrén, 牧主 mùzhǔ.

here /hɪə(r)/*adv* **1** 这〔這〕里〔裏〕zhèlǐ; 向这里 xiàng zhèlǐ; 在这里 zài zhèlǐ; 到这里 dào zhèlǐ;

Come ~. 到这里来. *I live* ~. 我住在这里. **2** 在这点[點]上 zài zhèdiǎn shàng: *H*~ *the speaker paused.* 演讲人说到这一点时停了一下. **3** ˌ~ *and* ˈ*there* 各处[處] gèchù, 到处 dàochù. ***neither*** ˌ~ ***nor*** ˈ***there*** [非正式用语]与[與]题目不相关[關] yǔ tímù bù xiānggūān. ~**aˈbouts** *adv* 在这里附近 zài zhèlǐ fùjìn. ~ˈ**after** *adv, n* [U] 此后[後] cǐhòu; 来[來]世 láishì. ~ˈ**with** *adv* 与此一道 yǔcǐ yídào.

her·ed·itary /hɪˈredɪtrɪ/ *adj* 世袭[襲]的 shìxíde; 遗传[傳]的 yíchuánde.

her·ed·ity /hɪˈredətɪ/ *n* [U] **1** 遗传[傳] yíchuán. **2** [C] 遗传特征[徵] yíchuán tèzhēng.

her·esy /ˈherəsɪ/ *n* [C, U] [*pl* -ies] 异[異]端 yìduān; 异教 yìjiào.

her·etic /ˈherətɪk/ *n* [C] 持异[異]端论[論]者 chí yìduānlùn zhě. 异教徒 yìjiàotú. ~**al** /hɪˈretɪkl/ *adj*

heri·tage /ˈherɪtɪdʒ/ *n* [C] 传[傳]统 chuántǒng, 遗产[產] yíchǎn.

her·mit /ˈhɜːmɪt/ *n* [C] 隐士 yǐnshì. ~**age** *n* [C] 隐士住处[處] yǐnshì zhùchù.

her·nia /ˈhɜːnɪə/ *n* [U] [医学] 疝 shān.

hero /ˈhɪərəʊ/ *n* [C] [*pl* ~es] **1** 英雄 yīngxióng; 勇士 yǒngshì. **2** 男主人公 nánzhǔréngōng. ˈ~**ism** /ˈherəʊɪzəm/ *n* [U] 英勇 yīngyǒng, 英雄行为[爲] yīngxióng xíngwéi. ~**ic** /hɪˈrəʊɪk/ *adj* **(a)** 英雄的 yīngxióngde, 英勇的 yīngyǒngde. **(b)** (语言)堂皇的 tánghuángde. ~**ics** *n pl* **(a)** 夸[誇]大的语言或意见 kuādàde yǔyán huò yìjiàn. **(b)** 英勇 yīngyǒng, 英勇的行为 yīngyǒngde xíngwéi. ~-**i·cally** /-ɪklɪ/ *adv*

her·oin /ˈherəʊɪn/ *n* [U] (药)海洛因 hǎiluòyīn.

her·oine /ˈherəʊɪn/ *n* [C] 女英雄 nǚyīngxióng.

heron /ˈherən/ *n* [C] 苍[蒼]鹭[鷺] cānglù.

her·ring /ˈherɪŋ/ *n* [C] [*pl*~] 鲱鱼 fēiyú. ˈ~**bone** *adj, n* [U] 人字形的 rénzìxíngde, 人字形 rénzìxíng. ˌ**red**ˈ~, ⇨ red.

hers /hɜːz/ ⇨ her.

her·self /həˈself 强式: hɜː-/ *pron* **1** [反身]: *She hurt* ~. 她自己受了伤. ***(all) by*** ~ **(a)** 她独[獨]自地 tā dúzìde. **(b)** 她独力地 tā dúlìde. **2** [用于加强语气]: *She told me* ~. 她亲自告诉了我. **3** *She's not quite* ~ *today.* 她今天不大舒服.

he's /hiːz/ = *he is, he has.*

hesi·tant /ˈhezɪtənt/ *adj* 犹[猶]豫的 yóuyùde, 踌[躊]躇的 chóuchúde.

hesi·tate /ˈhezɪteɪt/ *vi* 犹[猶]豫 yóuyù, 踌[躊]躇 chóuchú. **hesi·ta·tion** /-ˈteɪʃən/ *n* [C, U]

het·ero·gen·eous /ˌhetərəˈdʒiːnɪəs/ *adj* 由不同种[種]类[類]组成的 yóu bùtóng zhǒnglèi zǔchéng de. ⇨ homogeneous.

het·ero·sex·ual /ˌhetərəˈsekʃʊəl/ *adj* 异[異]性爱[愛]的 yìxìng'àide.

hey-day /ˈheɪ deɪ/ *n* [只用 *pl*] 全盛时[時]期 quánshèng shíqī.

H.H. = **1** Her (His) Highness. **2** His Holiness (the Pope).

hi·ber·nate /ˈhaɪbəneɪt/ *vi* 冬眠 dōngmián. **hi·berˈna·tion** *n* [U]

hic·cup, hic·cough /ˈhɪkʌp/ *vt, n* [C] 打呃 dǎ'è.

hid, hidden ⇨hide[1].

hide[1] /haɪd/ *vt/i* [*pt* hid /hɪd/; *pp* hidden /ˈhɪdn/ 或 hid] 隐藏 yǐncáng 遮掩 zhēyǎn: 把…隐藏起来[來] bǎ...yǐncáng qǐlái. □ *n* [C] [美语 = *blind*] (观察鸟兽动静的)隐蔽处[處] yǐnbìchù. ˈ~-**out** (或 -**away**) [非正式用语]隐藏处 yǐncángchù. **hid·ing** *n* ***be in***(或 ***go into***) ***hiding*** 隐藏起来 yǐncáng qǐlái. ***come out of hiding*** 出现 chūxiàn. ˈ**hiding-place** 隐藏处 yǐncángchù.

hide[2] /haɪd/ *n* [C] **1** 兽[獸]皮 shòupí. **2** [非正式用语](人)皮肤[膚] pífū. **hid·ing** *n* [C] 鞭打 biāndǎ.

hid·eous /ˈhɪdɪəs/ *adj* 丑[醜]陋的 chǒulòude; 可怕的 kěpàde. ~**ly** *adv*

hi·er·archy /ˈhaɪərɑːkɪ/ *n* [C] [*pl* -ies] 等级制度 děngjí zhìdù.

hi-fi /ˈhaɪ ˌfaɪ/ *adj* (high fidelity 的缩略形式)高保真度的 gāo bǎozhēndù de.

high[1] /haɪ/ *adj* [-er, -est] **1** 高的 gāode. *How* ~ *is Mt Qomolangma?* 珠穆朗玛峰有多高? ˌ~ ***and*** ˈ***dry*** 搁[擱]浅[淺] gēqiǎn, 孤立无[無]援 gūlì wúyuán. **2** 重要的 zhòngyàode. 高级的 gāojíde: *a* ~ *official* 高级官员. **3** (声音)尖的 jiānde. 高声调的 gāoshēngdiàode. **4** 高度的 gāodùde; 很大的 hěndàde; 非常的 fēichángde: ~ *prices* 高价, *in* ~ *spirits* 兴高采烈. **5** ~ *time* 正盛的时[時]间 zhèngshèngde shíjiān, 成熟的时机〔機〕 chéngshúde shíjī: *It's ~ time you started.* 现在是你应该出发的时候了. **6** 高尚的 gāoshàngde: *~ ideals* 高尚的理想. **7** (食物)有些腐坏〔壞〕的 yǒuxiē fǔhuài de. **8** [非正式用语]醉了的 zuìlede; 麻醉了的 mázuìlede. **'~brow** *n, adj* 有高度文化修养〔養〕的 yǒu gādù wénhuà xiūyǎngde. **,~-'class** *adj* 高级的 gāojíde, 第一流的 dìyīliúde. **'H~ Court** 高级法庭 gāojífǎtíng. **,~-fi'delity** *adj* 高保真度的(略作 **hi-fi**) gāo bǎozhēndù de. □ *n* [C] 高保真度音响〔響〕设备〔備〕gāo bǎozhēndù yīnxiǎng shèbèi. **'~-grade** *adj* 优〔優〕质〔質〕的yōuzhìde. **,-'handed** *adj* 专〔專〕横的 zhuānhéngde, 用高压〔壓〕手段的 yòng gāoyāshǒuduàn de. **'~land** [*pl*] 高原 gāoyuán; 高地 gāodì. **'~life** 豪华〔華〕的现代化生活方式 háohuáde xiàndàihuà shēnghuó fāngshì. **'~light (a)** [常用 *pl*](图画,照片等)光线〔線〕最强处〔處〕 guāngxiàn zuìqiángchù. **(b)** [喻]最突出部分 zuì tūchū bùfen;最精采〔彩〕场〔場〕面 zuì jīngcǎi chǎngmiàn: *the ~ of our holiday* 我们度假中最愉快的场面. □ *vt* 使显〔顯〕著 shǐ xiǎnzhù, 使突出 shǐ tūchū. **,~-'minded** *adj* 品格高尚的 pǐngé gāoshàng de. **,~-'powered** *adj* **(a)** 力量大的 lìliàng dà de. **(b)** 精力充沛的 jīnglì chōngpèi de. **'~-rise** *adj* (建筑)多楼〔樓〕层〔層〕的 duō lóucéng de. **,~'seas** *n pl* [与 *the* 连用]公海 gōnghǎi. **,~ so'ciety** 上流社会 shàngliú shèhuì, 上层阶〔階〕级 shàngcéng jiējí. **,~-'spirited** *adj* 勇敢的 yǒnggǎnde, 振奋〔奮〕的 zhèngfènde. **'~spot** 特点〔點〕 tèdiǎn. **'~street** 主要街道 zhǔyào jiēdào. **,~'tea** [英国英语] (下午五、六点钟时)正式茶点〔點〕 zhèngshì chádiǎn. **'~way**主要公路 zhǔyào gōnglù. **'~wayman** [旧词]拦〔攔〕路抢〔搶〕劫的强盗 lánlù qiǎngjié de qiángdào.

high² /haɪ/ *adv* 高 gāo. *run ~* (情绪)激动〔動〕起来〔來〕 jīdòng qǐlái.

high³ /haɪ/ *n* 高水准〔準〕 gāoshuǐzhǔn: *from* (*on*) ~自上天,自天堂.

high·ly /'haɪlɪ/ *adv* 高度地 gāodùde: *~ paid* 高薪的. *think ~ of sb* 器重某人 qìzhòng mǒurén.

high·ness /'haɪnɪs/ *n* **1** [U] (*lowness* 之对)高 gāo, 高贵 gāoguì. **2** [C] 王室成员的尊称〔稱〕 wángshì chéngyuán de zūnchēng: *His* (*Her*) *Royal H~* 殿下.

hi·jack /'haɪdʒæk/ *vt* 劫持 jiéchí; 劫机〔機〕 jiéjī. **2** 拦〔攔〕路抢〔搶〕劫 lánlù qiǎngjié. **~er** *n* [C]

hike /haɪk/ *vi, n* [C] [非正式用语]远〔遠〕足 yuǎnzú, 长〔長〕途徒步旅行 chángtú túbùlǚxíng. ⇨ hitch-hike.

hil·ari·ous /hɪ'leərɪəs/ *adj* 狂欢〔歡〕的 kuánghuānde; 热〔熱〕闹的 rènàode. **~ly** *adv* **hil·ar·ity** /hɪ'lærətɪ/ *n* [U] 欢闹 huānnào, 热闹 rènào.

hill /hɪl/ *n* [C] **1** 小山 xiǎoshān, 丘陵 qiūlíng, 山坡 shānpō. **2** 坡 pō. **3** 土堆 tǔduī: *'ant~s* 蚁〔蟻〕丘. **'~side** 山坡 shānpō, 山腰 shānyāo. **'~top** 小山山顶 xiǎoshān shāndǐng. **hilly** *adj* [-ier, -iest] 丘陵的 qiūlíngde, 多坡的 duōpōde.

hilt /hɪlt/ *n* [C] 剑〔劍〕柄 jiànbǐng. (*up*) *to the ~* 彻〔徹〕底地 chèdǐde, 完全地 wánquánde: *We support you to the ~.* 我们完全支持你.

him /hɪm/ *personal pron* [he 的宾格]: *Give ~ the money.* 把这钱给他.

him·self /hɪm'self/ *pron* **1** [反身]: *He cut ~.* 他割伤了自己. **(*all*) *by ~*** **(a)** 单独〔獨〕 dāndú, 孤独 gūdú. **(b)** 独力地 dúlìde. **2** [用以加强语气] 他亲〔親〕自 tā qīnzì; 他本人 tā běnrén: *Did you see the manager ~?* 你看见经理本人了吗? **3** *He's not quite ~ today* 他今天有些不舒服.

hind¹ /haɪnd/ *adj* 后〔後〕面的 hòumiànde, 后部的 hòubùde: *the ~ legs of a horse* 马的两只后腿. ⇨ fore. **'~most** *adj* 最后方的 zuì hòufāngde, 最后面的 zuì hòumiàn de. **'~sight** *n* [U] 事后聪〔聰〕明 shìhòu cōngming.

hind² /haɪnd/ *n* [C] 红色雌鹿 hóngsè cílù.

hin·der /'hɪndə(r)/ *vt* 阻碍〔礙〕 zǔ'ài, 阻止 zǔzhǐ.

hin·drance /'hɪndrəns/ *n* [C] 障碍 zhàng'ài; 妨碍的人 fáng'àide rén, 妨碍的物 fáng'àide wù.

Hindu /ˌhɪn'du:/ *n* [C] 印度教教徒 yìndùjiào jiàotú. □ *adj* 印度教的 yìndùjiàode. **H~ism** /ˌhɪndu:ɪzəm/ *n* [U] 印度教 yìndùjiào.

hinge /hɪndʒ/ *n* [C] **1** 铰链〔鏈〕 jiǎoliàn; 合页 héyè. **2** [喻]关〔關〕键 guānjiàn. □ *vt/i* **1** 给...安铰链 gěi...ān jiǎoliàn. **2** *~ on* (或 *upon*) [喻]随...而定 suí...ér dìng, 决定于 juédìng yú: *Success ~s on our armies.* 胜利要靠我们的

军队.

hint /hɪnt/ *n* [C] 暗示 ànshì, 提示 tíshì. □ *vt/i* **1** 暗示 ànshì. **2** ~ *at* 暗示 ànshì.

hip /hɪp/ *n* [C] 臀部 túnbù.

hippo /ˈhɪpəʊ/ *n* [C] [*pl* ~s] 河马[馬] (hippopotamus 的非正式缩略形式) hémǎ.

hip·po·pota·mus /ˌhɪpəˈpɒtəməs/ *n* [C] [*pl* ~es 或 -mi /-maɪ/] 河马[馬] hémǎ.

hire /ˈhaɪə(r)/ *vt* 租 zū, 雇 gù: ~ *a car* 租汽车. □ *n* [U] 租金 zūjīn, 工钱[錢] gōngqián. ˌ~-ˈ**purchase**, (略作: **HP**) 分期付款购[購]买[買]法 fēnqī fùkuǎn gòumǎifǎ.

his /hɪz/ *adj, pron* 他的 tāde: ~ *hand* 他的手, *a friend of* ~. 他的一位朋友.

hiss /hɪs/ *vt/i* **1** 发[發]嘶嘶声[聲] fā sīsī shēng. **2** 发嘘声反对[對] fā xūshēng fǎnduì. □ *n* [C] 嘶嘶声 sīsīshēng.

his·to·gram /ˈhɪstəgræm/ *n* [C] (统计学)直方图[圖] zhífāngtú, 矩形图 jǔxíngtú. ⇨ bar chart, bar graph.

his·tor·ian /hɪˈstɔːrɪən/ *n* [C] 历[歷]史学[學]家 lìshǐxuéjiā.

his·toric /hɪˈstɒrɪk/ *adj* 有历史意义[義]的 yǒu lìshǐ yìyì de: *a(n)* ~ *victory* 有历史意义的胜利.

his·tori·cal /hɪˈstɒrɪkl/ *adj* 历史的 lìshǐde: ~ *novels* 历史小说, ~ *studies* 历史研究. ~**ly** *adv*

his·tory /ˈhɪstrɪ/ *n* [*pl* -ies] **1** [U] 历[歷]史学[學] lìshǐxué, 历史 lìshǐ. **2** [C] 过[過]去事件的记载[載] guòqù shìjiàn de jìzǎi; 沿革 yángé. **3** [C] 某人或某物的事件记载 mǒurén huò mǒuwù de shìjiàn jìzǎi: *his medical* ~ 他的病历. ˌ**natural** ˈ~ 博物学[學] bówùxué.

hit /hɪt/ *vt/i* [*pt, pp* ~] [-tt-] **1** 打 dǎ, 打击[擊] dǎjī; (使)碰撞 pèngzhuàng: *He* ~ *me with a stick.* 他用棍子打我. *The car* ~ *a tree.* 这汽车撞到树上. ~ *the* ˌ*nail on the* ˈ*head* 说中 shuōzhòng; 打中要害 dǎzhòng yàohài. ~ *it* ˈ*off* **(*with sb, together*)** 相处[處]很好 xiāngchù hěnhǎo. **2** ~ *sb hard* 沉重打击 chénzhòng dǎjī: *People were* ~ *hard by the higher taxes.* 人们受到苛捐杂税的沉重打击. **3** 找到zhǎodào; 到达[達] dàodá: ~ *the right path* 走对了路. **4** ~ *out* **(*against*)** [喻]猛打 měngdǎ. **5** ~ *on* (或 *upon*) 碰巧找到 pèngqiǎo zhǎodào. □ *n* [C] **1** 打击 dǎjī. **2** 巨大的成功 jùdàde chénggōng: *His new play is a* ~. 他的新戏十分成功. ˈ~ **parade** 最流行的一批歌曲唱片 zuìliúxíngde yìpī gēqǔ chàngpiàn.

hitch /hɪtʃ/ *vt/i* **1** ~ *up* 急拉 jílā. **2** 钩住 gōuzhù, 拴住 shuānzhù. **3** [非正式用语] = hitch-hike. □ *n* [C] **1** 急拉 jílā; 急推 jítuī. **2** 索结 suǒjié. **3** 暂[暫]时[時]的困难[難] zhànshíde kùnnàn.

hitch-hike /ˈhɪtʃhaɪk/ *vi* 免费搭乘他人便车[車] miǎnfèi dāchéng tārén biànchē. ~**hiker** 免费搭乘他人便车的人 miǎnfèi dāchéng tārén biànchē de rén.

hive /haɪv/ *n* [C] **1** 蜂箱 fēngxiāng, 蜂群 fēngqún. **2** [喻]充满喧闹繁忙的人群的处[處]所 chōngmǎn xuānnào fánmáng de rénqún de chùsuǒ: ~ *of activity* 紧张繁忙的场所. □ *vi* ~ ***off (from)*** [喻]成为[爲]单[單]独[獨]的团[團]体[體] chéngwéi dāndúde tuántǐ.

H.K. = Hong Kong 香港 xiānggǎng.

H.M. = Her (His) Majesty.

H.M.S. = Her (His) Majesty's Ship 英舰[艦] yīngjiàn.

hoard /hɔːd/ *n* [C] 秘藏的钱[錢]财 mìcángde qiáncái. □ *vt/i* ~ **(*up*)** 积[積]攒 jīzǎn, 积聚 jījù.

hoard·ing /ˈhɔːdɪŋ/ *n* [C] 张[張]贴广[廣]告的临[臨]时[時]围[圍]篱[籬] zhāngtiē guǎnggào de línshí wéilí.

hoarse /hɔːs/ *adj* [-r, -st] 嘶哑[啞]的 sīyǎde. ~**ly** *adv* ~**ness** *n* [U]

hoax /həʊks/ *n* [C] 欺骗[騙] qīpiàn. 戏[戲]弄 xìnòng. □ *vt* 欺骗 qīpiàn, 戏弄 xìnòng.

hobble /ˈhɒbl/ *vt/i* **1** 跛行 bǒxíng, 蹒跚 pánshān. **2** 拴住 (马腿) shuānzhù. □ *n* [C] 跛行 bǒxíng.

hobby /ˈhɒbɪ/ *n* [C] [*pl* -ies] 业[業]余[餘]癖好 yèyú pǐhào.

hob·nail /ˈhɒbneɪl/ *n* [C] (钉在鞋底上的) 平头[頭]钉 píngdóudīng. ~**ed** *adj*

hockey /ˈhɒkɪ/ *n* [U] 曲棍球 qūgùnqiú. ˈ**ice** ~ 冰球 bīngqiú.

hod /hɒd/ *n* [C] 砖[磚]斗 zhuāndǒu.

hoe /həʊ/ *n* [U] 锄头[頭] chútou. □ *vt/i* [*pt, pp* ~d] 锄 chú.

hog /hɒg/ *n* [C] **1** 阉[閹]过[過]的公猪 yānguòde gōngzhū. **2** [喻]肮[骯]脏[髒], 贪吃的人 āngzāng, tānchī de rén. ***go the whole*** ~ 干〔幹〕到底 gàndàodǐ, 干彻〔徹〕底 gànchèdǐ: □ *vt* [-gg-] 过〔過〕多地拿取 guòduōde náqǔ. ~**gish** *adj*

Hog·ma·nay /ˈhɒgməneɪ/ *n* (苏格兰)除夕 chúxī, 大年夜 dàniányè.

hogs·head /ˈhɒgzhed/ *n* [C] 大啤酒桶 dàpíjiǔtǒng.

hoist /hɔɪst/ *vt* 升起 shēngqǐ, 扯起 chěqǐ, 绞起 jiǎoqǐ. □ *n* [C] **1** 起重〔重〕机〔機〕qǐzhòngjī, 升降机 shēngjiàngjī. **2**〔非正式用语〕向上推 xiàngshàngtuī.

hold[1] /həʊld/ *n* **1** [C, U] 抓 zhuā, 握 wò, 掌握 zhǎngwò. **2** [C] 用以把握的东〔東〕西 yòngyǐ bǎwò de dōngxi; 支撑点〔點〕zhīchēngdiǎn. ⇨ foothold. **3** (摔角等)擒拿法 qínnáfǎ.

hold[2] /həʊld/ *n* [C] 货舱〔艙〕huòcāng, 底层〔層〕舱 dǐcéngcāng.

hold[3] /həʊld/ *vt/i* [*pt, pp* held /held/] **1** 握 wò, 拿 ná, 抓住 zhuāzhù. ~ ***the line*** 不挂〔掛〕电〔電〕话 bú guà diànhuà. **2** ~ ***one's tongue*** 不说话 bù shuōhuà. ***There is no*** ~***ing*** **(*sb*)** 某人是管不住的 mǒurén shì guǎnbúzhùde. **3** 保持某一姿势〔勢〕bǎochí mǒuyì zīshì: *H~ your head up!* 抬起头! **4** 抓着 zhuāzhe: *the car ~s the road well.* 这汽车在路上走得平稳. **5** 支持 zhīchí: *That branch won't ~ you.* 那树枝吃不消你. **6** 装〔裝〕得下 zhuāngdéxià, 容得下 róngdéxià: *This box will ~ all my books.* 这箱子装得下我所有的书. **7** 吸引…的兴〔興〕趣 xīyǐn...de xìngqù: ~ *an audience* 吸引观众的兴趣. **8** 认为〔爲〕rènwéi: ~ *oneself responsible* 认为自己应该负责. **9** 守住 shǒuzhù. ~ ***one's ground*** **(*own*)** 坚〔堅〕持立场〔場〕jiānchí lìchǎng. **10** 拥〔擁〕有 yōngyǒu, 保有 bǎoyǒu: ~ *shares* 拥有股票. **11** 占〔佔〕有 zhànyǒu, 保持 bǎochí: ~ *office* 在职. **12** 举〔舉〕行 jǔxíng: ~ *a meeting* 举行会议. **13** 不破 búpò 不变〔變〕búbiàn: *The defences held.* 防线被守住. ⇨ 5 above. **14** ~ ***sth against sb*** 把某事作为〔爲〕对〔對〕某人的成见 bǎ mǒushì zuòwéi duì mǒurén de chéngjiàn. ~ ***back*** 踌〔躊〕躇 chóuchú. ~ ***sb*** **(*sth*)** ***back*** **(a)** 克制 kèzhì, 控制 kòngzhì: ~ *back a crowd* 控制群众. **(b)** 隐瞒 yǐnmán. ~***sb*** **(*sth*)** ***down*** **(a)** 压〔壓〕制 yāzhì. **(b)** 压低 yādī, 保持向下 bǎochí xiàngxià: ~ *prices down* 压低物价. ~ ***a job down*** 〔非正式用语〕保持住职〔職〕位 bǎochí zhù zhíwèi. ~ ***in*** 约束 yuēsù, 抑制 yìzhì. ~ ***off*** **(a)** 不使接近 bùshǐ jiējìn: ~ *off the enemy* 阻止敌人. **(b)** 拖延 tuōyán, 延缓 yánhuǎn. ~ ***on*** **(a)** 坚持 jiānchí. **(b)** (命令式)停止 tíngzhǐ. ~ ***on to*** **(a)** 抓住…不放 zhuāzhù...búfàng. **(b)** 不放手 bú fàngshǒu, 不卖〔賣〕掉 bú màidiào. ~ ***sth on*** 使固定 shǐ gùdìng: *a shelf held on by screws* 用螺丝固定的架子. ~ ***out*** **(a)** ~ ***out*** **(*against*)** 坚持 jiānchí, 不退让〔讓〕bú tuìràng. **(b)** 支持 zhīchí, 维持 wéichí: *Our food held out.* 我们的食物得以支持下去. ~ ***out for*** 不妥协 bù tuǒxié: ~ *out for higher wages* 坚持要提高工资. ~ ***sth over*** 延迟〔遲〕yánchí. ~ ***to sth*** **(a)** 忠于 zhōngyú, 坚持 jiānchí. **(b)** 保持 bǎochí: ~ *to a westerly course* 保持向西的路线. ~ ***sb to sth*** 使某人信守(诺言等) shǐ mǒurén xìnshǒu. ~ ***sb*** **(*sth*)** ***up*** **(a)** 支撑 zhīchēng. **(b)** 阻滞〔滯〕zǔzhì. **(c)** 抢〔搶〕劫 qiǎngjié: ~ *up a bank* 抢劫银行. **ˈhold·up** *n* [C] 抢劫 qiǎngjié.

hold-all /ˈhəʊld ɔːl/ *n* [C] 手提旅行包 shǒutí lǚxíngbāo.

hold·ing /ˈhəʊldɪŋ/ *n* [C] 土地 tǔdì, 土地的所有 tǔdìde suǒyǒu.

hold-up /ˈhəʊld ʌp/ *n* ⇨ hold[3]-(14).

hole /həʊl/ *n* [C] **1** 洞 dòng, 孔 kǒng. ***pick*** ~***s in*** 挑毛病 tiāo máobìng. **2** ***be in a*** ~ 〔非正式用语〕处〔處〕于困境 chǔyú kùnjìng. **3** 兽〔獸〕穴 shòuxué. **4**〔喻〕狭〔狹〕窄, 阴〔陰〕暗的房子 xiázhǎi yīnàn de fángzi. □ *vt/i* 打洞 dǎdòng, 穿孔 chuānkǒng.

holi·day /ˈhɒlədeɪ/ *n* [C] **1** 假日 jiàrì, 节〔節〕日 jiérì. ⇨ bank[2]. **2** 〔常用 *pl*〕假期 jiàqī. ***on*** ~ 在度假 zài dùjià. **ˈ~-maker** 度假的人 dùjiàde rén.

holi·ness /ˈhəʊlɪnɪs/ *n* **1** [U] 神圣 shénshèng. **2 His (Your) H~,** 陛下 (对罗马教皇的尊称) bìxià.

hol·low /ˈhɒləʊ/ *adj* **1** 空的 kōngde, 中空的 zhōngkōngde. **2** (声音)空洞的 kōngdòngde, 沉重的 chénzhòngde. **3** 〔喻〕虚假的 xūjiǎde: ~ *words* 虚假的言语; ~ *laughter* 假笑. **4** 凹陷的 āoxiànde, 凹的 āode. ~ *cheeks* 深陷的双颊. □ *n* [C] 洞 dòng, 穴 xué. □ *vt* 挖洞 wādòng: ~ *out a tree to make a boat* 把树凿空造

船.

holly /'hɒlɪ/ *n* [U] 冬青属[屬]植物 dōngqīngshǔ zhíwù.

holo·caust /'hɒləkɔ:st/ *n* [C] 大破坏[壞] dà pòhuài.

holo·gra·phy /hə'lɒgrəfɪ/ *n* [U] (物理)全息照相术[術] quánxī zhàoxiàngshù. **holo·gram** /'hɒləgræm/ *n* [C] (物理)全息图[圖] quánxītú.

hol·ster /'həulstə(r)/ *n* [C] 手枪[槍]皮套[套] shǒuqiāng pítào.

holy /'həulɪ/ *adj* [-ier, -iest] **1** 上帝的 shàngdìde, 与[與]宗教有关[關]的 yǔ zōngjiào yǒuguānde. **2** 献[獻]身于宗教的 xiànshēn yú zōngjiào de.

hom·age /'hɒmɪdʒ/*n* [U] 尊敬 zūnjìng, 敬重 jìngzhòng.

home¹ /həum/ *adv* **1** 在家 zàijiā, 回家 huíjiā: *go ~ from school* 从学校回家. **2** 中目标[標] zhòng mùbiāo: *His arrow flew ~.* 他的箭射中目标. ***bring ~ to sb, come ~ to sb*** 使...认[認]识[識]到 shǐ ... rènshi dào.

home² /həum/ *n* [C] **1** 家 jiā. ***at ~*** 在家里[裡] zài jiālǐ. ***make oneself (be*** 或 ***feel) at ~*** 无[無]拘束 wújūsù. **2** 养[養]育院 yǎngyùyuàn; 疗[療]养所 liáoyǎngsuǒ; 收容所 shōuróngsuǒ: *a children's ~* 儿童中心, *old·persons' ~* 敬老院. **3** 家庭生活 jiātíng shēnghuó. **4** (动植物)产地 chǎndì. □ *vt* (导弹, 飞机等)飞[飛]向(目标) fēixiàng. **,~-'grown** *adj* 本国[國]产[產]的 běnguó chǎnde; 本地产的 běndì chǎn de. **,~'help** 女佣人 nǚyòngrén. **'~land** 祖国 zǔguó. **,~-made** *adj* 家里做的 jiālǐ zuò de. **'H~ Office** 内政部 nèizhèngbù. **'~sick** *adj* 想家的 xiǎngjiāde. **'~sick·ness** *n* [U]. **,~'truth** 确[確]实[實]但使人不愉快的事实 quèshí dàn shǐ rén bù yúkuài de shìshí. **'~work** 家庭作业[業] jiātíng zuòyè. **~ward** *adj* 朝家走的 cháo jiā zǒu de. **~wards** *adv* 向家 xiàngjiā.

home·ly /'həumlɪ/ *adj* [-ier, -iest] **1** 简[簡]朴[樸]的 jiǎnpǔde; 家常的 jiāchángde. **2** 亲[親]切的 qīnqiède, 无[無]拘束的 wú jūsù de: *a ~ atmosphere* 亲切的气氛. **home·li·ness** *n* [U]

homi·cide /'hɒmɪsaɪd/*n* **1** [U] 杀[殺]人 shārén. **2** [C] 杀人者 shārénzhě. **homi·cidal** /-'saɪdl/ *adj*

hom·ing /'həumɪŋ/ *adj* **1** 有归[歸]家性的 yǒu guījiāxìng de. **2** 导[導]航的 dǎohángde.

ho·mo·gene·ous /,hɒmə'dʒi:nɪəs/ *adj* 同类[類]的 tónglèide; 同族的 tóngzúde. ⇨ heterogeneous.

homo·nym /'hɒmənɪm/ *n* [C] 同形异[異]义[義]词 tóngxíngyìyìcí, 同音异义词 tóngyīnyìyìcí.

homo·sex·ual /,hɒmə'sekʃuəl/ *adj* 同性恋[戀]的 tóngxìngliànde. □ *n* [C] 同性恋者 tóngxìngliànzhě. **~ity** /-'ælətɪ/ *n* [U]

Hon. = **1** The Honourable. **2** Honorary.

Hon. Sec. = Honorary Secretary 名誉[譽]秘书[書] míngyù mìshū.

hon·est /'ɒnɪst/ *adj* **1** 诚实[實]的 chéngshíde, 正直的 zhèngzhíde. **2** 显[顯]出诚意的 xiǎnchū chéngyì de, 由诚意产[產]生的 yóu chéngyì chǎnshēng de: *an ~ face* 诚实的面孔. **~ly** *adv* **~y** *n* [U]

honey /'hʌnɪ/ *n* **1** [U] 蜂蜜 fēngmì, 蜜 mì. **2** [C] [*pl* ~s] [非正式用语]亲[親]爱[愛]的人 qīn'àide rén; 宝[寶]贝儿[兒] bǎobèi'er. **'~comb** /-kəum/ *n* [C, U] 巢脾 cháopí, 蜂房 fēngfáng. □ *vt* 使充满孔洞 shǐ chōngmǎn kǒngdòng. **~suckle** *n* [U] [植物]忍冬属[屬] rěndōngshǔ.

honey·moon /'hʌnɪmu:n/ *n* [C] **1** 蜜月 mìyuè. **2** [喻] 共同事业[業]中关[關]系和谐的阶[階]段 gòngtóng shìyè zhōng guānxì héxiéde jiēduàn. □ *vi* 度蜜月 dù mìyuè.

honk /hɒnk/ *n* [C] 雁叫声[聲] yànjiàoshēng, 旧[舊]式汽车[車]喇叭声 jiùshì qìchē lǎbashēng. □ *vi* 发[發]雁叫声 fā yànjiàoshēng, 汽车喇叭响[響] qìchē lǎba xiǎng.

hon·or·ary /'ɒnərərɪ/ *adj* **1** (略作 ***Hon***) 名誉[譽]的 míngyùde, 义[義]务[務]的 yìwùde. **2** 名誉的(学位等) míngyùde.

hon·our [美语 = **honor**] /'ɒnə(r)/ *n* **1** [U] 尊敬 zūnjìng, 公众[衆]的尊重 gōngzhòngde zūnzhòng. **2** [U] 荣[榮]誉[譽] róngyù, 光荣 guāngróng: *a man of ~* 讲信誉的人. **3 Your (His) H~** (对某些法官等的尊称)阁[閣]下 géxià, 先生 xiānsheng. **4** [与 with *a*, *an*, 连用] 引以为[爲]光荣的人或事物 yǐn yǐwéi guāngróngde rén huò shìwù: *You are an ~ to the school.* 你是这个学校的光荣. **5** [*pl*] 荣誉的标志 róngyùde biāozhì, 爵位 juéwèi. **6** [*pl*] (大学)优[優]等成绩 yōuděng chéngjì. □ *vt* **1** 使增光 shǐ zēngguāng, 给以荣誉 gěiyǐ róngyù: *I feel ~ed to meet* *you.* 同你会面感到荣幸. **2** 承兑 chéngduì: ~ *a cheque* 承兑支票.

hon·our·able /'ɒnərəbl/ *adj* **1** 光荣〔榮〕的 guāngróngde, 荣誉〔譽〕的 róngyùde. **2** (略作 **Hon**) 尊敬的(对法官,贵族等的尊称)zūnjìngde. **hon·our·ably** *adv*

hood /hʊd/ *n* [C] **1** 头〔頭〕巾 tóujīn. **2** 形状〔狀〕或用途同头巾相仿之物 xíngzhuàng huò yòngtú tóng tóujīn xiāngfǎng zhī wù. **3** [美语] = bonnet(2). □ *vt* [主要用过去分词]用头巾包 yòng tóujīn bāo.

hoof /hu:f/ *n* [C] [*pl* ~s 或 hooves /hu:vz/] 蹄 tí.

hook /hʊk/ *n* [C] **1** 钩 gōu; 挂〔掛〕钩 guàgōu. **2** (拳击) 肘弯〔彎〕击〔擊〕zhǒuwānjī. □ *vt/i* **1** 钩住 gōuzhù, 用钩连〔連〕结 yòng gōu liánjié. **2** 弯成钩状〔狀〕wānchéng gōuzhuàng: ~ *one's finger* 弯起手指. **3** (高尔夫球) 击左曲球 jī zuǒ qūqiú. **~ed** *adj* 钩状的 gōuzhuàngde. **~*ed* (*on*)** [喻]吸毒成瘾的 xīdú chéngyǐn de.

hoo·li·gan /'hu:lɪgən/ *n* [C] 流氓 liúmáng, 恶〔惡〕少 èshào. **~·ism** *n* [U]

hoop /hu:p/ *n* [C] 箍 gū. □ *vt* 用箍箍(桶等) yòng gū gū.

hoo·ray /hu:'reɪ/ = hurrah.

hoot /hu:t/ *n* [C] **1** 猫头〔頭〕鹰〔鷹〕叫声〔聲〕māotóuyīng jiàoshēng. **2** 汽车〔車〕喇叭声 qìchē lǎbashēng; 雾〔霧〕角信号〔號〕声 wùjiǎo xìnhàoshēng. **3** 表示不同意的叫声 biǎoshì bù tóngyì de jiàoshēng. ***not care a ~*** (或 ***two ~s***) [俚语]毫不在乎 háobúzàihu. □ *vt/i* 向…叫嚣 (at) xiàng…jiàoxiāo, 轰〔轟〕赶〔趕〕hōnggǎn. **~·er** **(a)** 汽笛 qìdí. **(b)** 汽车喇叭 qìchē lǎba.

hooves /hu:vz/ *pl* of hoof.

hop[1] /hɒp/ *n* [C] 蛇麻草 shémácǎo.

hop[2] /hɒp/ *vt/i* [-pp-] **1** (人)单〔單〕脚跳 dānjiǎotiào, (鸟, 动物等)双〔雙〕脚跳 shuāngjiǎotiào. **2** ~ ***over*** (***to***) 作短途旅行 zuò duǎntú lǚxíng. ~ ***it*** [非正式用语]走开〔開〕zǒukāi. □*n* [C] **1** 单足跳 dānzútiào. **2** 短跳 duǎntiào. **3** 长距离〔離〕飞〔飛〕行中的一段 cháng jùlí fēixíng zhōng de yíduàn.

hope /həʊp/ *n* **1** [C, U] 希望 xīwàng, 信心 xìnxīn: *There is no ~ that they are alive.* 他们仍然活着的希望没有了. ***hold out some ~ (of sth)*** 抱某些希望 bào mǒuxiē xīwàng. ***hold out no (little) ~ (of sth)*** 不抱希望 búbào xīwàng. ***(be) beyond*** (或 ***past***) ~ 没有希望 méiyǒu xīwàng. ***raise sb's ~s*** 燃起某人的希望之火 ránqǐ mǒurénde xīwàng zhī huǒ. **2** [C] 寄予希望的人或物 jìyǔ xīwàng de rén huò wù. □ *vt/i* 希望 xīwàng, 盼望 pànwàng: *I ~ you win.* 我希望你胜利. **~ful** *adj* **(a)** 抱有希望的 bàoyǒu xīwàng de. **(b)** 有希望的 yǒu xīwàng de, 有前途的 yǒu qiántú de. **~fully** *adv* **~less** *adj* 没有希望的 méiyǒu xīwàng de. **~less·ly** *adv*

hop·per /'hɒpə(r)/ *n* [C] **1** 漏斗 lòudǒu, 送料斗 sòngliàodǒu. **2** 跳虫 tiàochóng.

horde /hɔ:d/ *n* [C] **1** 游牧部落 yóumù bùluò. **2** 群 qún: ~*s of football fans* 一帮足球迷.

hor·izon /hə'raɪzn/ *n* [C] **1** 地平线〔線〕dìpíngxiàn. **2** [喻]眼界 yǎnjiè, 视野 shìyě. **~tal** /ˌhɒrɪ'zɒntl/ *adj* 水平的 shuǐpíngde, 平的 píngde. ⇨ vertical. **~tally** *adv*

hor·mone /'hɔ:məʊn/ *n* [C] 荷尔〔爾〕蒙 hé'ěrméng, 激素 jīsù.

horn /hɔ:n/ *n* **1** [C] (兽)角 jiǎo. **2** [U] 角质〔質〕物 jiǎozhìwù. **3** [C] 角制〔製〕品 jiǎozhìpǐn. **4** [C] 喇叭 lǎba, 管 guǎn, 号〔號〕hào. **5** 号角 hàojiǎo: *a 'fog ~* 雾角. **horny** *adj* [-ier, -iest] 角制的 jiǎozhìde, 角形的 jiǎoxíngde.

hor·net/'hɔ:nɪt/ *n* [C] 大黄蜂 dà huángfēng.

hor·oscope /'hɒrəskəʊp/ *n* [C] 星占 xīngzhàn; 算命天宫图〔圖〕suànmìng tiāngōngtú.

hor·rible /'hɒrəbl/ *adj* **1** 可怕的 kěpàde, 恐怖的 kǒngbùde. **2** [非正式用语]讨厌〔厭〕的 tǎoyànde. *What a ~ party!* 多糟糕的聚会!

hor·ribly *adv*

hor·rid /'hɒrɪd/ *adj* **1** 可怕的 kěpàde. **2** [非正式用语]讨厌〔厭〕的 tǎoyànde. **~ly** *adv*

hor·rific /hə'rɪfɪk/ *adj* [非正式用语]非常可怕的 fēicháng kěpàde.

hor·rify /'hɒrɪfaɪ/ *vt* [*pt*, *pp* -ied] 使恐怖 shǐ kǒngbù, 使害怕 shǐ hàipà: *horrified by his death* 对他的死感到震惊.

hor·ror /'hɒrə(r)/ *n* [C, U] 恐怖 kǒngbù, 极〔極〕端厌〔厭〕恶〔惡〕jíduān yànwù. **'~ stories** 恐怖故事 kǒngbù gùshi. **'~ films** 恐怖电〔電〕影 kǒngbù diànyǐng. **'~-struck** *adj* (人)受惊吓的 shòu jīngxià de.

hors d'œuvres /ˌɔːˈdɜːvrə/ *n pl* 餐前的小吃 cānqiánde xiǎochī.

horse /hɔːs/ *n* **1** [C] 马〔馬〕mǎ. *be* (或 *get*) *on one's high* ~ 趾高气〔氣〕扬 zhǐgāoqìyáng, 盛气凌人 shèngqì língrén. ***(straight) from the*** ˌ**~'s** ˈ***mouth*** (情报)第一手的 dìyīshǒude. **2** [C] 支架 zhījià: *a clothes-~* 烘衣架. ˈ**~back** *n* (只用于) *on ~back* 骑〔騎〕马 qímǎ. ˈ**~power,** (略作 **hp**) 马力 mǎlì. ˈ**~shoe** 马蹄铁〔鐵〕mǎtítiě.

hor·ti·cul·ture /ˈhɔːtɪkʌltʃə(r)/ *n* [U] 园〔園〕艺〔藝〕yuányì. **hor·ti'cul·tural** *adj*

hose¹ /həʊz/ *n* [C, U] 输〔輸〕水软〔軟〕管 shūshuǐ ruǎnguǎn, 一段输水软管 yíduàn shūshuǐ ruǎnguǎn. □ *vt* 浇〔澆〕(园子) jiāo; 用水管冲洗 (汽车等) yòng shuǐguǎn chōngxǐ. ˈ**~pipe** 一段水龙软管 yíduàn shuǐlóng ruǎnguǎn.

hose² /həʊz/ *n* [U] 长统袜〔襪〕chángtǒngwà; 短统袜 duǎntǒngwà.

ho·sier /ˈhəʊzɪə(r)/ *n* [C] 内衣业〔業〕商人 nèiyīyè shāngrén. **ho·siery** *n* [U] 内衣业货品 nèiyīyè huòpǐn.

hos·pit·able /həˈspɪtəbl/ *adj* 好客的 hàokède, 招待周到的 zhāodài zhōudào de. **hos·pit·ably** *adv*

hos·pi·tal /ˈhɒspɪtl/ *n* [C] 医〔醫〕院 yīyuàn.

hos·pi·tal·ity /ˌhɒspɪˈtælətɪ/ *n* [U] 好客 hàokè 殷勤 yīnqín.

host¹ /həʊst/ *n* [C] 许多 xǔduō, 一大群 yídàqún: *a whole ~ of friends* 很多朋友.

host² /həʊst/ *n* [C] **1** 主人 zhǔrén. **2** 旅店老板 lǚdiàn lǎobǎn.

hos·tage /ˈhɒstɪdʒ/ *n* [C] 人质〔質〕rénzhì.

hos·tel /ˈhɒstl/ *n* [C] 校外出租给学〔學〕生的宿舍 xiàowài chūzū gěi xuéshēng de sùshè. ˈ**youth** ~ (有关当局为徒步或骑自行车旅行的青年设立的)招待所 zhāodàisuǒ.

host·ess /ˈhəʊstɪs/ *n* 女服务〔務〕员 nǚfúwùyuán, 女招待 nǚzhāodài; 女主人 nǚzhǔrén. ⇨ air hostess.

hos·tile /ˈhɒstaɪl/ *adj* **1** 敌〔敵〕方的 dífāngde, 敌对〔對〕的 díduìde. **2** 不友好的 bùyǒuhǎode. **~ly** *adv*

hos·til·ity /hɒˈstɪlətɪ/ *n* [*pl* -ies] **1** [U] 敌〔敵〕意 díyì, 敌视 díshì. **2** [*pl*] 战〔戰〕争 zhànzhēng, 战争行动〔動〕zhànzhēng xíngdòng.

hot /hɒt/ *adj* [-ter, -test] **1** 热〔熱〕的 rède. **2** 辣的 làde: *~ spices* 辣的调味品. **3** 强烈的 qiángliède, 猛烈的 měngliède; 暴躁的 bàozàode: *a ~ temper* 暴躁的脾气. **4** [用作副词] 新近的 xīnjìnde, 刚〔剛〕刚的 gānggāngde: *newspapers ~ off the press* 刚出版的报纸. **5** 紧〔緊〕跟的 jǐngēnde: *~ on his trail* 紧紧追踪着他. □ *vt/i* [-tt-] **~ (*sth*) *up*** [非正式用语] (使)变〔變〕热 biànrè; [喻]激动〔動〕起来〔來〕jīdòng qǐlái. ˌ**~ 'air** 空话 kōnghuà. ˌ**~-'blooded** *adj* 热情的 rèqíngde, 易激动的 yìjīdòngde. ˈ**~ dog** 红肠〔腸〕面包 hóngcháng miànbāo. ˈ**~foot** *adv* 匆忙地 cōngmángde: *follow the enemy ~foot* 紧急追赶敌人. □ *vi* ***~ foot (it)*** 急忙地走 jímángde zǒu. ˈ**~head** 急性子的人. ˌ**~-'headed** *adj* ˈ**~-house** 温室 wēnshì. ˈ**~ line** 热线〔線〕(直接联系的途径) rèxiàn. ˌ**~-'tempered** *adj* 易怒的 yìnùde. ˌ**~ 'water** [非正式用语] 困境 kùnjìng, 麻烦 máfan. *be in* (*get into*) *~ water* 陷入困境. **~ly** *adv* **(a)** 热烈地 rèliède; 热心地 rèxīnde. **(b)** 紧紧地 jǐnjǐnde. *~ly pursued* 紧追.

ho·tel /həʊˈtel/ *n* [C] 旅馆 lǚguǎn. **~ier** *n* [C] 旅馆老板 lǚguǎn lǎobǎn.

hound /haʊnd/ *n* [C] 猎〔獵〕狗 liègǒu. □ *vt* 追逼 zhuībī, 困扰〔擾〕kùnrǎo, 追逐 zhuīzhú: *~ed by the newspapers* 被记者纠缠.

hour /aʊə(r)/ *n* [C] **1** 小时〔時〕xiǎoshí. **2** 时刻 shíkè, 钟〔鐘〕点〔點〕zhōngdiǎn: *at all ~s* 任何时刻. **3** [*pl*] 固定时间〔間〕gùdìng shíjiān: *working ~s* 工作时间. **4** 特定时刻 tèdìng shíkè: *in the ~ of danger* 危险时刻. ˈ**~ hand** 时针 shízhēn. **~ly** *adj, adv* **(a)** 每小时的 měixiǎoshíde, 每小时地 měixiǎoshíde. **(b)** 时时刻刻 shíshíkèkè: *We expect news ~ly.* 我们时时刻刻在期待着消息. **(c)** 按小时 àn xiǎoshí: *paid ~ly* 按小时付费.

house¹ /haʊs/ *n* [C] [*pl* ~s /ˈhaʊzɪz/] **1** 房屋 fángwū. ⇨ home²(1). **2** 特定用途的建筑 tèdìng yòngtú de jiànzhù: *a* ˈ*hen~* 鸡〔鷄〕舍. **3** 议〔議〕院 yìyuàn, 议院大楼〔樓〕yìyuàn dàlóu: *the H-~s of Parliament* 国〔國〕会〔會〕两院. **4** 显〔顯〕贵家族 xiǎnguì jiāzú. **5** 观〔觀〕众〔衆〕guānzhòng, 听〔聽〕众 tīngzhòng: *a full ~* 满座, 客满. ***bring the*** ˈ***~ down*** 博得满堂喝采 bódé mǎntáng hècǎi. ***on the ~*** 由店家出钱 yóu diànjiā chūqián. ˈ**~bound** *adj* 闲居家中的 xiánjū jiāzhōng de. ˈ**~breaker** 入屋抢〔搶〕劫者 rùwū qiǎngjié zhě. '~**hold** 家庭 jiātíng, 家属〔屬〕 jiāshǔ. '~**holder** 住房者 zhùfángzhě, 房主 fángzhǔ. '~-**keeper** 女管家 nǚguǎnjiā. '~**keeping** (a) 家务〔務〕管理 jiāwù guǎnlǐ, 家政 jiāzhèng. (b) 家庭经〔經〕济〔濟〕 jiātíng jīngjì. '~-**master** (学生宿舍)舍监〔監〕 shèjiān. '~**proud** *adj* 关〔關〕心家事的 guānxīn jiāshì de. '~**wife** 做家务〔務〕的妇〔婦〕女 zuò jiāwù de fùnǚ. 家庭妇女 jiātíng fùnǚ. '~-**work** 家务劳〔勞〕动〔動〕 jiāwù láodòng. ⇨ homework

house² /haʊz/ *vt* 供给…房子住 gōngjǐ... fángzi zhù.

hous·ing /'haʊzɪŋ/ *n* **1** [U] 住房供给 zhùfáng gōngjǐ. **2** [C] (机器等的)遮盖物 zhēgàiwù. '~ **estate** 住宅区〔區〕 zhùzháiqū.

hove /həʊv/ *pt, pp* of heave.

hovel /'hɒvl/ *n* [C] 陋屋 lòuwū, 棚 péng, 茅屋 máowū.

hover /'hɒvə(r)/ *vi* **1** (鸟)盘旋 pánxuán, 翱翔 áoxiáng. **2** (人)逗留在附近 dòuliú zài fùjìn. **3** [喻] 徘徊 páihuái: ~ *between life and death* 处于生死关头. '~**craft** 气〔氣〕垫〔墊〕船 qìdiànchuán.

how /haʊ/ *adv* **1** (方法,方式)怎样〔樣〕 zěnyàng, 怎么〔麼〕 zěnme: *H~ does this machine work?* 这台机器是怎样运转的? **2** (程度,数量)多么 duōme, 如何 rúhé: *H~ old are you?* 你多大年纪? *H~ kind you are.* 你多好啊. **3** (健康情况)怎样 zěnyàng: *H~ are you?* 你身体好吗? *H~ do you do?* (正式介绍见面时用语) 你好 nǐhǎo. *H~* **about** …怎么样? …zěnmeyàng? …好吗? …hǎoma? *H~ about coming for a walk?* 出去散散步怎么样?

how·ever /haʊ'evə(r)/ *adv* 无〔無〕论〔論〕如何 wúlùn rúhé, 不管怎样〔樣〕 bùguǎn zěnyàng: *H~ hard I try, I cannot win.* 不管我怎样努力,我胜不了. □ *conj* 然而 ránér, 可是 kěshì.

howl /haʊl/ *n* [C] **1** (狼等)嗥叫 háojiào. **2** (痛苦时)哀号〔號〕 āiháo; (表示蔑视)狂笑 kuángxiào. **3** (风)怒吼 nùhǒu. □ *vt/i* 嗥叫 (at) háojiào, 哀号 āiháo, 狂笑 kuángxiào, 怒吼 nùhǒu.

h.p. = **1** horse-power. **2** hire purchase.

H.Q. = Headquarters.

hr(s). = hour(s).

hub /hʌb/ *n* [C] **1** 轮〔輪〕毂〔轂〕 lúngǔ. **2** [喻]活动中心 huódòng zhōngxīn.

hub·bub /'hʌbʌb/ *n* [U] 吵闹 chǎonào, 喧哗〔嘩〕 xuānhuá.

huddle /'hʌdl/ *vt/i* **1** 挤〔擠〕成一团〔團〕 jǐchéng yìtuán. **2** ~ *up against* 缩成一团 suōchéng yìtuán, □ *n* [C] 杂〔雜〕乱〔亂〕的一团 záluànde yìtuán.

hue¹ /hju:/ *n* [C] 颜色 yánsè, 色度 sèdù.

hue² /hju:/ *n* [C] ~ *and cry* 追捕罪犯时〔時〕的叫喊声〔聲〕 zhuīpǔ zuìfàn shí de jiàohǎnshēng.

huff /hʌf/ *n* **be in** (或 **get into**) **a** ~ 发〔發〕脾气〔氣〕 fāpíqì.

hug /hʌg/ *vt* [-gg-] **1** 紧〔緊〕抱 jǐnbào, 拥〔擁〕抱 yōngbào. **2** ~ *the shore* 紧紧地沿着 jǐnjǐnde yánzhe. □ *n* [C] 紧紧的拥抱 jǐnjǐnde yōngbào.

huge /hju:dʒ/ *adj* 巨大的 jùdàde, 庞〔龐〕大的 pángdàde. ~**ly** *adv* 非常地 fēichángde.

hulk /hʌlk/ *n* 废〔廢〕船 fèichuán. **2** 巨大笨重的人或物 jùdà bènzhòng de rén huò wù. ~**ing** *adj* 巨大而笨重的 jùdà ér bènzhòng de.

hull /hʌl/ *n* [C] 船体〔體〕 chuántǐ.

hullo /ˌhʌ'ləʊ/ *int* = hallo.

hum /hʌm/ *vt/i* [-mm-] **1** 发〔發〕哼哼声〔聲〕 fā hēnghēng shēng. **2** 哼曲子 hēngqǔzi. **3** 活跃〔躍〕 huóyuè, 忙碌 mánglù: *a factory ~-ming with activity* 忙碌的工厂. □ *n* [C] 哼哼声 hēnghēng shēng, 嗡嗡声 wēngweng shēng.

hu·man /'hju:mən/ *adj* **1** 人的 rénde, 人类〔類〕的 rénlèide. **2** 有人性的 yǒu rénxìng de, 有人情味的 yǒu rénqíngwèi de: *The manager is quite ~ really.* 这经理真富有人情味. □ *n* [C] 人 rén. ˌ~ '**rights** 人权〔權〕 rénquán ~**ly** *adv* 用人力 yòngrénlì, 人力所及地 rénlì suǒ jí de: *do everything ~ly possible to help* 尽人力之所及进行帮助.

hu·mane /hju:'meɪn/ *adj* 仁慈的 réncíde, 人道的 réndàode. ~**ly** *adv*

hu·man·ity /hju:'mænətɪ/ *n* [U] **1** 人类 rénlèi. **2** 仁慈 réncí, 仁爱〔愛〕 rén'ài.

humble /'hʌmbl/ *adj* [-r, -st] **1** 谦卑的 qiānbēide, 恭顺的 gōngshùnde. **2** 地位低下的 dìwèi dīxià de, 微贱〔賤〕的 wēijiànde. **3** 简〔簡〕陋的 jiǎnlòude: *a ~ house* 简陋的房子. □ *vt* 使卑下 shǐ bēixià, 贬抑 biǎnyì. **hum·bly** *adv*

hum·drum /'hʌmdrʌm/ *adj* 单〔單〕调的 dāndiàode, 枯燥的 kūzàode.

hu·mid /'hju:mɪd/ *adj* 湿〔濕〕的 shīde, 湿气〔氣〕的 shīqìde. ~**ity** /-'mɪdɪtɪ/ *n* [U] 湿度 shīdù, 空气湿度 kōngqì shīdù.

hu·mili·ate /hju:'mɪlɪeɪt/ *vt* 羞辱 xiūrǔ, 使丢脸〔臉〕 shǐ diūliǎn. **hu·mili'ation** *n* [C, U]

hu·mil·ity /hju:'mɪlətɪ/ *n* [U] 谦卑 qiānbēi, 谦恭 qiāngōng.

hu·mor·ist /'hju:mərɪst/ *n* [C] 幽默家 yōumòjiā, 幽默作家 yōumò zuòjiā.

hu·mor·ous /'hju:mərəs/ *adj* 幽默的 yōumòde, 有幽默感的 yǒu yōumògǎn de. ~**ly** *adv*

hu·mour [美语 = **hu·mor**] /'hju:mə(r)/ *n* [U] 幽默 yōumò, 诙谐 huīxié: *a sense of* ~ 幽默感. □ *vt* 迁〔遷〕就 qiānjiù, 使满足 shǐ mǎnzú.

hump /hʌmp/ *n* [C] 圆形隆起物 yuánxíng lóngqǐwù; 驼〔駝〕峰 tuófēng. □ *vt* **1** 使隆起成圆形 shǐ lóngqǐ chéng yuánxíng. **2** [非正式用语] 把…驼在背上 bǎ…tuó zài bèishàng.

hunch /hʌntʃ/ *n* [C] ***have a ~ that*** [俚语]预感到… yù gǎndào …, 总〔總〕感到… zǒng gǎndào…. □ *vt* 使隆起 shǐ lóngqǐ: ~ *one's shoulders* 耸起双肩. '~**-back** 驼背 tuóbèi, 驼背的人 tuóbèide rén. '~**-backed** *adj*

hun·dred /'hʌndrəd/ *adj, n* [C] 一百 yìbǎi, 一百个〔個〕 yìbǎigè. '~**weight,** (略作 **cwt**) [英国英语] 英担〔擔〕(衡名) yīngdàn. **hundredth** /'hʌndrədθ/ *adj, n* [C] (略作 *100th*) 百分之一 bǎifēn zhī yī; 第一百 dìyìbǎi.

hung /hʌŋ/ *pt, pp* of hang².

hun·ger /'hʌŋgə(r)/ *n* **1** [U] 饿 è. **2** [喻]渴望 kěwàng, 欲望 yùwàng. □ *vi* **1** 饿 è. **2** 渴望 kěwàng. '~**-strike** 绝食 juéshí.

hun·gry /'hʌŋgrɪ/ *adj* [-ier, -iest] 饥饿的 jī'ède, 表示饥饿的 biǎoshì jī'è de, 使饥饿的 shǐ jī'è de. **hun·grily** *adv*

hunk /hʌŋk/ *n* [C] 厚块 hòukuài, 大块 dàkuài: *a ~ of bread* 一大块面包.

hunt /hʌnt/ *vt/i* **1** 打猎〔獵〕 dǎliè, 猎取 lièqǔ. **2** ~ ***down*** 穷追…直至发〔發〕现 qióngzhuī … zhí zhì fāxiàn. ~ ***for*** 搜寻 sōuxún. □ *n* **1** [*sing* 与 *the, a* 或 *an* 连用] 狩猎 shòuliè; 搜寻 sōuxún. **2** 猎狐队〔隊〕 lièhúduì. 猎人 lièrén.

hurdle /'hɜ:dl/ *n* [C] **1** 跳栏〔欄〕 tiàolán. **2** [喻]障碍〔礙〕 zhàng'ài. □ *vt* 参〔參〕加跳栏比赛 cānjiā tiàolán bǐsài.

hurl /hɜ:l/ *vt* 猛掷〔擲〕 měngzhì, 猛投 měngtóu. □ *n* [C] 猛掷 měngzhì, 猛投 měngtóu.

hurly-burly /'hɜ:lɪ bɜ:lɪ/ *n* [U] 喧嚣 xuānxiāo, 喧哗〔嘩〕 xuānhuá.

hur·rah /hʊ'rɑ:/ *int* 好哇! hǎowa!

hur·ri·cane /'hʌrɪkən/ *n* [C] 飓〔颶〕风〔風〕 jùfēng. '~ **lamp** 风灯〔燈〕 fēngdēng.

hurry /'hʌrɪ/ *n* [U] 匆忙 cōngmáng, 仓〔倉〕促 cāngcù. ***in a*** ~ 急忙的 jímángde, 匆忙的 cōngmángde. □ *vt/i* [*pt, pp* -ied] (使)赶〔趕〕紧〔緊〕 gǎnjǐn, 匆忙 cōngmáng. ~ ***up!*** 赶紧! gǎnjǐn! **hurried** *adj* 匆促的 cōngcùde, 匆忙的 cōngmángde. **hur·ried·ly** *adv*

hurt /hɜ:t/ *vt/i* [*pt, pp* ~] **1** (使)受伤〔傷〕痛 shòu shāngtòng. **2** 伤…感情 shāng…gǎnqíng, 使…痛心 shǐ…tòngxīn. **3** 危害 wēihài, 损害 sǔnhài: *It won't ~ to wait.* 等一等没有妨碍. □ *n* [U] 伤害 shānghài, 危害 wēihài. ~**ful** *adj*

hurtle /'hɜ:tl/ *vi* 猛烈落下 měngliè luòxià, 猛烈碰撞 měngliè pèngzhuàng: *Rocks ~d down the mountain.* 岩石从山上飞滚下来.

hus·band /'hʌzbənd/ *n* [C] 丈夫 zhàngfu.

hush /hʌʃ/ *vt/i* (使)静下来〔來〕 jìng xiàlái. ~ ***sth up*** 保守秘密 bǎoshǒu mìmì. □ *n* [U] 沉默 chénmò, 寂静 jìjìng.

husk /hʌsk/ *n* [C] 荚〔莢〕 jiá. 外果壳〔殼〕 wàiguǒké. □ *vt* 去荚 qùjiá, 去壳 qùké.

husky /'hʌskɪ/ *adj* [-ier, -iest] 沙哑〔啞〕的 shāyǎde. □ *n* [C] [*pl* -ies] 爱〔愛〕斯基摩种〔種〕狗 àisījīmózhǒnggǒu. **husk·ily** *adv*

hustle /'hʌsl/ *vt/i* **1** 乱〔亂〕推 luàntuī. **2** 催促 cuīcù. □ *n* [只用 *sing*] 急速而有力的活动〔動〕 jísù ér yǒulì de huódòng.

hut /hʌt/ *n* [C] **1** 小棚屋 xiǎopéngwū. **2** 临〔臨〕时〔時〕木头〔頭〕营〔營〕房 línshí mùtou yíngfáng.

hutch /hʌtʃ/ *n* [C] 兔箱 tùxiāng, 兔笼〔籠〕 tùlóng.

hya·cinth /'haɪəsɪnθ/ *n* [C] [植物]风〔風〕信子 fēngxìnzǐ.

hy·æna /haɪ'i:nə/ ⇨ hyena.

hy·brid /'haɪbrɪd/ *n, adj* 杂〔雜〕种〔種〕 zázhǒng; 杂种的 zázhǒngde: *A mule is a ~ (animal).* 骡子是杂种(动物).

hy·drant /'haɪdrənt/ *n* [C] 取水管 qǔshuǐguǎn.

hy·drau·lic /haɪ'drɔ:lɪk/ *adj* 水

力的 shuǐlìde; 液力的 yèlìde; 液压〔壓〕的 yèyāde.

hy·dro·elec·tric /ˌhaɪdrəʊɪ'lektrɪk/ *adj* 水力发〔發〕电〔電〕的 shuǐlì fādiàn de.

hy·dro·foil /'haɪdrəfɔɪl/ *n* [C] 水翼艇 shuǐyìtǐng.

hy·dro·gen /'haɪdrədʒən/ *n* [U] 氢〔氫〕气〔氣〕(化学符号 **H**) qīngqì. '~ **bomb** 氢弹〔彈〕 qīngdàn.

hy·drom·eter /haɪ'drɒmɪtə(r)/ *n* [C] 液体〔體〕比重计 yètǐ bǐzhòngjì.

hy·ena, hy·æna /haɪ'i:nə/ *n* [C] 鬣狗 liègǒu.

hy·giene /'haɪdʒi:n/ *n* [U] 卫〔衛〕生 wèishēng. **hy'gienic** *adj* 卫生的 wèishēngde. **hy·gieni·cally** *adv*

hymn /hɪm/ *n* [C] (宗教)赞美诗 zànměishī, 圣〔聖〕歌 shènggē. □ *vt* 为〔爲〕...唱赞美诗 wèi...chàng zànměishī.

hy·per·market /'haɪpəmɑ:kɪt/ *n* [C] 大型超级市场〔場〕 dàxíng chāojí shìchǎng.

hy·phen /'haɪfn/ *n* [C] 连〔連〕字号 liánzìhào. □ *vt* 用连字号连接 yòng liánzìhào liánjiē. **~ate** /-eɪt/ *vt* = hyphen.

hyp·no·sis /hɪp'nəʊsɪs/ *n* [C] [*pl* -ses /-si:z/] 催眠状态〔態〕 cuīmián zhuàngtài; 催眠术〔術〕 cuīmiánshù. **hyp·notic** /hɪp'nɒtɪk/ *adj* **hyp·not·ism**/ 'hɪpnətɪzəm/ *n* [U] 催眠 cuīmián, 催眠状态 cuīmián zhuàngtài. **hyp·not·ist** *n* [C] **hyp·not·ize** /-aɪz/ *vt* 为〔爲〕...催眠 wèi...cuīmián.

hy·poc·risy /hɪ'pɒkrəsɪ/ *n* [C, U] [*pl* -ies] 伪〔僞〕善 wěishàn, 虚伪 xūwěi.

hyp·ocrite /'hɪpəkrɪt/ *n* [C] 伪〔僞〕君子 wěijūnzǐ. **hy·po'criti·cal** *adj*

hy·po·der·mic /ˌhaɪpə'dɜ:mɪk/ *adj* 皮下注射的 píxià zhùshè de.

hy·pot·en·use /haɪ'pɒtənju:z/ *n* [C] [数学]弦 xuán, 斜边〔邊〕 xiébiān.

hy·poth·esis /haɪ'pɒθəsɪs/ *n* [C] [*pl* -ses /-si:z/] (逻辑)前提 qiántí, 假说 jiǎshuō. **hy·po·theti·cal** /ˌhaɪpə'θetɪkl/ *adj*

hys·teria /hɪ'stɪərɪə/ *n* [U] **1** 歇斯底里 xiēsīdǐlǐ; 癔病 yìbìng. **2** 狂热〔熱〕 kuángrè. **hys·teri·cal** /hɪ'sterɪkl/ *adj* **hys·ter·ics** *n pl* 癔病发〔發〕作 yìbìng fāzuò.

I i

I[1] **i** /aɪ/ [*pl* I's i's /aɪz/] **1** 英语的第九个字母 yīngyǔde dìjiǔgè zìmǔ. **2** 罗马〔馬〕数字 I luómǎ shùzì yī.

I[2] /aɪ/ *personal pron* 我 wǒ.

i/c= in charge 负责 fùzé.

I.C.B.M.= Inter-Continental Ballistic Missile 洲际〔際〕弹〔彈〕道导〔導〕弹 zhōujì dàndào dǎodàn.

ice /aɪs/ *n* **1** [U] 冰 bīng. **2** [C] 冰制〔製〕食品 bīngzhì shípǐn. □ *vt/i* **1** 使冰冷 shǐ bīnglěng. **2** 用冰覆盖 yòng bīng fùgài. **3** 加糖霜于(糕点) jiā tángshuāng yú. ⇨ icing. '**I~ Age** 冰河时〔時〕期 bīnghé shíqī. '**~berg** 冰山 bīngshān, 流冰 liúbīng. ˌ**~-'cream** *n* [C, U] 冰淇淋 bīngqílín. '**~hockey** ⇨ hockey. '**~rink** 室内溜冰场〔場〕 shìnèi liūbīngchǎng. '**~-skate** (溜冰鞋上的) 冰刀 bīngdāo. □ *vi* 溜冰 liūbīng.

icicle /'aɪsɪkl/ *n* [C] 冰柱 bīngzhù.

icing /'aɪsɪŋ/ *n* [U] (糕饼表层上的)糖霜 tángshuāng; 糖衣 tángyī; 酥皮 sūpí.

icy /'aɪsɪ/ *adj* [-ier, -iest] **1** 冰冷的 bīnglěngde. **2** 盖着冰的 gàizhe bīng de. **3** [喻]冷冰冰的 lěngbīngbīngde, 不友好的 bù yǒuhǎo de: *an ~ stare* 冷冰冰的盯视. **icily** *adv*

I'd /aɪd/ = *I had* 或 *I would*.

idea /aɪ'dɪə/ *n* [C] **1** 思想 sīxiǎng, 概念 gàiniàn. **2** 计划〔劃〕 jìhuà, 主意 zhǔyi, 打算 dǎsuàn: *He's full of new ~s.* 他新主意满多. **3** 意见 yìjiàn. **4** 认〔認〕为〔爲〕某事可能发〔發〕生的感觉〔覺〕 rènwéi mǒushì kěnéng fāshēng de gǎnjué: *I have an ~ that she will be late.* 我认为她要迟到.

ideal /aɪ'dɪəl/ *adj* **1** 完美的 wánměide, 理想的 lǐxiǎngde: *The weather was ~.* 天气是理想的. **2** 想象中的 xiǎngxiàngzhōngde; 空想的 kōngxiǎngde: *an ~ world* 想象的世界. □ *n* [C] 理想 lǐxiǎng; 理想的事物 lǐxiǎngde shìwù. **~ist** 理想主义〔義〕者 lǐxiǎngzhǔyìzhě. **~'listic** *adj*

ideal·ize /aɪ'dɪəlaɪz/ *vt* 使理想化

shǐ lǐxiǎnghuà. **ideal·i'zation** *n* [U]

ident·ical /aɪ'dentɪkl/ *adj* **1** 同一的 tóngyīde. **2** 完全相似的 wánquán xiāngsì de, 完全相同的 wánquán xiāngtóng de: ～ *twins* 同卵双生. **～ly** *adv*

ident·ify /aɪ'dentɪfaɪ/ *vt* [*pt*, *pp* -ied] **1** 认〔認〕出 rènchū, 识〔識〕别 shíbié: *Can you ～ the man who attacked you?* 你能认出打你的人吗? **2 ～ with** 认为〔爲〕...与〔與〕...一致 rènwéi ... yǔ ... yízhì. **～ oneself with** 和...打成一片 hé...dǎchéng yípiàn. **identi·fi·ca·tion** /-fɪ'keɪʃn/ *n* **(a)** [U] 认出 rènchū, 识别 shíbié **(b)** [C] 身份证〔證〕明 shēngfèn zhèngmíng.

ident·ity /aɪ'dentətɪ/ *n* [*pl* -ies] **1** [U] 同一 tóngyī, 一致 yízhì. **2** [C, U] 身份 shēngfèn; 个〔個〕性 gèxìng, 特性 tèxìng: *prove one's ～* 证明某人的身份.

ideol·ogy /ˌaɪdɪ'ɒlədʒɪ/ *n* [*pl* -ies] [C] 思想 sīxiǎng, 思想体〔體〕系 sīxiǎng tǐxì, 意识〔識〕形态〔態〕yìshìxíngtài. **ideo'logi·cal** *adj*

idi·ocy /'ɪdɪəsɪ/ *n* [*pl* -ies] **1** [U] 极〔極〕端愚笨 jíduān yúbèn, 白痴〔癡〕báichī. **2** [C] 极愚蠢的言行 jí yúchǔn de yánxíng.

id·iom /'ɪdɪəm/ *n* [C] 习〔習〕语 xíyǔ, 成语 chéngyǔ, 惯用语 guànyòngyǔ. **～atic** /-'mætɪk/ *adj*

idio·syn·crasy /ˌɪdɪə'sɪŋkrəsɪ/ *n* [C] [*pl* -ies] (人的)特性 tèxìng; 癖性 pǐxìng. **idio·syn'cratic** *adj*

id·iot /'ɪdɪət/ *n* [C] **1** 白痴〔癡〕báichī. **2** 傻子 shǎzi. **～ic** /ˌɪdɪ'ɒtɪk/ *adj* 愚蠢的 yúchǔnde, 白痴的 báichīde.

idle /'aɪdl/ *adj* [-r, -st] **1** 闲〔閑〕着的 xiánzhede. **2** (时间)空闲的 kòngxiánde. **3** (人)懒的 lǎnde. **4** 无〔無〕用的 wúyòngde, 无根据〔據〕的 wúgēnjùde: ～ *gossip* 无聊的闲话. □ *vt/i* **1 ～ (away)** 虚度 xūdù. **2** 使(发动机)慢慢转〔轉〕动〔動〕而不发〔發〕出力量 shǐ mànmàn zhuǎndòng ér bù fāchū lìliàng. **idly** *adv*

idol /'aɪdl/ *n* [C] **1** 偶像 ǒuxiàng. **2** 宠〔寵〕儿 chǒng'ér; 宠物 chǒngwù; 崇拜的对〔對〕象 chóngbàide duìxiàng. **～ize** /'aɪdəlaɪz/ *vt* 崇拜 chóngbài.

idyl·lic /ɪ'dɪlɪk/ *adj* 质〔質〕朴〔樸〕宜人的 zhìpǔyírénde.

i·e· = that is 即 jí.

if /ɪf/ *conj* **1** 假使 jiǎshǐ, 如果 rúguǒ: *I～ you ask him, he will help you.* 假使你要求他帮你,他会帮助你的. *I～ I asked him for a loan, would he agree?* 如果我向他借钱,他会同意吗? *I～ they had started earlier, they would have arrived in time.* 如果他们早点动身的话,他们本来是能及时抵达的. **2** 当〔當〕dāng, 无〔無〕论〔論〕何时〔時〕wúlùn héshí: *I～ you mix yellow and blue you get green.* 把黄色同蓝色混合起来,就得到绿色. **3** 即使 jìshǐ, 纵〔縱〕使 zòngshǐ: *Even ～ he did say that, he ...* 即使他说了,他.... **4 (even) ～** 虽〔雖〕然 suīrán. *I'll do it, even ～ it takes me all day.* 虽然要花费我整天的时间,我还是要做. **5** 是否 shìfǒu: *Do you know ～ Mr Smith is at home?* 你知道史密斯先生是否在家里吗? **6 as ～** 好象 hǎoxiàng, 仿佛 fǎngfú. **7 ～ only** 要是...就好 yàoshi...jiùhǎo: *I～ only he had arrived in time!* 要是他及时到达该多好啊!

ig·loo /'ɪglu:/ *n* [C] [*pl* ～s] 爱〔愛〕斯基摩人用雪块〔塊〕砌成的小屋 àisījīmórén yòng xuěkuài qìchéng de xiǎowū.

ig·nite /ɪg'naɪt/ *vt/i* 点〔點〕燃 diǎnrán, 使燃烧〔燒〕shǐ ránshāo.

ig·ni·tion /ɪg'nɪʃn/ *n* **1** [U] 点〔點〕火 diǎnhuǒ, 着火 zháohuǒ. **2** [C] (机械)发〔發〕火装〔裝〕置 fāhuǒ zhuāngzhì.

ig·nor·ance /'ɪgnərəns/ *n* [U] 无〔無〕知 wúzhī, 愚昧 yúmèi.

ig·nor·ant /'ɪgnərənt/ *adj* **1** 无〔無〕知的 wúzhīde. **2** 粗鲁的 cūlǔde, 不客气〔氣〕的 búkèqìde: ～ *conduct* 粗鲁的行为. **～ly** *adv*

ig·nore /ɪg'nɔ:(r)/ *vt* 不顾〔顧〕búgù, 不理 bùlǐ.

I'll /aɪl/ = *I will* 或 *I shall.*

ill /ɪl/ *adj* **1** 有病的 yǒubìngde, 不健康的 bújiànkāngde. ***fall*** (或 ***be taken***) ～生病 shēngbìng. **2** 坏〔壞〕的 huàide, 恶劣的 èliède: ～ *health* 不健康. □ *n* **1** [U] 坏〔壞〕huài, 恶〔惡〕è: *do ～* 作恶. **2** [C] 不幸 búxìng, 灾祸 zāihuò. □ *adv* 不完美地 bùwánměide. **ˌ～ at 'ease** 不安 bù'ān, 不舒服 bùshūfu. **ˌ～-ad'vised** *adj* 不智的 búzhìde, 鲁莽的 lǔmǎngde. **ˌ～-'bred** *adj* 没有教养〔養〕的 méiyǒu jiàoyǎng de. **ˌ～-'feeling** 忿怒 fènnù, 妒忌 dùjì. **ˌ～-'na·tured** *adj* 脾气〔氣〕坏的 píqì huài de. **ˌ～-'treat** *vt* 虐待 nüèdài, 不友好 bùyǒuhǎo. **ˌ～ 'will** 恶意 èyì.

il·legal /ɪ'li:gl/ *adj* 不合法的 bùhéfǎde, 非法的 fēifǎde. **～ly** *adv* **～ity** /ˌɪlɪ'gælətɪ/ *n* [C, U]

il·leg·ible /ɪ'ledʒəbl/ *adj* 难〔難〕以辨认〔認〕的 nányǐ biànrèn de, 字迹不清的 zìjī bùqīng de.

il·legit·imate /ˌɪlɪ'dʒɪtɪmət/ *adj* **1** 违〔違〕法的 wéifǎde, 非法的 fēifǎde. **2** 私生的 sīshēngde. **~ly** *adv*

il·licit /ɪ'lɪsɪt/ *adj* 违〔違〕法的 wéifǎde. **~ly** *adv*

il·lit·er·ate /ɪ'lɪtərət/ *adj, n* [C] 文盲 wénmáng. **il·lit·er·acy** /-rəsɪ/ *n* [U]

ill·ness /'ɪlnɪs/ *n* **1** [U] 疾病 jíbìng. **2** [C] 某种〔種〕疾病 mǒuzhǒng jíbìng.

il·logi·cal /ɪ'lɒdʒɪkl/ *adj* 不合逻辑〔輯〕的 bùhé luójì de, 无〔無〕意义〔義〕的 wúyìyìde. **~ly** *adv* **~ity** /-'kælətɪ/ *n* [C ,U]

il·lumi·nate /ɪ'lu:mɪneɪt/ *vt* **1** 照亮 zhàoliàng, 照明 zhàomíng; 阐〔闡〕明 chǎnmíng. **2** 用灯装〔裝〕饰〔飾〕yòng dēng zhuāngshì. **il·lumi·nat·ing** *adj* 启发〔發〕性的 qǐfāxìngde: *an illuminating explanation* 有启发性的解释. **il·lumi'na·tion** *n* **(a)** [U] 照明 zhàomíng, 照亮 zhàoliàng; 阐明 chǎnmíng. **(b)** 灯〔燈〕彩装〔裝〕饰 dēngcǎi zhuāngshì.

il·lu·sion /ɪ'lu:ʒn/ *n* **1** [C] 幻象 huànxiàng, 错 cuò. **2** [U] 错觉〔覺〕cuòjué.

il·lu·sory /ɪ'lu:sərɪ/ *adj* 迷惑人的 míhuò rén de, 虚幻的 xūhuànde.

il·lus·trate /'ɪləstreɪt/ *vt* **1** 举〔舉〕例或以图〔圖〕表说明 jǔlì huò yǐ túbiǎo shuōmíng. **2** 配以插图 pèi yǐ chātú. **il·lus·tra·tor** /-tə(r)/ 插图作者 chātú zuòzhě. **il·lus'tra·tion** *n* **(a)** [U] 说明 shuōmíng, 图解 tújiě. **(b)** [C] 插图 chātú, 例证〔證〕lìzhèng. **il·lus·tra·tive** /'ɪləstrətɪv/ *adj* 用作说明的 yòngzuò shuōmíng de: *illustrative example* 解说性例证.

il·lus·tri·ous /ɪ'lʌstrɪəs/ *adj* 著名的 zhùmíngde. **~ly** *adv*

I'm /aɪm/ = *I am.* ⇨ be.

im·age /'ɪmɪdʒ/ *n* [C] **1** 像 xiàng, 偶像 ǒuxiàng. **2** 相象 xiāngxiàng: *He's the ~ of his brother.* 他活象他的兄弟. **3** 形像 xíngxiàng, 典型 diǎnxíng. **4** 映像 yìngxiàng, 影像 yǐngxiàng. **~ry** *n* [U]

im·agin·ary /ɪ'mædʒɪnərɪ/ *adj* 虚构的 xūgòude, 假想的 jiǎxiǎngde.

im·ag·ine /ɪ'mædʒɪn/ *vt* **1** 想象 xiǎngxiàng, 设想 shèxiǎng: *~ life on another planet* 想象另一个星球上存在生物. **2** 料想 liàoxiǎng, 以为〔為〕yǐwéi: *I ~ he arrived today.* 我想他是今天到的. **im·agin·able** /-əbl/ *adj* 可以想象得到的 kěyǐ xiǎngxiàng dédào de. **im·agin·ation** /-'neɪʃn/ *n* [C, U] **(a)** 想像力 xiǎngxiànglì. **(b)** 想象出的事物 xiǎngxiàngchūde shìwù. **im·agin·ative** /-ətɪv/ *adj* 想象的 xiǎngxiàngde, 有想象力的 yǒu xiǎngxiànglì de.

im·bal·ance /ˌɪm'bæləns/ *n* [C] 不平衡 bù pínghéng.

im·be·cile /'ɪmbəsi:l/ *adj, n* [C] 低能儿 dīnéng'ér, 笨人 bènrén.

I. M. F. = International Monetary Fund 国〔國〕际〔際〕货币〔幣〕基金组织〔織〕guójì huòbì jījīng zǔzhī.

imi·tate /'ɪmɪteɪt/ *vt* **1** 模仿 mófǎng, 仿效 fǎngxiào: *~ one's father* 模仿父亲. **2** 模拟〔擬〕mónǐ. **3** 看似 kànsì: *wood painted to ~ marble* 仿大理石油漆的木制品. **imi·ta·tor** /-tə(r)/ *n* [C] **imi'tation** *n* **(a)** [U] 模仿 mófǎng, 仿造 fǎngzào. **(b)** [C] 仿制品. fǎngzhìpǐn. **(c)** 人造〔用作定语〕rénzào: *imitation jewels* 人造宝石. **imi·tat·ive** /'ɪmɪtətɪv/ *adj* 模仿的 mófǎngde, 模拟〔擬〕的mónǐde.

im·macu·late /ɪ'mækjʊlət/ *adj* 纯洁〔潔〕的 chúnjiéde, 无瑕疵的 wúxiácīde. **~ly** *adv*

im·ma·terial /ˌɪmə'tɪərɪəl/ *adj* **1** 不重要的 búzhòngyàode: *His future is ~ to me.* 他的前途与我无关紧要. **2** 非物质〔質〕的 fēiwùzhìde; 无〔無〕形的 wúxíngde: *Man's soul is ~.* 人的灵魂是无形的.

im·ma·ture /ˌɪmə'tjʊə(r)/ *adj* 未成熟的 wèichéngshúde, 未完成的 wèiwánchéngde. **im·ma'tur·ity** *n* [U]

im·medi·ate /ɪ'mi:dɪət/ *adj* **1** 最接近的 zuìjiējìnde, 紧〔緊〕靠的 jǐnkàode: *my ~ neighbours* 我的紧邻. **2** 立即 lìjì: *~ action* 立即行动. **~ly** *adv* **(a)** 立即地 lìjìde. **(b)** 紧靠地 jǐnkàode, 紧密地 jǐnmìde: *follow ~ly behind* 紧跟. □ *conj* 一经…(立即) yījīng…: *go ~ly he arrives* 他一到…就走.

im·mense /ɪ'mens/ *adj* 广〔廣〕大的 guǎngdàde, 巨大的 jùdàde. **~ly** *adv* 非常 fēicháng: *enjoy it ~ly* 非常喜爱. **im·men·sity** /-ətɪ/ *n* [C, U]

im·merse /ɪ'mɜ:s/ *vt* **1** 沉浸 chénjìn. **2** *be ~ed (in)* 沉浸于 (in) chénjìn yú: *~d in one's work* 沉浸于工作. **im'mersion heater** 浸入式热〔熱〕水器 jìnrùshì rèshuǐqì.

im·mi·grant /'ɪmɪgrənt/*n* [C] 移

民 yímín, 侨〔僑〕民 qiáomín.
im·mi·grate /ˈɪmɪgreɪt/ *vi* 侨〔僑〕居 qiáojū. **im·miˈgra·tion** /-ʃn/ *n* [C, U]
im·mi·nent /ˈɪmɪnənt/ *adj* 迫近的 pòjìnde, 紧〔緊〕迫的 jǐnpòde. **~ly** *adv*
im·mo·bile /ɪˈməʊbaɪl/ *adj* 不机〔機〕动〔動〕的 bùjīdòngde, 不动的 búdòngde.
im·mo·bil·ity /ˌɪməˈbɪlətɪ/ *n* [U] 固定 gùdìng, 静止 jìngzhǐ.
im·mo·bi·lize /ɪˈməʊbəlaɪz/ *vt* 使固定 shǐ gùdìng, 使不机动 shǐ bùjīdòng. **im·mo·bii·iˈz·ation** *n* [U]
im·moral /ɪˈmɒrəl/ *adj* 不道德的 búdàodéde, 邪恶〔惡〕的 xié'ède. **~ity** /-ˈrælətɪ/ *n* [C,U]
im·mor·tal /ɪˈmɔːrtl/ *adj* **1** 不朽的 bùxiǔde. **2** 流芳百世的 liúfāngbǎishìde. □*n* [C] 不朽的 bùxiǔde. **~ity** /-ˈtælətɪ/ *n* [U] **~ize** /-aɪz/ *vt* 使不朽 shǐ bùxiǔ: *~ized in a novel* 在一本小说中成为不朽的人物.
im·mune /ɪˈmjuːn/ *adj* **~ (*from*)** 免除…的 miǎnchú…de; 安全的 ānquánde; 不受影响〔響〕的 búshòu yǐngxiǎng de. **im·mun·ity** *n* [U] **(a)** 安全 ānquán. **(b)** 免除 miǎnchú.
im·mu·nize /ˈɪmjʊnaɪz/ *vt* 使免除 (against) shǐ miǎnchú. **im·mu·niz·ation** /-ˈzeɪʃn/*n* [C, U]
imp /ɪmp/ *n* [C] **1** 小魔鬼 xiǎomóguǐ. **2** [非正式用语] 小淘气〔氣〕xiǎotáoqì, 顽童 wántóng.
im·pact /ˈɪmpækt/ *n* **1** [C] 碰撞 pèngzhuàng, 撞击〔擊〕zhuàngjī. **2** [U] 撞击力 zhuàngjīlì. **3** 影响 yǐngxiǎng, 效果 xiàoguǒ: *the ~ of the war* 战争的影响, *the ~ of his speech* 他的话的效果. □ *vt* /ɪmˈpækt/ 装〔裝〕紧 zhuāngjǐn.
im·pair /ɪmˈpeə(r)/ *vt* 损害 sǔnhài, 削弱 xiāoruò: *~ one's health* 损害健康. **~ment** *n* [U]
im·pale /ɪmˈpeɪl/ *vt* 刺穿 cìchuān: *~d on a spear* 用矛戳起的.
im·par·tial /ɪmˈpɑːʃl/ *adj* 公正的 gōngzhèngde, 公平的 gōngpíngde: *A judge must be ~.* 法官必须公正. **~ity** /-ʃiːˈælətɪ/ *n* [U]
im·pass·able /ɪmˈpɑːsəbl/ *adj* 不能通行的 bùnéng tōngxíng de.
im·pas·sioned /ɪmˈpæʃnd/ *adj* 充满热〔熱〕情的 chōngmǎn rèqíng de, 激动〔動〕的 jīdòngde: *an ~ appeal* 热情的呼吁.
im·pass·ive /ɪmˈpæsɪv/ *adj* 冷淡的 lěngdànde. **~ly** *adv*
im·pa·tience /ɪmˈpeɪʃns/ *n* [U] 急躁 jízào, 不耐烦 búnàifán.
im·pa·tient *adj* **im·pa·tient·ly** *adv*
im·peach /ɪmˈpiːtʃ/ *vt* **1** 非难〔難〕fēinàn, 指责 zhǐzé. **2** 控告…叛国〔國〕kònggào … pànguó.
im·pec·cable /ɪmˈpekəbl/ *adj* [正式用语] 无〔無〕瑕疵的 wúxiácīde.
im·pede /ɪmˈpiːd/ *vt* 妨碍〔礙〕fáng'ài, 阻碍 zǔ'ài.
im·pedi·ment /ɪmˈpedɪmənt/ *n* [C] **1** 口吃 kǒuchī. **2** 障碍〔礙〕zhàng'ài, 阻碍 zǔ'ài.
im·pen·etrable /ɪmˈpenɪtrəbl/ *adj* 穿不进〔進〕的 chuānbújìnde, 刺不进的 cìbújìnde.
im·pera·tive /ɪmˈperətɪv/ *adj* **1** 紧〔緊〕急的 jǐnjíde, 必要的 bìyàode. **2** 强制的 qiángzhìde, 命令的 mìnglìngde. **3** [语法] 祈使语气〔氣〕qǐshǐyǔqì. **~ly** *adv*
im·per·fect /ɪmˈpɜːfɪkt/ *adj* 不完整的 bùwánzhěngde, 不完美的 bùwánměide. **im·per·fec·tly** *adv*
im·per·fec·tion /-ˈfekʃən/ *n* **(a)** [U] 不完整 bùwánzhěng, 不完美 bùwánměi. **(b)** [C] 缺陷 quēxiàn.
im·per·ial /ɪmˈpɪərɪəl/ *adj* 帝国〔國〕的 dìguóde; 皇帝的 huángdìde. **~ly** *adv* **~ism** *n* [U] 帝国主义〔義〕dìguózhǔyì. **~ist** *adj* 帝国主义的 dìguózhǔyìde. □ *n* [C] 帝国主义者 dìguózhǔyìzhě.
im·per·sonal /ˌɪmˈpɜːsənl/ *adj* **1** 不受个〔個〕人感情影响〔響〕的 búshòu gèrén gǎnqíng yǐngxiǎng de, 不特指某个人的 bú tè zhǐ mǒugèrén de. **2** 不具人格的 bújù réngé de, 非人力的 fēi rénlì de: *~ forces* 非人力(指自然力等).
im·per·son·ate /ɪmˈpɜːsəneɪt/ *vt* 扮演 bànyǎn, 假扮 jiǎbàn. ~ the Prime Minister 扮演总理. **im·per·soˈn·ation** *n* [C, U]
im·per·ti·nent /ɪmˈpɜːtɪnənt/ *adj* **1** 不礼〔禮〕貌的 bùlǐmàode, 不客气〔氣〕的 búkèqìde. **im·per·ti·nence** /-nəns/ *n* [C, U]
im·perˈvi·ous /ɪmˈpɜːvɪəs/ *adj* **1** (材料)透不过〔過〕的 tòubúguòde, 穿不过的 chuānbúguòde. **2** **~ to** [喻]无〔無〕动〔動〕于衷的 wúdòngyúzhōngde; 不受影响〔響〕的 búshòu yǐngxiǎng de.
im·petu·ous /ɪmˈpetʃʊəs/ *adj* 鲁莽的 lǔmǎngde, 轻〔輕〕举〔舉〕妄动〔動〕的 qīngjǔwàngdòngde.
im·petu·os·ity /-ˈɒsətɪ/ *n* [C, U]
im·pe·tus /ˈɪmpɪtəs/ *n* [*pl* -es] **1** [U] 动〔動〕力 dònglì, 原动力 yuándònglì. **2** [C] 推动 tuīdòng, 激励〔勵〕jīlì: *an ~ to greater*

sales 推动销售的扩大.

im·pinge /ɪm'pɪndʒ/ *vi* ~ *(up) on* [正式用语]过[過]多占用 guòduō zhànyòng: ~ *on a person's time* 过多占用某人的时间. ~**ment** *n* [U]

imp·ish /'ɪmpɪʃ/ *adj* 小鬼的 xiǎoguǐde, 顽皮的 wánpíde. ~**ly** *adv*

im·plant /ɪm'plɑ:nt/ *vt* **1** 灌输 guànshū, 使树[樹]立 shǐ shùlì. **2** (医学)移植 yízhí. □ *n* /'ɪmplɑ:nt/ [C] 移植物 yízhíwù.

im·ple·ment[1] /'ɪmplәmәnt/ *n* [C] 工具 gōngjù, 器具 qìjù.

im·ple·ment[2] /'ɪmplәment/ *vt* 贯彻[徹] guànchè, 履行 lǚxíng: ~ *my ideas* 贯彻我的主张. ~**a·tion** /-'teɪʃәn/ *n* [U]

im·pli·cate /'ɪmplɪkeɪt/ *vt* 使(某人) 牵连[連]于罪行之中 shǐ qiānlián yú zuìxíng zhī zhōng.

im·pli·ca·tion /ˌɪmplɪ'keɪʃn/ *n* **1** [U] 牵连[連] (于罪行) qiānlián. **2** [C] 暗示 ànshì; 含意 hányì.

im·pli·cit /ɪm'plɪsɪt/ *adj* [正式用语] **1** 暗示的 ànshìde, 含蓄的 hánxùde. **2** 无[無]疑的 wúyíde, 无保留的 wúbǎoliúde: ~ *trust* 无保留的信任. ~**ly** *adv*

im·plore /ɪm'plɔ:(r)/ *vt* 恳[懇]求 kěnqiú, 乞求 qǐqiú: *I* ~ *you not to kill him.* 我恳求你不把他弄死. **im·plor·ing·ly** *adv*

im·ply /ɪm'plaɪ/ *vt* [*pt, pp* -ied] **1** 含有…的意思 hán yǒu … de yìsī: *Did he* ~ *that you were guilty?* 他的意思是说你有罪吗? **2** 必须具备[備] bìxū jùbèi.

im·po·lite /ˌɪmpә'laɪt/ *adj* 不客气[氣]的 búkèqìde. ~**ly** *adv* ~**ness** *n* [U]

im·port /ɪm'pɔ:t/ *vt* 进[進]口 jìnkǒu. □ *n* /'ɪmpɔ:t/ **1** [C] [常用] *pl* 进口货 jìnkǒuhuò. **2** [U] 进口 jìnkǒu. ~**a·tion** /-'teɪʃn/ *n* [C, U]

im·port·ance /ɪm'pɔ:tns/ *n* [U] 重要性 zhòngyàoxìng, 重要 zhòngyào, 重大 zhòngdà.

im·port·ant /ɪm'pɔ:tnt/ *adj* **1** 重要的 zhòngyàode, 重大的 zhòngdàde: *an* ~ *decision* 重要的决定. **2** (人)有权[權]力的 yǒu quánlì de. ~**ly** *adv*

im·pose /ɪm'pәʊz/ *vt/i* **1** 征[徵](税等) zhēng. **2** 把…强加于 bǎ … qiángjiā yú: ~ *one's ideas on* 把自己的意见强加于人. **3** ~ *(up) on sb* 利用 lìyòng. **im·pos·ing** *adj* 壮[壯]丽[麗]的 zhuànglìde, 堂皇的 tánghuángde. **im·pos·ing·ly** *adv*

im·po·si·tion /ˌɪmpә'zɪʃn/ *n* **1** [U] 征税 zhēngshuì: *the* ~ *of taxes* 征税. **2** [C] 加派之物 jiāpài zhī wù; 税 shuì, 负担[擔] fùdān. **3** 占便宜 zhàn piányì, 利用 lìyòng: *It's an* ~ *asking me to help you.* 要我帮你,这是想占便宜.

im·poss·ible /ɪm'pɒsәbl/ *adj* **1** 不可能的 bùkěnéngde. **2** 无[無]法忍受的 wúfǎ rěnshòu de: *an* ~ *situation* 不能忍受的局面. **im·possi'bil·ity** *n* [C, U]

im·po·tent /'ɪmpәtәnt/ *adj* **1** 无[無]力的 wúlìde, 软[軟]弱无能的 ruǎnruò wúnéng de. **2** (医学)阳[陽]萎的 yángwěide. **im·po·tence** /-tәns/ *n* [U] ~**ly** *adv*

im·pound /ɪm'paʊnd/ *vt* 没收 mòshōu

im·prac·ti·cal /ɪm'præktɪkl/ *adj* 不现实[實]的 búxiànshíde, 不切实际[際]的 bú qiè shíjì de.

im·preg·nable /ɪm'pregnәbl/ *adj* 坚[堅]不可摧的 jiān bùkěcuī de: *an* ~ *fort* 坚不可摧的堡垒.

im·preg·nate /'ɪmpregneɪt/ *vt* **1** 使怀[懷]孕 shǐ huáiyùn, 使妊娠 shǐ rènchén. **2** 灌注 guànzhù, 浸透 jìntòu: *cloth* ~*d with perfume* 浸过香水的布.

im·press /ɪm'pres/ *vt* **1** 压[壓] yā, 印 yìn, 盖印 gàiyìn. **2** 给以深刻的印象 gěiyǐ shēnkède yìnxiàng: *His honesty* ~*ed me.* 他的诚实给我以深刻的印象.

im·pres·sion /ɪm'preʃn / *n* **1** [C] 印记 yìnjì, 压[壓]痕 yāhén. **2** [C] 印次 yìncì, 印刷 yìnshuā: *the first* ~ *of a book* 某书的第一次印刷. **3** [C, U] 印象 yìnxiàng. *be under the* ~ *that* 记得好象… jìdé hǎoxiàng …. ~**ism** /-ɪzәm/ *n* [U] (绘画等)印象派 yìnxiàngpài, 印象主义[義] yìnxiàngzhǔyì.

im·pres·sion·able /ɪm'preʃәnәbl/ *adj* 可塑的 kěsùde, 易受影响[響]的 yìshòu yǐngxiǎng de.

im·pres·sive /ɪm'presɪv/ *adj* 感人的 gǎnrénde; 给人深刻印象的 gěi rén shēnkè yìnxiàng de: *an* ~ *performance* 给人以深刻印象的表演. ~**ly** *adv*

im·print /ɪm'prɪnt/ *vt* 印 yìn, 铭刻 míngkè: *memories* ~*ed on his brain* 铭刻于他的脑海的记忆. □ *n* /'ɪmprɪnt/ [C] **1** 印 yìn, 印记 yìnjì. **2** 书[書]籍内封或版权[權]页上关[關]于出版者名称[稱]等的标[標]识[識] shūjí nèifēng huò bǎnquányè shàng guānyú chūbǎnzhě míngchēng děng de biāo shí.

im·prison /ɪm'prɪzn/ *vt* 监〔監〕禁 jiānjìn, 关〔關〕押 guānyā. **~ment** *n* [U]

im·prob·able /ɪm'prɒbəbl/ *adj* 不大可能的 bú dà kěnéng de, 不大可能是真的 bú dà kěnéng shì zhēn de. **im·prob·ably** *adv* **ˌim-prob·a'bil·ity** *n* [C, U]

im·promptu /ɪm'prɒmptju:/ *adj, adv* 无〔無〕准〔準〕备〔備〕的(地) wúzhǔnbèide, 即兴〔興〕的(地) jìxìngde: *an ~ speech* 即席演讲.

im·proper /ɪm'prɒpə(r)/ *adj* **1** 不适〔適〕当〔當〕的 búshìdāngde, 不合适的 bùhéshìde: *~ behaviour* 不适当的举止; *~ dress* 不适当的衣服. **2** 不正确〔確〕的 búzhèngquède: *~ use of a word* 用字不正确. **3** 不道德的 búdàodéde, 不正派的 búzhèngpài de, 不合礼〔禮〕仪〔儀〕的 bù hé lǐyí de: *make ~ suggestions* 提出不礼貌的建议. **~ly** *adv*

im·prove /ɪm'pru:v/ *vt/i* 改进〔進〕gǎijìn, 改善 gǎishàn. **~ment** *n* **(a)** [U] 改进 gǎijìn, 改良 gǎiliáng. **(b)** [C] 改进措施 gǎijìn cuòshī, 经〔經〕改进的东〔東〕西 jīng gǎijìn de dōngxi.

im·pro·vise /'ɪmprəvaɪz/ *vt/i* **1** 即席创〔創〕作 jìxí chuàngzuò, 即席演奏 jìxí yǎnzòu. **2** 临〔臨〕时〔時〕凑成 línshí còuchéng: *~ a meal* 临时凑合的一顿饭. **im·pro·vis·ation** /-'zeɪʃn/ *n* [C, U]

im·pu·dence /'ɪmpjʊdəns/ *n* [U] 厚颜 hòuyán, 冒失 màoshi, 轻〔輕〕率 qīngshuài, 厚颜,冒失的言行 hòuyán, màoshi de yánxíng.

im·pu·dent /'ɪmpjʊdənt/ *adj* 厚颜的 hòuyánde, 冒失的 màoshide. **~ly** *adv*

im·pulse /'ɪmpʌls/ *n* **1** [C] 推动〔動〕tuīdòng, 冲〔衝〕力 chōnglì. **2** [C, U] 冲动 chōngdòng: *act on ~* 凭一时冲动行事.

im·pul·sive /ɪm'pʌlsɪv/ *adj* **1** (人) 凭感情冲动行事的 píng gǎnqíng chōngdòng xíngshì de. **2** (力) 冲击〔擊〕的 chōngjīde. **~ly** *adv* **~ness** *n* [U]

im·pun·ity /ɪm'pju:nətɪ/ *n* [U] *with ~* 不受损害 búshòu sǔnhài, 不受惩〔懲〕罚 búshòu chěngfá.

im·pure /ɪm'pjʊə(r)/ *adj* 不纯的 bùchúnde. **im·pur·ity** *n* [C, U]

in¹ /ɪn/ *adv* (同 *out* 相对) **1** *be ~* **(a)** 在家里〔裡〕zàijiālǐ: *Is your father ~?* 你父亲在家吗? **(b)** 到达〔達〕dàodá: *Is the train ~?* 火车到了吗? **(c)** (庄稼) 收割 shōugē. **(d)** (水果等) 上市 shàngshì, 当〔當〕令 dānglìng. **(e)** 时〔時〕兴〔興〕shíxīng: *Long skirts are ~ this year.* 今年时兴长裙子. **(f)** 当政 dāngzhèng, 执〔執〕政 zhízhèng: *The Labour Party is ~.* 工党执政. ***be* '~ *on*** [非正式用语] 参〔參〕预 cānyù. **2** *~ for* 遭到 zāodào. ***have it ~ for sb*** 伺机〔機〕报〔報〕复〔復〕某人 cìjī bàofù mǒurén.

in² /ɪn/ *prep* **1** (表示地点 ⇨ at): 在…里〔裡〕zài … lǐ: *~ Africa* 在非洲. **2** (表示方向) 朝… cháo: *~ this direction* 朝这个方向. **3** (表示动作) 进〔進〕入 jìnrù: *He put it ~ his pocket.* 他把它放进口袋. **4** (表示时间) 在… zài …: *~ 1970* (在) 1970 年; *~ the morning* (在) 早晨. ⇨ at (2). ⇨ on²(2). **5** (时间) 在…期间〔間〕zài … qījiān: *The work was done ~ a week.* 这工作在一星期内就完成了. 在…之后〔後〕zài … zhī hòu: *I will come ~ a few days.* 我过几天来. **6** (表示包含): *a man ~ his thirties* 一个三十几岁的男人. **7** 每 měi: *25p ~ the pound* 每英镑 (归还等) 二十五便士. **8** (服饰等) 穿着 chuānzhe: *dressed ~ white* 穿白衣服的. **9** (表示周围环境等) *~ the rain* 在雨中. **10** (表示情况) *~ a hurry* 匆忙, *~ love* 恋爱. **11** (表示方法方式) 用 yòng, 以 yǐ: *speak ~ English* 说英语 (用英语说), *pay ~ cash* 付现款 (用现款付). **12** (表示程度, 范围) 按 àn, 以 yǐ: *~ large quantities* 大量. *~ 'all* 全部 quánbù. **13** (表示职业等) 从〔從〕事于 cóngshì yú, 参〔參〕加 cānjiā: *He's ~ the army* 他是军人. **14** *~ that* 因为〔爲〕yīnwéi: *The chemical is dangerous ~ that it can kill.* 化学物品是危险的, 因为它能致命. *~ itself* 在他自身 zài tā zìshēn.

in³ /ɪn/ *n* (仅用于) **the ~s and outs** 详情 xiángqíng, 细节〔節〕xìjié.

in. = inch(s).

in·abil·ity /ˌɪnə'bɪlətɪ/ *n* [U] 无〔無〕能 wúnéng, 无力量 wú lìliàng.

in·ac·cess·ible /ˌɪnək'sesəbl/ *adj* [正式用语] 达〔達〕不到的 dábúdàode, 难〔艱〕接近的 nánjiējìnde 难得到的 nándédàode.

in·ac·cur·acy /ɪ'nækjʊrəsɪ/ *n* **1** [U] 不精密 bù jīngmì, 不准确〔確〕bù zhǔnquè. **2** [U] [*pl* -ies] 不精确的说明 bùjīngquède shuōmíng.

in·ac·curate /ɪ'nækjʊrət/ *adj* 不精密的 bùjīngmìde. 不准确〔確〕的

bùzhǔnquède. ~**ly** *adv*

in·ad·equate /ɪn'ædɪkwət/ *adj* 不适〔適〕当〔當〕的 búshìdāngde, 不充足的 bùchōngzúde. ~**ly** *adv*

in·admiss·ible /ˌɪnəd'mɪsəbl/ *adj* 不能接纳的 bùnéng jiēnà de; 不能承认〔認〕的 bùnéng chéngrèn de; 不允许的 bùyǔnxǔde: ~ *evidence* 不能承认的证据.

in·ad·ver·tent /ˌɪnəd'vɜːtənt/ *adj* 〔正式用语〕 **1** 不经〔經〕心的 bùjīngxīnde, **2** 疏忽的 shūhude. ~**ly** *adv*

in·alien·able /ɪn'eɪlɪənəbl/ *adj* 〔正式用语〕不可剥夺〔奪〕的 bùkě bōduó de, 不可让〔讓〕与〔與〕的 bùkě ràngyǔ de.

in·ane /ɪ'neɪn/ *adj* 愚蠢的 yúchǔnde. ~**ly** *adv*

in·ani·mate /ɪn'ænɪmət/ *adj* 无〔無〕生命的 wúshēngmìnde: *A statue is* ~. 塑像是无生命的.

in·ap·pli·cable /ɪn'æplɪkəbl/ *adj* ~ **(*to*)** 不适〔適〕用的 búshìyòngde.

in·ap·pro·pri·ate /ˌɪnə'prəʊprɪət/ *adj* 不适〔適〕当〔當〕的 búshìdāngde.

in·apt /ɪn'æpt/ *adj* 不适〔適〕当〔當〕的 búshìdāngde, 不合适的 bùhéshìde: ~ *remarks* 不适当的话.

in·ar·ticulate /ˌɪnɑː'tɪkjʊlət/ *adv* **1** 口齿〔齒〕不清的 kǒuchǐ bùqīng de. **2** 无〔無〕关〔關〕节〔節〕的 wúguānjiéde: *an* ~ *body* 无关节的躯体.

in·as·much as /ˌɪnəz'mʌtʃ əz/ *adv* 由于 yóuyú, 因为〔為〕yīnwéi.

in·aud·ible /ɪn'ɔːdəbl/ *adj* 听〔聽〕不见的 tīngbújiànde. **in·audi'bil·ity** *n* [U]

in·aug·ural /ɪ'nɔːgjʊrəl/ *adj* 就职〔職〕的 jiùzhíde, 开〔開〕幕的 kāimùde, 开始的 kāishǐde: *an* ~ *speech* 就职(开幕)演说.

in·aug·ur·ate /ɪ'nɔːgjʊreɪt/ *vt* **1** 为〔為〕... 举〔舉〕行就职〔職〕典礼〔禮〕 wèi... jǔxíng jiùzhí diǎnlǐ. **2** 为展览〔覽〕会〔會〕等揭幕 wèi zhǎnlǎn huì děng jiēmù. **3** 〔正式用语〕开〔開〕创〔創〕 kāichuàng: ~ *a new age of space travel* 开创了空间旅行的新时代. **in·aug·u'r·ation** *n* [C, U]

in·board /ˌɪn'bɔːd/ *adj* 在船内的 zài chuán nèide : *an* ~ *motor* 船内发动机.

in·born /ˌɪn'bɔːn/ *adj* 生来〔來〕的 shēngláide.

in·bred /ˌɪn'bred/ *adj* **1** 生来〔來〕的 shēngláide. **2** 近亲〔親〕繁殖的 jìnqīn fánzhí de.

in·breed·ing /ˌɪn'briːdɪŋ/ *n* [U] 近亲〔親〕繁殖 jìnqīn fánzhí.

inc. = Incorporatd 股份有限公司 gǔfèn yǒuxiàn gōngsī.

in·cal·cu·lable /ɪn'kælkjʊləbl/ *adj* 无〔無〕数〔數〕的 wúshùde, 数〔數〕不清的 shǔbùqīngde.

in·ca·pable /ɪn'keɪpəbl/ *adj* 无〔無〕能力的 wúnénglìde; 不会〔會〕的 búhuìde; 不能的 bùnéngde.

in·ca·paci·tate /ˌɪnkə'pæsɪteɪt/ *vt* 使无〔無〕能力 shǐ wú nénglì. **in·ca·pac·ity** *n* [U] 无能力 wú nénglì.

in·car·cer·ate /ɪn'kɑːsəreɪt/ *vt* 〔正式用语〕监〔監〕禁 jiānjìn. **in·car·ce'r·ation** *n* [U]

in·car·nate /ɪn'kɑːnət/ *adj* **1** 人体〔體〕化的 réntǐhuàde, 化身的 huàshēnde: *the Devil* ~ 魔王的化身. **2** (理想等)以人形显〔顯〕现的 yǐ rénxíng xiǎnxiàn de, 具体〔體〕化的 jùtǐhuàde. **in·car·na·tion** /-'neɪʃn/ *n* **the I**~ 耶稣之化为〔爲〕人 yēsū zhī huà wéi rén.

in·cen·di·ary /ɪn'sendɪərɪ/ *n* [C] [*pl* -ies] *adj* **1** 纵〔縱〕火者 zònghuǒzhě; 纵火的 zònghuǒde. **2** 煽动〔動〕者 shāndòngzhě, 煽动的 shāndòngde: *an* ~ *speech* 煽动性的演说. **3** (炸弹)燃烧〔燒〕的 ránshāode.

in·cense[1] /'ɪnsens/ *n* [U] 香 xiāng, 燃香时〔時〕发〔發〕出的烟气〔氣〕 ránxiāng shí fāchūde yānqì.

in·cense[2] /ɪn'sens/ *vt* 激怒 jīnù, 触〔觸〕怒 chùnù.

in·cen·tive /ɪn'sentɪv/ *n* [C, U] 鼓励 gǔlì, 激励 jīlì.

in·cess·ant /ɪn'sesnt/ *adj* 连〔連〕续〔續〕的 liánxùde, 不停的 bùtíngde: *his* ~ *complaints* 他的不停的埋怨. ~**ly** *adv*

in·cest /'ɪnsest/ *n* [U] 乱伦〔倫〕luànlún. ~**uous** /ɪn'sestjʊəs/ *adj*

inch /ɪntʃ/ *n* [C] **1** 英寸. **2** 少量 shǎoliàng, 一点〔點〕点 yìdiǎndiǎn: *within an* ~ *of death* 差点儿死了. □ *vt/i* (使)缓慢移动〔動〕 huǎnmàn yídòng.

in·ci·dence /'ɪnsɪdəns/ *n* [C] 发〔發〕生率 fāshēnglǜ; 影响〔響〕的方式 yǐngxiǎngde fāngshì.

in·ci·dent /'ɪnsɪdənt/ *n* [C] 事件 shìjiàn, 事变〔變〕 shìbiàn **2** (剧本或诗歌中的) 插曲 chāqǔ 枝节〔節〕 zhījié. ~**al** /-'dentl/ *adj* **(a)** 附带〔帶〕的 fùdàide, 伴随的 bànsuíde. **(b)** 零星的 língxīng xīngde: ~*al expenses* 杂费. ~**ally** *adv* 偶然地 ǒuránde, 顺便地 shùnbiànde.

in·cin·er·ate /ɪn'sɪnəreɪt/ *vt* 把…烧〔燒〕成灰 bǎ … shāochéng huī, 焚化 fénhuà. **in·cin·e'r·ation** *n* [U] **in·cin·er·ator** *n* [C] 焚化炉〔爐〕 fénhuàlú.

in·cipi·ent /ɪn'sɪpɪənt/ *adj* 开〔開〕始的 kāishǐde, 早期的 zǎoqīde.

in·cise /ɪn'saɪz/ *vt* 切开〔開〕 qiēkāi, 切入 qiērù. **in·ci·sion** /ɪn'sɪʒn/ *n* (a) [U] 切开 qiēkāi, 切入 qiērù. (b) [C] 切口 qiēkǒu. **in·cis·ive** *adj* (a) 锋利的 fēnglìde. (b) 尖锐的 jiānruìde: *incisive critisism* 尖锐的批评. **in·cis·ive·ly** *adv*

in·cisor /ɪn'saɪzə(r)/ *n* [C] 门〔門〕牙 ményá.

in·cite /ɪn'saɪt/ *vt* 激励 jīlì, 煽动〔動〕 shāndòng: ~ *a riot* 煽动骚乱. ~**ment** *n* [C, U]

incl.=including, inclusive 包括 bāokuò.

in·cli·na·tion /ˌɪnklɪ'neɪʃn/ *n* 1 [C] 弯〔彎〕曲 wānqū; 倾斜 qīngxié. 2 [C, U] 倾向 qīngxiàng; 爱〔愛〕好 àihào: *have no ~ to leave* 不想离开.

in·cline[1] /ɪn'klaɪn/ *vt/i* 1 (使)倾斜 qīngxié. 2 屈身 qūshēn, 低头〔頭〕 dītóu. 3 [常用被动语态]倾向于 qīngxiàngyú, 喜欢〔歡〕 xǐhuān: *He's ~d to be lazy.* 他爱懒散.

in·cline[2] /'ɪnklaɪn/ *n* [C] 斜坡 xiépō, 斜面 xiémiàn.

in·clude /ɪn'klu:d/ *vt* 包括 bāokuò, 包含 bāohán: ~ *John in the team* 把约翰包括在队里. **in·clu·sion** /-ʒn/ *n* [U] 包括 bāokuò: *his inclusion in the team* 他被包括在队里. **in·clus·ive** /-sɪv/ *adj* 包括的 bāokuòde, 包含的 bāohánde. **in·clus·ive·ly** *adv*

in·cog·nito /ˌɪnkɒg'ni:təʊ/ *adj*, *adv* 化名的 huàmíngde, 化名地 huàmíngde.

in·co·her·ent /ˌɪnkəʊ'hɪərənt/ *adj* 语无〔無〕伦〔倫〕次的 yǔwúlúncìde, 难〔難〕懂的 nándǒngde. ~**ly** *adv* **in·co·her·ence** *n* [U]

in·come /'ɪnkʌm/ *n* [C] 收入 shōurù, 所得 suǒdé. '~-**tax** 所得税 suǒdéshuì.

in·com·ing /'ɪnkʌmɪŋ/ *adj* 进〔進〕来〔來〕的 jìnláide: ~ *mail* 进来的邮件. ⇨ outgoing.

in·com·par·able /ɪn'kɒmprəbl/ *adj* 无〔無〕比的 wúbǐde.

in·com·pat·ible /ˌɪnkəm'pætəbl/ *adj* 不相容的 bùxiāngróngde, 不能共存的 bùnéng gòngcún de. **in·com·pati'bil·ity** *n* [U]

in·com·pe·tent /ɪn'kɒmpɪtənt/ *adj* 不胜〔勝〕任的 búshèngrènde, 不够格的 búgòugéde. **in·com·pe·tence** *n* [U]

in·com·plete /ˌɪnkəm'pli:t/ *adj* 不完全的 bùwánquánde. 不完善的 bùwánshànde. ~**ly** *adv*

in·com·pre·hen·sible /ˌɪnˌkɒmprɪ'hensəbl/ *adj* [正式用语]不能理解的 bùnéng lǐjiě de. **in·com·pre·hen·sion** /-ʃn/ *n* [U] 缺乏理解 quēfá lǐjiě.

in·con·ceiv·able /ˌɪnkən'si:vəbl/ *adj* 1 不能想象的 bùnéng xiǎngxiàng de. 2 [非正式用语]难〔難〕以相信的 nányǐ xiāngxìn de.

in·con·clus·ive /ˌɪnkən'klu:sɪv/ *adj* (证据, 证词等)不能使人信服的 bùnéng shǐrén xìnfú de. ~**ly** *adv*

in·con·gru·ous /ɪn'kɒŋgrʊəs/ *adj* 不适〔適〕宜的 búshìyíde: *Lions would be ~ in the Arctic.* 狮子不适宜在北极生活. **in·con·gru·ity** /-'gru:ətɪ/ *n* [C, U]

in·con·sid·er·ate /ˌɪnkən'sɪdərət/ *adj* (人)考虑〔慮〕不周的 kǎolǜ bùzhōu de, 粗心的 cūxīnde. ~**ly** *adv*

in·con·sist·ent /ˌɪnkən'sɪstənt/ *adj* 矛盾的 máodùnde, 不协调的 bùxiétiáode; 反复〔復〕无〔無〕常的 fǎnfù wúcháng de: *Their stories are ~.* 他们说的话互相矛盾. ~**ly** *adv* **in·con·sist·ency** /-tənsɪ/ *n* [C, U]

in·con·spicu·ous /ˌɪnkən'spɪkjʊəs/ *adj* 不显〔顯〕著的 bùxiǎnzhùde, 不引人注意的 bù yǐnrén zhùyì de. ~**ly** *adv*

in·con·ti·nent /ɪn'kɒntɪnənt/ *adj* 1 不能自制的 bùnéng zìzhì de, 无〔無〕节〔節〕制的 wújiézhìde. 2 [医学]失禁的 shījìnde. **in·con·ti·nence** /-nəns/ *n* [U]

in·con·ven·ience /ˌɪnkən'vi:nɪəns/ *n* [C, U] 不方便 bùfāngbiàn, 烦扰〔擾〕 fánrǎo, 不方便之事 bùfāngbiàn zhī shì. □ *vt* 打扰 dǎrǎo, 使感到不方便 shǐ gǎndào bù fāngbiàn.

in·con·ven·ient /ˌɪnkən'vi:nɪənt/ *adj* 不方便的 bùfāngbiànde, 烦扰〔擾〕的 fánrǎode. ~**ly** *adv*

in·cor·por·ate /ɪn'kɔ:pəreɪt/ *vt/i* 1 结合 jiéhé, 合并〔併〕 hébìng: ~ *all our ideas in one plan.* 把我们所有的想法合成一个计划. 2 [法律](使)组成公司 zǔchéng gōngsī,

(使)结成社团〔團〕 jiéchéng shètuán. **in·cor·po'r·ation** *n* [U]

in·cor·rect /ˌɪnkəˈrekt/ *adj* 不正确〔確〕的 búzhèngquède, 错误的 cuòwùde. **~ly** *adv* **~ness** *n* [U]

in·cor·ri·gible /ˌɪnˈkɒrɪdʒəbl/ *adj* (人)不可救药的 bùkě jiùyào de, 难〔難〕以改正的 nányǐ gǎizhèng de.

in·crease[1] /ˈɪnkriːs/ *n* **1** [U] 增加 zēngjiā, 增长〔長〕 zēngzhǎng. **2** [C] 增加量 zēngjiāliàng.

in·crease[2] /ɪnˈkriːs/ *vt/i* 增加 zēngjiā, 增长〔長〕 zēngzhǎng. **in·creas·ing·ly** *adv* 愈来〔來〕愈 yùláiyù, 日益 rìyì: *Travel is ~ly expensive.* 旅行费用愈来愈昂贵.

in·cred·ible /ɪnˈkredəbl/ *adj* **1** 难〔難〕以置信的 nányǐ zhìxìn de. **2** [非正式用语]惊〔驚〕人的 jīngrénde. **in·cred·ibly** *adv* ˌ**in·credi'bil·ity** *n* [U]

in·cre·ment /ˈɪnkrɪmənt/ *n* [C, U] 增值 zēngzhí, 增额 zēng'é.

in·crimi·nate /ɪnˈkrɪmɪneɪt/ *vt* 控告 kònggào, 显〔顯〕示某人有罪 xiǎnshì mǒurén yǒuzuì.

in·cu·bate /ˈɪnkjʊbeɪt/ *vt/i* 孵(卵) fū, 孵化 fūhuà. **in·cu'ba·tion** *n* [U] **in·cu·ba·tor** /-tə(r)/ *n* [C] **(a)** 孵化器 fūhuàqì. **(b)** 早产〔產〕婴儿〔兒〕保育箱 zǎochǎn yīngér bǎoyùxiāng.

in·cum·bent /ɪnˈkʌmbənt/ *adj* ***be ~ (up) on sb*** [正式用语] 负有责任的 fùyǒu zérèn de, 义〔義〕不容辞〔辭〕的 yìbùróngcíde. □ *n* [C] 任职〔職〕者 rènzhízhě.

in·cur /ɪnˈkɜː(r)/ *vt* [-rr-] 招致 zhāozhì, 遭受 zāoshòu: *~ heavy debts* 负债累累.

in·cur·able /ɪnˈkjʊərəbl/ *adj* 医〔醫〕不好的 yībùhǎode. □ *n* [C] 医不好的病人 yībùhǎode bìngrén. **in·cur·ably** *adv*

in·cur·sion /ɪnˈkɜːʃn/ *n* [C] 入侵 rùqīn, 侵犯 qīnfàn.

in·debted /ɪnˈdetɪd/ *adj* 负债的 fùzhàide, 蒙恩的 méng'ēnde.

in·de·cent /ɪnˈdiːsnt/ *adj* 下流的 xiàliúde; 粗鄙的 cūbǐde; 猥亵的 wěixiède. **~ly** *adv* **in·de·cency** /-snsɪ/ *n* [C, U]

in·de·cision /ˌɪndɪˈsɪʒn/ *n* [U] 优〔優〕柔寡断〔斷〕 yōuróu guǎduàn, 犹〔猶〕豫 yóuyù.

in·de·cis·ive /ˌɪndiˈsaɪsɪv/ *adj* 非决定性的 fēi juédìng xìng de. **~ly** *adv*

in·deed /ɪnˈdiːd/ *adv* **1** 真正地 zhēnzhèngde: *He is ~ a great man.* 他真是一位伟大的人. **2** [加强语气]确〔確〕实〔實〕 quèshí, 实在 shízài: *very good ~* 确实很好. **3** (表示惊讶,兴趣等) 真的 zhēnde, 真是 zhēnshì: '*Oh, ~!*' '啊,真的!'

in·de·fens·ible /ˌɪndɪˈfensəbl/ *adj* 无〔無〕法防御〔禦〕的 wúfǎ fángyù de, 无法辩护〔護〕的 wúfǎ biànhù de.

in·defi·nite /ɪnˈdefɪnət/ *adj* **1** 模糊的 móhude, 不明确〔確〕的 bùmíngquède: *an ~ outline* 模糊的轮廓. **2** 无〔無〕定限的 wúdìngxiànde: *an ~ period of time* 一段长短不确定的时间. **the ~ article** [语法] 不定冠词 búdìngguàncí. **~ly** *adv* 模糊地 móhude, 无定限地 wúdìngxiànde: *The meeting was postponed ~ly.* 会议无限期推迟.

in·del·ible /ɪnˈdeləbl/ *adj* 去不掉的 qùbúdiàode, 擦不掉的 cābúdiàode. **in·del·ibly** *adv*

in·dem·nify /ɪnˈdemnɪfaɪ/ *vt* [*pt*, *pp* -ied] **1** [法律]保障 bǎozhàng, 保护〔護〕 bǎohù: *~ a person against loss* 保障某人不受损失. **2** 赔偿〔償〕 péicháng; 补〔補〕偿 bǔcháng.

in·dem·nity /ɪnˈdemnətɪ/ *n* [*pl* -ies] [U] 保障 bǎozhàng, 保护 bǎohù; 赔偿 péicháng, 补偿 pǔcháng.

in·dent /ɪnˈdent/ *vt/i* 缩进〔進〕排字或书〔書〕写〔寫〕 suōjìn páizì huò shūxiě. **~a·tion** /-ˈteɪʃən/ *n* **(a)** [U] 缺刻 quēkè. **(b)** [C] 海岸线〔線〕的凹入处〔處〕 hǎi'ànxiànde āorùchù; 行首空格 hángshǒu kònggé.

in·de·pen·dent /ˌɪndɪˈpendənt/ *adj* **1** 独〔獨〕立的 dúlìde. **2** 不需要为〔爲〕维持生活而工作的 bùxūyào wèi wéichí shēnghuó ér gōngzuò de. **3** 独立自主的 dúlìzìzhǔde *~ nations* 独立的国家. **in·de·pen·dence** /-dəns/ *n* [U] **~ly** *adv*

in·de·scrib·able /ˌɪndɪˈskraɪbəbl/ *adj* 难〔難〕以形容的 nányǐ xíngróng de.

in·de·struct·ible /ˌɪndɪˈstrʌktəbl/ *adj* 破坏〔壞〕不了的 pòhuài bùliǎo de.

in·dex /ˈɪndeks/ *n* [C] [*pl* ~es 或 indices /ˈɪndɪsiːz/] **1** 指示物 zhǐshìwù; 指标〔標〕 zhǐbiāo; 指数〔數〕 zhǐshù: *price ~* 物价指数. **2** 索引 suǒyǐn. □ *vt* 作索引 zuò suǒyǐn. **'~ finger** 食指 shízhǐ.

In·dian /ˈɪndɪən/ *n* [C] *adj* **1** 印度的 yìndùde, 印度人 yìndùrén. 印地安人 yìndì'ānrén.

in·di·cate /ˈɪndɪkeɪt/ *vt* 指示 zhǐshì, 指出 zhǐchū, 表示 biǎoshì

in·di'ca·tion *n* (a) [U] 指示 zhǐshì, 指出 zhǐchū, 表示 biǎoshì. (b) [C] 象征〔徵〕xiàngzhēng.

in·dica·tive /ɪn'dɪkətɪv/ *adj* 指示的 zhǐshìde, 表示的 biǎoshìde, 象征的 xiàngzhēngde. **in·di·ca·tor** *n* [C] 指示者 zhǐshìzhě, 指示物 zhǐshìwù: *a 'traffic-~* (汽车)方向指示器.

in·di·ces /'ɪndɪsi:z/ *pl* of index.

in·dict /ɪn'daɪt/ *vt* [法律]控告 kònggào, 对〔對〕…起诉 duì … qǐsù. **~able** *adj* 可被控告的 kě bèi kònggào de: *an ~able offence* 刑事罪. **~ment** *n* [C, U]

in·dif·fer·ent /ɪn'dɪfrənt/ *adj* 1 不感兴〔興〕趣的 bù gǎnxìngqù de, 不关〔關〕心的 bùguānxīn de. 2 质〔質〕量不高的 zhìliàng bùgāo de: *an ~ meal* 一顿凑合饭. **~ly** *adv* **in·dif·fer·ence** /-frəns/ *n* [U]

in·digen·ous /ɪn'dɪdʒɪnəs/ *adj* 土生土长〔長〕的 tǔshēngtǔzhǎngde, 本土的 běntǔde: *the ~ peoples of Africa* 非洲本地人.

in·di·ges·tion /ˌɪndɪ'dʒestʃən/ *n* [U] 消化不良 xiāohuà bùliáng, 消化不良症 xiāohuà bùliáng zhèng.

in·dig·nant /ɪn'dɪgnənt/ *adj* 愤慨的 fènkǎide, 义〔義〕愤的 yìfènde. **~ly** *adv* **in·dig·na·tion** /-'neɪʃn/ *n* [U]

in·dig·nity /ɪn'dɪgnətɪ/ *n* [*pl* -ies] [C, U] 无〔無〕礼〔禮〕wúlǐ, 侮辱 wǔrǔ.

in·di·rect /ˌɪndɪ'rekt/ *adj* 1 间〔間〕接的 jiànjiēde, 迂回的 yúhuíde: *go by an ~ route* 走迂回路线. 2 (税)间接的 jiànjiēde. **,~-'speech** [语法] 间接引语 jiànjiē yǐnyǔ. **~ly** *adv*

in·dis·creet /ˌɪndɪ'skri:t/ *adj* 不慎重的 búshènzhòngde, 轻〔輕〕率 qīngshuài. **~ly** *adv* **in·dis·cre·tion** /ˌɪndɪ'skreʃn/ *n* (a) [U] 不慎重 búshènzhòng, 轻率 qīngshuài. (b) [C] 不检〔檢〕点〔點〕的言行 bùjiǎndiǎnde yánxíng.

in·dis·crimi·nate /ˌɪndɪ'skrɪmɪnət/ *adj* 不加区〔區〕别的 bùjiā qūbiéde: *~ praise* 一味恭维; *~ killing* 不分青红皂白地杀戮,滥杀. **~ly** *adv*

in·dis·pens·able /ˌɪndɪ'spensəbl/ *adj* 必需的 bìxūde, 必不可少的 bì bùkěshǎo de.

in·dis·posed /ˌɪndɪ'spəʊzd/ *adj* [正式用语] 1 有病的 yǒubìngde, 不舒服的 bùshūfude. 2 不愿〔願〕的 búyuànde: *~ to help* 不愿帮助.

in·dis·put·able /ˌɪndɪ'spju:təbl/ *adj* 无〔無〕可争辩的 wúkězhēngbiànde.

in·dis·tin·guish·able /ˌɪndɪ'stɪŋgwɪʃəbl/ *adj* 区〔區〕分不出的 qūfēn bùchū de, 难〔難〕分辨的 nánfēnbiànde: *~ from his brother* 不能把他同他的兄弟加以区分.

in·di·vid·ual /ˌɪndɪ'vɪdʒʊəl/ *adj* 个〔個〕人的 gèrénde; 个体〔體〕的 gètǐde; 个别的 gèbiéde. □ *n* [C] 个人 gèrén, 个体 gètǐ. **~ly** *adv* 单〔單〕独〔獨〕地 dāndúde. **~-ity** /-'ælətɪ/ *n* [*pl* -ies] (a) [U] 个性 gèxìng. (b) [C] 独立存在 dúlì cúnzài.

in·doc·tri·nate /ɪn'dɒktrɪneɪt/ *vt* 灌输〔輸〕guànshū. **in·doc·tri'na·tion** *n* [U]

in·do·lent /'ɪndələnt/ *adj* [正式用语]懒惰的 lǎnduòde. **in·dol·ence** /-ləns/ *n* [U]

in·door /ˌɪn'dɔ:(r)/ *adj* 在室内的 zài shìnèi de, 在屋内的 zài wūnèi de.

in·doors /ˌɪn'dɔ:z/ *adv* 在屋里〔裡〕zài wūlǐ, 进〔進〕屋里 jìn wūlǐ.

in·duce /ɪn'dju:s/ *vt* 引起 yǐnqǐ, 导〔導〕致 dǎozhì: *~ someone to stay* 使某人留下. **~ment** *n* [C, U] 诱因 yòuyīn: *a pay rise as an ~ment to stay* 促使人留下来的提高工资.

in·duc·tion /ɪn'dʌkʃn/ *n* [U] [逻辑]归〔歸〕纳法 guīnàfǎ. ⇨ deduction. **in·duc·tive** *adj*

in·dulge /ɪn'dʌldʒ/ *vt/i* 1 放纵〔縱〕(欲望等) fàngzòng: *~ one's children* 纵容孩子. 2 *~ in* 沉迷于 chénmí yú, 纵情于 zòngqíng yú. **in·dul·gent** /-ənt/ *adj* 纵容的 zòngróngde, 沉溺的 chénnìde. **in·dul·gence** *n* (a) [U] 沉溺 chénnì; 纵容 zòngróng, 娇〔嬌〕惯 jiāoguàn. (b) [C] 嗜好 shìhào, 着迷的事物 zháomíde shìwù.

in·dus·trial /ɪn'dʌstrɪəl/ *adj* 工业〔業〕的 gōngyède. **~ estate** 工业区〔區〕gōngyèqū. **~ism** /-ɪzəm/ *n* [U] 工业主义〔義〕gōngyèzhǔyì. **~ist** *n* [C] 实〔實〕业家 shíyèjiā.

in·dus·tri·ous /ɪn'dʌstrɪəs/ *adj* 勤奋〔奮〕的 qínfènde, 勤劳的 qínláode.

in·dus·try /'ɪndəstrɪ/ *n* [*pl* -ies] 1 [U] 勤奋 qínfèn. 2 [C, U] 工业 gōngyè; 产〔產〕业 chǎnyè, 行业 hángyè: *the coal ~* 采煤工业, *the steel ~* 钢铁工业.

in·ebri·ate /ɪ'ni:brɪeɪt/ *vt* 使醉 shǐ zhì, 灌醉 guàn zuì. □ /ɪ'ni:brɪət/ *n* [C], *adj* 酒鬼 jiǔguǐ, 醉鬼 zuìguī.

in·ed·ible /ɪn'edɪbl/ *adj* 不能食用的 bùnéng shíyòng de.

in·ef·fec·tive /ˌɪnɪ'fektɪv/ *adj* 无〔無〕效的 wúxiàode, 不起作用的 bùqǐ zuòyòng de. ~**ly** *adv* ~**ness** *n* [U]

in·ef·fec·tual /ˌɪnɪ'fektʃʊəl/ *adj* 无〔無〕效的 wúxiàode, 不成功的 bùchénggōngde: *an* ~ *manager* 不称职的经理.

in·ef·fi·cient /ˌɪnɪ'fɪʃnt/ *adj* **1** (人)无〔無〕能的 wúnéngde, 不称〔稱〕职〔職〕的 búchènzhíde. **2** (机器等)无效的 wúxiàode, 效率低的 xiàolǜdīde. ~**ly** *adv* **in·ef·fi·ciency** /-ʃnsɪ/ *n* [U]

in·eli·gible /ɪn'elɪdʒəbl/ *adj* 不合格的 bùhégéde. **in·eli·gi'bil·ity** *n* [U]

in·ept /ɪ'nept/ *adj* 不适〔適〕当〔當〕的 búshìdàngde: *an* ~ *comment* 不恰当的评论. ~**ly** *adv.* ~**i·tude** /-tɪtju:d/ *n* [C, U]

in·equal·ity /ˌɪnɪ'kwɒlətɪ/ *n* [*pl* -ies] [C, U] 不平等 bùpíngděng; 不平衡 bùpínghéng; 不平坦 bùpíngtǎn.

in·ert /ɪ'nɜ:t/ *adj* **1** 无〔無〕活动〔動〕能力的 wú huódòng nénglì de: ~ *matter* 无活动能力的物质. **2** [化学]惰性的 duòxìngde, 不活泼〔潑〕的 bùhuópode: ~ *gases* 惰性气体. **3** 呆滞〔滯〕的 dāizhìde, 迟〔遲〕钝的 chídùnde.

in·er·tia /ɪ'nɜ:ʃə/ *n* [U] **1** 呆滞〔滯〕 dāizhì, 迟〔遲〕钝 chídùn. **2** [物理]惯性 guànxìng.

in·es·cap·able /ˌɪnɪ'skeɪpəbl/ *adj* 逃避不了的 táobì bùliǎo de.

in·evi·table /ɪn'evɪtəbl/ *adj* **1** 不可避免的 bùkě bìmiǎn de. **2** [非正式用语]照例必有的 zhàolì bì yǒu de: *the tourist with his* ~ *camera* 照例携有照像机的游客. **in·evi·ta'bil·ity** *n* [U]

in·ex·cus·able /ˌɪnɪk'skju:zəbl/ *adj* 不可原谅的 bùkě yuánliàng de: ~ *behaviour* 不可原谅的行为, ~ *rudeness* 不可宽恕的粗鲁行为.

in·ex·pen·sive /ˌɪnɪk'spensɪv/ *adj* 花费不大的 huāfèi búdà de, 廉价〔價〕的 liánjiàde. ~**ly** *adv*

in·ex·pe·ri·ence /ˌɪnɪk'spɪərɪəns/ *n* [U] 缺乏经〔經〕验〔驗〕 quēfá jīngyàn.

in·ex·plic·able /ˌɪnɪk'splɪkəbl/ *adj* 费解的 fèijiěde, 不能说明的 bùnéng shuōmíng de.

in·fal·lible /ɪn'fæləbl/ *adj* **1** 不会〔會〕犯错误的 búhuì fàn cuòwù de. **2** 绝对〔對〕可靠的 juéduì kěkào de. *an* ~ *method* 绝对可靠的方法: **in·fal·li'bil·ity** *n* [U]

in·fa·mous /'ɪnfəməs/ *adj* 邪恶〔惡〕的 xié'ède, 可耻的 kěchǐde: *an* ~ *murderer* 可耻的杀人犯: **in·famy** *n* [*pl* -ies] **(a)** [U] 声〔聲〕名狼藉 shēngmínglángjí. **(b)** [C] 无耻的行为〔爲〕 wúchǐde xíngwéi.

in·fancy /'ɪnfənsɪ/ *n* [U] **1** 婴儿〔兒〕yīng'ér; 婴儿期 yīng'érqī. **2** 初期阶〔階〕段 chūqī jiēduàn: *Space travel is in its* ~. 空间旅行处于初期阶段.

in·fant /'ɪnfənt/ *n* [C] 婴儿〔兒〕 yīng'ér.

in·fan·tile /'ɪnfəntaɪl/ *adj* 婴儿〔兒〕的 yīng'érde.

in·fan·try /'ɪnfəntrɪ/ *n* [U] 步兵 bùbīng.

in·fatu·ate /ɪn'fætʃʊeɪt/ *vt* *be* ~*d with* (或 *by*) *sb* 迷恋〔戀〕某人 míliàn mǒurén. **in·fatu'ation** *n* [C, U]

in·fect /ɪn'fekt/ *vt* **1** 传〔傳〕染 chuánrǎn. **2** [喻]受影响〔響〕 shòu yǐngxiǎng, 受感染 shòu gǎnrǎn. **in·fec·tion** /-ʃn/ *n* **(a)** [U] 传染 chuánrǎn: *danger from* ~*ion* 传染的危险. ⇨ contagion. **(b)** [C] 传染病 chuánrǎnbìng. ~**ious** *adj* **(a)** 传染的 chuánrǎnde, 传染性的 chuánrǎnxìngde. ⇨ contagious. **(b)** [喻]感染性的 gǎnrǎnxìngde: ~*ious laughter* 感染性的笑声.

in·fer /ɪn'fɜ:(r)/ *vt* [-rr-] 推论〔論〕 tuīlùn, 推断〔斷〕 tuīduàn. ~**ence** /'ɪnfərəns/ *n* [C, U]

in·fer·ior /ɪn'fɪərɪə(r)/ *adj* 劣质〔質〕的 lièzhìde, 差的 chàde, 下等的 xiàděngde. □ *n* [C] 地位低的人 dìwèidīde rén; 能力低的人 nénglìdīde rén. ~**ity** /-'ɒrətɪ/ *n* [U]

in·fer·nal /ɪn'fɜ:nl/ *adj* 地狱般的 dìyùbānde, 恶〔惡〕魔般的 èmóbānde.

in·ferno /ɪn'fɜ:nəʊ/ *n* [C] [*pl* ~s] 地狱 dìyù, 恐怖的景象 kǒngbùde jǐngxiàng.

in·fer·tile /ˌɪn'fɜ:taɪl/ *adj* 贫瘠的 pínjíde, 不毛的 bùmáode: ~ *land* 不毛之地.

in·fest /ɪn'fest/ *vt* (老鼠,害虫等) 大批出现 dàpī chūxiàn.

in·fi·del /'ɪnfɪdəl/ *n* [C] 异〔異〕教徒 yìjiàotú.

in·fi·del·ity /ˌɪnfɪ'delətɪ/ *n* [C, U] [*pl* -ties] 不忠诚 bù zhōngchéng 背信 bèixìn.

in·fight·ing /'ɪnfaɪtɪŋ/ *n* [U] [非正式用语]暗斗〔鬥〕 àndòu.

in·fil·trate /ˈɪnfɪltreɪt/ *vt/i* **1** 悄悄穿越 qiāoqiāo chuānyuè: ~ *the enemy lines* 悄悄穿越敌人防线. **2** (思想)渗〔滲〕透 shèntòu. **in·fil'tra·tion** *n* [U]

in·fi·nite /ˈɪnfɪnət/ *adj* 无〔無〕限的 wúxiànde, 无穷〔窮〕的 wúqióngde. ~**ly** *adv*

in·fini·tive /ɪnˈfɪnətɪv/ *adj, n* [C] 〔英语语法〕不定式 búdìngshì.

in·fin·ity /ɪnˈfɪnətɪ/ *n* [U] 无〔無〕穷〔窮〕 wúqióng.

in·firm /ˌɪnˈfɜːm/ *adj* **1**〔书面语〕体〔體〕弱的 tǐruòde, 年老体衰的 niánlǎo tǐshuāi de. **2** 意志薄弱的 yìzhìbóruòde, 不坚〔堅〕定的 bùjiāndìngde. ~**ity** *n* [C, U] [*pl* -ties]

in·firm·ary /ɪnˈfɜːmərɪ/ *n* [C] [*pl* -ies] 医〔醫〕院 yīyuàn.

in·flame /ɪnˈfleɪm/ *vt/i* **1** (使)疼痛发〔發〕炎 téngtòng fāyán, (使)烦躁 fánzào: ~*d eyes* 红肿发炎的眼睛. **2** 激动 jīdòng, 激怒 jīnù.

in·flam·mable /ɪnˈflæməbl/ *adj* **1** 易燃的 yìránde. **2**〔喻〕易激动〔動〕的 yì jīdòng de.

in·flam·ma·tion /ˌɪnfləˈmeɪʃn/ *n* [C, U] 发〔發〕炎 fāyán.

in·flam·ma·tory /ɪnˈflæmətrɪ/ *adj* **1** 煽动〔動〕性的 shāndòngxìngde: ~ *remarks* 煽动性的话. **2** 炎性的 yánxìngde, 发炎的 fāyánde.

in·flate /ɪnˈfleɪt/ *vt* **1** 充气〔氣〕chōngqì, 使膨胀〔脹〕shǐ péngzhàng. **2** (财政)通货膨胀 tōnghuò péngzhàng. ⇨ deflate. **in·fla·tion** /-ʃn/ *n* [U] 通货膨胀 tōnghuò péngzhàng, 物价〔價〕上涨〔漲〕wùjià shàngzhǎng.

in·flec·tion /ɪnˈflekʃn/ *n* **1** [C, U]〔语法〕词形变〔變〕化 cíxíng biànhuà, 屈折形式 qūzhé xíngshì. **2** [U] 变〔變〕音 biànyīn, 转〔轉〕调 zhuǎndiào.

in·flex·ible /ɪnˈfleksəbl/ *adj* **1** 不可弯〔彎〕曲的 bùkě wānqū de. **2**〔喻〕坚〔堅〕定的 jiāndìngde, 固执〔執〕的 gùzhìde. **in·flex·ibly** *adv* **in·flexi'bil·ity** *n* [U]

in·flex·ion /ɪnˈflekʃn/ *n* = inflection.

in·flict /ɪnˈflɪkt/ *vt* **1** 使遭受(痛苦等) shǐ zāoshòu: ~ *punishment on him* 处罚他. **2** 强加 qiángjiā: ~ *one's presence on* 打扰(某人), 闯入. **in·flic·tion** /-ʃn/ *n* [C, U]

in·flow /ˈɪnfləʊ/ *n* [C, U] 流入 liúrù: *the* ~ *of refugees* 难民的流入.

in·flu·ence /ˈɪnflʊəns/ *n* **1** [U] 影响〔響〕力 yǐngxiǎnglì, 感化力 gǎnhuàlì; 影响 yǐngxiǎng, 感化 gǎnhuà. **2** [C] 有影响的人或事 yǒuyǐngxiǎngde rén huò shì: *He's a bad* ~ *on me.* 他是个对我有坏影响的人. **3** [U] 自然力的作用 zìránlìde zuòyòng. **4** [U] 势〔勢〕力 shìlì, 权〔權〕势 quánshì. □ *vt* 影响 yǐngxiǎng; 感化 gǎnhuà; 左右 zuǒyòu.

in·flu·en·tial /ˌɪnflʊˈenʃl/ *adj* 有影响〔響〕的 yǒuyǐngxiǎngde, 有权〔權〕势〔勢〕的 yǒuquánshìde. ~**ly** *adv*

in·flu·enza /ˌɪnflʊˈenzə/ *n* [U] 流行性感冒 liúxíngxìng gǎnmào.

in·flux /ˈɪnflʌks/ *n* [*pl* ~es] **1** [U] 流入 liúrù, 注入 zhùrù. **2** [C] 涌进〔進〕yǒngjìn: *an* ~ *of tourists* 大批游客涌进.

in·form /ɪnˈfɔːm/*vt/i* **1** 通知 tōngzhī, 告诉 gàosù. **2** 告发〔發〕gàofā. ~**ant** *n* [C] 提供消息或情报〔報〕的人 tígòng xiāoxī huò qíngbào de rén. ~**er** *n* [C] 告发人 gàofārén.

in·for·mal /ˌɪnˈfɔːml/ *adj* 非正规的 fēizhèngguīde, 非正式的 fēizhèngshìde, 不拘礼〔禮〕节〔節〕的 bùjū lǐjié de, 日常的 rìchángde. ~**ly** *adv* ~**ity** /-ˈmælətɪ/ *n* [C, U]

in·for·ma·tion /ˌɪnfəˈmeɪʃn/ *n* [U] **1** 通知 tōngzhī, 报〔報〕告 bàogào. **2** 消息 xiāoxī, 情报〔報〕qíngbào. ~**re'trieval** *n* 信息检〔檢〕索 xìnxī jiǎnsuǒ. ~**science** *n* 资料学〔學〕zīliàoxué, 信息学 xìnxīxué.

in·for·ma·tive /ɪnˈfɔːmətɪv/ *adj* 提供消息, 情报〔報〕的 tígòng xiāoxī, qíngbào de. ~**ly** *adv*

in·fre·quent /ɪnˈfriːkwənt/ *adj* 不常发〔發〕生的 bùcháng fāshēng de, 稀罕的 xīhande. ~**ly** *adv* **in·fre·quency** *n* [U]

in·fringe /ɪnˈfrɪndʒ/ *vt/i* **1** 违〔違〕反(规则等) wéifǎn, 触〔觸〕犯 chùfàn. **2** 侵犯 qīnfàn, 侵害 qīnhài: ~ *on his rights* 侵犯他的权利. ~**ment** *n* [C, U]

in·furi·ate /ɪnˈfjʊərɪeɪt/ *vt* 激怒 jīnù.

in·fuse /ɪnˈfjuːz/ *vt/i* 〔正式用语〕**1** 向某人灌输 (*with*) ... xiàng mǒurén guànshū ...: ~ *courage into soldiers* 鼓励兵士勇敢. **2** 泡(茶) pào, 浸渍 jìnzì. **in·fu·sion** /-ʒn/ *n* [C, U] 灌输 guànshū; 浸渍 jìnzì; 浸液 jìnyè.

in·geni·ous /ɪnˈdʒiːnɪəs/ *adj* **1** 机〔機〕灵〔靈〕的 jīlingde. **2** 制〔製〕作精巧的 zhìzuò jīngqiǎo de, 灵巧的 língqiǎode. ~**ly** *adv* **in·gen'uity** /ˌɪndʒɪˈnjuːətɪ/ *n* [U]

in·got /'ɪŋgət/ *n* [C] 锭 dìng, 铸〔鑄〕块〔塊〕 zhùkuài.

in·grained /ˌɪn'greɪnd/ *adj* (习惯等)根深蒂固的 gēnshēndìgùde.

in·grati·tude /ɪn'grætɪtjuːd/ *n* [U] 忘恩负义〔義〕 wàngēn-fùyì.

in·gredi·ent /ɪn'griːdɪənt/ *n* [C] 混合物的组成部分 hǔnhéwùde zǔchéngbùfen, 配料 pèiliào.

in·habit /ɪn'hæbɪt/ *vt* 居住于 jūzhù yú. **~able** /-əbl/ *adj* **~ant** 居民 jūmín.

in·hale /ɪn'heɪl/ *vt/i* 吸气〔氣〕 xīqì. **in·haler** 吸入器 xīrùqì.

in·her·ent /ɪn'hɪərənt/ *adj* 内在的 nèizàide, 固有的 gùyǒude: ~ *qualities in a design* 一项计划的固有的性质.

in·herit /ɪn'herɪt/ *vt/i* **1** 继〔繼〕承 jìchéng. **2** 经〔經〕遗传〔傳〕而得(特性等) jīng yíchuán ér dé. **~ance** /-təns/ *n* [U] **(a)** 继承 jìchéng. **(b)** [C] 继承物 jìchéngwù, 遗产〔產〕 yíchǎn.

in·hibit /ɪn'hɪbɪt/ *vt* 禁止 jìnzhǐ, 阻止 zǔzhǐ, 抑制 yìzhì. **in·hi·bi·tion** /-'bɪʃn/ *n* [C, U] 抑制 yìzhì.

in·hos·pi·table /ˌɪnhɒ'spɪtəbl/ *adj* 不适〔適〕于居住的 bú shìyú jūzhù de: *an* ~ *climate* 不适宜居住的气候,气候恶劣.

in·hu·man /ˌɪn'hjuːmən/ *adj* 野蛮〔蠻〕的 yěmánde, 残〔殘〕暴的 cánbào de, 无〔無〕情的 wúqíngde. **~·ity** /-'mænətɪ/ *n* [C, U] 野蛮 yěmán, 残酷无情 cánkù wúqíng.

in·hu·mane /ˌɪnhjuː'meɪn/ *adj* 无〔無〕人道的 wúréndàode, 残〔殘〕忍的 cánrěnde. **~ly** *adv*

in·itial /ɪ'nɪʃl/ *adj* 最初的 zuìchūde, 开〔開〕始的 kāishǐde. □ *n* [C] [*pl*] 人名的首字母 rénmíngde shǒuzìmǔ. □ *vt* [-ll-; 美语亦作 -l-] 签〔簽〕署姓名首字母于 qiānshǔ xìngmíng shǒuzìmǔ yú. **~ly** *adv* 开始 kāishǐ, 最初 zuìchū.

in·iti·ate /ɪ'nɪʃɪeɪt/ *vt* **1** 创〔創〕始 chuàngshǐ, 着手 zháoshǒu, 发〔發〕动〔動〕 fādòng. **2** 介绍某人为〔爲〕(会员等) jièshào mǒurén wéi. **3** 向某人传〔傳〕授基础知识〔識〕 xiàng mǒurén chuánshòu jīchǔ zhīshi. **in·iti'ation** *n* [U]

in·iti·at·ive /ɪ'nɪʃətɪv/ *n* **1** [U] 发〔發〕端 fāduān, 创〔創〕始 chuàngshǐ: *take the* ~ *in a discussion* 讨论中首先发言. **2** [U] 主动〔動〕性 zhǔdòngxìng. ***act* (*do sth*) *on one's own* ~** 主动〔動〕地 zhǔdòngde. ***have* (或 *take*) *the* ~** 带〔帶〕头〔頭〕 dàitóu.

in·ject /ɪn'dʒekt/ *vt* **1** 注射 zhùshè. **2** [喻; 非正式用语]注入 zhùrù, 灌入 guànrù: ~ *new life into the team* 给这个队输进新的生命. **in·jec·tion** /-ʃn/ *n* [C, U]

in·junc·tion /ɪn'dʒʌŋkʃn/ *n* [C] 法院的强制令 fǎyuànde qiángzhìlìng.

in·jure /'ɪndʒə(r)/ *vt* 伤〔傷〕害 shānghài, 损害 sǔnhài. **in·jured** *adj* 受伤害的 shòu shānghài de, 被触〔觸〕怒的 bèi chùnù de. □ *n* **the ~d** 受伤者 shòushāngzhě.

in·jury /'ɪndʒərɪ/ *n* [*pl* -ies] **1** [U] 伤〔傷〕害 shānghài, 损害 sǔnhài. **2** [C] 受伤处〔處〕 shòushāngchù. 伤害的行为〔爲〕 shānghàide xíngwéi.

in·jus·tice /ˌɪn'dʒʌstɪs/ *n* [U] 非正义〔義〕 fēi zhèngyì. 不公正 bùgōngzhèng; [C] 非正义的行为 fēi zhèngyì de xíngwéi.

ink /ɪŋk/ *n* [U] 墨水 mòshuǐ, 油墨 yóumò. **inky** *adj* [-ier, -iest] 黑的 hēide.

ink·ling /'ɪŋklɪŋ/ *n* [C] 模糊的想法 móhude xiǎngfǎ.

in·land /'ɪnlənd/ *adj* **1** 内地的 nèidìde, 内陆〔陸〕的 nèilùde. **2** 国〔國〕内的 guónèide: ~ *trade* 国内贸易. □ *adv* /ɪn'lænd/ 在内地 zài nèidì, 向内地 xiàng nèidì. **ˌI~ 'Revenue** 税务〔務〕局 shuìwùjú.

in-laws /'ɪnlɔːz/ *n pl* [非正式用语]姻亲〔親〕 yīnqīn.

in·let /'ɪnlet/ *n* [C] 海湾〔灣〕 hǎiwān, 小港 xiǎogǎng.

in·mate /'ɪnmeɪt/ *n* [C] 同住者(同狱犯人等) tóngzhùzhě.

inn /ɪn/ *n* [C] 小旅馆 xiǎolǚguǎn, 小客栈〔棧〕 xiǎokèzhàn. **'~-keeper** 小旅馆老板〔闆〕 xiǎolǚguǎnlǎobǎn.

in·nards /'ɪnədz/ *n pl* [非正式用语] **1** 内脏〔臟〕 nèizàng. **2** [非正式用语]内部结构〔構〕 nèibù jiégòu, 内部机〔機〕件 nèibù jījiàn: *the* ~ *of a car* 汽车的内部机件.

in·nate /ɪ'neɪt/ *adj* 天生的 tiānshēngde, 固有的 gùyǒude. **~ly** *adv*

in·ner /'ɪnə(r)/ 内部的 nèibùde, 里〔裡〕面的 lǐmiànde.

in·ning /'ɪnɪŋ/ *n* [C] **1** (棒球)一局 yìjú, 一盘〔盤〕 yìpán. **2** (板球) [*pl*] 一局 yìjú, 一盘 yìpán.

in·no·cent /'ɪnəsnt/ *adj* **1** [法律]无〔無〕罪的 wúzuìde. **2** 无害的 wúhàide: ~ *fun* 无害的玩笑. **3** 天真的 tiānzhēnde, 单〔單〕纯的 dānchúnde: ~ *children* 天真的儿童. **4** 无知的 wúzhīde, 轻〔輕〕易信任别人的 qīngyì xìnrèn biérén de. □ *n* [C] 天真无邪的人 tiānzhēn wúxié de rén. **in·no·cence** /-sns/ *n* [U] ~**ly** *adv*

in·nocu·ous /ɪ'nɒkjʊəs/ *adj* 无〔無〕害的 wúhàide.

in·no·vate /'ɪnəveɪt/ *vi* 创〔創〕新 chuàngxīn, 革新 géxīn. **in·no'va·tion** *n* [C, U]

in·nu·endo /ˌɪnjʊ'endəʊ/ *n* [C] [*pl* ~es]暗指 ànzhǐ, 影射 yǐngshè, 暗讽〔諷〕ànfěng.

in·numer·able /ɪ'nju:mərəbl/ *adj* 数〔數〕不清的 shǔbùqīngde.

in·ocu·late /ɪ'nɒkjʊleɪt/ *vt* 接种〔種〕(疫苗) jiēzhòng. **in·ocu'la·tion** *n* [C, U]

in·of·fen·sive /ˌɪnə'fensɪv/ *adj* 不触〔觸〕犯人的 bú·chùfàn rén de, 不粗野的 bùcūyěde.

in·op·por·tune /ˌɪn'ɒpətʃu:n/ *adj* 不合适〔適〕的 bùhéshìde, 不合时宜的 bùhé shíyí de: *an ~ moment* 不合适的时刻. ~**ly** *adv*

in·or·ganic /ˌɪnɔ:'gænɪk/ *adj* 无〔無〕机〔機〕的 wújīde: *Rocks are ~ materials.* 岩石是无机物.

in·put /'ɪnpʊt/ *n* [C] 输〔輸〕入 shūrù.

in·quest /'ɪnkwest/ *n* [C] 审〔審〕讯 shěnxùn, 审问〔問〕 shěnwèn.

in·quire /ɪn'kwaɪə(r)/ *vt/i* **1** 询问〔問〕xúnwèn. **2** 打听〔聽〕dǎting. ~ ***after sb*** 问起某人健康情况 wènqǐ mǒurén jiànkāng zhuàngkuàng. ~ ***into*** 调查 diàochá. **in·quir·ing** *adj* 爱〔愛〕打听的 ài dǎting de, 好询问的 hào xúnwèn de: *an inquiring mind* 爱探索的头脑〔腦〕.

in·quiry /ɪn'kwaɪərɪ/ *n* [*pl* -ies] **1** [U] 询问 xúnwèn, 打听〔聽〕dǎting. ***on*** ~ 经〔經〕查询 jīng cháxún. **2** [C] 质〔質〕询 zhìxún, 调查 diàochá.

in·qui·si·tion /ˌɪnkwɪ'zɪʃn/ *n* [C, U] 彻〔徹〕底调查或审〔審〕讯 chèdǐ diàochá huò shěnxùn.

in·quisi·tive /ɪn'kwɪzətɪv/ *adj* 爱〔愛〕打听〔聽〕别人事情的 ài dǎting biérén shìqing de. ~**ly** *adv*

in·road /'ɪnrəʊd/ *n* [C] **1** 突然袭〔襲〕击〔擊〕(一个国家) tūrán xíjī. **2**[喻]侵蚀 qīnshí, 花费 huāfèi: *make ~s into one's money* 花费了某人的钱.

in·sane /ɪn'seɪn/ *adj* **1** 疯〔瘋〕狂的 fēngkuáng de. **2**[非正式用语]愚蠢的 yúchǔnde. ~**ly** *adv* **in·san·ity** /ɪn'sænətɪ/ *n* [U] 疯狂 fēngkuáng.

in·scribe /ɪn'skraɪb/ *vt* 题写〔寫〕tíxiě. **in·scrip·tion** /ɪn'skrɪpʃn/ *n* [C] 铭刻 míngkè, 铭文 míngwén.

in·sect /'ɪnsekt/ *n* [C] 昆虫〔蟲〕kūnchóng. ~**i·cide** /ɪn'sektɪsaɪd/ *n* [C, U] 杀〔殺〕虫剂〔劑〕 shāchóngjì.

in·se·cure /ˌɪnsɪ'kjʊə(r)/ *adj* **1** 不安全的 bùānquánde, 不可靠的 bùkěkàode. **2** 得不到信任的 débúdào xìnrèn de. ~**ly** *adv* **in·se·cur·ity** *n* [U]

in·semi·nate /ɪn'semɪneɪt/ *vt* 授精 shòujīng **in·semi·nation** /ɪnˌsemɪ'neɪʃn/ *n* [U] 授精 shòujīng ˌ**artificial** ~ *n* 人工授精 réngōng shòujīng.

in·sen·sible /ɪn'sensəbl/ *adj* **1** 失去知觉〔覺〕的 shīqù zhījué de. **2** 不知道的 bùzhīdàode, 没觉察到的 *(of)* méi chájué dào de: *~ to the danger* 不知道危险. **in·sen·si'bil·ity** *n* [U]

in·sen·si·tive /ɪn'sensətɪv/ *adj* 不敏感的 bùmǐngǎnde, 不灵〔靈〕敏的 bùlíngmǐnde. ~**ly** *adv* **in·sen·si'tiv·ity** *n* [U]

in·sep·ar·able /ɪn'seprəbl/ *adj* 分不开〔開〕的 fēnbùkāide, 不可分割的 bùkě fēngē de: *~ friends* 好友.

in·sert /ɪn'sɜ:t/ *vt* 插入 (*in* 或 *into*) chārù: *~ a key in a lock* 把钥匙插进锁里. □ *n* /'ɪnsɜ:t/ [C] 插入物 chārùwù, 插页 chāyè. **in·ser·tion** /ɪn'sɜ:ʃn/ *n* [C, U]

in·set /'ɪnset/ *n* [C] **1** (大地图上的)小插图〔圖〕, 图表 xiǎochātú, túbiǎo. **2** (衣裳)镶边〔邊〕xiāngbian. □ *vt* /ɪn'set/ 插入 chārù, 镶入 xiāngrù.

in·shore /'ɪnʃɔ:(r)/ *adj, adv* 靠海岸的 kào hǎi'àn de. 沿海岸的 yán hǎi'ànde, 沿海岸 yánhǎi'àn.

in·side /ɪn'saɪd/ *n* [C] **1** 里〔裡〕面 lǐmiàn, 内部 nèibù. ˌ~'***out*** **(a)** 里面翻到外面 lǐmiàn fāndào wàimiàn. **(b)** 彻〔徹〕底地 chèdǐde: *know something ~ out* 透彻了解某事. **2**[非正式用语][常用 *pl*]肠〔腸〕胃 chángwèi, 肚子 dùzi. □*adj* /'ɪnsa:ɪd/ 里面的 lǐmiànde, 内幕的 nèimùde. □ *adv* **1** 在里面 zài lǐmiàn, 在内部 zài nèibù. **2** [英国俚语]在监狱里 zài jiānyù lǐ. □*prep.* 在…里面 zài … lǐmiàn, 在…内部 zài nèibù: *come ~ the house* 到屋里来.

in·sidi·ous /ɪn'sɪdɪəs/ *adj* 暗中为〔為〕害的 ànzhōng wéihài de, 阴〔陰〕险〔險〕的 yīnxiǎnde. ~**ly** *adv*

in·sight /'ɪnsaɪt/ *n* [C, U] 洞悉 dòngxī, 洞察 dòngchá; 见识〔識〕jiànshi: *~s into his character* 深刻了解他的性格.

in·sig·nia /ɪn'sɪgnɪə/ *n pl* 权〔權〕

威或荣〔榮〕誉〔譽〕的标〔標〕识〔識〕quánwēi huò róngyù de biāoshí.

in·sig·nifi·cant /ˌɪnsɪg'nɪfɪkənt/ *adj* 无〔無〕价〔價〕值的 wújiàzhíde, 无足轻〔輕〕重的 wúzúqīngzhòngde. ~**ly** *adv* **in·sig·nifi·cance** *n* [U]

in·sin·cere /ˌɪnsɪn'sɪə(r)/ *adj* 不真诚的 bùzhēnchéngde, 虚假的 xūjiǎde. ~**ly** *adv* **in·sin·cer·ity** /-'serətɪ/ *n* [U]

in·sinu·ate /ɪn'sɪnjʊeɪt/ *vt* **1** 巧妙地进〔進〕入 (*oneself* 或 *something*) qiǎomiàode jìnrù. **2** 暗示 ànshì, 暗讽〔諷〕ànfěng. **in·sinu'ation** *n* [C, U]

in·sipid /ɪn'sɪpɪd/ *adj* **1** 无〔無〕味的 wúwèide. **2** [喻]枯燥乏味的 kūzàofáwèide, 单〔單〕调的 dāndiàode. ~**ly** *adv*

in·sist /ɪn'sɪst/ *vt/i* ~ **(on, that)** **1** 坚〔堅〕决要求 jiānjué yāoqiú: *I ~ that you come with me.* 我坚决要求你同我一起走. **2** 坚决认〔認〕为〔為〕jiānjué rènwéi, 坚决地宣布 jiānjuéde xuānbù: *He ~s that he is innocent.* 他坚决认为他是无罪的. ~**ent** *adj* 要别人注意的 yào biérén zhùyì de, 显〔顯〕眼的 xiǎnyǎnde. ~**ence** *n* [U]

in·so·lent /'ɪnsələnt/ *adj* 蛮〔蠻〕横的 mánhéngde, 粗鲁的 cūlǔde. **in·so·lence** *n* [U]

in·sol·uble /ɪn'sɒljʊbl/ *adj* **1** 不能溶解的 bùnéng róngjiě de, 难〔難〕溶解的 nánróngjiěde. **2** 不能解决的 bùnéng jiějué de.

in·sol·vent /ɪn'sɒlvənt/ *n* [C] (人)无〔無〕偿债能力的 wú chángzhài nénglì de. **in·sol·vency** *n* [U]

in·som·nia /ɪn'sɒmnɪə/ *n* [U] 失眠 shīmián, 失眠症〔癥〕shīmiánzhèng. **in·som·niac** /-nɪæk/ 失眠者 shīmiánzhě.

in·spect /ɪn'spekt/ *vt* 检〔檢〕查 jiǎnchá, 审〔審〕查 shěnchá. **in·spec·tion** /-ʃn/ *n* [C, U]. ~**or** *n* [C] **(a)** 检查员 jiǎncháyuán, 督学〔學〕dūxué. **(b)** [英国英语]警察巡官 jǐngchá xúnguān.

in·spi·ra·tion /ˌɪnspə'reɪʃn/ *n* **1** [U] 灵〔靈〕感 línggǎn. **2** [C]鼓舞人心的人或事 gǔwǔ rénxīn de rén huò shì. **3** [C] [非正式用语]好主意 hǎo zhǔyi, 灵机〔機〕妙算 língjī-miàosuàn. **4** [U] 神灵的启示 shénlíngde qǐshì.

in·spire /ɪn'spaɪə(r)/ *vt* **1** 激励〔勵〕jīlì, 鼓励 gǔlì: ~ *confidence in her* 激起她的信心, ~ *success in her* 使她相信会成功. **2** 灌注以创〔創〕造力 guànzhù yǐ chuàngzàolì, 使有灵〔靈〕感 shǐ yǒu línggǎn.

in·sta·bil·ity /ˌɪnstə'bɪlətɪ/ *n* [U] 不稳定性 bùwěndìngxìng.

in·stall [美语亦作 **-stal**] /ɪn'stɔːl/ *vt* **1** 任命 rènmìn, 使…就职〔職〕shǐ … jiùzhí. **2** 安装〔裝〕ānzhuāng. **3** 安置 ānzhì, 安顿 āndùn. ~**a·tion** /ˌɪnstə'leɪʃn/ *n* [C, U]

in·stal·ment [美语亦作 **-stall-**] /ɪn'stɔːlmənt/ *n* [C] **1** 分期连〔連〕载〔載〕, 连演的一个部分 fēnqī liánzǎi, liányǎn de yígè bùfen: *a TV programme in 10 ~s* 共分十集的电视连续节目. **2** 分期支付的款子 fēnqīzhīfùde kuǎnzi.

in·stance /'ɪnstəns/ *n* [C] 例子 lìzi, 实〔實〕例 shílì. **for** ~ 例如 lìrú. □ *vt* 举〔舉〕…为〔爲〕例 jǔ … wéilì.

in·stant¹ /'ɪnstənt/ *adj* **1** 立即的 lìjìde, 紧〔緊〕迫的 jǐnpòde. **2** (食品)速溶的 sùróngde, 配制〔製〕好的 pèizhì hǎo de. ~**ly** *adv* 立即 lìjì.

in·stant² /'ɪnstənt/ *n* [C] **1** 时〔時〕刻 shíkè. **2** 瞬息 shùnxī, 霎时 shàshí: *I'll be there in an ~.* 我立刻就来. ~**aneous** /-'teɪnɪəs/ *adv*

in·stead /ɪn'sted/ *adv* 代替 dàitì, 顶替 dǐngtì. ~ **of** 代替 dàitì, 而不是 ér búshì: *drink tea ~ of coffee* 喝茶而不是喝咖啡.

in·step /'ɪnstep/ *n* [C] 脚背 jiǎobèi.

in·sti·gate /'ɪnstɪgeɪt/ *vt* 煽动〔動〕shāndòng, 教唆 jiàosuō: ~ *a riot* 煽动骚乱. **in·sti·ga·tor** 煽动者 shāndòngzhě, 教唆者 jiàosuōzhě. **in·sti'ga·tion** *n* [U]

in·stil /ɪn'stɪl/ *vt* [-ll-] 灌输〔輸〕(思想) guànshū: ~ *loyalty in troops* 向部队灌输效忠的思想.

in·stinct /'ɪnstɪŋkt/ *n* [C, U] 本能 běnnéng. ~**ive** /ɪn'stɪnktɪv/ *adj* 本能的 běnnéngde: *an ~ive reaction* 本能的反应. ~**ive·ly** *adv*

in·sti·tute¹ /'ɪnstɪtjuːt/ *n* [C] 学〔學〕会〔會〕xuéhuì; 协〔協〕会 xiéhuì; 学院 xuéyuàn; 研究所 yánjiūsuǒ.

in·sti·tute² /'ɪnstɪtjuːt/ *vt* **1** 着手 zhuóshǒu, 实〔實〕行 shíxíng. **2** 任命 rènmìn; (宗教) 授予…圣〔聖〕职〔職〕shòuyǔ … shèngzhí.

in·sti·tu·tion /ɪnstɪ'tjuːʃn/ *n* **1** [U] 建立 jiànlì, 制定 zhìdìng: *the ~ of rules (customs)* 制定规则(建立习惯). **2** [C] 制度 zhìdù; 惯例 guànlì. **3** [C] 慈善机〔機〕构〔構〕

或其建筑物 císhàn jīgòu huò qí jiànzhùwù. ~**al** *adj*

in·struct /ɪn'strʌkt/ *vt* **1** 教 jiāo, 教育 jiàoyù. **2** 指导〔導〕 zhǐdǎo, 指示 zhǐshì. **3** 通知 tōngzhī. ~**ive** *adj* ~**or** 教员 jiàoyuán, 指导者 zhǐdǎozhě. ~**ress** /-trɪs/ 女教员 nǚjiàoyuán, 女指导者 nǚzhǐdǎozhě.

in·struc·tion /ɪn'strʌkʃn/ *n* **1** [U] 教育 jiàoyù; 指导〔導〕 zhǐdǎo. **2** [*pl*] 指示 zhǐshì; 命令 mìnlìng; 教诲 jiàohuǐ.

in·stru·ment /'ɪnstrʊmənt/ *n* [C] **1** 仪〔儀〕器 yíqì; 器具 qìjù; 器械 qìjiè: *optical ~s* 光学仪器 *surgical ~s* 外科器械. '~ **flying** *n* 仪表飞〔飛〕行 yíbiǎo fēixíng '~ **panel** *n* 仪表板 yíbiǎobǎn **2** 乐〔樂〕器 yuèqì. ~**al** /-'mentl/ *adj* **(a)** 起作用的 qǐ zuòyòng de, 有助于 yǒu zhùyú: *You were ~al in his promotion.* 他的提升,你是出了力的. **(b)** 乐器的 yuèqìde, 为〔爲〕乐器谱写〔寫〕的 wèi yuèqì pǔxiě de. ~**al·ist** 乐器演奏者 yuèqì yǎnzòuzhě.

in·sub·or·di·nate /ˌɪnsə'bɔːdɪnət/ *adj* 不服从〔從〕的 bùfúcóngde, 不听〔聽〕话的 bùtīnghuàde. **in·sub·or·di'na·tion** *n* [C, U]

in·suf·fer·able /ˌɪn'sʌfrəbl/ *adj* 难〔難〕以忍受的 nányǐ rěnshòu de.

in·suf·fi·cient /ˌɪnsə'fɪʃnt/ *adj* 不足的 bùzúde, 不够的 búgòude. ~**ly** *adv* **in·suf·fi·ciency** *n* [U]

in·su·lar /'ɪnsjʊlə(r)/ *adj* **1** 岛屿〔嶼〕的 dǎoyǔde. **2** 思想狭〔狹〕窄的 sīxiǎng xiázhǎi de. ~**ity** /-'lærətɪ/ *n* [U]

in·su·late /'ɪnsjʊleɪt/ *vt* **1** 使绝缘 shǐ juéyuán; 使绝热〔熱〕 shǐ juérè: *~d wires* 绝缘电线. **2** 隔离〔離〕 gélí: *children ~d from harm* 受不到伤害的儿童. **in·su·la·tor** *n* [C] 绝缘体〔體〕 juéyuántǐ. **in·su'la·tion** *n* [U] 隔离 gélí, 绝缘 juéyuán; 绝缘材料 juéyuán cáiliào.

in·sult /ɪn'sʌlt/ *vt* 侮辱 wūrǔ, 凌辱 língrǔ. □ *n* /'ɪnsʌlt/ [C, U] 侮辱的言词或行为〔爲〕 wūrǔde yáncí huò xíngwéi. ~**ing** *adj*

in·sur·ance /ɪn'ʃʊərəns/ *n* **1** [U] 保险〔險〕 bǎoxiǎn. **2** [U] 保险费 bǎoxiǎnfèi; 保险金额 bǎoxiǎnjīn'é. **3** [C] 安全保障 ānquán bǎozhàng.

in·sure /ɪn'ʃʊə(r)/ *vt* 给…保险〔險〕 gěi...bǎoxiǎn.

in·sur·gent /ɪn'sɜːdʒənt/ *adj* 暴动〔動〕的 bàodòngde, 起义〔義〕的 qǐyìde, 造反的 zàofǎnde. □ *n* [C] 暴动者 bàodòngzhě, 起义者 qǐyìzhě.

in·sur·rec·tion /ˌɪnsə'rekʃn/ *n* [C, U] 暴动〔動〕 bàodòng, 起义 qǐyì, 造反 zàofǎn.

in·tact /ˌɪn'tækt/ *adj* 未受损的 wèishòusǔnde, 完整的 wánzhěngde.

in·take /'ɪnteɪk/ *n* **1** [C] (水,气等流入管子等的)入口 rùkǒu. **2** [C, U] 纳入量 nàrùliàng.

in·te·ger /'ɪntɪdʒə(r)/ *n* [C] 整数〔數〕 zhěngshù.

in·te·gral /'ɪntɪgrəl/ *adj* **1** 构〔構〕成整体〔體〕所必需的 gòuchéng zhěngtǐ suǒ bìxūde: *an ~ part of the machine* 机器的一个组成部分. **2** 完整的 wánzhěngde, 整体的 zhěngtǐde. ~**ly** *adv*

in·te·grate /'ɪntɪgreɪt/ *vt* **1** 使一体〔體〕化 shǐ yìtǐhuà. **2** 取消种〔種〕族隔离〔離〕 qǔxiāo zhǒngzú gélí. ~**d** '**circuit** *n* (无线电)集成电〔電〕路 jíchéng diànlù. **in·te'gra·tion** *n* [U]

in·teg·rity /ɪn'tegrətɪ/ *n* [U] 诚实〔實〕 chéngshí, 正直 zhèngzhí.

in·tel·lect /'ɪntəlekt/ *n* **1** [U] 智力 zhìlì, 才智 cáizhì. ~**ual** /-'lektʃʊəl/ *adj* **(a)** 智力的 zhìlìde, 理智的 lǐzhìde. **(b)** 有理解力的 yǒu lǐjiělì de, 有智力的 yǒu zhìlì de. □ *n* [C] 知识〔識〕分子 zhīshi fènzǐ. ~**ually** *adv*

in·tel·li·gence /ɪn'telɪdʒəns/ *n* [U] **1** 智力 zhìlì, 理解力 lǐjiělì. **2** 新闻〔聞〕 xīnwén, 情报〔報〕 qíngbào. **3** 政府情报机〔機〕构〔構〕 zhengfǔ qíngbào jīgòu. ~ **test** *n* 智力测验〔驗〕 zhìlì cèyàn. ~ **quotient** *n* (略作 **IQ**) 智力商数〔數〕 zhìlì shāngshù. **in·tel·li·gent** *adj* **in·tel·li·gent·ly** *adv*

in·tel·li·gible /ɪn'telɪdʒəbl/ *adj* 可理解的 kě lǐjiě de; 明白的 míngbaide.

in·tend /ɪn'tend/ *vt* 打算 dǎsuàn, 想要 xiǎngyào: *I ~ to leave now.* 我打算现在离开.

in·tense /ɪn'tens/ *adj* **1** 强烈的 qiángliède, 剧〔劇〕烈的 jùlìède. **2** (人)热〔熱〕情的 rèqíngde. ~**ly** *adv*

in·ten·sify /ɪn'tensɪfaɪ/ *vt/i* [*pt, pp* -ied] 加强 jiāqiáng, 加剧〔劇〕 jiājù.

in·ten·sity /ɪn'tensətɪ/ *n* [U] (感情等)强烈 qiángliè, 剧〔劇〕烈 jùliè; 强度 qiángdù.

in·ten·sive /ɪn'tensɪv/ *adj* 加强的 jiāqiángde, 深入细致的 shēnrù xìzhì de: *an ~ search* 深入细致的搜查. ~**ly** *adv*

in·tent[1] /ɪn'tent/ *adj* **1** (目光)不转

〔轉〕移的 bùzhuǎnyíde, 集中的 jízhōngde. **2**(人) 专〔專〕心的 zhuānxīnde, 坚〔堅〕决的 jiānjuéde. **~ly** *adv*

intent² /ɪn'tent/ *n* [U] 目的 mùdì, 意图〔圖〕yìtú: *shoot with ~ to kill* 射杀. *to* ˌ*all ~s and* ˈ*purposes* 实〔實〕质〔質〕上 shízhìshàng, 实际〔際〕上 shíjìshàng.

in·ten·tion /ɪn'tenʃn/ *n* [C, U] 意图〔圖〕yìtú, 目的 mùdì: *His ~ was to learn English.* 他打算学习英语. **~al** /-ʃənl/ *adj* 有意的 yǒuyìde, 故意的 gùyìde. **~al·ly** *adv*

in·ter /ɪn'tɜ:(r)/ *vt* [-rr-] 〔正式用语〕埋葬 máizàng.

in·ter·act /ˌɪntər'ækt/ *vi* 互相作用 hùxiāng zuòyòng: *These chemicals ~ when mixed.* 这些化学物品混合在一起时互相发生作用. **in·ter·ac·tion** /-ʃn/ *n* [C, U]

in·ter·cept /ˌɪntə'sept/ *vt* 拦〔攔〕截 lánjié, 截击 jiéjī, 截断〔斷〕jiéduàn. **in·ter·cep·tion** /-ʃn/ *n* [U]

in·ter·change /ˌɪntə'tʃeɪndʒ/ *vt* **1** 交换 jiāohuàn, 互换 hùhuàn. **2** 交换位置 jiāohuàn wèizhì. □ *n* [C] 交换 jiāohuàn, 交替 jiāotì. **~able** *adj*

in·ter·com /'ɪntəkɒm/ *n* (飞机, 轮船等内部使用的) 对〔對〕讲机〔機〕duìjiǎngjī: *receive a message on (over) the ~* 从对讲机上听到消息.

in·ter·con·ti·nen·tal /ˌɪntəˌkɒntɪ'nentl/ *adj* 洲际〔際〕zhōujì: *~ missiles* 洲际导弹.

in·ter·course /'ɪntəkɔ:s/ *n* [U] 交际〔際〕jiāojì, 往来〔來〕wǎnglái. **(sexual) ~** ⇨ sexual.

in·ter·est /'ɪntrəst/ *n* **1** [U] 兴〔興〕趣 xìngqù, 趣味 qùwèi: *take ~ in* 对〔對〕…有兴趣; *lose ~ in* 对…失去兴趣. **2** [U] 兴趣性 xìngqùxìng, 趣味性 qùwèixìng: *an idea of ~ to us* 我们感兴趣的一个主意. **3** [C] 爱〔愛〕好的事物 àihàode shìwù: *His great ~ is football* 他的一大爱好是足球. **4** [C] [常用 *pl*] 利益 lìyì, 好处〔處〕hǎochù: *It is in your ~(s) to work hard.* 勤奋努力是对你有好处的. **5** [C] 股份 gǔfèn: *have an ~ in a company* 在某公司有股份. **6** [U] 利息 lìxī: *rate of ~* 利率. **7** [常用 *pl*] 行业〔業〕hángyè: ˈ*business ~s* 商业界. *in the ~(s) of* 为〔爲〕了…的利益 wèile...de lìyì. □ *vt* 使注意 shǐ zhùyì, 使发〔發〕生兴趣 shǐ fāshēng xìngqù: *He is ~ed in shipping.* 他对航运业有兴趣. **~ed** *adj* (a) 有利害关〔關〕系的 yǒu lìhài guānxìde. (b) 表现出兴趣的 biǎoxiànchū xìngqù de. **~ing** *adj* 使人有兴趣的 shǐ rén yǒu xìngqù de.

in·ter·fere /ˌɪntə'fɪə(r)/ *vi* **1** 干预(他人的事) gānyù, 干涉 gānshè. **2** 触〔觸〕犯 chùfàn; 损害 sǔnhài: *~ with a machine* 乱弄机器. **3** 妨碍〔礙〕fáng'ài, 妨害 fánghài. **in·ter·fer·ence** /-rəns/ *n* [U]

in·terim /'ɪntərɪm/ *adj* 临〔臨〕时〔時〕的 línshíde; 暂〔暫〕时的 zànshíde: *an ~ payment* 暂付款. *an ~ report* 临时报告.

in·ter·ior /ɪn'tɪərɪə(r)/ *adj* **1** 在内的 zàinèide; 内部的 nèibùde. **2** 内地的 nèidìde; 内陆的 nèilùde. **3** 国〔國〕内的 (与 *foreign* 相对) guónèide. □ *n* [C] **1** 内部 nèibù. **2** 内地 nèidì.

in·ter·ject /ˌɪntə'dʒekt/ *vt* (他人讲话时)突然插话 tūrán chāhuà. **in·ter·jec·tion** /-ʃn/ *n* [C] 感叹〔嘆〕词 gǎntàncí.

in·ter·lock /ˌɪntə'lɒk/ *vt/i* (使)连〔連〕锁 liánsuǒ, (使)连结 liánjié.

in·ter·lude /'ɪntəlu:d/ *n* [C] 两事件中间〔間〕的时〔時〕间 liǎng shìjiàn zhōngjiān de shíjiān; 幕间 mùjiān.

in·ter·medi·ary /ˌɪntə'mi:dɪərɪ/ *n* [C] [*pl* -ies], *adj* 中人 zhōngrén; 调解人 tiáojiěrén; 居间〔間〕的(人或物) jūjiānde; 斡旋的 wòxuánde.

in·ter·medi·ate /ˌɪntə'mi:dɪət/ *adj, n* [C] (时间、空间、程度等)中间〔間〕的 zhōngjiānde; 中间物 zhōngjiānwù: *an ~ course* 中等课程. **~ly** *adv*

in·ter·mis·sion /ˌɪntə'mɪʃn/ *n* [C] 间〔間〕歇 jiānxiē; 幕间休息 mùjiān xiūxi.

in·ter·mit·tent /ˌɪntə'mɪtnt/ *adj* 间〔間〕歇的 jiānxiēde; 断〔斷〕断续〔續〕续的 duànduànxùxùde: *~ rain* 时下时停的雨. **~ly** *adv*

in·tern /ɪn'tɜ:n/ *vt* 拘留(俘虏等) jūliú. **~ment** *n* [U]

in·ter·nal /ɪn'tɜ:nl/ *adj* **1** 内部的 nèibùde; 在内部的 zài nèibùde: *~ injuries* 内伤. **2** 国〔國〕内的 guónèide; 内政的 nèizhèngde: *~ trade* 国内贸易. *~* **com'bustion** *n* 内燃(由气缸内气体的爆发而产生动力的方法) nèirán. **~ly** *adv*

in·ter·na·tional /ˌɪntə'næʃnəl /*adj n* [C] 国〔國〕际〔際〕的 guójìde 国际性组织〔織〕guójìxìng zǔzhī

in·ter·pose /ˌɪntə'pəʊz/ *vt/i* **1** 插嘴 chāzuǐ. **2** 调停 tiáoting: *~ between two arguing people* 调解两人的争执

in·ter·pret /ɪn'tɜ:prɪt/ *vt/i* **1** 解释

〔釋〕jiěshì; 说明 shuōmíng. **2** 认〔認〕为〔爲〕是…的意思 rènwéi shì… de yìsi: ~ *his silence as an expression of guilt* 认为他的沉默是有罪的表示. **3** 口译〔譯〕kǒuyì. ~**er** 口译者 kǒuyìzhě; 译员 yìyuán. ~**a·tion** /-'teɪʃn/ *n* [C,U]

in·ter·ro·gate /ɪn'terəgeɪt/ *vt* 审〔審〕问〔問〕shěnwèn; 询问 xúnwèn. **in·ter·ro'ga·tion** *n* [C, U] **in·ter·ro·ga·tor** 审问者 shěnwènzhě; 讯问者 xùnwènzhě.

in·ter·roga·tive /ˌɪntə'rɒgətɪv/ *adj* **1** 疑问〔問〕的 yíwènde; 质〔質〕问的 zhìwènde. **2** [语法]用于疑问句的 yòng yú yíwènjù de: ~ *pronouns(adverbs)* 疑问代词(副词)(例如 *who, why*). □ *n* [C] 疑问词 yíwèncí.

in·ter·rupt /ˌɪntə'rʌpt/ *vt/i* **1** 中断〔斷〕zhōngduàn; 阻碍〔礙〕zǔ'ài: ~ *a journey* 中断旅行. **2** 打断(讲话等) dǎduàn. **in·ter·rup·tion** /-ʃn/ *n* [C, U]

in·ter·sect /ˌɪntə'sekt/ *vt/i* **1** 横切 héngqiē, 横断〔斷〕héngduàn. **2** (指直线)交叉 jiāochā. **in·ter·sec·tion** /-ʃn/ *n* [C, U] 交叉点〔點〕jiāochādiǎn; 十字街口 shízhì jiēkǒu.

in·ter·val /'ɪntəvl/ *n* [C] **1** (两件事)间〔間〕隔的时〔時〕间 jiāngéde shíjiān; 间歇 jiānxiē. **2** 间隔 jiāngé.

in·ter·vene /ˌɪntə'vi:n/ *vi* **1** (指事件)插入 chārù; 介入 jièrù. **2** (指人)干涉 gānshè. **3** (指时间)介于 jièyú: *the intervening time before his death* 在他死去的前夕. **in·ter·ven·tion** /-'venʃn/ *n* [C, U]

in·ter·view /'ɪntəvju:/ *n* [C] **1** 接见 jiējiàn; 会〔會〕谈 huìtán. **2** 会见某求职〔職〕者 huìjiàn mǒu qiúzhízhě. □ *vt* 会见 huìjiàn; 访问 fǎngwèn.

in·tes·tate /ɪn'testeɪt/ *adj* 未留遗嘱〔囑〕的 wèi liú yízhǔ de: *die* ~ 未留遗嘱而死.

in·tes·tine /ɪn'testɪn/ *n* [C] [常用 *pl*] 肠〔腸〕cháng. **in·tes·ti·nal** /ɪn'testɪnl/ *adj*

in·ti·macy /'ɪntɪməsɪ/ *n* [*pl* -ies] **1** [U] 亲〔親〕密 qīnmì; 亲近 qīnjìn. **2** [*pl*] 接吻 jiēwěn.

in·ti·mate¹ /'ɪntɪmət/ *adj* **1** 亲〔親〕密的 qīnmìde: ~ *friends* 知己. **2** 私人的 sīrénde; 秘密的 mìmìde: ~ *details of his life* 他的琐碎的私生活上的事. **3** 精湛的 jīngzhànde; 熟悉的 shúxīde: ~ *knowledge of flowers* 熟悉花卉知识. ~**ly** *adv*

in·ti·mate² /'ɪntɪmeɪt/ *vt* 宣布〔佈〕xuānbù, 通知 tōngzhī; 暗示 ànshì. **in·ti'ma·tion** *n* [C,U]

in·timi·date /ɪn'tɪmɪdeɪt/ *vt* 恫吓〔嚇〕dònghè, 威胁〔脅〕wēixié. **in·timi'da·tion** *n* [U]

into /'ɪntə, 强式 'ɪntu:/ *prep* **1** 到…里〔裡〕dào…lǐ: *Come ~ the house* 到房屋里来. **2**(表示情况或结果的变化): *burst ~ tears* 潸然泪下. **3** 冲 chōng; 闯〔闖〕chuǎng: *crash ~ a tree* 撞在树上. **4** [数学]除 chú: *5 ~ 25 equals 5.* 五除二十五等于五.

in·tol·er·able /ɪn'tɒlərəbl/ *adj* 无〔無〕法容忍的 wúfǎ róngrěn de; 不能忍受的 bùnéng rěnshòu de. **in·tol·er·ably** *adv*

in·tol·er·ant /ɪn'tɒlərənt/ *adj* 不容忍的 bù róngrěn de; 偏狭的 piānxiáde. **in·tol·er·ance** /-rəns/ *n* [U]

in·ton·ation /ˌɪntə'neɪʃn/ *n* [U] 语调 yǔdiào; 声〔聲〕调 shēngdiào.

in·toxi·cate /ɪn'tɒksɪkeɪt/ *vt* **1** 使喝醉 shǐ hē zuì. **2** [喻]使陶醉 shǐ táozuì. **in·toxi'ca·tion** *n* [U]

in·tran·si·tive /ɪn'trænsɪtɪv/ *adj* [语法](指动词)不及物的 bùjíwùde ~**ly** *adv*

in·trepid /ɪn'trepɪd/ *adj* [正式用语]无〔無〕畏的 wúwèide. ~**ly** *adv*

in·tri·cacy /'ɪntrɪkəsɪ/ *n* [C, U] [*pl* -ies] 错综 cuòzōng; 复杂〔雜〕fùzá: *the ~ of a watch* 手表的复杂结构.

in·tri·cate /'ɪntrɪkət/ *adj* 复〔複〕杂〔雜〕的 fuzáde; 错综的 cuòzōngde. ~**ly** *adv*

in·trigue /ɪn'tri:g/ *vt/i* **1** 策划〔劃〕阴〔陰〕谋 cèhuà yīnmóu; 用诡计取得 yòng guǐjì qǔdé. **2** 引起…的兴〔興〕趣或好奇心 yǐnqǐ…de xìngqù huò hàoqíxīn. □ *n* /'ɪntri:g/ **1** [U] 密谋 mìmóu. **2** [C] 阴谋 yīnmóu; 私通 sītōng.

in·trin·sic /ɪn'trɪnsɪk/ *adj* (指价值,性质)固有的 gùyǒude; 内在的 nèizàide. ~**ally** *adv*

in·tro·duce /ˌɪntrə'dju:s/ *vt* **1** 提出 tíchū: ~ *a Bill before Parliament* 向国会提出法案. **2** ~ *(into)* 采〔採〕用 cǎiyòng; 引进〔進〕yǐnjìn. **3** 介绍相识〔識〕jièshào xiāngshí.

in·tro·duc·tion /ˌɪntrə'dʌkʃn/ *n* **1** [U] 采〔採〕用 cǎiyòng; 引进〔進〕yǐnjìn. **2** [C] 介绍相识〔識〕jièshào xiānashí. **3** [C] 引言 yǐnyán, 序言 xùyán. **4** [C] 入门 rùmén.

in·tro·duc·tory /ˌɪntrə'dʌktərɪ/

adj 介绍的 jièshàode; 导〔導〕言的 dǎoyánde: ~ *remarks* 绪言; 开场白.

in·tro·vert /ˌɪntrəˈvɜ:t/ *vt* 使(思想)内向 shǐ nèixiàng. □ *n* /ˈɪntrəvɜ:t/ [C] **1** 内向性格的人 nèixiàng xìnggé de rén. **2** [非正式用语]内倾者 nèiqǐngzhě. ⇨ extrovert.

in·trude /ɪnˈtru:d/ *vt/i* 闯〔闖〕入 chuǎngrù; 侵入 qīnrù. **in·truder** 闯入者 chuǎngrùzhě; 入侵者 rùqīnzhě. **in·tru·sion** /-ʒn/ *n* [C, U]

in·tu·ition /ˌɪntjʊˈɪʃn/ *n* **1** [U] 直觉〔覺〕zhíjué; 直观〔觀〕zhíguān. **2** [C] 直觉知识〔識〕zhíjué zhīshì. **inˈtu·itive** *adj* **in·tu·itive·ly** *adv*

in·un·date /ˈɪnʌndeɪt/ *vt* **1** 淹没 yānmò; 泛滥〔濫〕fànlàn. **2** [喻][用被动语态]压〔壓〕倒 yādǎo: ~*d with letters* 信件如雪片飞来. **in·unˈda·tion** *n* [C, U]

in·vade /ɪnˈveɪd/ *vt* **1** 侵略 qīnlüè, 侵入 qīnrù, 侵犯 qīnfàn. **2** [喻]蜂拥〔擁〕而至 fēng yōng ér zhì: *fans* ~*d the football pitch* 球迷们拥进了足球场. **in·va·sion** *n* [C, U]

in·valid¹ /ɪnˈvælɪd/ *adj* 无〔無〕效的 wúxiàode; 作废〔廢〕的 zuòfèide: *an* ~ *excuse* (*passport*) 无效的辩解(护照). ~**ate** *vt* 使无效 shǐ wúxiào; 使作废 shǐ zuòfèi. ~**a·tion** /-ˈdeɪʃən/ *n* [C, U]

in·va·lid² /ˈɪnvəli:d/ *adj* **1** 病弱的 bìngruòde; 伤〔傷〕残〔殘〕的 shāngcánde. **2** 病人用的 bìngrén yòng de: *an* ~ *car* 病人用的轮椅. □ *n* [C] 病人 bìngrén; 病弱者 bìngruòzhě; 伤病员 shāngbìngyuán. □ *vt* 因伤病而退伍 yīn shāngbìng ér tuìwǔ.

in·valu·able /ɪnˈvæljʊbl/ *adj* 无〔無〕价〔價〕的 wújiàde; 无法估价的 wúfǎ gūjià de.

in·vari·able /ɪnˈveərɪəbl/ *adj* 不变〔變〕的 búbiànde, 永不变的 yǒng búbiàn de: *an* ~ *temperature* 恒温. **in·vari·ably** *adv* 不变地 búbiànde; 永恒地 yǒnghéngde: *He's invariably late.* 他总是迟到.

in·vec·tive /ɪnˈvektɪv/ *n* [U] 抨击〔擊〕pēngjī; 谩骂〔罵〕mànmà.

in·vent /ɪnˈvent/ *vt* **1** 发〔發〕明 fāmíng; 创〔創〕造 chuàngzào. **2** 虚构〔構〕xūgòu, 捏造 niēzào: ~ *an excuse* 捏造借口. ~**or** 发明者 fāmíngzhě. **in·ven·tion** /-ʃn/ *n* **(a)** [U] 发明 fāmíng, 创造 chuàngzào. **(b)** [C] 发明物 fāmíngwù. ~**ive** *adj* 有发明才能的 yǒu fāmíng cáinéng de; 发明创造的 fāmíng chuàngzào de.

in·ven·tory /ˈɪnvəntrɪ/ *n* [C] [*pl* -ies] 详细目录〔錄〕xiángxì mùlù; 存货清单〔單〕cúnhuò qīngdān; 存货盘〔盤〕存 cúnhuò páncún.

in·vert /ɪnˈvɜ:t/ *vt* 倒转〔轉〕dàozhuǎn; 上下倒置 shàng xià dàozhì. ~**commas** 引号〔號〕(" "或' ') yǐnhào. **in·ver·sion** /-ʃn/ *n* [C, U]

in·vert·ebrate /ɪnˈvɜ:tɪbrət/ *adj, n* [C] [动物]无〔無〕脊椎的 wú jǐzhuī de.

in·vest /ɪnˈvest/ *vt/i* **1** ~ **(*in*)** 投资 tóuzī: ~ *in a new company* 对某新公司投资. **2** ~***in*** [非正式用语]购〔購〕买〔買〕gòumǎi. **3** ~ **(*with*)** 授予 shòuyǔ: ~ *power in the President* 授予总统权力. ~**ment** *n* **(a)** [U] 投资 tóuzī. **(b)** [C] 投资额 tóuzī'é. ~**or** 投资者 tóuzīzhě.

in·ves·ti·gate /ɪnˈvestɪgeɪt/ *vt* 调查 diàochá, 调查研究 diàochá yánjiū: ~ *a murder* 调查谋杀案. **in·ves·tiˈga·tion** *n* [C, U] **in·ves·ti·ga·tor** 调查者 diàocházhě.

in·ves·ti·ture /ɪnˈvestɪtʃə(r)/ *n* [C] 授职〔職〕(仪式) shòuzhí; 授爵 shòujué; 授权〔權〕shòuquán.

in·vigi·late /ɪnˈvɪdʒɪleɪt/ *vi* 监〔監〕考 jiānkǎo. **in·vigiˈla·tion** *n* [U] **in·vigi·la·tor** 监考员 jiānkǎoyuán.

in·vig·or·ate /ɪnˈvɪgəreɪt/ *vt* 鼓舞 gǔwǔ; 使活跃〔躍〕shǐ huóyue.

in·vin·cible /ɪnˈvɪnsəbl/ *adj* 无〔無〕敌〔敵〕的 wúdíde; 不能征服的 bù néng zhēngfú de. **in·vin·cibly** *adv*

in·viol·ate /ˌɪnˈvaɪələt/ *adj* 不受侵犯的 bú shòu qīnfàn de; 纯洁〔潔〕的 chúnjiéde.

in·vis·ible /ɪnˈvɪzəbəl/ *adj* 看不见〔見〕的 kàn bú jiàn de; 无〔無〕形的 wúxíngde. **in·visiˈbil·ity** *n* [U] **in·vis·ibly** *adv*

in·vi·ta·tion /ˌɪnvɪˈteɪʃn/ *n* **1** [U] 邀请 yāoqǐng: *admission by* ~ *only* 非请勿入. **2** [C] 请帖 qǐngtiě: *an* ~ *to a party.* 宴会等的请帖.

in·vite /ɪnˈvaɪt/ *vt* **1** 邀请 yāoqǐng. **2** 请求 qǐngqiú, 要求 yāoqiú: ~ *offers* 请人提出价钱, 请人报价. **in·vit·ing** *adj* 吸引人的 xīyǐn rén de, 诱人的 yòurénde. **in·vit·ing·ly** *adv*

in·vo·ca·tion /ˌɪnvəʊˈkeɪʃn/ *n* [U] 乞灵〔靈〕qǐlíng, [C] 祈祷 qídǎo.

in·voice /ˈɪnvɔɪs/ *vt, n* [C] 开

〔開〕发〔發〕票 kāi fāpiào; 发票 fāpiào; 装〔裝〕货清单〔單〕 zhuānghuò qīngdān.

in·voke /ɪnˈvəʊk/ *vt* **1** 祈求(上帝、法律等)帮〔幫〕助 qíqiú bāngzhù. **2** 恳〔懇〕求 kěnqiú, 乞求 qǐqiú. **3** (用法术)召唤 zhāohuàn.

in·vol·un·tary /ɪnˈvɒləntrɪ/ *adj* 不知不觉〔覺〕的 bùzhī bùjué de; 非本意的 fēi běnyì de: *an ~ movement* 不随意动作. **in·vol·un·tar·ily** *adv*

in·volve /ɪnˈvɒlv/ *vt* **1** 使陷入 shǐ xiànrù, 使卷〔捲〕入 shǐ juǎnrù. **2** 包含 bāohán; 必须包括 bìxū bāokuò. **in·volved** *adj* 复杂〔雜〕的 fùzáde. **~ment** *n* [C,U]

in·vul·ner·able /ɪnˈvʌlnərəbl/ *adj* 不会〔會〕受伤〔傷〕害的 bú huì shòu shānghài de.

in·ward /ˈɪnwəd/ *adj* **1** 内部的 nèibùde; 内在的 nèizàide: *a man's ~ nature.* 一个人内在的性情. **2** 向内的 xiàngnèide: *an ~ curve* 内弯. **~ly** *adv* 内心或精神方面 nèixīn huò jīngshén fāngmiàn. **inward(s)** *adv* **(a)** 向内 xiàngnèi. **(b)** 向着心灵〔靈〕 xiàng zhe xīnlíng.

iod·ine /ˈaɪədiːn/ *n* [U] [化学]碘 diǎn.

ion /ˈaɪən/ *n* [C] 离〔離〕子 lízǐ. **~ize** /-aɪz/ *vt* 电〔電〕离 diànlí.

I.O.U. = I owe you 借据〔據〕 jièjù.

I.Q. = intelligence quotient 智商 zhìshāng.

irate /aɪˈreɪt/ *adj* 发〔發〕怒的 fānùde, 愤怒的 fènnùde. **~ly** *adv*

iri·descent /ˌɪrɪˈdesnt/ *adj* [正式用语]彩虹的 cǎihóngde; 彩虹色的 cǎihóngsède.

iris /ˈaɪərɪs/ *n* [C] **1** 彩虹 cǎihóng; 虹膜 hóngmó. **2** 鸢〔鳶〕尾属植物 yuānwěishǔ zhíwù.

irk /ɜːk/ *vt* 使厌〔厭〕烦 shǐ yànfán; 使苦恼〔惱〕 shǐ kǔnǎo. **~some** *adj* 令人厌烦的 lìng rén yànfán de.

iron[1] /ˈaɪən/ *n* **1** [U] 铁〔鐵〕 (Fe) tiě. **2** [C] 熨斗 yùndǒu. **3** [*pl*] 镣铐 liàokào. **ˈ~monger** 五金商 wǔjīnshāng. **ˈ~mongery** 五金店 wǔjīndiàn.

iron[2] /ˈaɪən/ *vt/i* 熨 yùn. **~ out**, **(a)** 熨平 yùnpíng. **(b)** [喻]消除困难〔難〕等 xiāochú kùnnan děng. **ˈ~ing-board** 熨衣板 yùnyībǎn.

ironic /aɪˈrɒnɪk/ (亦作 **~al**) *adj* 讽〔諷〕刺的 fěngcìde; 反话的 fǎnhuàde. **~ally** *adv*

irony /ˈaɪərənɪ/ *n* [*pl* -ies] **1** [U] 反话 fǎnhuà; 冷嘲 lěngcháo. **2** [C] 讽刺性的事件, 情况等 fěngcìxìngde shìjiàn, qíngkuàng děng.

ir·ra·tional /ɪˈræʃənl/ *adj* **1** 无〔無〕理性的 wú lǐxìng de. **2** 不合理的 bù hélǐ de: *an ~ fear of water* 没有道理的怕水. **~ly** *adv*

ir·regu·lar /ɪˈregjʊlə(r)/ *adj* **1** 不规则的 bù guīzé de. **2** 不平坦的 bù píngtǎn de; 不整齐〔齊〕的 bù zhěngqí de: *an ~ surface* 不整齐的外表. **3** [语法]不规则变〔變〕化的 bù guīzé biànhuà de. **~ly** *adv* **~ity** /-ˈlærətɪ/ *n* [C,U]

ir·rel·evant /ɪˈreləvənt/ *adj* 离〔離〕题的 lítíde; 不相干的 bùxiānggān de.

ir·rep·ar·able /ɪˈrepərəbl/ *adj* (指损失、伤害等)不能弥〔彌〕补〔補〕的 bùnéng míbǔ de; 无〔無〕可挽救的 wú kě wǎnjiù de.

ir·re·place·able /ˌɪrɪˈpleɪsəbl/ *adj* 不能替代的 bùnéng tìdài de; 不能恢复原状的 bùnéng huīfù yuánzhuàng de.

ir·re·sist·ible /ˌɪrɪˈzɪstəbl/ *adj* (过于坚强, 令人愉快等而)不可抵抗的 bùkě dǐkàng de; 不能压〔壓〕制的 bùnéng yāzhì de.

ir·re·spec·tive /ˌɪrɪˈspektɪv/ *adj* ~ (*of*) 不考虑〔慮〕的 bù kǎolǜ de; 不顾〔顧〕的 búgùde: *~ of the danger* 不顾危险.

ir·re·spon·sible /ˌɪrɪˈspɒnsəbl/ *adj* 无〔無〕责任感的 wú zérèngǎn de; 不负责任的 bú fù zérèn de. **ir·re·spon·siˈbil·ity** *n* [U]

ir·rev·er·ent /ɪˈrevərənt/ *adj* 不虔诚的 bù qiánchéng de; 不尊敬的 bù zūnjìng de. **~ly** *adv* **ir·rev·er·ence** *n* [U]

ir·revo·cable /ɪˈrevəkəbl/ *adj* 不可改变〔變〕的 bùkě gǎibiàn de; 不可取消的 bùkě qǔxiāo de: *my ~ decision* 我的最后决定.

ir·ri·gate /ˈɪrɪgeɪt/ *vt* 灌溉(田地) guàngài. **ir·riˈga·tion** *n* [U]

ir·ri·table /ˈɪrɪtəbl/ *adj* 急躁的 jízàode; 易怒的 yìnùde. **ir·ri·taˈbil·ity** *n* [U]

ir·ri·tate /ˈɪrɪteɪt/ *vt* **1** 激怒 jīnù; 使烦躁 shǐ fánzào. **2** 使(身体某部)感到不适 shǐ gǎndào búshí. **ir·riˈta·tion** *n* [C, U]

is /ɪz/ ⇨ be.

Is·lam /ˈɪzlɑːm/ *n* 伊斯兰〔蘭〕教 Yīsīlánjiào; (总称) 伊斯兰教徒 Yīsīlánjiàotú; 穆斯林 mùsīlín. **~ic** *adj*

is·land /ˈaɪlənd/ *n* [C] **1** 岛〔島〕 dǎo, 岛屿〔嶼〕 dǎoyǔ. **2** 似岛之物 sì dǎo zhī wù: *a traffic ~* (马路上的)安全岛.

isle /aɪl/ *n* [C] 岛〔島〕 dǎo, 岛屿

〔嶼〕dǎoyǔ.

isn't ⇨ be.

iso·late /'aɪsəleɪt/ *vt* 隔离〔離〕gélí; 孤立 gūlì. **iso'la·tion** *n* [U]

isos·celes /aɪ'sɒsəli:z/ *adj* (指三角形)等边〔邊〕的 děngbiānde, 等腰的 děngyāode.

issue /'ɪʃu:/ *vt/i* **1** 分发〔發〕fēnfā: ~ *weapons* 分发武器. **2** 出版(书等) chūbǎn. **3** 发〔發〕行(邮票、钞票等) fāxíng. □ *n* **1** [C, U] 出版 chūbǎn; 发行 fāxíng: *two ~s of a newspaper* 两期(或早晚两版)报纸. **2** [C] 问〔問〕题 wèntí; 争端 zhēngduān. **3** [C] 结果 jiéguǒ; 后〔後〕果 hòuguǒ. **4** [U] [法律] 子女 zǐnǚ.

isth·mus /'ɪsməs/ *n* [*pl* ~es] 地峡 dìxiá.

it /ɪt/ *pron* [*pl* they /ðeɪ/, them /ðem/] **1** 它(指东西、动物) tā: *Where's my book?* 我的书在哪儿? *Have you seen ~?* 你看见它没有? **2** (用以指其后一组字): *Is ~ difficult to learn Chinese?* 学习汉语难吗? **3** (用以指明人或事): '*Who's that?*' '是谁?' — '*I~'s the postman.*' '是邮递员.' **4** [用作无人称动词主语]: *I~ is raining.* 下雨了. **5** [用作强调句中某一部分]: *I~ was work that exhausted him.* 工作使他疲劳不堪.

italic /ɪ'tælɪk/ *adj* (指字母)斜体〔體〕的 xiétǐde: *This is ~ type.* 这是斜体. □ *n* [*pl*] 斜体字母 xiétǐzìmǔ.

itch /ɪtʃ/ *n* [C] **1** 痒〔癢〕yǎng. **2** 渴望 kěwàng: *the ~ to travel* 渴望旅行. □ *vi* **1** 发〔發〕痒 fāyǎng. **2** 渴望 kěwàng. **itchy** *adj* [-ier, -iest] 发痒的 fāyǎngde; 渴望的 kěwàngde: *an ~y shirt* (因衣料粗糙)使人穿上骚痒的衣衫.

item /'aɪtəm/ *n* [C] **1** 条〔條〕款 tiáokuǎn, 项目 xiàngmù. **2** (新闻)一条 yìtiáo. **~ize** *vt* 分项列举〔舉〕fēnxiàng lièjǔ; 逐条列记 zhútiáo lièjì.

i·tin·er·ant /aɪ'tɪnərənt/ *adj* [正式用语]巡回的 xúnhuíde: ~ *musicians* 巡回乐师.

i·tin·er·ary /aɪ'tɪnərərɪ/ *n* [C] [*pl* -ies] 旅行计划〔劃〕lǚxíng jìhuà; 旅行日记 lǚxíng rìjì; 旅程 lǚchéng.

it'll /'ɪtl/ = *it will*.

it's /ɪts/ = *it is*; *it has*.

its /ɪts/ *adj* 它的 tāde: ~ *tail* 它的尾巴.

itself /ɪt'self/ *pron* **1** [反身]它自己 tā zìjǐ, 它本身 tā běnshēng: *The dog stretched ~.* 这只狗挺伸四肢. *by ~* **(a)** 独〔獨〕立地 dúlìde. **(b)** 单〔單〕独地 dāndúde; 孤零地 gūlíngde. **2** [用以加强语气]: *I saw the jewel ~.* 我看见了这件珠宝实物.

I've /aɪv/ = *I have*.

ivory /'aɪvərɪ/ *adj, n* [U] **1** 象牙 xiàngyá; 象牙制〔製〕品 xiàngyá zhìpǐng; 象牙制成的 xiàngyá zhìchéng de; 似象牙的 sì xiàngyá de. **2** 象牙色的 xiàngyásède; 乳白色的 rǔbáisède.

ivy /'aɪvɪ/ *n* [U]常春藤 chángchūnténg.

J j

J, j /dʒeɪ/ [*pl* J's, j's /dʒeɪz/] 英语的第十个〔個〕字母 yīngyǔ de dìshígè zìmǔ.

jab /dʒæb/ *vt/i* [-bb-] 刺 cì, 戳(与 *into* 连用) chuō; 猛击〔擊〕(与 *at* 连用) měngjī. □ *n* [C] **1** 猛刺 měngcì, 猛戳 měngchuō; 猛击 měngjī. **2** [非正式用语]臂上打针或接种〔種〕bì shàng dǎzhēn huò jiēzhòng.

jab·ber /'dʒæbə(r)/ *vt/i* 激动〔動〕地说 jīdòngde shuō. □ *n* [U] 喋喋不休 diédié bùxū.

jack /dʒæk/ *n* [C] **1** 支撑物 zhīchēngwù; 千斤顶 qiānjīndǐng. **2** (纸牌中的) 杰克(介于十点和王后之间) jiékè. **the ,Union 'J~** 英国〔國〕国旗 Yīngguó guóqí. □ *vt* (用千斤顶)顶起 dǐngqǐ: ~ *up a car* 把汽车顶起.

jackal /'dʒækɔ:l/ *n* [C] 豺 chái.

jack·ass /'dʒækæs/ *n* [C] **1** 公驴〔驢〕gōnglǘ. **2** 笨伯 bènbó.

jacket /'dʒækɪt/ *n* [C] **1** 短上衣 duǎn shàngyī, 夹〔夾〕克 jiákè. **2** (箱, 烟斗等的) 套 tào. **3** (马铃薯)皮 pí. **4** (亦作 '*dust* ~) (书籍的)护〔護〕封 hùfēng.

jack-knife /'dʒæk naɪf/ *n* [C] (可放袋内的)大折合刀 dà zhéhédāo. □ *vi* (货车在紧急煞车或滑动时)重叠〔疊〕chóngdié.

jack·pot /'dʒækpɒt/ *n* [C] (屡次得奖而积累的)大笔钱〔錢〕dàbǐqián.

jade /dʒeɪd/ *adj, n* [U] 玉制〔製〕的 yùzhìde; 绿玉色的 lǜyùsède; 玉 yù; 绿玉色 lǜyùsè.

jaded /'dʒeɪdɪd/ *adj* 精疲力竭的

jīng pí lì jié de.

jag·ged /ˈdʒægɪd/ *adj* 边〔邊〕缘不整齐〔齊〕的 biānyuán bù zhěngqí de; 参差不齐的 cēncī bù qí de.

jag·uar /ˈdʒægjʊə(r)/ *n* [C] 美洲虎 Měizhōuhǔ.

jail /dʒeɪl/ ⇨ gaol.

jam¹ /dʒæm/ *n* [U] 果酱〔醬〕guǒjiàng. **ˈ~-jar (-pot)** 果酱瓶(罐) guǒjiàngpíng.

jam² /dʒæm/ *vt/i* [-mm-] **1** 压〔壓〕紧〔緊〕yājǐn; 夹住 jiāzhù: *~ one's finger in a door* 手指夹在门缝里. **2** (指机器等)발〔發〕生故障 fāshēng gùzhàng. **3** 塞进〔進〕sāijìn, 挤〔擠〕进 jǐjìn: *~ clothes into a case* 把衣服塞进箱子里. **4** (无线电)干扰〔擾〕gānrǎo. □ *n* [C] **1** 阻塞物 zǔsèwù: *ˈtraffic-~* 交通堵塞. **2** [俚语]窘境 jiǒngjìng: *be in (get into) a ~* 陷入困境.

Jan. = January.

jangle /ˈdʒæŋgl/ *vt/i* 使发〔發〕出刺耳的金属〔屬〕声〔聲〕shǐ fāchū cìěrde jīnshǔshēng. □ *n* [U] 刺耳的金属声 cìěrde jīnshǔshēng.

jani·tor /ˈdʒænɪtə(r)/ *n* [C] 看门〔門〕人 kānménrén, 管门人 guǎnménrén.

Jan·uary /ˈdʒænjʊərɪ/ *n* 一月 yīyuè.

jar¹ /dʒɑ:(r)/ *n* [C] 罐子 guànzi; 坛〔罈〕子 tánzi; 广〔廣〕口瓶 guǎngkǒupíng.

jar² /dʒɑ:(r)/ *vt/i* [-rr-] **1** 发〔發〕出刺耳声〔聲〕fāchū cì'ěrshēng. **2** ~ **(on)** 使人产〔產〕生不愉快的感觉〔覺〕shǐ rén chǎnshēng bù yúkuài de gǎnjué: *His singing really ~s my nerves.* 他的歌声确实使我的神经受到刺激. **3** 摇动〔動〕yáodòng: *~ one's elbow* 摇晃胳膊肘. □ *n* [C] **1** 刺耳声 cì'ěrshēng; 轧〔軋〕轧声 yàyàshēng. **2** 震惊 zhènjīng. **~ring** *adj* 引起不调和的 yǐnqǐ bù tiáohé de.

jar·gon /ˈdʒɑ:gən/ *n* [U] 行话 hánghuà; 切口 qièkǒu: *medical ~* 医学用语.

jaun·dice /ˈdʒɔ:ndɪs/ *n* [U] 黄疸 huángdǎn. □ *vt* 〔常用 *passive*〕**1** 使患黄疸病 shǐ huàn huángdǎnbìng. **2** [喻]使妒忌 shǐ dùjì; 使有偏见 shǐ yǒu piānjiàn: *a ~d opinion* 偏见.

jaunt /dʒɔ:nt/ *n* [C] 短途游览〔覽〕duǎntú yóulǎn. □ *vi* 作短途游览 zuò duǎntú yóulǎn.

jaunty /ˈdʒɔ:ntɪ/ *adj* [-ier, iest] 洋洋得意的 yángyáng déyì de. **jauntily** *adv*

jav·elin /ˈdʒævlɪn/ *n* [C] 标〔標〕枪〔槍〕biāoqiāng.

jaw /dʒɔ:/ *n* [C] **1 lower (upper)** ~ 下(上)颚 xià'è. **2** [*pl*] [*sing*] 下巴 xiàba, 颌 hé. **3** [喻]危险〔險〕的境遇 wēixiǎnde jìngyù: *the ~s of a vice(death)* 鬼门关. □ *vi* 唠〔嘮〕叨 láodao. **ˈ~bone** 颚骨 ègǔ; 牙床骨 yáchuánggǔ.

jay /dʒeɪ/ *n* [C] [动物]一种爱叫的、羽毛鲜丽的鸟 yīzhǒng ài jiào de, yǔmáo xiānlì de niǎo.

jazz /dʒæz/ *n* [U] 爵士音乐〔樂〕juéshì yīnyuè. □ *vt* **1** 演奏或安排爵士乐 yǎnzòu huò ānpái juéshìyuè. **2** ~ *up* [喻]使活泼〔潑〕shǐ huópo. **~y** *adj* [-ier, -iest] [非正式用语] **(a)** 爵士音乐的 juéshì yīnyuè de. **(b)** 鲜明的 xiānmíngde: *a ~y tie* 花俏的领带.

jeal·ous /ˈdʒeləs/ *adj* **1** 妒忌的 dùjìde: *a ~ husband* 爱猜忌的丈夫. **2** ~ **(of sb,)** 妒羡的 dùxiànde. **3** 注意的 zhùyìde: *~ of one's rights* 爱护自己的权利. **jealously** *adv* **jeal·ousy** *n* [C, U] [*pl* -ies]

jeans /dʒi:nz/ *n pl* (斜纹布的)工装〔裝〕裤〔褲〕gōngzhuāngkù.

jeep /dʒi:p/ *n* [C] 吉普车〔車〕jípǔchē.

jeer /dʒɪə(r)/ *vt/i* 嘲笑 cháoxiào; 嘲弄 cháonòng. □ *n* [C] 讥〔譏〕笑的言语 jīxiàode yányǔ. **~ing·ly** *adv*

jelly /ˈdʒelɪ/ *n* [*pl* -ies] **1** [U] 冻〔凍〕子 dòngzi, 果子冻 guǒzidòng. **2** [C, U] 果冻甜食 guǒdòng tiánshí. **3** [U] 冻状物质 dòngzhuàng wùzhì. □ *vt/i* [*pt, pp* -ied] 使结冻 shǐ jiédòng. **ˈ~-fish** 水母 shuǐmǔ, 海蜇 hǎizhé.

jeop·ard·ize /ˈdʒepədaɪz/ *vt* 使受危害 shǐ shòu wēihài; 使陷险境 shǐ xiàn xiǎnjìng. **jeop·ardy** *n* [U] 危险 wēixiǎn: *The success of our plan is in jeopardy.* 我们的计划面临失败的危险.

jerk /dʒɜ:k/ *n* [C] 急动〔動〕jídòng; 急停 jítíng. □ *vt/i* 急动 jídòng. **jerky** *adj* [-ier, -iest]

jer·sey /ˈdʒɜ:zɪ/ *n* [*pl* ~s] [C] 毛织〔織〕紧〔緊〕身上衣 máozhī jǐnshēn shàngyī; 运〔運〕动〔動〕衫 yùndòngshān.

jest /dʒest/ *n* [C] 玩笑 wánxiào; 笑话 xiàohuà. **in ~** 开〔開〕玩笑地 kāi wánxiào de. □ *vi* 说笑话 shuō xiàohuà; 开玩笑 kāi wánxiào. **~er** *n* [C] (中世纪的)弄臣 nòngchén; 爱〔愛〕开玩笑的人 ài kāi wánxiào de rén.

jet¹ /dʒet/ *n* [C] **1** (气体,液体或火

焰的)喷射 pēnshè: ~ *engine* 喷气式发动机. **2** 喷射口 pēnshèkǒu; 喷嘴 pēnzuǐ. **3** □ *vt/i* [-tt-] **1** 喷出 pēnchū, 喷射 pēnshè. **2** 乘喷气式飞机旅行 chèng pēnqìshì fēijī lǚxíng. **'~lag** *n* 乘喷气式飞机飞越不同时〔時〕区〔區〕后的疲倦感 chéng pēnqìshì fēijī fēiyuè bùtóng shíqū hòu de píjuàngǎn. **'~plane (aircraft)** 喷气式飞机 pēnqìshì fēijī. **'~set** (经常乘喷气式客机的)富翁旅游团〔團〕 fùyōng lǚyóutuán.

jet² /ʤet/ *adj, n* [U] 黑色大理石制〔製〕的 hēisè dàlǐshí zhì de; 黑色大理石 hēisè dàlǐshí ˌ~ **'black** 乌黑发〔發〕亮的 wūhēi fāliàng de.

jet·ti·son /ˈʤetɪsn/ *vt* **1** (在紧急情况下)将〔將〕货物抛出船外 jiāng huòwù pāochū chuánwài. **2** 抛弃〔棄〕pāoqì; 丢弃 diūqì.

jetty /ˈʤetɪ/ *n* [C] [*pl* -ies] 栈〔棧〕桥〔橋〕 zhànqiáo; 码〔碼〕头〔頭〕 mǎtóu.

jewel /ˈʤu:əl/ *n* [C] **1** 宝〔寶〕石 bǎoshí. **2** 人造钻〔鑽〕石 rénzào zuànshí. **3** [喻] 被珍重的人或物 pèi zhēnzhòng de rén huò wù. □ *vt* [-ll-, 美语 -l-] 用宝石装〔裝〕饰 yòng bǎoshí zhuāngshì. **~ler** 珠宝商 zhūbǎoshāng. **~ry, ~lery** *n* [U] 珠宝 zhūbǎo.

jiffy /ˈʤɪfɪ/ *n* [C] [*pl* -ies] [非正式用语]瞬间〔間〕 shuènjiān. *in a ~* 马〔馬〕上 mǎshàng, 立刻 lìkè.

jig /ʤɪg/ *n* [C] 快步舞 kuàibùwǔ; 快步舞曲 kuàibù wǔqǔ. □ *vt/i* [-gg-] **1** 跳快步舞 tiào kuàibùwǔ. **2** 活泼〔潑〕地急跳 huópode jí tiào; 蹦跳 bèngtiào.

jig·saw /ˈʤɪgsɔ:/ *n* [C] (亦作 *'~ puzzle*) 拼图〔圖〕玩具 pīntú wánjù.

jilt /ʤɪlt/ *vt* 抛弃〔棄〕情人的女子 pāoqì qíngrén de nǚzǐ.

jingle /ˈʤɪŋgl/ *n* [C] **1** (硬币,小铃的)玎珰〔璫〕声〔聲〕 dīngdāngshēng **2** 具有韵律的诗句 jùyǒu yùnlǜ de shījù: *advertising ~s* 广告顺口溜. □ *vt/i* (使) 玎珰响〔響〕 dīngdāngxiǎng.

jinx /ʤɪŋks/ *n* [C] [俚语]不吉祥的人或物 bù jíxiáng de rén huò wù.

job /ʤɒb/ *n* [C] **1** 一件工作 yíjiàn gōngzuò. ***make a good ~ of sth*** 做得很好 zuò dé hěn hǎo. ***ˌodd-'~man*** 短工 duǎngōng. **2** [非正式用语]职〔職〕业〔業〕 zhíyè. **3** ***a good ~*** 幸运〔運〕的事 xìngyùnde shì.

jockey /ˈʤɒkɪ/ *n* [C] [*pl* ~s] 赛马〔馬〕的职〔職〕业〔業〕骑〔騎〕师〔師〕 sàimǎ de zhíyè qíshī. ⇨ disc jockey. □ *vt/i* 使人处〔處〕于有利地位 shǐ rén chùyú yǒulì dìwèi.

jog /ʤɒg/ *vt/i* [-gg-] **1** 轻〔輕〕推 qīngtuī; 轻撞 qīngzhuàng. ***~ sb's memory*** 唤起某人的记忆〔憶〕huànqǐ mǒurénde jìyì. **2** *~ along(on)* 缓步前进〔進〕 huǎnbù qiánjìn. **3** 慢跑 mànpǎo. □ *n* [C] **1** 轻推 qīngtuī; 轻撞 qīngzhuàng. **2** 慢跑 mànpǎo.

joggle /ˈʤɒgl/ *vt/i* 摇摆〔擺〕 yáobǎi; 摇动〔動〕 yáodòng. □ *n* [C] 轻〔輕〕摇 qīngyáo.

join /ʤɔɪn/ *vt/i* **1** 连〔連〕接(两点或物) liánjiē; 接合 jiēhé. ***~ forces (with)*** (同...) 联〔聯〕合 liánhé, (与...)通力合作 tōnglì hézuò. **2** 交会〔會〕 jiāohuì; 相连 xiānglián: *The two roads ~ here.* 两条路在这里连接. **3** 参〔參〕加 cānjiā, 加入 jiārù: *~ a club* 加入俱乐部. **4** 与〔與〕...在一起 yǔ... zài yìqǐ: *Please ~ us for a drink.* 请和我们一起喝点什么. □ *n* [C] 交叉点〔點〕 jiāochādiǎn; 连〔連〕接处〔處〕 liánjiēchù.

joiner /ˈʤɔɪnə(r)/ *n* [C] 细木工人 xìmù gōngrén. **join·ery** 细木工技术〔術〕或行业〔業〕 xìmùgōng jìshù huò hángyè.

joint¹ /ʤɔɪnt/ *adj* 共同的 gòngtóngde; 共有的 gòngyǒude: *~ responsibility* 共同的责任. ~ **account** 共同户头〔頭〕 gòngtóng hùtóu. **~ly** *adv*

joint² /ʤɔɪnt/ *n* [C] **1** 连〔連〕接处〔處〕 liánjiēchù; 接合点〔點〕 jiēhédiǎn: *~s on a pipe* 管道的连接处. **2** 关〔關〕节〔節〕 guānjié. **3** 带〔帶〕骨的腿肉 dài gǔ de tuǐròu. **4** [俚语]下流场〔場〕所(小酒馆) xiàliú chǎngsuǒ. **5** [俚语]含有大麻叶〔葉〕的烟〔煙〕卷 hányǒu dàmáyè de yānjuǎn.

joist /ʤɔɪst/ *n* [C] 小梁〔樑〕 xiǎoliáng; (地板等的)托梁 tuōliáng.

joke /ʤəʊk/ *n* [C] 笑话 xiàohuà; 玩笑 wánxiào. ***play a ~ on sb*** 戏〔戲〕弄某人 xìnòng mǒurén. □ *vi* 开〔開〕玩笑 kāi wánxiào. **jok·ing·ly** *adv* 玩笑地 wánxiàode.

joker /ˈʤəʊkə(r)/ *n* [C] **1** 喜开〔開〕玩笑的人 xǐ kāi wánxiào de rén. **2** (纸牌)百搭(可作任何点数的牌或王牌) bǎidā.

jolly /ˈʤɒlɪ/ *adj* [-ier, -iest] 高兴〔興〕的 gāoxìngde; 愉快的 yúkuàide. □ *adv* [非正式用语]很 hěn, 非常 fēicháng: *~ good!* 很好!

jolt /ʤəʊlt/ *vt/i* 使颠簸 shǐ diānbǒ; 颠簸而行 diānbǒ ér xíng. ☐ *n* [C] 颇[顛]簸 diānbǒ; 震摇 zhènyáo.

jostle /'ʤɒsl/ *vt/i* 推撞 tuīzhuàng; 拥[擁]挤[擠] yōngjǐ: *~ed in a crowded train* 挤在一列拥挤的火车里.

jot /ʤɒt/ *vt* [-tt-] ~ *sth down* 草草记下 cǎocǎo jì xià. '**~ter** 笔[筆]记本 bǐjìběn.

jour·nal /'ʤɜ:nl/ *n* [C] **1** 日报[報] rìbào; 定期刊物 dìngqī kānwù. **2** 日志[誌] rìzhì; 日记 rìjì. **~ism** /-ɪzəm/ 新闻[聞]工作 xīnwén gōngzuò. **~ist** *n* [C]

jour·ney /'ʤɜ:nɪ/ *n* [C] [*pl* ~s] 旅行 lǚxíng. ☐ *vi* 旅行 lǚxíng: ~ *across Africa* 穿越非洲的旅行.

jov·ial /'ʤəʊvɪəl/ *adj* [正式用语] 快活的 kuàihuóde; 愉快的 yúkuàide. **~ly** *adv* **~ity** /-'ælətɪ/ *n* [C,U]

jowl /ʤaʊl/ *n* [C] 下颚 xià'è.

joy /ʤɔɪ/ *n* **1** [U] 高兴[興] gāoxìng; 欢[歡]乐[樂] huānlè. **2** [C] 乐事 lèshì. **~ful** *adj* 十分喜悦的 shífēn xǐyuè de. **~ous** /'ʤɔɪəs/ *adj* 快乐的 kuàilède; 高兴的 gāoxìngde. **~ous·ly** *adv*

J.P. =Justice of the Peace.

jr.,jun. =junior.

ju·bi·lant /'ʤu:bɪlənt/ *adj* 喜气[氣]洋洋的 xǐqì yángyáng de. **~ly** *adv* **ju·bi'la·tion** *n* [C, U] 欢[歡]欣 huānxīn; 欢腾[騰]huānténg.

ju·bi·lee /'ʤu:bɪli:/ *n* [C] 有特定含义[義]的周年纪念 yǒu tèdìng hányì de zhōunián jìniàn. '**diamond** ~ 六十周年纪念 liùshí zhōunián jìniàn. '**golden** ~ 金婚纪念 jīnhūn jìniàn. '**silver** ~ 银婚纪念 yínhūn jìniàn.

judge /ʤʌʤ/ *n* [C] **1** 法官 fǎguān, 审[審]判员 shěnpànyuán. **2** 评判人 píngpànrén; 裁判人 cáipànrén. **3** 有判断[斷]功过[過]能力的人 yǒu pànduàn gōng guò nénglì de rén: *a good ~ of character* 善于鉴定人的优缺点的人. ☐ *vt/i* [*pres part* judging] **1** 审判 shěnpàn; 审理 shěnlǐ. **2** 评判 píngpàn; 裁判 cáipàn. **3** 断[斷]定 duàndìng; 判断 pànduàn.

judge·ment (法律 **judg·ment**) /'ʤʌʤmənt/ *n* **1** [U] 审[審]判 shěnpàn. **2** [C] (法官或法庭的)判决 pànjué. **3** [U] 判断[斷]力 pànduànlì. **4** [C,U] 意见 yìjiàn: *in my* ~ 就我看来. '**~Day, the** ,**Day of** '**J~** 上帝的最后[後]审判日 shàngdìde zuìhòu shěnpànrì

ju·di·cial /ʤu:'dɪʃl/ *adj* 法庭的 fǎtíngde; 法官的 fǎguānde; 审[審]判的 shěnpànde. **~ly** *adv*

ju·dici·ary /ʤu:'dɪʃərɪ/ *n* [C] [*pl* -ies] (总称)审[審]判员 shěnpànyuán; 法院系统或制度 fǎyuàn xìtǒng huò zhìdù.

ju·di·cious /ʤu:'dɪʃəs/ *adj* [正式用语]有见识[識]的 yǒu jiànshìde; 明智的 míngzhìde. **~ly** *adv*

judo /'ʤu:dəʊ/ *n* [U] (日本)柔道 róudào.

jug /ʤʌg/ *n* [C] **1** 壶[壺] hú; 罐 guàn. **2** 壶中物 hú zhōng wù; 罐中物 guàn zhōng wù: *a ~ of milk* 一罐牛奶.

jug·ger·naut /'ʤʌgənɔ:t/ *n* [C] **1** [喻] 摧毁一切的力量或物体[體] cuīhuǐ yíqiè de lìliàng huò wùtǐ. **2** [非正式用语] 大型长[長]途运[運]货车[車] dàxíng chángtú yùnhuòchē.

juggle /'ʤʌgl/ *vt/i* **1** (用球等)玩杂[雜]耍 wán záshuǎ; 变[變]戏[戲]法 biàn xìfǎ. **2** 耍花招 shuǎ huāzhāo, 欺骗[騙] qīpiàn: ~ *the accounts* 在帐目上耍花招. **jug·gler** 玩杂耍的人 wán záshuǎ de rén; 骗子 piànzi.

juice /ʤu:s/ *n* [C,U] 果汁 guǒzhī; 菜汁 càizhī; 肉汁 ròuzhī. **juicy** *adj* [-ier,-iest] 多汁液的 duō zhīyè de. **juici·ness** *n* [U]

juke-box /'ʤu:k bɒks/ *n* [C] 自动[動]电[電]唱机[機](投进硬币即放唱片) zìdòng diànchàngjī.

Jul.=July.

July /ʤu:'laɪ/ *n* 七月 qīyuè.

jumble /'ʤʌmbl/ *vt/i* ~ **(up)** 混杂[雜] hùnzá. ☐ *n* [C] 混乱[亂]的一堆 hùnluànde yìduī; 杂乱 záluàn. '**~-sale** 旧[舊]杂货拍卖[賣] jiù záhuò pāimài.

jumbo /'ʤʌmbəʊ/ *adj* 特大的 tèdàde; 巨大的 jùdàde: ~ *jets* 大型喷气式客机.

jump[1] /ʤʌmp/ *n* [C] **1** 跳 tiào; 惊[驚]跳 jīngtiào. **2** 猛增 měngzēng; 暴涨[漲] bàozhǎng: *a ~ in prices* 物价暴涨. **3** (需跳越的)障碍[礙]物 zhàng'àiwù.

jump[2] /ʤʌmp/ *vt/i* **1** 跳 tiào, 跳跃[躍] tiàoyuè: ~ *up in the air* 向上跳起来. **2** 跳过[過] tiàoguò; 越过 yuèguò: ~ *(over) a wall* 跳过一堵墙. **3** 暴涨[漲] bàozhǎng; 猛增 měngzēng: *prices ~ed.* 物价暴涨. **4** [俚语]攻击[擊] gōngjī. **5** ~ **at** 欣然接受 xīnrán jiēshòu. ~ **to conclusions** 匆匆作出结论[論] cōngcōng zuòchū jiélùn. **6** ~ **the queue** [喻]在未轮[輪]到前抢[搶]先获[獲]得某物 zài wèi lúndào qián qiǎngxiān huòde mǒuwù.

jumper /ˈdʒʌmpə(r)/ *n* [C] **1**（编织的）套头〔頭〕毛衣 tàotóu máoyī. **2** 跳跃的人、动〔動〕物或昆虫〔蟲〕tiàoyuède rén, dòngwù huò kūnchóng.

jumpy /ˈdʒʌmpɪ/ *adj* [-ier, -iest] 神经〔經〕过〔過〕敏的 shénjīng guòmǐn de.

Jun. = June.

junc·tion /ˈdʒʌŋkʃn/ *n* [C] 交叉点〔點〕jiāochādiǎn; 接合点 jiēhédiǎn.

junc·ture /ˈdʒʌŋktʃə(r)/ *n* [C] [正式用语] ***at this*** ~ 在此时〔時〕zàicǐshí.

June /dʒu:n/ *n* 六月 liùyuè.

jungle /ˈdʒʌŋgl/ *n* [C] 丛〔叢〕林 cónglín, 密林 mìlín.

jun·ior /ˈdʒu:nɪə(r)/ *n* [C], *adj* 较〔較〕年幼的 jiào niányòu de; 等级较低的 děngjí jiàodī de.

junk[1] /dʒʌŋk/ *n* [U] 废〔廢〕弃〔棄〕的旧〔舊〕物 fèiqìde jiùwù; 旧货 jiùhuò.

junk[2] /dʒʌŋk/ *n* [C] （平底）中国〔國〕帆船 Zhōngguó fānchuán.

junkie /ˈdʒʌŋkɪ/ *n* [C] [俚语] 吸毒的人 xīdúde rén.

junta /ˈdʒʌntə/ *n* [C] [*pl* ~s] 夺〔奪〕得政权的军人集团 duóde zhèngquán de jūnrén jítuán.

ju·ris·dic·tion /ˌdʒʊərɪsˈdɪkʃn/ *n* [U] 司法 sīfǎ; 司法权〔權〕sīfǎquán.

juror /ˈdʒʊərə(r)/ *n* [C] 陪审〔審〕员 péishěnyuán.

jury /ˈdʒʊərɪ/ *n* [C] [*pl* -ies] 陪审〔審〕团〔團〕（由十二人组成）péishěntuán. **~man** = juror.

just[1] /dʒʌst/ *adj* **1** 公平的 gōngpíngde; 公正的 gōngzhèngde: *a ~ decision* 公正的决定. **2** 应〔應〕得的 yīngdéde. **~ly** *adv*

just[2] /dʒʌst/ *adv* **1** 刚〔剛〕才 gāngcái, 方才 fāngcái: *I've ~ had dinner.* 我刚吃过饭. **2** 正好 zhènghǎo, 恰好 qiàhǎo: *It's ~ two o'clock.* 现在正好两点钟. **3** ~ ***as***, **(a)** 正如 zhèngrú: *Leave it ~ as you find it.* 让它保持原样. **(b)** 正当〔當〕…的时〔時〕候 zhèngdāng …de shíhòu: *He arrived ~ as I did.* 我到达时他也到了. **4** 此时 cǐshí; 那时 nàshí: *We're ~ leaving.* 我们正要离开. **5** 勉勉强强地 miǎnmiǎn qiǎngqiáng de: *We (only) ~ caught the train.* 我们刚好赶上火车. **6** [用于祈使句，以引起对某事物的注意]: *J~ a moment, please.* 请稍等一下. **7** 仅〔僅〕仅 jǐnjǐn, 只是 zhǐshì: *He's ~ an ordinary man.* 他仅仅是个普通人.

jus·tice /ˈdʒʌstɪs/ *n* **1** [U] 正义〔義〕zhèngyì; 公正 gōngzhèng, 公平 gōngpíng. **2** [U] 司法 sīfǎ; 审〔審〕判 shěngpàn. **3** [C]（英国）高等法院法官 gāoděng fǎyuàn fǎguān;（美国）最高法院法官 zuì gāo fǎyuàn fǎguān: *the Lord Chief J~* 高等法院的庭长或首席法官. ,**J~ of the 'Peace** 治安官 zhì'ānguān.

jus·tify /ˈdʒʌstɪfaɪ/ *vt* [*pt*, *pp* -ied] **1** 证明…是正当〔當〕的或有理的 zhèngmíng…shì zhèngdāngde huò yǒulǐde. **2** 为〔爲〕…辩护〔護〕wèi …biànhù. **jus·ti'fi·able** *adj* **jus·ti·fi·ably** *adv* 有充分理由 yǒu chōngfèn lǐyǒu: *justifiably proud* 理所当然地感到自豪. **jus·ti·fi·ca·tion** /-fɪˈkeɪʃn/ *n* [U]

jut /dʒʌt/ *vi* [-tt-] ~ ***out*** 突出 tūchū; 伸出 shēnchū.

jute /dʒu:t/ *n* [U] 黄麻 huángmá; 黄麻的纤〔纖〕维 huángmáde xiānwéi.

ju·ven·ile /ˈdʒu:vənaɪl/ *n* [C] 青少年 qīngshàonián. □ *adj* 青少年特有的 qīngshàonián tè yǒu de; 适〔適〕合于青少年的 shìhéyú qīngshàonián de. ,~ **de'linquency** 少年犯罪 shàonián fànzuì.

K k

K k /keɪ/ [*pl* K's, k's /keɪz/] 英语的第十一个〔個〕字母 Yīngyǔ de dìshíyīgè zìmǔ.

ka·leido·scope /kəˈlaɪdəskəʊp/ *n* [C] **1** 万〔萬〕花筒 wànhuātǒng. **2** [喻] 千变〔變〕万〔萬〕化的情景 qiānbiàn-wànhuàde qíngjǐng. **ka·leido·scopic** /-ˈskɒpɪk/ *adj*

kan·ga·roo /ˌkæŋgəˈru:/ *n* [C] 大袋鼠 dà dàishǔ.

karat /ˈkærət/ = carat.

ka·rate /kəˈrɑ:tɪ/ *n* [U] 日本的一种〔種〕徒手自卫〔衛〕武术〔術〕Rìběn de yìzhǒng túshǒu zìwèi wǔshù.

kayak /ˈkaɪæk/ *n* [C] 覆以帆布的独〔獨〕木舟 fù yǐ fānbùde dúmùzhōu.

K.C. = **1** King's Counsel (barrister 英国〔國〕王室法律顾〔顧〕问〔問〕

Yīngguó wángshì fǎlǜ gùwèn. **2** Knight Commander 英国高级爵士 Yīngguó gāojí juéshì.

ke·bab /kə'bæb/ *n* [C] 烤肉串 kǎo ròuchuàn.

keel /ki:l/ *n* [C] (船)龙〔龍〕骨 lónggǔ; 船脊骨 chuánjǐgǔ. *on an even* ~(船)平稳〔穩〕的 píngwěnde. □ *vt/i* ~ *over* 倾覆 qīngfù; (指人)病倒 bìngdǎo.

keen /ki:n/ *adj* [-er, -est] **1** (指边)锋利的 fēnglìde; 锐利的 ruìlìde. **2** [喻]尖锐的 jiānruìde: *a* ~ *wind* 刺骨的风. **3** (指兴趣等)强烈的 qiángliède. **4** 敏锐的 mǐnruìde: *a* ~ *sense of smell* 敏锐的嗅觉. **5** (指人)渴望的 kěwàngde. ~ *on* 渴望 kěwàng; 喜爱〔愛〕xǐ'ài. ~**ly** *adv* ~**ness** *n* [U]

keep[1] /ki:p/ *vt/i* [*pt, pp* kept/kept/] **1** 使(人或物)保持某一状〔狀〕态〔態〕shǐ bǎo chí mǒu yí zhuàngtài: ~ *(them) quiet* 使(他们)安静. ~ *an eye on* [非正式用语] 密切注视 mìqiè zhùshì. ~ *sth in mind* 记住(某事) jìzhù. **2** 阻止 zǔzhǐ: ~ *him from leaving* 不让他离开. **3** ~ *sth (back) from* **(a)** 不让〔讓〕他人知道 bú ràng tārén zhīdào. **(b)** 留下 liúxià; 保留 bǎoliú. ~ *sth to oneself* 不让他人分享 bú ràng tārén fēnxiǎng. ~ *a secret* ⇨ secret. **4** 履行 lǚxíng; 遵守 zūnshǒu: ~ *a promise* 遵守诺言. **5** 保卫〔衛〕bǎowèi; 保护〔護〕bǎohù: ~ *goal* 守球门. ⇨ goalkeeper. **6** 保有 bǎo yǒu; 保存 bǎocún: *K*~ *the change* 不要找钱了. **7** 赡养〔養〕shànyǎng: ~ *a family* 养〔養〕家. **8** 经售 jīngshòu. **9** ~ *house* 料理家务〔務〕liàolǐ jiāwù. ⇨ housekeeper. **10** 拥〔擁〕有 yōngyǒu; 经营〔營〕jīngyíng: ~ *a shop* 经营商店. **11** 记入 jìrù; 记录〔錄〕jìlù: ~ *a diary* 记日记. ⇨ bookkeeper. **12** 保持(某种方向、路线等) bǎochí: *K*~ *straight on.* 一直向前. **13** ~ *going* 不停止 bù tíngzhǐ; 不放弃〔棄〕bú fàngqì. **14** (食物)保持良好 bǎochí liánghǎo. **15** ~ *at sth* 不断〔斷〕地做 búduànde zuò. ~ *away (from)* 远〔遠〕离〔離〕yuǎnlí; 回避 huíbì. ~ *sb down* 压〔壓〕制 yāzhì. ~ *in with sb* 与〔與〕(某人)保持友谊 yǔ bǎochí yǒuyí. ~ *off* 不接近 bù jiējìn. ~ *on (doing sth)* 继〔繼〕续〔續〕做某事 jìxù zuò mǒushì. ~ *sth on* 穿(或戴)着… chuānzhuo… ~ *sb on* 继续雇〔僱〕用某人 jìxù gùyòng mǒurén. ~ *on at sb* 因一再抱怨而烦恼〔惱〕yīn yízài bàoyuàn ér fánnǎo. ~ *out (of)* 停留在外面 tíngliú zài wàimiàn. ~ *sb (sth) out (of)* 不让〔讓〕入内 búràng rùnèi. ~ *to sth,* **(a)** 履行诺言 lǚxíng nuòyán. **(b)** 限制自己 xiànzhì zìjǐ: ~ *to the subject* 把握讨论的主题(要点). ~ *(oneself) to one'self* 不与〔與〕人交往 bù yǔ rén jiāowǎng. ~ *up (with)* 跟上 gēnshàng. ~ *sb up* 使迟〔遲〕睡 shǐchíshuì. ~ *sth up,* **(a)** 振起 zhènqì; 使不低落 shǐ bù dīluò: ~ *prices up* 使价格不下跌. **(b)** 继续 jìxù: ~ *up an attack* 不断地攻击. **(c)** 使保持适〔適〕当〔當〕的状态 shǐ bǎochí shìdāngde zhuàngtài: ~ *up a large house* 维护好一所大房子. ~ *it up* 继续下去而不松〔鬆〕弛 jìxù xiàqù ér bù sōngchí.

keep[2] /ki:p/ *n* **1** [U] 生计 shēngjì; 生活所需的食粮〔糧〕shēnghuó suǒxū de shíliáng. **2** [C] 要塞 yàosài; (城堡的)高楼〔樓〕gāolóu. **3** *for* ~*s* [俚语]永远〔遠〕地 yǒngyuǎnde.

keeper /'ki:pə(r)/ *n* [C] 看守人 kānshǒurén; 看护〔護〕人 kānhùrén: *zoo-*~ (动物园的)饲养员; *goal*~ (足球等)守门员.

keep·ing /'ki:pɪŋ/ *n* [U] **1** 保管 bǎoguǎn: *the* ~ *of bees* 蜜蜂的饲养. *in safe* ~ 细心地保管 xìxīnde bǎoguǎn. **2** 一致 yízhì: *in* ~ *with his promises* 言行一致.

keep·sake /'ki:pseɪk/ *n* [C] 纪念品 jìniànpǐn.

keg /keg/ *n* [C] 小桶 xiǎotǒng.

ken·nel /'kenl/ *n* [C] **1** 狗舍 gǒushè, 狗窝〔窩〕gǒuwō. **2** [*pl*] 养〔養〕狗场〔場〕yǎnggǒuchǎng. □ *vt/i* [-ll-] 使进〔進〕狗窝 shǐ jìn gǒuwō.

kept /kept/ ⇨ keep[1].

kerb (亦作 **curb**) /kɜ:b/ *n* [C] (人行道的)边〔邊〕石 biānshí.

ker·nel /'kɜ:nl/ *n* [C] **1** (果)核 hé; 果仁 guǒrén; 谷〔穀〕粒 gǔlì. **2** [喻]核心 héxīn, 中心 zhōngxīn.

kes·trel /'kestrəl/ *n* [C] 茶隼(一种小鹰) chásǔn.

ketch·up /'ketʃəp/ *n* [U] 蕃茄酱〔醬〕fānqiéjiàng.

kettle /'ketl/ *n* [C] (烧开水用的)壶〔壺〕hú.

kettle·drum/'ketldrʌm/ *n* [C] 铜鼓 tónggǔ, 定音鼓 dìngyīngǔ.

key[1] /ki:/ *n* [C] **1** 钥〔鑰〕匙 yàoshi. **2** [喻](问题的)解答 jiědá. **3** 题解 tíjiě. **4** (打字机、钢琴等)键 jiàn. **5** (音乐)调 diào. **6** [喻](思想或表达的)调子 diàozi; 基调 jīdiào: *a low-~ speech* 低调讲话.7 [用作定语]支配的 zhīpèide; 基本的 jīběnde: *a ~ position* 险要位置; *~ industry* 基本工业. '**~board** 键盘[盤] jiànpán; 挂[掛]钥匙的板 guà yàoshi de bǎn.

key² /kiː/ *vt ~ up* [喻]激励[勵] jīlì; 准备[備]做某件事 zhǔnbèi zuò mǒujiànshì.

key·stone /'kiːstəʊn/ *n* [C] **1** 拱顶石 gǒngdǐngshí. **2** [喻]基本原理 jīběn yuánlǐ, 要旨 yàozhǐ.

Kg.=kilogram.

khaki /'kɑːkɪ/ *n* [U], *adj* 卡其布服装(尤指军服) kǎqíbù fúzhuāng; 黄褐色 huánghèsè; 黄褐色的 huánghèsède.

kick /kɪk/ *vt/i* **1** 踢 tī. *~ the bucket* [俚语] 死亡 sǐwáng. **2** (指枪)反冲 fǎnchōng. **3** *~ against* (或 *at*) 反对[對] fǎnduì; 抱怨 bàoyuàn. *~ off* (足球)开[開]球 kāiqiú. '**~-off** *n* [C] *~ up a fuss* (或 *row*) [非正式用语]大吵大闹 dàchǎo dànào; 起哄 qǐhòng. □ *n* [C] **1** 踢 tī. **2** [非正式用语]兴[興]奋[奮] xīngfèn; 快感 kuàigǎn: *take drugs for ~s* 服用兴奋剂.

kid¹ /kɪd/ *n* **1** [C] 小山羊 xiǎo shānyáng. **2** [U] 小山羊皮革 xiǎo shānyáng pígé. **3** [俚语]小孩 xiǎohái.

kid² /kɪd/ *vt* [-dd-] [俚语]欺骗[騙] qīpiàn; 哄骗 hǒngpiàn.

kid·nap /'kɪdnæp/ *vt* [-pp-] 诱拐(小孩) yòuguǎi; 绑架 bǎngjià. **~-per** 拐子 guǎizhi; 绑架者 bǎngjiàzhě.

kid·ney /'kɪdnɪ/*n* [C] [*pl* ~s] 肾[腎] shèn; (牛、羊等作为食用的)腰子 yāozi. ,**~'bean** 菜豆 càidòu; 肾形豆 shènxíngdòu.

kill /kɪl/ *vt/i* **1** 杀[殺]死 shāsǐ, 弄死 nòngsǐ. **2** 摧毁 cuīhuǐ; 毁掉 huǐdiào: *~ our hopes of winning* 使我们获胜的希望破灭. **3** 淹没 yānmò; 压[壓]倒 yādǎo: *~ her with kindness* 爱她反倒害她. □ *n* [仅用 *sing*] 杀[殺] shā; 猎[獵]获[獲]物 lièhuòwù. '**~joy** 扫[掃]兴[興]的人 sǎoxìngde rén. **~er** 凶[兇]手 xiōngshǒu, 杀人者 shārénzhě. ***make a ~ing*** 很快赚了一大笔钱[錢] hěn kuài zhuànle yí dàbǐ qián.

kiln /'kɪln/ *n* [C] 窑[窰] yáo.

kilo /'kiːləʊ/ *n* [C] [*pl* ~s]kilogram 的缩写[寫] *kilogram* de suōxiě.

kilo·gram(me) /'kɪləgræm/ *n* [C] 公斤 gōngjīn, 千克 qiānkè.

kilo·metre [美语 = **-meter**] /'kɪləmiːtə(r)/ *n* [C] 公里 gōnglǐ, 千米 qiānmǐ.

kilo·watt /'kɪləwɒt/ *n* [C] 千瓦 qiānwǎ, 瓩 qiānwǎ.

kilt /kɪlt/ *n* [C] (苏格兰高地男子穿的)褶迭短裙 zhědié duǎnqún.

kim·ono /kɪ'məʊnəʊ/ *n* [C] [*pl* ~s] (日本)和服 héfú; 和服式女晨衣 héfúshì nǚchényī.

kin /kɪn/ *n pl* 家族 jiāzú; 亲[親]属[屬] qīnshǔ. ***next of ~*** 最近的亲属 zuìjìnde qīnshǔ.

kind¹ /kaɪnd/ *adj* [-er, -est] 亲[親]切的 qīnqiède; 友爱[愛]的 yǒuàide.,**~-'hearted** *adj* 仁慈的 réncíde;好心的 hǎoxīnde. **~ly** *adv* **(a)** 亲切地 qīnqiède; 和善地 héshànde. **(b)** 自然地 zìránde: *He doesn't take ~ly to being cheated.* 他不容易受骗. **~ness** *n* **(a)** [U] 仁慈 réncí; 和气[氣] héqì. **(b)** [C] 友好的行为[爲] yǒuhǎode xíngwéi.

kind² /kaɪnd/ *n* [C] **1** (动植物的)类[類] lèi; 属[屬] shǔ: *man~* 人类. **2** 种[種]类 zhǒnglèi. ***a ~ of*** 一种 yìzhǒng; 一类 yílèi. (用以表示不肯定): *I had a ~ of suspicion that he was cheating.* 我有点怀疑他在欺骗. **3** ***in ~***, **(a)** 以货代款 yǐ huò dài kuǎn. **(b)** [喻]同样[樣]的方法或手段 tóngyàngde fāngfǎ huò shǒuduàn.

kin·der·gar·ten /'kɪndəgɑːtn/ *n* [C] 幼儿[兒]园[園] yòuéryuán.

kindle /'kɪndl/ *vt/i* **1** 点[點]燃 diǎnrán. **2** 引起 yǐnqǐ; 激发[發] jīfā.

kin·dred /'kɪndrɪd/ *n* [仅用 *sing*] [U] 血缘关[關]系 xuèyuán guānxì. □ *adj* **1** 同宗的 tóngzōngde; 同源的 tóngyuánde. **2** ***a ~ spirit*** 有同情感的人 yǒu tóngqínggǎn de rén.

kin·etic / kɪ'netɪk/ *adj* 运[運]动[動]的 yùndòngde;活动的 huódòngde:*~ energy* 动能.

king /kɪŋ/ *n* [C] **1** 国[國]王 guówáng. **2** 最有势[勢]力的人 zuì yǒu shìlì de rén: *an oil ~* 石油大王. **3** (国际象棋) 王 wáng; (西洋跳棋)王棋 wángqí. **4** 纸牌 K zhǐpái *K*. **5** 出众[衆]成员 chūzhòng chéngyuán: *the ~ of beasts* 狮(百兽之王). '**~pin, (a)** 中心立轴[軸] zhōngxīn lìzhóu. **(b)** [喻]中心人物 zhōngxīn rénwù; 主要成分 zhǔyào chéngfèn. '**~ size** *adj* 特大的 tèdàde; 特长[長]的 tèchángde: *~ size cigarettes* 特长香烟.

king·dom /'kɪŋdəm/ *n* [C] **1** 王国[國] wángguó. **2** 神政 shénzhèng. **3** 自然三界之一 zìrán sānjiè zhī yī: *the animal* ~ 动物界; *the vegetable* ~ 植物界; *the mineral* ~ 矿物界. **the U,nited 'K**~ 联[聯]合王国 liánhéwángguó.

kink /kɪŋk/ *n* [C] **1** (绳、索等)纽结 niǔjié. **2** [喻]奇想 qíxiǎng; 怪念头[頭] guàiniàntóu. □ *vt/i* 打结 dǎ jié; 绞缠[纏] jiǎochán. **kinky** *adj* [-ier, -iest] [非正式用语]不正当[當]的 bú zhèngdāngde.

kiosk /'ki:ɒsk/ *n* [C] **1** 报[報]摊[攤]等 bàotān děng. **2** 公用电[電]话间[間] gōngyòng diànhuàjiān.

kip·per /'kɪpə(r)/ *n* [C] 腌或熏[燻]的鲑鱼 yān huò xūn de guīyú; 鲱鱼 fēiyú.

kiss /kɪs/ *vt/i* 吻 wěn, 接吻 jiēwěn. □ *n* [C] 吻 wěn. ~ *of 'life* 急救呼吸 jíjiù hūxī.

kit /kɪt/ *n* **1** (士兵旅游者)所有的装[裝]备[備](尤指衣服) suǒyǒude zhuāngbèi. **2** [C] 工人、运[運]动[動]员的成套用具 gōngrén yùndòngyuán de chéngtào yòngjù. □ *vt* [-tt-] ~ *out (with sth)*, ~ *up (with sth)* 发[發]给装备 fāgěi zhuāngbèi.

kit·chen /'kɪtʃɪn/ *n* [C] 厨[廚]房 chúfáng. **~ette** /-'net/ *n* [C] 小厨房 xiǎo chúfáng.

kite /kaɪt/ *n* [C] **1** 鸢 yuān. **2** 风[風]筝 fēngzhēng.

kith /kɪθ/ *n* [仅用于] ,~ *and 'kin,* 亲[親]友 qīnyǒu.

kit·ten /'kɪtn/ *n* [C] 小猫[貓] xiǎomāo.

kiwi /'ki:wi:/ *n* [C] 鹬[鷸]鸵[鴕](产于新西兰的一种无翼鸟) yùtuó.

klep·to·mania /ˌkleptə'meɪnɪə/ *n* [U] 偷窃[竊]癖 tōuqièpǐ. **klep·to·maniac** /-nɪæk/ 有偷窃癖的人 yǒu tōuqièpǐ de rén.

Km=Kilometre.

knack /næk/ *n* [C] 诀窍[竅] juéqiào; 技巧 jìqiǎo.

knap·sack /'næpsæk/ *n* [C] 背包 bēibāo.

knead /ni:d/ *vt* **1** 揉(面粉和水)成团[團] róuchéng tuán. **2** 按摩(肌肉) ànmó.

knee /ni:/ *n* [C] 膝 qī; 膝盖 qīgài. *bring sb to his* ~*s* 迫使某人屈服 pò shǐ mǒurén qūfú. **'~cap** 膝盖骨 qīgàigǔ.

kneel /ni:l/ *vi* [*pt,pp* knelt /nelt/] 跪下 guìxià; 跪倒 guìdǎo.

knell /nel/ *n* [U] 钟[鐘]声[聲](尤指丧钟) zhōngshēng.

knelt /nelt/ ⇨ kneel.

knew /nju:/ ⇨ know.

knickers /'nɪkəz/ *n pl* = panties.

knick-knack /'nɪk næk/ *n* [C] 小装[裝]饰品 xiǎo zhuāngshìpǐn.

knife /naɪf/ *n* [C] [*pl* knives /naɪvz/] (有柄的)锋利小刀 fēnglì xiǎodāo. □ *vt* 用刀刺(人) yòng dāo cì. **'~-edge** 刀口 dāokǒu; 刀刃 dāorèn. *on a* ~*-edge* (指重要结果等)极[極]不肯定 jí bù kěndìng.

knight /naɪt/ *n* [C] **1** (欧洲中世纪)骑[騎]士 qíshì, 武士 wǔshì. **2** [现代用法]爵士(注意: 称号 *Sir* 用在教名前面.) juéshì. **3** (国际象棋中的)马[馬] mǎ. □ *vt* 封…为爵士 fēn … wéi juéshì. **'~hood** *n* [C, U] 爵士(骑士)的地位、身份 juéshìde dìwèi, shēn fèn.

knit /nɪt/ *vt/i* [*pt, pp* ~ted 或 knit] [-tt-]· **1** 编织[織](衣物等) biānzhī. **2** 紧[緊]密结合 jǐnmì jiéhé: *a closely-~ group of men* 紧密团结的一伙人. **~ting, (a)** 编织 biānzhī. **(b)** 编织物 biānzhīwù. **'~ting-needle** 编结用的织针 biānjié yòng de zhīzhēn.

knives /naɪvz/ *n pl* of knife.

knob /nɒb/ *n* [C] **1** (门、抽屉等)圆形把手 yuánxíng bǎshǒu. **2** [非正式用语](收音机的)旋钮 xuánniǔ; 调节[節]器 tiáojiéqì. **3** 圆形突出物 yuánxíng tūchūwù; 球块[塊] qiúkuài: *a* ~ *of butter* 一块黄油. **~bly** *adj* [-ier, -iest] 有圆形突出物的 yǒu yuánxíng tūchūwù de.

knock¹ /nɒk/ *n* [C] **1** 击[擊] jī, 打 dǎ; 敲 qiāo; 敲击声[聲] qiāojīshēng. **2** [俚语]指摘 zhǐzhāi; 财政损失 cáizhèng sǔnshī. **~er** 门[門]环[環] ménhuán.

knock² /nɒk/ *vt/i* **1** 敲 qiāo; 击[擊] jī, 打 dǎ: ~ *him over* 把他打翻在地. **2** (汽油发动机)发[發]出砰砰声[聲] fāchū pēngpēngshēng. **3** [俚语]找岔子 zhǎo cházi, 说坏[壞]话 shuō huàihuà. **4** ~ *sth back* [俚语]喝掉 hēdiào. ~ *sb down* 打倒 dǎdǎo; 击[擊]倒 jīdǎo. ~ *sth down*, **(a)** 拆除 chāichú. **(b)** 减[減]价[價] jiǎnjià, 降价 jiàngjià. ~ *off (work)* 停止(工作) tíngzhǐ. ~ *sth off*, **(a)** 扣除 kòuchú: ~ *£2 off the price* 减价两英镑. **(b)** [俚语]偷 tōu. ~ *sb out* 打昏 dǎhūn. ~ *sb up* [英国英语, 非正式用语]敲门[門]唤醒 qiāomén huànxǐng. ~ *sth up* 匆匆凑[湊]成 cōngcōng còuchéng: ~ *up a meal* 匆匆做好一顿饭. ,**~-'kneed** *adj* [医]膝内翻的 xīnèifānde. **'~out** *n, adj* [C] **(a)** (缩作 **KO**) (拳击)打倒对[對]手(的)

dǎdǎo duì shǒu. **(b)** 清除弱竞〔競〕争者的回合 qīngchú ruòjìngzhēngzhě de huíhé. **(c)** 引人注目的人 yǐn rén zhùmù de rén; 轰〔轟〕动〔動〕的事物 hōngdòngde shìwù.

knot /nɒt/ *n* [C] **1** (绳索等的) 结 jié. **2** [喻]结合 jiéhé: *the marriage* ~ 婚姻关系. **3** (树木或木板上的) 节〔節〕jié; 节疤 jiébā. **4** 海里 hǎilǐ, 浬 lǐ. **5** 一小群人 yìxiǎoqún rén. □ *vt/i* [-tt-] 打结 dǎjié; 成结 chéngjié. **~ty** *adj* [-ier, -iest] 多结的 duōjiéde; 多节的 duōjiéde. ***a ~ty problem*** 难〔難〕题 nántí.

know /nəʊ/ *vt/i* [*pt* knew /nju:/; *pp* ~n /nəʊn/] **1** 知道 zhīdào; 懂得 dǒngdé. **2** 认〔認〕识〔識〕 rènshi. **3** 经〔經〕历〔歷〕 jīnglì; 体〔體〕验〔驗〕 tǐyàn: *They* ~ *poverty.* 他们经历了贫困. **4** 分辨 fēnbiàn; 识〔識〕别 shíbié: *I'll* ~ *him when I see him.* 看到他时就会认出他. ~ ***the ropes*** 知道事情的内情 zhīdào shìqíngde nèiqíng. **5** ~ ***about*** (或 ***of***) 听〔聽〕说关〔關〕于…的事情 tīngshuō guānyú ... de shìqing. **'~-how** 实〔實〕际〔際〕知识〔識〕 shíjì zhīshì; 技能 jìnéng.

know·ing /'nəʊɪŋ/ *adj* 机〔機〕警的 jījǐngde; 狡猾的 jiǎohuáde. **~ing·ly** *adv* **(a)** 故意地 gùyìde. **(b)** 老练〔練〕地 lǎoliànde.

knowl·edge /'nɒlɪdʒ/*n* [U] **1** 了解 liǎojiě; 理解 lǐjiě. **2** 消息 xiāoxi; 知识〔識〕 zhīshi; 学〔學〕识 xuéshí: *human* ~ 人类知识. **~able** /-əbl/ *adj* 有知识的 yǒu zhīshi de; 渊〔淵〕博的 yuānbóde.

knuckle /'nʌkl/ *n* [C] 指节〔節〕 zhǐjié □ *vi* ~ ***down to*** 开〔開〕始认〔認〕真工作 kāishǐ rènzhēn gōngzuò.

ko·ala /kəʊ'ɑ:lə/ *n* [C] [动物]考拉 (澳大利亚产一种似小熊会攀树的动物) kǎolā.

Kt.=knight.

Kw.=kilowatt.

L l

L, l /el/ [*pl* L's l's /elz/] **1** 英语的第十二个〔個〕字母Yīngyǔ de dìshíèrgè zìmǔ. **2** 罗〔羅〕马〔馬〕数〔數〕字的 50 Luómǎ shùzì de 50.

L.=Latin.

l.=**1** left. **2** line. **3** litre.

Lab.=Labour (political party)

lab /læb/ *n* [C] [非正式用语] laboratory 的缩写〔寫〕*laboratory* de suōxiě.

label /'leɪbl/ *n* [C] **1** 标〔標〕签〔籤〕 biāoqiān; 签条〔條〕 qiāntiáo. **2** 称〔稱〕呼(用以描述人或事物) chēnghū: *the* ~ *of thief* 贼的称号. □ *vt* [-ll-, 美语 -l-] **1** 贴标签于 tiē biāoqiān yú. **2** 给…贴上标签 gěi ... tiēshàng biāoqiān.

la·bor /'leɪbə(r)/ *n* [美语] = labour.

lab·ora·tory /lə'bɒrətrɪ/ *n* [C] [*pl* -ies] 实〔實〕验〔驗〕室 shíyànshì.

la·bori·ous /lə'bɔ:rɪəs/ *adj* **1** (指工作等)吃力的 chīlìde. **2** 具见苦心的 jù jiàn kǔxīn de; 不流畅〔暢〕的 bù liúchàng de: *a* ~ *style* 矫揉造作的文体. **~ly** *adv*

la·bour [美语 =**la·bor**] /'leɪbə(r)/ *n* **1** [U] 劳〔勞〕动〔動〕 láodòng. **2** [C] 工作 gōngzuò. **3** [U] 劳工 láogōng. **4** [U] 分娩 fēnmiǎn: *a woman in* ~ 分娩中的妇女. □ *vt/i* **1** 劳动 láodòng. **2** 吃力地行动或呼吸 chīlìde xíngdòng huò hūxī, **3** ~ ***under*** 为〔爲〕…苦恼〔惱〕 wèi ... kǔnǎo: ~ *under a disadvantage* 因不利条件而吃苦头. **4** 仔细去做 zǐxì qù zuò: *to* ~ *a point* 仔细解释一个论点. **,hard'**~ 苦工 kǔgōng, 劳役 láoyì. **'L**~ **Party** 工党〔黨〕 Gōngdǎng. **~er** 劳动者 láodòngzhě; 工人 gōngrén.

lab·yr·inth /'læbərɪnθ/ *n* [C] **1** 迷宫 mígōng;曲径〔徑〕qūjìng. **2** [喻] (事情的)错综复〔復〕杂〔雜〕 cuòzōng fùzá; 曲折 qūzhé.

lace /leɪs/ *n* **1** [U] 花边〔邊〕 huābiān; 饰带〔帶〕 shìdài. **2** [C] 鞋带 xiédài; 带 dài. □ *vt/i* **1** 用带子束紧〔緊〕 yòng dàizi sù jǐn; 缚带子 fù dàizi. **2** 穿带于 chuān dài yū. **3** ~ ***with*** 搀〔攙〕酒于(饮料) chān jiǔ yú.

lac·er·ate /'læsəreɪt/ *vt* [正式用语]划〔劃〕破(肌肉等) huápò; 撕裂 sīliè. **lac·e'r·ation** *n* [C,U]

lack /læk/ *vt/i* **1** 没有 méiyǒu; 短少 duǎnshǎo. **2** ***be ~ing*** 缺乏 quēfá. □ *n* [U] 缺乏 quēfá, 不足 bùzú: ~ *of money* 缺钱.

lac·quer /'lækə(r)/ *n* [C, U] **1** 漆 qī. **2** 发〔髮〕膠 fàjiāo. □ *vt* 用漆涂〔塗〕 yòng qī tú.

la·crosse /lə'krɒs/ *n* [U] 长〔長〕曲棍球(运动) chángqūgùnqiú.

lacy /ˈleɪsɪ/ *adj* [-ier, -iest] 花边〔邊〕的 huābiānde; 似花边的 sì huābiān de; 带〔帶〕状〔狀〕的 dài zhuàngde.

lad /læd/ *n* [C] [非正式用语]少年 shàonián; 青年 qīngnián.

lad·der /ˈlædə(r)/ *n* [C] **1** 梯子 tīzi. **2** (长统袜上的)抽丝〔絲〕chōusī. **3** 阶〔階〕梯 jiētī: *the ~ of success* 成功的手段. □ *vi* (指袜子)抽丝 chōusī.

laden /ˈleɪdn/ *adj* 装〔裝〕满的 zhuāngmǎnde; 载〔載〕满的 zǎimǎnde.

ladle /ˈleɪdl/ *n* [C] 长〔長〕柄勺〔杓〕chángbǐngsháo; 勺子 sháozi. □ *vt* **1** (用勺)盛 chéng, 舀 yǎo. **2** ~ *out* [喻]分给 fēngěi; 提供 tígòng: ~ *out prizes* 发奖.

lady /ˈleɪdɪ/ *n* [C] [*pl* -dies] **1** 贵妇〔婦〕人 guìfùrén. **2** 风〔風〕度大方的妇女 fēngdù dàfāng de fùnǚ. **3** 女士 nǚshì. **4** [用作定语]女性的 nǚxìngde: *a ~ doctor* 女医生. **5** **L~** [英国英语](对贵族的妻女的尊称)夫人 fūrén; 小姐 xiǎojiě. **Our 'L~** 圣〔聖〕母玛〔瑪〕利亚〔亞〕shèngmǔ Mǎlìyǎ. **'~bird** 瓢虫〔蟲〕piáochóng. **'~like** 象贵妇人的 xiàng guìfùrěn de.

lag¹ /læg/ *vi* [-gg-] 走得慢 zǒu de màn; 落后〔後〕luòhòu: ~ *behind* 落在后面. □ *n* [C] (一个现象和另一相关现象中的)相隔〔隔〕时〔時〕间〔間〕xiānggé shíjiān: *a time* ~ 时间滞差.

lag² /læg/ *vt* [-gg-] 以隔〔隔〕热〔熱〕或隔冷材料包扎〔紮〕(水管等) yǐ gérè huò gélěng cáiliào bāozhā **~ging** 绝缘材料 juéyuán cáiliào.

la·ger /ˈlɑːgə(r)/ *n* [C, U] 淡啤酒 dànpíjiǔ.

la·goon /ləˈguːn/ *n* [C] 礁湖 jiāohú; 咸〔鹹〕水湖 xiánshuǐhú.

laid /leɪd/ *pt, pp* of lay².

lain /leɪn/ *pp* of lie².

lair /leə(r)/ *n* [C] 兽〔獸〕穴 shòuxuè; 兽窝〔窩〕shòuwō.

laity /ˈleɪətɪ/ *n* [C] [通常为 sing. 与the 连用] 俗人 súrén

lake /leɪk/ *n* [C] 湖 hú.

lamb /læm/ *n* **1** [C] 小羊 xiǎoyáng, 羔羊 gāoyáng; [U] 羔羊肉 gāoyángròu. **2** [C] 羔羊般柔弱的人 gāoyángbān róuruò de rén. *like a* ~ 温顺地 wēnshùnde □ *vi* 生小羊 shēng xiǎoyáng.

lame /leɪm/ *adj* [-r, -st] **1** 跛的 bǒde, 瘸的 quéde. **2** (指辩解)不能说服人的 bùnéng shuōfú rén de. □ *vt* 使跛 shǐ bǒ. ~ **duck** 财政困难〔難〕时〔時〕的企业〔業〕组织〔織〕cáizhèng kùnnan shí de qǐyè zǔzhī. **~ly** *adv* **~ness** *n* [U]

la·ment /ləˈment/ *vt/i* 悲痛 bēitòng. 哀悼 āidào. □ *n* [C] 挽〔輓〕歌 wǎngē; 挽诗 wǎnshī. **~able** /ˈlæməntəbl/ *adj* 可悲的 kěbēide; 令人惋惜的 lìng rén wǎnxī de. **~ably** *adv* **~a·tion** /-ˈteɪʃn/ *n* [C,U]

lami·nated /ˈlæmɪneɪtɪd/ *adj* 由薄片迭成的 yóu bópiàn diéchéng de.

lamp /læmp/ *n* [C] **1** 灯〔燈〕dēng. **2** 加热〔熱〕装置 jiārè zhuāngzhì. **'~-post** 路灯柱 lùdēngzhù. **'~-shade** 灯罩 dēngzhào.

lance¹ /lɑːns/ *n* [C] 骑〔騎〕兵用的长〔長〕矛 qíbīng yòngde chángmáo. **,~-'corporal** (英国陆军中的)一等兵 yīděngbīng.

lance² /lɑːns/ *vt* 用柳叶〔葉〕刀割开〔開〕yòng liǔyèdāo gēkāi.

lan·cet /ˈlɑːnsɪt/ *n* [C] [医学]柳叶〔葉〕刀 liǔ yèdāo; 刺血针 cìxuězhēn.

land¹ /lænd/ *n* **1** [U] 陆地 lùdì. **2** [U] 土地 tǔdì; 田地 tiándì: *work on the* ~ 务农. **3** [U] [有时用 *pl*] 地产〔產〕dìchǎn. **4** [C] 国〔國〕土 guótǔ; 国家 guójiā. **'~lady** 女房东〔東〕nǚ fángdōng; 女店主 nǚ diànzhǔ. **'~locked,** *adj* 内陆〔陸〕国家 nèilù guójiā. **'~lord,** **(a)** 房东 fángdōng. **(b)** (旅馆、酒店的)店主 diànzhǔ; 经〔經〕理 jīnglǐ. **'~mark, (a)** 界标〔標〕jièbiāo. **(b)** [喻]重大事件 zhòngdà shìjiàn. **'~owner** 土地所有者 tǔdì suǒyǒuzhě. **'~slide** 山崩 shānbēng; 塌方 tāfāng.

land² /lænd/ *vt/i* **1** 上岸 shàng'àn, 登陆〔陸〕dēnglù; 着陆 zhuólù. ~ *on one's feet* [喻]幸运〔運〕xìngyùn. **2** ~ *in* 处〔處〕于困难〔難〕中 chù yú kùnnàn zhōng. ~ *up* [非正式用语] 最后〔後〕落得 zuìhòu luòde: ~ *up in jail* 结果入狱. **3** 获〔獲〕得 huòdé: ~ *a good job* 找到好工作. **~ed** *adj* 有地的 yǒudìde; 不动〔動〕产〔產〕的 búdòngchǎnde.

land·ing/ˈlændɪŋ/*n* [C] **1** 登陆〔陸〕dēnglù; 着陆 zhuólù: *a crash-~* 紧急着陆. **2** 楼〔樓〕梯平台 lóutī píngtái. **'~-craft** 登陆艇 dēnglùtǐng. **'~-gear** (飞机)起落装〔裝〕置 qǐluò zhuāngzhì; 起落架 qǐluòjià. **'~-stage** 浮动〔動〕码〔碼〕头〔頭〕fúdòng mǎtóu.

land·scape /ˈlændskeɪp/ *n* **1** [C] 风〔風〕景 fēngjǐng; 景色 jǐngsè **2** [U] 风景画〔畫〕fēngjǐnghuà.

lane /leɪn/ *n* [C] **1** 小径〔徑〕xiǎojìng; 小路 xiǎolù. **2** 巷 xiàng. **3** 行车〔車〕道 xíngchēdào: *a three-~ motorway* 有三条车道的高速公路. **4** 航线〔線〕hángxiàn; 航道 hángdào.

lan·guage /'læŋgwɪdʒ/ *n* **1** [U] 语言 yǔyán. **2** [C] 一个〔個〕国〔國〕家或种〔種〕族的语言 yígè guójiā huò zhǒngzú de yǔyán: *the English ~* 英语. **3** [U] 专〔專〕门〔門〕术〔術〕语 zhuānmén shùyǔ: *the ~ of computers* 电子计算机用语. **4** 〔喻〕(感情的表示): *the ~ of love* 爱情的表示 **'~laboratory** 语言试验〔驗〕室 yǔyán shìyànshì.

lan·guid /'læŋgwɪd/ *adj* 没精打采〔彩〕的 méi jīng dǎ cǎi de; 倦怠的 juàndàide. **~ly** *adv*

lan·guish /'læŋgwɪʃ/ *vi* 变〔變〕得衰弱无〔無〕力 biànde shuāiruò wúlì de: *~ in jail* 在狱中折磨得衰弱无力.

lank /læŋk/ *adj* **1** (指头发)平直的 píngzhíde. **2** (指人)瘦长〔長〕的 shòuchángde.

lanky /'læŋkɪ/ *adj* [-ier, -iest] 瘦长〔長〕的 shòuchángde.

lan·tern /'læntən/ *n* [C] 灯〔燈〕笼〔籠〕dēnglóng; 提灯 tídēng.

lap[1] /læp/ *n* [C] (跑道的)一圈 yìquān. □ *vt* [-pp-] (赛跑中)比(某人)领先一圈 bǐ ... lǐngxiān yìquān.

lap[2] /læp/ *n* [C] (人坐着时)腰以下及大腿的前面部分 yāo yǐxià jí dàtuǐde qiánmiàn bùfen: *sitting with the baby on her ~* 她把婴儿抱在怀里坐着.

lap[3] /læp/ *vt/i* [-pp-] **1** *~ up* 舔 tiǎn. **2** *~up* 〔喻〕贪婪地喝或吃 tānlánde hē huò chī: *~ up praise* 爱听恭维. **3** (指水)轻〔輕〕拍 qīngpāi; 拍打 pādǎ. □ *n* [C] 舔 tiǎn; 水的轻拍声〔聲〕shuǐ de qīngpāishēng: *the ~ of waves* 波浪拍打声.

la·pel /lə'pel/ *n* [C] (西服上衣的)翻领 fānlǐng.

lapse /læps/ *n* [C] **1** 小错 xiǎocuò; 记错 jìcuò. **2** (指时间)流逝 liúshì; 间〔間〕歇 jiànxiē. **3** (法律)权〔權〕利终止 quánlì zhōngzhǐ; 权利失效 quánlì shīxiào. □ *vi* **1** *~* ***from*** (或 ***into***) 失足 shīzú; 堕落 duòluò. **2** (指时间)流逝 liúshì. **3** (指权利)终止 zhōngzhǐ; 失效 shīxiào.

lar·ceny /'lɑːsənɪ/ *n* [*pl* -ies] [C, U] 偷窃〔竊〕tōuqiè.

larch /lɑːtʃ/ *n* **1** [C] 落叶〔葉〕松 luòyèsōng. **2** [U] 落叶松木 luòyèsōngmù.

lard /lɑːd/ *n* [U] 猪油 zhūyóu. □ *vt* 涂〔塗〕猪油于 tú zhūyóu yú.

lar·der /'lɑːdə(r)/ *n* [C] 食橱 shíchú; 食物贮藏室 shíwù chǔcángshì.

large /lɑːdʒ/ *adj* [-r, -st] 大的 dàde, 巨大的 jùdàde. □ *n* [仅用于] ***at ~***, **(a)** 自由的 zìyóude. **(b)** 一般的 yìbānde: *the people at ~* 一般人民. □ *adv* ***by and ~***, ⇨ by[1] (2). **'~-scale** *adj* **(a)** 大规模的 dàguīmóde: *~-scale changes* 大规模变化. **(b)** 大比例尺绘〔繪〕制〔製〕的 dà bǐlìchǐ huìzhì de. **~ly** *adv* 大部分 dàbùfen. **~ness** *n* [U]

lark[1] /lɑːk/ *n* [C] 小鸣〔鳴〕禽(如云雀) xiǎomíngqín.

lark[2] /lɑːk/ *n* [C] 嬉戏〔戲〕xīxì; 欢〔歡〕乐〔樂〕huānlè. □ *vi* ***~ about*** 嬉戏 xīxì, 开〔開〕玩笑 kāi wánxiào.

larva /'lɑːvə/ *n* [C] [*pl* ~e/-viː/] 昆虫〔蟲〕的幼虫 kūnchóngde yòuchóng.

lar·yn·gi·tis /ˌlærɪn'dʒaɪtɪs/ *n* [U] 喉炎 hóuyán.

lar·ynx /'lærɪŋks/ *n* [C] 喉 hóu.

las·civ·ious /lə'sɪvɪəs/ *adj* 〔正式用语〕淫荡〔蕩〕的 yíndàngde; 猥亵〔褻〕的 wěixiède.

laser /'leɪzə(r)/ *n* [C] 激光 jīguāng; 激光器 jīguāngqì.

lash[1] /læʃ/ *n* [C] **1** 鞭子 biānzi; 鞭打 biāndǎ. **2** = eyelash.

lash[2] /læʃ/ *vt/i* **1** 鞭打 biāndǎ; 猛击〔擊〕měngjī. **2** *~* ***out (against, at)*** 猛打 měngdǎ; 痛斥 tòngchì. **3** 用绳〔繩〕等绑紧〔緊〕yòng shéng děng bǎngjǐn.

lash·ing /'læʃɪŋ/ *n* **1** [C] 捆绑用的绳〔繩〕子 kǔnbǎng yòng de shéngzi. **2** [C] 鞭打 biāndǎ. **3** [*pl*] 〔非正式用语〕许多 xǔduō: *~s of cream* 许多奶油.

lass /læs/ *n* [C] 〔非正式用语〕少女 shàonǚ, 小姑娘 xiǎogūniáng.

lasso /læ'suː/ *n* [C] [*pl* ~s, ~es] 套索 tàosuǒ. □ *vt* 用套索捕捉 yòng tàosuǒ bǔzhuō.

last[1] /lɑːst/ *adj, adv* **1** (与 *first* 相对; ⇨ late) 最后〔後〕的 zuìhòude; 最后地 zuìhòude: *the ~ Sunday in June* 六月的最后一个星期日. ***have the ~ word***, ⇨ word(2). **2** (与 *next* 相对) 刚〔剛〕过〔過〕去的 gāng guòqù de: *~ night* 昨夜. **3** 仅〔僅〕余〔餘〕的 jǐnyúde: *our ~ hope* 我们唯一的希望. □ *n* **the ~** 最后的人或事物 zuìhòude rén huò shìwù. ***at (long) ~*** 最后 zuìhòu; 终于 zhōngyú. **~ly** *adv* 最后 zuìhòu.

last[2] /lɑːst/ *vi* 继〔繼〕续〔續〕jìxù

持久 chíjiǔ. ~**ing** *adj* 持的久 chíjiǔde.

Lat.=Latin.

lat.=latitude.

latch /lætʃ/ *n* [C] 门[門]闩[閂] ménshuān. □ *vt/i* **1** 用门闩栓住 yòng ménshuān shuānzhù. **2** ~ *on (to)* [非正式用语]理解 lǐjiě.

late /leɪt/ *adj* [-r, -st], *adv* ⇨ last¹, latter. **1** (与 *early* 相对) 迟[遲]的 chíde; 迟 chí: *The train is ~.* 火车晚点. **2** 晚的 wǎnde: *in the ~ afternoon* 在下午晚些时候. **3** 近来[來]的 jìnláide; 近来 jìnlái: *the ~st news* 最新消息. **4** 以前的 yǐqiánde; 前任的 qiánrènde: *the ~ prime minister* 前任首相. **5** 已故的 yǐgùde: *her ~ husband* 她的已故的丈夫. **6** *of ~* 近来 jìnlái. ~**ly** *adv* 最近 zuìjìn.

latent /'leɪtnt/ *adj* 潜[潛]伏的 qiánfúde; 潜在的 qiánzàide: ~ *talent (energy)* 潜能

lat·eral /'lætərəl/ *adj* 侧面的 cèmiànde; 旁边[邊]的 pángbiānde.

lathe /leɪð/ *n* [C] 车[車]床 chēchuáng; 旋床 xuànchuáng.

lather /'lɑːðə(r)/ *n* [U] (肥皂) 泡沫 pàomò. □ *vt/i* 涂[塗]以皂沫 tú yǐ zàomò.

Latin /'lætɪn/ *adj, n* 拉丁文的 Lādīngwénde; 拉丁文 Lādīngwén.

lati·tude /'lætɪtjuːd/ *n* **1** [C] 纬[緯]度 wěidù. **2** [*pl*] 地区[區] dìqū. **3** [U] (言论、行动的) 自由 zìyóu.

la·trine /lə'triːn/ *n* [C] 厕所 cèsuǒ.

lat·ter /'lætə(r)/ *adj* **1** 近来[來]的 jìnláide; 末尾的 mòwěide: *the ~ part of his life* 他的晚年. **2** *the ~* 后[後]者 hòuzhě. ⇨ former. '~-**day** *adj* 现今的 xiànjīnde. ~**ly** *adv* 近来 jìnlái.

lat·tice /'lætɪs/ *n* [C] (板条制成的) 格子架 gézhijià.

laugh /lɑːf/ *vt/i* 笑 xiào; 发[發]笑 fāxiào. ~ *at* 因…有趣而发笑 yīn … yǒuqù ér fāxiào. **(b)** 嘲笑 cháoxiào. □ *n* [C] 笑 xiào; 笑声[聲] xiàoshēng. *have the last ~* 笑在最后[後], 获[獲]得最后胜[勝]利 xiào zài zuìhòu, huòdé zuìhòu shènglì. ~**able** /-əbl/ *adj* 可笑的 kěxiàode; 有趣的 yǒuqùde. ~**ably** *adv* ~**ter** *n* [U] 笑 xiào.

launch¹ /lɔːntʃ/ *vt/i* **1** 使 (船) 下水 shǐ xiàshuǐ; 发[發]射 (火箭) fāshè. **2** 开[開]始 kāishǐ; 开办[辦] kāibàn: ~ *an attack* 发动进攻. ~ *a new business* 创办新企业. **4** ~ *(out) into* 开始新的事情 kāishǐ xīnde shìqing: ~ *into an argument* 开始辩论. □ *n* [C] (船) 下水 xiàshuǐ. '~**ing-pad** (火箭等的) 发射台 fāshètái.

launch² /lɔːntʃ/ *n* [C] 汽艇 qìtǐng; 游艇 yóutǐng.

laun·der /'lɔːndə(r)/ *vt/i* 洗熨 (衣服) xǐ yùn.

laun·der·ette /ˌlɔːn'dret/ *n* [C] (设有自动洗衣机的) 洗衣店 xǐyīdiàn.

laun·dry /'lɔːndrɪ/*n* [*pl* -ies] **1** [C] 洗衣店 xǐyīdiàn. **2** *the ~* 所洗的衣物 suǒxǐde yīwù; 待洗的衣物 dàixǐde yīwù.

laurel /'lɒrəl/ *n* [C] 月桂树[樹] yuèguìshù. *look to one's ~s* 小心地保持已得的荣[榮]誉[譽] xiǎoxīnde bǎochí yǐdé de róngyù. *rest on one's ~s* 满足于已有的成就 mǎnzú yú yǐyǒude chéngjiù.

lava /'lɑːvə/ *n* [U] 熔岩 róngyán.

lava·tory /'lævətrɪ/ *n* [C[[*pl* -ies] 盥洗室 guànxǐshì; 厕所 cèsuǒ.

lav·en·der /'lævɪndə(r)/ *adj, n* [U] 薰衣草 xūnyīcǎo; 淡紫色 dànzǐsè; 淡紫色的 dànzǐsède.

lav·ish /'lævɪʃ/ *adj* **1** 慷慨的 kāngkǎide. **2** 过[過]度的 guòdùde; 大量的 dàliàngde: ~ *praise* 大肆吹捧. □ *vt* 慷慨地给予 kāngkǎide gěiyǔ. ~**ly** *adv*

law /lɔː/ *n* **1** [C] 法律 fǎlǜ. **2** *the ~* 法学[學] fǎxué: *study ~* 学法律; *obey the ~* 遵守法律. *ˌlay down the '~* 发[發]号[號]施令 fāhào shīlìng. **3** [U] ˌ~ *and 'order* 治安 zhì'ān. **4** (亦作 ~ *of nature* or *natural ~*) 自然法则 zìrán fǎzé: *the ~ of gravity* 地心引力定律. '~-**abiding** *adj* 守法的 shǒufǎde. '~**court** 法庭 fǎtíng, 法院 fǎyuàn. '~**suit** 诉讼 (案件) sùsòng. ~**ful** *adj* **(a)** 合法的 héfǎde. **(b)** 法定的 fǎdìngde. ~**fully** *adv* ~**less** *adj* 没有法律的 méiyǒu fǎlǜ de; 非法的 fēifǎde. ~**less·ness** *n* [U]

lawn¹ /lɔːn/ *n* [C] 草地 cǎodì, 草坪 cǎopíng. '~-**mower** 割草机[機] gēcǎojī. ˌ~'**tennis** 草地网[網]球 cǎodì wǎngqiú.

lawn² /lɔːn/ *n* [U] 上等细布 shàngděng xìbù; 上等细麻布 shàngděng xìmábù.

law·yer /'lɔːjə(r)/ *n* [C] 律师[師] lǜshī; 法学[學]家 fǎxuéjiā.

lax /læks/ *adj* 疏忽的 shūhude; 不严[嚴]格的 bù yángéde. ~**ity** *n* [C, U]

laxa·tive /'læksətɪv/ *n* [C], *adj* 轻

〔輕〕泻〔瀉〕剂〔劑〕qīngxièjì; 缓泻的 huǎnxiède.

lay¹ /leɪ/ *adj* **1** 凡俗的 fánsúde, 世俗的 shìsúde. ⇨ laity. **2** 外行的 wàihángde; 非专〔專〕业〔業〕性的 fēi zhuānyèxìng de. '**~man** 俗人 súrén; 外行 wàiháng.

lay² /leɪ/ *vt/i* [*pt, pp* laid/leɪd/] **1** 放 fàng, 放置 fàngzhì: ~ *a book on the table* 把书放在桌上. **2** ~ ***the blame (for sth) on sb*** 责怪某人 zéguài mǒurén. ~ ***sb to rest*** 埋葬 máizàng. **3** ~ ***sth bare*** 显〔顯〕示 xiǎnshì; 表露 biǎolù: ~ *bare one's feelings* 表露感情. ***be laid low*** 卧病在床 wòbìng zàichuáng. ~ ***oneself open to sth*** 使自己遭到(责难等) shǐ zìjǐ zāodào. ~ ***waste*** 损毁 sǔnhuǐ; 蹂躏〔躪〕róulìn. **4** 沉降 chénjiàng: ~ *dust with water* 洒水除尘. **5** 安置 ānzhì; 布〔佈〕置 bùzhì: ~ *the table* (饭前)摆好餐具. **6** 下蛋 xiàdàn. **7** ~ ***sth aside,*** **(a)** 储蓄(金钱) chǔxù. **(b)** 放下 fàngxià: ~ *a book aside* 放下书. ~ ***down one's life*** 献〔獻〕出生命 xiànchū shēngmìng. ~ ***into sb,*** **(a)** 攻击〔擊〕gōngjī. **(b)** 责骂〔罵〕zémà. ~ ***off*** [非正式用语] 停止工作或活动〔動〕tíngzhǐ gōngzuò huò huódòng; 休息 xiūxi: ~ *off for a week* 休假一周. *L~ off insulting him!* 不要侮辱他! ~ ***sb off*** (暂时)解雇〔僱〕jiěgù. '**~-off** *n* [C] ~ ***sth on,*** **(a)** 安装〔裝〕(水, 电, 煤气等) ānzhuāng. **(b)** [非正式用语] 提供 (食物, 运输等) tígòng. ~ ***sth out,*** **(a)** 展示 zhǎnshì; 摆〔擺〕开〔開〕bǎikāi. **(b)** 布〔佈〕置 bùzhì; 设计 shèjì. '**~-out** *n* [C] 布置 bùzhì; 设计 shèjì: *the ~-out of the factory* 工厂的布局. ***be laid up*** 被迫卧床 bèipò wòchuáng.

lay·about /'leɪəbaʊt/ *n* [C] [俚语] 不务〔務〕正业〔業〕的人 búwù zhèngyè de rén.

lay·by /'leɪbaɪ/ *n* [C] 路旁停车〔車〕场〔場〕lùpáng tíngchēchǎng.

layer /'leɪə(r)/ *n* [C] 层〔層〕céng.

lay·man ⇨ lay¹.

laze /leɪz/ *vt/i* 懒散 lǎnsǎn; 混日子 hùn rìzi.

lazy /'leɪzɪ/ *adj* [-ier, -iest] 懒惰的 lǎnduòde; 怠惰的 dàiduòde; 令人懒散的 lìng rén lǎnsǎn de. ⇨ idle. '**~-bones** 懒人 lǎnrén; 懒骨头〔頭〕lǎngǔtóu. **lazi·ly** *adv* **lazi·ness** *n* [U]

lb. = pound(s) in weight.

lead¹ /led/ *n* **1** [U] 铅 **(Pb)** qiān; 铅色 qiānsè. **2** [U] 石墨 shímò; 黑铅 hēiqiān. **3** [C] 铅锤 qiānchuí; 测锤 cèchuí. **~en** *adj* **(a)** 铅制〔製〕的 qiānzhìde. **(b)** 铅色的 qiānsède. **(c)** 沉重的 chénzhòngde.

lead² /li:d/ *n* **1** [*sing* 与 *the* 或 *a, an* 连用] 领导〔導〕lǐngdǎo; 率领 shuàilǐng; 指挥〔揮〕zhǐhuī. **2** [与 *the* 连用] 领先 lǐngxiān; [与 *a, an* 连用] 领先的距离〔離〕lǐngxiānde jùlí; *a ~ of 10 metres* 领先十米. **3** [C] 牵〔牽〕狗的绳〔繩〕索或链〔鏈〕子 qiāngǒude shéngsuǒ huò liànzi. **4** 电缆〔纜〕diànlǎn.

lead³ /li:d/ *vt/i* [*pt, pp* led /led/] **1** 引导〔導〕yǐndǎo. ~ ***the way (to)*** 引路 yǐnlù; 带〔帶〕路 dàilù. **2** 搀〔攙〕chān; 牵〔牽〕qiān: ~ *a blind man.* 搀扶一位盲人. ~ ***sb astray*** [喻]将〔將〕某人引入歧途 jiāng mǒurén yǐnrù qítú. **3** 领导 lǐngdǎo; 率领 shuàilǐng; 指挥〔揮〕zhǐhuī: ~ *a team of scientists* 率领一组科学家. **4** 领先 lǐngxiān: ~ *the race* 赛跑领先. **5** 影响〔響〕yǐnxiǎng: ~ *him to believe that* 使他相信… **6** 通 tōng; 达〔達〕dá: *Where does this road ~?* 这条路通往哪儿? **7** [喻]导致某种〔種〕结果 dǎozhì mǒuzhǒng jiéguǒ: *The plan led to confusion.* 这个计划导致混乱. ~ ***up to*** 作为〔爲〕…的准〔準〕备〔備〕zuòwéi … de zhǔnbèi. **8** 过〔過〕(生活等) guò: ~ *a miserable existence* 生活困苦. **~er** *n* [C] **(a)** 领导 lǐngdǎo: 领袖 lǐngxiù. **(b)** (报纸的)社论〔論〕shèlùn. **~er·ship** 领导 lǐngdǎo; 领导能力 lǐngdǎo nénglì. **~ing** *adj* 最主要的 zuìzhǔyàode. ,**~ing 'article** (报纸的)社论 shèlùn. ,**~ing 'question** 诱导性的提问〔問〕yòudǎoxìngde tíwèn.

leaf /li:f/ *n* [C] [*pl* leaves /li:vz/] **1** 叶〔葉〕yè; 叶子 yèzi. **2** (书刊等的)一张〔張〕(即正反两页) yì zhāng. ***turn over a ,new '~*** [喻] 改过〔過〕自新 gǎiguò zìxīn. **3** (支起来可增大桌面的) 活动〔動〕桌板 huódòng zhuōbǎn. **4** [U] 箔 bó: *gold ~* 金箔. **leafy** *adj* [-ier, -iest]

leaf·let /'li:flɪt/ *n* [C] 散页〔葉〕的印刷品 sǎnyède yìnshuāpǐn; 传〔傳〕单 chuándān.

league /li:g/ *n* [C] **1** 同盟 tóngméng; 联〔聯〕盟 liánméng; 盟约 méngyuē. ***in ~ with*** 与〔與〕…联盟 yǔ … liánméng; 和…联合 hé … liánhé. **2** (运动等) 竞〔競〕赛联合会〔會〕jìngsài liánhéhuì; 社团〔團〕shètuán: *the Football L~* 足

球联合会. □ *vt/i* 结盟 jiéméng; 联合 liánhé.

leak /li:k/ *n* [C] **1** 漏洞 lòudòng; 漏隙 lòuxì **2** [喻]泄漏 xièlòu: *a security* ~ 治安上的漏洞. □ *vt/i* **1** 漏 lòu. **2** (指秘密等)泄漏 xièlòu. '~**age** *n* [C, U] 漏 lòu; 泄漏 xièlòu. **leaky** *adj* [-ier, -iest].

lean[1] /li:n/ *adj* [-er, -est] **1** (指人和动物)瘦的 shòude; (指肉)无[無]脂肪的 wú zhīfáng de. **2** 贫乏的 pínfáde: *a* ~ *harvest* 歉收. □ *n* [U] 瘦肉 shòuròu. ~**ness** *n* [U]

lean[2] /li:n/ *vt/i* [*pt, pp* ~ed 或 ~t /lent/] **1** 倾斜 qīngxié: *Do not* ~ *out of the window.* 身子不要探出窗外. **2** ~ ***on*** (或 ***upon***) ***sth*** 倚 yǐ; 靠 kào. **3** 使倚靠 shǐ yǐkào; ~ *the ladder against the wall* 把梯子靠在墙上. **4** ~ ***towards*** 倾向 qīngxiàng. **5** ~ ***on*** (或 ***upon***) ***sb*** 依靠 yīkào. ~**ing** *n* [C] 倾向 qīngxiàng: *He has socialist* ~*ings.* 他倾向社会主义.

leap /li:p/ *vt/i* [*pt, pp* ~ed 或 ~t /lept/] = jump (普通用语). ~ ***at*** [喻]扑[撲]向 pūxiàng; 欣然接受 xīnrán jiēshòu: ~ *at an offer* 欣然接受建议. □ *n* [C] 跳 tiào; 跃[躍] yuè. '~-**frog** *n* [U] 跳背游戏[戲]tiàobèi yóuxì. □*vt*[-gg-] (蛙跳般地)跃过[過] yuèguò. '~ **year** 闰[閏]年 rùnnián.

learn /lɜ:n/ *vt/i* [*pt, pp* ~t /lɜ:nt/, ~ed] **1** 学[學] xué; 学习[習] xuéxí: ~ *French* 学法语; ~ *how to swim.* 学游泳. ~ ***sth by heart***, ⇨ heart(2). **2** 获[獲]悉 huòxī: *I* ~ *you're leaving us.* 我听说你要离开我们. ~**ed** /'lɜ:nɪd/ *adj* 有学问[問]的 yǒu xuéwèn de. ~**ing** *n* [U] 学问 xuéwèn; 知识[識] zhīshi.

lease /li:s/ *n* [C] (土地或房屋的)租约(租金称 *rent*) zūyuē. ***a* ˌ*new* ~ *of* '*life*** 重生 chóngshēng; 富于希望的新生 fùyú xīwàng de xīnshēng. □ *vt* 出租(土地等) chūzū; 租得 zūdé. '~**hold** *n* [U] *adj* 租借的 zūjiède. ⇨ freehold. '~**holder** 租借人 zūjièrén.

leash /li:ʃ/ *n* [C] = lead[2](3).

least /li:st/ *adj, n* [U] (与 *most* 相对; ⇨ less, little) 最小的 zuìxiǎode; 最少的 zuìshǎode. ***at*** ~ 至少 zhìshǎo: *at* ~ *five pounds* 至少五英镑. □ *adv* 最小 zuìxiǎo; 最少 zuìshǎo.

leather /'leðə(r)/ *n* [U] 皮革 pígé; 皮革制品 pígé zhìpǐn. **leathery** *adj* 似皮革的 sìpígéde.

leave[1] /li:v/ *vt/i* [*pt, pp* left /left/] **1** 离[離]开[開] líkāi: ~ *home* 离家. ~ ***for*** 动身去(某地) dòngshēn qù: *He left for Rome.* 他去罗马了. **2** 遗忘 yíwàng; 丢下 diūxià: *I left my books on the table.* 我把书忘在桌上了. ~ ***sb*** (或 ***sth***) ***behind*** 忘带[帶] wàngdài **3** 保持一定状[狀]态[態] bǎochí yídìng zhuàngtài: *Who left that window open?* 谁让窗户开着的? ~ ***sb*** (或 ***sth***) ***alone*** 不干涉某人(或某事) bù gānshè mǒurén. ~ ***off*** (使)停止 tíngzhǐ: ~ *off work for a while* 暂时停工. ~ ***sth*** (或 ***sb***) ***out*** 遗漏 yílòu. **4** 留下 liúxià; 剩下 shèngxià: *Three from seven* ~*s four.* 七减三剩四. **5** 委托 wěituō; 交给 jiāogěi: ~ *somebody in charge* 委托某人负责. **6** 遗赠 yízèng.

leave[2] /li:v/ *n* **1** [U] 许可 xǔkě. ***on*** ~ 休假 xiūjià. **2** [C] 假期 jiàqī; 休假 xiūjià. **3** ***take*** (***one's***) ~ (***of sb***) [正式用语]告别 gàobié.

leaves /li:vz/ *pl* of leaf.

lec·tern /'lektən/ *n* [C] (教堂中的)读[讀]经[經]台[臺] dújīngtái; 讲[講]台[臺] jiǎngtái.

lec·ture /'lektʃə(r)/ *n* [C] 讲[講]课 jiǎngkè; 演讲 yǎnjiǎng. □ *vt/i* **1** 讲课 jiǎngkè; 演讲 yǎnjiǎng. **2** 责骂[罵] zémà; 训斥 xùnchì. **lecturer** 讲师[師] jiǎngshī. ~**ship** 讲师的职[職]位 jiǎngshīde zhíwèi.

led /led/ *pt, pp* of lead[3].

ledge /ledʒ/ *n* [C] (自墙壁突出的)壁架 bìjià; 架状[狀]突出物 jiàzhuàng tūchūwù.

ledger /'ledʒə(r)/ *n* [C] 分类[類]帐[帳] fēnlèizhàng.

lee /li:/ *n* [C, U] 避风[風]处[處] bìfēngchù; 下风 xiàfēng. □ *adj* 避风处的 bìfēngchùde; 下风的 xiàfēngde.

leech /li:tʃ/ *n* [C] **1** 水蛭 shuǐzhì. **2** [喻]吸血鬼 xīxuěguǐ; 榨取他人脂膏者 zhàqǔ tārén zhīgāo zhě.

leek /li:k/ *n* [C] 韭[韮] jiǔ.

leer /lɪə(r)/ *n* [U] 斜眼一瞥(表示敌意等) xiéyǎn yìpiē. □ *vi* 斜眼看 xiéyǎn kàn.

left[1] *pt, pp* of leave.

left[2] /left/ *adj* **1** (与 *right* 相对) 左边[邊]的 zuǒbiānde; 左侧的 zuǒcède. **2** [政治]左翼的 zuǒyìde. □ *adv* 向左 xiàngzuǒ; 在左边 zài zuǒbian. □ *n* [U] **1** 左边 zuǒbiān; 左方 zuǒfāng. **2 the L**~ [政治] ⇨ the L~ (Wing) below. ˌ~'**hand** *adj* 左方的 zuǒfāngde; 左边的 zuǒbiānde. ˌ~'**handed**

adj （指人）惯用左手的 guànyòng zuǒshǒu de. **the L~ (Wing)** （政党等的）左翼 zuǒyì. **'~ist** *n* [C] *adj* 左派的人 zuǒpàide rén; 左派的 zuǒpàide.

leg /leg/ *n* [C] **1** 腿 tuǐ. ***pull sb's ~*** 愚弄某人 yúnòng mǒurén. ***not have a ,~ to 'stand on*** 站不住脚 zhàn bú zhù jiǎo. ***stretch one's ~s*** （久坐之后）散散步 sànsànbù. **2** （桌椅等的）腿脚 tuǐjiǎo. ***on its last ~s*** 摇摇欲坠〔墜〕 yáoyáo yù zuì. **3** 一段旅程 yíduàn lǚchéng.

leg·acy /'legəsɪ/ *n* [C] [*pl* -ies] **1** 遗产〔產〕 yíchǎn. **2**〔喻〕后〔後〕果 hòuguǒ; （劫后）残〔殘〕存事物 cáncún shìwù: *Famine was the ~ of the war* 饥荒是战争的遗物.

legal /'li:gl/ *adj* 法律的 fǎlǜde. **,~ 'tender** 法币〔幣〕 fǎbì; 法偿〔償〕 fǎcháng. **~ly** *adv* **~ity** /li:'gæləti/ *n* [C, U] 合法性 héfǎxìng.

legal·ize /'li:gəlaɪz/ *vt* 使合法化 shǐ héfǎhuà ~ *drugs* 使毒品合法化. **legal·iz·ation** /-'zeɪʃən/ *n* [U]

leg·ation /lɪ'geɪʃn/ *n* [C] 公使馆 gōngshǐguǎn; 公使馆全体〔體〕人员 gōngshǐguǎn quántǐ rényuán.

leg·end /'ledʒənd/ *n* **1** [C] 传〔傳〕说 chuánshuō; 传奇 chuánqí, **2** [U] 传奇文学〔學〕 chuánqí wénxué. **3** 地图〔圖〕的图例 dìtúde túlì; 插图的说明 chātúde shuōmíng. **~ary** *adj* 传奇的 chuánqíde; 传说的 chuánshuōde.

leg·ible /'ledʒəbl/ *adj* 易读〔讀〕的 yìdúde; 字迹〔跡〕清楚的 zìjì qīngchude. **leg·ibly** *adv* **legi'bil·ity** *n* [U]

legion /'li:dʒən/ *n* [C] **1** 古罗〔羅〕马〔馬〕军〔軍〕团〔團〕 gǔluómǎ jūntuán. **2** 众〔衆〕多 zhòngduō; 大批 dàpī. **~ary** *n* [C] [*pl* -ies], *adj* 军团的 jūntuánde; 退伍军人协〔協〕会〔會〕的 tuìwǔ jūnrén xiéhuì de.

legis·late /'ledʒɪsleɪt/ *vi* 立法 lìfǎ. **legis'la·tion** *n* [U]

legis·lat·ive /'ledʒɪslətɪv/ *adj* 立法的 lìfǎde: *a ~ assembly* 立法会议.

legis·la·tor /'ledʒɪsleɪtə(r)/ *n* [C] 立法机〔機〕关〔關〕的成员 lìfǎ jīguān de chéngyuán; 议〔議〕员 yìyuán.

legis·la·ture /'ledʒɪsleɪtʃə(r)/ *n* [C] 立法机〔機〕关〔關〕 lìfǎ jīguān.

le·git·imate/lɪ'dʒɪtɪmət/ *adj* **1** 合法的 héfǎde. **2** 由合法婚姻所生的 yóu héfǎ hūnyīn suǒshēng de. **~ly** *adv* **le·git·imacy** *n* [U]

lei·sure /'leʒə(r)/ *n* [U] 空闲〔閑〕 kòngxián, 闲暇 xiánxiá. **~ly** *adv* 从〔從〕容地 cóngróngde. □ *adj* 从容的 cóngróngde: *a ~ly walk* 漫步.

lemon /'lemən/ *n* [C] 柠〔檸〕檬树〔樹〕 níngméngshù; [U] 柠檬 níngméng. **~ade** /-'neɪd/ *n* [C,U] 柠檬水 níngméngshuǐ.

lend /lend/ *vt* [*pt, pp* lent/lent/] **1** 借出jièchū; 把…借给 bǎ … jiègěi: *L~ me £5, Peter.* 彼得，借给我五英镑. **2** 贡献〔獻〕 gòngxiàn: *music that ~s gaiety to the party* 给舞会造成了欢乐气氛的音乐. **3 ~ *itself to*** 有助于 yǒuzhùyú; 适〔適〕宜于 shìyíyú.

length /leŋθ/ *n* [C] **1** 长〔長〕cháng, 长度 chángdù. ***at ~,*** **(a)** 最后〔後〕 zuìhòu. **(b)** 长〔長〕时〔時〕间〔間〕地 chángshíjiānde; 详细地 xiángxìde: *speak at (great) ~* 长篇大论. **2** 物体〔體〕的长度 wùtǐde chángdù: *The horse won by a~.* 那马以一马身之差获胜. **3** 极〔極〕端行动〔動〕 jíduān xíngdòng: *go to any ~s to win* 竭尽全力取胜. **4** （一）段 duàn: *a 'dress ~* 一段衣料. **~en** *vt/i* 使延长 shǐ yáncháng; 变〔變〕长 biàncháng. **'~-wise** /-waɪz/, **'~ways** /-weɪz/ *adv, adj* 纵〔縱〕长地（的） zòngchángde. **lengthy** *adj* [-ier, -iest] 冗长的 rǒngchángde.

leni·ent /'li:nɪənt/ *adj* 宽大的 kuāndàde; 宽厚的 kuānhòude. **~ly** *adv* **leni·ency** *n* [U]

lens /lenz/ *n* [C] [*pl*~es] **1** 透镜 tòujìng **2** （眼球的）水晶体〔體〕 shuǐjīngtǐ.

lent /lent/ *pt, pp* of lend.

Lent /lent/ *n* （基督教）四旬斋〔齋〕 sìxúnzhāi.

len·til /'lentl/ *n* [C] 扁豆 biǎndòu

leop·ard /'lepəd/ *n* [C] 豹 bào **~ess** /-'des/ *n* [C] 母豹 mǔbào

leper /'lepə(r)/ *n* [C] 麻风〔風〕病患者 máfēngbìng huànzhě.

lep·rosy /'leprəsɪ/ *n* [U] 麻风〔風〕 máfēng. **lep·rous** /'leprəs/ *adj* 患麻风的 huàn máfēngde.

les·bian /'lezbɪən/ *n* [C] 搞同性爱〔愛〕的女子 gǎo tóngxìng'ài de nǚzi.

lesion /'li:ʒn/ *n* [C] 损伤〔傷〕 sǔnshāng.

less /les/ *adj* （与 *more* 相对） 较〔較〕少的 jiàoshǎode; 更少的 gèngshǎode: ~ *butter* 较少的黄油. □ *adv* **1** 较少地 jiàoshǎode 更少地 gèngshǎode: *Eat ~ and sleep more.* 少吃，多睡. **2** 不如 b rú: *Tom is ~ clever than me.* 汤姆不如我聪明. **3** ***none the ~*** 依然 yīrán; 仍然 réngrán: *Though he cannot go out, he is none the ~ busy.* 他虽然不能出去，但他仍然很忙. □ *n* [U] 较少的数〔數〕量、时〔時〕间〔間〕 jiàoshǎode shùliàng, shíjiān: *in ~ than an hour.* 不到一小时. □ *prep* 减去 jiǎnqù: *£50 a week ~ £10 for the rent.* 每周五十英镑减去十英镑租金.

les·sen /'lesn/ *vt/i* 减少 jiǎnshǎo; 变〔變〕少 biànshǎo.

les·ser /'lesə(r)/ *adj* 较〔較〕小的 jiàoxiǎode; 更少的 gèngshǎode: *choose the ~ evil* 两害取其轻.

les·son /'lesn/ *n* [C] **1** 课程 kèchéng; 功课 gōngkè. **2** 教训 jiàoxùn: *His death was a ~ to us.* 他的死对我们是个教训. **3** [宗教] 日课(礼拜时的《圣经》选读) rìkè.

lest /lest/ *conj* [过时用法][用于 be afraid, anxious 之后,起连接从句的作用,并无实际意思]: *afraid ~ he arrive late* 恐怕他会晚到.

let /let/ *vt/i* [*pt, pp* ~] [-tt-] **1** 允许 yúnxǔ; 让〔讓〕ràng: *We ~ him leave.* 我们让他走了. ~ ***oneself go*** 尽〔盡〕情 jìnqíng; 情不自禁 qíng bù zì jìn. ~***sb know*** 告诉某人 gàosù mǒurén. **2** [用于祈使句]: *L~'s go!* 我们走吧! **3** 出租（房屋、土地）chūzū: ~ *one's house* 出租房屋. ~ ***sth down*** 衣服放长 yīfu fàngcháng. ~***sb down*** [喻]使失望 shǐ shīwàng. **'~-down** *n* [C] 失望 shīwàng; 令人失望的事物 lìng rén shīwàng de shìwù. ~ ***sb in for*** 使陷入(困难、艰苦工作等) shǐ xiànrù. ~ ***sb into*** **(*in on*)** 让某人知道 ràng mǒurén zhīdào. ~ ***sb off*** 不惩〔懲〕罚 bù chéngfá. **'~-off** *n* [C] ~ ***sth off*** 放（炮、烟火等）fàng: ~ *off a bomb* 引爆炸弹. ~ ***'on (that)*** [非正式用语] 泄露秘密 xièlù mìmì: *Don't ~ on that you know.* 你不要把知道的秘密泄露出去. ~ ***up*** 減小 jiǎnxiǎo: *The rain began to ~ up.* 雨开始下小了. **'~-up,** *n* [C, U] [非正式用语].

le·thal /'li:θl/ *adj* 致命的 zhìmìngde; 致死的 zhìsǐde:

leth·argy /'leθəʤɪ/ *n* [U] 懒散 lǎnsǎn; 无〔無〕兴〔興〕趣 wú xìngqù. **leth·ar·gic** /lɪ'θɑ:ʤɪk/ *adj*

let's /lets/ = *let us.* ⇨ let¹(2).

let·ter /'letə(r)/ *n* [C] **1** 字母 zìmǔ. **2** 信 xìng; 函件 hánjiàn. **3** [*pl*] 文学〔學〕 wénxué; 学问〔問〕 xuéwèn: *a man of ~s* 文人. **'~-box** **(a)** 信箱 xìnxiāng. **(b)** 邮筒 yóutǒng. **~ing** *n* [U] 文字(尤指其字体和大小) wénzì.

let·tuce /'letɪs/ *n* [C, U] 莴〔萵〕苣 wōjù.

leu·ke·mia /lu:'ki:mɪə/ *n* [U] 白血病 báixuèbìng.

level¹ /'levl/ *adj* **1** 水平的 shuǐpíngde; 平的 píngde. **2** 同等的 tóngděngde; 相等的 xiāngděngde: *draw ~ with them* 与他们同等. ***do one's ~ best*** 全力以赴 quánlì yǐ fù. **,~ 'crossing** (铁路等的)平面交叉 píngmiàn jiāochā. **,~-'headed** *adj* 头〔頭〕脑〔腦〕冷静的 tóunǎo lěngjìng de.

level² /'levl/ *n* **1** [C] 水平线〔綫〕 shuǐpíngxiàn; 水平面 shuǐpíngmiàn. **2** 地位 dìwèi; 等级 děngjí; 比率 bǐlǜ: ~ *of pay* 工资等级. ~ *of output* 生产率. **3** ***on the ~*** [非正式用语]坦率 tǎnshuài; 公平 gōngpíng.

level³ /'levl/ *vt/i* [-ll- 美语 -l-] **1** 使成水平 shǐ chéng shuǐpíng. ~ ***off*** (或 ***out***) [喻]把…弄平 bǎ … nòngpíng: *The plane ~led off.* 飞机成水平飞行状态. *The price ~led off.* 物价趋稳. **2** 使地位同等 shǐ dìwèi tóngděng. **3** 把…对〔對〕准〔準〕 bǎ … duìzhǔn. **4** ~ ***with sb*** [非正式用语] 坦率诚实〔實〕地对待 tǎnshuài chéngshí de duìdài.

lever /'li:və(r)/ *n* [C] **1** 杆〔桿〕 gǎn; 杠〔槓〕杆 gànggǎn. **2** [喻]施加影响〔響〕的手段 shījiā yǐngxiǎng de shǒuduàn. □ *vt* 用杠杆移动〔動〕 yòng gànggǎn yídòng: ~ *it into position* 用杠杆将其移入位置. **~age** *n* [U] 杠杆作用 gànggǎn zuòyòng.

levy /'levɪ/ *vt/i* [*pt, pp* -ied] 征〔徵〕收 zhēngshōu; 征税 zhēngshuì: ~ *a tax* 征税. □ *n* [C] [*pl* -ies] 征收 zhēngshōu; 征税 zhēngshuì.

lewd /lu:d/ *adj* 淫荡〔蕩〕的 yíndàngde; 卑劣的 bēiluède: ~ *jokes* 下流的笑话. **~ly** *adv*

lexi·cal /'leksɪkl/ *adj* 词汇〔彙〕的 cíhuìde; 词典的 cídiǎnde. **~ly** *adv*

lexi·cogra·phy /,leksɪ'kɒgrəfɪ/ *n* [U] 词典学〔學〕 cídiǎnxué. **lexi·cogra·pher** *n* [C] 词典编纂者 cídiǎn biānzuǎn zhě.

lia·bil·ity /,laɪə'bɪlətɪ/ *n* [*pl* -ies] **1** [U] 义〔義〕务〔務〕 yìwù; 责任 zérèn. **2** [*pl*] 债务 zhàiwù. **3** [C] [非正式用语]不利 búlì; 阻碍〔礙〕 zǔ'ài: *Those machines are a ~, not an asset.* 这些机器不是得力助手，反而是碍事的.

liable /ˈlaɪəbl/ *adj* **1** 有责任的 yǒuzérèn de; 有义〔義〕务〔務〕的 yǒuyìwù de: ~ *for debts* 负债. **2** *be* ~ *to sth* 易于…的 yìyū … de. **3** *be* ~ *to do sth* 有…倾向的 yǒu … qīngxiàng de.

li·aison /lɪˈeɪzn/ *n* [U] 联〔聯〕络 liánluò.

liar /ˈlaɪə(r)/ *n* [C] 说慌的人 shuōhuǎngde rén.

lib /lɪb/ *n* [非正式用语] liberation 的缩写〔寫〕*liberation* de suōxiě. ,**women's** '~妇〔婦〕女解放 fùnǚ jiěfàng.

li·bel /ˈlaɪbl/ *n* [C, U] 诽谤 fěibàng □ *vt* [-ll-, 美语 -l-] (发表文章等)诽谤 fěibàng. ~**lous** [美语 **-belous**] *adj*

lib·eral /ˈlɪbərəl/ *adj* **1** 慷慨的 kāngkǎide; 大方的 dàfāngde: *a* ~ *supply* 大量的供应. **2** 胸怀〔懷〕宽大 xiōnghuái kuāndà; 无〔無〕偏见的 wú piānjiàn de. **3** (指教育)授与〔與〕广〔廣〕泛的知识〔識〕 shòuyǔ guǎngfànde zhīshì. **4** **L**~(英国等的)自由党〔黨〕的 zìyóudǎngde. □ *n* [C] **1** 自由主义〔義〕者 zìyóuzhǔyìzhě. **2** **L**~自由党党员 zìyóudǎng dǎngyuán. '**L**~ **Party** [英国英语]自由党 zìyóudǎng. ~**ism** /-ɪzəm/ *n* [U] 自由主义 zìyóu zhǔyì. ~**ize** *vt* 使自由主义化 shǐ zìyóu zhǔyì huà.

lib·er·ate /ˈlɪbəreɪt/ *vt* 解放 jiěfàng; 使获〔獲〕自由 shǐ huò zìyóu. **lib·er·ator** *n* [C] 解放者 jiěfàngzhě. **lib·e'r·ation** *n* [U] ⇨ lib.

lib·erty /ˈlɪbətɪ/ *n* [*pl* -ies] **1** [U] 自由 zìyóu; 自由权〔權〕 zìyóuquán. *at* ~ 自由 zìyóu; 闲〔閑〕着 xiánzhe. **2** [C, U] 冒昧 màomèi; 失礼〔禮〕 shīlǐ: *Don't take liberties with a young woman.* 不要对年轻妇女太随便.

li·brar·ian /laɪˈbreərɪən/ *n* [C] 图书馆长〔長〕 túshūguǎnzhǎng.

li·brary /ˈlaɪbrərɪ/ *n* [C] [*pl* -ies] 图〔圖〕书〔書〕馆〔館〕 túshūguǎn.

lice /laɪs/ *n pl* of louse.

li·cence [美语 =**li·cense**] /ˈlaɪsns/ *n* **1** [C, U] 许可 xǔkě; 特许 tèxǔ; 执〔執〕照 zhízhào. **2** [U] 放纵〔縱〕 fàngzòng, 放肆 fàngsì. '**off**-~ 准许出售瓶装〔裝〕酒的执〔執〕照 (不得在店里饮用) zhǔnxǔ chūshòu píngzhuāngjiǔde zhízhào.

li·cense (亦作 **li·cence**)/ˈlaɪsns/ *vt* 许可 xǔkě; 特许 tèxǔ **li·cen·see** /ˌlaɪsənˈsiː/ *n* [C] 领有执〔執〕照者 lǐng yǒu zhízhào zhě.

lick /lɪk/ *vt/i* **1** 舔 tiǎn: *The dog* ~*ed its paw.* 狗舔脚爪. **2** (火焰)卷〔捲〕过〔過〕 juǎnguò; (波浪)轻〔輕〕轻拍打 qīngqīng pāidǎ. **3** [非正式用语]克服 kèfú; □ *n* [C] 舔 tiǎn.

licor·ice /ˈlɪkərɪs/ *n* = liquorice.

lid /lɪd/ *n* [C] **1** 盖子 gàizi: *the* '*teapot* ~ 茶壶盖. **2** = eyelid.

lie[1] /laɪ/ *vi* [*pt, pp* ~d; *pres part* lying], *n* [C] 说谎 shuōhuǎng; 谎言 huǎngyán.

lie[2] /laɪ/ *vi* [*pt* lay /leɪ/; *pp* lain, /leɪn/, *pres part* lying] **1** 躺 tǎng; 平躺 píngtǎng. ~ '*in* 睡懒觉〔覺〕 shuì lǎnjiào. ,~-'**in** *n* ~ **low** [非正式用语] ⇨ low'(1). **2** 位于 wèiyú: *The town* ~*s on the coast.* 这座城镇位于海滨. **3** 处〔處〕于某种〔種〕状〔狀〕态〔態〕 chǔ yú mǒuzhǒng zhuàngtài: *money lying idle* 闲置的钱. **4** 展现 zhǎnxiàn; 伸展 shēnzhǎn: *The valley lay before us.* 山谷展现在我们前面. *see* **(***find out***)** *how the* '*land* ~*s* [喻]了解事情的状况 liǎojiě shìqíngde zhuàngkuàng. **5** (原因、根据等) 在于 zài yú: *The trouble* ~*s in the engine.* 故障发生在发动机. □ *n* [仅用 *sing*] 位置 wèizhì; 状态 zhuàngtài. *the* ~ *of the* '*land,* (a) 地势〔勢〕 dìshì. (b) [喻]情况 qíngkuàng.

lieu /luː/ *n* [仅用于] *in* ~ (*of*) 代替 dàitì.

Lieut., Lt. =Lieutenant.

lieu·ten·ant /lefˈtenənt/ *n* [C] **1** 陆〔陸〕军〔軍〕中尉 lùjūn zhōngwèi; 海军上尉 hǎijūn shàngwèi. **2** 副职〔職〕官员 fùzhí guānyuán; 代理官员 dàilǐ guānyuán.

life /laɪf/ *n* [*pl* lives /laɪvz/] **1** [U] 生命 shēngmìng. **2** [U] 生物 shēngwù: *Is there* ~ *on Mars?* 火星上有生物吗? **3** [U] 人生 rénshēng: *L*~ *is difficult for the poor* 穷人的生活是艰苦的. *come to* ~ 苏〔蘇〕醒过〔過〕来〔來〕 sūxǐng guòlái. **4** [C] 人 rén: *many lives were lost* 许多人丧生. *take sb's* ~ 杀〔殺〕死某人 shāsǐ mǒurén. *Not on your* ~! [非正式用语]绝对〔對〕不! juéduì bù! **5** [C] 一生 yìshēng; 一辈〔輩〕子 yíbèizi: *all my* ~ 我的一生. **6** [U] 社交活动〔動〕 shèjiāo huódòng: *There is not much* ~ *here.* 这里没有很多社交活动. *true to* ~ 逼真的 bīzhēnde. **7** [U] 生活方式 shēnghuó fāngshì: *town* ~ 城市生活方式. **8** [C] 传〔傳〕 zhuànjì. **9** [U] 活力 huólì: *full of* ~ 充满活力. **10** [C] 寿〔壽〕 shòumìng: *the* ~ *of a ship* 船的用年限. '~**belt** 救生带〔帶〕 j shēngdài; 安全带 ānquándài. '~-**boat** 救生艇 jiùshēngtǐng. '~**buoy** 救生圈 jiùshēngquān. '~ **cycle** 生命周期 shēngmìng zhōuqī: *the ~ cycle of a frog* 蛙的生命周期. '~**guard** 救生员 jiùshēngyuán. '~**-jacket** 救生衣 jiùshēngyī. '~**like** *adj* 逼真的 bīzhēnde: *a ~-like painting.* 栩栩如生的绘画. '~**line,** (a) 救生索 jiùshēngsuǒ. (b) [喻]生命源泉 shēngmìng yuánquán. '~**long** *adj* 毕[畢]生的 bìshēngde, 终身的 zhōngshēnde. '~**time** 一生 yìshēng, 终身 zhōngshēn. ~**less** *adj* (a) 无[無]生命的 wú shēngmìng de. (b) 死的 sǐde. (c) 无生气[氣]的 wú shēngqì de. ~**less·ly** *adv*

lift /lɪft/ *vt/i* **1** 举[舉]起 jǔqǐ; 提起 tíqǐ. ~ *off* (宇宙飞船)发[發]射 fāshè. '~**-off** *n* **2** 提高(声音) tígāo: ~ (*up*) *one's voice* 提高嗓门. **3** (指人的心情)变[變]为[爲]更愉快(有希望等) biànwéi gèng yúkuài: *The news ~ed her spirits.* 这条新闻提高了她的情绪. **4** (指云雾 等) 消散 xiāosàn. **5** 解除(封锁、禁令) jiěchú. □ *n* [C] **1** 举起 jǔqǐ; 抬起 táiqǐ. *give sb a ~* 让[讓]某人免费搭车[車] ràng mǒurénmiǎnfèi dāchē. **2** [美语 = *elevator*] 电[電]梯 diàntī.

liga·ment /'lɪgəmənt/ *n* [C] 韧[韌]带[帶] rèndài

light[1] /laɪt/ *adj* [-er, -est] (与 *dark* 相反) **1** (指地方) 明亮的 míngliàngde: *a ~ room* 明亮的房间. **2** 淡色的 dànsède; 浅[淺]色的 qiǎnsède: ˌ~-'*blue* 淡蓝色.

light[2] /laɪt/ *adj* [-er, -est] **1** 轻[輕]的 qīngde; 不重的 búzhòngde. **2** 轻微的 qīngwēide: *a ~ touch* 轻轻一拍. **3** (指啤酒、酒) 清淡的 qīngdànde; (食物)少量的 shǎoliàngde. **4** 不沉睡的 bù chénshuìde. **5**(书籍、音乐)轻松[鬆]的 qīngsōngde. **6** 不重要的 bú zhòngyào de: *a ~ attack of flu* 不严重的流行性感冒. *make ~ of* 轻视 qīngshì. □ *adv* 轻装[裝]地 qīngzhuāngde: *travel ~* 轻装旅行. ˌ~-'**headed** ˏ*adj* (a) 头[頭]昏眼花的 tóuhūn yǎnhuā de. (b) 轻浮的 qīngfúde. ˌ~-'**hearted** *adj* 轻松愉快的 qīngsōng yúkuài de. '~**weight** *n* [C], *adj* (a) 体[體]重在平均重量以下的人(或动物) tǐzhòng zài píngjūn zhòngliàng yǐxià de rén. (b) [非正式用语]无[無]足轻重的人 wú zú qīng-zhòng de rén. ~**ly** *adv* (尤指) *get off ~ly* [非正式用语]避免严[嚴]厉[厲]的惩[懲]罚 bìmiǎn yánlì de chéngfá. ~**ness** *n* [U]

light[3] /laɪt/ *n* (与 *darkness* 相反) **1** [U] 光 guāng; 光线[綫] guāngxiàn: *sun~* 阳光; *day~* 白昼. *in a good (bad)* ~ [喻]给人良好(不好)的印象 gěi rén liánghǎo de yìnxiàng: *describe him in a good ~* 说他的好话. **2** [C] 光源 guāngyuán; 发[發]光体[體] fāguāngtǐ. **3** [C] 火花 huǒhuā; 点[點]火物 diǎnhuǒwù: *Can you give me a ~, please?* 请借个火好吗? **4** [U] 眼睛明亮 yǎnjīng míngliàng. **5** *come/bring sth to ~* 显[顯]露 xiǎnlù; 揭露 jiēlù. *shed* (或 *throw*) *~ on* 使某事清楚明白地显[顯]示出来[來] shǐ mǒushì qīngchu míngbái de xiǎnshì chūlái. *in the ~ of* 根据[據] gēnjù: *in the ~ of this news* 根据这条新闻. **6** [C] 观[觀]点 guāndiǎn; 外观 wàiguān: *see things in a new ~* 用新观点看事物. **7** (绘画的)明亮部分 míngliàng bùfen. ⇨ highlight. '~**house** 灯[燈]塔 dēngtǎ. '~ **pen** *n* 光笔[筆](用于电子显示屏幕上书写勾画的笔状工具) guāngbǐ. '~ **show** *n* (流行歌曲音乐会上所用的) 彩色灯[燈]光效果 cǎisè dēngguāng xiàoguǒ. '~ **year** 光年 guāngnián.

light[4] /laɪt/ *vt/i* [*pt, pp* lit /lɪt/] **1** 点[點]燃 diǎnrán; 点(火) diǎn. **2** 供以光源 gòng yǐ guāngyuán: *a road lit by electricity* 用电灯照明的道路. **3** 使明亮 shǐ míngliàng: *The fire lit up the whole district.* 火光照亮了整个地区. **4** ~ *up,* (a) 开[開](电)灯[燈] kāi dēng. (b) [非正式用语]点[點]香烟[煙] diǎn xiāngyān. **5** ~ *up (with)* (指人的面部或表情)容光焕发[發] róngguāng huànfā.

lighten[1] /'laɪtn/ *vt/i* 减轻[輕] jiǎnqīng; 变[變]轻 biànqīng.

lighten[2] /'laɪtn/ *vt/i* 照亮 zhàoliàng; 发[發]亮 fāliàng.

lighter /'laɪtə(r)/ *n* [C] 打火机[機] dǎhuǒjī.

light·ning /'laɪtnɪŋ/ *n* [U] 闪[閃]电[電] shǎndiàn. '~**-rod** (~**-conductor**) 避雷针 bìléizhēn; 避雷装[裝]置 bìléi zhuāngzhì.

lik·able, like·able /'laɪkəbl/ *adj* 可爱[愛]的 kě'àide; 值得喜欢[歡]的 zhídé xǐhuān de.

like[1] /laɪk/ *adj* 相似的 xiāngsìde; 相同的 xiāngtóngde. ⇨ alike □ *conj* 如同 rútóng; 好象 hǎoxiàng: *She looks ~ her mother (does).* 她看着象她的母亲. □ *n* [C] 同样[樣]的人或事物 tóngyàngde rén huò shìwù: *Music, painting and the ~* 音乐、绘画等等. □ *prep* **1** 象 xiàng, 如 rú: *What is he ~?* 他是怎样的人? **2** ***feel ~*** 想要 xiǎngyào; 心情适〔適〕合 xīnqíng shìhé: *She felt ~ crying.* 她想哭. ***look ~*** 好象 hǎoxiàng; 似乎 sìhū: *It looks ~ rain.* 好象要下雨. **3** 表现出…的特点〔點〕biǎoxiànchū …de tèdiǎn: *just ~ a woman* 就象一个典型的女人. **4** 样〔樣〕子 yàngzi; 方式 fāngshì: *He drinks ~ a fish.* 他大口大口地喝. **5** ~' ***anything*** 〔俚语〕拼命地 pīnmìngde. ˌ~-'**minded** *adj* 志趣相投的 zhìqù xiāngtóu de.

like² /laɪk/ *vt/i* **1** 喜欢〔歡〕xǐhuān; 喜爱〔愛〕xǐ'ài: *Do you ~ fish?* 你爱吃鱼吗? **2** 〔用于否定句〕愿〔願〕意 yuànyì: *I didn't ~ to disturb you.* 我不愿打搅你. **3** ***would (should) ~*** 希望 xīwàng; 想 xiǎng: *She would ~ a cup of tea.* 她想喝一杯茶. **4** 更喜欢 gèng xǐhuān; 宁〔寧〕愿 níngyuàn: *How do you ~ your tea?* 你喜欢喝什么样的茶? □ *n* [*pl*] 〔仅用于〕ˌ**~s and 'dislikes** 好恶〔惡〕hàowù; 爱憎 àizèng.

like·li·hood /'laɪklɪhʊd/ *n* [U] 可能(性) kěnéng.

like·ly /'laɪklɪ/ *adj* [-ier, -iest] 似乎合理的 sìhū hélǐ de; 很可能的 hěn kěnéng de. □ *adv* ***most*** (或 ***very***) ~ 很可能 hěn kěnéng.

liken /'laɪkən/ *vt* ~ ***sth to sth*** 把…比做(拟) bǎ …bǐzuò

like·ness /'laɪknɪs/*n* **1** [C, U] 相象〔像〕xiāngxiàng; 类〔類〕似 lèisì. **2** [C] 复〔複〕制〔製〕品 fùzhìpǐn; 画〔畫〕像 huàxiàng; 照片 zhàopiàn.

like·wise /'laɪkwaɪz/ *adv* 同样〔樣〕地 tóngyàngde; 照样地 zhàoyàngde. □ *conj* 也 yě.

lik·ing /'laɪkɪŋ/ *n* [U] 喜欢〔歡〕xǐhuān; 爱〔愛〕好 ài'hào. ***have a ~ for*** 喜欢 xǐhuān. ***to one's ~*** 合某人的意 hé mǒurén de yì.

li·lac /'laɪlək/ *n* **1** [C] 紫丁香 zǐdīngxiāng. **2** [U] 淡紫色 dànzǐsè.

lilt /lɪlt/ *n* [C] 强节〔節〕奏的生动〔動〕乐〔樂〕曲 qiángjiézòude shēngdòng yuèqǔ. □ *vt/i* 轻〔輕〕快有节〔節〕奏地唱 qīngkuài yǒujiézòude chàng: *a ~ing voice* 轻快的声音. *a ~ing tune* 轻快的曲调.

lily /'lɪlɪ/ *n* [C] [*pl* -ies] 百合 bǎihé; 百合花 bǎihéhuā. ˌ~-'**white** *adj* 纯白的 chúnbáide.

limb /lɪm/ *n* [C] **1** 肢 zhī; 臂 bì; 翼 yì. **2** 大树〔樹〕枝 dà shùzhī.

lim·ber /'lɪmbə(r)/ *vt/i* ~ ***(oneself) up*** 使(肌肉)柔软〔軟〕shǐ … róuruǎn.

limbo /'lɪmbəʊ/ *n* [U] 中间状〔狀〕态〔態〕zhōngjiān zhuàngtài. ***in ~*** 〔非正式用语〕搁〔擱〕置一旁 gēzhì yìpáng: *The plan is in ~ until I decide what to do.* 在我决定做什么以前这一计划被搁置一旁.

lime¹ /laɪm/ *n* [U] 石灰 shíhuī. ***in the ~light*** 引人注目 yǐn rén zhùmù. '~**stone** 石灰石 shíhuīshí.

lime² /laɪm/ *n* [C] (亦作 *linden*) 菩提树〔樹〕pútíshù.

lime³ /laɪm/ *n* [C] 宜母子 yímǔzǐ; 宜母子树〔樹〕yímǔzǐshù.

lim·er·ick /'lɪmərɪk/ *n* [C] 五行打油诗 wǔháng dǎyóushī.

limit¹ /'lɪmɪt/ *n* [C] 界线〔線〕jièxiàn, 界限 jièxiàn. ***within ~s*** 在一定范〔範〕围〔圍〕内 zài yīdìng fàngwéi nèi; 适〔適〕当〔當〕地 shìdāngde: *you are free to spend money, within ~s.* 你在一定范围内可自由地化钱. □ *vt* 限制 xiànzhì; 限定 xiàndìng. ~**ed** *pp* 少的 shǎode; 有限的 yǒuxiànde. ˌ~**a·tion** /-'teɪʃn/ *n* **(a)** [U] 限制 xiànzhì. **(b)** [C] 限制的条〔條〕件、事实〔實〕xiànzhìde tiáojiàn, shìshí; 无〔無〕能 wúnéng.

limou·sine /'lɪməzi:n/ *n* [C] (前后座间用玻璃隔开的) 轿〔轎〕车〔車〕jiàochē.

limp¹ /lɪmp/ *adj* 柔软〔軟〕的 róuruǎnde; 软弱的 ruǎnruòde. ~**ly** *adv* ~**ness** *n* [U]

limp² /lɪmp/ *vt* 跛行 bǒxíng; 蹒跚 pánshān. □ *n* [U] 跛行 bǒxíng.

lim·pet /'lɪmpɪt/ *n* [C] 蝛 qī.

linch·pin /'lɪntʃpɪn/ *n* [C] **1** 车〔車〕辖 chēxiá; 制轮〔輪〕楔 zhìlúnxiē. **2** 〔喻〕能把一个〔個〕组搞在一起的人 néng bǎ yìgèzǔ gǎozài yìqǐ de rén.

lin·den /'lɪndən/ *n* ⇨ lime².

line¹ /laɪn/ *n* [C] **1** 线〔線〕xiàn; 索 suǒ; 绳〔繩〕shéng: *'telephone ~* 电话线路. **2** [C] 线条〔條〕xiàntiáo. **3** [U] (艺术等)线条的使用 xiàntiáode shǐyǒng: *a '~ drawing* 线条画. **4** 皱〔皺〕纹 zhòuwén: *the ~s on his face* 他脸上的皱纹. **5** [*pl*] 外形 wàixíng; 轮〔輪〕廓 lúnkuò. **6** (人或物的)排 pái; 行列 hángliè. ***in ~ for*** 即可得到 jìkědédào. ***stand in ~*** 排成一队〔隊〕páichéng yíduì. **7** 边〔邊〕界 biānjiè; 界线 jièxiàn. ***draw the ~ (at)*** ⇨ draw² (7). **8** 铁〔鐵〕路线 tiělùxiàn; 铁轨〔軌〕tiěguǐ: *The London to Oxford ~* 伦敦至牛津的路线. **9** 运〔運〕输〔輸〕公司 yùns gōngsī: *an 'air* ~ 航空公司. **10** 方向 fāngxiàng; 路线 lùxiàn: *~s of communication* 交通路线. ***in (out of) ~ (with)*** 跟…(不)一致 gēn…yízhì. ***toe the ~*** [喻] ⇨ toe *v* **11** 家系 jiāxì: *the royal ~* 皇家家系. **12** (文字的)一行 yìháng. ***drop sb a ~*** [非正式用语]给某人一短信 gěi mǒurén yì duǎnxìn. **13** 防线 fángxiàn.

line² /laɪn/ *vt/i* **1** 用线[線]标[標]示 yòng xiàn biāoshì; 划[劃]线于 huàxiàn yú. **2** *~* ***up*** 排成行列 páichéng hángliè. ⇨ ~-up. **3** 沿…排列 yán… páiliè: *a road ~d with trees* 两旁有树的道路.

line³ /laɪn/ *vt* **1** 加衬[襯]里[裡]于 jiā chènlǐ yú: *fur-~d gloves* 毛皮里的手套. **2** [喻]填(腰包) tián; 塞(肚皮) sāi. ⇨ lining.

lin·ear /'lɪnɪə(r)/ *adj* **1** 线[綫]的 xiànde; 直线的 zhíxiànde. **2** 长[長]度的 chángdùde: *~ measurement* 长度.

linen /'lɪnɪn/ *n* [U] 亚[亞]麻布 yàmábù; 亚麻布的制[製]品 yàmábùde zhìpǐng.

liner /'laɪnə(r)/ *n* [C] 班机[機] bānjī; 班轮[輪] bānlún.

lines·man /'laɪnzmən/ *n*[C] (球赛中的)巡边[邊]员 xúnbiānyuán.

line-up /'laɪn ʌp/ *n* [C] 整队[隊] zhěngduì; 排队 páiduì.

lin·ger /'lɪŋgə(r)/ *vi* 逗留 dòuliú, 徘徊 páihuái. **~ing** *adj* 长[長]久 chángjiǔ; 拖延的 tuōyánde; 逗留不去的 dòuliú búqù de: *a ~ing illness* 久病不愈. **~ly** *adv*

linge·rie /'lænʒəri:/ *n* [U] 女内衣 nǚ nèiyī.

lin·guist /'lɪŋgwɪst/ *n* [C] **1** 通晓外国[國]语言的人 tōngxiǎo wàiguó yǔyán de rén. **2** 语言学[學]家 yǔyánxuéjiā. **~tic** /-'gwɪstɪk/ *adj* 语言的 yǔyánde; 语言学的 yǔyánxuéde. **~ics** *n* [U] 语言学 yǔyánxué.

lini·ment /'lɪnɪmənt/ *n* [C, U] 涂[塗]抹剂[劑] túmǒjì.

lin·ing /'laɪnɪŋ/ *n* **1** [C, U] 衬[襯]里[裡] chènlǐ: *a fur ~*毛皮里.

link /lɪŋk/ *n* [C] **1** 链[鏈]环[環] liànhuán; 环 huán. **2** 链扣 liànkòu: *'cuff-~s* 衬衫袖口的链扣. **3** 连[連]系[繫] liánxì. □ *vt/i* 连接 liánjiē; 联[聯]系 liánxì.

lino /'laɪnəʊ/ *n* [U] linoleum 的缩写[寫] *linoleum* de suōxiě.

lino·leum /lɪ'nəʊlɪəm/*n* [U] 亚[亞]麻油地毡[氈] yàmáyóu dìzhān; 漆布 qībù.

lin·seed /'lɪnsɪd/ *n* [U] 亚[亞]麻子 yàmázǐ; 亚麻仁 yàmárén.

lint /lɪnt/ *n* [U] (作绷带等用的)软[軟]麻布 ruǎnmábù.

lion /'laɪən/ *n* [C] 狮[獅]子 shīzi. ***the ~'s share*** 最大部分 zuìdà bùfen. **~ess** /-nɪs/ *n* [C] 母狮 mǔshī. **~ize** /-aɪz/ *vt* 把…作为显[顯]要看待 bǎ… zuòwéi xiǎnyào kàndài.

lip /lɪp/ *n* [C] **1** 唇 chún. ***give (pay) '~-service to sth*** 口惠无[無]实[實] kǒuhuì wú shí; 不真诚的许诺 bù zhēnchéngde xǔnuò. ***keep a stiff upper ~*** 坚[堅]定不移 jiāndìng bùyí. ***lick*** (或 ***smack***) ***one's ~s*** 咂咂嘴唇 zázá zuǐchún. **2** (器皿或凹洞的)边[邊] biān. **'~-reading** 唇读[讀]法 chúndúfǎ. **'~-read** *vt* **'~stick** 口红 kǒuhóng.

liquefy /'lɪkwɪfaɪ/ *vt/i* [*pt, pp* -ied] 液化 yèhuà.

li·queur /lɪ'kjʊə(r)/ *n* [C, U] 味浓[濃]性烈的一种酒 wèinóng xìngliè de yìzhǒng jiǔ.

liquid /'lɪkwɪd/ *n* [C, U] 液体[體] yètǐ. □*adj* **1** 液体的 yètǐde **2** 透明的 tòumíngde; 清澈的 qīngchède: *~ eyes* 明亮的眼睛. **3** (声音)清脆的 qīngcuìde; 纯正的 chúnzhèngde. **4** (指经济) 易变[變]卖[賣]的 yìbiànmàide: *~ assets* 流动资产.

liqui·date /'lɪkwɪdeɪt/ *vt/i* **1** 清偿[償](债务) qīngcháng. **2** 清算(破产的企业等) qīngsuàn; 清理 qīnglǐ. **3** [非正式用语]除掉 (用暗杀等手段) chúdiào. **liqui'da·tion** *n* [U] **liqui·da·tor** 清算人 qīngsuànrén.

liquor /'lɪkə(r)/ *n* [C, U] 酒 jiǔ, 酒类[類] jiǔlèi.

liquor·ice [美语 = **licor·ice**] /'lɪkərɪs/ *n* [U] 甘草 gāncǎo.

lisp /lɪsp/ *vt/i* 咬舌儿[兒](指将 [s] [z] 发音作 [θ]) yǎoshé'ér. □ *n* [C] 口齿[齒]不清 kǒuchǐ bùqīng.

list¹ /lɪst/ *n* [C] 名单[單] míngdān; 目录[錄] mùlù; 表 biǎo. □ *vt* 编目录 biān mùlù; 造表 zàobiǎo; 列入表册(目录、名册) lièrù biǎocè.

list² /lɪst/ *vi* (尤指船只)倾侧 qīngcè; 倾斜 qīngxié. □ *n* [C] (船)倾侧 qīngcè.

lis·ten /'lɪsn/ *vi* **1** 听[聽] tīng; 留神听 liúshén tīng: *~ to a friend's story* 听一位朋友的讲述. *~* ***in (to)*** 听广[廣]播节[節]目 tīng guǎngbō jiémù. **2** 听从[從](忠告、建议) tīngcóng; 倾听 qīngtīng. **'~er** *n* [C]

list·less /'lɪstlɪs/ *adj* 无[無]精打采的 wú jīng dǎ cǎi de. **~ly** *adv*

~**ness** *n* [U]

lit /lɪt/ *pt, pp* of light[4].

liter /'li:tə(r)/ *n* [美语] = litre.

lit·er·acy /'lɪtərəsɪ/ *n* [U] 阅〔閱〕读〔讀〕和写〔寫〕作的能力 yuèdú hé xiězuò de nénglì.

lit·eral /'lɪtərəl/ *adj* **1** 原义〔義〕的 yuányìde: *a ~ translation* 直译〔譯〕zhíyì. **2** 采用词的常义的 cǎiyòng cí de chángyì de: *~ meaning of a word* 词的确切意思. ~**ly** /'lɪtrəlɪ/ *adv* **(a)** 逐字地 zhúzìde: *translate ~-ly* 逐字翻译. **(b)** [非正式用语]不夸〔誇〕张〔張〕地 bù kuāzhāng de.

lit·er·ary /'lɪtərərɪ/ *adj* 文学〔學〕的 wénxuéde; 作家的 zuòjiāde.

lit·er·ate /'lɪtərət/ *adj* **1** 有阅〔閱〕读〔讀〕和写〔寫〕作能力的 yǒu yuèdú hé xiězuò nénglì de. **2** 有文化的 yǒu wénhuà de; 有教养〔養〕的 yǒu jiàoyǎngde. □ *n* [C] 有文化的人 yǒu wénhuà de rén.

lit·era·ture /'lɪtrətʃə(r)/ *n* [U] **1** 文学〔學〕wénxué; 文学作品 wénxué zuòpǐn. **2** (某一国家或时期的文学)作品 zuòpǐn; (关于某一学科或专题的)文献〔獻〕wénxiàn; 著作 zhùzuò: *English ~* 英国文学. **3** [U] 说明书〔書〕shuōmíngshū; 印刷品(如小册子) yìnshuāpǐn.

lithe /laɪð/ *adj* (指人等)柔软〔軟〕的 róuruǎnde; 易弯〔彎〕曲的 yì wānqū de.

lit·mus /'lɪtməs/ *n* [U] 石蕊 shíruǐ.

litre [美语 = **liter**] /'li:tə(r)/ *n* [C] 升 (容量单位,约合 1 品脱) shēng.

Litt.D.=Doctor of Letters 文学〔學〕博士 wénxué bóshì.

lit·ter[1] /'lɪtə(r)/ *n* **1** [U] 杂〔雜〕乱〔亂〕物(纸屑、废瓶等) záluànwù. **2** [C] 一胎生下的小动〔動〕物 yìtāi shēngxià de xiǎodòngwù. □ *vt/i* 使杂乱 shǐ záluàn; 乱丢杂物 luàndiū záwù. '~-**basket** (或 -**bin**) 废〔廢〕物箱 fèiwùxiāng; 废纸篓 fèizhǐlǒu.

litter[2] /'lɪtə(r)/ *n* [C] 担〔擔〕架 dānjià.

little[1] /'lɪtl/ *adj* (⇨ less and least) **1** 小的 xiǎode: *the ~ finger* 小手指. **2** 微不足道的 wēi bù zú dào de: *a few ~ problems* 一些小问题. **3** (指时间、距离、身材)短的 duǎnde. **4** 年轻〔輕〕的 niánqīngde. **5** 很少的 hěnshǎode: *I have very ~ time for reading.* 我的读书时间很少. **6** [与 *a* 连用]少许的 shǎoxǔde: *He knows a ~ French.* 他懂一点法语. □ *adv* **1** (⇨ less, least) 少 shǎo: *He is ~ known.* 他不大出名. *a ~* 稍许 shāoxǔ: *a ~ afraid* 有点害怕. **2** 毫不 háobù: *L~ does he know that* 他一点不知道…

little[2] /'lɪtl/ *n* [U] (⇨ less, least) **1** 少量 shǎoliàng: *You have done very ~ for us.* 你为我们做的事情很少. ~ **by** ~ 逐渐〔漸〕zhújiàn. **2** [与 *a* 连用]少许 shǎoxǔ; 一点〔點〕yìdiǎn: *He knows a ~ of everything.* 他什么都懂一点.

liv·able /'lɪvəbl/ *adj* (房屋、气候等)适〔適〕于居住的 shìyú jūzhù de.

live[1] /laɪv/ *adj* **1** 活的 huóde; 有生命的 yǒu shēngmìng de. **2** 燃烧〔燒〕的 ránshāode: *~ coals* 燃烧着的煤,未用过〔過〕的 wèiyòngguòde: *a ~ match* 未用过的火柴,充电〔電〕的 chōngdiànde: *a ~ rail* 带电的铁轨. **3** 实〔實〕况播送的 shíkuàng bōsòng de. **4** 精力充沛的 jīnglì chōngpèi de; 现在重要的 xiànzài zhòngyàode: *a ~ issue* 当前的问题.

live[2] /lɪv/ *vt/i* **1** 活着 huózhe; 生存 shēngcún. **2** 继〔繼〕续〔續〕活着 jìxù huózhe: *The doctors don't think she will ~.* 医生认为她不能活了. ~ **through** 度过〔過〕dùguò; 经〔經〕受住 jīngshòuzhù: *~ through the war* 亲历战争(而幸存). **3** '~ **on, (a)** 以…为主食 yǐ … wéizhǔshí. **(b)** 靠…生活 kào … shēnghuó. **4** 居住 jūzhù: *Where do you ~?* 你住在哪儿? ~ **together, (a)** 同住一起 tóngzhù yìqǐ. **(b)** (未婚)同居 tóngjū. **5** 过 guò; 度过 dùguò: *He ~d a happy life.* 他过着幸福的生活. **6** ~ ***sth down*** 过〔過〕新的生活以忘却 (过去的丑行等) guò xīnde shēnghuó yǐ wàngquè ~ ***up to sth*** 与〔與〕…相等 yǔ … xiāngděng: *~ up to one's reputatio* 不负自己的声望. ~ ***with sth*** 接受 jiēshòu; 忍受 rěnshòu. **7** 享受人生 xiǎngshòu rénshēng. ~ ***it u*** 过着消遥的日子 guòzhe xiāoyáod rìzi.

live·li·hood /'laɪvlɪhʊd/ *n* [C] 生活 shēnghuó; 生计 shēngjì.

live·ly /'laɪvlɪ/ *adj* [-ier, -iest] **1** 充满生气〔氣〕的 chōngmǎn shēngqì de 活泼〔潑〕的 huópode. **2** (颜色)鲜明的 xiānmíngde; 明快的 míngkuàide. **live·li·ness** *n* [U]

liven /'laɪvn/ *vt/i* 使活泼〔潑〕shǐ huópo; 使有生气〔氣〕shǐ yǒu shēngqì: *~ up a party* 使晚会活跃起来.

liver /'lɪvə(r)/ *n* **1** [C] 肝 gān; 肝脏〔臟〕gānzàng. **2** [U] (供食

的鸡、牛等的)肝 gān.
lives /laɪvz/ *pl* of life.
live·stock /'laɪvstɒk/ *n* [U] (尤指)家畜 jiāchù; 牲畜 shēngchù.
livid /'lɪvɪd/ *adj* **1** 铅色的 qiānsède; 青灰色的 qīnghuīsède. **2** (指人)狂怒的 kuángnùde. ~**ly** *adv*
liv·ing[1] /'lɪvɪŋ/ *adj* **1** 活着的 huózhede; 现存的 xiàncúnde. ***within*** (或 ***in***) ~ ***memory*** 现今人们〔們〕记忆〔憶〕中的 xiànjīn rénmen jìyìzhōngde. **2** 强烈的 qiángliède; 生动〔動〕的 shēngdòngde: *a* ~ *faith* 强烈的信念. □ *n* **the** ~ 活着的人们〔們〕 huózhede rénmen.
liv·ing[2] /'lɪvɪŋ/ *n* **1** [C] 生活 shēnghuó; 生计 shēngjì: *earn a good* ~ 生活优裕. **2** [U] 生活方式 shēnghuó fāngshì: *a poor standard of* ~ 贫穷的生活. '~**-room** 起居室 qǐjūshì; 客厅〔廳〕 kètīng.
liz·ard /'lɪzəd/ *n* [C] 蜥蜴 xīyì.
ll. = lines
llama /'lɑːmə/ *n* [C] 美洲驼〔駝〕 Měizhōu tuó; 无〔無〕峰驼 wúfēngtuó.
LL.B. = Bachelor of Laws 法学〔學〕士 fǎxuéshì.
LL.D. = Doctor of Laws 法学〔學〕博士 fǎxué bóshì.
load[1] /ləʊd/ *n* [C] **1** 担〔擔〕子 dànzi; 重载〔載〕 zhòngzài. ~***s of*** [非正式用语]大量 dàliàng; 许多 xǔduō: ~*s of money* (*bottles*) 很多钱(瓶子). **2** [喻]负担 fùdān; 重任 zhòngrèn. ***take a*** ~ ***off sb's mind*** 解除某人忧〔憂〕虑〔慮〕 jiěchú mǒurén yōulǜ. **3** (电机、机器等的)负载 fùzài, 负荷 fùhé.
load[2] /ləʊd/ *vt/i* **1** 装〔裝〕载〔載〕 zhuāngzài: ~ *a van* (*ship*). 装车(船). ~ **(*sth*)** ***up*** 装载货物 zhuāngzài huòwù. **2** 把弹〔彈〕药〔藥〕装入(枪炮) bǎ dànyào zhuāngrù. **3** 把胶〔膠〕卷〔捲〕装入(照相机) bǎ jiāojuǎn zhuāngrù. **a** ~**ed question** 别有用心的问〔問〕题 biéyǒu yòngxīn de wèntí.
loaf[1] /ləʊf/ *n* [C] [*pl* loaves/ ləʊvz/] **1** 一块〔塊〕面〔麵〕包 yíkuì miànbāo. **2** [C, U] 块 kuài; 团〔團〕 tuán: *meat* ~ 烤肉糕. **3** [俚语]头 tóu. ***use one's*** ~ 动〔動〕脑〔腦〕筋 dòng nǎojīn.
loaf[2] /ləʊf/ *vt/i* ~ ***about*** 消磨(时间) xiāomó. ~**er** 游手好闲〔閒〕者 yóu shǒu hào xián zhě.
loan /ləʊn/ *n* [C] **1** 借出物 jièchūwù; 贷款 dàikuǎn. **2** [U] 借出 jièchū. □ *vt* [正式用语] = lend.
loath, loth /ləʊθ/ *adj* 不愿〔願〕意的 bú yuànyì de. ~ ***to do sth*** 不愿作某事 bú yuàn zuò mǒushì.
loathe /ləʊð/ *vt* 厌〔厭〕恶〔惡〕 yànwù, 不喜欢〔歡〕 bú xǐhuān. **loathing** *n* [U] 厌〔厭〕恶〔惡〕 yànwù. **loath·some** *adj* 可厌的 kěyànde.
loaves /ləʊvz/ *pl* of loaf.[1]
lob /lɒb/ *vt/i* [-bb-] (打网球、板球时)吊高球 diào gāoqiú. □ *n* [C] (网球)高球 gāoqiú; (板球)低球 dīqiú.
lobby /'lɒbɪ/ *n* [C] [*pl* -ies] **1** 门〔門〕廊 ménláng; 门厅〔廳〕 méntīng. **2** 院外活动〔動〕集团〔團〕 yuànwài huódòng jítuán: *the farming* ~ 农业院外活动集团. □ *vt/i* 对〔對〕(议员等)游说活动 duì ... yóushuì huódòng. '~**ist** 院外活动集团的成员 yuànwài huódòng jítuán de chéngyuán; 说客 shuōkè.
lobe /ləʊb/ *n* [C] 耳垂 ěrchuí.
lob·ster /'lɒbstə(r)/ *n* **1** [C] 龙〔龍〕虾〔蝦〕 lóngxiā. **2** [U] 龙虾肉 lóngxiāròu.
lo·cal /'ləʊkl/ *adj* **1** 地方的 dìfāngde; 当〔當〕地的 dāngdìde; 本地的 běndìde: ~ *elections* 地方选举. **2** 局部的 júbùde: *a* ~ *anaesthetic* 局部麻醉剂. □ *n* [C] **1** 当地居民 dāngdì jūmín. **2** [非正式用语]本地酒店 běndì jiǔdiàn. ,~ '**government** 地方政府 dìfāng zhèngfǔ. ~**ly** *adv*
lo·cal·ity /ləʊ'kælətɪ/ *n* [*pl* -ies] [C] 地区〔區〕 dìqū; 地方 dìfāng.
lo·cal·ize /'ləʊkəlaɪz/ *vt* 使限于局部 shǐ xiànyú júbù; 局部化 júbùhuà: ~ *a disease* 使疾病限于局部. **lo·cal·i'z·ation** *n* [U]
lo·cate /ləʊ'keɪt/ *vt* **1** 找出…的位置 zhǎochū ... de wèizhì. **2** 设置 shèzhì: ~ *the new offices in Pa is* 在巴黎设置新办公处. **lo·ca·tion** /-ʃn/ *n* **(a)** [U] 定位 dìngwèi. **(b)** [C] 位置 wèizhi. **(c)** ***on location*** 拍外景 pāi wàijǐng.
loch /lɒk/ *n* [C] [苏格兰语] **1** 狭〔狹〕长〔長〕的海湾〔灣〕 xiácháng de hǎiwān: *L*~ *Ness* (英国)内斯湖. **2** 湖 hú.
lock[1] /lɒk/ *n* [C] 一绺头〔頭〕发〔髮〕 yìliǔ tóufa.
lock[2] /lɒk/ *n* [C] **1** 锁 suǒ **2** [军事]枪〔槍〕机〔機〕 qiāngjī. ,~, ,***stock and 'barrel*** 完全地 wánquánde. **3** (运河或河流的)水闸〔閘〕 shuǐzhá. **4** [U] (驾驶汽车)方向盘〔盤〕转〔轉〕动〔動〕的限度 fāngxiàngpán zhuǎndòngde xiàndù. ,~-'**gate** 水闸〔閘〕 shuǐzhá; 水门〔門〕 shuǐmén. '~**jaw** 破伤〔傷〕风〔風〕 pòshāngfēng. '~**smith** 锁匠 suǒjiàng.

lock³ /lɒk/ *vt/i* **1** 锁 suǒ; 锁上 suǒshàng. ~ *sb in* 将某人锁在房内 jiāng mǒurén suǒzài fángnèi. ~ *sb out* 将某人关〔關〕在门〔門〕外 jiāng mǒurén guān zài ménwài. ⇨ ~-out. ~ *sth (sb) up*, **(a)** 上锁 shàngsuǒ; 锁好 suǒhǎo. **(b)** 关〔關〕锁房门〔門〕 guānsuǒ fángmén. **(c)** 〔非正式用语〕监〔監〕禁 jiānjìn. **2** 固定 gùdìng. **3** 揪扭 jiūniǔ: ~-*ed in battle* 打得难解难分. **'~-out** 雇主因争端封闭〔閉〕工厂〔廠〕 gùzhǔ yīn zhēngduān fēngbì gōngchǎng. ⇨ strike¹(1).

locker /'lɒkə(r)/ *n* [C] (公共场所供个人存放衣帽用的) 小橱柜〔櫃〕 xiǎochúguì.

locket /'lɒkɪt/ *n* [C] (挂在项链下的)保藏纪念品(画像、一绺头发等)的贵重小盒 bǎocáng jìniànpǐn de guìzhòng xiǎohé.

loco·mo·tion /ˌləʊkə'məʊʃn/ *n* [U] 移动〔動〕 yídòng; 运〔運〕动 yùndòng; 移动力 yídònglì; 运动力 yùndònglì.

loco·mo·tive /ˌləʊkə'məʊtɪv/ *adj* 运〔運〕动〔動〕的 yùndòngde; 移动的 yídòngde. □ *n* [C] 火车〔車〕头〔頭〕 huǒchētóu.

lo·cust /'ləʊkəst/ *n* [C] 蝗虫〔蟲〕 huángchóng.

lodge¹ /lɒdʒ/ *n* [C] **1** (花园宅第大门口的)仆〔僕〕人住房 púrén zhùfáng. **2** (狩猎期间居住用的)山林小屋 shānlín xiǎowū: *a 'skiing* ~ 滑雪时用的小屋.

lodge² /lɒdʒ/ *vt/i* **1** 供(某人)住宿 gòng ... zhùsù. **2** 寄宿 jìsù. **3** ~ *in* (子弹等)射入shèrù: *The bullet ~d in his head.* 这颗子弹打进他的头部. **4** 存放(金钱等) cúnfàng. **5** 提出(申诉、抗议等) tíchū: ~ *a complaint* 提出控诉. **lodger** 房客 fángkè; 寄宿人 jìsùrén.

lodg·ing /'lɒdʒɪŋ/ *n* [C] 〔通常用 *pl*〕公寓 gōngyù.

loft /lɒft/ *n* [C] **1** (屋顶下的)阁〔閣〕楼〔樓〕 gélóu. **2** (教堂、礼堂的)楼厢 lóuxiāng.

lofty /'lɒftɪ/ *adj* [-ier, -iest] **1** 极〔極〕高的 jígāode. **2** (指思想等)高尚的 gāoshàngde. **3** 高傲的 gāo'àode; 傲慢的 àomànde. **loft·ily** *adv*

log¹ /lɒg/ *n* [C] 原木 yuánmù; 圆木 yuánmù.

log² /lɒg/ *n* [C] **1** (船只的)测程仪〔儀〕 cèchéngyí; 计程仪 jìchéngyí. **2** = log-book(a). □ *vt* [-gg-] 把…记入航海 (或飞行) 日志〔誌〕 bǎ ... jìrù hánghǎi rìzhì. **'~-book**, **(a)** 航海日志 hánghǎi rìzhì. **(b)** 旅程记录〔錄〕 lǚchéng jìlù.

log³ /lɒg/ *n* [C] logarithm 的缩写〔寫〕 *logarithm* de suōxiě.

log·ar·ithm /'lɒgərɪðəm/ *n* [C] 对〔對〕数〔數〕 duìshù.

log·ger·heads/'lɒgəhedz/ *n* 〔仅用于〕 *at* ~ (与…)不和 bùhé; (与…)相争 xiāngzhēng.

logic /'lɒdʒɪk/*n* [U] **1** 逻〔邏〕辑〔輯〕 luójì; 逻辑学〔學〕 **2** luójìxué. **2** 逻辑性 luójìxìng; 条〔條〕理性 tiáolǐxìng. **~al** /-kl/ *adj* **(a)** 符合逻辑的 fúhé luójì de. **(b)** 推理 tuīlǐ. **~ally** *adv*

lo·gis·tics /lə'dʒɪstɪks/ *n* [U] 后〔後〕勤(学) hòuqín: *the ~ of North Sea oil drilling* 北海油井的后勤工作. **lo·gis·ti·cal** *adj* 后勤的 hòuqínde: ~ *support* 后勤支援.

loin /lɔɪn/ *n* **1** [*pl*] 腰 yāo, 腰部 yāobù. **2** [C] 腰肉 yāoròu. **'~-cloth** 缠〔纏〕腰布 chányāobù.

loi·ter /'lɔɪtə(r)/ *vt/i* 闲〔閒〕逛 xiánguàng; 消磨时〔時〕光 xiāomó shíguāng.

loll /lɒl/ *vt/i* 懒洋洋地休息 lǎnyángyángde xiūxì; 懒散地闲〔閒〕荡〔蕩〕 lǎnsǎnde xiándàng.

lol·li·pop /'lɒlɪpɒp/ *n* [C] 糖果 tángguǒ; 棒糖 bàngtáng.

lone /ləʊn/ *adj* 孤独〔獨〕的 gūdúde; 寂寞的 jìmòde.

lone·ly /'ləʊnlɪ/*adj* [-ier, -iest] **1** 孤独〔獨〕的 gūdúde; 寂寞的 jìmòde. **2** (指地方)偏僻的 piānpìde. **lone·li·ness** *n* [U]

lone·some /'ləʊnsəm/ *adj* = lonely(1).

long¹ /lɒŋ/ *adj* [-er, -est] **1** 长〔長〕的 chángde: *How ~ is the River Nile?* 尼罗河有多长? **2** (指时间长久的): *a ~ flight* 长时间的飞行. *in the'~ run*, ⇨ run¹(4). *in the ~ term* 长期 chángqī. **'~-term** *adj* **'~hand** 普〔普〕通写〔寫〕法 pǔtōng xiěfǎ. **ˌ~-play(ing) 'record** (缩作 **LP**)慢转〔轉〕密纹唱片 mànzhuàn mìwén chàngpiàn. **'~-range** *adj* 长期的 chángqīde; 远〔遠〕程的 yuǎnchéngde: *a ~-range rocket* 远程火箭. *a ~-range forecast* 长期预报. **ˌ~'sighted** *adj* **(a)** 远视的yuǎnshìde. **(b)**〔喻〕有远见的yǒu yuǎnjiànde. **ˌ~-'standing** *adj* 长期间〔間〕的 chángqījiānde: *a ~-standing agreement* 长期协议. **'~ wave** (无线电)长波(在 1000 公尺以上) chángbō. **ˌ~-'winded** *adj* 无〔無〕聊 wúliáo; 冗长的 rǒngchángde.

long² /lɒŋ/ *adv* **1** 长〔長〕期地 chángqīde; 长久 chángjiǔ. *as (so) ~ as* 只要 zhǐyào; 如果 rúguǒ. **2**

在长时〔時〕间〔間〕 zài chángshíjiān: ~ *ago* 很久以前. **3** 一直 yìzhí: *all day* ~ 整天 **4** *no* (*any, much*) ~*er* 不再 búzài. **'~-suffering** *adj* 长期忍受苦难〔難〕的 chángqī rěnshòu kǔnàn de.

long³ /lɒŋ/ *n* 〔仅用 *sing*〕长〔長〕时〔時〕间〔間〕 chángshíjiān. *before* ~ 不久 bùjiǔ.

long⁴ /lɒŋ/ *vi* 渴望 kěwàng. **~ing** *adj, n* [C, U] 渴望 kěwàng. **~ing·ly** *adv*

long. =longitude.

longi·tude /'lɒndʒɪtju:d/ *n* [C] 经〔經〕度 jīngdù.

long·ways /'lɒŋweɪz/, **long·wise** /'lɒŋwaɪz/ *adv* = lengthways.

look¹ /lʊk/ *n* [C] **1** 看 kàn; 望 wàng. *take a* ~ *at* 查看一下 chákàn yíxià. **2** 外表 wàibiǎo: *I don't like the* ~ *of him.* 我不喜欢他的外表. **3** [*pl*] 容貌 róngmào: *her good* ~*s* 她容貌很美.

look² /lʊk/ *vt/i* **1** 看 kàn; 瞧 qiáo: ~ (*up*) *at the ceiling* 看天花板. **2** 显〔顯〕得 xiǎndé; 好象 hǎoxiàng: ~ *sad* 面带悲容. **(not)** ~ *oneself* 看起来〔來〕和平常(不)一样〔樣〕 kànqǐlái hé píngcháng yíyàng. ~ *one's best* 显〔顯〕得最有吸引力 xiǎnde zuì yǒu xīyǐnlì. *L~ here!* 喂,瞧! ~ *well,* **(a)** 看上去健康 kàn shàngqù jiànkāng. **(b)** 看上去漂亮 kàn shàngqù piàoliàng: *Does this hat* ~ *well on me?* 我戴上这顶帽子好看吗? **3** ~ *like* (*as if*) 似乎是 sìhū shì: *It* ~*s like rain.* 天象是要下雨. **4** 注意 zhùyì: *L~ where you're going!* 走路当心! **5** ~ *about* (*for sth*) 四处〔處〕寻〔尋〕找 sìchù xúnzhǎo. ~ *after sb* (*sth*) 照顾〔顧〕 zhàogù. ~ *at sth* 检〔檢〕查 jiǎnchá: *Doctor, will you* ~ *at my ankle?* 大夫,请检查一下我的脚脖子好吗? ~ *back* (*on sth*) [喻]回顾 huígù. ~ *down on sb* 轻〔輕〕视qīngshì. ~ *for sb* (*sth*) 寻找 xúnzhǎo. ~ *forward to sth* 盼望 pànwàng. ~ *in* (*on sb*) (顺便)看望 kànwàng. ~ *into sth* 调查 diàochá; 检〔檢〕查 jiǎnchá. ~ *on sb as* 看待 kàndài. ~ *on to* 面向 miànxiàng. ~ *out* (*for sb, for sth*) 注意 zhùyì; 留神 liúshén. **'~-out,** *n* **(a)** 〔仅用 *sing*〕留神 liúshén; 注意 zhùyì. **(b)** [C] 守望者 shǒuwàngzhě. ~ *over sth* 检查 jiǎnchá. ~ *round,* **(a)** 慎重考虑 shènzhòng kǎolǜ. **(b)** 转〔轉〕头〔頭〕看 zhuǎntóu kàn. ~ *round sth* 观〔觀〕光 guānguāng. ~ *to sb for sth* (*to do sth*) 依赖 yīlài. ~ *up,* **(a)** 仰视 yǎngshì. **(b)** 繁荣〔榮〕 fánróng. ~ *sth up* 查(字典中的字) chá. ~ *sb up* 拜访 bàifǎng. ~ *up to sb* 尊敬 zūnjìng.

loom¹ /lu:m/ *n* [C] 织〔織〕布机〔機〕 zhībùjī.

loom² /lu:m/ *vi* **1** 隐〔隱〕隐呈现 yǐnyǐn chéngxiàn: *A figure* ~*ed up out of the mist in a threatening way.* 一个人在雾中隐约出现令人感到可怕. **2** ~ *large* [喻]显〔顯〕得突出 xiǎndé tūchū.

loop /lu:p/ *n* [C] **1** 环〔環〕状〔狀〕物 huánzhuàngwù. **2** (线,绳等打成的)圈 quān; 环 huán. □ *vt/i* 绕〔繞〕成圈 ràochéng quān.

loop·hole /'lu:phəʊl/ *n* [C] [喻] (法律等的)漏洞 lòudòng: ~*s in the law* 法律上的漏洞.

loose /lu:s/ *adj* [-r, -st] **1** 松〔鬆〕开〔開〕的 sōngkāide; 不受束缚的 bú shòu shùfù de. *break* ~ (挣脱束缚而)逃出 táochū; *get* ~ 逃脱 táotuō. **2** (衣服)宽松的 kuānsōngde. **3** 松弛的 sōngshíde; 不牢的 bùláode: *a* ~ *tooth* 松动的牙齿. *come*(*work*) ~ (结等)松掉 sōngdiào. **4** (指言行等)散漫的 sǎnmànde; 放荡〔蕩〕的 fàngdàngde. **5** 松散的 sōngsǎnde: ~ *soil* 松土. **6** 不准〔準〕确〔確〕的 bù zhǔnquè de: ~ *passing of the ball* 不准确的传球. **7** 淫荡〔蕩〕的 yíndàngde: *a* ~ *woman* 放荡的女人. **~ly** *adv* **loosen** /'lu:sn/ *vt/i* 使松 shǐ sōng; 放松 fàngsōng; 变〔變〕松 biànsōng.

loot /lu:t/ *n* [U] 掠夺〔奪〕物 lüèduówù; 战〔戰〕利品 zhànlìpǐn. □ *vt/i* 掠夺 lüèduó; 抢〔搶〕劫 qiǎngjié.

lop /lɒp/ *vt* [-pp-] 砍去(树枝等) kǎnqù.

lop-sided /ˌlɒp 'saɪdɪd/ *adj* 不平衡的 bù pínghéng de.

lord /lɔ:d/ *n* [C] **1** 君主 jūnzhǔ. **2** **L~** 上帝 Shàngdì; 基督 Jīdū: *The L~'s Prayer* 主祷文. **3** (表示惊奇等): *Good L~!* 天哪! **4** 贵族 guìzú. **5** 正式头〔頭〕衔 zhèngshì tóuxián: *L~ Mayor* 市长. **the House of 'L~s** 〔英国英语〕上议〔議〕院 shàngyìyuàn. **~ly** *adj* [-ier, -iest] **(a)** 高傲的 gāo'àode. **(b)** 贵族似的 guìzú sì de. **~ship** *n* **(a)** [U] 统治 tǒngzhì; 权〔權〕威(与 *over* 连用) quánwēi. **(b)** **His (Your) L~** 阁〔閣〕下(对贵族的尊称) géxià.

lorry /'lɒrɪ/ *n* [C] [*pl* -ies] 〔美语 = truck〕运〔運〕货汽车〔車〕 yùnhuò qìchē.

lose /lu:z/ *vt/i* [*pt, pp* lost /lɒst/] **1**

失去 shīqù; 丧〔喪〕失 sàngshī: ~ *one's money* 丢钱. ~ ***one's balance*** 跌倒 diēdǎo. ~ ***one's temper*** 发〔發〕怒 fānù, 发脾气〔氣〕fā píqì. **2** ***be lost*** 死去 sǐqù; 消失 xiāoshī. ~ ***oneself in sth*** 专〔專〕心于某事 zhuānxīn yú mǒushì. **3** 遗失 yíshī; 找不到 zhǎobúdào. ~ ***one's place*** 忘记上次读〔讀〕到的地方 wàngjì shàngcì dú dào de dìfang. ~ ***sight of sth,*** **(a)** 忽略 hūlüè: ~ *sight of the problems* 忽视这些问题. **(b)** 看不见 kànbújiàn. **4** 使(某人)损失 shǐ sǔnshī: *This will ~ you your job.* 这将使你失去工作. **5** 输〔輸〕shū; 失败 shībài: ~ *a game* 输一局. ***a lost cause*** 已失败的事业〔業〕等 yǐ shībài de shìyè děng. **6** (钟、表等) 走得慢 zǒu de màn. ~ ***out*** 输掉 shūdiào; 失败 shībài.

loss /lɒs/ *n* **1** [U] 损失 sǔnshī; 丧〔喪〕失 sàngshī: ~*of life in war* 在战争中丧生. **2**[U] 未保住 wèi bǎozhù: *a ~ of power* 丧失权力. **3**[U] 输〔輸〕shū; 未得到 wèi dédào: *the ~ of a game* 比赛失败; 赛输了. **4**[C] 损失物 sǔnshīwù. **5*(be) at a*** ~ 感到迷惑 gǎndào míhuò; 不知所措 bùzhī suǒ cuò: *at a ~ for words* 不知道说什么好.

lost /lɒst/ *pt, pp* of lose.

lot[1] /lɒt/ *n* [C] [非正式用语] **1** ***the*** ~ 全部 quánbù; 全体〔體〕quántǐ. **2** ***a ~(of); ~s (and ~s) (of)*** 许多 xǔduō. **3** 很多 hěnduō: *a ~ better* 好多了.

lot[2] /lɒt/ *n* [C] **1** 抽签〔簽〕法 chōuqiānfǎ. ***draw (cast) ~s*** 抽签 chōuqiān. **2** [C] 命运〔運〕mìngyùn; 运气〔氣〕yùnqì. **3** (拍卖品等)一批 yìpī; 一组 yìzǔ. **4** 一批(东西)yìpī: *a new ~ of coats* 新来的一批外衣. **5** 一块〔塊〕地 yíkuài dì.

loth /ləʊθ/ *adj* ⇨ loath.

lo·tion /'ləʊʃn/ *n* [C,U] (药)洗液 xǐyè; 洗剂〔劑〕xǐjì.

lot·tery /'lɒtərɪ/ *n* [C] [*pl* -ies] 抽彩给奖〔獎〕法 chōucǎi gěijiǎng fǎ.

lo·tus /'ləʊtəs/ *n* [C] [*pl* ~es] 莲〔蓮〕lián.

loud /laʊd/ *adj* [-er, -est] **1** 高声〔聲〕的 gāoshēngde; 响〔響〕亮的 xiǎngliàngde. **2** (指行为) 吵闹的 chǎonàode; (颜色)刺眼的 cìyǎnde. □ *adv* 大声〔聲〕地 dàshēngde. ,**~-'speaker,** (亦作 *speaker*) 扬〔揚〕声器 yángshēngqì. **~ly** *adv* **~ness** *n* [U]

lounge /laʊndʒ/ *vi* (懒洋洋地)坐着 zuòzhe; 站着 zhànzhe. □ *n* [C] **1** 懒洋洋的姿势〔勢〕lǎnyángyángde zīshì. **2** 休息室 xiūxìshì. **3** 酒店 jiǔdiàn. **'~-suit** 男子便服 nánzǐ biànfú.

louse /laʊs/ *n* [C] [*pl* lice /laɪs/] 虱〔蝨〕shī.

lousy /'laʊzɪ/ *adj* [-ier, -iest] **1** 多虱〔蝨〕的 duōshīde. **2** [非正式用语]坏〔壞〕的 huàide: *What a ~ meal!* 多糟糕的饭!

lout /laʊt/ *n* [C] 粗鄙的人 cūbǐde rén. **'~ish** *adj*

lov·able /'lʌvəbl/ *adj* 可爱〔愛〕的 kě'àide; 讨人喜欢〔歡〕的 tǎo rén xǐhuān de.

love /lʌv/ *n* **1** [U] 热〔熱〕爱〔愛〕rè'ài; 喜爱 xǐ'ài: *a mother's ~ for her children* 母爱. ***There's no ~ lost between them*** 他们互相讨厌〔厭〕tāmen hùxiāng tǎoyàn. ***for the ~of*** 为〔爲〕了…起见 wèi le … qǐ jiàn. **2** [U] 性爱 xìng'ài. ***be in ~ (with sb)*** (跟…)恋〔戀〕爱 liàn'ài. ***fall in ~ (with sb)*** 爱上(某人) ài shàng. ***make ~ (to sb)*** (与…)发〔發〕生性行为 fāshēng xìngxíngwéi. **3** 可爱的人 kě'àide rén. **4** (比赛)零分 língfēn. **'~-affair** 风〔風〕流韵事 fēngliú yùnshì. **'~sick** *adj* 害相思病的 hài xiāngsībìng de. □ *vt* **1** 爱 ài; 热爱 rè'ài:~ *one's wife* 爱妻子. **2** 崇拜 chóngbài: ~ *God* 崇敬上帝. **3** 爱好 àihào; 喜欢〔歡〕xǐhuān: ~ *ice-cream* 喜好冰激凌.

love·ly /'lʌvlɪ/ *adj* **1** 美丽〔麗〕的 měilìde; 好看的 hǎokànde. **2** [非正式用语]令人愉快的 lìng rén yúkuài de: *a ~ holiday* 愉快的假日. **3** 可爱〔愛〕的 kě'àide: *a ~ person* 可爱的人. **love·li·ness** *n* [U]

lover /'lʌvə(r)/ *n* [C] **1** 爱〔愛〕好者 àihàozhě: *a ~ of music* 音乐爱好者. **2** 风〔風〕流人物 fēngliú rénwù.

lov·ing /'lʌvɪŋ/ *adj* 爱〔愛〕的 àide; 表示爱的 biǎoshì ài de. **~ly** *adv*

low[1] /ləʊ/ *adj* [-er, -est] **1** 低的 dīde; 矮的 ǎide: ~ *hills* 小山. ***lie ~*** [非正式用语]隐〔隱〕匿 yǐnnì. **2** 低于通常高度的 dī yú tōngcháng gāodù de: ~ *pressure* 低压. **3** (指声音)不大的 búdàde; 不高的 bùgāode. **4** 低等的 dīděngde; 下层〔層〕的 xiàcéngde. **5** ***feel ~*** 情绪不高 qíngxù bù gāo. **6** ***have a ~ opinion of sb (sth)*** 不重视 bú zhòngshì; 轻〔輕〕视 qīngshì. **7** ***be (run) ~*** 减少 jiǎnshǎo

缺少 quēshǎo. '~-down *adj* [非正式用语] 卑鄙的 bēibǐde. □ *n* **get (give) sb the ~-down** [非正式用语]内幕 nèimù; 真相 zhēnxiàng. ,~'**key(ed)** *adj* [喻]低调的 dīdiàode. **~ness** *n* [U]

low² /ləʊ/ *adv* [-er, -est] 地位低地 dìwèi dī de; 卑微地 bēiwēide.

low³ /ləʊ/ *n* [C] 低水平 dī shuǐpíng: *Shares reached new ~s yesterday* 昨天股票落到新的低价.

low⁴ /ləʊ/ *n* [U] 牛叫声〔聲〕 niú jiàoshēng. □ *vt* (指牛)哞哞叫 mōumōujiào.

lower¹ /'ləʊə(r)/ *vt/i* **1** 降低 jiàngdī; 降下 jiàngxià: ~ *a flag* 降旗. **2** 减低 jiǎndī: ~ *the rent* 减低租金. **3** ~ *oneself* 贬低自己的身分 biǎndī zìjǐ de shēnfen.

low·ly /'ləʊlɪ/ *adj* [-ier, -iest] 谦逊〔遜〕的 qiānxùnde; 卑贱〔賤〕的 bēijiànde. **low·li·ness** *n* [U]

loyal /'lɔɪəl/ *adj* 忠诚的 zhōngchéngde. '**~ist** 忠臣 zhōngchén. **~ly** *adv* **~ty** *n* [*pl* -ies] **(a)** [U] 忠诚 zhōngchéng. **(b)** [*pl*] 忠实〔實〕 zhōngshí.

loz·enge /'lɒzɪndʒ/ *n* [C] **1** 菱形 língxíng. **2** 糖锭 tángdìng.

L.P. =long-playing (record) 密纹唱片 mìwén chàngpiān.

L.S.D. =lysergic acid diethylamide 麦〔麥〕角酸二乙基酰胺（一种麻醉药物） màijiǎosuānèryǐjīxiānàn.

Ltd. =limited.

lu·bri·cant /'lu:brɪkənt/ *n* [U] 润〔潤〕滑剂〔劑〕 rùnhuájì.

lu·bri·cate /'lu:brɪkeɪt/ *vt* **1** 使润〔潤〕滑 shǐ rùnhuá. **2** [喻]使…顺利 shǐ … shùnlì. **lu·bri'ca·tion** *n* [U]

lu·cid /'lu:sɪd/ *adj* **1** 清楚的 qīngchǔde; 易懂的 yìdǒngde. **2** 神志清醒的 shénzhì qīngxǐng de. **~ly** *adv* **~ity** /lu:'sɪdɪtɪ/ *n* [U]

luck /lʌk/ *n* [U] (好或坏的)运〔運〕气〔氣〕 yùnqì **Bad ~!** 倒霉! dǎo méi! **Good L~!** 好运气! hǎo yùnqì! **lucky** *adj* [-ier, -iest] 幸运〔運〕的 xìngyùnde. **~ily** *adv* 幸亏〔虧〕 xìngkuī.

lu·cra·tive /'lu:krətɪv/ *adj* 有利的 yǒulìde; 赚钱〔錢〕的 zhuànqiánde.

lu·di·crous /'lu:dɪkrəs/ *adj* 荒谬的 huāngmiùde; 可笑的 kěxiàode. **~ly** *adv*

lug /lʌg/ *vt* [-gg-] (用力)拉 lā, 拖 tuō.

lug·gage /'lʌgɪdʒ/ *n* [U] [美语= baggage] 行李 xínglǐ. '**~-van** 行李车〔車〕 xínglǐchē.

luke·warm /,lu:k'wɔ:m/ *adj* **1** (指液体)微温的 wēiwēnde. **2** [喻]不热〔熱〕情的 bú rèqíng de.

lull /lʌl/ *vt/i* 使安静 shǐ ānjìng; 变〔變〕平静 biàn píngjìng: ~ *a baby to sleep* 哄婴儿入睡 □ *n* [C] 间〔間〕歇 jiānxiē.

lull·aby /'lʌləbaɪ/ *n* [C] [*pl* -ies] 摇篮〔籃〕曲 yáolánqǔ; 催眠曲 cuīmiánqǔ.

lum·bago /lʌm'beɪgəʊ/ *n* [U] 腰部风〔風〕湿〔濕〕痛 yāobù fēngshītòng.

lum·ber¹ /'lʌmbə(r)/ *n* [U] **1** 木材 mùcái, 木料 mùliào. **2** 无〔無〕用杂〔雜〕物(如旧家具) wúyòng záwù. □ *vt* ~ **with** [非正式用语]留下(不要的东西)给别人 liúxià gěi biérén: *Don't ~ me with your mother tonight.* 今夜不要把你母亲留下来让我照管. '**~jack** 伐木者 fámùzhě.

lum·ber² /'lʌmbə(r)/ *vi* 笨重地移动〔動〕 bènzhòngde yídòng.

lu·mi·nous /'lu:mɪnəs/ *adj* 发〔發〕光的 fāguāngde, 发亮的 fāliàngde. **lu·min·os·ity** /-'nɒsətɪ/ *n* [U]

lump /lʌmp/ *n* [C] **1** 团〔團〕 tuán, 块〔塊〕 kuài. **a** ,~ '**sum** 总〔總〕数〔數〕 zǒngshù. **2** 肿〔腫〕块 zhǒngkuài □ *vt* **1** ~ *together* 合在一起 hé zài yìqǐ. **2** 结块 jiékuài. **lumpy** *adj* [-ier, -iest].

lu·nacy /'lu:nəsɪ/ *n* [U] 疯〔瘋〕狂 fēngkuáng; 精神错乱〔亂〕 jīngshén cuòluàn.

lu·nar /'lu:nə(r)/ *adj* 月的 yuède; 似月的 sìyuède.

lu·na·tic /'lu:nətɪk/ *n* [C] 疯〔瘋〕子 fēngzi. □ *adj* 疯的 fēngde; 极〔極〕端愚蠢的 jíduān yúchǔn de. '**~ asylum** 精神病院 jīngshénbìngyuàn.

lunch /lʌntʃ/ *n* [C] 午餐 wǔcān. □ *vt/i* 吃午餐 chī wǔcān; 为〔為〕…供应〔應〕午餐 wèi… gòngyìng wǔcān.

lunch·eon /'lʌntʃən/ *n* [正式用语] = lunch.

lung /lʌŋ/ *n* [C] 肺 fèi; 肺脏〔臟〕 fèizàng.

lunge /lʌndʒ/ *n* [C], *vi* [C] 猛冲〔衝〕 měngchōng; 冲刺 chōngcì.

lurch¹ /lɜ:tʃ/ *n* [仅用于] **leave sb in the ~** 在某人危难〔難〕时〔時〕舍弃〔棄〕不顾〔顧〕 zài mǒurén wēinàn shí shěqì búgù.

lurch² /lɜ:tʃ/ *n* [C] 突然倾斜 tūrán qīngxié. □ *vi* 蹒跚 pánshān; 东〔東〕倒西歪地向前 dōng dǎo xī wāi de xiàngqián.

lure /lʊə(r)/ *n* [C] **1** 诱饵 yòu'ěr. **2** [喻]诱惑物 yòuhuòwù. □ *vt* 诱

惑 yòuhuò: *~d away from work by a woman* 由于一位妇女的引诱而离开工作。

lu·rid /ˈlʊərɪd/ *adj* **1** 火红的 huǒhóngde; 紫红的 zǐhóngde. **2**〔喻〕耸〔聳〕人听〔聽〕闻〔聞〕的 sǒngrén tīng wén de: *~ details of his murder* 他被谋害的惊人详情.

lurk /lɜːk/ *vi* 潜〔潛〕伏 qiánfú; 埋伏 máifú、**luscious** /ˈlʌʃəs/ *adj* 香甜的 xiāngtiánde.

lush /lʌʃ/ *adj* (尤指草木)茂盛的 màoshèngde.

lust /lʌst/ *n* [C,U] 欲〔慾〕望(尤指色欲) yùwàng. □ *vi* ~ **for (after)** 贪求 tānqiú; 渴望 kěwàng. **~ful** *adj* **lusty** *adj*

lustre [美语= **lus·ter**] /ˈlʌstə(r)/ *n* [U] **1** 光泽〔澤〕 guāngzé; 光辉〔輝〕 guānghuī. **2**〔喻〕显〔顯〕赫 xiǎnhè. **lus·trous** *adj*

lute /luːt/ *n* [C] 琵琶 pípá.

lux·ur·iant /lʌgˈʒʊərɪənt/ *adj* **1** 丰〔豐〕富的 fēngfùde; 繁茂的 fánmàode: ~ *plants* 茂密的花草. **2** (文体)华〔華〕丽〔麗〕的 huálìde. **~ly** *adv* **lux·ur·iance** /-rɪəns/ *n* [U]

lux·ur·ious /lʌgˈʒʊərɪəs/ *adj* 非常舒适〔適〕的 fēicháng shūshì de. **~ly** *adv*

lux·ury /ˈlʌkʃərɪ/ *n* [*pl* -ies] **1** [U] 奢侈 shēchǐ: *a life of ~* 奢侈的生活. **2** [C] 奢侈品 shēchǐpǐn.

lynch /lɪntʃ/ *vt* 私刑处〔處〕死 sīxíng chǔsǐ.

lynch·pin /ˈlɪntʃpɪn/ *n* = linchpin.

lynx /lɪŋks/ *n* [C] 山猫 shānmāo.

lyre /ˈlaɪə(r)/ *n* [C] (古希腊的)竖〔竪〕琴 shùqín; 七弦琴 qīxuánqín.

lyric /ˈlɪrɪk/ *adj* **1** 适〔適〕合于演奏或歌唱的 shìhé yú yǎnzòu huò gēchàng de. **2** 抒情的 shūqíngde: ~ *poetry* 抒情诗. □ *n* [C] **1** 抒情诗 shūqíngshī. **2** [*pl*] 民歌的词句 míngēde cíjù. **~al** *adj* **(a)** = lyric. **(b)** 充满感情的 chōngmǎn gǎnqíng de. **~ally** *adv*

M m

M, m /em/ [*pl* M's, m's /emz/] **1** 英语的第十三个〔個〕字母 Yīngyǔ de dìshísāngè zìmǔ. **2** 罗〔羅〕马〔馬〕数〔數〕字的 1000 Luómǎ shùzì de 1000.

m. = **1** masculine. **2** married. **3** metre. **4** mile. **5** million. **6** minute(s).

ma /mɑː/ *n* [C] mamma, mother 的简〔簡〕体〔體〕 *mamma, mother* de jiǎntǐ.

M.A. = Master of Arts.

mac /mæk/ *n* mackintosh 的缩写〔寫〕 *mackintosh* de suōxiě.

ma·cabre /məˈkɑːbrə/ *adj* 可怕的 kěpàde; 令人毛骨悚然的 lìng rén máo gǔ sǒngrán de.

maca·roni /ˌmækəˈrəʊnɪ/ *n* [U] 通心粉 tōngxīnfěn; 通心面〔麵〕 tōngxīnmiàn.

mace[1] /meɪs/ *n* [C] **1** 钉头〔頭〕锤(中古时代武器) dīngtóuchuí. **2** 权〔權〕杖 quánzhàng.

mace[2] /meɪs/ *n* [U] 豆蔻香料(肉豆蔻的干皮) dòukòu xiāngliào.

Mach /mɑːk/ *n* [C] ˈ~ **number** *n* 马〔馬〕赫值(飞行速度与音速的比例值) mǎhèzhí: ~ *two* 二倍于音速.

ma·chete /məˈtʃetɪ/ *n* [C] (中南美人使用的)大砍刀 dà kǎndāo.

ma·chine /məˈʃiːn/ *n* [C] 机〔機〕器 jīqì; 机械 jīxiè. □ *vt* 机制 jīzhì. **~-gun** 机枪〔槍〕 jīqiāng. ~ ˈ**readable** *adj* (电脑)可用电〔電〕子计算机〔機〕处〔處〕理的 kěyòng diànzǐ jìsuànjī chǔlǐ de. ~ **tool** 机床 jīchuáng. **ma·chin·ist** 机械师〔師〕 jīxièshī; 机工 jīgōng.

ma·chin·ery /məˈʃiːnərɪ/ *n* [*pl* -ies] [U] **1** 机〔機〕器 jīqì; 机器的运〔運〕转〔轉〕部分 jīqìde yùnzhuǎn bùfen. **2** 方法 fāngfǎ; 组织〔織〕 zǔzhī: *the ~ of government* 政府机构.

mack·erel /ˈmækrəl/ *n* [C] [*pl* ~] 鲭鱼 qīngyú.

mack·in·tosh /ˈmækɪntɒʃ/ *n* [C] [英国英语] 雨衣 yǔyī.

mac·ro·biotic /ˌmækrəʊbaɪˈɒtɪk/ *adj* 延长〔長〕寿〔壽〕命的 yáncháng shòumìng de. ~ ˈ**food** *n* 延长寿命的食物(不借化学助力) yáncháng shòumìng de shíwù.

mac·ro·cosm /ˈmækrəʊkɒzəm/ *n* [C]宇宙 yǔzòu; 任何大而完整的实〔實〕体〔體〕 rènhé dà ér wánzhěng de shítǐ. ⇨ microcosm.

mad /mæd/ *adj* [-der, -dest] **1** 发〔發〕疯〔瘋〕的 fāfēngde; 发狂的 fākuángde. *drive (send) sb ~* 逼得人发疯 bī de rén fāfēng. **2** [非正式用语] 非常激动〔動〕的 fēicháng jīdòng de. **3** [非正式用语] 狂怒的 kuángnùde. ˈ**~man (woman)** (女)疯子 fēngzi. **~ly** *adv*

(a) 疯狂地 fēngkuángde. (b) [非正式用语]非常 fēicháng: *~ly in love* 热恋. ~**ness** *n* [U]

madam /'mædəm/ *n* **1**(对妇女的尊称)夫人 fūrén; 女士 nǚshì. **2** (用于书信中): *Dear M~* 亲爱的女士.

mad·den /'mædn/ *vt* 使发[發]疯[瘋] shǐ fāfēng; 使发狂 shǐ fākuáng.

made /meɪd/ *pt, pp* of make¹.

Ma·donna /mə'dɒnə/ *n* **the M~** 圣[聖]母(马利亚) shèngmǔ; 圣母像 shèngmǔ xiàng.

mad·ri·gal /'mædrɪgl/ *n* [C] 情歌 qínggē; 小曲 xiǎoqǔ.

mag /mæg/ *n* [C] [非正式用语] magazine 的缩写[寫] *magazine* de suōxiě.

maga·zine /ˌmægə'ziːn/ *n* [C] **1** 弹[彈]药[藥]库[庫] dànyàokù. **2** 弹仓[倉] dàncāng; 弹盒 dànhé. **3** 杂[雜]志[誌] zázhì; 期刊 qīkān.

ma·genta /mə'dʒentə/ *adj, n* [U] 洋红色的 yánghóngsède; 洋红 yánghóng.

mag·got /'mægət/ *n* [C] 蛆 qū. **mag·goty** *adj* 多蛆的 duōqūde.

magic /'mædʒɪk/ *adj* 魔术[術]的 móshùde; 巫术的 wūshùde. □ *n* [U] **1** 魔法 mófǎ; 巫术 wūshù. **2** 戏[戲]法 xìfǎ, 魔术 móshù. **3** [喻]魔力 mólì. ~**al** /-kl/ *adj* = magic. ~**ally** *adv* ~**ian** /mə'dʒɪʃn/ *n* [C] 魔术师[師] móshùshī.

magis·trate /'mædʒɪstreɪt/ *n* [C] 地方法官 dìfāng fǎguān.

mag·nani·mous /mæg'nænɪməs/ *adj* 慷慨的 kāngkǎide; 宽宏大量的 kuānhóng dàliàng de. ~**ly** *adv* **mag·na·nim·ity** /ˌmægnə'nɪmətɪ/ *n* [C,U]

mag·nate /'mægneɪt/ *n* [C] 达[達]官 dáguān; 显[顯]贵 xiǎnguì.

mag·net /'mægnɪt/ *n* [C] **1** 磁铁[鐵] cítiě; 磁石 císhí. **2** [喻]有吸引力的人或物 yǒu xīyǐnlì de rén huò wù ~**ic** /mæg'netɪk/*adj* 有磁性的 yǒu cíxìng de; 有吸引力的 yǒu xīyǐnlì de. ~ **'field** *n* 磁场 cíchǎng. ~**ic pole** 磁极[極] cíjí. ~**ic tape** (录音用的)磁带[帶] cídài. ~**i·cally** *adv* ~**ism** /'mægnɪtɪzəm/ *n* [U] **(a)** 磁学[學] cíxué. **(b)** [喻]魅力 mèilì; 吸引力 xīyǐnlì. ~**ize** *vt* **(a)** 使磁化 shǐ cíhuà, 使生磁性 shǐ shēng cíxìng. **(b)** [喻]吸引 xīyǐn.

mag·nifi·cent /mæg'nɪfɪsənt/ *adj* 壮[壯]丽[麗]的 zhuànglìde; 宏伟[偉]的 hóngwěide. ~**ly** *adv* **mag·nifi·cence** /-sns/ *n* [U]

mag·nify /'mægnɪfaɪ/ *vt* [*pt, pp* -ied] **1** 放大 fàngdà, 扩[擴]大 kuòdà. **2** 夸[誇]大 kuādà, 夸张[張] kuāzhāng: *~ the dangers* 夸大危险. '~**ing-glass** 放大镜 fàngdàjìng. **mag·ni·fi·ca·tion** /-fɪ'keɪʃn/ *n* [U] [尤指]放大 fàngdà; 放大率 fàngdàlǜ.

mag·ni·tude /'mægnɪtjuːd/ *n* [C] [正式用语] **1** 大小 dà xiǎo. **2** 重要性 zhòngyàoxìng.

mag·pie /'mægpaɪ/ *n* [C] 鹊[鵲] què.

ma·hog·any /mə'hɒgənɪ/ *n* [C, U] 桃花心木 táohuāxīnmù; 红木 hóngmù.

maid /meɪd/ *n* [C] **1** [文学]少女 shàonǚ. **2** [现代用法]女仆[僕] nǚpú.

maiden /'meɪdn/ *n* [C] [文学]少女 shàonǚ; 未婚女子 wèihūn nǚzǐ. □ *adj* **1** 未婚女子的 wèihūn nǚzǐ de. **2** 初次的 chūcìde: *a ship's ~ voyage* 轮船的处女航行. **3** 老处[處]女的 lǎochùnǚde. ~ **name** (已婚妇女的)本姓 běnxìng.

mail¹ /meɪl/ *n* [U] 铠[鎧]甲 kǎijiǎ.

mail² /meɪl/ *n* **1** [U] 邮[郵]政 yóuzhèng. **2** [C,U] 邮件 yóujiàn. □ *vt* [主美语]邮寄 yóujì. '~**-box** [美语]邮筒 yǒutǒng; 信箱 xìnxiāng. '~**-man** [美语]邮递员 yóudìyuán. ˌ~ **'order** 函购[購] hángòu; 邮购 yóugòu.

maim /meɪm/ *vt* 残[殘]害 cánhài; 使残废[廢] shǐ cánfèi.

main¹ /meɪn/ *adj* 主要的 zhǔyàode; 最重要的 zuì zhòngyào de. ˌ~**-frame com'puter** *n* 大型通用高速计算机[機] dàxíng tōngyòng gāosù jìsuànjī. '~**land** 大陆[陸] dàlù. '~**-spring, (a)** (钟表的)主发[發]条[條] zhǔfātiáo. **(b)** [喻]主要动[動]力 zhǔyào dònglì; 主要动机[機] zhǔyào dòngjī. '~**stay** [喻]主要的依靠 zhǔyàode yīkào: *He is the ~ stay of his family.* 他是他家庭的主要依靠. ~**ly** *adv*

main² /meɪn/ *n* **1** [C] (自来水、煤气等的)总[總]管道 zǒngguǎndào; 干线[綫] gànxiàn. **2** *in the ~* 大体[體]上 dàtǐshàng.

main·tain /meɪn'teɪn/ *vt* **1** 维持 wéichí; 继[繼]续[續] jìxù: *~ law and order* 维护法律和秩序. **2** 供养[養] gōngyǎng; 扶养 fúyǎng: *~ a wife and children* 扶养妻子和子女. **3** 坚[堅]持 jiānchí: *~ one's innocence* 坚持认为自己是无罪的. **4** 保养 bǎoyǎng, 维修 wéixiu: ~

a car 维修汽车. ~**able** /-əbe/ *adj*

main·ten·ance /'meɪntənəns/ *n* [U] 维持 wéichí; 扶养〔養〕fúyǎng; 生活费 shēnghuófèi.

maize /meɪz/ *n* [U] (亦作 *Indian corn*) 玉米 yùmǐ.

Maj. = Major.

ma·jes·tic /mə'dʒestɪk/ *adj* 威严〔嚴〕的 wēiyánde; 庄〔莊〕严的 zhuāngyánde. ~**ally** *adv*

maj·esty /'mædʒəstɪ/ *n* [*pl* -ies] **1** [U] 威严〔嚴〕的 wēiyánde; 庄〔莊〕严的 zhuāngyánde. **2 His (Her, Your)** ~ 陛下 bìxià.

ma·jor[1] /'meɪdʒə(r)/ *adj* ⇨ minor. 较〔較〕大的 jiǎodàde; 较重要的 jiǎozhòngyàode: ~ *roads* 干道;要道.

ma·jor[2] /'meɪdʒə(r)/ *n* [C] 陆〔陸〕军〔軍〕少校 lùjūn shàoxiào.

ma·jor·ity /mə'dʒɒrətɪ/ *n* [C] [*pl* -ies] **1** 多数〔數〕duōshù; 大半(与 *of* 连用) dàbàn. **2** 多得票数 duō de piàoshù: *win by a* ~ *of 20* 以二十票多数获胜. **3** 法定年龄〔齡〕fǎdìng niánlíng.

make[1] /meɪk/ *vt/i* [*pt, pp* made /meɪd/] **1** 建造 jiànzào; 制〔製〕造 zhìzào: ~ *bread* 做面包; ~ *a hole* 打洞. **2** 引起 yǐnqǐ; 产〔產〕生 chǎnshēng: ~ *trouble* 引起麻烦. **3** 使 shǐ; 使成为〔爲〕shǐ chéngwéi: *The news made her happy.* 这消息使她高兴. **4** 赚 zhuàn; 获〔獲〕得 huòdé: ~ *a profit* 获利. ~ *or break* 使成功或失败 shǐ chénggōng huò shībài. ~ *one's living (as, at, by, from)* 维持生活 wéichí shēnghuó. **5** (板球比赛中)得分 défēn. **6** 使(某事)发〔發〕生 shǐ fāshēng: *Can you* ~ *this old car start?* 你能发动这辆旧汽车吗? ~ *sth 'do;* ~ *'do with sth* 对〔對〕付 duìfù. **7** 估计 gūjì; 认〔認〕为 rènwéi: *What do you* ~ *the time?* 你看现在是几点钟? **8** 等于 děngyú; 合计 héjì: *A hundred pence* ~ *one pound.* 一百便士是一英镑. ~ **sense**, ⇨ sense(5). **9** 成为 chéngwéi, *She will* ~ *him a good wife.* 她将成为他的好妻子. **10** [非正式用语] 保持(某一速度) bǎochí; 到达〔達〕(某地) dàodá: *Can we* ~ *the station in time?* 我们能按时到达车站吗? **11** 选〔選〕举〔舉〕xuǎnjǔ; 任命 rènmìng: ~ *him King* 使他成为国王. **12** ~ *for sb (sth)*, **(a)** 走向 zǒuxiàng; 向…前进〔進〕xiàng … qiánjìn. **(b)** 贡献〔獻〕gòngxiàn: *Does exercise* ~ *for good health?* 锻炼有益于健康吗? ~ *sth (sb) into sth* 把…制〔製〕成 bǎ…zhìchéng; 使转〔轉〕变〔變〕为〔爲〕shǐ zhuǎnbiàn wéi. ~ *sth of* 了解 liǎojiě; 明白 míngbái: *I can* ~ *nothing of this letter.* 我不明白这封信. ~ *off* 逃走 táozǒu. ~ *off with sth* 携…而逃 xié … ér táo. *make sth out*, **(a)** 书〔書〕写〔寫〕shūxiě; 填写 tiánxiě: ~ *out a cheque* 开支票. **(b)** 辨认〔認〕出 biànrèn chū: ~ *out of his writing* 辨认出他的笔迹. ~ *sb out to be* 把…说成 bǎ…shuōchéng. ~ *sth up*, **(a)** 补〔補〕足 bǔzú; 弥〔彌〕补 míbǔ: *We need £5 to* ~ *up the sum.* 我们需要五英镑以补足总数. **(b)** 编造 biānzào; 虚构〔構〕xūgòu: *a made-up story* 编造的故事. **(c)** 组成 zǔchéng: *Are all animal bodies made up of cells?* 所有动物身体都是细胞组成的吗? **(e)** 准〔準〕备〔備〕(床铺) zhǔnbèi. ~ *sb (oneself) up* 化装〔裝〕huàzhuāng. '~-**up** *n* [U] ~ *up one's (sb's) mind* 下决心 xià juéxīn; 拿定主意 nádìng zhǔyì. ~ *up for sth* 补偿〔償〕bǔcháng; 弥补 míbǔ. ~ *it up to sb* 补偿某人损失 bǔcháng mǒurén sǔnshī. ~ *it up (with sb)* (与…)和解 héjiě. '~**shift** 权〔權〕宜之计 quányí zhī jì.

make[2] /meɪk/ *n* [C, U] 制〔製〕造(法) zhìzào; 样〔樣〕式 yàngshì: *cars of all* ~*s* 各种型号的汽车.

maker /'meɪkə(r)/ *n* [C] **the (our) M**~ [宗教]上帝 Shàngdì.

mak·ing /'meɪkɪŋ/ *n* ***be the*** ~ ***of*** 成功的原因 chénggōngde yuányīn. ***have the*** ~***s of*** 具有成为〔爲〕…所需要的素质〔質〕jùyǒu chéngwéi…suǒxūyào de sùzhì.

mal·adjusted /ˌmælə'dʒʌstɪd/ *adj* (指人)不适〔適〕应〔應〕环〔環〕境的 bú shìyìng huánjìng de. **mal·adjust·ment** *n* [U]

ma·laria /mə'leərɪə/ *n* [U] 疟〔瘧〕疾 nüèjì.

male /meɪl/ *adj* 男的 nánde; 雄的 xióngde. □ *n* [C] 男子 nánzǐ; 雄性动〔動〕物 xióngxìng dòngwù.

mal·ice /'mælɪs/ *n* [U] 恶〔惡〕意 èyì; 怨恨 yuànhèn. **ma·li·cious** /mə'lɪʃəs/ *adj* 恶意的 èyìde; 恶毒的 èdúde.

ma·lig·nant /mə'lɪgnənt/ *adj* **1** [正式用语]恶〔惡〕意的 èyìde; 恶毒的 èdúde. **2** (指疾病)恶性的 èxìngde. ~**ly** *adv*

mal·leable /'mælɪəbl/ *adj* **1** (指金属)可锻的 kěduànde; 有延展性的 yǒu yánzhǎnxìng de. **2** [喻](指性格)可训练〔練〕的 kě xùnliàn de 易适〔適〕应〔應〕的 yì shìyìng de.

mal·let /'mælɪt/ *n* [C] 木槌 mùchuí.

mal·nu·tri·tion /ˌmælnju:'trɪʃn/ *n* [U] 营〔營〕养〔養〕不良 yíngyǎng bù liáng.

malt /mɔ:lt/ *n* [U] 麦〔麥〕芽 màiyá. □ *vt/i* **1** 使成麦芽 shǐchéng màiyá; 制〔製〕麦芽 zhì màiyá. **2** 用麦芽调制 yòng màiyá tiáozhì.

mal·treat /ˌmæl'tri:t/ *vt* [正式用语]虐待 nüèdài. **~ment** *n* [U]

mamba /'mæmbə/ *n* [C] [*pl* ~s] 非洲毒蛇 Fēizhōu dúshé.

mam·mal /'mæml/ *n* [C] 哺乳动〔動〕物 bǔrǔ dòngwù.

mam·moth /'mæməθ/ *n* [C] 猛犸〔獁〕(已绝种的古代大象) měngmǎ. □ *adj* [非正式用语]巨大的 jùdàde.

man¹ /mæn/ *n* [C] [*pl* men /men/] **1** 男人 nánrén; 男子 nánzǐ. *the* ˌ*~ in the* '*street* 普通人 pǔtōngrén; 一般人 yìbānrén. **2** 人(指男人或女人) rén: *All men must die.* 所有人都得死. **3** 人类〔類〕 rénlèi: *the achievements of ~* 人类的成就. **4** 男佣人 nán yòngrén; 雇员 gùyuán; 士兵 shìbīng: *officers and men* 官兵. **5** 丈夫 zhàngfū: *~ and wife* 夫妇. **6** 棋子 qízǐ. **'~handle** *vt* **(a)** 用人力推动〔動〕 yòng rénlì tuīdòng. **(b)** [俚语]粗暴地对〔對〕付 cūbàode duìfù. **'~hole** (进)人孔 rénkǒng. **'~hood, (a)** (男子)成年 chéngnián; 成人期 chéngrénqī. ⇨ majority(3). **(b)** 男子气〔氣〕慨 nánzǐ qìgài. ˌ**~-'made** 人造的 rénzàode, 人工的 réngōngde: *~-made cloth* 人造织物. **'~-power** 人力 rénlì. **'~slaughter** 杀〔殺〕人 shārén; 误杀 wùshā.

man² /mæn/ *vt* [-nn-] 提供军〔軍〕事或防务〔務〕人员 tígòng jūnshì huò fángwù rényuán: *~ gun* 配备炮手 *~ machine* 配备机器操作人员.

man·acle /'mænəkl/ *n* [C] [常用 *pl*] 手铐 shǒukào; 足镣 zúliào. □ *vt* 上手铐 shàng shǒukào; 束缚 shùfù.

man·age /'mænɪdʒ/ *vt/i* **1** 控制 kòngzhì; 管理 guǎnlǐ: *~ a business* 经营事业. **2** 完成 wánchéng: *We can't ~ with these tools.* 我们不能使用这些工具. **3** [非正式用语]吃 chī: *Can you ~ another apple?* 你能再吃个苹果吗? **'~able** /-əbl/ *adj* 易管理的 yì guǎnlǐ de; 易处〔處〕理的 yì chǔlǐ de.

man·age·ment /'mænɪdʒmənt/ *n* **1** [U] 管理 guǎnlǐ; 经〔經〕营〔營〕 jīngyíng: *poor ~ of an industry* 糟糕的工业管理. **2** [U] 手段 shǒuduàn; 经营才能 jīngyíng cáinéng. **3** [C, U] (工商企业的)管理部门〔門〕 guǎnlǐ bùmén; 资方 zīfāng: *workers and ~* 劳资双方.

man·ager /'mænɪdʒə(r)/ *n* [C] 经〔經〕理 jīnglǐ; 管理人 guǎnlǐrén. **~ess** /-'res/ *n* [C] 女经理 nǚ jīnglǐ; 女管理人 nǚ guǎnlǐrén. **~ial** /-'dʒɪərɪəl/ *adj* 经理的 jīnglǐde; 管理人的 guǎnlǐrénde.

man·date /'mændeɪt/ *n* [C] **1** 命令 mìnglìng; 训令 xùnlìng. **2** (选民对选出的代表)授权〔權〕 shòuquán. **man·da·tory** /'mændətrɪ/ *adj* 命令的 mìnglìngde; 强制性的 qiángzhìxìngde.

man·do·lin /'mændəlɪn/ *n* [C] 曼陀林(琴) màntuólín.

mane /meɪn/ *n* [C] (马、狮等的)鬃毛 zōngmáo.

man·eu·ver /mə'nu:və(r)/ *n, v* [美语] = manoeuvre.

man·ful /'mænfl/ *adj* 勇敢的 yǒnggǎnde; 果断〔斷〕的 guǒduànde. **~ly** *adv*

mange /meɪndʒ/ *n* [U] 兽〔獸〕疥癣 shòu jièxuǎn **mangy** *adj* [-ier, -iest]

manger /'meɪndʒə(r)/ *n* [C] 马〔馬〕(或牛等的)槽 mǎcáo.

mangle¹ /'mæŋgl/ *n* [C] (洗衣用的)挤〔擠〕干〔乾〕机〔機〕 jǐgānjī. □ *vt* 将〔將〕(衣服等)送入挤干机挤压〔壓〕 jiāng... sòngrù jǐgānjī jǐyā.

mangle² /'mæŋgl/ *vt* 割碎 gésuì; 毁坏〔壞〕 huǐhuài; 弄糟 nòngzāo.

mango /'mæŋgəʊ/ *n* [C] [*pl* ~es 或~s] 芒果 mángguǒ; 芒果树〔樹〕 mángguǒshù.

mangy /'meɪndʒɪ/ ⇨ mange.

man·handle ⇨ man¹.

mania /'meɪnɪə/ *n* **1** [U] 疯〔瘋〕狂 fēngkuáng; 躁狂症 zàokuángzhèng. **2** 狂热〔熱〕 kuángrè; 癖好 pǐhào: *a ~ for motorbikes* 摩托车狂. **maniac** /'meɪnɪæk/ *n* [C] **(a)** 疯子 fēngzi. **(b)** [喻]躁狂者 zàokuángzhě. **~cal** /mə'naɪəkl/ *adj*

mani·cure /'mænɪkjʊə(r)/ *n* [U] 修指甲 xiū zhījia. □ *vt* 修…的指甲 xiū...de zhījia; 修剪 xiūjiǎn. **'mani·cur·ist** *n* [C]

mani·fest /'mænɪfest/ *adj* 明白的 míngbaide; 明显〔顯〕的 míngxiǎnde. □ *vt* 显示 xiǎnshì; 出现 chūxiàn: *No disease ~ed itself.* 未发生过疾病. **~ly** *adv* **~a·tion** /ˌmænɪfe'steɪʃn/ *n* [C, U]

mani·festo /ˌmænɪ'festəʊ/ *n* [C] [*pl* ~s 或 ~es] 宣言 xuānyán 声〔聲〕明 shēngmíng.

mani·fold /ˈmænɪfəʊld/ *adj* 多样〔樣〕的 duōyàngde; 种〔種〕种的 zhǒngzhǒngde: ~ *uses* 多种用途. □ *n* [C] 歧管 qíguǎn; 多支管 duōzhīguǎn.

ma·nipu·late /məˈnɪpjʊleɪt/ *vt* 熟练〔練〕地使用 shúliànde shǐyòng; 操纵〔縱〕 cāozòng: ~ *controls* (*people*) 操纵装置(人民). **ma·nipu'la·tion** *n* [C, U]

man·kind /ˌmænˈkaɪnd/ *n* [U] 人类〔類〕 rénlèi.

man·ly /ˈmænlɪ/ *adj* [-ier, -iest] 男子气〔氣〕概的 nánzǐ qìgài de; 适〔適〕合男子的 shìhé nánzǐ de. **man·li·ness** *n* [U]

man·ner /ˈmænə(r)/ *n* [C] **1** 方式 fāngshì; 方法 fāngfǎ. **2** [仅用 *sing*] 态〔態〕度 tàidù; 举〔舉〕止 jǔzhǐ: *I don't like his* ~. 我不喜欢他的举止态度. **3** [*pl*] 习〔習〕惯 xíguàn; 风〔風〕俗 fēngsú. **4** [*pl*] 礼〔禮〕貌 lǐmào; 规矩 guīju: *good* ~*s* 彬彬有礼. **5** (文艺上的)风格 fēngé; 手法 shǒufǎ. **6** 种〔種〕类〔類〕 zhǒnglèi. ***all* ~ *of*** 各种的 gèzhǒngde. ~**ed** *adj*: *good* (*'ill*)-~*ed* 有(无)礼貌的 yǒulǐmàode.

man·ner·ism /ˈmænərɪzəm/ *n* [C] (说话、举止等的)习〔習〕气〔氣〕 xíqì; 癖性 pǐxìng.

ma·noeuvre [美语 = **man·eu·ver**] /məˈnuːvə(r)/ *n* [C] **1**(部队的)调动〔動〕 diàodòng; 机〔機〕动 jīdòng; [*pl*] 演习〔習〕 yǎnxí. **2** 策略 cèlüè; 花招 huāzhāo. □ *vt/i* (使)调动 diàodòng; 演习 yǎnxí. **ma·noeuvr·able** /-vrəbl/ *adj* 可调动的 kě diàodòng de; 机动的 jīdòngde: *a manoeuvrable car* 容易操纵的汽车.

manor /ˈmænə(r)/ *n* [C] (ˈ~-*house*) 庄〔莊〕园〔園〕 zhuāngyuán; 庄园中的宅第 zhuāngyuánzhōngde zháidì.

man·sion /ˈmænʃn/ *n* [C] 大厦 dàshà; 官邸 guāndǐ.

mantel·piece /ˈmæntəlpiːs/ *n* [C] 壁炉〔爐〕台〔臺〕 bìlútái.

mantle /ˈmæntl/ *n* [C] **1** 斗篷 dǒupéng; 披风〔風〕 pīfēng. **2** [喻]覆盖物 fùgàiwù: *a* ~ *of snow* 一层雪. **3** (煤气灯的)白热〔熱〕罩 báirèzhào.

man·ual /ˈmænjʊəl/ *adj* 手工的 shǒugōngde; 用手的 yòngshǒude. □ *n* [C] 手册 shǒucè; 便览〔覽〕 biànlǎn. ~**ly** *adv*

manu·fac·ture /ˌmænjʊˈfæktʃə(r)/ *vt* (大量)制〔製〕造 zhìzào; 加工 jiāgōng. □ *n* **1** [U] (大量)制造 zhìzào. **2** [*pl*] 制造品 zhìzàopǐn, 产〔產〕品 chǎnpǐn.

ma·nure /məˈnjʊə(r)/ *n* [U] 粪〔糞〕肥 fènféi; 肥料 féiliào. □ *vt* 施肥 shīféi.

manu·script /ˈmænjʊskrɪpt/ *n* [C] (缩作 **MS**, *pl* **MSS**) 手稿 shǒugǎo; 原稿 yuángǎo.

many /ˈmenɪ/ *adj, n* (与 *few* 相对; ⇨ more, most) **1** (与 *pl nouns* 连用)许多的 xǔduōde; 多的 duōde. ***one too* ~** 多余〔餘〕的一个〔個〕 duōyúde yígè. **2** [与 *sing noun* 连用]: ~ *a man* (= many men) 许多人.

map /mæp/ *n* [C] 地图〔圖〕 dìtú; 天体〔體〕图 tiāntǐtú. **(*put sth*) *on the* ~** [喻]重视 zhòngshì. □ *vt* [-pp-] 绘〔繪〕制〔製〕...的地图〔圖〕 huìzhì...de dìtú.

mar /mɑː(r)/ *vt* [-rr-] 毁坏〔壞〕 huǐhuài; 弄糟 nòngzāo: *an accident* ~*red their holiday* 一场事故破坏了他们的假期.

Mar. = March.

mara·thon /ˈmærəθən/ *n* [C] **1** 马〔馬〕拉松长〔長〕跑(全长约 26 英里或 41.8 公里) mǎlāsōng chángpǎo. **2** [喻]耐力比赛 nàilì bǐsài. □ *adj* 马拉松式的 mǎlāsōngshìde: *a* ~ *debate* 长时间的辩论.

ma·raud /məˈrɔːd/ *vi* 抢〔搶〕劫 qiǎngjié; 掳〔擄〕掠 lǔlüè. ~**er** 抢劫者 qiǎngjiézhě; 掳掠者 lǔlüèzhě.

marble /ˈmɑːbl/ *n* **1** [U] 大理石 dàlǐshí **2** [C] (游戏用的玻璃做的)弹〔彈〕子 dànzi.

March /mɑːtʃ/ *n* 三月 sānyuè.

march /mɑːtʃ/ *n* **1** [U] 行进〔進〕 xíngjìn; 行军〔軍〕 xíngjūn. **2** [C] 行程 xíngchéng. **3** 进展 jìnzhǎn: *the* ~ *of time* 时间的推移. **4** [C] 进行曲 jìnxíngqǔ. □ *vt/i* (使)行进 xíngjìn; (使)行军 xíngjūn.

mar·chion·ess /ˌmɑːʃəˈnes/ *n* [C] 侯爵夫人 hóujué fūrén; 女侯爵 nǚ hóujué.

mare /meə(r)/ *n* [C] 母马〔馬〕 mǔmǎ; 牝驴〔驢〕 pìnlǘ.

mar·gar·ine /ˌmɑːdʒəˈriːn/ *n* [U] 人造黄油 rénzào huángyóu.

mar·gin /ˈmɑːdʒɪn/ *n* [C] **1** 页边〔邊〕的空白 yèbiānde kòngbái. **2** 边 biān; 缘 yuán. **3** (时间、金钱等)多余〔餘〕 duōyú; 过〔過〕量 guòliàng. ~**al** *adj* 很少的 hěnshǎode: *a* ~*al increase* 稍微的增加. ~**ly** *adv*

mari·juana, mari·huana /ˌmærɪˈwɑːnə/ *n* [U] 粉蓝〔藍〕烟草 fěnlányāncǎo; 大麻 dàmá.

ma·rina /məˈriːnə/ *n* [C] [*pl* ~s]

小船坞〔塢〕 xiǎochuánwù; 系船池 xìchuánchí.

mari·nade /ˌmærɪˈneɪd/ *n* [C, U] (一种酒、醋和香料合成的)腌〔醃〕泡汁 yānpàozhī. □ *vt* (亦作 **marinate** /ˈmærɪneɪt/) 用腌泡汁泡(或腌) yòng yānpàozhī pào.

mar·ine /məˈriːn/ *adj* **1** 海的 hǎide; 海产〔產〕的 hǎichǎnde: *~ life* 海生生物. **2** 海运〔運〕的 hǎiyùnde; 海军〔軍〕的 hǎijūnde. □ *n* **1** [U] (总称)船舶 chuánbó; 海运业〔業〕 hǎiyùnyè. **2** [C] 海军陆〔陸〕战〔戰〕队〔隊〕军官(或士兵) hǎijūn lùzhànduì jūnguān.

mari·tal /ˈmærɪtl/ *adj* 婚姻的 hūnyīnde; 丈夫的 zhàngfude.

mari·time /ˈmærɪtaɪm/ *adj* **1** 海上的 hǎishàngde; 海事的 hǎishìde. **2** 近海的 jìnhǎide; 沿海的 yánhǎide.

mark[1] /mɑːk/ *n* [C] **1** 痕迹〔跡〕 hénjì; 斑点〔點〕 bāndiǎn. **2** 记号〔號〕 jìhào; 特征〔徵〕 tèzhēng: *a ˈbirth ~* 胎痣. **3** 标〔標〕志〔誌〕 biāozhì: *~s of old age* 老年的标志. **4** 符号 fúhào: *ˌpunctuˈation ~s* 标点符号. **5** (考试的)分数〔數〕 fēnshù: *top ~s* 最高分. **6** 目标 mùbiāo. ***be (fall) wide of the ~*** 不准〔準〕确的 bù zhǔnquè de. **7** ***make one's ~*** 成名 chéngmíng. **8** 标准 biāozhǔn: *up to (below) the ~* 达到(低于)标准.

mark[2] /mɑːk/ *vt* **1** 作记号〔號〕(或符号) zuò jìhào; 标〔標〕明 biāomíng: *~ the price on clothes.* 在衣服上标价. **2** 标〔標〕示位置 biāoshì wèizhì: *A stone ~s his grave.* 一块石头标示他的坟墓的位置. **3** 批分数〔數〕 pī fēnshù. **4** 用记号表示某种事物 yòng jìhào biǎoshì mǒuzhǒng shìwù: *~ an answer wrong* 标出错误答案. **5** 注意 zhùyì. ***(You) ~ my words*** (你)留心听〔聽〕着! liúxīn tīngzhe! **6** 表示…的特征〔徵〕 biǎoshì…de tèzhēng: *qualities that ~ a leader* 领袖的特征. **7** 标志〔誌〕 biāozhì: *His death ~s the end of an era.* 他的逝世标志着一个时代的结束. ***~ time***, **(a)** 踏步 tàbù. **(b)** 〔喻〕停顿不前 tíngdùn bù qián. **8** ***~ sth off (out)*** 划〔劃〕分 huàfēn; 划出 huàchū. ***~ up*** 增加(商品)的价〔價〕格 zēngjiā...de jiàgé. **~ed** *adj* 明显〔顯〕的 míngxiǎnde: *a ~ed improvement in his health* 他的健康状况明显好转. **~ing** (兽皮、鸟羽等的)斑纹 bānwén.

marker /ˈmɑːkə(r)/ *n* [C] **1** 记分员 jìfēnyuán; 记分器 jìfēnqì. **2** 里程碑 lǐchéngbēi; 标〔標〕示物 biāoshìwù. **3** 打分数〔數〕的人 dǎ fēnshù de rén.

mar·ket /ˈmɑːkɪt/ *n* [C] **1** 市场〔場〕 shìchǎng. **2** 集市日 jíshìrì. **3** 单项商品交易 dānxiàng shāngpǐn jiāoyì: *the ˈcoffee ~* 咖啡市场. **4** 行情 hángqíng; 市价〔價〕 shìjià: *The ~ was steady.* 行情稳定. **5** 销路 xiāolù; 需要 xūyào: *There's no ~ for these goods.* 这些商品没有销路. **6** ***on the ~*** 销售 xiāoshòu. **7** 推销地区〔區〕 tuīxiāo dìqū: *foreign ~s for cars.* 销售汽车的外国市场. □ *vt/i* 销售 xiāoshòu. **ˌ~ reˈsearch** 研究人们〔們〕购〔購〕买〔買〕某些商品的原因 yánjiū rénmén gòumǎi mǒuxiē shāngpǐn de yuányīn. **~able** /-əbl/ *adj* **~ing** 销售(学) xiāoshòu.

marks·man /ˈmɑːksmən/ *n* [C] [*pl* -men /-mən/] 射手 shèshǒu; 神枪〔槍〕手 shénqiāngshǒu.

mar·ma·lade /ˈmɑːməleɪd/ *n* [U] 橘子酱〔醬〕 júzijiàng; 果酱 guǒjiàng.

ma·roon[1] /məˈruːn/ *adj, n* [U] 栗色 lìsè; 栗色的 lìsède.

ma·roon[2] /məˈruːn/ *vt* 将〔將〕(某人)放逐到孤岛〔島〕 jiāng ... fàngzhú dào gūdǎo.

mar·quee /mɑːˈkiː/ *n* [C] 大帐〔帳〕篷 dà zhàngpéng.

mar·quis, mar·quess /ˈmɑːkwɪs/ *n* 侯爵 hóujué. ⇨marchioness.

mar·riage /ˈmærɪdʒ/ *n* [C, U] 结婚 jiéhūn; 婚姻 hūnyīn. **~able** /-əbl/ *adj* (年龄)适〔適〕宜结婚的 shìyí jiéhūn de.

mar·ried /ˈmærɪd/ *adj* 已婚的 yǐhūnde; 夫妇〔婦〕的 fūfùde.

mar·row /ˈmærəʊ/ *n* **1** [U] 髓 suí; 骨髓 gǔsuí. **2** [C, U] [英国英语] 菜瓜 càiguā. [美语 = squash].

marry /ˈmærɪ/ *vt/i* [*pt, pp* -ied] **1** 结婚 jiéhūn; 嫁 jià; 娶 qǔ. **2** 正式结为夫妇〔婦〕 zhèngshì jié wéi fūfù: *married by the vicar* 牧师主持婚礼. **3** 嫁(女) jià: *He married his daughter to a rich man.* 他把女儿嫁给一个富翁.

marsh /mɑːʃ/ *n* [C, U] 沼泽〔澤〕 zhǎozé; 湿〔濕〕地 shīdì. **marshy** *adj* [-ier, -iest]

mar·shal[1] /ˈmɑːʃl/ *n* [C] **1** 元帅〔帥〕 yuánshuài; 高级军〔軍〕官 gāojí jūnguān. **2** 司仪〔儀〕 sīyí; 典礼〔禮〕官 diǎnlǐguān. **3** [美语]县〔縣〕的行政司法官 xiànde xíngzhèng sīfǎguān.

mar·shal[2] /ˈmɑːʃl/ *vt* [-ll-, 美语 -l-]

1 整理 zhěnglǐ; 排列 páiliè. 2 (按礼仪)引导[導] yǐndǎo.

mar·su·pial /mɑːˈsuːpɪəl/ *adj, n* [C] 有袋动[動]物的 yǒu dài dòngwù de; 有袋动物(如袋鼠等) yǒu dài dòngwù.

mar·tial /ˈmɑːʃl/ *adj* 1 军[軍]事的 jūnshìde; 战[戰]争的 zhànzhēngde. 2 尚武的 shàngwǔde. ,~ **'law** 军事管制法 jūnshì guǎnzhìfǎ. ~**ly** *adv*

mar·tin /ˈmɑːtɪn/ *n* [C] (亦作 *'house-~*) 一种[種]燕子 yìzhǒng yànzi.

mar·tyr /ˈmɑːtə(r)/ *n* [C] 烈士 lièshì; 殉难[難]者 xùnnànzhě. □ *vt* 杀[殺]害(坚持某种信仰者) shāhài; 折磨 zhémó. ~**dom** *n* [U] 牺[犧]牲 xīshēng; 殉难 xùnnàn.

mar·vel /ˈmɑːvl/ *n* [C] 令人惊[驚]奇的事 lìng rén jīngqí de shì. *work ~s* 做出惊人成绩 zuò chū jīngrén chéngjī; 创[創]造奇迹 chuàngzào qíjī. □ *vi* [-ll-] 惊异[異] jīngyì. ~**lous** [美语 = ~**ous**] *adj* ~**lous·ly** [美语 = ~**ous·ly**] *adv*

Marx·ist /ˈmɑːksɪst/ *n* [C] 马[馬]克思主义[義]者 Mǎkèsīzhǔyìzhě. **Marx·ism** *n* [U] 马克思主义 Mǎkèsī zhǔyì.

mar·zi·pan /ˈmɑːzɪpæn/ *n* [U] 杏仁糖果 xìngrén tángguǒ.

mas·cara /mæˈskɑːrə/ *n* [U] 染眉毛(或睫毛)油 rǎn méimáo yóu.

mas·cot /ˈmæskət/ *n* [C] 吉祥的人(或动物,东西) jíxiángde rén.

mas·cu·line /ˈmæskjʊlɪn/ *adj* 1 男性的 nánxìngde. 2 阳[陽]性的 yángxìngde: ~ *pronouns* 阳性代词. ⇨feminine. **mas·cu'lin·ity** *n* [U]

mash /mæʃ/ *n* [U] 1 一种牛马的饲料 yìzhǒng niúmǎ de sìliào. 2 糊状[狀]物(如捣烂的熟马铃薯) húzhuàngwù. □ *vt* 捣[擣]碎成糊状 dǎosuì chéng húzhuàng.

mask /mɑːsk/ *n* [C] 1 面具 miànjù; 假面具 jiǎmiànjù. 2 艺[藝]术[術]假面具 yìshù jiǎmiànjù. 3 口罩 kǒuzhào. □ *vt* 戴假面具 dài jiǎmiànjù. 2 遮蔽 zhēbì; 伪[僞]装[裝] wěizhuāng. **'gas-~** 防毒面具 fángdú miànjù.

maso·chism /ˈmæsəkɪzəm/ *n* [U] 受虐狂 shòunüèkuáng. **maso·chist** 受虐狂者 shòunüèkuángzhě. **maso·'chis·tic** *adj*

ma·son /ˈmeɪsn/ *n* [C] 1 石工 shígōng; 泥瓦工 níwǎgōng; 2= freemason. ~**ic** /məˈsɒnɪk/ *adj* 共济[濟]会[會]成员的 gòngjìhuì chéngyuán de; 共济会的 gòngjìhuìde. ~**ry, (a)** 石工 shígōng; 砖石建筑 zhuānshí jiànzhù. **(b)** = freemasonry.

mas·quer·ade /ˌmɑːskəˈreɪd/ *n* [C] 1 化装[裝]舞会[會] huàzhuāng wǔhuì. 2 [喻]伪[僞]装 wěizhuāng; 掩饰 yǎnshì. □ *vi* 假装 jiǎzhuāng; 乔[喬]装 qiáozhuāng: ~ *as a prince* 乔装王子.

mass /mæs/ *n* 1 [C] 块[塊]kuài, 堆 duī; 大量 dàliàng; 大堆 dàduī: *a ~ of clouds* 一块云. *a ~ of papers* 一堆纸. 2 **the ~es** 群众[衆] qúnzhòng; 民众 mínzhòng. 3 [物理] 质[質]量 zhìliàng. ⇨ size (1). □ *vt/i* 集中 jízhōng; 聚集 jùjí: *Troops are ~ing to attack.* 军队在集结准备进攻. ,~ **'media** 媒介 méijiè; 传[傳]播工具 (尤指报纸、电视) chuánbō gōngjù. ,~ **pro'duction** 大量生产[産] dàliàng shēngchǎn. ,~**-pro'duce** *vt*

mass·acre /ˈmæsəkə(r)/ *n* [C] 大屠杀[殺] dàtúshā; 残[殘]杀 cánshā. □ *vt* 大屠杀 dàtúshā.

mass·age /ˈmæsɑːʒ/ *n* [C, U] 按摩 ànmó; 推拿 tuīná. □ *vt* 按摩 ànmó; 推拿 tuīná.

mass·eur /mæˈsɜː(r)/ *n* [C] 男按摩师[師] nán ànmóshī.

mass·euse /mæˈsɜːz/ *n* [C] 女按摩师[師] nǚ ànmóshī.

mass·ive /ˈmæsɪv/ *adj* 1 大而重的 dà ér zhòng de; 粗大的 cūdàde. 2 [喻]巨大的 jùdàde: *a ~ effort* 巨大的努力.

mast /mɑːst/ *n* [C] 1 桅杆 wéigān; 樯[檣] qiáng. 2 天线[綫]塔 tiānxiàntǎ.

mas·ter /ˈmɑːstə(r)/ *n* [C] 1 店老板 diànlǎobǎn; 雇主 gùzhǔ. 2 男主人 nán zhǔrén. 3 (商船的) 船长[長] chuánzhǎng. 4 (狗马[馬]等的) 男主人 nán zhǔrén. 5 男教师[師] nán jiàoshī. 6 ~ *of* 精通 jīngtōng; 掌握 zhǎngwò. 7 大师 dàshī; 名家 míngjiā. ⇨ old master. 8 (唱片) 母片 mǔpiàn. □ *adj* 1 熟练[練]的 shúliànde; 精通的 jīngtōngde: *a ~ builder* 大建筑师. 2 原声[聲]带的 yuánshēngdàide. □ *vt* 做…的主人 zuò…de zhǔrén: ~ *a skill* 掌握一种技能. ,**M~ of 'Arts ('Science)** (缩作 **MA, MSc**) 文科(理科)硕士 wénkē shuòshì. **'~mind** *vt* 筹[籌]划[劃],指导[導]一项计划 chóuhuà, zhǐdǎo yíxiàng jìhuà. **'~piece** 杰[傑]作 jiézuò; 名著 míngzhù.

mas·ter·ful /ˈmɑːstəfl/ *adj* 1 专[專]横的 zhuānhèngde; 好支配人

的 hào zhīpèi rén de. 2 = masterly. ~fully *adv*

mas·ter·ly /ˈmɑːstəlɪ/ *adj* 巧妙的 qiǎomiàode; 精巧的 jīngqiǎode.

mas·tery /ˈmɑːstərɪ/ *n* [U] 熟练〔練〕shúliàn; 精通 jīngtōng.

mas·tur·bate /ˈmæstəbeɪt/ *vi* 手淫 shǒuyín. **mas·turˈba·tion** *n* [U]

mat[1] /mæt/ *n* [C] 1 席〔蓆〕子 xízi; 垫〔墊〕子 diànzi. 2 (花瓶、盘等的)小垫 xiǎodiàn. □ *vt/i* [-tt-] (使)缠结 chánjié ~*ted hair* 乱蓬蓬的头发.

mat[2], **matt** /mæt/ *adj* 暗淡的 àndànde; 无〔無〕光泽〔澤〕的 wú guāngzé de. ⇨ gloss.

mata·dor /ˈmætədɔː(r)/ *n* [C] 斗〔鬥〕牛士 dòuniúshì.

match[1] /mætʃ/ *n* [C] 火柴 huǒchái. ˈ~**box** 火柴盒 huǒcháihé.

match[2] /mætʃ/ *n* [C] 1 比赛 bǐsài; 竞〔競〕赛 jìngsài: *a ˈboxing-~* 拳击比赛. 2 对〔對〕手 duìshǒu; 敌〔敵〕手 díshǒu: *He's no ~ for me.* 他不是我的对手. 3 婚姻 hūnyīn. 4 配偶 pèi'ǒu: *a good ~* 一个好配偶. 5 相配的人或物 xiāngpèide rén huò wù: *The carpets and curtains are a good ~.* 地毯和窗帘很相称. □ *vt/i* 1 相当〔當〕xiāngdāng; 相等 xiāngděng: *~ him in strength* 力量和他相当. 2 (品质、颜色等)相配 xiāngpèi. ⇨clash(4). ~**less** *adj*

mate[1] /meɪt/ *n* 1 [非正式用语]伙伴 huǒbàn; 同事 tóngshì. ⇨ playmate. 2 大副 dàfù. 3 助手 zhùshǒu: *a plumber's ~* 管子工的助手. 4 鸟〔鳥〕兽〔獸〕的配偶 niǎo shòu de pèi'ǒu. □ *vt/i* (鸟兽)交配 jiāopèi.

mate[2] /meɪt/ *n, v* = checkmate.

ma·terial[1] /məˈtɪərɪəl/ *adj* 1 (与 *spiritual* 相对)物质〔質〕的 wùzhìde. 2 肉体〔體〕的 ròutǐde. 3 [法律]实〔實〕质〔質〕性的 shízhìxìngde: *~ evidence* 实证; 物证. ~**ly** *adv* 实质上 shízhìshàng.

ma·terial[2] /məˈtɪərɪəl/ *n* [C, U] 材料 cáiliào; 原料 yuánliào: *ˈdress ~s* 衣料.

ma·teri·al·ism /məˈtɪərɪəlɪzəm/ *n* [U] 1 唯物主义〔義〕wéiwùzhǔyì; 唯物论〔論〕wéiwùlùn. 2 实〔實〕利主义 shílì zhǔyì. **ma·teri·al·ist** *n* [C]

ma·teri·al·ize /məˈtɪərɪəlaɪz/ *vi* (使)具体〔體〕化 jùtǐhuà; 成为〔為〕事实〔實〕chéngwéi shìshí.

ma·ter·nal /məˈtɜːnl/ *adj* 1 母亲〔親〕的 mǔqīnde; 似母亲的 sìmǔqīnde. 2 母系的 mǔxìde; 母方的 mǔfāngde: *my ~ grandfather* 我的外祖父. ~**ly** *adv*

ma·tern·ity /məˈtɜːnətɪ/ *n* [U] 母性 mǔxìng; 母道 mǔdào. □ *adj* 产〔產〕妇〔婦〕的 chǎnfùde; 孕妇的 yùnfùde: *a ~ home* 产科医院.

math·emat·ics /ˌmæθəˈmætɪks/ *n* [U] 数〔數〕学〔學〕shùxué. **math·emat·ical** *adj* **math·ema'ti·cian** *n* [C] 数学家 shùxuéjiā.

maths [美语= **math**] /mæθs/ *n* mathematics 的缩写〔寫〕*mathematics* de suōxiě.

mati·née /ˈmætɪneɪ/ *n* [C] 午后〔後〕的演出 wǔhòude yǎnchū; 日戏〔戲〕rìxì.

matric. = matriculation.

ma·tricu·late /məˈtrɪkjʊleɪt/ *vt/i* [过时用法](大学中准许)注册入学〔學〕zhùcè rùxué. **ma·tricuˈla·tion** *n* [C, U]

mat·ri·mony /ˈmætrɪmənɪ/ *n* [U] 婚姻 hūnyīn; 结婚 jiéhūn; 婚姻生活 hūnyīn shēnghuó. **mat·riˈmo·nial** *adj*

ma·tron /ˈmeɪtrən/ *n* [C] 1 (学校等的)女总〔總〕管 nǚ zǒngguǎn. 2 护〔護〕士长〔長〕hùshìzhǎng. ~**ly** *adj*

matt /mæt/ *adj* = mat[2].

mat·ter[1] /ˈmætə(r)/ *n* 1 [U] 物质〔質〕wùzhì. 2 (书籍、讲话等的)内容 nèiróng; 素材 sùcái. 3 [U] 印刷品 yìnshuāpǐn: *ˈreading ~* 读物. 4 [C] 事务〔務〕shìwù; 事情 shìqíng; 问〔問〕题 wèntí: *ˈmoney ~s* 金钱方面的问题. ***a ˌ~ of ˈcourse*** 理所当〔當〕然的事 lǐsuǒdāngránde shì. ***as a ˌ~ of ˈfact*** 事实〔實〕上 shìshíshàng. 5 [U] 重要 zhòngyào; 要紧〔緊〕yàojǐn. ***no ~ ˈwho (ˈwhat, ˈwhere) etc*** 无〔無〕论〔論〕何人(什么、哪里等) wúlùn hérén. 6 ***What's the ~?*** 怎么〔麼〕啦? zěnmò lā? 7 ***a ~ of*** 大约 dàyuē: *within a ~ of hours* 大约几小时内. ˌ~-**of-ˈfact** *adj* (指人)讲〔講〕究实〔實〕际〔際〕的 jiǎngjiu shíjì de.

mat·ter[2] /ˈmætə(r)/ *vi* 关〔關〕系〔係〕重要 guānxì zhòngyào: *It doesn't ~.* 没关系.

mat·ting /ˈmætɪŋ/ *n* [U] 地席〔蓆〕dìxí; 草席 cǎoxí.

mat·tock /ˈmætək/ *n* [C] 丁字镐 dīngzìgǎo.

mat·tress /ˈmætrɪs/ *n* [C] 床垫〔墊〕chuángdiàn.

ma·ture /məˈtʃʊə(r)/ *vt/i* (使)成熟 chéngshú; (使)成长〔長〕chéngzhǎng. □ *adj* 成熟的 chéngshúde; 充分发〔發〕展的 chōngfèn fāzhǎn de. **~ly** *adv* **ma·tur·ity** *n* [U]

maul /mɔːl/ *vt* 伤〔傷〕害 shānghài; 虐打 nüèdǎ: *~ed by a lion* 受到狮子伤害.

mau·so·leum /ˌmɔːsəˈliːəm/ *n* [C] 陵墓 língmù; 壮〔壯〕丽〔麗〕的陵墓 zhuànglìde língmù.

mauve /məʊv/ *adj, n* [U] 淡紫色的 dànzǐsède; 淡紫色 dànzǐsè.

max. = maximum.

maxim /ˈmæksɪm/ *n* [C] 格言 géyán; 箴言 zhēnyán.

maxi·mize /ˈmæksɪmaɪz/ *vt* 增加到最大限度 zēngjiādào zuì dà xiàndù. **maxi·miˈza·tion** *n* [U]

maxi·mum /ˈmæksɪməm/ *n* [*pl* ~s 或 -ma /-mə/] 最大量 zuìdàliàng; 最大限度 zuìdà xiàndù; 极〔極〕限 jíxiàn.

may/meɪ/ *aux verb* [*pt* migth /maɪt/] [否定式 may not, mayn't 和 might not, mightn't] **1** 可能 kěnéng: *That ~ (might) be true.* 那可能是真的. **2** (表示许可)可以 kěyǐ: *M~ I come in?* 我可以进来吗? **3 ~ as well** 还〔還〕是…的好 háishì…de hǎo: *He's late, I ~ as well go home.* 他迟到了, 我还是回家吧. **4** (用于表示请求): *I think you might offer to help.* 我想你会帮帮忙的.

May /meɪ/ *n* 五月 wǔyuè.

may·be /ˈmeɪbɪ/ *adv* 大概 dàgài, 或许 huòxǔ.

may·on·naise /ˌmeɪəˈneɪz/ *n* [U] (用蛋黄、油、醋等制成的)蛋黄酱〔醬〕 dànhuángjiàng.

mayor /meə(r)/ *n* [C] 市长〔長〕 shìzhǎng. **~ess** /meəˈres/ *n* [C] 市长夫人 shìzhǎng fūrén; 女市长 nǚ shìzhǎng.

maze /meɪz/ *n* [C] 迷宫 mígōng; 曲径〔徑〕 qūjìng.

Mc. = megacycle(s) 兆周 zhàozhōu.

M.C. = Master of Ceremonies 典礼〔禮〕官 diǎnlǐguān.

M.Ch. = Master of Surgery 外科学〔學〕硕士 wàikēxué shuòshì.

M.D. = Doctor of Medicine 医〔醫〕学〔學〕博士 yīxué bóshì.

me /miː/ *personal pron* 我(I 的宾格) wǒ: *He saw ~.* 他看见了我.

meadow /ˈmedəʊ/ *n* [C, U] 草地 cǎodì; 牧草地 mùcǎodì.

meagre [美语 = **mea·ger**] /ˈmiːgə(r)/ *adj* **1** 瘦的 shòude. **2** 不足的 bùzúde; 贫乏的 pínfáde: *~ supplies* 供应不足. **~ly** *adv* **~ness** *n* [U]

meal¹ /miːl/ *n* [C] **1** 一餐 yìcān, 一顿(饭) yídùn. **2** 饭食 fànshí.

meal² /miːl/ *n* [U] 粗粉 cūfěn. **mealy** *adj* [-ier, -iest].

mean¹ /miːn/ *adj* [-er, -est] **1** 难〔難〕看的 nánkànde; 简〔簡〕陋的 jiǎnlòude. **2** 残〔殘〕酷的 cánkùde; 恶〔惡〕意的 èyìde. **3** 吝啬〔嗇〕的 lìnsède; 自私的 zìsīde: *~ with money* 花钱吝啬. **~ly** *adv* **~ness** *n* [U]

mean² /miːn/ *adj* 中间〔間〕的 zhōngjiānde; 中庸的 zhōngyōngde. □ *n* **1** [C] 中间 zhōngjiān; 中庸 zhōngyōng. **2** [数学] 平均数〔數〕 píngjūnshù; (比例)中项 zhōngxiàng.

mean³ /miːn/ *vi* [*pt, pp* ~t /ment/] **1** 意指 yìzhǐ, 意谓 yìwèi: *What does this word ~?* 这个词作什么解释? **2** 造成某种〔種〕结果 zàochéng mǒuzhǒng jiéguǒ: *This will ~ more work.* 这将有更多的工作. **3** 意欲 yìyù: *What do you ~ by saying that?* 你那样说是什么意思? **4** 决意 juéyì: *He ~s to succeed.* 他决心要获得成功. **5** 对〔對〕…是重要的 duì…shì zhòngyàode; 对…有价〔價〕值 duì … yǒu jiàzhí: *Your friendship ~s a lot to me.* 你的友谊对我很重要. **6** ˈ**~ well** 怀〔懷〕有好意 huáiyǒu hǎoyì. **~ing** *n* [C,U] 意义〔義〕 yìyì; 意图〔圖〕 yìtú. **~ing·ful** *adj* 富有意义的 fùyǒu yìyì de.

me·ander /mɪˈændə(r)/ *vi* **1** (指河川)蜿蜒 wānyán. **2** 漫步 mànbù; 闲〔閑〕荡〔蕩〕 xiándàng. **~·ings** /mɪˈændrɪŋz/ *n pl* 曲折小路 qūzhé xiǎo lù.

means¹ /miːnz/ *n pl* 方法 fāngfǎ; 手段 shǒuduàn: *(a) ~ of travel* 旅行方法. ***by ~s of*** 用 yòng; 依靠 yīkào. ***by all ~*** 当〔當〕然 dāngrán; 必定 bìdìng.

means² /miːnz/ *n pl* 金钱〔錢〕 jīnqián; 财富 cáifù: *a man of ~* 富有的人. ***live beyond one's ~*** 不量入为出. bú liàng rù wéi chū. ***live within one's ~*** 量入为〔爲〕出 liàng rù wéi chū.

meant /ment/ *pt, pp* of mean³.

mean·time /ˈmiːntaɪm/ *adv, n* [*sing*] 当〔當〕时〔時〕 dāngshí; 同时 tóngshí; 其间〔間〕 qíjiān.

mean·while /ˌmiːnˈwaɪl/ *adv* 当〔當〕时〔時〕 dāngshí; 同时 tóngshí: *I shall be back soon, ~ do some work.* 我很快就回来, 在我回来之前你可以干点活.

measles /ˈmiːzlz/ *n* [U] 麻疹 má

zhěn.

measure /'meʒə(r)/ *n* **1** [U] 量度 liàngdù; 分量 fènliàng; 尺寸 chǐcùn. ,*made to* '~ (衣服)定做的 dìngzuòde. **2** [C] 计量单〔單〕位 jìliàng dānwèi: *liquid* ~ 液量. *for good* ~ 作为〔爲〕额外增添 zuòwéi éwài zēngtiān. **3** [C] 量具 liángjù; 量器 liángqì: *a* '*tape*-~ 卷尺. **4** *beyond* ~ 极〔極〕度 jídù; 过〔過〕分 guòfèn. **5** [C] 行动〔動〕 xíngdòng; 步骤 bùzhòu: *take* ~*s against dangerous drivers* 对危险的司机采取措施. □ *vt/i* **1** 测量 cèliáng; 计量 jìliàng: ~ *a piece of wood* 量一块木头. **2** 有…长(或阔、高等) yǒu...cháng. **3** 标〔標〕出量过的数〔數〕量 biāochū liángguò de shùliàng: ~ *out a metre of cloth* 量出一米布. ~**ment** *n* **(a)** [U] 测量 cèliáng; 衡量 héngliáng. **(b)** [*pl*] 长(或宽、深) 度 chángdù; 大小 dàxiǎo.

meat /mi:t/ *n* **1** [U] 食用肉类〔類〕 shíyòng ròulèi. **2** [喻] 实〔實〕质〔質〕 shízhì; 要点〔點〕 yàodiǎn: *There's not much* ~ *in his argument.* 他的论点没有什么实质性的东西. **meaty** *adj* [-ier, -iest]

mech·anic /mɪ'kænɪk/ *n* [C] 技工 jìgōng; 机〔機〕械工 jīxiègōng; 机修工 jīxiūgōng. ~**al** /-kl/ *adj* **(a)** 机械的 jīxiède; 用机械的 yòng jīxiè de. **(b)** 机械似的 jīxièsìde; 呆板的 dāibǎnde. ~**ally** /-lɪk/ *adv*

mech·an·ics /mɪ'kænɪks/ *n* [U] **1** 力学〔學〕 lìxué; 机械学 jīxièxué. **2** [*pl*] 结构〔構〕 jiégòu; 构成法 gòuchéngfǎ; 技巧 jìqiǎo.

mech·an·ism /'mekənɪzəm/ *n* [C] **1** 机〔機〕械的活动〔動〕部件 jīxiède huódòng bùjiàn. **2** 机构〔構〕 jīgòu; 结构 jiégòu: *the* ~ *of government* 政府机构.

mech·an·ize /'mekənaɪz/ *vt* 使机〔機〕械化 shǐ jīxièhuà; 用机械装〔裝〕备〔備〕 yòng jīxiè zhuāngbèi. **mech·an·iz·ation** /-'zeɪʃən/ *n* [U]

medal /'medl/ *n* [C] 奖〔獎〕章 jiǎngzhāng; 勋〔勳〕章 xūnzhāng; 纪念章 jìniànzhāng. ~**list** [美语 =~**ist**] 奖章(或勋章)获〔獲〕得者 jiǎngzhāng huòdézhě.

me·dal·lion /mɪ'dælɪən/ *n* [C] 大奖〔獎〕章 dà jiǎngzhāng; 大纪念章 dàjìniàn zhāng.

meddle /'medl/ *vi* 干涉 gānshè; 干预 gānyù. **med·dler** 干涉者 gānshèzhě; 多事之徒 duōshì zhī tú.

me·dia /'mi:dɪə/ *n* [U] **the** ~ 宣传〔傳〕工具(如电视、广播、报纸) xuānchuán gōngjù.

medi·aeval /,medɪ'i:vl/ = medieval.

me·di·ate /'mi:dɪeɪt/ *vt/i* **1** ~ *(between)* 调停 tiáotíng; 斡旋 wòxuán. **2** 居间〔間〕促成 jū jiān cùchéng: ~ *a settlement* 居间促成一项解决办法. **me·di'a·tion** /-ʃn/ *n* [U] **me·dia·tor** /-tə(r)/ 调停者 tiáotíngzhě; 斡旋者 wòxuánzhě.

medic /'medɪk/ *n* [非正式用语] medical student 的缩写〔寫〕 *medical student* de suōxiě.

medi·cal /'medɪkl/ *adj* **1** 医〔醫〕学〔學〕的 yīxuéde; 医术〔術〕的 yīshùde: *a* ~ *student* 医科学生. **2** 内科的(与 *surgery* 相对) nèikēde. □ *n* [C] 体〔體〕格检〔檢〕查 tǐgé jiǎnchá. ~**ly** *adv*

medi·cate /'medɪkeɪt/ *vt* 加入药〔藥〕品 jiārù yàopǐn: ~*d shampoo.* 药物洗发剂. **medi'ca·tion** *n* [C, U] 药〔藥〕物 yàowù; 药剂 yàojì.

med·ici·nal /mɪ'dɪsɪnl/ *adj* 治疗〔療〕的 zhìliáode.

medi·cine /'medsn/ *n* **1** [U] 医〔醫〕学〔學〕 yīxué; 医术〔術〕 yīshù; 内科学 nèikēxué. **2** [C,U] 药〔藥〕 yào; 内服药 nèifúyào. **3** [U] [喻] 罪有应〔應〕得 zuì yǒu yīng dé. **4** [U] 魔法 mófǎ; 巫术 wūshù. '~-**man** = witch-doctor.

medi·eval (亦作 **medi·aeval**) /,medɪ'i:vl/ *adj* 中世纪的 zhōngshìjìde; 中古的 zhōnggǔde.

me·di·ocre /,mi:dɪ'əʊkə(r)/ *adj* 平庸的 píngyōngde; 平常的 píngchángde. **me·di·oc·rity** /,mi:dɪ'ɒkrətɪ/ *n* [C,U] [*pl* -ies]

medi·tate /'medɪteɪt/ *vt/i* **1** 深思 shēnsī. **2** ~ **on** 深思熟虑〔慮〕 shēnsī shúlǜ. **medi'ta·tion** *n* [C,U]

me·dium /'mi:dɪəm/ *n* [C] [*pl* ~s 或 media /'mi:dɪə/] **1** 媒介 méijiè: *Television is a* ~ *for advertising.* 电视是做广告的媒介. **2** 中庸 zhōngyōng; 适〔適〕中 shìzhōng. **3** 媒介物 méijièwù; 传〔傳〕导〔導〕体〔體〕 chuándǎotǐ. **4** 巫师〔師〕 wūshī. □ *adj* 中等的 zhōngděngde; 中庸的 zhōngyōngde. '~ **wave** [无线电] 中波 zhōngbō.

meek /mi:k/ *adj* [-er, -est] 温顺的 wēnshùnde; 谦逊的 qiānxùnde 忍耐的 rěnnàide. ~**ness** *n* [U]

meet[1] /mi:t/ *vt/i* [*pt, pp* met /met/] **1** 遇到 yùdào; 碰见 pèngjiàn. ~ **with** 遭受 zāoshòu; 碰到 pèngdào: ~ *with misfortune* 遭遇不幸. **2** 成为相识〔識〕 chéngwéi xiāngshí. **3** 迎接 yíngjiē. **4** 满足(要求等) mǎnzú: ~ *his wishes* 满足

他的愿望. ~ ***sb halfway*** [喻]为〔爲〕达〔達〕成一致而让〔讓〕步 wèi dáchéng yízhì ér ràngbù. **5** 接触〔觸〕jiēchù: *their lips met* 接吻.

meet² /mi:t/ *n* [C] [英国英语] (猎狐前) 猎〔獵〕人和猎犬的集合 lièrén hé lièquǎn de jíhé.

meet·ing /'mi:tɪŋ/ *n* [C] 集会〔會〕jíhuì; 会议〔議〕huìyì; 会合 huìhé.

mega·phone /'megəfəʊn/ *n* [C] 麦〔麥〕克风〔風〕màikèfēng; 喇叭筒 lǎbātǒng.

mega·ton /'megətʌn/ *n* [C] 百万〔萬〕吨级 (相当于一百万吨黄色炸药的爆炸威力) bǎiwàndūnjí.

mel·an·choly /'melənkɒlɪ/ *n* [U] 忧〔憂〕郁〔鬱〕yōuyù; 悲哀 bēi'āi. □ *adj* 忧郁的 yōuyùde; 令人伤〔傷〕感的 lìng rén shānggǎn de. **mel·an·cholic** /-'kɒlɪk/ *adj*

mel·low /'meləʊ/ *adj* [-er, -est] **1** 软〔輭〕而甜的 ruǎn ér tián de; 甘美的 gānměide. **2** (颜色)柔和的 róuhéde; (声音)圆润〔潤〕的 yuánrùnde. **3** 成熟的 chéngshúde; 老练〔練〕的 lǎoliànde. □ *vt/i* 使(变) 醇香 shǐ chúnxiāng; 使圆润 shǐ yuánrùn; 使(变)成熟 shǐ chéngshú. ~**ness** *n* [U]

mel·odic /mə'lɒdɪk/ *adj* 旋律的 xuánlǜde.

mel·odi·ous /mə'ləʊdɪəs/ *adj* 音调悦耳的 yīndiào yuè'ěr de; 旋律的 xuánlǜde.

melo·drama /'melədra:mə/ *n* **1** [C] 情节〔節〕剧〔劇〕qíngjiéjù. **2** [C] 激动〔動〕人心的事件或文章 jīdòng rénxīn de shìjiàn huò wénzhāng. ~**tic** /-drə'mætɪk/ *adj*

mel·ody /'melədɪ/ *n* [*pl* -ies] **1** [U] 音律 yīnlǜ. **2** [C] 歌曲 gēqǔ; 曲调 qǔdiào.

melon /'melən/ *n* [C] 瓜 guā.

melt /melt/ *vt/i* [*pt*, *pp* ~ed; *pp* of metal molten /'məʊltən/] **1** (使) 融化 rónghuà; (使)熔化 rónghuà: ~ *iron* 熔化铁. ~ *ice* 融化冰. ~ ***away*** 融掉 róngdiào; 消失 xiāoshī. ~ ***sth down*** 熔化 rónghuà; 熔毁 rónghuǐ. **2** (指软的食物)易于溶解或软〔輭〕化 yì yú róngjiě huò ruǎnhuà. **3** (指人心、态度) 变〔變〕软 biànruǎn. '~**ing-pot** [喻] (融合各种思想、各种人的) 熔炉〔爐〕rónglú.

mem·ber /'membə(r)/ *n* [C] **1** (团体、组织等的)成员 chéngyuán; 会〔會〕员 huìyuán. **2** [旧用法] 器官 qìguān; 肢体〔體〕zhītǐ. '~-**ship, (a)** [U] 会员资格 huìyuán zīgé; 成员资格 chéngyuán zīgé. **(b)** [C] 成员人数〔數〕chéngyuán rénshù; 会员人数 huìyuán rénshù.

mem·brane /'membreɪn/ *n* [C] 膜 mó; 薄膜 bómó.

mem·ento /mə'mentəʊ/ *n* [C] [*pl* ~s 或 ~es] 纪念品 jìniànpǐn; 令人回忆〔憶〕的东〔東〕西 lìng rén huíyì de dōngxī.

memo /'meməʊ/ *n* [C] [*pl* ~s] memorandum. 的缩写〔寫〕*memorandum* de suōxiě.

mem·oir /'memwa:(r)/ *n* [C] **1** 传〔傳〕记 zhuànjì. **2** [*pl*] 自传 zìzhuàn; 回忆〔憶〕录〔錄〕huíyìlù.

mem·or·able /'memərəbl/ *adj* 值得纪念的 zhíde jìniàn de; 值得注意的 zhíde zhùyì de. **mem·or·ably** *adv*

mem·or·an·dum /,memə'rændəm/ *n* [C] [*pl* -da /-də/ 或 ~s] **1** 备〔備〕忘录〔錄〕bèiwànglù. **2** 便函 biànhán. **3** 外交备〔備〕忘录 wàijiāo bèiwànglù.

mem·or·ial /mə'mɔ:rɪəl/ *n* [C] 纪念物 jìniànwù; 纪念日 jìniànrì; 纪念碑 jìniànbēi; 纪念仪〔儀〕式 jìniàn yíshì.

mem·or·ize /'meməraɪz/ *vt* 熟记 shújì; 记住 jìzhù.

mem·ory /'memərɪ/ *n* [*pl* -ies] **1** [C,U] 记忆〔憶〕jìyì; 记忆力 jìyìlì. ***commit sth to*** ~ 把某事记住 bǎ mǒushì jìzhù. **2** [U] 回忆期间〔間〕huíyì qījiān. ***within living*** ~ 现在留在人的记忆中 xiànzài liú zài rénde jìyì zhōng. **3** [C] 回忆 huíyì. **4** [U] 死后〔後〕的名声〔聲〕sǐhòude míngshēng. '~ **bank** 数〔數〕据〔據〕库〔庫〕shùjùkù.

men /men/ *n pl* of man¹(1).

men·ace /'menəs/ *n* [C,U] 危险〔險〕wēixiǎn; 威胁〔脅〕wēixié. □ *vt* 威胁 wēixié. **men·ac·ing·ly** *adv*

men·ag·erie /mɪ'nædʒərɪ/ *n* [C] (马戏团中)囚在笼〔籠〕中的兽〔獸〕群 qiú zài lóngzhōng de shòuqún.

mend /mend/ *vt/i* **1** 修理 xiūlǐ, 修补〔補〕xiūbǔ. **2** 改正 gǎizhèng, 纠正 jiūzhèng. **3** 痊愈 quányù. □ *n* [C] 修理部分 xiūlǐ bùfen. ***on the*** ~ (病情) 在好转〔轉〕中 zài hǎozhuǎn zhōng.

men·folk /'menfəʊk/ *n pl* (总称) 男人 nánrén; (家庭、社团中的)男成员 nán chéngyuán.

me·nial /'mi:nɪəl/ *adj* 低贱〔賤〕的 dījiànde: ~ *tasks* 低下的工作. ~**ly** *adv*

meno·pause /'menəpɔ:ʒ/ *n* [C] 经〔經〕绝(期) jīngjué.

men·stru·ate /'menstrʊeɪt/ *vi* 行经〔經〕xíngjīng; 来〔來〕月经 lái yuèjīng. **men·stru'ation** *n* [U] **men·strual** *adj*

men·tal /'mentl/ *adj* **1** 心理的 xīnlǐde; 智力的 zhìlìde. **2** 精神病的 jīngshénbìngde. '~ **home (hospital)** 精神病院 jīngshénbìngyuàn. ,~ '**illness** 精神病 jīngshénbìng. ~**ly** *adv*

men·tal·ity /men'tælətɪ/ *n* [*pl* -ies] **1** [U] 智力 zhìlì. **2** [C] 心理状〔狀〕态〔態〕xīnlǐ zhuàngtài: *a war* ~ 战争心理.

men·thol /'menθɒl/ *n* [U] 薄荷醇 bòhechún. ~**ated** /'menθəleɪtɪd/ *adj*

men·tion /'menʃn/ *vt* 说到 shuōdào; 写〔寫〕到 xiědào; 提及 tíjí. *Don't* ~ *it* 不用客气〔氣〕búyòng kèqì. □ *n* [C,U] 简〔簡〕要提及 jiǎnyào tíjí.

menu /'menju:/ *n* [C] 菜单〔單〕càidān.

mer·can·tile /'mɜ:kəntaɪl/ *adj* 贸易的 màoyìde; 商业〔業〕的 shāngyède, 商人的 shāngrénde.

mer·cen·ary /'mɜ:sɪnərɪ/ *adj* 唯利是图〔圖〕的 wéilì shì tú de; 为〔爲〕钱〔錢〕的 wèiqiánde. □ *n* [C] [*pl* -ies] 外国〔國〕雇佣兵 wàiguó gùyōngbīng.

mer·chan·dise /'mɜ:tʃəndaɪz/ *n* [U] 商品 shāngpǐn; 货物 huòwù. □ *vt/i* 买〔買〕卖〔賣〕mǎimai.

mer·chant /'mɜ:tʃənt/ *n* [C] **1** 商人 shāngrén. **2** [用作定语]海外贸易与〔與〕海上货运〔運〕hǎiwài màoyì yǔ hǎishàng huòyùn: ~ *ships* 商船.

mer·ci·ful /'mɜ:sɪfl/ *adj* 仁慈的 réncíde; 宽大的 kuāndàde. ~**ly** *adv*

mer·ci·less /'mɜ:sɪlɪs/ *adj* 冷酷无〔無〕情的 lěngkù wúqíng de; 残〔殘〕忍的 cánrěnde. ~**ly** *adv*

mer·cur·ial /mɜ:'kjʊərɪəl/ *adj* **1** 水银的 shuǐyínde; 汞的 gǒngde. **2** [喻]活泼〔潑〕的 huópode: *a* ~ *mind* 思想活泼. **3** (指人)易变〔變〕的 yìbiànde.

mer·cury /'mɜ:kjʊrɪ/ *n* [U] (亦作 *quicksilver*) 水银 shuǐyín; 汞 **(Hg)** gǒng.

mercy /'mɜ:sɪ/ *n* [*pl* -ies] **1** [U] 怜〔憐〕悯〔憫〕liánmǐn; 宽恕 kuānshù. *at the* ~ *of* 在…支配中 zài ... zhīpèi zhōng; 任凭〔憑〕…摆〔擺〕布 rènpíng...bǎibù. **2** [C] 幸运〔運〕xìngyùn.

mere /mɪə(r)/ *adj* [-r, -st] 仅〔僅〕仅 jǐnjǐn, 只不过〔過〕zhǐbúguò: *a* ~ *boy* 只是个孩子. ~**ly** *adv* 仅仅 jǐnjǐn, 不过 búguò.

merge /mɜ:dʒ/ *vt/i* **1** (企业等)合并〔併〕hébìng; 兼并 jiānbìng. **2** ~ *into* 渐〔漸〕渐消失 jiànjiàn xiāoshī: *Day* ~*d into night.* 日尽夜至. **merger** *n* [C,U] 合并 hébìng; 并吞 bìngtūn.

mer·id·ian /mə'rɪdɪən/ *n* [C] **1** 子午线〔線〕zǐwǔxiàn; 子午圈 zǐwǔquān. **2** (太阳或其他星球所达到的)最高点〔點〕zuìgāodiǎn; 正午 zhèngwǔ.

me·ringue /mə'ræŋ/ *n* [U] 蛋白酥皮 dànbái sūpí; [C] 蛋白甜饼 dànbái tiánbǐng.

merit /'merɪt/ *n* **1** [U] 价〔價〕值 jiàzhí; 优〔優〕点〔點〕yōudiǎn. **2** [C] 功绩 gōngjī. □ *vt* 应〔應〕受 yīngshòu; 值得 zhídé: ~ *a reward* 值得嘉奖.

mer·maid /'mɜ:meɪd/ *n* [C] (传说中的)美人鱼 měirényú.

merry /'merɪ/ *adj* [-ier, -iest] 愉快的 yúkuàide; 欢〔歡〕乐〔樂〕的 huānlède. '~-**go-round** (儿童玩乐用的)旋转〔轉〕木马〔馬〕xuánzhuǎn mùmǎ. **mer·rily** /'merəlɪ/ *adv* **mer·ri·ment** *n* [U]

mesh /meʃ/ *n* [C] **1** 网〔網〕眼 wǎngyǎn; 筛〔篩〕孔 shāikǒng. **2** [*pl*] 网 wǎng; 网状〔狀〕物 wǎngzhuàngwù: *the* ~*es of a spider's web* 蜘蛛网的网状组织. □ *vt/i* **1** 用网捕捉 yòng wǎng bǔzhuō. **2** (指齿轮)啮合 nièhé.

mess[1] /mes/ *n* [U] 混乱〔亂〕hùnluàn; 污垢 wūgòu; 杂〔雜〕乱 záluàn. □ *vt/i* **1** 弄乱 nòngluàn; 弄糟 nòngzāo. **2** ~ *about*, **(a)** 瞎忙 xiāmáng. **(b)** 草率处〔處〕理 cǎoshuài chǔlǐ; 随便应〔應〕付 suíbiàn yìngfù. ~ *up* 毁坏〔壞〕huǐhuài. **messy** *adj* [-ier, -iest].

mess[2] /mes/ *n* [C] **1** (尤指海陆军的)伙食团〔團〕huǒshítuán. **2** 食堂 shítáng, 餐厅〔廳〕cāntīng.

mess·age /'mesɪdʒ/ *n* [C] **1** 消息 xiāoxi; 音信 yīnxìn; 通讯 tōngxùn. **2** 启〔啓〕示 qǐshì. **mess·en·ger** /'mesɪndʒə(r)/ 送信者 sòngxìnzhě; 通信员 tōngxìnyuán.

mess·iah /mə'saɪə/ *n* **1** 宗教的新领袖 zōngjiàode xīn lǐngxiù. **2** 救世主 jiùshìzhǔ; 耶稣 Yēsū.

Messrs. = Mr. 的复〔復〕数〔數〕*Mr*. de fùshù.

met /met/ *pt, pp* of meet[1].

me·tab·olism /mɪ'tæbəlɪzəm/ *n* [U] 新陈〔陳〕代谢 xīn chén dàixiè. **meta·bolic** /,metə'bɒlɪk/ *adj*

metal /'metl/ *n* [C,U] 金属〔屬〕(如锡、铁) jīnshǔ; 金属制〔製〕品 jīnshǔ zhìpǐn. ~**lic** /mɪ'tælɪk/ *adj*

金属的 jīnshǔde; 金属制的 jīnshǔzhìde.

meta·phor /'metəfə(r)/ *n* [C,U] 隐〔隱〕喻 (一种修辞手法, 如 'I'll make him *eat* his words' 中的 eat) yǐnyù. **~i·cal** /,metə'fɒrɪkl/ *adj* 隐喻的 yǐnyùde, 含有隐喻的 hányǒu yǐnyù de. **~cally** *adv*

me·teor /'mi:tɪə(r)/ *n* [C] 流星 liúxīng. **~ic** /,mi:tɪ'ɒrɪk/ *adj* **(a)** 流星的 liúxīngde. **(b)** [喻]转〔轉〕瞬即逝的 zhuǎnshùn jì shì de: *a ~ic rise to power* 突然掌权. **~ite** /-raɪt/ *n* [C] 陨星 yǔnxīng.

me·teor·ol·ogy / mi:tɪə'rɒlədʒɪ/ *n* [U] 气〔氣〕象学〔學〕 qìxiàngxué. **me·teoro·logi·cal** /-'lɒdʒɪkl/ *adj* **,me·teo'r·ol·ogist** *n* [C] 气象学家 qìxiàngxuéjiā.

me·ter[1] /'mi:tə(r)/ *n* [C] 计量器 jìliàngqì; 仪〔儀〕表 yíbiǎo: *gas ~* 煤气表.

meter[2] /'mi:tə(r)/*n* [美语] =metre.

method /'meθəd/ *n* **1**[U] 条〔條〕理 tiáolǐ; 秩序 zhìxù. **2** [C] 方法 fāngfǎ; 办〔辦〕法 bànfǎ. **~i·cal** /mə'θɒdɪkl/ *adj* **(a)** 有方法的 yǒufāngfǎde. **(b)** 有条理的 yǒutiáolǐde. **~i·cally** *adv*

me·ticu·lous /mɪ'tɪkjʊləs/ *adj* 谨小慎微的 jǐn xiǎo shèn wēi de; 过〔過〕细的 guòxìde. **~ly** *adv*

metre[1] [美语 = **meter**] /'mi:tə(r)/ *n* [C] (公制长度单位) 米 mǐ; 公尺 gōngchǐ. **met·ric** /'metrɪk/ *adj* **'metric system** 十进〔進〕制 shíjìnzhì; 公制 gōngzhì. **metri'ca·tion** *n* [U] 十进化 shíjìnhuà; 公制化 gōngzhìhuà.

metre[2] [美语 = **meter**] /'mi:tə(r)/ *n* [C,U] (诗的)韵〔韻〕律 yùnlǜ; 格律 gélǜ.

me·trop·olis /mə'trɒpəlɪs/ *n* [C] [*pl* ~es] 大城市 dà chéngshì; 首府 shǒufǔ. **metro·poli·tan** /,metrə'pɒlɪtən/ *adj* 大城市的 dàchéngshìde; 首府的 shǒufǔde.

mettle /'metl/ *n* [U] 忍耐力 rěnnàilì; 勇气〔氣〕yǒngqì. ***be on his ~*** 奋〔奮〕发〔發〕 fènfā; ***put sb on his ~*** 激励〔勵〕某人 jīlì mǒurén.

mews /mju:z/ *n pl* (马厩改建的) 汽车〔車〕房 (或平房) qìchēfáng.

mg. = milligram(s) 毫克 (千分之一克) háokè.

mi·aow /mi:'aʊ/ *n* [C] 猫〔貓〕叫声〔聲〕māo jiàoshēng. □ *vi* 咪咪叫 mīmījiào; 喵喵叫 miāomiāojiào.

mice /maɪs/ *n pl* of mouse.

mickey /'mɪkɪ/ *n* ***take the ~(out of sb)*** [俚语]嘲弄 cháonòng; 讽〔諷〕刺 fěngcì.

mi·crobe /'maɪkrəʊb/ *n* [C] 微生物 wēishēngwù; 细菌 xìjūn.

micro·bi·ol·ogy /,maɪkrəʊbaɪ'ɒlədʒɪ/ *n* [U]微生物学〔學〕 wēishēngwùxué.

micro·chip /'maɪkrəʊtʃɪp/ *n* [C] 微集成电〔電〕路 wēijíchéng diànlù.

micro·com·puter /,maɪkrəʊkəm'pju:tə(r)/ *n* [C] 微型电〔電〕子计算机〔機〕wēixíng diànzǐ jìsuànjī. ⇨ minicomputer.

micro·cosm /'maɪkrəʊkɒzəm/ *n* [C] 微观〔觀〕世界 wēiguān shìjiè; (人类、社会等的) 缩影 suōyǐng. ⇨ macrocosm.

micro·dot /'maɪkrəʊdɒt/ *n* [C] 微粒照片 (缩小至微粒大小的相片) wēilì zhàopiàn.

micro-elec·tron·ics /,maɪkrəʊ,ɪlek'trɒnɪks/ *n* [U] 微电〔電〕子学〔學〕 wēidiànzǐxué.

micro·film /'maɪkrəʊfɪlm/ *n* [C, U] 微缩胶〔膠〕片 wēisuō jiāopiàn. □ *vt* 微缩摄影 wēisuō shèyǐng.

mi·cron /'maɪkrɒn/ *n* [C] 微米 (长度单位, 符号 μ, 等于百万分之一公尺) wēimǐ.

micro-or·gan·ism /,maɪkrəʊ'ɔ:gənɪzəm/ *n* [C] (仅在显微镜下才能看得见的) 微生物 wēishēngwù.

micro·phone /'maɪkrəfəʊn/ *n* [C] 麦〔麥〕克风〔風〕 màikèfēng; 扩〔擴〕音器 kuòyīnqì; 话筒 huàtǒng.

micro·scope /'maɪkrəskəʊp/ *n* [C] 显〔顯〕微镜 xiǎnwēijìng. **micro·scopic** /-'skɒpɪk/ *adj*

mid /mɪd/ *adj* 中间〔間〕的 zhōngjiānde; 中部的 zhōngbùde.

mid·day /,mɪd'deɪ/ *adj*, *n* [C] 正午 zhèngwǔ.

middle /'mɪdl/ *n* ***the ~*** 中间〔間〕zhōngjiān; 中部 zhōngbù. □ *adj* 中间的 zhōngjiānde; 中部的 zhōngbùde. **,~ 'age** 中年的 zhōngniánde. **,~-'aged** *adj* **the ,M~ 'Ages** 中世纪 zhōngshìjì. **,~ 'class** 中产〔產〕阶〔階〕级 zhōngchǎn jiējí. **,~-'class** *adj* **the ,M~ 'East** 中东〔東〕 zhōngdōng. **'~man** 经〔經〕纪人 jīngjìrén; 中人 zhōngrén.

midge /mɪdʒ/ *n* [C] 蠓 měng; 小蚊 xiǎowén.

midget /'mɪdʒɪt/ *n* [C] 侏儒 zhūrú; 矮人 ǎirén. □ *adj* 小型的 xiǎoxíngde.

mid·land /'mɪdlənd/ *adj*, *n* 中部地方的 zhōngbù dìfāng de; 内地的 nèidìde; (一国的)中部地方zhōngbù dìfāng. **the M~s** 英国〔國〕中部

Yīngguó zhōngbù.
mid·night /'mɪdnaɪt/ *adj, n* [C] 午夜 wǔyè; 子夜 zǐyè; 夜半 yèbàn.
mid·riff /'mɪdrɪf/ *n* [C] 横隔膜 hénggémó; 腹部 fùbù.
mid·sum·mer /,mɪd'sʌmə(r)/ *n* [U] 仲夏 zhòngxià.
mid·way /,mɪd'weɪ/ *adj, adv* 中途 zhōngtú: ~ *between Paris and Rome* 巴黎至罗马的中途.
mid·wife /'mɪdwaɪf/ *n* [C] [*pl* mid-wives /-waɪvz/] 助产[産]士 zhùchǎnshì; 接生婆 jiēshēngpó. **~ry** /'mɪdwɪfrɪ/ *n* [U] 产科学[學] chǎnkēxué; 助产学 zhùchǎnxué; 接生 jiēshēng.
might¹ /maɪt/ *pt* of may.
might² /maɪt/ *n* [U] 力量 lìliàng; 强权[權] qiángquán; 势[勢]力 shìlì. **mighty** *adj* [-ier, -iest] **(a)** 强大的 qiángdàde; 强有力的 qiáng yǒu lì de. **(b)** 巨大的 jùdàde; 浩大的 hàodàde: *the ~y oceans* 汪洋大海. ,*high and* '*~y* 趾高气[氣]扬[揚] zhǐ gāo qì yáng. □ *adv* [非正式用语] 非常 fēicháng; 很 hěn: *~y tired* 非常累. **~ily** *adv*
mi·graine /'mi:greɪn/ *n* [C] 周期性偏头[頭]痛 zhōuqīxìng piāntóutòng.
mi·grant /'maɪgrənt/ *n* [C] 移居者 yíjūzhě; 候鸟[鳥] hòuniǎo.
mi·grate /maɪ'greɪt/ *vi* **1** 迁[遷]移 qiānyí; 移居 yíjū. **2** (候鸟等) 定期移栖[棲] dìngqī yíqī. **mi'gration** *n* [C,U] **mi·gra·tory**/'maɪgrətrɪ/ *adj* 移居的 yíjūde; 漂泊的 piāobóde.
mike /maɪk/ *n* [C] [非正式用语] microphone 的缩写[寫] *microphone* de suōxiě.
mild /maɪld/ *adj* [-er, -est] **1** 温和的 wēnhéde; 温柔的 wēnróude: *a ~ punishment* 轻微的惩罚. *a ~ climate* 温和的气候. **2** (烟、酒、食物)味淡的 wèidànde. **~ly** *adv* **~ness** *n* [U]
mil·dew /'mɪldju:/ *n* [U] 霉 méi. □ *vt/i* 生霉 shēngméi; 发[發]霉 fāméi.
mile /maɪl/ *n* [C] 英里 yīnglǐ. **~·om·eter** /maɪ'lɒmɪtə(r)/ 里程表 lǐchéngbiǎo. **'~stone, (a)** 里程碑 lǐchéngbēi. **(b)** [喻]历[歷]史上的重大事件 lìshǐ shàng de zhòngdà shìjiàn.
mile·age /'maɪlɪdʒ/ *n* [C] **1** (旅行的)总[總]英里数[數] zǒng yīnglǐ shù; 里程 lǐchéng. **2** 按英里计算的旅行费. àn yīnglǐ jìsuàn de lǚxíngfèi.
mili·tant /'mɪlɪtənt/ *adj, n* [C] 战[戰]斗[鬥]的 zhàndòude; 好战的 hàozhànde: ~ *workers* 好斗的工人 **mili·tancy** *n* [U]
mili·tary /'mɪlɪtrɪ/ *adj* 军[軍]人的 jūnrénde; 军事的 jūnshìde. □ *n* **the ~** 军人 jūnrén; 军方 jūnfāng; 陆[陸]军 lùjūn.
mil·itia /mɪ'lɪʃə/ *n* [C] 民兵 mínbīng
milk¹ /mɪlk/ *n* [U] **1** 乳 rǔ; 牛奶 niúnǎi. **2** (植物、果实的)乳液 rǔyè. **'~man** 卖[賣](或送)牛奶的人 mài niúnǎi de rén. **'~shake** 牛奶和冰淇淋等的混合饮料 niúnǎi hé bīngqílíng děng de hùnhé yǐnliào. **milky** *adj* [-ier, -iest] **(a)** 牛奶的 niúnǎide; 搀[攙]奶的 chānnǎide. **(b)** (指液体)混浊[濁]不清的 hùnzhuó bùqīng de. **the ,M~y 'Way** = the Galaxy.
milk² /mɪlk/ *vt/i* **1** 挤[擠]奶 jǐnǎi. **2** [喻]榨取 zhàqǔ.
mill¹ /mɪl/ *n* **1** 磨粉机[機] mòfěnjī; 面粉厂[廠] miànfěnchǎng. ,***run-of-the-'~*** 通常的 tōngchángde; 普通的 pǔtōngde. **2** 工厂 gōngchǎng; 制[製]造厂 zhìzàochǎng: *a 'paper-~* 造纸厂. **3** 碾磨机 niǎnmòjī: *a 'pepper-~* 胡椒碾磨机. **'~-stone, (a)** 磨石 mòshí. **(b)** [喻]重担 zhòngdàn. **~er** *n* [C] 磨坊主 mòfángzhǔ; 磨坊工人 mòfáng gōngrén.
mill² /mɪl/ *vt/i* **1** 碾碎 niǎnsuì; 磨细 mòxì. **2** 在(硬币)上轧[軋]花边[邊] zài ... shàng zhá huābiān. **3** ***~ about (around)*** 乱[亂]哄[鬨]哄地推挤[擠] luànhōnghōngde tuījǐ.
mil·len·nium /mɪ'lenɪəm/ *n* [C] [*pl* -nia /-nɪə/ 或 ~s]. **1** 一千年 yìqiānnián; 千年间[間] qiānniánjiān. **2** [喻] 太平盛世 tàipíng shèngshì.
mil·let /'mɪlɪt/ *n* [U] 稷 jì; 黍 shǔ.
mil·liner /'mɪlɪnə(r)/ *n* [C] 女帽商 nǚmàoshāng; 妇[婦]女服饰商 fùnǚ fúshìshāng. **mil·lin·ery** /-nərɪ/ *n* [U] 女帽 nǚmào; 女帽业[業] nǚmàoyè.
mil·lion /'mɪlɪən/ *adj, n* [C] 百万[萬] bǎiwàn. **~aire** 百万富翁 bǎiwàn fùwēng. **~th** *adj, n* [C] 第一百万 dìyìbǎiwàn; 一百万分之一 yìbǎiwànfēn zhī yī.
mil·li·pede /'mɪlɪpi:d/ *n* [C] 千足虫[蟲] qiānzúchóng.
mime /maɪm/ *n* [C] 滑稽剧[劇] huájìjù; 丑角 chǒujiǎo; 模仿演员 mófǎng yǎnyuán. □ *vt/i* 扮演笑剧(哑剧) bànyǎn xiàojù.

mimic /'mɪmɪk/ *adj* 假装〔裝〕的 jiǎzhuāngde; 模仿〔倣〕的 mófǎngde: ~ *warfare* 摹拟战. □ *n* [C] 善于模仿的人 shàn yú mófǎng de rén. □ *vt* [*pt, pp* ~ked] **1** 模仿 mófǎng; 摹拟〔擬〕 mónǐ. **2** (指物品)酷似 kùsì. '**~ry** *n* [U]

min. = minimum.

min·aret /ˌmɪnə'ret/ *n* [C] 伊斯兰〔蘭〕教寺院的尖塔 Yīsīlánjiào sìyuàn de jiāntǎ.

mince /mɪns/ *vt/i* **1** 切碎 qiēsuì; 剁碎 duòsuì. **2** [过时用法]装〔裝〕腔作势〔勢〕 zhuāngqiāng zuòshì. □ *n* [U]碎肉 suìròu. '**~meat** 百果馅 bǎiguǒxiàn; 肉馅 ròuxiàn.

mind[1] /maɪnd/ *n* **1** [U] 记忆〔憶〕 jìyì. ***bear (keep) sth in*** ~ 记住某事 jìzhù mǒushì. ***bring*** (或 ***call***) ***sth to*** ~ 想起某事 xiǎngqǐ mǒushì. **2** [U] 意向 yìxiàng; 愿望 yuànwàng. ***be in two ~s about sth*** 犹〔猶〕豫不决 yóuyù bùjué. ***change one's*** ~ 改变〔變〕主意 gǎibiàn zhǔyì. ***have a ˌgood ~ to 'do sth*** 想做某事 xiǎngzuò mǒushì. ***have sth (sb) on one's*** ~ 为〔爲〕某事(某人)担忧〔憂〕 wèi mǒushì dānyōu. ***know one's own*** ~ 有自己的想法 yǒu zìjǐde xiǎngfǎ. ***make up one's*** ~ 下决心 xià juéxīn; 拿定主意 nádìng zhǔyì. ***speak one's*** ~ 直言不讳〔諱〕 zhíyán bú huì. **3** [C,U] 智力 zhìlì; 有才智的人 yǒu cáizhì de rén.

mind[2] /maɪnd/ *vt/i* **1** 留心 liúxīn: *Who's ~ing the baby?* 谁在照顾那个婴儿? ***ˌ~ your ˌown 'business*** 少管闲〔閒〕事 shǎo guǎn xiánshì. **2** 介意 jièyì; 反对〔對〕 fǎnduì: *Do you ~ if I smoke?* 我抽烟你不反对吧? ***Never*** ~ 不要紧〔緊〕 bú yàojǐn; 没关〔關〕系〔係〕 méi guānxi. ***M~'out!*** 小心 xiǎoxīn; 注意 zhùyì. **~er** 照料者 zhàoliàozhě; 看护〔護〕人 kànhùrén: '*baby ~er* 保姆;照看婴儿的人.

mind·ful /'maɪndfl/ *adj* ~ ***of*** 留意的 liúyìde; 注意的 zhùyìde.

mind·less /'maɪndlɪs/ *adj* **1** ~ ***of*** 不注意的 bú zhùyì de; 不留心的 bù liúxīn de. **2** 没头〔頭〕脑〔腦〕的 méi tóunǎo de. **~ly** *adv*

mine[1] /maɪn/ *possessive pron* 我的 wǒde: *Is this book yours or ~?* 这本书是你的还是我的?

mine[2] /maɪn/ *n* [C] **1** 矿〔礦〕 kuàng; 矿山 kuàngshān; 矿井 kuàngjǐng. **2** [喻]丰〔豐〕富的资源 fēngfùde zīyuán: *a ~ of information* 知识宝库. **3** 地雷 dìléi; 水雷 shuǐléi. '**~-detector** 探雷器 tànléiqì. **~field** 布雷区〔區〕 bùléiqū; 布雷场〔場〕 bùléichǎng. '**~-sweeper** 扫〔掃〕雷舰 sǎoléijiàn; 扫雷器 sǎoléiqì.

mine[3] /maɪn/ *vt/i* **1** 开〔開〕矿〔礦〕 kāikuàng; 采〔採〕掘 cǎijué. **2** 敷设地雷(或水雷) fūshè dìléi; (用雷)炸毁 zhàhuǐ. **miner** *n* [C] 矿工 kuànggōng.

min·eral /'mɪnərəl/ *n* [C] 矿〔礦〕物 kuàngwù; 矿石 kuàngshí. □ *adj* 矿物的 kuàngwùde; 矿质〔質〕的 kuàngzhìde. '~ **water, (a)** 矿泉水 kuàngquánshuǐ. **(b)** [英国英语]苏〔蘇〕打水 sūdáshuǐ.

min·er·al·ogy /ˌmɪnə'rælədʒɪ/ *n* [U] 矿〔礦〕物学〔學〕 kuàngwùxué. **min·er·al·ogist** *n* [C] 矿物学家 kuàngwùxuéjiā.

mingle /'mɪŋgl/ *vt/i* ~ ***(with)*** 混合 hùnhé: ~ *with the crowds* 混在人群中.

mini /'mɪnɪ/ *prefix* (表示"小"): *a '~bus* 微型公共汽车.

minia·ture /'mɪnɪtʃə(r)/ *n* **1** [C] 小画〔畫〕像 xiǎo huàxiàng. **2** [C] 缩图〔圖〕 suōtú; 缩小的东〔東〕西 suōxiǎode dōngxi. **minia·tur·ize** /-raɪz/ *vt* 使小型化 shǐ xiǎoxíng huà.

mini·com·puter /ˌmɪnɪkəm'pjuːtə(r)/ *n* [C] 小型电〔電〕子计算机〔機〕 xiǎoxíng diànzǐ jìsuànjī. ⇨ microcomputer.

mini·mal /'mɪnɪml/ *adj* 最小的 zuìxiǎode; 最低限度的 zuìdī xiàndù de.

mini·mize /'mɪnɪmaɪz/ *vt* 使减到最少 shǐ jiǎn dào zuìshǎo; 使缩到最小 shǐ suō dào zuìxiǎo.

mini·mum /'mɪnɪməm/ *n* [C] [*pl* ~s, -ma /-mə/] 最小量 zuì xiǎoliàng; 最低限度 zuìdī xiàndù.

min·ing /'maɪnɪŋ/ *n* [U] 采〔採〕矿〔礦〕 cǎikuàng; 矿业〔業〕 kuàngyè.

min·ion /'mɪnɪən/ *n* [C] 奴才 núcái.

min·is·ter[1] /'mɪnɪstə(r)/ *n* [C] 1 部长〔長〕 bùzhǎng; 大臣 dàchén. **2** 公使 gōngshǐ. **3** (基督教) 牧师〔師〕 mùshī. **~ial** /-'stɪərɪəl/ *ad*

min·is·ter[2] /'mɪnɪstə(r)/ *vi* ~ *t* 照顾〔顧〕 zhàogù; 给予帮〔幫〕助 gěiyǔ bāngzhù.

min·is·try /'mɪnɪstrɪ/ *n* [C] [*p* -ies] **1** (政府的) 部 bù. **2** 部长〔長〕的职〔職〕位(或职责) bùzhǎng de zhíwèi. **3** ***enter the*** ~ 当〔當〕牧师〔師〕 dāng mùshī.

mink /mɪŋk/ *n* [C,U] 水貂 shuǐdiāo; 貂皮 diāopí.

mi·nor /'maɪnə(r)/ *adj* ⇨ major **1** 较〔較〕小的 jiàoxiǎode; 次要的 cìyàode: ~ *problems* 次要问题. **2** 不重要的 bú zhòngyào de: *the* ~ *poets* 平凡的诗人. □ *n* [C]〔法律〕未成年者 wèichéngniánzhě.

mi·nor·ity /maɪ'nɒrətɪ/ *n* [*pl* -ies] **1** [U]〔法律〕未成年 wèi chéngnián. **2** 少数〔數〕shǎoshù; 少数票 shǎoshùpiào. ***be in the*** ~ 占少数 zhàn shǎoshù. **3** [C] 少数民族 shǎoshù mínzú.

min·ster /'mɪnstə(r)/ *n* [C] 寺院的教堂 sìyuànde jiàotáng; 大教堂 dà jiàotáng.

min·strel /'mɪnstrəl/ *n* [C] (中世纪的) 吟游诗人 yínyóu shīrén; 音乐〔樂〕家 yīnyuèjiā.

mint[1] /mɪnt/ *n* [U] 薄荷 bòhe; 薄荷属〔屬〕植物 bòheshǔ zhíwù.

mint[2] /mɪnt/ *n* [C] **1** 造币〔幣〕厂〔廠〕zàobìchǎng. ***make (earn) a*** ~〔非正式用语〕发〔發〕财 fācái; 致富 zhìfù. **2** ***in*** ~ ***condition*** 崭〔嶄〕新的 zhǎnxīnde. □ *vt* 铸〔鑄〕造(钱币) zhùzào.

min·uet /,mɪnjʊ'et/ *n* [C] 小步舞 xiǎobùwǔ; 小步舞曲 xiǎobùwǔqǔ.

minus /'maɪnəs/ *adj* **1** *the* '~ *sign* 负号〔號〕(−) fùhào; 减号 (−) jiǎnhào. **2** 负的 fùde: *a* ~ *quantity* 负数. □ *prep* **1** 减 jiǎn: *15−6 =9*. 十五减六等于九. **2**〔非正式用语〕缺少 quēshǎo; 无〔無〕wú: *He returned from the war* ~ *a leg.* 他作战回来,少了一条腿. □ *n* [C] 减号 jiǎnhào; 负号 fùhào; 负数 fùshù.

min·ute[1] /'mɪnɪt/ *n* [C] **1** 分 (一小时的六十分之一) fēn. ***in a*** ~ 马〔馬〕上 mǎshàng; 立刻 lìkè. ***the*** ~ ***(that)*** —…就 yī…jiù. **2** 分 (一度的六十分之一) fēn. **3** 备〔備〕忘录〔錄〕bèiwànglù **4** [*pl*] 会〔會〕议〔議〕记录 huìyì jìlù. □ *vt* 记录 jìlù. **,up-to-the-'**~ *adj* 最新的 zuìxīnde.

mi·nute[2] /maɪ'nju:t/ *adj* [-r, -st] **1** 微小的 wēixiǎode; 极〔極〕小的 jíxiǎode. **2** 细致〔緻〕的 xìzhìde; 精密的 jīngmìde: *a* ~ *account* 细帐. ~**ly** *adv*

mir·acle /'mɪrəkl/ *n* [C] 奇迹〔蹟〕qíjī; 令人惊〔驚〕奇的事 lìng rén jīngqíde shì. ***a*** ~ ***of*** 非凡的事例 fēifánde shìlì: *a* ~ *of modern science* 现代科学的奇迹. **mir·acu·lous** /mɪ'rækjʊləs/ *adj*

mi·rage /'mɪrɑ:ʒ/ *n* [C] 海市蜃楼〔樓〕hǎi shì shèn lóu; 蜃景 shènjǐng; [喻]幻想 huànxiǎng.

mire /'maɪə(r)/ *n* [U] 泥泞〔濘〕nínìng; 沼地 zhǎodì.

mir·ror /'mɪrə(r)/ *n* [C] **1** 镜 jìng. **2** [喻]真实〔實〕的反映 zhēnshíde fǎnyìng. □ *vt* 反映 fǎnyìng.

mis·ad·ven·ture /,mɪsəd'ventʃə(r)/ *n* [C, U] 不幸的事 búxìngde shì; 灾〔災〕难〔難〕zāinàn.

mis·ap·pro·pri·ate /,mɪsə'prəʊprɪeɪt/ *vt* 滥〔濫〕用 lànyòng; 误用 wùyòng: ~ *a person's money* 私吞或盗用别人的金钱.

mis·be·have /,mɪsbɪ'heɪv/ *vt/i* 行为〔爲〕不当〔當〕xíngwéi búdàng; 举〔舉〕止不端 jǔzhǐ bùduān. **mis·be·hav·iour** [美语 =-ior] /-ɪə(r)/ *n* [U]

misc. = miscellaneous.

mis·cal·cu·late /,mɪs'kælkjʊleɪt/ *vt/i* 误算 wùsuàn; 误估 wùgū; 判断〔斷〕错误 pànduàn cuòwù. **mis·cal·cu'la·tion** *n* [C,U]

mis·car·riage /'mɪskærɪdʒ/ *n* **1** [C,U] ~ *of justice* 审〔審〕判不公 shěnpàn bùgōng, 误判 wùpàn; 误罚 wùfá. **2** [C,U] 流产〔産〕liúchǎn, 小产 xiǎochǎn.

mis·carry /,mɪs'kærɪ/ *vi* [*pt*, *pp* -ied] **1** (计划等) 失败 shībài. **2** 流产〔産〕liúchǎn, 小产 xiǎochǎn.

mis·cel·laneous /,mɪsə'leɪnɪəs/ *adj* 混杂〔雜〕的 hùnzáde; 各种〔種〕的 gèzhǒngde.

mis·cel·lany /mɪ'selənɪ/ *n* [C] [*pl* -ies] 杂〔雜〕集 zájí.

mis·chance /,mɪs'tʃɑ:ns/ *n* [C,U] 不幸 búxìng; 灾〔災〕难〔難〕zāinàn.

mis·chief /'mɪstʃɪf/ *n* **1** [U] 伤〔傷〕害 shānghài; 损害 sǔnhài. ***do sb a*** ~ 伤害某人 shānghài mǒurén. **2** [U] 胡闹〔鬧〕húnào; 恶〔惡〕作剧〔劇〕èzuòjù: *Children are always up to some* ~. 孩子们总是搞点恶作剧. **mis·chiev·ous** *adj* **(a)** 有害的 yǒuhàide; 为〔爲〕害的 wéihàide. **(b)** 恶作剧的 èzuòjùde; 胡闹的 húnàode.

mis·con·ceive /,mɪskən'si:v/ *vt/i* 误解 wùjiě. **mis·con·cep·tion** /-'sepʃn/ *n* [C,U]

mis·con·duct /mɪs'kɒndʌkt/ *n* [U] **1** 不端行为〔爲〕bùduān xíngwéi. **2** 不善的管理 (经营) búshànde guǎnlǐ. □ *vt* /,mɪskən'dʌkt/ **1** 行为不端 xíngwéi bùduān. **2** 处置…不当 chǔzhì…búdàng; 管理不善 guǎnlǐ búshàn.

mis·deed /mɪs'di:d/ *n* [C] 不端行为〔爲〕bùduān xíngwéi; 罪行 zuìxíng.

miser /'maɪzə(r)/ *n* [C] 守财奴 shǒucáinú; 吝啬〔嗇〕鬼 lìngsèguǐ.

~ly *adj*

mis·er·able /'mɪzrəbl/ *adj* **1** 悲惨〔慘〕的 bēicǎnde; 痛苦的 tòngkǔde. **2** 使人难〔難〕受的 shǐ rén nánshòu de: ~ *weather* 讨厌的天气. **3** 粗劣的 cūliède; 不象样〔樣〕的 búxiàngyàngde. **mis·er·ably** *adv*

mis·ery /'mɪzərɪ/ *n* [*pl* -ies] **1** [U] 悲惨〔慘〕bēicǎn; 痛苦 tòngkǔ. **2** [*pl*] 痛苦的事 tòngkǔde shì.

mis·fire /ˌmɪs'faɪə(r)/ *vi* **1** (枪等)不发〔發〕火 bù fāhuǒ; 射不出 shè bùchū. **2** (笑话等)不奏效 bú zòuxiào.

mis·fit /'mɪsfɪt/ *n*. [C] 〔喻〕不适〔適〕应〔應〕环〔環〕境的人 bú shìyìng huánjìng de rén; 不称〔稱〕职〔職〕的人 bú chèngzhí de rén.

mis·for·tune /ˌmɪs'fɔːtʃuːn/ *n* [C, U] 不幸 búxìng; 灾〔災〕祸〔禍〕zāihuò.

mis·giv·ing /ˌmɪs'gɪvɪŋ/ *n* [C,U] 疑虑〔慮〕yílǜ; 怀〔懷〕疑 huáiyí.

mis·guided /ˌmɪs'gaɪdɪd/ *adj* 误入歧途的 wù rù qítú de.

mis·hap /'mɪshæp/ *n* **1** [C] 不幸的事 búxìngde shì. **2** [U] 不幸 búxìng; 灾祸〔禍〕zāihuò.

mis·judge /ˌmɪs'dʒʌdʒ/ *vt/i* 误断〔斷〕wùduàn; 估计错误 gūjì cuòwù: ~ *a distance* (*a person's character*) 错误估计距离 (某人的品格).

mis·lay /ˌmɪs'leɪ/ *vt* [*pt, pp* mislaid /-'leɪd/] 误放 wùfàng; 搁〔擱〕忘 gēwàng.

mis·lead /ˌmɪs'liːd/ *vt* [*pt, pp* misled /-'led/] 引入歧途 yǐn rù qítú; 领错 lǐngcuò.

mis·man·age /ˌmɪs'mænɪdʒ/ *vt* 管理不善 guǎnlǐ búshàn; 处〔處〕理错误 chǔlǐ cuòwù. **~ment** *n* [U]

mis·rep·re·sent /ˌmɪsˌreprɪ'zent/ *vt* 误传〔傳〕wùchuán; 歪曲 wāiqū; 曲解 qūjiě. **~a·tion** /-'teɪʃn/ *n* [C,U]

miss /mɪs/ *n* [C] **M~** (对未婚女子的称呼)小姐 xiǎojiě.

miss /mɪs/ *vt/i* **1** 未击〔擊〕中 wèi jīzhòng; 未得到 wèi dédào; 未达〔達〕到 wèi dádào; 未看见 wèi kànjiàn: *He ~ed the 9.30 train*. 他误了九点半那班火车. **2** 惦念 diànniàn; 想念 xiǎngniàn: *I'll ~ you when you go*. 你走了,我会怀念你. **3** *~ out (on sth)* 未得到某物 wèi dédào mǒuwù; 在某事上不成功 zài mǒushì shàng bù chénggōng. *miss sth out* 省掉 shěngdiào; 遗漏 yílòu. **~ing** *adj* 失去的 shīqùde; 下落不明的 xiàluò bùmíng de: *~ing persons* 失踪的人. ☐ *n* [C] 击不中 jī bú zhòng; 得不到 dé bú dào; 达不到 dá bú dào.

mis·sile /'mɪsaɪl/ *n* [C] 发〔發〕射物 fāshèwù; 导〔導〕弹〔彈〕dǎodàn; 飞〔飛〕弹 fēidàn: *guided* '~ 导弹.

mis·sion /'mɪʃn/ *n* [C] **1** 代表团〔團〕dàibiǎotuán; 使节〔節〕shǐjié. **2** 传〔傳〕教团 chuánjiàotuán; 传教机〔機〕构〔構〕chuánjiào jīgòu. **3** 传教地区〔區〕chuánjiào dìqū. **4** *one's ~ in life* 使命 shǐmìng; 天职〔職〕tiānzhí. **5** 使命 shǐmìng; 任务〔務〕rènwù. **~ary** /-rɪ/ *n* [C] [*pl* -ies] 传教士 chuánjiàoshì. ☐ *adj* 传教的 chuánjiàode; 传教士的 chuánjiàoshìde.

misspell /ˌmɪs'spel/ *vt* [*pt, pp* ~-ed 或 -spelt /'spelt/] 拼错 pīncuò. **~ing** *n* [C,U]

mis·spent /ˌmɪs'spent/ *adj* 误用的 wùyòngde; 浪费的 làngfèide; 虚〔虛〕度的 xūdùde: *a ~ youth* 虚度了的青春.

mist /mɪst/ *n* **1** [C,U] 薄雾〔霧〕bówù; 霭 ǎi. **2** [C] 朦胧〔朧〕ménglóng; 模糊 móhu. **3** 〔喻〕使(判断等)模糊之物 shǐ móhu zhī wù: *the ~s of time* 因时间消失而记不清或遗忘. ☐ *vt/i* 蒙上薄雾 méngshàng bówù. **misty** *adj* [-ier, iest] **(a)** 有薄雾的 yǒu bówù de. **(b)** 朦胧不清的 ménglóng bùqīng de; 模糊的 móhude: *have only a ~y idea* 只有模糊的概念.

mis·take /mɪ'steɪk/ *n* [C] 错误 cuòwù; 过〔過〕失 guòshī. *by ~* 误 wù; 由疏忽所致 yóu shūhu suǒ zhì. ☐ *vt/i* [*pt* mistook /mɪ'stʊk/, *pp* ~n /mɪ'steɪkn/] **1** 弄错 nòngcuò; 误解 wùjiě. **2** *~ sb (*或 *sth) for* 把…错认〔認〕为〔爲〕… bǎ … cuòrèn wéi…. **mis·taken** *adj* **(a)** 错误的 cuòwùde; 弄错的 nòngcuòde: *a case of ~n identity* 错认人的事件. **(b)** 判断〔斷〕错误的 pànduàn cuòwù de: *~n kindness* 错误的善意. **~nly** *adv*

mis·ter /'mɪstə(r)/ *n* [C] (书写作 **Mr**) (用于姓名前)先生 xiānshēng.

mistle·toe /'mɪsltəʊ/ *n* [U] 〔植物〕槲寄生 (用作圣诞节的装饰物) hújìshēng.

mis·took /mɪ'stʊk/ *pt* of mistake.

mis·tress /'mɪstrɪs/ *n* [C] **1** 〔正式用语〕女主人 nǚ zhǔrén; 主妇〔婦〕zhǔfù. ⇨ master(2). **2** 女教师〔師〕nǚ jiàoshī. **3** 情妇 qíngfù.

mis·trust /ˌmɪs'trʌst/ *vt* 不信任 bú xìnrèn; 怀〔懷〕疑 huáiyí. ☐ *n* [U] 不信任 bú xìnrèn; 怀疑 huái-

yí. ~**ful** *adj*
misty /'mɪstɪ/ ⇨ mist.
mis·un·der·stand /ˌmɪsˌʌndə'stænd/ *vt/i* [*pt, pp* -stood /-'stʊd/] 误解 wùjiě; 误会〔會〕wùhuì. ~**ing** *n* [C,U] 误解 wùjiě; 误会 wùhuì.
mis·use /ˌmɪs'juːz/ *vt* **1** 误用 wùyòng; 滥〔濫〕用 lànyòng: ~ *power* 滥用权力. **2** 虐待 nüèdài. ☐ /ˌmɪs'juːs/ *n* [C,U]
mi·ter /'maɪtə(r)/ *n* 〔美语〕= mitre.
miti·gate /'mɪtɪgeɪt/ *vt* 使缓和 shǐ huǎnhé; 使镇静 shǐ zhènjìng. **miti'ga·tion** *n* [U]
mitre 〔美语 = **mi·ter**〕/'maɪtə(r)/ *n* [C] 主教冠 zhǔjiàoguān.
mit·ten /'mɪtn/, **mitt** /mɪt/ *n* [C] 连〔連〕指手套(拇指分开,其他四指连在一起) liánzhǐ shǒutào.
mix /mɪks/ *vt/i* **1** 混合 hùnhé; 搀〔攙〕和 chānhuo. **2** (指人) 交往 jiāowǎng; 相处〔處〕xiāngchǔ. **3** ~ *up* 混淆 hùnxiáo. *be (get)* ~*ed up in* 卷入 juǎnrù; 牵连〔連〕qiānlián. ☐ *n* [C] (由几种成分配合的)调制〔製〕食品 tiáozhì shípǐn. ~**ed** *adj* 混合的 hùnhéde; 杂〔雜〕样〔樣〕的 záyàngde. ~**er** *n* [C] 混合者 hùnhézhě; 搅〔攪〕拌器 jiǎobànqì.
mix·ture /'mɪkstʃə(r)/ *n* **1** [U] 混合 hùnhé. **2** [C] 混合物 hùnhéwù.
mm. = millimetre(s) 毫米 (千分之一米) háomǐ.
M.O. = **1** medical officer 军〔軍〕医〔醫〕jūnyī. **2** money order 汇〔匯〕票 huìpiào.
moan /məʊn/ *n* [C], *vt/i* 呻吟声〔聲〕shēnyínshēng; 呜〔嗚〕咽声 wūyèshēng.
moat /məʊt/ *n* [C] (城堡的)护〔護〕城河 hùchénghé; 壕沟〔溝〕háogōu.
mob /mɒb/ *n* [C] **1** [蔑] 暴民 bàomín. **2** 一帮罪犯 yìbāng zuìfàn. ☐ *vt* [-bb-] 聚众〔衆〕袭〔襲〕击〔擊〕jù zhòng xíjī; 成群欢〔歡〕呼 chéngqún huānhū.
mo·bile /'məʊbaɪl/ *adj* **1** 易动〔動〕的 yìdòngde; 运〔運〕动的 yùndòngde; 可动的 kědòngde. **2** 易变〔變〕的 yìbiànde; 多变的 duōbiànde: *a* ~ *face* 表情多变的脸. ☐ *n* [C] 一种〔種〕带有能随风〔風〕飘〔飄〕动〔動〕的装〔裝〕饰品 yìzhǒng dàiyǒu néng suí fēng piāodòng de zhuāngshìpǐn. **mo·bil·ity** /məʊ'bɪlətɪ/ *n* [U]
mo·bi·lize /'məʊbɪlaɪz/ *vt/i* 动〔動〕员 dòngyuán: ~ *troops* 动员部队.
moc·ca·sin /'mɒkəsɪn/ *n* [C] 鹿皮鞋 lùpíxié.
mock /mɒk/ *vt/i* 嘲弄 cháonòng; 嘲笑 cháoxiào. ☐ *adj* 假的 jiǎde; 模拟〔擬〕的 mónǐde: *a* ~ *battle* 模拟战. ~**ery** *n* [*pl* -ies] **(a)** [U] 嘲笑 cháoxiào; 愚弄 yúnòng. **(b)** [C] 恶〔惡〕劣的事例 èliède shìlì: *a* ~ *of justice* 蔑视正义的恶例. *make a* ~*ery of* 嘲弄 cháonòng; 愚弄 yúnòng.
mo·dal /'məʊdl/ *adj* 〔语法〕语气〔氣〕的 yǔqìde; 情态〔態〕的 qíngtàide: ~ *auxiliaries* 情态动词 (如 *can, may*)
mode /'məʊd/ *n* [C] 方法 fāngfǎ; 样〔樣〕式 yàngshì.
model[1] /'mɒdl/ *n* [C] **1** 模型 móxíng; 原型 yuánxíng. **2** 模范〔範〕mófàn; 典型 diǎnxíng. **3** (为画家等服务的) 模特儿〔兒〕mótèr. **4** (为服装业服务的) 模特儿 mótèr: *a fashion* ~ 时装模特儿. **5** 模特儿穿戴的衣帽等 mótèr chuāndài de yī mào děng. **6** 样式 yàngshì: *the latest* ~*s of cars* 汽车的最新式样. ☐ *adj* 模范的 mófànde; 典型的 diǎnxíngde: *a* ~ *wife* 模范妻子.
model[2] /'mɒdl/ *vt/i* [-ll-, 美语 -l-] **1** 做…的模型 zuò…de móxíng. **2** 做模特儿〔兒〕zuò mótèr. **3** ~ *oneself on (upon) sb* 使模仿 shǐ mófǎng.
mod·er·ate[1] /'mɒdərət/ *adj* 适〔適〕度的 shìdùde; 适中的 shìzhōngde. ☐ *n* [C] 稳〔穩〕健的人 wěnjiànde rén; (政治上)温和派 wēnhépài. ~**ly** *adv*
mod·er·ate[2] /'mɒdəreɪt/ *vt/i* 缓和 huǎnhé; 节〔節〕制 jiézhì; 减轻〔輕〕jiǎnqīng.
mod·er·ation /ˌmɒdə'reɪʃn/ *n* [U] 适〔適〕度 shìdù; 温和 wēnhé. *in* ~ 适中地 shìzhōngde: *drink whisky in* ~ 喝适量的威士忌.
mod·ern /'mɒdn/ *adj* **1** 现代的 xiàndàide; 近代的 jìndàide. **2** 最新的 zuìxīnde. ~**ize** /-aɪz/ *vt* 使现代化 shǐ xiàndàihuà. ˌ~**ization** /-'zeɪʃn/ *n* [U]
mod·est /'mɒdɪst/ *adj* **1** 谦虚〔虛〕的 qiānxūde; 谦让〔讓〕的 qiānràngde. **2** 适〔適〕度的 shìdùde; 不大的 búdàde: *a* ~ *salary* 不高的工资. **3** 有礼〔禮〕貌的 yǒu lǐmào de: ~ *in behaviour* 举止端庄. ~**ly** *adv* **mod·esty** *n* [U]
mod·ify /'mɒdɪfaɪ/ *vt* [*pt, pp* -ied] **1** 修改 xiūgǎi; 更改 gēnggǎi. **2** 减轻〔輕〕jiǎnqīng: ~ *one's demands*

减少要求. 3〔语法〕修饰 xiūshì. ˌ**modi·fi·ca·tion** /-fɪ'keɪʃn/ *n* [C, U]

mod·ule /'mɒdju:l/ *n* [C] **1** 量度单位 liángdù dānwèi. **2** 建筑〔築〕用的标〔標〕准〔準〕部件 jiànzhù yòng de biāozhǔn bùjiàn. **3** (宇宙飞船上各个独立的)舱〔艙〕cāng.

mo·hair /'məʊheə(r)/ *n* [U] 马〔馬〕海毛 mǎhǎimáo; 马海毛织〔織〕物 mǎhǎimáo zhīwù.

Mo·ham·medan /mə'hɒmɪdən/ *n* ⇨ Muhammad.

moist /mɔɪst/ *adj* (尤指表面)潮湿〔濕〕的 cháoshīde; 湿润〔潤〕的 shīrùnde. **~en** /'mɔɪsn/ *vt/i* 弄湿 nòng shī; 变〔變〕潮湿 biàn cháoshī. **~ure** /-tʃə(r)/ *n* [U] 潮气〔氣〕cháoqì; 湿气 shīqì; 水气 shuǐqì.

mo·lar /'məʊlə(r)/ *n* [C], *adj* 臼齿〔齒〕jiùchǐ; 臼齿的 jiùchǐde.

mole[1] /məʊl/ *n* [C] 黑痣 hēizhì.

mole[2] /məʊl/ *n* [C] 鼹鼠 yǎnshǔ. '**~-hill** 鼹鼠窝〔窩〕yǎnshǔwō. ***make a mountain out of a ~-hill*** 小题大作 xiǎo tí dà zuò.

mol·ecule /'mɒlɪkju:l/ *n* [C] 分子 fēnzǐ. **mol·ecu·lar** /mə'lekjʊlə(r)/ *adj*

mo·lest /mə'lest/ *vt* 骚〔騷〕扰〔擾〕sāorǎo; 干扰 gānrǎo.

mol·lusc [美语= **mol·lusk**] /'mɒləsk/ *n* [C] 软〔軟〕体〔體〕动〔動〕物(如牡蛎、蜗牛等) ruǎntǐ dòngwù.

mol·ten /'məʊltən/ *adj* [*pp* of melt] 熔化的 rónghuàde; 熔融的 róngróngde.

mo·ment /'məʊmənt/ *n* [C] 瞬间〔間〕shùnjiān; 片刻 piànkè. □ *conj* ***the ~*** 一…就… yī…jiù…; 正当…的一刹那间 zhèngdāng … de yíchànà jiān: *Call me the ~ he arrives.* 他一到你就打电话给我. **~ary** *adj* 短暂〔暫〕的 duǎnzànde; 瞬息间的 shùnxījiānde. **~ar·ily** /-'trəlɪ/ *adv*

mo·men·tous /mə'mentəs/ *adj* 重要的 zhòngyàode; 重大的 zhòngdàde.

mo·men·tum /mə'mentəm/ *n* [U] **1**〔科学〕动〔動〕量 dòngliàng. **2**〔喻〕势〔勢〕头〔頭〕shìtóu.

mon·arch /'mɒnək/ *n* [C] 君主 jūnzhǔ; 最高统治者 zuìgāotǒngzhìzhě. **~ic** /mə'nɑ:kɪk/ *adj* **mon·archy** *n* **(a)** [U] 君主政体〔體〕jūnzhǔ zhèngtǐ. **(b)** [C] [*pl* -ies] 君主国〔國〕jūnzhǔguó.

mon·as·tery /'mɒnəstrɪ/ *n*[C] [*pl* -ies] 修道院 xiūdàoyuàn.

mon·as·tic /mə'næstɪk/ *adj* 修道院的 xiūdàoyuànde; 修道士的 xiūdàoshìde.

Mon·day /'mʌndɪ/ *n* 星期一 xīngqīyī.

mon·et·ary /'mʌnɪtrɪ/ *adj* 钱〔錢〕的 qiánde; 货币〔幣〕的 huòbìde.

money /'mʌnɪ/ *n* [U] 货币〔幣〕(硬币和纸币) huòbì; 钱 qián. '**~-box** 钱箱 qiánxiāng.

mon·grel /'mʌŋgrəl/ *adj*, *n* [C] (狗等)杂〔雜〕种〔種〕zázhǒng.

moni·tor /'mɒnɪtə(r)/ *n* [C] **1** 班长〔長〕bānzhǎng; 级长 jízhǎng. **2** (外国广播的)监〔監〕听〔聽〕员 jiāntīngyuán. **3** (放射性的)检〔檢〕验〔驗〕器 jiǎnyànqì; 监听器 jiāntīngqì. □ *vt/i* 监听(外国广播等) jiāntīng.

monk /mʌŋk/ *n* [C] 修道士 xiūdàoshì; 僧侣 sēnglǚ.

mon·key /'mʌŋkɪ/ *n* [C] [*pl* ~s] **1** 猴子 hóuzi; 猿 yuán. **2** 顽童 wántóng. □ *vi* ***~ about (with)*** 胡闹〔鬧〕húnào; 瞎弄 xiānòng. '**~ wrench** 活动〔動〕扳手 huódòng bānshou.

mono·chrome /'mɒnəkrəʊm/ *n* [C] 单〔單〕色画〔畫〕dānsèhuà. □ *adj* 单色的 dānsède.

mon·ocle /'mɒnəkl/ *n* [C] 单〔單〕片眼镜 dānpiàn yǎnjìng.

mon·og·amy /mə'nɒgəmɪ/ *n* [U] 一夫一妻制 yìfū yìqī zhì. ⇨polygamy. **mon·og·amous** *adj*

mono·gram /'mɒnəgræm/ *n* [C] 交织〔織〕字母 jiāozhī zìmǔ.

mono·logue /'mɒnəlɒg/ *n* [C]〔戏剧〕独〔獨〕白 dúbái; 滔滔不绝的话 tāotāo bù jué de huà.

mono·plane /'mɒnəpleɪn/ *n* [C] 单〔單〕翼(飞)机〔機〕dānyìjī.

mon·op·ol·ize /mə'nɒpəlaɪz/ *vt* 垄〔壟〕断〔斷〕lǒngduàn; 独〔獨〕占 dúzhàn; 专〔專〕利 zhuānlì.

mon·op·oly /mə'nɒpəlɪ/ *n* [C] [*pl* -ies] 垄〔壟〕断〔斷〕lǒngduàn; 专〔專〕卖〔賣〕权〔權〕zhuānmàiquán.

mono·rail /'mɒnəʊreɪl/ *n* [C] 单〔單〕轨〔軌〕铁路 dānguǐ tiělù.

mono·syl·lable /'mɒnəsɪləbl/ *n* [C] 单〔單〕音节〔節〕词 dānyīnjié cí. ˌ**mono·sy'l·labic** *adj*

mon·ot·on·ous /mə'nɒtənəs/ *adj* 单〔單〕调的 dāndiàode; 无〔無〕变〔變〕化的 wú biànhuà de: *a ~ voice* 单调的声音. **~ly** *adv* **mon·ot·ony** *n* [U]

mon·soon /mɒn'su:n/ *n* [C] 季风〔風〕(在印度洋和亚洲南部,夏为西南风,冬为东北风) jìfēng; (西南风带来的)雨季 yǔjì.

mon·ster /'mɒnstə(r)/ *n* [C] **1** 畸形的动〔動〕植物 jīxíngde dòngzhíwù; 怪物 guàiwù. **2** 恶〔惡〕人 èrén; 残〔殘〕忍的人 cǎnrěnde rén.

mon·stros·ity /mɒn'strɒsətɪ/ *n* [*pl* -ies] 怪物 guàiwù; 巨大的东〔東〕西 jùdàde dōngxi.

mon·strous /'mɒnstrəs/ *adj* **1** 巨大的 jùdàde. **2** 恐怖的 kǒngbùde: ~ *cruelty* 恐怖的暴行. **3**〔非正式用语〕可耻的 kěchǐde; 丢脸〔臉〕的 diūliǎnde. **~ly** *adv*

month /mʌnθ/ *n* [C] 月 yuè; 一个〔個〕月的时〔時〕间〔間〕 yígèyuède shíjiān. **~ly** *adj*, *adv* 每月的 měiyuède; 每月一次的(地) měiyuè yícì de. □ *n* [C] [*pl* -lies] 月刊 yuèkān.

monu·ment /'mɒnjʊmənt/ *n* [C] **1** 纪念碑 jìniànbēi; 纪念物 jìniànwù. **2** 不朽的文学〔學〕作品或科学文献〔獻〕 bùxiǔde wénxué zuòpǐn huò kēxué wénxiàn. **~al** /-'mentl/ *adj* **(a)** 纪念物的 jìniànwùde. **(b)** (指著作、绘画等)不朽的 bùxiǔde. **(c)** 巨大的 jùdàde.

moo /mu:/ *n* [C] 哞(牛叫声) mōu. □ *vi* (牛) 哞哞地叫 mōumōude jiào.

mood¹ /mu:d/ *n* [C] 心境 xīnjìng; 情绪 qíngxù: *in a bad* ~ 闹情绪.

moody *adj* [-ier, -iest] 心情易变〔變〕的 xīnqíng yìbiàn de, 喜怒无〔無〕常的 xǐ nù wúcháng de. **~-ily** *adv*

mood² /mu:d/ *n* [C] 〔语法〕 语气〔氣〕 yǔqì: *the imperative* ~ 祈使语气.

moon¹ /mu:n/ *n* [C] **1 the** ~ 月亮 yuèliàng, 月球 yuèqiú. **2** 行星的卫〔衛〕星 xíngxīngde wèixīng. ***once in a blue*** ~ 〔非正式用语〕罕有地 hǎnyǒude; 永无〔無〕地 yǒngwúde. **'~·beam** 月光 yuèguāng. **'~light** 月光 yuèguāng.

moon² /mu:n/ *vt/i* ~ ***about (around)*** 闲〔閑〕荡〔蕩〕 xiándàng; 出神 chūshén.

moor¹ /mʊə(r)/ *n* [C,U] 荒野 huāngyě; 旷〔曠〕野 kuàngyě. **'~land** 荒地 huāngdì.

moor² /mʊə(r)/ *vt/i* (使)停泊 tíngbó **~ings** *n pl* **(a)** 系〔繫〕泊用具 xì bó yòngjù. **(b)** 停船处〔處〕 tíngchuánchù.

moose /mu:s/ *n* [C] [*pl* ~ 或 ~s /-sɪz/] 麋 mí.

mop /mɒp/ *n* [C] **1** 拖把 tuōbǎ. **2** 蓬乱〔亂〕的头〔頭〕发〔髮〕 péngluànde tóufa. □ *vt* [-pp-] 用拖把拖洗 yòng tuōbǎ tuōxǐ; 擦 cā, 抹 mǒ.

mope /məʊp/ *vi* 忧〔憂〕郁 yōuyù; 闷〔悶〕闷不乐〔樂〕 mènmèn bú lè.

mo·ped /'məʊped/ *n* [C]〔英国英语〕机〔機〕动〔動〕脚踏车〔車〕 jīdòng jiǎotàchē.

moral¹ /'mɒrəl/ *adj* **1** 道德的 dàodéde; 道义〔義〕的 dàoyìde. **2** 善良的 shànliángde; 诚实〔實〕的 chéngshíde: *a* ~ *man* 有道德的人. **3** 道德教育的 dàodé jiàoyù de: *a* ~ *talk* 德育讲话. ***give sb*** ~ ***support*** 给某人道义上的支持 gěi mǒurén dàoyìshàngde zhīchí. **~ly**

moral² /'mɒrəl/ *n* [C] **1** 教训 jiàoxùn; 寓意 yùyì. **2** [*pl*] 道德 dàodé; 伦〔倫〕理 lúnlǐ; 品行 pǐnxíng.

mo·rale /mə'rɑ:l/ *n* [U] 士气〔氣〕 shìqì; 风〔風〕纪 fēngjì; 精神 jīngshén.

mor·al·ity /mə'rælətɪ/ *n* [*pl* -ies] **1** [U] 道德 dàodé; 美德 měidé. **2** [C] 某一伦〔倫〕理体〔體〕系 mǒuyī lúnlǐ tǐxì.

mor·al·ize /'mɒrəlaɪz/ *vt/i* ~ ***about (upon, on)*** 论〔論〕道德问〔問〕题 lùn dàodé wèntí; 说教 shuōjiào.

mor·bid /'mɔ:bɪd/ *adj* 疾病的 jíbìngde; 病态〔態〕的 bìngtàide: *a* ~ *sense of humour* 病态的幽默感. **~ly** *adv*

more /mɔ:(r)/ (与 *less* 和 *fewer* 相对; ⇨ many, most, much¹) *adj* 更多的 gèngduōde; 较〔較〕多的 jiàoduōde; 更高程度的 gènggāo chéngdù de: *I've got* ~ *money than he has.* 我的钱比他的多. □ *n* [U] 更多的数〔數〕量 gèngduōde shùliàng; 较多的数量 jiàoduōde shùliàng. □ *adv* **1** [much 的比较级, 常和两个音节以上的形容词或副词连用]: ~ *beautiful* (*than*...) (比...)更美丽. **2** 更多 gèngduō: *You need to sleep* ~. 你需要更多的睡眠. **3** 再 zài: *I shall not go there any* ~. 我再也不去那里了. **4** ~ ***and*** ~ 越来〔來〕越 ... yuè lái yuè ... ~ ***or less*** 左右 zuǒyòu; 大约 dàyuē: *£20,* ~ *or less* 大约二十英镑.

more·over /mɔ:r'əʊvə(r)/ *adv* 加之 jiāzhī; 而且 érqiě; 此外 cǐwài.

morgue /mɔ:g/ *n* [C] (待人认领尸体的)陈尸〔屍〕所 chénshīsuǒ. ⇨ mortuary.

morn·ing /'mɔ:nɪŋ/ *n* [C] 早晨 zǎochén; 上午 shàngwǔ. **'~ dress** 常礼〔禮〕服 chánglǐfú.

mo·ron /'mɔ:rɒn/ *n* [C] **1** 低能者 dīnéngzhě. **2**〔非正式用语〕蠢人 chǔnrén. **~ic** /mə'rɒnɪk/ *adj*

mo·rose /mə'rəʊs/ *adj* 郁闷〔悶〕的

yùmènde; 脾气〔氣〕不好的 píqì bùhǎo de. **~ly** *adv*

mor·phia /ˈmɔːfɪə/, **mor·phine** /ˈmɔːfiːn/ *n* [U] 吗〔嗎〕啡 mǎfēi.

Morse /mɔːs/ *n* (亦作 *the ~ code*) 摩尔〔爾〕斯电〔電〕码〔碼〕Mó'ěrsī diànmǎ.

mor·sel /ˈmɔːsl/ *n* [C] (食物的) 一口 yìkǒu; 一小片 yìxiǎopiàn.

mor·tal /ˈmɔːtl/ *adj* **1** (与 *immortal* 相对) 必有一死的 bì yǒu yì sǐ de; 死的 sǐde: *Man is ~.* 人是会死的; 人必有一死. **2** 致死的 zhìsǐde; 致命的 zhìmìngde: *a ~ wound* 致命的创伤. **3** [非正式用语] 极〔極〕端的 jíduānde; 极大的 jídàde: *in ~ fear* 极大的恐惧. □ *n* [C] [书面语] 凡人 fánrén. **~ly** *adv* **(a)** 致命地 zhìmìngde: *~ly wounded* 致命伤. **(b)** 极 jí, 非常 fēicháng. **~ity** /mɔːˈtæləti/ *n* [U] **(a)** 致命性 zhìmìngxìng; 必死性 bìsǐxìng. **(b)** 死亡数〔數〕sǐwángshù. **(c)** 死亡率 sǐwánglǜ.

mor·tar¹ /ˈmɔːtə(r)/ *n* [U] 灰浆〔漿〕huījiāng; 灰泥 huīní. □ *vt* 用灰泥黏接 yòng huīní niánjiē.

mor·tar² /ˈmɔːtə(r)/ *n* [C] **1** 臼 jiù; 研钵 yánbō. **2** 迫击〔擊〕炮 pǎijīpào.

mort·gage /ˈmɔːgɪdʒ/ *vt* 抵押 dǐyā. □ *n* [C] 抵押 dǐyā; 抵押单〔單〕据〔據〕dǐyā dānjù.

mor·tify /ˈmɔːtɪfaɪ/ *vt/i* [*pt, pp* -ied] **1** 使受辱 shǐ shòurǔ; 伤〔傷〕害(感情) shānghài. **2** ~ *the flesh* 禁欲 jìnyù; 克制 kèzhì. **mor·ti·fi·ca·tion** /-fɪˈkeɪʃn/ *n* [U]

mor·tu·ary /ˈmɔːtʃəri/ *n* [C] [*pl* -ies] (丧葬前的) 停尸〔屍〕房 tíngshīfáng; (医院的) 太平间〔間〕tàipíngjiān.

mo·saic /məʊˈzeɪɪk/ *n* [C], *adj* 镶嵌细工(的) xiāngqiàn xìgōng; 镶嵌工艺〔藝〕品 xiāngqiàn gōngyìpǐn; 嵌花式的 qiànhuāshìde.

Mos·lem /ˈmɒzləm/ *n, adj* 见 Muslim jiàn *Muslim.*

mosque /mɒsk/ *n* [C] 清真寺 qīngzhēnsì.

mos·quito /məˈskiːtəʊ/ *n* [C] [*pl* ~es] 蚊子 wénzi; 蚊虫〔蟲〕wénchóng.

moss /mɒs/ *n* [U] 苔藓 táixiǎn. **mossy** *adj* [-ier, -iest]

most /məʊst/ (与 *least* 和 *fewest* 相对; ⇨ many, more, much¹) *adj, n* **1** [加 *the*] 最多的 zuìduōde; 最高程度的 zuìgāo chéngdù de; 最多数〔數〕zuìduōshù; 最大量 zuìdàliàng. ***make the ~ of*** 充分利用 chōngfèn lìyòng; 尽〔盡〕量利用 jìnliàng lìyòng. ***for the ˈ~ part*** 通常地 tōngchángde. **2** [不加 *the*] 大多数 dàduōshù; 大部分 dàbùfen: *M~ people like him.* 大多数人喜欢他. □ *adv* **1** [much 的最高级, 和两个音节以上的形容词或副词连用]: *the ~ beautiful car* 最漂亮的汽车. **2** 最 zuì: *What is troubling you ~?* 什么事情最使你烦恼? **3** 很 hěn; 十分 shífēn: *a ~ useful book* 一本十分有用的书.

most·ly /ˈməʊstli/ *adv* 主要地 zhǔyàode; 通常 tōngcháng.

mo·tel /məʊˈtel/ *n* [C] 汽车〔車〕旅馆 qìchēlǚguǎn.

moth /mɒθ/ *n* [C] 蛾 é. **ˈ~-eaten** *adj* **(a)** 蠹蛀过〔過〕的 dùzhùguòde. **(b)** [喻] 过时〔時〕的 guòshíde; 破烂〔爛〕的 pòlànde.

mother /ˈmʌðə(r)/ *n* [C] **1** 母亲〔親〕mǔqīn. **2** 妇〔婦〕女宗教团〔團〕体〔體〕的女主持人 fùnǚ zōngjiào tuántǐ de nǚ zhǔchírén. □ *vt* (母亲般地) 照管 zhàoguǎn; 保护〔護〕bǎohù. **the ˈ~ country** 祖国〔國〕zǔguó. **~-in-law** *n* [C] (*pl* ~s-in-law) 岳母 yuèmǔ; 婆婆 pópo. **ˌ~ ˈtongue** 本国语言 běnguó yǔyán. **ˈ~hood** 母性 mǔxìng; 母亲身分 mǔqīn shēnfen; 母亲 mǔqīn. **~ly** *adj* 母亲的 mǔqīnde; 慈母般的 címǔbānde.

mo·tif /məʊˈtiːf/ *n* [C] (文艺作品的) 主题 zhǔtí; (图案的) 基本花纹 jīběn huāwén.

mo·tion /ˈməʊʃn/ *n* **1** [U] 运〔運〕动〔動〕yùndòng; 动态〔態〕dòngtài. ***put* (或 *set*) *sth in ~*** 使某物运转〔轉〕shǐ mǒuwù yùnzhuàn. **2** [C] 手势〔勢〕shǒushì; 眼色 yǎnsè; 姿势 zīshì: *signal with a ~ of the hand.* 打手势. ***go through the ~s*** [非正式用语] 敷衍了事 fūyǎn liǎoshì. **3** [C] 提议〔議〕tíyì; 动议 dòngyì. □ *vt/i* 以姿势示意 yǐ zīshì shìyì. **~less** *adj* 不动的 búdòngde, 静止的 jìngzhǐde.

mo·ti·vate /ˈməʊtɪveɪt/ *vt* 促动 cùdòng; 激发〔發〕jīfā. **mo·ti'v·ation** /-ʃn/ *n* [C,U]

mo·tive /ˈməʊtɪv/ *adj* 发〔發〕动〔動〕的 fādòngde; 运〔運〕动的 yùndòngde: *~ power* 动力. □ *n* [C] 动机〔機〕dòngjī.

mo·tor /ˈməʊtə(r)/ *n* [C] **1** 发〔發〕动〔動〕机〔機〕fādòngjī; 马〔馬〕达〔達〕mǎdá. **2** [过时用法] 汽车〔車〕qìchē. □ *vt/i* 乘汽车 chéng qìchē. **ˈ~bike (cycle)** 机动脚踏车. jīdòng jiǎotàchē; 摩托车 mótuōchē. **ˈ~cade** [美语] 汽车车队〔隊〕qìchē chēduì. **ˈ~-car** 汽车 qìchē.

'~way 高速公路 gāosù gōnglù. '~ist 驾〔駕〕驶〔駛〕汽车的人 jiàshǐ qìchē de rén; 乘汽车旅行者 chéng qìchē lǚxíngzhě. '~ize /-raɪz/ *vt* 用汽车装〔裝〕备〔備〕yòng qìchē zhuāngbèi; 使摩托化 shǐ mótuōhuà.

motto /'mɒtəʊ/ *n* [C] [*pl* ~es 或 ~s] 座右铭 zuòyòumíng; 箴言 zhēnyán.

mould¹ [美语 = **mold**] /məʊld/ *n* [C] **1** 模子 múzi; 模型 múxíng. **2** 模制〔製〕品 múzhìpǐn; 铸〔鑄〕造物 zhùzàowù. □ *vt* **1** 造型 zàoxíng; 塑造 sùzào. **2** [喻]对〔對〕…产〔產〕生影响〔響〕duì … chǎnshēng yǐngxiǎng: ~ *his character* 塑造他的性格.

mould² [美语 = **mold**]/məʊld/ *n* [U] 霉 méi; 霉菌 méijūn. **mouldy** *adj* [-ier, -iest]

moul·der[美语 =**mol·der**]/'məʊldə(r)/ *vi* 崩碎 bēngsuì; 腐朽 fǔxiǔ.

moult [美语 = **molt**] /məʊlt/*vt/i* **1** (指鸟)脱换(羽毛) tuōhuàn. **2** (指猫狗)脱毛 tuōmáo.

mound /maʊnd/ *n* [C] 土墩 tǔdūn; 土堆 tǔduī; 小山 xiǎoshān.

mount¹ /maʊnt/ *n* [C] (缩作 **Mt**) (用于专有名词前)山 shān.

mount² /maʊnt/ *vt/i* **1** 爬上 páshàng; 登上 dēngshàng. **2** 骑〔騎〕上(马等) qíshàng. **3** 增加 zēngjiā; 上升 shàngshēng: *Our expenses are ~ing (up)*. 我们的费用正在增多. **4** 贴(照片等) tiē: ~ *pictures* 画集上贴画片; 相册上贴照片. **5** ~ ***an offensive*** 攻击〔擊〕gōngjī; 发〔發〕动〔動〕攻势〔勢〕fādòng gōngshì. **6** 上演(戏剧) shàngyǎn. □ *n* [C] 乘 chéng; 骑〔騎〕qí.

moun·tain /'maʊntɪn/ *n* [C] 山 shān; 高山 gāoshān. **~eer** /-'nɪə(r)/ 登山家 dēngshānjiā. **~eering** *n* [U] 登山运〔運〕动 dēngshān yùndòng. **~ous** *adj* **(a)** 多山的 duōshānde. **(b)** 巨大的 jùdàde: ~*ous waves* 巨浪.

mourn /mɔːn/ *vt/i* ~ **(*for, over*)** 哀悼 āidào. **~er** 哀悼者 āidàozhě; 送葬者 sòngzàngzhě. **~ful** *adj* 悲哀的 bēi'āide; 哀痛的 āitòngde.

mourn·ing /'mɔːnɪŋ/ *n* [U] **1** 悲哀 bēi'āi. **2** 丧〔喪〕服 sàngfú; 戴孝 dàixiào.

mouse /maʊs/ *n* [C] [*pl* mice /maɪs/] **1** 鼠 shǔ; 耗子 hàozi. **2** [喻]胆小如鼠的人 dǎn xiǎo rú shǔ de rén.

mousse /muːs/ *n* [C,U] 奶油冻〔凍〕(一种点心) nǎiyóudòng.

mous·tache /mə'stɑːʃ/ *n* [C] (嘴上边的)胡〔鬍〕子 húzi; 髭 zī.

mousy /'maʊsɪ/ *adj* [-ier, -iest] **1** (尤指头发)棕褐色 zōnghèsè. **2** 胆小的 dǎnxiǎode.

mouth¹ /maʊθ/ *n* [C] [*pl* ~s /maʊðz/] **1** 嘴 zuǐ; 口 kǒu. **2** 河口 hékǒu; 瓶口 píngkǒu; 隧道口 suìdàokǒu. '~**-organ** 口琴 kǒuqín. '~**piece, (a)** 烟〔煙〕嘴口 yānzuǐkǒu; (乐器的)吹口 chuīkǒu. **(b)** 代言人 dàiyánrén. **~ful** /-fʊl/ *n* [C] [*pl* ~s] 一口(食物) yīkǒu.

mouth² /maʊð/ *vt/i* 做作地说 zuòzuode shuō; 夸〔誇〕大地说 kuādàde shuō.

mov·able /'muːvəbl/ *adj* 可移动〔動〕的 kěyídòngde; 动产〔產〕的 dòngchǎnde. ⇨ portable.

move¹ /muːv/ *n* [C] **1** 移动〔動〕yídòng; 迁〔遷〕居 qiānjū; (象棋)走棋 zǒuqí. **2** 步骤〔驟〕bùzòu; 措施 cuòshī: ~*s to end the strike* 结束罢工的措施. **3** ***on the*** ~ 在活动中 zài huódòng zhōng. ***get a*** ~ ***on*** [俚]赶〔趕〕快 gǎnkuài. ***make a*** ~, **(a)** 迁移 qiānyí. **(b)** 开〔開〕始行动〔動〕kāishǐ xíngdòng.

move² /muːv/ *vt/i* **1** 移动〔動〕yídòng; 搬动 bāndòng. **2** ~ ***house*** 搬家 bānjiā, 迁〔遷〕居 qiānjū. ~ ***in (out)*** 搬进〔進〕(出) bānjìn. **3** 感动 gǎndòng. **4** (在会上) 提议〔議〕tíyì; 动议 dòngyì. ⇨ motion(3).

move·ment /'muːvmənt/ *n* **1** [U] 运〔運〕动〔動〕yùndòng; 活动 huódòng. **2** [C] (部队等的)调动 diàodòng; 行进〔進〕xíngjìn. **3** [C] 机〔機〕件 jījiàn; [机械] 动程 dòngchéng. **4** [C] (群众性) 运动 yùndòng: *the peace* ~ 和平运动. **5** [C] [音乐]乐〔樂〕章 yuèzhāng.

movie /'muːvɪ/ *n* [C] [非正式用语][美语] **1** 电〔電〕影 diànyǐng. **2 the** ~**s** 电影 diànyǐng; 电影制〔製〕片业〔業〕diànyǐng zhìpiānyè; 电影院 diànyǐngyuàn.

mow /məʊ/ *vt* [*pt* ~ed; *pp* ~n /məʊn/ ~ed] **1** (用刈草机) 割 gé; 刈 yì. **2** ~ ***down*** (象刈草一样)刈倒 yìdǎo; 扫〔掃〕除 sǎochú. **~er** 刈割者 yìgézhě; 割草机〔機〕gécǎojī.

M.P. = **1** Member of Parliament (英国)下院议〔議〕员 xiàyuàn yìyuán. **2** military police 宪〔憲〕兵队〔隊〕xiànbīngduì.

m.p.g. = miles per gallon 英里/加仑〔侖〕yīnglǐ/jiālún.

m.p.h. = miles per hour 英里/时〔時〕yīnglǐ/shí.

Mr /'mɪstə(r)/ ⇨ mister.

Mrs /'mɪsɪz/ 夫人 fūrén.
M.Sc. = Master of Science.
Mt. = **1** mountain. **2** Mount.
much¹ /mʌtʃ/ [more, most. ⇨ little] *adj, n* [U] 许多 xǔduō; 大量 dàliàng: *There isn't ~ food in the house.* 家里食物不多了. ***be too ~*** 太多 tài duō. ***how ~,*** **(a)** 多少 duōshǎo. **(b)** 什么〔麽〕价〔價〕钱〔錢〕 shénme jiàqián. ***so ~ so that*** 到这〔這〕样〔樣〕程度以致 dào zhèyàng chéngdù yǐzhì. ***make ~ of,*** **(a)** 理解 lǐjiě; 明白 míngbai: *I didn't make ~ of that lecture.* 我不理解那篇演讲. **(b)** 重视 zhòngshì. ***not think ~ of*** 对〔對〕… 估价〔價〕不高 duì… gūjià bù gāo.
much² /mʌtʃ/ *adv* **1** 多 duō; 更 gèng: *work ~ harder* 更加努力地工作. *This is ~* (= by far) *the best.* 这是最好的了. **2** 很 hěn, 极〔極〕 jí, 非常 fēicháng: *I enjoyed it very ~.* 我很喜欢. **3** ***~ as*** 虽〔雖〕然 suīrán: *M~ as I want to, I cannot go.* 我虽然要去,但不能去. ***how ~*** 到什么〔麽〕程度 dào shénme chéngdu: *How ~ does it really matter?* 到底有多大关系?
muck /mʌk/ *n* [U] **1** 粪〔糞〕 fèn; 粪肥 fènféi. **2** 脏〔髒〕物 zāngwù; 污物 wūwù. □ *vt/i* **1** ***~ sth up*** [非正式用语]弄乱〔亂〕 nòng luàn; 弄坏〔壞〕nòng huài. **2** ***~ about***[俚语]混日子 hùn rìzi. **mucky** *adj* [-ier, -iest]
mu·cous /'mju:kəs/ *adj* 黏液的 niányède; 似黏液的 sìniányède. **the ~ membrane** 黏膜 niánmó.
mu·cus /'mju:kəs/ *n* [U] (由黏膜分泌的)黏液 niányè.
mud /mʌd/ *n* [U] 泥 ní. **'~-guard** (车子的)挡〔擋〕泥板 dǎngníbǎn. **'~dy** *adj* [-ier, -iest].
muddle /'mʌdl/ *vt/i* **1** 使混乱〔亂〕 shǐ hùnluàn; 弄糟 nòng zāo. **2** ***~ along*** **(*on*)** 混日子 hùn rìzi. ***~ through*** 混过〔過〕去 hùnguòqù. □ *n* [C] 混乱 hùnluàn; (头脑)糊涂〔塗〕 hútu: *in a ~* 乱糟糟; 混乱中. **'~-headed** *adj* 笨拙的 bènzhuóde; 头〔頭〕脑〔腦〕糊涂的 tóunǎo hútu de.
muff /mʌf/ *n* [C] (妇女防寒用的)皮手笼〔籠〕 píshǒulóng; 皮手筒 píshǒutǒng.
muffle /'mʌfl/ *vt* **1** 包 bāo; 裹 guǒ. **2** 将〔將〕某物(铃,鼓等)包住使其声〔聲〕音低沉 jiāng mǒuwù bāozhù shǐ qí shēngyīn dīchén. **muf·fler** *n* [C] **(a)** 围〔圍〕巾 wéijīn. **(b)** 消声器 xiāoshēngqì, 减〔減〕音器 jiǎnyīnqì.
mug¹ /mʌg/ *n* [C] **1** (有柄的)大杯 dàbēi; 一杯容量 yìbēi róngliàng. **2** [俚语]脸〔臉〕 liǎn.
mug² /mʌg/ *n* [C] [俚语]愚人 yúrén; 容易受骗〔騙〕的人 róngyì shòupiàn de rén.
mug³ /mʌg/ *vt* [-gg-] [俚语]猛烈袭〔襲〕击〔擊〕并抢〔搶〕劫(某人) měngliè xíjī bìng qiǎngjié. **~ger** *n* [C] **~ging** *n* [C,U]
Mu·ham·mad /mə'hæmɪd/ *n* 穆罕默德(伊斯兰教创始人) Mùhǎnmòdé. **~an** *adj, n* [C]
mul·berry /'mʌlbrɪ/ *n* [C] [*pl* -ies] 桑树〔樹〕 sāngshù; 桑葚 sāngshèn.
mule /mju:l/ *n* [C] 骡〔騾〕 luó. **mul·ish** *adj* 顽固的 wángùde; 执〔執〕拗的 zhíniùde.
mull¹ /mʌl/ *vt* 加糖和香料等后〔後〕温热〔熱〕(饮料) jiā táng hé xiāngliào děng hòu wēnrè.
mull² /mʌl/ *vt* ***~ sth over*** 深思 shēnsī; 熟虑〔慮〕 shúlǜ.
multi·lat·eral /ˌmʌltɪ'lætərəl/ *adj* 多边〔邊〕的 duōbiānde; 多国〔國〕参加的 duōguó cānjiā de: *~ aid* 多边援助.
multi·media /ˌmʌltɪ'mi:dɪə/ *adj* 媒介综合利用 méijiè zōnghé lìyòng: *~ language course* 综合媒介语言课程.
multiple /'mʌltɪpl/ *adj* 复〔複〕合的 fùhéde; 多样〔樣〕的 duōyàngde; 多重的 duōchóngde. □ *n* [C] 倍数〔數〕 bèishù.
multi·ply /'mʌltɪplaɪ/ *vt/i* [*pt, pp* -ied] **1** [数学]乘 chéng: *6 multiplied by 5 is 30.* 6 乘 5 等于 30. **2** 增加 zēngjiā; 增多 zēngduō. **3** 繁殖 fánzhí: *Rabbits ~ very quickly.* 兔子繁殖很快. **multi·pli·cation** /-plɪ'keɪʃn/ *n* [C,U]
multi·tude /'mʌltɪtju:d/ *n* [C] 大批 dàpī; 大群 dàqún; 众〔衆〕多 zhòngduō.
mum¹ /mʌm/ *n* ***M~'s the word*** 不可泄露 bù kě xièlòu.
mum² /mʌm/ *n* [C] [非正式用语] 妈〔媽〕妈 māma.
mumble /'mʌmbl/ *vt/i* 含糊地说 hánhúde shuō; 咕哝〔噥〕 gūnong.
mum·mify /'mʌmɪfaɪ/ *vt* [*pt, pp* -ied] 用香料保存(尸体) yòng xiāngliào bǎocún; (使)皱〔皺〕缩 zhòusuō.
mummy¹ /'mʌmɪ/ *n* [C] [*pl* -ies] 木乃伊 mùnǎiyī.
mummy² /'mʌmɪ/ *n* [C] [*pl* -ies] [非正式用语]妈〔媽〕妈 māma.
mumps /mʌmps/ *n* [U] 流行性腮腺炎 liúxíngxìng sāixiànyán.

munch /mʌntʃ/ *vt/i* 用力嚼 yòng lì jiáo.

mun·dane /mʌn'deɪn/ *adj* 世俗的 shìsúde; 世间〔間〕的 shìjiānde. ~**ly** *adv*

mu·nici·pal /mju:'nɪsɪpl/ *adj* 市的 shìde; 市政的 shìzhèngde; 市立的 shìlìde: ~ *elections* 市区选举. ~**ity** /-'pælətɪ/ *n* [C][*pl* -ies] 自治市、镇 zìzhìshì, zhèn; 市政当〔當〕局 shìzhèng dāngjú; 市政府 shìzhèngfǔ.

mu·ni·tion /mju:'nɪʃn/ *n* [*pl*] 军〔軍〕需品 jūnxūpǐn; 军火 jūnhuǒ.

mural /'mjʊərəl/ *adj* 墙〔牆〕壁的 qiángbìde; 墙壁上的 qiángbìshàngde. □ *n* [C] 壁画〔畫〕bìhuà; 壁饰 bìshì.

mur·der /'mɜ:də(r)/ *n* [C,U] 谋杀〔殺〕móushā; 谋杀案 móushā'àn. □ *vt* 谋杀 móushā. ~**er** 杀人犯 shārénfàn; 凶〔兇〕手 xiōngshǒu. ~**ess** 女杀人犯 nǚ shārénfàn; 女凶手 nǚ xiōngshǒu. ~**ous** *adj* 杀人的 shārénde; 行凶的 xíngxiōngde: *a* ~*ous look* 一副凶杀相. *a* ~*ous attack* 行凶的攻击.

murk /mɜ:k/ *n* [U] 黑暗 hēi'àn; 阴〔陰〕沉 yīnchén. **murky** *adj* [-ier, -iest]. ~**ily** *adv*

mur·mur /'mɜ:mə(r)/ *n* [C] **1** 低沉连〔連〕续〔續〕的声〔聲〕音 dīchén liánxù de shēngyīn. **2** 怨言 yuànyán: *suffer without a* ~ 受苦而无怨言. □ *vt/i* **1** 发〔發〕低沉连续声 fā dīchén liánxù shēng; 发牢骚〔騷〕fā láosāo. **2** 低声说 dīshēng shuō.

Mus. B. = Bachelor of Music 音乐〔樂〕学〔學〕士 yīnyuè xuéshì.

muscle /'mʌsl/ *n* **1** [C,U] 肌肉 jīròu. **2** [喻]力量 lìliàng.

mus·cu·lar /'mʌskjʊlə(r)/ *adj* **1** 肌肉的 jīròude. **2** 肌肉发〔發〕达〔達〕的 jīròu fādá de.

mu·seum /mju:'zɪəm/ *n* [C] 博物馆 bówùguǎn.

mush·room /'mʌʃrʊm/ *n* [C] **1** 蘑菇 mógu; 食用伞〔傘〕菌 shíyòng sǎnjùn. **2** 迅速发〔發〕展 xùnsù fāzhǎn: *the* ~ *growth of London* 伦敦的迅速发展. □ *vi* **1** 采〔採〕蘑菇 cǎi mógu. **2** 迅速发〔發〕展 xùnsù fāzhǎn; 迅速成长 xùnsù chéngzhǎng.

mu·sic /'mju:zɪk/ *n* [U] **1** 音乐〔樂〕yīnyuè. **2** 乐曲 yuèqǔ; 乐谱 yuèpǔ. ***face the*** ~ 勇敢地面对〔對〕麻烦或困难〔難〕 yǒnggǎnde miànduì máfán huò kùnnán. ~**al** *adj* 音乐的 yīnyuède; 爱〔愛〕好音乐的 àihào yīnyuè de; 精通音乐的 jīngtōng yīnyuè de. □ *n* [C] 音乐喜剧〔劇〕yīnyuè xǐjù; (电影的)音乐片 yīnyuèpiān. ~**ally** /-klɪ/ *adv*

mu·si·cian /mju:'zɪʃn/ *n* [C] 音乐〔樂〕家 yīnyuèjiā; 作曲家 zuòqǔjiā.

mus·ket /'mʌskɪt/ *n* [C] 滑膛枪〔槍〕huátángqiāng; 旧〔舊〕式步枪 jiùshì bùqiāng. ~**eer** /-'tɪə(r)/ 用滑膛枪装〔裝〕备〔備〕的步兵 yòng huátángqiāng zhuāngbèi de bùbīng.

Mus·lim /'mʊzlɪm/ *n* 伊斯兰〔蘭〕教徒 Yīsīlánjiàotú; 伊斯兰教的 Yīsīlánjiàode.

mus·lin /'mʌzlɪn/ *n* [U] 细薄棉布 xìbó miánbù.

mus·sel /'mʌsl/ *n* [C] 淡菜 dàncài.

must /məst 强式: mʌst/ *auxiliary verb* [否定式 must not 或 mustn't /'mʌsnt/] **1** (表示义务; *must not* 表示禁止): *You* ~ *do as you're told.* 你必须按照吩咐去做. *You* ~ *not hit him.* 你不许打他. **2** (表示一定): *If you try hard, you* ~ *win.* 如果你下苦功夫,你一定会胜利. **3** (表示必定、必然): *You* ~ *be hungry after your walk.* 你走路以后一定饿了. □ *n* [C] [非正式用语]必须做的事 bìxū zuò de shì: *His new play is a* ~. 他的新剧是一定要看的.

mus·tard /'mʌstəd/ *n* [U] **1** 芥 jiè; 芥子 jièzi. **2** 芥末 jièmò; 芥粉 jièfěn.

mus·ter /'mʌstə(r)/ *n* [C] 集合 jíhé; 检〔檢〕阅〔閱〕 jiǎnyuè. □ *vt/i* 集合 jíhé; 集中 jízhōng.

musty /'mʌstɪ/ *adj* [-ier, -iest] 霉的 méide; 霉臭的 méichòude. **musti·ness** *n* [U]

mu·ta·tion /mju:'teɪʃn/ *n* [C,U] 变〔變〕化 biànhuà; 变异〔異〕biànyì; 转〔轉〕变 zhuǎnbiàn.

mute /mju:t/ *adj* **1** 沉默的 chénmòde; 不出声〔聲〕的 bùchūshēngde. **2** 哑〔啞〕的 yǎde. □ *n* [C] **1** 哑巴 yǎba, 哑人 yǎrén. **2** 弱音器(装在乐器上使声音变柔和或减弱的装置) ruòyīnqì. □ *vt* 减弱或减低(乐器的)声音 jiǎnruò huò jiǎndī shēngyīn. ~**ly** *adv*

mu·ti·late /'mju:tɪleɪt/ *vt* 使断〔斷〕肢 shǐ duànzhī; 使残〔殘〕废〔廢〕shǐ cánfèi; 切去(手、足等) qiēqù. **mu·ti'la·tion** *n* [C,U]

mu·ti·nous /'mju:tɪnəs/ *adj* 叛变〔變〕的 pànbiànde; 反抗的 fǎnkàngde.

mu·tiny /'mju:tɪnɪ/ *n* [*pl* -ies]

[C,U] (尤指军人和水手) 叛变〔變〕pànbiàn; 兵变 bīngbiàn; 反抗 fǎnkàng. □ *vi* [*pt, pp* -ied] 叛变 pànbiàn; 反抗 fǎnkàng. **mu·ti'n·eer** 叛变者 pànbiànzhě; 反抗者 fǎnkàngzhě.

mut·ter /'mʌtə(r)/ *vt/i* 轻〔輕〕声〔聲〕低语 qīngshēng dīyú; 咕哝〔噥〕gūnong. □ *n* [C] 轻声低语 qīngshēng dīyǔ; 怨言 yuànyán.

mut·ton /'mʌtn/ *n* [U] 羊肉 yángròu.

mu·tual /'mju:tʃʊəl/ *adj* **1** 共有的 gòngyǒude. **2** 相互的 xiānghùde; 彼此的 bǐcǐde: ~ *aid* 互助. **3** 共同的 gòngtóngde: *our ~ friend* 我们共同的朋友. **~ly** *adv*

muzzle /'mʌzl/ *n* [C] **1**(狗等的)鼻和口 bí hé kǒu. **2** (动物的) 口套 kǒutào. **3** 枪〔槍〕口 qiāngkǒu; 炮口 pàokǒu. □ *vt* **1** 给(动物)上口络 gěi shàng kǒuluò. **2** [喻]禁止(人等)自由发〔發〕表意见 jìnzhǐ zìyóu fābiǎo yìjiàn.

my /maɪ/ *possessive adj* **1** 我的 wǒde: *Where's ~ hat?* 我的帽子在哪儿? **2** (用于称呼): *Yes, ~ dear.* 是的, 我亲爱的. **3** [用于感叹句中]: *M~ goodness!* 天哪!

my·opia /maɪ'əʊpɪə/ *n* [U] 近视 jìnshi. **my·opic** /maɪ'ɒpɪk/ *adj*

myr·iad /'mɪrɪəd/ *n* [C] 极〔極〕大数〔數〕量 jídà shùliàng.

myrrh /mɜ:(r)/ *n* [U] [药]没药 méiyào; 没药树〔樹〕méiyàoshù.

my·self /maɪ'self/ *pron* **1** [反身代词]: *I hurt ~.* 我伤了自己; 我把自己弄伤了. ***(all) by ~***, **(a)** 独〔獨〕自 dúzì; 单〔單〕独 dāndú. **(b)** 无〔無〕人帮助 wúrén bāngzhù. **2** [用以加强语气]: *I said so ~.* 我亲自这么说过. **3** *I'm not ~ today.* 我今天有点不舒服.

mys·teri·ous /mɪ'stɪərɪəs/ *adj* 神秘的 shénmìde; 不可思议〔議〕的 bùkě sīyì de. **~ly** *adv*

mys·tery /'mɪstərɪ/ *n* [*pl* -ies] **1** [C] 神秘的事物 shénmìde shìwù; 不可思议〔議〕的事物 bùkě sīyì de shìwù. **2** [U] 神秘 shénmì; 秘密 mìmì.

mys·tic /'mɪstɪk/ *adj* 神秘的 shénmìde; 引起惊〔驚〕奇的 yǐnqǐ jīngqí de. □ *n* [C] 神秘主义〔義〕者 shénmìzhǔyìzhě. **~al** *adj* **'~ism** /-sɪzəm/ *n* [U] 神秘主义 shénmìzhǔyì.

mys·tify /'mɪstɪfaɪ/ *vt* [*pt, pp* -ied]使神秘化 shǐ shénmìhuà; 迷惑 míhuò. **mys·ti·fi·ca·tion**/-fɪ'keɪʃn/ *n* [C,U]

mys·tique /mɪ'sti:k/ *n* [C] 神秘气〔氣〕氛 shénmì qìfēn; 神秘性 shénmìxìng; 奥妙 àomiào.

myth /mɪθ/ *n* **1** [C] 神话 shénhuà. **2** [U] 传〔傳〕说 chuánshuō. **3** [C] 虚构〔構〕的人或物 xūgòude rén hòu wù. **~i·cal** *adj* **(a)** 神话的 shénhuàde; 神话式的 shénhuàshìde. **(b)** 想象的 xiǎngxiàngde; 虚构的 xūgòude.

myth·ol·ogy /mɪ'θɒlədʒɪ/ *n* [*pl* -ies] **1** [U] 神话学〔學〕shénhuàxué. **2** [C] 神话集 shénhuàjí. **mytho·logi·cal** /-'lɒdʒɪkl/ *adj* 神话学的 shénhuàxuéde; 虚构的 xūgòude.

N n

N, n /en/ [*pl* N's, n's /enz/] 英语的第十四个〔個〕字母 Yīngyǔ de dìshísìgè zìmǔ.

N. = **1** North. **2** New.

n. = **1** neuter. **2** nominative. **3** noon. **4** noun.

nab /næb/ *vt* [-bb-] [非正式用语] 逮捕 dàibǔ; 捉住 zhuōzhù.

nag¹ /næg/ *n* [C] [非正式用语]小马〔馬〕xiǎomǎ.

nag² /næg/ *vt/i* [-gg] 唠〔嘮〕叨 láodao; 责骂〔罵〕不休 zémà bùxiū.

nail /neɪl/ *n* [C] **1** 指甲 zhǐjia. **2** 钉 dīng. ***hit the ~ on the head*** 说得中肯 shuōde zhōngkěn; 做得恰到好处〔處〕zuò de qià dào hǎochù; 一针见血 yìzhēn jiàn xiě. □ *vt* 用钉钉牢 yòng dīng dīngláo. **~ *sb down (to sth)*** 使人明说自己的打算 shǐ rén míngshuō zìjǐde dǎsuàn.

naive, (亦作**naïve**) /naɪ'i:v/ *adj* 天真的 tiānzhēnde; 幼稚的 yòuzhìde. **~ly** *adv*

naked /'neɪkɪd/ *adj* **1** 裸体〔體〕的 luǒtǐde. **2** 无〔無〕遮蔽的 wú zhēbì de: *a ~ light* 没有灯罩的灯. ***with the ~ eye*** 用肉眼 yòng ròuyǎn. **~ly** *adv* **~ness** *n* [U]

name /neɪm/ *n* **1** [C] 名字 míngzi; 姓 xìng; 名称〔稱〕míngchēng. ***in the ~ of***, **(a)**凭 ...: *stop in the ~ of the law* 以法律的名义阻止. **(b)** 为〔爲〕wèi: *in the ~ of peace* 了和平. ***call sb ~s*** 侮辱某人 w rǔ mǒurén. 2 [仅用 *sing*] 名誉〔譽〕míngyù; 名声〔聲〕míngshēng. ***make a ~ for oneself*** 成名 chéngmíng. □ *vt* 1 命名 mìngmíng; 取名 qǔmíng. ***~ sb after sb*** 以某人的名字命名 yǐ mǒuréndе míngzì mìngmíng. 2 说出…的名字 shuōchū ... de míngzi; 叫出 jiàochū. 3 指定 zhǐdìng; 说出 shuōchū: *Please ~ the day.* 请说定日期. **'~sake** 同姓名的人 tóng xìngmíng de rén. **'~less, (a)** 没有名字的 méiyǒu míngzi de. **(b)** 不知名的 bù zhīmíng de.

name·ly /'neɪmlɪ/ *adv* 即 jí, 也就是 yě jiùshì: *Two men, ~ Peter and Jim* 两个人,即彼得和吉姆.

nanny /'nænɪ/ *n* [C] [*pl* -ies] 保姆 bǎomǔ.

nanny-goat /'nænɪ gəʊt/ *n* [C] 雌山羊 cí shānyáng. ⇨ billy-goat.

nap[1] /næp/ *n* [C] 小睡 xiǎoshuì, 打盹 dǎdǔn. □ *vi* [-pp-] ***catch sb ~ping*** 乘某人不备〔備〕而抓住他的过〔過〕错等 chéng mǒurén bú bèi ér zhuāzhù tāde guòcuò děng.

nap[2] /næp/ *n* [U] (织物上面的一层)绒毛 róngmáo.

na·palm /'neɪpɑ:m/ *n* [U] 凝固汽油 nínggù qìyóu.

nape /neɪp/ *n* [C] 颈〔頸〕背 jǐngbèi; 后〔後〕颈 hòujǐng.

nap·kin /'næpkɪn/ *n* [C] 餐巾 cānjīn.

nappy /'næpɪ/ *n* [C] [*pl* -ies] 尿布 niàobù.

nar·cissus /nɑ:'sɪsəs/ *n* [C] [*pl* ~es 或 -cissi /-sɪsaɪ/] 水仙花 shuǐxiānhuā.

nar·cotic /nɑ:'kɒtɪk/ *n* [C], *adj* 麻醉剂〔劑〕mázuìjì; 麻醉的 mázuìde.

nar·rate /nə'reɪt/ *vt* 讲〔講〕(故事) jiǎng; 叙述 xùshù. **nar·rator** 讲述者 jiǎngshùzhě; 叙述者 xùshùzhě. **nar·ra·tion** *n* [C,U]

nar·ra·tive /'nærətɪv/ *n* **1** [C] 故事 gùshì; [U] 叙述 xùshù; 讲〔講〕述 jiǎngshù. 2 [用作定语]叙述的 xùshùde; 叙述体〔體〕的 xùshùtǐde.

nar·row /'nærəʊ/ *adj* [-er, -est] (与 *wide* 相对) **1** 狭〔狹〕xiá, 窄 zhǎi. 2 勉强的 miǎnqiángde: *a ~ escape* 九死一生. 3 偏狭 piānxiá; 狭隘 xiá'ài: *a ~ mind* 小心眼; 心胸狭窄. □ *vt/i* 变〔變〕狭 biàn xiá; 弄窄 nòng zhǎi. **,~-'minded** *adj* 气〔氣〕量小的 qìliàngxiǎode. **~ly** *adv* 勉强的 miǎnqiángde: *~ly escape* 勉强逃脱. **~ness** *n* [U]

na·sal /'neɪzl/ *adj* 鼻的 bíde; 鼻音的 bíyīnde. □ *n* [C] [语音]鼻音 bíyīn.

nas·tur·tium /nə'stɜ:ʃəm/ *n* [C] [*pl* ~s] 旱金莲〔蓮〕属〔屬〕植物 hànjīnliánshǔ zhíwù.

nasty /'nɑ:stɪ/ *adj* [-ier, -iest] **1** 令人作呕〔嘔〕的 lìng rén zuò'ǒu de; 令人不快的 lìng rén búkuài de. 2 淫猥的 yínwěide; 下流的 xiàliúde. **nas·tily** *adv* **nas·ti·ness** *n* [U]

na·tal /'neɪtl/ *adj* 出生的 chūshēngde; 诞生的 dànshēngde.

na·tion /'neɪʃn/ *n* [C] 民族 mínzú; 国〔國〕家 guójiā.

na·tion·al /'næʃnəl/ *adj* 民族的 mínzúde; 国〔國〕家的 guójiāde. □ *n* [C] 某国籍的人 mǒuguójíde rén; 国民 guómín. **,~ 'anthem** 国歌 guógē. **,~ 'service** 在军〔軍〕队〔隊〕服役期间〔間〕 zài jūnduì fúyì qījiān. **~ly** *adv* **'~ism** /-ɪzəm/ *n* [U] **(a)** 民族主义〔義〕mínzú zhǔyì; 国家主义 guójiā zhǔyì. **(b)** 政治独〔獨〕立运〔運〕动〔動〕zhèngzhì dúlì yùndòng. **~ist** *n* [C], *adj*

na·tion·al·ity /,næʃən'ælətɪ/ *n* [C,U] [*pl* -ies] 国〔國〕籍 guójí.

na·tion·al·ize /'næʃnəlaɪz/ *vt* 使国〔國〕有化 shǐ guóyǒuhuà; 收归〔歸〕国有 shōu guī guóyǒu. **na·tion·al·i'z·ation** /-ʃn/ *n* [U]

na·tive /'neɪtɪv/ *n* [C] **1** 本地人 běndìrén; 本国〔國〕人 běnguórén. 2 当〔當〕地产〔產〕的动〔動〕物或植物 dāngdìchǎnde dòngwù huò zhíwù. □ *adj* **1** 出生地的 chūshēngdìde. 2 本地的 běndìde; 土生的 tǔshēngde. 3 天生的 tiānshēngde: *~ charm* 天生的魅力.

na·tiv·ity /nə'tɪvətɪ/ *n* [C] [*pl* -ies] (尤指) **(the N~)** 诞生(尤指耶稣的诞生) dànshēng.

N.A.T.O. = North Atlantic Treaty Organization 北大西洋公约组织〔織〕Běidàxīyánggōngyuē zǔzhī.

natu·ral /'nætʃrəl/ *adj* **1** 自然的 zìránde; 自然界的 zìránjiède. 2 本能的 běnnéngde: *~ abilities* 本能. 3 生来〔來〕的 shēngláide: *a ~ orator* 天生的演说家. 4 正常的 zhèngchángde; 合乎自然规律的 héhū zìrán guīlǜ de: *It is ~ for a bird to fly.* 鸟会飞是自然的. 5 通常的 tōngchángde; 不做作的 bú zuòzuò de: *speak in a ~ voice* 用正常的声音讲话. 6 私生的 sīshēngde. □ *n* [C] ***a ~ (for sth)*** [非正式用语] 天生的专〔專〕

门〔門〕人才 tiānshēngde zhuānmén réncái. ˌ~ 'gas 天然气〔氣〕tiānránqì. ˌ~ 'history 博物学〔學〕bówùxué.

natu·ral·ist /'nætʃrəlɪst/ *n* [C] 博物学〔學〕家 bówùxuéjiā.

natu·ral·ize /'nætʃrəlaɪz/ *vt/i* (使)入国〔國〕籍 rù guójí. **natu·ral·i'z·ation** /-ʃn/ *n* [U]

nat·ur·ally /'nætʃrəlɪ/ *adv* 1 天然地 tiānránde; 天生地 tiānshēngde. 2 当〔當〕然 dāngrán: *N~ I'll help you.* 我当然要帮助你. 3 自然地 zìránde: *speak ~* 说话自然.

na·ture /'neɪtʃə(r)/ *n* 1 [U] 自然界 zìránjiè. 2 [U] 自然力 zìránlì: *the forces of nature* 自然力. 3 [U] 自然状〔狀〕态〔態〕 zìrán zhuàngtài; 原始状态 yuánshǐ zhuàngtài: *a return to ~* 回到自然. 4 [C,U] 本性 běnxìng; 天性 tiānxìng: *It is his ~ to tell lies.* 说慌是他的本性. ⇨ good/ill-natured. 5 种〔種〕类〔類〕 zhǒnglèi: *stories of that ~* 那一类故事

naughty /'nɔːtɪ/ *adj* [-ier, -iest] 1 顽皮的 wánpíde; 不听〔聽〕话的 bù tīnghuà de. 2 猥亵〔褻〕的 wěixiède; 下流的 xiàliúde. **naught·ily** *adv.* **naughti·ness** *n* [U]

nausea /'nɔːsɪə/ *n* [U] 噁〔噁〕心 ěxīn; 晕〔暈〕船 yùnchuán. **naus·eate** /'nɔːsɪeɪt/ *vt* 使噁心 shǐ ěxīn; 使作呕〔嘔〕 shǐ zuò'ǒu. **naus·eous** *adj*

nauti·cal /'nɔːtɪkl/ *adj* 航海的 hánghǎide; 船舶的 chuánbóde; 海员的 hǎiyuánde. ~ **mile** 浬 lǐ, 海里 hǎilǐ.

na·val /'neɪvl/ *adj* 海军〔軍〕的 hǎijūnde; 军舰〔艦〕的 jūnjiànde.

nave /neɪv/ *n* [C] 教堂中殿 jiàotáng zhōngdiàn.

na·vel /'neɪvl/ *n* [C] 肚脐〔臍〕 dùqí.

navi·gable /'nævɪgəbl/ *adj* 1 (指江河、海洋等) 可航行的 kěhángxíngde, 可通航的 kětōnghángde. 2 (指船等)适〔適〕航的 shìhángde. **navi·ga'bil·ity** *n* [U]

navi·gate /'nævɪgeɪt/ *vt/i* 1 航行 hángxíng. 2 驾〔駕〕驶〔駛〕船舶或飞〔飛〕机〔機〕 jiàshǐ chuánbó huò fēijī. **navi·gator** 驾驶员 jiàshǐyuán; 领航员 lǐnghángyuán. **navi'ga·tion** /-ʃn/ *n* [U]

navy /'neɪvɪ/ *n* [C] [*pl* -ies] 1 海军〔軍〕 hǎijūn. 2 海军人员 hǎijūn rényuán. ˌ~ '**blue** 藏青色 zàngqīngsè.

N.B. = note carefully 注意 zhùyì, 留心 liúxīn.

N.C.O. = non-commissioned officer 军〔軍〕士 jūnshì.

N.E. = north-east.

near[1] /nɪə(r)/ *adj* [-er, -est] 1 (空间、时间)近的 jìnde. 2 近亲〔親〕的 jìnqīnde; 亲密的 qīnmìde: *~ relations* 近亲. 3 (与 *off* 相对) (指车)左方的 zuǒfāngde. □ *vt/i* 走近 zǒujìn; 驶〔駛〕近 shǐjìn. ~**ness** *n* [U]

near[2] /nɪə(r)/ *adv* 接近 jiējìn; 近 jìn. ~ ***at hand,*** **(a)** 在近旁 zài jìnpáng. **(b)** 在不久的将〔將〕来〔來〕 zài bùjiǔde jiānglái. ~ ***by*** 附近的(地) fùjìnde. '~**side** 左边〔邊〕(的) zuǒbiān. ˌ~-'**sighted** *adj* = short-sighted.

near[3] /nɪə(r)/ *prep* (= *near to*) (空间、时间等)接近 jiējìn; 近 jìn: *Sit ~ me.* 靠近我坐下.

near·by /nɪə'baɪ/ *adj* 附近的 fùjìnde.

near·ly /'nɪəlɪ/ *adv* 1 几〔幾〕乎 jīhū ⇨ hardly, scarcely. 2 ***not*** ~ 相差很远〔遠〕 xiāngchà hěnyuǎn: *not ~ enough money* 钱远远不够.

neat /niːt/ *adj* [-er, -est 除第 4 义外] 1 整洁〔潔〕的 zhěngjiéde. 2 雅致的 yǎzhìde: *a ~ dress* 雅致的服装. 3 灵〔靈〕巧的 língqiǎode: *a ~ reply* 巧妙的回答. 4 (指酒)纯的 chúnde; 不掺〔摻〕水的 bù chān shuǐ de. ~**ly** *adv* ~**ness** *n* [U]

necess·ar·ily /ˌnesə'serəlɪ/ *adv* 必定 bìdìng, 必然 bìrán: *Big men are not ~ strong.* 大块头的人不一定就是强壮的人.

necess·ary /'nesəsərɪ/ *adj* 必要的 bìyàode; 必需的 bìxūde: *food is ~ for life.* 食物是生活的必需.

necessi·tate /nɪ'sesɪteɪt/ *vt* [正式用语]使成为必需 shǐ chéngwéi bìxū.

necess·ity /nɪ'sesətɪ/ *n* [*pl* -ies] 1 [U] 急需 jíxū. 2 [C] 必需品 bìxūpǐn: *Food is a ~ of life.* 食物为生活的必需品.

neck[1] /nek/ *n* [C] 1 颈〔頸〕 jǐng; 脖子 bózi. ˌ~ ***and*** '~ (赛马等) 并驾〔駕〕齐〔齊〕驱〔驅〕 bìng jià qí qū; 不分上下 bùfēn shàngxià. ***risk one's*** ~ [非正式用语]冒生命危险〔險〕 mào shēngmìng wēixiǎn. ***stick one's ~ out*** [非正式用语]招麻烦 zhāo máfán; 惹祸〔禍〕事 rě huòshì. 2 (物的) 颈状〔狀〕部分 jǐngzhuàng bùfen: *the ~ of a bottle* 瓶颈. '~**lace** /-lɪs/ 项链〔鍊〕 xiàngliàn. '~-**tie** 领带〔帶〕 lǐngdài.

neck² /nek/ *vi* [俚语]拥[擁]抱 yōngbào.

nec·tar /'nektə(r)/ *n* [U] **1** 花蜜 huāmì. **2** [喻] 任何美味的饮料 rènhé měiwèi de yǐnliào.

née /neɪ/ *adj* (法语)娘家姓…的(表示已婚妇女的娘家姓) niángjiāxìng … de: *Mrs J Smith, ~ Brown* 娘家姓布朗的史密斯夫人.

need¹ /ni:d/ *n* **1** [U] 需要 xūyào; 必要 bìyào: *the ~ to work hard* 努力工作的需要. **2** [*pl*] 需求 xūqiú; 需用的东[東]西 xūyòngde dōngxi: *His ~s are few.* 他几乎没有什么需要. **3** [U] 贫穷[窮] pínqióng; 不幸 búxìng. **~less** *adj* 不需要的 bù xūyào de. **~less·ly** *adv* **needy** *adj* [-ier, -iest] 贫困的 pínkùnde.

need² /ni:d/ *aux verb* (第三人称单数, 现在式以及否定句和疑问句用 need; need not 缩作needn't /'ni:dnt/) 需要 xūyào; 必须 bìxū: *N~ you go yet?* 你还需要去吗? *We ~n't have hurried.* 我们当时实在不必那么匆忙.

need³ /ni:d/ *vt* **1** 需要 xūyào; 必需 bìxū: *Does he ~ any help?* 他需要帮助吗? **2** 应[應]受 yīngshòu; 应得 yīngdé: *What he ~s is a slap!* 他应得一个耳光.

needle /'ni:dl/ *n* [C] **1** 针 zhēn; 缝衣针 féngyīzhēn. **2** 编织[織]针 biānzhīzhēn. **3** 注射针 zhùshèzhēn. **4** 唱针 chàngzhēn. □ *vt* [非正式用语]烦扰[擾] fánrǎo; 伤[傷]害 shānghài. **'~craft (work)** 刺绣 cìxù; 缝纫 féngrèn.

ne·ga·tion /nɪ'geɪʃn/ *n* [U] 否定 fǒudìng; 否认[認] fǒurèn.

nega·tive /'negətɪv/ *adj* **1** 否定的 fǒudìngde; 否认[認]的 fǒurènde. ⇨ affirmative. **2** 消极[極]的 xiāojíde: *~ criticism* 消极的批评. ⇨ positive(3). **3** [数学]负的 fùde. **4** [电学]阴[陰]性的 yīnxìngde; 负的 fùde: *a ~ terminal* 负电的接头. ⇨ positive (6). **5** [摄影]底片的 dǐpiànde. □ *n* [C] **1** 否定词 fǒudìngcí; 否定语 fǒudìngyǔ; 否定的观[觀]点[點] fǒudìngde guāndiǎn. **2** [摄影] 底片 dǐpiàn. **~ly** *adv*

ne·glect /nɪ'glekt/ *vt* **1** 忽视 hūshì; 忽略 hūlüè: *~ one's health* 忽视健康. **2** 搁[擱]置未做 gēzhì wei zuò. □ *n* [U] 忽略 hūlüè; 疏忽 shūhu. **~ful** *adj* 疏忽的 shūhude; 不注意的 bú zhùyì de. **~ful·ly** *adv.* **~ful·ness** *n* [U]

nég·ligé, neg·li·gee /'neglɪʒeɪ/ *n* [C,U] 便服 biànfú.

neg·li·gence /'neglɪdʒəns/ *n* [U] 疏忽 shūhu; 粗心大意 cūxīn dàyì. **neg·li·gent** *adj.* **neg·li·gent·ly** *adv*

neg·li·gible /'neglɪdʒəbl/ *adj* 微不足道的 wēi bù zú dào de; 可以忽视的 kěyǐ hūshì de.

ne·go·ti·able /nɪ'gəʊʃɪəbl/ *adj* **1** 可谈判的 kětánpànde; 可商议[議]的 kěshāngyìde: *a ~ contract* 可商议的合同. **2** 可兑换现金的 kě duìhuàn xiànjīn de: *~ shares* 可转让(兑现)的股票. **3** (道路、河流等)可通行的 kětōngxíngde.

ne·go·ti·ate /nɪ'gəʊʃɪeɪt/ *vt/i* **1** 谈判 tánpàn; 协[協]商 xiéshāng. **2** 商订 shāngdìng: *negotiating a treaty* 商订条约. **3** 转[轉]让[讓] zhuǎnràng; 兑现 (票证等) duìxiàn. **4** 越过[過](障碍) yuèguò. **ne·go·ti·ator** 谈判者 tánpànzhě; 协商者 xiéshāngzhě. **ne·go·ti'ation** *n* [C,U]

Ne·gress /'ni:gres/ *n* [C] 女黑人 nǚ hēirén.

Ne·gro /'ni:grəʊ/ *n* [C] [*pl* ~es] 黑人 hēirén.

neigh /neɪ/ *vi, n* [C] (马)嘶 sī; 马[馬]嘶声[聲] mǎsīshēng.

neigh·bour [美语 = **-bor**] /'neɪbə(r)/ *n* [C] **1** 邻[鄰]居 línjū. **2** 邻人 línrén; 邻国[國] línguó; 邻接的东[東]西 línjiēde dōngxi. □ *vt/i* 邻接 línjiē; 邻近 línjìn: *~ing towns* 邻近的市镇. **~ly** *adj* **~li·ness** *n* [U]

neigh·bour·hood [美语 = **-bor-**] /'neɪbəhʊd/ *n* [C] 邻[鄰]近 línjìn; 附近(地区) fùjìn; 周围[圍] zhōuwéi: *in the ~ of London* 在伦敦附近地区.

nei·ther /'naɪðə(r), 'ni:ð-/ *adj, pron* 两者都不 liǎngzhě dū bù: *N~ statement is true.* 两种说法都不真实. ⇨ either. □ *adv, conj* **1** *~ nor* 既不…也不 jìbù…yěbù: *N~ John nor I can go.* 约翰和我都不能去. **2** 也不 yěbù: *If you don't go, ~ shall I.* 假如你不去, 我也不去.

neon /'ni:ɒn/ *n* [U] 氖光灯[燈] nǎiguāngdēng; 霓虹灯 níhóngdēng.

nephew /'nevju:/ *n* [C] 侄子 zhízi; 外甥 wàisheng.

nep·ot·ism /'nepətɪzəm/ *n* [U] 裙带[帶]关[關]系[係] qúndài guānxi.

nerve /nɜ:v/ *n* **1** [C] 神经[經] shénjīng. **2** [*pl*] 神经质[質] shénjīngzhì; 神经紧[緊]张[張] shénjīng jǐnzhāng. *a bundle of ~s* 非常神经质的人 fēicháng shénjīngzhì de rén. ***get on one's ~s*** 使某人心烦 shǐ mǒurén xīnfán. **3** [U] 勇气〔氣〕yǒngqì. ***have the ~ to do sth,*** **(a)** 有勇气做某事 yǒu yǒngqì zuò mǒushì. **(b)** [非正式用语]厚颜 hòuyán. ***lose one's ~*** 失去勇气 shīqù yǒngqì. **'~-racking** 伤〔傷〕脑〔腦〕筋的 shāngnǎojīnde.

nerv·ous /'nɜːvəs/ *adj* **1** 神经〔經〕的 shénjīngde. **2** 神经质〔質〕的 shénjīngzhìde; 易激动〔動〕的 yì jīdòng de. **,~ 'breakdown** 神经衰弱 shénjīng shuāiruò. **'~ system** 神经系统 shénjīng xìtǒng. **~ly** *adv.* **~ness** *n* [U]

nervy /'nɜːvɪ/ *adj* [非正式用语]神经〔經〕质〔質〕的 shénjīngzhìde; 神经紧〔緊〕张〔張〕的 shénjīng jǐnzhāng de.

nest /nest/ *n* [C] **1** 鸟〔鳥〕巢 niǎocháo; 鸟窝〔窩〕 niǎowō **2** 舒适〔適〕的地方 shūshìde dìfāng. **3** 一套物件 yítào wùjiàn. □ *vi* 筑〔築〕巢 zhùcháo; 做窝 zuòwō. **'~-egg** 储备〔備〕金 chǔbèijīn.

nestle /'nesl/ *vt/i* **1 ~ (*down*)** 舒适〔適〕地安顿下来〔來〕 shūshìde āndùn xiàlái. **2 ~ *up* (*against, in*)** 偎依 wēiyī: *She ~d her head in the cushions.* 她把头依在靠垫上.

nest·ling /'nestlɪŋ/ *n* [C] (未离巢的)雏〔雛〕鸟〔鳥〕chúniǎo.

net[1] /net/ *n* [C,U] 网〔網〕 wǎng; 网状〔狀〕物 wǎngzhuàngwù: *'fishing-~s* 渔网. □ *vt* [-tt-] 用网捕 yòng wǎng bǔ. **'~ball** 类〔類〕似篮〔籃〕球的球戏〔戲〕 lèisì lánqiúde qiúxì. **'~work, (a)** 网状系统 wǎngzhuàng xìtǒng. **(b)** 连〔連〕成的系统 liánchéngde xìtǒng: *a spy ~work* 特务网.

net[2], **nett** /net/ *adj* 纯净的 chúnjìngde: *~ profit* 纯利,净利. □ *vt* [-tt-] 净得 jìngde; 净赚 jìngzhuàn.

net·ting /'netɪŋ/ *n* [U] **1** 结网〔網〕 jiē wǎng; 撒网 sā wǎng. **2** 网 wǎng; 网状〔狀〕物 wǎngzhuàngwù.

nettle /'netl/ *n* [C] 荨〔蕁〕麻 xúnmá.

net·work ⇨ net[1].

neur·ol·ogy /njʊə'rɒlədʒɪ/ *n* [U] 神经〔經〕病学〔學〕 shénjīngbìngxué. **neu·rologist** *n* [C] 神经病学家 shénjīngbìngxuéjiā.

neur·osis /njʊ'rəʊsɪs/ *n* [C] [*pl* -ses /-siːz/] 神经〔經〕(机能)病 shénjīngbìng; 精神神经病 jīngshén shénjīngbìng.

neur·otic /njʊ'rɒtɪk/ *adj* 神经〔經〕(机能)病的 shénjīngbìngde; 神经过〔過〕敏的 shénjīngguòmǐnde. □ *n* [C] 神经过敏者 shénjīngguòmǐnzhě; 神经病患者 shénjīngbìnghuànzhě.

neu·ter /'njuːtə(r)/ *adj* **1** [语法]中性的 zhōngxìngde. **2** 无〔無〕性的 wúxìngde. □ *n* [C] **1** 中性 zhōngxìng; 中性词 zhōngxìngcí. **2** 无性动〔動〕物 wúxìng dòngwù; 无性昆虫〔蟲〕 wúxìng kūnchóng. □ *vt* 阉〔閹〕割 yāngē.

neu·tral /'njuːtrəl/ *adj* **1** 中立的 zhōnglìde; 中立国〔國〕的 zhōnglìguóde. **2** 中性的 zhōngxìngde: *~ tints* 灰色. **3** (齿轮)空档〔檔〕的 kōngdǎngde. □ *n* [C] **1** 中立者 zhōnglìzhě; 中立国 zhōnglìguó. **2** [机械]空档 kōngdǎng. **~ity** /njuː'trælətɪ/ *n* [U] 中立 zhōnglì; 中性 zhōngxìng. **~ize** /-aɪz/ *vt* **(a)** 使中立 shǐ zhōnglì. **(b)** 使无〔無〕效 shǐ wúxiào; 中和 zhōnghé: *~ize a poison* 使毒品无效.

neu·tron /'njuːtrɒn/ *n* [C] 中子 zhōngzǐ. **~ 'bomb** *n* [C] 中子弹 zhōngzǐdàn.

never /'nevə(r)/ *adv* **1** 永不 yǒngbù; 未曾 wèicéng. **2 *N~ mind!*** 没关〔關〕系〔係〕 méiguānxi.

never·the·less /ˌnevəðə'les/ *adv, conj* 然而 rán'ěr; 不过〔過〕 búguò; 仍然 réngrán: *He was old and poor, ~ he was happy.* 他年老而且贫穷,然而很快乐.

new /njuː/ *adj* [-er, -est] **1** 新的 xīnde: *a ~ film* 新影片. **2** 新发〔發〕现的 xīn fāxiàn de: *learn ~ words* 学习新词. **3 ~ *to*** 不熟悉的 bù shúxī de: *I'm ~ to this job.* 我不熟悉这个工作. **4** 新制〔製〕的 xīnzhìde: *a ~ car* 一辆新汽车. **5** 重新的 chóngxīnde; 重新开〔開〕始的 chóngxīn kāishǐ de: *a ~ life* 新生活. □ *adv* 新近 xīnjìn; 最近 zuìjìn: *'~born* 新生. **'~-comer** 新来〔來〕的人 xīnláide rén. **~ness** *n* [U]. **~ly** *adv* **(a)** 新近 xīnjìn; 最近 zuìjìn: *~ly-arrived* 最近来到地. **(b)** 以新的方式 yǐ xīnde fāngshì: *~ly arranged furniture* 新布置的家俱. **'~ly-weds** *n pl* 新婚夫妇〔婦〕 xīnhūn fūfù.

news /njuːz/ *n pl* [U] 新闻〔聞〕 xīnwén; 新闻报〔報〕道 xīnwén bàodào: *The ~ of his death is shocking.* 他去世的消息令人震惊. **'~-agent** 报刊经〔經〕售人 bàokān jīngshòurén. **'~paper** 报纸 bàozhǐ.

newt /njuːt/ *n* [C] 蝾〔蠑〕螈 róngyuán.

next /nekst/ *adj, n* [U] **1** 其次的

qícìde; 邻〔鄰〕接的（位置）línjiēde: *Take the ~ turning to the right.* 前面向右转弯. **2** 贴近的 tiējìnde; 隔〔隔〕壁的 gébìde: *the chair ~ to mine* 靠近我的椅子的那把椅子. *~ door* 隔壁 gébì. *~ of kin* 近亲〔親〕jìnqīn; 至亲 zhìqīn. *~ to* 几〔幾〕乎 jīhū: *say ~ to nothing* 几乎什么也没说. □ *adv* 下次 xiàcì: *What are you going to do ~?* 下一步你要做什么?

nib /nɪb/ *n* [C] 钢〔鋼〕笔〔筆〕尖 gāngbǐjiān.

nibble /ˈnɪbl/ *vt/i* 啃 kěn; 一点〔點〕一点地咬 yìdiǎnyìdiǎnde yiǎo. □ *n* [C] 啃 kěn; 轻〔輕〕咬 qīngyiǎo.

nice /naɪs/ *adj* [-r, -st] **1** (与 *nasty* 相反) 令人愉快的 lìng rén yúkuài de; 和蔼的 hé'ǎide; 美好的 měihǎode: *a ~ day* 好天气; *a ~ little girl* 可爱的小女孩. *~ and...* 因…而舒适〔適〕宜人 yīn... ér shūshì yírén: *It's ~ and warm today.* 今天很暖和. **2** 须慎重对〔對〕待的 xū shènzhòng duìdài de; 细微的 xìwēide: *~ differences of meaning* 意义上细微的差别. **3** [非正式用语] 坏〔壞〕的 huàide; 糟的 zāode: *We're in a ~ mess!* 我们陷入困境. **~ly** *adv* **(a)** 美好地 měihǎode; 谨慎地 jǐnshènde. **(b)** [非正式用语] 很好地 hěnhǎode: *progressing ~ly* 进展良好. **~ness** *n* [U]

nicety /ˈnaɪsətɪ/ *n* [C] [*pl* -ies] 细微的区〔區〕别 xìwēide qūbié: *niceties of meaning* 意义上的细微区别.

niche /nɪtʃ/ *n* [C] **1** 壁龛〔龕〕bìkān. **2** [喻] 适〔適〕当〔當〕的地位 shìdàngde dìwèi: *my ~ in the company* 我在公司里的合适职务.

nick /nɪk/ *n* [C] **1** (V 形的) 小刻痕 xiǎo kèhéng. **2** *in the ,~ of 'time* 正是时〔時〕候 zhèngshì shíhòu. **3** [俚语] 监〔監〕狱 jiānyù. □ *vt* 刻痕于 kè hén yú; 弄缺 nòng quē.

nickel /ˈnɪkl/ *n* **1** [U] 镍 **(Ni)** niè. **2** [C] (美国的) 五分镍币〔幣〕wǔfēn nièbì. □ *vt* [-ll-, 美语 -l-] 镀镍于 dù niè yú.

nick·name /ˈnɪkneɪm/ *n* [C] 绰号〔號〕chuòhào; 浑〔渾〕名 húnmíng. □ *vt* 给…起绰号 gěi...qǐ chuòhào.

nic·otine /ˈnɪkətiːn/ *n* [U] 烟〔煙〕碱 yānjiǎn; 尼古丁 nígǔdīng.

niece /niːs/ *n* [C] 侄女 zhínǚ; 甥女 shēngnǚ.

night /naɪt/ *n* [C] 夜 yè, 夜间〔間〕yèjiān. *by ~* 在夜间 zài yèjiān. *have a good (bad) ~* 夜里睡得好(不好) yèlǐ shuì de hǎo. **'~dress** (妇女的) 睡衣 shuìyī. **'~fall** 黄昏 huánghūn. **'~ie, '~y** [非正式用语] = nightdress. **'~ life** 夜生活 yèshēnghuó. **'~mare** /-meə(r)/, **(a)** 恶〔惡〕梦〔夢〕èmèng. **(b)** 可怕的经〔經〕历〔歷〕kěpàde jīnglì. **,~-'watchman** 值夜班的人 zhíyèbānde rén; (专职的) 守夜人 shǒuyèrén. **~ly** *adj, adv* 每夜的 měiyède; 每夜 měiyè.

night·in·gale /ˈnaɪtɪŋgeɪl/ *n* [C] 夜莺〔鶯〕yèyīng.

nil /nɪl/ *n* 无〔無〕wú; 零 líng.

nimble /ˈnɪmbl/ *adj* [-r, -st] **1** 敏捷的 mǐnjiéde. **2** 机〔機〕智的 jīzhìde; 聪〔聰〕明的 cōngmingde. **nim·bly** *adv*

nine /naɪn/ *adj, n* [C] 九 jiǔ. **ninth** /naɪnθ/ *adj n* [C] (缩作 *9th*) 第九 dìjiǔ; 九分之一 jiǔfēn zhī yī.

nine·teen /ˌnaɪnˈtiːn/ *adj, n* [C] 十九 shíjiǔ. **nine·teenth** *adj, n* [C] (缩作 *19th*) 第十九 dìshíjiǔ; 十九分之一 shíjiǔfēn zhī yī.

ninety /ˈnaɪntɪ/ *adj, n* [C] 九十 jiǔshí. **nine·tieth** *adj, n* [C] (缩作 *90th*) 第九十 dìjiǔshí; 九十分之一 jiǔshífēn zhī yī.

nip /nɪp/ *vt/i* [-pp-] **1** 夹〔挾〕jiā; 钳 qián; 掐 qiā; 捏〔揑〕niē; 咬 yǎo. **2** (风、霜等) 摧残〔殘〕cuīcán; 伤〔傷〕害 shānghài. *~ sth in the bud* 在萌芽时〔時〕摘取 zài méngyáshí zhāiqǔ; 防患于未然 fánghuàn yú wèirán. **3** [非正式用语] 急忙 jímáng: *~ along to the shops* 急忙去商店. □ *n* [C] **1** 夹 jiā; 钳 qián; 掐 qiā; 捏 niē; 咬 yǎo. *a cold ~ in the air* 刺骨的寒气 cìgǔ de hánqì. **2** 小饮 (尤指酒类) xiǎo yǐn. ⇨ nippy.

nipple /ˈnɪpl/ *n* [C] **1** 奶头〔頭〕nǎitóu. **2** 橡皮奶头 xiàngpí nǎitóu.

nippy /ˈnɪpɪ/ *adj* [-ier, -iest] [非正式用语] **1** 寒冷刺骨的 hánlěng cìgǔ de. **2** 敏捷的 mǐnjiéde; 轻〔輕〕快的 qīngkuàide: *a ~ little car* 轻便汽车.

nit[1] /nɪt/ *n* [C] (虱等的) 卵 luǎn.

nit[2] /nɪt/ *n* [C] [非正式用语] = nitwit.

ni·tro·gen /ˈnaɪtrədʒən/ *n* [U] 氮 (N) dàn.

ni·tro·glycer·ine, -glycerin /ˌnaɪtrəʊˈglɪsəriːn/ *n* [U] 硝化甘油 xiāohuàgānyóu.

nit·wit /ˈnɪtwɪt/ *n* [C] [非正式用语] 傻〔傻〕瓜 shǎguā; 笨人 bènrén.

no /nəʊ/ *adj* **1** 没有 méiyǒu: *She had ~ money.* 她没有钱. **2** 决不是 juébúshì: *He's ~ friend of mine.* 他决不是我的朋友. **3** 不许 bùxǔ: *N~ smoking.* 禁止吸烟. ***be ~ good (use)*** 没用 méiyóng. ***by*** **'~ *means*** 决不 juébù. **,~-'go** [非正式用语]不成 bùchéng. **'~-man's-land** [军事] 无[無]人地带[帶] wúrén dìdài.

no² /nəʊ/ *adv* 毫不 háobù; 并不 bìngbù: *I have ~ more money.* 我没有更多的钱了. □*particle* (与'Yes'相对): *Is it six o'clock yet?* 已经六点了吗? *N~ it isn't.* 不, 不是六点. □ *n* [C] 不 bù; 否定 fǒudìng; 否认[認] fǒurèn. ***The noes*** 投反对[對]票的人 tóu fǎnduìpiào de rén.

No. = Number.

no·bil·ity /nəʊ'bɪlətɪ/ *n* [U] **1** 高贵 gāoguì; 高尚 gāoshàng. **2** 贵族 guìzú.

noble /'nəʊbl/ *adj* [-r, -st] **1** 贵族的 guìzúde; 高贵的 gāoguìde. **2** 高尚的 gāoshàngde; 崇高的 chónggāode: *~ sentiments* 高尚的情操. **3** 壮[壯]丽[麗]的 zhuànglìde; 宏伟[偉]的 hóngwěide: *a ~ building* 宏伟的建筑. □ *n* [C] 贵族 guìzú. **'~man** 贵族 guìzú. **nobly** *adv*

no·body /'nəʊbədɪ/ *pron* [*pl* -ies] **1**[U] 没有人 méiyǒu rén; 无[無]人 wúrén: *N~ could find him.* 没有人能找到他. **2** [C] 无足轻[輕]重的人 wú zú qīngzhòng de rén; 小人物 xiǎorénwù: *a mere ~* 无名之辈.

noc·tur·nal /nɒk'tɜ:nl/ *adj* 夜的 yède; 夜间[間]发[發]生的 yèjiān fāshēng de; 夜出的 yèchūde.

nod /nɒd/ *vt/i* [-dd-] **1** 点[點]头[頭](表示同意或打招呼) diǎntóu. **2** 打盹 dǎdǔn; 瞌睡 kēshuì. ***~ off*** 入睡 rùshuì. □ *n* [C] 点头 diǎntóu; 打盹 dǎdǔn.

noise /nɔɪz/ *n* [C,U] 噪声[聲] zàoshēng; 嘈杂[雜]声 cáozáshēng. **noisy** *adj* [-ier, -iest] 嘈杂的 cáozáde; 喧闹[鬧]的 xuānnàode. **nois·ily** *adv*

no·mad /'nəʊmæd/ *n* [C] 游牧民 yóumùmín; 流浪者 liúlàngzhě. **~ic** /nəʊ'mædɪk/ *adj*

nom·inal /'nɒmɪnl/ *adj* **1** 名义[義]上的 míngyìshàngde; 有名无[無]实[實]的 yǒumíng wúshí de: *the ~ ruler of the country* 名义上国家的统治者. **2** 极[極]微的 jíwēide: *a ~ rent* 象征性房租. **3** [语法] 名词性的 míngcíxìngde. **~ly** *adv*

nomi·nate /'nɒmɪneɪt/ *vt* **1** *~ sb (for)* 提名 tímíng; 推荐[薦] tuījiàn. **2** *~ sb (to)* 任命 rènmìng; 指定 zhǐdìng. **nomi'na·tion** *n* [C, U]

nomi·nee /,nɒmɪ'ni:/ *n* [C] 被提名者 bèitímíngzhě; 被任命者 bèirènmìngzhě.

non- /,nɒn/ *prefix* 无[無] wú; 非 fēi; 不 bù. **,~-com'missioned** *adj* 无[無]委任状[狀]的 wú wěirènzhuàng de; 未受任命的 wèishòu rènmìng de. **,~-com'mittal** *adj* 不表明意见的 bù biǎomíng yìjiàn de; (观点等)不明朗的 bù mínglǎng de. **~-'fiction** 非小说类[類]文学[學] 作品 (如传记、随笔等) fēi xiǎoshuōlèi wénxué zuòpǐn. **,~-'resident** *n* [C] 暂[暫]居的人 zànjūde rén. **,~-'stop** *adj, adv* 中途不停的 zhōngtú bùtíng de; 直达[達]的 zhídáde; 直达地 zhídáde: *a ~-stop train* 直达火车.

non·cha·lance /'nɒnʃələns/ *n* [U] 冷淡 lěngdàn; 漠不关[關]心 mòbù guānxīn. **non·cha·lant** *adj*

non·de·script /'nɒndɪskrɪpt/ *n* [C], *adj* 不易分类[類]的 búyì fēnlèi de; 没有特征[徵]的 méiyǒu tèzhēng de.

none /nʌn/ *pron* 没有人 méiyǒurén; 没有任何东[東]西 méiyǒu rènhé dōngxi: *N~ of them has (have) come back yet.* 他们当中还没有一个人回来. ***~ but*** 仅[僅] jǐn; 只 zhǐ: *I want ~ but the best.* 我只要最好的. ***~ the less*** ⇨ less. □ *adv* 一点[點]也不 yìdiǎn yě bù: *~ the worse for his experience* 他的经验并不坏.

non·en·tity /nɒn'entətɪ/ *n* [C] [*pl* -ties] 无[無]足轻[輕]重的人 (或物) wúzú qīngzhòng de rén.

non·plus /nɒn'plʌs/ *vt* [-ss-] 使迷惑 shǐ míhuò; 使狼狈 shǐ lángbèi.

non·sense /'nɒnsns/ *n* [U] 废[廢]话 fèihuà, 胡说 húshuō; 胡闹[鬧] húnào. **non'sen·si·cal** /-ɪkl/ *adj* 无[無]意义[義]的 wú yìyì de; 荒谬的 huāngmiùde.

noodle /'nu:dl/ *n* [常用 *pl*] 面[麵]条[條] miàntiáo; 鸡[鷄]蛋面 jīdànmiàn.

nook /nʊk/ *n* [C] 隐[隱]蔽处[處] yǐnbìchù; 角落 jiǎoluò: *search every ~ and cranny* 搜查每个角落.

noon /nu:n/ *adj, n* [C] 中午 zhōngwǔ; 正午 zhèngwǔ.

no-one, no one /'nəʊ wʌn/ *pron* = nobody(1).

noose /nu:s/ *n* [C] 套索 tàosuǒ; 绞索 jiǎosuǒ; 圈套 quāntào.

nor /nɔ:(r)/ *conj* (用在 *neither* 或 *not* 之后) 也不 yěbù: *I have neither time ~ money for pop festivals.* 我既没有时间也没有钱参加通俗音乐节.

norm /nɔ:m/ *n* **the ~** 标〔標〕准〔準〕biāozhǔn; 规范〔範〕guīfàn.

nor·mal /'nɔ:ml/ *adj* 正常的 zhèngchángde; 正规的 zhèngguīde; 常态〔態〕的 chángtàide. □ *n* 〔仅用 *sing*〕正常 zhèngcháng; 常态 chángtài. **~ly** *adv*

north /nɔ:θ/ *n* **1 the ~** 北 běi, 北方 běifāng, 北部 běibù. **2**〔用作定语〕北方的 běifāngde; 从〔從〕北面来〔來〕的 cóng běimiàn lái de: *a ~ wind* 北风. □ *adv* 向北方 xiàng běifāng; 在北方 zài běifāng. **,~'east, ,~'west (略 NE, NW)** *n, adj, adv* 东〔東〕北 dōngběi; 西北 xīběi; 东北的 dōngběide; 西北的 xīběide; 在(向)东北 zài dōngběi; 在(向)西北 zài xīběi. **~er·ly** /'nɔ:ðəlɪ/ *adj, adv* **(a)** (指风)来自北方(的) lái zì běifāng. **(b)** 向北方(的) xiàng běifāng. **~ern** /'nɔ:ðən/ *adj* 北方的 běifāngde; 在北方的 zài běifāng de; 来自北方的 lái zì běifāng de. **~ward** /-wəd/ *adj* 向北的 xiàngběide. **~wards** *adv*

Nos. = Numbers.

nose[1] /nəʊz/ *n* [C] **1** 鼻子 bízi. ***follow one's ~***, **(a)** 笔〔筆〕直走 bǐzí zǒu. **(b)** 凭〔憑〕本能行事 píng běnnéng xíngshì. ***keep one's ~ clean*** 避免麻烦. ***look down one's ~ at sb*** 瞧不起 qiáobùqǐ. ***pay through the ~*** 付出过〔過〕高的代价〔價〕fùchū guògāode dàijià. ***poke (stick) one's ~ into*** (*sb else's business*) 干涉 (别人的事) gānshè. ***turn one's ~ up at*** 瞧不起 qiáobùqǐ, 卑视 bǐshì. **2** 嗅觉〔覺〕xiùjué. **3 *a ~ (for sth)*** [喻]善于发〔發〕现 shànyú fāxiàn. ⇨ nose[2](2). **4** 鼻状〔狀〕物 (如飞机机首) bízhuàngwù. **'~dive** *n, vi* 俯冲 fǔchōng. **'~gay** 花束 huāsù.

nose[2] /nəʊz/ *vt/i* **1** 慎重地前进〔進〕shènzhòngde qiánjìn. **2 ~ *sth out*** 闻〔聞〕出 wénchū, 嗅出 xiùchū.

nosey, nosy /'nəʊzɪ/ *adj* [-ier, -iest] [俚语]好打听〔聽〕别人事情的 hàodǎting biérén shìqing de; 爱〔愛〕管闲〔閑〕事的 àiguǎn xiánshì de. **'~-parker** [非正式用语]爱管闲事的人 àiguǎn xiánshìde rén.

nos·tal·gia /nɒ'stælʤə/ *n* [U] 怀〔懷〕乡〔鄉〕病 huáixiāngbìng; 留恋〔戀〕过〔過〕去 liúliàn guòqù; 怀旧〔舊〕huáijiù. **nos·tal·gic** /-ʤɪk/ *adj* 怀乡的 huáixiāngde; 留恋过去的 liúliàn guòqù de; 怀旧的 huáijiùde.

nos·tril /'nɒstrəl/ *n* [C] 鼻孔 bíkǒng.

not /nɒt/ *adv* (常缩作 -n't /-ənt/, 如 *hasn't*) 不 bù: *He warned me ~ to be late.* 他警告我不要迟到. '*Can you come next week?*' '你下星期能来吗?' —'*I'm afraid ~.*' '我恐怕不能来.' **~ *at all*** /ˌnɒt ə 'tɔ:l/ (客套语)别客气 biékèqi: '*Thank you very much.*' '谢谢你.' — '*N~ at all.*' '不用客气.' **~ *that*** 并不是说 bìng bú shì shuō.

no·table /'nəʊtəbl/ *adj* 显〔顯〕著的 xiǎnzhùde; 著名的 zhùmíngde. □ *n* [C] 名人 míngrén; 显要人物 xiǎnyào rénwù. **no·tably** *adv* 显著地 xiǎnzhùde; 著名地 zhùmíngde.

no·tary /'nəʊtərɪ/ *n* [C] [*pl* -ies] (常作 **,~ 'public**) 公证人 gōngzhèngrén, 公证员 gōngzhèngyuán.

no·ta·tion /nəʊ'teɪʃn/ *n* [C,U] (数学、音乐等用的) 一套符号〔號〕yítào fúhào.

notch /nɒtʃ/ *n* [C] (V 字形) 槽口 cáokǒu; 缺口 quēkǒu. □ *vt* 给…开〔開〕槽 gěi …kāi cáo; 将〔將〕…切口 jiāng…qiē kǒu.

note /nəʊt/ *n* [C] **1** 笔〔筆〕记 bǐjì; 摘记 zhāijì. **2** 短笺〔箋〕duǎnjiān; 便条〔條〕biàntiáo. **3** 注释〔釋〕zhùshì; 注解 zhùjiě. ⇨ footnote. **4 *compare ~s*** 交换意见 jiāohuàn yìjiàn. **5** 票据〔據〕piàojù; 纸币〔幣〕zhǐbì: *'bank~s* 钞票. **6** 音调 yīndiào; 音符 yīnfú; 琴键 qínjiàn. **7** 语调 yǔdiào: *a ~ of warning in his speech* 他的讲话有一种警告的语气. **8** [U] 著名 zhùmíng; 重要 zhòngyào: *a family of ~* 显贵之家. **9** [U] 注意 zhùyì: *Take ~ of what he says.* 注意他说的话. □ *vt* **1** 注意 zhùyì. **2 ~ *sth down*** 记录〔錄〕jìlù; 记下 jìxià. **'~book** 笔记本 bǐjìběn. **'~paper** 信纸 xìnzhǐ. **noted** /'nəʊtɪd/ *adj* 著名的 zhùmíngde; 知名的 zhīmíngde. **~worthy** *adj* 值得注目的 zhídé zhùmù de; 显〔顯〕著的 xiǎnzhùde.

noth·ing /'nʌθɪŋ/ *n* 没有东〔東〕西 méiyǒu dōngxi; 没有什么〔麼〕méiyǒu shénme: *He's had ~ to eat yet.* 他还没有吃东西呢. ***for ~*** **(a)** 免费 miǎnfèi. **(b)** 没有报〔報〕

酬 méiyǒu bàochou; 无〔無〕结果 wú jiēguǒ. ***be ~ to,*** **(a)** 同…无关〔關〕 tóng...wúguān. **(b)** 少于 shǎo yú: *My losses are ~ to yours.* 我的损失和你的相比算不了什么. ***come to ~*** 失败 shībài. ***~ to do with*** 与…无关 yǔ...wúguān: *This has ~ to do with you.* 这同你没有关系. ***think ~ of*** 把…看成平常 bǎ... kànchéng píngcháng. □ *adv* 毫不 háobù; 一点〔點〕也不 yìdiǎn yěbù: *He's ~ like as good as Peter.* 他一点也不象彼得那样好.

no·tice /ˈnəʊtɪs/ *n* **1** [C] 通告 tōnggào; 布〔佈〕告 bùgào. **2** [U] 警告 jǐnggào; 通知 tōngzhī: *give her a month's ~ to leave* 通知她一个月后离开. ***(do sth) at short ~*** 急忙地(做某事) jímángde. **3** [U] 注意 zhùyì. ***bring sth (come) to sb's ~*** 引人注意 yǐnrén zhùyì. ***take no ~ (of)*** 不注意 bú zhùyì; 不理会〔會〕 bù lǐhuì. □ *vt/i* 注意 zhùyì. **~able** /-əbl/ *adj* 显〔顯〕而易见的 xiǎn ér yìjiàn de; 显著的 xiǎnzhùde. **~ably** *adv*

no·tify /ˈnəʊtɪfaɪ/ *vt* [*pt, pp* -ied] 报〔報〕告 bàogào; 通知 tōngzhī: *~ the police of an accident* 向警方报告出了事故. **no·ti·fi·ca·tion** /-fɪˈkeɪʃn/ *n* [C,U]

no·tion /ˈnəʊʃn/ *n* [C] 概念 gàiniàn; 观〔觀〕念 guānniàn.

no·tor·iety /ˌnəʊtəˈraɪətɪ/ *n* [U] 臭名昭著 chòumíng zhāozhù.

no·tori·ous /nəʊˈtɔːrɪəs/ *adj* 臭名昭著的 chòumíng zhāozhù de; 声〔聲〕名狼藉的 shēngmíng lángjí de: *a ~ murderer* 声名狼藉的杀人犯. **~ly** *adv*

nou·gat /ˈnuːgɑː/ *n* [U] 牛根糖(加入胡桃、花生等做成的糖果) niúgēntáng.

nought /nɔːt/ *n* [C] 无〔無〕 wú; 零 líng. ***come to ~*** 失败 shībài.

noun /naʊn/ *n* [C] [语法] 名词 míngcí.

nour·ish /ˈnʌrɪʃ/ *vt* **1** 养〔養〕育 yǎngyù. **2** [正式用语]怀〔懷〕有(希望等) huáiyǒu. **~ment** *n* [U] [正式用语]食物 shíwù.

Nov. = November.

no·va /ˈnəʊvə/ *n* [C] (*pl* ~s, -vae /-viː/)(天文)新星(在一段时间中突然增强其光度的星) xīnxīng.

novel[1] /ˈnɒvl/ *adj* 新奇的 xīnqíde; 新的 xīnde.

novel[2] /nɒvl/ *n* [C] 小说 xiǎoshuō. **ˈ~ist** 小说家 xiǎoshuōjiā.

nov·elty /ˈnɒvltɪ/ *n* [*pl* -ies] **1** [U] 新颖 xīnyǐng; 新奇 xīnqí. **2** [C] 新奇的事物 xīnqíde shìwù. **3** [*pl*] 廉价〔價〕物品(如玩具) liánjià wùpǐn.

No·vem·ber /nəʊˈvembə(r)/ *n* 十一月 shíyīyuè.

nov·ice /ˈnɒvɪs/ *n* [C] **1** 新手 xīnshǒu; 初学〔學〕者 chūxuézhě. **2** 见习〔習〕修道士(修女) jiànxí xiūdàoshì.

now /naʊ/ *adv* **1** 现在 xiànzài, 目前 mùqián: *Where are you living ~?* 你现在住在什么地方? **2** ***(every) ~ and then (again)*** 有时〔時〕候 yǒushíhòu; 时时刻刻 shíshí kèkè. **3** 立刻 lìkè, 马〔馬〕上 mǎshàng: *Do it (right) ~!* 马上就做! **4** [用以引起注意]: *N~, stop quarrelling and listen.* 喂! 别吵了, 听我说. □ *conj* 既然 jìrán; 由于 yóuyú: *N~ you're here, let's begin.* 既然你在这里, 那就开始吧.

now·adays /ˈnaʊədeɪz/ *adj* 现在 xiànzài, 当今 dāngjīn.

no·where /ˈnəʊweə(r)/ *adv* 什么〔麼〕地方都没有 shénme dìfāng dōu méiyǒu. ***get ~*** 一事无〔無〕成 yīshì wúchéng.

nox·ious /ˈnɒkʃəs/ *adj* 有害的 yǒuhàide; 有毒的 yǒudúde.

nozzle /ˈnɒzl/ *n* [C] 管嘴 guǎnzuǐ; 喷嘴 pēnzuǐ.

nr. = near.

N.T. = New Testament («圣经»的)«新约全书〔書〕» «Xinyuē Quánshū».

nu·ance /ˈnjuːɑːns/ *n* [C] (意义、意见、颜色等)细微差别 xìwēi chābié.

nu·clear /ˈnjuːklɪə(r)/ *adj* 原子核的 yuánzǐhéde; 原子能的 yuánzǐnéngde. **~ ˈbomb** *n* 核弹 hédàn. **ˌ~ ˈenergy** 原子能 yuánzǐnéng. **ˌ~ reˈactor** (原子)核反应〔應〕堆 héfǎnyìngduī.

nu·cleus /ˈnjuːklɪəs/ *n* [C] [*pl* nuclei /-klɪaɪ/] **1** (原子)核 hé. **2** 核 hé; 核心 héxīn.

nude /njuːd/ *adj* 裸体〔體〕的 luǒtǐde □ *n* [C] 裸体画〔畫〕 luǒtǐhuà. ***in the ~*** 赤裸裸的 chìluǒluǒde. **nu·dism** 裸体主义〔義〕luǒtǐzhǔyì; 裸体主义的实〔實〕行 luǒtǐzhǔyìde shíxíng. **nu·dist** *n* [C]. **nu·dity** 裸体 luǒtǐ.

nudge /nʌdʒ/ *vt* 用肘轻〔輕〕推(以引起注意) yòng zhǒu qīngtuī. □ *n* [C] 用肘轻推 yòng zhǒu qīngtuī.

nug·get /ˈnʌgɪt/ *n* [C] (天然)块〔塊〕金 kuàijīn; 矿〔礦〕块 kuàngkuài.

nui·sance /ˈnjuːsns/ *n* [C] 麻烦事 máfánshì; 讨厌〔厭〕的人 tǎoyàn de rén; 可厌物 kěyànwù.

null /nʌl/ *adj* ,~ **and 'void** [法律] 无〔無〕效的 wúxiàode. **~ify** /'nʌlɪfaɪ/ *vt* [*pt, pp* -ied] 使无效 shǐ wúxiào; 废〔廢〕弃〔棄〕fèiqì; 取消 qǔxiāo.

numb /nʌm/ *adj* [-er, -est] 麻木的 mámùde; 失去知觉〔覺〕的 shīqù zhījué de: ~ *with shock* 因触电而失去知觉的. ~ *with cold* 冻僵了的. □ *vt* 使麻木 shǐ mámù; 使失去知觉 shǐ shīqù zhījué. **~ly** *adv* **~ness** *n* [U]

num·ber /'nʌmbə(r)/ *n* [C] **1** 3, *13 and 103 are ~s.* 3, 13, 和 103 都是数字. **2** 数〔數〕目 shùmù; 总〔總〕数 zǒngshù: *a small ~ of people* 少量的人. **3** (报刊等的)期 qī. **4** (一个)节〔節〕目 jiémù; (歌剧的)部分 bùfen. □ *vt* **1** 给…编号〔號〕gěi...biānhào: ~ *cards from 1 to 9.* 给卡片编一至九的号码. **2** 总共 zǒnggòng: *We ~ed 20 in all.* 我们一共二十人. **3** 计入 jìrù; 算作 suànzuò: ~ *her among one's friends* 把她算作一个朋友. **4** [常用被动语态]在数目方面受到限制 zài shùmù fāngmiàn shòudào xiànzhì: *His days are ~ed.* 他活不长了.

nu·meral /'nju:mərəl/ *n* [C], *adj* 数〔數〕字 shùzì; 数词 shùcí; 数的 shùde.

nu·mer·ate /'nju:mərət/ *adj* 某人的数〔數〕学〔學〕基础〔礎〕好 mǒuréndе shùxué jīchǔ hǎo. ⇨ literate.

nu·meri·cal /nju:'merɪkl/ *adj* 数〔數〕字的 shùzìde; 用数字表示的 yòng shùzì biǎoshì de. **~ly** /-klɪ/ *adv*

nu·mer·ous /'nju:mərəs/ *adj* 许许多多的 xǔxǔduōduōde.

nun /nʌn/ *n* [C] 修女 xiūnǚ; 尼姑 nígū. **~nery** 女修道院 nǚxiūdàoyuàn; 尼姑庵 nígū'ān.

nurse /nɜ:s/ *n* [C] 护〔護〕士 hùshì. □ *vt* **1** 看护〔護〕kànhù; 护理(病人等) hùlǐ. **2** 哺乳 bǔrǔ; 给(婴儿)喂奶 gěi...wèinǎi. **3** 培养〔養〕péiyǎng; 养育 yǎngyù: ~ *young plants* 培养幼苗. **4** 怀〔懷〕有 huáiyǒu: ~ *feelings of revenge* 怀着报复心理.

nurs·ery /'nɜ:sərɪ/ *n* [C] [*pl* -ies] **1** 保育室 bǎoyùshì; 托儿〔兒〕所 tuō'érsuǒ; 儿童室 értóngshì. **2** 苗圃 miáopǔ. **'~ rhyme** 童谣 tóngyáo; 儿歌 érgē. **'~ school** 幼儿园〔園〕yòu'éryuán.

nurs·ing /'nɜ:sɪŋ/ *n* [U] 保育 bǎoyù; 护〔護〕理 hùlǐ. **'~-home** 小型私人医〔醫〕院 xiǎoxíng sīrén yīyuàn.

nur·ture /'nɜ:tʃə(r)/ *n* [U] [正式用语]养〔養〕育 yǎngyù; 培育 péiyù; 教养 jiàoyǎng. □ *vt* 养育 yǎngyù; 培育 péiyù; 教养 jiàoyǎng.

nut /nʌt/ *n* [C] **1** 坚〔堅〕果 jiānguǒ. **2** 螺母 luómǔ; 螺帽 luómào. **3** [俚语]脑〔腦〕袋 nǎodài. ***off one's ~*** [俚语]疯〔瘋〕狂的 fēngkuángde. **4** [俚语]疯子 fēngzi. **'~crackers** *n pl* 轧〔軋〕碎坚果的钳子 zháhuì jiānguǒ de qiánzi. **'~shell, (*put sth*) *in a ~shell*** [喻]用最少的几〔幾〕句话 yòng zuìshǎode jǐjù huà. **~ty** *adj* [-ier, -iest] **(a)** 有坚果味的 yǒu jiānguǒwèi de. **(b)** [俚语]疯的 fēngde; 狂的 kuángde.

nut·meg /'nʌtmeg/ *n* **1** [C] 肉豆蔻(树) ròudòukòu. **2** [U] 豆蔻末 dòukòumò.

nu·tri·ent /'nju:trɪənt/ *adj* [正式用语]营〔營〕养〔養〕的 yíngyǎngde; 滋养的 zīyǎngde.

nu·tri·tion /nju:'trɪʃn/ *n* [U] [正式用语]营〔營〕养〔養〕yíngyǎng; 营养学〔學〕yíngyǎngxué. **nu·tri·tious** *adj* [正式用语]营养的 yíngyǎngde; 滋养的 zīyǎngde.

nuts /nʌts/ *adj* [俚语]发〔發〕疯〔瘋〕的 fāfēngde; 疯狂的 fēngkuángde.

nuzzle /'nʌzl/ *vt/i* ~ ***(up against)*** 用鼻子推压〔壓〕yòng bízi tuīyā.

N.W. =north-west.

N.Y. = New York 纽约 Niǔyuē.

ny·lon /'naɪlɒn/ *n* **1** [U] 尼龙〔龍〕nílóng. **2** [*pl*] 尼龙长〔長〕袜〔襪〕nílóng chángwà.

nymph /nɪmf/ *n* [C] **1** (希腊罗马神话)居于山林、河上的仙女 jū yú shānlín héshàng de xiānnǚ. **2** [书面语]美女 měinǚ.

N.Z. = New Zealand 新锡兰〔蘭〕Xīnxīlán.

O o

O, o /əʊ/ [*pl* O's, o's /əʊz/] **1** 英语的第十五个〔個〕字母 Yīngyǔ de dìshíwǔgè zìmǔ. **2** ○形的符号〔號〕(尤指电话号码) ○ xíng de fúhào.

oak /əʊk/ *n* [C] 橡树〔樹〕 xiàngshù; [U] 橡木 xiàngmù.

oar /ɔ:(r)/ *n* [C] 桨〔槳〕 jiǎng; 橹 lǔ. ***put*** (或 ***stick***) ***one's*** ~ ***in*** 〔非正式用语〕干涉 gānshè; 干预 gānyù.

oasis /əʊ'eɪsɪs/ *n* [C] [*pl* -ses /-si:z/] (沙漠中的)绿洲 lǜzhōu.

oast /əʊst/ *n* [C] (啤酒花)烘炉〔爐〕 hōnglú. **'~house** 蛇麻子烘干〔乾〕所 shémázhǐ hōnggānsuǒ.

oat /əʊt/ *n* [C] [常用 *pl*] **1** 燕麦〔麥〕 yànmài; 燕麦属〔屬〕植物 yànmàishǔ zhíwù. **2** [*pl*] 麦片粥 màipiànzhōu; 燕麦粥 yànmàizhōu. **'~meal** 燕麦片 yànmàipiàn; 燕麦粥 yànmàizhōu.

oath /əʊθ/ *n* [C] [*pl* ~s /əʊðz/] **1** 誓言 shìyán; 誓约 shìyuē. ***be on*** (或 ***under***) ~ 发〔發〕誓 fāshì. **2** 诅咒 zǔzhòu.

O.A.U. = Organization for African Unity 非洲统一组织〔織〕 Fēizhōu Tǒngyī Zǔzhī.

ob. = died.

obedi·ent /ə'bi:dɪənt/ *adj* 服从〔從〕的 fúcóngde; 顺从的 shùncóngde. **~ly** *adv* **obedi·ence** *n* [U]

ob·elisk /'ɒbəlɪsk/ *n* [C] 方尖形的石碑 fāngjiānxíngde shíbēi; 方尖塔 fāngjiāntǎ.

obese /əʊ'bi:s/ *adj* (指人)非常肥胖的 fēicháng féipàng de; 肥大的 féidàde. **obes·ity** *n* [U]

obey /ə'beɪ/ *vt/i* 服从〔從〕 fúcóng; 听〔聽〕从 tīngcóng.

obitu·ary /ə'bɪtʃʊərɪ/ *n* [C] [*pl* -ies] 讣告 fùgào.

ob·ject[1] /'ɒbdʒɪkt/ *n* [C] **1** 物 wù, 物体〔體〕 wùtǐ. **2** 对象 duìxiàng; 目标〔標〕 mùbiāo: *an* ~ *of pity* 可怜的人(或物). **3** 目的 mùdì: *Our* ~ *is to win.* 我们的目的是要获胜. **4**〔语法〕宾〔賓〕语 bīnyǔ. **direct** ~ 直接宾语 (如'He took *the money*'.) zhíjiē bīnyǔ.

ob·ject[2] /əb'dʒekt/ *vi* ~ **(*to*)** 不赞成 bú zànchéng; 反对〔對〕 fǎnduì.

ob·jec·tion /əb'dʒekʃn/ *n* **1** [C,U] 厌〔厭〕恶〔惡〕 yànwù; 反对〔對〕 fǎnduì. **2** [C] 反对的理由 fǎnduìde lǐyóu. **~able** /-əbl/ *adj* 令人不愉快的 lìng rén bù yúkuài de. **~ably** *adv*

ob·jec·tive /əb'dʒektɪv/ *adj* **1**〔哲学〕客观〔觀〕的 kèguānde; 真实〔實〕的 zhēnshíde. ⇨ subjective. **2** 不受个〔個〕人感情影响〔響〕的 búshòu gèrén gǎnqíng yíngxiǎng de: *an* ~ *decision* 客观的决定. □ *n* [C] **1** 目标〔標〕 mùbiāo; 目的 mùdì. **2** (军语)出击〔擊〕目标〔標〕 chūjī mùbiāo. **~ly** *adv* 客观地 kèguānde. **ob·jec'tiv·ity** *n* [U]

ob·li·ga·tion /ˌɒblɪ'geɪʃn/ *n* [C] 义〔義〕务〔務〕 yìwù; 责任 zérèn. ***be (place) sb under an*** ~ 使某人负有义务 shǐ mǒurén fùyǒu yìwù.

ob·li·ga·tory /ə'blɪgətrɪ/ *adj* (法律上或道义上)必须的 bìxūde; 应〔應〕尽〔盡〕的 yīngjìnde.

ob·lige /ə'blaɪdʒ/ *vt* **1** 以誓言(或契约等)束缚(某人) yǐ shìyán shùfù. ***be*** **~*d*** ***to do sth*** 被迫做某事 bèi pò zuò mǒushì. **2** 施惠 shīhuì; 答应〔應〕...的请求 dāying...de qǐngqiú: *I'm much* ~*d to you.* 我非常感激你. **oblig·ing** *adj* 乐〔樂〕于助人的 lèyú zhùrén de. **oblig·ing·ly** *adv*

ob·lique /ə'bli:k/ *adj* 斜的 xiéde; 偏斜的 piānxiéde. **~ly** *adv*

ob·lit·er·ate /ə'blɪtəreɪt/ *vt* 抹掉 mǒdiào; 涂去 túqù. **ob·lit·e'r·ation** *n* [U]

ob·liv·ion /ə'blɪvɪən/ *n* [U] 被忘却的状〔狀〕态〔態〕 bèi wàngquè de zhuàngtài; 湮没 yānmò. ***sink*** (或 ***fall***) ***into*** ~ 湮没无〔無〕闻〔聞〕 yānmò wú wén.

ob·livi·ous /ə'blɪvɪəs/ *adj* ~ ***of*** 不在意的 bú zàiyì de; 忘却的 wàngquède.

ob·long /'ɒblɒŋ/ *n* [C], *adj* 长〔長〕方形 chángfāngxíng; 长方形的 chángfāngxíngde.

ob·nox·ious /əb'nɒkʃəs/ *adj* 非常讨厌〔厭〕的(与 *to* 连用) fēicháng tǎoyàn de; 可憎的 kězèngde.

oboe /'əʊbəʊ/ *n* [C] 双簧管 shuānghuángguǎn; (风琴的)欧〔歐〕巴音程 ōubā yīngchéng. **'obo·ist** 欧巴吹奏者 ōubā chuīzòuzhě.

ob·scene /əb'si:n/ *adj* (指文字、图画等)猥亵〔褻〕的 wěixiède; 淫秽〔穢〕的 yínhuìde. **~ly** *adv* **ob·scen·ity** /əb'senətɪ/ *n* [*pl* -ies] [C,U] 猥亵 wěixiè; 淫秽 yínhuì; 猥亵的言语、行为〔爲〕 wěixiède yányǔ, xíngwéi.

ob·scure /əb'skjʊə(r)/ *adj* **1** 暗的 àndе; 不清楚的 bù qīngchu de; 不明了〔瞭〕的 bù míngliǎo de. **2** 无〔無〕名的 wúmíngde: *an* ~ *poet* 无名诗人. □ *vt* 使阴〔陰〕暗 shǐ yīn'àn; 使不明了 shǐ bù míngliǎo. **~ly** *adv* **ob·scur·ity** *n* [*pl* -ies] **(a)** [U] 暗淡 àndàn; 含糊 hánhu; 默默无〔無〕闻〔聞〕 mòmò wú wén. **(b)** [C] 不明了的事物 bù míngliǎo de shìwù.

ob·serv·ance /əb'zɜ:vəns/ *n* **1**

[U](法律、习俗等的)遵守 zūnshǒu; 奉行 fèngxíng. 2 [C] 礼仪〔儀〕 lǐyí; 仪式 yíshì.

ob·serv·ant /əb'zɜ:vənt/ *adj* 善于观〔觀〕察的 shànyú guānchá de; 留心的 liúxīnde. **~ly** *adv*

ob·ser·va·tion /ˌɒbzə'veɪʃn/ *n* **1** [U] 观〔觀〕察 guānchá; 注意 zhùyì. ***be*** (或 ***come, keep***) ***under*** ~ 注意观察 zhùyì guānchá. **2** [U] 观察力 guānchálì: *a man of keen* ~ 观察力敏锐的人. **3** [常用 *pl*] 观察资料或报〔報〕告 guānchá zīliào huò bàogào. **4** [C] (观察后发表的)言论〔論〕 yánlùn: *a casual* ~ 漫评.

ob·serv·atory /əb'zɜ:vətrɪ/ *n* [C] [*pl* -ies] 天文台〔臺〕 tiānwéntái; 气〔氣〕象台 qìxiàngtái; 了〔瞭〕望台 liàowàngtái.

ob·serve /əb'zɜ:v/ *vt/i* **1** 看到 kàndào. **2** 遵守(规则等) zūnshǒu. **3** 庆〔慶〕祝(节日、生日等) qìngzhù. **4** 说 shuō; 评论〔論〕 pínglùn. **5** 观〔觀〕察 guānchá. **ob·server** 观察者 guāncházhě; 观察员 guāncháyuán; 奉行者 fèngxíngzhě.

ob·sess /əb'ses/ *vt* [常用 *passive*] ***be ~ed by*** (指恐惧等)缠〔纏〕住 chánzhù; 使烦扰〔擾〕 shǐ fánrǎo. **ob·ses·sion** /-ʃn/ *n* **(a)** [U] 缠住 chánzhù; 被困扰 bèi kùnrǎo. **(b)** [C] (观念等)固执〔執〕 gùzhí; 死脑〔腦〕筋 sǐ nǎojīn. **~ive** *adj* 束缚 shùfù.

ob·sol·escent /ˌɒbsə'lesnt/ *adj* 渐〔漸〕废〔廢〕的 jiànfèide; 逐渐过〔過〕时〔時〕的 zhújiàn guòshí de. **ob·sol·escence** *n* [U]

ob·sol·ete /'ɒbsəli:t/ *adj* 已废〔廢〕弃〔棄〕的 yǐfèiqìde; 过〔過〕时〔時〕的 guòshíde.

ob·stacle /'ɒbstəkl/ *n* [C] 障碍〔礙〕物 zhàng'àiwù; 妨碍 fáng'ài.

ob·stet·rics /əb'stetrɪks/ *n* [U] 产〔產〕科学〔學〕 chǎnkēxué; 助产术〔術〕 zhùchǎnshù. **ob·ste·tri·cian** /ˌɒbstə'trɪʃn/ *n* [C] 产科医〔醫〕生 chǎnkē yīshēng.

ob·sti·nate /'ɒbstɪnət/ *adj* **1** 顽固的 wángùde; 倔强的 juéjiàngde. **2** 不易屈服的 bú yì qūfú de: *an ~ disease* 难治的病. **~ly** *adv* **ob·sti·nacy** *n* [U]

ob·struct /əb'strʌkt/ *vt* **1** 阻塞 zǔsè; 堵塞 dǔsè: ~ *a road* 阻塞道路. **2** 妨碍〔礙〕 fáng'ài; 阻挡〔擋〕 zǔdǎng: ~ *justice* 阻碍审判. **ob·struc·tion** /-ʃn/ *n* **(a)** [U] 阻塞 zǔsè; 阻碍 zǔ'ài. **(b)** [C] 障碍物 zhàng'àiwù.

ob·tain /əb'teɪn/ *vt/i* 获〔獲〕得 huòdé; 买〔買〕到 mǎidào: *Where can I ~ the book?* 我从哪里可以买到这本书? **~able** /-əbl/ *adj*

ob·trus·ive /əb'tru:sɪv/ *adj* 突出的 tūchūde; 炫耀的 xuànyàode. **~ly** *adv*

ob·tuse /əb'tju:s/ *adj* **1** 迟〔遲〕钝的 chídùnde; 愚笨的 yúbènde: *an ~ remark* 愚钝的评论. **2** [数学] 钝角的 dùnjiǎode. **~ly** *adv* **~ness** *n* [U]

ob·vi·ous /'ɒbvɪəs/ *adj* 明显〔顯〕的 míngxiǎnde; 清楚的 qīngchude; 明白的 míngbaide. **~ly** *adv*

O.C. = officer commanding 指挥〔揮〕官 zhǐhuīguān.

oc·ca·sion /ə'keɪʒn/ *n* **1** [C] (发生特殊事情的)时〔時〕刻 shíkè; 机〔機〕会〔會〕 jīhuì. ***rise to the*** ~ 应〔應〕付自如 yìngfù zìrú. **2** [U] 理由 lǐyóu; 需要 xūyào: *You had no ~ to hit him.* 你没有必要打击他. □ *vt* [正式用语]引起 yǐnqǐ: *He ~ed me much worry.* 他使我大为烦恼.

oc·ca·sional /ə'keɪʒənl/ *adj* 偶然的 ǒuránde; 非经〔經〕常的 fēi jīngcháng de: *an ~ cigarette* 偶然抽的香烟. *an ~ visit* 偶然的拜访. **~ally** *adv* 偶然 ǒurán; 非经常地 fēi jīngcháng de.

oc·cu·pant /'ɒkjʊpənt/ *n* [C] 居住者 jūzhùzhě; 占〔佔〕有人 zhànyǒurén. **oc·cu·pancy** *n* [C] [*pl* -ies] 占有 zhànyǒu; 居住 jūzhù; 占有期间〔間〕 zhànyǒu qījiān.

oc·cu·pa·tion /ˌɒkjʊ'peɪʃn/ *n* **1** [U] 占〔佔〕有 zhànyǒu; 居住 jūzhù. **2** [U] 占有期 zhànyǒuqī; 居住期 jūzhùqī. **3** [C] 职〔職〕业〔業〕 zhíyè. **4** [C] 事业 shìyè. **~al** /-nl/ *adj* 职业的 zhíyède; 与〔與〕职业有关〔關〕的 yǔ zhíyè yǒuguān de.

oc·cu·pier /'ɒkjʊpaɪə(r)/ *n* [C] 占〔佔〕有人 zhànyǒurén; 占用者 zhànyòngzhě.

oc·cupy /'ɒkjʊpaɪ/ *vt* [*pt, pp* -ied] **1** 居住 jūzhù; 占〔佔〕有 zhànyǒu. **2** 占领 zhànlǐng; 占据〔據〕 zhànjù. **3** 占(空间、时间、心思) zhàn. **4** 担任(职务) dānrèn: ~ *a position* 担任职务.

oc·cur /ə'kɜ:(r)/ *vi* [-rr-] **1** 发〔發〕生 fāshēng. **2** ~ ***to*** 想起 xiǎngqǐ; 想到 xiǎngdào: *It ~red to me that we should leave.* 我想起我们该离开了. **3** 存在 cúnzài; 出现 chūxiàn: *Errors ~ on every page.* 每一页都有错误. **~rence** /ə'kʌrəns/ *n* [C] 发生 fāshēng; 出现 chūxiàn.

ocean /'əʊʃn/ *n* [C] 海洋 hǎiyáng; 海 hǎi. **~ic** /ˌəʊʃɪ'ænɪk/ *adj*

o'clock /ə'klɒk/ *particle* 点〔點〕钟〔鐘〕 diǎnzhōng: *It's five ~.* 五点钟.

Oct. = October.

oc·ta·gon /'ɒktəgən/ *n* [C] 〔数学〕八边〔邊〕形 bābiānxíng; 八角形物体〔體〕 bājiǎoxíng wùtǐ. **~al** /ɒk'tægənl/ *adj* 八边的 bābiānde.

oc·tane /'ɒkteɪn/ *n* [C,U] 〔化学〕辛烷 xīnwán.

oc·tave /'ɒktɪv/ *n* [C] 〔音乐〕八音度 bāyīndù; 高(或低)八度音 gāo bādùyīn.

Oc·to·ber /ɒk'təʊbə(r)/ *n* 十月 shíyuè.

oc·to·pus /'ɒktəpəs/ *n* [C] [*pl* ~-es] 章鱼 zhāngyú; 章鱼属〔屬〕动〔動〕物 zhāngyúshǔ dòngwù.

o.d. = (banking account) overdrawn 透支 tòuzhī.

odd /ɒd/ *adj* **1** 奇数〔數〕的 jīshùde: *1, 3, 5, and 7 are ~ numbers.* 一,三, 五, 七是奇数. **2** 单〔單〕只〔隻〕的 dānzhīde; 不成对〔對〕的 bù chéngduì de: *an ~ sock (shoe)* 单只袜子(鞋). **ˌ~ man 'out** 〔非正式用语〕(其余人成对后)剩下的一人 shèngxiàde yìrén. **3** 零头〔頭〕的 língtóude: *thirty-~ years* 三十来岁. **4** 临〔臨〕时〔時〕的 línshíde; 不固定的 bú gùdìng de: *doing ~ jobs* 打杂,做零工. **5** [-er, -est] 奇特的 qítède; 古怪的 gǔguàide. **~ly** *adv* 奇特地 qítède; 古怪地 gǔguàide. **~ity** *n* [*pl* -ies] **(a)** [U] 奇特 qítè; 古怪 gǔguài. **(b)** [C] 怪人 guàirén; 古怪的事(物) gǔguàide shì.

odd·ment /'ɒdmənt/ *n* [C] 残〔殘〕余的东〔東〕西 cányúde dōngxi.

odds /ɒdz/ *n pl* **1** 可能性 kěnéngxìng; 机〔機〕会〔會〕 jīhuì: *The ~ are you will win.* 你大概会赢. **2** *be at ~ (with sb) (over sth)* 与〔與〕…有争执〔執〕 yǔ...yǒu zhēngzhí. **~ and ends** 残〔殘〕剩(零星)的东〔東〕西 cánshèngde dōngxi.

ode /əʊd/ *n* [C] 颂诗 sòngshī; 颂歌 sònggē.

odour /'əʊdə(r)/ *n* [C] 气〔氣〕味 qìwèi; 香气 xiāngqì; 臭气 chòuqì.

od·ys·sey /'ɒdɪsɪ/ *n* [C] [*pl* ~s] 长〔長〕久的冒险〔險〕旅行 chángjiǔde màoxiǎn lǚxíng; 一连〔連〕串的冒险 yìliánchuànde màoxiǎn.

O.E.C.D. = Organization for Economic Co-operation and Development 经〔經〕济〔濟〕合作与〔與〕发〔發〕展组织〔織〕 jīngjì hézuò yǔ fāzhǎn zǔzhī.

of /əv, 强式 ɒv/ *prep* **1** (表示空间或时间的距离): *five miles south ~ Paris* 巴黎以南五英里. **2** (表示来源、作者): *the works ~ Shakespeare* 莎士比亚的著作. *with the help ~ my father* 由于父亲的帮助. **3** (表示原因): *die ~ hunger* 饿死. **4** (表示解除、分离): *cure her ~ a disease* 治愈她的病. **5** (表示材料): *a dress ~ silk* 丝绸衣服. **6** [构成定语,起修饰作用]: *the countries ~ Europe* 欧洲国家. *a case of measles* 麻疹的病例. **7** (表示属于,所属): *the leg ~ the table* 桌子腿. **8** (表示包含、分量): *a pint ~ milk* 一品脱牛奶. *few ~ us* 我们当中没什么人. **9** (表示其中的一部分): *a friend ~ mine* 我的一位朋友.

off[1] /ɒf/ *adj* **1** (与 *near* 相对)(车辆)右侧的 yòucède: *the '~-side wheel* 右侧的轮子. **2** (很小)可能的 kěnéngde. **on the '~ chance** 可能性极〔極〕小的 kěnéngxìng jíxiǎo de. **3** 闲〔閒〕着的 xiánzhede: *the '~ season* 淡季.

off[2] /ɒf/ *adv* **1** 离〔離〕开〔開〕 líkāi; 距离 jùlí: *The town is five miles ~.* 离城有五英里. *I'm ~ home.* 我离开家. **2** 取消 qǔxiāo: *Their engagement is (broken) ~.* 他们取消了婚约. **3** (与 *on* 相对)中断〔斷〕 zhōngduàn; 中止 zhōngzhǐ: *The electricity is ~.* 电停了. **4** 没事的 méishìde; 空闲〔閒〕的 kòngxiánde: *a day ~* 休假日. **5** (指食物)不新鲜 bù xīnxiān: *This meat is (has gone) ~.* 这块肉不新鲜了. **on and ~; ~ and on** 断〔斷〕断续〔續〕续地 duànduànxùxùde. **better (worse) ~,** ⇨ better, worse *adv.*

off[3] /ɒf/ *prep* **1** 离〔離〕开〔開〕 líkāi; 不在 búzài: *fall ~ a ladder* 从梯子上跌下来. **2** (指路)从…分岔 cóng...fēnchà: *a lane ~ the main road* 大路上的一条小巷. **3** 离… lí ...: *an island ~ the coast* 海岸外的岛屿. **4** 〔非正式用语〕不吃 bùchī; 不用 búyòng: *I'm ~ my food.* 我没有吃饭(胃口不好). **5** 不完全 bù wánquán; 不确〔確〕实〔實〕 bú quèshí: *'~white* 不很白. **(look) ~ colour** ⇨ colour[1](2). **~ duty** ⇨ duty(1).

of·fal /'ɒfl/ *n* [U] (动物被宰杀后的)内脏〔臟〕 nèizàng; 下水 xiàshui.

of·fence [美语 = **of·fense**] /ə'fens/ *n* **1** [C] 犯罪 fànzuì; 犯法 fànfǎ. **2** [U] 冒犯 màofàn; 触〔觸〕怒 chùnù. **3** [U] 攻击〔擊〕 gōngjī: *weapons of ~* 进攻性武器.

of·fend /ə'fend/ *vt/i* **1** 违〔違〕犯

wěifàn; 犯罪 fànzuì. 2 伤〔傷〕害…的感情 shānghài…de gǎnqíng. 3 使不愉快 shǐ bù yúkuài: *ugly buildings that ~ the eye* 难看的丑陋建筑物. **~er** 冒犯者 màofànzhě; 罪犯 zuìfàn.

of·fen·sive /ə'fensɪv/ *adj* **1** 冒犯的 màofànde; 唐突的 tángtūde: *~ language* 无礼语言. **2** 攻击〔擊〕的 gōngjīde; 进〔進〕攻的 jìngōngde. ⇨ defensive. □ *n* [C] 攻击 gōngjī; 攻势〔勢〕 gōngshì. ***take the ~*** 采〔採〕取攻势 cǎiqǔ gōngshì. **~ly** *adv*

of·fer /'ɒfə(r)/ *vt/i* **1** 提出 tíchū; 提供 tígòng: *~ him a good job* 给他个好工作. **2** *~ (up)* 奉献〔獻〕 fèngxiàn. **3** 表示 biǎoshì; 企图〔圖〕 qǐtú: *~ resistance* 企图抵抗. □ *n* [C] 提供 tígòng; 提议〔議〕 tíyì. **~ing** *n* [C] 提供 tígòng; 奉献 fèngxiàn.

off-hand /ˌɒf'hænd/ *adj* **1** 未经〔經〕准〔準〕备〔備〕的 wèijīng zhǔnbèi de. **2** 不客气〔氣〕的 bú kèqì de; 随便的 suíbiànde. □ *adv* 未经准备地 wèijīng zhǔnbèi de: *give an answer ~* 即席回答.

of·fice /'ɒfɪs/ *n* [C] **1** 〔常用 *pl*〕办〔辦〕公室 bàngōngshì; 事务〔務〕所 shìwùsuǒ; 营〔營〕业〔業〕所 yíngyèsuǒ. **2** 政府机〔機〕关〔關〕 zhèngfǔ jīguān. ***in ~*** 执〔執〕政 zhízhèng. **3** 公职〔職〕 gōngzhí; 官职 guānzhí: *the ~ of President* 总统职位. **'~-block** 办〔辦〕事处〔處〕集中的街区〔區〕 bànshìchù jízhōng de jiēqū.

of·fi·cer /'ɒfɪsə(r)/ *n* [C] **1** 军〔軍〕官 jūnguān. **2** 官员 guānyuán: *a customs ~* 海关官员. **3** 警官 jǐngguān.

of·fi·cial /ə'fɪʃl/ *adj* 公务〔務〕的 gōngwùde; 职〔職〕务上的 zhíwùshàngde. □ *n* [C] 官员 guānyuán; 行政人员 xíngzhèng rényuán. **~ly** *adv* 官方地 guānfāngde; 正式地 zhèngshìde.

of·fi·cious /ə'fɪʃəs/ *adj*〔正式用语〕过〔過〕分〔份〕殷勤的 guòfèn yīnqín de; 好管闲〔閒〕事的 hào guǎng xiánshì de. **~ly** *adv* **~ness** *n* [U]

off·ing /'ɒfɪŋ/ *n* ***in the ~*** 〔喻〕即将〔將〕发〔發〕生 jíjiāng fāshēng.

off-licence /'ɒf laɪsns/ *n* [C] 有卖〔賣〕酒执〔執〕照的商店(可把酒带走,不许在店内喝) yǒu màijiǔ zhízhào de shāngdiàn.

off-putting /ˌɒf'pʊtɪŋ/ *adj* 〔非正式用语〕令人泄气〔氣〕的 lìng rén xièqì de; 令人沮丧〔喪〕的 lìng rén jǔsàng de: *His rudeness was very ~.* 他的粗鲁令人十分沮丧. ⇨ *put sb off* at put(9).

off·set /'ɒfset/ *vt* [-tt-] 抵销 dǐxiāo; 补〔補〕偿〔償〕 bǔcháng.

off·shoot /'ɒfʃuːt/ *n* [C] **1** 分枝 fēnzhī; 分株 fēnzhū. **2** 〔喻〕(家族的)旁系 pángxì; 支脉 zhīmài.

off·shore /'ɒfʃɔː(r)/ *adj* **1** 离〔離〕岸的 lí'ànde: *~ breezes* 吹向海洋的微风. **2** 近海的 jìnhǎide: *~ islands* 近海岛屿.

off·side /ˌɒf'saɪd/ *adj, adv* 越位 yuèwèi

off·spring /'ɒfsprɪŋ/ *n* [C] [*pl* ~] 子孙 zǐsūn; 后〔後〕代 hòudài; 动〔動〕物的幼仔 dòngwùde yòuzǐ.

of·ten /'ɒfn/ *adv* [*more ~, most ~*] 时〔時〕常 shícháng; 常常 chángcháng: *We ~ go there.* 我们时常去那里. ***every so ~*** 时常 shícháng.

ogre /'əʊgə(r)/ *n* [C] (童话中)吃人的妖魔 chī rén de yāomó. **~ss** /'əʊgres/ 女妖魔 nǚ yāomó.

O.H.M.S. = On Her (His) Majesty's Service 为〔爲〕女王(英王)陛下效劳〔勞〕(英国公函免付邮费的戳记) wèi nǚwáng bìxià xiàoláo.

oil /ɔɪl/ *n* [C,U] **1** 油 yóu; 油类〔類〕 yóulèi. ***strike ~***, **(a)** 发〔發〕现油矿〔礦〕 fāxiàn yóukuàng. **(b)** 发大财 fā dàcái; 飞〔飛〕黄腾〔騰〕达〔達〕 fēihuáng téngdá. **2** [*pl*] 油画〔畫〕颜料 yóuhuà yánliào; 油画作品 yóuhuà zuòpǐn. □ *vt* 涂〔塗〕油于 tú yóu yú. **'~ colours** *n pl* 油画颜料 yóuhuà yánliào; 油漆 yóuqī. **'~-field** 油田 yóutián. **'~-painting, (a)** [U] 油画艺〔藝〕术 yóuhuà yìshù. **(b)** [C] 油画作品 yóuhuà zuòpǐn. **'~-rig** 石油钻〔鑽〕台 shíyóu zuàntái. **'~skin** [C U] 油布 yóubù; 油布雨衣 yóubù yǔyī. **'~ slick** (水面上的)浮油 fúyóu. **'~-well** 油井 yóujǐng. **oily** *adj* [-ier,-iest] **(a)** 油的 yóude; 似油的 sìyóude. **(b)** 涂〔塗〕满油的 túmǎnyóude; 浸透油的 jìntòuyóude. **(c)**(言行等)圆滑的 yuánhuáde; 讨好人的 tǎohǎo rén de.

oint·ment /'ɔɪntmənt/ *n* [C,U] 药〔藥〕膏 yàogāo; 油膏 yóugāo.

O.K. = all correct, agreed.

okay /ˌəʊ'keɪ/ *adj, adv* (一般缩作 **OK**) 〔非正式用语〕对〔對〕 duì; 好 hǎo; 可以 kěyǐ. □ *vt* 同意 tóngyì; 认〔認〕可 rènkě. □ *n* [C] 同意 tóngyì.

old /əʊld/ *adj* [-er, -est] ⇨ also elder[1], eldest. **1** (指年龄)…岁〔歲〕的… suìde: *He's forty years ~.* 他四十岁. *How ~ are you?* 你几

岁? 2 年老的 niánlǎode; 老的 lǎode: *He's too ~ to work.* 他太老了，不能工作. 3 旧〔舊〕的 jiùde; 用旧的 yòng jiù de: *~ habits* 旧习惯. *~ shoes* 旧鞋. 4 熟悉的 shúxíde: *an ~ friend* 老朋友. 5 旧时〔時〕的 jiùshíde: *~ boys* 老同学〔學〕, 校友. □ *n* [U] **1 the ~** 老人 lǎorén. **2 *of* ~** 从〔從〕前 cóngqián; 很久前 hěnjiǔ qián. ˌ**~ age 'pensioner** = senior citizen. ˌ**~-'fashioned** *adj* **(a)** 老式的 lǎoshìde; 过〔過〕时的 guòshíde. **(b)** 守旧的 shǒujiùde. **~ hand** 老手 lǎoshǒu; 熟手 shúshǒu. **~ master** 大画〔畫〕家 dà huàjiā; 古代大画家的作品 gǔdài dà huàjiā de zuòpǐn.

olden /'əʊldən/ *adj* [书面语]从〔從〕前的 cóngqiánde: *in ~ days* 往昔 wǎngxī.

ol·ive /'ɒlɪv/ *n* **1** [C] 橄榄〔欖〕 gǎnlǎn; 橄榄树〔樹〕 gǎnlǎnshù. **2** *~ branch* (作为和平象征的)橄榄枝 gǎnlǎnzhī. **3** [U] [亦作 *adj*] 橄榄色 gǎnlǎnsè; 橄榄色的 gǎnlǎnsède.

om·elette (亦作 **om·elet**) /'ɒmlɪt/ *n* [C] 煎蛋卷 jiāndànjuǎn.

omen /'əʊmen/ *n* [C,U] 预兆 yùzhào; 征〔徵〕兆 zhēngzhào.

om·in·ous /'ɒmɪnəs/ *adj* 不祥的 bùxiángde; 不吉的 bùjíde: *~ clouds* 不祥的阴影. **~ly** *adv*

omis·sion /ə'mɪʃn/ *n* **1** [U] 省略 shěnglüè; 忽略 hūlüè. **2** [C] 省略之物 shěnglüè zhī wù.

omit /ə'mɪt/ *vt* [-tt-] [正式用语] **1 ~ *to do* (或 *doing*) *sth*** 疏忽 shūhu; 忘记 wàngjì. **2** 遗漏 yílòu; 省略 shěnglüè.

om·ni·bus /'ɒmnɪbəs/ *n* [C] [*pl* ~es] 公共汽车〔車〕(以前的名称) gōnggòng qìchē.

on¹ /ɒn/ *adv* **1** (表示向前，继续下去): ***I'll follow ~.*** 我会跟上来的. ***and 'so ~*** ⇨ so²(1). ***later ~*** 后〔後〕来〔來〕 hòulái. ˌ***~ and '~*** 继〔繼〕续〔續〕不停地 jìxù bùtíng de. ***off and ~*** ⇨ off²(5). **2** (与…)在接触〔觸〕中 zài jiēchù zhōng: *Your hat is not ~ straight.* 你的帽子没有戴正. ***have nothing ~*, (a)** 赤裸裸 chìluǒluǒ. **(b)** 没有承诺 méiyǒu chéngnuò. **3** 使用中 shǐyòng zhōng; 进〔進〕行中 jìnxíng zhōng: *The lights were all ~.* 灯光全亮着. **4 *What's ~?*** 发〔發〕生了什么〔麼〕事? fāshēng le shénme shì? ***be '~ to*** 知道(某人的)意图〔圖〕 zhīdào yìtú. **5** 朝向 cháoxiàng: *crash head '~* 迎头冲撞.

on² /ɒn/ *prep* **1** 在…之上 zài…zhīshàng: *a carpet ~ the floor* 地板上的地毯. **2** (表示时间) **(a)** 在 zài: *~ Sunday(s)* 在星期日. *~ the 1st of May* 在五月一日. **(b)** 在…的时〔時〕候 zài… de shíhòu: *~ my arrival* 在我到达的时候. ***~ time*** 准〔準〕时 zhǔnshí. **3** 关〔關〕于 guānyú: *a lecture ~ Shakespeare* 关于莎士比亚的演讲. **4** (表示为…的成员): *He is ~ the committee.* 他是委员会中的一员. **5** (表示方向)向 xiàng: *turn one's back ~ her* 不理睬她. *march ~ Rome* 向罗马前进. **6** (表示理由): *arrested ~ a charge of theft* 被控偷窃而被捕. **7** (表示费用): *put a tax ~ tobacco* 征收烟草税. **8** 接近 jiējìn; 靠近 kàojìn: *a town ~ the coast* 海边的一个城市. **9** (表示活动、状态): *go to London ~ business* 出差去伦敦. *~ fire* 着火.

once /wʌns/ *adv* **1** 一次 yícì. ***~ more*** 再一次 zài yícì. ***~ in a while*** 有时〔時〕 yǒushí. ˌ***~ and for 'all*** ⇨all³(2). **2** 从〔從〕前 cóngqián; 曾经〔經〕 céngjīng: **(a)** *He ~ lived in Munich.* 他曾在慕尼黑住过. **(b)** (讲故事用语): *O~ upon a time* 从前. **3 *at* ~, (a)** 立刻 lìkè, 马〔馬〕上 mǎshàng. **(b)** 同时 tóngshí: *Don't all speak at ~!* 不要全体同时说! □ *conj* 一旦…(就…) yídàn: *O~ you know how, it's easy.* 你一旦知道如何，就容易了.

on·com·ing /'ɒnkʌmɪŋ/ *adj* 即将〔將〕来临〔臨〕的 jìjiāng láilín de; 接近的 jiējìnde: *~ traffic* 对向交通，迎面车流.

one¹ /wʌn/ *adj, n* [C] **1** 一 yī; 一个〔個〕 yígè. ***be ~ 'up (on sb)*** 优〔優〕于 yōu yú; 比…有利 bǐ…yǒulì. **2** (与 *a, an* 类同): *~ day* 一天. **3** (表示与 *the other, another* 相对): *I can't tell ~ car from the other.* 我说不出这辆汽车与那辆有什么区别. ***for '~ thing*** 举〔舉〕个理由 jǔ gè lǐyǒu. **4** 同样〔樣〕的 tóngyàngde: *They all went off in ~ direction.* 他们都往同一方向去了. ***in ~*** 合在一起 hé zài yìqǐ: *He is President and Secretary in ~.* 他一身兼会长和秘书二职. ˌ**~-'sided** *adj* **(a)** 单〔單〕方面的 dānfāngmiànde. **(b)** 不公平的 bù gōngpíng de: *a ˌ~-sided 'argument* 片面的论据. **'~-time** *adj* 从〔從〕前的 cóngqiánde. **'~-way** 单〔單〕行的 dānxíngde.

one² /wʌn/ *pron* **1 ~ *of*** (表示属于该种类之一，此处 *of* 相当于 *among*) *Mr Smith is not ~ of my customers*

史密斯先生并不是我的一个顾客. **2**[代替 *noun*]: *I haven't any stamps. Will you please give me* ~? 我没有邮票, 请你给我一张好吗? **3**[相当于 *that, those*]: *The blue hat is the* ~ *I like best.* 这顶蓝帽子就是我最喜欢的那一种. **4**[用在 *the, that,* 和 *adj* 之后]: *My cheap camera is just as good as John's expensive* ~. 我的廉价照像机和约翰昂贵的照相机一样好. **5**(表示某种人或物): *the little* ~*s* 小孩儿们. ~ ***another('s)*** 彼此 bǐcǐ; 互相 hùxiāng: *They don't like* ~ *another.* 他们彼此不喜欢. **6** [正式用语]任何人 rènhérén: *O*~ *cannot always find time for reading.* 人们不一定能经常找到读书的时间.

one·self /wʌn'self/ *pron* **1**[反身]自己 zìjǐ; 自身 zìshēn: *wash* ~ 洗澡. ***(all) by*** ~, **(a)** 独[獨]自 dúzì. **(b)** 无[無]帮[幫]助 wú bāngzhù. **2**[用于加强语气]: *To be sure, one ought to look at it* ~. 无疑地,他应当亲自去看看.

on·go·ing /'ɒngəʊɪŋ/ *adj* 继[繼]续[續]的 jìxùde: ˌ~ *re'search* 继续的研究.

onion /'ʌnɪən/ *n* [C,U] 洋葱 yángcōng.

on·looker /'ɒnlʊkə(r)/ *n* [C] 旁观[觀]者 pángguānzhě.

only¹ /'əʊnlɪ/ *adj* **1** 唯一的 wéiyīde: *Smith was the* ~ *person able to do it.* 史密斯是唯一能做那事的人. **2** 仅[僅]有的 jǐnyǒude: *We were the* ~ *people wearing hats.* 只有我们戴着帽子. **3** 最好的 zuìhǎode: *He's the* ~ *man for me.* 他是唯一支持我的人.

only² /'əʊnlɪ/ *adv* 仅[僅]仅 jǐnjǐn: *I* ˌ~ *saw 'Mary.* 我只见到了玛莉. ***if*** ~ ⇨ if (7). ~ ***too*** 很 hěn: ˌ~ *too 'pleased* 很高兴.

only³ /'əʊnlɪ/ *conj* 可是 kěshì; 不过[過] búguò: *I like the book,* ~ *it's expensive.* 我喜欢这本书,但是它很贵.

on·set /'ɒnset/ *n* [C] 进[進]攻 jìngōng; 开[開]始 kāishǐ: *the* ~ *of an illness* 疾病的发作.

on·shore /'ɒnʃɔː(r)/ *adj, adv* 朝着岸的 cháozhe àn de; 朝着岸 cháozhe àn: ~ *winds* 吹向陆地的风.

on·slaught /'ɒnslɔːt/ *n* [C] 猛攻 (与 on 连用) měnggōng.

onto /'ɒntə, 强式: 'ɒntuː/ *prep* 到…上 dào…shàng: *climb* ~ *a horse* 骑上马.

onus /'əʊnəs/ *n* [仅用 *sing*] 责任 zérèn; 负担[擔] fùdān: *the* ~ *is on you* 这个责任在你.

on·ward /'ɒnwəd/ *adj, adv* 向前的 xiàngqiánde; 向前 xiàngqián. □ *adv* (亦作 **on·wards**): *move* ~*s* 向前移动.

ooze /uːz/ *n* [U] 淤泥 yūní; 软[輭]泥 ruǎnní. □ *vt/i* **1** (指浓液)慢慢地流 mànmànde liú. **2** 流出 liúchū.

opac·ity /əʊ'pæsətɪ/ *n* [U] 不透明 bú tòumíng; 昏暗 hūn'àn.

opal /'əʊpl/ *n* [C] 蛋白石 dànbáishí.

opaque /əʊ'peɪk/ *adj* 不透光的 bú tòuguāng de; 不透明的 bú tòumíng de. ~**ly** *adv* ~**ness** *n* [U]

O.P.E.C. = Organization of Petroleum Exporting Countries 石油输[輸]出国[國]组织[織] shíyóu shūchū guó zǔzhī.

open¹ /'əʊpən/ *adj* **1** 开[開]的 kāide: ~ *doors* 开着的门. **2** 开阔[闊]的 kāikuòde: ~ *fields* 旷野. **3** 无[無]遮盖的 wú zhēgài de. ***in the*** ~ ***'air*** 在户外 zài hùwài. **4** 开放的 kāifàngde: *The flowers were all* ~. 那些花都开了. **5** 公开的 gōngkāide. ***keep*** ~ ***house*** 欢迎所有来客 huānyíng suǒyǒu láikè. **6** 未决定的 wèi juédìng de; 未解决的 wèijiějué de: *leave a matter* ~ 留下一件事没解决. ***have (keep) an*** ~ ***'mind (on sth)*** 敞开思想 chǎngkāi sīxiǎng. **7** (商店等)开着的 kāizhede: *Are the shops* ~ *yet?* 商店都开门了吗? **8** 无秘密的 wú mìmì de: *an* ~ *secret* 公开的秘密. **9** ~ ***to*** 易接受…的 yì jiēshòu…de: ~ *to criticism* 易受到批评. **10** 坦率的 tǎnshuàide: *an* ~ *face (discussion)* 坦率的面孔(讨论). □ *n* **the** ~ 户外 hùwài; 野外 yěwài. '~**-air** *adj* 户外的 hùwàide; 野外的 yěwàide. ~ **cheque** 普通支票 pǔtōng zhīpiào. ˌ~**-'ended** *adj* **(a)** 无[無]限制的 wú xiànzhì de; **(b)** 有许多可能答案的辩论[論] yǒu xǔduō kěnéng dá'àn de biànlùn. ~ **market** 自由市场[場] zìyóu shìchǎng. ˌ~**-'minded** *adj* 无偏见的 wú piānjiàn de. ~**ly** *adv* 公开地 gōngkāide; 坦率地 tǎnshuàide. ~**ness** *n* [U] 率直 shuàizhí; 公开 gōngkāi.

open² /'əʊpən/ *vt/i* **1** 开[開] kāi. **2** 开口 kāikǒu; 打通 dǎtōng: ~ *a road through a forest.* 通过森林开一条路. **3** ~ ***sth up*** 开展 kāizhǎn: ~ *up the forest* 开发森林. **4** 展开 zhǎnkāi: ~ *a book* 打开一本书. ~ ***one's mind (heart) to sb*** 对[對]某人吐露心意(真情) duì mǒurén tǔlù xīnyì. **5** 开始 kāishǐ: ~

an account (在银行)开个户头．～ *fire (at, on)* 开火 kāihuǒ．6 开业〔業〕kāiyè: ～ *a shop* 开一家商店．

open·ing /'əʊpənɪŋ/ *n* [C] **1** 口 kǒu; 孔 kǒng．**2** 开〔開〕始 kāishǐ; 开端 kāiduān．**3** 张〔張〕开 zhāngkāi: *the* ～ *of a flower* 花朵开放．**4** (职位的)空缺 kòngquē．□ *adj* 开头〔頭〕的 kāitóude: *his* ～ *words* 他的开场白．

op·era /'ɒprə/ *n* [*pl* ～s] **1** [C] 歌剧〔劇〕gējù．**2** [U] 歌剧作品 gējù zuòpǐn; 歌剧艺〔藝〕术〔術〕gējù yìshù．～**tic** /ˌɒpə'rætɪk/ *adj*

op·er·ate /'ɒpəreɪt/ *vt/i* **1** 操作 cāozuò; 运〔運〕转〔轉〕yùnzhuàn: ～ *a machine* 操作一部机器．**2** 动〔動〕手术〔術〕dòng shǒushù; 开刀 kāidāo．**3** 经〔經〕营〔營〕jīngyíng: *My company* ～*s abroad.* 我的公司在国外开业．**'operating table (theatre)** 手术台(示教室) shǒushùtái．

op·er·ation /ˌɒpə'reɪʃn/ *n* **1** [U] 操作 cāozuò; 运〔運〕转〔轉〕yùnzhuàn: *the* ～ *of a machine* 机器的运转．**2** [C] 工作 gōngzuò．**3** [常用 *pl*] 军〔軍〕事行动〔動〕jūnshì xíngdòng; 军事演习〔習〕jūnshì yǎnxí．**4** [C] (工业等的)有计划〔劃〕行动 yǒu jìhuà xíngdòng．**5** [C] 手术〔術〕shǒushù．～**al** *adj* **(a)** 操作的 cāozuòde; 手术的 shǒushùde．**(b)** 可使用的 kě shǐyòng de．

op·er·at·ive /'ɒpərətɪv/ *adj* **1** 操作的 cāozuòde; 有效的 yǒuxiàode．**2** 手术〔術〕的 shǒushùde．□ *n* [C] 技工 jìgōng; 工人 gōngrén．

op·er·ator /'ɒpəreɪtə(r)/ *n* [C] 操作者 cāozuòzhě．

op·er·etta /ˌɒpə'retə/ *n* [C] [*pl* ～s] (独幕或短而轻松的)小歌剧〔劇〕xiǎo gējù．

opin·ion /ə'pɪnɪən/ *n* **1** [C] 意见 yìjiàn; 看法 kànfǎ．***be of the*** ～ ***that*** 认〔認〕为〔為〕… rènwéi… **2** [U] 信念 xìnniàn; 见解 jiànjiě．**3** [C] (专家等的)鉴〔鑒〕定 jiàndìng: *a doctor's* ～ 医生的诊断．～**ated** *adj* 固执〔執〕己见的 gùzhí jǐjiàn de．

opium /'əʊpɪəm/ *n* [U] 鸦〔鴉〕片 yāpiàn．

opp. = opposite.

op·po·nent /ə'pəʊnənt/ *n* [C] 对〔對〕手 duìshǒu; 敌〔敵〕手 díshǒu; 反对者 fǎnduìzhě．

op·por·tune /'ɒpətjuːn/ *adj* [正式用语] **1** (指时间) 合适〔適〕的 héshìde; 恰好 qiàhǎo．**2** (指行动)及时〔時〕的 jíshíde; 适时的 shìshíde．～**ly** *adv*

op·por·tun·ity /ˌɒpə'tjuːnətɪ/ *n* [C,U] [*pl* -ies] 机〔機〕会〔會〕jīhuì; 时〔時〕机 shíjī．

op·pose /ə'pəʊz/ *vt* **1** 反对〔對〕fǎnduì; 反抗 fǎnkàng．**2** ***as*** ～***d to*** 与〔與〕…形成对照 yǔ…xíngchéng duìzhào．

op·po·site /'ɒpəzɪt/ *adj* **1** 对〔對〕面的 duìmiànde; 相对的 xiāngduìde: *the house* ～ *(to) mine* 我的房子的对面的那所房子．**2** 相反的 xiāngfǎnde; 对立的 duìlìde: *in the* ～ *direction* 朝相反的方向．***one's*** ˌ～ **'*number*** 与〔與〕对方地位相等或相当〔當〕的人 yǔ duìfāng dìwèi xiāngděng huò xiāngdāng de rén．□ *prep* 在…的对面 zài…de duìmiàn: ～ *the station* 在车站对面．□ *n* [C] 对立物 duìlìwù; 对立面 duìlìmiàn．

op·po·si·tion /ˌɒpə'zɪʃn/ *n* **1** [U] 反对〔對〕fǎnduì; 敌〔敵〕对 díduì: *great* ～ *to the new law* 同新法律大相径庭．**2 the O**～ 反对党〔黨〕fǎnduìdǎng．

op·press /ə'pres/ *vt* **1** 压〔壓〕迫 yāpò; 压制 yāzhì．**2** ***be (或 feel)*** ～***ed with sth*** [喻]压抑 yāyì; 使烦恼〔惱〕shǐ fánnǎo．**op·pres·sion** /-ʃn/ *n* [C, U]．～**ive** *adj* **(a)** 暴虐的 bàonüè de; 不公平的 bù gōngpíng de．**(b)** 难〔難〕以忍受的 nán yǐ rěnshòu de: ～*ive heat* 难以忍受的闷热．～**or** 压迫者 yāpòzhě．

opt /ɒpt/ *vi* **1** ～ ***for sth*** 选〔選〕择〔擇〕xuǎnzé; 挑选 tiāoxuǎn．～ ***out of*** 使退出 shǐ tuìchū．

op·tic /'ɒptɪk/ *adj* 视觉〔覺〕的 shìjuéde; 眼睛的 yǎnjīngde: *the* ～ *nerve* 视觉神经．～**al** *adj* 视觉的 shìjuéde．～**al illusion** 视力错觉 shìlì cuòjué．～**ian** /ɒp'tɪʃn/ *n* [C] 眼镜制造者 yǎnjìng zhìzàozhě; 眼镜商 yǎnjìngshāng．

op·ti·mism /'ɒptɪmɪzəm/ *n* [U] 乐〔樂〕观〔觀〕lèguān; 乐观主义 lèguān zhǔyì．**op·ti·mist** 乐观者 lèguānzhě; 乐观主义者 lèguānzhǔyìzhě．**op·ti'mis·tic** *adj*

op·ti·mum /'ɒptɪməm/ *adj* 最适〔適〕宜的 zuì shìyí de: *the* ～ *price* 最适宜的价格．

op·tion /'ɒpʃn/ *n* **1** [U] 选〔選〕择〔擇〕xuǎnzé; 选择权〔權〕xuǎnzéquán．**2** [C] 可挑选的事物 kě tiāoxuǎnde shìwù．～**al** *adj* 非强制的 fēi qiángzhì de．

or /ɔː(r)/ *conj* **1** (表示选择): *Is it green* ～ *blue?* 它是绿的还是蓝的? *Do you want tea, coffee* ～ *beer?* 你要喝茶，喝咖啡，还是喝啤酒? *ei* *ther* ~⇨ either ~ ***(else)***否则 fǒuzé: *Do it, ~ else I'll hit you!* 你去干，不然我要打你！ **2** 也就是 yě jiùshì: *a pound, ~ one hundred pence.* 一英镑，也就是一百便士. **4** ~ ***so*** 大约 dàyuē: *I'd like twenty ~ so.* 我想要二十个左右.

oral /'ɔ:rəl/ *adj* **1** 口头〔頭〕的 kǒutóude; 口述的 kǒushùde. **2**〔解剖〕口的 kǒude; 口部的 kǒubùde. □ *n* [C] 〔非正式用语〕口试 kǒushì. **~ly** *adv*

or·ange /'ɒrɪndʒ/ *adj, n* [C] 橘柑(树) júgān, 橙(树) chéng; 橘柑的 júgānde; 橙的 chéngde; [U] 橘色 júsè, 橙黄色 chénghuángsè.

orang-outang /ɔ:,ræŋ u:'tæŋ/ (亦作 **-utan, -outan** /-'tæn/) *n* [C] 猩猩 xīngxīng.

ora·tion /ɔ:'reɪʃn/ *n* [C] 正式演讲〔講〕 zhèngshì yǎnjiǎng; 演说 yǎnshuō.

ora·tor /'ɒrətə(r)/ *n* [C] 演说者(尤指出色的演说家) yǎnshuōzhě. **ora·tory** /'ɒrətrɪ/ *n* [U] 演说 yǎnshuō; 修辞〔辭〕 xiūcí.

or·bit /'ɔ:bɪt/ *n* [C] **1** (天体的)轨〔軌〕道 guǐdào. **2** 势〔勢〕力范〔範〕围〔圍〕 shìlì fànwéi. □ *vt/i* 沿轨道运〔運〕行 yán guǐdào yùnxíng. **~al** *adj*

or·chard /'ɔ:tʃəd/ *n* [C] 果园〔園〕 guǒyuán.

or·ches·tra /'ɔ:kɪstrə/ *n* [C] [*pl* ~s] 管弦乐〔樂〕队〔隊〕 guǎnxiányuè duì. **or·ches·tral** /ɔ:'kestrəl/ *adj* **~te** /-eɪt/ *vt* 为〔爲〕管弦乐队谱写〔寫〕(音乐) wèi guǎnxiányuè duì pǔxiě. **~tion** /-'streɪʃn/ *n* [C,U]

or·chid /'ɔ:kɪd/ *n* [C] 兰〔蘭〕花 lánhuā.

or·dain /ɔ:'deɪn/ *vt* **1** 任(某人为)牧师〔師〕 rèn wéi mùshī. **2** (指上帝、法律)命令 mìnglìng; 注定 zhùdìng.

or·deal /ɔ:'di:l/ *n* [C] (对品格或忍耐力的)严〔嚴〕格考验〔驗〕 yángé kǎoyàn.

or·der¹ /'ɔ:də(r)/ *n* **1** [U] 次序 cìxù; 顺序 shùnxù. ***in ~ of*** 照…排列 zhào…páiliè: *placed in ~ of size* 依大小次序排列. **2** [U] 有次序的状〔狀〕态〔態〕 yǒu cìxù de zhuàngtài. ***(not) in ~*** (无)有序 yǒu xù: *Your papers are in ~.* 你的文件很整齐. ***out of ~*** (指机器)出故障 chū gùzhàng; 不能起作用 bù néng qǐ zuòyòng. **3** [U] 遵守法律 zūnshǒu fǎlǜ. ⇨ disorder. ***law and ~*** ⇨ law(3). **4** [U] 会〔會〕议〔議〕规则 huìyì guīzé. ***on a point of ~*** 在程序问〔問〕题上 zài chéngxù wèntí shàng. **5** [C] 命令 mìnglìng. **6** [C] 定购〔購〕 dìnggòu; 定单〔單〕 dìngdān. ***on ~*** 已定购(货尚未到) yǐ dìnggòu. **7** [C] (尤指银行或邮局的)汇〔匯〕票 huìpiào. **8** ***in ~ to do sth*** 为〔爲〕了(作某事) wèile. ***in ~ that*** 为了 wèile. **9** [C] 属于某一特殊等级的一批人 shǔyú mǒuyī tèshū děngjí de yìpīrén: *the O~ of the Bath* 获得巴斯勋章的一批人. **10** ***take (holy) ~s*** 任牧师〔師〕 rèn mùshī. **11** [C] 种〔種〕 zhǒng; 类〔類〕 lèi: *ability of a high ~* 优等的才干.

or·der² /'ɔ:də(r)/ *vt* **1** 命令 mìnglìng; 定购〔購〕 dìnggòu; 汇〔匯〕寄 huìjì. ~ ***sb about*** 不断〔斷〕驱〔驅〕使某人 búduàn qūshǐ mǒurén. **2** 安排 ānpái; 指导〔導〕 zhǐdǎo: *~ one's life better* 更好地安排生活.

or·der·ly /'ɔ:dəlɪ/ *adj* **1** 有秩序的 yǒu zhìxù de; 整齐〔齊〕的 zhěngqíde. **2** 有条〔條〕不紊的 yǒu tiáo bù wěn de: *an ~ mind* 严谨的思想. **3** 守秩序的 shǒu zhìxù de; 守纪律的 shǒu jìlǜ de: *an ~ crowd* 守秩序的群众. □ *n* [C] [*pl* -ies] [军事]传〔傳〕令兵 chuánlìngbīng; 护〔護〕理员 hùlǐyuán. **or·der·li·ness** *n* [U]

or·di·nal /'ɔ:dɪnl/ *adj, n* [C] 顺序的 shùnxùde; 序数〔數〕 (如 *first, second, third*) xùshù. ⇨ cardinal¹.

or·di·nary /'ɔ:dɪnrɪ/ *adj* 普通的 pǔtōngde; 平常的 píngchángde. ***out of the ~*** 例外的 lìwàide. **or·di·nar·ily** /'ɔ:dənrəlɪ/ *adv* 平常地 píngchángde: *Ordinarily he leaves early.* 他通常动身很早.

ore /ɔ:(r)/ *n* [C,U] 矿〔礦〕石 kuàngshí; 矿砂 kuàngshā.

or·gan¹ /'ɔ:gən/ *n* [C] **1** 器官 qìguān. **2** 报〔報〕刊 bàokān; 传〔傳〕播工具 chuánbō gōngjù: *~s of public opinion* 舆论的喉舌.

or·gan² /'ɔ:gən/ *n* [C] 风〔風〕琴 fēngqín. **'~ist** 风琴演奏者 fēngqín yǎnzhòuzhě.

or·ganic /ɔ:'gænɪk/ *adj* **1** 器官的 qìguānde. **2** (与 *inorganic* 相对) 有机〔機〕的 yǒujīde. **3** 有组织〔織〕的 yǒu zǔzhī de: *an ~ structure* 有组织的结构. **~ally** /-klɪ/ *adv*

or·gan·ism /'ɔ:gənɪzəm/ *n* [C] **1** 生物 shēngwù; 有机〔機〕体〔體〕 yǒujītǐ. **2** 有机的组织〔織〕 yǒujīde zǔzhī.

or·gan·iz·ation /,ɔ:gənaɪ'zeɪʃn/ *n* **1** [U] 组织〔織〕 zǔzhī. **2** [C] 机构〔構〕 jīgòu; 团〔團〕体〔體〕tuántǐ.

or·gan·ize /'ɔ:gənaɪz/ *vt* **1** 组织〔織〕zǔzhī: ~ *workers* 组织工人. **2** 创〔創〕办〔辦〕chuàngbàn: ~ *a party* 组织政党.

orgy /'ɔ:dʒɪ/ *n* [C] [*pl* -ies] 狂欢〔歡〕kuánghuān; 纵〔縱〕酒宴乐〔樂〕zòngjiǔ yiànlè.

orient /'ɔ:rɪənt/ *n* **the O**~ [诗歌] 地中海以东〔東〕的国〔國〕家 Dìzhōnghǎi yǐ dōng de guójiā; 远〔遠〕东 yuǎndōng. □ *adj*[诗歌]东方的 dōngfāngde. ~**al** /,ɔ:rɪ'entl/ *adj, n* [C] 东方的 dōngfāngde; 东方人 dōngfāngrén.

orien·tate /'ɔ:rɪənteɪt/ *vt* **1** 定…的位 dìng...de wèi. **2** ~ *oneself* [喻]使认〔認〕清形势〔勢〕shǐ rènqīng xíngshì. **orien·ta·tion** *n* [U]

ori·fice /'ɒrɪfɪs/ *n* [C] 外孔 wàikǒng; 洞口 dòngkǒu; 口 kǒu.

ori·gin /'ɒrɪdʒɪn/ *n* [C,U] **1** 起源 qǐyuán; 开〔開〕端 kāiduān. **2** 出身 chūshēn; 血统 xuètǒng: *of English* ~ 英国血统.

orig·inal /ə'rɪdʒənl/ *adj* **1** 最初的 zuìchūde. **2** 新颖的 xīnyǐngde: ~ *designs* 别出心裁的设计. **3** 有独〔獨〕创〔創〕性的 yǒu dúchuàngxìng de: *an* ~ *thinker* 有创见的思想家. □ *n* [C] (1) 起源 qǐyuán; 原始 yuánshǐ. (2) 原物 yuánwù; 原作品 yuán zuòpǐn. ~**ly** *adv* **(a)** 最初 zuìchū; 新颖地 xīnyǐngde; 独特地 dútède. **(b)** 原先 yuánxiān: *His shirt was* ~*ly white.* 他的衬衫原先是白的. ~**al·ity** /-'nælətɪ/ *n* [U]

orig·inate /ə'rɪdʒɪneɪt/ *vt/i* **1** ~ *from* **(*with*)** 发〔發〕生 fāshēng, 发起 fāqǐ. **2** 创〔創〕始 chuàngshǐ; 发明 fāmíng. **orig·in·ator** *n* [C]

or·na·ment /'ɔ:nəmənt/ *n* **1** [U] 装〔裝〕饰 zhuāngshì. **2** [C] 装饰物 zhuāngshìwù: □ *vt* /'ɔ:nəment/ 装饰 zhuāngshì; 修饰 xiūshì. ~**al** /-'mentl/ *adj*

or·nate /ɔ:'neɪt/ *adj* **1** 装〔裝〕饰华〔華〕丽〔麗〕的 zhuāngshì huálì de. **2** (文体)华丽不实〔實〕的 huálì bùshí de. ~**ly** *adv* ~**ness** *n* [U]

or·ni·thol·ogy /,ɔ:nɪ'θɒlədʒɪ/ *n* [U] 鸟〔鳥〕类〔類〕学〔學〕niǎolèixué. **or·ni·thol·ogist** *n* [C] 鸟类学家 niǎolèixuéjiā.

or·phan /'ɔ:fn/ *n* [C] 孤儿〔兒〕gū'ér. □ *vt* 使成孤儿 shǐchéng gū'ér. '~**age** 孤儿院 gū'éryuàn.

or·tho·dox /'ɔ:θədɒks/ *adj* 正统的 zhèngtǒngde; 传〔傳〕统的 chuántǒngde. **or·tho·doxy** *n* [C,U] [*pl* -ies]

or·thogra·phy /ɔ:'θɒgrəfɪ/ *n* [U] 正字法 zhèngzìfǎ.

or·tho·paedic (亦作 **-pedic**) /,ɔ:θə'pi:dɪk/ *adj* 整形的 zhěngxíngde; 矫〔矯〕形术〔術〕的 jiǎoxíngshùde. **or·tho·paedics** (亦作 **-pedics**) *n* 整形外科 zhěngxíng wàikē; 整形术 zhěngxíngshù.

os·cil·late /'ɒsɪleɪt/ *vt/i* **1** 摆〔擺〕动〔動〕bǎidòng; 振动 zhèndòng. **2** [喻]踌〔躊〕躇 chóuchú; 犹〔猶〕豫 yóuyù. **os·cil'la·tion** /-ʃn/ *n* [C, U]

os·ten·sible /'ɒstensəbl/ *adj* [正式用语](指理由)表面的 biǎomiànde; 假装〔裝〕的 jiǎzhuāngde. **os·ten·sibly** *adv*

os·ten·ta·tion /,ɒsten'teɪʃn/ *n* [U] 夸〔誇〕耀 kuāyào; 卖〔賣〕弄 màinòng. **os·ten·ta·tious** *adj*

os·tra·cize /'ɒstrəsaɪz/ *vt* 排斥 páichì; 摈〔擯〕弃〔棄〕bìngqì.

os·trich /'ɒstrɪtʃ/ *n* [C] [*pl* ~es] 鸵〔鴕〕鸟〔鳥〕tuóniǎo.

O.T. = Old Testament («圣经»的) «旧〔舊〕约全书〔書〕» «Jiùyuē Quánshū».

other /'ʌðə(r)/ *adj, pron* 另外的 lìngwàide; 其他的 qítāde. **1 the** ~ [*sing*] (两个中) 另一个人或事物 lìngyígè rén huò shìwù: *on the* ~ *side of the street* 在街的另一边. ***on the*** '~ ***hand*** 另一方面 lìng yī fāngmiàn: *It's cheap, but on the* ~ *hand the quality is poor.* 它是便宜的,但另一方面,质量很差. **2 the** ~**s** [*pl*] 其余〔餘〕的人(或事物) qíyúde rén: *Six of them are mine; the* ~*s are John's.* 其中六个是我的; 其余是约翰的. **3** 剩下的 shèngxiàde: *Smith is better than any* ~ *member of the team.* 史密斯比工作班子里任何其他成员都强. **4** 更多的 gèngduōde; 额外的 éwàide: *Have you any* ~ *books?* 你没有其他书吗? ***every*** ~, **(a)** 所有其他的 suǒyǒu qítā de: *John is stupid; every* ~ *boy knows the answer.* 约翰愚钝,所有其他的男孩都知道这答案. **(b)** 间〔間〕隔的 jiàngéde: *Write only on every* ~ *line.* 务必隔行书写. ***or*** ~ (表示不肯定的意思): *some day or* ~ 过几天. ***the*** ~ ***day*** 几〔幾〕天前 jǐtiānqián. **5** 不同的 bùtóngde: *I do not wish her to be* ~ *than she is.* 我不希望她改变现状. □ *adv* =(*otherwise*) 用别的办〔辦〕法 yòng biéde bànfǎ: *I can't do it* ~ *than slowly.* 我只好慢慢地做那件事.

other·wise /'ʌðəwaɪz/ *adv* **1** 用其他方法 yòng qítā fāngfǎ; 不同地 bùtóngde: *You evidently think* ~.

你显然有不同想法. **2** 在其他方面 zài qítā fāngmiàn; 在不同的情况下 zài bùtóngde qíngkuàng xià: *The rent is high, but ~ the house is satisfactory.* 房租昂贵,但在其他方面这房子还令人满意. □ *conj* 否则 fǒuzé; 不然 bùrán: *Get out, ~ he'll be angry.* 走开,否则他要发怒了.

ot·ter /ˈɒtə(r)/ *n* [C] 水獭 shuǐtǎ; [U] 水獭皮 shuǐtǎpí.

ought /ɔːt/ *aux verb* (否定式 ought not 或 oughtn't /ˈɔːtnt/) **1** (表示责任或义务): *Such things ~ not to be allowed.* 不应该允许有这类事情. **2** (表示适当): *You ~* (= I advise you) *to see that new film.* 你应该去看那部新电影. **3**(表示可能性): *That ~ to be enough fish for three people.* 大概有够三个人吃的鱼.

ounce /aʊns/ *n* [C] (缩作 **oz**) 盎司 àngsī; 英两 yīngliǎng.

O.U.P. = Oxford University Press 牛津大学[學]出版社 Niújīn Dàxué Chūbǎnshè.

our /ɑː(r) 强式: ˈaʊə(r)/ *adj* 我们[們]的 wǒménde.

ours /ˈɑːʊəz/ *possessive pron* 我们[們]的(东西) wǒménde.

our·selves /ɑːˈselvz/ *pron* **1**[反身] 我们[們]自己 wǒmén zìjǐ: *It's no use worrying ~.* 我们烦恼是没用的. **(all) by ~, (a)** 单[單]独[獨]的 dāndúde. **(b)** 无[無]他人帮[幫]助的 wú tārén bāngzhù de. **2** [强调用法]: *We've often made that mistake ~.* 我们自己常常犯那个错误.

oust /aʊst/ *vt* **~ sb (from)** 驱[驅]逐(某人) qūzhú; 赶[趕]走 gǎnzǒu.

out[1] /aʊt/ *adv* (与 **in** 相对) **1** 离[離]去 líqù; 在外 zàiwài: *go ~* 外出. **2 be ~** (与 be 连用,表示不同的含义): *Mrs White is ~.* 怀特太太不在家. *The dockers are ~ again.* 码头工人又罢工了. *Short skirts are ~.* 短裙不时兴了. **be ~ to do, etc** 企图 qǐtú: *I'm not ~ to change the world.* 我并不打算改变世界. **3** 遥远地 yáoyuǎnde: *He lives ~ in the country.* 他住在乡下. **4** 脱离限制 tuōlí xiànzhì; 显[顯]露出来[來] xiǎnlù chūlái: *The sun is ~.* 太阳出来了. *The prisoner got ~.* 犯人出狱. **5** 耗尽[盡] hàojìn; 消灭[滅] xiāomiè: *Put that cigarette ~!* 把香烟熄掉! **6** 完全地 wánquánde: *I'm tired ~.* 我已精疲力尽. **have it ~ with sb** ⇨ have[3](8). **all ~** 竭尽全力 jiéjìn quánlì. **7** (表示错误): *I'm ~ in my calculations.* 我的计算错误. **8** (表示高声): *cry ~* 叫出声来. **~ loud** 大声[聲]地 dàshēngde. **9** (板球) (指击球员)出局 chūjú; 退场[場] tuìchǎng.

out[2] /aʊt/ *prep* **~ of** (与 *in, into* 相对) **1** 在…外 zài…wài; 离[離]开[開] líkāi: *Fish cannot live ~ of water.* 鱼离开水就不能活. **2**(指动作): *walk ~ of the shop* 从商店里走出来. **3** (表示动机): *They helped us ~ of kindness.* 他们出于好意帮助我们. **4**从[從]…(当中) cóng…: *in nine cases ~ of ten* 十之八九. **5** 用…(制成) yòng…: *made ~ of old planks* 用旧木板做的. **6** 缺乏 quēfá; 没有 méiyǒu: *~ of breath* 喘不过气来. **7** (表示起源): *drink ~ of a cup* 从一只杯里喝. **8** (表示结果): *talk him ~ of doing it* 劝他不做那件事. **9** 距 jù; 离[離] lí: *ten miles ~ of Hull* 距赫尔有十英里.

out·board /ˈaʊtbɔːd/ *adj* 在船外的 zài chuán wài de: *~ motor* 装于船尾外的马达.

out·break /ˈaʊtbreɪk/ *n* [C] 爆发[發] bàofā.

out·build·ing /ˈaʊtbɪldɪŋ/ *n* [C] 附属[屬]建筑[築]物 fùshǔ jiànzhùwù.

out·burst /ˈaʊtbɜːst/ *n* [C] (怒气等)爆发[發] bàofā.

out·cast /ˈaʊtkɑːst/ *n* [C], *adj* 被遗弃[棄]者 bèi yíqì zhě; 被逐出者 bèi zhúchū zhě; 被遗弃的 bèi yíqì de; 被放逐的 bèi fàngzhú de.

out·come /ˈaʊtkʌm/ *n* [C] 结果 jiéguǒ; 后[後]果 hòuguǒ.

out·crop /ˈaʊtkrɒp/ *n* [C] (岩石等)露头[頭] lùtóu; 露出地面的岩层[層] lùchū dìmiànde yáncéng.

out·cry /ˈaʊtkraɪ/ *n* [*pl* -ies] [C,U] 公开[開]反对[對] gōngkāi fǎnduì.

out·dated /aʊˈdeɪtɪd/ *adj* 过[過]时[時]的 guòshíde; 不流行的 bù liúxíng de: *~ customs* 旧风俗.

out·do /ɑːʊtˈduː/ *vt* [*pt* -did/-ˈdɪd/; *pp* -done /-ˈdʌn/] 胜[勝]过[過] shèngguò; 优[優]于 yōuyú: *~ one's rivals* 胜过竞争者.

out·door /ˈaʊtdɔː(r)/ *adj* 户外的 hùwàide. **out·doors** *adv* 户外 hùwài.

outer /ˈaʊtə(r)/ *adj* **1** 外的 wàide: *~ garments* 外衣. ⇨ inner. **2** 外面的 wàimiànde; 外部的 wàibùde: *the ~ suburbs* 远郊区. **,~ˈspace** 外层[層]空间[間] wàicéng kōngjiān. **ˈ~most** *adj* 最外面的 zuì wàimiàn de.

out·fit /ˈaʊtfɪt/ *n* [C] 装〔裝〕备〔備〕zhuāngbèi; 全部用品 quánbù yòngpǐn. □ *vt* [-tt-] 装备 zhuāngbèi. ~**ter** 服装商 fúzhuāng shāng; 旅行用品商店 lǚxíng yòngpǐn shāngdiàn.

out·flank /aʊtˈflæŋk/ *vt* 对(敌人)进〔進〕行翼侧包围〔圍〕duì...jìnxíng yìcè bāowéi.

out·go·ing /ˈaʊtgəʊɪŋ/ *adj* 外出的 wàichūde; 离〔離〕去的 líqùde: *the ~ President* 即将离任的总统. ⇨ incoming. **out·go·ings** *n pl* 开〔開〕支 kāizhī; 支出 zhīchū.

out·grow /aʊtˈgrəʊ/ *vt* [*pt* -grew /-ˈgru:/; *pp* -grown /-ˈgrəʊn/] **1** 过〔過〕大而不适〔適〕于 guòdà ér búshì yú. **2** 因年长〔長〕而放弃〔棄〕(坏习惯等)yīn niánzhǎng ér fàngqì.

out·house /ˈaʊthaʊs/ *n* [C] [*pl* ~s /-haʊzɪz/] 外屋 wàiwū; 附属〔屬〕的建筑〔築〕物 fùshǔde jiànzhùwù.

out·ing /ˈaʊtɪŋ/ *n* [C] 远〔遠〕足 yuǎnzú; 短途旅行 duǎntú lǚxíng.

out·land·ish /aʊtˈlændɪʃ/ *adj* 希奇古怪的 xīqí gǔguài de: *~ clothes* 奇装异服. ~**ly** *adv*

out·law /ˈaʊtlɔ:/ *n* [C] 被剥夺〔奪〕公民权〔權〕者 bèi bōduó gōngmínquán zhě. □ *vt* 禁止 jìnzhǐ: *~ the sale of guns* 禁止出售枪枝.

out·lay /ˈaʊtleɪ/ *n* [U] 开〔開〕支 kāizhī; [C] 花费 huāfèi.

out·let /ˈaʊtlet/ *n* [C] **1** (河流等的)出口 chūkǒu; 出路 chūlù. **2** [喻]发〔發〕泄〔洩〕(感情、精力等的)方法 fāxiè fāngfǎ.

out·line /ˈaʊtlaɪn/ *n* [C] **1** 轮〔輪〕廓 lúnkuò; 外形 wàixíng. **2** 大纲〔綱〕dàgāng; 纲要 gāngyào: *an ~ of the plans* 计划纲要. □ *vt* 画〔畫〕出…的轮廓 huàchū...de lúnkuò; 述要点〔點〕shù yàodiǎn.

out·live /aʊtˈlɪv/ *vt* 活得比…长〔長〕久 huóde bǐ...chángjiǔ: *~ one's children* 比自己的孩子活得久.

out·look /ˈaʊtlʊk/ *n* [C] **1** 景色 jǐngsè; 风〔風〕光 fēngguāng. **2** 展望 zhǎnwàng; 前景 qiánjǐng. **3** 看法 kànfǎ: *a hopeful ~ on life* 充满希望的人生观. ⇨ narrow(3).

out·lying /ˈaʊtlaɪɪŋ/ *adj* 远〔遠〕离〔離〕中心的 yuǎnlí zhōngxīn de: *~ villages* 偏僻的乡村、

out·num·ber /aʊtˈnʌmbə(r)/ *vt* 数〔數〕量上超过〔過〕shùliàng shàng chāoguò.

out-of-date /ˌaʊt əv ˈdeɪt/ *adj* = out of date. ⇨ date[1](2).

out-of-the-way /ˌaʊt əv ðə ˈweɪ/ *adj* 偏僻的 piānpìde; 罕见的 hǎnjiànde.

out·patient /ˈaʊtpeɪʃnt/ *n* [C] 门〔門〕诊病人 ménzhěn bìngrén.

out·post /ˈaʊtpəʊst/ *n* [C] **1** 前哨 qiánshào; 哨兵 shàobīng. **2** 边〔邊〕远〔遠〕地区〔區〕biānyuǎn dìqū.

out·put /ˈɑ:ʊtpʊt/ *n* [C] 产〔產〕量 chǎnliàng.

out·rage /ˈaʊtreɪdʒ/ *n* [C,U] **1** 暴行 bàoxíng; 残〔殘〕暴 cánbào. **2** 使舆〔輿〕论〔論〕震惊〔驚〕的行为〔爲〕shǐ yúlùn zhènjīng de xíngwéi. □ *vt* 对…施暴行 duì...shī bàoxíng. ~**ous** *adj* 残暴的 cánbàode; 蛮〔蠻〕横的 mánhèngde. ~**ous·ly** *adv*

out·right /ˈaʊtraɪt/ *adj* **1** 断〔斷〕然的 duànránde; 确实〔實〕的 quèshíde: *an ~ denial* 断然否认. **2** 明白无〔無〕误的 míngbái wúwù de: *the ~ winner* 明显的胜者. □ *adv* 立刻地 lìkède: *be killed ~* 立即致命.

out·set /ˈaʊtset/ *n* **at the ~** 在开〔開〕头〔頭〕时〔時〕zài kāitóu shí. **from the ~** 从〔從〕一开始 cóng yì-kāishǐ.

out·side /aʊtˈsaɪd/ *n* [C] (与 *inside* 相对)外部 wàibù; 外面 wàimiàn: *the ~ of the house* 房子外部. □ *adj* **1** 外面的 wàimiànde; 在外面的 zài wàimiàn de. **2** 局外的 júwàide: *~ help* 外援. **3** 未必可能的 wèibì kěnéng de: *an ~ chance* 不大可能的机会. □ *adv* 在外面 zài wàimiàn: *The car is waiting ~.* 汽车在外面等着. □ *prep* **1** 在…的外面 zài ...de wàimiàn: *~ the house* 在屋子外面. **2** 除了 chúle: *He has no interest ~ his work.* 除了工作,他没有别的兴趣.

out·sider /aʊtˈsaɪdə(r)/ *n* [C] **1** 局外人 júwàirén; 非会〔會〕员 fēi huìyuán. **2** 不大可能获〔獲〕胜〔勝〕的选〔選〕手或赛马〔馬〕bú dà kěnéng huòshèng de xuǎnshǒu huò sàimǎ.

out·size /aʊtˈsaɪz/ *adj* (尤指衣服)特大的 tèdàde.

out·skirts /ˈaʊtskɜ:ts/ *n pl* (尤指城市)郊区〔區〕jiāoqū.

out·spoken /aʊtˈspəʊkən/ *adj* 直言的 zhíyánde; 坦率的 tǎnshuàide.

out·stand·ing /aʊtˈstændɪŋ/ *adj* **1** 杰〔傑〕出的 jiéchūde; 显〔顯〕著的 xiǎnzhùde: *an ~ performance* 出色的演出. **2** (指工作等)未完成的 wèi wánchéng de. ~**ly** *adv*

out·strip /aʊtˈstrɪp/ *vt* [-pp-] 胜〔勝〕过〔過〕shèngguò; 超过 chāo guò: ～ *one's rivals* 胜过竞争者.

out·ward /'aʊtwəd/ *adj* **1** 外面的 wàimiànde; 外表的 wàibiǎode: ～ *appearence* 外表. **2** 外出的 wàichūde: *the* ～ *voyage* 出航. □ *adv* (亦作 **out·wards**) 向外 xiàngwài; 在外 zàiwài. **～ly** *adv* 外表上 wàibiǎoshàng.

out·weigh /aʊt'weɪ/ *vt* 比…更重 bǐ...gèng zhòng; 比…更重要 bǐ...gèng zhòngyào.

out·wit /aʊt'wɪt/ *vt* [-tt-] 智胜〔勝〕zhì shèng.

oval /'əʊvl/ *n* [C], *adj* 卵形的 luǎnxíngde; 椭圆形的 tuǒyuánxíngde.

ovary /'əʊvərɪ/ *n* [C] [*pl* -ies]〔解剖〕卵巢 luǎncháo. ⇨ ovum.

ova·tion /əʊ'veɪʃn/ *n* [C] 热〔熱〕烈欢〔歡〕迎 rèliè huānyíng; 欢呼 huānhū.

oven /'ʌvn/ *n* [C] 烤炉〔爐〕kǎolú; 烤箱 kǎoxiāng.

over[1] /'əʊvə(r)/ *adv* **1** 翻倒 fāndǎo; 翻转〔轉〕过〔過〕来 fānzhuǎnguòlái: *Knock a vase* ～. 把花瓶打翻. *Turn the page* ～. 把这一页翻过去. **2** (越)过〔過〕guò: *The milk boiled* ～. 牛奶潽了. **3** 从头〔頭〕至尾地 cóng tóu zhì wěi de: *think it* ～ 细想一下. **4** ,～ *and* '～ (*a'gain*) 反复〔復〕fǎnfù, 再三 zàisān. **5** 越过〔過〕(一段距离等) yuèguò: *Take this* ～ *to the post office.* 把这个送到邮局去. **6** 剩余〔餘〕shèngyú: *meat* (*left*) ～ 剩下的肉. **7** 更多 gèng duō: *children of fourteen and* ～ 十四岁以上的小孩们. **8** 结束 jiésù: *The meeting is* ～. 会开完了. **9** 全部地 quánbùde: *ache all* ～ 全身疼.

over[2] /'əʊvə(r)/ *prep* **1** 在…上面 zài...shàngmiàn: *He spilt oil* ～ *his clothes.* 他把油溅到自己的衣服上. **2** 在…之上 zài...zhī shàng: *the shelf* ～ *the table* 桌子上方的架子. **3** (表示职权、权力等在…之上): *He has no control* ～ *his students.* 他控制不了他的学生. **4** 遍及 biànjí: *travel all* ～ *Europe* 走遍欧洲. **5** 从〔從〕一边〔邊〕到另一边 cóng yībiān dào lìng yībiān: *Look* ～ *the hedge.* 看树篱的那一边. **6** (反义词 = *under*) 超过〔過〕chāoguò: *for* ～ *an hour* 一个多小时. ,～ *and a'bove* 加之 jiā zhī. **7** 关〔關〕于 guānyú: *an argument* ～ *methods* 关于方法的争论. **8** 依 yī: *hear it* ～ *the radio* (*telephone*) 从无线电广播(电话)中听到某事.

over[3] /'əʊvə(r)/ *n* [C] (板球)所投的球数〔數〕suǒtóude qiúshù.

over- /,əʊvə(r)/ *prefix* **1** 在…上面 zài...shàngmiàn: *overland* 经由陆路; 陆上的. *overhead* 在上; 头上的. **2** 太(多) tài: *,over-po'lite* 太多礼的.

over·all[1] /,əʊvər'ɔ:l/ *adj* 包括一切的 bāokuò yíqiè de; 全部的 quánbùde: ～ *measurements* (*control*) 全部衡量(控制).

over·all[2] /'əʊvərɔ:l/ *n* **1** [C] 罩衫 zhàoshān; 罩衣 zhàoyī. **2** [*pl*] 工装〔裝〕裤〔褲〕gōngzhuāngkù.

over·awe /,əʊvər'ɔ:/ *vt* 威慑〔懾〕wēishè; 吓〔嚇〕住 xiàzhù.

over·bal·ance /,əʊvə'bæləns/ *vt/i* 失去平衡 shīqù pínghéng.

over·bear·ing /,əʊvə'beərɪŋ/ *adj* 专〔專〕横的 zhuānhèngde; 傲慢的 àomànde. **～ly** *adv*

over·board /'əʊvəbɔ:d/ *adv* 从〔從〕船上落入水中 cóng chuánshàng luòrù shuǐ zhōng; 在船外 zài chuánwài.

over·cast /,əʊvə'kɑ:st/ *adj* 阴〔陰〕暗的 yīn'ànde; 多云〔雲〕的 duōyúnde.

over·charge /,əʊvə'tʃɑ:dʒ/ *vt/i* **1** 要价〔價〕过〔過〕高 yào jià guò gāo. **2** 装〔裝〕载〔載〕过多 zhuāngzài guò duō.

over·coat /'əʊvəkəʊt/ *n* [C] 大衣 dàyī.

over·come /,əʊvə'kʌm/ *vt* [*pt* -came /-'keɪm/; *pp* ～] **1** 压〔壓〕倒 yādǎo; 克服 kèfú. **2** 使无〔無〕能为〔爲〕力 shǐ wúnéng wéilì: ～ *by tiredness* 累倒了.

over·do /,əʊvə'du:/ *vt* [*pt* -did /-'dɪd/, *pp* -done /-'dʌn/] **1** 做得过〔過〕头〔頭〕zuòde guòtóu; 夸〔誇〕张〔張〕kuāzhāng. ～ *it* 竭尽〔盡〕其力 jiéjìn qílì.

over·dose /'əʊvədəʊs/ *n* [C] 用药过〔過〕量 yòng yào guòliàng.

over·draft /'əʊvədrɑ:ft/ *n* [C] 透支 tòuzhī; 透支额 tòuzhī'é.

over·draw /,əʊvə'drɔ:/ *vt/i* [*pt* -drew /-'dru:/; *pp* -drawn /-'drɔ:n/] 透支 tòuzhī; 超支 chāozhī.

over·due /,əʊvə'dju:/ *adj* 过〔過〕期(未付)的 guòqīde.

over·flow /'əʊvə'fləʊ/ *vt/i* [*pt, pp* ～ed] **1** 溢出 yìchū; 泛滥〔濫〕fànlàn: *The cup* ～*ed.* 杯子太满,溢出了. **2** 充满 chōngmǎn; 洋溢 yángyì. □ *n* /'əʊvəfləʊ/ [C] **1** 泛滥 fànlàn; 溢流 yìliú. **2** 排水管道 páishuǐ guǎndào.

over·grown /,əʊvə'grəʊn/ *adj* **1** 长〔長〕得太快的 zhǎngde tài kuàide: *an* ～ *boy* 长得太快的男孩. **2** 长满的 zhǎngmǎnde.

over·hang /,əʊvə'hæŋ/ *vt/i* [*pt*,

pp -hung /-'hʌŋ/] 悬〔懸〕于…之上 xuán yú…zhī shàng; 悬垂 xuánchuí; 伸出 shēnchū; 突出 tūchū. □ *n* /'əʊvəhæŋ/ [C] 悬垂物 xuánchuíwù; 伸出物 shēnchūwù.

over·haul /ˌəʊvə'hɔ:l/ *vt* **1** 彻〔徹〕底检〔檢〕修 chèdǐ jiǎnxiū. **2** 赶〔趕〕上 gǎnshàng; 追上 zhuīshàng: ~ *the leading driver* 赶上领头的司机. □ *n* /'əʊvəhɔ:l/ [C] 检修 jiǎnxiū; 详细检查 xiángxì jiǎnchá.

over·head /ˌəʊvə'hed/ *adv* 在空中 zài kōngzhōng; 在高处〔處〕 zài gāochù: *aircraft flew* ~ 飞机在空中飞行. □ *adj* /'əʊvəhed/ 高架的 gāojiàde: ~ *cables* 高架电缆.

over·heads /'əʊvəhedz/ *n pl* 企业〔業〕一般管理费 qǐyè yìbān guǎnlǐfèi.

over·hear /ˌəʊvə'hɪə(r)/ *vt* [*pt, pp* ~d/-'hɜ:d/] 偶然听〔聽〕到 ǒurán tīngdào; 偷听 tōutīng.

over·joyed /ˌəʊvə'dʒɔɪd/ *adj* 极〔極〕高兴〔興〕的 jí gāoxìng de.

over·land *adj* /'əʊvəlænd/, *adv* /-'lænd/ 陆〔陸〕上的 lùshàngde; 经〔經〕过〔過〕陆路的 jīngguò lùlù de *travel* ~ *to India* 从陆上旅行到印度.

over·lap /ˌəʊvə'læp/ *vt/i* [-pp-] **1** 部分重叠〔疊〕 bùfen chóngdié. **2** [喻]部分一致 bùfen yízhì. □ /'əʊvəlæp/ *n* [C,U] 重叠 chóngdié; 重叠部分 chóngdié bùfen.

over·load /ˌəʊvə'ləʊd/ *vt* 使超载〔載〕 shǐ chāozài; 使负荷过〔過〕重 shǐ fùhé guòzhòng.

over·look /ˌəʊvə'lʊk/ *vt* **1** 俯视 fǔshì; 俯瞰 fǔkàn. **2** 忽略 hūlüè; 忽视 hūshì. **3** 宽恕 kuānshù: ~ *a fault* 宽容错误.

over·night /ˌəʊvə'naɪt/ *adv* 一夜 yíyè; 在夜里 zài yèlǐ: *stay* ~ 过夜. □ /'əʊvənaɪt/ *adj* 一夜的 yíyède; 短途旅行的 duǎntú lǚxíng de: *an* ~ *bag* 短途旅行包.

over·power /ˌəʊvə'paʊə(r)/ *vt* 压〔壓〕服 yāfú; 制服 zhìfú. ~**ing** *adj* 极〔極〕强大的 jí qiángdà de; 压倒的 yādǎode: *an* ~*ing smell* 强烈的臭味.

over·rate /ˌəʊvə'reɪt/ *vt* 对〔對〕…估计过〔過〕高 duì…gūjì guògāo.

over·reach /ˌəʊvə'ri:tʃ/ *vt* ~ *oneself* 因不自量力而失败 yīn bú zì liàng lì ér shībài.

over·ride /ˌəʊvə'raɪd/ *vt* [*pt* -rode /-'rəʊd/; *pp* -ridden /-'rɪdn/] 不理(某人的愿望、要求等) bùlǐ; 不顾〔顧〕 búgù.

over·rule /ˌəʊvə'ru:l/ *vt* 否决 fǒujué; 驳〔駁〕回 bóhuí.

over·run /ˌəʊvə'rʌn/ *vt* [*pt* -ran /-'ræn/; *pp* ~] **1** 蔓延 mànyán; 占〔佔〕领 zhànlǐng: *A house* ~ *by spiders* 房子满布蛛网. **2** 超越(范围) chāoyuè.

over·seas /ˌəʊvə'si:z/ *adj, adv* 外国的 wàiguóde; 海外的 hǎiwàide; 在外国 zài wàiguó; 在海外 zài hǎiwài.

over·see /ˌəʊvə'si:/ *vt* [*pt* -saw /-'sɔ:/; *pp* -seen /-'si:n/] 监〔監〕视 jiānshì; 监督(工作、工人) jiāndū. '**over·seer** 监工 jiāngōng.

over·shadow /ˌəʊvə'ʃædəʊ/ *vt* **1** 投下阴〔陰〕影 tóu xià yīnyǐng. **2** [喻]使相形见绌 shǐ xiāng xíng jiàn chù.

over·shoot /ˌəʊvə'ʃu:t/ *vt* [*pt, pp* -shot /-'ʃɒt/] 射过〔過〕头〔頭〕 shè guòtóu; 超过(目标、界线) chāoguò.

over·sight /'əʊvəsaɪt/ *n* [C,U] 失察 shīchá; 忽略 hūlüè.

over·step /ˌəʊvə'step/ *vt* [-pp-] 逾越 yúyuè; 超过〔過〕 yuèguò: ~ *one's authority* 越权.

overt /'əʊvɜ:t/ *adj* 公开〔開〕的 gōngkāide; 明显〔顯〕的 míngxiǎnde: ~ *hostility* 公然的敌意. ~**ly** *adv*

over·take /ˌəʊvə'teɪk/ *vt* [*pt* -took /-'tʊk/; *pp* -taken /-'teɪkən/] **1** 赶〔趕〕上 gǎnshàng; 超过〔過〕 chāoguò. **2** (指暴风雨、麻烦等)突然降临〔臨〕 tūrán jiànglín.

over·throw /ˌəʊvə'θrəʊ/ *vt* [*p* -threw /-'θru:/; *pp* -thrown /-'θrəʊn/] 击〔擊〕败 jībài; 推翻 tuīfān; 使毁灭〔滅〕 shǐ huǐmiè: ~ *the government* 推翻政府. □ /ˌəʊvə θrəʊ/ *n* [C]

over·time /'əʊvətaɪm/ *n* [U] *adv* *adj* 超过〔過〕规定的时〔時〕间〔間 chāoguò guīdìng de shíjiān; 加班的时间 jiābānde shíjiān.

over·ture /'əʊvətʃə(r)/ *n* [C] [常用 *pl*] 提议〔議〕 tíyì; 建议 jiànyì. **2** 序曲 xùqǔ.

over·whelm /ˌəʊvə'welm/ *vt* 压〔壓〕倒 yādǎo; 淹没 yānmò.

over·wrought /ˌəʊvə'rɔ:t/ *adj* 过〔過〕分劳〔勞〕累的 guòfèn láol de; 过度兴〔興〕奋〔奮〕的 guòd xīngfèn de.

ovum /'əʊvəm/ *n* [C] [*pl* ov /'əʊvə/] 卵子 luǎnzǐ; 卵细胞 luǎ xìbāo.

owe /əʊ/ *vt/i* **1** 欠(债等) qiàn: *Y* ~ *me* £*50*. 你欠我五十英镑. **2** 激 gǎnjī. **3** 由于 yóuyú: *I* ~ *success to hard work.* 我的成功由努力工作.

ow·ing /ˈəʊɪŋ/ *adj* 未付的 wèifùde. ～ *to prep* 由于 yóuyú.
owl /aʊl/ *n* [C] 猫头〔頭〕鹰〔鷹〕 māotóuyīng.
own[1] /əʊn/ *adj* 自己的 zìjǐde: *with my ～ eyes* 亲眼. **(all) on one's ～,** (a) 独〔獨〕自地 dúzìde. (b) 独立地 dúlìde. *get one's ˈ～ back* 报〔報〕仇 bàochóu. ˌ*hold one's ˈ～,* (a) 坚〔堅〕守住 jiānshǒuzhù. (b) 支撑 zhīcheng.
own[2] /əʊn/ *vt/i* 1 有 yǒu; 拥〔擁〕有 yōngyǒu: ～ *a house* 拥有一所房子. 2 ～ *ˈup (to sth)* 爽快承认〔認〕 shuǎngkuài chéngrèn. ～**er** *n* [C] ～**ership** 所有权〔權〕 suǒyǒuquán.
ox /ɒks/ *n* [C] [*pl* ～en /ˈɒksn/] 1 牛 niú. 2 公牛 gōngniú.
oxy·gen /ˈɒksɪdʒən/ *n* [U] 氧 yǎng, 氧气〔氣〕 yǎngqì. ˈ～ **mask** *n* 氧气〔氣〕面具 yǎngqì miànjù. ˈ～**tent** *n* 氧气帐〔帳〕(罩于需要加量氧气的病人身上的小帐幕) yǎngqìzhàng.
oy·ster /ˈɔɪstə(r)/ *n* [C] 蚝〔蠔〕háo; 牡蛎〔蠣〕 mǔlì ˈ～**-catcher** 蛎鹬〔鷸〕 lìyù.
oz. = ounces.

P p

P p /piː/ [*pl* P's, p's /piːz/] 英语的第十六个〔個〕字母 Yīngyǔ de dìshíliùgè zìmǔ.
P = (car) park.
p. = 1 page. 2 past. 3 (new) penny.
P.A. = personal assistant (*to*) 私人助理 sīrén zhùlǐ.
pace /peɪs/ *n* [C] 1 一步 yíbù. 2 (走或跑的) 速度 sùdù. *keep ～ (with)* [喻]同速前进〔進〕tóngsù qiánjìn; 并驾〔駕〕齐〔齊〕驱〔驅〕 bìng jià qí qū. ˈ～**maker** *n* 定步速者 dìng bùsù zhě; 带〔帶〕步人 dàibùrén. **artificial** ～**maker** *n* 电〔電〕子心脏〔臟〕定调器 (用以纠正微弱的心跳) diànzǐ xīnzàng dìngtiáoqì. ☐ *vt/i* 1 慢慢地走 mànmànde zǒu. 2 ～ *off* (或 *out*) 步测 bùcè. 3 定…的步伐 dìng...de bùfá.
paci·fism /ˈpæsɪfɪzəm/ *n* [U] 和平主义〔義〕 hépíng zhǔyì. **paci·fist** *n* [C]
pac·ify /ˈpæsɪfaɪ/ *vt* [*pt, pp* -ied] 1 抚〔撫〕慰 fǔwèi; 平静píngjìng. 2 平定 píngdìng; 绥靖 suíjìng. **paci·fi·ca·tion** /-fɪˈkeɪʃn/ *n* [U]
pack[1] /pæk/ *n* [C] 1 包裹 bāoguǒ; 捆 kǔn. 2 (猎犬等)一群 yìqún. 3 大量 dàliàng: *a ～ of lies* 连篇谎话. 4 一副纸牌 yífù zhǐpái. 5 [美语] = packet.
pack[2] /pæk/ *vt/i* 1 捆扎 kǔnzhā; 包装 bāozhuāng. ～ *up* [非正式用语] (a) 停止工作 tíngzhǐ gōngzuò. (b) (机器)出故障 chū gùzhàng. 2 ～ *into* 挤〔擠〕满 jǐmǎn. 3 填塞 tiánsāi; 装〔裝〕满 zhuāngmǎn. 4 ～ *sb off, send sb ～ing* 打发〔發〕走 dǎfa zuǒ; 解雇〔僱〕 jiěgù. 5 把(肉、水果等)装罐 bǎ zhuāngguàn.
pack·age /ˈpækɪdʒ/ *n* [C] 捆 kǔn; 束 sù; 包 bāo. ☐ *vt* 包装〔裝〕 bāozhuāng. ˌ～ ˈ**deal** [非正式用语]一揽〔攬〕子交易 yìlǎnzi jiāoyì. ˌ～ ˈ**holiday** (或 ˈ**tour**) 包办〔辦〕旅行 bāobàn lǚxíng.
packet /ˈpækɪt/ *n* [C] 小包 xiǎobāo; 小捆 xiǎokǔn: *a ～ of cigarettes* 一包香烟.
pack·ing /ˈpækɪŋ/ *n* [U] 1 包装〔裝〕 bāozhuāng; 打包 dǎbāo. 2 包装材料 bāozhuāng cáiliào.
pact /pækt/ *n* [C] 协〔協〕定 xiédìng.
pad /pæd/ *n* [C] 1 垫〔墊〕子 diànzi. 2 拍纸簿 pāizhǐbù. 3 = launching-pad. 4 (板球用的) 护〔護〕垫 hùdiàn. 5 (指狗等)爪垫 zhǎodiàn; 肉趾 ròuzhǐ ☐ *vt* [-dd-] 1 步行 bùxíng; 走路 zǒulù. 2 ～ *sth out* 拉长〔長〕(句子、书等) lācháng; 添凑〔湊〕 tiāncòu. ～**ding** *n* [U] 填塞的材料 tiánsāide cáiliào; 添凑语 tiāncòuyǔ.
paddle[1] /ˈpædl/ *n* [C] 短桨〔槳〕 duǎnjiǎng. ☐ *vt/i* 用桨划动〔動〕 yòng jiǎng huádòng. ˈ～**-steamer** 明轮〔輪〕船 mínglúnchuán.
paddle[2] /ˈpædl/ *vi* 涉水 shèshuǐ.
pad·dock /ˈpædək/ *n* [C] 围〔圍〕场〔場〕(尤指遛马的草地) wéichǎng.
paddy /ˈpædɪ/ *n* [U] 稻 dào. ˈ～**-field** 稻田 dàotián.
pad·lock /ˈpædlɒk/ *n* [C] 挂〔掛〕锁. guàsuǒ. ☐ *vt* (用挂锁)锁上 suǒshàng.
paedi·at·rics /ˌpiːdɪˈætrɪks/ ⇨ pediatrics.
pa·gan /ˈpeɪgən/ *n* [C], *adj* 异〔異〕教徒 yìjiàotú.
page[1] /peɪdʒ/ *n* [C] 1 页 yè. 2 一面 yímiàn.

page[2] /peɪʤ/ *n* [C] **1** (作 '~ *boy*) 小侍从〔從〕xiǎo shìcóng **2** (婚礼上的)男宾〔賓〕相 nán bīnxiàng.

pag·eant /'pæʤənt/ *n* [C] **1** 露天表演 lùtiān biǎoyǎn. **2** 庆〔慶〕典 qìngdiǎn **~ry** *n* [U] 壮〔壯〕观〔觀〕zhuàngguān.

pa·goda /pə'gəʊdə/ *n* [C] [*pl* ~s] (印度、中国等)宝〔寶〕塔 bǎotǎ; 塔式建筑〔築〕物 tǎshì jiànzhùwù.

paid /peɪd/ ⇨ pay[2].

pail /peɪl/ *n* [C] 桶 tǒng.

pain /peɪn/ *n* **1** [U] 痛苦 tòngkǔ. **2** [C] (身体上的)痛 tòng. □ *vt* 使痛 shǐ tòng; 使痛苦 shǐ tòngkǔ. **~ed** *adj* 痛苦的 tòngkǔde: *a ~ed look* 一副痛苦相. **~ful** *adj* 使痛的 shǐ tòngde; 使痛苦的 shǐ tòngkǔde. **~less** *adj* 不痛的 bútòngde.

pains /peɪnz/ *n pl* 辛苦 xīnkǔ. ***be at ~ to do sth, take (great) ~ to do sth*** 尽〔盡〕力去做 jìnlì qù zuò. '**~taking** *adj* 极〔極〕小心的 jí xiǎoxīn de.

paint /peɪnt/ *n* **1** [U] 油漆 yóuqī; 涂〔塗〕料 túliào: *a coat of ~* 一层油漆. **2** [*pl*] (一套)颜料 yánliào. □ *vt/i* **1** 油漆 yóuqī; 着色 zhuósè. **2** 画〔畫〕huà; 绘〔繪〕画 huìhuà. ***~ the town red*** 狂欢〔歡〕kuánghuān. **~ing, (a)** [U] 绘画 huìhuà. **(b)** [C] 油画 yóuhuà; 画 huà.

painter /'peɪntə(r)/ *n* [C] **1** 画〔畫〕家 huàjiā; 绘〔繪〕画者 huìhuàzhě. **2** 油漆工 yóuqīgōng.

pair /peə(r)/ *n* [C] **1** 一双〔雙〕yìshuāng; 一对〔對〕yíduì: *a ~ of shoes* 一双鞋. **2** 一把 yìbǎ; 一条〔條〕yìtiáo; 一副 yífù: *a ~ of trousers* 一条裤子. **3** 两个〔個〕关〔關〕系〔係〕密切的人(如已婚夫妇) liǎnggè guānxi mìqiè de rén. □ *vt/i* 成对 chéngduì; 结婚 jiéhūn; 交配 jiāopèi.

pa·ja·mas /pə'ʤɑːməz/ *n pl* ⇨ pyjamas.

pal /pæl/ *n* [C] [非正式用语]朋友 péngyǒu.

pal·ace /'pælɪs/ *n* [C] **1** 官邸 guāndǐ; 宫殿 gōngdiàn. **2** 华〔華〕丽〔麗〕建筑〔築〕物 huálì jiànzhùwù.

pal·at·able /'pælətəbl/ *adj* **1** 可口的 kěkǒude; 美味的 měiwèide. **2** [喻]惬意的 qièyìde.

pal·ate /'pælət/ *n* [C] **1** 腭〔齶〕è. **2** 味觉〔覺〕wèijué.

pa·la·tial /pə'leɪʃl/ *adj* 象宫殿的 xiàng gōngdiàn de; 壮〔壯〕丽〔麗〕的 zhuànglìde.

pale[1] /peɪl/ *adj* [-r, -st] **1** (脸色)苍〔蒼〕白的 cāngbáide. **2** (颜色)暗淡的 àndànde. □ *vi* 失色 shīsè; 变〔變〕苍白 biàn cāngbái. **~ness** *n* [U]

pale[2] /peɪl/ *n* [C] (做栅栏用的)桩〔樁〕zhuāng; 栅栏〔欄〕zhàlan.

pal·ette /'pælɪt/ *n* [C] 调色板 tiáosèbǎn.

pal·ing /'peɪlɪŋ/ *n* [C,U] 木栅 mùzhà; 围〔圍〕篱〔籬〕wéilí.

pall[1] /pɔːl/ *n* [C] **1** 柩衣 jiùyī. **2** [喻](阴暗色的)遮盖物 zhēgàiwù: *a ~ of smoke* 一片浓烟. '**~bearer** (丧礼中)抬棺材的人 tái guāncái de rén.

pall[2] /pɔːl/ *vi* 厌〔厭〕倦 yànjuàn; 乏味 fáwèi.

pal·lid /'pælɪd/ *adj* 苍〔蒼〕白的 cāngbáide; 病状〔狀〕的 bìngzhuàngde. **pal·lor** /'pælə(r)/ *n* [U]

palm[1] /pɑːm/ *n* [C] 手掌 shǒuzhǎng; 手心 shǒuxīn. □ *vt* 藏(硬币、纸牌等)于掌中 cáng yú zhǎngzhōng. ***~ sth off (on sb)*** (用欺骗手段)把…硬塞给(或卖给) bǎ... yìng sāigěi.

palm[2] /pɑːm/ *n* [C] 棕榈〔櫚〕zōnglǘ; 棕榈树〔樹〕zōnglǘshù.

palm·ist /'pɑːmɪst/ *n* [C] 手相家 shǒuxiàngjiā. **~ry** *n* [U]

pal·pi·tate /'pælpɪteɪt/ *vi* **1** (指心脏)急速地跳动〔動〕jísùde tiàodòng. **2** (指人)颤抖 chàndǒu. **pal·pi·ta·tion** /-ʃn/ *n* [C,U]

pam·per /'pæmpə(r)/ *vt* 纵〔縱〕容 zòngróng; 娇〔嬌〕养〔養〕jiāoyǎng: *~ one's pet dog* 娇惯宠爱的狗.

pamph·let /'pæmflɪt/ *n* [C] 小册子 xiǎocèzi.

pan[1] /pæn/ *n* [C] **1** 平底锅〔鍋〕píngdǐguō. **2** 盘状器皿 pánzhuàng qìmǐn: *a 'bed~* 便盆. **3** 淘盘〔盤〕táopán. □ *vt/i* [-nn-] ~ ***out***, **(a)** 淘金 táojīn; 产〔產〕金 chǎnjīn. **(b)** [喻]成功 chénggōng: *How di[d] things ~ out?* 事情的结果怎么样? '**~cake** 薄煎饼 bójiānbǐng.

pan[2] /pæn/ *vt/i* (电影、电视)摇镜头〔頭〕yáo jìngtóu; 拍摄〔攝〕全景 pāishè quánjǐng. ⇨ zoom(2).

pan·creas /'pæŋkrɪəs/ *n* [C] 胰 yí; 胰腺 yíxiàn.

panda /'pændə/ *n* [C] [*pl* ~s] 熊猫 xióngmāo.

pan·de·mo·nium /ˌpændɪ'məʊnɪəm/ *n* [C,U] [*pl* ~s] 大混乱〔亂〕dà hùnluàn.

pan·der /'pændə(r)/ *vi* ~ ***to*** 迎合 yínghé; 怂〔慫〕恿 sǒngyǒng: *~ all his desires* 满足他的全部愿望.

pane /peɪn/ *n* [C] (窗上的)单〔單〕块〔塊〕玻璃 dānkuài bōli.

panel /'pænl/ *n* [C] **1** 镶板 xiāngbǎn; 嵌板 qiànbǎn. **2** 控制板 kòngzhìbǎn; 操纵〔縱〕盘〔盤〕cāozòngpán. **3** (广播、电视中)座谈小组 zuòtán xiǎozǔ; 答问〔問〕小组 dáwèn xiǎozǔ. □ *vt* [-ll-, *US* -l-] 镶板于 xiāngbǎn yú. **~ling** (墙壁等的)镶板 xiāngbǎn.

pang /pæŋ/ *n* [C] 一阵〔陣〕剧痛 yízhèn jùtòng; 悲痛 bēitòng.

panic /'pænɪk/ *n* [C,U] 惊〔驚〕慌 jīnghuāng; 恐慌 kǒnghuāng. □ *vi* [-ck-] 受惊 shòujīng; 惊慌 jīnghuāng. **~ky** *adj* [非正式用语]容易受惊的 róngyì shòujīng de. **'~-stricken** *adj* 惊慌失措的 jīnghuāng shīcuò de.

pan·nier /'pænɪə(r)/ *n* [C] 驮〔馱〕篮〔籃〕tuólán; 背篓〔簍〕bēilǒu.

pan·or·ama /ˌpænə'rɑːmə/ *n* [C] [*pl* ~s] 全景 quánjǐng. **pan·or·amic** /-'ræmɪk/ *adj*

pansy /'pænzɪ/ *n* [C] [*pl* -ies] 三色紫罗〔羅〕兰〔蘭〕sānsè zǐluólán.

pant /pænt/ *vt/i* **1** 气〔氣〕喘 qìchuǎn; 喘息 chuǎnxī. **2** 气喘吁吁地说 qìchuǎn xūxū de shuō. □ *n* [C] 气喘 qìchuǎn.

pan·ther /'pænθə(r)/ *n* [C] 豹 bào; 美洲狮〔獅〕Měizhōushī.

pan·ties /'pæntɪz/ *n pl* [非正式用语](妇女穿的)紧〔緊〕身短裤〔褲〕jǐnshēng duǎnkù.

pan·to·mime /'pæntəmaɪm/ *n* **1** [C,U] 哑〔啞〕剧〔劇〕yǎjù. **2** [U] 手势〔勢〕shǒushì.

pan·try /'pæntrɪ/ *n* [C] [*pl* -ies] **1** 餐具室 cānjùshì. **2** 食品室 shípǐnshì; 备〔備〕餐室 bèicānshì.

pants /pænts/ *n pl* **1** 内裤〔褲〕nèikù. **2** (尤指美语)裤子 kùzi.

papa /pə'pɑː/ *n* [C] (儿语)爸爸 bàba.

pa·pacy /'peɪpəsɪ/ *n* [C] [*pl* -ies] 罗〔羅〕马〔馬〕教皇的职〔職〕位 luómǎ jiàohuáng de zhíwèi.

pa·pal /'peɪpl/ *adj* 罗〔羅〕马〔馬〕教皇的 luómǎ jiàohuáng de.

pa·per /'peɪpə(r)/ *n* **1** [U] 纸 zhǐ. **2** [C] 报〔報〕纸 bàozhǐ. **3** [*pl*] 文件 wénjiàn. **4** [C] 考卷 kǎojuàn. □ *vt* 用纸裱糊 yòng zhǐ biǎohú: ~ *a room* 用纸裱糊房间. **'~back** 纸皮书〔書〕zhǐpíshū; 平装〔裝〕本 píngzhuāngběn. **'~clip** ⇨ clip[1].

pap·rika /'pæprɪkə/ *n* [U] 红辣椒 hónglàjiāo.

par /pɑː(r)/ *n* [U] **1** 平均数〔數〕量 píngjūn shùliàng; 一般标〔標〕准〔準〕yìbān biāozhǔn; 票面价〔價〕值 piàomiàn jiàzhí. *on a ~ with* 同等 tóngděng. **2** (高尔夫球)标准打数 biāozhǔn dǎshù.

par. = paragraph.

par·able /'pærəbl/ *n* [C] 寓言 yùyán; 比喻 bǐyù.

para·chute /'pærəʃuːt/ *n* [C] 降落伞〔傘〕jiàngluòsǎn. □ *vt/i* 用降落伞降落 yòng jiàngluòsǎn jiàngluò. **para·chut·ist** 跳伞者 tiàosǎnzhě; 伞兵 sǎnbīng.

par·ade /pə'reɪd/ *vt/i* **1** (为阅兵)整队〔隊〕zhěngduì. **2** 列队行进〔進〕lièduì xíngjìn; 游行 yóuxíng. **3** 夸〔誇〕耀 kuāyào; 炫示 xuánshì: ~ *one's wealth* 夸耀个人的财富. □ *n* [C,U] 行列 hángliè; 阅〔閱〕兵 yuèbīng.

para·dise /'pærədaɪs/ *n* **1** 天国〔國〕tiānguó. **2** 乐〔樂〕园〔園〕lèyuán; 极〔極〕乐 jílè.

para·dox /'pærədɒks/ *n* [C] 似非而是的论〔論〕点〔點〕sì fēi ér shì de lùndiǎn; 反论 fǎnlùn. **~i·cal** /-'dɒksɪkl/ *adj* **~i·cally** *adv*

par·af·fin /'pærəfɪn/ *n* [U] 石腊〔臘〕油 shílàyóu; 煤油 méiyóu. [美语 = *kerosene*].

para·graph /'pærəgrɑːf/ *n* [C] 段 duàn; 节〔節〕jié. □ *vt* 分段 fēnduàn.

para·keet /'pærəkiːt/ *n* [C] 长〔長〕尾小鹦〔鸚〕鹉〔鵡〕chángwěi xiǎoyīngwǔ.

par·al·lel /'pærəlel/ *adj* **1** 平行的 píngxíngde. **2** [喻]相当〔當〕的 xiāngdāngde: *a ~ job abroad* 国外相当的工作. □ *n* [C] **1** 类〔類〕似的人或事 lèisìde rén huò shì. **2** 比较〔較〕bǐjiào: *draw a ~ between* 在…之间作比较. □ *vt* [-l- 或 -ll-] 与〔與〕…相似 yǔ...xiāngsì: *His success ~s mine.* 他和我同样成功.

par·al·ysis /pə'ræləsɪs/ *n* [U] **1** 麻痹〔痺〕mábì; 瘫〔癱〕痪 tānhuàn. **2** [喻]完全无〔無〕力 wánquán wúlì. **para·lyt·ic** /ˌpærə'lɪtɪk/ *adj* **(a)** 麻痹的 mábìde; 瘫痪的 tānhuànde. **(b)** [喻]无〔無〕力的 wúlìde; 无助的 wúzhùde: *paralytic laughter* 不能自已的笑声. **(c)** [非正式用语]酩酊大醉 mǐngdǐng dàzuì. □ *n* [C] 麻痹的病人 mábì de bìngrén.

para·lyse [美语 =-lyze] /'pærəlaɪz/ *vt* **1** 使麻痹〔痺〕shǐ mábì; 使瘫〔癱〕痪 shǐ tānhuàn. **2** [喻]使无〔無〕力 shǐ wúlì: *~d with laughter* 笑得发呆.

para·mount /'pærəmaʊnt/ *adj* [正式用语]最高的 zuìgāode; 首要的

shǒuyàode: *of ~ importance* 最重要的.

para·noia /ˌpærəˈnɔɪə/ *n* [U] 妄想狂 wàngxiǎngkuáng; 偏执〔執〕狂 piānzhíkuáng. **para·noid** /ˈpærənɔɪd/ *n* [C], *adj* 患妄想狂的人 huàn wàngxiǎngkuáng de rén; 患妄想狂的 huàn wàngxiǎngkuángde.

para·pet /ˈpærəpɪt/ *n* [C] (屋顶、桥梁等边缘的)栏〔欄〕杆 lángān; 扶墙〔牆〕fúqiáng.

para·pher·nalia /ˌpærəfəˈneɪlɪə/ *n* [U] 随身用具 suíshēng yòngjù.

para·phrase /ˈpærəfreɪz/ *vt, n* [C] 释〔釋〕义〔義〕shìyì; 意译 yìyì.

para·site /ˈpærəsaɪt/ *n* [C] **1** 寄生虫〔蟲〕jìshēngchóng; 寄生植物 jìshēng zhíwù. **2** [喻]靠他人为〔爲〕生的人 kào tārén wéishēng de rén. **para·sitic** /ˌpærəˈsɪtɪk/ *adj*

para·sol /ˈpærəsɒl/ *n* [C] 阳〔陽〕伞〔傘〕yángsǎn.

para·troops /ˈpærətru:ps/ *n pl* 伞〔傘〕兵部队〔隊〕sǎnbīng bùduì. **para·trooper** *n* [C]

par·cel /ˈpɑ:sl/ *n* [C] 包 bāo; 包裹 bāoguǒ. □ *vt* [-ll-, 美语亦作 -l-] **1** *~ out* 分成数〔數〕分 fēn chéng shùfèn. **2** *~ up* 打包 dǎbāo; 捆扎 kǔnzhā.

parch /pɑ:tʃ/ *vt* 使干透 shǐ gāntòu; 烘 hōng; 烤 kǎo.

parch·ment /ˈpɑ:tʃmənt/ *n* **1** [C, U] 羊皮纸 yángpízhǐ. **2** [U] (羊皮纸似的)上等纸 shàngděngzhǐ.

par·don /ˈpɑ:dn/ *n* **1** [C,U] 原谅 yuánliàng; 宽恕 kuānshù. ***I beg your ~*** 对〔對〕不起 duìbùqǐ; 抱歉(不同意对方意见) bàoqiàn; 没听〔聽〕清楚,请再说一遍 méi tīng qīngchu, qǐng zàishuō yíbiàn. **2** 赦免 shèmiǎn. □ *vt* 原谅 yuánliàng; 饶〔饒〕恕 ráoshù.

pare /peə(r)/ *vt* **1** 剥 bō; 削 xiāo; 剥去(外皮) bōqù.

par·ent /ˈpeərənt/ *n* [C] 父母亲〔親〕fùmǔqīn; 双亲 shuāngqīn. **~al** /pəˈrentl/ *adj*

par·enth·esis /pəˈrenθəsɪs/ *n* [C] [*pl* -eses /-əsi:z/] **1** 插句 chājù; 插入语 chārùyǔ. **2** 圆括号〔號〕yuánkuòhào.

par·ish /ˈpærɪʃ/ *n* [C] 教区〔區〕jiàoqū. **~ioner** /pəˈrɪʃənə(r)/ *n* [C]

park /pɑ:k/ *n* [C] **1** 公园〔園〕gōngyuán. **2** (乡村别墅四围的)园林 yuánlín. ⇨ car park. □ *vt/i* 停放(车辆等) tíngfàng.

par·lia·ment /ˈpɑ:ləmənt/ *n* [C] 国〔國〕会〔會〕guóhuì; 议〔議〕会 yìhuì. **~ary** /-ˈmentrɪ/ *adj*

par·lour /ˈpɑ:lə(r)/ *n* [C] [过时用法]客厅〔廳〕kètīng; 会〔會〕客室 huìkèshì.

par·ochial /pəˈrəʊkɪəl/ *adj* **1** 教区〔區〕的 jiàoqūde. **2** [喻]有限的 yǒuxiànde; 狭〔狹〕小的 xiáxiǎode: *a ~ mind* 思想狭隘. **~ly** *adv*

par·ody /ˈpærədɪ/ *n* [*pl* -ies] **1** [C,U] 模仿滑稽作品 mófǎng huájī zuòpǐn. **2** [C] 拙劣的模仿 zhuōliède mófǎng: *a ~ of justice* 假装公正. □ *vt* [*pt, pp* -ied] 拙劣地模仿 zhuōliède mófǎng.

pa·role /pəˈrəʊl/ *n* [U] *on ~* 有条〔條〕件的释〔釋〕放 yǒutiáojiànde shìfàng; 假释 jiǎshì. □ *vt* 使(俘虏)宣誓后〔後〕释放 shǐ xuānshì hòu shìfàng; 假释 jiǎshì.

par·rot /ˈpærət/ *n* [C] 鹦〔鸚〕鹉〔鵡〕yīngwǔ. □ *vt/i* 鹦鹉学〔學〕舌般地复述 yīngwǔ xuéshébānde fùshù.

parry /ˈpærɪ/ *vt* [*pt, pp* -ied] 挡〔擋〕开〔開〕dǎngkāi; 回避 huíbì. □ *n* [C] 挡开 dǎngkāi; 回避 huíbì.

pars·ley /ˈpɑ:slɪ/ *n* [U] [植物]芫荽 yánsuī; 香菜 xiāngcài.

pars·nip /ˈpɑ:snɪp/ *n* [C] 防风〔風〕草根(可做蔬菜食用) fángfēngcǎogēn.

par·son /ˈpɑ:sn/ *n* [C] 教区〔區〕牧师〔師〕jiàoqū mùshī. **ˈ~age** (教区)牧师住所 mùshī zhùsuǒ.

part¹ /pɑ:t/ *n* [C] **1** 部分 bùfen; 局部 júbù. ***for the ˈmost ~*** ⇨ most(1). ***in ~*** 一部分 yíbùfen. **2** [*pl*] 地区〔區〕dìqū; 区域 qūyù. **3** …分之一 … fēn zhī yī; 等分 děngfen. **4** 职〔職〕责 zhízé; (剧中的)角色 juésè. ***play one's ~*** 尽〔盡〕本分 jìn běnfen. ***take ~ (in)*** 参加 cānjiā. **5** (争论中的)一方 yìfāng. ***take sb's ~*** 站在某人一方 zhàn zài mǒurén yìfāng. ***for ˈmy ~*** 就我来说 jiù wǒ lái shuō. **6** [音乐]音部 yīnbù; 乐〔樂〕曲的一部分 yuèqǔde yíbùfen. **7** 部件 bùjiàn; 组件 zǔjiàn: *spare ~s* 备用零件. □ *adv* 部分地 bùfende. **ˌ~-ˈtime** *adj* 非全日的 fēi quánrìde. **ˌ~ of ˈspeech** 词类〔類〕(如名词、动词、形容词等) cílèi.

part² /pɑ:t/ *vt/i* **1** 分开〔開〕fēnkāi; 分离〔離〕fēnlí: *the clouds ~ed* 云露出缝隙. *~ two boxers.* 把两名拳击者分开. ***~ company (with)***, **(a)** 各自东〔東〕西 gè zì dōng xī. **(b)** 意见不合 yìjiàn bùhé. **2** 放弃〔棄〕fàngqì; 离〔離〕开 líkāi: *~ with money* 花钱. **~ing** *n* **(a)** [C] (头发的)分缝 fēnfèng. **(b)** [C, U

分别 fēnbié; 离开 líkāi. ~**ly** *adv* 部分地 bùfende.

par·take /pɑ:ˈteɪk/ *vt/i* [*pt* -took /-ˈtʊk/; *pp* -taken/-ˈteɪkən/] [正式用语] *~of* (或 *in*) *sth* 参加 cānjiā; 参与〔與〕cānyǔ; 分享 fēnxiǎng.

par·tial /ˈpɑ:ʃl/ *adj* **1** 不完全的 bù wánquán de; 部分的 bùfende: *a ~ success* 部分成功. **2** ~ (*towards*) 偏袒的 piāntǎnde. **3** ~ *to* 偏爱〔愛〕的 piān'àide. ~**ly** *adv* **(a)** 部分地 bùfende; 不完全地 bù wánquán de. **(b)** 偏袒地 piāntǎnde. ~**ity** /-ˈælətɪ/ *n* **(a)** [U] 偏袒 piāntǎn. **(b)** [C] 喜爱 xǐ'ài.

par·tici·pate /pɑ:ˈtɪsɪpeɪt/ *vi* ~ (*in*) 参与〔與〕cānyù; 分享 fēnxiǎng. **par·tici·pant** 参与者 cānyùzhě; 共享者 gòngxiǎngzhě.

par·ti·ciple /ˈpɑ:tɪsɪpl/ *n* [C] 分词 fēncí: *'Hurrying' and 'hurried' are the present and past ~s of 'hurry'.* *Hurrying* 和 *hurried* 是 *hurry* 的现在分词和过去分词.

par·ticle /ˈpɑ:tɪkl/ *n* [C] **1** 粒子 lìzǐ; 微粒 wēilì: *~s of dust.* 尘埃. **2** [语法]小品词 xiǎopǐncí; 不变〔變〕词(如 *a, an, the*) búbiàncí.

par·ticu·lar /pəˈtɪkjʊlə(r)/ *adj* **1** 独〔獨〕特的 dútède: *in this ~ case* 在这种特殊情况下. **2** 特殊的 tèshūde; 特别的 tèbiéde: *of ~ interest* 特殊的兴趣. *in ~* 特别 tèbié; 尤其 yóuqí. **3** ~ (*about, over*) 讲〔講〕究的 jiǎngjiude; 挑剔的 tiāotìde. □ *n* [C] 细节〔節〕xìjié. ~**ly** *adv* 特别 tèbié; 尤其 yóuqí.

par·ti·san /ˌpɑ:tɪˈzæn/ *adj, n* [C] 党〔黨〕人 dǎngrén; 敌〔敵〕后〔後〕游击〔擊〕队〔隊〕员 díhòu yóujī duìyuán.

par·ti·tion /pɑ:ˈtɪʃn/ *n* **1** [U] 分开〔開〕fēnkāi; 分割 fēngé. **2** [C] 隔开物 gékāiwù; 隔墙〔牆〕géqiáng. □ *vt* ~ (*sth off*) 隔开 gékāi.

part·ner /ˈpɑ:tnə(r)/ *n* [C] **1** 合伙者 héhuǒzhě. **2** 舞伴 wǔbàn; (打网球等的)搭挡〔擋〕dādàng. **3** 夫或妻 fū huò qī. □ *vt* 同…合作 tóng…hézuò; 做…的伙〔夥〕伴 zuò…de huǒbàn. '~**ship** **(a)** [U] 合股 hégǔ; 合伙〔夥〕héhuǒ. **(b)** [C] 合股经〔經〕营〔營〕的商业〔業〕hégǔ jīngyíng de shāngyè.

par·took /pɑ:ˈtʊk/ ⇨ partake.

par·tridge /ˈpɑ:trɪdʒ/ *n* [C] 鹧〔鷓〕鸪〔鴣〕zhègū; [U] 鹧鸪肉 zhègūròu.

party /ˈpɑ:tɪ/ *n* [C] [*pl* -ies] **1** 党〔黨〕派 dǎngpài; 政党 zhèngdǎng: *the Labour ~* 工党. **2** (契约或争论的)一方 yìfāng; 当〔當〕事人 dāngshìrén. **3** (参加共同活动的)一组 yìzǔ, 一伙〔夥〕人 yìhuǒrén: *a ~ of tourists* 旅游团. **4** 聚会〔會〕jùhuì: *a birthday ~* 生日宴会. **5** 参与〔與〕者 cānyùzhě; 关〔關〕系人 guānxìrén: *be ~ to a decision* 参与决定.

pass¹ /pɑ:s/ *n* **1** [C] 穿过〔過〕chuānguò; 经〔經〕过 jīngguò. **2** [C] 及格 jígé; 考试通过 kǎoshì tōngguò. **3** [C] 通行证 tōngxíngzhéng; 入场〔場〕券 rùchǎngjuàn. **4** [C] 传〔傳〕球 chuánqiú. **5** [C] 关〔關〕口 guānkǒu. **6** *make a ~ at* (*a woman*) [俚语]勾引女性 gōuyǐn nǚxìng. '~**word** 口令 kǒulìng.

pass² /pɑ:s/ *vt/i* (比较 past¹) **1** 穿过〔過〕chuānguò; 通过 tōngguò (与 *along, through, down* 等连用): *~ through a village* 穿过村庄. *The two ships ~ed each other.* 两船相会, 背向而驶. **2** 经过 jīngguò: *Turn right after ~ing the post office.* 经过邮局后向右转. **3** 传〔傳〕递〔遞〕chuándì: *Please ~ (me) the butter.* 请把黄油递给我. **4** 过去 guòqù: *Six months ~ed.* 六个月过去了. **5** 消磨(时间) xiāomó: *How shall we ~ the evening?* 我们将怎样消磨今晚的时间? *~ the time of day with* 寒暄 hánxuān. **6** 说出 shuōchū: *~ a comment* 发表评论. **7** 通过(考试、检查等) tōngguò: *~ an examination* 考试及格. **8** 宣布(判决等) xuānbù; 表示(意见等) biǎoshì: *~ sentence on a prisoner* 判处犯人. **9** 使行进〔進〕shǐ xíngjìn: *He ~ed his fingers through his hair.* 他用手指拢头发. ~ *water* 小便 xiǎobiàn. **10** 传(球) chuán. **11** ~ *away* 死 sǐ; 逝世 shìshì. ~ *sb* (或 *sth*) *by* 忽视 hūshì. ~ *for sb* (或 *sth*) 被认〔認〕为〔爲〕bèi rènwéi: *He could ~ for a Frenchman.* 他可能被当成法国人. ~ *off* (事件等)发〔發〕生 fāshēng. ~ *sth off* 把注意力从〔從〕…转〔轉〕移他处〔處〕bǎ zhùyìlì cóng…zhuǎnyí tāchù. ~ *sth* (或 *sb*) *off as* 冒充 màochōng: *He ~ed the boy off as his son.* 他把这男孩子冒充他的儿子. ~ *on* 去世 qùshì. ~ *sth on* (*to*) 把(某物)交给(别人) bǎ jiāogěi. ~ *out* [非正式用语]=faint. ~ *over* 忽略 hūluè; 不注意 bú zhùyì. ~ *sth up* [非正式用语]拒绝(机会等) jùjué.

pass·able /ˈpɑ:səbl/ *adj* **1** (指道路等) 可通行的 kě tōngxíngde. 2 尚可的 shàngkěde; 过〔過〕得去的 guòdeqùde. **pass·ably** *adv*

pas·sage /'pæsɪdʒ/ *n* **1** [U] 通过〔過〕tōngguò; 经〔經〕过 jīngguò: *the ~ of time* 时间的推移. **2** [C] 航行 hángxíng. **3** [C] 通路 tōnglù. **4** [C] 走廊 zǒuláng. **5** [C] 一段 yíduàn; 一节〔節〕yìjié.

pas·sen·ger /'pæsɪndʒə(r)/ *n* [C] 乘客 chéngkè; 旅客 lǚkè.

passion /'pæʃn/ *n* [C,U] 激情 jīqíng; 强烈的情感 qiángliède qínggǎn. **the P~** (十字架上)耶稣的受难 Yēsūde shòunàn. **~ate** *adj* **~ate·ly** *adv*

pass·ive /'pæsɪv/ *adj* **1** 被动〔動〕的 bèidòngde; 消极〔極〕的 xiāojíde. **2** [语法]被动语态〔態〕bèidòng yǔtài. **the ~ (voice)** [语法]被动语态(如 'The letter *was written* yesterday.' 句中的 was written 就是被动语态) bèidòng yǔtài. **~ly** *adv* **~ness** *n* [U]

Pass·over /'pɑ:səʊvə(r)/ *n* 逾〔踰〕越节〔節〕(犹太人的宗教节日) yúyuèjié.

pass·port /'pɑ:spɔ:t/ *n* [C] **1** 护〔護〕照 hùzhào. **2** [喻]获〔獲〕得允准的手段 huòde yǔnzhǔn de shǒuduàn: *a ~ to success* 获得成功的保证.

pass·word ⇨ pass[1].

past[1] /pɑ:st/ *adj* 过〔過〕去的 guòqùde; 刚〔剛〕过去的 gāng guòqù de. □ *n* **1** (与 *the* 连用)过去 guòqù; 昔日 xīrì. **2** 往事 wǎngshì; 经〔經〕历〔歷〕jīnglì. **~ participle** [语法] ⇨ participle. **~ tense** [语法] ⇨ tense.[2]

past[2] /pɑ:st/ *prep* **1** (指时间)过〔過〕guò: *half ~ two* 两点半钟. **2** (在空间上)超过 chāoguò: *He walked ~ the house.* 他走过那间屋子. **3** 超过…的限制或权〔權〕力 chāoguò...de xiànzhì huò quánlì: *pain almost ~ bearing* 疼痛难忍. □ *adv* 过 guò: *go ~* 走过去.

pasta /'pæstə/ *n* [U] [意大利语] 干〔乾〕面〔麵〕食 gānmiànshi.

paste /peɪst/ *n* [U] **1** (做点心等用的)加油脂的面〔麵〕团〔團〕jiā yóuzhīde miàntuán. **2** 糊 hú; 酱〔醬〕jiàng. **3** 浆〔漿〕糊 jiànghú. □ *vi* (用浆糊)粘贴 zhāntiē.

pas·tel /'pæstl/ *n* [C] **1** 彩色粉笔 cǎisè fěnbǐ; 彩色腊〔臘〕笔 cǎisè làbǐ. **2** [用作定语]轻〔輕〕淡优〔優〕美的色彩 qīngdàn yōuměi de sècǎi.

pas·teur·ize /'pæstʃəraɪz/ *vt* 用巴斯德法对(牛奶等)消毒 yòng Bāsīdéfǎ duì...xiāodú. **pas·teur·iz·ation** /-'zeɪʃn/ *n* [U]

pas·tille /'pæstɪl/ *n* [C] 香锭 xiāngdìng; 锭剂〔劑〕dìngjì.

pas·time /'pɑ:staɪm/ *n* [C] 消遣 xiāoqiǎn; 娱乐〔樂〕yúlè.

pas·tor /'pɑ:stə(r)/ *n* [C] 牧师〔師〕mùshi.

pas·try /'peɪstrɪ/ *n* [*pl* -ies] **1** [U] (用油脂和面烤成的)点〔點〕心 diǎnxīn. **2** [C] 面〔麵〕粉制〔製〕的糕点 miànfěn zhì de gāodiǎn.

pas·ture /'pɑ:stʃə(r)/ *n* [C,U] 牧场〔場〕mùchǎng. □ *vt/i* **1** 放牧 fàngmù. **2** (牛等)吃草 chī cǎo.

pasty[1] /'peɪstɪ/ *adj* 面〔麵〕团〔團〕似的 miàntuánsìde.

pasty[2] /'pæstɪ/ *n* [C] [*pl* -ies] 肉馅饼 ròuxiànbǐng; 馅饼 xiànbǐng.

pat /pæt/ *vt/i* [-tt-] 轻〔輕〕拍 qīngpāi; 轻打 qīngdǎ. □ *n* [C] **1** 轻拍 qīngpāi. **2** (黄油等的)小块〔塊〕xiǎokuài.

patch /pætʃ/ *n* [C] **1** 补〔補〕钉 bǔding **2** (保护受伤眼睛的)眼罩 yǎnzhào. **3** (与周围颜色不同的)斑片 bānpiàn. **4** 小块〔塊〕土地 xiǎokuài tǔdì: *a ~ of ground* 一小块地. *not a ~ on* 远〔遠〕不如 yuǎn bù rú; 比不上… bǐ bú shàng... □ *vt* 补缀 bǔzhuì. **~ up** 修补 xiūbǔ. **~ up a quarrel** 平息一场〔場〕争吵 píngxī yìchǎng zhēngchǎo. **patchy** *adj* [-ier, -iest] 质地不均匀的 zhìdì bù jūnyún de. **~work** *n* [U] **(a)** 缝缀起来的各色布片 féngzhuì qǐlái de gèsè bùpiàn. **(b)** [喻] 拼凑的东〔東〕西 pīncòude dōngxi.

pâté /'pæteɪ/ *n* [U] 肉酱〔醬〕ròujiàng; 鱼酱 yújiàng.

pat·ent[1] /'peɪtnt/ *adj* **1** 明显〔顯〕的 míngxiǎnde. **2** 专〔專〕利的 zhuānlìde. **~ leather** 漆皮 qīpí. **~ly** *adv* 明显地 míngxiǎnde.

pat·ent[2] /'peɪtnt/ *n* [C] **1** 专〔專〕利 zhuānlì; 专利权〔權〕zhuānlìquán. **2** 专利品 zhuānlìpǐn. □ *vt* 取得…的专〔專〕利权〔權〕qǔde ...de zhuānlìquán.

pa·ter·nal /pə'tɜ:nl/ *adj* **1** 父亲〔親〕的 fùqīnde; 象父亲的 xiàng fùqīnde. **2** 父方的亲属〔屬〕fùfāngde qīnshǔ: *my ~ grandfather* 我的祖父. **~ly** *adv*

pa·ter·nity /pə'tɜ:nətɪ/ *n* [U] **1** 父系 fùxì. **2** 父系后〔後〕裔 fùxì hòuyì.

path /pɑ:θ/ *n* [C] [*pl* ~s /pɑ:ðz/] **1** 小路 xiǎolù; 小径〔徑〕xiǎojìng. ⇨ footpath. **2** 跑道 pǎodào; 轨〔軌〕道 guǐdào. '**~way** = path

(1)

pa·thetic /pə'θetɪk/ *adj* **1** 可怜[憐]的 kěliánde: *a ~ sight* 悲惨的景象. **2** 不适[適]当[當]的 bú shìdāng de: *a ~ attempt* 不适当的打算. **~ally** *adv*

pa·thol·ogy /pə'θɒlədʒɪ/ *n* [U] 病理学[學] bìnglǐxué. **pa'th·ol·ogist** *n* [C] **(a)** 病理学家 bìnglǐxuéjiā. **(b)** 研究病理学者 yánjiū bìnglǐxué zhě.

pa·thos /'peɪθɒs/ *n* [U] 引起怜[憐]悯[憫]的因素 yǐnqǐ liánmǐnde yīnsù.

pa·tience /'peɪʃns/ *n* [U] **1** 容忍 róngrěn; 忍耐 rěnnài. **2** 忍耐力 rěnnàilì. **3** [英国英语][美语=solitaire]单[單]人纸牌戏[戲] dānrén zhǐpáixì.

pa·tient¹ /'peɪʃnt/ *adj* 有耐性的 yǒu nàixìng de; 容忍的 róngrěnde. **~ly** *adv*

pa·tient² /'peɪʃnt/ *n* [C] 病人 bìngrén.

patio /'pætɪəʊ/ *n* [C] [*pl* ~s] 天井 tiānjǐng; 内院 nèiyuàn.

pa·tri·arch /'peɪtrɪɑːk/ *n* [C] **1** 家长[長] jiāzhǎng; 族长 zúzhǎng. **2** (东正教的)最高一级主教 zuìgāo yìjí zhǔjiào. **~al** /-'ɑːkəl/ *adj*

pa·triot /'peɪtrɪət/ *n* [C] 爱[愛]国[國]者 àiguózhě. **~ic** /-'ɒtɪk/ *adj.* **'~ism** *n* [U]

pa·trol /pə'trəʊl/ *vt/i* [-ll-] 巡逻[邏] xúnluó; 巡查 xúnchá. □ *n* **1** [U] 巡逻 xúnluó; 巡查 xúnchá. **2** [C] 巡逻兵 xúnluóbīng; 巡逻艇 xúnluótǐng; 巡逻机[機] xúnluójī.

pa·tron /'peɪtrən/ *n* [C] **1** 赞助人 zànzhùrén, 资助人 zīzhùrén. **2** 老顾[顧]客 lǎo gùkè; 主顾 zhǔgù. **,~ 'saint** 守护[護]神 shǒuhùshén. **~age** /'pætrənɪdʒ/ *n* [C] **(a)** 赞助 zànzhù, 资助 zīzhù. **(b)** 任命权[權] rènmìngquán. **(c)** 光顾 guānggù, 惠顾 huìgù.

pa·tron·ize /'pætrənaɪz/ *vt* **1** 赞助 zànzhù; 光顾[顧] guānggù. **2** 对[對]…以恩人自居 duì … yǐ ēnrén zìjū. **pat·ron·iz·ing** *adj*

pat·ter¹ /'pætə(r)/ *n* [U] 行话 hánghuà; 黑话 hēihuà; 切口 qièkǒu.

pat·ter² /'pætə(r)/ *n* [U] (急促的)嗒[噠]嗒声[聲] dādāshēng. □ *vi* 发[發]出嗒嗒声 fāchū dādāshēng.

pat·tern /'pætn/ *n* [C] **1** 模范[範] mófàn; 典型 diǎnxíng. **2** 式样[樣] shìyàng; 纸样 zhǐyàng. **3** 图[圖]案 tú'àn; 花样 huāyàng. **4** 方式 fāngshì: *the ~ of events* 事件的格局. □ *vt* 以图案装[裝]饰 yǐ tú'àn zhuāngshì.

paunch /pɔːntʃ/ *n* [C] 腹(尤指胖大的肚子) fù.

pause /pɔːz/ *n* [C] 中止 zhōngzhǐ, 暂[暫]停 zàntíng. □ *vi* 暂停 zàntíng; 停顿 tíngdùn.

pave /peɪv/ *vt* 铺(路等) pū. **~ *the way for*** ⇨ way(1). **'paving-stone** 铺路石 pūlùshí.

pave·ment /'peɪvmənt/ *n* [C] [英国英语][美语 = sidewalk] 人行道 rénxíngdào.

pa·vil·ion /pə'vɪlɪən/ *n* [C] **1** (运动场的)休息处[處] xiūxìchù. **2** (供音乐会等使用的)装[裝]饰华[華]美的建筑[築]物 zhuāngshì huáměi de jiànzhùwù. **3** 大帐[帳]篷 dà zhàngpéng.

paw /pɔː/ *n* [C] 脚爪 jiǎozhǎo; 爪子 zhuǎzi. □ *vt* **1** (用脚爪)抓 zhuā; 扒 bā. **2** (指人)粗鲁地摸弄 cūlǔde mōnòng.

pawn¹ /pɔːn/ *n* [C] **1** (西洋象棋)兵 bīng; 卒 zú. **2** 爪牙 zhǎoyá; 工具 gōngjù.

pawn² /pɔːn/ *vt* 典 diǎn, 当[當] dàng, 押 yā. **'~broker** 当铺老板 dàngpù lǎobǎn. **'~shop** 当铺 dàngpù.

pay¹ /peɪ/ *n* [U] 工资 gōngzī, 薪金 xīnjīn. **'~-off** [非正式用语]结算 jiésuàn. **'~-packet** 工资袋 gōngzīdài. **'~-phone** 公用电[電]话 gōngyòng diànhuà. **'~-roll** 工资名单 gōngzī míngdān.

pay² /peɪ/ *vt/i* [*pt, pp* paid /peɪd/ɜː] **1** 支付 zhīfù; 付给 fùgěi; 付款 fùkuǎn. **2** 有利 yǒulì: *It ~s to advertise.* 做广告是有利可图的. **3** 偿[償]还[還] chánghuán. **4** 给予(注意等) gěiyǔ. **~ *a visit*** 拜访 bàifǎng, 访问[問] fǎngwèn. **5 ~ *sth back*** 还债 huánzhài, 还钱[錢] huánqián. **~ *sb back (for sth)*** 向…报[報]复 xiàng…bàofù. **~ *for*, (a)** 付出…的代价[價] fùchū … de dàijià. **(b)** 因…受处[處](惩)罚 yīn…shòu chǔfá: *~ for one's crime* 因罪受罚. **~ *off*, (a)** 给薪解雇 gěixīn jiěgù. **(b)** 偿清(欠款) chángqīng. **~ *sth out*, (a)** 花费 huāfèi; 付出 fùchū. **(b)** 放松[鬆](绳子) fàngsōng. **~ *up*** 付清 fùqīng. **~-able** *adj* 应[應]付的 yīngfùde; 可支付的 kězhīfùde. **~'ee** *n* [C] 受款人 shòukuǎnrén. **~er** *n* [C] 付款人 fùkuǎnrén. **~ment** *n* **(a)** [U] 支付 zhīfù. **(b)** [C] 支付的款项 zhīfùde kuǎnxiàng. **(c)** [C, U] [喻]报应 bàoying; 惩[懲]罚 chéngfá.

P.C. = **1** police constable (英国)普

通警员 pǔtōng jǐngyuán. 2 Privy Council(lor) (英国)枢〔樞〕密院 shūmìyuàn.

p.c.=1 per cent. 2 postcard.

pd.=paid.

P.E.=physical education 体〔體〕育 tǐyù.

pea /pi:/ *n* [C] 豌豆 wāndòu.

peace /pi:s/ *n* [U] **1** 和平 hépíng. **2** (常作 **P~**) 和约 héyuē. **3** 安宁〔寧〕ānníng. ***keep the*** ~ 守法 shǒufǎ. ⇨ Justice of the Peace. **4** 安静 ānjìng; 宁静 níngjìng. ***at*** ~ **(*with*)** 处〔處〕于和平状〔狀〕态〔態〕chùyú hépíng zhuàngtài. **~ful** *adj* **(a)** 爱〔愛〕好和平的 àihào hépíng de. **(b)** 宁静的 níngjìngde; 安静的 ānjìngde. **~ful·ly** *adv* **~ful·ness** *n* [U]

peach /pi:tʃ/ *n* [C] 桃 táo; 桃树〔樹〕táoshù; 桃色 táosè.

pea·cock /ˈpi:kɒk/ *n* [C] (雄)孔雀 kǒngquè.

pea-hen /ˈpi:hen/ *n* [C] 雌孔雀 cíkǒngquè.

peak /pi:k/ *n* [C] **1** 山顶 shāndǐng; 山峰 shānfēng. **2** 帽檐 màoyán. **3** 最高点〔點〕zuìgāodiǎn; 顶端 dǐngduān: *Sales reached a new* ~. 销售额达到了新的高峰. ***off-~*** (交通等的)非高峰时间 fēi gāofēng shíjiān. □ *vi* 达〔達〕到高峰 dádào gāofēng. **~ed** *adj* 有峰的 yǒufēngde; 尖的 jiānde.

peal /pi:l/ *n* [C] **1** 钟〔鐘〕声〔聲〕zhōngshēng. **2** 洪亮的回响〔響〕声 hóngliàngde huíxiǎngshēng; 隆隆声 lónglóngshēng: *a ~ of thunder* 雷声隆隆. □ *vt/i* 使鸣〔鳴〕响 shǐ míngxiǎng.

pea·nut /ˈpi:nʌt/ *n* [C] 花生 huāshēng; 花生米 huāshēngmǐ.

pear /peə(r)/ *n* [C] 梨 lí; 梨树〔樹〕líshù.

pearl /pɜ:l/ *n* [C] **1** 珍珠 zhēnzhū. **2** 杰〔傑〕出的人 jiéchūde rén; 珍品 zhēnpǐn. □ *vi* 采〔採〕珍珠 cǎi zhēnzhū.

peas·ant /ˈpeznt/ *n* [C] (不用于英国、美国)农〔農〕民 nóngmín. **~ry** *n* [U] (总称)农民 nóngmín.

peat /pi:t/ *n* [U] 泥煤 níméi; 泥炭 nítàn. **peaty** *adj*

pebble /ˈpebl/ *n* [C] 卵石 luǎnshí; 小圆石 xiǎoyuánshí. **peb·bly** *adj*

peck /pek/ *vt/i* **1** 啄 zhuó. **2** ~ **(*at*)**[非正式用语]斯文地吃 sīwénde chī. **3** [非正式用语]匆忙地吻cōngmángde wěn. □ *n* [C] **1** 啄 zhuó; 凿〔鑿〕záo; 琢 zhuó. **2** [非正式用语]匆忙的一吻 cōngmángde yìwěn. **ˈ~ish** *adj* [非正式用语] 饥饿的 jī'ède.

pe·cu·liar /pɪˈkju:lɪə(r)/ *adj* **1** ~ **(*to*)** 特有的 tèyǒude: *habits ~ to him*. 他所特有的习惯. **2** 奇怪的 qíguàide; 罕见的 hǎnjiànde. **3** 特别的 tèbiéde, 特殊的 tèshūde: *of ~ interest*. 特殊兴趣. **~ly** *adv* **~ity** /-ˈærətɪ/ *n* [*pl* -ies] **(a)** [U] 特色 tèsè; 特质〔質〕tèzhì. **(b)** [C] 特殊的东〔東〕西 tèshūde dōngxi.

peda·gogy /ˈpedəgɒdʒɪ/ *n* [U] [正式用语]教育学〔學〕jiàoyùxué; 教学法 jiàoxuéfǎ. **peda'gog·ic(al)** *adj* **peda·gogue** [美语 = **-gog**] /-gɒg/ *n* [C] 教师〔師〕jiàoshī; 卖〔賣〕弄学问〔問〕的教师 màinòng xuéwènde jiàoshī.

pedal /ˈpedl/ *n* [C] (自行车、钢琴等的)脚蹬 jiǎodēng; 踏板 tàbǎn. □ *vt/i* [-ll-, 美语 -l-] 踩踏板 cǎi tàbǎn; 骑〔騎〕自行车〔車〕qí zìxíngchē.

ped·ant /ˈpednt/ *n* [C] 书〔書〕呆〔獃〕子 shūdāizi; 学〔學〕究 xuéjiū. **~ic** /pɪˈdæntɪk/ *adj*

peddle /ˈpedl/ *vt/i* 沿街叫卖〔賣〕yánjiē jiàomài; 挨户兜售 āihù dōushòu.

ped·estal /ˈpedɪstl/ *n* [C]柱脚 zhùjiǎo; 垫〔墊〕座 diànzuò. ***put*** **(或 *set*) *sb on a*** ~ 把某人当〔當〕偶像崇拜 bǎ mǒurén dàng ǒuxiàng chóngbài.

pe·des·trian /pɪˈdestrɪən/ *n* [C] 行人 xíngrén; 步行者 bùxíngzhě. □ *adj* **1** 步行的 bùxíngde. **2** 平淡的 píngdànde. ~ **crossing** 人行横道 rénxíng héngdào.

pedi·at·rics /ˌpi:dɪˈætrɪks/ *n pl* 小儿〔兒〕科xiǎo'érkē. **pedia·ˈtric·ian** *n* [C] 儿科医〔醫〕师〔師〕érkē yīshī.

pedi·gree /ˈpedɪgri:/ *n* [C, U] 家系 jiāxì; 系谱〔譜〕xìpǔ. □ *adj* 有血统来历〔歷〕的 yǒu xuètǒng láide.

ped·lar /ˈpedlə(r)/ *n* [C] (挨户兜售的)小贩 xiǎofàn; (沿街叫卖的)商贩 shāngfàn.

peek /pi:k/ *vi* ~ ***at*** 偷看 tōukàn 窥视 kuīshì. □ *n* [C] 一瞥 yīpiē

peel /pi:l/ *vt/i* **1** 剥(皮) bō; 削(皮) xiāo. **2** 剥落 bōluò; 脱皮 tuōpí *the paint is ~ing*. 油漆在剥落. □ *n* [U] (水果、蔬菜等的)皮 pí: *potato ~* 土豆皮.

peep /pi:p/ *vi*. *n* [C] 偷看 tōukàn 窥视 kuīshì.

peer[1] /pɪə(r)/ *n* [C] **1** 同等 tóngděng; 同辈〔輩〕tóngbèi. **2** (英国)贵族 guìzú. **~ess** **(a)** 女贵族 guìzú; 贵妇〔婦〕guìfù; **(b)** (上院)议〔議〕员夫人 yìyuán fūrén.

peer² /pɪə(r)/ *vi* ~ *at* (*into*) 凝视 níngshì; 盯着看 dīngzhekàn.
peer·age /ˈpɪərɪdʒ/ *n* [C,U] **1** 贵族 guìzú; 贵族爵位 guìzú juéwèi. **2** 贵族名册 guìzú míngcè.
peg /peg/ *n* [C] **1** (木或金属的)钉 dīng; 栓 shuān. **2** 桩〔樁〕zhuāng; (挂衣帽的)钉 dīng. □ *vt/i* [-gg-] **1** 用木钉钉 yòng mùdīng dīng. **2** 用短桩固定 yòng duǎnzhuāng gùdìng. **3** (商业用语)固定 gùdìng; 限定(价格等) xiàndìng.
pe·kin·ese /ˌpi:kɪˈni:z/ *n* [C] 小狮〔獅〕子狗 xiǎo shīzigǒu.
peli·can /ˈpelɪkən/ *n* [C] 鹈〔鵜〕鹕〔鶘〕(又名淘河) tíhú.
pel·let /ˈpelɪt/ *n* [C] **1** 小球 xiǎo qiú; 小团〔團〕xiǎo tuán. **2** 小弹〔彈〕丸 xiǎo dànwán.
pel·met /ˈpelmɪt/ *n* [C] 窗帘〔簾〕盒 chuānglіánhé.
pelt¹ /pelt/ *n* [C] 毛皮 máopí.
pelt² /pelt/ *vt/i* **1** ~ *sb with sth* 投掷〔擲〕tóuzhì; 投击〔擊〕tóujī. **2** (指雨等)急降 jíjiàng. □ *n at full* ~ 全速地 quánsùde.
pel·vis /ˈpelvɪs/ *n* [C] [解剖]骨盆 gǔpén. **pel·vic** *adj*
pen¹ /pen/ *n* [C] 笔〔筆〕bǐ. ⇨ fountain-pen. □ *vt* [-nn-] 写〔寫〕(信等) xiě. **ˈ~-friend** 笔友 bǐyǒu. **ˈ~knife** 小刀 xiǎodāo; 削铅笔刀 xiāo qiānbǐ dāo. **ˈ~-name** 笔名 bǐmíng.
pen² /pen/ *n* [C] **1** (家畜的)栏〔欄〕lán; 圈 juàn; 槛〔檻〕jiàn. **2** = play-pen. □ *vt* [-nn-] ~ *up* (或 *in*) 把…关〔關〕起来 bǎ … guānqǐlái.
penal /ˈpi:nl/ *adj* 刑事的 xíngshìde; 刑罚的 xíngfáde. ~ **servitude** 监〔監〕禁时〔時〕的劳〔勞〕役 jiānjìn shí de láoyì.
pe·nal·ize /ˈpi:nəlaɪz/ *vt* 处〔處〕罚 chǔfá; 对…处以刑事惩〔懲〕罚 duì … chǔ yǐ xíngshì chéngfá.
pen·alty /ˈpenltɪ/ *n* [C,U] [*pl* -ies] **1** 处〔處〕罚 chǔfá; 刑罚 xíngfá; 惩〔懲〕罚 chéngfá. **2** (运动)犯规的处罚 fànguīde chǔfá. **ˈ~ (kick)** (足球的)罚球 fáqiú.
pen·ance /ˈpenəns/ *n* [U] (赎罪的)惩〔懲〕罚 chéngfá; 苦行 kǔxíng.
pence /pens/ *n pl* ⇨ penny.
pen·cil /ˈpensl/ *n* [C] 笔〔筆〕bǐ-铅笔 qiānbǐ. □ *vt* [-ll-, 美语 -l-] 用铅笔写〔寫〕(或画) yòng qiānbǐ xiě.
pen·dant /ˈpendənt/ *n* [C](项链附着的)垂饰 chuíshì; 垂环〔環〕chuíhuán.
pend·ing /ˈpendɪŋ/ *adj* 未决定的 wèi juédìng de; 待解决的 dài jiějué de. □ *prep* 在…以前 zài … yǐqián: ~ *his decision* 在他决定以前.
pen·du·lum /ˈpendjʊləm/ *n* [C] [*pl* ~s] (钟等的)摆〔擺〕bǎi.
pen·etrate /ˈpenɪtreɪt/ *vt/i* **1** 穿过〔過〕chuānguò; 透过 tòuguò. **2**〔喻〕看穿 kànchuān; 识〔識〕破 shípò. **pen·etrat·ing** *adj* **(a)** 敏锐的 mǐnruìde; 透彻〔徹〕的 tòuchède. **(b)** (指声音)响〔響〕亮的 xiǎngliàngde. **pen·eˈtra·tion** *n* [U]
pen·guin /ˈpeŋgwɪn/ *n* [C] 企鹅〔鵝〕qǐ'é.
peni·cil·lin /ˌpenɪˈsɪlɪn/ *n* [U] 青霉素 qīngméisù; 盘〔盤〕尼西林 pánníxīlín.
pen·in·sula /pəˈnɪnsjʊlə/ *n* [C] [*pl* ~s]半岛〔島〕bàndǎo. **pen·in·su·lar** *adj*
pe·nis /ˈpi:nɪs/ *n* [C] 阴〔陰〕茎〔莖〕yīnjīng.
peni·tence /ˈpenɪtəns/ *n* [U] 后〔後〕悔 hòuhuǐ; 悔罪 huǐzuì. **peni·tent** *adj*
pen·nant /ˈpenənt/ *n* [C] (船上用的)尖旗 jiānqí; 三角旗 sānjiǎoqí.
pen·ni·less /ˈpenɪlɪs/ *adj* 身无〔無〕分文的 shēng wú fēnwén de; 穷〔窮〕的 qióngde.
penny /ˈpenɪ/ *n* [C] [*pl* pence /pens/ 指价值, 如 *ˈsixpence; pl* pennies /ˈpenɪz/ 指硬币的个数] (略作 **p**) (1971 年采用十进位币制后)(新) 辨士 (价值百分之一英镑) biànshì. *spend a* ~ [非正式用语] 上(公共)厕所 shàng cèsuǒ. *the* ~ *(has) dropped* 话已听〔聽〕明白 huà yǐ tīng míngbai.
pen·sion /ˈpenʃn/ *n* [C] 养〔養〕老金 yǎnglǎojīn, 退休金 tuìxiūjīn; 抚〔撫〕恤金 fǔxùjīn. □ *vt* ~ *sb off* 发〔發〕给某人养老金使其退休 fāgěi mǒurén yǎnglǎojīn shǐ qí tuìxiū. **ˈ~able** /-əbl/ *adj* 可领取抚恤金(或养老金)的 kě lǐngqǔ fǔxùjīn de **~er** 领抚恤金(或养老金)的人 lǐng fǔxùjīn de rén.
pen·sive /ˈpensɪv/ *adj* 沉思的 chénsīde; 忧〔憂〕郁的 yōuyùde. **~ly** *adv*
pen·ta·gon /ˈpentəgən/ *n* [C] 五角形 wǔjiǎoxíng; 五边〔邊〕形 wǔbiānxíng. **~al** /-ˈtægənl/ *adj*
pen·tath·lon /penˈtæθlən/ *n* [C] (奥林匹克运动会中)五项运〔運〕动〔動〕wǔxiàng yùndòng.
pent·house /ˈpenthaʊs/ *n* [C] (建于高楼屋顶的)房屋 fángwū.
pen·ul·ti·mate /penˈʌltɪmət/ *n* [C] *adj* 倒数〔數〕第二位 dàoshǔ

dì'èrwèi; 倒数第二的 dàoshǔ dì'èr de.

people /'pi:pl/ *n* [U] **1** 人 rén. **2** (某一地区、阶级的)人 rén; 人员 rényuán: *village* ~ 村民. **3** 平民 píngmín, 老百姓 lǎobǎixìng. **4** [*pl*] 种[種]族 zhǒngzú; 民族 mínzú: *the* ~*s of Asia* 亚洲各民族. □ *vt* 使住着(或住满)人 shǐ zhùzhe rén.

pep /pep/ *n* [U] [俚语]精力 jīnglì; 活力 huólì. □ *vt* [-pp-] [俚语]激励[勵] jīlì; 给…打气[氣] gěi...dǎqì. '~ **pill** 兴[興]奋[奮]药片 xīngfèn yàopiàn. '~ **talk** (对球员等)鼓励士气的讲[講]话 gǔlì shìqì de jiǎnghuà.

pep·per /'pepə(r)/ *n* **1** [U] 胡椒 hújiāo; 胡椒粉 hújiāofěn. **2** [C] 辣椒 làjiāo; 胡椒属[屬] hújiāoshǔ. □ *vt* 加胡椒粉于(食物) jiā hújiāofěn yú. '~**mint,** **(a)** 薄荷 bòhe; 薄荷油 bòheyóu. **(b)** 薄荷糖 bòhetáng.

per /pɜ:(r)/ *prep* 每 měi: *30 miles* ~ *gallon*(缩作**mpg**)每加仑油(汽车)可走三十英里. **as** ~ 按照 ànzhào: *work as* ~ *instructions* 按照指示工作. ˌ~ **'annum** 每年 měinián. ˌ~ **'cent** ⇨ cent.

per·am·bu·lator /pə'ræmbjʊleɪtə(r)/ *n* [C] [通常作]四轮[輪]婴儿[兒]车[車] sìlún yīng'érchē; 婴儿车 yīng'érchē.

per·ceive /pə'si:v/ *vt* [正式用语]察觉[覺] chájué, 发[發]觉 fājué; 看出 kànchū.

per·cen·tage /pə'sentɪdʒ/ *n* [C] **1** 百分数[數] bǎifēnshù; 百分率 bǎifēnlǜ. **2** 部分 bùfen; 比例 bǐlì.

per·cep·tible /pə'septəbl/ *adj* [正式用语] 察觉[覺]得到的 chájué dédào de; 看得出的 kàndéchūde: *a* ~ *change in colour* 看得出颜色的变化. **per·cep·tibly** *adv*

per·cep·tion /pə'sepʃn/ *n* [U] [正式用语]感觉[覺] gǎnjué; 知觉 zhījué.

per·cep·tive /pə'septɪv/ *adj* [正式用语]有知觉[覺]的 yǒu zhījué de; 有理解力的 yǒu lǐjiělì de. ~**ly** *adv*

perch[1] /pɜ:tʃ/ *n* [C] [*pl* ~] 河鲈[鱸] hélú.

perch[2] /pɜ:tʃ/ *n* [C] (鸟的)栖[棲]木 qīmù. □ *vt/i* **1** (指鸟)栖息 qīxī. **2** (指人)坐在高处[處] zuò zài gāochù. **3** (指建筑物)位于高处 wèi yú gāochù.

per·co·late /'pɜ:kəleɪt/ *vt/i* **1** 滤[濾](与*through* 连用) lǜ; 渗[滲]透 shèntòu. **2** [喻]透过[過] tòuguò; (消息等)走漏 zǒulòu: *The news* ~*d through to us*. 这一消息透露给我们. **per·co·lator** 咖啡过滤壶[壺] kāfēi guòlǜhú.

per·cus·sion /pə'kʌʃn/ *n* [U] **1** 碰撞 pèngzhuàng; 震动[動] zhèndòng. **2 the** ~ 打击[擊]乐[樂]器 dǎjī yuèqì.

per·en·nial /pə'renɪəl/ *adj* **1** 终年的 zhōngniánde, 四季不断[斷]的 sìjì búduàn de. **2** 持久的 chíjiǔde; 长[長]久的 chángjiǔde. **3** (指植物)多年生的 duōniánshēngde. □ *n* [C] 多年生植物 duōniánshēng zhíwù. ~**ly** *adv*

per·fect[1] /'pɜ:fɪkt/ *adj* **1** 完全的 wánquánde. **2** 无[無]瑕的 wúxiáde; 完美的 wánměide: *a* ~ *answer* 圆满的回答. **3** 正确[確]的 zhèngquède; 精确的 jīngquède: *a* ~ *circle* 一个正圆. **4** 绝对[對]的 juéduìde; 全然的 quánránde: *a* ~ *stranger* 完全陌生的人. ~ **tense** [语法]完成时[時] wánchéngshí. ~**ly** *adv* 完全地 wánquánde; 美好地 měihǎode: ~*ly fit* 非常合适.

per·fect[2] /pə'fekt/ *vt* 使完美 shǐ wánměi; 使精通 shǐ jīngtōng.

per·fec·tion /pə'fekʃn/ *n* [U] **1** 完成 wánchéng; 完善 wánshàn: *the* ~ *of a technique* 一项技术的完成. **2** 尽[盡]善尽美 jìnshàn jìnměi. ~**ist** *n* [C] [非正式用语]追求尽善尽美者 zhuīqiú jìnshàn jìnměi zhě.

per·for·ate /'pɜ:fəreɪt/ *vt/i* 穿孔于 chuānkǒng yū; 打洞于 dǎdòng yū. **per·fo'r·ation** *n* [C,U]

per·form /pə'fɔ:m/ *vt/i* **1** [正式用语]履行 lǚxíng; 执[執]行 zhíxíng. **2** 演出 yǎnchū; 表演 biǎoyǎn; 演奏 yǎnzòu. ~**ance** *n* **(a)** [U] 履行 lǚxíng; 执行 zhíxíng. **(b)** [C] 成绩 chéngjì; 功绩 gōngjī. **(c)** [C] 演出 yǎnchū; 演奏 yǎnzòu. ~**er** 表演者 biǎoyǎnzhě; 执行者 zhíxíngzhě.

per·fume /'pɜ:fju:m/ *n* [C,U] 香味 xiāngwèi; 香水 xiāngshuǐ. □ *vt* /pə'fju:m/ 使发[發]香 shǐ fāxiāng; 加香水于 jiā xiāngshuǐ yū.

per·haps /pə'hæps/ *adv* 也许 yěxǔ, 可能 kěnéng.

peril /'perəl/ *n* **1** [U] (严重的)危险[險] wēixiǎn. **2** [C] 危险的事物 wēixiǎnde shìwù. ~**ous** *adj*

per·imeter /pə'rɪmɪtə(r)/ *n* [C] 周边[邊] zhōubiān; 周长[長] zhōucháng; 周界 zhōujiè.

period /'pɪərɪəd/ *n* [C] **1** 期间[間] qījiān; 时[時]期 shíqī. **2** [美语]句号[號] jùhào, 句点[點](.) jùdiǎn. **3** [非正式用语] 月经[經] yuèjīng. ~**ic** /ˌpɪərɪ'ɒdɪk/ *adj* 周期的 zhōuqīde; 定期的 dìngqīde. ~**ical** /-ɪkl/ *adj* = periodic. □

n [C] 期刊 qīkān; 杂〔雜〕志〔誌〕 zázhì. **~ically** /-klɪ/ *adv* **(a)** 定期地 dìngqīde. **(b)** 偶然地 ǒuránde.

pe·riph·ery /pəˈrɪfərɪ/ *n* [C] [*pl* -ies] (圆体的)外面 wàimiàn; 周围〔圍〕 zhōuwéi. **pe·riph·eral** *adj*

peri·scope /ˈperɪskəʊp/ *n* [C] 潜〔潛〕望镜 qiǎnwàngjìng.

per·ish /ˈperɪʃ/ *vt/i* **1** 死亡 sǐwáng; 夭折 yāozhé. **2** 使痛苦 shǐ tòngkǔ: *~ed with cold (hunger)* 冻(饿)死. **3** 腐朽 fǔxiǔ. **~able** /-əbl/ *adj, n pl* (尤指食物)易坏〔壞〕的 yìhuàide.

per·jure /ˈpɜːdʒə(r)/ *vt* [反身] *~ oneself* 作伪〔僞〕证 zuò wěizhèng. **per·jury** *n* [C,U]

perk[1] /pɜːk/ *vt/i* *~ up* (指人)振作 zhènzuò; 活跃〔躍〕起来 huóyuè qǐlái. **perky** *adj* [-ier, -iest] 生龙〔龍〕活虎的 shēnglóng huóhǔ de.

perk[2] /pɜːk/ *n pl* [非正式用语]额外津贴 éwài jīntiē; 小帐〔賬〕xiǎozhàng.

perm /pɜːm/ *n* [C] [非正式用语] permanent wave 的缩写〔寫〕 *permanent wave* de suōxiě. □*vt* 电烫(头发) diàntàng.

per·ma·nence /ˈpɜːmənəns/ *n* [U] 永久 yǒngjiǔ; 持久 chíjiǔ.

per·ma·nent /ˈpɜːmənənt/ *adj* 永久的 yǒngjiǔde; 持久的 chíjiǔde. **~ magnet** *n* 永久磁石 yǒngjiǔ císhí. ⇨ temporary. **~ wave** 电烫的头发 diàntàngde tóufa. **~ly** *adv*

per·meate /ˈpɜːmɪeɪt/ *vt/i* ~ **(*through* 或 *among*)** 渗〔滲〕透 shèntòu; 透入 tòurù. **per·me·ˈation** *n* [U]

per·mis·sible /pəˈmɪsəbl/ *adj* 容许的 róngxǔde; 许可的 xǔkěde. **per·mis·sibly** *adv*

per·mis·sion /pəˈmɪʃn/ *n* [U] 允许 yǔnxǔ; 许可 xǔkě.

per·miss·ive /pəˈmɪsɪv/ *adj* 许可的 xǔkěde; 容许的 róngxǔde: *the ~ society* 性开放的社会. **~ness** *n* [U]

per·mit[1] /ˈpɜːmɪt/ *n* [C] 许可证〔證〕 xǔkězhèng.

per·mit[2] /pəˈmɪt/ *vt/i* [-tt-] 允许 yǔnxǔ; 许可 xǔkě.

per·pen·dicu·lar /ˌpɜːpənˈdɪkjʊlə(r)/ *adj* **1** 垂直的 chuízhíde, 成直角的 chéngzhíjiǎode. **2** 直立的 zhílìde. □ *n* [C] 垂直线〔線〕 chuízhíxiàn. ⇨ horizontal; vertical.

per·pet·ual /pəˈpetʃʊəl/ *adj* 永久的 yǒngjiǔde, 永恒的 yǒnghéngde: *~ complaints* 不停的抱怨,没完没了的叫苦. **~ly** *adv*

per·petu·ate /pəˈpetʃʊeɪt/ *vt* 使永存 shǐ yǒngcún; 使不朽 shǐ bùxiǔ. **per·petu·ˈation** *n* [U]

per·plex /pəˈpleks/ *vt* 困惑 kùnhuò; 迷惑 míhuò. **~ed** *adj*. **~ity** *n* [*pl -ies*] [正式用语] **(a)** [U] 困惑 kùnhuò; 窘困 jiǒngkùn. **(b)** [C] 令人困惑的事物 lìngrén kùnhuòde shìwù.

perpro. =on behalf of.

per·se·cute /ˈpɜːsɪkjuːt/ *vt* **1** (尤指因宗教信仰不同)迫害 pòhài. **2** 烦扰〔擾〕 fánrǎo. **per·se·cu·tor** 迫害者 pòhàizhě. **per·seˈcu·tion** *n* [C, U]

per·se·vere /ˌpɜːsɪˈvɪə(r)/ *vi* ~ **(*at* 或 *in* 或 *with*)** 坚〔堅〕持 jiānchí, 不屈不挠〔撓〕 bùqū bùnáo. **per·se·ver·ance** *n* [U].

per·sist /pəˈsɪst/ *vi* **1** ~ ***in sth(in doing sth)*** 坚〔堅〕持 jiānchí; 固执〔執〕 gùzhí. **2** ~ ***with*** 坚持努力工作 jiānchí nǔlì gōngzuò. **3** 持续〔續〕 chíxù; 存留 cúnliú: *Fog will ~ in most areas.* 大部分地区将继续有雾. **~ence** *n* [U] **~ent** *adj* 坚持的 jiānchíde; 固执的 gùzhíde: *persistent warnings* 一再警告. *~ attacks* 不停地进攻.

per·son /ˈpɜːsn/ *n* [C] **1** 人 rén. **2** 人身 rénshēn; 身体〔體〕 shēntǐ. *in ~* 亲〔親〕自 qīnzì. **3** [语法]人称〔稱〕 rénchēng: *the first ~* (I, we), *the second ~* (you) *and the third ~* (he, she, it, they). 第一人称 dìyī rénchēng, 第二人称 dìèr rénchēng, 第三人称 dìsān rénchēng. **~able** /-əbl/ *adj* 漂亮的 piàoliàngde; 风〔風〕度好的 fēngdùhǎode.

per·sonal /ˈpɜːsənl/ *adj* **1** 私人的 sīrénde; 个〔個〕人的 gèrénde. **2** 身体〔體〕的 shēntǐde: *~ cleanliness* 身体清洁. **3** 攻击〔擊〕人的 gōngjī rén de: *~ remarks.* 批评个人的言词. ˌ**~ ˈpronoun** 人称代词 rénchēng dàicí. **~ly** *adv* **(a)** 亲〔親〕自地 qīnzìde. **(b)** 就自己而言 jiù zìjǐ ér yán: *P~ly, I think you are mad.* 就我个人来说, 我认为你疯了.

per·son·al·ity /ˌpɜːsəˈnælətɪ/ *n* [*pl* -ies] **1** [C,U] 个〔個〕性 gèxìng. **2** [C] [现代用法] (有名的)人物 rénwù: *a TV ~* 电视明星.

per·son·ify /pəˈsɒnɪfaɪ/ *vt* [*pt, pp* -ied] **1** 拟〔擬〕(某物)为〔爲〕人 nǐ wéi rén. **2** 是…的化身 shì … de huàshēn: *He is kindness personified.* 他是仁慈的化身. **per·soni·fi·ca·tion** /-fɪˈkeɪʃn/ *n* [C, U]

per·son·nel /ˌpɜːsəˈnel/ *n* [U] [集合名词]职〔職〕员 zhíyuán; 人

员 rényuán. ~ **manager** (或 **officer**) 人事主任 rénshì zhǔrèn.

per·spec·tive /pə'spektɪv/ *n* **1** [U] 透视 tòushì; 透视画[畫]法 tòushìhuàfǎ. **2** [U] 一个[個]问[問]题的不同方面的关[關]系[係] yígè wèntí de bùtóng fāngmiàn de guānxì: *He sees things in their right* ~. 他正确地观察事物.

per·spex /'pɜːspeks/ *n* [U] 一种有机[機]玻璃(学名为甲基丙烯酸甲酯) yīzhǒng yǒujī bōli.

per·spire /pə'spaɪə(r)/ *vi* 出汗 chūhàn; 流汗 liúhàn. **per·spir·ation** /ˌpɜːspə'reɪʃn/ *n* [U]

per·suade /pə'sweɪd/ *vt* **1** ~ *sb that*, ~ *sb of sth* 说服(某人) shuōfú; 劝[勸]说 quànshuō. **2** 说服…(做某事) shuōfú…: ~ *her to marry you* 劝她同你结婚.

per·sua·sion /pə'sweɪʒn/ *n* **1** [U] 说服 shuōfú; 劝[勸]服 quànfú. **2** [C,U] 信念 xìnniàn; 信仰 xìnyǎng.

per·sua·sive /pə'sweɪsɪv/ *adj* 有说服力的 yǒu shuōfúlì de. ~**ly** *adv*

pert /pɜːt/ *adj* 无[無]礼[禮]的 wúlǐde; 冒失的 màoshīde. ~**ly** *adv* ~**ness** *n* [U]

per·tain /pə'teɪn/ *vi* ~ *to* [正式用语]从[從]属[屬] cóngshǔ, 附属 fùshǔ: *land* ~*ing to a farm* 属于农场的土地.

per·ti·nent /'pɜːtɪnənt/ *adj* [正式用语]贴切的 tiēqiède; 中肯的 zhōngkěnde.

per·turb /pə'tɜːb/ *vt* [正式用语]使不安 shǐ bù'ān; 烦扰[擾] fánrǎo.

per·vade /pə'veɪd/ *vt* [正式用语]弥[彌]漫 mímàn; 遍及 biànjí: *a smell* ~*d the room* 房间里充满一种气味. **per'va·sion** /-'veɪʒn/ *n* [U]

per·va·sive /pə'veɪsɪv/ *adj* 弥[彌]漫的 mímànde; 遍布的 biànbùde.

per·verse /pə'vɜːs/ *adj* **1** (指人)刚[剛]愎的 gāngbìde; 坚[堅]持错误的 jiānchí cuòwù de. **2** (指行为)反常的 fǎnchángde ~**ly** *adv*

per·ver·sion /pə'vɜːʃn/ *n* **1** [U] 堕落 duòluò; 败坏[壞] bàihuài. **2** [C] 反常 fǎncháng: *sexual* ~*s* 性变态.

per·ver·sity /pə'vɜːsətɪ/ *n* [*pl* -ies] [U] 刚[剛]愎 gāngbì; 任性 rènxìng; [C] 堕落 duòluò; 邪恶[惡] xié'è.

per·vert[1] /'pɜːvɜːt/ *n* [C] 堕落者 duòluòzhě; 反常者 fǎnchángzhě.

per·vert[2] /pə'vɜːt/ *vt* **1** 误用 wùyòng; 滥[濫]用 lànyòng: ~ *justice* 滥用法律制裁. **2** 使(人)堕落 shǐ duòluò; 使入邪路 shǐ rù xiélù.

pes·si·mism /'pesɪmɪzəm/ *n* [U] 悲观[觀] bēiguān; 悲观主义[義] bēiguān zhǔyì. **pes·si·mist** 悲观主义者 bēiguānzhǔyìzhě. **pes·si'mis·tic** *adj*

pest /pest/ *n* [C] **1** 有害动[動]物 yǒuhài dòngwù; 害虫[蟲] hàichóng; 有害的东[東]西 yǒuhàide dōngxi. **2** [非正式用语]讨厌[厭]的人 tǎoyànde rén.

pes·ter /'pestə(r)/ *vt* 烦扰[擾] fánrǎo; 纠缠[纏] jiūchán.

pes·ti·cide /'pestɪsaɪd/ *n* [C, U] 杀[殺]虫[蟲]剂[劑] shāchóngjì, 农[農]药 nóngyào.

pet /pet/ *n* **1** 宠[寵]物 chǒngwù; 爱[愛]物 àiwù. **2** 受宠爱的人 shòu chǒng'ài de rén. □ *vt* [-tt-] 接吻 jiēwěn; 爱抚[撫] àifǔ. ~ **name** 爱称[稱] àichēng.

petal /'petl/ *n* [C] 花瓣 huābàn.

peter /'piːtə(r)/ *vi* ~ *out* 渐[漸]渐消失 jiànjiàn xiāoshī; 逐渐枯竭 zhújiàn kūjié.

pe·ti·tion /pɪ'tɪʃn/ *n* [C] **1** 祈求 qíqiú; 请求 qǐngqiú. **2** 请愿 qǐngyuàn. **3** (向法院递交的)请求书[書] qǐngqiúshū. □ *vt/i* **1** 请愿[願] qǐngyuàn. **2** ~ *for* 祈求 qíqiú; 恳[懇]求 kěnqiú. ~**er** 请愿人 qǐngyuànrén; 请求者 qǐngqiúzhě; 原告 yuángào.

pet·rify /'petrɪfaɪ/ *vt/i* [*pt*, *pp* -ied] **1** 使石化 shǐ shíhuà. **2** [喻](因恐惧等而)发[發]呆 fādāi.

pet·rol /'petrəl/ *n* [U] [美语 = *gasoline*] 汽油 qìyóu.

pe·tro·leum /pɪ'trəʊlɪəm/ *n* [U] 石油 shíyóu.

pet·ti·coat /'petɪkəʊt/ *n* [C] 衬[襯]裙 chènqún.

petty /'petɪ/ *adj* [-ier, -iest] **1** 小的 xiǎode; 次要的 cìyàode. **2** 器量小的 qìliàngxiǎode: ~ *spite* 卑下的恶意. ~ **cash** [商业]小额现金收支 xiǎo'é xiànjīn shōuzhī. **pet·ti·ness** *n* [U]

petu·lant /'petjʊlənt/ *adj* [正式用语]脾气[氣]坏[壞]的píqì huài de; 易怒的 yìnùde. ~**ly** *adv* **petu·lance** *n* [U]

pew /pjuː/ *n* [C] (教堂内的)靠背长[長]凳[櫈] kàobèi chángdèng.

pew·ter /'pjuːtə(r)/ *n* [U] 白镴 báilà.

P.G.=paying guest 寄宿客 jìsùkè

phal·lus /'fæləs/ *n* [C] 男性生殖器形象 nánxìng shēngzhíqì xíngxiàng. **phal·lic** *adj*

phan·tasy /'fæntəsɪ/ *n* = fantasy

phan·tom /'fæntəm/ *n* [C] 幽灵

〔靈〕yōulíng，鬼怪 guǐguài.
Phar·aoh /'feərəʊ/ *n* [C]（古埃及君王称号）法老 fǎlǎo.
phar·ma·ceuti·cal /ˌfɑːmə'sjuːtɪkl/ *adj* 制〔製〕药〔藥〕的 zhìyàode；药物的 yàowùde.
phar·ma·cist /'fɑːməsɪst/ *n* [C] 药〔藥〕剂〔劑〕师〔師〕yàojìshī；药商 yàoshāng. ⇨ chemist.
phar·ma·col·ogy /ˌfɑːmə'kɒlədʒɪ/ *n* [U] 药〔藥〕物学〔學〕yàowùxué；药理学 yàolǐxué. **phar·ma·col·ogist** /-dʒɪst/ *n* [C] 药物学家 yàowùxuéjiā.
phar·macy /'fɑːməsɪ/ *n* [*pl* -ies] **1** [U] 制〔製〕药〔藥〕zhìyào；配药 pèiyào. **2** [C] 药房 yàofáng，药店 yàodiàn.［美语 = *drugstore*］.
phase /feɪz/ *n* [C] **1** 阶〔階〕段 jiēduàn；状〔狀〕态〔態〕zhuàngtài. **2**（指月亮）盈亏〔虧〕yíngkuī；变〔變〕象 biànxiàng. □ *vt* 使按计划〔劃〕进〔進〕行 shǐ àn jìhuà jìnxíng. ~ *in* 逐渐〔漸〕采〔採〕用 zhújiàn cǎiyòng. ~ *out* 逐渐淘汰 zhújiàn táotài.
Ph.D. =Doctor of Philosophy 哲学〔學〕博士 zhéxué bóshì.
pheas·ant /'feznt/ *n* [C] 雉 zhì；[U] 雉肉 zhìròu.
phe·nom·enal /fə'nɒmɪnl/ *adj* 非凡的 fēifánde，出众〔衆〕的 chūzhòngde: ~ *expense* 庞大的开支. ~ *strength* 非凡的力量. ~**ly** *adv*
phe·nom·enon /fə'nɒmɪnən/ *n* [C] [*pl* -ena /-nə/] **1** 现象 xiànxiàng. **2** 非凡的人 fēifánde rén；奇迹〔跡〕qíjī.
phi·lis·tine /'fɪlɪstaɪn/ *n* [C]［现代用法］兴〔興〕趣庸俗的人 xìngqù yōngsú de rén.
phil·os·opher /fɪ'lɒsəfə(r)/ *n* [C] **1** 哲学〔學〕家 zhéxuéjiā. **2**［非正式用语］达〔達〕观〔觀〕者 dáguānzhě.
phil·os·ophy /fɪ'lɒsəfɪ/ *n* [*pl* -ies] **1** [U] 哲学〔學〕zhéxué. **2** [C] 思想体〔體〕系〔係〕sīxiǎng tǐxì: *a religious* ~ 宗教哲理. **3** [U] 达〔達〕观〔觀〕dáguān；镇静 zhènjìng. **philo·sophi·cal** /ˌfɪlə'sɒfɪkl/ *adj* **(a)** 哲学的 zhéxuéde. **(b)** 达观的 dáguānde. **phil·os·ophize** /fɪ'lɒsəfaɪz/ *vi* 推究哲理 tuījiū zhélǐ；进〔進〕行哲学探讨 jìnxíng zhéxué tàntǎo.
phlegm /flem/ *n* [U] **1** 痰 tán. **2** 迟〔遲〕钝 chídùn；冷淡 lěngdàn.
phleg·matic /fleg'mætɪk/ *adj* 迟〔遲〕钝的 chídùnde；冷淡的 lěngdànde. ~**ally** *adv*
pho·bia /'fəʊbɪə/ *n* [C] [*pl* ~s]（病态的）恐惧 kǒngjù；憎恶〔惡〕zēngwù.
phone /fəʊn/ *n*, *vt*/*i* telephone 的缩写〔寫〕*telephone* de suōxiě. '~**-booth** (或**-box**) 电话间〔間〕diànhuàjiān.
pho·netic /fə'netɪk/ *adj* 语音的 yǔyīnde；语音学〔學〕的 yǔyīnxuéde. ~**ally** /-klɪ/ *adv* **pho·ne·tics** *n*［用 *sing verb*］**(a)** 语音学 yǔyīnxué. **(b)** 发〔發〕音学 fāyīnxué. ~**ian** /fəʊnɪ'tɪʃn/ *n* [C] 语音学家 yǔyīnxuéjiā.
pho·ney, phony /'fəʊnɪ/ *adj* [-ier, -iest]［俚语］假的 jiǎde；伪〔僞〕造的 wěizàode. □ *n* [C] 骗〔騙〕子 piànzi；假冒者 jiǎmàozhě.
pho·nol·ogy /fə'nɒlədʒɪ/ *n* [U] 音位学〔學〕yīnwèixué；音韵〔韻〕学 yīnyùnxué.
phos·pho·rescence /ˌfɒsfə'resns/ *n* [U] 磷光 línguāng. **phos·pho·rescent** *adj*
phos·phorus /'fɒsfərəs/ *n* [U] 磷 lín.
photo /'fəʊtəʊ/ *n* [C]［非正式用语］photograph 的缩写〔寫〕*photograph* de suōxiě.
photo·copy /'fəʊtəkɒpɪ/ *vt* [*pt*, *pp* -ied] 照相复〔複〕制 zhàoxiàng fùzhì. □ *n* [C] [*pl* -ies] 照相复制本 zhàoxiàng fùzhìběn.
photo·elec·tric /ˌfəʊtəʊɪ'lektrɪk/ *adj* ~ **cell** *n* 光电〔電〕管 guāngdiànguǎn，光电仪〔儀〕guāngdiànyí.
photo·genic /ˌfəʊtə'dʒenɪk/ *adj* 适〔適〕于拍照的 shì yú pāizhào de.
photo·graph /'fəʊtəgrɑːf/ *n* [C] 照片 zhàopiàn. □ *vt* 拍照 pāizhào. ~**er** /fə'tɒgrəfə(r)/ *n* [C] 摄〔攝〕影者 shèyǐngzhě. ~**ic** /-'græfɪk/ *adj* **pho·togra·phy** /fə'tɒgrəfɪ/ *n* [U] 摄〔攝〕影术〔術〕shèyǐngshù.
phrasal /'freɪzl/ *adj* 短语的 duǎnyǔde.
phrase /freɪz/ *n* [C] **1** 短语（如 *in the garden*）duǎnyǔ，词组 cízǔ. **2** 警句 jǐngjù. □ *vt* 用话表示 yòng huà biǎoshì. '~ **book** 短语集 duǎnyǔjí.
phras·eol·ogy /ˌfreɪzɪ'ɒlədʒɪ/ *n* [U] 措词 cuòcí；用语 yòngyǔ.
physi·cal /'fɪzɪkl/ *adj* **1** 物质〔質〕的 wùzhìde: *the* ~ *world* 物质世界. **2** 身体〔體〕的 shēntǐde；肉体的 ròutǐde: ~ *exercise* 体育活动. **3** 按自然法则的 àn zìrán fǎzé de: *a* ~ *impossibility* 自然法则上不可能的事. **4** 自然（界）的 zìránde；自然科学〔學〕的 zìrán kēxué de: ~ *geography* 地文学，自然地理学. ~**ly** /-klɪ/ *adv*

phys·ician /fɪ'zɪʃn/ *n* [C] 医〔醫〕生 yīshēng.
physi·cist /'fɪzɪsɪst/ *n* [C] 物理学〔學〕家 wùlǐxuéjiā.
phys·ics /'fɪzɪks/ *n* [U] 物理学〔學〕 wùlǐxué.
physi·ol·ogy /ˌfɪzɪ'ɒlədʒɪ/ *n* [U] 生理学〔學〕 shēnglǐxué. **physi·ol·ogist** *n* [C] 生理学家 shēnglǐxuéjiā. **physio·logi·cal** /-'lɒdʒɪkl/ *adj*
physio·ther·apy /ˌfɪzɪəʊ'θerəpɪ/ *n* [U] 物理疗〔療〕法 wùlǐliáofǎ. **physio·thera·pist** *n* [C]
phy·sique /fɪ'zi:k/ *n* [U]体〔體〕格 tǐgé: *a man of strong* ~ 体格健壮的人.
pi·ano /pɪ'ænəʊ/ *n* [C] [*pl* ~s] 钢〔鋼〕琴 gāngqín. **pia·nist** /'pɪənɪst/ *n* [C] 钢琴家 gāngqínjiā.
pic·colo /'pɪkələʊ/ *n* [C] [*pl* ~s] 短笛 duǎndí.
pick[1] /pɪk/ *n* [C] 挑选〔選〕 tiāoxǔn; 选择〔擇〕 xǔnzé: *take your* ~ 你自己选择. ***the*** ~ ***of*** 精华〔華〕 jīnghuá; 最好的部分 zuìhǎode bùfèn.
pick[2] /pɪk/ *n* [C] **1** (亦作 **'~-axe**) 镐 gǎo; 丁字镐 dīngzìgǎo. **2** (用来挖掘的)尖的小工具 jiānde xiǎo-gōngjù: *a 'tooth*~ 牙签.
pick[3] /pɪk/ *vt/i* **1** 摘 zhāi, 采〔採〕 cǎi. ~ ***sb's brains*** 窃〔竊〕取某人脑〔腦〕力劳〔勞〕动〔動〕的成果 qièqǔ mǒurén nǎolì láodòng de chéngguǒ. ~***sb's pocket*** 扒窃 páqiè; [口语]掏腰包 tāo yāobāo. **2** 撕 sī, 扯 chě; 剔 tì; 挖 wā: ~ *one's teeth* 剔牙. **3** 挑选〔選〕 tiāoxǔn; 选择〔擇〕 xǔnzé: ~ *a team* 挑选班子. ~ ***a quarrel with sb*** 找机〔機〕会〔會〕吵架 zhǎo jīhuì chǎojià. **4** 挖 wā, 凿〔鑿〕 záo, 掘 jué: ~ *a hole in a shirt* 在衬衣上挖一个洞. ~ ***holes in an argument*** [喻]在辩论〔論〕中找漏洞 zài biànlùn zhōng zhǎo lòudòng. **5** (指鸟)啄食 zhuóshí; (指人)少量地吃 shǎoliàngde chī. **6** ~ ***on sb*** 挑中(某人)(叫他干不愉快的事) tiāozhòng. ~ ***sb*** (或 ***sth***) ***out***, **(a)** 选出 xuǎnchū; 拣〔揀〕出 jiǎnchū. **(b)** 区〔區〕别出 qūbiéchū; 看出 kànchū: ~ *out a friend in a crowd* 在人群中认出一位朋友. ~ ***sth up***, **(a)** 拾起 shíqǐ; 捡〔撿〕起 jiǎnqǐ. **(b)** 获〔獲〕得 huòdé; 得到 dédào: ~ *up information* 得到消息. **(c)** 恢复(健康等) huīfù: *His health is* ~*ing up.* 他的健康正在恢复. ~ ***sb up***, **(a)** 结识〔識〕 jiéshí **(b)** 中途搭乘(车等) zhōngtú dāchéng: *I'll* ~ *you up at the station.* 我的车子在车站接你.
picket /'pɪkɪt/ *n* [C] **1** 桩〔樁〕 zhuāng; 尖桩 jiānzhuāng. **2** 哨兵 shàobīng **3** (罢工时工会派出的)纠察员 jiūcháyuán. ☐ *vt/i* **1** 派…担任警戒哨 pài...dānrèn jǐngjièshào. **2** 设置纠察 shèzhì jiūchá: ~ *a factory* 在工厂设置纠察.
pickle /'pɪkl/ *n* **1** [U] (腌肉、泡菜等的)盐〔鹽〕水 yánshuǐ; 泡菜水 pàocàishuǐ. **2** 泡菜 pàocài. ☐ *vt* 腌〔醃〕 yān; 泡 pào. ~**d** *adj* [俚语]醉的 zuìde.
pick·pocket /'pɪkpɒkɪt/ *n* [C] 扒手 páshǒu; 小偷 xiǎotōu. ⇨ pick[3](1).
pick-up /'pɪk ʌp/ *n* [C] [*pl* ~s] **1** (电唱机的)唱头〔頭〕 chàngtóu. **2** 小型轻〔輕〕便货车〔車〕 xiǎoxíng qīngbiàn huòchē.
pic·nic /'pɪknɪk/ *n* [C] 野餐 yěcān. ☐ *vi* [-ck-] 野餐 yěcān.
pic·tor·ial /pɪk'tɔ:rɪəl/ *adj* 绘〔繪〕画〔畫〕的 huìhuàde; 图〔圖〕片的 túpiànde; 图画似的 túhuàsìde.
pic·ture /'pɪktʃə(r)/ *n* [C] **1** 画〔畫〕 huà; 画像 huàxiàng; 照片 zhàopiàn. **2** 完美的事物(或人) wánměide shìwù. ***be the*** ˌ~ ***of 'health*** 看来很健康 kànlái hěn jiànkāng. **3** [喻]形象描写〔寫〕一个事件 xíngxiàng miáoxiě yígè shìjiàn. ***put sb in the*** ~ 把情况告诉某人 bǎ qíngkuàng gàosu mǒurén. **4** 影片 yǐngpiàn. ☐ *vt* **1** 画 huà. **2** 想象 xiǎngxiàng: ~*oneself as a rich man* 想象自己是个富人. **the** ~**s**, [非正式用语]电〔電〕影 diànyǐng.
pic·tur·esque /ˌpɪktʃə'resk/ *adj* **1** 似画〔畫〕的 sìhuàde. **2** 生动〔動〕的 shēngdòngde: ~ *language* 生动的语言.
pidgin /'pɪdʒɪn/ *n* [C] 混杂〔雜〕语言 hǔnzá yǔyán; 不纯粹的英语 bù chúncuì de yīngyǔ.
pie /paɪ/ *n* [C,U] (肉或水果的)馅饼 xiànbǐng.
pie·bald /'paɪbɔ:ld/ *adj* (指马)黑白斑的 hēibáibānde.
piece[1] /pi:s/ *n* [C] **1** 块〔塊〕 kuài; 片 piàn; 段 duàn. ***fall to*** ~***s*** 跌碎 diēsuì. ***go (all) to*** ~***s*** [非正式用语](指人)身体〔體〕(或精神上)垮下来〔來〕 shēntǐ kuǎxiàlái. ***a*** ˌ~ ***of 'cake*** 轻〔輕〕松的事 qīngsōngde shì. **2** 个〔個〕别的事例 gèbiéde shìlì: *a* ~ *of news* 一条新闻; *a* ~ *of advice* 一个忠告. ***give sb a*** ˌ~ ***of one's 'mind*** 对某人直言不讳〔諱〕 duì mǒurén zhíyán búhuì. **3** (音乐等)首 shǒu; 件 jiàn; 幅 fú. **4** (成套中的)件 jiàn; 个〔個〕 gè:

a chess ~ 棋子. **5** 硬币〔幣〕yìngbì: *a tenpence* ~ 十便士硬币.

piece² /pi:s/ *vt* ~ **(*together*)** 拼合 pīnhé; 拼凑 pīncòu.

piece·meal /'pi:smi:l/ *adv* 零碎地 língsuìde: *work done* ~ 零碎做出的工作. □ *adj* 零碎的 língsuìde.

pier /pɪə(r)/ *n* [C] **1** 码〔碼〕头〔頭〕mǎtóu. **2** 桥〔橋〕墩 qiáodūn.

pierce /pɪəs/ *vt/i* **1** 刺穿 cìchuān; 戳入 chuōrù. **2**〔喻〕(指寒冷等)刺入 cìrù; 感动〔動〕gǎndòng. **pierc·ing** *adj* (尤指寒冷、声音)尖锐的 jiānruìde; 刺穿的 cìchuānde. **pierc·ing·ly** *adv*

piety /'paɪətɪ/ *n* [U]〔正式用语〕虔诚 qiánchéng.

pig /pɪg/ *n* **1** [C] 猪 zhū; [U] 猪肉 zhūròu. ⇨ bacon, ham, pork. **2**〔非正式用语〕猪一般的人(指肮脏、贪吃、粗野的人) zhūyībānde rén. ***make a ~ of oneself*** 吃得过〔過〕多 chī de guòduō. ˌ~-'**headed** *adj* 顽固的 wángùde. '~**sty** /-staɪ/ 猪圈 zhūjuàn. '~**tail** 辫子 biànzi. ~**gy** *n* [C] [*pl* -ies] 小猪 xiǎo zhū.

pigeon /'pɪdʒɪn/ *n* [C] 鸽〔鴿〕子 gēzi. '~**hole** *n* [C] 文件架 wénjiànjià. □ *vt* 把…搁〔擱〕置 bǎ…gēzhì. ˌ~-'**toed** *adj* 足内翻的 zúnèifān de.

pig·let /'pɪglɪt/ *n* [C] 小猪 xiǎo zhū.

pig·ment /'pɪgmənt/ *n* **1** [U] 颜料 yánliào. **2** [U] 色素 sèsù.

pigmy /'pɪgmɪ/ *n* [C] = pygmy.

pike¹ /paɪk/ *n* [C] 长〔長〕矛 chángmáo; 长枪 chángqiāng.

pike² /paɪk/ *n* [C] 狗鱼 gǒuyú; 梭子鱼 suōziyú.

pil·chard /'pɪltʃəd/ *n* [C] 沙丁鱼 shādīngyú; 沙脑〔腦〕鱼 shānǎoyú.

pile¹ /paɪl/ *n* [C] **1** 堆 duī. **2** 大笔〔筆〕钱〔錢〕财 dàbǐ qiáncái: *make one's* ~ 发财.

pile² /paɪl/ *n* [C] 桩〔樁〕zhuāng. '~-**driver** 打桩机〔機〕dǎzhuāngjī; 打桩者 dǎzhuāngzhě.

pile³ /paɪl/ *n* [U] 绒毛 róngmáo; 软〔軟〕绒 ruǎnróng.

pile⁴ /paɪl/ *vt/i* **1** 堆起 duīqǐ; 堆叠 duīdié. **2** ~ ***up***, **(a)** 堆积〔積〕duījī: *My work began to* ~ *up.* 我的工作开始堆积起来. **(b)**(指汽车)碰撞 pèngzhuàng. '~-**up** *n* **3** ~ ***into sth*** 挤〔擠〕jǐ; 进〔進〕(入) jìn; ~ ***out of sth*** 走(出).

pil·fer /'pɪlfə(r)/ *vt/i* 小偷小摸 xiǎotōu xiǎomō.

pil·grim /'pɪlgrɪm/ *n* [C] 香客 xiāngkè; 朝拜圣〔聖〕地者 cháobài shèngdì zhě. '~**age** /-ɪdʒ/ 朝圣 cháoshèng.

pill /pɪl/ *n* [C] **1** 药〔藥〕丸 yàowán. **2 the** ~ 口服避孕药 kǒufú bìyùnyào.

pil·lar /'pɪlə(r)/ *n* [C] **1** 柱 zhù, 柱子 zhùzi. **2** 栋〔棟〕梁 dòngliáng; 支柱 zhīzhù: *a* ~ *of the Church* 教会的中坚. '~-**box** 邮〔郵〕筒 yóutǒng, 信筒 xìntǒng.

pil·lion /'pɪlɪən/ *n* [C] 摩托车〔車〕后〔後〕座 mótuōchē hòuzuò.

pil·low /'pɪləʊ/ *n* [C] 枕头〔頭〕zhěntou. □ *vt* 把…搁〔擱〕在枕上 bǎ…gē zài zhěn shàng. '~-**case** (或 **-slip**) 枕套 zhěntào.

pi·lot /'paɪlət/ *n* [C] **1** 领港员 lǐnggǎngyuán; 领航员 lǐnghángyuán. **2** 飞〔飛〕行员 fēixíngyuán, 飞机〔機〕驾〔駕〕驶〔駛〕员 fēijī jiàshǐyuán. **3**〔用作定语〕(小规模)试验〔驗〕性的 shìyànxìngde: *a* '~ *scheme* (小规模)试验计划. □ *vt* 领航 lǐngháng; 驾驶 jiàshǐ.

pim·ple /'pɪmpl/ *n* [C] 丘疹 qiūzhěn; 脓〔膿〕疱 nóngpào. **pim·ply** *adj* [-ier, -iest]

pin¹ /pɪn/ *n* [C] 大头〔頭〕针 dàtóuzhēn; 别针 biézhēn. ⇨ safety pin, drawing pin. ˌ~**s and 'needles** 发〔發〕麻 fāmá. '~**point** *vt* 〔喻〕精确〔確〕地发现目标〔標〕jīngquède fāxiàn mùbiāo. '~**stripe** (织物上的)细条〔條〕子 xìtiáozi.

pin² /pɪn/ *vt* [-nn-] **1** (用别针)别住 biézhù; 钉住 dīngzhù. **2** 使不能行动〔動〕shǐ bùnéng xíngdòng; 牵〔牽〕制 qiānzhì: *He was* ~*ned under a fallen tree.* 他被压在倒下的树下. ~ ***sb down***〔喻〕使某人作出承诺 shǐ mǒurén zuòchū chéngnuò.

pina·fore /'pɪnəfɔ:(r)/ *n* [C] 围〔圍〕涎 wéixián.

pin·cers /'pɪnsəz/ *n pl* (亦作 *a pair of* ~*s*) **1** 钳子 qiánzi. **2** 螯 áo.

pinch /pɪntʃ/ *vt/i* **1** 捏〔揑〕niē; 拧〔擰〕níng; 掐 qiā. **2** 夹痛 jiātòng; 紧〔緊〕压〔壓〕jǐnyā: *These shoes* ~. 这双鞋太紧. **3**〔非正式用语〕偷 tōu; 盗窃〔竊〕dàoqiè. □ *n* [C] **1** 捏 niē; 拧 níng; 夹 jiā. **2** 〔喻〕重压 zhòngyā; 压力 yālì: *feel the* ~ *of poverty* 感受贫困的重压. **3** 微量 wēiliàng: *a* ~ *of tobacco.* 一捏烟草. **4** ***at a*** ~ 必要时〔時〕bìyàoshí.

pine¹ /paɪn/ *n* [C] 松树〔樹〕sōngshù; [U] 松木 sōngmù.

pine² /paɪn/ *vi* **1** 消瘦 xiāoshòu; 衰弱 shuāiruò. **2** ~ ***for sth*** (或

to do sth) 渴望 kěwàng.

pine·apple /'paɪnæpl/ *n* [C] 凤〔鳳〕梨树〔樹〕fènglíshù; [U] 菠萝〔蘿〕bōluó.

ping·pong /'pɪŋpɒŋ/ *n* [C] = table tennis.

pin·ion /'pɪnɪən/ *n* [C] 小齿〔齒〕轮〔輪〕xiǎo chǐlún.

pink /pɪŋk/ *n, adj* **1** [U] 粉红色 fěnhóngsè; 粉红色的 fěnhóngsède. **2** [C] 石竹 shízhú; 石竹花 shízhúhuā. **3** *in the* ~ 〔非正式用语〕(健康)良好 liánghǎo.

pin·nacle /'pɪnəkl/ *n* [C] **1** 尖塔 jiāntǎ; 尖顶 jiāndǐng. **2** 山顶 shāndǐng; 山峰 shānfēng. **3**〔喻〕顶点〔點〕dǐngdiǎn: *the* ~ *of his career* 他事业的顶峰.

pin·point /'pɪn pɔɪnt/ ⇨ pin¹.

pin·stripe /'pɪn straɪp/ ⇨ pin¹.

pint /paɪnt/ *n* [C] **1** 品脱(液量名) pǐntuō. **2** 一品脱啤酒 yìpǐntuō píjiǔ.

pin-up /'pɪn ʌp/ *n* [C] 挂〔掛〕在墙〔牆〕上的漂亮女人照片 guà zài qiángshàng de piàoliàng nǚrén zhàopiàn.

pion·eer /ˌpaɪə'nɪə(r)/ *n* [C] 拓荒者 tuōhuāngzhě; 开〔開〕辟〔闢〕者 kāipìzhě; 先驱〔驅〕xiānqū. □ *vt/i* 当〔當〕先驱 dāng xiānqū; 开辟 kāipì.

pi·ous /'paɪəs/ *adj* 虔诚的 qiánchéngde; 虔敬的 qiánjìngde. ~**ly** *adv*

pip¹ /pɪp/ *n* [C] 种〔種〕子(尤指水果) zhǒngzhi.

pip² /pɪp/ *n* [C] (电话或广播中的)报〔報〕时〔時〕信号〔號〕bàoshí xìnghào.

pipe¹ /paɪp/ *n* [C] **1** 管子 guǎnzi. **2** 管乐〔樂〕器 guǎnyuèqì; 管状〔狀〕器官 guǎnzhuàng qìguān; (*pl*) = bagpipes. **3** 鸟〔鳥〕叫声〔聲〕niǎo jiàoshēng. **4** 烟〔煙〕斗 yāndǒu. ~**line** 管道 guǎndào; 油管 yóuguǎn. *in the* ~*line* 运〔運〕输〔輸〕中 yùnshū zhōng.

pipe² /paɪp/ *vt/i* **1** 用管道输〔輸〕送 yòng guǎndào shūsòng. **2** 用管乐〔樂〕器吹奏 yòng guǎnyuèqì chuīzòu. ~ *down* 〔非正式用语〕禁声〔聲〕jìnshēng.

pipe·line /'paɪplaɪn/ *n* ⇨ pipe¹.

piper /'paɪpə(r)/ *n* [C] 吹奏人 chuīzòurén.

pip·ette /pɪ'pet/ *n* [C] 吸量管 xīliàngguǎn.

pi·quant /'pi:kənt/ *adj* 辛辣的xīnlàde; 开〔開〕胃的 kāiwèide. ~**ly** *adv* **pi·quancy** *n* [U]

pi·racy /'paɪərəsɪ/ *n* [*pl* -ies] [C, U] **1** 海上掠夺〔奪〕hǎishàng lüèduó. **2** 侵犯版权〔權〕qīnfàn bǎnquán; 非法翻印 fēifǎ fānyìn.

pi·rate /'paɪərət/ *n* [C] **1** 掠夺〔奪〕者 lüèduózhě. **2** 侵犯版权〔權〕者 qīnfàn bǎnquán zhě. □ *vt* 非法翻印 fēifǎ fānyìn.

pir·ou·ette /ˌpɪrʊ'et/ *n* [C] (芭蕾)舞蹈中以脚尖急速旋转〔轉〕wǔdǎo zhōng yǐ jiǎojiān jísù xuánzhuàn. □ *vi* 用脚尖旋转 yòng jiǎojiān xúnzhuàn.

piss /pɪs/ *vt/i* △〔粗俗语〕小便 xiǎobiàn. □ *n*[U] 尿 niào. ~**ed** *adj* △〔粗俗语〕酩酊大醉 mǐngdǐng dà zuì.

pis·tol /'pɪstl/ *n* [C] 手枪〔槍〕shǒuqiāng.

pis·ton /'pɪstən/ *n* [C] 活塞 huósāi.

pit /pɪt/ *n* [C] **1** 坑 (如 *a 'coal-*~) kēng. **2** 躯〔軀〕体〔體〕凹部 qūtǐ āobù: *the* ~ *of the stomach* 心窝. ⇨ armpit. **3** 麻子 mázi; 天花疤痕 tiānhuā bāhén. **4** (*pl*) (赛车中途的)加油站 jiāyóuzhàn; 修理站 xiūlǐzhàn. **5** (剧场)楼〔樓〕下正厅〔廳〕(后座) lóuxià zhèngtīng. □ *vt* [-tt-] 使留下疤痕 shǐ liúxià bāhén. '~**fall** 隐藏着的危险 yǐncángzhede wēixiǎn

pitch¹ /pɪtʃ/ *n* [C] **1** (足球、板球等)球场〔場〕qiúchǎng. **2** 投掷〔擲〕tóuzhì. **3** 声〔聲〕音的高低度 shēngyīnde gāodīdù. **4** 程度 chéngdù: *a high* ~ *of excitement* 异常激动. **5** (指船)上下颠簸 shàngxià diānbǒ.

pitch² /pɪtʃ/ *n* [U] 沥〔瀝〕青 lìqīng. ˌ~-'**black** *adj* 漆黑的 qīhēide.

pitch³ /pɪtʃ/ *vt/i* **1** 搭(帐) dā; 扎(营) zhā. **2** 投 tóu, 掷〔擲〕zhì. **3** (音乐)为〔爲〕...定调 wèi...dìngdiào. **4** (头向下)坠〔墜〕落 zhuìluò; 向前倾跌 xiàngqián qīngdiē: *The car crashed and the driver was* ~*ed out.* 汽车撞坏,司机摔出车外. **5** (指船)上下颠簸 shàngxià diānbǒ. **6** ~ *in* 开〔開〕始努力工作 kāishǐ nǔlì gōngzuò. ~ *into*, **(a)** 猛烈攻击〔擊〕měngliè gōngjī. **(b)** 着手 zhuóshǒu. '~**fork** 长〔長〕柄叉 chángbǐngchā; 干〔乾〕草叉 gāncǎochā.

pitcher /'pɪtʃə(r)/ *n* [C] 大水罐 dàshuǐguàn.

pit·eous /'pɪtɪəs/ *adj* 〔正式用语〕令人哀怜〔憐〕的 lìng rén āilián de: *a* ~ *cry* 令人怜悯的哭声. ~**ly** *adv*

pit·fall /'pɪtfɔ:l/ ⇨ pit.

pith /pɪθ/ *n* [U] **1** 木髓 mùsuí. **2** 桔皮里面柔软〔軟〕的部分 júpí lǐmiàn róuruǎn de bùfen. **3**〔喻〕重

要部分 zhòngyào bùfen. **pithy** *adj* [-ier, -iest] **(a)** 多髓的 duōsuíde. **(b)** 简〔簡〕练〔練〕的 jiǎnliànde: *~y remarks* 简明的谈话. **~ily** *adv*

piti·able /'pɪtɪəbl/ *adj* 令人怜〔憐〕悯〔憫〕的 lìngrén liánmǐn de: *a ~ attempt* 可怜又可鄙的企图. **piti·ably** *adv*

piti·ful /'pɪtɪfl/ *adj* **1** 有同情心的 yǒu tóngqíngxīn de. **2** 可怜〔憐〕的 kěliánde; 令人同情的 lìng rén tóngqíngde. **3** = pitiable. **~ly** *adv*

piti·less /'pɪtɪls/ *adj* 无〔無〕情的 wúqíng de; 无怜〔憐〕悯〔憫〕心的 wú liánmǐnxīn de. **~ly** *adv*

pit·tance /'pɪtns/ *n* [C] 微薄的收入 wēibóde shōurù.

pity /'pɪtɪ/(*pl -ies*) **1** 怜〔憐〕悯〔憫〕liánmǐn, 同情 tóngqíng. ***have (take) ~ on sb*** 帮助不幸的人 bāngzhù búxìng de rén. ***out of ~*** 由于怜〔憐〕悯〔憫〕之情 yóuyú liánmǐn zhī qíng. **2** 表示遗憾的原因 biǎoshì yíhànde yuányīn: *What a ~ that you lost it!* 你丢掉它多么可惜! □ *vt* [*pt, pp* -ied] 同情 tóngqíng.

pivot /'pɪvət/ *n* [C] **1** 枢〔樞〕轴〔軸〕shūzhóu; 支点〔點〕zhīdiǎn. **2** [喻]辩论〔論〕的要点 biànlùnde yàodiǎn. □ *vt/i* 在枢轴上转〔轉〕动〔動〕zài shūzhóu shàng zhuàndòng **~al** *adj*

pixy, pixie /'pɪksɪ/ *n* [C] [*pl* -ies] 小妖精 xiǎo yāojīng.

pizza /'pi:tsə/ *n* [C,U] (意大利式)烘馅饼 hōngxiànbǐng.

pl. = **plural**.

plac·ard /'plækɑ:d/ *n* [C] 布〔佈〕告 bùgào; 招贴 zhāotiē. □ *vt* 贴布告于 tiē bùgào yú.

pla·cate /plə'keɪt/ *vt* = pacify.

place[1] /pleɪs/ *n* [C] **1** 地方 dìfang ***in (out of) ~*, (a)** 在(不在)适〔適〕当〔當〕的地位 zài shìdàngde dìwèi. **(b)** [喻]适合的 shìhéde; 不适合的 bú shìhé de: *his remarks were out of ~.* 他的话不恰当. ***in ~ of*** 代替 dàitì. ***put sb in his (proper) ~***, ⇨ put(2). ***take ~*** 发〔發〕生 fāshēng. **2** 城市 chéngshì; 镇 zhèn. **3** (有特定用途的)场〔場〕所 chǎngsuǒ: *a ~ of worship* 礼拜的场所, 教堂. **4** (社会上的)地位 dìwèi; 阶〔階〕级 jiējí. ***keep sb in his ~*** 使某人保持他的身分 shǐ mǒurén bǎochí tāde shēnfen. **5** (竞赛时获胜者的)名次 míngcì. **6** (辩论等的)步骤 bùzhòu: *in the first ~* 第一点. **7** 职〔職〕位 zhíwèi; 职责 zhízé: *a ~ in the team* 工作班子中的职位. **8** [非正式用语]住所 zhùsuǒ; 屋子 wūzi. **9** (用于专有名词)街道 jiēdào; 广〔廣〕场 guǎngchǎng: *St James's P~* 圣詹姆斯街. **10** 席位 xíwèi; (餐桌等的)座位 zuòwèi.

place[2] /pleɪs/ *vt* **1** 放置 fàngzhì, 放 fàng. **2** 任命 rènmìng. **3** 发〔發〕出(订单) fāchū. **4** 认〔認〕出 rènchū; 认定 rèndìng: *I know his face, but I can't ~ him.* 我熟悉他的面孔, 但不能确定他是谁.

pla·centa /plə'sentə/ *n* [C] [解剖] 胎盘〔盤〕tāipán.

pla·cid /'plæsɪd/ *adj* 平静的 píngjìngde; 安静的 ānjìngde. **~ly** *adv*

pla·giar·ize /'pleɪdʒəraɪz/ *vt* 剽窃 piáoqiè; 抄袭〔襲〕(别人的学说、著作等) chāoxí. **pla·giar·ism** /-rɪzəm/ *n* [C,U]

plague /pleɪg/ *n* [C,U] **1** 瘟疫 wēnyì. **2** [喻]麻烦 máfán; 祸〔禍〕患 huòhuàn: *a ~ of rats* 鼠灾, 鼠疫. □ *vt* **~(with)** 烦扰〔擾〕fánrǎo: *~d with questions* 被问得烦死了.

plaice /pleɪs/ *n* [C] 鲽 dié.

plaid /plæd/ *n* [C] (苏格兰高地人所披的)肩巾 jiānjīn.

plain[1] /pleɪn/ *adj* [-er, -est] **1** 清楚的 qīngchude; 明白的 míngbaide. **2** 简〔簡〕单〔單〕的 jiǎndānde; 朴〔樸〕素的 pǔsùde: *~ food* 便饭. ***in ~ clothes*** 穿着便衣 chuānzhe biànyī. **3** (指人)直率的 zhíshuàide; 坦白的 tǎnbáide. ***in ~ words*** 坦白地 tǎnbáide. **4** (指人的仪表)不好看的 bù hǎokànde: *a very ~ girl* 不漂亮的女孩. □ *adv* 清楚地 qīngchude. **,~-'spoken** *adj* 坦率的 tǎnshuàide. **~ly** *adv* **~ness** *n* [U]

plain[2] /pleɪn/ *n* [C] 平原 píngyuán; 平地 píngdì.

plain·tive /'pleɪntɪv/ *adj* 哀伤〔傷〕的 āishāngde; 忧〔憂〕愁的 yōuchóude. **~ly** *adv*

plait /plæt/ *vt* 把…编成辫 bǎ...biānchéng biàn. □ *n* [C] 发〔髮〕辫 fàbiàn; 辫状〔狀〕物 biànzhuàngwù.

plan /plæn/ *n* [C] **1** (建筑物、城市、花园等)略图〔圖〕lüètú. **2** (机器部件)图形 túxíng. **3** 计划〔劃〕jìhuà; 方案 fāng'àn: *make ~s for the holidays* 作度假计划. □ *vt* [-nn-] 计划 jìhuà.

plane[1] /pleɪn/ *n* [C] (a'~tree) 悬〔懸〕铃木属〔屬〕树〔樹〕木 xuánlíngmùshǔ shùmù.

plane[2] /pleɪn/ *n* [C] 刨刀 bàodāo. □ *vt* 刨平 bàopíng.

plane[3] /pleɪn/ *n* [C] **1** 平面 píngmiàn. **2** [非正式用语] = aeroplane. **3** [喻]水平 shuǐpíng; 阶〔階〕段 jiēduàn. □ *adj* 平的 píngde, 平坦的 píngtǎnde.

planet/'plænɪt/ *n* [C] 行星(如*Mars, Venus*) xíngxīng. ~**ary** /-trɪ/ *adj*

planet·ar·ium /ˌplænɪ'teərɪəm/ *n* [C] 天文馆 tiānwénguǎn.

plank /plæŋk/ *n* [C] 厚板 hòubǎn. '~**ing** *n* [U] 板材 bǎncái; 地板 dìbǎn.

plank·ton /'plæŋktən/ *n* [U] 浮游生物 fúyóu shēngwù.

plant[1] /plɑ:nt/ *n* [C] **1** 植物 zhíwù; 幼苗 yòumiáo. **2** 仪〔儀〕器 yíqì; 设备〔備〕shèbèi; **3** 工厂〔廠〕gōngchǎng.

plant[2] /plɑ:nt/ *vt* **1** 种植 zhòngzhí; 栽培 zāipéi. **2** [喻]灌输 guànshū. **3** 安插 ānchā. **4** [俚语]窝〔窩〕藏(赃物) wōcáng; 栽(赃) zāi.

plan·ta·tion /plæn'teɪʃn/ *n* [C] 种〔種〕植园〔園〕zhòngzhíyuán.

plaque /plɑ:k/ *n* [C] 饰板 shìbǎn.

plasma /'plæzmə/ *n* [U] 血浆〔漿〕xuèjiāng.

plas·ter /plɑ:stə(r)/ *n* **1** [U] 灰泥 huīní **2** [C] 膏药〔藥〕gāoyào. □ *vt* **1** 在…涂〔塗〕灰泥 zài...tú huīní. **2** 厚厚地涂抹 hòuhòude túmǒ: *hair ~ed with oil* 擦了油的头发. ˌ~ **of 'Paris** 石膏粉 shígāofěn. '~ **cast,** **(a)** 石膏绷带〔帶〕shígāo bēngdài. **(b)** 石膏像 shígāoxiàng. ~**er,** 泥水匠 níshuǐjiàng, 瓦工 wǎgōng.

plas·tic /'plæstɪk/ *adj* **1** 易塑的 yìsùde; 可塑的 kěsùde. **2** 塑料的 sùliàode; 塑料制的 sùliàozhìde. **3** 塑造的 sùzàode. □ *n* [C, U] 塑料 sùliào; 塑料制品 sùliào zhìpǐn. ˌ~'**surgery** 整形外科 zhěngxíng wàikē.

plas·ti·cine /'plæstɪsi:n/ *n* [U] 代用粘土 dàiyòng niántǔ.

plate /pleɪt/ *n* **1** [C] 盘〔盤〕子 pánzi. **2** [U] 金银餐具 jīn yín cānjù. **3** [C] (金属、玻璃)板 bǎn. **4** [印刷]印版 yìnbǎn; 图〔圖〕板 túbǎn; 整页插图 zhěngyè chātú. □ *vt* **1** 覆以金属〔屬〕板 fù yǐ jīnshǔbǎn. **2** 镀(金、银等) dù.

pla·teau /'plætəʊ/ *n* [C] [*pl* ~s 或 ~x /-təʊz/] 高原 gāoyuán.

plat·form /'plætfɔ:m/ *n* [C]**1** 月台〔臺〕yuètái, 站台 zhàntái. **2** 讲〔講〕台 jiǎngtái. **3** (政党的)政纲〔綱〕zhènggāng; 党〔黨〕纲 dǎnggāng.

plat·ing /'pleɪtɪŋ/ *n* [U] (尤指) 一层〔層〕极〔極〕薄的金属〔屬〕(如金、银等) yìcéng jíbóde jīnshǔ. ⇨ plate *vt* (2).

plati·num /'plætɪnəm/ *n* [U]白金 báijīn; 铂 **(Pt)**bó.

plati·tude /'plætɪtju:d/ *n* [C] 陈〔陳〕词滥〔濫〕调 chéncí làndiào.

pla·toon /plə'tu:n/ *n* [C] [军事]排 pái.

platy·pus /'plætɪpəs/ *n* [C] [*pl* ~-es /-pəsɪz/],**duck-billed**' ~ 鸭〔鴨〕嘴兽〔獸〕yāzuǐshòu.

plaus·ible /'plɔ:zəbl/ *adj* 似乎有理的 sìhū yǒulǐ de. **plaus·ibly** *adv*

play[1] /pleɪ/ *n* **1** [C] 剧〔劇〕本 jùběn; 戏〔戲〕剧 xìjù. **2** [U] 游戏 yóuxì; 消遣 xiāoqiǎn. ***a*** ˌ~ ***on 'words*** = pun. **3** [U] 运〔運〕动〔動〕yùndòng. ⇨ fair play. **4** [U] 闪〔閃〕动 shǎndòng; 跳动 tiàodòng: *the ~ of sunlight on water* 阳光在水面上闪烁. **5** [U] 自由活动 zìyóu huódòng; 自由活动的空间 zìyóu huódòng de kōngjiān: *a lot of ~ in a rope* 一条可以大大放开的绳子. '~**boy** 追求享乐〔樂〕者 zhuīqiú xiǎnglè zhě. '~**ground** 运动场〔場〕yùndòngchǎng. '~**house** = theatre. '~**mate** 游戏的伙伴 yóuxìde huǒbàn. '~**-pen** 供婴儿〔兒〕在内玩的围〔圍〕栏〔欄〕gòng yīng'ér zài nèi wán de wéilán. '~**thing,** **(a)** 玩具 wánjù. **(b)** 〔喻〕玩物 wánwù. '~**wright** 剧作家 jùzuòjiā.

play[2] /pleɪ/ *vt*/*i* [*pt,pp* ~ed /pleɪd/] **1** (与 *work* 相对) 玩 wán; 游戏〔戲〕yóuxì. **2** ~ ***(at doing sth)*** 假装〔裝〕jiǎzhuāng; 装扮 zhuāngbàn. **3** 做 zuò; 实〔實〕行 shíxíng: *He ~ed a trick on me.* 他捉弄了我. ~ ***it cool*** ⇨ cool[1](2). ~ ***into sb's hands*** ⇨ hand[1](2). ~ ***for time*** ⇨ time(3). ~ ***truant*** ⇨ truant. **4** 参加比赛 cānjiā bǐsài. **5** 打(球) dǎ; 踢(球) tī. **6** 移动〔動〕(棋子) yídòng; 出(牌) chū. ~ ***the game,*** **(a)** 遵守比赛规则 zūnshǒu bǐsài guīzé. **(b)** [喻]行动光明正大 xíngdòng guāngmíng zhèngdà. **7** 演奏 yǎnzòu; 弹〔彈〕tán; 拉 lā; 吹 chuī. ~ ***sth back*** (唱片、录音机等) 放音 fàngyīn. '~**-back** *n* ~ ***sth by ear*** ⇨ ear[1](2). **8** 演(戏) yǎn. ~ ***the fool*** ⇨ fool. **9** 闪〔閃〕动 shǎndòng; 飘〔飄〕动 piāodòng: *sunlight ~ing on the water* 水面上闪烁的阳光. **10** 喷出 pēnchū: *~ water on a burning building* 向燃烧的建筑物上喷水. **11** ~ ***at sth,*** **(a)** ⇨ 2 above. **(b)** 做事不认〔認〕真 zuòshì bú rènzhēn. ~ ***sth down*** 不太重视 bú tài zhòngshì. ~ ***on sth*** 利用 lìyòng. ~ ***up*** [非正式用语]顽皮的 wánpíde. ~ ***sth up*** 强调 qiángdiào. ~ ***sb up*** [非正式用语]使恼〔惱〕火 shǐ nǎohuǒ

~ *with sb (sth)*, (a) ⇨ 1 above.(b) 玩弄 wánnòng; (不认真地)对〔對〕待或考虑〔慮〕duìdài huò kǎolǜ.

player /'pleɪə(r)/ *n* [C] **1** 游戏〔戲〕的人 yóuxìde rén. **2** 演员 yǎnyuán. **3** 演奏者 yǎnzòuzhě. **4** 自动〔動〕演奏装置 zìdòng yǎnzòu zhuāngzhì: *a' record-*~ 唱机.

play·ful/'pleɪfl/ *adj* 顽皮的 wánpíde; 开〔開〕玩笑的 kāi wánxiào de. ~**ly** *adv* ~**ness** *n* [U]

plea /pli:/ *n* [C] **1**〔法律〕抗辩 kàngbiàn. **2** 恳〔懇〕求 kěnqiú; 请求 qǐngqiú: *a ~ for mercy* 恳求宽恕. **3** 托词 tuōcí; 口实〔實〕kǒushí.

plead /pli:d/ *vt/i* [*pt,pp* ~ed, 或美语 pled] **1** ~ *for sb* 为〔爲〕...辩护〔護〕wèi...biànhù; ~ *against sb* 反驳〔駁〕某人 fǎnbó mǒurén. **2** ~ *guilty* 服罪 fúzuì. ~ *not guilty* 不服罪 bù fúzuì. **3** 以...为借口 yǐ...wéi jièkǒu. **4** ~ (*with sb*) 恳求 kěnqiú.

pleas·ant /'pleznt/ *adj* 令人愉快的 lìng rén yúkuàide; 友爱〔愛〕的 yǒu'àide. ~**ly** *adv* ~**ness** *n* [U]

pleas·ant·ry /'plezntrɪ/ *n* [*pl* -ies]〔正式用语〕**1** [U] 幽默 yōumò. **2** [C] 打趣的话 dǎqùde huà.

please /pli:z/ *vt/i* **1** (客套话)请 qǐng: *Come in,* ~. 请进来. **2** 使高兴〔興〕shǐ gāoxìng; 使满意 shǐ mǎnyì. **3** 选〔選〕择〔擇〕xuǎnzé: *I shall do as I* ~. 我将做我高兴做的事情. **pleased** *adj* 高兴〔興〕的 gāoxìngde; 满意的 mǎnyìde. **pleas·ing** *adj* (a) 使人愉快的 shǐ rén yúkuàide (b) 可爱〔愛〕的 kě'àide.

pleas·ure /'pleʒə(r)/ *n* **1** [U] 愉快 yúkuài; 高兴〔興〕gāoxìng. **2** [U]〔正式用语〕愿〔願〕望 yuànwàng: *at your* ~ 随意, 随便. **3** [C] 乐〔樂〕事 lèshì; 乐趣 lèqù. **pleas·ur·able** /-rəbl/ *adj* 令人愉快的 lìng rén yúkuài de. **pleas·ur·ably** *adv*

pleat /pli:t/ *n* [C] 褶 zhě. □ *vt* 使打褶 shǐ dǎzhě.

plec·trum /'plektrəm/ *n* [C] (弹弦乐器用的)拨〔撥〕子 bōzi; 琴拨 qínbō.

pledge /pledʒ/ *n* **1** [C] 抵押品 dǐyāpǐn; 典当〔當〕物 diǎndàngwù. **2** [U] 抵押 dǐyā: *put (hold) goods in* ~ 以货物抵押. **3** [C] 象征〔徵〕xiàngzhēng. **4** [U] 保证 bǎozhèng. □ *vt* **1** 抵押 dǐyā; 典当 diǎndàng. **2** 保证 bǎozhèng.

plen·ti·ful /'plentɪfl/ *adj* 丰〔豐〕富的 fēngfùde; 多的 duōde: *a* ~ *supply* 充裕的供应. ~**ly** *adv*

plenty /'plentɪ/ *n* [U] ~ (*of*) 丰〔豐〕富 fēngfù; 大量 dàliàng.

pli·able /'plaɪəbl/ *adj* **1** 易弯〔彎〕的 yìwānde; 柔韧〔韌〕的 róurènde. **2** 易受影响〔響〕的 yì shòu yǐngxiǎng de. **pli·a'bil·ity** *n* [U]

pli·ers /'plaɪəz/ *n pl* (亦作 *a pair of* ~) 钳子 qiánzi; 老虎钳 lǎohǔqián.

plight /plaɪt/ *n* [C] 困境 kùnjìng; 苦境 kǔjìng.

plim·soll /'plɪmsəl/ *n* [C] 橡皮底帆布鞋 xiàngpídǐ fānbùxié [美语 = sneaker].

Plim·soll line /'plɪmsəl laɪn/ *n* [C] 载〔載〕重线〔線〕标〔標〕志 zǎizhòngxiàn biāozhì.

plinth /plɪnθ/ *n* [C] 底座 dǐzuò; 柱基 zhùjī.

plod /plɒd/*vt/i* [-dd-] **1** 沉重缓慢地走 chénzhòng huǎnmàn de zǒu. **2** 沉闷〔悶〕地苦干 chénmènde kǔgàn. ~**der**, (a) 拖着沉重步子走的人 tuōzhe chénzhòng bùzi zǒu de rén. (b) 沉闷苦干的人 chénmèn kǔgàn de rén. ~**ding** *adj*

plot[1] /plɒt/ *n* [C] 小块〔塊〕土地 xiǎokuài tǔdì. □ *vt/i* [-tt-] **1** 绘〔繪〕制...的图〔圖〕huìzhì...de tú. **2** 标〔標〕绘 biāohuì. **3** ~ (*out*) 把...划〔劃〕成小块地 bǎ...huà chéng xiǎo kuàidì.

plot[2] /plɒt/ *n* [C] **1** 阴〔陰〕谋 yīnmóu. **2** (故事的)情节〔節〕qíngjié. □ *vt/i* [-tt-] 密谋 mìmóu; 策划〔劃〕cèhuà. ~**ter** 密谋者 mìmóuzhě.

plough [美语 = **plow**] /plaʊ/ *n* [C] **1** 犁 lí. **2** 犁形器具 líxíng qìjù: *a snow* ~ 扫〔掃〕雪机〔機〕. **3 the P**~〔天文〕北斗七星 běidǒuqīxīng. □ *vt/i* **1** 犁(地) lí; 耕(田) gēng. **2** ~ (*back*)〔喻〕(把利润)再投资 zài tóuzī. **3** ~ *through* 开〔開〕路 kāilù; 跋涉 báshè.

plow /plaʊ/〔美语〕= plough.

ploy /plɔɪ/ *n* [C]〔非正式用语〕职〔職〕业〔業〕zhíyè; 消遣 xiāoqiǎn.

pluck /plʌk/ *vt/i* **1** 拔...的毛 bá...de máo. **2** 采 cǎi, 摘 zhāi. **3** ~ *at* 拉 lā; 扯 chě **4** ~ *up courage* 鼓起勇气〔氣〕gǔqǐ yǒngqì. □ *n* [U] 勇气 yǒngqì. **plucky** *adj* [-ier, -iest] 勇敢的 yǒnggǎnde.

plug /plʌg/ *n* [C] **1** 塞子 sāizi; 栓 shuān. **2** 插头〔頭〕chātóu. ⇨ sparking-plug. **3**〔俚语〕广〔廣〕告 guǎnggào. □*vt/i* [-gg-] **1** 塞 sāi; 堵 dǔ. **2** ~ (*sth*) *in* 插上插头接通电〔電〕源 chā shàng chātóu jiētōng diànyuán. **3**〔非正式用语〕~

away at 苦干 kǔgàn. 4[俚语]大肆宣传[傳] dàsì xuānchuán.

plum /plʌm/ *n* [C] 1 李属[屬]植物 lǐshǔ zhíwù; 李子 lǐzi; 梅子 méizi. 2[非正式用语][用作定语]佳品 jiāpǐn; 最好的东[東]西 zuìhǎode dōngxi: *a* ~ *job* 最好的职业; 理想的工作.

plum·age /'plu:mɪdʒ/ *n* [U] 鸟[鳥]羽 niǎoyǔ; 羽毛 yǔmáo.

plumb /plʌm/ *n* [C] (*a* '~*-line*) 铅锤 qiānchuí; 测锤 cèchuí. □ *adv* 恰恰 qiàqià; 正 zhèng: ~ *in the middle* 正在中间; 不偏不依. □ *vt* [喻]探测 tàncè; 查明 chámíng: ~ *the depths of a mystery* 探查神秘的底细.

plumber /'plʌmə(r)/ *n* [C] 管子工 guǎnzigōng.

plumb·ing /'plʌmɪŋ/ *n* [U] 1 铅管业[業] qiānguǎnyè; 管子工作 guǎnzi gōngzuò. 2 (总称) 管件 guǎnjiàn.

plume /plu:m/ *n* [C] 1 羽毛 yǔmáo; 羽饰 yǔshì. 2 羽状[狀]物 yǔzhuàngwù: *a* ~ *of smoke* 一缕烟.

plum·met /'plʌmɪt/ *vi* [-tt-] 骤[驟]然跌落 zhòurán diēluò.

plump[1] /plʌmp/ *adj* 丰[豐]满的 fēngmǎnde □ *vt/i* ~ **out** (**up**) 鼓起 gǔqǐ.

plump[2] /plʌmp/ *vt/i* 1 突然而沉重地落下 tūrán ér chénzhòng de luòxià. 2 ~ **for** 投票赞成 tóupiào zànchéng; 坚[堅]决拥[擁]护[護] jiānjué yōnghù. □ *adv* 突然 tūrán; 蓦[驀]地 mòdì. □ *n* [C] 坠[墜]落 zhuìluò.

plun·der /'plʌndə(r)/ *vt/i* 抢[搶]劫 qiǎngjié; 掠夺[奪] lüèduó. □ *n* [U] 掠夺 lüèduó; 掠夺物 lüèduówù.

plunge /plʌndʒ/ *vt/i* ~ **(into)** 投入 tóurù; 插入 chārù; 陷入 xiànrù. □ *n* [C] 投入 tóurù; 陷入 xiànrù; 跳入tiàorù. ***take the*** ~ [喻]冒险[險]尝[嘗]试 màoxiǎn chángshì. **plunger** 活塞 huósāi; 柱塞 zhùsāi.

plu·ral /'plʊərəl/ *n* [C], *adj* 复[複]数[數](的) fùshù: The ~ of *child* is *children*. *child* 的复数是 *children*.

plus /plʌs/ *prep* 加 jiā; 加上 jiāshàng: *Two* ~ *five is seven* 二加五等于七. □ *adj*: *a* ~ *quantity*[数学] 正的. ⇨ minus. □ *n* [C] [-ss-] 加号[號] jiāhào; 正号(+) zhènghào.

plush /plʌʃ/ *adj* [俚语] 奢侈豪华[華]的 shēchǐ háohuá de.

plu·to·nium /plu:'təʊnɪəm/ *n* [U] 钚 (**Pu**) bù.

ply[1] /plaɪ/ *n* [C] 1 厚度 hòudù; 层[層]片 céngpiàn. 2 (毛、绳等的) 绹 táo; 股 gǔ. '~**wood** 三夹[夾]板 sānjiābǎn; 合板 hébǎn.

ply[2] /plaɪ/ *vt/i* [*pt, pp* plied, *pres part* plying] 1 (车船等) 定期地往返或横渡 dìngqīde wǎngfǎn huò héngdù: *oil tankers* ~*ing the Indian Ocean* 在印度洋上往返航行的油船. 2 ~ *sb with sth* 不断[斷]供给…饮食 búduàn gōngjǐ yǐngshí.

P.M.=Prime Minister 总[總]理 zǒnglǐ; 首相 shǒuxiàng.

p.m.=1 after noon. 2 per month 每月 měiyuè.

P.M.G. =Postmaster-General 邮[郵]政总[總]长[長] yóuzhèng zǒngzhǎng.

pneu·matic /nju:'mætɪk/ *adj* 由压[壓]缩空气[氣]推动[動](或操作)的 yóu yāsuō kōngqì tuīdòng de: *a* ~ *drill* 风钻; *a* ~ *tyre* 气胎 ~**ally** *adv*

pneu·monia /nju:'məʊnɪə/ *n* [U] 肺炎 fèiyán.

P.O. =1 Petty Officer 海军[軍]军士 hǎijūn jūnshì. 2 Pilot Officer (英)空军少尉 Kōngjūn shàowèi. 3 postal order 邮[郵]政汇[匯]票 yóuzhèng huìpiào. 4 post office.

poach[1] /pəʊtʃ/ *vt* 水煮 (荷包蛋) shuǐzhǔ.

poach[2] /pəʊtʃ/ *vt/i* (侵入他人地界)偷猎[獵] tōuliè. ~**er** (侵入他人地界)偷猎者 tōulièzhě.

pock /pɒk/ *n* [C] 痘疱 dòupào; 痘痕 dòuhén. '~**-marked** 有痘痕的 yǒu dòuhén de.

pocket /'pɒkɪt/ *n* [C] 1 衣袋 yīdài; 口袋 kǒudài. 2[用作定语]小型的 xiǎoxíngde, 袖珍的 xiùzhēnde: *a* ~ *watch* 怀表. 3 矿[礦]穴 kuàngxué; 小矿藏 xiǎo kuàngcáng. 4(大气中的)气[氣]阱 qìjǐng: *an 'air*-~ 气阱 5 (被敌军占领的) 孤立地区[區] gūlì dìqū: ~*s of resistance* [军事] (被包围的) 孤立地区. □ *vt* 1 放入袋中 fàng rù dàizhōng. 2 侵吞 qīntūn '~**-money** 零用钱[錢] língyòngqián.

pod /pɒd/ *n* [C] 豆荚 dòujiá; 荚 jiá. □ *vt* [-dd-] 剥出 (豆等) 粒 bōchū lì.

podgy /'pɒdʒɪ/ *adj* [-ier, -iest] 矮胖的 ǎipàngde.

poem /'pəʊɪm/ *n* [C] 诗 shī; 韵文 yùnwén.

poet /'pəʊɪt/ *n* [C] 诗人 shīrén. ~**ic(al)** /pəʊ'etɪk(l)/ *adj* 诗的 shīde; 诗人的 shīrénde.

po·etry /'pəʊɪtrɪ/ *n* [U] 1 诗 shī;

诗歌 shīgē. 2 诗意 shīyì: *the ~ of dance.* 舞蹈的诗意.

poign·ant /ˈpɔɪnjənt/ *adj* [正式用语]伤[傷]人感情的 shāngrén gǎngqíng de; 痛切的 tòngqiède: *~ memories* 深刻的记忆. **~ly** *adv* **poig·nancy** *n* [U]

point¹ /pɔɪnt/ *n* **1** [C] (针、铅笔等)尖 jiān. **2** [C] 岬 jiǎ. **3** 点[點] diǎn ⇨ decimal point. **4** [C] (空间或时间上的)一点 yìdiǎn. ***at this ~*** 在此地 zài cǐdì; 在此刻 zài cǐkè. ***a ~ of view*** 观[觀]点 guāndiǎn. ***be on the ~ of doing sth*** 就要做某事 jiùyào zuò mǒushì. **5** [C] 刻度上的记号[號] kèdùshàngde jìhào: *ˈboiling-~* 沸点. **6** [C] (比赛等的)得分 défēn. **7** [C] 罗[羅]经[經]点 (罗盘上的三十二个刻度之一) luójīngdiǎn. **8** [C] 要点 yàodiǎn; 论[論]点 lùndiǎn. ***get (see, miss) the ~ of sth*** 明白 (不明白) 重点 míngbai zhòngdiǎn; 抓得(不)到要点 zhuā de dào yàodiǎn. ***make a ~ of doing sth*** 坚[堅]持做某事 jiānchí zuò mǒushì. ***take sb's ~*** 领会[會]某人的论点 lǐnghuì mǒurén de lùndiǎn. ***to the ~*** 中肯 zhòngkěn; 扼要 èyào. **9** [U] 目的 mùdì; 意义[義] yìyì: *There's no ~ in going.* 已经是毫无意义的了. **10** [C] 特点 tèdiǎn; 特征[徵] tèzhēng: *see his good ~s* 看他的优点(长处). **11** [英国英语] (电)插座 chāzuò; (插头等的) 接触[觸]点 jiēchùdiǎn. **12** [*pl*] (铁路的)岔尖 chàjiān.

point² /pɔɪnt/ *vt/i* **1** **~(to)** 指向 zhǐxiàng. **2** **~ *sth at*** (或 ***towards***) 把…对[對]准[準] bǎ…duìzhǔn. **3** **~ *sth out*** 指出 zhǐchū. **4** (用灰泥等)填补接缝 tiánbǔ jiēfèng; 勾抹 gōumǒ. **~ed** *adj* **(a)** 尖的 jiānde. **(b)** [喻]率直的 shuàizhíde: *~ed remarks* 明指某人的评论. **~ed·ly** *adv*

point-blank /ˌpɔɪnt ˈblæŋk/ *adj, adv* **1** 近距离[離]平射的 (地) jìn jùlí píngshè de. **2** [喻] 直截了当[當] 的 (地) zhíjié-liǎodàngde: *He refused ~.* 他直截了当地拒绝了.

pointer /ˈpɔɪntə(r)/ *n* [C] **1** 指示物 zhǐshìwù. **2** 指针 zhǐzhēn. **3** 一种[種]短毛大猎[獵]犬 yìzhǒng duǎnmáo dà lièquǎn.

point·less /ˈpɔɪntlɪs/ *adj* [喻]无[無]意义[義]的 wú yìyì de; 无目标[標]的 wú mùbiāo de. **~ly** *adv*

poise /pɔɪz/ *vt/i* 平衡 pínghéng; 保持均衡 bǎochí jūnhéng. □ *n* **1** [U] 平衡 pínghéng; 均衡 jūnhéng. **2** [C] (身体或头部的) 姿态[態] zītài. **3** [U] 泰然自若 tàirán zìruò; 自信 zìxìn.

poi·son /ˈpɔɪzn/ *n* [C,U] **1** 毒药[藥] dúyào; 毒物 dúwù. **2** [喻] 弊害 bìhài. □ *vt* **1** 放毒 fàngdú. **2** [喻] 败坏[壞] bàihuài; 玷污 diànwū. **~ous** *adj* **~ous·ly** *adv*

poke /pəʊk/ *vt/i* **1** (用棍棒等)拨[撥]弄 bōnòng; 碰 pèng. **2** 伸出 shēnchū; 把…推向 bǎ…tuīxiàng: *~ your head out of the window* 把你的头伸出窗外. **~ *fun at sb*** 嘲弄某人 cháonòng mǒurén. □ *n* [C] 拨 bō; 戳 chuō; 捅 tǒng.

poker¹ /ˈpəʊkə(r)/ *n* [C] 拨[撥]火棒 bōhuǒbàng, 火钳 huǒqián.

poker² /ˈpəʊkə(r)/ *n* [U] 扑[撲]克牌戏[戲] pūkèpáixì.

po·lar /ˈpəʊlə(r)/ *adj* **1** 南极[極]的 nánjíde; 北极的 běijíde; 近地极的 jìndìjíde. **2** 极端相反的 jíduān xiāngfǎn de. **~ bear** 北极熊 běijíxióng. **~ity** /pəʊˈlærətɪ/ *n* [U] 反向性 fǎnxiàngxìng; 极性 jíxìng.

po·lar·ize /ˈpəʊləraɪz/ *vt* (使)极[極]化 jíhuà: *An issue that ~d opinions.* 造成意见对立的问题. **po·lar·iz·ation** /-ˈzeɪʃn/ *n* [U]

pole¹ /pəʊl/ *n* [C] **1** (南、北) 极[極] jí: *the North (South) P~* 北(南)极. **2** 磁极 cíjí; 电[電]极 diànjí. **5** [喻]两个相反的原则之一 liǎnggè xiāngfǎn de yuánzé zhī yī. ***be ~s apart*** 截然相反 jiérán xiāngfǎn.

pole² /pəʊl/ *n* [C] 柱 zhù; 杆[桿] gǎn; 竿 gān. **ˈ~-vault** 撑竿跳 chēnggāntiào.

pole·cat /ˈpəʊlkæt/ *n* [C] 鸡[鷄]貂 jīdiāo.

po·lice /pəˈliːs/ *n* 警察 jǐngchá; 警察当[當]局 jǐngchá dāngjú: *The ~ are searching everybody.* 警察正在搜查每一个人. □ *vt* 维持…的治安 wéichí…de zhì'ān. **~man** 警察 jǐngchá. **~woman** 女警察 nǚ jǐngchá. **~ force** (总称)警察 jǐngchá; 警察力量 jǐngchá lìliàng. **~ station** 警察局 jǐngchájú.

pol·icy /ˈpɒləsɪ/ *n* [C] [*pl* -ies] **1** 政策 zhèngcè; 方针 fāngzhēn: *the Government's foreign ~* 政府外交政策. **2** 保险[險]单[單] bǎoxiǎndān: *an inˈsurance ~* 保险单.

po·lio /ˈpəʊlɪəʊ/ 亦作 **~mye·litis** /-maɪəˈlaɪtɪs/ *n* [U] 小儿[兒]麻痹症[癥] xiǎo'ér mábìzhèng.

polish /'pɒlɪʃ/ *vt/i* **1** 磨光 móguāng; 擦亮 cāliàng. **2** 润〔潤〕饰 rùnshì; 使优〔優〕美 shǐ yōuměi. **3** ~ *sth off* 草草做完 cǎocǎo zuòwán. □ *n* **1** [U] 磨光 móguāng; 擦亮 cāliàng. **2** [C] 擦光剂〔劑〕 cāguāngjì; 擦光油 cāguāngyóu. **3** [U] [喻]优美 yōuměi; 完善 wánshàn.

pol·ite /pə'laɪt/ *adj* 有礼〔禮〕貌的 yǒu lǐmào de; 文雅的 wényǎde. ~**ly** *adv* ~**ness** *n* [U]

poli·tic /'pɒlətɪk/ *adj* **1** (指人)精明的 jīngmíngde. **2** (指行为)得策的 décède; 明智的 míngzhìde.

pol·iti·cal /pə'lɪtɪkl/ *adj* **1** 政治的 zhèngzhìde; 政治上的 zhèngzhìshàngde. **2** 政治学〔學〕的 zhèngzhìxuéde: ~ *prisoners* 政治犯. ~**ly** /-klɪ/ *adv*

poli·ti·cian /ˌpɒlə'tɪʃn/ *n* [C] 政客 zhèngkè.

poli·tics /'pɒlətɪks/ *n* [U] 政治学〔學〕 zhèngzhìxué; 政见 zhèngjiàn; 政治活动〔動〕 zhèngzhì huódòng.

polka /'pɒlkə/ *n* [C] 波尔〔爾〕卡舞 bō'ěrkǎwǔ; 波尔卡舞曲bō'ěrkǎ wǔqǔ.

poll[1] /pəʊl/ *n* [C] **1** 选〔選〕举〔舉〕投票 xuǎnjǔ tóupiào; 投票人的名册 tóupiàorénde míngcè; 投票数 tóupiàoshù. *go to the ~s* 去投票处〔處〕投票 qù tóupiàochù tóupiào. **2** 民意测验〔驗〕 mínyì cèyàn.

poll[2] /pəʊl/ *vt/i* **1** 投票 tóupiào. **2** 得到(若干)选〔選〕票 dédào xuǎnpiào. '~**ing-booth (-station)** 投票处〔處〕 tóupiàochù, 投票站 tóupiàozhàn.

pol·len /'pɒlən/ *n* [U] 花粉 huāfěn.

pol·lin·ate /'pɒlɪneɪt/ *vt* 授以花粉 shòu yǐ huāfěn. **pol·li·na·tion** /-'neɪʃn/ *n* [U]

pol·lute /pə'lu:t/ *vt* 弄脏〔髒〕nòngzāng; 污染 wūrǎn: ~ *the atmosphere with fumes* 烟、汽等污染了大气.

pol·lu·tion /-ʃn/ *n* [U]

polo /'pəʊləʊ/ *n* [U] 马〔馬〕球 mǎqiú. ⇨ water-polo. '~**-neck** 圆翻领毛衣 yuán fānlǐng máoyī.

poly·gamy /pə'lɪgəmɪ/ *n* [U] 一夫多妻 yìfū duōqī. ⇨ monogamy. **poly·ga·mous** *adj*

poly·gon /'pɒlɪgən/ *n* [C] 多边〔邊〕形 duōbiānxíng; 多角形 duōjiǎoxíng.

poly·tech·nic /ˌpɒlɪ'teknɪk/ *n* [C] 综合性工艺〔藝〕学〔學〕校 zōnghéxìng gōngyì xuéxiào; 工业〔業〕学校(或大学) gōngyè xuéxiào.

poly·thene /'pɒlɪθi:n/ *n* [U] [化学] 聚乙烯 jùyǐxī.

pom·egran·ate /'pɒmɪgrænɪt/ *n* [C] 石榴 shíliu; 石榴树〔樹〕 shíliushù.

pom·mel /'pʌml/ *n* [C] 鞍头〔頭〕(鞍最前端翘起部分) āntóu.

pomp /pɒmp/ *n* [U] 华〔華〕丽〔麗〕 huálì; 壮〔壯〕观〔觀〕 zhuàngguān.

pom·pous /'pɒmpəs/ *adj* 自负〔負〕的 zìfùde; 夸〔誇〕大的 kuādàde. **pom·pos·ity** /pɒm'pɒsətɪ/ *n* [C, U] [*pl* -ies] 自负 zìfù; 夸大 kuādà.

pon·cho /'pɒntʃəʊ/ *n* [C] [*pl* ~s] 斗篷 dǒupéng; 雨披 yǔpī.

pond /pɒnd/ *n* [C] 池塘 chítáng.

pon·der /'pɒndə(r)/ *vt/i* 深思 shēnsī; 考虑〔慮〕 kǎolǜ.

pon·der·ous /'pɒndərəs/ *adj* **1** 沉重的 chénzhòngde; 笨重的 bènzhòngde. **2** (指文章)冗长〔長〕的 rǒngchángde. ~**ly** *adv*

pon·toon[1] /pɒn'tu:n/ *n* [C] 浮桥〔橋〕 fúqiáo; (架设浮桥用的)平底船 píngdǐchuán.

pon·toon[2] /pɒn'tu:n/ *n* [U] (二十一点)牌戏〔戲〕 páixì.

pony /'pəʊnɪ/ *n* [C] [*pl* -ies] 小马〔馬〕 xiǎomǎ.

poodle /'pu:dl/ *n* [C] 长〔長〕卷〔捲〕毛狗 chángjuǎnmáogǒu.

pool[1] /pu:l/ *n* [C] **1** 水塘 shuǐtáng. **2** 浮在表面的液体〔體〕 fú zài biǎomiànde yètǐ: *a ~ of blood* 血泊. **3** = swimming pool.

pool[2] /pu:l/ *n* [C] **1** (赌博者所下的)全部赌注 quánbù dǔzhù. **2** *the ~s* = football pools. **3** 联〔聯〕营〔營〕 liányíng; 合伙经〔經〕营 héhuǒ jīngyíng: *a 'typing ~* 联营打字行. **4** [U] [美语] = snooker. □ *vt* 合伙经营 héhuǒ jīngyíng.

poor /pʊə(r)/ *adj* [-er, -est] **1** 贫穷〔窮〕的 pínqióngde; 贫困的 pínkùnde. **2** 可怜〔憐〕的 kěliánde; 不幸的 búxìngde: *a ~ little puppy* 可怜的小狗. **3** 少量的 shǎoliàngde: *a ~ supply of teachers* 教师不足. **4** 质〔質〕劣的 zhìliède; 坏〔壞〕的 huàide: ~ *soil* 贫瘠的土壤.

poor·ly /'pʊəlɪ/ *adj* [非正式用语] 身体〔體〕不适〔適〕的 shēntǐ búshì de; 健康不佳的 jiànkāng bùjiā de. □ *adv* **1** 贫乏地 pínfáde; 拙劣地 zhuōliède. **2** ~ *off* 贫困的 pínkùnde; 没钱〔錢〕的 méiqiánde.

poor·ness /'pʊənɪs/ *n* [U] 贫乏 pínfá; 不足 bùzú: *the ~ of the* *soil* 土壤贫瘠。

pop[1] /pɒp/ *n* [C] **1** 短促爆裂声〔聲〕duǎncù bàolièshēng. **2**〔非正式用语〕有气〔氣〕的瓶装饮料(如汽水、啤酒等) yǒuqìde píngzhuāng yǐnliào. □ *adv* 砰地(一声) pēngde; 突然地 tūránde.

pop[2] /pɒp/ *n* [C]〔非正式用语〕= father.

pop[3] /pɒp/ *adj*〔非正式用语〕popular 的缩写〔寫〕*popular* de suōxiě: '~ *music* 流行音乐. □ *n*〔非正式用语〕[U] 流行音乐〔樂〕liúxíng yīnyuè; [C] 流行歌曲 liúxíng gēqǔ.

pop[4] /pɒp/ *vt/i* [-pp-] **1** 发〔發〕短促爆裂声〔聲〕fā duǎncù bàolièshēng. **2** ~ ***in (out)*** 来〔來〕去匆匆 lái qù cōngcōng. '**~corn** 爆玉米(花) bào yùmǐ. **~-eyed** *adj* (因惊讶等) 睁大眼睛的 zhēngdà yǎnjīng de.

pop. = population

pope /pəʊp/ *n* **the P~** (罗马天主教的)教皇 jiàohuáng.

pop·lar /'pɒplə(r)/ *n* [C] 白杨〔楊〕báiyáng; [U] 杨木 yángmù.

poppy /'pɒpɪ/ *n* [C] [*pl* -pies] 罂粟 yīngsù.

popu·lar /'pɒpjʊlə(r)/ *adj* **1** 民众〔衆〕的 mínzhòngde; 人民的 rénmínde. **2** 通俗的 tōngsúde; 普通的 pǔtōngde: *at ~ prices* 廉价. **3** 受欢〔歡〕迎的 shòu huānyíng de; 被爱〔愛〕戴的 bèi àidài de. ⇨ pop[3]. **~ly** *adv* **~ity** /-'lærətɪ/ *n* [U]

popu·late /'pɒpjʊleɪt/ *vt* 移民于 yímín yú; 居住于 jūzhù yú.

popu·la·tion /ˌpɒpjʊ'leɪʃn/ *n* [C] 人口 rénkǒu; 人口数〔數〕rénkǒushù.

por·ce·lain /'pɔːsəlɪn/ *n* [U] 瓷器 cíqì.

porch /pɔːtʃ/ *n* [C] 门〔門〕廊 ménláng; 走廊 zǒuláng.

por·cu·pine /'pɔːkjʊpaɪn/ *n* [C] 豪猪 háozhū; 箭猪 jiànzhū.

pore[1] /pɔː(r)/ *n* [C] 毛孔 máokǒng; 孔 kǒng.

pore[2] /pɔː(r)/ *vi* ~ ***over sth*** 钻〔鑽〕研 zuānyán; 熟读〔讀〕shúdú.

pork /pɔːk/ *n* [U] 猪肉 zhūròu. ⇨ bacon, ham(1).

porn /pɔːn/ *n* [U]〔非正式用语〕pornography 的缩写〔寫〕*pornography* de suōxiě.

por·nogra·phy /pɔː'nɒgrəfɪ/ *n* [U] 色情文学〔學〕sèqíng wénxué; 色情画〔畫〕sèqínghuà. **por·no·graphic** /ˌpɔːnə'græfɪk/ *adj*

po·rous /'pɔːrəs/ *adj* 多孔的 duōkǒngde; 能渗〔滲〕透的 néng shèntòu de.

por·poise /'pɔːpəs/ *n* [C] 海豚 hǎitún.

por·ridge /'pɒrɪdʒ/ *n* [U] 麦〔麥〕片粥 màipiànzhōu.

port[1] /pɔːt/ *n* [C] **1** 港 gǎng; 港口 gǎngkǒu. **2** 港市 gǎngshì; 口岸 kǒu'àn.

port[2] /pɔːt/ *n* [C]〔航海〕(船上的)舱〔艙〕门〔門〕cāngmén; (装卸货物的)舱口 cāngkǒu. '**~hole**, **(a)** (船侧供采光通气的)窗孔 chuāngkǒng. **(b)** 舷窗 xiánchuāng.

port[3] /pɔːt/ *n* [U]〔航海〕(船、飞机的)左舷 zuǒxián. ⇨ starboard.

port[4] /pɔːt/ *n* [U] (葡萄牙产的)葡萄酒 pútáojiǔ.

port·able /'pɔːtəbl/ *adj* 手提式的 shǒutíshìde; 便于携带〔帶〕的 biàn yú xiédài de.

por·ter /'pɔːtə(r)/ *n* [C] **1** 搬行李工人 bān xínglǐ gōngrén. **2** (旅馆等的)服务〔務〕员 fúwùyuán.

port·folio /pɔːt'fəʊlɪəʊ/ *n* [C] [*pl* ~s] **1** 公事包 gōngshìbāo; 文件夹〔夾〕wénjiànjiā. **2** 大臣职〔職〕dàchénzhí; 部长〔長〕职 bùzhǎngzhí.

port·hole *n* ⇨ port[2].

por·tion /'pɔːʃn/ *n* [C] **1** 一部分 yībùfen; 一份 yīfèn. **2** (食物的)一份 yīfèn; 一客 yīkè: *a small ~ of food* 少量食物. □ *vt* ~ ***sth out*** 将〔將〕…分成份 jiāng…fēnchéng fèn.

port·ly /'pɔːtlɪ/ *adj* 肥胖的 féipàngde; 魁梧的 kuíwúde.

port·man·teau /pɔːt'mæntəʊ/ *n* [C][*pl* ~s 或 ~x /-təʊz/] 旅行皮箱 lǚxíng píxiāng; 旅行皮包 lǚxíng píbāo.

por·trait /'pɔːtrɪt/ *n* [C] **1** 肖像 xiàoxiàng; 画〔畫〕像 huàxiàng. **2** 生动〔動〕的描写〔寫〕shēngdòngde miáoxiě.

por·tray /pɔː'treɪ/ *vt* **1** 描绘〔繪〕miáohuì; 画〔畫〕(人物、风景等) huà. **2** 描述 miáoshù; 描写〔寫〕miáoxiě. **3** 扮演 bànyǎn. **~al** *n* [C,U] 描绘 miáohuì; 画像 huàxiàng.

pose /pəʊz/ *vt/i* **1** (画像前)使人摆〔擺〕好姿势〔勢〕shǐ rén bǎihǎo zīshì. **2** ~ ***for*** (为摄影等)摆好姿势 bǎihǎo zīshì. **3** 提出 tíchū: ~ *a problem* 提出问题. **4** ~ ***as*** 假装〔裝〕jiǎzhuāng. □ *n* [C] **1** 姿势 zīshì; 姿态〔態〕zītài. **2** 装腔作势 zhuāngqiāng zuòshì. **poser** *n* [C] 难〔難〕题 nántí.

posh /pɒʃ/ *adj*〔非正式用语〕漂亮的

piàoliàngde; 第一流的 dìyīliúde.

po·si·tion /pəˈzɪʃn/ *n* **1** [C] 位置 wèizhi. **2** [U] 阵〔陣〕势〔勢〕zhènshì; 阵地 zhèndì: *manoeuvring for* ~ 阵地演习. **3** [C] 姿势 zīshì: *lie in a comfortable* ~ 舒适地躺着. **4** [C] 地位 dìwèi; 身份 shēnfen. **5** [C] 工作 gōngzuò; 职〔職〕业〔業〕zhíyè. **6** [C] 状〔狀〕况 zhuàngkuàng: *I am not in a* ~ (= am unable) *to help you.* 我无力帮助你. **7** [C] 见解 jiànjiě. □ *vt* 把…放在适当的位置 bǎ...fàng zài shìdàng de wèizhi.

posi·tive /ˈpɒzətɪv/ *adj* **1** 确定的 quèdìngde; 明确的 míngquède: ~ *instructions* 明确的指示. **2** (指人)确信的 quèxìnde; *I'm* ~ *he's here.* 我确信他在这里. **3** 实〔實〕际〔際〕的 shíjìde; 有用的 yǒuyòngde: ~ *suggestion* 积极的建议. **4** [非正式用语]完全的 wánquánde: *a* ~ *fool* 彻头彻尾的傻瓜. **5** [数学] 正的 zhèngde. **6** [电]阳〔陽〕性的 yángxìngde: *a* ~ *charge* 正电荷. □ *n* [C] 原级 yuánjí. ~**ly** *adv* 确定地 quèdìngde.

pos·sess /pəˈzes/ *vt* **1** 占〔佔〕有 zhànyǒu; 拥〔擁〕有 yōngyǒu. **2** 控制(思想) kòngzhì: ~*ed by fear* 陷于恐惧. ~**or** *n* [C] 所有人 suǒyǒurén; 占有人 zhànyǒurén.

pos·ses·sion /pəˈzeʃn/ *n* **1** [U] 所有 suǒyǒu; 拥〔擁〕有 yōngyǒu. **2** [C] [常用 *pl*] 财产〔產〕cáichǎn; 所有物 suǒyǒuwù.

pos·sess·ive /pəˈzesɪv/ *adj* **1** 占〔佔〕有的 zhànyǒude; 占有欲的 zhànyǒuyùde. **2** [语法] 所有格的 suǒyǒugéde. ~ **pronoun** (如 *yours, his*) 所有格代词 suǒyǒugé dàicí. ~**ly** *adv*

pos·si·bil·ity /ˌpɒsəˈbɪlətɪ/ *n* [*pl* -ies] **1** [U] 可能 kěnéng; 可能性 kěnéngxìng. **2** [C] 可能的事 kěnéngde shì; 可能发〔發〕生的事 kěnéng fāshēng de shì.

poss·ible /ˈpɒsəbl/ *adj* **1** 可能的 kěnéngde; 可能存在的 kěnéng cúnzài de. **2** 令人满意的 lìng rén mǎnyìde: *a* ~ *candidate* 适当的候选人. □ *n* [C] 可能的人或事物 kěnéngde rén huò shìwù. **poss·ibly** /-əblɪ/ *adv* **(a)** [用于强调]: *as soon as I possibly can* 我尽可能地快. **(b)** 或者 huòzhě: *I'll possibly come tomorrow.* 我明天也许来.

post[1] /pəʊst/ *n* [C] **1** 岗〔崗〕位 gǎngwèi; 哨所 shàosuǒ. **2** (部队的)驻〔駐〕地 zhùdì; 兵营〔營〕bīngyíng. ⇨ outpost. **3** 职〔職〕位 zhíwèi; 职守 zhíshǒu: *a* ~ *in the government* 政府里的职位. □ *vt* **1** 布置(岗哨等) bùzhì. **2** 任命 rènmìng; 派任 pàirèn.

post[2] [美语 = **mail**] /pəʊst/ *n* [C] **1** 邮〔郵〕政 yóuzhèng; 邮寄 yóujì. **2** 邮箱 yóuxiāng, 邮筒 yóutǒng; 邮局 yóujú. **3** 邮件 yóujiàn; 邮包 yóubāo. ˈ~**box** = post(2). ˈ~**card** 明信片 míngxìnpiàn. ˈ~**man** /-mən/ [美语 = mailman] 邮递〔遞〕员 yóudìyuán. ˈ~**mark** 邮戳 yóuchuō. □ *vt* 盖〔蓋〕邮戳于(信封等) gài yóuchuō yú. ˈ~ **office** 邮局 yóujú. ˈ~**office box**, (缩作 **PO Box**) 邮政信箱 yóuzhèng xìnxiāng.

post[3] [美语 = **mail**] /pəʊst/ *vt/i* 邮〔郵〕寄 yóujì; 投寄 tóujì. ˌ~ˈ**haste** *adv* 急速地 jísùde.

post[4] /pəʊst/ *n* [C] (木、金属等的)柱 zhù; 支柱 zhīzhù; 标〔標〕杆〔桿〕biāogān. ⇨ lamp-post. □ *vt* **1** 贴出(布告、通告等) tiēchū: ~ *the names of the team on a board* 张贴队员名单. **2** (用布告)宣布 xuānbù; 公告 gōnggào.

post·age /ˈpəʊstɪdʒ/ *n* [U] 邮〔郵〕费 yóufèi; 邮资 yóuzī. ˈ~ **stamp** 邮票 yóupiào.

postal /ˈpəʊstl/ *adj* 邮〔郵〕政的 yóuzhèngde; 邮局的 yóujúde. ˈ~ **order** 邮政汇〔匯〕票 yóuzhèng huìpiào.

post·date /ˌpəʊstˈdeɪt/ *vt* 把日期填迟〔遲〕bǎ rìqī tiánchí.

poster /ˈpəʊstə(r)/ *n* [C] **1** (贴在公共场所的)招贴 zhāotiē; 广〔廣〕告 guǎnggào. **2** 广告画 guǎnggàohuà.

pos·ter·ior /pɒˈstɪərɪə(r)/ *adj* **1** (时间上)以后〔後〕的 yǐhòude; (次序上)其次的 qícìde. ⇨ prior[1]. **2** 后面的 hòumiànde.

pos·ter·ity /pɒˈsterətɪ/ *n* [U] **1** 后〔後〕裔 hòuyì; 子孙 zǐsūn. **2** 后代 hòudài.

post·gradu·ate /ˌpəʊstˈgrædʒuət/ *adj* 大学〔學〕毕〔畢〕业〔業〕后〔後〕的 dàxué bìyè hòu de; 大学研究院的 dàxué yánjiūyuàn de. □ *n* [C] 研究生 yánjiūshēng.

post·hum·ous /ˈpɒstjʊməs/ *adj* **1** (指小孩)遗腹的 yífùde; 父死后〔後〕出生的 fù sǐhòu chūshēng de. **2** 死后的 sǐhòude; 身后的 shēnghòude: *a* ~ *award* 死后的奖赏. ~**ly** *adv*

post me·rid·iem /ˌpəʊst məˈrɪdɪəm/ *adj* (缩作 **pm**)午后〔後〕wǔhòu; 下午 xiàwǔ: *7.30 pm.* 午后七时半. ⇨ *am* at ante meridiem

post-mor·tem /ˌpəʊstˈmɔːtəm/ *n*

[C], *adj* **1** (医学检验)验[驗]尸[屍] yànshī; 尸体[體]解剖 shītǐ jiěpōo; 验尸的 yànshīde. **2** [非正式用语]事后[後]检[檢]查或评论[論] shìhòu jiǎnchá huò pínglùn.

post·pone /pə'spəʊn/ *vt* 推迟[遲] tuīchí; 延缓 yánhuǎn. **~ment** *n* [C,U]

post·script /'pəʊsskrɪpt/ *n* [C] (缩作 **PS**) (信件中)附笔[筆] fùbǐ; 附言 fùyán.

pos·ture /'pɒstʃə(r)/ *n* [C] **1** 姿势[勢] zīshì; 姿态[態] zītài. **2** 态度 tàidu.

posy /'pəʊzɪ/ *n* [C] [*pl* -ies] 小花束 xiǎo huāsù.

pot[1] /pɒt/ *n* [C] **1** 罐 guàn; 锅[鍋] guō; 壶[壺] hú. **2** *go to* ~ [俚语]变[變]坏[壞] biàn huài; 破灭[滅] pòmiè. *take* ,~'*luck* 吃便饭 chī biànfàn. **3** [非正式用语]大量 dàliàng: *~s of money* 一笔巨款. **4** [俚语] 大麻 dàmá. ,**~-'bellied** *adj* (指人)大腹便便的 dà fù piánpián de. '**~hole, (a)** (路上的)坑洼 kēngwā. **(b)** 壶[壺]穴 húxuè. '**~holer** 洞窟探测者 dòngkū tàncèzhě. '**~-shot** 近距离[離]射击[擊] jìn jùlí shèjī.

pot[2] /pɒt/ *vt/i* [-tt-] **1** 把 (肉、鱼等)放在罐(或锅)里[裡] bǎ...fàng zài guàn lǐ. **2** 栽在花盆里 zāi zài huāpén lǐ. **3** [非正式用语]近距离[離]射杀 jìn jùlí shèshā: ~ *a rabbit* 近距离射杀一只兔子.

po·tass·ium /pə'tæsɪəm/ *n* [U] [化学]钾 **(K)** jiǎ.

po·tato /pə'teɪtəʊ/ *n* [C,U] [*pl* ~-es] 马[馬]铃薯 mǎlíngshǔ; 土豆 tǔdòu.

po·tent /'pəʊtnt/ *adj* 有力的 yǒulìde; 有效的yǒuxiàode. **~ly** *adv* **po·tency** *n* [U]

po·ten·tial /pə'tenʃl/ *adj* 可能的 kěnéngde; 潜[潛]在的 qiánzàide. □ *n* [C,U] 潜能 qiánnéng; 潜力 qiánlì. **~ly** *adv* **~ity** /pə,tenʃɪ'ælətɪ/ *n* [C] [*pl* -ies] 潜力 qiánlì; 可能性 kěnéngxìng.

po·tion /'pəʊʃn/ *n* [C] (药等的)一剂[劑] yíjì; 一服 yífù.

pot·ter[1] /'pɒtə(r)/ *vt/i* ~ *about* 懒散而无[無]目的地工作 lǎnsǎn ér wú mùdì de gōngzuò; 无事忙 wúshìmáng.

pot·ter[2] /'pɒtə(r)/ *n* [C] 陶工 táogōng. **pot·tery** *n* [*pl* -ies] **(a)** [U] 陶器 táoqì. **(b)** [C] 陶器制[製]造厂[廠] táoqì zhìzàochǎng.

pouch /paʊtʃ/ *n* [C] **1** 小袋 xiǎo dài; 小包 xiǎo bāo. **2** (袋鼠等的)育儿[兒]袋 yù'érdài; 袋状[狀]物 dàizhuàngwù.

poul·tice /'pəʊltɪs/ *n* [C] 泥罨剂[劑] níyǎnjì.

poul·try /'pəʊltrɪ/ *n* **1** [*pl*] 家禽 jiāqín. **2** [U] 家禽肉 jiāqínròu.

pounce /paʊns/ *vi* ~ *on* **(at)** **1** 突然袭[襲]击[擊] tūrán xíjī. **2** [喻]抓住 zhuāzhù: *He ~d on the chance to win.* 他抓住取胜机会. □ *n* [C] 突袭 tūxí; 猛扑[撲] měngpū.

pound[1] /paʊnd/*n* [C] **1** 磅(重量单位) bàng. **2** 镑(英国等货币单位) bàng.

pound[2] /paʊnd/ *n* [C] [现代用法] (主人不详的) 动[動]物收容所 dòngwù shōuróngsuǒ.

pound[3] /paʊnd/ *vt/i* **1** ~ *(away)* (与 *at*, *on* 连用) 连[連]续[續]重击[擊] liánxù zhòngjī. **2** 捣[搗]碎 dǎosuì; 捣成粉 dǎo chéng fěn. **3** 沉重地跑 chénzhòngde pǎo; 沉重地走 chénzhòngde zǒu.

pour /pɔ:(r)/ *vt/i* **1** (指液体)灌 guàn; 注 zhù; 倒 dào. **2** [喻]流注 liúzhù; 流出 liúchū: *Tourists ~ into London.* 游客拥进伦敦. **3** (指雨)倾注 qīngzhù. **4** ~ *(out)* 倾吐 qīngtǔ; 诉说 sùshuō: ~ *out one's troubles* 倾诉苦恼.

pout /paʊt/ *vt/i* 撅嘴 juēzuǐ. □ *n* [C] 撅嘴 juēzuǐ.

pov·erty /'pɒvətɪ/ *n* [U] 贫穷[窮] pínqióng; 贫困 pínkùn. '**~-stricken** *adj* 贫穷的 pínqióngde; 贫困的 pínkùnde.

pow·der /'paʊdə(r)/ *n* [C,U] 粉末 fěnmò; 粉 fěn. ⇨ gunpowder. □ *vt/i* 洒[灑]粉于 sǎ fěn yú. '**~-room** (尤指美语)女用盥洗室 nǚyòng guànxǐshì; 化妆[妝]室 huàzhuāngshì. **pow·dery** *adj* 粉的 fěnde; 粉状[狀]的 fěnzhuàngde.

power /'paʊə(r)/ *n* **1** [U] 能力 nénglì. **2** [*pl*] 体[體]力 tǐlì; 精力 jīnglì. **3** [U] 力 lì; 力量 lìliàng. **4** [U] 动[動]力 dònglì: *e'lectric* ~ 电力. ⇨ horsepower. **5** [U] 权[權]力 quánlì; 势[勢]力 shìlì: *the ~ of the law* 法律的力量. *in* ~ (指政党)执[執]政的 zhízhèngde. **6** [C] 有权力的人 yǒu quánlì de rén; 有影响[響]的机[機]构[構] yǒu yǐngxiǎng de jīgòu. **7** [C] 强国[國] qiángguó: *a world* ~ 世界大(强)国. **8** [U] (光学上的)放大功能 fàngdà gōngnéng: *the ~ of a lens* 透镜的放大力. '**~boat** *n* 汽艇 qìtǐng. '**~ cut** *n* 停电[電] tíngdiàn. '**~ point** *n* 电插座 diànchāzuò. '**~ station** *n* (亦作 ~ **house**, ~ **plant**) 发[發]

电所 fādiànsuǒ. '~ **steering** *n* [U] (亦作 ~-assisted steering) 动力自动驾驶 dònglì zìdòng jiàshǐ. □ *vt* 供给动力 gōngjǐ dònglì: ~-*ed by steam* 用蒸汽作动力. **~ed** *adj* **(a)** 产[產]生机械能的 chǎnshēng jīxiènéng de: *a high-~ed car.* 高功能汽车. **(b)** [喻] 能力强的 nénglì qiáng de: *a high-~ed salesman* 能力强的推销员.

power·ful /'paʊəfl/ *adj* 强大的 qiángdàde; 强有力的 qiáng yǒulì de. **~ly** *adv*

power·less /'paʊəlɪs/ *adj* 无[無]力的 wúlìde; 无权[權]的 wúquánde; 无能为力的 wú néng wéi lì de: ~ *to act* 无力行动. **~ly** *adv*

p.p. = past participle.

pp. = pages.

pr. = pair.

prac·ti·cable /'præktɪkəbl/ *adj* 可实[實]行的 kěshíxíngde; 能用的 néngyòngde: ~ *ideas* 可行的意见. **prac·ti·cably** *adv*

prac·ti·cal /'præktɪkl/ *adj* **1** 实[實]际[際]的 (与 *theoretical* 相对) shíjìde. **2** (指人)注重实际的 zhùzhòng shíjì de. **3** 实用的 shíyòngde; 可行的 kěxíngde: *a ~ invention* 实用的发明. ,~ '**joke** 恶[惡]作剧[劇] èzuòjù. **~ly** *adv* **(a)** 实际地 shíjìde. **(b)** 几[幾]乎 jīhū: *~ly no time left* 几乎没有时间了. **~ity** /-'kælətɪ/ *n* [C] [*pl* -ies]

prac·tice (美语亦作 **-tise**) /'præktɪs/ *n* **1** [U] 实[實]行 (与 *theory* 相对) shíxíng; 实际 shíjì; 实践[踐] shíjiàn. **2** [C] 惯例 guànlì; 习[習]俗 xísú: *religious ~s* 宗教仪式. ***make a ~ of (sth)*** 经[經]常进[進]行 jīngcháng jìnxíng. **3** [U] 练[練]习 liànxí; 实习 shíxí: *~ makes perfect* 熟能生巧. ***in ~*** 在不断[斷]练习中 zài búduàn liànxí zhōng. ***out of ~*** 荒疏 huāngshū. **4** [U] (医生、律师的)业[業]务[務] yèwù; [C] (一批)主顾 zhǔgù.

prac·tise (美语亦作 **-tice**) /'præktɪs/ *vt/i* **1** 练[練]习[習] liànxí; 实[實]习 shíxí: ~ *the piano* 练习弹钢琴. **2** 惯做 guànzuò; 常为[爲] chángwéi. ~ ***what one preaches*** 以身作则 yǐ shēn zuò zé. **3** 以…为业[業] yǐ...wéi yè: ~ *medicine* 开业行医. **prac·tised** *adj* 熟练的 shúliànde.

prac·ti·tioner /præk'tɪʃənə(r)/ *n* [C] **1** 实[實]践[踐]者 shíjiànzhě; 从[從]事者 cóngshìzhě. **2** 开[開]业[業]者(尤指医生和律师) kāiyèzhě. ⇨ general practitioner.

prag·matic /præg'mætɪk/ *adj* 重实[實]效的 zhòngshíxiàode; 实际[際]的 shíjìde.

prairie /'preərɪ/ *n* [C] (指北美洲无森林的)大草原 dàcǎoyuán.

praise /preɪz/ *vt* **1** 赞[讚]扬[揚] zànyáng; 称[稱]赞 chēngzàn. **2** [宗教]赞美(上帝) zànměi. □ *n* [U] **1** 赞扬 zànyáng; 表扬 biǎoyáng. **2** 赞美 zànměi; 荣[榮]耀 róngyào. '~**worthy** /-wɜːðɪ/ *adj* 值得赞扬的 zhíde zànyáng de.

pram /præm/ *n* [C] [英国英语] perambulator 的缩写[寫] *perambulator* de suōxiě.

prance /prɑːns/ *vi* **1** ~ **(*about*)** (指马)腾[騰]跃[躍] téngyuè. **2** [喻]欢[歡]跃 huānyuè. □ *n* [C] (马的)腾跃 téngyuè; 欢跃 huānyuè.

prank /præŋk/ *n* [C] 恶[惡]作剧[劇] èzuòjù; 开[開]玩笑 kāi wánxiào.

prattle /'prætl/ *vi* 天真地说 tiānzhēnde shuō; 轻[輕]率地说 qīngshuàide shuō. □ *n* [U] 孩子气[氣]的话 háiziqìde huà.

prawn /prɔːn/ *n* [C] 对[對]虾[蝦] duìxiā; 明虾 míngxiā.

pray /preɪ/ *vt/i* ~ **(*to God*) (*for sth*)** 祈祷[禱] qídǎo; 祈求 qíqiú.

prayer /preə(r)/ *n* **1** [U] 祈祷[禱] qídǎo; 祈求 qíqiú. **2** [U] 祈祷式 qídǎoshì. **3** [C] 祈祷文 qídǎowén.

P.R.C. = People's Republic of China 中华[華]人民共和国[國] Zhōnghuá Rénmín Gònghéguó.

preach /priːtʃ/ *vt/i* **1** 传[傳]教 chuánjiào; 讲[講]道 jiǎngdào. **2** 劝[勸]诫 quànjiè. **3** 鼓吹 gǔchuī: ~ *war* 鼓吹战争. **~er** 传道士 chuándàoshì; 鼓吹者 gǔchuīzhě.

pre·amble /priː'æmbl/ *n* [C] (尤指正式文件的)序言 xùyán; 绪论[論] xùlùn.

pre·cari·ous /prɪ'keərɪəs/ *adj* 不稳[穩]定的 bù wěndìng de; 不安全的 bù ānquán de. **~ly** *adv*

pre·caution /prɪ'kɔːʃn/ *n* [C,U] 预防 yùfáng: *take ~s against illness* 预防疾病. **~ary** *adj*

pre·cede /prɪ'siːd/ *vt/i* 在前 zàiqián; 居前 jūqián; 领先 lǐngxiān. **pre·ced·ing** *adj* 在前的 zàiqiánde; 在先的 zàixiānde.

pre·ced·ence /'presɪdəns/ *n* [U] [正式用语]在前 zàiqián; 优[優]先 yōuxiān: *have* (或 *take*) ~ *(over)* 优先于.

pre·ced·ent /'presɪdənt/ *n* [C]

［正式用语］先例 xiānlì; 前例 qiánlì: *set a* ~ 创先例.

pre·cinct /'pri:sɪŋkt/ *n* [C] **1** (尤指教堂的)围［圍］地 wéidì; **2**[*pl*] 分界 fēnjiè; 范［範］围 fànwéi: *within the city* ~*s* 在市区内. **3**(美语)(城市内)警察局的管辖［轄］地段 jǐngchájúde guǎnxiá dìduàn. **4** 限定区域 xiàndìng qūyù: *a 'shopping* ~ 商业区.

pre·cious /'preʃəs/ *adj* 宝［寶］贵的 bǎoguìde; 珍贵的 zhēnguìde. □ *adv* ［非正式用语］很 hěn, 非常 fēicháng: ~ *little time* 极少的时间. ~**ly** *adv* ~**ness** *n* [C]

preci·pice /'presɪpɪs/ *n* [C] 悬［懸］崖 xuányá; 峭壁 qiàobì.

pre·cipi·tate /prə'sɪpɪteɪt/ *vt* **1** ［正式用语］猛然抛下 měngrán pāo xià; 猛抛 měngpāo. **2** 突然发［發］生 tūrán fāshēng; 加速 jiāsù: *illness* ~*d his death* 疾病加速他的死亡. **3** 使沉淀［澱］shǐ chéndiàn. □ *n* [C] 沉淀物 chéndiànwù. **pre·cipi'ta·tion** *n* **(a)** [C] (雨、霰、冰雹等)降下 jiàngxià. **(b)** [U] 急促 jícù; 鲁莽 lǔmǎng: *act with* ~ 仓卒地行动.

pré·cis /'preɪsi:/ *n* [C] [*pl* ~ /-si:z/] 摘要 zhāiyào; 概要 gàiyào. □ *vt* 摘要 zhāiyào; 写［寫］...的大意 xiě...de dàyì.

pre·cise /prɪ'saɪs/ *adj* **1** 精确［確］的 jīngquède, 准确的 zhǔnquède. **2** 讲［講］究精确的 jiǎngjiù jīngquè de. **3** 爱［愛］挑剔细节［節］的 ài tiāotì xìjié de. ~**ly** *adv* **(a)** 精确地 jīngquède. **(b)** 对［對］duì; 确实如此 quèshí rúcǐ. ~**ness** *n* [U]

pre·ci·sion /prɪ'sɪʒn/ *n* [U] 精确［確］(性) jīngquè; 精密 jīngmì; 精密度 jīngmìdù.

pre·co·cious /prɪ'kəʊʃəs/ *adj* (指人)早熟的 zǎoshúde. ~**ly** *adv* ~**ness** *n*

pre·con·ceive /ˌpri:kən'si:v/ *vt* 预想 yùxiǎng; 事先想好(意见等) shìxiān xiǎng hǎo. **pre·con·cep·tion** /ˌpri:kən'sepʃn/ *n* [C] 预想 yùxiǎng; 偏见 piānjiàn.

preda·tory /'predətrɪ/ *adj* ［正式用语］ **1** 掠夺［奪］的 lüèduóde: ~ *tribes* 以抢劫为生的部落. **2** (指动物)食肉的 shíròude. **pred·ator** *n* [C] 掠夺者 lüèduózhě.

pre·de·ces·sor /'pri:dɪsesə(r)/ *n* [C] 前任 qiánrèn.

pre·des·tined /pri:'destɪnd/ *adj* 命定的 mìngdìngde; 宿命的 sùmìngde.

pre·dica·ment /prɪ'dɪkəmənt/ *n* [C] 困境 kùnjìng.

predi·cate /'predɪkət/ *n* [C] ［语法］谓语 (如 '*Life is short*' 中的 '*is short*' 是谓语) wèiyǔ. **predi·cat·ive** /prɪ'dɪkətɪv/ *adj*

pre·dict /prɪ'dɪkt/ *vt* 预言 yùyán; 预示 yùshì. ~**able** /-əbl/ *adj* 可预言的 kě yùyán de. **pre·dic·tion** /-ʃn/ *n* [U] 预言 yùyán; [C] 被预言的事物 bèi yùyán de shìwù.

pre·dis·pose /ˌpri:dɪ'spəʊz/ *vt* ［正式用语］使倾向于 shǐ qīngxiàng yú; 使偏向于 shǐ piānxiàng yú: *His training* ~*d him to travel widely.* 他的训练使他爱好到处旅行. **pre·dis·posi·tion** /-pə'zɪʃn/ *n* [C]

pre·domi·nant /prɪ'dɒmɪnənt/ *adj* ［正式用语］主要的 zhǔyàode; 占［佔］优［優］势［勢］的 zhàn yōushì de: *a man's* ~ *features* 一个人的相貌特点. ~**ly** *adv* 主要地 zhǔyàode. **pre·domi·nance** *n* [U]

pre·domi·nate /prɪ'dɒmɪneɪt/ *vi* ~ **(over)** 统治 tǒngzhì; 支配 zhīpèi; 占［佔］优［優］势［勢］zhàn yōushì.

pre-emi·nent /pri:'emɪnənt/ *adj* ［正式用语］卓越的 zhuóyuède, 杰［傑］出的 jiéchūde. ~**ly** *adv* **pre-emi·nence** *n* [U]

preen /pri:n/ *vt* **1** (指鸟)用嘴整理(羽毛) yòng zuǐ zhěnglǐ. **2**［喻］装［裝］束 zhuāngshù; 打扮 dǎbàn.

pre·fab·ri·cate /ˌpri:'fæbrɪkeɪt/ *vt* 预先建造(如房屋、墙等) yùxiān jiànzào; 预制 yùzhì. **pre·fab·ri'ca·tion** *n* [U]

pref·ace /'prefɪs/ *n* [C] 序言 xùyán, 前言 qiányán. □ *vt* 开［開］始 kāishǐ; 作序 zuòxù. **prefa·tory** /'prefətrɪ/ *adj*

prefect /'pri:fekt/ *n* [C] **1** (学生的)级长［長］jízhǎng; 班长 bānzhǎng. **2** (法国的)地方行政长官 dìfāng xíngzhèng zhǎngguān.

pre·fer /prɪ'fɜ:(r)/ *vt* [-rr-] **1** 宁［寧］可 nìngkě; 更喜欢［歡］gèng xǐhuān: *I* ~ *tea to coffee.* 我喜欢茶,不喜欢咖啡. **2** 提出 tíchū: ~ *charges against somebody* 对某人提出控告. ~**able** /'prefrəbl/ *adj* 更好的 gènghǎode. ~**ably** *adv*

pref·er·ence /'prefrəns/ *n* **1** [C, U] 偏爱［愛］piān'ài; 优［優］先 yōuxiān. **2** [C] 偏爱物 piān'àiwù. **3** [C,U] (关税等)特惠 tèhuì.

pref·er·en·tial /ˌprefə'renʃl/ *adj* 优［優］先的 yōuxiānde; 优待的 yōudàide; 特惠的 tèhuìde: *get* ~ *treatment* 受优待.

pre·fix /'pri:fɪks/ *n* [C] 前缀 (如

pre-, co-) qiánzhuì; 词头〔頭〕cítóu. □ *vt* 给…加前缀 gěi…jiā qiánzhuì.

preg·nant /'pregnənt/ *adj* **1** 怀〔懷〕孕的 huáiyùnde; 怀胎的 huáitāide. **2**〔喻〕(言词、行动)意义〔義〕深远〔遠〕的 yìyì shēnyuǎn de. **preg·nancy** *n* [C,U]

pre·his·toric /ˌpriːhɪ'stɒrɪk/ *adj* 史前的 shǐqiánde. **pre·his·tory** /priː'hɪstrɪ/ *n* [U]

pre·judge /ˌpriː'dʒʌdʒ/ *vt* 预先判断〔斷〕yùxiān pànduàn. **~ment** *n* [C,U]

preju·dice /'predʒʊdɪs/ *n* **1**[C,U] 偏见 piānjiàn; 成见 chéngjiàn. **2** [U]〔法律〕损害 sǔnhài; 伤〔傷〕害 shānghài. □ *vt* **1** 使抱偏见 shǐ bào piānjiàn; 使有成见 shǐ yǒu chéngjiàn. **2** 损害 sǔnhài; 侵害 qīnhài; 不利于 búlì yú: ~ *his career* 损害他的事业. **preju·di·cial** /-'dɪʃl/ *adj*

prel·ate /'prelət/ *n* [C] 主教 zhǔjiào; 高级教士 gāojí jiàoshì.

pre·limi·nary /prɪ'lɪmɪnərɪ/ *adj* 初步的 chūbùde; 开〔開〕端的 kāiduānde: *a* ~ *study* (*report*) 初步研究(报告). □ *n* [C] [*pl* -ries] [通常用 *pl*] 初步的行动〔動〕chūbùde xíngdòng; 开〔開〕端 kāiduān.

prel·ude /'preljuːd/ *n* [C] **1** 序言 xùyán; 序幕 xùmù. **2** (音乐)序曲 xùqǔ; 前奏曲 qiánzòuqǔ.

pre·mari·tal /ˌpriː'mærɪtl/ *adj* 婚前的 hūnqiánde: ~ *sex* 婚前的性交.

pre·ma·ture /'premətjʊə(r)/ *adj* 早熟的 zǎoshúde; 过〔過〕早的 guòzǎode: ~ *birth* 早产. **~ly** *adv*

pre·medi·tate /priː'medɪteɪt/ *vt* 预先考虑 yùxiān kǎolǜ; 预先计划〔劃〕yùxiān jìhuà; 预谋 yùmóu: ~*d murder* 谋杀. **pre·medi'ta·tion** /-ʃn/ *n* [U]

pre·mier /'premɪə(r)/ *adj* 首要的 shǒuyàode; 首位的 shǒuwèide. □ *n* [C] 总〔總〕理 zǒnglǐ; 首相 shǒuxiàng. **'~ship** *n* [C]

pre·mière /'premɪeə(r)/ *n* [C] 首次公演 shǒucì gōngyǎn.

prem·ise /'premɪs/ *n* [C] **1**(亦作 **pre·miss**) 前提 qiántí. **2** [*pl*] 房屋(及其附属建筑和基地等) fángwū.

pre·mium /'priːmɪəm/ *n* [C] [*pl* ~s] **1** 保险〔險〕费 bǎoxiǎnfèi. **2** 额外费用(房租等) éwài fèiyòng.

pre·mon·ition /ˌpremə'nɪʃn/ *n* [C] 预感 yùgǎn; 预兆 yùzhào.

pre·oc·cu·pa·tion /ˌpriːˌɒkjʊ'peɪʃn/ *n* [U] 先占 xiānzhàn [C] 令人全神贯注的事物 lìng rén quán shén guànzhù de shìwù.

pre·oc·cupy /priː'ɒkjʊpaɪ/ *vt*[*pt,pp* -ied] 使对〔對〕…全神贯注 shǐ duì…quán shén guàn zhù.

prep·ara·tion /ˌprepə'reɪʃn/ *n* **1** [U] 准〔準〕备〔備〕zhǔnbèi; 预备 yùbèi: *work done without* ~ 无准备而完成的工作. **2** [C]〔通常用 *pl*〕准备的事物 zhǔnbèide shìwù. **3** [C] (特别配制的)药〔藥〕剂〔劑〕yàojì; 食物 shíwù.

pre·para·tory /prɪ'pærətrɪ/ *adj* 预备〔備〕的 yùbèide; 准〔準〕备的 zhǔnbèide: ~ *training* 预备性训练.

pre·pare /prɪ'peə(r)/ *vt/i* **1** ~ (*for*) 预备〔備〕yùbèi; 准〔準〕备 zhǔnbèi. **2** *be* ~*d to* 愿意 yuànyì; 乐〔樂〕于 lè yú.

prep·osi·tion /ˌprepə'zɪʃn/ *n* [C] 介词 (如 *in, from, to*) jiècí; 前置词 qiánzhìcí. **~al** *adj*

pre·pos·ter·ous /prɪ'pɒstərəs/ *adj* 反常的 fǎnchángde; 荒谬的 huāngmiùde. **~ly** *adv*

pre·roga·tive /prɪ'rɒgətɪv/ *n* [C] 特权〔權〕tèquán.

Pres. = President.

Pres·by·ter·ian /ˌprezbɪ'tɪərɪən/ *adj* (亦作 ~ *Church*) 长〔長〕老会〔會〕的 zhǎnglǎohuìde □ *n* [C] 长老会教徒 zhǎnglǎohuì jiàotú.

pre·scribe /prɪ'skraɪb/ *vt/i* 吩咐使用 fēnfù shǐyòng: ~ *medicine* 开药方. ~ *books* 指定阅读的书.

pre·scrip·tion /prɪ'skrɪpʃn/ *n* **1** [U] 规定 guīdìng; 指定 zhǐdìng; [C] 所规定的事物 suǒ guīdìngde shìwù. **2** (尤指)药〔藥〕方 yàofāng, 处〔處〕方 chùfāng.

pre·scrip·tive /prɪ'skrɪptɪv/ *adj* 规定的 guīdìngde; 指示的 zhǐshìde. ⇨ descriptive.

pres·ence /'prezns/ *n* [U] **1** 出席 chūxí; 到场 dàochǎng. **2** 风〔風〕采 fēngcǎi; 风度 fēngdù.

pres·ent[1] /'preznt/ *adj* **1** 出席的 chūxíde; 到场〔場〕的 dàochǎngde. ⇨ absent[1]. **2** 现在的 xiànzàide; 现存的 xiàncúnde: *the* ~ *government* 现政府. □ *n* **1 the** ~ 现在 xiànzài. **at** ~ 现在 xiànzài; 目前 mùqián. **2**〔语法〕= present tense. ~ **participle** 〔语法〕⇨ participle. ~ **tense** 〔语法〕⇨ tense[2].

pres·ent[2] /'preznt/ *n* [C] 礼〔禮〕物 lǐwù, 赠品 zèngpǐn.

pre·sent[3] /prɪ'zent/ *vt* **1** ~ *sth to sb*, ~ *sb with sth* 赠送…给某人 zèngsòng…gěi mǒurén. **2**〔反身〕出现 chūxiàn; 出席 chūxí: ~

oneself for trial 到场受审. **3** 呈现 chéngxiàn; 出示 chūshì. **4** 上演 shàngyǎn. **5** 在电〔電〕视或广〔廣〕播中介绍节〔節〕目 zài diànshì huò guǎngbō zhōng jièshào jiémù.

pre·sent·able /prɪ'zentəbl/ *adj* 拿得出的 nádechūde; 象样〔樣〕的 xiàngyàngde. **pre·sent·ably** *adv.*

pres·en·ta·tion /ˌprezən'teɪʃn/ *n* [U] 赠送 zèngsòng; [C] 表现方式 biǎoxiàn fāngshì.

pres·ent·ly /'prezntlɪ/ *adv* 不久 bùjiǔ: *I'll see you* ~. 我不久就去看你.

pres·er·va·tion /ˌprezə'veɪʃn/ *n* [U] **1** 保存 bǎocún; 保护〔護〕 bǎohù. **2** 保存状〔狀〕况 bǎocún zhuàngkuàng.

pre·serv·ative /prɪ'zɜːvətɪv/ *n* [C], *adj* 防腐剂〔劑〕 fángfǔjì; 防腐的 fángfǔde.

pre·serve /prɪ'zɜːv/ *vt* **1** 保护〔護〕 bǎohù; 防护 fánghù. **2** 保存 bǎocún; 保藏 bǎocáng: ~ *fruit* 蜜饯水果. **3** 保持(健康等)bǎochí. **4** 使留存 shǐ liúcún. □ *n* [C][通常用 *pl*] 果酱〔醬〕 guǒjiàng.

pre·side/prɪ'zaɪd/ *vi* ~ **(*at, over*)** 作会〔會〕议〔議〕的主席 zuò huìyì de zhǔxí; 指挥〔揮〕 zhǐhuī; 负责 fùzé.

presi·dency /'prezɪdənsɪ/ *n* [C] [*pl* -ies] **1 the** ~ 总〔總〕统(或大学校长,董事长,会长,总经理,总裁等) 的职〔職〕位 zǒngtǒngde zhíwèi. **2**上述各职位的任期shàngshù gè zhíwèi de rènqī.

presi·dent /'prezɪdənt/ *n* [C] **1** 总〔總〕统 (如美国) zǒngtǒng. **2** 政府部门〔門〕首长〔長〕 zhèngfǔ bùmén shǒuzhǎng; 商行、会〔會〕社等的首长 shāngháng huìshè děng de shǒuzhǎng. ~**ial** /-'denʃl/ *adj*

press[1] /pres/ *n* [C] **1** 压〔壓〕 yā; 按 àn; 挤〔擠〕 jǐ; 熨 yùn. **2** 压榨机〔機〕 yāzhàjī: *a wine* ~ 榨葡萄机. **3 the** ~ (总称) 报〔報〕纸 bàozhǐ; 期刊 qīkān; 新闻〔聞〕界 xīnwénjiè; 报界 bàojiè. **4** 出版界 chūbǎnjiè; 出版社 chūbǎnshè.

press[2] /pres/ *vt/i* **1** 压〔壓〕 yā; 按 àn; 挤〔擠〕 jǐ. **2** 压榨 yāzhà; 熨平 yùnpíng; 榨取(汁等) zhàqǔ. **3** ~ ***for*** 反复〔復〕请求 fǎnfù qǐngqiú; 迫切要求 pòqiè yāoqiú. **4** ***be*** ~***ed for*** 缺少 quēshǎo; 缺乏 quēfá: ~*ed for time* 时间紧迫. **5** 推进〔進〕 tuījìn; 拥〔擁〕挤 yōngjǐ. **6** 急迫 jípò; 紧〔緊〕迫 jǐnpò: *The matter is* ~*ing* 事情急迫. **7** ~ ***on (with sth)*** 决心继〔繼〕续〔續〕 juéxīn jìxù. ~**ing** *adj* 紧迫的 jǐnpòde; 迫切的 pòqiède: ~*ing business* 急事.

press·ure /'preʃə(r)/ *n* [C,U] **1** 压〔壓〕 yā; 按 àn ⇨ blood pressure. **2** 压力 yālì; 强制 qiángzhì. ***be(come) under*** ~ 在…的压力下 zài…de yālì xià. '~**-cooker** 高压锅〔鍋〕 gāoyāguō. '~ **gauge** *n* (测量液体或气体在某一点上压力的)压力计 yālìjì.

press·ur·ize /'preʃəraɪz/ *vt* **1** 在(飞机) 中保持正常气〔氣〕压〔壓〕 zài…zhōng bǎochí zhèngcháng qìyā: *a* ~*d cabin* (飞机的) 压力舱. **2** ~ ***sb (into doing sth)*** [非正式用语]施加压力 shījiā yālì; 说服 shuōfú.

pres·tige /pre'stiːʒ/ *n* [U] **1** 威信 wēixìn; 声〔聲〕望 shēngwàng. **2** (由于成功、财富等而产生的)显〔顯〕赫 xiǎnhè. **pres·tig·ious** /pre'stɪdʒəs/ *adj* 有威信的 yǒu wēixìn de; 有声望的 yǒu shēngwàng de.

pre·stressed /ˌpriː'strest/ *adj*(指混凝土)预力的 yùlìde. ~ *concrete* 预力混凝土.

pre·sum·ably /prɪ'zjuːməblɪ/ *adv* 假定地 jiǎdìngde; 也许 yěxǔ: *P*~ (= I suppose) *you will stay here.* 我想你将呆在这里.

pre·sume /prɪ'zjuːm/ *vt/i* **1** 假定 jiǎdìng; 假设 jiǎshè. **2** ~ ***(to do sth)*** [正式用语]敢于 gǎn yú; 冒…的危险〔險〕 mào… de wéixiǎn: *I wouldn't* ~ *to advise you.* 我不敢向你提出劝告.

pre·sump·tion /prɪ'zʌmpʃn/ *n* **1** [C] 假定 jiǎdìng; 推测 tuīcè. **2** [U] 无〔無〕理 wúlǐ; 傲慢 àomàn.

pre·sup·pose /ˌpriːsə'pəʊz/ *vt* **1** 预先假定 yùxiān jiǎdìng; 推测tuīcè. **2** 以…为先决条〔條〕件 yǐ…wéi xiānjué tiáojiàn: *Sleep* ~*s a peaceful mind.* 思想安静是入睡的前提. **pre·sup·po·si·tion** /-pə'zɪʃn/ *n* [C,U]

pre·tence (美语亦作 **pre·tense**) /prɪ'tens/ *n* **1** [U] 假装〔裝〕 jiǎzhuāng; 做作 zuòzuò. **2** [C] 借口 jièkǒu; 托词 tuōcí. ***false*** ~***s*** [法律]欺诈(手段) qīzhà.

pre·tend /prɪ'tend/ *vt/i* **1** 假装〔裝〕 jiǎzhuāng **2** 借口 jièkǒu: ~ *sickness.* 装病.

pre·ten·sion /prɪ'tenʃn/ *n* **1** [C] [常用 *pl*] 要求 yāoqiú, 主张〔張〕 zhǔzhāng; 权〔權〕利 quánlì. **2** [U] 自命 zìmìng; 自负 zìfù.

pre·ten·tious /prɪ'tenʃəs/ *adj* 自负的 zìfùde, 自命不凡的 zìmìng bùfán de. ~**ly** *adv* ~**ness** *n* [U]

pre·text /'pri:tekst/ *n*[C] 借〔藉〕口 jièkǒu, 托词 tuōcí.

pretty /'prɪtɪ/ *adj* [-ier, -iest] 漂亮的 piàoliàngde, 标〔標〕致的 biāozhìde, 俏的 qiàode. □ *adv* **1** 相当〔當〕xiāngdāng, *It's* ~ *cold.* 天气相当冷. **2**〔非正式用语〕很 hěn: *a* ~ *big car* 一辆很大的汽车. ~ **well** 几〔幾〕乎 jīhū. **prettily** *adv* **pret·ti·ness** *n* [U]

pre·vail /prɪ'veɪl/ *vi* **1** ~ **(*over, against*)** 获〔獲〕胜〔勝〕huòshèng; 战〔戰〕胜 zhànshèng. **2**流行 liúxíng, 盛行 shèngxíng. **3** ~ **(*up*) *on sb*** 劝〔勸〕说 quànshuō, 说服 shuōfú. ~**ing** *adj* 流行的 liúxíngde; 普遍的 pǔbiànde: ~*ing winds* (气象)盛行风.

pre·va·lent /'prevələnt /*adj*〔正式用语〕普遍的 pǔbiànde; 流行的 liúxíngde: ~ *diseases* 流行病. **pre·va·lence** *n* [U]

pre·vent /prɪ'vent/ *vt* 阻止 zǔzhǐ; 妨碍〔礙〕fáng'ài; 预防 yùfáng: ~ *an accident* 预防意外. **pre·ven·tion** /-ʃn/ *n* [U] ~**tive** *adj* 预防的 yùfángde; 妨碍的 fáng'àide: ~*ive medicine* 预防药物,预防医学.

pre·view /'pri:vju:/ *n* [C] 预观〔觀〕yùguān; 预演 yùyǎn; 预映 yùyìng. □ *vt* 预观 yùguān; 预演 yùyǎn; 预映 yùyìng.

pre·vi·ous /'pri:vɪəs/ *adj* 以前的 yǐqiánde; 先前的 xiānqiánde: *the* ~ *day* 前一天. ~**ly** *adv*

prey /preɪ/ *n* [仅用 *sing*] 被捕食的动〔動〕物 bèi bǔshí de dòngwù. □ *vi* ~ **(*up*) *on,*** **1** 捕食 bǔshí, 攫食 juéshí. **2** 掠夺〔奪〕lüèduó, 抢〔搶〕掠 qiǎnglüè: ~*ed on by bandits* 被土匪抢夺. **3** (指恐惧等)使苦恼〔惱〕shǐ kǔnǎo. ˌ**beast** (ˌ**bird**) **of** '~ 肉食兽〔獸〕(鸟) ròushí shòu.

price /praɪs/ *n* **1** [C] 价〔價〕格 jiàgé, 价钱〔錢〕jiàqián. **2** [U] 价值 jiàzhí. **3** [C] 代价 dàijià: *the* ~ *of freedom* 自由的代价. □ *vt* 给…定价 gěi … dìngjià; 给…标〔標〕价 gěi...biāojià. ~**less** *adj* 无〔無〕价的 wújiàde; 贵重的 guìzhòngde.

prick[1] /prɪk/ *n* [C] **1** 刺痕 cìhén; 刺孔 cìkǒng; 刺点〔點〕cìdiǎn. **2** 刺痛 cìtòng.

prick[2] /prɪk/ *vt/i* **1** 刺(穿) cì, 扎(穿) zhā, 戳(穿) chuō. **2** 刺伤〔傷〕cìshāng; 刺痛 cìtòng. **3**〔喻〕使不安 shǐ bù'ān: *His conscience* ~*ed him.* 他受到良心的谴责. **4** ~ ***up one's ears,*** **(a)** (指狗、马) 竖〔豎〕起耳朵 shùqǐ ěrduō. **(b)**〔喻〕(指人)密切注意 mìqiè zhùyì.

prickle /'prɪkl/ *n* [C] (动植物的皮上长出的)刺 cì. □ *vt/i* 刺痛 cìtòng; 感到刺痛 gǎndào cìtòng. **prick·ly** /'prɪklɪ/ *adj* **(a)** 多刺的 duōcìde **(b)**〔非正式用语〕易动〔動〕怒的 yì dòngnù de.

pride /praɪd/ *n* **1** [U] 自豪 zìháo; 得意 déyì. **2** [U] 自尊 zìzūn. **3** [U] 引以自豪的人(或事物) yǐn yǐ zìháo de rén: *His son is his* ~ *and joy.* 他的儿子使他感到自豪和愉快. **4** [U] 骄〔驕〕傲 jiāo'ào, 傲慢 àomàn, 自大 zìdà. **5** [C] (鸟、兽等的)群 qún: *a* ~ *of lions* 一群狮子. □ *vt* [反身] ~ ***oneself on sth*** 以…自豪 yǐ...zìháo.

priest /pri:st/ *n* [C] (基督教)教士 jiàoshì; 牧师〔師〕mùshī; 神父 shénfù. '~**hood**(教会的)全体〔體〕教士(牧师、僧侣) quántǐ jiàoshì.

prim /prɪm/ *adj* [-mer, -mest] **1** 整洁〔潔〕的 zhěngjiéde; 端正的 duānzhèngde: *a* ~ *garden* 整洁的园子. **2** (指人)一本正经〔經〕的 yì běn zhèng jīng de; 不喜欢〔歡〕粗鲁的bù xǐhuān cūlǔ de: *a* ~ *and proper lady* 一位规矩有礼的妇人.

pri·mar·ily /'praɪmərəlɪ/ *adv* 首先 shǒuxiān; 主要地 zhǔyàode.

pri·mary /'praɪmərɪ/ *adj* 最初的 zuìchūde; 第一的 dìyīde; 首要的 shǒuyàode. '~ **school**〔英国英语〕小学〔學〕xiǎoxué.

pri·mate[1] /'praɪmeɪt/ *n* [C]大主教 dàzhǔjiào.

pri·mate[2] /'praɪmeɪt/ *n* [C]灵〔靈〕长〔長〕类(包括人、猿等)língchánglèi.

prime[1] /praɪm/ *adj* **1** 主要的 zhǔyàode, 首要的 shǒuyàode. **2** 最好的 zuìhǎode, 第一流的 dìyīliúde: ~ *beef* 上等牛肉. **the** ˌ**P**~ '**Minister** 首相 shǒuxiàng.

prime[2] /praɪm/ *n* [U] 最好部分 zuìhǎo bùfen: *in the* ~ *of life* 正在壮年.

prime[3] /praɪm/ *vt* **1** 准〔準〕备〔備〕zhǔnbèi: ~ *a gun* 给枪装子弹. **2** 提供事实〔實〕tígòng shìshí. **3** 涂〔塗〕底漆 tú dǐqī.

primer /'praɪmə(r)/ *n* [C] **1** 雷管 léguǎn; 导〔導〕火线〔綫〕dǎohuǒxiàn. **2** 底漆 dǐqī.

primi·tive /'prɪmɪtɪv/ *adj* **1** 原始的 yuánshǐde; 远〔遠〕古的 yuǎngǔde: ~ *man* (*culture*) 原始人(文化). **2** 简〔簡〕单〔單〕的 jiǎndānde 古老的 gǔlǎode. □ *n* [C] 原始人 yuánshǐrén. ~**ly** *adv*

prim·rose /'prɪmrəʊz/ *n* [C] 樱草 yīngcǎo; 樱草花 yīngcǎohuā; [U

樱草色 yīngcǎosè; 淡黄色 dànhuángsè. □ *adj* 淡黄色的 dànhuángsède.

prince /prɪns/ *n* [C] **1** 君主 jūnzhǔ. **2** 王子 wángzǐ; 王孙〔孫〕wángsūn; 亲〔親〕王 qīnwáng. **~ly** *adj* [-ier, -iest] 王子的 wángzǐde; 与〔與〕王子相称〔稱〕的 yǔ wángzǐ xiāngchèng de; 豪华〔華〕的 háo huáde.

prin·cess /prɪn'ses/ *n* [C] 公主 gōngzhǔ; 王妃 wángfēi; 公爵夫人 gōngjué fūrén.

prin·ci·pal /'prɪnsəpl/ *adj* 主要的 zhǔyàode, 首要的 shǒuyàode, 最重要的 zuì zhòngyào de: *the ~ cities of England* 英国的主要城市. □ *n* [C] **1** 校长〔長〕xiàozhǎng; 首长 shǒuzhǎng. **2** 资本 zīběn; 本金 běnjīn. **~ly** /-plɪ/ *adv* 主要地 zhǔyàode.

prin·ci·pal·ity /ˌprɪnsə'pælətɪ/ *n* [C] [*pl* -ies] 公国〔國〕gōngguó; 侯国 hóuguó.

prin·ciple /'prɪnsəpl/ *n* [C] **1** 原理 yuánlǐ; 原则 yuánzé. **2** 主义〔義〕zhǔyì; 规则 guīzé. ***in*** ~ 原则上 yuánzéshàng; 理论〔論〕上 lǐlùnshàng. ***on*** ~ 根据〔據〕原则 gēnjù yuánzé: *refuse to do it on* ~ 根据原则拒绝去做.

print[1] /prɪnt/ *n* **1** [U] 印刷符号〔號〕yìnshuā fúhào; 印刷字体〔體〕yìnshuā zìtǐ. ***in*** ~ 已出版的 yǐ chūbǎn de; (书等)在销售的 zài xiāoshòu de. ***out of*** ~ (书等)已售完的 yǐ shòuwán de; 已绝版的 yǐ juébǎn de. **2** [C] 印迹〔跡〕yìnjì; 痕迹 hénjì: *'finger-~s* 指印, 指纹. **3** [C] 印出的图片 yìnchūde túpiàn. **4** (用底版)印出的相片 yìnchūde xiàngpiàn.

print[2] /prɪnt/ *vt/i* **1** 印刷 yìnshuā. **2** 用印刷体〔體〕写〔寫〕yòng yìnshuātǐ xiě. **3** 晒印(照片) shàiyìn; 复〔複〕制〔製〕(电影拷贝) fùzhì. **~er** 印刷工人 yìnshuā gōngrén; 印刷商 yìnshuāshāng.

prior /'praɪə(r)/ *adj* 较〔較〕早的 jiàozǎode; 在前的 zàiqiánde; 更重要的 gèng zhòngyào de: *a ~ claim* 优先要求权. a ~ *engagement* 优先的约会. ~ ***to*** *prep* 在…之前 zài...zhī qián.

pri·or·ity /praɪ'ɒrətɪ/ *n* [*pl* -ies] **1** [U] 优〔優〕先权〔權〕yōuxiānquán; 在先 zàixiān. **2** [C] 更重要的事物 gèngzhòngyàode shìwù.

prism /'prɪzəm/ *n* [C] **1** 棱〔稜〕柱 léngzhù. **2** 棱柱体〔體〕léngzhùtǐ; 棱镜 léngjìng. **~atic** /-'mætɪk/ *adj* **(a)** 棱柱的 léngzhùde; 棱镜的 léngjìngde. **(b)** 五光十色的 wǔguāng shísè de.

prison /'prɪzn/ *n* [C] **1** 监〔監〕狱 jiānyù; 牢房 láofáng. **2** [U] 监禁 jiānjìn: *escape from* ~ 逃出监狱, 越狱. **~er** 囚犯 qiúfàn; 俘虏〔虜〕fúlǔ; 失去自由的人(动物) shīqù zìyóu de rén.

priv·acy /'prɪvəsɪ/ *n* [U] **1** 隐〔隱〕退 yǐntuì; 隐居 yǐnjū. **2** 秘密(与 *publicity* 相对) mìmì.

pri·vate /'praɪvɪt/ *adj* **1** (与 *public* 相对) 私人的 sīrénde; 私有的 sīyǒude. **2** 秘密的 mìmìde, 保密的 bǎomìde. **3** 非官职〔職〕的 fēi guānzhí de; 个〔個〕人的 gèrénde: *a ~ visit* 私人访问. **4** 士兵的 shìbīngde. □ *n* **1** [C] 士兵 shìbīng. **2** ***in*** ~ 秘密的(地) mìmìde. **~ly** *adv*

privet /'prɪvɪt/ *n* [U] 水蜡〔蠟〕树〔樹〕shuǐlàshù.

pri·vi·lege /'prɪvəlɪdʒ/ *n* **1** [C] 特权〔權〕tèquán; 优〔優〕惠 yōuhuì. **2** [C] 特殊的荣〔榮〕幸 tèshūde róngxìng. **privi·leged** *adj* 有特权的 yǒu tèquán de; 特许的 tèxǔde.

prize[1] /praɪz/ *n* [C] **1** 奖〔獎〕品 jiǎngpǐn; 奖金 jiǎngjīn; 赠品 zèngpǐn. **2** [喻](值得)竞〔競〕争的目标〔標〕jìnzhēngde mùbiāo. □ *vt* 珍视 zhēnshì; 珍藏 zhēncáng.

prize[2] (亦作 **prise**) /praɪz/ *vt* 撬 (与 *open, up, off* 连用) qiào; 撬动〔動〕qiàodòng: ~ *a box open* 撬开箱子.

pro /prəʊ/ *n* [C] [*pl* ~s] [非正式用语] professional (player) 的缩写〔寫〕*professional (player)* de suōxiě.

pro- /ˌprəʊ/ *prefix* **1** (表示"亲", "赞成"): *pro-Chinese* 亲华的. **2** (表示"副", "代"): *pro-vice-chancellor* 代理副大臣(代理副总理, 代理副校长等). **the ˌ~s and ˈcons** 正反双〔雙〕方 zhèngfǎn shuāngfāng.

P.R.O.=Public Relations Officer 新闻〔聞〕发〔發〕布员 xīnwén fābù yuán.

pro.=professional.

prob·abil·ity /ˌprɒbə'bɪlətɪ/ *n* [*pl* -ies] **1** [U] 可能性 kěnéngxìng: *There's little ~ that you will win.* 你没有什么可能取胜. ***in all*** ~ 很可能 hěn kěnéng; 多半 duōbàn. **2** [C] 可能发〔發〕生的事 kěnéng fāshēng de shì; 可能的结果 kěnéngde jiéguǒ.

prob·able /'prɒbəbl/ *adj* 很可能的 hěn kěnéng de; 象〔像〕事实〔實〕

的 xiàng shìshí de. **prob·ably** *adj*

pro·ba·tion /prəˈbeɪʃn/ *n* [U] **1** 试用 shìyòng, 试读〔讀〕shìdú; 见习〔習〕jiànxí; 试用(试读、见习)期 shìyòngqī. **2**〔法律〕缓刑 huǎnxíng.

probe /prəʊb/ *n* [C] **1**〔医学〕探针 tànzhēn. **2**〔新闻〕调查(丑闻等)(与 *into* 连用) diàochá. **3** 探测器 tàncèqì; 宇宙探测飞〔飛〕船 yǔzhòu tàncè fēichuán. ☐ *vt* **1** 用探针(或探测器)探查 yòng tànzhēn tànchá. **2** 探求 tànqiú; 细察 xìchá.

prob·lem /ˈprɒbləm/ *n* [C] 问〔問〕题 wèntí; 难〔難〕题 nántí. **~atic** /-ˈmætɪk/ *adj* (尤指结果)成问题的 chéng wèntí de, 疑难的 yínánde.

pro·cedure /prəˈsi:dʒə(r)/ *n* [C,U] 过〔過〕程 guòchéng; 步骤〔驟〕bùzòu; 程序 chéngxù. **pro·cedural** *adj*

pro·ceed /prəˈsi:d/ *vi* **1** ~ *to (do) sth* 进〔進〕行 jìnxíng; 继〔繼〕续〔續〕jìxù. **2** 开〔開〕始 kāishǐ, 着手 zhuóshǒu. *He ~ed to attack me.* 他开始攻击我. **3** ~ ***against*** 起诉 qǐsù.

pro·ceed·ing /prəˈsi:dɪŋ/ *n* **1**[U] 程序 chéngxù; 进〔進〕程 jìnchéng. **2** [C] 活动〔動〕huódòng. **3** [*pl*]〔法律〕诉讼 sùsòng.

pro·ceeds /ˈprəʊsi:dz/ *n pl* 收入 shōurù; 收益 shōuyì.

pro·cess /ˈprəʊses/ *n* **1** [C] 变〔變〕化的过〔過〕程 biànhuàde guòchéng. **2** [C] 方法 fāngfǎ; 制〔製〕作法 zhìzuòfǎ. **3** ***in the ~ of*** 在…的过程中 zài ... de guòchéng zhōng: *a factory in the ~ of being built* 正在建造的工厂. **4** [C]〔法律〕手续〔續〕shǒuxù; 诉讼 sùsòng. ☐ *vt* **1** 加工贮〔貯〕藏(食物) jiāgōng zhùcáng. **2** (摄影术): *~ film* 冲洗胶卷.

pro·ces·sion /prəˈseʃn/ *n* **1** [C](人或车辆等的)行列 hángliè; 队〔隊〕伍 duìwǔ. **2** [U] (列队的)行进〔進〕xíngjìn. **~al** *adj*

pro·claim /prəˈkleɪm/ *vt* 宣告 xuāngào; 宣布〔佈〕xuānbù; 声〔聲〕明 shēngmíng. **proc·la·ma·tion** /ˌprɒkləˈmeɪʃn/ *n* **(a)** [U] 宣布 xuānbù; 声明 shēngmíng. **(b)** [C] 布告 bùgào; 宣言 xuānyán; 声明书〔書〕shēngmíngshū.

pro·cure /prəˈkjʊə(r)/ *vt*〔正式用语〕(努力)取得 qǔdé; 获〔獲〕得 huòdé.

prod /prɒd/ *vt/i* [-dd-] **1** 刺 cì, 戳 chuō. **2**〔喻〕激励〔勵〕jīlì; 促使 cùshǐ: *~ her into starting work* 鼓励她开始工作. ☐ *n* [C] 刺 cì, 戳 chuō.

prodi·gal /ˈprɒdɪgl/ *adj*〔正式用语〕挥〔揮〕霍的 huīhuòde, 浪费的 làngfèide, 奢侈的 shēchǐde.

pro·di·gious /prəˈdɪdʒəs/ *adj* 巨大的 jùdàde, 奇妙的 qímiàode. **~ly** *adv*

prod·igy /ˈprɒdɪdʒɪ/ *n* [C] [*pl* -ies] 奇迹〔跡〕qíjì; 奇事 qíshì; 奇才 qícái.

pro·duce¹ /ˈprɒdju:s/ *n* [U] 产〔產〕品 chǎnpǐn; 农〔農〕产品 nóngchǎnpǐn.

pro·duce² /prəˈdju:s/ *vt/i* **1** 提出 tíchū; 出示 chūshì: *~ one's railway ticket* 出示火车票. **2** 制〔製〕造 zhìzào; 生产 shēngchǎn; 出产 chūchǎn. **3** 生 shēng; 产(卵) chǎn. **4** 引起 yǐnqǐ; 导〔導〕致 dǎozhì: *success ~d by hard work* 由努力而获得的成功. **5** 演出 yǎnchū; 放映 fàngyìng.

pro·ducer /prəˈdju:sə(r)/ *n* [C] **1** 生产〔產〕者 shēngchǎnzhě; 制〔製〕造者 zhìzàozhě. **2** 演出者 yǎnchūzhě; 制片人 zhìpiānrén. ⇨ director.

prod·uct /ˈprɒdʌkt/ *n* [C] **1** 产〔產〕品 chǎnpǐn; 产物 chǎnwù. **2** 结果 jiéguǒ, 成果 chéngguǒ. **3**〔数学〕乘积〔積〕chéngjī, 积 jī.

pro·duc·tion /prəˈdʌkʃn/ *n* **1** [U] 生产〔產〕shēngchǎn; 制〔製〕造 zhìzào. ⇨ mass production. ~ **line** *n* 生产线 shēngchǎnxiàn. **2** [U] 产量 chǎnliàng. **3** [C] 作品 zuòpǐn; 著作 zhùzuò.

pro·duc·tive /prəˈdʌktɪv/ *adj* **1** 能生产〔產〕的 néng shēngchǎn de; 肥沃的 féiwòde: *~ land* 肥沃的土地. **2** 节〔節〕约地生产东〔東〕西 jiéyuēde shēngchǎn dōngxi. **~ly** *adv*

pro·duc·tiv·ity /ˌprɒdʌkˈtɪvətɪ/ *n* [U] **1** 生产〔產〕能力 shēngchǎn nénglì: *the ~ of the land* 土地的生产能力. **2** 生产率 shēngchǎnlǜ: *~ has fallen sharply* 生产率急剧下降.

Prof. =Professor.

pro·fane /prəˈfeɪn/ *adj* 渎〔瀆〕神的 dúshénde; 亵〔褻〕渎的 xièdúde: *~ acts in a church* 教堂里的渎神行为. *~ language* 不敬的话; 粗话. ☐ *vt* 亵渎 xièdú; 玷污 diànwū. **~ly** *adv* **pro·fan·ity** /prəˈfænətɪ/ *n* [C,U] [*pl* -ies] 渎神 dúshén; 亵渎的言语或行为〔爲〕xièdúde yányǔ huò xíngwéi.

pro·fess /prəˈfes/ *vt/i* **1** 承认〔認

chéngrèn; 声〔聲〕称〔稱〕shēngchēng. 2 自称 zìchēng. ~**ed** *adj* 自称的 zìchēngde; 公开〔開〕表示的 gōngkāi biǎoshì de.

pro·fes·sion /prə'feʃn/ *n* [C] **1** 职〔職〕业〔業〕zhíyè. **2** 表白 biǎobái; 声〔聲〕明 shēngmíng.

pro·fes·sional /prə'feʃnəl/ *adj* **1** 职〔職〕业〔業〕的 zhíyède; 专〔專〕业的 zhuānyède. **2** 职业性的 zhíyèxìngde; 非业余的 fēi yèyú de: ~ *sportsmen* 职业运动员. ⇨ amateur. □ *n* [C] 以某种〔種〕职业为〔爲〕生的人 yǐ mǒuzhǒng zhíyè wéishēng de rén; 专业人员 zhuānyè rényuán. ~**ism** /-ɪzəm/ *n* [U] **(a)** 职业特性 zhíyè tèxìng. **(b)** 职业化 zhíyèhuà.

prof·es·sor /prə'fesə(r)/ *n* [C] (大学) 教授 jiàoshòu. ~**ial** /ˌprɒfɪ'sɔːrɪəl/ *adj* ~**ship** 教授职〔職〕位 (或身分) jiàoshòu zhíwèi.

pro·fi·cient /prə'fɪʃnt/ *adj* 熟练〔練〕的 shúliànde, 精通的 jīngtōngde. **pro·fi·ciency** *n* [U]

pro·file /'prəʊfaɪl/ *n* [C] **1** 侧面 cèmiàn; 侧面像 cèmiànxiàng. **2** 轮〔輪〕廓 lúnkuò, 外形 wàixíng. **3** 传〔傳〕略 zhuànlüè; 人物简〔簡〕介 rénwù jiǎnjiè. □ *vt* 作…的侧面像 zuò ... de cèmiànxiàng; 描绘〔繪〕…的轮廓 miáohuì...de lúnkuò.

profit /'prɒfɪt/ *n* **1** [U] 利益 lìyì; 益处〔處〕yìchù. **2** [C,U] 利润〔潤〕lìrùn; 赢利 yínlì. □ *vt/i* ~ *from (by)* 得益 déyì; 有利 yǒulì. ~**able** /-əbl/ *adj* **(a)** 有益的 yǒuyìde; 获〔獲〕利的 huòlìde. **(b)** 〔喻〕有用的 yǒuyòngde: *a* ~*able discussion* 有益的讨论. ~**ably** *adv*

pro·found /prə'faʊnd/ *adj* **1** 〔正式用语〕深的 shēnde; 极〔極〕深的 jíshēnde: ~ *interest* 很大的兴趣. ~ *silence* 十分寂静. **2** 渊〔淵〕博的 yuānbóde, 造诣深的 zàoyìshēnde. **3** 深奥的 shēn'àode. ~**ly** *adv* 深深地 shēnshēnde: ~*ly hurt by his insults* 由于他的侮辱而深受伤害.

pro·fuse /prə'fjuːs/ *adj* 〔正式用语〕**1** 极〔極〕其丰〔豐〕富的 jí qí fēngfù de. **2** 很多的 hěnduōde; 大量的 dàliàngde: ~ *apologies.* 多次道歉. ~**ly** *adv* **pro·fu·sion** /-ʒn/ *n* [U] 〔正式用语〕丰〔豐〕富 fēngfù, 大量 dàliàng.

pro·gramme (美语 **-gram**) /'prəʊgræm/ *n* [C] **1** 节〔節〕目单〔單〕jiémùdān; 说明书〔書〕shuōmíngshū. **2** 计划〔劃〕jìhuà. **3** 程序 chéngxù. **4** (广播、电视) 节目 jiémù. □ *vt* 把…列入节目 bǎ ... lièrù jiémù; 为〔爲〕…制订计划 wèi ... zhìdìng jìhuà. ~**d 'course** *n* (教育) 编序课程 biānxù kèchéng. ~**d 'learning** *n* 编序教学〔學〕biānxù jiàoxué. **programming 'language** *n* 编序语言 (如 Basic, Fortran) biānxù yǔyán. **pro·gram·mer** 程序编制员 chéngxù biānzhìyuán.

prog·ress[1] /'prəʊgres/ *n* **1** [U] 前进〔進〕qiánjìn; 改进 gǎijìn; 发〔發〕展 fāzhǎn. *in* ~ 进展中 jìnzhǎn zhōng: *work in* ~ 工作在进行中.

pro·gress[2] /prə'gres/ *vi* 进〔進〕步 jìnbù; 前进 qiánjìn.

pro·gres·sion /prə'greʃn/ *n* [U] 前进〔進〕qiánjìn; 进步 jìnbù.

pro·gress·ive /prə'gresɪv/ *adj* **1** 进〔進〕步的 jìnbùde; 前进的 qiánjìnde. **2** 累进的 lěijìnde; 渐〔漸〕进的 jiànjìnde: ~ *taxes* 累进税. **3** 提倡改革的 tíchàng gǎigé de: ~ *policies* 进步政策. □ *n* [C] 进步人士 jìnbù rénshì. ~**ly** *adv*

pro·hibit /prə'hɪbɪt/ *vt* 禁止 jìnzhǐ; 阻止 zǔzhǐ.

pro·hib·ition /ˌprəʊɪ'bɪʃn/ *n* **1** [U] 禁止 jìnzhǐ. **2** [C] 禁令 jìnlìng; 禁律 jìnlǜ.

pro·hibi·tive /prə'hɪbətɪv/ *adj* 禁止的 jìnzhǐde; 抑制的 yìzhìde: ~ *tax* 寓禁税. ~ *prices* 高得使人不敢问津的价格.

pro·ject[1] /'prɒdʒekt/ *n* [C] 方案 fāng'àn; 计划〔劃〕jìhuà.

pro·ject[2] /prə'dʒekt/ *vt/i* **1** 设计 shèjì; 规划〔劃〕guīhuà. **2** ~ *sth on (to) sth* 投影 tóuyǐng; 投射 tóushè. **3** 抛 pāo; 投 tóu; 射 shè: ~ *missiles into space* 向太空发射导弹. **4** 突出 tūchū: *a balcony that* ~*s over the street* 伸到街上的阳台.

pro·jec·tile /prə'dʒektaɪl/ *n* [C] 抛射物 pāoshèwù; 射弹〔彈〕shèdàn.

pro·jec·tion /prə'dʒekʃn/ *n* [C] 突出 tūchū; 投射 tóushè; 发〔發〕射 fāshè.

pro·jec·tor /prə'dʒektə(r)/ *n* [C] (电影) 放映机〔機〕fàngyìngjī; 幻灯 huàndēng.

pro·let·ar·iat /ˌprəʊlɪ'teərɪət/ *n* [C] 〔现代用法〕无〔無〕产〔產〕阶〔階〕级 wúchǎn jiējí. **pro·let·ar·ian** *n* [C], *adj* 无产者 wúchǎnzhě; 无产阶级的 wúchǎn jiējí de.

pro·lif·er·ate /prə'lɪfəreɪt/ *vt/i* 〔正式用语〕**1** 增生 zēngshēng. **2** 〔喻〕激增 jīzēng. **pro·lif·e·r·ation** *n* [U]

pro·lific /prə'lɪfɪk/ *adj* 〔正式用语〕

多产〔產〕的 duōchǎnde; 丰〔豐〕富的 fēngfùde: ~ *writers* 多产作家.

pro·logue /'prəʊlɒg/ *n* [C] **1** 序诗 xùshī; 序言 xùyán. **2** [喻] (一系列事件的) 开〔開〕端 kāiduān; 序幕 xùmù.

pro·long /prə'lɒŋ/ *vt* 延长〔長〕yáncháng; 拖延 tuōyán. **~a·tion** /-'geɪʃn/ *n* [C,U]

prom·en·ade /ˌprɒmə'nɑːd/ *n* [C] (为散心或炫耀服饰的) 散步 sànbù; 骑〔騎〕马〔馬〕qímǎ; 散步场〔場〕所 sànbù chǎngsuǒ. □ *vt/i* 散步 sànbù; 骑马 qímǎ.

promi·nent /'prɒmɪnənt/ *adj* **1** 突出的 tūchūde; 显〔顯〕著的 xiǎnzhùde. **2** (指人) 著名的 zhùmíngde; 重要的 zhòngyàode. **~ly** *adv* **promi·nence** *n* **(a)** [U] 突出 tūchū; 显著 xiǎnzhù; 卓越 zhuóyuè. **(b)** [C] 突出物 tūchūwù; 突出部分 tūchū bùfen.

pro·mis·cu·ous /prə'mɪskjʊəs/ *adj* (性交) 随便的 suíbiànde. **~ly** *adv* **prom·is·cu·ity** /-'skjuːətɪ/ *n* [U]

prom·ise /'prɒmɪs/ *n* **1** [C] 诺言 nuòyán; 允诺 yǔnnuò. **2** [C] 允诺的东〔東〕西 yǔnnuòde dōngxi; 约定的事 yuēdìngde shì. **3** [C] 有良好结果的希望 yǒu liánghǎo jiéguǒ de xīwàng: *a writer of* ~ 有希望的作家. □ *vt/i* **1** 允诺 yǔnnuò; 答应〔應〕dāyìng. **2** 有…希望 yǒu…xīwàng; 预示 yùshì: *It ~s to be a warm day.* 天气可望转暖. **prom·is·ing** *adj* 有前途的 yǒu qiántú de.

prom·on·tory /'prɒməntrɪ/ *n* [C] [*pl* -ies] 海角 hǎijiǎo; 岬 jiǎ.

pro·mote /prə'məʊt/ *vt* **1** 提升 tíshēng; 升级 shēngjí. **2** 筹〔籌〕建 chóujiàn; 创〔創〕办〔辦〕chuàngbàn: ~ *a new company* 创办一家新公司. **3** 宣传〔傳〕新产〔產〕品 xuānchuán xīn chǎnpǐn. **pro·mo·ter** 创办人 chuàngbànrén.

pro·mo·tion /prə'məʊʃn/ *n* **1** [C, U] 提升 tíshēng; 创〔創〕立 chuànglì. **2** (商品等的) 宣传〔傳〕xuānchuán; 推销 tuīxiāo.

prompt¹ /prɒmpt/ *adj* 迅速的 xùnsùde; 敏捷的 mǐnjiéde: *a ~ reply* 迅速的答复. **~ly** *adv* **~ness** *n* [U]

prompt² /prɒmpt/ *vt* **1** 敦促 dūncù; 激励〔勵〕jīlì. **2** (为演员) 提词 tící, 提白 tíbái. □ *n* [C] (对演员的) 提词 tící, 提白 tíbái. **~er** 提词员 tícíyuán.

prone /prəʊn/ *adj* **1** 俯伏的 fǔfúde; 面向下的 miàn xiàngxià de. **2** ~ *to* 有…倾向的 yǒu…qīngxiàng de: ~ *to accidents* 易出事故.

prong /prɒŋ/ *n* [C] 叉尖 chājiān.

pro·noun /'prəʊnaʊn/ *n* [C] 代词 (如 *he, it, hers, me, them*) dàicí.

pro·nounce /prə'naʊns/ *vt/i* **1** 发〔發〕音 fāyīn. **2** 宣称〔稱〕xuānchēng; 宣告 xuāngào: *The doctor ~d him dead.* 医生宣布他已死亡. **pro·nounced** *adj* 明确〔確〕的 míngquède; 显〔顯〕著的 xiǎnzhùde. **~ment** *n* [C] 声〔聲〕明 shēngmíng, 公告 gōnggào.

pro·nun·ci·ation /prəˌnʌnsɪ'eɪʃn/ *n* **1** [U] 发〔發〕音 fāyīn; 发音法 fāyīnfǎ. **2** [C] 读〔讀〕法 dúfǎ.

proof¹ /pruːf/ *adj* ~ **(*against*)** 不能穿透的 bùnéng chuāntòu de; 能抵挡〔擋〕的 néng dǐdǎng de: ~ *against bullets*, *'bullet-~* 防弹的 ⇨ foolproof. □ *vt* 使防水 shǐ fángshuǐ; 使…不被穿透 shǐ … bú bèi chuāntòu.

proof² /pruːf/ *n* **1** [C,U] 证据〔據〕zhèngjù; 证词 zhèngcí; 证明 zhèngmíng. **2** [C] 考验〔驗〕kǎoyàn; 检〔檢〕验 jiǎnyàn: *Put it to the ~.* 进行检验. **3** [C] 校样〔樣〕jiàoyàng; 样张〔張〕yàngzhāng. **4** [U] (酒精、酒类的) 强度标〔標〕准〔準〕qiángdù biāozhǔn.

prop /prɒp/ *n* [C] **1** 支柱 zhīzhù; 撑材 chēngcái. **2** [喻] 支持者 zhīchízhě; 后〔後〕盾 hòudùn. □ *vt* [-pp-] 支持 zhīchí; 支撑 zhīcheng.

propa·ganda /ˌprɒpə'gændə/ *n* [U] 宣传〔傳〕xuānchuán; 宣传方法 xuānchuán fāngfǎ.

propa·gate /'prɒpəgeɪt/ *vt/i* [正式用语] **1** 繁殖 fánzhí; 增殖 zēngzhí. **2** 传〔傳〕播 chuánbō; 宣传 xuānchuán: ~ *knowledge* 传播知识. **propa'ga·tion** *n* [U]

pro·pel /prə'pel/ *vt* [-ll-] 推进〔進〕tuījìn; 推动〔動〕tuīdòng. **~ler** (轮船、飞机上的) 螺旋桨〔槳〕luóxuánjiǎng; 推进器 tuījìnqì.

proper /'prɒpə(r)/ *adj* **1** 正确〔確〕的 zhèngquède; 适〔適〕当〔當〕的 shìdàngde. **2** 有礼〔禮〕貌的 yǒu lǐmào de; 高尚的 gāoshàngde. **~ noun (name)** [语法] 专〔專〕有名词 (如 *Mary, Prague*) zhuānyǒu míngcí. **~ly** *adv* 正当地 zhèngdāngde; 适当地 shìdàngde.

prop·erty /'prɒpətɪ/ *n* [*pl* -ies] **1** [U] 财产〔產〕cáichǎn; 资产 zīchǎn. **2** [C] 地产 dìchǎn; 房产 fángchǎn. **3** 性质〔質〕xìngzhì; 特性 tèxìng: *chemical properties* 化学性质.

proph·ecy /'prɒfəsɪ/ *n* [*pl* -ies] [U] 预言能力 yùyán nénglì. **2** [C

预言 yùyán.

proph·esy /'prɒfɪsaɪ/ *vt/i* [*pt, pp* -ied] 预言 yùyán; 预示 yùshì.

prophet /'prɒfɪt/ *n* [C] **1** 先知 xiānzhī. **2** 预言家 yùyánjiā. **~ic** /prə'fetɪk/ *adj*

pro·por·tion /prə'pɔ:ʃn/ *n* **1** [U] 比率 bǐlǜ; 比例 bǐlì. ***in ~ to*** 与〔與〕...成比例 yǔ...chéng bǐlì: *paid in ~ to work done* 按完成的工作付酬. **2** [C] 部分 bùfen. **3** [*pl*] 大小 dàxiǎo; 容积〔積〕róngjī; 面积 miànjī: *trade of substantial ~s* 大量的贸易. □ *vt* 「正式用语」使成比例 shǐ chéng bǐlì. **~al** *adj* 〔正式用语〕成比例的 chéngbǐlìde.

pro·po·sal /prə'pəʊzl/ *n* **1** [U] 建议〔議〕jiànyì, 提议 tíyì. **2** [C] 计划〔劃〕jìhuà; 方案 fāng'àn. **3**[C] 求婚 qiúhūn.

pro·pose /prə'pəʊz/ *vt/i* **1** 提议〔議〕tíyì. 建议 jiànyì. **2** 求婚 qiúhūn. **3** 提名 tímíng; 推荐〔薦〕tuījiàn.

prop·osi·tion /ˌprɒpə'zɪʃn/ *n* [C] **1** 陈〔陳〕述 chénshù; 主张〔張〕zhǔzhāng. **2** (尤指商业)报〔報〕价〔價〕bàojià. **3** [非正式用语]猥亵〔褻〕的要求 wěixiède yāoqiú. □ *vt* [俚语] 向...提出(猥亵的)要求 xiàng...tíchū yāoqiú.

pro·pri·etary /prə'praɪətrɪ/ *adj* 独〔獨〕占〔佔〕的 dúzhànde; 专〔專〕利的 zhuānlìde: *a ~ name* 专利商标名(如 Kodak).

pro·pri·etor /prə'praɪətə(r)/ *n* [C] 所有人(尤指房屋、土地) suǒyǒurén; 业〔業〕主 yèzhǔ. **pro·pri·etress** /-trɪs/ *n* [C] 女所有人 nǚ suǒyǒurén; 女业主 nǚ yèzhǔ.

pro·pri·ety /prə'praɪətɪ/ *n* [*pl* -ies] [正式用语] **1** [C,U] 正当〔當〕的行为〔爲〕zhèngdàngde xíngwéi. **2** [U] 正当 zhèngdàng; 适〔適〕当 shìdàng: *I doubt the ~ of granting his request.* 我怀疑同意他的请求是否适当.

pro·pul·sion /prə'pʌlʃn/ *n* [U] 推进〔進〕tuījìn; 推进力 tuījìnlì.

pro·rata /ˌprəʊ 'rɑ:tə/ *adv* [拉丁语] 按比例 àn bǐlì; 成比例 chéng bǐlì.

pro·scribe /prəʊ'skraɪb/ *vt* 使失去法律保护〔護〕shǐ shīqù fǎlù bǎohù.

prose /prəʊz/ *n* [U] 散文 sǎnwén. ⇨ poetry.

pros·ecute /'prɒsɪkju:t/ *vt* 起诉 qǐsù, 告发〔發〕gàofā. **pros·e'cu·tion** 起诉 qǐsù, 告发 gàofā; 原告及其律师〔師〕yuángào jí qí lǜshī. ⇨defence(3). **pros·ecutor** *n* [C] 原告 yuángào, 起诉人 qǐsùrén.

pros·pect¹ /'prɒspekt/ *n* **1** [C] 景色 jǐngsè; 景象 jǐngxiàng. **2** [*pl*] 前景 qiánjǐng; 前程 qiánchéng.

pros·pect² /prə'spekt/ *vi* **~ (*for*)** 勘探 kāntàn; 寻〔尋〕找 xúnzhǎo: *~-ing for gold* 试掘金矿. **~or** *n* [C] (矿藏等的)勘探者 kāntànzhě.

pros·pec·tive /prə'spektɪv/ *adj* 预期的 yùqīde; 未来〔來〕的 wèiláide: *his ~ fortune* 他未来的好运.

pro·spec·tus /prə'spektəs/ *n* [C] [*pl*~es] 说明书〔書〕shuōmíngshū; (即将出版的书等的)简〔簡〕介 jiǎnjiè.

pros·per /'prɒspə(r)/ *vt/i* 成功 chénggōng **~ity** /prɒ'sperətɪ/ *n* [U] 成功 chénggōng; **~ous** *adj* 成功的 chénggōngde; 富裕的 fùyùde.

pros·ti·tute /'prɒstɪtju:t/ *n* [C] 妓女 jìnǚ, 娼妓 chāngjì. □ *vt* **1** [反身] 使沦〔淪〕为〔爲〕娼妓 shǐ lúnwéi chāngjì. **2** 滥〔濫〕用 lànyòng: *~ one's talents.* 滥用才能.
pros·ti'tu·tion *n* [U]

pros·trate /'prɒstreɪt/ *adj* 俯卧的 fǔwòde. □ *vt* /prɒ'streɪt/ **1** 使平卧 shǐ píngwò; 弄倒 nòngdǎo. **2** 使衰竭 shǐ shuāijié; 使疲惫〔憊〕shǐ píbèi.

pro·tag·on·ist /prəʊ'tægənɪst/ *n* [C] [正式用法](戏剧、小说等的)主角 zhǔjué; 主人公 zhǔrengong.

pro·tect /prə'tekt/ *vt* **~ *from* (*against*)** 保护〔護〕bǎohù; 防护 fánghù. **pro·tec·tion**/-ʃn/ *n* [U]**(a)** 保护 bǎohù. **(b)** [C] 保护者 bǎohùzhě; 保护物 bǎohùwù. **~ive** *adj* **(a)** 保护的 bǎohùde; 防护的 fánghùde. **(b)** ***~ive (towards)*** 有保护愿〔願〕望的 yǒu bǎohù yuànwàngde. **~or** *n* [C] 保护者 bǎohùzhě; 防御者 fángyùzhě.

pro·tec·tor·ate /prə'tektərət/ *n* [C] 保护〔護〕国〔國〕bǎohùguó; 保护领地 bǎohù lǐngdì.

pro·tégé /'prɒtɪʒeɪ/ *n* [C] 被保护〔護〕人 bèi bǎohù rén.

pro·tein /'prəʊti:n/ *n* [C,U] 蛋白质〔質〕dànbáizhì.

pro·tem.=for the time. 当〔當〕时〔時〕(的) dāngshí; 临〔臨〕时(的) línshí.

pro·test¹ /'prəʊtest/ *n* **1** [C,U] 抗议〔議〕kàngyì; 反对〔對〕fǎnduì. **2** [用作定语]表示抗议 biǎoshì kàngyì. *a ~ march* 抗议游行.

pro·test² /prə'test/ *vt/i* **1** 明言 míngyán; (坚决)表示 biǎoshì: *He ~ed his innocence.* 他申明自己无罪. **2** **~ (*against*)** 抗议〔議〕kàngyì; 反对〔對〕fǎnduì. ~**er** *n* [C]

Prot·es·tant /'prɒtɪstənt/ *n, adj* 新教徒 xīnjiàotú; 基督徒 jīdūtú; 新教徒的 xīnjiàotúde; 基督徒的 jīdūtúde.

pro·to·col /'prəʊtəkɒl/ *n* [U] 礼〔禮〕仪〔儀〕lǐyí; 外交礼节〔節〕wàijiāo lǐjié.

pro·ton /'prəʊtɒn/ *n* [C] 质〔質〕子 zhìzǐ. ⇨ electron.

pro·to·type /'prəʊtətaɪp/ *n* [C] 原型 yuánxíng.

pro·tract /prə'trækt/ *vt* 延长〔長〕yáncháng; 拖延 tuōyán: ~ *a discussion* 延长讨论. **pro·trac·tion** /-ʃn/ *n* [U]

pro·trac·tor /prə'træktə(r)/ *n* [C] 量角器 liángjiǎoqì, 分度规 fēndùguī.

pro·trude /prə'tru:d/ *vt/i* (使)伸出 shēnchū; 突出 tūchū. **pro·tru·sion** /-ʒn/ *n* [U] 伸出 shēnchū; 突出 tūchū; [C] 突起部 tūqǐbù.

pro·tu·ber·ant /prə'tju:bərənt/ *adj* [正式用语]隆起的 lóngqǐde; 突出的 tūchūde. **pro·tu·ber·ance** *n* [C,U] 隆起 lóngqǐ; 隆起部 lóngqǐbù; 突出 tūchū; 突出物 tūchūwù.

proud /praʊd/ *adj* [-er, -est] **1** ~ **(*of*)** 因…而自豪 yīn…ér zìháo; 以…为〔爲〕荣〔榮〕yǐ … wéiróng. **2** 妄自尊大的 wàng zì zūn dà de. **3** 辉〔輝〕煌的 huīhuángde: *a ~ day for the school.* 学校的光辉日子. ~**ly** *adv*

prove /pru:v/ *vt/i* [*pp* ~d 或 ~n /'pru:vn/] · **1** 证明 zhèngmíng; 证实〔實〕zhèngshí. **2** 检验〔驗〕jiǎnyàn; 考验 kǎoyàn: ~ *a man's worth* 检验一个人的价值. **3** 被发〔發〕现 bèi fāxiàn: *It ~d (to be) useless.* 发现无用.

prov·erb /'prɒvɜ:b/ *n* [C] 谚语(如 'It takes two to make a quarrel') yànyǔ, 格言 géyán. ~**ial** /prə'vɜ:bɪəl/ *adj* 众〔衆〕所周知的 zhòng suǒ zhōu zhī de.

pro·vide /prə'vaɪd/ *vt/i* **1** ~ ***for sb (sth)*** 准〔準〕备〔備〕zhǔnbèi; 满足…的需要 mǎnzú … de xūyào. **2** ~ ***sth for sb*** 供给 gōngjǐ; 供应〔應〕gōngyìng.

pro·vided /prə'vaɪdɪd/ *conj* 假如 jiǎrú.

pro·vid·ing /prə'vaɪdɪŋ/ *conj* = provided.

prov·ince /'prɒvɪns/ *n* [C] **1** 省 shěng. **2 the** ~s 地方(首都以外的全部地区) dìfāng. **3** (学术)领域 lǐngyù; (活动)范〔範〕围〔圍〕fànwéi. **prov·in·cial** /prə'vɪnʃl/ *adj* **(a)** 省的 shěngde; 地方的 dìfāngde. **(b)** 偏狭〔狹〕的 piānxiáde. □ *n* [C] 地方居民 dìfāng jūmín; 外省人 wàishěngrén.

pro·vi·sion /prə'vɪʒn/ *n* **1** [U] 准〔準〕备〔備〕zhǔnbèi; 防备 fángbèi: ~ *for future needs* 为将来需要作准备. **2** [C] 供应〔應〕gōngyìng; (一批)供应品 gōngyìngpǐn. **3** [*pl*] 食物 shíwù; 给养〔養〕jǐyǎng. **4** [C] 条〔條〕款 tiáokuǎn; 规定 guīdìng. □ *vt* 供应食物(或必需品) gōngyìng shíwù.

pro·vi·sional /prə'vɪʒənl/ *adj* 临〔臨〕时〔時〕的 línshíde; 暂〔暫〕时性的 zànshíxìngde: *a ~ government* 临时政府. ~**ly** *adv*

provo·ca·tion /ˌprɒvə'keɪʃn/ *n* **1** [U] 激怒 jīnù; 惹起 rěqǐ. **2** [C] 激怒的原因 jīnùde yuányīn.

pro·voca·tive /prə'vɒkətɪv/ *adj* 激怒的 jīnùde; 引起兴〔興〕趣(议论、争论等)的 yǐnqǐ xìngqù de. ~**ly** *adv*

pro·voke /prə'vəʊk/ *vt* **1** 激怒 jīnù **2** 惹起 rěqǐ; 引起 yǐnqǐ: ~ *laughter* 引起大笑. **pro·vok·ing** *adj* 使人烦恼的 shǐ rén fánnǎo de.

prow /praʊ/ *n* [C] 船首 chuánshǒu.

prowl /praʊl/ *vt/i* (野兽等)四处〔處〕觅食 sìchù mìshí; 潜〔潛〕行(想偷窃等) qiǎnxíng. □ *n* ***be on the ~*** 徘徊 páihuái; 潜行(想偷窃) qiǎnxíng.

prox. = of next (month).

prox·im·ity /prɒk'sɪmətɪ/ *n* [U] 最近 zuìjìn; 接近 jiējìn.

proxy /'prɒksɪ/ *n* [*pl* -ies] **1** [C, U] 代理权〔權〕dàilǐquán; 代表权 dàibiǎoquán; 代理 dàilǐ. **2** [C] 代理人 dàilǐrén; 代表者 dàibiǎozhě.

prude /pru:d/ *n* [C] 过〔過〕分拘谨的人 guòfèn jūjǐn de rén. **prud·ish** *adj* 过分拘谨的 guòfèn jūjǐn de.

pru·dent /'pru:dnt/ *adj* 谨慎的 jǐnshènde; 慎重的 shènzhòngde. ~**ly** *adv* **pru·dence** *n* [U]

prune[1] /pru:n/ *n* [C] 梅干〔乾〕méigān; 梅脯 méifǔ.

prune[2] /pru:n/ *vt* **1** 修剪(树枝等) xiūjiǎn. **2** [喻]删除 shānchú; 删节〔節〕shānjié.

pry /praɪ/ *vi* [*pt, pp* pried /praɪd/] ~ **(*into*)** 窥探 kuītàn; 探问〔問〕tànwèn. ~**ing·ly** *adv*

PS. = postscript.

psalm /sa:m/ *n* [C] 圣〔聖〕诗(大指圣经的诗篇 **the P~s**) shèngshī; 赞〔讚〕美诗 zànměishī; 圣歌 shènggē.

pseu·do·nym /'sju:dənɪm/ *n* [C] 假名 jiǎmíng; 笔〔筆〕名 bǐmíng.
psyche·delic /ˌsaɪkɪ'delɪk/ *adj* **1** (指毒品)引起幻觉〔覺〕的 yǐnqǐ huànjué de. **2** (音乐、灯光等)引起幻觉的 yǐnqǐ huànjué de.
psy·chia·try /saɪ'kaɪətrɪ/ *n* [U] 精神病学〔學〕 jīngshénbìngxué. **psy·chia·trist** *n* [C] 精神病医〔醫〕生 jīngshénbìng yīshēng; 精神病学者 jīngshénbìng xuézhě. **psy·chi·atric** /ˌsaɪkɪ'ætrɪk/ *adj*
psy·chic(al) /'saɪkɪk(l)/ *adj* **1** 精神的 jīngshénde; 灵〔靈〕魂的 línghúnde. **2** 超越自然规律的现象 chāoyuè zìrán guīlǜ de xiànxiàng.
psy·cho-an·aly·sis /ˌsaɪkəʊ ə'næləsɪs/ *n* [U] 精神分析 jīngshén fēnxī. **psy·cho-anal·yst** /-'ænəlɪst/ *n* [C] 精神分析学〔學〕家 jīngshén fēnxīxuéjiā. **psy·cho-an·al·yse**〔美语 = **-lyze**〕/-'ænəlaɪz/ *vt* 用精神分析法治疗〔療〕 yòng jīngshén fēnxīfǎ zhìliáo.
psy·chol·ogy /saɪ'kɒlədʒɪ/ *n* [U] 心理学〔學〕 xīnlǐxué. **psy·chol·ogist** *n* [C] 心理学家 xīnlǐxuéjiā. **psy·cho·logi·cal** /-'lɒdʒɪkl/ *adj*
psy·cho·path /'saɪkəʊpæθ/ *n* [C] 精神变〔變〕态〔態〕者 jīngshén-biàntài zhě. **~ic** *adj*
P.T.=physical training 体〔體〕育锻炼〔煉〕 tǐyù duànliàn.
pt.= **1** part. **2** pint. **3** port.
P.T.O.=please turn over 见下页 jiàn xiàyè.
pub /pʌb/ *n* [C] public house 的缩写〔寫〕 *public house* de suōxiě.
pu·berty /'pju:bətɪ/ *n* [U] 青春期 qīngchūnqī; 发〔發〕身 fāshēn.
pu·bic /'pju:bɪk/ *adj* 阴〔陰〕部的 yīnbùde; 阴毛的 yīnmáode.
pub·lic /'pʌblɪk/ *adj* (与 *private* 相对) 公众〔衆〕的 gōngzhòngde; 公共的 gōnggòngde. □ *n* **1 the ~** 公众 gōngzhòng; 民众 mínzhòng. *in* ~ 公开〔開〕地 gōngkāide. **2** (某一方面的)大众 dàzhòng; 群众 qúnzhòng: *the reading* ~ 读者大众. ˌ~ **con'veni·ence**(公共场所的)厕所 cèsuǒ. ˌ~ **'house** *n* [C]〔英国英语〕〔正式用语〕小酒店 xiǎo jiǔdiàn; 领有出售酒类执〔執〕照的酒馆 lǐng yǒu chūshòu jiǔlèi zhízhào de jiǔguǎn. ˌ~ **re'lations** *n pl* (通过宣传手段建立的) 与〔與〕公众的联〔聯〕系〔繫〕 yǔ gōngzhòng de liánxì. '~ **school**〔英国英语〕(英国的)公学〔學〕 gōngxué; (美国的)公立中学(或小学) gōnglì zhōngxué. **~ly** *adv*
pub·li·ca·tion /ˌpʌblɪ'keɪʃn/ *n* **1** [U] 发〔發〕表 fābiǎo; 公布〔佈〕 gōngbù; 出版 chūbǎn. **2** [C] 出版物 chūbǎnwù.
pub·lic·ity /pʌb'lɪsətɪ/ *n* [U] **1** 公开〔開〕 gōngkāi. **2** 广〔廣〕告 guǎnggào. **3** 宣传〔傳〕 xuānchuán.
pub·li·cize /'pʌblɪsaɪz/ *vt* 宣传〔傳〕 xuānchuán; 公布〔佈〕 gōngbù.
pub·lish /'pʌblɪʃ/ *vt* **1** 出版(书、期刊等) chūbǎn; 发〔發〕行 fāxíng. **2** 公布 gōngbù; 发布 fābù. **~er** 出版者 chūbǎnzhě; 发行人 fāxíngrén.
puck /pʌk/ *n* [C] 冰球(冰上曲棍球用的橡胶制圆盘) bīngqiú.
pucker /'pʌkə(r)/ *vt/i* 折〔摺〕叠〔疊〕 zhédié; 皱〔皺〕起 zhòuqǐ: ~ *up one's lips* 噘嘴.
pudding /'pʊdɪŋ/ *n* **1** [C,U] 布丁(一种松软的甜点心) bùdīng. **2** 腊〔臘〕肠〔腸〕 làcháng; 香肠 xiāngcháng.
puddle /'pʌdl/ *n* [C] 水坑 shuǐkēng; 泥潭 nítán.
puff[1] /pʌf/ *n* [C] **1** (呼吸、空气)喷送 pēnsòng; 吹气〔氣〕 chuīqì. **2** = powder-puff. **puffy** *adj* [-ier, -iest] 喘息的 chuǎnxīde.
puff[2] /pʌf/ *vt/i* **1** 喘息 chuǎnxī; 喷烟(而驶去) pēnyān. **2** 阵〔陣〕阵喷出 zhènzhèn pēnchū, 吹气〔氣〕 chuīqì. **3** ~ *sth out* 膨胀〔脹〕 péngzhàng.
puf·fin /'pʌfɪn/ *n* [C] 善知鸟〔鳥〕 shànzhīniǎo; 海鹦〔鸚〕 hǎiyīng.
pull[1] /pʊl/ *n* **1** [C] 拉 lā, 拖 tuō; 扯 chě. **2** [U] 爬高 págāo; 费力的攀登 fèilìde pāndēng: *a long ~ up the hill* 长时间而费力的爬山. **3** [U] 影响〔響〕 yǐngxiǎng: *a man with a lot of* ~ 一位很有影响的人.
pull[2] /pʊl/ *vt/i* **1** (与 *push* 相对) 拉 lā, 拖 tuō, 牵〔牽〕 qiān. ~ *sth to pieces*, **(a)** 把…撕成碎片 bǎ...sīchéng suìpiàn. **(b)** 〔喻〕把…攻击〔擊〕得一钱〔錢〕不值 bǎ ... gōngjīde yìqián bùzhí. **2** = row². ~ *one's weight* 尽〔盡〕应〔應〕尽之力 jìn yīngjìn zhī lì. **3** ~ *a muscle* 拉紧〔緊〕 lājǐn. **4** ~ *sth down* 摧毁 cuīhuǐ; 破坏〔壞〕 pòhuài. ~ *in*, **(a)** (指火车)进〔進〕站 jìnzhàn. **(b)** (指车辆)开〔開〕进来〔來〕 kāi jìnlái. ~ *sth off*, **(a)** 把汽车〔車〕开〔開〕到路旁 bǎ qìchē kāi dào lùpáng. **(b)** 努力实〔實〕现 nǔlì shíxiàn. ~ *out* *(of)*, **(a)** 驶〔駛〕出 shǐchū. **(b)** 分开 fēnkāi; 离〔離〕开 líkāi. ~ *(sb) out (of)* 脱离困境 tuōlí kùnjìng:

~ *out of a race* 退出比赛. ~ **(sth) over** (把车)开到路边〔邊〕kāi dào lùbiān. ~ **through** (使)恢复健康 huīfù jiànkāng. ~ **oneself together** 控制自己 kòngzhì zìjǐ. ~ **(sth) up** (使)停止 tíngzhǐ. ~ **sb up** 阻止 zǔzhǐ.

pul·let /'pʊlɪt/ *n* [C] 小母鸡〔鷄〕xiǎo mǔjī.

pul·ley /'pʊlɪ/ *n* [C] [*pl* ~s] 滑轮〔輪〕huálún; 滑车〔車〕huáchē.

pull·over /'pʊləʊvə(r)/ *n* [C] 套头〔頭〕衫（如羊毛套衫等）tàotóushān.

pulp /pʌlp/ *n* [U] **1** 果肉 guǒròu. **2** 木浆〔漿〕mùjiāng; 纸浆 zhǐjiāng. □ *vt/i* (使)成浆状〔狀〕chéng jiāngzhuàng.

pul·pit /'pʊlpɪt/ *n* [C] (教堂的)讲〔講〕坛〔壇〕jiǎngtán; 布道坛 bùdàotán.

pul·sar /'pʌlsɑ:(r)/ *n* [C] 脉冲星 màichōngxīng.

pul·sate /pʌl'seɪt/ *vt/i* (心脏、脉搏)跳动〔動〕tiàodòng; 震动 zhèndòng. **pul·sa·tion** *n* [C,U]

pulse /pʌls/ *n* [C] **1** 脉搏 màibó. **2** [喻](感情等的)激动〔動〕jīdòng; 步调 bùdiào: *the* ~ *of life* 生活的步伐. □ *vi* 跳动 tiàodòng; 搏动 bódòng.

pul·ver·ize /'pʌlvəraɪz/ *vt/i* 研磨成粉 yánmóchéng fěn; 粉碎 fěnsuì.

puma /'pju:mə/ *n* [C] [*pl* ~s] 美洲狮〔獅〕Měizhōu shī.

pump /pʌmp/ *n* [C] 泵 bèng, 抽水机〔機〕chōushuǐjī, 唧筒 jītǒng. □ *vt/i* **1** 用抽水机抽(液体) yòng chōushuǐjī chōu; 用唧筒打 yòng jītǒng dǎ. **2** [喻]盘〔盤〕问〔問〕pánwèn; 追问 zhuīwèn. **3** 灌注 guànzhù.

pump·kin /'pʌmpkɪn/ *n* [C,U] 南瓜 nánguā.

pun /pʌn/ *n* [C] (亦作 *a play on words*) 双关〔關〕语(如'The soldier laid down his *arms*') shuāngguānyǔ. □ *vi* [-nn-] 用双关语 yòng shuāngguānyǔ.

punch[1] /pʌntʃ/ *n* [C] **1** 打孔器 dǎkǒngqì; 钻孔机〔機〕zuānkǒngjī. **2** 打印器 dǎyìnqì. □ *vt* (用打孔器)打孔 dǎ kǒng.

punch[2] /pʌntʃ/ *n* [U] (果汁、糖、香料等搀和的) 混合饮料 hùnhé yǐnliào.

punch[3] /pʌntʃ/ *vt* 用拳猛击〔擊〕yòng quán měngjī. □ *n* **1** [C]拳打 quándǎ. **2** [U] [喻] 力量 lìliàng; 活力 huólì. '~**-up** 殴〔毆〕斗〔鬥〕ōudòu.

punc·tual /'pʌŋktʃʊəl/ *adj* 准〔準〕时〔時〕的 zhǔnshíde; 严〔嚴〕守时刻的 yánshǒu shíkè de. ~**ly** *adv* ~**ity** /-'ælətɪ/ *n* [U]

punc·tu·ate /'pʌŋktʃʊeɪt/ *vt* **1** 加标〔標〕点〔點〕于 jiā biāodiǎn yú. **2** 不时〔時〕打断〔斷〕bùshí dǎduàn. **punc·tu'ation** /-ʃn/ *n* [U] 标点 biāodiǎn.

punc·ture /'pʌŋtʃə(r)/ *n* [C] 小孔 xiǎo kǒng; (车胎等的)刺孔 cìkǒng. □ *vt/i* 穿孔 chuānkǒng; 穿刺 chuāncì.

pun·gent /'pʌndʒənt/ *adj* [正式用语]刺鼻的 cìbíde; 刺激性的 cìjīxìngde.

pun·ish /'pʌnɪʃ/ *vt* **1** 处〔處〕罚 chǔfá; 惩罚 chéngfá. **2** 折磨 zhémó. ~**ment** *n* [U] 处罚 chǔfá; [C] 刑罚 xíngfá.

pu·ni·tive /'pju:nɪtɪv/ *adj* 处〔處〕罚的 chǔfáde; 刑罚的 xíngfáde: ~ *measures* 惩罚措施. ~ *taxes* 惩罚性赋税.

punt[1] /pʌnt/ *n* [C] (用篙撑的)方头〔頭〕平底船 fāngtóu píngdǐchuán. □ *vt/i* 用篙撑 yòng gāo chēng; 用方头平底船运〔運〕载〔載〕yòng fāngtóu píngdǐchuán yùnzài.

punt[2] /pʌnt/ *vi* (在赛马中)对一马〔馬〕下赌注 duì yìmǎ xià dǔzhù. ~**er** *n* [C] 赌博者 dǔbózhě.

puny /'pju:nɪ/ *adj* [-ier, -iest] 弱小的 ruòxiǎode; 软〔輭〕弱的 ruǎnruòde. **pun·ily** *adv*

pup /pʌp/ *n* [C] = puppy.

pu·pil[1] /'pju:pl/ *n* [C] 学〔學〕生 xuésheng.

pu·pil[2] /'pju:pl/ *n* [C] [解剖]瞳孔 tóngkǒng; 瞳仁 tóngrén.

pup·pet /'pʌpɪt/ *n* [C] **1** 木偶 mù'ǒu. **2** ('*glove*-~)(套在手上表演的)布袋木偶 bùdài mù'ǒu. **3** 傀儡 kuǐlěi.

puppy /'pʌpɪ/ *n* [C] [*pl* -ies] 小狗 xiǎo gǒu; 幼犬 yòuquǎn.

pur·chase /'pɜ:tʃəs/ *n* **1** [U] 买〔買〕mǎi; 购〔購〕买 gòumǎi. **2** [C] [正式用语]所购物 suǒgòuwù. □ *vt* 买 mǎi, 购买 gòumǎi. **pur·chaser** 买主 mǎizhǔ, 购买人 gòumǎirén.

pure /pjʊə(r)/ *adj* [-r, -st 除第 5,6 义外] **1** 纯粹的 chúncuìde, 不搀〔攙〕杂〔雜〕的 bù chānzá de. **2** 纯血统的 chúnxuètǒngde; 纯种〔種〕的 chúnzhǒngde. **3** 无〔無〕罪的 wúzuìde; 无错的 wúcuòde. **4** (指声音) 清亮的 qīngliàngde; 圆润〔潤〕的 yuánrùnde. **5** 纯理论〔論〕的 (非实用的) chúnlǐlùnde: ~ *science* 纯科学. **6** 单〔單〕纯的 dānchúnde; 仅〔僅〕仅的 jǐnjǐnde: *a* ~

waste of time 纯粹浪费时间. ~**ly** *adv* (尤指) 仅仅地 jǐnjǐnde; 全然 quánrán.
pu·rée /ˈpjʊəreɪ/ *n* [C,U] 菜泥 càiní; 果泥 guǒní; 酱〔醬〕jiàng.
pur·ga·tory /ˈpɜːgətrɪ/ *n* [C] [*pl* -ies] **1**[宗教]炼〔煉〕狱 liànyù; 涤〔滌〕罪 dízuì. **2**[喻]暂〔暫〕时〔時〕受苦的地方 zànshí shòukǔ de dìfāng.
purge /pɜːdʒ/ *vt* **1** ~ *sb* (*of sth* 或 *from sth*) 净化 jìnghuà; 洗清 xǐqīng. **2**(用药物)通便 tōngbiàn; 使泻〔瀉〕shǐ xiè. **3**清洗 qīngxǐ. □ *n* [C] 清洗 qīngxǐ.
pu·rify /ˈpjʊərɪfaɪ/ *vt* [*pt, pp* -ied] 使纯净 shǐ chúnjìng; 使洁〔潔〕净 shǐ jiéjìng. **pu·ri·fi·ca·tion** /-fɪˈkeɪʃn/ *n* [U]
pu·rist /ˈpjʊərɪst/ *n* [C] 语言纯正癖者 yǔyán chúnzhèngpǐ zhě.
puri·tan /ˈpjʊərɪtən/ *adj, n* [C] **1** **P**~ 清教徒的 qīngjiàotúde; (基督教新教的一派)清教徒 qīngjiàotú. **2**拘谨的 jūjǐnde. 道德(或宗教)上极〔極〕端拘谨的人 dàodé shàng jíduān jūjǐn de rén; 道貌岸然的人 dàomào ànrán de rén. ~**-i·cal** /-ˈtænɪkl/ *adj*
pu·rity /ˈpjʊərətɪ/ *n* [U] 纯净 chúnjìng; 纯正 chúnzhèng; 纯洁〔潔〕chúnjié.
purl /pɜːl/ *n* [C] (编织中的)反针 fǎnzhēn; 倒针 dàozhēn. □ *vt/i* 用反针(或倒针)编织〔織〕yòng fǎnzhēn biānzhī.
purple /ˈpɜːpl/ *n* [U], *adj* 紫色 zǐsè; 紫色的 zǐsède.
pur·pose /ˈpɜːpəs/ *n* [C] **1**目的 mùdì; 意图〔圖〕yìtú. **2**[U] [正式用语]决心 juéxīn; 意志 yìzhì. **3** *on* ~ 故意地 gùyìde. ~**ful** *adj*
purr /pɜː(r)/ *vt/i* (指猫) 满足地呜呜叫 mǎnzúde wūwūjiào. □ *n* [C] (猫等)满足时〔時〕呜呜的叫声〔聲〕mǎnzú shí wūwū de jiàoshēng.
purse[1] /pɜːs/ *n* [C] **1**钱〔錢〕包 qiánbāo; 小钱袋 xiǎo qiándài. **2**金钱 jīnqián; 基金 jījīn. **3**[美语] = handbag. **purser** *n* [C] (轮船、班机等的)事务〔務〕长〔長〕shìwùzhǎng.
purse[2] /pɜːs/ *vt* 噘嘴 juēzuǐ.
pur·sue /pəˈsjuː/ *vt* **1**追赶〔趕〕zhuīgǎn; 追捕 zhuībǔ. **2**继〔繼〕续〔續〕做 jìxù zuò: ~ *one's studies* 继续研究. **3**以…为〔爲〕目的 yǐ…wéi mùdì: ~ *a teaching career* 谋求教师职业.
pur·suit /pəˈsjuːt/ *n* **1** [U] 追赶〔趕〕zhuīgǎn; 追求 zhuīqiú. **2** [C] 消遣 xiāoqiǎn.
pur·vey /pɜːˈveɪ/ *vt/i* [正式用语] 供应〔應〕(伙食等) gōngyìng; 供给 gōngjǐ. ~**or** 承办〔辦〕伙食者 chéngbàn huǒshí zhě; 伙食供应商 huǒshí gōngyìngshāng.
pus /pʌs/ *n* [U] 脓〔膿〕nóng; 脓液 nóngyè.
push[1] /pʊʃ/ *n* **1** [C] 推 tuī; 推动〔動〕tuīdòng. **2** [C] 奋〔奮〕力 fènlì; 奋进〔進〕fènjìn. **3**[U] 进取心 jìnqǔxīn. **4** *get the* ~ [非正式用语]被解雇〔僱〕bèi jiěgù.
push[2] /pʊʃ/ *vt/i* **1**(与 *pull* 相对) 推动〔動〕tuīdòng; 推进〔進〕tuījìn. **2**使引人注意 shǐ yǐn rén zhùyì. **3**贩卖〔賣〕(毒品) fànmài. ⇨ pusher below. **4** ~ *sb for sth* 逼迫 bīpò; 促使 cùshǐ: ~ *him for payment* 催逼他还钱. **5**按 àn: ~ *a button* 按电钮. **6** ~ *sb around* [非正式用语]欺侮(某人) qīrǔ; 摆〔擺〕布 bǎibù. ~ *off* [非正式用语]离〔離〕开〔開〕líkāi. ˈ~**-bike** 自行车〔車〕zìxíngchē. ˈ~**chair** 婴儿〔兒〕车 yīng'érchē. ~**er, (a)** 进〔進〕取的人 jìnqǔ de rén; 钻〔鑽〕营〔營〕的人 zuānyíng de rén. **(b)** [俚语] 贩卖毒品者 fànmài dúpǐn zhě. ~**ing** *adj* 有进取心的 yǒu jìnqǔxīn de; 爱〔愛〕出风〔風〕头〔頭〕的 àichū fēngtóu de.
pussy /ˈpʊsɪ/ *n* [C] [*pl* -ies] (ˈ~-*cat*) (儿语)猫咪 māomī.
put /pʊt/ *vt/i* [*pt, pp* ~; *pres part* ~ting] **1**放 fàng; 安置 ānzhì: *He* ~ *the book on the table.* 他把书放在桌子上. **2** ~ *sb in his* (*proper*) *place* 贬低 biǎndī. **3**使承受 shǐ chéngshòu: ~ *the blame on sb* 责备某人. ~ *pressure on sb* 向某人施加压力. **4** ~ *a stop to sth* 停止 tíngzhǐ. **5** ~ *sb at his ease* 使人感到轻松〔鬆〕自如 shǐ rén gǎndào qīngsōng zìrú. **6**使(人或物)成为〔爲〕shǐ chéngwéi: ~ *him to death* 杀死他; 处死他. ~ *sth right* 纠正 jiūzhèng. **7**写〔寫〕上 xiě shàng; 标〔標〕上 biāo shàng: ~ *a tick against a name* 在名字上作记号. **8** ~ *sth* (*to sb*) 提出 tíchū; 表示 biǎoshì: ~ *a proposal to the manager* 向经理提建议. **9** ~ *sth about* 散布 sànbù. ~ *sth across* (*to sb*) 有效地传〔傳〕达〔達〕yǒuxiàode chuándá. ~ *sth aside,* **(a)** 放下 fàngxià: ~ *work aside* 放下工作. **(b)** 储蓄 chǔxù: ~ *money aside* 把钱储蓄起来. ~ *sth away* 放好 fànghǎo; 贮〔貯〕存 zhùcún. ~ *sth back,* **(a)** 放回原处〔處〕fànghuí yuánchù. **(b)** 向后

〔後〕移 xiànghòu yí; 拨〔撥〕回 bōhuí: ~ *the clock back five minutes* 把时钟倒拨五分钟. **(c)** 〔喻〕延误 yánwù; 耽搁〔擱〕dāngé: *The strike ~ back production.* 罢工大大耽搁了生产. ~ ***sth by*** 储存…备〔備〕用 chǔcún ... bèiyòng. ~ ***(sth) down,*** **(a)** (使) 着陆〔陸〕zhuólù: ~ *a plane down.* 使飞机着陆. **(b)** 放下 fàngxià. **(c)** 平定 píngdìng; 镇压〔壓〕zhènyā: ~ *down a rebellion* 平定了叛乱. **(d)** 记下 jìxià; 写〔寫〕下 xiěxià. **(e)** 处〔處〕死(有病的动物) chǔsǐ. ~ ***sb down*** 使下车〔車〕shǐ xiàchē. ~ ***sth down to sth*** 归〔歸〕于 guī yú: *Can we ~ his failure down to his ignorance?* 我们能把他的失败归于他的无知吗?
~ ***sth forward,*** **(a)** 提出 tíchū: ~ *forward a new theory* 提出一种新理论. **(b)** 拨快(时钟) bōkuài; 把(时钟等)向前拨 bǎ ... xiàngqián bō: ~ *a clock forward ten minutes* 把时钟拨快十分钟. ~ ***in*** 做 zuò; 实〔實〕行 shíxíng: ~ *in an hour's work* 做一小时工作. ~ ***in for*** 申请 shēnqǐng. ~ ***sth off*** 延期 yánqī. ~ ***sb off (sth),*** **(a)** 推迟〔遲〕tuīchí; 延期 yánqī. **(b)** 阻止 zǔzhǐ; 劝〔勸〕阻 quànzǔ: ~ *a man off his game* 使一个人在自己的比赛中分散注意力. ~ ***sth on,*** **(a)** (与 *take off* 相对) 穿上 chuānshàng; 戴上 dàishàng. **(b)** 假装〔裝〕jiǎzhuāng; 装出 zhuāngchū: *Her modesty is all ~ on.* 她的谦虚全是假装的. **(c)** 增加 zēngjiā; 添上 tiānshàng: *He's ~ting on weight.* 他的体重在增加. **(d)** 安排 ānpái; 准〔準〕备〔備〕zhǔnbèi: ~ *on extra trains* 开加班火车. **(e)** 拨快 bōkuài: ~ *the clock on one hour* 把钟拨快一小时. **(f)** 打开〔開〕(电灯等) dǎkāi: ~ *the light on* 开灯.
~ ***a play on*** 上演(戏剧等) shàngyǎn. ~ ***sth out,*** **(a)** 熄灭〔滅〕xīmiè; 关〔關〕灭 guānmiè; 消灭 xiāomiè. **(b)** 发〔發〕行 fāxíng; 发布 fābù: ~ *out a warning* 发布警告. ~ ***sb out,*** **(a)** 麻烦 máfan; 打扰〔擾〕dǎrǎo. **(b)** 不方便 bù fāngbiàn. ~ ***sb (sth) through*** 接通(电话) jiētōng. ~ ***sb up*** 供膳宿 gōng shànsù. ~ ***sb up to sth*** 密谋 mìmóu. ~ ***sth up,*** **(a)** 举〔舉〕起 jǔqǐ: ~ *up one's hand* 举起手. **(b)** 建造(房屋等) jiànzào. **(c)** 提高 tígāo; 抬高 táigāo: ~ *up the rent* 提高租金. **(d)** 使成 shǐ chéng; 使达〔達〕到 shǐ dádào: ~ *up a good fight* 勇敢抵抗. **(e)** 供给 gōngjǐ; 捐献〔獻〕juānxiàn. ~ ***sb's back up,*** ⇨ back²(1). ~ ***up with sb (sth)*** 忍受 rěnshòu.

pu·trefy /ˈpjuːtrɪfaɪ/ *vt/i* [*pt, pp* -ied] (使)腐烂〔爛〕fǔlàn; (使)腐败 fǔbài. **pu·tre·fac·tion** /-ˈfækʃn/ *n* [C,U]

pu·trid /ˈpjuːtrɪd/ *adj* 腐烂〔爛〕的 fǔlànde; 腐败的 fǔbàide.

putt /pʌt/ *vt/i* 小心轻〔輕〕击〔擊〕(高尔夫)球 xiǎoxīn qīngjī qiú.

putty /ˈpʌtɪ/ *n* [U] 油灰 yóuhuī; 腻子 nìzi.

puzzle /ˈpʌzl/ *n* [C] **1** 难〔難〕题 nántí. **2** 测验〔驗〕智力的问〔問〕题(如 *a 'crossword ~*)或玩具(如 *a 'jigsaw ~*) cèyàn zhìlì de wèntí huò wánjù; 谜 mí. □ *vt/i* **1** 迷惑 míhuò; 苦思 kǔsī. **2** ~ ***over sth*** 动〔動〕脑〔腦〕筋思考 dòng nǎojīn sīkǎo. ~ ***sth out*** 苦思 kǔsī.

P.W.D.=Public Works Department 工务〔務〕局(香港) gōngwùjú; 公共事业〔業〕厅〔廳〕gōnggòng shìyè tīng.

pygmy, pigmy /ˈpɪgmɪ/ *n* [C] [*pl* -ies] **1** P~ (分布在中非等的身体矮小的)俾格米人 bǐgémǐrén; 侏儒 zhūrú. **2** 矮人 ǎirén.

py·ja·mas 〔美语 = **pa·ja·mas**〕/pəˈdʒɑːməz/ *n pl* (亦作 *a pair of ~*) (宽大的)睡衣裤〔褲〕shuìyīkù.

py·lon /ˈpaɪln/ *n* [C] 架高压〔壓〕电〔電〕缆〔纜〕的铁塔 jià gāoyā diànlǎn de tiětǎ.

pyra·mid /ˈpɪrəmɪd/ *n* [C] **1** (古代埃及的)金字塔 jīnzìtǎ. **2** 角锥 jiǎozhuī; 角锥体〔體〕jiǎozhuītǐ.

pyre /ˈpaɪə(r)/ *n* [C] 供燃烧〔燒〕的大堆木料 gōng ránshāode dàduī mùliào; 火葬用的柴堆 huǒzàng yòng de cháiduī.

py·thon /ˈpaɪθn/ *n* [C] 大蟒 dàmǎng.

Q q

Q, q /kjuː/ (*pl* Q's, q's /kjuːz/) 英语的第十七个〔個〕字母 Yīngyǔde dìshíqīgè zìmǔ.

Q.=Queen.

Q.C.=Queen's Counsel 英国〔國〕王室法律顾〔顧〕问〔問〕Yīngguó wángshì fǎlǜ gùwèn.

Q.E.D.=which had to be shown.

qr.=quarter.

qt.=quart(s).

quack[1] /kwæk/ *vi, n* (鸭子)嘎嘎地叫 gāgāde jiào; 鸭〔鴨〕子的叫声〔聲〕yāzide jiàoshēng.

quack[2] /kwæk/ *n* [C] 庸医〔醫〕yōngyī; 江湖医生 jiānghú yīshēng.

quad /kwɒd/ *n* [C] **1** = quadrangle. **2** = quadruplet.

quad·rangle /'kwɒdræŋgl/ *n* [C] **1** 四边〔邊〕形 sìbiānxíng. **2** (缩作 quad) (有建筑物围着的)方院fāngyuàn.

quad·ru·ped /'kwɒdruped/ *n* [C] 四足动〔動〕物 sìzú dòngwù.

quad·ruple /'kwɒdru:pl/ *adj* 由四部分组成的 yóu sìbùfen zǔchéng de. □ *n* [C] 四倍 sìbèi. □ *vt/i* (使)成四倍 chéng sìbèi; 以四乘 yǐ sì chéng.

quad·ru·plet /'kwɒdru:plet/ *n* [C] (缩作 *quad*) 四胞胎中的一个〔個〕孩子 sìbāotāi zhōng de yígè háizi.

quag·mire /'kwɒgmaɪə(r)/ *n* [C] 沼泽〔澤〕zhǎozé; 泥潭 nítán.

quail[1] /kweɪl/ *n* [C] 鹑〔鶉〕chún; 鹌〔鵪〕鹑 ānchún.

quail[2] /kweɪl/ *vi* ~ (*at, before*) 胆〔膽〕怯 dǎnqiè; 畏缩 wèisuō.

quaint /kweɪnt/ *adj* [-er, -est] 古雅的 gǔyǎde; 离〔離〕奇的 líqíde. **~ly** *adv*

quake /kweɪk/ *vi* 震动〔動〕zhèndòng; 颤动 chàndòng.

quali·fi·ca·tion /ˌkwɒlɪfɪ'keɪʃn/ *n* **1** [U]修饰 xiūshì; 限制 xiànzhì; [C] 修饰或限制之物 xiūshì huò xiànzhì zhī wù: *accept an offer with ~s* 有限度(有条件)地接受建议. **2** [C] 资格 zīgé; 条〔條〕件 tiáojiàn.

qual·ify /'kwɒlɪfaɪ/ *vt/i* [*pt, pp* -ied] **1** (使)具有资格 jùyǒu zīgé. **2** (使)合格 hégé; 具有必需的经验〔驗〕、能力、年龄等 jùyǒu bìxū de jīngyàn, nénglì, niánlíng děng. **3** 使不一般化 shǐ bú yìbānhuà. **4** [语法]修饰 xiūshì; 限定 xiàndìng. **quali·fied** /-faɪd/ *adj* **(a)** 合格的 hégéde. **(b)** 限制的 xiànzhìde: *a qualified statement* 有限度的说明.

quali·tat·ive /'kwɒlɪtətɪv/ *adj* 质〔質〕的 zhìde; 定性的 dìngxìngde. ⇨ quantitative.

qual·ity /'kwɒlətɪ/ *n* [*pl* -ies] **1** [C,U] 品质〔質〕pǐnzhì. **2** [C] 特质 tèzhì; 性质 xìngzhì: *One ~ of leadership is to be trusted.* 领导的一种特质是受到信任.

qualm/'kwa:m/ *n* [C] **1** 疑虑〔慮〕yílǜ; 不安 bù'ān. **2** 一阵〔陣〕恶〔惡〕心 yízhèn ěxin.

quan·dary /'kwɒndərɪ/*n* [C] [*pl* -ies] 窘境 jiǒngjìng; 困惑 kùnhuò.

quan·ti·tat·ive /'kwɒntɪtətɪv/ *adj* 量的 liàngde; 定量的 dìngliàngde. ⇨ qualitative.

quan·tity /'kwɒntətɪ/ *n* [*pl* -ies] **1** [U] 量(如大小、重量、数等) liàng. **2** [C] 数〔數〕量 shùliàng. **3** *an unknown* ~,**(a)**[数学]未知数 wèizhīshù. **(b)** [喻]不可测的人或物 bù kěcè de rén huò wù.

quar·an·tine /'kwɒrənti:n/ *n* [C, U] 检〔檢〕疫 jiǎnyì; 检疫期 jiǎnyìqī. □ *vt* 对...进〔進〕行检疫 duì ...jìnxíng jiǎnyì.

quark /kwa:k/ *n* [C] 夸克(一种最基本的粒子) kuākè.

quar·rel /'kwɒrəl/ *n* [C] **1** 争吵 zhēngchǎo; 争论〔論〕zhēnglùn. **2** 争吵的原因 zhēngchǎode yuányīn. ***pick a ~ (with sb)*** 寻〔尋〕衅 xúnxìn. □ *vi* [-ll-] **1** 争吵 zhēngchǎo; 争论 zhēnglùn. **2** 挑剔 tiāotì: *I ~ with your conclusions.* 我不同意你的结论. **'~some** *adj* 爱〔愛〕争吵的 àizhēngchǎode.

quarry[1] /'kwɒrɪ/ *n* [C] [*pl* -ies] 猎〔獵〕物(鸟、兽等) lièwù.

quarry[2] /'kwɒrɪ/ *n* [C] [*pl* -ies] 采〔採〕石场〔場〕cǎishíchǎng. □ *vt/i* [*pt,pp* -ied] 采(石) cǎi; 挖掘 wājué.

quart /kwɔ:t/ *n* [C] 夸脱 kuātuō.

quar·ter /'kwɔ:tə(r)/ *n* [C] **1** 四分之一 sìfēn zhī yī. **2** 一刻钟〔鐘〕yíkèzhōng: *a ~ to* [美语= *of*] *two* 差一刻两点. *a ~ past six* 六点一刻. **3** 季 jì; 三个〔個〕月 sāngè yuè. **4** (活的四肢动物的)一肢 yìzhī: *'fore-~s* (牛羊等)前半部. *'hind-~s* (牛羊等的)后臀和腿. **5** 区〔區〕域 qūyù: *the business ~* 商业区. **6** (供应、援助的)来〔來〕源 láiyuán. **7** [*pl*] 住所 zhùsuǒ; 寓所 yùsuǒ: *married ~s* 已婚者的住所. ⇨ headquarters. **8** ***at close ~s*** 接近地 jiējìnde. □ *vt* **1** 把...四等分 bǎ...sìděngfēn. **2** 使(部队)驻〔駐〕扎 shǐ ... zhùzhá. **'~master, (a)** (陆军)军〔軍〕需军官 jūnxū jūnguān. **(b)** (海军)航信士官 hángxìn shìguān.

quar·ter·ly /'kwɔ:təlɪ/ *adj, adv* 季度的(地) jìdùde. □ *n* [C] [*pl* -ies] 季刊 jìkān.

quar·tet, quar·tette /kwɔ:'tet/ *n* [C] 四重唱 sìchóngchàng; 四重奏 sìchóngzòu.

quartz /'kwɔ:ts/ *n* [U] 石英 shíyīng.

qua·sar /'kweɪzɑ:(r)/ *n* [C] (天文)

类〔類〕星体〔體〕(极远的无线电波或光波来源) lèixīngtǐ.

quash /kwɒʃ/ *vt* 废〔廢〕止 fèizhǐ; 撤销 chèxiāo; 使无〔無〕效 shǐ wúxiào: ~ *a revolt* 平息一场暴乱. ~*an appeal* 撤销上诉.

qua·ver /'kweɪvə(r)/ *vt/i* **1** (指声音)震动〔動〕zhèndòng; 颤抖 chàndǒu. **2** 用颤声〔聲〕唱 yòng chànshēng chàng; 用颤声说 yòng chànshēng shuō. □ *n* [C] 颤音 chànyīn.

quay /ki:/ *n* [C] 码〔碼〕头〔頭〕mǎtóu.

queasy /'kwi:zɪ/ *adj* [-ier, -iest] **1** (指胃)易呕〔嘔〕吐的 yì ǒutù de. **2** (指人)不舒服的 bù shūfu de.

queen /kwi:n/ *n* [C] **1** 女王 nǚwáng. **2** 王后 wánghòu. **3** (国际象棋中的)王后 wánghòu. **4** (纸牌中的)王后 wánghòu. **5** (蜜蜂、蚂蚁等的)女王 nǚwáng. ,~ **'mother** 母后 mǔhòu; 皇太后 huángtàihòu.

queer /kwɪə(r)/ *adj* [-er, -est] **1** 奇怪的 qíguàide; 不平常的 bù píngcháng de. **2** 可疑的 kěyíde. **3** [非正式用语]眩晕〔暈〕的 xuànyùnde; 不舒服的 bù shūfu de.

quell /kwel/ *vt* 镇压〔壓〕zhènyā; 平息 píngxī.

quench /kwentʃ/ *vt* **1** 熄灭〔滅〕xīmiè; 扑〔撲〕灭 pūmiè. **2** 解(渴) jiě.

query /'kwɪərɪ/ *n* [C] [*pl* -ies] **1** 问〔問〕题 wèntí. **2** 问号〔號〕wènhào. □ *vt* **1** ~ *whether* (或 *if*) 询问 xúnwèn. **2** 对〔對〕…表示怀〔懷〕疑 duì … biǎoshì huáiyí. **3** 加问号 jiā wènhào.

quest /kwest/ *n* [C] [正式用语]寻〔尋〕找 xúnzhǎo; 追求 zhuīqiú.

ques·tion[1] /'kwestʃən/ *n* [C] **1** 疑问〔問〕句 yíwènjù. **2** 查询 cháxún; 问题 wèntí. *in* ~ 正被谈论的 zhèng bèi tánlùn de: *the man in* ~ 谈论中的这个人. *out of the* ~ 不可能 bù kěnéng. **3** [U] 怀〔懷〕疑 huáiyí; 反对〔對〕fǎnduì: *There is no* ~ *about his honesty.* 他的诚实无可怀疑. **'~-mark** 问号〔號〕wènhào.

ques·tion[2] /'kwestʃən/ *vt* **1** 询问〔問〕xúnwèn; 审〔審〕问 shěnwèn. **2** 怀〔懷〕疑 huáiyí. **'~able** /-əbl/ *adj* 可疑的 kěyíde. **'~ably** *adv*

ques·tion·naire /ˌkwestʃə'neə(r)/ *n* [C] 问〔問〕题单 wèntídān; 调查表 diàochábiǎo; 征〔徵〕求意见表 zhēngqiú yìjiàn biǎo.

queue /kju:/ *n* [C] (人或车辆等的)行列 hángliè; 长〔長〕队〔隊〕chángduì: *a bus* ~ 一长列公共汽车. *jump the* ~ ⇨ jump[2] (7) □ *vi* ~ **(*up*)** **(*for*)** 排队等候 páiduì děnghòu.

quibble /'kwɪbl/ *n* [C] 遁辞 dùncí; 托词 tuōcí. □ *vi* ~ **(*over*)** 模棱两可地说 móléng liǎngkě de shuō.

quick /kwɪk/ *adj* [-er, -est] **1** 快的 kuàide; 迅速的 xùnsùde. **2** 活泼〔潑〕的 huópode; 敏捷的 mǐnjiéde: ~ *to seize an opportunity* 迅速掌握时机. □ *n* [U] (尤指指甲下的)活肉 huóròu; 伤〔傷〕口的嫩皮 shāngkǒude nènpí. ***cut (touch) sb to the*** ~ 损伤(某人的)感情 sǔnshāng gǎnqíng. □ *adv* [-er, -est] [非正式用语]= *quickly*. **~ly** *adv* 迅速地 xùnsùde. **~ness** *n* [U]

quicken /'kwɪkən/ *vt/i* **1** 加快 jiākuài. **2** 使活跃〔躍〕shǐ huóyuè.

quick·sand /'kwɪksænd/ *n* [C] 流沙(区) liúshā.

quick·sil·ver /'kwɪksɪlvə(r)/ *n* [U] = mercury.

quid /kwɪd/ *n* [C] [*pl* ~] [英国英语,俚语] = pound[1](2).

quiet /'kwaɪət/ *adj* [-er, -est] **1** 静止的 jìngzhǐde; 寂静的 jìjìngde. **2** 不激动〔動〕的bù jīdòng de; 不烦恼的 bù fánnǎode: *a* ~ *life*悠然自在的生活. **3** 温和的 wēnhéde. **4**(指颜色)朴〔樸〕素的 pǔsùde; 暗淡的 àndànde. **5** 秘密的 mìmìde. *keep sth* ~ 保守秘密 bǎoshǒu mìmì. *on the* ~ 秘密地 mìmìde. □ *n* [U] 静止 jìngzhǐ; 宁〔寧〕静 níngjìng. **~en** *vt/i* 使静 shǐ jìng; 静 jìng.

quill /kwɪl/ *n* [C] **1** 羽笔〔筆〕yǔbǐ; 鹅〔鵝〕毛笔 émáobǐ. **2** (豪猪的)刺 cì.

quilt /kwɪlt/ *n* [C] 被(子) bèi. ⇨ duvet. □ *vt* 缝(被) féng.

quin /kwɪn/ *n* [C] = quintuplet.

quin·ine /kwɪ'ni:n/ *n* [U] 奎宁〔寧〕kuíníng.

quin·tet, quin·tette /kwɪn'tet/ *n* [C] 五重唱 wǔchóngchàng; 五重奏 wǔchóngzòu.

quin·tu·plet /'kwɪntjʊplet/ *n* [C] (缩作 *quin*) 五胞胎中的一个〔個〕wǔbāotāi zhōng de yígè.

quip /kwɪp/ *n* [C] 妙语 miàoyǔ; 讽〔諷〕刺话 fěngcìhuà. □ *vi* [-pp-] 讥〔譏〕讽 jīfěng; 说妙语 shuō miàoyǔ.

quit /kwɪt/ *vt* [*pt* ~ted 或 ~] [-tt-] **1** 离〔離〕开〔開〕líkāi; 离去 líqù. **2** 停止 tíngzhǐ: ~ *work* 停止工作. □ *adj* 摆〔擺〕脱了…的 bǎituōle … de; 了结的 liǎojiéde:

We're ~ of all our problems. 我们摆脱了所有的难题.

quite /kwaɪt/ *adv* **1** 完全 wánquán; 彻〔徹〕底 chèdǐ: *I ~ agree.* 我完全同意. **2** 相当〔當〕 xiāngdāng. 或多或少 huò duō huò shǎo: *~ a good player* 一个相当不错的球员. **3** 真正 zhēnzhèng; 的确〔確〕 díquè: *She's ~ a beauty.* 她的确是个美人. **4** (用于表示同意等): A: *'It's a difficult situation'.* '是个困难的局面.' B: *'Q~ (so)!'* '的确如此.'

quiver¹ /'kwɪvə(r)/ *n* [C] 箭袋 jiàndài; 箭筒 jiàntǒng.

quiver² /'kwɪvə(r)/ *vt/i* 颤动〔動〕 chàndòng; 抖动 dǒudòng. □ *n* [C] 颤动 chàndòng; 颤声〔聲〕 chànshēng.

quiz /kwɪz/ *vt* [-zz-] 测验〔驗〕 cèyàn. □ *n* [C] [-zz-] [现代用法] 一般知识〔識〕测验 yìbān zhīshi cèyàn.

quiz·zi·cal /'kwɪzɪkl/ *adj* [正式用语] **1** 可笑的 kěxiàode. **2** 疑惑的 yíhuòde. **~ly** /-klɪ/ *adv*

quoit /kɔɪt/ *n* [C] (掷环游戏中用的)铁圈(或绳圈) tiěquān;[*pl*] 掷圈游戏〔戲〕 zhì quān yóuxì.

quota /'kwəʊtə/ *n* [C] [*pl* ~s] 分配额 fēnpèi'é; 限额 (尤指政府对进口货物或移民人数的控制额) xiàn'é.

quo·ta·tion /kwəʊ'teɪʃn/ *n* **1** [U] 引用 yǐnyòng; 引证 yǐnzhèng. **2** [C] 引文 yǐnwén; 引语 yǐnyǔ. **3** [C] 行情 hángqíng; 报〔報〕价〔價〕单〔單〕 bàojiàdān. **4** [C] 估价单 gūjiàdān. **~ marks** 引号〔號〕(即" ") yǐnhào.

quote /kwəʊt/ *vt* **1** ~ **(*from*)** 引用 yǐnyòng; 引述 yǐnshù. **2** 引证 yǐnzhèng. **3** 报〔報〕...的价〔價〕bào ... de jià.

R r

R,r /ɑ:(r)/ (*pl* R's, r's /ɑ:z/) 英语的第十八个〔個〕字母 Yīngyǔ de dìshíbāgè zìmǔ.

R. =1 Railway. 2 River.

r. =right.

R.A. =Royal Academy (英国) 皇家艺〔藝〕术〔術〕学〔學〕会〔會〕 Huángjiā Yìshù Xuéhuì.

rabbi /'ræbaɪ/ *n* [C] [*pl* ~s] 犹〔猶〕太法学〔學〕专〔專〕家 yóutài fǎxué zhuānjiā; 犹太教教士 yóutàijiào jiàoshì.

rab·bit /'ræbɪt/ *n* [C] 兔 tù. □ *vt* [-tt-] 猎〔獵〕兔 liè tù. **'~-warren** 养〔養〕兔场〔場〕 yǎngtùchǎng.

rabble /'ræbl/ *n* [C] 乌〔烏〕合之众〔衆〕 wū hé zhī zhòng. **'~-rousing** *adj* 激起暴徒的愤怒 jī qǐ bàotúde fènnù.

rabid /'ræbɪd/ *adj* **1** 狂犬病的 kuángquǎnbìngde. **2** [喻]狂热〔熱〕的 kuángrède.

ra·bies /'reɪbi:z/ *n* [U] 狂犬病 kuángquǎnbìng.

race¹ /reɪs/ *n* [C] **1** (速度上的)比赛 bǐsài; 竞〔競〕赛 jìngsài. **2** (江、海的)急流 jíliú. □ *vt/i* **1** ~ **(*with, against sb*)** 比速度 bǐ sùdù; 全速行进〔進〕 quánsù xíngjìn. **2** 拥〔擁〕有或训练赛马〔馬〕用的马 yōngyǒu huò xùnliàn sàimǎ yòngde mǎ. **'~-course** 赛马〔馬〕场〔場〕 sàimǎchǎng; 跑道 pǎodào. **'~-horse** 比赛用的马 bǐsài yòng de mǎ. **'~-track** (体育比赛用的)跑道 pǎodào.

race² /reɪs/ *n* **1** [C,U] 人种〔種〕 rénzhǒng; 种族 zhǒngzú. **2** [C] (生物的)族类〔類〕 zúlèi: 种属〔屬〕 zhǒngshǔ: *the human ~* 人类.

ra·cial /'reɪʃl/ *adj* 种〔種〕族的 zhǒngzúde; 人种的 rénzhǒngde. **~ly** *adv* **~ism** *n* [U] 种族偏见 zhǒngzú piānjiàn; 种族主义〔義〕 zhǒngzú zhǔyì. **~ist** *adj*, *n* [C]

ra·cily, raci·ness ⇨ racy.

rack¹ /ræk/ *n* [C] **1** 挂〔掛〕物架 guàwùjià; 搁〔擱〕物架 gēwùjià. **2** (火车、客机等座位上面的)行李架 xínglǐjià.

rack² /ræk/ *vt* **1** (指疾病)使痛苦 shǐ tòngkǔ; 折磨 zhémó: *~ed with pain* 被痛苦折磨. **2** *~ one's brains* 绞脑〔腦〕汁 jiǎo nǎozhī.

rack³ /ræk/ *n* [仅用于] ***go to ,~ and 'ruin*** 陷于毁灭〔滅〕 xiàn yú huǐmiè.

racket¹ /'rækɪt/ *n* **1** 吵闹〔鬧〕声〔聲〕 chǎonàoshēng. **2** [C] [非正式用语]敲诈 qiāozhà; 骗〔騙〕钱〔錢〕 piànqián. **~eer** /-'tɪə(r)/ *n* [C] 诈骗者 zhàpiànzhě.

racket², rac·quet /'rækɪt/ *n* [C] **1** (网球、羽毛球等的) 球拍 qiúpāi. **2** [*pl*] (在四周有围墙的院子里玩的)一种网〔網〕球戏〔戲〕 yìzhǒng wǎngqiúxì.

rac·quet *n* [C] = racket².

racy /'reɪsɪ/ *adj* 生动〔動〕的 shēngdòngde, 活泼〔潑〕的 huópode; 新鲜的 xīnxiānde.

ra·dar /ˈreɪdɑ:(r)/ *n* [U] 雷达〔達〕léidá. ˈ~ **beacon** *n* 雷达〔達〕信标〔標〕léidá xìnbiāo. ˈ~ **trap** *n* 雷达侦查车〔車〕速器(警察用它检查车速的仪器) léidá zhēnchá chēsù qì.

ra·di·ance /ˈreɪdɪəns/ *n* [U] 发〔發〕光 fāguāng; 光辉〔輝〕guānghuī.

ra·di·ant /ˈreɪdɪənt/ *adj* **1** 发〔發〕光的 fāguāngde; 光辉〔輝〕的 guānghuīde. **2** (指人)喜悦的 xǐyuède ~**ly** *adv*

ra·di·ate /ˈreɪdɪeɪt/ *vt*/*i* **1** 发〔發〕射光线〔線〕fāshè guāngxiàn. **2** 〔喻〕散发 sànfā; 发出 fāchū: ~ *happiness* 洋溢着快乐. **3** ~ ***from*** 向四方扩〔擴〕散 xiàng sìfāng kuòsàn.

ra·di·ation /ˌreɪdɪˈeɪʃn/ *n* **1** [U] 发〔發〕射 fāshè, 放射 fàngshè. **2** [C, U] [物理]辐〔輻〕射 fúshè. **3** [C] 放射物 fàngshèwù; 辐射线〔線〕fúshèxiàn; 辐射能 fúshènéng: *X-ray* ~*s*. X 光辐射线. ~ **sickness** 辐射症 fúshèzhèng.

ra·di·ator /ˈreɪdɪeɪtə(r)/ *n* [C] **1** 散热〔熱〕器 sànrèqì. **2** 冷却器 lěngquèqì.

rad·ical /ˈrædɪkl/ *adj* **1** 根本的 gēnběnde, 基本的 jīběnde: ~ *changes* 根本的(彻底的)改变. **2** [政治]激进〔進〕的 jījìnde. □ *n* [C] 激进分子 jījìn fènzǐ. ~**ly** *adv*

ra·dii /ˈreɪdɪaɪ/ *n pl* ⇨ radius.

ra·dio /ˈreɪdɪəʊ/ *n* [*pl* ~s] **1** [U] 无〔無〕线〔線〕电〔電〕wúxiàndiàn. **2** [U] 无线电广〔廣〕播 wúxiàndiàn guǎngbō. **3** [C] 无线电广播收发〔發〕装置 wúxiàndiàn guǎngbō shōufā zhuāngzhì. ~ **aˈstronomy** *n* [U] 射电天文学〔學〕shèdiàn tiānwénxué. ˈ~ **beacon** *n* 无线电导〔導〕航信标〔標〕(发信号以协助飞机驾驶员) wúxiàndiàn dǎoháng xìnbiāo. ˈ~ **beam** *n* 无线电导航信号(亦作 radar) wúxiàndiàn dǎoháng xìnhào. ˈ~ **station** *n* **1** 无线电台〔臺〕wúxiàn diàntái. **2** 组织〔織〕无线电公众〔衆〕娱乐〔樂〕节〔節〕目 zǔzhī wúxiàndiàn gōngzhòng yúlè jiémù. ~ ˈ**telescope** *n* 无线电望远镜 wúxiàndiàn wàngyuǎnjìng. ˈ~ **wave** *n* 无线电波 wúxiàn diànbō.

radio-/ˈreɪdɪəʊ/ *prefix* 光的 guāngde; 镭的 léide. ~·ˈ**ac·tive** *adj* (指镭和铀等金属) 放射性的 fàngshèxìngde; 有辐射能的 yǒu fúshènéng de: ~*active dust* 放射尘. ~·**ac·tive waste** *n* [U] 放射性废〔廢〕料 fàngshexìng fèiliào. ~·**ac·tivi·ty** *n* [U] **radi·ˈogra·phy** *n* [U] X 光摄〔攝〕影 X guāng shèyǐng. **radi·ˈogra·pher** *n* [C] X 光摄影师〔師〕 X guāng shèyǐngshī. **radi·ology** *n* [U] 放射学〔學〕fàngshèxué. **radi·ˈologist** *n* [C] 放射线〔線〕专〔專〕家 fàngshèxiàn zhuānjiā. **radio·ˈtherapy** *n* [U] 放射疗〔療〕法 fàngshèliáofǎ **radio-ˈthera·pist** *n* [C] 放射疗法专家 fàngshèliáofǎ zhuānjiā.

rad·ish /ˈrædɪʃ/ *n* [C] 萝〔蘿〕卜〔蔔〕(可放在色拉中生吃) luóbo.

ra·dius /ˈreɪdɪəs/ *n* [C] [*pl* radii /-dɪaɪ/] **1** 半径〔徑〕bànjìng. **2** 以半径〔徑〕度量的面积〔積〕yǐ bànjìng dùliàng de miànjī: *within a* ~ *of two miles from the house* 从房子起半径两英里的范围.

R.A.F. Royal Air Force (英国) 皇家空军〔軍〕huángjiā kōngjūn.

raf·fia /ˈræfɪə/ *n* [U] 酒椰纤维 jiǔyē xiānwéi.

raffle /ˈræfl/ *n* [C] 抽彩售货 chōucǎi shòuhuò. □ *vt* 以抽彩法出售 yǐ chōucǎifǎ chūshòu.

raft /rɑ:ft/ *n* [C] 木排 mùpái; 木筏 mùfá.

raf·ter /ˈrɑ:ftə(r)/ *n* [C] 椽 chuán.

rag[1] /ræg/ *n* [C] 破布 pòbù; 碎布 suìbù.

rag[2] /ræg/ *vt* [-gg-] [非正式用语] 和…开〔開〕玩笑 hé...kāi wánxiào. □ *n* [C] 恶〔惡〕作剧〔劇〕èzuòjù; 喧闹〔鬧〕xuānnào.

rage /reɪdʒ/ *n* **1** [C,U] 狂怒 kuángnù; 盛怒 shèngnù. **2** [C] 强烈的感情 qiángliède gǎnqíng: *a* ~ *for collecting butterflies* 喜爱收集蝴蝶. ⇨ craze. **3** ***be (all) the*** ~ [非正式用语]风〔風〕靡一时〔時〕fēngmí yìshí. □ *vi* **1** 大怒 dànù. **2** (指风雨等)狂暴 kuángbào.

rag·ged /ˈrægɪd/ *adj* **1** 褴〔襤〕褛〔褸〕的 lánlǚde. **2** 外形参差不齐〔齊〕的 wàixíng cēncī bùqí de. ~**ly** *adv*

raid /reɪd/ *n* [C] **1** (突然)袭〔襲〕击〔擊〕xíjī. **2** (警察的)突然搜查 tūrán sōuchá, 搜捕 sōubǔ. □ *vt*/*i* 袭击 xíjī; 侵入 qīnrù. ~**er** 袭击者 xíjīzhě; 侵入者 qīnrùzhě.

rail /reɪl/ *n* [C] **1** 横条〔條〕héngtiáo; 栏〔欄〕杆〔桿〕lángān. **2** (挂东西用的)横杆 hénggān: *a* ˈ*towel* ~ 挂毛巾用的横杆. **3** 铁〔鐵〕轨〔軌〕tiěguǐ. □ *vt* ~ ***off*** 用栏杆隔开〔開〕yòng lángān gékāi. ~ ***in*** 围〔圍〕以栏杆 wéi yǐ lángān ˈ~**way** [美语 = ~**road**], **(a)** 铁轨

tiěguǐ. **(b)** 铁路系统 tiělù xìtǒng. **~ing** *n* [C] [常用 *pl*] 栏杆 lángān.

rain[1] /reɪn/ *n* **1** [U] 雨 yǔ, 雨水 yǔshuǐ. **2** (雨点般的)落下 luòxià. *a ~ of arrows* 箭如雨落 **~bow** /ˈreɪnbəʊ/ 虹 hóng **~coat** 雨衣 yǔyī. **~fall** 降雨 jiàngyǔ, 雨量 yǔliàng.

rain[2] /reɪn/ *vt/i* **1** 下雨 xiàyǔ, 降雨 jiàngyǔ. **2** ~ **(down) on** 落下 luòxià; 降下 jiàngxià: *blows ~ed down on his head* 接连不断打击他的头部.

rainy /ˈreɪnɪ/ *adj* [-ier, -iest] 多雨的 duōyǔde. ***save sth for a ~ day*** 未雨绸缪 wèi yǔ chóumóu; 以备[備]不时[時]之需 yǐ bèi bùshí zhī xū.

raise /reɪz/ *vt* **1** 举[舉]起 jǔqǐ; 使升高 shǐ shēnggāo. ***~ sb's hopes*** 使人更有希望 shǐ rén gèngyǒu xīwàng. **2** 使升起 shǐ shēngqǐ; 使出现 shǐ chūxiàn: *~ a cloud of dust* 扬起一片灰尘. **3** 提出 tíchū: *~ a new point* 提出新论点. **4** 种[種]植 zhòngzhí; 饲养[養] sìyǎng; 养育 yǎngyù. **5** 筹[籌](款) chóu; 招(兵) zhāo; 集结 jíjié: *~ money* 筹款, 集资. **~ Cain** (或 **hell**) 引起大风[風]波 yǐnqǐ dà fēngbō.

raisin /ˈreɪzn/ *n* [C] 葡萄干[乾] pútáogān.

rake /reɪk/ *n* [C] (长柄的)耙子 pázi. □ *vt/i* **1** (用耙子)耙 pá; 耙松[鬆] pásōng. **2** 用耙子集拢[攏](某物) yòng pázi jílǒng. **~ *it in*** [喻]大赚一笔[筆] dà zhuàn yìbǐ. **~ *sth up*** 重新提起某事(尤指不愉快的事) chóngxīng tíqǐ mǒushì *~ up the past* 重提往事. **3** 扫[掃]射 sǎoshè; 纵[縱]射 zòngshè: *~ a ship* 扫射一船. **ˈ~-off** [俚语]佣金 yòngjīn; 回扣 huíkòu.

rally /ˈrælɪ/ *vt/i* [*pt, pp* -lied] **1** (重新)集合 jíhé; 重整 chóngzhěng: *~ an army* 重整军队. **2** 振作(精神等) zhènzuò; 恢复[復](元气等) huīfù. □ *n* [C] [*pl* -ies] **1** 集会[會] jíhuì: *a political ~* 政党集会. **2** 汽车[車]竞[競]赛会 qìchē jìngsàihuì. **3** (网球等)连[連]续[續]对[對]打 liánxù duìdǎ.

ram /ræm/ *n* [C] **1** 公羊 gōngyáng. **2** 撞锤 zhuàngchuí; 夯 hāng; 撞杆[桿] zhuànggǎn. **3** = battering ram. □ *vt* [-mm-] 锤击[擊] chuíjī; 撞击 zhuàngjī; 夯击 hāngjī: *~ a post into the ground.* 把桩打入地下.

ramble /ˈræmbl/ *vi* **1** 漫步 mànbù, 闲[閑]逛 xiánguàng. **2** [喻]漫谈 màntán. **3** (指物)蔓延 mànyán. □ *n* [C] 漫步 mànbù. **ram·bling** *adj* **(a)** (尤指建筑物)凌乱[亂]的 língluànde. **(b)** (说话等)不连[連]贯的 bù liánguàn de.

ramp /ræmp/ *n* [C] 斜坡 xiépō, 坡道 pōdào.

ram·page /ˈræmpeɪdʒ/ *vi* 横冲直撞 héngchōng-zhízhuàng □ *n* ***be*** (或 ***go***) ***on the ~*** 暴跳如雷 bàotiào rú léi; 横冲直撞 héngchōng-zhízhuàng.

ram·pant /ˈræmpənt/ *adj* **1** (指植物)繁茂的 fánmàode, 蔓生的 mànshēngde. **2** 不能控制的 bùnéng kòngzhìde.

ram·part /ˈræmpɑːt/ *n* [C] 壁垒[壘] bìlěi; 防御[禦]物 fángyùwù.

ram·shackle /ˈræmʃækl/ *adj* 要倒塌的 yào dǎotā de, 摇摇欲坠[墜]的 yáoyáo yùzhuì de.

ran /ræn/ *pt* of run[1].

ranch /rɑːntʃ/ *n* [C] (北美洲的)大牧场[場] dà mùchǎng; 大农[農]场 dà nóngchǎng. **~er** *n* [C]

ran·cid /ˈrænsɪd/ *adj* 陈[陳]腐的 chénfǔde; 有陈腐脂肪臭味的 yǒu chénfǔ zhīfáng chòuwèi de: *~ butter* 变味的黄油.

ran·cour [美语 = **-cor**] /ˈræŋkə(r)/ *n* [U] [正式用语]积[積]怨 jīyuàn; 深仇 shēnchóu. **ran·cor·ous** *adj*

ran·dom /ˈrændəm/ *n* [U] **1** ***at ~*** 随便 suíbiàn; 无[無]目的 wú mùdì: *choose at ~* 随便挑选. **2** [用作定语]随便的 suíbiànde, 任意的 rènyìde: *a ~ choice* 随意选择.

rang /ræŋ/ *pt* of ring[2].

range[1] /reɪndʒ/ *n* [C] **1** 排 pái; 行 háng; 系列 xìliè: *a ~ of mountains* 山脉. **2** 靶场[場] bǎchǎng; 射击[擊]场 shèjīchǎng. **3** 射程 shèchéng. **4** 两极限间[間]的距离[離] liǎng jíxiàn jiān de jùlí: *a ~ of temperature* 温差. **5** 炉[爐]灶[竈] lúzào.

range[2] /reɪndʒ/ *vt/i* **1** 排列 páiliè; 排列成行 páiliè chéng háng. **2** ~ ***through*** **(*over*)** 漫游 mànyóu; 徘徊 páihuái. **3** [喻]涉及 shèjí; 包括 bāokuò: *a talk ranging over many subjects.* 涉及许多问题的谈话. **4** (在一定范围内)变[變]化 biànhuà: *prices ranging from £7 to £10.* 从7英镑到10英镑的价格.

ranger /ˈreɪndʒə(r)/ *n* [C] 漫游者 mànyóuzhě, 巡逻[邏]骑[騎]兵 xúnluó qíbīng.

rank /ræŋk/ *n* **1** [C] 排 pái; 行列 hángliè. **2** ***the ~s*** 士兵 shìbīng.

3 [C,U] 军〔軍〕阶〔階〕 jūnjiē; 军衔 jūnxián: *the ~ of captain* 上尉军衔. □ *vt/i* 1 排列成行 páiliè chéng háng. 2 地位 dìwèi: *~ among the world's best* 处于世界最好之列.

rankle /ˈræŋkl/ *vi* 引起怨恨 yǐnqǐ yuànhèn; 使人痛恨 shǐ rén tònghèn.

ran·sack /ˈrænsæk/ *vt* 1 彻〔徹〕底搜索 chèdǐ sōusuǒ. 2 洗劫 xǐjié, 抢〔搶〕劫 qiǎngjié.

ran·som /ˈrænsəm/ *n* [U] 赎〔贖〕救 shújiù; [C] 赎金 shújīn. □ *vt* 赎出 shúchū; 赎回 shúhuí; 得赎金后释〔釋〕放某人 dé shújīn hòu shìfàng mǒurén.

rant /rænt/ *vt/i* 喧嚣夸〔誇〕张〔張〕地说 xuānxiāo kuāzhāng de shuō.

rap /ræp/ *n* [C] 1 敲击〔擊〕(声) qiāojī; 急拍(声) jípāi. 2 [俚语] 责备〔備〕 zébèi; 责骂〔罵〕 zémà. ***take the ~ (for sth)*** (尤指为别人)受责备 shòu zébèi. □ *vt/i* [-pp-] 敲击 qiāojī; 急拍 jípāi.

rape /reɪp/ *vt* 强奸 qiángjiān. □ *n* [C] 强奸 qiángjiān; 强奸罪 qiángjiānzuì. **ra·pist** 强奸犯qiángjiānfàn.

rapid /ˈræpɪd/ *adj* 快的 kuàide, 迅速的 xùnsùde. **~ity** /rəˈpɪdətɪ/ *n* [U] **~ly** *adv*

rap·ids /ˈræpɪdz/ *n pl* 急流 jíliú; 湍滩〔灘〕 chuāntān.

ra·pier /ˈreɪpɪə(r)/ *n* [C] (决斗或剑术中用的)轻〔輕〕剑〔劍〕 qīngjiàn.

rapt /ræpt/ *adj* 着迷的 zhuómíde; 全神贯注的 quán shén guànzhù de.

rap·ture /ˈræptʃə(r)/ *n* 1 [U] 着迷 zhuómí; 全神贯注 quán shén guànzhù. 2 [*pl*] ***be in ~s (over, about)*** 狂喜 kuángxǐ. **rap·tur·ous** *adj* 狂喜的 kuángxǐde: *rapturous applause* 欢喜若狂的喝采.

rare[1] /reə(r)/ *adj* [-r, -st] 稀有的 xīyǒude, 罕见的 hǎnjiànde. **~ly** *adv* 难〔難〕得 nándé; 非常地 fēichángde. **~ness** *n* [U]

rare[2] /reə(r)/ *adj* (指肉)半熟的 bànshúde; 煮得嫩的 zhǔ de nènde.

rarefy /ˈreərɪfaɪ/ *vt/i* [*pt, pp* -ied] 使(变)稀薄 shǐ xībó; 使(变)纯净 shǐ chúnjìng: *rarefied air* 稀薄空气.

rar·ity /ˈreərətɪ/ *n* [*pl* -ies] 1 [U] 稀有 xīyǒu; 稀薄 xībó. 2 [C] 罕见的东〔東〕西 hǎnjiànde dōngxi.

ras·cal /ˈrɑːskl/ *n* [C] 1 流氓 liúmáng, 无〔無〕赖 wúlài. 2 小淘气〔氣〕 xiǎo táoqì.

rash[1] /ræʃ/ *adj* 鲁莽的 lǔmǎngde; 急躁的 jízàode. **~ly** *adv* **~ness** *n* [U]

rash[2] /ræʃ/ *n* [C] 1 疹子 zhěnzi. 2 [喻]迅速扩〔擴〕展 xùnsù kuòzhǎn: *a ~ of strikes* 工潮的迅速蔓延.

rasher /ˈræʃə(r)/ *n* [C] 咸肉(或火腿)薄片 xiánròu buópiàn.

rasp /rɑːsp/ *n* [C] 1 粗锉 cūcuò. 2 锉磨的声〔聲〕音 cuò mó de shēngyīn. □ *vt/i* 1 用粗锉刀锉 yòng cū cuòdāo cuò. 2 ***~ out*** 粗声粗气〔氣〕地说 cūshēng cūqì de shuō. 3 发〔發〕出刺耳的声音 fāchū cì'ěr de shēngyīn.

rasp·berry /ˈrɑːzbrɪ/ *n* [C] [*pl* -ies] 1 木莓 mùméi; 山莓 shānméi. 2 [俚语] (表示憎恶, 嘲笑, 不赞成等的)咂舌声〔聲〕(或姿势) zāshéshēng.

rat /ræt/ *n* [C] 1 鼠 shǔ; 耗子 hàozi. 2 ***smell a ~*** 感到有可疑之处〔處〕 gǎn dào yǒu kěyí zhī chù. 3 [俚语]叛徒 pàntú; 可耻的人 kěchǐde rén. □ *vt* [-tt-] 1 捕鼠 bǔshǔ. 2 ***~ (on sb)*** 密告(或背弃)某人 mìgào mǒurén. **the ˈ~ race** 激烈的竞〔競〕争 jīliède jìngzhēng. **~ty** *adj* [-ier, -iest] [非正式用语]易怒的 yìnùde.

rate[1] /reɪt/ *n* 1 [C] 比率 bǐlǜ; 率 lǜ: *the ˈbirth-~* 出生率. 2 ***at ˈthis (ˈthat) ~*** 这〔這〕(那)样〔樣〕的话 zhèyàngde huà. ***at ˈany ~*** 无〔無〕论〔論〕如何 wúlùn rúhé. 3 ***the ~s*** [英国英语]房地产〔產〕税 fángdìchǎn shuì 4 速度 sùdù; 速率 sùlǜ. 5 等级 děngjí: *first ~* 一等.

rate[2] /reɪt/ *vt/i* 1 对〔對〕...估价〔價〕 duì...gūjià. 2 [英国英语] 为〔爲〕征〔徵〕税而估计(财产)的价值 wèi zhēngshuì ér gūjì...de jiàzhí.

rather /ˈrɑːðə(r)/ *adv* 1 宁〔寧〕可 níngkě; 宁愿〔願〕 níngyuàn: *I'd ~ go.* 我宁愿走. 2 更确〔確〕切地 gèng quèqiè de: *last night or ~ early this morning* 昨天夜里, 或者更确切地说, 今天凌晨. 3 相当〔當〕 xiāngdāng, 颇 pō: *a ~ surprising result* 一个相当惊人的结果.

rat·ify /ˈrætɪfaɪ/ *vt* [*pt, pp* -ied] 批准 pīzhǔn; 认〔認〕可 rènkě. **ˌrati·fi·ca·tion** /-fɪˈkeɪʃn/ *n* [U]

rat·ing /ˈreɪtɪŋ/ *n* 1 [C] (广播、电视的)收看(听)率 shōukànlǜ. 2 [U] 为〔爲〕缴税对财产〔產〕的估价〔價〕 wèi jiǎoshuì duì cáichǎn de gūjià. 3 [海军](非军官的)水手 shuǐshǒu.

ratio /ˈreɪʃɪəʊ/ *n* [C] [*pl* ~s] 比 bǐ; 比率 bǐlǜ: *The ~ of boys to girls was 3 to 1.* 男孩和女孩的比率是三

比一

ra·tion /'ræʃn/ *n* [C] (食物的)定量 dìngliàng. □ *vt* 定量供应[應] dìngliàng gōngyìng.

ra·tion·al /'ræʃnəl/ *adj* 1 有推理能力的 yǒu tuīlǐ nénglì de. 2 合理的 hélǐde. ~**ly** *adv*

ra·tion·al·ize /'ræʃnəlaɪz/ *vt* 1 合理地说明或处[處]理 hélǐde shuōmíng huò chǔlǐ: ~ *one's fears* 对自己的忧虑作出合理解释. 2 合理化地改革(工业等) hélǐhuàde gǎigé. **ration·al·iz·ation** /-'zeɪʃn/ *n* [U]

rattle /'rætl/ *vt/i* 1 (使)发[發]出嘎嘎声[聲] fāchū gāgāshēng: *coins ~d in his pocket* 硬币在他的口袋里嘎嘎作响. 2 ~ ***sth off*** 喋喋不休 diédié bùxiū. 3 [非正式用语]使紧[緊]张[張] shǐ jǐnzhāng. □ *n* 1[U] 格格声 gégéshēng. 2 [C] 拨[撥]浪鼓(一种玩具) bōlànggǔ. '~**snake** 响[響]尾蛇 xiǎngwěishé.

ratty ⇨ rat.

rau·cous /'rɔ:kəs/ *adj* 沙哑[啞]的 shāyǎde; 粗声[聲]的 cūshēngde. ~**ly** *adv*

rav·age /'rævɪdʒ/ *vt/i* 1 毁坏[壞] huǐhuài; 蹂躏[躪] róulìn. 2(指军队等)抢[搶]劫 qiǎngjié; 掠夺[奪] lüèduó. □ *n* [*pl*] 破坏的结果 pòhuàide jiēguǒ: *the ~s of time* 岁月的摧残(如妇女的年老色衰).

rave /reɪv/ *vi* 1 胡言乱[亂]语 húyán luànyǔ. 2 ~ ***about*** 热[熱]衷地谈论[論] rèzhōngde tánlùn. □ *n* [C] 1 [非正式用语]热情的赞扬[揚] rèqíngde zànyáng: *a ~ review* 非常好的评论. 2 [俚语]令人兴[興]奋[奮]的晚会[會] lìng rén xīngfènde wǎnhuì. **raving** *adj, adv* 语无[無]伦[倫]次的 yǔ wú lúncì de; 疯[瘋]狂地 fēngkuángde: *raving mad* 狂怒.

raven /'reɪvn/ *n* [C] 1 渡乌[烏]鸦[鴉] dùwūyā. 2 [用作定语]乌黑的 wūhēide.

rav·en·ous /'rævənəs/ *adj* 极[極]饿的 jí'ède; 贪婪的 tānlánde. ~**ly** *adv*

ra·vine /rə'vi:n/ *n* [C] 深谷 shēngǔ; 峡[峽]谷 xiágǔ.

rav·ish /'rævɪʃ/ *vt* 使狂喜 shǐ kuángxǐ; 使陶醉 shǐ táozuì. ~**ing** *adj*

raw /rɔ:/ *adj* 1 未煮过[過]的 wèi zhǔguò de; 生的 shēngde. 2 未加工的 wèi jiāgōng de; 处[處]于自然状[狀]态[態]的 chù yú zìrán zhuàngtài de: ~ *materials* 原料. 3 (指人)未受训练[練]的 wèishòu xùnliàn de; 无[無]经验[驗]的 wú jīngyàn de. 4 (指天气)阴[陰]冷的 yīnlěngde; 湿[濕]冷的 shīlěngde. 5 疼痛 téngtòng.

ray[1] /reɪ/ *n* [C] 1 光线[綫] guāngxiàn; 射线 shèxiàn. 2 [喻]微量 wēiliàng: *a ~ of hope* 一线希望.

ray[2] /reɪ/ *n* [C] 魟鱼 hóngyú.

rayon /'reɪɒn/ *n* [U] 人造丝 rénzàosī; 人造丝织[織]物 rénzàosī zhīwù.

raze, rase /reɪz/ *vt* 摧毁 cuīhuǐ; 夷为[爲]平地 yí wéi píngdì.

razor /'reɪzə(r)/ *n* [C] 剃刀 tìdāo; 刮胡子刀 guā húzi dāo.

R.C. =1 Red Cross 红十字(会) hóngshízì. 2 Roman Catholic.

Rd.=road.

reach /ri:tʃ/ *vt/i* 1 伸出(手等) shēnchū; 伸手取(某物) shēnshǒu qǔ. 2 把…递来 bǎ … dìlái: *R~ me my coat.* 递给我大衣. 3 抵达[達] dǐdá, 到达 dàodá: ~ *London* 到达伦敦. 4 延伸 yánshēn: *My land ~es to the river.* 我的土地延伸到河边. □ *n* 1 [U] 伸 shēn; 伸出 shēnchū. 2 [C] 河段 héduàn: *the lower ~es of the Thames* 泰晤士河下游.

re·act /rɪ'ækt/ *vi* 1 ~ **(up)on** 起作用 qǐ zuòyòng; 有影响[響] yǒu yǐnxiǎng. 2 ~ ***to*** 起反应[應] qǐ fǎnyìng. 3 ~ ***against*** 反抗 fǎnkàng; 反对[對] fǎnduì. 4 ~ ***on*** 起化学[學]反应 qǐ huàxué fǎnyìng.

re·ac·tion /rɪ'ækʃn/ *n* [C,U] 1 反作用 fǎn zuòyòng. 2 反动[動] fǎndòng. 3 反应[應] fǎnyìng. 4 化学[學]反应 huàxué fǎnyìng; (核子)反应 ~**ary** *adj, n* [C] [*pl* -ies] fǎnyìng. 反动的 fǎndòngde; 反动分子 fǎndòng fènzǐ.

re·ac·tor /rɪ'æktə(r)/ *n* = nuclear reactor.

read /ri:d/ *vt/i* [*pt, pp* read /red/] 1 读[讀] dú, 阅[閱]读 yuèdú: ~ *a book* 读书. 2 朗读 lǎngdú. 3 研究 yánjiū. 4 解释[釋] jiěshì; 解答 jiědá: ~ *a person's thoughts* 了解某人的思想. 5 ~ ***between the lines*** 体[體]会[會]字里行间[間]的言外之意 tǐhuì zìlǐ-hángjiān de yán wài zhī yì. 6 (指仪器)指示 zhǐshì. ~**able** /-əbl/ *adj* 易读的 yìdúde; 使人爱[愛]读的 shǐ rén àidú de.

reader /'ri:də(r)/ *n* [C] 1 读[讀]者 dúzhě. 2 [英国英语](某些英国大学中)讲[講]师[師] jiǎngshī. 3 教科书[書] jiàokēshū. '~**ship** (报刊等的)读者总[總]数[數] dúzhě zǒngshù.

read·ily, readi·ness ⇨ ready.

read·ing /'ri:dɪŋ/ *n* **1** [U] 阅〔閱〕读〔讀〕 yuèdú. **2** [U] 知识〔識〕(尤指书本知识) zhīshì: *a man of wide* ~ 学识渊博的人. **3** [C] 见解 jiànjiě; 解释〔釋〕 jiěshì: *My* ~ *of the situation is* ... 我对形势的看法是... **4** [C] 仪〔儀〕器指示数〔數〕 yíqì zhǐshìshù.

ready /'redɪ/ *adj* [-ier, -iest] **1** 准〔準〕备〔備〕好的 zhǔnbèi hǎo de; 愿〔願〕意的 yuànyìde: ~ *for work* 准备好,可以工作. ***make*** ~ 准备好 zhǔnbèi hǎo. **2** 快的 kuàide, 迅速的 xùnsùde: *a* ~ *answer* 脱口而出的回答. **3** 有效的 yǒuxiàode; 可用的 kěyòngde: *keep a revolver* ~ 身边备有一只左轮手枪. **4** 预先准备好 yùxiān zhǔnbèi hǎo: *buy food* ~*-cooked* 购买熟食 □ *n* [仅用于] ***at the*** ~ 预备射击〔擊〕 yùbèi shèjī. ,~-**'made** *adj* 现成的 xiànchéngde. **read·ily** *adv* **(a)** 不迟〔遲〕疑地 bù chíyí de. **(b)** 无〔無〕困难〔難〕地 wú kùnnan de. **readi·ness** /'redɪnɪs/ *n* [U] **(a)** ***in readiness(for)*** 准备就绪 zhǔnbèi jiù xù. **(b)** 愿〔願〕意 yuànyì: *readiness to work* 情愿工作.

real /rɪəl/ *adj* 真实〔實〕的 zhēnshíde; 实际〔際〕的 shíjìde. '~ **estate** [法律]不动〔動〕产〔產〕 búdòngchǎn; 房地产 fángdìchǎn.

real·ism /'rɪəlɪzəm/ *n* [U] **1** (文艺的)现实〔實〕主义〔義〕 xiànshí zhǔyì; 写〔寫〕实主义 xiěshí zhǔyì. **2** 务〔務〕实〔實〕能力 wùshí nénglì. **real·ist** *n* [C] **real·is·tic** /-'lɪstɪk/ *adj*

re·al·ity /rɪ'ælətɪ/ *n* [*pl* -ies] **1** [U] 真实〔實〕 zhēnshí; 实际〔際〕存在 shíjì cúnzài. ***in*** ~ 事实上 shìshíshàng; 实际上 shíjìshàng. **2** [C] 真正看到或体〔體〕验〔驗〕到的东西 zhēnzhèng kàndào huò tǐyàn dào de dōngxi: *the realities of war* 战争的实情. **3** [U] 现实 xiànshí: *escape from* ~ 逃避现实.

real·ize /'rɪəlaɪz/ *vt* **1** 认〔認〕识〔識〕到 rènshi dào; 了解 liǎojiě. **2** 使(计划等)实〔實〕现 shǐ shíxiàn. **3** 把(产业等)变〔變〕为〔爲〕现钱〔錢〕 bǎ...biànwéi xiànqián. **real·iz·ation** /-'ʒeɪʃn/ *n* [U]

really /'rɪəlɪ/ *adv* **1** 事实〔實〕上 shìshíshàng. **2** (表示兴趣、惊讶等): *'We're leaving next month.'* '我们下个月就走了'. — 'Oh, ~!' '啊,真的吗!'

realm /relm/ *n* [C] **1** [喻]世界 shìjiè. *the* ~ *of fantasy* 幻想的世界. **2** [喻]王国〔國〕 wángguó.

reap /ri:p/ *vt/i* **1** 收割 shōugē; 收获〔獲〕 shōuhuò. **2** [喻]获得 huòdé; 得到 dédào: ~ *the reward of hard work* 得到努力工作的报酬.

rear[1] /rɪə(r)/ *n* [C] **1** 后〔後〕部 hòubù; 后面 hòumiàn. **2** [用作定语]后部的 hòubùde; 后面的 hòumiànde. **3** ***bring up the*** ~ 殿后 diànhòu. '~**guard** 后卫〔衛〕 hòuwèi.

rear[2] /rɪə(r)/ *vt/i* **1** 培植 péizhí; 饲养〔養〕 sìyǎng: ~ *cattle* 饲养家畜. ⇨ raise(4). **2** (尤指马)后〔後〕腿站立 hòutuǐ zhànlì. **3** 举〔舉〕起 jǔqǐ; 竖〔竪〕起 shùqǐ: ~ *one's head* 抬起头.

rea·son[1] /'ri:zn/ *n* **1** [C,U] 理由 lǐyóu; 原因 yuányīn: *The* ~ *why he's late is that* 他迟到的原因是... **2**[U] 理智 lǐzhì; 理性 lǐxìng. ***lose one's*** ~ 发〔發〕疯〔瘋〕 fāfēng. **3** [U] 明智 míngzhì; 常识〔識〕 chángshí. ***do anything (with) in*** ~ 作合情合理的事 zuò héqíng hélǐ de shì. ***it stands to*** ~ ***(that)*** 按照常情 ànzhào chángqíng.

rea·son[2] /'ri:zn/ *vt/i* **1** 思考 sīkǎo; 推理 tuīlǐ. **2** ~ ***with sb*** 劝〔勸〕说 quànshuō; 说服 shuōfú. **3** ~ ***(that)*** 辩论〔論〕 biànlùn. ~**ing** *n* [U] 推理 tuīlǐ.

rea·son·able /'ri:znəbl/ *adj* **1** 有普通常识〔識〕的 yǒu pǔtōng chángshí de; 明智的 míngzhìde. **2** 公平的 gōngpíngde; 公道的 gōngdàode: *a* ~ *price* 公道的价格. **rea·son·ably** *adv*

re·as·sure /,ri:ə'ʃʊə(r)/ *vt* 使放心 shǐ fàngxīn; 使消除疑虑〔慮〕 shǐ xiāochú yílǜ. **re·as·sur·ance** *n* [U]

re·bate /'ri:beɪt/ *n* [C] 折扣 zhékòu; 债务〔務〕,租税可获〔獲〕减免的款额 zhàiwù, zūshuì kě huò jiǎnmiǎn de kuǎn'é.

rebel[1] /'rebl/ *n* [C] 反叛者 fǎnpànzhě; 反抗者 fǎnkàngzhě.

re·bel[2] /rɪ'bel/ *vi* [-ll-] **1** 反抗 fǎnkàng; 对〔對〕抗 duìkàng. **2** 强烈抗议〔議〕 qiángliè kàngyì. ~**lion** /-lɪen/ *n* [C,U] 反抗 fǎnkàng; 对抗 duìkàng. ~**li·ous** *adj* **(a)** 反叛的 fǎnpànde; 反抗的 fǎnkàngde. **(b)** 不易控制的 búyì kòngzhì de.

re·birth /,ri:'bɜ:θ/ *n* [C] **2** 再生 zàishēng; 复兴〔興〕 fùxīng: *the* ~ *of learning* 文艺复兴.

re·bound /'ri:baʊnd/ *vi* **1** 弹〔彈〕回 tánhuí; 跳回 tiàohuí. **2** ~***(up)on*** 报〔報〕应〔應〕 bàoyìng.

re·buff /rɪ'bʌf/ *n* [C] 断〔斷〕然拒

绝 duànrán jùjué. □ *vt* 断然拒绝 duànrán jùjué.

re·buke /rɪ'bjuːk/ *vt* [正式用语]指责 zhǐzé; 非难〔難〕fēinàn. □ *n* [C] 指责 zhǐzé; 非难 fēinàn.

re·call /rɪ'kɔːl/ *vt* **1** ~ *sb* **(***from***,** *to***)** 召回 zhàohuí. **2** 回想 huíxiǎng; 回忆〔憶〕huíyì. □ *n* **1** [C] 召回(大使) zhàohuí. **2** [U] 回忆 huíyì, 回想 huíxiǎng.

re·cap·itu·late /ˌriːkə'pɪtʃʊleɪt/ *vt/i* 扼要重述 èyào chóngshù. **re·cap·itu'la·tion** /-ʃn/ *n* [C,U]

recd. =received.

re·cede /rɪ'siːd/ *vi* **1** 后〔後〕退 hòutuì **2** 向后倾斜 xiànghòu qīngxié: *a receding chin* 向后倾斜的下巴.

re·ceipt /rɪ'siːt/ *n* **1** [U] 收到 shōudào: *the* ~ *of your cheque* 收到你的支票. **2** [*pl*] 收到的款项 shōudàode kuǎnxiàng; 进〔進〕款 jìnkuǎn. **3** [C] 收据〔據〕shōujù, 收条〔條〕shōutiáo.

re·ceive /rɪ'siːv/ *vt/i* **1** 收到 shōudào; 接到 jiēdào. **2** 受到 shòudào; 得到 dédào: ~ *a knife wound* 受刀伤. **3** 准〔準〕予进〔進〕入 zhǔn yǔ jìnrù: ~ *him into the Church* 准许他入教. **re·ceiver** *n* [C] **(a)** 收受者 shōushòuzhě; 收件人 shōujiànrén. **(b) R**~ 破产〔產〕案产〔產〕业〔業〕管理人 pòchǎn'àn chǎnyè guǎnlǐrén. **(c)** 受话器 shòuhuàqì; 电〔電〕话听〔聽〕筒 diànhuà tīngtǒng.

re·cent /'riːsnt/ *adj* 最近的 zuìjìnde; 近来〔來〕的 jìnláide. ~**ly** *adv* 最近地 zuìjìnde; 近来地 jìnláide.

re·cep·tacle /rɪ'septəkl/ *n* [C] 容器 róngqì.

re·cep·tion /rɪ'sepʃn/ *n* **1** [C] 招待会〔會〕zhāodàihuì; 宴会 yànhuì. **2** [C] 欢〔歡〕迎 huānyíng; 接待 jiēdài: *get a warm* ~ 受到热情的欢迎. **3** [U] (无线电等信号的)接收 jiēshōu; 接收力 jiēshōulì. **4** (旅馆等的)柜〔櫃〕台〔臺〕guìtái; 接待处〔處〕jiēdàichù. ~**ist** (旅馆等的)接待员 jiēdàiyuán.

re·cep·tive /ri'septɪv/ *adj* (对新思等)善于接受的 shàn yú jiēshòu de.

re·cess /rɪ'ses/ *n* [C] **1** [美语 = *vacation*] 休息 xiūxi; 短暂〔暫〕的休假 duǎnzhànde xiūjià; 休会〔會〕xiūhuì. **2** (墙的)凹进〔進〕处〔處〕āojìnchù; 壁龛〔龕〕bìkān. **3** 幽深处 yōushēnchù. *vt* 置于隐〔隱〕秘处〔處〕zhì yú yǐnmìchù.

re·ces·sion /rɪ'seʃn/ *n* **1** [U] 后〔後〕退 hòutuì; 撤回 chèhuí. **2** [C] (工商业的)衰退 shuāituì; (价格的)暴跌 bàodiē.

recipe /'resəpɪ/ *n* [C] 烹饪法 pēngrènfǎ; 食谱 shípǔ.

re·cipi·ent /rɪ'sɪpɪənt/ *n* [C] [正式用语]接受者 jiēshòuzhě.

re·cip·ro·cal /rɪ'sɪprəkl/ *adj* 相互的 xiānghùde; 互惠的 hùhuìde: ~ *affection* 相互喜爱. ~**ly** /-klɪ/ *adv*

re·cital /rɪ'saɪtl/ *n* [C] **1** 详述 xiángshù **2** 演奏会〔會〕yǎnzòuhuì; 独〔獨〕奏会 dúzòuhuì; 独唱会 dúchànghuì.

re·cite /rɪ'saɪt/ *vt/i* **1** 背诵 bèisòng; 朗诵 lǎngsòng. **2** 列举〔舉〕(名字、事实等) lièjǔ. **reci·ta·tion** /ˌresɪ'teɪʃn/ *n* [C]

reck·less /'reklɪs/ *adj* 鲁莽的 lǔmǎngde; 不顾〔顧〕后〔後〕果的 búgù hòuguǒ de. ~**ly** *adv* ~**ness** *n* [U]

reckon /'rekən/ *vt/i* **1** 计算 jìsuàn. **2** ~ *with sb*, **(a)** 清算 qīngsuàn; 处〔處〕理 chǔlǐ. **(b)** 将〔將〕…加以考虑 jiāng…jiā yǐ kǎolǜ: *a man to be* ~*ed with* 一个不可忽视的人. **3** ~ **(***up***)***on* 依赖 yīlài **4** 认〔認〕为〔爲〕rènwéi: *She's* ~*ed to be beautiful.* 她被认为是漂亮的. ~**ing** *n* **(a)** *day of* ~*ing* 报〔報〕应〔應〕来〔來〕到的日子 bàoyìng láidào de rìzi; 清算日 qīngsuànrì. **(b)** [U] 计算 jìsuàn.

re·claim /rɪ'kleɪm/ *vt* **1** 开〔開〕拓 kāituò; 开垦〔墾〕kāikěn. **2** 要求归〔歸〕还〔還〕yāoqiú guīhuán. **rec·la·ma·tion** /ˌreklə'meɪʃn/ *n* [U]

re·cline /rɪ'klaɪn/ *vt/i* 斜倚 xiéyǐ; 躺 tǎng.

re·cluse /rɪ'kluːs/ *n* [C] 隐〔隱〕士 yǐnshì.

rec·og·nize /'rekəgnaɪz/ *vt* **1** 认〔認〕识〔識〕rènshi; 认出 rènchū. **2** 承认 chéngrèn: *refuse to* ~ *a new government* 拒绝承认一新政府. ~ *one's faults* 承认错误. **3** 公认 gōngrèn: ~ *someone as a great poet* 公认某人是位伟大的诗人. **rec·og·niz·able** /-əbl/ *adj* **rec·og·ni·tion** /-'nɪʃn/ *n* [U]

re·coil /rɪ'kɔɪl/ *vi* **1** ~ **(***from***)** 跳回 tiàohuí; 退缩 tuìsuō. **2** 弹〔彈〕回 tánhuí; (枪等)产〔產〕生后〔後〕坐力 chǎnshēng hòuzuòlì. □ /'riːkɔɪl/ *n* [C] 退缩 tuìsuō; 跳回 tiàohuí; 弹回 tánhuí.

rec·ol·lect /ˌrekə'lekt/ *vt/i* 回忆〔憶〕huíyì; 想起 xiǎngqǐ. **rec·ol·lec·tion** /-ʃn/ *n* **(a)** [U] 回忆 huíyì; 记忆力 jìyìlì. **(b)** [C] 往事 wǎngshì.

rec·om·mend /ˌrekə'mend/ *vt* **1** 推荐〔薦〕tuījiàn; 介绍 jièshào. **2** 劝〔勸〕告 quàngào; 建议 jiànyì: *I ~ leaving* 我建议动身离开. *I ~ you to leave early.* 我劝你早点走. **~a·tion** /-'deɪʃn/*n* **(a)** [U] 推荐 tuījiàn; 介绍 jièshào. **(b)** [C] 介绍信 jièshàoxìn.

rec·om·pense /'rekəmpens/ *vt* [正式用语]报〔報〕酬 bàochóu; 回报 huíbào. □ *n* [C, U] [正式用语] 报酬 bàochóu; 酬金 chóujīn.

rec·on·cile /'rekənsaɪl/ *vt* **1** 使和解 shǐ héjiě; 使复交 shǐ fùjiāo. **2** 调解 tiáojiě; 调停 tiáotíng. **3** 使一致 shǐ yīzhì: *~ two accounts (statements)* 使两种说法一致. **4** *~ oneself to sth* 接受 jiēshòu. **rec·on·cili·ation** /-sɪlɪ'eɪʃn/ *n* [C,U]

re·con·nais·sance /rɪ'kɒnɪsns/ *n* [C,U] 侦察 zhēnchá.

re·con·noitre /ˌrekə'nɔɪtə(r)/ *vt/i* 侦察 zhēnchá.

rec·ord[1] /'rekɔ:d/ *n* **1** [C] 记录〔録〕jìlù; 记载〔載〕jìzǎi. **2** [U] 文字记录的情况 wénzì jìlù de qíngkuàng: *go on ~* 公开声明. *off the ~* [非正式用语]不公开〔開〕的 bù gōngkāi de; 不能发〔發〕表的 bùnéng fābiǎo de. **3** [C] (人的)履历〔歷〕或事情经〔經〕过〔過〕的记载 lǚlì huò shìqing jīngguò de jìzǎi **4** [C] 唱片 chàngpiān. ⇨ recording. **6**[C] (指运动)最高记录 zuì gāo jìlù: *the world high-jump ~* 世界跳高纪录. **'~-player** 电〔電〕唱机〔機〕diànchàngjī.

re·cord[2] /rɪ'kɔ:d/ *vt* **1** 记录〔録〕jìlù; 记载〔載〕jìzǎi. **2** (指仪器)在刻度上指示 zài kèdù shàng zhǐshì.

re·corder /rɪ'kɔ:də(r)/ *n* [C] **1** (英国某些市镇的)首席法官 shǒuxí fǎguān. **2** 记录〔録〕器 jìlùqì. 录音机〔機〕lùyīnjī. ⇨ tape recorder. **3** 直笛 zhídí.

re·cord·ing /rɪ'kɔ:dɪŋ/ *n* [C] 录〔録〕音的节〔節〕目 lùyīnde jiémù.

re·count[1] /rɪ'kaʊnt/ *vt* [正式用语] 详述 xiángshù; 描述 miáoshù.

re-count[2] /ˌri:'kaʊnt/ *vt/i* 重新计算 chóngxīn jìsuàn. □ *n* [C] 重算 chóngsuàn.

re·coup /rɪ'ku:p/ *vt* 赔偿〔償〕péicháng; 补〔補〕偿 bǔcháng.

re·cover /rɪ'kʌvə(r)/ *vt/i* **1** 重新找到 chóngxīn zhǎodào. **2** *~ from* 复原 fùyuán; 痊愈〔癒〕quányù. **3** 恢复原状〔狀〕huīfù yuánzhuàng. **re·cov·ery** *n* [U]

rec·re·ation /ˌrekrɪ'eɪʃn/ *n* [C,U] 消遣 xiāoqiǎn; 娱〔娛〕乐〔樂〕yúlè.

re·cruit /rɪ'kru:t/ *n* [C] 新兵 xīnbīng; 新成员 xīn chéngyuán. □ *vt/i* 吸收(新成员) xīshōu; 征募(新兵) zhēngmù. **~ment** *n* [U]

rec·tangle /'rektæŋgl/ *n*[C] 长〔長〕方形 chángfāngxíng; 矩形 jùxíng. **rec·tangu·lar**/rek'tæŋgjʊlə(r)/*adj*

rec·tify /'rektɪfaɪ/ *vt* [*pt, pp* -ied] 纠正 jiūzhèng; 矫〔矯〕正 jiǎozhèng: *~ an error* 纠正错误.

rec·tor /'rektə(r)/ *n* [C] **1** (英国教会的)教区〔區〕长〔長〕 jiàoqūzhǎng. ⇨ vicar. **2** (某些学校、学院、大学的)校长 xiàozhǎng. **rec·tory** *n* [C] [*pl* -ies] 教区长(或校长)的住宅 jiàoqūzhǎngde zhùzhái.

rec·tum /'rektəm/ *n* [C] [*pl* ~s] [解剖]直肠〔腸〕zhícháng.

re·cu·per·ate /rɪ'ku:pəreɪt/ *vt/i* 复原 fùyuán; 恢复健康 huīfù jiànkāng. **re·cu·pe'r·ation** *n* [U]

re·cur /rɪ'kɜ:(r)/ *vi* [-rr-] 再发〔發〕生 zài fāshēng; 重现 chóngxiàn: *The error ~red in his work.* 他工作中再次出现这个错误. **~rence** /rɪ'kʌrəns/ *n* [C,U] 再发生 zài fāshēng; 复发 fùfā. **~rent** *adj*

re·cycle /ˌri:'saɪkl/ *vt* (使)再循环〔環〕zài xúnhuán.

red /red/ *adj* [-der, -dest] **1** 红色的 hóngsède. *see ~* 怒不可遏 nù bù kě è. **2** 苏〔蘇〕联〔聯〕人 Sūlián rén; 共产〔產〕党〔黨〕人 gòngchǎndǎngrén. □ *n* **1** [C,U] 红色 hóngsè. **2** 红衣 hóngyī: *dressed in ~* 穿红衣服的. **3** [非正式用语]赞成共产主义〔義〕的人 zànchéng gòngchǎnzhǔyì de rén. **4** *be (get) into the ~* 亏〔虧〕损 kuīsǔn; 负债 fùzhài. **'~head** 红头〔頭〕发〔發〕的人 hóng tóufa de rén. **ˌ~ 'herring** 转〔轉〕移注意力的事 zhuǎnyí zhùyìlì de shì. **ˌR~ 'Indian** 北美印第安人 běiměi yìndì'ānrén. **ˌ~ 'tape** 官样〔樣〕文章 guānyàng wénzhāng.

red·den /'redn/ *vt/i* 使红 shǐ hóng; 变〔變〕红 biàn hóng.

re·deem /rɪ'di:m/ *vt* **1** 买〔買〕回 mǎihuí; 赎〔贖〕回 shúhuí. **2** 补〔補〕偿〔償〕bǔcháng; 补救 bǔjiù: *his ~ing feature* 能弥补他的缺点的特质. **the R~er** 救世主 jiùshìzhǔ 耶稣基督 Yēsū Jīdū. **re·demp·tion** /rɪ'dempʃn/ *n* [U]

re·dress /rɪ'dres/ *vt* **1** 纠正 jiūzhèng; 矫〔矯〕正 jiǎozhèng. *~ the 'balance* 使再平衡 shǐ zài pínghéng. □ *n* [U] 补偿〔償〕bǔcháng.

re·duce /rɪ'dju:s/ *vt* **1** 减少 jiǎnshǎo; 减小 jiǎnxiǎo. **2** 使处〔處〕于(某种状态) shǐ chùyú: ~ *a girl to tears* 使一女孩流泪. **re·duc·tion** /rɪ'dʌkʃn/ *n* **(a)** [C,U] 减少 jiǎnshǎo; 减小 jiǎnxiǎo: *huge price ~s.* 大减价. **(b)** [C] 地图〔圖〕照相等的缩版 dìtú zhàoxiàng děng de suōbǎn.

re·dun·dant /rɪ'dʌndənt/ *adj* **1** 过〔過〕多的 guòduōde. **2** 过剩的 guòshèngde; 多余〔餘〕的 duōyúde. **re·dun·dancy** *n* [C,U]

reed /ri:d/ *n* **1** [C] 芦〔蘆〕苇〔葦〕lúwěi; 芦杆 〔稈〕lúgān. **2** [C] (乐器的)簧 huáng.

reef /ri:f/ *n* [C] 礁 jiāo; 暗礁 ànjiāo.

reek /ri:k/ *n* [U] 臭气〔氣〕 chòuqì; 臭味 chòuwèi. □ *vi* ~ *of* 发〔發〕臭气 fā chòuqì.

reel[1] /ri:l/ *n* [C] **1** (电线、棉纱等的)卷〔捲〕轴〔軸〕 juǎnzhóu; 卷筒 juǎntǒng. **2** (电影胶片)一盘 yìpán. □ *vt* **1** 卷 juǎn; 绕〔繞〕rào. **2** ~ *sth off* 滔滔不绝地讲〔講〕tāotāo bù jué de jiǎng.

reel[2] /ri:l/ *vi* **1** 震颤 zhènchàn. **2** 摇晃 yáohuàng; 蹒跚 pánshān.

re·fec·tory /rɪ'fektərɪ/ *n* [C] [*pl* -ies] 食堂 shítáng, 餐厅〔廳〕 cāntīng.

re·fer /rɪ'fɜ:(r)/ *vt/i* [-rr-] **1** 把…提交 bǎ…tíjiāo; 把…委托 bǎ…wěituō: *I'll ~ you to my secretary.* 我把你交给我的秘书. **2** ~ *to* 谈到 tándào; 提到 tídào; 涉及 shèjí: *I ~ to your last letter.* 我指的是有关你最近的来信.

ref·eree /ˌrefə'ri:/ *n* [C] **1** 仲裁人 zhòngcáirén; 公断〔斷〕人 gōngduànrén. **2** (运动)裁判员 cáipànyuán. ⇨ umpire. **3** 鉴〔鑒〕定人 jiàndìngrén; 审〔審〕查人 shěncharén. □ *vt/i* 裁判 cáipàn.

ref·er·ence /'refrəns/ *n* **1** [C,U] 参〔參〕考 cānkǎo. *ˌterms of* '~' 职〔職〕权〔權〕范〔範〕围〔圍〕 zhíquán fànwéi. **2** [C] (关于品行、能力的)证明 zhèngmíng;证明书〔書〕zhèngmíngshū. **3** [C] 出处〔處〕 chūchù; 参照 cānzhào. **4** [U] *in* (*with*) ~ *to* 关〔關〕于 guānyú. '~ **book** 参考书(如词典) cānkǎoshū.

ref·er·en·dum /ˌrefə'rendəm/ *n* [C] [*pl* ~s, -da /-də/] 公民投票 gōngmíng tóupiào; 复决权〔權〕 fùjuéquán.

re·fill /ˌri:'fil/ *vt* 再装〔裝〕满 zài zhuāng mǎn; 再灌满 zài guàn mǎn. □ *n* [C] /'ri:fil/ 新补〔補〕充物 xīn bǔchōngwù.

re·fine /rɪ'faɪn/ *vt/i* **1** 精炼〔煉〕jīngliàn; 提纯 tíchún. **2** 使文雅 shǐ wényǎ; 变〔變〕得优〔優〕雅 biàn de yōuyǎ. ~**ment** *n* **(a)** [U] 精炼 jīngliàn; 提纯 tíchún. **(b)** [U] 优美 yōuměi; 文雅 wényǎ. **(c)** [C] 改良 gǎiliáng; 巧妙的发〔發〕挥〔揮〕 qiǎomiàode fāhuī. ~**ry** *n* [C] 精炼厂〔廠〕(如炼油厂、制糖厂) jīngliànchǎng.

re·flect /rɪ'flekt/ *vt/i* **1** 反射(光、热、声) fǎnshè; 反映 fǎnyìng. **2** 表达〔達〕biǎodá; 表现 biǎoxiàn: *Her sad looks ~ed her thoughts.* 她忧愁的面容反映出她的思想. **3** ~ *(up)on* 带〔帶〕给 dàigěi; 招致 zhāozhì. **4** 考虑 kǎolǜ; 想到 xiǎngdào. ~**or** *n* [C] 反射物 fǎnshèwù; 反射器 fǎnshèqì.

re·flec·tion (英国英语亦作 **reflexion**) /rɪ'flekʃn/ *n* **1** [U] 反射 fǎnshè: *the ~ of light* 光的反射. **2** [C] 映像 yìngxiàng; 倒影 dàoyǐng. **3** *on ~* 再三考虑 zàisān kǎolǜ.

re·flex /'ri:fleks/ *n* [C] (亦作 '~ **action**) 反射作用 fǎnshè zuòyòng.

re·flexion /rɪ'flekʃn/ *n* = reflection.

re·flex·ive /rɪ'fleksɪv/ *adj*, *n* [C] 〔语法〕反身的 fǎnshēngde; 反身代词(动词) fǎnsheng dàicí. ~ **pronoun** 反身代词(如 *myself, themselves*) fǎnshēng dàicí. ~ **verb** 反身动〔動〕词(如 *He cut himself.*) fǎnshēng dòngcí.

re·form[1] /rɪ'fɔ:m/ *vt/i* 改革 gǎigé; 改良 gǎiliáng: ~ *a prisoner (one's character)* 改造犯人 (一个人的性格). □ *n* [C,U] 改革 gǎigé; 改良 gǎiliáng. ~**er** 改革者 gǎigézhě; 改良者 gǎiliángzhě.

re-form[2] /ˌri: 'fɔ:m/ *vt/i* 重新形成 chóngxīn xíngchéng; 重新编队〔隊〕chóngxīn biānduì: *The army ~ed and attacked.* 军队重新编队以后发起了进攻.

ref·or·ma·tion /ˌrefə'meɪʃn/ *n* **1** [U] 改革 gǎigé; [C] (社会、政治、宗教事务的)革新 géxīn. **2** the **R~** 宗教改革(十六世纪改革罗马天主教会的运动,结果产生了新教) zōngjiào gǎigé.

re·fract /rɪ'frækt/ *vt* 使折射 shǐ zhéshè. **re·frac·tion** /-ʃn/ *n* [U]

re·frain[1] /rɪ'freɪn/ *n* [C] 〔正式用语〕= chorus(2).

re·frain[2] /rɪ'freɪn/ *vi* ~ (*from*) 〔正式用语〕抑制 yìzhì; 制止 zhìzhǐ; 戒除 jièchú.

re·fresh /rɪ'freʃ/ *vt* **1** 使精力恢复 shǐ jīnglì huīfù; 使精神振作 shǐ jīngshén zhènzuò. **2** ~ *one's memory* 唤起记忆〔憶〕 huànqǐ jìyì. ~**er course** 进〔進〕修课程 jìnxiū kèchéng. ~**ing** *adj* **(a)** 使精力恢复的 shǐ jīnglì huīfù de. **(b)** 使人耳目一新的 shǐ rén ěr mù yìxīn de. ~**ment** *n* **(a)** [U] 爽快 shuǎngkuài. **(b)** [*pl*] 点〔點〕心 diǎnxin; 饮料 yǐnliào.

re·frig·er·ate /rɪ'frɪdʒəreɪt/ *vt* 冷冻〔凍〕 lěngdòng; 冷藏 lěngcáng. **re·frig·er·ant** /-ənt/ *n, adj* 冰冻剂〔劑〕 bīngdòngjì; 冷冻的 lěngdòngde. **re·frig·er·ation** /-'reɪʃn/ *n* [U] (尤指)(食物的)冷藏 lěngcáng. **re·frig·er·ator** *n* [C] (缩作 **fridge**) 冰箱 bīngxiāng.

re·fuel /ˌriː'fjuːəl/ *vt* [-ll-, 美语亦作 -l-] 加燃料 jiā ránliào.

ref·uge /'refjuːdʒ/ *n* [C, U] 避难〔難〕 bìnàn; 庇护〔護〕 bìhù.

refu·gee /ˌrefjʊ'dʒiː/ *n* [C] 避难〔難〕者 bìnànzhě; 难民 nànmín.

re·fund /rɪ'fʌnd/ *vt* 归〔歸〕还〔還〕 guīhuán; 偿〔償〕还 chánghuán. □ /'riːfʌnd/ *n* [C,U] 归还 guīhuán; 归还额 guīhuán'é.

re·fusal /rɪ'fjuːzl/ *n* **1** [C,U] 拒绝 jùjué. **2** *first* ~ 优〔優〕先取舍〔捨〕权〔權〕 yōuxiān qǔshěquán; 购〔購〕买〔買〕权 gòumǎiquán.

ref·use[1] /'refjuːs/ *n* [U] 废〔廢〕物 fèiwù; 垃圾 lājī.

re·fuse[2] /rɪ'fjuːz/ *vt/i* 拒绝 jùjué; 谢绝 xièjué: ~ *permission* 拒绝要求. ~ *to help* 拒绝帮助.

re·gain /rɪ'geɪn/ *vt* 恢复 huīfù; 重回 chónghuí: ~ *strength* 恢复力量.

re·gal /'riːgl/ *adj* 国〔國〕王的 guówángde; 王室的 wángshìde. ~**ly** *adv*

re·galia /rɪ'geɪlɪə/ *n pl* 王权〔權〕的标〔標〕志(如王冠等) wángquánde biāozhì.

re·gard[1] /rɪ'gɑːd/ *n* **1** [U] 注意 zhùyì; 关〔關〕心 guānxīn: *with no ~ for my safety* 不顾到我的安全. **2** [U] 尊重 zūnzhòng; 敬意 jìngyì: *hold a person in high ~* 十分尊敬某人. **3** [*pl*] 问〔問〕候 wènhòu; 致意 zhìyì. **4** *in (with) ~ to* 关于 guānyú. ~**less** *adj* ~*less of* 不注意 bú zhùyì; 不顾〔顧〕 búgù.

re·gard[2] /rɪ'gɑːd/ *vt* **1** ~ *sb (sth) as* 把…看作 bǎ…kànzuò; 把 … 认〔認〕为〔爲〕 bǎ…rènwéi: *I ~ him as a fool.* 我把他当作傻子. *as ~s;* ~*ing* 关〔關〕于 guānyú.

re·gatta /rɪ'gætə/ *n* [C] [*pl* ~s] 赛船会〔會〕 sàichuánhuì.

re·gency /'riːdʒənsɪ/ *n* [C] [*pl* -ies] 摄〔攝〕政期 shèzhèngqī.

re·gen·er·ate /rɪ'dʒenəreɪt/ *vt/i* 新生 xīnshēng; 更新 gēngxīn. **re·gen·er·ation** /-'reɪʃn/ *n* [U]

re·gent /'riːdʒənt/ *n* [C] 摄〔攝〕政者 shèzhèngzhě: *the Prince R~* 摄政王.

re·gime, ré·gime /reɪ'ʒiːm/ *n*[C] 政体〔體〕 zhèngtǐ; 政制 zhèngzhì; 政权〔權〕 zhèngquán.

regi·ment /'redʒɪmənt/ *n* [C] (陆军) 团〔團〕 tuán. □ *vt* 编成团 biānchéng tuán; 组织〔織〕 zǔzhī. ~**al** /-mentl/ *adj*

re·gion /'riːdʒən/ *n* **1** [C] 地区〔區〕 dìqū; 地带〔帶〕 dìdài: *desert ~s* 沙漠区. **2** [*pl*] 地方 dìfāng; 区域 qūyù. ~**al** *adj*

reg·is·ter[1] /'redʒɪstə(r)/ *n* [C] **1** 登记簿 dēngjìbù; 花名册 huāmíngcè. **2** 音域 yīnyù. ⇨ cash register.

reg·is·ter[2] /'redʒɪstə(r)/ *vt/i* **1** 登记 dēngjì; 注册 zhùcè. **2** (仪表) 指示 zhǐshì: *The thermometer ~s 15 Centigrade.* 温度计上是十五摄氏度. **3** 显〔顯〕示 xiǎnshì; 表达〔達〕 biǎodá. **4** 挂〔掛〕号〔號〕(信或包裹) guàhào.

reg·is·trar /ˌredʒɪ'strɑː(r)/ *n* [C] 登记员 dēngjìyuán; 记录〔録〕员 jìlùyuán.

reg·is·tra·tion /ˌredʒɪ'streɪʃn/ *n* **1** [U] 登记 dēngjì; 注册 zhùcè. **2** [C] 登记项目 dēngjì xiàngmù; 事实〔實〕记录 shìshí jìlù. ˌ~ **number (plate)** (汽车等的) 牌照号〔號〕码〔碼〕 páizhào hàomǎ.

re·gret[1] /rɪ'gret/ *n* [C,U] 懊悔 àohuǐ; 悔恨 huǐhèng. ~**ful** *adj* 懊悔的 àohuǐde; 遗憾的 yíhànde.

re·gret[2] /rɪ'gret/ *vt* [-tt-] **1** 懊悔 àohuǐ; 悔恨 huǐhen. **2** 抱歉 bàoqiàn; 遗憾 yíhàn: *We ~ to say that you lost* 我们遗憾地说, 你输了. ~**table** /-əbl/ *adj* 令人遗憾的 lìng rén yíhàn de. ~**tably** *adv*

Regt.=Regiment.

reg·ular /'regjʊlə(r) / *adj* **1** 整齐〔齊〕的 zhěngqíde; 匀称〔稱〕的 yúnchèngde. **2** 有规律的 yǒu guīlǜ de; 习〔習〕惯性的 xíguànxìngde: *a ~ customer* 老主顾. **3** 专〔專〕职〔職〕的 zhuānzhíde; 职业〔業〕的 zhíyède: ~ *soldiers* 常备兵. **4** 恰当〔當〕的 qiàdàngde: ~ *procedure (methods)* 合乎标准的程序(方法). **5**[语法] (指*verbs, nouns* 等)按规则变〔變〕化的 àn guīzé biànhuà de. □*n* [C] **1** 正规兵 zhèngguībīng. **2** [非正式用语]老主顾〔顧〕 lǎozhǔgù; 常客 chángkè. ~**ity** /-'lærətɪ

n [U] 整齐 zhěngqí; 规律 guīlǜ. ~**ly** *adv* 有规律地 yǒuguīlǜde.
regu·late /ˈregjʊleɪt/ *vt* **1** 控制 kòngzhì; 管理 guǎnlǐ. **2** 调整 tiáozhěng; 校准〔準〕jiàozhǔn.
regu·la·tion /ˌregjʊˈleɪʃn/ *n* **1** [U] 管理 guǎnlǐ; 控制 kòngzhì. **2** [C] 规则 guīzé; 法规 fǎguī. **3** [用作定语] 规定的 guīdìngde; 正式的 zhèngshìde.
re·ha·bili·tate /ˌriːəˈbɪlɪteɪt/ *vt* **1** 恢复…的地位 huīfù ... de dìwèi. **2** 使(残废者)恢复正常生活 shǐ ... huīfù zhèngcháng shēnghuó. **re·ha·bili'ta·tion** *n* [U]
re·hearse /rɪˈhɜːs/ *vt/i* 排练〔練〕páiliàn; 排演 páiyǎn. **re·hearsal** *n* [C,U]
reign /reɪn/ *n* [C] 君主统治 jūnzhǔ tǒngzhì; 统治时〔時〕期 tǒngzhì shíqī. □ *vi* **1** (君主等)统治 tǒngzhì. **2** 存在 cúnzài: *the ~ing champion* 当前的冠军.
re·im·burse /ˌriːɪmˈbɜːs/ *vt* 偿〔償〕还〔還〕chánghuán; 付还 fùhuán. ~**ment** *n* [C,U]
rein /reɪn/ *n* [C] [常用 *pl*] 缰绳〔繩〕jiāngshéng. □ *vt* (用缰绳)勒住 lēizhù; 驾〔駕〕驭〔馭〕jiàyù.
re·in·car·nate /ˌriːɪnkɑːˈneɪt/ *vt* 赋予(灵魂)新的肉体 fùyú xīnde ròutǐ. □ *adj* /ˌriːɪnˈkɑːnət/ 使再生 shǐ zàishēng. **re·in·car'na·tion** *n* [C,U]
rein·deer /ˈreɪndɪə(r)/ *n* [C] [*pl* ~] 驯〔馴〕鹿 xúnlù.
re·in·force /ˌriːɪnˈfɔːs/ *vt* 增援 zēngyuán; 加强 jiāqiáng. ~**ment** *n* [U] **(a)** 增援 zēngyuán; 加强 jiāqiáng. **(b)** [尤指 *pl*] 援军〔軍〕yuánjūn.
re·in·state /ˌriːɪnˈsteɪt/ *vt* 使复原位 shǐfù yuánwèi; 恢复原职〔職〕huīfù yuánzhí. ~**ment** *n* [C,U]
re·iter·ate /riːˈɪtəreɪt/ *vt* 反复做 fǎnfù zuò; 反复讲〔講〕fǎnfù jiǎng. **re·ite'r·ation** *n* [C,U]
re·ject /rɪˈdʒekt/ *vt* **1** 抛弃〔棄〕pāoqì; 丢掉 diūdiào. **2** 拒绝 jùjué; 不受 búshòu. □ /ˈriːdʒekt/ *n* [C] 被抛弃的东〔東〕西 bèi pāoqìde dōngxi. **re'jec·tion** /-ʃn/ *n* [C,U] 抛弃 pāoqì; 拒绝 jùjué; 被抛弃的东西 bèi pāoqìde dōngxi.
re·joice /rɪˈdʒɔɪs/ *vt/i* 欣喜 xīnxǐ; 高兴〔興〕gāoxìng. **re·joic·ing** *n* [U] 欢〔歡〕庆〔慶〕huānqìng; 高兴 gāoxìng.
re·ju·ven·ate /riːˈdʒuːvəneɪt/ *vt/i* (使)返老还〔還〕童 fǎn lǎo huán tóng. **re·ju·ve'n·ation** *n* [U]
re·lapse /rɪˈlæps/ *vi* (病等) 复发〔發〕fùfā. □ *n* [C] 旧〔舊〕病复发〔發〕jiùbìng fùfā.
re·late /rɪˈleɪt/ *vt/i* **1** [正式用语] 叙述 xùshù; 讲〔講〕jiǎng. **2** (思想上)有关〔關〕联〔聯〕yǒu guānlián. **3** ~ *to* 有关系 yǒu guānxi. **4** *be ~d (to)* 有亲〔親〕戚关系〔係〕yǒu qīnqì guānxì.
re·la·tion /rɪˈleɪʃn/ *n* **1** [U] 叙述 xùshù. **2** [U] 关〔關〕系〔係〕guānxì. *the ~ between work and money* 工作与金钱的关系. *in* (或 *with*) *~ to* 关于 guānyú. **3** [*pl*] 事务〔務〕shìwù; 交往 jiāowǎng: *business ~s* 商业交往. ⇨ public relations. **4** [C] 和…有关 hé ... yǒuguān. ~**ship** *n* [C] 关系 guānxi; 亲〔親〕属〔屬〕关系 qīnshǔ guānxi.
rela·tive /ˈrelətɪv/ *adj* **1** 比较的 bǐjiàode; 相对〔對〕的 xiāngduìde: *~ prices* 比较价格. **2** ~ *to* 有关〔關〕系〔係〕的 yǒu guānxìde. □ *n* [C] **1** 关系词 (尤指关系代词) guānxìcí. **2** 亲〔親〕属〔屬〕qīnshǔ; 亲戚 qīnqī. ~ **clause** 关系从〔從〕句 (用关系代词或关系副词联接) guānxì cóngjù. ~ **pronoun** 关系代词(如 'the man who saw you' 中的 *who*) guānxì dàicí. ~**ly** *adv* 比较地 bǐjiàode; 相对地 xiāngduìde: *~ly cheap food* 比较便宜的食物.
re·lax /rɪˈlæks/ *vt/i* **1** 松〔鬆〕弛 sōngchí; 放松 fàngsōng: *~ one's grip* 放松控制. **2** 使轻〔輕〕松 shǐ qīngsōng; 停止工作 tíngzhǐ gōngzuò. ~**ation** /-ˈseɪʃn/ *n* **(a)** [U] 松弛 sōngchí; 放松 fàngsōng **(b)** [C,U] 娱乐〔樂〕yúlè; 消遣 xiāoqiǎn.
re·lay /ˈriːleɪ/ *n* [C] **1** 接替人员 jiētì rényuán; 替班 tìbān. **2** (广播)中继〔繼〕zhōngjì; 转〔轉〕播 zhuǎnbō. **3** 接力赛跑 jiēlì sàipǎo. □ *vt* /rɪˈleɪ/ [*pt, pp* ~ed] 转播 (无线电节目) zhuǎnbō; 传〔傳〕递〔遞〕chuándì. ˈ~ **race** 接力赛跑 jiēlì sàipǎo.
re·lease /rɪˈliːs/ *vt* **1** 释〔釋〕放 shìfàng; 放松〔鬆〕fàngsōng. **2** 发〔發〕表(消息等) fābiǎo; 发行(书、影片等) fāxíng. □ *n* [C,U] 释放 shìfàng; 免除 miǎnchú; 发行 fāxíng: *his ~ from jail* 释放他出狱.
rel·egate /ˈrelɪgeɪt/ *vt* 使降位 shǐ jiàngwèi; 使降级 shǐ jiàngjí. **rel·e'ga·tion** *n* [U]
re·lent /rɪˈlent/ *vi* 变〔變〕温和 biàn wēnhé; 变宽厚 biàn kuānhòu. ~**less** *adj* 无〔無〕情的 wúqíngde; 不仁慈的 bù réncí de: *~less persecution* 残酷的迫害.

rel·evant /'reləvənt/ *adj* 有关〔關〕的 yǒuguānde; 切题的 qiètíde; 中肯的 zhōngkěnde. **~ly** *adv* **relevance** *n* [U]

re·li·able /rɪ'laɪəbl/ *adj* 可靠的 kěkàode; 可信赖的 kě xìnlài de. **re·li·ably** *adv* **re·lia'bil·ity** *n* [U]

re·li·ance /rɪ'laɪəns/ *n* [U] 信任 xìnrèn; 信赖 xìnlài. **re·li·ant** *adj* 信赖的 xìnlàide.

relic /'relɪk/ *n* [C] **1** 圣〔聖〕骨 shènggǔ; 圣物 shèngwù; 遗骸 yíhái. **2** 遗物 yíwù; 纪念物 jìniànwù.

re·lief[1] /rɪ'li:f/ *n* [U] **1** (痛苦等的)减轻〔輕〕jiǎnqīng; 解除 jiěchú. **2** 救济〔濟〕jiùjì; 救济品 jiùjìpǐn. **3** 换班 huànbān; 换班的人 huànbānde rén.

re·lief[2] /rɪ'li:f/ *n* [C,U] 浮雕 fúdiāo. **~ map** 地形图〔圖〕dìxíngtú; 立体地图 lìtǐ dìtú.

re·lieve /rɪ'li:v/ *vt* **1** 救济〔濟〕jiùjì; 援助 yuánzhù. **2** 换班 huànbān; 接替 jiētì. **3 ~ *sb of sth*,** **(a)** 从〔從〕某人手中接取某物 cóng mǒurén shǒu zhōng jiēqǔ mǒuwù. **(b)** 解除 jiěchú.

re·lig·ion /rɪ'lɪdʒən/ *n* **1** [U] 宗教信仰 zōngjiào xìnyǎng. **2** [C] 宗教 zōngjiào.

re·lig·ious /rɪ'lɪdʒəs/ *adj* **1** 宗教的 zōngjiàode. **2** 虔诚的 qiánchéngde; 信奉宗教的 xìnfèng zōngjiào de. **~ly** *adv*

re·lin·quish /rɪ'lɪŋkwɪʃ/ *vt* 放弃〔棄〕fàngqì; 撤回 chèhuí: *~ power* (*one's grip*) 放弃权力(控制).

rel·ish /'relɪʃ/ *n* **1** [C,U] 风〔風〕味 fēngwèi; 美味 měiwèi. **2** [U] 爱〔愛〕好 àihào. □ *vt* 享受 xiǎngshòu; 爱好 àihào: *I ~ the idea of staying in bed.* 我喜欢躺在床上的主意.

re·luc·tant /rɪ'lʌktənt/ *adj* 不愿〔願〕的 búyuànde; 勉强的 miǎnqiǎngde. **~ly** *adv* **re·luc·tance** *n* [U]

rely /rɪ'laɪ/ *vi* [*pt, pp* -lied] ~ **(*up*)*on*** 依赖 yīlài; 信赖 xìnlài.

re·main /rɪ'meɪn/ *vi* **1** 剩下 shèngxià; 余〔餘〕留 yúliú. **2** 继〔繼〕续〔續〕存在 jìxù cúnzài: *~ silent* 保持沉默. **~der** *n* [C,U] 剩余物 shèngyúwù; 剩下的人 shèngxiàde rén. **re·mains** *n pl* **(a)** 残〔殘〕存者 cáncúnzhě; 剩下的东〔東〕西 shèngxiàde dōngxi. **(b)** 遗体〔體〕yítǐ.

re·mark /rɪ'mɑ:k/ *vt/i* **1** 说起 shuōqǐ; 谈到 tándào. **2 ~ (*up*)*on*** 评论〔論〕pínglùn. □ *n* **1** [U] 注意 zhùyì; 觉〔覺〕察 juéchá: *nothing worthy of ~* 没有什么值得注意的. **2** [C] 评论 pínglùn; 谈论 tánlùn: *a few rude ~s* 粗鲁的谈话. **~able** /-əbl/ *adj* 不平常的bù píngcháng de; 值得注意的 zhíde zhùyì de. **~ably** *adv*

re·medial /rɪ'mi:dɪəl/ *adj* 治疗〔療〕的 zhìliáode; 补〔補〕救的 bǔjiùde.

rem·edy /'remədɪ/ *n* [C,U] [*pl* -ies] 治疗〔療〕zhìliáo; 补〔補〕救 bǔjiù; 纠正 jiūzhèng. □*vt* [*pt, pp* -ied] 治疗 zhìliáo; 补救 bǔjiù; 纠正 jiūzhèng.

re·mem·ber /rɪ'membə(r)/ *vt/i* **1** 记得 jìdé; 回忆〔憶〕起 huíyì qǐ. **2** 记住 jìzhù; 不忘 búwàng: '*~ to phone me*'. '别忘了给我打电话'. **3** 送礼〔禮〕给… sònglǐ gěi…; 遗赠财产〔產〕给 … yízèng cáichǎn gěi…: *I hope you'll ~ me in your will.* 我希望你在遗嘱中对我有所遗赠. **4 ~ *sb to sb*** 问〔問〕候 wènhòu; 致意 zhìyì. **re·membrance** *n* **(a)** [U] 记忆 jìyì; 回忆 huíyì. **(b)** [C] 纪念物 jìniànwù; 纪念 jìniàn.

re·mind /rɪ'maɪnd/ *vt* 提醒 tíxǐng; 使想起 shǐ xiǎngqǐ. **~er** 提醒物(如信件) tíxǐngwù; 令人回忆〔憶〕的东〔東〕西 lìng rén huíyì de dōngxì.

remi·nisce /ˌremɪ'nɪs/ *vi* ~ **(*about*)** 回忆〔憶〕huíyì; 话旧〔舊〕huàjiù. **remi·nis·cence** /-sns/ *n* **(a)** [U] 回忆 huíyì; 怀〔懷〕旧 huáijiù. **(b)** [*pl*] 回忆录〔錄〕huíyìlù; 怀旧谈 huáijiù tán. **remi·nis·cent** /-snt/ *adj* 回忆往事的 huíyì wǎngshì de; 话旧的 huàjiùde.

re·mis·sion /rɪ'mɪʃn/ *n* **1** [U] 宽恕 kuānshù; 赦免 shèmiǎn. **2** [C,U] 免除(处罚) miǎnchú.

re·mit /rɪ'mɪt/ *vt/i* [-tt-] **1** 豁免(债务等) huōmiǎn; 免除 (处罚) miǎnchú. **2** 汇〔匯〕款 huìkuǎn. **~-tance** *n* [U] 汇款 huìkuǎn; [C]汇款额 huìkuǎn'é.

rem·nant /'remnənt/ *n* [C] 残〔殘〕余〔餘〕cányú; 剩余 shèngyú.

re·mon·strate /'remənstreɪt/ *vi* ~ ***with sb*** 规劝〔勸〕guīquàn. 告诫 gàojiè.

re·morse /rɪ'mɔ:s/ *n* [U] 懊悔 àohuǐ; 悔恨 huǐhèn. **~ful** *adj* 懊悔的 àohuǐde; 悔恨的 huǐhènde. **~less** *adj* 不懊悔的 bú àohuǐ de.

re·mote /rɪ'məʊt/ *adj* [-r, -st] ~ **(*from*)** **1** 久远〔遠〕的 jiǔyuǎnde; 遥远的 yáoyuǎnde. **2** 关〔關〕系

〔係〕远的 guānxì yuǎn de: *ideas too ~ from the subject* 离主题太远的意见 **3** 冷淡的 lěngdànde. **4** 很少的 hěnshǎode: *a ~ possibility* 极小的可能性. ~ **control** 遥控 yáokòng. ~**ly** *adv* ~**ness** *n* [U]

re·move /rɪ'muːv/ *vt/i* **1** 移动〔動〕 yídòng; 搬开〔開〕 bānkāi. **2** 除去 chúqù; 排除 páichú: ~ *oil* 去掉油渍; ~ *stains* 除去污斑; ~ *doubts* 消除疑虑. **3** 免职〔職〕 miǎnzhí; 开除 kāichú. **4** 迁〔遷〕移 qiānyí; 搬家 bānjiā. **5** ~**d** *from* 远〔遠〕离〔離〕的 yuǎnlíde; 疏远的 shūyuǎnde. **re·mover** *n* [C] 去污剂〔劑〕 qùwūjì: *a 'stain ~*退渍物质. **re·moval** *n* [C,U] 移动 yídòng; 除掉 chúdiào.

re·mun·er·ate /rɪ'mjuːnəreɪt/ *vt* [正式用语]报〔報〕酬 bàochóu; 酬劳〔勞〕chóuláo. **re·mun·e'r·ation** *n* [C,U] 报酬 bàochóu. **re·mun·er·ative** /-rətɪv/ *adj* 有利的 yǒulìde; 有报酬的 yǒu bàochóu de.

re·nais·sance /rɪ'neɪsns/ *n* **1 the R~**(欧洲十四至十六世纪的)文艺〔藝〕复〔復〕兴〔興〕 wényì fùxīng. **2** [C] 复兴 fùxīng.

re·nal /'riːnl/ *adj* [解剖]肾〔腎〕脏〔臟〕的 shènzàngde.

ren·der /'rendə(r)/ *vt* **1** 提供(帮助等) tígòng; 报〔報〕答 bàodá: *a reward for services ~ed* 对服务的酬金. **2** 开〔開〕出(帐单) kāichū. **3** 使成 shǐ chéng; 致使 zhìshǐ: *~ed helpless with laughter* 笑得不行了. **4** 表演 biǎoyǎn; 演奏 yǎnzòu: 翻译〔譯〕 fānyì. ~**ing** *n* [C] 表演 biǎoyǎn; 翻译 fānyì.

ren·dez·vous /'rɒndɪvuː/ *n* [C] [*pl* ~] **1** 约会〔會〕 yuēhuì; 集会 jíhuì; 约会地 yuēhuìdì. **2** 聚会的地方 jùhuìde dìfāng. □ *vi* (在指定地点)集合(或聚会、相见) jíhé.

ren·di·tion /ren'dɪʃn/ *n* [C] [正式用语](歌曲等的)解释〔釋〕 jiěshì; 演唱 yǎnchàng; 演奏 yǎnzòu; 翻译(与 *of* 连用) fānyì.

ren·egade /'renɪgeɪd/ *n* [C] 背教者 bèijiàozhě; 叛党〔黨〕者 pàndǎngzhě.

re·new /rɪ'njuː/ *vt* **1** 使新 shǐ xīn; 更新 gēngxīn. **2** 再得 zàidé; 再做 zàizuò: ~ *a contract* 续订契约. ~ *an attack* 再行攻击. **3** 换新 huànxīn; 补〔補〕充 bǔchōng: ~ *one's supplies* 更换补给品. ~**al** *n* [C, U]

re·nounce /rɪ'naʊns/ *vt* **1** 正式宣称〔稱〕(与某人或某事)断〔斷〕绝关〔關〕系〔係〕 zhèngshì xuānchēng duànjué guānxì: ~ *one's faith* 弃绝信仰. **2** 同意放弃〔棄〕(要求、权利) tóngyì fàngqì.

reno·vate /'renəveɪt/ *vt* 修理 xiūlǐ, 恢复〔復〕(旧房屋、油画)成良好状况 huīfù chéng liánghǎo zhuàngkuàng. **reno'va·tion** *n* [C,U]

re·nown /rɪ'naʊn/ *n* [U] 名望 míngwàng; 声〔聲〕誉〔譽〕 shēngyù. ~**ed** *adj*

rent[1] /rent/ *n* [C,U] 租金 zūjīn, 租费 zūfèi. □ *vt/i* **1** 租入 zūrù, 租用 zūyòng. **2** 租出 zūchū. ~**al** /'rentl/ *n* [C] 租费 zūfèi.

rent[2] /rent/ *n* [C] (衣服等的)破裂处〔處〕 pòlièchù; 裂缝 lièfèng.

re·nunci·ation /rɪˌnʌnsɪ'eɪʃn/ *n* [U] 放弃〔棄〕 fàngqì; 拒绝承认〔認〕 jùjué chéngrèn; 自制 zìzhì.

re·or·gan·ize /riː'ɔːgənaɪz/ *vt/i* 改组 gǎizǔ; 改编 gǎibiān; 改革 gǎigé.

rep /rep/ *n* [C] [非正式用语] repertory(company)或 representative 的缩写〔寫〕 *repertory (company)* huò *representative* de suōxiě.

re·pair /rɪ'peə(r)/ *vt* 修理 xiūlǐ; 修补〔補〕 xiūbǔ. □ *n* **1** [U] 修理 xiūlǐ; 修补 xiūbǔ. **2** 修理、补救的工作(过〔過〕程) xiūlǐ bǔjiù de gōngzuò: *road ~s* 道路修理. **3** [U] 维修状〔狀〕况 wéixiū zhuàngkuàng: *in good ~*维修良好.

rep·ar·ation /ˌrepə'reɪʃn/ *n* [C, U] 补〔補〕偿〔償〕 bǔcháng.

re·pat·ri·ate /riː'pætrɪeɪt/ *vt* 遣返 qiǎnfǎn; 遣回 qiǎnhuí. **re·pat·ri'ation** *n* [U]

re·pay /rɪ'peɪ/ *vt/i* [*pt, pp* -paid] **1** 付还〔還〕(钱) fùhuán; 偿〔償〕还 chánghuán. **2** 报〔報〕答 bàodá; 回敬 huíjìng: *How can I ~ your kindness?* 我怎样报答你的盛意呢? ~**ment** *n* [C,U]

re·peal /rɪ'piːl/ *vt* 撤销 chèxiāo; 废〔廢〕除(法令等) fèichú. □ *n* [C, U] 撤销 chèxiāo; 废除 fèichú.

re·peat /rɪ'piːt/ *vt/i* **1** 重说 chóngshuō; 重做 chóngzuò **2** 转〔轉〕述 zhuǎnshù. □ *n* [C] 重复〔複〕 chóngfù; 重演 chóngyǎn. ~**ed·ly** *adv* 反复〔復〕 fǎnfù; 再三 zàisān.

re·pel /rɪ'pel/ *vt* [-ll-] **1** 击〔擊〕退 jītuì; 驱〔驅〕逐 qūzhú: ~ *an invasion* 击退入侵. **2** 使厌〔厭〕恶〔惡〕 shǐ yànwù; 使反感 shǐ fǎncǎn. ~**lent** *adj* 讨厌的 tǎoyànde. □ *n* [C] 令人厌〔厭〕恶之物 lìng rén yànwù zhī wù: *'insect ~* 驱虫剂.

re·pent /rɪ'pent/ *vt/i* ~ (*of*) 悔悟 huǐwù; 后〔後〕悔 hòuhuǐ. ~**ance**

n [U] 悔悟 huǐwù; 后悔 hòuhuǐ. ~**ant** *adj*

re·per·cus·sion /ˌri:pəˈkʌʃn/ *n* [C] [通常用 *pl*] 反响〔響〕fǎnxiǎng; 反应〔應〕fǎnyìn; 影响 yǐngxiǎng.

rep·er·toire /ˈrepətwɑ:(r)/ *n* [C] 全部剧〔劇〕目 quánbù jùmù; 全部节〔節〕目 quánbù jiémù.

rep·er·tory /ˈrepətrɪ/ *n* [C] [*pl* -ies] = repertoire. ˈ~ **company** 定期换演剧〔劇〕目的剧团〔團〕dìngqī huànyǎn jùmù de jùtuán. ~ **theatre** (缩作 **rep**) 某剧团定期换演剧目的剧场〔場〕mǒujùtuán dìngqī huànyǎn jùmù de jùchǎng.

rep·eti·tion /ˌrepəˈtɪʃn/ *n* [C,U] 重复〔複〕chóngfù; 重说 chóngshuō; 重做 chóngzuò. **re·peti·tive** /rɪˈpetətɪv/ *adj* 重复的 chóngfùde; 反复的 fǎnfùde.

re·phrase /ri:ˈfreɪz/ *vt* 再措辞〔辭〕zài cuòcí; 改变〔變〕措辞 gǎibiàn cuòcí.

re·place /rɪˈpleɪs/ *vt* **1** 放回 fànghuí. **2** 代替 dàitì; 取代 qǔdài. ~**ment** *n* [U] 代替 dàitì; [C] 代替者 dàitìzhě; 替换物 tìhuànwù.

re·plen·ish /rɪˈplenɪʃ/ *vt* [正式用语]再装〔裝〕满 zài zhuāngmǎn; 补〔補〕充 bǔchōng.

rep·lica /ˈreplɪkə/ *n* [C] [*pl* ~s] 复〔復〕制〔製〕品 fùzhìpǐn.

re·ply /rɪˈplaɪ/ *vt/i* [*pt, pp* -ied] 回答 huídá, 答复〔復〕dáfù. □ *n* [C] 回答 huídá, 答复 dáfù.

re·port[1] /rɪˈpɔ:t/ *n* **1** [C] 报〔報〕告 bàogào; 报道 bàodào. **2** [C, U] 谣〔謠〕言 yáoyán; 传〔傳〕闻〔聞〕chuánwén. **3** [C] 爆炸声〔聲〕bàozhàshēng.

re·port[2] /rɪˈpɔ:t/ *vt/i* **1** 报〔報〕道 bàodào. **2** ~ *(up)on* 报告 bàogào; 汇〔匯〕报 huìbào. ~ *sb (to sb)* 告发〔發〕gàofā; 控告 kònggào. ~**ed speech** = indirect speech. ~**er** 记者 jìzhě; 通讯员 tōngxùnyuán.

re·pose /rɪˈpəʊz/ *vt/i* [正式用语] 休息 xiūxi. □ *n* [U] [正式用语] 休息 xiūxi; 睡眠 shuìmián.

rep·re·sent /ˌreprɪˈzent/ *vt* **1** 表示 biǎoshì; 象征〔徵〕xiàngzhēng: *symbols that ~ people* 代表着人物的象征. **2** 声〔聲〕称〔稱〕shēngchēng: *He ~ed himself as an expert.* 他声称自己是一位专家. **3** 代表 dàibiǎo. ~**a·tion** /-ˈteɪʃən/ *n* [C, U]

rep·re·sen·ta·tive/ˌreprɪˈzentətɪv/ *adj* **1** 代表的 dàibiǎode; 代表性的 dàibiǎoxìngde: *a ~ sample* 有代表性的样品. **2** 代议〔議〕制的 dàiyìzhìde: ~ *goverment* 代议政体. □ *n* [C] **1** 典型(与 *of* 连用) diǎnxíng. **2** 代表 dàibiǎo.

re·press /rɪˈpres/ *vt* 镇压〔壓〕zhènyā; 抑制 yìzhì: ~ *emotions* 抑制情绪. ~ *a nation* 镇压一个民族. **re·pres·sion** /-ʃn/ *n* [U] ~-**ive** *adj*

re·prieve /rɪˈpri:v/ *vt* **1** 缓处〔處〕死刑 huǎnchǔ sǐxíng. □ *n* [C] 缓刑 huǎnxíng; 暂〔暫〕缓 zànhuǎn.

re·pri·mand /ˌreprɪˈmɑ:nd/ *vt* 惩〔懲〕戒 chěngjiè; 谴责 qiǎnzé. □ *n* /ˈreprɪmɑ:nd/ [C] 惩戒 chěngjiè; 谴责 qiǎnzé.

re·prisal /rɪˈpraɪzl/ *n* **1** [C,U] 报〔報〕复〔復〕bàofù; 报复行为〔爲〕bàofù xíngwéi.

re·proach /rɪˈprəʊtʃ/ *vt* ~ *sb (for sth)* 责备〔備〕zébèi; 指责 zhǐzé. □ *n* **1** [U] 责备 zébèi; 指责 zhǐzé. **2** [C] 责备〔備〕的言词 zébèide yáncí. *above (beyond)* ~ 无〔無〕可指责 wúkě zhǐzé.

re·pro·duce /ˌri:prəˈdju:s/ *vt/i* **1** 复〔復〕制〔製〕fùzhì; 翻版 fānbǎn; 重演 chóngyǎn. **2** 繁殖 fánzhí; 生殖 shēngzhí. **re·pro·duc·tion** /ˌri:prəˈdʌkʃn/ *n* [C,U] **re·pro·duc·tive** *adj*

rep·tile /ˈreptaɪl/ *n* [C] 爬行动〔動〕物(如蜥蜴、蛇) páxíng dòngwù; 爬虫〔蟲〕páchóng. **rep·til·ian** /repˈtɪlɪən/ *adj*

re·pub·lic /rɪ pʌblɪk/ *n* [C] 共和国〔國〕gònghéguó; 共和政体〔體〕gònghé zhèngtǐ. ~**an** *adj* 共和国的 gònghéguóde; 共和政体的 gònghé zhèngtǐ de. □ *n* [C] **(a)** 拥〔擁〕护〔護〕共和政体者 yōnghù gònghé zhèngtǐ zhě. **(b) R**~ (美国)共和党党员 gònghédǎng dǎngyuán.

re·pug·nant /rɪˈpʌɡnənt/ *adj* [正式用语]令人厌〔厭〕恶〔惡〕的 lìng rén yànwù de; 使人反感的 shǐ rén fǎngǎn de. **re·pug·nance** *n* [U]

re·pulse /rɪˈpʌls/ *vt* **1** 打退(敌人) dǎtuì. **2** 拒绝 jùjué. **re·pul·sion** /-ʃn/*n* [U] **(a)** 厌〔厭〕恶〔惡〕yànwù; 反感 fángǎn. **(b)** [物理]排斥 páichì; 斥力 chìlì. **re·pul·sive** *adj*

repu·table /ˈrepjʊtəbl/ *adj* 声〔聲〕誉〔譽〕好的 shēngyù hǎo de.

repu·ta·tion /ˌrepjʊˈteɪʃn/ *n* [U] 名誉〔譽〕míngyù; 名声〔聲〕míngshēng.

re·pute /rɪˈpju:t/ *vt* *be ~d to be* 称〔稱〕为〔爲〕chēngwéi; 认〔認〕

为 rènwéi. □ *n* [U] **1** 名誉〔譽〕míngyù; 名声〔聲〕míngshēng. **2** 美名 měimíng; 声望 shēngwàng: *a doctor of* ~ 名医. ~**d·ly** /-ədlɪ/ *adv* 一般认为 yìbān rènwéi; 号〔號〕称〔稱〕地 hàochēngde.

re·quest /rɪ'kwest/ *n* **1** [U] 请求 qǐngqiú, 要求 yāoqiú: ~*s for help* 请求帮助. ~*s for more money* 请求更多的资助. **2** [C] 要求的事物 yāoqiúde shìwù. □ *vt* 请求 qǐngqiú, 要求 yāoqiú.

re·quire /rɪ'kwaɪə(r)/ *vt* **1** 需要 xūyào: *My car* ~*s some attention.* 我的汽车需要修理一下 **2** [正式用语]命令 mìnglìng; 要求 yāoqiú: *be~ed to pay a fine* 被命令交罚款. ~**ment** *n* [C][正式用语] 需要 xūyào; 需要的东〔東〕西 xūyàode dōngxi.

requi·site/'rekwɪzɪt/ *n* [C], *adj* 必需品 bìxūpǐn; 需要的 xūyàode; 必要的 bìyàode.

res. = **1** residence. **2** resigned. **3** reserved.

res·cue /'reskju:/ *vt* 援救 yuánjiù; 营〔營〕救 yíngjiù; 挽救 wǎnjiù. □ *n* [C, U] 援救 yuánjiù; 营救 yíngjiù.

re·search /rɪ'sɜ:tʃ/ *n* [C,U] 调查 diàochá; 研究 yánjiū. □ *vi* ~ **(*into*)** 调查 diàochá, 研究 yánjiū. ~**er** 调查者 diàocházhě; 学〔學〕术〔術〕研究者 xuéshù yánjiū zhě.

re·sem·blance /rɪ'zembləns/*n* [C, U] 相似 xiāngsì; 类〔類〕似 lèisì.

re·semble /rɪ'zembl/ *vt* 象 xiàng, 类〔類〕似 lèisì.

re·sent /rɪ'zent/ *vt* 对〔對〕... 不满 duì ... bùmǎn; 怨恨 yuànhèn: ~ *his success* 对他的成功心怀怨恨. ~**ful** *adj* ~**ment** *n* [U]

res·er·va·tion/ˌrezə'veɪʃn/ *n* **1** [C,U] 保留 bǎoliú: *accept a plan with* ~*s* 有保留的接受一项计划. **2** [C] 保留地 bǎoliúdì; 专〔專〕用地 zhuānyòngdì: *the Indian* ~*s* 印第安人保留地. **3** [C] 预定 (如火车票、旅馆房间等) yùdìng.

re·serve /rɪ'zɜ:v/ *n* **1** [C] 保存bǎocún. **2** [用 *sing* 或 *pl*][军事]后〔後〕备〔備〕军〔軍〕hòubèijūn; 预备队〔隊〕yùbèiduì. **3** [U] *in* ~储备 chǔbèi. **4** [C] 专〔專〕用地 zhuānyòngde; 保留地 bǎoliúde: *a 'game* ~ 狩猎保留地. **5** [U] 自我克制 zì wǒ kèzhì; 缄默 jiānmò. **6** (体育)预备队员 yùbèi duìyuán. □ *vt* **1** 储备 chǔbèi; 保存 bǎocún. **2** 预定 yùdìng: ~ *a seat on a train* 预定火车座位. **re·served** *adj* 保留的 bǎoliúde; 缄默的 jiānmòde.

res·er·voir /'rezəvwa:(r)/ *n* [C] 水库〔庫〕shuǐkù; 蓄水池 xùshuǐchí.

re·side /rɪ'zaɪd/ *vi* [正式用语] **1** ~ **(*in, at*)** 居住 jūzhù. **2** ~ *in* (权力等) 属〔屬〕shǔ; 归〔歸〕guī.

resi·dence /'rezɪdəns/ *n* [正式用语] **1** [U] 居住 jūzhù. ***in*** ~, **(a)** (官员)住在任所的 zhù zài rènsuǒ de. **(b)** (大学)住校的 zhùxiàode. **2** 住处〔處〕zhùchù; 住宅 zhùzhái.

resi·dent /'rezɪdənt/ *adj* 居住的 jūzhùde: *the* ~ *population* 居民人口. □ *n* [C] 居民 jūmín. ~**ial** /-'denʃl/ *adj* 住宅的 zhùzháide: ~*ial parts of town* 城镇的住宅区.

re·sid·ual /rɪ'zɪdjʊəl/ *adj* 剩余〔餘〕的 shèngyúde; 残〔殘〕留的 cánliúde.

resi·due /'rezɪdju:/ *n* [C] 残〔殘〕余〔餘〕cányú; 剩余 shèngyú; 留数〔數〕liúshù.

re·sign /rɪ'zaɪn/ *vt/i* **1** 放弃〔棄〕fàngqì; 辞〔辭〕去 cíqù. **2** ~ ***oneself to sth*** 听〔聽〕任 tīngrèn; 顺从〔從〕shùncóng. ~**ed** *adj* 屈从的 qūcóngde; 顺从的 shùncóngde.

res·ig·na·tion /ˌrezɪg'neɪʃn/ *n* **1** [C,U] 放弃〔棄〕fàngqì; 辞〔辭〕职〔職〕cízhí; 辞职书〔書〕cízhíshū. **2** [U] 听〔聽〕从〔從〕tīngcóng; 顺从 shùncóng: *accept failure with* ~ 无可奈何地接受失败.

re·sil·ience /rɪ'zɪlɪəns/ *n* **1** [U] 回弹〔彈〕huítán; 弹性 tánxìng; 回能 huínéng; 弹能 tánnéng. **2** [喻] 恢复〔復〕力 huīfùlì; 复原力 fùyuánlì. **re·sil·ient** *adj*

resin /'rezɪn/ *n* [C,U] 树〔樹〕脂 shùzhī; 松香 sōngxiāng.

re·sist /rɪ'zɪst/ *vt/i* **1** 抵抗 dǐkàng; 反抗 fǎnkàng. **2** 不受 ... 的影响〔響〕búshòu ... de yǐngxiǎng: *glass that* ~*s heat* 耐热玻璃. **3** 抵制 dǐzhì; 抗拒 kàngjù: ~ *temptation* 不受引诱. ~**ance** *n* **(a)** [U] 抵抗 dǐkàng; 反抗 fǎnkàng. **(b)** **(c)** [U] 抵抗力 dǐkànglì; 阻力 zǔlì: *wind* ~*ance* 风的阻力. ~**ant** *adj* 抵抗的 dǐkàngde; 反抗的 fǎnkàngde.

re·sis·tor /rɪ'zɪstə(r)/ *n* [C] 电〔電〕阻 diànzǔ; 电阻器 diànzǔqì.

res·ol·ute /'rezəlu:t/ *adj* [正式用语]坚〔堅〕决的 jiānjuéde; 坚定的 jiāndìngde. ~**ly** *adv* ~**ness** *n* [U]

res·ol·ution /ˌrezə'lu:ʃn/ *n* **1** [U] 坚〔堅〕决 jiānjué; 坚定 jiāndìng. **2** [C] 决议〔議〕juéyì; 决定 juédìng. **3** [C] 决心 juéxīn. **4** [U] 解

决 jiějué. ⇨ resolve(3). 5 [U] 分解 fēnjiě: *the ~ of white light into the colours of the spectrum.* 将白色的光分解成光谱的各种颜色.

re·solve /rɪ'zɒlv/ *vt/i* 1 决定 juédìng; 决心 juéxīn. 2 议〔議〕决 yìjué. 3 解决(疑问、困难等) jiějué. □ *n* [C] 已决定的事物 yǐ juédìngde shìwù.

res·on·ant /'rezənənt/ *adj* 反响〔響〕的 fǎnxiǎngde; 共鸣〔鳴〕的 gòngmíngde. **res·on·ance** *n* [U] 回声〔聲〕 huíshēng; 共鸣 gòngmíng.

re·sort /rɪ'zɔːt/ *vi* ~ *to* 求助 qiúzhù; 凭〔憑〕借〔藉〕 píngjiè. □ *n* 1 *in the* (*as a*) *last* ~ 孤注一掷〔擲〕 gū zhù yí zhì; (一切失败后)作为最后〔後〕的手段 zuòwéi zuìhòude shǒuduàn2 [C] 常去的地方 chángqùde dìfāng; *a 'seaside* ~ 海滨胜地.

re·sound /rɪ'zaʊnd/ *vt/i* 回响〔響〕 huíxiǎng; 反响 fǎnxiǎng. ~**ing** *adj* (a) 响〔響〕亮的 xiǎngliàngde: *~ing cheers* 响亮的欢呼. (b) 重大的 zhòngdàde: *a ~ing success.* 重大的成功.

re·source /rɪ'sɔːs/ *n* 1 [*pl*] 资源 zīyuán; 富源 fùyuán. 2 [C] 有助于做某事的东〔東〕西 yǒuzhù yú zuò mǒushì de dōngxi. 3 [U] 机〔機〕智 jīzhì; 应〔應〕变〔變〕之才 yìngbiàn zhī cái. ~**ful** *adj* 机智的 jīzhìde; 善于随机应变的 shànyú suí jī yìngbiàn de. ~**fully** *adv*

resp. = respectively.

re·spect /rɪ'spekt/ *n* 1 [U] 尊敬 zūnjìng; 敬重 jìngzhòng. 2 [U] 考虑 kǎolǜ: *show ~ for his wishes* 重视他的愿望. 3 *with ~ to* 关〔關〕于 guānyú: *with ~ to your request* 关于你的要求 4 [C] 细节 xìjié. *in some ~s* 在某些方面 zài mǒuxiē fāngmiàn. 5 [*pl*] 敬意 jìngyì; 问〔問〕候 wènhòu: *give her my ~s* 请代我向她致意. □ *vt* 尊敬 zūnjìng; 尊重 zūnzhòng.

re·spect·able /rɪ'spektəbl/ *adj* 1 值得尊敬的 zhídé zūnjìng de. 2 高尚的 gāoshàngde; 有身分的 yǒu shēngfen de. 3 体〔體〕面 的tǐmiànde. 4 相当〔當〕大的 xiāngdāngdà de; 可观〔觀〕的 kěguānde: *a ~ income* 可观的收入. **re·spect·ably** *adv*

re·spect·ful /rɪ'spektfl/ *adj* [正式用语]尊敬的 zūnjìngde. ~**ly** *adv*

re·spect·ive /rɪ'spektɪv/ *adj* 个〔個〕别的 gèbiéde; 各个的 gègèi de: *We went to our ~ homes.* 我们都回到各自的家里. ~**ly** *adv* 个别地 gèbiéde; 各自地 gèzìde.

res·pir·ation /ˌrespə'reɪʃn/ *n* [U] 呼吸 hūxī; [C] 一次呼吸 yícì hūxī.

res·pite /'respaɪt/ *n* [C] 休息 xiūxi; 中止 zhōngzhǐ.

re·splen·dent /rɪ'splendənt/ *adj* 灿〔燦〕烂〔爛〕的 cànlànde; 辉〔輝〕煌的 huīhuángde. ~**ly** *adv*

re·spond /rɪ'spɒnd/ *vi* 1 ~(*to*) 回答 huídá. 2 响〔響〕应〔應〕 xiǎngyìng. 3 反应〔應〕 fǎnyìng: *~ to treatment* 治疗生效.

re·sponse /rɪ'spɒns/ *n* 1 [C] 回答 huídá. 2 [C,U] 反应〔應〕 fǎnyìng.

re·spon·si·bil·ity /rɪˌspɒnsə'bɪlətɪ/ *n* [*pl* -ies] 1 [U] 责任 zérèn. 2 [C] 职〔職〕责 zhízé; 义〔義〕务〔務〕 yìwù.

re·spon·sible /rɪ'spɒnsəbl/ *adj* 1 负责任的 fùzérènde. 2 有责任的 yǒu zérèn de. 3 可信赖的 kě xìnlài de; 可靠的 kěkàode: *a ~ man* 可靠的人. **re·spon·sibly** *adv*

re·spon·sive /rɪ'spɒnsɪv/ *adj* (对…) 易于或迅速反应〔應〕的 yìyú huò xùnsù fǎŋyìng de: *~ to treatment* 对治疗易起反应的.

rest[1] /rest/ *n* 1 [U] 休息 xiūxi; 睡眠 shuìmián. *at ~*, (a) 静止 jìngzhǐ; 安静 ānjìng. (b) 安息 ānxī, 长〔長〕眠 chángmián. 2 [C] 撑架 chēngjià; 支座 zhīzuò; 托 tuō: *an 'arm-~* 扶手. 3 [C] [音乐] 休止 xiūzhǐ; 休止符 xiūzhǐfú. ~**ful** *adj* 使平静的 shǐ píngjìng de. ~**less** *adj* 没有休息的 méiyǒu xiūxi de; 不安定的 bù āndìng de.

rest[2] /rest/ *vt/i* 1 平静 píngjìng; 静止 jìngzhǐ. 2 (使)休息 xiūxi. 3 支撑 (与 *on, against* 连用) zhīcheng; 搁〔擱〕 gē:

rest[3] /rest/ *vi* 1 依然 yīrán: *You may ~ assured that* 你尽可放心. 2 ~ *with* 由 … 负责 yóu … fùzé. *The decision ~s with you.* 全由你来决定. 3 ~ (*up*)*on* 依赖 yīlài; 依靠 yīkào.

rest[4] /rest/ *n* (*the* ~) 1 其余〔餘〕 qíyú; 剩余部分 shèngyú bùfen. 2 [用 *pl verb*] 其余的人 qíyúde rén.

res·taur·ant /'restrɑːnt/ *n* [C] 饭店 fàngdiàn, 餐馆 cānguǎn, 菜馆 càiguǎn.

res·ti·tu·tion /ˌrestɪ'tjuːʃn/ *n* [U] 1 归〔歸〕还〔還〕 guīhuán; 赔偿〔償〕 péicháng. 2 = reparation.

res·tive /'restɪv/ *adj* (指人) 不耐烦的 bú nàifán de; 不安静的 bù ānjìng de. ~**ly** *adv*

res·to·ra·tion /ˌrestə'reɪʃn/ *n* 1

[U] 恢复〔復〕huīfù; 复原 fùyuán. **2** [C] 修建 xiūjiàn; 重建 chóngjiàn.

re·stora·tive /rɪ'stɔːrətɪv/ *adj* 恢复〔復〕健康（或体力）的 huīfù jiànkāng de. ☐ *n* [C,U] 营〔營〕养〔養〕食品 yíngyǎng shípǐn; 补〔補〕药〔藥〕bǔyào.

re·store /rɪ'stɔː(r)/ *vt* **1** 归〔歸〕还〔還〕guīhuán; 交还 jiāohuán: ~ *stolen goods* 归还偷窃的货物. **2** 恢复〔復〕huīfù; 复原 fùyuán. **3** 修复 xiūfù; 重建 chóngjiàn. **4** 复职〔職〕fùzhí; 复位 fùwèi: ~ *the monarchy* 恢复君主政体. **~er** 修补〔補〕者(尤指使旧油画复原的专家) xiūbǔzhě; 修补物 xiūbǔwù.

re·strain /rɪ'streɪn/ *vt* 抑制 yìzhì; 制止 zhìzhǐ. **~ed** *adj* 受约束的 shòuyuēshùde. **re·straint** *n* [C, U] 抑制 yìzhì; 约束 yuēshù.

re·strict /rɪ'strɪkt/ *vt* 限制 xiànzhì; 约束 yuēshù. **re'stric·tion** /-ʃn/ *n* [C,U] **~ive** *adj* 限制的 xiànzhìde; 约束的 yuēshùde.

re·sult /rɪ'zʌlt/ *vi* **1** ~ (*from*) 起因 qǐyīn; 由来〔來〕yóulái. **2** ~*in* 导〔導〕致 dǎozhì; 终归〔歸〕zhōngguī. ☐ *n* **1** [C,U] 结果 jiéguǒ; 效果 xiàoguǒ. **2** [C] [数学]（计算）结果 jiéguǒ; 答案 dá'àn. **3**（体育）比分 bǐfēn. **~ant** *adj* 结果的 jiéguǒde.

re·sume /rɪ'zjuːm/ *vt* **1** 重新开〔開〕始 chóngxīn kāishǐ; 继〔繼〕续〔續〕jìxù. **2** 重新占〔佔〕用 chóngxīn zhànyòng: ~ *one's seat* 回到原座.

ré·sumé /'rezuːmeɪ/ *n* [C] 摘要 zhāiyào; 梗概 gěnggài.

re·sump·tion /rɪ'zʌmpʃn/ *n* [C, U] 再开〔開〕始 zài kāishǐ; 恢复〔復〕huīfù; 重新占〔佔〕用 chóngxīn zhànyòng.

res·ur·rect /ˌrezə'rekt/ *vt/i*（使）复〔復〕活 fùhuó; 复兴〔興〕fùxīng; 恢复 huīfù. **res·ur'rec·tion** /-ʃn/ *n* [U] **(a)** **the R~ion**（基督教）耶稣复〔復〕活 Yēsū fùhuó;（上帝最后审判日）全体〔體〕死者的复活 quántǐ sǐzhě de fùhuó. **(b)** 复活 fùhuó; 复兴〔興〕fùxīng; 恢复 huīfù.

re·sus·ci·tate /rɪ'sʌsɪteɪt/ *vt/i*（使）恢复〔復〕知觉〔覺〕huīfù zhījué;（使）苏〔蘇〕醒 sūxǐng. **re·sus·ci'ta·tion** *n* [U]

re·tail /'riːteɪl/ *n* [C] 零售 língshòu, 零卖〔賣〕língmài. ⇨wholesale. ☐ *adv* 按照零售 ànzhào língshòu. ☐ *vt/i* 零售 língshòu, 零卖 língmài. **~er** 零售商 língshòushāng.

re·tain /rɪ'teɪn/ *vt* **1** 保持 bǎochí; 保有 bǎoyǒu. **2** 聘请（律师）pìnqǐng. **~er** *n* [C] **(a)** 律师〔師〕费 lǜshīfèi. **(b)**（旧用法）侍从〔從〕shìcóng; 仆〔僕〕人 púrén.

re·tali·ate /rɪ'tælɪeɪt/ *vi* 报〔報〕复〔復〕bàofù; 还〔還〕击〔擊〕huánjī; 回敬 huíjìng. **re·tali'ation** *n* [U]

re·tard /rɪ'tɑːd/ *vt* 阻止 zǔzhǐ; 妨碍〔礙〕fáng'ài.

retch /retʃ/ *vi* 干〔乾〕呕〔嘔〕gān'ǒu.

re·ten·tion /rɪ'tenʃn/ *n* [U] 保持 bǎochí; 保留 bǎoliú.

re·ten·tive /rɪ'tentɪv/ *adj* 保持的 bǎochíde; 有保持力的 yǒu bǎochílì de: *a ~ memory* 强的记忆力.

reti·cent /'retɪsnt/ *adj* 沉默寡言的 chénmò guǎyán de; 言不尽〔盡〕意的 yán bú jìn yì de. **reti·cence** *n* [C,U]

ret·ina /'retɪnə/ *n* [C] [*pl* ~s 或 -nae /-niː/] [解剖] 视网〔網〕膜 shìwǎngmó.

reti·nue /'retɪnjuː/ *n* [C]（高级官员等的）随员 suíyuán.

re·tire /rɪ'taɪə(r)/ *vt/i* **1** 退下 tuìxià; 离〔離〕开〔開〕líkāi; 撤退 chètuì. **2** [正式用语] 就寝〔寢〕jiùqǐn. **3** 退休 tuìxiū; 退职〔職〕tuìzhí; 退役 tuìyì. **4** 使（某人）退休 shǐ ... tuìxiū. **re·tired** *adj* 退休的 tuìxiūde; 退职的 tuìzhíde; 退役的 tuìyìde. **re·tir·ing** *adj* 孤独〔獨〕的 gūdúde; 缄默的 jiānmòde. **~ment** *n* [U]

re·tort /rɪ'tɔːt/ *vt/i* 反驳〔駁〕fǎnbó; 反击〔擊〕fǎnjī. ☐ *n* [C, U] 反驳 fǎnbó.

re·trace /rɪː'treɪs/ *vt* **1** 折回 zhéhuí; 折返 zhéfǎn: ~ *one's steps* 走回头路. **2** 回忆〔憶〕huíyì; 回顾〔顧〕huígù.

re·tract /rɪ'trækt/ *vt/i* **1** 撤回 chèhuí; 收回 shōuhuí. **2** 缩进〔進〕suōjìn; 缩回 suōhuí: *A cat can ~ its claws.* 猫能缩回它的爪子. **~able** /-əbl/ *adj* 能收回的 néng shōuhuí de; 能缩进的 néng suōjìn de, **re'trac·tion** /-ʃn/ *n* [C,U]

re·treat /rɪ'triːt/ *vi*（尤指军队）退却 tuìque, 后〔後〕退 hòutuì. ☐ *n* **1** [C,U] 撤退 chètuì; 退却 tuìquè. **2** [C] 退却号〔號〕tuìquèhào, 降旗号 jiàngqíhào; 归〔歸〕营〔營〕号 guīyínhào. **3** [C,U] 一段安静和休息时〔時〕间〔間〕yíduàn ānjìng hé xiūxi shíjiān; 宁〔寧〕静的休息处〔處〕níngjìngde xiūxichù.

ret·ri·bu·tion /ˌretrɪ'bjuːʃn/ *n*

[U] 惩〔懲〕罚 chěngfá; 报〔報〕应〔應〕bàoying.

re·trieve /rɪ'triːv/ *vt/i* **1** 再获〔獲〕得 zài huòdé. **2** ~ ***sth*** **(*from*)** 挽回 wǎnhuí; 挽救 wǎnjiù. **3** (猎犬) 找回 zhǎohuí; 衔回 (被击中的猎物) xiánhuí. **re·trieval** *n* [U] 补〔補〕偿〔償〕bǔcháng; 补救的行动〔動〕bǔjiùde xíngdòng. **re·triever** 衔回猎〔獵〕物的猎犬 xiánhuí lièwù de lièquǎn.

retro·grade /'retrəgreɪd/ *adj* 后〔後〕退的 hòutuìde; 退步的 tuìbùde; 退化的 tuìhuàde.

retro·gres·sion /ˌretrə'greʃn/ *n* [U] 倒退 dàotuì; 退步 tuìbù; 退化 tuìhuà. **retro·gres·sive** /-sɪv/ *adj*

retro·spect /'retrəspekt/ *n* ***in*** ~ 回顾〔顧〕huígù; 回想 huíxiǎng. **ret-ro·spec·tion** /-'spekʃn/ *n* [C,U] ~**ive** /-'spektɪv/ *adj*

re·turn[1] /rɪ'tɜːn/ *n* **1** [C,U] 回来〔來〕huílái; 返回 fǎnhuí: *our ~ from holiday* 我们度假归来. ***in*** ~ **(*for*)** 作为〔爲〕...的报〔報〕答 zuò: wéi...de bàodá. **2** [C] 〔常 *pl*〕利润〔潤〕lìrùn; 利润率 lìrùnlǜ. **3** [C] 报〔報〕告(书) bàogào; 报告表 bàogàobiǎo: *fill in one's tax ~* 填写税单. ~ **ticket** 〔美语 = *round-trip ticket*〕来回票 láihuípiào.

re·turn[2] /rɪ'tɜːn/ *vt/i* **1** 回来〔來〕huílái; 返回 fǎnhuí. **2** 回复〔復〕huífù; 恢复 huīfù. **3** 送回 sònghuí; 归〔歸〕还〔還〕guīhuán: *~ damaged goods to the shop* 将破损货物退回商店. **4** (选区) 选〔選〕举〔舉〕xuǎnjǔ; 选出 xuǎnchū.

re·un·ion /ˌriː'juːnɪən/ *n*, **1** [U] 再结合 zài jiéhé; 再联〔聯〕合 zài liánhé. **2** [C] (尤指) 重聚 chóngjù; 团〔團〕聚 tuánjù.

Rev. = Reverend

re·veal /rɪ'viːl/ *vt* **1** 展现 zhǎnxiàn; 露出 lùchū. **2** 揭示 jiēshì; 揭露 jiēlù: *~ a secret* 泄露秘密.

revel /'revl/ *vi* [-ll-, 美语亦作 -l-] ~ ***in*** 着迷 zháomí; 深爱〔愛〕shēn'ài: *~ in his success* 他因成功而扬扬得意.

rev·el·ation /ˌrevə'leɪʃn/ *n* **1** [U] 揭露 jiēlù; 泄〔洩〕露 xièlù. **2** [C] 揭露的事物 jiēlùde shìwù.

re·venge /rɪ'vendʒ/ *vt* 报〔報〕仇 bàochóu; 报复〔復〕bàofù. ⇨ avenge. □ *n* [U] 报仇 bàochóu; 报复 bàofù: *take ~ on* 向...报仇.

rev·enue /'revənjuː/ *n* [U] (国家的) 岁〔歲〕入 suìrù; 税收 shuìshōu. ⇨Inland Revenue.

re·ver·ber·ate /rɪ'vɜːbəreɪt/ *vt/i* 反响〔響〕fǎnxiǎng; 回响 huíxiǎng. **re·ver·be'r·ation** *n* [U] 回响 huíxiǎng; [*pl*] 反响 fǎnxiǎng.

re·vere /rɪ'vɪə(r)/ *vt* 崇敬 chóngjìng; 尊敬 zūnjìng.

rev·er·ence /'revərəns/ *n* [U] 崇敬 chóngjìng; 尊敬 zūnjìng.

rev·er·end /'revərənd/ *adj* 应〔應〕受尊敬的 yīng shòu zūnjìng de. □ *n* **the R**~ (缩作 **Revd**) 牧师〔師〕(或神父等) 的尊称〔稱〕mùshīde zūnchēng.

rev·er·ent /'revərənt/ *adj* 恭敬的 gōngjìngde; 虔诚的 qiánchéngde. ~**ly** *adv*

re·ver·sal /rɪ'vɜːsl/ *n* [C,U] 反转〔轉〕fǎnzhuǎn; 倒转 dàozhuǎn.

re·verse /rɪ'vɜːs/ *adj* 相反的 xiāngfǎnde; 颠倒的 diāndǎode: *in ~ order* 倒序地. □ *n* **1** [U] 〔与 *the* 连用〕相对〔對〕xiāngduì; 相反 xiāngfǎn. **2** [C] (机械) 逆转〔轉〕(倒退) 装置 nìzhuǎn zhuāngzhì: *~ gear* 倒车档. **3** [C] 失败 shībài; 倒霉 dǎoméi. □ *vt/i* 反转〔轉〕fǎnzhuǎn; 颠倒 diāndǎo. **2** (使) 倒退 dàotuì: *~ car* 倒车. **3** 撤消 chèxiāo; 取消 qǔxiāo: *~ a decision* 撤消一项决定.

re·vert /rɪ'vɜːt/ *vi* ~ **(*to*)** **1** 回复〔復〕huífù. **2** 〔法律〕(财产等) 归〔歸〕还〔還〕guīhuán; 归属 guīshǔ.

re·view /rɪ'vjuː/ *vt/i* **1** 回顾〔顧〕huígù; 再检〔檢〕查 zài jiǎnchá; 复审〔審〕fùshěn: *~ the past* 回顾过去. *~ a decision* 复查一项决定. **2** 检〔檢〕阅〔閲〕jiǎnyuè. **3** 评论〔論〕pínglùn. □ *n* **1** [C,U] 检查 jiǎnchá; 回顾 huígù; 复习 fùxí; 复审 fùshěn. **2** [C] 检阅 jiǎnyuè; 阅兵 yuèbīng. **3** [C] 评论 pínglùn. **4** [C] 评论性刊物 pínglùnxìng kānwù. ~**er** 评论家 pínglùnjiā.

re·vise /rɪ'vaɪz/ *vt/i* **1** 重新考虑〔慮〕chóngxīn kǎolǜ: *~ an opinion* 改变主意. **2** 复〔復〕习〔習〕fùxí: *~ a lesson (for an exam)* 复习功课 (为预备考试). **re·vi·sion** /rɪ'vɪʒn/ *n* **(a)** [C,U] 修订 xiūdìng; 校订 jiàodìng; 修改 xiūgǎi. **(b)** [C] 修订本 xiūdìngběn.

re·vive /rɪ'vaɪv/ *vt/i* **1** 苏〔蘇〕醒 sūxǐng; 复〔復〕活 fùhuó. **2** 复兴〔興〕fùxīng; 再流行 zài liúxíng: *~ old customs* 旧风俗再流行. **re·vival** *n* [C,U]

re·voke /rɪ'vəʊk/ *vt/i* 废〔廢〕除 fèichú; 撤销 chèxiāo; 取消(法令、允诺等) qǔxiāo.

re·volt /rɪ'vəʊlt/ *vt/i* **1** 反抗 fǎnkàng; 起义〔義〕qǐyì; 反叛 fǎnpàn **2** ~ ***against*** **(*at, from*)** 厌〔厭〕恶

〔惡〕yànwù; 反感 fǎngǎn. 3 使…厌恶 shǐ...yànwù; 使…起反感 shǐ...qǐ fǎngǎn. □ *n* [C,U] 反抗 fǎnkàng; 起义 qǐyì; 反叛 fǎnpàn. ~**ing** *adj* 令人厌恶的 lìng rén yànwù de.

rev·ol·ution /ˌrevəˈluːʃn/ *n* 1 [C] 旋转〔轉〕xuánzhuǎn; 绕〔繞〕转 ràozhuǎn: *10 ~s of a wheel* 一个轮子旋转十次. 2 [C, U] 革命 gémìng. ~**ary** /-rɪ/ *adj* (a) 革命的 gémìngde. (b) 大变〔變〕革的 dàbiàngé de. □ *n* [C] 革命者 gémìngzhe. ~**ize** *vt* 变革 biàngé: *~ize travel between countries* 彻底改革各国之间的旅行状况.

re·volve /rɪˈvɒlv/ *vt/i* (使)旋转〔轉〕xuánzhuǎn; (使)绕〔繞〕转 ràozhuǎn.

re·volver /rɪˈvɒlvə(r)/ *n* [C] 左轮〔輪〕手枪〔槍〕zuǒlún shǒuqiāng.

re·vue /rɪˈvjuː/ *n* [C,U] (有小型歌舞的)时〔時〕事讽〔諷〕刺剧〔劇〕shíshìfěngcìjù; 活报〔報〕剧 huó bàojù.

re·vul·sion /rɪˈvʌlʃn/ *n* [U] (感情等的)突变〔變〕tūbiàn; 厌〔厭〕恶〔惡〕yànwù.

re·ward /rɪˈwɔːd/ *n* 1 [U] 报〔報〕酬 bàochóu; 报答 bàodá. 2 [C] 酬金 chóujīn; 奖〔獎〕赏 jiǎngshǎng. □ *vt* 酬劳〔勞〕chóuláo; 奖赏 jiǎngshǎng.

rhap·sody /ˈræpsədɪ/ *n* [C] [*pl* -ies] 1 狂文 kuángwén; 狂诗 kuángshī; 狂言 kuángyán. 2 [音乐]狂想曲 kuángxiǎngqǔ.

rhet·oric /ˈretərɪk/ *n* [U] 1 修辞〔辭〕学〔學〕xiūcíxué. ~**al** /rɪˈtɒrɪkl/ *adj* 修辞的 xiūcíde; 修辞学的 xiūcíxuéde. ~**al question** (不必回答，只为加强印象或取得效果的)反问〔問〕fǎnwèn.

rheu·ma·tism /ˈruːmətɪzəm/ *n* [U] 风〔風〕湿〔濕〕病 fēngshībìng.

rheu·matic /ruːˈmætɪk/ *adj, n* [C]

rhino /ˈraɪnəʊ/ *n* [C] [非正式用语] rhinoceros 的缩写〔寫〕*rhinoceros* de suōxiě.

rhi·noc·eros /raɪˈnɒsərəs/ *n* [C] [*pl* ~es 或 ~] 犀牛 xīniú.

rhu·barb /ˈruːbɑːb/ *n* [U] [植物] 大黄 dàhuáng; 大黄属〔屬〕植物 dàhuángshǔ zhíwù.

rhyme /raɪm/ *n* 1 [U] 韵〔韻〕yùn; 同韵的词 (如尾音相同的) tóngyùnde cí. 2 [C] 押韵的词 yāyùnde cí. 3 [C] 有韵诗 yǒuyùnshī. ⇨ nursery rhyme. 4 [U] 押韵 yāyùn. □ *vt/i* 1 (使)押韵 yāyùn. 2 押韵 yāyùn.

rhythm /ˈrɪðəm/ *n* 1 [C,U] 韵〔韻〕律 yùnlǜ; 格律 gélǜ. 2 [C,U] 有规律的反复 (循环) yǒu guīlǜ de fǎnfù; 周期性 zhōuqīxìng: *the ~ of the tides* 潮汐的涨落. ~**ic(al)** /ˈrɪðmɪk(l)/ *adj*

rib /rɪb/ *n* [C] 1 肋骨 lèigǔ; 肋条〔條〕lèitiáo. 2 类〔類〕似肋骨的东〔東〕西 lèisì lèigǔ de dōngxi. ~**bed** *adj* 呈肋状〔狀〕的 chéng lèizhuàng de.

rib·bon /ˈrɪbən/ *n* [C,U] 缎带〔帶〕duàndài; 丝带 sīdài; 带子 dàizi.

rice /raɪs/ *n* [U] 稻 dào; 米 mǐ; 饭 fàn.

rich /rɪtʃ/ *adj* [-er, -est] 1 富的 fùde, 富裕的 fùyùde. 2 (指服装、首饰等)贵重的 guìzhòngde, 富丽〔麗〕的 fùlìde. 3 ~ *in* 丰〔豐〕富的 fēngfùde; 多产〔產〕的 duōchǎnde: *a country ~ in gold* 金矿丰富的国家. 4 (指食物)味浓〔濃〕的 wèinóngde. 5 (色彩)浓〔濃〕艳〔艷〕的 nóngyànde; (声音)圆润的 yuánrùnde; 低沉的 dīchénde. □ *n* **the** ~ 富人 fùrén. ~**ly** *adv* ~**ness** 富饶〔饒〕fùráo; 丰富 fēngfù; 浓厚 nónghòu. ~**es** *n pl* 财富 cáifù; 财宝〔寶〕cáibǎo.

rick·ety /ˈrɪkətɪ/ *adj* 佝偻病的 gōulóubìngde; 患佝偻病的 huàn gōulóubìng de.

rick·shaw /ˈrɪkʃɔː/ *n* [C] 人力车〔車〕rénlìchē; 黄包车 huángbāochē.

rico·chet /ˈrɪkəʃeɪ/ *n* [C, U] (指子弹等)飞〔飛〕蹦 fēibèng; 滑飞 huáfēi. □ *vt/i* [-t- 或 -tt-] (子弹等) 飞蹦 fēibèng; 滑飞 huáfēi.

rid /rɪd/ *vt* [*pt, pp* rid] ~ *of* 摆〔擺〕脱 bǎituō; 去掉 qùdiào: *~ a country of disease* 消除一个国家里的疾病. **be (get) ~ of** 摆脱 bǎituō; 去掉 qùdiào.

rid·dance /ˈrɪdns/ *n* [U] (常用 *good* ~)摆〔擺〕脱 bǎituō; 清除 qīngchú.

rid·den /ˈrɪdn/ 受压〔壓〕迫的 shòu yāpò de. *a po'lice- ~ state* 受警察压迫的国家.

riddle[1] /ˈrɪdl/ *n* [C] 1 谜 mí, 谜语 míyǔ. 2 难〔難〕以捉摸的人 nán yǐ zhuōmó de rén; 莫名其妙的事物 mò míng qí miào de shìwù.

riddle[2] /ˈrɪdl/ *n* [C] 粗筛〔篩〕cūshāi. □ *vt* 1 筛(土、灰等) shāi. 2 穿孔 chuānkǒng; 打许多洞在…上 dǎ xǔduō dòng zài ... shàng: *a body ~d with bullets* 满身弹洞.

ride[1] /raɪd/ *n* [C] 骑〔騎〕qí; 乘 chéng.

ride[2] /raɪd/ *vt/i* [*pl* rode /rəʊd/;

pp ridden /'rɪdn/] **1** 骑〔騎〕马〔馬〕(或自行车等) qímǎ. **2** 乘车〔車〕chéngchē. **3** 漂浮 piāofú: *a ship riding the waves* 一艘乘风破浪的船. ***let sth*** ~[非正式用语]听〔聽〕其自然 tīng qí zìrán. **4** ***ride up*** (衣服、领子、领带等穿着时)往上滑 wǎngshàng huá. **rider** *n* [C] **(a)** 骑手 qíshǒu. **(b)** 附文 fùwén.

ridge /rɪʤ/ *n* [C] **1** 脊 jǐ. **2** 山脊 shānjǐ; 岭〔嶺〕lǐng.

ridi·cule /'ridɪkju:l/ *n* [U] 嘲笑 cháoxiào; 嘲弄 cháonòng. □ *vt* 嘲笑 cháoxiào; 嘲弄 cháonòng.

rid·icu·lous /rɪ'dɪkjʊləs/ *adj* 可笑的 kěxiàode; 荒谬的 huāngmiùde. ~**ly** *adv*

rife /raɪf/ *adj* 流行的 liúxíngde; 普遍的 pǔpiànde.

rifle[1] /'raɪfl/ *vt* 在(枪、枪管、枪膛)内制〔製〕来〔來〕复线〔綫〕zài...nèi zhì láifùxiàn. □ *n* [C] 步枪〔槍〕bùqiāng, 来复枪 láifùqiāng.

rifle[2] /'raɪfl/ *vt* 搜劫 sōujié, 抢〔搶〕劫 qiǎngjié, 掠夺〔奪〕lüèduó.

rift /rɪft/ *n* [C] **1** 裂缝 lièfèng; 空隙 kòngxì. **2** [喻]分裂 fēnliè; 不和 bùhé. '~**-valley** 裂谷 liègǔ.

rig[1] /rɪg/ *vt* [-gg-] **1** 给(船)装〔裝〕上帆(或桅杆等) gěi zhuāngshàng fān. **2** ~ ***sb out*** **(*with sth*)** 为〔爲〕(某人)提供必需的衣服(装备等) wèi tígòng bìxū de yīfu. **3** ~ ***sth up*** 草草做成 cǎocǎo zuòchéng. □*n* [C] **1** 船具装置方法 chuánjù zhuāngzhì fāngfǎ. **2** 成套〔套〕装备〔備〕chéngtàozhuāngbèi. ⇨ oil-rig. '~**-out** [非正式用语]个〔個〕人衣物等 gèrén yīwù děng. ~**ging** *n* [U] 帆缆〔纜〕fānlǎn; 索具 suǒjù.

rig[2] /rɪg/ *vt* [-gg-] (用欺骗手段)操纵〔縱〕cāozòng; 控制 kòngzhì: ~ *an election* 控制选举.

right[1] /raɪt/ *adj* **(1** 至 **3** 义与 *wrong* 相对) **1** 公正的 gōngzhèngde; 正当〔當〕的 zhèngdàngde. **2** 正确〔確〕的zhèngquède; 对〔對〕的 duìde: *the* ~ *answer* 正确答案. ***put sth*** ~ 使恢复〔復〕正常 shǐ huīfù zhèngcháng. **3** 最合适〔適〕的 zuì héshì de: *the* ~ *man for the job* 最适宜做这工作的人. **4** 健康的 jiànkāngde: *Do you feel all* ~? 你觉得怎么样? **5** (指角)直角的 zhíjiǎode. ~**ly** *adv* 公正地 gōngzhèngde; 正确地 zhèngquède. ~**ness** *n* [U]

right[2] /raɪt/ *adv* **1** 正好 zhènghǎo; 恰好 qiàhǎo: *Put it* ~ *in the middle.* 把它放在正中间. ~ ***away (now)*** 立刻 lìkè. **2** 全程地 quánchéngde: *Go* ~ *to the end of this road.* 走这条路，一直走到头. **3** 公正地 gōngzhèngde; 正确地 zhèngquède. ***It serves him*** ~ 他活该; 这是他的报应.

right[3] /raɪt/ *n* **1** [U] 正确〔確〕zhèngquè; 公正 gōngzhèng; 正当〔當〕zhèngdàng. ***be in the*** ~ 站在正义〔義〕的一边〔邊〕zhàn zài zhèngyìde yìbiān. **2** [U] 权〔權〕利 quánlì. **3** [C] 法权 fǎquán: *human* ~*s* 人权. ⇨ human. ***by*** ~***(s)*** 正当〔當〕地 zhèngdàngde. ***in one's ,own*** '~ 凭〔憑〕本人的资格 píng běnrénde zīgé. ,~ ***of*** '***way*** **(a)** 通行权 tōngxíngquán. **(b)** 优〔優〕先通行权 yōuxiān tōngxíngquán. ***set*** **(**或 ***put)*** ***things to*** ~***s*** 使某事恢复〔復〕正常 shǐ mǒushì huīfù zhèngcháng.

right[4] /raɪt/ *vt* 纠正 jiūzhèng; 使恢复〔復〕正常 shǐ huīfù zhèngcháng: ~ *an injustice* 纠正一项非正义的行为. *The ship* ~*ed herself.* 船自行恢复平稳.

right[5] /raɪt/ *adj* (与 *left* 相对)右边〔邊〕的 yòubiānde; 右方的 yòufāngde. □ *adv* 在右边 zài yòubiān; 向右 xiàng yòu. □ *n* [U] **1** 右边 yòubiān; 右方 yòufāng. **2** [政治] **the R**~ ⇨ Right Wing. ,~-'**handed** *adj* 惯用右手的 guànyòng yòushǒu de. **the R**~ **(Wing)** 右翼 yòuyì; 保守派 bǎoshǒupài.

right·eous /'raɪʧəs/ *adj* **1** 正直的 zhèngzhíde; 正当〔當〕的 zhèngdàngde. **2** 公正的 gōngzhèngde; 正义〔義〕的 zhèngyìde: ~ *anger* 义愤. ~**ly** *adv* ~**ness** *n* [U]

right·ful /'raɪtfl/ *adj* 合法的 héfǎde; 公正的 gōngzhèngde: *the* ~ *owner* 合法所有人. ~**ly** *adv* ~**ness** *n* [U]

rigid /'rɪʤɪd/ *adj* **1** 僵硬的 jiāngyìngde; 不易弯〔彎〕的 bú yì wān de. **2** 严〔嚴〕格的 yángéde. ~**ly** *adv* ~**ity** /rɪ'ʤɪdətɪ/ *n* [U]

rig·or·ous /'rɪgərəs/ *adj* **1** 严〔嚴〕格的 yángéde; 严厉〔厲〕的 yánlìde: ~ *discipline* 严格的纪律. **2** 酷烈的 kùliède: *a* ~ *climate* 严酷的气候. ~**ly** *adv*

rig·our [美语 = **rigor**]/'rɪgə(r)/ *n* **1** [U] 严〔嚴〕厉〔厲〕yánlì; 严格 yángé; 严峻 yánjùn. **2** [常用 *pl*] (生活)艰〔艱〕苦 jiānkǔ; (气候)严〔嚴〕酷 yánkù.

rim /rɪm/ *n* [C] 边〔邊〕biān; 边缘 biānyuán; 轮〔輪〕辋〔輞〕lúnwǎng: *the* ~ *of a cup* 杯口. □ *vt* [-mm-] 装〔裝〕以轮辋 zhuāng yǐ lúnwǎng; 给...装边 gěi...zhuāngbiān.

rind /raɪnd/ *n* [C,U] 皮 pí; 树〔樹

皮 shùpí; 果皮 guǒpí.

ring[1] /rɪŋ/ *n* [C] 1 环〔環〕huán; 戒指 jièzhi: *an 'ear~* 耳环. 2 环状〔狀〕物 huánzhuàngwù. 3 圈状 quānzhuàng; 环状 huánzhuàng: *a ~ of light* 光环. 4 集团〔團〕jítuán: *a spy ~* 特务集团.5 (亦作 *'circus-~*) 马〔馬〕戏〔戲〕团的圆形场〔場〕地 mǎxìtuánde yuánxíng chǎngdì. 6 拳击〔擊〕场 quánjīchǎng. □ *vt/i* [*pt, pp ~ed*] 1 包围〔圍〕bāowéi; 围拢 wéilǒng. 2 装〔裝〕牛鼻圈 zhuāng niúbíquān; 给鸟〔鳥〕腿套小环 gěi niǎotuǐ tào xiǎo huán. 3 (用铅笔) 圈出 quānchū. **'~leader** 头〔頭〕目 tóumù; 魁首 kuíshǒu. **'~ road** 环城公路 huánchéng gōnglù, 环形道路 huánxíng dàolù.

ring[2] /rɪŋ/ *vt/i* (*pt* rang /ræŋ/; *pp* rung /rʌŋ/) 1 (钟、铃等)鸣〔鳴〕míng; 响〔響〕xiǎng. 2 *~ 'true* 似乎真诚 sìhū zhēnchéng. 3 按铃 ànlíng; 摇铃 yáolíng. 4 回响 huíxiǎng: *The room rang with laughter.* 室内笑声洋溢. 5 *~ sb (up)* [美语 = *call up*] 打电〔電〕话给某人 dǎ diànhuà gěi mǒurén. *~ off* 挂〔掛〕断〔斷〕电话 guàduàn diànhuà □ *n* 1 [仅用 *sing*] 铃声〔聲〕língshēng. 2 [仅用 *sing*] (表示某种性质的) 声调 shēngdiào; 口气〔氣〕kǒuqì: *a ~ of truth* 真实的声调. 3 [C] 鸣响 míngxiǎng; 铃声 língshēng; 钟〔鐘〕声 zhōngshēng. 4 打电话 dǎ diànhuà.

ring·let /'rɪŋlɪt/ *n* [C] 卷〔鬈〕发〔髮〕juǎnfà.

rink /rɪŋk/ *n* [C] 溜冰场〔場〕liūbīngchǎng; 滑冰场 huábīngchǎng.

rinse /rɪns/ *vt* 冲洗 chōngxǐ; 漂清 piǎoqīng. □*n* [C] 1 冲洗 chōngxǐ; 漂清 piǎoqīng. 2 染发〔髮〕液 rǎnfàyè.

riot/'raɪət/ *n* 1 [C] 暴乱〔亂〕bàoluàn; 骚〔騷〕动〔動〕sāodòng. 2 [U] 放纵〔縱〕fàngzòng; 狂闹〔鬧〕kuángnào. *run ~,* **(a)** 肆无〔無〕忌惮 sìwújìdàn. **(b)** (植物) 茂盛 màoshèng. 3 (色彩) 丰〔豐〕富 fēngfù: *a ~ of colour* 色彩缤纷. □ *vi* 骚扰〔擾〕sāorǎo; 闹事 nàoshì. **~ous** *adj* 暴乱的 bàoluànde; 骚动的 sāodòngde; 放纵〔縱〕的 fàngzòngde. **~ous·ly** *adv*

rip /rɪp/ *vt/i* [-pp-] 撕裂 sīliè; 扯破 chěpò. □ *n* [C] 裂缝 lièfèng; 裂口 lièkǒu. **'~-cord** 开〔開〕伞〔傘〕索 kāisǎnsuǒ.

R.I.P. = May he (she, they) be at rest. 愿〔願〕灵〔靈〕安眠 (墓碑用语) yuàn líng ānmián.

ripe /raɪp/ *adj* [-r, -st] 1 熟的 shúde; 成熟的 chéngshúde. 2 适〔適〕于食用的 shìyú shíyòng de: *~ cheese* 已制成的干酪. 3 成年的 chéngniánde; 老练〔練〕的 lǎoliànde: *a person of ~ years* 成年人. 4 *~ for* 准〔準〕备〔備〕好的 zhǔnbèi hǎode. **~ness** *n* [U]

ripen /'raɪpən/ *vt/i* (使)成熟 chéngshú.

ripple /'rɪpl/ *n* [C] 涟〔漣〕漪 liányī; 波纹 pōwén. □ *vt/i* (使)起细浪 qǐ xìlàng.

rise[1] /raɪz/ *n* [C] 1 小山 xiǎo shān; 岗 gǎng; 斜坡 xiépo. 2 上涨〔漲〕shàngzhǎng; 增长〔長〕zēngzhǎng: *a wage ~* [美语 = *raise*] 增加工资. 3 (地位等的) 升高 shēnggāo: *a ~ in social position* 社会地位提高. 4 *give ~ to* 引起 yǐnqǐ.

rise[2] /raɪz/ *vi* [*pt* rose /rəʊz/; *pp* risen /'rɪzn/] 1 (指太阳、月亮、星)升起 shēngqǐ ⇨ set[2](1). 2 起立 qǐlì. 3 起床 qǐchuáng. 4 上涨〔漲〕shàngzhǎng; 增长〔長〕zēngzhǎng: *The river has ~n two feet.* 河水上涨两英尺. *Prices continue to ~.* 物价继续上涨. 6 渐〔漸〕高 jiàngāo: *rising ground* 丘. 7 增强 zēngqiáng: *The wind is rising.* 风势在增强. 8 地位升高 dìwèi shēnggāo. 9 起源 qǐyuán; *The river ~s here.* 河发源于这里. *~ to the occasion* 妥善处〔處〕理难〔難〕题 tuǒshàn chǔlǐ nántí. 10 *~ against* 反叛 (政府等) fǎnpàn. **ris·ing** (尤指) 武装〔裝〕暴动〔動〕wǔzhuāng bàodòng; 叛乱〔亂〕pànluàn. ⇨ uprising.

risk /rɪsk/ *n* 1 [C, U] 危险〔險〕wēixiǎn; 风〔風〕险 fēngxiǎn. *at ~* 处〔處〕于险境 chǔ yú xiǎnjìng. *run a (the) ~ of, take ~s* 冒险 màoxiǎn. 2 [C] 保险对象 (人和物) bǎoxiǎn duìxiàng: *a good (poor) ~* 条件很好 (风险很大)的保险对象. □ *vt* 1 使冒危险 shǐ mào wēixiǎn. 2 冒…的危险 mào …de wēixiǎn: *~ getting wet* 冒淋雨的危险. **risky** *adj* [-ier, -iest] 危险的 wēixiǎnde; 冒险的 màoxiǎnde.

ris·sole /'rɪsəʊl/ *n* [C] 炸肉卷〔捲〕zháròujuǎn.

rite /raɪt/ *n* [C] (宗教) 仪〔儀〕式 yíshì; 典礼〔禮〕diǎnlǐ.

rit·ual /'rɪtʃʊəl/ *n* [C,U] 1 (宗教)仪〔儀〕式 yíshì; 典礼〔禮〕diǎnlǐ. 2 (宗教) 仪式的程序 yíshìde chéngxù. □*adj* (宗教)仪式的 yíshìde; 典礼的 diǎnlǐde.

ri·val /'raɪvl/ *n* [C] 竞〔競〕争者 jìngzhēngzhě; 对〔對〕手 duìshǒu. □ *vt* [-ll-, 英语亦作 -l-] 同…竞争 tóng...jìngzhēng. **~ry** *n* [C, U] [*pl* -ies].

river /'rɪvə(r)/ *n* [C] 江 jiāng; 河 hé. **'~-bed** 河床 héchuáng.

rivet /'rɪvɪt/ *n* [C] 铆钉 mǎodīng. □ *vt* **1** 铆接 mǎojiē; 铆牢 mǎoláo. **2** [喻]集中(目光、注意力) jízhōng.

R.N. = Royal Navy (英国) 皇家海军〔軍〕 huángjiā hǎijūn.

road /rəʊd/ *n* [C] **1** 公路 gōnglù; 道路 dàolù. **2 ~ to** 途径〔徑〕 tújìng: *the ~ to ruin* 毁灭之路. **'~-block** 路障 lùzhàng. **'~hog** 妨碍〔礙〕其他车〔車〕辆〔輛〕行驶〔駛〕的司机〔機〕 fáng'ài qítā chēliàng xíngshǐ de sījī. **'~worthy** *adj* (适于)在道路上用的 zài dàolùshàng yòng de.

roam /rəʊm/ *vt*/*i* 漫步 mànbù; 漫游 mànyóu.

roar /rɔː(r)/ *n* [C] (狮等) 吼叫 hǒujiào; 轰〔轟〕鸣〔鳴〕声〔聲〕 hōngmíngshēng. □ *vt*/*i* **1** 吼叫 hǒujiào; 呼啸〔嘯〕 hūxiào; 轰鸣 hōngmíng. **2 ~ sth out** 大声地说 dàshēngde shuō; 高唱 gāochàng. **~ing** *adj* **(a)** 喧闹〔鬧〕的 xuānnàode; 狂暴的 kuángbàode. **(b)** 兴〔興〕旺的 xīngwàngde; 兴隆的 xīnglóngde: *do a ~ing trade* 生意兴隆. □ *adv* 非常 fēicháng; 甚 shèn; 很 hěn: *~ing drunk* 大醉.

roast /rəʊst/ *vt*/*i* 烤 kǎo; 烘 hōng; □ *adj* 烤过〔過〕的 kǎoguòde. □ *n* [C] 烤肉 kǎoròu.

rob /rɒb/ *vt* [-bb-] 抢〔搶〕劫 qiǎngjié, 劫掠 jiélüè; 盗取 dàoqǔ. **~ber** 强盗 qiángdào, 盗贼 dàozéi. **~bery** *n* [C, U] [*pl* -ries].

robe /rəʊb/ *n* [C] **1** 长〔長〕袍 chángpáo; 长衣 chángyī: *a 'bath~* 浴衣. **2** [常用 *pl*] 礼〔禮〕服 lǐfú; 官服 guānfú; 法衣 fǎyī. □ *vt* 穿上长袍 chuān shàng chángpáo; 披上法衣 pī shàng fǎyī.

robin /'rɒbɪn/ *n* [C] 欧〔歐〕鸲〔鴝〕ōuqú; 知更鸟〔鳥〕 zhīgēngniǎo.

ro·bot /'rəʊbɒt/ *n* [C] 机〔機〕器人 jīqìrén.

ro·bust /rəʊ'bʌst/ *adj* 强健的 qiángjiànde; 健康的 jiànkāngde. **~ly** *adv* **~ness** *n* [U]

rock[1] /rɒk/ *n* **1** [U] 岩〔巖〕 yán. **2** [C,U] 岩石 yánshí. ***on the ~s*** [喻] **(a)** 很可能以离〔離〕婚而告终(的婚姻) hěn kěnéng yǐ líhūn ér gàozhōng. **(b)** 放有小冰块〔塊〕的饮料 fàng yǒu xiǎo bīngkuài de yǐnliào. **3** [C] 石头〔頭〕 shítou, 石块〔塊〕 shíkuài. **4** [英国英语]硬糖 yìngtáng. **,~-'bottom** 最低点〔點〕 zuìdīdiǎn. **~ery** 种〔種〕植岩石植物的岩石公园〔園〕 zhòngzhí yánshí zhíwù de yánshí gōngyuán.

rock[2] /rɒk/ *vt*/*i* 摇 yáo; 摇动〔動〕 yáodòng. **~ *the boat*** [喻] 捣乱〔亂〕 dǎoluàn. **~er, (a)** (摇椅脚下摇动用的)摇板 yáobǎn. **(b)** = rocking-chair. **(c)** ***off one's ~er*** [俚语]发〔發〕疯〔瘋〕 fāfēng. **'~ing-chair** 摇椅 yáoyǐ.

rock[3] /rɒk/ *n* [U] 摇摆〔擺〕舞(曲) yáobǎiwǔ. □ *vi* 跳摇摆舞 tiào yáobǎiwǔ.

rock-'n-roll /ˌrɒk ən 'rəʊl/ *n* [U] (亦作 *rock and roll*) = rock[3].

rocket /'rɒkɪt/ *n* [C] 火箭 huǒjiàn; 烟〔煙〕火 yānhuǒ. □ *vi* 飞〔飛〕速上升 fēisù shàngshēng: *Prices are ~ing.* 物价飞涨.

rocky /'rɒkɪ/ *adj* [-ier, -iest] **1** 岩〔巖〕石的 yánshíde; 多岩石的 duōyánshí de. **2** [非正式用语]不稳〔穩〕的 bùwěnde: *The table is rather ~.* 这张桌子不稳.

rod /rɒd/ *n* [C] 杆〔桿〕 gān; 竿 gān; 棒 bàng: *a 'fishing-~* 钓鱼竿.

rode /rəʊd/ *pt* of ride[2].

ro·dent /'rəʊdnt/ *n* [C] 啮〔嚙〕齿〔齒〕动〔動〕物(如鼠、兔等) nièchǐ dòngwù.

ro·deo /'rəʊdɪəʊ/ *n* [C] [*pl* ~s] **1** (美国西部) 驱〔驅〕集牛马〔馬〕 qūjí niúmǎ. **2** 竞〔競〕技表演 jìngjì biǎoyǎn.

roe[1] /rəʊ/ *n* [C,U] 鱼卵 yúluǎn; 鱼子 yúzǐ.

roe[2] /rəʊ/ *n* [C] 牝麅鹿 pìntiānlù. **'~buck** (雄)獐 zhāng.

rogue /rəʊg/ *n* [C] **1** 流氓 liúmáng, 无〔無〕赖 wúlài. **2** 凶〔兇〕猛而离〔離〕群的野兽〔獸〕 xiōngměng ér líqún de yěshòu. **roguish** *adv*

role, rôle /rəʊl/ *n* [C] **1** 角色 juésè. **2** 任务〔務〕 rènwù; 作用 zuòyòng.

roll[1] /rəʊl/ *n* [C] **1** (一) 卷〔捲〕 juǎn; 卷状〔狀〕物 juǎnzhuàngwù: *a ~ of film* 一卷胶卷. **2** 滚〔滾〕动〔動〕 gǔndòng; 摇晃 yáohuàng; 翻滚 fāngǔn. **3** 名册 míngcè; 名单 míngdān. **4** 隆隆声〔聲〕 lónglóngshēng: *the ~ of thunder* 雷声隆隆. **'~ing-mill** *n* 碾压〔壓〕机〔機〕 niǎnyājī; 碾压工厂〔廠〕

niǎnyā gōngchǎng.

roll² /rəʊl/ *vt/i* **1** 滚〔滾〕动〔動〕gǔndòng; 转〔轉〕动 zhuǎndòng. **2** 卷(成筒形或球形) juǎn. **3** 滚动 gǔndòng: *The clouds ~ed away.* 云散了. **4** 辗〔輾〕niǎn; 辊〔輥〕gǔn: *~ a lawn* 把草地压平. **5**(使)摇晃或摆〔擺〕动 yáohuàng huò bǎidòng: *The ship was ~ing heavily.* 船摇晃得很厉害. **6** 发〔發〕出隆隆声〔聲〕fāchū lónglóngshēng: *The thunder ~ed in the distance.* 远处雷声隆隆. **7 ~ in** 滚滚而来〔來〕gǔngǔn ér lái. ***roll up***, **(a)** 卷〔捲〕起 juǎnqǐ: *He ~ed up his sleeves.* 他卷起袖子. **(b)** 乘车〔車〕抵达〔達〕chéngchē dǐdá: *Two or three late-comers ~ed up.* 两三个后来者乘车到达.

roller /ˈrəʊlə(r)/ *n* [C] 滚〔滾〕子 gǔnzi; 滚轴〔軸〕gǔnzhóu; 滚筒 gǔntǒng. **ˈ~-skate** 有轮〔輪〕溜冰鞋 yǒu lún liūbīngxié.

roll·ing /ˈrəʊlɪŋ/ *adj* 颠簸的 diānbǒde; 起伏的 qǐfúde: *~ waves* 波浪起伏. **ˈ~-pin** 擀面棍 gǎnmiàngùn.

Ro·man /ˈrəʊmən/ *adj, n* [C] (古)罗〔羅〕马〔馬〕的 Luómǎde; 古罗马人 gǔluómǎrén. **R~ Catholic** *adj, n* [C] 罗马天主教的 Luómǎ tiānzhǔjiào de; 罗马天主教徒 Luómǎ tiānzhǔjiàotú. **,~ ˈnumeral** 罗马数〔數〕字(如 I, IV, XL, M 等) Luómǎ shùzì.

ro·mance /rəˈmæns/ *n* **1** [C] 冒险〔險〕故事 màoxiǎn gùshì; 爱〔愛〕情故事 àiqíng gùshì. **2** [C] 风〔風〕流韵事 fēngliú yùnshì. **3** [U] 爱情与〔與〕冒险 àiqíng yǔ màoxiǎn: *travel in search of ~* 寻找不平凡经历的旅行.

ro·man·tic /rəˈmæntɪk/ *adj* **1** 浪漫的 làngmànde; 空想的 kōngxiǎngde. **2** 传〔傳〕奇(式)的 chuánqíde; 富于浪漫色彩的 fù yú làngmàn sècǎi de. **3** (文艺)浪漫主义〔義〕的 làngmàn zhǔyì de. □ *n* [C] 浪漫的人 làngmànde rén; 浪漫主义作家 làngmàn zhǔyì zuòjiā. **~ally** /-klɪ/ *adv*

romp /rɒmp/ *vi* (尤指儿童)嬉闹〔鬧〕玩耍 xīnào wánshuǎ. □ *n* [C] 喧闹嬉戏〔戲〕的一段时〔時〕间〔間〕xuānnào xīxì de yíduàn shíjiān.

roof /ruːf/ *n* [C] [*pl* ~s] **1** 屋顶 wūdǐng; 车〔車〕顶 chēdǐng. **2** 顶 dǐng; 顶部 dǐngbù: *the ~ of the mouth* 上颚. □ *vt* [*pp* ~ed /ruːft/] 给…盖上屋顶 gěi…gài shàng wūdǐng. **~ing** 盖屋顶的材料 gài wūdǐngde cáiliào.

rook¹ /rʊk/ *n* [C] 白嘴鸦〔鴉〕báizuǐyā. **~ery** 白嘴鸦结巢处〔處〕báizuǐyā jiécháochù.

rook² /rʊk/ *vt* [俚语] 敲诈(顾客) qiāozhà.

rook³ /rʊk/ *n* [C] (国际象棋的)车〔車〕(亦作 *castle*) jū.

room /ruːm/ *n* **1** [C] 室 shì, 房间〔間〕fángjiān. **2** [*pl*] 一套房间 yítào fángjiān, 寓所 yùsuǒ. **3** [U] 空间 kōngjiān: *Is there ~ for me in the car?* 车里还有我坐的空位吗? **4** [U] 余〔餘〕地 yúdì; 机〔機〕会〔會〕jīhuì: *~ for improvement* 改进的余地. **roomy** *adj* [-ier, -iest] 宽〔寬〕敞的 kuānchǎngde.

roost /ruːst/ *n* [C] 栖木 qīmù; 鸡〔雞〕棚 jīpéng. ***rule the ~*** 当〔當〕家 dāngjiā; 称〔稱〕雄 chēngxióng. □ *vi* 栖息 qīxī; 歇息 xiēxi.

rooster /ˈruːstə(r)/ *n* [C] 公鸡〔雞〕gōngjī.

root¹ /ruːt/ *n* [C] **1** 根 gēn. **2** 发〔髮〕根 fàgēn; 齿〔齒〕根 chǐgēn. **3** [喻]基础〔礎〕jīchǔ; 根源 gēnyuán: *Is money the ~ of all evil?* 金钱是万恶之源吗? **4** [语法] 词根 cígēn; 根词 gēncí. **ˈ~ sign** [数学]根(符号 √) gēn.

root² /ruːt/ *vt/i* **1** (使)生根 shēnggēn. **2** (使)固定 gùdìng: *~ed to the spot by fear* 吓得一动不动地呆在那里. **3** [主要用 *pp*] (指观念等)根深蒂固 gēn shēn dì gù. **4 ~ *sth out*** 根除 gēnchú; 铲〔鏟〕除 chǎnchú.

rope /rəʊp/ *n* **1** [C, U] 绳〔繩〕shéng; 索 suǒ. **2** ***give sb (plenty of) ~*** 任其自由行动 rèn qí zìyóu xíngdòng. ***know the ~s*** 熟悉内情、规则等 shúxī nèiqíng, guīzé děng. □ *vt* **1** 用绳系〔繫〕住 yòng shéng xìzhù. **2 ~ *sb in*** 拉某人参加 lā mǒurén cānjiā. **ropey** *adj* [俚语]破旧〔舊〕的 pòjiùde; 蹩脚的 biéjiǎode.

ro·sary /ˈrəʊzərɪ/ *n* [C] [*pl* -ies] **1** 念珠祈祷〔禱〕niàn zhū qídǎo. **2** (一串)念珠(共一百六十五颗) niànzhū.

rose¹ /rəʊz/ *pt* of rise².

rose² /rəʊz/ *n* **1** [C] 玫瑰 méiguì; 蔷〔薔〕薇 qiángwēi. **2** [U] 玫瑰色 méiguìsè; 玫瑰红 méiguìhóng.

ro·sette /rəʊˈzet/ *n* [C] 玫瑰形饰物 méiguìxíng shìwù; 玫瑰形的雕饰 méiguìxíngde diāoshì.

ros·trum /ˈrɒstrəm/ *n* [C] [*pl* ~s 或 -tra /-trə/] 讲〔講〕台〔臺〕jiǎngtái; 讲坛〔壇〕jiǎngtán.

rosy /ˈrəʊzɪ/ *adj* [-ier, -iest] **1** 玫瑰色的 méiguìsède; 玫瑰红的 méiguìhóngde. **2**[喻]美好的 měihǎode; 光明的 guāngmíngde: ~ *prospects* 光明的前途.

rot /rɒt/ *n* [U] **1** 腐烂〔爛〕 fǔlàn; 腐朽 fǔxiǔ; 腐败 fǔbài. **2** 胡说 húshuō. □ *vt/i* [-tt-] **1** 腐坏〔壞〕 fǔhuài; 烂〔爛〕 làn. **2** [喻] (在狱中) 消瘦 xiāoshòu; 憔悴 qiáocuì. **3** 使腐烂 shǐ fǔlàn; 使腐朽 shǐ fǔxiǔ.

rota /ˈrəʊtə/ *n* [C] [*pl* ~s] [英国英语]花名册 huāmíngcè; 值勤人员表 zhíqín rényuánbiǎo.

ro·tary /ˈrəʊtərɪ/ *adj* 旋转〔轉〕的 xuánzhuǎngde; 转动〔動〕的 zhuǎndòngde.

ro·tate /rəʊˈteɪt/ *vt/i* **1** (使)旋转〔轉〕 xuánzhuǎng; 转动〔動〕zhuǎndòng. **2** 轮〔輪〕流 lúnliú; 交替 jiāotì: ~ *crops* 轮种庄稼. **ro'tation (a)** [U] 旋转 xuánzhuǎng: *the rotation of the earth* 地球的自转. **(b)** [C] 轮流 lúnliú.

ro·tor /ˈrəʊtə(r)/ *n* [C] (直升飞机的)水平旋翼 shuǐpíng xuányì.

rot·ten /ˈrɒtn/ *adj* **1** 腐烂〔爛〕的 fǔlànde; 腐朽的 fǔxiǔde. **2** [俚语] 糟糕的 zāogāode; 蹩脚的 biějiǎode: *What* ~ *luck!* 真倒霉!

rouge /ru:ʒ/ *n* [U] 胭脂 yānzhi. □ *vt* 擦胭脂 cā yānzhi.

rough¹ /rʌf/ *adj* [-er, -est] **1** (表面)不平的 bùpíngde; 粗糙的 cūcāode. **2** 粗鲁的 cūlǔde; 粗暴的 cūbàode; 粗野的 cūyěde. **3** 粗略的 cūlüède; 大致的 dàzhìde: *a* ~ *sketch* 草图. ˌ~ **and** ˈ**ready** 粗糙但尚能用的 cūcāo dàn shàng néngyòng de. **4** (指声音) 刺耳的 cì'ěr de. □ *adv* 粗暴地 cūbàode *live* ~ 过〔過〕简〔簡〕陋生活 guò jiǎnlòu shēnghuó. □ *n* **1** [U] 高低不平的地面 gāodī bùpíng de dìmiàn. **2** [U] 未加工状〔狀〕态〔態〕 wèi jiāgōng zhuàngtài; 粗制〔製〕品 cūzhìpǐng: *notes in* ~ 粗略的草稿. ⇨ rough¹(3). **~ly** *adv* **(a)** 粗暴地 cūbàode. **(b)** 粗略地 cūlüède: *It's* ~*ly 2 metres long.* 大约两米长. **~ness** *n* [U]

rough² /rʌf/ *vt* **1** ~ *sb* **up** [俚语] 粗暴对待 cūbào duìdài. **2** ~ *it* 过〔過〕艰〔艱〕苦生活 guò jiānkǔ shēnghuó.

roughen /ˈrʌfn/ *vt/i* (使)变〔變〕粗糙 biàn cūcāo: (使) 变毛糙 biàn máocāo.

rou·lette /ru:ˈlet/ *n* [U] 轮〔輪〕盘〔盤〕赌 lúnpándǔ.

round¹ /raʊnd/ *adj* **1** 圆的 yuánde; 球形的 qiúxíngde. **2** 来〔來〕回的 láihuíde: ~ *trip* 往返的旅行. **3** 完整的 wánzhěngde; 十足的 shízúde: *a* ~ *dozen* 整整一打. ˌ~-ˈ**shouldered** *adj* 曲背 qūbèi. **~ness** *n* [U]

round² /raʊnd/ *adv* **1** 朝反方向 cháo fǎn fāngxiàng; 转〔轉〕过〔過〕来〔來〕 zhuǎn guòlái: *Turn your chair* ~. 把你的椅子转过来. **2** 循环〔環〕地 xúnhuánde: *the hands of a clock go* ~ 钟的指针周而复始地走动. **3** 在周围〔圍〕 zài zhōuwéi: *A crowd gathered* ~ 一群人围了上来. *spin* ~ 旋转. **4** 逐一 zhúyī; 挨次 āicì: *Please hand these papers* ~. 请把这些文件分发给大家. ***go*** ~ 供给每个〔個〕人 gōngjǐ měigèrén. **5** 迂回地 yúhuíde; 绕〔繞〕道地 ràodàode: *a long way* ~ 绕远路. **6** 到某(指定)地点〔點〕 dào mǎo dìdiǎn: *Come* ~ *and see me.* 请过来看我.

round³ /raʊnd/ *n* [C] **1** 圆形物 yuánxíngwù. **2** 职〔職〕责 zhízé; 环〔環〕行路 huánxínglù: *the postman's* ~ 邮递员的投递路线. **3** (比赛等)(一)局 jú; (一)回合 huíhé: *a boxing-match of ten* ~*s* 一次十回合的拳击比赛. **4** 一份 yífèn; (一套或一组中的)一个〔個〕 yígè: *a* ~ *of drinks* 全座一巡酒. **5** (弹药的) (一) 发〔發〕 fā: *three* ~*s of ammunition* 三发弹药.

round⁴ /raʊnd/ *prep* **1** 环〔環〕 huán; 绕〔繞〕 rào: *The earth moves* ~ *the sun.* 地球绕着太阳转. **2** 绕过〔過〕 ràoguò: *walk* ~ *a corner.* 步行绕过拐弯处. ~ ***the bend*** [俚语]疯〔瘋〕狂 fēngkuáng. **3** 在…周围〔圍〕 zài...zhōuwéi: *a fence* ~ *the field* 农田周围的篱笆. **4** 在各处〔處〕 zài gèchù: *He looked* ~ *the room.* 他朝房间里四下看看.

round⁵ /raʊnd/ *vt/i* **1** 成圆形 chéng yuánxíng: *stones* ~*ed by the wind* 风化成圆形的石头. **2** 绕〔繞〕行 ràoxíng: *He* ~*ed a corner.* 他绕着拐角走. **3** ~ ***sth off*** 使圆满结束 shǐ yuánmǎn jiésù. ~ ***up*** 使集拢 shǐ jílǒng; 驱〔驅〕集 qūjí; 聚拢 jùlǒng: ~ *up cattle* 把牛赶到一起. ~ ***up*** 将〔將〕(数目)调整为〔爲〕整数〔數〕 jiāng tiáozhěng wéi zhěngshù.

round·about /ˈraʊndəbaʊt/ *adj* 迂回的 yúhuíde: *a* ~ *trip* 绕道的旅程. □ *n* [C] **1** 旋转〔轉〕木马〔馬〕 xuánzhuǎn mùmǎ. **2** 道路交叉处〔處〕的环〔環〕形路 dàolù jiāochāchùde huánxínglù.

roun·ders /ˈraʊndəz/ *n* *pl* 圆场

〔場〕棒球 yuánchǎng bàngqiú.
rouse /raʊz/ *vt/i* 〔正式用语〕 **1** 唤醒 huànxǐng; 唤起 huànqǐ. **2** 激励〔勵〕jīlì; 激起 jīqǐ.
rout /raʊt/ *n* [C] 溃败 kuìbài, 溃退 kuìtuì. □ *vt* 打败 dǎbài, 击〔擊〕败 jībài.
route /ru:t/ *n* [C] 路线〔綫〕 lùxiàn; 路程 lùchéng; 航线 hángxiàn. □ *vt* 按规定路线发〔發〕送 àn guīdìng lùxiàn fāsòng.
rou·tine /ru:'ti:n/ *n* [C,U] 例行公事 lìxíng gōngshì; 惯例 guànlì; 常规 chángguī.
row[1] /rəʊ/ *n* [C] 行列 hángliè; 排 pái.
row[2] /rəʊ/ *vt/i* 划(船) huá. □ *n* [C] 划船 huáchuán; 划船游览〔覽〕 huáchuán yóulǎn. '**~ing-boat** 划艇 huátǐng.
row[3] /raʊ/ *n* [C,U] 吵闹〔鬧〕 chǎonào; 争吵 zhēngchǎo. □ *vt/i* 吵闹 chǎonào; 争吵 zhēngchǎo.
rowdy /'raʊdɪ/ *adj* [-ier, -iest] 粗暴的 cūbàode; 吵闹〔鬧〕的 chǎonàode. □ *n* [C] [*pl* -ies] 好吵闹的人 hào chǎonào de rén. **rowdily** *adv* **row·di·ness** *n* [U]
royal /'rɔɪəl/ *adj* 王的 wángde; 女王的 nǚwángde; 王室的 wángshìde. **~ly** *adv* 威严〔嚴〕地 wēiyánde; 高贵地 gāoguìde. **~ist** *n* [C] 保皇党人 bǎohuángdǎngrén; 保皇主义〔義〕者 bǎohuángzhǔyìzhě.
roy·alty /'rɔɪəltɪ/ *n* [*pl* -ies] **1** [U] 王族 wángzú; 皇亲〔親〕 huángqīn. **2** [U] 王位 wángwèi; 王权〔權〕 wángquán. **3** [C] 版税 bǎnshuì; 专〔專〕利权税 zhuānlìquánshuì.
R.P.M. =revolutions per minute 每分钟〔鐘〕转〔轉〕数〔數〕měifēnzhōng zhuǎnshù.
Rs.=rupees 卢〔盧〕比（印度货币单位）lúbǐ.
R.S.P.C.A.= Royal Society for the Protection of Cruelty to Animals（英国）皇家防止虐待动〔動〕物协〔協〕会〔會〕Huángjiā Fángzhǐ Nüèdài Dòngwù Xiéhuì.
R.S.V.P. =Please reply（请帖等用语）请答复 qǐng dáfù.
Rt.Hon. =Right Honourable 对〔對〕有爵位（或高级官员）的尊称〔稱〕duì yǒu juéwèi de zūnchēng.
rub[1] /rʌb/ *n* [C] 摩擦 mócā; 擦 cā.
rub[2] /rʌb/ *vt/i* [-bb-] **1** 摩擦 mócā; 擦（净、干等）cā. **2** ~ *sb (oneself) a horse down*（用毛巾）用力擦干〔乾〕净 yònglì cā gānjìng. ~ *sth down* 磨平 mópíng. ~ *sth in*（或 *into*) *sth*, **(a)** 把…用力擦入 bǎ...yònglì cārù. **(b)** 反复〔復〕讲〔講〕(令人不愉快的事) fǎnfù jiǎng. ~ *sth out* 擦掉 cādiào; 磨去 móqù.
rub·ber[1] /'rʌbə(r)/ *n* **1** [U] 橡胶〔膠〕 xiàngjiāo. **2** [C] 橡皮(擦子) xiàngpí.
rub·ber[2] /'rʌbə(r)/ *n* [C]（牌戏中）连〔連〕续〔續〕三局比赛 liánxù sānjú bǐsài.
rub·bish /'rʌbɪʃ/ *n* [U] **1** 垃圾 lājī; 废〔廢〕物 fèiwù. **2** 废话 fèihuà. **rub·bishy** *adj* 无〔無〕价〔價〕值的 wú jiàzhí de.
rubble /'rʌbl/ *n* [U] 碎石 suìshí; 碎砖〔磚〕suìzhuān; 破瓦 pòwǎ.
ruby /'ru:bɪ/ *n* [C] [*pl* -ies] 红宝〔寶〕石 hóngbǎoshí. □ *adj*, *n* [U] 红宝石色(的) hóngbǎoshísè.
ruck·sack /'rʌksæk/ *n* [C] 帆布背包 fānbù bēibāo.
rud·der /'rʌdə(r)/ *n* [C]（船的）舵 duò;（飞机等的）方向舵 fāngxiàngduò.
ruddy /'rʌdɪ/ *adj* [-ier, -iest] **1** 红润〔潤〕的 hóngrùnde; 有血色的 yǒu xuèsè de. **2** 红的 hóngde.
rude /ru:d/ *adj* [-r, -st] **1** 粗鲁的 cūlǔde; 无〔無〕礼〔禮〕的 wúlǐde. **2** 骇〔駭〕人听〔聽〕闻〔聞〕的 hàirén tīngwén de; *get a* ~ *shock* 受到剧烈的震动. **~ness** *n* [U]
ru·di·ment /'ru:dɪmənt/ *n* [*pl*] 初步 chūbù, 入门〔門〕rùmén; 基本 jīběn. **~ary** /-'mentrɪ/ *adj* 初步的 chūbùde; 基本的 jīběnde.
ruff /rʌf/ *n* [C]（硬而宽的轮状）皱〔皺〕领 zhòulǐng.
ruf·fian /'rʌfɪən/ *n* [C] 暴徒 bàotú, 流氓 liúmáng.
ruffle /'rʌfl/ *vt/i* ~ *(up)* 扰〔擾〕乱〔亂〕rǎoluàn; 打扰 dǎrǎo.
rug /rʌg/ *n* [C] **1**（小）地毯 dìtǎn. **2** 毛毯 máotǎn.
rug·ged /'rʌgɪd/ *adj* **1** 不平的 bùpíngde; 多岩石的 duōyánshí de. **2** 有皱〔皺〕纹的 yǒu zhòuwén de: *a* ~ *face* 有皱纹的脸. **~ly** *adv* **~ness** *n* [U]
ruin /'ru:ɪn/ *n* **1** [U] 毁灭〔滅〕 huǐmiè; 崩溃 bēngkuì. **2** [C] 毁坏〔壞〕huǐhuài; 废〔廢〕墟 fèixū: *The house is in* ~*s.* 这座房子已成废墟. **3** [U] 祸〔禍〕因 huòyīn: *Drink was his* ~. 饮酒是他的祸根. **4** 破产 pòchǎn. □ *vt* 使毁灭 shǐ huǐmiè; 毁坏 huǐhuài. **~ous** /-əs/ *adj* 毁灭性的 huǐmièxìngde; 破坏性的 pòhuàixìngde.
rule /ru:l/ *n* **1** [C] 规则 guīzé, 章程 zhāngchéng, 条〔條〕例 tiáolì.

work to ~ (故意) 死扣规章而减低生产〔產〕 sīkòu guīzhāng ér jiǎndī shēngchǎn. **2** [C] 习〔習〕惯 xíguàn. ***as a*** ~ 通常 tōngcháng. **3** [U] 管〔管〕理 guǎnlǐ; 统治 tǒngzhì: *under foreign* ~ 在外国的统治下. **4** [C] 尺 chǐ. □ *vt/i* **1** 统治 tǒngzhì; 管理 guǎnlǐ. **2** 支配 zhīpèi; 控制 kòngzhì. **3** 裁决 cáijué. ~ ***sth out*** 拒绝考虑某事 jùjué kǎolù mǒushì. **4** (用尺)在纸上划〔劃〕(直线) zài zhǐshàng huà. **ruler** *n* [C] **(a)** 统治者 tǒngzhìzhě. **(b)** 尺 chǐ; 直尺 zhíchǐ. **rul·ing** *n* [C] 裁决 cáijué; 裁定 cáidìng.

rum /rʌm/ *n* [C,U] 朗姆酒 lángmǔjiǔ; (甘蔗汁制的)糖酒 tángjiǔ.

rumble /ˈrʌmbl/ *vt/i* 发〔發〕出隆隆声〔聲〕 fāchū lónglóng shēng. □ *n* [U] 隆隆声 lónglóngshēng: *the* ~ *of lorries* 卡车的隆隆声.

rum·mage /ˈrʌmɪdʒ/ *vt/i* (使) 隆隆响〔響〕 lónglóngxiǎng.

ru·mour /ˈruːmə(r)/ *n* **1** [U] 传〔傳〕闻〔聞〕 chuánwén; 传说 chuánshuō. **2** [C] 谣〔謠〕言 yáoyán. □ *vt* 谣传 yáochuán.

rump /rʌmp/ *n* [C] (鸟的) 尾部 wěibù; (兽的) 臀部 túnbù. ˌ~-ˈ**steak** 后〔後〕腿部的牛排 hòutuǐbùde niúpái.

rumple /ˈrʌmpl/ *vt* 弄皱〔皺〕 nòngzhòu; 弄乱〔亂〕 nòngluàn.

rum·pus /ˈrʌmpəs/ *n* [仅用 *sing*] [非正式用语]吵闹〔鬧〕 chǎonào; 喧嚷 xuānrǎng.

run[1] /rʌn/ *n* [C] **1** 跑 pǎo. ***on the*** ~ 逃跑 táopǎo. **2** [C] 短期旅行 duǎnqī lǚxíng. **3** [C] (车船等的)路线〔綫〕 lùxiàn; 航线 hángxiàn. **4** 一段时〔時〕间〔間〕 yíduàn shíjiān; 连〔連〕续〔續〕 liánxù: *a* ~ *of bad luck* 一连串的不幸. ***in the*** ˈ***long*** ~ 结局 jiéjú; 归〔歸〕根到底 guī gēn dào dǐ. **5** 饲养〔養〕场〔場〕 sìyǎngchǎng. **6** (板球、棒球的)得分单〔單〕位 défēn dānwèi; 一分 yìfēn. **7** [非正式用语] ***get (give) sb the*** ~ ***of sth*** 准〔準〕许自由使用 zhǔnxǔ zìyóu shǐyòng. ˌ~**-of-the-**ˈ**mill** 一般性的 yìbānxìngde; 不突出的bù tūchū de.

run[2] /rʌn/ *vt/i* [*pt* ran /ræn/, *pp* ~; -nn-] **1** 跑 pǎo, 奔 bēn. **2** 逃跑 táopǎo. **3** 跑步 pǎobù; 赛跑 sàipǎo. **4** ~ ***for*** 竞〔競〕选〔選〕 jìngxuǎn: ~ *for President* 竞选总统. **5** 使遭受 shǐ zāoshòu; 易受 yìshòu: ~ *the risk of losing* 冒失败的危险. **6** 行驶〔駛〕xíngshǐ: *The train ran past the signal.* 火车从信号旁边通过. ~ ***aground*** 使 (船) 搁〔擱〕浅〔淺〕 shǐ gēqiǎn. **7** 在活动〔動〕中 zài huódòng zhōng: *Don't leave the engine* ~*ning.* 不要让发动机空转. **8** (公共汽车等) 行驶 xíngshǐ. **9** 组织〔織〕 zǔzhī; 管〔管〕理 guǎnlǐ: ~ *a business* 经营一商店. **10** 运〔運〕载〔載〕 yùnzài: *I'll* ~ *you back home.* 我用车送你回家. ~ ***arms*** 私运军〔軍〕火 sīyùn jūnhuǒ. **11** 通过〔過〕 tōngguò: ~ *a comb through one's hair* 用梳子拢头发. **12** 使进〔進〕入 shǐ jìnrù; 使与〔與〕...接触〔觸〕 shǐ yǔ...jiēchù: *to* ~ *a car into a tree.* 开车撞上一棵树. **13** (指液体、沙等)流 liú; 滴 dī: *a river that* ~*s to the sea* 一条入海的河流. **14** 蔓延 mànyán. **15** 变〔變〕成 biànchéng: *Supplies are* ~*ning short.* 供应品渐渐短缺. **16** 伸展 shēnzhǎn; (演出)连〔連〕续〔續〕 liánxù: *The play ran for six months.* 这个剧连续演出了六个月. **17** 有倾向 yǒu qīngxiàng: *Yellow hair* ~*s in the family.* 这一家人都是黄头发. **18** (针织品)脱针 tuōzhēn; 脱线〔綫〕 tuōxiàn. **19** ~ ***across sb (sth)*** 不期而迁〔遇〕(某人或某物)bù qī ér yù. ~ ***after sb (sth),*** **(a)** 追捕 zhuībǔ; 跟踪 gēnzōng. **(b)** 追求 zhuīqiú: *She's always* ~*ning after men.* 她总是追求男人. ~ ***against sb*** 与某人赛跑 yǔ mǒurén sàipǎo. ~ ***away*** 潜〔潛〕逃 qiántáo; 私奔 sībēn. ~ ***down,*** **(a)** (指钟表)停止 tíngzhǐ. **(b)** (指电池)用完 yòngwán. ~***-down*** (指人)衰弱 shuāiruò; 筋疲力尽〔盡〕 jīnpí lìjìn. ~ ***sb (sth) down*** 撞倒 zhuàngdǎo. ~ ***into sb*** 偶遇 ǒuyù. ~ ***sth off,*** **(a)** 使流掉 shǐ liúdiào. **(b)** 印出 yìnchū: ~ *off* 2[illegible] *copies of a notice* 印出二十份通知. ~***out,*** **(a)** 消退 xiāotuì. **(b)** 期满 qīmǎn. **(c)** (供应品)用尽 yòngjìn. ~ ***over*** 溢出 yìchū. ~ ***over sb, run sb over*** (指车辆)辗〔輾〕过 niǎnguò. ~ ***to sth,*** **(a)** 达〔達〕到 (某量、数等) dádào. **(b)** (指钱) 足够做某事 zúgòu zuò mǒushì: *My wages don't* ~ *to* [illegible] *new car.* 我的薪水不够买一辆新汽车. ~ ***sth up,*** **(a)** 抬高 táigāo, 升起 shēngqǐ. **(b)** 迅速增长〔長〕 xùnsù zēngzhǎng: ~ *up a big bill* 迅速积欠一大笔帐. ~ ***up against sth*** 遭遇(障碍、危险) zāoyù.

rung[1] /rʌŋ/ *n* [C] 梯级 tījí.

rung[2] /rʌŋ/ *pp* of ring[2].

run·ner /ˈrʌnə(r)/ *n* [C] **1** 奔跑者 bēnpǎozhě. **2** 送信者 sòngxìn zhě. 3 走私者 zǒusīzhě: *'gun-~s* 军火走私者. 4 滑行装〔裝〕置 huáxíng zhuāngzhì: *the ~s of a sledge* 雪橇的滑行板. ,~-'**up** 亚〔亞〕军〔軍〕yàjūn.

run·ning /'rʌnɪŋ/ *n* [U] 跑 pǎo. ***make the*** ~ 先跑 xiānpǎo; 带〔帶〕头〔頭〕dàitóu. □ *adj* **1** 跑着做的 pǎozhe zuò de: *a ~ jump* 急行跳. **2** 连〔連〕续〔續〕的 liánxùde: *a ~ fire of questions* 一连串发问. **3** 接连的 jiēliánde: *win three times* ~ 连胜三次. **4** (指水) 流动〔動〕的 liúdòngde.

run·way /'rʌnweɪ/ *n* [C] 飞〔飛〕机〔機〕跑道 fēijī pǎodào.

rup·ture /'rʌptʃə(r)/ *n* [C,U] 破裂 pòliè. **2** [C,U] 决裂 juéliè; 绝交 juéjiāo. **3** [C] 疝 shàn. □ *vt/i* 破裂 pòliè.

ru·ral /'rʊərəl/ *adj* 农〔農〕村的 nóngcūnde, 乡〔鄉〕村的 xiāngcūnde. ⇨ urban.

ruse /ru:z/ *n* [C] 诡计 guǐjì; 计策 jìcè.

rush[1] /rʌʃ/ *n* **1** [C,U] 急速行进〔進〕jísù xíngjìn; 冲 chōng; 突进 tūjìn. **2** [C] 急需 jíxū: *the Christmas* ~ 圣〔聖〕诞节〔節〕(前夕) 的购〔購〕买〔買〕热〔熱〕潮 shèngdànjié de gòumǎi rècháo. **the '~-hour** 拥〔擁〕挤〔擠〕时〔時〕间〔間〕yōngjǐ shíjiān.

rush[2] /rʌʃ/ *n* [C] 灯〔燈〕心草 dēngxīncǎo; 灯心草属〔屬〕植物 dēngxīncǎoshǔ zhíwù.

rush[3] /rʌʃ/ *vt/i* **1** 匆忙地做(去, 来) cōngmángde zuò. **2** 冲〔衝〕过〔過〕chōngguò; 冲进〔進〕chōngjìn: *~ the gates* 挤进大门. **3** 仓〔倉〕促行动〔動〕cāngcù xíngdòng: *Don't ~me.* 不要催我.

rusk /rʌsk/ *n* [C] 面〔麵〕包干〔乾〕miànbāogān; 脆饼干 cuì bǐnggān.

rust /rʌst/ *n* [U] 锈 xiù. □ *vt/i* 生锈 shēngxiù. **rusty** *adj* [-ier, -iest] **(a)** 生锈的 shēngxiùde; 发〔發〕锈的 fāxiùde. **(b)** 落伍的 luòwǔde; 荒疏的 huāngshūde.

rustle /'rʌsl/ *vt/i* **1** (叶子、绸衣等) 沙沙作响〔響〕shāshā zuò xiǎng. **2** 凑集 còují; 供应〔應〕gōngyìng: *~ up some food* 准备些食品. **3** 偷(牛马) tōu. □ *n* [U] 沙沙声〔聲〕shāshāshēng.

rut /rʌt/ *n* [C] 车〔車〕辙〔轍〕chēzhé. ***be in (get into) a ~*** 墨守成规 mò shǒu chéngguī. □ *vt* [-tt-] 留下辙迹 liúxià zhéjì.

ruth·less /'ru:θlɪs/ *adj* 残〔殘〕忍的 cánrěnde; 无〔無〕情的 wúqíngde. **~ly** *adv*

rye /raɪ/ *n* [U] **1** 黑麦〔麥〕hēimài; 裸麦 luǒmài **2** 黑麦威士忌酒 hēimài wēishìjìjiǔ.

S s

S, s /es/ [*pl* S's, s's /'esɪz/] 英语的第十九个〔個〕字母 Yīngyǔ de dìshíjiǔgè zìmǔ.

S.=**1** saint. **2** south.

s.=**1** second. **2** singular. **3** son.

S.A.=**1** Salvation Army (基督教) 救世军〔軍〕jiùshìjūn. **2** South Africa 南非 nánfēi.

Sab·bath /'sæbəθ/ *n* 安息日 ānxīrì.

sab·otage /'sæbətɑ:ʒ/ *n* [U] 故意毁坏〔壞〕gùyì huǐhuài; 阴〔陰〕谋破坏 yīnmóu pòhuài. □ *vt* 破坏 pòhuài; 捣〔搗〕乱〔亂〕dǎoluàn.

sab·oteur /,sæbə'tɜ:(r)/ *n* [C] 破坏者 pòhuàizhě; 怠工者 dàigōngzhě.

sabre [美语 = **sa·ber**] /'seɪbə(r)/ *n* [C] 军〔軍〕刀 jūndāo, 马〔馬〕刀 mǎdāo.

sachet /'sæʃeɪ/ *n* [C] 香袋 xiāngdài; 香粉 xiāngfěn.

sack[1] /sæk/ *n* [C] 粗布袋 cūbùdài; 麻袋 mádài. **'~cloth** 麻袋布 mádàibù; 粗麻布 cūmábù. **~-ing** = sackcloth.

sack[2] /sæk/ *n* [非正式用语] (与 *the* 连用) 解雇 jiěgù. □ *vt* 解雇 jiěgù.

sack[3] /sæk/ *vt* 劫掠 jiélüè; 洗劫 (被攻陷的城市等) xǐjié. □ *n* 劫掠 jiélüè.

sac·ra·ment /'sækrəmənt/ *n* [C] (基督教) 圣〔聖〕礼〔禮〕shènglǐ; 圣事 (如洗礼等) shèngshì. **~al** /-'mentl/ *adj*

sacred /'seɪkrɪd/ *adj* **1** 上帝的 shàngdìde; 宗教的 zōngjiàode. **2** 神圣〔聖〕的 shénshèngde. **~ly** *adv* **~ness** *n* [U]

sac·ri·fice /'sækrɪfaɪs/ *n* **1** [C,U] 献〔獻〕祭 xiànjì; 祭品 jìpǐn. **2** [C,U] 牺〔犧〕牲 xīshēng; 牺牲品 xīshēngpǐn. □ *vt/i* 献祭 xiànjì; 牺牲 xīshēng: *~ one's life for a friend* 为朋友牺牲生命. **sac·ri·fi·cial** /,sækrɪ'fɪʃl/ *adj*

sac·ri·lege /'sækrɪlɪdʒ/ *n* [U] 渎〔瀆〕圣〔聖〕dúshèng; 亵〔褻〕渎

xièdú. **sac·ri'legious** *adj*

sad /sæd/ *adj* [-der, -dest] **1** 悲哀的 bēi'āide; 令人悲痛的 lìng rén bēitòng de. **2** (指颜色) 黯淡的 àndànde. **~ly** *adv* **~ness** *n* [U]

sad·den /'sædn/ *vt/i* (使)悲哀 bēi-āi; (使)悲痛 bēitòng.

saddle /'sædl/ *n* [C] **1** 马[馬]鞍 mǎ'ān; 鞍座 ānzuò; (自行车) 车[車]座 chēzuò. **2** 鞍状[狀]山脊 ānzhuàng shānjǐ. □ *vt* **1** 给(马)装[裝]鞍 gěi zhuāng ān. **2** ~ *sb with sth* 使负担 shǐ fùdān. **'~-bag** 鞍囊 ānnáng; 马[馬]褡裢[褳] mǎdālián.

sa·dism /'seɪdɪzəm/ *n* [U] 性虐待狂 xìngnüèdàikuáng; 施虐淫 shī nüèyín. **sa·dist** 性虐待狂者 xìngnüèdàikuángzhě; 施虐淫者 shī nüèyín zhě. **sa·dis·tic** /sə'dɪstɪk/ *adj*

sa·fari /sə'fɑːrɪ/ *n* [C,U] (尤指在非洲的)旅行 lǚxíng; 狩猎[獵]远[遠]征 shòuliè yuǎnzhēng.

safe¹ /seɪf/ *adj* [-r, -st] **1** ~ **(***from***)** 安全的 ānquánde; 无[無]危险[險]的 wú wēixiǎn de. **2** 未受伤[傷]害的 wèishòu shānghài de: *a ~ journey* 平安旅行. ~ *and 'sound* 安然无[無]事 ānrán wúshì. **3** 不致危害的 búzhì wēihài de. **4** (指地方等)给予安全的 gěiyǔ ānquán de; 不会[會]有危险的 búhuì yǒu wēixiǎn de. **5** 谨慎的 jǐnshènde; 稳[穩]健的 wěnjiànde: *a ~ driver* 谨慎的司机. **'~guard** *n* [C] 保护[護]措施 bǎohù cuòshī; 安全装[裝]置 ānquán zhuāngzhì. □ *vt* 保护 bǎohù; 维护 wéihù. **~-'keeping** 保管 bǎoguǎn; 保护 bǎohù. **~ly** *adv*

safe² /seɪf/ *n* [C] 保险[險]箱 bǎoxiǎnxiāng.

safety /'seɪftɪ/ *n* [U] 安全 ānquán; 保险[險] bǎoxiǎn. **'~ belt** = seat belt. **'~ pin** (安全) 别针 biézhēn. **'~ valve, (a)** 安全阀[閥] ānquánfá. **(b)** [喻]使人息怒的方法 shǐ rén xīnù de fāngfǎ.

sag /sæg/ *vi* [-gg-] (中部) 下垂 xiàchuí; 下陷 xiàxiàn. □ *n* [C] 下垂 xiàchuí; 下陷 xiàxiàn.

saga /'sɑːgə/ *n* [C] [*pl* ~s] **1** 英雄故事 yīngxióng gùshì **2** 家世小说 jiāshì xiǎoshuō.

sage¹ /seɪdʒ/ *n* [C] 哲人 zhérén; 贤[賢]人 xiánrén. □ *adj* 贤明的 xiánmíngde; 明智的 míngzhìde.

sage² /seɪdʒ/ *n* [U] 鼠尾草 shǔwěicǎo; 蒿属[屬]植物 hāoshǔ zhíwù.

sago /'seɪgəʊ/ *n* [U] 西米 xīmǐ; 西谷椰子属[屬]植物 xīgǔ yēzishǔ zhíwù.

said /sed/ *pt, pp* of say.

sail¹ /seɪl/ *n* **1** [C,U] 帆 fān; 篷 péng. *set ~* **(***from, to, for***)** 出航 chūháng, 启[啓]航 qǐháng. **2** [C] (风车的)翼板 yìbǎn.

sail² /seɪl/ *vt/i* **1** 扬[揚]帆行驶[駛] yángfān xíngshǐ; 航行 hángxíng. **2** 启[啓]航 qǐháng, 开[開]船 kāichuán. **3** 航行于 hángxíng yú: *~ the sea* 在海上航行. **4** 驾[駕]驶(船只) jiàshǐ: *Do you ~?* 你会驾驶船吗? **5** [喻]平稳[穩]地行进 píngwěnde xíngjìn. **~or** *n* [C] 水手 shuǐshǒu; 海员 hǎiyuán.

saint /seɪnt [英国英语] 弱式: snt/ *n* [C] **1** 圣[聖]人 shèngrén; 圣徒 shèngtú. **2** (缩作 **St**) 进[進]入天国[國]的死者 jìnrù tiānguó de sǐzhě. **~ly** *adj* (亦作 **~like**) 圣人似的 shèngrén sì de; 圣洁[潔]的 shèngjiéde.

sake /seɪk/ *n for the ~ of* 为[爲]…起见 wèi...qǐjiàn.

salad /'sæləd/ *n* [C, U] (西餐)色拉 sèlā; 凉拌菜 liángbàncài. **'~-dressing** 拌色拉的调味汁 bànsèlāde tiáowèizhī.

sa·lami /sə'lɑːmɪ/ *n* [U] (腌制并以大蒜调味的)意大利香肠[腸] Yìdàlì xiāngcháng; 色拉米香肠 sèlāmǐ xiāngcháng.

sal·ary /'sælərɪ/ *n* [C] [*pl* -ies] 薪水 xīnshuǐ, 薪金 xīnjīn. ⇨ wage. **sal·ar·ied** *adj*

sale /seɪl/ *n* **1** [C,U] 卖[賣] mài, 出售 chūshòu. *for ~* 待售 dàishòu. *on ~* 出售的 chūshòude; 上市的 shàngshìde. **2** [C] 廉售 liánshòu, 贱[賤]卖 jiànmài. **'~s·man, '~s-woman** (女) 售货员 shòuhuòyuán. **'~s·man·ship** 推销术[術] tuīxiāoshù; 售货术 shòuhuòshù.

sa·line /'seɪlaɪn/ *adj* 咸的 xiánde 含盐[鹽]的 hányánde.

sal·iva /sə'laɪvə/ *n* [U] 口水 kǒushuǐ, 唾液 tuòyè.

sal·low /'sæləʊ/ *adj* [-er, -est] (面色、气色)灰黄色的 huīhuángsède.

salmon /'sæmən/ *n* [C] [*pl* ~] 鲑 guī; 大马[馬]哈鱼 dàmǎhāyú; [U] 鲑肉 guīròu; 鲑肉色 guīròusè; 橙红色 chénghóngsè.

salon /'sælɒn/ *n* [C] 沙龙[龍] shālóng; 大会[會]客室 dà huìkèshì.

sa·loon /sə'luːn/ *n* [C] **1** (轮船旅馆等) 交谊室 jiāoyìshì; 大厅[廳] dàtīng. **2** [美语]酒吧间[間] jiǔbājiān. **3** [英国英语] (亦作 ~

car) (供四人坐的)轿〔轎〕车〔車〕 jiàochē.

S.A.L.T. = Strategic Arms Limitation Talks 限制战〔戰〕略武器会〔會〕谈 xiànzhì zhànlüè wǔqì huìtán.

salt /sɔ:lt/ *n* **1** [U] 盐〔鹽〕 yán. ***take sth with a pinch of*** ~ 对〔對〕…有所怀〔懷〕疑 duì...yǒu suǒ huáiyí. **2** [C] 〔化学〕盐类〔類〕 yánlèi. **3** [*pl*] 泻〔瀉〕盐 xièyán. □ *vt* 加盐于(食物) jiā yán yú. **'~-cellar** (餐桌上的)盐瓶 yánpíng. **,~-'water** *adj* 咸〔鹹〕水的 xiánshuǐde. **~iness** *n* [U] **salty** *adj* [-ier, -iest]

salt·petre [美语 = **-pe·ter**] /sɔ:lt'pi:tə(r)/ *n* [U] 硝石 xiāoshí; 硝酸钾 xiāosuānjiǎ.

sa·lute /sə'lu:t/ *n* [C] 行礼〔禮〕 xínglǐ; 敬礼 jìnglǐ; 礼炮 lǐpào. □ *vt/i* **1** 行礼 xínglǐ. **2** 致敬 zhìjìng.

sal·vage /'sælvɪdʒ/ *n* [U] **1** (从火灾及其它灾难中) 抢〔搶〕救财物 qiǎngjiù cáiwù; 救助 jiùzhù. **2** 救出的财产〔產〕 jiùchūde cáichǎn. **3** 废〔廢〕物利用 fèiwù lìyòng. □ *vt* (从火灾等中)抢救 qiǎngjiù; 援救 yuánjiù.

sal·va·tion /sæl'veɪʃn/ *n* [U] **1** 〔宗教〕拯救 zhěngjiù; 救世 jiùshì. **2** 救助 jiùzhù; 拯救 zhěngjiù.

sal·ver /'sælvə(r)/ *n* [C] (银)托盘〔盤〕 tuōpán; 盘子 pánzi.

salvo /'sælvəʊ/ *n* [C] [*pl* ~s, ~es] 齐〔齊〕射 qíshè; 齐发〔發〕 qífā; 齐投 qítóu.

same /seɪm/ *adj, pron* **1** 同一的 tóngyīde: *He's the ~ age as his wife.* 他同妻子同年. **2** 同样〔樣〕的事物 tóngyàngde shìwù: *We must all say the ~.* 我们大家必须说相同的话. ***be all the ~ to*** 对〔對〕…说来〔來〕都一样 duì...shuō lái dōu yíyàng. **3** 刚〔剛〕才提到(或想到)的 gāngcái tídào de; 上述的 shàngshùde: *I was ill Monday. On that ~ day, the office was bombed.* 星期一我病了, 就在那一天办公室被炸. □ *adv* ***all the*** ~, ⇨ all². **~ness** 同一 tóngyī; 同样 tóngyàng; 单〔單〕调 dāndiào.

sample /'sɑ:mpl/ *n* [C] 样〔樣〕品 yàngpǐn; 试样 shìyàng; 货样 huòyàng. □ *vt* 从〔從〕…采〔採〕样 cóng...cǎiyàng; 从…取样 cóng...qǔyàng.

sana·tor·ium /,sænə'tɔ:rɪəm/ *n* [C] [*pl* ~s] 疗〔療〕养〔養〕院 liáoyǎngyuàn.

sanc·ti·moni·ous /,sæŋktɪ'məʊnɪəs/ *adj* 假装〔裝〕神圣〔聖〕的 jiǎzhuāng shénshèng de. **~ly** *adv*

sanc·tion /'sæŋkʃn/ *n* **1** [U] 认〔認〕可 rènkě; 批准 pīzhǔn; 赞许 zànxǔ. **2** [C] 制裁 zhìcái. □ *vt* 认可 rènkě; 批准 pīzhǔn; 同意 tóngyì.

sanc·tity /'sæŋktətɪ/ *n* [C,U] [*pl* -ies] 神圣〔聖〕 shénshèng; 圣洁〔潔〕 shèngjié; 尊严〔嚴〕 zūnyán.

sanc·tu·ary /'sæŋktʃʊərɪ/ *n* [*pl* -ies] **1** [C] 圣〔聖〕地 shèngdì; 教堂 jiàotáng; 寺院 sìyuàn. **2** [C] 避难〔難〕所 bìnànsuǒ; 庇护〔護〕所 bìhùsuǒ. **3** [U] 庇护 bìhù. *be offered* ~ 受到庇护. **4**[C] 鸟〔鳥〕类〔類〕禁猎〔獵〕区〔區〕 niǎolèi jìnlièqū.

sand /sænd/ *n* **1** [U] 沙 shā. **2** [常用 *pl*] 沙滩〔灘〕 shātān; 沙地 shādì; 沙洲 shāzhōu. □ *vt* **1** 覆以沙 fù yǐ shā. **2** 用沙纸磨光 yòng shāzhǐ móguāng. **'~bag** 沙袋 shādài; 沙包 shābāo. **'~dune** 沙丘 shāqiū. **'~paper** 沙纸 shāzhǐ. □ *vt* 用沙纸擦 yòng shāzhǐ cā. **'~stone** 沙岩 shāyán. **sandy** *adj* [-ier, -iest] **(a)** 覆有沙的 fù yǒu shā de; 沙质〔質〕的 shāzhìde. **(b)** (毛发)沙色的 shāsède; 黄中带〔帶〕红的 huáng zhōng dài hóng de.

san·dal /'sændl/ *n* [C] 凉鞋 liángxié; 便鞋 biànxié.

sand·wich /'sænwɪdʒ/ *n* [C] 三明治 sānmíngzhì; 夹心面〔麵〕包片 jiāxīn miànbāopiàn. □ *vt* 夹入 jiārù; 挤〔擠〕入 jǐrù.

sane /seɪn/ *adj* [-r, -st] **1** 神智正常的 shénzhì zhèngcháng de; 心智健全的 xīnzhì jiànquán de. **2** 明智的 míngzhìde. **~ly** *adv*

sang /sæŋ/ *pt* of sing.

sani·tary /'sænɪtrɪ/ *adj* **1** 清洁〔潔〕的 qīngjiéde. **2** 保健的 bǎojiànde; 卫〔衛〕生的 wèishēngde.

sani·ta·tion /,sænɪ'teɪʃn/ *n* [U] 卫〔衛〕生 wèishēng; 卫生设备〔備〕 wèishēng shèbèi.

san·ity /'sænətɪ/ *n* [U] **1** 心智健全 xīnzhì jiànquán; 神志正常 shénzhì zhèngcháng. **2** 判断〔斷〕正确 pànduàn zhèngquè.

sank /sæŋk/ *pt* of sink².

sap¹ /sæp/ *vt/i* [-pp-] 使伤〔傷〕元气〔氣〕 shǐ shāng yuánqì; 使衰弱 shǐ shuāiruò; 耗竭 hàojié.

sap² /sæp/ *n* [U] 树〔樹〕液 shùyè; 树浆〔漿〕 shùjiāng. **~ling** 树苗 shùmiáo.

sap·phire /'sæfaɪə(r)/ *n* **1** [C] 蓝〔藍〕宝〔寶〕石 lánbǎoshí. **2** [U]

宝石蓝(色) bǎoshílán.

sar·casm /'sɑ:kæzəm/ *n* [U] 讽〔諷〕刺 fěngcì; 挖苦 wākǔ; 嘲笑 cháoxiào. **sar'cas·tic** *adj*

sar·copha·gus /sɑ:'kɒfəgəs/ *n* [C] [*pl* -gi /-gaɪ/, ~es] 石棺 shíguān.

sar·dine /sɑ:'di:n/ *n* [C] 沙丁鱼 shādīngyú; 鳁鱼 wēnyú.

sari /'sɑ:rɪ/ *n* [C] [*pl* ~s] (印度妇女的)莎丽〔麗〕服 shālìfú; (印度女服)卷〔捲〕布 juǎnbù.

sa·rong /sə'rɒŋ/ *n* [C] 沙龙〔龍〕 shālóng; 围〔圍〕裙(马来民族服装) wéiqún.

sash[1] /sæʃ/ *n* [C] 腰带〔帶〕 yāodài; 彩带 cǎidài, 饰带 shìdài; 肩带 jiāndài. ~ **window** 上下推拉窗 shàngxià tuīlā chuāng.

Sat. = Saturday.

sat /sæt/ *pt, pp* of sit.

Satan /'seɪtn/ *n* 撒旦 sādàn, 魔鬼 móguǐ. ~**ic** /sə'tænɪk/ *adj*

satchel /'sætʃl/ *n* [C] 书〔書〕包 shūbāo; 小背包 xiǎo bēibāo.

sat·el·lite /'sætəlaɪt/ *n* [C] **1** 卫〔衛〕星 wèixīng. **2** 人造卫星 rénzào wèixīng. **3** [喻] 卫星国〔國〕 wèixīngguó; 仆〔僕〕从〔從〕 púcóng.

satin /'sætɪn/ *n* [U] 缎子 duànzi. □ *adj* 缎子般的 duànzibānde.

sat·ire /'sætaɪə(r)/ *n* **1** [U] 讽〔諷〕刺 fěngcì. **2** [C] 讽刺作品 fěngcì zuòpǐn. **sa·tiri·cal** /sə'tɪrɪkl/ *adj*

sat·is·fac·tion /ˌsætɪs'fækʃn/ *n* **1** [U] 满意 mǎnyì, 满足 mǎnzú. **2** [C] 乐〔樂〕事 lèshì, 快事 kuàishì. **3** [U] 报〔報〕复〔復〕 bàofù; 赔偿〔償〕 péicháng.

sat·is·fac·tory /ˌsætɪs'fæktərɪ/ *adj* **1** 令人满意的 lìng rén mǎnyì de. **2** 良好的 liánghǎode. **sat·is·fac·tor·ily** *adv*

sat·isfy /'sætɪsfaɪ/ *vt/i* [*pt, pp* -ied] **1** (使)满足 mǎnzú, (使)满意 mǎnyì. **2** 达〔達〕到 (要求等) dádào. **3** 消除(怀疑) xiāochú.

satu·rate /'sætʃəreɪt/ *vt* **1** 浸透 jìntòu; 浸湿〔濕〕 jìnshī. **2** 使满 shǐ mǎn; 使饱和 shǐ bǎohé: *The car market is ~d.* 汽车市场已经饱和. **satu'ra·tion** *n* [U]

Sat·ur·day /'sætədɪ/ *n* 星期六 xīngqīliù.

sauce /sɔ:s/ *n* **1** [C,U] 调味汁 tiáowèizhī; 酱〔醬〕油 jiàngyóu. **2** [U] [非正式用语] 莽撞 mǎngzhuàng; 冒失 màoshi. **saucy** *adj* [-ier, -iest] 莽撞的 mǎngzhuàngde; 冒失的 màoshide. **sauc·ily** *adv*

sauce·pan /'sɔ:spən/ *n* [C] (长柄有盖的)深平底锅〔鍋〕 shēn píngdǐguō.

saucer /'sɔ:sə(r)/ *n* [C] 茶托 chátuō; 茶碟 chádié.

sauna /'sɔ:nə/ *n* [C] [*pl* ~s] 蒸气〔氣〕浴 zhēngqìyù.

saun·ter /'sɔ:ntə(r)/ *vi* 闲〔閑〕逛 xiánguàng; 逍遥 xiāoyáo. □*n*[C] 漫步 mànbù; 闲逛 xiánguàng.

saus·age /'sɒsɪdʒ/ *n* [C,U] 香肠〔腸〕 xiāngcháng; 腊〔臘〕肠 làcháng.

sav·age /'sævɪdʒ/ *adj* **1** 野蛮〔蠻〕的 yěmánde; 未开〔開〕化的 wèi kāihuà de. **2** 凶〔兇〕猛的 xiōngměngde; 残〔殘〕酷的 cánkùde. □ *n* [C] (以渔猎为生) 原始时〔時〕代的人 yuánshǐ shídài de rén. □ *vt* 袭〔襲〕击〔擊〕xíjī; 乱〔亂〕咬 luànyǎo; 乱踩 luàncǎi: *~d by a dog* 被狗咬. ~**ly** *adv* ~**ry** *n* [U] 原始状〔狀〕态〔態〕 yuánshǐ zhuàngtài; 未开化状态 wèi kāihuà zhuàngtài.

save[1] /seɪv/ *vt/i* **1** ~ *sb(sth)* (*from*) 援救 yuánjiù; 拯救 zhěngjiù; 保全 bǎoquán. ~ (*one's*) *face*, ⇨ face (2). **2** ~ (*up*) (*for*) *sth* 储存 chǔcún; 储蓄 chǔxù: ~ (*up*) *to buy a house* 存钱买房. **3** 节〔節〕省 jiéshěng: *That will ~ you a lot of trouble.* 那将省去你许多麻烦. □ *n* [C] (足球等) 救球 jiùqiú. **sav·ing** *adj* (尤指) 补〔補〕偿〔償〕的 bǔchángde; 弥〔彌〕补的 míbǔde: *his saving grace* 他的唯一长处(弥补缺点等). □ *n* **(a)** [C] 救助 jiùzhù. **(b)** [*pl*] 储蓄 chǔxù; 储金 chǔjīn. **'savings account** 储蓄存款户头〔頭〕 chǔxù cúnkuǎn hùtóu.

save[2] /seɪv/ (亦作 **sav·ing**/ 'seɪvɪŋ/) *prep* 除…以外 chú…yǐwài: *all died ~ him* 除他以外都死了.

sav·iour [美语 = **-ior**] /'seɪvɪə(r)/ *n* [C] **1** 救助者 jiùzhùzhě; 挽救者 wǎnjiùzhě. **2 The S~** [宗教]救世主 jiùshìzhǔ; 耶稣基督 Yēsū jīdū.

sa·vour [美语 = **-or**] /'seɪvə(r)/ *n* [C,U] 滋味 zīwèi; 味道 wèidào; 风〔風〕味 fēngwèi. □ *vt* 玩味 wánwèi; 欣赏 xīnshǎng: ~ *wine* 品酒.

sa·voury [美语 = **-ory**] /'seɪvərɪ/ *adj* **1** 美味可口的 měiwèi kěkǒde; 有香味的 yǒu xiāngwèi de. 咸〔鹹〕的 xiánde. □ *n* [C] [*pl* -ies] (餐前或餐后吃的) 开〔開〕胃的菜肴 kāiwèide càiyáo.

saw[1] /sɔ:/ *pt* of see[1].

saw² /sɔː/ *n* [C] 锯 jù; 锯床 jùchuáng. □ *vt/i* [*pt* ~ed; *pp* ~n /sɔːn/] **1** 锯 jù; 锯开〔開〕jùkāi. ~ *sth up* 把某物锯成小段 bǎ mǒuwù jùchéng xiǎoduàn. **2** 可被锯开 kě bèi jùkāi: *This wood ~s easily*. 此木材容易锯开. '~-**dust** 锯屑 jùxiè; 木屑 mùxiè. '~-**mill** 锯木厂〔廠〕jùmùchǎng.

saxo·phone /'sæksəfəʊn/ *n* [C] [音乐]萨〔薩〕克斯管 sākèsīguǎn.

say /seɪ/ *vt/i* [*pt, pp* said /sed/] **1** 说 shuō; 讲〔講〕jiǎng: *Did you ~ anything?* 你说过什么话吗? *go without ~ing*, ⇨ go without. **2** 说明 shuōmíng, 宣称〔稱〕xuānchēng: *It ~s here that he was killed*. 这里宣称, 他被杀害. **3** 提供情况 tígòng qíngkuàng: *She spoke for an hour but didn't ~ much*. 她讲了一小时, 但是没提供很多情况. **4** 发〔發〕表意见 fābiǎo yìjiàn. **5** 估计 gūjì: *It's difficult to ~ where he is*. 很难说他在何处. *be hard to ~* 难〔難〕以估计 nán yǐ gūjì. □ *n have one's ~* 表示意见 biǎoshì yìjiàn. ~**ing** *n* [C] 谚语 yànyǔ; 格言 géyán.

scab /skæb/ *n* [C] **1** 痂 jiā. **2** [非正式用语]拒不参加罢〔罷〕工者 jù bù cānjiā bàgōng zhě.

scab·bard /'skæbəd/ *n* [C] 鞘 qiào.

scaf·fold /'skæfəʊld/ *n* [C] 断〔斷〕头〔頭〕台〔臺〕duàntóutái; 绞刑架 jiǎoxíngjià. ~**ing** /'skæfəldɪŋ/ *n* [U] (建筑)脚手架 jiǎoshǒujià.

scald /skɔːld/ *vt* 烫〔燙〕伤〔傷〕tàngshāng. □ *n* [C] 烫伤 tàngshāng.

scale¹ /skeɪl/ *n* **1** [C] 鳞 lín, 鱼鳞 yúlín. **2** [C] 鳞状〔狀〕物 línzhuàngwù; 鳞屑 línxiè; 铁〔鐵〕屑 tiěxiè. □ *vt/i* 刮去…的鳞片 guāqù...de línpiàn. **scaly** *adj* [-ier, -iest]

scale² /skeɪl/ *n* [C] **1** 尺度 chǐdù; 刻度 kèdù; 标〔標〕度 biāodù. **2** 等级 děngjí; 级别 jíbié: *a ~ of wages* 工资等级. **3** (实物与图表等之间的)比例 bǐlì: *a ~ of 1 inch to 1 mile* 用一英寸代表一英里的比例. **4** 规模 guīmó; 相对〔對〕的大小 xiāngduìde dàxiǎo: *war on a large ~* 大规模战争. **5** [音乐] 音阶〔階〕yīnjiē. □ *vt ~ up (down)* 按比例增加(减低) àn bǐlì zēngjiā.

scale³ /skeɪl/ *n* [C] **1** 天平盘〔盤〕tiānpíngpán; 秤盘 chèngpán. **2** [*pl*, 或 *a pair of ~s*] 天平 tiānpíng; 秤 chèng.

scale⁴ /skeɪl/ *vt* 攀登 (悬崖等) pāndēng.

scal·lop /'skɒləp/ *n* [C] 扇贝 shànbèi.

scalp /skælp/ *n* [C] (人的)头〔頭〕皮 tóupí □ *vt* 剥去…的头皮 bōqù...de tóupí.

scal·pel /'skælpəl/ *n* [C] 解剖刀 jiěpōudāo; (外科用)小刀 xiǎodāo.

scam·per /'skæmpə(r)/ *vi* (儿童等)跳跳蹦蹦 tiàotiàobèngbèng; (动物)惊惶奔跑 jīnghuāng bēnpǎo. □ *n* [C] 蹦跳 bèngtiào; 奔跑 bēnpǎo.

scampi /'skæmpɪ/ *n pl* 大虾〔蝦〕dàxiā.

scan /skæn/ *vt/i* [-nn-] **1** 细看 xìkàn; 细察 xìchá. **2** 粗略地看 cūlüède kàn; 浏〔瀏〕览〔覽〕liúlǎn: ~ *the newspapers* 浏览报纸. **3** 测定(诗句的) 韵〔韻〕律 cèdìng yùnlǜ. **4** (指诗)合韵律 hé yùnlǜ. **5** (雷达)扫〔掃〕描 sǎomiáo. ~**ner** *n* [C]

scan·dal /'skændl/ *n* **1** [C,U] 冒犯或引起反感的行动〔動〕màofàn huò yǐnqǐ fǎngǎnde xíngdòng. **2** [U] 流言 liúyán; 诽谤 fěibàng. '~**ize** /-aɪz/ *vt* 引起…反感 yǐnqǐ...fǎngǎn; 使愤慨 shǐ fènkǎi: *His behaviour ~ized the village*. 他的行为引起村里的反感. '~**ous** *adj*

scant /skænt/ *adj* 不足的 bùzúde; 缺乏的 quēfáde. **scanty** *adj* [-ier, -iest] 不够多的 búgòu duō de; 不够大的 búgòu dà de. ~**ily** *adv*

scape·goat /'skeɪpgəʊt/ *n* [C] 替罪羊 tìzuìyáng.

scar /skɑː(r)/ *n* [C] **1** 伤〔傷〕疤 shāngbā; 伤痕 shānghén. **2** [喻] (内心的) 创〔創〕伤 chuàngshāng. □ *vt/i* [-rr-] **1** 使留下伤痕 shǐ liúxià shānghén; 结疤 jiēbā. **2** [喻]创〔創〕伤〔傷〕chuàngshāng.

scarce /skeəs/ *adj* [-r, -st] 缺乏的 quēfáde, 不足的 bùzúde: *food was ~ in winter* 冬天食物不足. ~**ly** *adv* 仅〔僅〕仅 jǐnjǐn; 几〔幾〕乎不 jīhū bù: *~ly enough food* 勉强够吃的食物. **scarc·ity** *n* [C,U] [*pl* -ies] 缺乏 quēfá, 不足 bùzú.

scare /skeə(r)/ *vt/i* 惊〔驚〕吓〔嚇〕jīngxià; 恐慌 kǒnghuāng. □ *n* [C] 惊恐 jīngkǒng; 恐慌 kǒnghuāng. '~**crow** 稻草人 dàocǎorén. **scary** /'skeərɪ/ *adj* [-ier, -iest] [非正式用语] 引起惊慌的 yǐnqǐ jīnghuang de.

scarf /skɑːf/ *n* [C] [*pl* scarves /skɑːvz/ 或 ~s] 围〔圍〕巾 wéijīn; 头〔頭〕巾 tóujīn.

scar·let /'skɑːlət/ *n* [U], *adj* 鲜

红色xiānhóngsè; 鲜红的 xiānhóngde. ,~ 'fever 猩红热〔熱〕xīnghóngrè.

scath·ing /'skeɪðɪŋ/ *adj* 严〔嚴〕厉〔厲〕的 yánlìde; 苛刻的 kēkède. ~**ly** *adv*

scat·ter /'skætə(r)/ *vt/i* **1** 驱〔驅〕散 qūsàn; 打散 dǎsàn. **2** 撒播 sǎbō; 撒布 sǎbù: ~ *seed* 播种. '~**-brain** 注意力不集中的人 zhùyìlì bù jízhōng de rén; 浮躁的人 fúzàode rén. '~**-brained** *adj* ~**ed** *adj* 分散的 fēnsànde; 散乱〔亂〕的 sǎnluànde: ~*ed villages* 分散的村落.

scav·enge /'skævɪndʒ/ *vt/i* 清除(垃圾等) qīngchú. **scav·en·ger** *n* [C] **(a)** 以腐尸〔屍〕为食的动〔動〕物yǐ fǔshī wéi shí de dòngwù. **(b)** 清扫〔掃〕工 qīngsǎogōng.

scen·ario /sɪ'nɑːrɪəʊ/ *n* [C] [*pl* ~s] 电〔電〕影剧〔劇〕本 diànyǐng jùběn; 剧情说明 jùqíng shuōmíng.

scene /siːn/ *n* [C] **1** (事件)发〔發〕生地点〔點〕fāshēng dìdiǎn. **2** 现实〔實〕生活中的事件 xiànshí shēnghuó zhōng de shìjiàn: *There were horrible ~s during the fire.* 火灾过程中有些可怕的情景. **3** 吵闹〔鬧〕chǎonào; 发〔發〕脾气〔氣〕fā píqì: *She made a ~.* 她大吵大闹. **4** 景色 jǐngsè; 景象 jǐngxiàng: *The sunrise made a beautiful ~.* 日出形成美丽的景色. **5** (缩作 **Sc**) (戏剧等中短于一幕的)一场〔場〕yìchǎng; 一景 yìjǐng; (一场、一景中的)一段情节〔節〕yíduàn qíngjié. **6** 布景 bùjǐng; 道具 dàojù. ***behind the ~s,*** **(a)** 在幕后〔後〕zài mùhòu; 在后台〔臺〕zài hòutái. **(b)** [喻](指人)秘密左右(某一)事件的 mìmì zuǒyòu shìjiàn de. ~**ry** /-ərɪ/ *n* [U] **(a)** 风〔風〕景 fēngjǐng; 景色 jǐngsè. **(b)** 舞台〔臺〕布景 wǔtái bùjǐng. **scenic** *adj*

scent /sent/ *n* **1** [C,U] 气〔氣〕味 qìwèi; 香味 xiāngwèi: ~ *of lavender* 熏衣草的香味. **2** [U] 香水 xiāngshuǐ. **3** [C] (猎物的)遗臭 yíchòu, 臭迹〔跡〕chòujī. **4** [U] (犬的)嗅觉〔覺〕xiùjué. □ *vt* **1** 嗅出 xiùchū, 闻〔聞〕到 wéndào. **2** 察觉 chájué; 怀〔懷〕疑有 huáiyí yǒu: ~ *a crime* 察觉一项罪行. **3** 使变〔變〕香 shǐ biànxiāng.

scep·tic [美语 = **skep·tik**] /'skeptɪk/ *n* [C] 怀〔懷〕疑论〔論〕者 huáiyílùnzhě. ~**al** *adj* ~**ism** /'skeptɪsɪzəm/ *n* [U] 怀疑主义〔義〕huáiyí zhǔyì; 怀疑态〔態〕度 huáiyí tàidù.

sceptre [美语 = **scep·ter**] /'septə(r)/ *n* [C] 君主的节〔節〕杖(权位的象征) jūnzhǔde jiézhàng.

sch. = school.

sched·ule /'ʃedjuːl/ *n* [C] 一览〔覽〕表 yìlǎnbiǎo; 时〔時〕间〔間〕表 shíjiānbiǎo; 计划〔劃〕表 jìhuàbiǎo. ***on (behind)*** ~ 按照(落后)预定时间 ànzhào yùdìng shíjiān. □ *vt* 将〔將〕...列表 jiāng...lièbiǎo; 将...列入计划表(或程序表、时间表等) jiāng...lièrù jìhuàbiǎo.

scheme /skiːm/ *n* [C] **1** 安排 ānpái; 配置 pèizhì: *a 'colour ~* 色彩的调配. **2** 计划〔劃〕jìhuà. **3** 阴〔陰〕谋 yīnmóu; 诡计 guǐjì. □ *vt/i* 设计 shèjì; 策划 cèhuà.

schizo·phrenia /,skɪtsəʊ'friːnɪə/ *n* [U] 精神分裂症 jīngshénfēnlièzhèng. **schizo·phrenic** /-'frenɪk/ *adj* □ *n* [C] 精神分裂症患者 jīngshénfēnlièzhèng huànzhě.

schnor·kel /'snɔːkl/ *n* = snorkel.

scholar /'skɒlə(r)/ *n* [C] **1** 公费生 gōngfèishēng; 津贴生 jīntiēshēng. **2** 学〔學〕者 xuézhě. ~**ly** *adj* ~**ship** *n* **(a)** [U] 学识〔識〕xuéshí, 学问〔問〕xuéwèn. **(b)** [C] 奖〔獎〕学金 jiǎngxuéjīn.

school[1] /skuːl/ *n* **1** [C] 学〔學〕校 xuéxiào. **2** 上学 shàngxué: *Is he old enough for ~?* 他到了上学年龄吗? **3** 授课 shòukè: *S~ begins at 9 am.* 上午九点开始上课. **4** [与 *the* 连用]全校学生 quánxiào xuéshēng. **5** [C] 学院 xuéyuàn: *medical ~* 医学院. **6** [C] 学派 xuépài, 流派 liúpài: *the 'Dutch ~ of painting* 荷兰画派. □ *vt* 培养〔養〕péiyǎng, 训练〔練〕xùnliàn; 约束 yuēshù. '~**master (mistress)** (女)教师〔師〕jiàoshī. '~**mate** 同学 tóngxué; 校友 xiàoyǒu.

school[2] /skuːl/ *n* [C] 鱼群 yúqún.

schoo·ner /'skuːnə(r)/ *n* [C] **1** 纵〔縱〕帆船 zòng fānchuán; 双桅帆船 shuāngwéi fānchuán. **2** 大啤酒杯 dà píjiǔ bēi.

science /'saɪəns/ *n* **1** [U]科学〔學〕kēxué. **2** [C,U] 学科 xuékē. ⇨ art(2). ,~ '**fiction** 科学幻想小说 kēxué huànxiǎng xiǎoshuō. **scien·tist** /'saɪəntɪst/ 科学家 kēxuéjiā. **scien·ti·fic** /,saɪən'tɪfɪk/ *adj*

scin·til·late /'sɪntɪleɪt/ *vi* **1** [... 〔閃〕烁〔爍〕shǎnshuò; 闪耀 shǎnyào. **2** [喻]言谈机〔機〕敏 yántán jīmǐn.

scis·sors /'sɪzəz/ *n pl* (亦作 *a pair of ~s*) 剪刀 jiǎndāo; 剪子 jiǎnzi.

scoff /skɒf/ *vi* 嘲笑 cháoxiào; 嘲弄 cháonòng. □ *n* [C] 嘲笑 cháoxiào; 嘲弄 cháonòng.

scold /skəʊld/ *vt/i* 责骂〔駡〕 zémà; 申斥 shēnchì.

scol·lop /'skɒləp/ *n* = scallop.

scone /skɒn/ *n* [C] 烤饼 kǎobǐng.

scoop /sku:p/ *n* [C] **1** 勺〔杓〕sháo; 铲〔鏟〕子 chǎnzi. **2** 戽斗 hùdǒu. **3** [非正式用语]独〔獨〕家新闻〔聞〕 dújiā xīnwén. □ *vt* **1** ~ *sth out (up)* 刬〔剷〕起 chǎnqǐ; 舀出 yǎochū. **2** 挖空 wākōng.

scooter /'sku:tə(r)/ *n* [C] **1** (亦作 *'motor-~*) (低座)小摩托车〔車〕 xiǎo mótuōchē. **2** (儿童游戏用的)踏板车 tàbǎnchē.

scope /skəʊp/*n* [U] **1** 机〔機〕会〔會〕 jīhuì: ~ *for improvement* 改进的机会. **2** 范〔範〕围〔圍〕fànwéi; 眼界 yǎnjiè.

scorch /skɔ:tʃ/*vt/i* 烧〔燒〕焦 shāojiāo, 烤焦 kǎojiāo; (使)枯萎 kūwěi. □ *n* [C] 烧焦 shāojiāo; 焦痕 jiāohén.

score[1] /skɔ:(r)/ *n* [C] **1** 刻痕 kèhén; 伤〔傷〕痕 shānghén. **2** 鞭痕 biānhén. **3** *pay (settle) an old* ~ 报〔報〕仇 bàochóu. **4** (比赛中的)得分 défēn; 得分记录〔錄〕 défēn jìlù. **5** *on 'that* ~ 在那点〔點〕上 zài nàdiǎn shàng. **6** [音乐]总〔總〕谱 zǒngpǔ; 乐〔樂〕谱 yuèpǔ. **7** [过时用法]二十 èrshí.

score[2] /skɔ:(r)/ *vt/i* **1** 刻痕(于) kèhén; 划〔劃〕线〔綫〕(号) huàxiàn. **2** (在比赛中)记分 jìfēn. **3** 得分 défēn: ~ *a goal* 进一球, 赢球得分. ~ *an advantage over* 获〔獲〕得一分 huòdé yìfēn. **4** 为〔爲〕…谱曲 wèi … pǔqǔ; 为…配乐〔樂〕 wèi … pèiyuè. **scorer**, **(a)** 记分员 jìfēnyuán. **(b)** 得分者 défēnzhě.

scorn /skɔ:n/ *n* [U] 轻〔輕〕蔑 qīngmiè; 蔑视 mièshì. □ *vt* 轻蔑 qīngmiè; 蔑视 mièshì; 不屑做 búxiè zuò. ~**ful** *adj* ~**fully** *adv*

scor·pion /'skɔ:pɪən/ *n* [C] 蝎子 xiēzi.

Scot /skɒt/ *n* [C] 苏〔蘇〕格兰〔蘭〕人 Sūgélánrén.

scot-free /ˌskɒt 'fri:/ *adj* 免于受罚的 miǎn yú shòufá de: *He escaped* ~. 他安然逃跑.

Scotch /skɒtʃ/ *n* [C,U] 苏〔蘇〕格兰〔蘭〕威士忌酒 Sūgélán wēishìjìjiǔ.

Scots /skɒts/ *adj* 苏〔蘇〕格兰〔蘭〕的 Sūgélánde; 苏格兰人的 Sūgélánrénde. **'S~·man ('S~woman)** 苏格兰男(女)人 Sūgélán nánrén.

Scot·tish /'skɒtɪʃ/ *adj* 苏〔蘇〕格兰〔蘭〕的 Sūgélánde; 苏格兰人的 Sūgélánrénde.

scoun·drel /'skaʊndrəl/ *n* [C] 恶〔惡〕棍 ègùn, 无〔無〕赖 wúlài.

scour /'skaʊə(r)/ *vt/i* **1** 擦亮 cāliàng; 擦净 cājìng. **2** 冲刷 chōngshuā; 冲出 chōngchū. **3** 搜索 sōusuǒ: ~ *the area for the thief* 在这个地区搜捕窃贼. □ *n* [C] 擦 cā; 冲刷 chōngshuā. ~**er** 刷锅〔鍋〕用的尼龙〔龍〕或金属〔屬〕网垫〔墊〕 shuāguō yòng de nílóng huò jīnshǔ wǎngdiàn.

scourge /skɜ:dʒ/ *n* [C] **1** [旧用法]鞭 biān. **2** 苦难〔難〕的原因 kǔnàn de yuányīn: *the* ~ *of war* 战祸. □ *vt* **1** (旧用法)鞭打 biāndǎ; 鞭笞 biānchī. **2** 使痛苦 shǐ tòngkǔ.

scout /skaʊt/ *n* [C] **1** 侦察员 zhēncháyuán; 侦察机〔機〕 zhēnchájī; 侦察舰 zhēnchájiàn. **2** **S~** 童子军〔軍〕 tóngzǐjūn. □ *vi* ~ ***about*** (或 ***around***)(***for sb*** 或 ***sth***)到处〔處〕搜索 dàochù sōusuǒ; 寻〔尋〕找 xúnzhǎo.

scowl /skaʊl/ *n* [C] 苦脸〔臉〕 kǔliǎn; 怒容 nùróng. □ *vi* ~ *(at)* 皱〔皺〕眉头〔頭〕 zhòu méitóu; 怒视 nùshì.

scrabble /'skræbl/ *vi* ~ *about (for sth)* (摸索着)寻〔尋〕找某物 xúnzhǎo mǒuwù; 抓拢〔攏〕 zhuālǒng.

scram /skræm/ *vi* [-mm-] [俚语]走开〔開〕 zǒukāi; 滚〔滾〕开 gǔnkāi.

scramble /'skræmbl/ *vt/i* **1** 爬行 páxíng; 向上爬 xiàngshàng pá. **2** ~ *for sth* 争夺〔奪〕 zhēngduó; 抢〔搶〕夺 qiǎngduó. **3** 炒(蛋) chǎo. **4** 在电〔電〕话上用暗语传〔傳〕递〔遞〕信息 zài diànhuà shàng yòng ànyǔ chuándì xìnxī. □ *n* [C] **1** 摩托车〔車〕越野比赛 mótuōchē yuèyě bǐsài. **2** 争夺 zhēngduó, 抢夺 qiǎngduó: *a* ~ *for seats on the train* 在火车上抢座位.

scrap[1] /skræp/ *n* **1** [C] 碎片 suìpiàn; 碎屑 suìxiè. **2** [喻]少许 shǎoxǔ; 小量 xiǎoliàng: ~*s of information* 零零星星一点儿信息. **3** [U] 废〔廢〕料 fèiliào; 废品 fèipǐn. □ *vt*[-pp-] 废弃〔棄〕 fèiqì. ~**book** 剪贴簿 jiǎntiēbù. **'~ heap** 废物堆 fèiwùduī, 垃圾堆 lājīduī. ~**py** *adj*[-ier,-iest]散漫的 sǎnmànde; 不连〔連〕贯的 bù liánguàn de: *a* ~ *idea* 散漫的思想.

scrap[2] /skræp/ *n* [C] [非正式用语]打架 dǎjià; 吵架 chǎojià. □ *vi* [-pp-] 打架 dǎjià; 吵架 chǎojià.

scrape /skreɪp/ *vt/i* **1** 刮 guā; 削 xiāo; 擦 cā; 刮落 guāluò. **2** 擦伤〔傷〕 cāshāng: *He* ~*d his arm on the wall.* 他在墙上擦伤了手臂. **3**

挖空 wākōng; 挖成 wāchéng: ~ *(out) a hole* 挖洞. **4** 擦过[過] cāguò: *branches scraping against the window* 擦着窗子的树枝. **5** ~ *sth together* **(up)** 积[積]攒 jīzǎn: ~ *up the money for a holiday* 为度假而积攒钱. □ *n* [C] **1** 刮 guā; 削 xiāo; 刮削声[聲] guāxiāoshēng. **2** 刮痕 guāhén; 擦伤 cāshāng. **3** 困境 kùnjìng.

scrappy /'skræpɪ/ *adj* ⇨ scrap[1].

scratch[1] /skrætʃ/*n* **1** [C] 抓痕 zhuāhén; 擦伤[傷] cāshāng. **2** [仅用 *sing*] 抓 zhuā; 搔 sāo. **3** *start from* ~ 起跑线[綫] qǐpǎoxiàn. *up to* ~ [喻]情况良好 qíngkuàng liánghǎo. **scratchy** *adj* [-ier, -iest] 发[發]刮擦声[聲]的 fā guācā-shēng de.

scratch[2] /skrætʃ/ *vt/i* **1** 抓 zhuā; 搔 sāo. **2** ~ *sth out* 勾掉 gōudiào; 划[劃]去 huàqù. **3** (为止痒而)搔(皮肤) sāo. **4** 挖 wā: ~ *(out) a hole* 挖出一个洞.

scrawl /skrɔ:l/ *vt/i* 潦草地写[寫] liǎocǎode xiě; 乱[亂]涂[塗] luàntú. □ *n* [C,U] 潦草书[書]写 liǎocǎo shūxiě; 潦草写成的东[東]西 liǎocǎo xiěchéng de dōngxi.

scream /skri:m/ *vt/i* **1** 尖叫 jiānjiào. **2** 尖声[聲]叫喊 jiānshēng jiàohǎn. **3** (风、机器等) 发[發]尖叫声 fā jiānjiàoshēng. □ *n* [C] 尖叫声 jiānjiàoshēng.

screech /skri:tʃ/ *vt/i* **1** 发[發]出尖叫声[聲] fāchū jiānjiàoshēng. **2** (愤怒或痛苦地)尖叫 jiānjiào. □ *n* [C] 尖叫 jiānjiào: *a* ~ *of brakes* 刹车的嘎吱声.

screen /skri:n/ *n* [C] **1** 屏 píng; 幕 mù; 帘[簾] lián; 帐[帳] zhàng. **2** 掩蔽物 yǎnbìwù. **3** (幻灯、电影的)银幕 yínmù. **4** (电视的)屏幕 píngmù. **5** 纱窗 shāchuāng; 纱门[門] shāmén. □ *vt/i* **1** 遮蔽 zhēbì; 掩护[護] yǎnhù. **2** 审[審]查 shěnchá; 甄别 zhēnbié. **3** 放映(电影) fàngyìng; 拍摄[攝] pāishè.

screw /skru:/ *n* [C] **1** 螺丝 luósī; 螺(丝)钉 luódīng; 螺旋 luóxuán. **2** (螺旋式的)旋转[轉] xuánzhuǎn. **3** (船的)螺旋桨[槳] luóxuánjiǎng. □ *vt/i* **1** (用螺钉)钉住 dìngzhù; (用螺丝)拧[擰]紧[緊] níngjǐn. **2** 拧[擰]转[轉] nǐngzhuàn; 使紧[緊] shǐ jǐn: ~ *up one's eyes* 眯着眼睛. *have one's head* ~*ed on (right)* 头[頭]脑[腦]清醒明智 tóunǎo qīngxǐng míngzhì; 有判断[斷]力 yǒu pànduànlì. ~**driver** 旋凿[鑿] xuánzáo.

scribble /'skrɪbl/ *vt/i* **1** 潦草地书[書]写[寫] liáocǎo de shūxiě. **2** 乱[亂]涂[塗] luàntú. □ *n* [U] 乱写 luànxiě; [C] 潦草书写成的东[東]西 liáocǎo shūxiě chéng de dōngxi.

scribe /skraɪb/ *n* [C] (古代)抄写[寫]员chāoxiěyuán; 书[書]记 shūji.

script /skrɪpt/ *n* **1** [U] 手迹[跡] shǒujì; 笔[筆]迹 bǐjì. **2** [C] 手稿 shǒugǎo; 剧[劇]本(原稿) jùběn; 广[廣]播(原)稿 guǎngbōgǎo. ~**writer** 广播(电视)节[節]目的撰稿人 guǎngbō jiémù de zhuàngǎorén.

scrip·ture /'skrɪptʃə(r)/ *n* **1 The (Holy) S~s** 圣[聖]经[經] shèngjīng. **2** 经文 jīngwén; 圣典 shèngdiǎn. **scrip·tural** *adj*

scroll /skrəʊl/ *n* [C] **1** 卷轴[軸] juǎnzhóu; 纸卷 zhǐjuǎn. **2** (石刻上的)漩涡[渦]饰 xuánwōshì.

scrounge /skraʊndʒ/ *vt/i* [非正式用语] 偷 tōu; 骗[騙]取 piànqǔ. **scroun·ger** 偷者 tōuzhě; 骗取者 piànqǔzhě.

scrub[1] /'skrʌb/ *n* [U] 矮树[樹] ǎishù; 灌木 guànmù.

scrub[2] /skrʌb/ *vt/i* [-bb-] **1** 擦洗 cāxǐ; 擦净 cājìng. **2** ~ **(out)** 取消 qǔxiāo: ~ *plans to go abroad* 取消出国计划. □ *n* [C] 擦洗 cāxǐ; 擦净 cājìng. '~**bing-brush** 硬毛刷子 yìngmáo shuāzi.

scruff /skrʌf/ *n* [仅用于] *the* ~ *of the neck* 颈[頸]背 jǐngbèi.

scruffy /'skrʌfɪ/ *adj* [-ier, -iest] [非正式用语]肮[骯]脏[髒]的 āngzāng de; 不整洁[潔]的 bù zhěngjié de.

scruple /'skru:pl/ *n* [C,U] 顾[顧]忌 gùjì; 顾虑[慮] gùlǜ; 不安bù'ān: *have no* ~*s about robbing him* 抢劫他是无所顾忌的.

scru·pu·lous /'skru:pjʊləs/ *adj* 审[審]慎的 shěnshènde; 小心翼翼的 xiǎoxīn yìyì de. ~**ly** *adv*

scru·ti·nize /'skru:tɪnaɪz/ *vt* 细察 xìchá; 考查 kǎochá.

scru·tiny /'skru:tɪnɪ/ *n* [*pl* -ies] [C,U] 细察 xìchá; 调查 diàochá.

scuff /skʌf/ *vt/i* **1** 拖着脚走 tuōzhe jiǎo zǒu. **2** 磨损 mósǔn.

scuffle /'skʌfl/ *vi, n* [C] 扭打 niǔdǎ; 混战[戰] hùnzhàn.

sculpt /skʌlpt/ *vt/i* = sculpture.

sculp·tor /'skʌlptə(r)/ *n* [C] 雕刻家 diāokèjiā. **sculp·tress** /'skʌlptrɪs/ *n* [C] 女雕刻家 nǚ diāokèjiā.

sculp·ture /'skʌlptʃə(r)/ *n* **1** [U] 雕刻 diāokè; 雕塑 diāosù. **2** [C, U] 雕刻品 diāokèpǐn; 雕塑品 diāosùpǐn. □ *vt* 雕刻 diāokè; 雕

塑 diāosù: ~ *a figure in marble* 雕刻大理石雕像.

scum /skʌm/ *n* [U] **1** 泡沫 pàomò; 浮垢 fúgòu. **2 the** ~ [喻]渣滓 zhāzǐ, 糟粕 zāopò.

scurry /ˈskʌrɪ/ *vi* [*pt, pp* -ied] 快跑 kuàipǎo; 疾走 jízǒu. □ *n* [U] 快跑 kuàipǎo; 疾走 jízǒu; 疾走声〔聲〕jízǒushēng.

scurvy /ˈskɜːvɪ/ *n* [U] 坏〔壞〕血病 huàixuèbìng.

scythe /saɪð/ *n* [C] 长〔長〕柄镰 chángbǐnglián. □ *vt* 用长柄镰割 yòng chángbǐnglián gē.

S.E. =south-east.

sea /siː/ *n* **1 the** ~ 海 hǎi, 海洋 hǎiyáng. **2** (用于专有名词)海 hǎi; 内海 nèihǎi: *the Caspian S~* 里海. **3** *at* ~ 在海上 zài hǎishàng. *completely at* ~[喻]茫然 mángrán, 迷惑 míhuò. *by* ~ 由海路 yóu hǎilù; 乘船 chéngchuán. *go to* ~ 当水手 dāng shuǐshǒu. *put to* ~ 离〔離〕港 lígǎng; 出航 chūháng. **4** 海的动〔動〕态〔態〕hǎide dòngtài: *a heavy* ~ 海上波涛汹涌. *a calm* ~ 海上平静. **5** 大量 dàliàng: *a* ~ *of faces* 人山人海. '~**faring** /-feərɪŋ/ *adj* 航海的 hánghǎide; 水手的 shuǐshǒude. '~**food** 海味 hǎiwèi. '~**front** 滨〔濱〕海区〔區〕bīnhǎiqū. '~**-going** *adj* (指船)适〔適〕于远〔遠〕洋航行的 shì yú yuǎnyáng hángxíng de. '~**gull** 海鸥〔鷗〕hǎi'ōu. '~**-horse** 海马〔馬〕hǎimǎ; 龙〔龍〕落子 lóngluòzi; 马头〔頭〕鱼 mǎtóuyú. '~**-level** 海平面 hǎipíngmiàn; (高低潮间的)平均海面 píngjūn hǎimiàn. '~ **lion** 海狮〔獅〕hǎishī. '~**man** 海员 hǎiyuán; 水手 shuǐshǒu. '~**man·ship** 航海术〔術〕hánghǎishù. '~**plane** 水上飞〔飛〕机〔機〕shuǐshàng fēijī. '~**shore** 海岸 hǎi'àn; 海滨〔濱〕hǎibīng. '~**sick** *adj* 晕〔暈〕船的 yùnchuánde. '~**side** 海边〔邊〕的 hǎibiānde; 海滨的 hǎibīngde. '~**ward** /-wəd/ *adj* 向海的 xiànghǎide; 朝海的 cháohǎide. '~**weed** 海草 hǎicǎo; 海藻 hǎizǎo. '~**worthy** *adj* (指船)适于航海的 shì yú hánghǎi de.

seal[1] /siːl/ *n* [C] 海豹 hǎibào. □ *vi* 捕海豹 bǔ hǎibào. '~**skin** 海豹皮 hǎibàopí.

seal[2] /siːl/ *n* [C] **1** 封蜡 fēnglà; 封铅 fēngqiān; 火漆〔漆〕huǒqī. **2** 印记 yìnjì; 图〔圖〕章 túzhāng. **3** ~ *of* [喻]保证 bǎozhèng; 证明 zhèngmíng: *Your plan has the manager's* ~ *of approval.* 你的计划得到经理的批准. **4** 密封垫〔墊〕mìfēngdiàn: *an airtight* ~ 密封垫; 密封圈. □ *vt* **1** 封 fēng; 加封腊 jiā fēnglà. **2** ~ **(*up*)** 密封 mìfēng. **3** ~ *off* 把…封锁起来〔來〕bǎ … fēngsuǒ qǐlái: *The police* ~*ed off the building.* 警察把这座建筑封锁起来. **4** 决定 juédìng: *His fate is* ~*ed!* 他的命运已定. '~**ing-wax** 封腊 fēnglà; 火漆 huǒqī.

seam /siːm/ *n* [C] **1** 线〔綫〕缝 xiànfèng; 接缝 jiēfèng. **2** 层〔層〕céng; 矿〔礦〕层 kuàngcéng.

sé·ance /ˈseɪɑːns/ *n* [C] 集会〔會〕jíhuì; 降神会 jiàngshénhuì.

search /sɜːtʃ/ *vt/i* 搜查 sōuchá; 搜索 sōusuǒ. □ *n* [C,U] 搜查 sōuchá; 搜索 sōusuǒ. '~**light** 探照灯〔燈〕tànzhàodēng. '~**-warrant** 搜查证 sōucházhèng. ~**ing** *adj* **(a)** (指目光)锐利的 ruìlìde. **(b)** (搜寻、检查)彻〔徹〕底的 chèdǐde.

sea·son /ˈsiːzn/ *n* [C] **1** 季 jì. **2** 季节〔節〕jìjié; 时〔時〕节 shíjié: *the 'holiday* ~ 休假(旅行)旺季. *in* ~ (水果等)当〔當〕令的 dānglìngde. *out of* ~ 不合时令的 bùhé shílìng de. □ *vt/i* **1** 使适〔適〕应〔應〕shǐshìyìng: ~*ed wood* 干燥材. **2** 调味 tiáowèi. '~**-ticket** 月季票 yuèjìpiào; 定期车〔車〕票 dìngqī chēpiào; 长〔長〕期票 chángqīpiào. ~**able** /-əbl/ *adj* **(a)** (指天气)合时令的 hé shílìng de. **(b)** (帮助等)及时的 jíshíde. ~**al** *adj* 季节性的 jìjiéxìngde: ~*al trade* 季节性生意. ~**ally** *adv* ~**ing** 调味品 tiáowèipǐn; 作料 zuóliao.

seat /siːt/ *n* [C] **1** 座 zuò, 座位 zuòwèi. *take a* ~ 坐下 zuòxià. **2** (椅等的)座部 zuòbù. **3** 臀部 túnbù: *the* ~ *of his trousers* 裤子后裆. **4** 中心地 zhōngxīndì; 所在地 suǒzàidì: *the* ~ *of government* 政府所在地. **5** 邸宅 dǐzhái; 别墅 biéshù. **6** 席位 xíwèi: *a* ~ *in Parliament* 在议会中的席位. □ *vt* **1** [正式用语] *be* ~*ed* 坐下 zuòxià; 就座 jiùzuò. **2** 供给…座位 gōngjǐ … zuòwèi: *The cinema* ~*s 200 people.* 这个影院可坐二百人. '~**-belt** (系于汽车、飞机座位上的)安全带〔帶〕ānquándài.

S.E.A.T.O. =South East Asia Treaty Organization 东〔東〕南亚〔亞〕条〔條〕约组织〔織〕Dōngnányà Tiáoyuē Zǔzhī.

Sec. =Secretary.

seca·teurs /ˈsekətɜːz/ *n pl* 剪枝刀 jiǎnzhīdāo.

se·cede /sɪˈsiːd/ *vi* (指团体)脱离〔離〕tuōlí; 退出 tuìchū. **se·ces·sion** /sɪˈseʃn/ *n* [C,U] 脱离 tuōlí;

退出 tuìchū.

se·clude /sɪ'klu:d/ *vt* 使隔离〔離〕shǐ gélí; 使孤立 shǐ gūlì; 使隐〔隱〕退 shǐ yǐntuì. **se·cluded** *adj* 僻静的 pìjìngde. **se·clu·sion** /-ʒn/ *n* [U] 隔离 gélí; 隐居 yǐnjū.

sec·ond¹ /'sekənd/ *adj* (缩作 *2nd*) **1** 第二的 dì'èrde;次等的 cìděngde. **2** 另一 lìngyī; 又一yòuyī: *Take a ~ pair of shoes.* 请拿另一双鞋. □ *adv* 第二 dì'èr; 次要地 cìyàode: *The English swimmer came* (*in*) *~.* 那位英国游泳家获得第二名. **,~-'best** *adj, n* 居第二位的 jū dì'èrwèi de; 居第二位 jū dì'èrwèi. **,~-'hand** *adj* **(a)** 用过〔過〕的 yòngguòde; 旧〔舊〕的 jiùde. **(b)** (新闻)第二手的 dì'èrshǒude; 间〔間〕接的 jiànjiēde. **,~'nature** 第二天性 dìèr tiānxìng. **,~-'rate** *adj* 二等的 èrděngde; 二流的 èrliúde. **,~ 'thoughts** 重新考虑〔慮〕后〔後〕的决定 chóngxīn kǎolǜ hòu de juédìng. **~ly** *adv* 第二 dì'èr; 其次 qícì.

sec·ond² /'sekənd/ *n* [C] **1** 第二名 dì'èrmíng; 第二位 dì'èrwèi. **2** [*pl*] 次货 cìhuò; 二等品 èrděngpǐn. **3** (决斗中的)助手 zhùshǒu.

sec·ond³ /'sekənd/ *n* [C] **1** 秒 miǎo. **2** 片刻 piànkè; 瞬间〔間〕shùnjiān: *Wait a ~!* 稍等一会儿! **'~-hand** (钟表的)秒针 miǎozhēn.

se·cond⁴ /'sekənd/ *vt* **1** 支持 zhīchí. **2** 赞成(提案等) zànchéng; 附议〔議〕fùyì. **~er** 附议者 fùyìzhě.

se·cond⁵ /sɪ'kɒnd/ *vt* 调任 diàorèn; 调派 diàopài. **~ment** *n* [U]

sec·ond·ary /'sekəndrɪ/ *adj* **1** 第二的 dì'èrde; 中级的 zhōngjíde: *~ schools* 中等学〔學〕校. **2** 次要的 cìyàode: *~symptoms* 次要征兆.

se·crecy /'si:krəsɪ/ *n* [U] 秘密 mìmì; 机〔機〕密 jīmì.

se·cret /'si:krɪt/ *adj* **1** 秘密的 mìmìde. ***keep sth ~*** **(*from*)** 不把某事告诉某人 bùbǎ mǒushì gàosu mǒurén. **2** 隐〔隱〕蔽的 yǐnbìde; 暗藏的 àncángde. □ *n* **1** [C] 秘密 mìmì. ***keep a ~*** 保守秘密 bǎoshǒu mìmì. **2** [C] 秘诀 mìjué: *the ~ of success* 成功的秘诀. **3** [U] ***in ~*** 秘密地 mìmìde. **4** [C] 神秘 shénmì. **,~ 'agent** 特务〔務〕tèwù. **the ,~'service** (政府的)特务〔務〕机〔機〕构〔構〕tèwù jīgòu. **~ly** *adv*

sec·re·tary /'sekrətrɪ/ *n* [C] [*pl* -ies] **1** 秘书〔書〕mìshū. **2** 干〔幹〕事 gànshi; 文书 wénshū. **S~ of State, (a)** [英国英语]国〔國〕务〔務〕大臣 guówù dàchén. **(b)** [美语]国务卿 guówùqīng.

sec·re·tar·ial /ˌsekrə'teərɪəl/ *adj*

se·crete /sɪ'kri:t/ *vt* **1** 分泌 fēnmì. **2** 隐〔隱〕藏 yǐncáng.

se·cre·tion /sɪ'kri:ʃn/ *n* [U] 分泌 fēnmì; [C] 分泌物(如唾液) fēnmìwù.

se·cret·ive /'si:krətɪv/ *adj* 遮遮掩掩的 zhēzhē yǎnyǎn de; 守口如瓶的 shǒu kǒu rú píng de. **~ly** *adv*

sect /sekt/ *n* [C] 派别 pàibié; 宗派 zōngpài. **~ar·ian** /sek'teərɪən/ *n* [C], *adj* 宗派主义〔義〕者 zōngpàizhǔyìzhě; 宗派的 zōngpàide.

sect.=section.

sec·tion /'sekʃn/ *n* [C] **1** 部分 bùfen; 零件 língjiàn. **2** 剖面 pōumiàn; 截面 jiémiàn; 横断〔斷〕面 héngduànmiàn. **~al** *adj* **(a)** 由各部分组合而成的 yóu gèbùfen zǔhé ér chéng de. **(b)** 社会〔會〕各阶〔階〕层〔層〕或不同部分 shèhuì gèjiēcéng huò bùtóng bùfen: *~al interests* 社会各阶层的不同利益.

sec·tor /'sektə(r)/ *n* [C] **1** 战〔戰〕区〔區〕zhànqū; 防区 fángqū. **2** (工业等)部门〔門〕bùmén: *the private ~*私有部分. *the public ~* 公有部分.

secu·lar /'sekjʊlə(r)/ *adj* 现世的 xiànshìde; 世俗的 shìsúde; 非宗教的 fēi zōngjiào de.

se·cure /sɪ'kjʊə(r)/ *adj* [rarely -r, -st] **1** 安心的 ānxīnde; 无〔無〕忧〔憂〕虑〔慮〕的 wú yōulǜ de. **2** 可靠的 kěkàode: *a ~ job* 可靠的工作. *~ future* 可靠的将来. **3** 牢固的 láogùde; 结实〔實〕的 jiēshide; 系〔繫〕紧〔緊〕的 xìjǐnde. **4** *~***(*from, against*)** 安全的 ānquánde. □ *vt* **1** 关〔關〕紧 guānjǐn; 扣紧 kòujǐn: *~ all the doors* 紧闭门户. **2** *~* ***sth*** **(*against, from*)** 防护〔護〕fánghù; 保卫〔衛〕bǎowèi: **3** 获〔獲〕得 huòdé: *~ a job* 找到工作. **~ly** *adv*

se·cur·ity /sɪ'kjʊərətɪ/ *n* [*pl* -ies] **1** [C,U] 安全 ānquán; 无〔無〕危险〔險〕wú wēixiǎn. **2** [C,U] 抵押品 dǐyāpǐn. **3** [C] 产〔產〕权〔權〕证明 chǎnquán zhèngmíng; 证券 zhèngquàn; 债券 zhàiquàn.

se·date /sɪ'deɪt/ *adj* 安静的 ānjìngde; 严〔嚴〕肃〔肅〕的 yánsùde. **~ly** *adv*

se·da·tion /sɪ'deɪʃn/ *n* [U] 镇静作用 zhènjìng zuòyòng.

seda·tive /'sedətɪv/ *n* [C], *adj* 镇静剂〔劑〕zhènjìngjì; 镇静的 zhènjìngde.

sed·en·tary /'sedntrɪ/ *adj* **1** (指工作)坐着的 zuòzhède. **2** (指人)坐惯的 zuòguànde; 久坐的 jiǔzuòde.

sedi·ment /'sedɪmənt/ *n* [U] 沉积〔積〕物 chénjīwù; 沉淀 chéndiàn. ~**ary** /-'mentrɪ/ *adj*

se·duce /sɪ'dju:s/ *vt* **1** 引诱 yǐnyòu; 诱惑 yòuhuò. **2** 诱奸〔姦〕yòujiān, 勾引 gōuyǐn. **se·duc·tion** /sɪ'dʌkʃn/ *n* [C,U] **se·duc·tive** /sɪ'dʌktɪv/ *adj* 诱惑的 yòuhuòde; 吸引人的 xīyǐn rén de.

see¹ /si:/ *vt/i* [*pt* saw /sɔ:/; *pp* ~n /si:n/] **1** [常与 *can, could* 连用]看见 kànjiàn: *If you shut your eyes you can't* ~. 如果你闭上眼睛,你就看不见. **2** [常与 *can, could* 连用]看出 kànchū; 见到 jiàndào: *I saw him put the key in the lock.* 我看到他把钥匙插入锁中. ***be*** ~***ing things*** 在幻觉〔覺〕中看见 zài huànjué zhōng kànjiàn. **3** [用于祈使句中]看 kàn; 瞧 qiáo: *S~ page 4.* 请看第四页. **4** 了解 liǎojiě; 明白 míngbai: *He didn't* ~ *the joke.* 他不明白那笑话的可笑之处. **5** 得知 dézhī; 获〔獲〕悉 huòxī: *I* ~ *that the Prime Minister is in China.* 我了解首相在中国. **6** 经〔經〕历〔歷〕jīnglì; 阅〔閱〕历 yuèlì: ~ *life* 见世面. **7** 会〔會〕见 huìjiàn; 访问〔問〕fǎngwèn: ~ *a doctor* 去看医生. **8** 留神 liúshén: *S~ that the windows are shut.* 务必把窗户关好. **9** ~ ***about sth*** 处〔處〕理(某事) chǔlǐ; 照料(某事) zhàoliào. ~ ***sb about sth*** 向某人请教(某事) xiàng mǒurén qǐngjiào. ~ ***sb back (home)*** 送某人回家 sòng mǒurén huíjiā. ~ ***sb off*** 为〔爲〕某人送行 wèi mǒurén sòngxíng. ~ ***through sb (sth)*** 看透(某人或某物) kàntòu. ,~ ***sth 'through*** 把某事进〔進〕行到底 bǎ mǒushì jìnxíng dàodǐ. ~ ***to sth*** 注意 zhùyì; 留心 liúxīn.

see² /si:/ *n* [C] 主教的辖〔轄〕区〔區〕zhǔjiàode xiáqū; 主教的地位 zhǔjiàode dìwèi.

seed /si:d/ *n* [C] [*pl* ~s or ~] **1** 种〔種〕子 zhǒngzi. ***run*** (或 ***go***) ***to*~**, **(a)** 花谢结子 huāxiè jiézǐ. **(b)** [喻]变〔變〕得不修边〔邊〕幅 biàndé bùxiū biānfú; 不再注意服饰外表 búzài zhùyì fúshì wàibiǎo. **2** 根源(与 *of* 连用) gēnyuán. **3** (运动)种子选手 zhǒngzi xuǎnshǒu. ⇨ 3 below. □ *vt/i* **1** (植物)结实〔實〕jiēshí; 生子 shēngzǐ. **2** 播种 bōzhǒng. **3** (尤指网球) 抽出种子选手 chōuchū zhǒngzi xuǎnshǒu. ~**ling** 幼苗 yòumiáo. **seedy** *adj* [-ier, -iest] **(a)** 多种子的 duō zhǒngzi de. **(b)** [非正式用语]褴〔襤〕褛〔褸〕的 lánlǚde. ~**ily** *adv*

seek /si:k/ *vt* [*pt, pp* sought /sɔ:t/] **1** 寻〔尋〕找 xúnzhǎo; 探寻 tànxún. **2** 请求 qǐngqiú: ~ *advice* 请教. **3** ***(much) sought after*** 供不应〔應〕求 gōng bú yìng qiú.

seem /si:m/ *vi* 好象 hǎoxiàng; 似乎 sìhū: *This book* ~*s interesting.* 这本书似乎有趣. ~**ing** *adj* 表面上的 biǎomiànshàngde; 似乎真实〔實〕的 sìhū zhēnshí de. ~**ing·ly** *adv*

seem·ly /'si:mlɪ/ *adj* [-ier, -iest] (指行为)适〔適〕宜的 shìyíde; 得体〔體〕的 détǐde.

seen /si:n/ *pp* of see¹.

seep /si:p/ *vi* (指液体)渗〔滲〕出 shènchū; 漏出 lòuchū. ~**age** /-ɪdʒ/ *n* [U] 渗出 shènchū; 漏出 lòuchū.

see·saw /'si:sɔ:/ *n* [C,U] **1** 跷〔蹺〕跷板 qiàoqiàobǎn. **2** [喻]反复的活动〔動〕fǎnfùde huódòng. □ *vi* **1** 玩跷跷板 wán qiàoqiàobǎn. **2** [喻]上下运〔運〕动〔動〕shàngxià yùndòng.

seethe /si:ð/ *vt/i* ~ ***(with)*** 激动〔動〕jīdòng; 激昂 jī'áng.

seg·ment /'segmənt/ *n* [C] **1** 部分 bùfen; 切片 qiēpiàn. **2** 段 duàn; 节〔節〕jié; 弓形 gōngxíng; 圆缺 yuánquē: *a* ~ *of an orange* 一瓣桔子. □ *vt/i* /seg'ment/ 分割 fēngē; 分裂 fēnliè.

seg·re·gate /'segrɪgeɪt/ *vt* 分离〔離〕fēnlí; 隔开〔開〕gékāi: ~ *boys from girls* 分开男孩女孩. **seg·re'ga·tion** /-ʃn/ *n* [U]

seis·mic /'saɪzmɪk/ *adj* 地震的 dìzhènde.

seis·mo·graph /'saɪzməgrɑ:f/ *n* [C] 地震仪〔儀〕(记录地震的强度) dìzhènyí.

seize /si:z/ *vt/i* **1** 抓住 zhuāzhù; 夺〔奪〕取 duóqǔ. **2** 抓住(时机等) zhuāzhù: ~ *an opportunity* 抓住机会. **3** (指机器)停住 tíngzhù.

seiz·ure /'si:ʒə(r)/ *n* **1** [C,U] 依法律占〔佔〕有、没收、查封等的实〔實〕例 yī fǎlǜ zhànyǒu, mòshōu, cháfēng děng de shílì. **2** [C] (疾病的)发〔發〕作 fāzuò.

sel·dom /'seldəm/ *adv* 很少 hěnshǎo; 不常 bùcháng.

se·lect /sɪ'lekt/ *vt* 选〔選〕择〔擇〕xuǎnzé; 挑选 tiāoxuǎn. □ *adj* **1** 精选的 jīngxuǎnde. **2** 选择成员严〔嚴〕格的 xuǎnzé chéngyuán yángé de: *a* ~ *audience* 经过挑选的观众. **se'lec·tion** /-ʃn/ *n* **(a)** [U] 选择 xuǎnzé; 挑选 tiāoxuǎn. **(b)** [C] 精选物 jīngxuǎnwù; 选集 xuǎnjí. ~**ive** *adj* **(a)** 有选择力的 yǒu xuǎnzélì de. (b) 选拔的 xuǎnbáde.

self /self/ *n* [*pl* selves /selvz/] [U] 本性 běnxìng; 本质〔質〕 běnzhì; 自己 zìjǐ; 自我 zìwǒ.

self- /self/ *prefix* 表示"自","自身","自我","自动〔動〕"biǎoshì"zì","zìshēn","zìwǒ", "zìdòng".,**~-'confident** *adj* 自信的 zìxìnde. ,**~-'conscious** *adj* 自觉〔覺〕的 zìjuéde;自我意识〔識〕的 zìwǒ yìshì de. ,**~-'consciousness** *n* [U] ,**~-con'tained** *adj* (a) (指人)不依赖他人的 bù yīlài tārén de. (b) (尤指公寓式住宅)设备〔備〕齐〔齊〕全的 shèbèi-qíquán de. ,**~-con'trol** 自制 zìzhì; 克己 kèjǐ. ,**~-de'fence** 自卫〔衛〕 zìwèi. ,**~-em'ployed** *adj* 自己开〔開〕业〔業〕(经营)的 zìjǐ kāiyè de. ,**~-'evident** *adj* 自明的 zìmíngde; 不言而喻的 bù yán ér yù de. ,**~-im'portant** *adj* 自大的 zìdàde. ,**~-im'portance** *n* [U] ,**~-in'dulgent** *adj* 放纵〔縱〕自己的 fàngzòng zìjǐ de. ,**~-'interest** 自私自利 zìsī-zìlì. ,**~-pos'sessed** *adj* 冷静的 lěngjìngde; 沉着的 chénzhuóde. ,**~-re'spect** 自尊 zìzūn; 自重 zìzhòng. ,**~-'righteous** *adj* 自以为〔爲〕公正善良的 zì yǐwéi gōngzhèng shànliáng de. '**~-same** *adj* 同一的 tóngyīde. ,**~-'service** 自助餐馆 zìzhù cānguǎn. ,**~-'willed** *adj* 固执〔執〕己见的 gùzhí jǐjiàn de.

self·ish /'selfɪʃ/ *adj* 自私的 zìsīde; 利己的 lìjǐde. **~ly** *adv* **~ness** *n* [U]

sell /sel/ *vt/i* [*pt, pp* sold /səʊld/] **1** 卖〔賣〕 mài, 销 xiāo. **2** 经〔經〕售 jīngshòu: *Do you ~ needles?* 你卖针吗? **3** 使接受 shǐ jiēshòu: *~ him an idea* 说服他接受某个主张. '**~ oneself** (a) 自我宣传〔傳〕 zìwǒ xuānchuán. (b) 出卖自己 chūmài zìjǐ. **4 ~ off** 廉售(存货) liánshòu.

selves /selvz/ *pl* of self.

sem·an·tic /sɪ'mæntɪk/ *adj* 语义〔義〕的 yǔyìde; 语义学〔學〕的 yǔyìxuéde. **sem·an·tics** *n* [U] 语义学 yǔyìxué.

sema·phore /'seməfɔː(r)/ *n* [U] 信号〔號〕 xìnhào; 旗语 qíyǔ. □ *vt/i* 打信号 dǎ xìnhào; 打旗语 dǎ qíyǔ.

sem·blance /'sembləns/ *n* [C] 外表 wàibiǎo; 外貌 wàimào.

se·men /'siːmən/ *n* [U] 精液 jīngyè.

semi- /semɪ/ *prefix* 半 bàn; 部分的 bùfende. '**~circle** 半圆 bànyuán. ,**~-'colon** 分号〔號〕(即;) fēnhào. **~-'conductor** 半导〔導〕体〔體〕 bàndǎotǐ. ,**~-de'tached** *adj* (指房屋)一侧与〔與〕他屋相连〔連〕的 yícè yǔ tāwū xiānglián de. ,**~-'final** 半决赛(的) bànjuésài.

semo·lina /,semə'liːnə/ *n* [U] (做布丁、通心粉等用的)粗面粉 cūmiànfěn.

Sen. =**1** Senate. **2** Senator. **3** Senior.

sen·ate /'senət/ *n* [C] **1** (美、法等的)参〔參〕议〔議〕院 cānyìyuàn; 上院 shàngyuàn. **2** (大学的)评议会〔會〕 píngyìhuì. **sena·tor** 参议员 cānyìyuán; 上议员 shàngyìyuán.

send/send/ *vt/i* [*pt, pp* sent] **1** 寄 jì; 送 sòng: *~ a letter* 寄信. *~ a message* 送口信. ⇨ take. **2** 使变〔變〕成 shǐ biànchéng: *This noise is ~ing me crazy.* 这闹声快使我发疯了. **3 *~ sb away*** 解雇 jiěgù. ***~ away for sth*** 邮〔郵〕寄订货单〔單〕 yóujì dìnghuòdān. ***~ for sb (sth)*** 派人去叫 pài rén qù jiào; 派人去拿 pài rén qù ná. ***~ sth on,*** (a) 预送 yùsòng. (b) 转〔轉〕送 zhuǎnsòng. ***~ sth out,*** (a) 放出 fàngchū: *The sun ~s out light.* 太阳发出光. (b) 发〔發〕出 fāchū; 长〔長〕出 zhǎngchū: *plants that ~ out shoots* 长出芽的作物.

se·nile /'siːnaɪl/ *adj* 老年的 lǎoniánde; 衰老的 shuāilǎode. **sen·il·ity** /sɪ'nɪlətɪ/ *n* [U].

sen·ior /'siːnɪə(r)/ *adj* (与 *junior* 相对) **1 ~ (*to*)** 年长〔長〕的 niánzhǎngde; 地位高的 dìwèigāode. **2** (缩作 **Snr, Sen** 或 **Sr**) (同名的父子二人中的)长者(用于姓名后) zhǎngzhě. □ *n* [C] 年长者 niánzhǎngzhě; 资历〔歷〕较〔較〕深者 zīlì jiàoshēn zhě. ,**~ 'citizen** 老年人 lǎoniánrén. **~ity** /,siːnɪ'ɒrətɪ/ *n* [U] 年长 niánzhǎng; 资历深 zīlì shēn; 职〔職〕位高 zhíwèi gāo.

sen·sa·tion /sen'seɪʃn/ *n* **1** [C,U] 感觉〔覺〕 gǎnjué; 知觉 zhījué. **2** [C,U] 感动〔動〕 gǎndòng; 激动 jīdòng. **~al** *adj* (a) 感觉的 gǎnjuéde. (b) (指报纸等)耸〔聳〕人听〔聽〕闻〔聞〕的 sǒng rén tīngwén de.

sense /sens/ *n* [C] **1** 官能 guānnéng; 感官 gǎnguān; 感觉〔覺〕 gǎnjué. **2** [*pl*] 心智健全 xīnzhì jiànquán. ***bring sb to his ~s*** 使醒悟 shǐ xǐngwù; 使神智恢复〔復〕正常 shǐ shénzhì huīfù zhèngcháng. ***take ,leave of one's '~s*** 发〔發〕疯〔瘋〕 fāfēng. **3** [不用 *pl*] 辨别力 (与 *of* 连用) biànbiélì; 意识〔識〕 yìshí: *a ~ of humour* 幽默感. **4** [U] 好的判断〔斷〕力 hǎode pànduànlì: *There's no ~ in doing that.* 做那件事没有道理. ⇨ common sense. 5 [C] 意义〔義〕yìyì. **make** ~有意义 yǒu yìyì. □ *vt* 感觉 gǎnjué; 意识到 yìshí dào: ~ *danger* 意识到有危险.

sense·less /'senslɪs/ *adj* 1 愚蠢的 yúchǔnde: *a* ~ *idea* 愚蠢的主意. 2 无〔無〕知觉的 wú zhījué de: *fall* ~ 昏倒. ~**ly** *adv* ~**ness** *n* [U]

sen·sible /'sensəbl/ *adj* 可感觉〔覺〕的 kě gǎnjué de; 切合实〔實〕际〔際〕的 qièhéshíjìde: *a* ~ *person* 聪明人. *a* ~ *idea* 明智的主意. **sen·sibly** *adv*

sen·si·tive /'sensətɪv/ *adj* 1 ~ (*to*) 敏感的 mǐngǎnde. 2 过〔過〕敏的 guòmǐnde; 容易生气〔氣〕的 róngyì shēngqì de. 3 (指仪器)灵〔靈〕敏的 língmǐnde. 4 感光的 gǎnguāngde. ,**sen·si·'tiv·ity** *n* [U] 敏感性 mǐnggǎnxìng; 灵敏性 língmǐnxìng; 感光度 gǎnguāngdù.

sen·si·tize /'sensɪtaɪz/ *vt* 使敏化 shǐ mǐnhuà.

sen·sual /'senʃʊəl/ *adj* 1 肉欲的 ròuyùde. 2 淫荡〔蕩〕的 yíndàngde. ~**ity** /-'ælətɪ/ *n* [U] 淫荡 yíndàng.

sen·su·ous /'senʃʊəs/ *adj* 引起美感的 yǐnqǐ měigǎn de; 影响〔響〕感觉〔覺〕的 yǐnxiǎng gǎnjué de.

sent /sent/ *pt, pp* of send.

sen·tence /'sentəns/ *n* [C] 1 判决 pànjué; 宣判 xuānpàn: *pass* ~ (*on him*) 判(他)刑. 2 [语法]句子 jùzi. □ *vt* 判决 pànjué; 宣判 xuānpàn: ~ *him to death* 判他死刑.

sen·ti·ment /'sentɪmənt/ *n* 1 [C, U] 情操 qíngcāo; 思想感情 sīxiǎng gǎnqíng. 2 [U] 情绪 qíngxù. 3 [*pl*] 意见 yìjiàn.

sen·ti·men·tal /,sentɪ'mentl/ *adj* 1 感情的 gǎnqíngde. 2 感情用事的 gǎnqíng yòngshì de; 多愁善感的 duōchóu shàngǎn de. ~**ity** /-'tælətɪ/ *n* [U] 多愁善感 duōchóu shàngǎn; 伤〔傷〕感 shānggǎn. ~**ly** *adv*

sen·try /'sentrɪ/ *n* [C] [*pl* -ies] 哨兵 shàobīng; 步哨 bùshào. '~-**box** 岗〔崗〕亭 gǎngtíng.

sep·ar·ate[1] /'seprət/ *adj* 分离〔離〕的 fēnlíde; 分开〔開〕的 fēnkāide: ~ *beds* 一对单人床. ~ *rooms* 独用房间. ~**ly** *adv*

sep·ar·ate[2] /'sepəreɪt/ *vt/i* 1 分离〔離〕fēnlí; 分开〔開〕fēnkāi. 2 分手 fēnshǒu. **sep·ar·ation** /-'reɪʃn/ *n* [C,U]

Sept. = September.

Sep·tem·ber /sep'tembə(r)/ *n* 九月 jiǔyuè.

sep·tic /'septɪk/ *adj* 使腐败的 shǐ fǔbài de. ,~ '**tank** 污水净化槽 wūshuǐ jìnghuàcáo.

sep·ulchre [美语 = -**ul·cher**] /'sepəlkə(r)/ *n* [C] 坟墓 fénmù; 冢〔塚〕zhǒng.

se·quel /'si:kwəl/ *n* [C] 1 后〔後〕续〔續〕hòuxù; 结果 jiéguǒ; 结局 jiéjú. 2 续集 xùjí; 续篇 xùpiān.

se·quence /'si:kwəns/ *n* [C,U] (事件、观念等的)系列 xìliè; 顺序 shùnxù; 关〔關〕联〔聯〕guānlián.

se·quin /'si:kwɪn/ *n* [C] (衣服上作饰物用的)小金属片 xiǎo jīnshǔpiàn.

ser·en·ade /,serə'neɪd/ *n* [C] 夜曲 yèqǔ; 小夜曲 xiǎoyèqǔ. □ *vt* (向…)歌唱(或弹奏)小夜曲 gēchàng xiǎoyèqǔ.

ser·ene /sɪ'ri:n/ *adj* 晴朗的 qínglǎngde; 宁〔寧〕静的 níngjìngde. ~**ly** *adv* **ser·en·ity** /sɪ'renətɪ/ *n* [U]

ser·geant /'sɑ:dʒənt/ *n* [C] 1 军〔軍〕士 jūnshì; 中士 zhōngshì. 2 警官 jǐngguān.

Sergt., Sgt. = Sergeant.

ser·ial /'sɪərɪəl/ *adj* 1 连〔連〕续〔續〕的 liánxùde; 一系列的 yíxìliède. 2 连载〔載〕的 liánzǎide. □ *n* [C] 连载小说 liánzǎi xiǎoshuō. ~**ize** /-laɪz/ *vt* 连载 liánzǎi.

series /'sɪəri:z/ *n* [C] [*pl* ~] 连〔連〕续〔續〕liánxù; 系列 xìliè.

seri·ous /'sɪərɪəs/ *adj* 1 严〔嚴〕肃〔肅〕的 yánsùde; 庄〔莊〕重的 zhuāngzhòngde: *a* ~ *face* 严肃的面孔. 2 严重的 yánzhòngde; 危急的 wēijíde: *a* ~ *illness* 重病. 3 认〔認〕真的 rènzhēnde: *a* ~ *worker* 认真工作的人. ~**ly** *adv* ~**ness** *n* [U]

ser·mon /'sɜ:mən/ *n* [C] 讲〔講〕道 jiǎngdào; 说教 shuōjiào.

ser·pent /'sɜ:pənt/ *n* [C] 蛇 shé.

ser·rated /se'reɪtɪd/ *adj* 有锯齿〔齒〕的 yǒu jùchǐ de.

serum /'sɪərəm/ *n* [*pl* ~s] 1 [U] 浆〔漿〕液 jiāngyè. 2 [C,U] 血清 xuèqīng.

ser·vant /'sɜ:vənt/ *n* [C] 1 仆〔僕〕人 púrén; 雇工 gùgōng. 2 **public** ~ 公仆 gōngpú; 政府官员 zhèngfǔ guānyuán. ⇨ civil servant.

serve /sɜ:v/ *vt/i* 1 服务〔務〕fúwù. 2 (为…)尽〔盡〕责 jìnzé: ~ *one's country* 为国家服务. 3 招待(顾客) zhāodài; 端上(饭菜) duānshàng. 4 ~ (*for, as sth*) 适〔適〕合 shìhé; 合用 héyòng. 5 ~ *one right* 遭受应〔應〕有的不幸 zāoshòu yīngyǒude búxìng. 6 (在任期内)供职〔職〕gòngzhí. ~ *time as a manager* 履行

经理任内职责. 7 ~ *time*, ~ *a sentence* 服刑 fúxíng. 8 [法律]送交(传票等) sòngjiāo. 9 (网球等)发[發](球) fā. □ *n* [C] (网球等)发球 fāqiú.

ser·vice /'sɜːvɪs/ *n* 1 [U] 帮佣 bāngyōng. 2 [C] 机[機]关[關]部门[門] jīguān bùmén; 服务机构[構] fúwù jīgòu. ⇨ civil service. 3 [C] 服务 fúwù; 帮助 bāngzhù. 4 [U] 利益 lìyì; 有用 yǒuyòng; 好处[處] hǎochù: *I am at your* ~ 我随时为你效劳. 5 [C] 公共需要的供应[應]系统 gōnggòng xūyào de gōngyìng xìtǒng: *a 'bus* ~ 公共汽车公司. 6 [C] [宗教]礼[禮]拜式 lǐbàishì. 7 [C] (全套)食器 shíqì: *a dinner* ~ 一套餐具. 8 [U] 招待 zhāodài; 上菜 shàngcài; 上饮料 shàng yǐnliào. 9 [U] (厂商出售物品后给予顾客的)检[檢]修 jiǎnxiū; 维修 wéixiū; 保养[養] bǎoyǎng. 10 (网球等)发[發]球 fāqiú. □ *vt* 检修 jiǎnxiū; 维修 wéixiū; 保养 bǎoyǎng (⇨ 9 above). '~ **charge** 小费 xiǎofèi. '~ **station** 加油站 jiāyóuzhàn. ~**able** /-əbl/ *adj* (a) 耐用的 nàiyòngde. (b) 有用的 yǒuyòngde.

ser·vi·ette /ˌsɜːvɪ'et/ *n* [C] = napkin.

ser·vile /'sɜːvaɪl/ *adj* 奴隶[隸]的 núlìde; 奴隶般的 núlìbānde.

ses·sion /'seʃən/ *n* [C] 1 开[開]庭 kāitíng; 开庭期 kāitíngqī. 2 [苏格兰语,美语](大学的)学[學]期 xuéqī. 3 (为某种目的所举行的)集会[會] jíhuì: *a re'cording* ~ 录音时间.

set¹ /set/ *n* [C] 1 (一)套 tào; (一)副 fù; (一)组 zǔ: *a* ~ *of spanners* 一套扳手. 2 (一批)同道 tóngdào: *the literary* ~ 文艺界. 3 (无线电)接收机[機] jiēshōujī. 4 (网球等)(一)盘[盤] pán. 5 (舞台、电影等的)布[佈]景 bùjǐng.

set² /set/ *vt/i* [-tt-, *pt*, *pp* ~] 1 (日、月等)落 luò; 下沉 xiàchén. 2 放 fàng: ~ *pen to paper* 动笔,下笔. ~ *light (fire) to sth* 使某物开[開]始燃烧[燒] shǐ mǒuwù kāishǐ ránshāo. ~ *foot in* 进[進]入 jìnrù. 3 使处[處]于某种[種]状[狀]态[態] shǐ chǔyú mǒuzhǒng zhuàngtài. ~ *sb free* 释[釋]放 shìfàng. *be all* ~ 准[準]备[備]就绪 zhǔnbèi jiùxù. 4 使开(啟)动[動] shǐ kāidòng: ~ *machinery going* 开动机器. 5 搁[擱] gē; 竖[豎] shù: *She* ~ *the food on the table.* 她把食物放在桌上. 6 提出 tíchū; 规定 guīdìng: *I have* ~ *myself a task.* 我为自己安排了一件工作. ~ *(sb) an example* 树[樹]立榜样[樣] shùlì bǎngyàng: 7 ~ *one's heart (hopes) on sth* 极[極]欲 jíyù; 决心要得到 juéxīn yào dédào. ~ *eyes on* 看 kàn. 8 使固定 shǐ gùdìng: ~ *a (broken) bone* 接合断骨. ~ *one's hair* 卷[捲]头[頭]发[髮] juǎn tóufa. ~ *the scene* 描述戏[戲]剧[劇]等中的地点[點]及参与[與]活动的人 miáoshù xìjù děng zhōng de dìdiǎn jí cānyǔ huódòng de rén. ~ *sail* 启[啟]航 qǐháng. 9 镶 xiāng; 嵌 qiàn. ~ *a diamond in gold* 在黄金上镶钻石. 10 ~ *sth (to sth)* 为[爲]...配曲 wèi ... pèiqǔ: ~ *words to music* 为词谱曲. 11 (使)凝固 nínggù; (使)凝结 níngjié: *The cement has* ~. 水泥已凝固. 12 [*pp*] 不变[變]的 búbiànde; 固执[執]的 gùzhíde: ~ *in one's ways* 生活习惯不变的, 一成不变的. 13 ~ *about sth* 着手 zhuóshǒu; 开始 kāishǐ. ~ *sth back*, (a) 拨[撥]回 bōhuí. (b) 置于远[遠]处[處] zhì yú yuǎnchù. ~ *sb (sth) back* 阻碍[礙] zǔ'ài; 阻止 zǔzhǐ. ~ *in* 开始 kāishǐ. ~ *off* 出发[發] chūfā. ~ *sth off*, (a) 使(地雷等)爆炸 shǐ bàozhà. (b) 平衡 pínghéng; 抵销 dǐxiāo: ~ *off gains against losses* 得失相抵. ~ *on sb* 攻击[擊] gōngjī. *be* ~ *on sth* 决心做某事 juéxīn zuò mǒushì. ~ *out* 出发 chūfā; 启程 qǐchéng. ~ *out to do sth* 为了某个[個]目标[標]而努力 wèile mǒugè mùbiāo ér nǔlì. ~ *sth out* 装[裝]饰 zhuāngshì: ~ *out flowers on a table* 把花摆在桌上. ~ '*to* 开始积[積]极[極]地做 kāishǐ jījíde zuò. ~ *sth up*, (a) 设立 shèlì; 建立 jiànlì. (b) 开办[辦] kāibàn. '~-**up** *n* [非正式用语]组织[織] zǔzhī; 结构[構] jiégòu. ~ *(oneself) up as*, (a) 从[從]事(经营)某种[種]行业[業] cóngshì mǒuzhǒng hángyè. (b) 打算成为 dǎsuàn chéngwéi.

set·back /'setbæk/ *n* [C] 挫折 cuòzhé; 倒退 dàotuì.

set-square /'set skweə(r)/ *n* [C] 三角板 sānjiǎobǎn.

set·tee /se'tiː/ *n* [C] = sofa.

set·ter /'setə(r)/ *n* [C] 塞特种[種]猎[獵]狗 sàitèzhǒng liègǒu.

set·ting /'setɪŋ/ *n* [C] 1 镶嵌 xiāngqiàn. 2 环[環]境 huánjìng; 背景 bèijǐng. 3 (日、月的) 沉落 chénluò.

settle /'setl/ *vt/i* 1 定居 dìngjū; 安

家 ānjiā. 2 停息 tíngxī; 停留 tíngliú: *The bird ~d on the branch.* 鸟歇落在枝上. 3 使平静 shǐ píngjìng; 使安宁〔寧〕 shǐ ānníng: ~ *his nerves* 使他镇静下来. 4 解决 jiějué; 决定 juédìng: ~ *an argument* 结束争论. 5 支付 zhīfù; 结算 jiésuàn: ~ *a bill* 付帐. 6 (使)沉淀〔澱〕 chéndiàn; (使)澄清 chéngqīng. 7 ~ *down* 定居 dìngjū. ~ *(down) to sth* 专〔專〕心致志于 zhuānxīn-zhìzhì yú. ~ *for sth* 勉强接受 miǎnqiǎng jiēshòu. ~ *(sb) in* 迁〔遷〕入(新居) qiānrù. ~ *on (upon) sth* 决定 juédìng; 选〔選〕择〔擇〕 xuǎnzé. ~ *(up) (with sb)* 付清 fùqīng. **settled** *adj* **(a)** 固定的 gùdìngde; 不变〔變〕的 búbiànde. **(b)** 付清的 fùqīngde. **~ment** *n* **(a)** [C,U] 解决 jiějué. **(b)** [C] 赠与〔與〕财产〔產〕的文书〔書〕 zèngyǔ cáichǎn de wénshū; 所赠与的财产 suǒ zèngyǔde cáichǎn. **(c)** [C,U] 殖民 zhímín **set·tler** *n* [C] 移居者 yíjūzhě; 移民 yímín.

seven /'sevn/ *adj, n* [C] 七 qī. **~th** *adj, n* [C] (缩作 *7th*) 第七 dìqī; 七分之一 qīfēn zhī yī.

seven·teen /ˌsevn'ti:n/ *adj, n* [C] 十七的 shíqīde; 十七 shíqī. **~th** *adj, n* [C] (缩作 *17th*) 第十七 dìshíqī; 十七分之一 shíqīfēn zhī yī.

sev·enty /'sevntɪ/ *adj, n* [C] 七十的 qīshíde; 七十qīshí. **seven·ti·eth** *adj, n* [C] (缩作 *70th*) 第七十 dìqīshí; 七十分之一 qīshífēn zhī yī.

sever /'sevə(r)/ *vt/i* 1 切断〔斷〕 qiēduàn; 割断 gēduàn: ~ *an artery* 切断一条动脉. 2 [喻]断绝 duànjué; 中断 zhōngduàn: ~ *relations* 断绝关系. **~ance** *n* [U]

sev·eral /'sevrəl/ *adj* 1 几〔幾〕个〔個〕 jǐgè; 数〔數〕个 shùgè. 2 个别的 gèbiéde; 各自的gèzìde: *They went their ~ ways.* 他们各走各的路. □ *pron* 几个 jǐgè; 数个 shùgè. **~ly** *adv*

se·vere /sɪ'vɪə(r)/ *adj* 1 严〔嚴〕厉〔厲〕的 yánlìde; 严肃〔肅〕的 yánsùde. 2 (指天气、疾病等) 严重的 yánzhòngde; 剧〔劇〕烈的 jùliède. **~ly** *adv*

se·ver·ity /sɪ'verətɪ/*n* [*pl* -ies] [正式用语] **(a)** [U] 严〔嚴〕厉〔厲〕yánlì; 严肃〔肅〕 yánsù. **(b)** [*pl*] 严厉的对待 yánlìde duìdài; 艰〔艱〕苦的经〔經〕验〔驗〕 jiānkǔ de jīngyàn.

sew /səʊ/ *vt/i* [*pt* ~ed; *pp* ~n /səʊn/] 缝制〔製〕 féngzhì; 缝合 fénghé; 缝 féng.

sew·age /'sju:ɪdʒ/ *n* [U] 污水 wūshuǐ; 污物 wūwù.

sewer /'sju:ə(r)/ *n* [C] 下水道 xiàshuǐdào, 阴〔陰〕沟〔溝〕 yīngōu.

sewn /səʊn/ *pp* of sew.

sex /seks/ *n* 1 [U] 性 xìng; 性别 xìngbié. 2 [C] (总称)男性 nánxìng; 女性 nǚxìng. 3 [U] 性的活动〔動〕 xìngde huódòng. **sexy** *adj* [-ier, -iest] 色情的 sèqíngde.

sex·tant /'sekstənt/ *n* [C] 六分仪〔儀〕 liùfēnyí.

sex·ton /'sekstən/ *n* [C] 教堂司事(管理教堂、敲钟、挖掘墓地等) jiàotáng sīshì.

sex·ual /'sekʃʊəl/ *adj* 性的 xìngde; 两性的 liǎngxìngde. **~'intercourse** 性交 xìngjiāo. **~ity** /ˌ'ælətɪ/ *n* [U] 性欲 xìngyù.

sgd.=signed.

shabby /'ʃæbɪ/ *adj* [-ier, -iest] 1 破旧〔舊〕的 pòjiùde; 褴〔襤〕褛〔褸〕的 lánlǚde. 2 (指行为) 卑鄙的 bēibǐde; 不公平的 bù gōngpíng de. **shab·bily** *adv*

shack /ʃæk/ *n* [C] 简〔簡〕陋的小木屋 jiǎnlòude xiǎomùwū; 棚屋 péngwū.

shackle /'ʃækl/ *n* [C] 1 镣铐 liàokào; 手铐 shǒukào; 脚镣 jiǎoliào. 2 [喻]束缚 shùfù; 枷锁 jiāsuǒ. □ *vt* 加镣铐于 jiā liàokào yú; 束缚 shùfù.

shade /ʃeɪd/ *n* 1 [U] 荫〔蔭〕 yīn; 阴〔陰〕暗 yīn'àn. 2 [U] (图画等的)阴暗部分 yīn'àn bùfen. 3 [C] (色彩的)浓〔濃〕淡 nóngdàn: *four ~s of blue.* 四种深浅不同的蓝色. 4 [C] (意义)细微差别 xìwēi chābié: *~s of meaning* 意义上的细微差别. 5 遮光物 zhēguāngwù: *a 'lamp~* 灯罩. □ *vt/i* 1 遮蔽 zhēbì, 荫蔽 yīnbì: ~ *one's eyes* 遮目. 2 遮(光、灯等) zhē. 3 画〔畫〕阴影于 huà yīnyǐng yú. 4 渐〔漸〕变〔變〕 jiànbiàn: *green shading into blue* 由绿渐变为蓝.

shadow /'ʃædəʊ/ *n* 1 [C] 影子 yǐngzi; 阴〔陰〕影 yīnyǐng. 2 [*pl*] 阴暗部分 yīn'àn bùfen. 3 [C] 黑斑 hēibān: *~s under the eyes* 眼睛周围有黑圈 (因缺乏睡眠或疾病而造成). 4 微量 wēiliàng: *beyond a ~ of doubt* 没有丝毫的怀疑. □ *vt* 1 遮暗 zhē'àn; 遮蔽 zhēbì. 2 尾随 wěisuí, 钉梢 dīngshāo. **shad·owy** *adj*

shady /'ʃeɪdɪ/ *adj* [-ier, -iest] 1 多荫〔蔭〕的 duōyīnde; 荫凉的 yīnliángde. 2 可疑的 kěyíde; 靠不住的 kàobúzhùde: *a ~ salesman* 靠不住的店员.

shaft /'ʃɑ:ft/ *n* [C] **1** 箭(杆) jiàn; 矛(柄)máo. **2** 斧柄 fǔbǐng; 长〔長〕柄 chángbǐng. **3** 车〔車〕杠 chēgāng, 辕〔轅〕yuán. **4** 矿〔礦〕井 kuàngjǐng; 竖〔豎〕井 shùjǐng; 升降井 shēngjiàngjǐng. **5** (机械的)轴〔軸〕zhóu. **6** 光线〔綫〕guāngxiàn.

shaggy /'ʃægɪ/ *adj* [-ier, -iest] **1** (指毛发)蓬乱〔亂〕的 péngluànde. **2** 覆有粗浓〔濃〕的毛发 fù yǒu cūnóngde máofà.

shake[1] /ʃeɪk/ *n* [C] 摇动〔動〕yáodòng; 震动 zhèndòng.

shake[2] /ʃeɪk/ *vt/i* (*pt* shook /ʃʊk/; *pp* ~n /'ʃeɪkən/) **1** 摇 yáo; 摇动〔動〕yáodòng; 抖动 dǒudòng. **2** 震惊〔驚〕zhènjīng: *We were ~n by his death.* 他的逝世使我们震惊. **3** 发〔發〕颤音 fā chànyīn. **4** ~ *sb off* 摆〔擺〕脱 bǎituō. ~ *sth off* 除去 chúqù. ~ *sth up* 摇匀 yáoyún. ~ *sb up* 摇醒 yáoxǐng. '**~-up** *n* **shaky** *adj* [-ier, -iest] **(a)** (指人)衰弱的 shuāiruòde; 不稳〔穩〕的 bùwěnde. **(b)** 不安全的 bù ānquán de. **shak·ily** /-əlɪ/ *adv*

shale /ʃeɪl/ *n* [U] 页岩〔巖〕yèyán.

shall /ʃəl 强式: ʃæl/ *aux verb* (常简略为 **'ll;** shall not 常简略为 **shan't** /ʃɑ:nt/; *pt* **should** /ʃʊd 弱式: ʃəd/; *should not* 常简略为 **shouldn't** /'ʃʊdnt/) **1** (表示将来): *We ~ (We'll) arrive tomorrow.* 我们将于明日到达. **2** (表示义务): *I say you '~ do it.* 我说你就该做. **3** (表示允诺或威胁): *You shan't beat me so easily next time.* 你下次不会那样容易地赢我了. **4** (表示责任、命令和(否定式中)禁止): *S~ I open the window?* 我可以把窗子打开吗? *You should have been more careful.* 你不应该如此粗心大意. **5** (表示期望): *They should be there by now.* 他们现在就该到那里了.

shal·lot /ʃə'lɒt/ *n* [C] 青葱 qīngcōng.

shal·low /'ʃæləʊ/ *adj* [-er, -est] **1** 浅〔淺〕的 qiǎnde: *a ~ river* 浅河. **2** [喻]浅薄的 qiǎnbóde, 肤〔膚〕浅的 fūqiǎnde: *a ~ thinker* 肤浅的思想家. □ *n* [C] 〔常用 *pl*〕浅滩〔灘〕qiǎntān.

sham /ʃæm/ *vt/i* [-mm-] 假装〔裝〕jiǎzhuāng: ~ *illness* 装病. □ *n* [C] **1** 假冒者 jiǎmàozhě; 赝品 yànpǐn. **2** [U] 托词 tuōcí; 口实〔實〕kǒushí. □ *adj* 假的 jiǎde; 虚伪〔僞〕的 xūwěide: *a ~ fight* 模拟战.

shamble /'ʃæmbl/ *vi* 蹒跚 pánshān. □ *n* [C] 蹒跚 pánshān; 拖沓的步子 tuōtàde bùzi.

shambles /'ʃæmblz/ *n* [U] 混乱〔亂〕hùnluàn; 废〔廢〕墟 fèixū.

shame /ʃeɪm/ *n* [U] **1** 羞耻 xiūchǐ; 羞愧 xiūkuì. **2** 羞耻心 xiūchǐxīn: *He has no ~.* 他不知羞耻. **3** [U] 耻辱 chǐrǔ: *bring ~ on one's parents* 给某人的父母带来耻辱. **4** 遗憾的事 yíhànde shì: *It's (What a) ~ you can't come with us.* 你不能同我们一起去真是遗憾. □ *vt* **1** 使羞愧 shǐ xiūkuì. **2** ~ *sb into doing sth* 使(某人)因羞愧而做某事 shǐ yīn xiūkuì ér zuò mǒushì. '**~-faced** *adj* 害羞的 hàixiūde; 惭〔慚〕愧的 cánkuìde. **~ful** *adj* 可耻的 kěchǐde; 淫猥的 yínwěide. **~fully** /-fəlɪ/ *adv* **~less** *adj* 无〔無〕耻的 wúchǐde; 伤〔傷〕风〔風〕败俗的 shāng fēng bài sú de.

sham·poo /ʃæm'pu:/ *n* [C,U] 洗发〔髮〕xǐfà; 洗发剂〔劑〕xǐfàjì. □ *vt* 洗(发) xǐ.

sham·rock /'ʃæmrɒk/ *n* [C] 〔植物〕白花酢浆〔漿〕草(爱尔兰的国花) báihuācùjiāngcǎo.

shandy /'ʃændɪ/ *n* [C,U] 啤酒和柠〔檸〕檬水混合的饮料 píjiǔhé níngméngshuǐ hùnhé de yǐnliào.

shank /ʃæŋk/ *n* [C] **1** 胫〔脛〕jìng; 小腿 xiǎotuǐ; 胫骨 jìnggǔ. **2** (工具的)柄 bǐng; 杆〔桿〕gǎn.

shan't /ʃɑ:nt/ = *shall not.* ⇨ shall.

shanty /'ʃæntɪ/ *n* [C] [*pl* -ies] 小屋 xiǎowū; 棚屋 péngwū. '**~-town** 棚户区〔區〕pénghùqū; 贫民窟 pínmínkū.

shape /ʃeɪp/ *n* **1** [C,U] 形状〔狀〕xíngzhuàng, 形态〔態〕xíngtài; 外形 wàixíng. *take ~* 成形 chéngxíng; 具体〔體〕化 jùtǐhuà. **2** [喻] 方式 fāngshì: *I had help in the ~ of a friend.* 我得到了朋友式的帮助. **3** 情况 qíngkuàng; 状态 zhuàngtài: *He's in good ~.* 他情况良好. □ *vt/i* **1** (使)成形 chéngxíng; 塑造 sùzào. **2** 发〔發〕展 fāzhǎn: *Our plans are shaping well.* 我们的计划进展顺利. **~ly** *adj* [-ier, -iest] 匀称〔稱〕的 yúnchènde; 样〔樣〕子好的 yàngzi hǎo de.

share /ʃeə(r)/ *n* **1** [C] 一份 yífèn; 份儿〔兒〕fènr. **2** [U] 份额 fèn'é; 负担量 fùdānliàng: *your ~ of the blame* 你的一份过失. **3** [C] 股份 gǔfèn. □ *vt/i* **1** ~ *sth (out)* 均分 jūnfēn; 分配 fēnpèi. **2** ~ *(with)* 共有 gòngyǒu; 共用 gòngyòng: ~ *a house with someone* 同某人共有(或合用)一所房子. **3** ~ *(in) sth* 分享 fēnxiǎng. '**~holder** 股东〔東〕gǔdōng.

shark /ʃɑ:k/ *n* [C] **1** 鲨鱼 shāyú. **2** [喻]骗[騙]子 piànzi.

sharp /ʃɑ:p/ *adj* [-er, -est] **1** 锋利的 fēnglìde; 尖锐的 jiānruìde: *a ~ knife* 快刀. **2** 明显[顯]的míngxiǎnde; 鲜明的 xiānmíngde: *a ~ outline*鲜明的轮廓. **3** 急转[轉]的 jízhuǎnde; 陡的 dǒude; 急剧[劇]的 jíjùde. **4** (指声音)刺耳的 cì'ěrde. **5** 敏锐的 mǐnruìde; 机[機]警的 jījǐngde: *He's got a ~ mind.* 他思想敏捷. **6** (指感觉、味道)强烈的 qiángliède; 辛辣的 xīnlàde. **7** 苛刻的 kēkède; 刻薄的 kèbóde: *~ words* 刻薄言词. **8** [音乐]升半音的 shēngbànyīnde. □ *n* [C] [音乐]升(半)音 shēngyīn; 升号[號] (即 ♯) shēnghào. □ *adv* **1** 准[準]时[時]地 zhǔnshíde: *at seven (o'clock) ~* 七时整. **2** 突然 tūrán: *turn ~ left* 向左急转. **~en** *vt/i* 使(变)尖锐 shǐ jiānruì; 使(变)急剧[劇] shǐ jíjù. **~ener** 削刀 xiāodāo; 磨床 móchuáng. **~ly** *adv* **~ness** *n* [U]

shat·ter /'ʃætə(r)/ *vt/i* 粉碎 fěnsuì; 毁损 huǐsǔn.

shave /ʃeɪv/ *vt/i* [*pt, pp* ~d 或用作定语 ~n /'ʃeɪvn/] **1** 剃 tì; 刮(胡子等) guā. **2** *~ sth off* 削 xiāo; 刨 bào. **3** 掠过[過] lüèguò; 擦过 cāguò. □ *n* [C] **1** 修面 xiūmiàn; 刮脸[臉] guāliǎn. **2** *a close ~* 幸免于难[難] xìngmiǎn yú nàn. **shaver** 电[電]动[動]剃刀 diàndòng tìdāo. **shav·ings** *n pl* 刨花 bàohuā; 削片 xiāopiàn; 薄片 bópiàn.

shawl /ʃɔ:l/ *n* [C] 披巾 pījīn; 围[圍]巾 wéijīn.

she /ʃi:/ *pron* (⇨ her; they) **1** 她 tā; 它 tā: *My sister says ~ is going for a walk.* 我的姐姐说她要去散步. **2** 女性 nǚxìng; 雌性 cíxìng: *a '~-goat* 雌山羊.

sheaf /ʃi:f/ *n* [C] [*pl* sheaves /ʃi:vz/] **1** (收割后的小麦、大麦等的)捆 kǔn; 束 shù. **2** (箭等的)束 shù.

shear /ʃɪə(r)/ *vt* (*pt,* ~ed; *pp* shorn /ʃɔ:n/ 或 ~ed) 剪 jiǎn; 剪(羊)毛 jiǎn máo; 修剪 xiūjiǎn. **shears** /ʃɪəz/ *n pl* (亦作 *a pair of* ~) 大剪刀 dà jiǎndāo.

sheath /ʃi:θ/ *n* [C] [*pl* ~s /ʃi:ðz/] 鞘 qiào; 套 tào.

sheathe /ʃi:ð/ *vt* 插…入鞘 chā…rùqiào.

sheaves /ʃi:vz/ ⇨ sheaf.

shed[1] /ʃed/ *n* [C] 棚 péng; 货棚 huòpéng; 车[車]库[庫] chēkù.

shed[2] /ʃed/ *vt* [*pt, pp* ~] [-dd-] **1** 脱落 tuōluò. **~ *blood,*** (a) 流血 liúxuè; 杀[殺]戮 shālù. (b) 使他人流血 shǐ tārén liúxuè. ⇨ bloodshed. **~ *tears*** = cry. **2** 脱去 tuōqù: *~ clothes* 脱掉衣服. **3** 放射 fàngshè: *~ light* 发出光. ***~ light on*** (*fig*) ⇨ light[3](5).

she'd /ʃi:d/ = *she had; she would.*

sheep /ʃi:p/ *n* [C] [*pl*~] 羊 yáng; 绵羊 miányáng. **'~dog** 护[護]羊犬 hùyángquǎn. **'~skin** 羊皮 yángpí; 羊皮衣 yángpíyī; 羊皮纸 yángpízhǐ. **'~ish** *adj* (a) 害羞的 hàixiūde. (b) 胆怯的 dǎnqiède.

sheer /ʃɪə(r)/ *adj* **1** 全然的 quánránde; 绝对[對]的 juéduìde: *~ nonsense* 纯粹的胡说八道. **2** (指织物)极[極]薄的 jíbóde. **3** 陡峭的 dǒuqiàode: *a ~ drop* 陡落. □ *adv* 垂直地 chuízhíde.

sheet /ʃi:t/ *n* [C] **1** 被单[單] bèidān. **2** 薄板 bóbǎn; 薄片 bópiàn. **3** 大片 dàpiàn.

sheik(h) /ʃeɪk/ *n* [C] (阿拉伯)酋长[長] qiúzhǎng; 族长 zúzhǎng. **~dom** *n* [C]

shelf /ʃelf/ *n* [C] [*pl* shelves /ʃelvz/] **1** 架子 jiàzi; 搁[擱]板 gēbǎn. **2** 突出的扁平岩[巖]石 tūchūde biǎnpíng yánshí.

shell /ʃel/ *n* [C] **1** 壳[殼] qiào; 果壳 guǒqiào. **2** (房屋等)框架 kuàngjià; (船的)壳板 qiàobǎn. **3** 炮弹[彈] pàodàn; 猎[獵]枪[槍]子弹 lièqiāng zǐdàn. □ *vt/i* **1** 剥…的壳 bō…de ké; 脱壳 tuō ké: *~ peas* 剥豌豆. **2** 炮击[擊] pàojī. **'~fish** 水生贝壳类[類]动[動]物 shuǐshēng bèiqiàolèi dòngwù.

she'll /ʃi:l/ = *she will; she shall.*

shel·ter /'ʃeltə(r)/ *n* **1** [U] 掩蔽 yǎnbì, 遮蔽 zhēbì; 庇护[護] bìhù. **2** [C] 隐[隱]蔽处[處] yǐnbìchù; 避难[難]所 bìnànsuǒ. □ *vt/i* **1** 庇护 bìhù, 保护 bǎohù; 掩蔽 yǎnbì. **2** 躲避 duǒbì; 避难 bìnàn: *~ from the rain under a tree* 在树下避雨.

shelve[1] /ʃelv/ *vt* **1** 把…放在架上 bǎ…fàngzài jiàshàng. **2** [喻](问题等)搁[擱]置 gēzhì; 暂[暫]缓考虑[慮] zànhuǎn kǎolǜ.

shelve[2] /ʃelv/ *vi* (渐次)倾斜 qīngxié; 成斜坡 chéng xiépō.

shelves /ʃelvz/ *pl* of shelf.

shep·herd /'ʃepəd/ *n* [C] 牧羊人 mùyángrén, 羊倌 yángguān. □ *vt* 照看 zhàokàn; 带[帶]领 dàilǐng. **~ess** *n* [C] 女牧羊人 nǚ mùyángrén.

sher·iff /'ʃerɪf/ *n* [C] **1** (亦作 *High* ~) 郡长[長] jùnzhǎng; 行政司法长官 xíngzhèn sīfǎ zhǎngguān. 2 [美语]县[縣]的行政司法长官 xiànde xíngzhèng sīfǎ zhǎngguān.

sherry /'ʃerɪ/ *n* [U] (西班牙、塞浦路斯等地所产黄色或褐色的)葡萄酒 pútáojiǔ; 雪利酒 xuělìjiǔ.

shied /ʃaɪd/ ⇨ shy².

shield /ʃi:ld/ *n* [C] **1** 盾 dùn. **2** 盾形徽章 dùnxíng huīzhāng. **3** [喻]保护[護]者 bǎohùzhě; 保护物 bǎohùwù. □ *vt* 保护 bǎohù; 庇护 bìhù.

shift¹ /ʃɪft/ *n* [C] **1** 位置的转[轉]移 wèizhìde zhuǎnyí; 性格的转变[變] xìnggéde zhuǎnbiàn. **2** [C] 轮[輪]班 lúnbān. **3** (无腰围的)宽松[鬆]女衣 kuānsōng nǚyī.

shift² /ʃɪft/ *vt/i* 转[轉]移 zhuǎnyí; 移动[動] yídòng; 转变[變] zhuǎnbiàn. **shifty** *adj* [-ier, -iest] 不老实[實]的 bù lǎoshí de; 善变的 shànbiànde.

shil·ling /'ʃɪlɪŋ/ *n* [C] 先令(1971年以前英国货币单位，二十先令为一镑，十二便士为一先令) xiānlìng.

shim·mer /'ʃɪmə(r)/ *vi, n* [U] 发[發]微光 fā wēiguāng; 发闪[閃]光 fā shǎnguāng; 微光 wēiguāng; 闪光 shǎnguāng.

shin /ʃɪn/ *n* [C] 胫[脛] jìng; 胫骨 jìnggǔ. □ *vi* [-nn-] ~ ***up*** 爬 pá, 攀 pān.

shine /ʃaɪn/ *vt/i* (*pt, pp* shone/ʃɒn/) **1** (使)发[發]光 fāguāng; (使)发亮 fāliàng. **2** [喻]出类[類]拔萃 chū lèi bá cuì. *He ~s in English.* 他的英语很出色. **3** [非正式用语] [*pp* ~d] 擦亮 cāliàng: ~ *shoes* 擦皮鞋. □ *n* [仅用 *sing*] 擦(亮) cā; 光(亮) guāng: *Give your shoes a ~.* 把你的鞋擦一下. **shiny** *adj* [-ier, -iest] 擦亮的 cāliàngde; 发亮的 fāliàngde.

shingle /'ʃɪŋgl/ *n* [U] (海滩)圆卵石 yuánluǎnshí. **shin·gly** /-glɪ/ *adj*

ship¹ /ʃɪp/ *n* [C] **1** 海船 hǎichuán; 客轮[輪] kèlún; 货船 huòchuán. **2** 飞[飛]机[機] fēijī; 飞艇 fēitǐng; 宇宙飞船 yǔzhòu fēichuán. **'~mate** 同船水手 tóngchuán shuǐshǒu. **'~shape** *adj* 整齐[齊]的 zhěngqíde; 井井有条[條]的 jǐngjǐng yǒu tiáo de. **'~wreck** *n* [C, U] 船只[隻]失事 chuánzhī shīshì. □ *vi* 使(船只)失事 shǐ shīshì. **'~yard** 船坞 chuánwù; 造船厂[廠] zàochuánchǎng.

ship² /ʃɪp/ *vt/i* [-pp-] **1** 装[裝]上船 zhuāngshàng chuán; 用船运[運] yòng chuán yùn. **2** 装运 zhuāngyùn; 运送 yùnsòng. **~ment** *n* 装货 zhuāng huò; 装船 zhuāng chuán; 装运 zhuāngyùn. **~per** 货物装运调度员 huòwù zhuāngyùn diàodùyuán. **~ping** *n* [U] (一国或一海港的)船舶 chuánbó; 船舶吨[噸]数[數] chuánbó dūnshù.

shire /ʃə(r)/ *suffix* 郡 jùn: *York~* 约克郡.

shirk /ʃɜ:k/ *vt/i* 逃避(义务、责任等) táobì; 回避 huíbì. **~er** 逃避(义务)者 táobìzhě.

shirt /ʃɜ:t/ *n* [C] (男式)衬[襯]衫 chènshān; 衬衣 chènyī. **shirty** *adj* [-ier, -iest] [俚语]发[發]怒的 fānùde; 烦恼[惱]的 fánnǎode.

shiver /'ʃɪvə(r)/ *vi* 颤抖 chàndǒu; 哆嗦 duōsuō. □ *n* [C] 颤抖 chàndǒu.

shoal /ʃəʊl/ *n* [C] 鱼群 yúqún. □ *vi* (鱼等)成群 chéngqún; 群集 qúnjí.

shock /ʃɒk/ *n* **1** [C] 冲击[擊] chōngjī; 震动 zhèndòng. **2** [C] 电[電]震 diànzhèn. **3** [C,U] 震惊[驚] zhènjīng; 震扰[擾] zhènrǎo: *His friend's death was a great ~.* 他朋友的逝世是个很大的震惊. □ *vt* 使震惊 shǐ zhènjīng. **~ing** *adj* **(a)** 极[極]坏[壞]的 jíhuàide, 糟糕的 zāogāode: *~ing behaviour* 恶劣的行为. **(b)** 令人震惊的 lìng rén zhènjīng de.

shod /ʃɒd/ *pt, pp* of shoe.

shoddy /'ʃɒdɪ/ *adj* [-ier, -iest] 质[質]劣的 zhìluède: ~ *work* 次品.

shoe /ʃu:/ *n* [C] **1** 鞋 xié. **2** = horseshoe. **3** (轮部的)刹车[車] shāchē. □ *vt* [*pt, pp* shod /ʃɒd/] 给…穿上鞋 gěi...chuānshàng xié; 给(马)钉蹄铁 gěi...dīng títiě. **'~horn** 鞋拔 xiébá. **'~lace** 鞋带[帶] xiédài. **'~string** [美语] = ~lace. ***do sth on a ~ string*** 以极[極]少的钱[錢]做某事 yǐ jíshǎode qián zuò mǒushì.

shone /ʃɒn/ *pt, pp* of shine.

shoo /ʃu:/ *int* 嘘(驱赶鸟兽等的声音) xū. □ *vt* [*pt, pp* ~ed] 发[發]嘘声[聲]赶[趕]走 fā xūshēng gǎnzǒu.

shook /ʃʊk/ *pt* of shake.

shoot¹ /ʃu:t/ *n* [C] **1** 芽 yá; 苗 miáo; 嫩枝 nènzhī. **2** 射猎[獵](队) shèliè.

shoot² /ʃu:t/ *vt/i* [*pt, pp* shot /ʃɒt/] **1** 突然或迅速地动[動](送) tūrán huò xùnsù de dòng: *Pain shot up his arm.* 他的臂膀突然感到一阵剧痛. **2** (植物)发[發]芽 fāyá; 生枝 shēngzhī. **3** 射击[擊] shèjī; 射伤[傷]shèshāng; 射死 shèsǐ. **4** 拍摄[攝]pāishè. **5** (足球)射门[門] shèmén. **~ing 'star** 流星 liúxīng.

shop /ʃɒp/ *n* [C] **1** 商店 shāngdiàn, 店铺 diànpù. [美语= *store*]. **2** *talk* ~ 谈论〔論〕本行事情 tánlùn běnháng shìqing. **3** = workshop. □ *vi* [-pp-] 到商店购〔購〕物(通常用 *go shopping*) dào shāngdiàn gòuwù. **'~-assistant** 店员 diànyuán **'~keeper** 店主 diànzhǔ. **'~-lifter** 商店扒手 shāngdiàn páshǒu. **'~-lifting** *n* [U] **,~-'steward** 工厂〔廠〕的工人代表 gōngchǎngde gōngrén dàibiǎo. **~per** 顾〔顧〕客 gùkè. **~ping** *n* [U]: *do one's ~ping* 买东西.

shore¹ /ʃɔ:(r)/ *n* [C] 岸 àn.

shore² /ʃɔ:(r)/ *vt* ~ *sth up* 支持 zhīchí; 撑住 chēngzhù.

shorn /ʃɔ:n/ ⇨ shear.

short¹ /ʃɔ:t/ *adj* [-er, -est] **1** (与 *long* 相对) 短的 duǎnde; 短暂〔暫〕的 duǎnzànde: *a ~ stick* 短手杖. *a ~ journey* 短途旅行. **2** (与 *tall* 相对) 矮的 ǎide: *a ~ man* 矮人. **3** 短缺的 duǎnquēde, 不足的 bùzúde. *get ~ change* 被别人占了小便宜. ~ *of*, **(a)** 短少 duǎnshǎo: ~ *of money* 缺钱. **(b)** 远〔遠〕离〔離〕yuǎnlí: *five miles ~ of the garage* 离修车厂有五英里路. **4** *in ~* 总〔總〕之 zǒngzhī; 简〔簡〕言之 jiǎnyánzhī. **5** 松〔鬆〕脆的 sōngcuìde. **'~bread** 脆饼 cuìbǐng; 松饼 sōngbǐng. **,~-'circuit** *n* [C] (电) 短路 duǎnlù. □ *vt/i* 短路 duǎnlù. **'~ cut** 近路 jìnlù; 捷径〔徑〕jiéjìng. **'~hand** 速记 sùjì. **,~-'handed** 人手不足的 rénshǒu bùzú de. **'~list** 供最后挑选〔選〕的求职〔職〕者名单 gōng zuìhòu tiāoxuǎn de qiúzhízhě míngdān. **'~-list** *vt* **,~-'lived** *adj* 短命的 duǎnmìngde; 短暂的 duǎnzànde. **~ sight, (a)** 近视 jìnshì. **(b)** 〔喻〕目光短浅〔淺〕mùguāng duǎnqiǎn. **,~-'sighted** *adj* **,~-'tempered** *adj* 急性子的 jíxìngzide; 脾气〔氣〕暴躁的 píqì bàozào de. **'~-term** *adj, n* 短期(的) duǎnqī. **'~wave** (无线电) 短波 duǎnbō. **~ly** *adv* **(a)** 不久 bùjiǔ; 立刻 lìkè: *We leave ~ly.* 我们很快就离开. **(b)** 简〔簡〕短地 jiǎnduǎnde. **~ness** *n* [U]

short² /ʃɔ:t/ *adv* **1** 突然 tūrán: *stop ~* 突然停止. ~ *of* 除去 chúqù: *do anything ~ of murder* 除了谋杀以外什么事都做. **2** *fall ~ of* 不足地 bùzúde. *cut sth* (或 *sb*) ~ 打断〔斷〕dǎduàn. *go ~ (of)* 无〔無〕需 wúxū; 使自己没有 shǐ zìjǐ méiyǒu.

short·age /'ʃɔ:tɪdʒ/ *n* [C,U] 不足 bùzú, 缺少 quēshǎo.

shorten /'ʃɔ:tn/ *vt/i* 弄短 nòngduǎn, 缩短 suōduǎn. ~ *a dress* 改短衣服.

shorts /ʃɔ:ts/ *n* [*pl*] 短裤〔褲〕duǎnkù.

shot /ʃɒt/ *n* **1** [C] 射击〔擊〕shèjī; 开〔開〕枪〔槍〕kāiqiāng; 射击声〔聲〕shèjīshēng. *like a ~* 立刻 lìkè. **2** [C] 射门〔門〕shèmén; 投篮〔籃〕tóulán. *have a ~ (at sth)* 试试看 shìshìkàn. **3** [C] 铅球 qiānqiú. **4** [U] (亦作 *lead ~*) 霰弹〔彈〕xiàndàn. **5** [C] 射手 shèshǒu; 枪手 qiāngshǒu: *He's a poor ~.* 他是差劲的射手. **6** [C] 拍摄〔攝〕pāishè; 镜头〔頭〕jìngtóu; 景 jǐng. **7** = injection (of a drug). **8** *a 'big ~* [俚语]要人 yàorén; 大人物 dàrénwù. **'~-gun** 猎〔獵〕枪 lièqiāng.

should /ʃʊd 弱式 ʃəd/ *v* ⇨ shall.

shoul·der /'ʃəʊldə(r)/ *n* [C] **1** 肩 jiān, 肩膀 jiānbǎng. **2** [*pl*] 上背部 shàngbèibù. **3** 肩状〔狀〕物 jiānzhuàngwù. ⇨hard shoulder. □ *vt* **1** 肩负 jiānfù: ~ *a burden* 肩负重担. ~ *a responsibility* 承担责任. **2** 用肩膀推 yòng jiānbǎng tuī. **'~-blade** 肩胛骨 jiānjiǎgǔ.

shout /ʃaʊt/ *n* [C] 呼喊 hūhǎn; 喊叫声〔聲〕hǎnjiàoshēng. □ *vt/i* **1** 呼喊 hūhǎn; 喊叫 hǎnjiào: *Don't ~ at me!* 不要对我叫喊! **2** 大声说 dàshēngshuō; 嚷 rǎng: ~ *(out) one's orders* 高声发出命令.

shove /ʃʌv/ *vt/i* [非正式用语]推 tuī. □ *n* [C] 推 tuī.

shovel /'ʃʌvl/ *n* [C] 铲〔鏟〕chǎn; 铁锹 tiěxiān. □ *vt* [-ll-, 美语 -l-] 铲 chǎn; 铲起 chǎnqǐ.

show¹ /ʃəʊ/ *n* **1** [U] 表示 biǎoshì; 显〔顯〕示 xiǎnshì: *vote by (a) ~ of hands* 举手表决. **2** [C] 展览〔覽〕zhǎnlǎn; 展览会〔會〕zhǎnlǎnhuì. *on ~* 展览中 zhǎnlǎn zhōng. **3** [C] 公众〔衆〕娱乐〔樂〕gōngzhòng yúlè; 表演(如戏剧、电视等) biǎoyǎn. **4** [C] [非正式用语]表现 biǎoxiàn: *put up a good ~* 某事做得很漂亮. **5** 外观〔觀〕wàiguān, 外表 wàibiǎo: *a ~ of resistance* 抵抗的样子. **6** [U] 炫耀 xuànyào, 卖〔賣〕弄 màinòng: *She does it for ~.* 她为了炫耀而做. **'~-business** 娱乐性行业〔業〕yúlèxìng hángyè. **'~down** [俚语]摊〔攤〕牌 tānpái. **'~-jumping** 骑〔騎〕马〔馬〕越障的技术〔術〕表演 qímǎ yuèzhàng de jìshù biǎoyǎn. **showy** *adj* [-ier, -iest] 显眼的 xiǎnyǎnde; 夸〔誇〕示的 kuāshìde.

show² /ʃəʊ/ *vt/i* [*pt* ~ed; *pp* ~n

/ʃəʊn/] **1** 出示 chūshì: ~ *your ticket at the barrier.* 在入口处出示你的门票. **2** 给看 gěikàn; 展示 zhǎnshì. **3** 给 gěi; 给予 gěiyǔ: *He ~ed me great kindness.* 他对我极为亲切. **4** 表明 biǎomíng; 显〔顯〕示 xiǎnshì: *She ~ed great courage.* 她表现得很有勇气. **5** 引导〔導〕yǐndǎo; 带〔帶〕领 dàilǐng: *S~ him in* 领他进来. **6** 说明 shuōmíng: *He ~ed me how to do it.* 他向我说明怎样做那件事. **7** ~ *off* 炫耀 xuànyào, 卖〔賣〕弄 màinòng. ~ ***sb*** **(*sth*)** ***up,*** 揭露 jiēlù; 揭穿 jiēchuān. ~ ***up,*** **(a)** 显眼 xiǎnyǎn; 易见 yìjiàn: *The lines ~ed up in the light.* 轮廓在亮光下很显眼. **(b)** 出席 chūxí, 到场〔場〕dàochǎng: *All the guests ~ed up.* 所有的客人都到了. **'~-off** 爱〔愛〕炫耀的人 ài xuànyào de rén. **~ing** *n* [C] 表现 biǎoxiàn; 外表 wàibiǎo.

shower /'ʃaʊə(r)/ *n* [C] **1** 阵〔陣〕雨 zhènyǔ; 暴雨 bàoyǔ. **2** 淋浴 línyù. **3** 大量涌到的事物 dàliàng yǒngdào de shìwù: *a ~ of stones* 一阵(投来的)石块. □ *vt/i* **1** 大量地给予 dàliàngde gěiyǔ. **2** 阵雨般降落 zhènyǔbān jiàngluò. **3** 淋浴 línyù. **show·ery** *adj* (指天气)多阵雨的 duō zhènyǔ de.

shown /ʃəʊn/ *pp* of show².

shrank /ʃræŋk/ *pt* of shrink.

shrap·nel /'ʃræpnəl/ *n* [U] 榴霰弹〔彈〕liúxiàndàn; 弹片 dànpiàn.

shred /ʃred/ *n* [C] **1** 碎片 suìpiàn. **2** [喻]最少量 zuì shǎoliàng: *not one ~ of proof* 没有一点证据. □ *vt* [-dd-] 撕碎 sīsuì.

shrewd /ʃru:d/ *adj* [-er, -est] **1** 敏锐的 mǐnruìde; 精明的 jīngmíngde. **2** 准确的 zhǔnquède: *a ~ guess* 准确的猜测. **~ly**

shriek /ʃri:k/ *vt/i* **1** 尖声〔聲〕叫喊 jiānshēng jiàohǎn. **2** 以尖叫声说出 yǐ jiānjiàoshēng shuōchū. □ *n* [C] 尖叫 jiānjiào.

shrill /ʃrɪl/ *adj* [-er, -est] (指声音)尖锐的 jiānruìde; 刺耳的 cì'ěrde. **~ness** *n* [U]

shrimp /ʃrɪmp/ *n* [C] 小虾〔蝦〕xiǎo xiā. □ *vi* 捕虾 bǔ xiā.

shrine /ʃraɪn/ *n* [C] **1** 圣〔聖〕骨墓 shènggǔmù; 圣骨匣 shènggǔxiá. **2** 圣地 shèngdì; 神圣场〔場〕所 shénshèng chǎngsuǒ.

shrink /ʃrɪŋk/ *vt/i* [*pt* shrank /ʃræŋk/, 或 shrunk /ʃrʌŋk/; *pp* shrunk, 或用作定语 shrunken /'ʃrʌŋkən/] **1** 收缩 shōusuō; 皱〔皺〕缩 zhòusuō. **2** ~ ***from*** **(*back*)** 退缩 tuìsuō; 畏缩 wèisuō. **'~age** /-ɪdʒ/ *n* [U] 收缩 shōusuō; 收缩量 shōusuōliàng.

shrivel /'ʃrɪvl/ *vt/i* [-ll-, 美语亦作 -l-] ~ **(*up*)** (使)皱〔皺〕缩 zhòusuō; (使)枯萎 kūwěi.

shroud /ʃraʊd/ *n* [C] **1** 尸〔屍〕布 shībù, 寿〔壽〕衣 shòuyī. **2** 遮蔽物 zhēbìwù; 幕 mù; 罩 zhào: *a ~ of mist* 雾的笼罩. □ *vt* **1** 用尸布裹尸体〔體〕yòng shībù guǒ shītǐ. **2** 覆盖〔蓋〕fùgài; 遮蔽 zhēbì: *~ed in mystery* 隐蔽在神秘中.

shrub /ʃrʌb/ *n* [C] 灌木 guànmù. **~bery** *n* [C] [*pl* -ies] 灌木丛〔叢〕guànmùcóng.

shrug /ʃrʌg/ *vt* [-gg-] 耸〔聳〕肩 sǒngjiān. ~ ***sth off*** 对〔對〕某事不屑一顾〔顧〕duì mǒushì búxiè yígù. □ *n* [C] 耸肩 sǒngjiān.

shrunk /'ʃrʌŋk/, **shrunken** /'ʃrʌŋkən/ ⇨ shrink.

shud·der /'ʃʌdə(r)/ *vi* 发〔發〕抖 fādǒu; 战〔戰〕栗 zhànlì. □ *n* [C] 发抖 fādǒu; 战栗 zhànlì.

shuffle /'ʃʌfl/ *vt/i* **1** 拖着(脚)走 tuōzhe zǒu. **2** 洗(纸牌) xǐ. □ *n* [C] **1** 拖着脚走 tuōzhe jiǎo zǒu. **2** 改组 gǎizǔ; 混合 hùnhé.

shun /ʃʌn/ *vt* [-nn-] 避免 bìmiǎn; 避开〔開〕bìkāi: ~ *publicity* 避免出风头. ~ *his company* 躲开他.

shunt /ʃʌnt/ *vt/i* 使(火车)转〔轉〕轨〔軌〕shǐ zhuǎnguǐ; (火车)调轨 tiáoguǐ.

shut /ʃʌt/ *vt/i* [*pt, pp* ~] [-tt-] **1** 关〔關〕guān, 闭〔閉〕bì. ~ ***one's eyes to*** 假装〔裝〕没看见 jiǎzhuāng méi kànjiàn. **2** 关上 guānshàng, 闭上 bìshàng: *The door won't ~.* 这门关不上. **3** ~ **(*sth*)** ***down*** 关闭 guānbì; 停工 tínggōng. **'~-down** *n* [C] ~ ***sth off*** 停闭(水、煤气等) tíngbì. ~ ***sth up,*** **(a)** 关闭门〔門〕窗 guānbì mén chuāng. **(b)** 妥藏 tuǒcáng: ~ *up one's jewels* 将某人的珠宝妥藏. ~ **(*sb*)** ***up*** 使不开〔開〕口 shǐ bù kāikǒu.

shut·ter /'ʃʌtə(r)/ *n* [C] **1** 百叶〔葉〕窗 bǎiyèchuāng; 窗板 chuāngbǎn. **2** (照相机的)快门〔門〕kuàimén. □ *vt* 装〔裝〕窗板(或快门) zhuāng chuāngbǎn.

shuttle /'ʃʌtl/ *n* [C] **1** 梭 suō. **2** (缝纫机的)滑梭 huásuō. □ *vt/i* 穿梭般往返移动〔動〕chuānsuōbān wǎngfǎn yídòng. **'~cock** 羽毛球 yǔmáoqiú; 毽球 jiànqiú. **'~ service** (火车、公共汽车等的)短程往返行驶〔駛〕duǎnchéng wǎngfǎn xíngshǐ.

shy[1] /ʃaɪ/ *adj* [-er, -est] **1** 害羞的

hàixiūde, 怕羞的 pàxiūde. 2 易受惊〔驚〕的yì shòujīng de. 3 ~ *of* 迟〔遲〕疑的 chíyíde. ~**ly** *adv* ~**ness** *n* [U]

shy² /ʃaɪ/ *vi* [*pt, pp* shied /ʃaɪd/] (马等)惊〔驚〕退 jīngtuì; 惊跳 jīngtiào.

sick /sɪk/ *adj* 1 *be* ~ 嗯〔噁〕心的 ěxīnde; 要呕〔嘔〕吐的 yào ǒutù de. 2 有病的 yǒubìngde, 患病的 huànbìngde. 3 ~ **(and 'tired) of** [非正式用语] 十分厌〔厭〕倦 shífēn yànjuàn: *I'm ~ of your complaints.* 我听够了你的抱怨. 4 **feel ~ at (about)** [非正式用语]遗憾 yíhàn. 5 [现代用法]不正当〔當〕的 bú zhèngdàng de; 反常的 fǎnchángde: ~ *jokes* 下流的笑话. '~**-bay** 船上诊所 chuánshàng zhěnsuǒ; (学校等)医〔醫〕务〔務〕室 yīwùshì.

sicken /'sɪkən/ *vt/i* 1 ~ **(for sth)** (使)生病shēngbìng. 2 (使)厌〔厭〕恶〔惡〕yànwù. ~**ing**/'sɪkənɪŋ/ *adj* 令人厌恶的 lìng rén yànwù de: *a ~ing murder* 令人厌恶的谋杀.

sickle /'sɪkl/ *n* [C] 镰刀 liándāo.

sick·ly /'sɪklɪ/ *adj* [-ier, -iest] 1 多病的 duōbìngde. 2 令人作呕〔嘔〕的 lìng rén zuò'ǒu de: *a ~ taste* 令人作呕的味道. *a ~ atmosphere* 令人作呕的气氛.

sick·ness /'sɪknɪs/ *n* 1 [C,U] 病 bìng, 疾病 jíbìng. 2 [U] 呕〔嘔〕吐 ǒutù, 作呕 zuò'ǒu.

side¹ /saɪd/ *n* [C] 1 面 miàn. 2 侧面 cèmiàn: *the ~ of the house* 房子的侧面. 3 [数学]边〔邊〕biān. 4 胁〔脅〕xié; (身体的)侧边(尤指腋至肋的部分) cèbiān: *sit at my left ~* 坐在我的左边. ,~ **by** '~ 并肩地 bìngjiānde. 5 半面 bànmiàn; 半边 bànbiān: *the sunny ~ of the street* 街道的向阳面. **on (from) all ~** 在各方面 zài gèfāngmiàn; 四面八方 sìmiàn bāfāng. **put sth on one ~** 不理会〔會〕某事 bù lǐhuì mǒushì. 6 一方 yìfāng; 一派 yípài. **take ~s (with)** 支持(某人) zhīchí. ⇨ side². 7 方面 fāngmiàn; 观〔觀〕点〔點〕guāndiǎn: *study all ~s of a question* 研究问题的各个方面. '~**board** 餐具桌 cānjùzhuō; 餐具柜〔櫃〕cānjùguì. '~**-burns (-boards)** 连〔連〕鬓〔鬢〕胡〔鬍〕子 liánbìn húzi. '~ **effect** (药物等的)副作用 fùzuòyòng. '~**-line** 兼职〔職〕jiānzhí; 副业〔業〕fùyè. '~**-road** 小路 xiǎolù; 叉路 chàlù. '~**step** *n* [C] (拳击中为避免打击而走的)侧步 cèbù; 横步 héngbù. □ *vt/i* [-pp-] **(a)** (拳击时为躲避打击)走侧步 zǒu cèbù. **(b)** [喻]回避(问题) huíbì. '~**-track** *vt* 转〔轉〕移(某人)目标〔標〕zhuǎnyí mùbiāo. '~**walk** [美语] = pavement. '~**wards,** '~**ways** *adv* 横 héng; 斜 xié; 傍 páng.

side² /saɪd/ *vi* ~ **with** 支持 zhīchí; 袒护〔護〕tǎnhù.

sid·ing /'saɪdɪŋ/ *n* [C] (铁路的)侧线〔綫〕cèxiàn; 旁轨〔軌〕pángguǐ.

siege /siːdʒ/ *n* [C,U] 围〔圍〕困 wéikùn; 围城 wéichéng; 围攻期间〔間〕wéigōng qījiān. **lay ~ to** 包围 bāowéi; 围攻 wéigōng.

sieve /sɪv/ *n* [C] (细)筛〔篩〕shāi; 滤〔濾〕网〔網〕lǜwǎng. □ *vt* 筛 shāi; 筛分 shāifēn; 滤 lǜ.

sift /sɪft/ *vt/i* 1 筛〔篩〕shāi; 筛分 shāifēn; 过〔過〕滤〔濾〕guòlǜ. 2 [喻]详审〔審〕xiángshěn; 细察 xìchá: ~ *the evidence* 细审证据.

sigh /saɪ/ *vt/i* 1 叹〔嘆〕气〔氣〕tànqì, 叹息 tànxī. 2 叹息地说 tànxīde shuō. □ *n* [C] 叹气 tànqì, 叹息 tànxī; 叹息声〔聲〕tànxīshēng.

sight /saɪt/ *n* 1 [U] 视力 shìlì; 视觉〔覺〕shìjué. 2 [U] 看 kàn. **at first ~** 初见 chūjiàn; 乍一看 zhà yíkàn. **catch ~ of** 看到 kàndào; 发〔發〕现 fāxiàn. **lose ~ of** 不再看见 búzài kànjiàn. 3 [U] 视域 shìyù: *out of ~* 在视程之外,看不见. 4 [C] 情景 qíngjǐng; 奇观〔觀〕qíguān; [*pl*] 名胜〔勝〕míngshèng: *see the ~s of London* 看看伦敦的名胜. 5 [C] 瞄准〔準〕miáozhǔn; 瞄准器 miáozhǔnqì. 6 滑稽可笑的景象 huájī kěxiào de jǐngxiàng: *You look a ~!* 你的样子真怪! □ *vt* 看见 kànjiàn. '~**-seeing** 观光 guānguāng; 游览〔覽〕yóulǎn.

sign /saɪn/ *n* [C] 1 记号〔號〕jìhào; 符号 fúhào: *mathematical ~s* 数学符号(如+). 2 告示 gàoshì; 标〔標〕记 biāojì; 指示牌 zhǐshìpái: *'traffic ~s* 交通标志. 3 征〔徵〕兆 zhēngzhào; 迹〔跡〕象 jìxiàng: *the ~s of suffering on his face* 他脸上痛苦的痕迹. 4 信号 xìnhào. 5 招牌 zhāopái. '~**post** 路标 lùbiāo. □ *vt/i* 签〔簽〕名 qiānmíng; 签字 qiānzì. ~ **off, (a)** (信件末尾的)签名 qiānmíng. **(b)** (电台、电视)停播 tíngbō. ~ **sb on (up)** 签约雇用 qiānyuē gùyòng.

sig·nal /'sɪgnəl/ *n* [C] 1 信号〔號〕xìnhào. 2 直接起因 zhíjiē qǐyīn: *His arrival was the ~ to cheer.* 他的到来引起了欢呼. 3 播出或接受的声〔聲〕音或电〔電〕视图〔圖〕象 bōchū huò jiēshòu de shēngyīn huò diànshì túxiàng. □ *vt/i* [-ll-, 美语 -l-] 发〔發〕信号 fā xìnhào;

用信号通知 yòng xìnhào tōngzhī. '~**-box** (铁路上的)信号所 xìnhàosuǒ; 信号塔 xìnhàotǎ. '~**man** 信号员 xìnhàoyuán.

sig·na·tory /'sɪgnətrɪ/ *n* [C] [*pl* -ies] (协议、条约等)签[簽]字人 qiānzìrén; 签约国[國] qiānyuēguó.

sig·na·ture /'sɪgnətʃə(r)/ *n* [C] 签[簽]名 qiānmíng, 署名 shǔmíng.

sig·net /'sɪgnɪt/ *n* [C] 图[圖]章 túzhāng; 私章 sīzhāng. '~**-ring** 图章戒指 túzhāng jièzhǐ.

sig·ni·fi·cance /sɪg'nɪfikəns/ *n* [U] 意义[義] yìyì; 重要性 zhòngyàoxìng. **sig·ni·fi·cant** *adj* 意义深长[長]的 yìyì shēncháng de; 重要的 zhòngyàode. **sig·ni·fi·cant·ly** *adv*

sig·nify /'sɪgnɪfaɪ/ *vt/i* [*pt, pp* -ied] [正式用语] **1** 表示 biǎoshì; 意味 yìwèi. **2** [正式用语]有重要性 yǒu zhòngyàoxìng: *It signifies little.* 那不大重要.

si·lence /'saɪləns/ *n* [U] **1** 寂静 jìjìng; 无[無]声[聲] wúshēng. **2** 沉默 chénmò. *in* ~ 沉默地 chénmòde. □ *vt* 使沉默 shǐ chénmò; 使安静 shǐ ānjìng. **si·lencer** 消音器 xiāoyīnqì; 减音器 jiǎnyīnqì.

si·lent /'saɪlənt/ *adj* **1** 寂静的 jìjìngde. **2** 沉默的 chénmòde; 无[無]声[聲]的 wúshēngde. **3** 不发[發]音的 bù fāyīn de: *a* ~ *letter* 不发音的字母(如 *doubt* 中的 *b*). ~**ly** *adv*

sil·hou·ette /ˌsɪlu:'et/ *n* [C] 侧影 cèyǐn; 剪影 jiǎnyǐn. □ *vt* [被动语态]使现出轮[輪]廓 shǐ xiànchū lúnkuò.

sili·con /'sɪlɪkən/ *n* [U] 硅 (旧称矽) guī ~ '**chip** *n* [C] (用以制造集成电路的)硅片 guīpiàn.

silk /sɪlk/ *n* [U] 丝[絲] sī; 丝织[織]品 sīzhīpǐn. '~**worm** 蚕[蠶] cán. ~**en** *adj* 柔软[軟]光滑的 róuruǎn guānghuá de. **silky** *adj* [-ier, -iest] 柔软的 róuruǎnde; 有光泽[澤]的 yǒu guāngzé de; 似丝的 sìsīde.

sill /sɪl/ *n* [C] 窗台[臺] chuāngtái; 槛[檻] jiàn.

silly /'sɪlɪ/ *adj* [-ier, -iest] 傻[傻]的 shǎde; 愚蠢的 yúchǔnde.

silt /sɪlt/ *n* [U] 淤泥 yūní; 淤沙 yūshā. □ *vt/i* ~ **(sth) up** (使)淤塞 yūsè.

sil·ver /'sɪlvə(r)/ *n* [U] **1** 银 **(Ag)** yín. **2** 银具 yínjù; 银币[幣] yínbì. **3** [用作定语]银白色 yínbáisè. □ *vt/i* **1** 镀银 dùyín. **2** 变[變]成银白色 biànchéng yínbáisè. ˌ~'**paper** [非正式用语]锡纸 xīzhǐ. '~**plate** 银器 yínqì. '~**smith** 银匠 yínjiàng. ˌ~ '**wedding** 银婚(二十五周年) yínhūn. **silvery** *adj* 似银的 sìyínde.

simi·lar /'sɪmɪlə(r)/ *adj* 类[類]似的 lèisìde; 相象的 xiāngxiàngde. ~**ly** *adv*

simi·lar·ity /ˌsɪmɪ'lærətɪ/ *n* [*pl* -ies] [U] 类[類]似 lèisì; 相似 xiāngsì; [C] 类似点[點] lèisìdiǎn.

sim·ile /'sɪmɪlɪ/ *n* [C,U] 直喻 zhíyù; 明喻 míngyù (如 *He is as brave as a lion.*).

sim·mer /'sɪmə(r)/ *vt/i* **1** 煨 wēi, 燉 dùn. **2** ~ ***down*** [喻]平静下来[來] píngjìng xiàlái.

simple /'sɪmpəl/ *adj* [-r, -st] **1** 简[簡]单[單]的 jiǎndānde; 简易的 jiǎnyìde: *a* ~ *machine* 简单的机器. **2** 朴[樸]素的 pǔsùde; 简朴的 jiǎnpǔde: ~ *food* 粗茶淡饭. **3** 非高度发[發]展的 fēi gāodù fāzhǎn de: ~ *forms of life* 低级的生命形态. **4** 易懂的 yìdǒngde: *written in* ~ *English* 用简易英语写的. **5** 单纯的 dānchúnde;天真的 tiānzhēnde: *as* ~ *as a child* 象小孩一样的单纯. **6** 易受骗[騙]的 yì shòupiàn de. **sim·ply** *adv* **(a)** 朴素地 pǔsùde; 简朴地 jiǎnpǔde. **(b)** 绝对[對]地 juéduìde: *I simply refuse.* 我绝对拒绝. **(c)** 仅[僅]仅 jǐnjǐn: *He is simply a workman.* 他只是一名工人.

sim·plic·ity /sɪm'plɪsɪtɪ/ *n* [U] [正式用语]简[簡]单[單] jiǎndān; 简易 jiǎnyì.

sim·plify /'sɪmplɪfaɪ/ *vt* [*pt, pp* -ied] 简[簡]化 jiǎnhuà; 使单[單]纯shǐ dānchún; 使易做shǐ yìzuò; 使易懂 shǐ yìdǒng. **sim·pli·fi·ca·tion** /-fɪ'keɪʃn/ *n* [C,U]

simu·late /'sɪmjʊleɪt/ *vt* [正式用语]假装[裝] jiǎzhuāng; 伪[僞]装 wěizhuāng. **simu'la·tion** *n* [C,U]

simu·la·tor /'sɪmjʊˌleɪtə(r)/ *n* [C] (做试验用的)摹拟[擬]仪[儀]器 mónǐ yíqì.

sim·ul·ta·neous /ˌsɪməl'teɪnɪəs/ *adj* 同时[時]发[發]生的 tóngshí fāshēng de; 同时的 tóngshíde; 一齐[齊]的 yìqíde. ~**ly** *adv*

sin /sɪn/ *n* **1** [U] (宗教上的)罪 zuì, 罪恶[惡] zuì'è. **2** [C] 不道德行为[爲] bú dàodé xíngwéi. □ *vi* [-nn-] 犯罪 fànzuì; 违[違]过[過] wěiguò. ~**ner** /'sɪnə(r)/ (宗教道德上的)罪人 zuìrén. ~**ful** /-fl/ *adj* 有错的 yǒucuòde; 邪恶的 xié'ède. ~**ful·ness** *n* [U]

since /sɪns/ *adv* [与完成时连用](在过去某日期、事件等之后,在现在以前): *He left home in 1970 and has* *not been seen* ~. 他在一九七〇年离开家，此后再没有见到他. **ever** ~ 从〔從〕那时〔時〕起一直到现在 cóng nàshí qǐ yìzhí dào xiànzài. □ *prep* 〔与完成时连用〕从…以来〔來〕cóng … yǐlái; 自从 zìcóng: *She hasn't been home* ~ *her marriage.* 她结婚以来未曾回过家. □ *conj* **1** …以来 … yǐlái; …以后〔後〕… yǐhòu: *How long is it* ~ *you were here?* 你在这里有多久了? **2** 因为〔爲〕yīnwèi; 既然 jìrán: *S*~ *we've no money, we can't buy it.* 因为我们没钱，我们不能买它.

sin·cere /sɪn'sɪə(r)/ *adj* **1** (感情) 真挚〔摯〕的 zhēnzhìde. **2** 真诚的 zhēnchéngde; 诚恳〔懇〕的 chéngkěnde. ~**ly** *adv* 真诚地 zhēnchéngde; 诚恳地 chéngkěnde. *Yours* ~*ly* 您的忠诚的(致友人等信末署名前的客套语) nínde zhōngchéngde. **sin·cer·ity** /sɪn'serətɪ/ *n* [U]

sinew /'sɪnjuː/ *n* [C] 腱 jiàn. **sin·ewy** *adj* 坚〔堅〕韧〔韌〕的 jiānrènde.

sing /sɪŋ/ *vt*/*i* (*pt* sang /sæŋ/; *pp* sung /sʌŋ/) **1** 唱 chàng; 歌唱 gēchàng. **2** 发〔發〕嗡嗡声〔聲〕fā wēngwēngshēng; 发鸣〔鳴〕叫声 fā míngjiàoshēng: *The kettle was* ~*ing.* 水壶发出响声. ~**er** *n* [C] 歌唱家 gēchàngjiā, 歌手 gēshǒu. ~**ing** *n* [U]

singe /sɪndʒ/ *vt*/*i* 烧〔燒〕焦 shāojiāo; 烫〔燙〕焦 tàngjiāo. □ *n* [C] 轻〔輕〕微的烧〔燒〕焦 qīngwēide shāojiāo.

single /'sɪŋgl/ *adj* **1** 单〔單〕一的 dānyīde: *a* ~ *ticket* 单程票. **2** 未婚的 wèihūnde; 独〔獨〕身的 dúshēnde. **3** 单人的 dānrénde: *a* ~ *bed* 单人床. □ *n* [C] **1** (球类运动)单打 dāndǎ. **2** 单程票 dānchéngpiào. □ *vt* ~ *sb* (*sth*) *out* 挑选〔選〕tiāoxuǎn. ,~-'**handed** *adj, adv* 独立的(地) dúlìde; 无〔無〕助的(地) wúzhùde. ,~-'**minded** *adj* 一心一意的 yìxīn yíyì de. **sing·ly** /'sɪŋglɪ/ *adv* 个别地 gèbiéde; 单独的 dāndúde.

sing·song /'sɪŋsɒŋ/ *n* [C] 即席演唱会〔會〕jíxí yǎnchànghuì; (朋友们聚在一起的) 歌咏会 gēyǒnghuì.

sin·gu·lar /'sɪŋgjʊlə(r)/ *adj* **1** 〔正式用语〕非凡的 fēifánde; 卓越的 zhuóyuède: *a man of* ~ *courage* 勇敢非凡的人. **2** 〔语法〕单〔單〕数〔數〕dānshù. □ *n* [C] 〔语法〕单数 dānshù. ~**ly** *adv* 〔正式用语〕奇异〔異〕地 qíyìde.

sin·is·ter /'sɪnɪstə(r)/ *adj* 不吉祥的 bù jíxiáng de; 邪恶〔惡〕的 xié'è de: *a* ~ *plan* 阴险的计划.

sink[1] /sɪŋk/ *n* [C] (厨房内)洗涤〔滌〕槽 xǐdícáo.

sink[2] /sɪŋk/ *vt*/*i* (*pt* sank /sæŋk/; *pp* sunk /sʌŋk/, 用作定语 sunken /'sʌŋkən/) **1** 下沉 xiàchén; 沉没 chénmò. **2** 变〔變〕低 biàndī; 变弱 biànruò. **3** 掘 jué, 挖 wā: ~ *a well* 掘井. **4** ~ **in(into)**, **(a)** (指液体)渗〔滲〕入 shènrù. **(b)** 被了解 bèi liǎojiě. **5** 〔喻〕丧〔喪〕失信心、失望等 sàngshī xìnxīn, shīwàng děng: *His heart sank.* 他精神沮丧. **6** 投(资) tóu.

sinus /'saɪnəs/ *n* [C] [*pl* ~es] 〔解剖〕窦〔竇〕dòu.

sip /sɪp/ *vt*/*i* [-pp-] 呷 xiā; 啜 chuò. □ *n* [C] 呷 xiā; 啜 chuò.

si·phon /'saɪfən/ *n* [C] **1** 虹吸管 hóngxīguǎn. **2** 虹吸瓶 hóngxīpíng; 压〔壓〕力瓶 yālìpíng. □ *vt*/*i* ~ *sth* **off (out)** 用虹吸管抽出(液体) yòng hóngxīguǎn chōuchū.

sir /sɜː(r)/ *n* **1** 先生 xiānshēng; 阁〔閣〕下 géxià (对人表示礼貌的称呼). **2** (用于信件): *Dear S*~ 亲爱的先生. **3** 用于爵士或准男爵的名之前 yòng yú juéshì huò zhǔnnánjué de míng zhī qián: *Sir* ,*Winston* '*Churchill* 温斯顿·邱吉尔爵士.

sire /'saɪə(r)/ *n* [C] 动〔動〕物的雄亲〔親〕dòngwùde xióngqīn. □ *vt* (尤指马)为〔爲〕…的雄亲 wéi…de xióngqīn.

si·ren /'saɪərən/ *n* [C] 警报〔報〕器 jǐngbàoqì; 汽笛 qìdí.

sir·loin /'sɜːlɔɪn/ *n* [C,U] 最好的牛腰肉 zuìhǎode niúyāoròu.

sis·ter /'sɪstə(r)/ *n* [C] **1** 姐 jiě; 妹 mèi. **2** 〔英国英语〕高级护〔護〕士 gāojí hùshì; 护士长〔長〕hùshìzhǎng. **3** 修女 xiūnǚ; 尼姑 nígū. ~**hood** *n* [C] (宗教的)妇〔婦〕女团〔團〕体〔體〕fùnǚ tuántǐ. ~**ly** *adj* 姐妹般的 jiěmèibānde.

sit /sɪt/ *vt*/*i* (*pt, pp* sat /sæt/) [-tt-] **1** 坐 zuò. ~ **tight**, **(a)** 坐稳〔穩〕zuòwěn. **(b)** 固执〔執〕己见 gùzhí jǐjiàn. **2** (议会等)开〔開〕会〔會〕kāihuì; (法院)开庭 kāitíng. **3** (衣服)合身 héshēn: *The coat* ~*s badly across the shoulders.* 那上衣肩部不合适. **4** ~ **down** 坐下 zuòxià; 就座 jiùzuò. ~ **for**, **(a)** 参〔參〕加考试 cānjiā kǎoshì. **(b)** 坐着由人画〔畫〕像 zuòzhe yóu rén huàxiàng. ,~ **in** (工人、学生等)室内静坐抗议 shìnèi jìngzuò kàngyì. '~-**in** *n* ~ **in on** *sth* (作观察员)列席(讨论会) lièxí. ~ **on** *sth* (陪审团、委员会等的)成员 chéngyuán. ~

up 迟〔遲〕睡 chíshuì; 熬夜 áoyè. ~ *(sb) up* 坐正 zuòzhèng; 坐起 zuòqǐ.

site /saɪt/ *n* [C] 位置 wèizhì; 场〔場〕所 chǎngsuǒ. □ *vt* 设置 shèzhì; 定...的位置 dìng...de wèizhi.

sit·ting /ˈsɪtɪŋ/ *n* [C] **1** (议会等)开〔開〕会〔會〕kāihuì; (法院)开庭 kāitíng. **2** 坐着供人画〔畫〕像 zuòzhe gōng rén huàxiàng. **3** 就座(进食等) jiùzuò. ˌ~ ˈ**duck** 容易击〔擊〕中的目标〔標〕róngyì jīzhòng de mùbiāo. ˈ~**-room** 起居室 qǐjūshì.

situ·ated /ˈsɪtjʊeɪtɪd/ *adj* **1** (城镇、建筑物等)坐落在...的 zuòluò zài...de. **2** (指人)处〔處〕于某种境地的 chǔ yú mǒuzhǒng jìngdì de: *I'm badly ~ at the moment.* 我此刻处境很坏.

situ·ation /ˌsɪtjʊˈeɪʃn/ *n* [C] **1** (建筑物、城镇等的)位置 wèizhi; 场〔場〕所 chǎngsuǒ. **2** 形势〔勢〕xíngshì; 情况 qíngkuàng; 局面 júmiàn: *the economic ~* 经济形势. **3** 工作 gōngzuò; 职〔職〕业〔業〕zhíyè: *~s vacant* 空缺招人.

six /sɪks/ *adj, n* [C] 六 liù. **~th** /sɪksθ/ *adj, n* [C] (缩作 *6th*) 第六 dìliù; 六分之一 liùfēn zhī yī.

six·teen /sɪkˈstiːn/ *adj, n* [C] 十六 shíliù. **~th** *adj, n* [C] (缩作 *16th*) 第十六 dìshíliù; 十六分之一 shíliùfēn zhī yī.

sixty /ˈsɪkstɪ/ *adj, n* [C] 六十 liùshí. **six·ti·eth** *adj, n* [C] (缩作 *60th*) 第六十 dìliùshí; 六十分之一 liùshífēn zhī yī.

size /saɪz/ *n* **1** [U] 大小 dàxiǎo; 尺寸 chǐcùn: *the ~ of a car* 汽车的大小. **2** [C] (服装等的)尺码〔碼〕chǐmǎ: *~ five shoes* 五号鞋. □ *vt* **1** 按大小排列 àn dàxiǎo páiliè. **2** ~ *sb (sth) up* [非正式用语]估量 gūliàng. **~able** /-əbl/ *adj* 相当〔當〕大的 xiāngdāng dà de.

sizzle /ˈsɪzl/ *vi, n* [C] [非正式用语]发〔發〕咝〔嗞〕咝声〔聲〕fā sīsīshēng; 咝咝声 sīsīshēng.

skate /skeɪt/ *n* [C] 冰鞋 bīngxié. ⇨roller-skate. □ *vi* 滑冰 huábīng; 溜冰 liūbīng. ˈ**skat·ing-rink** 滑冰场〔場〕huábīngchǎng; 溜冰场 liūbīngchǎng.

skel·eton /ˈskelɪtn/ *n* [C] **1** 骨骼 gǔgé. **2** (建筑物、计划等)骨架 gǔjià; 纲〔綱〕要 gāngyào. ˈ~ **key** 万〔萬〕能钥〔鑰〕匙wànnéng yàoshi. ~ **staff (crew, service, etc)** 基干〔幹〕人员 jīgàn rényuán.

sketch /sketʃ/ *n* [C] **1** 草图〔圖〕cǎotú; 素描 sùmiáo. **2** 简〔簡〕述 jiǎnshù. **3** (滑稽的)短剧〔劇〕duǎnjù. □ *vt/i* **1** 绘〔繪〕草图 huì cǎotú; 作简短的描述 zuò jiǎnduǎn de miáoshù. ~ *sth out* 草拟〔擬〕cǎonǐ. **sketchy** *adj* [-ier, -iest] 粗略的 cūlüède; 大概的 dàgàide.

skewer /ˈskjuːə(r)/ *n* [C] (烤肉用的)串肉扦 chuànròuqiān; 烤肉叉 kǎoròuchā. □ *vt* (用串肉扦等)串 chuàn.

ski /skiː/ *n* [C] [*pl* ~ or ~s] 滑橇 huáqiāo; 滑雪屐 huáxuějī. □ *vi* [*pt, pp* ~'d, *pres part* ~ing] 滑雪 huáxuě.

skid /skɪd/ *n* [C] **1** 车〔車〕轮〔輪〕的打滑 chēlúnde dǎhuá. **2** 刹车 shāchē; 制轮器 zhìlúnqì. □ *vi* [-dd-] (汽车等)打滑 dǎhuá; 滑向一侧 huáxiàng yícè.

skies /skaɪz/ *pl* of sky.

skil·ful [美语 = **skillful**] /ˈskɪlfl/ *adj* 灵〔靈〕巧的 língqiǎode; 熟练〔練〕的 shúliànde. **~ly** *adv*

skill /skɪl/ *n* [C,U] **1** 技能 jìnéng; 熟练〔練〕shúliàn. **~ed** *adj* 有技能的 yǒu jìnéng de; 熟练的 shúliànde.

skim /skɪm/ *vt/i* [-mm-] **1** 撇 piē; 撇去 piēqù; 撇清 piēqīng; 抹去 mǒqù. **2** 掠过〔過〕lüèguò; 擦过 cāguò. **3** ~ *through sth* 浏〔瀏〕览〔覽〕liúlǎn; 略读〔讀〕lüèdú.

skin /skɪn/ *n* **1** [U] 皮 pí, 皮肤〔膚〕pífū. *save one's ~* 免受损伤〔傷〕miǎnshòu sǔnshāng; 安然逃脱 ānrán táotuō. *by the ˌ~ of one's ˈteeth* 幸免于难〔難〕xìngmiǎn yú nàn. **2** [C] 兽〔獸〕皮 shòupí; 毛皮 máopí; 皮革 pígé. **3** [C,U] 果皮 guǒpí. **4** [C,U] 奶皮(指煮沸的牛奶上结成的薄层) nǎipí. □ *vt/i* [-nn-] 剥皮 bōpí; 去皮 qùpí. ˌ~-ˈ**deep** *adj* 肤浅〔淺〕的 fūqiǎnde. ˈ~**-diving** 潜〔潛〕游运〔運〕动〔動〕qiǎnyóu yùndòng. ˈ~**-flint** = miser. ˌ~-ˈ**tight** *adj* 紧〔緊〕身的 jǐnshēnde. **~ny** *adj* [-ier, -iest] 皮包骨的 píbāogǔde; 精瘦 jīngshòu.

skip[1] /skɪp/ *vt/i* [-pp-] **1** 跳 tiào; 蹦 bèng. **2** 跳绳〔繩〕tiàoshéng. **3** 急速离〔離〕开〔開〕jísù líkāi: *~ the country* 匆匆离开这个国家. **4** 迅速改变〔變〕xùnsù gǎibiàn. **5** 略过〔過〕lüèguò; 遗漏 yílòu: *~ two chapters of a book* 一本书略过两章未看. □ *n* [C] 轻〔輕〕跳 qīngtiào; 略过 lüèguò; 看漏 kànlòu.

skip[2] /skɪp/ *n* [C] 箕斗 jīdǒu.

skip·per /ˈskɪpə(r)/ *n* [C] 船长〔長〕chuánzhǎng; 队〔隊〕长 duì

zhǎng. □ *vt* 担任船长(队长等) dānrèn chuánzhǎng.

skirt /skɜːt/ *n* [C] 裙子 qúnzi. □ *vt/i* 在…的边[邊]缘 zài...de biānyuán; 沿…走 yán...zǒu. '~**ing-board** 壁脚板 bìjiǎobǎn.

skittles /'skɪtlz/ *n pl* 九柱戏[戲] jiǔzhùxì; 撞柱戏(沿球道以球击倒数个瓶状木柱的游戏) zhuàngzhùxì.

skulk /skʌlk/ *vi* 躲藏 duǒcáng; 偷偷摸摸地走 tōutōumōmōde zǒu.

skull /skʌl/ *n* [C] 头[頭]盖骨 tóugàigǔ; 头颅[顱] tóulú.

skunk /skʌŋk/ *n* [C] 臭鼬(北美产) chòuyòu.

sky /skaɪ/ *n* [C] [*pl* skies /skaɪz/] 天 tiān, 天空 tiānkōng. '~**light** 天窗 tiānchuāng. '~**line** (建筑物、山等)以天空为[爲]背景映出的轮[輪]廓 yǐ tiānkōng wéi bèijǐng yìngchū de lúnkuò. '~**lark** 云[雲]雀 yúnquè. '~**scraper** 摩天楼[樓] mótiānlóu.

slab /slæb/ *n* [C] (石、木等的)板 bǎn; 片 piàn.

slack[1] /slæk/ *adj* [-er, -est] **1** 懈怠的 xièdàide. **2** 萧[蕭]条[條]的 xiāotiáode; 呆滞[滯]的 dāizhìde: *Trade is* ~. 生意不好; 买卖萧条. **3** 不紧[緊]的 bùjǐnde; 松[鬆]弛的 sōngchíde: *a* ~ *rope* 松弛的绳子. □ *vi* **1** ~ **(off)** 怠惰 dàiduò; 偷懒 tōulǎn. **2** 放松(绳等) fàngsōng. ~**ness** *n* [U]

slack[2] /slæk/ *n* **the** ~ (绳等)松[鬆]垂部分 sōngchuí bùfen.

slacken /'slækən/ *vt/i* **1** 放慢 fàngmàn; 缓慢 huǎnmàn, 停滞[滯] tíngzhì. **2** 放松[鬆] fàngsōng.

slacks /slæks/ *n pl* [旧用法]宽松[鬆]的裤[褲]子 kuānsōngde kùzi.

slag /slæg/ *n* [U] 矿[礦]渣 kuàngzhā; 炉[爐]渣 lúzhā; 熔渣 róngzhā. '~**-heap** 熔渣堆 róngzhāduī.

slam /slæm/ *vt/i* [-mm-] **1** 使劲[勁]关[關] shǐjìn guān; 砰地关上 pēngde guānshàng. **2** 猛投 měngtóu; 猛击[擊] měngjī. **3** [非正式用语]抨击 pēngjī. □ *n* [C] 砰然声[聲] pēngránshēng.

slan·der /'slɑːndə(r)/ *n* [C,U] 诽谤 fěibàng, 污蔑 wūmiè. □ *vt* 诽谤 fěibàng, 污蔑 wūmiè. ~**ous** *adj*

slang /slæŋ/ *n* [U] 俚语 lǐyǔ. □ *vt* 用粗话骂[罵] yòng cūhuà mà.

slant /slɑːnt/ *vt/i* **1** 倾斜 qīngxié. **2** 根据某种[種]观[觀]点[點]提供情况 gēnjù mǒuzhǒng guāndiǎn tígòng qíngkuàng. □ *n* [C] **1** 倾斜 qīngxié; 斜面 xiémiàn. **2** [非正式用语]看法 kànfǎ.

slap /slæp/ *vt* [-pp-] **1** 掌击[擊] zhǎngjī; 掴[摑] guāi; 拍打 pāidǎ. **2** 啪的一声[聲]放下 pāde yìshēng fàngxià. □ *n* [C] 掌击 zhǎngjī; 掴 guāi; 拍 pāi. □ *adv* 直接地 zhíjiēde; 一直地 yìzhíde: *The car ran* ~ *into the wall.* 车子直撞在墙上. '~**dash** *adj, adv* 粗心的(地) cūxīnde; 草率的(地) cǎoshuàide. '~**-up** *adj* [俚语]上等的 shàngděngde; 第一流的 dìyīliúde; 极[極]好的 jíhǎode: *a* ~*-up dinner* 上等大餐

slash /slæʃ/ *vt/i* **1** 猛砍 měngkǎn; 乱[亂]砍 luànkǎn. **2** [非正式用语]削减 xuējiǎn; 减低 jiǎndī: ~ *prices* 大减价. □ *n* [C] 猛砍 měngkǎn; 乱砍 luànkǎn.

slat /slæt/ *n* [C] 条[條]板 tiáobǎn; 铁条 tiětiáo.

slate /sleɪt/ *n* [C,U] 板岩 bǎnyán; [C] 石板 shíbǎn. *a clean* ~ 行为[爲]良好的记录[録] xíngwei liánghǎo de jìlù. □ *vt* **1** 用石板瓦盖[蓋](屋顶等) yòng shíbǎnwǎ gài. **2** [非正式用语]严[嚴]厉[厲]的评论[論] yánlìde pínglùn.

slaugh·ter /'slɔːtə(r)/ *n* [U] **1** 屠宰 túzǎi. **2** 屠杀[殺] túshā. □ *vt* 屠杀 túshā; 杀戮 shālù. '~**-house** 屠宰场[場] túzǎichǎng.

slave /sleɪv/ *n* [C] **1** 奴隶[隸] núlì. **2** 苦工 kǔgōng. **3** 摆[擺]脱不了某种[種]习[習]惯的人 bǎituō bùliǎo mǒuzhǒng xíguàn de rén: *a* ~ *to drink* 酒鬼. □ *vi* ~ **(away)** **(at** *sth***)** 努力工作 nǔlì gōngzuò. ~**ry** *n* [U]

sled /sled/ *n* = **sledge**.

sledge /sledʒ/ *n* [C] 雪橇 xuěqiāo. □ *vt/i* 乘雪橇 chéng xuěqiāo; 用雪橇运[運]送 yòng xuěqiāo yùnsòng.

sledge-hammer /'sledʒ hæmə(r)/ *n* [C] 大锤 dà chuí.

sleek /sliːk/ *adj* [-er, -est] **1** (毛发、毛皮等)柔滑而发[發]亮的 róuhuá ér fāliàng de. **2** 有柔软[軟]而发亮的毛发[髮]的 yǒu róuruǎn ér fāliàngde máofà de: *a* ~ *cat* 毛皮光滑的猫. **3** 光滑的 guānghuáde. □ *vt* 使光滑 shǐ guānghuá.

sleep[1] /sliːp/ *n* **1** [U] 睡眠 shuìmián, 睡觉[覺] shuìjiào. **2** 睡眠时[時]间[間] shuìmián shíjiān. **3** *go to* ~ 入睡 rùshuì.

sleep[2] /sliːp/ *vt/i* [*pp, pt* slept/slept/] **1** 睡 shuì, 睡眠 shuìmián, 睡着 shuìzháo. **2** ~ *sth off* 用睡眠消除(头痛等) yòng shuìmián xiāochú. ~ *on* 继[繼]续[續]睡觉 jìxù shuìjiào. ~ *on sth* 把问〔問〕题等留到第二天解决 bǎ wèntí děng liúdào dì'èrtiān jiějué. ~ *through sth* 未被(某事)吵醒 wèi bèi chǎoxǐng. ~ *with sb* 与〔與〕某人发〔發〕生性关〔關〕系〔係〕 yǔ mǒurén fāshēng xìngguānxì. ~**er** *n* [C] (a) 睡眠者 shuìmiánzhě. (b) [铁路]枕木 zhěnmù. (c) 卧铺 wòpù. '~**ing-car** 卧车 wòchē. '~**less** 失眠 shīmián. **sleepy** *adj* [-ier, -iest] (a) 想睡的 xiǎng shuì de, 瞌睡的 kēshuìde; 困乏的 kùnfáde. (b) 寂静的(地方等) jìjìngde; 不活泼〔潑〕的 bù huópo de. ~**ily** *adv*

sleet /sliːt/ *n* [U] 雨夹〔夾〕雪 yǔjiāxuě. □ *vi* 下雨夹雪 xià yǔjiāxuě.

sleeve /sliːv/ *n* [C] 1 袖子 xiùzi. *have sth up one's* ~ 暗中已有打算,办〔辦〕法等 ànzhōng yǐ yǒu dǎsuàn, bànfǎ děng. 2 唱片套 chàngpiàntào.

sleigh /sleɪ/ *n* [C] (尤指用马拉的)雪车〔車〕 xuěchē.

sleight /slaɪt/ *n* ~ *of hand* (变戏法等)手法熟练〔練〕 shǒufǎ shúliàn.

slen·der /'slendə(r)/ *adj* [-er, -est] 1 细长〔長〕的 xìchángde. 2 (指人)苗条〔條〕的 miáotiáode, 纤〔纖〕弱的 xiānruòde. 3 微小的 wēixiǎode, 微薄的 wēibóde: *have a ~ chance* 机会极微小. ~**ness** *n* [U]

slept /slept/ *pt, pp* of sleep.

slice /slaɪs/ *n* [C] 1 片 piàn, (尤指面包,肉)薄片 bópiàn. 2 部分 bùfen: *take a ~ of the credit* 获得一份荣誉. 3 餐刀 cāndāo; 菜刀 càidāo. □ *vt/i* ~ (*up*) 切片 qiēpiàn.

slick /slɪk/ *adj* [非正式用语] 1 光滑的 guānghuáde, 平滑的 pínghuáde. 2 圆滑而有效地完成的 yuánhuá ér yǒuxiàode wánchéng de. 3 (指人)狡猾的 jiǎohuáde, 圆滑的 yuánhuáde. ⇨oil slick.

slide[1] /slaɪd/ *n* [C] 1 滑 huá, 滑动〔動〕 huádòng. 2 滑道 huádào, 滑坡 huápō, 滑梯 huátī. 3 幻灯〔燈〕片 huàndēngpiān. 4 (显微镜的)承物玻璃片 chéng wù bōlipiàn. 5 = landslide.

slide[2] /slaɪd/ *vt/i* [*pt, pp* slid /slɪd/] 1 (使)滑动〔動〕 huádòng. 2 (使)偷偷地行动 tōutōude xíngdòng: *He slid out of the room.* 他偷偷地溜出房间. '~-**rule** 计算尺 jìsuànchǐ.

slight[1] /slaɪt/ *adj* [-er, -est] 1 细长〔長〕的 xìchángde, 苗条〔條〕的 miáotiáode, 纤〔纖〕弱的 qiànruòde, 瘦小的 shòuxiǎode. 2 轻〔輕〕微的 qīngwēide; 不重要的 bú zhòngyào de: *a ~ headache* 轻微的头痛. ~**ly** *adv* (a) 细长地 xìchángde: *a ~ly built boy* 身材瘦长的男孩. (b) 稍微 shāowēi, 略 lüè: *feel ~ly better* 觉得略为好些. ~**ness** *n* [U]

slight[2] /slaɪt/ *vt* 轻〔輕〕视 qīngshì, 怠慢 dàimàn. □ *n* [C] 轻蔑 qīngmiè, 怠慢 dàimàn.

slim /slɪm/ *adj* [-mer, -mest] 1 细长〔長〕的 xìchángde, 苗条〔條〕的 miáotiáode. 2 [非正式用语]微小的 wēixiǎode; 稀少的 xīshǎode: *a ~ chance of success* 成功希望不大的机会. □ *vi* [-mm-] (用减食等办法)减轻〔輕〕体〔體〕重 jiǎnqīng tǐzhòng. ~**ness** *n* [U]

slime /slaɪm/ *n* [U] 1 软〔軟〕泥 ruǎnní, 黏土 niántǔ. 2 (蜗牛等的)黏液 niányè. **slimy** *adj* [-ier, -iest] (a) 黏性的 niánxìngde, 泥泞〔濘〕的 nínìngde. (b) [喻]令人讨厌〔厭〕的 lìng rén tǎoyàn de; 谄媚的 chǎnmèide: *a slimy young man* 令人讨厌的年轻人.

sling /slɪŋ/ *n* [C] 1 吊索 diàosuǒ, 吊带〔帶〕 diàodài. 2 投石器 tóushíqì. 3 掷〔擲〕 zhì, 投 tóu, 抛 pāo. □ *vt/i* [*pt, pp* slung /slʌŋ/] (用力)掷 zhì, 抛 pāo: *We slung him out of the bar.* 我们把他扔出酒吧间.

slink /slɪŋk/ *vi* [*pt, pp* slunk /slʌŋk/] 溜走 liūzǒu, 悄悄地走 qiāoqiāode zǒu.

slip[1] /slɪp/ *n* [C] 1 滑 huá, 溜 liū; 失足 shīzú, 失误 shīwù; 疏忽 shūhū, 小错 xiǎocuò. 2 = pillow-slip. 3 衬〔襯〕衣 chènyī, 内衣 nèiyī. 4 年轻〔輕〕而细长〔長〕的人 niánqīng ér xìcháng de rén: *a ~ of a girl* 一个瘦长的女孩. 5 [*pl*] (修造船只的)船台 chuántái. '~-**road** (汽车道)支路 zhīlù, 叉道 chādào. '~-**stream** (飞机的)向后〔後〕气〔氣〕流 xiànghòu qìliú. '~-**up** [非正式用语]错误 cuòwù, 疏忽 shūhū.

slip[2] /slɪp/ *vt/i* [-pp-] 1 滑倒 huádǎo, 失足 shīzú. 2 溜走 liūzǒu, 悄悄地过〔過〕去 qiāoqiāode guòqù. 3 滑落 huáluò, 松〔鬆〕脱 sōngtuō: *The plate ~ped from my hand.* 盘〔盤〕子从我手中滑落. *let sth ~* (a) 放走 fàngzǒu; 错过〔過〕 cuòguò. (b) 无〔無〕意中泄漏(秘密等) wúyìzhōng xièlòu. ~ *one's mind* (姓名消息等)被遗忘 bèi yíwàng. 4 匆忙地穿衣或脱衣 cōngmángde chuānyī huò tuōyī: ~ *a coat on* 匆忙穿上外衣. 5 容许(小错等)发〔發〕生 róngxǔ fāshēng. ~ *up* [非正式用语]出错 chūcuò, 失误 shī wù.

slip·por /'slɪpə(r)/ *n* [C] 拖鞋 tuōxié, 便鞋 biànxié.

slip·pery /'slɪpərɪ/ *adj* [-ier, -iest] **1** (表面)光滑的 guānghuáde; 易滑脱的 yì huátuō de. **2** [喻](指人)不老实[實]的 bù lǎoshi de, 不可靠的 bù kěkào de.

slit /slɪt/ *n* [C] 狭长[長]的切口 xiáchángde qiēkǒu, 裂缝 lièfèng. ☐ *vt* [*pt*, *pp* ~] [-tt-] 切开[開] qiēkāi, 撕裂 sīliè.

slither /'slɪðə(r)/ *vi* 不稳[穩]地滑动[動] bùwěnde huádòng.

sliver /'slɪvə(r)/ *n* [C] 薄片 báopiàn, 碎片 suìpiàn.

slog /slɒg/ *vt*/*i* [-gg-] 艰[艱]难[難]地行走 jiānnánde xíngzǒu; 辛勤地工作 xīnqínde gōngzuò. ☐ *n* [U] [非正式用语]苦干[幹] kǔgàn.

slo·gan /'sləʊgən/ *n* [C] 标[標]语 biāoyǔ; 口号[號] kǒuhào.

slop /slɒp/ *vt*/*i* [-pp-] **1** 溢出 yìchū, 溅[濺]出 jiànchū. **2** 使溢出 shǐ yìchū. **3** 弄脏[髒] nòng zāng: ~ *paint all over the floor* 地板上到处溅上了油漆. ☐ *n* **1** [*pl*] 脏水 zāngshuǐ, 污水 wūshuǐ. **2** [U] (喂猪)泔脚 gānjiǎo.

slope /sləʊp/ *n* **1** [C,U] 斜线[綫] xiéxiàn; 斜度 xiédù. **2** 倾斜面 qīngxiémiàn, 斜坡 xiépō. ☐ *vt*/*i* (使)倾斜 qīngxié, (使)有斜度 yǒu xiédù.

sloppy /'slɒpɪ/ *adj* [-ier, -iest] **1** [非正式用语]草率的 cǎoshuàide, 粗心的 cūxīnde. **3** [非正式用语]感情用事的 gǎnqíng yòng shì de; 伤[傷]感的 shānggǎnde: *a* ~ *love story* 伤心的爱情故事. **slop·pily** *adv* 草率地 cǎoshuàide, 粗心地cūxīnde. **slop·pi·ness** *n* [U]

slosh /slɒʃ/ *vt*/*i* **1** [俚语] 打击[擊] dǎjī. **2** 溅[濺] jiàn, 泼[潑] pō; 溅着泥水行走 jiànzhe níshuǐ xíngzǒu. ~**ed** *adj* [非正式用语]喝醉的 hēzuìde.

slot /slɒt/ *n* [C] **1** 狭[狹]缝 xiáfèng. **2** 槽沟[溝] cáogōu. **3** [非正式用语](在计划, 程序单中的)适[適]当[當]位置 shìdàng wèizhi: ~*s for advertisements on TV* 电视节目中插入广告的位置. ☐ *vt*[-tt-] 开[開]槽于[於] kāi cáo yú; 放入缝中 fàngrù fèng zhōng. '~ **machine** *n* [C] [非正式用语]自动[動]售货机[機] zìdòng shòuhuòjī, 吃角子老虎 chī jiǎozi lǎohǔ. ⇨ vending machine.

sloth /sləʊθ/ *n* **1** [U] 懒惰 lǎnduò, 懒散 lǎnsǎn. **2** [C] (南美洲)树[樹]獭 shùtǎ. ~**ful** *adj*

slouch /slaʊtʃ/ *vi* 懒散地站, 坐或行动[動] lǎnsǎnde zhàn, zuò huò xíngdòng. ☐ *n* [C] 没精打彩的姿态[態] méi jīng dǎ cǎi de zītài, 懒洋洋的走动 lǎnyángyángde zǒudòng.

sloven·ly /'slʌvnlɪ/ *adj* 不整洁[潔]的 bù zhěngjié de, 邋遢的 lātāde.

slow[1] /sləʊ/ *adj* [-er, -est] **1** 慢的 mànde, 缓慢的 huǎnmànde. **2** 迟[遲]钝的 chídùnde, 笨的 bènde. **3** 不立即发[發]作的 bú lìjí fāzuò de: ~ *to anger* 不轻易发怒. **4** (钟表)慢了的 mànlede. **5** 乏味的 fáweìde, 不精采的 bù jīngcǎi de: *a* ~ *film* 乏味的电影.

slow[2] /sləʊ/ *adv* [-er, -est] 缓慢地 huǎnmànde, 慢慢地 mànmànde. *go* ~ (工人)怠工 dàigōng. ,**go-'**~ *n* [C] 怠工 dàigōng.

slow[3] /sləʊ/ *vt*/*i* ~ *up* (或 *down*) (使)慢下来[來] mànxiàlái.

sludge /slʌdʒ/ *n* [U] 烂[爛]泥 lànní, 淤泥 yūní.

slug /slʌg/ *n* [C] 蛞蝓 kuòyú.

slug·gish /'slʌgɪʃ/ *adj* 不活泼[潑]的 bù huópo de, 呆滞[滯]的 dāizhìde.

sluice /slu:s/ *n* [C] **1** 水闸[閘] shuǐzhá. **2** 排水沟[溝] páishuǐgōu; 洗矿[礦]槽 xǐkuàngcáo. '~**-gate** = sluice(1).

slum /slʌm/ *n* [C] 陋巷 lòuxiàng, 贫民窟 pínmínkū. ☐ *vi* [-mm-] [非正式用语]简[簡]陋地生活着 jiǎnlòude shēnghuózhe. ~**my** *adj*

slum·ber /'slʌmbə(r)/ *vt*/*i* [书面语]安眠 ānmián. ☐ *n* [C] 睡眠 shuìmián.

slump /slʌmp/ *vi* **1** 猛然落下 měngrán luòxià, 颓然倒下 tuírán dǎoxià. **2** (物价, 贸易等)暴跌 bàodiē. ☐ *n* [C] (市面)不景气[氣] bù jǐngqì, 衰退 shuāituì.

slung /slʌŋ/ *pt*, *pp* of sling.

slunk /slʌŋk/ *pt*, *pp* of slink.

slur /slɜ:(r)/ *vt*/*i* [-rr-] 含糊不清地发[發]音 hánhù bùqīng de fāyīn; 模糊地写[寫] móhude xiě. ☐ *n* [C] **1** 污辱 wūrǔ, 毁谤 huǐbàng: *a* ~ *on his name* 对他名声的污辱. **2** 含糊发音 hánhu fāyīn: *speak in a* ~ 说话时发音含糊不清.

slush /slʌʃ/ *n* [U] **1** 半融雪 bàn róng xuě, 雪泥 xuění. **2** [喻]愚痴的伤[傷]感 yúchīde shānggǎn. '~ **fund** 行贿钱[錢] xínghuìqián.

slut /slʌt/ *n* [C] 不正经[經]的女人 bú zhèngjing de nǚrén, 荡[蕩]妇[婦] dàngfù. ~**tish** *adj*

sly /slaɪ/ *adj* [-er, -est] 狡猾的 jiǎohuáde, 狡诈的 jiǎozhàde; 偷偷摸

摸的 tōutōumōmōde. ~ly *adv* ~-ness *n* [U]

smack[1] /'smæk/ *n* [C] **1** 拍击〔擊〕pāijī, 拍击声 pāijīshēng. □ *vt* **1** (用掌)拍击 pāijī. **2** 咂嘴 zā zuǐ. □ *adv* 猛烈地 měngliède; 不偏不倚地 bùpiān bùyǐ de: *hit* ~ *in the eye* 猛击眼睛.

smack[2] /'smæk/ *n* [C] 小渔船 xiǎo yúchuán.

smack[3] /'smæk/ *vi* ~ *of* 带〔帶〕有(某种)风〔風〕味 dài yǒu fēngwèi.

small /smɔ:l/ *adj* [-er, -est] (*large* 的反义词)**1** 小的 xiǎode, 少的 shǎode. **2** 小规模(经营)的 xiǎo guīmó de: ~ *farmers* 小农. **3** 不重要的 bú zhòngyào de, 微不足道的 wēi bùzúdào de: *a* ~ *problem* 小问题. □ *n* 狭〔狹〕小部分 xiáxiǎo bùfen: *the* ~ *of the back* 腰背部. '~-**arms** *n* [*pl*] 轻〔輕〕武器 qīng wǔqì. '~-**holding** [英国英语]五十英亩〔畝〕以下的小片地 wǔshí Yīngmǔ yǐxià de xiǎopiàndì. **the** ~ **hours** *n pl* 半夜后三,四点〔點〕钟〔鐘〕bànyè hòu sān, sì diǎnzhōng. '~**pox** *n* [U]天花 tiānhuā. '~ **talk** 闲〔閒〕聊 xiánliáo. ~**ness** *n* [U]

smart[1] /smɑ:t/ *adj* [-er, -est] **1** 漂亮的 piàoliangde; 整洁〔潔〕的 zhěngjiéde. **2** 时〔時〕髦的 shímáode. **3** 聪〔聰〕明的 cōngmingde, 伶俐的 línglìde. **4** 轻〔輕〕快的 qīngkuàide, 敏捷的 mǐnjiéde, 活泼〔潑〕的 huópode: *a* ~ *pace* 轻快的脚步. **5** 剧〔劇〕烈的 jùliède; 严〔嚴〕厉〔厲〕的 yánlìde: *a* ~ *slap* 一记猛烈的耳光. ~**ly** *adv* ~**ness** *n* [U]

smart[2] /smɑ:t/ *vt*, *n* [U] (感觉)剧〔劇〕痛 jùtòng, 刺痛 cìtòng.

smarten /'smɑ:tn/ *vt/i* 使漂亮 shǐ piàoliang; 使活泼〔潑〕shǐ huópo.

smash /smæʃ/ *vt/i* **1** 打碎 dǎ suì, 打破 dǎ pò: ~ *a cup on the floor* 在地上摔碎一只杯子. **2** [与 *into*. *through* 等连用] 猛冲〔衝〕měng chōng, 撞入 zhuàngrù. **3** 击〔擊〕溃 jīkuì. **4** [网球]猛叩 měngkòu. □ *n* [C] **1** 粉碎 fěnsuì, 破碎 pòsuì. **2** [网球]叩球 kòuqiú, 杀〔殺〕球 shāqiú. □ *adv* 碰撞地 pèngzhuàngde; 破碎地 pòsuìde: *drive* ~ *into a wall* 驾车撞墙. '~-**up** 撞车 zhuàngchē.

smat·ter·ing /'smætərɪŋ/ *n* 肤〔膚〕浅〔淺〕的知识〔識〕fūqiǎnde zhīshi, 一知半解 yīzhī-bànjiě.

smear /smɪə(r)/ *vt/i* **1** 涂〔塗〕抹(油腻) túmǒ. **2** [喻]诽谤 fěibàng, 毁坏〔壞〕(名誉) huǐhuài. □ *n* [C] 污点〔點〕wūdiǎn, 污迹〔跡〕wūjī.

smell[1] /smel/ *n* **1** [U] 嗅觉〔覺〕xiùjué. **2** [C,U] 气〔氣〕味 qìwèi. **3** 嗅 xiù, 闻〔聞〕wén.

smell[2] /smel/ *vt/i* [*pt*, *pp* smelt /smelt/] **1** [常与 *can*, *could* 连用] 嗅出 xiùchū, 闻〔聞〕到 wéndào. ~ *a rat* ⇨ rat(2). **2** 嗅 xiù, 闻 wén: ~ *the flowers* 闻一闻这些花. **3** 有嗅觉〔覺〕yǒu xiùjué: *Can fishes* ~? 鱼有嗅觉吗? **4** 发〔發〕出…气〔氣〕味 fāchū … qìwèi: *That food* ~*s good*. 那食物好香. **5** 发〔發〕出臭味 fāchū chòuwèi: *your feet* ~ 你的脚发臭. **smelly** *adj* [-ier, -iest] [非正式用语]有臭味的 yǒu chòuwèi de.

smelt[1] /smelt/ *vt* 熔炼〔煉〕rónglìàn.

smelt[2] *pp*, *pt* of smell[2].

smile /smaɪl/ *n* [C] 微笑 wēixiào, 笑容 xiàoróng. □ *vt/i* 微笑 wēixiào.

smirk /smɜ:k/ *vi*, *n* [C] 傻笑 shǎxiào; 得意的笑 déyìde xiào.

smock /smɒk/ *n* [C] 罩衫 zhàoshān, 工作服 gōngzuòfú.

smog /smɒg/ *n* [U] 烟雾〔霧〕yānwù.

smoke[1] /sməʊk/ *n* **1** [U] 烟 yān, 烟尘〔塵〕yānchén. **2** [C] 吸烟 xī yān. '~-**screen** **(a)** 烟幕 yānmù. **(b)** [喻] 蒙〔矇〕骗〔騙〕人的话 mēngpiàn rén de huà. ~**less zone** *n* [C] 无〔無〕烟地区〔區〕wú yān dìqū. **smoky** *adj* [-ier, -iest].

smoke[2] /sməʊk/ *vt/i* **1** 冒烟 mào yān, 起烟雾〔霧〕qǐ yānwù. **2** 抽烟 chōuyān, 吸烟 xīyān. ~ *a pipe* 吸烟斗. **3** 熏〔燻〕制〔製〕(鱼、肉) xūnzhì. **4** 熏黑 xūn hēi, 熏脏〔髒〕xūn zāng: ~*d glass* 熏黑的玻璃(用以观察太阳). **smoker** 吸烟者 xīyānzhě.

smooth /smu:ð/ *adj* [-er, -est] **1** 光滑的 guānghuáde, 平滑的 pínghuáde. **2** 平稳〔穩〕的 píngwěnde, 不摇晃〔搖〕的 bù yáohuàng de. **3** 调匀的 tiáoyúnde, 不结块〔塊〕的 bù jié kuài de. **4** 柔和的 róuhéde, 温和的 wēnhéde. **5** 奉承的 fèngchengde, 有礼〔禮〕貌的 yǒu lǐmào de. □ *vt/i* 使光滑 shǐ guānghuá, 把…弄平 bǎ…nòngpíng; 使平稳 shǐ píngwěn, 使平静 shǐ píngjìng, 使缓和 shǐ huǎnhé. ~**ly** *adv* ~**ness** *n* [U]

smother /'smʌðə(r)/ *vt* **1** 使窒息 shǐ zhìxī, 把…闷〔悶〕死 bǎ…mēnsǐ. **2** 闷住(火) mēnzhù, 闷熄 mēnxī. **3** ~ *sth* (*in*) 覆盖〔蓋〕fùgài: *bread* ~*ed in butter* 涂黄油的面包. **4** 抑制 yìzhì, 忍住 rěnzhù: ~

yawn 忍住呵欠.

smoul·der [美语 = **smol-**] /'sməʊldə(r)/ *vi* **1** 用文火闷烧[燒] yòng wénhuǒ mēnshāo. **2** [喻](情绪等)闷在心里[裏] mēn zài xīnlǐ. □ *n* [U] 闷烧 mēnshāo.

smudge /smʌdʒ/ *n* [C] 污点[點] wūdiǎn, 污迹[跡] wūjī. □ *vt/i* **1** 弄脏 nòng zāng, 涂[塗]污 túwū. **2** (墨水等)形成污迹 xíngchéng wūjī.

smug /smʌg/ *adj* [-ger, -gest] 自满的 zìmǎnde, 沾沾自喜的 zhānzhān zìxǐ de. **~ly** *adv* **~ness** *n* [U]

smuggle /'smʌgl/ *vt* **1** 私运[運] sīyùn, 走私 zǒusī. **2** 偷带[帶](人或物) tōudài: *~ a letter into a prison* 把一封信偷偷地带进监狱. **smug·gler** /'smʌglə(r)/ 走私者 zǒusīzhě.

smut /smʌt/ *n* **1** [C] 煤尘[塵] méichén, 一片黑污 yípiàn hēiwū. **2** [U] 淫词 yíncí, 秽[穢]语 huìyǔ. **smutty** *adj*

snack /snæk/ *n* [C] 小吃 xiǎochī, 快餐 kuàicān.

snag /snæg/ *n* [C] [非正式用语]意外的困难[難] yìwàide kùnnan.

snail /sneɪl/ *n* [C] 蜗牛 wōniú.

snake /sneɪk/ *n* [C] **1** 蛇 shé. **2** [喻]阴[陰]险[險]的人 yīnxiǎnde rén. □ *vi* 蜿蜒前进[進] wānyán qiánjìn, 蛇行 shéxíng.

snap /snæp/ *vt/i* [-pp-] **1** *~ at sth* 咬住 yǎozhù. **2** [喻]攫夺[奪] juéduó. *~ sth up* 抢[搶]购[購] qiǎnggòu. **3** 啪地一声[聲]折断[斷] pāde yìshēng zhéduàn, 啪地一声关[關]上或打开[開] pāde yìshēng guānshàng huò dǎkāi. **4** 厉[厲]声说 lìshēng shuō, 急促地说 jícùde shuō. *~ at sb* 对[對]人厉声说话 duì rén lìshēng shuōhuà. **5** 拍照 pāi zhào. **6** *~ out of it* 突然改变[變]情绪,习[習]惯等 tūrán gǎibiàn qíngxù, xíguàn děng. □ *n* **1** [C] 猛咬 měng yǎo; 折断声 zhéduànshēng. **2** [C] = snapshot. **'~shot** 快照 kuàizhào. **~py** *adj* [-ier, -iest] **(a)** 活泼[潑]的 huópode, 敏捷的 mǐnjiéde. **(b)** 急躁的 jízàode; 过[過]敏的 guòmǐnde.

snare /sneə(r)/ *n* [C] 罗[羅]网[網] luówǎng, 陷阱 xiànjǐng. □ *vt* 诱捕 yòupǔ, 陷害 xiànhài.

snarl[1] /snɑ:l/ *vt/i* **1** (指狗)嗥[嘷]叫 háojiào. **2** (指人)咆哮 páoxiāo. □ *n* [C] 嗥叫 háojiào; 咆哮 páoxiāo

snarl[2] /snɑ:l/ *vt/i* (使)缠[纏]结 chánjié; (使)混乱[亂] hùnluàn: *The traffic was ~ed up.* 交通混乱. **'~-up** *n* [C] 缠结 chánjié; 混乱 hùnluàn.

snatch /snætʃ/ *vt/i* **1** 抢[搶] qiǎng, 夺[奪]取 duóqǔ. **2** 迅速获[獲]得 xùnsù huòdé; 趁机[機]取得 chènjī qǔdé: *~ a kiss* 趁机一吻. □ *n* [C] **1** 抢 qiǎng, 夺 duó. **2** 片段 piànduàn; 短时 duǎn shí: *~es of conversation* 谈话的片段.

sneak /sni:k/ *vt/i* 偷偷地走 tōutōude zǒu, 偷偷摸摸地行动[動] tōutōumōmōde xíngdòng. □ *n* [C] [非正式用语]鬼鬼祟祟的人 guǐguǐsuìsuìde rén. **~ing** *adj* **(a)** 偷偷摸摸的 tōutōumōmōde, 诡秘的 guǐmìde: *have a ~ing respect for him* 私下里对他尊敬. **(b)** 含糊的 hánhude, 不明确[確]的 bù míngquè de: *a ~ing suspicion* 隐藏在心中的猜疑.

sneer /snɪə(r)/ *vi* *~ (at)* 嘲笑 cháoxiào, 讥[譏]笑 jīxiào; 说轻[輕]蔑话 shuō qīngmiè huà. □ *n* [C] 嘲笑 cháoxiào, 讥笑 jīxiào.

sneeze /sni:z/ *n* [C] 喷嚏 pēntì. □ *vi* 打喷嚏 dǎ pēntì.

sniff /snɪf/ *vt/i* **1** (有声音地)以鼻吸气[氣] yǐ bí xīqì. **2** 嗤之以鼻 chī zhī yǐ bí. **3** *~ (at) sth* 闻[聞](香味) wén. □ *n* [C] **1** 吸气声 xīqìshēng, 嗅 xiù. **2** 吸入的东[東]西 xīrùde dōngxi: *a ~ of gas* 闻到煤气.

snig·ger /'snɪgə(r)/ *n* [C] 窃[竊]笑 qièxiào, 暗笑 ànxiào. □ *vi* 窃笑 qièxiào, 暗笑 ànxiào.

snip /snɪp/ *vt/i* [-pp-] 剪 jiǎn, 剪去 jiǎnqù. □ *n* [C] **1** 剪下的东[東]西 jiǎnxiàde dōngxi. **2** [非正式用语]便宜货 piányihuò.

snipe /snaɪp/ *vt/i* 伏击[擊] fújī, 狙击 jūjī. **sniper** 狙击手 jūjīshǒu.

snip·pet /'snɪpɪt/ *n* [C] **1** (切下的)小片 xiǎopiàn. **2** [*pl*] (新闻等)片段 piànduàn.

snivel /'snɪvl/ *vi* [-ll-, 美语 -l-] 哭诉 kūsù.

snob /snɒb/ *n* [C] 势利的人 shìlìde rén. **~bish** *adj* **~bery** 势利 shìlì.

snooker /'snu:kə(r)/ *n* [U] 落袋撞击[擊]球 luò dài zhuàngjī qiú.

snoop /snu:p/ *vi* 打听[聽] dǎting.

snooze /snu:z/ *vi, n* [C] [非正式用语]小睡 xiǎoshuì, 午睡 wǔshuì.

snore /snɔ:(r)/ *vi* 打鼾 dǎhān. □ *n* [C] 鼾声[聲] hānshēng.

snor·kel, schnor·kel /'snɔ:kl/ *n* [C] (潜水用)通气[氣]管 tōngqìguǎn.

snort /snɔ:t/ *vt/i* **1** 喷鼻息 pēn bíxī. **2** 发[發]哼声[聲] fā hēngshēng. □ *n* [C] 喷鼻息 pēn bíxī, 鼻息声 bíxīshēng.

snout /snaʊt/ *n* [C] (动物的)口鼻部 kǒubíbù; (尤指)猪鼻 zhūbí.

snow[1] /snəʊ/ *n* [U] 雪 xuě, 积〔積〕雪 jīxuě. '**~ball** *n* [C] 雪球 xuěqiú. □ *vt/i* 似雪片飞〔飛〕来〔來〕 shì xuěpiàn fēilái. '**~drift** (被风吹成的)雪堆 xuěduī. '**~drop** [植物]雪莲〔蓮〕xuělián. '**~man** 雪人 xuěrén. '**~-plough** [美语 = **-plow**] 扫〔掃〕雪机〔機〕sǎoxuějī.

snow[2] /snəʊ/ *vt/i* **1** 下雪 xiàxuě, 降雪 jiàngxuě. ***be ~ed in*** (或 ***up***) 被大雪封住 bèi dàxuě fēngzhù. **2** ~ ***under*** 压〔壓〕倒 yādǎo, 淹没 yānmò: *~ed under with presents* 礼物多不胜收. **snowy** *adj* [-ier, -iest].

snub /snʌb/ *vt* [-bb-] 冷落 lěngluò, 怠慢 dàimàn. □ *n* [C] 冷落的言词或态〔態〕度 lěngluòde yáncí huò tàidù.

snub nose /'snʌb nəʊz/ *n* [C] 狮〔獅〕子鼻 shīzibí. '**~-nosed** *adj*

snuff[1] /snʌf/ *n* [U] 鼻烟 bíyān.

snuff[2] /snʌf/ *vt/i* 熄灭〔滅〕(蜡烛) xīmiè; 剪烛〔燭〕花 jiǎn zhúhuā.

snug /snʌg/ *adj* [-gg-] **1** 温暖的 wēnnuǎnde, 舒适〔適〕的 shūshìde. **2** 整洁〔潔〕的 zhěngjiéde: *a ~ cabin* 整洁的船舱. **3** 紧〔緊〕贴的 jǐntiēde, 紧身的 jǐnshēnde: *a ~ jacket* 紧身短上衣. **~ly** *adv*

snuggle /'snʌgl/ *vt/i* 舒服地蜷伏 shūfude quánfú; 挨紧〔緊〕āijǐn, 偎依 wēiyī.

so[1] /səʊ/ *adv* (表示程度、大小)那么〔麼〕nàme, 这〔這〕么 zhème: *It is not ~ big as I thought.* 它并没有我想象的那么大.

so[2] /səʊ/ *adv* **1** (表示方式,方法)这〔這〕样〔樣〕zhèyàng, 那样 nàyàng, 如此 rúcǐ: *Kick the ball ~.* 这样踢球. ***and*** '**~ *on*** 等等 děngděng. **2** ~ ***that*** **(a)** 为〔爲〕的是 wèi de shì, 以便 yǐbiàn, 使得 shǐdé: *Shout ~ that they hear you.* 大声叫喊,以使他们听到你. **(b)** 以致 yǐzhì, 结果是 jiéguǒ shì: *Nothing was heard of him, ~ that people thought he was dead.* 没有听到他的消息,以致人们以为他死了. ~ ***as to*** 为的是 wèi de shì, 以便 yǐbiàn, 使得 shǐdé. **3** [用于代替词语]这样 zhèyàng, 如此 rúcǐ: *I told you ~!* 我对你这样讲过! **4** (表示赞同)是的 shìde, 不错 búcuò: *A: "It was cold yesterday".* "昨天很冷." *B: "S~ it was."* "是的." **5** 同样 tóngyàng, 也 yě: *You are young and ~ am I.* 你年轻,我也年轻. **6** 非常 fēicháng, 极〔極〕jí, 很 hěn: *He's ~ tired.* 他十分疲劳. '**~-called** 所谓的 suǒwèide: *~-called friends* 所谓的朋友. **~-and-~** /'səʊ n səʊ/ 某人 mǒurén; 某事 mǒushì.

so[3] /səʊ/ *conj* 所以 suǒyǐ, 因而 yīn'ér: *He was hurt ~ I helped him.* 他受伤了,所以我帮助他.

soak /səʊk/ *vt/i* **1** 浸 jìn, 泡 pào. **2** 使浸透 shǐ jìntòu, 使吸收 shǐ xīshōu. **3** (指雨等)淋湿〔濕〕línshī, 湿透 shītòu. □ *n* [C] 浸 jìn, 泡 pào.

soap /səʊp/ *n* [U] 肥皂 féizào. □ *vt* 用肥皂(擦洗) yòng féizào. **soapy** *adj* [-ier, -iest]

soar /sɔː(r)/ *vi* **1** (鸟)高飞〔飛〕gāofēi, 翱〔翺〕翔 áoxiáng **2** [喻]高涨〔漲〕gāozhǎng, 猛增 měngzēng: *Prices are ~ing.* 物价高涨.

sob /sɒb/ *vt/i* [-bb-] **1** 呜〔嗚〕咽 wūyè, 啜泣 chuòqì. **2** ~ ***sth out*** 哭诉 kūsù. □ *n* [C] 哭泣 kūqì, 哭泣声〔聲〕kūqìshēng.

so·ber /'səʊbə(r)/ *adj* **1** 严〔嚴〕肃〔肅〕的 yánsùde, 认〔認〕真的 rènzhēnde: *a ~ decision* 严肃而认真的决定. **2** 清醒的 qīngxǐngde, 未醉的 wèi zuì de. □ *vt/i* **1** ~ **(*sb*) (*down*)** (使)变〔變〕严肃 biàn yánsù. **2** ~ **(*sb*) *up*** 使清醒 shǐ qīngxǐng, 清醒起来〔來〕qīngxǐng qǐlái. **~ly** *adv*

Soc. = Society.

soc·cer /'sɒkə(r)/ *n* [U] 英式足球 Yīngshì zúqiú.

so·ciable /'səʊʃəbl/ *adj* 友好的 yǒuhǎode; 好交际〔際〕的 hào jiāojì de. **so·ciably** *adv*

so·cial /'səʊʃl/ *adj* **1** 群居的 qúnjūde. **2** 人与〔與〕社群关〔關〕系〔係〕的 rén yǔ shèqún guānxì de: *~ customs* 社会风俗. **3** 社会〔會〕的 shèhuìde, 社会上的 shèhuìshàngde: *one's ~ equals* 同一阶层者. **4** 社交的 shèjiāode, 交际〔際〕的 jiāojìde: *a* '*~ club* 联谊会. **5** = sociable. □ *n* [C] 联欢〔歡〕会 liánhuānhuì, 交谊会 jiāoyìhuì. ,**~ se'curity** 社会保险〔險〕shèhuì bǎoxiǎn. '**~ worker** 社会服务〔務〕者 shèhuì fúwùzhě. **~ly** *adv*

so·cial·ism /'səʊʃəlɪzəm/ *n* [U] 社会〔會〕主义〔義〕shèhuìzhǔyì. **so·cial·ist** *adj*, *n* [C]

so·ciety /sə'saɪətɪ/ *n* [*pl* -ies] [U] 社会〔會〕制度 shèhuì zhìdù. [C] 社会 shèhuì. **3** [U] 上流社会 shàngliú shèhuì, 社交界 shèjiāojiè. ⇨ high society. **4** [C] (为某种目的组成的)团〔團〕体〔體〕tuán tǐ, 协〔協〕会 xiéhuì.

so·ci·ol·ogy /ˌsəʊsɪˈɒlədʒɪ/ *n* [U] 社会〔會〕学〔學〕shèhuìxué. **so·ci·ol·ogist** *n* [C] 社会学家 shèhuìxuéjiā. **so·cio'logi·cal** /-ˈlɒdʒɪkl/ *adj*

sock¹ /sɒk/ *n* [C] 短袜〔襪〕duǎn wà. ***pull one's ~s up*** 鼓起劲〔勁〕来〔來〕gǔqǐ jìn lái.

sock² /sɒk/ *n* [C] [俚语]拳打 quándǎ, 殴〔毆〕打 ōudǎ. □ *vt* [俚语] 拳打 quándǎ, 殴打 ōudǎ.

socket /ˈsɒkɪt/ *n* [C] 孔 kǒng, 穴 xué; 插口 chākǒu, 插座 chāzuò.

sod /sɒd/ *n* [C,U] 草地 cǎodì, 草皮 cǎopí.

soda /ˈsəʊdə/ *n* [U] 苏〔蘇〕打 sūdá, 碳酸钠 tànsuānnà. **'~-water** 汽水 qìshuǐ.

sod·den /ˈsɒdn/ *adj* 浸透了的 jìntòulede.

so·dium /ˈsəʊdɪəm/ *n* [U] [化学] 钠 **(Na)** nà. **~(-vapour) lamp** *n* [C] 钠灯〔燈〕nàdēng.

sofa /ˈsəʊfə/ *n* [C] 沙发〔發〕shāfā.

soft /sɒft/ *adj* [-er, -est] **1** 软〔軟〕的 ruǎnde, 柔软的 róuruǎnde: *a ~ pillow* 柔软的枕头. **2** (表面)柔滑的 róuhuáde, 软滑的 ruǎnhuáde: *~ cotton* 柔滑的棉布. **3** (光线、色彩)柔和的 róuhéde. **4** (声调)轻〔輕〕柔的 qīngróude. **5** (轮廓、线条)不明显〔顯〕的 bù míngxiǎn de, 模糊的 móhude. **6** (回答、语言)温和的 wēnhéde, 文雅的 wényǎde. **7** (指水质)软性的 ruǎnxìngde. **8** 发〔發〕软音的 fā ruǎnyīn de: *C is ~ in "city" and hard in "cat".* "city" 中的 "c" 为软音,而 "cat" 中的 "c" 为硬音. **9** 轻〔輕〕松〔鬆〕的 qīngsōngde, 容易的 róngyìde: *have a ~ job* 担任轻松的工作. **10** 软弱的 ruǎnruòde, 不坚〔堅〕强的 bù jiānqiángde. **'~ drink** 无〔無〕酒精饮料 wú jiǔjīng yǐnliào. **ˌ~-'hearted** *adj* 心肠〔腸〕软的 xīncháng ruǎn de, 心慈的 xīn cí de. **'~ware** [计算机]软件 ruǎnjiàn. ⇨ hardware. **~ly** *adv* **~ness** *n* [U]

sof·ten /ˈsɒfn/ *vt/i* **1** (使)软〔軟〕化 ruǎnhuà, 变〔變〕软弱 biàn ruǎnruò, 使柔和 shǐ róuhé, 使温和 shǐ wēnhé. **2** 使容易 shǐ róngyì, 使轻〔輕〕松〔鬆〕shǐ qīngsōng.

soggy /ˈsɒgɪ/ *adj* [-ier, -iest] (尤指地面)浸水的 jìn shuǐ de, 湿〔濕〕透的 shī tòu de. **sog·gi·ness** *n* [U]

soil /sɔɪl/ *n* [C,U] 泥土 nítǔ, 土壤 tǔrǎng. □ *vt/i* 弄脏〔髒〕nòng zāng, 弄污 nòng wū.

sol.=Solicitor.

so·lar /ˈsəʊlə(r)/ *adj* 太阳〔陽〕的 tàiyángde, 日光的 rìguāngde. **~-'cell** *n* [C] 太阳能电〔電〕池 tàiyángnéng diànchí. **the '~ system** 太阳系 tàiyángxì.

sold /səʊld/ *pt, pp* of sell.

sol·der /ˈsɒldə(r)/ *n* [U] 焊料 hànliào. □ *vt* 焊接 hànjiē. **'~ing-iron** 烙铁〔鐵〕làotie.

sol·dier /ˈsəʊldʒə(r)/ *n* [C] 士兵 shìbīng, 军〔軍〕人 jūnrén. □ *vi* 当〔當〕兵 dāng bīng, 从〔從〕军 cóng jūn. **ˌ~ 'on** 坚〔堅〕持下去 jiānchí xiàqù.

sole¹ /səʊl/ *n* [C] 鲽(鱼) dié.

sole² /səʊl/ *n* [C] 脚底 jiǎodǐ; 鞋底 xiédǐ; 袜〔襪〕底 wàdǐ. □ *vt* (给鞋等)配底 pèi dǐ.

sole³ /səʊl/ *adj* 单〔單〕独〔獨〕的 dāndúde, 唯一的 wéiyīde: *the ~ owner* 唯一的所有者. **~ly** *adv* 单独地 dāndúde, 唯一地 wéiyīde, 孤独地 gūdúde.

sol·emn /ˈsɒləm/ *adj* **1** 庄〔莊〕严〔嚴〕的 zhuāngyánde, 严肃〔肅〕的 yánsùde, 隆重的 lóngzhòngde. **2** 表情严肃的 biǎoqíng yánsùde, 一本正经〔經〕的 yìběn zhèngjīng de. **~ly** *adv* **~ness** *n* [U]

sol·em·nity /səˈlemnətɪ/ *n* [*pl* -ies] [正式用语] **1** [U] 庄〔莊〕严〔嚴〕zhuāngyán, 严肃〔肅〕yánsù, 隆重 lóngzhòng. **2** [C] 庄重的仪〔儀〕式 zhuāngzhòngde yíshì.

sol·icit /səˈlɪsɪt/ *vt/i* **1** 请求 qǐngqiú, 恳〔懇〕求 kěnqiú, 乞求 qǐqiú. **2** (妓女)拉客 lā kè.

sol·ici·tor /səˈlɪsɪtə(r)/ *n* [C] [英国英语](初级)律师〔師〕lǜshī. ⇨ barrister.

solid /ˈsɒlɪd/ *adj* **1** 固体〔體〕的 gùtǐde. **2** 实〔實〕心的 shíxīnde. **3** 坚〔堅〕固的 jiāngùde, 牢固的 láogùde. **4** 可靠的 kěkàode: *~ arguments* 有根据的论点. **5** 纯质的 chúnzhìde, 单〔單〕一的 dānyīde: *~ gold* 赤金. **6** 连〔連〕续〔續〕的 liánxùde: *sleep ten hours ~* 连续睡十个小时. **7** [数学]立体的 lìtǐde. □ *n* [C] **1** 固体 gùtǐ. **2** [数学] 立体 lìtǐ. **~ly** *adv* **~ity** /səˈlɪdətɪ/ *n* [U]

soli·dar·ity /ˌsɒlɪˈdærətɪ/ *n* [U] 团〔團〕结一致 tuánjié yízhì.

sol·id·ify /səˈlɪdɪfaɪ/ *vt/i* [*pt, pp* -ied] (使)团〔團〕结 tuánjié; (使)坚〔堅〕固 jiāngù.

soli·tary /ˈsɒlɪtrɪ/ *adj* **1** 独〔獨〕居的 dújūde, 孤独的 gūdúde. **2** 唯一的 wéiyīde: *a ~ visitor* 唯一的客人. **3** 荒凉的 huāngliángde, 冷落的 lěngluòde.

soli·tude /'sɒlɪtju:d/ *n* [U] 孤独〔獨〕gūdú, 隐〔隱〕居 yǐnjū.
solo /'səʊləʊ/ *n* [C] [*pl* ~s] **1** 独〔獨〕奏曲 dúzòuqǔ, 独唱曲 dúchàngqǔ. **2** 独奏 dúzòu, 独唱 dúchàng, 单〔單〕独表演 dāndú biǎoyǎn. '**~ist** 独唱者 dúchàngzhě, 独奏者 dúzòuzhě.
sol·stice /'sɒlstɪs/ *n* [C] [天文]至点〔點〕zhìdiǎn. ⇨ equinox.
sol·uble /'sɒljʊbl/ *adj* **1** 可溶解的 kě róngjiě de. **2** = solvable. **solu'bil·ity** *n* [U]
sol·ution /sə'lu:ʃn/ *n* **1** [C] 解答(问题等) jiědá, 解决(困难) jiějué. **2** [U] 解决的过〔過〕程或方法 jiějuéde guòchéng huò fāngfǎ. **3** [U] 溶解 róngjiě. **4** [C,U] 溶液 róngyè.
solv·able /'sɒlvəbl/ *adj* 可解答的 kě jiědá de, 可解决的 kě jiějué de: *the problem is* ~ 问题是可以解答的.
solve /sɒlv/ *vt* 解答(问题等) jiědá, 解释〔釋〕jiěshì.
sol·vent /'sɒlvənt/ *adj* 能偿〔償〕还〔還〕的 néng chánghuán de. □ *n* [C] 溶剂〔劑〕róngjì. **sol·vency** *n* [U] 偿付能力 chángfù nénglì.
sombre [美语 = **som·ber**] /'sɒmbə(r)/ *adj* 暗色的 ànsède; 昏暗的 hūnànde, 阴〔陰〕沉的 yīnchénde. **~ly** *adv* **~ness** *n* [U]
some¹ /sʌm, 弱式: səm/ *adj* **1** 一些 yīxiē, 若干 ruògān, 几〔幾〕个〔個〕jǐgè: *Please give me ~ milk.* 请给我一点牛奶. *There are ~ children outside.* 外面有几个孩子. ⇨ any. **2** [用于疑问句,希望得到肯定的答复]: *Aren't there ~ stamps in that drawer?* 抽斗里不是还有些邮票吗? **3** [用于邀请]: *Will you have ~ cake?* 请吃些糕饼吧? **4** 某一 mǒuyī: *He's living at ~ place in East Africa.* 他现在住在东非某地. **5** 大约 dàyuē, 大概 dàgài: *~ twenty years ago* 大约在二十年以前. **6** 大量的 dàliàngde, 很大的 hěndàde: *for ~ time* 很久.
some² /sʌm/ *pron* 一些 yìxiē, 若干 ruògān, 几〔幾〕个〔個〕jǐgè: *S~ of these books are quite useful.* 这些书中有几种是很有用的.
some·body /'sʌmbədɪ/, **some·one** /'sʌmwʌn/ *pron* **1** 某人 mǒurén, 有人 yǒurén: *There's ~ at the door.* 有人敲门. [注意: 在疑问句或否定句中用 *anybody* 或 *anyone*]. **2** 要人 yàorén, 大人物 dàrénwù: *become ~ (in one's country, town, etc)* (在本国或在自己城镇等处)成为重要人物.
some·how /'sʌmhaʊ/ *adv* 以某种〔種〕方式 yǐ mǒuzhǒng fāngshì: *We shall get there ~.* 我们会设法到达那里的.
some·one /'sʌmwʌn/ *n* = somebody.
som·er·sault /'sʌməsɔ:lt/ *n* [C] 筋斗 jīndǒu. □ *vi* 翻筋斗 fān jīndǒu.
some·thing /'sʌmθɪŋ/ *pron* 某物 mǒuwù, 某事 mǒushì: *I want ~ to eat.* 我要吃点东西. [注意: 在疑问、否定句中用 *anything*].
some·time /'sʌmtaɪm/ *adv* 在某一时〔時〕候 zài mǒuyī shíhòu: *I saw him ~ in May.* 我在五月份见到过他.
some·times /'sʌmtaɪmz/ *adv* 有时〔時〕yǒushí, 时常 shícháng: *I ~ receive letters from him.* 我时常收到他的来信.
some·what /'sʌmwɒt/ *adv* 有点〔點〕儿〔兒〕yǒu diǎnr: *I was ~ surprised.* 我有点惊讶.
some·where /'sʌmweə(r)/ *adv* 在某处〔處〕zài mǒuchù; 到某地 dào mǒudì: *It must be ~ near here.* 它一定在附近某处. [注意: 在疑问、否定句中用 *anywhere*].
son /sʌn/ *n* [C] 儿〔兒〕子 érzi. '**~-in-law** *n* [C] [*pl* ~s-in-law] 女婿 nǚxù.
so·nata /sə'nɑ:tə/ *n* [C] [*pl* ~s] [音乐]奏鸣〔鳴〕曲 zòumíngqǔ.
song /sɒŋ/ *n* **1** [U] 歌唱 gēchàng, 声〔聲〕乐〔樂〕shēngyuè. **2** [C] 歌词 gēcí. '**~bird** 鸣〔鳴〕禽 míngqín.
sonic /'sɒnɪk/ *adj* 声〔聲〕音的 shēngyīnde; 音速的 yīnsùde. ⇨ supersonic.
son·net /'sɒnɪt/ *n* [C] 十四行诗 shísìhángshī.
soon /su:n/ *adv* [-er, -est] **1** 不久 bùjiǔ, 即刻 jíkè: *We shall ~ be home.* 我们很快就要到家了. **2** 早 zǎo; 快 kuài: *How ~ can you be ready?* 你什么时候能准备好? **3** *as ~ as* 一…就 yī…jiù; 立即 lìjí: *He started as ~ as he received the news.* 他听到消息后立即动身. **4** [用于比较结构中]: *The ~er the better.* 愈快愈好. ***~er … than*** 宁〔寧〕愿〔願〕…而不 nìngyuàn … ér bù: *He would ~er die than marry you.* 他宁死不愿同你结婚.
soot /sʊt/ *n* [U] 烟灰 yānhuī, 煤灰 méihuī. □ *vt* 用煤灰覆盖〔蓋〕yòng méihuī fùgài, 涂〔塗〕以黑灰 tú yǐ hēi huī. **sooty** *adj* [-ier -iest] 被煤灰弄脏〔髒〕的 bèi méihuī nòng zāng de.

soothe /suːð/ *vt* **1** 使平静 shǐ píngjìng, 使镇定 shǐ zhèndìng. **2** 减轻〔輕〕(痛苦) jiǎn qīng. **sooth·ing** *adj*

soph·is·ti·cated /səˈfɪstɪkeɪtɪd/ *adj* **1** 老练〔練〕的 lǎoliànde, 世故的 shìgùde, 有经〔經〕验〔驗〕的 yǒu jīngyàn de. **2** 尖端的 jiānduānde: ~ *weapons* 尖端武器. **soph·is·ti·ˈca·tion** /-ʃn/ *n* [U]

soppy /ˈsɒpɪ/ *adj* [-ier, -iest] 〔非正式用语〕过〔過〕于〔於〕伤〔傷〕感的 guòyú shānggǎn de.

so·prano /səˈprɑːnəʊ/ *n* [C] [*pl* ~s] *adj* 女高音 nǚgāoyīn.

sor·cerer /ˈsɔːsərə(r)/ *n* [C] 男巫 nán wū; 男魔术〔術〕师〔師〕 nán móshùshī. **sor·cer·ess** /-ɪs/ *n* [C] 女巫 nǚ wū; 女魔术师 nǚ móshùshī. **sor·cery** *n* [*pl* -ies] [U] 巫术 wūshù.

sor·did /ˈsɔːdɪd/ *adj* **1** 肮〔骯〕脏〔髒〕的 āngzāngde, 破烂〔爛〕的 pòlànde; 悲惨〔慘〕的 bēicǎnde. **2** (指人)卑鄙的 bēibǐde, 下贱〔賤〕的 xiàjiànde. ~**ly** *adv* ~**ness** *n* [U]

sore /sɔː(r)/ *adj* [-r, -st] **1** 疼痛的 téngtòngde, 一碰就痛的 yípèng jiù tòng de. **2** 使人痛苦的 shǐ rén tòngkǔde, 使人烦恼〔惱〕的 shǐ rén fánnǎo de. *a* ~ *point* 伤〔傷〕心事 shāngxīn shì, (感情上的)痛处〔處〕 tòngchù. **3** 恼火的 nǎohuǒde: *feel* ~ 感到恼火. □ *n* [C] (身上的)痛处 tòngchù, 伤处 shāngchù. ~**ly** *adv* 极〔極〕 jí, 非常 fēicháng: ~*ly needed* 急需. ~**ness** *n* [U]

sor·row /ˈsɒrəʊ/ *n* [C,U] 悲哀(的原因) bēi'āi, 伤〔傷〕心事 shāngxīn shì. □ *vi* [与 *at*, *for*, *over* 连用] 感到悲伤 gǎndào bēishāng. ~**ful** *adj*

sorry /ˈsɒrɪ/ *adj* **1** 后〔後〕悔的 hòuhuǐde; 难〔難〕过〔過〕的 nánguòde. ***be*** (或 ***feel***) ~ ***for sb*** 同情 tóngqíng, 怜〔憐〕悯〔憫〕 liánmǐn **2** 对〔對〕不起 duìbùqǐ, 抱歉 bàoqiàn: *"Can you lend me a pound?"* "你能借我一镑钱吗?"— *"Sorry, but I can't."* "很抱歉,我无能为力." **3** [-ier, -iest] 可怜的 kěliánde: *in a* ~ *state* 在可怜的状况之中.

sort¹ /sɔːt/ *n* [C] 种〔種〕类〔類〕 zhǒnglèi, 类别 lèibié.

sort² /sɔːt/ *vt/i* ~ ***sth*** (***out***) 分类〔類〕 fēnlèi; 拣〔揀〕选〔選〕 jiǎnxuǎn. ~ ***sth out*** 〔非正式用语〕 **(a)** 整理 zhěnglǐ: ~ *out a drawer* 整理抽斗. **(b)** 解决 jiějué: ~ *out a problem* 解决一个问题. **(c)** 消除误会〔會〕 xiāochú wùhuì.

S.O.S. /ˈesəʊˈes/ *n* (无线电)呼救信号〔號〕 hūjiù xìnhào.

souf·flé /ˈsuːfleɪ/ *n* [C] 〔法语〕蛋奶酥 dànnǎisū.

soul /səʊl/ *n* [C] **1** 灵〔靈〕魂 línghún. **2** 精神 jīngshén, 精力 jīnglì, 热〔熱〕情 rèqíng: *put* ~ *into one's work* 全神贯注地工作. **3** 化身 huàshēn; 典型 diǎnxíng: *the* ~ *of honour* 光荣的化身. **4** (死者的)幽灵 yōulíng, 鬼魂 guǐhún. **5** 人 rén: *not a* ~ *to be seen* 一个人影也看不到. ~**ful** *adj* 热情的 rèqíngde, 深情的 shēnqíngde. ~**fully** *adv* ~**less** *adj* 无〔無〕情的 wúqíngde.

sound¹ /saʊnd/ *adj* [-er, -est] **1** 健康的 jiànkāngde, 健全的 jiànquánde. **2** 可靠的 kěkàode, 忠实〔實〕的 zhōngshíde: *a* ~ *worker* 一个扎实的工人. **3** 彻〔徹〕底的 chèdǐde, 充分的 chōngfènde: *be a* ~ *sleeper* 是一个酣睡的人. □ *adv* 彻底地 chèdǐde, 充分地 chōngfènde. ~**ly** *adv* 彻底地 chèdǐde, 充分地 chōngfènde; 健全地 jiànquánde; 可靠地 kěkàode. ~**ness** *n* [U]

sound² /saʊnd/ *n* [C,U] **1** 声〔聲〕音 shēngyīn. **2** [仅用 *sing*] 语气〔氣〕 yǔqì; 笔〔筆〕调 bǐdiào: *I don't like the* ~ *of it.* 我不喜欢这种语气. ˈ~ **barrier** 声障 shēngzhàng, 音障 yīnzhàng. ˈ~**-track** (影片上的)声带〔帶〕 shēngdài. ˈ~**-wave** 声波 shēngbō.

sound³ /saʊnd/ *vt/i* **1** (使)发〔發〕声〔聲〕 fā shēng. **2** 发…的音 fā…de yīn: *Don't* ~ *the "b" in "dumb".* "dumb" 中的 "b" 不要发音. **3** 通知 tōngzhī, 宣告 xuāngào: ~ *the alarm* 发布警报. **4** [喻]似乎 sìhū, 听〔聽〕起来〔來〕 tīngqǐlái: *His explanation* ~*s all right.* 他的解释似乎有道理.

sound⁴ /saʊnd/ *vt/i* **1** 测(海等)深度 cè shēndù. **2** ~ ***sb*** (***out***) (***about sth***), ~***sb*** (***out***) (***on sth***) 试探某人对某事的意见 shìtàn mǒurén duì mǒushì de yìjiàn.

sound⁵ /saʊnd/ *n* [C] 海峡〔峽〕 hǎixiá.

soup /suːp/ *n* [U] 汤〔湯〕 tāng, 羹 gēng.

sour /ˈsaʊə(r)/ *adj* **1** 酸的 suānde, 酸味的 suānwèide. **2** 酸臭的 suānchòude, 酸腐的 suānfǔde: ~ *milk* 发酸了的奶. **3** [喻] 脾气〔氣〕坏〔壞〕的 píqì huài de. □ *vt/i* (使)变〔變〕酸 biàn suān. ~**ly** *adv* ~**ness** *n* [U]

source /sɔːs/ *n* [C] 源头〔頭〕 yuántóu, 来〔來〕源 láiyuán, 出处〔處〕 chūchù: *the* ~ *of a river* 河流的源

头. *the ~ of an idea* 思想的来源. *the ~ of a disease* 疾病的根源.

south /saʊθ/ *n* **1** the ~ 南 nán, 南方 nánfāng, 南部 nánbù. **2** [用作 *adj*] 南方的 nánfāngde; 向南的 xiàngnánde; 来[來]自南方的 lái zì nánfāng de. □ *adv* 向南 xiàngnán. ,~'**east** (缩作 **SE**) *n*, *adj*, *adv* 东[東]南 dōngnán. ,~-'**west** (缩作 **SW**) *n*, *adj*, *adv* 西南 xīnán. ~**er·ly** /'sʌðəlɪ/ *adj*, *adv* 来自南方 lái zì nánfāng; 向南 xiàng nán; 在南方 zài nánfāng. ~**ern** /'sʌðən/ *adj* (世界,国家等)南方的 nánfāngde, 南部的 nánbùde; 来自南方的 lái zì nánfāng de. ~**ward** /-wəd/ *adj* 向南方 xiàng nánfāng. ~**wards** *adv*

sou·venir /,su:və'nɪə(r)/ *n* [C] 纪念品 jìniànpǐn.

sov·er·eign /'sɒvrɪn/ *adj* 最高的 zuìgāode, 无[無]上的 wúshàngde, 有最高权[權]力的 yǒu zuìgāo quánlì de. □ *n* [C] **1** 君主 jūnzhǔ, 国[國]王 guówáng, 女王 nǚwáng. **2** 英国[國]硬币[幣]金镑(面值一镑) Yīngguó yìngbì jīnbàng. ~**ty** 君权 jūnquán; 统治权 tǒngzhìquán, 主权 zhǔquán.

so·viet /'səʊvɪət/ *n* [C] 苏[蘇]维埃 Sūwéi'āi.

sow[1] /saʊ/ *n* [C] 大母猪 dà mǔzhū.

sow[2] /səʊ/ *vt/i* [*pt* ~ed; *pp* ~n /səʊn/ 或 ~ed] 播种[種] bōzhòng.

soya /sɔɪə/ *n* [U] (亦作 '**soya-bean**) 大豆 dàdòu, 黄豆 huángdòu.

spa /spɑ:/ *n* [C] [*pl* ~s] 矿[礦]泉(疗养地) kuàngquán.

space /speɪs/ *n* **1** [U] 空间[間] kōngjiān, 太空 tàikōng: *travel into ~* 太空旅行. **2** [C,U] 间隔 jiàngé, 距离[離] jùlí. **3** [C,U] (空地)面积[積] miànjī. **4** [U] 空地 kòngdì, 余[餘]地 yúdì; 未被占用之处[處] wèi bèi zhànyòng zhī chù: *There's not enough ~ here.* 这里没有足够的地位了. **5** 一段时[時]间 yíduàn shíjiān: *within the ~ of a day* 一天之内. □ *vt* ~ *sth out* 把…分隔开[開] bǎ…fēnggékāi. '~ **age** *n* [C] 太空时代 tàikōng shídài. '~ **craft**, '~ **ship** *n* [C] 太空船 tàikōngchuán, 宇宙飞[飛]船 yǔzhòu fēichuán. '~-**rocket** *n* [C] 宇宙火箭 yǔzhòu huǒjiàn. '~-**suit** *n* [C] 太空服 tàikōngfú, 宇宙服 yǔzhòufú. '~-**shuttle** *n* [C] 航天飞机[機] hángtiān fēijī.

spa·cious /'speɪʃəs/ *adj* 广[廣]阔[闊]的 guǎngkuòde, 宽敞的 kuānchangde. ~**ness** *n* [U]

spade /speɪd/ *n* [C] **1** 铲[鏟]chǎn, 铁[鐵]锹 tiěqiāo. **2**(纸牌)黑桃 hēitáo. □ *vt* 铲 chǎn, 用铁锹掘 yòng tiěqiāo jué. '~**work** [喻]艰[艱]苦的基础[礎]工作 jiānkǔde jīchǔ gōngzuò.

spa·ghetti /spə'getɪ/ *n* [U] 细圆面[麵]条[條] xì yuán miàntiáo.

span /spæn/ *n* [C] **1** 一拃宽 yìzhǎ kuān. **2** 跨度 kuàdù. **3** 自始至终 zì shǐ zhì zhōng: *the life ~ of man* 人的寿命. □ *vt* [-nn-] 跨过[過] kuàguò, 跨越 kuàyuè.

spangle /'spæŋgl/ *n* [C] (衣服上用作装饰的)小金属[屬]片 xiǎo jīnshǔpiàn. □ *vt* 用小金属片装饰 yòng xiǎo jīnshǔpiàn zhuāngshì.

span·iel /'spænɪəl/ *n* [C] 一种[種]长[長]毛垂耳狗 yìzhǒng cháng máo chuí ěr gǒu.

spank /spæŋk/ *vt/i* 打(小孩)屁股 dǎ pìgǔ. ~**ing** *n* [C]

span·ner /'spænə(r)/ [美语 = *wrench*] *n* [C] 扳头[頭] bāntóu, 扳手 bānshǒu.

spar[1] /spɑ:(r)/ *n* [C] (用作桅杆等的)圆材 yuáncái.

spar[2] /spɑ:(r)/ *vi* [-rr-] **1** 拳斗[鬪] quándòu. **2** [喻]争吵 zhēngchǎo, 争论[論] zhēnglùn.

spare[1] /speə(r)/ *adj* **1** 剩余[餘]的 shèngyúde; 空闲[閑]的 kòngxiánde. **2** (指人)瘦的 shòude. □ *n* [C] 备[備]用件 bèiyòngjiàn.

spare[2] /speə(r)/ *vt/i* **1** 饶[饒]恕 ráoshù, 赦免 shèmiǎn: *~ a prisoner's life* 饶犯人一命. **2** 抽出(时间) chōuchū; 让[讓]给(金钱) rànggěi: *Can you ~ me a few minutes?* 你能给我几分钟时间吗? *~ a thought for* 考虑[慮](下决心) kǎolù. **spar·ing** *adj* 节[節]省的 jiéshěngde; 谨慎的 jǐnshènde. **sparing·ly** *adv*

spark /spɑ:k/ *n* [C] **1** 火星 huǒxīng, 火花 huǒhuā. **2** [喻]生气[氣] shēngqì, 活力 huólì. □ *vt*, **1** 发[發]火花 fā huǒhuā, 飞[飛]火星 fēi huǒxīng. **2** ~ *sth o*… [喻]为[為]…的直接原因 wéi … de zhíjiē yuányīn, 导[導]致 dǎozhì. '~**ing-plug** (内燃机)火花塞 huǒhuāsāi.

sparkle /'spɑ:kl/ *vi* 闪[閃]光 shǎnguāng, 闪耀 shǎnyào. □ [C] 闪光 shǎnguāng, 闪耀 shǎnyào. ~**ling** /'spɑ:klɪŋ/ *adj*

spar·row /'spærəʊ/ *n* [C] 麻雀 máquè.

sparse /spɑ:s/ *adj* **1** 稀少的 xīshǎode: ~ *population* 人口稀少.

稀疏的 xīshūde: ~ *grass* 稀疏的草皮. ~**ly** *adv* ~**ness** *n* [U]

spasm /'spæzəm/ *n* [C] **1** 抽筋 chōujīn, 痉〔痙〕挛〔攣〕 jìngluán. **2** 一阵〔陣〕发〔發〕作 yízhèn fāzuò. ~**odic** /spæz'mɒdɪk/ *adj* **(a)** 间〔間〕歇的 jiānxiēde, 阵发性的 zhènfāxìngde. **(b)** 痉挛引起的 jìngluán yǐnqǐ de. ~**odi·cally** *adv*

spas·tic /'spæstɪk/ *n* [C], *adj* 痉〔痙〕挛〔攣〕的(人) jìngluánde; 患大脑〔腦〕麻痹的(人) huàn dànǎo mábì de.

spat /spæt/ *pt, pp* of spit.

spate /speɪt/ *n* [C,U] **1** 洪水 hóngshuǐ, (河水的)猛涨〔漲〕 měngzhǎng. **2** (营业等)突然涌来〔來〕 tūrán yǒnglái.

spa·tial /'speɪʃl/ *adj* 空间〔間〕的 kōngjiānde, 关〔關〕于〔於〕空间的 guānyú kōngjiān de. ~**ly** *adv*

spat·ter /'spætə(r)/ *vt/i* 溅〔濺〕 jiàn, 洒〔灑〕 sǎ, 泼〔潑〕 pō. □ *n* [C] 一阵〔陣〕洒〔灑〕落 yízhèn sǎluò: *a* ~ *of rain* 一阵雨.

spat·ula /'spætjʊlə/ *n* [C] [*pl* ~s] (涂敷用的)抹刀 mòdāo, 刮铲〔鏟〕 guāchǎn.

spawn /spɔːn/ *n* [U] (鱼,蛙等的)卵 luǎn, 子 zǐ. □ *vt/i* **1** (使鱼等)产〔產〕卵 chǎn luǎn. **2** 大量生产 dàliàng shēngchǎn.

speak /spiːk/ *vt/i* [*pt* spoke /spəʊk/; *pp* spoken /'spəʊkən/] **1** 说 shuō, 说话 shuōhuà: *I was* ~*ing to him about my plans.* 我正在和他讲我的打算. ~ *for sb* **(a)** 为〔爲〕某人说话 wèi mǒurén shuōhuà, 陈述某人的意见 chénshù mǒurén de yìjiàn. **(b)** 为某人作证〔證〕 wèi mǒurén zuòzhèng. **2** 表达〔達〕意见 biǎodá yìjiàn: *Actions* ~ *louder than words.* 行动胜于言辞. **3** 能说(某种语言) néng shuō: ~ *French* 讲法语. **4** 演说 yǎnshuō, 发〔發〕言 fā yán. **5** 说明 shuōmíng, 说出 shuōchū: ~ *the truth* 说真话. ~**er** **(a)** 演讲人 yǎnjiǎngrén, 演说家 yǎnshuōjiā. **(b)** (loudspeaker 的缩写) 扬〔揚〕声〔聲〕器 yángshēngqì.

spear /spɪə(r)/ *n* [C] 矛 máo, 枪〔槍〕 qiāng. □ *vt* (用矛)刺 cì. '~**head** *n* [C] [喻]先头〔頭〕突击〔擊〕部队〔隊〕 xiāntóu tūjī bùduì, 先锋 xiānfēng. □ *vt* 当〔當〕...的先锋 dāng...de xiānfēng.

spear·mint /'spɪəmɪnt/ *n* [U] [植物]留兰〔蘭〕香 liúlánxiāng.

spe·cial /'speʃl/ *adj* **1** 特别的 tèbiéde, 特殊的 tèshūde; 专〔專〕门〔門〕的 zhuānménde. **2** 格外的 géwàide, 额外的 éwàide: ~ *treatment* 额外待遇. □ *n* [C] 临〔臨〕时〔時〕列车〔車〕 línshí lièchē; 特刊 tèkān, 号〔號〕外 hàowài. ~**ly** *adv* 特别地 tèbiéde; 专门地 zhuānménde: *I came* ~*ly to see you.* 我特地来看你. ~**ist** 专家 zhuānjiā.

spe·ci·al·ity /ˌspeʃɪ'ælətɪ/ *n* [C] [*pl* -ies] **1** 特性 tèxìng, 特质〔質〕 tèzhì. **2** 特制〔製〕品 tèzhìpǐn, 特产〔產〕 tèchǎn; 特长〔長〕 tècháng.

spe·cial·ize /'speʃəlaɪz/ *vt/i* 成为专〔專〕家 chéngwéi zhuānjiā; 专门〔門〕研究 zhuānmén yánjiū. **spe·cial·iz·ation** /-'zeɪʃn/ *n* [C,U]

spe·cies /'spiːʃiːz/ *n* [C] [*pl* ~] **1** (生物的)种〔種〕 zhǒng. **2** 种类〔類〕 zhǒnglèi.

spe·ci·fic /spə'sɪfɪk/ *adj* **1** 具体〔體〕的 jùtǐde, 明确〔確〕的 míngquède: ~ *orders* 明确的命令. **2** 特有的 tè yǒu de, 特种的 tèzhǒngde, 特定的 tèdìngde: *for a* ~ *purpose* 为一个特定的目的. ~**ally** /-klɪ/ *adv*

spec·ifi·ca·tion /ˌspesɪfɪ'keɪʃn/ *n* **1** [U] 载〔載〕明 zàimíng, 详述 xiáng shù. **2** [C] [常用 *pl*] 规格 guīgé; 清单〔單〕 qīngdān; 说明书〔書〕 shuōmíngshū.

spec·ify /'spesɪfaɪ/ *vt* [*pt, pp* -ied] 指定 zhǐdìng; 载明 zàimíng, 详述 xiáng shù.

speci·men /'spesɪmɪn/ *n* [C] **1** 标〔標〕本 biāoběn. **2** 样〔樣〕品 yàngpǐn, 样张〔張〕 yàngzhāng: *a* ~ *of his work* 他的工作质量的一个样品. **3** 试样 shìyàng: *a* ~ *of urine* 尿的试样.

speck /spek/ *n* [C] **1** 斑点〔點〕 bāndiǎn, 微粒 wēilì. **2** [喻]缺点 quēdiǎn, 污点 wūdiǎn.

speckle /'spekl/ *n* [C] (尤指皮毛上的)小斑点〔點〕 xiǎo bāndiǎn. **speckled** *adj*

spec·tacle /'spektəkl/ *n* [C] **1** 公开〔開〕展示 gōngkāi zhǎnshì; 场〔場〕面 chǎngmiàn. **2** 景象 jǐngxiàng, 奇观〔觀〕 qíguān, 壮〔壯〕观 zhuàngguān. **3** [*pl*] (亦作 *a pair of* ~*s*) 眼镜 yǎnjìng.

spec·tacu·lar /spek'tækjʊlə(r)/ *adj* 壮〔壯〕观〔觀〕的 zhuàngguānde, 洋洋大观的 yángyáng dà guān de. ~**ly** *adv*

spec·ta·tor /spek'teɪtə(r)/ *n* [C] 观〔觀〕众〔衆〕 guānzhòng, 旁观者 pángguānzhě.

spec·tro·scope /'spektrəskəʊp/ *n* [C] 分光镜 fēnguāngjìng. **spec·tro·scopic** /ˌspektrə'skɒpɪk/ *adj* 分光镜的 fēnguāngjìngde; 用分光镜的 yòng fēnguāngjìng de: ~*anal-*

ysis 光谱分析 guāngpǔ fēnxī.

spec·trum /'spektrəm/ *n* [C] [*pl* -tra /-trə/] **1** 光谱 guāngpǔ. **2** [喻]系列 xìliè: *a ~ of opinions* 一系列的不同意见.

specu·late /'spekjʊleɪt/ *vi* **1** 思索 sīsuǒ, 推测 tuīcè. **2** 投机[機] tóujī. **specu'la·tion** *n* [C,U] **specu·lat·ive** *adj*

sped /sped/ *pt, pp* of speed.

speech /spi:tʃ/ *n* **1** [U] 说话 shuōhuà; 说话方式或能力 shuōhuà fāngshì huò nénglì. **2** [C] 演说 yǎnshuō, 发[發]言 fāyán. **~less** *adj* 说不出话的 shuō bù chū huà de.

speed /spi:d/ *n* **1** [U] 快 kuài, 迅速 xùnsù. **2** [C,U] 速度 sùdù. □ *vt/i* **1** [*pt, pp* sped] 迅速前进[進] xùnsù qiánjìn, 快行 kuàixíng. **2** [*pt, pp* ~ed] ~ **(*sth*) *up*** 加速 jiā sù, 加快 jiā kuài: *~ up production* 加快生产. **~om·eter** /spi:'dɒmɪtə(r)/ 速度计 sùdùjì. **speedy** *adj* [-ier, -iest] 快的 kuàide, 迅速的 xùnsùde.

spell¹ /spel/ *n* [C] **1** 咒语 zhòuyǔ, 符咒 fúzhòu. **2** 吸引力 xīyǐnlì, 迷惑力 míhuòlì. **'~bound** *adj* 被迷惑的 bèi míhuò de, 入迷的 rùmíde.

spell² /spel/ *n* [C] 一段时[時]间[間] yíduàn shíjiān.

spell³ /spel/ *vt/i* [*pt,pp* ~ed /speld/ 或 spelt /spelt/] **1** 用字母拼 yòng zìmǔ pīn, 拼写[寫] pīnxiě. **2** ~ ***sth out*** 讲[講]清楚 jiǎng qīngchu, 说明 shuōmíng. **3** 招致 zhāozhì, 带[帶]来[來] dàilái: *Does laziness always ~ failure?* 懒惰总是招致失败吗? **~ing** 拼法 pīnfǎ, 拼写法 pīnxiěfǎ.

spelt ⇨ spell³.

spend /spend/ *vt/i* [*pt, pp* spent /spent/] **1** 用(钱) yòng, 花费 huāfèi. **2** 用尽[盡] yòng jìn, 消耗 xiāohào: *Their ammunition was spent.* 他们的弹药已用尽. **3** 消磨(时间) xiāomó, 过[過](日子) guò. **'~thrift** 挥[揮]金如土的人 huī jīn rú tǔ de rén.

sperm /spɜ:m/ *n* [U] 精液 jīngyè, 精子 jīngzǐ.

spew /spju:/ *vt/i* = vomit.

sphere /sfɪə(r)/ *n* [C] **1** 球 qiú, 球面 qiúmiàn; 天体[體] tiāntǐ. **2** (兴趣, 活动, 势力等的)范[範]围[圍] fànwéi, 领域 lǐngyù. **spheri·cal** /'sferɪkl/ *adj* 球形的 qiúxíngde.

spice /spaɪs/ *n* **1** [C,U] 香料 xiāngliào, 调味品 tiáowèipǐn. **2** [U] [喻]趣味 qùwèi; 风[風]味 fēngwèi: *add ~ to a story* 增添故事的兴味. □ *vt* 加香料于[於] jiā xiāngliào yú. **spicy** *adj* [-ier, -iest] **(a)** 加香料的 jiā xiāngliào de, 香的 xiāngde. **(b)** [喻]因下流而有刺激性的 yīn xiàliú ér yǒu cìjīxìng de.

spick /spɪk/ *adj* [仅用于] **,~ and 'span** 崭[嶄]新的 zhǎnxīnde; 干[乾]净的 gānjìngde, 整洁[潔]的 zhěngjiéde.

spi·der /'spaɪdə(r)/ *n* [C] 蜘蛛 zhīzhū. **spid·ery** *adj* (书法)笔[筆]划[劃]细长[長]的 bǐhuà xìcháng de.

spied /spaɪd/ *pt, pp* of spy.

spike /spaɪk/ *n* [C] **1** 尖端 jiānduān; 尖钉 jiān dīng. **2** 穗 suì. □ *vt* 用尖钉刺 yòng jiān dīng cì. **spiky** *adj* [-ier, -iest]

spill /spɪl/ *vt/i* [*pt,pp* spilt /spɪlt/ 或 ~ed] (使)溢出 yìchū, (使)溅[濺]出 jiànchū. □ *n* [C] (从马, 车等上)摔[跸]下 shuāixià.

spin /spɪn/ *vt/i* [*pt* spun /spʌn/ 或 span /spæn/; *pp* spun] [-nn-] **1** 纺(纱,线) fǎng, 纺绩 fǎngjì. **2** 编结 biānjié: *Spiders ~ webs.* 蜘蛛结网. **3** [喻]编造(故事) biānzào. **~ *sth out*** 尽[盡]量使某物持续[續] jìnliàng shǐ mǒuwù chíxù, 延长[長] yáncháng. **4** 使(某物)旋转[轉] shǐ xuánzhuǎn. □ *n* **1** [U] 旋转 xuánzhuǎn. **2** [C] 乘汽车[車]兜一圈 chéng qìchē dōu yìquān **,~-'drier** 旋转式脱水机[機] xuánzhuǎnshì tuōshuǐjī, 甩干[乾]机 shuǎigānjī. **'~ning-wheel** 纺车 fǎngchē.

spin·ach /'spɪnɪdʒ/ *n* [U] 菠菜 bōcài.

spi·nal /'spaɪnl/ *adj* [解剖]脊椎骨的 jǐzhuīgǔde.

spindle /'spɪndl/ *n* [C] **1** 纺锤 fǎngchuí, 锭子 dìngzǐ. **2** 轴[軸] zhóu. **spin·dly** /'spɪndlɪ/ *adj* [-ier, -iest] 细长[長]的 xìchángde: *spindly legs* 细长腿.

spine /spaɪn/ *n* [C] **1** = backbone. **2** (植物的)针 zhēn, 刺 cì. **3** 书[書]脊 shūjǐ. **~less** *adj* **(a)** 无[無]脊骨的 wú jǐgǔ de. **(b)** [喻]无骨气[氣]的 wú gǔqì de, 无勇气的 wú yǒngqì de. **spiny** *adj* [-ier, -iest] 多刺的 duō cì de, 棘手的 jíshǒude.

spin·ster /'spɪnstə(r)/ *n* [C] 未婚女子 wèi hūn nǚzǐ, 老处[處]女 lǎo chùnǚ.

spi·ral /'spaɪərəl/ *adj, n* [C] 螺旋形(的) luóxuánxíng: *A snail's shell* *is* ~. 蜗牛的壳是螺旋形的. □ *vi* [-ll-, 美语亦作 -l-] 盘〔盤〕旋 pánxuán, 螺旋形移动〔動〕luóxuánxíng yídòng.

spire /ˈspaɪə(r)/ *n* [C] (尤指教堂的)塔尖 tǎjiān, 尖顶 jiāndǐng.

spirit /ˈspɪrɪt/ *n* **1** [C,U] 精神 jīngshén, 心灵〔靈〕xīnlíng. **2** [C] 灵魂 línghún, 鬼怪 guǐguài. **3** [C] 人 rén, 人物 rénwù: *What a generous* ~! 多么慷慨的人啊! **4** [U] 勇气 yǒngqì, 生气 shēngqì: *Put more* ~ *into your work.* 在你的工作中拿出更多的勇气来. **5** [仅用 *sing*] 态〔態〕度 tàidu. *It depends on the* ~ *in which it was done.* 那要看是抱什么态度干的. **6** [U] 精神实〔實〕质〔質〕jīngshén shízhì: *obey the* ~, *not the letter, of the law.* 服从法律的精神,而不是它的字句. **7** [*pl*] 情绪 qíngxù, 心情 xīnqíng, 兴〔興〕致 xìngzhì: *in high* ~*s* 兴高采烈. **8** [常用 *pl*] 烈酒 liè jiǔ. □ *vt* ~ ***sth (sb) away*** (或 ***off***) 迅速而神秘地带〔帶〕走 xùnsù ér shénmì de dàizǒu, 拐带 guǎidài. ~**ed** *adj* (a) 有勇气的 yǒu yǒngqì de, 有生气的 yǒu shēngqì de. (b) 有…情绪的 yǒu…qíngxù de, 心情…的 xīnqíng…de: *high* ~*ed* 高兴的. *low* ~*ed* 沮丧的.

spiri·tual /ˈspɪrɪtʃʊəl/ *adj* **1** 精神的 jīnshénde, 心灵〔靈〕的 xīnlíngde; 宗教的 zōngjiàode, 神圣〔聖〕的 shénshèngde. **2** 鬼魂的 guǐhúnde, 超自然的 chāo zìrán de. □ *n* [C] 美国〔國〕黑人的圣歌 Měiguó hēirén de shènggē. ~**ly** *adv*

spirt /spɜːt/ *vi, n* [C] = spurt.

spit[1] /spɪt/ *n* [C] **1** 烤肉叉 kǎoròuchā. **2** 伸入海中的狭〔狹〕长〔長〕陆〔陸〕地 shēnrù hǎizhōng de xiácháng lùdì.

spit[2] /spɪt/ *vt/i* [*pt, pp* spat /spæt/] [-tt-] **1** 吐(唾沫) tǔ. **2** ~ ***sth (out)*** 吐出(某物) tǔchū. **3** (雨,雪)霏霏下降 fēifēi xiàjiàng. □ *n* **1** [U] = saliva. **2** ***the*** ~***ting image of*** 同…一模一样〔樣〕tóng… yìmó yíyàng.

spite /spaɪt/ *n* [U] 恶〔惡〕意 èyì, 意欲造成痛苦 yìyù zàochéng tòngkǔ. ***in*** ~ ***of*** 不管 bùguǎn, 不顾〔顧〕búgù: *They went out in* ~ *of the rain.* 尽管下雨,他们仍然外出. □ *vt* 恶意对〔對〕待 èyì duìdài, 刁难〔難〕diāonàn. ~**ful** *adj*

splash /splæʃ/ *vt/i* **1** 溅〔濺〕(水) jiàn, 泼〔潑〕(水) pō. **2** 显〔顯〕示 xiǎnshì; 鼓吹 gǔchuī: ~ *his name all over the newspapers* 在报纸上为他大力鼓吹. □ *n* [C] 溅 jiàn; 飞〔飛〕溅声〔聲〕fēijiànshēng; 溅污的斑点〔點〕jiànwū de bāndiǎn.

splen·did /ˈsplendɪd/ *adj* **1** 壮〔壯〕丽〔麗〕的 zhuànglìde, 辉〔輝〕煌的 huīhuángde. **2** [非正式用语] 极〔極〕好的 jíhǎode, 令人满意的 lìng rén mǎnyì de: *a* ~ *performance* 极好的演出. ~**ly** *adv*

splen·dour [美语 = **-dor**] /ˈsplendə(r)/ *n* [U] 壮〔壯〕丽〔麗〕zhuànglì, 光辉〔輝〕guānghuī.

splice /splaɪs/ *vt* **1** 绞接(绳头) jiǎojiē. **2** 拼接(木板等) pīnjiē. □ *n* [C] 拼接 pīnjiē; 绞接 jiǎojiē.

splint /splɪnt/ *n* [C] (正骨用)夹〔夾〕板 jiābǎn.

splin·ter /ˈsplɪntə(r)/ *n* [C] (木,玻璃等)碎片 suìpiàn. □ *vt/i* (使)裂成碎片 liè chéng suìpiàn. ˈ~ **group** (自原政党〔黨〕)分裂出来的派别 fēnliè chūlái de pàibié.

split /splɪt/ *vt/i* [*pt, pp* ~] [-tt-] **1** 劈开〔開〕pīkāi, (使)裂开 lièkāi. **2** ~ ***hairs*** 作细致的剖析 zuò xìzhìde pōuxī. ~ ***one's sides*** 捧腹大笑 pěng fù dà xiào. ~ ***up*** 分裂 fēnliè. **3** (使)分开 fēnkāi, (使)分离〔離〕fēnlí: *Arguments* ~ *the party.* 争论使党分裂. □ *n* [C] **1** 劈开 pīkāi, 裂开 lièkāi; 裂缝 lièfèng. **2** 分裂 fēnliè, 分开 fēnkāi, 分化 fēnhuà. **3** ***the*** ~***s*** 劈叉 pǐchà. ˌ~ ˈ**second** 一刹那 yíchànà.

splut·ter /ˈsplʌtə(r)/ *vt/i* **1** (因激动等)急促地乱〔亂〕说 jícùde luànshuō. **2** 发〔發〕劈啪声 fā pīpāshēng, 作爆裂声 zuò bàolièshēng: *The fire* ~*ed and died.* 这火劈劈啪啪地烧起来,然后熄灭了. □ *n* [U] 劈啪声 pīpāshēng, 爆裂声 bàolièshēng.

spoil /spɔɪl/ *vt/i* [*pt, pp* ~t 或 ~ed] **1** 破坏〔壞〕pòhuài, 损害 sǔnhài. **2** 宠〔寵〕坏 chǒng huài, 溺爱〔愛〕nì'ài. **3** (食物)变〔變〕坏 biàn huài, 腐败 fǔbài. □ *n pl* 赃〔贓〕物 zāngwù; (分得的)利益 lìyì. ˈ~**sport** 扫〔掃〕兴〔興〕的人 sǎoxìngde rén.

spoke[1] /spəʊk/ *n* [C] 轮〔輪〕辐〔輻〕lúnfú.

spoke[2], **spoken** /spəʊk, spəʊkən/ ⇨ speak.

spokes·man /ˈspəʊksmən/ *n* [C] [*pl* -men /-mən/] 发〔發〕言人 fāyánrén.

sponge /spʌndʒ/ *n* **1** [C] 海绵 hǎimián. **2** 海绵状〔狀〕物 hǎimiánzhuàng wù. **3** = sponge-cake. □ *vt/i* **1** 用海绵揩拭 yòng hǎimián kāishì. **2** ˈ~ ***on*** (或 ***off***) ***sh*** [非

正式用语]乞讨 qǐtǎo; 骗[騙]取 piànqǔ. '~**-cake,** 松[鬆]糕 sōnggāo. **sponger** 寄生虫[蟲] jìshēngchóng, 食客 shíkè. **spongy** *adj* [-ier, -iest]

spon·sor /'spɒnsə(r)/ *n* [C] **1** 负责人(如教父) fùzérén. **2** 发[發]起人 fāqǐrén, 主办[辦]人 zhǔbànrén. 资助人 zīzhùrén. □ *vt* 发起 fāqǐ, 主办 zhǔbàn.

spon·ta·neous /spɒn'teɪnɪəs/ *adj* 自发[發]的 zìfāde, 自然产[產]生的 zìrán chǎnshēng de. ~**ly** *adv* **spon·ta·neity** /,spɒntə'neɪətɪ/ *n* [U]

spool /spu:l/ *n* [C] 线[綫]轴[軸] xiànzhóu, 卷轴 juǎnzhóu.

spoon /spu:n/ *n* [C] 匙 chí, 调羹 tiáogēng. □ *vt* 用匙舀取 yòng chí yǎoqǔ. '~**feed** *vt* (对某人)作填鸭[鴨]式灌输[輸] zuò tiányāshì guànshū.

spor·adic /spə'rædɪk/ *adj* 偶而发[發]生的 ǒu'ěr fāshēng de. ~**-ally** /-klɪ/ *adv*

spore /spɔ:(r)/ *n* [C] [植物]孢子 bāozǐ.

sport /spɔ:t/ *n* **1** [C,U] 娱乐[樂] yúlè, 游戏[戲] yóuxì. **2** [*pl*] 运[運]动[動]会[會] yùndònghuì. **3** [非正式用语]公正的人 gōngzhèngde rén; 和善的人 héshànde rén. □ *vt/i* **1** 开[開]玩笑 kāiwánxiào. **2** [非正式用语]炫耀 xuànyào, 夸[誇]示 kuāshì: *He came in ~ing a new suit.* 他炫耀着他的新衣服走进来. '**sportscar** 比赛用汽车[車] bǐsài yòng qìchē, 高速汽车 gāo sù qìchē. '**sportsman** 运动员 yùndòngyuán. '**sportsman·ship** *n* [U] 运动道德 yùndòng dàodé, 体[體]育道德 tǐyù dàodé. ~**ing** *adj* **(a)** 运动的 yùndòngde, 喜爱[愛]运动的 xǐ'ài yùndòng de. **(b)** 有失败危险[險]的 yǒu shībài wēixiǎn de: *a ~ing chance* 一个带有冒险性的机会. ~**ing·ly** *adv*

spot /spɒt/ *n* [C] **1** 点[點] diǎn, 斑点 bāndiǎn. **2** 污点 wūdiǎn, 污迹[跡] wūjī. **3** (皮肤上的)小红痣 xiǎo hóng zhì. **4** 一点点 yìdiǎndiǎn, 少量 shǎoliàng: *a ~ of tea* 一小杯茶. **6** 地点 dìdiǎn, 场[場]所 chǎngsuǒ: *the ~ where he died* 他死去的地方. ***on the ~*** **(a)** 在场 zàichǎng. **(b)** 立即 lìjí, 当[當]场 dāngchǎng: *killed on the ~* 当场杀死. □ *vt/i* [-tt-] **1** (使)有斑点 yǒu bāndiǎn, (使)沾上污点 zhānshàng wūdiǎn. **2** 认[認]出 rènchū, 发[發]现 fāxiàn. ~**ted** *adj* 有斑点的 yǒu bāndiǎn de, 有污点的 yǒu wūdiǎn de. ~**less** *adj* 无[無]斑点的 wú bāndiǎn de, 纯洁[潔] 的 chúnjiéde. ~**ty** *adj* [-ier, -iest] (皮肤)有斑点的 yǒu bāndiǎn de.

spot·light /'spɒtlaɪt/ *n* [C] 聚光灯[燈] jùguāngdēng. □ *vt* 聚光照明 jùguāng zhàomíng; 使显[顯]著 shǐ xiǎnzhù.

spouse /spaʊs/ *n* [C] [法律]配偶 pèi'ǒu.

spout /spaʊt/ *n* [C] **1** 喷管 pēnguǎn; (茶壶的)嘴 zuǐ. **2** 水柱 shuǐzhù, 喷流 pēnliú. □ *vt/i* **1** 喷出 pēnchū, 喷射 pēnshè. **2** [非正式用语]滔滔不绝地讲[講] tāotāo bùjué de jiǎng.

sprain /spreɪn/ *vt* 扭伤[傷] niǔshāng. □ *n* [C] 扭伤 niǔshāng.

sprang /spræŋ/ *pt* of spring[3].

sprat /spræt/ *n* [C] 西鲱(鱼) xīfēi.

sprawl /sprɔ:l/ *vi* **1** 伸开[開]手足躺或坐 shēn kāi shǒu zú tǎng huò zuò. **2** (植物)蔓生 mànshēng; (城市)无[無]计划[劃]地延伸 wú jìhuà de yánshēn. □ *n* [C] 伸开四肢的躺卧姿势[勢] shēnkāi sìzhī de tǎngwò zīshì; 蔓生 mànshēng; 散乱[亂] sǎnluàn.

spray[1] /spreɪ/ *n* [C] 小花枝 xiǎo huāzhī, 枝状[狀]饰物 zhīzhuàng shìwù.

spray[2] /spreɪ/ *n* **1** [U] 水花 shuǐhuā, 飞[飛]沫 fēimò, 浪花 lànghuā. **2** [C,U] 用作喷洒[灑]的液体[體] yòngzuò pēnsǎ de yètǐ. **3** [C] 喷雾器 pēnwùqì. □ *vt* 喷射 pēnshè.

spread /spred/ *vt/i* [*pt*, *pp* ~] **1** 展开[開] zhǎnkāi, 铺开 būkāi. **2** 涂[塗] tú, 敷 fū, 抹 mǒ: *~ butter on bread* 在面包上抹黄油. **3** (使)传[傳]播 chuánbō, 散布[佈] sànbù: *~ knowledge* 传播知识. *~ disease* 传布疾病. **4** (使)延长[長] yáncháng, (使)展开[開] zhǎnkāi. □ *n* [C] **1** 范[範]围[圍] fànwéi, 广[廣]度 guǎngdù. **2** 传播 chuánbō, 散布 sànbù. **3** [非正式用语]丰[豐]盛的酒席 fēngshèngde jiǔxí, 宴会[會] yànhuì. **4** 涂抹用的食品 túmǒ yòng de shípǐn. '~**-eagle** *vt* [反身]手脚伸展着躺卧 shǒu jiǎo shēnzhǎnzhe tǎngwò.

spright·ly /'spraɪtlɪ/ *adj* [-ier, -iest] 活泼[潑]的 huópode, 轻[輕]快的 qīngkuàide. **spright·liness** *n* [U]

spring[1] /sprɪŋ/ *n* [C] **1** 跳 tiào, 跳跃[躍] tiàoyuè. **2** 泉 quán, 源泉 yuánquán. **3** 弹[彈]簧 tánhuáng, 发〔發〕条〔條〕 fātiáo. 4 [U] 弹性 tánxìng, 弹力 tánlì. **springy** *adj* [-ier, -iest]

spring² /sprɪŋ/ *n* [C] 春天 chūntiān, 春季 chūnjì. ˌ~-'**clean** *vt* 彻〔徹〕底打扫(房屋) chèdǐ dǎsǎo. ˌ~-'**cleaning** *n* 大扫除 dàsǎochú.

spring³ /sprɪŋ/ *vt/i* [*pt* sprang /spræŋ/; *pp* sprung /sprʌŋ/] **1** 跳 tiào, 跳跃〔躍〕 tiàoyuè. **2** ~ **(*up*)** (植物)生长〔長〕 shēngzhǎng, 发〔發〕芽 fāyá. **3** 突然出现 tūrán chūxiàn. **4** ~ ***sth on sb*** 突然提出 tūrán tíchū: *He sprang a surprise on me.* 他使我吃一惊. **5** 使发动〔動〕 shǐ fādòng, 开〔開〕动 kāidòng: ~ *a trap* 触动捕兽机. **6** ~ ***a leak*** (船)发生漏缝 fāshēng lòufèng.

sprinkle /'sprɪŋkl/ *vt* 洒〔灑〕 sǎ, 撒布〔佈〕 sànbù. **sprink·ler** /-klə(r)/ [尤指]洒水器 sǎshuǐqì, 喷水设备〔備〕 pēn shuǐ shèbèi.

sprint /sprɪnt/ *vi* 全速奔跑 quánsù bēnpǎo, 冲〔衝〕刺 chōngcì. □ *n* [C] 快跑 kuàipǎo.

sprout /spraʊt/ *vt/i* **1** 发〔發〕芽 fāyá; 开〔開〕始生长〔長〕 kāishǐ shēngzhǎng. **2** 发展 fāzhǎn. □ *n* [C] **1** 新芽 xīn yá, 嫩枝 nèn zhī. **2** = Brussels sprout.

sprung /sprʌŋ/ *pp* of spring³.

spun /spʌn/ *pp* of spin.

spur /spɜ:(r)/ *n* [C] **1** 踢马〔馬〕刺 tīmǎcì. **2** [喻]刺激物 cìjīwù, 鼓励〔勵〕品 gǔlìpǐn. ***on the ~ of the moment*** 一时〔時〕冲〔衝〕动〔動〕之下 yìshí chōngdòng zhī xià. **3** 山嘴 shānzuǐ; 横岭〔嶺〕 héng lǐng. □ *vt/i* [-rr-] ~ ***sb* (*on*)** 用踢马刺催促 yòng tīmǎcì cuīcù, 鞭策 biāncè.

spurn /spɜ:n/ *vt* 轻〔輕〕蔑地拒绝 qīngmiède jùjué; 唾弃〔棄〕 tuòqì.

spurt /spɜ:t/ *vi* **1** (液体,火焰等)喷射 pēnshè, 喷出 pēnchū. **2** 突然拼命努力 tūrán pīnmìng nǔlì, 冲〔衝〕刺 chōngcì. □ *n* [C] 突然喷射 tūrán pēnshè; 爆发〔發〕 bàofā.

sput·ter /'spʌtə(r)/ *vt/i* 连〔連〕续〔續〕发〔發〕出喷溅〔濺〕唾沫声〔聲〕 liánxù fāchū pēnjiàn tuòmò shēng.

spy /spaɪ/ *n* [C] [*pl* spies] **1** 间〔間〕谍 jiàndié, 特务〔務〕 tèwù. **2** 侦探 zhēntàn, 密探 mìtàn. □ *vt/i* **1** ~ ***on sth* (*sb*)** 侦查 zhēnchá, 暗中监〔監〕视 ànzhōng jiānshì. **2** 察看 chákàn; 发〔發〕现 fāxiàn.

sq. = square.

squabble /'skwɒbl/ *vi, n* [C] 争吵 zhēngchǎo, 口角 kǒujiǎo.

squad /skwɒd/ *n* [C] 小组 xiǎozǔ, 班 bān.

squad·ron /'skwɒdrən/ *n* [C] **1** 骑〔騎〕兵中队〔隊〕 qíbīng zhōngduì, (工兵,装甲兵等)连〔連〕 lián. **2** (海军)中队 zhōngduì; (空军)中队 zhōngduì.

squalid /'skwɒlɪd/ *adj* 肮〔骯〕脏〔髒〕的 āngzāngde; 贫穷〔窮〕的 pínqióngde; 无〔無〕人照顾〔顧〕的 wú rén zhàogù de. ~**ly** *adv*

squall /skwɔ:l/ *n* [C] **1** 高声〔聲〕叫喊 gāoshēng jiàohǎn; 啼哭 tíkū. **2** 大风〔風〕 dàfēng, 狂风 kuángfēng. □ *vi* 高声叫喊 gāoshēng jiàohǎn; 啼哭 tíkū.

squalor /'skwɒlə(r)/ *n* [U] 肮〔骯〕脏〔髒〕 āngzāng; 贫穷〔窮〕 pínqióng.

squan·der /'skwɒndə(r)/ *vt* 浪费(时间,金钱) làngfèi.

square¹ /skweə(r)/ *adj* **1** 正方形的 zhèngfāngxíngde. **2** 成直角的 chéng zhíjiǎo de: *a ~ chin* 方下巴. **3** 平方的 píngfāngde: *The ~ of 3 is 9.* 三的平方是九. **4** ***a ~ meal*** 一顿丰盛的饭菜 yídùn fēngshèngde fàncài. **5** 公平的 gōngpíngde, 公正的 gōngzhèngde: ~ *dealings* 公平交易. **6** (指人)守旧〔舊〕的 shǒujiùde. ***all ~*** 不分上下 bùfēn shàng xià, 势〔勢〕均力敌〔敵〕 shìjūn-lìdí. □ *adv* 成直角地 chéng zhíjiǎo de. ~**ly** *adv* **(a)** 成直角地 chéng zhíjiǎo de. **(b)** 公平地 gōngpíngde, 公正地 gōngzhèngde. **(c)** 面对〔對〕面地 miàn duì miàn de, 直接地 zhíjiēde: *I looked him ~ly in the eye.* 我直瞪瞪地逼视他的眼睛. ~**ness** *n* [U]

square² /skweə(r)/ *n* [C] **1** 正方形 zhèngfāngxíng. **2** 正方形物 zhèngfāngxíng wù. **3** 广〔廣〕场〔場〕 guǎngchǎng. **4** 平方 píngfāng. **5** 守旧〔舊〕的人 shǒujiùde rén.

square³ /skweə(r)/ *vt/i* **1** (使)成方形 chéng fāngxíng. **2** (使)成直角 chéng zhíjiǎo, (使)垂直 chuízhí. **3** 自乘 zìchéng. **4** ~ ***sth off*** 把某物划〔劃〕成方形 bǎ mǒuwù huà chéng fāngxíng. **5** ~ **(*up*) (*with sb*)** (与某人)结算 jiésuàn, 清帐〔賬〕 qīngzhàng.

squash¹ /skwɒʃ/ *vt/i* **1** 压〔壓〕扁 yā biǎn, 压平 yā píng. **2** 挤〔擠〕 jǐ, 挤进〔進〕 jǐjìn. **3** [非正式用语] (以压服性的反驳)使(人)沉默 shǐ chénmò. **4** 镇压(叛乱) zhènyā. □ *n* [C] **1** 拥〔擁〕挤的人群 yōngjǐde rénqún. **2** [C,U] 果子汁 guǒzizhī.

squash[2] /skwɒʃ/ *n* [U] (亦 '~-*rackets*) (在围墙内用小网拍玩的)小橡皮球戏〔戲〕 xiǎo xiàngpíqiú xì.

squat /skwɒt/ *vi* [-tt-] **1** 蹲坐 dūnzuò. **2** 非法占〔佔〕用(空屋,土地) fēifǎ zhànyòng. □ *adj* 矮胖的 ǎipàngde. **~ter** 非法占用(空屋,土地)者 fēifǎ zhànyòngzhě.

squaw /skwɔ:/ *n* [C] 北美印地安妇女 Běiměi Yìndì'ān fùnǚ.

squawk /skwɔ:k/ *vi, n* [C] (鸟类发出)粗厉〔厲〕的叫声〔聲〕 cūlìde jiàoshēng.

squeak /skwi:k/ *n* [C] **1** 短促刺耳的尖叫声〔聲〕 duǎncù cì'ěrde jiānjiàoshēng. **2** *a narrow* ~ 幸免于〔於〕难〔難〕 xìngmiǎn yú nàn. □ *vt/i* 发〔發〕短促的尖声 fā duǎncùde jiānshēng. **squeaky** *adj* [-ier, -iest]

squeal /skwi:l/ *n* [C] 长〔長〕声〔聲〕尖叫 chángshēng jiānjiào. □ *vt/i* 发〔發〕长而尖的叫声 fā cháng ér jiān de jiàoshēng.

squeam·ish /'skwi:mɪʃ/ *adj* 易呕〔嘔〕吐的 yì ǒutù de **~ly** *adv* **~ness** *n*[U]

squeeze /skwi:z/ *vt/i* **1** 挤〔擠〕jǐ, 榨 zhà. **2** *~ sth (from),~ sth (out of)* (从…中)榨取 zhàqǔ. **3** (指人)挤进〔進〕 jǐjìn. **4** *~ sth out of sb.* 向某人榨取(或勒索)某物 xiàng mǒurén zhàqǔ mǒuwù. □ *n* [C] **1** 压〔壓〕榨 yāzhà, 挤 jǐ. **2** [U] [非正式用语]财政困难〔難〕时〔時〕期 cáizhèng kùnnan shíqī.

squelch /skweltʃ/ *vt/i* (使)咯吱咯吱作响〔響〕 gēzī gēzī zuò xiǎng. □ *n* [C] 咯吱声〔聲〕 gēzīshēng.

squid /skwɪd/ *n* [C] 鱿鱼 yóuyú.

squint /skwɪnt/ *vi* **1** 斜着眼看 xiézhe yǎn kàn. **2** 眯着眼看 mīzhe yǎn kàn. □ *n* [C] 斜视 xiéshì; 斜视眼 xiéshìyǎn.

squirm /skwɜ:m/ *vi* (因痛苦,窘迫而)扭曲身子 niǔqū shēnzi; 局〔侷〕促不安 júcù bù'ān. □ *n* [C] 扭曲 niǔqū.

squir·rel /'skwɪrəl/ *n* [C] 松鼠 sōngshǔ.

squirt /skwɜ:t/ *vt/i* (液体,粉末)喷出 pēnchū. □ *n* [C] 细的喷流 xìde pēnliú.

Sr.= Senior.

S.S.= Steam-ship.

St.= **1** Saint, **2** Strait, **3** Street.

stab /stæb/ *vt/i* [-bb-] **1** (用刀,尖物)刺 cì, 刺伤〔傷〕 cìshāng. **2** 感觉〔覺〕刺痛 gǎnjué cìtòng: *a ~bing pain* 刀刺般的剧痛. □ *n* [C] **1** 刺 cì, 戳 chuō, 刺痛 cìtòng. **2** [非正式用语]企图〔圖〕 qǐtú; 尝〔嘗〕试 chángshì: *have a ~ at it* 试做此事.

stable[1] /'steɪbl/ *adj* [-er, -est] 稳〔穩〕定的 wěndìngde, 坚〔堅〕固的 jiāngùde. **sta·bil·ity** /stə'bɪlətɪ/ *n* [U]. **sta·bil·ize** /'steɪbəlaɪz/ *vt* 使稳定 shǐ wěndìng, 使坚固 shǐ jiāngù. **sta·bi·lizer** 使稳定者 shǐwěndìngzhě, 稳定器 wěndìngqì, 安定剂〔劑〕 āndìngjì.

stable[2] /'steɪbl/ *n* [C] 厩 jiù, 马棚 mǎpéng. □ *vt* (把…)拴进〔進〕马厩 shuān jìn mǎjiù.

stack /stæk/ *n* [C] **1** (稻草等)堆 duī, 垛 duǒ. **2** 一堆(书报,木材等) yìduī. **3** 烟囱群 yāncōng qún. □ *vt* 堆起 duīqǐ, 堆放 duīfàng.

sta·dium /'steɪdɪəm/ *n* [C] [*pl* ~s] (有看台的)露天运〔運〕动〔動〕场〔場〕 lùtiān yùndòngchǎng.

staff /stɑ:f/ *n* [C] **1** 拐杖 guǎizhàng, 木棍 mùgùn. **2** 杆 gān; 支柱 zhīzhù: *a 'flag~* 旗杆. **3** (全体)工作人员 gōngzuò rényuán. **4** 参谋人员 cānmóu rényuán. **5** [*pl staves* /'steɪvz/] [音乐]五线〔綫〕谱 wǔxiànpǔ. □ *vt* (为…)配备〔備〕工作人员 pèibèi gōngzuò rényuán.

stag /stæg/ *n* [C] 牡鹿 mǔlù.

stage /steɪdʒ/ *n* [C] **1** 舞台 wǔtái. **2** *be* (或 *go*) *on the ~* 当〔當〕演员 dāng yǎnyuán. **3** [喻]出事地点〔點〕 chūshì dìdiǎn. **4** (进展的)时〔時〕期 shíqī, 阶〔階〕段 jiēduàn. **5** 站 zhàn; 二站间〔間〕的距离〔離〕 èr zhàn jiān de jùlí. □ *vt* 上演 shàngyǎn: *~ a play* 上演一个戏剧. **'~-coach** 公共马〔馬〕车〔車〕 gōnggòng mǎchē.

stag·ger /'stægə(r)/ *vt/i* **1** (指行走)摇晃 yáohuàng, 蹒跚 pánshān. **2** (指新闻等)使震惊〔驚〕 shǐ zhènjīng. **3** 错开〔開〕 cuòkāi: *~ed holidays* 错开的休假日. □ *n* [*sing*] 摇晃 yáohuàng, 蹒跚 pánshān.

stag·nant /'stægnənt/ *adj* **1** 不流动〔動〕的 bù liúdòngde. **2** [喻]不变〔變〕的 búbiànde; 迟〔遲〕钝的 chídùnde; 不景气〔氣〕的 bù jǐngqì de.

stag·nate /stæg'neɪt/ *vi* **1** 停滞〔滯〕 tíngzhì, 不流动〔動〕 bù liúdòng. **2** [喻]迟〔遲〕钝 chídùn, 不活泼〔潑〕 bù huópo. **stag'nation** /-ʃn/ *n* [U]

staid /steɪd/ *adj* 沉着的 chénzhuóde, 严〔嚴〕肃〔肅〕的 yánsùde. **~ly** *adv*

stain /steɪn/ *vt/i* **1** 沾污 zhānwū, 污染 wūrǎn. **2** (给木材,织物等)着色 zhuósè, 染色 rǎnsè. □ *n* **1** [U]染料 rǎnliào, 着色剂〔劑〕 zhuósèjì

2 [C]污点〔點〕wūdiǎn, 沾污处〔處〕zhānwūchù. ~**ed glass** 彩色玻璃 cǎisè bōlí. ~**less** *adj* (尤指钢)不锈的 bú xiù de.

stair /steə(r)/ *n* [C] 楼〔樓〕梯lóutī. ***a flight of ~s*** 一段楼梯 yíduàn lóutī. ⇨downstairs, upstairs. '~-**case** (或 **way**) 楼梯间〔間〕lóutījiān.

stake/steɪk/ *n* [C] **1** 木桩〔樁〕mùzhuāng. **2** 火刑柱 huǒxíngzhù. **3** 赌注 dǔzhù, 赌金 dǔjīn. ***at ~*** 得失攸关〔關〕dé shī yōuguān; 在危险〔險〕中 zài wēixiǎnzhōng. **4** 利害关系〔係〕lì hài guānxì; 关心之事 guānxīn zhī shì: *I have a ~ in her future.* 我关心她的前途. ☐ *vt* **1** 用桩撑住 yòng zhuāng chēngzhù. **2** 立桩标〔標〕出 lì zhuāng biāochū: *~ out a claim* 立界标以表明(土地)所有权. **3** (用金钱等)打赌 dǎdǔ.

stale /steɪl/ *adj* **1** (指食品)不新鲜的 bù xīnxiānde. **2** 陈〔陳〕旧〔舊〕的 chénjiùde: *~ jokes* 陈旧的笑话. **3** (运动员等)因过〔過〕劳〔勞〕而表现不佳的 yīn guò láo ér biǎoxiàn bù jiā de. ☐ *vi* 变〔變〕得无〔無〕味 biànde wú wèi; 变陈旧 biàn chénjiù. ~**ness** *n* [U]

stale·mate / 'steɪlmeɪt/ *n*[C,U] **1** (国际象棋)王棋受困 wángqí shòu kùn. **2** [喻]僵局 jiāngjú, 对〔對〕峙 duìzhì.

stalk[1] /stɔ:k / *n* [C]茎〔莖〕jīng, 花梗 huāgěng; 叶〔葉〕柄 yèbǐng.

stalk[2] /stɔ:k/ *vt/i* **1** 高视阔〔闊〕步 gāo shì kuò bù, 大踏步走 dà tàbù zǒu. **2** 偷偷走近(野兽等) tōutōu zǒu jìn: *~ deer* 潜近鹿群. ~**er** 潜〔潛〕随〔隨〕猎〔獵〕物者 qián suí lièwù zhě.

stall /stɔ:l/ *n* [C] **1** (畜舍内的)分隔栏 〔欄〕 fēngélán. **2** 售货摊〔攤〕 shòuhuòtān. **3** [*pl*] (戏院正厅)前排座位 qiánpái zuòwèi. ☐ *vt/i* **1** (汽车等)发〔發〕生故障 fāshēng gùzhàng. **2** (飞机)失速而无〔無〕法控制 shī sù ér wúfǎ kòngzhì. **3** 拖延(时间) tuōyán.

stal·lion /'stælɪən/ *n* [C] 雄马〔馬〕(尤指种马) xióngmǎ.

stam·ina /'stæmɪnə/ *n* [U] 持久力 chíjiǔlì, 耐力 nàilì.

stam·mer /'stæmə(r)/ *vt/i* **1** 结结巴巴地说 jiējiēbābāde shuō. **2** ***~ sth (out)*** 结结巴巴地说出某事 jiējiēbābāde shuōchū mǒushì. ☐ *n* [C] 口吃 kǒuchī.

stamp[1] /stæmp/ *n* [C] **1** 顿足 dùn zú, 跺脚 duò jiǎo. **2** 图〔圖〕章 túzhāng, 印 yìn. **3** 印记 yìnjì, 图记 tújì, 标〔標〕记 biāojì. **4** (亦作 '*postage ~*) 邮〔郵〕票 yóupiào; 印花 yìnhuā. '~-**album** 集邮簿 jíyóu bù.

stamp[2] /stæmp/ *vt/i* **1** (用脚)踩踏 cǎità. **2** ***~ sth out*** 毁掉 huǐdiào, 捣〔搗〕碎 dǎosuì, 扑〔撲〕灭〔滅〕pūmiè. **3** ***~ sth on, ~ with sth*** 印(图案,字样等)于〔於〕yìn yú. **4** 贴邮〔郵〕票于 tiē yóupiào yú. **5** [喻]给予印象 gěiyú yìnxiàng: *to ~ one's personality on something* 在某事中留下个人性格的痕迹.

stam·pede /stæm'pi:d/ *n* [C] 惊〔驚〕跑 jīngpǎo, 奔窜〔竄〕bēncuàn. ☐ *vt/i* (使)惊跑 jīngpǎo; (使)溃散 kuìsàn.

stance /stæns/ *n* [C] (高尔夫球等)击〔擊〕球姿势〔勢〕jī qiú zīshì.

stand[1] /stænd/ *n* [C] **1** ***make a~*** 准〔準〕备〔備〕战〔戰〕斗〔鬥〕zhǔnbèi zhàndòu. **2** 架 jià, 台〔臺〕tái: *a 'music-~* 乐谱架. **3** 售货摊〔攤〕 shòuhuòtān, 陈〔陳〕列架 chénlièjià. **4** 看台 kàntái. **5** [美语] = witness-box. '~**point** 立场〔場〕lìchǎng, 观〔觀〕点〔點〕guāndiǎn.

stand[2] /stænd/ *vt/i* [*pt*, *pp* stood /stʊd/] **1** 站 zhàn, 立 lì. **2** ***~ (up)*** 站起来〔來〕zhàn qǐlái. **3** 坚〔堅〕持 jiānchí, 维持原状〔狀〕wéichí yuánzhuàng: *My decision ~s.* 我的决心不变. ***~ firm*** (或 ***fast***) 不改变〔變〕bù gǎibiàn, 不放弃〔棄〕bú fàngqì. **4** 处〔處〕于〔於〕某种状态〔態〕 chù yú mǒuzhǒng zhuàngtài: *As affairs now ~* 目前的情况是.... **5** 使直立 shǐ zhílì, 竖〔豎〕起 shùqǐ: *S~ the ladder against the wall.* 把梯子靠墙竖立. **6** 忍受 rěnshòu, 顶住 dǐngzhù: *He can't ~ hot weather.* 他不能忍受炎热的天气. **7** 为...付帐〔賬〕wèi...fù zhàng: *~ a friend a good dinner* 请朋友吃一顿美餐. **8** ***It ~s to reason (that)*** ⇨ reason[1] (3). **9** ***~ by (a)*** 袖手旁观〔觀〕xiù shǒu páng guān. ⇨ bystander. **(b)** 准〔準〕备〔備〕行动〔動〕 zhǔnbèi xíngdòng. ***~ by sb*** 支持某人 zhīchí mǒurén. ***~ by sth*** 信守(诺言等) xìn shǒu '~**by** *n* **(a)** 作好准备 zuòhǎo zhǔnbèi. **(b)** 可依靠的人或物 kě yīkào de rén huò wù. ***~ for sth*** **(a)** 代表 dàibiǎo, 表示 biǎoshì: *PO ~s for Post Office. PO* 代表 *Post Office.* **(b)** [英国英语] 作...的候选〔選〕人 zuò...de hòuxuǎnrén: *~ for Parliament* 做国会议员候选人. **(c)** [非正式用语]允许 yǔnxǔ, 容忍 róngrěn: *She doesn't ~ for disobedience.* 她不容

许对她不服从. ~ *in* (*for sb*) 代替(某人) dàitì. '~-**in** *n* [C] 替身 tìshēn. ~ *off* 远[遠]离[離] yuǎnlí, 疏远 shūyuǎn. ~ *out* **(a)** 突出 tūchū, 显[顯]著 xiǎnzhù. ⇨ outstanding. **(b)** 继[繼]续[續]抵抗 jìxù dǐkàng: ~ *out against the enemy* 坚持抵抗敌人. ~ *up*⇨ 本条释义(2)~ *sb up* [非正式用语]不遵守同…的约定 bù zūnshǒu tóng …de yuēdìng. ~ *up for sb* 支持 zhīchí, 拥[擁]护[護] yōnghù. ~ *up to sth* (物料)经[經]用 jīng yòng, 耐久 nài jiǔ.

stan·dard /'stændəd/ *n* [C] **1** 旗 qí, 旗帜[幟] qízhì. **2** 标[標]准[準] biāozhǔn, 规格 guīgé: *a high ~ of living* 高的生活水平. *a ~ metre* 标准米尺. '~ **lamp** 落地灯[燈] luò dì dēng. ~**ize** /-daɪz/ *vt* 使标准化 shǐ biāozhǔnhuà, 使合规格 shǐ hé guīgé.

stand·ing /'stændɪŋ/ *n* **1** [U] 持续[續] chíxù; 期间[間] qījiān: *debts of long ~* 长期债务. **2** [C, U] 身份 shēnfèn, 地位 dìwèi, 名望 míngwàng. □ *adj* 永存的yǒngcúnde, 常备[備]的 chángbèide: *a ~ing army* 常备军.

stank /stæŋk/ *pt* of stink.

stan·za /'stænzə/ *n* [C] [*pl* ~s] (诗的)节[節] jié.

staple[1] /'steɪpl/ *n* [C] **1** U形钉 U xíngdīng, 骑马[馬]钉 qímǎdīng. **2** 钉书[書]钉 dìngshūdīng. □ *vt* 用骑马钉钉住 yòng qímǎdīng dīngzhù. **stapler** *n* [C] 钉书机[機] dìngshūjī.

staple[2] /'steɪpl/ *n* **1** [C] 主要产[產]品 zhǔyào chǎnpǐn, 名产míngchǎn. **2** [U]纤[纖]维 xiānwéi. **3** [用作定语]主要成分zhǔyào chéngfèn: ~ *diet* 主食 zhǔshí.

star /stɑ:(r)/ *n* [C] **1** 星 xīng. **2** 星状[狀]物 xīngzhuàngwù; 星号[號] xīnghào. **3** (指演员等)明星 míngxīng. □ *vt/i* [-rr-] **1** 用星状物装[裝]饰 yòng xīngzhuàngwù zhuāngshì; 打上星号 dǎshàng xīnghào. **2** 当(电影等)主角 dāng zhǔjué. '~**dom** /-dəm/ 明星的地位 míngxīngde dìwèi. '~**fish** 海星 hǎixīng. ~**ry** *adj*

star·board /'stɑ:bɔ:d/ *n* [U] (船, 飞机的)右舷 yòuxián. ⇨ port[3].

starch /stɑ:tʃ/ *n* [U] **1** 淀[澱]粉 diànfěn. **2** (浆棉布用的)浆[漿]粉 jiāngfěn. □ *vt* 给(衣服)上浆 gěi shàng jiāng. **starchy** *adj* [-ier, -iest]

stare /steə(r)/ *vt/i* ~ (*at*) 凝视 níngshì, 睁大(眼睛) zhēngdà. □ *n* [C] 凝视 níngshì, 盯 dīng.

stark /stɑ:k/ *adj* 完全的 wánquánde, 十足的 shízúde: ~ *madness* 十足的疯狂. □ *adv* 完全 wánquán: ~ *naked* 赤裸的.

star·ling /'stɑ:lɪŋ/ *n* [C] 欧[歐]椋鸟[鳥] ōuliángniǎo, 燕八哥yànbāgē.

starry /'stɑ:rɪ/ ⇨ star.

start[1] /stɑ:t/ *n* [C] **1** 出发[發] chūfā, 起点[點] qǐdiǎn, 开[開]端 kāiduān, 着手 zhuóshǒu. **2** [仅用单数] 优[優]先起跑的时[時]间[間]或距离[離] yōuxiān qǐpǎo de shíjiān huò jùlí. **3** 惊[驚]起 jīngqǐ, 惊动[動] jīngdòng.

start[2] /stɑ:t/ *vt/i* **1** ~ (*out*) 出发[發] chūfā, 动[動]身 dòngshēn. **2** 开[開]始 kāishǐ, 着手 zhuóshǒu. **3** 惊[驚]起 jīngqǐ, 惊动[動] jīngdòng. **4** 创[創]办[辦] chuàngbàn, 发起 fāqǐ: ~ *a business* 创办一个事业. **5** ~ *off* 出发 chūfā, 开始活动 kāishǐ huódòng. ~ *out* (*to do sth*)[非正式用语]着手(进行某事) zhuóshǒu. ~ *sth up* 开动(机器等) kāidòng, 发动 fādòng. ~-**er** **(a)** 起动装[裝]置 qǐdòng zhuāngzhì, 启[啟]动器 qǐdòngqì. **(b)** [非正式用语]第一道菜 dìyīdào cài. **(c)** 起跑发令员 qǐpǎo fālìngyuán.

startle /'stɑ:tl/ *vt* 使大吃一惊[驚] shǐ dà chī yì jīng.

starve /stɑ:v/ *vt/i* **1** (使)挨饿 āi'è, (使)饿死 è sǐ. *be ~d of* [喻]渴望 kěwàng, 急需 jíxū. **2** 觉[覺]得饥[饑]饿 juédé jī'è: *I'm starving*. 我饿了. **star·va·tion** /-'veɪʃn/ *n* [U]

state[1] /steɪt/ *n* [C] **1** 状[狀]态[態] zhuàngtài, 状况 zhuàngkuàng, 情形 qíngxíng: *in a poor ~ of health* 健康不佳. **2** [常用 S~] 国[國]家 guójiā; 领土 lǐngtǔ; (美国的)州 zhōu: *The United States* 美国. **3** [U] 政府 zhèngfǔ: *Church and S~* 教会和政府. **4** [U] 仪[儀]式 yíshì, 礼[禮]仪 lǐyí: *received in ~* 隆重的接待. **5** [用作定语]仪式上的 yíshìshàngde, 礼仪用的 lǐyí yòng de: *the ~ apartments* 举行仪式用的大厅. ~**ly** *adj* [-ier, -iest] 庄[莊]严[嚴]的 zhuāngyánde, 高贵的 gāoguìde.

state[2] /steɪt/ *vt* 陈[陳]述 chénshù, 说明 shuōmíng. ~**ment** **(a)** [C] 陈述 chénshù, 声[聲]明 shēngmíng, 声明书[書] shēngmíngshū. **(b)** 财务[務]报[報]表 cáiwù bàobiǎo: *a bank ~ment* 银行结单.

states·man /'steɪtsmən/ *n* [C] [*p*

-men] 政治家 zhèngzhìjiā. '~-ship *n* [U] 政治家的才能 zhèngzhìjiāde cáinéng, 政治家风〔風〕度 zhèngzhìjiā fēngdù.

static /'stætɪk/ *adj* 静止的 jìngzhǐde, 固定的 gùdìngde: *~ electricity* 静电. □ *n* [U] 天电〔電〕干扰〔擾〕tiāndiàn gānrǎo.

sta·tion /'steɪʃn/ *n* [C] **1** 岗〔崗〕位 gǎngwèi, 所 suǒ, 台〔臺〕tái, 局 jú, 站 zhàn: *a po'lice ~* 警察派出所. *a 'bus-~* 公共汽车站. **2** 火车〔車〕站 huǒchēzhàn. **3** 社会〔會〕地位 shèhuì dìwèi, 身分 shēnfèn. □ *vt* 配备〔備〕pèibèi, 驻〔駐〕扎 zhùzhā. '~**-wagon** 旅行汽车 lǚxíng qìchē.

sta·tion·ary /'steɪʃənrɪ/ *adj* **1** 定置的 dìngzhìde, 固定的 gùdìngde: *a ~ engine* 固定式发动机. ⇨ mobile(1). **2** 不变〔變〕动的 bú biàndòng de, 不移动的 bù yídòng de.

sta·tioner /'steɪʃnə(r)/ *n* [C] 文具商 wénjùshāng. **sta·tion·ery** *n* [U] 文具 wénjù.

stat·is·tics /stə'tɪstɪks/ *n* **1** [*pl*] 统计 tǒngjì, 统计数〔數〕字 tǒngjì shùzì. **2** [U] 统计学〔學〕tǒngjìxué. **stat·is·ti·cal** /-kl/ *adj* **stat·is·ti·cian** /ˌstætɪ'stɪʃn/ *n* [C] 统计学家 tǒngjìxuéjiā, 统计员 tǒngjìyuán.

statue /'stætʃuː/ *n* [C] 雕像 diāoxiàng, 塑像 sùxiàng, 铸〔鑄〕像 zhùxiàng. ~**tte** /ˌstætʃʊ'et/ 小雕像 xiǎo diāoxiàng, 小塑像 xiǎo sùxiàng.

stat·ure /'stætʃə(r)/ *n* [U] **1** 身材 shēncái, 身高 shēngāo. **2** [喻] (道德, 才能等)发〔發〕展成长〔長〕的高度 fāzhǎn chéngzhǎng de gāodù.

status /'steɪtəs/ *n* [U] 身分 shēnfèn, 地位 dìwèi. '~ **symbol** 表示地位高的东〔東〕西 biǎoshì dìwèi gāo de dōngxī.

stat·ute /'stætʃuːt/ *n* [C] 法令 fǎlìng, 法规 fǎguī. **statu·tory** /-trɪ/ *adj* 法定的 fǎdìngde, 依法的 yīfǎde.

staunch /stɔːntʃ/ *adj* 忠诚的 zhōngchéngde, 坚〔堅〕定的 jiāndìngde. ~**ly** *adv*

stave[1] /steɪv/ *n* [C] **1** 桶板 tǒngbǎn. **2** [音乐] = staff(5).

stave[2] /steɪv/ *vt/i* [*pt, pp* ~d 或 stove /stəʊv/] **1** ~ *sth in* 击〔擊〕穿 jīchuān, 凿〔鑿〕孔于〔於〕záo kǒng yú. **2** ~ *sth off* 避开〔開〕bìkāi; 延缓 yánhuǎn.

stay[1] /steɪ/ *vt/i* **1** 停留 tíngliú; 保持 bǎochí: ~ *at home* 呆在家里. ~ *sober* 保持清醒. ~ *up* 不睡觉〔覺〕bú shuìjiào. **2** ~ **'put** [非正式用语] 留在原处〔處〕不动〔動〕liúzài yuánchù búdòng. **3** 制止 zhìzhǐ, 抑止 yìzhǐ; 延缓 yánhuǎn: ~ *the progress of a disease* 阻止疾病的发展. **4** 坚〔堅〕持 jiānchí, 持久 chíjiǔ: '~*ing power* 持久力. □ *n* [C] **1** 停留时〔時〕间〔間〕tíngliú shíjiān, 逗留期 dòuliúqī: *a long ~ in hospital*. 长期住医院. **2** [法律]延期 yánqī, 缓期 huǎnqī: *a ~ of execution* 缓期执行.

stay[2] /steɪ/ *n* [C] (支持桅杆等的)绳〔繩〕索 shéngsuǒ.

stead·fast /'stedfɑːst/ *adj* 固定的 gùdìngde, 不变〔變〕的 búbiànde, 不动〔動〕摇的 bú dòngyáo de. ~**ly** *adv*

steady /'stedɪ/ *adj* [-ier, -iest] **1** 坚〔堅〕固的 jiāngùde, 牢靠的 láokàode; 平衡的 pínghéngde. **2** 稳〔穩〕定的 wěndìngde, 平稳的píngwěnde: *a ~ speed* 稳定的速度. **3** 可靠的 kěkàode, 扎实〔實〕的 zhāshide: *a ~ worker* 扎实的工人. **4** 不变〔變〕的 búbiànde: *a ~ purpose* 不变的目标. □ *adv* = steadily. □ *vt/i* (使)稳定 wěndìng; (使)坚固 jiāngù. **stead·ily** *adv* 稳定地 wěndìngde, 不变地 búbiànde.

steak /steɪk/ *n* [C,U] 肉片 ròupiàn; 鱼片 yúpiàn; 牛(猪)排 niúpái.

steal /stiːl/ *vt/i* (*pt* stole /stəʊl/; *pp* stolen /'stəʊlən/) **1** 偷 tōu, 窃〔竊〕取 qièqǔ. **2** 偷袭〔襲〕tōuxí; 巧取 qiǎoqǔ: ~ *a kiss* 偷吻. **3** 偷偷地行动〔動〕tōutōude xíngdòng.

steam /stiːm/ *n* [U] **1** 蒸汽 zhēngqì. **2** 蒸汽压〔壓〕力 zhēngqì yālì. **3** [喻][非正式用语]气〔氣〕力 qìlì, 精力 jīnglì. *let off ~* 放掉蒸汽 fàngdiào zhēngqì; 发〔發〕泄〔洩〕精力或感情 fāxiè jīnglì huò gǎnqíng. □ *vt/i* **1** 蒸发 zhēngfā, 冒热〔熱〕气 mào rèqì. **2** 用蒸汽开〔開〕动〔動〕yòng zhēngqì kāidòng. **3** 蒸煮 zhēngzhǔ. **4** ~ *up* (使)有蒸汽 yǒu zhēngqì. '~**-engine** 蒸汽机〔機〕zhēngqìjī. '~**ship** 汽船 qìchuán, 轮〔輪〕船 lúnchuán. ~**er** (a) = steamship. (b) 蒸笼〔籠〕zhēnglóng, 汽锅〔鍋〕qìguō. **steamy** *adj* [-ier, -iest]

steel /stiːl/ *n* [U] 钢〔鋼〕gāng. □ *vt* 使坚〔堅〕硬 shǐ jiānyìng, 钢化 gāngchuà: ~ *oneself (against pity)* 硬着心肠(不同情). '~ **mill** *n* [C] 炼〔煉〕钢厂〔廠〕liàngāngchǎng.

steep[1] /stiːp/ *adj* [-er, -est] **1** 陡峭的 dǒuqiàode. **2** [非正式用语] 过〔過〕分的 guòfènde; 不合理的 bù hélǐ de: ~ *prices* 不合理的价格. ~**ly** *adv* ~**ness** *n* [U]

steep[2] /stiːp/ *vt/i* **1** 浸 jìn, 泡 pào. **2** [喻]精通 jīngtōng.

steeple /ˈstiːpl/ *n* [C] (教堂的)尖顶 jiāndǐng. ˈ~**chase** 障碍〔礙〕赛跑或赛马〔馬〕 zhàng'ài sàipǎo huò sàimǎ. ˈ~**jack** 烟囱或尖塔等的修理工人 yāncōng huò jiāntǎ děng de xiūlǐ gōngrén.

steer /stɪə(r)/ *vt/i* 驾〔駕〕驶〔駛〕jiàshǐ. ~ *clear of* [喻]避开〔開〕bìkāi. ˈ~**ing-wheel** 方向盘〔盤〕fāngxiàngpán.

stem[1] /stem/ *n* [C] **1** 茎〔莖〕jīng. **2** (高酒杯等的) 脚 jiǎo. □ *vi* [-mm-] ~ *from* 起源于〔於〕qǐyuán yú.

stem[2] /stem/ *vt* [-mm-] 堵塞 dǔsāi, 挡〔擋〕住 dǎngzhù.

stench /stentʃ/ *n* [C] 恶臭 èchòu.

sten·cil /ˈstensl/ *n* [C] 模板 móbǎn. □ *vt* [-ll-, 美语亦作 -l-] 用模板印刷 yòng móbǎn yìnshuā.

step[1] /step/ *n* **1** (脚)步 bù, 步幅 bùfú. ˌ~ *by* ˈ~ 逐步地 zhúbùde. *watch one's* ~ 小心 xiǎoxīn, 慎重 shènzhòng. **2** 脚步声〔聲〕jiǎobùshēng; 步态〔態〕bùtài. **3** *be* (或 *get*) *in* ~ (*with*) (a) 与〔與〕...的脚步取齐〔齊〕yǔ...de jiǎobù qǔqí. (b) 与...的步调一致 yǔ...de bùdiào yízhì. *be* (或 *get*) *out of* ~ (*with*) (a) 与...的脚步不齐 yǔ ... de jiǎobù bù qí. (b) 与...的步调不一致 yǔ...de bùdiào bù yízhì. **4** 步骤〔驟〕bùzhòu, 措施 cuòshī: *take* ~*s to increase output* 为增产采取措施. **5** 台〔臺〕阶〔階〕táijiē, 梯级 tījí. **6** 等级 děngjí; 升级 shēngjí. **7** [*pl*] = step-ladder. ˈ~-**ladder** 折梯 zhétī, 梯凳 tīdèng.

step[2] /step/ *vt/i* [-pp-] **1** 走 zǒu, 踏步 tàbù, 步行 bùxíng: ~ *across a stream* 跨过一条小河. **2** ~ *aside* [喻]退让〔讓〕tuìràng; 离〔離〕题 lítí. ~ *down* [喻]辞〔辭〕职〔職〕cízhí, 下台〔臺〕xiàtái. ~ *in* [喻]插手 chāshǒu, 干涉 gānshè. ~ *sth up* 逐步增加 zhúbù zēngjiā. ˈ~**ping-stone** 垫〔墊〕脚石 diànjiǎoshí.

step- /step/ *prefix*(表示"继"、"后"). ˈ~**son** (**daughter**) 前妻或前夫所生子(女) qiánqī huò qiánfū suǒ shēng zǐ.

stereo /ˈsterɪəʊ/ *adj,n* [*pl* ~s] **1** [U] *stereophonic* 的缩写〔寫〕*stereophonic* de suōxiě. **2** [C] 立体〔體〕声〔聲〕录〔錄〕音机〔機〕 lìtǐshēng lùyīnjī.

stereo·phonic /ˌsterɪəˈfɒnɪk/ *adj* 立体〔體〕声〔聲〕的 lìtǐshēngde.

stereo·type /ˈsterɪətaɪp/ *n* [C] 典型的榜样〔樣〕diǎnxíngde bǎngyàng: *the* ~ *of a good husband* 好丈夫的典型.

ster·ile /ˈsteraɪl/ *adj* **1** 不结果实〔實〕的 bù jié guǒshí de, 不育的 búyùde. **2** (指土地)贫瘠的 pínjíde, 不毛的 bùmáode. **3** [喻]无〔無〕结果的 wú jiéguǒ de: *a* ~ *argument* 无结果的辩论. **4** 无菌的 wú jùn de. **ste·ril·ity** /stəˈrɪlətɪ/ *n* [U]. **ster·il·ize** /ˈsterəlaɪz/ *vt* 使不结果实 shǐ bù jié guǒshí; 使绝育 shǐ juéyù; 使无效 shǐ wúxiào; 杀〔殺〕菌 shā jūn.

ster·ling /ˈstɜːlɪŋ/ *adj* **1** (指金银)标〔標〕准〔準〕成分的 biāozhǔn chéngfèn de. **2** [喻]货真价〔價〕实〔實〕的 huòzhēn-jiàshí de, 纯正的 chúnzhènde. □ *n* [U] 英国〔國〕货币〔幣〕Yīngguó huòbì.

stern[1] /stɜːn/ *adj* [-er, -est] 严〔嚴〕厉〔厲〕的 yánlìde, 严格的 yángéde. ~**ly** *adv*

stern[2] /stɜːn/ *n* [C] 船尾 chuánwěi.

stetho·scope /ˈsteθəskəʊp/ *n* [C] 听〔聽〕诊器 tīngzhěnqì.

stew /stjuː/ *vt/i* 炖〔燉〕dùn, 煨 wēi, 焖〔燜〕mèn. □ *n* **1** [C,U] 炖肉 dùn ròu. **2** *be in a* ~ [非正式用语]着急 zháojí, 烦恼〔惱〕fánnǎo.

stew·ard /ˈstjuːəd/ *n* [C] **1** 乘务〔務〕员 chéngwùyuán, 服务员 fúwùyuán. **2** (赛马, 舞会等的) 干事 gànshi, 组织〔織〕者 zǔzhīzhě.

stew·ard·ess /ˌstjuːəˈdes/ *n* [C] 女乘务员 nǚ chéngwùyuán, 女服务员 nǚ fúwùyuán.

stg.=sterling.

stick[1] /stɪk/ *n* [C] **1** 枝条〔條〕zhītiáo; 枯枝 kūzhī. **2** 木棍 mùgùn: *a* ˈ*walking*-~ 手杖. **3** (细圆的)条状〔狀〕物 (如粉笔等) tiáozhuàngwù.

stick[2] /stɪk/ *vt/i* [*pt*, *pp* stuck /stʌk/] **1** [与 *into*, *through* 等连用]刺 cì, 戳 chuō. **2** (使) 粘住 zhānzhù, 粘贴 zhāntiē. **3** [非正式用语]插牢 chā láo; 放置 fàngzhì: *He stuck his hands in his pockets.* 他把手插在口袋里. **4** 陷住 xiànzhù 卡住 qiǎzhù: *The key stuck in the lock.* 钥匙卡在锁中了. **5** [非正式用语]忍受 rěnshòu, 容忍 róngrěn: *I can't* ~ *it.* 我不能容忍. **6** ~ *around* [非正式用语]在附近逗留

zài fùjìn dòuliú. ～ at sth 继〔繼〕续〔續〕做某事 jìxù zuò mǒushì. ～ sth out (使)突出 tūchū, 伸出 shēnchū: ～ one's tongue out 吐出舌头. ～ out for sth 坚〔堅〕持索取 jiānchí suǒqǔ. ～ to sb (sth) 忠于〔於〕(理想,朋友等) zhōngyú. ～ up (使)竖〔豎〕起 shùqǐ, (使)直立 zhílì. ～ sb (sth) up [俚语]威吓〔嚇〕...以便抢〔搶〕劫 wēihè...yǐbiàn qiǎngjié. '～-up n [C]'～ up for sb (oneself, sth) 维护〔護〕wéihù, 支持 zhīchí. ～er n [C] (背面)有粘胶〔膠〕的标〔標〕签〔簽〕yǒu zhānjiāo de biāoqiān. ～ing plas·ter n [C,U] ⇨ plaster(2).
sticky adj [-ier, -iest] (a) 粘住的 zhānzhùde. (b) [非正式用语]困难〔難〕的 kùnnande: a ～y situation 艰难的处境.
stiff /stɪf/ adj [-er, -est] 1 坚〔堅〕硬的 jiānyìngde, 不易弯〔彎〕曲的 bú yì wānqū de. 2 难〔難〕于〔於〕移动〔動〕的 nán yú yídòng de, 不灵〔靈〕活的 bù línghuó de. 3 难的 nánde, 费劲〔勁〕的 fèijìngde: a ～ climb 艰难的攀登. 4 拘谨的 jūjǐnde, 冷淡的 lěngdànde, 生硬的 shēngyìngde. 5 强烈的 qiánglìede, 猛烈的 měngliède: a ～ breeze 强劲的风. a ～ drink 烈酒. □ adv 彻〔徹〕底地 chèdǐde: scared ～ 极度惊恐. ～ly adv ～ness n [U]
stif·fen /'stɪfn/ vt/i (使)变〔變〕硬 biàn yìng; (使)变呆板 biàn dāibǎn; (使)变僵硬 biàn jiāngyìng.
stifle /'staɪfl/ vt/i 1 (使)窒息 zhìxī, 闷〔悶〕死 mēnsǐ. 2 抑制 yìzhì, 镇压〔壓〕zhènyā: ～ a yawn 忍住呵欠. ～ a rebellion 镇压叛乱.
stigma /'stɪgmə/ n [C] [pl ～s] [喻]耻辱 chǐrǔ, 污点〔點〕wūdiǎn.
stile /staɪl/ n [C] (供人越过篱或墙的)踏级 tàjí.
still[1] /stɪl/ adj, adv 不动〔動〕的 búdòngde, 静止的 jìngzhǐde; 无〔無〕声〔聲〕的 wú shēng de. □ vt 使平静 shǐ píngjìng, 止住 zhǐzhù. ～ness n [U] '～-born adj (a) 死产〔產〕的 sǐchǎnde. (b) [喻]不成功的 bù chénggōng de; 流产的 liúchǎnde.
still[2] /stɪl/ adv 1 还〔還〕hái, 仍旧〔舊〕réngjiù: He is ～ busy. 他还很忙. 2 还要 háiyào, 更 gèng: Tom is tall but Mary is ～ taller. 汤姆很高,而玛丽更高. 3(虽然...)还是 háishì.
still[3] /stɪl/ n [C] 蒸馏器 zhēngliúqì.
stilt /stɪlt/ n [C] 高跷〔蹺〕gāoqiāo. '～ed adj (文体等)生硬的 shēngyìngde, 不自然的 bú zìrán de.
stimu·lant /'stɪmjʊlənt/ n [C] 兴〔興〕奋〔奮〕剂〔劑〕xīngfènjì.
stimu·late /'stɪmjʊleɪt/ vt 刺激 cìjī, 促进〔進〕cùjìn: ～ interest in a new car 激发对新汽车的兴趣. **stimu·lat·ing** adj
stimu·lus /'stɪmjʊləs/ n [C] [pl -li /-laɪ/] 刺激物 cìjīwù, 鼓励〔勵〕gǔlì: a ～ to hard work 对勤奋工作的鼓励.
sting[1] /stɪŋ/ n 1 [C] (昆虫的)刺 cì, 螫针 shìzhēn. 2 (植物的)刺毛 cìmáo. 3 [C] 刺痛 cìtòng, 刺伤〔傷〕cìshāng.
sting[2] /stɪŋ/ vt/i [pt, pp stung /stʌŋ/] 1 刺 cì, 螫 shì. 2 刺痛 cìtòng.
stingy /'stɪndʒɪ/ adj [-ier, -iest] 吝啬〔嗇〕的 lìnsède, 小气〔氣〕的 xiǎoqìde. **stin·gily** /-əlɪ/ adv
stink /stɪŋk/ vt/i [pt stank /stæŋk/ 或 stunk /stʌŋk/, pp stunk] 1 发〔發〕恶〔惡〕臭 fā èchòu. 2 ～ sth out 充满臭气〔氣〕chōngmǎn chòuqì. □ n [C] 臭气 chòuqì.
stint /stɪnt/ vt/i ～ sb (of sth) 限制 xiànzhì, 节〔節〕制 jiézhì. □ n [C] (工作)定额 dìng'é.
stipu·late /'stɪpjʊleɪt/ vt/i 规定 guīdìng, 约定 yuēdìng. **stipu'la·tion** n [C] 规定 guīdìng, 约定 yuēdìng.
stir /stɜː(r)/ vt/i [-rr-] 1 (使)移动〔動〕yídòng. 2 搅〔攪〕拌 jiǎobàn. 3 激起 jīqǐ, 鼓动 gǔdòng: speakers ～ring up the crowd 鼓动群众的演说者. □ n 骚〔騷〕动 sāodòng; 激动 jīdòng. ～ring adj 激动的 jīdòngde, 鼓舞人心的 gǔwǔ rénxīn de.
stir·rup /'stɪrəp/ n [C] 马〔馬〕镫 mǎdèng.
stitch /stɪtʃ/ n 1 [C] 缝 féng, 缝纫 féngrèn. 2 缝线〔綫〕féngxiàn, 针脚 zhēnjiǎo. 3 (胁部)突然剧〔劇〕痛 tūrán jùtòng. □ vt/i 缝 féng, 缝合 fénghé.
stoat /stəʊt/ n [C] 鼬 yòu.
stock[1] /stɒk/ n 1 [C,U] 存货 cúnhuò, 现货 xiànhuò. in ～ 有存货 yǒu cúnhuò. out of ～ 无〔無〕存货 wú cúnhuò. take ～ of [喻] 估量 gūliàng, 观〔觀〕察 guānchá. 2 [C,U] 供给 gōngjǐ; 储备〔備〕chǔbèi. 3 [U] = livestock. 4 [C,U] 公债 gōngzhài; 股本 gǔběn. 5 [U] 汤〔湯〕料 tāngliào. '～broker 证〔證〕券经〔經〕纪人

zhèngquàn jīngjìrén. '~ **exchange** 证券交易所 zhèngquàn jiāoyìsuǒ. '~**holder** [主美语] = shareholder. '~ **market** 证券市场[場] zhèngquàn shìchǎng. '~**pile** *vi* 堆料 duīliào, 贮[貯]存物资 zhùcún wùzī. ,~'**still** *adv* 静止的 jìngzhǐde, 不动的 búdòngde. '~**taking** 盘[盤]货 pánhuò.

stock² /stɒk/ *vt* 供应[應] gōngyìng; 备货 bèihuò.

stock·ade /stɒ'keɪd/ *n* [C] 栅栏[欄] zhàlan.

stock·ings /'stɒkɪŋz/ *n pl* (长统)袜[襪] wà.

stocky /'stɒkɪ/ *adj* [-ier, -iest] 矮胖的 ǎipàngde, 粗壮[壯]的 cūzhuàngde. **stock·ily** *adv*

stodge /stɒdʒ/ *n* [U] [俚语]浓[濃]厚油腻的食物 nónghòu yóunì de shíwù. **stodgy** *adj* 厚腻的 hòunìde, 不好消化的 bùhǎo xiāohuà de.

stoic /'stəʊɪk/ *n* [C] 禁欲[慾]主义[義]者 jìnyù zhǔyì zhě. ~**al** *adj* ~**ally** /-klɪ/ *adv* ~**ism** /'stəʊɪsɪzəm/ *n* [U] 禁欲主义 jìnyù zhǔyì.

stoke /stəʊk/ *vt/i* ~ *sth up* 给(锅炉等)添燃料 gěi tiān ránliào.

stole¹ /stəʊl/ *n* [C] 披肩 pījiān; 圣[聖]带[帶] shèngdài.

stole², stolen *pt, pp* of steal.

stom·ach /'stʌmək/ *n* 1 [C] 胃 wèi. 2 [U] 胃口 wèikǒu, 食欲[慾] shíyù. ***have no ~ for sth*** 对[對]做某事无[無]兴[興]趣 duì zuò mǒushì wú xìngqù. □ *vt* 忍耐 rěnnài, 忍受 rěnshòu.

stone /stəʊn/ *n* 1 [U] 石头[頭] shítou. 2 [C] 石块[塊] shíkuài. ***within a '~'s throw (of)*** 在短距离[離]内 zài duǎn jùlí nèi. 3 [C] (亦作 *'precious* ~) = jewel. 4 [C] (特殊用途的)石料 shíliào: *a 'grave~* 墓碑. 5 [C]果核 guǒhé. 6 [*pl* ~] 呎(英国重量名,等于14 磅) shí. □ *vt* 1 向…扔石头 xiàng... rēng shítou. 2 去…的核 qù...de hé. '**S~ Age** 石器时[時]代 shíqì shídài. ,~-'**deaf** *adj* 完全聋[聾]的 wánquán lóng de. '~**ware** 粗陶器 cū táoqì.

stoned /stəʊnd/ *adj* [非正式用语] 麻醉的 mázuìde; (药物) 中毒的 zhòngdúde. 2 醉熏熏的 zuìxūnxūnde.

stony /'stəʊnɪ/ *adj* [-ier, -iest] 1 多石的 duō shí de. 2 冷酷无[無]情的 lěngkù wúqíng de: *a ~ face* 铁板的脸孔. *a ~ look* 冷漠的神态. **ston·ily** /-əlɪ/ *adv*

stood /stʊd/ *pt, pp* of stand².

stool /stu:l/ *n* [C] 凳子 dèngzi.

stoop /stu:p/ *vt/i* 1 弯[彎]腰 wān yāo, 俯身 fǔ shēn. 2 ~ *to sth* [喻]屈从[從] qūcóng; 堕落 duòluò: ~ *to begging for food* 沦为乞丐. □ *n* [C] 弯腰 wān yāo, 曲身 qū shēn.

stop¹ /stɒp/ *n* [C] 1 停止 tíngzhǐ, 中止 zhōngzhǐ: *He came to a ~.* 他停了下来. 2 车[車]站 chēzhàn. 3 (风琴等的) 音栓 yīnshuān. 4 = full stop. ***put a ~ to*** 使停止 shǐ tíngzhǐ, 制止 zhìzhǐ. '~**cock** 活塞 huósāi. '~**gap** 临[臨]时[時]代替者 línshí dàitì zhě: '~-**press** (报纸付印时加入的) 最新消息 zuì xīn xiāoxī.

stop² /stɒp/ *vt/i* [-pp-] 1 停止 tíngzhǐ, 停住 tíngzhù. 2 ~ ***sb (from) (doing sth)*** 阻止某人(做某事) zǔzhǐ mǒurén. 3 中止 (做某事) zhōngzhǐ. 4 停下 tíngxià. 5 塞住 sāizhù, 堵塞 dǔsāi. 6 断[斷]绝 duànjué; 扣留 kòuliú: ~ (*payment of*) *a cheque* 止付支票. 7 ~ ***off (at, in)***; ~ ***over*** 中途停留 zhōngtú tíngliú. '~-**over** *n* [C]. ~**page** /-pɪdʒ/ *n* [C] **(a)** 阻碍[礙] zǔ'ài. **(b)** 中断工作 zhōngduàn gōngzuò. ~**per** *n* [C] 塞子 sāizi.

stor·age /'stɔ:rɪdʒ/ *n* [U] 仓[倉]库[庫] cāngkù, 货栈[棧] huòzhàn.

store /stɔ:(r)/ *n* 1 [C] 贮[貯]藏 zhùcáng; 库[庫]存量 kùcúnliàng. 2 [U] ***in*** ~ **(a)** 准[準]备[備]着 zhǔnbèizhe. **(b)** [与 *for* 连用]必将[將]发[發]生 bìjiāng fāshēng: *What's in ~ for us today?* 今天会发生什么事? 3[C] 仓[倉]库 cāngkù, 栈[棧]房 zhànfáng. 4 [C] 百货商店 bǎihuò shāngdiàn. 5 [U] ***set great ~ by*** 非常重视 fēicháng zhòngshì. ***set not much ~ by*** 不太重视 bú tài zhòngshì. □ *vt* ~ ***sth (up)*** 1 储[儲]备 chǔbèi, 贮藏 zhùcáng. 2存(家具等)入仓库 cúnrù cāngkù.

storey [美语 = **story**] /'stɔ:rɪ/ *n* [*pl* ~s] (房屋的) 一层 [層] yìcéng.

stork /stɔ:k/ *n* [C] 鹳[鸛] guàn.

storm /stɔ:m/ *n* 1 [C] 风[風]暴 fēngbào, 暴风雨 bàofēngyǔ. 2(感情上的) 激动 [動] jīdòng, 暴发[發] bàofā. 3 ***take by*** ~ 攻占 gōngzhàn, 强夺 [奪] qiángduó □ *vt/i* 1 暴怒 bàonù. 2 猛攻 měnggōng, 袭[襲]取 xíqǔ. **stormy** *adj* [-ier, -iest]

story¹ /'stɔ:rɪ/ *n* [C] [*pl* -ies] 1

历〔歷〕史 lìshǐ, 事迹〔蹟〕shìjī. 2 故事 gùshi, 传〔傳〕奇 chuánqí.

story² /'stɔːrɪ/ *n* [美语] = storey.

stout /staʊt/ *adj* [-er, -est] 1 粗壮〔壯〕的 cūzhuàngde, 结实〔實〕的 jiēshide. 2 坚〔堅〕定的 jiāndìngde, 勇敢的 yǒnggǎnde. ˌ~-'**hearted** *adj* 3 (指人)胖的 pàngde. □ *n* [U] 烈性黑啤酒 lièxìng hēi píjiǔ. ~**ly** *adv*

stove¹ /stəʊv/ *n* [C] 火炉〔爐〕huǒlú.

stove² /stəʊv/ *pt, pp* of stave².

stow /stəʊ/ *vt* ~ *sth* (*away*) 堆装〔裝〕duīzhuāng. '~**away** (船, 飞机的)偷乘者 tōuchéngzhě.

straddle /'strædl/ *vt/i* 叉开〔開〕腿坐或站立 chākāi tuǐ zuò huò zhànlì.

straight¹ /streɪt/ *adj* 1 直的 zhíde, 笔〔筆〕直的 bǐzhíde. 2 水平的 shuǐpíngde. 3 整齐〔齊〕的 zhěngqíde, 有条〔條〕理的 yǒu tiáolǐ de. 4 正直的 zhèngzhíde, 坦率的 tǎnshuàide. 5 *keep a* ~ *face* 板起面孔 bǎnqǐ miànkǒng. 6 (指酒等)不搀〔攙〕水的 bù chān shuǐ de. ~**ness** *n* [U]

straight² /streɪt/ *adv* 1 直 zhí; 直接地 zhíjiēde: *Keep* ~ *on.* 继续前进. 2 一直地 yìzhíde; 立即地 lìjíde: *Come* ~ *home.* 直接回家. 3 ˌ~ '*away* 立刻 lìkè, 马〔馬〕上 mǎshàng.

straight³ /streɪt/ *n* [C] (尤指跑道的)直线〔線〕部分 zhíxiàn bùfèn.

straighten /'streɪtn/ *vt/i* 使直 shǐ zhí; (使)变〔變〕平整 biàn píngzhěng.

straight·for·ward /streɪt'fɔːwəd/ *adj* 1 正直的 zhèngzhíde, 坦率的 tǎnshuàide, 老实〔實〕的 lǎoshide. 2 易懂的 yì dǒng de; 易做的 yì zuò de. ~**ly** *adv*

strain¹ /streɪn/ *n* 1 [C,U] 拉紧〔緊〕lā jǐn, 紧张〔張〕jǐnzhāng; 拉力 lālì: *put* ~ *on a rope* 把绳子拉紧. 2 [C,U] 考验〔驗〕力量之物 kǎoyàn lìliàng zhī wù, 费力之物 fèilì zhī wù. 3 [U] 劳〔勞〕累 láolèi, 过〔過〕分疲劳 guòfèn píláo: *suffering from* ~ 苦于劳累. 4 [C] = sprain. 5 (动物的)种〔種〕zhǒng.

strain² /streɪn/ *vt/i* 1 [与 at 连用]拉紧 lā jǐn. 2 尽〔盡〕量利用 jǐnliàng lìyòng: ~ *every nerve* (*to do it*) 全力以赴. 3 扭伤〔傷〕niǔshāng. 4 过〔過〕滤〔濾〕guòlǜ. 5 [*pp*] (尤指行为)勉强的 miǎnqiǎngde: *a* ~*ed laugh* 勉强的笑. ~**er** 滤器 lǜqì.

strait /streɪt/ *n* [C] 1 海峡〔峽〕hǎixiá: *the S*~*s of Gilbraltar* 直布罗陀海峡. 2 [*pl*] 困难〔難〕kùnnan, 窘迫 jiǒngpò: *in terrible* ~*s* 在极度困难中.

strait-jacket /'streɪt dʒækɪt/ *n* [C] (给疯人等用的)拘束衣 jūshùyī. □ *vt* (用拘束衣)束缚 shùfù.

strait-laced /ˌstreɪt 'leɪsd/ *adj* 拘谨的 jūjǐnde, 严〔嚴〕谨的 yánjǐnde.

strand¹ /strænd/ *vt/i* 1 (使)搁〔擱〕浅〔淺〕gēqiǎn. 2 *be* (或 *left*) ~*ed* [喻]处〔處〕于〔於〕困境 chù yú kùnjìng.

strand² /strænd/ *n* [C] 1 (线, 绳等的)(一)股 gǔ. 2 [喻] (故事等的)发〔發〕展线〔線〕索 fāzhǎn xiànsuǒ.

strange /streɪndʒ/ *adj* [-r, -st] 1 陌生的 mòshēngde. 2 ~ *to sth* 对〔對〕某事生疏 duì mǒushì shēngshū, 不习〔習〕惯于 … bù xíguàn yú: *He was* ~ *to city life.* 他不习惯于城市生活. ~**ly** *adv* ~**ness** *n* [U] ~**er** *n* [C] 陌生人 mòshēngrén, 异〔異〕乡〔鄉〕人 yìxiāngrén.

strangle /'stræŋgl/ *vt* 勒死 lēisǐ, 绞死 jiǎosǐ. '~**hold** [常喻](致命的)紧〔緊〕扼 jǐn è, 束缚 shùfù: *They have a* ~*hold on the economy.* 他们有力地控制着经济.

strap /stræp/ *n* [C] 带〔帶〕dài, 皮带 pídài. □ *vt* [-pp-] 1 用带束住 yòng dài shùzhù, 捆〔綑〕扎〔紮〕kǔnzhā. 2 用皮带抽打 yòng pídài chōudǎ.

strata /'strɑːtə/ ⇨ stratum.

stra·tegic(al) /strə'tiːdʒɪk(l)/ *adj* 战〔戰〕略的 zhànlüède. ~**ally** /-klɪ/ *adv*

strat·egy /'strætədʒɪ/ *n* 1 [U] 战略 zhànlüè. 2 [U] 策略 cèlüè. 3 [C] 计谋 jìmóu. **strat·egist** 战略家 zhànlüèjiā.

strato·sphere /'strætəsfɪə(r)/ *n* [C] 平流层〔層〕píngliúcéng, 同温层 tóngwēncéng.

stra·tum /'strɑːtəm/ *n* [C] [*pl* -ta /-tə/] 1 地层 dìcéng. 2 (社会)阶〔階〕层 jiēcéng.

straw /strɔː/ *n* 1 [U] 稻草 dàocǎo; 麦〔麥〕杆〔稈〕màigǎn. 2 [C] (一根)稻草 dàocǎo. *the ˌlast* '~ 终于〔於〕使人不能忍受的因素 zhōng yú shǐ rén bùnéng rěnshòu de yīnsù. 3 [C] (喝汽水等用的)吸管 xīguǎn.

straw·berry /'strɔːbrɪ/ *n* [C] [*pl* -ies] 草莓 cǎoméi.

stray /streɪ/ *vi* [*pt, pp* ~ed] 走离〔離〕zǒulí, 迷路 mílù. □ *n* 迷失的动〔動〕物 míshīde dòngwù.

streak /stri:k/ *n* [C] **1** 条〔條〕纹 tiáowén, 线〔線〕条 xiàntiáo. **2**〔与 *of* 连用〕(性格上的) 特征〔徵〕tèzhēng: *a ~ of cruelty* 残忍的性格. **3** 短时〔時〕间〔間〕duǎn shíjiān, 一阵〔陣〕子 yízhènzi: *a ~ of good luck* 一阵好运气. □ *vt/i* **1** 在…上加条纹 zài...shàng jiā tiáowén. **2**〔非正式用语〕飞〔飛〕跑 fēipǎo. **streaky** *adj* [-ier, -iest] 有条〔條〕纹的 yǒu tiáowén de.

stream /stri:m/ *n* [C] **1** 小河 xiǎohé, 溪流 xīliú. **2** 水流 shuǐliú; 流动〔動〕liúdòng: *caught in the ~* 陷于潮流不能自拔. **3** 一连〔連〕串 yìliánchuàn, 川流不息 chuān liú bù xī: *a ~ of abuse* 一连串的辱骂. **4** 学〔學〕生的智力水平(的划分) xuéshēngde zhìlì shuǐpíng. □ *vi* **1** 流 liú, 流出 liúchū. **2** (在风中)飘〔飄〕扬〔揚〕piāoyáng. '**~line** *vt* (精简…) 使效率更高 shǐ xiàolǜ gènggāo. '**~lined** *adj* **(a)** 流线〔線〕型的 liúxiànxíngde. **(b)** 效率高的 xiàolǜ gāo de. **~er** 狭〔狹〕长〔長〕的纸带〔帶〕xiáchángde zhǐdài, 飘带 piāodài.

street /stri:t/ *n* [C] 街道 jiēdào. *the ˌman in the '~* 普通市民 pǔtōng shìmín. '**~s ahead of**〔非正式用语〕前面很远〔遠〕qiánmiàn hěnyuǎn. '**~-car**〔美语〕= tram.

strength /streŋθ/ *n* [U] **1** 力 lì, 力量 lìliàng. **on the ~ of** 因为〔爲〕yīnwéi; 凭〔憑〕借 píngjiè: *buy it on the ~ of his advice* 由于他的劝告而买它. **2** 实〔實〕力 shílì, 兵力 bīnglì: *The army is below ~.* 这支军队不足额定兵员. **~en** *vt/i* 加强 jiāqiáng, (使)巩〔鞏〕固 gǒnggù.

strenu·ous /'strenjʊəs/ *adj* 费劲〔勁〕的 fèijìnde, 用力的 yònglìde. **~ly** *adv* **~ness** *n* [U]

stress /stres/ *n* **1** [U] 压〔壓〕力 yālì, 重压 zhòngyā. **2** [U] 重点〔點〕zhòngdiǎn; 重视 zhòngshì, 强调 qiángdiào: *put ~ on the need to improve* 强调改进的需要. **3** [C, U] 重读〔讀〕zhòngdú, 重音 zhòngyīn. □ *vt* 着重 zhuózhòng, 强调 qiángdiào.

stretch /stretʃ/ *vt/i* **1** 伸展 shēnzhǎn, 扩〔擴〕大 kuòdà, 拉长〔長〕lācháng. **2 ~ out** 直躺 zhí tǎng. **3** 曲解(字义, 法律等) qūjiě. **4** 滥〔濫〕用 lànyòng: *~ one's powers* 滥用权力. **5** 延伸 yánshēn, 连〔連〕绵 liánmián: *fields ~ing for miles* 连绵数英里的田野. □ *n* [C] **1** 伸展 shēnzhǎn, 扩大 kuòdà, 拉长 lācháng. **2** 一段持续〔續〕时〔時〕间〔間〕yíduàn chíxù shíjiān; 一大片田野 yídàpiàn tiányě: *twelve hours at a ~* 持续十二个小时.

stretcher /'stretʃə(r)/ *n* [C] 担〔擔〕架 dānjià.

stricken /'strɪkən/ *adj* 受害的 shòuhàide, 受灾〔災〕的 shòuzāide: *'terror-~* 受恐怖折磨的.

strict /strɪkt/ *adj* [-er, -est] **1** 严〔嚴〕格的 yángéde, 严厉〔厲〕的 yánlìde. **2** 明确〔確〕的 míngquède, 确切的 quèqiède: *the ~ sense of a word* 词的确切含义. **~ly** *adv* **~ness** *n* [U]

stride /straɪd/ *vt/i* [*pt* strode /strəʊd/; *pp* 罕用 stridden /'strɪdn/] **1** 大踏步走 dà tàbù zǒu. **2 ~ over** (或 **across**) **sth** 跨过〔過〕某物 kuàguò mǒuwù. □ *n* [C] 大步 dàbù, 阔〔闊〕步 kuòbù. **take sth in one's ~** 轻〔輕〕易地做某事 qīngyìde zuò mǒushì.

strife /straɪf/ *n* [U] 争吵 zhēngchǎo, 冲〔衝〕突 chōngtū.

strike[1] /straɪk/ *n* [C] **1** 罢〔罷〕工 bàgōng. **be (out) on ~** 参〔參〕加罢工 cānjiā bàgōng. ⇨ general strike. **2** (油田等的) 发〔發〕现 fāxiàn.

strike[2] /straɪk/ *vt/i* (*pt, pp* struck /strʌk/) **1** 打击〔擊〕dǎjī, 攻击 gōngjī. **2** 擦出(火) cāchū, 打出 dǎchū: *~ a match* 擦火柴. **3** 发〔發〕现 fāxiàn, 找到 zhǎodào: *~ oil* 找到油(田). **~ it rich** 发横财 fā hèngcái. **4** (钟等)敲 qiāo, (使)响〔響〕xiǎng: *The clock struck (four)* 钟敲(四下). **5** 罢〔罷〕工 bàgōng. ⇨ strike[1](1). **6** 给…以印象 gěi ... yǐ yìnxiàng: *He ~s me as a clever boy.* 他给我的印象是一个聪明的孩子. **7** 铸〔鑄〕造 zhùzào: *~ a medal* 铸制纪念章. **8** 完成 wánchéng, 达〔達〕成 dáchéng: *~ bargain* 成交. **9 ~ (out)** 走向 zǒuxiàng. **10** 使(某人)突然成为〔爲〕shǐ tūrán chéngwéi: *be struck blind* 突然瞎了. **11 ~ camp** 拔营〔營〕bá yíng. **12 ~ sth off (sth)** 抹去 mǒqù, 取消 qǔxiāo. **~ out (a)** (用力)打击 dǎjī. **(b)** 创〔創〕新 chuàngxīn, 自成一格 zì chéng yìgé.

strik·ing /'straɪkɪŋ/ *adj* 引人注目的 yǐn rén zhùmù de, 显〔顯〕著的 xiǎnzhùde. **~ly** *adv*

string[1] /strɪŋ/ *n* **1** [C,U] 线〔綫〕xiàn, 细绳〔繩〕xìshéng, 带〔帶〕子 dàizi. **2** [C] (乐器等的) 弦 xián: *~ instruments* 弦乐器. **3** [C]〔常 *pl*〕(操纵木偶的)线 xiàn. **pull ~s** 操纵〔縱〕(他人的行动) cāozòng.

with no* ~s *(attached) [非正式用语]无[無]附带条[條]件 wú fùdài tiáojiàn. **4** [C] (一) 串 chuàn: *a ~ of beads* 一串珠子. **5** 一系列 yíxìliè: *a ~ of curses* 不断的咒骂. *a ~ of accidents* 一连串的事故. **stringy** *adj* [-ier, -iest] 象[像]线的 xiàng xiàn de; 多筋的 duō jīn de.

string² /strɪŋ/ *vt/i* [*pt, pp* strung /strʌŋ/] **1** 装弦于[於](提琴,球拍等) zhuāng xián yú. **2** [*pp*] ***strung (up)*** (指人)(使)紧[緊]张[張] jǐnzhāng; (使)有准[準]备[備] yǒu zhǔnbèi. **3** (用线)穿 chuān, 串起 chuànqǐ. **4** (用线,绳)缚,扎[紮]或吊起 fù, zā huò diàoqǐ. **5** ~ ***out*** 成串地展开[開] chéng chuàn de zhǎnkāi.

strip /strɪp/ *vt/i* [-pp-] **1** 剥去 bōqù, 脱去 tuōqù, 除去 chúqù. ~ ***sth down*** 拆卸(机器等) chāixiè. **2** ~***sb of sth*** 剥夺[奪]某人的财产[產]等 bōduó mǒurén de cáichǎn děng. □ *n* [C] 狭[狹]长[長]的一片 (材料, 土地等) xiáchángde yípiàn. ⇨ airstrip, comic strip. ~ **cartoon** 连[連]环[環]画[畫] liánhuánhuà. ~ **'lighting** *n* [C] (舞台用)长条[條]照明灯[燈] chángtiáo zhàomíngdēng. **'~ mill** *n* [C] 带[帶]钢[鋼]厂[廠] dàigāngchǎng. **~-'tease** 脱衣舞 tuōyīwǔ. **~per** 表演脱衣舞的女人 biǎoyǎn tuōyīwǔ de nǚrén.

stripe /straɪp/ *n* [C] **1** 条[條]纹 tiáowén. **2** (军队的)阶[階]级臂章(通常为V字形) jiējí bìzhāng. **striped** *adj* 有条纹的 yǒu tiáowén de. **stripy** *adj*

strive /straɪv/ *vi* [*pt* strove /strəuv/; *pp* striven /'strɪvn/] **1** ~ ***with*** (或 ***against***) 斗[鬥]争 dòuzhēng, 反抗 fǎnkàng. **2** ~ ***for*** (或 ***to do***) ***sth*** 努力 nǔlì, 奋[奮]斗 fèndòu.

stro·bo·scope /'strəubəskəup/ *n* [C] (缩作 **strobe**) 频闪[閃]观[觀]测器 pínshǎn guàncèqì.

strode /strəud/ *pt* of stride.

stroke¹ /strəuk/ *n* [C] **1** (一)击[擊] jī, 打击 dǎjī. **2** (划船,游泳等的)一划 yìhuá. **3** (网球,板球等的)打法 dǎfǎ. **4** ***at a*** ~ 一下子 yíxiàzi, 一次努力 yícì nǔlì. **5** (写字)一笔[筆] yìbǐ, 一画[畫] yíhuà. **6** (钟的)鸣[鳴]声[聲] míngshēng. **7** 中风[風] zhòngfēng. ⇨ sunstroke.

stroke² /strəuk/ *vt* (用手)抚[撫]摸 fǔmō. □ *n* [C] 抚摸 fǔmō.

stroll /strəul/ *n* [C] 散步 sànbù, 溜达[達] liūda. □ *vi* 散步 sànbù, 溜达 liūda.

strong /strɒŋ/ *adj* [-er, -est] **1** 强壮[壯]的 qiángzhuàngde, 坚[堅]固的 jiāngùde, 强大的 qiángdàde. **2** 浓[濃]厚的 nónghòude: ~ *coffee* 浓咖啡. **3** ***going*** ~ [非正式用语] 有力继[繼]续[續](运动等) yǒu lì jìxù; (体力)强健 qiángjiàn. **4** (人数等)达[達]到…的 dádào...de: *an army 2000* ~ 两千大军. **'~-box** 保险[險]箱 bǎoxiǎnxiāng. ~ **drink** 烈性饮料 lièxìng yǐnliào. **'~hold** (a) 堡垒[壘] bǎolěi, 要塞 yàosài. (b) [喻]据[據]点[點] jùdiǎn, 根据地 gēnjùdì. **~ly** *adv*

strove /strəuv/ *pt* of strive.

struck /strʌk/ *pt, pp* of strike².

struc·tural /'strʌktʃərəl/ *adj* 结构[構]的 jiégòude, 构造的 gòuzàode. **~ly** *adv*

struc·ture /'strʌktʃə(r)/ *n* **1** [U] 构[構]造 gòuzào, 结构 jiégòu, 组织[織] zǔzhī. **2** [C] 构造物 gòuzàowù, 建筑[築]物 jiànzhùwù.

struggle /'strʌgl/ *vi* 斗[鬥]争 dòuzhēng, 奋[奮]斗 fèndòu, 努力 nǔlì. □ *n* [C] 斗争 dòuzhēng, 奋斗 fèndòu.

strum /strʌm/ *vt/i* [-mm-] ~ ***(on)*** 乱[亂]弹[彈](琴等) luàntán. □ *n* [C] 乱弹(声) luàntán.

strung /strʌŋ/ *pt, pp* of string².

strut¹ /strʌt/ *n* [C] (构架的)支柱 zhīzhù, 撑杆[桿] chēnggān.

strut² /strʌt/ *vi* [-tt-] 大摇大摆[擺]地走 dàyáo dàbǎi de zǒu. □ *n* [C] 高视阔[闊]步 gāoshì-kuòbù.

stub /stʌb/ *n* [C] **1** (铅笔)头[頭] tóu; (烟)蒂 dì. **2** (支票)存根 cúngēn. □ *vt* [-bb-] **1** 绊 bàn, 碰 pèn: ~ *one's toe* 碰踢 pèngtī, 绊脚 bàn jiǎo. **2** ~ ***sth out*** 捻熄(香烟) niǎnxī.

stubble /'stʌbl/ *n* [U] **1** 茬 chá, 残[殘]株 cán zhū. **2** 短髭 duǎn zī. **stub·bly** /'stʌblɪ/ *adj*

stub·born /'stʌbən/ *adj* 顽固的 wángùde, 坚[堅]定的 jiāndìngde. **~ly** *adv* **~ness** *n* [U]

stubby /'stʌbɪ/ *adj* [-ier, -iest] 短粗的 duǎn cū de, 矮胖的 ǎi pàng de.

stuck /stʌk/ *pt, pp* of stick².

stud¹ /stʌd/ *n* [C] (衬衫)领扣 lǐngkòu. □ *vt* [-dd-] [常 *pp*] 满布[佈] mǎn bù, 点[點]缀 diǎnzhuì.

stud² /stʌd/ *n* [C] 马[馬]群 mǎqún; 种马 zhǒngmǎ.

stu·dent /'stju:dnt/ *n* [C] **1** [英国英语]大学[學]生 dàxuéshēng. **2** 学者 xuézhě, 研究者 yánjiūzhě.

stu·dio /'stju:dɪəu/ *n* [C] [*pl* ~s]

1 (画家，摄影者的) 工作室 gōngzuòshì. 2 (电影) 摄影棚 shèyǐngpéng; 播音室 bōyīnshì; (电视) 播送室 bōsòngshì.

stu·di·ous /'stju:dɪəs/ *adj* [正式用语]好学[學]的 hàoxuéde, 用功的 yònggōngde. ~**ly** *adv*

study[1] /'stʌdɪ/ *n* [*pl* -ies] 1 [U] [*pl*] 学[學]习[習] xuéxí, 研究 yánjiū. 2 [C] 学科 xuékē, 研究项目 yánjiū xiàngmù. 3 [C] 书房 shūfáng. 4 [C] 习作 xízuò, 试作 shìzuò; 练[練]习曲 liànxíqǔ.

study[2] /'stʌdɪ/ *vt/i* [*pt, pp* -ied] 1 学[學] xué, 学习 xuéxí, 研究 yánjiū: ~ *medicine* 学医. 2 细看 xì kàn; 细想 xì xiǎng: ~ *the map* 仔细察看地图.

stuff[1] /stʌf/ *n* 1 [C,U] 原料 yuánliào, 材料 cáiliào, 资料 zīliào. 2 [U] [喻] 素质[質] sùzhì, 本质 běnzhì: *the ~ heroes are made of* 英雄本色. 3 [U] 物质 wùzhì. 4 东[東]西 dōngxi, 物品 wùpǐn: *Put your ~ in your room.* 把你的东西放在你的房间里. ***know one's ~*** 精通(自己的)业[業]务[務] jīngtōng yèwù; 内行 nèiháng.

stuff[2] /stʌf/ *vt* 1 把…装满 bǎ…zhuāngmǎn, 塞进[進] sāijìn. 2 把馅塞入(待烹煮的鸡，鸭等肚中) bǎ xiàn sāirù. 3 剥制[製](标本) bōzhì. ~**ing** *n* [U] 填料 tiánliào, 填充剂[劑] tiánchōngjì.

stuffy /'stʌfɪ/ *adj* [-ier, -iest] 1 通风[風]不良的 tōng fēng bù liáng de, 闷[悶]热[熱]的 mēnrède. 2 [非正式用语](指人)易受惊[驚]的 yì shòujīng de; 拘谨的 jūjǐnde. **stuffily** /-əlɪ/ *adv* **stuffi·ness** *n* [U]

stumble /'stʌmbl/ *vi* 1 绊跌 bàndiē, (几乎) 绊倒 bàndǎo. ~ ***across*** **(或 *on, upon*)** ***sth*** [喻] 偶然发[發]现(某事物) ǒurán fāxiàn. 2 结结巴巴地说话 jiējiēbābā de shuōhuà. □ *n* [C] 绊跌 bàndiē; 结巴 jiēba. **'stum·bling block** 障碍[礙]物 zhàng'àiwù, 绊脚石 bànjiǎoshí.

stump /stʌmp/ *n* [C] 1 树[樹]桩[樁] shùzhuāng. 2 残[殘]余[餘]部分 cányú bùfen. 3 [板球] 三柱门[門]的柱 sānzhùménde zhù. □ *vt/i* 1 笨重地行走 bènzhòngde xíngzǒu. 2 [非正式用语]难[難]住 nánzhù, (使)困惑 kùnhuò. **stumpy** *adj* [-ier, -iest] 短粗的 duǎn cū de.

stun /stʌn/ *vt* [-nn-] 1 把…打晕[暈] bǎ … dǎyūn. 2 使震惊[驚] shǐ zhènjīng. 使不知所措 shǐ bùzhī suǒcuò. ~**ning** *adj* [非正式用语]漂亮的 piàoliangde, 极[極]好的 jíhǎode.

stung /stʌŋ/ *pt, pp* of sting[2].

stunk /stʌŋk/ *pp* of stink.

stunt[1] /stʌnt/ *n* [C] [非正式用语] 惊[驚]人之举[舉] jīng rén zhī jǔ, 绝技 juéjì, 噱头[頭] xuétóu. '~**man** (拍危险镜头时) 当演员替身的杂[雜]技演员 dāng yǎnyuán tìshēn de zájì yǎnyuán.

stunt[2] /stʌnt/ *vt* 阻碍[礙]…的发[發]育成长[長] zǔ'ài…de fāyù chéngzhǎng.

stu·pen·dous /stju:'pendəs/ *adj* 巨大的 jùdàde, 惊[驚]人的 jīngrénde. ~**ly** *adv*

stu·pid /'stju:pɪd/ *adj* 笨的 bènde, 愚蠢的 yúchǔnde. ~**ly** *adv* ~**ity** /-'pɪdətɪ/ *n* [C,U]

stu·por /'stju:pə(r)/ *n* [C,U] 昏迷 hūnmí, 不省人事 bù xǐng rénshì.

sturdy /'stɜ:dɪ/ *adj* [-ier, -iest] 强健的 qiángjiànde, 坚[堅]实[實]的 jiānshíde. **stur·dily** /-əlɪ/ *adv*

stut·ter /'stʌtə(r)/ *vt/i, n* = stammer.

sty[1] /staɪ/ *n* [C] [*pl* sties] = pigsty.

sty[2] (亦作 **stye**) /staɪ/ *n* [C] [*pl* sties, styes] 睑[瞼]腺炎 jiǎnxiànyán; 麦[麥]粒肿[腫] màilìzhǒng.

style /staɪl/ *n* 1 [C,U] 风[風]格 fēnggé, 作风 zuòfēng, 风度 fēngdù; 文体[體] wéntǐ. 2 [U] 优[優]越性 yōuyuèxìng, 优势[勢] yōushì. 3 [C,U] (特指衣服等)式样[樣] shìyàng, 时[時]式 shíshì, 时髦 shímáo. □ *vt* 设计 shèjì. **styl·ish** *adj* 时髦的 shímáode, 漂亮的 piàoliangde. **sty·list** *n* [C] **(a)** 文体家 wéntǐjiā. **(b)** (服装等)设计师[師] shèjìshī. **sty'lis·tic** *adj* 风格(上)的 fēnggéde; 文体(上)的 wéntǐde.

sty·lus /'staɪləs/ *n* [C] [*pl* ~es] (唱机的) 唱针 chàngzhēn; 尖笔[筆] jiānbǐ.

suave /swa:v/ *adj* 温和的 wēnhéde, 文雅的 wényǎde.

sub(s). = **1** subscription, **2** substitute.

sub·con·scious /ˌsʌb'kɒnʃəs/ *adj* 潜[潛]意识[識]的 qiányìshíde. □ *n* **the** ~ 潜意识 qiányìshí. ~**ly** *adv* ~**ness** *n* [U]

sub·di·vide /ˌsʌbdɪ'vaɪd/ *vt/i* (把…)再分 zài fēn, 细分 xì fēn. **sub·di·vi·sion** /-dɪ'vɪʒn/ *n* [C,U]

sub·due /səb'dju:/ *vt* 1 使屈服 shǐ qūfú, 征服 zhēngfú; 克制 kèzhì. 2 使柔和 shǐ róuhé, 使安静 shǐ ānjìng: ~*d lighting* 柔和的灯

光.

sub·ject[1] /'sʌbdʒɪkt/ *adj, adv* ~ *to* **1** 隶〔隸〕属〔屬〕的 lìshǔde, 受支配的 shòu zhīpèi de: ~ *to the law* 受法律约束. **2** 在…条〔條〕件下 zài ... tiáojiàn xià; 依照 yīzhào: ~ *to confirmation* 须经过批准.

sub·ject[2] /'sʌbdʒɪkt/ *n* [C] **1** 国〔國〕民 guómín, 臣民 chénmín. **2** 题目 tímù, 主题 zhǔtí. **3** [语法] 主语 zhǔyǔ.

sub·ject[3] /səb'dʒekt/ *vt* **1** 征服 zhēngfú, 使服从〔從〕 shǐ fúcóng. **2** 使遭受 shǐ zāoshòu: ~ *a man to torture* 使人受折磨. **sub·jec·tion** /-ʃn/ *n* [U]

sub·jec·tive /səb'dʒektɪv/ *adj* 主观〔觀〕的 zhǔguānde. ⇨ objective. ~**ly** *adv* **sub·jec'tiv·ity** *n* [U]

sub·lime /sə'blaɪm/ *adj* 最大的 zuìdàde, 伟〔偉〕大的 wěidàde, 至高无〔無〕上的 zhì gāo wú shàng de: ~ *happiness* 无比的幸福. ~**ly** *adv*

sub·mar·ine /ˌsʌbmə'ri:n/ *adj* 水下的 shuǐxiàde, 海底的 hǎidǐde. □ *n* [C] 潜〔潛〕水艇 qiánshuǐtǐng.

sub·merge /səb'mɜ:dʒ/ *vt/i* **1** 放于〔於〕水下 fàng yú shuǐxià. 进〔進〕入水中 jìnrù shuǐzhōng. **2** (使)沉没 chénmò. **sub·mer·sion** /səb'mɜ:ʃn/ *n* [U] 浸没 jìnmò, 淹没 yānmò, 潜〔潛〕入水中 qiánrù shuǐzhōng.

sub·mis·sion /səb'mɪʃən/ *n* **1** [U] 投降 tóuxiáng, 归〔歸〕顺 guīshùn. **2** [U] 服从〔從〕 fúcóng. **3** [C,U] [法律]建议〔議〕 jiànyì, 意见 yìjiàn.

sub·miss·ive /səb'mɪsɪv/ *adj* 服从〔從〕的 fúcóngde, 顺从的 shùncóngde. ~**ly** *adv* ~**ness** *n* [U]

sub·mit /səb'mɪt/ *vt/i* [-tt-] **1** (使)服从〔從〕 fúcóng, (使) 屈服 qūfú. **2** 提出 tíchū, 提交 tíjiāo. **3** [法律]提议〔議〕 tíyì, 提出声〔聲〕辩 tíchū shēngbiàn. **4** ~ **(to)** 服从 fúcóng, 投降 tóuxiáng.

sub·or·di·nate /sə'bɔ:dɪnət/ *adj* 下级的 xiàjíde; 次要的 cìyàode, 从〔從〕属〔屬〕的 cóngshǔde. □ *n* [C] 部下 bùxià, 下级职〔職〕员 xiàjí zhíyuán. □ *vt* /sə'bɔ:dɪneɪt/ 把…列为〔爲〕下级 bǎ...lièwéi xiàjí, 使在次要地位 shǐ zài cìyào dìwèi.

sub·scribe /səb'skraɪb/ *vt/i* **1** 认〔認〕捐(款项) rènjuān, 捐助 juānzhù. **2** ~ *to sth* **(a)** 订阅〔閱〕(杂志等) dìngyuè. **(b)** 同意 tóngyì, 赞成 zànchéng. **sub·scriber** *n* [C] **sub·scrip·tion** /səb'skrɪpʃn/ *n* **(a)** [U] 捐助 juānzhù; 订阅 dìngyuè; 签〔簽〕署 qiānshǔ. **(b)** [C] 捐款 juānkuǎn; 预订费 yùdìngfèi.

sub·se·quent /'sʌbsɪkwənt/ *adj* ~ *(to)* 后〔後〕来〔來〕的 hòuláide, 随〔隨〕后的 suíhòude. ~**ly** *adv* 接着 jiēzhe, 然后 ránhòu.

sub·ser·vi·ent /səb'sɜ:vɪənt/ *adj* 奉承的 fèngchéngde, 谄媚的 chǎnmèide.

sub·side /səb'saɪd/ *vt* **1** (指洪水) 退落 tuìluò. **2** (指土地)下沉 xiàchén. **3** (指建筑物) 沉降 chénjiàng. **4** (指风等) 平息 píngxī, 平静 píngjìng. **sub·sid·ence** /səb'saɪdns/ *n* [C,U] 降落 jiàngluò, 下沉 xiàchén; 平息 píngxī.

sub·sidi·ary /səb'sɪdɪərɪ/ *adj* 辅〔輔〕助的 fǔzhùde, 补〔補〕充的 bǔchōngde, 次要的 cìyàode, 附属(屬)的 fùshǔde: *a* ~ *role* 配角. *a* ~ *industry* 辅助性产业. □ *n* [C] [*pl* -ies] 子公司 zǐgōngsī, 附属机〔機〕构〔構〕 fùshǔ jīgòu.

sub·si·dize /'sʌbsɪdaɪz/ *vt* 资助 zīzhù, 津贴 jīntiē.

sub·sidy /'sʌbsədɪ/ *n* [C] [*pl* -ies] 补〔補〕助金 bǔzhùjīn, 津贴费 jīntiēfèi.

sub·stance /'sʌbstəns/ *n* **1** [C,U] 物质〔質〕 wùzhì. **2** [U] 实〔實〕质 shízhì, 本质 běnzhì, 要义〔義〕 yàoyì. **3** [U] 牢固 láogù, 坚〔堅〕实 jiānshí. **4** [U] 财产〔產〕 cáichǎn, 财物 cáiwù: *a man of* ~ 有财产的人. **sub·stan·tial** /səb'stænʃl/ *adj* **(a)** 坚固的 jiāngùde, 结实的 jiēshide. **(b)** 巨大的 jùdàde, 大量的 dàliàngde: *a substantial meal* 丰盛的一餐. **(c)** 富有的 fùyǒude, 有相当〔當〕财产的 yǒu xiāngdāng cáichǎn de: *a substantial business* 殷实的商行. **sub·stan·tially** *adv*

sub·stan·ti·ate /səb'stænʃɪeɪt/ *vt* 证〔證〕实〔實〕 zhèngshí, 证明 zhèngmíng. **sub·stan·ti'ation** *n* [U]

sub·sti·tute /'sʌbstɪtju:t/ *n* [C] 代替人 dàitìrén, 代用品 dàiyòngpǐn. □ *vt/i* 代替 dàitì, 作代替者 zuò dàitìzhě. **sub·sti'tu·tion** *n* [C,U]

sub·ter·ranean /ˌsʌbtə'reɪnɪən/ *adj* [正式用语] = underground.

sub·title /'sʌbtaɪtl/ *n* [C] **1** (书籍的)副标〔標〕题 fù biāotí. **2** (印在外国影片下方的) 译〔譯〕文字幕 yìwén zìmù.

subtle /'sʌtl/ *adj* **1** 微妙的 wēimiàode, 难〔難〕以捉摸的 nán yǐ zhuōmō de: *a* ~ *difference* 细微的不同. **2** 精明的 jīngmíngde; 巧妙

的 qiǎomiàode: *a ~ joke* 一个巧妙的玩笑. **~ty** *n* [C,U] [*pl* -ies]

sub·tract /səb'trækt/ *vt* 减去 jiǎnqù; 扣除 kòuchú. **sub·trac·tion** /-ʃn/ *n* [C,U]

sub·urb /'sʌbɜ:b/ *n* [C] 市郊 shìjiāo, 郊区〔區〕 jiāoqū. **~an** /sə'bɜ:bən/ *adj* **~ia** /sə'bɜ:bɪə/ *n* [U] 郊区居民的生活 jiāoqū jūmín de shēnghuó.

sub·vert /sʌb'vɜ:t/ *vt* 颠覆(政府) diānfù. **sub·ver·sion** /-ʃn/ *n* [U] **sub·vers·ive** *adj* 颠覆性的 diānfùxìngde.

sub·way /'sʌbweɪ/ *n* [C] **1** 地道 dìdào. **2**〔美语〕= underground(1).

suc·ceed /sək'si:d/ *vt/i* **1** ~ (*in*) 成功 chénggōng, 完成 wánchéng. **2** 继〔繼〕续〔續〕 jìxù, 继任 jìrèn: *Who ~ed Kennedy as President?* 谁继肯尼迪出任总统? **3** ~ (*to*) 继承 jìchéng.

suc·cess /sək'ses/ *n* **1** [C,U] 成功 chénggōng. **2** [U] 获〔獲〕得财富 huòdé cáifù, 发〔發〕迹 fājī. **3** [C] 取得成功的人或事 qǔdé chénggōng de rén huò shì. **~ful** *adj* **~fully** *adv*

suc·ces·sion /sək'seʃn/ *n* **1** [U] 连〔連〕续〔續〕 liánxù, 继〔繼〕续 jìxù. *in ~* 连接地 liánjiēde, 连续地 liánxùde. **2** [C] 一连串 yìliánchuàn. **3** [U] 继承(权) jìchéng. **suc·cess·ive** *adj* 连续的 liánxùde, 接连的 jiēliánde. **suc·ces·sor** *n* [C] 继承人 jìchéngrén, 接班人 jiēbānrén, 后〔後〕继者 hòujìzhě.

suc·cinct /sək'sɪŋkt/ *adj* 简明的 jiǎnmíngde. **~ly** *adv* **~ness** *n* [U]

suc·cu·lent /'sʌkjʊlənt/ *adj* **1** 多汁的 duō zhī de, 有味的 yǒu wèi de. **2** (指植物) 肉质〔質〕的 ròuzhì de.

suc·cumb /sə'kʌm/ *vi* ~ *to* 屈服 qūfú, 屈从〔從〕 qūcóng; 死 sǐ.

such /sʌtʃ/ *adj* **1** [与 *as* 连用] 同类〔類〕的 tónglèide, 这〔這〕种〔種〕的 zhèzhǒngde: *poets ~ as Keats and Shelley* 象济慈和雪莱这样的诗人. **2** ~ (...) *that* 如此(...)以致 rúcǐ (...) yǐzhì: *His behaviour was ~ that everyone disliked him.* 他的行为使人人都嫌恶他. **3** 这样〔樣〕zhèyàng, 那样 nàyàng: *Don't be in ~ a hurry.* 不要这样匆忙. □ *pron* **1** 这(个) zhè, 那(个) nà; 这些 zhèxiē, 那些 nàxiē: *S~ were his words.* 那些正是他的话. *as ~* 照此 zhào cǐ.

suck /sʌk/ *vt/i* **1** 吸 xī, 啜 chuò. **2** 舔 tiǎn, 舐食 shìshí. **3** ~ *sth up* 吸收(某物) xīshōu. **4** 卷〔捲〕入 juǎnrù, 吸入 xīrù: *The strong current ~ed him under the water.* 强大的洪流把他卷入水中. □ *n* [C] 吸 xī, 啜 chuò; 舐 shì, 舔 tiǎn. **~er** *n* [C] **(a)** (动物的)吸盘〔盤〕 xīpán. **(b)** 橡皮吸子 xiàngpí xīzi. **(c)**〔非正式用语〕容易受骗〔騙〕的人 róngyì shòu piàn de rén.

suckle /'sʌkl/ *vt* 哺乳 bǔ rǔ, 喂奶 wèi nǎi.

suc·tion /'sʌkʃn/ *n* [U] **1** 吸 xī, 吸入 xīrù. **2** 互相吸住 hùxiāng xīzhù.

sud·den /'sʌdn/ *adj* 突然的 tūránde; 急速的 jísùde. **~ly** *adv* **~ness** *n* [C]

suds /sʌdz/ *n pl* 肥皂泡沫 féizào pàomò.

sue /sju:/ *vt/i* ~ *for* **1** 控诉 kòngsù, 控告 kònggào. **2** 请求 qǐngqiú.

suede, suède /sweɪd/ *n* [U] 软〔軟〕羔皮 ruǎn gāopí.

suet /'su:ɪt/ *n* [U] 板油 bǎnyóu.

suf·fer /'sʌfə(r)/ *vt/i* **1** 受苦 shòu kǔ; 受害 shòu hài, 受损失 shòu sǔnshī. **2** 遭受 zāoshòu, 蒙受 méngshòu; 经〔經〕历〔歷〕 jīnglì. **3** 忍受 rěnshòu, 忍耐 rěnnài: *I can't ~ his insolence.* 我不能忍受他的侮辱.

suf·fi·cient /sə'fɪʃnt/ *adj* 足够的 zúgòude, 充分的 chōngfènde. **~ly** *adv* **suf·fi·ciency** /-nsɪ/ *n* 充足 chōngzúde, 足量 zú liàng.

suf·fix /'sʌfɪks/ *n* [C] 后〔後〕缀 hòuzhuì, 词尾 cíwěi.

suf·fo·cate /'sʌfəkeɪt/ *vt/i* **1** (使)窒息 zhìxī, (使)呼吸困难〔難〕 hūxī kùnnan. **2** (把...)闷〔悶〕死 mēnsǐ. **suf·fo'ca·tion** *n* [U]

sugar /'ʃʊgə(r)/ *n* [U] 糖 táng. □ *vt* 加糖于〔於〕 jiā táng yú, 使甜 shǐ tián. '**~ beet** (制糖用的)甜菜 tiáncài. **sugary** *adj*

sug·gest /sə'dʒest/ *vt* **1** 提议〔議〕 tíyì, 建议 jiànyì. **2** 启〔啟〕发〔發〕 qǐfā, 提醒 tíxǐng, 暗示 ànshì. **sug·ges·tion** /-tʃn/ *n* **(a)** [U] 建议 jiànyì, 提议 tíyì, 启发 qǐfā, 暗示 ànshì. **(b)** [C] (所提)意见, 计划〔劃〕等 yìjiàn, jìhuà děng. **~ive** *adj* 提醒的 tíxǐngde, 暗示的 ànshìde. **~ly** *adv*

sui·cide /'sju:ɪsaɪd/ *n* **1** [C,U] 自杀〔殺〕 zìshā: *commit ~* 自杀. [C] 自杀者 zìshāzhě. **2** [U] 自取灭〔滅〕亡 zì qǔ mièwáng. **sui·cidal** *adj*

suit[1] /su:t/ *n* [C] 一套衣服 yítào yīfu. 一组同花纸牌 yìzǔ tónghuā zhǐpái. *follow* ~ 〔喻〕学〔學〕样〔樣〕xué yàng, 照着做 zhàozhe zuò. '~**case** 衣箱 yīxiāng.

suit² /su:t/ *vt/i* **1** (使)满意 mǎnyì, 合适〔適〕héshì. ~ *oneself* 自便 zìbiàn, 自主 zìzhǔ. **2** (尤指衣服等)相配 xiāngpèi, 合式 héshì: *That hat ~s you.* 那顶帽子对你正合适. **3** *be ~ed* (*to, for*) 适宜于〔於〕shìyí yú, 有资格 yǒu zīgé, **~able** /əbl/ *adj* 合适的 héshìde, 适当〔當〕的 shìdāngde. **~ably** *adv* **~a'bil·ity** *n* [U]

suite /swi:t/ *n* [C] **1** 一套家具 yītào jiājù. **2** 一套房间〔間〕yítào fángjiān.

sulk /sʌlk/ *vi* 生气〔氣〕而不说话 shēngqì ér bù shuōhuà. **sulky** *adj* [-ier, -iest]

sul·len /'sʌlən/ *adj* 生气〔氣〕的 shēngqìde, 闷〔悶〕闷不乐〔樂〕的 mènmèn bú lè de. **~ly** *adv* **~ness** *n* [U]

sul·phur 〔美语 = **sulfur**〕/'sʌlfə(r)/ *n* [U] 〔化学〕硫 (**S**) liú. **~ic** /sʌl'fjʊərɪk/ *adj*

sul·tan /'sʌltən/ *n* [C] 苏〔蘇〕丹(某些伊斯兰国家统治者) sūdān.

sul·tana /sʌl'tɑ:nə/ *n* [C] [*pl* ~s] 无〔無〕核小葡萄(干) wú hé xiǎo pútáo.

sul·try /'sʌltrɪ/ *adj* [-ier, -iest] **1** (指天气)闷〔悶〕热〔熱〕的 mēnrède. **2** (指人)热情的 rèqíngde, 易激动〔動〕的 yì jīdòng de. **sul·trily** *adv*

sum /sʌm/ *n* [C] **1** (亦作 ~ **total**) 总〔總〕数〔數〕zǒngshù; 〔数学〕和 hé. **2** 算术〔術〕题 suànshùtí. **3** 金额 jīn'é. □ *vt/i* [-mm-] ~ (*sb, sth*) *up* **1** 计算…的总数 jìsuàn...de zǒngshù, 合计 héjì. **2** 概述 gàishù, 概括 gàikuò. **3** 形成对…的判断〔斷〕或意见 xíngchéng duì...de pànduàn huò yìjiàn.

sum·mary /'sʌmərɪ/ *adj* 〔正式用语〕 **1** 概括的 gàikuòde, 扼要的 èyàode. **2** 即时〔時〕的 jíshíde, 速决的 sùjuéde: *a ~ execution* 立即处决. □*n* [C] [*pl* -ies] 摘要 zhāiyào, 概要 gàiyào. **sum·mar·ize** /-raɪz/ *vt* 概述 gàishù, 摘要 zhāiyào.

sum·mer /'sʌmə(r)/ *n* [C,U] 夏季 xiàjì. **sum·mery** *adj* 如夏季的 rú xiàjì de, 适〔適〕合夏季的 shìhé xiàjì de.

sum·mit /'sʌmɪt/ *n* [C] 顶点〔點〕dǐngdiǎn. '~ **talks** (或 **meeting**) 最高级会谈 zuìgāojí huìtán.

sum·mon /'sʌmən/ *vt* **1** ~ *sb* 召唤 zhāohuàn, 传〔傳〕唤 chuánhuàn. **2** ~ *sth up* 鼓起 gǔqǐ, 聚集 jùjí: ~ *up courage* 鼓起勇气.

sum·mons /'sʌmənz/ *n* [C] [*pl* ~es] (法庭)传〔傳〕票 chuánpiào. □ *vt* 把传票送达〔達〕(某人) bǎ chuánpiào sòngdá.

sun /sʌn/ *n* **1** *the* ~ 太阳〔陽〕tàiyáng. **2** *the* ~ 阳光 yángguāng, 日光 rìguāng. **3** [C] (有卫星的)恒星 héngxīng. □ *vt* [-nn-] 晒〔曬〕shài. '~**bathe** *vi* 沐日光浴 mù rìguāngyù '~**beam** (一道)日光 rìguāng. '~**burn** 日炙 rìzhì, 晒黑 shàihēi. '~**burnt** *adj* '~**dial** 日晷 rìguǐ. '~**shade** 遮阳伞〔傘〕zhēyángsǎn. '~**shine** 阳光 yángguāng, 日光 rìguāng. '~**stroke** 中暑 zhòngshǔ, 日射病 rìshèbìng. '~**tan** 晒黑 shàihēi. ~**ny** *adj* [-ier, -iest] **(a)** 阳光充足的 yángguāng chōngzú de. **(b)** 快乐〔樂〕的 kuàilède, 愉快的 yúkuàide.

Sun. = Sunday.

Sun·day /'sʌndɪ/ *n* 星期日 xīngqīrì.

sun·dries /'sʌndrɪz/ *n pl* 各式各样〔樣〕的 gèshì gèyàng de.

sung /sʌŋ/ *pp* of sing.

sunk /sʌŋk/ *pt, pp* of sink².

sunk·en /'sʌŋkən/ *pp* of sink².

super /'su:pə(r)/ *adj* 〔非正式用语〕特级的 tèjíde, 极〔極〕好的 jíhǎode.

su·perb /su:'pɜ:b/ *adj* 壮〔壯〕丽〔麗〕的 zhuànglìde; 头〔頭〕等的 tóuděngde. **~ly** *adv*

super·fi·cial /ˌsu:pə'fɪʃl/ *adj* **1** 表面的 biǎomiànde, 表皮的 biǎopíde. **2** 肤〔膚〕浅〔淺〕的 fūqiǎnde, 浅薄的 qiǎnbóde: *a ~ knowledge of* 对…一知半解. **~ly** *adv*

su·per·flu·ous /su:'pɜ:flʊəs/ *adj* 过剩的 guòshèngde, 多余〔餘〕的 duōyúde, 不必要的 bú bìyào de. **~ly** *adv*

super·hu·man /ˌsu:pə'hju:mən/ *adj* (力气,身材等)超过〔過〕常人的 chāoguò chángrén de, 超人的 chāorénde.

super·im·pose /ˌsu:pərɪm'pəʊz/ *vt* 把…放在另一物之上 bǎ...fàngzài lìng yí wù zhī shàng; 添加 tiānjiā, 附加 fùjiā: ~ *two photographs* 把两张照片叠印在一起.

super·in·tend /ˌsu:pərɪn'tend/ *vt/i* 监〔監〕督 jiāndū; 指挥〔揮〕(工作等) zhǐhuī. **~ent** *n* [C] **(a)** 监督人 jiāndūrén; 指挥者 zhǐhuīzhě. **(b)** 警察长〔長〕jǐngcházhǎng.

su·per·ior /sə'pɪərɪə(r)/ *adj* **1** 优〔優〕越的 yōuyuède, 优良的 yōuliángde, 较〔較〕高的 jiàogāode. **2** 较多的 jiàoduōde. **3** ~ *to* **(a)** 胜〔勝〕过〔過〕shèngguò, 优于〔於〕yōu yú. **(b)** (地位)高于 gāo yú. **4**

势〔勢〕利的 shìlìde. □ *n* [C] **1** 长〔長〕者 zhǎngzhě; 上级 shàngjí; 占〔佔〕优势者 zhàn yōushì zhě. **2** 修道院院长 xiūdàoyuàn yuànzhǎng: *the Father S~* 男修道院院长. **~·ity** /-'ɒrətɪ/ *n* [U]

su·per·la·tive /su:'pɜ:lətɪv/ *adj* **1** 最高的 zuìgāode, 无〔無〕上的 wúshàngde. **2** [语法] 最高级的 zuìgāojíde. □ *n* [C] 最高级 zuìgāojí.

super·mar·ket /'su:pəmɑ:kɪt/ *n* [C] 超级市场〔場〕chāojí shìchǎng, 自选〔選〕商场 zìxuǎn shāngchǎng.

super·natu·ral /ˌsu:pə'nætʃrəl/ *adj* 超自然的 chāo zìrán de, 神奇的 shénqíde, 不可思议〔議〕的 bùkě sīyì de.

super·sede /ˌsu:pə'si:d/ *vt* 代替 dàitì, 接替 jiētì.

super·sonic /ˌsu:pə'sɒnɪk/ *adj* 超声〔聲〕的 chāoshēngde, 超音速的 chāoyīnsùde.

super·sti·tion /ˌsu:pə'stɪʃn/ *n* [C, U] 迷信 míxìn, 迷信行为〔爲〕míxìn xíngwéi. **super·sti·tious** *adj*

super·struc·ture /'su:pəstrʌktʃə(r)/ *n* [C] 上层〔層〕建筑〔築〕shàngcéng jiànzhù, (船舰的)上层结构〔構〕shàngcéng jiégòu.

super·vise /'su:pəvaɪz/ *vt/i* 监〔監〕督 jiāndū, 管理 guǎnlǐ, 指导〔導〕zhǐdǎo. **super·vi·sion** /ˌsu:pə'vɪʒn/ 监督 jiāndū, 管理 guǎnlǐ, 指导 zhǐdǎo. **super·vi·sor** *n* [C]

sup·per /'sʌpə(r)/ *n* [C,U] 晚餐 wǎncān.

supple /'sʌpl/ *adj* [-r, -st] 易弯曲的 yì wānqū de, 柔软〔軟〕的 róuruǎnde.

supple·ment /'sʌplɪmənt/ *n* [C] **1** 增补〔補〕zēngbǔ, 补遗 bǔyí. **2** (报刊的) 增刊 zēngkān. □ *vt* /'sʌpləment/ 补充 bǔchōng, 增补 zēngbǔ. **~ary** /-'mentrɪ/ *adj* 补充的 bǔchōngde, 附加的 fùjiāde.

supply /sə'plaɪ/ *vt* [*pt, pp* -ied] **1** 供给 gōngjǐ, 供应〔應〕gōngyìng. **2** 满足 (需要) mǎnzú. □ *n* **1** [U] 供给 gōngjǐ, 供应 gōngyìng; [C] [*pl* -ies] 供应品 gōngyìngpǐn. **2** [*pl*] (尤指) 生活必需品 shēnghuó bìxūpǐn. **sup·lier** 供应者 gōngyìngzhě, 供应厂〔廠〕商 gōngyìng chǎngshāng.

sup·port /sə'pɔ:t/ *vt* **1** 支撑 zhīchēng; 支持 zhīchí. **2** 供养〔養〕gōngyǎng, 维持 wéichí: *~ a family* 养家. **3** 拥〔擁〕护〔護〕yōnghù, 赞助 zànzhù, 鼓励〔勵〕gǔlì: *~ a motion* 支持一项提议. *~ a political party* 拥护某一政党. □ *n* **1** [U] 支持 zhīchí, 支撑 zhīchēng; 供养 gōngyǎng; 拥护 yōnghù, 赞助 zànzhù. **2** [C] 支撑物 zhīchēngwù; 支持者 zhīchízhě; 供养者 gōngyǎngzhě; 赞助人 zànzhùrén. **sup·port·er** *n* [C]

sup·pose /sə'pəʊz/ *vt* **1** 假定 jiǎdìng, 认〔認〕定 rèndìng: *Let us ~ (that) the news is true.* 让我们假定这消息是正确的. **2** 猜测 cāicè, 想象 xiǎngxiàng: *Do you ~ he's gone?* 你猜想他已经走了吗? **3** *be ~d to* **(a)** 被期望 bèi qīwàng; 应〔應〕该 yīnggāi. **(b)** [非正式用语] [用于否定] 被允许 bèi yǔnxǔ: *You're not ~d to leave early.* 你不许早走. **sup·pos·ing** *conj* 假使 jiǎshǐ, 倘若 tǎngruò. **~d·ly** /-ɪdlɪ/ *adv* 想象上 xiǎngxiàngshàng, 恐怕 kǒngpà.

sup·po·si·tion /ˌsʌpə'zɪʃn/ *n* **1** [U] 假定 jiǎdìng, 想象 xiǎngxiàng. **2** [C] 猜测 cāicè.

sup·press /sə'pres/ *vt* **1** 镇压〔壓〕zhènyā, 平定 píngdìng. **2** 抑制 yìzhì; 隐〔隱〕瞒 yǐnmán: *~ the truth* 隐瞒真相. **sup·pres·sion** /-ʃn/ *n* [U]

su·preme /sʊ'pri:m/ *adj* **1** 最高的 zuìgāode, 至上的 zhìshàngde. **2** 最大的 zuìdàde; 最重要的 zuì zhòngyào de: *make the ~ sacrifice* 作出最大的牺牲. **~ly** *adv* 最高地 zuìgāode; 最重要地 zuì zhòngyào de; 极〔極〕大地 jídàde. **su·prem·acy** /sʊ'preməsɪ/ *n* [U]

Supt. = superintendent.

sur·charge /'sɜ:tʃɑ:dʒ/ *n* [C] 额外费 éwàifèi, 过〔過〕高的要价〔價〕guògāode yàojià. □ *vt* 向…收取额外费 xiàng...shōuqǔ éwàifèi, 处〔處〕…以附加罚款 chù ... yǐ fùjiā fákuǎn.

sure /ʃʊə(r)/ *adj* **1** 无〔無〕疑的 wúyíde, 一定的 yīdìngde, 确〔確〕信的 quèxìnde: *I think he's coming but I'm not quite ~.* 我想他会来的, 但我还不十分肯定. ***be*** (或 ***feel***) ***~ (about sth)*** 对…有把握 duì...yǒu bǎwò. ***be ~ to*** 一定会〔會〕yídìng huì. **2** 可靠的 kěkào de, 稳〔穩〕妥的 wěntuǒde: *a ~ cure for colds* 治感冒的良药. **~ly** *adv* **(a)** 确实〔實〕地 quèshíde, 无疑地 wúyíde: *slowly but ~ly* 缓慢但是踏实地. **(b)** 一定 yídìng, 谅必 liàngbì: *S~ly you know him* 你一定认识他.

surety /'ʃʊərətɪ/ *n* [C,U] [*pl* -ies] **1** 担〔擔〕保品 dānbǎopǐn. **2** 保证〔證〕人 bǎozhèngrén.

surf /sɜ:f/ *n* [U] 拍岸浪 pāi à

làng. '~-**board** 冲〔衝〕浪板 chōnglàngbǎn. ~**ing** 冲浪(运动) chōnglàng.

sur·face /'sɜːfɪs/ *n* [C] **1** 面 miàn, 表面 biǎomiàn. **2** 水面 shuǐmiàn, 液面 yèmiàn. **3** 外表 wàibiǎo, 外观〔觀〕wàiguān. **4**〔用作 *adj*〕表面的 biǎomiànde, 水面上的 shuǐmiànshàngde, 外表上的 wàibiǎoshàngde. ⇨ superficial. □ *vt/i* **1** 进〔進〕行表面处〔處〕理 jìnxíng biǎomiàn chùlǐ. 使成平面 shǐ chéng píngmiàn: *surfacing the roads* 铺路面. **2**(使)浮出水面 fúchū shuǐmiàn. '~ **mail** 普通邮〔郵〕件 pǔtōng yóujiàn.

sur·feit /'sɜːfɪt/ *n* [C] 过〔過〕量 guòliàng, 过度 guòdù, (尤指)饮食过度 yǐnshí guòdù.

surge /sɜːdʒ/ *vi* 波动〔動〕bōdòng, 汹〔洶〕涌〔湧〕xiōngyǒng, 澎湃 péngpài. □ *n* [C] 波浪起伏 bōlàng qǐ fú, 汹涌 xiōngyǒng, 澎湃 péngpài.

sur·geon /'sɜːdʒən/ *n* [C] 外科医〔醫〕生 wàikē yīshēng.

sur·gery /'sɜːdʒərɪ/ *n* [*pl* -ies] **1** [U] 外科 wàikē, 外科手术〔術〕wàikē shǒushù. **2** [C]〔英国英语〕手术室 shǒushùshì.

sur·gi·cal /'sɜːdʒɪkl/ *adj* 外科的 wàikēde, 外科手术〔術〕的 wàikē shǒushù de. ~**ly** /-klɪ/ *adv*

sur·ly /'sɜːlɪ/ *adj* [-ier, -iest] 粗暴的 cūbàode, 不友好的 bù yǒuhǎo de.

sur·mount /sə'maʊnt/ *vt* **1** 克服(困难) kèfú; 越过〔過〕yuèguò. **2** *be ~ed by* (或 *with*) 在…顶上有 zài … dǐngshàng yǒu, 装〔裝〕在…顶上 zhuāngzài … dǐngshàng: *a church ~ed by a tower* 有尖塔的教堂.

sur·name /'sɜːneɪm/ *n* [C] 姓 xìng. ⇨ first name, Christian name.

sur·pass /sə'pɑːs/ *vt*〔正式用语〕超越 chāoyuè, 胜〔勝〕过〔過〕shèngguò.

sur·plus /'sɜːpləs/ *n* **1** [C] 余〔餘〕款 yúkuǎn, 盈余 yíngyú. **2** 剩余(物资) shèngyú, 过〔過〕剩 guòshèng.

sur·prise /sə'praɪz/ *n* [C,U] 惊〔驚〕奇 jīngqí; 使人惊奇的事物 shǐ rén jīngqí de shìwù. □ *vt* **1** 使惊奇 shǐ jīngqí. **2** 感到惊奇 gǎndào jīngqí: *We were ~d to learn ....* 我们得知…感到惊奇. **3** 意外地发〔發〕现 yìwàide fāxiàn, 撞见 zhuàngjiàn: ~ *a burglar* 撞见一个窃贼. **sur·pris·ing** *adj* **sur·pris·ing·ly** *adv*

sur·ren·der /sə'rendə(r)/ *vt/i* **1** ~ (*to*) 投降 tóuxiáng, 自首 zìshǒu, 投案 tóu'àn. **2** 放弃〔棄〕fàngqì, 交出 jiāochū. **3** ~ (*oneself*) *to* 屈服于〔於〕(习惯, 感情等) qūfú yú, 陷于 xiàn yú. □ *n* [U] 屈服 qūfú, 投降 tóuxiáng; 放弃 fàngqì.

sur·round /sə'raʊnd/ *vt* 包围〔圍〕bāowéi, 围绕〔繞〕wéirào: *A river ~s the city.* 一条河流围绕城市. □ *n* [C] 围绕物 wéiràowù; 地毯四周(与墙之间)的地板 dìtǎn sìzhōu de dìbǎn. ~**ing** *adj* ~**ings** *n* [*pl*] 周围的事物 zhōuwéide shìwù, 环〔環〕境 huánjìng.

sur·veil·lance /sɜː'veɪləns/ *n* [U] 监〔監〕视 jiānshì, 监督 jiāndū: *under* ~ 置于监视下.

sur·vey /sə'veɪ/ *vt* **1** 环〔環〕视 huánshì, 眺望 tiàowàng. **2** 测量(土地) cèliáng, 勘定 kāndìng. **3** 检〔檢〕查 jiǎnchá, 调查 diàochá. □ *n* /'sɜːveɪ/ [C] **1** 概观〔觀〕gàiguān, 考察 kǎochá. **2** 测量(图或记录) cèliáng. ~**or** /sə'veɪə(r)/ *n* [C]

sur·vival /sə'vaɪvl/ *n* [C,U] 幸存 xìncún, 残〔殘〕存 cáncún; 幸存者 xìncúnzhě, 残存物 cáncúnwù.

sur·vive /sə'vaɪv/ *vt/i* 活下来〔來〕huóxiàlái, 残〔殘〕存 cáncún; 比…活得长〔長〕bǐ… huóde cháng: ~ *an earthquake* 在地震中幸免于死. *She ~d her husband.* 丈夫死后她还活着. **sur·vivor** 幸存者 xìncúnzhě, 逃生者 táoshēngzhě.

sus·cep·tible /sə'septəbl/ *adj* **1** 易受感动〔動〕的 yì shòu gǎndòng de, 敏感的 mǐngǎnde. **2** ~ *to* 易受…感动的 yì shòu…gǎndòng de: ~ *to cold* 容易感冒. **sus·cep·ti·'bil·ity** *n* [C,U] [*pl* -ies]

sus·pect /sə'spekt/ *vt* **1** 疑有 yíyǒu, 觉〔覺〕得 juéde, 猜想 cāixiǎng: *We ~ that he's dead.* 我们猜想他死了. **2** 觉得可疑 juéde kěyí, 怀〔懷〕疑 huáiyí: ~ *the truth of an account* 怀疑报导的真实性. **3** ~ *sb* (*of sth*) 怀疑某人(有罪等) huáiyí mǒurén. □ *n* /'sʌspekt/ [C] 嫌疑犯 xiányífàn, 可疑分子 kěyí fènzǐ. □ *adj* /'sʌspekt/ 可疑的 kěyíde.

sus·pend /sə'spend/ *vt* **1**〔与 *from* 连用〕吊 diào, 悬〔懸〕挂〔掛〕xuánguà. **2**(在空中或水面上)悬浮 xuánfú. **3** 推迟〔遲〕tuīchí, 中止 zhōngzhǐ, 暂〔暫〕停 zàntíng: ~ *judgement* 缓期宣判. **4** 暂令停职〔職〕等 zàn lìng tíngzhí děng: *They ~ed two boys from school.* 他们暂令两个孩子停学.

sus·penders /sə'spendəz/ *n pl* (亦作 *a pair of* ~) **1**[英国英语]吊袜〔襪〕带〔帶〕diàowàdài. **2**[美语] = braces[1](3).

sus·pense /sə'spens/ *n* [U] (有关新闻、决定等)不确〔確〕定 bú quèdìng; 悬〔懸〕而未决 xuán ér wèi jué.

sus·pen·sion /sə'spenʃn/ *n* [U] 悬〔懸〕挂〔掛〕xuánguà; 悬浮 xuánfú; 暂〔暫〕停 zàntíng. ~ **bridge** 吊桥〔橋〕diàoqiáo.

sus·pi·cion /sə'spɪʃn/ *n* **1** [C,U] 怀〔懷〕疑 huáiyí, 疑心 yíxīn, 嫌疑 xiányí: *He was arrested on* ~ *of murder.* 他因杀人嫌疑而被捕. **2** 一点〔點〕儿 yīdiǎnr: *a* ~ *of sadness* 有点伤心. **sus·pi·cious** *adj* 可疑的 kěyíde, 疑心的 yíxīnde. **sus·pi·cious·ly** *adv*

sus·tain /sə'steɪn/ *vt* **1** 支撑 zhīchēng, 承受住 chéngshòu zhù. **2** 支持 zhīchí, 维持 wéichí: ~*ing food* 维持体力的食物. **3** 蒙受 méngshòu, 遭受 zāoshòu: ~ *an injury* 受伤.

sus·ten·ance /'sʌstɪnəns/ *n* [U] [正式用语] 食物 shíwù; 营〔營〕养〔養〕yíngyǎng.

swab /swɒb/ *n* [C] **1** (擦地板用)拖把 tuōbǎ. **2** (医用)棉花球 miánhuāqiú; 拭子 shìzi. □ *vt* [-bb-] (用拖把)擦洗 chāxǐ.

swag·ger /'swægə(r)/ *vi* 昂首阔〔闊〕步 ángshǒu kuòbù, 摆〔擺〕架子 bǎi jiàzi. □ *n* [C] 昂首阔步 ángshǒu kuòbù, 摆架子 bǎijiàzi.

swal·low[1] /'swɒləʊ/ *n* [C] 燕子 yànzi.

swal·low[2] /'swɒləʊ/ *vt/i* **1** 吞下 tūnxià, 咽〔嚥〕下 yànxià. **2** ~ **(*up*)** 吞没 tūnmò, 用尽〔盡〕yòng jìn: *earnings* ~*ed up by bills* 被欠帐耗尽的收入. **3**[喻]: ~ *an insult* 忍受侮辱. □ *n* [C] 吞 tūn, 咽 yàn; 一次吞咽量 yícì tūnyànliàng.

swam /swæm/ *pt of* swim.

swamp /swɒmp/ *n* [C,U] 沼泽〔澤〕地 zhǎozédì. □ *vt* **1** 使淹没 shǐ yānmò. **2**[喻]使应〔應〕接不暇 shǐ yìngjiē bù xiá; 使不知所措 shǐ bù zhī suǒ cuò: ~*ed with requests* 请求多得应接不暇. **swampy** *adj* [-ier, -iest] (多)沼泽的 zhǎozéde.

swan /swɒn/ *n* [C] 天鹅〔鵝〕tiān'é. □ *vi* [-nn-] [非正式用语]闲〔閒〕荡〔蕩〕xiándàng, 游逛 yóuguàng. '~-**song** 诗人, 音乐〔樂〕家的最后作品 shīrén, yīnyuèjiā de zuìhòu zuòpǐn.

swap /swɒp/ *vt/i* [-pp-] = swop.

swarm /swɔ:m/ *n* [C] (昆虫等)一大群 yí dà qún. □ *vi* **1** (蜜蜂)成群飞〔飛〕舞 chéng qún fēiwǔ. **2** (指地方)拥〔擁〕挤〔擠〕yōngjǐ: *The beaches were* ~*ing with people.* 海滩上到处都是人. **3** 蜂拥而进〔進〕fēngyōng ér jìn, 涌〔湧〕入 yǒngrù: *The crowds* ~*ed into the cinemas.* 观众蜂拥而入电影院.

swat /swɒt/ *vt* [-tt-] 重拍 zhòng pāi, 拍死 pāi sǐ: ~ *a fly* 拍苍蝇. □ *n* [C] (苍蝇)拍子 pāizi.

sway /sweɪ/ *vt/i* **1** (使)摇摆〔擺〕yáobǎi, (使)摆动〔動〕bǎidòng. **2** 统治 tǒngzhì, 支配 zhīpèi, 影响〔響〕yǐngxiǎng: *a speech that* ~*ed the voters* 说服了投票人的演讲. □ *n* [U] **1** 摇摆 yáobǎi, 摇动 yáodòng. **2** 统治 tǒngzhì, 支配 zhīpèi, 影响 yǐngxiǎng: *under the* ~ *of friends* 在朋友们的影响下.

swear /sweə(r)/ *vt/i* (*pt* swore /swɔ:(r)/; *pp* sworn /swɔ:n/) **1** 郑〔鄭〕重地说 zhèngzhòngde shuō, 强调 qiángdiào; 发〔發〕誓 fāshì: *He swore to tell the truth.* 他发誓要说实话. **2** (使某人)宣誓 xuānshì. **3** ~ ***by sth*** 使用并〔並〕深信 shǐyòng bìng shēnxìn: *He* ~*s by strictness for discipline.* 他深信严厉的办法能整顿纪律. **4** 诅咒 zǔzhòu, 咒骂〔罵〕zhòumà. '~-**word** 诅咒 zǔzhòu, 骂人话 màrénhuà.

sweat /swet/ *n* **1** [U] 汗 hàn: *wipe the* ~ *off one's brow.* 擦去额上的汗. **2** 出汗 chū hàn, 一身汗 yìshēn hàn: *be in a* ~ 满身大汗. □ *vt/i* (使)出汗 chū hàn. ,~**ed** '**labour** 工资低的苦工 gōngzī dī de kǔgōng. **sweaty** *adj* [-ier, -iest] 汗湿〔濕〕透的 hàn shītòu de.

sweater /'swetə(r)/ *n* [C] 厚运〔運〕动〔動〕衫 hòu yùndòngshān, 毛线〔線〕衫 máoxiànshān, 卫〔衛〕生衫 wèishēngshān.

swede /swi:d/ *n* [C,U] [植物]瑞典芜〔蕪〕菁 Ruìdiǎn wújīng.

sweep[1] /swi:p/ *n* [C] **1** 扫〔掃〕sǎo, 扫除 sǎochú: *Give the room a good* ~. 把房间好好打扫一下. ***make a clean*** ~ ***of sth*** 彻〔徹〕底扫除 chèdǐ sǎochú, 清除 qīngchú. **2** 扫动〔動〕sǎodòng, 挥〔揮〕动 huīdòng: *with one* ~ *of his arm* 挥动一下他的手臂. **3** (一扫的)空间〔間〕kōngjiān, (一挥的)范〔範〕围〔圍〕fànwéi: *The radar has a* ~ *of 100 miles.* 这部雷达有100英里的扫描范围. **4** 连〔連〕绵区〔區〕域 liánmián qūyù; (道路等)弯〔彎〕曲处〔處〕wānqūchù: *a fine* ~ *of country* 一片美丽的乡村地区. **5** 激

流 jīliú: *the ~ of the tide* 潮水的激流. 6 = chimney-sweep. '~-**stake** 赌金独〔獨〕得的跑马〔馬〕比赛 dǔjīn dú dé de pǎomǎ bǐsài, 独赢 dúyíng.

sweep[2] /swi:p/ *vt/i* [*pt, pp* swept /swept/] 1 扫 sǎo, 扫除 sǎochú: *~ the floor* 扫地. *~ up the crumbs* 扫去面包屑. 2 带〔帶〕走 dàizǒu, 席卷〔捲〕xíjuǎn: *The current swept the logs along.* 洪水将木料冲走了. *~ sb off his feet* 使某人大为激动 shǐ mǒurén dà wéi jīdòng. 3 掠过〔過〕lüèguò, 扫过 sǎoguò: *A huge wave swept over the deck.* 大浪掠过甲板. 4 威仪〔儀〕地走动〔動〕wēiyíde zǒudòng. 5 连〔連〕绵 liánmián, 延伸 yánshēn: *The coast ~s northwards.* 海岸向北方延伸. **~er** 扫除的人或物 sǎochúde rén huò wù: *'street ~ers* 街道清扫工. **~ing** *adj* **(a)** 广〔廣〕泛的 guǎngfànde, 彻〔徹〕底的 chèdǐde: *~ing changes* 彻底的改变. *~ing reforms* 广泛的改革. **(b)** 总〔總〕括的 zǒngkuòde: *a ~ing statement* 概括的陈述.

sweet /swi:t/ *adj* [-er, -est] 1 甜的 tiánde, 甜味的 tiánwèide. ***have a ~ tooth*** 喜欢〔歡〕吃甜食 xǐhuan chī tiánshí. 2 新鲜而纯净的 xīnxiān ér chúnjìng de: *keep a room clean and ~* 保持房间整洁和空气清新. 3 香的 xiāngde, 芬芳的 fēnfāngde: *Don't the roses smell ~!* 多香的玫瑰花! 4 可爱〔愛〕的 kě'àide, 漂亮的 piàoliangde: *a ~ face* 讨人喜欢的脸庞. □ *n* [C] 1 糖果 tángguǒ. 2 甜品 tiánpǐn, 甜食 tiánshí. '~**bread** (供食用的小牛, 小羊)胰脏〔臟〕yízàng. '~**heart** [旧时用法]情人 qíngrén: *John and his ~heart* 约翰和他的情人. **~ly** *adv* **~ness** *n* [U]. **~en** *vt/i* (使)变〔變〕甜 biàn tián; (使)变香 biàn xiāng; (使)变得可爱 biànde kě'ài.

swell /swel/ *vt/i* [*pt* ~ed /sweld/; *pp* swollen /'swəulən/] 1 (使)膨胀〔脹〕péngzhàng, (使)增强 zēngqiáng, (使)壮〔壯〕大 zhuàngdà: *Wood often ~s when wet.* 木材浸湿后往往膨胀. 2 (使)隆起 lóngqǐ, (使)鼓起 gǔqǐ: *The wind ~ed the sails.* 风使船帆鼓起. □ *n* [亦用 *sing*] (海上的)浪涛〔濤〕làngtāo. **~ing** (尤指)身上的肿〔腫〕处〔處〕shēnshàngde zhǒngchù.

swel·ter /'sweltə(r)/ *vi* 酷热〔熱〕kùrè.

swept /swept/ *pt, pp* of sweep[2].

swerve /swɜ:v/ *vt/i* (使)突然转〔轉〕向 tūrán zhuǎnxiàng: *The car ~d to avoid the boy.* 汽车突然转向以躲开那孩子. □ *n* [C] 转向 zhuǎnxiàng.

swift[1] /swɪft/ *adj* [-er, -est] 快的 kuàide, 迅速的 xùnsùde: *a ~ reply* 敏捷的回答. **~ly** *adv* **~ness** *n* [U]

swift[2] /swɪft/ *n* [C] 雨燕 yǔyàn.

swill /swɪl/ *vt/i* 1 冲洗 chōngxǐ, 冲涮 chōngshuàn: *~ out a dirty tub* 洗涮脏盆子. 2 [非正式用语] 大口地喝 dà kǒu de hē, 痛饮 tòngyǐn: *The workmen were ~ing tea.* 工人们正在大口地喝茶. □ *n* 1 [C] 冲洗 chōngxǐ; 痛饮 tòngyǐn. 2 [U] 泔脚 gānjiǎo, 猪饲料 zhū sìliào.

swim /swɪm/ *vt/i* [*pt* swam /swæm/; *pp* swum /swʌm/] [-mm-] 1 游泳 yóuyǒng, 游水 yóushuǐ: *Fishes ~.* 鱼游水. 2 游过〔過〕yóuguò: *~ the English Channel* 游过英吉利海峡. 3 [与 *with* 连用]浸 jìn, 泡 pào; 覆盖〔蓋〕fùgài: *meat ~ming in gravy* 浸泡在浓汤中的肉. 4 摇晃 yáohuàng, 眼花 yǎnhuā, 眩晕〔暈〕xuànyūn: *His head swam.* 他头晕. □ *n* [C] 游泳 yóuyǒng, 游水 yóushuǐ: *have* (或 *go for*) *a ~* 去游泳. ***be in the ~*** 合乎时代潮流 gǎnshàng shídài cháoliú. **~mer** 游泳者 yóuyǒngzhě. '**~ming bath** (或 **pool**) 游泳池 yóuyǒngchí. '**~ming costume**, '**~-suit** (女用)游泳衣 yóuyǒngyī. '**~ming-trunks** *n pl* (男用)游泳裤〔褲〕yóuyǒngkù.

swindle /'swɪndl/ *vt/i* 诈取 zhàqǔ, 骗〔騙〕取 piànqǔ. □ *n* [C] 诈骗 zhàpiàn, 骗局 piànjú; 诈骗犯 zhàpiànfàn. **swin·dler** 骗子 piànzi.

swing /swɪŋ/ *vt/i* [*pt, pp* swung /swʌŋ/] 1 (使)摆〔擺〕动〔動〕bǎidòng, (使)摇摆 yáobǎi: *His arms swung as he walked.* 他走路时两臂摆动着. 2 (使)旋转〔轉〕xuánzhuǎn, (使)转向 zhuǎnxiàng: *~ round the corner* 在街角处拐弯. □ *n* [C] 1 摆动 bǎidòng, 摇摆 yáobǎi; 旋转 xuánzhuǎn; 转向 zhuǎnxiàng: *the ~ of the pendulum* 钟摆的摆动. 2 强的节〔節〕奏 qiángde jiézòu, 旋律 xuánlǜ. ***in full ~*** 活跃〔躍〕huóyuè; 正全力进〔進〕行中 zhèng quánlì jìnxíngzhōng. 3 秋〔鞦〕千〔韆〕qiūqiān. '**~-wing** *adj* (指飞机)变〔變〕翼的 biàn yì de.

swipe /swaɪp/ *vt* [俚语] 1 猛击〔擊〕měngjī. 2 [俚]偷 tōu. □ *n* [C] 猛击 měngjī: *take a ~ at the ball* 猛击球.

swirl /swɜːl/ *vt/i* (使)打旋 dǎxuán, (使)旋动〔動〕xuándòng: *dust ~ing about the streets* 街上打着旋的尘土. □ *n* [C] 旋动 xuándòng, 涡〔渦〕旋 wōxuán.

swish /swɪʃ/ *vt/i* 嗖地挥〔揮〕动〔動〕sōude huīdòng; (使)作窸窣声〔聲〕zuò xīsūshēng. □ *n* [C] 嗖嗖声 sōusōushēng, 窸窣声 xīsūshēng, 沙沙声 shāshāshēng.

switch /swɪtʃ/ *n* [C] **1** [铁路]转〔轉〕辙〔轍〕器 zhuǎnzhéqì, 道岔 dàochà. **2** (电路)开〔開〕关〔關〕kāiguān, 电〔電〕闸〔閘〕diànzhá: *a 'light-~* 电灯开关. **3** 转变〔變〕zhuǎnbiàn, 转换 zhuǎnhuàn. *a ~ from Liberal to Labour* 从自由党到工党的转变. □ *vt/i* **1** [与 *on* 连用]接通(电路) jiē tōng; [与 *off* 连用] 关断〔斷〕(电路) guān duàn: *~ the light on* 开灯. *~ the light off* 关灯. **2** (使)(火车等)转辙 zhuǎnzhé, 扳道岔 bān dàochà. **3** 转变 zhuǎnbiàn, 变换 biànhuàn: *~ to a Socialist Government* 转换成社会党政府.

swivel /'swɪvl/ *n* [C] (链的)转〔轉〕节〔節〕zhuǎnjié, 旋转接头〔頭〕xuánzhuǎn jiētóu. □ *vt/i* [-ll-, 美语亦作 -l-] (用转节等)旋转 xuánzhuǎn: *He ~led round in his chair.* 他在转椅中转过身来.

swob /swɒb/ *n, vt* [-bb-] = swab.

swol·len /'swəʊlən/ *pp* of swell: *a ~ ankle* 肿踝.

swoop /swuːp/ *vi* (飞下)猛扑〔撲〕měngpū, 猝然攻击〔擊〕cùrán gōngjī: *The eagle ~ed down on the rabbit.* 鹰猛扑兔子. □ *n* [C] 猛扑 měngpū, 突袭〔襲〕tūxí.

swop (亦作 **swap**) /swɒp/ *vt/i* [-pp-] [非正式用语]交换 jiāohuàn, 做交易 zuò jiāoyì: *~ foreign stamps* 交换外国邮票. *~ places with sb* 与〔與〕某人交换座位等 yǔ mǒurén jiāohuàn zuòwèi děng. □ *n* [C] 交换 jiāohuàn.

sword /sɔːd/ *n* [C] 剑〔劍〕jiàn; 刀 dāo. '**~fish** 旗鱼 qíyú.

swore, sworn ⇨ swear.

swum /swʌm/ *pp* of swim.

swung /swʌŋ/ *pt, pp* of swing.

syca·more /'sɪkəmɔː(r)/ *n* [C] [植物]埃及榕树〔樹〕Āijí yóngshù; [U] (埃及榕的)珍贵木材 zhēnguì mùcái.

syl·lable /'sɪləbl/ *n* [C] 音节〔節〕yīnjié: *'Arithmetic' has four ~s.* "Arithmetic" 一词有四个音节. **syl·labic** /sɪ'læbɪk/ *adj*

syl·la·bus /'sɪləbəs/ *n* [C] [*pl* ~es] 教学〔學〕大纲〔綱〕jiàoxué dàgāng, (学习)提纲 tígāng.

sym·bol /'sɪmbl/ *n* [C] 符号〔號〕fúhào, 记号 jìhào; 象征〔徵〕xiàngzhēng: *mathematical ~s* 数学符号. **~ic** /sɪm'bɒlɪk/ *adj* 符号的 fúhàode, 用作记号的 yòngzuò jìhào de; 象征性的 xiàngzhēngxìngde. **~ically** *adv* **~ize** /'siːmbəlaɪz/ *vt* 用符号表示 yòng fúhào biǎoshì; 作为...的象征 zuòwéi ... de xiàngzhēng.

sym·me·try /'sɪmətrɪ/ *n* [U] 对〔對〕称〔稱〕duìchèn; 匀称 yúnchen; 对称美 duìchèn měi: *mathematical ~* 数学对称. **sym·met·ric(al)** /sɪ'metrɪk(l)/ *adj*

sym·path·etic /ˌsɪmpə'θetɪk/ *adj* 同情的 tóngqíngde, 有同情心的 yǒu tóngqíngxīn de: *~ looks (words)* 表示同情的样子(语言). **~ally** *adv*

sym·path·ize /'sɪmpəθaɪz/ *vi* [与 *with* 连用]同情 tóngqíng, 表示同情 biǎoshì tóngqíng. **sym·path·izer** 同情者 tóngqíngzhě, 赞同者 zàntóngzhě, 支持者 zhīchízhě.

sym·pathy /'sɪmpəθɪ/ *n* [*pl* -ies] **1** [U] 同情 tóngqíng, 怜〔憐〕悯〔憫〕liánmǐn; 慰问〔問〕wèiwèn: *send her a letter of ~* 寄给她一封慰问信. **2** [*pl*] 同感 tónggǎn, 赞同 zàntóng, 同意 tóngyì: *My sympathies are with the miners in this dispute.* 在这场争执中我赞同矿工的主张.

sym·phony /'sɪmfənɪ/ *n* [C] [*pl* -ies] 交响〔響〕乐〔樂〕曲 jiāoxiǎngyuèqǔ. **sym·phonic** /sɪm'fɒnɪk/ *adj*

symp·tom /'sɪmptəm/ *n* [C] **1** 症〔癥〕状〔狀〕zhèngzhuàng, 症候 zhènghòu: *~s of measles* 出麻疹的症状. **2** 征兆 zhēngzhào: *~s of political discontent* 政治上不满的征兆. **~atic** /-'mætɪk/ *adj* 症状的 zhèngzhuàngde, 征兆的 zhēngzhàode.

syna·gogue /'sɪnəgɒg/ *n* [C] 犹〔猶〕太教堂 Yóutài jiàotáng.

syn·chron·ize /'sɪŋkrənaɪz/ *vt/i* (使)同时〔時〕发〔發〕生 tóngshí fāshēng, (使)同步 tóngbù: *~ clocks* 校正时钟.

syn·di·cate /'sɪndɪkət/ *n* [C] **1** 报〔報〕业〔業〕辛迪加 bàoyè xīndíjiā, 报业联〔聯〕合组织〔織〕bàoyè liánhé zǔzhī. **2** [经济]辛迪加 xīndíjiā, 企业联合组织 qǐyè liánhé zǔzhī. □ *vt* /'sɪndɪkeɪt/ 通过〔過〕报业辛迪加(在多家报纸上)发〔發〕表(文章等) tōngguò bàoyè xīndíjiā fābiǎo.

syn·drome /'sɪndrəʊm/ *n* [C] [医药]综合症候 zōnghé zhènghòu.
syn·onym /'sɪnənɪm/ *n* [C] 同义〔義〕词 tóngyìcí. **~ous** /sɪ'nɒnɪməs/ *adj*
syn·op·sis /sɪ'nɒpsɪs/ *n* [C] [*pl* -opses /-si:z/] (书, 剧本的)提要 tíyào.
syn·tax /'sɪntæks/ *n* [U] 造句(法) zàojù. **syn·tac·tic** /sɪn'tæktɪk/ *adj* of syntax.
syn·thesis /'sɪnθəsɪs/ *n* [C,U] [*pl* -theses /-si:z/] 综合 zōnghé, 合成(法) héchéng; 合成物 héchéngwù. **syn·thetic** /sɪn'θetɪk/ *adj*
syphon *n* = siphon.
syr·inge /sɪ'rɪndʒ/ *n* [C] 注射器 zhùshèqì: *a hypodermic* ~ 皮下注射器. □ *vt* (用注射器等)注射 zhùshè; 灌洗 guànxǐ.
syrup /'sɪrəp/ *n* [U] 糖浆 tángjiāng.
sys·tem /'sɪstəm/ *n* [C] **1** 系统 xìtǒng: *the nervous* ~ 神经系统. *a railway* ~ 铁路系统. **2** 体〔體〕制 tǐzhì, 制度 zhìdù, 体系 tǐxì: *a ~ of government* 政体. **3** [U] 秩序 zhìxù, 规律 guīlǜ, 组织〔織〕zǔzhī: *work with* ~ 有条不紊地工作. **~atic** /-'mætɪk/ *adj* 有系统的 yǒu xìtǒng de, 有秩序的 yǒu zhìxù de, 有规律的 yǒu guīlǜ de, 有组织的 yǒu zǔzhī de: *a ~atic analysis* 有系统的分析. **~ati·cally** *adv*

T t

T,t /ti:/ [*pl* T's, t's /ti:z/] 英语的第二十个字母 Yīngyǔde dì'èrshíge zìmǔ. **'T-shirt** 短袖圆领男汗衫 duǎn xiù yuán lǐng nán hànshān. **'T-square** 丁字尺 dīngzìchǐ.
t. =ton(s).
ta /tɑ:/ *int* [非正式用语]谢谢 xièxie.
tab /tæb/ *n* [C] (服装上装饰用的)垂片 chuípiàn. ***keep ~s on*** 记录〔錄〕jìlù; 注意 zhùyì; 监〔監〕视 jiānshì.
table /'teɪbl/ *n* [C] **1** 桌子 zhuōzi. **2** 一桌人 yìzhuōrén: *jokes that amused the whole* ~ 使满座欢悦的笑谈. **3** 项目表 xiàngmùbiǎo. **4** ***turn the ~s on sb*** 从〔從〕劣势〔勢〕转〔轉〕为〔爲〕优〔優〕势 cóng lièshì zhuǎn wéi yōushì. □ *vt* **1** (把…)列入议〔議〕程 lièrù yìchéng, 提出(讨论) tíchū: *~ a motion* 提议. **2** 列表 liè biǎo. **'~cloth** 桌布 zhuōbù. **'~mat** (热〔熱〕菜盘〔盤〕下的)垫〔墊〕子 diànzi. **'~spoon** 大汤〔湯〕匙 dà tāngchí. **'~spoon·ful** 一大汤匙的容量 yí dà tāngchí de róngliàng. **'~ tennis** 乒乓球 pīngpāngqiú. **'~ware** 餐具 cānjù.
tab·let /'tæblɪt/ *n* [C] **1** 碑 bēi; 书〔書〕板 shūbǎn. **2** 肥皂块〔塊〕féizào kuài. **3** 药片 yàopiàn: *two aspirin ~s* 两片阿司匹林.
ta·boo /tə'bu:/ *n* [C,U] (宗教迷信的)禁忌 jìnjì. □ *adj* 禁忌的 jìnjìde, 禁止的 jìnzhǐde: *Unkind gossip ought to be* ~. 刻薄的闲话应该避讳. □ *vt* 禁止 jìnzhǐ, 禁用 jìnyòng.
tabu·late /'tæbjʊleɪt/ *vt* 把…列成表 bǎ…liè chéng biǎo. **tabu'la·tion** *n* [U]
tacit /'tæsɪt/ *adj* 心照不宣的 xīnzhào bùxuān de: *~ consent* 默许. *~ agreement* 默契. **~ly** *adv*
tack /tæk/ *n* [C] **1** 平头〔頭〕钉 píngtóudīng. **2** 粗缝 cū fèng. **3** (帆船的)航向 hángxiàng. ***on the right (wrong) tack*** [喻]方针正确〔確〕(错误) fāngzhēn zhèngquè. □ *vt/i* **1** (用平头钉)钉住 dīngzhù; (用粗针脚)缝 féng. **2** 改变〔變〕航向 gǎibiàn hángxiàng.
tackle /'tækl/ *n* **1** [C,U] 滑车〔車〕huáchē, 复〔複〕滑车 fù huáchē. **2** [U] 用具 yòngjù, 装〔裝〕备〔備〕zhuāngbèi: *'fishing* ~ 渔具. **3** [C] [橄榄球]擒抱(对方带球球员) qínbào. □ *vt/i* **1** 处〔處〕理 chùlǐ, 解决 jiějué, 对〔對〕付 duìfù. ***~ sb about*** (或 ***over***) ***sth*** 对某人坦白地谈论〔論〕某事 duì mǒurén tǎnbáide tánlùn mǒushì. **2** 抓住 zhuāzhù: *~ an intruder* 抓住闯进来的人. **3** [橄榄球]擒抱 qínbào.
tact /tækt/ *n* [U] 老练〔練〕lǎoliàn, 机〔機〕智 jīzhì, 圆滑 yuánhuá: *show* (或 *have*) *great* ~ 显得十分老练. **~ful** /-fl/ *adj* 老练的 lǎoliànde, 机智的 jīzhìde, 圆滑的 yuánhuáde. **~fully** *adv* **~less** *adj* 不老练 bù lǎoliàn, 不机智 bù jīzhì, 不圆滑 bù yuánhuá. **~less·ly** *adv*
tac·tic /'tæktɪk/ *n* [C] **1** 策略 cèlüè. **2** [*pl*] 战〔戰〕术〔術〕zhànshù. **~al** /-kl/ *adj* of tactics: *a ~al error* 战术上的错误.
tac·ti·cian /tæk'tɪʃn/ *n* [C] 战〔戰〕术〔術〕家 zhànshùjiā.
tad·pole /'tædpəʊl/ *n* [C] 蝌蚪

kēdǒu.

tag /tæg/ *n* [C] **1** (鞋带,绳子等的)包头〔頭〕bāotóu. **2** 标〔標〕签〔簽〕biāoqiān. **3** [U] (儿童)捉人游戏〔戲〕zhuō rén yóuxì □ *vt/i* [-gg-] **1** 贴标签 tiē biāoqiān. **2** ~ ***along*** (或 ***behind, after***) 紧〔緊〕跟 jǐngēn, 尾随〔隨〕wěisuí.

tail /teɪl/ *n* [C] **1** 尾巴 wěiba: *Dogs wag their ~s.* 狗摆动尾巴. ***turn*** ~ 逃跑 táopǎo. **2** 尾状〔狀〕物 wěizhuàngwù, 尾部 wěibù: *the ~ of an aircraft* 飞机的尾部. **3** [*pl*] 钱〔錢〕币〔幣〕的背面 qiánbìde bèimiàn. ⇨ head[1](2). **4** [非正式用语] (盯梢的)特务〔務〕 tèwù, 暗探 àntàn. □ *vt/i* **1** ~ ***sb*** 跟踪(某人) gēnzōng. **2** ~ ***off*** (或 ***away***) **(a)** 变〔變〕少 biàn shǎo; 缩小 suō xiǎo. **(b)** (讲话等)不得要领地结束 bùdé yàolǐngde jiéshù. ˌ~-ˈ**end** 结尾 jiéwěi, 末端 mòduān. ˈ~-**light** (车的)尾灯〔燈〕wěidēng. ˈ~-**spin** *n* (飞机的)尾旋 wěixuán. ~**less** *adj*

tailor /ˈteɪlə(r)/ *n* [C] 裁缝 cáifeng, 成衣匠 chéngyījiàng. □ *vt* **1** 裁制〔製〕(衣服) cáizhì: *a well-~ed suit* 裁制得好的一套衣服. **2** 适〔適〕应〔應〕(特定目的) shìyìng. ˌ~-ˈ**made** *adj* **(a)** 定制的 dìngzhìde, 特制的 tèzhìde. **(b)** [喻]合适的 héshìde: *He is ~-made for the job.* 他干这个工作合适.

taint /teɪnt/ *n* [C,U] 污点〔點〕wūdiǎn, 感染的迹〔跡〕象 gǎnrǎnde jìxiàng: *a ~ of insanity in the family* 家族中的精神病迹象. □ *vt/i* (使)感染 gǎnrǎn, (使)腐败 fǔbài.

take[1] /teɪk/ *vt/i* [*pt* took /tʊk/; *pp* taken /ˈteɪkən/] **1** 拿 ná, 取 qǔ, 握 wò, 抱 bào: ~ *her hand* 握住她的手. *He took her in his arms.* 他拥抱她. **2** 占〔佔〕领 zhànlǐng; 获〔獲〕胜〔勝〕huòshèng: ~ *a town* 占领一个城镇. *He took the first prize.* 他获得头奖. ***be ~n ill*** 得病 dé bìng. **3** 拿走 názǒu, 偷去 tōuqù, (不告)自取 zì qǔ: *Who has ~n my bicycle?* 谁拿走了我的自行车? **4** 带〔帶〕走 dàizǒu, 带领 dàilǐng: ~ *letters to the post* 带信件去邮寄. ~ *a friend home* 把朋友带回家去. **5** 享有 xiǎngyǒu; 吃喝 chī hē: ~ *a holiday* 休假. ~ *a bath* 洗个澡. *T~ sugar in coffee.* 咖啡中加糖. **6** 接受 jiēshòu, 收取 shōuqǔ: *Will you ~ £450 for the car?* 你愿以 450 镑的代价出售此车吗? *T~ advice (orders).* 接受劝告(命令). ***be able to ~ it; can ~ it*** 能经〔經〕受得住(刑罚, 攻击等) néng jīngshòu dé zhù. **7** 订购〔購〕dìnggòu, 订阅〔閱〕dìngyuè: *Which newspapers do you ~?* 你订阅哪些报纸? **8** 记录〔録〕jìlù: ~ *notes* 记笔记. ~ *a photograph.* 拍摄照片. **9** 需要 xūyào; 花费 huāfèi: *The work took four hours.* 这工作花了四个小时. ~ ***one's time (over sth)*** 慢慢做(某事) mànmàn zuò. **10** 以为 yǐwéi, 看作 kànzuò, 当〔當〕作 dàngzuò: *Do you ~ me for a fool?* 你把我当傻瓜吗? **11** 找出 zhǎochū, 量出 liángchū: *The doctor took my temperature.* 医生量我的体温. **12** 处〔處〕理 chǔlǐ: ~ *it (things) easy* 从容, 不紧张. **13** 负起…责任 fùqǐ … zérèn, 承担〔擔〕chéngdān: ~ *a class* 负责一个班级. **14** 有效 yǒuxiào, 奏效 zòuxiào: *That smallpox injection did not ~.* 那种天花注射并不奏效. **15** 乘 chéng, 搭 dā: *I always ~ the bus to work.* 我经常乘公共汽车上班. ***be ~n aback*** ⇨ aback. ~ ***after sb*** 象某人 xiàng mǒurén. ~ ***sth apart*** 拆开〔開〕某物 chāikāi mǒuwù. ~ ***away*** **(a)** [数学]减去 jiǎnqù: *4 ~ away 2 is 2.* 4 减去 2 剩 2. **(b)** 带回家去吃(的饭菜) dài huí jiā qù chī. ˈ~-**away** *adj*: ~-*away meals* 带回家吃的饭菜. ~ ***sth (sb) away*** 移开 yíkāi, 拿走 názǒu, 使离〔離〕去 shǐ líqù. ~ ***sth back*** **(a)** 撤回自己的话 chèhuí zìjǐde huà. **(b)** (同意)收回 shōuhuí, 取回 qǔhuí: *Shops usually ~ back damaged goods.* 商店通常同意退回损坏的货物. ~ ***sb back (to)*** 使回忆〔憶〕shǐ huíyì. ~ ***sth down*** **(a)** 记录下来〔來〕jìlù xiàlái. **(b)** 拆卸 chāixiè, 拆除 chāichú: ~ *down a building* 拆除一座建筑物. ~ ***sth in*** **(a)** (在家)承接(活计) chéngjiē: *She earns money by taking in sewing.* 她在家靠承接缝纫活赚钱. **(b)** 改小(衣服等)尺寸 gǎi xiǎo chǐcùn; 卷〔捲〕起(风帆) juǎnqǐ: ~ *in a dress* 改小一件衣服. **(c)** 包含 bāohán, 包括 bāokuò. **(d)** 领会〔會〕lǐnghuì, 理解 lǐjiě. **(e)** 把…尽〔盡〕收眼底 bǎ…jìn shōu yǎndǐ: *She took in every detail of the scene.* 她把那片景色的每个部分都看到了. ~ ***sb in*** 欺骗〔騙〕qīpiàn: *Don't be ~n in by him.* 不要被他欺骗. ~ ***off*** (飞机)起飞〔飛〕qǐfēi. ˈ~-**off** *n* [C] ~ ***sth off*** **(a)** 除去 chúqù, 脱去 tuōqù: ~ *off one's hat* 脱帽. **(b)** 取消(火车班次等) qǔxiāo. **(c)** 减去 jiǎnqù: ~ *50p off the price* 减价 50 便士. ~ ***sb off*** **(a)** 带走 dàizǒu

He was ~n off to prison. 他被送进监狱. **(b)** 学[學]…的模样[様] xué…de móyàng: *Alice is clever at taking off the headmistress.* 阿莉斯善于模仿女校长以取乐. **~ *sth on*** **(a)** 接受(工作等) jiēshòu, 承担 chéngdān. **(b)** 现出(性质, 外表) xiànchū, 装[裝]出 zhuāngchū. **~ *sb on*** **(a)** 接受…作为[爲]对[對]手 jiēshòu…zuòwéi duìshǒu. **(b)** 雇用 gùyòng. **(c)** (指火车等)准许进[進]入 zhǔnxǔ jìnrù: *The bus stopped to ~ on some children.* 公共汽车停下来装载几个孩子. **~ *sth out*** **(a)** 去掉 qùdiào, 除去 chúqù: *have a tooth ~n out* 拔掉一个牙齿. **(b)** 取得 qǔdé, 领取 lǐngqǔ: *~ out an insurance policy* 领到保险单. **~ *sb out*** 带…出去 dài…chūqù: *~ the children out for a walk.* 带孩子们出去散步 **~ *it out of sb*** 使某人疲乏 shǐ mǒurén pífá. **~ *it out on sb*** 向某人出气[氣] xiàng mǒurén chūqì. **~ *sth over*** 接管(某事) jiēguǎn. **'~over** *n* [C] 接管. **~ *over (from sb)*** 接任(某人的)职[職]务[務] jiērèn zhíwù. **~ *to sth*** **(a)** 养[養]成…的习[習]惯 yǎngchéng … de xíguàn; 沉湎于[於] chénmiǎn yú: *~ to gardening when one retires* 退休后从事园艺. **(b)** (以…作为)逃避 táobì, 逃入 táorù: *~ to the woods to avoid capture* 逃入森林以免被捕. **~ *to sth (sb)*** 喜欢[歡] xǐhuan, 亲[親]近 qīnjìn. **~ *sth up*** **(a)** 拿起 náqǐ, 举[舉]起 jǔqǐ. **(b)** 对…有兴[興]趣 duì…yǒu xìngqǔ, 从[從]事: *~ up photography* 从事摄影. **(c)** 继[繼]续[續] jìxù. **(d)** 占去(时间, 地位) zhànqù: *This table ~s up too much space.* 这张桌子占去太多空间. **(e)** 接受 jiēshòu, 接纳 jiēnà. **~ *sth up with sb*** 与…交往 yǔ…jiāowǎng. **~ *sth upon oneself*** 承担 chéngdān, 担任 dānrèn.

take² /teɪk/ *n* **1** [C] 收入 shōurù. **2** [电影]镜头[頭] jìngtóu.

tak·ing /'teɪkɪŋ/ *adj* 吸引人的 xīyǐn rén de. □ *n* [*pl*] 收入 shōurù, 进[進]款 jìnkuǎn.

tal·cum powder /'tælkəm paʊdə(r)/ *n* [C] 爽身粉 shuǎngshēnfěn.

tale /teɪl/ *n* [C] **1** 故事 gùshi: *~s of adventure.* 冒险故事. **2** 报[報]告 bàogào; 记述 jìshù. ***tell ~s*** 搬弄是非 bānnòng shìfēi, 揭人隐[隱]私 jiē rén yǐnsī. **3** 谣言 yáoyán, 流言蜚语 liúyán-fēiyǔ.

tal·ent /'tælənt/ *n* [C,U] 天才 tiāncái, 才能 cáinéng: *have a ~ for music* 有音乐天才. **~ed** *adj* 有才能的 yǒu cáinéng de, 有才干[幹]的 yǒu cáigàn de.

talk¹ /tɔːk/ *n* **1** [C, U] 交谈 jiāotán, 谈话 tánhuà. ⇨ small talk. **2** [C] (非正式的)演讲[講] yǎnjiǎng. **3** 闲[閑]聊 xiánliáo, 闲谈 xiántán.

talk² /tɔːk/ *vt/i* **1** 说话 shuōhuà, 谈话 tánhuà: *He was ~ing to a friend.* 他正在和一个朋友谈话. ***be ~ed about*** 成为[爲]话题 chéngwéi huàtí. **~ *down to sb*** 高人一等地对[對]某人讲话 gāo rén yìděng de duì mǒurén jiǎnghuà. **~ *sth over*** 商量 shāngliàng, 讨论[論]tǎolùn. **~ *round sth*** 兜圈子谈(问题) dōu quānzi tán. **2** 有讲话能力 yǒu jiǎnghuà nénglì: *Can the baby ~ yet?* 这婴孩能讲话了吗? **3** 能使用(一种语言) néng shǐyòng: *~ English (Spanish)* 能讲英语(西班牙语). **4** 讨论 tǎolùn, 谈论 tánlùn: *We ~ed music all evening.* 我们整个晚上在谈论音乐. **5 ~ *sb into (out of) doing sth*** 说服某人做(不做)某事 shuōfú mǒurén zuò mǒushì. **6** 闲聊 xiánliáo, 闲谈 xiántán. **7** 招供 zhāogòng: *Has the prisoner ~ed yet?* 犯人已招供了吗? **'~ing point** 讨论的题目 tǎolùnde tímù. **'~ing-to** 责备[備] zébèi, 斥责 chìzé. **'~a·tive** *adj* 健谈的 jiàntánde, 多嘴的 duōzuǐde.

tall /tɔːl/ *adj* [-er, -est] **1** (身材)高的 gāode: *She is ~er than her sister.* 她比她的妹妹高些. **2** 有某种高度的 yǒu mǒuzhǒng gāodù de: *Tom is six foot ~.* 汤姆身高六英尺. **3 *a ~ order*** 难[難]完成的任务[務] nán wánchéng de rènwù, 苛求 kēqiú. ***a ~ story*** 难以相信的故事 nán yǐ xiāngxìn de gùshi.

tally /'tælɪ/ *vi* [*pt, pp* -ied] 符合 fúhé, 吻合 wěnhé: *The two lists do not ~.* 两张单子不相符.

talon /'tælən/ *n* [C] (猛禽的)爪 zhuǎ.

tam·bour·ine /ˌtæmbə'riːn/ *n* [C] 铃鼓 línggǔ.

tame /teɪm/ *adj* [-er, -est] **1** 驯[馴]服了的 xúnfúlede: *a ~ monkey* 驯服的猴子. **2** (指人)顺从[從]的 shùncóngde, 听[聽]话的 tīnghuàde: *Her husband is a ~ little man.* 她的丈夫是一个温顺的小个子. **3** 沉闷[悶]的 chénmènde, 平淡的 píngdànde, 乏味的 fáwèide: *The film has a ~ ending.* 那电影的结局平淡无味. □ *vt* 驯服 xúnfú, 使顺

从 shǐ shùncóng: ～ *a lion* 驯狮. **tamer** 驯〔馴〕兽〔獸〕者 xúnshòuzhě: *a 'lion-～r* 驯狮者. **～ly** *adv* **～ness** *n* [U]

tam·per /'tæmpə(r)/ *vi* 干预 gānyù; 乱〔亂〕弄 luàn nòng: ～ *with the lock* 撬锁.

tan /tæn/ *n* [C], *adj* 棕黄色 zōnghuángsè; 晒〔曬〕黑的皮色 shàihēide písè: ～ *leather shoes* 棕黄色皮鞋. *get a good* ～ 晒得很黑. □ *vt/i* [-nn-] **1** 鞣(革) róu, 硝(皮) xiāo. ～ *sb's hide* [俚语] 狠狠鞭打某人 hěnhěn biāndǎ mǒurén. **2** (皮肤)晒成棕褐色 shài chéng zōnghèsè: *Some people* ～ *quickly.* 有些人容易晒黑. **～ner** 制〔製〕革工人 zhì gé gōngrén. **～nery** /'tænərɪ/ 制革厂〔廠〕zhìgéchǎng.

tan·dem /'tændəm/ *n* [C] 前后〔後〕双〔雙〕座自行车〔車〕qián hòu shuāngzuò zìxíngchē. □ *adv* 一前一后地 yìqián yíhòu de: *ride* ～ 一前一后地骑车.

tang /tæŋ/ *n* [C] 强烈的气〔氣〕味 qiángliède qìwèi.

tan·gent /'tændʒənt/ *n* [C] 切线〔綫〕qiēxiàn; [数学]正切 zhèngqiē. *go* (或 *fly*) *off at a* ～ [喻]思想行动〔動〕等突然改变〔變〕sīxiǎng xíngdòng děng tūrán gǎibiàn.

tan·ger·ine /ˌtændʒə'ri:n/ *n* [C]红橘 hóngjú, 小蜜橘 xiǎo mìjú.

tan·gible /'tændʒəbl/ *adj* **1** 可触〔觸〕知的 kě chùzhīde. **2** 明确〔確〕的 míngquède, 确实〔實〕的 quèshíde: ～ *proof* 明确的证据. **tangibly** /-əblɪ/ *adv*

tangle /'tæŋgl/ *n* [C] **1** (线, 头发等的)缠〔纏〕结 chánjié. **2** 混乱〔亂〕hùnluàn: *The traffic was in a* ～. 交通混乱. □ *vt/i* **1** (使)缠结 chánjié, (使)混乱 hùnluàn: ～*d hair* 乱蓬蓬的头发. **2** [非正式用语] (与人)争吵 zhēngchǎo: *Don't* ～ *with Peter.* 不要和彼得争吵.

tango /'tæŋgəʊ/ *n* [C] [*pl* ～s] 探戈舞(曲) tàngēwǔ.

tank /tæŋk/ *n* [C] **1** (盛液体或气体的)大容器 dà róngqì. **2** 坦克 tǎnkè. **～er** (车、船的)液体〔體〕舱〔艙〕yètǐcāng.

tank·ard /'tæŋkəd/ *n* [C] 大酒杯 dà jiǔbēi.

tan·ner, tan·nery ⇨ tan.

tan·ta·lize /'tæntəlaɪz/ *vt* (引起兴趣而不给予满足的)逗弄 dòunòng, 使干〔乾〕着急 shǐ gānzháojí.

tan·trum /'tæntrəm/ *n* [C] [*pl* ～s] 发〔發〕脾气〔氣〕fā píqì.

tap[1] /tæp/ *n* (液体或气体管道的)龙〔龍〕头〔頭〕lóngtóu. *on* ～ [喻] 现成的 xiànchéngde, 就在手头的 jiù zài shǒutóu de. □ *vt* [-pp-] **1** 使(从龙头中)流出 shǐ liúchū. **2** 切开〔開〕树〔樹〕皮以汲取(树液) qiēkāi shùpí yǐ jíqǔ. **3** 开发〔發〕kāifā, 获〔獲〕取 huòqǔ: ～ *a country's resources* 开发国家资源. ～ *a telephone* 窃〔竊〕听〔聽〕电〔電〕话 qiètīng diànhuà.

tap[2] /tæp/ *n* [C] **1** 轻〔輕〕打 qīng dǎ, 轻拍 qīng pāi; 轻敲声〔聲〕qīng qiāo shēng. □ *vt/i* [-pp-] 轻打 qīng dǎ, 轻拍 qīng pāi, 轻敲 qīng qiāo: ～ *a man on the shoulder* 拍拍一个人的肩膀. **'～-dancing** 踢踏舞 tītàwǔ.

tape /teɪp/ *n* [C,U] **1** 狭〔狹〕带〔帶〕xiá dài, 带尺 dàichǐ; 磁带 cídài. ⇨ magnetic tape, red tape. **2** (赛跑)终点〔點〕线〔綫〕zhōngdiǎnxiàn. □ *vt* **1** 用带子捆扎〔紮〕yòng dàizi kǔnzhá. **2** 用磁带录〔錄〕音 yòng cídài lùyīn. **3** *have sth (sb)* ～*d* [非正式用语] 了解某事物 liáojiě mǒu shìwù. **'～-measure** 卷〔捲〕尺 juǎnchǐ, 带尺 dàichǐ. **'～ recorder** 磁带录音机 cídài lùyīnjī.

taper[1] /'teɪpə(r)/ *n* [C] 细蜡〔蠟〕烛〔燭〕xì làzhú.

taper[2] /'teɪpə(r)/ *vt/i* 逐渐〔漸〕变〔變〕细 zhújiàn biàn xì, 渐尖 jiàn jiān.

tap·es·try /'tæpɪstrɪ/ *n* [C,U] [*pl* -ies] 花毯 huā tǎn, 挂〔掛〕毯 guàtǎn.

tapi·oca /ˌtæpɪ'əʊkə/ *n* [U] (食用)木薯淀〔澱〕粉 mùshǔ diànfěn.

tar /tɑ:(r)/ *n* [U] 煤渣méitǎ, 焦油 jiāoyóu, 沥〔瀝〕青 lìqīng.□ *vt* [-rr-] 涂〔塗〕焦油 tú jiāoyóu, 铺沥青 pū lìqīng. ˌ*～red with the* ˌ*same* '*brush* 是一路货色 shì yílù huòsè, 是一丘之貉 shì yìqiū zhī hé. **'～mac** (铺路用)碎石沥青混合料 suìshí lìqīng hùnhé liào.

ta·ran·tula /tə'ræntjʊlə/ *n* [C] (产于南欧的)一种毒蜘蛛 yìzhǒng dú zhīzhū.

tar·get /'tɑ:gɪt/ *n* **1** 靶 bǎ, 标〔標〕的 biāodì. **2** (被批评的)对〔對〕象 duìxiàng. **3** (生产等的)指标 zhǐbiāo.

tar·iff /'tærɪf/ *n* [C] **1** (旅馆等的)价〔價〕目表 jiàmùbiǎo. **2** 关〔關〕税率 guānshuìlǜ.

tar·mac /'tɑ:mæk/ *n* ⇨ tar.

tarn /tɑ:n/ *n* [C] 山中小湖 shān zhōng xiǎo hú.

tar·nish /'tɑ:nɪʃ/ *vt/i* **1** (尤指金属

表面)(使)失去光泽[澤] shīqù guāngzé: *Brass ~es easily.* 铜器容易失去光泽. **2**[喻]玷污 diànwū; 降低 jiàngdī: *His reputation is ~ed.* 他的名誉受到玷污. □ *n* [U] 晦暗 huì'àn, 无[無]光泽 wú guāngzé.

tar·pau·lin /tɑ:'pɔ:lɪn/ *n* [C, U] 防水帆布 fáng shuǐ fānbù, 油布 yóubù.

tart[1] /tɑ:t/ *adj* **1** 酸的 suānde; 辛辣的 xīnlàde: *a ~ flavour* 酸味. **2**[喻]刻薄的 kèbóde, 尖刻的 jiānkède: *a ~ reply* 尖刻的回答. **~ly** *adv* **~ness** *n* [U]

tart[2] /tɑ:t/ *n* [C] 果馅[餡]饼 guǒxiànr bǐng.

tart[3] /tɑ:t/ *n* [C] [俚语](举止)轻[輕]佻的女子 qīngtiāode nǚzǐ. □ *vt* **~ sth (sb) up** [非正式用语]把…装[裝]饰起来[來] bǎ…zhuāngshì qǐlái.

tar·tan /'tɑ:tn/ *n* [U] 苏[蘇]格兰[蘭]格子呢 Sūgélán gézìní. [C] 格子图[圖]案 gèzi tú'àn.

tar·tar /'tɑ:tə(r)/ *n* [U] **1** 牙垢 yágòu. **2**[化学]酒石 jiǔshí.

task /tɑ:sk/ *n* [C] 任务[務] rènwù, 工作 gōngzuò, 功课 gōngkè. ***take sb to ~ (about, for sth)*** (为某事)责备[備]某人 zébèi mǒurén, **'~-force** 特遣部队[隊] tèqiǎn bùduì. **'~-master (-mistress)** 工头[頭] gōngtóu, 监[監]工 jiāngōng.

tas·sel /'tæsl/ *n* [C] (旗, 帽等上的)缨 yīng, 流苏[蘇] liúsū.

taste[1] /teɪst/ *n* **1** [U] 味觉[覺] wèijué: *sweet (sour) to the ~* 尝起来是甜(酸)的. **2** [C, U] 味道 wèidào, 滋味 zīwèi: *Sugar has a sweet ~.* 糖有甜味. **3** 一口 yìkǒu, 一点[點]儿[兒] yìdiǎnr. **4** [C,U] 鉴[鑒]赏力 jiànshǎnglì, 判断[斷]力 pànduànlì: *good ~ in music (clothes)* 对音乐(衣着)有很好的鉴赏力. **~ful** *adj* 有鉴赏力的 yǒu jiànshǎnglì de, 有判断力的 yǒu pànduànlì de. **~fully** *adv* **~less** *adj* **(a)** (指食物)无[無]味的 wúwèide. **(b)** 无鉴赏力的 wú jiànshǎnglì de, 无判断力的 wú pànduànlì de. **~less·ly** *adv* **tasty** *adj* [-ier, -iest] 美味的 měiwèide, 可口的 kěkǒude.

taste[2] /teɪst/ *vt/i* **1** 品尝[嘗] pǐncháng, 辨(味) biàn: *Can you ~ anything strange in this soup?* 你吃得出这汤里有什么特别的东西吗? **2** 有…味道 yǒu…wèidào: *~ sour (bitter)* 有酸(苦)味. **3** 试…的味道 shì…de wèidào: *She ~d the soup.* 她试试汤的味道. **4** 体[體]验[驗] tǐyàn, 感受 gǎnshòu: *~ happiness (freedom)* 感到幸福(自由).

tat·ters /'tætəz/ *n pl* (撕下的)破布条[條] pò bùtiáo; 碎纸片 suì zhǐpiàn.

tat·too[1] /tə'tu:/ *n* [C] [*pl* ~s] **1** (军队)归[歸]营[營]号[號] guīyínghào. **2** [C]连[連]续[續]的鼓声[聲] liánxùde gǔshēng. **3** [C] (军队)表演操 biǎoyǎncāo.

tat·too[2] /tə'tu:/ *vt* (皮肤上)刺花纹 cì huāwén. □ *n* [C][*pl* ~s] 文身 wénshēn.

taught /tɔ:t/ *pt, pp* of teach.

taunt /tɔ:nt/ *n* [C] 辱骂[罵] rǔmà, 侮辱 wǔrǔ. □ *vt* 辱骂 rǔmà, 侮辱 wǔrǔ.

taut /tɔ:t/ *adj* (绳索等)拉紧[緊]的 lā jǐn de; (神经)紧张[張]的 jǐnzhāngde: *pull a rope ~* 拉紧绳索. **~ly** *adv* **~ness** *n* [U]

taut·ol·ogy /tɔ:'tɒlədʒɪ/ *n* [C,U] [*pl* -ies] 同义[義]反复[復] tóngyì fǎnfù, 赘述 zhuìshù. **tauto·logi·cal** /-'lɒdʒɪkl/ *adj*

tav·ern /'tævən/ *n* [C] [旧用法]酒店 jiǔdiàn; 小旅馆 xiǎo lǚguǎn.

tawny /'tɔ:nɪ/ *adj* 黄褐色的 huánghèsède, 茶色的 chásède.

tax /tæks/ *n* **1** [C,U] 税 shuì, 税收 shuìshōu: *income ~* 所得税. **2** *a ~ on* 负担[擔] fùdān, 压[壓]力 yālì: *a ~ on one's patience* 对耐心的一种压力. □ *vt* **1** 对[對]…征税 duì … zhēng shuì: *~ rich and poor alike* 对富人和穷人同样地征税. **2** 使负重担 shǐ fù zhòng dàn, 使受压力 shǐ shòu yālì: *~ my patience* 考验我的耐心. ,**~-'free** *adj* 免税的 miǎnshuìde. ,**~-collector** 税务[務]员 shuìwùyuán. **'~-payer** 纳税人 nàshuìrén. **~-able** /-əbl/ *adj* 可征税的 kě zhēngshuì de, 应[應]纳税的 yīng nàshuì de: *~able income* 应课税的收入. **~ation** /tæk'seɪʃən/ *n* [U] 税制 shuìzhì; 税项 shuìxiàng.

taxi /'tæksɪ/ *n* [C] [*pl* ~s] 出租汽车[車] chūzūqìchē, 计程车 jìchéngchē. □ *vt/i* (指飞机)(使)滑行 huáxíng. **'~-cab** (缩作 *cab*) = taxi. **'~ rank** 出租汽车停车处[處] chūzū qìchē tíngchēchù.

T.B. = tuberculosis.

tea /ti:/ *n* **1** [U] 茶 chá, 茶叶[葉] cháyè. ***not my cup of ~*** 不合我口味的东[東]西 bù hé wǒ kǒuwèi de dōngxi. **2** [C, U] (午后)茶点[點] chádiǎn. ⇨ high tea. **'~ bag** 茶叶袋 cháyèdài. **'~-caddy** 茶叶罐 cháyèguàn. **'~-chest** (出口用)茶叶箱 cháyexiāng.

'~**cloth** 茶具布 chájùbù. '~**cup** 茶杯 chábēi. *a ˌstorm in a* '~*cup* 小事引起的风〔風〕波 xiǎo shì yǐnqǐde fēngbō. '~**pot** 茶壶〔壺〕 cháhú. '~**-service** (或 **-set**) 一套茶具 yītào chájù. '~**spoon** 茶匙 cháchí. '~**spoon·ful** 一茶匙容量 yìcháchí róngliàng. '~**-strainer** 滤〔濾〕茶器 lǜcháqì. '~**-time** (下午)吃茶点时〔時〕间〔間〕 chī chádiǎn shíjiān.

teach /tiːtʃ/ *vt/i* [*pt, pp* taught /tɔːt/] 教学〔學〕 jiàoxué, 讲〔講〕授 jiǎngshòu: ~ *French* 教法文. ~ *history* 讲授历史. ~ *a child* (*how*) *to swim* 教孩子游泳. ~**er** 教员 jiàoyuán, 教师〔師〕 jiàoshī. ~**ing** **(a)** [U] 教学 jiàoxué, 讲授 jiǎngshòu: *earn a living by* ~*ing* 以教书为生. **(b)** [*pl*] 教义〔義〕 jiàoyì, 教导〔導〕 jiàodǎo: *the* ~*ings of Jesus* 耶稣的教导 '~**ing aid** *n* 教具 jiàojù.

teak /tiːk/ *n* [C] 柚木树〔樹〕 yòumù shù. [U] 柚木 yòumù.

team /tiːm/ *n* [C] **1** (拉车的)一组牛,马〔馬〕等 yìzǔ niú, mǎ děng. **2** (一)队〔隊〕 duì, (一)组 zǔ: *a football* ~ 足球队. *a* ~ *of surgeons* 军医小组. □ *vi* ~ *up* (*with*) [非正式用语]与〔與〕…合作 yǔ … hézuò. '~**-work** 配合 pèihé, 合作 hézuò. '~**-mate** 队员 duìyuán, 组员 zǔyuán. ˌ~ '**spirit** 协〔協〕作精神 xiézuò jīngshén.

tear[1] /tɪə(r)/ *n* [C] 眼泪〔淚〕 yǎnlèi: *burst into* ~*s* 哭起来了. '~**-drop** 泪珠 lèizhū. '~**-gas** 催泪性毒气〔氣〕 cuīlèixìng dúqì. ~**ful** *adj* 哭泣的 kūqìde, 含泪的 hánlèide: *a* ~*ful face* 眼泪纵横的脸. ~**fully** *adv*

tear[2] /teə(r)/ *vt/i* [*pt* tore /tɔː(r)/; *pp* torn /tɔːn/] **1** (把…)撕开〔開〕 sīkāi, 撕裂 sīliè; 戳破 chuōpò: ~ *a sheet of paper* 撕破一张纸. ~ *sth up* 撕碎某物 sīsuì mǒuwù. **2** 拉掉 lādiào, 撕去 sīqù: ~ *a page out of a book* 撕下一页书. **3** 破坏〔壞〕…的安宁〔寧〕 pòhuài … de ānníng, 扰〔擾〕乱〔亂〕 rǎoluàn: *a country torn by civil war* 因内战而动乱不安的国家. *torn between* (在两种选择之间)不能决择〔擇〕 bùnéng juézé. **4** (被)撕破 sīpò, (易)撕碎 sīsuì: *Paper* ~*s easily.* 纸容易被撕破. **5** 飞〔飛〕跑 fēipǎo, 狂奔 kuángbēn, 冲〔衝〕 chōng: *He tore home.* 他飞奔回家. □ *n* [C] 撕破处〔處〕 sīpòchù, 裂缝 lièfèng. '~**away** *n* [C] 行动〔動〕莽撞的青年 xíngdòng mǎngzhuàng de qīngnián.

tease /tiːz/ *vt* **1** 取笑 qǔxiào, 嘲笑 cháoxiào: *She* ~*d him about his beard.* 她取笑他的胡子. **2** 戏〔戲〕弄 xìnòng, 惹恼〔惱〕 rě nǎo: *Molly was teasing the cat.* 莫莉在逗弄猫. **3** 梳理 shūlǐ, 使起毛 shǐ qǐ máo: ~ *flax* 梳理亚麻. □ *n* [C] 戏弄别人的人 xìnòng biérén de rén. **teaser** 爱戏弄别人的人 ài xìnòng biérén de rén.

teat /tiːt/ *n* [C] 乳头〔頭〕 rǔtóu, 奶头 nǎitóu.

Tech. = Technical (College).

tech·ni·cal /ˈteknɪkl/ *adj* **1** 技术〔術〕的 jìshùde, 工艺〔藝〕的 gōngyìde. **2** 有关〔關〕专〔專〕门〔門〕技术的 yǒuguān zhuānmén jìshù de: *a* '~ *college* 高等技术专科学校. ~**ly** /-klɪ/ *adv*

tech·ni·cal·ity /ˌteknɪˈkælətɪ/ *n* [C] [*pl* -ies] 术语 shùyǔ; 专业〔業〕事项 zhuānyè shìxiàng: *legal technicalities* 法律事项.

tech·ni·cian /tekˈnɪʃn/ *n* [C] 技术人员 jìshù rényuán, 技师〔師〕 jìshī.

tech·nique /tekˈniːk/ *n* **1** [U] (工艺,音乐等方面的)技术〔術〕 jìshù, 技巧 jìqiǎo. **2** [C] 技能 jìnéng, 行家手法 hángjiā shǒufǎ.

tech·noc·racy /tekˈnɒkrəsɪ/ *n* [C, U] [*pl* -cies] 专〔專〕家政治 zhuānjiā zhèngzhì. '**tech·no·crat** /ˈteknəkræt/ *n* [C] 专家治国〔國〕论〔論〕者 zhuānjiā zhìguólùn zhě.

tech·nol·ogy /tekˈnɒlədʒɪ/ *n* [U] 工艺〔藝〕学〔學〕 gōngyìxué. **tech·no·logi·cal** /ˌteknəˈlɒdʒɪkl/ *adj* **tech'nol·ogist** *n* [C]

tedi·ous /ˈtiːdɪəs/ *adj* 沉闷〔悶〕的 chénmènde, 乏味的 fáwèide, 厌〔厭〕烦的 yànfánde: *a* ~ *lecture* 冗长乏味的演说. ~ *work* 令人厌烦的工作. ~**ly** *adv*

tee /tiː/ *n* [C] [高尔夫球]发〔發〕球处〔處〕 fāqiúchù, 球座 qiúzuò. □ *vt/i* **1** ~ **(up)** 置球在球座上 zhì qiú zài qiúzuòshàng. **2** ~ *off* (从球座)发球 fāqiú.

teem[1] /tiːm/ *vi* **1** 大量出现 dàliàng chūxiàn, 涌〔湧〕现 yǒngxiàn: *Fish* ~ *in this river.* 这条河中有很多鱼. **2** ~ *with* 富于〔於〕 fù yú, 充满 chōngmǎn: ~*ing with ideas* 有很多主意.

teem[2] /tiːm/ *vi* (雨水)倾盆而下 qīngpén ér xià.

teen·age /ˈtiːneɪdʒ/ *adj* (十几岁)青少年的 qīngshàoniánde: ~ *fashion* 青年式.

teen·ager /ˈtiːneɪdʒə(r)/ *n* [C] (十

三至十九岁的)男女青少年 nán nǚ qīngshàonián.

teens /tiːnz/ *n pl* 十三至十九岁之间 shísān zhì shíjiǔ suì zhī jiān: *girls in their* ~ 少女们.

tee-shirt /'tiː ʃɜːt/ *n* [C] = T-shirt.

tee·ter /'tiːtə(r)/ *vi* 摇摇欲坠〔墜〕yáoyáo yù zhuì; 步履不稳〔穩〕地行走 bùlǚ bùwěn de xíngzǒu.

teeth /tiːθ/ *pl* of tooth.

teethe /tiːð/ *vi* 出乳牙 chū rǔyá. **'teething troubles** [喻]事情开〔開〕始时〔時〕遇到的麻烦 shìqing kāishǐ shí yùdào de máfan, 头〔頭〕难〔難〕tóunán.

tee·to·tal /tiː'təʊtl/ *adj* 戒酒的 jiè jiǔ de, 反对〔對〕饮酒的 fǎnduì yǐn jiǔ de. ~**ler** *n* [C]

tel. = telephone.

tele·com·muni·ca·tions /ˌtelɪkəˌmjuːnɪ'keɪʃnz/ *n pl* 电〔電〕信 diànxìn; 电信学〔學〕diànxìnxué.

tele·gram /'telɪɡræm/ *n* [C] 电〔電〕报〔報〕diànbào, 电信 diànxìn.

tele·graph /'telɪɡrɑːf/ *n* [C] 电〔電〕报〔報〕diànbào; 电报机〔機〕diànbàojī. □ *vt/i* 打电报 dǎ diànbào. ~**ic** /ˌtelɪ'ɡræfɪk/ *adj* 电报的 diànbàode, 由电报发〔發〕送的 yóu diànbào fāsòng de.

tel·epa·thy /tɪ'lepəθɪ/ *n* [U] 心灵〔靈〕感应〔應〕xīnlíng gǎnyìng. **tele·pathic** /ˌtelɪ'pæθɪk/ *adj*

tele·phone /'telɪfəʊn/ *n* (缩作 *phone*) [C,U] 电〔電〕话 diànhuà; 电话机〔機〕diànhuàjī: *answer the* ~ 接电话. □ *vt/i* 打电话 dǎ diànhuà, 通电话 tōng diànhuà. **'~ booth** (亦作 *'call-box*) (公用)电话间〔間〕diànhuàjiān. **'~ directory** ([非正式用语] = *'phone book*) 电话簿 diànhuàbù. **'~ exchange** 电话局 diànhuàjú, 电话交换机 diànhuà jiāohuànjī.

tel·ephon·ist /tɪ'lefənɪst/ *n* [C] 电话接线〔綫〕员 diànhuà jiēxiànyuán.

tele·prin·ter /'telɪprɪntə(r)/ *n* [C] 电〔電〕传〔傳〕打字电报〔報〕机〔機〕diàn chuán dǎzì diànbàojī.

tele·scope /'telɪskəʊp/ *n* [C] 望远〔遠〕镜 wàngyuǎnjìng. □ *vt/i* (使)嵌进〔進〕qiàn jìn, (使)套入 tào rù: *When the trains collided, the first two cars were* ~*d*. 火车相撞时, 前二节车箱撞挤在一起了. **tele·scopic** /ˌtelɪ'skɒpɪk/ *adj*

tele·vi·sion /'telɪvɪʒn/ *n* (缩作 TV) **1** [U] 电〔電〕视 diànshì. **2** [C] (亦作 *'~ set*) 电视机〔機〕diànshìjī. **tele·vise** /'telɪvaɪz/ *vt* 电视播送 diànshì bōsòng.

telex /'teleks/ *n* **1** [U] 电〔電〕报〔報〕用户直通电路 diànbào yònghù zhítōng diànlù. **2** [C] 用户电报 yònghù diànbào.

tell /tel/ *vt/i* [*pt, pp* told /təʊld/] **1** 告诉 gàosù, 告知 gàozhī: *I told him my name*. 我把我的名字告诉他. *I told you so* 如我所言 rú wǒ suǒyán. **2** 讲〔講〕述 jiǎngshù, 说 shuō: ~ *a lie* 说谎. ~ *a story* 讲故事. *tell tales* ⇨ tale(2). **3** 吩咐 fēnfu, 命令 mìnglìng: *T*~ *him to wait*. 叫他等着. **4** 辨别 biànbié, 分辨 fēnbiàn: *Can you* ~ *Tom from his twin brother?* 你能分得出汤姆和他的孪生兄弟吗? **5** 知道 zhīdào, 断〔斷〕定 duàndìng: *How do you* ~ *which key to use?* 你怎么知道用哪一个钥匙? ~ *the time* (看钟表)说出时〔時〕刻 shuōchū shíkè: *Can you* ~ *me what time it is?* 你能告诉我现在是什么时候吗? *there is no* ~*ing* 难〔難〕以预料 nán yǐ yùliào, 不可能知道 bùkěnéng zhīdào. **6** ~ *sb off* [非正式用语]斥责某人 chìzé mǒurén. **7** 产〔產〕生效果 chǎnshēng xiàoguǒ, 发〔發〕生影响〔響〕fāshēng yǐngxiǎng: *All this hard work is* ~*ing on him*. 所有这些艰难的工作都在影响着他的健康. **8** [非正式用语]说坏〔壞〕话 shuō huàihuà: *John told on his sister*. 约翰说他姐姐(妹妹)的坏话. **9** 泄露(秘密) xièlù: *You promised not to* ~. 你答应不泄露秘密. ~**er (a)** (银行)出纳员 chūnàyuán. **(b)** 点〔點〕票员 diǎnpiàoyuán. ~**ing** *adj* 有效的 yǒuxiàode, 有力的 yǒulìde: *a* ~*ing argument* (*blow*) 有力的论证(一击).

tell·tale /'telteɪl/ *n* [C] 搬弄是非者 bānnòng shìfēi zhě, 谈论〔論〕别人私事者 tánlùn biérén sīshì zhě. □ *adj* 暴露内情的 bàolù nèiqíng de: *a* ~ *blush* 暴露隐情的脸红.

telly /'telɪ/ *n* [非正式用语] (television 的缩写) 电〔電〕视 diànshì; 电视机〔機〕diànshìjī.

temp. = **1** temperature. **2** temporary (secretary).

tem·per[1] /'tempə(r)/ *n* [C] **1** 心情 xīnqíng, 情绪 qíngxù: *in a good* (*bad*) ~ 心情好(不佳)的. **2** 怒气〔氣〕nùqì, 脾气 píqì. *get* (或 *fly*) *into a* ~ 发〔發〕怒 fānù. *keep one's* ~ 忍住性子(不使发作) rěnzhù xìngzi. *lose one's* ~ 发脾气 fā píqi. **3** [C] (指钢等)韧〔韌〕度 rèndù, 硬度 yìngdù. **-tem·pered** /'tempəd/ *suffix* (表示"有某种性

情的"): *a ˌbad-~ed 'man* 脾气不好的人.

tem·per² /'tempə(r)/ *vt/i* **1** (使金属等)回火 huíhuǒ; 炼〔煉〕至所需要的硬度 liànzhì suǒ xūyào de yìngdù. **2** (使)软〔軟〕化 ruǎnhuà; (使)缓和 huǎnhé: ~ *justice with mercy* 恩威兼施.

tem·pera·ment /'temprəmənt/ *n* **1** [C,U] 性情 xìngqíng, 气〔氣〕质〔質〕qìzhì: *a girl with a nervous* ~ 神经质的女孩. **2** [U] 容易激动〔動〕róngyì jīdòng. **~al** /-'mentl/ *adj* **(a)** 气质的 qìzhìde, 性格的 xìnggéde: *a ~al dislike for study* 本质上不喜欢读书. **(b)** 敏感的 mǐngǎnde; 多变〔變〕的 duō biàn de: *a ~al tennis player* 不稳定的网球运动员. **~ally** *adv*

tem·per·ate /'tempərət/ *adj* **1** 有节〔節〕制的 yǒu jiézhì de, 不过〔過〕分的 bú guòfèn de. **2** (气候)温和的 wēnhéde. **~ly** *adv*

tem·pera·ture /'temprətʃə(r)/ *n* [C,U] 温度 wēndù: *The nurse took my* ~. 护士为我量体温. ***have*** (或 ***run***) ***a*** ~ 发〔發〕烧〔燒〕fāshāo.

tem·pest /'tempɪst/ *n* [C] 暴风〔風〕雨 bàofēngyǔ.

temple¹ /'templ/ *n* [C] 神殿 shéndiàn, 庙〔廟〕宇 miàoyǔ, 寺院 sìyuàn.

temple² /'templ/ *n* [C] [解剖]太阳〔陽〕穴 tàiyángxué.

tempo /'tempəʊ/ *n* [C] [*pl* ~s] **1** (行动,活动的)速度 sùdù: *the* ~ *of city life* 城市生活的节拍. **2** [音乐]速度 sùdù, 拍子 pāizi.

tem·poral /'tempərəl/ *adj* **1** [正式用语]暂〔暫〕时〔時〕的 zànshíde; 时间上的 shíjiānshàngde. **2** 世俗的 shìsúde, 现世的 xiànshìde.

tem·por·ary /'temprərɪ/ *adj* 暂〔暫〕时〔時〕的 zànshíde, 临〔臨〕时的 línshíde: ~ *employment* 临时工作: *a* ~ *bridge* 临时桥. **tem·por·ar·ily** /'temprərəlɪ/ *adv*

tempt /tempt/ *vt* **1** 引诱(某人干坏事) yǐnyòu, 勾引 gōuyǐn: *Nothing could* ~ *him to tell lies.* 没有什么东西能诱使他说谎. **2** 吸引 xīyǐn, 诱导〔導〕yòudǎo: *The warm weather ~ed us to go for a swim.* 暖和的天气诱使我们去游泳. **~ing** *adj* 吸引人的 xīyǐnrénde: *a ~ing offer* 吸引人的提议.

temp·ta·tion /temp'teɪʃn/ *n* **1** [U] 引诱 yǐnyòu, 诱惑 yòuhuò: *yield* (或 *give way*) *to* ~ 受诱惑. **2** [C] 诱惑物 yòuhuòwù.

ten /ten/ *n* [C] *adj* 十 shí. **'~fold** *adv* 十倍 shíbèi. **'~pence** *n* [C,U] (英国货币)十便士币〔幣〕shí biànshì bì. **tenth** /tenθ/ *n* [C] *adj* (缩作 *10th*) 第十 dìshí; 十分之一(的) shífēn zhī yī.

ten·able /'tenəbl/ *adj* **1** 可防守的 kě fángshǒu de, 守得住的 shǒudézhùde: *His theory is not* ~. 他的理论站不住脚. **2** 可保持的 kě bǎochí de, 可维持的 kě wéichí de: *The lectureship is* ~ *for three years.* 讲座可持续三年.

ten·acious /tɪ'neɪʃəs/ *adj* [正式用语]抓紧〔緊〕的 zhuājǐnde; 顽强的 wánqiángde: *a* ~ *memory* 强的记忆力. **ten·ac·ity** /tɪ'næsətɪ/ *n* [U]

ten·ancy /'tenənsɪ/ *n* [U] **1** 租赁 zūlìn, 租佃 zūdiàn. **2** 租期 zūqī: *hold a 'life* ~ *of a house* 持有房屋的终身租赁权. **'ten·ant** *n* [C] 承租人 chéngzūrén, 佃户 diànhù.

tend¹ /tend/ *vt* 照管 zhàoguǎn, 照料 zhàoliào: *shepherds ~ing their flocks* 照管羊群的牧羊人.

tend² /tend/ *vi* **1** 趋〔趨〕向 qūxiàng 走向 zǒuxiàng: *Prices are ~ing upwards.* 物价趋涨. **2** (有…)倾向 qīngxiàng, 易于〔於〕yì yú: *He* ~ *to make too many mistakes.* 他常常错误百出.

ten·dency /'tendənsɪ/ *n* [C] [*pl* -ies] 趋〔趨〕向 qūxiàng, 趋势〔勢〕qūshì: *a* ~ *to improve* 改进的趋势.

ten·der¹ /'tendə(r)/ *adj* [-er, -est] **1** 脆弱的 cuìruòde, 易损坏〔壞〕的 yì sǔnhuài de: ~ *flowers* 娇嫩的花朵. *a* ~ *heart* 脆弱的心. **2** (指肉)嫩的 nènde: *a* ~ *steak* 嫩肉片. **3** 温和的 wēnhéde; 亲〔親〕切的 qīnqiède: ~ *looks* 温柔的表情. **~ly** *adv* **~ness** *n* [U]

ten·der² /'tendə(r)/ *vt/i* **1** 提供 tígōng, 提出 tíchū: *He ~ed his resignation.* 他提出辞呈. **2** 投标〔標〕tóubiāo: ~ *for the construction of new motorway* 投标承建一条新的高速公路. □ *n* [C] 投标 tóubiāo 建议〔議〕jiànyì: *invite ~s for new bridge.* 招标建造新桥. • legal tender.

ten·don /'tendən/ *n* [C] 筋 jīn, 腱 jiàn.

ten·ement /'tenəmənt/ *n* [C] (多家合住的)经〔經〕济〔濟〕公寓 jīngjì gōngyù.

ten·nis /'tenɪs/ *n* [U] 网〔網〕球 wǎngqiú. **'~-court** 网球场〔場〕wǎngqiúchǎng.

tenor /'tenə(r)/ *n* [C] **1** [音乐]高音 nángāoyīn; 次中音部 cì zhōngyīnbù; 男高音乐〔樂〕曲 nángāoyīn yuèqǔ. 2 次中音乐器 cì zhōngyīn yuèqì: *a ~ saxophone* 次中音萨克斯管.

tense[1] /tens/ *adj* [-r, -st] 拉紧[緊]的 lā jǐn de, 紧张[張]的 jǐnzhāngde: *~ nerves* 紧张的神经. *a ~ moment* 紧张的时刻. □ *vt/i* (使)拉紧 lā jǐn, (使)紧张 jǐnzhāng: *He ~d his muscles for the effort.* 他紧绷着肌肉使劲. **~ly** *adv*

tense[2] /tens/ *n* [C,U] [语法]时[時]态[態] shítài: *the present (past, future) ~* 现在(过去,将来)时.

ten·sion /'tenʃn/ *n* [U] **1** 拉紧[緊] lā jǐn; [物理]张[張]力 zhānglì, 拉力 lālì: *the ~ of the rope* 这条绳索的拉力. **2** (情绪, 神经等的)紧张 jǐnzhāng, 激动[動] jīdòng. **3** 紧张(局势) jǐnzhāng, 不安(状态) bù'ān: *political ~* 政治紧张的局势. **4** 电[電]压[壓] diànyā: *high ~ wires* 高压线.

tent /tent/ *n* [C] 帐[帳]篷 zhàngpeng.

ten·tacle /'tentəkl/ *n* [C] (动物的)触[觸]角 chùjiǎo, 触须[鬚] chùxū.

ten·ta·tive /'tentətɪv/ *adj* 试验[驗]性的 shìyànxìngde, 暂[暫]时的 zànshíde: *make a ~ offer* 作试验性的建议. **~ly** *adv*

tenth /tenθ/ *n, adj* ⇨ ten

tenu·ous /'tenjuəs/ *adj* [正式用语] 单[單]薄的 dānbóde, 纤[纖]细的 xiānxìde: *the ~ web of a spider* 纤细的蛛网. **2** 内容贫乏的 nèiróng pínfá de, 无[無]实[實]质[質]的 wú shízhì de.

tepid /'tepɪd/ *adj* 温热[熱]的 wēnrède.

term /tɜ:m/ *n* [C] **1** 期 qī, 期间[間] qījiān, 限期 xiànqī: *a long ~ of imprisonment* 长期监禁. *~ of office* 任期. **2** 学[學]期 xuéqī: *end-of-~ exams* 期终考试. **3** [*pl*] 条[條]件 tiáojiàn, 条款 tiáokuǎn: *~s of surrender* 投降的条件. *~s of a contract* 合同的条款. ⇨ reference(1). ***come to ~s (with sb)*** (与某人)达[達]成协[協]议[議] dáchéng xiéyì. ***come to terms with sth*** 终于[於]接受 zhōng yú jiēshòu: *come to ~s with a difficult situation* 逆来顺受. **4** ***be on good ~s (with sb)*** (同某人)关系好 guānxì hǎo. **5** (有特定意义的)词 cí, 术[術]语 shùyǔ: *technical ~s* 专业名词. **6** [*pl*] 说法 shuōfǎ, 措辞[辭] cuòcí: *speak in abusive ~s* 口出恶言. □ *vt* 称[稱]呼 chēnghu: *~ him a professor* 称他为教授.

ter·minal /'tɜ:mɪnl/ *adj* **1** 每期的 měiqīde, 定期的 dìngqīde; 学[學]期的 xuéqīde: *~ examinations* 学期考试. *~ accounts* 按期结帐. **2** 末端的 mòduānde, 终点[點]的 zhōngdiǎnde: *~ cancer* 后期癌症. □ *n* [C] **1** (铁路,公共汽车等)终点站 zhōngdiǎnzhàn; (城市中的)航空集散站 hángkōng jísànzhàn. **2** (电路)接线[綫]头[頭] jiēxiàntóu: *the ~s of a battery* 电池的接头. **~ly** *adv*

ter·min·ate /'tɜ:mɪneɪt/ *vt/i* 终止 zhōngzhǐ, 结束 jiéshù: *~ his contract* 终止他的合约. **ter·mi'na·tion** *n* [C,U] 终止 zhōngzhǐ, 终点[點] zhōngdiǎn; 结束 jiéshù, 结局 jiéjú: *the termination of a contract* 合约的终止.

ter·mi·nol·ogy /ˌtɜ:mɪ'nɒlədʒɪ/ *n* [C,U] [*pl* -ies] 术[術]语 shùyǔ, 专[專]业[業]名词 zhuānyè míngcí: *medical ~* 医学名词.

ter·mi·nus /'tɜ:mɪnəs/ *n* [C] [*pl* -ni /-naɪ/ 或 ~es] (铁路, 公路, 公共汽车的)终点[點](站) zhōngdiǎn.

ter·mite /'tɜ:maɪt/ *n* [C] 白蚁[蟻] báiyǐ.

ter·race /'terəs/ *n* [U] **1** 斜坡地 xiépōdì; 台[臺]地 táidì, 梯田 tītián. **2** 看台 kàntái, (露天)大阶[階]梯 dà jiētī. **3** (斜坡上的)一排房屋 yīpái fángwū. □ *vt* 使成阶梯 shǐ chéng jiētī, 使成梯田 shǐ chéng tītián, 筑[築]台 zhù tái: *a ~d lawn* 有梯层的草地. *a ~d houses* (斜坡或高于街道的)成排的房屋.

ter·rain /te'reɪn/ *n* [C] 地面 dìmiàn, 地形 dìxíng, 地带[帶] dìdài: *difficult ~ for walking* 步行困难的地形.

ter·res·trial /tɪ'restrɪəl/ *adj* **1** 陆[陸]地(上)的 lùdìde: *the ~ parts of the world* 地球的陆地部分. **2** (同 *celestial* 相对) 地球(上)的 dìqiúde.

ter·rible /'terəbl/ *adj* **1** 可怕的 kěpàde, 骇[駭]人的 hàirénde; 令人极[極]不舒服的 lìngrén jí bù shūfú de: *a ~ war (accident)* 可怕的战争(意外事件). **2** [非正式用语] 极坏[壞]的 jíhuàide, 很糟的 hěn zāo de: *What ~ food!* 伙食多么糟糕啊! **ter·ribly** *adv* [非正式用语]非常 fēicháng, 极端地 jíduānde: *How terribly boring!* 多么烦人啊!

ter·rier /'terɪə(r)/ *n* [C] 㹴(一种狗) gēng.

ter·rific /tə'rɪfɪk/ *adj* **1** 可怕的 kěpàde, 骇〔駭〕人的 hàirénde. **2** [非正式用语]非常的 fēichángde, 极〔極〕度的 jídùde: *driving at a ~ pace* 以极高的速度驾驶. **~ally** *adv* 非常 fēicháng, 极端地 jíduānde.

ter·rify /'terɪfaɪ/ *vt* [*pt*, *pp* -ied] 使恐怖 shǐ kǒngbù, 恐吓〔嚇〕kǒnghè: *He was terrified of dogs.* 他怕狗.

ter·ri·torial /ˌterɪ'tɔːrɪəl/ *adj* 领土的 lǐngtǔde, 领地的 lǐngdìde: *~ possessions* 领地. ~ **'waters** 领海 lǐnghǎi.

ter·ri·tory /'terɪtrɪ/ *n* [*pl* -ies] **1** [C,U] 领土 lǐngtǔ, 版图〔圖〕bǎntú: *Is this American ~?* 这是美国的领土吗? **2** [U] 地区〔區〕dìqū, 区域 qūyù: *a salesman's ~* 售货员的推销区域. *a lion's ~* 狮子的活动地区.

ter·ror /'terə(r)/ *n* **1** [U] 恐怖 kǒngbù, 惊〔驚〕骇〔駭〕jīnghài: *run away in ~* 惊慌地逃走. **2** [C] 引起恐怖的事物 yǐnqǐ kǒngbù de shìwù: *have a ~ of fire* 怕火. **'~ism** /-rɪzəm/ *n* [U] 恐怖主义〔義〕kǒngbù zhǔyì. **'~ist** *n* [C] 恐怖分子 kǒngbù fènzǐ. **'~ize** /-raɪz/ *vt* 充满恐怖 chōngmǎn kǒngbù, 使恐惧〔懼〕shǐ kǒngjù, 恐吓〔嚇〕kǒnghè.

terse /tɜːs/ *adj* (说话,文笔等)精练〔練〕的 jīngliànde, 简〔簡〕明的 jiǎnmíngde. **~ly** *adv* **~ness** *n* [U]

test /test/ *n* [C] 试验〔驗〕shìyàn, 测验 cèyàn: *a 'blood ~* 验血. *a 'driving ~* 驾驶考试. □ *vt* 测验 cèyàn, 试验 shìyàn, 检〔檢〕验 jiǎnyàn: *have one's eyes ~ed* 检查眼睛. *The long climb ~ed our strength.* 长距离爬山考验我们的持久力. **'~ flight** (新飞机)试飞〔飛〕shìfēi. **'~ match** (板球,橄榄球等的)国〔國〕际〔際〕比赛 guójì bǐsài. **'~-tube** 试管 shìguǎn.

tes·ta·ment /'testəmənt/ *n* **1** [C] (常用 *last Will and T~*) = will[5](5). **2 Old T~, New T~** [基督教]《旧〔舊〕约全书〔書〕》Jiùyuē Quánshū, 《新约全书》Xīnyuē Quánshū.

tes·ticle /'testɪkl/ *n* [C] 睾丸 gāowán.

tes·tify /'testɪfaɪ/ *vt/i* [*pt*, *pp* -ied] **1** 证〔證〕明 zhèngmíng, 证实〔實〕zhèngshí; 声〔聲〕明 shēngmíng: *He testified under oath that he had not stolen the bike.* 他发誓声明他并没有偷自行车. **2** 成为〔爲〕...的证据〔據〕chéngwéi ... de zhèngjù: *Her tears testified her grief.* 她的眼泪证明了她的悲伤.

tes·ti·mo·nial /ˌtestɪ'məʊnɪəl/ *n* [C] **1** (能力,资格,品德等的)证〔證〕明书〔書〕zhèngmíngshū, **2** 鉴〔鑒〕定书 jiàndìngshū; 奖〔獎〕品 jiǎngpǐn, 奖状〔狀〕jiǎngzhuàng.

tes·ti·mony /'testɪmənɪ/ *n* [U] 证〔證〕据〔據〕zhèngjù, 证言 zhèngyán.

tether /'teðə(r)/ *n* [C] (拴牲口的)系绳〔繩〕xìshéng, 系链〔鏈〕xìliàn. ***at the end of one's ~*** [喻]智穷〔窮〕力竭 zhìqióng-lìjié. □ *vt* (用绳,链)拴 shuān: *He ~ed his horse to the fence.* 他把马拴在篱笆上.

text /tekst/ *n* **1** [U] 正文 zhèngwén, 本文 běnwén. **2** [C] 原文 yuánwén. **3** [C] (尤指《圣经》中的)经〔經〕文 jīngwén, 经句 jīngjù. **'~book** 教科书〔書〕jiàokēshū: *an algebra ~book* 代数学教科书. **~ual** /'tekstʃʊəl/ *adj* 正文的 zhèngwénde; 原文的 yuánwénde; 在正文中的 zài zhèngwén zhōng de; 在教科书内的 zài jiàokēshū nèi de: *~ual errors* 原文的错误.

tex·tile /'tekstaɪl/ *adj* 纺织〔織〕的 fǎngzhīde: *the ~ industry* 纺织工业. □ *n* [C] 纺织品 fǎngzhīpǐn.

tex·ture /'tekstʃə(r)/ *n* [C,U] **1** (织物的)组织〔織〕zǔzhī, 结构〔構〕jiégòu: *cloth with a loose ~* 质地稀松的布. **2** (材料等的)构造 gòuzào, 结构 jiégòu: *the ~ of a mineral* 矿石的结构.

than /ðən, 强式: ðæn/ *conj* 比 bǐ: *John is taller ~ me.* 约翰比我高. **sooner than** ⇨ soon(4).

thank /θæŋk/ *vt* 道谢 dàoxiè, 感谢 gǎnxiè: *~ a person for his help* 为某人的帮助而向他道谢. ***Thank you*** 谢谢你 xièxie nǐ. ***No, thank you*** 不了, 谢谢你. bùle, xièxie nǐ. □ *n* [*pl*] 谢意 xièyì, 谢忱 xièchén: *give ~s to God* 感谢上帝. ***thanks to*** 由于〔於〕yóuyú, 因 yīn 幸亏〔虧〕xìngkuī: *T~s to you, we won.* 幸亏你,我们赢了. ˌ**~'giving (a)** 感恩 gǎn'ēn, 感恩祈祷〔禱〕. **(b)** [美语] (亦作 ˌ*T~s'giving Day*) [基督教]感恩节〔節〕Gǎn'ēnjié. **~ful** *adj* 感谢的 gǎnxiède, 感激的 gǎnjīde; 欣慰的 xīnwèide: *be ~ful that you have escaped* 为你逃脱而感到欣慰. **~fully** *adv* **~less** *adj* 不感谢的 bù gǎnxiè de; 徒劳〔勞〕的 túláode: *a ~less task* 吃力不讨好的工作.

that[1] /ðæt/ *adj*, *pron* [*pl* those /ðəʊz/] 那 nà, 那个〔個〕nàge: *Look at ~ man (those men).* 看那个人 (那些人). □ *adv* [非正式用法] 那样

〔樣〕nàyàng, 那么〔麼〕nàme: *I can't walk ~ far.* 我不能走那么远.

that² /ðət, 强式: ðæt/ *conj* **1**〔引导各种从句〕: *She said (~) she would come.* 她说她要来. *The play was so bad ~ we left.* 戏不好,我们不看了. **2** *so that; in order that: Bring it nearer so ~ I can see it better.* 把它带近些,以使我看得比较清楚.

that³ /ðət, 强式: ðæt/ *relative pron* [*pl* ~] **1**〔在从句中作动词的主语〕: *You're the only person ~ can help me.* 你是唯一能帮助我的人. **2**〔在从句中作动词的宾语〕: *The pen (~) you gave me is very nice.* 你给我的那支笔非常好.

thatch /θætʃ/ *n* [U] 茅屋顶 máowūdǐng. □ *vt* 用茅草盖〔蓋〕(屋顶) yòng máocǎo gài.

thaw /θɔ:/ *vt/i* **1** (冰, 雪等) 融化 rónghuà. **2** 使化成水 shǐ huàchéng shuǐ; 使软〔軟〕化 shǐ ruǎnhuà: *~ frozen food* 化开冰冻的食物. **3** (指人, 行为等) (使)变〔變〕得友善 biàndé yǒushàn; (使) 缓和 huǎnhé: *After a good dinner he began to ~.* 吃过一顿好饭以后,他开始变得友好了. □ *n* (指天气) 解冻〔凍〕jiědòng: *Let's go skating before a ~ sets in.* 趁着未解冻,我们去溜冰吧.

the /ðə, 强式: ði:/ *definite article* **1** (指特定的或独一的人或事物): *Please close ~ window.* 请关窗 (指开着的窗). *~ sun* 太阳. *~ moon* 月亮. *~ year 1989* 1989年. *~ universe* 宇宙. **2**〔用于形容词, 副词的最高级前〕: *~ best way to get there* 去那里的最好方法. **3**〔用于地理名称前〕: *~ Mediterranean* 地中海. *~ Atlantic (Ocean)* 大西洋. *~ Suez Canal* 苏伊士运河. **4** (指一类中的所有分子): *~ rich* 富有者. *~ dead* 死者. **5**〔用于乐器前〕: *play ~ piano* 弹钢琴. *play ~ violin* 拉提琴. *play ~ guitar* 奏吉他. [但是, 运动名称前不加 *the*, 如: *play tennis* 打网球. *play football* 踢足球]. **6**〔与名词连用, 表示一单位〕: *thirty miles to ~ gallon* 一加仑油可跑三十英里. □ *adv*〔用于形容词, 副词比较级前〕愈 yù, 越 yuè: *T~ more he has ~ more he wants.* 他有的愈多, 他愈想要.

the·atre [美语 = **theater**] /ˈθɪətə(r)/ *n* [C] **1** 戏〔戲〕院 xìyuàn, 剧〔劇〕场〔場〕jùchǎng. **2** 讲〔講〕堂 jiǎngtáng, 会〔會〕场 huìchǎng. **3** 手术〔術〕室 shǒushùshì. **4** 现场 xiànchǎng, 场所 chǎngsuǒ: *a ~ of war* 战场. **5** 剧本的写〔寫〕作和演出 jùběnde xiězuò hé yǎnchū: *the Greek ~* 希腊戏剧. **ˈ~-goer** 戏迷 xìmí. **the·atri·cal** /θɪˈætrɪkl/ *adj* **(a)** 剧场的 jùchǎngde; 戏剧的 xìjùde. **(b)** 不自然的 bú zìrán de; 戏剧性的 xìjùxìngde: *theatrical behaviour* 戏剧性的行为.

theft /θeft/ *n* [C,U] 偷盗 tōudào.

their /ðeə(r)/ *adj* 他们的 tāmende; 她们的 tāmende; 它们的 tāmende: *They have lost ~ dog.* 他们的狗丢失了.

theirs /ðeəz/ *possessive pron* 他们的(东西) tāmende; 她们的 (东西) tāmende: *That dog is ~s, not ours.* 那只狗是他们的,不是我们的.

them /ðəm, 强式: ðem/ *personal pron* [*they* 的宾格]: *Give ~ to me.* 把它们给我. *It was kind of ~.* 他们很客气.

theme /θi:m/ *n* [C] **1** 题目 tímù, 主题 zhǔtí. **2**〔音乐〕主题 zhǔtí, 主旋律 zhǔ xuánlǜ. **ˈ~ song** 主题歌 zhǔtígē.

them·selves /ðəmˈselvz/ *pron* **1**〔反身〕他们自己 tāmen zìjǐ; 她们自己 tāmen zìjǐ, 它们本身 tāmen běnshēn: *They hurt ~.* 他们伤害了自己. *They kept some for ~.* 他们为自己保存了一些. **(all) by ~ (a)** 亲〔親〕自 qīnzì. **(b)** 独〔獨〕自 dúzì. **2**〔加强语气〕: *They ~ have often made that mistake.* 他们自己也常犯那个错误.

then /ðen/ *adv* **1** 当〔當〕时〔時〕dāngshí; 届时 jièshí: *I was still unmarried ~.* 那时我还未结婚. **(every) ˌnow and ˈthen** ⇨ now(2). **2**〔用于介词之后〕: *until ~* 到那时. *since ~* 自那时以来. **3** 然后〔後〕ránhòu, 接着 jiēzhe, 于〔於〕是 yúshì: *We stayed in Rome and ~ in Naples.* 我们先住在罗马, 然后住在那不勒斯. **4** 那么〔麼〕nàme: *A: "It isn't here." "它不在这儿". — B: "T~ it must be in the next room." "那么, 它一定在隔壁房间。"* **5** 而且 érqiě, 还〔還〕有 huányǒu, 另外 lìngwài.

the·ol·ogy /θi:ˈɒlədʒɪ/ *n* [U] 神学〔學〕shénxué. **theo·lo·gian** /ˌθɪəˈləʊdʒən/ *n* [C] 神学家 shénxuéjiā. **theo·logi·cal** /ˌθi:əˈlɒdʒɪkl/ *adj*

the·ory /ˈθɪərɪ/ *n* [*pl* -ies] **1** [C, U] 理论〔論〕lǐlùn, 原理 yuánlǐ: *The ~ of music* 音乐原理. **2** [C] 学〔學〕说 xuéshuō, 论 lùn: *Darwin's ~ of evolution.* 达尔文的进化论. **3** [C] 意见 yìjiàn, 想法 xiǎngfǎ. **the·or·etic(al)** /-ˈretɪk(l)/ *adj*

thera·peutic /ˌθerəˈpjuːtɪk/ *adj* 治疗〔療〕的 zhìliáode, 疗法的 liáofǎde.

ther·apy /ˈθerəpɪ/ *n* [U] 治疗〔療〕zhìliáo, 疗法 liáofǎ. **thera·pist** *n* [C]

there¹ /ðeə(r)/ *adv* **1** 在那里〔裏〕zài nàlǐ; 往那里 wàng nàlǐ: *We shall soon be* ~. 不久我们就去那里. **2** [用以引起注意, 加强语气]: *T~'s the bell for lunch.* 午饭铃响了. **3** 在那点〔點〕上 zài nàdiǎn shàng, 在那个〔個〕方面 zài nàge fāngmiàn: *Don't stop* ~! 别在那地方停住! **4** *here and* ~ ⇨ here(3). ~ *and back* 到那里再回来 dào nàlǐ zài huílái: *Can I go* ~ *and back in one day?* 一天之内我能往返吗?

there² /ðeə(r)/ *adv* [引导句子, 其动词, 尤其是 *be*, 一般在主语之前]: *T~'s a man at the door.* 门口有人. *T~ seems (to be) no doubt about it.* 此事看来无可怀疑.

there³ /ðeə(r)/ *int* **1** (表示安慰): *T~! T~! You'll soon feel better.* 好啦! 好啦! 你马上会好的. **2** (表示同意, 胜利或沮丧等): *T~, now! You've upset the ink!* 哎呀! 你把墨水打翻了! **ˈ~aˈbout(s)** *adv* 在那附近 zài nà fùjìn, 左右 zuǒyòu, 前后 qiánhòu; 大约 dàyuē. *in 1978 or ~abouts* 在 1978 年前后. **~ˈafter** *adv* [正式用语] = afterwards. **~by** *adv* [正式用语]借以 jièyǐ, 从〔從〕而 cóng'ér **ˈ~fore** *adv* 所以 suǒyǐ, 因此 yīncǐ.

ther·mal /ˈθɜːml/ *adj* 热〔熱〕的 rède, 热量的 rèliàngde. □ *n* [C] (上升的)暖气〔氣〕流 nuǎn qìliú.

ther·mom·eter /θəˈmɒmɪtə(r)/ *n* [C] 温度计 wēndùjì, 寒暑表 hánshǔbiǎo.

ther·mos /ˈθɜːməs/ *n* [C] [*pl* ~es] (亦作 ˈ~ *flask*) 热〔熱〕水瓶 rèshuǐpíng.

thermo·stat /ˈθɜːməstæt/ *n* [C] 恒温器 héngwēnqì.

the·sau·rus /θɪˈsɔːrəs/ *n* [C] [*pl* ~es 或 -ri /-raɪ/] (尤指) 词典 cídiǎn.

these /ðiːz/ *pl* of this.

the·sis /ˈθiːsɪs/ *n* [C] [*pl* theses /-siːz/] 论〔論〕文 lùnwén, (尤指)学〔學〕位论文 xuéwèi lùnwén.

they /ðeɪ/ *personal pron* **1** [主格] 他们 tāmen; 她们 tāmen; 它们 tāmen: *T~ came home late.* 他们回家晚了. **2** 人们 rénmen: *T~ say that the government will resign.* 据说内阁将辞职. ⇨ them.

thick /θɪk/ *adj* [-er, -est] **1** (同 *thin* 相对)厚的 hòude; 粗的 cūde: *a ~ line* 粗线. *ice three metres ~* 三米厚的冰. **2** 密的 mìde, 密集的 mìjíde, 茂密的 màomìde: *~ hair* 浓密的头发. *a ~ forest* 茂密的森林. **3** (指液体)浓〔濃〕的 nóngde, 稠的 chóude, 半固体〔體〕的 bàn gùtǐ de: *~ soup* 浓汤. (指大气等)阴〔陰〕霾的 yīnmáide, 不清明的 bù qīngmíng de: *a ~ fog* 浓雾. **4** [非正式用语]愚笨的 yúbènde, 迟〔遲〕钝的 chídùnde. **5** *lay it on ~* 过〔過〕份恭维或责备〔備〕guòfèn gōngwéi huò zébèi. □ *n* [U] **1** 最密集的部分 zuì mìjíde bùfen; 最活跃〔躍〕的部分 zuì huóyuède bùfen: *in the ~ of the battle* 在酣战中. *through ~ and ˈthin* 在任何情况下 zài rènhé qíngkuàngxià. **2** 最厚的部分 zuì hòude bùfen, 最粗的部分 zuì cūde bùfen; 最浓密部分 zuì nóngmì bùfen: *the ~ of the thumb* 拇指的最粗大处. □ *adv* 厚厚地 hòuhòude, 密集地 mìjíde, 浓稠地 nóngchóude: *You spread the butter too ~.* 你抹的奶油太厚了. **ˌ~-ˈheaded** *adj* 笨的 bènde. **ˌ~-ˈskinned** *adj* [喻] 脸〔臉〕皮厚的 liǎnpí hòu de, 感觉〔覺〕迟钝的 gǎnjué chídùn de. **~ly** *adv* **~ness (a)** [U] 厚 hòu, 厚度 hòudù; 浓 nóng, 浓度 nóngdù: *four centimetres in ~ness* 四厘米厚. **(b)** [C] (一)层〔層〕céng: *two ~nesses of cloth.* 两层布.

thicken /ˈθɪkən/ *vt/i* (使)变〔變〕厚 biàn hòu, (使) 变浓〔濃〕biàn nóng, (使) 变密集 biàn mìjí: *~ the gravy* 使肉汁变浓.

thicket /ˈθɪkɪt/ *n* [C] 灌木丛〔叢〕guànmùcōng.

thief /θiːf/ *n* [C] [*pl* thieves /θiːvz/] 贼 zéi.

thieve /θiːv/ *vt/i* 偷窃〔竊〕tōuqiè 做贼 zuò zéi.

thigh /θaɪ/ *n* [C] 大腿 dàtuǐ, 股 gǔ.

thimble /ˈθɪmbl/ *n* [C] 顶针箍 dǐngzhēngū.

thin /θɪn/ *adj* [-ner, -nest] **1** (*thick* 的反义词)薄的 bóde; 细的 xìde: *a ~ sheet of paper* 一张薄纸. **2** 稀少的 xīshǎode, 稀疏的 xīshūde: *~ hair* 稀疏的头发. *a ~ audience* 稀少的观众. **3** (同 *fat* 相对) 瘦的 shòude: *~ in the face* 脸庞消瘦. **4** 稀薄的 xībóde, 淡的 dànde: *~ soup* 淡汤. *~ blood* 稀薄的血液. *a ~ mist* 薄雾. **5** 贫乏的 pínfáde, 浅〔淺〕薄的 qiǎnbóde, 空洞的 kōngdòngde: *a ~ excuse* 勉强的借口. *a ~ disguise* 易被识破的伪装

□ *adv* 薄 bó, 稀 xī, 细 xì, 疏 shū: *You've spread the butter very* ~. 你把奶油涂得太薄了. □ *vt/i* [-nn-] (使)变〔變〕薄 biàn bó, (使)变稀 biàn xī, (使)变淡 biàn dàn; (使)变细 biàn xì, (使)变瘦 biàn shòu: *At last the crowd* ~*ned.* 最后, 群众散开了. ,~-'**skinned** *adj* 〔喻〕脸〔臉〕皮薄的 liǎnpí bó de, 敏感的 mǐngǎnde. ~**ly** *adv* 薄薄地 bóbóde, 稀疏地 xīshūde, 淡淡地 dàndànde: *Sow the seed* ~*ly.* 稀疏地播下种子. ~**ness** *n* [U]

thing /θɪŋ/ *n* [C] **1** 物 wù, 事物 shìwù, 东〔東〕西 dōngxi: *What are those* ~*s on the table?* 桌子上的东西是什么? **2** [*pl*] 用品 yòngpǐn, 用具 yòngjù; 所有物 suǒyǒuwù: *Bring your swimming* ~*s.* 带上你的游泳用品. **3** 题目 tímù, 主题 zhǔtí: *There's another* ~ *I want to ask you about.* 我还有一件事要问你. **4** 局势〔勢〕júshì, 情况 qíngkuàng; 事件 shìjiàn, 事情 shìqing: *That only makes* ~*s worse.* 那只有使情况更糟. *for* '*one* ~ 首先 shǒuxiān, 一则 yīzé: *For one* ~, *I haven't any money; for another* ...— 则, 我没有钱; 再则... **5** (指人或动物) 东西 dōngxi, 家伙 jiāhuo: *She's a sweet little* ~. 她是个可爱的小东西. **6** 最适〔適〕合的东西 zuì shìhé de dōngxi: *A holiday will be the very* ~ *for you.* 休假将对你最为适宜. **7** *the* ,~ '*is* 问〔問〕题是 wèntí shì. *a near* ~ 死里逃生 sǐlǐ táoshēng, 极〔極〕险〔險〕的事 jí xiǎn de shì.

think¹ /θɪŋk/ *vt/i* [*pt, pp* thought /θɔːt/] **1** 想 xiǎng, 思索 sīsuǒ, 考虑〔慮〕kǎolǜ: *Do you* ~ *in English when you speak English?* 你说英语时, 是用英语来想的吗? ~ *aloud* 自言自语 zìyán-zìyǔ. **2** 认〔認〕为〔爲〕rènwéi, 以为 yǐwéi: *Do you* ~ *it will rain?* 你以为天会下雨吗? ~ *fit* ⇨ fit¹(2). **3** 想象 xiǎngxiàng: *I can't* ~ *what you mean.* 我想象不出你的意思是什么. **4** 打算 dǎsuàn, 想要 xiǎng yào: *I* ~ *I'll go for a swim.* 我打算去游泳. **5** 想起 xiǎngqǐ, 回想 huíxiǎng: *She was* ~*ing about her life.* 她在回顾她的一生. **6** 料想 liàoxiǎng, 预料 yùliào: *I thought he would arrive.* 我料想他会来到. ~ *about sth* 考虑 kǎolǜ; 审〔審〕查 shěnchá. ~ *of sth* **(a)** 考虑 kǎolǜ, 思考 sīkǎo: *We're* ~*ing of going to Venice.* 我们正考虑去威尼斯. **(b)** 想象 xiǎngxiàng, 想一想 xiǎng yī xiǎng: *Just* ~ *of the cost (danger)!* 想一想那费用(危险)吧! **(c)** 想起 xiǎngqǐ, 记起 jìqǐ: *I can't* ~ *of his name.* 我记不起他的名字了. ~ *nothing of* 看不起 kànbùqǐ, 轻〔輕〕视 qīngshì. ~ *sth out* 想出 xiǎngchū, 想通 xiǎngtōng. ~ *sth over* 仔细考虑 zǐxì kǎolǜ. ~ *sth up* 想出 xiǎngchū, 设计出 shèjìchū.

think² /θɪŋk/ *n* 〔非正式用语〕想 xiǎng, 想法 xiǎngfǎ.

thinker /'θɪŋkə(r)/ *n* [C] 思想家 sīxiǎngjiā: *a great* ~ 伟大的思想家.

think·ing /'θɪŋkɪŋ/ *adj* 思想的 sīxiǎngde, 有思想的 yǒu sīxiǎng de: *all* ~ *men* 凡是有思想的人. □ *n* [U] 思想 sīxiǎng, 想法 xiǎngfǎ: *do some hard* ~ 深思.

third /θɜːd/ *adj, n* [C] (缩作 *3rd*) 第三 dìsān. ,~ **de'gree** 疲劳〔勞〕讯问 píláo xùnwèn, 逼供 bīgòng. ,~ '**party** 第三者 dìsānzhě: ,~-*party in'surance* 对被保险人以外的第三者有承诺的保险. ,~-'**rate** *adj* 三等的 sānděngde, 下等的 xiàděngde. **the** ,**T**~ '**World** 第三世界 dìsān shìjiè. ~**ly** *adv*

thirst /θɜːst/ *n* [U] **1** 渴 kě, 口渴 kǒukě: *They died of* ~. 他们是渴死的. **2** 〔喻〕渴望 kěwàng, 热〔熱〕望 rèwàng: *a* ~ *for knowledge* 求知欲. □ *vt* **1** 口渴 kǒukě. **2** 〔与 *for* 连用〕渴望 kěwàng, 热望 rèwàng: ~ *for revenge* 渴望复仇. **thirsty** *adj* [-ier, -iest] 渴的 kěde, 使人口渴的 shǐ rén kǒukě de; 渴望的 kěwàngde: *be* (或 *feel*) ~*y* 口渴.

thir·teen /,θɜː'tiːn/ *adj, n* [C] 十三 shísān. **thir·teenth** /,θɜː'tiːnθ/ *adj, n* [C] (缩作 *13th*) 第十三 dìshísān; 十三分之一 shísānfēn zhī yī.

thirty /'θɜːtɪ/ *adj, n* [C] 三十 sānshí. **thir·ti·eth** /'θɜːtɪəθ/ *adj, n* [C] (缩作 *30th*) 第三十 dìsānshí; 三十分之一 sānshífēn zhī yī.

this /ðɪs/ *adj, pron* [*pl* these /ðiːz/] **1** 这〔這〕zhè, 这个〔個〕zhège: *Look at* ~ *box* (*these boxes*). 看这个(这些)盒子. **2** 某 mǒu, 某个 mǒuge: *Then* ~ *man came in.* 接着, 有人进来了. □ *adv* 〔非正式用语〕如此 rúcǐ, 这样地 zhèyàngde: *It's about* ~ *high.* 它大约有这么高.

thistle /'θɪsl/ *n* [C] 〔植物〕蓟 jì.

thong /θɒŋ/ *n* [C] 皮条〔條〕pítiáo, 皮鞭 píbiān.

thorn /θɔːn/ *n* **1** [C] 刺 cì, 棘 jí. *a* ~ *in one's flesh* (或 *side*) 〔喻〕经〔經〕常使人烦恼〔惱〕的事物 jīngcháng shǐ rén fánnǎo de shìwù. **2** [C,U] 荆棘 jīngjí, 有荆棘

的树〔樹〕yǒu jīngjí de shù. **thorny** *adj* [-ier, -iest] **(a)** 有刺的 yǒu cì de, 多刺的 duō cì de. **(b)** 〔喻〕棘手的 jíshǒude, 多困难〔難〕的 duō kùnnan de: *a ~y problem* 棘手的问题.

thor·ough /'θʌrə/ *adj* 彻〔徹〕底的 chèdǐde, 完善的 wánshànde, 周到的 zhōudàode, 详尽〔盡〕的 xiángjìnde: *a ~ worker* 一丝不苟的工作者. '**~-going** *adj* 彻底的 chèdǐde, 十足的 shízúde: *a ,~-going re'vision* 彻底修订. **~ly** *adv* **~ness** *n* [U]

thor·ough·bred /'θʌrəbred/ *n* [C] *adj* (犬,马等) 良种〔種〕的 liángzhǒngde, 纯种的 chúnzhǒngde.

thor·ough·fare /'θʌrəfeə(r)/ *n* [C] 大街 dàjiē, 通道 tōngdào.

those /ðəʊz/ *pl* of that.

though /ðəʊ/ *conj* **1** (亦作 **al·though** /ɔ:l'ðəʊ/) 虽〔雖〕然 suīrán, 尽〔儘〕管 jǐnguǎn: *T~ they are poor, they are happy.* 他们虽然穷, 他们是快乐的. **2** 可是 kěshì, 然而 rán'ér, 不过〔過〕búguò: *I'll try to come, ~ I don't think I can.* 我会尽量来的,不过,看来我来不了. □ *adv* 可是 kěshì, 然而 rán'ér: *He said he would come; he didn't, ~.* 他说他会来,可是他并没有来.

thought¹ /θɔ:t/ *pt, pp* of think¹.

thought² /θɔ:t/ *n* **1** [U] 思想 sīxiǎng; 思维能力 sīwéi nénglì: *He was lost (deep) in ~.* 他陷入沉思中. **2** [U] 关〔關〕心 guānxīn, 顾〔顧〕虑〔慮〕gùlǜ, 挂〔掛〕念 guàniàn: *He often acts without ~.* 他常常鲁莽行事. **3** [C,U] 观〔觀〕念 guānniàn, 意图〔圖〕yìtú, 想法 xiǎngfǎ. ***food for ~*** ⇨ food(2). ***on second ~s*** 进〔進〕一步考虑后〔後〕jìnyíbù kǎolǜ hòu. ***give sth a ~*** 考虑一下 kǎolǜ yíxià. **~ful** *adj* **(a)** 深思的 shēnsīde, 思考的 sīkǎode: *~ful looks* 沉思的表情. **(b)** 关心的 guānxīnde, 体〔體〕贴的 tǐtiēde: *It was ~ful of you to help me.* 你帮助我, 太关心我了. **~fully** *adv* **~less** *adj* 粗心的 cūxīnde, 疏忽的 shūhūde; 不关心别人的 bù guānxīn biérén de: *It was ~less of you to leave without me.* 你不和我一起离开, 太轻率了. **~lessly** *adv*

thou·sand /'θaʊznd/ *adj, n* [C] **1** 千 qiān. **2** 许许多多 xǔxǔduōduō, 无〔無〕数〔數〕wúshù: *A ~ thanks.* 多谢. ***one in a ~*** 千里挑一 qiānlǐ tiāo yī, 难〔難〕得的人或物 nándéde rén huò wù. **~th** /'θaʊzənθ/ *adj, n* [C] (缩作 *1000th*) 第一千 dìyìqiān; 千分之一 qiānfēn zhī yī.

thrash /θræʃ/ *vt/i* **1** (用鞭, 棍等) 痛打 tòngdǎ. **2** [非正式用语] 打败 dǎbài, 胜〔勝〕过〔過〕shèngguò. **3 ~ *sth out*** **(a)** 研讨解决 (问题) yántǎo jiějué. **(b)** 通过讨论获〔獲〕得 tōngguò tǎolùn huòdé. **4** (使)颠簸 diānbò; 猛烈移动〔動〕měngliè yídòng: *She ~ed about in the water.* 她在水中来回游动. **~ing (a)** 鞭打 biāndǎ, 痛打 tòngdǎ. **(b)** (在比赛中)失败 shībài.

thread /θred/ *n* **1** [C,U] (一段)线〔線〕xiàn: *a needle and ~* 一根穿了线的针. **2** 细细的一条〔條〕xìxìde yìtiáo: *A ~ of light* 一线亮光. **3** [C] 头〔頭〕绪 tóuxù,思路 sīlù,线索 xiànsuǒ: *lose the ~ of one's argument* 争论中乱了头绪. **4** 螺纹 luówén. □ *vt* **1** 穿线于〔於〕chuān xiàn yú; '(把珍珠等) 穿成一串 chuānchéng yíchuàn. **2 ~ *one's way through*** 挤〔擠〕过〔過〕(人群等) jǐguò. '**~bare** *adj* (指衣服) 穿旧〔舊〕的 chuānjiùde.

threat /θret/ *n* [C] **1** 恐吓〔嚇〕kǒnghè, 威胁〔脅〕wēixié: *carry out a ~* 把恐吓付诸实施. **2** 坏〔壞〕兆头〔頭〕huài zhàotou, 凶兆 xiōngzhào. **3** 造成威胁的事物 zàochéng wēixié de shìwù: *He is a ~ to society.* 他是一个有害社会的危险分子.

threaten /'θretn/ *vt/i* **1** 恐吓〔嚇〕kǒnghè, 威胁〔脅〕wēixié. **2** 预示 yùshì: *The clouds ~ed rain.* 乌云预示要下雨. **3** 似将〔將〕发〔發〕生 sì jiāng fāshéng, 可能来〔來〕临〔臨〕kěnéng láilín: *danger ~ed* 随时有危险发生. **4** 是一种威胁 shì yìzhǒng wēixié. *Terrorism ~s our society.* 恐怖主义是我们社会的一种威胁. **~ing** *adj*: *a ~ing sky* 要变坏的天气. **~ing·ly** *adv*

three /θri:/ *adj, n* [C] 三 sān. ,**~-di'mensional** *adj* 三维的 sānwéide, 三度的 sāndùde.

thresh /θreʃ/ *vt/i* 打麦,谷〔穀〕等 dǎ mài, gǔ děng: *~ corn by hand* 用手打谷.

thresh·old /'θreʃhəuld/ *n* [C] **1** 门〔門〕槛〔檻〕ménkǎn: *cross the ~* 跨过门槛. **2** 〔喻〕开〔開〕始 kāishǐ, 开端 kāiduān, 入门 rùmén: *the ~ of his career* 他的事业的开端.

threw /θru:/ *pt* of throw¹.

thrift /θrɪft/ *n* [U] 节〔節〕约 jiéyuē. **thrifty** *adj* [-ier, -iest] 节约的 jiéyuēde.

thrill /θrɪl/ *n* [C] (一阵)激动〔動〕jīdòng; 刺激性 cìjīxìng; 震颤感 zhènchàngǎn: *a ~ of joy (pleasure, horror)* 一阵高兴 (愉快, 恐怖).

□ *vt/i* (使) 激动 jīdòng; (使)震颤 zhènchàn: *The film* ~*ed the audience.* 那电影使观众激动. ~**er** 引起激动的人或物 yǐnqǐ jīdòng de rén huò wù; 富于〔於〕刺激性的小说,戏〔戲〕剧〔劇〕,电〔電〕影等 fùyú cìjīxìng de xiǎoshuō, xìjù, diànyǐng děng.

thrive /θraɪv/ *vi* 繁荣〔榮〕fánróng, 兴〔興〕旺 xīngwàng; 茁壮〔壯〕成长〔長〕 zhuózhuàng chéngzhǎng: *Children* ~ *on good food.* 儿童靠良好的食物而茁壮成长. *a thriving business* 生意兴隆的买卖.

throat /θrəʊt/ *n* [C] **1** [解剖] 颈〔頸〕前 jǐngqián. **2** 咽喉 yānhóu. ***stick in one's*** ~ [喻]使人难〔難〕于接受 shǐ rén nányú jiēshòu.

throb /θrɒb/ *vi* [-bb-] (心脏,脉搏等)跳动〔動〕tiàodòng, 悸动 jìdòng. □ *n* [C] 跳动 tiàodòng, 悸动 jìdòng, 震动 zhèndòng. ~**bing** *adj* 跳动的 tiàodòngde, 悸动的 jìdòngde: *a* ~*bing headache* 一跳一跳的头痛.

throne /θrəʊn/ *n* [C] **1** 宝〔寶〕座 bǎozuò, 御座 yùzuò. **2 the** ~ 王位 wángwèi, 帝位 dìwèi, 王权〔權〕 wángquán: *come to the* ~ 即王位.

throng /θrɒŋ/ *n* [C] 人群 rénqún, 群众〔衆〕qúnzhòng. □ *vt/i* 群集 qúnjí, 拥〔擁〕挤〔擠〕yōngjǐ: *People* ~*ed to see him.* 人们蜂拥着去看他.

throttle /ˈθrɒtl/ *vt/i* **1** 掐死 qiāsǐ, 勒死 lēisǐ. **2** (使发动机)节〔節〕流 jiéliú, 减速 jiǎnsù. □ *n* [C] (发动机的)节流阀〔閥〕jiéliúfá.

through[1] [美语 = **thru**] /θru:/ *adv* **1** 穿过〔過〕 chuānguò, 通过 tōngguò: *He slept the whole night* ~. 他一觉睡到天亮. *The nail went* ~ *the wood.* 这钉子穿透木头了. ***all*** ~ 一直 yìzhí, 从〔從〕来〔來〕就 cónglái jiù, 老是 lǎoshì. **2** 到最后〔後〕 dào zuìhòu, 到底 dào dǐ. ***be*** ~ ***(with)*** **(a)** 完成 wánchéng, 结束 jiéshù. **(b)** [非正式用语] 对〔對〕...已经〔經〕厌〔厭〕烦 duì ... yǐjīng yànfán: *I'm* ~ *with this job.* 我对这工作已经厌烦. **(c)** [非正式用语]嫌弃〔棄〕xiánqì, 绝爱〔愛〕jué'ài: *I'm* ~ *with her.* 我和她断绝关系. ~ ***and*** ~ 彻〔徹〕头〔頭〕彻尾地 chètóu chèwěi de: *He's a reliable man* ~ *and* ~. 他是一个完全可靠的人. **3** 直达〔達〕地 zhídáde, 全程地 quánchéngde: *This train goes* ~ *to Paris.* 这列车直达巴黎. **4** [用作 *adj*]: *a* ~ *train to Paris* 直达巴黎的列车. ~ *traffic* 过境交通. **5** 接通 (电话) jiētōng: *I will put you* ~ 我将为你接通(电话).

through[2] [美语 = **thru**] /θru:/ *prep* **1** 穿过〔過〕 chuānguò, 通过 tōngguò: *look* ~ *a telescope* 用望远镜观看. **2** (指时间) 从〔從〕头〔頭〕到尾经〔經〕过 cóngtóu dàowěi jīngguò: *He won't live* ~ *the night.* 他不会活过今晚了. **3** 由于〔於〕yóuyú, 因为〔爲〕yīnwéi: *The accident happened* ~ *no fault of yours.* 这个意外事件的发生, 并非由于你的过错. **4** (穿过 ...) 未停 wèi tíng: *Drive* ~ *a red light.* (驾车) 闯红灯〔燈〕.

through·out /θru:ˈaʊt/ *adv* 各方面 gèfāngmiàn, 到处〔處〕dàochù; 始终 shǐzhōng: *The house needs painting* ~. 这房子需要全部油漆. □ *prep* 遍及 biànjí, 贯穿 guànchuān: ~ *the country (the year)* 全国(年).

throw[1] /θrəʊ/ *vt/i* [*pt* threw /θru:/; *pp* thrown /θrəʊn/] **1** 抛 pāo, 掷〔擲〕zhì, 投 tóu, 扔 rēng: *Don't* ~ *stones!* 不要扔石子! **2** [与 *on*, *off* 连用] 匆匆穿上或脱下 cōngcōng chuānshàng huò tuōxià: ~ *on a coat* 匆匆穿上外套. **3** 用力移动〔動〕yònglì yídòng: ~ *one's head back* 用力向后仰头. **4** 摔倒 shuāidǎo, 摔下 shuāixià: *The horse threw its jockey.* 这马摔下它的骑师. **5** [喻] 投向 tóuxiàng: *He threw me an angry look.* 他对我怒目而视. **6** [非正式用语] ~ ***a party*** 举〔舉〕行宴会 jǔxíng yànhuì. **7** ~ ***sth about*** 乱〔亂〕扔 luàn rēng, 撒布〔佈〕sànbù. ~ ***money about*** [喻]乱花钱〔錢〕luàn huā qián. ~ ***sth away*** **(a)** 浪费掉 làngfèidiào: ~ *away an opportunity* 放过一个机会. **(b)** 处〔處〕理掉 chǔlǐdiào, 扔掉 rēngdiào: ~ *away old clothes* 扔掉旧衣服. ~ ***oneself down*** 平躺下 píng tǎngxià. ~ ***sth in*** 额外增添 éwài zēngtiān, 免费添加 miǎnfèi tiānjiā. ~ ***in the towel*** [非正式用语]认〔認〕输〔輸〕rènshū. ~ ***oneself into sth*** 投身于〔於〕(工作) tóushēn yú. ~ ***sb (sth) off*** 摆〔擺〕脱 bǎituō, 甩掉 shuǎidiào. ~ ***oneself on*** 依赖 yīlài, 听〔聽〕命于〔於〕tīngmìng yú: ~ *oneself on the mercy of the court* 听从法院处置. ~ ***sth out*** **(a)** 拒绝 jùjué; 否决 fǒujué. **(b)** 撵〔攆〕走 niǎnzǒu; 扔掉 rēngdiào. ~ ***sb over*** 放弃〔棄〕fàngqì, 抛弃 pāoqì: ~ *over one's girlfriend* 遗弃女朋友. ~ ***sth together*** 匆匆拼凑

成 cōngcōng pīncòu chéng. ~ ***sth up*** **(a)** 呕〔嘔〕吐 ǒutù. **(b)** 辞〔辭〕去 cíqù: ~ *up one's job* 辞职.
throw up one's hands (in horror) 举〔舉〕起双〔雙〕手(表示恐怖) jǔqǐ shuāng shǒu. ~ ***oneself upon*** = throw on.

throw² /θrəʊ/ *n* [C] 投掷〔擲〕tóuzhì; 投掷的距离〔離〕tóuzhìde jùlí: *a ~ of 70 metres* 投掷距离为七十米. ***within a stone's ~ (of)*** ⇨ stone(2).

thrush /θrʌʃ/ *n* [C] 画〔畫〕眉鸟〔鳥〕huàméiniǎo.

thrust /θrʌst/ *vt/i* [*pt, pp* ~] 猛推 měng tuī, 冲〔衝〕chōng; 刺 cì, 戳 chuō. □ *n* **1** [C] 猛推 měng tuī, 冲 chōng; 刺 cì, 戳 chuō. **2** [C] 冲锋 chōngfēng, 突击〔擊〕tūjī. **3** [U] 推力 tuīlì: *the ~ of a jet-engine* 喷气机的推力.

thud /θʌd/ *n* [C] 重击〔擊〕(软物)声〔聲〕zhòngjīshēng. □ *vi* [-dd-] 发〔發〕出重击声 fāchū zhòngjīshēng; 砰地落下 pēngde luòxià.

thug /θʌg/ *n* [C] 暴徒 bàotú, 恶〔惡〕棍 ègùn.

thumb /θʌm/ *n* [C] 大拇指 dàmǔzhǐ. ***under sb's ~*** 在某人的控制下 zài mǒurén de kòngzhìxià. ***rule of ~*** 单〔單〕凭〔憑〕经〔經〕验〔驗〕的作法 dān píng jīngyàn de zuòfǎ. □ *vt* **1** 翻阅〔閱〕(书页) fānyuè; 以拇指翻动〔動〕而弄脏〔髒〕yǐ mǔzhǐ fāndòng ér nòngzāng: ~ *the pages of a dictionary* 翻查词典. **2** ~ ***a lift*** = hitchhike.

thump /θʌmp/ *vt/i* **1** 重击〔擊〕zhòngjī, 拳击 quánjī: *He ~ed (on) the door.* 他用力捶门. **2** 剧〔劇〕烈跳动〔動〕jùliè tiàodòng: *His heart ~ed with excitement.* 他兴奋得心头怦怦直跳. □ *n* [C] 重击声 zhòngjīshēng, 砰然声 pēngránshēng: *Give him a friendly ~ on the back.* 在他背上给一下友好但很重的拍打.

thun·der /ˈθʌndə(r)/ *n* [U] **1** 雷 léi, 雷声〔聲〕léishēng. **2** (似雷的)轰〔轟〕隆声 hōnglōngshēng: *the ~ of the guns* 大炮的隆隆声. ***steal sb's ~*** 抢〔搶〕先做某人要做的事(来破坏他的计划) qiǎngxiān zuò mǒurén yào zuò de shì. □ *vt/i* **1** 打雷 dǎléi: *It was ~ing and lightenig.* 当时正在电闪雷鸣. **2** 发〔發〕出雷鸣般的隆隆声 fāchū léimíngbānde lōnglōngshēng. **3** 大声说话 dà shēng shuōhuà. '~**bolt** **(a)** 雷电交加 léidiàn jiāojiā. **(b)** 〔喻〕意外的可怕事件 yìwàide kěpà shìjiàn, 晴天霹雳〔靂〕qíng tiān pīlì. '~**clap** 雷响〔響〕léixiǎng, 霹雳 pīlì. '~**storm** 雷暴雨 léibàoyǔ. ~**ous** *adj* 雷声似的 léishēng sì de: ~*ous applause* 雷鸣般的掌声.

Thurs. = Thursday.

Thurs·day /ˈθɜːzdɪ/ *n* 星期四 xīngqīsì.

thus /ðʌs/ *adv* 如此 rúcǐ; 因而 yīn'ér.

thyme /taɪm/ *n* [U] 〔植物〕百里香 bǎilǐxiāng.

thy·roid /ˈθaɪrɔɪd/ *n* [C] (亦作'~ *gland*) 甲状〔狀〕腺 jiǎzhuàngxiàn.

ti·ara /tɪˈɑːrə/ *n* [C] [*pl* ~s] **1** 妇〔婦〕女的冠状〔狀〕头〔頭〕饰 fùnǚde guānzhuàng tóushì. **2** 罗〔羅〕马〔馬〕教皇的三重冠 Luómǎ Jiàohuáng de sānchóngguān.

tick¹ /tɪk/ *n* [C] **1** (尤指钟表等的)滴答声〔聲〕dīdāshēng. **2** [非正式用语] 一刹那 yíchànà, 片刻 piànkè: *I'll be with you in a ~.* 我一会儿就来陪你. **3** (核对帐目等用的)记号〔號〕(常用✓) jìhào. □ *vt/i* **1** (钟表等)滴答作响〔響〕dīdā zuòxiǎng. **2** 标〔標〕以(✓)记号 biāo yǐ jìhào: ~ *off a name* 把名字勾出. ~ ***sb off*** [非正式用语] 责备〔備〕zébèi, 斥责 chìzé.

tick² /tɪk/ *n* [C] [动物] 扁虱〔蝨〕biǎnshī.

ticker /ˈtɪkə(r)/ *n* [C] **1** 自动〔動〕收报〔報〕机〔機〕zìdòng shōubàojī. '~**-tape** 自动收报机纸条〔條〕zìdòng shōubàojī zhǐtiáo. **2** [俚语] 心脏〔臟〕xīnzàng.

ticket /ˈtɪkɪt/ *n* [C] **1** 票 piào, 车〔車〕票 chēpiào, 入场〔場〕券 rùchǎngquàn. **2** (货物上的)标〔標〕签〔簽〕biāoqiān. **3** (给违反交通规则者的)传〔傳〕票 chuánpiào. □ *vt* 加上标签 jiāshàng biāoqiān. '~**-collecter** (火车)收票员 shōupiàoyuán.

tickle /ˈtɪkl/ *vt/i* **1** 搔痒〔癢〕sāoyǎng. **2** 逗乐〔樂〕dòulè, 使高兴〔興〕shǐ gāoxìng. **3** (使)觉〔覺〕得痒 juédé yǎng: *My nose ~s.* 我的鼻子发痒. **tick·lish** /ˈtɪklɪʃ/ *adj* **(a)** (指人)怕痒的 pà yǎng de. **(b)** (指问题等)困难〔難〕的 kùnnande, 棘手的 jíshǒude.

ti·dal /ˈtaɪdl/ *adj* 潮汐的 cháoxīde 有潮的 yǒu cháo de. '~ **wave** 潮浪 cháolàng; 海啸〔嘯〕hǎixiào.

tide /taɪd/ *n* **1** [C,U] 潮汐 cháoxī **2** [C] (指舆论, 公众情绪等) 潮流 cháoliú, 趋〔趨〕势〔勢〕qūshì. □ *vt* ~ ***sb over (sth)*** 帮助某人渡过(难关) bāngzhù mǒurén dùguò:

loan to ~ me over until pay-day. 一笔贷款帮我克服困难直到发薪.'~-**mark** 涨〔漲〕潮点〔點〕zhǎngcháodiǎn.

tid·ings /'taɪdɪŋz/ *n pl* 〔书面语〕消息 xiāoxī, 音信 yīnxìn: *glad ~* 好消息.

tidy /'taɪdɪ/ *adj* [-ier, -iest] **1** 整洁〔潔〕的 zhěngjiéde: *a ~ room (boy)* 整洁的房间(男孩). **2**〔非正式用语〕相当〔當〕大的 xiāngdāng dà de: *a ~ sum of money* 相当大的一笔钱. □ *n* [C] [*pl* -ies] 装〔裝〕零碎东〔東〕西的容器 zhuāng língsuì dōngxi de róngqì. □ *vt/i* 使整洁 shǐ zhěngjié: *~ (up) the room* 整理房间. **ti·dily** *adv* **ti·di·ness** *n* [U]

tie[1] /taɪ/ *n* [C] **1** (结扎用的)带〔帶〕子 dàizi, 绳〔繩〕子 shéngzi. **2**〔喻〕关〔關〕系〔係〕guānxì, 联〔聯〕系 liánxì: *family ~s* 家庭关系. **3** 束缚 shùfù, 牵〔牽〕累 qiānlěi: *Small children can be a ~.* 小孩子可能成为一种牵累. **4** (比赛中)不分胜〔勝〕负 bùfēn shèng fù, 平局 píngjú. **5** = neck-tie.

tie[2] /taɪ/ *vt/i* [*pres part* tying; *pt, pp* tied] **1** (用带, 绳等)捆扎〔紮〕kǔnzhā, 系〔繫〕jì, 结 jié: *~ a man up* 将一个人绑起来. *~ on a label* 结上标签. **2** (把带子等)打结 dǎjié: *~ one's shoelaces* 系鞋带. *~ a knot* 打一个结. **3** 结起 jiéqǐ, 打结 dǎjié: *Does this dress ~ in front?* 这衣服是在前面打结的吗? **4** 打成平局 dǎ chéng píngjú: *The two teams ~d.* 两队打成平局. *~ sb down* 约束某人 yuēshù mǒurén. **be ~d up (with sth, sb)** (与某人, 某事)有关〔關〕系〔係〕yǒu guānxì.

tier /tɪə(r)/ *n* [C] 一排(座位) yìpái.

tiff /tɪf/ *n* [C] 小口角 xiǎo kǒujiǎo.

ti·ger /'taɪgə(r)/ *n* [C] 虎 hǔ.

ti·gress /'taɪgrɪs/ *n* [C] 母虎 mǔhǔ.

tight /taɪt/ *adj* [-er, -est] **1** 紧〔緊〕的 jǐnde, 牢固的 láogùde: *a ~ knot* 死结. **2** 紧密的 jǐnmìde, 密封的 mìfēngde: *,water-'~* 不漏水的. *,air-'~* 不透气的. **3** 装〔裝〕满的 zhuāng mǎn de, 装紧的 zhuāng jǐn de, 挤〔擠〕满的 jǐ mǎn de: *The bags are packed ~.* 袋子装得满满的. **4**〔非正式用语〕醉醺醺的 zuì xūnxūn de: *He gets ~ every pay-day.* 他每逢领薪水的日子总是喝得酩酊大醉. **5** 绷紧的 bēng jǐn de, 拉紧的 lā jǐn de: *a ~ rope* 绷紧的绳索. **6** 紧身的 jǐn shēn de, 贴身的 tiē shēn de: *a ~ shirt* 贴身的衬衫. *in a ~* **corner** (或 **spot**)〔喻〕处〔處〕于〔於〕困境 chù yú kùnjìng. *a ~ **squeeze*** 挤满 jǐ mǎn, 塞紧 sāi jǐn. **7** (指钱)难〔難〕得到的 nán dédào de; 银根紧的 yíngēn jǐn de. □ *adv* 紧紧地 jǐnjǐnde: *squeeze (hold) it ~* 紧紧地压挤(握住)它. ***sit ~*** ⇨ sit(1). **,~-'fisted** 吝啬〔嗇〕的 lìnsède, 小气〔氣〕的 xiǎoqìde. **'~rope** (走钢丝用的)绷索 bēngsuǒ. **~ly** *adv* **~ness** *n* [U]

tighten /'taɪtn/ *vt/i* (使)变〔變〕紧〔緊〕biàn jǐn, (使)绷紧 bēng jǐn: *~ (up) the screws* 拧紧螺丝钉.

tights /taɪts/ *n pl* 紧身衣 jǐnshēn yī.

tile /taɪl/ *n* [C] 瓦 wǎ, 瓦片 wǎpiàn. ***be (out) on the ~s*** 〔俚语〕寻〔尋〕欢〔歡〕作乐〔樂〕xínhuān-zuòlè, 花天酒地 huātiān-jiǔdì. □ *vt* 用瓦铺(屋顶) yòng wǎ pū.

till[1] /tɪl/ (亦作 **until** /ʌn'tɪl/) *conj, prep* 直到…为〔爲〕止 zhídào…wéizhǐ: *Wait ~ I arrive!* 一直等到我来到!

till[2] /tɪl/ *n* [C] (帐台中)放钱〔錢〕的抽屉〔屜〕fàng qián de chōutì.

till[3] /tɪl/ *vt* 耕种〔種〕gēngzhòng.

tiller /'tɪlə(r)/ *n* [C] 舵柄 duòbǐng.

tilt /tɪlt/ *vt/i* (使)倾斜 qīngxié: *Don't ~ the table.* 不要让桌子倾斜. □ *n* [C] 倾斜 qīngxié; 斜坡 xiépō. ***at full ~*** 全速地 quánsùde.

tim·ber /'tɪmbə(r)/ *n* **1** [U] 木材 mùcái, 木料 mùliào. **2** [U] 树〔樹〕木 shùmù, 树林 shùlín, 木材林 mùcáilín: *acres of ~* 几亩地的树林. **3** [C] 栋〔棟〕木 dòngmù, 支架 zhījià. **~ed** *adj*

time[1] /taɪm/ *n* **1** [U] 时〔時〕间〔間〕shíjiān: *The world exists in space and ~.* 世界存在于空间和时间中. **2** [U] 一段时间 yíduàn shíjiān: *What a (long) ~ you have been!* 你花了多么长的时间啊! ***all the ~*** 始终 shǐzhōng, 一直 yìzhí: *It rained all the ~ we were out.* 我们出门后一直下雨. ***behind ~*** 迟〔遲〕到 chídào, 晚 wǎn. ***for the ~ being*** ⇨ be[1](3). ***on ~*** 按时 ànshí, 准〔準〕时 zhǔnshí. ***in no ~*** 立刻 lìkè, 很快 hěn kuài. ***play for ~*** 为〔爲〕争取时间而拖延 wèi zhēngqǔ shíjiān ér tuōyuán. **3** [U] 时候 shíhòu, 时刻 shíkè: *What ~ is it?* 什么时候了? **4** [U] (作某事所费的)时间 shíjiān: *The winner's ~ was 11 seconds.* 获胜者用了十一秒钟. ***pass the ~ of day (with …)*** (与…)打招呼 (如说"你早"等) dǎ zhāohu. **5** [C,U] (发生某事的)时候 shíhòu, 时机〔機〕shíjī:

It's lunch-~. 是午餐的时候了. *It's* ~ *for me to go.* 我该走了. ***at the same*** ~ **(a)** 同时 tóngshí, 一起 yìqǐ. **(b)** 然而 rán'ér: *He's mad, but at the same* ~ *I like him.* 他是疯了, 然而我喜欢他. ***from*** ~ ***to*** ~; ***at*** ~***s*** 有时 yǒushí, 时时 shíshí. ***at all*** ~***s*** 经〔經〕常 jīngcháng, 无〔無〕论〔論〕何时 wúlùn hé shí. ***in*** ~ **(a)** 及时 jíshí, 还〔還〕早 hái zǎo, 不晚 bùwǎn. **(b)** 总〔總〕有一天 zǒng yǒu yìtiān, 最后〔後〕zuìhòu, 早晚 zǎowǎn: *You will learn how to do it in* ~. 你总有一天会学会做此事. ***do*** ~ 〔非正式用语〕服徒刑 fú túxíng. **6** [C] 次 cì, 回 huí: *this (that, next, another)* ~. 这(那, 下, 另一)次. ~ ***and again*** 反复〔復〕地 fǎnfùde, 多次 duō cì. **7** [*pl*] 倍 bèi; 乘 chéng: *Three* ~*s five is (are) fifteen.* 三乘五得十五. **8** [C] 〔常作 *pl*〕时代 shídài, 时期 shíqī: *in ancient* ~*s* 在古代. *in prehistoric* ~*s* 在史前时期. **9** [C] 〔常作 *pl*〕某一时期的生活状〔狀〕况 mǒuyī shíqī de shēnghuó zhuàngkuàng: *The terrible* ~*s during the war.* 战争年代的可怕的生活. ***behind the*** ~***s*** 旧〔舊〕式的 jiùshìde, 过〔過〕时的 guòshíde, 落伍的 luòwǔde. ***have a*** ˌ***good*** ˈ~ 过得愉快 guòdé yúkuài. ***the*** ˌ~ ***of one's*** ˈ***life*** 〔非正式用语〕一生中最愉快的一段时期 yìshēng zhōng zuì yúkuài de yíduàn shíqī. **10** 〔音乐〕拍子 pāizi, 节〔節〕拍 jiépāi: *beat* ~ 打拍子. ~ ***and motion study*** *n* 提高工作效率的研究 tígāo gōngzuò xiàolǜ de yánjiū. ˈ~**-bomb** 定时炸弹〔彈〕dìngshí zhàdàn. ˈ~**-limit** 期限 qīxiàn. ˈ~**-signal** (电台的)报〔報〕时信号〔號〕bào shí xìnhào. ˈ~**-switch** 定时开〔開〕关〔關〕dìng shí kāiguān. ˈ~**table** 时刻表 shíkèbiǎo.

time² /taɪm/ *vt* **1** 安排 … 的时间〔間〕ānpái … de shíjiān, 为…选〔選〕择〔擇〕时机〔機〕wèi … xuǎnzé shíjī: *He* ~*d his journey so that he arrived early.* 他适当安排旅程的时间, 因而及早到达了. **2** 计算 … 的时间 jìsuàn … de shíjiān.

time·ly /ˈtaɪmlɪ/ *adj* [-ier, -iest] 及时〔時〕的 jíshíde, 适〔適〕时的 shìshíde.

timid /ˈtɪmɪd/ *adj* 胆〔膽〕怯的 dǎnqiède: *He's as* ~ *as a rabbit.* 他象兔子一样胆小. ~**ity** /tɪˈmɪdətɪ/ *n* [U] ~**ly** *adv*

tin /tɪn/ *n* **1** [U] 锡(Sn) xī. **2** [C] 罐头〔頭〕guàntou, 听〔聽〕tīng: *a* ~ *of beans* 一听蚕〔蠶〕豆. □ *vt* [-nn-] **1** 镀锡 dù xī, 包锡 bāo xī. **2**(= *can*) 装〔裝〕…罐头 zhuāng … guàntou: ~*ned peaches* 罐头桃子. ˈ~**foil** 锡纸 xīzhǐ. ˈ~**-opener** 开〔開〕罐头刀 kāi guàntou dāo; ~**ny** *adj* [-ier, -iest] 锡的 xīde; (声音)细弱无〔無〕力的 xìruò wú lì de: *a* ~ *piano* 声音细弱的钢琴.

tinge /tɪndʒ/ *vt* **1** (较淡地) 着色于〔於〕zhuó sè yú, 染 rǎn. **2** 〔喻〕使带〔帶〕…气〔氣〕息 shǐ dài … qìxī: *admiration* ~*d with envy* 含有妒意的赞美. □ *n* [C] (淡淡的)色彩 sècǎi; (些微的)气息 qìxī: *a* ~ *of sadness in her voice* 她的声音中略带悲伤.

tingle /ˈtɪŋgl/ *vi* **1** 感到刺痛 gǎn dào cìtòng: *His fingers* ~*d with the cold.* 他的手指冻得刺痛. **2** 激动〔動〕jīdòng, 兴〔興〕奋〔奮〕xìngfèn. □*n* [C] 刺痛 cìtòng; 激动 jīdòng.

tinkle /ˈtɪŋkl/ *vt/i* (使)发〔發〕丁当〔當〕声〔聲〕fā dīngdāngshēng. □ *n* [*sing*] 丁当声 dīngdāngshēng, 丁丁声 dīngdīngshēng: *the* ~ *of a bell* 铃声丁当.

tint /tɪnt/ *n* [C] 颜色的浓〔濃〕淡 yánsède nóng dàn, 色彩 sècǎi, (尤指)浅〔淺〕色 qiǎn sè. □ *vt* 着色于〔於〕zhuó sè yú, 给 … 染色 gěi … rǎn sè.

tiny /ˈtaɪnɪ/ *adj* [-ier, -iest] 极〔極〕小的 jíxiǎode.

tip¹ /tɪp/ *n* [C] **1** 尖端 jiānduān, 末端 mòduān: *the* ˈ*finger-*~*s* 手指尖. ***(have sth) on the*** ˌ~ ***of one's*** ˈ***tongue*** 即将〔將〕想起(某事) jíjiāng xiǎngqǐ, (某事)就在嘴边〔邊〕jiù zài zuǐbiān. **2** 附加在顶端的小物件 fùjiā zài dǐngduān de xiǎo wùjiàn: *cigarettes with filter-*~*s* 有过滤嘴的香烟. □ *vt* [-pp-] 装〔裝〕上尖头〔頭〕或附加物 zhuāngshàng jiāntóu huò fùjiāwù: ~*ped cigarettes* 过滤嘴香烟. ˈ~**toe** *adv* ***on*** ~-***toe*** 踮着脚尖 diànzhe jiǎojiān. □ *vi* 踮着脚尖走 diànzhe jiǎojiān zǒu: *She* ~*toed out.* 她踮着脚尖走出去了. ˌ~-ˈ**top** *adj, adv* 〔非正式用语〕第一流的(地) dìyīliúde.

tip² /tɪp/ *vt/i* [-pp-] **1** ~ ***(sth) up*** (使)倾斜 qīngxié: *The table* ~*ped up.* 桌子倾斜了. ~ ***sth (over)*** (使)翻倒 fāndǎo, (使)倾覆 qīngfù. ~ ***the scale*** **(a)** 〔喻〕起决定性作用 qǐ juédìngxìng zuòyòng. **(c)** 称〔稱〕量 chēngliáng: *He* ~*ped the scale at 70 kilos.* 他体重七十公斤. **2** 倾泻〔瀉〕qīngxiè, 倒 dào

□ *n* [C] **1** 倒垃圾处〔處〕dào lājī chù: *a 'refuse* ~ 垃圾堆. **2** (煤矿等的)废〔廢〕料堆积〔積〕场〔場〕fèiliào duījīchǎng. **3** [非正式用语]脏〔髒〕地方 zāng dìfang.

tip³ /tɪp/ *vt* [-pp-] **1** 轻〔輕〕触〔觸〕qīng chù, 轻拍 qīng pāi. **2** 给小费 gěi xiǎofèi: ~ *the waiter* 给侍者小费. ~ *sb off* [非正式用语]告诫某人 gàojiè mǒurén, 提示某人 tíshì mǒurén. '~-**off** *n* [C] 提示 tíshì, 告诫 gàojiè. □ *n* [C] **1** (给侍者等的) 小费 xiǎofèi. **2** 劝〔勸〕告 quàngào, 提示 tíshì. **3** 轻打 qīng dǎ, 轻拍 qīng pāi.

tipple /'tɪpl/ *n* [U] 烈酒 liè jiǔ: *My favourite* ~ *is sherry.* 我喜爱的是雪利酒.

tipsy /'tɪpsɪ/ *adj* [非正式用语]微醉的 wēi zuì de.

tire /'taɪə(r)/ *vt/i* (使) 疲劳〔勞〕píláo, (使) 疲倦 píjuàn: *The long walk* ~*ed him out.* 走这趟远路把他累坏了. **be** ~**d of** 对…感到厌〔厭〕烦 duì...gǎndào yànfán: *be* ~*d of boiled eggs* 煮蛋吃腻烦了. **tired** *adj* 疲劳的 píláode, 累的 lèide. ~**less** *adj* **(a)** 不易疲倦的 bùyì píjuàn de, 不累的 búlèide. **(b)** 不停的 bùtíngde, 持久的 chíjiǔde: ~*less energy* 持久的精力. '~**some** *adj* 令人厌倦的 lìng rén yànjuànde, 讨厌的 tǎoyànde.

tis·sue /'tɪʃu:/ *n* **1** [C,U] [生理] 组织〔織〕zǔzhī: '*muscular* ~ 肌肉组织. **2** [C,U] (亦作 '~ *paper*) 薄纸 bó zhǐ, 棉纸 mián zhǐ. **3** [C, U] 织物 zhīwù. **4** [C] [喻] 一套 yītào, 一连〔連〕串 yī liánchuàn: *a* ~ *of lies* 一连串的谎话.

tit¹ /tɪt/ *n* [C] 山雀 shānquè.

tit² /tɪt/ *n* [仅用于] ~ *for tat* 针锋相对〔對〕zhēn fēng xiāng duì, 以牙还〔還〕牙 yǐ yá huán yá.

tit³ /tɪt/ *n* [俚语]奶头〔頭〕nǎitóu.

tit·bit /'tɪtbɪt/ *n* [C] (少量而吸引人的) 珍品 zhēnpǐn, 珍闻〔聞〕zhēnwén.

titi·vate (亦作 **titti-**) /'tɪtɪveɪt/ *vt/i* [非正式用语]装〔裝〕饰 zhuāngshì, 打扮 dǎbàn.

title /'taɪtl/ *n* **1** [C] 标〔標〕题 biāotí, 题目 tímù. **2** [C] 称〔稱〕号〔號〕chēnghào, 头〔頭〕衔 tóuxián. **3** [C,U] [法律] 权〔權〕利 quánlì, 所有权 suǒyǒuquán: *Has he any* ~ *to the land?* 他对此土地有任何权利吗? '~-**role** (戏剧中其名字被用作剧名的)剧〔劇〕名角色 jùmíng juésè. '~-**deed** 地契 dìqì. **titled** *adj* 有贵族头衔的 yǒu guìzú tóuxián de: *a* ~*d lady* 命妇 (如女公爵).

tit·ter /'tɪtə(r)/ *vt, n* [C] 窃〔竊〕笑 qièxiào, 傻〔傻〕笑 shǎxiào.

TNT /,ti: en 'ti:/ *n* [U] 褐色炸药〔藥〕hèsè zhàyào.

to¹ /tu:/ *adv* (尤指门窗等)关〔關〕上 guānshàng: *Push the door* ~. 把门关上.

to² /tə, 强式: tu:/ *particle* **1** [构成动词不定式]: *He wants* ~ *go.* 他要去. **2** (表示目的, 效果, 结局): *They came (in order)* ~ *help me.* 他们来(为了要)帮助我. *He lived* ~ *be 90.* 他活到九十岁. **3** [用来代替动词不定式以避免重复]: *We didn't want to go but we had* ~. 我们不想去,但必须去.

to³ /tə, 强式: tu:/ *prep* **1** 向 xiàng, 对〔對〕duì, 往 wàng: *walk* ~ *work* 步行去上班. **2** [引导间接宾语]: *I gave it* ~ *Peter.* 我把它给了彼得. **3** 到 dào, 达〔達〕到 dádào: *from beginning* ~ *end* 自始至终. **4** 在…之前 zài ... zhī qián: *a quarter* ~ *six.* 六点差一刻钟. **5** 直到 … 为〔爲〕止 zhídào ... wéi zhǐ: *stay* ~ *the end* 坚持到底. **6** (表示比较): *I prefer walking* ~ *climbing.* 我喜欢步行, 不愿爬山. *We won by six goals* ~ *three.* 我们以六比三获胜.

T.O. = turn over.

toad /təʊd/ *n* [C] [动物] 蟾蜍 chánchú. '~**stool** [植物]毒蕈 dúxùn.

toast¹ /təʊst/ *n* [U] 烤面〔麵〕包 kǎo miànbāo. □ *vt/i* **1** 烤 (面包等) kǎo. **2** 烤火 kǎo huǒ. ~**er** 烤面包器 kǎo miànbāo qì.

toast² /təʊst/ *vt* 为〔爲〕... 祝酒 wèi ... zhùjiǔ: ~ *the bride and bridegroom* 举杯祝贺新郎新娘. □ *n* [C] 祝酒 zhùjiǔ: *propose a* ~ 敬酒. *drink a* ~ 干杯.

to·bacco /tə'bækəʊ/ *n* [U] 烟草 yāncǎo, 烟叶〔葉〕yānyè. ~**nist** 烟草商 yāncǎoshāng, 香烟店 xiāngyāndiàn.

to·bog·gan /tə'bɒgən/ *n* [C] 平底雪橇 píng dǐ xuěqiāo. □ *vi* 坐雪橇滑行 zuò xuěqiāo huáxíng.

to·day /tə'deɪ/ *adv, n* [U] **1** (在) 今天 jīntiān: *T*~ *is Sunday.* 今天是星期日. **2** 现在 xiànzài; 当〔當〕代 dāngdài: *the writers of* ~ 当代的作家们. *the young people of* ~ 现在的年轻人.

toddle /'tɒdl/ *vi* (如小孩的)蹒跚行走 pánshān xíngzǒu. **tod·dler** /'tɒdlə(r)/ 学〔學〕走的小孩 xué zǒu de xiǎohái.

toe /təʊ/ *n* [C] **1** 脚趾 jiǎozhǐ.

tread (或 *step*) *on sb's ~s* [喻]触[觸]怒某人 chù nù mǒurén. *on one's ~s* [喻]警觉[覺]的 jǐngjué-de, 准[準]备[備]行动[動]的 zhǔn-bèi xíngdòng de. **2** (鞋, 袜等的)脚尖部 jiǎojiānbù. □ *vt* 用脚趾触及 yòng jiǎozhǐ chùjí. *~ the line* [喻]听[聽]从[從]命令 tīngcóng mìnglìng. '**~nail** 脚趾甲 jiǎozhǐ-jiǎ.

tof·fee /'tɒfɪ/ *n* [C,U] 乳脂糖 rǔ-zhītáng, 太妃糖 tàifēitáng.

to·gether /tə'geðə(r)/ *adv* **1** 共同 gòngtóng, 一起 yìqǐ: *They went for a walk ~.* 他们一起出去散步. *~ with* 和 hé, 加之 jiāzhī, 连[連]同 liántóng. **2** (结合)在一起 zài yìqǐ, 集拢[攏]地 jílǒngde: *Tie the ends ~.* 把末端绑在一起. *put your (our) heads ~* 在一起商量 zài yìqǐ shāng-liang. **3** 同时[時] tóngshí: *All his troubles happened ~.* 他所有的麻烦事同时来临了. **~ness** *n* [U] 友谊 yǒuyì; 团[團]结性 tuánjiéxìng.

toil /tɔɪl/ *vi* 辛劳[勞]地工作 xīn-láode gōngzuò; 艰[艱]难[難]地行动[動] jiānnánde xíngdòng. □ *n* [U] 苦工 kǔgōng; 难事 nánshì: *after long ~* 在长时间的辛劳之后.

toilet /'tɔɪlɪt/ *n* [C] **1** 梳妆[粧] shūzhuāng, 打扮 dǎbàn. **2** 盥洗室 guànxǐshì. '**~-paper** 卫[衛]生纸 wèishēng zhǐ. '**~-roll** 卫生卷纸 wèishēng juǎnzhǐ.

to·ken /'təʊkən/ *n* [C] **1** 标[標]志 biāozhì, 记号[號] jìhào, 象征[徵] xiàngzhēng: *a ~ of my affection* 我的深情的象征. ⇨ book token. **2** [用作定语] 象征性的 xiàngzhēngxìngde: *a ~ payment* 象征性的偿付. ˌ**~ 'strike** (数小时的)象征性罢[罷]工 xiàngzhēng-xìng bàgōng.

told /təʊld/ *pt, pp* of tell.

tol·er·ance /'tɒlərəns/ *n* [U] 容忍 róngrěn, 宽恕 kuānshù: *religious (racial) ~* 宗教(种族)上的宽容. **tol·er·ant** *adj* 容忍的 róngrěnde, 宽恕的 kuānshùde. **tol·er·ant·ly** *adv*

tol·er·ate /'tɒləreɪt/ *vt* **1** 忍受 rěn-shòu, 容忍 róngrěn, 宽恕 kuān-shù: *I won't ~ your impudence.* 我不能容忍你的无礼. **2** 容许和…交往 róngxǔ hé…jiāowǎng: *How can you ~ that girl?* 你怎么竟和那个女孩子来往? **tol·er·able** /'tɒlə-rəbl/ *adj* [正式用语] 可忍受的 kě rěnshòu de, 可容许的 kě róngxǔ de; 尚好的 shànghǎode: *tolerable food* 还可以的食物. **tol·er·ably** *adv* **tol·er·ation** /-'reɪʃn/ 容忍 róngrěn, 宽恕 kuānshù.

toll¹ /təʊl/ *n* [C] **1** (道路, 桥梁等的)通行费 tōngxíngfèi. **2** [喻] 损失 sǔnshī; 代价[價] dàijià: *The war took a heavy ~.* 战争付出了巨大的代价. '**~-bar (-gate)** 收税关[關]卡 shōushuì guānkǎ.

toll² /təʊl/ *vt/i* (缓慢而有规律地)敲钟[鐘] qiāo zhōng. □ *n* [仅用 *sing*] 钟声 zhōngshēng.

tom·ato /tə'mɑːtəʊ/ *n* [C] [*pl* ~es] 西红柿 xīhóngshì.

tomb /tuːm/ *n* [C] 坟墓 fénmù. '**~stone** 墓碑 mùbēi.

tom·boy /'tɒmbɔɪ/ *n* [C] (男孩似的)顽皮姑娘 wánpí gū'niang.

tom·cat /'tɒmkæt/ *n* [C] 雄猫 xióngmāo.

to·mor·row /tə'mɒrəʊ/ *adv, n* [C, U] (在)明天 míngtiān.

ton /tʌn/ *n* [C] **1** (重量单位) 吨 (英吨 = 2240 磅, 公吨 = 1000 公斤) dūn. **2** [非正式用语] 大量 dàliàng; 沉重 chénzhòng: *~s of money* 许多钱.

tone¹ /təʊn/ *n* **1** [C] 声[聲]音 shēngyīn; (尤指)音质[質] yīnzhì, 音调 yīndiào: *the sweet ~(s) of a violin* 小提琴的悦耳的声音. *a serious ~ of voice* 说话的语气严肃. **2** [仅用 *sing*] 风[風]气[氣] fēng-qì, 气氛 qìfèn: *The ~ of the school is excellent.* 校风极好. **3** [C] 色调 sèdiào; 光度 guāngdù. **4** [C] [音乐]全音程 quán yīnchéng. **5** [U] 健康状[狀]况 jiànkāng zhuàng-kuàng: *good muscular ~* 肌肉结实. **~less** *adj* 单[單]调的 dāndiàode, 沉闷[悶]的 chénmènde.

tone² /təʊn/ *vt/i* **1** (给 …) 定调子 dìng diàozi. **2** *~ (sth) down* (使)减轻[輕] jiǎn qīng, (使) 缓和 huǎnhé. **3** *~ (sth) up* (使) 提高 tígāo, (使)加强 jiāqiáng.

tongs /tɒŋz/ *n pl* (亦作 *a pair of ~*) 钳 qián, 夹[夾]子 jiāzi: *'sugar ~* 糖块夹子.

tongue /tʌŋ/ *n* **1** [C] 舌头[頭] shétou. *have one's ~ in one's cheek* 毫无[無]诚意地说话 háo wú chéngyì de shuōhuà. *hold one's ~* 不开[開]口 bù kāikǒu, 缄默 jiānmò. **2** [C] 语言 yǔyán: *one's mother ~* 本国语. **3** [C,U] (动物的)舌头(作食品用者) shétou. **4** 舌状[狀]物(如鞋舌,火舌等) shé-zhuàngwù. '**~-tied** *adj* 张[張]口结舌的 zhāngkǒu-jiéshé de, 不愿[願]说话的 bú yuàn shuōhuà de. '**~-twister** 拗口令 àokǒulìng.

tonic /'tɒnɪk/ *n* [C], *adj* **1** 滋补

〔補〕品 zībǔpǐn, 补药〔藥〕 bǔyào; 滋补的 zībǔde, 强身的 qiángshēnde. **2** = tonic water: *a gin and* ~ 奎宁杜松子酒. '~ **water** (瓶装)奎宁〔寧〕水 kuíníngshuǐ.

to·night /tə'naɪt/ *adv, n* [U] (在)今晚 jīnwǎn.

ton·nage /'tʌnɪdʒ/ *n* [U] **1** (船的)登记吨位 dēngjì dūnwèi. **2** (一国商船的)总〔總〕吨数〔數〕 zǒng dūnshù.

ton·sil /'tɒnsl/ *n* [C] 扁桃体〔體〕 biǎntáotǐ, 扁桃腺 biǎntáoxiàn. ~**itis** /-'aɪtɪs/ *n* [U] 扁桃体炎 biǎntáotǐ yán.

too /tu:/ *adv* **1** 也 yě, 又 yòu, 还〔還〕hái: *I,* ~, *have been to Paris.* 我也去过巴黎. **2** 此外 cǐwài, 而且 érqiě: *There was frost last night, and in May* ~! 昨晚降霜了,而且是在五月里呢! **3** 太 tài, 过〔過〕分 guòfèn: *You're driving* ~ *fast.* 你(开车)开得太快了. **all** ~ **soon (quickly,** *etc***)** 太早(快,等) tài zǎo.

took /tʊk/ *pt* of take[1].

tool /tu:l/ *n* [C] **1** 工具 gōngjù, 用具 yòngjù. **2** 走狗 zǒugǒu, 傀儡 kuǐlěi.

tooth /tu:θ/ *n* [C] [*pl* teeth /ti:θ/] **1** 牙齿〔齒〕 yáchǐ. ***in the teeth of*** 对〔對〕抗 duìkàng, 面对 miànduì. ***armed to the teeth*** 武装〔裝〕到牙齿 wǔzhuāng dào yáchǐ. ***long in the*** ~ 年纪大 niánjì dà. ***fight*** ,~ ***and 'nail*** 猛烈战〔戰〕斗〔鬥〕 měngliè zhàndòu. ***get one's teeth into sth*** 死死抓住 sǐsǐ zhuāzhù. **2** (梳, 锯, 耙等的) 齿 chǐ. '~**ache** 牙痛 yátòng. '~**brush** 牙刷 yáshuā. '~**paste (powder)** 牙膏(粉) yágāo. '~**pick** 牙签〔簽〕 yáqiān. ~**less** *adj* 没有牙齿的 méiyǒu yáchǐ de: *a* ~*less grin* 不露牙齿的咧嘴微笑.

top[1] /tɒp/ *n* **1** 顶部 dǐngbù, 顶端 dǐngduān: *at the* ~ *of the hill* 在山顶. **on** ~ **of (a)** 在…的上面 zài …de shàngmiàn, 在…之上 zài… zhī shàng. **(b)** 除…之外 chú… zhī wài, 还〔還〕有 háiyǒu. ***from*** ,~ ***to 'bottom*** 从〔從〕头〔頭〕到底 cóng tóu dào dǐ, 全部地 quánbùde. **2** [C] (物的)上面 shàngmiàn, 上边〔邊〕 shàngbiān: *the* ~ *of a table* 桌面. ***on*** ~ ***of things (one's work)*** [非正式用语] 熟练〔練〕掌握 shúliàn zhǎngwò, 胜〔勝〕任 shèngrèn. **3** [C] 最高地位 zuìgāo dìwèi, 首位 shǒuwèi: ~ *of the class* 班级中名列前茅者. ***reach (be) at the*** ~ ***of the ladder (tree)*** (在本行业中)达〔達〕到(处于)领导〔導〕地位 dádào lǐngdǎo dìwèi. **4** [C] 最高级 zuìgāojí, 最高度 zuìgāodù: *at the* ~ *of one's voice* 大声(叫喊). **5** [用作定语]最高的 zuìgāode; 最大的 zuìdàde: *at* ~ *speed* 全速地. *charge* ~ *prices* 要高价. ,~'**brass** [非正式用语]要员 yàoyuán, 高级管理人员 gāojí guǎnlǐ rényuán. '~**-coat** 大衣 dàyī. ,~'**dog** [俚语] 主人 zhǔrén; 优〔優〕胜者 yōushèngzhě. ,~'**hat** 大礼〔禮〕帽 dà lǐmào. ,~-'**heavy** *adj* 头重脚轻〔輕〕的 tóuzhòng jiǎoqīng de. '~**most** *adj* 最高的 zuìgāode, 至上的 zhìshàngde. ,~ '**secret** 绝密的 juémìde. '~ **soil** 表土层〔層〕 biǎotǔcóng. ~**less** *adj* (指妇女服装)袒胸的 tǎn xiōng de.

top[2] /tɒp/ *vt* [-pp-] **1** 给…加顶 gěi…jiā dǐng, 盖〔蓋〕 gài: *a cake* ~*ped with icing* 敷糖霜的饼. **2** ~ ***(sth) up*** 装〔裝〕满 (未满的容器) zhuāng mǎn: ~ *up with oil* 加足油. ~ *up a drink* 斟满酒. **3** 超过〔過〕 chāoguò, 胜〔勝〕过 shèngguò, 高于〔於〕 gāo yú: *Our exports have just* ~*ped £80000.* 我们的出口额已经超过八万镑. **4** (为植物)打顶 dǎ dǐng: ~ *carrots* 为胡萝卜打顶.

top[3] /tɒp/ *n* [C] 陀螺 tuóluó. ***sleep like a*** ~ 熟睡 shúshuì.

topic /'tɒpɪk/ *n* [C] 论〔論〕题 lùntí, 话题 huàtí. ~**al** /-kl/ *adj* 当〔當〕前有关〔關〕的 dāngqián yǒuguān de: ~*al news* 时事.

topple /'tɒpl/ *vt/i* (使)倒塌 dǎotā; 推翻 tuīfān: ~ *the government* 颠覆政府.

torch /tɔ:tʃ/ *n* [C] **1** 手电〔電〕筒 shǒudiàntǒng. **2** 火把 huǒbǎ, 火炬 huǒjù. '~**light** 火炬光 huǒjùguāng: *a* ~*light procession* 火炬游行.

tore /tɔ:(r)/ *pt* of tear[2].

tor·ment /'tɔ:ment/ *n* [C,U] 剧〔劇〕烈痛苦 jùliè tòngkǔ, 折磨 zhémó; 烦恼〔惱〕(的原因) fánnǎo. □ *vt* /tɔ:'ment/ 使受剧烈痛苦 shǐ shòu jùliè tòngkǔ, 折磨 zhémó: ~*ed with pain (hunger)* 受疼痛(饥饿)之苦. ~**or** 使人痛苦的人或物 shǐ rén tòngkǔ de rén huò wù.

torn /tɔ:n/ *pp* of tear[2].

tor·nado /tɔ:'neɪdəʊ/ *n* [C] [*pl* ~es] 飓〔颶〕风〔風〕 jùfēng, 龙〔龍〕卷〔捲〕风 lóngjuǎnfēng.

tor·pedo /tɔ:'pi:dəʊ/ *n* [C] [*pl* ~es] 鱼雷 yúléi. □ *vt* 用鱼雷袭〔襲〕击〔擊〕 yòng yúléi xíjī.

tor·rent /ˈtɒrənt/ *n* [C] **1** 激流 jīliú, 洪流 hóngliú: *mountain* ~*s* 山洪. **2**〔喻〕爆发〔發〕bàofā, 迸发 bèngfā: *a* ~ *of abuse* 连续不断的谩骂. ~**ial** /təˈrenʃl/ *adj* 激流的 jīliúde, 激流似的 jīliú shìde: ~*ial rain* 暴雨.

tor·toise /ˈtɔːtəs/ *n* [C] 乌〔烏〕龟〔龜〕wūguī.

tor·tu·ous /ˈtɔːtʃʊəs/ *adj* **1** 弯〔彎〕弯曲曲的 wānwānqūqū de, 曲折的 qūzhéde: *a* ~ *path* 弯弯曲曲的小径. **2**〔喻〕不正当〔當〕的 bù zhèngdāng de; 不正直的 bù zhèngzhí de, 拐弯〔彎〕抹角的 guǎiwān-mòjiǎo de: *a* ~ *argument* 拐弯抹角的议论. ~**ly** *adv*

tor·ture /ˈtɔːtʃə(r)/ *vt* 拷打 kǎodǎ, 折磨 zhémó, 使受剧〔劇〕烈痛苦 shǐ shòu jùliè tòngkǔ. □ *n* **1** [U] 拷打 kǎodǎ, 折磨 shémó, 严〔嚴〕刑 yánxíng: *instruments of* ~ 刑具. **2** [C,U] 剧烈痛苦 jùliè tòngkǔ. ~**er** 拷问〔問〕者 kǎowènzhě.

Tory /ˈtɔːrɪ/ *n* [C] [*pl* -ies] = Conservative.

toss /tɒs, 美语: tɔːs/ *vt/i* **1** 扔 rēng, 抛 pāo, 掷〔擲〕zhì; 突然举〔舉〕起 tūrán jǔqǐ: *He* ~*ed the beggar a coin.* 他扔给乞丐一文钱. *The horse* ~*ed its head.* 那马突然扬起头. ~ ***sb for sth*** 掷钱〔錢〕币〔幣〕以决定某事 zhì qiánbì yǐ juédìng mǒushì: *Who's to pay for the drinks?* 谁付酒钱? — *Let's* ~ *for it.* 让我们掷钱币取决吧. **2** (使)摇摆〔擺〕yáobǎi, (使)动〔動〕荡〔蕩〕dòngdàng: *The ship (was)* ~*ed about on the stormy sea.* 船在汹涌的海浪中颠簸着. □ *n* [C] **1** 扔 rēng, 抛 pāo, 掷 zhì; 摇摆 yáobǎi, 动荡 dòngdàng; 举起 jǔqǐ: *a* ~ *of the head* 把头一扬. **2** ***win (lose) the*** ~ 掷钱币猜赢(猜输). zhì qiánbì cāi yíng. ˈ~**-up** 掷钱币(以决定某事) zhì qiánbì; 有疑问〔問〕或碰运〔運〕气〔氣〕的事 yǒu yíwèn huò pèng yùnqì de shì.

tot¹ /tɒt/ *n* [C] **1** 小孩 xiǎohái. **2**〔非正式用语〕一小杯(酒) yì xiǎo bēi.

tot² /tɒt/ *vt/i* [-tt-] ~ ***(sth) up***〔非正式用语〕合计 héjì, 总〔總〕计 zǒngjì.

to·tal /ˈtəʊtl/ *adj* 全部的 quánbùde, 完全的 wánquánde: ~ *silence* 寂静. □ *n* [C] 总〔總〕数〔數〕zǒngshù, 全体〔體〕quántǐ, 合计 héjì: *a* ~ *of £20* 总额二十英镑. □*vt/i* [-ll-] 计算…的总数 jìsuàn-…de zǒngshù; 总数达〔達〕zǒngshù dá: *The number of visitors* ~*led 15000.* 参观者总共一万五千人. ~**ly** *adv* 完全地 wánquánde, 全部地 cuánbùde: ~*ly blind* 全盲的. ~**ity** /təʊˈtælətɪ/ *n* [U] 全体 quántǐ, 总数 zǒngshù.

to·tali·tar·ian /ˌtəʊˌtælɪˈteərɪən/ *adj* 极〔極〕权〔權〕主义〔義〕的 jíquán zhǔyì de.

tot·ter /ˈtɒtə(r)/ *vi* **1** 蹒跚 pánshān, 踉跄〔蹌〕liàngqiàng. **2** 摇摇欲坠〔墜〕yáoyáo yù zhuì: *The tree* ~*ed and then fell.* 那树摇晃着, 然后倒下了.

touch¹ /tʌtʃ/ *n* **1** [C] 触〔觸〕chù, 接触 jiēchù: *I felt a* ~ *on my arm.* 我觉得手臂被人碰了一下. **2** [U] 触觉〔覺〕chùjué: *soft to the* ~ 手感柔软. **3** [C] 笔〔筆〕触 bǐchù, 一笔 yibǐ. **4** [C] 少许 shǎoxǔ, 微量 wēiliàng: *a* ~ *of frost in the air* 空气中有一点轻霜. **5** [C] 风〔風〕格 fēnggé, 格调 gédiào, 作风 zuòfēng: *have a light* ~ *on a piano* 轻弹钢琴. ***in*** ~ ***(with)*** (与…)交往 jiāowǎng, 有(…的)消息 yǒu xiāoxī. ***out of*** ~ ***(with)*** (与…)不交往 bù jiāowǎng, 没有(…的)消息 méiyǒu xiāoxī. ***lose*** ~ ***(with)*** (与…)失去联〔聯〕系 shīqù liánxì. **6**〔足球〕边〔邊〕线〔線〕区〔區〕域 biānxiàn qūyù: *The ball is in* ~. 球在边线区域. ˌ~**-and-ˈgo** *adj* 危险〔險〕的 wēixiǎnde; 无〔無〕把握的 wú bǎwò de.

touch² /tʌtʃ/ *vt/i* **1** (使)接触〔觸〕jiēchù, (使)碰到 pèngdào: *A branch is* ~*ing the water.* 一条树枝碰到水面. *His hand* ~*ed mine.* 他的手触及我的手. ~ ***wood*** 摸摸木头〔頭〕(以避免灾祸) mōmō mùtou. **2** 比得上 bǐdéshàng, 及得上 jídéshàng: *No one can* ~ *him as an actor.* 作为一个演员, 没有人能及得上他. **3** 吃 chī; 喝 hē: *He hasn't* ~*ed food for two days.* 他两天没有吃东西了. **4** 感动〔動〕gǎndòng; 关〔關〕心 guānxīn: *The sad story* ~*ed us (our hearts).* 那悲惨的故事感动我们. **5** 涉及 shèjí, 提到 tídào: *I refuse to* ~ *that kind of work.* 我不愿涉及那种工作. **6** (轻微地)损害 sǔnhài: *The house was not* ~*ed by the fire.* 火灾没有波及这栋房屋. **7** [*pp* ~**ed**] (轻微地)发〔發〕疯〔瘋〕fāfēng: *He seems to be a bit* ~*ed.* 他似乎有一点精神错乱. **8** 对〔對〕付 duìfu; 起作用于〔於〕qǐ zuòyòng yú: *Nothing will* ~ *these grease spots.* 什么东西都去不掉这些油渍. ~ ***down*** (飞机)着陆〔陸〕zhuólù. ˈ~**-down** *n* [C] (飞

机)降落 jiàngluò. ~ *sth off* [喻]触发 chùfā, 激起 jīqǐ: *His action ~ed off a riot.* 他的行动触发了一次暴动. ~ *on sth* (简要地)论[論]及 lùnjí, 谈到 tándào. ~ *sth up* 润[潤]色(图画, 文章等) rùnsè.

touch·ing /ˈtʌtʃɪŋ/ *adj* 动[動]人的 dòngrénde, 使人感伤[傷]的 shǐ rén gǎnshāng de: *a ~ request* 感人的恳求.

touchy /ˈtʌtʃɪ/ *adj* [-ier, -iest] 易怒的 yì nù de, 暴躁的 bàozàode.

tough /tʌf/ *adj* [-er, -est] 1 (指肉)咬不动[動]的 yǎo bú dòng de. 2 坚[堅]韧[韌]的 jiānrènde, 不易切开[開]或打破的 bú yì qiēkāi huò dǎpò de: *as ~ as leather* 坚韧得象皮革一样. 3 强壮[壯]的 qiángzhuàngde, 坚强的 jiānqiángde, 能耐劳[勞]的 néng nàiláo de: *~ soldiers* 能吃苦耐劳的士兵. 4 (指人)粗暴的 cūbàode, 凶[兇]恶[惡]的 xiōng'ède: *a ~ criminal* 凶恶的罪犯. 5 倔强的 juéjiàngde, 顽固的 wángùde: *The employers got ~ with their workers.* 雇主们对他们的工人毫不让步. 6 困难[難]的 kùnnande, 难对[對]付的 nán duìfu de: *a ~ job (problem)* 棘手的工作(问题). ,~ ˈ**luck** [非正式用语]恶运[運] èyùn. ~**ly** *adv* ~**ness** *n* [U]

toughen /ˈtʌfn/ *vt/i* (使)变[變]坚[堅]韧[韌] biàn jiānrèn; (使)变坚强 biàn jiānqiáng; (使)变困难 biàn kùnnan.

tou·pee /ˈtu:peɪ/ *n* [C] 假发[髮] jiǎfà.

tour /tʊə(r)/ *n* [C] 1 旅游 lǚyóu: *a round-the-world ~* 环球旅行. 2 参观[觀] cānguān: *a ~ of the palace* 参观宫殿. 3 (海外)任职[職]期 rènzhíqī: *a ~ of three years in Africa* 在非洲三年的服务期. □ *vt/i* 旅游 lǚyóu: *~ western Europe* 漫游西欧. ~**ing** *n, adj*: *a ˈ~ing party* 旅行团.

tour·ism /ˈtʊərɪzəm/ *n* [U] 旅游事业[業] lǚyóu shìyè. **tour·ist** *n* [C] 旅游者 lǚyóuzhě: *a ˈ~ agency* 旅行社.

tour·na·ment /ˈtʊənəmənt/ *n* [C] 比赛 bǐsài, 联[聯]赛 liánsài: *a ˈtennis (ˈchess) ~* 网球(象棋)比赛.

tour·ni·quet /ˈtʊənɪkeɪ/ *n* [C] [医学]止血带[帶] zhǐxiědài, 压[壓]脉器 yāmàiqì.

tout /taʊt/ *n* [C] 推销员 tuīxiāoyuán, 兜售者 dōushòuzhě: *a ˈticket ~* 入场券兜售者. □ *vi* 招徕(生意) zhāolái, 兜售 dōushòu.

tow /təʊ/ *vt* (用绳索)拖 tuō, 拉 lā: *~ a damaged car to the garage* 拖一辆损坏的汽车去修车厂. □ *n* [C, U] 拖 tuō, 拉 lā: *Can we give you a ~?* 我们能拉你一把吗? *in ~* [非正式用语]在一起 zài yìqǐ, 在身边[邊] zài shēnbiān. *on ~* 被拖拉着 bèi tuōlā zhe.

to·ward(s) /təˈwɔ:d(z)/ *prep* 1 向 xiàng, 对[對] duì, 朝 cháo: *walking ~ the sea* 向大海走去. 2 对于[於] duìyú, 关[關]于 guānyú: *my feelings ~ the plan* 我对那个计划的看法. 3 为[爲]了 wèile, 有助于 yǒu zhù yú: *save money ~ the children's education* 为了孩子们的教育而节省开支. 4 (指时间)接近 jiējìn, 将[將]近 jiāngjìn: *~ noon* 将近中午.

towel /ˈtaʊəl/ *n* [C] 毛巾 máojīn, 手巾 shǒujīn: *a ˈbath-~* 一条浴巾. *throw in the towel* ⇨ throw¹(7). □ *vt* [-ll-, 美语 -l-] 用毛巾擦干[乾] yòng máojīn cāgān. ~**ling** *n* [U] 毛巾布 máojīnbù.

tower /ˈtaʊə(r)/ *n* [C] 1 塔 tǎ, 塔状[狀]建筑[築] tǎzhuàng jiànzhù. 2 *a ~ of strength* [喻]可信赖的人 kě xìnlài de rén. □ *vi* 屹立 yìlì, 高耸[聳] gāosǒng. ~ *above sb* [喻](指能力)胜[勝]过[過] shèngguò, 超出 chāochū. ˈ~-**block** 高楼[樓]大厦 gāolóu dàshà.

town /taʊn/ *n* 1[C] 市镇 shìzhèn, 城镇 chéngzhèn. *paint the town red* ⇨ paint. 2 [U] 市区[區] shìqū, 商业[業]中心区 shāngyè zhōngxīnqū ⇨ downtown. *go out on the ~* 在城里寻[尋]欢[歡]作乐[樂] zài chénglǐ xúnhuān zuòlè. *go to ~* [俚语]无[無]节[節]制地去做 wú jiézhì de qù zuò. 3 [U] 都市 dūshì, 主要城市 zhǔyào chéngshì: *He's gone up to ~ for the weekend.* 他已上城去度周末. 4[U] 市民 shìmín, 镇民 zhènmín: *The whole ~ knew.* 满镇上的人都知道. 5 *the ~* 城市 chéngshì: *Farm workers leave the country to work in the ~.* 农场工人离开乡间去城里工作. ,~ ˈ**clerk** 城镇书[書]记 chéngzhèn shūjì. ,~ ˈ**council** 镇议[議]会[會] zhèn yìhuì. ,~ ˈ**hall** 镇公所 zhèn gōngsuǒ, 市政厅[廳] shìzhèngtīng. ˈ**towns·folk** 镇民 zhènmín, 市民 shìmín.

toxin /ˈtɒksɪn/ *n* [C] (尤指细菌的)毒素 dúsù. **toxic** /ˈtɒksɪk/ *adj* 有毒的 yǒu dú de, 中毒的 zhòngdúde. **toxicity** /tɒk'sɪsɪtɪ/ *n* [U] 毒性 dúxìng, 毒力 dúlì.

toy /tɔɪ/ *n* [C] **1** 玩具 wánjù. **2** [用作定语]: ~ *dog* (*spaniel*) 供玩赏的小狗(长耳狗). □ *vi* **1** 不很认〔認〕真地考虑〔慮〕 bù hěn rènzhēn de kǎolǜ: *He ~ed with the idea* 他心不在焉地想着这个意见. **2** 玩弄 wánnòng, 戏〔戲〕耍 xìshuǎ: *~ing with a pencil* 耍弄一支铅笔. '**~shop** 玩具店 wánjùdiàn.

trace[1] /treɪs/ *n* [C] **1** 痕迹〔跡〕 hénjì, 足迹 zújì: *~s of an ancient civilization* 古代文明的遗迹. **2** 微量 wēiliàng, 少量 shǎoliàng: *There were ~s of poison in his blood.* 他的血中有少量的毒素.

trace[2] /treɪs/ *vt/i* **1** 描绘〔繪〕miáohuì, 勾出…的轮〔輪〕廓 gōuchū … de lúnkuò: *tracing* (*out*) *one's route on a map* 在地图上划出路线. **2** 摹写〔寫〕 móxiě, 映描 yìngmiáo. **3** 追踪 zhuīzōng, 跟踪 gēnzōng: *I cannot ~ the letter.* 我找不到那封信. **4** 找出 zhǎochū, 探索 tànsuǒ. **trac·ing** (地图,图案等的)复〔復〕制〔製〕 fùzhì, 摹绘 móhuì.

tra·chea /trə'kɪə/ *n* [C] [*pl* ~e /-kiː/] [解剖] = windpipe.

track /træk/ *n* [C] **1** 行踪 xíngzōng, 踪迹〔跡〕 zōngjì, 足迹 zújì: *~s in the snow* 雪地上的足迹. ***cover one's ~s*** 隐〔隱〕匿行踪 yǐnnì xíngzōng. ***keep*** (***lose***) ***~ of sb*** (***sth***) 跟上(跟不上)…的发〔發〕展 gēnshàng-…de fāzhǎn; 保持(失去)对〔對〕…的联〔聯〕系 bǎochí duì…de liánxì. ***make ~s*** 匆匆离〔離〕去 cōngcōng líqù. ***off the ~*** [喻]出轨〔軌〕 chū guǐ; 离题 lí tí; 误入歧途 wùrù qítú. ⇨ beaten. **2** 行程 xíngchéng, 路线〔綫〕 lùxiàn: *the ~ of a storm* 暴风雨的路线. *the ~ of a spacecraft* 宇宙飞船的轨道. **3**(火车等的)轨道 guǐdào: *The train left the ~.* 火车出轨. **4** 跑道 pǎodào. **5** = caterpillar(2). □ *vt* 跟踪 gēnzōng, 尾随〔隨〕 wěisuí: *~ an animal* 追踪一只动物. *~ sb* (*sth*) *down* 追踪而发现 zhuīzōng ér fāxiàn, 追捕到 zhuībǔ dào. '**~ suit** 运〔運〕动〔動〕外套 yùndòng wàitào. '**~ing station** (宇航的)跟踪站 gēnzōngzhàn. **~-er** 追捕者 zhuībǔzhě.

tract /trækt/ *n* [C] **1** 一片土地 yípiàn tǔdì, 地带〔帶〕 dìdài: *wide ~s of desert* 广阔的沙漠地带. **2** [解剖]道 dào, 束 shù, 系统 xìtǒng: *the di'gestive ~* 消化系统.

trac·tion /'trækʃn/ *n* [U] 拖 tuō, 牵〔牽〕引 qiānyǐn; 牵引力 qiānyǐnlì: *electric* (*steam*) ~ 电力(蒸汽)牵引.

trac·tor /'træktə(r)/ *n* [C] 拖拉机〔機〕 tuōlājī.

trade[1] /treɪd/ *n* **1** [C,U] 贸易 màoyì, 商业〔業〕 shāngyè: *T~ was good last year.* 去年的贸易良好. *He's in the 'furniture ~.* 他做家具生意. **2** [C,U] 职〔職〕业 zhíyè, 行业 hángyè; 手艺〔藝〕 shǒuyì: *He's a carpenter by ~.* 他是木匠. '**~mark** 商标〔標〕 shāngbiāo. '**~ name** 商品名称〔稱〕 shāngpǐn míngchéng. '**trades·man** 店主 diànzhǔ, 商人 shāngrén. ,**~(s)-'union** 工会〔會〕 gōnghuì. ,**~-'unionist** 工会会员 gōnghuì huìyuán.

trade[2] /treɪd/ *vt/i* **1** 从〔從〕事贸易 cóngshì màoyì, 做买〔買〕卖〔賣〕 zuò mǎimài: *Britain ~s with Europe.* 英国和欧洲进行贸易. **2** 交换 jiāohuàn, 交易 jiāoyì: *The boy ~d his skates for a ball.* 那男孩用他的冰鞋换一只球. **3** *~ sth in* (以旧物)折价〔價〕购〔購〕物 shéjià gòu wù. **4** 利用 lìyòng: *~ on her sympathy* 利用她的同情心. **trader** 商人 shāngrén.

tra·di·tion /trə'dɪʃn/ *n* **1** [U] 传〔傳〕统 chuántǒng. **2** [C] 传统的信仰, 习〔習〕惯等 chuántǒngde xìnyǎng, xíguàn děng. **~al** *adj*

traf·fic /'træfɪk/ *n* [U] **1** 交通 jiāotōng, 通行 tōngxíng, 往来〔來〕 wǎnglái. **2** 运〔運〕输〔輸〕业〔業〕务〔務〕 yùnshū yèwù, 交通事业 jiāotōng shìyè. **3** (非法)交易 jiāoyì: *the 'drug ~* 毒品买卖. □ *vi* [-ck-] 做交易 zuò jiāoyì, 做生意 zuò shēngyì: *~king in drugs* 做药物生意. '**~ island** (交通)安全岛〔島〕 ānquándǎo. '**~-light(s)** 交通管理灯〔燈〕 jiāotōng guǎnlǐ dēng, 红绿灯 hónglǜdēng. '**~ warden** 停车〔車〕场〔場〕管理员 tíngchēchǎng guǎnlǐyuán.

tra·gedy /'trædʒədɪ/ *n* [*pl* -ies] **1** [C] (一出)悲剧〔劇〕 bēijù. **2** [U] 悲剧 (戏剧的一种类型) bēijù. **3** [C,U] 惨〔慘〕事 cǎnshì, 惨案 cǎn'àn.

tra·gic /'trædʒɪk/ *adj* of tragedy: *a ~ actor* 悲剧演员. *a ~ accident* 悲惨的事故. **~ally** *adv*

trail /treɪl/ *n* [C] **1** 痕迹〔跡〕 hénjì, 足迹 zújì: *a ~ of destruction* 破坏的残迹. ***hot on the ~*** (***of***) 紧〔緊〕跟 jǐn gēn. **2** (荒野中的)小径〔徑〕 xiǎojìng. □ *vt/i* **1** 拖 tuō, 拉 lā: *Her long skirt was ~ing along the floor.* 她的长裙拖着地. **2**

= track. **3** (植物的)蔓延 mànyán: *roses ~ing over the walls* 蔓生在墙上的蔷薇花. **~er (a)** 拖车〔車〕tuōchē. **(b)** 蔓生植物 mànshēng zhíwù. **(c)** (电影的)预告片 yùgàopiān.

train[1] /treɪn/ *n* **1** [C] 列车〔車〕lièchē, 火车 huǒchē: *'passenger ('goods) ~s* 客(货)车. *travel by ~* 乘火车旅行. **2** (人, 动物等的)队〔隊〕列 duìliè. **3** 一系列 yíxìliè, 一连〔連〕串 yìliánchuàn: *~ of thoughts* 一系列的想法. **4** 拖裙 tuōqún.

train[2] /treɪn/ *vt/i* **1** 训练〔練〕xùnliàn, 培养〔養〕péiyǎng: *~ a horse (football team)* 训练一匹马(足球队). **2** 使(植物)沿着一定方向生长〔長〕shǐ yánzhe yídìng fāngxiàng shēngzhǎng: *~ roses against a wall* 使玫瑰沿墙生长. **3** 瞄准〔準〕miáozhǔn, 对〔對〕准 duìzhǔn: *~ a gun on the enemy* 把枪口对准敌人. **~ee** /treɪ'ni:/ 受训者 shòuxùnzhě. **~er** 教练员 jiàoliànyuán; 驯〔馴〕兽〔獸〕人 xúnshòurén. **~ing** 训练 xùnliàn, 锻炼〔煉〕duànliàn.

trait /treɪt/ *n* [C] 特性 tèxìng, 品质 pǐnzhì.

trai·tor /'treɪtə(r)/ *n* [C] 叛徒 pàntú, 卖〔賣〕国〔國〕贼 màiguózéi.

tram /træm/ *n* [C] [美语 = *'street-car*] (亦作 *'~car*) 有轨〔軌〕电〔電〕车〔車〕yǒuguǐ diànchē.

tramp /træmp/ *vt/i* **1** 用沉重的脚步走 yòng chénzhòng de jiǎobù zǒu. **2** 徒步远〔遠〕行 túbù yuǎnxíng: *~ through the mountains* 徒步穿越山岭. □ *n* **1** 重步声〔聲〕zhòng bù shēng: *the ~ of marching soldiers* 行军的重步声. **2** [C] 徒步旅行 túbù lǚxíng, 长〔長〕途步行 chángtú bùxíng. **3** [C] 流浪者 liúlàngzhě. **'~-steamer** 航线〔綫〕不定的货轮〔輪〕hángxiàn búdìng de huòlún.

trample /'træmpl/ *vt/i* **1** 踩 cǎi, 践〔踐〕踏 jiàntà. **2** [喻]蔑视 mièshì; 粗暴地对〔對〕待 cūbàode duìdài: *~ on his feelings* 蔑视他的感情. □ *n* [C] 践踏 jiàntà; 践踏声〔聲〕jiàntàshēng.

tram·po·line /'træmpəli:n/ *n* [C] (杂技表现用的) 蹦床 〔牀〕bèngchuáng.

trance /trɑ:ns/ *n* [C] 恍惚 huǎnghū, 失神 shīshén: *be (fall, go) into a ~* 进入昏迷状态.

tran·quil /'træŋkwɪl/ *adj* [正式用语]平静的 píngjìngde, 安宁〔寧〕的 ānníngde: *a ~ life* 安静的生活. **~ly** *adv* **~lity** /træŋ'kwɪlətɪ/ *n* [U] 安静 ānjìng, 平静 píngjìng.

tran·quil·lize [美语亦作 **tran·quil·ize**] /'træŋkwɪlaɪz/ *vt* 使安静 shǐ ānjìng, 使安定 shǐ āndìng. **tran·quil·li·zer** *n* [C] 镇静剂〔劑〕zhènjìngjì.

trans·act /træn'zækt/ *vt* [正式用语]办〔辦〕理 bànlǐ, 处〔處〕理 chùlǐ, 执〔執〕行 zhíxíng.

trans·ac·tion /træn'zækʃn/ *n* **1** [U] 办〔辦〕理 bànlǐ, 处〔處〕理 chùlǐ, 执〔執〕行 zhíxíng: *the ~ of business* 处理事务. **2** [C] 事务〔務〕shìwù, 事项 shìxiàng, 交易 jiāoyì: *cash ~s* 现金交易. **3** [*pl*] 议〔議〕事录〔録〕yìshìlù, 会〔會〕报〔報〕huìbào.

trans·at·lan·tic /ˌtrænzət'læntɪk/ *adj* 大西洋彼岸的 Dàxīyáng bǐ'àn de; 横渡大西洋的 héngdù Dàxīyáng de: *a ~ treaty* 与大西洋彼岸签订的协定. *a ~ flight* 横渡大西洋的飞行.

tran·scend /træn'send/ *vt* 超出 chāochū, 超过〔過〕chāoguò: *~ human knowledge* 超出人类的知识.

trans·con·ti·nen·tal /ˌtrænzˌkɒntɪ'nentl/ *adj* 横贯大陆〔陸〕的 héngguàn dàlù de.

tran·scribe /træn'skraɪb/ *vt* **1** 抄写〔寫〕chāoxiě, 照抄 zhàochāo. **2** 改写成(特定形式) gǎixiě chéng: *~d into phonetic symbols* 用音标记录. **tran·script** /'trænskrɪpt/ *n* [C] 抄本 chāoběn, 副本 fùběn. **tran'scrip·tion** /-ʃn/ *n* [C,U]

trans·fer[1] /'trænsfɜ:(r)/ *n* **1** [C, U] 转〔轉〕移 zhuǎnyí, 传〔傳〕递〔遞〕chuándì, 调动〔動〕diàodòng; 过〔過〕户 guòhù. **2** [C] 转让〔讓〕证〔證〕书〔書〕zhuǎnràng zhèngshū, 过户凭〔憑〕单〔單〕guòhù píndān; 转印的图〔圖〕表等 zhuǎnyìnde túbiǎo děng.

trans·fer[2] /træns'fɜ:(r)/ *vt/i* [-rr-] **1** 转〔轉〕移 zhuǎnyí, 调动〔動〕diàodòng. **2** 让〔讓〕渡(财产等) ràngdù, 转让 zhuǎnràng: *~ rights to a son* 让渡权利给儿子. **3** 转印 zhuǎnyìng, 转抄 zhuǎnchāo. **4** 转车〔車〕zhuǎnchē, 换车 huànchē. **5** 调任 diàorèn, 转业〔業〕zhuǎnyè: *He ~red to the Sales Department.* 他调到营业部去任职. **~able** /-əbl/ *adj* 可转让的 kě zhuǎnràng de: *~able tickets* 可换车使用的车票. **~ence** /'trænsfərəns/ *n* [U]

trans·form /træns'fɔ:m/ *vt* 改变〔變〕(形状, 性质等) gǎibiàn: *Success ~ed him.* 成功使他变了样. **~ation** /ˌtrænsfə'meɪʃn/ *n* **(a)**

[U] 变形 biànxíng; 变性biànxìng. (b) [C] 转〔轉〕变 zhuǎnbiàn, 变化 biànhuà. ~**er** 促使变化的人或物 cùshǐ biànhuà de rén huò wù; (尤指)变压〔壓〕器 biànyāqì.

trans·fuse /træns'fju:z/ *vt* (尤指)给…输〔輸〕血 gěi ... shūxuè. **trans·fusion** /-ʒn/ *n* [C,U]

trans·gress /trænz'gres/ *vt/i* [正式用语] **1** 超越(限度) chāoyuè. **2** 违〔違〕反(法律,规则等) wéifǎn. ~**ion** /-ʃn/ *n* [C,U]

tran·sis·tor /træn'zɪstə(r)/ *n* [C] **1** 晶体〔體〕管 jīngtǐguǎn. **2**晶体管收音机〔機〕 jīngtǐguǎn shōuyīnjī. ~**ized** /-aɪzd/ *adj* 装〔裝〕有晶体管的 zhuāng yǒu jīngtǐguǎn de.

tran·sit /'trænsɪt/ *n* [U] 运〔運〕输〔輸〕 yùnshū, 搬运 bānyùn: *goods damaged in* ~ 运输中损坏的货物.

tran·si·tion /træn'zɪʃn/ *n* [C,U] 转〔轉〕变〔變〕 zhuǎnbiàn, 过〔過〕渡 guòdù. ~**al** /-nl/ *adj*

tran·si·tive /'trænsətɪv/ *adj* [语法] 及物的 jíwùde.

trans·late /trænz'leɪt/ *vt* **1** 翻译〔譯〕fānyì: ~ *a book into French* 把一本书译成法文. **2** 解释〔釋〕jiěshì, 说明 shuōmíng. **trans·la·tor** /-tə(r)/ 翻译者 fānyìzhě.

trans·la·tion /ˌtrænz'leɪʃn/ *n* [U] 翻译〔譯〕fānyì; [C] 译文 yìwén: *a* ~ *into French* 法文译文.

trans·lu·cent /trænz'lu:sənt/ *adj* 透明的 tòumíngde; 半透明的 bàn tòumíng de.

trans·mis·sion /trænz'mɪʃn/ *n* **1** [U] 传〔傳〕送 chuánsòng, 播送 bōsòng: *the* ~ *of a TV programme* 电视节目的播出. **2** [C] (汽车的)传动〔動〕系统 chuándòng xìtǒng.

trans·mit /trænz'mɪt/ *vt* [-tt-] **1** 传〔傳〕送 chuánsòng, 传达〔達〕 chuándá; 播送 bōsòng: ~ *a message by radio* 由无线电传送讯息. **2** 传导〔導〕 chuándǎo; 通过〔過〕tōngguò: *Iron* ~*s heat.* 铁传热. ~**ter** 传送者 chuánsòngzhě, 播送者 bōsòngzhě; (无线电)发〔發〕射机〔機〕fāshèjī; 送话器 sònghuàqì.

trans·par·ency /træn'spærənsɪ/ *n* [*pl* -ies] **1** [U] 透明 tòumíng; 透明度 tòumíngdù. **2** [C] 透明的软〔軟〕片, 图〔圖〕片等 tòumíngde ruǎnpiàn, túpiàn děng.

trans·par·ent /træn'spærənt/ *adj* **1** 透明的 tòumíngde: *Glass is* ~. 玻璃是透明的. **2** (性格) 开〔開〕朗的 kāilǎngde; 显〔顯〕而易见的 xiǎn ér yì jiàn de: *a man of* ~ *honesty* 非常忠实的人. ~**ly** *adv*

trans·plant /træns'plɑ:nt/ *vt/i* **1** 移植 yízhí, 移种〔種〕yízhòng. **2** 人工移植(心,肾等) réngōng yízhí. **3** [喻]迁〔遷〕移 qiānyí. □ /'trænsplɑ:nt/ *n* [C] (心,肾的)人工移植 réngōng yízhí.

trans·port /'trɑ:nspɔ:t/ *n* **1** [U] 运〔運〕输〔輸〕 yùnshū, 搬运 bānyùn: *the* ~ *of troops by air* 空运军队. *London's* ~ *system* 伦敦的运输系统. □ /trɑ:n'spɔ:t/ *vt* 运输 yùnshū: ~ *goods by lorry* 用卡车运货. ~**a·tion** /-'teɪʃn/ *n* [U] ~**er** *n* [C] 运输者 yùnshūzhě; 转〔轉〕运机 zhuǎnyùnjī.

trans·pose /træn'spəʊz/ *vt* **1** 使互换位置 shǐ hùhuàn wèizhì. **2** [音乐]使变〔變〕调 shǐ biàn diào. **trans·po·si·tion** /ˌtrænspə'zɪʃn/ *n* [C,U]

trans·verse /'trænzvɜ:s/ *adj* 横向的 héngxiàngde, 横断〔斷〕的 héngduànde, 横放的 héngfàngde. ~**ly** *adv*

trap /træp/ *n* [C] **1** (捕兽的)陷阱 xiànjǐng, 捕捉机〔機〕bǔzhuōjī: *a 'mouse*~ 捕鼠机. **2** [喻](陷人的)圈套 quāntào, 诡计 guǐjì. **3** (U 形) 存水弯〔彎〕头〔頭〕 cún shuǐ wāntóu. **4** 双〔雙〕轮〔輪〕轻〔輕〕便马〔馬〕车〔車〕 shuāng lún qīngbiàn mǎchē. □ *vt* [-pp-] **1** (设陷阱)捕捉 bǔzhuō. **2** 诱捕yòubǔ, 使堕〔墮〕入圈套 shǐ duòrù quāntào. '~**door** 地板活门〔門〕 dìbǎn huómén. ~**per** (设陷阱)捕兽〔獸〕者 bǔshòuzhě.

tra·peze /trə'pi:z/ *n* [C] (杂技表演用)吊架 diàojià.

trash /træʃ/ *n* [U] 废〔廢〕物 fèiwù, 糟粕 zāopò. **trashy** *adj* [非正式用语]毫无〔無〕价〔價〕值的 háowú jiàzhí de.

trauma /'trɔ:mə/ *n* [C] **1** 损伤〔傷〕 sǔnshāng. **2**精神创〔創〕伤 jīngshén chuāngshāng. ~**tic** /trɔ:'mætɪk/ *adj*

travel /'trævl/ *vt/i* [-ll-] **1** 旅行 lǚxíng: ~ *round the world* 环球旅行. **2** 作旅行推销 zuò lǚxíng tuīxiāo: *He* ~*s in cotton goods.* 他旅行推销棉织品. **3** 移动〔動〕yídòng, 行进〔進〕xíngjìn: *Light* ~*s faster than sound.* 光比声快. □ *n* **1** [U] 旅行 lǚxíng, 旅游 lǚyóu: *fond of* ~ 喜欢旅游. ~ *agent* 旅行社. **2** [*pl*] 旅行笔〔筆〕记 lǚxíng bǐjì, 游记 yóujì: *write about one's* ~*s* 写游记. ~**led** *adj* 富于〔於〕旅行经〔經〕验〔驗〕的 fù yú lǚxíng jīngyàn de: *a* ~*led man* 旅行经验丰富的人. ~**ler** (a) 旅行者 lǚxíngzhě, 旅客 lǚkè. (b) = commercial traveller. '~**ler's cheque** 旅行支票 lǚxíng zhīpiào.

tra·verse /'trævɜːs/ *vt* [正式用语] 横越 héngyuè, 穿过[過] chuānguò: *Searchlights ~d the sky.* 探照灯在天空扫射.

trav·esty /'trævəstɪ/ *n* [C] [*pl* -ies] 歪曲的模仿 wāiqūde mófǎng: *a ~ of justice* 对法律正义的歪曲.

trawl /trɔːl/ *vt/i* 拖网[網]捕鱼 tuōwǎng bǔ yú. **~er** 拖网捕鱼者 tuōwǎng bǔyúzhě; 拖网船tuōwǎngchuán.

tray /treɪ/ *n* [C] 碟 dié, 盘[盤] pán, 托盘 tuōpán.

treach·er·ous /'tretʃərəs/ *adj* **1** 背信弃[棄]义[義]的 bèixìn-qìyì de, 不忠实[實]的 bù zhōngshí de. **2** 不可靠的 bù kěkào de: *~ weather* 靠不住的天气. **~ly** *adv*

treach·ery /'tretʃərɪ/ *n* [C] [*pl* -ies].

treacle /'triːkl/ *n* [U] 糖浆[漿] tángjiāng. **treacly** *adj*

tread /tred/ *vt/i* [*pt* trod /trɒd/; *pp* trodden /'trɒdn/] **1** 走 zǒu, 踏 tà, 踩 cǎi: *Don't ~ on the flowers.* 不要踩着花朵. **2** 践[踐]踏 jiàntà, 踩碎 cǎisuì: *~ grapes* (制酒时)踩碎葡萄. **3** 踏成 tàchéng, 踩出(一条小路) cǎichū. **~ water** 踩水 cǎishuǐ. □ *n* [C] **1** 步法 bùfǎ; 脚步声[聲] jiǎobùshēng: *with a heavy (loud)~* 脚步沉重(响亮)地. **2** (楼梯的)踏板 tàbǎn. **3** (轮胎的)胎面 tāimiàn.

treadle /'tredl/ *n* [C] (自行车,缝纫机等的)踏板 tàbǎn. □ *vi* 踩动[動]踏板 cǎidòng tàbǎn.

Treas. = Treasurer.

trea·son /'triːzn/ *n* [U] 叛逆 pànnì, 谋反 móufǎn. **~able** /-əbl/ *adj*

treas·ure /'treʒə(r)/ *n* **1** [C,U] 金银财宝[寶] jīn yín cáibǎo, 财富 cáifù. **2** 被珍爱[愛]的人或物 bèi zhēn'ài de rén huò wù. □ *vt* 珍重 zhēnzhòng, 重视 zhòngshì: *He ~s the watch she gave him.* 他珍爱她送给他的表. '**~-trove** 地下宝藏 dìxià bǎozàng.

treas·urer /'treʒərə(r)/ *n* [C] 掌管财务[務]的人 zhǎngguǎn cáiwù de rén.

treas·ury /'treʒərɪ/ *n* [*pl* -ies] **1 the T~** (英国)财政部 cáizhèngbù. **2** [C] 经[經]费 jīngfèi; 金库[庫] jīnkù.

treat /triːt/ *vt/i* **1** 对[對]待 duìdài: *He ~s his wife badly.* 他虐待他的妻子. **2** 当[當]作 dāngzuò, 看作 kànzuò: *~ it as a joke* 把它当作笑话. **3** 治疗[療] zhìliáo: *~ a patient* 给病人治病. **4** 处[處]理 chǔlǐ: *~ wood with creosote.* 用杂酚油处理木材. **5** 请(客) qǐng, 款待 kuǎndài: *I shall ~ you to dinner.* 我要请你吃饭. □ *n* **1** [C] 乐[樂]事 lèshì: *It's a great ~ to go to the cinema.* 看电影是一大乐事. **2** 请客 qǐngkè, 款待 kuǎndài: *This is my ~.* 这次我请客.

treat·ise /'triːtɪz/ *n* [C] (专题)论[論]文 lùnwén.

treat·ment /'triːtmənt/ *n* [C,U] 对[對]待 duìdài, 待遇 dàiyù, 处[處]理 chǔlǐ; 治疗[療] zhìliao: *a new ~ for cancer* 治疗癌症的一种新方法.

treaty /'triːtɪ/ *n* [*pl* -ies] [C,U] [正式用语]条[條]约 tiáoyuē, 协[協]定 xiédìng: *a 'peace ~* 和平条约.

treble[1] /'trebl/ *adj, n* [C] 三倍(的) sān bèi, 三重(的) sān chóng: *He earns ~ my salary.* 他挣的薪水是我的三倍. □ *vt/i* 使成三倍 shǐ chéng sān bèi, 使增加二倍 shǐ zēngjiā èr bèi: *He has ~d his earnings.* 他的收入已增加二倍.

treble[2] /'trebl/ *n* [C] [音乐]最高音部 zuìgāo yīnbù.

tree /triː/ *n* [C] **1** 树[樹] shù, 乔[喬]木 qiáomù. **2** = family tree. **~less** *adj* 无[無]树木的 wú shùmù de.

trek /trek/ *vi* [-kk-] *n* [C] 牛车[車]旅行 niúchē lǚxíng; 长[長]途跋涉 chángtú báshè.

trel·lis /'trelɪs/ *n* [C] (葡萄等)架 jià, 棚 péng.

tremble /'trembl/ *vi* **1** 发[發]抖 fādǒu, 哆嗦 duōsuo. **2** 震颤 zhènchàn: *The bridge ~d as the heavy lorry crossed it.* 那辆重卡车驶过时,桥在震颤. **3** 焦虑[慮] jiāolǜ, 担[擔]忧[憂] dānyōu: *I ~ for his safety.* 我担心他的安全. □ *n* [C] 发抖 fādǒu; 震颤 zhènchàn: *a ~ in his voice* 他的声音有点发抖.

tre·men·dous /trɪ'mendəs/ *adj* **1** 极[極]大的 jídàde, 巨大的 jùdàde: *a ~ explosion* 巨大的爆炸. **2** [非正式用语]非常的 fēichángde; 极好的 jíhǎode: *a ~ meal* 一顿美餐. **~ly** *adv* 非常 fēicháng, 极度地 jídùde: *~ly grateful* 非常感谢.

tremor /'tremə(r)/ *n* [C] 发[發]抖 fādǒu; 震动[動] zhèndòng: *'earth ~s* 地面的震动.

trench /trentʃ/ *n* [C] 地沟[溝] dìgōu, 战[戰]壕 zhànháo. □ *vt/i* 用战壕防御[禦] yòng zhànháo fángyù.

trend /trend/ *n* [C] 倾向 qīngxiàng, 趋〔趨〕势〔勢〕 qūshì: *The ~ of prices is still upwards.* 物价的趋势仍在上涨. ***set the ~*** 开〔開〕风〔風〕气〔氣〕之先 kāi fēngqì zhī xiān. **'~-setter** *n* [C] 时〔時〕髦款式带〔帶〕头〔頭〕者 shímáo kuǎnshì dàitóu zhě. □ *vi* 向着 xiàngzhe, 趋向 qūxiàng, 倾向qīngxiàng. **trendy** *adj* [-ier, -iest] [非正式用语] 时髦的 shímáode.

tres·pass /'trespəs/ *vt* **1**非法侵入(私地) fēifǎ qīnrù. **2** 侵夺〔奪〕 qīnduó, 侵占〔佔〕 qīnzhàn: *~ on my time.* 占去我的时间. □ *n* [C, U] 非法侵入 fēifǎ qīnrù. **~er** 非法侵入者 fēifǎ qīnrù zhě.

tress /tres/ *n* [C] [诗] **1** [*pl*] (尤指女人的)头〔頭〕发〔髮〕 tóufa. **2** 一绺头发 yìliǔ tóufa.

trestle /'tresl/ *n* [C] 支架 zhījià, 搁〔擱〕凳 gēdèng. **,~-'table** 搁板桌 gēbǎnzhuō.

trial /'traɪəl/ *n* **1** [C,U] 试验〔驗〕 shìyàn, 试用 shìyòng: *give a new typist a ~* 试用一位新来的打字员. ***on ~*** 试验性的 shìyànxìngde, 为〔爲〕了试验 wèile shìyàn: *Take the machine on ~.* 试用那部机器. ***,~ and 'error*** 反复〔復〕试验 fǎnfù shìyàn. **2** [C,U] 审〔審〕讯shěnxùn, 受审 shòushěn: *The ~ lasted a week.* 审讯持续了一个星期. ***be*** (或 ***go***) ***on ~; stand ~ (for sth)*** (因…而)受审 shòushěn. **3** [C] 讨厌〔厭〕的人(或物) tǎoyànde rén.

tri·angle /'traɪæŋgl/ *n* [C] **1** 三角 sānjiǎo, 三角形 sānjiǎoxíng. **2** 三角关〔關〕系〔係〕 sānjiǎo guānxì. ***the eternal ~*** 三角恋〔戀〕爱〔愛〕 sānjiǎo liàn'àn. **tri·angu·lar** /traɪ'æŋgjʊlə(r)/ *adj*

tribe /traɪb/ *n* [C] 部落 bùluò, 宗族 zōngzú: *the Indian ~s of America* 美洲的印第安人部落. **tri·bal** *adj* 部落的 bùluòde, 宗族的 zōngzúde. **'tribes·man** 部落中的一员 bùluò zhōng de yìyuán.

tri·bu·nal /traɪ'bju:nl/ *n* [C] 审〔審〕判员 zhěnpànyuán. 法官 fǎguān; 法庭fǎtíng: *a rent ~* 法官意见不一致的法庭.

tribu·tary /'trɪbjʊtrɪ/ *adj, n* [C] 支流(的) zhīliú.

trib·ute /'trɪbju:t/ *n* [C,U] 贡献〔獻〕 gòngxiàn, 贡品 gòngpǐn; 赞〔讚〕扬〔揚〕 zànyáng: *pay ~ to his courage* 赞扬他的勇气.

trick /trɪk/ *n* [C] **1** 诡计 guǐjì, 骗〔騙〕局 piànjú: *He got the money from me by a ~.* 他施诡计骗取我的钱财. **2** 恶〔惡〕作剧〔劇〕 èzuòjù: *The children are always playing amusing ~s.* 孩子们常常玩恶作剧游戏. **3** 技艺〔藝〕 jìyì, 窍〔竅〕门〔門〕 qiàomén: *conjuring ~s* 戏法. ***do the ~*** [俚语]做好工作 zuò hǎo gōngzuò; 达〔達〕到目的 dádào mùdì. **4** 一圈(牌) yìquān. □ *vt* 哄骗 hōngpiàn: *He ~ed the poor girl out of her money.* 他骗去那可怜的女孩子的钱. **~ery** 诡计 guǐjì, 欺骗 qīpiàn. **tricky** *adj* [-ier, -iest] **(a)** 狡猾的 jiǎohuáde, 奸诈的 jiānzhàde: *a ~y politician* 奸诈的政客. **(b)** 困难〔難〕的 kùnnande; 复〔復〕杂〔雜〕的 fùzáde: *a ~y problem* (*job*) 棘手的问题(工作).

trickle /'trɪkl/ *vt/i* (使)滴流 dīliú, (使)细流 xìliú: *The tears ~d down her cheeks.* 眼泪从她的脸上滴下来. □ *n* [C] 滴流 dīliú, 细流 xìliú: *~ of blood* 血滴.

tri·cycle /'traɪsɪkl/ *n* [C] 三轮〔輪〕车〔車〕 sānlúnchē.

tried /traɪd/ ⇨ try[1].

trifle /'traɪfl/ *n* **1** [C] 小事 xiǎo shì; 无〔無〕价〔價〕值的东〔東〕西 wú jiàzhí de dōngxi. **2** [C] 少量的钱 shǎoliàngde qián. **3** ***a ~*** *adv* 稍微 shāowēi, 有一点〔點〕儿 yǒu yìdiǎnr: *a ~ too short* 稍微短了一些. **4** [C,U] 甜食 tiánshí; 糕点 gāodiǎn. □ *vt/i* 开〔開〕玩笑 kāiwánxiào, 玩弄 wánnòng: *~ with the girl's affections* 玩弄那女孩子的感情. **'trif·ling** *adj* 不重要的 bú zhòngyàode, 微不足道的 wēi bù zú dào de: *a trifling error* 小错误.

trig·ger /'trɪgə(r)/ *n* [C] (尤指枪的)扳机〔機〕 bānjī. □ *vt* ***~ sth off*** 引起 yǐnqǐ, 激发〔發〕 jīfā.

trill /trɪl/ *n* [C] **1** 颤抖声〔聲〕 chàndǒushēng; (鸟的) 啭〔轉〕鸣〔鳴〕 zhuànmíng. **2** [音乐] 颤音 chànyīn. □ *vt/i* 用颤音唱或奏 yòng chànyīn chàng huò zòu.

tril·ogy /'trɪlədʒɪ/ *n* [C] [*pl* -ies] (戏剧,小说等的)三部曲 sānbùqǔ.

trim /trɪm/ *adj* [-mer, -mest] 整洁〔潔〕的 zhěngjiéde, 整齐〔齊〕的 zhěngqíde. □ *n* [U] 整洁 zhěngjié; 准〔準〕备〔備〕 zhǔnbèi, 齐备 qíbèi: *Everything was in good* (*proper*) *~.* 一切都已准备就绪. □ *vt/i* [-mm-] **1** 使整洁 shǐ zhěngjié, 整理 zhěnglǐ, 修剪 xiūjiǎn: *~ one's beard* 修剪胡子. **2** 装〔裝〕饰 (衣帽等) zhuāngshì. **3** 装稳〔穩〕(船只,飞机等) zhuāngwěn; 调整(风帆) tiáozhěng. **~ming** *n* [C] [常用 *pl*] 装饰物 zhuāngshìwù: *lace ~mings* 花边装饰.

trin·ity /'trɪnətɪ/ *n* [C] [*pl* -ies] 三个〔個〕一组 sāngè yìzǔ, 三位一体〔體〕 sānwèi yìtǐ. **the T~** [基督教](圣父,圣子,圣灵) 三位一体 sānwèi yìtǐ.
trin·ket /'trɪŋkɪt/ *n* [C] 小件饰物 xiǎo jiàn shìwù.
trio /'tri:əʊ/ *n* [C] [*pl* ~s] **1** 三个〔個〕一组 sāngè yìzǔ, 三位一体〔體〕 sānwèi yìtǐ. **2** [音乐]三重奏 sānchóngzòu; 三人合唱 sānrén héchàng.
trip /trɪp/ *vt/i* [-pp-] **1** ~ *over sth* (被…)绊倒 bàndǎo. ~ *(sb) up* **(a)** (使…)失足 shīzú, (使…)摔倒 shuāidǎo. **(b)** [喻]使犯错误 shǐ fàn cuòwù. **2** 轻〔輕〕快地走动〔動〕 qīngkuàide zǒudòng: *She came ~ping down the path.* 她轻快地从小径跑来. □ *n* [C] **1** 旅行 lǚxíng, 远〔遠〕足 yuǎnzú. **2** 绊倒 bàndǎo, 失足 shīzú. **3** (吸麻醉毒品者的)幻觉〔覺〕 huànjué. **~per** 远足者 yuǎnzúzhě, (短程)旅行者 lǚxíngzhě.
tri·par·tite /,traɪ'pɑ:taɪt/ *adj* 有三份的 yǒu sānfènde, 一式三份的 yíshì sānfèn de.
tripe /traɪp/ *n* [U] **1** (食用)牛肚 niúdǔ. **2** [俚语]废〔廢〕话 fèihuà.
triple /'trɪpl/ *adj* 三部分合成的 sānbùfèn héchéng de, 三方的 sānfāngde. □ *vt/i* 使增至三倍 shǐ zēng zhì sānbèi: ~ *one's income* 收入增加到三倍.
trip·let /'trɪplɪt/ *n* [*pl*] 三胞胎 sānbāotāi.
trip·li·cate /'trɪplɪkət/ *adj* 一式三份的 yíshì sānfèn de. □ *n* [C] 一式三份中的一份 yíshì sānfèn zhōng de yífèn: *a letter typed in ~* 打成一式三份的信. □ *vt* /'trɪplɪkeɪt/ (把…)作一式三份 zuò yíshì sānfèn.
tri·pod /'traɪpɒd/ *n* [C] 三脚架 sānjiǎojià.
trip·per /'trɪpə(r)/ *n* ⇨ trip.
trite /traɪt/ *adj* (言论等) 平凡的 píngfánde, 陈〔陳〕腐的 chénfǔde.
tri·umph /'traɪʌmf/ *n* [C,U] 凯〔凱〕旋 kǎixuán, 成功 chénggōng: *return home in ~* 凯旋归来. □ *vi* [与 *over* 连用]获〔獲〕胜〔勝〕 huòshèng, 击〔擊〕败 jībài: ~ *over a defeated enemy* 战胜敌人而凯旋. **~al** /traɪ'ʌmfl/ *adj* **~ant** /traɪ'ʌmfnt/ *adj* (庆祝)胜利的 shènglìde. **~ant·ly** *adv*
triv·ial /'trɪvɪəl/ *adj* **1** 不重要的 bú zhòngyào de, 琐〔瑣〕屑的 suǒxiède: *a ~ offence* 小过失. **2** 平常的 píngchángde, 平凡的 píngfánde; 乏味的 fáwèide: *a ~ speech* 乏味的演说. **~ly** *adv* **~ity** /-'ælətɪ/ *n* [U] 平凡 píngfán, 琐屑 suǒxiè. [C] [*pl* -ies] 琐事 suǒshì; 平凡的意见 píngfánde yìjiàn.
trod, trod·den /trɒd, 'trɒdn/ ⇨ tread.
trol·ley /'trɒlɪ/ *n* [C] [*pl* ~s] **1** 手推车〔車〕 shǒutuīchē. **2** [铁路]查道车 chádàochē. **3** (用以送食物，书籍等的)小台〔檯〕车 xiǎo táichē.
trom·bone /trɒm'bəʊn/ *n* [C] [音乐]长〔長〕号〔號〕 chánghào. **trom·bon·ist** 长号吹奏者 chánghào chuīzòu zhě.
troop /tru:p/ *n* [C] **1** 一群 (人或动物) yìqún. **2** [*pl*] 军〔軍〕队〔隊〕 jūnduì, 部队 bùduì. **3** 骑〔騎〕兵队 qíbīngduì. □ *vt/i* 成群结队而行 chéngqún jiéduì ér xíng: *children ~ing out of school* 成群地从学校出来的儿童. **~er** 骑兵 qíbīng. *swear like a ~er* 破口大骂〔罵〕 pò kǒu dà mà.
trophy /'trəʊfɪ/ *n* [C] [*pl* -ies] **1** 胜〔勝〕利纪念品 shènglì jìniànpǐn. **2** 奖〔獎〕品 jiǎngpǐn: *'tennis trophies* 网球奖.
tropic /'trɒpɪk/ *n* **1** [C] [天文]回归〔歸〕线〔線〕 huíguīxiàn: *T~ of Cancer* 北回归线. *T~ of Capricorn* 南回归线. **2 the ~s** 热〔熱〕带〔帶〕 rèdài. **~al** *adj* of the tropics.
trot /trɒt/ *vt/i* [-tt-] **1** (马)小跑 xiǎopǎo. **2** (人) 快步走 kuàibù zǒu. **3** ~ *sth out* 说出 shuōchū: ~ *out an excuse* 提出一个借口. □ *n* **1** (马的)小跑 xiǎopǎo; (人的)快步 kuàibù: *go at a steady ~* 一路以快步走去. *on the ~* [俚语]一个〔個〕接一个地 yígè jiē yígè de, 不断〔斷〕地 búduànde; *five whiskies on the ~* 一连五杯威士忌酒.
trouble /'trʌbl/ *vt/i* **1** (使)烦恼〔惱〕 fánnǎo, (使)忧〔憂〕虑〔慮〕 yōulǜ, (使)不安 bù'ān: *be ~d by bad news* 为坏消息而忧虑. **2** (用于有礼貌的请求等): *May I ~ you for a match?* 麻烦你给我火柴好吗? **3** 烦劳〔勞〕 fánláo, 费心 fèixīn: *Don't ~ to meet me at the station.* 不必劳驾到车站接我. **4** [尤用 *pp*] 苦恼 kǔnǎo, 受折磨 shòu zhémó: *~d looks* 苦恼的表情. □ *n* **1** [C,U] 烦恼 fánnǎo, 忧虑 yōulǜ; 困难〔難〕 kùnnan, 麻烦 máfan: *She's always making ~ for her friends.* 她常常为她的朋友们带来麻烦. **ask** (或 **look**) **for ~** [非正式用语]自找麻烦 zì zhǎo

máfan. ***get into*** ~ 招致责罚 zhāozhì zéfá; 陷入困境 xiàn rù kùnjìng. ***get a girl into*** ~ [非正式用语] 使女孩子怀孕 shǐ nǚháizi huáiyùn. **2** [U] 不方便 bù fāngbiàn, 麻烦 máfan: *Did the work give you much* ~? 那工作给你添不少麻烦吗? **3** [C,U] 不安 bù'ān, 扰[擾]乱[亂] rǎoluàn: *industrial* ~*(s)* 产业纠纷(如罢工). **4** [C,U] 疾病 jíbìng: *'liver* ~ 肝病. **'~-maker** 闹[鬧]事者 nàoshìzhě. **'~some** *adj* 令人烦恼的 lìng rén fánnǎo de, 讨厌[厭]的 tǎoyànde.

trough /trɒf/ *n* [C] **1** 饲料槽 sìliàocáo; 水槽 shuǐcáo. **2** [物理] 波谷 bōgǔ. **3** [气象] 低压[壓]槽 dīyācáo.

troupe /tru:p/ *n* [C] 剧[劇]团[團] jùtuán, 戏[戲]班 xìbān.

trousers /'traʊzəz/ *n pl* [常用 *a pair of* ~] 裤[褲]子 kùzi, 长[長]裤 chángkù. **trouser** *adj* 裤子的 kùzide: *'~ pockets* 裤袋.

trout /traʊt/ *n* [C] 鳟鱼 zūnyú.

trowel /'traʊəl/ *n* [C] **1** 抹泥刀 mònídāo. **2** 泥铲[鏟]子 níchǎnzi.

tru·ant /'tru:ənt/ *n* [C] 逃学[學]者 táoxuézhě, 旷[曠]课者 kuàngkèzhě: *play* ~ 逃学. **tru·ancy** /'tru:ənsɪ/ *n* [U]

truce /tru:s/ *n* [C] 休战[戰] xiūzhàn.

truck /trʌk/ *n* [C] **1** [英国英语] [铁路]敞篷货车[車] chǎngpéng huòchē. **2** [美语]货车 huòchē, 卡车 kǎchē.

trudge /trʌdʒ/ *vi* 履步艰[艱]难[難]地走 lǚbù jiānnán de zǒu: *trudging through the deep snow* 在深雪中跋涉. □ *n* [C] 长[長]途跋涉 chángtú báshè.

true /tru:/ *adj* [-r, -st] **1** 真实[實]的 zhēnshíde, 确[確]实的 quèshíde: *Is the news* ~? 这消息确实吗? ***come*** ~ (希望等) 实现 shíxiàn. **2** 忠实的 zhōngshíde, 忠诚的 zhōngchéngde: *be* ~ *to one's promise* 信守诺言. **3** 真正的 zhēnzhèngde: *T~ friendship* 真正的友谊. **4**(指安装等)正的 zhèngde, 准[準]的 zhǔnde: *Is the wheel* ~? 那车轮装准了吗? **5** 确切的 quèqiède, 正确的 zhèngquède: *a* ~ *copy* 正确的抄本. □ *n* ***out of*** ~ (部位)不正 bú zhèng: *The door is out of* ~. 门装歪了.

truly /'tru:lɪ/ *adv* **1** 真实[實]地 zhēnshíde, 确[確]实地 quèshíde. **2** 忠诚地 zhōngchéngde, 忠实地 zhōngshíde, 诚恳[懇]地 chéngkěnde: *feel* ~ *grateful* 诚挚地感谢. **3** 真正 zhēnzhèng: *a* ~ *brave action* 真正勇敢的行为.

trump /trʌmp/ *n* [C] 王牌 wángpái: *Hearts are* ~*s*. 红心是王牌. ***turn up*** ~***s*** [非正式用语] 结果较[較]预期的为[爲]好 jiéguǒ jiào yùqīde wéi hǎo. □ *vt/i* **1** 打出王牌 dǎ chū wángpái. **2** 捏造(借口等) niēzào: *a* ~*ed-up charge* 捏造的罪名.

trum·pet /'trʌmpɪt/ *n* [C] **1** 喇叭 lǎba. **2** 喇叭声[聲] lǎbashēng, 似喇叭声 sì lǎbashēng: *the* ~ *of a elephant* 象的吼声. □ *vt/i* (尤指象的)吼叫 hǒujiào. **~er** 吹喇叭者 chuī lǎba zhě, 号[號]兵 hàobīng.

trun·cheon /'trʌntʃən/ *n* [C] 短粗的棍棒 duǎncūde gùnbàng, 警棍 jǐnggùn.

trunk /trʌŋk/ *n* [C] **1** 树[樹]干[幹] shùgàn. **2** 躯[軀]干 qūgàn. **3** 大衣箱 dà yīxiāng. **4** 象鼻 xiàngbí. **5** [*pl*] 男游泳衣 nán yóuyǒngyī. **6** [美语] = boot(2). **'~ call** 长[長]途电[電]话 chángtú diànhuà. **'~ line** (铁路,通讯等的)干线[線] gànxiàn. **'~ road** 干道 gàndào.

truss /trʌs/ *n* [C] **1** [英国英语] (干草等的)捆 kǔn, 束 shù. **2** 桁架 héngjià. **3** (疝气) 托带[帶] tuōdài. □ *vt* 捆扎 kǔnzā: ~ *up a chicken* (烹烤前) 把鸡翅扎好.

trust[1] /trʌst/ *n* **1** [U] 信任 xìnrèn, 信赖 xìnlài: *A child has* ~ *in its mother.* 小孩子信赖母亲. ***on*** ~ **(a)** 不加证[證]明地 bù jiā zhèngmíng de 不作深究地 bù zuò shēnjiū de: *He took my statement on* ~. 他不深究地信任我的陈述. **(b)** 赊帐[賬] shēzhàng: *supply goods on* ~ 赊帐供应物品. **2** [U] 责任 zérèn, 职[職]责 zhízé: *a position of great* ~ 责任重大的职位. **3** [U] [法律]托管 tuōguǎn. [C] 受托管的财产[產] shòu tuōguǎn de cáichǎn. **4** [C][经济]托拉斯 tuōlāsī. **~ful, ~ing** *adj* 信任的 xìnrènde, 不疑的 bùyíde. **~fully, ~ing·ly** *adv*

trust[2] /trʌst/ *vt/i* **1** 信任 xìnrèn, 相信 xiāngxìn: ~ *one's friends* 相信朋友. **2** 信仰 xìnyǎng: ~ *in God* 信仰上帝. **3** (对某人) 放心 fàngxīn: *I* ~ *you with my new car.* 我放心你使用我的新车. **4** 希望 xīwàng, 盼望 pànwàng: *I* ~ *you are not hurt.* 我希望你没有受伤.

trustee /trʌ'sti:/ *n* [C] 受托管者 shòu tuōguǎn zhě.

trust·worthy /'trʌstwɜ:ðɪ/ *adj* 可信赖的 kě xìnlài de, 可靠的 kěkàode.

truth /tru:θ/ *n* [*pl* ~s /tru:ðz/] **1** [U] 真实[實] zhēnshí, 真实性 zhēnshíxìng: *There's no ~ in what he says.* 他所说的毫不真实. **2** [U] 事实 shìshí, 真相 zhēnxiàng: *tell the ~* 说真话. **3** [C] 真理 zhēnlǐ, 真义[義] zhēnyì: *scientific ~s* 科学的真理. **~ful** *adj* **(a)** (指人) 诚实的 chéngshíde, 说真话的 shuō zhēnhuà de. **(b)** (指叙述) 真实的 zhēnshíde, 如实的 rúshíde. **~fully** *adv* **~ful·ness** *n* [U]

try[1] /traɪ/ *vt/i* [*pt, pp* tried] **1** 试做 shì zuò, 尝[嘗]试 chángshì: *He tried to escape.* 他试图逃跑. **2** 试验[驗] shìyàn, 试用 shìyòng: *Why not ~ this new glue.* 为什么不试用这种新的胶水. **~ *sth on*** **(a)** 试穿(衣服等) shì chuān. **(b)** [非正式用语] (为试探某事可否被忍受而)玩弄花招 wánnòng huāzhāo. **~ *sth out*** 试验(某物) shìyàn: *~ out a new car* 试新车. **3** 审[審]问[問] shěnwèn, 审判shěnpàn: *He was tried and found guilty of murder.* 他以杀人受审, 并判决有罪. **4** 考验 kǎoyàn, 磨炼[煉] móliàn: *His courage was severely tried.* 他的勇气受到严厉的考验.

try[2] /traɪ/ *n* [C] [*pl* tries] **1** 试验[驗] shìyàn, 尝[嘗]试 chángshì: *He had three tries and failed each time.* 他试验了三次, 每次都失败. **2** (橄榄球赛中)在对[對]方球门[門]线[綫]后[後]面带[帶]球触[觸]地 zài duìfāng qiúménxiàn hòumiàn dài qiú chù dì.

tsetse /'tsetsɪ/ *n* [C] (亦作 *'~-fly*) [动物](非洲)采采蝇[蠅] cǎicǎiyíng.

T.U. = Trade Union.

tub /tʌb/ *n* [C] **1** 桶 tǒng; 盆 pén. **2** = tubful. **3** [非正式用语]浴盆 yùpén, 浴缸 yùgāng. **'~ful** /-fʊl/ 一桶的容量 yìtǒngde róngliàng.

tuba /'tju:bə/ *n* [C] [*pl* ~s] [音乐]大号[號] dàhào.

tubby /'tʌbɪ/ *adj* [-ier, -iest] 矮胖的 ǎipàngde, 肥圆的 féiyuánde.

tube /tju:b/ *n* [C] **1** 管 guǎn, 管道 guǎndào. **2** (金属)软[軟]管 ruǎnguǎn: *a ~ of toothpaste* 一管牙膏. **3** (伦敦) 地下铁道 dìxià tiědào. **4** [解剖]管 guǎn: *the bronchial ~s* 支气管. **tub·ing** *n* [U] 管形材料 guǎnxíng cáiliào.

tu·ber /'tju:bə(r)/ *n* [C] [植物]块[塊]茎[莖] kuàijīng.

tu·ber·cu·lo·sis /tju:,bɜ:kjʊ'ləʊsɪs/ *n* [U] (缩作 **TB**) 结核(病) jiéhé.

tu·bu·lar /'tju:bjʊlə(r)/ *adj* 管形的 guǎnxíngde, 由管构[構]成的 yóu guǎn gòuchéng de.

tuck /tʌk/ *n* **1** [C] (衣服的)缝褶 féngzhě, 褶裥[襇] zhějiǎn. **2** [U] [俚语]食物 shíwù. □ *vt/i* **1** 打褶裥 dǎ zhějiǎn, 缩拢[攏] suōlǒng; 塞置于[於] sāizhì yú: *~ your shirt in to your trousers* 把你的衬衫塞进裤子里去. **2** *~ in* [过时用法]大吃 dà chī, 尽[盡]情地吃 jìnqíngde chī.

Tues. = Tuesday.

Tues·day /'tju:zdɪ/ *n* 星期二 xīngqī'èr.

tuft /tʌft/ *n* [C] (羽毛,草等)一束 yíshù, 一簇 yícù.

tug /tʌg/ *vt/i* [-gg-] [与 *at* 连用]用力拉 yòng lì lā. □ *n* [C] **1** 猛拉 měng lā, 拖拉 tuōlā **2** (亦作 *'~-boat*) 拖船 tuōchuán.

tu·ition /tju:'ɪʃn/ *n* [U] 教学[學] jiàoxué; 学费 xuéfèi: *have private ~* 请私人教学.

tu·lip /'tju:lɪp/ *n* [C] [植物]郁[鬱]金香 yùjīnxiāng; 山慈姑 shāncígū.

tumble /'tʌmbl/ *vt/i* **1** 跌倒 diēdǎo, 跌落 diēluò: *tumbling down the stairs* 从楼梯上跌下来. **2** 打滚 dǎ gǔn, 乱[亂]动[動] luàn dòng: *The puppies were tumbling about.* 小狗在打滚. **3** 摇摇欲坠[墜] yáoyáo yù zhuì: *The old barn is tumbling down.* 那旧谷仓要倒坍. **4** 使跌倒 shǐ diēdǎo, 使倾覆 shǐ qīngfù. **5** *~ to sth* [非正式用语]了解 liáojiě, 明白 míngbái: *At last he ~d to what I meant.* 他终于明白了我的意思. □ *n* [C] 跌倒 diēdǎo, 跌落 diēluò: *have a nasty ~* 重重地跌一交. **'~down** 摇摇欲坠的 yáoyáo yù zhuì de, 要倒塌的 yào dǎotā de.

tum·bler /'tʌmblə(r)/ *n* [C] **1** 平底无[無]把酒杯 píngdǐ wú bǎ jiǔbēi. **2** (锁的)制栓 zhìshuān.

tummy /'tʌmɪ/ *n* [C] [*pl* -ies] [非正式用语]胃 wèi, 肚子 dùzi.

tu·mour [美语 = **tu·mor**] /'tju:mə(r)/ *n* [C] 肿[腫]瘤 zhǒngliú.

tu·mult /'tju:mʌlt/ *n* [C,U] **1** 吵闹[鬧] chǎonào, 喧哗[嘩] xuānhuá: *the ~ of battle* 战争的喧嚣. **2** 激动[動] jīdòng; 混乱[亂] hùnluàn: *be in a ~* 激动的. **~u·ous** /tju:'mʌltʃʊəs/ *adj* [正式用语]吵闹的 chǎonàode, 喧哗的 xuānhuáde; 激动的 jīdòngde: *a ~uous welcome* 喧嚣的欢迎. **~u·ous·ly** *adv*

tuna /'tju:nə/ *n* [C] 金枪〔槍〕鱼 jīnqiāngyú.

tune /tju:n/ *n* **1** [C] 曲调 qǔdiào **2** [U] 明显〔顯〕的旋律 míngxiǎnde xuánlǜ. **3** [U] *in* ~ 和谐 héxié, 合拍 hépāi. *out of* ~ 走调 zǒu diào. **4** [U] [喻]协〔協〕调 xiétiáo, 调和 tiáohé: *be in ~ with one's companions* 与同伴协调一致. *change one's* ~ 改变〔變〕态〔態〕度 gǎibiàn tàidù. *to the ~ of* 达〔達〕到…数〔數〕量 dádào … shùliàng: *He was fined to the ~ of £30.* 他被罚款达三十镑. □ *vt/i* **1** 为〔爲〕…调音 wèi…tiáo yīn: ~ *a guitar* 调准吉他的音. **2** ~ *in (to)* (无线电)调谐 tiáoxié, 收听〔聽〕 shōutīng: ~ *in to the BBC* 收听英国 BBC 电台. **3** (机器)调整 tiáozhěng, 调节〔節〕 tiáojié. **~ful** *adj* (曲调)悦耳的 yuè'ěrde, 和谐的 héxiéde. **~fully** *adv* **'tuning-fork** 音叉 yīnchā.

tuner /'tju:nə(r)/ *n* 调音师〔師〕 tiáoyīnshī.

tu·nic /'tju:nɪk/ *n* [C] **1** (警察,士兵的)紧〔緊〕身上衣 jǐn shēn shàngyī. **2** (系带的)宽大外衣 kuāndà wàiyī.

tun·nel /'tʌnl/ *n* [C] 隧道 suìdào, 地道 dìdào. □ *vt/i* [-ll-, 美语亦作 -l-] 掘地道 jué dìdào.

tunny /'tʌnɪ/ *n* [C] = tuna.

tur·ban /'tɜ:bən/ *n* [C] **1** (某些亚洲国家)男用头〔頭〕巾 nányòng tóujīn. **2** (女用)无〔無〕沿帽 wúyánmào.

tur·bine /'tɜ:baɪn/ *n* [C] 涡〔渦〕轮〔輪〕机 wōlúnjī, 透平 tòupíng.

turbo- /,tɜ:bəʊ/ *prefix* (表示"涡轮推动的"). **'~car** *n* [C] 涡〔渦〕轮〔輪〕机〔機〕汽车〔車〕 wōlúnjī qìchē. **~'charger** *n* [C] 涡轮增压〔壓〕器 wōlún zēngyāqì. **~'jet (engine)** *n* [C] 涡轮喷气〔氣〕飞〔飛〕机〔機〕(发动机) wōlún pēnqì fēijī. **~'prop (engine)** *n* [C] 涡轮螺旋桨〔槳〕飞机(发动机) wōlún luóxuánjiǎng fēijī.

tur·bu·lent /'tɜ:bjʊlənt/ *adj* 狂暴的 kuángpàode, 骚〔騷〕乱〔亂〕的 sāoluànde: ~ *waves* 汹涌的波涛. ~ *passions* 狂烈的情感. **~ly** *adv* **tur·bu·lence** *n* [U]

tu·reen /tjʊ'ri:n/ *n* [C] (盛汤的)大盖〔蓋〕碗 dà gàiwǎn.

turf /tɜ:f/ *n* **1** [U] 草地 cǎodì, 草皮 cǎopí. **2** [C] 草皮块〔塊〕 cǎopíkuai. □ *vt* **1** 铺草皮 pū cǎopí. **2** ~ *(sb, sth) out* [俚语]赶〔趕〕出(某人) gǎnchū, 抛出(某物) pāochū.

tur·key /'tɜ:kɪ/ *n* [C] [*pl* ~s] 火鸡〔鷄〕 huǒjī.

Tur·kish bath /,tɜ:kɪʃ 'bɑ:θ/ *n* [C] 土耳其浴 Tǔ'ěrqí yù, 蒸汽浴 zhēngqì yù.

tur·moil /'tɜ:mɔɪl/ *n* [C,U] 骚〔騷〕动〔動〕 sāodòng, 混乱〔亂〕 hùnluàn.

turn¹ /tɜ:n/ *n* [C] **1** 转〔轉〕动〔動〕 zhuàndòng, 旋转 xuánzhuǎn: *a few ~s of the handle* 把手的数次转动. *done to a* ~ 烹煮得恰到好处〔處〕 pēngzhǔde qiàdào hǎochù. **2** 转弯〔彎〕 zhuǎnwān, 转向 zhuǎnxiàng: *sudden ~s in the road* 路的急转弯. *at every* ~ [喻]经〔經〕常地 jīngchángde. **3** 变〔變〕化 biànhuà, 转折 zhuǎnzhé: *a ~ for the better (worse.)* 好转(变坏). **4** 机〔機〕会〔會〕 jīhuì; 轮〔輪〕值 lúnzhí: *It's your ~ to read now, John.* 约翰, 现在轮到你读了. *in* ~ 依次 yīcì, 轮流 lúnliú. *out of* ~ 不依顺序地 bù yī shùnxù de; 不合时〔時〕宜地 bù hé shíyí de. *take ~s at sth* 轮流做某事 lúnliú zuò mǒushì. **5** (影响别人的)举〔擧〕动 jǔdòng: *do her a good* ~ 做一件有利于她的事. **6** (戏院的)短节〔節〕目 duǎn jiémù.

turn² /tɜ:n/ *vt/i* **1** (使)旋转〔轉〕 xuánzhuǎn, (使)转向 zhuǎnxiàng: *The earth ~s round the sun.* 地球绕着太阳转. *He ~ed to look at me.* 他转过来看着我. ~ *one's hand to sth* 着手做某事 zhuóshǒu zuò mǒushì. ~ *one's attention to sth* 把注意力转向某事 bǎ zhùyìlì zhuǎnxiàng mǒushì. **2** (使)改变〔變〕(性质,状况等) gǎibiàn, (使)成为〔爲〕 chéngwéi: *Frost ~s water into ice.* 严寒使水结成冰. *Caterpillars ~ into butterflies.* 毛毛虫蜕化为蝴蝶. ~ *sb's head* 使人狂妄自负 shǐ rén kuángwàng zìfù. **3** 达〔達〕到并超过〔過〕 dádào bìng chāoguò: *He has ~ed fifty.* 他已过五十岁了. **4** (在车床上)车〔車〕(某物) chē: ~ *a bowl on a potter's wheel* 在旋盘上车一个碗. ~ *(sb) against sb* (使某人)对〔對〕…变为敌〔敵〕对 duì … biànwéi díduì: ~ *the children against their mother* 唆使孩子们反抗他们的母亲. ~ *(sb) away* 转过脸〔臉〕去 zhuǎnguò liǎn qù, 拒绝接纳 jùjué jiēnà: *She ~ed away in disgust.* 她感到厌恶地把脸转过去. *We had to ~ away hundreds of fans.* 我们只好谢绝了成千上百的狂热者. ~ *(sb, sth) back* (使)折回去 zhé huíqù. ~ *(sth) down* **(a)** (使)翻下 fānxià. **(b)** 关〔關〕小(灯

光,水流等) guānxiǎo. ~ ***sb (sth) down*** 拒绝(建议等) jùjué. ~ ***in*** [非正式用语]睡觉[覺]去 shuìjiàoqù. ~ ***sb in*** [非正式用语]告发[發] gàofā, 告密 gàomì. ~ ***off*** 避开[開] bìkāi, 让[讓](路) ràng. ~ ***sth off*** 关掉(灯光,水流等) guāndiào: ~ *off the TV* 关掉电视. ~ ***(sb) off*** [俚语](使)厌[厭]烦 yànfán. ~ ***sth on*** 打开(灯光,水流等) dǎkāi: *T~ the radio on.* 打开收音机. ~ ***(sb) on*** [俚语]使生快感 shǐ shēng kuàigǎn. ~ ***on sb*** 攻击[擊] gōngjī, 反对 fǎnduì. ~ ***out (well, etc)*** 证[證]明(为) zhèngmíng, 结果(是) jiéguǒ: *Everything ~ed out well.* 结果一切都很好. ~ ***sth out*** **(a)** 关掉 guāndiào, 熄灭[滅] xīmiè: *Please ~ out the lights.* 请熄灯. **(b)** 翻出 fānchū, 出空 chūkòng: ~ *out one's pockets* 把口袋翻出来. ~ ***sb out (of, from sth)*** 逐出 zhúchū, 把…赶[趕]走 bǎ...gǎnzǒu. ~ ***sb (sth) out*** 培养[養] péiyǎng, 生产[產] shēngchǎn. ~ ***(sb) out*** (使)出来[來]集合 chūlái jíhé: *Not many men ~ed out to watch the match.* 没有多少人出来看比赛. **'~-out** 集合的人群 jíhéde rénqún. ~ ***(sb, sth) over*** (使)打翻 dǎ fān, (使)翻转 fānzhuǎn: *He ~ed over in bed.* 他在床上翻身. ~ ***sth (sb) over (to sb)*** 移交 yíjiāo, 交给 jiāogěi: *The thief was ~ed over to the police.* 那贼已被送交警察. ~ ***sth over*** 营[營]业[業]额达[達] yíngyè'é dá: *His business ~s over £500 a week.* 他的商店每星期做五百镑生意. **'~over** (某一时期的)营业额 yíngyè'é. ~ ***to*** 求助于[於] qiú zhù yú. ~ ***up*** **(a)** 到达 dàodá: *He ~ed up late.* 他迟到了. **(b)** 被发[發]现 bèi fāxiàn: *The book you've lost may ~ up.* 你遗失的书会找到的. ~ ***(sth) up*** **(a)** (使)卷[捲]起 juǎnqǐ, 折起 zhéqǐ: ~ *up one's shirt sleeves* 卷起衬衫袖子. **(b)** 发掘出 fājuéchū, 使暴露 shǐ bàolù: *He ~ed up some buried treasure.* 他发掘出若干埋藏的珍宝. **'~-up** **(a)** (裤腿的)卷边[邊] juǎnbiān. **(b)** 意外的事 yìwàide shì.

turn·stile /'tɜ:nstaɪl/ *n* [C] 旋转[轉]式栅门[門] xuánzhuǎnshì zhàmén.

turner /'tɜ:nə(r)/ *n* [C] 车[車]工 chēgōng; 旋工 xuàngōng.

turn·ing /'tɜ:nɪŋ/ *n* [C] (路的)转弯[彎]处[處] zhuǎnwānchù. **'~-point** [喻] 转折点[點] zhuǎnzhédiǎn, 转机[機] zhuǎnjī: *reach a ~-point in one's life* 到达一生的转折点.

tur·nip /'tɜ:nɪp/ *n* [C] 萝[蘿]卜[蔔] luóbo.

tur·quoise /'tɜ:kwɔɪz/ *n* [C,U] 绿松石 lǜsōngshí; 绿蓝[藍]色 lǜlánsè.

tur·ret /'tʌrɪt/ *n* [C] **1** 角楼[樓] jiǎolóu, 小塔 xiǎotǎ. **2** [C] 炮塔 pàotǎ.

turtle /'tɜ:tl/ *n* [C] 海龟[龜] hǎiguī.

tusk /tʌsk/ *n* [C] (象,野猪等的)獠牙 liáoyá.

tussle /'tʌsl/ *n* [C], *vi* [与 *with* 连用]扭打 niǔdǎ, 争斗[鬥] zhēngdòu.

tut /tʌt/, **tut-tut** /,tʌt 'tʌt/ *int* (表示不耐烦)嘘 xū! 啧 zé!

tu·tor /'tju:tə(r)/ *n* [C] **1** 私人教师[師] sīrén jiàoshī, 家庭教师 jiātíng jiàoshī. **2** [英国英语] (大学)导[導]师 dǎoshī. □ *vt* (个别地)教学[學] jiàoxué; 当[當]…的导师 dāng...de dǎoshī. **~ial** /tju:'tɔ:rɪəl/ *adj* 家庭教师的 jiātíng jiàoshī de; (大学)导师的 dǎoshīde: *~ial classes* 家庭教师的课. □ *n* [C] (教师的)个别指导期 gèbié zhǐdǎoqī.

T. V. = television.

twang /twæŋ/ *n* [C] **1** 拨[撥]弦声[聲] bōxiánshēng: *the ~ of a guitar* 吉他的弦声. **2** 鼻声 bíshēng, 鼻音 bíyīn. □ *vt/i* (使)发[發]拨弦声 fā bōxiánshēng.

tweak /twi:k/ *vt* 拧[擰] níng, 扭 niǔ, 捏 niē: ~ *a child's nose* 捏小孩儿的鼻子. □ *n* [C] 拧 níng, 扭 niǔ, 捏 niē.

tweed /twi:d/ *n* **1** [U] 花呢 huāní: *a ~ coat* 花呢外衣. **2** [*pl*] (一套)花呢衣服 huāní yīfu.

tweez·ers /'twi:zəz/ *n pl* (亦作 *a pair of ~*) 镊[鑷]子 nièzi.

twelfth /twelfθ/ *n* [C], *adj* (缩作 *12th*) 第十二 dì shí'èr; 十二分之一 shí'èrfēn zhī yī.

twelve /twelv/ *n* [C] *adj* 十二 shí-èr.

twenty /'twentɪ/ *n* [C], *adj* 二十 èrshí. **twen·ti·eth** *n* [C], *adj* (缩作 *20th*) 第二十 dì èrshí; 二十分之一 èrshífēn zhī yī.

twice /twaɪs/ *adv* 两次 liǎngcì; 两倍 liǎngbèi: ~ *as much (as many)* 两倍之多. ***think ~ about*** 重新考虑[慮] chóngxīn kǎolǜ, 仔细考虑 zǐxì kǎolǜ.

twiddle /'twɪdl/ *vt/i* 抚[撫]弄 fǔnòng, 把玩 bǎwán: ~ *one's thumbs* 抚弄大拇指.

twig[1] /twɪg/ *n* [C] 细枝 xìzhī, 嫩枝 nènzhī.

twig[2] /twɪg/ *vt/i* [-gg-] [非正式用语]懂得 dǒngdé, 了解 liǎojiě: *I soon ~ged what he mean*. 我很快就明白了他的意思.

twi·light /'twaɪlaɪt/ *n* [U] **1** 曙光 shǔguāng, 黎明 límíng; 黄昏 huánghūn.

twill /twɪl/ *n* [U] 斜纹布 xiéwénbù.

twin /twɪn/ *n* **1** [C] 孪[孿]生儿[兒]之一 luánshēng'ér zhī yī: ,~ '*brothers* 孪生兄弟. **2** [用作定语]完全相象的 wánquán xiāngxiàng de: ,~ '*beds* 两张相同的单人床.

twinge /twɪndʒ/ *n* [C] 剧[劇]痛 jùtòng, 刺痛 cìtòng: *a ~ of toothache* 一阵牙痛. □ *vi* 刺痛 cìtòng.

twinkle /'twɪŋkl/ *vi* **1** 闪[閃]烁[爍] shǎnshuò, 闪耀 shǎnyào: *stars twinkling in the sky* 天上闪烁着的星星. **2** (眼睛)闪闪发[發]光 shǎnshǎn fā guāng. □ *n* **1** [U] 闪光 shǎn guāng, 闪烁 shǎnshuò. **2** (眼睛的)闪亮 shǎnliàng; 眨眼 zhǎyǎn.

twirl /twɜːl/ *vt/i* **1** (使)快速旋转[轉] kuàisù xuánzhuǎn: *He sat ~ing his thumbs*. 他坐着,交互地转动着他的两个大拇指. **2** 扭转 niǔzhuǎn, 捻弄 niǎnnòng: *He ~ed his moustache*. 他捻弄他的小胡子. □ *n* [C] 旋转 xuánzhuǎn.

twist /twɪst/ *vt/i* **1** 捻 niǎn, 搓 cuō: *~ thread into a rope* 把线搓成绳子. **2** (尤指用力)扭转[轉] niǔzhuǎn, 拧[擰] níng: *~ the cap off a tube of toothpaste*. 拧开一管牙膏的盖子. *He ~ed his ankle*. 他扭伤了脚踝. *~ sb's arm* [喻]强迫某人 qiángpò mǒurén. **3** 曲解 qūjiě: *The police tried to ~ his words*. 警察试图曲解他的话. **4** 盘[盤]旋 pánxuán, 曲折 qūzhé: *The road ~s up the mountain*. 那条路盘旋上山. □ *n* **1** [C] 搓 cuō, 扭 niǔ, 拧 níng: *Give the rope a ~*. 把绳子搓一下. **2** [C] 扭卷[捲]而成之物 niǔjuǎn ér chéng zhī wù: *a rope full of ~s* 纠结很多的绳子. **3** 怪僻 guàipì: *He has a criminal ~ in him*. 他有犯罪僻. *~er* 不诚实[實]的人 bù chéngshí de rén.

twit /twɪt/ *n* [C] [俚语]傻[傻]瓜 shǎguā.

twitch /twɪtʃ/ *n* [C] **1** (肌肉的)抽搐 chōuchù. **2** 急速拉动[動] jísù lādòng, 急扯 jíchě. □ *vt/i* (使)抽搐 chōuchù.

twit·ter /'twɪtə(r)/ *vi* **1** (指鸟)吱吱地叫 zhīzhīde jiào. **2** (指人)因兴[興]奋[奮]而快速地说 yīn xìngfèn ér kuàisùde shuō. □ *n* [C] 鸣[鳴]啭[囀] míngzhuàn.

two /tuː/ *adj*, *n* [C] 二 èr, 两 liǎng. *put ,~ and ,~ to'gether* 推理 tuīlǐ. ,*~-'faced adj* [喻]两面派的 liǎngmiànpàide. '*~fold adj*, *adv* 二倍的 èrbèide; 两倍地 liǎngbèide. '*~-,way adj* 双[雙]向的 shuāngxiàngde, 双通道的 shuāngtōngdàode.

ty·coon /taɪ'kuːn/ *n* [C] [现代非正式用语]实[實]业[業]界巨头[頭] shíyèjiè jùtóu.

type[1] /taɪp/ *n* **1** [C] 典型 diǎnxíng, 模范[範] mófàn: *Pele was a fine ~ of player*. 皮尔是选手中的模范. **2** [C] 型 xíng, 类[類]型 lèixíng: *men of this ~* 这一类型的人. **3** [U] [印刷]活字 huózì, 铅字 qiānzì. [C] (一个)铅字 qiānzì. '*~-script* 打字文件 dǎzì wénjiàn. '*~writer* 打字机[機] dǎzìjī.

type[2] /taɪp/ *vt/i* **1** 打字 dǎzì: *~ a letter* 打一封信. **2** 测定…的类型 cèdìng…de lèixíng: *~ a virus* 测定一种病毒的类型. **typ·ing** *n* [C] 打字 dǎzì. **ty·pist** /'taɪpɪst/ 打字员 dǎzìyuán.

type·cast /'taɪpkɑːst/ *vt* [*pt*, *pp* ~] 根据类型分配角色 gēnjù lèixíng fēnpèi jiǎosè.

ty·phoid /'taɪfɔɪd/ *n* [U] (亦作 *~ fever*) 伤[傷]寒 shānghán.

ty·phoon /taɪ'fuːn/ *n* [C] 台风[風] táifēng.

ty·phus /'taɪfəs/ *n* [U] 斑疹伤[傷]寒 bānzhěn shānghán.

typi·cal /'tɪpɪkl/ *adj* 典型的 diǎnxíngde, 代表性的 dàibiǎoxìngde. *~ly adv*

typ·ify /'tɪpɪfaɪ/ *vt* [*pt*, *pp* -ied] 作…的模范[範] zuò … de mófàn.

ty·pist /'taɪpɪst/ *n* [C] ⇨ type[2].

ty·ran·ni·cal /tɪ'rænɪkl/ *adj* 暴君的 bàojūnde, 专[專]制的 zhuānzhìde.

tyr·an·nize /'tɪrənaɪz/ *vt/i* 施暴政 shī bàozhèng, 暴虐统治 bàonüè tǒngzhì.

tyr·anny /'tɪrənɪ/ *n* [*pl* -ies] **1** [C,U] 暴虐 bàonüè, 暴行 bàoxíng, 残[殘]暴 cánbào. **2** [C,U] 暴政(国家) bàozhèng.

ty·rant /'taɪrənt/ *n* [C] 暴君 bàojūn.

tyre /taɪə(r)/ *n* [C] 轮[輪]胎 lúntāi.

U u

U,u /juː/ [*pl* U's, u's /juːz/] 英语的第二十一个〔個〕字母 Yīngyǔde dì'èrshíyīgè zìmǔ
U.A.E. = United Arab Emirates 阿拉伯联〔聯〕合酋长〔長〕国〔國〕Ālābó Liánhé Qiúzhǎngguó.
U.A.R. = United Arab Republic 阿拉伯联〔聯〕合共和国〔國〕Ālābó Liánhé Gònghéguó.
ud·der /'ʌdə(r)/ *n* [C] (牛,羊的)乳房 rǔfáng.
U.F.O. = unidentified flying object 飞〔飛〕碟 fēidié.
ugly /'ʌglɪ/ *adj* [-ier, -iest] **1** 丑〔醜〕陋的 chǒulòude, 难〔難〕看的 nánkànde. **2** 险〔險〕恶〔惡〕的 xiǎnède: *The situation looks* ~. 局势看来是险恶的. **ug·li·ness** *n* [U]
U.H.F. = ultra-high frequency 超高频 chāogāopín.
U.K. = United Kingdom (England, Wales, Scotland, N. Ireland) 联〔聯〕合王国〔國〕Liánhé Wángguó.
ul·cer /'ʌlsə(r)/ *n* [C] 溃疡〔瘍〕kuìyáng. **~ate** *vt/i* (使)生溃疡 shēng kuìyáng. **~ous** *adj*
ul·ti·mate /'ʌltɪmət/ *adj* 最后〔後〕的 zuìhòude; 最远〔遠〕的 zuìyuǎnde: *the* ~ *deterrent* 最终的威慑手段(指核武器). **~ly** *adv* 最后 zuìhòu.
ul·ti·ma·tum /ˌʌltɪ'meɪtəm/ *n* [C] 最后〔後〕通牒 zuìhòu tōngdié, 哀的美敦书〔書〕āidíměidūnshū.
ultra·vio·let /ˌʌltrə'vaɪələt/ *adj* 紫外线〔綫〕的 zǐwàixiànde.
um·bili·cal /ʌm'bɪlɪkl/ *adj* (亦作 ~ *cord*) 脐〔臍〕带〔帶〕qídài.
um·brella /ʌm'brelə/ *n* [C] [*pl* ~s] **1** 雨伞〔傘〕yǔsǎn. **2** [喻]保护〔護〕伞 bǎohùsǎn: *under the* ~ *of the UNO* 在联合国组织的保护下.
um·pire /'ʌmpaɪə(r)/ *n* [C] 仲裁人 zhòngcáirén, 裁判员 cáipànyuán. □ *vt/i* 裁判 cáipàn.
U.N. = The United Nations 联〔聯〕合国〔國〕Liánhéguó.
un·able /ʌn'eɪbl/ *adj* 不能的 bùnéngde, 不会〔會〕的 búhuìde.
un·ac·count·able /ˌʌnə'kaʊntəbl/ *adj* 无〔無〕法解释〔釋〕的 wúfǎ jiěshì de. **un·ac·count·ably** *adv*
un·ac·cus·tomed /ˌʌnə'kʌstəmd/ *adj* **1** 不习〔習〕惯的 bù xíguàn de: ~ *to speaking in public* 不习惯于在大庭广众中说话. **2** 不平常的 bù píngcháng de, 奇怪的 qíguàide: *an* ~ *silence* 反常的沉默.
unani·mous /juː'nænɪməs/ *adj* 一致同意的 yízhì tóngyì de: *a* ~ *decision* 全体一致同意的决定. **una·nim·ity** /ˌjuːnə'nɪmətɪ/ *n* [U]
un·an·swer·able /ʌn'ɑːnsərəbl/ *adj* (尤指)不〔無〕可辩〔辯〕驳〔駁〕的 wú kě biànbó de.
un·armed /ʌn'ɑːmd/ *adj* 非武装〔裝〕的 fēi wǔzhuāng de.
un·as·sum·ing /ˌʌnə'sjuːmɪŋ/ *adj* 不摆〔擺〕架子的 bù bǎi jiàzi de, 谦逊〔遜〕的 qiānxùnde.
un·at·tended /ˌʌnə'tendɪd/ *adj* 无〔無〕陪伴的 wú péibàn de, 没人照顾〔顧〕的 méirén zhàogù de: *Never leave a baby* ~. 不要把婴孩留下无人照顾.
un·avoid·able /ˌʌnə'vɔɪdəbl/ *adj* 不可避免的 bùkě bìmiǎn de.
un·aware /ˌʌnə'weə(r)/ *adj* 不知道的 bù zhīdào de, 没察觉〔覺〕到的 méi chájuédào de: ~ *of the danger* 没有察觉到危险. **un·awares** *adv* 意外地 yìwàide, 突然 tūrán: *taken* ~*s* 被突然袭击.
un·bal·anced /ʌn'bælənst/ *adj* 不正常的 bù zhèngcháng de, 失常的 shīchángde.
un·bear·able /ʌn'beərəbl/ *adj* 忍受不了的 rěnshòu bù liǎo de. **un·bear·ably** *adv*
un·beaten /ʌn'biːtn/ *adj* (尤指)未被击〔擊〕败的 wèi bèi jībài de: *an* ~ *record* 未被打破的纪录.
un·be·com·ing /ˌʌnbɪ'kʌmɪŋ/ *adj* 不适〔適〕当〔當〕的 bú shìdàng de, 不相称〔稱〕的 bù xiāngchèn de.
un·bi·as·sed (亦作 **-biased**) /ʌn'baɪəst/ *adj* 无〔無〕偏见的 wú piānjiàn de, 公正的 gōngzhèngde.
un·born /ʌn'bɔːn/ *adj* 未诞生的 wèi dànshēng de.
un·bro·ken /ʌn'brəʊkən/ *adj* (尤指) **1** (马)未驯〔馴〕服的 wèi xúnfú de. **2** 不中断〔斷〕的 bù zhōngduàn de: *six hours of* ~ *sleep* 六小时不间断的睡觉. **3** (纪录等)未被打破的 wèi bèi dǎpò de.
un·called-for /ʌn'kɔːld fɔː(r)/ *adj* 没有理由的 méiyǒu lǐyóu de; 不适〔適〕宜的 bú shìyí de: ~ *comments* 不适当的评语.
un·canny /ʌn'kænɪ/ *adj* 不自然的 bú zìrán de; 神秘的 shénmìde.

un·cer·tain /ʌn'sɜ:tn/ *adj* **1** 靠不住的 kàobúzhùde, 易变〔變〕的 yì biàn de: ~ *weather* 易变的天气. **2** 不确〔確〕定的 bú quèdìng de, 不明确的 bù míngquè de: *be* (或 *feel*) ~ *about the future* 对前途不明确. ~**ty** *n* [C,U] [*pl* -ies]

un·chari·table /ʌn'tʃærɪtəbl/ *adj* (尤指)严〔嚴〕厉〔厲〕的 yánlìde, 无〔無〕情的 wúqíngde.

un·checked /ˌʌn'tʃekt/ *adj* **1** 未被制止的 wèi bèi zhìzhǐde. **2** 未经检〔檢〕查的 wèi jīng jiǎnchá de.

un·civil /ʌn'sɪvl/ *adj* 不礼〔禮〕貌的 bù lǐmào de, 不文明的 bù wénmíng de.

uncle /'ʌŋkl/ *n* [C] 伯父 bófù; 叔父 shūfù; 舅父 jiùfù; 姑丈 gūzhàng; 姨夫 yífu.

un·com·fort·able /ʌn'kʌmftəbl/ *adj* 不舒服的 bù shūfu de.

un·com·mon /ʌn'kɒmən/ *adj* 不普通的 bù pǔtōng de, 不平常的 bù píngcháng de. ~**ly** *adv* (尤指)显〔顯〕著地 xiǎnzhùde: ~*ly intelligent* 非常聪明的.

un·com·pro·mis·ing /ʌn'kɒmprəmaɪzɪŋ/ *adj* 不妥协〔協〕的 bù tuǒxié de, 坚〔堅〕定的 jiāndìngde.

un·con·cerned /ˌʌnkən'sɜ:nd/ *adj* 无〔無〕忧〔憂〕虑〔慮〕的 wú yōulǜ de; 漠不关〔關〕心的 mò bù guānxīn de: ~ *about the future* 对前途漠不关心.

un·con·di·tional /ˌʌnkən'dɪʃənl/ *adj* 绝对〔對〕的 juéduìde, 无〔無〕条〔條〕件的 wú tiáojiàn de: ~ *surrender* 无条件投降.

un·con·scious /ʌn'kɒnʃəs/ *adj* 无〔無〕意识〔識〕的 wú yìshí de, 不知道的 bù zhīdào de, 失去知觉〔覺〕的 shīqù zhījué de: *knocked* ~ 被打昏过去. ~ *of danger* 不知道有危险. ~**ly** *adv*

un·couple /ʌn'kʌpl/ *vt* 解开〔開〕jiěkāi: ~ *a locomotive* 使机车脱钩.

un·couth /ʌn'ku:θ/ *adj* (人,动作等)粗野的 cūyěde; 笨拙的 bènzhuōde.

un·cover /ʌn'kʌvə(r)/ *vt* **1** 移去…的覆盖〔蓋〕物 yíqù...de fùgàiwù. **2**〔喻〕揭露 jiēlù; 宣布〔佈〕xuānbù: ~ *a plot* 揭露一件阴谋.

U.N.C.T.A.D. = United Nations Conference on Trade Development 联〔聯〕合国〔國〕贸易和发〔發〕展会〔會〕议〔議〕Liánhéguó Màoyì hé Fāzhǎn Huìyì.

un·daunted /ʌn'dɔ:ntɪd/ *adj* 无〔無〕畏的 wúwèide, 大胆〔膽〕的 dàdǎnde.

un·de·cided /ˌʌndɪ'saɪdɪd/ *adj* 未定的 wèidìngde, 未决的 wèijuéde.

un·de·ni·able /ˌʌndɪ'naɪəbl/ *adj* 确〔確〕实〔實〕的 quèshíde, 不能否认〔認〕的 bùnéng fǒurèn de.

un·der /'ʌndə(r)/ *adv* 在下面 zài xiàmiàn; 往下 wàngxià: *The ship went* ~. 船下沉了. □ *prep* **1** 在…之下 zài...zhī xià; (位置)低于〔於〕dīyú: *The cat was* ~ *the table.* 猫在桌子下面. **2** 被…遮蔽着 bèi...zhēbìzhe: *He hid* ~ *the bedclothes.* 他藏在被窝里. **3** 少于 shǎoyú; (级别等)低于 dīyú: *children* ~ *fourteen years* 不满十四岁的儿童. *no one* ~ (*the rank of*) *captain* 没有人(的阶级)低于上尉. ~ *'age* 未成年的 wèi chéngnián de. ~ *re'pair* 在修理中的 zài xiūlǐzhōng de. ~ *dis'cussion* 在讨论〔論〕中的 zài tǎolùnzhōng de. *be* ~ *the impression that* 相信 xiāngxìn, 以为〔爲〕yǐwéi.

under·car·riage /'ʌndəkærɪdʒ/ *n* [C] (飞机的)起落架 qǐluòjià.

under·charge /ˌʌndə'tʃɑ:dʒ/ *vt* 少讨…的价〔價〕钱〔錢〕shǎo tǎo...de jiàqián.

under·clothes /'ʌndəkləʊðz/ *n pl* (贴身)内衣 nèiyī.

under·cover /ˌʌndə'kʌvə(r)/ *adj* 秘密的 mìmìde, 暗中进〔進〕行的 ànzhōng jìnxíng de: *an* ~ *agent* 密探.

under·cur·rent /'ʌndəkʌrənt/ *n* [U] **1** 潜流 qiánliú. **2**〔喻〕(思想,情绪的)暗流 ànliú: *an* ~ *of hatred* 一股仇恨的暗流.

under·cut /ˌʌndə'kʌt/ *vt* [*pt*, *pp* ~] [-tt-] 削低(商品)价〔價〕格 xuēdī jiàgé.

under·de·vel·oped /ˌʌndədɪ'veləpt/ *adj* 不太发〔發〕达〔達〕的 bútài fādá de, 未充分开〔開〕发的 wèi chōngfèn kāifā de.

under·dog /'ʌndədɒg/ *n* [C]〔喻〕竞〔競〕争中处〔處〕于〔於〕劣势〔勢〕者 jìngzhēngzhōng chǔyú lièshì zhě.

under·done /ˌʌndə'dʌn/ *adj* (尤指肉)不太熟的 bú tài shú de.

under·esti·mate /ˌʌndər'estɪmeɪt/ *vt* 低估 dīgū, 看轻〔輕〕kànqīng: ~ *the enemy's strength* 低估敌人的力量.

under·fed /ˌʌndə'fed/ *adj* 吃得太少的 chīde tài shǎo de.

under·foot /ˌʌndə'fʊt/ *adv* 在脚下 zài jiǎoxià: *The grass was wet* ~. 脚下的草地是湿的.

under·go /ˌʌndə'gəʊ/ *vt* [*pt* -went, *pp* -gone] 经〔經〕历〔歷〕jīnglì, 遭受 zāoshòu: ~ *an operation* 经受一次手术. ~ *repairs* 经过整修.

under·grad·uate /ˌʌndəˈgrædʒʊət/ *n* [C] 大学〔學〕肄业〔業〕生 dàxué yìyèshēng.

under·ground /ˌʌndəgraʊnd/ *adj, adv* **1** 地下的 dìxiàde; 在地下 zài dìxià: ~ *caves* 地窖. **2** 秘密的 mìmìde; 隐〔隱〕蔽地 yǐnbìde. □ *n* **1 the U~** (伦敦) 地下铁〔鐵〕道 dìxià tiědào. **2** 秘密政治活动〔動〕mìmì zhèngzhì huódòng.

under·growth /ˈʌndəgrəʊθ/ *n* [U] (生在大树下的)下层〔層〕林丛〔叢〕xiàcóng líncóng.

under·line /ˌʌndəˈlaɪn/ *vt* **1** 划〔劃〕线〔綫〕于〔於〕…之下 huá xiàn yú … zhī xià. **2** [喻]强调 qiángdiào, 使突出 shǐ tūchū. □ *n* /ˈʌndəlaɪn/ [C] 划在下面的线 huà zài xiàmiàn de xiàn.

under·man·ned /ˌʌndəˈmænd/ *adj* (船, 矿等)人员不足的 rényuán bùzú.

under·mine /ˌʌndəˈmaɪn/ *vt* **1** (在…下)挖坑道 wā kēngdào. **2** (暗中)破坏〔壞〕pòhuài; (逐渐)削弱 xuēruò: *His health was ~d by drink.* 他的健康被酗酒逐渐损害了.

under·neath /ˌʌndəˈni:θ/ *adv, prep* 在(…)下面 zài xiàmiàn, 在(…)底下 zài dǐxià.

under·pants /ˈʌndəpænts/ *n pl* (男用)衬裤〔褲〕chènkù.

under·pass /ˈʌndəpɑ:s/ *n* [C] 地下过〔過〕道 dìxià guòdào.

under·privi·leged /ˌʌndəˈprɪvəlɪdʒd/ *adj* (阶级, 民族等)被剥夺〔奪〕基本社会〔會〕权〔權〕利的 bèi bōduó jīběn shèhuì quánlì de.

under·rate /ˌʌndəˈreɪt/ *vt* 低估 dīgū.

under·signed /ˌʌndəˈsaɪnd/ *pp* (在文件末尾)签〔簽〕名 qiānmíng: *We, the ~* … 我们, 在下面签名的人们, ….

under·skirt /ˈʌndəskɜ:t/ *n* [C] 衬裙 chènqún.

under·stand/ˌʌndəˈstænd/ *vt/i* [*pt, pp* -stood] **1** 懂得 dǒngdé, 了解 liáojiě, 领会〔會〕lǐnghuì: ~ *him* 了解他. ~ *French* 懂得法语. **2** 获〔獲〕悉 huòxī; 听〔聽〕说 tīngshuō: *I ~ that you are married.* 我听说你结婚了. **~able** /-əbl/ *adj* 可懂的 kědǒngde, 可理解的 kě lǐjiěde. **~ing** *adj* 了解的 liǎojiěde; 有理解力的 yǒu lǐjiělì de. □ *n* **(a)** [U] 理解力 lǐjiělì; 判断〔斷〕力 pànduànlì. **(b)** [C] 谅解 liàngjiě; 协〔協〕议〔議〕xiéxì: *reach an ~ing with the manager* 和经理达成谅解.

under·state /ˌʌndəˈsteɪt/ *vt* 没有充分地陈〔陳〕述 méiyǒu chōngfèn de chénshù: *They ~d the enemy's power.* 他们没有充分报道敌人的力量. **~ment** *n* [C,U]

under·study /ˈʌndəstʌdɪ/ *n* [C] [*pl* -ies] 候补〔補〕人员 hòubǔ rényuán, (尤指)预备〔備〕演员 yùbèi yǎnyuán. □ *vt* [*pt, pp* -ied] (学习某角色以便)当〔當〕预备演员 dāng yùbèi yǎnyuán: *He is ~ing Macbeth.* 他正在研究"马克白"以便当替角.

under·take /ˌʌndəˈteɪk/ *vt* [*pt* -took, *pp* -taken] **1** 同意 tóngyì, 答应〔應〕(做某事) dāying: *He undertook to leave by Friday.* 他答应星期五以前离开. **2** 着手做 zhuóshǒu zuò. **under·tak·ing** /ˌʌndəˈteɪkɪŋ/ *n* [C] **(a)** 任务〔務〕rènwù; 事业〔業〕shìyè. **(b)** 答应 dāying, 保证 bǎozhèng.

under·taker /ˈʌndəteɪkə(r)/ *n* [C] 承办〔辦〕殡〔殯〕葬者 chéngbàn bìnzàng zhě.

under·took /ˌʌndəˈtʊk/ *pt* of undertake.

under·value /ˌʌndəˈvælju:/ *vt* 低估…的价〔價〕值 dī gū…de jiàzhí.

under·water /ˈʌndəwɔ:tə(r)/ *adj* 在水面下的 zài shuǐmiànxià de: ~ *swimming* 潜泳. ~ *film* 水下摄制的电影.

under·wear /ˈʌndəweə(r)/ *n* [U] 内衣 nèiyī.

under·went /ˌʌndəˈwent/ *pt* of undergo.

under·world /ˈʌndəwɜ:ld/ *n* [C] **1** [神话]阴〔陰〕间 yīnjiān, 地狱 dìyù. **2** 下流社会〔會〕xiàliú shèhuì, 黑社会 hēi shèhuì.

under·write /ˌʌndəˈraɪt/ *vt* [*pt* -wrote /-ˈrəʊt/; *pp* -written /-ˈrɪtn/] 给…保险〔險〕gěi…bǎoxiǎn; 同意赔款(尤指海上保险) tóngyì péikuǎn.

un·de·sir·able /ˌʌndɪˈzaɪərəbl/ *adj* 不受欢〔歡〕迎的 bú shòu huānyíng de 不合需要的 bù hé xūyào de. □ *n* [C] 不受欢迎的人 bú shòu huānyíng de rén.

un·de·vel·oped /ˌʌndɪˈveləpt/ *adj* 不发〔發〕达〔達〕的 bù fādá de, 未开〔開〕发的 wèi kāifā de.

un·did /ʌnˈdɪd/ *pt* of undo.

un·dies /ˈʌndɪz/ *n pl* [非正式用语] (女用)内衣 nèiyī.

undo /ʌnˈdu:/ *vt* [*pt* undid; *pp* undone] **1** 解开〔開〕jiěkāi, 使松〔鬆〕开 shǐ sōngkāi. **2** 败坏〔壞〕(名声, 成果等) bàihuài: *He has undone all my good work.* 他已经败坏了我所有的良好成就. **~ing** 败坏(的原因) bàihuài: *Drink was his*

~*ing*. 酗酒是他失败的原因.

un·doubted /ʌn'daʊtɪd/ *adj* 无〔無〕疑的 wúyíde, 肯定的 kěndìngde, 真正的 zhēnzhèngde. ~**ly** *adv*

un·dress /ʌn'dres/ *vt/i* **1** 脱去(…的)衣服 tuōqù yīfu: *Jane ~ed her doll.* 珍妮替她的娃娃脱去衣服. **2** 宽衣 kuān yī.

un·due /ʌn'dju:/ *adj* 过〔過〕分的 guòfènde, 过度的 guòdùde: *with ~ haste* 过分匆忙地. **un·duly** *adv*

un·dy·ing /ʌn'daɪɪŋ/ *adj* 不朽的 bùxiǔde, 永恒的 yǒnghéngde: *~ love* 永恒的爱情.

un·earth /ʌn'ɜ:θ/ *vt* 发〔發〕掘 fājué, 发现 fāxiàn.

un·earth·ly /ʌn'ɜ:θlɪ/ *adj* **1** 神秘的 shénmìde; 鬼怪的 guǐguàide: *~ screams* 怪声尖叫. **2**〔非正式用语〕不合理的 bù hélǐ de, 荒谬的 huāngmiùde: *at this ~ hour* (不早不晚)偏偏在这不合适的时刻.

un·easy /ʌn'i:zɪ/ *adj* [-ier, -iest] (身,心)不舒畅的 bù shūchàng de, 不自在的 bú zìzài de, 不安的 bù'ānde. **un·eas·ily** *adv* **un·easi·ness** *n* [U]

un·em·ployed /ˌʌnɪm'plɔɪd/ *adj* **1** 失业〔業〕的 shīyède: *~ men* 失业的人们. **2** 未用的 wèi yòng de: *~ capital* 游资. □ *n* **the ~** 失业者 shīyèzhě. **un·em·ploy·ment** *n* [U]

un·equal /ʌn'i:kwəl/ *adj* **1** 不平等的 bù píngděng de, 不相等的 bù xiāngděng de: *two ~ sides* 不相等的两边. **2** (尤指工作)不一律的 bù yīlǜ de, 不均匀的 bù jūnyún de. **3** 不胜〔勝〕任的 bú shèngrèn de; 不够坚〔堅〕强的 búgòu jiānqiáng de: *I feel ~ to the task.* 我觉得不能胜任这项工作. ~**ly** *adv*

U.N.E.S.C.O. = United Nations Educational, Scientific and Cultural Organization 联〔聯〕合国〔國〕教育科学〔學〕及文化组织〔織〕 Liánhéguó Jiàoyù Kēxué jí Wénhuà Zǔzhī.

un·even /ʌn'i:vən/ *adj* 不平坦的 bù píngtǎn de; 不均匀的 bù jūnyún de.

un·fair /ʌn'feə(r)/ *adj* 不公平的 bù gōngpíng de, 不公正的 bù gōngzhèng de: *~ remarks (competition)* 不公正的评论(比赛). ~**ly** *adv*

un·faith·ful /ʌn'feɪθfl/ *adj* 不忠实〔實〕的 bù zhōngshí de, (尤指对丈夫或妻子)不贞洁〔潔〕的bù zhēnjié de.

un·fam·il·iar /ˌʌnfə'mɪlɪə(r)/ *adj* **1** 陌生的 mòshēngde, 生疏的 shēngshūde: *That face is ~ to me.* 那张脸对我是陌生的. **2** 不熟悉的 bù shúxī de, 外行的 wàihángde: *He is ~ with this district.* 他对这个地区并不熟悉.

un·fit /ʌn'fɪt/ *adj* 不合适〔適〕的 bù héshì de, 不适当〔當〕的 bú shìdàng de: *He is ~ for the army.* 他不适宜于参军.

un·fold /ʌn'fəʊld/ *vt/i* **1** 展开〔開〕 zhǎnkāi, 打开 dǎkāi: *~ a newspaper* 打开一份报纸. **2** 显〔顯〕露 xiǎnlù, 表明 biǎomíng: *as the story ~s* 正如事件经过所表明的.

un·for·get·table /ˌʌnfə'getəbl/ *adj* 难〔難〕忘的 nánwàngde.

un·for·tu·nate /ʌn'fɔ:tʃʊnət/ *adj* **1** 不幸的 búxìngde: *an ~ expedition* 一次不走运的探险. **2** 令人遗憾的 lìngrén yíhàn de: *an ~ remark* 令人遗憾的话.

un·founded /ʌn'faʊndɪd/ *adj* 无〔無〕根据〔據〕的 wú gēnjù de: *~ rumours* 无稽的谣言.

un·friend·ly /ʌn'frendlɪ/ *adj* 不友好的 bù yǒuhǎo de.

un·furl /ʌn'fɜ:l/ *vt/i* 展开〔開〕 zhǎnkāi, 打开 dǎkāi: *~ the sails* 张开风帆.

un·fur·nished /ʌn'fɜ:nɪʃt/ *adj* 无〔無〕家具设备〔備〕的 wú jiājù shèbèi de.

un·gain·ly /ʌn'geɪnlɪ/ *adj* 笨拙的 bènzhuōde; 难〔難〕看的 nánkànde.

un·god·ly /ʌn'gɒdlɪ/ *adj* **1** 不敬神的 bú jìng shén de. **2**〔非正式用语〕不合理的 bù hélǐ de; 不讲〔講〕道理的 bù jiǎng dàolǐ de: *at this ~ hour* 在这不合适的时刻.

un·grate·ful /ʌn'greɪtfl/ *adj* 不领情的 bù lǐngqíng de.

un·happy /ʌn'hæpɪ/ *adj* [-ier, -iest] 不快乐〔樂〕的 bú kuàilè de.

un·healthy /ʌn'helθɪ/ *adj* **1** 有损健康的 yǒu sǔn jiànkāng de. **2** 不健康的 bú jiànkāng de.

un·heard /ʌn'hɜ:d/ *adj* 未听〔聽〕到的 wèi tīngdào de. **~-of** /ʌn'hɜ:d əv/ *adj* 没有前例的 méiyǒu qiánlì de, 空前的 kōngqiánde: *~-of wealth* 空前未有的财富.

U.N.I.C.E.F. = United Nations International Children's Emergency Fund 联〔聯〕合国〔國〕儿〔兒〕童基金会〔會〕Liánhéguó Értóng Jījīnhuì.

uni·corn /'ju:nɪkɔ:n/ *n* [C]〔神话〕似马〔馬〕的独〔獨〕角兽〔獸〕 shì mǎ de dújiǎoshòu.

un·iden·ti·fied /ˌʌnaɪ'dentɪfaɪd/ *adj* 不能识〔識〕别的 bùnéng shíbié de, 未查明的 wèi chámíng de.

uni·form /'ju:nɪfɔ:m/ *adj* 不变〔變〕

的 búbiànde, 一贯的 yīguànde: ~ *temperature* 恒温. □ *n* [C, U] 制服 zhìfú.

uni·form·ity /ˌjuːnɪ'fɔːmətɪ/ *n* [U] 一样〔樣〕 yīyàng, 一律 yīlǜ, 一致 yízhì.

unify /'juːnɪfaɪ/ *vt* [*pt*, *pp* -ied] 统一 tǒngyī, 使一致 shǐ yīzhì. **uni·fi·ca·tion** /-fɪ'keɪʃn/ *n* [U]

uni·lat·eral /ˌjuːnɪ'lætrəl/ *adj* 单〔單〕方面的 dānfāngmiàn de, 片面的 piànmiànde: *a* ~ *declaration of independence* 单方面的宣佈独立.

un·in·hib·ited /ˌʌnɪn'hɪbɪtɪd/ *adj* 无〔無〕人居住的 wúrén jūzhù de.

union /'juːnɪən/ *n* **1** [C,U] 联〔聯〕合 liánhé, 合并〔併〕 hébìng: *the* ~ *of the three towns* 三个市镇的合并. **2** [C,U] 一致 yīzhì, 融洽 róngqià: *a happy* ~ 美满的婚姻. **3** [C] 协〔協〕会〔會〕 xiéhuì, 联合会 liánhéhuì. ⇨ trade-union. **the U~ 'Jack** 英国〔國〕国旗 Yīngguó guóqí.

unique /juː'niːk/ *adj* 唯一的 wéiyīde, 独〔獨〕一无〔無〕二的 dúyī-wú-èr de. **~ly** *adv*

uni·son /'juːnɪsn/ *n* [U] *in* ~ 一致 yīzhì, 调和 tiáohé: *sing in* ~ 齐声歌唱.

unit /'juːnɪt/ *n* [C] **1** 单〔單〕位(指构成整体的人,物,团体等) dānwèi. **2** (计量)单位 dānwèi: *The metre is a* ~ *of length.* 米是长度单位. **3** (最小的整数)一 yī.

unite /juː'naɪt/ *vt*/*i* **1** (使)联〔聯〕合 liánhé, (使)合并〔併〕 hébìng; (使)团〔團〕结 tuánjié. **2** 联合行动〔動〕 liánhé xíngdòng, 协〔協〕力 xiélì.

unity /'juːnətɪ/ *n* [*pl* -ies] **1** [C, U] 联〔聯〕合 liánhé; 统一 tǒngyī; 协〔協〕调 xiétiáo: *the* ~ *of the painting* 画面的协调. **2** [U] 一致 yīzhì: *political* ~ 政治上的团结一致.

Univ. = University.

uni·ver·sal /ˌjuːnɪ'vɜːsl/ *adj* 普遍的 pǔbiànde; 全体〔體〕的 quántǐde: *War causes* ~ *misery.* 战争引起普遍的苦难. **~ly** *adv*

uni·verse /'juːnɪvɜːs/ *n* **the U~** 宇宙 yǔzhòu.

uni·ver·sity /ˌjuːnɪ'vɜːsətɪ/ *n* [C] [*pl* -ies] **1** 大学〔學〕 dàxue. **2** 大学人员 dàxué rényuán.

un·kind /ʌn'kaɪnd/ *adj* 不和善的 bù héshàn de, 不客气〔氣〕的 bú kèqì de; 刻薄的 kèbóde.

un·known /ʌn'nəʊn/ *adj* 不知道的 bù zhīdào de, 未知的 wèizhīde.

un·leash /ʌn'liːʃ/ *vt* 〔喻〕解开〔開〕…的束缚 jiěkāi…de shùfú, 释〔釋〕放 shìfàng: ~ *a dog* 放开一条狗.

un·less /ən'les/ *conj* 除非 chúfēi, 如果不 rúguǒ bù: *You will fail* ~ *you work harder.* 你如果不更加努力工作,你将失败.

un·like /ʌn'laɪk/ *adj*, *prep* 不相同的 bù xiāngtóng de; 和…不同 hé…bùtóng.

un·like·ly /ʌn'laɪklɪ/ *adj* 未必的 wèibìde, 靠不住的 kàobúzhùde.

un·load /ʌn'ləʊd/ *vt*/*i* **1** (从…)卸下货物 xièxià huòwù: ~ *a ship* 从船上卸货. **2** 解除 jiěchú, 摆〔擺〕脱 bǎituō.

un·lock /ʌn'lɒk/ *vt* 开〔開〕锁〔鎖〕 kāi suǒ.

un·lucky /ʌn'lʌkɪ/ *adj* [-ier, iest] 不幸的 búxìngde, 倒霉的 dǎoméide.

un·man·ned /ʌn'mænd/ *adj* 无〔無〕人员的 wú rényuán de: *an* ~ *spacecraft* 无人驾驶宇宙飞船.

un·mask /ʌn'mɑːsk/ *vt*/*i* **1** 撕下假面具 sīxià jiǎmiànjù. **2** 〔喻〕揭露 jiēlù: ~ *a traitor.* 揭露叛徒的伪装.

un·men·tion·able /ʌn'menʃənəbl/ *adj* 说不出口的 shuō bù chū kǒu de: ~ *crimes* 说不出口的罪行.

un·mis·tak·able /ˌʌnmɪ'steɪkəbl/ *adj* 不会〔會〕错的 búhuì cuò de, 不会被怀〔懷〕疑的 bùhuì bèi huáiyí de. **un·mis·tak·ably** /-əblɪ/ *adv*

un·moved /ʌn'muːvd/ *adj* (尤指)无〔無〕动〔動〕于〔於〕衷的 wú dòng yú zhōng de, 冷淡的 lěngdànde: ~ *by her tears* 没有被她的眼泪打动.

un·natu·ral /ʌn'nætʃrəl/ *adj* 不自然的 bú zìrán de, 反常的 fǎnchángde.

un·nec·ess·ary /ʌn'nesəsrɪ/ *adj* 不必要的 bú bìyào de, 不需要的 bù xūyào de.

un·nerve /ʌn'nɜːv/ *vt* 使丧〔喪〕失勇气〔氣〕 shǐ sàngshī yǒngqì.

un·not·iced /ʌn'nəʊtɪst/ *adj* 未被注意的 wèi bèi zhùyì de, 被忽视的 bèi hūshì de.

U.N.O. = United Nations Organization 联〔聯〕合国〔國〕组织〔織〕 Liánhéguó Zǔzhī.

un·ob·trus·ive /ˌʌnəb'truːsɪv/ *adj* 不引人注意的 bù yǐn rén zhùyì de.

un·of·fi·cial /ˌʌnə'fɪʃl/ *adj* 非官方的 fēi guānfāng de.

un·pack /ʌn'pæk/ *vt*/*i* 打开〔開〕(包裹等) dǎkāi: ~ *a suitcase* 打开衣箱.

un·pleas·ant /ʌn'pleznt/ *adj* 使人不愉快的 shǐ rén bù yúkuài de. ~ness *n* [C,U]

un·prece·dented /ʌn'presɪdentɪd/ *adj* 前所未有的 qián suǒ wèi yǒu de, 空前的 kōngqiánde: ~ *wealth* 前所未有的财富.

un·quali·fied /ʌn'kwɒlɪfaɪd/ *adj* **1** 无〔無〕限制的 wú xiànzhì de, 无条〔條〕件的 wú tiáojiàn de: ~ *praise* 绝口称赞. **2** 不合格的 bù hégé de, 无资格的 wú zīgé de: ~ *to teach* 不能胜任教学工作.

un·ques·tion·able /ʌn'kwestʃənəbl/ *adj* 毫无〔無〕疑问〔問〕的 háowú yíwèn de, 确〔確〕实〔實〕的 quèshíde.

un·ravel /ʌn'rævl/ *vt/i* [-ll-, 美语 -l-] **1** 拆散(线团等) chāisǎn: *The cat has ~led the knitting.* 那猫弄散了编织物. **2** 解决 jiějué; 阐〔闡〕明 chǎnmíng: ~ *a mystery* 阐明一件神秘的事.

un·real /ʌn'rɪəl/ *adj* 虚构〔構〕的 xūgòude, 不真实〔實〕的 bù zhēnshí de.

un·reas·on·able /ʌn'ri:zənəbl/ *adj* 不合理的 bù hélǐ de; 不讲〔講〕道理的 bù jiǎng dàolǐ de.

un·re·li·able /ˌʌnrɪ'laɪəbl/ *adj* 靠不住的 kàobúzhùde.

un·rest /ʌn'rest/ *n* [U] 不安 bù'ān, 动〔動〕乱〔亂〕dòngluàn: *political* ~ 政治动乱.

un·re·stricted /ˌʌnrɪ'strɪktɪd/ *adj* 无〔無〕限制的 wú xiànzhì de, 不受约束的 bú shòu yuēshù de.

un·ruffled /ʌn'rʌfld/ *adj* 平静的 píngjìngde, 不混乱〔亂〕的 bù hùnluàn de.

un·ruly /ʌn'ru:lɪ/ *adj* [-ier, -iest] 难〔難〕控制的 nán kòngzhì de; 不守规矩的 bù shǒu guīju de.

un·sa·voury [美语 = **-sa·vory**] /ʌn'seɪvərɪ/ *adj* (尤指)不好的 bùhǎode; 令人厌〔厭〕恶〔惡〕的 lìng rén yànwù de.

un·scathed /ʌn'skeɪðd/ *adj* 未受伤〔傷〕害的 wèi shòu shānghài de.

un·scru·pu·lous /ʌn'skru:pjʊləs/ *adj* 无〔無〕耻的 wúchǐde, 不讲〔講〕道德的 bù jiǎng dàodé de.

un·seat /ʌn'si:t/ *vt* **1** 使去职〔職〕shǐ qùzhí, 使退位 shǐ tuìwèi: ~ *the President* 罢免总统. **2** 使落马〔馬〕shǐ luòmǎ.

un·settle /ʌn'setl/ *vt* 使不安定 shǐ bù āndìng, 扰〔擾〕乱〔亂〕rǎoluàn: *~d weather* 不稳定的天气.

un·sight·ly /ʌn'saɪtlɪ/ *adj* 难〔難〕看的 nánkànde.

un·sound /ʌn'saʊnd/ *adj* **1** 不健全的 bú jiànquán de, 不健康的 bú jiànkāng de; 不稳〔穩〕固的 bù wěngù de: *an ~ building* 不坚固的建筑物. **2** *of ~ mind* 精神错乱〔亂〕的 jīngshén cuòluàn de.

un·speak·able /ʌn'spi:kəbl/ *adj* 说不出的 shuō bùchū de, 无〔無〕法形容的 wúfǎ xíngróng de: ~ *joy* (*sadness*) 无法形容的快乐(悲哀).

un·stuck /ʌn'stʌk/ *adj* **1** 未粘住的 wèi zhānzhù de, 松〔鬆〕开〔開〕的 sōngkāide. **2** *come* ~ 失败 shībài.

un·suit·able /ʌn'su:təbl/ *adj* 不合适〔適〕的 bù héshì de, 不适当〔當〕的 bú shìdàng de.

un·swerv·ing /ʌn'swɜ:vɪŋ/ *adj* 不改变〔變〕的 bù gǎibiàn de, 坚〔堅〕定的 jiāndìngde: ~ *loyalty* 始终不渝的忠诚.

un·tidy /ʌn'taɪdɪ/ *adj* [-ier, -iest] 不整洁〔潔〕的 bù zhěngjié de.

un·tie /ʌn'taɪ/ *vt* [*pres part* untying; *pt, pp* untied] 解开〔開〕(绳结等) jiěkāi.

un·til /ən'tɪl/ *prep, conj* ⇨ till[1].

un·told /ʌn'təʊld/ *adj* (尤指)无〔無〕数〔數〕的 wúshùde, 数不清的 shǔ bù qīng de: ~ *wealth* 数不清的财富.

un·used[1] /ʌn'ju:zd/ *adj* 未用过〔過〕的 wèi yòngguò de, 新的 xīnde.

un·used[2] /ʌn'ju:st/ *adj* ~ *to* 不习〔習〕惯于〔於〕bù xíguàn yú: ~ *to city life* 不习惯于城市生活.

un·usual /ʌn'ju:ʒl/ *adj* 不平常的 bù píngcháng de; 奇怪的 qíguàide. ~**ly** *adv*

un·veil /ʌn'veɪl/ *vt/i* **1** 除去(…的)面纱或幕布等 chúqù miànshā huò mùbù děng. **2** 揭露 jiēlù.

un·wieldy /ʌn'wi:ldɪ/ *adj* 难〔難〕操纵〔縱〕的 nán cāozòng de; 笨重的 bènzhòngde.

un·wind /ʌn'waɪnd/ *vt/i* [*pt, pp* -wound] **1** 解开〔開〕(毛线团等) jiěkāi. **2** [非正式用语](使)放松〔鬆〕fàngsōng.

un·wrap /ʌn'ræp/ *vt/i* [-pp-] 打开〔開〕dǎkāi, 解开 jiěkāi.

up /ʌp/ *adv* (与 *down* 相对) **1** 趋〔趨〕向或处〔處〕于〔於〕直立姿势〔勢〕qūxiàng huò chùyú zhílì zīshì, 起来〔來〕qǐlái: *He's already* ~. 他已起床. *Stand* ~! 站起来! **2** 向上 xiàngshàng, 在上面 zài shàngmiàn, 在较〔較〕高处 zài jiào gāochù: *Lift your head* ~. 抬起头来. *Prices are going* ~. 物价在上涨. ***pull one's socks up*** ⇨ sock[1] **3** 往较重要的地方 wàng jiào zhòng yào de dìfāng; 向北 xiàngběi: *go ~ to London* 去伦敦. **4** 向目的地 xiàng mùdìdì; 向说话者所在处 xiàng shuōhuàzhě suǒzàichù: *He came ~ (to me) and asked the time.* 他走过来询问时间. **5** 完全地 wánquánde, 彻〔徹〕底地 chèdǐde: *The stream has dried ~.* 溪水全干涸了. **6** (表示强度等的增加): *Speak (Sing) ~!* 说(唱)大声些! **7** *~ against (it)* 面临〔臨〕或对〔對〕付(困难,阻碍等) miànlín huò duìfu. ,*~ and 'down* (a) 来来往往 láiláiwǎngwǎng, 往返地 wǎngfǎnde: *walking ~ and down the station platform.* 在月台上来回走动. (b) 上上下下 shàngshàng xiàxià, 起伏地 qǐfúde: *The boat bobbed ~ and down on the water.* 那船在水面上上下浮动. *~ for* (a) 接受(审判) jiēshòu. (b) 提供 tígòng; 提名 tímíng. *The house is ~ for sale.* 房屋待售. *~ to* (a) 忙于〔於〕 mángyú, 从〔從〕事于 cóngshì yú: *What's he ~ to?* 他在干什么? (b) 适〔適〕于 shìyú, 胜〔勝〕任 shèngrèn: *I don't feel ~ to going to work.* 我不适于去工作. (c) 直到 zhídào: *~ to now* 直到现在. (d) 该由… gāiyóu…, 轮〔輪〕到… lúndào…: *It's ~ to us to help.* 该由我们去帮助. □ *prep*: *climb ~ a mountain* 爬山. *walk ~ the stairs* 上楼梯. **,~-and-'coming** *adj* (指人在事业上)可能成功的 kěnéng chénggōng de. **,~s and 'downs** 〔喻〕多变〔變〕的命运〔運〕 duō biàn de mìngyùn.

up·bring·ing /'ʌpbrɪŋɪŋ/ *n* [U] 抚〔撫〕育 fǔyù, 教养〔養〕 jiàoyǎng.

up·date /ʌp'deɪt/ *vt* 使现代化 shǐ xiàndàihuà: *~ sales figures* 把销售数字结算到最近.

up·heaval /ʌp'hi:vl/ *n* [C] 激剧〔劇〕变〔變〕动〔動〕 jījù biàndòng: *political ~s* 政治大动荡.

up·held /ʌp'held/ *pt, pp* of uphold.

up·hill /'ʌphɪl/ *adj* **1** 上坡的 shàngpōde: *an ~ road* 上坡路. **2** 〔喻〕艰〔艱〕难〔難〕的 jiānnánde: *an ~ task* 艰难的任务. □ *adv* 往上坡 wǎng shàngpō: *walk ~* 往上坡走.

up·hold /ʌp'həʊld/ *vt* [*pt, pp* upheld] **1** 支持 zhīchí, 赞成 zànchéng. **2** 确〔確〕认〔認〕(决议等) quèrèn.

up·hol·ster /ʌp'həʊlstə(r)/ *vt* (为沙发,椅子等)装〔裝〕上垫〔墊〕子,弹〔彈〕簧,套子等 zhuāngshàng diànzi, tánhuáng, tàozi děng. **~er** *n* [C]. **up·hol·stery** /-strɪ/ *n* [U] 室内装璜 shìnèi zhuānghuáng, 室内装璜业〔業〕 shìnèi zhuānghuáng yè.

up·keep /'ʌpki:p/ *n* [U] 保养〔養〕(费) bǎoyǎng, 维修(费) wéixiū: *the ~ of a house* 房屋的维修费.

up·land /'ʌplənd/ *n* [C] 高地 gāodì.

up·most /'ʌpməʊst/ *adj* = uppermost.

upon /ə'pɒn/ *prep* = on.

up·per /'ʌpə(r)/ *adj* 在上面的 zài shàngmiàn de: *the ~ lip* 上唇. *the ~ arm* 上臂. □ *n* [C] 鞋帮 xiébāng. **the '~ class** 上流社会〔會〕 shàngliú shèhuì. **'~most** /-məʊst/ *adj* 最高的 zuìgāode; 最主要的 zuì zhǔyào de: *thoughts ~most in their minds* 他们心中主要的想法. □ *adv* 最高 zuìgāo, 最上 zuìshàng.

up·right /'ʌpraɪt/ *adj* **1** 垂直的 chuízhíde, 直立的 zhílìde: *an ~ post* 立柱. **2** 正直的 zhèngzhíde: *an ~ judge* 正直的法官. □ *n* [C] 立柱. lìzhù.

up·ris·ing /ʌp'raɪzɪŋ/ *n* [C] 叛乱〔亂〕 pànluàn.

up·roar /'ʌprɔ:(r)/ *n* [U] 吵闹〔鬧〕 chǎonào, 骚〔騷〕动〔動〕 sāodòng: *The meeting ended in (an) ~.* 会议在一片吵闹声中结束. **~i·ous** /ʌp'rɔ:rɪəs/ *adj*

up·root /ʌp'ru:t/ *vt* 连〔連〕根拔 lián gēn bá.

up·set /ʌp'set/ *vt/i* [*pt, pp* ~] [-tt-] **1** 倾覆 qīngfù, 打翻 dǎfān: *Don't ~ the boat.* 不要把船弄翻了. **2** 打乱〔亂〕 dǎluàn; 使不安 shǐ bù'ān: *~ the enemy's plan* 打乱敌人的计划. *~ one's stomach* 使胃不舒服. □ *n* /'ʌpset/ [C] **1** 倾覆 qīngfù, 翻倒 fāndǎo; 混乱 hùnluàn: *have a 'stomach ~* 胃不舒服. **2** [运动]意外的结果 yìwàide jiéguǒ.

up·shot /'ʌpʃɒt/ *n* **the ~** 结果 jiéguǒ, 结局 jiéjú.

up·side-down /,ʌpsaɪd 'daʊn/ *adv* **1** 颠倒的 diāndǎode. **2** [喻]混乱〔亂〕的 hùnluànde: *The house was turned ~ by the burglars.* 那屋子被窃贼翻得乱七八糟.

up·stairs /ʌp'steəz/ *adv, adj* 往楼〔樓〕上 wǎng lóushàng; 在楼上 zài lóushàng: *go (walk) ~* 上楼. *an ~ room* 楼上的房间.

up·stand·ing /ʌp'stændɪŋ/ *adj* **1** 直立的 zhílìde; 强健的 qiángjiànde. **2** 诚实〔實〕的 chéngshíde.

up·stream /ʌp'stri:m/ *adv* 在上游 zài shàngyóu; 向上游 xiàng shàngyóu.

up-to-date /,ʌp tə 'deɪt/ *adj* 现代的

xiàndàide, 时〔時〕新的 shíxīnde: ~ *methods* 最新的方法.

up·ward /'ʌpwəd/ *adj* 向上的 xiàngshàngde, 上升的 shàngshēngde: *an ~ glance* 向上的一瞥. □ *adv* (常作 **up·wards**) 向上地 xiàngshàngde, 上升地 shàngshēngde.

ura·nium /jʊ'reɪnɪəm/ *n* [U] 〔化学〕铀 **(U)** yóu.

ur·ban /'ɜ:bən/ *adj* 城市的 chéngshìde, 都市的 dūshìde.

ur·chin /'ɜ:tʃɪn/ *n* [C] **1** 顽童 wántóng. **2** (无家可归的)穷〔窮〕孩子 qióng háizi.

urge /ɜ:dʒ/ *vt* **1** 推进〔進〕tuījìn, 驱〔驅〕策 qūcè: *The crowd ~d him on to win.* 群众激励他去争取胜利. **2** 催促 cuīcù, 力劝〔勸〕lìquàn: *I ~ you to go.* 我劝你走. □ *n* [C] 强烈的欲望 qiángliède yùwàng.

ur·gent /'ɜ:dʒənt/ *adj* 紧〔緊〕急的 jǐnjíde, 急迫的 jípòde. **~ly** *adv*

uri·nate /'jʊərɪneɪt/ *vi* 排尿 pái niào, 小便 xiǎobiàn.

urine /'jʊərɪn/ *n* [U] 尿 niào.

urn /ɜ:n/ *n* [C] **1** 骨灰瓮 gǔhuīwèng. **2** (金属)大茶壶 dà cháhú.

us /əs, 强式: ʌs/ *pron* 〔*we* 的宾格〕我们〔們〕wǒmen: *We hope you will visit ~ soon.* (我们)希望你很快来看望我们.

U.S., U.S.A. = United States (of America) 美国〔國〕Měiguó.

usage /'ju:zɪdʒ/ *n* **1** [U] 用法 yòngfǎ: *rough ~* 用得不小心. **2** [C,U] 习〔習〕惯 xíguàn; 〔语言〕惯用法 guànyòngfǎ: *Such ~s are not acceptable.* 这种(惯)用法是不能接受的.

use[1] /ju:s/ *n* **1** [U] 用 yòng, 使用 shǐyòng, 运〔運〕用 yùnyòng: *the ~ of gas for cooking* 煤气用来做饭. ***in*** ~在使用着 zài shǐyòngzhe. ***come into*** ~开〔開〕始被使用 kāishǐ bèi shǐyòng. ***out of*** ~ (目前)不使用 bù shǐyòng. **2** [C,U] 用途 yòngtú, 用处〔處〕yòngchù: *a tool with many ~s* 有多种用途的工具. **3** [U] 价〔價〕值 jiàzhí; 效用 xiàoyòng: *Is this paper of any ~?* 这张纸有用吗? **4** [U] 使用的能力 shǐyòngde nénglì: *lose the ~ of one's legs* 失去双腿的功能. **5** [U] 使用权〔權〕shǐyòngquán: *You can have the ~ of my car.* 你可以使用我的汽车. **~ful** /'ju:sfl/ *adj* 有帮助的 yǒu bāngzhù de, 有用的 yǒuyòngde: *a ~ful tool* 实用的工具. **~fully** *adv* **~less** *adj* **(a)** 无〔無〕用的 wúyòngde, 无价〔價〕值的 wú jiàzhí de. **(b)** 无效的 wúxiàode; 无结果的 wú jiéguǒde: *It's ~less to argue with them.* 和他们辩论是不会有结果的. **~less·ly** *adv*

use[2] /ju:z/ *vt* [*pt*, *pp* ~d /ju:zd/] **1** 用 yòng, 使用 shǐyòng, 应〔應〕用 yīngyòng: ~ *a pen to write* 用钢笔写字. **2** 消耗 xiāohào, 用尽〔盡〕yòngjìn: *He has ~d up all his strength.* 他已经筋疲力尽. **3** 对〔對〕待 duìdài: *U~ others badly.* 待别人不好. **used** *adj* 旧〔舊〕的 jiùde: *~d cars* 旧汽车. **user** 使用者 shǐyòngzhě; 使用物 shǐyòngwù.

used /ju:st/ *v* 过〔過〕去常常 guòqù chángcháng: *That's where I ~ to live when I was a child.* 那就是我小时候常住的地方.

used to /'ju:st tə, 元音前: tu:/ *adj* 习〔習〕惯于 xíguàn yú: *You will soon be (get) ~ the weather.* 你不久将会习惯于这种天气的.

usher /'ʌʃə(r)/ *n* [C] (戏院, 公共场所等的)引座员 yǐnzuòyuán. □ *vt* **1** 引导〔導〕yǐndǎo: *The girl ~ed me to my seat.* 女郎引导我入座. **2** 展示 zhǎnshì; 预报〔報〕yùbào; 引进〔進〕yǐnjìn: *Oil ~ed in a period of prosperity.* 石油引来了一个繁荣的时期. **~ette** /ˌʌʃə'ret/ 女引座员 nǚ yǐnzuòyuán.

U.S.S.R. = Union of Soviet Socialist Republics 苏〔蘇〕维埃社会〔會〕主义〔義〕共和国〔國〕联〔聯〕盟 Sūwéi'āi Shèhuìzhǔyì Gònghéguó Liánméng.

usual /'ju:ʒl/ *adj* 通常的 tōngchángde, 平常的 píngchángde, 惯常的 guànchángde: *He arrived later than ~.* 他到得比平常晚些. **~ly** /'ju:ʒəlɪ/ *adv*

usurp /ju:'zɜ:p/ *vt* 篡夺〔奪〕cuànduó, 侵占〔佔〕qīnzhàn. **~er** *n* [C]

uten·sil /ju:'tensl/ *n* [C] 器皿(尤指家庭用具) qìmǐn.

uterus /'ju:tərəs/ *n* [C] [*pl* ~es] 〔解剖〕子宫 zǐgōng.

util·ity /ju:'tɪlətɪ/ *n* [*pl* -ies] **1** [U] 有用 yǒuyòng, 实〔實〕用 shíyòng: '*~ van* 多种用途(通用)搬运车. **2** [C] 公用事业〔業〕gōngyòng shìyè.

util·ize /'ju:tɪlaɪz/ *vt* 利用 lìyòng. **util·iz·ation** /-'zeɪʃn/ *n* [U]

ut·most /'ʌtməʊst/ *adj* 最远〔遠〕的 zuìyuǎnde; 最大的 zuìdàde; 极〔極〕度的 jídùde: *with the ~ care* 极其小心地. □ *n* [仅用 *sing*] 极端 jíduān; 最大限度 zuìdà xiàndù: *I shall do my ~.* 我将尽最大努力.

ut·ter[1] /'ʌtə(r)/ *adj* 完全的 wánquánde, 十足的 shízúde: ~ *darkness*

漆黑. ~**ly** *adv* 完全地 wánquánde.

ut·ter²/'ʌtə(r)/ *vt* 用口发出(声音) yòng kǒu fāchū; 说(话) shuō: *the last words he ~ed* 他的临终遗言. ~**ance** [C,U] 话 huà, 言词 yáncí.

V v

V,v /vi:/ [*pl* V's, v's] **1** 英语的第二十二个[個]字母 Yīngyǔde dì-èrshí'èrgè zìmǔ. **2** 罗[羅]马[馬]数[數]字五 (V) Luómǎ shùzì wǔ.

V. = volt(s).

v. = **1** see. **2** verse. **3** versus.

va·cancy /'veɪkənsɪ/ *n* [*pl* -ies] **1** [U] 空 kōng, 空白 kòngbái; 空虚 kōngxū. **2** [C] 空地 kòngdì; 空间[間] kōngjiān; 空缺 kòngquē.

va·cant /'veɪkənt/ *adj* **1** 空的 kōngde, 未被占[佔]用的 wèi bèi zhànyòng de: *a ~ room* 空房间. *a ~ position* 空缺. **2** (头脑)空虚的 kōngxūde; 无[無]表情的 wú biǎoqíng de: *a ~ expression* 茫然的表情. ~**ly** *adv*

va·cate /veɪ'keɪt/ *vt* 使空出 shǐ kòngchū, 搬出 bānchū: *~ a house* 腾出屋子. *~ one's seat* 让出座位.

va·ca·tion /və'keɪʃn/ *n* [C] 假期 jiàqī, 休假 xiūjià.

vac·ci·nate /'væksɪneɪt/ *vt* 给(某人)种[種]牛痘 gěi zhòng niúdòu. **vac·ci'na·tion** /-ʃn/ *n* [C, U]

vac·cine /'væksi:n/ *n* [C,U] 牛痘苗 niúdòumiáo.

vac·uum /'vækjʊəm/ *n* [C] [*pl* ~s 或 vacuua /-jʊə/] 真空 zhēnkōng. '~ **cleaner** 真空吸尘[塵]器 zhēnkōng xīchénqì. '~ **flask** 保温瓶 bǎowēnpíng. '~-**packed** 真空包装[裝]的 zhēnkōng bāozhuāng de.

vaga·bond /'vægəbɒnd/ *adj*, *n* [C] 流浪的 liúlàngde; 流浪者 liúlàngzhě.

va·gina /və'dʒaɪnə/ *n* [C] [*pl* ~s] [解剖]阴[陰]道 yīndào.

va·grant /'veɪgrənt/ *adj*, *n* [C] 流浪的 liúlàngde; 流浪者 liúlàngzhě: *~ tribes* 生活无定居的部落. **va·grancy** *n* [C,U]

vague /veɪg/ *adj* [-r, -st] **1** 模糊的 móhude, 不清楚的 bù qīngchu de: *a ~ outline (idea)* 模糊的轮廓(思想). **2** (指人)暧[曖]昧的 àimèide, 不明的 bùmíngde. ~**ly** *adv* ~**ness** *n* [U]

vain /veɪn/ *adj* [-er, -est] **1** 徒劳[勞]的 túláode, 无[無]效果的 wú xiàoguǒ de: *a ~ attempt* 徒劳的尝试. **2** *in* ~ (a) 徒劳 túláo, 徒然 túrán. (b) 不尊敬地 bù zūnjìng de, 轻[輕]慢地 qīngmànde: *take a person's name in ~* 不尊敬地用一个人的名字. **3** 自负的 zìfùde, 自视过[過]高的 zì shì guògāo de. ~**ly** *adv*

vale /veɪl/ *n* [C] [书面语] = valley.

val·en·tine /'væləntaɪn/ *n* [C] (在二月十四日圣瓦伦丁节所祝贺的)情人 qíngrén.

valet /'vælɪt/ *n* [C] (被雇来)洗烫[燙]衣服的人 xǐtàng yīfu de rén. □ *vt* 为[為]...洗烫衣服 wèi...xǐtàng yīfu.

valid /'vælɪd/ *adj* **1** [法律]有效的 yǒuxiàode. **2** 有根据[據]的 yǒu gēnjù de; 正当[當]的 zhèngdāngde; 有力的 yǒulìde: *raise ~ objections* 提出有力的反驳. ~**ity** /və'lɪdətɪ/ *n* [U] 有效 yǒuxiào; 正当 zhèngdāng. ~**ate** /'vælɪdeɪt/ *vt* 使有效 shǐ yǒuxiào; 证[證]实[實] zhèngshí: *~ a claim* 使某一要求有效.

val·ley /'vælɪ/ *n* [C] [*pl* ~s] 溪谷 xīgǔ, 山谷 shāngǔ.

valu·able /'væljʊəbl/ *adj*, *n* [C] 贵重的 guìzhòngde, 值钱[錢]的 zhíqiánde; 有用的 yǒuyòngde: *a ~ discovery* 有价值的发现.

valu·ation /ˌvæljʊ'eɪʃn/ *n* **1** [U] 定价[價] dìngjià, 估价 gūjià. **2** [C] 评定的价值 píngdìngde jiàzhí: *put a high ~ on the house* 对那所房屋开高价.

value /'vælju:/ *n* **1** [U] 价[價]值 jiàzhí; 实[實]用性 shíyòngxìng: *the ~ of walking as an exercise* 散步运动的益处. **2** [C,U] 价格 jiàgé: *the ~ of my house is £10000* 我的房屋的价格是一万镑. **3** [U] 价值(与价格相比较而言) jiàzhí: *I offered £350 for the car but its ~ is higher.* 这辆汽车我出价三百五十镑, 但它的实际价值更高些. **4** [音乐]音的长[長]短 yīnde cháng duǎn. **5** [*pl*] 标[標]准[準] biāozhǔn: *moral ~s* 道德价值. □ *vt* **1** 估价 gūjià, 评价 píngjià. **2** 重视 zhòngshì, 尊重 zūnzhòng: *I ~ my secretary.* 我尊重我的秘书. ~**less** *adj* 无[無]价值的 wú jiàzhí de, 无用的 wúyòngde. **valuer** 估价者 gūjiàzhě.

valve /vælv/ *n* [C] **1** 阀[閥] fá, 活门[門] huómén. **2** (心,血管)瓣

膜 bànmó. 3 电〔電〕子管 diànzǐguǎn.

vam·pire /'væmpaɪə(r)/ *n* [C] 吸血鬼 xīxiěguǐ. '~ **bat** 吸血蝙蝠 xīxuě biānfú.

van /væn/ *n* [C] 大篷货车〔車〕 dàpéng huòchē.

van·dal /'vændl/ *n* [C] 故意破坏〔壞〕(他人)财物者 gùyì pòhuài cáiwù zhě. ~**ism** /-ɪzəm/ *n* [U] 故意破坏财物的行为〔爲〕 gùyì pòhuài cáiwù de xíngwéi.

vane /veɪn/ *n* [C] 1 风〔風〕向标〔標〕 fēngxiàngbiāo. 2 (风车,螺旋桨等的)叶〔葉〕片 yèpiàn.

va·nilla /və'nɪlə/ *n* 1 [C] [植物]香草 xiāngcǎo. 2 [U] 香草香精 xiāngcǎo xiāngjīng.

van·ish /'vænɪʃ/ *vi* 突然不见 tūrán bújiàn; 逐渐〔漸〕消失 zhújiàn xiāoshī.

van·ity /'vænətɪ/ *n* [*pl* -ies] 1 [U] 自大 zìdà, 虚荣〔榮〕心 xūróngxīn. 2 [U] 无〔無〕价〔價〕值 wú jiàzhí; 空虚 kōngxū: *the* ~ *of pleasure* 寻欢作乐的空虚性.

van·quish /'væŋkwɪʃ/ *vt* 征服 zhēngfú, 击〔擊〕败 jībài.

va·por·ize /'veɪpəraɪz/ *vt/i* (使)汽化 qìhuà.

va·pour /'veɪpə(r)/ *n* [U] 蒸气 zhēngqì: '*water* ~ 水蒸气.

vari·able /'veərɪəbl/ *adj* 变〔變〕化的 biànhuàde, 可变的 kěbiànde: ~ *winds* 变化不定的风. □ *n* [C] 可变物 kěbiànwù; 变量 biànliàng. **vari·ably** *adv*

vari·ant /'veərɪənt/ *adj* 不同的 bùtóngde, 变〔變〕异〔異〕的 biànyìde: ~ *spellings of a word* 词的不同拼法. □ *n* [C] 变体〔體〕 biàntǐ, 异体 yìtǐ.

vari·ation /ˌveərɪ'eɪʃn/ *n* 1 [C,U] 变〔變〕化 biànhuà, 改变 gǎibiàn: ~(*s*) *of temperature* 温度的变化. 2 [C,U] 变异〔異〕 biànyì, 变量 biànliàng.

vari·cose vein /ˌværɪkəʊs 'veɪn/ *adj* 静脉〔脈〕曲张〔張〕 jìngmài qūzhāng.

var·ied /'veərɪd/ *adj* 1 各种〔種〕各样〔樣〕的 gèzhǒng gèyàng de: ~ *scenes* 各式各样的情景. 2 多变〔變〕化的 duō biànhuà de: *a* ~ *career* 多变化的生涯.

var·iety /və'raɪətɪ/ *n* [*pl* -ies] 1 [U] 多样〔樣〕化 duōyànghuà: *a life full of* ~ 多样化的生活. 2 [仅用 *sing*] 种〔種〕种 zhǒngzhǒng: *for a* ~ *of reasons* 由于种种原因. 3 [C] 变〔變〕种 biànzhǒng, 变体〔體〕 biàntǐ: *rare varieties of birds* 鸟类的稀有品种. 4 [U] (音乐,舞蹈,杂耍等的)联〔聯〕合演出 liánhé yǎnchū: *a* '~ *act* 一幕杂耍表演.

vari·ous /'veərɪəs/ *adj* 不同的 bùtóngde, 各式各样〔樣〕的 gèshì gèyàng de: *for* ~ *reasons* 由于种种原因. ~**ly** *adv*

var·nish /'vɑ:nɪʃ/ *n* [C,U] 清漆 qīngqī. □ *vt* 给…涂〔塗〕清漆 gěi … tú qīngqī.

vary /'veərɪ/ *vt/i* [*pt, pp* -ied] (使)变〔變〕化 biànhuà; (使)不同 bùtóng: *They* ~ *in weight.* 它们的重量不等.

vase /vɑ:z/ *n* [C] 花瓶 huāpíng.

vast /vɑ:st/ *adj* 巨大的 jùdàde; 广〔廣〕大的 guǎngdàde: *a* ~ *desert* 大沙漠. ~**ly** *adv*: ~*ly improved* 很大改进的. ~**ness** *n* [U]

vat /væt/ *n* [C] 大桶 dàtǒng; 大缸 dàgāng.

V.A.T. = value added tax 附加价〔價〕值税 fùjiā jiàzhí shuì.

vault[1] /vɔ:lt/ *n* [C] 1 拱顶 gǒngdǐng. 2 地窖 dìjiào: *a* '*bank* ~ 银行保险库.

vault[2] /vɔ:lt/ *vt/i* (以手撑物)跳跃〔躍〕 tiàoyuè: ~ (*over*) *a fence* 跳过篱笆. □ *n* [C] (撑物)跳跃 tiàoyuè. ⇨ pole-vault. ~**er** (撑物)跳跃者 tiàoyuèzhě: *a* '*pole*-~*er* 撑竿跳运动员.

V.C. = 1 Vice-Chancellor (英国)副(财政)大臣 fù dàchén. 2 Victoria Cross (英国)维多利亚〔亞〕十字勋章 Wéiduōlìyà shízì xūnzhāng.

veal /vi:l/ *n* [U] (食用)小牛肉 xiǎo niúròu.

veer /vɪə(r)/ *vi* 改变〔變〕方向 gǎibiàn fāngxiàng.

veg·etable /'vedʒtəbl/ *adj* 植物的 zhíwùde; 蔬菜的 shūcàide: ~ *oils* 植物油. □ *n* [C] 植物 zhíwù; (尤指)蔬菜 shūcài.

veg·etar·ian /ˌvedʒɪ'teərɪən/ *n* [C] 吃素的人 chī sù de rén.

veg·etate /'vedʒɪteɪt/ *vi* 过〔過〕枯燥单〔單〕调的生活 guò kūzào dāndiào de shēnghuó.

veg·eta·tion /ˌvedʒɪ'teɪʃn/ *n* [U] 植被 zhíbèi.

ve·he·ment /'vi:əmənt/ *adj* 1 [正式用法](感情)强烈的 qiángliède 热〔熱〕烈的 rèliède. 2 (指人,言词等)有强烈感情的 yǒu qiángliè gǎnqíng de: ~ *passions* 热烈的感情. ~**ly** *adv*

ve·hicle /'vi:ɪkl/ *n* [C] 1 车〔車〕辆〔輛〕 chēliàng. 2 (传递思想等的)工具 gōngjù: *Art is a* ~ *for propaganda.* 艺术是一种宣传工具.

veil /veɪl/ *n* [C] **1** 面纱 miànshā. **2** [喻]掩饰物 yǎnshìwù; 借[藉]口 jièkǒu: *a ~ of mist* 一层雾. □ *vt* 蒙上面纱 méngshàng miànshā, [喻]掩盖[蓋] yǎngài, 隐[隱]蔽 yǐnbì.

vein /veɪn/ *n* [C] **1** 静脉[脈] jìngmài. **2** 叶[葉]脉 yèmài; 翅脉 chìmài. **3** (石头的)纹理 wénlǐ. **4** 矿[礦]脉 kuàngmài: *a ~ of gold* 黄金矿脉.

vel·oc·ity /və'lɒsətɪ/ *n* [正式用语] = speed.

vel·vet /'velvɪt/ *n* [U] 丝绒 sīróng 天鹅[鵝]绒 tiān'éróng. **vel·vety** *adj* (天鹅绒般)柔软[軟]光滑的 róuruǎn guānghuá de.

Ven. = Venerable.

vend /vend/ *vt* 出售 chūshòu. '~ **machine** *n* 自动[動]售货机[機] zìdòng shòuhuòjī. ⇨ slot machine.

ve·neer /vɪ'nɪə(r)/ *n* **1** [C,U] (镶饰表面用的)贴面板 tiēmiànbǎn. **2** [喻](掩盖真情的)外表 wàibiǎo, 虚饰 xūshì: *a ~ of kindness* 和善的外表. □ *vt* 给…贴面板 gěi … tiē miànbǎn.

ven·er·able /'venərəbl/ *adj* (因年老等而)值得尊敬的 zhídé zūnjìng de: *a ~ abbot* 尊敬的修道院院长.

ven·er·ate /'venəreɪt/ *vt* 崇敬 chóngjìng, 崇拜 chóngbài. **vene'r·ation** *n* [U]

ve·nereal /vɪ'nɪərɪəl/ *adj* 性交的 xìngjiāode: *~ diseases* 性病.

ven·geance /'vendʒəns/ *n* [U] **1** 报[報]仇 bàochóu: *take ~ on an enemy* 向敌人报仇. **2** *with a ~* 猛烈地 měngliède; 彻[徹]底地 chèdǐde: *The rain came down with a ~.* 大雨滂沱.

venge·ful /'vendʒfl/ *adj* 有复[復]仇心的 yǒu fùchóuxīn de, 报[報]复的 bàofùde.

ven·ison /'venɪzn/ *n* [U] 鹿肉 lùròu.

venom /'venəm/ *n* [U] **1** (毒蛇的)毒液 dúyè. **2** [喻]恶[惡]意 èyì; 怨恨 yuànhèn. **~ous** /'venəməs/ *adj* 有毒的 yǒudúde.

vent /vent/ *n* [C] **1** (气,水等的)出口 chūkǒu. **2** (感情的)发[發]泄[洩] fāxiè. *give ~ to* 发泄 fāxiè, 吐露 tǔlù: *He gave ~ to his feelings.* 他发泄自己的情绪. □ *vt* 发泄(感情) fāxiè. *He ~ed his anger on his wife.* 他拿他的妻子出气.

ven·ti·late /'ventɪleɪt/ *vt* 使(空气)流通 shǐ liútōng: *~ a room* 使房间通风. **ven·ti·la·tor** 通风设备[備] tōngfēng shèbèi. **ven·ti'la·tion** *n* [U]

ven·ture /'ventʃə(r)/ *n* [C,U] 冒险[險] màoxiǎn, 冒险事业[業] màoxiǎn shìyè: *a 'business ~* 商业投机. □ *vt/i* **1** (使)冒险 màoxiǎn; (使)遭受危险或损失 zāoshòu wēixiǎn huò sǔnshī: *~ too near a cliff* 冒险靠近悬崖. **2** 敢于[於] gǎnyú: *~ an opinion* 提出一个意见看看.

ve·ran·dah, ve·randa /və'rændə/ *n* [C] 走廊 zǒuláng; 阳[陽]台 yángtái.

verb /vɜ:b/ *n* [C] [语法]动[動]词 dòngcí.

ver·bal /'vɜ:bl/ *adj* **1** 言语的 yányǔde; 字句的 zìjùde. **2** 口头[頭]的 kǒutóude: *a ~ statement* 口头声明. **~ly** *adv* 口头上 kǒutóushàng.

ver·bose /vɜ:'bəʊs/ *adj* 噜苏[蘇]的 lūsūde, 冗长[長]的 rǒngchángde: *a ~ speaker* 噜苏的演讲者. **ver·bos·ity** /vɜ:'bɒsətɪ/ *n* [U]

ver·dict /'vɜ:dɪkt/ *n* [C] **1** (陪审团的)裁决 cáijué: *a ~ of guilty (not guilty)* 判决有罪(无罪). **2** 定论[論] dìnglùn; 意见 yìjiàn: *The popular ~ was against the strike.* 公众的意见是反对罢工.

verge /vɜ:dʒ/ *n* **1** [C] 边[邊]缘 biānyuán; 边界 biānjiè. **2** *be on the ~ of* 接近于[於] jiējìn yú, 濒于 bīnyú: *on the ~ of war* 处于战争的边缘. □ *vi* 接近 jiējìn, 濒临[臨] bīnlín.

ver·ify /'verɪfaɪ/ *vt* [*pt, pp* -ied] 证[證]实[實] zhèngshí, 查对[對] cháduì, 核实 héshí: *~ a report* 核实一份报告. **veri·fi·ca·tion** /-fɪ'keɪʃn/ *n* [U]

veri·table /'verɪtəbl/ *adj* 名副其实[實]的 míng fù qí shí de, 确[確]实的 quèshíde: *a ~ liar* 十足的说谎者.

ver·min /'vɜ:mɪn/ *n* [U] **1** 害兽[獸] hàishòu; 害虫[蟲] hàichóng. **2** [喻]害人虫 hàirénchóng, 歹徒 dǎitú.

ver·nacu·lar /və'nækjʊlə(r)/ *adj* 用本国[國]语的 yòng běnguóyǔ de; 用方言的 yòng fāngyán de: *a ~ poet* 方言诗人. □ *n* [C] 本国语 běnguóyǔ; 方言 fāngyán, 白话 báihuà.

ver·sa·tile /'vɜ:sətaɪl/ *adj* 多才多艺[藝]的 duō cái duo yì de: *a ~ mind* 多才多艺的人. *a ~ invention* 一项可多方面适用的发明.

verse /vɜ:s/ *n* **1** [U] 诗 shī, 诗体[體] shītǐ, 韵文 yùnwén: *prose and*

～ 散文和韵文. **2** [C] 诗节〔節〕shījé. **3** [C] 诗句 shījù. **4** (《圣经》的)节 jié.

versed /vɜːst/ *adj* **～d in** 精通 jīngtōng, 熟练〔練〕shúliàn.

ver·sion /ˈvɜːʃn/ *n* [C] **1** 描述 miáoshù, 说法 shuōfǎ: *There were three ～s of what happened.* 关于所发生的事有三种说法. **2** 译〔譯〕文 yìwéng, 译本 yìběn: *a new ～ of the Bible.* 《圣经》的新译本.

ver·sus /ˈvɜːsəs/ *prep* (印刷时缩作 v)(诉讼,比赛中)对〔對〕duì: *England v Brazil* 英国对巴西.

ver·te·bra /ˈvɜːtɪbrə/ *n* [C] [*pl* ～e /-briː/] [解剖]脊椎骨 jǐzhuīgǔ. **～te** /ˈvɜːtɪbrɪt/ *n* [C], *adj* 脊椎动〔動〕物 jǐzhuī dòngwù; 有脊椎的 yǒu jǐzhuī de.

ver·ti·cal /ˈvɜːtɪkl/ *adj* 垂直的 chuízhíde. □ *n* [C] 垂直线〔綫〕chuízhíxiàn. **～ly** *adv*

very[1] /ˈverɪ/ *adj* **1** 恰好的 qiàhǎode, 同一的 tóngyīde: *At that ～ moment the phone rang.* 正在那个时候电话铃响了. **2** 极〔極〕端的 jíduānde, 末端的 mòduānde: *at the ～ end* 在结束之际.

very[2] /ˈverɪ/ *adv* **1** 很 hěn, 甚 shèn; 颇 pō: *～ quickly (little)* 很快(小). **～ well** 好吧 hǎoba: *V～ well, doctor, I'll give up smoking.* 好吧, 大夫, 我将戒烟. **2** 极〔極〕其 jíqí, 最 zuì: *at the ～ latest* 最迟.

vessel /ˈvesl/ *n* [C] **1** 容器 róngqì, 器皿 qìmǐn. **2** 船 chuán, 舰〔艦〕jiàn. ⇨ blood-vessel.

vest[1] /vest/ *n* [C] **1** [英国英语]汗衫 hànshān. **2** [美语] = waistcoat.

vest[2] /vest/ *vt* 授予 shòuyǔ, 给予 gěiyǔ: *～ a man with authority* 授权给某人.

ves·tige /ˈvestɪdʒ/ *n* [C] 痕迹〔跡〕hénjī, 遗迹 yíjī: *There is not a ～ of truth in the report.* 这个报告一点也不真实.

vet[1] /vet/ *n* [C] [非正式用语] (veterinary surgeon 的缩写)兽〔獸〕医〔醫〕shòuyī.

vet[2] /vet/ *vt* [-tt-] [非正式用语]检〔檢〕查 jiǎnchá, 审〔審〕查 shěnchá.

vet·eran /ˈvetərən/ *n* [C] **1** 老练〔練〕者 lǎoliànzhě, 老手 lǎoshǒu, 老兵 lǎobīng: *a war ～* 老战士. **2** (1916 年以前制造的)老式汽车〔車〕lǎoshì qìchē: *a ～ Rolls Royce* 一辆罗尔斯·劳埃牌的老式汽车

vet·erin·ary /ˈvetrɪnrɪ/ *adj* 兽〔獸〕医〔醫〕的 shòuyīde: *a ～ surgeon* 兽医.

veto /ˈviːtəʊ/ *n* [C] [*pl* ～es] 否决 fǒujué; 禁止 jìnzhǐ; 否决权〔權〕fǒujuéquán: *exercise a power of ～* 行使否决权. □ *vt* 否决 fǒujué; 禁止 jìnzhǐ: *～ a proposal* 否决一项提案.

vex /veks/ *vt* [正式用语]使烦恼〔惱〕shǐ fánnǎo, 使苦恼 shǐ kǔnǎo: *He was ～ed at his failure.* 他因失败而苦恼. **～ation** /-ˈseɪʃn/ *n* [C,U]

v.f. = very fair.

V.H.F. = very high frequency 甚高频 shèn gāopín.

via /ˈvaɪə/ *prep* 经〔經〕过〔過〕jīngguò, 经由 jīngyǒu: *travel ～ Dover* 旅行经过多佛.

vi·able /ˈvaɪəbl/ *adj* 能活的 néng huó de, 能生存的 néng shēngcún de: *make a business ～* 使商店能维持下去. **vi·abil·ity** /-ˈbɪlətɪ/ *n* [U]

vi·aduct /ˈvaɪədʌkt/ *n* [C] 高架桥〔橋〕gāojiàqiáo, 栈〔棧〕道 zhàndào.

vi·brate /vaɪˈbreɪt/ *vt/i* **1** (使)摆〔擺〕动〔動〕bǎidòng, (使)摇动 yáodòng: *The house ～s whenever a heavy lorry passes.* 当重型卡车经过时, 那房屋晃动. **2** 颤动 chàndòng, 振动 zhèndòng: *The strings of a piano ～.* 钢琴的琴弦振动. **viˈbration** *n* [C,U] 摆动 bǎidòng, 摇动 yáodòng, 颤动 chàndòng, 振动 zhèndòng.

vicar /ˈvɪkə(r)/ *n* [C] 教区〔區〕牧师〔師〕jiàoqū mùshī. **～age** *n* [C] 教区牧师的住宅 jiàoqū mùshī de zhùzhái.

vice[1] /vaɪs/ *n* [C,U] 罪恶〔惡〕zuìè, 不道德行为〔爲〕bú dàodé xíngwéi: *Smoking is a ～.* 吸烟是坏习惯.

vice[2] /vaɪs/ *n* [C] 老虎钳 lǎohǔqián.

vice- /vaɪs-/ *prefix* 副的 fùde, 次的 cìde, 代理的 dàilǐde: *～-president* 副总统.

vice versa /ˌvaɪsə ˈvɜːsə/ *adj* [拉丁语]反过〔過〕来〔來〕(也是一样) fǎnguòlái: *We gossip about them and ～.* 我们议论他们, 反过来, 他们也同样议论我们.

vi·cin·ity /vɪˈsɪnətɪ/ *n* [C,U] [*pl* -ies] 邻〔鄰〕近 línjìn, 附近 fùjìn: *There isn't a good school in the ～.* 附近没有好学校.

vi·cious /ˈvɪʃəs/ *adj* **1** 邪恶〔惡〕的 xié'ède, 堕落的 duòluòde: *a ～ life* 堕落的生活. **2** 恶意的 è'yìde, 恶毒的 èdúde: *a ～ kick* 凶恶的踢一脚. ˌ**～ ˈcircle** 循环〔環〕影响〔響〕xúnhuán yǐngxiǎng, 恶性

循环 èxìng xúnhuán. ~ly *adv*

vic·tim /'vɪktɪm/ *n* [C] **1** 牺〔犧〕牲 xīshēng. **2** 受害者 shòuhàizhě, 牺牲者 xīshēngzhě: *the ~s of the earthquake* 地震的受害者. **~ize** /-maɪz/ *vt* 使牺牲 shǐ xīshēng, 使受害 shǐ shòuhài. **~iz·ation** /-'zeɪʃn/ *n* [U]

vic·tor /'vɪktə(r)/ *n* [C] 胜〔勝〕利者 shènglìzhě, 战〔戰〕胜者 zhànshèngzhě. **~i·ous** /vɪk'tɔːrɪəs/ *adj* 胜利的 shènglìde, 战胜的 zhànshèngde. **~i·ous·ly** *adv*

vic·tory /'vɪktərɪ/ *n* [C,U] [*pl* -ies] 胜〔勝〕利 shènglì, 战〔戰〕胜 zhàngshèng.

video /'vɪdɪəʊ/ [C,U] *adj* 电〔電〕视的 diànshìde; 影象〔像〕的 yǐngxiàngde: *~ cassettes* 录象带.

view¹ /vjuː/ *n* **1** [U] 看 kàn, 观〔觀〕察 guānchá; 视力 shìlì; 视野 shìyě: *in full ~ of the crowd* 在大家都能看得见的地方. *in ~ of* 考虑到 kǎolǜdào, 鉴〔鑒〕于〔於〕jiànyú: *In ~ of the facts ...* 考虑到这些事实.... *on ~* 展览〔覽〕着 zhǎnlǎnzhe, 陈〔陳〕列着 chénlièzhe: *clothes on ~ in the big shops* 在大商店里展览的服装. *come into ~* 出现在眼前 chūxiàn zài yǎnqián. **2** [C] 看见的东〔東〕西 kànjiànde dōngxi; (尤指)风〔風〕景 fēngjǐng, 景色 jǐngsè: *a house with a fine ~ of the mountains* 一幢可以看见美丽的山景的房屋. **3** [C] 意见 yìjiàn, 观点〔點〕guāndiǎn: *She had strong ~s on the subject.* 她对这个问题很有意见. **4** *with a ~ to* 以...为〔爲〕目的 yǐ...wéi mùdì, 为了要 wèile yào. **'~-finder** [摄影]取景器 qǔjǐngqì. **'~point** = point of view.

view² /vjuː/ *vt* 看 kàn, 观〔觀〕察 guānchá; 检〔檢〕查 jiǎnchá; 考虑 kǎolǜ: *The subject may be ~ed in various ways.* 这个问题可用不同的方式去考虑. **~er** 观察者 guāncházhě; (尤指)看电〔電〕视者 kàn diànshìzhě.

vigil /'vɪdʒɪl/ *n* [C,U] 值夜 zhíyè, 守夜 shǒuyè.

vigi·lant /'vɪdʒɪlənt/ *adj* 警戒的 jǐngjiède, 警惕的 jǐngtìde. **~ly** *adv* **vigi·lance** *n* [U]

vig·our [美语 = **vigor**] /'vɪgə(r)/ *n* [U] 力量 lìliàng, 体〔體〕力 tǐlì; 活力 huólì, 精力 jīnglì. **vig·or·ous** *adj* 强有力的 qiángyǒulìde, 精力充沛的 jīnglì chōngpèi de. **vig·or·ous·ly** *adv*

vile /vaɪl/ *adj* [-r, -st] **1** 卑鄙的 bēibǐde, 讨厌〔厭〕的 tǎoyànde: *~ habits* 讨厌的恶习. *~ language* 粗鄙的语言. **2** [非正式用语]坏〔壞〕透的huài tòu de, 恶〔惡〕劣的 èliède: *~ weather* 恶劣的天气. **~ly** /'vaɪllɪ/ *adv*

villa /'vɪlə/ *n* [C] [*pl* ~s] 别墅 biéshù.

vil·lage /'vɪlɪdʒ/ *n* [C] 乡〔鄉〕村 xiāngcūn, 村庄〔莊〕cūnzhuāng. **vil·lager** 村民 cūnmín.

vil·lain /'vɪlən/ *n* [C] 坏〔壞〕人 huàirén, 恶〔惡〕棍 ègùn.

vin·di·cate /'vɪndɪkeɪt/ *vt* 为〔爲〕...辩白 wèi... biànbái, 证〔證〕明...正确〔確〕zhèngmíng... zhèngquè: *~ a claim (one's actions)* 证明一项权利(某人的行为). **vin·di'ca·tion** *n* [C,U]

vin·dic·tive /vɪn'dɪktɪv/ *adj* 有报〔報〕复〔復〕心的 yǒu bàofùxīn de. **~ly** *adv* **~ness** *n* [U]

vine /vaɪn/ *n* [C] 藤本植物 téngběn zhíwù; 葡萄树〔樹〕pútáoshù. **~yard** /'vɪnjəd/ 葡萄园〔園〕pútáoyuán.

vin·egar /'vɪnɪgə(r)/ *n* [C] 醋 cù. **vin·egary** *adj* 似醋的 sì cù de, 酸溜溜的 suānliūliūde.

vin·tage /'vɪntɪdʒ/ *n* **1** [C] [罕用 *pl*] 收获〔穫〕葡萄(季节) shōuhuò pútáo. **2** [C,U] 某一年所产〔產〕的葡萄 mǒuyìnián suǒchǎn de pútáo; (该年葡萄所酿的)葡萄酒 pútáojiǔ. *of the ~ of 1973* 一九七三年所产葡萄酿的. **3** [用作定语] 古老而品质优〔優〕良的 gǔlǎo ér pǐnzhì yōuliáng de: *a ~ car* 一辆老牌汽车.

vi·nyl /'vaɪnɪl/ *n* [C,U] [化学]乙烯基 yǐxījī.

vi·ola /vɪ'əʊlə/ *n* [C] 中提琴 zhōng tíqín.

vi·ol·ate /'vaɪəleɪt/ *vt* **1** 违〔違〕犯(誓言,条约等) wéifàn. **2** 侵犯 qīnfàn, 冒犯 màofàn: *~ a person's privacy* 侵犯个人自由(闯入私室). **vi·o'la·tion** *n* [C,U]

vi·ol·ence /'vaɪələns/ *n* [U] 猛烈 měngliè; 暴行 bàoxíng: *robbery with ~* 行凶的抢劫.

vi·ol·ent /'vaɪələnt/ *adj* **1** 猛烈的 měngliède, 凶〔兇〕暴的 xiōngbàode: *a ~ wind* 暴风. *a ~ attack* 猛攻. **2** 由暴力引起的 yóu bàolì yǐnqǐ de: *a ~ death* 横死. **3** 强烈的 qiángliède, 厉〔厲〕害的 lìhàide: *~ pain* 剧痛. **~ly** *adv*

vi·olet /'vaɪələt/ *n* **1** [C] 紫罗〔羅〕兰〔蘭〕zǐluólán. **2** [U] 紫罗兰色 zǐluólánsè, 紫色 zǐsè.

vi·olin /ˌvaɪə'lɪn/ *n* [C] 小提琴 xiǎo tíqín. **~ist** 小提琴手 xiǎo tíqínshǒu.

V.I.P. = very important person 要人 yàorén.

vi·per /ˈvaɪpə(r)/ *n* [C] 蝰蛇 kuíshé, 毒蛇 dúshé.

vir·gin /ˈvɜːdʒɪn/ *n* [C] 处〔處〕女 chùnǚ. □ *adj* **1** 处女的 chùnǚde, 童贞的 tóngzhēnde; 纯洁〔潔〕的 chúnjiéde: ~ *snow* 洁白的雪. **2** 未开〔開〕发〔發〕的 wèi kāifā de, 原始的 yuánshǐde: ~ *soil* 处女地. **~ity** /vəˈdʒɪnətɪ/ *n* [U] 处女性 chùnǚxìng, 童贞 tóngzhēn; 纯洁 chúnjié.

vir·ile /ˈvɪraɪl/ *adj* **1** 强有力的 qiáng yǒulì de; 有男子气概的 yǒu nánzǐ qìgài de, 雄纠纠的 xióngjiūjiūde. **2** 有男性生殖力的 yǒu nánxìng shēngzhílì de. **vir·il·ity** /vɪˈrɪlətɪ/ *n* [U]

vir·tual /ˈvɜːtʃʊəl/ *adj* 实〔實〕际〔際〕上的 shíjìshàngde, 事实上的 shìshíshàngde: *a* ~ *defeat* (*confession*) 一次实际上的失败(忏悔). **~ly** /-tʃʊəlɪ/ *adv*

vir·tue /ˈvɜːtʃuː/ *n* **1** [C,U] 善良 shànliáng, 德行 déxíng, 美德 měidé; 长〔長〕处〔處〕 chángchù: *Patience is a* ~. 忍耐是一种美德. **2** [U] (尤指妇女的)贞操 zhēncāo. **3** 效力 xiàolì, 功效 gōngxiào: *The great* ~ *of the scheme* ...规划的巨大功效. **4** *by* ~ *of* 由于〔於〕 yóuyú, 因为〔爲〕 yīnwèi, 凭〔憑〕借〔藉〕 píngjiè. **vir·tu·ous** /ˈvɜːtʃʊəs/ *adj* 善良的 shànliángde, 有德行的 yǒu déxíng de.

vi·rus /ˈvaɪərəs/ *n* [C] [*pl* ~es] 病毒 bìngdú.

visa /ˈviːzə/ *n* [C] [*pl* ~s] 签〔簽〕证〔證〕 qiānzhèng.

vis·count /ˈvaɪkaʊnt/ *n* [C] 子爵 zǐjué. **~ess** /-ɪs/ *n* [C] 子爵夫人 zǐjué fūren; 女子爵 nǚ zǐjué.

vis·ible /ˈvɪzəbl/ *adj* 看得见的 kàndejiànde, 可见的 kějiànde. **vis·ibly** *adv* 明显〔顯〕地 míngxiǎnde: *She was visibly annoyed*. 她显然被惹恼了. **vis·ibil·ity** /-ˈbɪlətɪ/ *n* [U] (尤指)能见度 néngjiàndù.

vi·sion /ˈvɪʒn/ *n* **1** [U] 视力 shìlì, 视觉〔覺〕 shìjué; 洞察力 dòngchálì: *the field of* ~ 视野. **2** 幻想 huànxiǎng, 想象 xiǎngxiàng: *a man of* ~ 富于想象的人. **3** [C] 看见或想象的东〔東〕西 kànjiàn huò xiǎngxiàng de dōngxi: ~*s of great wealth* 发财的梦想.

vi·sion·ary /ˈvɪʒənrɪ/ *adj* **1** 梦幻的 mènghuànde, 想象的 xiǎngxiàngde: ~ *schemes* 空想的计划. **2** 好空想的 hào kōngxiǎng de, 有幻想的 yǒu huànxiǎng de.

visit /ˈvɪzɪt /*vt*/*i* **1** 访问〔問〕 fǎngwèn; 参观〔觀〕 cānguān, 游览〔覽〕 yóulǎn: ~ *a friend* 访问朋友. ~ *Rome* 游览罗马. **2** 视察 shìchá, 巡视 xúnshì. □ *n* [C] 访问 fǎngwèn; 参观 cānguān, 游览 yóulǎn; 视察 shìchá: *pay a* ~ *to a friend* 访问朋友.

visi·tor /ˈvɪzɪtə(r)/ *n* [C] 访问〔問〕者 fǎngwènzhě, 来〔來〕宾〔賓〕 láibīn; 游客 yóukè, 参观〔觀〕者 cānguānzhě.

vi·sor /ˈvaɪzə(r)/ *n* [C] **1** (古时盔的)面甲 miànjiǎ, 假面具 jiǎmiànjù. **2** 帽舌 màoshé.

vista /ˈvɪstə/ *n* [C] [*pl* ~s] **1** 远〔遠〕景 yuǎnjǐng. **2** [喻](对往事)一连〔連〕串的追忆〔憶〕 yìliánchuànde zhuīyì; (对前景)一系列的展望 yíxìliède zhǎnwàng: *Scientific discoveries give us new* ~*s of the future*. 科学的发现为我们带来新的远景.

vis·ual /ˈvɪʒʊəl/ *adj* 看的 kànde, 看得见的 kàndejiànde; 用于〔於〕看的 yòngyú kàn de: ~ *aids* 视觉教具. ~ **disˈplay unit** *n* (缩作 **VDU**) 荧〔熒〕光数〔數〕字显〔顯〕示器 yíngguāng shùzì xiǎnshìqì. **~ly** *adv*. **~ize** /-laɪz/ *vt* 使形象化 shǐ xíngxiàng huà; 想象 xiǎngxiàng.

vi·tal /ˈvaɪtl/ *adj* **1** 生命的 shēngmìngde; 必需的 bìxūde. **2** 极〔極〕端重要的 jíduān zhòngyào de, 必不可少的 bì bùkě shǎo de: *of* ~ *importance* 极其重要的. **~ly** *adv*

vi·tal·ity /vaɪˈtælətɪ/ *n* [U] **1** 生命力 shēngmìnglì. **2** 活力 huólì, 生气〔氣〕 shēngqì: *the* ~ *of young children* 小孩子们的蓬勃生气.

vi·tal·ize /ˈvaɪtəlaɪz/ *vt* 给与〔與〕活力 gěiyǔ huólì, 赋以生命力 fùyǐ shēngmìnglì.

vit·amin /ˈvɪtəmɪn/ *n* [C] 维生素 wéishēngsù.

vi·va·cious /vɪˈveɪʃəs/ *adj* 活泼〔潑〕的 huópode, 有生气〔氣〕的 yǒu shēngqì de: *a* ~ *girl* 活泼的女孩子. **~ly** *adv*

vivid /ˈvɪvɪd/ *adj* **1** (色彩,光线等)鲜艳〔艷〕的 xiānyànde, 强烈的 qiángliède: *a* ~ *colour* 鲜艳的色彩. **2** 活泼〔潑〕的 huópode, 有生气〔氣〕的 yǒu shēngqì de: *a* ~ *imagination* 活跃的想象力. **3** 清晰的 qīngxīde; 生动〔動〕的 shēngdòngde: *have* ~ *memories* 有着清楚的记忆. **~ly** *adv*

vivi·sec·tion /ˌvɪvɪˈsekʃn/ *n* [C, U] 活体〔體〕解剖 huótǐ jiěpōu.

vixen /ˈvɪksn/ *n* [C] **1** 雌狐 cí hú. **2** 泼〔潑〕妇〔婦〕 pōfù.

viz. = namely.

vo·cabu·lary /və'kæbjʊlərɪ/ *n* [C] [*pl* -ies] **1** 词汇〔彙〕 cíhuì, 总〔總〕词汇量 zǒng cíhuìliàng. **2** [C,U] (某人,某行业所用的)词汇 cíhuì, 语汇 yǔhuì: *a writer with a large* ~ 语汇丰富的作家. **3** [C] 词汇表 cíhuìbiǎo.

vo·cal /'vəʊkl/ *adj* 声〔聲〕音的 shēngyīnde, 有声的 yǒushēngde, 发〔發〕音的 fāyīnde: *the* ~ *organs* 发音器官. ~**ly** *adv* ~**ist** *n* [C] 声乐〔樂〕家 shēngyuèjiā, 歌唱家 gēchàngjiā.

vo·ca·tion /vəʊ'keɪʃn/ *n* **1** [U] 天职〔職〕 tiānzhí, 使命 shǐmìng: *Nursing is a* ~. 护理是一种天职. **2** [U] [与 *for* 连用] 才能 cáinéng; 适〔適〕宜性 shìyíxìng. **3** [C] 行业〔業〕 hángyè, 职业 zhíyè. ~**al** *adj* 职业的 zhíyède, 业务〔務〕的 yèwùde: ~*al courses* 专业教程.

vodka /'vɒdkə/ *n* [C,U] 伏特加(酒) fútèjiā.

vogue /vəʊg/ *n* [C] 流行物 liúxíngwù, 时〔時〕髦 shímáo: *Are earrings still the* ~? 耳环还时髦吗?

voice /vɔɪs/ *n* **1** [U] 说话声〔聲〕 shuōhuàshēng, 嗓音 sǎngyīn. **2** [C] 发〔發〕音能力 fāyīn nénglì: *He has lost his* ~ 他嗓子哑了. **3** [C,U] 声音 shēngyīn; (尤指)声音的质〔質〕量 shēngyīnde zhìliàng: *in a loud (soft)* ~大(柔)声地. ***at the top of one's*** ~ 大声地 dàshēngde. **4** [U] ***have (demand) a*** ~ ***in sth*** (对某事)有(要求)发言权〔權〕 yǒu fāyánquán. □ *vt* (用言语)表达〔達〕 biǎodá, 说出 shuōchū: *The spokesman* ~*d the feelings of the crowd.* 发言人表达了群众的情绪.

void /vɔɪd/ *adj* **1** 空的 kōngde; 空虚的 kōngxūde. **2** ~ ***of*** 没有 méiyǒu, 缺乏 quēfá: *a subject* ~ *of interest* 乏味的题目. **3** ,***null and*** '~ [法律]无〔無〕效 wúxiào. □ *n* [C] 空间〔間〕 kōngjiān, 空位 kōngwèi; 真空 zhēnkōng. □ *vt* [法律]使无效 shǐ wúxiào.

vol. = volume.

vol·atile /'vɒlətaɪl/ *adj* **1** (液体等)易挥〔揮〕发〔發〕的 yì huīfā de. **2** (指人等)反复〔覆〕无〔無〕常的 fǎnfù wúcháng de.

vol·cano /vɒl'keɪnəʊ/ *n* [C] [*pl* ~es 或 ~s] 火山 huǒshān. **vol·canic** /vɒl'kænɪk/ *adj*

vol·ley /'vɒlɪ/ *n* [C] **1** (箭,子弹等)齐〔齊〕射 qíshè. **2** (咒骂,质问等)齐发〔發〕 qífā, 迸发 bèngfā. **3** [网球] (球落地前的) 截击〔擊〕 jiéjī. □ *vt/i* **1** (指枪炮)齐发 qífā. **2** (在球落地前)截击 jiéjī.

volt /vəʊlt/ *n* [C] (缩作 **v**) (电压单位)伏特 fútè. ~**age** *n* [C,U] 电〔電〕压〔壓〕 diànyā, 伏特数〔數〕 fútè shù.

vol·uble /'vɒljʊbl/ *adj* (言词)流利的 liúlìde, 健谈的 jiàntánde. **vol·ubly** *adv*

vol·ume /'vɒlju:m/ *n* [C] **1** (一)册 cè; (一)卷 juàn. **2** [U] 容积〔積〕 róngjī; 体〔體〕积 tǐjī. **3** [C] 大量 dàliàng, 许多 xǔduō: *a large* ~ *of work* 大量的工作. **4** [U] 音量 yīnliàng, 响〔響〕度 xiǎngdù: *Your radio has a* '~ *control.* 你的收音机装有音量控制.

vol·umi·nous /və'lu:mɪnəs/ *adj* [正式用语] **1** 长〔長〕篇的 chángpiānde, 多卷的 duōjuànde, 大部头〔頭〕的 dà bùtóu de. **2** (体积)庞〔龐〕大的 pángdàde: ~ *skirts* 宽大的裙子.

vol·un·tary /'vɒləntrɪ/ *adj* **1** 自愿〔願〕的 zìyuànde, 志愿的 zhìyuànde: ~ *work (helpers)* 自愿的工作(帮助者). **2** 有意的 yǒuyìde, 故意的 gùyìde. **vol·un·tar·ily** /'vɒləntrəlɪ/ *adv*

vol·un·teer /,vɒlən'tɪə(r)/ *n* [C] **1** 自愿参加者 zìyuàn cānjiāzhě. **2** 志愿军〔軍〕 zhìyuànjūn. □ *vt/i* 自愿做(某事) zìyuàn zuò: *He* ~*ed some information* 他自动提供某些信息. ~ *for the army* 志愿参军.

vo·lup·tu·ous /və'lʌptʃʊəs/ *adj* 骄〔驕〕奢淫逸的 jiāoshēyínyì de; 色情的 sèqíngde: *a* ~ *girl* 妖娆的女郎. ~**ly** *adv*

vomit /'vɒmɪt/ *vt/i* **1** 呕〔嘔〕吐 ǒutù. **2** 大量喷出 dàliàng pēnchū: *chimneys* ~*ing smoke* 大量喷烟的烟囱. □ *n* [U] 呕吐物 ǒutùwù.

vote /vəʊt/ *n* [C] **1** 选〔選〕举〔舉〕(权) xuǎnjǔ, 投票(权) tóupiào, 表决(权) biǎojué: *record (cast) my* ~ 投我的一票. *a* ~ *of thanks* 鼓掌表示感谢. **2** 选票数〔數〕 xuǎnpiàoshù: *Will the Labour* ~ *increase?* 工党的选票将增加吗? □ *vt/i* **1** ~ ***for (against) sb (sth)*** 投票赞成(反对)某人(某事) tóupiào zànchéng mǒurén; 对〔對〕某问〔問〕题进〔進〕行表决 duì mǒuwèntí jìnxíng biǎojué. **2** [与 *to* 连用](为某用途所议决的)拨〔撥〕款 bōkuǎn: *voting money for Education* 投票通过教育经费. **voter** 选举人 xuǎnjǔrén, 投票者 tóupiàozhě.

vouch /vaʊtʃ/ *vi* ~ ***for sb (sth)*** 担〔擔〕保某人(某物) dānbǎo mǒurén: ~ *for him* 替他担保. ~ *for his ability* 保证他的能力.

voucher /'vaʊtʃə(r)/ *n* [C] 收据〔據〕shōujù; 凭〔憑〕单〔單〕píngdān.
vow /vaʊ/ *n* [C] 誓约 shìyuē, 许愿〔願〕xǔyuàn: *'marriage ~s* 婚誓. □ *vt* 起誓 qǐshì, 许愿 xǔyuàn.
vowel /'vaʊəl/ *n* [C] **1** 元音 yuányīn. **2** 元音字母 yuányīn zìmǔ.
voy·age /'vɔɪɪdʒ/ *n* [C] 航海 hánghǎi, 航行 hángxíng. □ *vi* 航海 hánghǎi, 航行 hángxíng. **voy·ager** *n* [C] 航海者 hánghǎizhě, 航行者 hángxíngzhě.
vs. = versus.
vul·gar /'vʌlgə(r)/ *adj* **1** 粗俗的 cūsúde, 粗陋的 cūlòude, 粗鄙的 cūbǐde: ~ *language* 粗俗的语言. **2** 趣味不高的 qùwèi bùgāo de; 通俗的 tōngsúde, 庸俗的 yōngsúde: ~ *patterns on the carpets* 地毯上的庸俗图案. **~ity** /vʌl'gærətɪ/ *n* [*pl* -ies] **(a)** [U] 粗俗(的行为) cūsú, 庸俗(的趣味) yōngsú. **(b)** [*pl*] 粗野(的动作) cūyě, 粗俗(的言词) cūsú. **~ly** *adv*
vul·ner·able /'vʌlnərəbl/ *adj* 易受攻击〔擊〕的 yì shòu gōngjī de: *a ~ position* 易受攻击的地位. **vul·ner·abil·ity** /-'bɪlətɪ/ *n* [U]
vul·ture /'vʌltʃə(r)/ *n* [C] **1**〔动物〕秃鹫〔鷲〕tūjiù. **2**〔喻〕贪婪而残〔殘〕酷的人 tānlán ér cánkù de rén.
vv. = verses.

W w

W, w /'dʌblju:/ [*pl* W's, w's /'dʌblju:z/] 英语的第二十三个〔個〕字母 Yīngyǔde dì'èrshísāngè zìmǔ.
W. = **1** West. **2** watt(s).
w. = **1** wife. **2** with. **3** width.
wad /wɒd/ *n* [C] **1** (软质)填料 tiánliào: *~s of cotton-wool* 一团团棉花. **2** (钞票等)一卷 yījiàn, 一迭 yīdié. □ *vt* [-dd-] (用填料)填塞 tiánsāi.
waddle /'wɒdəl/ *vi* (如鸭子般地)蹒跚而行 pánshān ér xíng. □ *n* [C] 蹒跚 pánshān.
wade /weɪd/ *vt/i* **1** 跋涉 báshè, 蹚(水) tāng. **2** 缓慢地通过〔過〕huǎnmànde tōngguò: ~ *through a long book* 啃完一本厚书. ~ ***into sth*** 猛烈攻击〔擊〕(某事物) měngliè gōngjī. **wader** 〔动物〕涉禽 shèqín.
wa·fer /'weɪfə(r)/ *n* [C] **1** 薄脆饼 bócuìbǐng. **2** (圣餐用的)圣饼 shèngbǐng.
waffle[1] /'wɒfl/ *n* [C] 蛋奶烘饼 dànnǎi hōngbǐng.
waffle[2] /'wɒfl/ *vi* 〔非正式用语〕唠〔嘮〕叨 láodāo, 胡扯 húchě. □ *n* [U] 无〔無〕聊话 wúliáohuà.
waft /wɒft/ *vt* 使飘〔飄〕荡〔蕩〕shǐ piāodàng: *The scent ~ed into the room.* 香气飘进屋子里来了. □ *n* [C] 一阵〔陣〕(风,气味等) yīzhèn.
wag /wæg/ *vt/i* [-gg-] (使)摇摆〔擺〕yáobǎi, (使)摇动〔動〕yáodòng: *The dog ~ged its tail.* 狗摇动尾巴. □ *n* [C] 摇摆 yáobǎi, 摇动 yáodòng.
wage[1] /weɪdʒ/ *n* [C] (按周计算的)工资 gōngzī: *His ~s are £50 a week.* 他的工资是每周五十镑. **'~-freeze** 工资冻〔凍〕结 gōngzī dòngjié.
wage[2] /weɪdʒ/ *vt* 从〔從〕事(战争等) cóngshì.
wa·ger /'weɪdʒə(r)/ *n* [C] 赌注 dǔzhù. □ *vt/i* 押(赌注) yā, 打赌 dǎdǔ.
waggle /'wægl/ *vt/i* = wag.
wag·gon 〔美语常作 **w gon**〕/'wægən/ *n* [C] **1** (四轮)运〔運〕货车〔車〕yùnhuòchē. **2** (铁路)货车 huòchē.
wail /weɪl/ *vt/i* **1** (大声)哀号〔號〕āiháo, 恸〔慟〕哭 tòngkū: *a ~ing child* 哭叫的孩子. **2** 尖啸〔嘯〕jiānxiào, 呼啸 hūxiào. □ *n* [C] 恸哭 tòngkū; 呼啸 hūxiào.
waist /weɪst/ *n* [C] **1** 腰 yāo. **2** 中间〔間〕细的部分 zhōngjiān xìde bùfen: *the ~ of a violin* 小提琴的腰部. **'~coat** /'weɪskəʊt/ 背心 bèixīn, 马〔馬〕甲 mǎjiǎ. **'~line** 腰围〔圍〕yāowéi.
wait[1] /weɪt/ *n* [C] **1** 等待 děngdài; 等待的时〔時〕间〔間〕děngdàide shíjiān. **2** [U] ***lie in ~ for*** 埋伏以待 máifú yǐ dài.
wait[2] /'weɪt/ *vt/i* **1** 等 děng, 期待 qīdài: *We are ~ing for John to come.* 我们正在等约翰来到. **2** 准〔準〕备〔備〕好 zhǔnbèi hǎo: *He is ~ing his opportunity.* 他正在等待着机会. **3** ~ ***on sb*** 服侍(某人) fúshì. **4** ~ ***at*** 伺候 cìhòu: ~ *at table* 伺候开饭. **'~ing list** 待任命者的名单〔單〕dài rènmìngzhě de míngdān. **'~ing room** 候车〔車〕室 hòuchēshì; 候诊室 hòuzhěnshì. **~er** 服务〔務〕员 fúwùyuán. **~ress** 女服务员 nǚ fúwùyuán.
wake[1] /weɪk/*vt/i* [*pt* woke/wəʊk/; *pp*

woken /'wəʊkən/] **1** (使)醒来〔來〕 xǐnglái: *He woke up with a start.* 他突然惊醒了. **2** 使认〔認〕识〔識〕到 shǐ rènshídào, 使惊〔驚〕觉〔覺〕 shǐ jīngjué: ~ *him up to the danger* 使他认识到危险性. **wak·ing** *adj* 醒着的 xǐngzhede: *his waking hours* 他清醒的时候.

wake² /weɪk/ *n* [C] (船的)尾波 wěibō, 航迹〔跡〕 hángjì. *in the* ~ *of* 在…之后〔後〕 zài … zhīhòu, 随〔隨〕着…而来〔來〕 suízhe … ér lái.

walk¹ /wɔ:k/ *n* [C] **1** 走 zǒu, 步行 bùxíng. **2** 走步的姿态〔態〕 zǒubùde zītài, 步法 bùfǎ: *a slow* ~ 慢步走. **3** 行走的道路 xíngzǒude dàolù, 人行道 rénxíngdào, 散步场〔場〕所 sànbù chǎngsuǒ: *my favourite* ~*s in the area* 在附近我所喜欢散步的地方. **4** ~ *of life* 行业〔業〕 hángyè, 职〔職〕业 zhíyè.

walk² /wɔ:k/ *vt/i* **1** 走 zǒu, 步行 bùxíng. **2** 使行走 shǐ xíngzǒu: *He* ~*ed his horse up the hill.* 他让马慢步上山. **3** 走过〔過〕 zǒuguò, 步行于〔於〕 bùxíng yú: *I have* ~*ed this district many times.* 我好几次走过这个地区. **4** ~ *away with sth* 轻〔輕〕易取胜〔勝〕 qīngyì qǔshèng. ~ *in* 走进〔進〕 zǒujìn. *walk into* 遇到 yùdào, 遭受 zāoshòu: ~ *into an ambush* 遭到伏击. ~ *off with sth* 取走 qǔzǒu, 偷走 tōuzǒu: *He has* ~*ed off with my umbrella.* 他拿走了我的伞. *walk out* 罢〔罷〕工 bàgōng. '~**-out** *n* [C] 罢工 bàgōng. ~ *out on sb* [非正式用语] (正当某人需要帮助时)遗弃〔棄〕某人 yíqì mǒurén. ~ *over sb* [非正式用语] 轻易胜过〔過〕某人 qīngyì shèngguò mǒurén. '~**-over** *n* [C] 轻易取得的胜利 qīngyì qǔdéde shènglì.

wall /wɔ:l/ *n* **1** 墙 qiáng, 壁 bì. *go up the* ~ [俚语] 大怒 dà nù. *go to the* ~ 失败 shībài; (尤指经济)破产〔產〕 pòchǎn. **2** [喻]似墙之物 sì qiáng zhī wù: *a* ~ *of fire* 一道火墙. *the abdominal* ~ 腹壁. □ *vt* **1** 用墙围〔圍〕住 yòng qiáng wéizhu: *a* ~*ed garden* 有围墙的花园. **2** ~ *sth up (off)* (用砖等)堵塞 dǔsāi: ~ *up a window* 堵塞窗口 '~**flower** (常栽在墙上的)墙花 qiáng huā. '~**paper** 糊壁纸 húbìzhǐ.

wal·let /'wɒlɪt/ *n* [C] 皮夹〔夾〕子 píjiāzi, 钱〔錢〕包 qiánbāo.

wal·low /'wɒləʊ/ *vi* **1** (在泥水中)打滚 dǎ gǔn. **2** [喻] 沉迷于〔於〕 chénmí yú: ~*ing in success* 沉醉于成功之中.

wal·nut /'wɔ:lnʌt/ *n* **1** [C] 胡桃 hútáo; 胡桃树〔樹〕 hútáoshù. **2** 胡桃木 hútáomù.

wal·rus /'wɔ:lrəs/ *n* [C] [*pl* ~es] 海象 hǎixiàng.

waltz /wɔ:ls/ *n* [C] 华〔華〕尔〔爾〕兹舞 huá'ěrzī wǔ; 圆舞曲 yuánwǔqǔ.

wand /wɒnd/ *n* [C] 魔杖 mózhàng.

wan·der /'wɒndə(r)/ *vt/i* **1** 漫游 mànyóu, 徘徊 páihuái. **2** 迷路 mílù, 离〔離〕开〔開〕正道 líkāi zhèngdào: *We* ~*ed (for) miles in the mist.* 我们在雾中走离正道有几英里. **3** 离题 lí tí: *His mind is* ~*ing.* 他心不在焉. ~**er** 漫游者 mànyóuzhě, 徘徊者 páihuáizhě; 迷路的人或动〔動〕物 mílùde rén huò dòngwù. ~**ings** *n pl* **(a)** 长〔長〕途旅行 chángtú lǚxíng. **(b)** 胡言乱〔亂〕语 húyán-luànyǔ.

wane /weɪn/ *vi* **1** (指月亮)变〔變〕小 biàn xiǎo, 亏〔虧〕 kuī. ⇨ wax². **2** 衰退 shuāituì, 减弱 jiǎnruò: *His strength is waning.* 他的精力正在衰退.

wangle /'wæŋgl/ *vt* [俚语]使用诡计 shǐyòng guǐjì: ~ *an extra week's holiday* 不正当地取得一星期的额外假期. □ *n* [C] 欺骗〔騙〕行为〔爲〕 qīpiàn xíngwéi, 不正当〔當〕手段 búzhèngdàng shǒuduàn.

want¹ /wɒnt/ *n* **1** [U] 缺少 quēshǎo, 缺乏 quēfá: *die from* ~ *of water* 因缺水而死. **2** [U] 需要 xūyào: *in* ~ *of repair* 需要修理. **3** [C] [常用 *pl*]需要的东〔東〕西 xūyàode dōngxi, 必需品 bìxūpǐn: *We can supply all your* ~*s.* 我们可以供给你所需要的一切.

want² /wɒnt/ *vt/i* **1** 需要 xūyào, 缺乏 quēfá: *That man* ~*s help.* 那个人需要帮助. **2** 想要 xiǎng yào, 希望 xīwàng: *She* ~*s to go home.* 她想要回家. **3** 通缉 tōngjī: *He is* ~*ed by the police.* 他被警察局通缉. **4** 应〔應〕该 yīnggāi; 需要 xūyào: *Your hair* ~*s cutting.* 你的头发该剪了. *be found* ~*ing* 发〔發〕现不充分 fāxiàn bù chōngfèn, 觉〔覺〕得不适〔適〕当〔當〕 juédé bú shìdàng, 查明不合格 cháming bù hégé. **5** ~ *for nothing* 具有所需要的一切 jùyǒu suǒ xūyàode yíqiè.

war /wɔ:(r)/ *n* [C,U] **1** 战〔戰〕争 zhànzhēng, 战争状〔狀〕态〔態〕 zhànzhēng zhuàngtài. *at* ~ 处于战争状态 chù yú zhànzhēng zhuàngtài. *have been in the* ~*s* [非正式用语]受过〔過〕创〔創〕伤〔傷〕 shòuguò chuāngshāng; 吃过苦头

〔頭〕chīguò kǔtóu. **2**〔喻〕冲〔衝〕突 chōngtū, 斗争 dòuzhēng, 竞〔競〕争 jìngzhēng: *the ~ against poverty* 同贫穷作斗争. *a ~ of nerves* 神经战. □ *vi* [-rr-] 战斗 zhàndòu, 作战 zuòzhàn. **~fare** /ˈwɔːfeə(r)/ 战争 zhànzhēng, 交战 jiāozhàn. **ˈ~head** 弹〔彈〕头 dàntóu. **~like** *adj* **(a)** 准〔準〕备〔備〕作战的 zhǔnbèi zuòzhàn de, 军〔軍〕事的 jūnshìde: *~like preparations* 军备. **(b)** 好战的 hàozhànde: *a ~like people* 好战的民族. **ˈ~path** 〔仅用于〕 ***on the ~path*** 准备作战或争吵 zhǔnbèi zuòzhàn huò zhēngchǎo. **ˈ~ship** 军舰〔艦〕 jūnjiàn. **ˈ~ time** 战时〔時〕zhànshí.

warble /ˈwɔːbl/ *vt/i* 用柔和的颤音唱歌 yòng róuhéde chànyīn chànggē. **war·bler** 〔动物〕鸣〔鳴〕禽 míngqín.

ward /wɔːd/ *n* **1** [C] (房屋中的)隔间〔間〕géjiān; (尤指)病房 bìngfáng. **2** [C] 行政区〔區〕划〔劃〕xíngzhèng qūhuà. **3** [C] 受监〔監〕护〔護〕者 shòu jiānhùzhě. □ *vt* ***~ sth off*** 避开〔開〕bìkāi, 防止 fángzhǐ: *~ off a blow (danger)* 避开打击(危险) bìkāi dǎjī.

war·den /ˈwɔːdn/ *n* [C] 管理员 guǎnlǐyuán; 监〔監〕护〔護〕人 jiānhùrén: *the ~ of a youth hostel* 青年招待所的管理人. ⇨traffic warden.

war·der /ˈwɔːdə(r)/ *n* [C] 狱吏 yùlì, 看守 kānshǒu. **ward·ress** 女看守 nǚ kānshǒu.

ward·robe /ˈwɔːdrəʊb/ *n* [C] **1** 衣柜〔櫃〕yīguì, 衣橱 yīchú. **2** (某人的)全部衣服 quánbù yīfu. **3** (剧场的)戏〔戲〕装〔裝〕xìzhuāng, 行头〔頭〕xíngtou.

ware /weə(r)/ *n* **1** 器皿 qìmǐn; 制〔製〕造品zhìzàopǐn: *ˈsilver~* 银器. **2** [*pl*] 商品 shāngpǐn, 货物 huòwù: *sell one's ~s* 出售货物. **~house** /ˈweəhaʊs/ *n* [C] 仓〔倉〕库〔庫〕cāngkù, 货栈〔棧〕huòzhàn. □ *vt* /-haʊz/ 把…存放在仓库中 bǎ … cúnfàng zài cāngkù zhōng.

warm[1] /wɔːm/ *adj* [-er, -est] **1** 温和的 wēnhéde, 温暖的 wēnnuǎnde. **2** 保暖的 bǎonuǎnde: *~ clothes* 保暖的衣服. **3** 暖色的 nuǎnsède: *Red and yellow are ~ colours.* 红和黄是暖色. **4** 热〔熱〕烈的 rèliède, 热诚的 rèchéngde: *a ~ welcome* 热烈的欢迎. **5** 同情的 tóngqíngde; 热情的 rèqíngde: *a ~ heart* 热情的心. **ˌ~-ˈblooded (a)** (指动物) 温血的 wēnxiěde. **(b)** (指人)热情的 rèqíngde. **ˌ~-ˈhearted** 热情的 rèqíngde, 富于〔於〕同情心的 fùyú tóngqíngxīn de. **~ly** *adv*

warm[2] /wɔːm/ *vt/i* (使)变〔變〕暖 biàn nuǎn: *~ one's hands by the fire* 烤火使手暖和. **~ up (a)** 使温暖 shǐ wēnnuǎn, 使热〔熱〕shǐ rè. **(b)**(运动员在比赛前) 做准〔準〕备〔備〕动〔動〕作 zuò zhǔnbèi dòngzuò, 热身 rèshēn. □ *n* 暖 nuǎn, 取暖 qǔ nuǎn.

warmth /wɔːmθ/ *n* [U] 温暖 wēnnuǎn; 热〔熱〕烈 rèliè, 亲〔親〕切 qīnqiè.

warn /wɔːn/ *vt* 警告 jǐnggào, 告诫 gàojiè. **~ing** *adj* 警告的 jǐnggàode, 告诫的 gàojiède. □ *n* [C] 警告 jǐnggào; 警报〔報〕jǐngbào: *He didn't listen to my ~ing.* 他不听我的告诫.

warp /wɔːp/ *vt/i* **1** (使)翘〔翹〕起 qiàoqǐ, (使)变〔變〕弯〔彎〕biàn wān: *Some wood ~s in hot weather.* 有些木材在炎热的天气中变得弯翘. **2**〔喻〕使有偏见 shǐ yǒu piānjiàn; 作不公正(判断) zuò bùgōngzhèng, 歪曲(事实等) wāiqū: *His judgement is ~ed by suffering.* 由于痛苦, 他的判断变得不公正了. □ *n* [C] **1** (木材等)弯曲 wānqū, 翘曲qiáoqū. **2** (布的)经〔經〕纱 jīngshā.

war·rant /ˈwɒrənt/ *n* [C] 授权〔權〕证〔證〕shòuquánzhèng; 委任状〔狀〕wěirènzhuàng. □ *vt* 〔常用 *pp*〕证明为〔爲〕正当〔當〕zhèngmíng wéi zhèngdāng, 辩明为有理 biànmíng wéi yǒulǐ: *His anger is not ~ed.* 他的发怒是没有道理的. **war·ranty** (书面) 担〔擔〕保 dānbǎo, 保证书〔書〕bǎozhèngshū.

war·ren /ˈwɒrən/ *n* [C] **1** 养〔養〕兔场〔場〕yǎngtùchǎng. **2**〔喻〕拥〔擁〕挤〔擠〕的地区〔區〕或房屋 yōngjǐde dìqū huò fángwū.

war·rior /ˈwɒrɪə(r)/ *n* [C] 〔书面语〕战〔戰〕士 zhànshì.

wart /wɔːt/ *n* [C] 疣 yóu, 瘊子 hóuzi.

wary /ˈweərɪ/ *adj* [-ier, -iest] 谨慎的 jǐnshènde, 小心的 xiǎoxīnde: *be ~ of strangers* 提防陌生人. **war·ily** *adv*

was /wəz, 强式: wɒz/ ⇨be[1].

wash[1] /wɒʃ/ *n* [C,U] **1** 洗 xǐ, 洗涤〔滌〕xǐdí: *give the car a ~*把汽车冲洗一下. **2** 洗涤的衣服等 xǐdíde yīfu děng. **3** (水的)流动〔動〕liúdòng; 冲〔衝〕击〔擊〕chōngjī: *the ~ of the waves* 波涛的冲击.

wash[2] /wɒʃ/ *vt/i* **1** 洗 xǐ, 洗涤〔滌〕xǐdí: *~ one's hands (clothes)* 洗手(衣服). ***wash one's hands of*** ⇨

hand¹(1). **2** (布料等)耐洗 nài xǐ: *Does this material ~ well?* 这布料耐洗吗? **3** [喻](论点等)经[經]得起考验[驗] jīngdeqǐ kǎoyàn: *That argument (excuse) will not ~.* 那个论据(辩解)站不住脚. **4** 流过[過] liúguò; 冲[衝]击[擊] chōngjī: *The sea ~es the base of the cliffs.* 海水冲击悬崖的底部. **5** 冲走 chōngzǒu, 卷[捲]去 juǎnqù: *He was ~ed overboard by a huge wave.* 他被一个巨浪从甲板上卷走. **~ *sth away*** 洗去 xǐqù, 洗掉 xǐdiào: *~ away stains* 洗掉污点. ***be ~ed away*** 被(海水等)冲走 bèi chōngzǒu. **~ *sth down* (a)** 冲洗 chōngxǐ: *~ down a car* 冲洗汽车. **(b)** (用水)吞下 tūnxià: *bread and cheese ~ed down with beer.* 用啤酒下面包和乳酪. **~ *sth out*** 洗去 xǐqù, 淘汰 táotài. ***~ed out* (a)** [喻] 筋疲力尽[盡] jīnpí-lìjìn. **(b)** (比赛因大雨而)被取消 bèi qǔxiāo. **~ *sth up*** (餐后) 洗餐具 xǐ cānjù. **the ,~ing-'up** *n* (碗碟等的)洗涤 xǐdí **'~-basin** 脸[臉]盆 liǎnpén. **'~-out** *n* [非正式用语]惨[慘]败cǎnbài. **'~room** [美语]盥洗室 guànxǐshì. **'~-tub** 洗衣盆 xǐyīpén.

wash·able /ˈwɒʃəbl/ *adj* 可洗的 kěxǐde.

washer /ˈwɒʃə(r)/ *n* [C] **1** 洗衣机[機] xǐyījī, 洗涤[滌]机 xǐdíjī. **2** [机械]垫[墊]圈 diànquān.

wash·ing /ˈwɒʃɪŋ/ *n* [U] **1** 洗 xǐ, 洗涤 [滌] xǐdí. **2** 洗的衣服 xǐdeyīfu. **'~-machine** 洗衣机 xǐyījī.

wasp /wɒsp/ *n* [C] [动物]黄蜂 huángfēng.

wast·age /ˈweɪstɪdʒ/ *n* [U] 消耗量 xiāohàoliàng, 损耗量 sǔnhàoliàng; 废[廢]物 fèiwù.

waste¹ /weɪst/ *adj* **1** (指土地)无[無]法利用的 wúfǎ lìyòngde, 荒芜[蕪]的 huāngwúde. ***lay sth ~*** ⇨ lay²(3). **2** 无用的 wúyòngde, 废弃[棄]的 fèiqìde: *,~ 'paper* 废纸. □ *n* **1** [U] 浪费 làngfèi, 消耗 xiāohào: *It's a ~ of time.* 那是浪费时间. ***go* (或 *run*) *to ~*** 浪费掉 làngfèidiào. **2** [U] 废物 fèiwù, 废料 fèiliào. **3** 荒地 huāngdì, 原野 yuányě: *the ~s of the Sahara* 撒哈拉沙漠 **,~-'paper-basket** 字纸篓[簍] zìzhǐlǒu. **'~-pipe** 排水管 páishuǐguǎn. **~ful** *adj* 浪费的 làngfèide: *~ful processes* 浪费的制作法. **~fully** *adv*

waste² /weɪst/ *vt/i* **1** 浪费 làngfèi, 未充分利用 wèi chōngfèn lìyòng: *~ one's time and money* 浪费时间和金钱. **2** 使(土地)荒芜[蕪] shǐ huāngwú. **3** (使)消耗 xiāohào; (使)消瘦 xiāoshòu: *~d by illness* 因生病而消瘦.

watch¹ /wɒtʃ/ *n* **1** [U] 观[觀]看 guānkàn; 看守 kānshǒu, 监[監]视 jiānshì; 注意 zhùyì. **2** (船上的)当[當]班(四或二小时) dāngbān. ***keep ~*** 值班 zhíbān, 守望 shǒuwàng. **'~-dog** 看门[門]狗 kānméngǒu. **'~man** 警卫[衛]员 jǐngwèiyuán; 守夜者 shǒuyèzhě. **~ful** *adj* (尤指)警惕的 jǐngtìde, 警戒的 jǐngjiède. **~word** /wɜːd/ 口令 kǒulìng, 口号[號] kǒuhào.

watch² /wɒtʃ/ *vt/i* 观[觀]看 guānkàn; 注视 zhùshì; 看守 kānshǒu: *W~ me carefully.* 仔细看看我. ***~ one's step*** [喻]谨慎小心 jǐnshèn-xiǎoxīn. **~ *out*** 密切注意 mìqiè zhùyì, 警戒 jǐngjiè. **~er** 看守人 kānshǒurén, 监[監]视者 jiānshìzhě.

watch³ /wɒtʃ/ *n* [C] 怀[懷]表[錶] huáibiǎo; 手表 shǒubiǎo.

water¹ /ˈwɔːtə(r)/ *n* **1** [U] 水 shuǐ. ***by ~*** 乘船 chéng chuán, 由水路 yóu shuǐlù. ***under ~*** 淹在水中的 yān zài shuǐzhōng de. ***be in* (或 *get into*) *hot ~*** 陷于[於]困境 xiànyú kùnjìng. ***hold ~*** (指理论)站得住脚 zhàndezhù jiǎo. ***keep one's head above ~*** 避免(尤指经济的)困难[難] bìmiǎn kùnnan; 不借债 bú jièzhài. ***throw cold ~ on*** 对[對]…泼[潑]冷水 duì … pō lěngshuǐ. ***tread water*** ⇨ tread *v* (3). **2** [U] 潮 cháo, 水位 shuǐwèi: *at high (low) ~* 在高(低)潮. **3** [*pl*] 领海 lǐnghǎi; 近海 jìnhǎi: *enemy ~s* 敌人控制的海域. **4** [常用 *pl*] 水体[體] shuǐtǐ, 大片的水 dàpiànde shuǐ: *the ~s of the Nile* 尼罗河的水. **'~-closet** (缩作 **WC**) 厕所 cèsuǒ. **'~-colour** [美语= **-color**] **(a)** [*pl*] 水彩颜料 shuǐcǎi yánliào. **(b)** 水彩画[畫] shuǐcǎihuà. **'~cress** [植物]水田芥 shuǐtiánjiè. **'~fall** 瀑布 pùbù. **'~front** (城市中的)滨[濱]水区[區] bīnshuǐqū. **'~-level** 水位 shuǐwèi. **'~logged** *adj* 浸满水的 jìn mǎn shuǐ de. **'~-main** 总[總]水管 zǒng shuǐguǎn. **'~mill** 水力磨坊 shuǐlì mòfáng. **'~-polo** 水球 shuǐqiú. **'~proof** *adj* 防水的 fángshuǐde: *~proof material* 防水材料. □ *n* [C] 雨衣 yǔyī. □ *vt* 使不透水 shǐ bú tòushuǐ. **'~shed (a)** 分水岭[嶺] fēnshuǐlǐng. **(b)** [喻]界限 jièxiàn. **'~ ski** *n* [C] 滑水橇 huáshuǐqiāo. *vi* 用滑水橇滑

行 yòng huáshuǐqiāo huáxíng. '~ **skiing** *n* [U]. '~**-supply** 供水 gōng shuǐ, 自来〔來〕水 zìláishuǐ. '~ **table** 地下水位 dìxià shuǐwèi. '~**tight** *adj* **(a)** 不漏水的 bú lòu shuǐ de: *~tight boots* 不漏水的靴. **(b)** 〔喻〕(指合约等) 严〔嚴〕密的 yánmìde, 无〔無〕懈可击〔擊〕的 wú xiè kě jī de. '~**way** 水路 shuǐlù, 航道 hángdào. '~**-wheel** 水轮〔輪〕 shuǐlún, 水车〔車〕 shuǐchē. '~**works** 供水系统 gōngshuǐ xìtǒng.

water² /'wɔ:tə(r)/ *vt/i* **1** 浇〔澆〕水 jiāoshuǐ, 灌溉 guàngài: *~ the lawn* 在草地上洒水. **2** 供水 gōng shuǐ, 加水 jiā shuǐ, 使饮水 shǐ yǐn shuǐ: *~ the horses* 饮马. **3** 流泪〔淚〕 liú lèi; 淌口水 tǎng kǒushuǐ: *The smoke made my eyes ~.* 烟熏得我流泪. **4 ~ sth down (a)** 搀〔攙〕水 chānshuǐ, 冲淡 chōngdàn: *This whisky has been ~ed (down).* 这威士忌酒已搀过水. **(b)** 〔喻〕减弱 jiǎn ruò, 打折扣 dǎ zhékòu: *The story was ~ed down.* 故事的生动性被冲淡了. '~**ing-can** 洒〔灑〕水壶 sǎshuǐhú.

wat·ery /'wɔ:tərɪ/ *adj* [-ier, -iest] **1** 水的 shuǐde; 象〔像〕水的 xiàng shuǐ de: *~ soup* 稀薄的汤. **2** (指颜色)淡的 dànde. **3** 流着水的 liúzhe shuǐ de, 水汪汪的 shuǐwāngwāngde.

watt /wɒt/ *n* [C] 瓦特(电功率单位) wǎtè.

wave /'weɪv/ *vt/i* **1** (使)波动〔動〕 bōdòng, (使)飘〔飄〕扬〔揚〕 piāoyáng: *branches waving in the wind* 迎风摆动的树枝. **2** 挥〔揮〕手(向…)示意 huī shǒu shìyì: *He ~d us away.* 他挥手叫我们走开. **~ sth aside** 〔喻〕对〔對〕…置之不理 duì …zhì zhī bùlǐ, 丢弃〔棄〕 diūqì: *My objections were ~d aside.* 我的反对意见被置之不理. **3** (使)成波浪形 chéng bōlàngxíng: *She's had her hair permanently ~d.* 她烫了头发. □ *n* [C] **1** 波浪 bōlàng, 波涛〔濤〕 bōtāo. **2** 波动 bōdòng; 挥动 huīdòng: *with a ~ of his hand* 他挥动一下手. **3** 鬈曲 quánqǔ, 波纹 bōwén: *the ~s in her hair* 她头发上的波纹. **4** 高涨〔漲〕 gāozhǎng, 高潮 gāocháo: *a ~ of hatred* 仇恨的高涨. ⇨ heatwave. **5** (热, 光, 声或电的) 波 bō. '~**-length** 波长〔長〕 bōcháng. **wavy** *adj* [-ier, -iest] 成波浪形的 chéng bōlàng xíng de, 有波纹的 yǒu bōwén de: *a wavy line* 波纹线. *wavy hair* 鬈发.

wa·ver /'weɪvə(r)/ *vi* **1** 摇摆〔擺〕 yáobǎi, 摇晃 yáohuàng: *~ing flames* 摇曳的火焰. **2** 动〔動〕摇 dòngyáo: *His courage ~ed.* 他的勇气动摇了. **3** 犹〔猶〕豫不决 yóuyù bùjué, 踌〔躊〕躇 chóuchú: *~ between two opinions* 在两种意见之间犹豫不决. **~er** 动摇的人 dòngyáode rén, 犹豫不决者 yóuyù bùjué zhě.

wax¹ /wæks/ *n* [U] 蜡〔蠟〕 là; 蜂蜡 (*'bees ~*) fēnglà. ⇨ sealing-wax. □ *vt* 给…上蜡 gěi…shànglà: *~ furniture* 在家具上打蜡.

wax² /wæks/ *vi* (指月亮)渐〔漸〕圆 jiàn yuán. ⇨ wane.

way /weɪ/ *n* **1** [C] 路 lù, 道路 dàolù: *a ~ across the fields* 穿过田野的路. ***pave the ~ for*** 〔喻〕为〔爲〕…作准〔準〕备〔備〕工作 wèi… zuò zhǔnbèi gōngzuò. **2** [C] 路线〔綫〕 lùxiàn, 路途 lùtú: *Which is the quickest ~ there?* 哪一条是去那里最快的路? ***go out of one's ~ (to do sth)*** 特地(去做某事) tèdì, 故意(去做某事) gùyì. ***lead the ~*** **(a)** 带〔帶〕路 dài lù, 引路 yǐn lù. **(b)** 示范〔範〕 shìfàn. ***pay one's ~*** **(a)** 不负债 bú fùzhài. **(b)** 支付生活费用 zhīfù shēnghuó fèiyòng. ***by ~ of*** 经〔經〕由 jīng yóu, 经过〔過〕 jīngguò: *He came by ~ of Dover.* 他经由多佛来此. **3 *on the (one's) ~*** 在(来的或去的)路上 zài lùshàng. ***by the ~*** 〔喻〕顺便说 shùnbiàn shuō, 附带说说 fùdài shuōshuō. **4** [C] 方法 fāngfǎ, 方式 fāngshì: *the right ~ to do something* 做某事的正确方法. ***have* (或 *get*) *one's own ~*** 随〔隨〕心所欲 suí xīn suǒ yù, 为所欲为 wéi suǒ yù wéi. ***go one's own ~*** 独〔獨〕断〔斷〕独行 dú duàn dú xíng. **5** 〔仅用 *sing*〕 距离〔離〕 jùlí: *It's a long ~ from here.* 离这儿很远. **6** [C] 方向 fāngxiàng: *He went the other ~.* 他向另一边走去. **7** [U] 开〔開〕动 kāidòng; 进〔進〕行 jìnxíng. ***be (get) under way*** 正在(开始)进行 zhèngzài jìngxíng. **8** [U] 前进〔進〕的自由 qiánjìnde zìyóu: *Don't stand in the (my) ~.* 不要挡住(我的)去路. ***out of harm's ~*** 在安全的地方 zài ānquánde dìfāng. ***give ~ (to sth, sb)*** ⇨ give¹(6). ***make ~ (for)*** (为…) 让〔讓〕路 rànglù. **9** [C] 习〔習〕惯 xíguàn; 作风〔風〕 zuòfēng: *Chinese ~ of life* 中国人的生活方式. *I don't like the ~ he looks at me.* 我不喜欢他那样地看我. ***mend one's ~s*** 改过 gǎiguò, 改进作风 gǎijìn zuòfēng.

10 [C] 方面 fāngmiàn, (某)点〔點〕diǎn: *He's a clever man in some ~s.* 在某些方面他是一个聪明人. **11** [C] 情形 qíngxíng, 状〔狀〕况 zhuàngkuàng, 程度 chéngdù: *She's in a bad ~.* 她的景况不佳. **by ~ of** 当〔當〕作 dāngzuò, 作为 zuòwéi: *say something by ~ of an introduction* 说几句话作为开场白. **,~-a'head** *adj* 〔非正式用语〕与〔與〕众〔衆〕不同的 yǔ zhòng bùtóng de. **,~-'out** *adj* 〔非正式用语〕= way-ahead: *,~-out 'clothes* 奇装异服.

way·lay /weɪˈleɪ/ *vt* [*pt, pp* -laid] 伏击〔擊〕fújī, 拦〔攔〕路抢〔搶〕劫 lán lù qiǎngjié; 拦住问〔問〕讯 lánzhù wènxùn.

way·ward /ˈweɪwəd/ *adj* 任性的 rènxìngde, 倔强的 juéjiàngde: *a ~ child* 任性的孩子.

w.c. = water-closet.

we /wiː/ *pron* (⇨ us) 〔主格〕我们〔們〕wǒmen: *Can ~ all come to visit you?* 我们可以都来看你吗?

weak /wiːk/ *adj* [-er, -est] **1** 虚弱的 xūruòde, 脆弱的 cuìruòde, 无〔無〕力的 wúlìde: *too ~ to walk* 太虚弱不能走路. *a ~ team* 弱队. *a ~ argument* 无力的论点. **2** 衰弱的 shuāiruòde, 懦弱的 nuòruòde: *a ~ heart* 衰弱的心脏. **3** 淡薄的 dànbóde, 多水份的 duō shuǐfèn de: *~ tea (beer)* 淡茶(啤酒). **4** 差的 chàde, 不行的 bùxíngde: *~ in spelling* 对拼写不行. **,~-'kneed** *adj* 〔喻〕易屈服的 yì qūfú de, 不坚〔堅〕定的 bù jiāndìngde. **~ling** 体〔體〕弱的人或动〔動〕物 tǐruòde rén huò dòngwù. **~ly** *adv* 虚弱地 xūruòde, 脆弱地 cuìruòde. □ *adj* (身体)虚弱的 xūruòde: *a ~ly child* 不健壮的孩子. **~ness** *n* **(a)** [U] 虚弱 xūruò, 脆弱 cuìruò. **(b)** [C] 弱点〔點〕ruòdiǎn, 缺点 quēdiǎn: *We all have our little ~nesses.* 我们都有些小缺点. **(c)** 嗜好 shìhào: *a ~ness for ice-cream* 特别喜欢吃冰淇淋.

weaken /ˈwiːkən/ *vt/i* (使)变〔變〕弱 biàn ruò.

wealth /welθ/ *n* [U] **1** 财富 cáifù, 财产〔產〕cáichǎn: *a man of ~* 富人. **2** 丰〔豐〕富 fēngfù, 大量 dàliàng: *a book with a ~ of illustrations* 有大量插图的书. **wealthy** *adj* [-ier, -iest] 富的 fùde, 丰富的 fēngfùde.

wean /wiːn/ *vt* **1** 使断〔斷〕奶 shǐ duànnǎi. **2 ~ from** 〔喻〕使戒掉 shǐ jièdiào.

weapon /ˈwepən/ *n* [C] 武器 wǔqì. **~ry** *n* [U] 武器(总称) wǔqì.

wear[1] /weə(r)/ *n* [U] **1** 穿 chuān; 戴 dài: *This coat looks the worse for ~.* 这件外衣显得很旧了. **2** 用坏〔壞〕yòng huài, 损耗 sǔnhào: *The carpet is showing signs of ~.* 这条地毯看来已经磨损了. **,~ and 'tear** 损耗 sǔnhào, 磨损 mósǔn. **3** 耐用性 nàiyòngxìng, 耐久性 nàijiǔxìng: *There's not much ~ left in these shoes.* 这双鞋穿不了多久了. **4** 衣服 yīfu, 服装〔裝〕fúzhuāng: *'under ~* 内衣. *'ladies' ~* 女式服装.

wear[2] /weə(r)/ *vt/i* [*pt* wore /wɔː(r)/; *pp* worn /wɔːn/] **1** 穿 chuān; 戴 dài: *He was ~ing heavy shoes.* 他穿着一双笨重的鞋. *He was ~ing a ring.* 他戴了一只戒指. **2** (脸上)带〔帶〕着 dàizhe, 显〔顯〕出 xiǎnchū: *~ a smile* 带着微笑. **3** (使)磨损 mósǔn, 用旧〔舊〕yòng jiù: *I have worn my socks into holes.* 我的袜子已穿破了. **4** 磨擦成 mócā chéng: *~ holes in a rug* 地毯上磨出洞来了. *The river wore the rocks smooth.* 河水把石头磨得很光滑. **5** 耐用 nàiyòng, 耐久 nàijiǔ: *Good leather will ~ for years.* 好的皮革可以穿用多年不坏. **~ away** **(a)** 磨损 mósǔn, 磨灭〔滅〕mómiè. **(b)** (时间)消逝 xiāoshì, 消磨(时间) xiāomó: *as the evening wore away* 当黄昏慢慢消失的时候. **~ down** 磨损 mósǔn, 损耗 sǔnhào: *These shoes are ~ing down.* 这双鞋快穿破了. **~ sb (sth) down** 使…筋疲力尽〔盡〕shǐ … jīnpí-lìjìn. **~ off** 消失 xiāoshī, 消逝 xiāoshì: *The pain soon ~s off.* 痛苦不久就消失了. **~ on** (时间)消逝 xiāoshì: *Evening wore on.* 黄昏过去了. **~ (sth) out** (把…)用坏〔壞〕yòng huài, (使)耗损 hàosǔn: *Cheap shoes soon ~ out.* 廉价的鞋不耐穿. **~ sb out** 使某人筋疲力尽 shǐ mǒurén jīnpí-lìjìn. **,worn-'out** *adj*: *a ,worn-out 'coat* 穿破了的外套.

weary /ˈwɪərɪ/ *adj* [-ier, -iest] **1** 疲倦的 píjuànde, 困乏的 kùnfáde. **2** 使人疲倦的 shǐ rén píjuàn de, 令人厌〔厭〕倦的 lìng rén yànjuàn de: *a ~ journey* 令人厌倦的旅程. □ *vt/i* (使)疲乏 pífá, (使)厌烦 yànfán. **wear·ily** /-əlɪ/ *adv* **weariness** *n* [U]

wea·sel /ˈwiːzl/ *n* [C] 〔动物〕黄鼬 huángyòu.

weather[1] /ˈweðə(r)/ *n* [C] 天气〔氣〕tiānqì. **under the ~** 〔非正式用语〕不舒服 bù shūfu. **make heavy ~ of sth** 发〔發〕现某事棘

手fāxiàn mǒushì jíshǒu. '~**-beaten** *adj* 饱经〔經〕风〔風〕霜的 bǎojīng fēngshuāng de. '**weather forecast** ⇨ forecast. '~**proof** *adj* 不受气候影响〔響〕的 bú shòu qìhòu yǐngxiǎng de. '~**-station** 气象站 qìxiàngzhàn. '~**-vane** = vane(1).

weather² /'weðə(r)/ *vt/i* **1** (平安)渡过〔過〕dùguò, 经〔經〕受住 jīngshòuzhù: ~ *a storm* 战胜暴风雨. ~ *a crisis* 渡过一次危机. **2** 曝露 pùlù, 晒〔曬〕干〔乾〕shài gān, 风〔風〕干 fēng gān: ~ *wood before use* 使用前风干木材. **3** (因风吹雨打而使)受侵蚀 shòu qīnshí: *rocks* ~*ed by wind and rain* 受风雨侵蚀的岩石.

weave /wi:v/ *vt/i* [*pt* wove /wəʊv/; *pp* woven /'wəʊvn/] **1** 织〔織〕(布) zhī. **2** 编制〔製〕biānzhì: ~ *flowers into a wreath* 用鲜花编成一个花圈. **3** [喻]编排 biānpái: ~ *a plot* 编排情节. **4** (使)迂回〔迴〕行进〔進〕yūhuí xíngjìn: ~ *through the traffic* 在行人和车辆中迂回穿行. □ *n* [C]编织的式样〔樣〕biānzhīde shìyàng: *a loose* (*tight*) ~ 松〔鬆〕编法. **weaver** 织布工 zhībùgōng, 编织者 biānzhīzhě.

web /web/ *n* [C] **1** (蜘蛛等的)网〔網〕wǎng **2** [常作喻]一套 yítào, 一堆 yìduī: *a* ~ *of lies* 一套谎话. **3** 蹼 pǔ. ,~-'**footed** *adj* 蹼足的 pǔzúde. ~**bed** /webd/ *adj* 有蹼的 yǒupǔde.

Wed. = Wednesday.

wed /wed/ *vt/i* [*pt* ~ded; *pp* ~ded 或罕 ~] **1** (使)结婚 jiéhūn. **2** (使)结合 jiéhé: *simplicity* ~*ded to beauty* 既朴素又美丽.

we'd /wi:d/ = *we had; we would.*

wed·ding /'wedɪŋ/ *n* [C] 婚礼〔禮〕hūnlǐ. '~**-ring** 结婚戒指 jiéhūn jièzhi.

wedge /wedʒ/ *n* [C] **1** 楔子 xiēzi. ***the thin end of the*** ~ [喻]可能有重大后〔後〕果的小事 kěnéngyǒu zhòngdà hòuguǒ de xiǎoshì. **2** 楔形物 xiēxíngwù: ~ *heels* (*on shoes*) (鞋的)楔形后跟. □ *vt* 把…楔住 bǎ...xiēzhù; 挤〔擠〕进〔進〕jǐjìn: ~ *a door open* 把敞开的门楔住. ~*d between two fat women on the bus* 在公共汽车上挤在两个胖女人之间

wed·lock /'wedlɒk/ *n* [U] 婚姻 hūnyīn.

Wed·nes·day /'wenzdɪ/ *n* 星期三 xīngqīsān.

wee /wi:/ *adj* 极〔極〕小的 jíxiǎode

weed /wi:d/ *n* [C] **1** 杂〔雜〕草 zácǎo. **2** [喻]瘦高个〔個〕子 shòu gāo gèzi. □ *vt/i* **1** 除草 chú cǎo: ~ *the garden* 除去花园内的杂草. **2** 除去 chúqù, 剔出 tīchū: ~ *out the lazy students* 淘汰不用功的学生. **weedy** *adj* [-ier, -iest] **(a)** 杂草丛〔叢〕生的 zácǎo cóngshēng de. **(b)** 瘦弱的 shòuruòde.

week /wi:k/ *n* [C] **1** 星期 xīngqī, 周 zhōu: *the working* ~ 工作周(通常为星期一到星期五) gōngzuòzhōu. ~ *in*, ~ *out* 接连〔連〕几〔幾〕个〔個〕星期 jiēlián jǐgè xīngqī. **2** 一星期的工作日 yìxīngqīde gōngzuòrì. '~**day** 星期天以外的任何一天 xīngqītiān yǐwài de rènhé yìtiān. ,~'**end** *n* [C] 周末 zhōumò. □ *vi* 度周末 dù zhōumò: *I'm* ~*ending in London.* 我正在伦敦度周末. ~**ly** *adj, adv* 每周一次(的) měizhōu yícì: ~*ly visits* 每周一次的访问. □ *n* [C] [*pl* -ies] 周刊 zhōukān.

weep /wi:p/ *vt/i* [*pt, pp* wept] 哭泣 kūqì. ~**ing** *adj* (指树)有垂枝的 yǒu chuízhī de.

weft /weft/ *n* [C] (布的)纬〔緯〕纱 wěishā.

weigh /weɪ/ *vt/i* **1** 称〔稱〕…的重量 chēng...de zhòngliàng: *He* ~*ed himself on the scales.* 他在体重器上量体重. ~ ***sth out*** 称出 chēngchū, 量出 liángchū. ~ ***in (with)*** (在讨论中)提出(论点等) tíchū. **2** 重(若干) zhòng: ~ *10 kilos* (*a ton*) 重十公斤(一吨). **3** (指机械等)能称…重量 néngchēng...zhòngliàng: *This machine will* ~ *up to 10 kilos.* 这台机器可称起十公斤. **4** 对〔對〕比 duìbǐ; 权〔權〕衡 quánhéng: ~ *one plan against another* 权衡一个计划与另一个计划的优劣. ~ ***sth (up)*** 估量 gūliàng, 考虑〔慮〕kǎolǜ: ~ (*up*) *the consequences* 考虑后果. **5** ~ ***anchor*** 起锚 qǐmáo, 起航 qǐháng. ~ ***sth down*** 压〔壓〕下去 yāxiàqù: *The fruit* ~*ed the branches down.* 果实压弯了树枝. ~ ***sb down*** 使疲倦 shǐ píjuàn; 使沮丧〔喪〕shǐ jǔsàng. ~ ***on sb (sth)*** 使担〔擔〕心 shǐ dānxīn, 使成负担 shǐ chéng fùdān.

weight /weɪt/ *n* **1** [U] 重 zhòng, 重量 zhòngliàng: *My* ~ *is 70 kilos.* 我的体重是七十公斤. ***over*** ~ 过〔過〕重 guòzhòng. ***under*** ~ 份量不足 fènliàng bùzú. ***pull one's weight*** ⇨ pull² (2). ***put on*** ~ 体〔體〕重增加 tǐzhòng zēngjiā. ***throw one's*** ~ ***about*** [非正式用语]仗势〔勢〕欺人 zhàngshì qīrén. **2** 负担〔擔〕fùdān: *The pillars have a great* ~ *to bear.* 这

些柱子支撑着很大压力. *That's a great ~ off my mind.* 那是我去掉的重大精神负担. 3 [U] 重要 zhòngyào, 重要性 zhòngyàoxìng; 影响〔響〕yǐngxiǎng, 影响力 yǐngxiǎnglì: *opinions that carry ~* 有重大影响的意见. 4 [C] 砝码〔碼〕fǎmǎ, 秤砣 chèngtuó: *an ounce (100 grammes) ~* 一英两重(一百克重)的砝码. 5 [C] 重物 zhòngwù: *a 'paper~* 镇纸. □ *vt* 1 加重量于〔於〕jiā zhòngliàng yú,加砝码于 jiā fǎmǎ yú: *~ a pendulum in a clock* 在钟内加一个摆. 2 [喻] 给予好处〔處〕gěiyú hǎochù: *Circumstances are ~ed in his favour.* 形势对他有利. 3 *~ sb down* 使某人负重担 shǐ mǒurén fù zhòngdàn: *~ed down with suitcases* 负着过多的箱子. **'~-lifting** 举〔舉〕重 jǔzhòng. **~less** *adj* 失重的 shīzhòngde. **weighty** *adj* [-ier, -iest] (a) 重的 zhòngde. (b) [喻] 重大的 zhòngdàde, 重要的 zhòngyàode.

weir /wɪə(r)/ *n* [C] 堰 yàn, 鱼梁〔樑〕yúliáng.

weird /wɪəd/ *adj* 1 超自然的 chāo zìrán de, 怪诞的 guàidànde: *~ shrieks* 怪诞的尖叫. 2 [非正式用语]离〔離〕奇的 líqíde, 古怪的 gǔguàide: *~ ideas* 古怪的念头. **~ly** *adv* **~ness** *n* [U]

wel·come /'welkəm/ *adj* 1 受欢〔歡〕迎的 shòu huānyíng de: *a ~ visitor (rest)* 受欢迎的来宾(休息). 2 *~ to* 欣然允许的 xīnrán yǔnxǔ de: *You are ~ to borrow my bicycle.* 欢迎你借用我的自行车. 3 [用作感叹词] 欢迎 huānyíng: *W~ home!* 欢迎你(们)回来! *W~ to England!* 欢迎到英国来! □ *n* [C] 欢迎 huānyíng, 接待 jiēdài: *They gave us a warm ~.* 他们给予我们热烈的欢迎. □ *vt* 欢迎 huānyíng: *~ a friend* 欢迎一位朋友. *~ a suggestion* 欢迎一项建议.

weld /weld/ *vt/i* 焊接 hànjiē. □ *n* [C] 焊接 hànjiē. **~er** 焊工 hàngōng.

wel·fare /'welfeə(r)/ *n* [U] 幸福 xìngfú, 福利 fúlì. **the ,W~ 'State** 福利国〔國〕家 fúlì guójiā.

well[1] /wel/ *n* [C] 1 井 jǐng. 2 楼〔樓〕梯井 lóutījǐng. □ *vi* 流出 liúchū. *~ over* 溢出 yìchū. *~ up (in)* 涌〔湧〕出 yǒngchū: *Tears ~ed up in her eyes.* 眼泪从她的眼眶中涌出.

well[2] /wel/ *adj* [better, best] 1 健康的 jiànkāngde: *feel (get) ~* 感到(恢复)健康. 2 满意的 mǎnyìde, 良好的 liánghǎode: *All's ~ that ends ~.* 凡是结果好的,一切都好. 3 恰当〔當〕的 qiàdàngde, 适〔適〕宜的 shìyíde: *It would be ~ to start early.* 早一点动身为好.

well[3] /wel/ [better, best] *adv* 1 好 hǎo, 对〔對〕duì, 令人满意地 lìng rén mǎnyì de: *The children behaved ~.* 孩子们很乖. *W~ done!* 干得好! *do ~* 做得好 zuòde hǎo; 取得进〔進〕步 qǔdé jìnbù. *do ~ out of* 从〔從〕…中得利cóng…zhōng délì. 2 赞扬〔揚〕地 zànyángde: *think (speak) ~ of a person* 认为(表扬)某人好. 3 幸运〔運〕地 xìngyùnde. *,~ 'off* 富裕的 fùyùde, 幸运的 xìngyùnde. *come off ~* 交好运 jiāo hǎoyùn, 幸运 xìngyùn. 4 有理由地 yǒu lǐyóu de; 恰当〔當〕地 qiàdàngde: *You may ~ be surprised.* 你很可能会大吃一惊的. 5 *may as ~* ⇨ may(3). *be just as ~* 还〔還〕是…好 háishì…hǎo, 没有坏〔壞〕处〔處〕méiyǒu huàichù: *It's just as ~ I didn't lend him the money.* 我不会后悔没有借钱给他. 6 彻〔徹〕底地 chèdǐde, 充分地 chōngfènde: *Examine the account ~ before you pay it.* 你在付款前要仔细核对帐目. 7 很 hěn, 颇 pō, 相当 xiāngdāng: *His name is ~ up in the list.* 他的名字列在相当前面. 8 *as ~ (as)* 也 yě, 又 yòu, 此外 cǐwài. 9 *pretty well* ⇨ pretty *adv*

well[4] /wel/ *int* (表示惊讶,快慰,同意等): *W~, ~!* 好啦,好啦! *W~, here we are at last!* 好了,我们终于到了! *W~, you may be right.* 唔,你可能是对的.

well- /wel-/ *prefix* (表示幸运,正当,彻底等). **,~-ad'vised** *adj* 明智的 míngzhìde; 谨慎的 jǐnshènde: *You'd be ~-advised to apologize.* 你表示道歉,那就是明智之举. **'~-being** 幸福 xìngfú; 健康 jiànkāng; 福利 fúlì: *the ~-being of the nation* 国家的福利. **,~-'bred** *adj* 教养〔養〕良好的 jiàoyǎng liánghǎo de. **,~-con'nected** *adj* 出身名门〔門〕的 chūshēn míngmén de. **,~-'earned** *adj* 应〔應〕得的 yīngdéde, 正当〔當〕的 zhèngdāngde: *a ,~-earned 'rest* 应得的休息. **,~-in'formed** *adj* (a) 见多识〔識〕广〔廣〕的 jiànduō shíguǎng de. (b) 消息灵〔靈〕通的 xiāoxī língtōng de. **,~-in'tentioned** *adj* 善意的 shànyìde, 好心的 hǎoxīnde. **,~-'known** *adj* 出名的 chūmíngde. **,~-'meaning** *adj* = well-intentioned. **,~-'read** *adj* 读〔讀〕书〔書〕多的 dúshū duō de, 博学〔學〕的 bóxuéde. **,~-'spoken** *adj* 善于〔於〕词令的 shànyú cílìng de; 言语谦恭的 yányǔ qiāngōng de. ,~-'**timed** *adj* 正合时〔時〕宜的 zhènghé shíyí de; 准〔準〕时的 zhǔnshíde. ,~-**to-'do** *adj* 富有的 fùyǒude. '~-**wisher** 表示良好祝愿的人 biǎoshì liánghǎo zhùyuàn de rén.

we'll /wi:l/ = *we shall; we will.*

wel·ling·ton /'welɪŋtən/ *n* [C] (亦作 ,~ '*boot*) 惠灵〔靈〕顿长〔長〕靴 huìlíngdùn chángxuē.

went /went/ *pt* of go¹.

wept /wept/ *pt, pp* of weep.

were /wɜ:(r)/ *pt* of be¹.

we're /wɪə(r)/ = *we are.*

were·wolf /'wɜ:wʊlf/ *n* [C] [*pl* -wolves /-wʊlvz/] [神话] 狼人 lángrén.

weren't /wɜ:nt/ = *were not.*

west /west/ *n* **1 the** ~ 西 xī, 西部 xībù, 西方 xīfāng. **2** [用作定语]西方的 xīfāngde, 来〔來〕自西方的 lái zì xīfāng de: *the* ~ *wind* 西风. □ *adv* 向西 xiàngxī. *go* ~ 上西天 shàng xītiān, 死 sǐ. **the W~ (a)** 西方(西欧和美国) xīfāng. **(b)** (国家的) 西部 xībù. ~**er·ly** *adj, adv* 西方的 xīfāngde, 从〔從〕西面来的 cóng xīmiàn lái de; 向西 xiàngxī. ~**ward** *adj* 向西的 xiàngxīde. ~**ward(s)** *adv*

west·ern /'westən/ *adj* 西的 xīde, 西方的 xīfāngde, 西部的 xībùde, 来自西方的 lái zì xīfāng de. □ *n* [C] (美国的)西部电〔電〕影或小说 xībù diànyǐng huò xiǎoshuō. ~**er** 西方人 xīfāngrén; (尤指) 美国西部人 Měiguó xībùrén. ~**ize** /-naɪz/ *vt* (使)西洋化 xīyánghuà, (使)欧化 Ōuhuà.

wet /wet/ *adj* [~ter, ~test] **1** 湿〔濕〕的 shīde, 潮的 cháode: ~ *clothes (roads)* 湿的衣服(马路). *Did you get* ~ 你淋湿了吗? ~ *through* 浑〔渾〕身湿透 húnshēn shītòu. **2** 下雨的 xiàyǔde, 多雨的 duōyǔde: ~ *weather* 雨天. □ *n* **1 the** ~ 雨 yǔ. **2** [U] 湿气〔氣〕 shīqì, 水分 shuǐfèn. □ *vt* [*pt, pp* ~ 或 ~ ted] [-tt-] 把…弄湿 bǎ...nòngshī. ,~ '**blanket** [非正式用语]扫〔掃〕兴〔興〕的人 sǎoxìngde rén.

we've /wi:v/ = *we have.*

whack /wæk/ *vt* 重击〔擊〕 zhòngjī, 用力打 yòng lì dǎ, 击败 jībài. □ *n* [C] **1** 重击(声) zhòngjī. **2** [俚语]一份 yífèn: *Have you all had a fair* ~? 你们都已得到公平的一份吗? ~**ed** *adj* [非正式用语] 筋疲力尽〔盡〕的 jīnpí-lìjìn de. ~**ing** *n* [C] 打击 dǎjī: *give a child a* ~*ing* 把小孩打一顿. □ *adj* [非正式用语]特大的 tèdàde, 极〔極〕大的 jídàde: *a* ~*ing lie* 弥天大谎.

whale /weɪl/ *n* [C] **1** [动物] 鲸 jīng. **2** *have a* ~ *of a (good) time* 玩得极〔極〕愉快 wánde jí yúkuài. □ *vi* 捕鲸 bǔ jīng. **whaler** 捕鲸者 bǔjīngzhě; 捕鲸船 bǔjīngchuán.

wharf /wɔ:f/ *n* [C] [*pl* ~s 或 wharves /wɔ:vz/] 码〔碼〕头〔頭〕 mǎtóu.

what /wɒt/ *adj* **1** (表示疑问) 什么〔麼〕 shénme; 哪些 nǎxiē: *W~ books have you read on this subject?* 你读过哪些关于这方面的书? *W~ time is it?* 现在是什么时候? **2** (表示感叹)多么 duōme, 何等 héděng: *W~ a good idea!* 多么好的主意! **3** 所有…的 suǒyǒu...de, 任何…的 rènhé ... de: *Give me* ~ *books you have.* 把你所有的书都给我. □ *pron* **1** 什么(东西) shénme: *Tell me* ~ *happened.* 告诉我发生了什么事. ~ *for* 为〔爲〕什么(目的) wèishénme: *W~ is this tool used for?* 这工具是作什么用的? *W~ did you do that for?* 你做那事为的什么? *what if* 如果…将〔將〕会〔會〕怎样〔樣〕 rúguǒ ... jiāng huì zěnyàng: *W~ if it rains tomorrow?* 如果明天下雨怎么办? *what about* (或 *of*) **(a)** 关〔關〕于〔於〕…有什么消息 guānyú... yǒu shénme xiāoxī. **(b)** ⇨ about²(3). **2** [关系代词] (= that which): *W~ he says is not important.* 他所说的话并不重要.

what·ever /wɒt'evə(r)/ *adj* **1** [加强 *what* 的语气]任何(种类,程度)的 rènhéde, 无〔無〕论〔論〕什么样〔樣〕 的 wúlùn shénmeyàng de: *W~ he says you believe it.* 无论他说些什么你总相信. **2** [强调否定]: *There can be no doubt* ~ *about it.* 关于那件事是毫无疑问的. □ *pron* **1** 不论什么 bùlùn shénme: *Keep calm,* ~ *happens.* 无论发生什么事, 都要保持冷静. **2** 任何事物 rènhé shìwù: *Do* ~ *you like.* 你爱干什么, 就干什么吧,随你的便.

wheat /wi:t/ *n* [U] 小麦〔麥〕 xiǎomài.

wheel /wi:l/ *n* [C] **1** 轮〔輪〕 lún, 车〔車〕轮 chēlún. *at the* ~ 控制 kòngzhì. *put one's shoulder to the* ~ 努力工作 nǔlì gōngzuò. **2** [C] 旋转〔轉〕运〔運〕动〔動〕 xuánzhuǎn yùndòng: *a right (left)* ~ 右(左)转弯. □ *vt/i* **1** 推(或拉)动车轮 (前进) tuīdòng chēlún: ~ *a bike up a hill* 推自行车上山. **2** (使) 旋转 xuánzhuǎn, (使) 转动 zhuàndòng. '~**barrow** 手推车

shǒutuīchē. '~**chair** 轮椅 lúnyǐ.

wheeze /wi:z/ *vt/i* **1** 喘气〔氣〕chuǎn qì, 喘息 chuǎnxī. **2** 喘息着说 chuǎnxīzhe shuō: *The man ~d out a few words.* 那人喘息着说出几个字. □ *n* [C] 喘息声〔聲〕chuǎnxīshēng. **wheezy** *adj* [-ier, -iest].

whelk /welk/ *n* [C] 〔动物〕峨螺 éluó.

when /wen/ *adv* **1** 在什么时〔時〕候 zài shénme shíhòu: *W~ can you come?* 你什么时候能来? *W~ did that happen?* 那事是在什么时候发生的? **2** 什么时候 shénme shíhòu: *Since ~ has he been missing?* 他是从什么时候不见了的? □ *adv* 在那时 zài nàshí, 当〔當〕时 dāngshí: *Sunday is the day ~ I am least busy.* 星期天是我最不忙的日子. □ *conj* **1** 当…时 dāng … shí, 在…时候 zài …shíhòu: *It was raining ~ we arrived.* 我们到达的时候正下着雨. **2** 虽〔雖〕然 suīrán, 可是 kěshì, 尽〔盡〕管 jìnguǎn: *He walks ~ he might take a taxi.* 他尽可坐出租汽车, 不过他还是步行了. **3** 既然 jìrán; 考虑〔慮〕到 kǎolǜdào: *How can I help ~ they won't listen?* 既然他们不听, 我怎么能帮助他们?

when·ever /wen'evə(r)/ *adv* **1** 不论〔論〕何时〔時〕búlùn héshí: *I'll discuss it ~ you like.* 我要同你讨论那件事, 随便你什么时候都行. **2** 每当〔當〕měi dāng, 每逢 měi féng: *I go ~ I can.* 我有空就去.

where /weə(r)/ *adv* 在哪里 zài nǎlǐ, 在何方 zài héfāng; 往哪里 wǎng nǎlǐ: *I wonder ~ he lives.* 我想知道他住在哪里. *W~ does he come from?* 他是哪里人? □ *adv* **1** [以 *place* 等为先行词]在那里 zài nàlǐ: *That's the place ~ the accident occurred.* 这就是出事地点. **2** 在…的地方 zài…de dìfang; 到…的地方 dào…de dìfang: *I found my books ~ I had left them.* 我在原处找到了我的书. *That's ~ you are mistaken.* 你就错在那一点上. ,~**a'bouts** *adv* 在哪里 zài nǎlǐ; 靠近哪里 kàojìn nǎlǐ: *W~ abouts did you find it?* 你是在哪儿找到它的? □ *n* ('~*abouts*) 所在 suǒzài, 下落 xiàluò: *Her ~abouts is (are) unknown.* 她的下落不明. ,~**'as** *conj* **(a)** 鉴〔鑒〕于〔於〕jiànyú. **(b)** 反之 fǎnzhī: *I like meat, ~as others hate it.* 我爱吃肉, 而有的人则厌恶它. ,~**'by** *adv* 凭〔憑〕什么〔麼〕píng shénme, 靠那个〔個〕kào nàge: *He devised a plan ~by he might escape.* 他想出一个可以逃走的办法.

wher·ever /,weər'evə(r)/ *adv* (究竟)在哪里 zài nǎlǐ, (究竟)到哪里 dào nǎlǐ; 无〔無〕论〔論〕在哪里 wúlùn zài nǎlǐ, 无论到哪里 wúlùn dào nǎlǐ: *Sit ~ you like.* 你随便坐吧.

where·withal /'weərwɪðɔ:l/ *n* **the ~** 〔非正式用语〕必要的钱〔錢〕财 bìyàode qiáncái.

whet /wet/ *vt* [-tt-] **1** 磨(刀, 斧等) mó. **2** [喻]刺激 cìjī, 促进〔進〕(食欲, 欲望等) cùjìn.

whether /'weðə(r)/ *conj* 是否 shìfǒu: *I don't know ~ to accept or refuse.* 我不知道接受好呢, 还是拒绝好.

which /wɪtʃ/ *adj* **1** 哪一个〔個〕nǎyīgè; 哪一些 nǎyīxiē: *W~ way shall we go?* 我们将走哪一条路? **2** (而)这〔這〕个 zhège; (而) 这些 zhèxiē: *Don't call at 1 o'clock, at ~ time I'm busy.* 不要在一点钟来看我, 此时我正忙着. □ *pron* 哪一个 nǎyīgè; 哪一些 nǎyīxiē: *W~ of the boys is the tallest?* 哪一个男孩子最高? □ *relative pron* (仅指物, 不指人) **1** 那一个 nàyīgè; 那一些 nàyīxiē: *the book ~ is lying on that table* 在那张桌上放着的书. **2** (指一个子句或句子): *He said he had lost the book, ~ was untrue.* 他说他遗失了那本书, 那是瞎说.

which·ever /wɪtʃ'evə(r)/ *adj, pron* **1** 随〔隨〕便哪一个 suíbiàn nǎyīge, …中的一个 … zhōng de yīge: *Take ~ you like best.* 你最喜欢哪一个, 就随便拿吧. **2** 不论哪一个 búlùn nǎyīgè: *W~ way you travel, it is expensive.* 你不论采取什么方式旅行, 都是很费钱的.

whiff /wɪf/ *n* [C] [与 *of* 连用]一阵〔陣〕(轻微的)气〔氣〕味 yīzhèn qìwèi: *the ~ of a cigar* 一股雪茄烟的气味.

while /waɪl/ *n* [C] 一会〔會〕儿〔兒〕yīhuìr, 一段时〔時〕间〔間〕yīduàn shíjiān: *Stay a ~.* 呆一会儿. **once in a ~** 偶尔〔爾〕ǒu'ěr, 有时 yǒushí. **worth (one's) ~** 值得(某人去花时间)的 zhídéde. □ *vt* **~ away** 消磨(时间) xiāomó. □ *conj* **1** 当〔當〕…的时候 dāng…de shíhòu: *He fell asleep ~ (he was) reading his book.* 他在看书的时候睡着了. **2** 但是 dànshì, 然而 rán'ér, 而 ér: *Jane is tall ~ Mary is short.* 珍妮是高个儿, 而玛丽是矮个儿. **3** 虽〔雖〕然 suīrán: *W~ I want to help I don't think I can.* 虽然我要去帮助, 但我觉得我帮不了.

whilst /waɪlst/ *conj* = while.

whim /wɪm/ *n* [C] 一时〔時〕的兴〔興〕致 yìshíde xìngzhì, 突然的念头〔頭〕 tūránde niàntou.

whim·per /'wɪmpə(r)/ *vt/i* **1** 呜〔嗚〕咽 wūyè, 啜泣 chuòqì. **2** 啜泣地说 chuòqìde shuō. □ *n* [C] 呜咽声〔聲〕 wūyèshēng, 啜泣声 chuòqìshēng.

whine /waɪn/ *n* [C]哀鸣〔鳴〕声〔聲〕 āimíngshēng, 呜呜声 wūwūshēng. □ *vt/i* **1** 发〔發〕哀鸣声 fā āimíngshēng, 作呜呜声 zuò wūwūshēng: *The dog was whining to come in.* 那狗呜呜地叫着要进来. **2** 抱怨 bàoyuàn, 哀诉 āisù: *a child that never stops whining* 不断哀叫的孩子.

whinny /'wɪnɪ/ *n* [C] [*pl* -ies] 马〔馬〕嘶 mǎsī. □ *vi* [*pt, pp* -ied] 马嘶声 mǎsīshēng.

whip[1] /wɪp/ *n* [C] **1** 鞭子 biānzi. **2** 政党〔黨〕的组织秘书〔書〕 zhèngdǎngde zǔzhī mìshū; 发〔發〕给本党议〔議〕员(要求参加辩论或选举)的命令 fāgěi běndǎng yìyuán de mìnglìng. **3** (用蛋奶搅打成的) 甜食 tiánshí.

whip[2] /wɪp/ *vt/i* [-pp-] **1** 鞭笞 biānchī, 抽打 chōudǎ: *~ a horse* 策马. *~ a child* 鞭打孩子. **2** 搅〔攪〕打(蛋, 奶油等) jiǎodǎ: *~ped cream* 搅打过的奶油. **3** [非正式用语]击〔擊〕败 jībài. **4** 突然移动〔動〕 tūrán yídòng: *He ~ped out a knife.* 他突然抽出一把刀. **~ping** 鞭打 biāndǎ. **'~ping-boy** 代人受罚者 dài rén shòufázhě.

whirl /wɜːl/ *vt/i* **1** (使) 旋转〔轉〕 xuánzhuǎn: *The wind ~ed the dead leaves about.* 风吹得落叶到处旋转. **2** 眩晕〔暈〕 xuànyūn: *His head ~ed.* 他的头发晕. □ *n* [仅用 *sing*] **1** 旋转 xuánzhuǎn: *a ~ of dust* 尘土的纷飞. **2** 繁忙 fánmáng: *the ~ of modern life* 现代生活的纷扰. **'~-pool** 旋涡〔渦〕 xuánwō. **'~wind** 旋风〔風〕 xuánfēng.

whirr /wɜː(r)/ *n* [仅用 *sing*] 呼呼声〔聲〕 hūhūshēng, 飕〔颼〕飕声 sōusōushēng: *the ~ of a helicopter's propellers* 直升飞机螺旋桨的呼呼声. □ *vi* [-rr-] 发〔發〕呼呼声 fā hūhūshēng, 作飕飕声 zuò sōusōushēng.

whisk /wɪsk/ *n* [C] **1** 打蛋器 dǎdànqì. **2** 掸〔撣〕dǎn, 拂 fú. □ *vt/i* **1** (轻快地)掸扫〔掃〕 dǎnsǎo, 挥〔揮〕动〔動〕 huīdòng: *~ the flies off* 赶走苍蝇. **2** 掸 dǎn, 拂 fú: *The cow ~ed her tail.* 母牛拂动它的尾巴. **3** 突然带〔帶〕走 tūrán dàizǒu: *They ~ed him off to prison.* 他们突然把他带进监牢. **4** =whip (2): *~ eggs* 打蛋.

whisker /'wɪskə(r)/ *n* **1** [*pl*] 连〔連〕鬓〔鬢〕胡〔鬍〕子 lián bìn húzi. **2** (动物的)须〔鬚〕xū.

whisky [美语 =**whiskey**] /'wɪskɪ/ *n* [C,U] [*pl* -ies] 威士忌酒 wēishìjì jiǔ.

whis·per /'wɪspə(r)/ *vt/i* **1** 耳语 ěryǔ, 低声〔聲〕说话 dīshēng shuōhuà. **2** 私下说话 sīxià shuōhuà, 秘密传〔傳〕闻〔聞〕 mìmì chuánwén: *It is ~ed that he is ill.* 人们私下传说他病了. **3** (树叶) 沙沙地响〔響〕shāshāde xiǎng; 风(風)发〔發〕飒〔颯〕飒声 fā sàsàshēng. □ *n* [C] **1** 低声 dīshēng; (树叶, 风等的)沙沙声 shāshāshēng: *answer in a ~* 低声回答. **2** 耳语 ěryǔ, 私语 sīyǔ; 传闻 chuánwén.

whistle /'wɪsl/ *n* [C] **1** 口哨声〔聲〕 kǒushàoshēng; 汽笛声 qìdíshēng, 哨子声 shàozishēng; (鸟)啭〔囀〕鸣〔鳴〕声 zhuànmíngshēng. **2** 哨子 shàozi, 汽笛 qìdí: *the referee's ~* 裁判员的哨子. □ *vt/i* **1** 吹口哨 chuī kǒushào, 吹哨子 chuī shàozi, 发〔發〕汽笛声 fā qìdíshēng: *whistling at the girls* 对姑娘们吹口哨. **2** (使)发啸〔嘯〕声行进〔進〕 fā xiàoshēng xíngjìn: *The bullets ~d past our ears.* 子弹飕飕地在我们耳边飞过.

white /waɪt/ *adj* [-r, -st] 白的 báide, 白色的 báisède, 雪白的 xuěbáide: *as ~ as a sheet* (脸色)苍白如纸. □ *n* **1** [U] 白色 báisè. **2** [C] 白种〔種〕人 báizhǒngrén. **3** [C,U] 蛋白 dànbái; 眼白 yǎnbái. **'~ ant** 白蚁〔蟻〕 báiyǐ. **,~-'collar** *adj* 白领阶〔階〕层〔層〕的 báilǐng jiēcéng de: *,~-collar 'workers* 白领工人. **,~ 'coffee** 牛奶咖啡 niúnǎi kāfēi. **,~ 'elephant** 无〔無〕用的财物 wúyòngde cáiwù. **,~ 'heat** 白热〔熱〕 báirè, 白炽〔熾〕 báichì. **the 'W~ House** (美国) 白宫 Báigōng. **,~ 'lie** (无恶意的)小谎言 xiǎo huǎngyán. **'~ man** 白种人 báizhǒngrén. **'~wash (a)** (刷白用的) 粉水 fěnshuǐ. **(b)** [喻]粉饰 fěnshì, 美化 měihuà. □ *vt* **(a)** 刷白灰水于〔於〕 shuā báihuīshuǐ yú. **(b)** [喻] 粉饰 fěnshì, 掩盖〔蓋〕(错误) yǎngài. **~ness** *n* [U]

whittle /'wɪtl/ *vt/i* 切 qiē, 削 xuē. **~ *sth down* (a)** 将〔將〕某物切小 jiāng mǒuwù qiē xiǎo. **(b)** [喻] (逐渐)削减 xuējiǎn: *Our membership is being slowly ~d down.* 我们的会员正在逐渐减少.

whiz /wɪz/ *vi* [-zz-], *n* [U] 作飕〔颼〕飕声〔聲〕 zuò sōusōushēng

飕飕声 sōusōushēng: *The bullets ~zed past.* 子弹飕飕地飞过.

whizz-kid /ˈwɪz kɪd/ *n* [C] [俚语]神童 shéntóng.

W.H.O. = World Health Organization 世界卫〔衛〕生组织〔織〕shìjiè wèishēng zǔzhī.

who /huː/ *pron* **1** 谁 shuí: *W~ is that man (are those men)?* 那人(那些人)是谁? **2**[可用 *whom* 代替]: *W~ did you give it to?* 你把那东西给谁了? □ *relative pron* **1**[有时可用 *that* 代替 *who*]: *This is the man ~ wanted to see you.* 这就是要见你的那个人. **2**[不可用 *that* 代替 *who*]: *My wife, ~ has been ill, hopes to see you soon.* 我的妻子希望能很快见到你,她病了.

who·ever /huːˈevə(r)/ *pron* 无〔無〕论〔論〕谁 wúlùn shuí, 任何人 rènhérén: *W~ says that is wrong.* 不管那话是谁说的,反正是错误的.

whole /həʊl/ *adj* **1** 完全的 wánquánde; 未受伤〔傷〕的 wèi shòushāng de; 未损坏〔壞〕的 wèi sǔnhuài de: *She swallowed the sweet ~.* 她把糖囫囵吞下去了. **2** 全部的 quánbùde, 整个〔個〕的 zhěnggèrde: *I waited for her a ~ half hour.* 我等了她整整半个小时. *the ~ truth* 全部真相. □ *n* [*sing*] 完整之物 wánzhěng zhī wù, 全部 quánbù, 整体〔體〕zhěngtǐ: *Four quarters make a ~.* 四个四分之一构成一个整体. **on the ~** 总〔總〕的来〔來〕看 zǒngde lái kàn. ˌ**~-ˈhearted(ly)** *adj, adv* 全心全意的(地) quánxīnquányì de. ˌ**~ ˈnumber** 整数〔數〕zhěngshù. **wholly** /ˈhəʊllɪ/ *adv* 完全地 wánquánde, 全部地 quánbùde: *I wholly agree with you.* 我完全同意你.

whole·sale /ˈhəʊlseɪl/ *n* [U] 批发〔發〕pīfā. □ *adj, adv* **1** 批发的 pīfāde; 大批地 dàpīde. **2**[喻]大规模的(地) dà guīmó de: *a ~ slaughter of animals* 大规模捕杀动物. **ˈwhole·saler** 批发商 pīfāshāng.

whole·some /ˈhəʊlsəm/ *adj* 健康的 jiànkāngde; 有益于〔於〕健康的 yǒuyì yú jiànkāng de: *~ food (exercise)* 有益于健康的食物(运动).

who'll /huːl/ = *who shall; who will.*

whom /huːm/ ⇨ who.

whoop /huːp/ *n* [C] **1** 大叫 dà jiào, 高呼 gāo hū: *~s of joy* 欢呼. **2** 哮喘声〔聲〕xiàochuǎnshēng. □ *vt/i* 大叫 dà jiào, 高呼 gāo hū: *~ with joy* 欢呼. **ˈ~ing-cough** (小儿)百日咳 bǎirìké.

who're /ˈhuːə(r)/ = *who are.*

whore /hɔː(r)/ *n* [C] 妓女 jìnǚ.

who's /huːz/ = *who is; who has.*

whose /huːz/ *possessive pron* (⇨ who, which) 谁的 shuíde: *W~ house is that?* 那是谁的房子?

why /waɪ/ *adv* 为〔為〕什么〔麼〕wèishénme: *W~ was he late?* 他为什么迟到? *This is ~ I left.* 这就是我为什么离开的原因.

wick /wɪk/ *n* [C,U] 烛〔燭〕芯 zhúxīn, 灯〔燈〕芯 dēngxīn.

wicked /ˈwɪkɪd/ *adj* **1** 坏〔壞〕的 huàide, 邪恶〔惡〕的 xié'ède. **2** 有恶意的 yǒu èyìde: *a ~ blow* 恶意的一击. **3** 恶作剧〔劇〕的 èzuòjùde, 淘气〔氣〕的 táoqìde: *a ~ look* 淘气地看一下. **~ly** *adv* **~ness** *n* [U]

wicker /ˈwɪkə(r)/ *adj* 柳条〔條〕编制〔製〕的 liǔtiáo biānzhì de: *a ~ chair* 柳条椅.

wicket /ˈwɪkɪt/ *n* [C] [板球]三柱门〔門〕sānzhùmén; 三柱门之间〔間〕的场〔場〕地 sānzhùmén zhī jiān de chǎngdì.

wide /waɪd/ *adj* [-r, -st] **1** 宽广〔廣〕的 kuānguǎngde, 宽阔〔闊〕的 kuānkuòde: *a ~ river* 宽阔的河流. *twelve metres ~* 十二米宽的. **2** [喻]广大的 guǎngdàde, 广泛的 guǎngfànde: *~ interests* 广泛的兴趣. *a ~ selection* 广泛的选择. **3** 充分张〔張〕开〔開〕的 chōngfèn zhāngkāi de: *Open your mouth ~.* 张大你的嘴. **4** 远〔遠〕离〔離〕目标〔標〕的 yuǎnlí mùbiāo de: *a ~ shot* 一次远未打中目标的射击. □ *adv* **1** 离目标很远地 lí mùbiāo hěnyuǎn de: *The arrow fell ~.* 箭落在离目标很远的地方. **2** 充分地 chōngfènde: *He was ~ awake* 他是完全清醒的. *~ open* 大开着. **3** 广大地 guǎngdàde: *travel far and ~* 到处旅行. ˌ**~-aˈwake** *adj* [喻]机〔機〕警的 jījǐngde. **ˈ~-spread** *adj* (尤指)流传〔傳〕广的 liúchuán guǎng de, 普及的 pǔjíde. **~ly** *adv* **(a)** 间〔間〕隔大地 jiàngé dà de: *~ly distributed* 散布很广的. **(b)** 大大地 dàdàde: *~ly different* 相差很远.

widen /ˈwaɪdn/ *vt/i* (使)变〔變〕宽 biàn kuān, 扩〔擴〕大 kuòdà.

widow /ˈwɪdəʊ/ *n* [C] 寡妇〔婦〕guǎfu. **~er** 鳏夫 guānfū.

width /wɪtθ/ *n* **1** [U] 宽阔〔闊〕kuānkuò. **2** [C] 宽度 kuāndù: *a ~ of 10 metres* 十米宽.

wield /wiːld/ *vt* 使用 shǐyòng: *~ an axe* 挥动斧头. *~ power* 行使权力.

wife /waɪf/ *n* [C] [*pl* wives /waɪvz/] 妻 qī; 已婚妇〔婦〕女 yǐhūn fùnǚ: *Mr Smith and his* ~ 史密斯夫妇. *my* ~ 我的妻子.

wig /wɪg/ *n* [C] 假发〔髮〕jiǎfà.

wiggle /'wɪgl/ *vt/i* (使)摆〔擺〕动〔動〕bǎidòng, 扭动 niǔdòng: *The baby was wiggling its toes.* 那婴儿正在扭动脚趾头. □ *n* [C] 摆动 bǎidòng, 扭动 niǔdòng.

wild /waɪld/ *adj* [-er, -est] **1** 野生的 yěshēngde: ~ *flowers* 野花. ~ *birds* 野鸟. **2** (指人)未开〔開〕化的 wèi kāihuà de, 野蛮〔蠻〕的 yěmánde. **3** (指土地等) 荒芜〔蕪〕的 huāngwúde, 无人居住的 wú rén jūzhù de. **4** 暴风〔風〕雨的 bàofēngyǔde: *a* ~ *night* 暴风雨之夜. **5** 激动〔動〕的 jīdòngde, 狂热〔熱〕的 kuángrède: ~ *laughter* 狂笑. ~ *with anger* 狂怒. ***drive sb*** ~ 激得某人狂怒 jīde mǒurén kuángnù. **6 *be* ~ *about*** 热衷于〔於〕rèzhōng yú. **7** 失去控制的 shīqù kòngzhì de, 放荡〔蕩〕的 fàngdàngde: *a* ~ *party* 放荡的聚会. ***run*** ~ 变得野蛮 biànde yěmán, 放肆起来〔來〕fàngsì qǐlái. **8** 轻〔輕〕率的 qīngshuàide, 鲁莽的 lǔmǎngde: *a* ~ *guess* 乱猜. □ *adv* 轻率地 qīngshuàide, 胡乱〔亂〕地 húluànde: *shoot* ~ 乱射. **'~cat (a)** [动物] 野猫 yěmāo. **(b)** [喻] 暴戾的人 bàolìde rén. □ *adj* 未经官方允许的 wèi jīng guānfāng yǔnxǔ de: *a* ,~*-cat 'strike* (未经工会批准)工人自发进行的罢工. **'~life** 野生动物 yěshēng dòngwù. **~ly** *adv* 狂暴地 kuángbàode, 激动地 jīdòngde; 轻率地 qīngshuàide: *rush about* ~*ly* 匆促地跑来跑去. *a* ~*ly exaggerated story* 大大夸张的传闻. **~ness** *n* [U]

wil·der·ness /'wɪldənɪs/ *n* [C] 荒地 huāngdì.

wile /waɪl/ *n* [C] [常用 *pl*] 诡计 guǐjì: *the* ~*s of the Devil* 恶魔的奸计.

wil·ful [美语亦作 **will-**] /'wɪlfl/ *adj* **1** 任性的 rènxìngde; 固执〔執〕的 gùzhíde. **2** 故意的 gùyìde, 存心的 cúnxīnde: ~ *murder* 蓄意的谋杀. **~ly** *adv*

will[1] /wɪl/ *aux verb* [在口语中常用 'll; 否定式 will not 或 **won't;** *pt* **would,** 在口语中常用 **'d;** 否定式 would not 或 **wouldn't**] **1** (表示将来)将〔將〕要 jiāngyào: *He* ~ (或 *He'll*) *be here tomorrow.* 他明天将在这儿. **2** (表示意愿,建议,应允) 愿〔願〕yuàn, 要 yào: *We won't do it again.* 我们不愿再干了. **3** (表示疑问, 请求): *W* ~ *you come in?* 请进来好吗? **4** (表示坚持,不可避免) 必须 bìxū, 应〔應〕yīng: *He* '~ *have his own way.* 他坚持一意孤行. *Accidents* '~ *happen.* 意外事件总会发生. **5** (表示习惯,经常性)惯于〔於〕guànyú, 总〔總〕是 zǒngshì: *He'll sit there hour after hour.* 他常常坐在那里好几个钟头. **6** (表示可能性) 可能 kěnéng, 该是 gāishì: *This* ~ *be the book you wanted.* 这可能是你所需要的书. **'would-be** *adj* 想要成为〔爲〕...的xiǎngyào chéngwéi...de: ,*would-be 'authors* 希望成为作家的人.

will[2] /wɪl/ *vt/i* [*pt, pp* ~ed] **1** 意欲 yìyù, 决心要 juéxīn yào: *We cannot achieve success merely by* ~*ing it.* 我们仅仅凭愿望是不能取得成功的. **2** 用意志力使 yòng yìzhìlì shǐ: *God* ~*s that man should be happy.* 上帝的意旨是要人快乐. **3** 遗赠(财产)与〔與〕(某人) yízèng yǔ

will[3] /wɪl/ *n* [U] **1** 意志 yìzhì. **2** [C] 自我控制 zìwǒ kòngzhì, 自制力 zìzhìlì: *He has a strong (weak)* ~. 他的意志坚强(薄弱). **3** [仅用 *sing*] 决心 juéxīn: *the* ~ *to live* 求生的决心. ***of one's own free*** ~ 自愿〔願〕地 zìyuànde. **4** [*sing*] 活力 huólì; 热〔熱〕情 rèqín *work with a* ~ 起劲地干 **5** [C] (亦作 *last W*~ *and Testament*) 遗嘱〔囑〕yízhǔ. **~ful** *ad* [美语] = wilful.

will·ing /'wɪlɪŋ/ *adj* **1** 愿〔願〕意的 yuànyìde, 乐〔樂〕意的 lèyìde: ~ *workers* 自愿的工作人员. **2** 心甘情愿的 xīngān-qíngyuàn de: ~ *obedience* 心甘情愿的服从. **~ly** *ad* **~ness** *n* [C]

wil·low /'wɪləʊ/ *n* [C] 柳 liǔ, 柳树〔樹〕liǔshù. [U] 柳木 liǔmù 柳条〔條〕liǔtiáo.

wilt /wɪlt/ *vt/i* **1** (使) 枯萎 kūwě **2** [喻](指人) (使) 颓丧〔喪〕tu sàng.

wily /'waɪlɪ/ *adj* [-ier, -iest] 狡猾的 jiǎohuáde.

win /wɪn/ *vt/i* [*pt, pp* won /wʌn [-nn-] **1** 赢得 yíngdé, 获〔獲〕胜〔勝〕huòshèng, 取得成功 qǔdé chénggōng: ~ *a race (a battle)* 赛跑(战斗)获胜. ~ ***hands down*** [非正式用语] 轻〔輕〕易地取得成功 qīngyìde qǔdé chénggōng. **2** 说服 shuōfú; 影响 yǐngxiǎng; 争取 zhēngqǔ: *We won him over to our view.* 我们说服他赞成我们的观点 □ *n* [C] 成功 chénggōng, 胜利 shènglì. **~ner** 获胜者 huòshèngzhě. **~ning** *adj* **(a)** 胜利的 shèn lìde, 获胜的 huòshèngde: *the ~-ning horse* 获胜的马. **(b)** 动〔動〕人的 dòngrénde, 迷人的 mírénde: *a ~ning smile* 动人的微笑. **~nings** *n pl* 赢得的钱〔錢〕yíngdéde qián.

wince /wɪns/ *vi* (因疼痛而)退缩 tuìsuō, 退避 tuìbì: *He ~d at the insult.* 他因受辱而退缩. ☐ *n* [C] 退缩 tuìsuō, 退避 tuìbì.

winch /wɪntʃ/ *n* [C] 绞车〔車〕jiǎochē. ☐ *vt* 用绞车拉动〔動〕yòng jiǎochē lādòng.

wind[1] /wɪnd/ *n* **1** [C,U] 风〔風〕fēng: *a north ~* 北风. ***put the ~ up sb*** [俚语]使某人害怕 shǐ mǒurén hàipà. **2** [U] 呼吸 hūxī, 喘息 chuǎnxī. **3** [U] 气〔氣〕味 qìwèi. ***get ~ of*** [喻]听〔聽〕到…的风声〔聲〕tīngdào … de fēngshēng. **4** [U] 肠〔腸〕气 chángqì, 屁 pì. ***break ~*** 放屁 fàng pì. **5** 管乐〔樂〕器 guǎnyuèqì: *the 'wood~* 木管乐器. **'~fall (a)** 被风吹落的果实〔實〕bèi fēng chuīluòde guǒshí. **(b)** [喻]意外的收获〔獲〕yìwàide shōuhuò, 横财 hénɡcái. **'~mill** 风车〔車〕fēngchē. **'~pipe** 气管 qìguǎn. **'~-screen** [美语 = **'~shield**] 挡〔擋〕风玻璃 dǎng fēng bōli. **'~swept** *adj* 当〔當〕风的 dāngfēngde; 被强风吹的 bèi qiángfēng chuī de. **windy** *adj* [-ier, -iest] 有风的 yǒngfēngde, 多风的 duōfēngde: *a ~y day* 多风的日子.

wind[2] /wɪnd/ *vt* [*pt, pp* ~ed] 使喘息 shǐ chuǎnxī: *~ed by the long climb* 由于长时间攀登而喘气.

wind[3] /waɪnd/ *vt/i* (*pt, pp* wound /waʊnd/) **1** (使)迂回〔迴〕前进〔進〕yūhuí qiánjìn: *The river ~s (its way) to the sea.* 那条河蜿蜒地流入大海. **2** 绕〔繞〕(线球) rào, 卷〔捲〕绕 juǎnrào. **3** 包 bāo, 抱 bào, 裹 guǒ: *~ a shawl round a baby* 用围巾裹着婴儿. **4** 上(钟, 表的)弦〔絃〕shàng xián. **5** ***be wound up (to)*** 使紧〔緊〕张〔張〕shǐ jǐnzhāng, 使兴〔興〕奋〔奮〕shǐ xìngfèn. ⇨ unwind. **6** 结束 jiéshù: *~ up a speech* 结束演讲. ☐ *n* [C] 一圈 yīquān, 一转〔轉〕yīzhuǎn.

win·dow /'wɪndəʊ/ *n* [C] 窗 chuāng, 窗口 chuāngkǒu. **'~-box** 窗槛〔檻〕花箱 chuāngkǎn huāxiāng. **'~-dressing** 橱窗布置 chúchuāng bùzhì. **'~-pane** 窗玻璃 chuāngbōli. **'~-sill** ⇨ sill.

windy /'wɪndɪ/ ⇨ wind[1].

wine /waɪn/ *n* [C,U] 葡萄酒 pútaojiǔ; 果子酒 guǒzijiǔ. ☐ *vt* [常作] ***~ and dine sb*** 以吃喝款待某人 yǐ chīhē kuǎndài mǒurén.

wing /wɪŋ/ *n* [C] **1** 翼 yì, 翅膀 chìbǎng. ***take sb under one's ~*** 庇护〔護〕某人 bìhù mǒurén. **2** 侧厅〔廳〕cètīng, 边〔邊〕房 biānfáng: *add a new ~ to a hospital* 给一所医院新建一座侧楼. **3** (军队的)侧翼 cèyì. **4** (政党中的)派别 pàibié: *the left (right) ~* (某政党的)左(右)翼. **5** [*pl*] (舞台的)两侧 liǎng cè. **6** ***on the ~*** 在飞〔飛〕行中 zài fēixíng zhōng. ***take ~*** 起飞 qǐfēi. **7** (亦作 **winger**) [足球, 曲棍球]翼 yì. ☐ *vt/i* **1** 飞行 fēixíng: *The planes ~ed over the Alps.* 飞机飞越阿尔卑斯山. **2** 打伤〔傷〕(鸟)翼 dǎshāng yì. **3** [非正式用语]打伤(人)臂 dǎshāng bì. **'~-span (-spread)** 翼展 yìzhǎn.

wink /wɪŋk/ *vt/i* **1** ~ **(at)** 眨眼 zhǎyǎn, 使眼色 shǐ yǎnsè: *She ~ed at me.* 她向我使眼色. **2** (星光等)闪〔閃〕耀 shǎnyào, 闪烁〔爍〕shǎnshuò. ☐ *n* [C] **1** 眨眼 zhǎyǎn, 眨眼示意 zhǎyǎn shìyì. **2** 霎时〔時〕shàshí, 瞬息 shùnxī: *I didn't sleep a ~.* 我没有合过眼. ***have forty ~s*** 小睡 xiǎo shuì, 打盹 dǎdǔn.

winkle /'wɪŋkl/ *n* [C] (食用)海螺 hǎiluó. ☐ *vt* [与 *out* 连用]挑出 tiāochū, 拔出 báchū.

win·ner, win·ning ⇨ win.

win·ter /'wɪntə(r)/ *n* [C] 冬季 dōngjì. ☐ *vi* 过〔過〕冬 guò dōng, 越冬 yuè dōng: *~ in the south* 在南方过冬. **win·tery, win·try** /'wɪntrɪ/ *adj*

wipe[1] /waɪp/ *n* [C] 擦 cā, 揩 kāi, 抹 mǒ.

wipe[2] /waɪp/ *vt/i* 擦 cā, 揩 kāi, 抹 mǒ. ***~ sth away*** 擦去 cāqù. ***~ sth off*** **(a)** 擦掉 cādiào. **(b)** 清除 qīngchú, 除去 chúqù: *~ off a debt* 了结债务. ***~ sb out*** [俚语]杀〔殺〕掉某人 shādiào mǒurén. ***~ sth out*** **(a)** 擦洗…的内部 cāxǐ…de nèibù: *~ out a jug* 擦洗瓶子. **(b)** 消灭〔滅〕xiāomiè, 毁灭 huǐmiè: *war ~d out the whole village* 战争毁灭了整个村庄. ***~ sth up*** **(a)** 擦净(餐具等) cājìng. **(b)** 擦干〔乾〕(水污等) cāgān.

wire /'waɪə(r)/ *n* **1** [C, U] 金属〔屬〕线〔綫〕jīnshǔxiàn: *'telephone ~(s)* 电话线. **2** [C] [美语]—telegram: *send off a ~* 发电报. ☐ *vt/i* **1** 用金属线捆绑 yòng jīnshǔxiàn kǔnbǎng. **2** (在建筑物中)安装〔裝〕电〔電〕线 ānzhuāng diànxiàn 3［美语］= telegraph. **wir·ing**（尤指）电线系统 diànxiàn xìtǒng. **wiry** *adj* [-ier, -iest] **(a)** 似金属丝的 sì jīnshǔsī de. **(b)** 瘦长〔長〕而结实〔實〕的（人） shòucháng ér jiēshi de rén.

wire·less /ˈwaɪəlɪs/ *adj, n* [C]［旧用法］= radio.

wis·dom /ˈwɪzdəm/ *n* [U] **1** 智慧 zhìhuì, 才智 cáizhì. **2** 明智的思想, 言论〔論〕等 míngzhìde sīxiǎng, yánlùn děng. **ˈ~-tooth** 智牙 zhìyá.

wise /waɪz/ *adj* [-r, -st] 有知识〔識〕的 yǒu zhīshìde, 聪〔聰〕明的 cōngmíngde, 明智的 míngzhìde: *~ men* 聪明人. *~ acts* 明智的行为. ***be none the ~r***（和以前一样）不明白 bù míngbai: *After the lecture he was none the ~r.* 他听课后还是不明白. **~ly** *adv*

wish /wɪʃ/ *vt/i* **1** 想要 xiǎng yào, 希望 xīwàng, 但愿〔願〕 dànyuàn: *I ~ I knew what was happening.* 但愿我知道正在发生什么事. **2** 祝 zhù, 祝愿 zhùyuàn: *~ her a pleasant journey.* 祝愿她旅途愉快. **3** 问〔問〕候 wènhòu, 向…致意 xiàng …zhìyì: *~ him good morning* 向他道早安. **4** *~ for*（热切）盼望 pànwàng. □ *n* **1** [C, U] 欲望 yùwàng, 愿望 yuànwàng: *He ignored his father's ~es.* 他不顾他父亲的心愿. **2** [C] 所盼望的事物 suǒ pànwàng de shìwù: *She got her ~.* 她如愿以偿了. **~ful** /-fl/ 有希望的 yǒu xīwàng de, 愿望的 yuànwàngde. ***~ful thinking*** 如意算盘〔盤〕 rúyì suànpán. **~fully** *adv*

wisp /wɪsp/ *n* [C] 小捆 xiǎokǔn, 小把 xiǎobǎ, 小束 xiǎoshù: *a ~ of hair* 一绺头发. *a ~ of smoke* 一缕青烟. **wispy** *adj* [-ier, -iest] 小捆似的 xiǎokǔn sìde; 纤〔纖〕细的 xiānxìde.

wit /wɪt/ *n* **1** [C] 智力 zhìlì, 才智 cáizhì, 理智 lǐzhì: *He hadn't the ~s to realize what to do.* 他没有应付事件的才能. ***at one's ~'s end*** 不知所措 bùzhī suǒ cuò. ***have*** (或 ***keep***) ***one's ~s about one*** 保持机〔機〕警 bǎochí jījǐng. **2** [U] 机智而幽默的措辞〔辭〕 jīzhì ér yōumò de cuòcí: *writings full of ~* 情趣横溢的作品. **3** [C] 富于〔於〕机智的人 fùyú jīzhì de rén, 才子 cáizǐ. **~tily** *adv* 机智地 jīzhìde; 幽默地 yōumòde. **~ticism** /ˈwɪtɪsɪzəm/ *n* [C] 妙语 miàoyǔ, 打趣话 dǎqùhuà. **~ty** *adj* [-ier -iest] 幽默的 yōumòde, 诙谐的 huīxiéde.

witch /wɪtʃ/ *n* [C] 女巫 nǚwū, 巫婆 wūpó. **ˈ~craft** 巫术〔術〕 wūshù, 魔法 mófǎ. **ˈ~-doctor** 巫医〔醫〕 wūyī. **ˈ~-hunt**［非正式用法］政治迫害 zhèngzhì pòhài.

with /wɪð/ *prep* **1** 具有 jùyǒu, 带〔帶〕有 dàiyǒu: *a coat ~ two pockets* 有两个口袋的外衣. *a girl ~ blue eyes* 蓝眼睛的女孩子. **2**（表示方法或工具）用 yòng, 以 yǐ: *write ~ a pen* 用钢笔写字. *see it ~ your own eyes* 用你自己的眼睛看它. **3** 和…(一起) hé…, 跟… gēn…: *live ~ one's parents* 和父母在一起生活. *in ~* 与〔與〕…友好 yǔ… yǒuhǎo: *She's in ~ the wrong people.* 她和坏人在一起. **4**（表示反对, 敌对）对〔對〕… duì…, 与〔與〕… yǔ …: *fight (argue) ~ them* 和他们打架(辩论). **5** 因为〔爲〕 yīnwéi, 由于〔於〕 yóuyú: *trembling ~ fear (cold)* 因恐惧(寒冷)而发抖. **6**（表示态度）: *fight ~ courage* 英勇地战斗. **7**（表示同方向或同时间）随〔隨〕着 suízhe: *A tree's shadow moves ~ the sun.* 树影随着太阳移动. **8**（表示照顾, 管理, 保有）: *Leave the child ~ its aunt.* 把孩子留给他的姑妈照顾. **9** 对于 duìyú, 关〔關〕于 guānyú: *be patient ~ them* 对他们忍耐. *sympathize ~ her* 同情她. **10**（表示分离）: *He has broken ~ his best friend.* 他已和他最好的朋友绝交了. **11** 赞同 zàntóng, 拥〔擁〕护〔護〕 yōnghù; 有利于 yǒulìyú: *vote ~ the majority* 投票支持大多数. **ˈ~ it**［俚语］时〔時〕髦的 shímáode, 流行的 liúxíngde: *ˈ~-it clothes* 时装. **12** 尽〔儘〕管 jìnguǎn, 虽〔雖〕有 suīyǒu: *W~ all her faults he still liked her.* 尽管她有许多缺点, 他仍然喜欢她.

with·draw /wɪðˈdrɔː/ *vt/i* [*pt* -drew /-ˈdruː/; *pp* -drawn /-ˈdrɔːn/] **1** 收回 shōuhuí, 取回 qǔhuí; 拿开〔開〕 nákāi: *~ money from the bank* 从银行取款. *~ one's labour* 罢工. **2** 撤回 chèhuí, 撤销 chèxiāo: *He refused to ~ (the remark).* 他拒绝撤回(他的话). **3**（使）撤退 chètuì, （使）退出 tuìchū: *~ troops from the battle* 从战斗中撤退军队. **~al** *n* [C,U] 收回 shōuhuí, 撤销 chèxiāo, 撤退 chètuì. **with·drawn** *adj* 孤独〔獨〕的 gūdúde; 向内性的 xiàngnèixìngde.

wither /ˈwɪðə(r)/ *vt/i* **1**（使）枯萎 kūwěi, （使）雕〔凋〕谢 diāoxiè: *The hot summer ~ed (up) the grass.* 盛夏炎热使草枯萎了. **2** 使（人）感觉〔覺〕羞惭〔慚〕或迷惑 shǐ gǎnjué xiūcán huò míhuò: *a ~ing look*

人感觉难堪的一瞥.

with·hold /wɪð'həʊld/ *vt* [*pt, pp* -held /-'held/] 制止 zhìzhǐ, 扣留 kòuliú, 不给 bùgěi: *I shall ~ my consent.* 我将不予同意.

with·in /wɪð'iːn/ *prep* 在…里面 zài…lǐmiàn, 不超出 bù chāochū: *~ call* (*reach*) 在附近.

with·out /wɪð'aʊt/ *prep* **1** 没有 méiyǒu: *You can't buy things ~ money.* 你没有钱就买不了东西. *~ doubt* 无〔無〕疑 wúyí, 一定 yīdìng. *~ fail* 一定 yīdìng. *do without* ⇨ do¹(9). **2** 不 bù: *He can't speak German ~ making mistakes.* 他每说德语必有错误. *go ~ saying* 不消说 bùxiāoshuō.

with·stand /wɪð'stænd/ *vt* [*pt, pp* -stood /-'stʊd/] 抵抗 dǐkàng, 反抗 fǎnkàng: *~ a siege* 抵抗围攻. *~ hard wear* 耐穿.

wit·ness /'wɪtnɪs/ *n* [C] **1** (常作 *'eye-~*) 目击〔擊〕者 mùjīzhě, 见证〔證〕人 jiànzhèngrén. *bear ~ to sth* 证明某事 zhèngmíng mǒushì: *acts that bear ~ to her courage* 证明她有勇气的行为. **2** [法律]证人 zhèngrén; 连〔連〕署人 liánshǔrén. **3** 证明 zhèngmíng, 证据〔據〕 zhèngjù, 见证 jiànzhèng: *My clothes are a ~ to my poverty.* 我的衣服是我贫穷的证明. □ *vt/i* **1** 亲〔親〕见 qīnjiàn, 目击 mùjī: *~ an accident* 亲眼看见一次意外事件. **2** (在法庭)作证 zuòzhèng. **3** 作证人 zuò zhèngrén; 作连署人 zuò liánshǔrén: *~ a signature* 在签字旁连署. *'~-box* 证人席 zhèngrénxí.

wit·ti·cism /'wɪtɪsɪzəm/ ⇨ wit.

wives /waɪvz/ *n pl* of wife.

wiz·ard /'wɪzəd/ *n* [C] **1** 男巫 nánwū, 术〔術〕士 shùshì. **2** 奇才 qícái: *a financial ~* 生财有道的人.

wiz·ened /'wɪznd/ *adj* 枯萎的 kūwěide, 干〔乾〕瘪〔癟〕的 gānbiěde: *a ~ tree* (*apple*) 干枯的树(苹果).

wobble /'wɒbl/ *vt/i* (使)摇摆〔擺〕 yáobǎi, (使)晃动〔動〕 huàngdòng: *The old table ~d as he touched it.* 当他碰那张旧桌子时, 它晃动了.

wob·bly /'wɒbəlɪ/ *adj* [-ier, -iest] 摇摆的 yáobǎide, 不稳〔穩〕的 bùwěnde: *a wobbly chair* 摇晃不稳的椅子.

woe /wəʊ/ *n* 〔诗〕 **1** [U] 悲哀 bēi'āi, 悲痛 bēitòng: *a tale of ~* 悲惨的故事. **2** [*pl*] 灾〔災〕难〔難〕 zāinàn, 不幸 búxìng: *poverty and other ~s.* 贫穷和其他灾难. *~ful adj*

woke, woken *pt, pp* of wake¹.

wolf /wʊlf/ *n* [C] [*pl* wolves /wʊlvz/] 狼 láng. *cry ~* 发〔發〕假警报〔報〕 fā jiǎ jǐngbào. □ *vt* 狼吞虎咽〔嚥〕 lángtūn-hǔyàn: *~ down one's dinner* 狼吞虎咽地吃饭.

woman /'wʊmən/ *n* [*pl* women /'wɪmɪn/] **1** 成年女子 chéngnián nǚzǐ, 妇〔婦〕女 fùnǚ. **2** [用作定语]: *a ~ driver* (*doctor*) 女司机(医生). **3** 女性 nǚxìng, 女人 nǚrén: *W~ is as capable as man.* 女人和男人一样能干. **4** 女性的感情 nǚxìngde gǎnqíng, 女人气〔氣〕质〔質〕 nǚrén qìzhì: *There is something of the ~ in him.* 他有些女人气. **5** [C] 有女人气质的男子 yǒu nǚrén qìzhì de nánzǐ. *'~hood* /-hʊd/ **(a)** 女子(的总称) nǚzǐ, 妇女界 fùnǚjiè. **(b)** 女子的状〔狀〕态〔態〕和特性 nǚzǐde zhuàngtài hé tèxìng: *reach ~hood* 长成为成年女子. *,~'kind* 女子(的总称) nǚzǐ. **women·folk** /'wɪmɪnfəʊk/ *n pl* (尤指一个家庭的)妇女们〔們〕 fùnǚmen.

womb /wuːm/ *n* [C] 子宫 zǐgōng.

won /wʌn/ *pt, pp* of win.

won·der /'wʌndə(r)/ *n* **1** [U] 惊〔驚〕奇 jīngqí, 惊叹〔嘆〕 jīngtàn. *no* (或 *little, small*) *wonder* 不足为〔為〕奇 bù zú wéi qí; 难〔難〕怪 nánguài. **2** [C] 奇迹〔蹟〕 qíjī, 奇事 qíshì, 奇观〔觀〕 qíguān: *Space travel is the ~ of our times.* 太空旅行是我们时代的奇观. *work ~s* 创〔創〕造奇迹 chuàngzào qíjī, 取得惊人的成就 qǔdé jīngrénde chéngjiù. □ *vt/i* **1** (感到)惊奇 jīngqí, 惊叹 jīngtàn. **2** (感到)奇怪 qíguài; 想知道 xiǎng zhīdào: *I ~ who he is.* 我想知道他是谁. *~ful adj* 惊人的 jīngrénde, 奇妙的 qímiàode: *~ful weather* 非常好的天气. *~fully adv*

won't /wəʊnt/ = will not.

woo /wuː/ *vt* [*pt, pp* ~ed] 追求 zhuīqiú, 求取 qiúqǔ: *~ voters* 争取投票人.

wood /wʊd/ *n* **1** [U] 木头〔頭〕 mùtou, 木材 mùcái: *Tables are usually made of ~.* 桌子通常是用木头做的. *Teak is a hard ~.* 柚木是硬木材. **2** [C] [常用 *pl*] 树〔樹〕林 shùlín. *out of the ~s* 〔喻〕脱离〔離〕困境 tuōlí kùnjìng. *be unable to see the ~ for the trees* 〔喻〕只见树木不见森林 zhǐjiàn shùmù bújiàn sēnlín. *'~land* 森林地区〔區〕 sēnlín dìqū. *'~pecker* 啄木鸟〔鳥〕 zhuómùniǎo.

'~wind 木管乐[樂]器 mùguǎn yuèqì. '~work (a) 木制[製]品 mùzhìpǐn. (b) 木工活 mùgōnghuó. '~worm 钻[鑽]木虫[蟲] zuānmùchóng. ~ed adj 多树木的 duō shùmù de: *a thickly ~ed country* 树木茂密的乡村. ~en /'wʊdn/ adj (a) 木制的 mùzhìde. (b) 呆板的 áibǎnde, 笨拙的 bènzhuōde: *a ~en smile* 呆板的笑容. **woody** adj [-ier, -iest] (a) 多树木的 duō shùmù de: *a ~y hillside* 多树木的山坡. (b) 木质[質]的 mùzhìde; 似木头的 sì mùtou de.

woof /wʊf/ n [C] (狗的)低吠声[聲] dī fèi shēng.

wool /wʊl/ n [U] **1** 羊毛 yángmáo; 毛线[綫] máoxiàn, 毛织[織]品 máozhīpǐn. ***pull the '~ over sb's eyes*** 蒙蔽某人 méngbì mǒurén. **2** 羊毛状[狀]物 yángmáozhuàng wù: *cotton-~* 原棉. ~**len** [美语 = **woollen**] /'wʊlən/ adj 羊毛制的 yángmáo zhì de. ~**lens** [美语 = **wool·ens**] n pl 毛织品 máozhīpǐn, 毛料 máoliào. ~**ly** [美语亦作 **wooly**] /'wʊlɪ/adj [-ier, -iest] (a) 羊毛制的 yángmáo zhìde; 羊毛状的 yángmáozhuàngde: *a ~ly coat* 羊毛外衣. (b) [喻]模糊的 móhude, 不清的 bùqīngde. □ n [pl -ies] [非正式用语]毛线衣 máoxiànyī.

word /wɜːd/ n [C] **1** 词 cí, 单[單]词 dāncí. ,~ ***for*** '~ 逐字地 zhúzìde, 一字不变[變]地 yīzì búbiàn de: *translate ~ for ~* 直译. ***in a ~*** 简言之 jiǎnyánzhī, 总[總]之 zǒngzhī. ***by ,~ of 'mouth*** 口头[頭]地 kǒutóude. **2** [C] 话 huà, 言词 yáncí: *He didn't say a ~ about it.* 他对那件事只字未提. ***eat one's ~s*** 承认[認]错误 chéngrèn cuòwù, 收回前言 shōuhuí qiányán. ***have a ~ with sb*** 和某人谈话 hé mǒurén tánhuà. ***have the last ~*** (在辩论中)作最后[後]说明 zuò zuìhòu shuōmíng. ***the last ~ (in sth)*** (在某方面)最新式者 zuìxīnshìzhě. **3** 消息 xiāoxī, 音讯 yīnxùn: *Please send me ~ of your safe arrival.* 请将你平安到达的消息告诉我. **4** 诺言 nuòyán, 保证[證] bǎozhèng. ***take sb's ~ for it*** 相信某人的话 xiāngxìn mǒurén de huà. **5** 命令 mìnglìng, 口令 kǒulìng: *The officer gave the ~ to fire.* 军官下令开火. **6** [基督教]圣[聖]经[經] Shèngjīng; (尤指)福音书[書] Fúyīnshū. □ vt 说 shuō, 以言词表达[達] yǐ yáncí biǎodá: *a well-~ed letter* 一封措辞良好的信. ,~-'**perfect** adj 能背诵的 néng bèisòng de. '~ **processing** n [U] 文字(信息)处[處]理 wénzì chùlǐ. '~ **processor** n [C] 文字处理器 wénzì chùlǐqì. ~**ing** n [仅作 sing] 措辞[辭] cuòcí. **wordy** adj [-ier, -iest] 多言的 duōyán de, 唠[嘮]叨的 láodaode.

wore /wɔː(r)/ pt of wear².

work¹ /wɜːk/ n **1** [U] 劳[勞]动[動] láodòng, 工作 gōngzuò: *Are you fond of hard ~?* 你喜欢费力的工作吗? ***set*** (或 ***get***) ***to ~*** 着手工作 zhuóshǒu gōngzuò. ***all in the day's ~*** 正常的 zhèngchángde, 一般的 yìbānde. **2** [U] 职[職]业[業] zhíyè, 业务[務] yèwù: *The men were on their way to ~.* 那些人是在上班途中. ***in*** (***out of***) ***~*** 在(失)业 zàiyè. ***at ~*** 在工作 zài gōngzuò, 忙于[於] mángyú. **3**[U] 待做的事 dài zuò de shì; 作业 zuòyè: *I have plenty of ~ in my garden.* 我在庭园中有许多要做的工作. **4** [U] 制[製]作品 zhìzuòpǐn; 工艺[藝]品 gōngyìpǐn: *The ~ of famous sculptors* 著名雕刻家的作品. **5** [pl] 著作 zhùzuò, 作品 zuòpǐn: *the ~s of Shakespeare* 莎士比亚的著作. **6** [pl] 活动的机[機]件 huódòngde jījiàn. [pl] 工场[場] gōngchǎng, 工厂[廠] gōngchǎng: *an'iron-~s* 铁工厂. ,~ **of 'art** 艺术[術]品 yìshùpǐn. '~**bench** 工作台 gōngzuòtái. '~**day** 工作日 gōngzuòrì. '~**force** (全厂的)劳动力 láodònglì. '~**man** 劳动者 láodòngzhě, 劳工 láogōng. '~**man·like** adj 工作熟练[練]的 gōngzuò shúliàn de. '~**man·ship** 手艺 shǒuyì, 技艺 jìyì: *poor* (*excellent*) *~manship* 拙劣的(极好的)手艺. '~**shop** 车[車]间[間] chējiān, 工场 gōngchǎng. '~**-shy** adj 不愿[願]工作的 búyuàn gōngzuò de, 懒惰的 lǎnduò de.

work² /wɜːk/ vt/i [pt, pp ~ed] 或 wrought. **1** 工作 gōngzuò, 劳[勞]动[動] láodòng, 做 zuò: *I've been ~ing hard all day.* 我辛苦地工作一整天. ***~ to rule*** ⇨ rule(1). 运[運]转[轉] yùnzhuǎn, 活动 huódòng; 起作用 qǐ zuòyòng: *The lift is not ~ing.* 电梯失灵了. *Will your plan ~?* 你的计划行得通吗? **3** 使工作 shǐ gōngzuò; 使运转 shǐ yùnzhuǎn: *The machine ~s by electricity.* 这机器是电动的. **4** (通过努力)造成 zàochéng: *~ wonders* 造成奇迹. *~ a cure* 使获得痊愈. **5** 经[經]营[營] jīngyíng, 管理 guǎnlǐ: *~ a mine* 经营一处矿山

6 (使)缓慢地进〔進〕行 huǎnmànde jìnxíng: *One of the screws has ~ed loose.* 一个螺钉已经松动了. 7 锤炼〔煉〕chuílàn; 捏成 niēchéng: *~ clay* 捏黏土. *~ dough* 揉面团. ***~ away (at sth)*** 继〔繼〕续〔續〕工作 jìxù gōngzuò. ***~ sth off*** (好不容易)排除 páichú; (做工)偿〔償〕清(债务) chángqīng: *~ off a debt* (做工)清偿债务. *~ off excess weight* 消除过多的体重. ***~ out*** **(a)** 有(预期的)结果 yǒu jiéguǒ: *The situation ~ed out quite well.* 形势发展的结果很好. **(b)** (比赛前体育选手)锻炼 duànliàn. **'~-out** *n* [C] 锻炼(方式和时期) duànliàn. ***~ sth out*** **(a)** 计算出 jìsuànchū: *~ out the new price* 算出新的价格. **(b)** 作出 zuòchū, 设计出 shèjìchū: *They've ~ed out a new plan.* 他们已经制订出新的计划. **(c)** 解答 jiědá, 解决 jiějué: *He was ~ing out a problem.* 他正在解决一个问题. **(d)** 用尽〔盡〕yòng jìn, 枯竭 kūjié: *That silver-mine is now ~ed out.* 那银矿现已采掘完了. ***~ up to sth*** 逐渐发〔發〕展成 zhújiàn fāzhǎn chéng: *The orchestra was ~ing up to a crescendo.* 管弦乐队正在形成一个高潮. ***work sth up*** 激起 jīqǐ; 激动 jīdòng.

work·able /'wɜ:kəbl/ *adj* 可操作的 kě cāozuò de, 可运〔運〕转〔轉〕的 kě yùnzhuǎn de, 可使用的 kě shǐyòng de.

worker /'wɜ:kə(r)/ *n* [C] 工人 gōngrén, 劳〔勞〕动〔動〕者 láodòngzhě. **~ant** 工蚁〔蟻〕gōngyǐ. **~ bee** 工蜂 gōngfēng. ⇨ drone.

work·ing /'wɜ:kɪŋ/ *n* **1** [C] 矿〔礦〕坑 kuàngkēng; 采〔採〕石场〔場〕cǎishíchǎng; (矿内)巷道 hàngdào. **2** [C] 运〔運〕转〔轉〕yùnzhuǎn, 操作 cāozuò, 作用 zuòyòng: *the ~s of the human mind* 人脑的活动. **3** [用作定语]: *~ majority* (指议会票数)足够的多数〔數〕zúgòude duōshù. ***the ~ day*** 工作日 gōngzuòrì. ***in ~ order*** 能正常运行 néng zhèngcháng yùnxíng. ☐ *adj* 从〔從〕事工作的 cóngshì gōngzuò de, 劳〔勞〕动〔動〕的 láodòngde. **the ~ classes** 工人阶〔階〕级 gōngrén jiējí. **'~-class** *adj*. **'~ party** (尤指)专〔專〕题调查委员会〔會〕zhuāntí diàochá wěiyuánhuì.

world /wɜ:ld/ *n* [C] **1** 地球 dìqiú; 世界 shìjiè; (与地球相似的)天体〔體〕tiāntǐ: *make a journey round the ~* 作环球旅行. ***a ~ language*** 世界性语言. **2** 人世间〔間〕rénshìjiān: *this ~ and the next* 人世与阴间. **3** ***think the ~ of sb*** 极〔極〕其重视某人 jíqí zhòngshì mǒurén, 高度评价〔價〕某人 gāodù píngjià mǒurén. ***be*** (或 ***feel***) ***on ˌtop of the '~*** 兴〔興〕高采烈的 xìnggāo-cǎiliè de. ***out of this ~*** 极其动〔動〕人的 jíqí dòngrén de, 非常好的 fēicháng hǎo de. ***a ~ of sth*** 大量 dàliàng, 许多 xǔduō: *My holiday did me a ~ of good.* 假期对我大有好处. **4** 世事 shìshì, 人世生活 rénshì shēnghuó: *a man of the ~* 老于〔於〕世故的人 lǎoyú shìgù de rén. **5** ...界 ...jiè: *the ~ of sport (art)* 体育(艺术)界. **ˌ~-'famous** *adj* 世界闻〔聞〕名的 shìjiè wénmíng de. **ˌ~-'power** 世界强国〔國〕shìjiè qiángguó. **'~-wide** 遍及全球的 biànjí quánqiú de, 世界性的 shìjièxìngde. **~ly** *adj* **(a)** 物质〔質〕的 wùzhìde: *my ~ly goods* 我的财产. **(b)** 世俗的 shìsúde, 尘〔塵〕世的 chénshìde. **~li·ness** *n* [U]

worm /wɜ:m/ *n* [C] **1** 虫〔蟲〕chóng, 蠕虫 rúchóng. ⇨ earthworm. **2** [用作某些幼虫, 昆虫的名称]: *'silk~* 蚕. *'glow~* 萤火虫. **3** [喻]小人物 xiǎorénwù, 可怜〔憐〕虫 kěliánchóng. ☐ *vt* 使蠕行 shǐ rúxíng, 小心缓慢地爬行 xiǎoxīn huǎnmàn de páxíng: *He ~ed his way through the undergrowth.* 他缓慢爬过树丛.

worn /wɔ:n/ *pp* of wear².

worry /'wʌrɪ/ *vt/i* [*pt, pp* -ied] **1** (使)烦恼〔惱〕fánnǎo, (使)困扰〔擾〕kùnrǎo: *The traffic worried her.* 交通困扰着她. **2** 焦虑〔慮〕jiāolǜ, 不安 bù'ān: *You have no cause to ~.* 你没有理由担忧. **3** 撕咬 sīyǎo: *The dog was ~ing the rat.* 狗撕咬着耗子. ☐ *n* [*pl* -ies] **1** [U] 烦恼 fánnǎo, 焦虑 jiāolǜ, 困扰 kùnrǎo: *show signs of ~* 显出焦虑的样子. **2** [C] 烦恼的原因 fánnǎode yuányīn; 令人担忧〔憂〕的事 lìngrén dānyōu de shì: *Money has always been a ~.* 金钱常常是一桩烦恼事. **wor·ried** *adj* 烦恼的 fánnǎode, 焦虑的 jiāolǜde. **~ing** *adj* 使人烦恼的 shǐrén fánnǎo de, 令人不安的 lìngrén bù'ān de: *have a ~ing time.* 度过一段烦恼的时间.

worse /wɜ:s/ *adj* [⇨ bad, worst] **1** 更坏〔壞〕的 gènghuài de; 更差的 gèngchà de; 更恶〔惡〕劣的 gèng èliè de: *Your work is bad but mine is much ~.* 你的工作不好,

但我的更差. *the ~ for wear* 破旧〔舊〕不堪 pòjiù bùkān. 2 (病情)更重 gèngzhòng: *The doctor says she is much ~ today.* 医生说,她的病情今天更重了. □ *adv* (⇨ badly, worst) 1 更坏 gènghuài, 更糟 gèngzāo; (病)更重 gèngzhòng: *He is behaving ~ than ever.* 他的行为比过去更坏. *none the ~* 并不更差 bìngbú gèngchà, 仍然 réngrán, 还〔還〕是 háishì: *I like him none the ~.* 我还是喜欢他的. *~ off* 情况更坏 qíngkuàng gènghuài, 处〔處〕境更糟 chùjìng gèngzāo. 2 更 gèng, 更加 gèngjiā: *It's raining ~ than ever.* 雨越下越大. □ *n* 更坏的事 gènghuàide shì: *I have ~ to tell.* 我有更坏的事要讲.

worsen /ˈwɜːsn/ *vt/i* (使)变〔變〕坏〔壞〕biàn huài, (使)恶化 èhuà.

wor·ship /ˈwɜːʃɪp/ *n* [U] 1 礼〔禮〕拜 lǐbài. 2 崇拜 chóngbài, 敬仰 jìngyǎng: *ˈhero ~* 英雄崇拜. □ *vt/i* [-pp-; 美语 -p-] 崇拜 chóngbài, 尊敬 zūnjìng: *~ God* 崇拜上帝. **~per** [美语 = **~er**] 崇拜者. chóngbàizhě.

worst /wɜːst/ *adj* (⇨ bad, worse) 最坏〔壞〕的 zuìhuàide, 最差的 zuìchàde, 最恶〔惡〕劣的 zuì èliè de: *the ~ storm for five years* 五年来最厉害的暴风雨. □ *adv* (⇨ badly, worse) 最坏地 zuìhuàide. □ *n* **the ~** 最坏的部分 zuìhuàide bùfen, 最坏者 zuìhuàizhě: *You must be prepared for the ~* 你必须作最坏的打算. *get the ~ of* 忍受最大的痛苦 rěnshòu zuìdàde tòngkǔ.

worth /wɜːθ/ *adj* 1 值…的 zhí…de, 相当〔當〕于〔於〕…价〔價〕值的 xiāngdāng yú…jiàzhí de: *It's not ~ more than two pounds.* 它的价值不超过两英镑. ***worth (one's) while*** ⇨ while. 2 拥〔擁〕有…价值财产〔產〕的 yōng yǒu … jiàzhí cáichǎn de: *What's the old man ~?* 那老人有多少财产? *for all one is ~* [非正式用语]尽〔儘〕力 jìnlì, 拼命 pīnmìng: *He was running for all he was ~.* 他正在拼命地跑. 3 值得…的 zhíde…de: *The book is well ~ reading.* 这本书很值得一读. □ *n* [U] 1 价值 jiàzhí: *know a friend's ~* 了解一位朋友的品质. 2 (值…价钱的)份量 fènliàng: *a ˈpound's ~ of apples* 一英镑钱的苹果(份量). **~less** *adj* 无〔無〕价值的 wú jiàzhí de. ˌ**~ˈwhile** *adj* 值得(花时间,精力)的 zhídéde, 合算的 hésuànde.

worthy /ˈwɜːðɪ/ *adj* [-ier, -iest] 1 值得的 zhídéde; 相称〔稱〕的 xiāngchènde: *a cause ~ of support* 值得支持的事业. 2 有价〔價〕值的 yǒu jiàzhí de; 可尊敬的 kě zūnjìng de: *a ~ gentleman* 一位可敬的先生.

would ⇨ will[1].

wound[1] /wuːnd/ *n* [C] 1 伤〔傷〕shāng, 伤口 shāngkǒu: *a ˈbullet ~* 枪伤. 2 (感情)痛苦 tòngkǔ, (精神)创〔創〕伤 chuāngshāng. □ *vt* 使受伤 shǐ shòushāng, 伤害 shānghài: *~ed in battle* 在战斗中受伤.

wound[2] /waʊnd/ *pt, pp* of wind[3].

wove, wo·ven ⇨ weave.

w.p. = weather permitting 遇雨顺延 yù yǔ shùn yán.

w.p.m. = words per minute 每分钟〔鐘〕…字 měi fēn zhōng …zì

wrangle /ˈræŋgl/ *vi, n* [C] 争吵 zhēngchǎo, 口角 kǒujiǎo.

wrap /ræp/ *vt/i* [-pp-] 缠〔纏〕绕〔繞〕chánrǎo; 包 bāo, 裹 guǒ: *~ a child in a shawl* 把小孩裹在围巾里. ***be ~ped up in*** **(a)** [喻]被隐〔隱〕藏于〔於〕…之中 bèi yǐncáng yú … zhōng: *The affair is ~ped (up) in mystery.* 这件事被隐藏于神秘之中. **(b)** 埋头〔頭〕于 máitóu yú, 全神贯注于 quán shén guànzhù yú: *He was ~ped up in his work.* 他埋头于他的工作. □ *n* [C] 外套 wàitào, 罩件(如围巾,披风等) zhàojiàn. **~per** (尤指)包装〔裝〕纸 bāozhuāng zhǐ, 封皮 fēngpí. **~ping** [C, U] 包装材料 bāozhuāng cáiliào.

wreath /riːθ/ *n* [C] [*pl* ~s /riːðz/] 花圈 huāquān, 花环〔環〕huāhuán.

wreathe /riːð/ *vt/i* 覆盖〔蓋〕fùgài, 包围〔圍〕bāowéi: *hills ~d in mist* 隐藏在雾中的群山.

wreck /rek/ *n* 1 [C,U] 破坏〔壞〕pòhuài; (尤指船只等)失事 shīshì: *save a ship from ~* 营救一只遇难的船. 2 [C] 失事的船只等 shīshìde chuánzhī děng. 3 [U] [喻](希望等的)破灭〔滅〕pòmiè. 4 [C] 健康极〔極〕度受损的人 jiànkāng jídù shòusǔnde rén. □ *vt* 使破坏 shǐ pòhuài; 使失事 shǐ shīshì: *The ship (train) was ~ed.* 那轮船(火车)失事了. **~age** /ˈrekɪdʒ/ *n* [U] (被毁物的)残〔殘〕骸 cánhái.

wren /ren/ *n* [C] [动物]鹪〔鷦〕鹩〔鷯〕jiāoliáo.

wrench /rentʃ/ *n* [C] 1 猛扭 měng niǔ; 猛拉 měng lā. 2 (离别时的)一阵〔陣〕悲痛 yízhèn bēitòng. 3 扳钳 bānqián, 扳手 bānshǒu. □ *vt* 1 猛扭 měng niǔ; 拉 měng lā: *~ the door open* 用力把门拉开. 2 扭伤〔傷〕(足踝等) niǔshāng.

wrestle /'resl/ *vi* **1** 摔角 shuāijiǎo, 角力 jiǎolì. **2**[喻] 斗[鬪]争 dòuzhēng; 努力 nǔlì: ~ *with a problem* 努力解决一个问题. **wrestler** /'reslə(r)/ 摔角运[運]动[動]员 shuāijiǎo yùndòngyuán.

wretch /retʃ/ *n* [C] 不幸的人 búxìngde rén, 可怜[憐]的人 kěliánde rén.

wretched /'retʃɪd/ *adj* **1** 不幸的 búxìngde, 可怜[憐]的 kěliánde: ~ *poverty* 可怜的贫困. **2** 使人不幸的 shǐ rén búxìng de, 令人难[難]受的 lìng rén nánshòu de: ~ *houses* 肮脏破旧的房屋. **3**[非正式用语]恶[惡]劣的 èliède, (质量)差的 chàde: ~ *weather* (*food*) 恶劣的天气(食物). **~ly** *adv* **~ness** *n* [U]

wriggle /rɪgl/ *vt/i* 蠕动[動] rúdòng, 扭动 niǔdòng, 蜿蜒而行 wānyán ér xíng: *The snake* ~*d out of my fingers.* 蛇从我的手指缝间滑走了. □ *n* [C] 蠕动 rúdòng, 扭动 niǔdòng, 蜿蜒 wānyán.

wring /rɪŋ/ *vt* [*pt*, *pp* wrung /rʌŋ/] **1** 拧[擰] níng; 绞出 jiǎochū: ~ *a hen's neck* 扭住母鸡的脖子. ~ *out wet clothes* 把湿衣服拧干. ~ *one's hands* · 扭手(表示悲痛等) niǔ shǒu. ~*ing wet* 湿[濕]得可拧出水来[來]的 shīde kě níngchū shuǐlái de. **2**[喻]勒索(钱财) lèsuǒ, 逼取(口供) bīqǔ. **~er** 绞衣机[機] jiǎoyījī.

wrinkle /'rɪŋkl/ *n* [C] 皱[皺]纹 zhòuwén: ~*s round her eyes* 她眼角周围的皱纹. □ *vt/i* (使)起皱纹 qǐ zhòuwén: ~ *up one's forehead* 皱起眉头. ~*d with age* 老得脸上起皱纹. **wrinkly** /'rɪŋklɪ/ *adj*

wrist /rɪst/ *n* [C] 腕 wàn; 腕关[關]节[節] wànguānjié. **'~-band** 袖口 xiùkǒu; 护[護]腕 hùwàn. **'~watch** 手表[錶] shǒubiǎo.

writ /rɪt/ *n* [C] **1** (法院的)令状[狀] lìngzhuàng. **2 Holy W~** 圣[聖]经[經] Shèngjīng.

write /raɪt/ *vt/i* [*pt* wrote /rəʊt/; *pp* written /'rɪtn/] **1** 书[書]写[寫] shūxiě, 写字 xiě zì: *learn to read and* ~ 学习读书和写字. **2** 写出 xiěchū, 填写 tiánxiě: ~ *one's name* 写出自己的名字. ~ *a cheque* 开支票. **3** 写作 xiězuò, 编写 biānxiě: ~ *a novel* 写小说. **4** 写信给 xiě xìn gěi, 函告 hángào: *He promised to* ~ (*to*) *me every week.* 他答应每星期写信给我. **5** [常用被动语态]显[顯]露 xiǎnlù, 明白表示 míngbái biǎoshì: *He had pain written on his face.* 他的脸上显露出痛苦. ~ *sth down* 写下 xiěxià, 记下 jìxià. ~ *off* (*for sth*) 去信定购(某物) xiě xìn yóugòu: ~ *off for an application form* 函索一份申请表格. ~ *sth off* 注销 zhùxiāo, 勾销 gōuxiāo, 报[報]销 bàoxiāo: ~ *off a debt* 勾销一笔债务. *write off a new car* 彻底损坏了一辆新汽车. **'write-off** *n*: *The car was a complete* ~*-off.* 那辆汽车完全报销了. ~ *sth out* 全部写出 quánbù xiěchū: ~ *out a copy of an agreement* 誊写一份合约. ~ *sth up* (补写)完成 wánchéng: ~ *up one's diary* 写完日记. **'~-up** (事件的)记录[錄] jìlù.

writer /'raɪtə(r)/ *n* [C] **1** 书[書]写[寫]人 shūxiěrén: *the* ~ *of this letter* 这封信的发信人. **2** 作家 zuòjiā.

writhe /raɪð/ *vi* (因痛苦而)翻滚 fāngǔn, 折腾[騰] zhēteng.

writ·ing /'raɪtɪŋ/ *n* **1** [U] 书[書]写[寫] shūxiě; 文件 wénjiàn: *put something down in* ~ 把某事记录在卷. **2** = handwriting. **3** [*pl*] (文学)作品 zuòpǐn, 著作 zhùzuò: *the* ~*s of Swift* 斯威夫特的作品. **'~-paper** (尤指)信纸 xìnzhǐ.

writ·ten /'rɪtn/ ⇨ write.

wrong /rɒŋ/ *adj* (与 *right* 相对) **1** 不道德的 bú dàodé de, 不正当[當]的 bú zhèngdāng de; 非法的 fēifǎde: *It is* ~ *to steal.* 偷窃是不道德的. **2** 错误的 cuòwùde, 不正确[確]的 bú zhèngquède: *He has six* ~ *answers.* 他有六个错误的答案. *We caught the* ~ *train.* 我们乘错了火车. **3** 失常的 shīchángde; 不健全的 bú jiànquán de: *There's nothing* ~ *with the engine.* 发动机没有毛病. □ *adv* 不正当地 bú zhèngdāng de; 错误地 cuòwùde; 失常地 shīchángde: *You've spelt my name* ~. 你把我的名字拼错了. **go** ~ **(a)** 走错路 zǒu cuò lù, 误入歧途 wù rù qítú. **(b)** 结果不好 jiéguǒ bùhǎo, 失败 shībài: *All our plans went* ~. 我们所有的计划都失败了. **(c)** [非正式用语](机器等)损坏[壞] sǔnhuài, 出毛病 chū máobìng. □ *n* **1** [U] 邪恶[惡] xié'è. [C] 罪行 zuìxíng: *know the difference between right and* ~ 明辨是非. *do* ~ *to her* 对不起她. **2** *in the* ~ 犯错误 fàn cuòwù, 有罪 yǒu zuì. □ *vt* 虐待 nüèdài; 冤屈 yuānqū; 对[對]…不公正 duì…bù gōngzhèng. **~ful** *adj* 不正当的 bú zhèngdāng de; 非法的 fēifǎde: ~*ful dismissal* 不合法的解雇. **~fully** *adv* **~ly** *adv*:

~*ly accused* 不公正地被控告.

wrong·doer /ˈrɒŋduːə(r)/ *n* [C] 做坏[壞]事的人 zuò huàishì de rén, 犯罪者 fànzuìzhě.

wrote /rəʊt/ ⇨ write.

wrought /rɔːt/ *pt, pp* of work². 锤炼[煉]成 chuíliàn chéng: ~ *iron* 熟(锻)铁.

wrung /rʌŋ/ ⇨ wring.

wry /raɪ/ *adj* [wrier, wriest] 扭歪的 niǔ wāi de, 歪斜的 wāixiéde: *a ~ smile* 苦笑. ~**ly** *adv*

wt. = weight.

X x

X,x /eks/ [*pl* X's, x's /ˈeksɪz/] **1** 英语的第二十四个[個]字母 Yīngyǔde dì'èrshísìgè zìmǔ. **2** 罗[羅]马[馬]数[數]字十 (X) Luómǎ shùzì shí. **3** [代数]第一个未知数 dìyīgè wèizhīshù.

xeno·phobia /ˌzenəˈfəʊbɪə/ *n* [U] 对[對]外国人(或事物)的憎恨或畏惧[懼] duì wàiguórén de zēnghèn huò wèijù.

Xmas /ˈkrɪsməs/ *n* (Christmas 的缩写).

X-ray /ˈeks reɪ/ *n* [C] X 射线[綫] X shèxiàn, X 光 X guāng; X 光照片 X guāng zhàopiàn. □ *vt* 用 X 光检[檢]查 yòu X guāng jiǎnchá. ~ **therapy** *n* [U] X 光治疗[療]法 X guāng zhìliáofǎ.

xylo·phone /ˈzaɪləfəʊn/ *n* [C] [音乐]木琴 mùqín.

Y y

Y,y /waɪ/ [*pl* Y's, y's /waɪz/] 英语的第二十五个[個]字母 Yīngyǔde dì'èrshíwǔgè zìmǔ.

yacht /jɒt/ *n* [C] **1** (竞赛用)小帆船 xiǎo fānchuán, 快艇 kuàitǐng. **2** 游艇 yóutǐng. □ *vi* 乘游艇(旅行) chéng yóutǐng, 驾[駕]快艇(竞赛) jià kuàitǐng. ~**ing** 驾驶[駛]快艇的技术[術] jiàshǐ kuàitǐng de jìshù.

yank /jæŋk/ *vt* 突然猛拉 tūrán měnglā: ~ *out a tooth* 猛力拔出一颗牙齿.

yap /jæp/ *vi* [-pp-] **1** (尤指狗)狂吠 kuángfèi. **2** [俚语]吵嚷 chǎorǎng; 瞎谈 xiātán. □ *n* [C] (狗的)狂吠 kuángfèi.

yard¹ /jɑːd/ *n* [C] **1** 院子 yuànzi: *a ˈfarm~* 农家的场院. **2** 工作场[場]地 gōngzuò chǎngdì: *the ˈrailway ~* 铁路调车场

yard² /jɑːd/ *n* [C] **1** 码(=3英尺) mǎ. **2** 帆桁 fānhéng. ˈ~**stick** [喻]衡量的标[標]准[準] héngliángde biāozhǔn.

yarn /jɑːn/ *n* **1** [U] 纱线[綫] shāxiàn. **2** [C] [非正式用语]故事 gùshì, 奇谈 qítán. *spin a ~* 讲[講]故事 jiǎng gùshi. □ *vi* 讲故事 jiǎng gùshi.

yawn /jɔːn/ *vi* **1** 打呵欠 dǎ hēqiàn. **2** 张[張]开[開] zhāngkāi, 裂开 lièkāi: *a ~ing hole* 敞着口的洞. □ *n* [C] 打呵欠 dǎ hēqiàn.

yd(s). = yard(s).

year /jɜː(r)/ *n* [C] **1** (太阳)年 nián. **2** (亦作 *calendar* ~) (历)年 nián. ~ ˌ*in* ~ ˈ*out* 一年一年地 yìnián yìnián de. ˌ*all the* ˌ~ ˈ*round* 一年到头[頭] yìnián dào tóu. **3** (与某事物相关连的)一年 yìnián, 年度 niándù: *the academic ~* 学年. ~**ly** *adj, adv* 每年 měinián, 每年一次 měinián yīcì.

yearn /jɜːn/ *vi* 想念 xiǎngniàn, 渴望 kěwàng: *He ~ed for home.* 他想家了. ~**ing** *n* [U] [亦用 *pl*] 怀[懷]念 huáiniàn, 渴望 kěwàng.

yeast /jiːst/ *n* [C] 酵母 xiàomǔ.

yell /jel/ *vt/i* **1** 叫喊 jiàohǎn, 叫嚷 jiàorǎng: ~ *with fright* 因惊恐而大叫. ~ *with laughter* 大笑大叫. **2** 喊出 hǎnchū, 大声[聲]说出 dàshēng shuōchū: ~ *(out) an order* 大声发出命令. □ *n* [C] 大喊 dàhǎn, 大叫 dàjiào.

yel·low /ˈjeləʊ/ *n* [U], *adj* **1** 黄 huáng, 黄色 huángsè; 黄色的 huángsède. **2** [俚]胆怯的 dǎnqiède; 卑鄙的 bēibǐde. □ *vt/i* (使)变[變]黄色 biàn huángsè: *The pages had ~ed with age.* 书页因年久而发黄. ~**ish** *adj* 淡黄色的 dàn huángsè de.

yelp /jelp/ *vi,n* [C] (因痛苦, 愤怒等)叫喊 jiàohǎn.

yes /jes/ *particle* (与 *no* 相对) 是 shì, 是的 shìde: *"Can you read this?"* "你能读出这个吗?" — *"Y~."* "是,我能." □ *n* [C]: *Answer 'Y~' or 'No'.* 明确回答"是"

或"不是"。

yes·ter·day /'jestədɪ/ *adv, n* [C] (在)昨天 zuótiān: *He arrived* ~. 他昨天到达。

yet /jet/ *adv* **1** 到此时〔時〕dào cǐshí, 到那时 dào nàshí: *They are not here* ~. 他们到现在还没有来。**2** 更加 gèngjiā, 比…还〔還〕要 bǐ ... háiyào: ~ *more accidents* 更多的事故。**3** 还 hái, 尚 shàng, 仍然 réngrán: *There is* ~ *time to do it.* 还来得及去做它。**4** 在未来〔來〕某一时间〔間〕zài wèilái mǒuyī shíjiān, 早晚 zǎowǎn: *He may surprise us all* ~. 他总有一天会使我们吃惊的。**5** *as* ~ 到目前为〔爲〕止 dào mùqián wéizhǐ; 到当〔當〕时为止 dào dāngshí wéizhǐ: *As* ~ *we do not know.* 到目前为止我们还不知道。□ *conj* 然而 rán'ér, 可是 kěshì: *He worked hard and* ~ *he failed.* 他工作很努力,可是他失败了。

yew /ju:/ *n* [C] (亦作 '~-*tree*) [植物]紫杉 zǐshān. [U] 紫杉木材 zǐshān mùcái.

yield /ji:ld/ *vt/i* **1** 生产〔產〕shēngchǎn, 生长〔長〕出 shēngzhǎngchū: *trees that* ~ *fruit* 结果实的树。**2**[与 *to* 连用]让〔讓〕与〔與〕ràngyǔ, 给与 gěiyǔ; 投降 tóuxiáng, 屈服 qūfú: *He* ~*ed to temptation.* 他在诱惑之下屈服了。□ *n* [C,U] 产量 chǎnliàng, 收获〔獲〕量 shōuhuòliàng: *a good* ~ *of wheat* 小麦丰收。~**ing** *adj* **(a)** 易弯〔彎〕曲的 yì wānqū de. **(b)** [喻]不固执〔執〕的 bú gùzhí de, 顺从〔從〕的 shùncóng de.

Y.M.C.A. = Young Men's Christian Association 基督教青年会〔會〕Jīdūjiào qīngniánhuì.

yoga /'jəʊgə/ *n* [U] 瑜伽(古代印度哲学的一派) yújiā.

yo·gurt, yo·ghurt, yo·ghourt /'jɒgət/ *n* [U] 酸乳酪 suān rǔlào.

yoke /jəʊk/ *n* [C] **1** 牛轭〔軛〕niú'è. **2** [喻]屈从的象征〔徵〕qūcóngde xiàngzhēng: *throw off the* ~ 拒绝服从。**3** 轭状〔狀〕扁担〔擔〕èzhuàng biǎndàn. **4** (女服)上衣的抵肩 shàngyīde dǐjiān. □ *vt/i* 加轭于(牛) jiā è yú.

yolk /jəʊk/ *n* [C,U] 蛋黄 dànhuáng.

yon·der /'jɒndə(r)/ *adj, adv* [书面语]那边〔邊〕的 nàbiānde, 远〔遠〕处〔處〕的 yuǎnchùde; 在那边 zài nàbiān, 在远处 zài yuǎnchù.

you /ju:/ *pron* **1** 你 nǐ; 你们〔們〕nǐmen: *Y*~ *are my friend.* 你是我的朋友。**2** [非正式用语]一个〔個〕人 yígè rén, 任何人 rènhé rén: *You can't live without food.* 没有食物,谁也活不了。

you'd /ju:d/ = *you had; you would.*

you'll /ju:l/ = *you will.*

young /jʌŋ/ *adj* [-er, -est] **1** (与 *old* 相对)年轻〔輕〕的 niánqīngde, 幼小的 yòuxiǎode; 初期的 chūqīde: *a* ~ *woman (nation)* 年轻的妇女(国家)。*The evening is still* ~. 夜晚刚开始不久。**2** [用于称呼]: *Now listen to me,* ~ *man!* 现在听我说,年轻人! **3** 没有经〔經〕验〔驗〕的 méiyǒu jīngyàn de, 未成熟的 wèi chéngshú de: ~ *in crime* 无犯罪经验的。□ *n* **1** *the* ~ 青年们〔們〕qīngniánmen; 小孩子们 xiǎoháizimen. **2** [U] 仔 zǎi, 雏〔雛〕chú: *The cat fought to defend its* ~. 那猫为保护它的幼仔而战斗。~**ish** *adj* 还〔還〕年轻的 hái niánqīng de, 还幼小的 hái yòuxiǎo de. ~**ster** /'jʌŋstə(r)/ 年轻人 niánqīngrén, 小伙子 xiǎohuǒzi; 小孩 xiǎoháir.

your /jɔ:(r)/ *adj* 你的 nǐde; 你们〔們〕的 nǐmende: *Show me* ~ *hands.* 把你的手给我看。

you're /jɔ:(r)/ = *you are.*

yours /jɔ:z/ *adj, pron* **1** 你的(东西) nǐde; 你们〔們〕的(东西) nǐmende: *Is that book* ~? 那本书是你的吗? **2** [用在信尾具名前]: ~ *faithfully (truly, sincerely)* 你的忠实的。

your·self /jɔ:'self/ *pron* [*pl* -selves /-'selvz/] **1** [反身]你自己 nǐ zìjǐ: *Did you hurt* ~? 你弄伤(自己)了吗? **2** [用以加强语气]你亲〔親〕自 nǐ qīnzì, 你本人 nǐ běnrén: *You said so* ~. 你亲自这样说的。**(all) by yourself (a)** 你独〔獨〕自地 nǐ dúzì de. **(b)** 全靠(你)自己 quánkào zìjǐ, 独力地 dúlìde.

youth /ju:θ/ *n* [*pl* ~s /ju:ðz/] **1** [U] 青春 qīngchūn, 青年时〔時〕期 qīngnián shíqī: *in my* ~ 我年轻的时候。**2** [C] 青年 qīngnián; 少年 shàonián: *Half a dozen* ~*s* 六个年轻人。**3** [U] 青年们〔們〕qīngniánmen, 青年男女 qīngnián nán nǚ: *a* '~ *club* 青年俱乐部。*the* ~ *of today* 现在的年轻〔輕〕人。~**ful** *adj* 年轻的 niánqīngde, 青春的 qīngchūnde, 青年的 qīngniánde: *a* ~*ful appearance* 青春的外貌。~**fully** *adv* ~**ful·ness** *n* [U]

you've /ju:v/ = *you have.*

yr(s). = **1** year(s). **2** your(s).

yule /ju:l/ *n* [过时用法] 圣〔聖〕诞节〔節〕Shèngdànjié.

Y. W. C. A. = Young Women's Christian Association 基督教女青年会〔會〕Jīdūjiào nǚ qīngniánhuì.

Z z

Z,z /zed/ [*pl* Z's, z's /zeds/] 英语的第二十六个〔個〕字母 Yīngyǔde dìèrshíliùgè zìmǔ.

zeal /zi:l/ *n* [U] 热〔熱〕心 rèxīn, 热情 rèqíng. **~ous** /'zeləs/ *adj* 热心的 rèxīnde, 热情的 rèqíngde.

zebra /'zi:brə/ *n* [C] 〔动物〕斑马〔馬〕 bānmǎ. ,~ **'crossing** 人行横道线〔綫〕 rén xíng héngdàoxiàn.

zen·ith /'zenɪθ/ *n* [C] **1**〔天文〕天顶 tiāndǐng. **2**〔喻〕(名誉,幸运等的)顶峰 dǐngfēng.

zero /'zɪərəʊ/ *n* [C] **1** 零 líng. **2** 零点〔點〕 língdiǎn, 零位 língwèi, (尤指)零度 língdù. **'~ hour** 〔军事〕行动〔動〕开〔開〕始时〔時〕刻 xíngdòng kāishǐ shíkè.

zest /zest/ *n* [U] **1** 兴〔興〕趣 xìngqù, 乐〔樂〕趣 lèqù. **2** (辛辣的)滋味 zīwèi, 风〔風〕味 fēngwèi: *Garlic adds ~ to a stew.* 大蒜增添了炖肉的风味.

zig·zag /'zɪgzæg/ *n* [C] 之字形(线条,道路等) zhīzìxíng; 锯齿〔齒〕形物 jùchǐxíng wù: *a ~ path up the hillside* 通往山坡上的一条曲折小径. □ *adv* 曲折地 qūzhéde, 盘〔盤〕旋地 pánxuánde. □ *vi* [-gg-] 曲折地前进〔進〕 qūzhéde qiánjìn.

zinc /zɪŋk/ *n* [U] 〔化学〕锌 **(Zn)** xīn.

zip /zɪp/ *n* [C] **1** (子弹的)尖啸〔嘯〕声〔聲〕 jiānxiàoshēng. **2** = zip-fastener. □ *vt* [-pp-] 将〔將〕拉链〔鏈〕打开〔開〕或扣上 jiāng lāliàn dǎkāi huò kòushàng. **~-fastener** /'zɪp fɑ:snə(r)/ *n* [C] 拉链 lāliàn.

zither /'zɪðə(r)/ *n* [C] 齐〔齊〕特儿〔兒〕琴 qítèr qín.

zo·diac /'zəʊdɪæk/ *n* 〔天文〕黄道带〔帶〕 huángdàodài: *the signs of the* ~ 黄道十二宫.

zone /zəʊn/ *n* [C] **1** 环〔環〕状〔狀〕带〔帶〕 huánzhuàng dài, 腰带 yāodài. **2** 地带 dìdài. **3** 地区〔區〕 dìqū, 区域 qūyù: *the war* ~ 战争地区. *the 'danger* ~ 危险地区. **4** (美国城市中的)邮〔郵〕区 yóuqū. □ *vt* 划〔劃〕分成地区 huàfēn chéng dìqū.

zoo /zu:/ *n* [C] [*pl* ~s] 动〔動〕物园〔園〕 dòngwùyuán.

zo·ol·ogy /zəʊ'ɒlədʒɪ/ *n* [U] 动〔動〕物学〔學〕 dòngwùxué. **zo·ologi·cal** /,zəʊə'lɒdʒɪkl/ *adj* 动物学的: ~ *gardens* 动物园〔園〕 dòngwùyuán. **zo·ol·ogist** /zəʊ'ɒlədʒɪst/ *n* [C] 动物学家 dòngwùxuéjiā.

zoom /zu:m/ *n* [U] (低沉的)嗡嗡声〔聲〕 wēngwēngshēng. □ *vi* **1** (飞机)陡直上升〔昇〕 dǒuzhí shàngshēng. **2** (摄影机)迅速移向或移离〔離〕目标〔標〕 xùnsù yíxiàng huò yílí mùbiāo: ~ *in* (*out*) (镜头)移向(移离)目标. **'~ lens** 可变〔變〕焦距镜头〔頭〕 kěbiàn jiāojù jìngtóu.

汉 英 词 典

Chinese-English Dictionary

用 法 说 明

一、**条目**。1. 本词典所收单字(打头字)条目按汉语拼音字母次序排列。同音同调的单字按起笔丶(点)一(横)丨(直)丿(撇)乛(折,包括亅乚㇆𠃋等笔形)的顺序排列。

2. 多字条目按第一个字分别列于单字条目之下。各多字条目亦按汉语拼音字母次序排列。

3. 简化汉字除"讠""门""纟""贝""见""钅""饣""车""马""鱼"等常用偏旁构成的字外,在圆括号( )内注明繁体字。

二、**注音**。1. 汉语拼音的声调符号(ˉ阴平,ˊ阳平,ˇ上声,ˋ去声)标在音节的主要母音上。轻声不标符号。

2. 儿化音在词的基本读音后加"r"。

3. 单字另有其他不同读音时,在该条目最后(另起一行)注明"see also..."。

三、**释义**。1. 单字和复词条目(除结构形式和成语词组外)一般注明语法词类,词类略语套以圆括号( )。

2. 不同词类,除少数可以合并释义者外,用罗马数字分开,并分项进行释义。

3. 条目一般用英语对应词释义。不用英语对应词的和有关语法特征、使用范围等的说明,以方括号[ ]表示。

4. 修辞略语套以尖括号〈 〉。

5. 汉语特有名词(无英语对应词)用汉语拼音(不加调号)对译,并用斜体字表示。

四、**检字法**。本词典正文前有新式部首与汉语拼音对照检字表。检字方法:①根据字的部首在表(一)内查到该部首的号码;②在表(二)内按部首号码和字的笔画(字的笔画数不含其部首)查到该字的汉语拼音。

略 语 表

(名)名词 noun	(动)动词 verb
(形)形容词 adjective	(副)副词 adverb
(介)介词 preposition	(数)数词 numeral
(代)代词 pronoun	(叹)叹词 interjection
(量)量词 classifier	(象)象声词 onomatope
〈敬〉敬词 polite expression	〈套〉套语 polite formula
〈谦〉谦词 self-depreciatory	〈书〉书面语 literary
〈口〉口语 colloquial	〈贬〉贬义 derogatory
〈旧〉旧时用法 archaic	〈简〉简称 abbreviation

部首检字表

(一)部首目录

部首左边的号码表示部首的次序

一 画

1 丶
2 一
3 丨
4 丿
5 乙(一㇆乚)

二 画

6 亠
7 冫
8 冖
9 讠(言)
10 二
11 十
12 厂
13 匚
14 卜(⺊)
15 刂
16 冂
17 八(丷)
18 人(入)
19 亻
20 勹
⺈(见刀)
21 儿
22 几(𠘨)
23 厶
24 又(㕛)
25 廴
26 卩(㔾)
27 阝(在左)
28 阝(在右)
29 凵
30 刀(⺈)
31 力
㔾(见卩)

三 画

32 氵
33 忄(⺗)
34 宀
35 丬(爿)
36 广
37 门(門)
38 辶(辵)
39 工
40 土
41 士
42 艹
43 大
44 廾(在下)
45 尢
46 寸
47 弋
48 扌
49 小(⺌)
50 口
51 囗
52 巾
53 山
54 彳
55 彡
56 夕
57 夂
58 犭
59 饣(食)
60 彐(彐⺕)
61 尸
62 己(巳)
63 弓
64 屮
65 女
66 幺
67 子(孑)
68 纟(糹)
69 马(馬)
70 巛

四 画

71 灬
72 斗
73 文
74 方
75 火
76 心
77 户
78 礻(示)
79 王
80 韦(韋)
81 木
82 犬
83 歹
84 车(車)
85 戈
86 比
87 瓦
88 止
89 支
90 日
91 曰(⺜)
92 贝(貝)
93 见(見)
94 父
95 牛(牜⺧)
96 手
97 毛
98 气
99 攵
100 片
101 斤
102 爪(爫)
103 月(⺝)
104 欠
105 风(風)
106 殳
⺗(见忄)
107 肀(聿⺻)
爿(见丬)
108 毋(母)
109 水(氺)

五 画

110 穴
111 立
112 疒
113 衤
114 示(⺬见礻)
115 石
116 龙(龍)
117 业
118 目
119 田
120 罒
121 皿
122 钅(釒)
123 矢
124 禾
125 白
126 瓜
127 鸟(鳥)
128 用
氺(见水)
129 矛
聿(见肀)
艮(见艮)
130 疋(⺪)
131 皮
母(见毋)

六 画

132 衣
133 羊(⺶⺷)
134 米
135 耒
136 老
137 耳
138 臣
139 西(覀)
140 页(頁)
141 虍
142 虫
143 缶
144 舌
145 竹(⺮)
146 臼
147 自
148 血
149 舟
150 羽
聿(见肀)
151 艮(⺄)
152 糸(糹见纟)

七 画

153 辛
154 言(訁见讠)
155 麦(麥)
156 走
157 赤
158 豆
車(见车)
159 酉
160 辰
161 豕
162 卤(鹵)
163 里
貝(见贝)
見(见见)
164 足(⻊)
165 豸
166 谷
167 采
168 身
169 角

八 画

170 青
171 其
172 雨(⻗)
173 齿(齒)
174 黾(黽)
食(见饣)
175 金(釒见钅)
176 隹
177 鱼(魚)
門(见门)

九 画

178 音
179 革
頁(见页)
180 骨
181 食(⻞见饣)
182 鬼
風(见风)
韋(见韦)

十 画

183 鬥
184 髟
馬(见马)

十一画

185 麻
186 鹿
麥(见麦)
鹵(见卤)
鳥(见鸟)
魚(见鱼)

十二画以上

187 黑
黽(见黾)
188 鼠
189 鼻
齒(见齿)
龍(见龙)

（二）检字表

(1)
丶部

义 yì
丸 wán
之 zhī
为 wéi; wèi
头 tóu
主 zhǔ
半 bàn
州 zhōu
农 nóng
良 liáng
举 jǔ
叛 pàn

(2)
一部

一 yī

一至二画

七 qī
丁 dīng
三 sān
千 qiān
于 yú
下 xià
上 shàng
丈 zhàng
兀 wù
与 yǔ; yù
才 cái

三画

丰 fēng
夭 yāo
夫 fū
开 kāi
井 jǐng
无 wú
专 zhuān
丐 gài
五 wǔ
不 bù
丑 chǒu
屯 tún
互 hù
牙 yá

四画

平 píng
击 jī
未 wèi
末 mò
正 zhēng; zhèng
甘 gān
世 shì
且 qiě
可 kě
丙 bǐng
册 cè
东 dōng
丝 sī

五画

夹 gā; jiā; jiá
亚 yà
再 zài
吏 lì
百 bǎi
而 ér
尧 yáo
丞 chéng

六画

来 lái
严 yán
巫 wū
丽 lì
甫 fǔ
更 gēng, gèng
束 shù
两 liǎng
(夾) gā; jiā; jiá
求 qiú

七画

表 biǎo
(長) cháng; zhǎng
(亞) yà
(來) lái
(東) dōng
事 shì
枣 zǎo
(兩) liǎng

八画

韭 jiǔ
甚 shèn
巷 xiàng
柬 jiǎn
歪 wāi
面 miàn
昼 zhòu

九至十三画

艳 yàn
哥 gē
焉 yān
(棗) zǎo
棘 jí
(壽) shòu
(爾) ér

十四画以上

(憂) yōu
噩 è
整 zhěng
臻 zhēn
囊 náng

(3)
丨部

三至六画

丰 fēng
中 zhōng; zhòng
内 nèi
北 běi
凸 tū
旧 jiù
甲 jiǎ
申 shēn
电 diàn
由 yóu
且 qiě
冉 rǎn
史 shǐ
央 yāng
凹 āo
出 chū
师 shī
曳 yè
曲 qū; qǔ
肉 ròu
串 chuàn

七画以上

非 fēi
畅 chàng
(臨) lín
(暢) chàng

(4)
丿部

一至二画

九 jiǔ
乃 nǎi
匕 bǐ
千 qiān
川 chuān
么 me; mò
久 jiǔ
及 jí

三画

乏 fá
午 wǔ
夭 yāo
升 shēng
长 cháng; zhǎng
币 bì
反 fǎn
丹 dān
氏 shì
鸟 niǎo

四画

乎 hū
生 shēng
失 shī
乍 zhà
丘 qiū
卮 zhī
甩 shuǎi
氐 dǐ
乐 lè; yuè

五画

兆 zhào
年 nián
朱 zhū
丢 diū
乔 qiáo
乓 pāng
乒 pīng
向 xiàng
后 hòu

六至八画

我 wǒ
每 měi
囱 cōng
卵 luǎn
龟 guī
系 jì; xì
垂 chuí
乖 guāi
秉 bǐng
质 zhì
周 zhōu
拜 bài
重 chóng; zhòng
复 fù

九画以上

乘 chéng;
(師) shī
弑 shì
甥 shēng
(喬) qiáo
舞 wǔ
毓 yù
睾 gāo
孵 fū
疑 yí
靠 kào
(舉) jǔ
(歸) guī
釁 xìn
爨 cuàn

(5)
乙(乛フ乚)部

乙 yǐ

一至三画

刁 diāo
了 le; liǎo; liào
习 xí
也 yě
飞 fēi
乞 qǐ
孓 jué
孑 jié
乡 xiāng
以 yǐ
予 yú
尺 chǐ
(弔) diào
丑 chǒu
巴 bā
孔 kǒng
书 shū

四画以上

司 sī
民 mín
弗 fú
疋 pǐ
电 diàn
发 fā; fà
买 mǎi
尽 jìn
乱 luàn
肃 sù
乳 rǔ
承 chéng
亟 jí; qì
癸 guǐ
昼 zhòu
咫 zhǐ
(飛) fēi
(發) fā fà
(肅) sù
(亂) luàn
豫 yù

(6)
亠部

一至五画

亡 wáng
六 liù
亢 kàng
市 shì
玄 xuán

产 chǎn
交 jiāo
亦 yì
充 chōng
亥 hài
亩 mǔ
亨 hēng
弃 qì

六至七画

变 biàn
京 jīng
享 xiǎng
卒 zú
夜 yè
氓 máng; méng
帝 dì
彦 yàn
亭 tíng
亮 liàng
哀 āi

八画

旁 páng
衰 shuāi
(畝) mǔ
衷 zhōng
高 gāo
离 lí

九画

(産) chǎn
商 shāng
毫 háo
烹 pēng
孰 shú
袤 mào
率 lǜ; shuài

十至十一画

亵 xiè
就 jiù
(棄) qì
(裏) lǐ
禀 bǐng
雍 yōng

十二至十四画

(齊) qí
豪 háo
膏 gāo
裹 guǒ
褒 bāo

十五画以上

(齋) zhāi
(褻) xiè
襄 xiāng
嬴 yíng
羸 léi

(7)
冫部

一至五画

习 xí
冲 chōng; chòng
次 cì
决 jué
冰 bīng
冻 dòng
况 kuàng
冷 lěng
冶 yě

六至八画

冽 liè
净 jìng
凉 liáng; liàng
凌 líng
(凍) dòng
凄 qī
准 zhǔn
凋 diāo
凑 còu
减 jiǎn
寒 hán
凛 lǐn
凝 níng

(8)
冖部

冗 rǒng
写 xiě
军 jūn
罕 hǎn
冠 guān; guàn
冢 zhǒng
冥 míng
冤 yuān
幂 mì

(9)
讠(言)部

二画

计 jì
订 dìng
讣 fù
认 rèn
讥 jī

三画

讦 jié
讧 hòng
讨 tǎo
让 ràng
讯 xùn
讪 shàn
议 yì
讫 qì
(託) tuō
训 xùn
记 jì

四画

访 fǎng
讲 jiǎng
讳 huì
讴 ōu
讵 jù
讶 yà
讷 nè
论 lún; lùn
讼 sòng
许 xǔ
讹 é
讽 fěng
设 shè
诀 jué

五画

评 píng
证 zhèng
诃 hē
诅 zǔ
识 shí
诎 qū
诊 zhěn
诈 zhà
诉 sù
诋 dǐ
诌 zhōu
译 yì
词 cí
诏 zhào

六画

诧 chà
该 gāi
详 xiáng
诨 hùn
诓 kuāng
试 shì
诗 shī
诘 jié
(誇) kuā
诙 huī
诚 chéng
诠 quán
诛 zhū
话 huà
诞 dàn
诟 gòu
诡 guǐ
询 xún
诣 yì
诤 zhèng
诩 xǔ

七画

说 shuì; shuō
诫 jiè
(誌) zhì
诬 wū
语 yǔ; yù
诮 qiào
误 wù
诰 gào
诱 yòu
诲 huì
诳 kuáng
诵 sòng
(認) rèn

八画

谊 yì
谅 liàng
谆 zhūn
谈 tán
请 qǐng
诸 zhū
诺 nuò
读 dú
诼 zhuó
诽 fěi
课 kè
谂 shěn
(論) lún; lùn
诿 wěi
谁 shuí
谀 yú
调 diào; tiáo
谄 chǎn

九画

谛 dì
谙 ān
谚 yàn
(諮) zī
谜 mí
谎 huǎng
谋 móu
谌 chén
谍 dié
谏 jiàn
谐 xié
谑 xuè
谓 wèi
谕 yù
谗 chán
(諱) huì

十画

谤 bàng
谥 shì
谦 qiān
谧 mì
(講) jiǎng
谠 dǎng
谟 mó
谣 yáo
谢 xiè
(謅) zhōu

十一画

谨 jǐn
(謳) ōu
谩 màn
谬 miù

十二画

(識) shí;
谰 lán
谱 pǔ
谮 zèn
(證) zhèng
谲 jué
(譏) jī

十三至十四画

(議) yì
(護) hù
谴 qiǎn
(譯) yì
谵 zhān

十五画以上

(讀) dú
(讓) ràng
谶 chèn
(讒) chán
(讜) dǎng

(10)
二部

二 èr
干 gān; gàn
于 yú
亏 kuī
五 wǔ
开 kāi
井 jǐng
元 yuán
无 wú
云 yún
些 xiē
叆 ài
叇 dài

(11)
十部

十 shí

二至六画

支 zhī
卉 huì
古 gǔ
考 kǎo
毕 bì
华 huá
协 xié
克 kè
卒 zú
丧 sāng; sàng
卓 zhuō
直 zhí
卑 bēi
阜 fù

卖 mài
(協) xié

七至十画

南 nán
真 zhēn
(喪) sāng; sàng
嗇 sè
乾 qián
(乾) gān
博 bó

十一画以上

(準) zhǔn
(榦) gàn
(嗇) sè
斡 wò
兢 jīng
嘏 gǔ
翰 hàn
矗 chù

(12) 厂部

厂 chǎng

二至六画

厅 tīng
仄 zè
历 lì
厄 è
厉 lì
压 yā; yà
厌 yàn
励 lì
厕 cè

七至十画

厘 lí
厚 hòu
厝 cuò
原 yuán
厢 xiāng
厩 jiù
厥 jué
厨 chú
厦 shà
雁 yàn

十一画以上

厮 sī
(厲) lì
(廠) chǎng
(厭) yàn
(歷) lì
赝 yàn
(壓) yā; yà

(13) 匚部

二至五画

区 qū
匹 pǐ
巨 jù
叵 pǒ
匝 zā
匡 kuāng
匠 jiàng
匣 xiá
医 yī

六画以上

匦 guǐ
匿 nì
匪 fěi
匾 biǎn
匮 kuì
(區) qū
(匯) huì
颐 yí

(14) 卜(⺊)部

卜 bǔ

二至四画

卡 kǎ; qiǎ
占 zhàn
外 wài
贞 zhēn

五画以上

卦 guà
卧 wò
卓 zhuō
桌 zhuō

(15) 刂部

二至四画

刈 yì
刊 kān
刑 xíng
刓 wán
列 liè
划 huá; huà
刚 gāng
则 zé
创 chuāng; chuàng
刎 wěn

五画

判 pàn
别 bié; biè
利 lì
删 shān
刨 bào; páo
刭 jǐng

六画

剂 jì
刻 kè
刺 cì
到 dào
刽 guì
刹 chà; shā
制 zhì
刮 guā
剁 duò
刷 shuā; shuà

七画

前 qián
剃 tì
荆 jīng
剋 kè; kēi
剌 là
(剄) jǐng
削 xiāo; xuē
剐 guǎ
剑 jiàn

八画

剜 wān
剖 pōu
(剛) gāng
剔 tī
(剮) guǎ
剥 bāo; bō
剧 jù

九至十一画

副 fù
割 gē
(創) chuāng; chuàng
剩 shèng
剽 piāo
剿 jiǎo

十二画以上

劄 zhā; zhá
(劃) huá; huà
(劇) jù
(劍) jiàn
(劊) guì
(劑) jì

(16) 冂部

冈 gāng
冉 rǎn
同 tóng
网 wǎng
肉 ròu
罔 wǎng
(岡) gāng
周 zhōu

(17) 八(丷)部

八 bā

二至五画

兮 xī
公 gōng
分 fēn; fèn
兰 lán
半 bàn
只 zhī; zhǐ
兴 xīng; xìng
关 guān
并 bìng
共 gòng
兑 duì
兵 bīng
弟 dì

六至八画

卷 juǎn; juàn
(並) bìng
具 jù
单 dān
典 diǎn
养 yǎng
前 qián
酋 qiú
首 shǒu
真 zhēn
益 yì
兼 jiān

九至十五画

黄 huáng
兽 shòu
普 pǔ
奠 diàn
曾 céng; zēng
(義) yì
(與) yǔ; yú; yù
(養) yǎng
舆 yú
冀 jì
(興) xīng; xìng
蠲 juān

(18) 人(入)部

人 rén
入 rù

一至三画

个 gè
今 jīn
从 cōng; cóng
介 jiè
以 yǐ
仓 cāng
令 lǐng; lìng
丛 cóng

四至五画

伞 sǎn
全 quán
会 huì; kuài
合 hé
企 qǐ
众 zhòng
汆 cuān
含 hán
余 yú
巫 wū
(夾) jiā; jiá

六至九画

舍 shě; shè
命 mìng
臾 yú
俞 yú
俎 zǔ
衾 qīn
(倉) cāng
拿 ná
(龕) kān
盒 hé

十画以上

禽 qín
舒 shū
翕 xī
(傘) sǎn
(會) huì; kuài
(龕) kān

(19) 亻部

一至二画

亿 yì
仁 rén
什 shén; shí
仃 dīng
仆 pú
仇 chóu
仍 réng
化 huā; huà
仅 jǐn

三画

们 men; mén
仕 shì
仗 zhàng
付 fù
代 dài
仙 xiān
仪 yí
仟 qiān
他 tā
仞 rèn
仔 zǐ

四画

伫 zhù
仿 fǎng
伉 kàng
伙 huǒ
伪 wěi
伕 fū

传 chuán;
zhuàn
伟 wěi
休 xiū
伎 jì
伍 wǔ
伏 fú
伛 yǔ
优 yōu
伐 fá
仲 zhòng
价 jià; jie
伦 lún
份 fèn
伧 cāng
仵 wǔ
件 jiàn
任 rèn
伥 chāng
伤 shāng
仰 yǎng
似 shī; sì
伊 yī

五画

(佇) zhù
位 wèi
住 zhù
伴 bàn
佞 nìng
估 gū
体 tǐ
何 hé
佐 zuǒ
佑 yòu
(佈) bù
(佔) zhàn
攸 yōu
但 dàn
伸 shēn
佃 diàn
伶 líng
佚 yì
作 zuō;
zuó;
zuò
伯 bó; bǎi
佣 yōng; yòng
低 dī
佝 gōu
你 nǐ
伺 cì; sì
佛 fó; fú
伽 jiā

六画

侘 chà
佼 jiǎo
侪 chái
依 yī
佯 yáng
(併) bìng
侬 nóng
侠 xiá
佳 jiā
侍 shì
佶 jí
佬 lǎo
供 gòng
使 shǐ
佰 bǎi
例 lì
侄 zhí
侥 jiǎo
侦 zhēn
侣 lǚ
侃 kǎn
侧 cè
侩 kuài
佻 tiāo
侏 zhū
侨 qiáo
侈 chǐ
佩 pèi
侔 móu

七画

信 xìn
俦 chóu
俨 yǎn
俪 lì
便 biàn; pián
俩 liǎ; liǎng
(俠) xiá
俏 qiào
修 xiū
俚 lǐ
保 bǎo
俘 fú
俭 jiǎn
俗 sú
俐 lì
俄 é
侮 wǔ
(係) xì
俑 yǒng
俊 jùn
俟 sì
侵 qīn
侯 hóu
侷 jú

八画

倌 guān
倍 bèi
俯 fǔ
(倣) fǎng
倦 juàn
俸 fèng
倩 qiàn
债 zhài
(倀) chāng
借 jiè
偌 ruò
值 zhí
(倆) liǎ;
liǎng
倚 yǐ
俺 ǎn
倒 dǎo; dào
倾 qīng
倘 tǎng
(絛) tiáo
俱 jù
倡 chàng
(個) gè
僶 mǐn
候 hòu
(倫) lún
倭 wō
倪 ní
俾 bǐ
倜 tì
健 jiàn
倨 jù
倔 jué; juè

九画

停 tíng
偻 lóu
偾 fèn
做 zuò
偃 yǎn
偕 xié
偿 cháng
偶 ǒu
偎 wēi
偷 tōu
傀 kuí
假 jiǎ; jià
(偉) wěi

十画

傢 jiā
傧 bīn
傍 bàng
(傚) xiào
储 chǔ
傲 ào
(備) bèi
傅 fù
傥 tǎng
(傖) cāng;
(傑) jié

十一画

(傭) yōng;
yòng
(僅) jǐn
(傳) chuán;
zhuàn
催 cuī
(傷) shāng
傻 shǎ
像 xiàng

十二画

僮 tóng
僧 sēng
(僱) gù
(僥) jiǎo
儆 jǐng
僚 liáo
僭 jiàn
(僕) pú
(僞) wěi
(僑) qiáo

十三至十四画以上

(億) yì
(儀) yí
僵 jiāng
(價) jià;
jie
(儂) nóng
(儍) shǎ
(儉) jiǎn
(儈) kuài
僻 pì
(儐) bīn
(儕) chái
儒 rú
(儔) chóu
(優) yōu
(償) cháng
儡 lěi
(儘) jǐn
(儷) lì
(儼) yǎn

(20)
勹部

一至四画

勺 sháo
匀 yún
勿 wù
勾 gōu; gòu
句 jù
匆 cōng
包 bāo
旬 xún
匈 xiōng

五画以上

匍 pú
(芻) chú
匐 fú
够 gòu
(夠) gòu

(21)
儿部

儿 ér
兀 wù
元 yuán
允 yǔn
兄 xiōng
充 chōng
光 guāng
(兇) xiōng
兑 duì
先 xiān
克 kè
(兒) ér
党 dǎng
兜 dōu
兢 jīng

(22)
几(⺇)部

几 jī; jǐ
凡 fán
凤 fèng
夙 sù
凫 fú
壳 ké; qiào
秃 tū
凯 kǎi
凭 píng
凰 huáng
(凱) kǎi
(凴) píng
(鳳) fèng
凳 dèng

(23)
厶部

允 yǔn
去 qù
弁 biàn
台 tái
牟 móu
县 xiàn
矣 yǐ
叁 sān
参 cān; cēn;
shēn
畚 běn
能 néng

(24)
又(⺀)部

又 yòu

一至六画

叉 chā; chǎ
支 zhī
友 yǒu
反 fǎn

双 shuāng
劝 quàn
圣 shèng
对 duì
发 fā; fà
戏 xì
观 guān
欢 huān
变 biàn
取 qǔ
叔 shū
受 shòu
艰 jiān

七画以上

爰 yuán
叙 xù
叟 sǒu
难 nán; nàn
叠 dié
(叢) cóng
(雙) shuāng
矍 jué

(25)
廴部

廷 tíng
延 yán
建 jiàn

(26)
卩(㔾)部

卫 wèi
叩 kòu
卮 zhī
印 yìn
卯 mǎo
危 wēi
却 què
即 jí
卷 juǎn; juàn
卺 jǐn
卸 xiè
卿 qīng

(27)
阝(在左)部

二至四画

队 duì
阡 qiān
防 fáng
阱 jǐng
阵 zhèn
阳 yáng
阶 jiē
阴 yīn

五画

陀 tuó
陆 liù; lù
际 jì
阿 ā; ɑ; ē
陈 chén
阻 zǔ
附 fù
陂 pí

六至七画

陋 lòu
陌 mò
降 jiàng; xiáng
限 xiàn
院 yuàn
陡 dǒu
陛 bì
陨 yǔn
险 xiǎn
除 chú

八至九画

陪 péi
(陸) liù; lù
陵 líng
陲 chuí
陶 táo
陷 xiàn
(隊) duì
随 suí
(階) jiē
(陽) yáng
隅 yú
(陰) yīn
隆 lóng
隐 yǐn

十画以上

隘 ài
隔 gé
隙 xì
障 zhàng
(際) jì
隧 suì
(隨) suí
(險) xiǎn
(隱) yǐn
隳 huī

(28)
阝(在右)部

二至六画

邦 bāng
邪 xié; yé
那 nà
邮 yóu
邻 lín
邱 qiū
邸 dǐ
郊 jiāo
郑 zhèng
郎 láng
耶 yē
郁 yù

七至十二画以上

郤 què
郡 jùn
部 bù
郭 guō
都 dū
(郵) yóu
(鄉) xiāng
鄙 bì
(鄰) lín
(鄭) zhèng

(29)
凵部

凶 xiōng
击 jī
出 chū
凸 tū
凹 āo; wā
画 huà
函 hán
幽 yōu
凿 záo; zuò

(30)
刀(⺈)部

刀 dāo

一至六画

刃 rèn
切 qiē; qiè
分 fēn; fèn
召 zhāo
刍 chú
危 wēi
负 fù
争 zhēng
色 sè; shǎi
初 chū
龟 guī; jūn
奂 huàn
免 miǎn
券 quàn
兔 tù

七画以上

剪 jiǎn
象 xiàng
赖 lài
劈 pī
(龜) guī; jūn
(釁) xìn

(31)
力部

力 lì

二至六画

办 bàn
劝 quàn
功 gōng
夯 hāng
加 jiā
务 wù
动 dòng
劣 liè
劫 jié
劳 láo
励 lì
助 zhù
男 nán
劬 qú
劲 jìn; jìng
劭 shào
努 nǔ
劾 hé
势 shì

七至十画以上

勃 bó
(勁) jìn; jìng
勋 xūn
勉 miǎn
勇 yǒng
勘 kān
(動) dòng
(勞) láo
(勢) shì
勤 qín
(勵) lì
(勳) xūn
(勸) quàn

(32)
氵部

二至三画

汁 zhī
汀 tīng
汇 huì
汉 hàn
汗 hàn
污 wū
江 jiāng
汛 xùn
汐 xī
汲 jí
池 chí
汝 rǔ
汤 tāng

四画

沆 hàng
沁 qìn
沉 chén
汪 wāng
沄 yún
沐 mù
沛 pèi
汰 tài
沤 ōu; òu
沥 lì
沌 dùn
沏 qī
沙 shā
汩 gǔ
泛 fàn
汹 xiōng
沦 lún
沧 cāng
汽 qì
沃 wò
沟 gōu
没 méi; mò
泐 lè

五画

沱 tuó
泣 qì
注 zhù
泫 xuàn
泌 mì
泻 xiè
泳 yǒng
沫 mò
浅 qiǎn
法 fǎ
泔 gān
泄 xiè
沽 gū
河 hé
沾 zhān
泪 lèi
沮 jǔ
油 yóu
泅 qiú
泊 bó; pō
沿 yán; yàn
泡 pào
泽 zé
泾 jīng
治 zhì
泥 ní; nì
泯 mín
沸 fèi
泓 hóng
波 bō
沼 zhǎo
泼 pō

六画

浏 liú
济 jǐ; jì
洲 zhōu
洋 yáng

浑 hún
浒 hǔ
浓 nóng
浃 jiā
洼 wā
洁 jié
洪 hóng
洒 sǎ
洌 liè
浇 jiāo
泚 cǐ
浊 zhuó
洞 dòng
洇 yīn
洄 huí
测 cè
洽 qià
洗 xǐ
活 huó
涎 xián
洫 xù
派 pài
津 jīn

七画

浣 huàn
流 liú
润 rùn
涧 jiàn
涕 tì
浪 làng
涛 tāo
涝 lào
浦 pǔ
酒 jiǔ
(浹) jiā
涟 lián
(涇) jīng
消 xiāo
涉 shè
涅 niè
浬 lǐ
涓 juān
涡 wō
涔 cén
浮 fú
涂 tú
浴 yù
浩 hào
海 hǎi
涤 dí
涣 huàn
涌 yǒng
浚 jùn
涘 sì
浸 jìn
涨 zhǎng; zhàng
涩 sè

八画

淙 cóng
淀 diàn
淳 chún
淬 cuì
液 yè
淤 yū
淡 dàn
(淚) lèi
深 shēn
清 qīng
添 tiān
渚 zhǔ
鸿 hóng
淇 qí
淋 lín; lìn
淅 xī
渎 dú
淹 yān
涯 yá
渐 jiàn
渠 qú
(淺) qiǎn
淌 tǎng
淑 shū
淖 nào
混 hún; hùn
涸 hé
(渦) wō
淫 yín
(淪) lún
淆 xiáo
渊 yuān
渔 yú
淘 táo
渗 shèn
涮 shuàn
涵 hán

九画

渲 xuàn
湾 wān
渡 dù
游 yóu
滋 zī
湛 zhàn
港 gǎng
滞 zhì
湖 hú
渣 zhā
渺 miǎo
(湯) tāng
湿 shī
温 wēn
渴 kě
渭 wèi
溃 kuì
湍 tuān
溅 jiàn
湃 pài
(淵) yuān
溲 sōu
(湧) yǒng
溉 gài
渥 wò
湣 mǐn

十画

滓 zǐ
溶 róng
滨 bīn
滂 pāng
滚 gǔn
溏 táng
溢 yì
溯 sù
(溝) gōu
满 mǎn
漠 mò
(滅) miè
源 yuán
滤 lǜ
滥 làn
溷 hùn
滔 tāo
溪 xī
(滄) cāng
滗 bì
(滌) dí
溴 xiù
溜 liū; liù
滩 tān
溺 nì

十一画

演 yǎn
滴 dī
漩 xuán
(漢) hàn
(滿) mǎn
(滯) zhì
潇 xiāo
漆 qī
漕 cáo
漱 shù
(漚) ǒu; òu
漂 piāo
漫 màn
潴 zhū
漪 yī
(滲) shèn
漏 lòu
(漲) zhǎng; zhàng

十二画

澈 chè
澜 lán
(澇) lào
(潔) jié
潜 qián
(澆) jiāo
澎 pēng
潮 cháo
潸 shān
潭 tán
潦 lǎo; liǎo
(潛) qián
(潷) bì
澳 ào
澄 chéng
(潑) pō
潺 chán

十三画

濛 méng
濑 lài
濒 bīng
(濃) nóng
澡 zǎo
(澤) zé
(濁) zhuó
激 jī
澹 dàn
(澱) diàn

十四画至十六画

(濱) bīn
(濟) jǐ; jì
濡 rú
(濤) tāo
(濫) làn
(濕) shī
(瀏) liú
濯 zhuó
(濶) kuò
(澀) sè
(瀉) xiè
(瀆) dú
(濾) lǜ
瀑 pù
(濺) jiàn
瀛 yíng
(瀝) lì
瀚 hàn
(瀟) xiāo

十七画以上

灌 guàn
(灘) tān
(灑) sǎ
(灣) wān

(33)

忄(小)部

一至三画

忆 yì
忙 máng
忖 cǔn
忏 chàn

四画

忭 biàn
忱 chén
忝 tiǎn
怃 wǔ
怄 òu
怀 huái
忧 yōu
怅 chàng
忡 chōng
怆 chuàng
忤 wǔ
忾 kài
快 kuài
忸 niǔ

五画

怦 pēng
怯 qiè
怙 hù
怖 bù
怏 yàng
怜 lián
性 xìng
怕 pà
怪 guài
怡 yí

六画

恼 nǎo
恸 tòng
恃 shì
恭 gōng
恒 héng
恢 huī
恍 huǎng
恫 dòng
恻 cè
恰 qià
恬 tián
恤 xù
恪 kè
恨 hèn

七画

悯 mǐn
悦 yuè
悌 tì
悖 bèi
悚 sǒng
悟 wù
悄 qiao
悭 qiān
悍 hàn
悔 huǐ
悛 quān

八画

惋 wǎn
惊 jīng
悴 cuì

惦 diàn
惓 juàn
惮 dàn
惬 qiè
情 qíng
悻 xìng
(悵) chàng
惜 xī
惭 cán
悼 dào
惘 wǎng
惧 jù
惕 tì
悸 jì
惟 wéi
惆 chóu
惨 cǎn
惯 guàn

九画

(愜) qiè
愤 fèn
慌 huāng
惰 duò
愠 yùn
惺 xīng
愦 kuì
愕 è
惴 zhuì
愣 lèng
愉 yú
愎 bì
惶 huáng
愧 kuì
慨 kǎi
(惱) nǎo

十画至十二画

慑 shè
慕 mù
慎 shèn
慄 lì
(愴) chuàng
(愾) kài
慵 yōng
慷 kāng
(慪) òu
(慳) qiān
慢 màn
(慟) tòng
(慘) cǎn
憧 chōng
(憐) lián
憎 zèng
懂 dǒng
憬 jǐng
(憚) dàn
(憮) wǔ
憔 qiáo
懊 ào

十三画以上

(憶) yì
懒 lǎn
憾 hàn
懈 xiè
懦 nuò
懵 měng
(懷) huái
(懺) chàn
(懾) shè
(懼) jù

(34)
宀部

二至四画

宁 níng; nìng
它 tā
宇 yǔ
守 shǒu
宅 zhái
安 ān
字 zì
灾 zāi
完 wán
宏 hóng
牢 láo

五画

实 shí
宝 bǎo
宗 zōng
定 dìng
宠 chǒng
宜 yí
审 shěn
宙 zhòu
官 guān
宛 wǎn

六至八画

宣 xuān
宦 huàn
室 shì
宫 gōng
宪 xiàn
客 kè
宰 zǎi
害 hài
宽 kuān
宧 huàn
家 jiā
宵 xiāo
宴 yàn
宾 bīn
密 mì
寇 kòu
寄 jì
寂 jì
宿 sù; xiǔ
(寃) yuān

九至十一画

寒 hán
富 fù
寓 yù
寐 mèi
寝 qǐn
塞 sāi; sài; sè
寞 mò
(寧) níng; nìng
蜜 mì
寨 zhài
赛 sài
(賓) bīn
寡 guǎ
察 chá
寥 liáo
寤 wù
(寢) qǐn
(實) shí

十二画以上

寮 liáo
(審) shěn
(寫) xiě
(憲) xiàn
寰 huán
(寵) chǒng
(寶) bǎo

(35)
丬(爿)部

壮 zhuàng
(壯) zhuàng
妆 zhuāng
(妝) zhuāng
状 zhuàng
(狀) zhuàng
戕 qiāng
将 jiāng; jiàng
(將) jiāng; jiàng

(36)
广部

广 guǎng

二至五画

庄 zhuāng
庆 qìng
应 yīng; yìng
庐 lú
床 chuáng
庋 guǐ
库 kù
庇 bì
序 xù
庞 páng
庙 miào
府 fǔ
底 dǐ
庖 páo
废 fèi

六至九画

度 dù; duó
庭 tíng
席 xí
座 zuò
唐 táng
廊 láng
庶 shù
庵 ān
庸 yōng
康 kāng
赓 gēng

十至十三画以上

廓 guō
廉 lián
(廣) guǎng
腐 fǔ
廚 chú
(廟) miào
(廠) chǎng
(廢) fèi
(慶) qìng
(應) yīng; yìng
膺 yīng
鹰 yīng
(龐) páng
(廬) lú
(廳) tīng

(37)
门(門)部

门 mén
(門) mén

一至五画

闩 shuān
闪 shǎn
闭 bì
问 wèn
闯 chuǎng
闷 mēn; mèn
闰 rùn
(開) kāi
闱 wéi
闲 xián
间 jiān; jiàn
闹 nào
闸 zhá

六至十一画以上

阂 hé
闺 guī
闻 wén
闾 lǘ
阀 fá
阁 gé
阅 yuè
阄 jiū
阐 chǎn
阉 yān
阍 hūn
阎 yán
阔 kuò
(闈) wéi
阙 què
阖 hé
(關) guān
(闡) chǎn
(鬮) jiū

(38)
辶(辵)部

二至三画

边 biān
辽 liáo
迂 yū
达 dá
迈 mài
过 guò
迅 xùn
迁 qiān
迄 qì
巡 xún

四至五画

这 zhè; zhèi
进 jìn
远 yuǎn
运 yùn
违 wéi
还 hái; huán
连 lián
迓 yà
迕 wǔ
近 jìn
返 fǎn
迎 yíng
迟 chí
述 shù
迪 dí
迥 jiǒng
迭 dié
迤 yí; yǐ
迫 pǎi; pò
迩 ěr
迢 tiáo

六画

迹 jì
送 sòng
迸 bèng
迷 mí
逆 nì

荣 róng
荤 hūn
荦 luò
荚 jiá
荆 jīng
茸 róng
茬 chá
荐 jiàn
草 cǎo
茧 jiǎn
茵 yīn
茴 huí
荟 huì
茶 chá
荏 rěn
茗 míng
荫 yīn; yìn
茹 rú
荔 lì
药 yào

七画

莞 wǎn
莘 shēn
莹 yíng
莺 yīng
(華) huá
莽 mǎng
(莢) jiá
莲 lián
(莖) jīng
莫 mò
莠 yǒu
莓 méi
莅 lì
荷 hé; hè
获 huò

八画

萍 píng
菠 bō
菅 jiān
菩 pú
萤 yíng
营 yíng
萦 yíng
菁 jīng
菱 líng
著 zhù; zhuó
黄 huáng
(菴) ān
菲 fēi
菽 shū
菓 cuǒ
荫 yīn; yìn
萝 luó
菌 jūn; jùn
(萵) wō
菜 cài
萎 wěi
菊 jú
萄 táo
萧 xiāo
萨 sà
菇 gū

九画

落 là; luò
蒂 dì
(葉) yè
葬 zàng
募 mù
葺 qì
(萬) wàn
葛 gě
董 dǒng
葆 bǎo
葩 pā
葡 pú
葱 cōng
葵 kuí
(葦) wěi

十画

蒲 pú
(蒞) lì
蓉 róng
蓑 suō
蒿 hāo
蒺 jí
蓄 xù
蒙 mēng; méng; měng
蒜 suàn
(蓋) gài
蓝 lán
墓 mù
幕 mù
蓦 mù
(夢) mèng
(蒼) cāng
蓖 bì
蓬 péng
蓓 bèi
(蔭) yīn; yìn
蒸 zhēng

十一画

蓿 xu
蔗 zhè
蔽 bì
蔼 ǎi
蔷 qiáng
蔫 niān
暮 mù
摹 mó
慕 mù
蔓 màn
蔑 miè
蔚 wèi

十二画

(蕩) dàng
蕊 ruǐ
蕨 jué
蕃 fān; fán
(蕪) wú
蕉 jiāo
蔬 shū
蕴 yùn

十三画

薄 báo; bó
薪 xīn
(薦) jiàn
薮 sǒu
蕾 lěi
(薔) qiáng
薑 jiāng
薤 xiè
(蘋) píng
薨 hōng
薯 shǔ
(薈) huì
薇 wēi
(獲) huò
(蕭) xiāo
(薩) sà
薅 hāo

十四画至十五画

藉 jí; jiè
藍 lán
藏 cáng; zàng
藐 miǎo
薰 xūn
(舊) jiù
藓 xiǎn
藩 fān
藕 ǒu
(藝) yì
(藪) sǒu
(繭) jiǎn
(藥) yào
藤 téng

十六画以上

藻 zǎo
蘑 mó
(蘆) lú
(蘇) sū
(蘭) lán
蘼 mí
(蘿) luó
蘸 zhàn

(43)
大部

大 dà; dài

一至五画

太 tài
央 yāng
夯 hāng
夹 gā; jiā; jiá
夸 kuā
夺 duó
尖 jiān
夷 yí
奁 lián
(夾) ga; jiā; jiá
奉 fèng
奈 nài
奔 bēn; bèn
奇 jī; qí
奄 yǎn
奋 fèn

六画

奖 jiǎng
奕 yì
美 měi
牵 qiān
契 qì
奎 kuí

七至九画

套 tào
奚 xī
匏 páo
奢 shē
爽 shuǎng
奠 diàn
欹 qī
奥 ào

十一画以上

(奩) lián
(奪) duó
(獎) jiǎng
樊 fán
(奮) fèn

(44)
廾(在下部)

卉 huì
弁 biàn
异 yì
弃 qì
弄 nòng
舁 yú
弊 bì
彝 yí

(45)
尢部

尤 yóu
尬 gà
尴 gān
(尷) gān

(46)
寸部

寸 cùn

二至六画

对 duì
寺 sì
寻 xín; xún
导 dǎo
寿 shòu
将 jiāng; jiàng
封 fēng
耐 nài

七画以上

(剋) kè
辱 rǔ
射 shè
(專) zhuān
尉 wèi
尊 zūn
(尋) xún
(對) duì
(導) dǎo

(47)
弋部

弋 yì
弍 èr
式 shì
忒 tè; tēi; tuī
鸢 yuān
贰 èr
弑 shì

(48)
扌部

一至三画

扎 zā; zhā; zhá
打 dá; dǎ
扑 pū
扒 bā; pá
扔 rēng
扩 kuò
扪 mén
扞 hàn
扛 káng
扣 kòu
托 tuō
执 zhí
扫 sǎo; sào
扬 yáng

四画

抖 dǒu
抗 kàng

护 hù
扶 fú
抚 fǔ
技 jì
抠 kōu
扰 rǎo
扼 è
拒 jù
找 zhǎo
批 pī
扯 chě
抄 chāo
扮 bàn
抢 qiāng; qiǎng
折 zhē; zhé; shé
抓 zhuā
扳 bān
投 tóu
抑 yì
抛 pāo
拟 nǐ
抒 shū
抉 jué
扭 niǔ
把 bǎ; bà
报 bào

五画

拧 níng; nǐng; nìng
拉 lā; lá;
拄 zhǔ
拦 lán
拌 bàn
抨 pēng
抹 mā; mǒ; mò
拓 tà; tuò
拔 bá
拢 lǒng
拣 jiǎn
拈 niān
担 dān; dàn
押 yā
抽 chōu
拐 guǎi
拙 zhuō
拎 līn
拖 tuō
拍 pāi
拆 cā; chāi
拥 yōng
抵 dǐ
拘 jū
抱 bào
择 zé; zhái
拚 pàn; pīn
抬 tái
抿 mǐn
拂 fú
披 pī
招 zhāo
拨 bo
拗 ào; niù
拇 mǔ

六画

挖 wā
按 àn
挤 jǐ
拼 pīn
挥 huī
挟 jiā; xié
拭 shì
挂 guà
持 chí
拮 jié
拷 kǎo
拱 gǒng
挞 tà
挎 kuà
挠 náo
挡 dǎng
拽 zhuài
拴 shuān
拾 shí
挑 tiāo; tiǎo
挺 tǐng
括 kuò
指 zhī; zhǐ
挣 zhēng; zhèng
挪 nuó
拯 zhěng

七画

捞 lāo
捕 bǔ
捂 wǔ
(挾) jiā; xié
振 zhèn
捎 shāo
捍 hàn
捏 niē
捉 zhuō
捆 kǔn
捐 juān
损 sǔn
挹 yì
捌 bā
捋 luō
捡 jiǎn
捣 dǎo
换 huàn
挽 wǎn
捅 tǒng
挨 āi; ái

八画

控 kòng
接 jiē
掠 lüě; lüè
掂 diān
掷 zhì
(捲) juǎn
掸 dǎn
捩 liè
掮 qián
探 tàn
捧 pěng
(掛) guà
措 cuò
描 miáo
捺 nà
掩 yǎn
捷 jié
排 pái
掉 diào
捋 lǚ
授 shòu
(採) cǎi
捻 niǎn
(捨) shě
捶 chuí
推 tuī
掀 xiān
掬 jū
掏 tāo
掐 qiā
(掃) sǎo; sào
据 jù
掘 jué
掼 guàn

九画

搅 jiǎo
搁 gē
搓 cuō
搂 lōu; lǒu
揍 zòu
搽 chá
搭 dā
(揀) jiǎn
揩 kāi
揽 lǎn
提 dī; tí
(揚) yáng
揖 yī
揭 jiē
揣 chuāi; chuǎi
援 yuán
揿 qìn
揪 jiū
插 chā
(揑) niē
搜 sōu
搀 cān
搔 sāo
揆 kuí
揉 róu
摒 bìng
握 wò

十画

摈 bìn
搞 gǎo
搪 táng
(搧) shān
摄 shè
摸 mō; mó
搏 bó
摁 èn
摆 bǎi
摇 yáo
(搶) qiǎng
携 xié
(搗) dǎo
搬 bān
摊 tān

十一画

摘 zhāi
摔 shuāi
撇 piē; piě
(摳) kōu
(摟) lōu; lǒu
撂 liào
摧 cuī

十二画

撞 zhuàng
撤 chè
撙 zǔn
(撈) lāo
撵 niǎn
(撻) tà
(撓) náo
撕 sī
撒 sā; sǎ
撩 liāo; liáo
撅 juē
撑 chēng
(撲) pū
撮 zuō
(撣) dǎn
擒 qín
播 bō
撬 qiào
(撫) fǔ
(撥) bō
撰 zhuàn

十三画

擅 shàn
(擁) yōng
擂 lēi; léi; lèi
擀 gǎn
撼 hàn
(擋) dǎng
(據) jù
(擄) lǔ
操 cāo
(擇) zé
(撿) jiǎn
(擔) dān; dàn

十四画

(擰) níng; nǐng; nìng
(擯) bìn
擦 cā
(擠) jǐ
(擴) kuò
(擲) zhì
(擡) tái
擤 xǐng
(擬) nǐ
擢 zhuó

十五至十七画

(擾) rǎo
(擺) bǎi
(攏) lǒng
攘 rǎng
攒 zǎn
(攙) chān
(攔) lán

十八画以上

(攝) shè
(攤) tān
攥 zuàn
攫 jué
(攪) jiǎo
(攬) lǎn

(49)
小(⺌)部

小 xiǎo

一至四画

少 shǎo; shào
尔 ěr
尘 chén
尖 jiān
光 guāng
劣 liè
当 dāng; dàng
肖 xiāo; xiào

五至八画

尚 shàng
尝 cháng
省 shěng; xǐng
党 dǎng
堂 táng
常 cháng
雀 què

九至十画

(囈) yì
(囑) zhǔ

(51)
囗部

〇 líng
二至四画
囚 qiú
四 sì
团 tuán
因 yīn
回 huí
囱 cōng
园 yuán
围 wéi
困 kùn
囤 dùn; tún
囵 lún
囫 hú
五至七画
国 guó
固 gù
囹 líng
图 tú
圃 pǔ
圄 yǔ
圆 yuán
八至十一画
圈 juān; juàn; quān
啬 sè
圉 yǔ
(國) guó
(圇) lún
(圍) wéi
(園) yuán
(嗇) sè
(團) tuán
(圖) tú

(52)
巾部

巾 jīn
一至四画
币 bì
市 shì
布 bù
帅 shuài
师 shī
吊 diào
帆 fān
希 xī
帐 zhàng
五至七画
帘 lián
帖 tiē; tiě; tiè
帜 zhì
帕 pà
帛 bó
帚 zhǒu
帑 tǎng
帝 dì
帮 bāng
带 dài
帧 zhèng
(帥) shuài
(師) shī
八至十画
(帳) zhàng
(帶) dài
常 cháng
帷 wéi
幅 fú
帽 mào
幄 wò
幕 mù
幌 huǎng
十一至十三画以上
(幣) bì
幔 màn
幢 chuáng; zhuàng
(幟) zhì
幡 fān
(幫) bāng
(歸) guī

(53)
山部

山 shān
三至四画
屿 yǔ
屹 yì
岁 suì
岌 jí
屺 qǐ
岂 qǐ
岐 qí
岗 gāng; gǎng
岑 cén
岔 chà
岙 ào
岛 dǎo
岚 lán
五至六画
岸 àn
岩 yán
岿 kuī
(岡) gāng
(岬) jiǎ
岭 lǐng
岳 yuè
岱 dài
峦 luán
峡 xiá
峙 shì; zhì
炭 tàn
峥 zhēng
幽 yōu
七至九画
(豈) qǐ
(峽) xiá
峭 qiào
峪 yù
峨 é
(島) dǎo
峰 fēng
峻 jùn
崇 chóng
崎 qí
崖 yá
崭 zhǎn
(崗) gāng; gǎng
崩 bēng
崛 jué
嵯 cuó
嵌 qiàn
(歲) suì
崴 wēi; wěi
嵎 yú
嵬 wéi
十至十七画以上
嵩 sōng
嶂 zhàng
嶙 lín
(嶼) yǔ
(嶺) lǐng
(嶽) yuè
巅 diān
巍 wēi
巉 chán
(巋) kuī
(巒) luán
(巖) yán

(54)
彳部

彳 chì
三至五画
行 háng; xíng
彷 fǎng
彻 chè
役 yì
往 wǎng; wàng
征 zhēng
径 jìng
彿 fú
彼 bǐ
六至七画
衍 yǎn
徉 yáng
待 dāi; dài
徊 huái; huí
徇 xùn
律 lǜ
很 hěn
(後) hòu
徒 tú
(徑) jìng
徐 xú
八至九画
(術) shù
徜 cháng
徘 pái
徙 xǐ
得 dé; děi
(從) cōng; cóng
衔 xián
街 jiē
御 yù
(復) fù
徨 huáng
循 xún
十至十三画以上
徬 páng
衙 yá
微 wēi
徭 yáo
(徹) chè
德 dé
(徵) zhēng; zhǐ
(衛) wèi
衡 héng
徽 huī
衢 qú

(55)
彡部

形 xíng
杉 shā; shān
彤 tóng
衫 shān
参 cān, cēn; shēn
彦 yàn
须 xū
彬 bīn
彪 biāo
彩 cǎi
(參) cān; cēn; shēn
彰 zhāng
影 yǐng
(鬱) yù

(56)
夕部

夕 xī
舛 chuǎn
名 míng
岁 suì
多 duō
罗 luō; luó
(夠) gòu
梦 mèng
夤 yín
(夢) mèng
夥 huǒ

(57)
夂部

冬 dōng
处 chǔ; chù
务 wù
各 gè
条 tiáo
备 bèi
复 fù
夏 xià
惫 bèi
(愛) ài
(憂) yōu

(58)
犭部

二至五画
犯 fàn
犷 guǎng
狄 dí
狂 kuáng
犹 yóu
狈 bèi
狞 níng
狙 jū
狐 hú
狗 gǒu
六至七画
狩 shòu
狡 jiǎo
狱 yù
狭 xiá
狮 shī
独 dú
狰 zhēng
狠 hěn
狼 láng
狸 lí
狷 juàn
八至九画
猝 cù
猜 cāi

猪 zhū
猎 liè
猫 máo
猖 chāng
猛 měng
(猶) yóu
猢 hú
猩 xīng
猥 wěi
猾 huá
猴 hóu

十至十五画以上

猿 yuán
(獅) shī
(獄) yù
(獨) dú
(獰) níng
(獷) guǎng
(獵) liè

(59)
饣(食)部

二至五画

饥 jī
饨 tún
饪 rèn
饭 fàn
饮 yǐn
饯 jiàn
饰 shì
饱 bǎo
饲 sì

六至七画

饺 jiǎo
饼 bǐng
饵 ěr
饶 ráo
蚀 shí
饷 xiǎng
馁 něi
馀 yú
饿 è

八至九画

馆 guǎn
(餞) jiàn
馄 hún
餚 yáo
餬 hú
馈 kuì
馊 sōu
馋 chán

十画以上

馐 xiū
馍 mó
馏 liú
馑 jǐn
馒 mán
(饒) ráo
馔 zhuàn
(饑) jī
(饞) chán

(60)
彐(⺕彑)部

归 guī
刍 chú
寻 xún
当 dāng; dàng
灵 líng
帚 zhǒu
录 lù
彗 huì
(尋) xún
彘 zhì
彝 yí
(歸) guī

(61)
尸部

尸 shī

一至四画

尺 chǐ
尹 yǐn
尻 kāo
尼 ní
尽 jǐn; jìn
层 céng
屁 pì
尾 wěi
局 jú
尿 niào

五至六画

屉 tì
居 jū
届 jiè
屈 qū
昼 zhòu
咫 zhǐ
屏 bǐng; píng
屎 shǐ
(屍) shī
屋 wū

七至十四画以上

展 zhǎn
屑 xiè
屐 jī
屠 tú
屡 lǚ
犀 xī
属 shǔ; zhū
孱 càn; chán
(屢) lǚ
(層) céng
履 lǚ
(屬) shǔ

(62)
己(巳)部

己 jǐ
已 yǐ
巴 bā
包 bāo
异 yì
导 dǎo
岂 qǐ
忌 jì
巷 hàng; xiàng

(63)
弓部

弓 gōng

一至五画

引 yǐn
(弔) diào
弗 fú
弘 hóng
弛 chí
张 zhāng
弦 xián
弧 hú
弥 mí
弩 nǔ

六至十一画以上

弯 wān
弭 mǐ
弱 ruò
弹 dàn; tán
(張) zhāng
粥 zhōu
弼 bì
强 qiáng; qiǎng
(發) fā; fà
(彈) dàn; tán
(彌) mí
疆 jiāng
(彎) wān

(64)
屮部

(芻) chú

(65)
女部

女 nǚ

二至三画

奶 nǎi
奴 nú
妆 zhuāng
妄 wàng
奸 jiān
如 rú
妇 fù
妃 fēi
她 tā
好 hǎo; hào
妈 mā

四画

妨 fáng
妒 dù
妍 yán
妩 wǔ
妓 jì
妪 yù
妣 bǐ
妙 miào
妥 tuǒ
妊 rèn
妖 yāo
姊 zǐ
妞 niū
(妝) zhuāng

五画

妾 qiè
妹 mèi
姑 gū
妻 qī
姐 jiě
妯 zhóu
姓 xìng
委 wěi
姗 shān
始 shǐ
姆 mǔ

六画

姹 chà
姣 jiāo
姿 zī
姜 jiāng
姘 pīn
娄 lóu
娃 wá
姥 lǎo
娅 yà
要 yāo; yào
威 wēi
耍 shuǎ
姨 yí
娆 ráo
姻 yīn
姝 shū
娇 jiāo
(姸) yán
(姙) rèn
姦 jiān

七画

娑 suō
娴 xián
娘 niáng
娠 shēn
娌 lǐ
娱 yú
娟 juān
娩 miǎn
娓 wěi
婀 ē

八画

婆 pó
婶 shěn
婉 wǎn
婵 chán
婊 biǎo
婭 yà
娶 qǔ
婪 lán
娼 chāng
(婁) lóu
婴 yīng
婢 bì
婚 hūn
(婦) fù

九至十画

媒 méi
媪 ǎo
嫂 sǎo
婿 xù
媚 mèi
嫁 jià
嫔 pín
嫉 jí
嫌 xián
媾 gòu
媳 xí
媲 pì

十一至十四画以上

(嫗) yù
嫖 piáo
嫦 cháng
(嬈) ráo
(嬋) chán
嬉 xī
(嫵) wǔ
嬖 bì
(嬪) pín
(嬸) shěn
孀 shuāng

(66)
幺部

幺 yāo
乡 xiāng
幻 huàn
幼 yòu
兹 cí; zī

幽 yōu
(幾) jī; jǐ
畿 jī

(67)
子(子)部

子 zǐ; zi
孓 jué
孑 jié

一至四画

孔 kǒng
孕 yùn
存 cún
孙 sūn
孖 mā
孝 xiào
孚 fú
孜 zī

五至九画以上

学 xué
享 xiǎng
孟 mèng
孤 gū
孢 bāo
孥 nú
孪 luán
孩 hái
(孫) sūn
孰 shú
孳 zī
(學) xué
(孿) luán
孺 rú

(68)
纟(糸)部

一至三画

纠 jiū
纡 yū
红 hóng
纤 qiàn; xián
约 yāo; yuē
纨 wán
级 jí
纪 jì

四画

纹 wén; wèn
纺 fǎng
纬 wěi
纯 chún
纱 shā
纲 gāng
纳 nà
纵 zòng
纶 lún
纷 fēn
纴 rèn
纸 zhǐ
纾 shū
纽 niǔ

五画

绊 bàn
线 xiàn
练 liàn
组 zǔ
绅 shēn
细 xì
织 zhī
绌 chù
终 zhōng
绉 zhòu
绎 yì
经 jīng; jìng
绐 dài
绍 shào

六画

绞 jiǎo
统 tǒng
绑 bǎng
绒 róng
结 jiē; jié
绕 rào
绘 huì
给 gěi; jǐ
(紝) rèn
绗 háng
绛 jiàng
络 luò
绚 xuàn
绝 jué
(絲) sī

七画

继 jì
绠 gěng
(經) jīng; jìng
绢 juàn
绥 suí
绣 xiù
绦 tāo

八画

综 zōng
绽 zhàn
绩 jī
绪 xù
续 xù
绮 qǐ
(綫) xiàn
绱 shàng
绯 fēi
绰 chuò
(網) wǎng
(綱) gāng
绳 shéng
绶 shòu
(綸) lún
维 wéi
绵 mián
绷 bēng; běng; bàng
绸 chóu
缀 zhuì
绿 lù; lù

九画

缔 dì
缕 lǚ
编 biān
(練) liàn
缄 jiān
缅 miǎn
缆 lǎn
缉 jī; qī
缓 huǎn
缎 duàn
缏 biàn; pián
缐 xiàn
(緯) wěi
缘 yuán

十至十一画

缟 gǎo
缤 bīn
缠 chán
缢 yì
缜 zhěn
缚 fù
(緻) zhì
缝 féng; fèng
(縐) zhòu
(縴) qiàn
缩 suō
缥 piāo
(縷) lǚ
缨 yīng
(總) zǒng
(縱) zòng
缪 miù; móu
缫 sāo

十二画

(織) zhī
缮 shàn
(繞) rào
(繐) suì
缭 liáo
(繩) shéng

十三至十五画以上

缰 jiāng
(繹) yì
(繪) huì
缴 jiǎo
(繡) xiù
(繽) bīn
(繼) jì
(纏) chán
(續) xù
纍 lěi
(變) biàn
(纖) xiān
(纔) cái
(纜) lǎn

(69)
马(馬)部

马 mǎ
(馬) mǎ

二至四画

驭 yù
闯 chuǎng
驮 duò; tuó
驯 xùn
驰 chí
驴 lǘ
驱 qū
驳 bó

五画

驼 tuó
驻 zhù
驶 shǐ
驷 sì
驸 fù
驹 jū
驿 yì
骀 dài; tái
驽 nú
驾 jià

六至八画

骇 hài
骂 mà
骄 jiāo
骆 luò
骋 chěng
验 yàn
骑 qí

九至十四画以上

骗 piàn
骚 sāo
骛 wù
腾 téng
(驅) qū
骡 luó
(驚) jīng
(驕) jiāo
(驛) yì
(驗) yàn
骤 zhòu
(驢) lǘ

(70)
巛部

(災) zāi
巢 cháo

(71)
灬部

四至七画

杰 jié
点 diǎn
羔 gāo
烈 liè
热 rè
(烏) wū
烹 pēng
焉 yān

八至九画

煮 zhǔ
(爲) wéi; wèi
(無) wú
焦 jiāo
然 rán
煎 jiān
蒸 zhēng
煦 xù
照 zhào
煞 shā; shà

十画以上

熬 áo
熙 xī
熏 xūn
熊 xióng
(熱) rè
熹 xī
燕 yàn

(72)
斗部

斗 dǒu; dòu
料 liào
斜 xié
斟 zhēn
斡 wò

(73)
文部

文 wén
齐 qí
吝 lìn
斋 zhāi
虔 qián
紊 wěn
斑 bān
斌 bīn
斐 fěi
齑 jī

(74)
方部

方 fāng
房 fáng
(於) yú
放 fàng
施 shī
旁 páng
旄 máo
旅 lǚ
旌 jīng
族 zú
旋 xuán; xuàn
旗 qí

(75)
火部

火 huǒ

一至三画

灭 miè
灰 huī
灯 dēng
灾 zāi
灶 zào
灿 càn
灸 jiǔ
灼 zhuó
灵 líng
(災) zāi

四画

炕 kàng
炎 yán
炉 lú
炬 jù
炖 dùn
炒 chǎo
炙 zhì
炊 chuī

五画

炫 xuàn
烂 làn
荧 yíng
炳 bǐng
炼 liàn
炽 chì
炭 tàn
炯 jiǒng
炸 zhá; zhà
炮 páo; pào
烁 shuò

六至七画

烫 tàng
烤 kǎo
耿 gěng
烘 hōng
烦 fán
烧 shāo
烛 zhú
烟 yān
烩 huì
烬 jìn
焊 hàn
烽 fēng
焕 huàn

八至十画

焙 bèi
焚 fén
焰 yàn
煸 biān
煤 méi
(煉) liàn
煨 wēi
煅 duàn
煌 huáng
熔 róng
(熒) yíng
(榮) róng
煽 shān
熄 xī
熘 liū

十一至十二画

熨 yùn
(燙) tàng
(熾) chì
燧 suì
(營) yíng
(燒) shāo
燎 liáo; liǎo
燃 rán
(燄) yàn
(燈) dēng

十三至十五画以上

(燦) càn
燥 zào
(燭) zhú
(燴) huì
燻 xūn
(燼) jìn
爆 bào
(爍) shuò
(爐) lú
(爛) làn
爨 cuàn

(76)
心部

心 xīn

一至三画

必 bì
忘 wàng
闷 mèn
忑 tè
志 zhì
忐 tǎn
忌 jì
忍 rěn

四至五画

态 tài
忠 zhōng
怂 sǒng
念 niàn
忿 fèn
忽 hū
总 zǒng
毖 bì
思 sī
怎 zěn
怨 yuàn
急 jí
怠 dài
怒 nù

六画

恋 liàn
恣 zī
恙 yàng
恚 huì
恐 kǒng
恶 ě; è; wù
虑 lǜ
恩 ēn
恁 nèn
息 xī
恳 kěn
恕 shù

七至八画

悬 xuán
患 huàn
悉 xī
悠 yōu
您 nín
恿 yǒng
(惡) ě; è; wù
惹 rě
惠 huì
惑 huò
悲 bēi
崽 zǎi
惩 chéng
惫 bèi

九画

意 yì
慈 cí
想 xiǎng
感 gǎn
愚 yú
(愛) ài
愈 yù
愁 chóu
愆 qiān
愍 mǐn

十至十一画

愿 yuàn
(態) tài
(慶) qìng
憋 biē
慧 huì
憃 chōng
(憂) yōu
(慮) lǜ
(慫) sǒng
憨 hān
慰 wèi

十二至十四画以上

(憲) xiàn
(憑) píng
憩 qì
(憊) bèi
懑 mèn
(應) yīng; yìng
懋 mào
(懇) kěn
(懲) chéng
(懸) xuán
懿 yì
(戀) liàn

(77)
户部

户 hù

一至六画以上

启 qǐ
戽 hù
房 fáng
戾 lì
肩 jiān
所 suǒ
扁 biǎn; piān
扇 shān; shàn
扈 hù
扉 fēi
雇 gù

(78)
礻(示)部

一至四画

礼 lǐ
社 shè
祀 sì
视 shì
祈 qí
祇 qí; zhǐ

五至七画

祛 qū
祖 zǔ
神 shén
祝 zhù
祗 zhī
祠 cí
祥 xiáng
祷 dǎo
祸 huò

八画以上

禅 chán; shàn
祺 qí
(禍) huò
禄 lù
福 fú
(禪) chán; shàn
(禮) lǐ
(禱) dǎo

(79)
王部

王 wáng

一至四画

主 zhǔ
玉 yù
全 quán
弄 lòng; nòng
玖 jiǔ
玛 mǎ
玩 wán
环 huán
现 xiàn
玫 méi

五至六画

珐 fà
玲 líng
珍 zhēn
皇 huáng
珊 shān
玻 bō
班 bān
莹 yíng
珠 zhū
玺 xǐ

七至八画

琉 liú
望 wàng
琅 láng
球 qiú
琐 suǒ
理 lǐ
琼 qióng
斑 bān
琵 pí
琴 qín
琶 pá

琳 líng
琢 zhuó; zuó
琥 hǔ
九至十画
瑟 sè
(聖) shèng
瑞 ruì
瑜 yú
瑰 guī
瑕 xiá
瑙 nǎo
璃 lí
瑶 yáo
十一画以上
(瑩) yíng
璀 cuǐ
噩 è
璨 càn
(環) huán
(璽) xǐ
(瓊) qióng
璧 bì

(80)
韦(韋)部

韦 wéi
(韋) wéi
韧 rèn
(韌) rèn
韫 yùn
(韞) yùn
韬 tāo
(韜) tāo

(81)
木部

木 mù
一至二画
术 shù
本 běn
未 wèi
末 me; mò
札 zhá
朽 xiǔ
朴 pǔ
杀 shā
朱 zhū
机 jī
朵 duǒ
杂 zá
权 quán
三画
床 chuáng
杆 gān; gǎn
杠 gàng
杜 dù
杖 zhàng
村 cūn
材 cái
杏 xìng
束 shù
杉 shān
条 tiáo
极 jí
杈 chā; chà
杨 yáng
李 lǐ
四画
杰 jié
杭 háng
枕 zhěn
枉 wàng
林 lín
枝 zhī
枢 shū
杯 bēi
柜 guì
杪 miǎo
枣 zǎo
杳 yǎo
果 guǒ
(東) dōng
枘 ruì
采 cǎi
枞 cōng; zōng
松 sōng
枪 qiāng
杵 chǔ
枚 méi
析 xī
板 bǎn
枭 xiāo
枫 fēng
构 gòu
杼 zhù
(牀) chuáng
五画
柒 qī
染 rǎn
柠 níng
亲 qīn
柱 zhù
柿 shì
栏 lán
栈 zhàn
标 biāo
荣 róng
柑 gān
某 mǒu
枯 kū
柄 bǐng
柩 jiù
栋 dòng
柬 jiǎn
查 chá; zhā
相 xiāng; xiàng
枵 xiāo
柚 yòu
栅 shān; zhà
柏 bǎi
柳 liǔ
栎 lì
树 shù
柔 róu
枷 jiā
架 jià
六画
案 àn
桨 jiǎng
校 jiào; xiào
桩 zhuāng
核 hé; hú
样 yàng
框 kuāng; kuàng
椰 yē
桔 jié; jú
栽 zāi
桓 huán
栖 qī; xī
栗 lì
桎 zhì
档 dàng
柴 chái
桌 zhuō
桐 tóng
桃 táo
(殺) shā
株 zhū
桥 qiáo
桁 héng
格 gé
桅 wéi
栩 xǔ
桑 sāng
根 gēn
七画
渠 qú
梁 liáng
梳 shū
梯 tī
械 xiè
彬 bīn
梵 fàn
梗 gěng
梢 sào; shāo
检 jiǎn
梏 gù
梨 lí
梅 méi
桶 tǒng
梭 suō
八画
棕 zōng
棺 guān
(棄) qì
棒 bàng
棱 lēng; léng
棋 qí
椰 yē
植 zhí
森 sēn
椟 dú
(棟) dòng
椅 yǐ
(棲) qī
(棧) zhàn
椒 jiāo
棹 zhào
棵 kē
棍 gùn
棘 jí
弑 shì
椎 zhuī
集 jí
棉 mián
棚 péng
椭 tuǒ
(極) jí
九画
榇 chèn
榈 lǘ
楼 lóu
楔 xiē
楂 chá
楚 chǔ
楷 kǎi
(業) yè
(楊) yáng
楫 jí
槐 huái
槌 chuí
楹 yíng
概 gài
椽 chuán
十画
寨 zhài
榨 zhà
榜 bǎng
槁 gǎo
(榮) róng
榛 zhēn
(構) gòu
毂 gǔ
(槓) gàng
模 mó; mú
槛 jiàn; kǎn
榻 tà
(槍) qiāng
榫 sǔn
榭 xiè
槃 pán
榴 liú
十一画
樟 zhāng
(樣) yàng
樯 qiáng
横 héng; hèng
槽 cáo
(樞) shū
(標) biāo
(樓) lóu
樱 yīng
(樂) lè; yuè
(樅) cōng; zōng
槲 hú
橡 xiàng
橄 gǎn
(橢) tuǒ
(槳) jiǎng
十二画
樽 zūn
(樹) shù
橐 tuó
橛 jué
橱 chú
(樸) pǔ
橇 qiāo
(橋) qiáo
樵 qiáo
橹 lǔ
橙 chén
橘 jú
(機) jī
十三至十四画
檀 tán
(檣) qiáng
(檔) dàng
(檢) jiǎn
檄 xí
(檸) níng
(櫃) guì
(檻) jiàn; kǎn
十五画以上
(櫝) dú
(櫟) lì
(櫬) chèn
(權) quán
(欄) lán
(鬱) yù

(82)
犬部

状 zhuàng
戾 lì
轶 yì
(狀) zhuàng
哭 kū
臭 chòu; xiù
猷 yóu
献 xiàn
(獃) dāi
(獸) shòu
(獻) xiàn

(83)
歹部

歹 dǎi

二至五画

列 liè
死 sǐ
夙 sù
歼 jiān
殁 mò
残 cán
殂 cú
殃 yāng
殆 dài

六画以上

毙 bì
殊 shū
殉 xùn
殓 liàn
殚 dān
(殘) cán
殛 jí
殡 bìn
(斃) bì
(殭) jiāng
(殮) liàn
(殯) bìn
(殲) jiān

(84)
车(車)部

车 chē; jū
(車) chē; jū

一至四画

轧 gá; yà; zhá
军 jūn
轨 guǐ
轩 xuān
转 zhuǎn; zhuàn
轭 è
轮 lún
斩 zhǎn
软 ruǎn
轰 hōng

五至七画

轱 gū
轶 yì
轴 zhóu
轻 qīng
较 jiào
载 zǎi; zài
轿 jiào
辄 zhé
辅 fǔ
辆 liàng
(輕) qīng
(輓) wǎn

八至九画

辇 niǎn
辈 bèi
(輛) liàng
辉 huī
(輪) lún
辍 chuò
辎 zī
毂 gū; gǔ
辐 fú
输 shū

十至十二画以上

辖 xiá
辕 yuán
輿 yú
辗 zhǎn
辘 lù
(轉) zhuǎn; zhuàn
辙 zhé
(轎) jiào
(轟) hōng

(85)
戈部

戈 gē

一至三画

戋 jiān
戊 wù
划 huá; huà
戎 róng
戍 shù
成 chéng
戏 xì
戒 jiè
我 wǒ

四至八画

或 huò
戕 qiāng
(戔) jiān
哉 zāi
战 zhàn
咸 xián
威 wēi
栽 zāi
载 zǎi
戛 jiá
戚 qī
裁 cái
(幾) jǐ

九至十一画以上

戡 kān
戥 děng
截 jié
臧 zāng
戮 lù
畿 jī
(戰) zhàn
戴 dài
(戲) xì
戳 chuō

(86)
比部

比 bǐ
毕 bì
毖 bì
毙 bì
皆 jiē

(87)
瓦部

瓦 wǎ; wà

三至九画

瓩 qiān wǎ
瓮 wèng
瓷 cí
瓶 píng
甄 zhēn
(甕) wèng

(88)
止部

止 zhǐ
正 zhèng
此 cǐ
步 bù
武 wǔ
歧 qí
肯 kěn
歪 wāi
耻 chǐ
(歲) suì
(歷) lì
(歸) guī

(89)
攴部

敲 qiāo

(90)
日部

日 rì

一至三画

旦 dàn
旧 jiù
早 zǎo
旬 xún
旭 xù
旷 kuàng
旱 hàn
时 shí

四画

旺 wàng
昙 tán
昔 xī
杳 yǎo
昆 kūn
昌 chāng
明 míng
昏 hūn
昂 áng

五画

春 chūn
昧 mèi
是 shì
显 xiǎn
映 yìng
星 xīng
昨 zuó
昵 nì
昭 zhāo

六至七画

晏 yàn
晕 yūn
晖 huī
(時) shí
晋 jìn
晓 xiǎo
晃 huǎng; huàng
晌 shǎng
匙 chí; shi
晤 wù
晨 chén
晦 huì
晚 wǎn
昼 zhòu

八画

晾 liàng
普 pǔ
景 jǐng
晴 qíng
暑 shǔ
晰 xī
量 liáng; liàng
暂 zàn
晶 jīng
智 zhì
晷 guǐ

九至十一画

暄 xuān
暗 àn
暖 nuǎn
暌 kuí
暇 xiá
暮 mù
暧 ài
暴 bào; pù

十二至十四画以上

(曇) tán
(曉) xiǎo
曚 méng
曙 shǔ
(曖) ài
(曠) kuàng
(韙) wěi
曝 pù
曦 xī
曩 nǎng
(曬) shài

(91)
曰(⺜)部

曰 yuē

二至八画

曲 qǔ
旨 zhǐ
曳 yè
者 zhě
沓 dá; tà
(者) zhě
冒 mào
曷 hé
書 shū
(勗) xù
冕 miǎn
曾 céng; zēng
替 tì
最 zuì
(嘗) cháng

(92)
贝(貝)部

贝 bèi
(貝) bèi

二至四画

贞 zhēn
则 zé
负 fù
贡 gòng
财 cái
员 yuán
贮 zhù
责 zé

贤 xián
贪 tān
贬 biǎn
货 huò
质 zhì
贩 fàn
购 gòu
贯 guàn

五画

(貯) zhù
貳 èr
贱 jiàn
贲 bēn; bì
貼 tiē
贵 guì
(買) mǎi
贷 dài
贸 mào
贻 yí
费 fèi
贺 hè

六至七画

赃 zāng
资 zī
赅 gāi
贼 zéi
贾 gǔ; jiǎ
贿 huì
赁 lìn
赂 lù
(賓) bīn
(實) shí
赈 zhèn
赊 shē

八画

赔 péi
赋 fù
(賣) mài
赌 dǔ
赍 jī
赎 shú
(賢) xián
(賤) jiàn
赏 shǎng
赐 cì
(質) zhì

九画以上

赖 lài
赛 sài
赚 zhuàn
赘 zhuì
(購) gòu
赠 zèng
赞 zàn
赡 shàn
(贓) zāng
(贜) zāng
(贖) shú

(93)
见(見)部

见 jiàn; xiàn

二至七画

观 guān; guàn
视 shì
现 xiàn
规 guī
觅 mì
觉 jiào; jué
览 lǎn
觊 jì
舰 jiàn

八画以上

觍 tiǎn
(親) qīn
靦 miǎn
覦 yú
(覬) jì
觐 jìn
觑 qù
(覺) jiào; jué
(覽) lǎn
(觀) guān; guàn

(94)
父部

父 fù
爷 yé
斧 fǔ
爸 bà
爹 diē
(爺) yé

(95)
牛(⺧牜)部

牛 niú

二至四画

牝 pìn
牟 móu
牢 láo
牡 mǔ
告 gào
牦 máo
牧 mù
物 wù

五至九画以上

荦 luò
牯 gǔ
牵 qiān
牲 shēng
牴 dǐ
特 tè
牺 xī
(牽) qiān
犁 lí
犊 dú
犄 jī
犀 xī
犒 kào
(犖) luò
靠 kào
犟 jiàng
(犢) dú
(犧) xī

(96)
手部

手 shǒu

四至八画

承 chéng
拜 bài
挛 luán
拳 quán
挈 qiè
挚 zhì
拿 ná
挲 sā; suō
掌 zhǎng
掰 bāi
掣 chè

九画以上

摩 mā; mó
(摯) zhì
擎 qíng
(擊) jī
(擘) bāi
攀 pān
(攣) luán

(97)
毛部

毛 máo

三至九画以上

尾 wěi
毡 zhān
耄 mào
毫 háo
(毬) qiú
毯 tǎn
毹 shū
麾 huī
氅 chǎng
(氈) zhān

(98)
气部

气 qì
氕 piē
氘 dāo
氖 nǎi
氙 xiān
氛 fèn
氢 qīng
氨 ān
氧 yǎng
(氣) qì
(氫) qīng
氮 dàn

(99)
攵部

二至五画

收 shōu
攻 gōng
改 gǎi
孜 zī
放 fàng
败 bài
政 zhèng
故 gù
畋 tián

六至七画

效 xiào
致 zhì
敌 dí
敝 bì
(敧) qī
赦 shè
教 jiāo; jiào
敕 chì
救 jiù
敛 liǎn
敏 mǐn
敢 gǎn

八至十一画以上

敦 dūn
散 sǎn; sàn
敬 jìng
敞 chǎng
数 shǔ; shù; shuò
(敵) dí
敷 fū
(數) shǔ; shù; shuò
整 zhěng
(斂) liǎn
(變) biàn
(黴) méi

(100)
片部

片 piān; piàn
版 bǎn
牍 dú
(牋) jiān
牒 dié
牌 pái
(牘) dú

(101)
斤部

斤 jīn
斥 chì
斩 zhǎn
斧 fǔ
所 suǒ
欣 xīn
断 duàn
斯 sī
新 xīn
斫 zhuó
(斷) duàn

(102)
爪(爫)部

爪 zhǎo; zhuǎ
妥 tuǒ
孚 fú
受 shòu
采 cǎi
觅 mì
(爭) zhēng
爬 pá
乳 rǔ
爱 ài
(爲) wéi; wèi
舀 yǎo
奚 xī
(愛) ài
(亂) luàn
孵 fū
爵 jué

(103)
月(⺝)部

月 yuè

一至三画

有 yǒu
肌 jī
肋 lē; lèi
肓 máng
肝 gān
肛 gāng
肚 dǔ; dù
肘 zhǒu
肖 xiāo; xiào
肠 cháng

四画

肪 fáng

肮 āng
育 yù
肩 jiān
肤 fū
肢 zhī
肺 fèi
肯 kěn
肾 shèn
肿 zhǒng
肴 yáo
胀 zhàng
朋 péng
股 gǔ
肥 féi
服 fú; fù
胁 xié

五画

胖 pàng
脉 mài;mò
胡 hú
胚 pēi
背 bēi; bèi
胪 lú
胆 dǎn
胃 wèi
胄 zhòu
胜 shēng; shèng
胞 bāo
胫 jìng
胎 tāi

六画

脐 qí
胶 jiāo
脊 jí; jǐ
脑 nǎo
脏 zāng; zàng
朕 zhèn
朔 shuò
朗 lǎng
脓 nóng
胰 yí
脍 kuài
(脈) mài; mò
脆 cuì
胸 xiōng
脂 zhī
能 néng
(脅) xié

七画

望 wàng
脱 tuō
脖 bó
脚 jiǎo
脯 fǔ
(脣) chún
豚 tún
(脛) jìng
脸 liǎn

八画

腔 qiāng
腕 wàn
腋 yè
腑 fǔ
(勝) shèng
(脹) zhàng
期 qī
腊 là
朝 cháo; zhāo
(腎) shèn
腌 ā; yān
腓 féi
腴 yú
脾 pí
腱 jiàn

九画

腾 téng
腰 yāo
(腸) cháng
腥 xīng
腮 sāi
(腫) zhǒng
腺 xiàn
鹏 péng
腿 tuǐ
(腦) nǎo

十画

膀 bǎng; pàng
膏 gāo
膂 lǚ
膜 mó
膊 bó
膈 gé
膝 xī
膘 biāo
(膚) fū
(膠) jiāo
膳 shàn
膨 péng

十三画以上

臆 yì
膺 yīng
臃 yōng
(騰) téng
朦 méng
(膿) nóng
臊 sāo; sào
(膾) kuài
(臉) liǎn
膽 dǎn
臀 tún
臂 bì
(臍) qí
(臘) là
(朧) lóng
(臚) lú
(臟) zàng

(104)
欠部

欠 qiàn

二至八画

次 cì
欢 huān
欤 yú
欧 ōu
软 ruǎn
欣 xīn
欬 kài
欷 xī
欲 yù
款 kuǎn
欺 qī

九画以上

歇 xiē
歉 qiàn
歌 gē
(歐) ōu
歔 xū
(歟) yú
(歡) huān

(105)
风(風)部

风 fēng
(風) fēng
飒 sà
飓 jù
飕 sōu
飘 piāo
飙 biāo
(飆) biāo

(106)
殳部

殳 shū

四至八画

殴 ōu
殁 mò
段 duàn
(殺) shā
般 bān
殷 yīn
(殼) ké; qiào
(發) fā; fà

九画以上

彀 gòu
毁 huǐ
殿 diàn
毅 yì
(毆) ōu

(107)
肀(⺻聿)部

聿 yù
隶 lì
(書) shū
肃 sù
(晝) zhòu
(畫) huà
肆 sì
肄 yì
肇 zhào
(肅) sù
(盡) jǐn; jìn

(108)
毋(母)部

毋 wú
母 mǔ
每 měi
毒 dú
贯 guàn

(109)
水(氺)部

水 shuǐ

一至六画以上

永 yǒng
求 qiú
汞 gǒng
录 lù
尿 niào
沓 dá; tà
泰 tài
泵 bèng
泉 quán
浆 jiāng; jiàng
黎 lí
(漿) jiāng; jiàng

(110)
穴部

穴 xué

一至五画

穷 qióng
究 jiū
空 kōng; kòng
帘 lián
穹 qióng
突 tū
窃 qiè
穿 chuān
窍 qiào
容 róng
窄 zhǎi
窈 yǎo

六至七画

窒 zhì
窕 tiǎo
窑 yáo
窜 cuàn
窝 wō
窖 jiào
窗 chuāng
窘 jiǒng

八画以上

窥 kuī
窦 dòu
窠 kē
(窩) wō
窟 kū
(窪) wā
(窮) qióng
(竅) qiào
(竄) cuàn
(竈) zào
(竇) dòu
(竊) qiè

(111)
立部

立 lì

一至六画

产 chǎn
妾 qiè
亲 qīn
竖 shù
彦 yàn
飒 sà
站 zhàn
竞 jìng
章 zhāng
(產) chǎn
翌 yì

七画以上

竦 sǒng
童 tóng
竣 jùn
靖 jìng
(豎) shù
意 yì
竭 jié
端 duān
(競) jìng

(112)
疒部

二至四画

疔 dīng
疖 jiē
疗 liáo

疟 nüè; yào
疝 shàn
疙 gē
疚 jiù
疡 yáng
疬 lì
疥 jiè
疮 chuāng
疯 fēng
疫 yì
疤 bā

五画

症 zhēng; zhèng
疴 kē
病 bìng
疽 jū
疹 zhěn
疾 jí
疼 téng
痈 yōng
疱 pào
痉 jìng
疲 pí
痂 jiā

六至七画

痒 yǎng
痔 zhì
痍 yí
疵 cī
痊 quán
痕 hén
痧 shā
痣 zhì
痘 dòu
痨 láo
痞 pǐ
(痙) jìng
痢 lì
痛 tòng

八至九画

瘁 cuì
痰 tán
痱 fèi
痼 gù
痹 bì
痴 chī
瘌 là
(瘧) nüè; yào
(瘍) yáng
瘟 wēn
瘦 shòu
瘊 hóu

十至十一画

瘼 mò
(瘡) chuāng
瘪 biē; biě
瘢 bān
瘤 liú
瘫 tān
瘴 zhàng
瘰 luǒ
瘳 chōu
瘾 yǐn
瘸 qué

十二至十四画以上

(癆) láo
癍 bān
(療) liáo
癌 ái
癔 yì
癞 lài
(癤) jiē
癖 pǐ
(癢) yǎng
(癟) biē; biě
癣 xuǎn
癫 diān
(癧) lì
(癮) yǐn
(癰) yōng
(癱) tān

(113) 衤部

二至四画

补 bǔ
初 chū
衬 chèn
衫 shān
衩 chǎ; chà
袄 ǎo
袂 mèi

五至六画

袜 wà
袒 tǎn
袖 xiù
袍 páo
被 bèi
袴 kù
裆 dāng

七至八画

裤 kù
(補) bǔ
裕 yù
裙 qún
裱 biǎo
褂 guà
裨 bì

九画以上

褊 biǎn
褙 bèi
褐 hè
(複) fù
褓 bǎo
褪 tuì
褥 rù
褴 lán
褫 chǐ
褶 zhě
(襖) ǎo
襁 qiǎng
襟 jīn
襠 dāng
(襪) wà
(襤) lán
(襯) chèn

(114) 示部

示 shì
奈 nài
祟 suì
票 piào
祭 jì
禀 bǐng
禁 jīn; jìn
(禦) yù

(115) 石部

石 shí

二至四画

矿 kuàng
矾 fán
码 mǎ
研 yán
砖 zhuān
砌 qì
砂 shā
砚 yàn
砭 biān
斫 zhuó
砍 kǎn
泵 bèng

五画

砣 tuó
砰 pēng
砝 fǎ
砸 zá
砺 lì
砻 lóng
砧 zhēn
础 chǔ
砥 dǐ
砲 pào
砾 lì
破 pò

六至七画

硅 guī
硕 shuò
硫 liú
硬 yìng
硝 xiāo
确 què

八画

碇 dìng
碗 wǎn
碎 suì
碰 pèng
碍 ài
碘 diǎn
碑 bēi
硼 péng
碉 diāo
碌 lù

九画

磋 cuō
磁 cí
碧 bì
碟 dié
碴 chā; chá
碱 jiǎn
碳 tàn

十至十二画

磅 bàng; páng
(確) què
磕 kē
磊 lěi
磐 pán
碾 niǎn
磨 mó; mò
磬 qìng
磺 huáng
(磚) zhuān
磷 lín
礁 jiāo

十三画以上

(礎) chǔ
(礦) kuàng
(礪) lì
(礙) ài
(礫) lì
(礱) lóng
(礮) pào

(116) 龙(龍)部

龙 lóng
(龍) lóng
垄 lǒng
(壟) lǒng
砻 lóng
(礱) lóng
袭 xí
(襲) xí
龛 kān
(龕) kān

(117) 业部

业 yè
凿 záo; zuò
(業) yè

(118) 目部

目 mù

二至四画

盯 dīng
盲 máng
眈 dān
相 xiāng; xiàng
眄 miàn
盹 dǔn
眇 miǎo
省 shěng; xǐng
眨 zhǎ
盼 pàn
看 kān; kàn
眉 méi

五至七画

眩 xuàn
眠 mián
眯 mī; mí
眶 kuàng
眺 tiào
睁 zhēng
眸 móu
眼 yǎn
睐 lài
睒 shǎn
睑 jiǎn
鼎 dǐng

八画

睛 jīng
睦 mù
睹 dǔ
瞄 miáo
(睞) lài
睫 jié
督 dū
睬 cǎi
睡 shuì
睨 nì
睥 pì

九至十一画

瞅 chǒu
睽 kuí
瞎 xiā
瞑 míng
瞌 kē
瞒 mán
瞥 piē
(瞞) mán
(縣) xiàn
瞟 piǎo

瞠 chēng
瞰 kàn

十二画以上

瞳 tóng
(瞭) liǎo;liào
瞬 shùn
瞧 qiáo
瞩 zhǔ
瞽 gǔ
矇 mēng;méng
瞼 jiǎn
瞻 zhān
(矚) zhǔ

(119)
田部

田 tián
甲 jiǎ
申 shēn
由 yóu
电 diàn

二至四画

亩 mǔ
町 tǐng
甸 diàn
男 nán
备 bèi
思 sī
畎 quǎn
畏 wèi
毗 pí
胃 wèi
禺 yú
界 jiè
畋 tián
畈 fàn

五至六画

(畝) mǔ
畜 chù; xù
畔 pàn
(畢) bì
留 liú
畚 běn
畦 qí
(異) yì
略 lüè
累 léi;lěi;lèi

七至十一画以上

富 fù
畴 chóu
番 fān
(畫) huà
畸 jī
(當) dāng; dàng
畿 jī
(奮) fèn
(壘) lěi
(疇) chóu
纍 léi; lěi
(疊) déi

(120)
罒部

四 sì

二至八画

罗 luō;luó
罚 fá
罢 bà
罝 jū
詈 lì
(買) mǎi
署 shǔ
置 zhì
罪 zuì
罩 zhào
蜀 shǔ

九画以上

(罰) fá
(罵) mà
(罷) bà
罹 lí
羁 jī
(羅) luō; luó
蠲 juān

(121)
皿部

皿 mǐn

三至五画

盂 yú
孟 mèng
(盃) bēi
盅 zhōng
盆 pén
盈 yíng
益 yì
盏 zhǎn
盐 yán
盍 hé
盎 àng

六画

盗 dào
盖 gài
盔 kuī
盛 shèng
蛊 gǔ
盒 hé
盘 pán

八画以上

(盞) zhǎn
盟 méng
(監) jiān
(盡) jìn
(盤) pán
盥 guàn
(盪) dàng
蠲 juān
(蠱) gǔ
(鹽) yán
(豔) yàn

(122)
钅(金)部

一至三画

针 zhēn
钉 dīng; dìng
钌 liào
钏 chuàn
钓 diào
钗 chāi

四画

钙 gài
钜 jù
钝 dùn
钞 chāo
钟 zhōng
钠 nà
钢 gāng
钧 jūn
钥 yào;yuè
钦 qīn
钩 gōu
钨 wū
钮 niǔ

五画

钱 qián
钳 qián
钵 bō
钹 bó
钺 yuè
钻 zuān; zuàn
钾 jiǎ
铃 líng
铁 tiě
铅 qiān
铆 mǎo
铄 shuò

六画

铵 ǎn
铲 chǎn
铰 jiǎo
铳 chòng
铐 kào
铛 chēng; dāng
铝 lǚ
铜 tóng
铠 kǎi
铡 zhá
铢 zhū
铣 xǐ; xiǎn
铤 tǐng
铧 huá
铬 gè
铮 zhēng
银 yín

七画

锌 xīn
锐 ruì
锑 tī
铸 zhù
铺 pù
链 liàn
销 xiāo
锁 suǒ
铿 kēng
锄 chú
锅 guō
锉 cuò
锈 xiù
锋 fēng

八画

锭 dìng
(錶) biǎo
错 cuò
锚 máo
(錢) qián
(鋼) gāng
锡 xī
锣 luó
(鍋) guō
锤 chuí
锥 zhuī
锦 jǐn
锨 xiān
键 jiàn
(録) lù
锯 jù
锰 měng

九至十画

锵 qiāng
镀 dù
镁 měi
镂 lòu
锲 qiè
(鍼) zhēn
(鍾) zhōng
锻 duàn
镑 bàng
镐 gǎo
镊 niè
(鏵) huá
镇 zhèn
(鎧) kǎi
镍 niè
(鎢) wū
镌 juān

十一至十二画

镜 jìng
(鏟) chǎn
(鏗) kēng
镖 biāo
(鏤) lòu
镘 màn
(鏘) qiāng
(鐘) zhōng
(鐐) liào
(鐫) juān
镫 dèng

十三至十五画

镰 lián
镭 léi
(鐵) tiě
(鐺) chēng; dāng
镯 zhuó

十四画以上

(鑄) zhù
(鑑) jiàn
镳 biāo
(鑠) shuò
镴 là
镶 xiāng
(鑰) yào; yuè
镵 chán
(鑷) niè
(鑼) luó
鑽 zuān; zuàn

(123)
矢部

矢 shǐ
矣 yǐ
知 zhī
矩 jǔ
矫 jiáo;jiǎo
矧 shěn
短 duǎn
矮 ǎi
雉 zhì
(矯) jiáo; jiǎo

(124)
禾部

禾 hé

二至三画

利 lì
秃 tū
秀 xiù
私 sī
秆 gǎn
和 hé;hè huó;hu

秉 bǐng
委 wěi
季 jì

四画

科 kē
秋 qiū
秕 bǐ
秒 miǎo
香 xiāng
种 zhǒng; zhòng

五画

秘 bì; mì
秤 chèng
秣 mò
乘 chéng
租 zū
秧 yāng
积 jī
秩 zhì
称 chèn; chēng

六至七画

秾 nóng
秸 jiē
秽 huì
移 yí
税 shuì
稍 shāo
(稈) gǎn
程 chéng
稀 xī
黍 shǔ

八画

稔 rěn
稚 zhì
稗 bài
稠 chóu
颓 tuí
稣 sū
颖 yǐng

九至十一画

(稱) chèn; chēng
(種) zhǒng; zhòng
稳 wěn
稼 jià
稿 gǎo
(穀) gǔ
稽 jī; qǐ
稷 jì
稻 dào
黎 lí
(積) jī
穑 sè
穆 mù

十二画以上

穗 suì
黏 nián
(穫) huò
(穡) sè
(穢) huì
馥 fù
(穠) nóng
(穩) wěn

(125)
白部

白 bái

一至三画

百 bǎi
皂 zào
帛 bó
的 de; dí

四至十画以上

皇 huáng
皆 jiē
皈 guī
泉 quán
皎 jiǎo
皑 ái
皓 hào
皙 xī
魄 pò
(皚) ái

(126)
瓜部

瓜 guā
瓞 dié
瓠 hù
瓢 piáo
瓣 bàn
瓤 ráng

(127)
鸟(鳥)部

鸟 niǎo
(鳥) niǎo

二至四画

鸡 jī
鸢 yuān
鸣 míng
(鳳) fèng
鸩 zhèn
鸥 ōu
鸦 yā
鸨 bǎo

五画

鸵 tuó
莺 yīng
鸪 gū
鸭 yā
鸯 yāng
鸳 yuān
鶵 chú

六至八画

鸿 hóng
鸾 luán
鸽 gē
鹄 gǔ; hú
鹅 é
鹉 wǔ
鹊 què
鹏 péng
鹌 ān

九画以上

鹜 wù
(鶯) yīng
鹤 hè
(鷄) jī
(鶵) chú
(鷗) ōu
鹦 yīng
鹫 jiù
鹰 yīng
鹳 guàn
(鸞) luán

(128)
用部

用 yòng
甩 shuǎi
甫 fǔ
甭 béng

(129)
矛部

矛 máo
柔 róu
矜 jīn
(務) wù
蟊 máo

(130)
疋(𤴓)部

疋 pǐ
蛋 dàn
疏 shū
楚 chǔ
疑 yí

(131)
皮部

皮 pí
皱 zhòu
皲 jūn
颇 pō
皴 cūn
(皺) zhòu

(132)
衣部

衣 yī

二至六画

表 biǎo
衰 shuāi
衷 zhōng
袅 niǎo
袭 xí
袋 dài
装 zhuāng
裁 cái
裂 liè
亵 xiè
裒 póu

七画以上

裘 qiú
(裏) lǐ
裔 yì
(裝) zhuāng
裹 guǒ
(製) zhì
褒 bāo
(褻) xiè
襄 xiāng
(襲) xí

(133)
羊(⺶⺷)部

羊 yáng

一至四画

养 yǎng
差 chā; chà; chāi; cī
美 měi
姜 jiāng
羔 gāo
恙 yàng
羞 xiū

五画以上

着 zhāo; zháo; zhe; zhuó
盖 gài
羚 líng
羡 xiàn
善 shàn
翔 xiáng
(義) yì
群 qún
(養) yǎng
羹 gēng
羸 léi

(134)
米部

米 mǐ

二至四画

籴 dí
类 lèi
娄 lóu
屎 shǐ
籽 zǐ
料 liào
粉 fěn

五至八画

粒 lì
粘 nián; zhān
粗 cū
粜 tiào
粪 fèn
粟 sù
粥 zhōu
粱 liáng
粮 liáng
粳 jīng
粹 cuì
精 jīng
粼 lín

九画以上

糊 hū; hú; hù
糖 táng
糕 gāo
糙 cāo
糜 méi; mí
糠 kāng
糟 zāo
(糞) fèn
(糧) liáng
糯 nuò
(糴) dí
鬻 yù
(糶) tiào

(135)
耒部

耒 lěi
耔 zǐ
耕 gēng
耘 yún
耗 hào
耙 bà; pá

(136)
老部

老 lǎo
考 kǎo
耆 qí
耄 mào
耋 dié

(137)
耳部

耳 ěr

二至四画

取 qǔ
耶 yé
闻 wén
耷 dā

耿 gěng
耽 dān
耻 chǐ
耸 sǒng

五至七画

聋 lóng
职 zhí
聆 líng
聊 liáo
联 lián
聒 guō
(聖) shèng
聘 pìn

八画以上

聚 jù
聪 cōng
聩 kuì
(聲) shēng
(聰) cōng
(聳) sǒng
(聯) lián
(職) zhí
(聾) lóng
(聽) tīng

(138)
臣部

臣 chén
卧 wò
(臨) lín

(139)
西(覀)部

西 xī
要 yāo;yào
栗 lì
票 piào
粟 sù
(覆) fù

(140)
页(頁)部

页 yè
(頁) yè

二至三画

顶 dǐng
顷 qǐng
项 xiàng
顺 shùn
须 xū

四至五画

颃 háng
烦 fán
顾 gù
顿 dùn
颂 sòng
颁 bān
预 yù
硕 shuò
颅 lú
领 lǐng
颈 jǐng
颇 pō

六至八画

颊 jiá
颌 gé;hé
颐 yí
(頭) tóu
(頰) jiá
(頸) jǐng
频 pín
颔 hàn
颓 tuí
颖 yǐng
颗 kē

九至十画

额 é
颜 yán
题 tí
颚 è
(類) lèi
颠 diān
(願) yuàn
颡 sǎng

十一画以上

(顧) gù
嚣 xiāo
颤 chàn;zhàn
颥 rú
(顯) xiǎn
颦 pín
(顱) lú
颧 quán

(141)
虍部

二至五画

虎 hǔ
虏 lǔ
虐 nüè
虔 qián
虑 lù
虚 xū
(處) chǔ;chù
彪 biāo

六画以上

虞 yú
(號) hào
(虜) lǔ
(慮) lù
(膚) fū
(戲) xì
(虧) kuī

(142)
虫部

虫 chóng

一至四画

虱 shī
虻 méng
虾 xiā
虹 hóng
虽 suī
蚁 yǐ
蚤 zǎo
蚂 mǎ
蚊 wén
蚌 bàng
蚕 cán
蚓 yǐn
蚝 háo

五画

蛇 shé; yí
蛀 zhù
蚶 hān
蛆 qū
蛊 gǔ
蚱 zhà
蚯 qiū
蛋 dàn

六至七画

蛮 mán
蛟 jiāo
蛙 wā
蛐 qū
蛔 huí
蛤 gé; há
蛛 zhū
蜈 wú
蜗 wō
蛾 é
蜂 fēng
蛹 yǒng

八画

蜜 mì
蜿 wān
蜷 quán
蝉 chán
蜻 qīng
蜡 là
蜚 fēi
蝇 yíng
(蝸) wō
蜘 zhī
蜢 měng

九画

蝙 biān
蝶 dié
蝴 hú
蝠 fú
(蝨) shī
蝎 xiē
蝌 kē
蝮 fù
蝗 huáng
蝥 máo
(蝦) xiā

十至十一画

螃 páng
(螢) yíng
螟 míng
螯 áo
蟒 mǎng
蟆 má
融 róng
蟀 shuài
螳 táng
蟋 xī
蟊 máo

十二画以上

(蟲) chóng
(蠅) yíng
(蟬) chán
蠃 luǒ
(蟻) yǐ
蟾 chán
蟹 xiè
(蠔) háo
蠕 rú
蠢 chǔn
蠡 lí
(蠟) là
蠹 dù
(蠱) gǔ
(蠶) cán
(蠻) mán

(143)
缶部

缶 fǒu
缸 gāng
缺 quē
罂 yīng
罄 qìng
罅 xià
罐 guàn

(144)
舌部

舌 shé
乱 luàn
舍 shě;shè
舐 shì
甜 tián
舒 shū
辞 cí
舔 tiǎn
(舖) pù
(舘) guǎn

(145)
竹(⺮)部

竹 zhú

二至四画

竿 gān
竽 yú
笈 jí
笃 dǔ
笔 bǐ
笑 xiào
笋 sǔn

五画

笠 lì
笺 jiān
笨 bèn
笼 lóng;
lǒng
笛 dí
笙 shēng
符 fú
笞 chī
第 dì
笤 tiáo

六画

筴 jiā
筐 kuāng
等 děng
筑 zhù
策 cè
筚 bì
筛 shāi
筒 tǒng
答 dā; dá
筏 fá
筵 yán
筋 jīn
筍 sǔn
筝 zhēng
(筆) bǐ

七画

筷 kuài
简 jiǎn
筹 chóu
签 qiān
(節) jiē; jié

八画

箔 bó
管 guǎn
箧 qiè
箸 zhù;zhuó
箕 jī
箍 gū
(箋) jiān
算 suàn
箩 luó
箠 chuí
箫 xiāo

九画

篓 lǒu
箭 jiàn

篇 piān
(篋) qiè
箱 xiāng
(範) fàn
箴 zhēn
篑 kuì
篁 huáng
篆 zhuàn
十画
篙 gāo
篱 lí
篝 gōu
(築) zhù
篮 lán
篡 cuàn
(篳) bì
(篩) shāi
篦 bì
篷 péng
十一至十二画
簏 lù
簇 cù
簖 duàn
簧 huáng
(簍) lǒu
篾 miè
簪 zān
十三至十四画
簿 bù
(簾) lián
簸 bǒ; bò
籁 lài
(簽) qiān
(簫) xiāo
籍 jí;jiè
(籌) chóu
(籃) lán
纂 zuǎn
十五画以上
(籠) lóng; lǒng
(籤) qiān
(籪) duàn
(籬) lí
(籮) luó
(籲) yù

(146)
臼部

臼 jiù
臾 yú
(兒) ér
舀 yǎo
舂 chōng
(與) yú;yǔ; yù
舅 jiù
(舉) jǔ
(舊) jiù

(147)
自部

自 zì
息 xī
臭 chòu;xiù

(148)
血部

血 xiě;xuè
衄 nù
衅 xìn
(衆) zhòng

(149)
舟部

舟 zhōu
三至四画
舢 shān
舫 fǎng
航 háng
舰 jiàn
舱 cāng
舨 bǎn
般 bān
五画以上
舵 duò
舷 xián
舸 gě
盘 pán
舶 bó
船 chuán
艇 tǐng
艘 sōu
(盤) pán
(艙) cāng
(艦) jiàn

(150)
羽部

羽 yǔ
三至六画
扇 shàn
翅 chì
翁 wēng
翎 líng
(習) xí
翔 xiáng
翘 qiáo; qiào
翕 xī
八画以上
翠 cuì
翡 fěi
翩 piān
翰 hàn
翮 hé
翱 áo
翼 yì
(翹) qiáo; qiào
翻 fān
(翺) áo

(151)
艮(艮)部

良 liáng
艰 jiān
即 jí
垦 kěn
恳 kěn
既 jì
暨 jì
(艱) jiān

(152)
糸部

一至五画
系 xì; jì
紊 wěn
素 sù
索 suǒ
紧 jǐn
萦 yíng
累 léi;lěi;lèi
六画以上
紫 zǐ
絮 xù
(緊) jǐn
(縈) yíng
(縣) xiàn
縻 mí
繁 fán
纂 zuǎn
(纍) léi;lěi;lèi

(153)
辛部

辛 xīn
辜 gū
辞 cí
辟 bì; pì
辣 là
辨 biàn
辩 biàn
(辦) bàn
辫 biàn
(辭) cí
瓣 bàn
(辮) biàn
(辯) biàn

(154)
言部

言 yán
訇 hōng
(這) zhè
詈 lì
誉 yù
誊 téng
誓 shì
警 jǐng
(譽) yù
譬 pì

(155)
麦(麥)部

麦 mài
(麥) mài
麸 fū
(麪) miàn
麴 qū
(麵) miàn

(156)
走部

走 zǒu
赴 fù
赳 jiū
赶 gǎn
起 qǐ
越 yuè
趁 chèn
趋 qū
超 chāo
(趕) gǎn
趣 qù
趟 tàng
(趨) qū

(157)
赤部

赤 chì
赦 shè
赧 nǎn
赫 hè
赭 zhě

(158)
豆部

豆 dòu
豇 jiāng
(豈) qǐ
壹 yī
短 duǎn
登 dēng
豌 wān
(豎) shù
(頭) tóu
(豐) fēng
(艷) yàn

(159)
酉部

酉 yǒu
二至四画
酋 qiú
酊 dīng
酒 jiǔ
酌 zhuó
配 pèi
酝 yùn
酗 xù
五至七画
酣 hān
酢 zuò
酥 sū
酱 jiàng
酬 chóu
酩 míng
酪 lào
酿 niáng; niàng
酵 jiào
酶 méi
酸 suān
八至九画
醇 chún
醉 zuì
醋 cù
醒 xǐng
(醞) yùn
(醜) chǒu
十一画以上
(醫) yī
(醬) jiàng
醺 xūn
(釀) niáng; niàng
(釁) xìn

(160)
辰部

辰 chén
辱 rǔ
唇 chún
晨 chén
(農) nóng

(161)
豕部

豕 shǐ
家 jiā
象 xiàng
豪 háo
豫 yù
燹 xiǎn

(162)
卤(鹵)部

卤 lǔ
(鹵) lǔ
(鹹) xián

(163)
里部

里 lǐ
厘 lí
重 chóng; zhòng
野 yě
量 liáng; liàng

(164)
足(⻊)部

足 zú

二至五画

趴 pā
距 jù
趾 zhǐ
跄 qiàng
跃 yuè
践 jiàn
跋 bá
跌 diē
跑 pǎo
跛 bǒ

六画

跻 jī
(跡) jī
跨 kuà
跷 qiāo
跳 tiào
跣 xiǎn
路 lù
跺 duò
跪 guì
跟 gēn

七至八画

踉 liàng
踌 chóu
踊 yǒng
跼 jú
踪 zōng
踮 diǎn
踯 zhí
(踐) jiàn
踝 huái
踢 tī
踩 cǎi
踟 chí
踏 tà

九画

蹄 tí
踱 duó
蹉 cuō
蹀 dié
踹 chuài
踵 zhǒng
踽 jǔ
(踴) yǒng
蹂 róu

十至十一画

蹑 niè
蹒 pán
蹈 dǎo
蹊 qī
蹌 qiàng
蹠 zhí
蹩 bié
(蹟) jī
蹰 chú
蹙 cù
蹚 tāng
蹦 bèng
(蹤) zōng

十二画

蹴 cù
蹲 cún; dūn
蹭 cèng
(蹺) qiāo
(躉) dǔn
蹶 jué; juě
蹯 fán

十三画以上

躁 zào
(躋) jī
(躑) zhí
(躊) chóu
(躍) yuè
(躕) chú
躔 chán
(躚) xiān
(躡) niè

(165)
豸部

豸 zhì
豺 chái
豹 bào
貂 diāo
貉 háo; hé
貌 mào
貔 pí
(貛) huān

(166)
谷部

谷 gǔ
欲 yù
豁 huō;huò
谿 xī

(167)
釆部

悉 xī
番 fān
釉 yòu
释 shì
(釋) shì

(168)
身部

身 shēn
射 shè
躬 gōng
(躭) dān
躯 qū
躲 duǒ
躺 tǎng
(軀) qū

(169)
角部

角 jiǎo; jué
斛 hú
觞 shāng
觥 gōng
触 chù
解 jiě;jiè
(觴) shāng
(觸) chù

(170)
青部

青 qīng
靖 jìng
静 jìng
靛 diàn

(171)
其部

其 qí
甚 shèn
基 jī
斯 sī
期 qī
欺 qī

(172)
雨(⻗)部

雨 yǔ

二至五画

雪 xuě
(雲) yún
雳 lì
(電) diàn
雷 léi
雾 wù
雹 báo

六至八画

霁 jì
需 xū
霈 pèi
震 zhèn
霄 xiāo
霎 shà
霖 lín
霍 huò
霓 ní

九画以上

霜 shuāng
霪 yín
霞 xiá
霭 ǎi
(霧) wù
霸 bà
露 lòu; lù
霹 pī
(霽) jì
(靂) lì
(靈) líng

(173)
齿(齒)部

齿 chǐ
(齒) chǐ
龀 chèn
龃 jǔ
龄 líng
(齣) chū
龆 tiáo
龇 zī
龈 yín
龉 yǔ
龋 qǔ
(齷) wō

(174)
黾(黽)部

黾 miǎn
(黽) miǎn
(鼇) áo

(175)
金部

金 jīn
鉴 jiàn
錾 zàn
(鑒) jiàn
(鑿) záo; zuò

(176)
隹部

隹 zhuī
隼 sǔn
隽 juàn; jùn
难 nán; nàn
(隻) zhī
雀 què
售 shòu
焦 jiāo
雇 gù
集 jí
雁 yàn
雄 xióng
雅 yǎ
雍 yōng
雉 zhì
雌 cí
雕 diāo
(雖) suī
(雜) zá
(離) lí
(雞) jī
(雙) shuāng
(雛) chú
(難) nán; nàn

(177)
鱼(魚)部

鱼 yú
(魚) yú

四至六画

鲁 lǔ
鲅 bà
稣 sū
鲍 bào
鲜 xiān; xiǎn
鲞 xiǎng
鲑 guī
鲟 xún
鲨 shā
鲠 gěng
鲢 lián
鲤 lǐ
鲫 jì

八画以上

鲸 jīng
鳄 è
鳊 biān
鳏 guān
鳙 yōng
鳍 qí
鳖 biē
鳕 xuě
鳔 biào
鳗 mán
鳘 mǐn
鳝 shàn
鳟 zūn
鳜 guì
(鱘) xún
(鱷) è

(178)
音部

音 yīn

章 zhāng
竟 jìng
韵 yùn
(韻) yùn
(響) xiǎng

(179)
革部

革 gé
二至八画
勒 lè; lēi
靴 xuē
靶 bǎ
鞍 ān
鞋 xié
(鞏) gǒng
靼 dá
鞘 qiào; shāo
鞠 jū
九画以上
鞦 qiū
鞭 biān
鞣 róu
(韃) dá
(韁) jiāng
韆 qiān

(180)
骨部

骨 gú;gǔ
三至八画
(骯) āng
骷 kū
骶 dǐ
骸 hái
骼 gé
九画以上
髖 kuān
(髒) zāng
髓 suǐ
(體) tǐ

(181)
食部

食 shí; sì
餐 cān
餮 tiè
饕 tāo
饜 yàn

(182)
鬼部

鬼 guǐ
魁 kuí
魅 mèi
魂 hún
魄 pò
魎 liǎng
魍 wǎng
魑 chī
魔 mó

(183)
鬥部

(鬥) dòu
(鬭) dòu
(鬧) nào
(鬩) xì

(184)
髟部

(髮) fà
髭 zī
鬃 zōng
鬈 quán
鬓 bìn
(鬚) xū
(鬢) bìn

(185)
麻部

麻 mā; má
麼 me;mó
麾 huī
摩 mā; mó
磨 mó; mò
糜 mí
靡 mí; mǐ
魔 mó

(186)
鹿部

鹿 lù
(塵) chén
麋 mí
麒 qí
麟 lín
麓 lù
(麗) lì
鏖 áo
麝 shè

(187)
黑部

黑 hēi
墨 mò
默 mò
黔 qián
黜 chù
黛 dài
黝 yǒu
黠 xiá
黥 qíng
(黨) dǎng
黧 lí
黯 àn
(黷) dú

(188)
鼠部

鼠 shǔ

(189)
鼻部

鼻 bí
鼾 hān
齁 hōu

A a

阿 ā [used before a pet name, a surname or a title of family and other relationships]: ～宝 A Bao. ～大 the eldest. ～哥 elder brother. ～婆 granny

阿飞(飛) āfēi (名) hoodlum; hooligan; street rowdy

阿訇 āhōng (名) ahung; imam

阿拉伯 Ālābó (名) Arab; Arabian; Arabic: ～人 Arab. ～半岛 the Arabian Peninsula; Arabia. ～国家 Arab countries. ～数字 Arabic numerals. ～语 Arabic

阿门(門) āmén amen

阿摩尼亚(亞) āmóníyà (名) ammonia

阿司匹林 āsīpǐlín (名) aspirin

阿姨 āyí (名) 1 a child's form of address for any woman of its mother's generation; auntie 2 nursemaid 3 nanny; baby-sitter

啊 ā (叹) [a cry of surprise or amazement]: ～! 这地方多美哇! Oh, what a beautiful place!

腌 ā see also yān

腌臜 āza (形) filthy; dirty

啊 á (叹) [pressing for an answer or asking for something to be repeated]: ～? 你说什么? Pardon?

啊 ǎ (叹) [expressing surprise]: ～,你怎么啦? Gosh, what's the matter with you?

啊 à (叹) [expressing sudden realization]: ～, 原来是你! Ah, so it's you.

啊 a (助) 1 [used at the end of a sentence to convey a feeling of admiration or an undertone of warning]: 多好的天儿～! What a fine day! 你可要小心～! Do be careful! 这是真的～? Is this really true? 2 [used before a pause in order to attract attention]: 你～,这样下去可不行! Look! You can't go on like this. 3 [used after each item of a series of things]: 桃～,梨～,苹果～,我们都有. We have all sorts of fruit — peaches, pears, apples.

哀 āi (名) 1 grief; sorrow: 喜怒～乐 joy, anger, grief and happiness 2 mourning: 志～ express one's mourning for the deceased 3 pity: ～怜 have pity on sb.

哀悼 āidào (动) mourn or grieve for the deceased; lament over sb.'s death: 向死者家属表示深切的～ express one's heartfelt condolences to the family of the deceased

哀号(號) āiháo (动) cry with sorrow; wail

哀鸣 āimíng (名) a plaintive whine; wail

哀求 āiqiú (动) entreat; implore: 苦苦～ piteously beg

哀伤(傷) āishāng (形) grieved; saddened

哀思 āisī (名) sad memories (of the deceased); grief: 寄托～ give expression to one's grief

哀叹(嘆) āitàn (动) sigh sorrowfully (for)

哀痛 āitòng (名) grief; deep sorrow

哀乐(樂) āiyuè (名) funeral music; dirge

哎 āi (叹)[showing surprise or discontent]: ～! 是老王啊! Why, it's old Wang! ～,你怎么不早跟我说呢? But why didn't you tell me sooner?

哎呀 āiyā (叹) [expressing surprise]: ～! 我的笔丢了. Oh, dear! I've lost my pen. ～,这瓜真甜哪! Ah, this melon is really sweet!

埃 āi (名) 1 dust 2 angstrom (Å)

挨 āi (动) 1 get close to; be next or near to: ～着我坐 sit by my side. 那两座房子紧～着. The two houses are next to each other. 2 in sequence; by turns: ～家～户 from door to door. ～个儿 one by one. ～次 one after another. 还没～到你呢. It isn't your turn yet. see also ái

唉 āi (叹) [a verbal response to inquiry]: ～,来啦! Yes, I'm coming. see also ài

唉声(聲)叹(嘆)气(氣) āishēng-tànqì sigh in despair

癌 ái (名) cancer; carcinoma: ～转移 metastasis. ～扩散 carcinomatous infiltration. 致～

物质 cancerogenic substance
癌细胞 áixìbāo (名) cancer cell
癌症 áizhèng (名) cancer
呆 ái
see also dāi
呆板 áibǎn (形) rigid; inflexible; stereotyped: 这些规定也太～了. These regulations are a bit too rigid.
皑(皚) ái (形)〈书〉pure white (snow or frost)
皑皑 ái'ái (形) pure white: 白雪～ an expanse of snow
挨 ái (动) 1 suffer; endure: ～饿 suffer from hunger; go hungry. ～骂 get a scolding. ～打 take a beating; be spanked. ～批评 be criticized sharply 2 drag out: ～日子 drag out a miserable existence 3 delay; stall: ～时间 play for time
see also āi
霭 ǎi (名)〈书〉mist; haze: 暮～ evening haze
蔼 ǎi (形) friendly; amiable: 和～可亲 kindly; amiable; affable
嗳(噯) ǎi (叹) [expressing disagreement]: ～,别客气了. Come on. Don't be too polite. ～,你搞混啦. No, no, you got it all mixed up. ～,不是这种茶. No, it's not this kind of tea.
see also ài
矮 ǎi (形) 1 short (of stature) 2 low: 一堵～墙 a low wall. 他在大学里～我一级. He was one class my junior at college.
矮小 ǎixiǎo (形) undersized (of stature or house): 身材～ short and of slight build
矮子 ǎizi (名) a short person; dwarf; pygmy
矮墩墩 ǎidūndūn (形) dumpy, stumpy.
隘 ài I (形) narrow: 狭～ narrow; narrow-minded II (名) pass: 要～ a strategic pass. 关～ (mountain) pass
艾 ài (名) 1 Chinese mugwort: ～绒 moxa 2〈书〉end; stop: 方兴未～ be just unfolding
碍(礙) ài (动) hinder; obstruct; be in the way of: 有～健康 be harmful (or detrimental) to health. ～于情面 for fear of hurting sb.'s sensibilities
碍口 àikou (形) too embarrassing to bring up
碍事 àishì stand in the way: 这箱子太～了. This box is very much in the way.
碍手碍脚 àishǒu-àijiǎo be in the way; be a hindrance
唉 ài (叹) 1 [a sigh of sadness or regret]: ～,太晚了! Oh, It's too late! 2 sound of sighing
see also āi
爱(愛) ài (动、名) 1 love; affection: ～祖国 love one's country. 母～ maternal love 2 like; be fond of: ～看电影 like watching movies 3 be apt to; be in the habit of: ～发脾气 be apt to lose one's temper
爱…不… ài...bù... [used before reduplicated verbs meaning 'do as you like']: 爱信不信 believe it or not. 他爱去不去. He can go or not, for all I care.
爱不释(釋)手 ài bù shìshǒu so delighted with sth. that one can scarcely take one's eyes off it
爱称(稱) àichēng (名) term of endearment; pet or affectionate name
爱戴 àidài (名) love and esteem: 受到人民的～ enjoy the love and esteem of the people
爱抚(撫) àifǔ (动) show tender care for; caress
爱国(國) àiguó love one's country; be patriotic: ～者 patriot. ～主义 patriotism
爱好 àihào I (动) love; like; be keen on: ～和平 be peace-loving. ～运动 be keen on sports. 足球～者 football fan II (名) interest; hobby: 种花是我的～ gardening is my hobby
爱护(護) àihù (动) cherish; treasure; protect: ～公物 take good care of public property
爱恋(戀) àiliàn (动) fall in love with
爱面子 ài miànzi be intent on saving face
爱莫能助 ài mò néng zhù willing and yet unable to help; be willing to lend a hand but unable to do so
爱慕 àimù (动) adore; admire fondly
爱情 àiqíng (名) love (between man and woman)
爱人 àiren (名) 1 spouse; husband or wife 2 sweetheart
爱惜 àixī (动) treasure; cherish: ～时间 not waste one's time
嗳(噯) ài (叹) [ejaculation showing regret or an-

noyance]: ～，早知如此，我就不去了. Oh! Had I known what it would be like, I wouldn't have gone there at all.
see also ǎi

暧(曖) ài (形)〈书〉(of daylight) dim

暧昧 àimèi (形) 1 ambiguous; equivocal: 在这个问题上，他的态度～. He takes an ambiguous stand on this matter. 2 shady; dubious: 关系～. Their relationship is dubious.

安 ān I (动) 1 put sb. in a suitable position: ～插 assign a job to sb. 2 install; fix; fit: ～电话 have a telephone installed 3 harbour (an intention): ～坏心 harbour evil intentions II (形) 1 peaceful; quiet; tranquil; calm: 心神不～ feel worried (about sth.) 2 tranquillize; stabilize: ～神 make sb. calm and peaceful 3 be content or satisfied: ～之若素 not feel upset or annoyed despite adversity III (名) safety: 转危为～ turn danger into safety; be out of danger

安 ān interrogative word〈书〉1 where; what: 其故～在? What is the cause? 2 how: ～能若无其事? How can you behave as if nothing had happened?

安瓿 ānbù (名) ampoule

安插 ānchā (动) place in a certain position; assign to a job; plant: ～亲信 plant one's supporters in key positions

安定 āndìng I (形) stable; settled: 那里局势不～. The situation there is not stable. II (动) stabilize; maintain: ～人心 reassure the public

安顿 āndùn (动) help settle in; find a place for; arrange properly for: 你～好了吗? Have you settled in yet?

安放 ānfàng (动) lay; place with: 烈士墓前～着花圈. Wreaths were laid at the martyr's tomb.

安分 ānfèn (形) honest and dutiful: ～守己 law-abiding and well-behaved

安抚(撫) ānfǔ (动) console; reassure

安好 ānhǎo (形) safe and sound; well: 全家～，请勿挂念. You may rest assured that everyone in the family is fine.

安家 ānjiā (动) settle in; make one's home in a place

安静 ānjìng (形) quiet; peaceful: 病人需要～. The patient needs peace and quiet. 保持～. Keep quiet!

安居乐(樂)业(業) ānjū-lèyè live in peace and work contentedly

安乐(樂) ānlè (名) peace and comfort: ～窝 cosy nest. ～椅 easy chair

安眠 ānmián sleep peacefully: ～药 sleeping pill (or tablet); soporific

安宁(寧) ānníng (形) 1 peaceful; tranquil: 保持心情～ maintain the peace of mind 2 calm; composed; free from worry

安排 ānpái (动) arrange; plan; fix up: 为游客～旅行日程 arrange itineraries for the tourists

安培 ānpéi (名) ampere: ～计 ammeter; amperemeter. ～小时 ampere-hour

安全 ānquán (形、名) safe; secure: ～到达 arrive safe and sound. 交通～ traffic safety. ～带 safety belt (or strap); seat belt. ～岛 safety (or pedestrian) island. ～阀 safety valve. ～帽 safety helmet. ～门 emergency exit. ～梯 fire escape. ～灯 safety lamp

安全理事会(會) Ānquán Lǐshìhuì (名) The (U.N.) Security Council

安然 ānrán (形) 1 safely: ～无事 safe and sound; without a slight hitch 2 peacefully; at rest: 只有把真相告诉他，他心里才会～. You can only set his mind at rest by telling him the whole truth.

安如泰山 ānrú tàishān as secure as Mount Tai

安设 ānshè (动) install; set up: ～气象观测站 set up a weather station

安身 ānshēn (动) take shelter: 无处～ have nowhere to live; have no roof over one's head

安神 ānshén calm (or soothe) the nerves

安生 ānshēng (形) 1 peaceful; free from worry 2 quiet; still: 这孩子一会儿也不～. The child simply won't keep quiet.

安适(適) ānshì (形) quiet and comfortable: ～的生活 a life of ease and comfort

安危 ān-wēi (名) safety and danger; safety: 不顾个人～ despite the danger to oneself

安慰 ānwèi (动) 1 comfort; console 2 reassuring: ～奖 consolation prize

安稳 ānwěn （形）safe and steady
安息 ānxī （动） 1 rest; go to sleep 2 rest in peace: 烈士们，～吧！May our martyrs rest in peace!
安闲(閒) ānxián （形） carefree; leisurely
安详 ānxiáng （形） calm; composed; placid: 举止～ behave with quiet dignity
安歇 ānxiē （动） 1 go to bed; retire for the night 2 take a rest
安心 ānxīn feel at ease; set one's mind at rest: ～工作 work single-mindedly
安逸 ānyì （形）carefree and comfortable: 生活～ live in comfort
安营(營) ānyíng （动） set up a camp; camp out
安葬 ānzàng （动）bury (the dead)
安之若素 ān zhī ruò sù be imperturbable
安置 ānzhì （动）find a place for; help settle down; arrange for: ～新来的学生 find accomodation for the new student
安装(裝) ānzhuāng （动） install: ～电话 have a telephone installed

鞍 ān （名）saddle
鞍马(馬) ānmǎ （名）1 pommelled horse; side horse 2 saddle and horse
鞍子 ānzi （名）saddle

氨 ān （名）ammonia

谙 ān （动）〈书〉know well: 不～水性 be no swimmer

庵 ān （名） 1 hut 2 nunnery; Buddhist convent

鹌 ān
鹌鹑 ānchún （名）quail

俺 ǎn （代） I; we [referring only to the speakers themselves]: ～爹 my father. ～村 our village

铵 ǎn （名）ammonium

案 àn （名） 1 case; law case: 破～ clear up a criminal case 2 record; file: 有～可查 be on record (or file) 3 a plan submitted for consideration; proposal: 提～ proposal; motion. 决议草～ a draft resolution
案板 ànbǎn （名） kneading or chopping board
案件 ànjiàn （名）law case; case: 行凶抢劫～ a case of robbery with violence
案卷 ànjuàn （名） records; files; archives
案情 ànqíng （名） details of a case; case: 了解～ make a thorough investigation of the case
案头(頭) àntóu （名） on one's desk: ～日历 desk calendar
案验(驗) ànyàn （动）〈书〉 investigate criminal evidence
案子 ànzi （名） 1〈口〉case; law case 2 long table; counter: 肉～ meat counter

按 àn I （动） 1 press; push down: ～电钮 press (or push) a button 2 hold sth. back; shelve 3 restrain; control: ～不住心头怒火 be unable to restrain (or control) one's temper 4 in accordance with; in the light of; on the basis of: ～我说的办. Do as I told you. 5 check; refer to II （名）note: 编者～ editor's note
按脉 ànmài （动） feel (or take) the pulse
按摩 ànmó （动）massage
按劳(勞)分配 àn láo fēnpèi distribution according to work
按理 ànlǐ according to reason; normally: ～说他不应该管她的事. He is not supposed to interfere in her affairs.
按兵不动 àn bīng bù dòng hold the troops in readiness for combat; bide one's time; take no action
按部就班 ànbù-jiùbān observe the proper order of doing things; act according to the usual procedure
按捺 ànnà （动）restrain; contain: ～不住激动的心情 be unable to contain one's excitement
按钮 ànniǔ （名）push button
按期 ànqī （副） on schedule; on time: ～出发 start on time
按时(時) ànshí （副）on time; on schedule: ～到达 arrive on time
按说 ànshuō （副）in the ordinary course of events; normally: ～这时候该下雪了. Normally it should be snowing by now (or this time of the year).
按需分配 àn xū fēnpèi distribution according to need
按语 ànyǔ （名）note; comment
按照 ànzhào （副） according to; in accordance with; in the light of; on the basis of: ～预定计划完成任务 fulfil the task on schedule

黯 àn （形）dim; gloomy
黯淡 àndàn see "暗淡" àndàn

黯然 ànrán （形）〈书〉1 dim; faint: ～失色 be pale into insignificance 2 in low spirits; sadly: ～泪下 shed tears sadly

暗 àn （形）1 dark; dim; dull: 天色渐～. It's getting dark. 2 hidden; secret: 明人不做～事. One who is aboveboard does nothing on the sly. 3 hazy: 情况若明若～. The situation is a little murky.

暗暗 àn'àn （副）secretly; inwardly; to oneself: 他觉得有人～跟踪. He felt he was being shadowed.

暗藏 àncáng （动）hide; conceal: ～的敌人 a hidden enemy

暗娼 ànchāng （名）unlicensed prostitute

暗淡 àndàn （形）dim; faint; dismal; gloomy: 前途～ a gloomy future. 灯光～ The light is dim.

暗地里(裏) àndìli （副）secretly; on the sly

暗害 ànhài （动）1 murder; incriminate 2 stab in the back

暗号(號) ànhào （名）secret signal (or sign)

暗箭 ànjiàn （名）a stab in the back: ～难防. It is hard to guard against snipers.

暗礁 ànjiāo （名）submerged reef (or rock)

暗杀(殺) ànshā （动、名）assassinate; assasination

暗示 ànshì （动）1 drop a hint; hint: 他用眼睛～我，让我走开. The look on his face suggested that I was in the way.

暗室 ànshì （名）darkroom

暗算 ànsuàn （动）plot against; entrap

暗锁 ànsuǒ （名）built-in lock

暗滩(灘) àntān （名）hidden shoal

暗探 àntàn （名）detective; secret agent

暗无(無)天日 àn wú tiānrì dark days; total absence of justice

暗箱 ànxiāng （名）camera bellows; camera obscura

暗语 ànyǔ （名）code word

暗中 ànzhōng （副）1 in the dark: ～摸索 grope in the dark 2 in secret; surreptitiously: ～操纵 pull strings from behind the scenes

岸 àn （名）bank; shore; coast: 江～ a river bank. 海～ coast; seashore. 上～ go ashore

岸然 ànrán （形）in a solemn manner: 道貌～ look dignified

肮(骯) āng

肮脏(髒) āngzāng （形）dirty; filthy; foul: ～的勾当 dirty deal; foul play

昂 áng I（动）hold (one's head) high II（形）high; soaring: 雄赳赳，气～～ fearless and militant

昂贵 ángguì （形）very expensive; costly

昂然 ángrán （形）upright and fearless

昂首阔步 ángshǒu-kuòbù stride forward

昂扬(揚) ángyáng （形）high-spirited: 斗志～ have high morale

盎 àng （名）an ancient vessel with a big belly and a small mouth

盎然 àngrán （形）abundant; full; overflowing: 春意～. Spring is in the air.

凹 āo （形）concave; hollow; sunken; dented: ～凸不平 rugged

凹透镜 āotòujìng （名）concave lens

凹陷 āoxiàn （形）hollow; sunken; depressed: 双颊～ sunken (or hollow) cheeks

鏖 áo （动）〈书〉engage in fierce battle

鏖战(戰) áozhàn （动）〈书〉fight hard; engage in fierce battle

熬 áo （动）1 boil; stew: ～粥 cook gruel. ～药 decoct medicinal herbs 2 endure (pain or hardships)

熬煎 áojiān （名）suffering; torture: 受尽～ be subjected to all kinds of suffering

熬夜 áoyè （动）stay up late; burn the mid-night oil

遨 áo （动）stroll; saunter

遨游 áoyóu （动）roam; wander

嗷 áo

嗷嗷 áo'áo 〈象〉: 疼得～叫 scream with pain

翱 áo （动）〈书〉take wing

翱翔 áoxiáng （动）hover; soar: 雄鹰在空中～. Eagles hover in the sky.

袄(襖) ǎo （名）a short Chinese-style coat or jacket: 皮～ a fur coat. 棉～ a cotton-padded jacket

媪 ǎo （名）〈书〉old woman

傲 ào I (形) proud; haughty II (动) refuse to yield to; brave; defy

傲岸 ào'àn (形) 〈书〉 supercilious; haughty: ～不群 proud and aloof

傲骨 àogǔ (名) lofty and unyielding character

傲慢 àomàn (形) arrogant; haughty: 态度～ be arrogant; put on airs

傲气(氣) àoqì (名) air of arrogance; haughtiness: ～十足 extremely haughty or arrogant

傲然 àorán (副) loftily; unyieldingly

傲视 àoshì (动) turn up one's nose at; scorn; treat with disdain

奥 ào (形) profound; abstruse; difficult to understand

奥秘 àomì (名) profound mystery

奥妙 àomiào (形) profound; subtle; secret

澳 ào an inlet of the sea; bay

懊 ào (形) 1 regretful; remorseful 2 annoyed; vexed

懊悔 àohuǐ (动) regret; repent: 我～捅了这么大的漏子. I regret having made such a blunder.

懊恼(惱) àonǎo (形) annoyed; vexed; upset: 他心里很～. He was quite upset.

懊丧(喪) àosàng (形) dejected; depressed

拗 ào

see also niù

拗口 àokǒu (形) hard to pronounce; awkward-sounding: ～话 tongue-twister

Bb

捌 bā (数) eight [used for the simpler, though normal, form 八 on cheques, etc. to avoid mistakes or alterations]

八 bā (数) eight

八宝(寶) bābǎo (名) eight treasures(choice ingredients of certain special dishes): ～饭 eight-treasure rice pudding

八成 bāchéng 1 eighty percent: ～新 eighty percent new; practically new. 事情有了～啦. We stand a fair chance of success. 2 most probably; most likely: ～他不来了. Most likely he won't come at all.

八方 bāfāng (名) all quarters; all around: 四面～ in all directions; from all quarters

八股 bāgǔ (名) 1 eight-legged style (a literary style prescribed for the imperial civil service examinations during Ming and Qing Dynasties) 2 stereotyped writing

八路军 Bālùjūn (名) the Eighth Route Army (led by the Chinese Communist Party during the War of Resistance Against Japan)

八面玲珑(瓏) bāmiàn línglóng (形) be slick (in social intercourse); try to please everybody or offend nobody

八仙 Bāxiān (名) the Eight Immortals (in the legend): ～过海, 各显神通 like the Eight Immortals soaring over the ocean, each showing his or her special skill

八仙桌 bāxiānzhuō (名) a big square table for eight people

八月 bāyuè (名) 1 August 2 the eighth month of the lunar year; the eight moon: ～节 the Mid-Autumn Festival (15th day of the 8th lunar month)

八字 bāzì (名) character 八: ～还没见一撇儿. Nothing tangible is in sight yet.

扒 bā (动) 1 hold on to: ～墙头儿 hold on to the top of the wall 2 dig up; rake; pull down: ～房 pull down the house 3 push aside: ～开芦苇 push aside the reeds 4 strip off; take off:把鞋袜一～,光着脚蹚水. Taking off his shoes and socks, he waded across barefoot.

see also pá

扒拉 bāla (动) touch lightly: 把钟摆～一下 set the pendulum swinging

巴 bā I (动) 1 hope earnestly; look forward to: 朝～夜望 be waiting anxiously day and night. 2 cling to; stick to: 爬山虎～在墙上. The ivy climbs over the wall. 粥～锅了. The porridge has stuck to the pot. 3 be close to; be next to: 前不～村, 后不着店 with neither villages ahead nor inns behind —

stranded in an out-of-the-way place
巴不得 bābùdé 〈口〉 be only too glad (to do sth.); eagerly look forward to; earnestly wish: 他～立刻开始工作. He is only too glad to get down to work at once.
巴结 bājié I (动) fawn on; curry favour with: ～某人 try to win sb's favour II (形) hard-working: 他工作很～. He is very hard-working.
巴黎公社 Bālí Gōngshè the Paris Commune
巴掌 bāzhang (名) palm; hand: 打他一～ slap him on the cheek
疤 bā (名) scar
疤痕 bāhén (名) scar
芭 bā
芭蕉 bājiāo (名) bajiao banana
芭蕾舞 bālěiwǔ (名) ballet
吧 bā 1 〈象〉: ～的一声,把树枝折断了. The branch broke with a snap. 2 (动) 〈口〉 draw on (one's pipe, etc.)
see also ba
拔 bá (动) 1 pull out; winkle out: ～草 pull up weeds. ～牙 pull out (or extract) a tooth 2 suck out (usually something poisonous) 3 choose; select (usually people of talent): 选～ select (from candidates) 4 lift; raise: ～起嗓子 raise one's voice 5 stand out; surpass: 出类～萃 be outstanding 6 capture; seize: 连～敌人五个据点 capture five enemy strongholds in succession 7 cool in water: 把西瓜放在冰水里～一～ cool a watermelon in ice water
拔除 báchú (动) wipe out; remove: ～障碍 remove an obstacle
拔海 báhǎi (名) elevation (above sea level): ～五千米 at an elevation of 5,000 metres; 5,000 metres above sea level
拔河 báhé (名) tug-of-war
拔尖儿 bájiānr I (形) 〈口〉 tip-top; top-notch: 他们种的花生是～的. The peanuts they grow are top-notch. II (动) push oneself to the front
拔节(節) bájié (名) jointing
拔苗助长(長) bá miáo zhù zhǎng try to help the saplings grow by pulling them upward — spoil things by excessive enthusiasm
拔腿 bátuǐ step forward: ～就跑 dash off
跋 bá I (动) trudge over mountains: ～山涉水 travel across mountains and rivers II (名) postscript
跋扈 báhù (形) domineering; bossy
跋涉 báshè (动) trudge; trek: 长途～ trudge over a long distance; trek; make a long arduous journey
靶 bǎ (名) target: 打～ shooting (or target) practice
靶场(場) bǎchǎng (名) shooting range; range
靶子 bǎzi (名) target
把 bǎ I (动) 1 hold; grasp; grip: 他紧紧地～住我的手. He held my hand tightly. 2 hold (a baby while it relieves itself) 3 control; monopolize; dominate: 不要什么都～着不放手. Do not keep such a tight control on things. 4 guard; watch: ～门 guard a gate II (名) 1 handle (of a pushcart, etc.): 自行车～ the handlebar of a bicycle 2 bundle; bunch: 草～ a bundle of hay III (量) 1 [of an instrument with a handle]: 一～刀 a knife. 一～茶壶 a teapot. 一～椅子 a chair. 2 [of a handful of sth.]: 一～米 a handful of rice. 一～花 a bunch of flowers 3 [used with certain abstract nouns]: 有一～年纪 be getting on in years. 有～力气 be quite strong. 加～劲 make a special effort; put on a spurt 4 [used to indicate an offer to lend sb. a hand]: 拉他一～ give (or lend) him a hand 5 about; or so: 个～月 about a month; a month or so. 百～人 some hundred people IV (介) [The usage of '把' often causes inversion with the object placed before the verb]: 请～门带上. Shut the door, please. ～水搅浑 muddy the water; create confusion. 这一趟可～他累坏了. That trip really tired him out.
另见 bà
把柄 bǎbǐng (名) handle: 给人抓住～ give sb. a handle
把持 bǎchí (动) control; dominate; monopolize: ～机构内一切重要位置 occupy all the key positions in the institution
把风(風) bǎfēng (动) stand guard; keep watch
把关(關) bǎguān (动) 1 guard a pass 2 check on: 层层～

make checks at all levels. 把好质量关 make a careful check of the quality (of goods)

把酒 bǎjiǔ (动) 1 raise one's wine cup 2 fill a wine cup for sb.: ～言欢 converse cheerfully over a glass of wine

把式 bǎshi (名) 〈口〉 1 *wushu* (武术): 练～ practise wushu (martial arts) 2 person skilled in a trade: 车～ carter 3 skill

把守 bǎshǒu (动) guard: 分兵～各个关口 divide up one's forces to guard the passes

把手 bǎshou (名) handle; grip; knob

把头(頭) bǎtóu (名) labour contractor; gangmaster

把稳(穩) bǎwěn (形) trustworthy; dependable: 办事～ be a conscientious worker

把握 bǎwò I (动) hold; grasp: ～时机. seize the opportunity II (名) assurance; certainty: 有成功的～. Success is as good as assured.

把戏(戲) bǎxì (名) 1 acrobatics; jugglery 2 trick: 耍鬼～ play tricks

把兄弟 bǎxiōngdì (名) sworn brothers

霸 bà I (名) 1 chief of feudal princes; overlord 2 tyrant; despot; bully: 恶～ local tyrant (or despot) 3 hegemonist power: 反～斗争 the struggle against hegemonism. 超级大国争～世界. The superpowers are contending for world hegemony. II (动) dominate; lord it over; tyrannize over: 各～一方 each lording it over his own sphere of influence

霸道 bàdào (名) (feudal) rule by force

霸道 bàdao 1 savage; high-handed: 横行～ ride roughshod over 2 (of liquor, medicine, etc.) strong; potent

霸权(權) bàquán (名) hegemony; supremacy: ～主义 hegemonism

霸占 bàzhàn (动) forcibly occupy; illegally take possession of: ～别国领土 forcibly occupy the territory of another country

坝(壩) bà (名) 1 dam 2 dyke; embankment 3 sandbar 4 flatland; plain

罢(罷) bà (动) 1 stop; cease: 作～ let the matter drop. 欲～不能 cannot but carry on 2 dismiss: ～职 remove from office; dismiss 3 finish: 吃～晚饭 after finishing supper

罢黜 bàchù (动) 〈书〉 1 dismiss from office 2 ban; reject

罢工 bàgōng (名) strike; go on strike

罢官 bàguān (动) dismiss from office

罢课 bàkè (名) students' strike

罢了 bàle (助) [used at the end of a statement to indicate something not worth mentioning]: 这有什么, 我不过做了我应该做的事～. I have only done what I ought to. That's all.

罢了 bàliǎo [used to indicate reluctance or displeasure on the part of the speaker]: 他不愿来也就～. Well, if he doesn't want to come, it can't be helped.

罢免 bàmiǎn (动) recall: ～权 right of recall; recall

罢市 bàshì (名) shopkeepers' strike

罢手 bàshǒu (动) give up; stop: 不试验成功,决不～. We will go on with the experiment until we succeed.

罢休 bàxiū (动) give up; let the matter drop [often used in a negative sentence]: 不达目的,决不～. We'll keep on trying until we reach our goal.

鲅 bà

鲅鱼(魚) bàyú (名) Spanish mackerel

耙 bà I (名) harrow II (动) draw a harrow over (a field); harrow

see also pá

把 bà (名) 1 grip; handle: 茶壶～儿 the handle of a teapot. 枪～儿 rifle butt 2 stem (of a leaf, flower or fruit)

see also bǎ

把子 bàzi (名) handle: 刀～ the handle of a knife

爸 bà (名) pa; dad; father

爸爸 bàba (名) papa; dad; father

吧 ba (助) 1 [used at the end of a sentence to indicate suggestion, request or command]: 帮帮他～. Let's give him a hand. 2 [used at the end of a sentence to indicate agreement or approval]: 好～,我答应你了. O.K. I promise. 3 [used at the end of a sentence to indicate

doubt or conjecture]: 他今天大概不来了～? He is not likely to come today, is he? 4 [used to indicate a pause suggesting a dilemma]: 走～,不好,不走～,也不好. It's no good if we go; if we don't, it's no good either.
see also bā

掰 bāi (动) break off with the fingers and thumb: 把饼～成两半 break the cake in two

白 bái I (形) 1 snow-white: 一件～府绸衬衫a white poplin shirt 2 clear; made clear: 真相大～. The whole truth is out. 3 pure; plain; blank: ～开水 plain boiled water. ～卷 a blank paper II (副) 1 in vain; to no effect: ～跑一趟 make a fruitless trip. ～费力气 It's a waste of effort 2 free of charge; gratis: ～送 be given gratis (or as a gift). ～送我都不要. I wouldn't have it as a gift. III (名) 1 White (as a symbol of reaction): ～军 the White army 2 spoken part in opera, etc.: 独～ soliloquy; monologue. 对～ dialogue IV (动) state; explain: 自～ confessions

白班儿 báibānr (名) 〈口〉 day shift

白报(報)纸 báibàozhǐ (名) newsprint

白璧微瑕 báibì wēi xiá a spot in white jade — a slight blemish or small failing of a person's character; a minor defect of anything that would otherwise be perfect

白布 báibù (名) plain white cloth; calico

白菜 báicài (名) Chinese cabbage

白痴 báichī (名) 1 idiocy 2 idiot

白炽(熾) báichì (形) white heat; incandescence: ～灯 incandescent lamp

白搭 báidā 〈口〉 no use; no good: 和他争辩也是～. It's no use arguing with him.

白垩(堊) bái'è (名) chalk

白费 báifèi (动) waste: ～唇舌 waste one's breath. ～心思 bother one's head for nothing

白宫 Bái Gōng (名) the White House

白果 báiguǒ (名) ginkgo; gingko

白鹤 báihè (名) white crane

白喉 báihóu (名) diphtheria

白话 báihuà (名) unrealizable wish or unfounded argument: 空口说～ make empty promise

白话 báihuà (名) the written form of modern Chinese (putonghua): ～诗 free verse written in the vernacular

白金 báijīn (名) platinum

白净 báijìng (形) (of skin) fair and clear

白酒 báijiǔ (名) spirit usu. distilled from sorghum or maize; white spirit

白茫茫 báimángmáng (形) (of cloud, mist, snow, floodwater, etc.) a vast expanse of whiteness: 在辽阔的田野上铺了一层雪，～的一眼望不到尽头. The fields covered with snow became a vast expanse of whiteness stretching to infinity.

白米 báimǐ (名) (polished) rice: ～饭 (cooked) rice

白面(麵) báimiàn (名) wheat flour; fine flour

白面书生 báimiàn shūshēng (名) a young handsome scholar

白描 báimiáo (名) 1 line drawing in the traditional ink and brush style 2 simple, straightforward style of writing

白内障 báinèizhàng (名) cataract

白热(熱) báirè (名) white heat; incandescence

白热化 báirèhuà (形) white-hot: 争论达到了～的程度 The debate became white-hot.

白人 báirén (名) white man or woman

白刃 báirèn (名) naked sword: ～战 bayonet charge; hand-to-hand combat

白日做梦(夢) báirì zuòmèng daydream; indulge in wishful thinking: 这是～. This is day dreaming.

白色 báisè I (形) white (colour) II (名) White (as a symbol of reaction) ～恐怖 the white terror

白手起家 báishǒu qǐjiā start from scratch

白薯 báishǔ (名) sweet potato

白糖 báitáng (名) (refined) white sugar

白天 báitiān (名) daytime; day

白铁(鐵) báitiě (名) galvanized iron

白头(頭) báitóu (名) hoary head; old age

白头偕老 báitóu xiélǎo live in conjugal bliss to a ripe old age

白血病 báixuèbìng (名) leukaemia

白血球 báixuèqiú (名) white

blood cell
白眼 báiyǎn (名) contemptuous look: 遭人～ be treated with disdain
白杨(楊) báiyáng (名)white poplar
白银 báiyín (名) silver
白纸黑字 báizhǐ-hēizì (written) in black and white
白昼(晝) báizhòu (名) daytime
白字 báizì (名) wrongly written or mispronounced character; wrong word; malapropism: ～连篇 full of malapropisms
百 bǎi (数) **1** hundred **2** numerous; all kinds of: ～花盛开. A hundred flowers are in full bloom.
百般 bǎibān (副) in a hundred and one ways; in every possible way; by every means: ～抵赖 try by every means imaginable to deny
百倍 bǎibèi (数) a hundredfold; a hundred times
百尺竿头(頭),更进(進)一步 bǎi chǐ gāntóu, gèng jìn yī bù forge further ahead; make still further progress
百发(發)百中 bǎifā-bǎizhòng (as in archery and shooting)every shot hits the target
百废(廢)俱兴(興) bǎi fèi jù xīng get all neglected projects started at once
百分比 bǎifēnbǐ (名) percentage: 按～计算 in terms of percentage
百分之百 bǎifēn zhī bǎi (副) a hundred per cent; absolutely: 有～的把握 be a hundred per cent sure; be absolutely certain
百花齐(齊)放,百家争鸣 bǎihuā qífàng, bǎijiā zhēngmíng let a hundred flowers blossom and a hundred schools of thought contend
百货 bǎihuò (名) general merchandise: 日用～ articles of daily use;basic commodities.～商店 department store; general store
百科全书(書) bǎikē quánshū (名) encyclopaedia
百孔千疮(瘡) bǎikǒng-qiānchuāng be riddled with holes; afflicted with social ills; be seriously damaged
百炼(煉)成钢(鋼) bǎi liàn chéng gāng be tempered into steel; be tempered into a person of iron will
百年 bǎinián (名) **1** a hundred years; a very long period **2** lifetime: ～之后〈婉〉 when sb. has passed away; after sb's death
百年大计 bǎinián dàjì (名) a project of vital and lasting importance; an undertaking of great moment and long-range significance
百万(萬) bǎiwàn (数) million: ～富翁 millionaire
百闻不如一见(見) bǎi wén bùrú yī jiàn it is better to see once than hear a hundred times; seeing is believing
百无(無)聊赖 bǎi wú liáolài (形) languish in boredom; overcome with boredom
百姓 bǎixìng (名) common people
百叶(葉)窗 bǎiyèchuāng (名) shutter; blind; jalousie
百依百顺 bǎiyī-bǎishùn (形) docile and obedient; all obedience
百战(戰)百胜(勝) bǎizhàn-bǎishèng (形) fight a hundred battles, win a hundred victories; invincible
百折不挠(撓) bǎi zhé bù náo (形) not flinch despite repeated reverses; be undaunted by repeated setbacks; be indomitable
佰 bǎi (数) hundred [used for the simpler, though normal, form 百 on cheques, etc. to avoid mistakes or alterations]
柏 bǎi (名) cypress
柏树(樹) bǎishù (名) cypress
柏油 bǎiyóu (名) pitch; tar; asphalt
摆(擺) bǎi I (动) **1** put; place; arrange: 把东西～好 put the things in order. ～事实,讲道理 present the facts and reason things out **2** put on; assume: ～架子 put on airs. **3** sway; wave: 他向我直～手. He kept waving his hand at me. II (名) pendulum
摆布 bǎibu (动) order about; manipulated: 任人～ allow others to lord it over oneself
摆动(動) bǎidòng (动) swing; sway: 树枝迎风～. The branches of the trees swayed in the breeze.
摆渡 bǎidù **1** (名) ferry; ferryboat **2** (动) ferry across (a river)
摆弄 bǎinòng (动) **1** move back and forth; fiddle with: 不要～那架打字机了. Don't fiddle with the typewriter. **2** twist(someone) round one's little finger
摆设 bǎishè (动)furnish and dec-

orate (a room): 屋里～得很美观. The room is beautifully furnished.
摆设 bǎishe (名) furnishings
摆脱 bǎituō (动) get rid of (restraint, difficulty, or any other undesirable state of things): ～困境 extricate oneself from an awkward predicament. ～羁绊 to shake off the yoke. ～旧的传统 break away from the old tradition

败 bài (动) **1** be defeated in battle or beaten in a contest: ～下阵来 lose a battle. 主队以二比三～于客队. The home team lost to the visitors 2 to 3. **2** defeat (enemy): 大～侵略军 inflict a severe defeat on the aggressor troops **3** fail: 不能以成～论英雄. Success or failure is no measure of a person's ability. **4** spoil: 成事不足,～事有余 be unable to accomplish anything but quite capable of spoiling the whole show **5** counteract: ～毒 counteract a toxin **6** decay; wither: 枯枝～叶 dead twigs and withered leaves
败北 bàiběi (动) 〈书〉 suffer defeat; be defeated
败笔(筆) bàibǐ (名) **1** a faulty stroke in calligraphy or painting **2** a faulty expression in writing
败坏(壞) bàihuài (动) ruin; undermine: ～某人的名誉 blacken sb.s good name; damage sb.'s reputation. 道德～ degenerate; be depraved
败家子 bàijiāzǐ (名) spendthrift; wastrel; prodigal
败类(類) bàilèi (名) scum of a community; degenerate; renegade: 民族～ scum of a nation
败露 bàilù (动) (of a plot, etc.) be discovered or exposed: 阴谋终于～. The conspiracy was eventually uncovered
败落 bàiluò (动) be on the decline: 家道～ The family lived in reduced circumstances.
败兴(興) bàixìng (形) in low spirits: 他乘兴而来,～而归. He came in ebullient good spirits but went back very much disappointed.
败阵 bàizhèn (动) be defeated on the battlefield: ～而逃 lose the field and take to flight
败子 bàizi (名) spendthrift, wastrel: ～回头了. The prodigal has returned.

拜 bài I (动) **1** make a courtesy call: 回～ pay a return call **2** form ceremoniously a certain relationship with sb.: ～他为师 respectfully offer oneself as sb.'s disciple; ceremoniously acknowledge sb. as one's master II 〈敬〉 [used before a verb]: ～读大作 respectfully peruse your work
拜把子 bài bǎzi become sworn brothers
拜辞(辭) bàicí bid farewell to
拜倒 bàidǎo (动) prostrate oneself; fall on one's knees; grovel: ～在某人脚下 grovel (or lie prostrate) at the feet of sb.
拜访 bàifǎng (动) pay a visit; pay a call on: 正式～ official visit
拜会(會) bàihuì (动) pay an official call; call on
拜见(見) bàijiàn (动) **1** pay a formal visit; call to pay respects **2** meet one's senior or superior
拜年 bàinián (动) pay a New Year call
拜托 bàituō (动)〈敬〉 request sb. to do sth.: ～您捎个信给他. Would you kindly take a message to him?
拜谒 bàiyè (动) **1** pay a formal visit; call to pay respects **2** pay homage (at a monument, mausoleum, etc.)

稗 bài I (名) barnyard grass II (形) 〈书〉 insignificant; unofficial
稗官野史 bàiguān-yěshǐ unofficial histories
稗子 bàizi (名) barnyard grass; barnyard millet

斑 bān I (名) spot; speck; speckle: 油～ oil stains. 雀～ speckles II (形) spotted; striped
斑白 bānbái (形) grizzled; greying: 两鬓～ greying at the temples; with greying temples
斑驳 bānbó (形) 〈书〉 mottled; motley: ～陆离 variegated
斑点(點) bāndiǎn (名) spot; stain
斑斓 bānlán (形) gorgeous; bright-coloured; multicoloured: 五彩～ a blaze of multifarious colours
斑马(馬) bānmǎ (名) zebra
斑纹 bānwén (名) stripe; streak

瘢 bān (名) abnormal pigmentary deposits on the skin; flecks

班 bān I (名) 1 class; team: 学习～ study class. 作业～ work team 2 shift; duty: 日夜三～倒 work round the clock in three shifts 3 squad II (量) 1[used of a group of people]: 这～青年人真了不起. They're a fine bunch of young people. 2 [used to indicate the number of runs in transportation]: 搭下一～汽车进城 take the next bus to town III (形) regularly-run; regular; scheduled: ～车 regular bus service

班车(車) bānchē (名) regular bus (service)

班次 bāncì (名) 1 order of classes or grades at school: 她～比我高. She was in a higher class than me. 2 number of runs of flights: 增加货车～ increase the number of runs of freight trains

班底 bāndǐ 1 ordinary members of a theatrical troupe 2 core members of an organization

班房 bānfáng (名)〈口〉jail: 坐～ be (put) in jail

班门(門)弄斧 Bān mén nòng fǔ show off one's skill with the axe before Lu Ban (the ancient master carpenter); show off one's scanty knowledge in the presence of an expert

班长(長) bānzhǎng (名) 1 class monitor 2 squad leader 3 (work) team leader

班主任 bānzhǔrèn (名) grade adviser; a teacher in over-all charge of a class

班子 bānzi (名) 1 (old use) theatrical troupe 2 group; team: 领导～ a leading body (or group). 生产～ a production team

扳 bān (动) pull; turn: ～倒 pull down. ～着指头算 count on one's fingers

扳机(機) bānjī (名) trigger

扳手 bānshou (名) 1 spanner; wrench 2 lever (on a machine)

扳子 bānzi (名) spanner; wrench

颁 bān (动) promulgate; issue

颁布 bānbù (动) promulgate; issue; publish: ～法令 promulgate a decree

颁发(發) bānfā (动) 1 issue; promulgate: ～命令 issue an order (or directive) 2 award: ～奖章 award a medal (or a certificate of commendation)

颁行 bānxíng (动、名) promulgate; promulgation

般 bān (名) kind; way; like: 百～ in a hundred ways. 暴风雨～的掌声 thunderous applause

瘢 bān (名) scar

瘢痕 bānhén (名) scar

搬 bān (动) 1 take away; move; remove: 把东西～走 take the junk away 2 move (house): 他早就～走了. He moved away long ago. 3 apply indiscriminately: 生～硬套 copy mechanically and apply indiscriminately

搬家 bānjiā (动) move (house)

搬弄 bānnòng (动) 1 move sth. about; fiddle with: ～枪栓 fiddle with the rifle bolt 2 show off; display: ～学问 show off one's erudition 3 instigate; incite: ～是非 sow the seeds of dissension

搬运(運) bānyùn (动) carry; transport: ～货物 transport goods. ～工人 (of railway station, airport, etc.) porter; docker

坂 bǎn (名)〈书〉slope

板 bǎn I (名) 1 board; plank; plate: 切菜～ chopping block. 钢～ steel plate 2 shutter: 上～儿 put up the shutters 3 clappers 4 an accented beat in traditional Chinese music; time; measure II (形) 1 hard: 地～了,不好锄. The ground is too hard to hoe. 2 stiff; unnatural: 他们都那样活泼,显得我太～了. I looked a bit stiff while they were so lively. III (动) look serious: 他～着脸不说话. He put on a grave expression, saying nothing.

板凳 bǎndèng (名) wooden bench or stool

板胡 bǎnhú (名) a bowed stringed instrument with a thin wooden soundboard

板栗 bǎnlì (名) Chinese chestnut

板刷 bǎnshuā (名) scrubbing brush

板牙 bǎnyá (名) 1 front tooth; incisor 2 molar

板眼 bǎnyǎn (名) 1 measure in traditional Chinese music 2 orderliness: 他说话有板有眼. He is always concise in whatever he says.

板滞 bǎnzhì (形) stiff; dull

板子 bǎnzi (名) 1 board; plank 2 bamboo or birch for corporal

punishment

版 bǎn (名) **1** printing plate (or block): 铜～ copperplate. 制～ plate making **2** edition: 初～ first edition. 绝～ out of print **3** page (of a newspaper): 头～新闻 front-page news

版本 bǎnběn (名) edition

版次 bǎncì (名) the order in which a book is printed; impression

版画(畫) bǎnhuà (名) etching

版面 bǎnmiàn (名) **1** space of a whole page **2** layout (or make-up) of a printed sheet: ～设计 layout

版权(權) bǎnquán (名) copyright: ～所有 all rights reserved

版式 bǎnshì (名) format: 以新的～重版 reissued in a new format

版税 bǎnshuì (名) royalty (on books)

版图(圖) bǎntú (名) domain; territory: ～辽阔 be vast in territory

瓣 bàn (名) **1** petal **2** segment or section (of a tangerine, etc.); clove (of garlic) **3** valve; lamella: 三尖～ tricuspid valve. 鳃～ gill lamella **4** (量) as applied to a petal, a leaf or a fragment of fruit: 把苹果切成四～儿 cut the apple in four

瓣膜 bànmó (名) valve

半 bàn (形) **1** half; semi-: ～小时 half an hour. 一个～月 one and a half months. ～机械化 semi-mechanized **2** in the middle; halfway: ～夜 midnight. ～山腰 halfway up a hill **3** very little; the least bit: 一星～点 a wee bit **4** partly; about half: 房门～开着. The door was half open.

半…半… bàn...bàn... [used before two corresponding words to indicate that two opposing ideas exist simultaneously]: 半推半就 yield with a show of reluctance. 半心半意 half-hearted. 半信半疑 half-believing, half-doubting. 半吞半吐 ambiguous. 半明半暗 murky

半辈子 bànbèizi the first or second half of one's lifetime; half one's lifetime

半成品 bànchéngpǐn (名) semi-manufactured goods; semi-finished articles or products

半导(導)体 bàndǎotǐ (名) semiconductor: ～集成电路 semiconductor integrated circuit ～收音机 transistor radio

半岛 bàndǎo (名) peninsula

半封建 bànfēngjiàn (形) semi-feudal

半工半读(讀) bàngōng-bàndú part work, part study: 出国～ go abroad on a work-study programme

半截 bànjié (形) half (a section) of sth.: 他话只说了～儿. He stopped short when he had scarcely finished what he had to say.

半斤八两(兩) bànjīn-bāliǎng six of one and half a dozen of the other; tweedledum and tweedledee

半径(徑) bànjìng (名) radius

半决赛 bànjuésài (名) (of sports) semifinals

半路 bànlù (副) halfway; on the way: 走到～天就黑了. It was already dark when we had scarcely got halfway.

半路出家 bànlù chūjiā switch to new profession or a new field of study late in life

半票 bànpiào (名) half-price ticket; half fare

半瓶醋 bànpíngcù (名) a person who has just a little learning; smatterer

半旗 bànqí (名) half-mast: 下～ fly a flag at half-mast

半球 bànqiú (名) hemisphere: 东～ the Eastern hemisphere. 北～ the Northern hemisphere

半晌 bànshǎng (名) quite a while: 他想了～才想起来. It was quite some time before he recalled it.

半身不遂 bànshēn bùsuí (名) paralysis of one side of the body; hemiplegia

半数(數) bànshù (名) half the number; half: ～以上 more than half

半天 bàntiān **1** half of the day: 前～ morning. 后～ afternoon **2** a long time; quite a while: 等了～他才来. We waited and waited till he came.

半途而废(廢) bàntú ér fèi give up halfway

半夜 bànyè (名) midnight; in the middle of the night: 会议一直开到～. The meeting lasted until midnight.

半夜三更 bànyè-sāngēng in the depth of night; late at night

半圆 bànyuán (名) semicircle

半殖民地 bànzhímíndì (名) semi-colony: ～半封建社会 semicolonial, semi-feudal society

拌 bàn (动) mix: 给牲口～饲料 mix fodder for animals

拌种(種) bànzhǒng (名) seed dressing

拌嘴 bànzuǐ (动) bicker; squabble; quarrel

伴 bàn I (名) companion; partner: 旅～ fellow-traveller. 作～ keep sb. company II (动) accompany: ～奏 accompaniment

伴唱 bànchàng (名) vocal accompaniment

伴侣 bànlǚ (名) companion; mate; partner: 结为终身～ become lifelong partners; become man and wife

伴奏 bànzòu (动) accompany (with musical instruments): 钢琴～ piano accompaniment

绊 bàn (动) (cause to) stumble; trip: ～手～脚 be in the way. ～了一交 trip over sth.

绊脚石 bànjiǎoshí (名) stumbling block; obstacle

扮 bàn (动) 1 play the part of; disguise oneself as: 他在戏里～一位老渔翁. In the opera he plays the part of an old fisherman. 2 put on (an expression): ～鬼脸 make grimaces; make faces

扮相 bànxiàng (名) the make-up of an actor or actress

扮演 bànyǎn (动) play the part of; act

办(辦) bàn (动) 1 handle; manage; attend to: 怎么办? What is to be done? ～公 attend to one's routine duties 2 set up; run: 村里新～了一所中学. A new middle school has been set up in the village. 3 purchase; get sth. ready: ～酒席 prepare a feast; give a banquet 4 punish (by law); bring to book: 严～ punish severely

办案 bàn'àn (动) handle a case

办报(報) bànbào (动) run a newspaper

办法 bànfǎ (名) way; means; measure; ways and means: 她有～解决这个问题. She is capable of tackling the problem.

办公 bàngōng (动) handle official business

办理 bànlǐ (动) handle; conduct; transact: ～手续 go through the formalities (or procedure). 这些事情你可以斟酌～. You may handle these matters at your own discretion.

办事 bànshì (动) handle affairs; work: ～认真 work conscientiously

邦 bāng (名) nation; state; country: 邻～ a neighbouring country; neighbour state

邦交 bāngjiāo (名) relations between two countries; diplomatic relations: 建立(断绝, 恢复)～ establish (sever, resume) diplomatic relations

邦联(聯) bānglián (名) confederation

梆 bāng I (名) watchman's bamboo or wooden clapper II knocking

梆子 bāngzi (名) 1 watchman's clapper 2 wooden clappers with bars of unequal length

帮(幫) bāng I (动) help; assist: 互～互学 learn from and help each other. ～他一点忙 help him out II (名) 1 outer leaf (of cabbage, etc.) 2 gang; band; clique: 匪～ bandit gang III (量) [often said of a group of people]: 他带来了一～小朋友. He brought with him a group of children.

帮办(辦) bāngbàn I (动) assist in managing: ～军务 assist in handling military affairs II (名) deputy: 副国务卿～ Deputy Under Secretary (of the U.S. Department of State)

帮倒忙 bāng dàománg (动) do sb. a disservice

帮工 bānggōng I (动) lend a hand with farmwork II (名) farmhand; farm labourer

帮会(會) bānghuì (名) secret society; underworld gang

帮忙 bāngmáng (动) help; give (or lend) a hand; do a favour

帮派 bāngpài (名) faction: ～斗争 factional strife

帮腔 bāngqiāng (动) chime in with similar ideas

帮手 bāngshou (名) assistant

帮闲(閑) bāngxián (名) serve the rich and powerful by literary hack work, etc.: ～文人 literary hack

帮凶 bāngxiōng (名) accomplice; accessary

帮助 bāngzhù (动) help; assist: 互相～ mutual aid

榜 bǎng (名) 1 a list of names posted up: 光荣～ honour

roll. 发～ publish the list of successful candidates 2 (old use) notice; proclamation

榜样 bǎngyàng good example; model: 为别人作出～ set a good example to the others

膀 bǎng 1 shoulder: ～阔腰圆 broad-shouldered and solidly-built; of a powerful build 2 wing (of a bird)

see also páng

膀臂 bǎngbì (名) 1 upper arm 2 reliable assistant; right-hand man

膀子 bǎngzi (名) 1 upper arm; arm: 光着～ naked to the waist 2 wing: 鸭～ duck wings

绑 bǎng (动) tie up; truss up

绑架 bǎngjià (动) kidnap

绑票 bǎngpiào (动) kidnap sb. and hold him to ransom

绑腿 bǎngtuǐ (名) leg wrappings

谤 bàng (动) slander; defame; vilify

磅 bàng I (名) 1 pound 2 scales: 搁在～上称一称. Put sth. on the scale. II (动) weigh: ～体重 weigh oneself or sb.

see also páng

磅秤 bàngchèng (名) platform scale; platform balance

镑 bàng (名) pound sterling

傍 bàng (动) draw near; be close to: 依山～水 situated at the foot of a hill with a stream nearby

傍晚 bàngwǎn (副) toward evening; at nightfall; at dusk

棒 bàng I (名) stick; club; cudgel: 垒球～ softball bat II (形) 〈口〉 strong, good, excellent: ～小伙子 a strong young fellow. 功课～ do well in one's studies

棒槌 bàngchui (名) wooden club (used to beat clothes in washing)

棒球 bàngqiú (名) baseball

棒子 bàngzi (名) 1 stick; club; cudgel 2 maize; corn 3 ear of maize (or corn); corncob: ～面 corn-meal

蚌 bàng (名) freshwater mussel; clam

褒 bāo (动) praise; honour; commend

褒贬 bāo-biǎn (动) pass judgment on; appraise: ～人物 pass judgment on personages. 不加～ make neither commendatory nor censorious remarks; neither praise nor censure

褒贬 bāobian (动) criticize; condemn: 别在背地里～人. Don't speak ill of anybody behind his back.

褒义(義) bāoyì (名) commendatory: ～词 commendatory term

包 bāo I (动) 1 wrap: 把东西～起来 wrap things up (with a piece of paper or cloth or something else) ～饺子 make *jiaozi* (dumplings) 2 surround; encircle; envelop: 火苗～住了这座建筑物. The building was enveloped in flames. 3 include; contain: 无所不～ all-inclusive; all-embracing 4 undertake to fulfil the assignment 5 assure; guarantee: ～你满意. You'll like it, I assure you. 6 hire; charter: ～一只船 hire (or charter) a boat. ～机 a chartered plane II (名) 1 bundle; package; pack; packet; parcel: 邮～ parcel 2 bag: 书～ satchel; school bag 3 (量) [used of packages, bundles, etc.]: 一～香烟 a packet (or pack) of cigarettes. 一～棉纱 a bale of cotton yarn

包办(辦) bāobàn (动) 1 take sole charge of: 这件事你一个人～了吧. You'd better do it all by yourself. 2 do things or make decisions without consulting others in any collective enterprise

包庇 bāobì (动) shield; harbour; cover up: ～坏人坏事 shield evil-doers and cover up their evil deeds

包藏 bāocáng (动) contain; harbour; conceal: ～祸心 harbour evil intentions

包产(產)到户 bāochǎn dào hù fix farm output quotas for each household

包场(場) bāochǎng (动) book all or most of the seats in the theatre or cinema; make a block booking

包抄 bāochāo (动) outflank; envelop: 分三路～过去 outflank the enemy in three directions

包袱 bāofu (名) 1 cloth-wrapper 2 a bundle wrapped in cloth 3 load; weight; burden: 我的思想～丢掉了. It's a load (or weight) off my mind.

包干 bāogān (动) undertake to do a job until it is completed: 分片～ assign a task to an individual or group to be completed within a time limit

包工 bāogōng I (动) undertake to perform work within a time limit and according to specifications; contract for a job II (名) job contract: ~制 job contract system

包裹 bāoguǒ I (动) wrap up; bind up II (名) bundle; package; parcel: 邮政~ postal parcel. ~单 parcel form

包含 bāohán (动) contain; embody; imply: 这句话~好几层意思. This statement has several implications.

包涵 bāohan (动) 〈套〉 excuse; forgive: 我英文讲得不好，请多多~. Excuse (me for) my poor English.

包括 bāokuò (动) include; consist of; comprise; incorporate: ~我在内，大家都有责任. All of us, including myself, are to blame.

包揽(攬) bāolǎn (动) monopolize all work to serve private ends: ~词讼 engage in pettifoggery

包罗(羅) bāoluó cover (usually a wide range); embrace (usually many or all aspects)

包罗(羅)万(萬)象 bāoluó wànxiàng embrace a wide spectrum of ideas, subjects, etc.: ~,美不胜收 contain everything that's fine and fascinating

包容 bāoróng I (形) tolerant; magnanimous II (动) contain; hold

包围(圍) bāowéi (动) surround; encircle

包厢 bāoxiāng (名) box at the theatre, opera house, etc.

包扎 bāozā (动) wrap up; bind up; pack: ~伤口 bind up (or dress) a wound

包装 bāozhuāng (名) pack; package: ~车间 packing department. ~箱 packing box (or case)

包子 bāozi (名) steamed stuffed bun

炮 bāo (动) 1 quick-fry; sauté: ~羊肉 quick-fried mutton 2 dry by heat

see also páo; pào

苞 bāo (名) bud; unopened flower: 含~待放 be in bud

龅(齙) bāo

龅牙 bāoyá (名) bucktooth

胞 bāo I (名) afterbirth II (形) born of the same parents: ~兄弟 full brothers

孢 bāo

孢子 bāozǐ (名) spore

剥 bāo (动) shell; peel; skin: ~花生 shell peanuts. ~洋葱 skin an onion. ~桔子 peel a tangerine

see also bō

雹 báo (~子) (名) hail; hailstone

薄 báo (形) 1 thin; flimsy: ~纸 thin paper 2 weak; light: ~酒 a light wine 3 coldly; shabbily: 待他不~ treat him quite generously 4 infertile: ~田 infertile land

see also bó

薄板 báobǎn (名) sheet metal; sheet: 不锈钢~ stainless sheet steel

宝(寶) bǎo I (名) treasure: 粮食是~中之~. Grain is the treasure of treasures. II (形) precious; treasured: ~刀 a treasured sword III 〈敬〉 [said of a friend's family, etc. in old days]: ~眷 your good wife and children; your family

宝贝(貝) bǎobèi (名) 1 treasured object; treasure 2 darling; baby 3 a person with fantastic or absurd ideas: 这人真是个~! What a crank he is!

宝贵 bǎoguì I (形) valuable; precious: ~意见 valuable suggestion II (动) value; treasure; set store by: 这是极~的经验 This is a very valuable (or rewarding) experience.

宝剑(劍) bǎojiàn (名) a double-edged sword

宝库(庫) bǎokù (名) treasure-house

宝石 bǎoshí (名) precious stone; gem

宝塔 bǎotǎ (名) pagoda

宝藏 bǎozàng (名) precious (mineral) deposits: 发掘地下~ tap mineral resources

宝座 bǎozuò (名) throne

保 bǎo I (动) 1 protect; defend; safeguard: ~家卫国 protect our homes and defend our country; safeguard our homeland 2 keep; maintain; preserve: ~温 keep (sth.) warm or hot 3 guarantee; ensure: ~质~量 ensure both quality and quantity 4 go bail for sb.: ~外就医 be bailed out for medical treatment II (名) guarantor: 作～ stand guarantor (or surety) for sb.

保安 bǎo'ān (动) 1 ensure public security; maintain law and order 2 ensure safety (for workers engaged in production)

保镖 bǎobiāo (名) bodyguard

保不住 bǎobuzhù (副) most likely; more likely than not: ～会下雨. Most probably it's going to rain.

保藏 bǎocáng (动) keep in store; preserve (sth.) from damage or loss

保持 bǎochí (动) keep; maintain: ～安静 keep quiet. ～冷静的头脑 keep a cool head; keep cool. 跟群众～密切联系 keep close to the masses. ～中立 remain neutral; maintain neutrality. ～警惕 maintain vigilance; be on the alert

保存 bǎocún (动) preserve; conserve; keep: ～优良传统 preserve the fine traditions. ～得很完整 be well preserved; be kept intact

保单(單) bǎodān (名) guarantee slip

保管 bǎoguǎn I (动) take care of: ～图书 take care of library books II (副) certainly; surely: 他～不知道 He certainly doesn't know.

保护(護) bǎohù (动) protect; safeguard: ～国家财产 protect state property. ～人民的利益 safeguard the people's interests. ～关税 protective tariff. ～国 protectorate. ～贸易主义 protectivism. ～人 guardian

保皇党(黨) bǎohuángdǎng (名) royalists

保驾 bǎojià (动) (jocular) escort the Emperor: 放心吧,我给你～. Don't worry. I'll escort you.

保健 bǎojiàn (名) health protection; health care: 妇幼～ maternal and child hygiene; mother and child care

保留 bǎoliú (动) 1 retain: 仍然～他年轻时的工作作风 still retain the work style of his youthful days 2 hold (or keep) back; reserve: ～以后再答复的权利 reserve the right to reply at a later date. 持～意见 have reservations. ～剧目 repertory; repertoire. ～条款 reservation clause

保密 bǎomì (动) maintain secrecy; keep sth. secret: 这事绝对～. This is strictly confidential.

保姆 bǎomǔ (名) 1 (children's) nurse or domestic help 2 child-care worker

保全 bǎoquán (动) 1 save from damage; preserve: ～面子 save face 2 maintain; keep in good repair

保墒 bǎoshāng (名) preservation of soil moisture

保释(釋) bǎoshì (动) release on bail; bail: 准予(不准)～ accept (refuse) bail

保守 bǎoshǒu I (动) guard; keep: ～国家机密 guard state secrets II (形) conservative: ～思想 conservative ideas (or thinking)

保送 bǎosòng (动) recommend sb. for admission to school, etc.

保卫(衛) bǎowèi (动) defend; safeguard: ～祖国 defend one's country

保温 bǎowēn (动) keep warm; heat preservation

保险(險) bǎoxiǎn I (名) insurance: 人寿(海损)～ life(maritime) insurance. ～公司 insurance company II (形) 1 safe: 这样做可不～. It wouldn't be safe to pursure such a course. 你还是带上雨衣吧,～点儿. You'd better take your raincoat with you, to be on the safe side. 2 be bound to: 他明天～会来. He is sure to come tomorrow.

保险(險)刀 bǎoxiǎndāo (名) safety razor

保险(險)丝 bǎoxiǎnsī (名) fuse; fuse-wire

保修 bǎoxiū (名) guarantee to keep sth. in good repair: ～一年 a year's guarantee

保养(養) bǎoyǎng (动) 1 take good care of (or conserve) one's health: 他～得好. He is well preserved. 2 maintain; keep in good repair: 机器～ maintenance (or upkeep) of machinery

保佑 bǎoyòu (动) bless and protect

保育 bǎoyù (名) child care; child welfare: ～员 child-care worker; nurse

保障 bǎozhàng (动) ensure; guarantee; safeguard: ～人民言论自由 guarantee freedom of speech for the people. ～国家安全 assure national security

保证(證) bǎozhèng I (动) pledge; guarantee; assure; ensure: ～完成任务 pledge (or guarantee) to fulfil the task. ～履行 pledge to fulfil (obligation, etc.) II (名) guarantee: 党的领导是我们胜利的～. Party leadership is the guarantee of our victory.

保证(證)人 bǎozhèngrén (名) 1 guarantor 2 bail

保重 bǎozhòng (动) take care of oneself: 多多～. Take good care of yourself.

堡 bǎo (名) fort; fortress

堡垒(壘) bǎolěi (名) fort; fortress; stronghold; blockhouse

葆 bǎo 〈书〉 I (名) luxuriant growth II (动) preserve; retain: 永～青春 keep alive at all times one's youthful fervour

饱(飽) bǎo I (形) 1 have eaten one's fill; be full: 我～了. I am full. 2 full; plump: 谷粒很～. The grains are quite plump. II (副) fully; to the full: ～尝旧日的辛酸 taste to the full the bitter hardships of the old days. ～经忧患 suffer untold tribulations III (动) satisfy: 一～眼福 enjoy to the full watching a show, match, performance, etc.

饱和 bǎohé (名) saturation

饱经(經)风(風)霜 bǎo jīng fēngshuāng having had one's fill of hardships and difficulties

饱满(滿) bǎomǎn (形) full; plump: 颗粒～的小麦 plump-eared wheat. 精神～ vigourous; energetic

饱学(學) bǎoxué (形) learned; erudite; scholarly: ～之士 a learned scholar; a man of great erudition

报(報) bào I (动) 1 announce; declare: ～告 report. ～名 enter one's name 2 reply; respond; requite: ～以热烈的掌声 respond with warm applause. 以怨～德 requite kindness with ingratitude; return evil for good II (名) 1 newspaper 2 periodical; journal: 画～ pictorial. 周～ weekly. 学～ college journal. 3 bulletin; report: 喜～ report of success, a happy event, etc.; glad tidings; good news 4 telegram; cable: 发～机 transmitter

报案 bào'àn (动) report to the police an act violating the law or endangering social security

报表 bàobiǎo (名) forms for reporting to the higher organizations

报仇 bàochóu (动) avenge; revenge: ～雪恨 avenge a gross injustice

报酬 bàochou (名) reward; remuneration; pay: 不计～ not think in terms of remuneration

报答 bàodá (动) repay; requite: ～党的关怀 repay the Party for its kindness

报到 bàodào (动) report for work; check in; register: 向大会秘书处～ check in at the secretariat of the congress

报道 bàodào I (动) report (news); cover: ～会议情况 cover the conference II (名) news reporting; story: 他们写了一篇关于小麦丰收的～. They wrote an article describing the bumper harvest of wheat.

报恩 bào'ēn (动) pay a debt of gratitude; repay a person for his kindness

报废(廢) bàofèi (动) (any article or equipment which is no longer useful); scrap

报复(復) bàofù (名) reprisal; retaliation: 图谋～ nurse thoughts of revenge; contemplate retaliation

报告 bàogào I (动) report; make known: 向上级～ report to the higher authorities II (名) report; speech; lecture: 总结～ summing-up report. ～文学 reportage

报关(關) bàoguān (动) apply to customs to comply with import or export regulations

报国(國) bàoguó (动) dedicate one's life to the cause of the country

报户口 bào hùkǒu (动) apply for a residence permit; report at the police station

报捷 bàojié (动) report a success; announce a victory

报界 bàojiè (名) the press; journalistic circles; the journalists

报警 bàojǐng (动) 1 report (an imminent danger) to the police 2 give an alarm

报刊 bàokān (名) newspapers and periodicals; the press

报考 bàokǎo (动) enter (oneself) for the examination

报名 bàomíng (动) enter one's name; sign up: ～参加百米赛跑 sign up to participate in the 100-metre dash

报幕 bàomù (动) announce the items on a (theatrical) programme: ～员 announcer

报社 bàoshè (名) newspaper office
报失 bàoshī (动) report lost property to the authorities
报时(時) bàoshí (动) give the correct time (particularly referring to the correct time given by the radio station or telephone bureau to all inquirors)
报数 bàoshù (动) number off
报务(務)员 bàowùyuán (名) telegraph operator; radio operator
报喜 bàoxǐ (动) report a success worthy of celebration
报销 bàoxiāo (动) 1 ask for reimbursement: 向财务科～ submit an expense account to the cashier's office for reimbursement 2 submit a list of expended articles to the higher authorities 3 〈口〉 write off; wipe out
报晓(曉) bàoxiǎo (动) (of a cock, bell, etc.) herald the break of day; be a harbinger of dawn
报效 bàoxiào (动) render service to repay sb.'s kindness
报信 bàoxìn (动) pass on a message to (sb.)
报应(應) bàoyìng (名) retribution; judgment (on sb.)
报章 bàozhāng (名) newspapers: ～杂志 newspapers and magazines
报纸 bàozhǐ (名) 1 newspaper 2 newsprint
暴 bào (形) 1 sudden and violent: ～雨 torrential rain. ～饮～食 eat and drink immoderately 2 cruel; savage: 残～ atrocious 3 short-tempered; hot-tempered: 脾气～ have a hot temper
暴病 bàobìng (名) a sudden serious illness: 得～ suddenly fall gravely ill
暴跌 bàodiē (动) steep fall (in price); slump
暴动(動) bàodòng (名) insurrection; rebellion
暴发(發) bàofā (动) 1 break out: 山洪～. Torrents of water swept down the mountain. 2 suddenly become wealthy and powerful: ～户 upstart
暴风(風) bàofēng (名) 1 storm wind 2 storm (force 11 wind)
暴风(風)雨 bàofēngyǔ (名) rainstorm; storm; tempest: ～般的掌声 thunderous applause
暴风(風)骤雨 bàofēng-zhòuyǔ (名) violent storm; hurricane; tempest
暴光 bàoguāng (名) exposure
暴君 bàojūn (名) tyrant; despot
暴力 bàolì (名) violence; force; brute force
暴利 bàolì (名) huge ill-gotten gains: 牟取～ reap staggering (or colossal) profits
暴戾 bàolì (形) 〈书〉 ruthless and tyrannical; cruel and ferocious
暴露 bàolù (动) expose; reveal; lay bare: ～身分 reveal one's identity. ～无遗 be thoroughly exposed
暴乱(亂) bàoluàn (名) rebellion; revolt: 平定～ suppress (or put down, quell) a rebellion
暴虐 bàonüè (形) ruthless; tyrannical: ～无道 reign tyrannically and defy all ethical principles
暴殄天物 bàotiǎn tiānwù wilfully destroy Mother Nature's belongings — recklessly waste what is given to us by nature
暴跳如雷 bàotiào rú léi stamp with fury; fly into a rage
暴徒 bàotú (名) ruffian; thug; hooligan
暴行 bàoxíng (名) outrage; atrocity
暴雨 bàoyǔ (名) torrential rain; rainstorm
暴躁 bàozào (形) irascible; irritable: 性情～ easily get into a violent temper
暴涨(漲) bàozhǎng (动) (of floods, prices, etc.) rise suddenly or sharply
暴政 bàozhèng (名) tyranny; despotic rule
暴卒 bàozú (动) die suddenly
爆 bào (动) 1 explode; burst: 车胎～了. The tyre's burst. 2 quick-fry; quick-boil: ～羊肉 quick-fried mutton
爆发(發) bàofā (动) erupt; burst out; break out: 火山～. The volcano exploded (or erupted). 战争～. War broke out.
爆破 bàopò (动) blow up; demolish; dynamite; blast
爆炸 bàozhà (动) explode; blow up; detonate
爆竹 bàozhú (名) firecracker: 放～ let off firecrackers
豹 bào (名) leopard; panther
抱 bào I (动) 1 hold or carry in one's arms; embrace; hug 2 have one's first child or grandchild 3 adopt (a child) 4 hang together: ～成一团 gang up; hang together 5 cherish;

harbour: 不～幻想 cherish no illusions **6** hatch (eggs); brood **II** (量) [indicating quantity of material as being held by both arms]: 一～草 an armful of hay

抱病 bàobìng be ill; be in poor health: 长期～ have been ill for a long time

抱不平 bào bùpíng feel indignant at the injustice suffered by another: 打～ put up a fight against an injustice on sb.'s behalf

抱残(殘)守缺 bàocán-shǒuquē stick to old-fashioned ideas and refuse to change; be a stick-in-the-mud

抱负 bàofù (名) aspiration; ambition: 很有～ have high aspirations; be very ambitious

抱恨 bàohèn (动) be weighed down with a deep sense of regret: ～终天 be a victim of lifelong remorse

抱歉 bàoqiàn (动) be sorry; regret: 到迟了，很～。I'm sorry, I'm late.

抱头(頭)鼠窜(竄) bàotóu shǔcuàn (动) cover one's head with both hands and run away like a rat; flee helter-skelter

抱头(頭)痛哭 bàotóu tòngkū (动) weep in each other's arms; cry on each other's shoulder

抱怨 bàoyuàn (动) complain; grumble

刨

bào **I** (动) plane sth. down; plane: ～木板 plane a board **II** (名) plane; planer; planing machine

see also páo

刨床 bàochuáng (名) planer; planing machine

刨子 bàozi (名) plane

鲍

bào

鲍鱼 bàoyú (名) **1** abalone **2** 〈书〉 salted fish

杯

bēi (名) **1** cup: 茶～ teacup. 一～茶 a cup of tea. 一～水 a glass of water **2** (prize) cup; trophy: 银～ silver cup

杯弓蛇影 bēigōng-shéyǐng mistake the reflection of a bow in the wine cup for a snake — be too panicky and often get unnecessarily scared

杯水车(車)薪 bēishuǐ-chēxīn try to put out a burning cartload of faggots with a cup of water — make a ridiculously inadequate effort to save a grave situation

杯子 bēizi (名) cup; glass

悲

bēi (形) sad; sorrowful; melancholy: ～不自胜 be overwhelmed with grief. 慈～ compassionate; merciful

悲哀 bēi'āi (形) grieved; sorrowful

悲惨 bēicǎn (形) miserable; tragic: ～景象 a tragic scene or spectacle

悲悼 bēidào (动) mourn; grieve over sb.'s death

悲愤 bēifèn (名) grief and indignation

悲歌 bēigē **I** (名) **1** sad melody; stirring strains **2** elegy; dirge **II** (动) sing with solemn fervour

悲观(觀) bēiguān (形) pessimistic: ～情绪 pessimism

悲欢(歡)离(離)合 bēi-huān-lí-hé (名) the meetings and partings, the joys and sorrows — generally referring to varied and often bitter experiences of life

悲剧(劇) bēijù (名) tragedy

悲泣 bēiqì (动) weep with grief

悲伤(傷) bēishāng (形) sad; miserable

悲叹(嘆) bēitàn (动) bemoan; lament

悲天悯人 bēitiān-mǐnrén feel both grieved and indignant at the depravity of human society and the suffering of the teeming masses

悲痛 bēitòng (名) grief; sorrow: 感到深切的～ be deeply grieved; be overcome with sorrow

悲喜交集 bēi-xǐ jiāojí have mixed feelings; feel grief and joy intermingled

悲壮(壯) bēizhuàng (形) solemn and stirring

背

bēi (动) **1** carry on one's back; **2** bear; shoulder: 这个责任我还～得起。I presume I am up to this job.

see also bèi

背包 bēibāo (名) **1** knapsack; rucksack; field pack **2** blanket roll

背包袱 bēi bāofu (动) have a weight (or load) on one's mind

背负 bēifù (动) bear; carry on one's back; have on one's shoulder

背黑锅(鍋) bēi hēiguō (动) 〈口〉 take the blame for the fault of others; be made a scapegoat

背债 bēizhài (动) be in debt; be saddled with debts

卑 bēi (形) **1** low: 地势~湿. The terrain is low-lying and damp **2** inferior: ~不足道 too inferior to be worth mentioning **3** 〈书〉 modest; humble: ~辞厚礼 send a humble message along with expensive gifts

卑鄙 bēibǐ (形) base; ammoral; despicable: ~无耻 devoid of any sense of shame; shameless. ~龌龊 base and vile

卑躬屈节(節) bēigōng-qūjié be spineless and servile; bow and scrape

卑贱(賤) bēijiàn (形) **1** low, humble: 出身~ be of humble station or origin (in the old society) **2** mean and low

卑劣 bēiliè (形) base; mean; despicable: ~行径 base conduct. ~手法 a mean (or despicable) trick

卑怯 bēiqiè (形) weak-kneed; abject: ~行为 abject behaviour

卑微 bēiwēi (形) petty and low; mean

卑污 bēiwū (形) depraved

卑下 bēixià (形) base; low

碑 bēi (名) an upright stone tablet; stele: 人民英雄纪念~ the Monument to the People's Heroes. 墓~ tombstone

碑帖 bēitiè (名) a rubbing from a stone inscription (usu. as a model for calligraphy)

碑文 bēiwén (名) an inscription on a tablet

北 běi I (名) north: ~风 a north wind. 城~ north of the city. 华~ north China. ~屋 a room with a southern exposure II (形) 〈书〉 be defeated: 连战皆~ be defeated in one battle after another

北半球 běibànqiú (名) the Northern Hemisphere

北冰洋 Běibīngyáng (名) the Arctic (Ocean)

北斗星 běidǒuxīng (名) the Big Dipper; the Plough

北方 běifāng (名) **1** north **2** the northern part of the country, esp. the area north of the Yellow River; the North: ~话 northern dialect. ~人 Northerner

北国(國) běiguó (名) 〈书〉 the northern part of the country; the North

北极(極) běijí (名) **1** the North Pole; the Arctic Pole **2** the north magnetic pole

北京 Běijīng (名) Beijing (Peking)

北京人 Běijīngrén (名) Peking Men (Sinanthropus pekinensis)

北美洲 Běi Měizhou (名) North America

北纬(緯) běiwěi (名) north (or northern) latitude

北温带(帶) běiwēndài (名) the north temperate zone

焙 bèi (形) bake over a slow fire: ~干 dry over a fire. ~制 cure sth. by drying it over a fire

焙烧(燒) bèishāo (动) roast; bake

倍 bèi I (名) times: -fold: 四~ four times; fourfold. 二的五~是十. Five times two is ten. 增长了五~ increase by 500%; register a 500% increase; be six times as much. 产量成~增长. Output has doubled and redoubled. II (形) double; twice as much: 事半功~ get twice the result with half the effort

倍数 bèishù (名) multiple

蓓 bèi

蓓蕾 bèilěi (名) bud

悖 bèi (形) 〈书〉 **1** be contrary to; go against: ~理 contrary to reason. 并行不~ be parallel and not contrary to each other; not be mutually exclusive; can be carried out simultaneously without affecting each other

悖谬 bèimiù (形) 〈书〉 absurd; preposterous

悖入悖出 bèirù-bèichū ill-gotten, ill-spent; easy come, easy go

辈 bèi (名) **1** people of kindred interest; people of one kind or another: 无能之~ mediocre people **2** generation: 他比我长(小)一~. He's one generation my senior (junior). 他俩同~. They belong to the same generation. **3** lifetime: 后半~儿 the latter part of one's life

辈出 bèichū (动) come forth in large numbers: 人材~ Large numbers of talented people are coming to the fore.

辈分 bèifen (名) seniority in the family or clan; position in the family hierarchy

背 bèi I (名) **1** the back of the body; the back of an object **2** at the back: ~山面海

with hills behind and the sea in front II (动) 1 hide sth. from view; do sth. behind sb.'s back: 没有什么～人的事 have nothing to hide from anyone 2 recite from memory; learn by heart (or by rote): ～台词 recite the words of an actor's part; speak one's lines 3 act contrary to; violate; break: ～约 break one's promise; go back on one's word III (形)1 out-of-the-way: ～街 back street; side street 2 hard of hearing 3 <口> unlucky see also bēi

背道而驰 bèi dào ér chí run in opposite directions; run counter to; be diametrically opposed to

背地里(裏) bèidìli (副) behind sb.'s back; in private; on the sly

背光 bèiguāng (动) be shaded from the sun; be sheltered from direct light

背后(後) bèihòu (副) 1 behind; at the back; in the rear: 门～ behind the door. 房子～ at the back of the house 2 behind sb.'s back: 有话当面说，不要～乱说. Speak openly when you've got anything to say, but don't gossip behind anybody's back.

背井离(離)乡(鄉) bèijǐng-líxiāng leave one's native place to earn a livelihood elsewhere (esp. against one's will)

背景 bèijǐng (名) background; backdrop: 历史～ historical background (or setting)

背静 bèijing (形) quiet and secluded

背离(離) bèilí (动) deviate from; depart from: ～原意 deviate from one's original intentions

背面 bèimiàn (名) the reverse side of an object: 信封的～ the back of an envelope

背叛 bèipàn (动) betray; forsake: ～原来的阶级 forsake one's original class; rebel against one's own class

背弃(棄) bèiqì (动) abandon; desert; renounce: ～自己的诺言 go back on one's word

背时(時) bèishí (形) 1 behind the times 2 ill-fated; unfortunate

背书(書) bèishū I (动) recite a book from memory II (名) endorsement (on a cheque); signature or seal on the back of a cheque

背水一战(戰) bèi shuǐ yí zhàn fight with one's back to the river — fight to win or die in the attempt

背诵 bèisòng (动) recite from memory

背心 bèixīn (名) a sleeveless garment: 汗～ vest; singlet. 毛～ sleeveless woollen sweater

背信弃(棄)义(義) bèixìn-qìyì break faith with sb.; be perfidious: ～的行为 a breach of faith; an act of perfidy

背阴(陰) bèiyīn (形) (a spot) entirely shaded from the sun

背影 bèiyǐng (名) a view of sb.'s back; a figure viewed from behind

背约 bèiyuē (动) break an agreement; go back on one's word; fail to keep one's promise

褙

bèi (动) stick one piece of cloth or paper on top of another

贝(貝)

bèi (名) 1 shellfish 2 cowrie

贝壳(殼) bèiké (名) shell

贝类(類) bèilèi (名) shellfish; molluscs

备(備)

bèi I (动) 1 be equipped with; have: 德才兼～ have both political integrity and professional knowledge 2 prepare; get ready: ～而不用 get things ready not for immediate use, but for future occasions 3 provide (or prepare) against; take precautions against: 以～万一 prepare against all eventualities II (名) equipment: 军～ military equipment; armaments III (副) fully; in every possible way: ～受欢迎 be given a rousing welcome

备案 bèi'àn (动) report to the higher organization a case to be put on record (or on file) for future reference

备查 bèichá (名) for future reference

备耕 bèigēng (动) get things ready for ploughing and sowing

备荒 bèihuāng (动) prepare against natural disasters

备件 bèijiàn (名) spare parts

备考 bèikǎo (名) appendices or notes supplied for reference

备课 bèikè (动) (of a teacher or student) prepare lessons

备料 bèiliào (动) 1 get the raw materials ready 2 prepare feed (for livestock)

备忘录(錄) bèiwànglù (名) 1 memorandum; aide-memoire 2 memorandum book
备用 bèiyòng (名) reserve; spare: ~轮胎 a spare tyre
备战(戰) bèizhàn (动) 1 prepare for war: 扩军~ arms expansion and war preparations 2 be prepared against war
备至 bèizhì (副) to the utmost; in every possible way: 关怀~ show sb. every consideration
备注 bèizhù (名) remarks (a column reserved for additional information in a form)

惫(憊) bèi (形) exhausted; fatigued

被 bèi I (名) quilt: 棉~ cotton-wadded quilt II (介) [introducing the agent in a passive sentence]: 他~蛇咬伤. He was bitten by a snake. III (助) [used before a notional verb to indicate that the subject is the receiver]: ~捕 be arrested; be under arrest. ~选为主席 be elected chairman
被剥削阶(階)级 bèibōxuējiējí (名) the exploited class
被单(單) bèidān (名) (bed) sheet
被动(動) bèidòng (形) passive: 陷于~地位 land oneself in a passive position. ~语态 passive voice
被服 bèifú (名) bedding and clothing (esp. for army use)
被告 bèigào (名) defendant; the accused
被害人 bèihàirén (名) the injured party; the victim
被里(裏) bèilǐ (名) the underneathside of a quilt
被面 bèimiàn (名) the facing of a quilt
被迫 bèipò (动) be compelled; be forced; be constrained: ~作出这个决定 be compelled to make this decision
被褥 bèirù (名) bedding; bedclothes
被套 bèitào (名) 1 bedding bag 2 (bag-shaped) quilt cover 3 cotton wadding for a quilt
被选(選)举(舉)权(權) bèixuǎnjǔquán (名) the right to be elected
被压(壓)迫民族 bèiyāpò mínzú (名) oppressed nation
被子 bèizi (名) quilt

呗 bei (助) 1 [indicating that the idea is simple and easy to understand]: 你不会骑车就学~. You can't ride a bike? Well, learn to. 2 [indicating agreement with reluctance]: 你一定要去,就去~. Well, go if you insist.

贲 bēn see also bì
贲门(門) bēnmén (名) cardia

奔 bēn (动) 1 run quickly: ~驰 gallop; run about 2 hurry: ~走 dash around (on business) 3 flee: 东~西窜 flee helter-skelter
see also bèn
奔波 bēnbō (动) rush about; hurry back and forth
奔驰 bēnchí (动) run fast; speed: 火车~而过. The train sped past.
奔放 bēnfàng (形) bold and unrestrained; untrammelled; uninhibited: 热情~ brimming over with deep emotion
奔流 bēnliú I (动) flow at great speed; pour: ~入海 empty into the sea. 铁水~ molten iron comes pouring out II (名) racing current; running stream
奔忙 bēnmáng (动) be dashing about all day
奔命 bēnmìng (动) dash around on business: 疲于~ be run off one's feet
奔跑 bēnpǎo (动) run
奔丧(喪) bēnsāng (动) hasten home for the funeral of a parent
奔逃 bēntáo (动) flee; run away: 四散~ flee in all directions; flee helter-skelter; stampede
奔腾 bēnténg (动) 1 gallop: 犹如万马~ like ten thousand galloping horses 2 surge forward; roll on in waves
奔泻(瀉) bēnxiè (动) (of torrents) rush down; pour down
奔走 bēnzǒu (动) rush about; be busy running about: ~相告 run around telling people the news; lose no time in passing on the news

锛 bēn I (名) (~子) adze II (动) cut with an adze

本 běn I (名) 1 the root or stem of a plant 2 foundation; basis; origin: 舍~逐末 attend to trifles and neglect essentials 3 capital; principal: 还~付息 pay back the capital (or principal) plus interest 4 book: 帐~儿 account book. 日记~ diary. 照相~ photograph album 5 edition; version: 普及～ popular edition II (形) 1 original: ～意 original idea; real intention. 我～想不去. Originally I didn't mean to go. 2 one's own: ～厂 this factory 3 this; current; present: ～周(月) this week (month); the current week (month) 4 fountain: 每句话都有所～. Every statement is well-founded. III (量) [used of books, albums, etc.]: 两～书 two books

本草 běncǎo (名) a book on Chinese (herbal) medicine: «～纲目» Compendium of Materia Medica

本初子午线 běnchū zǐwǔxiàn (名) the first meridian; the prime meridian

本地 běndì (名) this locality: ～口音 local accent

本分 běnfèn I (名) one's duty: 尽～ do one's duty (or part) II (形) contented with one's lot

本国(國) běnguó (名) homeland; one's own country: ～资源 national resources

本行 běnháng (名) one's line; one's own profession

本家 běnjiā (名) a member of the same clan; a distant relative with the same family name

本届 běnjiè (形) current; this year's: ～毕业生 this year's graduates

本金 běnjīn (名) capital; principal

本科 běnkē (名) undergraduate course; regular college course: ～学生 undergraduate

本来 běnlái I (形) original: ～的面貌 true features II (副) 1 originally; at first: ～他身体不好, 现在很结实了. Originally he was in poor health but is quite strong now. 2 it goes without saying; of course: ～就该快办. Of course we should act promptly.

本领 běnlǐng (名) skill; ability; capability: ～高强 of superb skill

本末 běn-mò (名) 1 the whole course of an event from beginning to end; ins and outs: 详述～ recount the whole story in detail 2 the fundamental and the incidental: ～倒置 take the branch for the root; put the incidental before the fundamental

本能 běnnéng (名) instinct

本钱 běnqián (名) capital

本人 běnrén (名) 1 oneself; in person: 这事还是由他～来谈吧. He had better bring up the matter himself. 2 I (me, myself)

本色 běnsè (名) 1 true (or inherent) qualities; distinctive character: 军人的～ inherent qualities of a soldier 2 natural colour: ～棉毛衫 a sweater of natural colour

本身 běnshēn (代) itself: 这幅画～并没有什么价值. The painting itself is of very little value.

本事 běnshì (名) 1 ability 2 source material; original story: 莎氏乐府～ Tales from Shakespeare

本题 běntí (名) the subject under discussion; the point at issue: 这一段文章与～无关, 应该删去. This paragraph should be crossed out as it is irrelevant to the point at issue.

本土 běntǔ (名) one's native place

本位 běnwèi (名) 1 standard: 金～ gold standard 2 one's own department or unit: ～主义 departmental selfishness

本文 běnwén (名) 1 this essay, article, the present paper, etc. 2 the main body of a book; the original (or source) text

本性 běnxìng (名) a person's character; innate quality; nature; inherent quality: ～难移. It is difficult to alter one's character.

本义 běnyì (名) original meaning; literal sense

本意 běnyì (名) original idea; real intention: 他的～是好的. He meant well.

本质(質) běnzhì (名) essence; true nature

本子 běnzi (名) book; notebook: 笔记～ notebook

本族语 běnzúyǔ (名) native language; mother tongue

畚 běn (动) scoop up with a dustpan

畚箕 běnjī (名) 1 a bamboo or wicker scoop 2 dustpan

奔 bèn (动) 1 go straight towards; head for: 直～办公室 head straight for the office 2 <口> approach: 他是～六十的人了. He's getting on for sixty.

see also bēn

奔命 bènmìng <口> be in a des

perate hurry

奔头(頭)儿 bèntour (名) 〈口〉 prospect

笨 bèn (形) 1 slow; stupid; thick: 愚～ stupid; slow-witted 2 clumsy; awkward: 他这人～手～脚. He is clumsy. 3 cumbersome; unwieldy: 家具太～搬起来很不方便. The furniture is too cumbersome to move.

笨蛋 bèndàn (名) fool; idiot

笨鸟(鳥)先飞(飛) bèn niǎo xiān fēi A slow bird should make an early start

笨重 bènzhòng (形) heavy; cumbersome: ～的体力劳动 heavy manual labour

笨拙 bènzhuō (形) clumsy; awkward; stupid: 动作～ clumsy (or awkward) in movement. ～的伎俩 stupid tricks

崩 bēng (动) 1 collapse: 山～ landslide; landslip 2 burst: 这次会谈已经谈～了. The talks have broken down. 3 hit by bursting: 爆竹～了他的手. The firecracker went off in his hand. 4 〈口〉 execute by shooting; shoot 5 (of an emperor) die

崩溃 bēngkuì (名、动) collapse; breakdown; crumble

崩裂 bēngliè (动) burst (or break) apart; crack: 炸药轰隆一声,山石～. Boom! The dynamite sent the rocks flying.

崩塌 bēngtā (动) collapse; crumble

崩陷 bēngxiàn (动) fall in; cave in

嘣 bēng (象) (the sound of sth. throbbing or bursting): 我心里兴奋得～～直跳. My heart is throbbing with excitement.

绷 bēng I (动) 1 stretch tight or straight: 把绳子～直了. The rope is stretched taut. 2 spring; bounce: 弹簧～飞了. The spring jumped out. II (名) baste; tack; pin see also běng; bèng

绷带 bēngdài (名) bandage

绷子 bēngzi embroidery frame; hoop; tambour

甭 béng (动) don't; needn't: ～再说了. Don't say any more. ～管他. Leave him alone.

绷 běng (动) 〈口〉 1 ～着脸 pull a long face 2 strain oneself: ～住劲 strain all one's muscular strength see also bēng; bèng

迸 bèng (动) spout; spurt; burst forth: 火星乱～. The sparks are flying all around. 沉默了半天,他才～出几句话来. He kept quiet for a little while before he blurted out a few words.

迸发(發) bèngfā (动) burst forth; burst out: 笑声从四面八方～出来. There was an outburst of laughter from all sides.

迸裂 bèngliè (动) split; burst (open)

泵 bèng (名) pump: 离心～ centrifugal pump

蹦 bèng (动) leap; jump; spring: 他不用使劲一～就过了沟. He leaped over the ditch without effort.

绷 bèng (动) 1 split open; crack: ～了一条缝儿. There is a crack in it. 2 (副) 〈口〉 [used before such adjectives as 'hard', 'straight', 'bright', etc. to indicate superior degree.] very: ～硬 very hard; extremely stiff see also bēng; běng

逼 bī (动) 1 force; compel; drive: ～得她走投无路. She was driven into a corner. 2 press for; extort: ～债 dun. ～租 press for payment of rent 3 press on towards; press up to; close in on: 直～城下 press up to the city wall

逼宫 bīgōng (动) (of ministers, etc.) force the king or emperor to abdicate

逼供 bīgòng (动) extort a confession (usually by torture)

逼近 bījìn (动) press on towards; close in on; approach; draw near: 天色～黄昏. It is approaching dusk.

逼迫 bīpò (动) force; compel; pressurize

逼上梁山 bī shàng Liángshān be driven to join the Liangshan Marsh rebels; be driven to revolt; be forced to make a desperate move

逼债 bīzhài (动) press for payment of debts; dun

逼真 bīzhēn (形) 1 lifelike; true to life: 这幅画画得十分～. This is really a life-like picture 2 distinctly; clearly: 听得～ hear distinctly

荸 bí

荸荠(薺) bíqi (名) water chestnut (eleocharis tuberosa)

鼻 bí (名) nose

鼻孔 bíkǒng (名) nostril

鼻梁 bíliáng (名) bridge of the nose

鼻腔 bíqiāng (名) nasal cavity

鼻青脸(臉)肿(腫) bíqīng-liǎnzhǒng a bloody nose and a swollen face; badly battered: 打得～ be beaten black and blue

鼻儿 bír (名) 1 a hole in an article, utensil, etc. large enough for sth. to pass; eye: 针～ the eye of a needle. 门～ bolt staple 2 〈口〉 whistle

鼻涕 bítì (名) nasal mucus; snivel: 流～ have a running nose

鼻息 bíxī (名) breath: 仰人～ be totally dependent on sb. and allow oneself to be dictated to

鼻音 bíyīn (名) nasal sound: 说话带～ speak with a twang

鼻子 bízi (名) nose: 鹰钩～ aquiline nose. 牵着～走 lead a person by the nose

鼻祖 bízǔ (名) the earliest ancestor; originator (of a tradition, school of thought, etc.)

鄙 bǐ (形) 1 low; mean; vulgar: 卑～ mean; despicable 2 〈谦〉 my: ～意 in my poor (or humble) opinion II (动) 〈书〉 despise; disdain; scorn: 可～ despicable

鄙薄 bǐbó I (动) despise; scorn II (形) uncouth

鄙俚 bǐlǐ (形)〈书〉vulgar; boorish

鄙吝 bǐlìn (形) 〈书〉 1 coarse 2 stingy; miserly; mean

鄙陋 bǐlòu (形) superficial; shallow: ～无知 shallow and ignorant; superficial and ill-informed; illiterate

鄙弃(棄) bǐqì (动) disdain; loathe: ～这种庸俗作风 disdain such philistine practices

鄙人 bǐrén (代)〈谦〉 your humble servant

鄙视 bǐshì (动) despise; disdain; hold in contempt

鄙俗 bǐsú (形) coarse; philistine

笔(筆) bǐ I (名) 1 pen: 圆珠～ ball-point pen. 钢～ pen. 自来水～ fountain pen. 毛～ writing brush. 2 technique of writing, calligraphy or drawing: 文～ style of writing. 3 stroke; touch: 这个字的第一～ the first stroke of the character. 你给他写信时，替我带一～. Give him my best regards when you write to him. II (量) [amount (of money)]: 一～钱 a sum of money; a fund

笔触(觸) bǐchù (名) brush stroke in Chinese painting and calligraphy; style of writing: 简练的～ simple skilful strokes; a terse style

笔底下 bǐdǐxia (名) ability to write: ～不错 write well. ～来得快 write with ease (or facility)

笔调 bǐdiào (名) (of writing) tone; style: 讽刺的～ (in) a satirical style

笔法 bǐfǎ (名) technique of writing, calligraphy or drawing

笔锋 bǐfēng (名) 1 the tip of a writing brush 2 vigour of style in writing; stroke; touch

笔杆 bǐgǎn (名) 1 the shaft of a pen or writing brush; penholder 2 pen: 耍～ 〈口〉 wield the pen

笔画(畫) bǐhuà (名) strokes of a Chinese character

笔迹 bǐjì (名) a person's handwriting; hand

笔记 bǐjì (名) 1 take down (in writing) 2 notes: 记～ take notes 3 a type of literature consisting mainly of random notes ～本 notebook. ～小说 literary sketches

笔力 bǐlì (名) vigour of stroke in calligraphy or drawing; vigour of style in literary composition: ～雄健 powerful strokes; vigorous style

笔录(錄) bǐlù I (动) put down (in writing); take down II (名) notes; record

笔名 bǐmíng (名) pen name; pseudonym

笔墨 bǐmò (名) pen and ink; words; writing: 我们的感受不是用～可以形容的. Words can not describe how I felt. 操～生涯 earn a living by the pen

笔顺 bǐshùn (名) order of strokes observed in calligraphy

笔试 bǐshì (名) written examination

笔挺 bǐtǐng (形) 1 (standing) very straight; bolt upright 2 well-pressed; trim: 衣服～ immaculately dressed

笔头(頭) bǐtóu 1 nib; pen point 2 ability to write; writing skill 3 written; in written form: ～练习 written exercises

笔误 bǐwù (名) slip of the pen

笔译(譯) bǐyì (名) written translation

笔者 bǐzhě (名) [often referring to the author himself] the author; the present writer

笔直 bǐzhí (形) perfectly straight; bolt upright: ～的马路 straight avenue. 身子挺得～stand straight; sit bolt upright

俾 bǐ〈书〉in order to; so that: ～众周知 so that this may be made known to the public

匕 bǐ (名) an ancient type of spoon

匕首 bǐshǒu (名) dagger

比 bǐ (动) 1 compare; emulate: ～得上 compare favourably with. 我哪能～得了您. How can I compare with you? ～先进 emulate the advanced 2 as... as; compare to: 坚～金石 as solid as a rock 3 make a gesture: 连说带～ gesticulate 4 copy; model after: ～着旧衣裁新衣 pattern a new garment on an old one II (介) 1 [indicating difference in manner or degree by comparison]: 他～我学得好. He has done better than I. 2 [indicating difference in quantity]: 这一带水稻产量～小麦大二倍 The output of rice is 3 times that of wheat in this area. 3 [indicating the different scores won by two contestants or contesting teams]: 甲队以二～一胜乙队. Team A beat team B (by a score of) two to one. 现在几～几? What's the score?

比比 bǐbǐ (副) 1 frequently; many times 2 everywhere: ～皆是 can be found everywhere; be legion

比方 bǐfang I (动) likened to: 他的品德只宜用松柏来～. His integrity can only be compared to the pine and cypress. II (名) analogy; instance: 打～ draw an analogy. 拿盖房子作～ take for instance the building of a house

比分 bǐfēn (名) score: 场上～是三比二. The score is 3 to 2.

比画(劃) bǐhua (动) gesture; gesticulate: 他～着讲. He managed to make himself understood by gesticulating.

比价(價) bǐjià (名) price relations; parity; rate of exchange: 工农业产品～ the price parities between industrial and agricultural products

比较 bǐjiào I (动) compare; contrast: 有～才能鉴别. Only by comparing can we distinguish. II (名) comparison; contrast III (介) [to indicate difference in manner or degree]: 煤产量～去年有显著的增长. Coal output shows a marked increase as compared with last year. IV (副) fairly; comparatively; relatively; quite; rather: 我～爱看电影. Relatively speaking, I like films. 这篇文章写得～好. This article is comparatively well-written.

比例 bǐlì (名) 1 ratio; proportion: 3 与 4 的～等于 9 与 12 的～. The ratio of three to four is nine to twelve. 按～地协调发展 a proportionate and co-ordinated growth 2 scale: 按～绘制 be drawn to scale

比例尺 bǐlìchǐ (名) 1 scale: 这张地图的～是四十万分之一. The scale of the map is 1:400,000. 2 architect's scale; engineer's scale

比邻(鄰) bǐlín I (名) neighbour; next-door neighbour II (形) near; next to: 跟我们～的国家 the neighbour states of our country

比率 bǐlǜ (名) ratio; rate

比拟(擬) bǐnǐ I (动) compare: 无可～ be incomparable. 难以～ be hardly comparable II (名) analogy; metaphor; comparison: 这种～是不恰当的. It is inappropriate to draw such a parallel.

比热(熱) bǐrè (名) specific heat

比如 bǐrú for example; for instance; such as

比赛 bǐsài (名) match; competition: 足球～ football match. 象棋～ chess tournament. 演说～ speech (oratorial) contest. ～项目 event

比翼 bǐyì (动) fly wing to wing: ～齐飞 fly side by side. ～鸟 a pair of lovebirds — a devoted couple

比喻 bǐyù (名) metaphor; analogy; figure of speech: 打个～ by way of analogy. 这只是一个～的说法. This is only a metaphor.

比照 bǐzhào (动) 1 copy; model on 2 contrast

比值 bǐzhí (名) specific value; ratio: 8:4 的～(比率)为2:1. The ratio of 8 to 4 is 2 to 1.

比重 bǐzhòng (名) 1 proportion: 工业在整个国民经济中的～ the proportion of industry in the national economy as a whole 2 specific gravity

秕 bǐ (形) (of grain) not plump; blighted

秕糠 bǐkāng (名) 1 chaff 2 worthless stuff

秕子 bǐzi (名) blighted grain

妣 bǐ (名)‹书› one's deceased mother

彼 bǐ (代) 1 that; those; the other; another: ～时 at that time. 由此及～ proceed from one to the other 2 the other party: 知己知～ know one's opponent as well as oneself

彼岸 bǐ'àn (名) the other shore; Faramita

彼此 bǐcǐ (代) 1 each other; one another 2 ‹套› [often said twice to show that both sides are in the same position]: 您辛苦啦！——～～！ You have been working very hard! — So have you!

愎 bì (形) wilful; obstinate; perverse: 刚～ self-willed

闭 bì (动) 1 shut; close: ～上眼 close one's eyes. ～口不谈 refuse to say anything about; remain silent. ～嘴! Hold your tongue! (Shut up!) 2 stop up; obstruct: ～住气 hold one's breath

闭关(關)自守 bìguān zì shǒu close the country to international intercourse

闭门羹 bìméngēng [often used in phr.]: 飨以～ slam the door in sb.'s face. 吃～ be denied admittance

闭门(門)思过(過) bì mén sī guò shut oneself up and ponder over one's mistakes

闭门(門)造车(車) bì mén zào chē make a cart behind closed doors; divorce oneself from reality and act blindly

闭幕 bìmù (动) 1 the curtain falls 2 close; conclude: 会议已胜利～. The conference has come to a successful close. ～词 closing address (or speech). ～式 closing ceremony

闭塞 bìsè I (动) stop up; block: 管道～. The pipes were blocked. II (形) 1 hard to get to; out-of-the-way; inaccessible: 以前这一带交通～. In the past this district was difficult of access. 2 ill-informed

闭音节(節) bìyīnjié (名) closed syllable

敝 bì (形) 1 ‹书› shabby; worn-out; ragged: ～衣 ragged clothing; shabby (or worn-out) clothes 2 ‹谦› my; our; this: ～处 my place

敝屣 bìxǐ (名) ‹书› worn-out shoes; a worthless thing: 弃之如～ discard sth. like a pair of worn-out shoes

敝帚自珍 bìzhǒu zì zhēn cherish sth. of one's own for sentimental reasons

蔽 bì (动) cover; shelter; hide: 掩～ screen; cover. 隐～ conceal; take cover. 浮云～日. Floating clouds hid the Sun.

弊 bì (名) 1 fraud; abuse; malpractice: 舞～ practise fraud; engage in corrupt practices 2 disadvantage; harm: 有利有～. There are both advantages and disadvantages. 兴利除～ promote what is beneficial and abolish what is harmful

弊病 bìbìng (名) drawback; disadvantage

弊端 bìduān (名) abuse; corrupt practice

必 bì I (副) certainly; surely; necessarily: ～不可少 absolutely necessary; indispensable II (动) must; have to; be bound to: 事～躬亲 attend to everything personally

必定 bìdìng (副) certainly; surely: 他～会来. He is sure to come. 我以前～见过你. Surely I have met you before.

必恭必敬 bìgōng-bìjìng (形) reverent and respectful; extremely deferential

必然 bìrán I (形) inevitable; certain: ～结果 inevitable outcome. ～趋势 inexorable trend II (名) necessity: ～规律 inexorable law. ～性 necessity; inevitability; certainty

必修课 bìxiūkè (名) a required (or obligatory) course

必须 bìxū (动) must; have to: ～向大家讲明. It must be made clear to all. ～有耐心. It is imperative to have patience.

必需 bìxū (形) necessary; indispensable: 空气是生活所～的. Air is indispensable to life. 日用～品 daily necessities

必要 bìyào (形) requisite; necessary; indispensable: 为一个企业提供～的资金 provide the requisite capital for an enterprise. 没有～再讨论了. There's no need to discuss it any more. ～劳动 necessary labour. ～前提 prerequisite; precondition. ～条件 essential condition; prerequisite. ～性 necessity

毖 bì (名) caution: 惩前～后 learn from past mistakes to avoid future ones

秘 bì 见"便秘" biànbì
see also mì

碧 bì I (名)<书> emerald II (形) bluish green; blue: ～海 the blue sea. ～空 a clear blue sky; an azure sky. ～草 green grass

碧绿 bìlǜ (形) dark green

碧血 bìxuè (名) blood shed in a just cause

碧玉 bìyù (名) jasper

贲 bì (形) <书> beautifully adorned
see also bēn

贲临(臨) bìlín (形) <书> your gracious presence

庇 bì (动) shelter; protect; shield

庇护(護) bìhù (动) shelter; shield; take under one's wing

庇荫(蔭) bìyìn (动) 1 (of a tree, etc.) give shade 2 shield

毕(畢) bì I (动) finish; accomplish; conclude: 阅～请放回原处. Please replace after reading. II (副) <书> fully; altogether; completely: 原形～露 show one's true colours

毕竟 bìjìng (副) after all; all in all; in the final analysis

毕生 bìshēng (副) all one's life; lifetime

毕肖 bìxiào (形) <书> resemble closely; be the very image of: 画得神情～ paint a lifelike portrait of sb.

毕业(業) bìyè graduate; finish school

哔(嗶) bì

哔叽(嘰) bìjī (名) serge

筚(篳) bì (名) a bamboo or wicker fence

筚路蓝(藍)缕(縷) bìlù-lánlǚ <书> drive a cart in ragged clothes to break fresh ground — endure great hardships in pioneer work

毙(斃) bì 1 die; get killed 2 <口> execute; shoot

毙命 bìmìng (动) meet violent death; get killed

陛 bì (名) <书> a flight of steps leading to a palace hall

陛下 bìxià [a title for addressing or speaking of a king or queen] Your Majesty; His or Her Majesty

裨 bì (名)<书> benefit; advantage: 无～于事. It won't help matters.

裨益 bìyì (名) <书> benefit; advantage; profit: 大有～ be of great benefit

婢 bì (名) slave girl; servant-girl

婢女 bìnǚ (名) slave girl; servant-girl

币(幣) bì money; currency: 硬～ hard currency. 银～ silver coin. 纸～ paper money; bank-notes

币值 bìzhí (名) currency value: ～稳定. The currency is stable.

蓖 bì

蓖麻 bìmá (名) castor-oil plant

篦 bì (动) comb: ～头 comb one's hair

篦子 bìzi (名) a bamboo comb with fine teeth on both sides

辟 bì I (名) <书> monarch; sovereign: 复～ restore a monarchy; restoration II (动) <书> ward off
see also pì

辟邪 bìxié (动) exorcise evil spirits

避 bì (动) 1 avoid; evade; shun: ～风头 lie low. ～而不谈 evade the question; avoid the subject. ～风雨 seek shelter from wind and rain. 不～艰险 defy hardships and dangers 2 prevent; keep away; repel: ～孕 contraception

避风(風)港 bìfēnggǎng (名) haven

避雷针 bìléizhēn (名) lightning rod

避免 bìmiǎn (动) avoid; refrain from; avert: ～主观地看问题 avoid looking at problems subjectively

避难(難) bìnàn (动) take refuge; seek asylum: ～所 refuge; sanctuary; asylum; haven

避嫌 bìxián (动) avoid doing anything that may cause misunderstanding; avoid arousing suspicion

避重就轻(輕) bì zhòng jiù qīng 1 evade major tasks and choose minor ones 2 avoid major issues while dwelling on irrelevant details

璧 bì (名) an ancient piece of jade, round, flat and with a hole in its centre

璧还(還) bìhuán (动)‹敬› return sth. to its owner or decline a gift

壁 bì (名) 1 wall: 容器～ the wall of a container 2 cliff: 峭～ a precipitous cliff; precipice

壁橱 bìchú (名) a built-in wardrobe or cupboard; closet

壁画(畫) bìhuà (名) mural painting; fresco

壁垒(壘) bìlěi (名) rampart; camp: ～分明. There is a clear line of demarcation between the two schools of thought. ～森严 closely guarded; strongly fortified; sharply divided

壁立 bìlì (of cliffs, etc.) stand like a wall; rise steeply

壁炉(爐) bìlú (名) fireplace

壁毯 bìtǎn (名) wall tapestry

臂 bì (名) 1 arm: 左～ the left arm. 助一～之力 give sb. a hand 2 upper arm

臂膀 bìbǎng (名) arm

臂章 bìzhāng (名) 1 armband; armlet 2 shoulder emblem

弼 bì (动)‹书› assist

煸 biān (动) stir-fry before stewing

蝙 biān

蝙蝠 biānfú (名) bat

鳊 biān

鳊鱼(魚) biānyú (名) bream

编 biān I (动) 1 weave; plait: ～竹筐 plait bamboo baskets 2 organize; arrange 3 edit; compile: ～词典 edit or compile a dictionary 4 write; compose: ～剧本 write plays 5 fabricate; invent; make up; cook up: 瞎～ sheer fabrication II (名) part of a book; book; volume

编导(導) biāndǎo I (动) write and direct (a play, film, etc.) II (名) ‹戏剧› playwright-director; ‹舞剧› choreographer-director; ‹电影› scenarist-director

编队(隊) biānduì I (动) form into columns; organize into teams II (名) ～飞行 formation flight (or flying)

编号(號) biānhào I (动) number II (名) serial number

编辑 biānjí I (动) edit; compile II (名) editor; compiler: 总～ editor-in-chief; chief editor. ～部 editorial staff

编剧(劇) biānjù I (动) write a play, scenario, etc. II (名)‹戏剧› playwright; ‹电影› screenwriter; scenarist

编码 biānmǎ (动) coding

编目 biānmù I (动) make a catalogue; catalogue II (名) catalogue; list

编年史 biānniánshǐ (名) annals; chronicle

编排 biānpái (动) arrange; lay out: 文字和图片的～ the layout of pictures and articles

编审(審) biānshěn I (动) read and edit II (名) copy editor

编写(寫) biānxiě (动) 1 compile: ～教科书 compile a textbook 2 write; compose: ～剧本 write plays

编译(譯) biānyì (动) translate and edit

编造 biānzào (动) 1 compile; draw up; work out: ～预算 draw up a budget 2 fabricate; invent: ～谎言 fabricate lies. ～情节 invent a story 3 create out of the imagination: 古代人民～的神话 myths invented by the ancients

编者 biānzhě (名) editor; compiler: ～按 editor's note; editorial note

编织(織) biānzhī (动) weave; knit; plait: ～毛衣 knit a sweater

编制 biānzhì I (动) 1 weave; plait; braid: ～竹器 plait bamboo articles 2 work out; draw up: ～生产计划 work out a production plan. ～教学大纲 draw up a syllabus II (名) authorized strength; establishment: 部队～ establishment (for army units). 缩小～ reduce the staff

编纂 biānzuǎn (动) compile: ～词典 compile (or edit) a dictionary

鞭 biān I (名) 1 an iron staff (used as a weapon in ancient China) 2 sth. resembling a whip: 教～ (teacher's) pointer 3 a string of small firecrackers II (动) flog; whip; lash: ～马 whip a horse

鞭策 biāncè (动、名) spur on; urge on; encourage: 这是对我们的～. This is an encouragement to us.

鞭长(長)莫及 biān cháng mò j

beyond the reach of one's power; too far away to be helpful

鞭笞 biānchī (动) <书> flog; lash

鞭打 biāndǎ (动) whip; lash; flog; thrash

鞭炮 biānpào (名) 1 firecrackers 2 a string of small firecrackers

鞭辟入里(裏) biān pì rù lǐ (形) penetrating; incisive; in-depth

鞭挞(撻) biāntà (动) <书> lash; castigate

鞭子 biānzi (名) whip

边(邊) biān (名) 1 side: 海～ seaside. 河～ riverside 2 border (as an ornament): 花～儿 lace border 3 frontier; border: 守卫～疆 guard the border 4 limit; bound: 无～无际 boundless 5 close by (an object): 站在窗～ stand by the window

边(邊) bian (suffix of a noun of locality): 这～ here. 东～ in the east. 左～ on the left. 前～ in front. 里～ inside

边…边… biān...biān... [used before two verbs respectively to indicate simultaneous actions]: 边干边学 train on the job

边陲 biānchuí (名) <书> border area; frontier

边防 biānfáng (名) guarding the border: ～部队 frontier guards

边际(際) biānjì (名) limit; bound; boundary: 汪洋大海，漫无～. a boundless sea; a vast expanse of water. 不着～ wide of the mark

边疆 biānjiāng (名) border; borderland; frontier; frontier region

边界 biānjiè (名) boundary; border: 划定～ delimit boundaries. 越过～ cross a boundary; cross the border. ～事件 border incident. ～线 boundary line. ～争端 boundary dispute

边境 biānjìng (名) border; frontier: 封锁～ close the frontiers; seal off the borders

边卡 biānqiǎ (名) border checkpoint or checkpost

边区(區) biānqū (名) border area (or region)

边塞 biānsài (名) frontier fortress

边线(綫) biānxiàn (名) 1 sideline 2 <棒、垒球> foul line

边沿 biānyán (名) border; frontier: ～地带 borders; areas near the frontier

边缘 biānyuán (名) 1 edge; fringe; verge; brink 2 marginal; borderline: ～科学 frontier science

边远(遠) biānyuǎn remote; outlying: ～地区 remote region

扁 biǎn (形) flat: 一只～盒子 a flat box. 纸箱子压～了. The cardboard box was crushed.

see also piān

扁担 biǎndan (名) carrying pole; shoulder pole

扁豆 biǎndòu (名) hyacinth bean

扁圆 biǎnyuán (形) oblate

褊 biǎn (形) <书> narrow; cramped

褊急 biǎnjí (形) <书> narrow-minded and short-tempered

褊狭(狹) biǎnxiá (形) <书> narrow: 气量～ narrow-minded

匾 biǎn (名) 1 a horizontal board inscribed with words of praise (occasionally a silk banner embroidered for the same purpose): 绣金～ embroidering a silk banner in letters of gold 2 a big round shallow basket

匾额 biǎn'é (名) a horizontal inscribed board

贬 biǎn (动) 1 demote 2 reduce; devalue: ～价出售 sell at a reduced price 3 censure; condemn

贬斥 biǎnchì 1 (动) <书> demote 2 denounce

贬低 biǎndī (动) deliberately underestimate; play down

贬义(義) biǎnyì (名) derogatory sense: ～词 derogatory term

贬谪 biǎnzhé (动) banish from the court

贬值 biǎnzhí I (动) (of currency) devalue; devaluate; depreciate II (名) 1 devaluation 2 depreciation

辨 biàn (动) differentiate; distinguish; discriminate: 明～是非 discriminate between right and wrong. 不～真伪 fail to distinguish between truth and falsehood

辨别 biànbié (动) differentiate; distinguish; discriminate: ～真伪 distinguish the true from the false. ～方向 take one's bearings

辨认(認) biànrèn (动) identify; recognize: ～面貌 recognize one's face

辨析 biànxī (动) differentiate and analyse; discriminate

辩(辯) biàn (动) argue; dispute; debate: 我同她争～过好几次. I've argued with her many times.

辩白 biànbái (动) try to justify oneself
辩驳 biànbó (动、名) dispute; refute
辩才 biàncái (名)〈书〉eloquence; oratory
辩护(護) biànhù (动) 1 speak in defence of; try to justify or defend: 不要替他～了. Don't try to defend him. 2 plead; defend: 为被告人～ plead for the accused. ～权 right to defence. ～人 defender; counsel
辩解 biànjiě (动) make excuses
辩论(論) biànlùn (动) argue; debate: ～会 a debate
辩证(證) biànzhèng (形) dialectical: ～的统一 dialectical unity. 事物发展的～规律 the dialectical law of the development of things. ～法 dialectics. ～逻辑 dialectical logic
辩证(證)法 biànzhèngfǎ (名) dialectics: 唯物～materialist dialectics. ～的世界观 the dialectical world outlook
辩证(證)唯物主义 biànzhèng wéiwùzhǔyì (名) dialectical materialism: ～观点 a dialectical materialist point of view. ～者 dialectical materialist

辫(辮) biàn (名) plait; braid; pigtail: 梳小～儿wear pigtails. 蒜～ a braid of garlic
辫子 biànzi (名) plait; braid; pigtail: 梳～ wear one's hair in braids. 把问题梳梳～ sort out the problems

忭 biàn (形)〈书〉glad; happy

变(變) biàn I (动) 1 change; become different: 情况～了. The situation has changed. 2 transform; change; turn: ～农业国为工业国 turn an agricultural country into an industrial power II (名) an unexpected turn of events: 事～ incident. ～乱 turmoil
变本加厉(厲) biàn běn jiā lì (动) worsen; be further intensified
变电(電)站 biàndiànzhàn (名) (transformer) substation
变动(動) biàndòng (名) change; alteration: 人事～ change of personnel. 国际形势发生了很大的～. The world situation has undergone a great change.
变法 biànfǎ (名) political reform
变革 biàngé (动、名) transform; change: 社会～ social change
变更 biàngēng (动) change; alter; modify: ～作息时间 alter the daily timetable. 我们的计划稍有～. We have modified our plan.
变故 biàngù (名) an unforeseen event; catastrophe
变卦 biànguà (动) suddenly change one's mind; go back on one's word
变化 biànhuà (名、动) change; vary: 化学～ chemical change. 他的战术～多端. His tactics are varied.
变幻 biànhuàn (动) change irregularly; fluctuate: ～莫测 changeable; unpredictable. 风云～fast-changing situation
变换 biànhuàn (动) vary; alternate: ～手法 vary one's tactics
变节(節) biànjié (动、名) betray one's country or party: ～分子 traitor; renegade
变乱(亂) biànluàn (名) turmoil; social upheaval
变卖(賣) biànmài (动) sell off (one's property)
变迁(遷) biànqiān (名) changes; vicissitudes: 人事～ personnel changes
变色 biànsè (动) 1 change colour 2 discolour 3 show signs of displeasure or anger
变色龙(龍) biànsèlóng (名) chameleon
变态(態) biàntài I (名) metamorphosis II (形) abnormal; anomalous: ～心理 abnormal psychology
变天 biàntiān (名) 1 change of weather 2 euphemism for restoration of reactionary rule
变通 biàntōng (动) make changes according to specific conditions
变戏(戲)法 biàn xìfǎ (动) perform conjuring tricks; conjure; juggle
变相 biànxiàng (形) in disguised form; covert: ～贪污 a disguised form of corruption
变心 biànxīn (动) cease to be faithful
变形 biànxíng (动) be out of shape; warp: 这箱子压得～了. The box has been crushed out of shape. 这些木板已经～. These boards have warped.
变压(壓)器 biànyāqì (名) transformer
变异(異) biànyì (名) variation
变质(質) biànzhì (动) 1 go bad; be intrinsically changed for the worse: 这肉～了. The meat has gone bad. 蜕化～ become degen-

erate

变种(種) biànzhǒng (名) 1 mutation; variety 2 variety; variant

遍 biàn I (副) all over; everywhere: 我们的朋友～天下. We have friends all over the world. II (量) [indicating the process of an action from beginning to end]: 这本书我从头到尾看过两～. I've read the book twice from cover to cover. 请再说一～. Please say it again.

遍布 biànbù (动) be found everywhere; spread all over

遍地 biàndì (副) everywhere; all over: ～都是 be found everywhere. ～开花 (of good things) spring up all over the place

遍及 biànjí (动) extend (or spread) all over

遍体鳞伤(傷) biàntǐ línshāng be covered all over with cuts and bruises

便 biàn I (形) 1 convenient; handy: 顾客称～. Customers find this very convenient. 2 if it is considered proper: 悉听尊～ please yourself; act at one's own discretion 3 informal; plain; ordinary: ～宴 an informal dinner. ～装 ordinary (or everyday) clothes II (名) piss or shit; urine or excrement: 粪～ excrement; night soil III (副) then: 如果她这次又不来,她～没有什么借口了. If she doesn't appear this time, then she won't have any excuse. IV (连)[showing possible concession]: 只要依靠群众,～是最大的困难,也能克服. So long as we can rely on the masses, we can overcome any difficulty, however great it may be.

see also pián

便秘 biànbì (名) constipation

便池 biànchí (名) urinal

便当(當) biàndang (形) simple; easy: 这个房间收拾起来很～. There isn't any trouble tidying up the room.

便道 biàndào (名) 1 shortcut: 抄～走 take a shortcut 2 pavement; sidewalk: 行人走～. Pedestrians walk on the pavement.

便饭 biànfàn (名) a homely meal; potluck

便服 biànfú (名) 1 everyday clothes; informal dress 2 civilian clothes

便函 biànhán (名) an informal letter sent by an organization

便壶 biànhú (名) urinal; chamber pot

便笺(箋) biànjiān (名) notepaper; memo; memo pad

便览(覽) biànlǎn (名) brief guide: 旅游～ tourist guide

便利 biànlì (形) 1 convenient; easy: 交通～ have convenient communications; be conveniently located 2 render services to: 日夜商店～群众. A shop that is open round the clock saves the customers a lot of trouble.

便桥(橋) biànqiáo (名) a makeshift bridge

便条(條) biàntiáo (名) 1 a brief note 2 notepaper

便鞋 biànxié (名) slippers

便血 biànxiě (名) having (or passing) blood in one's stool

便宴 biànyàn (名) informal dinner: 设～招待 give a dinner for sb.

便衣 biànyī (名) 1 civilian clothes; plain clothes: ～公安人员 plainclothes public security personnel; public security personnel in plain clothes 2 plainclothesman

便宜行事 biànyí xíng shì act at one's discretion; act as one sees fit

便于 biànyú (形) easy to; convenient for: ～计算 easy to calculate; easily calculable

便中 biànzhōng (副) at one's convenience: ～请告知. Please let me know at your convenience.

弁 biàn (名) 1 a man's cap used in ancient times 2 a low-ranking officer in old China

弁言 biànyán (名) <书> foreword; preface

镳 biāo (名) 1 <书> bit (of a bridle): 分道扬～ part company each pursuing his own course 2 see "镖" biāo

标(標) biāo (名) 1 mark; sign: 商～ trade mark. 路～ road sign. 2 put a mark, tag or label on; label: 商品都～了价格. Every article has a price tag on it. 3 prize; award; championship 4 outward sign; symptom: 治～不如治本 would rather seek a permanent cure than temporary relief 5 tender; bid: 招～ invite tenders

标榜 biāobǎng (动) 1 brag about; parade: ～学术自由 brag about academic freedom 2 boost; excessively praise: 互相～ boost

each other
标本 biāoběn (名) specimen; sample: 昆虫～ insect specimen
标兵 biāobīng (名) 1 parade guards(usu. spaced out along parade routes) 2 example; pacesetter: 树立～ set a good example
标尺 biāochǐ (名) 1 surveyor's rod; staff 2 staff gauge 3 rear sight
标点(點) biāodiǎn (名、动) punctuation; punctuate: ～符号 punctuation mark
标定 biāodìng (动) demarcate: ～边界线 demarcate a boundary by setting up boundary markers (done jointly by the two parties concerned)
标记 biāojì (名) sign; mark; symbol
标价(價) biāojià I (动) mark a price II (名) marked price
标明 biāomíng (动) mark; indicate: 时刻表～火车七时开. The timetable indicates that the train leaves at seven.
标签(簽) biāoqiān (名) label; tag: 贴上～ stick on a label. 价目～ price tag
标枪(槍) biāoqiāng (名) javelin
标题 biāotí (名) title; heading; headline; caption: 通栏大字～ banner headline; banner
标新立异(異) biāoxīn-lìyì try to be deliberately unconventional; put forward novel ideas just to show one is different from the ordinary run
标语 biāoyǔ (名) slogan; poster
标志 biāozhì I (名) sign; mark;symbol:兴旺发达的～ a sign of prosperity II (动) indicate; mark; symbolize: ～着时代的开始 mark the beginning of a new era
标致 biāozhi (形) (usu. of women) pretty
标准 biāozhǔn (名) standard; criterion: 合乎～ up to standard. 实践是真理的唯一～. Practice is the sole criterion of truth. ～时 standard time. ～音 standard pronunciation

镖 biāo (名) a dartlike weapon

膘 biāo (名) fat (of an animal): 长～ get fat; put on flesh

飑(颮) biāo (名) violent wind; whirlwind

彪 biāo (名)〈书〉young tiger

彪炳 biāobǐng 〈书〉shine: ～千古 shine through the ages
彪形大汉(漢) biāoxíng dàhàn (名) burly chap; hefty fellow

表 biǎo I (名) 1 surface; outside; external: 由～及里 proceed from the outside to the inside 2 model; example 3 table; form; list: 时间～ timetable; schedule; form. 申请～ application form 4 meter; gauge: 温度～ thermometer 5 watch: 手～ (wrist) watch 6 the relationship between the children or grandchildren of a brother and a sister or of sisters: ～兄 cousin (see"姑表" gūbiǎo; "姨表" yíbiǎo) 7 memorial to an emperor II (动) show; express: 深～同情 show deep sympathy. 聊～微意 so as to express one's appreciation; as a token of one's gratitude
表白 biǎobái (动) vindicate; show: ～诚意 show one's sincerity
表册 biǎocè (名) statistical forms; book of tables or forms: 公文报告～ documents, written reports and statistical forms
表达(達) biǎodá (动) express (thoughts and feelings)
表带 biǎodài (名) watchband; watch strap
表格 biǎogé (名) form; table: 空白～ a blank form. 填写～ fill in a form
表决 biǎojué (动) decide by vote; vote: 付～ put to the vote; take a vote. ～权 right to vote; vote
表里如一 biǎo lǐ rú yī behave exactly in the same way as one thinks one ought to; think and act in one and the same way
表露 biǎolù (动) show; reveal: 他并没有～出焦急的心情. He didn't reveal his anxiety.
表蒙子 biǎoméngzi (名) watch glass; crystal
表面 biǎomiàn (名) surface; face outside; appearance: 地球的～ the surface of the earth. ～价值 face value
表面化 biǎomiànhuà (动) come to the surface; surface: 矛盾～了. The contradiction has surfaced.
表明 biǎomíng (动) make known make clear; state clearly; indicate: ～立场 state one's position ～决心 declare one's determination
表亲(親) biǎoqīn (名) 1 cousin 2 cousinship
表情 biǎoqíng I (动) express

one's feelings II (名) expression: 面部～ facial expression
表示 biǎoshì (动) show; express; indicate: ～关切 show concern. ～热烈欢迎 extend a warm welcome
表率 biǎoshuài (名) example; model: 老师要做学生的～. The teacher should set a good example to his pupils.
表态(態) biǎotài (动) make known one's position
表现 biǎoxiàn I (名) expression; manifestation: 反对机会主义的各种～ oppose opportunism in all its manifestations II (动) 1 show; display; manifest: ～出极大的勇敢和智慧 display great courage and wisdom 2 show off: 好～ like to show off
表演 biǎoyǎn I (动) perform act; play: ～节目 give a performance; put on a show II (名) performance; exhibition: 杂技～ acrobatic performance
表扬(揚) biǎoyáng (动) praise; commend: ～信 commendatory letter
表语 biǎoyǔ (名) predicative
表彰 biǎozhāng (动) cite (in dispatches); commend
裱 biǎo (动) mount (a picture, a painting, etc.)
裱糊 biǎohú (动) paper (a wall, ceiling, etc.)
婊 biǎo
婊子 biǎozi (名) prostitute; bitch
鳔 biào (名、动) 1 swim bladder; air bladder 2 fish glue
瘪(癟) biē
see also biě
瘪三 biēsān (名) a wretched-looking tramp who lives by begging or stealing
憋 biē (动) 1 suppress; hold back; restrain: ～不住 be unable to hold oneself back. ～着一肚子火 bottle up one's anger. ～着一肚子气 have pent-up grievances 2 suffocate; feel oppressed: 屋里太闷,～得人透不过气来. The room is so stuffy that one is not able to breathe freely.
鳖 biē (名) soft-shelled turtle
蹩 bié (动) sprain (one's ankle or wrist)
蹩脚 biéjiǎo (形) inferior; shoddy: ～货 shoddy work
别 bié I (名) 1 leave: 告～ take leave (of). 久～重逢 meet again after a long separation 2 other; another: ～人 other people; others. ～处 another place; elsewhere 3 difference; distinction: 天渊之～ a world of difference. 性～ sex II (动) 1 differentiate; distinguish: ～其真伪 determine whether it's true or false 2 fasten with a pin or clip: 把表格～在一起 pin (or clip) the forms together. ～针 safety pin 3 stick in: 腰里～着手枪 with a pistol stuck in one's belt 4 don't: ～忘了. Don't forget ～忙; No hurry. Take your time. III [used with "是" to express difference]: 他怎么还没来,～是病了吧? Why hasn't he come yet? I hope he's not ill.
see also biè
别出心裁 bié chū xīncái start something unique; deliberately adopt a different approach
别号(號) biéhào (名) alias
别具一格 bié jù yī gé have a unique (or distinctive) style
别开(開)生面 bié kāi shēngmiàn develop a new style; break fresh ground
别名 biémíng (名) alternative name
别人 biéren (名) other people; others; people: ～想法不同 other people think differently.
别墅 biéshù (名) villa
别有用心 bié yǒu yòngxīn have ulterior motives; have an axe to grind
别致 biézhì (形) novel; delightful: 这座房子的建筑结构非常～. The architecture of the house is uniquely delightful.
别字 biézì (名) incorrectly written or mispronounced character; malapropism
瘪(癟) biě (形) shrivelled; shrunken; deflated: 车胎～了. The tyre is flat.
see also biē
别 biè
see also bié
别扭 bièniu (形) 1 awkward; clumsy difficult: 这个人脾气真～. He is temperamentally unpredictable. 2 cannot see eye to eye: 闹～ be at odds. 两个人素来有些别别扭扭的. The two of them are often at loggerheads with each other.
濒 bīn (动) 1 be close to (the sea, a river, etc.); border on: 东～大海 overlook the sea on

the east 2 be on the point of: ～死 on the verge of death; dying
濒临(臨) bīnlín (动) be close to; border on; be on the verge of: 这个国家～太平洋. The country is on the pacific coast.
濒于 bīnyú be on the brink of: ～破产 teeter on the edge of bankruptcy
宾(賓) bīn (名) guest: 贵～ distinguished guest; guest of honour
宾馆 bīnguǎn (名) guesthouse
宾客 bīnkè (名) guests; visitors
宾语(語) bīnyǔ (名) object: 直接～ direct object. 间接～ indirect object
宾至如归(歸) bīn zhì rú guī (of a hotel or guesthouse)where guests feel at home; a home (away) from home
滨(濱) bīn (名) 1 bank; brink; shore: 海～ beech; seashore 2 be close to(the sea, a river, etc.): ～海 by the sea; coastal
傧(儐) bīn
傧相 bīnxiàng (名) attendant of the bride or bridegroom at a wedding: 男～ best man. 女～ bridesmaid
缤(繽) bīn
缤纷 bīnfēn ‹书› in riotous profusion: 五彩～ multi-coloured. 落英～ a profusion of falling petals
彬 bīn
彬彬有礼(禮) bīnbīn yǒu lǐ (形) courteous; urbane
鬓(鬢) bìn (名) temples; hair on the temples
鬓发(髮) bìnfà (名) hair on the temples: ～灰白 greying at the temples
殡(殯) bìn (动) carry a coffin to the burial place (or a crematory)
殡仪(儀)馆 bìnyíguǎn (名) funeral parlour (or home)
殡葬 bìnzàng (名) funeral and interment
摈(擯) bìn (动) ‹书› discard; get rid of: ～弃不用 reject
摈斥 bìnchì (动) reject: ～异己 dismiss those who hold different opinions
摈弃(棄) bìnqì (动) abandon; discard

冰 bīng I (名) ice II (动)coo[l] in the ice; ice: 把那瓶汽水～上. Have that bottle of lemonade iced.
冰雹 bīngbáo (名) hail
冰场(場) bīngchǎng (名) skating (or ice) rink
冰川 bīngchuān (名) glacier
冰刀 bīngdāo (名) (ice) skates
冰点(點) bīngdiǎn (名) freezing point
冰冻(凍) bīngdòng (动) freeze: ～三尺,非一日之寒. The fact tha[t] the water has frozen up canno[t] be attributed to the coldness o[f] one single day — the trouble is deeprooted.
冰棍儿 bīnggùnr (名) ice-lolly, popsicle; ice-sucker; frozen sucker
冰窖 bīngjiào (名) ice cell
冰冷 bīnglěng (形) ice-cold
冰淇淋 bīngqílín (名) ice cream
冰球 bīngqiú (名) 1 ice hockey 2 puck
冰山 bīngshān (名) iceberg
冰释(釋) bīngshì (动) ‹书› (o[f] misgivings, misunderstandings etc.) disappear or vanish withou[t] a trace
冰霜 bīngshuāng (名) 1 symbo[l] of moral integrity 2 symbol o[f] gravity: 冷若～ look frosty
冰糖 bīngtáng (名) rock sugar
冰天雪地 bīngtiān-xuědì (名) a world of forzen ice and drifting snow; a mass of ice and snow
冰箱 bīngxiāng (名)icebox; refrigerator; freezer
冰鞋 bīngxié (名) skating boots skates
冰镇 bīngzhèn (形) iced: ～西瓜 iced watermelon
兵 bīng (名) 1 soldier: 当～ enlist in the army, navy o[r] air force. 新～ recruit 2 weapon ～器 weaponry; arms 3 army troops 4 military strategy: 纸上谈～ be an armchair strategist
兵变(變) bīngbiàn (名) mutiny
兵不厌(厭)诈 bīng bù yàn zh[à] nothing is too deceitful in war all's fair in war
兵法 bīngfǎ (名)art of war; mil[i]tary strategy and tactics
兵工厂(廠) bīnggōngchǎng (名) munitions (or ordnance) factor[y]
兵贵神速 bīng guì shénsù speed a factor of incalculable valu[e] in war; lightning speed is th[e] essence of the art of war
兵荒马(馬)乱(亂) bīnghuāng-mǎluà[n]

the chaos of war;the turbulence of war
兵家 bīngjiā (名) military strategist in ancient China; (in wartime) military commander: ～必争之地 a strategic stronghold
兵力 bīnglì (名) military strength
兵马(馬) bīngmǎ (名) military forces
兵强马(馬)壮(壯) bīngqiáng-mǎzhuàng a well-trained and well-equipped army
兵权(權) bīngquán (名) military power; military leadership
兵士 bīngshì (名) ordinary soldier
兵团(團) bīngtuán (名) a large military unit consisting of several armies or divisions; corps: 主力～ main force
兵役 bīngyì (名) military service: 服～ serve in the armed force. ～制 conscription
兵营(營) bīngyíng (名) military camp; barracks
兵站 bīngzhàn (名) military depot
兵种(種) bīngzhǒng (名) arm of the services

禀 bǐng (动) 1 report (to one's superior); petition 2 receive; be endowed with
禀承 bǐngchéng see "秉承" bǐngchéng
禀赋 bǐngfù (名) natural endowment; gift: ～聪明 gifted or talented
禀告 bǐnggào (动) report (to one's superior)
禀性 bǐngxìng (名) natural disposition

饼 bǐng (名) 1 cake: 月～ moon cake. 烙～ pancake 2 shaped like a cake: 铁～ discus
饼干(乾) bǐnggān (名) biscuit; cracker

屏 bǐng (动) 1 hold (one's breath) 2 reject; abandon
see also píng
屏弃(棄) bǐngqì (动) discard; throw away
屏息 bǐngxī (动) hold one's breath: 听众～静听. The audience listened intently with bated breath.

丙 bǐng (名) 1 the third of the ten Heavenly Stems 2 third: ～等 the third grade; grade C. ～种维生素 vitamin C

炳 bǐng (形)〈书〉bright; splendid; remarkable

柄 bǐng (名) 1 handle: 刀～ the handle of a knife 2 stem (of a flower, leaf of fruit)

秉 bǐng (动)〈书〉1 grasp; hold: ～烛 hold a candle 2 control; preside over: ～政 hold political power
秉承 bǐngchéng (动)〈书〉act on (sb.'s advice or instructions)
秉公 bǐnggōng (副) justly; impartially

病 bìng I (形) ill; sick: 生～ fall ill II (名) 1 disease; ailment: 心脏～ heart trouble; heart disease. 流行～ epidemic disease 2 fault; defect: 语～ faulty expression
病变(變) bìngbiàn (名) pathological changes
病虫(蟲)害 bìng-chónghài (名) plant diseases and insect pests
病床(牀) bìngchuáng (名) 1 hospital bed 2 sickbed
病毒 bìngdú (名) virus
病笃 bìngdǔ (形)〈书〉be gravely ill
病房 bìngfáng (名) ward (of a hospital); sickroom: 隔离～ isolation ward. 内科～ medical ward
病根 bìnggēn (名) 1 an old complaint 2 the root cause of a trouble
病故 bìnggù (动) die of illness
病号(號) bìnghào (名) sick person; patient: 他是个老～. He is a valetudinarian.
病假 bìngjià (名) sick leave: 请～ ask for sick leave
病菌 bìngjūn (名) pathogenic bacteria; germs
病理 bìnglǐ (名) pathology
病历(歷) bìnglì (名) medical record; case history
病例 bìnglì (名) case (of illness)
病情 bìngqíng (名) state of an illness; patient's condition
病人 bìngrén (名) patient; invalid
病入膏肓 bìng rù gāohuāng the disease is beyond cure
病态(態) bìngtài (名) morbid (or abnormal) state: ～心理 morbid psychology (or mentality)
病危 bìngwēi (形) be critically ill
病因 bìngyīn (名) cause of disease; pathogeny
病愈 bìngyù (动) recover (from an illness)
病院 bìngyuàn (名) a specialized hospital: 精神～ mental hospital. 传染～ isolation hospital

并(併、並) bìng I (动) combine; merge;

incorporate II (副) **1** simultaneously; side by side **2** (not) at all [used before a negative for emphasis]: 这件毛衣～不便宜. This sweater is not at all cheap. III (连) and: 我同意～拥护这个报告. I agree with and endorse this report.

并驾齐(齊)驱(驅) bìngjià-qíqū run neck and neck; keep pace with sb.

并肩 bìngjiān shoulder to shoulder; side by side: ～作战 fight shoulder to shoulder

并立 bìnglì (动) exist side by side; be on a par

并列 bìngliè (动) stand side by side: ～句 compound sentence

并排 bìngpái (副) side by side; abreast

并且 bìngqiě (连) and; besides; moreover; furthermore

并吞 bìngtūn (动) swallow up; annex: ～别国领土 annex part or the whole of another country's territory

并行不悖 bìngxíng bù bèi not be mutually exclusive

拨(撥)

bō **1** (动) turn, move with finger, stick etc.; stir; poke: ～船 row a boat. ～电话号码 dial a telephone number **2** set aside; assign; allocate: ～出一大笔款子供基本建设用 appropriate a large sum for capital construction II (量) group; batch: 已经去了两～人了. Two groups of people have been sent there.

拨款 bōkuǎn I (动) allocate funds II (名) appropriation: 军事～ military appropriations

拨乱(亂)反正 bō luàn fǎn zhèng bring order out of chaos; set things to rights

拨弄 bōnong (动) **1** fiddle with: ～火盆里的木炭 poke the charcoal in the brazier. ～琴弦 pluck the strings of a fiddle **2** stir up: ～是非 stir up trouble; make trouble **3** manipulate

播

bō (动) **1** sow **2** broadcast

播送 bōsòng (动) broadcast; transmit; beam: ～新闻 broadcast news

播音 bōyīn (动) transmit; broadcast: ～室 broadcasting studio ～员 announcer

播种(種) bōzhǒng (动、名) sow seeds: ～机 seeder; planter. ～面积 sown area

钵

bō (名) **1** earthen bowl **2** alms bowl (of a Buddhist monk)

波

bō (名) **1** wave; ripples: 微～ micro-wave **2** an unexpected turn of events: 风～ disturbance; scene

波长(長) bōcháng (名) wavelength

波动(動) bōdòng I (动、名) fluctuate; be unstable: 物价～ price fluctuation II (名) wave motion

波段 bōduàn (名) wave band

波及 bōjí (动) spread to; engulf; affect: 经济危机～整个西方世界. The economic crisis affected the entire Western world.

波澜 bōlán (名) great waves; billows: ～起伏 with one climax following another. ～壮阔 surging forward with great momentum

波浪 bōlàng (名) wave

波涛(濤) bōtāo (名) great waves; billows: ～汹涌 roaring waves

波纹 bōwén (名) **1** ripple **2** corrugation

波折 bōzhé (名) twists and turns; setback

菠

bō

菠菜 bōcài (名) spinach

菠萝(蘿) bōluó (名) pineapple

玻

bō

玻璃 bōli (名) glass: 雕花～ cut glass; crystal. 教堂里的彩色～ stained glass. 有机～ organic glass; plastic

剥

bō

see also bāo

剥夺(奪) bōduó (动) deprive; expropriate; strip: ～政治权利 deprive sb. of political rights. ～权力 divest sb. of his power

剥离(離) bōlí (动) (of tissue, skin, covering, etc.) come off; peel off

剥落 bōluò (动) peel off: 墙上的石灰已～了. The plaster on the walls has peeled off.

剥削 bōxuē I (动) exploit II (名) exploitation: ～阶级 exploiting class. ～者 exploiter

脖

bó (名) neck

脖子 bózi (名) neck: 骑在某人的～上 lord it over sb.

勃

bó (副) suddenly

勃勃 bóbó (形) thriving; vigorous; exuberant: 生气～ full of vigor. 兴致～ in high spirits. 野心～ full of ambition

勃发(發) bófā (动) 1 thrive; prosper 2 break out: 战争～. War broke out.

勃然 bórán (副) agitatedly; excitedly: ～变色 show signs of displeasure; show a sudden change of countenance. ～大怒 fly into a rage; flare up; raise the roof

博 bó I (形) rich; abundant; plentiful: 地大物～ vast territory and rich natural resources II (动) win; gain: 聊～一笑 just for your amusement

博爱(愛) bó'ài (名) fraternity; brotherhood; universal love

博得 bódé (动) win; gain: ～同情 enlist one's sympathy. ～赞扬 win praise. ～好评 have a favourable reception; be well received

博古通今 bógǔ-tōngjīn have an extensive knowledge of the past and present; erudite and well-informed

博览(覽) bólǎn (动) read extensively: ～群书 well-read

博览(覽)会(會) bólǎnhuì (名) (international) fair; trade fair

博取 bóqǔ (动) gain; try to court: ～欢心 curry favour. ～信任 try to win sb.'s confidence

博士 bóshì (名) 1 doctor 2 court academician (in feudal China): ～学位 doctorate

博闻强记 bówén-qiángjì have wide knowledge and a retentive memory

博物 bówù (名) natural science: ～学家 naturalist

博物馆 bówùguǎn (名) museum: 历史～ the Museum of History

博学(學) bóxué (形) learned; erudite: ～之士 learned scholar; a walking dictionary

薄 bó I (形) 1 slight; meagre; small: ～酬 small reward 2 ungenerous; unkind; mean: ～待 treat frivolously II (动) 1 despise; belittle: 鄙～ despise; scorn 2 ‹书› approach; near: 日～西山 like the setting sun over the western hills; in one's declining years
see also báo

薄利 bólì (名) small profits

薄命 bómìng (形) (usu. of women) born under an unlucky star; ill-fated

薄膜 bómó (名) 1 membrane 2 film: 塑料～ plastic film

薄暮 bómù (名) ‹书› dusk; twilight

薄情 bóqíng (形) inconstant in love; fickle

薄弱 bóruò (形) weak; frail: ～环节 a weak link. 意志～ weak willed

薄雾(霧) bówù (名) mist; haze

薄饼 bóbǐng (名) thin pancake

搏 bó I (动) 1 wrestle; fight; combat; struggle: 肉～ hand-to-hand fight (or combat) 2 pounce on II (名) beat; throb: 脉～ pulse

搏动(動) bódòng (动) beat rhythmically; throb

搏斗(鬥) bódòu (动) wrestle; fight; struggle: 与风浪～ battle with the tempestuous waves

膊 bó (名) arm: 赤～ naked to the waist

钹 bó (名) cymbals

泊 bó (动) anchor a ship; be at anchor; moor: 停～ lie at anchor. 飘～ drift along
see also pō

泊位 bówèi (名) berth: 深水～ deepwater berth

泊船 bóchuán (动) moor a boat

箔 bó (名) 1 screen (of reeds, sorghum stalks, etc.): 苇～ reed screen 2 bamboo tray for raising silkworms 3 foil; tinsel: 金～ gold foil (or leaf) 4 paper tinsel (burnt as paper currency for the dead)

帛 bó (名) ‹书› silks: 布～ silk and satin. ～画 painting on silk. ～书 (ancient) characters inscribed on silk; book copied on silk

伯 bó (名) 1 father's elder brother; uncle 2 the eldest of brothers 3 earl; count

伯父 bófù (名) father's elder brother; uncle

伯爵 bójué (名) earl; count: ～夫人 countess

伯母 bómǔ (名) aunt; wife of father's elder brother

舶 bó (名) seagoing vessel of considerable size: 船～ ship. ～来品 imported goods

驳 bó I (动) refute; contradict: 反～ retort. 辩～ repel by argument. II (形) ‹书› of different colours: 斑～ parti-coloured; variegated

驳斥 bóchì (动) refute; denounce

驳船 bóchuán (名) barge; light-

er
驳倒 bódǎo (动) demolish sb.'s argument; succeed in refuting: 这个观点是驳不倒的. This argument is irrefutable.
驳回 bóhuí (动) reject; turn down; overrule
驳运(運) bóyùn (动) transport by lighter; lighter

跛 bǒ (形) lame: ～了一只脚 lame in one leg; crippled
跛子 bǒzi (名)lame person; cripple

簸 bǒ (动) winnow with a fan; fan: ～谷 winnow away the chaff
see also bò
簸扬(揚) bǒyáng (动) winnow

簸 bò
see also bǒ
簸箕 bòji (名) 1 dustpan 2 winnowing fan 3 loop (of a fingerprint)

擘 bò (名)〈书〉 thumb: 巨～ an authority in a certain field
擘画(畫) bòhuà (动)〈书〉 plan; arrange: 机构新立，一切均待～. We have to do a lot of planning as this is a new organization.

逋 bū (动)〈书〉 flee: ～逃 flee; abscond

捕 bǔ (动) catch; seize; arrest: ～鱼 catch fish. 被～ be arrested; be under arrest
捕风(風)捉影 bǔfēng-zhuōyǐng speak or act on hearsay evidence; make groundless charges
捕获(獲) bǔhuò (动) catch; capture; seize: 当场～ be caught red-handed. ～量 catch (of fish etc.)
捕捞(撈) bǔlāo (动) fish for (aquatic animals and plants); catch
捕食 bǔshí (动) catch and feed on; prey on
捕捉 bǔzhuō (动) catch; seize: ～害虫 catch harmful insects. ～逃犯 capture an escapee

哺 bǔ I (动) feed (a baby); nurse II (名)〈书〉 the food in one's mouth
哺乳 bǔrǔ (动) breast-feed: ～动物 mammal
哺育 bǔyù (动) 1 feed: ～雏鸟 (of mother birds) feed young birds 2 nurture; foster; bring up

卜 bǔ I (名) divination; fortune-telling: ～卦 divine by the Eight Diagrams II (动) 1〈书〉 foretell; predict: 胜败可～. Victory or defeat can be predicted. 2〈书〉 select; choose: ～居 make one's home
卜辞(辭) bǔcí (名)oracle inscriptions of the Shang Dynasty (c. 16th — 11th century B.C.) on tortoise shells or animal bones

补(補) bǔ I (动) 1 mend; patch; repair: ～袜子 darn socks. ～车胎 fix a tyre 2 fill; supply; make up for: 弥～损失 retrieve a loss 3 nourish: ～品 tonics II (名)〈书〉 benefit; use; help: 不无小～. not be without some advantage; be of some help. 无～于事 won't help
补白 bǔbái (名) filler(in a newspaper or magazine)
补偿(償) bǔcháng (动) compensate; make up: ～某人所受的损失 make compensation for sb.'s loss. ～差额 make up a deficiency. ～贸易 compensation trade
补充 bǔchōng I (动) replenish; supplement; complement; add: ～人力 replenish manpower. ～库存 replenish the stock. ～两点意见 have two more points. 互相～ complement each other; be mutually complementary II (形) additional; complementary; supplementary: ～读物 supplementary reading material. ～规定 additional regulations. ～说明 additional remarks
补丁 bǔding (动) patch: 打～ put (or sew) a patch on; patch up worn-out clothes
补发(發) bǔfā (动) supply again (sth. lost, etc.); reissue; issue or distribute behind schedule: ～增加的工资 pay increased wages retroactively. 通知～. Notice will be forwarded subsequently.
补给 bǔjǐ (名) supply: ～品 supplies
补救 bǔjiù (名) remedy: ～办法 corrective measures; remedy. 无可～ be past (or beyond) remedy; irremediable; irreparable
补考 bǔkǎo (名) make-up examination
补课 bǔkè (动) give tutorials to students who have missed classes; private tutoring; touch up sth. not done properly
补品 bǔpǐn (名) tonic; restoratives
补缺 bǔquē (动) 1 fill a vacancy 2 supply a deficiency
补税 bǔshuì (动) 1 pay a tax one has evaded 2 pay an overdue tax

补贴 bǔtiē （名）subsidy; allowance: 粮食～ grain subsidy. 生活～ living allowances. 地区～ weighting (allowance)

补习(習) bǔxí （动）take lessons after school or work

补选(選) bǔxuǎn （名）by-election: ～人民代表 hold a by-election for a people's deputy

补养(養) bǔyǎng （动）take a tonic or nourishing food to build up one's health

补药(藥) bǔyào （名）tonic

补遗 bǔyí （名）addendum

补益 bǔyì （名）〈书〉benefit; help: 有所～ be of some help (or benefit)

补语 bǔyǔ （名）complement

补助 bǔzhù （名）subsidy; allowance: ～金 grant-in-aid; subsidy

补缀 bǔzhuì （动）mend (clothes); patch: 缝连～ mend and darn

补足 bǔzú （名）bring up to full strength; make up a deficiency

部 bù I （名）**1** part; section: 分为三～ divide into three parts (or sections). 南～ the southern part **2** unit; ministry; department; board: 外交～ the Ministry of Foreign Affairs. 编辑～ editorial board (or office). **3** headquarters: 团～ regimental headquarters **4** 〈书〉command: 所～ troops under one's command II （量）: 一～电影 a film. 一～好作品 a fine work of literature

部队(隊) bùduì （名）**1** army; armed forces **2** troops; force; unit

部分 bùfen （名）part; section; share: 脸的上半～ the upper part of the face. 居民中的大～人 a large section of the inhabitants. 一本分为三～的小说 a novel in three parts

部件 bùjiàn （名）parts; components; assembly

部落 bùluò （名）tribe: ～社会 tribal society

部门 bùmén （名）department; branch: 政府各～ various departments of the government. 有关～ the departments concerned

部首 bùshǒu （名）radicals by which characters are arranged in traditional Chinese dictionaries

部署 bùshǔ （动）dispose; deploy: ～兵力 deploy troops for battle. 战略～ a strategic plan; strategic deployment

部位 bùwèi （名）position; place; location

部下 bùxià （名）**1** troops under one's command **2** subordinate

部长(長) bùzhǎng （名）minister; head of a department: 外交部～ Minister of Foreign Affairs. ～会议 Council of Ministers. ～助理 assistant minister

埠 bù （名）**1** wharf; pier **2** port: 本～ this port. 外～ other ports. 商～ a commercial (or trading) port

不 bù （副）**1** [used to form a negative]: ～严重 not serious. ～正确 incorrect. ～合法 illegal. ～可能 impossible. ～小心 careless. 拿～动 too heavy to carry. 睡～好 not sleep well. **2** [used as a negative answer]: 他知道吧？—～，他不知道. He knows, doesn't he? — No, he doesn't. **3** [used at the end of a sentence to form a question]: 你明儿来～？Are you coming tomorrow? **4** [inserted in reiterative locutions, usually preceded by 什么, to indicate indifference]: 什么难学～难学，我一定学会. No matter how hard it is, I'll learn how to do it. **5** [used together with 就 to indicate a choice]: 他这会儿～是在车间就是在实验室. He's either in the workshop or in the laboratory.

不安 bù'ān （形）**1** intranquil; unstable: 动荡～ unstable and unsettling **2** uneasy; disturbed; worried: 坐立～ restless. 听了这消息我心里很～. I was rather disturbed by the news.

不白之冤 bù bái zhī yuān （名）gross injustice

不败之地 bù bài zhī dì （名）invincible position: 立于～ be in an invincible position

不备(備) bùbèi （形）unprepared; off guard: 乘其～ catch sb. off guard

不必 bùbì （副）need not; not have to: ～紧张. Take it easy. There is nothing to be nervous about.

不便 bùbiàn （形）**1** inconvenient; inappropriate; unsuitable: 交通～ poor transport facilities. 如果对你没有什么～的话，我想提早办. I'd like to make it earlier, if that's not inconvenient to you. **2** 〈口〉short of cash: 手头～ be short of cash; be hard up

不…不… bù...bù... **1**[used to make an emphatic negative form of two words identical or similar in meaning]: 不骄不躁 not conceited or rash; free from arrogance and rashness. 不慌不忙 unhurried; calm; leisurely. 不知不觉 unawares 2 [used with two words of opposite meanings to indicate an intermediate state]: 不大不小 neither too big nor too small; just right. 不冷不热 neither cold nor hot. 不死不活 neither dead nor alive; half-dead. 3 [the first 不 is the condition of the second 不]: 不见不散 We won't leave until we meet.

不测 bùcè (名) accident; mishap; contingency: 以防～ be prepared for any eventuality. 险遭～ have a narrow escape

不成 bùchéng (动) 1 won't do; not going to succeed: 盲目按照他的指令办事，那是～的. To follow his instructions blindly won't lead you anywhere. 2 (助) [used at the end of a tag question]: 难道就这样算了～? How can we let it go at that?

不成文法 bùchéngwénfǎ (名) unwritten law

不逞之徒 bùchěng zhī tú (名)desperado

不齿(齒) bùchǐ (动)<书> despise: ～于人类 held in contempt by all.

不耻下问 bù chǐ xià wèn not feel ashamed to solicit advice from one's inferiors; modest enough to consult one's subordinates

不出所料 bù chū suǒ liào as expected; within one's expectations

不辞(辭)而别 bù cí ér bié leave without saying good-bye; take French leave

不辞(辭)辛苦 bù cí xīnkǔ make nothing of hardships; stint no effort

不错 bùcuò (形) 1 correct; right: 一点儿～ perfectly correct; quite right 2[to indicate what has been said is right]: ～,他明天来这儿. Yes, he will come tomorrow. 3 <口> not bad; pretty good: 他的中文挺～. His Chinese is not bad.

不但 bùdàn (连) not only: 我～听到过,而且看见过. I not only heard about it, but actually saw it.

不打自招 bù dǎ zì zhāo (动)confess without being pressed; make a confession without duress

不大 bùdà (副) 1 not very; not too: ～自然 not very natural. ～清楚 not too clear 2 not often: 他最近～来. He has made himself scarce recently.

不当(當) bùdàng (形) unsuitable; improper; inappropriate: 处理～ not be handled properly. 措词～ wrong choice of words; inappropriately worded

不倒翁 bùdǎowēng (名) tumbler; "survivor"

不道德 bùdàodé (形) immoral

不得 bùdé (动) must not; may not; not be allowed: ～在剧场抽烟. Smoking is not allowed in the theatre.

不得 bùdé [used after a verb indicating that such an action cannot or should not be taken]: 去～ must not go. 马虎～ mustn't (or can't afford to) be careless

不得不 bùdé bù (动) have no choice (or option) but to; cannot but; have to: 时间不早了,我～走了. It's getting late. I'm afraid I have to leave now.

不得了 bùdéliǎo I (形) desperately serious; disastrous: 没有什么～的事. There's nothing seriously wrong. II [used after 得 as a complement] extremely; exceedingly: 高兴得～ be extremely happy; be wild with joy III (叹) Good heavens!

不得人心 bù dé rénxīn (形) not enjoy popular support; be unpopular

不得要领 bù dé yàolǐng fail to grasp the essence; miss the main points; unable to get the hang of sth.

不得已 bùdéyǐ (动) act against one's will; have no alternative but to; can not help but: ～而求其次 have to choose the second best; have to give up one's first choice. 实在～,他只好走着去火车站. He had no alternative but to walk to the railway station.

不等 bùděng (动) vary; differ: 长短～ vary in length. 大小～ differ (or vary) in size

不迭 bùdié [used only after a verb to indicate haste] 1 cannot afford to: 后悔～ look back with regret, but it's too late 2 incessantly: 叫苦～complain endlessly

不定 bùdìng I (副) not sure: 他一天～来多少次. He comes I don't know how many times a day. II (形) indefinite: ～冠词

indefinite article. ～式 infinitive
不动(動)产(產) bùdòngchǎn (名) real estate; immovable property; immovables
不动(動)声(聲)色 bù dòng shēngsè maintain one's composure; not betray one's feelings
不冻(凍)港 bùdònggǎng (名) ice-free port; open port
不端 bùduān (形) improper; dishonourable: 品行～ dishonourable behaviour; immoral conduct
不断(斷) bùduàn (形) unceasing; uninterrupted; continuous; constant: 在医院时，～有人来看他. While he was in hospital, people kept on coming to see him.
不对(對) bùduì I (形) incorrect; wrong: 这样做～. It's wrong to act like that. II [indicating what has been said is wrong]: ～，我可没那么说. No, I didn't say so actually.
不…而… bù...ér... [indicate a result without a direct cause or condition]: 不谋而合 agree without prior consultation
不二法门(門) bù èr fǎmén the only correct approach; the only proper course to take
不乏 bùfá 〈书〉 there is no lack of: ～先例. There is no lack of precedents. ～其人. Such people are not rare.
不法 bùfǎ (形) lawless; illegal; unlawful: ～之徒 a lawless person. ～行为 unlawful practice; an illegal act
不凡 bùfán (形) out of the ordinary; out of the common run: 自命～ consider oneself a person of no ordinary talent; have an unduly high opinion of oneself
不妨 bùfāng there is no harm in; might as well: ～一试. There is no harm in trying. 你～先同他联系一下. You might as well contact him first.
不费吹灰之力 bù fèi chuī huī zhī lì (副) with the slightest effort; effortlessly
不分青红皂白 bù fēn qīng-hóng-zào-bái (副) indiscriminately
不分胜(勝)负 bù fēn shèng-fù tie; draw; come out even
不服 bù fú (动) refuse to obey (or comply): ～输 refuse to take defeat lying down. ～主席的裁决 refuse to accept the chairman's ruling
不服水土 bù fú shuǐtǔ (of a stranger) not accustomed to the climate or the particular type of food of a new place
不符 bùfú (动) not agree (or tally, square) with; not conform to; be inconsistent with: 言行～. One's deeds do not match one's words. 与事实～ be inconsistent (or at variance) with the facts
不干不净 bùgān-bùjìng (形) unclean; filthy: 嘴里～ be foul-mouthed
不甘 bùgān (动) unreconciled to; not resigned to; unwilling: ～落后 unwilling to lag behind. ～寂寞 unwilling to remain obscure; fond of the limelight
不甘心 bù gānxīn (动)not reconciled to; not resigned to
不敢当(當) bùgǎndāng 〈谦〉 [a polite expression in reply to a compliment] I wish I could deserve your compliment; you flatter me
不共戴天 bù gòng dài tiān (形) will not live under the same sky (with one's enemy) — absolutely irreconcilable: ～的敌人 sworn enemy
不苟 bùgǒu (形) not lax; not casual; careful; conscientious: 工作一丝～ work most conscientiously
不够 bùgòu (形) not enough; insufficient; inadequate: 我们的教室～. We don't have enough classrooms. 分析～深入 The analysis lacks depth. or This is not quite an in-depth analysis.
不顾(顧) bùgù (动) in spite of; regardless of: ～后果 regardless of the consequences. ～自身安危 never think of one's own safety
不管 bùguǎn (动) no matter (what, how, etc.); regardless of: ～结果如何 whatever the results. ～怎样 in any case; anyway
不轨(軌) bùguǐ (名) acting against the law or discipline: 图谋～ contemplate conspiratorial activities
不过(過) bùguò I [used after an adjective to form the superlative degree]: 那就再好～了! It could not be better! *or* That would be superb. II (副) only; merely; no more than: 这本字典不过 10 美元钱. This dictionary costs no more than ten dollars. III (连) but; however; only: 病人精神还不错，～胃口不大好. The patient feels pretty well, but he

hasn't much of an appetite.

不含糊 bù hánhu (形)<口> 1 unambiguous; unequivocal; explicit: 以毫～的语言作出回答 answer in unequivocal terms; answer explicitly 2 not ordinary; really good: 他这活儿做得真～. He's really done a good job.

不寒而栗(慄) bù hán ér lì tremble with fear; make one's blood run cold

不好意思 bù hǎoyìsi (形) 1 feel bashful; be ill at ease 2 find it embarrassing (to do sth.): ～再提要求 hesitate to make another request

不合 bùhé (动) not conform to; unsuitable for; be out of keeping with: ～规定 in disagreement with the rules. ～标准 not up to the (required) standard; below the mark. 脾气～ be temperamentally incompatible. ～时宜 behind the times; unseasonable; out of step with modern life

不和 bùhé (动) 1 be at loggerheads; be at odds 2 discord: 制造～ sow discord

不怀(懷)好意 bù huái hǎoyì harbour evil designs; harbour malicious intentions; be up to no good

不欢(歡)而散 bùhuān ér sàn part in displeasure or anger; (of a meeting, etc.) break up in discord

不讳(諱) bùhuì <书>without concealing anything: 供认～ candidly confess; make a clean breast of something. 直言～ speak bluntly; be outspoken

不会(會) bùhuì (动) 1 be unlikely; will not (act, happen, etc.): 她～不知道. It's not likely that she doesn't know. 2 have not learned to; be unable to: 他～开车.He cannot drive a car. 3[used to show displeasure]: 你就～打个电话问一问? Couldn't you have phoned up and asked?

不羁 bùjī (形)<书> unconventional

不及 bùjí (形) 1 not as good as; inferior to: 这本书～那本书有趣. This book is not as interesting as that one. 2 find it too late: 躲避～ be too late to dodge; could not avoid getting into trouble

不即不离(離) bùjí-bùlí (形) be neither too intimate nor too distant; keep sb. at a respectful distance

不计其数(數) bù jì qí shù (形) countless; innumerable

不假思索 bù jiǎ sīsuǒ (副) without thinking; without hesitation; readily (also "不加思索")

不见得 bù jiànde (副) not necessarily; not likely: ～合逻辑 not necessarily logical. 他今晚～会来. It seems unlikely that he will come tonight.

不结盟 bùjiéméng (形) nonalignment: ～国家 nonaligned countries ～政策 policy of nonalignment

不解 bùjiě I (动) not understand: 迷惑～ be puzzled II (形) indissoluble: ～之缘 an indissoluble bond

不禁 bùjīn (动) can't help (doing sth.); can't refrain from: 他难过得～哭了起来. He felt so sad that he couldn't help crying.

不仅(僅) bùjǐn 1 not the only one: 这～是我一个人的主张. I'm not the only one who holds this view. 2 not only: ～如此 not only that; nor is this all; moreover

不景气(氣) bù jǐngqì (名) 1 depression; recession; slump 2 depressing state

不胫(脛)而走 bù jìng ér zǒu (动) get round fast; spread far and wide

不久 bùjiǔ (副) 1 soon; before long: 我们～就要毕业了. We'll soon graduate from this school. 2 not long after; soon after: 种完树～就下了一场雨. It rained soon after we had planted the trees.

不咎既往 bù jiù jìwǎng (动) not censure sb. for his past misdeeds; let bygones be bygones

不拘 bùjū (动) 1 not stick to; not confine oneself to: ～小节 not bother about trivialities; not be punctilious. 字数～ No limit is set on the length (for an article). 2 whatever: ～什么工作我都愿意接受. I'm ready to accept whatever job comes along.

不倦 bùjuàn (形) tireless; untiring; indefatigable: 诲人～ be tireless in teaching; teach with tireless zeal

不堪 bùkān (动) 1 cannot bear; cannot stand: ～设想 dreadful to contemplate. ～入耳 unpleasant to the ear; disgusting 2 utterly; extremely: 疲惫～ extremely tired; exhausted. 狼狈～ be embarrassed beyond endurance

不亢不卑 bùkàng-bùbēi (形) neither overbearing nor servile; be neither humble nor disrespectful

不可 bùkě (动) 1 cannot; should not; must not: 两者～偏废. Neither can be neglected. ～剥夺的权利 an inalienable right 2 [used together with 非 to indicate what one is set to do]: 这部电影太精彩了,我非看～. The film is extremely good; I just cannot miss it.

不可救药(藥) bùkě jiù yào (形) incorrigible; beyond cure; hopeless; past praying for

不可开(開)交 bùkě kāijiāo [used only after 得 as its complement to indicate what one cannot free oneself from]: 忙得～ be up to one's eyes in work; be awfully (or terribly) busy

不可磨灭(滅) bùkě mómiè (形) indelible: ～的印象 indelible (everlasting) impressions

不可收拾 bùkě shōushi (形) irremediable; unmanageable; out of hand

不可思议(議) bùkě sīyì (形) inconceivable; unimaginable

不可同日而语 bùkě tóngrì ér yǔ cannot be mentioned in the same breath

不可一世 bùkě yīshì (形) consider oneself second to none in the world

不可逾越 bùkě yúyuè (动) impassable; insurmountable; insuperable: ～的鸿沟 an impassable chasm. ～的障碍 an insurmountable (or insuperable) barrier

不可知论(論) bùkězhīlùn (名) agnosticism

不可终日 bùkě zhōng rì be unable to carry on even for a single day; be in a desperate situation: 惶惶～ be very worried; full of anxiety

不客气(氣) bù kèqi I (形) impolite; rude; blunt: 说句～的话 to put it bluntly II 〈套〉 (in reply to one's thanks) you're welcome; don't mention it; not at all III 〈套〉 [used to express gratitude for sb.'s offer] please don't bother; I'll help myself

不快 bùkuài (形) 1 be unhappy; be displeased; be in low spirits 2 be indisposed; feel under the weather

不愧 bùkuì (动) be worthy of; deserve to be called; prove oneself to be: 他～为英雄. He has proved himself to be a hero.

不劳(勞)而获(獲) bù láo ér huò reap without sowing; live off the labour of others

不理 bùlǐ (动) refuse to acknowledge; pay no attention to; take no notice of; ignore

不力 bùlì (动) not do one's best; ineffective: 办事～ prove incompetent in one's work. 领导～ not exercise effective leadership

不利 bùlì (形) 1 unfavourable; disadvantageous; harmful; detrimental: ～条件 unfavourable conditions 2 unsuccessful: 首战～ lose the first battle

不良 bùliáng (形) bad; harmful; unhealthy: ～倾向 unhealthy trends. ～影响 harmful (or adverse) effects. 存心～ harbour evil intentions

不了了之 bùliǎo liǎo zhī (动) let the matter take its own course; end up without any tangible results

不料 bùliào (副) unexpectedly; to one's surprise

不灵(靈) bùlíng (动) not work; be ineffective: 这架收音机～了. The radio doesn't work. 老太太耳朵有点～了. The old lady is hard of hearing.

不露声(聲)色 bù lù shēngsè not show one's feelings, intentions, etc.

不伦(倫)不类(類) bùlún-bùlèi (形) neither fish nor fowl; nondescript: ～的比喻 an incongruous metaphor; a far-fetched analogy

不论(論) bùlùn (连) no matter (what, who, how, etc.); whether ... or ...; regardless of: ～性别年龄 regardless (or irrespective) of sex and age

不落窠臼 bù luò kējiù not follow the beaten track; have an original style

不满(滿) bùmǎn (形) resentful; discontented; dissatisfied: 心怀～ nurse a grievance

不忙 bùmáng there's no hurry; take one's time: 你～就走. No need to leave in such a hurry.

不毛之地 bù máo zhī dì (名) barren land; desert

不免 bùmiǎn (形) unavoidable: 忙中～有错. We tend to make mistakes when we do things in a hurry.

不妙 bùmiào (形) (of a turn of events) not too encouraging; far from good; anything but reassuring

不明 bùmíng (形) not clear; unknown: 失踪的士兵至今下落～. We don't know yet the whereabouts of the missing soldiers.

不谋而合 bù móu ér hé (动) agree without prior consultation; happen to hold identical views: 我们的意见～. Our views happened to coincide.

不偏不倚 bùpiān-bùyǐ (形) evenhanded; impartial; unbiased

不平 bùpíng I (名) injustice; unfairness; wrong; grievance II (形) indignant; resentful: 愤愤～ very indignant; deeply resentful

不平等条(條)约 bùpíngděng tiáoyuē (名) unequal treaty

不平衡 bùpínghéng (名) disequilibrium: 工农业发展～ the disequilibrium between the development of industry and agriculture

不期而遇 bù qī ér yù (动) meet by chance; have a chance encounter

不巧 bùqiǎo (副) unfortunately

不切实(實)际(際) bùqiè shíjì (形) unrealistic; unpractical; impracticable: ～的设想 an impracticable idea; an unrealistic notion

不求甚解(解) bù qiú shèn jiě (动) seek no perfect understanding; be content with imperfect understanding

不屈 bùqū (动) never give in; never yield

不屈不挠(撓) bùqū-bùnáo (形) unyielding; indomitable

不然 bùrán 1 not so: 其实～. Actually this is not so. 2 [used at the beginning of a sentence to indicate disagreement] no: ～, 事情没有那样简单. No, it's not as simple as that. 3 (连) or else; otherwise; if not: 你得更用功一点, ～考试就会不及格. You ought to work a bit harder, or you'll fail in the exams.

不仁 bùrén (形) 1 not benevolent; heartless 2 benumbed: 麻木～ apathetic

不忍 bùrěn (动) cannot bear to: 母亲～再听他对她的孩子批评如此严厉. The mother couldn't bear to hear him speak so harshly of her child any more.

不日 bùrì 〈书〉 within the next few days; in a few days

不如 bùrú not as good as; inferior to: 我画图～他. I can't draw as well as he does.

不三不四 bùsān-bùsì (形) 1 dubious; shady: ～的人 a person of dubious (or shady) character 2 neither one thing nor the other; neither fish nor fowl: 说些～的话 make frivolous remarks

不善 bùshàn (形) 1 bad; ill: 来意～ come with evil intentions. 处理～ not handle properly; mishandle 2 not good at: ～管理 not good at managing things. ～辞令 not eloquent, not good at speeches

不胜(勝) bùshèng (动) 1 [inserted between two duplicate verbs to indicate that one is unable to do anything]: 防～防 be open to attack from any quarters 2 very; extremely: ～感激 be very grateful; appreciate it very much

不胜(勝)枚举(舉) bùshèng méi jǔ (形) too numerous to enumerate

不失时(時)机(機) bù shī shíjī let slip no opportunity; lose no time; make hay while the sun shines

不识(識)时(時)务(務) bù shí shíwù 1 show no understanding of the times 2 not be sensible 3 fail to make use of available chances

不时(時) bùshí (副) from time to time

不识(識)抬举(舉) bù shí táiju fail to appreciate sb.'s kindness

不是 bùshi (名) fault; blame: 这就是你的～了. It's your fault.

不适(適) bùshì (形) unwell; indisposed: 略感～ be feeling a bit out of sorts

不速之客 bù sù zhī kè (名) uninvited (or unexpected) guest

不通 bùtōng (形) 1 be obstructed; be blocked up; be impassable: 水池堵塞～了. The sink is blocked. 此路～. Not a Through Road. 电话～. The line's dead. 行～ won't work; won't do 2 not make sense; be illogical; be ungrammatical: 文章写得～. The article is full of grammar and other errors.

不同 bùtóng (形) different from; as distinct from

不同凡响(響) bùtóng fánxiǎng (形) outstanding; out of the ordinary

不痛不痒(癢) bùtòng-bùyǎng (形) not in-depth; superficial; perfunctory: ～的批评 superficial criti-

cism
不妥 bùtuǒ (形) improper; inappropriate: 措词～ inappropriate wording. 处理～ an improper way of handling the matter
不外 bùwài not beyond the scope of; nothing other than: 周末,他们～是看部电影、逛逛公园. At weekends they do nothing but go to the pictures or take a stroll in the park.
不闻不问 bùwén-bùwèn be indifferent to sth.
不问 bù wèn (动) 1 pay no attention to; disregard; ignore: ～宗教信仰 irrespective of religious belief 2 let go unpunished; let off
不务(務)正业(業) bù wù zhèngyè 1 not engage in honest work 2 ignore one's proper occupation; not attend to one's proper duties
不惜 bùxī (动) 1 stint no effort; not spare: ～工本 spare neither effort nor money 2 not scruple (to do sth.)
不相干 bù xiānggān (形) be irrelevant; have nothing to do with: ～的话 irrelevant remarks. 这事跟你们～. It has nothing to do with you.
不相上下 bù xiāng shàng-xià (形) equally matched; roughly the same: 水平～ be nearly identical in quality (level)
不详 bùxiáng (形)〈书〉 1 not in detail 2 not quite clear: 他的家庭背景情况～. Little is known about his family background.
不祥 bùxiáng (形) ominous; inauspicious: ～之兆 an ill omen
不象话 bù xiànghuà (形) 1 unreasonable: 要你们自己掏钱喝酒就～了. It would be unreasonable to have drinks on you 2 shocking; outrageous: 这种行为真～. Such behaviour is downright shocking.
不象样 bù xiàngyàng (形) 1 unpresentable: 这件大衣太～. This overcoat is hardly presentable. 2 beyond recognition: 破得～ worn to shreds
不肖 bùxiào (形)〈书〉 unworthy: ～子孙 unworthy descendants
不屑 bùxiè (动) disdain to do sth.; not consider sth. worth doing: ～一顾 scorn to take a look
不懈 bùxiè (形) untiring; unremitting; indefatigable: 坚持～ persevere unremittingly
不兴(興) bùxīng (形) 1 out of fashion; outmoded 2 impermissible; not allowed: ～这样做. That's not allowed.
不行 bùxíng 1 won't do; be out of the question 2 be no good; won't work: 这个计划～. This plan just won't work.
不省人事 bù xǐng rénshì (形) fall into a state of unconsciousness; be in a coma
不幸 bùxìng I (名) misfortune; adversity: 遭～ meet with a misfortune II (形) unfortunate; sad: ～的遭遇 unfortunate experience III(副) unfortunately: 他的话～而言中. His remarks have unfortunately proved correct.
不休 bùxiū [used as adverbial modifier] endlessly; ceaselessly: 争论～ argue endlessly; keep on arguing
不修边(邊)幅 bù xiū biānfú (形) untidy; be untidy in dress
不朽 bùxiǔ (形) immortal: ～的著作 an immortal masterpiece. 人民英雄永垂～! Eternal glory to the people's heroes!
不学(學)无(無)术(術) bùxué-wúshù (形) have neither learning nor skill; be ignorant and incompetent; lack neither knowledge nor ability
不言而喻 bù yán ér yù it goes without saying; it is self-evident
不要 bùyào don't: ～那样傲慢. Don't be so arrogant.
不要脸(臉) bù yàoliǎn (形) have no sense of shame; shameless: 真～! What a nerve!
不一 bùyī (动) vary; differ: 色彩～ vary in colour. 大小～ differ in size
不宜 bùyí (形) unsuitable; inadvisable: ～操之过急. It's no use trying to get everything done overnight.
不遗余(餘)力 bù yí yúlì spare no effort; do one's utmost
不已 bùyǐ (副) endlessly; incessantly: 赞叹～ praise repeatedly
不以为(爲)然 bù yǐ wéi rán (动) show disapproval of sth.
不义(義)之财 bùyì zhī cái (名) ill-gotten gains
不翼而飞(飛) bù yì ér fēi (动) disappear mysteriously; melt into thin air; vanish
不用 bùyòng (动) need not: ～惊慌. You needn't panic. *or* There is no need to panic.
不由得 bùyóude cannot help;

cannot but

不由自主 bù yóu zìzhǔ can't help; unrestrainedly: ～地流下眼泪 couldn't refrain from tears

不约而同 bù yuē ér tóng (动) agree with one another without prior consultation

不在 bù zài not be in; be out: 他～，我能帮你做什么呢？He is not in at the moment. What can I do for you?

不在乎 bùzàihu not mind; not care: 满～ couldn't care less

不在意 bù zàiyì 1 pay no attention to; take no notice of; not mind 2 negligent; careless

不择(擇)手段 bù zé shǒuduàn by fair means or foul; by hook or by crook; unscrupulously

不怎么(麼) bù zěnme not very; not particularly: 他～能干. He is not particularly capable.

不折不扣 bùzhé-bùkòu 1 to the letter: ～地贯彻政策 carry out the policy to the letter 2 out-and-out

不知不觉(覺) bùzhī-bùjué unconsciously; unwittingly; without being aware of it

不知死活 bù zhī sǐ-huó act recklessly

不知所措 bù zhī suǒ cuò be at a loss; be at one's wits' end

不知所云 bù zhī suǒ yún not know what sb. is talking about or what one has said

不值 bùzhí (形) not worth: ～一文 not worth a penny; worthless. ～一提 not worth mentioning

不只 bùzhǐ not only; not merely

不治之症 bùzhì zhī zhèng (名) incurable disease

不置可否 bù zhì kě-fǒu (动) decline to comment; neither confirm nor deny; be noncommittal; hedge: 他对此问题采取～的态度. He refused to say yes or no on this matter.

不中用 bù zhōngyòng (形) unfit for anything; no good; useless: 这把刀～，去换一把吧. This knife is no good. Go and fetch another one.

不中意 bù zhòngyì not to one's liking

不准 bùzhǔn (动) not allow; forbid; prohibit: 此处～吸烟 Smoking is not allowed here. *or* No Smoking!

不着边际(際) bù zhuó biānjì (形) not to the point; wide of the mark; entirely irrelevant

不足 bùzú (形) 1 not enough; insufficient; inadequate: 给养～ be short of supplies. 资金～ lack funds. 人手～ be understaffed 2 not worth: ～道 not be worth mentioning; of no consequence. ～为奇 not at all surprising; nothing out of the common; nothing to speak of 3 cannot; should not: ～为训 not to be taken as an established rule; not to be regarded as an example to be followed

布 bù I (名) cloth: ～鞋 cloth shoes. 花～ cotton prints II (动) 1 declare; announce; publish; proclaim: 公～于众 make known to the public; be made public 2 spread; disseminate: 控制疾病传～ check the spread of disease. 小水电站遍～全国 Small hydropower station can be found all over the country. 3 dispose; arrange; deploy: 在楼前～上岗哨 deploy sentinels in front of the building

布帛 bùbó (名) cloth and silk; cotton and silk fabrics

布道 bùdào (动) preach

布防 bùfáng (动) send soldiers to guard a place

布告 bùgào (名) notice; bulletin; proclamation: 张贴～ put up a notice. ～栏 notice board; bulletin board

布谷鸟 bùgǔniǎo (名) cuckoo

布景 bùjǐng (名) 1 composition (of a painting) 2 setting; scenery

布局 bùjú (名) 1 overall arrangement; layout; distribution: 新市区的～ layout of a new urban district 2 composition (of a picture, piece of writing, etc.)

布雷 bùléi (动) lay mines; mine: 在港口～ mine a harbour

布施 bùshī (名) <书> alms; charities

布匹 bùpǐ (名) cloth; piece goods

布置 bùzhì (动) 1 fix up; arrange; decorate: ～房间 arrange a room 2 assign; make arrangements for; give instructions about: ～工作 assign work; give instructions about an assignment

怖 bù (动) fear; be afraid of: 恐～ terror; horror. 可～ horrible; frightful

簿 bù (名) book: 练习～ exercise book. 帐～ account book. 登记～ register

簿记 bùjì (名) bookkeeping
簿子 bùzi (名) notebook; book
步 bù I (名) 1 step; pace: 邮局离这儿只有几~路. The post office is only a few steps away. 快~走 walk at a quick pace 2 stage; step: 撤军工作分两~进行. The troops will be pulled out in two stages. 3 condition; situation; state: 事情怎么发展到这一~? How did things get into such a mess? II (动) walk; go on foot: 散~ take a walk
步兵 bùbīng (名) 1 infantry; foot 2 infantryman; foot soldier
步调 bùdiào (名) pace; step: ~一致 keep in step. 统一~ synchronize their (our, your) steps
步伐 bùfá (名) step; pace: 加快~ quicken one's pace. 跟上时代的~ keep abreast of the times
步履维艰(艱) bùlǚ wéi jiān 〈书〉 have difficulty moving about; plod along
步枪(槍) bùqiāng (名) rifle
步人后(後)尘(塵) bù rén hòuchén follow in other people's footsteps
步行 bùxíng (动) go on foot; walk
步骤 bùzhòu (名) step; move; measure: 这是改善我们工作的具体~. This is a practical move to improve our work. 采取适当的~ take proper steps

Cc

擦 cā (动) 1 put (or spread) on: 在脸上~油 put (or smooth) some cream on the face. ~药 apply medical lotion to a wound 2 rub: ~火柴 strike a match. 手上~破一点皮 just a scratch on the hand. 3 clean; wipe: ~桌子 wipe the table. ~地板 mop (or scrub) the floor. ~皮鞋 polish shoes 4 pass lightly over or touch lightly against: ~肩而过 brush past sb. 燕子~水飞过 swallows skimming the water 5 scrape into shreds
嚓 cā 〈象〉 汽车~的一声停住了. The car screeched to a stop.
猜 cāi (动) guess; speculate: 你~谁来了? Guess who's here.
猜测 cāicè (名) guess; conjecture: 那不过是~. That's only guesswork.
猜忌 cāijì (动) be suspicious and resentful
猜谜儿 cāimeir (动) guess a riddle
猜拳 cāiquán (名) a finger-guessing game
猜想 cāixiǎng (动) suppose; guess
猜疑 cāiyí (动) suspect
裁 cái 1 cut (paper, cloth, etc.): ~纸 cut paper. ~衣服 cut out a new garment 2 cut down; reduce 3 judge; decide 4 check; sanction: 经济制~ economic sanction
裁定 cáidìng (名) ruling
裁缝 cáifeng (名) tailor; dressmaker
裁减 cáijiǎn (动、名) cut down; reduce: ~人员 cut down the staff of an organization. ~军费 reduction of military expenditure
裁剪 cáijiǎn (动) cut out: ~衣服 cut out garments
裁决 cáijué (名) ruling; verdict: 依法~ adjudicate according to law
裁军 cáijūn (名) disarmament
裁判 cáipàn (名) 1 judgment 2 referee
才 cái (名) 1 ability; talent; gift: 文~ literary talent. 人~ a person of talent. 2 people of a certain type: 蠢~ fool. 奴~ flunkey
才(纔) cái (副) 1 [used before a verb to indicate that sth. has just happened or is rather late by general standards]: 我~喂了孩子. I've just fed the baby. 他四十岁~结婚. He got married (as late as) when he was forty. 你怎么~来? Why are you so late? 2 [used in the main clause of a complex sentence to indicate that the condition stated in the subordinate clause is a prerequisite]: 等客人都走了, 她~坐下来休息. She sat down for a rest only after all the guests had left. 只有用功, ~能通过考试 One must work hard if he wishes to pass the exam. 3 [used before a phrase to indicate that the number is small] only: 她~五岁. She is only five year's

old. 怎么～三本书? How come that there are only three books? 4 [used for emphasis]: 你不知道～怪呢? It would be strange if you didn't know! 我～不去呢! I am (certainly) not going!

才干(幹) cáigàn (名) ability; competence

才华(華) cáihuá (名) (literary or artistic) talent: 一位很有～的演员 a gifted actor.

才能 cáinéng (名) ability; talent

才气(氣) cáiqì literary talent: ～横溢 highly gifted

才疏学(學)浅(淺) cáishū-xuéqiǎn 〈谦〉 have little talent and less learning; be an indifferent scholar

才学(學) cáixué (名) talent and learning; scholarship

才智 cáizhì (名) ability and intelligence

才子 cáizǐ gifted scholar: ～佳人 gifted scholars and beautiful ladies (in Chinese romances)

材 cái (名) material: 木～ timber. 教～ teaching material

材料 cáiliào (名) material; date: 建筑～ building material! 原～ raw material.

财 cái (名) wealth.

财宝(寶) cáibǎo money and valuables

财产(產) cáichǎn (名) property: 公共～ public property

财团(團) cáituán (名) financial group: 国际～ consortium

财务(務) cáiwù (名) financial affairs

财物 cáiwù (名) property; belongings: 个人～ personal effects

财政 cáizhèng (名) (publ'c) finance: ～收支平衡 balance of revenue and expenditure. ～赤字 financial deficits. ～年度 financial (or fiscal) year

财主 cáizhu (名) rich man; moneybags

采(採) cǎi (动) 1 pick; pluck; gather: ～花 pick flowers. ～药 cull medicinal herbs 2 mine; extract: ～煤 mine coal

采伐 cǎifá (动) (of trees) fell

采访 cǎifǎng (动) (of a reporter) gather material; cover: ～新闻 cover news. ～一位名作家 interview a famous writer.

采购(購) cǎigòu (动) purchase: ～员 purchasing agent

采集 cǎijí (动) gather; collect: ～标本 collect specimens

采矿(礦) cǎikuàng (名) mining: 露天～ opencut (or opencast) mining

采煤 cǎiméi (名) coal mining

采纳 cǎinà (动) accept; adopt

采取 cǎiqǔ (动) adopt; take: ～紧急措施 take emergency measures. ～强制手段 resort to high-handed measures (or compulsion)

采撷 cǎixié (动) 〈书〉 1 pick; pluck 2 gather

采用 cǎiyòng (动) employ; adopt; use: ～新技术 adopt new techniques

采油 cǎiyóu (名) oil extraction

采摘 cǎizhāi (名) pluck; pick

睬 cǎi (动) pay attention to; take notice of: 别～他. Take no notice of him.

踩 cǎi (动) step on; tread; trample

彩 cǎi 1 colour: 五～缤纷 colourful 2 coloured silk: 张灯结～ decorate with lanterns and coloured ribbons 3 applause; cheer: 喝～ acclaim; cheer 4 variety; splendour: 丰富多～ rich and varied 5 prize: 中～ win a prize (in a lottery, etc.)

彩虹 cǎihóng (名) rainbow

彩礼(禮) cǎilǐ (名) betrothal gifts (from the man's to his fiancée's family)

彩排 cǎipái (名) dress rehearsal

彩票 cǎipiào (名) lottery ticket

彩色 cǎisè multicolour; colour: ～电视 colour television. ～胶片 colour film

菜 cài (名) 1 vegetable: 蔬～ vegetable. 咸～ pickles 2 dish; course: 荤～ meat dish. 素～ vegetable dish. 一道～ a course

菜单(單) càidān (名) menu

菜刀 càidāo (名) kitchen knife

菜花 càihuā (名) cauliflower

菜市场(場) càishìchǎng (名) food market

菜肴 càiyáo (名) cooked food (usu. meat dishes)

菜油 càiyóu (名) rape oil

菜园(園) càiyuán (名) vegetable garden; vegetable farm

菜籽 càizǐ (名) 1 vegetable seeds 2 rapeseed

餐 cān I (名) food; meal: 中～ Chinese food. 西～ Western food. 一顿美～ a delicious meal. 午～ lunch. 野～ picnic. II (动) eat: 聚～ have

a Dutch treat
餐车(車) cānchē (名) dining car
餐巾 cānjīn (名) napkin
餐具 cānjù (名) tableware; cutlery
参(參) cān (动) 1 join; take part in: ～军 join the army; enlist. ～战 enter war 2 refer; consult: ～阅 consult; read for reference
see also cēn; shēn
参观(觀) cānguān (动) visit (place, exhibition, etc.): ～游览 visit places of interest; go sightseeing
参加 cānjiā (动) join; attend; take part in: ～示威游行 join the demonstration. ～会议 attend a meeting. ～会谈 take part in talks
参见(見) cānjiàn (动) 1 see also; cf.: ～第九章 See also Chapter 9. 2 pay one's respects to (a superior, etc.)
参看 cānkàn (动) 1 see also; cf: ～下面注释 see note below 2 consult; read sth. for reference
参考 cānkǎo I (动) consult; refer to II (名) reference: 仅供～ for reference only. ～书 reference book
参谋 cānmóu (名) 1 staff officer 2 adviser: ～长 chief of staff
参议(議)员 cānyìyuán (名) senator
参与(與) cānyù (动) participate in: ～各项活动 take part in various activities
参赞 cānzàn (名) counsellor: 商务～ commercial counsellor. 文化～ cultural counseller
参照 cānzhào (动) consult; refer to
参酌 cānzhuó (动) consider (a matter) in the light of actual conditions
惭 cán (名) shame: 大言不～ brag brazenly
惭愧 cánkuì (形) feel ashamed or abashed.
蚕(蠶) cán (名) silkworm
蚕茧(繭) cánjiǎn (名) silkworm cocoon
蚕食 cánshí (动) nibble (at another country's territory)
蚕丝(絲) cánsī (名) natural silk; silk
残(殘) cán (形) 1 incomplete; deficient: ～品 substandard goods 2 remnant; remaining: ～兵败将 remnants of a routed army. ～冬 the last days of winter 3 maimed; crippled 4 savage; 凶～ cruel
残暴 cánbào (形) brutal; cruel and ferocious
残存 cáncún (形) remnant; remaining; surviving
残废(廢) cánfèi I (形) crippled; maimed II (名) a maimed person; cripple
残羹剩饭 cángēng-shèngfàn (名) remains of a meal; leftovers
残骸 cánhái (名) remains; wreckage: 敌机～ the wreckage of an enemy plane
残害 cánhài (动) cruelly injure or kill:
残疾 cánji (名) deformity: 身体有～的人 a person with a misshapen body or limb; a handicapped person
残局 cánjú (名) 1 the final phase of a chess game 2 the situation resulting from the failure of an undertaking: 收拾～ clear up the mess
残酷 cánkù (形) cruel; brutal; ruthless
残缺 cánquē (形) incomplete; fragmentary: 这套茶具～不全. This tea set is incomplete.
残忍 cánrěn (形) cruel; ruthless
残杀(殺) cánshā (动) slaughter; massacre; 自相～ mutual slaughter
残余(餘) cányú (名) remnants; survivals; 封建～ survivals of feudalism
残渣余(餘)孽 cánzhā-yúniè (名) dregs of society; old diehards
惨(慘) cǎn I (形) 1 miserable; pitiful; tragic: ～不忍睹 too horrible to look at. ～遭不幸 die a tragic death 2 cruel; savage. ～无人道 brutal; inhuman II (副) to a serious degree; disastrously: 输得很～ suffer a devastating defeat in a match
惨案 cǎn'àn tragic incident; massacre
惨白 cǎnbái (形) pale: 脸色～ look ghostly pale
惨败 cǎnbài (名) crushing defeat
惨淡 cǎndàn (形) gloomy; dismal; bleak. 月光～ dim moonlight. ～经营 take great pains in one's difficult enterprise
惨痛 cǎntòng (形) grievous; bitter; painful: ～的教训 a bitter lesson
惨重 cǎnzhòng (形) heavy; di-

sastrous: 损失～ suffer heavy losses. 伤亡～ suffer heavy casualties
惨状(狀) cǎnzhuàng (名) miserable condition; pitiful sight

灿(燦) càn
灿烂(爛) cànlàn (形) bright; magnificent; splendid: ～的阳光 brilliant sunshine ～的未来 bright future

璨 càn (名) gem; precious stone

仓(倉) cāng (名) storehouse; warehouse: 粮～ granary
仓促 cāngcù (副) hurriedly; hastily: 时间～ time is pressing. 走得～ leave in a hurry
仓皇 cānghuáng (副) in panic; in a hurry: ～失措 be panic-stricken. ～逃窜 flee in panic
仓库 cāngkù (名) warehouse; storehouse: 清理～ take stock

沧(滄) cāng (形)(of the sea) dark blue
沧海 cānghǎi (名) the blue sea; the sea
沧海一粟 cānghǎi yī sù a drop in the ocean
沧桑 cāngsāng (名) 饱经～ have experienced many vicissitudes of life

苍(蒼) cāng (形) 1 dark green or blue: ～松 green pines. ～天 the blue sky 2 grey; ashy: ～白 pale
苍翠 cāngcuì (形) dark green; verdant: ～的山峦 green mountains
苍劲(勁) cāngjìng (形) 1 old and strong 2 (of calligraphy or painting) vigorous; bold
苍老 cānglǎo (形) (of look) old; aged
苍凉 cāngliáng (形) desolate; bleak
苍茫 cāngmáng (形) 1 vast; boundless: ～大地 vast land 2 indistinct; hazy: 暮色～ gathering dusk
苍蝇(蠅) cāngyíng (名) fly: ～拍子 flyswatter

舱(艙) cāng (名) cabin: 客～ (passenger) cabin. 货～ hold

藏 cáng (动) 1 hide; store 2 store; lay by
藏匿 cángnì (动) conceal; hide
藏身 cángshēn (动) hide oneself; lie low: ～之处 shelter
藏书(書) cángshū (名) a collection of books
藏拙 cángzhuō (名) hide one's inadequacy by keeping quiet

糙 cāo (形) rough; coarse: ～米 brown rice; unpolished rice. 粗～ rough; slipshod

操 cāo 1 (动) hold; grasp 2 drill; exercise 3 act; do; operate: ～之过急 act with undue haste; be overhasty 4 speak (a language or dialect): ～本地口音 speak with a local accent
操场(場) cāochǎng (名) playground; sports ground
操持 cāochí (动) manage: ～家务 manage household affairs
操劳(勞) cāoláo (动) work hard: ～过度 overwork oneself.
操练(練) cāoliàn (名) drill; practice
操心 cāoxīn (动) 1 concern; worry about
操行 cāoxíng (名) (of a student) moral conduct
操纵(縱) cāozòng (动) 1 operate; control: 培养～机器的工人 train workers to operate new machines. 无线电～ radio control 2 manipulate: 幕后～ manipulate from behind the scenes; pull strings. ～市场 rig the market
操作 cāozuò (动) operate (a machine)

槽 cáo (名) 1 trough; manger. 2 groove; slot

嘈 cáo (名) noise; din
嘈杂(雜) cáozá (形) noisy: 人声～ a hubbub of voices

草 cǎo I (名) grass; straw II (形) careless; rough; hasty III (动) draft: 起～文件 draft a document
草案 cǎo'àn (名) draft (of a plan, law, etc.): 决议～ a draft
草包 cǎobāo (名) 1 straw bag 2 blockhead; good-for-nothing
草草 cǎocǎo (副) hastily; carelessly: ～了事 hurry through the work. ～收场 wind up the affair in great haste
草地 cǎodì (名) grassland; meadow; lawn
草稿 cǎogǎo (名) manuscript; draft
草菅人命 cǎojiān rénmìng treat human life as if it were not worth a straw; treat human life like dirt
草料 cǎoliào (名) forage; fodder
草莽 cǎomǎng (名) uncultivated

land; wilderness: ~英雄 greenwood hero

草帽 cǎomào (名) straw hat

草木皆兵 cǎo mù jiē bīng be panic-stricken; feel exceedingly nervous

草坪 cǎopíng (名) lawn

草书(書) cǎoshū (名) rapid, cursive style of writing; grass writing

草率 cǎoshuài (形) careless; rash: ~从事 take hasty action; act rashly or carelessly

草图(圖) cǎotú (名) sketch; draft

草席 cǎoxí (名) straw mat

草鞋 cǎoxié (名) straw sandals

草药(藥) cǎoyào (名) medicinal herbs; herbal medicine

草原 cǎoyuán (名) steppe; grasslands; prairie

测

cè (动) 1 survey; measure 2 predict: 变化莫~ unpredictable; constantly changing

测定 cèdìng (动) survey and determine

测绘(繪) cèhuì (动) survey and draw

测量 cèliáng (动) survey; measure

测验(驗) cèyàn (动、名) test

恻

cè (形) sorrowful: 凄~ sad; grieved: ~隐 compassion; pity

厕

cè (名) lavatory; toilet; W.C.: 公~ public lavatory. 男~ men's (room, toilet). 女~ women's (room, toilet)

厕所 cèsuǒ (名) lavatory; toilet; W.C.

侧

cè I (名) side; flank: 两~ on both sides II (动) lean; incline

侧面 cèmiàn (名) side; profile: ~像 profile

侧记 cèjì (名) sidelights

侧重 cèzhòng (动) lay emphasis on; stress

策

cè (名) plan; scheme; strategy: 献~ present a strategy

策动(動) cèdòng (动) instigate; stir up; engineer: 阴谋~政变 plot a coup d'état

策划(劃) cèhuà (动) plan; plot: ~阴谋 hatch a plot. 幕后~ scheme behind the scenes

策略 cèlüè I (名) tactics: II (形) tactful

策源地 cèyuándì (名) source; place of origin: 战争~ a source of war

册

cè I (名) volume; 这套书共四~. This book is in four volumes. II ‹量› copy: 一千~ 1,000 copies (of a book)

参(參)

cēn

see also cān; shēn

参差 cēncī (形) uneven; not uniform.

曾

céng (副) once; formerly; sometime ago: 他~教过我英文. He once taught me English. 我未~去过意大利. I haven't been to Italy.

see also zēng

曾几(幾)何时(時) céng jǐ hé shí ‹书› before long; not long after

曾经(經) céngjīng (副) once; formerly: 他们~是好友, 现在不是了. They were good friends but are no longer so now.

曾经(經)沧(滄)海 céng jīng cānghǎi have much experience of life; have seen the world

层(層)

céng (名) 1 layer; stratum: 一~油漆 a coat of paint 2 storey; floor: 五~大楼 a five-storey building. 二楼 the first floor (Am: second floor)

层层 céngcéng (副) layer upon layer: ~把关 check at each level

层出不穷(窮) céng chū bù qióng (动) emerge in an endless stream; come thick and fast

层次 céngcì (名) 1 arrangement of ideas, colours etc.: 这篇文章~分明. The essay is well-organized 2 administrative levels.

层峦(巒)迭(叠)嶂 céngluán-diézhàng peaks rising one upon another

蹭

cèng (动) 1 rub; scrape: 他摔倒时把膝盖~破了. He scraped his knee when he slipped and fell. 2 be smeared with: 小心~油漆 Mind the fresh paint; wet paint 3 dillydally; loiter: 磨~ dawdle; dillydally

差

chā (名) 1 difference; discrepancy; dissimilarity: 时~ time difference 2 mistake: 偏~ deviation

see also chà; chāi

差别 chābié (名) difference; disparity: 年龄~ disparity in age

差错 chācuò (名) 1 mistake; error; slip: 他的工作很少出~. He has hardly made any mistake in his work. 2 mishap; accident: 万一这孩子出了~怎么办? What if anything should happen to the child?

差额 chā'é (名) balance; difference; margin: 补足～ make up the balance (or difference)

差距 chājù (名) gap; disparity; difference: 他说的跟做的有很大的～. There is a big gap between what he says and what he does.

差强人意 chā qiáng rényì (形) not too disappointing; passable

差异(異) chāyì (名) difference; divergence; discrepancy: 这两个地区气候～很大. These two regions differ greatly in climate.

喳 chā

see also zhā

喳喳 chāchā (名、动) whispering sound; whisper: 她在他耳边～两句. She whispered a few words in his ear.

插 chā (动) 1 stick in; insert; thrust: ～花瓶 put flowers in a vase. 2 interpolate; insert: ～入几句话 put in a few additional words

插翅难(難)飞(飛) chā chì nán fēi can hardly escape even if one grew a pair of wings; be unable to escape even if given wings

插话 chāhuà (动) chip in

插曲 chāqǔ (名) 1 interlude 2 songs in a film or play 3 episode

插入 chārù (动) 1 insert 2 plug in

插手 chāshǒu (动) 1 take part: 这事他们自己能对付，用不着我～. I don't have to join in since they can manage it by themselves. 2 have a hand in; poke one's nose into; meddle in

插图(圖) chātú (名) illustration; plate

插销 chāxiāo (名) 1 bolt (for a door, window, etc.) 2 plug

插秧 chāyāng (动) transplant rice seedlings

插嘴 chāzuǐ (动) interrupt; chip in: 插不上嘴 cannot get a word in edgeways

插座 chāzuò (名) socket

叉 chā I (名) 1 fork: 干草～ hayfork; pitchfork 2 cross: 在每个错字上打个～ put a cross on each wrongly spelt word II (动) work with a fork; fork: ～鱼 spear fish

see also chǎ

杈 chā (名) wooden fork; hayfork; pitchfork

see also chà

茬 chá (名) stubble: 麦～ wheat stubble 2 crop; batch: 二～韭菜 the second crop of Chinese chives

茶 chá (名) 1 tea: 沏～ make tea. 浓(淡)～ strong (weak) tea. 红(绿)～ black (green) tea. 2 certain kinds of drink or liquid food: 杏仁～ almond paste

茶杯 chábēi (名) teacup

茶房 cháfáng (名) waiter; steward

茶馆(館) cháguǎn (名) teahouse

茶壶(壺) cháhú (名) teapot

茶话会(會) cháhuàhuì (名) tea party

茶几 chájī (名) tea table; teapoy

茶具 chájù (名) tea set

茶叶(葉) cháyè (名) tea; tea-leaves

茶余(餘)饭后(後) cháyú-fànhòu over a cup of tea or after a meal: 作为～谈笑的题材 as a topic for after-dinner chit-chat

搽 chá (动) put on or rub into the skin; apply: ～雪花膏 put on vanishing cream. ～药 apply ointment, lotion, etc.

查 chá (动) 1 check; examine; inspect: ～谣言 chase down a rumour. ～血 have a blood test 2 look into; investigate; find out 3 look up; consult: ～字典 look up a word in the dictionary. ～档案 look into the archives

查办(辦) chábàn (动) investigate and deal with accordingly: 撤职～ dismiss a person from office and prosecute him

查抄 cháchāo (动) make an inventory of a criminal's possessions and confiscate them

查点(點) chádiǎn (动) check the number or amount of; make an inventory of

查对(對) cháduì (动) check; verify: ～材料 check the data. ～原文 check the version against the original

查访 cháfǎng (动) go around and make inquiries; investigate

查封 cháfēng (动) seal up; close down

查获(獲) cháhuò (动) hunt down and seize; ferret out; track down

查禁 chájìn (动) ban; prohib[it]

查究 chájiū (动) investigate an[d] ascertain (cause, responsibility etc.): ～责任 find out wh[o] should be held responsible fo[r] what has happened

查看 chákàn (动) look over; inspect; examine: ～帐目 examine the accounts

查明 chámíng (动) prove through investigation; find out; ascertain: 事实真相已经～. The truth of the matter has been established through investigation.

查票 chápiào (动) check tickets

查询 cháxún (动) inquire about: ～地址 inquire sb.'s address

查阅 cháyuè (动) consult; look up: ～技术资料 consult technical data; look up technical literature

查帐(帳) cházhàng (动) check(or audit, examine) accounts

楂 chá (名) short, bristly hair or beard; stubble

碴 chá (动) be cut (by broken glass, china, etc.)

碴儿 chár (名) 1 broken pieces; fragments: 冰～ small pieces of ice. 玻璃～ fragments of glass 2 the cause of a quarrel; quarrel: 找～打架 pick a quarrel (with sb.)

察 chá (动) examine; look into; scrutinize; observe: ～其言,观其行 examine his words and watch his deeds, check what he says against what he does

察觉(覺) chájué (动) become aware of; discover; perceive

察看 chákàn (动) inspect; look carefully at; observe: ～地形 survey the terrain

察言观(觀)色 cháyán-guānsè try to read sb.'s thoughts from his words and facial expression; weigh up sb.'s words and watch the expression on his face

叉 chǎ (动) part in the shape of a fork: ～腿站着 stand with one's legs apart
see also chā

诧 chà (动) be surprised

诧异(異) chàyì (动) be surprised; be astonished

姹 chà (形) <书> beautiful

姹紫嫣红 chàzǐ-yānhóng deep purples and bright reds; a riot of brilliant purple and tender crimson

差 chà I (动) differ from; fall short of: ～得远 a far cry. II (形) 1 <口> wrong: 这你可说～了. You're wrong there. 2 wanting; short of: ～五分两点 five (minutes) to two. ～两个人 two people short. 我还～你多少钱? How much more do I owe you? 3 not up to standard; poor: 质量不算太～. The quality is not too bad.
see also chā; chāi

差不多 chàbùduō I (副) almost; nearly: 他走了～两年了. It's nearly two years since he left. II (形) 1 about the same; similar: 她俩～大. They are about the same age. 2 just about right (or enough); not far off; not bad 3 almost used up: 鸡蛋吃得～了. There aren't many eggs left.

差点(點)儿 chàdiǎnr I (形) not good enough; not quite up to the mark II (副) almost; nearly; on the verge of: 她～摔倒. She very nearly fell.

差劲(勁) chàjìn (形) no good; disappointing: 这活干得太～. This work was too poorly done.

刹 chà (名) Buddhist temple
see also shā

刹那 chànà (名) instant: 一～ in an instant; in a flash; in the twinkling of an eye

岔 chà (动) 1 branch off; fork: 三～路口 a fork in the road; a junction of three roads 2 turn off

岔开(開) chàkāi (动) 1 branch off: 公路在这儿～了. The highway branches here. 2 diverge to (another topic); change (the subject of conversation) 3 stagger: 把我们的休假日～ stagger our days off

岔子 chàzi (名) accident; trouble: 机器出了什么～? What's wrong with the machine?

杈 chà (名) branch (of a tree)
see also chā

衩 chà (名) vent (or slit) in the sides of a garment

差 chāi I (动) send on an errand; dispatch: ～人去送封信 send a letter by messenger. 出～ be away on business trip II (名) errand; job: 兼～ hold more than one job concurrently; moonlight
see also chā; chà

差遣 chāiqiǎn (动) send sb. on an errand or mission; dispatch; assign: 你可～别人去干. You can assign somebody else to do the job.

差使 chāishǐ （名） official post; billet; commission

差事 chāishi （名） errand; assignment

差役 chāiyì （名） 1 corvée 2 runner or bailiff in a feudal *yamen*

拆 chāi （动） 1 take apart; tear open: ～信 open a letter. ～机器 disassemble a machine; take a machine apart 2 pull down; demolish: ～房子 pull down an old house

拆除 chāichú （动） demolish; dismantle; remove: ～军事基地 dismantle military bases

拆穿 chāichuān （动） expose; reveal; unmask: ～骗局 expose a fraud

拆毁 chāihuǐ （动） demolish; destroy

拆伙 chāihuǒ （动） dissolve a partnership; part company

拆开(開) chāikāi （动） take apart; open; separate

拆散 chāisǎn （动） break (a set)

拆散 chāisàn （动） break up (a marriage, family, etc.)

拆台(臺) chāitái （动） let sb. down; cut the ground from under sb.'s feet; pull away a prop

拆线(綫) chāi xiàn （动） take out stitches

拆卸 chāixiè （动） dismantle; disassemble; dismount

钗 chāi （名） hairpin (formerly worn by women for adornment)

柴 chái （名） firewood

柴草 cháicǎo （名） firewood; faggot

柴米油盐(鹽) chái-mǐ-yóu-yán （名） fuel, rice, oil and salt — basic daily necessities

柴油 cháiyóu （名） diesel oil: ～机车 diesel locomotive. ～机 diesel engine

豺 chái （名） jackal

豺狼 cháiláng （名） jackals and wolves — cruel and evil people

搀(攙) chān （动） 1 support or help sb. ～着病人进屋 help the patient by the arm into the room. 2 mix; blend: 往沙子里～石灰 mix lime into sand

搀扶 chānfú （动） support sb. with one's hand

搀和 chānhuo （动） mix

搀假 chānjiǎ （动） adulterate

搀杂(雜) chānzá （动） mix; mingle

缠(纏) chán （动） 1 twine; wind: ～线球 wind yarn into a ball 2 tangle; tie up; pester: ～住不放 stick to one like a burr. 我女儿～住我给她讲故事. My daughter has been pestering me to tell her a story.

缠绵 chánmián （形） 1 lingering (of illness or feelings) 2 touching; moving

缠绕(繞) chánrǎo （动） 1 twine; bind; wind 2 worry; harass

禅(禪) chán （名） 1 deep meditation; dhyana: 坐～ sit in meditation 2 Buddhist: ～堂 meditation room. see also shàn

婵(嬋) chán

婵娟 chánjuān （形）〈书〉 1 lovely [used in ancient writings to describe women] 2 the moon

蝉(蟬) chán （名） cicada

蝉联(聯) chánlián continue to hold a post or title

蟾 chán

蟾蜍 chánchú （名）〈书〉 1 toad 2 the moon

谗(讒) chán （动） slander; backbite

谗言 chányán （名） slanderous report; calumny; false charge

馋(饞) chán （形） greedy; gluttonous: 嘴～ fond of good food; greedy

馋涎欲滴 chánxián yù dī start drooling

馋嘴 chánzuǐ （形） gluttonous

孱 chán （形） frail; weak

孱弱 chánruò （形） frail; delicate (in health)

潺 chán

潺潺 chánchán （动） murmur; babble; purl: ～流水 a murmuring stream

产(產) chǎn I （动） 1 give birth to: ～卵 lay eggs 2 produce; yield: ～棉区 cotton-producing area II （名） 1 product; produce: 土特～ local speciality 2 property; estate 房地～ real estate. 家～ family possessions

产地 chǎndì （名） place of production

产妇(婦) chǎnfù （名） lying-in woman

产科 chǎnkē (名) 1 obstetrical (or maternity) department 2 obstetrics: ～医生 obstetrician
产量 chǎnliàng (名) output; yield: 煤～ output of coal
产卵 chǎnluǎn (动) (of birds) lay eggs; (of fish) spawn
产品 chǎnpǐn (名) product; produce: 农～ farm produce. 畜～ livestock product
产权(權) chǎnquán (名) property right
产生 chǎnshēng (动) 1 produce; engender; bring about; give rise to: ～好的结果 yield good results. ～坏的影响 exert a bad influence 2 emerge; come into being: 问题～了. Problems have emerged.
产物 chǎnwù (名) outcome; result
产销 chǎn-xiāo (名) production and marketing
产业(業) chǎnyè (名) 1 estate; property 2 industrial: ～革命 the Industrial Revolution
产值 chǎnzhí (名) output value

铲(鏟) chǎn I (名) shovel: 锅～ slice II (动) shovel: ～煤 shovel coal. 把地～平 scrape the ground even; level the ground with a shovel or spade
铲除 chǎnchú (动) root out; eradicate
铲子 chǎnzi (名) shovel

阐(闡) chǎn (动) explain; interpret
阐明 chǎnmíng (动) expound; clarify: ～观点 clarify one's views
阐释(釋) chǎnshì (动) explain; expound; interpret
阐述 chǎnshù (动) expound; elaborate; set forth: 各方～了自己对这一问题的立场. Each side set forth its position on this question.

谄 chǎn (动) flatter; fawn on; toady
谄媚 chǎnmèi flatter; fawn on; toady
谄谀 chǎnyú (动) flatter

颤 chàn quiver; tremble; vibrate: 他激动得说话声音都发～了. His voice quivered with emotion.
颤动(動) chàndòng (动) vibrate; quiver: 树叶在微风中～. The leaves quivered in the breeze.
颤抖 chàndǒu (动) shake; tremble; quiver; shiver: 冻得全身～ shiver all over with cold
颤音 chànyīn (名) trill; shake

忏(懺) chàn (动) repent
忏悔 chànhuǐ (动) 1 repent; 2 confess (one's sins)

昌 chāng (形) prosperous; flourishing
昌盛 chāngshèng (形) prosperous: 把中国建设成为一个繁荣～的社会主义国家 Build China into a prosperous socialist country.

猖 chāng
猖獗 chāngjué (形) rampant; unbridled; run wild
猖狂 chāngkuáng (形) outrageous; furious: ～反扑 counterattack with unbridled fury

娼 chāng (名) prostitute
娼妇(婦) chāngfù (名) bitch; whore
娼妓 chāngjì (名) prostitute; streetwalker

尝(嘗) cháng I (动) taste; experience: 艰苦备～ endure all hardships II (副) ever: 未～晤面 have never met before
尝试 chángshì (动、名) attempt; try

偿(償) cháng (动) repay; compensate: 补～损失 compensate for the loss
偿还(還) chánghuán (动) pay back: ～债务 pay one's debts
偿命 chángmìng (动) pay with one's life (for a murder)
偿清 chángqīng (动) clear off: ～债务 clear off all one's debts

裳 cháng (名) skirt (worn in ancient China)

常 cháng I (形) 1 ordinary; common; normal: 人情之～ normal in human relationships. 反～ unusual; abnormal. 习以为～ be used (or accustomed) to sth. 2 invariable: 四季～青 evergreen II (副) frequently; often: 这里你～来吗? Do you often come here?
常常 chángcháng (副) frequently; often; usually; generally: ～得到老师表扬 be often praised by the teacher
常规 chángguī (名) convention; routine; common practice: ～武器 conventional weapons
常会(會) chánghuì (名) regular meeting (or session)
常年 chángnián (副) 1 all the year round; for a very long period of time 2 year in year

out

常情 chángqíng (名) common sense; normal practice: 按照～,他会准时回来的. Under normal circumstances he would be back in time.

常任 chángrèn (形) permanent; standing: 安理会～理事国 permanent member of the Security Council

常设 chángshè (形) standing; permanent: ～机构 standing body; permanent organization

常识(識) chángshí (名) 1 general knowledge 2 common sense

常态(態) chángtài (名) normality; normal state of affairs: 恢复～ come back to normal

常务(務) chángwù (形) day-to-day business; routine: ～委员会 standing committee

常言 chángyán (名) saying; aphorism

常驻 chángzhù resident; permanent: ～记者 resident correspondent. ～联合国代表 permanent representative to the United Nations

嫦 cháng

嫦娥 cháng'é (名) the goddess of the moon

长(長) cháng I (形) long: ～袍 long gown; robe. ～跑 long-distance running. ～篇大论 make a lengthy speech; write a lengthy article. ～寿 longevity II (名) 1 length: 全～ the overall length 2 of long duration; lasting 3 strong point; forte: 取～补短 overcome one's shortcomings by learning from others' strong points

长城 chángchéng (名) the Great Wall

长处(處) chángchù (名) good qualities; strong points

长度 chángdù (名) length

长短 chángduǎn (名) 1 length: 这两条裙子～差不多. The two skirts are about the same length. 这件上衣～对他不合适. The jacket doesn't fit him. 2 merits and demerits; strong and weak points: 议论别人～ gossip about sb. 3 accident; mishap

长工 chánggōng (名) hired farmhand

长江 chángjiāng (名) the Changjiang (Yangtze) River

长久 chángjiǔ (形) lasting; permanent: ～之计 long-term planning; lasting solution

长空 chángkōng (名) vast sky

长眠 chángmián (名) demise; death

长年 chángnián (副) all the year round

长期 chángqī (形) over a long period of time; long-term: ～共存,互相监督 long-term co-existence and mutual supervision

长衫 chángshān (名) gown; long gown

长寿(壽) chángshòu (名) long life; longevity: 祝您健康～. I wish you good health and a long life.

长叹(嘆) chángtàn (动) heave a deep sigh

长途 chángtú (名) long-distance: ～旅行 make a long journey. ～电话 long-distance (or trunk) call. ～汽车 long-distance bus; coach

长远(遠) chángyuǎn (形) long-term; long-range: ～利益 long-term interests. ～规划 long-term (or long-range) plan

长征 chángzhēng (名) 1 expedition; long march 2 the Long March

长足 chángzú (形) rapid; speedy: ～的进步 rapid progress

场(場) cháng (名) 1 level open ground (usually used for threshing grains) 2 fair; market place 3 (量) [said of something which has happened]: 一～大雨 a heavy fall of rain

see also chǎng

肠(腸) cháng (名) intestines

肠断(斷) chángduàn (形) broken-hearted

场(場) chǎng (名) 1 site, spot; 会～ conference hall. 战～ battlefield. 篮球～ basketball court 2 farm: 农～ farm. 养鸡～ chicken farm 3 stage: 登～ come on the stage; appear on the scene 4 (of drama) scene: 第二幕第一～ Act II, Scene 1 5 (量) [of sports and recreation]: 一～电影 a film show. 一～球赛 a ball game 6 field: 电(磁)～ electric (magnetic) field

see also cháng

场地 chǎngdì (名) place; site

场合 chǎnghé (名) occasion: 在某种～ on certain occasions

场面 chǎngmiàn (名) 1 scene (in drama, fiction, etc.) event;

occasion **2** appearance; front; facade

场所 chǎngsuǒ (名) place (for certain activities): 公共～ a public place

厂(廠) chǎng (名) factory; mill; plant; works: 汽车～ car factory. 机床～ machine tool plant. 钢铁～ iron and steel works. 造船～ shipyard. 炼油～ oil refinery

厂房 chǎngfáng (名) **1** factory building **2** workshop

厂矿(礦) chǎng-kuàng (名) factories and mines

厂商 chǎngshāng (名) firm: 承包～ contractor

厂长(長) chǎngzhǎng (名) director of a factory

敞 chǎng (形) **1** open; uncovered: ～着门 leave the door open **2** spacious: 宽～ spacious; roomy

敞开(開) chǎngkāi (动) open wide: 大门～着. The gate was wide open. ～供应 unlimited supply. ～思想 speak one's mind.

氅 chǎng (名) cloak: 大～ overcoat

唱 chàng (动) **1** sing: ～歌 sing a song **2** call; cry: 鸡～三遍. The cock has crowed for the third time.

唱高调 chàng gāodiào use high-sounding words

唱段 chàngduàn (名) aria: 京剧～ an aria from a Beijing opera

唱机(機) chàngjī (名) gramophone; record player

唱片 chàngpiàn (名) record; disc: 放～ play a gramophone record. 灌～ cut a disc

唱腔 chàngqiāng (名) music for voices in a Chinese opera

唱戏(戲) chàngxì (动)〈口〉 act in an opera

倡 chàng (动) initiate; advocate

倡导(導) chàngdǎo (动) initiate; propose

倡议(議) chàngyì (动) recommend; propose: ～书 written proposal; proposal

怅(悵) chàng (形) disappointed; sorry: 走访不遇为～. Sorry not to have found you at home.

怅然 chàngrán (形) disappinted; upset: ～而返 come away disappointed

怅惘 chàngwǎng (形) depressed; dispirited

畅(暢) chàng (形) **1** smooth; unimpeded: ～通无阻 proceed without hindrance. 流～ fluent **2** free; uninhibited: ～饮 drink one's fill. ～谈 talk animatedly

畅快 chàngkuài (形)happy; carefree

畅所欲言 chàng suǒ yù yán speak one's mind freely

畅通 chàngtōng (形) unblocked; unimpeded

畅销 chàngxiāo sell well; sell like hot cakes: 中国丝绸～国外. Chinese silk fabrics sell well on foreign markets. ～书 best seller

畅叙 chàngxù (动) chat cheerfully: ～旧日友情 relive an old friendship

畅游 chàngyóu (动) enjoy a good swim or a sightseeing trip

抄 chāo (动) **1** copy; transcribe: ～稿件 make a fair copy of the manuscript. **2** plagiarize **3** search and confiscate **4** go by a more direct way: ～近路 take a shortcut **5** fold (one's arms): ～着手站在一边 stand by with folded arms

抄本 chāoběn (名) hand-copied book; transcript

抄获(獲) chāohuò (动) search and seize; ferret out

抄件 chāojiàn (名) duplicate; copy; carbon copy or copies [usually in abbreviated form c. c.]

抄袭(襲) chāoxí (动) **1** plagiarize **2** follow other people's example regardless objective condition **3** attack the enemy by making a detour

抄写(寫) chāoxiě (动) make a clear copy

钞 chāo (名) bank note; paper money: 现～ cash

钞票 chāopiào(名) bank note

超 chāo I (动) exceed; surpass; overtake II [used as prefix]: ultra-; super-; extra-: ～自然的 supernatural

超产(產) chāochǎn (动) overfulfil a production target

超车(車) chāochē (动) overtake other vehicles (in violation of traffic regulations)

超出 chāochū (动) overstep; go beyond; exceed: ～范围 go beyond the scope (or bounds)

超短波 chāoduǎnbō (名) ultrashort wave

超短裙 chāoduǎnqún (名) mini-

skirt
超额 chāo'é (动) overfulfil the quota
超过(過) chāoguò (动) outstrip; surpass; exceed
超级 chāojí (形) super: ～大国 superpower. ～市场 supermarket
超假 chāojià (动) overstay one's leave
超龄(齡) chāolíng (名) overage
超群 chāoqún (形) outstanding; superb
超然 chāorán (形) aloof; neutral
超声(聲)波 chāoshēngbō (名) supersonic (wave)
超脱 chāotuō I (形) unbiased; unconventional II (动) stand aloof: ～现实 dissociate oneself from one's social environment
超音速 chāoyīnsù (名) supersonic speed
超越 chāoyuè (动) surmount; transcend; surpass: ～职权范围 overstep one's authority
超载 chāozài (名) overload
超支 chāozhī (动) overspend
超重 chāozhòng (名) overweight: ～行李 excess luggage
朝 cháo I (名) 1 dynasty: 唐～ the Tang Dynasty. 改～换代 dynastic changes 2 court: ～臣 court official II facing; towards: 这门～外开. This door opens outwards. 这房子～南. This house has a southern exposure.
see also zhāo
朝拜 cháobài (动) pay respects to (a sovereign); pay religious homage to; worship
朝代 cháodài (名) dynasty
朝贡 cháogòng (动) pay tribute (to an imperial court)
朝圣(聖) cháoshèng (名) pilgrimage; hadj
朝廷 cháotíng (名) royal (or imperial) court
潮 cháo I (名) 1 tide: 涨(落)～了. The tide is in (on the ebb). 2 upsurge: 学～ student's movement II damp; moist: 受～ get damp
潮流 cháoliú (名) 1 tide 2 trend: 历史～ historical trend
潮湿(濕) cháoshī (名) moist; damp
潮水 cháoshuǐ (名) tidewater
潮汐 cháoxī (名) morning and evening tides; tide
嘲 cháo (动) ridicule; mock: 冷～热讽 sarcastic remarks
嘲讽(諷) cháofěng (动) sneer at; taunt
嘲弄 cháonòng (动) mock; poke fun at
嘲笑 cháoxiào (动) laugh at; ridicule
巢 cháo (名) nest: 鸟～ bird's nest. 匪～ nest (or den) of robbers; bandits' lair
巢穴 cháoxué (名) lair; den; nest; hideout
炒 chǎo (动) stir-fry; fry: 蛋～饭 fried rice with eggs. ～鸡蛋 scrambled eggs
吵 chǎo (动) 1 make a noise 2 disturb 3 quarrel; wrangle; squabble: 为一些小事～嘴 bickering over small matters
吵架 chǎojià (动) quarrel; have a row
吵闹(鬧) chǎonào I(动) wrangle; kick up a row II (名) make a lot of noise
吵嘴 chǎozuǐ (动) quarrel; bicker
车(車) chē I (名) 1 vehicle: ～水马龙 heavy traffic 2 wheeled machine or instrument: 纺～ spinning wheel. 水～ waterwheel 3 machine II (动) 1 lathe; turn 2 lift water by waterwheel
see also jū
车床(牀) chēchuáng (名) lathe
车次 chēcì (名) train number
车费 chēfèi (名) fare
车工 chēgōng (名) turner; lathe operator
车轱辘 chēgulū (名) <口> wheel (of a vehicle)
车祸(禍) chēhuò (名) traffic (or road) accident
车间 chējiān (名) workshop; shop
车库 chēkù (名) garage
车辆(輛) chēliàng (名) vehicle; car
车轮(輪) chēlún (名) wheel (of a vehicle)
车票 chēpiào (名) train or bus ticket; ticket
车速 chēsù (名) speed of a motor vehicle
车胎 chētāi (名) tyre
车厢 chēxiāng (名) railway carriage; railroad car
车站 chēzhàn (名) station; stop
扯 chě (动) 1 pull: ～后腿 hold sb. back (from action); be a drag on sb. 2 tear: 把信～得粉碎 tear a letter to pieces 3 chat; gossip: ～家常 chat about everyday domestic details. 别～远了. Don't wander from the subject.
扯淡 chědàn (动) talk nonsense

扯谎 chěhuǎng (动) tell a lie; lie
扯皮 chěpí (动) dispute over trifles; wrangle
澈 chè (形) (of water) clear; limpid: 清～ crystal clear
撤 chè (动) remove; take away: 把盘子、碗～了. clear away the dishes 2 withdraw: ～退 retreat. ～回 withdraw
撤兵 chèbīng (动) withdraw or pull back troops
撤除 chèchú (动) dismantle: ～军事设施 dismantle military installations
撤换 chèhuàn (动) dismiss and replace
撤回 chèhuí (动) 1 recall; withdraw: ～大使 recall an ambassador. ～声明 retract a statement
撤离(離) chèlí (动) withdraw from; evacuate; leave
撤退 chètuì (动) withdraw; pull out; retreat
撤销 chèxiāo (动) cancel; revoke: ～其职务 dismiss a person from his post. ～处分 rescind a penalty
撤职(職) chèzhí (动) dismiss or discharge sb. from his post; remove sb. from office
彻(徹) chè (形) thorough; penetrating: 透～的了解 perfect understanding
彻底 chèdǐ (形) thorough; thoroughgoing
彻骨 chègǔ (副) to the bone: 寒风～. The bitter wind chills one to the bone.
彻头(頭)彻尾 chètóu-chèwěi (形) out and out: 那是～的谎言. That's a lie, pure and simple.
彻夜 chèyè (副) all through the night: ～不眠 lie awake all night
掣 chè (动) 1 pull; tug 2 draw
嗔 chēn (动) be angry; be displeased; be annoyed
嗔怪 chēnguài (动) blame; disapprove of
嗔怒 chēnnù (动) get angry; be angered
瞋 chēn (动) <书> stare angrily; glare: ～目而视 stare at sb. angrily
沉 chén I (动) 1 sink: 星～月落. The stars have become indistinct and the moon is down. 2 be calm; concentrate 3 lower: 把脸一～ pull a long face II (形) 1 deep; profound: 睡得很～be sound asleep. ～醉 dead drunk; be intoxicated 2 heavy: 这张桌子真～! How heavy this desk is!
沉沉 chénchén (形) deep: 暮气～ lifeless; apathetic
沉甸甸 chéndiāndiān (形) heavy
沉淀(澱) chéndiàn (动、名) sediment; precipitate: 溶液里有～. There is some sediment in the solution.
沉积(積) chénjī (动) deposit; precipitate
沉寂 chénjì (形) 1 quiet; still: 四面一片～. All is still. 2 (of news) entirely blocked: 消息～. There is absolutely no news.
沉浸 chénjìn (动) immerse; steep: ～在幸福的回忆中 be immersed in happy memories
沉静 chénjìng (形) 1 quiet; calm: ～下来 grow quiet and still 2 (of one's character, mood or appearance) calm; peaceful; placid
沉闷 chénmèn (形) 1 (of weather, atmosphere, etc.) oppressive 2 depressed; in low spirits: 心情～ feel depressed 3 (of one's character) dull
沉湎 chénmiǎn (动) <书> wallow in; abandon oneself to
沉没 chénmò (动) sink
沉默 chénmò 1 reticent; uncommunicative: ～寡言的人 a person of few words 2 silent: 保持～ keep silent
沉溺 chénnì (动) indulge in: ～于享乐 indulge in pleasure
沉睡 chénshuì (动) be fast asleep
沉思 chénsī (动) be lost in thought; ponder; contemplate
沉痛 chéntòng I (名) profound grief; deep remorse: ～的哀悼 profound condolences. ～的教训 bitter lesson II (形) bitter
沉吟 chényín (动) hesitate and mutter to oneself; be unable to make up one's mind and think aloud
沉冤 chényuān (名) gross injustice; unrighted wrong: ～莫白 suffered grievous wrongs
沉重 chénzhòng (形) heavy: ～的打击 a heavy blow. 心情～ with a heavy heart
沉住气(氣) chénzhùqì (动) keep calm; keep one's head; be steady
沉着 chénzhuó (形) cool-headed; composed; calm; steady: 勇敢～ brave and steady
沉醉 chénzuì (动) become in-

toxicated

忱 chén (名) 〈书〉 sincere feeling: 热～ zeal; warmheartedness

辰 chén (名) 1 celestial bodies: 星～ stars 2 time; day; occasion: 诞～ birthday

辰时(時) chénshí (名) the period of the day from 7 a.m. to 9 a.m.

晨 chén (名) morning: 清～ dawn; early morning. ～光熹微 first faint rays of the morning sun

晨星 chénxīng (名) stars at dawn: 寥若～ as few as stars in the morning sky

橙 chén (～子) (名) orange

臣 chén (名) official under a feudal ruler; subject; minister

臣服 chénfú (动) submit oneself to the rule of; acknowledge allegiance to

臣民 chénmín (名) subjects (of a feudal ruler)

尘(塵) chén (名) 1 dust; dirt: 一～不染 spotless 2 this human world

尘埃 chén'āi (名) dust: 放射性～ radioactive dust

尘土 chéntǔ (名) dust

尘嚣 chénxiāo (名) hubbub; uproar

陈(陳) chén I (动) 1 put on display 2 state; explain II (形) old; stale: ～酒 aged wine. ～醋 mature vinegar

陈兵 chénbīng (动) mass (station) troops: ～百万 deploy a million troops

陈词滥(濫)调 chéncí-làndiào (名) hackneyed phrase; platitude; cliché: 满口～ mouth the bromide

陈腐 chénfǔ (形) stale; antiquated: ～观念 outworn concept

陈规 chénguī (名) outmoded conventions: 打破～ abolish outmoded conventions

陈货 chénhuò (名) old stock; shopworn goods

陈迹 chénjì (名) a thing of the past; relic

陈旧(舊) chénjiù (形) out-of-date; outmoded; obsolete; old-fashioned

陈列 chénliè (动) display; exhibit: ～馆 exhibition hall. ～品 exhibit

陈设 chénshè (名) furnishings: 房间里的～朴素大方. The room was furnished simply and in good taste.

陈述 chénshù (动) state: ～自己的意见 state one's views; make one's suggestions

衬(襯) chèn I (动) 1 line; place sth. underneath: ～上一层纸 put a piece of paper underneath 2 serve as a contrast: 绿叶～红花 red flowers set off by the green leaves II (名) lining; liner: 丝～里 silk-lining

衬裤 chènkù (名) underpants

衬衫 chènshān (名) shirt

衬托 chèntuō (动) set off; serve as a foil to

衬衣 chènyī (名) underclothes; shirt

趁 chèn I (动) take advantage of; avail oneself of: ～这个机会讲几句话 take this opportunity to say a few words. ～火打劫 loot a burning house; fish in troubled waters II (副) while: ～热打铁 strike while the iron's hot

趁机(機) chènjī (动) take advantage of the occasion; seize the chance

趁早 chènzǎo (副) as early as possible; before it is too late

称(稱) chèn (动) fit; match; suit: 领带跟上衣很相～. The tie matches the jacket.
see also chēng

称心 chènxīn (动) to one's liking; just as one wishes: 这事办得大家都～如意. This matter was settled to the satisfaction of all parties.

称职(職) chènzhí (形) be competent; fill a post with credit

撑 chēng (动) 1 support; prop up: ～起帐篷 put up a tent 2 maintain; keep up: 累了就休息一下,别硬～着. Take a rest when you are tired. Don't stick it out. 3 punt with a pole: ～船 pole a boat 4 open: ～伞 unfold an umbrella 5 overfill: 我吃得太～了. I'm too full.

撑腰 chēngyāo (动) support; back up

瞠 chēng (动) 〈书〉 stare: ～目结舌 wild-eyed and tongue-tied; dumbfounded

称(稱) chēng I (动) 1 call name: 我们都～他王大叔. We all call him uncle Wang. 2 weigh; scale 3 acclaim; praise II (名) name: 四川有天府之国之～. Sichuan is known as the heavenly land of plenty. 俗～ popular name.

see also chèn

称霸 chēngbà (动) seek hegemony; dominate

称道 chēngdào (动) speak approvingly of

称得起 chēngdeqǐ (动) be worthy of the name of: 万里长城真～为天下奇观. The Great Wall really deserves to be called a world wonder.

称号(號) chēnghào (名) title; designation

称呼 chēnghū I (动) call; address: 我该怎么～她? How should I address her? II (名) form of address

称快 chēngkuài (动) express one's gratification: 拍手～ clap one's hands to show one's desire is gratified.

称王称霸 chēngwáng-chēngbà (动) lord it over; ride roughshod over; domineer

称羡 chēngxiàn (动) express one's admiration; envy

称雄 chēngxióng (动) rule over a region like a sovereign

称赞(讚) chēngzàn (动) praise; acclaim; commend

成 chéng I (动) 1 become; turn into: 积水～河. Water accumulated turns into a river. 2 accomplish; succeed: 事情没有搞～. The task remains unfulfilled. II (名) achievement; result: 坐享其～ sit idle and enjoy the fruits of others' labour III (形) 1 fully developed; fully grown: ～人 adult 2 established; ready-made: ～衣 readymade clothes. 既～事实 established fact; fait accompli 3 in considerable numbers or amounts: ～千上万的人 tens of thousands of people. ～倍 (increase) by several times. ～群 in groups; in large numbers. ～批 in batches; one group after another 4 all right; O.K.: ～! 就这么办吧. O.K. Go ahead. 你不去可不～. No, you must go. 5 one tenth: 增产两～ a 20% increase in output. 这件衣服有九～新. This jacket is 90 percent new.

成败 chéng-bài (名) success or failure: ～在此一举. Success or failure hinges on this final move.

成本 chéngběn (名) cost: 生产～ production cost. ～核算 cost accounting

成材 chéngcái (动) 1 grow into useful timber 2 become a useful person

成分 chéngfèn (名) 1 composition; component part; ingredient: 化学～ chemical composition 2 one's class status or family background

成风(風) chéngfēng (动) become a common practice; prevail: 蔚然～ become the order of the day

成功 chénggōng (名、动) succeed; success

成规 chéngguī (名) established practice; set rules; conventions: 墨守～ stick to conventions

成果 chéngguǒ (名) positive result; accomplishment

成绩 chéngjī (名) achievement; success: 学习～ school record

成家 chéngjiā (动) 1 (of a man) get married: ～立业 get married and start one's career 2 become expert

成见(見) chéngjiàn (名) preconceived idea; prejudice

成交 chéngjiāo (动) strike a bargain; conclude a transaction; clinch a deal

成就 chéngjiù (名) achievement; accomplishment; attainment; success

成立 chénglì (动、名) 1 set up; found; establish: 中华人民共和国～ the founding of the People's Republic of China 2 be tenable; hold water: 这个论点不能～. That argument is untenable.

成名 chéngmíng (动) become famous: ～成家 establish one's reputation as an authority

成年 chéngnián I (动) grow up; come of age II (副) year after year

成品 chéngpǐn (名) end (or finished) product

成器 chéngqì (动) grow up to be a useful person

成全 chéngquán (动) help sb. to achieve his aim

成色 chéngsè (名) 1 the percentage of gold or silver in a coin, etc. 2 quality

成熟 chéngshú (形) ripe; mature: 庄稼～了. The crops are ripe. 他思想还不～. He is still immature.

成亲(親) chéngqīn (动) get married
成套 chéngtào (名) whole (or complete) set: ～设备 complete sets of equipment
成为(爲) chéngwéi (动) become; turn into: ～海军基地 become a naval base
成问题 chéng wèntí be a problem; be open to doubt
成效 chéngxiào (名) effect; result: 显著的～ marked success
成性 chéngxìng (副) by nature
成药(藥) chéngyào (名) patent medicine
成衣 chéngyī (名) ready-made clothes
成语 chéngyǔ (名) idiom; proverb; set phrase
成员 chéngyuán (名) member: ～国 member state
成灾(災) chéngzāi (动) cause disaster: 暴雨～. The heavy rainstorm caused serious damage.
成长(長) chéngzhǎng (动) grow up

诚 chéng I (形) sincere; honest II (副) <书> really; indeed
诚恳(懇) chéngkěn (形) sincere: ～听取意见 listen to criticisms with an open mind
诚实(實) chéngshí (形) honest
诚心诚意 chéngxīn chéngyì (名) sincerity; good faith
诚挚(摯) chéngzhì (形) sincere; cordial: ～友好的气氛 a sincere and friendly atmosphere

城 chéng (名) 1 city 2 city wall; wall: 长～ the Great Wall 3 town: ～乡差别 the difference between town and country
城堡 chéngbǎo (名) castle
城池 chéngchí (名) city wall and moat; city
城防 chéngfáng (名) the defence of a city: ～部队 city garrison
城关(關) chéngguān (名) the area just outside a city gate
城郊 chéngjiāo (名) outskirts of a town
城楼(樓) chénglóu (名) a tower over a city gate; gate tower
城门(門) chéngmén (名) city gate
城墙(牆) chéngqiáng (名) city wall
城区(區) chéngqū (名) the city proper: ～和郊区 the city proper and the suburbs
城市 chéngshì (名) town; city
城镇 chéngzhèn (名) cities and towns

盛 chéng (动) 1 ladle; dish out: ～饭 fill a bowl with rice 2 hold; contain: 罐子太小,～不下这么多奶. The jar is too small to hold this much milk.
盛器 chéngqì (名) vessel; receptacle

呈 chéng I (动) 1 appear; assume (form, colour etc.): 叶～椭圆形. The leaf is oval in shape. 2 submit; present
呈报(報) chéngbào (动) submit a report
呈递(遞) chéngdì (动) present; submit: ～国书 present credentials
呈文 chéngwén (名) document submitted to a superior; memorial; petition
呈现 chéngxiàn (动) present (a certain appearance); appear; emerge: 我国各条战线～着一片大好形势. A good situation prevails on all fronts in our country.

程 chéng (名) 1 rule; regulation: 章～ rules; constitution 2 order; procedure: 议～ agenda 3 journey; 启～ set out on a journey 4 distance: 路～ distance of travel. 射～ range
程度 chéngdù (名) level; degree; extent: 技术～ technical level. 在一定～上 to a greater or lesser extent. 在不同～上 in varying degrees
程序 chéngxù (名) 1 order; procedure; course; 法律～ legal procedure. 符合～ be in order 2 programme

乘 chéng (动) 1 ride: ～公共汽车 go by bus. ～火车(飞机、船)旅行 travel by train (plane, boat) 2 take advantage of 3 multiply: 五～三等于十五. Five times three is fifteen. *or* 5 multiplied by 3 is 15.
乘法 chéngfǎ (名) multiplication
乘机(機) chéngjī (动) seize the opportunity: ～反攻 seize the opportunity to counterattack
乘客 chéngkè (名) passenger
乘凉 chéngliáng (动) enjoy the cool
乘人之危 chéng rén zhī wēi take advantage of the precarious position of others
乘胜(勝) chéngshèng (动) exploit a victory: ～前进 advance on the crest of a victory
乘务(務)员 chéngwùyuán (名) attendant on a train

乘兴(興) chéngxìng (名) spurred on by momentary enthusiasm

乘虚 chéngxū (动) take advantage of a weak point; act when sb. is off guard

惩(懲) chéng (动) punish; penalize

惩办(辦) chéngbàn (动) punish: ～罪犯 punish criminals

惩罚(罰) chéngfá (动) punish; penalize

惩前毖后(後) chéngqián-bìhòu learn from past mistakes to avoid future ones

澄 chéng (形) clear; transparent

澄清 chéngqīng I (形) clear; transparent II (动) clear up; clarify: ～事实 clarify certain facts

橙 chéng (名) 1 orange 2 orange colour: ～黄 orange (colour)

承 chéng (动) 1 bear; hold; carry 2 undertake; contract (to do a job): ～做各式家具 undertake to make all kinds of furniture 3 〈套〉 be indebted: ～您过奖. You flatter me. ～贵国政府热情接待. We feel indebted to your government for the kind hospitality accorded us.

承办(辦) chéngbàn (动) undertake

承包 chéngbāo (动) contract: ～商 contractor

承担(擔) chéngdān (动) assume; undertake: ～义务 fulfil an obligation. ～一切费用 bear the cost

承蒙 chéngméng 〈套〉 be indebted to; be granted a favour

承诺 chéngnuò (动) promise to undertake

承认(認) chéngrèn (动) 1 admit; acknowlege; recognize: ～错误 acknowledge one's mistake. 2 give diplomatic recognition; recognize

承受 chéngshòu (动) 1 bear; sustain; withstand; endure: ～极大的痛苦 endure great pain. ～种种考验 undergo every kind of test

承袭(襲) chéngxí (动) 1 adopt; follow (a tradition, etc.) 2 inherit (a peerage, etc.)

丞 chéng (名) assistant officer (in ancient China)

丞相 chéngxiàng (名) prime minister (in ancient China)

逞 chěng (动) 1 show off; flaunt: ～英雄 play the hero. ～威风 flaunt one's power 2 carry out; succeed in an evil design: 得～ succeed in one's schemes 3 indulge, give free rein to: ～性子 be wilful

骋 chěng (动) 〈书〉 gallop: 驰～文坛 play a major part in the literary world

骋怀(懷) chěnghuái 〈书〉 give free rein to one's thoughts and feelings

秤 chèng (动) steelyard; scale

痴(癡) chī (形) 1 silly; idiotic: ～人说梦 a tale told by an idiot. 白～ idiot 2 crazy about: 书～ bookworm

痴呆 chīdāi (形) dull-witted; stupid

痴情 chīqíng (名) passionate but often unrequited love

痴心 chīxīn (名) infatuation: ～妄想 wishful thinking; day dream

吃 chī (动) 1 eat; take: ～药 take medicine 2 eat at: ～馆子 eat at a restaurant 3 live on: 靠山～山 those living on a mountain live off the mountain 4 wipe out: 又～掉敌军一个团 annihilate another enemy regiment. ～一个子儿 take a piece (in chess) 5 exhaust; be a strain 6 absorb; soak up: 这种纸不～墨. This kind of paper does not absorb ink. 7 suffer; incur

吃不开(開) chībùkāi (形) be unpopular: 不懂英文的人在这个公司是～的. This company has no use for people who don't know English.

吃不消 chībuxiāo (形) be unable to stand (exertion, fatigue, etc.): 怕他的身体～. We are afraid he won't be able to stand the strain. 全天工作她恐怕～. A full-time job may be too much for her.

吃穿 chī-chuān (名) food and clothing: ～不愁 not have to worry about food and clothing

吃醋 chīcù (形) be jealous (usu. about rivalry in love)

吃得开(開) chīdekāi be popular; be much sought after

吃得消 chīdexiāo be able to stand (exertion, fatigue, etc.)

吃饭 chīfàn (动) 1 eat; have a meal: ～了吗? Have you had

your meal? 2 make a living: 靠捕鱼～ make a living by fishing

吃喝玩乐(樂) chī-hē-wán-lè eat, drink and be merry; idle away one's time in pleasure-seeking

吃紧(緊) chījǐn (形) tense; critical; tense (of political, military, financial situation)

吃惊(驚) chījīng (动) be startled; be shocked; be amazed; be taken aback: 大吃一惊 greatly surprised

吃苦 chīkǔ (动) bear hardships: ～耐劳 endure hardships and be capable of hard work

吃苦头(頭) chī kǔtou (动) suffer: 蛮干是要～的. If you act rashly you are bound to suffer.

吃亏(虧) chīkuī (动) 1 stand to lose; get the worst of it: 跟他作生意你是要～的. You will stand to lose if you do business with him. 2 at a disadvantage

吃老本 chī lǎoběn (动) live off one's past gains; rest on one's laurels

吃力 chīlì (形) strenuous; difficult: ～不讨好的差使 a thankless but demanding job

吃奶 chīnǎi (动) suck the breast: ～的孩子 sucking child; suckling

吃素 chīsù (动) avoid eating meat and fish; be a vegetarian

吃闲(閒)饭 chī xiánfàn lead an idle life; be a loafer or sponger

吃香 chīxiāng (形) <口> be very popular; be much sought after; be in vogue

吃一堑,长一智 chī yi qiàn, zhǎng yi zhì a fall into the pit, a gain in your wit

笞 chī (动) <书> beat with a stick, cane, etc.: 鞭～ flog; whip

嗤 chī (动) sneer: ～笑 laugh at; sneer at. ～之以鼻 snort; give an impatient snort

迟(遲) chí (形) 1 late: 他来～了. He's late. 2 slow; tardy

迟迟 chíchí (形) slow; tardy: ～不决 hesitate for a long time without making a decision

迟到 chídào (形) be late: 他上班从不～. He is never late for work.

迟钝 chídùn (形) slow-witted

迟缓 chíhuǎn (形) slow; sluggish: 进展～ make slow progress

迟疑 chíyí (动、名) hesitate; hesitation: 毫不～ without hesitation

迟早 chízǎo (副) sooner or later; early or late

持 chí (动) 1 hold; grasp: ～枪 hold a gun 2 keep; maintain: ～中立态度 maintain a neutral attitude 3 support; keep; maintain: 维～ maintain 4 manage; run: 主～ be in charge of. 操～ manage; handle 5 oppose: 相～不下 be locked in stalemate

持家 chíjiā (动) run one's home: 勤俭～ be thrifty in running one's home

持久 chíjiǔ (形) lasting; enduring: ～和平 lasting peace. ～战 protracted war

持续(續) chíxù (形) continued; sustained: 产量～稳定上升 a steady increase in output

持有 chíyǒu (动) hold: ～外交护照 hold a diplomatic passport. ～不同意见 hold differing views

持之以恒 chí zhī yǐ héng persevere

持重 chízhòng (形) prudent; cautious; discreet: 老成～ experienced and prudent

匙 chí (名) spoon: 汤～ soup spoon

踟 chí

踟蹰 chíchú (动) hesitate; waver

池 chí (名) 1 pool; pond: 游泳～ swimming pool. 养鱼～ fishpond 2 an enclosed space with raised sides: 舞～ dance floor. 乐～ orchestra pit

池塘 chítáng (名) pond; pool

弛 chí (动) <书> relax; slacken: 一张一～ tension alternating with relaxation

弛缓 chíhuǎn (动) relax; calm down

驰 chí (动) 1 speed; gallop 2 spread: ～名 well-known

驰骋 chíchěng (动) <书> gallop

驰名 chímíng (形) well-known; famous: ～中外 enjoy a high reputation both at home and abroad

耻 chǐ (名) shame; disgrace; humiliation: 不知～ have no sense of shame. 引以为～ regard sth. as a disgrace

耻辱 chǐrǔ (名) shame; disgrace; humiliation

耻笑 chǐxiào (动) sneer at; ridicule

齿(齒) chǐ (名) **1** tooth **2** a tooth-like part of anything
齿冷 chǐlěng (动) <书> laugh scornfully: 令人～ inspire cold disdain
齿轮(輪) chǐlún (名) gear wheel; gear
侈 chǐ (形) <书> extravagant; wasteful: ～谈 talk glibly about. 奢～ luxurious; extravagant
褫 chǐ (动) <书> strip; deprive
褫夺(奪) chǐduó (动) strip; deprive: ～公权 deprive sb. of civil rights
尺 chǐ (名) **1** *chi*, a unit of length (1/3 of a metre) **2** ruler
尺寸 chǐcùn (名) size; measurement; dimensions: 量～ take sb.'s measurements
尺度 chǐdù (名) yardstick; criterion
炽(熾) chì (形) flaming; ablaze: ～烈 raging scorching. ～热 red-hot; sweltering
赤 chì (形) **1** red: 面红耳～ be red in the face; be flushed **2** loyal; sincere: ～胆忠心 utter devotion; whole-hearted dedication **3** bare: ～足 barefoot
赤道 chìdào (名) the equator
赤金 chìjīn (名) pure gold
赤裸裸 chìluǒluǒ (形) **1** stark-naked **2** undisguised; naked
赤贫 chìpín (形) utterly destitute
赤字 chìzì (名) deficit
翅 chì (名) wing: ～膀 wing. 鱼～ shark's fins
叱 chì (动) rebuke: 怒～ rebuke angrily. ～骂 curse; scold roundly
斥 chì (动) shout; scold; denounce: 痛～ vehemently denounce; shout at (sb.) angrily
斥责 chìzé (动) rebuke; denounce
饬(飭) chì (动) <书> **1** put in order; readjust: 整～ put in order; strengthen (discipline, etc.) **2** (old use) order: 严～ issue strict orders
充 chōng I (形) ample; full; sufficient II (动) **1** pose as; pass sth. off as: ～好人 pretend to be kind-hearted **2** serve as; act as: ～向导 serve as a guide **3** fill; charge: ～电 charge (a battery)
充斥 chōngchì (动) flood; be full of: 外国商品～市场. The market was glutted with goods from abroad.
充当(當) chōngdāng (动) act as; serve as; play the part of
充耳不闻 chōng ěr bù wén turn a deaf ear to
充分 chōngfèn (形) full; ample; abundant: 有～的信心 be full of confidence. ～证据 ample evidence
充公 chōnggōng (动) confiscate
充饥(饑) chōngjī (动) allay (or appease) one's hunger
充沛 chōngpèi (形) plentiful; abundant; full of: 精力～ vigorous; energetic
充任 chōngrèn (动) fill the post; hold the position of: 聘请他～顾问 ask him to be our adviser
充塞 chōngsè (动) fill (up); cram
充实(實) chōngshí I (形) substantial; rich: 内容～ substantial in content II (动) substantiate; enrich: ～领导班子 strengthen the leadership.
充数 chōngshù (动) merely make up the number: 滥竽～ be hardly qualified for the job
充裕 chōngyù (形) abundant; plentiful: 时间～ have ample (or plenty of) time
充足 chōngzú (形) adequate; ample; sufficient; abundant: 证据～ have ample evidence. 阳光～ full of sunshine; sunny
舂 chōng (动) pound; pestle: ～米 husk rice with mortar and pestle
冲(衝) chōng I (动) **1** pour boiling water on: ～茶 make tea **2** rinse; flush; wash away: ～厕所 flush the toilet. **3** charge; rush; dash: ～锋陷阵 charge forward **4** clash; collide: ～突 conflict **5** develop: ～胶卷 develop a piece of film II (名) important hub see also chòng
冲冲 chōngchōng (副) excitedly: 怒气～ in a towering temper
冲淡 chōngdàn (动) dilute; water down; weaken; play down: ～戏剧效果 weaken the dramatic effect
冲动(動) chōngdòng I (名) impulse: 出于一时～ act on impulse II get excited; be impetuous: 别～. Don't get excited.
冲击(擊) chōngjī I (动) lash;

pound: 海浪～着岩石. The waves lashed at the rocks. II (名)impact
冲积(積) chōngjī (名) alluviation
冲剂(劑) chōngjì (名) (of medicine) mixture to be taken with boiling water, wine, etc.
冲垮 chōngkuǎ (动) wash away; shatter
冲破 chōngpò (动)break through; breach
冲散 chōngsàn (动) break up; scatter; disperse
冲杀(殺) chōngshā (动) charge forward; rush ahead
冲晒(曬) chōngshài (动) develop and print
冲刷 chōngshuā (动) erode; wash away
冲天 chōngtiān (形) towering; soaring: 干劲～ with boundless enthusiasm. 怒气～ in a towering rage
冲突 chōngtū (名) conflict; clash: 武装～ an armed conflict
冲撞 chōngzhuàng (动) **1** collide; bump; ram **2** offend

憧 chōng

憧憧 chōngchōng (形) flickering; moving: 人影～ people's shadows moving back and forth
憧憬 chōngjǐng (动) long for; visualize: ～着光明的未来 visualize a bright future

忡 chōng

忡忡 chōngchōng (形) grieved: 忧心～ very worried; full of anxiety

虫(蟲) chóng (名) insect; worm: ～害 insect pest

崇 chóng I (形) high; lofty II (动) esteem; worship

崇拜 chóngbài (动) worship: adore: 英雄～ hero worship
崇高 chónggāo (形) lofty; high: ～的理想 a lofty ideal. ～的威望 high prestige
崇敬 chóngjìng (动) respect; revere: 受到人民的～ be held in high esteem by the people

重 chóng I (副) over again: 老调～弹 harp on the same old tune. ～访英伦 revisit England II (动) repeat III (名) layer: 万～山 ranges of hills. 双～领导 dual leadership

see also zhòng
重版 chóngbǎn (名) reprint
重唱 chóngchàng (名) a piece of music for two or more performers: 二～ duet
重重 chóngchóng (形) layer upon layer: 困难～ endless difficulties. 顾虑～ full of misgivings
重蹈覆辙 chóng dǎo fùzhé follow the track of the overturned cart; follow the same old road to ruin
重迭(叠) chóngdié (形) overlapping: 精简～的行政机构 streamline the administrative structure
重返 chóngfǎn (动) return
重逢 chóngféng (动) meet again: 旧友～ meeting of old friends (after a long separation)
重复(複) chóngfù (动) repeat; duplicate
重婚 chónghūn (名) bigamy
重申 chóngshēn (动) reaffirm; reiterate; restate: ～我们的立场 reaffirm our stand
重围(圍) chóngwéi (名) tight encirclement by the enemy
重温旧(舊)梦(夢) chóng wēn jiùmèng revive an old dream; recall or relive an old experience
重新 chóngxīn (副) again; anew; afresh: ～开始 start afresh. ～考虑 reconsider
重演 chóngyǎn (动) **1** repeat a performance or put on an old play **2** recur: 历史的～ history repeating itself
重洋 chóngyáng (名) the seas and oceans: 远涉～ travel across the oceans
重整旗鼓 chóng zhěng qígǔ rally one's forces (after a defeat)
重奏 chóngzòu (名) ensemble: 四～ quartet

宠(寵) chǒng (动) spoil; dote on: 得～ be in sb.'s good graces. 失～ fall from grace. 这孩子给～坏了. The child is spoiled.

宠爱(愛) chǒng'ài (动) make a pet of sb.; dote on
宠儿(兒) chǒng'ér (名) pet; favourite
宠信 chǒngxìn (动) favour and trust unduly (a subordinate)

冲 chòng I (副)〈口〉with force; dynamically; vigorously: 他干活真～. He works with vim and vigour. 烟味真～. The tobacco smells strong. II (介) facing; towards: 窗户～南开 The window faces south. 那话不是～你说的. That remark wasn't directed at you.

see also chōng

抽 chōu (动) 1 take out (from in beween): 从书架上～出一本书 take a book from the shelf 2 sprout; bud: 小麦～穗了. The wheat is coming into ear. 小树～出了嫩芽. The saplings are budding. 3 draw: ～水 draw water (from the well, etc.) 4 shrink: 这种布一洗就～. Washing shrinks this kind of cloth. 5 lash; whip; thrash

抽搐 chōuchù (动) twitch

抽打 chōudǎ (动) lash; whip; thrash

抽调 chōudiào (动) transfer

抽筋 chōujīn (动) cramp: 腿～ have a cramp in the leg

抽空 chōukōng (动) manage to find time

抽泣 chōuqì (动) sob

抽签(籤) chōuqiān (动) draw (or cast) lots

抽纱 chōushā (名) drawnwork

抽身 chōushēn (动) get away (from one's work)

抽屉(屜) chōuti (名) drawer

抽象 chōuxiàng (形) abstract: ～的概念 an abstract concept. 不要这样～地谈问题. Don't speak in such abstract terms.

抽烟 chōuyān (动) smoke (a cigarette or a pipe)

畴(疇) chóu (名)〈书〉 1 kind, division: 范～ category 2 farmland

踌(躊) chóu

踌躇 chóuchú (动) hesitate; shilly-shally: ～不前 mark time; hesitate to make a move

筹(籌) chóu (动) prepare; plan: 统～ overall planning. ～款 raise money (or funds). ～办 make preparations; make arrangements

筹备(備) chóubèi (动) prepare; arrange

筹措 chóucuò (动) raise (money): ～旅费 raise money for travelling expenses

筹划(劃) chóuhuà (动) plan to do sth.: 这里正在～建设一座水力发电站. We are planning to build a hydroelectric station here.

筹集 chóují (动) raise (money): ～基金 raise funds

筹建 chóujiàn (动) prepare to construct or establish sth.

筹码 chóumǎ (名) chip; counter: 作为这场政治交易的～ used as bargaining counters in the politicl deal

酬 chóu I (名) reward; payment: 稿～ payment for an article or book written II fulfil; realize: 壮志未～ with one's ambitions unfulfilled

酬报(報) chóubào (名) reward; renumeration

酬金 chóujīn (名) monetary reward; remuneration

酬劳(勞) chóuláo (名) recompense; reward

酬谢 chóuxiè (动) present sb. with a gift as a reward or as a token of one's appreciation

愁 chóu (动) worry; be anxious

愁肠(腸) chóucháng (名) pent-up feelings of sadness: ～百结 feel melancholy deep down in one's heart

愁眉 chóuméi (名) knitted brows; worried look: ～不展 knit one's brows. ～苦脸 look worried and miserable; have a worried look; pull a long face

愁闷 chóumèn (动) feel gloomy; be depressed

愁容 chóuróng (名) worried look

愁绪 chóuxù (名)〈书〉 pensive melancholy

仇 chóu (名) 1 hatred; enmity: animosity 2 enemy; foe: 亲痛～快 sadden one's own folk and gladden one's enemies

仇敌(敵) chóudí (名) foe; enemy

仇恨 chóuhèn (名) hatred; hostility

仇人 chóurén (名) personal enemy

仇视 chóushì (动) look upon with hatred; be hostile to

惆 chóu

惆怅(悵) chóuchàng (名) melancholy; sadness

稠 chóu (形) 1 thick: 粥太～了. The porridge is too thick. 2 dense

稠密 chóumì (形) dense: 人烟～ densely populated

绸 chóu (名) silk fabric; silk

绸缎 chóuduàn (名) silk and satins

瞅 chǒu (动) glimpse; glance: 我周围瞧了一下,一眼～见她. I looked around and glimpsed her.

丑(醜) chǒu (形) 1 ugly 2 disgraceful; shameful;

scandalous: 出～ make a fool of oneself

丑八怪 chǒubāguài (名)〈口〉a very ugly person

丑恶(惡) chǒu'è (形) ugly; hideous; despicable: ～嘴脸 ugly features

丑化 chǒuhuà (动) uglify; vilify

丑角 chǒujué (名) clown; buffoon

丑陋 chǒulòu (形) ugly

丑态(態) chǒutài (名) ugly (or ludicrous) performance; disgusting manner: ～百出 act like a buffoon

丑闻 chǒuwén (名) scandal

臭 chòu (形) 1 smelly; stinking; foul: ～鸡蛋 a rotten egg 2 disgusting: 摆～架子 put on lousy airs
see also xiù

臭虫(蟲) chòuchóng (名) bedbug

臭骂(罵) chòumà (动) curse angrily: 挨了一顿～ get a dressing down

臭名昭著 chòumíng zhāozhù (形) notorious; infamous

臭气(氣) chòuqì (名) bad smell; stink

初 chū I (名) beginning II (形) 1 early: ～冬 early winter 2 first (in order): ～雪 first snow. ～三 the third day of a lunar month 3 for the first time: ～露锋芒 display one's talent for the first time 4 elementary; rudimentary: ～中 junior middle school 6 original: ～衷 original intention

初版 chūbǎn (名) first edition

初步 chūbù (形) initial; preliminary; tentative: ～意见 tentative opinion (proposal)

初出茅庐(廬) chū chū máolú at the beginning of one's career; young and inexperienced: ～的作家 fledgling writer

初次 chūcì (副) the first time: ～见面 see sb. for the first time

初等 chūděng (形) elementary; primary: ～教育 primary education

初级 chūjí (形) elementary; primary: ～产品 primary products

初交 chūjiāo (名) new acquaintance

初期 chūqī (名) initial stage; early days: 革命～ in the early days of the revolution

初生之犊(犢) chū shēng zhī dú newborn calf: ～不畏虎. Newborn calves do not fear tigers — young people are fearless.

初试 chūshì (名) preliminary examination

初旬 chūxún (名) in the first ten days of a month

初诊 chūzhěn (名) first consultation

出 chū I (动) 1 go or come out: ～太阳了. The sun's come out. ～国 go abroad. ～狱 be released from prison 2 issue; put forth: ～主意 offer advice. ～通知 put up a notice. ～证明 issue a certificate 3 produce: 这个厂～的汽车 the cars made by this factory. ～新书 publish new books 4 arise; happen; occur: ～事故 There was an accident. ～问题 go wrong 5 exceed; go beyond: 不～三年 within three years. 怎么多～三个人? How come that there are three more people? 6 vent: ～气 vent one's spleen ～疹子 have measles II (量) a dramatic piece: 一～戏 an opera; a play

出 chū [used after a verb to indicate outward movement or completed action]: 拿～证件 produce one's papers. 选～新主席 elect a new chairman. 我说不～口. I find it too embarrassing to mention it. 他答不～这道题. He can't answer this question. 2 indicating identification: 我看不～他有多大年纪. I can't tell how old he is. 你能听～这是谁的声音? Can you identify this voice?

出版 chūbǎn (动) publish: ～社 publishing house. ～物 publication

出殡(殯) chūbìn (动) hold a funeral procession

出兵 chūbīng (动) dispatch troops (to a place)

出差 chūchāi (动) be on a business trip

出产(產) chūchǎn (动) produce; manufacture

出岔子 chūchàzi run into trouble; go wrong

出场(場) chūchǎng (动) 1 come on the stage; appear on the scene 2 enter the arena

出车(車) chūchē (动) dispatch a vehicle

出丑(醜) chūchǒu (动) make a fool of oneself; cut a sorry figure

出处(處) chūchù (名) source (of a quotation or allusion)

出错 chūcuò (动) make mistakes

出动(動) chūdòng (动) 1 go

into action: 全校～扫雪. The whole school turned out to sweep the snow. 2 send out; dispatch: ～军舰 dispatch warships. ～警察驱散示威队伍. The police were called out to break up the demonstration.
出尔(爾)反尔(爾) chū ěr fǎn ěr(动) go back on one's word; contradict oneself
出发(發) chūfā (动) 1 set out; start off: 我们六点～. We'll set out at six. 2 start from; proceed from: 从长远利益～ from the long-range view
出轨 chūguǐ (动) 1 be derailed; 2 overstep the bounds: ～行为 an act deviating from normal practice
出海 chūhǎi (动) put to sea
出汗 chūhàn (动) perspire; sweat: 出一身汗 sweat all over
出乎意料 chūhū yìliào (形) unexpectedly: 他的去世太～了. His death was really too sudden and unexpected.
出活 chūhuó (动) be efficient
出击(擊) chūjī (动) launch an attack
出家 chūjiā (动) become a Buddhist monk or nun
出嫁 chūjià (动) (of a woman) get married
出界 chūjiè (副) out-of-bounds; outside
出借 chūjiè (动) lend; loan
出境 chūjìng (动) leave the country: ～签证 exit visa. 驱逐～ deport. ～许可证 exit permit
出口 chūkǒu I (动) 1 speak; utter 2 export II (名) exit
出来(來) chūlai (动) come out; emerge: 月亮～了. The moon has come out.
出来(來) chūlái [used after a verb to indicate outward movement or completed action]: 他从屋里走～. He came out of the room. 论文写～了. The thesis is completed.
出类(類)拔萃 chūlèi-bácuì (形) preeminent; outstanding: ～的人物 an outstanding figure
出力 chūlì (动) contribute one's strength; exert oneself
出笼(籠) chūlóng (动) 1 come out of the steamer of cooking 2 〈贬〉come forth; appear; come out into the open
出路 chūlù (名) way out; outlet
出马(馬) chūmǎ (动) go into action; take the field: 亲自～ take up the matter oneself; take personal charge of the matter
出卖(賣) chūmài (动) 1 offer for sale; sell 2 betray; sell out
出毛病 chū máobìng go wrong; be out of order
出面 chūmiàn (动) act in one's own capacity or on sb.'s behalf: 这事得你亲自～. You'll have to take up the matter personally. ～调停 act as a mediator
出名 chūmíng (形) famous; well-known
出没 chūmò (动) appear and disappear; haunt: ～无常 appear or disappear unpredictably
出谋划(劃)策 chūmóu-huàcè (动) give counsel; mastermind: 在幕后～ mastermind a scheme from behind the scenes
出纳 chūnà (名) cashier; the work of a cashier
出品 chūpǐn I (动) produce; manufacture; make II (名) product
出其不意 chūqíbùyì take sb. by surprise
出奇 chūqí (形) extraordinary; exceptional [usu. used as an adverbial adjunct or a complement]: 今天真是～地热. It's unusually hot today.
出奇制胜(勝) chū qí zhì shèng win by a surprise attack
出气(氣) chūqì (形) give vent to one's spleen
出勤 chūqín (动) 1 turn out for work: 全体～ full attendance 2 be out on duty
出去 chūqu (动) go out; get out: ～走走 go out for a walk
出去 chuqu [used after a verb to indicate outward movement]: 把烟放～. Let out the smoke. 侵略者被赶～了. The invaders were driven off.
出让(讓) chūràng (动) sell (one's own things): 自行车减价～ sell one's bicycle at a reduced price
出人头(頭)地 chū rén tóu dì stand out among one's fellows
出任 chūrèn (动)〈书〉take up the post of
出入 chūrù I (动) come in and go out II (名) discrepancy; divergence: 他说的和事实有～. What he says does not square with the facts. ～证 pass (identifying a staff member, etc.)
出色 chūsè (形) outstanding; remarkable; splendid
出身 chūshēn (名) 1 family background 2 one's previous occu-

pation
出神 chūshén (动) be lost in thought; be spellbound: 想得～ be in a trance
出生 chūshēng (动) be born: ～地 birthplace. ～证 birth certificate
出生入死 chūshēng-rùsǐ go through fire and water; brave countless dangers
出师(師) chūshī (动) 1 finish one's apprenticeship 2 dispatch troops to fight; send out an army
出使 chūshǐ (动) serve as an envoy abroad; be sent on a diplomatic mission
出示 chūshì (动) show; produce: ～证件 produce one's papers
出事 chūshì (动) have an accident: 出了什么事? What's wrong?
出售 chūshòu (动) offer for sale; sell
出庭 chūtíng (动) appear in court: ～作证 appear in court as a witness
出头(頭) chūtóu I (动) 1 raise one's head; free oneself (from misery) 2 appear in public; come to the fore II [used after a round mumber]: a little over; odd: 他刚四十～. He's just a little over forty.
出头(頭)露面 chūtóu-lùmiàn make a public appearance; be in the limelight
出土 chūtǔ (动) be unearthed; be excavated: ～文物 unearthed historical relics
出席 chūxí (动) attend; be present: (at a meeting, banquet, etc.)
出息 chūxī (名) (of a person) promise: 有～ promising. 没～ good-for-nothing
出现(現) chūxiàn (动) appear; emerge: ～了一个新问题. A new problem has arisen.
出游 chūyóu (动) go on a (sightseeing) tour
出于(於) chūyú (动) start from: ～自愿 of one's own accord
出院 chūyuàn (动) leave hospital; be discharged from hospital after recovery
出诊 chūzhěn (动) (of a doctor) make a house call
出征 chūzhēng (动) go on an expedition
出众(衆) chūzhòng (形) outstanding: 人才～ a talented person; a person of outstanding talent
出租 chūzū (动) hire out; rent out; lease out: ～汽车 taxicab; taxi

厨 chú (名) kitchen
厨房 chúfáng (名) kitchen: ～用具 kitchen ware; cooking utensils
厨师(師) chúshī (名) cook; chef

橱 chú (名) cabinet; closet: 壁～ built-in cabinet. 衣～ wardrobe. 书～ bookcase. 碗～ cupboard
橱窗 chúchuāng (名) show window; showcase; shopwindow
橱柜(櫃) chúguì (名) cupboard

除 chú I (动) 1 get rid of; do away with; remove 2 divide: 五～十得二. 10 divided by 5 is 2. II (连) 1 except: ～此而外 with the exception of this (see 除了) 2 besides (see also 除了)
除草 chúcǎo (动) weed: ～机 weeder. ～剂 weed killer; herbicide
除法 chúfǎ (名) division
除非 chúfēi (连) [often used in conjunction with 才, 否则, 不然, etc. to indicate that what follows is a necessary condition]: only if; unless: ～动手术,否则她就没救了. She will die unless she has an operation. ～你亲自去请他,不然他是不会来的. Only when you go and ask him personally will he come.
除根 chúgēn (动) 1 dig up the roots; root out 2 cure once and for all
除了 chúle (介) except: ～她,谁也不会唱这支歌. No one can sing this song except her. 她～接电话以外, 还要打字. She does typing besides answering phone calls.
除外 chúwài (动) be excepted; not including: 博物馆每天开放, 星期一～. The museum is open every day except Monday.
除夕 chúxī (名) New Year's Eve

锄 chú I (名) hoe II (动) 1 work with a hoe; hoe: ～草 weed with a hoe 2 uproot; eliminate; wipe out: ～奸 eliminate traitors
锄头(頭) chútou (名) hoe

刍(芻) chú (名) <书> hay; fodder: 反～ ruminate; chew the cud
刍议(議) chúyì (名) <谦> a modest proposal

雏(雛) chú (名) 1 young (bird) 2 nestling; fledgling

雏形 chúxíng (名) microcosm; embryonic form

储 chǔ (动) 1 store up: 冬～白菜 cabbages stored for the winter.

储备(備) chǔbèi I (动) store; reserve; put by II (名) reserve: 黄金～ gold reserve. 外汇～ foreign exchange reserve

储藏 chǔcáng I (动) keep in custody; preserve: 鲜果～ preservation (or storage) of fresh fruit II (名) deposit: 丰富的石油～ abundant oil deposits. ～室 storeroom

储存 chǔcún (动)store; put away: ～余粮 store up surplus grain. ～核武器 stockpile nuclear weapons

储量 chǔliàng (名) reserves

储蓄 chǔxù (动、名) save; deposit: ～所 savings bank. 活期(定期)～ current (deposit) account

楚 chǔ I (形) clear; neat: 一清二～ perfectly clear. 衣冠～～ immaculately dressed II (名)〈书〉 suffering: 苦～ distress; suffering

础(礎) chǔ (名) plinth: ～石 the stone base of a column; plinth. 基～ foudation; base

处(處) chǔ (动) 1 get along (with sb.): ～得来 be on good terms; get along well 2 deal with; handle: ～事 handle affairs; manage matters 3 be in a certain position: ～于困难地位 be in a difficult position. 设身～地 put oneself in another's position.
see also chù

处罚(罰) chǔfá (动) punish; penalize

处方 chǔfāng (名) prescription; recipe

处分 chǔfèn (名) disciplinary action; punishment: 警告～ disciplinary warning. 免予～ exempt sb. from punishment. 行政～ administrative disciplinary measure

处境 chǔjìng (名) (usu.) unfavourable situation; plight: ～尴尬 be in an embarrassing situation. ～危险 be in a dangerous (or precarious) situation; be in peril

处决 chǔjué (动) execute: 依法～ execute in accordance with the law; implement a death sentence

处理 chǔlǐ (动) 1 handle; attend to; dispose of: ～国家大事 attend to state affairs. ～废物 waste disposal 2 treat by a special process: 热～ heat treatment 3 sell at a reduced price: ～价格 reduced price; bargain price. ～品 goods sold at reduced or sale prices

处女 chǔnǚ (名) virgin: ～地 virgin soil

处世 chǔshì (动) conduct oneself in social life

处死 chǔsǐ (动) put to death; execute

处心积(積)虑(慮) chǔxīn-jīlǜ deliberately scheme or plan (sth. evil)

处于(於) chǔyú (动) be in a certain condition (state): ～优势 be in a favourable condition

处置 chǔzhì (动) deal with; handle: ～得宜 handle matters with propriety

畜 chù (名) domestic animal; livestock
see also xù

畜生 chùsheng (名) 1 domestic animal 2 beast; dirty swine

怵 chù (动) fear: ～场 feel apprehensive

矗 chù (动)〈书〉 stand tall and upright: ～立 tower over

处(處) chù (名) 1 place: 住～ dwelling place; apartment. 停车～ parking lot; car park. 长～ strong point. 共同之～ common feature. 心灵深～ in the recesses of the heart. 几～人家 several homesteads 2 department; office: 秘书～ secretariat. 总务～ general affairs department
see also chǔ

处处 chùchù (副) everywhere; in all respects

黜 chù (动)〈书〉 remove sb. from office; dismiss: 罢～ dismiss (a government official)

绌 chù (形)〈书〉 inadequate; insufficient: 相形见～ prove inferior by comparison; be outshone

触(觸) chù (动) 1 touch: 抵～ contradict 2 move: ～景生情 The sight strikes a chord in one's heart.

触电(電) chùdiàn (动) get an electric shock: 小心～! Danger! Electricity!

触动(動) chùdòng (动) 1 touch; move slightly 2 stir up sb.'s

feelings
触发(發) chùfā (动) touch off; trigger
触犯 chùfàn (动) offend; violate: 我什么地方～了你? What have I done to offend you? ～法律 violate (or break) the law
触目惊(驚)心 chùmù-jīngxīn (形) startling; shocking
触怒 chùnù (动) make angry; enrage
触角 chùjiǎo (名) feeler; antenna
揣 chuāi (动) keep sth. in one's clothes: 把孩子～在怀里 hold a baby in arms
see also chuǎi
揣 chuǎi (动) <书> estimate; conjecture: ～测 guess. ～摩 try to figure out
踹 chuài (动) 1 kick: 一脚把门～开 kick the door open
穿 chuān 1 wear; put on: ～上大衣 put on your coat. 她～绿裙子. She is in a green skirt. 2 pierce through; penetrate: 看～ see through 3 pass through; cross: ～过马路 cross a street
穿插 chuānchā I (副) do alternately II (动) insert III (名) episode; interlude
穿戴 chuāndài (名) what one wears: ～整齐 be neatly dressed
穿孔 chuānkǒng I (动) bore (or punch) a hole II (名) perforation
穿梭 chuānsuō (动) shuttle back and forth: ～外交 shuttle diplomacy
穿越 chuānyuè (动) pass through; cut across
穿针引线(綫) chuānzhēn-yǐnxiàn act as a go-between
穿着 chuānzhuó (名) dress; what one wears
穿凿(鑿) chuānzuò give a farfetched (or strained) interpretation; read too much into sth.: ～附会 give strained interpretations and draw farfetched analogies
川 chuān (名) 1 river: 山～ mountains and rivers 2 plain; lowland area
川流不息 chuān liú bù xī flow past in an endless stream; come in a never-ending stream
椽 chuán (名) rafter
传(傳) chuán (动) 1 pass; pass on 2 spread: 消息很快～开了. The news runs apace. 3 hand down: 祖～秘方 a secret recipe handed down from the ancesters 4 summon: ～证人 summon a witness 5 transmit; conduct: ～热 transmit heat 6 infect; catch 7 convey; express: ～神 bring out the true meaning
传播 chuánbō (动) propagate; disseminate; popularize: ～先进技术 popularize advanced technique
传布 chuánbù (动) disseminate; spread
传抄 chuánchāo (动) copy privately
传达(達) chuándá (动) pass on; relay: ～信息 relay a message. ～会议精神 transmit the spirit of the meeting. ～室 reception office
传单(單) chuándān (名) leaflet; handbill
传导(導) chuándǎo (动、名) conduct; conduction
传递(遞) chuándì (动) transmit; deliver; transfer: ～信息 transmit messages
传呼 chuánhū (of a public telephone custodian) notify sb. of a phone call: ～电话 neighbourhood telephone service
传教 chuánjiào (动) teach and spread the Christian religion abroad; do missionary work: ～士 missionary
传票 chuánpiào (名) (court) summons; subpoena
传奇 chuánqí (名) 1 legend: ～式的英雄 legendary hero 2 romances of the Tang and Song dynasties (618—1279) 3 poetic dramas of the Ming and Qing dynasties (1368—1911)
传染 chuánrǎn (动) infect; be contagious: ～病 infectious (or contagious) disease
传神 chuánshén (形) vivid; lifelike: ～之笔 a fine vivid touch (in writing or painting)
传声(聲)筒 chuánshēngtǒng (名) 1 megaphone; mouthpiece 2 parrot
传授 chuánshòu (动) pass on (knowledge, skill, etc.); impart
传说 chuánshuō (名) 1 rumour has it; people say 2 lore; legend: 民间～ folklore
传诵 chuánsòng (动) circulated; be widely read
传统 chuántǒng (名) tradition; conventions: ～观念 traditional

ideas
传闻 chuánwén (名) hearsay; rumour: ～失实. The rumour proves unfounded.
传扬(揚) chuányáng (动) spread: 他的声名～四方. His reputation spread far and wide.
传阅 chuányuè (动) pass round or circulate
传真 chuánzhēn (名) facsimile
船 chuán (名) boat; ship: 上～ board a ship; go on board; embark. 下～ disembark. ～上交货 free on board
船舶 chuánbó (名) shipping
船舱(艙) chuáncāng (名) cabin
船坞(塢) chuánwù (名) dock; shipyard: 浮～ floating dock
船员(員) chuányuán (名) (ship's) crew
船长(長) chuánzhǎng (名) captain; skipper
船只(隻) chuánzhī (名) ship; vessel
喘 chuǎn (名) breathe with difficulty; pant: 哮～ asthma
喘气(氣) chuǎnqì (动) 1 pant; gasp: 喘不过气来 be out of breath 2 take a breather; have a break: 喘口气儿再干. Let's take a breather before we go on.
喘息 chuǎnxī (动) 1 pant; gasp for breath 2 breathing space
舛 chuǎn (名)〈书〉error; mishap: 命途多～ suffer many a setback during one's life. ～误 error; mishap
串 chuàn I (动) 1 string together: 把鱼～起来 string the fish together 2 get things mixed up: 电话～线. The lines have crossed. 3 go from place to place; run about: ～亲戚 go around visiting one's relatives II (量) string; cluster: 一～珠子 a string of beads. 一～钥匙 a bunch of keys. 一～葡萄 a cluster of grapes
串联(聯) chuànlián I (动) make contact II (名) series connection: ～电阻 series resistance
串通 chuàntōng (动) gang up; collaborate; collude: ～一气 act in collusion
窗 chuāng (名) window: 玻璃～ glass window. ～明几净. The window is bright and the desk clean.
窗户 chuānghu (名) opening in a wall for letting in air and light; window
窗口 chuāngkǒu (名) 1 the place near a window: 她就站在～. She is standing by the window. 2 wicket; window (for tickets, etc.)
窗帘(簾) chuānglián (名) (window) curtain
窗台(臺) chuāngtái (名) windowsill
疮(瘡) chuāng (名) sore; running sore: ～疤 scar
创(創) chuāng (名) wound: ～伤 a damaged place in the body; wound; trauma. ～痕 scar
see also chuàng
幢 chuáng (名) a stone pillar inscribed with Buddha's name or Buddhist scripture
幢幢 chuángchuáng (动)〈书〉flicker; swing from side to side: 人影～ shadows of people flickered
床(牀) chuáng (名) 1 bed: 单人～ single bed. 双人～ double bed. 折叠～ folding bed. 马上上～睡觉去 get straight into bed 2 (量): 一～被子 one quilt
床单(單) chuángdān (名) sheet
床铺(鋪) chuángpù (名) bed
闯 chuǎng (动) rush; force one's way in or out: 横冲直～ dash around madly; jostle and elbow one's way. ～出一条新路子. break a new path; blaze a trail
闯祸(禍) chuǎnghuò (动) get into trouble or cause disaster
闯将(將) chuǎngjiàng (名) bold general; pathbreaker
闯劲(勁) chuǎngjìn (名) heroic effort; pioneering spirit
怆(愴) chuàng (形)〈书〉very sad: ～然泪下 shed tears in sadness
创(創) chuàng (动) initiate; achieve (sth. for the first time): ～办 set up. ～记录 set a record
see also chuāng
创见(見) chuàngjiàn (名) originality; original idea
创建 chuàngjiàn (动) found; establish: ～新的机构 found a new organization
创举(舉) chuàngjǔ (名) pioneering work; something that has never been undertaken
创立 chuànglì (动) found; originate
创始 chuàngshǐ (动) originate; initiate: ～人 founder; founder member; founding father

创新 chuàngxīn (动) discard old ideas and bring forth new ones; blaze new trails

创业(業) chuàngyè (动) start an undertaking; do pioneering work: 有～精神 have the spirit of a pathbreaker

创造 chuàngzào (动) create; produce: ～新记录 make a record. ～奇迹 create miracles; work wonders. ～力 creative power. ～性 creativeness; creativity

创作 chuàngzuò I (动) create (write literary works): ～经验 creative experience II (名) literary and artistic creation

炊 chuī (动) cook: ～具 cooking utensils. ～事 cooking; kitchen work. ～烟 smoke from a kitchen chimney

吹 chuī (动) 1 blow; exhale: 把蜡烛～灭 blow out the candle. ～哨 whistle. ～一口气 breathe out. 雨打风～ weather beaten. ～起床号 sound the reveille 2 play (wind instruments): ～笛子 play the flute 3 〈口〉 brag; boast: 自～自擂 blow one's own trumpet. ～得天花乱坠 give an extravagant account of. ～～拍拍 flatter and toady 4 〈口〉 break off; break up; fall through: 她跟她的男朋友～了. She has broken with her boy friend. 原来的计划告～了. The original plan has fallen through.

吹打 chuīdǎ (动) perform with wind and percussion instruments

吹风(風) chuīfēng (动) 1 get in a draught 2 dry (hair, etc.) with a blower: ～器 hair dryer 3 diliberately let out inside information in an informal way: 给大家吹吹风 give people a briefing (usually matters of some importance)

吹拂 chuīfú (动) (of breeze) gently pass; flicker away

吹鼓手 chuīgǔshǒu (名) trumpeter; eulogist

吹灰之力 chuī huī zhī lì with the least effort: 不费～ be as easy as blowing off dust; require little effort

吹毛求疵 chuī máo qiú cī find fault; split hairs; nitpick

吹牛 chuīniú (动) boast; brag: ～拍马 boast and flatter

吹捧 chuīpěng (动) flatter; lavish praise on: 互相～ flatter each other; engage in mutual flattery so as to boost each other's importance

吹嘘 chuīxū (动) brag; lavish praise on oneself or others: 自我～ self-praise

吹奏 chuīzòu (动) play any musical instrument

槌 chuí (名) mallet; beetle: 碾～ pestle. 鼓～儿 drumstick

垂 chuí (动) 1 hang down; droop; let fall: ～柳 drooping willow. ～泪 shed tears 2 〈书〉 approaching: ～老 getting on in years.

垂钓 chuídiào (动) fish with a hook and line; go angling

垂暮 chuímù (名) dusk; before sundown: ～之年 evening of life

垂青 chuíqīng (动)〈书〉 look upon sb. with special favour

垂死 chuísǐ (形) moribund; dying: ～挣扎 put up a last-ditch struggle

垂头(頭)丧(喪)气(氣) chuítóusàngqì (形) crestfallen; dejected; depressed

垂危 chuíwēi (形) critically ill; at one's last gasp

垂涎 chuíxián (动) covet; slaver: ～三尺 drool with envy

垂直 chuízhí (形) vertical

捶 chuí (动) bang; pound: ～背 pound sb.'s back (as in massage). ～胸顿足 beat one's breast and stamp one's feet (in deep sorrow, etc.); be mad with grief

锤 chuí (名) hammer

锤炼(煉) chuíliàn (动) 1 temper 2 polish

春 chūn (名) 1 spring: ～风 spring breeze. ～意 savour of springtime 2 life; vitality: 妙手回～. Expert medical knowledge brings the dying back to life. 3 love; lust; stirrings of love

春播 chūnbō (名) spring sowing

春耕 chūngēng (名) spring ploughing

春光 chūnguāng (名) scenes of spring: ～明媚 the enchanting beauty of springtime

春季 chūnjì (名) the spring season; spring

春节(節) Chūnjié (名) the Spring Festival

春秋 chūnqiū (名) 1 spring and autumn; year 2 age: ～正富 in the prime of youth

春色 chūnsè (名) spring scenery: ～满园 a garden permeated with

the charms of springtime
春天 chūntiān (名) spring; springtime

淳 chún (形)〈书〉 pure; honest: ～厚 kind and honest. ～朴 simple-hearted and honest

醇 chún I (名)〈书〉 mellow wine; good wine II (形) pure; mellow; rich: 酒味～. The wine is mellow.

唇 chún (名) lip: 上(下)～ upper (lower) lip
唇膏 chúngāo (名) lipstick
唇枪(槍)舌剑(劍) chúnqiāng-shéjiàn cross verbal swords; argue heatedly
唇舌 chúnshé (名) argument: 费一番～ take a lot of explaining or arguing. 白费～ a waste of breath

纯 chún (形) 1 pure; unmixed: ～毛 pure wool 2 pure and simple: ～系无稽之谈. It's nonsense, pure and simple. 3 accomplished: 工夫不～. The skill is far from accomplished.
纯粹 chúncuì (形) 1 pure; unadulterated 2 simply; purely: 这～是为目前打算. This is purely meant to serve the present purposes.
纯洁(潔) chúnjié (形) pure; unselfish and honest: 心地～ pure in thought
纯净 chúnjìng (形) pure; clean
纯利 chúnlì (名) net profit
纯朴(樸) chúnpǔ (形) simple; unsophisticated: ～敦厚 simple and honest
纯熟 chúnshú (形) skilful; well versed: 技术～ highly skilled
纯真 chúnzhēn (形) pure; sincere: ～无邪 pure and innocent
纯正 chúnzhèng (形) pure; unadulterated: 酒味～. The wine has a pure taste. 动机～ have no selfish motives
纯种(種) chúnzhǒng (名) purebred ～牛 purebred cattle

蠢 chǔn (形) stupid; foolish: ～笨 clumsy; awkward. ～货 idiot; fool
蠢动(動) chǔndòng (动) 1 wriggle 2 create disturbances

戳 chuō (动) jab; poke; thrust: 在纸上～个洞 poke a hole in the paper
戳穿 chuōchuān (动) 1 puncture 2 lay bare; expose: ～谎言 give the lie to sth.
戳子 chuōzi (名)〈口〉 stamp; seal

辍 chuò (动)〈书〉 stop; cease: ～学 discontinue one's studies

啜 chuò (动) sob: ～泣 sob

绰 chuò (形)〈书〉 ample; spacious: ～～有余 more than enough
绰号(號) chuòhào (名) nickname

疵 cī (名) flaw; defect: ～点 flaw; fault

呲 cī 〈口〉 give a tongue-lashing: 挨了一顿～儿 get a good talking-to

瓷 cí (名) porcelain; china: ～器 porcelain; chinaware

慈 cí I (形) kind; loving
慈爱(愛) cí'ài (名) kindly affection
慈悲 cíbēi (名) mercy; benevolence; pity: 发～ have pity; be merciful
慈母 címǔ (名) loving mother
慈善 císhàn (形) charitable; benevolent; philanthropic: ～事业 charities
慈祥 cíxiáng (形) kindly: ～的面容 a kindly face

磁 cí (名) 1 magnetism: ～铁 magnet. ～场 magnetic field 2 porcelain; china
磁带 cídài (名) tape: ～录音机 tape recorder

雌 cí (名) female
雌雄 cí-xióng (名) male and female: 决一～ have a showdown (to see which side will emerge victorious)

辞(辭) cí I(名) 1 diction; phraseology: 修～ rhetoric 2 a form of classical Chinese II (动) 1 take leave 2 decline 3 dismiss; resign 4 shirk: 不～劳苦 spare no effort
辞别 cíbié (动) bid farewell to; say good-bye to
辞呈 cíchéng (名) (written) resignation: 提出～ submit (or hand in) one's resignation
辞典 cídiǎn (名) dictionary; lexicon
辞令 cílìng (名) language appropriate to the occasion: 外交～ diplomatic language. 善于～ good at speech; eloquent
辞让(讓) círàng (动) politely decline
辞退 cítuì (动) dismiss; discharge
辞谢 cíxiè (动) decline with

thanks
辞行 cíxíng (动) say good-bye to friends or relatives before setting out on a journey
辞藻 cízǎo (名) flowery language; rhetoric
辞职(職) cízhí (动) resign
词 cí (名) 1 〈语〉 word; term: 同义～ synonym. 反义～ antonym. 技术～ technical term 2 speech; statement: 开幕～ opening speech. 台～ lines (of an opera or play) 3 classical poetry conforming to a definite pattern: 宋～ such poems of the Song Dynasty
词典 cídiǎn (名) dictionaty; lexicon
词法 cífǎ (名) morphology
词汇(匯) cíhuì (名) vocabulary
词句 cíjù (名) words and phrases; expressions
词类(類) cílèi (名) part of speech
词序 cíxù (名) word order
词义(義) cíyì (名) the meaning of a word
词源 cíyuán (名) etymology
词藻 cízǎo (名) rhetoric
词缀 cízhuì (名) affix
词组 cízǔ (名) word group; phrase
祠 cí (名) ancestral temple: ～堂 ancestral hall
此 cǐ (代) this: ～处 this place; here. ～人 this man. ～等 this kind. ～辈 such people
此后(後) cǐhòu (副) after this; hereafter
此刻 cǐkè (副) at this moment; now
此路不通 cǐ lù bù tōng (名) 1 Not a Through Road (road sign) 2 blind alley
此起彼伏 cǐqǐ-bǐfú (动) rise and fall alternately; recur
此时(時) cǐshí (副) right now: ～此刻 at this very moment. ～此地 here and now
此外 cǐwài (副) besides; moreover; in addition
此致 cǐzhì greetings written at the end of a letter addressed to somebody by name
次 cì I (名) order; sequence: 依～ one by one in due order. 车～ train number. 五～列车 train No. 5 II (形) 1 second; next: ～日 next day 2 second-rate; inferior: ～品 goods of poor quality; defective goods III (量): 三～ three times. 首～ first time
次大陆(陸) cìdàlù (名) subcontinent
次等 cìděng (形) second-class; inferior
次品 cìpǐn (名) substandard products; defective goods
次数(數) cìshù (名) number of times; frequency: ～不多 not very often
次序 cìxù (名) order; sequence
次要 cìyào (形) less important; secondary; minor
刺 cì I (名) thorn; splinter: 鱼～ small bone of a fish. 手上扎了个～ get a thorn (or splinter) in one's hand. 她说话带～. There was a ring of sarcasm in her words. II (动) 1 prick; stab 2 assassinate: 被～ be assassinated 3 irritate; criticize: 讽～ satirize
刺刀 cìdāo (名) bayonet
刺耳 cì'ěr (形) ear-piercing; unpleasant to the ear: ～的话 harsh words
刺骨 cìgǔ (形) cut to the bone; piercing
刺激 cìjī I (名) stimulate; shock: 物质～ material incentive II (动) upset; irritate: 这一不幸的消息给了她很大的～. She was upset by the bad news.
刺杀(殺) cìshā (名) 1 assassination 2 bayonet charge
刺探 cìtàn (动) make secret inquiries; pry; spy: ～军情 gather military intelligence
刺猬 cìwèi (名) hedgehog
刺绣 cìxiù (名) embroidery
刺眼 cìyǎn (形) dazzling; offending to the eye: 亮得～ dazzlingly bright. 打扮得～ be loudly dressed
赐 cì (名) grant; favour; gift: 赏～ grant (or bestow) a reward. 请即～复. Be so kind as to give me a prompt reply.
伺 cì
see also sì
伺候 cìhou (动) wait on; serve: 难～ hard to please; fastidious
聪(聰) cōng
聪慧 cōnghuì (形) bright; intelligent
聪明 cōngmíng (形) intelligent; bright; clever: ～能干 bright and capable
聪颖 cōngyǐng (形) intelligent; bright

匆 cōng (副) hurriedly; hastily: 来去～～ pay sb. a flying visit; make hurried visits

匆促 cōngcù (副) hastily; in a hurry: 时间～ be pressed for time

匆忙 cōngmáng (副) hastily; in a hurry: 走得很～ leave in a hurry

葱 cōng (名) 1 onion; scallion: 大～ green Chinese onion. 小～ spring onion. 洋～ onion 2 green

葱翠 cōngcùi (形) fresh green

葱花 cōnghuā (名) chopped spring onion

葱绿 cōnglǜ (形) pale yellowish green

从(從) cōng

see also cóng

从容 cōngróng (形) calm; unhurried; leisurely:～不迫 remain cool-headed and steady. 时间很～. There's still plenty of time.

淙 cóng

淙淙 cóngcóng (象) gurgling: 流水～ a gurgling stream

从(從) cóng I (介) [used to indicate the starting point] from; pass by: ～现在起 from now on. 河水～桥下流过. The river flows by under the bridge. 火车～这个隧道通过. The train passes through this tunnel. ～东到西 from east to west. ～昏迷中醒过来 regain consciousness (from a coma). ～理论上讲 theoretically speaking II (副) [equivalent to 从来 when used before a negative word] ever: 我～没去过意大利. I've never been to Italy. III (动) 1 follow; obey; adopt: ～命 comply with sb.'s wish. ～宽处理 treat leniently 2 join: ～军 join the army; enlist IV(名) 1 follower; attendant: 随～ attendant 2 secondary; accessary: 主～ the primary and the secondary

see also cōng

从此 cóngcǐ (副) from now on; since then; henceforth

从…到… cóng...dào... (介) from ... to ... : 从早到晚 from morning till night. 从古到今 from ancient times to the present. 从头到尾 from beginning to end. 从上到下 from top to bottom; from the higher levels to grass roots

从而 cóng'ér (连) thus; thereby

从犯 cóngfàn (名) accessary

从简 cóngjiǎn conform to the principle of simplicity

从句 cóngjù (名) subordinate clause

从来(來) cónglái (副) always; all along: 他～没提过这事. He's never mentioned this before.

从略 cónglüè (动) be omitted: 此处引文～. The quotation is omitted here.

从前 cóngqián (副) before; in the past; formerly: 他～不是这样. He wasn't like this before.

从事 cóngshì (动) 1 go in for; be engaged in: ～科研工作 be engaged in scientific research. ～文学创作 take up writing as a profession; be engaged in literary work. ～技术革新 work on technical innovations. 2 deal with: 慎重～ act cautiously; steer a cautious course

从属(屬) cóngshǔ (形) subordinate: ～地位 subordinate status

从速 cóngsù (副) as soon as possible; without delay: ～处理 attend to the matter as soon as possible

从小 cóngxiǎo (副) from childhood:他～就喜欢画画. He's loved painting ever since he was a child.

从中 cóngzhōng (副) out of; from among; therefrom: ～渔利 profit from. ～吸取教训 draw a lesson from it

丛(叢) cóng (名) 1 clump; thicket: 树～ bush; shrubbery 2 a group of people or things

丛林 cónglín (名) jungle; forest

丛生 cóngshēng (动) grow thickly: 荆棘～ be overgrown with brambles

丛书(書) cóngshū (名) a series of books; collection: 自学～ self-study series

凑 còu (动) 1 put (or gather) together; pool: ～在一起 crowd together. ～钱 raise a fund 2 happen by chance; take advantage of: 正～上是个星期天. It happened to be a Sunday. 3 move close to

凑合 còuhe I (动) 1 gather together 2 make do: 有什么就～着用什么吧. Let's make do with what we have. II (形) passable: 他的英文还～. His English is not too bad.

凑巧 còuqiǎo (副) luckily; by coincidence; as luck would have it: 真不～! 他出去了. What bad luck! He's not in.
凑趣儿 còuqùr (动) show a similar interest (just to please sb.)
凑热(熱)闹 còu rènào (动) 1 join in the fun 2 add trouble to: 他们够忙的了,别再去～了. They're busy enough as it is. Leave them alone.
凑数(數) còushù (动) make up the number or amount
粗 cū I (形) 1 thick: ～绳 a thick rope 2 coarse; crude; rough: ～沙纸 coarse sandpaper. ～盐 crude salt. 活干得很～. The work is crudely done. 3 husky; hoarse (of sb.'s voice): ～声～气 with a gruff voice 4 careless; negligent: ～疏 be careless. ～心大意 be negligent 5 rude; coarse; unrefined: ～人 a blunt man. ～里～气 rough II (副) roughly: ～具规模 roughly put sth. into shape
粗暴 cūbào (形) rude; rough; brutal (of behaviour)
粗笨 cūbèn (形) clumsy; unwieldy
粗糙 cūcāo (形) rough; coarse; crude: 皮肤～ rough skin. 作工～ crudely made; of poor workmanship
粗茶淡饭 cūchá-dànfàn (名) homely meal
粗犷(獷) cūguǎng (形) 1 rugged; straightforward and uninhibited 2 rough; boorish
粗话 cūhuà (名) coarse language
粗活 cūhuó (名) heavy manual labour; unskilled work
粗粮(糧) cūliáng (名) coarse food grain (e.g. maize, sorghum, millet, etc. as distinct from wheat and rice)
粗劣 cūliè (形) of poor quality
粗陋 cūlòu (形) coarse and crude
粗鲁 cūlǔ (形) rude; boorish
粗略 cūlüè (形) rough; sketchy: ～的了解 some rough ideas about sth.
粗浅(淺) cūqiǎn (形) superficial; shallow
粗疏 cūshū (形) careless; inattentive
粗率 cūshuài (形) rough and careless; ill-considered: ～的决定 an ill-considered decision
粗俗 cūsú (形) coarse; unrefined
粗心 cūxīn (形) careless; thoughtless: ～大意 negligent; careless; inadvertent
粗野 cūyě (形) rude; boorish
粗壮(壯) cūzhuàng (形) 1 sturdy; brawny; strong: 身材～ be sturdily built 2 deep and resonant (of sb.'s voice)
粗枝大叶(葉) cūzhī-dàyè (形) crude and careless; sloppy; slapdash
粗制滥(濫)造 cūzhì-lànzào (动) manufacture in a crude and slipshod way
猝 cù (形) <书> sudden; abrupt; unexpected
猝然 cùrán (副) suddenly; abruptly; unexpectedly
簇 cù I (量) cluster; bunch: 一～鲜花 a bunch of flowers II (动) form a cluster; pile up: 花团锦～ rich multicoloured decorations
簇新 cùxīn (形) brand new
醋 cù (名) 1 vinegar 2 jealousy (as in love affairs): 吃～ feel jealous. ～意 (feeling of) jealousy
促 cù I (动) promote; urge II (形) hurried; urgent: 呼吸短～ pant; be short of breath
促成 cùchéng (动) help to bring about; facilitate
促进(進) cùjìn (动) promote; accelerate: ～贸易 promote trade
促使 cùshǐ (动) impel; spur; encourage: ～他人作出更大努力 impel others to greater efforts
促膝谈心 cù xī tánxīn sit side by side and talk intimately; have a heart to heart talk
蹿(躥) cuān (动) leap up
窜(竄) cuān (动) flee; scurry: 东逃西～ flee in all directions. 鼠～ scurry like rats
窜犯 cuānfàn (动) raid: ～边境的匪徒 the bandits that invaded the border area
窜扰(擾) cuànrǎo (动) harass: ～活动 harassment
篡 cuàn (动) usurp: ～权 usurp power. ～位 usurp the throne
篡改 cuàngǎi (动) tamper with; falsify: ～历史 distort history
篡夺(奪) cuànduó (动) usurp; seize
摧 cuī (动) destroy: ～折 break; snap: 无坚不～ all-conquering
摧残(殘) cuīcán (动) wreck; destroy; devastate: ～身体 ruin one's health

摧毁 cuīhuǐ (动) shatter; smash; destroy
摧枯拉朽 cuīkū-lāxiǔ (as easy as) crushing dryweeds and smashing rotten wood

催 cuī (动) hurry; urge; press; speed up: ～办 press sb. to expedite some business matter
催促 cuīcù (动) urge; press; hasten

璀 cuǐ
璀璨 cuǐcàn (形)〈书〉bright: ～夺目 dazzling

淬 cuì (动) temper by dipping in water, oil, etc.; quench: ～火 quench
淬砺(礪) cuìlì (动)〈书〉temper oneself through severe trials

瘁 cuì (名)〈书〉overworked; tired: 心力交～ be physically and mentally tired from overwork

粹 cuì I (形) pure II (名) essence; the best: 精～ essence

啐 cuì (动) spit: ～他一口 spit at him

翠 cuì (形) emerald green; green
翠绿 cuìlǜ (形) emerald green; jade green

脆 cuì (形) 1 fragile; brittle: 这纸太～. This kind of paper is too fragile. 2 crisp: ～梨 crisp pear 3 (of voice) clear: 嗓音～ a crisp voice
脆弱 cuìruò (形) fragile; frail; weak (of health or feelings): 感情～ emotionally fragile

村 cūn (名) village: ～庄 village; hamlet
村镇 cūnzhèn (名) villages and small towns

皴 cūn (形)(of skin) chapped (from the cold); cracked: 孩子的手～了. The child's hands were chapped from the cold.

存 cún (动) 1 exist; live; survive 2 store; keep; preserve: ～粮过冬 store up grain for the winter 3 place sth. for safe keeping; deposit: 把钱～在银行里 put money in a bank. ～自行车 park one's bicycle. ～行李 check one's luggage 4 cherish; harbour: 不～幻想 harbour no illusions
存车(車)处(處) cúnchēchù (名) parking lot (for bicycles)
存档(檔) cúndàng (动) keep in the archives; file
存放 cúnfàng (动) leave in sb's care
存根 cúngēn (名) counterfoil; stub: 支票～ cheque stub
存户 cúnhù (名) depositor
存货 cúnhuò (名) goods in stock: 减价出清～ a clearance sale
存款 cúnkuǎn (名) deposit; bank savings: 活期～ current account. 定期～ deposit or savings account
存亡 cún-wáng live or die; survive or perish: 生死～的战斗 a life-and-death struggle
存心 cúnxīn (副) intentionally; deliberately; on purpose: 我不是～这么做的. I didn't do it on purpose.
存疑 cúnyí (动) leave a question open
存折(摺) cúnzhé (名) deposit book; bankbook

忖 cǔn (动) turn over in one's mind: ～度 ponder; speculate

寸 cùn I (名) *cun*, a unit of length (= 1/30 metre) II (形) little; small: ～进 a little progress. 得～进尺 be insatiable
寸步 cùnbù (名) a tiny step; a single step: ～难行 unable to move a single step. ～不离 follow sb. closely; keep close to sb. ～不让 refuse to yield

磋 cuō (名) consult
磋商 cuōshāng (动) consult: 我们将与有关部门～后决定. We'll make a decision after consultation with the departments concerned.

搓 cuō (动) rub with the hands
搓板 cuōbǎn (名) washboard

蹉 cuō
蹉跎 cuōtuó (动) waste time: ～岁月 idle away one's time

撮 cuō I (动) scoop up II (量) pinch: 一～盐 a pinch of salt. 一小～匪徒 a handful of bandits
撮合 cuōhé (动) make a match; act as go-between
撮弄 cuōnòng (动) 1 make fun of; play a trick on; tease 2 abet; instigate; incite

措 cuò (动) arrange; manage; handle: ～置得当 be handled properly. 惊慌失～ be seized with panic. 不知所～ be at a loss what to do; be at one's wit's end
措辞(辭) cuòcí (名) wording;

diction: ～不当 inappropriate wording. ～强硬 strongly worded

措施 cuòshī (名) measure; suitable action:采取重大～ adopt an important measure

措手不及 cuò shǒu bù jí be caught unprepared: 打他个～ make a surprise attack on them

措置 cuòzhì (动) handle; manage; arrange: ～得当 be handled properly

错 cuò I (名) mistake; error; fault: 她没～,别怪她. It's not her fault, don't blame her. II (形) 1 wrong; mistaken; erroneous: ～字 wrong character. 你弄～了. You've got it wrong. 东西拿～了 take sth. by mistake 2 interlocked and jagged: 犬牙交～ jigsaw-like; interlocking. ～综复杂 intricate; complex III (动) 1 alternate; stagger: 把他们的假期～开. Stagger their holidays. 2 grind; rub: ～牙 grind one's teeth

错爱(愛) cuò'ài 〈名〉〈谦〉 undeserved kindness

错怪 cuòguài (动) blame sb. wrongly

错过(過) cuòguò (动) miss; let slip: ～机会 miss an opportunity

错觉(覺) cuòjué 〈名〉 illusion; misconception: 这样会给人造成～. This will give people a false impression.

错乱(亂) cuòluàn (形) in disorder: 精神～ insane

错落 cuòluò strewn at random: ～不齐 scattered here and there

错误 cuòwù I (名) mistake; error: 犯～ make a mistake; commit an error. ～百出 full of mistakes II (形) wrong; mistaken; erroneous: ～的结论 wrong conclusion

错综复(複)杂(雜) cuòzōng-fùzá (形) intricate; complex

挫 cuò (动) 1 frustrate; defeat 2 subdue; lower: ～其锋芒 blunt the edge of one's advance. ～敌人的锐气 deflate the enemy's arrogance

挫败 cuòbài (动)frustrate;thwart; defeat

挫伤(傷) cuòshāng I (名) bruise II (动) discourage

挫折 cuòzhé (名) setback; reverse: 遭受～ suffer setbacks

锉 cuò I (名) file: ～刀 file II (动)make smooth with a file; file

Dd

搭 dā (动) 1 put up; build: ～桥 put up a bridge. ～帐篷 pitch a tent 2 hang over; put over 3 come into contact; join: 他们已经～上了关系. They have established contact. 4 add; chip in: 我现在只能～上二三十元钱. I can only afford to put in some twenty or thirty *yuan* at the moment. 5 carry: 请你把我这台电视机～回家吧. Please help carry this T.V. set home (in your car). 6 take (a ship, plane, etc.); travel (or go) by: ～火车去上海 go to Shanghai by train. ～长途汽车 travel by coach. 你～我的车吧. Let me give you a lift in my car.

搭档(檔) dādàng I (动) cooperate; team up II (名) partner:老～ old partner

搭伙 dāhuǒ (动) 1 join as one the party going somewhere 2 eat regularly in (a mess, etc.)

搭救 dājiù (动) rescue; go to one's rescue

搭配 dāpèi I (动) arrange (in pairs or group); combine II (名) collocation

搭腔 dāqiāng (动) answer; respond: 我提醒他约会时间,但他没有～. I reminded him of the appointment, but he didn't make any response.

搭讪 dāshàn (动) strike up a conversation with sb.; make some humorous remarks to save face

答 dā

see also dá

答理 dāli (动) [often used in a negative sentence] respond; acknowledge sb.'s greeting, etc.:他甚至不～我. He didn't even return my greeting.

答应(應) dāying (动) 1 answer; reply; respond: 我敲了几下门,但没人～. I knocked at the door several times, but there was no answer. 2 promise; agree: 他～帮我的忙. He promised to help me.

耷 dā (形)〈书〉big-eared

耷拉 dāla (动) droop; hang down: 他～着肩膀. His shoulders drooped.

达(達) dá (动) 1 reach; attain: 我们不～目的决不罢休. We will never give up until we achieve our goal. 总数已～三千. The total figure has reached 3,000. 2 express; convey; communicate: 下～命令 give orders. 词不～意. Words fail to convey one's ideas. 通情～理 be understanding and reasonable 3 extend: 铁路四通八～. The railways extend in all directions.

达成 dáchéng (动) reach; conclude: ～一项协议 reach an agreement. ～交易 strike a bargain

达旦 dádàn (副) until dawn

达到 dádào (动) achieve; attain; reach: ～目的 achieve (or attain) the goal. ～要求 meet the requirements. ～高潮 come to a climax

达官贵人 dáguān-guìrén (名) high-ranking officials; dignitaries

打 dá (量) dozen: 一～袜子 a dozen socks. 论～出售 sell by the dozen

see also dǎ

答 dá (动) 1 answer; reply; respond: ～非所问 make an irrelevant reply 2 return (a visit, etc.); reciprocate: ～礼 return a salute

see also dā

答案 dá'àn (名) answer; solution; 问题的～ solution to the problem. 练习～ key to an exercise

答辩(辯) dábiàn (名) reply (to a charge, query or an argument): ～会 oral examination for M.A. or Ph.D. candidates, etc.

答复(復) dáfù (动、名) reply (formally)

答谢 dáxiè (动) extend appreciation (for sb.'s kindness or hospitality): ～宴会 a return banquet

沓 dá (量) pile (of paper; etc.); pad: 一～报纸 a pile of newspapers. 一～信纸 a pad of letter paper

see also tà

打 dǎ (动) 1 stride; hit; beat: ～稻子 thresh rice 2 break; smash. 碗～了. The bowl is broken. 3 fight; attack: ～仗 fight a battle. ～游击 fight as a guerrilla 4 construct; build: ～坝 construct a dam. ～基础 lay a foundation 5 make (in a smithy); forge: ～首饰 make jewellery. ～刀 forge a knife 6 knit; weave: ～草鞋 plait straw sandals. ～毛衣 knit a sweater 7 make a mark on; draw: ～手印 put one's fingerprint (on a document). ～印 mimeograph. ～问号 put a question mark. ～格子 draw squares (on paper etc.) 8 tie up: ～行李 pack one's luggage; pack up 9 spray; spread: ～农药 spray insecticide. 在地板上～蜡 wax the floor 10 dig; bore: ～井 dig (or sink) a well. 11 raise; hoist: ～伞 hold (or put) up an umbrella. ～起精神来 raise one's spirits 12 send; dispatch: ～电报 send a telegram. ～电话 make a phone call. ～信号 give a signal. ～枪 fire a gun 13 remove; get rid of: ～旁杈 prune the side branches 14 draw; fetch: ～开水 fetch boiled water. 从井里～水 draw water from a well 15 collect; reap: ～柴 gather firewood. ～了一千斤粮食 get in 1,000 *jin* of grain 16 buy: ～油 buy oil. ～饭 buy food and take it out from a canteen 17 catch; hunt: ～渔 catch fish. ～鸟 shoot a bird 18 work out; draw: ～草稿 draw a draft 19 do; engage in: ～短工 work as a seasonal labourer. ～夜班 be on the night shift 20 play: ～篮球 play basketball. ～太极拳 do *taiji* (shadow boxing). ～扑克 play cards. 21[indicate certain body movements]: ～哆嗦 shiver. ～手势 make a gesture. ～喷嚏 sneeze 22 adopt; use: ～个比方(喻) draw an analogy 23 from; since: 你～哪儿来? Where did you come from? ～那以后 since then 24 estimate; reckon: 成本～二百块钱 estimate the cost at 200 *yuan*

see also dá

打败 dǎbài (动) 1 defeat; beat 2 suffer a defeat; be defeated

打扮 dǎban (动) dress up; make up; deck out

打抱不平 dǎ bàobùpíng interfere on behalf of the injured party

打草惊(驚)蛇 dǎ cǎo jīng shé act rashly and alert the enemy: 不要～. Let the sleeping dogs lie.

打岔 dǎchà (动) interrupt; cut in: 别～吧，我还没说完呢. Don't interrupt me, please! I haven't finished yet.

打场(場) dǎcháng (动) thresh grain

打成一片 dǎchéng yīpiàn become one with; identify oneself with

打倒 dǎdǎo (动) overthrow; down with

打得火热(熱) dǎde huǒrè be very thick with each other

打动(動) dǎdòng (动) move; touch: 这番话～了他的心. He was moved by these words.

打赌 dǎdǔ (动) bet; wager: 我敢～，他明天准来. I bet he'll come tomorrow.

打发(發) dǎfa (动) 1 send; dispatch: 赶快～人去请医生. Send for a doctor at once. 2 dismiss; send away: 他把孩子们～走了. He sent the children away. 3 while away (one's time)

打翻 dǎfān (动) overturn; capsize: 一个大浪把小船～了. A huge wave capsized the boat.

打断(斷) dǎduàn (动) 1 break 2 interrupt: ～思路 interrupt sb.'s train of thought. ～别人的话 cut sb. short

打盹儿 dǎdǔnr (动) doze off; take a nap

打躬作揖 dǎgōng-zuōyī bow and scrape

打官腔 dǎ guānqiāng speak in bureaucratic jargon

打官司 dǎ guānsi I (动) go to law II (名) <口> squabble

打鼾 dǎhān (动) snore

打火 dǎhuǒ (动) strike sparks from a flint: ～机 lighter

打击(擊) dǎjī I (动) hit; strike; attack II (名) blow; attack

打架 dǎjià (动) engage in a brawl; come to blows; fight

打交道 dǎ jiāodao (动) have dealings with; come into contact with: 那个人容易～. That chap is easy to get along with.

打搅(攪) dǎjiǎo (动) disturb; trouble: 请别～. Please do not disturb.

打劫 dǎjié (动) rob; plunder; loot: 趁火～ loot a burning house

打开(開) dǎkāi (动) 1 open; unfold: ～窗户 open the window. 把盖子～ take off the lid. ～天窗说亮话 frankly speaking 2 turn on; switch on: ～收音机(电灯) turn on the radio (light)

打瞌睡 dǎ kēshuì (动) doze off; nod

打捞(撈) dǎlāo (动) get out of the water; salvage: ～沉船 salvage a sunken ship

打量 dǎliang (动) measure with the eye; size up: 上下～ look sb. up and down

打猎(獵) dǎliè (动) go hunting

打乱(亂) dǎluàn (动) throw into confusion; upset: ～计划 disrupt a plan; upset a scheme

打落水狗 dǎ luòshuǐgǒu completely crush a defeated enemy

打马虎眼 dǎ mǎhuyǎn pretend to be ignorant of sth. (in order to gloss it over); act dumb

打埋伏 dǎ máifu (动) 1 lie in ambush; set an ambush; ambush 2 hold sth. back for one's own use

打破 dǎpò (动) break; smash: ～僵局 break a deadlock. ～记录 break a record. ～沙锅问到底 insist on getting to the bottom of the matter

打气(氣) dǎqì (动) 1 inflate; pump up: 给车胎～ inflate (or pump up) a tyre. ～筒 tyre pump 2 bolster up (or boost) the morale; encourage

打趣 dǎqù (动) tease; make fun of

打扫(掃) dǎsǎo (动) clean; sweep: ～房间 clean a room

打手 dǎshǒu (名) hired roughneck (or thug); hatchet man

打算 dǎsuàn I (动) plan; intend II (名) plan; intention

打碎 dǎsuì (动) break into pieces; smash: 花瓶～了. The vase is smashed to pieces.

打胎 dǎtāi (动) have an (induced) abortion

打铁(鐵) dǎtiě (动) forge iron: 趁热～ strike while the iron's hot

打听(聽) dǎting (动) ask about; inquire about: 你可以去附近派出所～一下. You can make inquiries at the police station nearby.

打通 dǎtōng (动) get through; open up: 湖底～一条甬道. A passage was tunelled under the lake. ～思想 talk sb. round

打退堂鼓 dǎ tuìtánggǔ beat a retreat; back out

打消 dǎxiāo (动) give up; dispel: 她～了出国的念头. She gave up the idea of going abroad.

打油诗 dǎyóushī (名) doggerel;

ragged verse
打杂(雜)儿 dǎzár (动) do odds and ends
打战(戰) dǎzhàn (动) shiver; tremble; shudder: 她吓得浑身～. She trembled with fear.
打仗 dǎzhàng (动) fight a battle; go to war
打招呼 dǎ zhāohū (动) 1 greet sb. (by word or gesture) 2 notify; inform; give sb. a tip
打折扣 dǎ zhékòu (动) 1 sell at a discount; give a discount 2 fall short of a requirement or promise
打针 dǎzhēn (动) give or receive an injection
打主意 dǎ zhǔyì (动) 1 think of a plan: 打定主意 make up one's mind 2 try to obtain; seek: 他正在打你的主意,要你帮忙呢. He is thinking of enlisting your help.
打字 dǎzì (动) typewrite; type: ～机 typewriter. ～员 typist
打坐 dǎzuò (动)(of a Buddhist or Taoist monk) sit in meditation
大 dà I (形) 1 big; large; great: ～房间 a large room. ～问题 a big problem. ～团结 great unity 2 heavy; strong: ～风～雨 heavy rain and strong wind 3 loud: 声音太～ too loud 4 of age: 你的孩子多～了? How old is your child? 5 eldest: ～哥 eldest brother. 老～ the eldest among the brothers and sisters 6 main; major; general: ～路 main road. ～手术 major operation 7 size: 你穿多～的鞋? What size shoes do you wear? II (副) 1 greatly; fully; in a big way; on a large scale: ～笑 laugh heartily. ～哭 cry bitterly. ～闹一场 make big scene 2 [used to give force to a time word or expression]: ～白天 in broad daylight. ～清早 early in the morning 3 [used after "不" to indicate low degree or frequency] not very; seldom: 她不～会说英语. She doesn't speak much English. 我不～出门. I seldom go out.
see also dài
大白 dàbái (动) come out; become known: 真相～. The truth has been brought to light.
大半 dàbàn I (名) more than half; most: 来客中～是妇女. Most of the guests were women. II (副) very likely; most probably: 天气又阴又冷, ～要下雪. It's so cloudy and cold that it's likely to snow.
大本营(營) dàběnyíng (名) base camp; headquarters
大便 dàbiàn (名) bowel movement; shit: ～不通 (suffer from) constipation
大伯 dàbó (名) father's elder brother; uncle
大部 dàbù (名) greater part
大材小用 dàcái xiǎo yòng waste one's talent on a petty job
大臣 dàchén (名) minister (of a monarchy)
大处(處)落墨 dàchù luò mò concentrate on the key points
大吹大擂 dàchuī-dàlèi make a great fanfare; make a big noise
大慈大悲 dàcí-dàbēi (形) infinitely merciful
大打出手 dà dǎ chūshǒu strike violently; attack brutally
大大 dàdà (副) greatly; enormously: 生产效率～提高. Productivity has risen greatly.
大…大… dà…dà… [placed before related nouns, verbs or adjectives as an intensifier]: 大红大绿 loud colours. 大吵大闹 make a scene; set up a terrific racket. 大吃大喝 eat and drink immoderately. 大鱼大肉 plenty of meat and fish
大大咧咧 dàdaliēliē (of a person) careless; casual
大胆(膽) dàdǎn (形) bold; daring; audacious
大刀阔斧 dàdāo-kuòfǔ (副) boldly and resolutely; drastically
大道 dàdào (名) 1 broad road 2 the way to a bright future
大抵 dàdǐ (副) generally speaking; in the main
大地 dàdì (名) the earth: ～回春. Spring returns to the earth.
大典 dàdiǎn (名) grand ceremony
大动(動)脉(脈) dàdòngmài (名) main artery
大豆 dàdòu (名) soybean
大都 dàdū (副) for the most part; mostly
大度 dàdù 〈书〉 magnanimous: ～宽容 magnanimous and tolerant
大队(隊) dàduì (名) 1 production brigade (of a rural people's commune); brigade 2 a large body of: ～人马 large contingent of troops
大多 dàduō (副) for the most

part; mostly
大多数(數) dàduōshù (名) great majority; vast majority; the bulk:
大发(發)雷霆 dà fā léitíng (动) fly into a violent rage
大凡 dàfán (副) generally; in most cases
大方 dàfang (形) natural and poised; unaffected: 举止～ behave with grace and ease. 这衣服款式很～. The style of this dress is in good taste.
大放厥词 dàfàng jué cí (动) spout a stream of empty rhetoric; be full of sound and fury
大粪(糞) dàfèn (名) human excrement; night soil
大腹便便 dàfù piánpián (形) pot-bellied; big-bellied
大概 dàgài I (形) general; rough; approximate: 一个～印象 a general impression. ～数字 an approximate figure II (副) probably: 他～病了. He is probably ill. III (名) general idea: 我只记了个～. I have only some rough idea.
大纲(綱) dàgāng (名) general outline
大公无(無)私 dàgōng-wúsī (形) selfless; unselfish
大功 dàgōng (名) great merit; extraordinary service: 立了～ have performed exceptionally meritorious services. ～告成 be crowned with success
大观(觀) dàguān (名) grand sight: 洋洋～ spectacular; grandiose; imposing
大规模 dàguīmó (副) large-scale; extensive; massive: ～生产 mass production. ～地植树 plan trees on a large scale
大锅(鍋)饭 dàguōfàn (名) food prepared in a big pot: 吃～ with everybody eating from the same big pot
大海捞(撈)针 dàhǎi lāo zhēn look for a needle in a haystack
大好 dàhǎo (形) very good: ～时机 golden opportunity
大合唱 dàhéchàng (名) cantata; chorus
大亨 dàhēng (名) magnate
大话 dàhuà (名) big talk; boast: 说～ talk big; brag
大计 dàjì (名) a programme of lasting importance: 百年～ a matter of fundamental importance for generations to come
大家 dàjiā (名) 1 all; everybody 2 great master; authority: 书法～ a great master of calligraphy
大街 dàjiē (名) main street; avenue; street: 逛～ have a look round in the business centre; go window-shopping
大惊(驚)小怪 dàjīng-xiǎoguài make a fuss over: 有什么值得～的? What's all the fuss about?
大局 dàjú (名) 1 overall public interest: 顾全～ take the interests of the whole into account 2 overall situation: ～已定. There is no doubt about the overall situation.
大快人心 dà kuài rénxīn gratify the popular feeling; to the immense satisfaction of the masses
大力 dàlì (副) vigorously; energetically: ～提倡 make strenuous efforts to promote
大量 dàliàng (名) 1 a large number; a great quantity: ～情报 a vast amount of information. ～财富 enormous wealth. ～事实 a host of facts 2 generous; magnanimous: 宽宏～ magnanimous; large-minded
大楼(樓) dàlóu (名) large building: 居民～ apartment house; block of flats
大陆(陸) dàlù (名) continent; mainland: ～架 continental shelf
大略 dàlüè (副) generally; roughly
大名鼎鼎 dàmíng dǐngdǐng (形) famous; well-known; celebrated
大模大样(樣) dàmú-dàyàng (副) in an ostentatious manner; with a swagger
大逆不道 dà nì bú dào (名) high treason and heresy; worst offence
大年 dànián (名) 1 good year; bumper year; (of fruit trees) on-year 2 lunar year
大批 dàpī (形) large quantities or number: ～工厂 a large number of factories. ～金钱 a large sum (or amount) of money
大气(氣) dàqì (名) 1 atmosphere; air: ～层 atmospheric layer 2 heavy breathing: 跳得直喘～ breathe heavily from running
大权(權) dàquán (名) power over major issues; authority: ～独揽 concentrate power in one man's hands
大人 dàrén (名) 1 adult; grown-up 2 <旧>Your Excellency
大人物 dàrénwù (名) big shot;

dignitary
大扫(掃)除 dàsǎochú (名) thorough clean up
大厦 dàshà (名) large building
大赦 dàshè (名) amnesty; general pardon
大声(聲)疾呼 dàshēng jíhū utter fervent words of warning (usually against danger)
大失所望 dà shī suǒ wàng greatly disappointed
大师(師) dàshī (名) 1 great master: 国画～ a great master of traditional Chinese painting
大师(師)傅 dàshīfu (名) cook; chef
大使 dàshǐ (名) ambassador: ～馆 embassy
大事 dàshì I (名) major event; important matter: 头等～ a matter of vital importance II (副) in a big way: ～渲染 grossly embellish; exaggerate
大势(勢) dàshì (名) general trend of events: ～所趋 the trend of the times. ～已去. The game is up. *or* The situation is hopeless.
大肆 dàsì (副) without restraint; wantonly: ～宣扬 propagate unrestrainedly. ～吹嘘 boast
大…特… dà...tè... [each placed before the same verb or adjective as an intensifier]: 大错特错 be grievously mistaken. 大书特书 write volumes about
大提琴 dàtíqín (名) violoncello; cello
大体(體) dàtǐ I (副) on the whole; by and large; roughly: ～相同 more or less the same II (名) general interest; fundamental principle: 识～,顾大局 keep both the cardinal principles and the overall situation in mind
大庭广(廣)众(衆) dàtíng-guǎngzhòng a big crowd in a big courtyard; in public; openly before everybody
大同小异(異) dàtóng-xiǎoyì (形) similar in major principles but different on minor points
大王 dàwáng (名) king; magnate:
大显(顯)身手 dà xiǎn shēnshǒu display all one's skill or ability
大显(顯)神通 dà xiǎn shéntōng give full play to one's power or remarkable skill
大相径(徑)庭 dà xiāng jìng tíng <书> be widely divergent; seriously contradict each other
大小 dàxiǎo (名) 1 size: 这鞋我穿上～正合适. These shoes are just my size. 2 big or small: ～五个图书馆 five libraries of varying sizes 3 degree of seniority: 说话没个～ speak bluntly to elderly people 4 adults and children: 全家～五口. There are five people in the family altogether.
大写(寫) dàxiě (名) 1 the capital form of a Chinese numeral 2 capitalization: ～字母 capital letter
大修 dàxiū (名) overhaul; heavy repair
大选(選) dàxuǎn (名) general election
大学(學) dàxué (名) university; college: ～生 university (or college) student
大言不惭 dàyán bù cán (动) brag unblushingly
大业(業) dàyè (名) great cause; great undertaking
大衣 dàyī (名) overcoat; topcoat
大义(義)凛然 dàyì lǐnrán be awe-inspiring in defence of a just cause
大义(義)灭(滅)亲 dàyì miè qīn punish one's relatives severely according to law in order to uphold justice
大意 dàyì (名) general idea; main points; gist
大意 dàyi (形) careless: 粗心～ be negligent
大有文章 dà yǒu wénzhāng there's something intricate behind all this apparent simplicity
大有作为(爲) dà yǒu zuòwéi there is plenty of room for one to display one's talents
大约 dàyuē (副) approximately; about: 这部电影～要演两小时. This film will last about two hours.
大张(張)旗鼓 dà zhāng qí-gǔ give wide publicity to sth.; in a big way
大丈夫 dàzhàngfu (名) true man; real man; man
大志 dàzhì (名) lofty aim: 胸怀～ have a great ambition
大致 dàzhì (副) generally; roughly; approximately; more or less
大智若愚 dàzhì ruò yú a man of great wisdom often looks like a dullard
大众(衆) dàzhòng (名) the masses; the people: ～化 popular;

in a popular style. ～歌曲 popular songs for the masses

呆 dāi I (形) 1 slow-witted; dull: ～子 idiot. ～滞 dull, slow-moving. ～头～脑 dull-looking 2 blank; wooden: 吓得发～ be stupefied. ～若木鸡 struck dumb as a wooden chicken; be dumbstruck; transfixed (with fear or amazement) II (动) stay: ～在家里 stay at home

待 dāi (动) ‹口› stay: 他在那里～了三天. He stayed there for three days.
see also dài

歹 dǎi (形) bad; evil; vicious: 为非作～ do evil

歹徒 dǎitú (名) ruffian; evildoer

逮 dǎi (动) capture; catch: 猫～老鼠. Cats catch mice.
see also dài

戴 dài (动) 1 put on; wear: ～上帽子 put on one's hat. ～眼镜 wear glasses 2 respect; honour: 爱～ love and respect

戴罪立功 dàizuì lìgōng atone for one's crimes by doing good deeds

带(帶) dài I (名) 1 belt; girdle; ribbon; band; tape: 皮～ leather belt. 丝～ silk ribbon. 录音～ recording tape. 鞋～ shoelaces 2 tyre: 自行车～ bicycle tyre 3 zone; area; belt: 热～ tropical zone. 这一～ in these areas II (动) 1 take; bring; carry: ～上雨衣. Take your raincoat along. 我能～孩子来吗? Can I bring my children with me? 我没～钱. I haven't any money on me. 2 [suggesting doing sth.at an opportune moment]: 上街时请给～点茶叶来. When you go out, please get me some tea. 3 bear; have; with: 一件～帽的雨衣 a raincoat with a hood. 他面～笑容看着我. He looked at me with a smile. 这梨～点酸味. This pear tastes a bit sour. 4 lead; head: ～队 lead a group of people. ～兵 be in command of troops 5 look after; bring up; raise: ～孩子 look after children. 他是他奶奶～大的. He was brought up by his grandmother.

带劲(勁) dàijìn (形) 1 in high spirits; energetic; forceful 2 interesting; exciting; wonderful: 这场足球赛真～. This football match is terrifically exciting.

带领 dàilǐng (动) lead; guide

带路 dàilù (动) lead the way; act as a guide

带头(頭) dàitóu (动) take the lead; take the initiative; set an example: 起～作用 play a leading role

带孝 dàixiào (动) wear mourning for a parent; be in mourning

带子 dàizi (名) belt; girdle; ribbon; band; tape

大 dài
see also dà

大夫 dàifu (名) doctor; physician

代 dài I (动) take the place of; act for (or on behalf of) others: 我～他去. I'll go in his stead. ～课 take over a class for an absent teacher. 请～我向他问好. Please give him my regards. II (形) acting: ～主任 acting director III (名) 1 historical period: 古～ ancient times. 汉～ the Han Dynasty 2 generation: 元宵节在中国～～相传. The Lantern Festival has been observed in China from generation to generation.

代办(辦) dàibàn I (动) do or act for others: 这件事请你～吧. Could you do this for me? II (名) chargé d'affaires: 临时～ chargé d'affaires ad interim

代表 dàibiǎo I (名) representative; deputy; delegate II (动) represent; stand for: ～时代精神 embody the spirit of the era. 他～学校热烈欢迎我们. He gave us a warm welcome on behalf of their school. ～人物 representative figure (or personage). ～团 delegation; mission. ～大会 congress

代词 dàicí (名) pronoun

代号(號) dàihào (名) code name

代价(價) dàijià (名) price; cost: 不惜任何～ at any cost; at all costs

代劳(勞) dàiláo (动) do sth. for sb.; take trouble on sb.'s behalf: 这事请你～一下. Will you do this for me, please?

代理 dàilǐ (动) 1 act on sb.'s behalf; act for: ～厂长 acting manager of a factory 2 act as agent (or proxy, procurator)

代理人 dàilǐrén (名) agent; deputy; proxy

代替 dàitì (动) replace; substitute (for); take the place of

代言人 dàiyánrén (名) spokesman; mouthpiece

袋 dài (名) 1 bag; sack: 麻～ sack. 外交信～ diplomatic pouch. 邮～ mailbag. 工具～ tool kit 2 (量): 一～面粉 a sack of flour

袋装(裝) dàizhuāng in bags: ～奶粉 milk powder in bags

贷 dài I (名) 1 loan: ～方 credit side. ～款 provide a loan; loan; credit 2 shift (responsibility); shirk: 责无旁～ be duty-bound

待 dài (动) 1 treat; deal with: 平等～人 treat people as one's equals. ～人接物 the way one gets along with people 2 wait for; await: 等～时机 wait for an opportunity to take action; bide one's time. 有～改进 remain to be improved 3 going to; about to: 她到飞机场时,飞机正～起飞. The plane was about to take off when she arrived at the airport.
see also dāi

待续(續) dàixù (动) to be continued

待遇 dàiyù (名) 1 treatment: 最惠国～most-favoured-nation treatment 2 pay; wages; salary: ～优厚 excellent pay and conditions

怠 dài (形) idle; slack

怠惰 dàiduò (形) idle; lazy; indolent

怠工 dàigōng (动) slow down; go slow: 消极～ go slow

怠慢 dàimàn (名) 1 cold-shoulder; slight: 受到～ suffer slights. 不要～了客人. See that none of the guests are neglected. 2 〈套〉 [used as an apology for not having properly entertained a visitor]: ～了! I'm afraid I have been a poor host.

殆 dài I (名)〈书〉 danger: 危～ in great danger II (副) nearly; almost: 敌人伤亡～尽. The enemy were practically wiped out.

逮 dài (名)〈书〉 reach: 力有未～ beyond one's reach
see also dǎi

逮捕 dàibǔ (动) arrest; take into custody: ～证 arrest warrant

单(單) dān I (形) 1 one; single: ～人床 single bed. ～行道 single track. ～裤 unlined trousers 2 odd: ～日 odd days. ～数 odd number II (副) 1 singly; separately; alone: ～人独马 single-handed. 这几张照片要～放着. Keep these photos in a separate place. 2 only; solely; alone: ～凭热情还不够 to work by enthusiasm alone isn't enough. III (名) 1 sheet: 床～ bed sheet 2 bill; list: 名～ name list. 菜～ menu. 帐～ bill

单薄 dānbó (形) 1 (of clothing) thin: 穿得～ be thinly dressed 2 thin and weak; frail 3 poor; flimsy: 论据～ a feeble argument. 内容～ thin in content

单纯 dānchún (形) 1 simple; pure: 思想～ simple-minded 2 alone; merely; purely: 别～追求数量. Don't strive for quantity alone.

单词 dāncí (名) word (as opposite of phrase or sentence)

单打 dāndǎ (名) single: 男子(女子)～ men's (women's) singles

单刀直入 dāndāo zhí rù come straight to the point

单调 dāndiào (形) monotonous; full; drab: 声音～ in a monotonous tone. 色彩～ dull colouring

单独(獨) dāndú (副) alone; by oneself; on one's own: 她～住一套房子. She has a flat to herself. 我要和他～谈一谈. I want to have a talk with him alone.

单据(據) dānjù (名) bill; receipt; voucher

单身 dānshēn (形) 1 single; unmarried 2 live alone: ～汉 bachelor. ～宿舍 quarters for single men or women

单位 dānwèi (名) 1 unit of measurement: 长度～ a unit of length 2 unit of an organization: 行政～ administrative unit. 基层～ grass-roots unit. 你在哪个～工作? Where do you work?

单相思 dānxiāngsī (名) unrequited love

单行本 dānxíngběn (名) offprint; separate edition

单元 dānyuán (名) unit: 二号楼五～ Entrance No. 5, Building 2

单子 dānzi (名) 1 list: 开个～ make out a list 2 bed sheet

单字 dānzì (名) individual character; separate word

殚(殫) dān (动)〈书〉exhaust: ～精竭虑 rack one's brains

耽 dān

耽搁 dānge (名) 1 stop over;

stay: 我在去纽约途中，要在旧金山～一两天. I'll stop over in San Francisco for a day or two on my way to New York. 2 delay: 这项调查不能～. This investigation must not be delayed.

耽误 dānwù （动） hinder; hold up; spoil sth. because of delay: ～功夫 waste time. 别把病～了. Seek medical advice in time.

担(擔) dān （动） 1 carry on a shoulder pole: ～水 carry water 2 take on; undertake: ～风险 take (or run) risks. 承～全部责任 take on full responsibility

see also dàn

担保 dānbǎo （动） assure; guarantee: 出口信贷～ export credit guarantees. ～人 guarantor; guarantee

担当(當) dāndāng （动） take on; undertake; assume: 我情愿～这个责任. I am willing and ready to shoulder the responsibility.

担负 dānfù （动） bear; shoulder; take on: ～一项任务 take on a task. ～费用 bear the expenses

担架 dānjià （名） stretcher; litter

担惊(驚)受怕 dānjīng-shòupà be stricken with anxiety and fear

担任 dānrèn （动） hold the post of; take charge of: ～领导职务 assume a leading position. ～会议主席 take the chair

担心 dānxīn （动） worry; feel anxious: ～她的健康 worry about her health

丹 dān （形） red

丹青 dānqīng （名） 〈书〉painting: ～妙笔 superb artistry (in painting)

丹田 dāntián （名） the pubic region: ～之气 deep breath controlled by the diaphragm

丹心 dānxīn （名） a loyal heart; loyalty

掸(撣) dǎn （动） brush lightly; whisk: ～掉身上的雪花 brush the snow off one's coat

掸子 dǎnzi （名） duster: 鸡毛～ feather duster

胆(膽) dǎn （名） 1 gallbladder 2 courage; guts; bravery: 壮～ fortify sb.'s spirit 3 inner container: 热水瓶～ the glass liner of a thermos flask

胆大 dǎndà （形） bold; audacious: ～包天 extremely daring; foolhardy. ～妄为 reckless and defiant

胆敢 dǎngǎn （动） dare; venture; have the courage to: ～一试 dare to try

胆寒 dǎnhán （动） be terrified; be struck with terror

胆量 dǎnliàng （名） courage; guts: 很有～ have a lot of guts

胆略 dǎnlüè （名） courage and resourcefulness: ～过人 be exceptionally courageous and resourceful

胆怯 dǎnqiè （形） timid; shy

胆小 dǎnxiǎo （形） chicken-hearted; timid; cowardly: ～鬼 coward

胆战(戰)心惊(驚) dǎnzhàn-xīnjīng （动） tremble with fear

胆子 dǎnzi （名） courage; nerve: 好大的～! What a nerve!

惮(憚) dàn （名） 〈书〉 fear; dread

弹(彈) dàn （名） 1 ball; pellet 2 bullet; bomb: ～坑 shell crater. ～药 ammunition. ～头 warhead

see also tán

弹道 dàndào （名） trajectory: ～导弹 ballistic missile. ～火箭 ballistic rocket

弹药 dànyào （名） ammunition: ～库 ammunition depot (or storehouse)

弹子 dànzi （名） 1 a pellet shot from a slingshot 2 marble: 打～ play marbles 3 billiards

淡 dàn （形） 1 thin; light: 天高云～. The sky is high; the clouds are pale. ～绿 light (or pale) green 2 tasteless; weak: ～茶 weak tea. ～而无味 tasteless 3 indifferent; apathetic: 冷～ cold; distant 4 slack; dull: 生意清～. Business is slack. 5 meaningless; trivial: 扯～ talk nonsense

淡泊 dànbó （形） not seek fame and wealth

淡薄 dànbó （形） 1 thin; light 2 (of feelings, interest, etc.) flag: 他对象棋的兴趣逐渐～了. His interest in chess has begun to flag. 3 (of impression) faint; dim; hazy: 他童年的印象已经～了. His childhood memories have grown dim.

淡季 dànjì （名） off season

淡漠 dànmò （形） 1 indifferent; apathetic 2 faint; dim; hazy

淡水 dànshuǐ （名） fresh water

淡雅 dànyǎ （形） simple and in

good taste

啖 dàn (动)〈书〉 1 eat 2 feed 3 entice; lure

氮 dàn (名) nitrogen: ～肥 nitrogenous fertilizer

诞 dàn I (名) 1 birth 2 birthday II (形) absurd; fantastic: 荒～ fantastic

诞辰 dànchén (名) birthday

诞生 dànshēng (动) be born; come into being; emerge

旦 dàn (名) 1〈书〉 dawn; daybreak: 元～ New Year's Day 2 the female character type in Beijing opera, etc.

旦夕 dànxī 〈书〉 in a short while: 危在～ in imminent danger

担(擔) dàn (名) 1 *dan*, a unit of weight (50 kilograms) 2 a carrying pole and the loads on it; load;burden see also dān

担子 dànzi (名) load; burden; task: 他的工作～重. His workload is heavy.

但 dàn (连) but; yet; nevertheless

但是 dànshì (连) but; yet; still; nevertheless

但书(書) dànshū (名) proviso

但愿 dànyuàn if only; I wish: ～他能及时赶到. If only he could arrive in time! ～如此. I wish it were true!

蛋 dàn (名) 1 egg 2 an egg-shaped thing: 泥～儿 mud ball

蛋白 dànbái (名) egg white

蛋白质(質) dànbáizhì (名) protein

蛋糕 dàngāo (名) cake

蛋黄 dànhuáng (名) yolk

当(當) dāng I (动) 1 work as; serve as: 他想～教员. He wants to be a teacher. 2 bear; accept; deserve: 敢做敢～ be ready to act boldly and take full responsibility for it 3 manage; be in charge of: ～家 run the household 4 should; ought to II (形) equal: 实力相～ nearly equal in strength III (副) 1 in sb.'s presence; to sb.'s face: ～着大家谈一谈. Let's hear what you have to say. 2 when; just at a certain place: 当…的时候 [used at the beginning of a sentence as an adverbial adjunct] when …; at the time…
see also dàng

当兵 dāngbīng (动) get into uniform; join the army

当场(場) dāngchǎng (副) on the spot; then and there: ～抓住 catch red-handed

当初 dāngchū (副) originally; in the beginning; in the first place: ～这儿是一片沙漠. This area was a desert in the past. 记得～怎么对你讲的? Remember what I told you, eh?

当代 dāngdài (名) the present age: ～文学 contemporary literature

当道 dāngdào I (名) the middle of the road: 别在～站着. Don't stand in the way. II (动) be in power; hold sway

当地 dāngdì (形) in the locality; local: ～人 local people. ～时间 local time

当机(機)立断(斷) dāng jī lì duàn (动) make a prompt and timely decision

当即 dāngjí (副) at once; right away

当家作主 dāngjiā zuòzhǔ be master in one's own house

当今 dāngjīn (副) now; at present; nowadays: ～之世 in the world of today

当局 dāngjú (名) the authorities: 政府～ the government authorities

当空 dāngkōng (副) high above in the sky: 皓月～. A bright moon is hanging high up in the sky.

当面 dāngmiàn (副) to sb.'s face; in sb.'s presence: ～撒谎 tell a barefaced lie; speak with one's tongue in one's cheek

当年 dāngnián (副) 1 in those years (or days) 2 the prime of life: 他正～.He is in his prime. see also dàngnián

当前 dāngqián (副) 1 present; current: ～的国际形势 the current (or present) international situation 2 be faced with: 大敌～ be confronted by a formidable enemy

当权(權) dāngquán (动) be in power

当然 dāngrán (形) of course; without doubt: 朋友有困难,～要帮助. It goes without saying that we should help a friend in difficulty. ～同盟军 natural ally. 理所～. That is just as it should be. *or* This is a matter of course.

当仁不让(讓) dāng rén bù ràng be ready to tackle anything one is capable of; decline no responsibility that one thinks one ought to bear

当时(時) dāngshí (副) then; at that time

当头(頭) dāngtóu (副) right overhead; 烈日～照. The sun is shining overhead. ～一棒 a head-on blow

当务(務)之急 dāng wù zhī jí a burning issue of the moment; a top priority

当心 dāngxīn (动) look out; take care; be careful: ～, 汽车来了. Look out! there is a car coming. ～路滑. Watch your steps. The road is slippery. ～危险 Look out!

当政 dāngzhèng (动) be in power

当之无愧 dāng zhī wú kuì (动) be worthy of; fully deserve

当众(衆) dāngzhòng (副) in the presence of all; in public

裆(襠) dāng (名) crotch (of trousers)

铛(鐺) dāng (象) clank; clang

see also chēng

挡(擋) dǎng I (动) 1 block; keep off: ～道 block the road; get in the way. ～雨 keep off the rain 2 cover: ～亮 cover the light II (名) gear: 高速(低速)～ top (bottom) gear

挡驾 dǎngjià (动) turn away a visitor with some excuse; decline to see a guest

挡箭牌 dǎngjiànpái (名) 1 shield 2 excuse; pretext

党(黨) dǎng (名) 1 political party: 入～ join the party 2 gang; clique; faction: 死～ sworn follower

党报(報) dǎngbaò (名) 1 party newspaper 2 the Party organ

党纲(綱) dǎnggāng (名) party programme

党籍 dǎngjí (名) party membership: 开除～ expel from the party

党纪 dǎngjì (名) party discipline

党派 dǎngpài (名) political parties and groups

党徒 dǎngtú (名) 1 member of a reactionary political party 2 henchmen

党委 dǎngwěi (名) party committee

党性 dǎngxìng (名) Party spirit

党羽 dǎngyǔ (名) adherents; henchmen

党员 dǎngyuán (名) party member

当(當) dàng I (动) 1 treat as; regard as; take for: 她把他～作自己的亲生儿子. She treats him as her own son. 2 equal to: 他一个人能～两个人用. He can do the work of two persons. 3 think: 我～你不知道. I thought you didn't know. 4 pawn: ～衣服 pawn one's clothes II (形) proper; right: 用词不～ not properly worded; inappropriate wording; wrong choice of words

see also dāng

当年 dàngnián (副) the same year; that very year

当铺 dàngpù (名) pawnshop

当日 dàngrì (副) the same day; that very day: ～有效 valid for the date of issue only

当时(時) dàngshí (副) right away; at once; immediately: 听到这消息, 她～就昏了过去. She fainted the moment she heard the news.

当天 dàngtiān (副) the same day; that very day

当真 dàngzhēn I (副) 1 take seriously: 我只是开个玩笑, 何必～呢? I was only joking. Why take it so seriously? 2 really: 她说想要买一架钢琴, 后来～买了. She said she wanted to buy a piano, and she did. II (形) true: 这话～? Is it really true?

荡(蕩) dàng I (动) 1 swing; sway: ～秋千 play on a swing. ～桨 pull on the oars. 2 loaf: 游～ loaf about 3 clear away; sweep off: ～涤 cleanse; wash away. 扫～ mopping up II (形) of loose morals: 放～ dissolute; dissipated. 淫～ lustful; lascivious III (名) shallow lake; marsh: 芦苇～ a reed marsh

荡漾 dàngyàng (动) ripple; undulate

档(檔) dàng (名) 1 files; archives: 查～ consult the files 2 grade: 高～商品 high-grade goods 3 crosspiece (of a table, etc.)

档案 dàng'àn (名) files; archives; record: ～管理员 archivist

刀 dāo (名) 1 knife; sword ～子 pocketknife 2 sth shaped like a knife: 冰～ ice skates

刀叉 dāo-chā (名) knife and fork

刀口 dāokǒu (名) 1 the edge of a knife 2 the crucial point

cut; incision
刀山火海 dāoshān-huǒhǎi fire and water: 为了正义事业～也敢闯 would go through fire and water for the cause of justice.
刀枪(槍) dāo-qiāng (名) sword and spear; weapons
祷(禱) dǎo (动) pray: ～告 pray; say one's prayers
蹈 dǎo (动) 1 ‹书› tread; step: 赴汤～火 go through fire and water; defy all difficulties and dangers. 循规～矩 observe rules docilely; conform to convention 2 skip: 舞～ dance
倒 dǎo (动) 1 fall; topple: 墙～了. The wall has fallen down. 摔～ fall over. 风把树刮～了. The gale uprooted the tree. 2 collapse; be overthrown; close down: ～台 fall from power. 那家工厂～了. That factory has gone bankrupt. 3 change; exchange: ～车 change trains or buses. ～班 work in shifts
see also dào
倒闭 dǎobì (动) close down; go bankrupt: 银行～ bankruptcy of a bank
倒戈 dǎogē (动) turn one's coat; transfer one's allegiance
倒霉 dǎoméi (形) have bad luck; get into trouble
倒塌 dǎotā (动) collapse; topple down
岛(島) dǎo (名) island: ～国 island country. ～屿 islands
捣(擣) dǎo (动) pound with a pestle, etc.; beat; smash
捣蛋 dǎodàn (动) make trouble: 调皮～ be mischievous
捣鬼 dǎoguǐ (动) play underhand tricks
捣毁 dǎohuǐ (动) smash up; destroy
捣乱(亂) dǎoluàn (动) make trouble; create a disturbance
导(導) dǎo (动) 1 lead; guide; divert 2 transmit; conduct: ～电 electric conduction
导弹(彈) dǎodàn (名) guided missile
导航 dǎoháng (名) navigation
导火线(線) dǎohuǒxiàn (名) 1 (blasting) fuse 2 an apparently insignificant incident leading to a big conflict: 战争的～ an incident that touches off a war
导师(師) dǎoshī (名) 1 tutor; teacher 2 guide of a great cause; teacher
导体(體) dǎotǐ (名) conductor: 非～ nonconductor. 超～ superconductor
导言 dǎoyán (名) introduction; introductory remarks; foreword
导演 dǎoyǎn I (动) direct (a film, play, etc.) II (名) director
导游 dǎoyóu I (名) tourist guide II (动) guide a tour: ～图 tourist map
导致 dǎozhì (动) lead to; result in; bring about; cause: 恶劣的卫生条件常常～许多疾病. Bad sanitary conditions always breed diseases of various kinds.
盗 dào I (动) steal; rob II (名) thief; robber: ～贼 robbers; bandits
盗匪 dàofěi (名) bandits; robbers
盗汗 dàohàn (名) night sweat
盗卖(賣) dàomài (动) steal and sell (public property)
盗窃 dàoqiè (动) steal: ～犯 thief; burglar
盗用 dàoyòng (动) usurp: ～公款 embezzle public funds
悼 dào (动) mourn; grieve: 哀～死者 mourn for the deceased
悼词 dàocí (名) memorial speech; funeral oration: 致～ deliver a funeral oration
悼念 dàoniàn (动) mourn; grieve over: 沉痛～ mourn with deep grief
道 dào I (名) 1 road; way; path: 山间小～ a mountain path. 河～ the course of a river 2 line 划一条红～ draw a red line. 斜～ a slanting line 3 way; method: 养生之～ the way to keep fit. 头头是～ closely reasoned and well argued 4 doctrine; principle 5 Taoism; Taoist: ～观 a Taoist temple. 老～ a Taoist priest II (动) 1 say; speak; talk: 说长～短 idly chatter; gossip: 能说会～ have a glib tongue. 常言～ as the saying goes 2 think; suppose III (量) 1 [for anything in the form of a line]: 一～缝儿 a crack. 两～门 two successive doors. 三～防线 three lines of defence 2 [of orders or questions]: 一～命令 an order. 四～数学题 four maths questions 3 course of dish: 上四～菜 serve four cour-

ses

道德 dàodé (名) morals; morality: ～败坏 degenerate

道贺 dàohè (动) congratulate

道家 Dàojiā (名) Taoist school

道教 Dàojiào (名) Taoism

道具 dàojù (名) stage properties; props

道理 dàoli (名) **1** principle; truth **2** reason; sense; argument: 讲～ appeal to reason

道路 dàolù (名) road; way; path: 为两国首脑会谈铺平～ pave the way for summit talks between the two countries

道貌岸然 dàomào ànrán pose as a person of high morals; look dignified

道歉 dàoqiàn (动) apologize

道谢 dàoxiè (动) express one's gratitude; thank

道义(義) dàoyì (名) morality and justice: ～上的支持 moral support

道听(聽)途说 dàotīng-túshuō (名) hearsay; rumour; gossip

到 dào I (动) **1** arrive; reach: 火车三点钟～. The train arrives at three o'clock. **2** go to; leave for: ～南方去 go to the south. ～我家来 come to (or drop in at) my home. 他～过欧洲. He has been to Europe. II (形) thoughtful; considerate: 不～之处请原谅. Please excuse me if I have not been thoughtful enough. III [used after a verb as a complement to indicate success]: 买～ have bought sth. 找～ find sth. 办得～ can be done. 说～做～ be as good as one's word. 想不～你来了. I didn't expect you would come. IV (介) up until; up to: 从星期一～星期五 from Monday to Friday. ～目前为止 up to the present; so far

到场(場) dàochǎng (动) be present; show up; turn up

到处(處) dàochù (副) at all places; everywhere: 烟头不要～乱扔. Don't drop cigarette ends about.

到达(達) dàodá (动) arrive; get to; reach

到底 dàodǐ (副) **1** to the end; to the finish: 打～ fight to the finish **2** at last; finally; in the end: 可他～还是没去. But he still didn't go in the end. **3** after all; in the final analysis: 他～还是个孩子. After all, he's only a child. **4** [used in an interrogative sentence to indicate an attempt to get to the bottom of the matter]: 你～是什么意思? What on earth do you mean? 你～去不去? Are you going or not?

到来(來) dàolái (名) arrival; advent

到期 dàoqī become due; expire: 这本杂志今天～. The magazine is due for return today. 签证下月～. The visa expires next month.

倒 dào I (动) **1** turn upside down; move backward; reverse; invert: 把瓶子～过来 turn the bottle upside down. ～车 back a car. ～装词序 inverted order **2** pour; tip; dump: ～一杯茶 pour a cup of tea. ～垃圾桶 empty the dustbin II (副) **1** [indicating an opposite effect. cf. 反而]: 我明白你是想帮忙, 但这一来事情～更麻烦了. I know you meant to help but you've made the matter even more complicated. 我看他～还不错. As I see it, he is rather a nice chap. 别看他八十多了, 身体～很结实. Though he is over eighty, he's as sound as a bell. **2** [indicating that while one admits the merits of sth. he points out a drawback]: 那本小说～是有意思, 可太长了. That novel is fairly interesting but too long. 他～没说他不喜欢她. He didn't say (straight away) that he didn't like her. 说起来～容易, 做起来难啊! It's easier said than done. **3** [indicating impatience]: 你～是去呀, 还是不去? Are you going or are you not?
see also dǎo

倒彩 dàocǎi (名) booing; hooting: 喝～ make catcalls

倒打一耙 dào dǎ yī pá make unfounded countercharges; recriminate

倒立 dàolì (动) stand upside down

倒数 dàoshǔ (动) count backwards: ～第三行 the third line from the bottom. ～第二行 the last line but one

倒退 dàotuì (动) go backwards

倒行逆施 dàoxíng-nìshī I (动) go against the historical trend; push a reactionary policy; try to put the clock back II (名) perverse acts

倒置 dàozhì (动) place upside down: 本末～ put the unimportant before the important. 小心轻放,请勿～! Handle with care! This side up!

稻 dào (名) rice; paddy: ～草 rice straw. ～田 paddy field

得 dé (动) **1** get; gain; obtain: ～病 fall ill. 取～经验 gain experience. 二三～六 Twice three is six. ～分 score **2** be finished; be ready: 饭～了 Dinner is ready.

see also de; děi

得不偿(償)失 dé bù cháng shī The loss outweighs the gain.

得逞 déchěng (动) have one's way; succeed (in doing evil)

得宠(寵) déchǒng (动) find favour with sb.; be in sb.'s good graces

得寸进(進)尺 dé cùn jìn chǐ give him an inch and he'll take an ell; reach for a yard after getting an inch

得当(當) dédàng (形) proper; suitable; fitting: 安排～ be properly arranged. 措词～ aptly worded

得到 dédào (动) get; obtain; gain; receive

得法 défǎ (副) do sth. in the proper way; have the knack (of doing sth.): 学习不～ fail to learn in the proper way

得过(過)且过 dé guò qiě guò (动) muddle along; drift along; get by however one can

得力 délì (形) capable; competent: ～助手 capable assistant; right-hand man. 办事～ get things done promptly

得胜(勝) déshèng (动) win victory: ～归来 return in triumph (or with flying colours)

得失 dé-shī (名) gain and loss; advantages and disadvantages: 个人～ personal gain or loss. 各有～ each has its advantages and disadvantages

得势(勢) déshì (动) get the upper hand; be in power

得体(體) détǐ (形) (words or behaviour) proper; appropriate: 讲话～ speak in appropriate terms

得天独(獨)厚 dé tiān dú hòu abound in gifts of nature

得心应(應)手 déxīn-yìngshǒu handle with ease; be in one's element

得宜 déyí (形) proper; appropriate; suitable: 处置～ handle properly

得意 déyì (形) complacent: ～扬扬 be immensely proud of oneself. ～忘形 allow our achievements to turn one's head; get dizzy with success

得志 dézhì (动) achieve one's ambition: 少年～ have a successful career at an early age

得罪 dézuì (动) offend

德 dé (名) **1** virtue; morals: 品～ moral character. ～才兼备 have both ability and moral integrity; be both capable and noble-minded **2** heart; mind: 同心同～ be of one heart and one mind **3** kindness; favour: 以怨报～ return evil for good

德高望重 dégāo-wàngzhòng be held in high esteem for one's moral integrity or intellectual achievement; be of whole character and high prestige

德行 déxíng (名) moral integrity; moral conduct

德育 déyù (名) moral education

地 de (助) [used after an adjective, a noun or a phrase to form an adverbial adjunct before the verb]: 狐狸偷偷～跑进果园. The fox sneaked into the orchard. 他喝醉酒似～叫嚷. He shouted as if he were drunk.

see also dì

的 de (助) I used after an adjectival **1** [as an attribute, used after a noun]: 花～颜色 the colour of the flower **2** [used after a verb as an attribute]: 讨论～问题 matter for discussion **3** [used after an adjective]: 聪明～孩子 clever child [when the adjective is preceded by an intensifier or when it is in a reduplicated form, 的 is obligatory; as in 很高～山 very high mountains. 大大～眼睛 very big eyes] **4** [used after a pronoun]: 我～爸爸 my father **5** [used after a numeral]: 出一身～汗 sweat all over. 两天～时间 two days' time [when a numeral is combined with an ordinary classifier rather than a noun classifier, 的 is usually not to be used, as in 三个孩子 three children or 四匹马 four horses] **6** [used after a phrase, 的 is obligatory in this case]: 我对这个问题～看法 my views on this issue. 我刚听到～消息 the news I heard just now II other situations in which 的 is used **1** [used between the subject noun and the verb, functioning similarly as "of"]: 谣言～传播很惊人. The spread of the rumour is shocking. 2 [used between a verb and its object for emphatic purposes]: 他写～书. It was he who wrote the book. 她是去年买～这条裙子. It was last year that she bought this skirt. 3 [used between a personal pronoun and a noun to indicate one's role or the fact that one is the receiver of the action]: 今天的会谁～主席? Who is the chairman of today's meeting? 这部电影是我姐姐～主角. My sister plays the leading role in this film. 开她～玩笑 play a joke on her 4 [used after words belonging to the same parts of speech with a function similar to that of "soon" or "etc."]: 我不喜欢花儿草儿～! I don't like flowers, grass and things like that! 她尽说吃啊穿啊～. She talks about nothing but food and clothing, etc. 5 [attached to a verb, a noun, a pronoun or an adjective as a nominalizer]: 卖书～ the book-seller. see also dí

得 de 1 [used between a verb or an adjective and its complement to indicate result, possibility or degree]: 走～快 walk fast. 唱～好 sing well. 办～到 it can be done. 拿～动 can carry it. 雪下～大. It snowed heavily. 病～厉害 be very ill. 好～很 very good. 冷～打哆嗦 shiver with cold 2 [used after certain verbs to indicate possibility]: 这种蘑菇吃～. This kind of mushroom is edible. 衬衣太短,穿不～了. The shirt is too short for me now. 这话可说不～. We (you) mustn't say such things like this.
see also dé; děi

得 děi (动) 1 need: 写这篇文章至少～一个月. It will take at least a month to complete this article. 2 must; have to: 我～走了. I must go now. 我～事先告诉他. I have to tell him in advance. 3 will be sure to: 要不快走,你就～迟到了. Hurry up or you'll be late.
see also dé; de

灯(燈) dēng (名) lamp; light: 煤油～ kerosene lamp. 电～ electric light.

灯光 dēngguāng (名) 1 lamplight 2 (stage) lighting: 舞台～ stage lights. ～球场 floodlit court, field, etc.

灯火 dēnghuǒ (名) lights: ～辉煌 brilliantly illuminated. ～管制 blackout

灯笼(籠) dēnglong (名) lantern

灯谜 dēngmí (名) riddles written on lanterns; lantern riddles

灯泡 dēngpào (名) light bulb

灯塔 dēngtǎ (名) lighthouse; beacon

登 dēng (动) 1 ascend; mount; scale (a height): ～山 mountaineering. ～上讲台 mount the platform. ～上峰顶 reach the summit 2 publish; record; inter: ～广告 advertise (in a newspaper). ～消息 publish news (in a newspaper)

登场(塲) dēngchǎng (动) come on stage

登峰造极(極) dēngfēng-zàojí (of skill, learning, etc.) reach the peak of perfection; reach the pinnacle of scholastic attainment

登基 dēngjī (动) be enthroned

登记 dēngjì (动) register; enter one's name: 结婚～ marriage registration. 在旅馆～住宿 check in at a hotel

登陆(陸) dēnglù (动) land; disembark (from a ship)

登台(臺) dēngtái (动) come on stage; mount a platform: ～表演 put on a show

登载 dēngzǎi (动) carry (in newspapers or magazines)

等 děng I (名) grade; class; rank: 一～奖 first prize. 头～票 first class ticket. 一～品 top quality goods II (形) equal: 长短相～ be equal in length III (动) wait; await: ～车 wait for a bus. ～上级批准 await approval by the higher authorities IV (代) 1 [used after a personal pronoun or a noun to indicate plural number]: 老李～三人 Lao Li and two others. 我～五人 the five of us 2 and so on; etc.: 梨、苹果、葡萄～ pears, apples, grapes and so on 3 [used to end an enumeration]: 北京、上海、广州～大城市 big cities such as Beijing, Shanghai, and Guangzhou.

等待 děngdài (动) wait; await: ～时机 bide one's time

等到 děngdào (连) by the time; when

等等 děngděng and so on; and so on and so forth; etc.

等号(號) děnghào (名) equality

sign
等候 děnghòu (动) wait; await; expect: ～命令 wait for instructions; await orders
等级 děngjí (名) 1 grade; rank 2 order and degree; social stratum: ～制度 hierachy. ～观念 the concept of (social) status
等量齐(齊)观(觀) děngliàng-qíguān equate; put on a par
等同 děngtóng (动) equate; treat as equivalent
等外 děngwài (名) substandard: ～品 substandard product
等闲(閑) děngxián (形) ordinary; unimportant: ～视之 treat lightly
等于 děngyú (动) 1 be equal to; be equivalent to: 三加二～五. Three plus two is five. 2 be the same as; amount to; be tantamount to
澄 dèng (动) (of liquid) be clear: ～清 become clear; clarify
see also chéng
瞪 dèng (动) open one's eyes wide; stare; glare: 我～了他一眼. I gave him a stare. 干～眼 look on helplessly
凳 dèng (名) stool; bench: 方～ square stool. 长～ bench
滴 dī I (动) drip: 他脸上的汗水直往下～. Sweat kept dripping from his face. ～眼药 put drops in one's eyes II (量) drop: 一～眼泪 a drop of tear
滴答 dīdā (象) tick; ticktack: 钟摆～～的响声 the ticktack of the clock. 雨～～地敲着窗口. The rain kept pattering against the windows.
滴答 dīda (动) drip: 屋顶～着水. The roof is dripping water.
滴水穿石 dī shuǐ chuān shí little strokes fell big oaks; constant dripping wears away stone
堤 dī (名) dyke; embankment: ～岸 embankment. ～坝 dykes and dam. ～防 dyke
提 dī
see also tí
提防 dīfáng (动) guard against; take precautions against
低 dī I (形) low: ～地 low land. ～潮 low tide; low ebb. ～声 in a low voice II (动) let droop; hang down: ～头 lower one's head
低沉 dīchén (形) 1 overcast: ～的天空 an overcast sky 2 (of voice) low and deep 3 low-spirited; downcast
低估 dīgū (动) underestimate; underrate
低级 dījí (形) 1 elementary; rudimentary; lower 2 vulgar; low: ～趣味 vulgar taste
低廉 dīlián (形) (of price) cheap; reasonable
低劣 dīliè (形) inferior; low-grade
低落 dīluò (形) low; downcast: 情绪～ be depressed; in sagging spirits
低三下四 dīsān-xiàsì (形) humble; servile
低洼 dīwā (形) (of land) low-lying
低下 dīxià (形) (of status) low; lowly; humble
涤(滌) dí (动) wash; cleanse
涤荡(蕩) dídàng (动) wash away; clean up
涤纶(綸) dílún (名) polyester fibre
嘀 dí
嘀咕 dígu (动) 1 talk in whispers; talk in a low voice 2 have misgivings about sth.: 我心里一直～这件事. It's been on my mind all the while.
嫡 dí (形) of lineal descent; closely related
嫡亲(親) díqīn (名) blood relations
嫡系 díxì (名) direct line of descent: ～部队 troops under one's direct control
笛 dí (名) 1 (～子) flute 2 whistle: 汽～ air siren
敌(敵) dí I (名) enemy; foe: 劲～ a formidable enemy. ～机 an enemy plane II (动) fight; resist; withstand: 寡不～众 be outnumbered
敌对(對) díduì (形) hostile; antagonistic: ～情绪 a hostile attitude
敌忾(愾) díkài (名) hatred towards the enemy: 同仇～ share a bitter hatred of the enemy
敌情 díqíng (名) the enemy's situation
敌视 díshì (动) be hostile (or antagonistic) to
敌手 díshǒu (名) rival; opponent
敌特 dítè (名) enemy agent
敌意 díyì (名) hostility; animo-

sity

的 dí

see also de

的确 díquè (副) indeed; really: 这本书～很好. This book is really good.

的确良 díquèliáng (名) dacron

籴(糴) dí (动) buy in (grain)

底 dǐ (名) 1 bottom; base: 海～ sea bed 2 end: 年～ the end of a year 3 the heart of a matter; ins and outs: 刨根问～ get to the bottom of the matter 4 a copy or duplicate kept as a record: 留个～儿 keep a copy on file 5 background: 蓝～白花 white flowers on a blue background 6 end: 干到～ carry sth. through to the end. 你到～在这儿干什么? What on earth are you doing here?

底层(層) dǐcéng (名) 1 (英) ground floor; (美) first floor 2 bottom; the lowest rung of the ladder: 在社会的最～ at the bottom of society

底稿 dǐgǎo (名) draft; manuscript

底片 dǐpiàn (名) negative; photographic plate

底细 dǐxì (名) ins and outs; exact details

底下 dǐxià (副) 1 under; below; beneath: 床～ under the bed 2 next; later; afterwards: 我们～再谈吧. We can discuss it later.

底子 dǐzi (名) 1 bottom; base: 鞋～ the sole of a shoe 2 foundation: 他的英语语法～好. He has a good grounding in English grammar. 3 rough draft or sketch: 画画儿得先打个～. Make a rough sketch before you draw. 4 master copy 5 remnant: 货～ remnants of stock

诋 dǐ (动) <书> slander; defame

诋毁 dǐhuǐ (动) slander; vilify

抵 dǐ (动) 1 support; sustain: 重盖前先用东西把这片墙～住. Prop something against the wall before it is re-built. 2 resist; withstand 3 compensate for; make good: ～命 a life for a life 4 mortgage: 用房屋作～ mortgage a house 5 be equal to 6 <书> arrive; reach: 六日～京 arrive in Beijing on the 6th

抵偿(償) dǐcháng (动) compensate

抵触(觸) dǐchù (动、名) conflict; contradict: 与法律相～ go against the law. ～情绪 resentment; feeling of antagonism

抵达(達) dǐdá (动) arrive; reach

抵挡(擋) dǐdǎng (动) keep out; ward off; check; withstand: ～风沙 keep out wind and dust

抵抗 dǐkàng (动) resist; stand up to: 奋起～ put up a stubborn resistance

抵赖 dǐlài (动) deny: 不容～ undeniable

抵消 dǐxiāo (动) offset; cancel; balance: ～药物的作用 counteract the effect of a medicine

抵押 dǐyā (动) mortgage: ～品 security; pledge

抵御(禦) dǐyù (动) resist; withstand: ～自然灾害 withstand natural calamities

抵制 dǐzhì (动) resist; boycott

抵罪 dǐzuì (动) be punished for a crime

邸 dǐ (名) the residence of a high official: 官～ official residence

帝 dì (名) 1 the supreme Being: 上～ God 2 emperor: 称～ proclaim oneself emperor

帝国(國) dìguó (名) empire: 罗马～ the Roman Empire

帝国(國)主义(義) dìguózhǔyì (名) imperialism

帝王 dìwáng (名) emperor; monarch

帝制 dìzhì (名) monarchy

谛 dì (副)<书> carefully; attentively: ～听 listen attentively. ～视 examine closely; scrutinize

蒂 dì (名) the base of a fruit: 根深～固 deep-rooted; inveterate

缔 dì

缔交 dìjiāo (动) 1 make friends with 2 establish diplomatic relations

缔结 dìjié (动) conclude: ～条约 conclude a treaty

缔约 dìyuē (动) conclude (or sign) a treaty: ～国 signatory to a treaty. ～双方 both contracting parties

缔造 dìzào (动) found; create (a party, state, or school of thought)

弟 dì (名) younger brother: ～～ younger brother. ～兄 brothers. ～子 disciple; pupil follower

第 dì [prefix for ordinal numbers]: ～三世界 the third world

第一 dìyī (形) first; primary; foremost: 获得～名 come out first in the competition with a championship

第一线(綫) dìyīxiàn (名) forefront; front line: 战斗在～ be in the forefront of the fighting; be in the van of the struggle

递(遞) dì I (动) hand over; pass; give: 把书～给我. Give the book. ～眼色 wink at sb. II (副) successively; in sequential order: ～增(减) increase (decrease) by degrees

递交 dìjiāo (动) present; submit: ～国书 (of an ambassador) present one's credentials

递送 dìsòng (动) send; deliver

地 dì (名) 1 the earth 2 land; soil: 高～ highland. 盐碱～ saline and alkaline land (or soil) 3 field: 麦～ wheat field 4 ground; floor: 水泥～ cement floor 5 place; locality 6 position; situation: 立于不败之～ entrench oneself in an invincible position 7 background 8 distance: 十里～ a distance of ten *li*

see also de

地板 dìbǎn (名) (wooden) floor

地步 dìbù (名) 1 condition; situation; plight (usu. unfavourable) 2 extent: 兴奋到不能入睡的～ be too excited to fall asleep

地大物博 dìdà-wùbó vast in territory and rich in resources

地带(帶) dìdài (名) region; zone: 危险～ a danger zone

地道 dìdào (名) tunnel

地道 dìdao (形) 1 pure; genuine: ～的中国花茶 genuine Chinese jasmine tea 2 〈口〉 up to standard; fine: 这活干得真～. They have done an excellent job of work.

地点(點) dìdiǎn (名) place; site

地段 dìduàn (名) a section of an area

地方 dìfāng (名) locality (as distinct from the central administration): ～政府 local government

地方 dìfang (名) 1 place: 你住什么～? Where do you live? 2 space; room: 这张桌子太占～. That desk takes up too much space 3 part; respect: 他也有对的～. He is also partly right.

地基 dìjī (名) 1 ground 2 foundation

地窖 dìjiào (名) cellar

地界 dìjiè (名) the boundary of a piece of land

地雷 dìléi (名) land mine

地理 dìlǐ (名) geography

地面 dìmiàn (名) the earth's surface; ground

地盘(盤) dìpán (名) territory under one's control; domain

地皮 dìpí (名) land for building

地痞 dìpǐ (名) local ruffian

地平线(綫) dìpíngxiàn (名) horizon

地契 dìqì (名) title deed for land

地壳 dìqiào (名) the earth's crust

地勤 dìqín (名) ground service

地球 dìqiú (名) the earth; the globe: ～卫星 earth satellite. ～物理学 geophysics. ～仪 (terrestrial) globe

地区(區) dìqū (名) area; district; region: 森林～ forest area

地权(權) dìquán (名) land ownership

地热(熱) dìrè (名) terrestrial heat

地上 dìshàng (副) on the ground: 从～拣起 pick up from the ground

地势(勢) dìshì (名) physical features of a place; relief

地毯 dìtǎn (名) carpet; rug

地图(圖) dìtú (名) map

地位 dìwèi (名) position; status: 政治～ political position. 国际～ international status. 平等～ on an equal footing

地峡 dìxiá (名) isthmus

地下 dìxià (名) underground: ～宫殿 underground palace. ～核试验 underground nuclear test. ～室 basement; cellar. ～铁道 underground railway; tube; subway. ～工作 underground work

地心 dìxīn (名) the earth's core: ～引力 terrestrial gravity; gravity

地形 dìxíng (名) topography; terrain

地狱(獄) dìyù (名) hell; inferno: 打入十八层～ be cast into outer darkness

地域 dìyù (名) region; district

地震 dìzhèn (名) earthquake; seism: ～预报 seismic forecast

地址 dìzhǐ (名) address

地质(質) dìzhì (名) geology
地主 dìzhǔ (名) landlord: 恶霸～ despotic landlord
地租 dìzū (名) land rent
颠 diān I (动) totter; tumble; fall II (名) top; summit
颠簸 diānbǒ (动) jolt; bump; toss: 船在海上～着. The boat was tossed about in the sea.
颠倒 diāndǎo I (动) put upside down; reverse; invert: 画挂～了. The picture is upside down. 把次序～就行了. Reverse the order, and it will be alright. II (形) confused: 神魂～ be in a trance; be infatuated
颠倒黑白 diāndǎo hēi-bái (动) confound black and white; confuse right and wrong
颠覆 diānfù (动) overturn; subvert: ～活动 subversive activities
颠来(來)倒去 diānlái-dǎoqù over and over: ～没个完 keep harping on sth.
颠沛流离(離) diānpèi-liúlí go tramping; drift from place to place
颠扑(撲)不破 diānpū bù pò (形) irrefutable; indisputable: ～的真理 irrefutable truth
颠三倒四 diānsān-dǎosì (形) disorganized; incoherent; disorderly
癫 diān (形) insane; mentally deranged: ～痫 epilepsy
巅 diān (名) mountain peak; summit
掂 diān (动) weigh in the hand: ～～这有多重. Weigh this in your hand.
掂量 diānliàng (动) 1 weigh in the hand 2 think over; weigh up: 你～着办. Just do as you think fit.
踮 diǎn (动) tiptoe
点(點) diǎn I (名) 1 drop: 雨～ raindrops 2 dot; spot; speck: 污～ stain 3 point: 沸～ boiling point. 优～ strong point. 一～五 one point five (1.5) 4 aspect; feature: 特～ characteristic feature II (动) 1 put a dot 2 touch on briefly: ～一下就行了 have only to touch on it briefly 3 drip: ～眼药 put drops in the eyes 4 check; check to see that the number is correct 5 select; choose: ～菜 order dishes (in a restaurant) 6 hint; point out: 一～他就明白了. He quickly took the hint. 7 light; kindle: ～灯 light a lamp III (量) 1 a little; some: 吃一～东西 have something to eat. 她好～了. She is a bit better now. 2 [used to indicate time]: 五～钟 five o'clock. 几～了? What time is it now? 到～了! It's time. 误～ behind time; late
点火 diǎnhuǒ (动) 1 light a fire 2 stir up trouble
点名 diǎnmíng (动) 1 call the roll 2 mention somebody specifically: 他～要你去. He mentioned you as the person he specifically wanted.
点破 diǎnpò (动) show up sth. (particulary a secret) in a few words
点燃 diǎnrán (动) light; kindle
点头(頭) diǎntóu (动) nod (as a sign of greeting, approval, etc.): 他～了. He nodded agreement (approval).
点头(頭)哈腰 diǎntóu-hāyāo (动) bow and scrape
点心 diǎnxīn (名) light refreshments
点缀 diǎnzhuì (动) 1 embellish; adorn
点子 diǎnzi (名) 1 drop; speck 2 beat: 鼓～ drumbeat 3 key point: 他这话说到～上了. He has come to the point. 4 idea: 他～多. He's full of ideas. 鬼～ tricks
典 diǎn I (名) 1 standard work: 词～ dictionary. 引经据～ quote from classics; quote great masters 2 allusion; literary quotation 3 ceremony: 盛～ a grand ceremony II (动) mortgage
典当(當) diǎndàng (动) mortgage; pawn
典范(範) diǎnfàn (名) model; paragon
典故 diǎngù (名) allusion
典籍 diǎnjí (名) ancient books and records
典礼(禮) diǎnlǐ (名) ceremony celebration
典型 diǎnxíng I (名) typical case model II (形) typical; representative: ～人物 a typical character
典雅 diǎnyǎ (形) (of diction etc.) refined; elegant
碘 diǎn (名) iodine (I): ～酒 tincture of iodine

淀(澱) diàn I (动) settle; precipitate II (名) shallow lake
淀粉 diànfěn (名) starch
靛 diàn (名) indigo: ～青 indigo-blue
奠 diàn (动) 1 establish; settle 2 make offerings to the spirits of the dead
奠定 diàndìng (动) establish; settle: ～基础 lay the groundwork
奠基 diànjī (动) lay a foundation
垫(墊) diàn I (名) pad; cushion; mat: 椅～ chair cushion. 鞋～ insole. 床～ mattress II (动) 1 put sth. under sth. else to raise it or make it level; pad 2 pay for sb. and expect to be repaid later: 我先给你～上吧. Let me pay it for you now (you can pay me back later).
垫肩 diànjiān (名) shoulder pad
垫平 diànpíng (动) level up: 把路～ level a road
垫子 diànzi (名) mat; pad; cushion
店 diàn (名) 1 shop; store 2 inn: 住～ stop at an inn
店铺 diànpù (名) shop; store
店员 diànyuán (名) shop assistant; salesman: 女～ saleswoman
惦 diàn (动) continue to think about
惦记 diànjì (动) keep thinking about
惦念 diànniàn (动) be anxious about; worry about
玷 diàn (名) a flaw in a piece of jade
玷辱 diànrǔ (动) bring disgrace on
玷污 diànwū (动) stain; sully: ～某人的名誉 sully sb.'s reputation
电(電) diàn I (名) electricity: ～报 telegram II (动) give or get an electric shock
电报(報) diànbào (名) telegram; cable: ～挂号 cable address
电表 diànbiǎo (名) ammeter
电冰箱 diànbīngxiāng (名) refrigerator; fridge
电波 diànbō (名) electric wave
电场(場) diànchǎng (名) electric field
电唱机(機) diànchàngjī (名) gramophone; record player
电车(車) diànchē (名) trolleybus
电池 diànchí (名) battery
电磁 diàncí (名) electromagnetism
电灯(燈) diàndēng (名) electric light
电动(動) diàndòng (名) power-driven
电镀 diàndù (名) electroplate
电工 diàngōng (名) electrician
电焊 diànhàn (名) electric welding
电话 diànhuà (名) telephone: 长途～ long distance call. 打～ make a phone call. ～簿 telephone directory. ～分机 extension
电汇(匯) diànhuì (名) remittance by telegram
电机(機) diànjī (名) generator; electric motor
电极(極) diànjí (名) electrode
电缆(纜) diànlǎn (名) electric cable
电力 diànlì (名) electric power; power
电疗(療) diànliáo (名) electrotherapy
电铃 diànlíng (名) electric bell
电流 diànliú (名) electric current
电炉(爐) diànlú (名) 1 electric stove; hot plate 2 electric furnace
电路 diànlù (名) circuit: 集成～ integrated circuit
电码 diànmǎ (名) (telegraphic) code
电钮 diànniǔ (名) push button: 按～ press a button
电气(氣) diànqì (名) electric: ～机车 electric locomotive. ～化 electrification
电器 diànqì (名) electrical equipment (or appliance)
电容 diànróng (名) electric capacity; capacitance: ～器 capacitor
电扇 diànshàn (名) electric fan
电视 diànshì (名) television; TV: ～发射机 television transmitter. ～屏幕 television screen. ～塔 television tower. ～台 television station. ～转播 television relay. ～转播卫星 television transmission satellite
电台(臺) diàntái (名) 1 transmitter-receiver; transceiver 2 radio station
电梯 diàntī (名) lift; elevator
电筒 diàntǒng (名) (electric) torch; flashlight
电网(網) diànwǎng (名) electrified wire netting
电文 diànwén (名) text (of a

telegram)
电线(綫) diànxiàn (名) (electric) wire
电信 diànxìn (名) telecommunications
电讯 diànxùn (名) (telegraphic) dispatch; telecommunication
电压(壓) diànyā (名) voltage
电唁 diànyàn (动) send a telegram of condolence
电影 diànyǐng (名) film; movie: 有声(无声)～ sound (silent) film. 立体～ three-dimensional film. ～院 cinema. ～制片厂 (film) studio
电源 diànyuán (名) power source; mains: 接上～ connect with the mains
电子 diànzǐ (名) electron: ～管 electron tube; valve. ～计算机 computer
电阻 diànzǔ (名) resistance

佃 diàn (动) rent land (from a landlord)
佃户 diànhù (名) tenant (farmer)
佃农(農) diànnóng (名) tenant farmer
佃租 diànzū (名) land rent

殿 diàn (名) hall; palace: 佛～ Buddhist temple
殿下 diànxià (名) Your Highness; His or Her Highness

貂 diāo (名) marten

凋 diāo (动) wither; languish; decay
凋零 diāolíng (形) wither; fall into decay
凋谢 diāoxiè (动) (of trees or flowers) wither or fall

碉 diāo
碉堡 diāobǎo (名) pillbox

雕 diāo I (动) carve; engrave: 浮～ relief. ～梁画栋 with rich interior decorations II (名) vulture
雕虫小技 diāo chóng xiǎojì trifling skill
雕花 diāohuā (名) carving: ～家具 carved furniture
雕刻 diāokè (动) carve; engrave: 玉石～ jade carving
雕塑 diāosù (名) sculpture
雕像 diāoxiàng (名) statue: 大理石～ marble statue. 半身～ bust
雕琢 diāozhuó (动) chisel and carve

刁 diāo (形) tricky; artful; sly
刁悍 diāohàn (形) cunning and fierce
刁滑 diāohuá (形) sly
刁难(難) diāonàn (动) make things difficult for sb.: 百般～ try by all means to create difficulties for sb.

叼 diāo (动) hold in the mouth

调 diào I (动) 1 transfer; shift: ～任 be transferred to another post. ～军队 move troops 2 allocate ～来一批新货 a batch of new goods was allocated to us. II (名) 1 accent: 东北～儿 Northeast accent 2 melody; tune 3 tone; tune: 升～ rising tone (or tune). 降～ falling tone (or tune)
see also tiáo
调兵遣将(將) diàobīng-qiǎnjiàng dispatch officers and men
调拨(撥) diàobō (动) allocate; allot
调查 diàochá (动) investigate; survey: 农村～ rural survey
调动(動) diàodòng (动) 1 transfer; shift: ～工作 transfer sb. to another post 2 move (troops) 3 bring into play; mobilize: ～一切积极因素 bring every positive factor into play
调度 diàodù (动) 1 dispatch (trains, buses, etc.) 2 manage; control: 生产～ production management. ～室 control room. ～员 controller
调换 diàohuàn (动) exchange; change; swop
调回 diàohuí (动) recall (troops, etc.)
调集 diàojí (动) assemble; muster: ～兵力 concentrate large forces
调配 diàopèi (动) allocate; deploy
调遣 diàoqiǎn (动) dispatch; assign: ～军队 dispatch troops
调子 diàozi (名) 1 tune; melody 2 tone (of speech); note: 定～ set the tone

掉 diào (动) 1 fall; drop: 扣子～了. The botton has come off. ～眼泪 shed tears 2 lose; be missing: 这段～了几个字. A few words are missing from this paragraph. 我的提包～了. I've lost my handbag. 3 fall behind: 他～在后面了. He is lagging behind. 4 exchange: ～座位 change (or exchange) seats 5 turn: 把车头～过来 turn the

car round **6** [used as a complement after certain verbs]: 扔～ throw away. 擦～ wipe off
掉队(隊) diàoduì (动) drop out; fall behind
掉色 diàoshǎi (动) lose colour; fade
掉头(頭) diàotóu (动) turn round; turn about
掉以轻(輕)心 diào yǐ qīngxīn dismiss sth. as of no consequence; treat sth. lightly
掉转(轉) diàozhuǎn (动) turn round: ～身子 turn round
吊 diào (动) **1** hang; suspend **2** lift up or let down with a rope **3** condole; mourn; send one's condolences to **4** revoke; withdraw: ～销 revoke (a licence, etc.)
吊车(車) diàochē (名) crane
吊灯(燈) diàodēng (名) pendent lamp
吊环(環) diàohuán (名) rings
吊桥(橋) diàoqiáo (名) suspension bridge
吊死 diàosǐ (动) be hanged by the neck; hang oneself
吊唁 diàoyàn (动) offer one's condolences: ～函电 messages of condolence
钓 diào (动) angle; fish with hook and bait
钓饵 diào'ěr (名) bait
钓竿 diàogān (名) fishing rod
钓钩 diàogōu (名) fishhook
钓具 diàojù (名) fishing tackle
钓鱼(魚) diàoyú (动) angle; go fishing
跌 diē (动) **1** fall; tumble: 他～了一交. He tripped and fell down. **2** drop; fall: 物价下～. Prices have dropped.
跌倒 diēdǎo (动) fall; tumble
跌跌撞撞 diēdiēzhuàngzhuàng (动) stagger along; dodder
跌交 diējiāo (动) **1** trip (or stumble) and fall; fall **2** make a mistake; meet with a setback
跌落 diēluò (动) fall; drop
爹 diē (名) 〈口〉 dad; daddy: ～娘 father and mother; mum and dad. ～～ dad.
谍 dié (名) **1** espionage: ～报 intelligence **2** spy: 间～ spy. 从事间～活动 engaged in espionage activities
碟 dié (名) small dish: ～子 small dish
喋 dié
喋喋不休 diédié bù xiū (动) rattle away; talk endlessly
喋血 diéxuè (名) bloodshed
蝶 dié (名) butterfly: 蝴～ butterfly. ～泳 butterfly stroke
牒 dié (名) official document or note: 最后通～ ultimatum
迭 dié I (动) alternate; change: 更～ alternate II (副) repeatedly: ～起 happen repeatedly
叠(疊) dié I (动) **1** pile up; overlap: 重～ overlap **2** fold: 把信～好 fold a letter II (名) layer upon layer
叠字 diézì (名) reduplication
丁 dīng (名) **1** man: 壮～ able-bodied man. 园～ gardener **2** members of a family; population **3** fourth: ～种维生素 vitamin D **4** small cubes of meat or vegetable; cubes: 辣子肉～ diced pork with chilli
丁当(當) dīngdāng 〈象〉 tinkle; jingle
丁冬 dīngdōng 〈象〉 dingdong
丁香 dīngxiāng (名) **1** lilac **2** clove
丁字 dīngzì (形) T-shaped
疔 dīng (名) malignant boil
叮 dīng (动) **1** sting; bite: 一个虫子～了我一下. An insect stung me. **2** ask again; make sure: 我又～了他一句. I asked him again.
叮当(當) dīngdāng see 丁当
叮咛(嚀) dīngníng (动) exhort; urge
叮嘱(囑) dīngzhǔ (动) warn repeatedly; exhort
盯 dīng (动) gaze at; stare at; fix one's eyes on: 大家的眼睛都～住了靶心. All eyes were fixed on the bull's-eye.
盯梢 dīngshāo (动) tail sb.; shadow sb.
钉 dīng I (名) nail; tack II (动) **1** follow closely; tail **2** urge; press: 你要经常～着他一点,免得他忘了. You'll have to remind him from time to time lest he should forget.
see also dìng
钉梢 dīngshāo (动) shadow sb.; tail sb.
钉子 dīngzi (名) **1** nail **2** snag: 碰～ meet with a flat refusal

顶 dǐng I (名) top; peak; summit: 山～ mountaintop. 屋～ roof II (动) 1 carry on the head 2 retort: ～撞 contradict sb. 3 go against; brave: ～风 brave the wind 4 push from below; prop up: 嫩芽把土～起来了. The sprouts have pushed through the earth. 5 take the place of; substitute; replace: ～别人的名字 assume sb. else's name 6 equal; be equivalent to III (量) [for sth. with a top]: 一～帽子 a hat. 一～帐子 a mosquito net IV (副) very; most: ～有用 most useful. 那个～小的盆 that smallest pot

顶点(點) dǐngdiǎn (名) summit pinnacle; end

顶端 dǐngduān (名) top; peak; apex

顶多 dǐngduō (副) at (the) most; at best

顶峰 dǐngfēng (名) peak; summit; pinnacle

顶梁柱 dǐngliángzhù (名) pillar; backbone

顶事 dǐngshì (形) be useful; serve the purpose: 多穿件毛线衣也还～. It does serve the purpose to put on another woollen sweater.

顶替 dǐngtì (动) take sb.'s place; replcae: 冒名～ pass oneself off as somebody else with an assumed name

顶天立地 dǐngtiān-lìdì of gigantic stature; of indomitable spirit

顶头(頭)上司 dǐngtóu shàngsi (名) one's immediate superior

顶用 dǐngyòng (副) be of use (or help); serve the purpose: 孩子太小,不～. The child is too young to help.

顶住 dǐngzhù (动) withstand; stand up to: ～巨大的外部压力 withstand tremendous outside pressure

顶嘴 dǐngzuǐ (动) talk back

鼎 dǐng (名) an ancient cooking vessel; tripod

鼎鼎大名 dǐngdǐng dàmíng of high reputation; celebrated; famous

鼎沸 dǐngfèi (形) noisy and confused: 人声～ confused and loud noises

定 dìng (动) 1 decide; fix; set: ～计划 draw up a plan. ～时间 fix a time 2 calm down: 心神不～ be absent-minded; be perturbed 3 〈书〉 surely; certainly; definitely

定案 dìng'àn I (动) make a verdict; decide on a plan II (名) verdict; final decision

定额 dìng'é (名) quota; norm: 生产～ production quota

定价(價) dìngjià I(动) fix a price II (名) fixed price; price

定见(見) dìngjiàn (名) definite opinion

定睛 dìngjīng (动) fix one's eyes upon; gaze at: ～细看 scrutinize

定居 dìngjū (动) settle down: ～点 settlement

定局 dìngjú I (名) foregone conclusion II (动) settle finally: 事情还没～. The matter isn't settled yet.

定理 dìnglǐ (名) theorem: 基本～ fundamental theorem

定量 dìngliàng (名) ration; fixed quantity: ～供应 rationing

定律 dìnglǜ (名) law: 万有引力～ the law of universal gravitation

定论(論) dìnglùn (名) final conclusion: 这个问题还没有～. It remains an open question.

定期 dìngqī I (形) regular; at regular intervals; periodical: ～检查 regular check-ups. ～刊物 periodical publication II (动) fix (or set) a date

定然 dìngrán (副) certainly; definitely

定神 dìngshén (动) 1 collect oneself; pull oneself together 2 concentrate one's attention

定时(時)炸弹(彈) dìngshí zhàdàn (名) time bomb

定型 dìngxíng (动) finalize the design; become fixed

定性 dìngxìng (动) determine the nature of sth.: ～分析 qualitative analysis

定义(義) dìngyì (名) definition: 下～ give a definition; define

定语 dìngyǔ (名) attribute: ～从句 attributive clause

定罪 dìngzuì (动) declare sb. guilty

定做 dìngzuò (动) have sth. made to order (or measure): ～的衣服 tailor-made clothes

碇 dìng (名) a heavy stone used as an anchor; killick

锭 dìng (名) 1 ingot-shaped tablet 2 spindle

订 dìng (动) 1 conclude; draw up: ～条约 conclude a treaty. ～合同 enter into a contract. ～日期 fix a date. ～生产

指标 set a production target 2 subscribe to; book; order: ～报纸 subscribe to a newspaper. ～票 book a ticket. ～一桌酒席 order a dinner 3 make corrections; revise: 修～ revise 4 staple together

订购(購) dìnggòu (动) order goods

订户 dìnghù (名) subscriber

订婚 dìnghūn (动) be engaged (or betrothed)

订货 dìnghuò (动) order goods

订立 dìnglì (动) conclude (a treaty, agreement, etc.)

订阅 dìngyuè (动) subscribe to (a newspaper, periodical, etc.)

订正 dìngzhèng (动) make corrections

钉 dìng (动) 1 nail: ～钉子 drive in a nail 2 sew on: ～扣子 sew a button on

see also dīng

丢 diū (动) 1 lose; be missing: 我的笔～了. I've lost my pen. 2 throw; cast; toss: ～个石头到水里 throw a stone into the water 3 put (or lay) aside; dismiss (from one's mind): 只有一件事～不开. There is only one thing I cannot easily dismiss from my mind.

丢掉 diūdiào (动) 1 lose 2 throw away; discard; get rid of: ～官僚主义习气 get rid of bureaucracy

丢脸(臉) diūliǎn (动) lose face; be disgraced: 你这样做真～! You ought to be ashamed of what you did!

丢面子 diū miànzi (动) lose face

丢弃(棄) diūqì (动) abandon; discard

丢三落四 diūsān-làsì (形) be always forgetting things

丢失 diūshī (动) lose; let slip; miss

东(東) dōng (名) 1 east: ～郊 eastern suburbs 2 master; owner: 房～ landlord 3 host: 做～ stand treat; play the host

东半球 dōngbànqiú (名) the Eastern Hemisphere

东道 dōngdào (名) host: ～国 host country. ～主 host

东家 dōngjiā (名) master; boss

东经(經) dōngjīng (名) east longitude

东拉西扯 dōnglā-xīchě (动) drag in irrelevant matters; talk at random; ramble

东拼西凑 dōngpīn-xīcòu (动) scrape together; knock together: 那篇文章是～的. That article is a hodge-podge.

东山再起 dōngshān zài qǐ stage a comeback

东西 dōng-xī (名) east and west; from east to west

东西 dōngxi (名) 1 thing: 我没买什么～. I didn't buy anything. 2 [expressing a feeling of affection or hatred for a person or animal] thing; creature: 这小～真可爱. What a sweet little thing! 真不是～! What a despicable creature!

东…西… dōng ... xī ... here ... here: 东张西望 look around. 东奔西跑 dash around. 东一句, 西一句 talk incoherently

冬 dōng (名) winter: ～季 (or ～天) winter

冬眠 dōngmián (名) winter sleep; hibernation

董 dǒng

董事 dǒngshì (名) director; trustee: ～会(企业) board of directors (or trustees). ～长 chairman of the board

懂 dǒng (动) understand; know: 我不～你谈的什么. I don't understand what you are driving at. ～法文 know French. ～礼貌 have good manners

懂行 dǒngháng (动) know the business; know the ropes

懂事 dǒngshì (形) sensible; perceptive: ～的孩子 a sensible child

动(動) dòng I (动) 1 move; stir: 别～! Don't move! 2 act; get moving: 群众普遍地～起来了. The masses all got moving. 3 use: ～脑筋 use one's head 4 change; alter: 改～ change 5 touch (one's heart); arouse: ～感情 be carried away by emotion; get worked up II [used as a complement after a verb] be moved: 旗帜在风中飘～. The flag is fluttering in the wind.

动不动 dòngbudòng (副) easily; frequently: ～就发脾气 be apt to lose one's temper; be liable to flare up at any moment

动产(產) dòngchǎn (名) movable property

动词 dòng cí (名) verb

动荡(蕩) dòngdàng (名) turbulence; upheaval; unrest

动画(畫)片 dònghuàpiàn (名) animated cartoon; cartoon
动机(機) dòngjī (名) motive; intention: ～好，效果不一定好. The result may not be necessarily satisfactory, though you act with the best of intentions.
动静 dòngjìng (名) sound of people speaking or moving about: 屋子里静悄悄的，一点～也没有. It is quiet and still in the room. There is absolutely nothing stirring in there.
动力 dònglì (名) 1 power 2 driving force; motivation; impetus
动乱(亂) dòngluàn (名) turmoil; disturbance; upheaval: 十年～时期 the decade of turmoil. 社会～ social upheaval
动脉(脈) dòngmài (名) artery
动气(氣) dòngqì (动) <口> take offence; get angry
动情 dòngqíng (动) 1 feel excited 2 fall in love
动人 dòngrén (形) moving; touching: ～的情景 a moving scene
动身 dòngshēn (动) set out on a journey; leave
动手 dòngshǒu (动) 1 touch: 请勿～! Please don't touch! 2 start work; get to work: 大家一齐～! Everybody get to work! 3 raise a hand to strike; hit out: 谁先动的手? Who struck the first blow?
动手术(術) dòngshǒushù (动) 1 perform an operation; operate on sb. 2 undergo an operation; be operated on
动态(態) dòngtài (名) tendency; trends; developments: 科技新～ recent developments in science and technology
动听(聽) dòngtīng (形) interesting or pleasant to the ear
动武 dòngwǔ (动) use force; start a fight; come to blows
动物 dòngwù (名) animal: ～园 zoo. ～学 zoology. ～志 fauna
动向 dòngxiàng (名) trend; tendency: 密切注意敌人～. Keep a close watch on the enemy's movements.
动心 dòngxīn (动) be attracted by; one's desire, interest or enthusiasm is aroused
动摇 dòngyáo (动) move; shake; waver: ～分子 wavering element
动议(議) dòngyì (名) motion: 紧急～ an urgent motion
动用 dòngyòng (动) employ; draw on (resources, funds, etc.): ～库存 draw on stock
动员 dòngyuán (动) mobilize; arouse
动辄 dòngzhé (副) <书>easily; at every turn
动作 dòngzuò (名) movement; action: ～敏捷(缓慢) quick (slow) in one's movements

冻(凍) dòng I (动) 1 freeze: ～肉 frozen meat 2 feel very cold: 我～坏了. I'm freezing. 手～了. One's hands numbed with cold. II (名) jelly: 肉～儿 jellied meat
冻冰 dòngbīng (动) freeze: 河上～了. The river is frozen.
冻僵 dòngjiāng (形) frozen stiff; numb with cold
冻结 dòngjié (动) freeze: 工资～ wage freeze. ～的资产 frozen assets

栋(棟) dòng (量): 一～楼房 a building
栋梁 dòngliáng (名) 1 ridgepole and beam 2 pillar of the state

洞 dòng (名) hole; cavity; cave
洞察 dòngchá (动) see through clearly; have an insight into: ～力 insight; discernment
洞若观(觀)火 dòng ruò guān huǒ see something as clearly as a flazing fire
洞悉 dòngxī (动) know clearly; understand thoroughly
洞穴 dòngxué (名) cave; cavern

恫 dòng (名) fear
恫吓(嚇) dònghè (动) threaten; intimidate

都 dōu (副) 1 all; both: 这些我～喜欢. I like them all. 我俩～想去. Both of us want to go. 2 all [referring to causes]: ～是你多嘴，看她生气了. Look, she is annoyed. It's all because of your unsolicited remarks. 3 already: ～八点了，你怎么还不走? It's already eight o'clock, why are you still here? 我～十八岁了，别把我当小孩子. Don't treat me like a child. I'm already eighteen. 4 even: 这种事连小孩～知道. Even a child knows all this. 我中学～没上过. I didn't even go to middle school.
see also dū

兜 dōu I（名）pocket; bag: 网～儿 string bag II（动）1 wrapped up in a piece of cloth, etc.: 用手绢～着一些葡萄 carry some grapes wrapped up in a handkerchief 2 move round: 我们开车在城里～了一圈. We went for a drive around in town. 说话别～圈子. Come straight to the point. Don't beat about the bush.

兜风(風) dōufēng（动）go for a drive

兜揽(攬) dōulǎn（动）canvass; solicit: ～生意 solicit business

兜售 dōushòu（动）peddle; hawk

斗 dǒu（名）1 *dou*, measurement of capacity (10 litres) 2 an object shaped like a cup or dipper: 烟～ (tobacco) pipe. 漏～ funnel

see also dòu

斗胆 dǒudǎn（动）〈谦〉make bold; venture: 我～说一句，这件事您做错了. May I venture to say that you were wrong here.

斗笠 dǒulì（名）bamboo hat

斗篷 dǒupeng（名）cape; cloak

斗室 dǒushì（名）〈书〉a small room

抖 dǒu（动）1 shake: ～掉雨衣上的雪. Shake the snow off one's raincoat. 2 tremble; shiver; quiver: 浑身直～ tremble all over. 冷得发～ shiver with cold 3 rouse; stir up: ～起精神 pluck up one's spirits 4 get on in the world: 他现在～起来了. His star is rising.

抖动(動) dǒudòng（动）shake; tremble; vibrate

抖擞(擻) dǒusǒu（动）enliven; rouse: 精神～ full of energy; full of vim and vigour

陡 dǒu I（形）steep; precipitous: ～坡 abrupt slope. 悬崖～壁 precipice; cliff II（副）suddenly; abruptly: 天气～变. The weather changed suddenly.

陡峻 dǒujùn（形）high and precipitous

陡峭 dǒuqiào（动）precipitous

斗(鬥) dòu（动）1 fight; struggle against: 与风浪搏～ battle with the winds and waves 2 contest with; contend with: ～智 duel of wits. 我～不过你. I'm not your match. 3 (of cocks, crickets, etc.) fight: ～鸡 cockfighting

see also dǒu

斗争 dòuzhēng I（动）1 struggle; fight; combat 2 strive for; fight for: 为祖国的现代化而～ fight for the modernization of the motherland II（名）struggle

斗志 dòuzhì（名）fighting will; morale: ～昂扬 have high morale

豆 dòu（名）bean: 咖啡～ coffee beans. 蚕～ broad beans. 豌～ peas. ～角 French beans

豆腐 dòufu（名）bean curd

豆制品 dòuzhìpǐn（名）bean products

痘 dòu（名）smallpox

痘苗 dòumiáo（名）(bovine) vaccine

逗 dòu I（动）1 play with; tease; tantalize: ～孩子玩 tantalize a child 2 attract; charm; amuse: ～人发笑 set people laughing. 这小女孩很～人喜欢. She's a charming little girl. 3 stay; stop II（形）funny: 这话真～! What a funny remark!

逗号(號) dòuhào（名）comma (,)

逗留 dòuliú（名）stay; stop: 中途在东京～两小时 stop over at Tokyo for two hours

逗趣儿 dòuqùr（动）set people laughing; amuse

都 dū（名）1 capital 2 big city: 通～大邑 big cities

see also dōu

都城 dūchéng（名）capital

都会(會) dūhuì（名）chief city; capital city

都市 dūshì（名）big city

嘟 dū（动）1〈象〉honk: 汽车喇叭～～响. The car tooted. 2 pout: ～起了嘴 pout

嘟囔 dūnang（动）mutter to self; mumble

督 dū（动）superintend and direct

督察 dūchá（动）superintend; supervise

督促 dūcù（动）supervise sb. and urge him to go ahead

毒 dú I（名）1 poison; toxin: 病～ virus. 服～自杀 commit suicide by taking poison 2 narcotics: 吸～ take drugs II（形）1 poisonous; noxious 2 malicious; cruel: 这人心肠真～ What a cruel man! III（动）kill with poison; poison IV（副）fiercely; cruelly: ～打 give sb. a good beating

毒草 dúcǎo（名）1 poisonous

weeds; 2 harmful speech, writing, etc.

毒害 dúhài (动) poison (sb.'s mind)

毒计 dújì (名) ruthless scheme; deadly plot

毒辣 dúlà (形) vicious; murderous

毒气(氣) dúqì (名) poison gas

毒蛇 dúshé (名) poisonous snake; viper

毒手 dúshǒu (名) murderous scheme: 下~ lay murderous hands on sb.; prepare a treacherous trap for sb.

毒药(藥) dúyào (名) poison; toxicant

渎(瀆) dú (动) ‹书› show disrespect or contempt: 亵~ blaspheme

渎职(職) dúzhí (名) malfeasance; dereliction of duty

读(讀) dú (动) 1 read; read aloud: 你~过这本书吗? Have you read this book? 请你~给我听. Could you read it (aloud) for me, please? 2 go to school or college: 他~完大学后就在这里开始工作. He started to work here after finishing college.

读本 dúběn (名) textbook; reader

读书(書) dúshū (动) 1 read; study 2 attend school: ~人 an intellectual

读数(數) dúshù (名) reading: 标度~ scale reading

读物 dúwù (名) reading material: 通俗~ popular literature

读音 dúyīn (名) pronunciation

读者 dúzhě (名) reader: ~来信 readers' letters; letters to the editor

黩(黷) dú (动) 1 blacken; defile 2 act wantonly

黩武 dúwǔ militaristic; warlike; bellicose: 穷兵~ engage in unjust military ventures

犊(犢) dú (名) calf

牍(牘) dú (名) 1 wooden tablets or slips for writing (in ancient times) 2 documents; archives; correspondence

髑 dú

髑髅(髏) dúlóu (名) ‹书› skull (of a dead person)

独(獨) dú I (形) only; sole: ~(生)子 only son II (副) alone: ~往~来 seldom go anywhere in company

独霸 dúbà (动) dominate exclusively; monopolize

独白 dúbái (名) soliloquy; monologue

独裁 dúcái (名) dictatorship; autocratic rule: ~者 autocrat; dictator. ~政治 autocracy

独唱 dúchàng (名) (vocal) solo

独出心裁 dú chū xīncái show originality; be original

独创(創) dúchuàng (名) original creation: ~一格 create a style all one's own. ~性 originality

独当(當)一面 dú dāng yī miàn be capable of handling affairs of a whole department

独到 dúdào (形) original: ~之处 originality

独断(斷)独行 dúduàn-dúxíng act autocratically

独夫 dúfū (名) autocrat: ~民贼 autocrat and traitor to the people

独角戏(戲) dújiǎoxì (名) monodrama; one-man show

独揽(攬) dúlǎn (动) arrogate; monopolize: ~大权 arrogate all powers to oneself

独立 dúlì I (动) stand alone II (名) independence III (形) independent; on one's own: ~思考 think independently

独木桥(橋) dúmùqiáo (名) single-plank bridge; difficult path

独幕剧(劇) dúmùjù (名) one-act play

独身 dúshēn (动) 1 live apart from one's family 2 unmarried; single; celibate

独树(樹)一帜(幟) dú shù yī zhì start a separate school of thought

独特 dútè (形) unique; distinctive: ~的风格 a unique style

独一无二 dúyī-wú'èr (形) unique; unparalleled; unmatched

独占 dúzhàn (动) enjoy exclusively; monopolize

独奏 dúzòu (名) (instrumental) solo: 钢琴~ piano solo

堵 dǔ I (动) 1 stop up; block up: 路~住了. The road is blocked. 别~着门! Don't stand in the doorway! 2 feel suffocated; oppressed; stiffed II (量): 一~墙 a wall

堵塞 dǔsè (动) stop up; block up: 交通~ traffic jam

堵嘴 dǔzuǐ (动) silence sb.

睹 dǔ (动) see: 目～ witness. 目～者 eye witness. 熟视无～ turn a blind eye to

赌 dǔ (动) 1 gamble: ～博 gambling. ～场 gambling den. ～棍 gambler 2 bet: 打～ make a bet; bet

赌气(氣) dǔqì (动) feel wronged or frustrated and act rashly: ～走了 dash off in a fit of pique

赌钱(錢) dǔqián (动) (for money) gamble; play

赌咒 dǔzhòu (动) take an oath; swear

赌注 dǔzhù (名) stake

笃 dǔ (形) 1 sincere; earnest: ～志 tenacious of purpose 2 (of an illness) serious; critical: 病～ be terminally ill

笃信 dǔxìn (动) sincerely believe in; be a loyal adherent of

笃学(學) dǔxué (形) diligent in study; devoted to study; studious

肚 dǔ (～子)(名) tripe

see also dù

度 dù I (名) 1 degree: 长～ length. 温～ temperature. 硬～ hardness. 湿～ humidity 2 [a unit or measurement for angles, temperature, etc.] degree: 九十～的角 an angle of 90 degrees. 摄氏一百～ 100°C. 一～电 one kilowatt-hour 3 limit; extent; degree: 劳累过～ overwork oneself 4 tolerance; magnanimity: 大～ be magnanimous 5 consideration: 把生死置之～外 give no thought to personal safety II (动) spend; pass: 欢～佳节 joyously celebrate a festival. ～假 spend one's holidays III (量) occasion; time: 再～ once more. 一年一～ once a year

see also duó

度量 dùliàng (名) tolerance; magnanimity: ～大 broad-minded. ～小 narrow-minded

度量衡 dùliànghéng (名) length, capacity and weight; weights and measures

度日 dùrì (动) do for a living: ～如年 drag on a miserable existence

渡 dù I (动) 1 cross (a river, the sea, etc.): ～江 cross a river 2 tide over; pull through: ～过难关 tide over a difficulty II (名) ferry

渡船 dùchuán (名) ferryboat; ferry

渡口 dùkǒu (名) ferry

镀 dù (名) plating 电～: galvanizing. ～金 gold-plating; gilding

杜 dù (动) prevent; eradicate: 以～流弊 so as to put an end to any abuse or malpractice

杜绝 dùjué (动) stop; prevent; put an end to: ～贪污和浪费 prevent corruption and waste

杜撰 dùzhuàn (动) fabricate; make up

肚 dù (名) belly

see also dǔ

肚皮 dùpí (名) belly

肚脐(臍) dùqí (名) navel; belly button

妒 dù (动) be jealous (or envious) of; envy

妒忌 dùjì (动) be jealous (or envious) of; envy

端 duān I (名) 1 end; extremity: 笔～ the tip of a writing brush 2 beginning: 开～ beginning 3 reason; cause: 无～ without reason; unwarranted II (形) upright; proper: ～庄 dignified. 品行不～ misbehaviour III (动) hold sth. level with both hands; carry: ～托盘 carry a tray. ～饭菜 bring food in

端量 duānliáng (动) look sb. up and down

端倪 duānní (名) clue; inkling: 略有～ have some clues

端详 duānxiáng I (动) scrutinize; look sb. up and down II (名) details III (形) dignified and serene: 举止～ behave with dignity

端正 duānzhèng I (形) 1 upright; regular: 五官～ have regular features. 坐得～ sit straight in one's seat 2 proper; correct: 品行～ correct in behaviour; respectable II (动) rectify; correct: ～态度 make sure one's attitude is correct

短 duǎn I (形) short; brief II (动) 1 lack; be short of: 只～两个人. Only two people are absent. 2 owe: 你还～我三元钱. You still owe me three *Yuan*. III (名) weak point; fault: 揭人的～儿 pick on sb.'s weakness. 说长道～ gossip

短兵相接 duǎnbīng xiāng jiē fight at close quarters

短波 duǎnbō (名) short wave

短处(處) duǎnchù (名) short-

coming; weakness; fault
短促 duǎncù (形) very brief; short: 时间～ pressed for time. 呼吸～ short of breath
短见(見) duǎnjiàn (名) **1** short-sighted view **2** suicide: 寻～ attempt suicide; commit suicide
短路 duǎnlù (名) short circuit
短命 duǎnmìng (动) die young; be short-lived
短跑 duǎnpǎo (名) dash; sprint
短篇小说 duǎnpiān xiǎoshuō (名) short story
短期 duǎnqī (名) short-term; short period: ～贷款 short-term loan
短浅(淺) duǎnqiǎn (形) narrow and shallow: 目光～ shortsighted. 见识～ badly informed and superficial
短缺 duǎnquē (名) shortage; deficiency
短小 duǎnxiǎo (形) short and small: 身材～ of small stature
短小精悍 duǎnxiǎo jīnghàn (形) short but well-built; short and pithy
短语 duǎnyǔ (名) phrase
短暂 duǎnzàn (形) of short duration; brief: 生命是～的. Life is short.

断(斷) duàn I (动) **1** break; snap; cut: 绳子～了. The rope snapped. 桥～了. The bridge is broken. ～电 cut off electricity. 联系中～ lose contact (with) **2** judge; decide: 当机立～ make a prompt decision II (副) 〈书〉 [used only in negative sentences] absolutely; decidedly: ～无此理 absolutely absurd; the height of absurdity
断肠(腸) duàncháng (形) heart-broken; broken-hearted
断炊 duànchuī (动) run out of food and fuel; can't keep the pot boiling
断定 duàndìng (动) form a judgment; conclude
断断续(續)续 duànduànxùxù (副) intermittently: 他～在这里住了五年. He has lived here off and on for five years.
断根 duàngēn (动) (of an illness) be completely cured
断后(後) duànhòu (动) **1** cover the retreat **2** have no progeny
断句 duànjù (动) punctuate
断绝 duànjué (动) break off; cut off; sever: ～关系 break off all relationship. ～交通 cut off all communications
断气(氣) duànqì (动) breathe one's last; die
断然 duànrán I (形) resolute; drastic: 采取～措施 take drastic measures II (副) absolutely
断送 duànsòng (动) forfeit (one's life, future, etc.); ruin
断头(頭)台(臺) duàntóutái (名) guillotine
断言 duànyán (动) assert
断章取义(義) duàn zhāng qǔ yì quote one's words out of context; distort a statement, etc.

段 duàn (量) section; part: 一～路 certain distance. 一～话 a passage from a speech. 一～时间 a period of time
段落 duànluò (名) **1** paragraph **2** phase; stage

煅 duàn (动) forge: ～铁 forge iron

锻 duàn (动) forge
锻工 duàngōng (名) forging; forger
锻炼(煉) duànliàn (动) **1** take physical exercise **2** temper; steel; toughen

缎 duàn (名) satin

堆 duī I (动) pile; stack: 粮食～满仓. The granary was piled high with grain. II (名) heap; pile; stack: 土～ mound. 草～ haystack III (量) heap; pile; crowd: 一～人 a crowd of people
堆放 duīfàng (动) heap; stack
堆积(積) duījī (动) pile up; heap up
堆砌 duīqì (动) **1** pile up (hewn rocks, etc.) **2** write in a florid language

兑 duì (动) exchange; convert
兑换 duìhuàn (动) exchange; convert: ～率 rate of exchange. ～处 moneychanger
兑现 duìxiàn (动) **1** cash (a cheque, etc.) **2** realize; fulfil

对(對) duì I (动) **1** treat; against: 她～我很好. She treats me well. ～付 cope with. 反～ be against **2** face: ～着镜子看 look at oneself in the mirror. 把枪口～准敌人 aim one's gun at the enemy. ～坐 sit face to face **3** compare; check: 校～ proofread **4** adjust: ～表 adjust (or set) the watch. ～距离 (of a camera) adjust the distance **5**

bring two things into contact; fit one into the other: ～暗号 exchange code words. ～火儿 (of smoking). Give me a light, please **6** mix; add: 牛奶里～水了. The milk has been adulterated with water. **7** answer; reply **8** suit; agree: ～口味儿 suit one's taste II (形) correct; right: 你说得～. What you said is correct. 是他的不～. It's his fault. III (量) pair; couple: 一～花瓶 a pair of vases. 一～夫妇 a married couple IV (介):她～我说的. She said this to me. 我～他笑. I smiled at him. 这是我～她的看法. This is my opinion of her. ～某事的态度(one's) attitude towards sth.

对白 duìbái (名) dialogue (in a novel, film or play)

对半 duìbàn (副) half-and-half; fifty-fifty

对比 duìbǐ (动) contrast; compare: 形成鲜明的～ form a sharp contrast

对不起 duìbuqǐ **1** 〈套〉 I'm sorry; excuse me; pardon me; I beg your pardon **2** let sb. down; be unfair to sb.

对策 duìcè (名) countermeasure

对称(稱) duìchèn (名) symmetry

对答 duìdá (动) answer; reply: ～如流 answer fluently

对待 duìdài (动) treat; approach; handle

对得起 duìdeqǐ be worthy of; not let sb. down; treat sb. fairly (also as "对得住")

对等 duìděng (名) reciprocity; equity: 在～的基础上 on a reciprocal basis

对方 duìfāng (名) opposite side; the other party

对付 duìfù (动) **1** deal with; cope with; tackle: ～敌人 deal with the enemy **2** make do; get by: 这把伞还可以～着用. The umbrella is still serviceable.

对号(號) duìhào (动) check the number: ～入座 sit in the right seat

对话 duìhuà (名) dialogue

对劲(勁) duìjìn (形) **1** be to one's liking; suit one: 这支笔写起字不～. This writing brush is not easy to handle when you use it. 他俩很～. The two of them are getting along well. **2** normal; right: 他今天有些不～. He is not quite himself today.

对开(開) duìkāi I (动) **1** (of trains, buses or ships) run from opposite directions **2** divide into two halves; go fifty-fifty II (名) folio

对抗 duìkàng I (名) confrontation II (动) resist; oppose

对口 duìkǒu (动) fit in with one's training or speciality: 工作～ a job one is trained for

对立 duìlì (名) antagonism; antithesis; opposition: ～面 opposites

对联(聯) duìlián (名) antithetical couplet (written on scrolls, etc.)

对门(門) duìmén (名) the house opposite

对面 duìmiàn (形) **1** opposite: 加油站在学校～. The petrol station is opposite the school. **2** right in front: 一辆车从～开过来. A car is coming towards us. **3** face to face

对牛弹(彈)琴 duì niú tánqín play the lute to a cow; talk over sb.'s head; address the wrong audience

对手 duìshǒu (名) **1** opponent; adversary **2** match; equal: 他不是你的～. He's no match for you.

对台(臺)戏(戲) duìtáixì (名) rival performance or show: 唱～ put on a rival show

对头(頭) duìtóu (形) **1** correct; on the right track **2** normal; right: 你的脸色不～. You're not looking well.

对头(頭) duìtou (名) **1** enemy: 死～ sworn enemy **2** opponent; adversary

对外 duìwài (形) external; foreign: ～贸易 foreign trade

对象 duìxiàng (名) **1** target; object: 研究～ objective of a research project **2** boy or girl friend

对应(應) duìyìng (形) corresponding

对于(於) duìyú (介) 大家～这个问题的看法是一致的. Their views on this problem are identical. ～我来说，这没什么关系. As far as I am concerned, it doesn't matter.

对照 duìzhào (动) compare; collate: ～检查 make self-criticism. 把新本与旧本～一下. Collate the new copy with the old one.

对症下药(藥) duì zhèng xià yào decide on measures to solve problems according to specific

circumstances
对质(質) duìzhì (名) confrontation (in court)
对峙 duìzhì (动) confront each other: 武装～ military confrontation
队(隊) duì (名) 1 team; group: 篮球～ basketball team. 军乐～ military band. 游击～ guerrilla forces 2 a row (or line) of people: 排成两～ fall into two lines
队伍 duìwǔ (名) 1 troops 2 ranks; contingent: 游行～ procession; parade
队形 duìxíng (名) formation: ～飞行 formation flying. 战斗～ in battle formation
队长(長) duìzhǎng (名) group leader; team leader
敦 dūn (形) honest; sincere: ～请 cordially invite; earnestly request
敦促 dūncù (动) urge; press
敦厚 dūnhòu (形) honest and sincere
敦实(實) dūnshi (形) sturdy: 这人长得很～. He has a powerful build, though short in stature.
墩 dūn (名) block: 土～mound. 菜～(子) chopping board. 树～ stump. 桥～ pier (of a bridge)
墩布 dūnbù (名) mop
吨(噸) dūn (名) ton (t.)
吨位 dūnwèi (名) tonnage
蹲 dūn (动) 1 squat 2 stay: ～在家里 stay at home
蹲点(點) dūndiǎn (动) (of cadres) stay at a selected grassroots unit to help improve the work and gain firsthand experience
盹 dǔn (动) doze: 打～儿 doze off; get a wink of sleep
炖 dùn (动) 1 stew: ～牛肉 stewed beef 2 warm sth.: ～酒 warm (up) wine
顿 dùn I (动) 1 pause 2 arrange; settle: 安～ arrange for; settle in 3 stamp: ～脚 stamp one's foot II (名) pause III (量) 三～饭 three meals. 挨了一～骂 get a scolding IV(副) suddenly: 茅塞～开 be suddenly enlightened
顿时(時) dùnshí (副) immediately; at once
顿挫 dùncuò (名) pause and transition in rhythm or melody: 抑扬～ modulation in tone
顿号(號) dùnhào (名) a slight-pause mark used to set off items in a series(、)
囤 dùn (名) a grain bin see also tún
钝 dùn (形) 1 blunt; dull: ～刀 a blunt knife 2 stupid: 迟～ dull-witted; slow
盾 dùn (名) shield: ～牌 shield
遁 dùn (动) escape; flee; fly
遁词 dùncí (名) subterfuge; quibble
咄 duō
咄咄逼人 duōduō bī rén (形) aggressive; overbearing
咄咄怪事 duōduō guàishì (名) inconceivable absurdity
多 duō I (形) 1 many; much; more: 很～人 many people. 这菜油太～. The dish is too rich. 更～的帮助 more help 2 odd; over; more than: 五十～岁 over fifty year's old. 一个～月 more than a month. 三十～年 thirty-odd years 3 much more; far more: 病人今天好～了. The patient is much better today. 这部电影比那部要有意思～了. Compared with that film, this one is far more interesting. 这样做就容易～了. It is much easier to do it this way. 4 too many; too much; excessive: ～了十张票. There are ten tickets too many. 我在那里～住了几天. I stayed there a few days longer. II (副) [indicating degree or extent]: 这孩子～大了? How old is this child? 他要在这里呆～久? How long is he going to stay here? 我倒想看看她有～能干! I'd like to see how capable she is!
多半 duōbàn I (形) the greater part; most; mostly: 他们之中～是大学生. Most of them are students. II (副) probably; most likely: 瞧! 这天～要下雨. Look at the sky. It's most likely going to rain.
多边(邊) duōbiān (形) multilateral: ～会谈 multilateral talks. ～贸易 multilateral trade
多才多艺(藝) duōcái-duōyì (形) versatile: ～的人 a man (woman) of parts
多愁善感 duōchóu-shàngǎn (形) sentimental
多此一举(舉) duō cǐ yī jǔ make an unnecessary move: 何必～?

Why take the trouble to do that?

多次 duōcì (副) many times; repeatedly

多多益善 duōduō yì shàn the more the better

多方 duōfāng (副) in many ways; in every way: ～设法 try every possible means

多寡 duō-guǎ (名) number; amount: ～不等 vary in amount or number

多亏(虧) duōkuī (副) thanks to; luckily [indicating the result in which a misfortune has been avoided]: 这孩子没受伤～了你的帮助. Thanks to your help, the child is unhurt.

多么 duōme (副) [used in an exclamatory or a compound sentence indicating high degree] how; what; however: ～美的地方! What a beautiful place! 他跑得～快啊! How fast he runs! 不管天气～冷,他都坚持户外锻炼. However cold it was, he never stopped taking outdoor exercises.

多面手 duōmiànshǒu (名) a versatile person

多谋善断(斷) duōmóu-shànduàn(形) resourceful and decisive

多情 duōqíng (形) susceptible

多少 duōshǎo (名) somewhat; more or less; to some extent: 他讲的～有点道理. There's something in what he says. 他～有点不高兴. He's not entirely happy about it.

多少 duōshao (形) 1 how many; how much: 有～人来参加晚会? How many people are coming to the party? 他干了～了? How much has he done? 2 how many; how much [used to indicate an uncertain quantity]: 我说过～遍了,叫你别去那儿! Didn't I tell you not to go there! 他懂～! How much does he know!

多事 duōshì (形) 1 meddlesome: 怪我～. I shouldn't have meddled in this. 2 eventful

多数(數) duōshù (名) majority; most: 绝大～ an overwhelming majority

多谢 duōxiè 〈套〉 many thanks; thanks a lot

多心 duōxīn (形) oversensitive

多余(餘) duōyú (形) 1 extra; surplus: 有～的一份. There is an extra copy. ～农产品 surplus farm products 2 unnecessary; superfluous: 你这话是～的. What you said is unnecessary.

多云(雲) duōyún (形) cloudy

多种(種)经(經)营(營) duōzhǒng jīngyíng diversified economy

多嘴 duōzuǐ (动) speak out of turn: ～多舌 gossipy; long-tongued. 别～! Shut up!

哆 duō

哆嗦 duōsuo (动) tremble; shiver: 气得直～ tremble with rage. 冷得打～ shiver with cold

掇 duō (动) pick up: 拾～ tidy up

度 duó (动)〈书〉 surmise; estimate

see also dù

度德量力 duódé-liànglì estimate one's own political and professional competence; make an appraisal of one's own position

踱 duó (动) pace; stroll: ～来～去 pace to and fro; pace up and down

夺(奪) duó (动) 1 take by force; seize: ～权 seize power 2 strive for; win: ～高产 strive for high yields. ～金牌(try) to win a gold medal 3 force one's way: ～门而出 force one's way out. 眼泪～眶而出. Tears welled out from one's eyes.

夺目 duómù (动) dazzle the eyes: 光彩～ dazzling; brilliant

夺取 duóqǔ (动) capture; seize; wrest

朵 duǒ 〈量〉: 一～花 a flower. 一～云 a cloud

垛 duǒ (名) 1 buttress 2 battlements

see also duò

躲 duǒ (动) avoid; hide; dodge: 你怎么老～着他?Why do you always try to avoid him?～雨 take shelter from the rain

躲避 duǒbì (动) 1 hide (of person or animal) 2 avoid; dodge; evade: ～开人群 keep away from the crowd

躲藏 duǒcáng (动) hide (or conceal) oneself; go into hiding

躲闪 duǒshǎn (动) dodge; evade: 躲躲闪闪 be evasive; equivocate

惰 duò (形) lazy; indolent: 懒～ lazy

惰性 duòxìng (名) inertia

堕(墮) duò (动) fall; sink

堕落 duòluò (动) (of mind; behavior) be corrupted; degenerate

堕胎 duòtāi (名) abortion

舵 duò (名) rudder; helm

舵手 duòshǒu (名) steersman; helmsman

垛 duò I (动) pile up neatly; stack: 把木头～起来 pile up the logs II (名) pile; stack: 麦～ a stack of wheat

剁 duò (动) chop; cut: ～肉馅 chop up (or mince) meat

see also duǒ

跺 duò (动) stamp (one's foot)

E e

阿 ē (动) cater for

see also ā

阿弥(彌)陀佛 Ēmítuófó Amitabha; may Buddha preserve us; merciful Buddha

阿谀奉承 ēyú fèngcheng (动) fawn on; flatter

婀 ē

婀娜 ēnuó (形) (of a woman's bearing) graceful

额 é (名) **1** forehead **2** quota; a fixed number or amount: 超～ above quota. 贸易～ volume of trade

额定 édìng (形) specified (number or amount): ～人数 the maximum number of persons allowed. ～工资 regular pay

额外 éwài (形) extra; additional: ～开支 extra expenses. ～负担 additional burden

峨 é (形) <书> high: 巍～ towering; lofty

鹅 é (名) goose

鹅卵石 éluǎnshí (名) cobblestone; cobble

鹅毛 émáo (名) goose feather: ～大雪 snow in big flakes

娥 é (名) pretty young woman: 宫～ palace maid

娥眉 éméi (名) **1** delicate eyebrows **2** beautiful woman

蛾 é (名) moth

讹 é I (动) extort; blackmail II (名) error: 以～传～ pass on a wrong message from one person to another; inconnectedly relay a wrong message

讹传(傳) échuán (名) unfounded rumour

讹诈 ézhà (动) blackmail: 核～ nuclear blackmail. ～钱财 extort money under false pretences

恶(惡) ě

see also è; wù

恶心 ěxin I (动) feel sick II (形) disgusting; nauseating

恶(惡) è I (名) evil; vice; wickedness: 无～不作 stop at no evil II (形) **1** vicious; fierce;ferocious: 一场～战 a fierce battle. ～狼 a ferocious wolf **2** evil; wicked: ～人 evildoer

see also ě; wù

恶霸 èbà (名) local tyrant (or despot)

恶臭 èchòu (名) foul smell; stench

恶毒 èdú (形) vicious; malicious; venomous: ～攻击 make vicious attacks against. 手段～ vicious means

恶感 ègǎn (名) ill feeling; malice; resentment

恶贯满盈 è guàn mǎnyíng be guilty of too numerous crimes to escape punishment

恶棍 ègùn (名) ruffian; scoundrel; bully

恶果 èguǒ (名) evil consequence; disastrous effect

恶狠狠 èhěnhěn (形) fierce; ferocious

恶化 èhuà (动) worsen; deteriorate: 病情～了. The patient's condition has worsened. 形势不断～. The situation has steadily deteriorated.

恶劣 èliè (形) bad; evil; disgusting: 品质～ be morally corrupt. ～手段 despicable means. ～气候 inclement climate

恶魔 èmó (名) demon; devil

恶习(習) èxí (名) bad habit

恶性 èxìng (形) malignant; pernicious: ～循环 vicious circle. ～肿瘤 malignant tumour

恶意 èyì (名) evil (or ill) intentions; malice

恶作剧(劇) èzuòjù (名) practical joke; mischief

噩 è (形) shocking; upsetting

噩耗 èhào (名) sad news (of someone's death)

噩梦(夢) èmèng (名) nightmare

厄 è (名)〈书〉 1 disaster; adversity 2 strategic point: 险～ a strategic pass

厄运(運) èyùn (名) misfortune

扼 è (动) 1 clutch; grip 2 guard; control

扼杀(殺) èshā (动) strangle; smother

扼守 èshǒu (动) hold (a strategic point); guard

扼要 èyào (形) concise; to the point: 简明～ brief and precise

呃 è

呃逆 ènì (名) hiccup (also as 打呃)

遏 è (动) check; hold back: 怒不可～ cannot restrain one's anger; be fired with indignation; be in a towering rage

遏止 èzhǐ (动) check; hold back

遏制 èzhì (动) restrain; contain; keep within limits

愕 è (形) stunned; astounded

愕然 èrán (形) stunned; astounded: 消息传来，大家为之～. We were rather taken aback by the news.

颚 è (名) 1 jaw: 上(下)～ upper (lower) jaw 2 palate

腭 è (名) palate: 硬(软)～ hard (soft) palate

鳄(鱷) è (名) crocodile; alligator

鳄鱼 èyú (名) crocodile; alligator: ～的眼泪 crocodile tears

饿(餓) è I (形) hungry: 挨～ go hungry II (动) starve: ～死 starve to death

欸 ē (叹) [used to attract attention]: ～,你快来! Hey! Come over here. ～, 你说什么? Eh? What did you say?

see also ǎi; é; ě; è

欸 é or éi (叹) [used to express surprise]: ～,怎么停电了! Why, the electricity is off!

see also ǎi;ē; ě; è

欸 ě or ěi (叹) [usedto express disapproval]: ～, 可不能这样说哇. I'm afraid you can't talk like that.

see also ěi; ē; é; è

欸 è or èi (叹) [used to indicate response or agreement]: ～,来了! Yes, I'm coming. ～,我就给他送去. All right, I'll send it over to him immediately.

see also ǎi;ē;é;ě

恩 ēn (名) 1 kindness; favour; grace: 报～ repay a person for his kindness 2 matrimonial happiness

恩爱(愛) ēn'ài (名) conjugal love

恩赐 ēncì I (动) bestow (favours, charity, etc.) II (名) favour; charity

恩德 ēndé (名) favour; kindness; grace

恩惠 ēnhuì (名) favour; kindness; grace

恩将(將)仇报(報) ēn jiāng chóu bào return evil for good

恩情 ēnqíng (名) great kindness

恩人 ēnrén (名) benefactor

恩怨 ēn-yuàn (名) feeling of gratitude or resentment: 不计较个人～ never let personal feeling of gratitude or resentment interfere wtih matters

摁 èn (动) press (with the hand or finger): ～电钮 press (or push) a button

摁钉儿 èndīngr (名)〈口〉 drawing pin

摁扣儿 ènkòur (名)〈口〉 snap fastener

而 ér (连) 1 express coordination: 美丽～善良 beautiful and kind-hearted. 朴素～大方 simple and with good taste 2 [similar to 'but' or 'yet']: 华～不实 flashy without substance. 这颜色艳～不俗. This colour is bright but not garish. 3 [connect cause and effect; aim and means or action]: 因病～辞职 resign on health grounds. 为找工作～奔跑 hunting for a job. 匆匆～来 come in a hurry 4 [indicate change from one state to another]: 由远～近 approach from afar. 由上～下 from top to bottom

而今 érjīn (副) now; at the present time

而且 érqiě (连) and also; moreover; in addition: 他不但很懂画，～自己画得也不错. He knows a lot about painting, and he paints well himself. 不仅下了雪，～下得很大. It not only snowed but also snowed heavily.

而已 éryǐ (助) that is all; nothing more: 不过开个玩笑～. It's only a joke.

儿(兒) ér I (名) 1 son 2 child: 小～ little child 3 youngster; youth II (后缀) 小猫～ kitten

儿歌 érgē (名) nursery rhymes; children's song

儿化 érhuà (名) [a phonetic phenomenon — the retroflex ending 'r']: 猫～(māor) cat. 花～(huār) flower. 他火～了. He got angry.
儿科 érkē (名) paediatrics: ～医生 paediatrician
儿女 ér-nǚ (名) sons and daughters; youth: ～情长 Love between man and woman is long.
儿孙(孫) ér-sūn (名) children and grandchildren; descendants
儿童 értóng (名) children
儿媳妇(婦)儿 érxífur (名) daughter-in-law
儿戏(戲) érxì (名) trifling matter: 这可不是～. It's no trifling matter.
儿子 érzi (名) son

耳 ěr I (名) ear II (形) on both sides; flanking; side: ～房 side rooms
耳背 ěrbèi (形) hard of hearing
耳边(邊)风(風) ěrbiānfēng (名) sth. goes in at one ear and out at the other: 把某事当作～ turn a deaf ear to sth.
耳聪(聰)目明 ěrcōng-mùmíng clear-headed and clear-sighted
耳朵 ěrduo (名) ear: ～尖 have sharp ears. ～软 credulous; easily influenced
耳光 ěrguāng (名) a slap on the ear
耳环(環) ěrhuán (名) earrings
耳机(機) ěrjī (名) earphone
耳鸣 ěrmíng (名) tinnitus; ringing in the ear
耳目 ěrmù (名) ears and eyes: ～一新 find everything fresh and new. ～闭塞 ill-informed. ～众多have many people serving as one's eyes and ears; have many spies
耳闻 ěrwén (动) hear of (or about): ～目睹 what one sees and hears
耳语 ěryǔ (动) whisper

饵(餌) ěr (名) bait

尔(爾) ěr I (代)〈书〉1 you 2 that
尔后(後) ěrhòu (副)〈书〉thereafter; subsequently
尔虞我诈 ěryú-wǒzhà mutual deception; each trying to cheat and outwit the other

二 èr I (数) two: ～十 twenty. ～两茶叶 two *liang* of tea. ～楼(英) first floor; (美) second floor II (形) different: ～心 disloyalty; half-heartedness
二百五 èrbǎiwǔ (名)〈口〉a stupid person
二重唱 èrchóngchàng (名)〈乐〉(vocal) duet
二重性 èrchóngxìng (名) dual character; duality
二等 èrděng (形) second class; second-rate
二话 èrhuà (名) demur; objection: ～不说 without demur
二极(極)管 èrjíguan (名) diode
二流子 èrliúzi (名) loafer; idler; hooligan
二元论(論) èryuánlùn (名)dualism
二月 èryuè (名) February

贰 èr two [used for the numeral 二 on cheques, banknotes, etc. to avoid mistakes or alterations]

F f

发(發) fā I (动) 1 send out; issue; dispatch; distribute: ～电报 send a telegram (or cable). ～通知 issue a notice. ～炮 fire a cannon. ～工资 pay wages 2 utter: ～言 take the floor. ～议论 comment on sth. 3 come into existence; occur: 旧病复～ have another attack of one's old illness. ～了大水. A flood occurred. 4 become; get into a certain state: ～红 turn red. ～臭become smell (or off). ～潮 get damp. ～胖 become fat. ～酸 turn sour. ～面 let the dough rise 5 feel: 腿～麻 have pins and needles in one's leg. ～怒 get angry. ～痒 itch II (量) [for ammunition]: 两～炮弹 two shells
发榜 fābǎng (动) publish a list of successful candidates
发报(報) fābào (动) transmit messages by radio: ～机 telegraph transmitter
发表 fābiǎo (动) publish; issue: ～文章 publish an article. ～声明 issue (or make) a statement. ～意见 state one's views. ～演说 make a speech
发布(佈) fābù (动) issue; release: ～命令 issue orders. ～新闻 release news

发财 fācái (动) get rich; make a good deal of money
发愁 fāchóu (动) worry; be anxious
发出 fāchū (动) 1 send out; issue: ～稿 send a manuscript to the press. ～命令 give an order 2 give off: ～香味 give off a fragrant smell
发达(達) fādá (形) developed; flourishing: ～国家 developed country
发呆 fādāi (动) stare blankly; be stupified
发电(電) fādiàn (动) generate electricity: ～站 power station. ～厂 power plant; power station. ～机 generator
发动(動) fādòng (动) 1 start; launch: ～战争 launch a war. ～机器 start a machine. ～机 engine; motor 2 arouse; mobilize: ～群众 arouse (or mobilize) the masses
发抖 fādǒu (动) shiver; shake; tremble: 冷得～ shiver with cold. 气得～ shake with anger
发放 fāfàng (动) grant; provide: ～贷款 grant a loan
发奋(奮) fāfèn (动) 1 make a determined effort 2 work energetically
发愤 fāfèn (动) see 发奋: ～图强 make a determined effort to help revitalize the nation
发疯(瘋) fāfēng (动) go mad; lose one's senses; be out of one's mind
发福 fāfú (动) put on weight; grow stout
发光 fāguāng (动) give out light; shine; be luminous
发汗 fāhàn (动) induce perspiratino (as by drugs): ～药 sudorific; diaphoretic
发号(號)施令 fāhào-shīlìng (动) issue orders; order people about
发慌 fāhuāng (动) feel nervous; get flustered
发挥 fāhuī (动) 1 give play to; bring into play: ～群众的积极性 bring the initiative of the masses into full play. ～专长 give full play to sb's professional knowledge or skill 2 develop (an idea, a theme, etc.); elaborate: 借题～ seize on a minor incident to make an issue of it
发昏 fāhūn (动) feel dizzy; lose one's head; become confused
发火 fāhuǒ (动) get angry; flare up; lose one's temper
发迹 fājī (动) (of a poor man) gain fame and wealth
发家 fājiā (动) build up a family fortune
发奖(獎) fājiǎng (动) award prizes
发酵 fājiào (动) ferment
发觉(覺) fājué (动) find; realize; discover
发掘 fājué (动) excavate; unearth; explore: ～古墓 excavate an ancient tomb. ～潜力 explore the latent potential of sb. or sth.
发狂 fākuáng (动) go mad; go crazy
发愣 fālèng (动)〈口〉 be in a daze
发亮 fāliàng (动) shine
发霉 fāméi (动) go mouldy
发明 fāmíng (动、名) invent; invention: 印刷术是中国首先～的. Printing was first invented by the Chinese. ～家 inventor
发脾气(氣) fā píqi (动) lose one's temper; fly into a rage
发票 fāpiào (名) invoice; bill; receipt: 开～ make out a bill; write a receipt
发起 fāqǐ (动) 1 initiate; sponsor: ～人 sponsor; initiator 2 start; launch: ～进攻 launch an attack
发情 fāqíng (名) oestrus: ～期 heat period; oestrus
发球 fāqiú (动) serve a ball: 换～! Change service!
发人深省 fā rén shēn xǐng thought provoking; provide food for thought
发烧(燒) fāshāo (动) run a fever; have a temperature
发射 fāshè (动) launch; project; discharge; fire: ～宇宙飞船 launch a space-ship
发生 fāshēng (动) happen; occur; take place
发誓 fāshì (动) take an oath; vow; pledge
发售 fāshòu (动) sell; put on sale
发条(條) fātiáo (名) clockwork spring
发问 fāwèn (动) ask or raise a question
发现 fāxiàn (动) find; discover
发泄 fāxiè (动) give vent to; vent: ～怨气 give vent to one's grievances
发信 fāxìn (动) post a letter: ～人 addresser
发行 fāxíng (动) (of currency, books, etc.) issue; publish; dis-

tribute: ～纸币 issue paper money. ～书刊 publish books and magazines. ～影片 release a film

发芽 fāyá (动) sprout

发言人 fāyánrén (名) spokesman: 政府～ government spokesman

发炎 fāyán (动、名) inflammation: 伤口～了 The wound has become inflamed.

发扬(揚) fāyáng (动) 1 (of spirit, tradition, etc.) develop; foster; carry on

发音 fāyīn (名) pronunciation: ～器官 vocal organs

发育 fāyù (名) growth; development: ～健全 physically well developed

发源 fāyuán (动) originate: ～地 place of origin; source

发展 fāzhǎn (动) 1 develop; expand; grow: ～大好形势 The situation which is very good as it is calls for further expansion. 2 recruit: ～新党员 recruit new Party members

发展中国家 fāzhǎnzhōng guójiā(名) developing country

发作 fāzuò (动) 1 break out; show effect: 酒性～ The effect of the liquor is being felt. 2 flare up: 歇斯底里大～ have a bad fit of hysterics

罚(罰) fá (动) punish; penalize: 赏～分明 be fair in the administration of the law; be fair in passing critical judgment

罚款 fákuǎn (动) fine

罚球 fáqiú (篮球) penalty shot; (足球) penalty kick

乏 fá I (动) lack: ～味 tasteless; dull II (形) tired; weary: 走～了 feel dog-tired from a long walk

伐 fá (动) 1 fell; cut down: ～木 felling; lumbering 2 strike; attack: 征～ send a punitive expedition

阀 fá (名) 1 a powerful person or family: 军～ warlord. 财～ financial magnate 2 valve: ～门 valve. 安全～ safety valve

筏 fá (名) raft: 橡皮～ rubber raft

法 fǎ (名) 1 law: 守～ observe the law; be law-abiding. 违～ break the law 2 method; way: 作～ way of doing. 教学～ teaching method; pedagogical methodology

法案 fǎ'àn (名) proposed law; bill

法办(辦) fǎbàn (动) deal with according to law; punish by law; bring to justice

法宝(寶) fǎbǎo (名) a magic weapon

法场(場) fǎchǎng (名) execution ground

法典 fǎdiǎn (名) code; statute book

法定 fǎdìng (形) legal; statutory: ～汇率 official rate (of exchange); pegged rate of exchange. ～年龄 legal age. ～期限 legal time limit

法官 fǎguān (名) judge; justice

法规 fǎguī (名) laws and regulations; rules

法纪 fǎjì (名) law and discipline: 目无～ act in complete disregard of law and discipline

法警 fǎjǐng (名) bailiff

法郎 fǎláng (名) franc (currency)

法令 fǎlìng (名) laws and decrees; decree

法律 fǎlǜ (名) law: ～保护 legal protection. ～承认 de jure recognition. ～根据 legal basis. ～规定 legal provisions. ～手续 legal procedure. ～效力 legal effect. ～制裁 legal sanction

法术(術) fǎshù (名) magic touch

法庭 fǎtíng (名) court

法网(網) fǎwǎng (名) the web of justice; the arm of the law

法西斯 fǎxīsī (名) fascist: ～主义 fascism

法学(學) fǎxué (名) the science of law: ～家 jurist

法医(醫) fǎyī (名) coroner; forensic medical examiner

法院 fǎyuàn (名) court of justice; law court; court: 最高～ the Supreme Court

法则 fǎzé (名) rule; law: 自然～ law of nature

法治 fǎzhì (名) rule by law

法制 fǎzhì (名) legal system; legal institutions

法子 fǎzi (名) way; method

砝 fǎ

砝码 fǎmǎ (名) weight [used on a scale]

珐 fà

珐琅 fàláng (名) enamel: ～质 enamel

发(髮) fà (名) hair: 理～ haircut

see also fā

发型 fàxíng (名) hair style
发指 fàzhǐ boil with anger: 令人～ make one's hair bristle with anger

帆 fān (名) sail
帆布 fānbù (名) canvas
帆船 fānchuán (名) sailing boat; junk sail

番 fān (量) 1 kind: 别有一～风味 have an altogether different flavour 2 for actions which take time or effort: 下了一～功夫 put in a lot of effort. 三～五次 time and again
番号(號) fānhào (名) number of designation
番茄 fānqié (名) tomato: ～酱 tomato ketchup. ～汁 tomato juice
番薯 fānshǔ (名) sweet potato

幡 fān (名) long narrow flag; streamer

翻 fān (动) 1 turn (over; up, upside down, etc.): ～车了. The car turned over. 船～了. The ship capsized. 把领子向上～ turn the collar up. ～到第二十页 turn to p. 20 2 cross; get over: ～墙 climb over a wall. ～山越岭 cross over mountain after mountain. 3 rummage; search: ～箱倒柜 rummage through chests and cupboards 4 translate: 把书～成中文 translate the book into Chinese 5 increase two-fold; double: 粮食产量～了一番. The grain output is doubled. ～两番 be quadrupled 6 <口> fall out; break up: 他们闹～了. They quarrelled and split up. *or* They fell out.
翻案 fān'àn (动) reverse a verdict
翻版 fānbǎn (名) reprint; reproduction
翻地 fāndì (动) plough
翻斗 fāndǒu (名) tipping bucket; skip bucket
翻跟头(頭) fān gēntou (动) turn a somersault
翻滚 fāngǔn (动) roll; tumble: 波浪～. The waves rolled furiously.
翻悔 fānhuǐ (动) back out (of a commitment, promise, etc.); fail to make good one's promise
翻来(來)复(復)去 fānlái-fùqù (动) 1 toss from side to side: 他～睡不着. He tossed and turned in bed, unable to sleep. 2 again and again; repeatedly: ～地想一件事 mull over a problem
翻脸(臉) fānliǎn (动) fall out; suddenly turn hostile: ～不认人 turn against a friend. 两人吵～了脸. The two of them fell out.
翻然 fānrán (副) (change) quickly and completely: ～悔悟 wake up to one's error
翻身 fānshēn (动) 1 turn over (one's body) 2 free oneself; be liberated: ～农奴 emancipated serfs
翻腾 fānténg (动) 1 seethe; rise; surge: 波浪～ seething waves 2 rummage
翻天覆地 fāntiān-fùdì (形) earth-shaking: ～的变化 an earth-shaking change
翻胃 fānwèi (名) gastric disorder
翻新 fānxīn (动) renovate; make over: 工厂～ the renovation of the factory
翻修 fānxiū (动) rebuild: ～马路 repair the roads
翻译(譯) fānyì I (动) translate; interpret: ～电码 decode; decipher II (名) translator; interpreter: ～片 dubbed film
翻印 fānyìn (动) reprint; reproduce
翻阅 fānyuè (动) browse; leaf through

烦 fán I (形) 1 vexed; irritated; annoyed: 心～ feel vexed. 真～人! How annoying! 2 tired of: 厌～ be fed up with II (动) trouble: 麻～你帮我寄一封信好吗? Could I ask you to post a letter for me?
烦劳(勞) fánláo (动) trouble sb.; bother
烦闷 fánmèn (形) unhappy; be worried; depressed
烦恼(惱) fánnǎo (形) worried; vexed: 自寻～ worry oneself for nothing
烦扰(擾) fánrǎo (动) 1 bother; disturb 2 feel disturbed
烦琐 fánsuǒ (形) overelaborate; loaded down with trivial details: ～的手续 overelaborate procedure; tedious formalities
烦琐哲学 fánsuǒ zhéxué (名) 1 scholasticism 2 <口> overelaboration
烦躁 fánzào (形) irritable; agitated

繁 fán (形) numerous; manifold: ～星满天 a starry sky. 头绪纷～ have too many things to attend to
繁华(華) fánhuá (形) flourishing; bustling; busy: ～的街道 busy

street

繁忙 fánmáng (形) busy: 工作～ be very busy with one's work

繁茂 fánmào (形) lush: 草木～ a lush growth of trees and grass

繁荣(榮) fánróng (形) flourishing; prosperous; booming: 经济～ a prosperous economy. ～昌盛 thriving and prosperous

繁盛 fánshèng (形) thriving; flourishing; prosperous

繁体(體)字 fántǐzì (名) the original complex form of a simplified Chinese character

繁杂(雜) fánzá (形) numerous and diverse; miscellaneous: ～的日常事务 daily chores of all sorts; trivialities of everyday life

繁殖 fánzhí (动) breed; reproduce: ～力 reproductive capacity; fertility. ～率 breeding rate

繁重 fánzhòng (形) heavy; strenuous: ～的工作 strenuous work. ～的任务 arduous task

凡 fán I (形) commonplace; ordinary: 非～ extraordinary II (名) this mortal world; the earth: 天仙下～ a celestial beauty come down to earth III (副) every; any; all

凡人 fánrén (名) 1 ordinary person 2 mortal

凡士林 fánshìlín (名) vaseline

凡事 fánshì (名) everything

凡是 fánshì (副) every; any; all: ～去过北京的人都说北京很美. Those who have been to Beijing all say it's beautiful.

凡庸 fányōng (形) commonplace; ordinary

矾 fán (名) vitriol; alum

反 fǎn I (动) 1 turn over: 易如～掌 as easy as turning one's hand over. ～败为胜 turn defeat into victory 2 oppose, be against: ～叛 revolt; rebel. ～革命 counter-revolutionary. ～法西斯 anti-fascist. ～问 ask in retort II (副) 1 in an opposite direction; inside out: 大衣穿～了 wear one's coat inside out 2 on the contrary; instead

反霸 fǎnbà (形) anti-hegemonist

反比例 fǎnbǐlì (名) inverse proportion

反驳 fǎnbó (动) refute; retort; rebut

反常 fǎncháng (形) unusual; abnormal

反刍(芻) fǎnchú (动) ruminate; chew the cud: ～动物 ruminant

反帝 fǎndì anti-imperialist

反动(動) fǎndòng (名) reactionary

反对(對) fǎnduì (动) oppose; be against; fight; combat: ～殖民统治的斗争 fight against colonial rule. ～不正之风 combat unhealthy trends. ～意见 objection (to a decision, resolution, etc.). ～党 opposition party; the Opposition. ～派 opposition faction

反而 fǎn'ér (连) instead; on the contrary: 风不但没停,～越刮越大了. Instead of abating, the wind is blowing even harder.

反封建 fǎn fēngjiàn anti-feudal

反复(復) fǎnfù I (副) repeatedly; again and again; over and over again II (形) changeable; fickle: ～无常 capricious; changeable III (名) relapse; reversal: 他的病最近有～. He relapsed into his old illness recently.

反感 fǎngǎn (形) be averse to; repugnant; disgusted with (sb. or sth.)

反革命 fǎngémìng (名) counter-revolutionary

反攻 fǎngōng (名) counterattack; counteroffensive: ～倒算 counterattack to settle old scores; retaliate

反光 fǎnguāng (名) reflection of light: ～镜 (or 板) reflector

反过(過)来(來) fǎnguolai (副) conversely; the other way round: ～也是一样. It's the same the other way round.

反话 fǎnhuà (名) irony

反悔 fǎnhuǐ (动) go back on one's word (or promise)

反击(擊) fǎnjī (动) strike back; counterattack: 自卫～ counterattack in self-defence

反间 fǎnjiàn (动) sow distrust or dissension among one's enemies (by spreading rumours, etc.)

反抗 fǎnkàng (动) resist; revolt: ～精神 rebellious spirit

反馈 fǎnkuì (名) feedback

反面 fǎnmiàn (名) 1 back; reverse side; wrong side: 唱片的～ the reverse side of a disc. 料子的～ the wrong side of the cloth 2 negative side; a opposed to positive: ～角色 negative role; villain. ～的教训 lesson learnt from negative experience 3 opposite; the other side of the matter

反扑(撲) fǎnpū (动) attack in re

taliation
反射 fǎnshè I (动) reflect: 月亮～到水里. The moon is reflected in the water. ～板 (of traffic) reflector II (名) reflection; reflex: 条件～ conditioned reflex
反特 fǎntè (名) anti-espionage
反问 fǎnwèn I (动) ask (a question) in reply II (名) rhetorical question
反响(響) fǎnxiǎng (名) repercussion
反省 fǎnxǐng (名) introspection; self-examination
反咬 fǎnyǎo (动) invent a charge against sb.: ～一口 make a false countercharge
反义(義)词 fǎnyìcí (名) antonym
反应(應) fǎnyìng I (名) reaction: 化学～ chemical reaction. ～堆 reactor. 连锁～ chain reaction. 阳性(阴性)～ positive (negative) reaction II (动) react; respond
反映 fǎnyìng (动) 1 reflect; mirror; portray; depict: 这封信～了她的真实看法. The letter reflects her real views. ～当地居民生活的绘画 paintings depicting the life of the local people 2 report; make known: 向上级～ report to the higher level
反证(證) fǎnzhèng (动) disproof; give counterevidence
反正 fǎnzhèng (副) anyway; anyhow; in any case: 不管你怎么说,～不会同意. Whatever you say, I won't agree to it.
反之 fǎnzhī (连) otherwise; conversely; on the contrary
反作用 fǎnzuòyòng (名) counteraction; reaction
返 fǎn (动) return: ～回 return; go back. 一去不复～ be gone forever
返潮 fǎncháo (动) get damp
返工 fǎngōng (动) do a poorly done job over again
返航 fǎnháng (动) make a return voyage (or flight)
返老还(還)童 fǎnlǎo-huántóng (动) recover one's youthful vigour; feel rejuvenated
返青 fǎnqīng (动) (of winter crops or transplanted seedlings) turn green
泛 fàn I (动) 1 <书> float: ～舟西湖 go boating on the West Lake 2 be suffused with; spread: 脸上～出红晕 bring a blush into her cheeks. 广～ extensive; wide 3 flood; inundate
泛泛 fànfàn (形) general; not deepgoing: ～而谈 talk in general terms. ～之交 casual acquaintance
泛滥 fànlàn (动) 1 be in flood; overflow: 河水～. The river was in flood. 2 spread unchecked: ～成灾 run rampant; run wild
泛指 fànzhǐ (动) make a general reference; be used in a general sense
范 fàn (名) 1 model; example; pattern: 典～ example. 示～ demonstrate 2 limits
范畴(疇) fànchóu (名) category
范例 fànlì (名) example; model
范围(圍) fànwéi (名) scope; limits; range
范文 fànwén (名) model essay
梵 fàn (名) Buddhist: ～文 Sanskrit
贩 fàn (动) peddle; buy for resale: ～毒 traffic in narcotics. 小～ pedlar; vendor
贩卖(賣) fànmài (动) peddle; traffic; sell: ～军火 traffic in arms
贩运(運) fànyùn (动) transport goods for sale; traffic
贩子 fànzi (名) dealer; monger: 战争～ warmonger. 马～ horse dealer
饭(飯) fàn (名) cooked rice; meal: 米～ (cooked) rice
饭菜 fàncài (名) food
饭店 fàndiàn (名) 1 hotel 2 restaurant
饭馆(館) fànguǎn (名) restaurant
饭盒 fànhé (名) lunch-box
饭量 fànliàng (名) appetite; an amount of food eaten at one time
饭厅(廳) fàntīng (名) dining room; dining hall
饭桶 fàntǒng (名) 1 rice bucket 2 big eater 3 good-for-nothing (person)
饭碗 fànwǎn (名) 1 rice bowl 2 job; means of livelihood: 丢～ lose one's job
犯 fàn I (动) 1 violate; offend (against law, etc.) 2 attack; invade 3 have an attack of (an old illness): 他的心脏病又～了. He had a heart attack again. 4 commit (a mistake, crime, etc.): ～错误 make a mistake II (名) criminal: 杀人～ murderer. 战～ war criminal
犯病 fànbìng (动) have an attack of one's old illness; fall ill again

犯不着 fànbuzháo 〈口〉not worthwhile

犯愁 fànchóu (动) worry; be anxious

犯得着 fàndezháo worthwhile [usu. in rhetorical question]: 为这点小事～生气吗? Is it worthwhile getting angry over such a trifling matter?

犯法 fànfǎ (动) violate (or break) the law

犯规 fànguī (名) foul

犯人 fànrén (名) convict; prisoner

犯罪 fànzuì (动) commit a crime (or an offence): ～分子 offender; criminal

方 fāng I (形) square: ～桌 square table II (名) 1 direction: 东～ the east. 前～ the front. 四面八～ in all directions. 远方 a faraway place 2 side; party: 双～ both sides (or parties) 3 method; way: 想～设法 try every means possible. 千～百计 in a hundred and one ways; by every conceivable means. 领导有～ exercise good leadership 4 prescription: 处～ prescription III (副) just: 年～二十 be just twenty years old. ～兴未艾 be in the ascendant; be in full swing IV (量) 1 [for square objects]: 一～砚台 one ink-stone 2 (short for 平方 or 立方): 一～土 a cubic metre of earth

方案 fāng'àn (名) plan; scheme; programme: 提出初步～ put forward a preliminary plan

方便 fāngbiàn I (形) 1 convenient: 在你～的时候 (do this) at your convenience 2 proper: 在这儿谈私事不大～. It's not proper to talk about private matters here. II (动) 1 go to the lavatory: 你要不要～一下? Do you want to use the lavatory? 2〈婉〉 have money to spare: 手头不～ have little money to spare

方才 fāngcái (副) just now: 她～还在这儿. She was here just a moment ago.

方程 fāngchéng (名) equation: ～式 equation

方法 fāngfǎ (名) method; way; means

方法论(論) fāngfǎlùn (名) methodology

方格 fānggé (名) check

方面 fāngmiàn (名) aspect; respect; side: 在这～ in this respect. 问题的不同～ different aspects of a matter

方式 fāngshì (名) way; fashion; pattern: 生活～ way of life; lifestyle. 斗争～ form of struggle. 领导～ style of leadership

方位 fāngwèi (名) position; direction

方向 fāngxiàng (名) direction; orientation: ～盘〈汽车〉 steering wheel. ～舵〈航空〉 rudder

方言 fāngyán (名) dialect

方圆 fāngyuán (名) 1 neighbourhood 2 circumference

方针 fāngzhēn (名) guiding principle; policy

方子 fāngzi (名) prescription: 开～ write out a prescription

芳 fāng I (形) fragrant; sweet-smelling: ～草 fragrant grass II (名) good name or reputation; virtue: 流～百世 leave a good name to posterity

芳香 fāngxiāng (形) fragrant: ～剂 aromatic

房 fáng (名) 1 house: 平～ bungalow. 楼～ a building of two or more storeys 2 room: 书～ study. 客～ guest room. 病～ ward

房产(産) fángchǎn (名) house property

房地产(産) fángdìchǎn (名) real estate

房顶 fángdǐng (名) roof

房东(東) fángdōng (名) landlord or landlady

房间 fángjiān (名) room: 一套～ an apartment; a flat; a suite

房客 fángkè (名) tenant (of a room or house); lodger

房事 fángshì (名) sexual intercourse (between a married couple)

房屋 fángwū (名) houses; buildings

房檐 fángyán (名) eaves

房子 fángzi (名) 1 house; building 2 room

房租 fángzū (名) rent (for a house, flat, etc.)

坊 fáng workshop; mill: 作～ workshop. 油～ small oil mill

防 fáng I (动) guard against; prevent: 预～ prevent sth from happening; take precautions. ～患未然 take preventive measures. ～微杜渐 nip an evil in the bud. 以～万一 be prepared for all eventualities II (名) defence: 国～ national defence. 堤～ dyke; embankment

防备(備) fángbèi (动) guard against; take precautions against
防不胜(勝)防 fáng bùshèng fáng impossible to put up an all-round effective defence
防潮 fángcháo (形) dampproof
防尘(塵) fángchén (形) dustproof
防磁 fángcí (形) antimagnetic
防弹(彈) fángdàn (形) bulletproof; shellproof
防盗 fángdào (动) guard against theft; take precautions against burglars
防冻(凍) fángdòng (动) prevent frostbite
防毒 fángdú (名) gas defence: ～面具 gas mask
防范(範) fángfàn (动) be on guard; keep a lookout
防风(風)林 fángfēnglín (名) windbreak; shelterbelt
防腐 fángfǔ (形) antiseptic; anticorrosive
防洪 fánghóng (动) prevent or control flood
防护(護) fánghù (动) protect; shelter
防火 fánghuǒ I (动) prevent fire II (形) fireproof
防空 fángkōng (名) air defence; antiaircraft: ～壕 air-raid dugout. ～警报 air raid warning. ～洞 air-raid shelter
防涝(澇) fánglào (名) prevent waterlogging
防区(區) fángqū (名) defence area
防守 fángshǒu (动) defend; guard
防暑 fángshǔ (名) heatstroke (or sunstroke) prevention
防水 fángshuǐ (形) waterproof
防卫(衛) fángwèi (动) defend
防务(務) fángwù (名) defence
防线(綫) fángxiàn (名) defence line
防锈 fángxiù (形) antirust
防汛 fángxùn (名) flood prevention or control
防疫 fángyì (名) epidemic prevention: ～针 inoculation
防御(禦) fángyù (名) defence
防震 fángzhèn I (动) take precautions against earthquakes II (形) shockproof
防止 fángzhǐ (动) prevent; guard against; avoid
防治 fángzhì (名) prevention and cure (illness)

妨 fáng (动) hinder; hamper; impede; obstruct
妨碍(礙) fáng'ài (动) hinder; hamper; impede; obstruct
妨害 fánghài (动) impair; jeopardize; be harmful to

访 fǎng (动) visit; call on: ～友 call on a friend. 回～ a return visit. 互～ exchange visits
访问 fǎngwèn (动) **1** visit; call on **2** interview. 采～ (of a reporter) gather material; cover; interview

仿(倣) fǎng (动) **1** imitate; copy **2** resemble; be like: 相～ be similar
仿佛 fǎngfú I (动) seem; as if [see 好象] II (形) be more or less the same; be alike: 这两个姑娘的性格相～. These two girls are very much alike in character.
仿效 fǎngxiào (动) imitate; follow suit
仿造 fǎngzào (动) copy; be modelled on
仿照 fǎngzhào (动) imitate; copy; follow
仿制 fǎngzhì (动) copy; be modelledon: ～品 imitation

舫 fǎng (名) boat: 画～ a gaily-painted pleasure-boat

纺 fǎng (动) spin
纺车(車) fǎngchē (名) spinning wheel
纺锤 fǎngchuí (名) spindle
纺纱 fǎngshā (名) spinning: ～工人 spinner. ～机 spinning machine
纺织(織) fǎngzhī (名) spinning and weaving: ～厂 textile mill. ～品 textile; fabric

放 fàng (动) **1** put; place: 把杯子～在桌子上 put the glass on the table. 菜里少～点盐. Don't put too much salt in the dish. ～回原处 put it where it belongs **2** let go; set free; release: 释～ set free. 把水～掉 let the water out. ～开他! Let go of him! **3** let oneself go; give way to: ～开嗓子唱 try to sing loudest. ～声痛哭 cry unrestrainedly **4** give off: ～光 shine **5** shoot: ～枪 fire a gun **6** let off: ～鞭炮 let off firecrakers **7** blossom; open: 百花齐～ a hundred flowers blossom **8** put out to pasture: ～牛 graze cattle. ～鸭 tend ducks. ～羊娃 shepherd **9** lay aside: 这事不急,先～一～再说. This matter is not urgent. Let's put it aside for the moment. **10** expend; make larger or longer: 把裙子～长二英寸 let the skirt out two inches at the edge **11** readjust to a certain extent: 声音～轻些! Lower your voice! 速度～慢点儿 slow down a bit **12** show; play (film, radio, etc.) ～电影 show a film. ～录音 play a tape recorder

放出 fàngchū (动) give out; let out; emit

放大 fàngdà (动) enlarge; magnify; amplify: ～镜 magnifying glass. ～照片 have a photograph enlarged; blow up

放荡(蕩) fàngdàng (形) **1** dissipated; dissolute **2** unconventional: ～不羁 unconventional and unrestrained

放电(電) fàngdiàn (名) (electric) discharge

放风(風) fàngfēng (动) **1** let in fresh air **2** let prisoners out for exercise or to relieve themselves **3** leak information; spread rumours

放工 fànggōng (动) (of workers) knock off

放过(過) fàngguò (动) let off; let slip: 不要～这个好机会. Don't let slip this good opportunity.

放火 fànghuǒ (动) set fire to; commit arson

放假 fàngjià (动) have a holiday or vacation; have a day off

放空炮 fàng kōngpào talk big; make empty promises; indulge in idle boasting

放宽 fàngkuān (动) relax rules or restrictions: ～期限 extend a time limit. ～条件 modify the terms.

放牧 fàngmù (动) herd; graze

放屁 fàngpì I (动) break wind; fart II (名) bullshit; crap

放弃(棄) fàngqì (动) abandon; give up; renounce: ～权利 relinquish one's right

放晴 fàngqíng (动) (of weather) clear up

放任 fàngrèn (动、名) **1** let pass unchecked: ～自流 let things drift (or slide) **2** laissez-faire

放哨 fàngshào (动) stand sentry

放射 fàngshè (动、名) radiate; radiation: ～疗法 radiotherapy. ～性 radioactivity

放手 fàngshǒu (动) **1** let go; release one's hold **2** have a free hand: 你～干吧. Just go ahead boldly with your work.

放肆 fàngsì (形) audacious; unbridled; wanton: 胆敢如此～! How dare you take such liberties!

放松(鬆) fàngsōng (动) relax; slacken; loosen: ～警惕性 relax one's vigilance

放心 fàngxīn (动) feel relieved; set one's mind at rest; be at ease: ～不下 feel anxious

放行 fàngxíng (动) let sb. or sth. pass

放学(學) fàngxué (动) school is over (for the day)

放映 fàngyìng (动) show; project: ～机 (film) projector

放债 fàngzhài (动) lend money for interest

放置 fàngzhì (动) put; place: ～不用 lay up; lay aside

放逐 fàngzhú (动) send into exile; exile

放纵(縱) fàngzòng (动) **1** give free rein to **2** indulge

非 fēi I (名) wrong; evildoing: 混淆是～ confuse right and wrong. 为～作歹 do evil II (形) un, non, etc.: ～正义 unjust. ～正式 informal III (副) **1** not; no: ～同小可 no small matter. 答～所问 give an irrelevant answer **2** insist on; simply must: 我～要你去. I insist on your going. 这工作今天～得完成. This work simply must be done today.

非…不… fēi...bù... possible only if ...: 非工作人员不得入内 for staff members only. 他非你不见. He will see nobody but you. 该票非特许不得转让. This ticket is not transferable unless with special permission.

非…不可 fēi...bùkě [an emphatic expression] must; have to; will inevitably: 我非要试试不可. I simply must have a try. 你不听我的话非倒楣不可. If you don't listen to me, you are bound to run into trouble.

非常 fēicháng I (形) extraordinary; unusual: ～时期 unusual times. ～措施 emergency measures II (副) very; extremely; highly: ～抱歉 awfully (or terribly) sorry. ～必要 highly necessary. ～精彩 simply marvellous

非但 fēidàn (连) not only ..., but

非得 fēiděi (动) must; have got to: 你～亲自去一趟. You have

to go in person.
非法 fēifǎ (形) illegal; unlawful: ～活动 unlawful (or illegal) activities. ～收入 illicit income
非凡 fēifán (形) outstanding; extraordinary; uncommon: ～的人物 an outstanding person
非金属(屬) fēijīnshǔ (名) non-metal
非礼(禮) fēilǐ (形)〈书〉rude
非难(難) fēinàn (名) blame; censure; reproach
非人 fēirén (形) inhuman: ～待遇 inhuman treatment
非议(議) fēiyì (名) reproach; censure: 无可～ beyond (or above) reproach
非正式 fēizhèngshì (形) unofficial; informal
非洲 Fēizhōu (名) Africa
扉 fēi (名) door leaf
扉页(頁) fēiyè (名) title page
蜚 fēi
蜚声(聲) fēishēng (动)〈书〉make a name; become famous: ～文坛 become famous in the literary world
绯 fēi (形) red
绯红 fēihóng (形) bright red; crimson: 脸羞得～ blush with shame
飞(飛) fēi I (动) fly; hover; flutter II (副) swiftly: ～奔 dash. ～驰 speed along
飞船 fēichuán (名) airship
飞地 fēidì (名) enclave
飞蛾投火 fēi'é tóu huǒ seek one's own destruction like a moth darting toward a fire
飞黄腾达(達) fēihuáng téngdá become a rising star in the political world
飞机(機) fēijī (名) aircraft; aeroplane; plane: 直升～ helicopter. ～场 airport. ～库 hangar
飞溅(濺) fēijiàn (动) splash: 浪花～到岩石上. The waves splashed on the rocks.
飞快 fēikuài I (副) very fast; at lightning speed: ～前进 march ahead at full speed II (形) extremely sharp: 这把刀～. This knife is razor-sharp.
飞轮(輪) fēilún (名) 1 flywheel 2 free wheel (of a bicycle)
飞毛腿 fēimáotuǐ (名) fleet-footed runner
飞禽 fēiqín (名) birds: ～走兽 birds and beasts; fauna
飞舞 fēiwǔ (动) dance in the air; flutter: 雪花～. Snowflakes are dancing in the wind.
飞翔 fēixiáng (动) circle in the air; hover
飞行 fēixíng (名) flight; flying
飞檐 fēiyán (名) upturned eaves (on Chinese buildings)
飞扬(揚) fēiyáng (动) fly upward; rise: 尘土～. Clouds of dust are rising. 歌声～. The sound of singing is floating in the air.
飞扬(揚)跋扈 fēiyáng-báhù arrogant and domineering
飞跃(躍) fēiyuè (动、名) leap: ～地发展 develop by leaps and bounds
飞涨(漲) fēizhǎng (动) (of prices, etc.) soar; shoot up: 物价～. Prices are spiralling.
妃 fēi (名) 1 imperial concubine 2 the wife of a prince
妃子 fēizi (名) imperial concubine
腓 féi (名) calf (of the leg): ～骨 fibula
肥 féi I (形) 1 fat: ～猪 a fat big. ～肉 fat meat; fat 2 (of land; soil) fertile; rich 3 loose; wide: 裤腿太～了. The trousers are too fat in the leg (or too baggy). II (名) fertilizer; manure: 化～ chemical fertilizer. 绿～ green manure
肥厚 féihòu (形) plump; fleshy
肥力 féilì (名) fertility (of soil)
肥料 féiliào (名) fertilizer; manure: 有机～ organic fertilizer
肥胖 féipàng (形) fat: ～病 obesity
肥缺 féiquē (名) lucrative post
肥硕 féishuò (形) big and fleshy
肥田 féitián (动) enrich the soil
肥沃 féiwò (形) fertile; rich
肥皂 féizào (名) soap: 洗脸～ toilet soap
肥壮(壯) féizhuàng (形) stout and strong
诽 fěi (动) slander: ～谤 slander
菲 fěi
菲薄 fěibó I (形) humble: ～的礼物 a small gift II (动) belittle; despise: 不宜妄自～. You should not go so far as to depreciate your real ability or achievement.

匪 fěi I (名) bandit; robber II (副)〈书〉 not: 获益～浅 reap no little benefit
匪帮 fěibāng (名) bandit gang
匪巢 fěicháo (名) bandits' lair
匪军(軍) fěijūn (名) bandit troops
匪徒 fěitú (名) gangster; bandit
吠 fèi (动) (of a dog) bark
废(廢) fèi I (动) give up; abolish: 半途而～ give up halfway. ～寝忘食 (so absorbed in a book as to) forget to eat and sleep II (形) waste; useless; disused: ～物处理 waste disposal
废除 fèichú (动) abolish; abrogate (law, treaty, rule, etc.)
废黜 fèichù (动) dethrone; depose
废话 fèihuà (名) superfluous words; nonsense: ～连篇 pages and pages of nonsense
废料 fèiliào (名) waste material
废品 fèipǐn (名) 1 reject 2 scrap; waste: ～回收 waste recovery
废弃(棄) fèiqì (动) discard; abandon; cast aside: ～陈规旧习 discard outdated regulations and customs
废人 fèirén (名) 1 disabled person 2 good-for-nothing
废铁(鐵) fèitiě (名) scrap iron
废物 fèiwù (名) 1 waste material; trash 2 good-for-nothing
废墟 fèixū (名) ruins
废止 fèizhǐ (动) abolish; put an end to
废纸 fèizhǐ (名) waste paper
废置 fèizhì (动) put aside as useless
肺 fèi (名) lungs: ～癌 lung cancer. ～病 pulmonary disease; tuberculosis (TB)
肺腑 fèifǔ (名) the bottom of one's heart: 出自～ from the depths of one's heart
肺活量 fèihuóliàng (名) vital capacity
肺结核 fèijiéhé (名) tuberculosis (TB)
肺炎 fèiyán (名) pneumonia
痱 fèi
痱子 fèizi (名) prickly heat: ～粉 prickly-heat powder
沸 fèi (动) boil
沸点(點) fèidiǎn (名) boiling point
沸腾 fèiténg (动) 1 boil 2 seethe with excitement: 热血～ one's blood boils
费 fèi I (动) cost; spend; consume (too much money, time, energy, etc.): ～尽心机 rack one's brains in scheming; leave no stone unturned to do sth. II (名) fee; charge; dues; expenses: 学～ tuition fees; tuition. 会～ membership dues. 生活费 living expense. 房租～ rent. 车～ fare III (形) consuming too much; wasteful: 用电热器太～电. An electric heater consumes too much electricity.
费工 fèigōng (动) take a lot of work; require a lot of labour
费工夫 fèi gōngfu (动) take time and energy
费解 fèijiě (形) hard to understand; obscure; unintelligible
费劲(勁) fèijìn (形) energy-consuming; strenuous
费力 fèilì (动) require great effort, be strenuous: ～不讨好 do a hard but thankless job
费钱(錢) fèiqián (形) costly; expensive
费神 fèishén (套) may I trouble you (to do sth.)
费事 fèishì (动) give or take a lot of trouble
费心 fèixīn (动) take the trouble: 她为组织这次晚会费了不少心. She took a lot of trouble to organize this party.
费用 fèiyòng (名) cost; expenses; expenditure: 生产～ production cost. 生活～ cost of living; living expenses
分 fēn I (动) 1 divide; separate; part: 剧～三场演出. This play is divided into three scenes. ～而治之 divide and rule. 难舍难～ be reluctant to part with each other 2 distribute; allot; assign: 我～到了一个新任务. I was assigned a new task. 3 distinguish; tell one from another: 不～青红皂白 make no distinction between black and white (right and wrong). 我总是～不清他和他的弟弟. I can never tell him from his brother. II (名) 1 branch (of an organization): ～公司 a branch company 2 fraction: 四～之三 three-fourths. 二～之一 half 3 point; mark: 甲队又得了两～! Team A scores another two points! III (量) 1 (of time or degree) minute (= 1/60 of an hour o

degree) **2** (of money) *fen* (= 1/100 of a *yuan*) **3** (of weight) *fen* (= 1/2 gram) **4** (of area) *fen* (= 66.666 sq. metres) **5** (of length) *fen* (= 1/3 centimetre) see also fèn

分崩离(離)析 fēnbēng-líxī (动) disintegrate; fall to pieces; come apart

分辨 fēnbiàn (动) distinguish; differentiate: ～真假善恶 distinguish truth from falsehood and good from evil

分辩(辯) fēnbiàn (动) defend oneself (against a charge); offer an explanation: 不容～ refuse to hear any explanation

分别 fēnbié I (动) **1** part; say good bye to each other **2** distinguish; differentiate II (副) **1** differently: ～对待 treat differently **2** respectively; separately: 两案～处理. The two cases will be dealt with separately.

分布 fēnbù (动) distribute; spread; scatter: 这些民族主要～在四川、云南境内. These ethnic groups are mainly distributed over Sichuan and Yunnan provinces.

分寸 fēncùn (名) sense of propriety: 他措词很有～. He chose his words very carefully. 在公共场合讲话,有时不易掌握～. On public occasions, it is sometimes difficult to know what is proper to say and what is not.

分道扬(揚)镳 fēndào yángbiāo (动) part company, each going his own way

分等 fēnděng (动) grade; classify

分发(發) fēnfā (动) distribute; hand out; issue

分赴 fēnfù (动) leave for (different destinations)

分割 fēngē (动) cut apart; separate; carve up

分隔 fēngé (动) separate; partition

分工 fēngōng (名) division of labour: 有～也有协作. There is division of work as well as coordination of effort.

分号(號) fēnhào (名) **1** semicolon **2** branch of a firm etc.

分红 fēnhóng (动) share out extra profits

分洪 fēnhóng (名) flood diversion

分化 fēnhuà (动) become divided; break up; split up: 贫富两极～ polarization of rich and poor. ～瓦解 disintegrate

分会(會) fēnhuì (名) branch society, association, etc.; sub-committee

分机(機) fēnjī (名) extension (telephone): ～号码 extension number

分家 fēnjiā (动) divide up family property among children

分解 fēnjiě (动) resolve; decompose; break down

分界线(線) fēnjièxiàn (名) demarcation line; boundary

分居 fēnjū (动、名) (usu. of a married couple) separate; separation

分开(開) fēnkāi (动) separate; part

分类(類) fēnlèi (动、名) classify; classification

分离(離) fēnlí (动) separate: 理论不可与实践～. Theory cannot be separated from practice.

分裂 fēnliè (动、名) split; break up: ～工党的根本原因是显而易见的. The causes that split the Labour Party are obvious. 细胞～ cell division

分米 fēnmǐ (名) decimetre (dm)

分泌 fēnmì (动) secrete

分娩 fēnmiǎn (名) childbirth

分明 fēnmíng I (形) clearly distinguished; distinct: 事情的是非必须～. The rights and wrongs of the case are to be distinguished. II (副) clearly; plainly; evidently

分派 fēnpài (动) assign (to different persons)

分配 fēnpèi I (动) allocate; assign; distribute: 给大学毕业生～工作 assign jobs to college graduates II (名) distribution; allocation

分批 fēnpī (副) in batches; in groups

分期 fēnqī (副) by stages: ～付款 payment by instalments

分歧 fēnqí (名) dispute; difference; divergence: 意见～. The views are divergent. 制造～ sow dissension

分清 fēnqīng (动) distinguish; draw a clear line between

分散 fēnsàn (动) disperse; scatter; decentralize: ～注意力 divert attention. ～精力 diffuse one's energies

分身 fēnshēn (动) spare time to attend to sth. else

分手 fēnshǒu (动) part company,

say good-bye
分数(數) fēnshù (名) 1 fraction 2 mark; grade
分水岭(嶺) fēnshuǐlǐng (名) watershed; line of demarcation
分摊(攤) fēntān (动) share: ～费用 share the expenses
分庭抗礼(禮) fēntíng-kànglǐ stand up to sb. as an equal
分头(頭) fēntóu (副) separately; severally
分文 fēnwén (名) a single penny
分析 fēnxī (动、名) analyse; analysis: 深入～ in-depth analysis
分享 fēnxiǎng (动) share (joy, rights, etc.): ～胜利的喜悦 share the joys of success
分晓(曉) fēnxiǎo (名) outcome; solution: 此事还未见～. The outcome of the matter is still uncertain.
分心 fēnxīn (动) 1 divert one's attention 2 claim attention: 这件事您多～了. This would claim a good deal of your attention.
分野 fēnyě (名) dividing line: 两种学派的～ the dividing line between the two schools of thought
分忧(憂) fēnyōu (动) share sb.'s worries; help solve difficult problems
分赃(贓) fēnzāng (动) divide the spoils; share the booty (or loot)
分支 fēnzhī (名) branch of any organization or main part
分子 fēnzǐ (名) 1 numerator of a fraction 2 molecule
分组 fēnzǔ (动) divide into groups

芬
fēn (名) sweet smell; fragrance
芬芳 fēnfāng (形) fragrant; sweet

吩
fēn
吩咐 fēnfu (动) tell; bid; order; instruct

纷
fēn (形) numerous; confused: 大雪～飞. The snow is falling thick and fast.
纷繁 fēnfán (形) numerous and complicated: 头绪～ too many loose ends to tidy up
纷纷 fēnfēn (副) 1 one after another; in succession: 他们～要求发言. They all clamoured to take the floor. 2 numerous and confused: 落叶～. The leaves are falling in profusion.
纷乱(亂) fēnluàn (形) numerous and disorderly: ～的说话声 hullabaloo
纷扰(擾) fēnrǎo (名) confusion; turmoil: 内心～ feel perturbed
纷纭 fēnyún (形) diverse and confused: 众说～, 莫衷一是. There is no general agreement as opinions differ widely.
纷至沓来(來) fēnzhì-tàlái come thick and fast; keep pouring in

坟(墳)
fén (名) grave; tomb
坟地 féndì (名) graveyard; cemetery
坟墓 fénmù (名) grave; tomb

焚
fén (动) burn: ～香 burn incense. 忧心如～. Anxiety gnaws one's heart.
焚膏继(繼)晷 fén gāo jì guǐ (动) burn the midnight oil
焚化 fénhuà (动) burn; cremate
焚毁 fénhuǐ (动) destroy by fire; burn down
焚烧(燒) fénshāo (动) burn

粉
fěn I (名) 1 powder: 磨成～grind into powder; pulverize. 花～ the pollen of flowers. 奶～ powdered milk. 面～ flour. 香～ face powder 2 vermicelli (made from bean or sweet potato starch) II (形) 1 white washed: ～墙 white-washed wall 2 pink: ～色 pink colour
粉笔(筆) fěnbǐ (名) chalk
粉墨登场(場) fěnmò dēngchǎng make oneself up and go on stage; embark on a political venture
粉身碎骨 fěnshēn-suìgǔ (of human body) be smashed to pieces; be crushed to a pulp
粉饰 fěnshì (动) gloss over; whitewash
粉刷 fěnshuā (动) whitewash
粉碎 fěnsuì (动) 1 smash; shatter; crush: ～军事进攻 shatter an offensive 2 broken to pieces 茶杯摔得～. The cup broke into smithereens.

粪(糞)
fèn (名) excrement; dung; droppings
粪便 fènbiàn (名) excrement and urine; night soil; stool
粪肥 fènféi (名) manure; dung
粪土 fèntǔ (名) dung and dirt muck: 视如～ look upon as dirt be considered worthless

愤
fèn (名) anger; indignation: 公～ public indignation
愤愤不平 fènfèn bùpíng (动) feel indignant
愤恨 fènhèn (动) indignantly resent; detest

愤激 fènjī (形) excited and indignant; roused
愤慨 fènkǎi (名) righteous indignation
愤懑 fènmèn (动) go into a huff; be resentful
愤怒 fènnù (名) indignation; anger; wrath
愤世嫉俗 fènshì-jísú detest the unjust practices of human society; detest the ways of the world; be cynical

奋(奮) fèn (动) exert oneself; act vigorously: 振～ rouse oneself. ～不顾身 charge forward regardless of personal safety
奋斗(鬥) fèndòu (动) fight to achieve a certain goal; struggle; strive: 艰苦～ work arduously
奋发(發) fènfā (动) rouse oneself; exert oneself: ～图强 work hard for the prosperity of one's country; go all out to make the country strong
奋力 fènlì (动) do all one can; spare no effort
奋起 fènqǐ (动) rise vigorously: ～反抗 rise up in resistance
奋勇 fènyǒng (动) summon up one's courage: ～前进 advance bravely; forge ahead courageously
奋战(戰) fènzhàn (动) fight bravely: ～到底 fight to the bitter end

分 fèn I (名) 1 component: 水～ moisture content 2 what is within the scope of one's rights or obligations: 本～ one's duty II (形) simple and honest. 过～ excessive; going too far; over-done
see also fēn
分量 fènliang (名) weight: 他这话说得很有～. What he has just said is no casual comment.
分内 fènnèi (形) duty-bound: 照顾她姨妈是她～的事. It's her duty to look after her aunt.
分外 fènwài I (形) outside the scope of one's duty II (副) particularly; especially: ～激动 very excited. ～美丽 extremely beautiful
分子 fènzǐ (名) member; element: 积极～ activist. 知识～ intellectual

忿 fèn see "愤" fèn

份 fèn I (名) share; portion: 股～ stock; share II (量): 一～礼品 a gift. 一～报纸 a copy of a newspaper. 一～《中国日报》 a copy of *China Daily*
份额 fèn'é (名) share; portion
份子 fènzi (名) one's share of expenses for a joint undertaking: 凑～ club together to present a gift to sb.

丰(豐) fēng (形) 1 plentiful: ～衣足食 have ample food and clothing 2 great: ～功伟绩 great achievements; magnificent contributions
丰碑 fēngbēi (名) monument
丰产(產) fēngchǎn (名) high yield; bumper crop
丰富 fēngfù I (形) rich; abundant; plentiful: 资源(或物产)～ rich in natural resources II (动) enrich: ～精神生活 enrich one's spiritual life. ～多采 rich and varied
丰厚 fēnghòu (形) rich and generous: ～的礼品 generous gifts
丰满(滿) fēngmǎn (形) 1 full and round; well-developed; full-grown: 体形～ a well-shaped body. 羽毛～ full-fledged 2 plentiful
丰茂 fēngmào (形) lush; luxuriant: 水草～ lush pasture
丰年 fēngnián (名) bumper harvest year; good year
丰沛 fēngpèi (形) plentiful: 雨水～ have plenty of rain
丰盛 fēngshèng (形) 1 rich; sumptuous: ～的酒席 a sumptuous dinner 2 lush
丰收 fēngshōu (名) bumper harvest: ～在望 A good harvest is in sight.
丰硕 fēngshuò (形) plentiful and enormous: ～的成果 rich harvest; great success
丰裕 fēngyù (形) in plenty: 生活～ live in plenty; be comfortably off

封 fēng I (动) 1 seal: 把信～好 seal a letter. 大雪～山. Heavy snow has sealed off the mountain passes. 2 confer (a title, territory, etc.) upon: ～官许愿 offer high posts and make lavish promises II (量) 三～信 three letters. 一～饼干 a pack of biscuits
封闭 fēngbì (动) 1 seal up: 用蜡～瓶口 seal a bottle with wax 2 close down: 一家出版社被～

了. One publishing house was closed down.

封存 fēngcún (动) seal up for safekeeping

封底 fēngdǐ (名) (of a book) back cover

封建 fēngjiàn (形) feudal: ～主义 feudalism

封口 fēngkǒu (动) 1 seal: 信～了吗? Is the letter sealed? 2 heal: 腿上的伤已经～了. The leg wound has healed. 3 shut up; speak with a tone of finality

封面 fēngmiàn (名) (of a book) front cover

封锁 fēngsuǒ (动) blockade; block; seal off: 消息～ news blockade. ～边境 close the border. 经济～ economic blockade

封条(條) fēngtiáo (名) a strip of paper bearing an official seal and the date for the sealing of doors, drawers, etc.

烽 fēng (名) beacon

烽火 fēnghuǒ (名) 1 a signal fire used to give the border alarm in ancient China; beacon: ～台 beacon tower 2 flames of war: ～连天 raging flames of war

烽烟 fēngyān (名) beacon-fire

蜂 fēng (名) bee; wasp: 蜜～ honeybee

蜂房 fēngfáng (名) honeycomb

蜂蜜 fēngmì (名) honey

蜂窝(窩) fēngwō (名) beehive

蜂拥(擁) fēngyōng (动) swarm; flock: ～而至 come in swarms

峰 fēng (名) 1 peak; summit: 山～ mountain peak. 攀登科学高～ scale the heights of science 2 hump: 驼～ camel's hump

峰峦(巒) fēngluán (名) ridges and peaks

锋 fēng (名) 1 the cutting edge of a knife or a sword 2 van: 先～ vanguard

锋利 fēnglì (形) 1 (of knives, etc.) sharp; keen 2 (of style) incisive

锋芒 fēngmáng (名) 1 sharp edge of a sword; spearhead 2 outward show of one's talent and dynamism: ～毕露 make a display of one's talent; show off one's ability

风(風) fēng (名) 1 wind; draft: ～雨无阻 regardless of the weather. ～平浪静 the wind has subsided and the waves have calmed down; calm and peaceful 2 style; practice; custom: 不正之～ unhealthy trend. 文～ style of writing 3 scene; view: ～景 scenery; landscape 4 news; information: 走～ leak news. 闻～而动 act without delay upon hearing the news.

风暴 fēngbào (名) windstorm; storm

风波 fēngbō (名) disturbance

风采 fēngcǎi (名) charisma

风潮 fēngcháo (名) agitation; political unrest

风车(車) fēngchē (名) windmill

风尘(塵) fēngchén (名) travel fatigue: ～仆仆 endure the hardships of a long journey; be travel-worn

风驰电(電)掣 fēngchí-diànchè (形) swift as lightning

风传(傳) fēngchuán (名) hearsay; rumour

风吹草动(動) fēngchuī-cǎodòng (名) slight disturbance

风度 fēngdù (名) elegant manners: 有～ behave with grace and ease

风干(乾) fēnggān (动) air-dry

风格 fēnggé (名) style: 独特～ unique style

风光 fēngguāng (名) scene; view; sight: 大好～ a wonderful sight

风寒 fēnghán (名) chill; cold

风和日暖 fēnghé-rìnuǎn It is warm and sunny.

风华(華) fēnghuá (名) charisma and talent: ～正茂 in the flower of youth

风化 fēnghuà I (名) morals; decency: 有伤～ be offensive to general standards of behaviour II (动) weather: 岩石～. Rocks weather.

风景 fēngjǐng (名) scenery; landscape: ～如画 picturesque. ～区 scenic spot. ～优美 scenic beauty

风镜 fēngjìng (名) goggles

风口 fēngkǒu (名) draught: 站在～ stand in the draught

风浪 fēnglàng (名) stormy waves

风雷 fēngléi (名) wind and thunder

风力 fēnglì (名) wind force; wind power

风凉话 fēngliánghuà (名) sarcastic remarks: 说～ make critical comments from the sidelines

风流 fēngliú (名) 1 talented and meritorious: ～人物 legen

dary figures; truly great men 2 gifted and unconventional 3 romantic

风流云(雲)散 fēngliú-yúnsàn drift apart; dispersed by the wind and scattered like the clouds — (of old companions) separated and scattered

风帽 fēngmào (名) hood

风貌 fēngmào (名) characteristic style and features

风靡一时(時) fēngmǐ yìshí (形) fashionable for a time; à la mode

风起云(雲)涌 fēngqǐ-yúnyǒng surging and fast-changing

风气(氣) fēngqì (名) general mood; common practice; atmosphere

风琴 fēngqín (名) organ (musical instrument)

风情 fēngqíng (名) flirtatious expressions: 卖弄～ coquettish

风趣 fēngqù (名) humour; wit: 一句很有～的话 a witty remark

风骚 fēngsāo I (名)〈书〉literary excellence II (形) coquettish

风沙 fēngshā (名) dust storm

风扇 fēngshàn (名) electric fan

风尚 fēngshàng (名) prevailing custom or practice

风声(聲) fēngshēng (名) news; rumour: 听到～ get wind of sth. ～很紧. The situation is tense. 走漏～ leak information

风声(聲)鹤唳 fēngshēng-hèlì the whining of the wind and the cry of cranes — a fleeing army's suspicion of danger at the slightest sound; the fear of a fleeing panic-stricken army that danger is lurking everywhere.

风湿(濕) fēngshī (名) rheumatism

风霜 fēngshuāng (名) hardships, experienced in life or on a journey: 饱经～ weather-beaten

风水 fēngshui (名) geomantic omen

风俗 fēngsú (名) social customs: ～画 genre painting; genre

风调雨顺 fēngtiáo-yǔshùn favourable weather (for the crops)

风头(頭) fēngtou (名) 1 a straw in the wind: 避避～ lie low before the dust has settled 2 public attention: 想出～ seek publicity

风土 fēngtǔ: ～人情 local conditions and customs

风味 fēngwèi (名) distinctive flavour; local colour: 这首诗有民歌～. This poem has the distinctive flavour of a ballad.

风闻 fēngwén (动) learn through hearsay; get wind of

风险(險) fēngxiǎn (名) risk: 冒～ run risks

风箱 fēngxiāng (名) bellows

风向 fēngxiàng (名) wind direction: 看～ see which way the wind blows

风行 fēngxíng (动) be in fashion; become prevalent: ～一时 be popular for a while

风雅 fēngyǎ (形) polite; refined: 举止～ have refined social manners

风言风语 fēngyán-fēngyǔ (名) gossip; groundless talk

风衣 fēngyī (名) windbreak; wind coat

风雨 fēngyǔ (名) trials and hardships: ～飘摇 unstable; tottering. ～同舟 stand together through thick and thin

风云(雲) fēngyún fast-changing situation: ～变幻 a changeable situation. ～人物 influential man; man of the hour

风韵 fēngyùn (名) (of a woman) graceful bearing; charm

风筝 fēngzheng (名) kite: 放～ fly a kite

风烛(燭)残(殘)年 fēngzhú cánnián aging and ailing like a candle guttering in the wind

风姿 fēngzī (名) graceful bearing; charisma

疯(瘋) fēng (形) mad; insane; crazy

疯癫 fēngdiān (形) insane; mad

疯狗 fēnggǒu (名) mad dog

疯狂 fēngkuáng (形) wild, crazy, frenzied: ～反扑 a desperate counterattack

疯人院 fēngrényuàn (名) madhouse; lunatic asylum

疯子 fēngzi (名) lunatic; madman

枫(楓) fēng (名) maple

逢 féng (动) come across; meet; chance upon: 每～佳节 on every festive occasion. 久别重～ meet again after a long separation. ～场作戏 join in the fun on occasion

逢集 féngjí (名) market day

逢年过(過)节(節) féng nián guò jié on New Year's Day or other festivals

逢凶化吉 féng xiōng huà jí turn danger into safety

缝 féng (动) sew; stitch: ～扣子 sew on a button. ～被子 stitch a quilt
see also fèng
缝补(補) féngbǔ (动) sew and mend
缝合 fénghé (动) of a wound; sew up; suture
缝纫 féngrèn (名) sewing; tailoring: ～机 sewing machine
讽(諷) fěng (动) mock; satirize: 冷嘲热～ sarcasm
讽刺 fěngcì (动,名) satirize; mock; sarcasm
讽喻 fěngyù (名) parable; allegory
奉 fèng (动) 1 present or receive with respect: ～上年历一本 send with respect a calendar. ～上级指示 be instructed by higher authorities 2 esteem; revere: ～为典范 look upon as a model. 信～基督教 believe in Christianity. 侍～ attend to or look after sb. with respect
奉承 fèngcheng (动) flatter; fawn upon; toady
奉告 fènggào (动) have the honour to inform: 无可～. No comment.
奉公守法 fènggōng-shǒufǎ be law-abiding
奉还(還) fènghuán (动) return sth. with thanks
奉命 fèngmìng (动) receive orders or instructions
奉陪 fèngpéi (动)〈敬〉 keep sb. company: 恕不～. Sorry not to be able to keep you company.
奉劝(勸) fèngquàn (动)〈敬〉 give advice to sb.; advise
奉送 fèngsòng (动)〈敬〉 offer as a gift
奉献(獻) fèngxiàn (动) offer as a tribute; present with all respect
奉行 fèngxíng (动) pursue (a policy, etc.)
俸 fèng (名) pay; salary: 薪～ an official's salary
凤(鳳) fèng (名) phoenix: ～凰 phoenix
缝 fèng (名) seam; crack; slit: 无～钢管 seamless steel tube. 裤～ crease. ～隙 chink; crack
see also féng
佛 fó (名) 1 Buddha 2 Buddhism 3 statue of Buddha
佛教 Fójiào (名) Buddhism: ～徒 Buddhist
佛经(經) fójīng (名) Buddhist Scripture
佛龛(龕) fókān (名) niche for a statue of Buddha
佛门(門) fómén (名) Buddhism: ～弟子 followers of Buddhism; Buddhists
佛堂 fótáng (名) family hall for worshipping Buddha
佛像 fóxiàng (名) statue (or image) of Buddha
佛学(學) fóxué (名) Buddhism
佛爷(爺) fóye (名) Buddha
否 fǒu (动) 1 deny; negate: ～认 deny 2 no: 是～ yes or not; whether or not
否定 fǒudìng (动) negate; deny
否决 fǒujué (动) vote against; veto: 提案被～了. The motion was voted down. ～权 veto power; veto
否则 fǒuzé (连) otherwise; if not; or else: 咱们现在就干,～就晚了. Let's get down to work right away, otherwise it'll be too late.
夫 fū (名) 1 husband 2 man: 匹～ ordinary man. 船～ boatman. 农～ farmer; peasant
夫妇(婦) fū-fù (名) husband and wife: 新婚～ newly married couple; newlyweds
夫妻 fū-qī (名) man and wife
夫人 fūren (名) Mrs.; Madame; Lady: 某某～ Madame So-and-so. 大使及其～ the ambassador and his wife
夫子 fūzǐ (名) a Confucian scholar
麸(麩) fū (名): ～皮 (wheat) bran. ～子 (wheat) bran
肤(膚) fū (名) skin
肤皮潦草 fūpí liáocǎo (形) cursory; casual; perfunctory
肤浅(淺) fūqiǎn (形) skin-deep; superficial; shallow
肤色 fūsè (名) colour of skin; complexion
敷 fū (动) 1 apply (powder, ointment, etc.): 外～ for external application 2 be sufficient for: 入不～出 unable to make both ends meet
敷衍 fūyǎn (动) be perfunctory: ～了事 do sth. perfunctorily; muddle through one's work. ～塞责 perform one's duty in a perfunctory manner

孵 fū (动) hatch; incubate: ～小鸡 hatch chickens
孵化 fūhuà (名) hatching; incubation: 人工～ artificial incubation
孵卵 fūluǎn (动) hatch; brood; incubate

芙 fú
芙蓉 fúróng (名) 1 cottonrose hibiscus 2 lotus

扶 fú (动) 1 support with the hand: ～着盲人过马路 help the blind man across the road by taking his arm. ～着梯子! Hold the ladder! ～某人站起来; assist sb. to his feet 2 help; relieve: 救死～伤 heal the wounded and rescue the dying
扶病 fúbìng (副) in spite of illness: ～出席 turn up in spite of illness
扶持 fúchí (动) help; support
扶老携幼 fúlǎo-xiéyòu helping the old and the young by the hand (on a journey)
扶手 fúshou (名) 1 rail; banisters 2 armrest: ～椅 armchair
扶梯 fútī (名) staircase
扶养(養) fúyǎng (动) bring up; foster: ～成人 bring up (a child)
扶植 fúzhí (动) foster; prop up: ～傀儡政权 prop up a puppet regime
扶助 fúzhù (动) help; assist; support: ～病残 help the sick and the disabled

福 fú (名) good fortune; blessing; happiness
福利 fúlì (名) welfare; well-being: ～国家 welfare state. 群众～ the well-being of the masses
福气(氣) fúqi (名) happy lot; good fortune
福星 fúxīng (名) lucky star
福音 fúyīn (名) 1 Gospel 2 glad tidings

辐 fú (名) spoke: 轮～ spoke of a wheel
辐射 fúshè (名) radiation

幅 fú I (名) width of cloth; size of a painting, photographs, etc. II (量) [used of cloth, painting, etc.]: 一～画 a picture; a painting
幅度 fúdù (名) range; scope; extent: 大～增长 increase by a big margin
幅员 fúyuán (名) the size of a country: ～广大 vast in territory

蝠 fú (名) bat

浮 fú I (动) 1 float: ～萍 floating duckweed 2 swim 3 exceed: 人～于事 have an excessive number of staff; be overstaffed II (形) on the surface; superficial; flighty; frivolous: ～土 dust on the surface. 她这个人有点～. She is a bit flighty.
浮标(標) fúbiāo (名) buoy
浮财 fúcái (名) movable property
浮沉 fúchén (动) now sink, now emerge; drift along: 与世～ swim with the tide
浮雕 fúdiāo (名) relief (sculpture)
浮动(動) fúdòng (动) 1 float; drift 2 be unsteady; fluctuate: ～汇率 floating exchange rate
浮华(華) fúhuá (形) showy; flashy; ostentatious
浮夸(誇) fúkuā (形) boastful; untruthful: 他这人作风～. He is given to boasting.
浮力 fúlì (名) buoyancy
浮桥(橋) fúqiáo (名) pontoon (or floating) bridge
浮现 fúxiàn (动) appear in one's mind: 往事～在我眼前. My mind flashed back to scenes of the past.
浮躁 fúzào (形) impetuous; impulsive
浮肿(腫) fúzhǒng (名) dropsy; edema

俘 fú I (动) capture; take prisoner II (名) prisoner of war; captive
俘虏(虜) fúlǔ I (动) capture; take prisoner II (名) captive; prisoner of war (P.O.W.)

伏 fú I (动) 1 bend over 2 lie with one's face downward 3 subside; go down: 此起彼～ rise and fall; be rising everywhere 4 hide: 昼～夜出 hide by day and come out at night. 埋～ lie in ambush II (名) hot season; dog days
伏笔(筆) fúbǐ (名) a remark suggestive of later developments in a story, etc.
伏兵 fúbīng (名) troops in ambush
伏击(擊) fújī (名) ambush: 遭到～ fall into an ambush
伏特 fútè (名) volt
伏天 fútiān (名) hot summer days; dog days
伏贴 fútiē (动) 1 (of clothes) fit perfectly; comfortable 2 (of a person) be docile; obedient; submissive

符 fú I (名) symbol: 音～ musical notes II (动) tally with; square with: 与事实不～ not square with the facts
符号(號) fúhào (名) 1 symbol; mark; sign: 标点～ punctuation mark 2 insignia
符合 fúhé (动) accord with; conform to; be in line with: ～要求 accord with the demands. ～实际情况 tally with the actual situation
符咒 fúzhòu (名) Taoist magic figures or incantations
凫(鳧) fú (名) wild duck
服 fú I (名) clothes: 制～ uniform. 军～ army uniform. 工作～ work clothes II (动) 1 take (medicine): 日～三次, 每次两片. To be taken three times a day, two (tablets) each time. 2 serve: ～兵役 serve in the army (navy, airforce, etc.). ～刑 serve a sentence 3 be convinced; obey: 以理～人 convince by reasoning 4 be accustomed to: 水土不～ not accustomed to the climate
see also 䏎
服从(從) fúcóng (动) obey; be subordinated to: ～命令 obey orders. 少数～多数. The minority should submit to the majority.
服毒 fúdú (动) take poison
服气(氣) fúqì (动) be convinced: 他是错的, 但很难叫他～. He is wrong, but it is difficult to convince him.
服丧(喪) fúsāng (动) be in mourning (for the death of a kinsman, etc.)
服饰(飾) fúshì (名) dress and personal adornment
服侍 fúshi (动) wait upon; attend: ～病人 attend the sick
服输 fúshū (动) admit (or acknowledge) defeat
服帖 fútiē (形) 1 obedient; submissive 2 properly; smoothly: 事情都弄得服服帖帖. Everything has been done properly.
服务(務) fúwù (动) give service to; serve: ～很周到. The service is very good. ～行业 service trades. ～员 attendant. ～台 service desk (or counter); information and reception desk
服役 fúyì (动) be on active service; enlist (in the armed forces)
服装(裝) fúzhuāng (名) dress; garment; costume: 民族～ national costume
服罪 fúzuì (动) plead guilty
拂 fú (动) 1 touch: 春风～面. The spring breeze touched my cheeks. 2 whisk; flick
拂拭 fúshì (动) whisk or wipe off
拂晓(曉) fúxiǎo (名) dawn; daybreak
府 fǔ (名) 1 government office: 首～ capital 2 official residence; mansion: 总统～ presidential palace 3 ‹敬› your home: 贵～ your home 4 prefecture
府上 fǔshang (名) ‹敬› your home; your family: ～在哪里? Where is your home?
腐 fǔ I (形) rotten; stale; corroded: 流水不～. Running water is never stale. II (名) bean curd
腐败 fǔbài (形) 1 rotten; decayed 2 corrupt
腐化 fǔhuà (形) corrupt; degenerate; depraved: 贪污～ corrupt and degenerate
腐烂(爛) fǔlàn (形) 1 decomposed 2 corrupt; rotten: 极端～ rotten to the core
腐蚀(蝕) fǔshí (动) corrupt; corrode: ～剂 corrosive
腐朽 fǔxiǔ (形) rotten; decayed; decadent
腐殖质(質) fǔzhízhì (名) humus
俯 fǔ (动) bend; lower; bow: ～视 overlook. ～冲 (of a bird or an aeroplane) dive
俯瞰 fǔkàn (动) look down at; overlook
俯拾即是 fǔ shí jí shì can be found anywhere; be very common
俯视 fǔshì (动) look down at; overlook
俯首帖耳 fǔshǒu tiē ěr (动) be obedient; be submissive; be servile
抚(撫) fǔ (动) 1 stroke 2 comfort; console: 安～ appease; pacify 3 nurture; foster: ～养 bring up; foster; raise
抚爱(愛) fǔ'ài (动) caress; fondle
抚摩 fǔmó (动) stroke
抚弄 fǔnòng (动) stroke; fondle
抚慰 fǔwèi (动) comfort; console; soothe
抚恤 fǔxù (动) comfort and compensate the family of a person

who was hurt at work and / or died as a consequence: ～金 pension or compensation

抚育 fǔyù (动) foster; nurture; tend: ～子女 bring up children

甫 fǔ (副)〈书〉just; only: 年～二十 have just reached the age of twenty

辅 fǔ (动) assist; complement; supplement: 相～相成 complement each other; be complementary (to each other)

辅导(導) fǔdǎo (动) coach; give tutorials to: ～员 assistant; instructor

辅音 fǔyīn (名) consonant

辅助 fǔzhù I (动) assist II (形) supplementary; subsidiary: ～教材 supplementary reading material. ～机构 auxiliary body

脯 fǔ (名) 1 preserved fruit: 梨～ preserved pears 2 dried meat

斧 fǔ (名)(～子) axe

斧头(頭) fǔtou (名) axe; hatchet

釜 fǔ (名) cauldron: ～底抽薪 take a drastic measure to deal with an emergency. ～底游鱼 a person whose fate is as good as sealed

父 fù (名) 1 father: ～亲 father 2 male relative: 伯～ one's father's elder brother; uncle. 祖～ grandfather

父老 fùlǎo (名) elders (of a country or district)

父母 fù-mǔ (名) father and mother; parents

父系 fùxì (名) paternal line

缚 fù (动) tie up: 束～ tie; bind up

富 fù (形) rich; wealthy; abundant

富贵 fùguì (名) wealth and rank: 荣华～ wealth and honours

富豪 fùháo (名) rich and powerful people

富庶 fùshù (形) rich and populous

富翁 fùwēng (名) a very wealthy man

富有 fùyǒu (形) rich in; full of: ～代表性 highly representative. ～生命力 be full of vitality

富丽(麗)堂皇 fùlì tánghuáng (形) splendid; magnificent

富农(農) fùnóng (名) rich peasant

富强 fùqiáng (形) prosperous and powerful

富饶(饒) fùráo (形) richly endowed; abundant: ～的土地 a land of plenty

富裕 fùyù (形) well-to-do; prosperous; well-off: ～中农 well-to-do middle peasant

富余(餘) fùyu (形) have enough and to spare

富足 fùzú (形) rich; plentiful; abundant

副 fù I (形) 1 deputy; assistant; vice-: ～主任 deputy director: ～经理 assistant manager. ～主席 vice-chairman. ～教授 associate professor 2 auxiliary; subsidiary; secondary: ～品 substandard goods II (量) 1 pair; set: 一～眼镜 a pair of glasses. 两～手套 two pairs of gloves 2 [of facial expression]: 一～笑脸 a smiling face. 一～庄严的面孔 a dignified appearance

副本 fùběn (名) duplicate; transcript; copy

副产(產)品 fùchǎnpǐn (名) by-product

副词 fùcí (名) adverb

副官 fùguān (名) adjutant; aide-de-camp

副刊 fùkān (名) supplement: 文学～ literary supplement

副食 fùshí (名) non-staple food (including meat, vegetables, etc.): ～商店 grocer's; grocery

副手 fùshǒu (名) assistant

副题 fùtí (名) sub-title

副业(業) fùyè (名) sideline; side occupation

副作用 fùzuòyòng (名) (of medicine) side effect; by-effect

讣 fù (名) obituary

讣告 fùgào (名) obituary notice

赴 fù (动) go to; attend: ～宴 attend a banquet

赴难(難) fùnàn (动) join in the effort to save the nation

赴任 fùrèn (动) go to one's post; leave for an assignment

赴汤(湯)蹈火 fùtāng dǎohuǒ go through fire and water

赋 fù I (名) tax II (动) 1 bestow on; endow with: ～予 bestow; endow. 禀～ natural endowments 2 compose (a poem): ～诗一首 compose a poem

赋税 fùshuì (名) taxes; levy

赋闲(閑) fùxián (形) (of an official, etc.) be unemployed

复(複、復) fù I (动) 1 turn around; turn back; repeat: 反～无常 capricious. ～写 duplicate. 旧病～发 have a relapse 2 answer: 电～ cable reply 3 recover; resume: 康～ (of health) recover. 收～国土 recover one's motherland. 官～原职 restored to one's official post 4 revenge: 报～ retaliate. ～仇 revenge II (副) again: 周而～始 go round and begin again. 一去不～返 leave never to return; gone for ever

复辟 fùbì (动) restore a dethroned monarch; stage a comeback

复查 fùchá (动) check; reexamine

复工 fùgōng (动) return to work (after a strike or layoff)

复古 fùgǔ (动) restore ancient ways

复合 fùhé (名) compound; complex: ～词 compound word

复核 fùhé (动) check; reexamine

复会(會) fùhuì (动) resume a session

复活 fùhuó I (动) bring back to life; revive II (名) Resurrection: ～节 Easter

复旧(舊) fùjiù (名) restoration (or revival) of old ways; return to the past

复刊 fùkān (动) resume publication

复述 fùshù (动) repeat; retell

复数(數) fùshù (名) plural number

复苏(蘇) fùsū (动) come back to life (or consciousness)

复习(習) fùxí (动) review; revise: 总～ general revision (of one's lessons)

复信 fùxìn I (动) write a letter in reply II (名) letter in reply; reply

复兴(興) fùxīng (动) revive: 文艺～ the Renaissance

复姓 fùxìng (名) two-character surname

复印 fùyìn (动) photocopy; duplicate; xerox

复员 fùyuán (动、名) demobilize; demobilization: ～军人 demobilized soldier; ex-serviceman

复原 fùyuán (动) recover from an illness; be restored to health

复杂(雜) fùzá (形) complicated; complex

复制 fùzhì (动) duplicate; reproduce; copy: ～品 replica; reproduction

覆 fù (动) 1 cover 2 overturn: 前车之～,后车之鉴. The upset of the cart ahead is a warning to the cart behind.

覆盖(蓋) fùgài (动) cover: 积雪～着地面. The ground is covered with a layer of snow.

覆灭(滅) fùmiè (名) destruction; complete collapse

覆没 fùmò (动) 1 〈书〉 capsize and sink 2 (of troops) be annihilated: 敌人全军～. The enemy troops were entirely wiped out.

覆亡 fùwáng (名) (of a nation) fall

覆水难(難)收 fù shuǐ nán shōu It is no use crying over spilt milk.

覆辙 fùzhé (名) the track of an overturned cart: 重蹈～ follow the same disastrous course

蝮 fù

蝮蛇 fùshé (名) Pallas pit viper

馥 fù (名)〈书〉 fragrance

馥郁 fùyù (名)〈书〉 strong fragrance; heavy perfume

腹 fù (名) belly; abdomen; stomach

腹背受敌(敵) fù-bèi shòu dí be attacked front and rear

腹地 fùdì (名) hinterland

腹稿 fùgǎo (名) a draft worked out in one's mind

腹腔 fùqiāng (名) abdominal cavity

腹痛 fùtòng (名) abdominal pain

腹泻(瀉) fùxiè (名) diarrhoea

付 fù (动) 1 pay: ～帐 pay a bill. ～税 pay taxes. ～息 pay interest. 分期～款 pay in installments 2 hand (or turn) over to: ～印 send to the press. 托～ entrust. ～之一炬 commit to the flames. ～诸实施 put into practice

付出 fùchū (动) pay out; expend: ～代价 pay a price. ～辛勤的劳动 put in a lot of hard work

付诸东(東)流 fù zhū dōng liú (of efforts) have proven futile; have been wasted

咐 fù see "吩咐" fēnfu; "嘱咐" zhǔfu

附 fù (动) 1 add; attach; enclose: 依～ be sb.'s protégé; sponge on sb. ～笔 add a postscript. ～寄一张照片 enclose a photo 2 get close to; be near

～耳交谈 talk in whispers
附带(帶) fùdài I (副) in passing; incidentally: ～说一下 mention in passing; by the way II (动) attach: 不～条件 with no conditions (or strings) attached
附和 fùhè (动) (of opinion) echo; parrot: ～别人的意见 parrot other people's views
附加 fùjiā I (动) add; attach II (形) additional; attached; appended: ～条款 additional article; memorandum clause
附件 fùjiàn (名) 1 appendix; annex 2 (of a machine) accessory; attachment
附近 fùjìn (形) nearby; close to; in the vicinity: ～的城镇 neighbouring towns. 住在～ live nearby. 就在公园～ (It is) in the vicinity of the park.
附录 fùlù (名) appendix
附上 fùshàng (动) enclose herewith: 随信～商品目录一份. A catalogue of commodities is enclosed herewith.
附设 fùshè (动) have as an attached institution: 这个学院～一所中学. There is a middle school attached to the institute.
附属(屬) fùshǔ (形) affiliated; attached: 医学院～医院 a hospital attached to a medical college. ～机构 affiliated organization
附言 fùyán (名) postscript (P.S.)
附议(議) fùyì (动) second a motion
附庸 fùyōng (名) a vassal kingdom; dependency
附注 fùzhù (名) notes appended to a book; annotations

驸 fù

驸马(馬) fùmǎ (名) emperor's son-in-law

阜 fù

I (名)〈书〉mound II (形) abundant: 物～民丰 products abound and the people live in plenty

服 fù

(量) (for Chinese medicine) dose: 一～药 a dose of medicine

see also fú

负 fù

I (动) 1 carry on the back or shoulder; bear: 肩～重任 shoulder heavy responsibilities. 如释重～ feel a heavy load off one's mind; feel greatly relieved 2 owe: ～债 be in debt 3 fail in one's duty or obligation; betray: ～约 break a promise. 忘恩～义 be ungrateful 4 lose (a battle, game, etc.); be defeated: 不分胜～ end in a draw; break even 5 suffer: ～伤 be wounded; be injured 6 rely on: ～险固守 put up a stubborn defence by relying on one's strategic position II (名) minus; negative: ～一点五 minus one point five (−1.5). ～号 negative sign
负担(擔) fùdān I (动) bear (a burden); shoulder: ～旅费 bear travel expenses II (名) burden; load: 思想～ mental burden. 家庭～ family burden
负荷 fùhè (名) load
负极(極) fùjí (名) negative pole
负数(數) fùshù (名) negative number
负隅顽抗 fùyú wánkàng (of an enemy) put up a stubborn resistance
负责 fùzé I (动) be responsible for; be in charge of: 这里谁～? Who is in charge here? 我～校对. I'll be responsible for proofreading. 一切后果将由你～. You will be held responsible for all the consequences. II (形) 1 responsible: ～人 person in charge 2 conscientious: 对工作很～ be very conscientious in one's work

妇(婦) fù

(名) 1 woman: ～幼 (or 孺) women and children 2 married woman: 少～ young married woman 3 wife: 夫～ husband (or man) and wife
妇产(產)科 fùchǎnkē (名) (department of) gynaecology and obstetrics
妇女 fùnǚ (名) woman
妇人 fùrén (名) married woman
妇科 fùkē (名) (department of) gynaecology: ～医生 gynaecologist

Gg

夹(夾) gā

see also jiā; jiá
夹肢窝(窩) gāzhiwō (名) armpit

嘎 gā

嘎巴 gābā 〈象〉crack; snap

嘎嘎 gāgā 〈象〉 quack

咖 gā see also kā

咖喱 gālí (名) curry: ～牛肉 beef curry

该 gāi I (助) should; ought to: 他早～到了. He should have arrived. 这人～受惩罚. This chap ought to be punished. II (动) 1 be one's turn to do sth.: ～你了. It's your turn now. 下一个～谁发言? Who's the next speaker? 2 owe: 我～你多少钱? How much do I owe you? III (代) this, that; it; the above-mentioned: 这是本地最大的医院, ～医院有七百张病床. This is the biggest hospital in the locality. It has 700 beds. IV (副) [used for emphasis]: 你瞧,这么晚了,妈妈又～唠叨了! Look! It's late. Mother will grumble again. 要是我能跟你一块去, 那～多好哇! How nice it would be if I could go with you!

该死 gāisǐ 〈口〉 [used to express anger]: 你这～的笨蛋! You damn fool! ～的天气! What wretched weather! ～! 我忘带钥匙了. Damn it! I've forgotten my key.

改 gǎi (动) 1 change; transform: 把卧室～成起居室 convert a bedroom into a sitting room. 河流～道. The river changed its course. ～朝换代 dynastic changes 2 alter; correct: ～裙子 alter a skirt. ～缺点 overcome one's shortcomings. ～作业 correct (or go over) students' homework (or papers)

改编 gǎibiān (动) 1 adapt; rewrite: 这部电影是由一本小说～的. This film is adapted from a novel. 2 (of troops) reorganize

改变(變) gǎibiàn (动) change; alter; transform: ～主意 change one's mind

改道 gǎidào (动) change one's route; (of a river) change its course

改掉 gǎidiào (动) give up; drop: ～坏习惯 give up bad habits

改动(動) gǎidòng (动) change; modify: 这篇文章我只～了一些词句. I have only changed a few words and sentences in this article. *or*, I have only made a few changes in the wording of this article.

改革 gǎigé (动) reform: 土地～ land reform. 文字～ reform of a writing system

改观(觀) gǎiguān (动) take on a new look; change in appearance

改过(過) gǎiguò (动) correct one's errors: ～自新 mend one's ways; turn over a new leaf

改行 gǎiháng (动) change one's profession (or occupation)

改换 gǎihuàn (动) change; replace

改嫁 gǎijià (动) (of a woman) remarry

改进(進) gǎijìn (动) improve; make better: ～企业管理 improve business management

改口 gǎikǒu (动) correct oneself (in conversation); change one's tone

改良 gǎiliáng (动) improve; ameliorate; reform: ～主义 reformism

改期 gǎiqī (动) change the date: 会议～举行. The meeting has been postponed.

改日 gǎirì (副) another day; some other day

改善 gǎishàn (动) improve; better: ～生活条件 improve living conditions

改头(頭)换面 gǎitóu-huànmiàn (动) change the appearance but not the substance; dish up in a new form

改弦更张(張) gǎixián-gēngzhāng start afresh

改邪归(歸)正 gǎixié-guīzhèng (动) turn over a new leaf

改写(寫) gǎixiě (动) rewrite; adapt

改选(選) gǎixuǎn (动) reelect

改造 gǎizào (动) transform; reform; remould: ～自然 transform nature

改正 gǎizhèng (动) correct; amend; put right: ～错误 correct one's mistakes

改组 gǎizǔ (动) reorganize; reshuffle: ～内阁 reshuffle the cabinet

盖(蓋) gài I (名) lid; cover: 茶壶～ teapot lid II (动) 1 cover: 遮～ cover up. ～章 put the chop (a seal) on 2 overwhelm: 欢呼声～过了他的叫声. Cheers drowned his shouting. 3 build: ～房子 build houses. ～楼房 put up a building

盖棺论(論)定 gài guān lùn dìng only when a person is dead can final judgment be passed on him

盖世 gàishì (形) unparalleled:

～无双 peerless·
盖章 gàizhāng （动） affix one's seal; seal; stamp
盖子 gàizi （名） lid; cover: 揭～ take the lid off
丐 gài （名） beggar: 乞～ beggar
钙 gài （名） calcium (Ca)
概 gài （形） 1 general; approximate: 梗～ outline 2 without exception; categorically: ～不追究 no action will be taken (against sb. for his past offences). 商品售出，～不退换. Articles sold may not be returned.
概况 gàikuàng （名） general situation; brief account of sth.
概括 gàikuò （动） summarize; generalize: ～地说 generally speaking; briefly
概率 gàilǜ （名） probability
概略 gàilüè （名） outline; summary: 这只是故事的～. This is only a synopsis.
概论(論) gàilùn （名） outline
概念 gàiniàn （名） concept; conception; notion; idea
概算 gàisuàn （名） budgetary estimate
概要 gàiyào （名） essentials; outline
干(乾) gān I （形） 1 dry; dried: ～毛巾 dry towel. ～果 dried fruits 2 empty: 酒瓶～了. The wine bottle is empty. 外强中～ outwardly strong but inwardly weak 3 relatives not linked by blood: ～爹 father by affection. ～儿子 adopted son II （副） with no result; in vain: ～打雷不下雨 all thunder and no rain. 我～等了他半天. I wasted a lot of time waiting for him (and he didn't turn up). ～着急 be worried but unable to do anything III （名） concern: 与你何～？ What has it to do with you?
干巴 gānba （形） dried up; shrivelled; wizened: 树叶都晒～了. The leaves have dried up under the sun. ～的皮肤 wizened skin
干巴巴 gānbābā （形） 1 dried up; wizened 2 dull and dry: 文章写得～的. The article is dull.
干瘪(癟) gānbiě （形） shrivelled; wizened
干草 gāncǎo （名） hay: ～垛 haystack
干杯 gānbēi （动） drink a toast; cheers; "bottoms up!"
干脆 gāncuì （形、副） 1 frank and straightforward: 他这人很～. He is frank and straightforward. 回答～点！ Give me a simple, clear-cut answer! 2 simply; just: 他～一直保持沉默. He simply kept silent all the time. 你～亲自跟他谈谈吧. You'd better talk to him yourself.
干电(電)池 gāndiànchí （名） dry battery
干戈 gāngē （名） weapons: 动～ take up arms; go to war
干旱 gānhàn （形） (of weather or soil) arid; dry
干涸 gánhé （动） (of a river) dry up; run dry
干净 gānjìng I （形） clean: ～利落 neat and tidy II （副） completely; totally: 把责任推得一干二净 absolutely refuse to accept any responsibility
干粮(糧) gānliang （名） dry ready food
干枯 gānkū （形） dried-up; withered: 地上落满了～的树叶. The ground is covered with withered fallen leaves.
干酪 gānlào （名） cheese
干扰(擾) gānrǎo （动） disturb; interfere; obstruct
干涉 gānshè （动） 1 interfere; intervene; meddle: 互不～内政 noninterference in each other's internal affairs 2 be related to: 二者了无～. The two of them have nothing to do with each other.
干瘦 gānshòu （形） skinny; bony
干洗 gānxǐ （动、名） dry-clean; dry cleaning
干预 gānyù （动） intervene; meddle
干燥 gānzào （形） dry; arid: 沙漠地方气候很～. The climate is very dry in the desert area.
杆(桿) gān （名） pole; post: 旗～ flagstaff; flagpole.
see also gǎn
竿 gān （名） pole; rod: 竹～ bamboo pole. 钓鱼～ fishing rod
肝 gān （名） liver: ～癌 liver cancer. ～炎 hepatitis
肝胆(膽) gāndǎn （名） 1 openheartedness; sincerity: ～相照，荣辱与共 treating each other with all sincerity and sharing weal or woe 2 heroic spirit
肝功能 gāngōngnéng （名） liver

function

肝火 gānhuǒ (名) irascibility; spleen: 动～ vent one's spleen; get worked up. ～旺 hot-tempered; irascible

肝脏(臟) gānzàng (名) liver

甘 gān (形) 1 sweet; pleasant: ～泉 sweet spring water 2 willingly; of one's own accord: 不～ unwilling

甘拜下风(風) gān bài xiàfēng candidly acknowledge one's inferiority; willingly yield to sb.'s superior knowledge or skill

甘苦 gānkǔ (名) 1 joys and sorrows: 同甘共苦 share the joys and sorrows 2 hardships and difficulties experienced in work

甘露 gānlù (名) sweet dew; superior drink

甘美 gānměi (形) (of water) sweet and refreshing

甘薯 gānshǔ (名) sweet potato

甘心 gānxīn (副) willingly; readily

甘休 gānxiū (动) be willing to give up; take it lying down

甘油 gānyóu (名) glycerine

甘愿(願) gānyuàn (副) willingly

甘蔗 gānzhe (名) sugarcane

泔 gān

泔水 gānshuǐ (名) swill; slops

柑 gān (名) mandarin orange

柑橘 gānjú (名) oranges and tangerines

尴(尷) gān

尴尬 gāngà (形) awkward; embarrassed: 处境～ be in an awkward position

赶(趕) gǎn (动) 1 catch up with: ～上世界先进水平 catch up with the world advanced levels 2 hurry; rush: ～路 hurry on one's way. 我们必须～回去. We must hurry back. ～任务 rush through one's job 3 take; catch: ～头班车 catch the first bus 4 drive: 把牛～上山 drive the cattle up the hill. ～大车 drive a cart. 把敌人～走 drive the enemy away 5 happen to: 他～巧在家. He happened to be at home. 今天正～上是母亲的生日. Today happens to be mother's birthday.

赶集 gǎnjí (动) go to the local market (or a village fair)

赶紧(緊) gǎnjǐn (动) lose no time; hasten

赶快 gǎnkuài (副) hasten; at once; quickly: 时间不早了,我们～走吧. It's getting late. Let's leave at once.

赶忙 gǎnmáng (形) hurry; make haste: 他～道歉. He hastened to apologize.

赶巧 gǎnqiǎo (动) happen to; it so happened that

赶时(時)髦 gǎn shímáo (动) follow the fashion

杆(桿) gǎn I (名) the shaft or arm of sth.: 秤～ the arm of a steelyard. 钢笔～儿 penholder. 枪～ the barrel of a rifle II (量) [used of sth. with a shaft]: 一～秤 a steelyard. 一～枪 a rifle

see also gān

秆(稈) gǎn (名) stalk: 麦～ wheat stalk. 高粱～ sorghum stalk

擀 gǎn (动) roll (dough): ～面杖 rolling pin. ～面条 make noodles

感 gǎn I (动) 1 feel; sense: 深～力不从心. I feel keenly that my ability falls short of my wishes. 2 move; touch: 深有所～ be deeply moved II (名) sense; feeling: 责任～ sense of responsibility. 自卑～ inferiority complex

感触(觸) gǎnchù (名) thoughts and feelings aroused by what one sees or hears

感到 gǎndào (动) feel: 我～有些冷. I feel a bit chilly.

感动(動) gǎndòng (动) move; touch: ～得流下眼泪 be moved to tears

感恩 gǎn'ēn (动) feel grateful; be thankful

感官 gǎnguān (名) sense organs

感光 gǎnguāng (名) sensitization

感化 gǎnhuà (动) reform a misguided person through persuasion, etc.; send an erring person for corrective training

感激 gǎnjī (动) feel grateful; be thankful; feel indebted: 不胜～ be deeply grateful

感觉(覺) gǎnjué I (名) feeling; sense; perception; sensation II (动) feel; sense; perceive

感慨 gǎnkǎi (动) sigh with deep feeling

感冒 gǎnmào (名) cold; flu: 患～ catch cold; have a touch of flu

感情 gǎnqíng (名) 1 feelings; emotion; sentiment: 动～ be

carried away by one's emotions. ～用事 act impetuously. 伤～ hurt sb.'s feelings 2 affection; love

感染 gǎnrǎn (动) 1 infect: 细菌～ bacterial infection 2 influence; affect: 艺术～力 artistic appeal

感受 gǎnshòu I (动) catch (disease): ～风寒 catch a chill II (名) understanding; impression: ～很深 be deeply impressed

感叹(嘆) gǎntàn (动) sigh over sth. that strikes a chord: ～词 interjection. ～号 exclamation mark

感想 gǎnxiǎng (名) reflections; thoughts; impressions

感谢 gǎnxiè (动) thank; be grateful: 衷心的～ heartfelt thanks

感性 gǎnxìng (形) (of knowledge) perceptual

感召 gǎnzhào (动) move and inspire

敢 gǎn I (动) dare: 我～说他要试一试. I dare say he'd like to have a try. II (形) bold; daring: 果～ courageous and resolute

敢于(於) gǎnyú (动) dare to; have the courage to: 他～同不健康的现象作斗争. He has the courage to combat unhealthy trends.

橄 gǎn

橄榄(欖) gǎnlǎn (名) olive: ～球 rugby

干(幹) gàn I (名) 1 trunk; main part: 树～ tree-trunk; trunk. 骨干 backbone 2 short form for 干部: 高～ senior cadre (or official) II (动) do; work: ～活儿 work; do manual labour. 你想～什么? What do you want to do?

see also gān

干部 gànbù (名) cadre: 各级领导～ leading cadres at all levels. ～学员 mid-career student

干掉 gàndiào (动) 〈口〉 kill; get rid of

干劲(勁) gànjìn (名) vigour; drive; enthusiasm: ～冲天 with soaring enthusiasm. ～十足 be full of vigour

干练(練) gànliàn (形) capable and experienced

干吗 gànmá 〈口〉 1 why; why on earth: ～这么大惊小怪? Why all this fuss? 2 what to do: 你明天打算～? What are you going to do tomorrow?

干事 gànshì (名) person in charge of a particular kind of work

干线(綫) gànxiàn (名) main line: 交通～ main lines of communication

缸 gāng (名) big jar or crock: 水～ water vat. 金鱼～ goldfish bowl

缸子 gāngzi (名) mug; bowl

肛 gāng (名) anus

肛门(門) gāngmén (名) anus

冈(崗) gāng (名) ridge (of a hill)

刚(剛) gāng I (副) 1 just; exactly: 这件雨衣我穿上～好. This raincoat fits me perfectly. 大小～合适 just the right size 2 just, only a short while ago: 电影～开始. The film has just started. 他～～还在这儿. He was here only a moment ago. 我～来的时候觉得有些孤独. I felt a bit lonely when I first came here. 3 just; only at this moment: 我～想给他打电话,他就来了. He came just as I was about to call him. 他～要走. He is just about to leave. 我～进屋就下雨了. I had hardly come into the room when it began to rain. 4 just; no more than: ～够 just (or barely) enough. 这条裙子～过膝. The skirt comes just below my knees. II (形) firm; strong; hard: 柔中有～. Strength is hidden under an appearance of gentleness.

刚愎自用 gāngbì zìyòng (形) self-willed; opinionated

刚才 gāngcái (副) just now; a moment ago: ～你说什么来着? What did you say just now?

刚刚 gānggāng (副) just; only; exactly

刚好 gānghǎo (副) 1 just; exactly: 时间～. The time is just about right. 2 it so happened that: 我俩～在同一个班里. We happened to be in the same class.

刚健 gāngjiàn (形) (of character, style, bearing, etc.) vigorous; forceful; bold; robust

刚劲(勁) gāngjìng (形) (of handwriting) forceful and vigorous

刚…就… gāng…jiù… as soon as; no sooner than; immediately: 他刚搬进来就又想搬出去. No sooner had he moved in than he wanted to move out again.

刚强 gāngqiáng (形) (of charac-

ter, will) firm; staunch; unyielding
刚巧 gāngqiǎo (副) happen; it so happened that
刚毅 gāngyì (形) resolute and steadfast
刚正 gāngzhèng (形) staunch and upright
刚直 gāngzhí (形) outspoken and upright
钢(鋼) gāng (名) steel: 炼～ steelmaking. 不锈～ stainless steel
钢笔(筆) gāngbǐ (名) fountain pen
钢材 gāngcái (名) steel products
钢管 gāngguǎn (名) steel tube: 无缝～ seamless steel tube
钢筋 gāngjīn (名) reinforcing bar: ～混凝土 reinforced concrete
钢精锅(鍋) gāngjīngguō (名) aluminium pan
钢盔 gāngkuī (名) steel helmet
钢琴 gāngqín (名) piano: 弹～ play the piano
钢丝(絲) gāngsī (名) steel wire: 走～ high-wire walking (acrobatics). ～床 spring bed
钢铁(鐵) gāngtiě (名) iron and steel; steel
纲(綱) gāng (名) 1 the headrope of a fishing net 2 key link; guiding principle 3 class: 哺乳动物～ the class of mammals
纲领 gānglǐng (名) guiding principle; programme
纲目 gāngmù (名) detailed outline
纲要 gāngyào (名) outline; essentials
港 gǎng (名) port; harbour
港口 gǎngkǒu (名) port; harbour
港湾(灣) gǎngwān (名) bay; harbour
港务(務)局 gǎngwùjú (名) port office
岗(崗) gǎng (名) 1 hillock; mound 2 sentry; post: 站～ stand sentry
岗楼(樓) gǎnglóu (名) watchtower
岗哨 gǎngshào (名) sentry post; sentry
岗位 gǎngwèi (名) post
杠 gàng (名) 1 thick stick; bar: 单～ horizontal bar. 双～ parallel bars 2 thick line drawn as a mark
杠杆(桿) gànggǎn (名) lever
高 gāo (形) 1 tall; high: ～个子男人 a tall man. 这堵墙有三米～. This wall is three metres high. ～温 high temperature. ～喊 shout at the top of one's voice 2 advanced; superior: ～等教育 higher education. ～中 senior high school. ～水平 advanced level. ～见 wise idea
高矮 gāo'ǎi (名) height
高昂 gāo'áng (形) 1 high; elated 2 dear; expensive; costly
高傲 gāo'ào (形) supercilious; arrogant; haughty
高不可攀 gāo bùkě pān too high to reach; unattainable
高产(產) gāochǎn (名) high yield
高超 gāochāo (形) superb; excellent: 技艺～ superb skill
高潮 gāocháo (名) 1 high tide 2 upsurge; climax: 全剧的～ the climax of a play
高大 gāodà (形) tall and big
高档(檔) gāodàng (形) of top grade quality: ～商品 expensive goods
高等 gāoděng (形) higher: ～学院 institution of higher learning
高低 gāodī (名) 1 height: 估不出山崖的～ have no idea how high the cliff is. 声调的～ the pitch of a voice 2 difference in degree: 难分～ hard to tell which is better 3 sense of propriety; appropriateness: 不知～ have no sense of propriety
高地 gāodì (名) highland
高调 gāodiào (名) high-sounding words: 唱～ mouth high-sounding words
高度 gāodù I (名) altitude; height: 飞行～ flying altitude II (副) highly; to a high degree: ～赞扬 speak highly of. ～重视 attach great importance to
高峰 gāofēng (名) peak; summit; height: ～时间 peak (or rush) hours
高高在上 gāogāo zài shàng stand high above the masses; hold oneself aloof from the masses
高阁 gāogé (名) 1 mansion 2 shelf: 束之～ be shelved
高贵 gāoguì (形) 1 noble; high: ～品质 noble quality 2 privileged
高呼 gāohū (动) shout loudly: 振臂～ raise one's arm and shout at the top of one's voice
高级 gāojí (形) 1 senior; high-ranking; high-level: ～官员 high-ranking official 2 high-grade; high-quality: ～化妆品 de luxe cosmetics

高价(價) gāojià (名) high price
高峻 gāojùn (形) high and steep
高亢 gāokàng (形) loud and sonorous; resounding
高空 gāokōng (名) high altitude; upper air: ～作业 do a high-wire act
高利贷 gāolìdài (名) usury
高粱 gāoliang (名) sorghum
高龄(齡) gāolíng (名) advanced in years
高楼(樓)大厦 gāolóu-dàshà (名) huge buildings
高炉(爐) gāolú (名) blast furnace
高论(論) gāolùn (名)〈敬〉brilliant remarks
高帽子 gāomàozi (名) 1 tall paper hat (worn as a sign of humiliation) 2 flattery
高妙 gāomiào (形) ingenious; masterly: 手艺～ superb craftsmanship
高明 gāomíng I (形) wise; brilliant: 见解～ brilliant ideas II (名) wise or skillful person: 另请～. Find a better qualified person (for the job).
高攀 gāopān (动) make friends or forge ties of kinship with someone of a higher social position: 不敢～. I dare not aspire to the honour.
高频 gāopín (名) high frequency
高强 gāoqiáng (形) excel in; be skilled in: 武艺～ excel in martial arts
高跷(蹺) gāoqiāo (名) stilts: 踩～ walk on stilts
高尚 gāoshàng (形) noble; lofty
高烧(燒) gāoshāo (名) high fever: 发～ have (or run) a high fever
高射炮 gāoshèpào (名) antiaircraft gun (or artillery)
高深 gāoshēn (形) advanced; profound
高视阔步 gāoshì-kuòbù (动) stalk; strut; prance
高手 gāoshǒu (名) master-hand; ace: 象棋～ an ace at chess
高寿(壽) gāoshòu (名) 1 longevity: 祝你～ wish you a long life 2〈敬〉your venerable age
高耸(聳) gāosǒng (动) stand tall and erect; tower: ～入云 tower into the clouds
高速 gāosù (名) high speed: ～前进 advance at high speed
高谈阔论(論) gāotán-kuòlùn (名) indulge in lengthy and empty talk
高温 gāowēn (名) high temperature
高兴(興) gāoxìng (形) glad; happy; pleased; cheerful
高血压(壓) gāoxuèyā (名) hypertension; high blood pressure
高压(壓) gāoyā (名) 1 high pressure 2 high voltage 3 high-handed: ～政策 high-handed policy
高原 gāoyuán (名) highland; plateau
高瞻远(遠)瞩(矚) gāozhān-yuǎnzhǔ stand high and see far; show great foresight
高涨(漲) gāozhǎng (动) rise; upsurge
高招 gāozhāo (名) wise move
高枕无(無)忧(憂) gāo zhěn wú yōu sit back and relax; sleep soundly without any worries
高姿态(態) gāozītài (名) lofty stance (showing oneself capable of tolerance and generosity)

膏 gāo (名) 1 cream; ointment; paste: 牙～ toothpaste 2 fat
膏药(藥) gāoyao (名) plaster: 贴～ apply a plaster to

篙 gāo (名) punt-pole

羔 gāo (名) lamb
羔羊 gāoyáng (名) lamb; kid

糕 gāo (名) cake; pudding: 蛋～ cake
糕点(點) gāodiǎn (名) cake; pastry

睾 gāo
睾丸 gāowán (名) testis; testicle

搞 gǎo (动) 1 do: ～工作 do work. ～生产 engage in production. 你在这儿～什么名堂? What are you up to here? ～几个菜 prepare a few dishes. ～阴谋诡计 go in for intrigue and conspiracy. ～一个图书馆 set up a library 2 get hold of: ～几个人来帮助搬家 get some people to help move house. 你能～两张歌剧票吗? Can you get me two tickets for the opera?

镐 gǎo (名) pick; pickaxe

稿 gǎo (名) 1 draft; sketch: 初～ first draft. 这不过是个初～. This is only a first draft. 2 manuscript; original text: 定～ finalize a text
稿费 gǎofèi (名) payment for an article or book written
稿件 gǎojiàn (名) manuscript;

contribution

缟 gǎo (名) thin white silk

缟素 gǎosù (名) mourning dress

告 gào (动) 1 tell; inform; notify: 电～ inform by telegraph; cable 2 accuse; sue: 到法院去～某人 sue sb. for sth. 3 ask for; request: ～假 ask for leave 4 announce; declare: 宣～ declare; proclaim. 自～奋勇 volunteer to do sth. 大功～成. The task is at last accomplished.

告别 gàobié (动) take leave of; say good-bye to: ～家乡 bid farewell to one's home town. 向遗体～ pay one's last respects to the deceased

告辞(辭) gàocí (动) take leave of one's host

告发(發) gàofā (动) inform against (sb. to the police); accuse sb. (of an offence)

告急 gàojí (动) report the emergency to the higher level

告假 gàojià (动) ask for leave

告捷 gàojié (动) 1 win victory: 初战～ win the first battle 2 report a victory

告诫 gàojiè (动) warn; exhort

告密 gàomì (动) inform against sb.

告示 gàoshì (名) official notice; bulletin

告诉 gàosù (动) tell; let know: 请你～他，今天晚上七点钟开会. Please tell him that the meeting is fixed for seven o'clock this evening.

告知 gàozhī (动) inform; notify

告终 gàozhōng (动) come to an end; end up: 以失败～ end in failure

告状(狀) gàozhuàng (动) 1 bring a lawsuit against sb. 2 lodge a complaint against sb. (with his superior)

割 gē (动) cut: ～草 cut grass; mow. ～草机 (lawn) mower

割爱(愛) gē'ài (动) give up what one treasures

割断(斷) gēduàn (动) cut off; sever

割据(據) gējù (动) set up a separatist regime by force of arms: 封建～ feudal separatist rule.

割裂 gēliè (动) (of abstract matters) cut apart; separate; isolate: 不要把这两个问题～开来. Don't separate these two issues.

割让(讓) gēràng (动) cede: ～领土 cession of territory

哥 gē (名) (elder) brother

哥哥 gēgē (名) (elder) brother

哥儿(兒) gēr (名) brothers; boys: 你们～几个? How many boys are there altogether in your family?

哥儿(兒)们 gērmen 〈口〉 1 brothers 2 buddies; pals

歌 gē I (名) song II (动) sing

歌唱 gēchàng (动) sing (usu. in praise): ～家 singer; vocalist

歌功颂德 gēgōng-sòngdé (动) eulogize; sing the praises of sb.

歌喉 gēhóu (名) singing voice: 婉转的～ a beautiful voice

歌剧(劇) gējù (名) opera

歌曲 gēqǔ (名) song

歌手 gēshǒu (名) singer; vocalist

歌颂 gēsòng (动) sing the praises of; extol; eulogize

歌舞 gēwǔ (名) song and dance: ～升平 put on a façade of peace and prosperity

歌谣 gēyáo (名) ballad; folk song

歌咏 gēyǒng (名) singing

戈 gē (名) dagger-axe (an ancient weapon)

疙 gē

疙瘩 gēda (名) 1 pimple; lump; knot 2 misunderstanding; misgivings: 解开他心上的～ dispel his misgivings

鸽 gē (名) pigeon; dove: 通信～ carrier pigeon

咯 gē 〈象〉

咯咯 gēgē 〈象〉 chuckle; titter

咯吱 gēzhī 〈象〉 creak

胳 gē

胳臂 gēbei (名) arm

胳膊 gēbo (名) arm: ～肘儿 elbow

搁 gē (动) 1 put 2 put aside; shelve: 这件事得～一～再办. We'll have to put the matter aside for the time being.

搁浅(淺) gēqiǎn (动) be stranded: 船～了. The ship got stranded.

搁置 gēzhì (动) lay aside; shelve

革 gé I (名) leather; hide: ～制品 leather goods. 制～厂 tannery II (动) change; transform

革除 géchú (动) 1 get rid of; abolish: ～陈规陋习 abolish outmoded regulations and practices 2 dismiss; remove from office

革命 gémìng I (名) revolution II

(动) make revolution: ～家 revolutionary
革新 géxīn (名) innovation: 技术～ technological innovation
革职(職) gézhí (动) remove from office; dismiss; sack
嗝 gé (名) 1 belch 2 hiccup
膈 gé (名) diaphragm
膈膜 gémó (名) diaphragm
隔(隔) gé (动) 1 separate; partition: 把一间屋～成两间 partition a room into two 2 at a distance from; at an interval of: 相～甚远 be very far away from each other. 你～些时候再来吧. Come again some other time. ～一天一次 once every other day
隔岸观(觀)火 gé àn guān huǒ watch a fire from the other side of the river; look on unconcerned at troubles elsewhere
隔壁 gébì (名) next door: 住在～ live next door. ～邻居 next-door neighbour
隔断(斷) géduàn (动) cut off; separate
隔阂 géhé (名) estrangement; misunderstanding: 语言～ language barrier
隔绝 géjué (动) completely cut off; isolated: 和外界～ be cut off from the outside world
隔离(離) gélí (动) keep apart; isolate: 种族～ racial segregation; apartheid. ～病房 isolation ward
隔膜 gémó (名) lack of mutual understanding
隔墙有耳 gé qiáng yǒu ěr walls have ears; beware of eavesdroppers
隔音 géyīn (名) sound insulation: ～室 soundproof room
蛤 gé (名) clam
蛤蜊 géli (名) clam
阁 gé (名) 1 pavilion 2 (short for 内阁) cabinet: 组～ form a cabinet
阁楼(樓) gélóu (名) attic; loft; garret
阁下 géxià (名) ‹敬› Your Excellency; His or Her Excellency
格 gé (名) 1 line: 横～纸 ruled paper. 打～ draw lines on the paper 2 squares; check: ～子窗帘布 checked curtain 3 shelf: 这书架有三～. This bookcase has three shelves. 每服一小～. Dose: one measure each time. 4 standard; pattern; style: 合～ up to standard. 别具一～ have a style of its own 5 case: 主～ the nominative case. 宾～ the objective case
格调 gédiào (名) (literary or artistic) style
格斗(鬥) gédòu (名) wrestle; fistfight
格格不入 gégé bù rù be incompatible with; be like a square peg in a round hole
格局 géjú (名) pattern; setup; structure: 这篇文章写得很乱，简直不成个～. This essay is badly organized; it hardly holds together.
格律 gélǜ (名) set rules for tonal patterns and rhyme scheme in classical Chinese verse and poetic drama
格式 géshì (名) form; pattern: 公文～ various forms in documentary language
格外 géwài ‹副› especially; exceptionally: 你要～小心. You can't be too careful. 今年冬天～冷. This winter is exceptionally cold.
格言 géyán (名) maxim; motto
格子 gézi (名) check: ～布 checked fabric
舸 gě (名) barge
个(個) gè ‹量› 1 [the measure word most extensively used esp. before nouns which do not have special measure words of their own]: 一～人 one person. 两～桃 two peaches. 三～星期 three weeks. 四～问题 four problems 2 [used between a verb and its object]: 洗～澡 have a bath. 理～发 have a haircut 3 [used before a numeral to indicate approximation]: 有～二十分钟就够了. About twenty minutes would be enough. 这手艺得干～三年才能学会. One will need about three years to learn the skill. 4 [used between a verb and its complement]: 他说～不停. He talked on and on. 明天我们要玩～痛快. We'll have a wonderful time tomorrow.
个别 gèbié (形) 1 individual: ～辅导 individual tutorial. 跟学生～谈话 have private talks with individual students 2 very few; rare: 这只是～人的事. This mat-

ter is of concern to a couple of people only.

个个 gègè (名) each; every one; all: 你的孩子～都很聪明. All your children are very bright.

个儿 gèr (名) 1 size; height; stature 2 persons or things taken singly: 挨～握手问好 shake hands with and greet them one by one

个人 gèrén (名) 1 individual: ～私事 private affairs. ～项目 individual events. ～主义 individualism. ～崇拜 personality cult 2 oneself: 在我～看来 in my opinion

个体(體) gètǐ (名) individual: ～经济 individual economy

个性 gèxìng (名) individual character; individuality; personality

个子 gèzi (名) height; stature build

各 gè (形) each; every: "～位先生，女士" "Ladies and gentlemen". ～国 each country. ～奔前程 each follows his own career. ～持己见 each sticks to his own view. ～行其是 each goes his own way. ～得其所 each is properly provided for; each has a role to play

各…各… gè...gè... 1 each ... his own ...: 各走各的路 each goes his own way. 2 all kinds of: 各行各业 all walks of life. 各式各样 of various kinds

各个(個) gègè (形) each; every; one by one: ～方面 every aspect. ～击破 destroy one by one

各级 gèjí (名) different levels: ～领导机关 leading bodies at all levels

各界 gèjiè (名) all circles: ～人士 personalities of various circles

各色 gèsè (形) of all kinds; of every description: ～货物 goods of all kinds

各位 gèwèi (名) 1 everybody (a term of address): ～请注意. Attention please, everybody. 2 every: ～代表 fellow delegates

各有千秋 gè yǒu qiānqiū each has his merits (or strong points); each has something to recommend him

各自 gèzì (名) each; respective: 既要～努力,也要彼此帮助. This calls for both individual effort and mutual help.

各自为(爲)政 gèzì wéi zhèng each acts wilfully regardless of over-all interest

给 gěi I (动) 1 give: 他～我三本书. He gave me three books. 把孩子～我. Give me the child. 2 let; allow: ～我看看. Let me have a look. 我～你看一件东西. Let me show you something. II (介) 1 [used immediately after a verb to indicate the handing over of certain things] give: 把大衣交～他 give him the coat. 把钥匙留～我 leave the key with me. 请把杯子递～我 please pass me the glass 2 [introducing the object of one's service] for; to: 她～孩子们唱了一支歌. She sang a song for the children. 我～你讲个故事吧. Let me tell you a story. 他～她送去一束花. He sent her a bunch of flowers. 3 [as a passive indicator, as 被]: 我的钱包～偷走了. I had my wallet stolen. 报纸～风吹走了. The newspaper was blown away by the wind. III (助) [used before the main verb of the sentence, often concurrently with 叫, or 让 or 把 for emphasis]: 我差点把这事～忘了. I almost forgot this altogether.

给以 gěiyǐ (动) [followed by a direct object, usually an abstract noun] give; grant: 模范工作者应该～适当奖励. Model workers should be duly awarded.

根 gēn I (名) 1 root: 扎～ take root. 连～拔 pull up by the root 2 root; foot; base: 舌～ the root of the tongue. 城～ the foot of a city wall 3 cause; origin; source; root: 祸～ the root of trouble. 刨～问底 get to the root of a matter II (副) thoroughly; completely: ～除 completely do away with; eradicate III 〈量〉 [used of long and thin objects] 一～火柴 a match. 两～筷子 a pair of chopsticks

根本 gēnběn I (形) basic; fundamental; essential: ～利益 fundamental interest. ～原因 root cause. ～原则 cardinal principle II (名) foundation; base: 应从～上考虑解决问题的方法. We must seek a permanent solution to the problem. III (副) 1 [often used in the negative] at all; simply: 你～就不明白. You don't understand it at all. 这事我～不知道. I have absolutely no idea about this matter. 2 radically; thoroughly: ～改变这

种状况 thoroughly change the situation

根除 gēnchú (动) root out; eradicate

根底 gēndǐ (名) 1 foundation: 他的英文～很好. He has a good grounding in English. 2 cause; root: 追问～ inquire into the cause of the matter

根基 gēnjī (名) foundation; basis: 打好～ lay a solid foundation

根据(據) gēnjù I (动) on the basis of; according to: 这部电影是～一个真实故事写成的. This film is based on a true story. ～具体情况 in the light of specific conditions II (名) basis; grounds: 这话有～吗? Is this statement based on facts? 毫无～ utterly groundless

根绝 gēnjué (动) eradicate; exterminate

根深蒂固 gēnshēn-dìgù (形) deep-rooted: ～的偏见 deep rooted prejudice

根由 gēnyóu (名) cause; origin

根源 gēnyuán (名) source; origin; root: 历史～ historical roots

根治 gēnzhì (动) (of disease, etc.) effect a permanent cure

跟 gēn I (动) follow: 他后面～着一群人. He was followed by a crowd. II (名) heel: 鞋后～ the heel of a shoe. III (介) 1 [denoting the same function as that of "和","同"] and; with: 我～他一样高. He and I are of the same height. 我～你一起去. I'll go with you. 2 to; towards [as "向", "对"]: 这事你最好～他谈. You'd better discuss this with him. 别～我过不去! Don't be difficult with me!

跟班 gēnbān (动) join a regular shift or class

跟前 gēnqián (副) in front of; near: 到我～来! Come closer!

跟随 gēnsuí (动) follow: 孩子～父亲出去了. The boy has gone out with his father.

跟踪 gēnzōng (动) tail; follow closely: ～追击 be in hot pursuit

羹 gēng (名) a thick soup: 鸡蛋～ egg custard

羹匙 gēngchí (名) soup spoon; tablespoon

耕 gēng (动) plough; till: 春～ spring ploughing. 精～细作 intensive and careful cultivation

耕畜 gēngchù (名) farm animal

耕地 gēngdì I (名) arable land II (动) plough

耕耘 gēngyún (名) ploughing and weeding: 着意～, 自有收获. Set your mind on ploughing, and you will reap a good harvest.

耕种(種) gēngzhòng (动) till; cultivate

耕作 gēngzuò (名) cultivation; farming

更 gēng I (动) change; replace: ～新 update; refresh II (名) one of the five two-hour periods into which the night was formerly divided: 打～ beat the watches. 三～半夜 in the dead of night

see also gèng

更迭 gēngdié (动) alternate; change: 内阁～ a change of cabinet

更动(動) gēngdòng (动) change; alter: 人事～ personnel change

更番 gēngfān (副) alternately; by turns

更改 gēnggǎi (动) change; alter: 在细节安排上有一点～. There is a little change about the details of the arrangement.

更换 gēnghuàn (动) change; replace: ～衣裳 change one's clothes

更替 gēngtì (动) replace; substitute

更衣 gēngyī (动) change one's clothes: ～室 changeroom; locker room

更正 gēngzhèng I (动) make corrections (of errors in statements or newspaper articles) II (名) corrigenda

耿 gěng (形) dedicated; honest and just

耿耿 gěnggěng (形) 1 devoted; dedicated: 忠心～ loyal; dedicated 2 have sth. on one's mind, be troubled: ～于怀 take sth. to heart

耿直 gěngzhí (形) honest and frank; upright: 秉性～ be upright by nature

埂 gěng (名) 1 a low bank of earth between fields [also as 田埂] 2 an earth dyke (or embankment)

梗 gěng I (名) (of plants) stalk; stem II (动) 1 straighten; straighten up one's neck 2 obstruct; block: 从中作～ make it difficult for sb. to go ahead with sth.

梗概 gěnggài (名) outline; gist; highlight

梗塞 gěngsè (动) clog; block;

obstruct: 交通～ traffic jam. 心肌～ myocardial infarction

梗阻 gěngzǔ (动) block; hamper

哽 gěng (动) choke (with emotion); feel a lump in one's throat: ～咽 choke with sobs

更 gèng 〈副〉 even; more; still more; further: 这本书比那本书～有趣. This book is even more interesting than that one. ～重要的是… What is more important …. ～大的成功 still greater success

see also gēng

更加 gèngjiā 〈副〉 more; still more; even more: 天色渐亮,晨星～稀少了. At daybreak, the stars were becoming even more sparse.

工 gōng (名) 1 worker; workman; the working class: 熟练～ skilled worker. 矿～ miner 2 work; labour: 上～去 go to work. 这事很费～. It requires a lot of hard work. 3 (construction) project: 动～ begin a project. 竣～ complete a project 4 industry: 化～ chemical industry 5 man-day: 这项工程需要几个～? How many man-days will it take to complete this project?

工本 gōngběn (名) cost (of production): 不惜～ spare no expense

工笔(筆) gōngbǐ (名) a type of traditional Chinese painting characterized by fine brushwork and close attention to detail

工厂(廠) gōngchǎng (名) factory; mill; plant; works

工场(場) gōngchǎng (名) workshop

工程 gōngchéng (名) engineering; project: 土木～ civil engineering. 水利～ water conservancy project. ～师 engineer

工段 gōngduàn (名) 1 a section of a construction project 2 workshop section

工夫 gōngfu (名) 1 time: 五天的～ five days' time. 有～再来吧. Come again when you have time. 2 effort; work; labour: 花了好大～ put in a lot of work 3 workmanship; skill; art: 练～ (of actors, athletes, etc.) practise. 这画～真到家. This painting shows superb skill.

工会(會) gōnghuì (名) trade union

工件 gōngjiàn (名) workpiece

工具 gōngjù (名) tool; instrument: 生产～ implements of production. 运输～ means of transport. ～书 reference book; dictionary

工力 gōnglì (名) skill; craftsmanship: ～深厚 remarkable craftsmanship

工龄(齡) gōnglíng (名) length of service; standing

工钱(錢) gōngqián (名) 1 payment for odd jobs 2 〈口〉 wages; pay

工人 gōngrén (名) worker; workman: ～阶级 the working class

工伤(傷) gōngshāng (名) injury incurred during work

工商界 gōng-shāngjiè (名) industrial and commercial circles; business circles

工商业(業) gōng-shāngyè (名) industry and commerce

工时(時) gōngshí (名) man-hour

工事 gōngshì (名) defence works

工头(頭) gōngtóu (名) foreman

工效 gōngxiào (名) work efficiency

工业(業) gōngyè (名) industry: 轻(重)～ light (heavy) industry. ～革命 the Industrial Revolution. ～化 industrialization

工艺(藝) gōngyì (名) technology; craft: 手～ handicraft. ～美术 arts and crafts

工整 gōngzhěng (形) careful and neat: 他字写得～极了. He writes a very neat hand.

工资 gōngzī (名) wages; salary: ～表 payroll; pay sheet. ～级别 wage scale

工作 gōngzuò I (名) work; job: ～服 work clothes. ～证 employee's card II (动) work: ～早餐 working breakfast. ～语言 working language. ～日 working day

工作者 gōngzuòzhě (名) people who do a particular type of job: 文艺～ literary and art workers; writers and artists. 医务工作～ a medical worker

攻 gōng (动) 1 attack; take the offensive: ～城 lay siege to a city. ～下敌人的桥头堡 capture the enemy bridgehead 2 study; specialize in: 他是专～地质学的. He specializes in geology.

攻打 gōngdǎ (动) attack; assault

攻读(讀) gōngdú (动) study; make a study of: 他正～博士学位. He is trying for a Ph. D.

攻击(擊) gōngjī (动) 1 attack;

assault: 发起总～ launch a general offensive 2 slander; vilify
攻坚(堅) gōngjiān (动) assault fortified positions
攻势(勢) gōngshì (名) offensive: 采取～ take the offensive. 冬季～ winter offensive
攻陷 gōngxiàn (动) storm; capture: ～一个城市 capture a city
功 gōng (名) 1 meritorious deeds; merit; achievement: 记一大～ be cited for one's outstanding service 2 skill (of dancers, gymnasts, etc.): 练～ practise one's skill
功败垂成 gōng bài chuí chéng suffer defeat on the verge of success
功臣 gōngchén (名) a person who has rendered outstanding service to his country
功德 gōngdé (名) meritorious and beneficent deeds
功夫 gōngfu see "工夫"
功绩 gōngjī (名) merits and achievements; contribution
功课 gōngkè (名) schoolwork; homework
功亏(虧)一篑 gōng kuī yī kuì fall short of one's goal for want of a final effort
功劳(勞) gōngláo (名) credit; contribution (to a cause)
功利 gōnglì (名) utility; material gain
功名 gōngmíng (名) scholarly honour or official rank (in feudal times)
功能 gōngnéng (名) function: ～性障碍 functional disorder
功效 gōngxiào (名) efficacy; effect
功勋(勳) gōngxūn (名) meritorious service
功业(業) gōngyè (名) exploits; achievements
供 gōng (动) supply; provide: ～水 water supply. ～电 power supply. ～不上 be in short supply. ～不应求 supply falls short of demand
see also gòng
供给 gōngjǐ (动) supply; provide; furnish
供求 gōng-qiú (名) supply and demand: ～平衡 balance between supply and demand
供销 gōng-xiāo (动) supply and marketing: ～(合作)社 supply and marketing cooperative
供养(養) gōngyǎng (动) support; provide for (one's parents or elders)
供应(應) gōngyìng (名) supply: 市场～ market supplies
恭 gōng (形) respectful; reverent: ～贺 congratulate. ～候光临 request the pleasure of one's company.
恭敬 gōngjìng (形) respectful
恭顺 gōngshùn (形) respectful and submissive
恭维 gōngwéi (动) flatter; compliment: ～话 flattery; compliments
恭喜 gōngxǐ (名)〈套〉congratulations
公 gōng I (名) official business: 办～ do office or administrative work. 非～莫入 no admittance except on business II (形) 1 public; state-owned: ～私合营 joint state-private ownership 2 fair; just: 办事不～ unjust in handling affairs 3 metric: ～制 metric system 4 male (animal): ～鸡 cock; rooster. ～鸭 drake. ～牛 bull III (动) make public: ～之于世 make known to the public; be made publ c
公安 gōng'ān (名) public security: ～局 public security bureau. ～人员 public security officer
公案 gōng'àn (名) controversial or mysterious case
公报(報) gōngbào (名) communiqué; bulletin: 联合～ joint communiqué. 新闻～ press communiqué
公布 gōngbù (动) make public; announce: ～法令 promulgate a decree
公差 gōngchāi (名) official duty: 出～ go on official business
公尺 gōngchǐ (名) metre (m)
公道 gōngdào I (名) justice: 主持～ uphold justice II (形) fair; impartial
公敌(敵) gōngdí (名) public enemy
公断(斷) gōngduàn (名) 1 arbitration 2 impartial verdict
公费 gōngfèi (名) at public (or state) expense: ～医疗 free medical care (services)
公分 gōngfēn (名) 1 centimetre (cm) 2 gram (g)
公愤 gōngfèn (名) public indignation
公干(幹) gōnggàn (名) business: 有何～? What important business brings you here?
公告 gōnggào (名) announcement; proclamation
公共 gōnggòng (形) public; com-

mon; communal: ～财产 public property. ～厕所 public conveniences. ～卫生 public health (or hygiene). ～汽车 bus
公海 gōnghǎi (名) high seas
公害 gōnghài (名) environmental pollution
公函 gōnghán (名) official letter
公家 gōngjiā (名) the state; the public: ～的财产 public property
公斤 gōngjīn (名) kilogram (kg)
公爵 gōngjué (名) duke
公开(開) gōngkāi I (形) open; overt; public: ～露面 make public appearances. ～的秘密 an open secret. ～信 open letter. II (动) make public: ～化 come out into the open
公款 gōngkuǎn (名) public fund
公里 gōnglǐ (名) kilometre (km)
公理 gōnglǐ (名) 1 universally accepted truth 2 axiom
公历(歷) gōnglì (公) the Gregorian calendar
公立 gōnglì (形) established and maintained by the government: ～学校 state-run school
公粮(糧) gōngliáng (名) agricultural tax paid in grain
公路 gōnglù (名) highway: 高速～ motorway
公论(論) gōnglùn (名) public opinion
公民 gōngmín (名) citizen: ～权 civil rights. ～投票 referendum; plebiscite
公墓 gōngmù (名) cemetery
公平 gōngpíng (形) fair; just; impartial; equitable: ～合理 fair and reasonable. ～交易 fair deal
公婆 gōng-pó (名) husband's father and mother
公仆(僕) gōngpú (名) public servant
公顷 gōngqǐng (名) hectare (ha)
公然 gōngrán (副) openly; brazenly
公认(認) gōngrèn (形) generally recognized; universally acknowledged
公社 gōngshè (名) commune: 原始～ primitive commune. 人民公社 people's commune
公审(審) gōngshěn (名) public (or open) trial
公式 gōngshì (名) formula
公式化 gōngshìhuà I (名) formulism (in art and literature) II (形) stereotyped
公事 gōngshì (名) public affairs; official business: ～公办 business is business
公司 gōngsī (名) company; firm; corporation
公诉 gōngsù (名) public prosecution: ～人 public prosecutor
公文 gōngwén (名) official document
公务(務) gōngwù (名) official duty
公物 gōngwù (名) public property
公休 gōngxiū (名) official holiday
公演 gōngyǎn (动) perform in public
公益 gōngyì (名) public welfare
公用 gōngyòng (形) for public use; communal: ～电话 public telephone
公有 gōngyǒu (形) publicly-owned: ～制 public ownership
公寓 gōngyù (名) apartment house; block of flats
公元 gōngyuán (名) A.D.; the Christian era: ～前 B.C.
公园(園) gōngyuán (名) park
公约 gōngyuē (名) 1 pact; convention: 北大西洋～ the North Atlantic Treaty 2 joint pledge
公允 gōngyǔn (形) fair and proper: 持论～ be just and fair in passing judgement
公债 gōngzhài (名) government bonds; treasury bonds
公章 gōngzhāng (名) official seal
公正 gōngzhèng (形) just; fair; impartial
公证(證) gōngzhèng (名) notarization: ～人 notary public; notary
公职(職) gōngzhí (名) public employment
公众(衆) gōngzhòng (名) the public
公主 gōngzhǔ (名) princess
公子 gōngzǐ (名) son of a feudal prince or high official

弓 gōng I (名) bow: ～箭 bow and arrow. ～弦 bowstring II (动) bend; arch: ～着腿坐着 sit with one's legs crossed
弓子 gōngzi (名) 1 bow (of a stringed instrument) 2 anything bow-shaped

躬 gōng I (动) bow II (副) <书> personally: ～逢其盛 be present on the grand occasion

宫 gōng (名) palace: 皇～ imperial palace. 少年～ children's palace. 工人文化～ the Workers' Cultural Palace
宫殿 gōngdiàn (名) palace
宫廷 gōngtíng (名) 1 palace 2

royal or imperial court

巩(鞏) gǒng (动) consolidate

巩固 gǒnggù I (动) [often used in figurative sense] consolidate; strengthen; solidify II (形) firm; solid; stable

汞 gǒng (名) mercury (Hg)

拱 gǒng I (动) 1 join hands: ～手 make an obeisance by joining hands with one's forearms slightly raised 2 hunch; arch: 猫～了～腰. The cat arched its back. 3 push without using one's shoulder 4 (of pigs, etc.) dig earth with the snout 5 sprout up through the earth II (名) arch

拱门(門) gǒngmén (名) arched door; arch

拱桥(橋) gǒngqiáo (名) arch bridge

贡 gòng (动) tribute: 进～ pay tribute (to an imperial court)

贡品 gòngpǐn (名) articles of tribute

贡献(獻) gòngxiàn I (动) contribute; dedicate; devote II (名) contribution

共 gòng I (动) share: 同甘苦, ～患难 share weal and woe II (形) common; general: ～性 common characteristic III (副) 1 together: 和平～处 peaceful coexistence 2 in all; altogether: 一～四十人 altogether forty people

共产(産)党(黨) gòngchǎndǎng (名) the Communist Party

共产(產)主义(義) gòngchǎnzhǔyì (名) communism

共处(處) gòngchǔ (动、名) coexist; coexistence: 和平～ peaceful coexistence

共存 gòngcún (动) coexist

共和 gònghé (名) republic: ～国 republic

共计 gòngjì (动) amount to; add up to; total

共鸣 gòngmíng (名) 1 resonance 2 sympathetic response: 引起～ strike a responsive chord

共青团(團) gòngqīngtuán (名) (short for 共产主义青年团) the Communist Youth League

共事 gòngshì (动) work together

共同 gòngtóng I (形) common: ～关心的问题 matter of common concern II (副) together; jointly: ～努力 make joint efforts. ～点 common ground. ～市场 the Common Market

共同体(體) gòngtóngtǐ (名) community: 欧洲经济～ the European Economic Community

供 gòng I (动) 1 lay (offerings) 2 confess; own up: 口～ oral confession

see also gōng

供词 gòngcí (名) confession; deposition

供奉 gòngfèng (动) enshrine and worship

供认(認) gòngrèn (动) confess: ～不讳 candidly confess

供职(職) gòngzhí (动) hold office

篝 gōu

篝火 gōuhuǒ (名) bonfire; campfire

勾 gōu (动) 1 tick: 把你想去的地方～出来. Tick (off) the places you are interested in. 2 cancel; cross out, strike out [usu. followed by 掉, 销, 去, etc.]: 把他的名字～掉. Cross out his name. 把旧帐一笔～销. Write off all the debts at one stroke. 3 draw; delineate: ～出轮廓 draw an outline of sth. 4 evoke, call to mind: 这游戏～起了我对童年的回忆. This game reminds me of my childhood.

see also gòu

勾搭 gōuda (动) 1 engage jointly in wrong-doing: 他跟贼～上了. He ganged up with some thieves. 2 seduce

勾画(畫) gōuhuà (动) sketch out

勾结 gōujié (动) collude with; conspire with

勾通 gōutōng (动) work hand in glove with

勾销 gōuxiāo (动) liquidate; strike out: write off at one stroke

勾引 gōuyǐn (动) tempt; seduce; lure

沟(溝) gōu (名) 1 ditch; trench; channel 2 groove; rut; furrow

沟壑 gōuhè (名) gully; ravine

沟渠 gōuqú (名) irrigation canals

沟通 gōutōng (动) link up; connect

钩 gōu I (名) hook: 钓鱼～ fishhook. 挂衣～ clothes-hook II (动) 1 tick (as a check mark) 2 catch hold of with a hook: 她的裙边给钉子～住了. The edge of her skirt caught on a nail. 3 crochet: ～织品 cro-

chet. ～花边 crochet lace. ～针 crochet hook
勾心斗(鬥)角 gōuxīn-dòujiǎo I(名) (political) in fighting II (动) intrigue against each other
苟 gǒu (形) careless; negligent: 一丝不～ be scrupulous about every detail
苟安 gǒu'ān (动) seek transient peace
苟活 gǒuhuó (动) survive in humiliation
苟且 gǒuqiě (动) drift along; muddle along: ～偷安 seek transient peace by hook or by crook
苟全 gǒuquán (动) preserve one's humble existence at all costs
苟同 gǒutóng (动) [used in negative sentences] readily agree: 未敢～ beg to differ
苟延残喘 gǒuyán-cánchuǎn be on one's last leg; be at one's last gasp
狗 gǒu (名) 1 dog 2 damned; cursed
狗胆(膽)包天 gǒudǎn bāo tiān (名) monstrously audacious
狗急跳墙 gǒu jí tiào qiáng a cornered beast will bite indiscriminately or do something desperate; when a person is driven into a corner, he is capable of anything
狗屁 gǒupì (名) bullshit; nonsense: ～不通 unreadable rubbish
狗腿子 gǒutuǐzi (名)〈口〉lackey; henchman
狗尾续(續)貂 gǒuwěi xù diāo a wretched sequel to a fine work
狗血喷头(頭) gǒuxuè pēn tóu: 骂得～ let loose a stream of savage invective against sb.
狗仗人势(勢) gǒu zhàng rén shì be a bully who has the backing of a powerful person
媾 gòu (动)〈书〉1 wed: 婚～ marriage 2 reach agreement: ～和 make peace 3 coition: 交～ copulate
媾和 gòuhé (动) make peace: 单独～ make peace without consulting one's allies; make a separate peace
诟 gòu I (名)〈书〉shame; humiliation II (动) revile; talk abusively
诟病 gòubìng (动)〈书〉denounce; castigate: 为世～ become an object of universal condemnation
诟骂 gòumà (动) curse; abuse
垢 gòu I (名) 1 dirt; filth: 油～ grease; stain. 2〈书〉disgrace; humiliation: 含～忍辱 endure contempt and insults, II (形) dirty; filthy
够 gòu I(形) enough; sufficient; adequate: 她昨晚没睡～. She didn't have enough sleep last night. 这些钱～交学费了吗? Is this money enough for the tuition fee? II (动) reach; be up to (a certain standard, etc.) III (副) rather; really; quite: 这房子可真～大的. This house is really big. 他今天～累的了. He is rather tired today.
够呛(嗆) gòuqiàng (形) hard to bear; terrible: 忙得～ be terribly busy. 疼得～ unbearably painful. 这个人真～! This man is just impossible!
够格 gòugé (动) be qualified; be up to standard
够味儿 gòuwèir〈口〉just the right flavour; quite satisfactory
勾 gòu
see also gōu
勾当(當) gòudang (名) (dirty) deal
构(構) gòu (动) form; compose; construct: ～词 form a word. 虚～ fabrication
构成 gòuchéng (动) form; constitute; make up: ～威胁 pose (or constitute) a threat. 这台机器是由三个主要部分～的. This machine is made up of three major parts.
构件 gòujiàn (名) component part
构思 gòusī (动) (of writers or artists) work out the plot of a story or the composition of a painting
构造 gòuzào (名) structure: 人体～ the structure of the human body
购(購) gòu (动) buy; purchase
购买(買) gòumǎi (动) purchase; buy: ～力 purchasing power
购销 gòu-xiāo (名) purchase and sale
购置 gòuzhì (动) purchase
沽 gū
沽名钓誉(譽) gūmíng-diàoyù angle for fame and compliments; crave popular acclaim
辜 gū (名) guilt; crime: 无～ not guilty; innocent. 死有余～. Death could not atone for all his crimes.
辜负 gūfù (动) fail to live up

to; disappoint; let down; be unworthy of

轱 gū

轱辘 gūlu (名) wheel

咕 gū 〈象〉 (of hens, etc.) cluck

咕咚 gūdōng 〈象〉 splash; plump: ~一声掉进水里 fall into the water with a splash

咕嘟 gūdu 〈象〉 gurgle

咕噜 gūlū 〈象〉 1 rumble; gurgle; roll 2 murmur; whisper

咕哝(噥) gūnong (动) mutter; grumble: 他在~些什么? What is he muttering about?

估 gū (动) estimate; appraise; reckon: 低~ underestimate

估计 gūjì (动) estimate; appraise; reckon: ~形势 make an appraisal of the situation. 我们必须~到这种可能性. We must take this possibility into consideration. 我~他会接受这项工作. I reckon he will accept this job.

估价(價) gūjià I (动) evaluate; appraise II (名) estimated price

估量 gūliàng (动) appraise; assess: 不可~的损失 an incalculable loss

姑 gū I (名) 1 aunt (father's sister) 2 sister-in-law (husband's sister) 3 nun: 尼~ Buddhist nun. 道~ Taoist nun II (副) tentatively; for the time being

姑娘 gūniang (名) girl

姑且 gūqiě 〈副〉 tentatively; for the time being: 此事~不谈. We will leave the matter aside for the time being.

姑嫂 gū-sǎo (名) sisters-in-law

姑妄听(聽)之 gū wàng tīng zhī you must take it with a pinch of salt

姑妄言之 gū wàng yán zhī these are random remarks

姑息 gūxī (动) appease; endulge: ~养奸 to condone evil is to foster its growth

菇 gū (名) mushroom

箍 gū I (名) hoop; band II (动) bind round; hoop

呱 gū

呱呱 gūgū (名)〈书〉 the cry of a baby

孤 gū (形) lonely; isolated; solitary: ~岛 an isolated island

孤傲 gū'ào (形) aloof and arrogant

孤单(單) gūdān (形) 1 alone: ~一人 all alone; a lone soul 2 lonely; friendless

孤独(獨) gūdú (形) lonely; solitary: 过着~的生活 live in solitude

孤儿(兒) gū'ér (名) orphan

孤芳自赏 gūfāng zì shǎng indulge in self-admiration; be narcissistic

孤寂 gūjì (形) lonely

孤家寡人 gūjiā-guǎrén (名) a person alienated from the masses

孤苦伶仃 gūkǔ-língdīng (形) lonely and helpless

孤立 gūlì I (形) 1 isolated: 处于~地位 find oneself in an isolated position II (动) isolate: ~敌人 isolate the enemy

孤零零 gūlínglíng (形) all alone; lone

孤陋寡闻 gūlòu-guǎwén (形) superficial and ill-informed

孤僻 gūpì (形) unsociable and eccentric

孤掌难(難)鸣 gūzhǎng nán míng it's difficult to succeed without support

孤注一掷(擲) gūzhù yī zhì risk everything on one attempt; put all one's eggs in one basket

骨 gú (名) bone

see also gǔ

骨头(頭) gútou 〈名〉 bone: 懒~ lazybones. 软~ a spineless creature; be chicken-hearted. ~架子 skeleton

鼓 gǔ I (名) drum: 打~ beat a drum. ~点 drumbeats II (动) 1 rouse; agitate: ~起勇气 pluck up one's courage 2 blow with bellows, etc.: ~风 work a bellows

鼓吹 gǔchuī (动) advocate; preach; play up

鼓动(動) gǔdòng (动) agitate; arouse; instigate

鼓励(勵) gǔlì (动) encourage; urge

鼓舞 gǔwǔ (动) inspire; hearten: 形势很~人心. The situation is most inspiring. ~士气 boost the morale of the soldiers

鼓噪 gǔzào (动) make an uproar; clamour

鼓掌 gǔzhǎng (动) clap one's hands; applaud: ~通过 approve by acclamation

古 gǔ (名) ancient: ~时候 in ancient times. ~画 ancient

painting. ～籍 antiquarian books
古板 gǔbǎn (形) conservative and obdurate
古代 gǔdài (名) ancient times; antiquity: ～文化 ancient civilization
古典 gǔdiǎn (名) classical
古董 gǔdǒng (名) antique: ～商 antiquarian
古怪 gǔguài (形) odd; eccentric: 脾气～ eccentric character. 样子～ queer-looking
古话 gǔhuà (名) old saying
古迹 gǔjì (名) historic site; place of historic interest
古籍 gǔjí (名) ancient books: ～商人 an antiquarian bookseller
古老 gǔlǎo (形) ancient; age-old
古人 gǔrén (名) the ancients; our forefathers
古色古香 gǔsè-gǔxiāng (形) antique; quaint
古玩 gǔwán (名) antiques; curios: ～铺 a curiosity shop
古往今来(來) gǔwǎng-jīnlái from ancient times to the present age; from time immemorial
古文 gǔwén (名) 1 classical Chinese 2 ancient Chinese prose
古物 gǔwù (名) historical relics
古稀 gǔxī (名) seventy years of age: 年近～ approaching seventy
古雅 gǔyǎ (形) quaint

牯 gǔ (名) bull: ～牛 bull

贾 gǔ I (名) merchant II (动) 1 go into business 2 〈书〉court: ～祸 court disaster

蛊(蠱) gǔ (名) legendary venomous insect: ～惑人心 excite popular feelings; resort to demagogy

骨 gǔ (名) 1 bone 2 character; spirit: 傲～ lofty and unyielding character
see also gú
骨干(幹) gǔgàn (名) backbone; mainstay
骨骼 gǔgé (名) skeleton
骨灰 gǔhuī (名) ashes (of a dead body): ～盒 cinerary casket
骨架 gǔjià (名) skeleton; framework: 小说的～ the framework of the novel
骨牌 gǔpái (名) dominoes
骨气(氣) gǔqì (名) moral integrity
骨肉 gǔròu (名) flesh and blood; kindred: 亲生～ one's own flesh and blood. ～兄弟 blood brothers
骨髓 gǔsuǐ (名) marrow
骨子里 gǔzilǐ 〈口〉 in one's bones; in one's heart

谷 gǔ (名) 1 valley; gorge: 深～ a deep valley 2 (穀) cereal; grain 3 millet
谷仓(倉) gǔcāng (名) granary; barn
谷草 gǔcǎo (名) straw
谷物 gǔwù (名) cereal; grain
谷子 gǔzi (名) 1 millet 2 unhusked rice

鹄 gǔ (名)〈书〉target (in archery): 中～ hit the target
see also hú
鹄的 gǔdì (名) 1 target 2 aim

股 gǔ I (名) 1 thigh 2 (of an organization) section II (量) 1 [of strand-like things]: 一～泉水 stream of spring water. 三～毛线 three-ply wool 2 [for smell, air, energy, etc.]: 一～香味儿 a whiff of delicious smell. 一～烟 a puff of smoke. 一～劲儿 a burst of energy 3 group: 一～敌人 a group of enemy soldiers
股本 gǔběn (名) capital stock
股东(東) gǔdōng (名) shareholder; stockholder
股份 gǔfèn (名) share; stock
股金 gǔjīn (名) money paid for shares (in a partnership or cooperative)
股票 gǔpiào (名) share; stock: ～交易所 stock exchange. ～经纪人 stockbroker; stockjobber
股息 gǔxī (名) dividend

汩 gǔ
汩汩 gǔgǔ 〈象〉 gurgle: ～流水 gurgling water

雇(僱) gù (动) hire; employ
雇工 gùgōng (名) hired labourer
雇农(農) gùnóng (名) hired farmhand
雇佣(傭) gùyōng (动) employ; hire: ～军 mercenary army. ～劳动 wage labour
雇员 gùyuán (名) employee
雇主 gùzhǔ (名) employer

顾(顧) gù (动) 1 turn round and look at: 环～四周 look around 2 attend to: 只～自己 think only in terms of one's own interest. 兼～ give consideration to both sides. 不～个人安危 with no thought for personal safety. ～全大局 take the whole situation into consideration. 这么多事你～得过来吗？ Can you manage so many things by yourself?

顾此失彼 gùcǐ-shībǐ cannot attend to one thing without losing sight of the other

顾及 gùjí (动) take into account; give consideration to

顾忌 gùjì (名) scruple; misgivings: 毫无～ be unscrupulous; have no scruples

顾客 gùkè (名) customer; client

顾虑(慮) gùlǜ (名) worry; misgivings; apprehension: ～重重 be full of misgivings

顾名思义(義) gù míng sī yì as the term or title suggests

顾盼 gùpàn (动) look around

顾全 gùquán (动) show consideration for: ～大局 take the overall interests into account

顾问 gùwèn (名) adviser; consultant

故 gù I (名) 1 reason; cause: 无～缺席 be absent without reason. 不知何～ not know why 2 incident: 事～ accident 3 friend; acquaintance: 非亲非～ neither relative nor friend II (副) on purpose: ～弄玄虚 deliberately complicate a simple issue; purposely make a mystery of simple things. ～作惊讶 put on a show of surprise. 明知～犯 wilfully violate (a law or rule) III (形) old; former: 依然如～ the same as before IV (动) die: 病～ die of illness V (连) therefore

故步自封 gù bù zì fēng be contented with the existing state of affairs and refuse to forge ahead

故都 gùdū (名) ancient capital

故宫 gùgōng (名) the Imperial Palace: ～博物院 the Palace Museum

故技 gùjì (名) stock trick: ～重演 play the same old trick

故居 gùjū (名) former residence

故人 gùrén (名) old friend

故事 gùshi (名) 1 story; tale: 民间～ folk tale 2 plot: ～情节 the plot of a story

故土 gùtǔ (名) native land

故乡(鄉) gùxiāng (名) native place; hometown

故意 gùyì (副) purposely; intentionally; deliberately: 他～这么做的. He did it on purpose. 我不是～要刺伤你. I didn't mean to hurt your feelings. ～刁难 deliberately make things difficult for sb.

故障 gùzhàng (名) trouble; something wrong (with a machine): 机器出了～. The machine has broken down.

固 gù I (形) firm; solid: 加～ strengthen; reinforce II (副) firmly; resolutely: ～辞 resolutely refuse; firmly decline

固定 gùdìng I (动) fix; regularize: 把业余学习～下来 set a regular time for spare-time study II (形) fixed; regular: 没有～的想法 have no fixed idea. ～职业 a permanent job. ～资产 fixed assets

固然 gùrán (副) [used to acknowledge a fact in order to make a contrary statement which is the speaker's real purpose] no doubt; it is true: 她的嗓子～不错，但是她不会唱. True, she has a good voice but she doesn't know how to sing.

固守 gùshǒu (动) 1 defend tenaciously 2 stick to

固体(體) gùtǐ (名) solid: ～燃料 solid fuel

固有 gùyǒu (形) intrinsic; inherent; innate: ～属性 intrinsic properties

固执(執) gùzhí (形) stubborn; obstinate: ～已见 stick stubbornly to one's own opinion

痼 gù

痼疾 gùjí (名) chronic illness

梏 gù (名) wooden handcuffs: 桎～ fetters; shackles

瓜 guā (名) melon, gourd: 西～ watermelon. 南～ pumpkins. 黄～ cucumber

瓜分 guāfēn (动) carve up: ～别国领土 carve up the territory of another country

瓜葛 guāgě (名) connection; involvement

瓜熟蒂落 guāshú-dìluò things will be easily settled once conditions are ripe

瓜子 guāzǐ (名) melon seeds

呱 guā

呱呱 guāguā 〈象〉 (of ducks) quack; (of frogs) croak; (of crows) caw

呱呱叫 guāguājiào (形)〈口〉 very good indeed; first-rate

刮 guā (动) 1 scrape: ～鱼鳞 scale a fish. ～胡子 shave

2 blow ～大风了. It's blowing hard.

刮脸(臉) guāliǎn (动) shave (the face): ～刀 razor

刮目相看 guāmù xiāng-kàn (动) look at sb. with new eyes; treat sb. with increased respect

寡 guǎ (形) 1 few; scant: 沉默～言 reticent; uncommunicative. ～不敌众 be hopelessly outnumbered 2 tasteless: 索然～味 dull and monotonous. 清汤～水 watery and insipid 3 widowed: 守～ live in widowhood. ～妇 widow

寡廉鲜耻 guǎlián-xiǎnchǐ (形) lost to shame; shameless

寡人 guǎrén (名) I the sovereign; we [used by a royal person in proclamations instead of I]

寡头(頭) guǎtóu (名) oligarch: 金融～ financial oligarchy

剐(剮) guǎ (动) cut to pieces: 千刀万～ be hacked to pieces

褂 guà (名) gown: 大～儿 long gown. ～子 short gown

挂(掛) guà I (动) 1 hang; put up; suspend: 墙上～着一幅画. A picture is hanging on the wall. 一轮明月当空～着. A bright moon hung in the sky. 2 get caught: 钉子把裙子～住了. Her skirt got caught on a nail. 3 call; ring up: 我要给他～电话. I'll phone him up. 4 hang up (the receiver): 他把电话～上了. He's hung up. 5 be concerned about: 别把这事～在心上. Don't worry about it. 6 register (at a hospital): ～外科 register for surgery. II (量) [for things in strings]: 一～拖车 a trailer. 几～鞭炮 several strings of firecrackers

挂彩 guàcǎi (动) 1 be wounded in battle 2 decorate for festive occasions

挂齿(齒) guàchǐ (动) mention: 这点小事,何足～. Such a trifling matter is not worth mentioning.

挂钩 guàgōu (动) 1 couple (two railway coaches) 2 get in touch with; establish contact with

挂号(號) guàhào (动) 1 register (at a hospital) 2 send by registered mail: ～信 registered letter

挂面(麵) guàmiàn (名) fine dried noodles; vermicelli

挂名 guàmíng (形) nominal; only in name

挂念 guàniàn (动) worry about; miss: 十分～ miss sb. very much

挂失 guàshī (动) report the loss of sth.

挂帅(帥) guàshuài (动) take command

挂毯 guàtǎn (名) tapestry

挂羊头(頭),卖(賣)狗肉 guà yángtóu, mài gǒuròu engage in dishonest business by putting up a façade of honesty

挂一漏万 guà yī lòu wàn the list is by no means exhaustive

卦 guà (名) divinatory symbols: 占～ divination

乖 guāi I (形) 1 (of a child) well-behaved; obedient: 真是个～孩子. There's a dear. 2 clever

乖谬 guāimiù (形) absurd; aberrant

乖僻 guāipì (形) eccentric; odd

乖巧 guāiqiǎo (形) 1 clever 2 cute; lovely

拐 guǎi (动) 1 turn: 往左～ turn to the left. ～进一条胡同 turn into an alley 2 limp: 一～一～地走 limp along; hobble along 3 abduct; kidnap

拐棍 guǎigùn (名) walking stick; cane

拐角 guǎijiǎo (名) (at a street) corner, turning

拐骗 guǎipiàn (动) 1 abduct 2 swindle: ～钱财 swindle money (out of sb.)

拐弯(彎) guǎiwān (动) 1 turn a corner; turn 2 turn round; pursue a new course

拐弯(彎)抹角 guǎiwān-mòjiǎo talk in a roundabout way; beat about the bush

拐杖 guǎizhàng (名) 1 walking stick 2 cane

怪 guài I (形) strange; odd; queer; unusual; peculiar II (动) blame: 这不能～他,只～我没交代清楚. This is not his fault. I am to blame for not having made the whole thing clear to him. III (名) monster; demon; evil being: 鬼～ demons; ghosts IV (副) quite; rather: 这箱子～沉的. The suitcase is rather heavy.

怪不得 guàibude no wonder; so that's why: 原来她父母都是钢琴家,～她弹得这么好! So her parents are both pianists! No wonder she plays the piano so well.

怪诞 guàidàn (形) strange; weird
怪话 guàihuà (名) cynical remark; complaint: 说～ make cynical remarks
怪模怪样 (樣) guàimú-guàiyàng (形) odd; bizarre; grotesque
怪僻 guàipì (形) (of a person or his behaviour) eccentric
怪物 guàiwù (名) 1 monster 2 an eccentric person
怪异(異) guàiyì (形) strange; unusual
怪罪 guàizuì (动) blame (sb.)

官 guān (名) 1 government official; officer: 外交～ diplomat. ～兵 officers and men 2 official: ～办 run by the government 3 organ: 感～ sense organ
官场(場) guānchǎng (名) officialdom
官邸 guāndǐ (名) official residence
官方 guānfāng (形) official: ～消息 official sources
官话 guānhuà (名) 1 mandarin 2 bureaucratic jargon
官吏 guānlì (名) government officials (in feudal society)
官僚 guānliáo (名) bureaucrat; government official
官僚主义(義) guānliáozhǔyì (名) bureaucracy: ～作风 bureaucratic style of work; bureaucratic way of doing things
官能 guānnéng (名) (organic) function; sense: 视、听、嗅、味、触这五种～ the five senses of sight, hearing, smell, taste and touch
官腔 guānqiāng (名) official jargon: 打～ speak in bureaucratic jargon
官司 guānsi (名) lawsuit: 打～ go to law against sb.
官衔 guānxián (名) official title
官员 guānyuán (名) official

棺 guān (名) coffin: ～材 coffin

倌 guān (名) 1 herdsman: 羊～儿 shepherd. 马～儿 groom 2 a hired hand in certain service trades: 堂～儿 waiter

关(關) guān I (动) 1 shut; close: ～窗户 shut the window 2 turn off: ～电灯 turn off the light 3 lock up: ～进监狱 put in prison 4 close down: 昨天又有两家工厂～了. Two more factories closed down yesterday. 5 concern; involve: 这事与你无～. It's none of your business. 事～大局 The matter is of concern to the overall situation. II (名) 1 pass; check 2 barrier; critical juncture: 技术难～ a technical difficulty 3 customs house
关闭 guānbì (动) 1 close; shut 2 (of a shop or factory) close down; shut down
关怀(懷) guānhuái (动) pay serious attention to; be concerned about
关键 guānjiàn (名) key; crux: 问题的～ the crux of the matter. ～时刻 at the critical moment
关节(節) guānjié (名) joint: ～炎 arthritis
关口 guānkǒu (名) 1 strategic pass 2 juncture
关联(聯) guānlián (动) be related; be connected: 国家的外交政策和经济政策是相互～的. The foreign and economic policies of a country are interrelated.
关门(門) guānmén (动) 1 close; shut: 随手～ shut the door after you. 商店几点～? When does the shop close? 2 refuse to accept or tolerate different views
关切 guānqiè (动) be deeply concerned
关税 guānshuì (名) customs duty; tariff: 保护～ protective tariff. 特惠～ preferential tariff. ～壁垒 tariff barrier. ～豁免 exemption from customs duties
关头(頭) guāntóu (名) juncture; moment: 紧要～ a critical moment or juncture
关系 guānxì I (名) 1 relation; relationship: 外交～ diplomatic relations. 夫妻～ relations between husband and wife. 他俩的～不好. They are not on good terms with each other. or They don't get along. 2 ties; connections: 社会～ one's social connections 3 bearing: 没～. It doesn't matter. ～不大. It doesn't make much difference. 4 [indicating cause or condition]: 由于时间～, 就谈到这里吧. Since time is limited, I'll leave it at that. II (动) concern; affect; involve: 这是个原则问题, ～到我们所有的人. This is matter of principle which concerns all of us.
关心 guānxīn (动) be concerned about; concern oneself with; pay great attention to: 我们应当～青年一代的思想教育. We

should pay great attention to the moral education of the younger generation.
关押 guānyā (动) put in prison; take into custody
关于 (於) guānyú (介) about; on; with regard to; concerning: 一本～中国的书 a book about China. ～你的要求，我们准备在会上讨论一下。As for your request, we have decided to discuss it at the meeting.
关照 guānzhào (动) look after; keep an eye on: 我走后请你多～我的孩子。While I'm away, will you please keep an eye on my children? 你～他们一声，我一会儿就回来。Please bring them the message that I'll be back soon.
关注 guānzhù (动) attention; interest: 承蒙～，深以为感。I am very grateful for the trouble you have taken on my behalf.

鳏 guān (形) wifeless; widowered
鳏夫 guānfū (名) bachelor or widower

冠 guān (名) hat; crest; crown: 衣～整齐 be neatly dressed. 树～ the crown of a tree. 鸡～ cock's comb; crest
see also guàn
冠冕堂皇 guānmiǎn tánghuáng (形) high-sounding
冠心病 guānxīnbìng (名) coronary heart disease

观(觀) guān I (动) look at; watch; observe II (名) 1 sight; view: 奇～ wonderful sight; wonder. 改～ change in appearance 2 conception of the nature of things; way of looking at things: 世界～ world outlook
观测 guāncè (动) observe and survey: ～气象 make weather observations
观察 guānchá (动) observe; examine: ～地形 survey the terrain; topographical survey. ～家(员) observer. ～所 observation post
观点(點) guāndiǎn (名) viewpoint; standpoint
观感 guāngǎn (名) impressions of a visit
观光 guānguāng (动) be on a sightseeing trip
观看 guānkàn (动) watch; view: ～动静 watch what is happening. ～一场比赛 watch a game
观摩 guānmó (动) view and learn from each other's work; watch and emulate
观念 guānniàn (名) idea; concept
观赏 guānshǎng (动) watch and enjoy: 我～了演员的表演。I watched and enjoyed the performance of the actors
观望 guānwàng (动) 1 look around 2 wait and see
观众(衆) guānzhòng (名) audience; spectator; viewer

管 guǎn I (名) tube; pipe: 血～ blood vessel. 电子～ electron tube. 水～ water pipe. 单簧～ clarinet II (量) [used of tube-shaped things]: 一～牙膏 a tube of toothpaste III (动) 1 be in charge of; run; be responsible for: ～家 run the house. 他是～实验室的。He is in charge of the laboratory. 2 control; take care of: 这些孩子得～～了。These children must be taken in hand. 这件事你来～。Will you take care of this matter? 3 mind; attend to; bother about: 别～他 leave him alone. 我才不～呢！ I can't be bothered. 别～人家怎么说。Never mind what other people say. IV (介) [in conjunction with 叫]: 他们～我叫小胖子。They call me "little fatty".
管保 guǎnbǎo (动) guarantee; assure: 这外套～很合适。I can assure you that this jacket will fit you perfectly.
管道 guǎndào (名) pipeline
管教 guǎnjiào (动) take sb. in hand; subject sb. to discipline
管理 guǎnlǐ (动) manage; administer; run: ～部门 administrative. 企业～ business management
管事 guǎnshì (动) 1 be in charge: 这里谁～？Who's in charge here? 2 effective; of use: 这药很～儿。This medicine is very effective. 问他不～。It's no use asking him.
管束 guǎnshù (动) restrain; control: 严加～ keep sb. under strict control
管辖 guǎnxiá (名) control over: 在～范围之内 come within the jurisdiction of. ～权 jurisdiction
管弦乐(樂) guǎnxiányuè (名) orchestral music: ～队 orchestra
管乐(樂)器 guǎnyuèqì (名) wind instrument
管制 guǎnzhì (名) 1 control: 军事～ military control. 灯火～

blackout 2 (of criminals) under surveillance

管子 guǎnzi (名) tube; pipe

馆(館) guǎn (名) house; hall; shop: 旅～ hotel. 宾～ guesthouse. 理发～ barbershop. 茶～ teahouse. 饭～ restaurant. 照相～ photo studio. 博物～ museum. 展览～ exhibition hall. 美术～ art gallery. 体育～ gymnasium. 图书～ library

馆子 guǎnzi (名) restaurant: 下～ eat at a restaurant; dine out

冠 guàn

see also guān

冠军 guànjūn (名) champion

灌 guàn (动) 1 irrigate: 引水～田 irrigate the fields 2 fill; pour: 暖瓶都～满了. The thermos flasks have all been filled. ～醉 get sb. drunk

灌唱片 guàn chàngpiàn (动) make a gramophone record

灌溉 guàngài (动) irrigate: ～面积 irrigated area. ～渠 irrigation canal

灌木 guànmù (名) bush; shrub

灌输 guànshū (动) instil into; imbue with

灌注 guànzhù (动) pour into; fill

罐 guàn (名) jar; canister; tin: 一～茶叶 a canister of tea. 一～纸烟 a tin of cigarettes. 水～ water pitcher

罐头(頭) guàntóu (名) tin; can: ～食品 tinned (or canned) food

鹳 guàn (名) stork

盥 guàn (动)〈书〉 wash

盥洗 guànxǐ (动) wash one's hands and face: ～室 washroom. ～用具 toilet articles

贯 guàn (动) 1 pass through: 学～古今 combine classical training with modern scholarship 2 follow in a continuous line: 鱼～而入 enter one after another

贯彻(徹) guànchè (动) carry through (or out); implement: ～一项决议 put a decision into effect

贯穿 guànchuān (动) run through

贯通 guàntōng (动) 1 have a perfect understanding of: 豁然～ feel suddenly enlightened 2 link up: 这条铁路已全线～. The whole railway line has been joined up.

贯注 guànzhù (动) concentrate on: 全神～ be wholly absorbed

惯 guàn (动) 1 be used to; be in the habit of: 我过不～这里的生活. I'm not used to the life here. 2 spoil; indulge: 别把孩子～坏了. Don't spoil the child.

惯匪 guànfěi (名) repeat offender

惯技 guànjì (名) old trick

惯例 guànlì (名) usual practice; convention: 国际～ international practice

惯性 guànxìng (名) inertia

光 guāng I (名) 1 light; ray: 月～ moonlight. 太阳～ sunshine. 爱克斯～ X ray 2 brightness; lustre: 这只银盘闪闪发～. This silver plate has a fine lustre. 两眼无～ dull eyed 3 glory; honour: 为祖国争～ win honour for one's country 4 scenery: 春～明媚 the savoury scene of spring-time. 观～ on a sightseeing trip II (形) 1 smooth; glossy; polished 2 bare; naked: ～着脚 be barefoot 3 used up: 钱用～了. I've spent all my money. 4 solely; only; merely; alone: ～有好的意愿还不够. Good intention alone is not enough.

光彩 guāngcǎi (名) splendour; brilliance; radiance: ～夺目 dazzlingly brilliant

光复(復) guāngfù (动) recover (lost territory, etc.)

光顾(顧) guānggù (动) welcome to our shop

光怪陆(陸)离(離) guāngguài-lùlí (形) bizarre and gaudy

光棍 guānggùn (名) unmarried man; bachelor

光滑 guānghuá (形) smooth; glossy; sleek

光辉 guānghuī (名) radiance; brilliance; glory: 太阳的～ the brilliance of the sun

光洁(潔) guāngjié (形) polished and spotless

光景 guāngjǐng I (名) 1 circumstances 2 scene: 我童年时代的～在脑海里闪过. Scenes of my childhood flashed through my mind. II (副) about; around: 他父亲有60岁～. His father is about 60 years old.

光亮 guāngliàng (形) bright; shiny

光临(臨) guānglín (名)〈敬〉 gracious presence (of a guest, etc.): 敬请～. Your presence is cordially requested.

光溜溜 guāngliūliū (形) 1 smooth; slippery: ～的地板 well polished floor 2 bare; naked: 孩子们脱得～的在河里洗澡. The children are bathing naked in the river.

光芒 guāngmáng (名) rays of light; radiance

光明 guāngmíng I (名) light: 从黑暗走向～ go through darkness to the light II (形) 1 bright; promising: ～的前途 bright future 2 openhearted: ～磊落 open and aboveboard

光荣(榮) guāngróng (名) glory; honour; credit: ～称号 a title of honour. ～传统 a glorious tradition

光润 guāngrùn (形) (of skin) smooth

光头(頭) guāngtóu (名) bareheaded

光秃秃 guāngtūtū (形) bald; bare; barren

光线(綫) guāngxiàn (名) light; ray: ～不好 poor light

光耀 guāngyào (名) 1 brilliant light 2 glorious; honourable

光阴(陰) guāngyīn (名) time: ～似箭. Time flies.

光泽(澤) guāngzé (名) lustre; gloss; sheen

光照 guāngzhào (名) illumination

光宗耀祖 guāngzōng-yàozǔ bring honour to one's ancesters.

广(廣) guǎng I (形) broad; vast; extensive: 见多识～ have wide experience and extensive knowledge. 消息流传很广. The news has spread far and wide. II (动) broaden; spread

广播 guǎngbō (动) broadcast: ～电台 broadcasting station. 实况～ live broadcast. ～员 radio announcer

广博 guǎngbó (形) (of one's knowledge) extensive; wide

广场(場) guǎngchǎng (名) public square

广大 guǎngdà (形) 1 vast; wide; extensive: 幅员～ vast in territory 2 numerous: ～群众 the broad masses of the people

广度 guǎngdù (名) scope; range: ～和深度 scope and depth

广泛 guǎngfàn (形) extensive; wide-ranging; widespread: ～的兴趣 a wide range of interest. ～地征求意见 solicit opinions from all quarters

广告 guǎnggào (名) advertisement: 做～ advertise. ～画 poster. ～牌 bill-board

广阔 guǎngkuò (形) vast; wide; broad: ～的田野 a vast stretch of country. ～的前景 broad prospects

广袤 guǎngmào (名)〈书〉 length and breadth of land

广义(義) guǎngyì (名) broad sense: ～地说 in a broad sense; broadly speaking

犷(獷) guǎng (形) rustic; shaggy and uncouth: ～悍 tough and intrepid

逛 guàng (动) stroll; roam: ～商店 go windowshopping. ～大街 stroll around the streets

逛荡(蕩) guàngdang (动) loaf about

规 guī I (名) rule; regulation: 校～ school regulations II (动) 1 plan; map out: ～划 plan 2 admonish; advise: ～劝 admonish

规程 guīchéng (名) rules; regulations: 操作～ rules of operation

规定 guīdìng I (动) 1 stipulate: 宪法～男女平等 the Constitution stipulates that men and women are equal 2 fix; set: 在～的时间内 within the fixed time. ～的指标 a set quota II (名) rule; stipulation

规范(範) guīfàn (名) standard; norm: 合乎～ conform to the standard

规格 guīgé (名) specifications; standards: 统一的～ unified standards. 不合～ not be up to standard

规划(劃) guīhuà (名) plan; programme: 长远～ long-term planning. 全面～ comprehensive programme

规矩 guīju I (名) rule; established practice: 按老～办事 do things according to the old custom II (形) well-behaved; well-disciplined: ～点! Behave yourself

规律 guīlǜ (名) law; regular pattern: 客观～ objective law

规模 guīmó (名) scale; scope; dimensions: ～宏大 broad in scale

规劝(勸) guīquàn (动) admonish; advise

规则 guīzé I (名) rule; regulation: 交通～ traffic regulation II (形) regular

规章 guīzhāng (名) rule; regulation: ～制度 rules and regulations

闺 guī (名) boudoir

闺房 guīfáng (名) boudoir

闺女 guīnü (名) 1 girl; maiden 2 ‹口› daughter

硅 guī (名) silicon (Si)

鲑 guī (名) salmon

归(歸) guī I (动) 1 go back to; return: ～国华侨 returned overseas Chinese. ～期 date of return. 无家可～ be homeless 2 converge; come together: 条条大河～大海. All rivers lead to the sea. 这几本书应～为一类. These books ought to be put under one category. 3 turn over to; put under sb.'s care: ～国家所有 be turned over to the state. 这事应～你管. This matter comes within your jurisdiction. II (介) [used between reduplicated verbs] despite: 吵架～吵架, 可他俩还是很相爱. They love each other despite their frequent quarrels.

归案 guī'àn (动) bring to justice: 捉拿～ arrest and bring to justice

归并(併) guībìng (动) incorporate into; merge into

归根结蒂 guīgēn-jiédì (副) in the final analysis: ～, 人民的意志是不可抗拒的. In the final analysis the will of the people is irresistible.

归功 guīgōng (动) [usu. used with 于] give the credit to; attribute the success to: 我们的一切成就都～于正确的政策. We owe all our success to correct policy.

归还(還) guīhuán (动) give back; return: 你要按时把书～给图书馆. You must return this book to the library on time.

归结 guījié (动) sum up; put in a nutshell: 问题虽很复杂, ～起来不外三个方面. The questions, though very complicated, may be summed up as coming under three categories.

归咎 guījiù (动) lay the blame on; blame: 不能把一切错误都～于他. We can't put all the blame on him alone.

归拢(攏) guīlǒng (动) put together

归纳 guīnà (动) sum up; conclude: ～大意 sum up the main ideas. ～法 inductive method; induction

归侨(僑) guīqiáo (名) (short for 归国华侨) returned overseas Chinese

归属(屬) guīshǔ (动) belong to

归顺 guīshùn (动) pledge allegiance

归宿 guīsù (名) a place where a person really belongs; natural end: 人生的～the end of life's journey

归向 guīxiàng (动) turn towards: 人心～ the trend of the popular feelings

归心似箭 guīxīn sì jiàn be anxious to return

归于(於) guīyú (动) belong to; be attributed to: 光荣～英雄的人民. Glory goes to the heroic people. 经过磋商, 大家的意见已经～一致了. We reached the identity of views after consultation.

归罪 guīzuì (动) lay the blame on

瑰 guī (形) marvellous

瑰宝(寶) guībǎo (名) rarity; treasure

瑰丽(麗) guīlì (形) extremely beautiful; magnificent

龟(龜) guī (名) tortoise; turtle

龟缩 guīsuō (动) withdraw into passive defence; hole up

庋 guǐ (动)‹书› 1 shelf 2 keep; preserve: ～藏 store up; preserve

晷 guǐ (名) 1 ‹书› a shadow cast by the sun 2 ‹书› time: 余～ spare time 3 sundial

鬼 guǐ (名) 1 devil; ghost; spirit 2 [a term of abuse]: 懒～ lazy bones. 胆小～ coward. 酒～ drunkard 3 sinister plot; dirty trick: 心里有～ have something on one's conscience II (形) 1 stealthy; surreptitious: ～头～脑 stealthy; sneaky 2 damnable: ～地方 a lousy place 3 ‹口› clever; quick: 这孩子真～. What a clever child!

鬼把戏(戲) guǐbǎxì (名) dirty trick: 玩弄～ play a dirty trick

鬼怪 guǐguài (名) ghosts and monsters; forces of evil

鬼鬼祟祟 guǐguǐsuìsuì (形) sneaking; stealthy; furtive

鬼话 guǐhuà (名) damned lie

鬼魂 guǐhún (名) ghost; spirit; apparition

鬼混 guǐhùn (动) fool around

鬼脸(臉) guǐliǎn (名) wry face; grimace: 做～ make faces; make grimaces

鬼神 guǐshén(名) ghosts and supernatural beings

鬼胎 guǐtāi (名) ulterior motive; sinister design: 心怀～ harbour evil intentions

鬼蜮 guǐyù (名) demon: ～伎俩 evil tactics

轨 guǐ (名) 1 rail; track: 单(双)～ single (double) track. 出～ be derailed 2 order; regularity: 常～ normal practice. 走上正～ get onto the right path. 越～ overstep the bounds of propriety

轨道 guǐdào (名) 1 track 2 orbit: 卫星～ the orbit of a satellite 3 course: 生产已走上～. Production has come to normal.

诡 guǐ (形) deceitful; tricky

诡辩 guǐbiàn (名) sophistry; quibbling

诡称(稱) guǐchēng (动) falsely allege; pretend

诡计 guǐjì (名) trick; cunning scheme: ～多端 be very crafty; be full of tricks

诡谲 guǐjué (形)〈书〉fantastic

诡秘 guǐmì (形) mysterious; secretive: 行踪～ mysterious in one's movements

诡诈 guǐzhà (形) crafty; cunning; treacherous

桂 guì (名) 1 cassiabarktree 2 laurel 3 sweet osmanthus

桂冠 guìguàn (名) laurel

桂花 guìhuā (名) sweet-scented osmanthus

柜(櫃) guì (名) cupboard; cabinet: 书～ bookcase. 五斗～ chest of drawers

柜台(臺) guìtái (名) sales counter: 站～ serve behind the counter

贵 guì (形) 1 expensive; costly; dear: 这地方东西很～. Things are expensive here. 2 precious; valuable: 人～有自知之明. Self-knowledge is wisdom. 3 noble; honoured: ～客 guest of honour 4〈敬〉your: ～国 your country. ～姓? May I ask your name?

贵宾(賓) guìbīn (名) distinguished guest: ～室 VIP's room

贵重 guìzhòng (形) valuable; precious: ～物品 valuables

贵族 guìzú (名) noble; aristocrat; aristocracy

跪 guì (动) kneel

跪拜 guìbài (动) worship on bended knees

跪倒 guìdǎo (动) go down on one's knees

刽(劊) guì (动) cut off; chop of

刽子手 guìzishǒu (名) 1 executioner 2 slaughterer

滚 gǔn (动) 1 roll: 球～进洞里. The ball rolled into the hole. 眼泪顺着脸颊～下来. Tears were rolling down her cheeks. 2 [a term of abuse]: ～出去! Get out of here! ～开! get away! 3 boil: 水～了. The water is boiling.

滚动(動) gǔndòng (动) roll; trundle

滚瓜烂(爛)熟 gǔnguā lànshú (recite, etc.) fluently

滚滚 gǔngǔn (动) roll; surge: 大江～东去. The Great River surges eastward in billowing waves.

滚烫(燙) gǔntàng (形) boiling hot: scalding hot

滚圆 gǔnyuán (形) round as a ball

滚珠 gǔnzhū (名) ball: ～轴承 ball bearing

棍 gùn (名) 1 rod; stick 2 scoundrel: 恶～ ruffian rascal. 赌～ gambler

棍棒 gùnbàng (名) club; cudgel stick

棍子 gùnzi (名) rod; stick

郭 guō (名) the outer wall of a city

聒 guō (形) noisy: ～噪 noisy clamorous

锅(鍋) guō (名) pot; pan cooker: 炒菜～ frying pan

锅巴 guōbā (名) rice crust

锅炉(爐) guōlú (名) boiler

国(國) guó (名) country state; nation: 全～各地 all over the country. ～营 state-run. 收归～有 be nationalized. ～旗 national flag. ～画 traditional Chinese painting

国策 guócè (名) national policy

国产(產) guóchǎn (形) made in one's own country

国耻 guóchǐ (名) national humiliation

国都 guódū (名) national capital

国度 guódù (名) state; nation

国法 guófǎ (名) national law
国防 guófáng (名) national defence
国歌 guógē (名) national anthem
国徽 guóhuī (名) national emblem
国会(會) guóhuì (名) parliament; (美) Congress; (日) the Diet
国货 guóhuò (名) goods produced in one's own country
国籍 guójí (名) nationality: 双重～ dual nationality
国计民生 guójì-mínshēng (名) the national economy and the people's livelihood
国际(際) guójì (名) international: ～地位 international status. ～形势 the international (or world) situation. ～影响 international repercussions
国际(際)歌 Guójìgē (名) *The Internationale*
国际(際)主义(義) guójì zhǔyì (名) internationalism
国家 guójiā (名) country; state; nation
国教 guójiào (名) state religion
国界 guójiè (名) national boundaries
国境 guójìng (名) territory; border: ～线 boundary line
国君 guójūn (名) monarch
国库 guókù (名) national treasury: ～券 treasury bonds
国立 guólì (形) state-run: ～大学 state university
国民 guómín (形) national: ～收入 national income. ～生产总值 gross national product (GNP)
国难(難) guónàn (名) national calamity
国内 guónèi (形) internal; domestic: ～战争 civil war. ～市场 domestic (or home) market. ～贸易 domestic trade
国旗 guóqí (名) national flag
国情 guóqíng (名) national conditions: ～咨文(美) State of the Union Message
国庆(慶) guóqìng (名) National Day (celebrations)
国事 guóshì (名) state affairs: ～访问 state visit
国书(書) guóshū (名) (diplomatic) credentials
国体(體) guótǐ (名) 1 state system 2 national prestige
国土 guótǔ (名) national territory; land: 神圣的～ our sacred land
国外 guówài (形) external; overseas; abroad: ～市场 overseas (or foreign) market. 去～ go abroad
国王 guówáng (名) king
国务(務)院 guówùyuàn (名) 1 the State Council 2 (美) the State Department
国宴 guóyàn (名) state banquet
国营(營) guóyíng (形) state-operated; state-run: ～经济 state-owned economy. ～农场 state farm. ～企业 state enterprise
国有化 guóyǒuhuà (名) nationalization
国葬 guózàng (名) state funeral
国债 guózhài (名) national debt; the internal and external debts of a nation

果 guǒ I (名) 1 fruit: 开花结～ blossom and bear fruit. 水～ fruit. 干～ dried fruit 2 result; consequence: 自食其～ reap what one has sown. 恶～ a disastrous result II (形) resolute; determined III (副) really; as expected: ～不出所料 just as one expected
果断(斷) guǒduàn (形) resolute; decisive: 采取～措施 take decisive measures
果敢 guǒgǎn (形) courageous and resolute
果酱(醬) guǒjiàng (名) jam
果木 guǒmù (名) fruit tree
果品 guǒpǐn (名) fruit
果然 guǒrán (副) really; as expected; sure enough: ～是他. It was him as expected. 眼见为实, 这回我去西湖, 发现～不错. Seeing is believing. I visited the West Lake this time and found it really worth seeing.
果实(實) guǒshí (名) fruit; gains: ～累累 fruit growing in close clusters
果树(樹) guǒshù (名) fruit tree
果园(園) guǒyuán (名) orchard
果真 guǒzhēn (副) really; truly
果子 guǒzi (名) fruit: ～露 (or 汁) fruit syrup

裹 guǒ (动) wrap; bind: 用毛巾把孩子～起来 wrap the baby in a towel
裹足不前 guǒ zú bù qián hesitate to move forward; mark time

过(過) guò I (动) 1 pass; cross: ～河 cross a river. ～马路 cross the road. 从这条街上～ pass through this street 2 make sth. go through a process: 我们来把这些练习再～一遍. Let's go over these exercises once again. 先～秤 weigh (it) first. ～数 count (them) 3 spend (life, time): 假期～得怎么样? How did you spend your holiday? ～生日 celebrate one's birthday. ～日子 live one's life. 我妈妈跟我们～. My mother lives with us. 4 exceed; go beyond: 日产～万吨. The output per day is over 10,000 tons. 水深～膝. The water is more than knee-deep. II [used after a verb as a complement] 1 past; through; over: 跳～篱笆墙 jump over a fence. 闪电划～天空. Lightning flashed across the sky. 走～树林 walk past the wood 2 finished; over: 会已经开～了. The meeting is over. 钱已经付过了. The bill has been paid. 3 turn; over: 翻～这一页. turn this page over. 转～身 turn round 4 better than: 我说不～她. I can't outargue her. 谁也跑不～他. No one can run as fast as he can. III (副) after: ～了冬天再去吧. Let's go there after winter. 要～三天才知道结果. The result will come out three days later. 我～两天再来. I'll come again in a couple of days. IV (名) error; fault: 功～ merits and faults. 记～ record one's demerits. 改～ correct one's mistakes

过(過) guò (助) [used as a grammatical suffix to indicate aspect] 1 expressing the completion of action: 我吃～午饭就去. I'll go right after lunch. 房间已经打扫～. The room has been cleaned. 2 [indicating completion of action as an experience]: 我读～这本书. I have once read this book. 你去～伦敦吗? Have you been to London? 他以前当～兵. He was once a soldier. 她从来没生～病. She has never been ill. 天气从来没有这么冷～. It has never been so cold.

过磅 guòbàng (动) weigh (on the scales)

过不去 guòbuqù (动) 1 cannot get through: 路太窄, 车子～. The road is too narrow for the car to get through. 2 find fault with; be hard on: 别老是跟我～. Don't always try to find fault with me. 3 feel apologetic: 叫你等了这半天, 我心里真～. I'm awfully sorry to have kept you waiting so long. 面子上～ feel ashamed or disgraced

过场(塲) guòchǎng (名) 1 (of drama) interlude 2 (of Chinese operas) cross the stage 3 走～ do sth. as a mere formality

过程 guòchéng (名) process; course

过错 guòcuò (名) fault; mistake: 这不是你的～. That's not your fault.

过道 guòdào (名) corridor

过得去 guòdeqù (动) 1 be able to get through 2 so-so; passable; not too bad: 他的字写的还～. His handwriting is not too bad. 他们之间的关系～. They are on fairly good terms, as it is. 3 feel at ease: 我心里怎么能～呢? How can I feel at ease?

过度 guòdù (形) excessive; undue; over-: 饮酒～ drink immoderately. ～疲劳 be overworked; be dog-tired

过渡 guòdù (动) transition

过分 guòfèn (形) excessive; undue: going too far: ～的要求 excessive demands. ～着重 put undue emphasis on

过关(關) guòguān (动) pass a barrier; pass a test; reach a standard: 蒙混～ get by under false pretences. 这项新产品的质量还没～. The quality of this new product is not yet up to standard.

过河拆桥(橋) guòhé chāiqiáo pull down the bridge after crossing the river — cold-shoulder a person who has helped one tide over a difficulty be ungrateful

过后(後) guòhòu (副) afterwards later

过户 guòhù (名) transfer ownership

过活 guòhuó (动) make a living live

过火 guòhuǒ (形) carry thing too far; overdo: 你玩笑开得大～了. This is going beyond joke.

过激 guòjī (形) too drastic; extremist: ～言论 extremist opinions

过继(繼) guòjì (动) adopt young relative

过奖(獎) guòjiǎng (动) overpraise pay undeserved complimen

to: 您～了. You flatter me.

过节(節) guòjié (动) celebrate a festival

过境 guòjìng (动) pass through the territory of a country; be in transit: ～签证 transit visa

过来(來) guòlái [used after a verb and often preceded by "得" or "不" to show sufficiency of time; ability or quantity]: 图书馆里好书太多, 简直看不～. There are too many good books in the library for me to read. 你一个人忙得～吗? Can you manage by yourself?

过来(來) guòlai (动) come over; come up: 请～! Will you come over here please?

过来(來) guolai 1 [used after a verb to indicate moving towards the speaker]: 一个老头正朝我走～. An old man is coming towards me. 把那本书拿～. Bring me that book. 2 [used after a verb to indicate turning around towards the speaker]: 他转过身来对我说话. He turned round and spoke to me. 把那一页翻～. Turn that page back. 3 [used after a verb to indicate returning to the normal state]: 她从昏迷中醒～了. She came to. *or* She regained her consciousness.

过量 guòliàng (形) excessive; over: 饮酒～ drink beyond sensible limits

过虑(慮) guòlǜ (动) be over-anxious

过滤(濾) guòlǜ (动) filter; infiltrate: ～器 filter. ～嘴 filter tip (of a cigarette)

过敏 guòmǐn (名) allergy: 她对烟味～. She is allergic to smoke.

过目 guòmù (动) look over (for check or approval) 这是名单, 请您～. Here's the list for you to go over.

过年 guònián (动) celebrate (or spend) the New Year

过期 guòqī (动) expire; be overdue: ～作废 invalid after the specified date. 合同明年～. The contract expires next year. ～杂志 back number of a magazine. 你从图书馆借来的书, 早就～了. The books you borrowed from the library have long been overdue for return.

过谦 guòqiān (形) too modest: 你～了. You are being too modest.

过去 guòqù(形、名) past; former; previous: 请不要再提～了. Let us forget about the past. ～的事就让它～吧. Let bygones be bygones. 这个地方～很穷. This place was poverty-stricken in the past. 她比～活泼多了. She is much more lively than she used to be.

过去 guòqù (动) go over; pass by: 他刚从这儿～. He has just passed by. 我～看看. I'll go over and see how it is.

过去 guòqu 1 [used after a verb to indicate moving away from the speaker]: 把球给他扔～. Toss him the ball. 她向海滩跑～. She ran towards the beach. 2 [used after a verb to indicate turning the side away from the speaker]: 她转过身去, 望着大海. She turned back and looked at the sea. 把这一页翻～. Turn this page over. 3 [used after a verb to indicate loss of consciousness]: 她晕～了. She has fainted. 4 through: 这儿太挤, 我过不去. It's too crowded here, I can't get through. 大家都知道他, 他骗不～. People know him only too well to be kidded.

过人 guòrén (形) surpass; excel: 才华～ be outstanding in talent. ～的记忆力 remarkable memory

过日子 guòrìzi (动) live; get along: 勤俭～ live a frugal life

过甚 guòshèn (动) exaggerate: ～其词 overstate the case

过剩 guòshèng (动) excess; surplus: 生产～ overproduction

过失 guòshī (名) fault; error; slip

过时(時) guòshí (形) out-of-date; outmoded; out of fashion: 这是～的说法. This is a dated expression.

过头(頭) guòtóu (副) go beyond the limit; overdo: 他的话说～了. He has gone too far in his statement. 聪明～ be too clever by half

过问 guòwèn (动) take an interest in; concern oneself with; bother about: 亲自～ look into a matter, personally

过夜 guòyè (动) spend the night; stay overnight; put up for the night

过意不去 guòyì bùqù feel sorry; feel apologetic: 这事给你添不少麻烦, 真～. I'm very sorry to have put you to so much trouble.

过瘾(癮) guòyǐn (动) satisfy a craving; enjoy oneself to the full; do sth. to one's heart's content: 今天晚上玩得真～. I had an absolutely wondeful time tonight.

过硬 guòyìng (形) have a perfect mastery of sth.; be truly proficient in sth.: 他的技术还不～. His technique (or skill) is still far from perfect.

过于 guòyú 〈副〉 too; unduly; excessively: ～劳累 overtired. ～谨慎 be over-cautious

H h

哈 hā (动) 1 breathe out (with the mouth open) 2 〈象〉:～～大笑 laugh heartily; roar with laughter 3 [indicating complacency or satisfaction]: ～～,我猜着了. Aha, I've got (or guessed) it. ～～,这回可输给我了. Aha, you've lost to me for once.

哈欠 hāqiàn (名、动) yawn: 打～ give a yawn

哈腰 hāyāo (动)〈口〉 1 bend one's back; stoop 2 bow: 点头～ bow and scrape

蛤 há

see also gé

蛤蟆 háma (名) 1 frog 2 toad

嗨 hāi

嗨哟 hāiyō 〈叹〉 heave ho; yo-heave-ho; yo-ho

咳 hāi 〈叹〉 [indicating regret or surprise]: ～,我怎么这样糊涂! Dammit! How stupid I was!

see also ké

骸 hái (名) 1 bones of the body; skeleton 2 body: 形～ the human body. 遗～ (dead) body; corpse; remains

骸骨 háigǔ (名) human bones; skeleton

孩 hái (名) child: 小女～儿 a little girl

孩子 háizi (名) 1 child: 男～ boy. 女～ girl 2 son or daughter; children: 她有两个～. She has two children.

孩子气(氣) háiziqì (形) childish: 他越来越～了. He is getting more childish than ever.

还(還) hái (副) 1 still; yet: ～有一些具体细节要安排. Some details have yet to be worked out. 2 even more; still more: 今天比昨天～冷. It's even colder today than yesterday. 3 also; too; in addition: 他们参观了这所学校,～参观了工厂和医院. They visited some factories, hospitals as well as the school. 4 rather; fairly: 屋子收拾的倒～干净. The room is kept quite clean and tidy. 5 even: 你跑那么快～赶不上他,何况我呢? If a good runner like you can't catch up with him, how can I? 6 [used for emphasis]: 那～用说! That goes without saying. 7 [indicating that something quite unexpected has happened]: 他～真有办法. He really is resourceful.

see also huán

还是 háishì I (副) 1 still; nevertheless; all the same: 尽管下雨,运动会～照常进行. The sports meet went on as planned despite the rain. 2 had better: 你～戒烟吧. 吸烟对身体不好. You had better quit smoking. It's harmful to your health. II (连) or: 你是去加拿大,～去美国? Are you going to Canada or the United States? III [indicating that something unexpected has happened]: 我没想到这事儿～真难办. I didn't realize that the matter was so difficult to handle.

海 hǎi (名) 1 sea or big lake 2 a great number of people or things coming together: 人～ a sea of people; crowds of people. 林～ a vast stretch of forest 3 extra large; of great capacity

海岸 hǎi'àn (名) seacoast; coast; seashore: ～线 coastline

海拔 hǎibá (名) height above sea level; elevation: ～四千米 4,000 metres above sea level; with an elevation of 4,000 metres

海报(報) hǎibào (名) playbill; poster

海滨(濱) hǎibīn (名) seashore; seaside: ～胜地 seaside resort

海产(産) hǎichǎn (名) marine

products
海盗 hǎidào (名) pirate; sea rover: ～船 pirate ship. ～行为 piracy
海底 hǎidǐ (名) the bottom of the sea; seabed; sea floor: ～捞月 engage in an impossibly difficult undertaking; a forlorn hope. ～捞针 look for a needle in a haystack. ～油田 offshore oilfield. ～资源 seabed resources; submarine resources. ～电缆 submarine cable
海港 hǎigǎng (名) seaport; harbour: ～设备 harbour installations
海关(關) hǎiguān (名) customs house; customs: ～人员 customs officer. ～手续 customs formalities
海疆 hǎijiāng (名) coastal areas and territorial seas
海角 hǎijiǎo (名) cape; promontory: 天涯～ the four corners of the earth; (to) the end of the earth
海军 hǎijūn (名) navy: ～基地 naval base
海口 hǎikǒu (名) 1 seaport 2 [often used in conjunction with 夸]: 夸～ make a wild boast
海枯石烂(爛) hǎikū-shílàn (even if) the seas run dry and the rocks crumble: ～此心不移. I will never change no matter what happens. or I remain forever loyal
海阔天空 hǎikuò-tiānkōng as boundless as the sea and sky; unrestrained and far-ranging: ～地聊个没完 chat about everything under heaven with great gusto
海量 hǎiliàng (名) 1 <敬> magnanimity 2 enormous capacity for alcoholic drinks
海轮(輪) hǎilún (名) seagoing (or oceangoing) vessel
海绵 hǎimián (名) 1 sponge 2 foam rubber
海内 hǎinèi (名) within the four seas; throughout the country
海鸥(鷗) hǎi'ōu (名) sea gull
海市蜃楼(樓) hǎishì shènlóu (名) mirage
海誓山盟 hǎishì-shānméng (名) (make) swear an oath of eternal fidelity; vow eternal love
海滩(灘) hǎitān (名) seabeach; beach
海豚 hǎitún (名) dolphin
海外 hǎiwài (副) overseas; abroad: ～华侨 overseas Chinese
海湾(灣) hǎiwān (名) bay; gulf
海味 hǎiwèi (名) choice seafood
海峡(峽) hǎixiá (名) strait; channel: 台湾～ the Taiwan Straits
海啸(嘯) hǎixiào (名) tsunami; tidal wave
海洋 hǎiyáng (名) seas and oceans; ocean: ～性气候 maritime (or marine) climate. ～资源 marine resources
海域 hǎiyù (名) sea area; maritime space
海员 hǎiyuán (名) seaman; sailor: ～俱乐部 seamen's club
海运(運) hǎiyùn (名) sea transportation
海蜇 hǎizhé (名) jellyfish
害 hài I (名) evil; harm; calamity: 灾～ calamity; disaster. 两～相权取其轻 of the two evils choose the lesser II (形) harmful; destructive; injurious: ～鸟 harmful bird III (动) 1 do harm to; impair; cause trouble to: ～人不浅 do people great harm 2 kill; murder: 遇～ be murdered or assassinated 3 contract (an illness); suffer from: ～了一场大病 fall gravely ill 4 feel: ～羞 feel ashamed
害处(處) hàichù (名) harm: ～多, 好处少 do more harm than good
害怕 hàipà (动) fear; be afraid; be scared; 他们什么也不～. They have nothing to fear.
害群之马(馬) hài qún zhī mǎ (名) one who brings disgrace on or constitutes a danger to his group; a rotten apple in the barrel
害臊 hàisào (动) <口> feel ashamed; be bashful
害羞 hàixiū (动) be bashful; be shy: 她有些～. She was a bit shy.
骇 hài (动) be astonished; be shocked
骇人听(聽)闻 hài rén tīngwén (形) shocking; appalling
骇异(異) hàiyì (动) be shocked; be astonished
鼾 hān (动) snore: ～声 snore
憨 hān (形) 1 foolish; silly: ～痴 idiotic 2 naive; honest
憨厚 hānhòu (形) honest and good-natured
憨直 hānzhí (形) frank and straightforward
酣 hān (形) (drink, etc.) to one's heart's content: ～饮 drink one's fill. ～歌 lusty singing

酣畅(暢) hānchàng grow merry on wine; be sound asleep
酣睡 hānshuì (动) sleep soundly; be fast asleep

寒 hán (形) 1 cold: ～风刺骨. The cold wind cut one to the marrow. 他受了点～. He caught a chill. 2 afraid; fearful: 胆～ be terrified 3 poor; needy: 贫～ impoverished
寒潮 háncháo (名) cold wave
寒带(帶) hándài (名) frigid zone
寒噤 hánjìn (动) tremble (with cold or fear): 使人打～ send shivers down one's spine
寒冷 hánlěng (形) cold; icy
寒流 hánliú (名) cold current
寒暑表 hánshǔbiǎo (名) thermometer
寒酸 hánsuān (形) (of a poor intellectual in the old days) humble and shabby; unmannerly and acerbic
寒微 hánwēi (形)〈书〉of low station: 出身～ of humble origin
寒心 hánxīn (形) bitterly disappointed;
寒暄 hánxuān (动) exchange of greetings
寒意 hányì (名) a nip (or chill) in the air

含 hán (动) 1 keep in the mouth: ～一口水 hold some water in the mouth. 2 contain: ～着眼泪 fill with tears 3 nurse; suggest: ～恨 nurse grievances. 她脸上～怒. Her expression suggested anger.
含苞 hánbāo (动)〈书〉be budding: ～待放 be in bud
含垢忍辱 hángòu-rénrǔ (动) endure contempt and insults
含糊 hánhu (形) 1 ambiguous; vague: ～不清 equivocal. ～其词 talk evasively 2 careless; perfunctory: 这事一点儿也不能～. This matter should be handled with great care.
含混 hánhùn (形) equivocal; evasive: 言词～,令人费解. The wording is too ambiguous to be readily intelligible.
含沙射影 hán shā shè yǐng attack sb. by innuendo; make insinuating remarks
含笑 hánxiào have a smile on one's face: ～点头 nod with a smile
含辛茹苦 hánxīn-rúkǔ (动) suffer hardships and privations
含蓄 hánxù I (动) contain; embody II (形) 1 implicit; veiled: ～的批评 veiled criticism 2 reserved
含义(義) hányì (名) meaning; implication: 这句话的～不是很清楚. The implication of this remark is far from explicit.
含冤 hányuān suffer a gross injustice

函 hán (名) letter: 公～ official letter. 复～ a reply
函购(購) hángòu (名) purchase by mail; mail order: ～部 mail-order department
函件 hánjiàn (名) letters; correspondence
函授 hánshòu (动) teach by correspondence; give a correspondence course: ～学校 correspondence school

涵 hán I (动) contain II (名) culvert: 桥～ bridges and culverts
涵洞 hándòng (名) culvert
涵养(養) hányǎng (名) ability to control oneself; self-restraint: 他很有～. He never allows himself to be provoked.

罕 hǎn (副) rarely; seldom: ～见 rare. ～闻 seldom heard of. 人迹～至 show little trace of human habitation

喊 hǎn (动) 1 shout; cry out; yell: ～口号 shout slogans. 贼～捉贼 thief shouting "Stop thief!" 2 call (a person): 请～他一声. Give him a yell, please.
喊叫 hǎnjiào (动) shout; cry out

汗 hàn (名) sweat; perspiration: 出～ sweat; perspire. ～流浃背 streaming with sweat; soaked with sweat
汗马(馬)功劳(勞) hàn mǎ gōngláo (名) 1 distinctions won on the battlefield; war exploits 2 one's notable achievements in any discipline or project or any kind of constructive work
汗毛 hànmáo (名) fine hair on the human body
汗衫 hànshān (名) undershirt; T-shirt
汗颜 hànyán (形)〈书〉blush with shame

旱 hàn (名) 1 dry spell; drought: 抗～ combat drought. 久～逢甘雨. A soothing rain falls on the parched earth. 2 dryland: ～稻 dry rice 3 on land: ～路 overland route (as opposed to waterway)
旱季 hànjì (名) dry season
旱情 hànqíng (名) drought

damage caused by a drought
旱灾(災) hànzāi (名) drought
悍 hàn (形) 1 brave; bold: 一员～将 a brave general 2 intrepid; ferocious: 凶～ fierce and intrepid; ferocious
悍然 hànrán (副) outrageously; brazenly; flagrantly; without any scruples: ～入侵 outrageously invade.
焊 hàn (动) weld; solder: 气～ gas welding
焊接 hànjiē (名) welding; soldering
捍 hàn (动) defend; guard
捍卫(衛) hànwèi (动) defend; guard; protect: ～国家主权 uphold state sovereignty. ～民族利益 protect national interests
汉(漢) hàn (名) 1 the Han nationality 2 Chinese (language) 3 man: 好～ true man; hero
汉奸 hànjiān (名) traitor (to China): ～卖国贼 traitor and collaborator; quisling
汉学(學) Hànxué (名) 1 the Han school of classical philology 2 Sinology: ～家 Sinologist
汉语 hànyǔ (名) Chinese (language): ～拼音字母 the Chinese phonetic alphabet
汉字 Hànzì (名) Chinese character: 简化～ simplified Chinese characters
汉族 Hànzú (名) the Han nationality, China's main nationality
翰 hàn (名)〈书〉 writing brush: 挥～ write (a poem, a letter, etc. with a brush)
翰墨 hànmò (名)〈书〉 brush and ink — writing, painting, or calligarphy
瀚 hàn (形)〈书〉 vast: 浩～ vast; immense
憾 hàn (名) regret: 引以为～ consider it a matter for regret
撼 hàn (动) shake: 摇～ shake violently. 震～天地 shake the world
夯 hāng I (名) rammer; tamper II (动) ram; tamp; pound
吭 háng (名) throat: 引～高歌 sing lustily
see also kēng
航 háng I (名) boat; ship II (动) navigate (by water or air): ～线 air or shipping line; route. 夜～ night navigation. 首～ maiden voyage or flight
航班 hángbān (名) scheduled flight; flight number
航标(標) hángbiāo (名) navigation mark; buoy
航程 hángchéng (名) voyage; passage; distance travelled
航道 hángdào (名) channel; waterway; course: 主～ the main channel
航海 hánghǎi (名) navigation: ～日志 logbook; log
航空 hángkōng (名) aviation: 民用～ civil aviation. ～公司 airline company; airways. ～货运 airfreight. ～母舰 aircraft carrier. ～协定 air transport agreement. ～信 airmail letter; air letter; airmail
航路 hánglù (名) air or sea route: ～标志 route markings
航天 hángtiān (名) spaceflight: ～飞机 space shuttle. ～通信 space communication (SPACECOM). ～站 spaceport. ～工业部 Ministry of Space Industry
航向 hángxiàng (名) course (of a ship or plane): 改变～ change course
航行 hángxíng (动) 1 navigate by water; sail: 内河～ inland navigation 2 navigate by air; fly: 空中～ aerial navigation
航运(運) hángyùn (名) shipping: ～公司 shipping company
行 háng (名) 1 line; row: 排成两～ fall into two lines. 一路上杨柳成～. The roads are lined with willows. 2 seniority among brothers and sisters: 你～几? —我～三. Where do you come among your brothers and sisters? — I'm the third. 3 trade; profession; line of business: 各～各业 all trades and professions; all walks of life. 改～ change one's profession; switch to a new profession 4 business firm: 银～ bank 5〈量〉: [of anything forming a line]: 一～树 a row of trees. 四～诗句 four lines of verse
see also xíng
行家 hángjia (名) expert; specialist
行列 hángliè (名) ranks: 参加革命～ join the ranks of the revolution
行情 hángqíng (名) quotations (on the market); prices: ～表

quotations list
行市 hángshi (名) quotations (on the market); prices
行业(業) hángyè (名) trade; profession; industry: 服务～ service trades
绗 háng (动) sew with long stitches: ～被子 sew on the quilt cover with long stitches
巷 hàng
see also xiàng
巷道 hàngdào (名) tunnel
豪 háo I (名) a person of outstanding talent: 文～ a literary giant II (形) **1** forthright; unrestrained: ～气 undaunted spirit **2** despotic; bullying: 土～ local despot. 巧取～夺 take away by force or fraud
豪放 háofàng (形) uninhibited: ～不羁 unconventional and uninhibited
豪富 háofù I (形) powerful and wealthy (名) II powerful and wealthy people
豪华(華) háohuá (形) luxurious; sumptuous: ～的饭店 a luxury hotel. ～版 a de luxe edition
豪杰(傑) háojié (名) person of outstanding talent; hero
豪迈(邁) háomài (形) bold; heroic: ～的气概 heroic spirit
豪门(門) háomén (名) rich and powerful family; wealthy and influential clan
豪气(氣) háoqì (名) heroism; heroic spirit
豪强 háoqiáng I (形) despotic; tyrannical II (名) despot; bully
豪情 háoqíng (名) lofty sentiments: ～壮志 lofty sentiments and aspirations
豪爽 háoshuǎng (形) outspoken and straightforward
豪兴(興) háoxìng (名) ebullient high spirits; exhilaration; keen interest
豪言壮(壯)语 háoyán-zhuàngyǔ (名) brave words; proud remarks
壕 háo (名) **1** moat **2** trench: 掘～ dig trenches; dig in. 防空～ air-raid dugout
壕沟(溝) háogōu (名) **1** trench **2** ditch
嚎 háo (名) howl; wail
嚎啕 háotáo (动) cry loudly; wail
毫 háo I (名) **1** fine long hair: 羊～笔 a writing brush made of goat's hair **2** writing brush **3** milli-: ～米 millimetre. ～升 millilitre II (副) [used in the negative] in the least; at all: ～不犹豫 without the slightest hesitation. ～无诚意 without the least sincerity. ～无二致 without any noticeable difference
毫厘 háolí (名) the least bit; an iota: ～不差 without the slightest error; perfectly accurate
毫毛 háomáo (名) [often used figuratively] soft hair on the body: 不准你动他一根～. You are not allowed to do the least harm to him.
蚝(蠔) háo (名) oyster: ～油 oyster sauce
号(號) háo (动) **1** howl; roar: 北风怒～. A north wind is howling. **2** wail; cry piteously
see also hào
号啕 háotáo (动) cry loudly: ～大哭 wail bitterly
嗥 háo (名) (of a jackal or wolf) howl
好 hǎo I (形) **1** good; fine; nice: ～天气 nice weather. ～脾气 good-natured. 这本小说很～. This is an excellent novel. 这话说得太～了. This is a very apt remark. 你还是别答应～. You'd better make no promise. **2** be in good health; get well: 他身体一直很～. He's been in good health. 他的病～了. He's recovered from his illness. **3** friendly; kind: ～朋友 good friend. **4** [as a polite formula]: 你～! Hello! ～睡! Good night! **5** [used after a verb to indicate the completion of an action]: 计划定～了. The plan's been drawn up. 坐～吧, 要开会了. Please be seated. The meeting is going to begin. **6** [indicating praise, approval or dissatisfaction]: ～, 就这么办. O.K., it's settled. ～了, 不要再说了. All right, let's leave it at that. II (副) **1** [used before a verb as an adverb]: 这问题～解决 The problem can be easily solved. 那篇文章～懂. That essay is easy to read. **2** [used before 多, 久, 长, etc.] a good many: ～久 quite long. 他学了～几年英语. He's been learning English for quite a few years. **3** [used before certain adjectives

to indicate high degree]: ～深的一条河! What a deep river! 街上～热闹! What a busy street! 你这个人～糊涂! You are such a fool! 前些日子我～忙了一阵. I was quite busy some time ago. III [used as an adverb] may, can: 你留个电话，有事我～跟你联系. Give me your telephone number so that I can contact you when necessary. 别忘了带伞,下雨～用. Don't forget to take your umbrella in case it rains. IV (名) 1 [indicating acclamation]: 观众连声叫～. The audience broke into loud cheers. 2 [indicating a greeting]:向你的父母问～. Give my love to your parents. 你去见着他,别忘了给我捎个～儿. Don't forget to convey my regards, when you see him.

好办(辦) hǎobàn (形) easy to do: 这事～. That's easy.

好比 hǎobǐ (动) can be compared to; like: 军民关系～鱼和水的关系. The people are to the army what water is to fish.

好吃 hǎochī (形) nice; delicious

好处(處) hǎochù (名) 1 benefit; advantage: 对我们都有～ be of benefit to us all. 这对你们有～. It will do you good. 2 gain, profit: 没有人会从中得到～. Nobody will profit from it.

好歹 hǎo dǎi I (名) 1 what's good and what's bad: 不知～ unable to appreciate a favour 2 most unfortunate happening [usually referring to the death of a person]: 万一他有个～,这可怎么办? What if something should happen to her? II (副) in any case; whatever: 她要是在这里，～也能拿个主意. If she were here, she would give us a word of advice in any case.

好多 hǎoduō 1 a good many; a good deal; a lot of 2 how many; how much: 剩下～? How much is left?

好感 hǎogǎn (名) good impression: 对他有～ have a soft spot for him

好汉(漢) hǎohàn (名) brave man; true man; hero

好好儿 hǎohǎor (副) 1 in a proper way; when every thing is in order: ～地照顾他 take good care of him 2 to one's heart's content; to the best of one's ability: 咱们～聊一聊. Let's have a good chat.

好话 hǎohuà (名) 1 a good word: 给他说句～ put in a good word for him 2 word of praise: 爱听～ be fond of praise

好家伙 hǎojiāhuo my goodness; good heavens: ～,这真贵呀! My goodness, it's really expensive.

好看 hǎokàn (形) 1 fine; nice 2 interesting: 这本小说很～. This novel is very interesting. 3 honoured; proud: 儿子得了金牌,我的脸上也～. I'm proud of my son who has won a gold medal. 4 an embarrassing situation: 让我上台表演，这不是要我～吗? You're putting me on the spot if you want me to perform on the stage.

好评 hǎopíng (名) favourable comment; high opinion: 这部小说博得读者～. This novel was well received by the reading public.

好容易 hǎoróngyì (副) not without great difficulty: 他们～才找到我这儿. They had no small difficulty finding my place. 又作"好不容易"

好事多磨 hǎoshì duō mó the road to happiness is strewn with setbacks

好似 hǎosì (动) seem; be like: ～秋风扫落叶 like the autumn wind scuttling fallen leaves

好听(聽) hǎotīng (形) pleasing to the ear: ～的话 fine words. 这支歌～. This is a very pleasant song.

好象 hǎoxiàng (动) seem; be like: ～要下雨. It looks like rain. 到这儿就～到了自己家一样. You'll feel as if you were at home while here. 他今天～不怎么舒服. It seems that he is not quite himself today.

好笑 hǎoxiào (形) laughable; funny; ridiculous: 这有什么～的? What's so funny?

好心 hǎoxīn (名) good intention: 一片～ with the best of intentions

好意 hǎoyì (名) good intention; kindness: 谢谢您的～. Thank you for your kindness. 不怀～ harbour ulterior motives

好意思 hǎoyìsi (形) have the cheek: 亏他～说出这种话来! He had even the cheek to say such things! 脸上有点不～ look a little embarrassed

好转(轉) hǎozhuǎn (动) turn for the better; improve: 形势～.

The situation took a favourable turn.

耗 hào I (动) **1** consume; cost: ~费时间的工作 a time-consuming job **2** waste time; dawdle: 别~着了，快走吧. Stop dawdling and get going. II (名) bad news: 噩~ the passing away (of a friend or a relative or someone we love and respect)

耗费 hàofèi (动) consume; expend: ~人力物力 spend both manpower and material resources. 在这项工程上~了大量金钱. They spent a great amount of money on the project.

耗竭 hàojié (动) exhaust; use up: 资源~ be drained of natural resources

号(號) hào (名) **1** name: 国~ the name of a dynasty. 绰~ nickname **2** alias; assumed name; alternative name **3** business house: 银~ banking house, 分~ branch (of a firm, etc.) **4** mark; sign; signal: 问~ question mark. 击掌为~ clap as a signal **5** number: 五~楼 Building No.5. 编~ serial number **6** size: 大(中、小)~ large (medium, small) size: 你要几~的鞋? What size shoe would you like? **7** date: 今天几~? ——十三~. What date is it today? —The 13th. **8** order: 发~施令 issue orders **9** any brass wind instrument: 军~ bugle. 小~ trumpet **10** anything used as a horn: 螺~ conch-shell trumpet; conch **11** bugle call; any call made on a bugle: 熄灯~ the lights-out. 吹起床~ sound the reveille
see also háo

号称(稱) hàochēng (动) **1** be known as: 四川~天府之国. Sichuan is known as a land of plenty. **2** claim to be: 敌人的这个师~一万二千人. The enemy division claimed to be twelve thousand strong.

号角 hàojiǎo (名) **1** bugle; horn **2** bugle call

号令 hàolìng (动) command; order: ~三军 issue orders to the three services

号码 hàomǎ (名) number: 电话~ telephone number

号外 hàowài (名) extra (of a newspaper)

号召 hàozhào (名) call; appeal

浩 hào (形) great; vast; grand

浩大 hàodà (形) very great; huge; vast: 工程~. It's a project of great magnitude.

浩荡(蕩) hàodàng (形) vast and mighty: ~的长江 the mighty Changjiang (Yangtse) River

浩瀚 hàohàn (形) vast; immense: ~的沙漠 a vast expanse of desert

浩劫 hàojié (名) disaster; calamity; catastrophe

浩气(氣) hàoqì (名) noble spirit: ~长存. Imperishable is the noble spirit.

浩如烟(煙)海 hào rú yān hǎi (of data, etc.) vast in scope like the boundless sea

皓 hào (形) **1** white: ~首 hoary head **2** bright; luminous: ~月当空. A bright moon hung in the sky.

好 hào (动) **1** like; love; be fond of: ~学 eager to learn. ~管闲事 be meddlesome or nosy **2** be liable to: ~伤风 easily catch cold. ~发脾气 apt to lose one's temper
see also hǎo

好吃懒做 hàochī-lǎnzuò (形) be fond of food but averse to work

好大喜功 hàodà-xǐgōng have a passion for the grandiose; crave for grandeur and success

好高骛远(遠) hàogāo-wùyuǎn aim too high

好客 hàokè (形) be hospitable

好奇 hào qí (形) be curious: ~心 curiosity

好强 hàoqiáng (形) eager to put one's best foot forward

好胜(勝) hàoshèng (形) eager to excel in everything

好事 hàoshì (形) meddlesome: ~之徒 busybody; mischief-maker

好恶(惡) hào-wù (名) likes and dislikes

好逸恶(惡)劳(勞) hàoyì-wùláo (形) love ease and comfort but hate to work

好战(戰) hàozhàn (形) warlike: ~分子 hawkish elements; warmongers

诃 hē (动) scold

呵 hē (动) **1** breathe out (with the mouth open): ~一口气 breathe out; exhale **2** scold: ~责 scold sb. severely; give sb. a dressing down

呵斥 hēchì (动) berate; excoriate

呵呵 hēhē 〈象〉 guffaw: ~大笑 laugh heartily; roar with laughter; guffaw

嗬 hē 〈叹〉[indicating astonishment] ah; oh: ～,真了不得! Oh, it's really terrific!

喝 hē (动) 1 drink: ～茶 drink tea. ～酒 drink wine 3 drink alcoholic liquor: 爱～ be fond of drinking. ～醉了 be drunk
see also hè

涸 hé (动)〈书〉dry up

阂 hé (动) cut off from; not in communication with: 隔～ misunderstanding; estrangement. 语言～ language barrier

核 hé (名) 1 pit; stone: 桃～ peach-pit; peach-stone. 无～水果 stoneless fruit 2 nucleus: 原子～ atomic nucleus 3 examine; check: ～准 approve; ratify
see also hú

核弹(彈)头(頭) hédàntóu (名) nuclear warhead

核定 hédìng (动) check and ratify; appraise and decide

核对(對) héduì (动) check: ～数字 check figures. ～事实 check the facts

核讹诈 hé'ézhà (名) nuclear blackmail

核计 héjì (动) assess; calculate

核能 hénéng (名) nuclear energy

核实(實) héshí (动) verify; check: ～的产量 verified output

核算 hésuàn (名) business accounting: 成本～cost accounting

核桃 hétao (名) walnut

核武器 héwǔqì (名) nuclear weapon

核心 héxīn (名) nucleus; core; kernel; the heart of the matter: ～力量 force at the core. ～人物 key person; key figure

劾 hé (动) expose sb.'s misdeeds or crimes: 弹～ impeach

翮 hé (名) 1 shaft of a feather; quill 2 wing (of a bird): 振～高飞 flap the wings and soar into the sky

河 hé (名) river

河床(牀) héchuáng (名) riverbed

河谷 hégǔ (名) river valley

河流 héliú (名) rivers: ～沉积 fluvial (or fluviatile) deposit

河渠 héqú (名) rivers and canals; waterways

河山 héshān (名) rivers and mountains; land; territory: 锦绣～ the beautiful land of one's country

河网(網) héwǎng (名) a network of waterways

何 hé 〈书〉 1 [denoting interrogation]: ～人 who. ～时 what time; when. ～处 what place; where 2 [often used in rhetorical questions]: 谈～容易 Could it be that easy? 有～不可? What's wrong with it?

何必 hébì (副) there is no need; why: 既然不会下雨,～带伞. Why take the umbrella with you if it is not going to rain?

何不 hébù (副) why not: 既然有事,～早说? Since you have a previous engagement, why didn't you say so?

何尝(嘗) hécháng [used in a negative sentence, often in the form of a question]: 我～不想去,只是没工夫罢了. Not that I have no inclination to go; I just haven't got the time.

何等 héděng (形) 1 what kind: 你知道他是～人物? Have you any idea what sort of person he is? 2 [used in an exclamatory sentence to indicate something extraordinary]: 这是～巧妙的技术! What superb skill!

何妨 héfáng why not; might as well: ～试试? Why not have a try?

何苦 hékǔ why bother; is it worth the trouble: 你～在这些小事上伤脑筋? Why bother about such trifles?

何况 hékuàng (连) much less; let alone: 他在生人面前都不习惯讲话,～要到大庭广众之中. He is not used to talking with a stranger, let alone before a big audience.

何其 héqí [indicating disagreement] how; what: ～糊涂! How silly!

何去何从(從) héqù-hécóng what course to follow: ～,速作抉择. You must quickly decide for yourselves as to what course to take.

何如 hérú how about: 请试验一下～? You'll try it out first, won't you?

何谓 héwèi 〈书〉what is meant by: ～幸福? What does happiness mean?

何许 héxǔ 〈书〉 where; what kind of: 他是～人? Where is he from? *or* What sort of person is he?

何以 héyǐ (副)〈书〉1 how:～教我? How would you advise me? 2 why: ～变卦? Why all this sudden change?

何在 hézài (副) where: 理由～? For what reason?

何止 hézhǐ far more than: 例子～这些. These are merely a few instances.

荷 hé (名) lotus

see also hè

荷包 hébāo (名) 1 small bag (for carrying money and odds and ends); pouch 2 pocket (in a garment): ～蛋 fried eggs

荷花 héhuā (名) lotus

曷 hé (副)〈书〉 1 how; why 2 when

合 hé (动) 1 close; shut: 把书～上 close a book. 她听到这个消息笑得～不拢嘴来. She grinned from ear to ear at the good news. 2 join; combine: ～力 make a joint effort 3 suit; agree: 正～我意. That exactly falls in with what I have in mind. 4 be equal to; add up to: 一公顷～十五市亩. A hectare is equal to 15 *mu*.

合办(辦) hébàn (动) jointly run

合并(併) hébìng (动) combine: 这三个提议可以合并以便讨论. These three proposals can be combined to facilitate discussion.

合唱 héchàng (名) chorus: ～团 chorus

合成 héchéng (动) compose; compound: 由重要原料～be compounded of important raw materials. ～洗涤剂 synthetic detergent. ～纤维 synthetic fibre

合法 héfǎ (形) legal; lawful; legitimate; rightful: ～地位 legal status. ～手段 legitimate means

合格 hégé (形) qualified; up to standard: ～的教师 a qualified teacher. 质量检查～ quality checked

合乎 héhū (动) conform with (or to); correspond to; accord with; tally with: ～规律 conform to the laws. ～要求 measure up to the requirement

合伙 héhuǒ (动) form a partnership: ～经营 go in for a joint venture

合计 héjì (动) amount to; add up to; total

合计 héji (动) 1 think over; figure out: 他一天到晚心里老～这件事. He thought the matter over and over all day. 2 consult: 大家～～这个问题该怎么处理. Let's put our heads together and decide how the problem is to be tackled.

合金 héjīn (名) alloy: ～钢 alloy steel

合理 hélǐ (形) rational; reasonable; equitable: ～使用 rational utilization. 他说的话很～. What he says is very reasonable.

合理化 hélǐhuà (动、名) rationalize: ～建议 rationalization proposal

合力 hélì (动) make a concerted effort

合龙(龍) hélóng (名) 1 closure (of a dam, dyke, etc.) 2 join the two sections of a bridge, etc.

合谋 hémóu I (动) conspire; plot together II (名) conspiracy

合拍 hépāi (动) in time; in step; in harmony: 与时代～ in step with the times

合群 héqún (形) get on well with others; sociable

合身 héshēn (形) fit: 这件上衣很～. This jacket fits well.

合适(適) héshì (形) suitable; appropriate; becoming; right: 这个字用在这里不～. This is not the proper word to use here.

合算 hésuàn (形) paying; worthwhile

合同 hétóng (名) contract: 签订～ sign a contract. 撕毁～ tear up a contract

合意 héyì (动) suit; be to one's liking (or taste)

合影 héyǐng (名) group photo (or picture): ～留念 have a group photo taken to mark the occasion

合作 hézuò (动) cooperate; collaborate; work together: 互相～ cooperate with each other. ～经济 cooperative economy; cooperative sector of the economy. ～社 cooperative; co-op

颌 hé (名)〈书〉 jaw: 上(下)～ the upper (lower) jaw

盒 hé (名) box; case: 一～火柴 a box of matches. 铅笔～ pencil case; pencil box

禾 hé (名) standing grain (esp. rice)

禾苗 hémiáo (名) seedlings of cereal crops

和 hé I (形) 1 gentle; mild; kind 2 harmonious; on

good terms: ～睦相处 be on friendly terms II (名) **1** peace: 讲～ make peace **2** draw; tie: 那盘棋～了. The game of chess ended in a draw. III (副) together with: ～衣而卧 sleep in one's clothes IV (介) [denoting relations, comparison, etc.]: ～这件事没有关系 have nothing to do with the matter. 他～我一样高. He's as tall as I. V sum: 两数之～ the sum of the two numbers
see also hè; huó; huò

和蔼 hé'ǎi (形) kindly; good-natured: ～可亲 amiable

和畅(暢) héchàng (形) (of a wind) gentle: 春风～ The spring wind is gentle and caressing.

和好 héhǎo (形) become reconciled: ～如初 be on good terms as ever; restore good relations

和缓 héhuǎn I (形) gentle; mild II (动) ease up; relax: ～一下气氛 relax the tense atmosphere. 语气～ speak in mild terms

和解 héjiě (形) conciliatory

和局 héjú (名) drawn game; draw; tie

和睦 hémù (形) harmonious; amicable: ～关系 have amicable relations with

和暖 hénuǎn (形) pleasantly warm; genial: 天气～. The weather is getting warm.

和盘(盤)托出 hé pán tuōchū (动) reveal the whole truth; make a clean breast of something

和平 hépíng I (名) peace: 保卫世界～safeguard world peace. ～共处 peaceful coexistence II (形) mild: 中药药性～. Chinese herbal medicine is mild.

和气(氣) héqì (形) gentle; kind; polite; good-natured: 别为小事伤了～. Don't let this trifling matter affect our good relationship.

和善 héshàn (形) kind and gentle; amiable

和尚 héshàng (名) Buddhist monk

和声(聲) héshēng (名) harmony

和事佬 héshìlǎo (名) peacemaker

和谈 hétán (名) peace talks

和谐 héxié (形) harmonious

和颜悦色 héyán-yuèsè be kindly and genial

和约 héyuē (名) peace treaty

和衷共济(濟) hézhōng-gòngjì work with a concerted effort; act in concert with each other

鹤

hè (名) crane

鹤发(髮)童颜 hèfà-tóngyán (形) white-haired but healthy-looking; hale and hearty

鹤立鸡(鷄)群 hè lì jīqún (形) stand out most conspicuously among his peers

赫

hè I (形) conspicuous; grand: 显～ distinguished and influential; illustrious II (名) hertz: 千～ kilohertz. 兆～ megahertz

赫赫 hèhè (形) illustrious; very impressive: ～有名的人物 a person of great renown

赫然 hèrán (形) **1** impressively; awesomely **2** terribly (angry): ～而怒 get into a furious temper; fly into a rage

荷

hè I (动) <书> carry on one's shoulder or back II (名) burden; responsibility: 肩负重～ shoulder heavy responsibilities III [often used in letter writing] be granted a favour: 感～ feel grateful
see also hé

壑

hè (名) gully; big pool: 千山万～ an interminable range of mountains and valleys

吓(嚇)

hè I (动) threaten; intimidate II (叹) [expressing annoyance]: ～, 怎么能这样呢? My goodness, how could it be like that?
see also xià

褐

hè I (名) coarse cloth or clothing II (形) brown

褐煤 hèméi (名) brown coal; lignite

喝

hè (动) shout loudly; yell: 大～一声 give a loud shout
see also hē

喝采 hècǎi (动) acclaim; cheer: 齐声～ cheer in chorus

喝倒采 hè dàocǎi make catcalls

和

hè (动) **1** join in the singing **2** compose a poem in reply to a friend, using the same rhyme sequence
see also hé; huó; huò

贺

hè (动) congratulate: ～词 speech (or message) of congratulation; congratulations; greetings. ～电 message of congratulation; congratulatory telegram. ～信 letter of congratulation

贺年 hènián (动) extend New Year greetings: ～片 New Year

card

贺喜 hèxǐ (动) congratulate sb. on a happy occasion (e.g. a wedding, the birth of a child, etc.)

黑 hēi (形) 1 black: ～板 blackboard 2 dark: 天～了. It's getting dark. ～马 dark horse 3 secret; shady: ～交易 shady deal 4 wicked; sinister: ～心 evil-minded

黑暗 hēi'àn (形) dark: ～的角落里 in a dark corner. 在～的旧社会 in the dark old society. ～时期 Dark Ages (in Europe)

黑白 hēi-bái (动) black and white; right and wrong: 混淆～ confound black and white; confuse right and wrong

黑话 hēihuà (名) 1 (bandits') argot; (thieves') cant 2 double-talk; malicious words

黑货 hēihuò (名) smuggled goods; contraband

黑名单(單) hēimíngdān (名) blacklist

黑幕 hēimù (名) inside story of a plot: 揭穿～ expose a sinister plot

黑人 hērén (名) 1 Black people; Black; Negro 2 a person who has no residence card

黑市 hēishì (名) black market

黑压(壓)压 hēiyāyā (形) a dense or dark mass of: 广场上～地站满了人. Masses of people crowded the square.

黑油油 hēiyōuyōu (形) jet-black; shiny black: ～的头发 shiny black hair

嘿 hēi (叹) hey: ～! 快走吧! Hey, hurry up! ～,下雪了! Why, it's snowing!

痕 hén (名) mark; trace: 刀～ a scar left by a knife-cut. 泪～ tear stains

痕迹 hénjì (名) mark; trace; vestige: 旧日的～几乎完全消失了. The vestiges of bygone days have almost entirely disappeared.

很 hěn (副) very; quite; awfully: ～高兴 very happy. ～满意 feel very pleased. ～有价值 be of great value. 我～知道他是个怎样的人. I know very well what sort of person he is.

狠 hěn (形) 1 ruthless; relentless: 凶～ ferocious and ruthless 2 suppress (one's feelings); harden (the heart): 我～着心把泪止住. I made a terrific effort to refrain from tears. 3 firm; resolute: ～～的批评 severe criticism

狠毒 hěndú (形) vicious; venomous

狠心 hěnxīn (形、名) 1 cruel-hearted; heartless; merciless 2 (make) a determined effort

恨 hèn I (动) hate: ～之入骨 cherish bitter hatred for sb. ～铁不成钢 be unusually strict with sb. and anxious to see him make instant progress II (名) regret: 遗～ eternal regret

亨 hēng (形) smooth

亨通 hēngtōng (形) smooth; and prosperous: 万事～. One is blessed with good fortune in every thing. *or* Everything goes well.

哼 hēng (动) 1 groan; moan: 痛得直～～ groan with pain 2 hum; croon: ～着曲子 hum a tune

see also hng

恒 héng I (形) 1 permanent; lasting: 永～ eternal; everlasting 2 usual; common; constant: ～言 common saying II (名) perseverance: 持之以～ go on with perseverance

恒温 héngwēn (名) constant temperature

恒心 héngxīn (名) perseverance; constancy: 她这人有志气,有～. She is ambitious and tenacious of purpose.

恒星 héngxīng (名) (fixed) star

横 héng I (形) 1 horizontal; transverse: ～梁 horizontal beam. 纵～ vertical and horizontal 2 across; sideways: ～写 write words sideways. 一队飞机～过我们的头顶. A squadron of planes flew past overhead. 3 move crosswise; traverse: 这条铁路～贯五省. The railway traverses five provinces. II (副) 1 unrestrainedly; turbulently: 老泪～流. Tears streamed down one's old cheeks. 2 violently; fiercely; flagrantly: ～加阻挠 obstruct. ～冲直撞 dash around madly; run amok

see also hèng

横生 héngshēng (动) 1 grow wild: 荆棘～ be overgrown with brambles 2 be overflowing with; be full of: 妙趣～ brim with wit and humour

横行 héngxíng (动) run wild; run amok: ～一时 run wild for

a time. ～霸道 ride roughshod (over)
横征暴敛(斂) hèngzhēng-bàoliǎn (动) extort excessive taxes and levies

桁 héng (名) purlin
桁架 héngjià (名) truss: ～桥 truss bridge

衡 héng I (名) weighing apparatus II (动) weigh; measure; judge: ～情度理 judging by common sense
衡量 héngliáng (动) weigh; measure; judge: ～得失 weigh the pros and cons
衡器 héngqì (名) weighing apparatus

横 hèng (形) 1 harsh and unreasonable; perverse: ～话 harsh, unreasonable words. 2 unexpected: ～祸 unexpected calamity
see also héng
横财 hèngcái (名) ill-gotten wealth (or gains): 发～ get rich by foul means
横死 hèngsǐ (动) die a violent death

哼 hng (叹) [expressing dissatisfaction or doubt] humph: ～, 你信他的! Humph! you belive him?
see also hēng

烘 hōng (动) 1 dry or warm by the fire: 把湿衣服～干 dry the wet clothes by the fire 2 set off: ～托 set off by contrast
烘焙 hōngbèi (动) cure (tea or tobacco leaves)
烘烤 hōngkǎo (动) toast; bake
烘托 hōngtuō (动) 1 (in Chinese painting) add shading in ink around an object to make it stand out 2 set off by contrast; throw into sharp relief

哄 hōng 1 (象) roars of laughter 2 hubbub
see also hǒng; hòng
哄传(傳) hōngchuán (动) (of rumours) circulate widely
哄动(動) hōngdòng (动) cause a sensation; make a stir
哄抬(擡) hōngtái (动) drive up (prices)
哄堂大笑 hōngtáng dàxiào set the whole room roaring with laughter; explode into loud laughter

轰(轟) hōng I (象) bang; boom: ～的一声, 震得山鸣谷应. The hills resounded with a bang. II (动) 1 rumble; bombard; explode: 万炮齐～ cannonade 2 shoo away; drive off: ～下台 oust sb. from office; hoot sb. off the stage
轰动(動) hōngdòng (动) cause a sensation; make a stir: ～全国 cause a nationwide sensation. 全场～ make a stir in the audience
轰轰烈烈 hōnghōnglièliè (形) on a grand and spectacular scale; vigorous; dynamic
轰击(擊) hōngjī (动) shell; bombard: ～敌人阵地 shell enemy positions
轰隆 hōnglōng (动)〈象〉 rumble; roll
轰鸣 hōngmíng (动) thunder; roar: 马达～ Motors roared
轰炸 hōngzhà (动) bomb: ～机 bomber

鸿 hóng I (名) 1 swan; wild goose 2〈书〉letter: 远方来～ a letter from afar II (名) great; grand: ～图 grand plan; grand design
鸿沟(溝) hónggōu (名) wide gap; chasm: 不可逾越的～ an unbridgeable gap; an impassable chasm
鸿雁 hóngyàn (名) wild goose

虹 hóng (名) rainbow

红 hóng I (形) 1 red: ～铅笔 red pencil 2 revolutionary; red: ～军 the Red Army II (名) 1 red cloth worn as a sign of festivity, etc. 2 symbol of success: ～运 good luck 3 bonus; dividend
红茶 hóngchá (名) black tea
红尘(塵) hóngchén (名) human society: 看破～ see through the vanity of human life
红光满面 hóngguāng mǎnmiàn glowing with health; in the pink of health
红利 hónglì (名) bonus; extra dividend
红领巾 hónglǐngjīn (名) 1 red scarf (worn by Young Pioneers) 2 Young Pioneer
红绿灯(燈) hónglǜdēng (名) traffic light; traffic signal
红旗 hóngqí (名) red flag or banner: 工业战线上一面～ a pacesetter on the industrial front
红人 hóngrén (名) favourite follower (of a person in power); a rising star
红润 hóngrùn (形) ruddy; rosy: 脸色～ ruddy complexion; rosy

cheeks
红烧(燒) hóngshāo (动) braise in soy sauce: ～肉 pork braised in brown sauce
红十字会(會) Hóngshízìhuì (名) the Red Cross
红薯 hóngshǔ (名) sweet potato
红外线(綫) hóngwàixiàn (名) infrared ray
红血球 hóngxuěqiú (名) red blood cell
红药(藥)水 hóngyàoshuǐ (名) mercurochrome
红晕 hóngyùn (名) blush; flush: 脸上泛出～ one's face blushing scarlet
红肿(腫) hóngzhǒng (形) red and swollen
洪 hóng (名) 1 big; vast: ～涛 turbulent waves 2 flood: 防～ control or prevent flood
洪峰 hóngfēng (名) flood peak; peak water level
洪亮 hóngliàng (形) loud and clear; sonorous: ～的回声 loud reverberations
洪流 hóngliú (名) mighty torrent; powerful current
洪水 hóngshuǐ (名) flood; floodwater
宏 hóng (形) great; grand; magnificent
宏大 hóngdà (形) grand; great: 规模～ on a great scale; vast in scope
宏观(觀) hóngguān (形) macroscopic: ～经济 macroeconomics
宏论(論) hónglùn 〈敬〉 esteemed opinion
宏伟(偉) hóngwěi (形) magnificent; grand: ～建筑 magnificent building
宏愿(願) hóngyuàn (名) great aspirations; noble ambition
宏旨 hóngzhǐ (名) main theme; cardinal principle: 无关～ not a matter of cardinal principle
弘 hóng I (形) great; grand; magnificent II (动) enlarge; expand
弘大 hóngdà (形) grand
泓 hóng I (形) (of water) deep II 〈量〉: 一～秋水 an expanse of autumn water
哄 hǒng (动) 1 fool; humbug: 你这是～我. You're kidding me. 2 coax; humour: 她很会～孩子. She knows how to coax children to do one thing or another.
see also hōng; hòng
哄骗 hǒngpiàn (动) cheat; coax; humbug; hoodwink
哄 hòng (名) uproar: 一～而散 scatter in an uproar
see also hōng; hǒng
侯 hóu (名) 1 marquis: ～爵 marquis 2 a nobleman or a high official
瘊 hóu (名) wart: ～子 wart
喉 hóu (名) larynx; throat
喉咙(嚨) hóulóng (名) throat: ～痛 have a sore throat
喉舌 hóushé (名) mouthpiece: 人民的～ the mouthpiece of the people
猴 hóu (名) monkey: ～子 monkey
吼 hǒu (名) 1 roar; howl: 狮子～ the roar of a lion 2 (of wind, siren etc.) howl, whistle, thunder: 风浪的～声 the roar of the wind and waves
厚 hòu I (形) 1 thick: ～棉衣 a heavy padded coat 2 deep; profound: 深情～谊 great kindness and cordiality 3 kind; magnanimous: 忠～ honest and kind-hearted 4 large; generous: ～利 substantial gains. ～酬 handsome reward 5 rich or strong in flavour II (名) favour; stress: ～此薄彼 be prejudiced in favour of one and against the other
厚薄 hòubó (名) thickness
厚道 hòudào (形) kind and sincere
厚度 hòudù (名) thickness
厚脸(臉)皮 hòuliǎnpí (形) thick-skinned; brazen; shameless: 厚着脸皮说 have the cheek to say
厚望 hòuwàng (名) great expectations: 不负～ live up to sb.'s expectations; not let sb. down
厚颜 hòuyán (形) impudent; brazen: ～无耻 shameless
厚意 hòuyì (名) good will; kindness: 多谢你的～. Thank you for your kindness.
候 hòu I (动) 1 wait; await: 请稍～一会儿. Please wait a moment. 2 inquire after: 致～ send one's regards II (名) time; season: 时～ time 2 condition; state: 症～ symptom
候补(補) hòubǔ (名) a candidate (for a vacancy); an alternate member
候车(車)室 hòuchēshì (名) waiting room (in a railway or bus station)

候鸟(鳥) hòuniǎo (名) migratory bird; migrant
候选(選)人 hòuxuǎnrén (名) candidate: 提出～ nominate candidates
候诊 hòuzhěn (动) wait for one's turn to see the doctor: ～室 waiting room (in a hospital)

后 hòu (名) empress; queen

后(後) hòu I(副) 1 behind; at the back: 屋～ behind (or at the back of) a house. ～排 back row 2 after; afterwards; later: 不久以～ soon afterwards; before long II (名) offspring: 无～ without male offspring; without issue
后备(備) hòubèi (名) reserve: 留有～ keep sth. in reserve. ～基金 reserve fund. ～军 reserve forces
后辈 hòubèi (名) 1 younger generation 2 posterity
后尘(塵) hòuchén ‹书›: 步人～ follow in sb.'s footsteps
后代 hòudài (名) 1 later periods (in history) 2 later generations; descendants
后盾 hòudùn (名) backing; support: 坚强的～ powerful backing
后方 hòufāng (名) rear: ～勤务 rear service; logistics (service)
后顾(顧) hòugù (动) 1 give attention to what is left back at home: 无暇～ cannot attend to what is left behind 2 look back: ～与前瞻 sum up the past and plan for the future
后果 hòuguǒ (名) consequence; aftermath: 承担～ be responsible for the consequences
后患 hòuhuàn (名) future trouble: ～无穷 a source of endless trouble
后悔 hòuhuǐ (动) regret; repent; ～莫及 repent bitterly; no use crying over spilt milk
后继(繼) hòujì (动) succeed; carry on: ～无人 with nobody to carry on the work
后进(進) hòujìn (名) 1 laggard 2 junior member of a profession
后劲(勁) hòujìn (名) 1 aftereffect: 这酒～大. This kind of liquor has a strong delayed effect. 2 reserve strength; stamina
后来(來) hòulái (副) afterwards; later
后来(來)居上 hòu lái jū shàng those who come later on the scene often surpass their predecessors
后路 hòulù (名) 1 communication lines to the rear; route of retreat: 切断敌人的～ cut off the enemy's route of retreat 2 room for manoeuvre
后门(門) hòumén (名) 1 back door (or gate): 大院的～ the back gate of a compound 2 "back door" dealings
后面 hòumian (副) 1 at the back; in the rear; behind 2 later
后起 hòuqǐ (of people of talent) of the younger generation: ～之秀 a promising young person
后勤 hòuqín (名) rear service; logistics: ～部 rear-service department; logistics department (or command). ～基地 logistics base; rear supply base. ～支援 logistic support
后人 hòurén (名) 1 future generations 2 posterity; descendants
后生可畏 hòushēn kě wèi the younger generation deserves respect
后世 hòushì (名) 1 later ages 2 later generations
后事 hòushì (名) [often seen in novels or narratives in chronological order] later developments 2 funeral affairs: 料理～ make arrangements for a funeral
后台(臺) hòutái (名) 1 backstage 2 backstage supporter; behind-the-scenes backer: ～很硬 have very strong backing
后天 hòutiān I (名) day after tomorrow II (形) postnatal; acquired
后退 hòutuì (动) draw back; fall back; retreat
后卫(衛) hòuwèi (名) 1 rear guard 2 full back: 左～ left back. 右～ right back 3 guard
后遗症 hòuyízhèng (名) sequelae
后裔 hòuyì (名) descendant; offspring
后者 hòuzhě (名) the latter
后缀 hòuzhuì (名) suffix

糊 hū (动) plaster: 用灰把墙缝～上 plaster up cracks in the wall. ～一层泥 spread a layer of mud
see also hú; hù

乎 hū 1 (助) ‹书› [expressing doubt or conjuncture]: 有朋自远方来，不亦乐～? Is it not delightful to have friends coming from afar? 2 [verbal suffix]: 出～意料 exceed one's expectations;

come to one as a surprise. 超～寻常 be out of the ordinary run 3 [suffix of adjective or adverb]: 确～重要 very important indeed; of unmistakable importance. 迥～不同 entirely different

呼 hū (动) 1 breathe out; exhale 2 shout; cry out: ～口号 shout slogans 3 call: ～之即来 call one's name, and one will instantly appear; be at one's beck and call 4 〈象〉北风～～地吹. A north wind is shrieking.

呼喊 hūhǎn (动) call out; shout

呼号(號) hūháo (动) wail; cry out in distress: 奔走～ go about campaigning for a cause

呼号(號) hūhào (名) 1 call sign; call letters 2 catchword (of an organization)

呼唤 hūhuàn (动) call; shout to: 远处有人在～我们. Somebody is calling us in the distance.

呼叫 hūjiào (动) 1 call out; shout 2 call: ～信号 calling signal

呼救 hūjiù (动) call for help

呼噜 hūlu (动)〈口〉snore: 打～ snore

呼声(聲) hūshēng (名) cry; voice: 群众的～ the popular demand. 世界舆论的～ world opinion

呼吸 hūxī I (动) breathe: 出去～新鲜空气 go out for a breath of fresh air. ～困难breathe with difficulty II (名) respiration; breathing: 口对口～ mouth-to-mouth respiration. 人工～ artificial respiration. 他的～迟缓而困难. His breathing is laboured.

呼啸(嘯) hūxiào (动) whistle; scream: 歹徒～而遁. The hooligans broke up amidst loud shouts and screams.

呼应(應) hūyìng (动) echo; work in concert with: 遥相～ echo each other from afar

呼吁(籲) hūyù (动) appeal; call on: ～援助灾区难民 appeal for assistance to refugees from affected areas

忽 hū I (动) neglect; overlook; ignore II (副) suddenly: ～发奇想 have a brainwave

忽而 hū'ér (动) now ... now ... [often before similar constructive verbs or adjectives]: ～说～笑 talk and laugh by turns

忽略 hūlüè (动) neglect; overlook; lose sight of: 错误虽小,但不可～. The mistake may be small, but it should not be overlooked.

忽然 hūrán 〈副〉suddenly; all of a sudden

忽视 hūshì (动) ignore; overlook; neglect

壶(壺) hú (名) 1 kettle; pot: 水～ kettle. 茶～ teapot. 油～ oil can 2 bottle; flask: 暖～ thermos bottle (or flask)

胡 hú I (名) 1 non-Han nationalities living in the north and west in ancient times 2 introduced from the northern and western nationalities or from abroad: ～萝卜 carrot. ～椒 pepper II (副) recklessly; outrageously: ～闹 act outrageously. ～说 talk nonsense III (鬍)(名) moustache, beard or whiskers

胡话 húhuà (名) ravings; wild talk

胡搅(攪) hújiǎo (动) 1 pester sb.; annoy sb. with unreasonable demands 2 buttonhole sb. and argue one's case most unreasonably and incoherently: ～蛮缠 pester sb. endlessly

胡来(來) húlái (动) 1 mess things up 2 run wild; invite trouble

胡乱(亂) húluàn (副) carelessly; casually; at random: ～写了几行 scribble a few lines. ～猜测 make wild guesses

胡闹 húnào (动) act wilfully and make a scene.

胡琴 húqín (名) *huqin,* two-stringed

胡说 húshuō (动) 1 talk nonsense; drivel 2 nonsense: ～八道 sheer nonsense; rubbish

胡思乱(亂)想 húsī-luànxiǎng (动) give free rein to fancy

胡同 hútòng (名) lane; alley; *hutong*

胡须(鬚) húxū (名) beard, moustache or whiskers

胡言乱(亂)语 húyán-luànyǔ (动) talk arrant nonsense; rave

胡诌(謅) húzhōu (名) tall story; fabrication

胡子 húzi (名) beard, moustache or whiskers

胡作非为(爲) húzuò-fēiwéi (动) act in defiance of the law or public opinion; act wantonly

湖 hú (名) lake

湖滨(濱) húbīn (名) lakeside

湖泊 húpō (名) lakes

糊 hú I (名) paste II (动) stick with paste; paste: ～窗户 paste a sheet of paper over a lattice window. ～墙 paper a wall

see also hū; hù

糊涂(塗) hútu (形) muddle-headed; confused; bewildered: ～思想 muddled thinking 一时～ in a moment of aberration

蝴 hú

蝴蝶 húdié (名) butterfly

猢 hú

猢狲(猻) húsūn (名) a kind of monkey; macaque: 树倒～散. When a person falls from power, his fellowers scatter.

煳(餬) hú (名) mush

煳口 húkǒu (动) keep body and soul together; eke out a living; make ends meet

核 hú

see also hé

核儿 húr (名)〈口〉 1 stone; pit; core: 杏～ apricot stone. 梨～ pear core 2 sth. resembling a fruit stone: 煤～ partly burnt coals or briquets

囫 hú

囫囵(圇) húlún (形) whole: ～吞下 swallow sth. whole. ～吞枣 accept book knowledge without real understanding or analysis

鹄(鵠) hú (名) swan

鹄候 húhòu (动)〈书〉 await respectfully; expect: ～回音 I am looking forward to an early reply from you

鹄望 húwàng (动) eagerly look forward to

狐 hú (名) fox

狐臭 húchòu (名) body odour; bromhidrosis

狐假虎威 hú jiǎ hǔ wēi act outrageously on the strength of one's powerful connections

狐狸 húli (名) fox: 露出～尾巴 show a person's evil intentions; show the cloven hoof

狐媚 húmèi (动) bewitch by cajolery; entice by flattery

狐群狗党(黨) húqún-gǒudǎng (名) a pack of rogues; a gang of scoundrels

狐疑 húyí (名) doubt; suspicion: 满腹～ be full of misgivings; be very suspicious

弧 hú (名) arc

弧光 húguāng (名) arc light; arc: ～灯 arc lamp; arc light

弧形 húxíng (名) arc; curve

浒 hǔ (名) waterside

虎 hǔ I (名) tiger II (形) brave; vigorous: ～～有生气 be full of vigour

虎口 hǔkǒu (名) tiger's mouth—jaws of death: ～余生 escape from the clutches of the enemy

虎视眈眈 hǔ shì dāndān (动) glare like a tiger eyeing its prey; look with covetous eyes

虎头(頭)蛇尾 hǔtóu-shéwěi a fine start and poor finish

虎穴 hǔxué (名) tiger's den

琥 hǔ

琥珀 hǔpò (名) amber

唬 hǔ (动)〈口〉 bluff: 你别～人. Quit bluffing.

糊 hù (名) paste: 辣椒～ chilli paste. 玉米～ (cornmeal) mush

see also hū; hú

糊弄 hùnong (动) kid; deceive; hoodwink: 你别～我. Don't kid me.

户 hù (名) 1 door: 门～ door 2 household; family: 全村有好几百～. There are several hundred households in the village. 3 (bank) account: 存～ (bank) depositor

户籍 hùjí (名) 1 census register; household register 2 registered permanent residence

户口 hùkǒu (名) 1 number of households and total population 2 registered permanent residence: 迁～ report to the local authorities for change of domicile. 报～ register or apply for permanent residence. ～普查 census. ～登记本 household registraion book

户枢(樞)不蠹 hùshū bù dù a door-hinge is never worm-eaten

户头(頭) hùtóu (名) (bank) account: 开～ open an account

户主 hùzhǔ (名) head of a household

护(護) hù (动) 1 protect; guard; shield: ～航 escort; convoy 2 shield from censure: ～短 speak in defence

of what is wrong
护持 hùchí (动) shield and sustain
护短 hùduǎn (动) shield a shortcoming or fault; attempt to justify one's mistakes
护理 hùlǐ (动) nurse; tend: ～伤病员 nurse the sick and the wounded
护士 hùshi (名) (hospital) nurse
护送 hùsòng (动) escort; convoy
护养(養) hùyǎng (动) 1 cultivate; nurse; rear: ～秧苗 cultivate seedlings; nurse young plants 2 maintain: ～公路 maintain a highway
护照 hùzhào (名) passport: 外交～ diplomatic passport. 公务～ service passport

扈 hù (名) 〈书〉 retinue: ～从 retinue; retainer

怙 hù (动) 〈书〉 rely on

怙恶(惡)不悛 hù è bú quān persist in an iniquitous course and refuse to mend

互 hù (形) mutual; each other: ～通有无 exchange of needed goods. ～不干涉 mutual nc n nterference. ～不侵犯 mutual nonaggression
互访 hùfǎng (名) exchange visits
互惠 hùhuì (形) mutually beneficial; reciprocal: 平等～ equality and mutual benefit
互利 hùlì (形) mutually beneficial; of mutual benefit
互相 hùxiāng (副) mutual; mutually: ～排斥 be mutually exclusive. ～尊重 mutual respect. ～支持 mutual support. ～勾结 work in collusion
互助 hùzhù (动) help each other: ～合作 mutual aid and cooperation

化 huā (动) spend; expend: ～钱不少 spend a good deal money; cost a lot of money.
see also huà

花 huā I (名) 1 flower; blossom; bloom: ～盆 flower pot. 献～ floral tribute 2 anything resembling a flower: 火～ spark. 雪～ snowflakes. 3 fireworks: 放～ a show of fireworks 4 pattern; design: 白地蓝～ blue patterns on a white surface II (形) 1 multicoloured; coloured; variegated 2 (of eyes) blurred; dim 3 wounded: 挂～ get wounded in battle III (动) spend; expend: ～了不少钱 spend a lot of money. 很～时间 take a lot of time; be time-consuming
花白 huābái (形) (of hair) grey; grizzled: 头发～ with greying hair; grey-haired
花瓣 huābàn (名) petal
花边(邊) huābiān (名) 1 decorative border; floral border 2 lace 3 fancy borders in printing
花茶 huāchá (名) scented tea: 茉莉～ jasmine tea
花朵 huāduǒ (名) flower
花费 huāfèi (动) spend: ～心血 go to great pains
花费 huāfei (名) expenditure; expenses
花岗(崗)岩 huāgāngyán (名) granite
花好月圆 huāhǎo-yuèyuán (形) (as a congratulatory message for wedding in old days) the flowers are in bloom, and the moon is full — perfect conjugal felicity
花花公子 huāhuā gōngzǐ (名) dandy; coxcomb; fop; playboy
花花绿绿 huāhuālǜlǜ (形) brightly coloured
花花世界 huāhuā shìjiè (名) a community dazzling with a myriad temptations; vanity fair
花环(環) huāhuán (名) garland
花卉 huāhuì (名) 1 flowers and plants 2 traditional Chinese painting of flowers and plants
花甲 huājiǎ (名) a cycle of sixty years: 年逾～ over sixty years old
花篮(籃) huālán (名) a basket of flowers
花名册 huāmíngcè (名) register (of names); membership roster; muster roll
花木 huāmù (名) flowers and trees (in parks or gardens)
花鸟(鳥) huāniǎo (名) traditional Chinese painting of flowers and birds: ～画 flower-and-bird painting
花圃 huāpǔ (名) flower nursery
花腔 huāqiāng (名) florid ornamentation in Chinese opera singing; coloratura: ～女高音 coloratura soprano; coloratura 2 crafty talk: 耍～ talk craftily
花圈 huāquān (名) wreath: 献～ lay a wreath
花色 huāsè (名) 1 design and colour 2 (of merchandise) variety of designs, sizes, colours etc.: ～繁多 a great variety o

designs and colours

花哨 huāshuo (形) **1** garish; gaudy **2** no lack of variety

花生 huāshēng (名) peanut; groundnut

花饰(飾) huāshì (名) ornamental design

花束 huāshù (名) a bunch of flowers; bouquet

花天酒地 huātiān-jiǔdì wine, women and song; a dissipated life

花团(團)锦簇 huātuán-jǐncù rich multicoloured decorations

花纹 huāwén (名) decorative pattern; figure

花絮 huāxù (名) titbits (of news); sidelights

花言巧语 huāyán-qiǎoyǔ (名) fine and pleasant words

花样(樣) huāyàng (名) **1** kind; variety **2** trick: 玩~ play tricks. ~滑冰 figure skating

花园(園) huāyuán (名) flower garden; garden

花招 huāzhāo (名) **1** apparently skilful movement in *wushu* (武术); flourish **2** trick; game: 玩弄~ play tricks

花枝招展 huāzhī zhāozhǎn (形) (of women) be gaudily dressed

哗(嘩) huā 〈象〉: 铁门~的一声关上了. The iron gate was shut with a clang. 流水~~地响. The water was gurgling. see also huá

哗啦 huālā 〈象〉~一声墙倒了. The wall fell with a crash.

划(劃) huá (动) **1** paddle; row: ~船 paddle (or row) a boat; go boating **2** scratch; cut: ~火柴 strike a match. 手上~了一个口子 get a scratch on one's hand; cut one's hand **3** to one's profit; pay: 老实一点总~得来. It pays to be honest. see also huà

划拳 huáquán (动) finger-guessing game — a drinking game

划算 huásuàn (动) **1** calculate; weigh: ~来,~去 weigh the pros and cons **2** be to one's profit; pay

滑 huá I (形) **1** slippery; smooth: 又圆又~的小石子 smooth, round pebbles. 路面有雪~得很. The road is slippery with snow. **2** cunning; crafty; as slippery as an eel

滑冰 huábīng (名) skate; ice skating; skating: ~场 skating rink

滑稽 huáji (形) funny; farcical; comical

滑溜 huáliu (形)〈口〉smooth: 缎子被面摸着挺~. The satin quilt cover feels soft and smooth

滑轮(輪) huálún (名) pulley; block

滑腻 huánì (形) (of the skin) soft; velvety; creamy

滑头(頭) huátóu (名) **1** slippery fellow; sly old fox **2** foxy; sly; slick

滑翔 huáxiáng (动) glide: ~机 glider; sailplane

滑行 huáxíng (动) slide; coast: 飞机在跑道上~. The plane taxied along the runway.

滑雪 huáxuě (名) skiing: ~板 skis

华(華) huá I (形) **1** brilliant; magnificent; splendid: ~丽 magnificent; gorgeous **2** prosperous; flourishing: 繁~ flourishing; thriving II (名) **1** best part; cream: 精~ the cream; the essence **2** China: 来~正式访问 come to China on an official visit **3** flashy; extravagant: 奢~ extravagant; luxurious **4** grizzled; grey: ~发 grey hair

华而不实(實) huá ér bù shí showy and superficial

华贵 huáguì (形) luxurious; sumptuous; costly

华丽(麗) huálì (形) magnificent; resplendent; gorgeous: 服饰~ gaudily dressed. ~的词藻 florid language; ornate style

华侨(僑) huáqiáo (名) overseas Chinese

华夏 huáxià (名) an ancient name for China

华裔 huáyì (名) a person of Chinese descent

哗(嘩) huá (形) noise; clamour: 寂静无~ silent and still; very quiet see also huā

哗变(變) huábiàn (名) mutiny

哗然 huárán (副) in an uproar; in commotion: 舆论~. There was a public clamour.

哗众(衆)取宠(寵) huá zhòng qǔ chǒng win transient popularity with claptrap; play to the gallery

铧(鏵) huá (名) ploughshare: 双~犁 double-shared plough; double-furrow plough

话 huà I (名) word; remark: 说几句~ say a few words;

make a few remarks II (动) talk about; speak about: ～家常 engage in chitchat

话别 huàbié (动) talk with a friend on the eve of his departure; say good-bye; bid farewell

话柄 huàbǐng (名) subject for ridicule

话锋 huàfēng (名) course of conversation: 把～一转 switch to another topic

话剧(劇) huàjù (名) modern drama; stage play

话题 huàtí (名) theme of conversation

话筒 huàtǒng (名) 1 microphone 2 telephone transmitter 3 megaphone

画(畫) huà I (动) draw; paint: ～画 draw a picture. ～饼充饥 draw cakes to stay hunger — indulge in self-delusion. ～一张草图 make a sketch II (名) drawing; painting; picture: 年～ New Year picture. 油～ oil painting III (形) be decorated with paintings or pictures: ～栋雕梁 painted pillars and carved beams (of a magnificent building)

画报(報) huàbào (名) illustrated magazine or newspaper; pictorial

画册 huàcè (名) album

画家 huàjiā (名) painter; artist

画卷 huàjuǎn (名) picture scroll

画廊 huàláng (名) 1 painted corridor 2 (picture) gallery

画龙(龍)点(點)睛 huà lóng diǎn jīng put the finishing touches to a piece of writing

画面 huàmiàn (名) 1 general appearance of a picture; tableau 2 frame

画蛇添足 hàu shé tiān zú draw a snake and add feet to it — spoil the show by doing sth. quite superfluous

画室 huàshì (名) an artist's studio

画图(圖) huàtú I (动) draw designs, maps, etc. II (名) picture

画像 huàxiàng I (动) draw a portrait; portray: II (名) portrait; portrayal: 巨幅～ huge portrait. 自～ self-portrait

画展 huàzhǎn (名) art exhibition; exhibition of paintings

划(劃) huà I (动) 1 delimit; differentiate: ～界 delimit a boundary 2 appropriate; assign: ～款 appropriate a sum of money 3 plan: ～策 mastermind; instigate II (名) stroke (of a Chinese character)
see also huá

划拨(撥) huàbō (动) transfer; appropriate

划分 huàfēn (动) 1 divide: ～成小组 divide into groups 2 differentiate: ～两种不同类型的错误 differentiate the two different types of errors

划清 huàqīng (动) draw a clear line of demarcation; make a clear distinction

划时(時)代 huàshídài (形) epoch-making: 具有～的意义 have epoch-making significance

划一 huàyī (形) standardized; uniform

化 huà I (动) 1 change; turn; transform: ～险为夷 turn danger into safety. ～害为利 turn harm into good; turn a disadvantage into an advantage 2 melt; dissolve: 用水～开 dissolve in water 3 digest; get rid of: ～痰 reduce phlegm 4 burn up: 火～ cremate II [added to an adjective or noun to form a verb] -ize; -ify: 机械～ mechanize. 工业～ industrialize. 现代～ modernize. 知识～和专业～ become more educated and more competent
see also huā

化肥 huàféi (名) chemical fertilizer

化合 huàhé (名) chemical combination: ～物 chemical compound

化名 huàmíng (名) an assumed name; pseudonym

化脓(膿) huànóng (动) fester; suppurate: 伤口～了. The wound is festering.

化身 huàshēng (名) incarnation; embodiment: 正义的～ the embodiment of justice

化石 huàshí (名) fossil

化为乌(烏)有 huà wéi wūyǒu vanish completely; come to naught

化纤(纖) huàxiān (名) chemical fibre

化学(學) huàxué (名) chemistry 应用～ applied chemistry. 理论～ theoretical chemistry. ～成分 chemical composition. ～反应 chemical reaction

化验(驗) huàyàn (名) chemical examination; laboratory test ～单 laboratory test report. ～室 laboratory

化妆(妝) huàzhuāng (动) put on make-up; make up: ～品 cosmetics

化装(裝) huàzhuāng (动) 1 (of actors) make up 2 disguise oneself: ～跳舞会 masquerade

怀(懷) huái I (名) 1 bosom: 她把孩子搂在～里. She held the child in her arms. 2 mind: 襟～坦白 frank and straitforward II (动) 1 keep in mind; cherish: 少～大志 begin to cherish lofty aspirations in his youth. 不～好意 harbour evil intentions 2 think of; yearn for: ～友 think about a friend 3 conceive (a child): ～了孩子 be expecting a baby

怀抱 huáibào I (名) 1 bosom: 回到祖国的～ return to one's homeland II (动) cherish: ～着全心全意为人民服务的理想 cherish the idea of serving the people whole-heartedly

怀恨 huáihèn (动) cherish hatred; bear ill will; nurse grievances

怀旧(舊) huáijiù (动) miss old times or old friends

怀念 huáiniàn (动) cherish the memory of: ～故乡 think of one's hometown with nostalgic longing

怀疑 huáiyí (动、名) doubt; suspect: 引起～ arouse suspicion. 我～他今天来不了. I have a hunch that he won't be able to come today.

怀孕 huáiyùn (动) be pregnant; conceived: ～期 period of pregnancy

槐 huái (名) Chinese scholartree; locust tree

踝 huái (名) ankle: ～骨 anklebone

坏(壞) huài I (形) bad: 不～ not bad. ～人～事 evildoers and evil deeds II (动) go bad; spoil; ruin: 鱼～了. The fish has gone bad. III (副) badly; awfully; very: 吓～了 be badly scared. 累～了 dog-tired. 渴～了 parched IV (名) evil idea; dirty trick: 使～ play a dirty trick

坏处(處) huàichu (名) harm; disadvantage: 这对你没有～. It won't do you any harm.

坏蛋 huàidàn (名)〈口〉bad egg; scoundrel; bastard

坏话 huàihuà (名) malicious remarks; unpleasant words; vicious talk: 讲别人～ speak ill of others

坏事 huàishì (名) 1 bad thing; evil deed 2 ruin sth.; make things worse: 急躁只能～. Impetuosity will only make things worse.

欢(歡) huān (副) 1 joyfully; merrily: ～呼 shout joyfully; cheer. ～唱 sing merrily. ～声雷动 There was a burst of thunderous applause. 2 cheerfully; with a vengeance; in full swing: 雨下得正～. The rain is coming down with a vengeance.

欢畅(暢) huānchàng (形) have a wonderful time; thoroughly enjoy oneself

欢度 huāndù (动) spend (an occasion) joyfully: ～佳节 celebrate a festival with jubilation

欢聚 huānjù (动) happily gather: ～一堂 be gathered here

欢快 huānkuài (形) cheerful; light; lively: ～的乐曲 light music; a lively melody

欢乐(樂) huānlè (形) happy and gay; merry: ～的心情 (in) a merry mood

欢庆(慶) huānqìng (动) celebrate with jubilation

欢送 huānsòng (动) send off (usually referring to a collective affair): ～会 farewell party; send-off meeting.

欢腾 huānténg (名) great rejoicing; jubilation

欢天喜地 huāntiān-xǐdì wild with joy; overjoyed: ～迎新年 greet the New Year with boundless joy

欢喜 huānxǐ I (形) joyful; happy; delighted: 满心～ be overjoyed II (动) like; be fond of; delight in: 她～弹钢琴. She likes to play the piano.

欢心 huānxīn (名) favour; liking; love: 博取～ curry someone's favour

欢欣 huānxīn (形) joyous; elated: ～鼓舞 feel greatly encouraged; be elated

欢迎 huānyíng (动) welcome; greet: ～贵宾 welcome distinguished guests. 这部小说深受读者～. This novel is well received. ～词 welcoming speech; address of welcome

还(還) huán (动) 1 go (or come) back: ～家 return home. 2 give back; return; repay: 到期要～的书 a book due for return. ～债 repay a debt. ～嘴 talk back; re-

tort 3 give or do sth. in return: ～礼 send a present in return; return a salute
see also hái
还本 huánběn (名) repayment of principal (or capital): ～付息 repay capital with interest
还击(擊) huánjī (动) fight back; return fire; counterattack: 自卫～ fight back in self-defence
还价(價) huánjià (动) counter-offer; counter-bid: 讨价～ bargain; haggle
还俗 huánsú (of Buddhist monks and nuns or Taoist priests) resume secular life; secularize
还原 huányuán (动) (of things) be restored to the original state or shape
环(環) huán I (名) 1 ring; hoop: 光～ halo. 耳～ earring 2 link: 最薄弱的一～ the weakest link II (动) surround; encircle; hem in: 四面～山 be surrounded on all sides by mountains
环抱 huánbào (动) surround; encircle; hem in
环顾(顧) huángù (动) ‹书› look about (or round); look all round
环节(節) huánjié (名) 1 link: 主要～ a key link 2 segment
环境 huánjìng (名) environment; surroundings; circumstances: 换换～ go elsewhere for a change. 如～许可 if circumstances permit. ～保护 environmental protection. ～污染 pollution (of the environment)
环球 huánqiú (名) 1 round the world: ～旅行 transglobe expedition; a round-the-world tour 2 the earth; the whole world
环绕(繞) huánrǎo (动) surround; encircle; revolve around: 地球～太阳旋转. The earth revolves round the sun.
环视 huánshì (动) look around
环行 huánxíng (动) going in a ring: ～一周 make a circuit. ～公路 ring road; belt highway
缓 huǎn I (形) slow; unhurried: ～流 flow slowly. ～步 walk in a leisurely way; walk at a relaxed pace II (动) 1 delay; postpone; put off: ～兵之计 play stalling tactics 2 recuperate; revive; come to: 过了好一阵他才～过来. It was a long time before he came to.
缓冲(衝) huǎnchōng (名) buffer; cushion: ～地带 buffer zone. ～国 buffer state
缓和 huǎnhé I (动) 1 relax; ease up; mitigate; alleviate: ～紧张局势 relax the tension 2 calm down: 那个激动的青年人逐渐～下来了. The excited young man gradually calmed down. II (名) détente
缓急 huǎnjí (名) greater or lesser urgency: 分别轻重～加以处理 handle matters in the order of importance and urgency
缓慢 huǎnmàn (形) slow: 行动～ slow to act. 进展～make slow progress; proceed at a snail's pace
缓期 huǎnqī (动) postpone a deadline; suspend: ～付款 delay (or defer) payment
缓刑 huǎnxíng (名) suspended sentence; reprieve
浣 huàn (动) ‹书› wash: ～衣 wash clothes
宦 huàn (名) 1 official 2 eunuch
宦官 huànguān (名) eunuch
宦海 huànhǎi (名) officialdom; official circles: ～升沉 political ups and downs
宦途 huàntú (名) career as a government official
患 huàn I (名) 1 trouble; peril; disaster: 防～于未然 take preventive measures; provide against a rainy day 2 anxiety; worry: 何～之有. There's no cause for anxiety. II (动) contract; suffer from: ～病 suffer from an illness; fall ill; be ill
患得患失 huàndé-huànshī worry about personal loss; be swayed by considerations of gain or loss
患难(難) huànnàn (名) trials and tribulations; adversity; trouble: ～之交 a friend in need; a rough-weather friend. ～与共 go through thick and thin together; share weal and woe
涣 huàn (动) melt; vanish
涣然 huànrán (动) melt away; disappear; vanish
涣散 huànsàn (形) lax; slack: 纪律～ be lax in discipline. ～斗志 sap sb.'s morale; demoralize
焕 huàn (形) shining; glowing
焕发(發) huànfā (动) shine; glow; irradiate: 精神～ be full of vim and vigour
焕然一新 huànrán yī xīn take on an entirely new look

换 huàn (动) 1 exchange; barter; trade: ～货 exchange goods; barter 2 change: ～衣服 change one's clothes. ～车 change buses (trains)
换班 huànbān (动) 1 change shifts 2 relieve a person on duty
换季 huànjì (动) change garments for a new season
换取 huànqǔ (动) give sth. in exchange for; get in return
换算 huànsuàn (名) conversion: ～表 conversion table
换汤(湯)不换药(藥) huàn tāng bù huàn yào offer the same old stuff but with a different label
换文 huànwén (名) exchange of notes (or letters)

唤 huàn (动) call out: 呼～ call; shout
唤起 huànqǐ (动) 1 arouse: ～民众 arouse the masses of the people 2 call; attract: ～人们的注意 attract people's attention
唤醒 huànxǐng (动) wake up; awaken

幻 huàn I (形) unreal; imaginary; illusory: 虚～ unreal; illusory; imaginary II (动) undergo a surprising change: 变～莫测 change unpredictably
幻灯(燈) huàndēng (名) slide show: 放～ show slides. ～机 slide projector
幻境 huànjìng (名) dreamland; fairyland
幻觉(覺) huànjué (名) illusion; hallucination
幻灭(滅) huànmiè (动) melt into thin air
幻术(術) huànshù (名) magic; conjuring art
幻想 huànxiǎng (名) illusion; figment of one's imagination: 不抱～ have no illusions
幻象 huànxiàng (名) optical illusion; phantom; phantasm

荒 huāng I (形) 1 waste: 地～了. The land lies uncultivated. 2 desolate; barren: ～岛 desert (or uninhabited) island. ～山 barren hill II (动) neglect; be out of practice: 别把学业～了. Don't neglect your studies. III (名) 1 wasteland; uncultivated land: 垦～ open up (or reclaim) wasteland 2 shortage; scarcity: 房～ housing shortage. 3 famine; crop failure: 储粮备～ store up grain against famine
荒诞 huāngdàn (形) preposterous; absurd; ludicrous: ～的想法 a fantastic idea
荒地 huāngdì (名) wasteland; uncultivated (or undeveloped) land
荒废(廢) huāngfèi (动) 1 leave uncultivated; lie waste 2 waste: ～时间 waste time 3 (of studies, lessons, etc.) neglect; be out of practice
荒凉 huāngliáng (形) bleak and desolate; wild: 一片～ a scene of desolation
荒谬 huāngmiù (形) absurd; preposterous: ～的论点 a preposterous proposition
荒漠 huāngmò (名) desert; wilderness
荒年 huāngnián (名) famine (or lean) year
荒僻 huāngpì (形) desolate and out-of-the-way
荒疏 huāngshū (形) rusty: 他的古典文学有点～了. He is a bit rusty on classical literature.
荒唐 huāngtáng (形) absurd; fantastic; preposterous: ～可笑 ridiculous; absurd
荒芜(蕪) huāngwú (形) lie waste; overgrown with weeds
荒淫 huāngyín (形) debauched: ～无耻 dissipated and unashamed; given to debauchery

慌 huāng (形) nervous; scared: 不要～! Don't panic! ～了神 be scared out of one's wits. ～了手脚 be scared and not know what to do; be flustered
慌乱(亂) huāngluàn (副) flurried; in a hurry
慌忙 huāngmáng (副) in a great rush; in a flurry; hurriedly
慌张(張) huāngzhāng (形) flurried; flustered; confused: 神色～ be in a fluster

黄 huáng I (形) yellow; sallow II (名) short for the Yellow River: 治～ harness the Yellow River
黄道吉日 huángdào jírì (名) propitious (or auspicious) date; lucky day
黄澄澄 huángdēngdēng (形) golden: ～的麦穗儿 golden ears of wheat
黄豆 huángdòu (名) soya bean; soybean
黄瓜 huángguā (名) cucumber
黄花鱼(魚) huánghuāyú (名) yellow croaker

黄昏 huánghūn (名) dusk
黄金 huángjīn (名) gold: ～储备 gold reserve. ～时代 golden age
黄酒 huángjiǔ (名) yellow rice wine
黄粱美梦(夢) huángliáng měimèng pipe dream; a fool's paradise
黄牛 huángniú (名) ox
黄色 huángsè (名) 1 yellow 2 decadent; obscene; pornographic: ～电影 pornographic movie; sex film
黄铜 huángtóng (名) brass
黄土 huángtǔ (名) loess: ～高原 loess plateau
黄油 huángyóu (名) 1 butter 2 lubricating grease (or oil)
黄种(種) huángzhǒng (名) the yellow race

磺 huáng (名) sulphur
磺胺 huáng'àn (名) sulphanilamide (SN)

簧 huáng (名) 1 reed: ～乐器 reed instrument 2 spring: 弹～称 spring balance

皇 huáng (名) emperor; sovereign: 女～ empress
皇帝 huángdì (名) emperor
皇宫 huánggōng (名) (imperial) palace
皇后 huánghòu (名) empress
皇室 huángshì (名) imperial family (or house)
皇太子 huángtàizǐ (名) crown prince

惶 huáng (名) fear; anxiety: ～悚 sudden fear; fright
惶惶 huánghuáng (副) alarmed: ～不可终日 get scared and fidgety all day; be on tenterhooks
惶惑 huánghuò (形) perplexed
惶恐 huángkǒng (形) terrified; frightened

煌 huáng (形) bright; brilliant: 明星～～. The stars are bright.

蝗 huáng (名) locust: ～灾 plague of locusts
蝗虫(蟲) huángchóng (名) locust

谎 huǎng (名) lie; falsehood
谎话 huǎnghuà (名) lie; falsehood: 说～ tell a lie; lie
谎言 huǎngyán (名) lie; falsehood

恍 huǎng (副) 1 suddenly 2 [used in combination with "如","若"] seem; as if: ～如梦境 (all this happened) as if in a dream
恍惚 huǎnghū (形、副) 1 in a trance; absent-minded: 精神～ be absent-minded 2 dimly; faintly; seemingly: ～记得 have a hazy notion
恍然大悟 huǎngrán dàwù suddenly realize; suddenly see the light

晃 huǎng (动) 1 shine bright 2 flash past
see also huàng

幌 huǎng
幌子 huǎngzi (名) 1 shop sign; signboard 2 pretence; pretext; façade

晃 huàng (动) sway; rock
see also huǎng
晃荡(蕩) huàngdàng (动) rock; shake; sway: 小船在水里直～. The small boat rocked to and fro on the water.
晃动(動) huàngdòng (动) rock; sway: 别～桌子. Don't wobble the desk.
晃悠 huàngyou (动) shake from side to side; hobble; stagger: 他晃晃悠悠往前走. He was hobbling along.

麾 huī I (名) standard of a commander [used in ancient times] II (动) despatch: ～军前进 order an army to push ahead

挥 huī (动) 1 wave; wield: ～手 wave one's hand. 2 wipe off: ～泪 wipe one's eyes 3 despatch (an army) 4 scatter; disperse: ～金如土 squander money; play ducks and drakes with money
挥动(動) huīdòng (动) brandish; wave: ～大棒 brandish a big stick. ～拳头 shake one's fist
挥发(發) huīfā (动) volatilize
挥霍 huīhuò (动) spend freely; squander: ～无度 spend one's money recklessly
挥手 huīshǒu (动) wave one's hand; wave: ～告别 wave farewell; wave good-bye to sb.
挥舞 huīwǔ (动) wave; wield; brandish: ～花束表示欢迎 wave bouquets in welcome

辉 huī I (名) brightness; splendour II (动) shine
辉煌 huīhuáng (形) brilliant; splendid; glorious: 灯火～ brilliantly illuminated; ablaze with lights
辉映 huīyìng (动) shine; reflect: 灯光月色,交相～. The lanterns and the moon vied with each other for radiance.

晖 huī (名) sunshine; sunlight

灰 huī I (名) 1 ash: 炉～ ashes from a stove 2 dust: 积了厚厚的一层～ accumulate a thick layer of dust 3 lime; (lime) mortar: ～墙 plastered wall II (形) 1 grey: ～马 a grey horse 2 discouraged; 心～意懒 disillusioned

灰暗 huī'àn (形) murky grey; gloomy: ～的天空 a gloomy (or overcast) sky

灰白 huībái (形) greyish white; ashen; pale: 脸色～ look pale

灰尘(塵) huīchén (名) dust; dirt: 掸掉桌上的～ dust the table

灰浆(漿) huījiāng (名) mortar

灰烬(燼) huījìn (名) ashes: 化为～ be reduced to ashes

灰溜溜 huīliūliū (形) gloomy; dejected; crestfallen: 他看起来有点～的样子. He looked a little depressed.

灰蒙蒙 huīmēngmēng (形) dusky; gloomy; misty

灰色 huīsè (形) 1 grey; ashy 2 pessimistic; gloomy

灰心 huīxīn (动) lose heart; be discouraged; be disappointed

恢 huī (形) extensive; vast

恢复(復) huīfù (动) 1 resume; renew; regain: ～邦交 resume diplomatic relations. ～青春 regain youthful vigour 2 recover; regain: ～健康 recover one's health 3 restore; reinstate; rehabilitate: ～名誉 (of a person's reputation) rehabilitate. ～秩序 restore order. ～期 convalescence

恢恢 huīhuī (形)〈书〉extensive; vast; 天网～ justice has long arms

诙 huī

诙谐 huīxié (形) humorous; jocular

徽 huī (名) emblem; badge; insignia: 国～ national emblem. 校～ school badge. 帽～ cap insignia

徽号(號) huīhào (名) title of honour

徽章 huīzhāng (名) badge; insignia

隳 huī (动)〈书〉destroy; ruin

回 huí I (动) 1 return; go back: ～家 return home. ～乡 return to one's home village. 放～原处 put back where it was 2 turn round: ～过身来 turn round 3 answer; reply: ～信 send one a reply; write back II (量) 1 chapter: 这部小说共一百二十～. This novel contains 120 chapters. 2 [used to indicate frequency of action]: 来过一～ have been here once

回报(報) huíbào (动) 1 report back 2 repay; requite; reciprocate: ～他的盛情 repay him for his hospitality or kindness 3 retaliate; pay sth. in his own coin

回避 huíbì (动) evade; dodge; avoid (meeting sb.): ～要害问题 evade the crucial issue

回春 huíchūn (动) 1 return of spring: 大地～. Spring returns to the earth. 2 bring back to life: ～灵药 a miraculous cure; a wonderful remedy

回答 huídá (动) answer; reply; response

回荡(蕩) huídàng (动) resound; reverberate

回访 huífǎng (动) pay a return call

回复(復) huífù (动) reply (to a letter)

回顾(顧) huígù (动) look back; review: ～过去 look back on the past

回光返照 huíguāng fǎnzhào 1 the momentary recovery of a dying person 2 a sudden spurt of activity prior to collapse

回归(歸)线(綫) huíguīxiàn (名) the Tropic of Capricorn or Cancer

回合 huíhé (名) round; bout: 第一个～的胜利 a first-round victory

回话 huíhuà (名) reply; answer

回击(擊) huíjī (动) fight back; return fire; counterattack

回见(見) huíjiàn (动)〈套〉see you later (or again); cheerio

回教 Huíjiào (名) Islam

回敬 huíjìng (动) return a compliment; do or give sth. in return

回绝 huíjué (动) decline; refuse: 一口～ flatly refuse

回来(來) huílai (动) return; come back; be back: 他就～. He'll be back in a minute.

回笼(籠) huílóng (动) 1 steam again 2 withdraw surplus money from circulation

回民 Huímín (名) the Huis; the Hui people

回去 huíqu (动) return; go back; be back

回去 huíqu [used after a verb to indicate returning to where sth. came from]: 请把这封信给他退～. Please return the l tter to him.

回升 huíshēng (动) rise again (after a fall); pick up: 贸易～. Trade is picking up again. 气温～. The temperature has gone up again.

回声(聲) huíshēng (名) echo

回收 huíshōu (动) collect; recycle

回首 huíshǒu (动) 1 turn one's head; turn round 2 〈书〉 look back upon; recollect

回溯 huísù (动) recall; look back upon: ～过去,瞻望未来 recall the past and look ahead

回头(頭) huítóu (动) 1 turn one's head; turn round 2 repent: 浪子～ return of the prodigal son. 现在～还不算晚. It's not too late to repent. ～是岸. Repentance is salvation. 3 〈口〉 later: ～再谈. We'll disscuss it later. ～见! See you later! Bye now!

回味 huíwèi (动) 1 aftertaste 2 call sth. to mind and ponder over it: ～他刚看过的电影 ponder over what he saw in the film

回响(響) huíxiǎng (动) reverberate; echo; resound: 歌声在山谷中激起了～. The valley echoed with the sound of singing.

回想 huíxiǎng (动) think back; recollect; recall

回心转(轉)意 huíxīn-zhuǎnyì come around to the correct way of thinking

回信 huíxìn I (动) write in reply; write back: 望早日～. I look forward to hearing from you soon. II (名) 1 a reply 2 a verbal message in reply; reply

回旋 huíxuán (动) 1 circle round: 飞机在上空～. The aeroplane is circling overhead. 2 manoeuvre: 还有～余地. There is still room for manoeuvre.

回忆(憶) huíyì (动) call to mind; recollect; recall: ～录 reminiscences; memoirs; recollections

回音 huíyīn (名) 1 echo 2 reply: 立候～ await an early reply

洄

huí 〈书〉 (of water) whirl

洄游 huíyóu (名) migration of fish

茴

huí

茴香 huíxiāng (名) fennel: ～油 fennel oil

蛔

huí

蛔虫(蟲) huíchóng (名) roundworm

悔

huǐ (动) regret; repent: ～不当初 regret not having pursued a different course. ～改 repent and mend one's ways

悔过(過) huǐguò (动) repent one's error; be repentant: ～自新 repent and turn over a new leaf

悔恨 huǐhèn (动) deeply regret; be filled with remorse

悔悟 huǐwù (动) realize one's error and bitterly regret it

悔罪 huǐzuì (动) show penitence

毁

huǐ (动) 1 destroy; ruin; damage 2 burn up: 焚～ destroy by fire; burn down 3 defame; slander: 诋～ vilify; slander

毁谤 huǐbàng (动) slander; malign; calumniate

毁坏(壞) huǐhuài (动) destroy; damage: ～庄稼 damage the crops

毁灭(滅) huǐmiè (动) destroy; exterminate; wipe out

毁损 huǐsǔn (名) damage; impair

毁誉(譽) huǐ-yù (名) praise or blame; praise or censure: 不计～ regardless of praise or censure

汇(滙)

huì I (动) 1 converge: 百川所～ where a hundred streams converge 2 gather together: ～印成书 collect relevant articles and have them published in book form 3 remit: ～款 remit money. 电～ telegraphic transfer II (名) things collected; assemblage; collection: 词～ vocabulary; lexical items

汇报(報) huìbào (动) report; give an account of: ～工作 report to sb. on one's work

汇编 huìbiān (名) compilation; collection; corpus: 资料～工作 compilation of reference material. 文件～ a collection of documents

汇合 huìhé (动) converge; join; flow together: 这两条河在什么地方～? Where do the two rivers converge?

汇集 huìjí (动) 1 collect; compile: ～材料 collect all relevant data 2 come together; converge; assemble

汇款 huìkuǎn (动、名) 1 remit

money; make a remittance 2 remittance. 收到一笔～ receive a remittance. ～单 money order

汇率 huìlǜ (名) exchange rate: 固定～ fixed (exchange) rate. 浮动～ floating (exchange) rate

汇票 huìpiào (名) draft; bill of exchange; money order: 银行～ bank draft. 邮政～ postal money order

汇总(總) huìzǒng (动) gather; collect; pool: 把材料～上报 submit the collected data to the leadership

讳(諱) huì I (动) avoid as taboo: ～莫如深 refuse to breathe a word about the matter. 隐～ cover up. 直言不～ speak bluntly; call a spade a spade II (名) forbidden word; taboo

讳疾忌医(醫) huìjí-jìyī seek no medical advice lest one should be known as a victim of disease — conceal one's fault for fear of criticism

讳言 huìyán (动) dare not or would not speak up: 毫不～ make no bones about telling the truth

彗 huì (名)〈书〉 broom

彗星 huìxīng (名) comet

慧 huì (形) intelligent; bright: 智～ wisdom; intelligence

慧眼 huìyǎn (名) 1 a mind which perceives both past and future 2 mental discernment (or perception); insight

卉 huì (名) (various kinds of) grass: 奇花异～ rare flowers and plants

惠 huì (名) favour; kindness; benefit: 受～ receive kindness (or favour); be favoured. 互～ mutual benefit

惠存 huìcún 〈敬〉 please keep (this photograph, book, etc. as a souvenir); presented to so-and-so

惠临(臨) huìlín 〈敬〉 your gracious presence: 敬请～. Your presence is requested.

喙 huì (名) 1 beak or snout 2 mouth: 不容置～ admit of no intervention

秽(穢) huì (形) 1 dirty: 污～ filthy. ～土 dirt; refuse 2 ugly; abominable: ～行 abominable behaviour; immoral conduct

贿 huì (动) bribe: 受～ accept (or take) bribes

贿赂 huìlù (名) 1 bribe 2 bribery

会(會) huì I (动) 1 get together; assemble: 下午在校门口～齐. We'll assemble at the school gate this afternoon. 2 meet; see: 上星期你～着他没有? Did you meet him last week? II (名) 1 meeting; gathering; party; get-together; conference: 欢迎～ welcoming party. 年～ annual meeting (or convention) 2 association; society; union: 帮～ secret society. 工～ trade union. ～址 the site of an association or society 3 chief city; capital: 都～ city; metropolis. 省～ provincial capital 4 moment; an opportune moment: 机～ opportunity. 适逢其～ happen to be present on the occasion at the right moment

会(會) huì (动) 1 understand; grasp: 误～ misunderstand 2 can; be able to: ～使筷子 can use chopsticks. ～英语 know English 3 be likely to; be sure to: 他不～不来. He is sure to come. 4 be good at; be skilful in: 能说～道 have a smooth tongue. 我不太～下棋. I am not very good at chess.

see also kuài

会餐 huìcān (动) dine together among friends or colleagues; have a dinner party (usually sponsored by an organization)

会场(場) huìchǎng (名) meeting-place; conference (or assembly) hall

会费 huìfèi (名) membership dues

会合 huìhé (动) join forces; meet; converge; assemble

会话 huìhuà (名) conversation (as in a language course)

会见(見) huìjiàn (动) meet with

会客 huìkè (动) receive a visitor (or guest): ～时间 visiting hours. ～室 reception room

会面 huìmiàn (动) meet; come together

会儿 huìr 〈口〉 moment: 一～ little while. 等～. Wait a moment. 我去一～就回来. I won't be long.

会商 huìshāng (动) hold a conference or consultation

会师(師) huìshī (动) join forces

会谈 huìtán (动) talks: 双边～ bilateral talks. 最高级～ summit meeting. ～纪要 minutes of talks;

summary of a conversation
会堂 huìtáng (名) assembly hall; hall: 人民大～ the Great Hall of the People
会同 huìtóng (动) (handle an affair) jointly: ～有关部门办理 handle the matter jointly with other organizations concerned
会晤 huìwù (动) meet: 两国外长定期～. The foreign ministers of the two countries meet regularly.
会心 huìxīn (形) understanding; knowing: ～的微笑 a knowing smile
会演 huìyǎn (名) joint performence (by a number of theatrical troupes, etc.): 文艺～ theatrical festival
会议(議) huìyì (名) meeting; conference: 全体～ plenary session
会员 huìyuán (名) member: 正式～ full (or full-fledged) member. ～人数 membership. ～国 member state (or nation). ～证 membership card. ～资格 the status of a member; membership; credentials
会诊 huìzhěn (名) consultation of doctors; (group) consultation
烩(燴) huì (动) 1 braise: ～虾仁 braised shrimp meat 2 cook (rice or shredded pancakes) with meat, vegetables and water
荟(薈) huì (名)〈书〉 luxuriant growth (of plants)
荟萃 huìcuì (动)(of distinguished people) gather together; assemble: 人才～ a galaxy of talent
绘(繪) huì (动) paint; draw
绘画(畫) huìhuà (名) drawing; painting
绘声(聲)绘色 huìshēng-huìsè (形) vivid; lively: ～的描述 a vivid description
绘制 huìzhì (动) draw (a design, plan or blueprint, etc.)
诲 huì (动) teach; instruct: ～人不倦 teach with tireless zeal. ～淫～盗 propagate sex and violence
晦 huì (形) dark; obscure; gloomy
晦气(氣) huìqì (形) unlucky: 自认～ be resigned to one's bad luck
晦涩 huìsè (形) hard to understand; obscure: ～的语言 obscure language (in poetry, drama, etc.)
荤 hūn (名) meat or fish: ～菜 meat dishes. ～油 lard. 她不吃～. She's a vegetarian.
昏 hūn I (名) dusk: 晨～ at dawn and dusk II (形) 1 dark; dim 2 confused; muddled: 利令智～ be blinded by lust for gain III (动) lose consciousness; faint: ～迷 in a coma. ～倒 fall down in a faint; fall unconscious
昏暗 hūn'àn (形) dim; dusky: ～的灯光 a dim light
昏沉 hūnchén (形) 1 murky: 暮色～ dusk falls after sunset 2 dazed; befuddled: 头脑～ feel in a daze
昏花 hūnhuā (形) blurred; dim-sighted: 老眼～ dim-sighted from old age
昏黄 hūnhuáng (形) yellow; faint; dim: 月色～ faint moonlight. ～的灯光 a dim light
昏厥 hūnjué (动) faint; swoon: ～过去 fall into a coma; faint away
昏聩 hūnkuì (形) decrepit and muddleheaded
昏乱(亂) hūnluàn (形) dazed and confused; befuddled
昏迷 hūnmí (名) stupor; coma: 处于～状态be in a state of unconsciousness; be in a coma. ～不醒 remain unconscious
昏睡 hūnshuì (名) a deep slumber; lethargy
昏天黑地 hūntiān-hēidì (形) 1 pitch-dark 2 dizzy: 我觉得～. I suddenly felt everything went black. 3 decadent: ～的生活 a dissipated life
昏眩 hūnxuàn (形) dizzy; giddy
昏庸 hūnyōng (动) fatuous; muddleheaded; imbecile; stupid
阍 hūn I (动)〈书〉 tend or guard a gate: 司～ gatekeeper; janitor II (名) palace gate
婚 hūn (动、名) 1 wed; marry 2 marriage; wedding
婚配 hūnpèi (动) marry: 他们尚未～. They are not married yet.
婚礼(禮) hūnlǐ (名) wedding ceremony; wedding
婚事 hūnshì (名) marriage; wedding
婚姻 hūnyīn (名) marriage; matrimony: ～自由 freedom of marriage. 美满的～a happy marriage; conjugal felicity. ～法 marriage law. ～介绍所 marriage brokering centre; match-making

centre

婚约 hūnyuē (名) marriage contract; engagement: 解除～ break off one's engagement

浑(渾) hún (形) 1 muddy; turbid: ～水 muddy water 2 foolish; stupid 3 simple and natural; unsophisticated 4 whole; all over

浑蛋 húndàn (名) blackguard; wretch; scoundrel; bastard; skunk

浑厚 húnhòu (形) 1 simple and honest 2 (of writing, painting, etc.) simple and vigorous; (of handwriting) bold and vigorous

浑浑噩噩 húnhún'è'è (形) ignorant; muddleheaded

浑然一体(體) húnrán yī tǐ (名) an integral entity

浑身 húnshēn (副) from head to foot; all over: 吓得～发抖 tremble all over with fear. ～湿透 be wet through. ～是劲 bursting with energy

浑水摸鱼 húnshuǐ mō yú fish in troubled waters

浑浊(濁) húnzhuó (形) muddy; turbid

魂 hún (名) 1 soul 2 mood; spirit: 神～不定 feel distracted 3 the lofty spirit of a nation

魂不附体(體) hún bù fù tǐ be scared out of one's wits

魂魄 húnpò (名) soul

馄(餛) hún

馄饨(飩) húntun (名) *wonton*; dumpling soup

混 hùn (动) 1 mix; confuse: ～为一谈 lump together; confuse one thing with another. 不要搞～了. don't mix them up. 2 pass for; pass off as: 鱼目～珠 pass off the sham as genuine 3 muddle along; drift along: ～日子 drift along aimlessly; idle away one's time 4 get along with sb.: 同他们～得很熟 get familiar with them

混纺 hùnfǎng (名) blending: ～织物 blend fabric

混合 hùnhé (动) mix; blend; mingle: ～物 mixture. ～双打 mixed doubles

混乱(亂) hùnluàn (名) confusion; chaos: 陷于～ be thrown into confusion

混凝土 hùnníngtǔ (名) concrete: ～结构 concrete structure

混同 hùntóng (动) confuse; mix up

混淆 hùnxiáo (动) obscure; blur; confuse; mix up: ～黑白 mix up black and white. ～视听 mislead the public; confuse public opinion

混血儿 hùnxuè'ér (名) half-breed; a person whose parents are of different races

混杂(雜) hùnzá (动) mix; mingle: 鱼龙～ good and bad people get mixed up

混帐(帳) hùnzhàng (名) scoundrel; bastard; son of a bitch: ～话 impudent remark

混浊(濁) hùnzhuó (形) muddy; turbid: ～的空气 foul (or stale) air

诨 hùn (名) joke; jest: 打～ make gags

诨名 hùnmíng (名) nickname

豁 huō I (名) slit; break; crack: ～了一个口子 make an opening II (动) give up; sacrifice: ～出去了 be ready to pay any price

see also huò

活 huó I (动) live: ～到老,学到老. One is never too old to learn. II (形) 1 alive; living: 在他～着的时候 during his lifetime. ～捉 capture alive. ～字典 a walking dictionary 2 vivid; lively: 脑子很～ be resourceful 3 movable; moving: ～水 flowing water III (副) exactly; simply: ～象 look exactly like IV (名) 1 work: 针线～儿 needlework. 庄稼～ farm work 2 product: 这批～儿做得好. This batch of products is well made.

活宝(寶) huóbǎo (名) a bit of a clown; a funny fellow; a rare crank

活动(動) huódòng I (动) move about; exercise: 出去～～. Go out and stretch your limbs. II (形) 1 shaky; unsteady; loose: 这个螺丝～了. This screw is loose. 2 movable; mobile; flexible: ～房屋 mobile home III (名) 1 activity; manoeuvre: 户外～ outdoor activities. 政治～ political activities. ～余地 room for manoeuvre 2 use personal influence or irregular means: 替他～～ put in a word for him; use one's influence on his behalf

活该 huógāi (动)〈口〉 serve sb. right

活计 huójì (名) 1 handicraft work; manual labour 2 handiwork; work
活力 huólì (名) vigour; vitality; energy: 充满青春的~ brim with youthful vigour
活灵(靈)活现 huólíng-huóxiàn (形) vivid; lifelike
活路 huólù (名) 1 means of subsistence; way out 2 workable method
活命 huómìng (动) 1 earn a bare living; scrape along; eke out an existence 2 〈书〉 save sb.'s life
活泼(潑) huópo (形) lively; vivacious; vivid: 天真~的孩子. lively children. 文字~written in a lively style
活期 huóqī (名) current: ~储蓄 current deposit; demand deposit
活受罪 huóshòuzuì 〈口〉 have a hell of a life
活象 huóxiàng (动) look exactly like; be the spit and image of; be an exact replica of: 他长得~他父亲. He is the very spit (or image) of his father.
活页 huóyè (名) loose-leaf: ~笔记本 loose-leaf notebook
活跃(躍) huóyuè I (形) brisk; active; dynamic: 市场~. Business is brisk. II (动) enliven; animate; invigorate: ~气氛 enliven the atmosphere

和 huó (动) mix (powder) with water, etc.: ~点儿灰泥 prepare some plaster. ~面 knead dough
see also hé; hè

火 huǒ I (名) 1 fire: 生~ make a fire 2 firearms; ammunition: 交~ exchange fire 3 anger; temper: 心头~起 flare up II (形) 1 fiery; flaming: ~红 red as fire; flaming 2 urgent; pressing: ~急 extremely urgent
火把 huǒbǎ (名) torch
火并(倂) huǒbìng (动) open fight between factions
火柴 huǒchái (名) match: ~盒 matchbox
火车(車) huǒchē (名) train: ~票 railway ticket. ~站 railway station. ~头 (railway) engine; locomotive. ~时刻表 railway timetable; train schedule
火红 huǒhóng (形) red as fire; fiery; flaming: ~的太阳 a flaming sun
火花 huǒhuā (名) spark: ~四溅 sparks flying off in all directions
火化 huǒhuà (名) cremation
火急 huǒjí (形) urgent; pressing: 十万~ most urgent
火箭 huǒjiàn (名) rocket: 发射~ launch a rocket
火警 huǒjǐng (名) fire alarm
火炬 huǒjù (名) torch: ~赛跑 torch race
火坑 huǒkēng (名) abyss of suffering: 跳出~ escape from the living hell
火辣辣 huǒlàlà (形) burning: ~的太阳 a scorching sun. 脸上觉得~的 feel one's cheeks burning (as with shame)
火力 huǒlì (名) firepower; fire
火炉(爐) huǒlú (名) (heating) stove
火苗 huǒmiáo (名) tongues of flame; flames
火器 huǒqì (名) firearms
火上加油 huǒshàng jiā yóu pour oil on the flames
火烧(燒)眉毛 huǒ shāo méimao extremely urgent: ~的事 a matter of the utmost urgency
火石 huǒshí (名) flint
火速 huǒsù (副) at top speed; posthaste
火腿 huǒtuǐ (名) ham
火险(險) huǒxiǎn (名) fire insurance
火线(綫) huǒxiàn (名) battle (or firing, front) line
火星 huǒxīng (名) 1 spark: ~迸发 a shower of sparks 2 Mars
火性 huǒxìng (名)〈口〉 bad temper; hot temper
火焰 huǒyàn (名) flame: ~喷射器 flamethrower
火药(藥) huǒyào (名) gunpowder: ~库 powder magazine. ~桶 powder keg
火灾(災) huǒzāi (名) fire (as a disaster); conflagration
火葬 huǒzàng (名) cremation: ~场 crematorium; crematory
火中取栗 huǒzhōng qǔ lì pull sb.'s chestnuts out of the fire
火种(種) huǒzhǒng (名) kindling material; kinkling; tinder
火烛(燭) huǒzhú (名) anything that may cause a fire: 小心~! Be careful about fires!

伙 huǒ I (名) 1 mess; board; meals: 包~ get or supply meals at a fixed rate; board 2 partner; mate 3 partnership; company: 合~ enter into partnership II 〈量〉一~强盗 a band

of robbers
伙伴 huǒbàn (名) partner; companion
伙房 huǒfáng (名) kitchen (in a school, factory, etc.)
伙计 huǒji (名) 1 partner 2 <口> fellow; mate: ～,上哪儿去? Where are you going, man? 3 salesman; salesclerk; shop assistant
伙食 huǒshi (名) mess; food; board; meals: 管理～ handle messing arrangements. ～补助 food allowance.
伙同 huǒtóng (动) be in league with; act in collusion with
夥 huǒ (形)<书> much; a great deal; many; numerous: 获益甚～ have derived much benefit
豁 huò I (形) clear; open; open-minded; generous: ～达大度 large-minded II (动) exempt; remit: ～免 exempt; remit
see also huō
豁然贯通 huòrán guàntōng feel suddenly enlightened
豁然开(開)朗 huòrán kāilǎng suddenly see the light; be enlightened all of a sudden
祸(禍) huò I (名) misfortune; disaster; calamity: 车～ traffic accident II (动) bring disaster upon; ruin
祸不单(單)行 huò bù dān xíng misfortunes never come singly
祸端 huòduān (名) <书> the source of the disaster; the cause of the trouble
祸根 huògēn (名) the root of the trouble
祸国(國)殃民 huòguó-yāngmín bring calamity to the country and the people
祸害 huòhai I (名) disaster; curse; scourge II (动) damage; destroy
祸患 huòhuàn (名) disaster; calamity
祸首 huòshǒu (名) arch-criminal; chief culprit
祸胎 huòtāi (名) the root of the trouble; the cause of the disaster
祸心 huòxīn (名) evil intent: 包藏～ harbour malicious intentions
霍 huò (副) suddenly; quickly
霍乱(亂) huòluàn (名) cholera
霍然 huòrán (副) 1 suddenly; quickly: 手电筒～一亮. Suddenly somebody flashed an electric torch. 2 (of an ailment) be quickly restored to health
获(獲) huò (动) 1 capture; catch: 捕～ capture 2 obtain; win; reap: ～利 make a profit; reap profits. 3 get in; harvest: 收～ get in
获得 huòdé (动) gain; obtain; acquire; win; achieve: ～独立 win independence. ～宝贵经验 gain valuable experience
获胜(勝) huòshèng (动) win victory; be victorious; triumph
获悉 huòxī (动) <书> learn (of an event)
或 huò I (副) perhaps; maybe; probably: 代表团明晨～可到达. The delegation will probably arrive tomorrow morning. II (连) or; either ... or ...: 你～他必须参加这个会. Either you or he must attend the meeting. ～多～少卷了进去 more or less involved in the affair
或然 huòrán (形) probable: ～率 probability
或许 huòxǔ (副) perhaps; maybe: ～她已经改变了主意. Maybe, she has changed her mind.
或者 huòzhě I (副) perhaps; maybe: 快点走,～还赶得上末班车. Hurry up, and we may catch the last bus. II (连) or; either ...or...: 请把这个口信转达给李先生～他的夫人. Please pass on this oral message to Mr. or Mrs. Li.
惑 huò (动) 1 be puzzled; be bewildered: 大～不解 be greatly puzzled 2 delude; mislead: 造谣～众 create rumours to misguide the public
货 huò (名) 1 goods; commodity: 送～ delivery of goods. ～畅其流 ensure the smooth flow of commodities 2 money: 通～ currency 3 blockhead: 蠢～ blockhead; idiot
货币(幣) huòbì (名) money; currency: 周转～ vehicle currency. 自由兑换～ convertible currency. ～危机 monetary crisis
货舱(艙) huòcāng (名) (cargo) hold; cargo bay (of a plane)
货车(車) huòchē (名) 1 goods train; freight train 2 goods van (or wagon); freight car (or wagon) 3 lorry; truck
货船 huòchuán (名) freighter; cargo ship; cargo vessel: 定期

～ cargo liner
货单(單) huòdān (名) manifest; waybill; shipping list
货款 huòkuǎn (名) money for buying or selling goods; payment for goods
货色 huòsè (名) 1 goods: ～齐全. We offer goods of every specification. 2 junk; trash; rubbish
货物 huòwù (名) goods; commodity; merchandise
货样(樣) huòyàng (名) sample goods; sample
货源 huòyuán (名) source of goods; supply of goods: ～充足 an ample supply of goods
货运(運) huòyùn (名) freight transport: ～单 waybill. ～费 shipping cost; freight charges
货栈(棧) huòzhàn (名) warehouse
货真价(價)实(實) huòzhēn-jiàshí (形) 1 the goods are genuine and the price is fair 2 through and through; out-and-out; dyed-in-the-wool: ～的好战分子 out-and-out hawkish elements

J j

激 jī I (动) 1 surge; dash: 海水冲击礁石,～起高高的浪花. The waves broke against the rocks, sending up a fountain of spray. 2 arouse; stimulate; excite: ～于义愤 aroused by a sense of justice or by righteous indignation II(形) sharp; fierce; violent: ～流 strong currents. ～战 fierce fighting
激昂 jī'áng (形) impassioned: ～慷慨 speak fervour and with indignat on
激荡(蕩) jīdàng (动) agitate; surge; rage: 海水～的声音 the sound of surging waves
激动(動) jīdòng (动) excite; stir: ～人心的场面 a stirring scene. ～得流下眼泪 be moved to tears
激发(發) jīfā (动) arouse; stimulate; set off: ～群众的积极性 arouse popular enthusiasm
激愤 jīfèn (动、形) be roused to anger; indignant
激光 jīguāng (名) laser: ～束 laser beam
激化 jīhuà (动) sharpen; intensify; become acute: 矛盾进一步～. The contradictions further intensified.
激进(進) jījìn (形) radical: ～派 radicals
激励(勵) jīlì (动) encourage; impel; urge: ～战士 give a pep talk to officers and men. ～士气 boost the morale
激烈 jīliè (形) (of action and argument) intense; sharp; fierce; acute: 大家争论得很～. We (they) all argued heatedly.
激怒 jīnù (动) enrage; infuriate; exasperate
激切 jīqiè (形) <书> blunt and vehement: 言辞～ in blunt vehement terms
激情 jīqíng (名) strong emotion; enthusiasm: 他充满欢乐的～. He is bursting with joy.
激素 jīsù (名) hormone
激增 jīzēng (动) increase sharply; soar; shoot up: 价格～. Prices are rocketing.
跻(躋) jī (动) <书> ascend; mount: 使国家的科学～于世界先进之列 raise the country's science to the world's advanced level
迹(跡) jì (名) 1 mark; trace: 足～ footprint. 血～ bloodstain 2 remains; ruins; vestige: 古～ relics of historical interest
迹象 jìxiàng (名) sign; indication: 有～表明情况将进一步改善. There are indications that the situation will further improve.
绩 jì (名) achievement; accomplishment; merit: 战～ military achievement (or exploits). 功～ merits and achievements; contributions
积(積) jī I (动) amass; store up; accumulate: ～少成多. Many a little makes a mickle. II (形) long-standing; long-pending; age-old: ～案 a long-pending case. ～弊 age-old malpractice
积极(極) jījí (形) 1 positive: ～因素 positive factor. ～作用 positive role 2 active; energetic; vigorous: ～分子 activist ～性 zeal; initiative; enthusiasm
积聚 jījù (动) gather; accumulate; build up: ～财富 accumulate wealth. ～力量 build up strength

积劳(勞)成疾 jī láo chéng jí break down under the strain of long years of strenuous work; fall ill from prolonged overwork
积累 jīlěi (动、名) accumulate: ～经验 accumulate experience
积木 jīmù (名) toy bricks
积习(習) jīxí (名) old habit; long-standing practice: ～难改. It is very difficult to change one's old habit.
积蓄 jīxù (名) savings
积压(壓) jīyā (动) keep long in stock; overstock
积怨 jīyuàn (名) bottled up rancour; piled-up grievances
积攒 jīzǎn (动)〈口〉save (or collect) bit by bit: ～肥料 collect farmyard manure
积重难(難)返 jī zhòng nán fǎn unhealthy old customs die hard

击(擊) jī (动) 1 beat; hit; strike: ～鼓 beat a drum 2 attack; assault: 声东～西 make a feint to the east and attack in the west
击败 jībài (动) defeat; beat; vanquish
击毙(斃) jībì (动) shoot dead; kill
击毁 jīhuǐ (动) smash; wreck; shatter; destroy
击剑(劍) jījiàn (名) fencing
击溃 jīkuì (动) rout; annihilate; crush
击落 jīluò (动) shoot down; bring down; down: ～敌机七架 bring down seven enemy planes
击破 jīpò (动) break up; destroy; rout
击中 jīzhòng (动) hit: ～目标 hit the target. ～要害 hit the nail on the head; strike home

基 jī I (名) base; foundation: 路～ roadbed; bed. 奠～ lay a foundation II (形) basic; key; primary; cardinal: ～调 keynote. ～数 cardinal number 3〈化〉radical; base; group
基本 jīběn (形) 1 basic; fundamental: ～要求 basic requirements. ～原则 fundamental principles. ～知识 rudimentary knowledge. 2 main; essential: ～条件 principal conditions. ～词汇 basic vocabulary; basic word-stock. ～工资 basic wage (or salary). ～建设 capital construction
基层(層) jīcéng (名) basic level; primary level; grass-roots unit
基础(礎) jīchǔ (名) foundation; base; basis: 打～ lay a foundation. 物质～ material base. ～工业 basic industries. ～教育 elementary education. ～科学 basic science. ～课 basic courses (of a college curriculum). ～设施 infrastructure (such as energy and transport)
基地 jīdì (名) base: 军事～ military base. 工业～ industrial base. 原料～ source of raw materials
基点(點) jīdiǎn (名) basic point; starting point; centre
基调 jīdiào (名) 1 fundamental key; main key 2 keynote: 他讲话的～是团结. The keynote of his speech was unity.
基督 jīdū (名) Christ: ～教 Christianity; the Christian religion. ～徒 Christian
基金 jījīn (名) fund: ～会 foundation
基石 jīshí (名) foundation stone; cornerstone
基数(數) jīshù (名) 1 cardinal number 2 base: 以一九六五年的产量为～ taking the output of 1965 as the base
基因 jīyīn (名) gene
基于(於) jīyú (副) according to; in view of: ～以上理由我不赞成他的意见. For reasons mentioned above, I do not agree with him.

奇 jī (形) odd (number): ～数 odd number
see also qí

畸 jī 1 lopsided; unbalanced 2 irregular; abnormal
畸形 jīxíng I (名) deformity; malformation II (形) lopsided; unbalanced; abnormal: ～发展 lopsided development. ～现象 abnormal phenomenon

犄 jī
犄角 jījiǎo (名) corner: 屋子～ a corner of the room
犄角 jījiao (名) horn: 牛～ ox horn

羁(羈) jī I (名)〈书〉1 bridle; headstall: 无～之马 a horse without a bridle 2 restriction; restraint: 放荡不～ lead a Bohemian life II (动) stay; stop over; detain
羁绊 jībàn〈书〉trammels; fetters; yoke
羁押 jīyā (动)〈书〉detain; take into custody

稽 jī (动) 1 check; examine; investigate: 无～之谈 a tall

tale. **2** stay; stop over
see also qǐ

稽核 jīhé (动) check; examine: ～帐目 audit accounts

稽留 jīliú (动)〈书〉delay; detain: 因事～ be detained by business

几

jī I (名) a small table: 茶～儿 tea table; teapoy II (副) nearly; almost; practically: 到会者～三千人. Nearly 3,000 people attended the meeting.
see also jǐ

几乎 jīhū (副) nearly; almost; practically: 我～忘了. I very nearly forgot all about it. 他～一夜没睡. He lay awake practically the whole night.

讥(譏)

jī (动) laugh at; ridicule

讥讽(諷) jīfěng (动) satirize; hold sb. up to ridicule

讥诮 jīqiào (动)〈书〉sneer at; make gibes about; speak ironically about

讥笑 jīxiào (动) ridicule; sneer at

机(機)

jī I (名) **1** machine; engine: 缝纫～ sewing machine. ～床 machine tool. 影印 ～ photostat **2** aircraft; aeroplane; plane: 客～passenger plane. 运输～ transport plane **3** crucial point; pivot; key link: 转～a turning point **4** chance; occasion; opportunity:趁～ take advantage of the occasion; seize the opportunity (or chance). 随～应变 act according to circumstances II (形) **1** organic: 有～体 organism. 无～化学 inorganic chemistry **2** flexible; quickwitted: ～智 clever; resourceful

机场(場) jīchǎng (名) airport; airfield; aerodrome

机车(車) jīchē (名) locomotive; engine: 内燃(电力,蒸汽)～ diesel (electric, steam) locomotive

机动(動) jīdòng (形) **1** power-driven; motorized: ～车 motor-driven (or motor) vehicle **2** flexible; expedient; mobile: ～处置 deal with sth. flexibly. ～性 mobility; flexibility **3** in reserve; for emergency use: ～力量 reserve force. ～费 reserve fund

机构(構) jīgòu (名) **1** mechanism: 传动～ transmission mechanism **2** organization; setup: 政府～ government organization. 精简～ simplify (or streamline) the administrative structure

机关(關) jīguān (名) **1** mechanism; gear: 起动～ starting gear **2** office; organ; body: 领导～ leading bodies. ～报 official newspaper of a party, government, etc.; organ **3** intrigue; ruse: 识破～ see through a ruse

机会(會) jīhuì (名) chance; opportunity: 千载一时的好～ a rare opportunity in a lifetime

机会(會)主义(義) jīhuìzhǔyì (名) opportunism

机警 jījǐng (形) alert; sharp-witted; vigilant

机密 jīmì I (形) secret; classified; confidential: ～文件 classified papers; confidential documents II (名) secret: 严守国家～ strictly guard state secrets

机敏 jīmǐn (形) alert and resourceful

机能 jīnéng (名) function

机器 jīqì (名) machine; machinery; apparatus: 安装新～ install new machinery. 国家～ state apparatus (or machine). ～人 robot. ～油 lubricating oil; lubricant

机械 jīxiè I (名) machinery; machine; mechanism: ～故障 mechanical failure (or breakdown). ～工程学 mechanical engineering II (形) mechanical; inflexible; rigid: ～地照搬别人的经验 apply other people's experience mechanically

机械化 jīxièhuà (动、名) mechanize: 农业～ mechanization of agriculture; mechanization of farm work. ～部队 mechanized force (or troops, unit)

机要 jīyào (形) confidential: ～工作 confidential work. ～秘书 confidential secretary

机宜 jīyí (名) guiding principles guidelines: 面授～ brief sb. on how to act under certain circumstances; give confidential instructions in person

机遇 jīyù (名) good fortune; opportunity

机缘 jīyuán (名) good luck; opportunity: ～凑巧 as luck would have it; by chance; by a concatenation of lucky events

机智 jīzhì (形) quick-witted resourceful

机组 jīzǔ (名) **1** unit; set: 发电～ generating unit (or set) aircrew; flight crew

叽(嘰)

jī (象): 小鸟～～叫 Little birds chirp.

叽咕 jīgu (动) talk in a lo

voice; whisper; mutter: 他们俩叽叽咕咕不知谈了多久. The two of them have been talking in whispers for God knows how long.

叽叽喳喳 jījizhāzhā (象) (of birds) chirp; twitter

肌

jī (名) muscle; flesh

肌肤(膚) jīfū (名) (human) skin

肌腱 jījiàn (名) tendon

肌理 jīlǐ (名) 〈书〉 skin texture: ～细腻 fine-textured skin

肌肉 jīròu (名) muscle: ～发达 muscular

肌体(體) jītǐ (名) human body; organism

饥(饑)

jī I (动) be hungry; starve; be famished II (名) famine; crop failure: ～民 famine victims

饥不择(擇)食 jī bù zé shí a hungry person is not choosy about his food

饥肠(腸) jīcháng (名) 〈书〉 empty stomach

饥饿 jī'è (名) hunger; starvation

饥寒交迫 jī-hán jiāopò suffer hunger and cold; live in hunger and cold; be poverty-stricken

饥荒 jīhuāng I (名) famine; crop failure II (形) 〈口〉 be hard up

饥馑(饉) jījǐn (名) famine; crop failure

汲

jī (动) draw (water): 从井里～水 draw water from a well

汲汲 jījí 〈书〉 anxious; avid: ～于名利 avid for fame and wealth

汲取 jīqǔ (动) draw; derive: ～营养 derive nourishment from. 从中～教训 draw a lesson from it

鸡(鷄)

jī (名) chicken: 公～ cock; rooster. 母～ hen. 雏～ chick; chicken. ～窝 roost; henhouse

鸡蛋 jīdàn (名) (hen's) egg: ～糕 (sponge) cake

鸡飞(飛)蛋打 jīfēi-dàndǎ suffer a loss both ways

鸡肋 jīlèi (名) 〈书〉 things of little value which one is not particularly keen on but reluctant to throw away

鸡毛蒜皮 jīmáo-suànpí trivialities

鸡犬不宁(寧) jī-quǎn bù níng there is a scene of general turmoil —everybody is disturbed one way or the other

鸡尾酒 jīwěijiǔ (名) cocktail: ～会 cocktail party

屐

jī (名) 1 clogs 2 shoes in general

缉

jī (动) seize; arrest

缉拿 jīná (动) seize; arrest; apprehend: ～凶手 apprehend the murderer

缉私 jīsī (动) seize smugglers or smuggled goods; suppress smuggling: ～人员 anti-contraband personnel

疾

jí I (名) 1 disease; sickness; illness: 眼～ eye trouble 2 suffering; pain; difficulty: ～苦 sufferings; hardships II (动) hate; abhor: ～恶如仇 hate evils and evildoers like sworn enemies III (形) fast; quick: ～驰而过 gallop off; speed past

疾病 jíbìng (名) disease; illness: 治～ treatment of disease

疾风(風)劲(勁)草 jífēng jìncǎo sturdy grass withstands strong winds; misfortune is a test for a person's character

疾言厉(厲)色 jíyán-lìsè (名) look stern and speak harshly

嫉

jí (动) 1 be jealous; be envious 2 hate

嫉妒 jídù (动) be jealous of; envy

嫉恨 jíhèn (动) envy and hate; hate out of jealousy

脊

jí

see also jǐ

脊梁 jíliang (名) back (of the human body): ～骨 backbone; spine

瘠

jí (形) 〈书〉 1 lean; thin and weak 2 barren; poor; lean: ～土 poor soil; barren land

瘠薄 jíbó (形) (of land) barren; unproductive

吉

jí (形) lucky; auspicious; propitious: 万事大～. All is well. *or* Everything is fine.

吉卜赛人 jíbǔsàirén (名) Gypsy

吉利 jílì (形) lucky; auspicious; propitious

吉庆(慶) jíqìng (形) auspicious; propitious; happy

吉他 jítā (名) guitar

吉祥 jíxiáng (形) lucky; auspicious; propitious

吉凶 jí-xiōng (名) good or ill luck; fate

吉兆 jízhào (名) good omen; propitious sign

佶 jí (形)〈书〉robust and sturdy

佶屈聱牙 jíqū áoyá difficult to articulate: ～之词 tongue twister

籍 jí (名) 1 book; record: 古～ ancient books. 国～ nationality; citizenship. 党～ party affiliation 2 native place; home town; birthplace: 祖～ one's ancestral birthplace 3 membership

籍贯 jíguàn (名) the place of one's birth or origin

棘 jí (名) 1 sour jujube 2 thorn bushes; brambles

棘手 jíshǒu (形) thorny; difficult to handle; knotty: ～的问题 a thorny problem; a hard nut to crack

楫 jí〈书〉oar: 舟～ boat

辑 jí I (动) collect; compile; edit: 编～ edit; compile II (名) part; volume; division

辑录(錄) jílù (动) compile

集 jí I (动) gather; assemble: ～各家之长 incorporate the strong points of various schools. 惊喜交～ astonishment mingled with joy II (名) 1 fair; market: 赶～ go to market 2 collection; anthology: 诗～ a collection of poems. 影～ an album of pictures 3 volume; part: 这部影片分上、下两～,今晚放映. The film which is in two parts will be shown tonight.

集成电(電)路 jíchéng diànlù (名) integrated circuit

集合 jíhé (动) gather; assemble; muster; call together: ～地点 assembly place. 我们在校门口～. We shall assemble at the gate.

集会(會) jíhuì (名) assembly; rally; gathering; meeting

集结 jíjié (动) mass; concentrate; build up: 军队～待命. Troops are massing to await orders.

集锦 jíjǐn (名) a collection of choice specimens: 花鸟画～ outstanding examples of flower-and-bird paintings

集权(權) jíquán (名) centralization of state power; concentration of power

集散地 jísàndì (名) collecting and distributing centre; distributing centre

集思广(廣)益 jísī-guǎngyì let us pool our ideas; let us put our heads together

集体(體) jítǐ (名、形) collective: ～创作 collective effort. ～领导 collective leadership. ～化 collectivization. ～农场 collective farm. ～安全 collective security. ～舞 group dancing

集团(團) jítuán (名) group; clique; circle; bloc: 统治～ the ruling clique; the ruling circle. 军事～ a military bloc

集训 jíxùn (动) bring people together for training

集腋成裘 jí yè chéng qiú many a little makes a mickle; pool small resources to help accomplish a big project

集邮(郵) jíyóu (名) stamp collecting; philately: ～簿 stamp-album

集中 jízhōng (动) concentrate; centralize; focus; amass; put together: ～精力 concentrate one's efforts. ～大量财富 amass vast material resources. ～管理 centralized management. ～营 concentration camp

集装(裝)箱 jízhuāngxiāng (名) container: ～船 container ship. ～海港 container port. ～运输 container shipment

及 jí I (动) reach; come up to; attain: 力所能～ what is in one's power II (副) in time for: ～时 timely; in time III (连)[connecting nouns and noun phrases, the coordinate '及' is preceded by a noun or nouns of greater importance] and: 词典～其它参考书 dictionaries and other reference books

及格 jígé (动) pass a test, examination, etc.; pass; be up to the standard

及时(時) jíshí (副) 1 timely; in good time: ～的忠告 timely advice 2 promptly; without delay: 有问题就～解决. Problems, if any, should be solved without delay.

及早 jízǎo (副) at an early date; as soon as possible; before it is too late: 有病要～治. It is necessary to see a doctor at once when you are ill.

极(極) jí I (名) 1 the utmost point; extreme: 无所不用其～ go to any lengths. 荒谬之～ be the height of absurdity. ～而言之 talk in extreme terms 2 pole: 北(南)～ the North (South) Pole II (副) extremely; exceedingly: ～为重要 of the utmost importance. 冷

～了 extremely cold
极点(點) jídiǎn (名) the limit; the extreme: 我们忍耐到了～. Our tolerance has reached its limit.
极度 jídù (形) extreme; exceeding: ～困难 exceedingly difficult. ～兴奋 be elated
极端 jíduān (形) extreme; exceeding: ～仇视 show extreme hatred for. ～腐败 rotten to the core. ～左倾分子 extreme left lements; ultra-leftists
极乐(樂)世界 jílè shìjiè (名) <佛> Sukhavati; Pure Land; Western Paradise
极力 jílì (动) do one's utmost; spare no effort: ～劝阻 try very hard to dissuade sb. from doing sth. ～否认 deny vehemently
极其 jíqí (副) most; extremely; exceedingly: ～深刻 extremely profound. ～艰巨 exceptionally arduous
极权(權)主义(義) jíquánzhǔyì (名) totalitarianism
极盛 jíshèng (名) heyday; zenith; acme
极刑 jíxíng (名) capital punishment; the death penalty
岌 jí (形) <书> (of a mountain) lofty; towering
岌岌 jíjí (形) <书> precarious: ～可危 be in imminent danger
级 jí (名) 1 level; rank; grade: 高～ higher level. 部长～会谈 talks at ministerial level. 七～地震 an earthquake of magnitude 7 (on the Richter scale) 2 grade: 同～不同班 of the same grade but not of the same class 3 step: 石～ stone steps
级别 jíbié (名) rank; level; grade; scale: 工资～ wage scale; grade on the wage scale
急 jí I (形) 1 impatient; anxious: ～着要到前线去 be impatient to leave for the front 2 worrying: 火车快开了,他还不来,实在～人. It is really exasperating that he has not turned up when the train is about to leave. 3 irritated; annoyed; nettled: 没说上几句话他就～了. He had not spoken a few words when he got heated. 4 fast; rapid; violent: 水流很～. The current is swift. *or* It's a strong current. ～风暴雨 violent storm; tempest; hurricane 5 urgent; pressing: ～电 urgent telegram. 他走得很～. He left in a hurry. II (动) be eager to help: ～公好义 be jealous for the commonweal. ～功好利 crave instant success and benefit
急促 jícù (形) 1 hurried; rapid: ～的脚步声 hurried footsteps. 呼吸～ be panting 2 (of time) short; pressing: 时间很～, 要速作决定. Time presses, and we must make a quick decision.
急件 jíjiàn (名) urgent document or dispatch
急救 jíjiù (名) first aid; emergency treatment: ～药箱 first-aid kit. ～站 first-aid station
急剧(劇) jíjù (形) rapid; sharp; sudden: ～的变化 drastic change. ～转折 abrupt turn
急遽 jíjù (形) rapid; sharp; sudden
急流 jíliú (名) 1 torrent; rapid stream; rapids 2 jet stream; jet flow
急流勇退 jíliú yǒngtuì make a resolute decision to retire at the height of one's career
急忙 jímáng (副) in a hurry; in haste; hurriedly; hastily: 他穿上大衣,～赶去车站. He put on his overcoat and hurried to the station.
急难(難) jínàn I (名) <书> misfortune; time of trouble; grave danger II (动) be anxious to help (those in grave danger)
急迫 jípò (形) urgent; pressing; imperative: 最～的任务 the most pressing task. 形势～ critical juncture
急起直追 jíqǐ-zhízhuī hurry and catch up with; do one's utmost to overtake
急切 jíqiè (形) 1 eager; impatient: ～地盼望 eagerly look forward to; wait impatiently for 2 in a hurry; in haste
急速 jísù (副) very fast; at high speed; rapidly: ～行驶 drive at high speed. 情况～变化. The situation changed fast.
急性子 jíxìngzi (形、名) of impatient disposition; quick-tempered
急需 jíxū (名) 1 be badly in need of: 提供～的资金 provide much-needed funds 2 urgent need: 以应～ so as to meet an urgent need
急于(於) jíyú (形) eager; anxious; impatient: ～回去 anxious go

back. ～求成 overanxious for quick results; impatient for success

急躁 jízào (形) 1 irritable; irascible 2 impetuous; rash; impatient: 防止～情绪 guard against impetuosity

急诊 jízhěn (名) emergency call; emergency treatment: ～病人 emergency case. ～室 emergency ward

急中生智 jízhōng shēng zhì suddenly hit upon a way out at the last minute; show resourcefulness in an emergency

急转(轉)直下 jízhuǎn-zhíxià (of situation, plot of a play, style, etc.) develop rapidly and smoothly after taking a sudden turn for the better

即 jí I (动) 1 approach; reach; be near: 可望而不可～ be within sight but inaccessible 2 assume; undertake: ～位 ascend the throne; assume office 3 be; mean; namely: 此陌生人～约翰生教授. This stranger is no other than professor Johnson. II (形、副) 1 at present; in the immediate future: 成功在～. Success is within reach. ～日生效 come into effect beginning this very day (as of today) 2 prompted by the occasion: ～景诗 occasional verse 3 promptly; at once: 闻过～改 correct one's mistake as soon as it is pointed out

即便 jíbiàn (连) even; even if; even though: ～你当头,也不该摆架子. You shouldn't put on airs even if you were in charge.

即将(將) jíjiāng (副) be about to; be on the point of: 理想～实现. The ideal is about to come true. 春节～来临. The Spring Festival is just around the corner.

即景生情 jíjǐng shēng qíng the scene touches a responsive chord in one's heart

即刻 jíkè (副) at once; immediately; instantly

即时(時) jíshí (副) immediately; forthwith

即使 jíshǐ (连) even; even if; even though

即席 jíxí (形)〈书〉1 impromptu; extemporaneous: ～讲话 speak impromptu; make an impromptu (or extemporaneous) speech 2 take one's seat (at a dinner table, etc.)

即兴(興) jíxìng (形) impromptu; extemporaneous: ～之作 an improvisation.

亟 jí (副)〈书〉urgently; anxiously; earnestly: ～盼 earnestly hope. ～待解决 demand prompt solution

see also qì

殛 jí (动)〈书〉kill: 雷～ be struck dead by lightning

脊 jǐ (名) 1 spine; backbone 2 ridge: 山～ the ridge of a hill or mountain. 屋～ the ridge of a roof

see also jí

脊背 jǐbèi (名) back (of a human being or any other vertebrate)

脊椎 jǐzhuī (名) vertebra: ～动物 vertebrate. ～骨 vertebra; spine

济(濟) jǐ

see also jì

济济 jǐjǐ (形) (of people) many; numerous: 人才～ an abundance of talented people; a galaxy of talent

挤(擠) jǐ (动) 1 squeeze; press: ～牙膏 squeeze toothpaste out of a tube. ～牛奶 milk the cow 2 jostle; push against: ～进去 force (or elbow, shoulder, push) one's way in; sqeeze in. 人多～不进去. There are so many people there that it is impossible to squeeze in. 3 crowd; pack; cram: ～做一团 pressed close together; packed like sardines. 礼堂已经～满了. The assembly hall is filled to capacity.

几(幾) jǐ 1 how many: ～点钟了? What's the time? 你能在这里住～天? How many days can you stay here? 2 a few; several; some: 说～句话 say a few words. ～十 tens; dozens; scores. 十～岁的孩子 teenager. 二十～个人 twenty odd people. 所剩无～. There is not much left.

see also jī

几分 jǐfēn (形) a bit; somewhat; rather: 她说的有～道理. There is a grain of truth in what she said. ～怀疑 be somewhat suspicious. 有～醉意 be a bit tipsy

几何 jǐhé I〈书〉how much; how many: 不知尚有～ have yet to know how much is left II (名) geometry ～图形 geometric figure

几何学(學) jǐhéxué (名) geometry:

解析～ analytic geometry. 立体～ solid geometry. 平面～ plane geometry

几时(時) jǐshí (副) what time; when: 你们～回来? What time will you come back?

几许 jǐxǔ (副) 〈书〉 how much; how many: 不知～. No one can tell how much.

己 jǐ (名、形) oneself; one's own; personal: 舍～为公 make personal sacrifices for the public good. 引为～任 consider oneself duty-bound to; regard as one's duty. 请各抒～见. Everybody is requested to air his own views.

己方 jǐfāng (名) one's own side

给 jǐ I (动) supply; provide: 自～自足 self-sufficiency II (形) ample; well provided for: 家～户足. Every household is comfortably off.
see also gěi

给养(養) jǐyǎng (名) provisions; victuals: ～充足 be abundantly provisioned

给予 jǐyǔ (动) 〈书〉 give; render: ～支持 offer support. ～同情 show sympathy

寂 jì (形) 1 quiet; still; silent: 万籁俱～. All is quiet and still. 2 lonely; lonesome; solitary: 枯～ lonely and bored stiff

寂静 jìjìng (形) quiet; still; silent: 在～的深夜里 in the still of the night

寂寞 jìmò (形) lonely; lonesome: 感到～ feel lonely

寂然 jìrán (形) 〈书〉 silent; still

济(濟) jì (动) 1 cross a river: 同舟共～ make a concerted effort to tide over the difficulty 2 save: 缓不～急 slow action cannot save a critical situation. 3 be of help; benefit: 无～于事 not help matters; be of no benefit
see also jǐ

剂(劑) jì I (名) a pharmaceutical or other chemical preparation: 针～ injection. 片～ tablet. 防腐～ preservative; antiseptic II (量): 一～中药 a dose of Chinese herbal medicine

剂量 jìliàng (名) dosage; dose

计 jì I (动) count; compute; calculate; estimate: 不～其数 countless; innumerable II (名) 1 meter; gauge: 雨量～ rain gauge 2 idea; stratagem; plan: 中～ fall into a trap. 长远之～ from a long-term point of view

计策 jìcè (名) stratagem; plan

计划(劃) jìhuà I (名) plan; project; programme: 可行的～ a feasible(or workable) plan. 五年～ five-year plan II(动) map out; plan: 我们～周末去纽约. We plan to go to New York at the weekend. ～经济 planned economy. ～生产 planned production. ～生育 family planning; birth control

计件 jìjiàn (动) reckon by the piece: ～工资 piece rate wage. ～工作 piecework

计较 jìjiào (动) 1 haggle over; fuss about: 斤斤～ be too calculating 2 argue; dispute: 我不同你～,等你气平了再说. I won't argue with you until you have calmed down.3 think over; plan: 从不～个人名利 give no thought to personal fame and gain

计量 jìliàng (动) measure; calculate; estimate: 不可～ inestimable

计谋 jìmóu (名) scheme; stratagem

计算 jìsuàn (动、名) 1 count; compute; calculate: ～产值 calculate the output value. ～尺 slide rule 2 consideration; planning: 做事不能没个～. We shouldn't do anything without a plan.

计算机(機) jìsuànjī (名) computer; calculator: ～程序设计 computer programming. ～存储器 computer storage. ～软件 computer software. ～硬件 computer hardware

计议(議) jìyì (动) deliberate; talk over; consult: 从长～ discuss the matter at leisure

髻 jì (名) hair worn in a bun or coil

技 jì (名) skill; ability; trick: ～巧 technique. 有一～之长 be good at one branch of knowledge or one type of skill

技工 jìgōng (名) 1 skilled worker 2 mechanic; technician

技能 jìnéng (名) technical ability; occupational skills; mastery of a skill or technique: 生产～ skill in production

技师(師) jìshī (名) technician

技术(術) jìshù (名) technology;

skill; technique: ～水平 technical competence. ～革新 technological innovation; technical innovation. ～工人 skilled worker. ～力量 technical force; technical personnel. ～员 technician. ～知识 technological know-how; technical knowledge. ～资料 technical data; technological data. ～开发中心 centres for technological development. ～标准 technical norms

技艺(藝) jìyì (名) skill; artistry: ～精湛 highly skilled; masterly

伎 jì (名) 1 ruse; trick: 故～重演 be up to one's old tricks again; play the same old trick 2 a sing-song girl in ancient China

伎俩 jìliǎng (名) trick; intrigue; manoeuvre

妓 jì (名) prostitute: ～女 prostitute. ～院 brothel; whorehouse

寄 jì (动) 1 send; post; mail: ～信 post a letter; mail a letter. ～包裹 send a parcel by post 2 entrust; deposit; place: ～希望于青年 place hopes on the youth 3 depend on: ～食 live with a relative or friend for want of financial support

寄存 jìcún (动) deposit; leave with; check: 把大衣～在衣帽间 check one's overcoat at the cloakroom. 行李～处 left-luggage office; checkroom

寄放 jìfàng (动) leave with; leave in the care of: 我要外出一段时间,这些书可以～在你那里吗? I'll be away for some time. May I leave these books with you?

寄卖(賣) jìmài consign for sale on commission; put on sale in a secondhand shop: ～商店 commission shop

寄人篱(籬)下 jì rén líxià have to depend on sb. for a living

寄生 jìshēng (名) parasitism: ～生活 parasitic life

寄生虫(蟲) jìshēngchóng (名) parasite

寄宿 jìsù (动) 1 lodge: 我暂时～在朋友家里. I am staying at a friend's house for the time being. 2 (of students) board: ～生 resident student; boarder. ～学校 boarding school; residential college

寄托 jìtuō (动) 1 send to the care of sb.; leave with sb.: 把孩子～在邻居家里 entrust one's child to the care of a neighbour 2 place (hope, etc.) on: 作者把自己的思想感情～在剧中主人翁身上. The author projects his own thoughts and feelings into the personality of the hero of his play.

寄养(養) jìyǎng (动) entrust one's child to the care of sb.

寄予 jìyǔ (动) 1 place (hope, etc.) on: 国家对青年一代～很大的希望. The state places great hopes on the younger generation. 2 show; express: ～深切的同情 be extremely sympathetic to

骥 jì (名) 〈书〉 a thoroughbred horse

觊(覬) jì (动) 〈书〉 attempt; hope

觊觎 jìyú (动) 〈书〉 covet

稷 jì (名) 1 millet 2 the god of grains worshipped by ancient emperors: 社～ country

季 jì (名) 1 season: 一年四～ all the year round. 雨～ rainy season; monsoon. 旱～ dry season. 2 the end of an epoch: 清～ the end of the Qing dynasty 3 the last month of a season: ～春 the last month of spring

季度 jìdù (名) quarter (of a year): ～报告 a quarterly report

季风(風) jìfēng (名) monsoon: ～气候 monsoon climate

季节(節) jìjié (名) season: ～性 seasonal. ～工 seasonal worker

悸 jì (动) 〈书〉 (of the heart) throb with fear: 心有余～ shake with lingering fear

祭 jì (动) 1 hold a memorial ceremony for 2 offer a sacrifice to: ～天 offer a sacrifice to Heaven; worship Heaven

祭奠 jìdiàn (动) hold a memorial ceremony for

祭祀 jìsì (动) (of old customs) offer sacrifices to gods or ancestors

祭文 jìwén (名) funeral oration, elegiac address

际(際) jì (名) 1 border; boundary; edge: 天～ horizon. 无边无～ boundless 2 between; among; inter-: 星～旅行 space travel. 国～ international 3 inside: 脑～ in one's head (or mind) 4 occasion; time: 临别之～ at parting 5 one's lot: 遭～ unfavourable turns in life; misfortune

鲫 jì (名) crucian carp

系(繫) jì （动） tie; fasten; do up; button up: ～安全带 fasten one's seatbelt. 把衣服扣子～上 button up a jacket. ～着领带 wear ties
see also xì

系泊 jìbó （动） moor (a boat)

既 jì I（副） already: ～成事实 fait accompli; accomplished fact. ～得利益 vested interests II（连） 1 since; as; now that: ～来之，则安之. Since you are here, you may as well stay on and enjoy yourself. 2 [often used together with such adverbs as "且""又""也"] both ... and; as well as: 这本书～有趣，又有教育意义. This book is both interesting and instructive.

既然 jìrán （连） since; as; now that: ～如此 such being the case; under these circumstances

既往不咎 jìwǎng bù jiù let bygones be bygones

暨 jì （连）〈书〉 1 and 2 up to; till: ～今 up till now

记 jì I（动） 1 remember; bear in mind: ～忆 remember. ～不清 cannot recall exactly. 我们要牢牢～住这点. We must bear this firmly in mind. 2 write (or jot, take) down; record: ～在笔记本上 write it down in a notebook. ～下这些号码 jot down these numbers II（名） 1 notes; record: 游～ travel notes. 大事～ a chronicle of events 2 mark; sign: 暗～儿 secret mark 3 birthmark: 他左边眉毛上方有块～. There is a birthmark just above his left eyebrow. III（量）: 一～耳光 a slap in the face

记得 jìde （动） remember: 过了这些年，我都记不得他的名字了. After so many years, I don't quite remember his name.

记分 jìfēn （动） 1 keep the score; record the points (in a game) 2 register a student's marks 3 record workpoints: ～册 (teacher's) markbook. ～牌 scoreboard

记功 jìgōng （动） cite sb. for meritorious service; record a merit

记过(過) jìguò （动） record a demerit

记号(號) jìhao （名） mark; sign: 做个～ make a sign; mark out

记录(錄) jìlù I（动） take notes; keep the minutes; record: 教授堂上讲的我都～下来了. I took careful notes of the professor's lecture. II（名） 1 minutes; notes; record: 会议～ the minutes of a meeting. 会谈～ a transcript of talks. 逐字～ verbatim record 2 note-taker: 这次讨论请你做～好吗？Would you take notes at the discussion? 3 record: 创～ set a record; chalk up a record. 打破～ break a record. ～本 minute book. ～片 documentary film; documentary

记述 jìshù （动） record and narrate

记性 jìxing （名） memory: ～好 have a good (retentive) memory. ～坏 have a poor memory

记叙 jìxù （动） narrate: ～文 narration; narrative

记忆(憶) jìyì （动） remember; recall: 就我～所及 to the best of my memory. ～力 the faculty of memory; memory

记忆(憶)犹(猶)新 jìyì yóu xīn still remain fresh in one's memory (mind)

记载 jìzǎi （动、名） 1 put down in writing; record 2 record; account

记者 jìzhě （名） reporter; correspondent; newsman; journalist: 新闻～ newspaper reporter; newsman. 特派～ special correspondent. ～招待会 press conference

忌 jì I（动） 1 be jealous of: 猜～ suspicious and jealous 2 avoid; shun; abstain from: ～生冷 avoid eating any uncooked food 3 quit; give up: ～酒 give up alcohol; abstain from drinking. ～烟 quit(give up) smoking II（名） fear; dread; scruple: 横行无～ ride roughshod; act without scruples

忌辰 jìchén （名） the anniversary of the death of a parent, ancestor, or anyone else held in esteem

忌惮(憚) jìdàn （名） dread; fear: 肆无～ act wildly in defiance of law and public opinion; be unscrupulous

忌妒 jìdu （动） be jealous of; envy

忌讳(諱) jìhui （名、动） 1 taboo: 犯～ violate (or break) a taboo 2 avoid as taboo: 他～人家叫他的外号. He resents being called by his nickname. 3 avoid as harmful; abstain from: 在学习上，最～的是有始无终. In study the worst danger is give up halfway.

忌口 jìkǒu (动) abstain from certain food (as when one is ill); be on a diet

纪 jì (名) 1 discipline: 军～ military discipline. 党～国法 party discipline and the law of the land. 违法乱～ break the law and violate discipline 2 put down in writing; record: ～事 chronicle 3 age; epoch: 中世～ the Middle Ages

纪律 jìlǜ (名) discipline: 遵守～ observe discipline. 劳动～ labour discipline; labour regulations. 违反～ breach of discipline. ～松弛. Discipline is lax.

纪念 jìniàn I (动) commemorate; mark: ～大会 commemoration meeting. ～国际儿童节 observe International Children's Day II (名) 1 souvenir; keepsake; memento: 这张照片给你作个～吧. Keep this photo as a souvenir. 2 commemoration day; anniversary: 一百周年～ centenary. ～册 autograph book; autograph album. ～品 souvenir; keepsake; memento. ～日 commemoration day. ～章 souvenir badge. ～碑 monument; memorial tablet. ～馆 memorial hall. ～堂memorial hall

纪行 jìxíng (名) travel notes: 西伯利亚～ Siberian travel notes

纪要 jìyào (名) summary of minutes; summary: 会谈～ summary of conversations (or talks)

纪元 jìyuán (名) 1 the beginning of an era (e.g. an emperor's reign) 2 epoch; era: 世界历史的新～ a new era in world history

继(繼) jì I (动) continue; succeed; follow: 前赴后～ advance wave upon wave II (副) then; afterwards: 他初感头晕,～又呕吐. feeling dizzy, he began to vomit.

继承 jìchéng (动) inherit; carry on: ～财产 inherit property. ～权 right of inheritance

继承人 jìchéngrén (名) heir; successor; inheritor: 直系～ lineal successor. 法定～ heir at law; legal heir

继而 jì'ér (副) then; afterwards

继父 jìfù (名) stepfather

继母 jìmú (名) stepmother

继任 jìrèn (动) take over sb.'s job: ～首相 succeed sb. as prime minister

继往开(開)来(來) jìwǎng-kāilái carry forward the cause of the older generation and break new ground

继续(續) jìxù (动) continue; go on: ～学习 continue with his studies. ～执政 continue in office; remain in power. ～有效 remain in force; be still valid. 战斗～到第二天凌晨. The fighting went on till the small hours of the next morning.

家 jiā I (名) 1 family; household: 他～一共有四口人. They're four people in his family. ～事 family matters; domestic affairs 2 home: 回～ go (come) home. 3 a person or family engaged in a certain profession: 行～ professional; expert 4 a specialist in a certain field: 科学～ scientist. 画～ painter 5 a school of thought; school: 百～争鸣. A hundred schools of thought contend. II <谦> [used to address one's senior in age]: ～父 my father. ～兄 my elder brother III (形)domestic; tamed: ～畜 domestic animal; livestock IV (量) [used to count the number of families and enterprises]: 两～饭馆 two restaurants. 一～电影院 a cinema. 两～人家 two families

家产(產) jiāchǎn (名) family property

家常 jiācháng (名) 1 domestic trivia: ～便饭 pot luck; homely meal 2 common occurrence ～话 small talk; chitchat

家丑(醜) jiāchǒu (名) family scandal; the skeleton in the cupboard (or closet): ～不可外扬. Don't wash your dirty linen in public.

家传(傳) jiāchuán (形) handed down from the older generations of the family: ～秘方 a secret recipe handed down from the ancestors

家当(當) jiādang (名)<口> family belongings; property

家底 jiādǐ (名) family property or savings

家伙 jiāhuo (名) <口> 1 tool; utensil; weapon: 他从口袋中拔出一把～. He pulled a dagger out of his pocket. 2 fellow; guy: 小～ little chap; kid. 你认识那～吗? Do you happen to know that chap?

家教 jiājiào (名) family education; upbringing
家境 jiājìng (名) domestic financial situation; family circumstances: ～困难 live in straitened family circumstances
家具 jiāju (名) furniture: 一套～ a set of furniture
家眷 jiājuàn (名) **1** wife and children; one's family **2** wife **3** dependents
家谱 jiāpǔ (名) family tree; genealogical tree; genealogy
家禽 jiāqín (名) domestic fowl; poultry
家书(書) jiāshū (名) **1** a letter home **2** a letter from home
家属(屬) jiāshǔ (名) family members; (family) dependents
家庭 jiātíng (名) family; household: ～背景 family background. ～成员 family members. ～出身 family origin. ～负担 family responsibilities. ～妇女 housewife. ～副业 household sideline production. ～收入 family income. ～作业 homework. ～教师 private tutor
家务(務) jiāwù (名) household duties: ～劳动 housework; household chores
家乡(鄉) jiāxiāng (名) hometown; native place
家小 jiāxiǎo (名) 〈口〉 wife and children
家信 jiāxìn (名) a letter to or from one's family
家用 jiāyòng (名) family expenses; housekeeping money
家喻户晓(曉) jiāyù-hùxiǎo widely known; known to all: 斯诺这个名字在中国已～. The name Snow is a household word in China.
家园(園) jiāyuán (名) home; homeland: 重建～ rebuild one's homeland; rebuild one's village or town. 重返～ return to one's homeland
家长(長) jiāzhǎng (名) **1** the head of a family; patriarch **2** the parent or guardian of a child
家族 jiāzú (名) clan; family

夹(夾)

jiā I (动) **1** press from both sides; place in between: 把枫叶～在书里. Put the maple leaves in between the pages. 用筷子～菜 pick up food with chopsticks. 他被汽车门～住了. He was caught in the door of a bus. **2** mix; mingle; intersperse: ～在人群里 be in the midst of a crowd. ～心巧克力 stuffed chocolate II (名) clip, clamp, folder, etc.: 纸～ paper clip. 发～ hairpin. 衣～ clothes peg

see also gā; jiá
夹带(帶) jiādài (动) carry secretly; smuggle: 邮寄包裹不能～信件. Don't put a letter in anything you send by parcel post.
夹缝 jiāfèng (名) crack; crevice
夹攻 jiāgōng (动) attack from both sides; converging attack; pincer attack: 受到两面～ be under a pincer attack; be under attack from both sides
夹杂(雜) jiāzá (动) be mixed up with; be mingled with
夹子 jiāzi (名) **1** clip; tongs: 弹簧～ spring clip **2** folder; wallet: 文件～ folder; binder. 皮～ wallet; pocketbook

佳

jiā (形) good; fine; beautiful: ～景 fine landscape; beautiful view. 成绩甚～ achieve very good results. ～节 happy festive occasion; festival. ～宾 a welcome guest. ～肴 delicacies
佳话 jiāhuà (名) an anecdote or a good deed which is very much on everybody's lips; a much-told tale
佳境 jiājìng (名) 〈书〉 state of ecstasy
佳期 jiāqī (名) wedding (or nuptial) day
佳人 jiārén (名) 〈书〉 beautiful woman; beauty
佳音 jiāyīn (名) welcome news; glad tidings; favourable reply

加

jiā (动) **1** add; plus: 二～三等于五. Two and three makes five. ～强 strengthen; reinforce **2** increase; augment: 要求～工资 demand a raise in one's pay **3** put in; add; append: 汤里～点盐 put some salt in the soup. ～大压力 increase the pressure. ～注解 add explanatory notes to **4** [used to indicate the taking of a certain action]: 大～赞扬 praise highly; lavish praise on. 不～考虑 give no consideration to
加班 jiābān (动) work overtime; work an extra shift: ～费 overtime emolument
加倍 jiābèi (形) double; redouble: ～努力 redouble one's efforts. 产量可以在五年内～. The output will double in five years.
加法 jiāfǎ (名) addition
加工 jiāgōng (名、动) **1** process:

食品～ food processing. 这篇文章需要～. This article needs touching up a little bit. **2** machining; working: 冷～ cold working. 机～ machining. ～厂 processing factory

加害 jiāhài (动) injure; do harm to; incriminate

加紧(緊) jiājǐn (动) step up; speed up; intensify: ～生产 step up production

加剧(劇) jiājù (动) aggravate; intensify; exacerbate: ～紧张局势 aggravate tension

加快 jiākuài (动) quicken; accelerate; pick up speed: ～步子 quicken one's pace

加强 jiāqiáng (动) strengthen; enhance; augment; reinforce: ～纪律 strengthen discipline. ～控制 tighten one's control. ～兵力 reinforce the army

加入 jiārù (动) **1** add; mix; put in **2** join; accede to: ～联合国 join the United Nations

加深 jiāshēn (动) deepen: ～理解 get a better grasp of sth. ～印象 make a deeper impression on sb.

加速 jiāsù (动) quicken; speed up; accelerate; expedite: ～发展工业 speed up the development of industry. ～植物的生长 hasten the growth of plants

加以 jiāyǐ **1** [used to indicate how to deal with the matter previously mentioned]: 原计划须～小小修改. It is necessary to make some minor changes in the original plan. **2** (连) in addition; moreover: 天气太冷，～孩子也病了，今天我就不来了. I won't come today. It's too cold, and what's more, my child is ill.

加油 jiāyóu (动) **1** oil; lubricate: 这台机器该～了. This machine needs oiling. **2** refuel: 空中～ in flight (or air) refueling **3** make an extra effort: ～干 work with added vigour. ～站 filling (or petrol, gas) station

加重 jiāzhòng (动) **1** make or become heavier; increase the weight of: ～工作量 add to one's workload **2** make or become more serious; aggravate: 病情～了 The patient's condition worsened.

痂

jiā (名) scab; crust: 结～ form a scab; crust

嘉

jiā (形) **1** good; fine: ～宾 honoured guest; welcome guest **2** praise; commend: 他的精神可～. The spirit he has shown is worthy of praise.

嘉奖(奬) jiājiǎng (动) bestow praise, honour or reward

嘉许 jiāxǔ (动) 〈书〉 praise; approve

茄

jiā

see also qié

茄克 jiākè (名) jacket

枷

jiā (名) cangue

枷锁 jiāsuǒ (名) yoke; chains; shackles; fetters: 摆脱～ throw off the yoke

夹(夾)

jiá (形) double-layered; lined: ～袄 lined jacket

see also gā; jiā

颊(頰)

jiá (名) cheek: 两～红润rosy cheeks

甲

jiǎ (名) **1** the first of the ten Heavenly Stems **2** first: ～级 first rate; Class A. 桂林山水～天下. The landscape of Guilin is the finest under heaven. **3** [used as a substitute] ～方和乙方 the first party and the second party **4** shell; carapace: 龟～ tortoise shell **5** nail: 手指～ fingernail **6** armour: 装～车 armoured car

甲板 jiǎbǎn (名) deck

甲骨文 jiǎgǔwén (名) inscriptions on oracle bones of the Shang Dynasty (c. 16th — 11th century B.C.)

甲壳 jiǎqiào (名) crust: ～动物 crustancean

甲鱼 jiǎyú (名) soft-shelled turtle

岬

jiǎ (名) **1** cape; promontory **2** a narrow passage between mountains: ～角 cape; promontory

钾

jiǎ (名) potassium(K)

钾肥 jiǎféi (名) potash fertilizer

假

jiǎ I (形) false; fake; sham; phoney; artificial: ～话 falsehood. ～发 wig. ～牙 false tooth. ～肢 artificial limb II (动) borrow; loan: 久～不归 keep a borrowed article for a long period of time with no thought of returning it III (连) if; suppose: ～令 in case

see also jià

假扮 jiǎbàn (动) disguise oneself as

假充 jiǎchōng (动) pretend to be; pose as: ～内行 pass for a professional

假定 jiǎdìng I (动) suppose; assume; grant; presume: ～他明天起程，后天就可以到达上海. Suppose he sets out tomorrow, he will be in Shanghai the following day. II (名) hypothesis

假公济(濟)私 jiǎ gōng jì sī seek personal gain at public expense

假话 jiǎhuà (名) lie; falsehood: 说～ tell lies

假借 jiǎjiè (动) make use of: ～外力 make use of outside forces. ～名义 under the guise of; in the name of; under false pretences

假冒 jiǎmào (动) pass oneself off as; palm off (a fake as genuine): 谨防～ Beware of imitations

假面具 jiǎmiànjù (名) mask; false front

假仁假义(義) jiǎrén-jiǎyì (名) hypocrisy; sham kindness

假如 jiǎrú (连) if; supposing; in case: ～天下雨，我就不来了. If it rains, I won't come.

假若 jiǎruò (连) if; supposing; in case

假设 jiǎshè I (动) suppose; assume; grant; presume II (名) hypothesis: 科学～ a scientific hypothesis

假使 jiǎshǐ (连) if; in case; in the event that: ～他同意,那就很好. If he agrees, well and good.

假手 jiǎshǒu (动) do evil through another person: ～于人 make use of sb. to achieve one's malicious purpose

假说 jiǎshuō (名) hypothesis

假托 jiǎtuō (动) 1 make a pretext: 他～家里有事，站起来就走了. He stood up and strode off on the pretence that he had something to attend to at home. 2 under sb. else's name 3 by means of; through the medium of

假想 jiǎxiǎng (名、形) 1 imagination; hypothesis; supposition 2 imaginary; hypothetical; fictitious: ～敌 imaginary enemy

假象 jiǎxiàng (名) false appearance; false impression; false front

假惺惺 jiǎxīngxīng (副) hypocritically; unctuously

假意 jiǎyì (名、副) 1 unction; insincerity; hypocrisy 2 deliberately; affectedly; insincerely: 他～笑着问，刚来的这位是谁呢? He smirked, asking "who is the person who just came in?"

假造 jiǎzào (动) 1 forge; counterfeit: ～证件 forge a certificate 2 invent; fabricate: ～理由 cook up an excuse

假装(裝) jiǎzhuāng (动) pretend; feign; simulate; make believe: ～不知道 pretend to know nothing; feign ignorance

稼 jià 1 sow (grain): 耕～ ploughing and sowing; farm work. ～穑 sowing and reaping; farming; farm work 2 cereals; crops: 庄～ crops

嫁 jià 1 (of a woman) marry 2 shift; transfer: ～祸于人 shift the misfortune onto sb.

嫁接 jiàjiē (动) grafting

嫁娶 jiàqǔ (名) marriage

嫁妆(妝) jiàzhuang (名) dowry; trousseau

价(價) jià (名) 1 price: 要～ the asking price 2 value: 等～交换 exchange of equal values. 估～ estimate the value of; evaluate 3 valence: 氢是一～的元素. Hydrogen is a one-valence element.
see also jie

价格 jiàgé (名) price: 批发(零售)～ wholesale (retail) price. ～补贴 price subsidies from the state

价值 jiàzhí (名) 1 value: 使用～ use value. ～规律 law of value 2 worth; value: ～二百万元的援助 two million yuan worth of aid. 毫无～ worthless

价值连城 jià zhí liánchéng invaluable; priceless

价目 jiàmù (名) marked price; price: ～表 price list

价钱(錢) jiàqian (名) price: 讲～ bargain. ～公道 a fair (or reasonable) price

假 jià (名) holiday; vacation: 请～ask for leave. 寒～ winter vacation. 病～ sick leave. 学术～ sabbatical leave
see also jiǎ

假期 jiàqī (名) 1 vacation 2 period of leave

假日 jiàrì (名) holiday; day off

架 jià I (名) frame; rack; shelf; stand: 窗～ window frame. 行李～ luggage-rack. 衣～ clothes hanger. 书～ bookshelves II (动) 1 put up; erect: ～桥 put up (or build) a bridge. ～起接收天线 set up a receiving antenna 2 fend off; ward off; withstand 3 support; prop; help: ～着拐走 walk on crutches 4 kidnap; take sb. away forcibly 5 fight; quarrel: 劝～ try to part quarrelling parties III (量): 一～电视机 a T.V. set

架空 jiàkōng I (形) impracticable; unpractical II (动) make sb. a mere figurehead

架设 jiàshè (动) erect; put up (above ground or water level, as on stilts or posts): ～帐篷 erect a tent. ～输电线路 erect power transmission lines

架势(勢) jiàshi (名) 〈口〉 posture; stance; manner: 摆出一副盛气凌人的～ assume a domineering posture

架子 jiàzi (名) 1 frame; stand; rack; shelf: 脸盆～ washstand 2 framework; skeleton; outline: 写文章搭个～ make an outline for an essay. 3 airs; haughty manner: 摆～ put on airs 4 posture; stance

驾 jià (动) 1 harness; draw (a cart, etc.) 2 drive (a vehicle); pilot (a plane); sail (a boat)

驾轻(輕)就熟 jiàqīng-jiùshú drive a light carriage on a familiar road; have no difficulty handling familiar matters

驾驶 jiàshǐ (动) drive (a vehicle); pilot (a ship or plane): ～盘 steering wheel. ～室 driver's cab. ～员(车辆的) driver; (飞机的) pilot. ～执照 driving (or driver's) license

驾驭 jiàyù (动) 1 drive (a cart, horse, etc.): 这匹马不好～. This horse is difficult to control. 2 control; master: ～形势 take the situation in hand

煎 jiān (动) 1 fry in shallow oil: ～鱼 fried fish 2 simmer in water; decoct: ～药 decoct medicinal herbs

煎熬 jiān'áo (名) suffering; torture; torment

兼 jiān (形) 1 double; twice: ～旬 twenty days 2 simultaneously; concurrently: ～管 be concurrently in charge of; also look after. ～而有之 have both (merits and defects; advantages and disadvantages) at the same time. 身～数职 hold several posts simultaneously

兼备(備) jiānbèi (动) have both qualities; be in possession of both: 德才～ have both political integrity and ability

兼并(併) jiānbìng (动) annex (territory, property, etc.)

兼程 jiānchéng (动) travel at double speed: 日夜～ travel day and night

兼顾(顧) jiāngù (动) give consideration to (or take account of) two or more things; consider the needs of both parties: 统筹～ make overall plans and take all factors into consideration

兼任 jiānrèn (动) 1 hold a concurrent job 2 part-time: ～教师 part-time teacher

兼收并(並)蓄 jiānshōu-bìngxù incorporate into something factors of diverse nature

兼职(職) jiānzhí (动、名) 1 moonlight; hold two or more posts concurrently: ～过多 hold too many posts at the same time 2 concurrent post; moonlighting

间 jiān I (介) between; among: 劳资之～ between labour and capital II (副) within a definite time or space: 世～ (in) the world. 田～ (in) the fields. 晚～ (in the) evening; (at) night III (名) room: 洗澡～ bathroom. 衣帽～ cloakroom IV (量): 一～卧室 a bedroom see also jiàn

间不容发(髮) jiān bù róng fà be in imminent danger

肩 jiān I (名) shoulder: 并～战斗 fight shoulder to shoulder II (动) take on; undertake; shoulder; bear: 身～重任 shoulder heavy responsibilities

肩膀 jiānbǎng (名) shoulder

肩负 jiānfù (动) take on; undertake; shoulder; bear: ～伟大任务 undertake a great task

肩章 jiānzhāng (名) 1 shoulder ornament 2 epaulet

笺(箋) jiān (名) 〈书〉 1 writing paper: 信～ letter paper 2 letter 3 annotation; commentary

笺注 jiānzhù (名) 〈书〉 notes and commentary on ancient texts

歼(殲) jiān (动) annihilate; exterminate; wipe out

歼灭(滅) jiānmiè (动) annihilate; wipe out; destroy: ～敌军 wipe out enemy troops. ～战 war or battle of annihilation

缄 jiān (动) seal; close: ～封 seal a letter

缄口 jiānkǒu (动) 〈书〉 hol

one's tongue
缄默 jiānmò (动) keep silent; be reticent
缄札 jiānzā (名) a letter
监(監) jiān (动) 1 supervise; inspect; watch 2 prison; jail
监察 jiānchá (动) supervise; control: ～制度 supervisory system
监督 jiāndū I (动) supervise; superintend; control: 国际～ international control II (名) supervisor: ～权 authority to supervise
监工 jiāngōng (动、名) 1 supervise work; oversee 2 overseer; supervisor
监护(護) jiānhù (名) guardianship: ～人 guardian
监禁 jiānjìn (动) take into custody; imprison; put in jail (or prison)
监牢 jiānláo (名) prison; jail
监视 jiānshì (动) keep watch on; keep an eye on: 严密～ keep a close watch. ～敌人的行动 keep watch on the movements of the enemy
监守 jiānshǒu (动) have custody of; guard; take care of
监听(聽) jiāntīng (名) monitor
监狱 jiānyù (名) prison; jail
坚(堅) jiān I (形) hard; solid; firm; strong: ～冰 solid ice; hard ice. ～果 hard nut II (名) a heavily fortified point; fortification; stronghold: 攻～ storm strongholds III (副) firmly; steadfastly; resolutely: ～信 firmly believe. ～不吐实 refuse to tell the truth
坚壁清野 jiānbì-qīngyě strenthen defence works, evacuate noncombatants, hide provisions and livestock, and clear away all surrounding trees and cabins
坚不可摧 jiān bùkě cuī (形) indestructible; impregnable
坚持 jiānchí (动) persist in; persevere in; uphold; insist on; stick to; adhere to: ～原则 adhere (or stick) to principle. ～己见 hold on to one's own views. ～不懈 persevere
坚定 jiāndìng (形) firm; staunch; steadfast: ～不移 firm and unshakable; unswerving. ～的立场 a firm stand
坚固 jiāngù (形) firm; solid; sturdy; strong: ～耐用 strong and durable
坚决 jiānjué (形) firm; resolute, determined: ～支持 firmly support; stand firmly by. ～反对 resolutely oppose
坚苦卓绝 jiānkǔ zhuōjué (形) showing the utmost fortitude
坚强 jiānqiáng I (形) strong; firm; staunch: 意志～ strong-willed. ～不屈 staunch and unyielding II (动) strengthen
坚忍 jiānrěn (形) steadfast and persevering (in face of difficulties)
坚韧 jiānrèn (形) firm and tenacious
坚如磐石 jiān rú pánshí (形) as firm as a rock; rock-firm
坚实(實) jiānshí (形) solid; substantial: ～的基础 a solid foundation
坚毅 jiānyì (形) firm and persistent; tenacious of purpose
坚硬 jiānyìng (形) hard; solid
坚贞 jiānzhēn (形) faithful; constant: ～不屈 remain loyal and unyielding
尖 jiān I (名) 1 point; tip; top: 针～ the point of a needle or pin; pinpoint. 指～ fingertip. 塔～ the pointed top of a tower 2 the best of its kind; the pick of the bunch; the cream of the crop: 拔～儿的 topnotch II (形) 1 pointed; tapering: ～下巴 a pointed chin. 削～铅笔 sharpen a pencil 2 shrill; sharp: ～叫 scream. 耳朵～ have sharp ears. 鼻子～ have an acute sense of smell. ～嗓子 shrill voice
尖兵 jiānbīng (名) 1 <军> point 2 trailblazer; pathbreaker; pioneer; vanguard
尖端 jiānduān (名) 1 pointed end; acme; the highest point; peak: 科学的～ the pinnacle of science 2 most advanced; sophisticated: ～科学 most advanced branches of science; frontiers of science. ～武器 sophisticated weapons
尖刻 jiānkè (形) acrimonious; caustic; biting: 说话～ speak with sarcasm; make caustic remarks
尖利 jiānlì (形) 1 sharp; keen; cutting: ～的钢刀 a sharp knife 2 shrill; piercing: ～的叫声 a shrill cry
尖锐 jiānruì (形) 1 sharp-pointed 2 penetrating; incisive; sharp: 看问题很～ make a penetrating analysis of problems 3 shrill;

piercing: ～的哨声 the shrill sound of a whistle 4 intense; acute; sharp: ～的对立 be directly opposed to each other. ～的斗争 acute struggle

尖酸 jiānsuān (形) acrid; acrimonious; tart: ～刻薄 acerbic and bitterly sarcastic

艰(艱) jiān (形) difficult; hard

艰巨 jiānjù (形) arduous; extremely difficult: ～的任务 a difficult task. 付出～的劳动 make tremendous efforts

艰苦 jiānkǔ (形) arduous; difficult; hard; tough: ～的年代 hard times. ～朴素 hard work and plain living

艰难(難) jiānnán (形) difficult; hard: 步履～ walk with difficulty; plod along; dodder

艰涩(澀) jiānsè (形) involved and abstruse; intricate and obscure: 文词～ involved and abstruse writing

艰深 jiānshēn (形) difficult to understand; abstruse

艰险(險) jiānxiǎn (名) hardships and dangers: 不避～ brave hardships and dangers

艰辛 jiānxīn (名) hardships: 历尽～ experience all kinds of hardships

奸 jiān I (形) 1 wicked; evil; treacherous: ～计 an evil plot 2 self-seeking and wily II (名) 1 traitor: 内～ a secret enemy agent within one's ranks; hidden traitor. 汉～ traitor to the Chinese nation; traitor 2 illicit sexual relations: 通～ have illicit sexual relations; commit adultery

奸猾 jiānhuá (形) treacherous; crafty; deceitful

奸佞 jiānnìng (形、名) 〈书〉 1 crafty and fawning 2 crafty sycophant

奸污 jiānwū (动) rape or seduce

奸细 jiānxi (名) spy; enemy agent

奸险(險) jiānxiǎn (形) wicked and crafty; treacherous; malicious

奸邪 jiānxié (形、名) 〈书〉 1 crafty and evil; treacherous 2 a crafty and evil person

奸淫 jiānyín I (形) illicit sexual relations; adultery II (动) rape or seduce

奸诈 jiānzhà (形) fraudulent; crafty; treacherous

简 jiǎn I (形) simple; simplified; brief: ～而言之 in brief; in short; to put it in a nutshell II (名) 1 bamboo slips [used as a kind of paper in ancient times] 2 letter: 书～ letters; correspondence III (动) 〈书〉 select; choose: ～拔 select and promote

简报(報) jiǎnbào (名) bulletin; brief report: 会议～ conference bulletin; brief reports on conference proceedings

简编 jiǎnbiān (名) [often used in books' titles] short course; concise book

简便 jiǎnbiàn (形) simple and convenient; handy: ～的方法 a simple and convenient method; a handy way. 烹调～ easy to cook. 手续～ simple procedures

简称(稱) jiǎnchēng 1 the abbreviated form of a name; abbreviation 2 be called sth. for short

简单(單) jiǎndān (形) 1 simple; uncomplicated: ～明了 brief and to the point; simple and clear; concise and explicit. 解释～明了. Explanations are simple but clear. 2 rough and plain; casual: ～粗暴 rough and rude. 头脑～ simpleminded

简短 jiǎnduǎn (形) brief: 他的文章～有力. His article was brief and forceful.

简化 jiǎnhuà (动) simplify: ～工序 simplify working processes. ～手续 reduse the formalities

简化汉(漢)字 jiǎnhuà hànzì 1 simplify Chinese characters (i.e. reduce the number of strokes and eliminate complicated variants) 2 simplified Chinese characters

简洁(潔) jiǎnjié (形) succinct; terse; pithy: ～生动的语言 terse and lively language. 文笔～ written concisely

简历(歷) jiǎnlì (名) biographical notes; resume

简练(練) jiǎnliàn (形) terse; succinct; pithy

简陋 jiǎnlòu (形) simple and crude: 设备～ simple and crude equipment; crudely appointed

简略 jiǎnlüè (形) simple (in content); brief; sketchy: 他提供的材料过于～. The information he gave is too brief.

简明 jiǎnmíng (形) simple and clear, concise: ～扼要 brief and

to the point. ～新闻 news in brief

简朴(樸) jiǎnpǔ (形) simple and unadorned. plain: 生活～ a simple life-style; plain living

简写(寫) jiǎnxiě (动) 1 write a Chinese character in simplified form 2 simplify a book for beginners: ～本 simplified edition

简讯 jiǎnxùn (名) news in brief

简要 jiǎnyào (形) concise and to the point; brief: ～的介绍 a brief discription; briefing

简易 jiǎnyì (形) 1 simple and easy: ～的办法 a simple and easy method 2 simple constructed; simply equipped; unsophisticated: ～读物 easy reader

简章 jiǎnzhāng (名) general regulations

简直 jiǎnzhí (副) simply; at all: 这一队轿车,一辆跟着一辆,～没个完. The procession of cars, one following another, was simply endless.

剪

jiǎn I (名) scissors; shears; clippers II (动) 1 cut (with scissors); clip; trim: ～发 have a haircut. ～羊毛 shear a sheep 2 wipe out; exterminate: ～除 wipe out; annihilate; remove

剪裁 jiǎncái (动) 1 cut out (a garment); tailor 2 cut out unwanted material (from a piece of writing)

剪彩 jiǎncǎi (动) cut the ribbon at an opening ceremony

剪除 jiǎnchú (动) wipe out; annihilate; exterminate

剪刀 jiǎndāo (名) scissors; shears: ～差 price scissors

剪辑 jiǎnjí (名) 1 film editing 2 selected photos, recordings, etc. after editing

剪票 jiǎnpiào (动) punch a ticket

剪影 jiǎnyǐng (名) 1 paper-cut silhouette 2 outline; sketch

茧(繭)

jiǎn (名) 1 cocoon: 蚕～ silkworm cocoon. ～绸 pongee 2 callus: 老～ thick callus

柬

jiǎn (名) card; note; letter: 请～ invitation card

拣(揀)

jiǎn (动) 1 choose; select; pick out: ～最重要的说. Pick out the most essential you have got to say. 2 see "捡" jiǎn

拣选(選) jiǎnxuǎn (动) select; choose

减

jiǎn (动) 1 subtract; deduct: 五～二得三. Five minus two is three. or Two from five is three. 2 reduce; decrease; cut: ～半 reduce by half. ～价 reduce prices; at a reduced rate. ～产 decrease (or drop) in output. ～速 slow down

减法 jiǎnfǎ (名) subtraction

减免 jiǎnmiǎn (动) 1 mitigate or annul (a punishment) 2 reduce or remit (taxation, etc.)

减轻(輕) jiǎnqīng (动) lighten; ease; alleviate; mitigate: ～工作 cut down on one's workload. ～痛苦 alleviate pain

减色 jiǎnsè (动) lose lustre; become less attractive; detract from the merit of: 有些节目取消了,使集会气氛大为～. The fact that several items were cut greatly reduced the lively atmosphere of the gathering.

减少 jiǎnshǎo (动) reduce; decrease; lessen; cut down: ～开支 cut down expenditure; retrench expenses

减退 jiǎntuì (动) drop; go down: 视力(记忆力)～. One's eyesight (memory) is failing.

碱

jiǎn (名) 1 alkali 2 soda: 纯～ soda (ash). ～地 alkaline land

检(檢)

jiǎn (动) 1 check up; inspect; examine: ～定 examine and determine 2 restrain oneself; be careful in one's conduct: 行为不～ depart from correct conduct; improper conduct; misdemeanour

检查 jiǎnchá (动) 1 check; inspect; examine: ～工作 check up on work. ～质量 check the quality. ～身体 have a physical examination; have a medical check-up 2 self-criticism: 作～ criticize oneself. ～哨 checkpost. ～站 checkpoint; checkpost; inspection station

检察 jiǎnchá (名) procuratorial work: ～官 public procurator (or prosecutor)

检点(點) jiǎndiǎn (动) 1 examine; check: ～行李 check the luggage 2 be cautious (about what one says or does): 言行有失～ be careless about one's words and acts; be indiscreet in one's speech and conduct

检举(舉) jiǎnjǔ (动) report (an offence) to the authorities; inform against (an offender): ～信

letters of accusation
检讨 jiǎntǎo (名) self-criticism: 作~ make a self-criticism
检修 jiǎnxiū (动) examine and repair; overhaul: ~汽车 overhaul a car
检验(驗) jiǎnyàn (动) test; examine; inspect: 商品~ commodity inspection
检疫 jiǎnyì (名) quarantine
检阅 jiǎnyuè (动) review (troops, etc.); inspect: ~仪仗队 review a guard of honour
捡(撿) jiǎn (动) pick up; collect; gather: ~破烂 collect waste
睑(瞼) jiǎn: 眼~ eyelid
俭(儉) jiǎn (形) thrifty; frugal
俭朴(樸) jiǎnpǔ (形) thrifty and simple; economical: 生活~ lead a thrifty and simple life. 衣着~ dress simply
俭省 jiǎnshěng (形) economical; thrifty: ~过日子 live a frugal life
渐 jiàn (副) gradually; by degrees: 天气~冷. It is getting cold.
渐变(變) jiànbiàn (名) gradual change
渐渐 jiànjiàn (副) gradually; by degrees; little by little
渐进(進) jiànjìn (动) advance gradually; progress step by step: 循序~ advance by stages
间(間) jiàn I (名) space in between; opening: 团结无~ closely united II (动) 1 separate: ~隔 be separated from. 黑白相~ chequered with black and white 2 sow discord see also jiān
间谍 jiàndié (名) spy: ~活动 espionage
间断(斷) jiànduàn (动) be disconnected; be interrupted: 从不~ without interruption
间隔 jiàngé (名) interval; intermission: 幼苗~匀整. The seedlings are evenly spaced.
间或 jiànhuò (副) occasionally; now and then; sometimes; once in a while: 大家聚精会神地听着, ~有人笑一两声. Everybody listened intently; once or twice somebody broke into a laugh.
间接 jiànjiē (形) indirect; second-hand: ~经验 indirect experience. ~选举 indirect election
间隙 jiànxì (名) interval; gap; space
间歇 jiànxiē (名) intermittence; intermission
谏 jiàn 〈书〉 remonstrate with (one's superior or friend); expostulate with; admonish: ~止 admonish against sth.; advise sb. to refrain from doing sth.
践(踐) jiàn (动) 1 trample; tread 2 act on; carry out: ~诺 keep one's promise (or word)
践踏 jiàntà (动) tread on; trample underfoot
践约 jiànyuē (动) keep a promise; keep an appointment
贱(賤) jiàn (形) 1 low-priced; inexpensive; cheap: ~卖 cheap sale 2 lowly; humble: 贫~ poor and lowly 3 mean; base; despicable: 下~ shameless; base
溅(濺) jiàn (动) splash; spatter: ~落 splash down
饯(餞) jiàn (动) give a farewell dinner: 为人~行 give a farewell dinner for sb.
荐(薦) jiàn (动) recommend: ~举 recommend sb. for a post. 毛遂自~ volunteer one's services
鉴(鑒) jiàn I (名) 1 ancient bronze mirror 2 warning; object lesson: 引以为~ take warning from it II (动) 1 reflect; mirror: 水清可~. The water is so clear that it shines like a mirror. 2 inspect; scrutinize; examine: 请~核. Please check.
鉴别 jiànbié (动) distinguish; differentiate; judge: 有比较才能~. Only by comparing can one distinguish. ~真假 judge whether it is sham or genuine; distinguish between the false and the true
鉴赏 jiànshǎng (动) appreciate: ~能力 ability to appreciate (painting, music, etc.); connoisseurship
鉴于(於) jiànyú (副) in view of; seeing that: ~上述原因 for the above-mentioned reasons
鉴定 jiàndìng I (名) appraisal (of a person's strong and weak points): 工作~ an evaluation of one's work II (动) appraise; identify; authenticate; determine: ~文物年代 determine the date of a cultural relic

鉴戒 jiànjiè (名) warning; object lesson

见(見) jiàn I (动) **1** see; catch sight of: 所～所闻 what one sees and hears. ～义勇为 never hesitate to fight for justice **2** meet with; be exposed to: 冰～热就化. Ice melts with heat. **3** show evidence of; appear to be: ～诸行动 be translated into action. 病已～轻. The patient's condition has improved. **4** refer to; see; vide: ～第三十六页 see page 36 **5** meet; call on; see: 你～到他了没有? Did you meet him? II (名) view; opinion: 依我之～ in my opinion; to my mind. 真知灼～ profound understanding and penetrating insight

见长(長) jiàncháng (形) be good at; be expert in

见得 jiànde (动) [only used in negative statements or questions] seem; appear: 怎么～他来不了? Why do you think he won't come?

见地 jiàndì (名) insight; judgment: 很有～ have keen insight; show sound judgment

见风(風)使舵 jiàn fēng shǐ duò trim one's sails; act as the occasion dictates

见怪 jiànguài (动) mind; take offence: 事情没给您办好,请不要～. I hope you will forgive me for not having fulfilled your mission.

见鬼 jiànguǐ (形) **1** fantastic; preposterous; absurd: 这真是～,他怎么一转眼就不见了. That's fantastic. He's vanished in the twinkling of an eye. **2** go to hell

见好 jiànhǎo (形) (of a patient's condition) get better; mend: 她的病～了. She's mending.

见机(機) jiànjī as befits the occasion; according to circumstances: ～行事 do as one thinks fit

见解 jiànjiě (名) view; opinion; understanding: 相同～ identical views

见面 jiànmiàn (动) meet; see: 他们多年没有～了. They haven't seen each other for years. *or* It's many years since they parted.

见仁见智 jiànrén-jiànzhì different people have different views even about the same question

见世面 jiàn shìmiàn see the world; enrich one's experience

见识(識) jiànshi (名) experience; general knowledge: 长～ enrich one's knowledge; broaden one's horizons.

见外 jiànwài (动) regard sb. as an outsider: 你对我这样客气,倒有点～了. You stand so much on ceremony that you make me feel like a stranger.

见闻 jiànwén (名) what one sees and hears; knowledge; information: 增长～ add to one's knowledge and experience. ～广 well-informed

见习(習) jiànxí (动) learn on the job; be on probation: ～技术员 technician on probation. ～医生 intern

见效 jiànxiào (形) become effective; produce the desired result: 我们的一切努力均未～. All our efforts proved fruitless.

见笑 jiànxiào (动) laugh at (me or us): 我手拙,您可别～. Now don't laugh at me for my clumsiness.

见异(異)思迁(遷) jiàn yì sī qiān be inconstant or irresolute: 他这个人～. He changes his mind every time he sees something different.

见证(證) jiànzhèng (名) witness; testimony: ～人 eyewitness; witness

舰(艦) jiàn (名) warship; naval vessel: ～队 fleet; naval force

舰艇 jiàntǐng (名) naval ships and boats; naval vessels

剑(劍) jiàn (名) sword; sabre: ～柄 the handle of a sword; hilt. ～鞘 scabbard

剑拔弩张(張) jiànbá-nǔzhāng be at daggers drawn; sabre-rattling

箭 jiàn (名) arrow: ～在弦上,不得不发. The arrow is on the bowstring, and there is no turning back.

箭步 jiànbù (名) a sudden big stride forward

件 jiàn I (量) [indicating those things which can be counted]: 一～衬衫 a shirt. 两～事情 two things. 三～行李 three pieces of luggage II (名) letter; correspondence; paper; document: 信～ letters; mail. 来～ a communication, document, etc. received. 密～ confidential (or classified) documents; secret papers

建 jiàn (动) 1 build; construct; erect: ～电站 build a power station. 重～家园 rebuild one's homeland 2 establish; set up; found: ～都 make (a place) the capital. ～党 found a party 3 propose; advocate: ～议 make a suggestion

建交 jiànjiāo (动) establish diplomatic relations

建立 jiànlì (动) build; establish; set up; found: ～友谊 forges tie of friendship; make friends with. ～统一战线 form a united front. ～信心 build up one's confidence

建设 jiànshè (动) build; construct: 把中国～成现代化强国 build China into a powerful modern country. 社会主义～ socialist construction

建设性 jiànshèxìng (形) constructive: ～的意见 constructive suggestions

建树(樹) jiànshù (动)〈书〉make a contribution; contribute

建议(議) jiànyì (动、名) 1 propose; suggest; recommend: 他们～休会. They propose that the meeting be adjourned. 2 proposal; suggestion; recommendation: 有益的～ constructive suggestions. 合理化～ rationalization proposal

建造 jiànzào (动) build; construct; make: ～船只 ship building

建制 jiànzhì (名) organizational system: 部队～ the organizational system of the army

建筑(築) jiànzhù (动、名) 1 build; construct; erect: ～地下铁道 build a subway (or an underground railway) 2 building; structure; edifice: 古老的～ an ancient building. 宏伟的～ a magnificent structure 3 architecture: ～材料 building materials. ～工地 construction site

键 jiàn (名) key: 琴～ a piano key

键盘(盤) jiànpán (名) keyboard; fingerboard

毽 jiàn (名) shuttlecock

毽子 jiànzi (名) shuttlecock: 踢～ kick the shuttlecock (as a game)

健 jiàn I (形) healthy; strong II (动) 1 strengthen; toughen; invigorate: ～身 build up one's strength. ～胃 be good for the stomach 2 be strong in; be good at: ～谈 be good at casual conversation; be a magnificent conversationalist

健步 jiànbù (动) walk with vigorous strides: ～如飞 walk fast and with springy steps

健儿(兒) jiàn'ér (名) 1 valiant fighter 2 good athlete: 乒坛～ skillful ping-pong players

健将(將) jiànjiàng (名) master sportsman; top-notch player: 运动～ master sportsman

健康 jiànkāng I (名) health; physique: ～状况 state of health; physical condition II (形) healthy; sound: 身体～ be in good health. 祝你～! I wish you good health. 情况基本上是～的. The situation is basically sound.

健美 jiànměi (形) strong and handsome; vigorous and graceful

健全 jiànquán I (形) sound; perfect: 体魄～ sound in body and mind. 组织～ organizationally perfect II (动) strengthen; amplify; perfect: ～规章制度 make necessary amendments to the rules and regulations

健忘 jiànwàng (形) forgetful; having a failing memory: ～症 amnesia

健在 jiànzài (形)〈书〉(of a person of advanced age) be still living and in good health; still going strong

健壮(壯) jiànzhuàng (形) healthy and strong; robust

腱 jiàn (名) tendon

腱鞘 jiànqiào (名) tendon sheath

将(將) jiāng I (动) 1 do sth.; handle (a matter): 慎重～事 handle a matter with care 2〈象棋〉check 3 put sb. on the spot 4 incite sb. to action; challenge; prod: 他做事稳重,你～他也没用. It's no use trying to prod him, he is so steady and calm. II (介) 1 with; by means of; by: ～功折罪 make amends for one's crime by good deeds 2 [after 将 comes the object to be followed by *vt*. to form inversion]: ～革命进行到底. Carry the revolution through to the end. III (助) 1 be going to; be about to; will; shall: 明晨～有霜冻. Frost is expected tomorrow morning. 必～以失败告终 be certain to end in failure 2 ～信～疑 half believing, half doubting 3 [used in between the verb and the complement of direction]: 传～出去 (of news,

etc.) spread abroad
see also jiàng
将计就计 jiāng jì jiù jì turn the opponent's stratagem to one's own advantage
将近 jiāngjìn (副) close to; nearly; almost: ～一百人 close to a hundred people. ～完成 nearing completion. 他～四十岁了. He is close on forty.
将就 jiāngjiu make do with; make the best of; put up with: 衣服稍微小了点，你～着穿吧. This coat is a bit too tight, but perhaps you could make do with it.
将来(來) jiānglái (名) future: 在不远的～ in not too distant future
将息 jiāngxī (动) rest; recuperate
将要 jiāngyào (助) be going to; will; shall: 会议～在大厅举行. The meeting will be held in the main hall.

浆(漿) jiāng I (名) thick liquid: 糖～ syrup. 纸～ pulp II (动) starch: ～衣服 starch clothes. ～洗 wash and starch
see also jiàng

江 jiāng (名) 1 river 2 the Changjiang (Yangtze) River: ～南 south of the lower reaches of the river
江河日下 jiāng-hé rì xià deteriorate with each passing day; go from bad to worse.
江湖 jiānghú (名) 1 rivers and lakes 2 all corners of the country: 流落～ drift about homeless
江湖 jiānghu (名) 1 itinerant entertainers, quacks, etc. 2 trade of such people: ～骗子 swindler; charlatan. ～医生 quack; mountebank
江山 jiāngshān (名) 1 rivers and mountains; land; landscape: ～如画 a picturesque landscape; beautiful scenery. ～易改，本性难移. It's easy to change rivers and mountains but hard to alter a person's nature. *or* A fox may grow grey, but never good. 2 country; state power

豇 jiāng
豇豆 jiāngdòu (名) cowpea

僵 jiāng (形) 1 stiff; numb: 他的手足都冻～了. His limbs became stiff with cold. 2 deadlocked: 事情搞～了. Things have come to a deadlock.
僵持 jiāngchí (动) (of both parties) refuse to budge; reach a deadlock: 双方～好久. For quite some time, neither party was willing to compromise.
僵化 jiānghuà (动) become rigid; inflexible; ossify: 思想～ a rigid (or ossified) way of thinking
僵局 jiāngjú (名) deadlock; impasse; stalemate: 打破～ break a deadlock. 谈判陷入～. The negotiations have reached an impasse.
僵尸 jiāngshī (名) corpse
僵死 jiāngsǐ (形) stiff and dead; ossified
僵硬 jiāngyìng (形) 1 stiff: 觉得四肢～ feel stiff in the limbs 2 rigid; inflexible: ～的态度 a stiff manner

疆 jiāng (名) boundary; border
疆场(場) jiāngchǎng (名) battlefield
疆界 jiāngjiè (名) boundary; border
疆土 jiāngtǔ (名) territory
疆域 jiāngyù (名) territory; domain

缰 jiāng (名) reins; halter: ～绳 reins; halter

姜 jiāng (名) ginger: ～汁酒 ginger ale

桨(槳) jiǎng (名) oar

奖(獎) jiǎng I (动) encourage; praise; reward: ～许 praise; give encouragement to. 有功者～. Anyone who has distinguished himself by his performance will be rewarded. ～勤罚懒 reward the deligent and punish the lazy II (名) award; prize; reward: 发～ give awards; give prizes. 得～ win a prize
奖杯 jiǎngbēi (名) cup (as a prize)
奖惩 jiǎng-chéng (名) rewards and punishments: ～制度 system of rewards and penalties
奖金 jiǎngjīn (名) money award; bonus; premium
奖励(勵) jiǎnglì (名、动) encourage and reward; award; reward: 物质～ material reward. ～发明 give awards to innovators or inventors as an encouragement; encourage innovations. ～制度 bonus system
奖品 jiǎngpǐn (名) prize; award; trophy
奖赏 jiǎngshǎng (动) award; re-

ward

奖券 jiǎng quàn (名) lottery ticket

奖学(學)金 jiǎng xúe jīn (名) scholarship

奖章 jiǎngzhāng (名) medal; decoration

奖状(狀) jiǎngzhuàng (名) certificate of merit; citation

耩 jiǎng (动) sow with a drill

讲(講) jiǎng (动) 1 speak; say; tell: ～故事 tell stories. ～几句话 say a few words. ～几点意见 make a few remarks 2 explain; make clear; interpret: ～明立场 state one's stand in explicit (or unequivocal) terms. 这个字有几个～法. This word is capable of several interpretations. 3 bargain; negotiate: ～价钱 bargain over the price; negotiate the terms 4 stress; pay attention to; be particular about: ～质量 stress quality; be quality conscious

讲稿 jiǎnggǎo (名) the draft or text of a speech; lecture notes

讲和 jiǎnghé (动) make peace; settle a dispute

讲话 jiǎnghuà I (动) speak; talk; address: 他在会上讲了话. He addressed the meeting. II (名) 1 speech; talk: 鼓舞人心的～ an inspiring speech 2 [often used with the title of a book] guide; introduction: 《政治经济学～》 *A Guide to Political Economy*

讲解 jiǎngjiě (动) explain: ～要点 expound the essential points

讲究 jiǎngjiu I (动) be particular about; pay attention to; stress; strive for: ～效率 strive for efficiency II (形) exquisite; tasteful: 这个旅馆布置得很～. This hotel is beautifully furnished (well appointed). III (名) careful study: 这篇社论大有～. The leading article needs careful study.

讲课 jiǎngkè (动) teach; lecture

讲理 jiǎnglǐ (动) 1 argue things out 2 be reasonable: 蛮不～ be utterly unreasonable; be impervious to reason

讲明 jiǎngmíng (动) explain; make clear; state explicitly

讲情 jiǎngqíng (动) intercede; plead for sb.

讲师(師) jiǎngshī (名) lecturer

讲授 jiǎngshòu (动) lecture; instruct; teach

讲述 jiǎngshù (动) tell about; give an account of; narrate; relate

讲台(臺) jiǎngtái (名) lecture platform; rostrum

讲坛(壇) jiǎngtán (名) 1 platform; rostrum 2 forum

讲学(學) jiǎngxué (动) give lectures (on an academic subject): 应邀来我校～ come on invitation to give lectures at our college

讲演 jiǎngyǎn (名) lecture; speech

讲义(義) jiǎngyì (名) (mimeographed or xoroxed) teaching materials

讲座 jiǎngzuò (名) a course of lectures; series of lectures

酱(醬) jiàng (名) 1 a thick sauce made from soya beans, flour, etc.: ～油 soya sauce 2 cooked or pickled in soy sauce: ～肉 pork cooked in soy sauce; braised pork seasoned with soy sauce 3 sauce; paste; jam: 芝麻～ sesame jam. 番茄～ tomato sauce

酱菜 jiàngcài (名) vegetables pickled in soy sauce; pickles

酱园(園) jiàngyuán (名) a shop making and selling sauce, pickles, etc.; sauce and pickle shop

将(將) jiàng (名) 1 general 2 commander in chief, the chief piece in Chinese chess

see also jiāng

将官 jiàngguān (名) 〈口〉 high-ranking military officer; general

将领 jiànglǐng (名) high-ranking military officer; general

将士 jiàngshì (名) 〈书〉 officers and men; commanders and fighters

浆(漿) jiàng

see also jiāng

浆糊 jiànghu (名) paste

匠 jiàng (名) craftsman; artisan: 能工巧～ skilled craftsmen. 铁～ blacksmith

匠人 jiàngrén (名) artisan; craftsman

匠心 jiàngxīn (名) 〈书〉 ingenuity; craftsmanship: 独具～ show distinctive ingenuity

降 jiàng (动) fall; drop; lower: ～雨 a fall of rain; rainfall. ～价 cut prices. 许多消费品价格已经～了. The prices of many consumer goods have dropped. ～级 demote; reduce to a lower rank

see also xiáng

降低 jiàngdī (动) reduce; cut down; drop; lower: ～生产成本 reduce production costs

降格 jiànggé (动)〈书〉lower one's standard or status: ～以求 have to be content with a second best

降临(臨) jiànglín (动) befall; arrive; come: 夜色～. Darkness (or night) fell.

降落 jiàngluò (动) descend; land: 飞机的～ the landing of aircraft. 强迫～ forced landing. ～伞 parachute

降水 jiàngshuǐ (名) precipitation: 人工～ artificial precipitation. ～量 precipitation

降温 jiàngwēn (动、名) 1 lower the temperature (as in a workshop) 2 drop in temperature: ～设备 cooling system

绛 jiàng (形) deep red; crimson

绛紫 jiàngzǐ (名) dark reddish purple

强 jiàng (形) stubborn; unyielding: 倔～ stubborn; obstinate see also qiáng; qiǎng

强嘴 jiàngzuǐ (动) reply defiantly; answer back; talk back

犟 jiàng (形) obstinate; stubborn; self-willed

浇(澆) jiāo (动) 1 pour liquid on; sprinkle water on: 大雨～得他全身都湿透了. He was soaked. 2 irrigate; water: ～花 water flowers. ～地 irrigate the fields

浇灌 jiāoguàn (动) 1 water; irrigate 2 pour: ～混凝土 pour concrete

浇铸(鑄) jiāozhù (名) casting; pouring: ～机 casting machine

交 jiāo I (动) 1 hand in; give up; turn over; deliver: ～还 give back; return. ～税 pay tax. ～作业 hand in one's homework 2 (of places or periods of time) meet; join: ～界 line of demarcation 3 reach (a certain hour or season): ～冬以后 since winter set in 4 cross; intersect: 圆周内两直径必相～. Any two diameters of a circle intersect each other. 5 associate with: ～朋友 make friends 6 have sexual intercourse; mate; breed: 杂～ crossbreed II (名) 1 friend; acquaintance; friendship; relationship: 结～ make friends with. 点头之～ a nodding acquaintance. 建～ establish diplomatic relations 2 business transaction; deal; bargain: 成～ strike a bargain; conclude a transaction; clinch a deal III (形) 1 mutual; reciprocal; each other: ～换 exchange 2 both; together; simultaneous: 饥寒～迫 be plagued by hunger and cold

交班 jiāobān (动) hand over to the next shift; hand over one's official duties

交叉 jiāochā (动) 1 intersect; cross; crisscross: ～路口 an intersection 2 overlap: 他们的意见有点～. Their views overlap.

交差 jiāochāi (动) report to one's immediate superior when his mission has been duly accomplished

交错 jiāocuò I (动) interlock; crisscross II (形) staggered

交代 jiāodài (动) 1 hand over: ～工作 hand over work to one's successor; brief one's successor on his work 2 explain; make clear; brief; tell: ～任务 brief sb. on his task 3 account for: 这次你又怎么～? What excuse can you offer this time? 4 confess: ～罪行 confess a crime. also as "交待"

交底 jiāodǐ (动) explain what the matter really is

交锋 jiāofēng (动) cross swords; engage in a battle or contest

交付 jiāofù (动) 1 pay: ～佣金 pay commission 2 hand over; deliver; consign: ～表决 put to the vote. ～使用 be made available to the users

交割 jiāogē (动) complete a business transaction

交公 jiāogōng (动) hand over to the collective or the state

交媾 jiāogòu (名) sexual intercourse

交互 jiāohù (副) 1 each other; mutual 2 alternately; in turn: 两种策略～使用 use the two tactics alternately

交换 jiāohuàn (动) exchange; swop: ～意见 exchange views; compare notes. ～房子 exchange homes. 实物～ barter. ～留学生 exchange students between two countries

交货 jiāohuò (名) delivery: 即期～ prompt delivery. 分批～ partial delivery. ～港 port of delivery. ～期 date of delivery

交集 jiāojí (动) (of different feelings) be mixed; occur simultaneously: 悲喜～ have mixed feelings of grief and joy

交际(際) jiāojì (名) social intercourse; communication: 语言是人们～的工具. Language is the means by which people communicate with each other. 他不善于～. He is not sociable. ～场合 social occasion

交加 jiāojiā (动) <书> (of two things) occur simultaneously: 风雨～ Wind and rain raged. 悲喜～ Grief mingled with joy.

交接 jiāojiē (动) **1** join; connect **2** hand over and take over: ～班 relief of a shift. ～手续(仪式) handing over procedure (ceremony) 新老干部的～ the smooth succession of younger cadres to old ones

交界 jiāojiè (名) (of two or more places) have a common boundary: 三省～的地方 a place where three provinces meet; the juncture of three provinces

交卷 jiāojuàn (动) **1** hand in an examination paper **2** fulfil one's task; carry out an assignment

交口称(稱)誉(譽) jiāokǒu chēngyù (动) unanimously praise; sing sb's praises: 群众～ be held in high esteem by the public

交流 jiāoliú I (动、名) exchange; interflow; interchange: ～经验 exchange experiences; draw on each other's experience. 文化～ cultural exchange II (形) alternating: ～电 alternating current

交纳 jiāonà (动) pay (to the state or an organization); hand in: ～会费 pay membership dues

交配 jiāopèi (名) mating; copulation: ～期 mating season

交情 jiāoqing (名) friendship; friendly relations; acquaintanceship

交融 jiāoróng (动) blend; mingle: 水乳～ be in perfect harmony

交涉 jiāoshè (动) negotiate; make representations: 办～ carry on negotiations with; take up a matter with. 口头～ verbal representations

交谈 jiāotán (动) converse; chat; have chitchat

交替 jiāotì I (动) supersede; replace: 新旧～. The new takes the place of the old. II (副) alternately; in turn: ～使用 use alternately

交通 jiāotōng (名) traffic; communications: ～规则 traffic regulations. 公路～ highway traffic. ～事故 traffic (or road) accident. ～阻塞 traffic jam (or block)

交头(頭)接耳 jiāotóu-jiē'ěr speak in each other's ears; whisper to each other

交往 jiāowǎng (名) social contact

交尾 jiāowěi (名) mating; pairing; coupling

交响(響)乐(樂) jiāoxiǎngyuè (名) symphony; symphonic music: ～队 symphony orchestra; philharmonic orchestra

交易 jiāoyì (名) business; deal; trade; transaction: 现款～ cash transaction. 商品～会 trade fair; commodities fair. 政治～ a political deal. 做～ make a deal

交易所 jiāoyìsuǒ (名) exchange: 证券～ stock exchange

交谊 jiāoyì (名) <书> friendship; friendly relations

交游 jiāoyóu (名) <书> be friends: ～甚广 have a wide circle of acquaintances

交战(戰) jiāozhàn (动) be at war; wage war: ～状态 state of war. ～双方 the two belligerent parties

交帐(帳) jiāozhàng (动) **1** hand over the accounts **2** account for

交织(織) jiāozhī (动) interweave; intertwine; mingle

胶(膠)

jiāo I (名) **1** glue; gum **2** rubber II (动) stick with glue; glue III (形) gluey; sticky; gummy

胶版 jiāobǎn (名) offset plate: ～印刷 offset printing

胶布 jiāobù (名) **1** rubberized fabric **2** adhesive tape

胶卷 jiāojuǎn (名) roll film; film

胶片 jiāopiàn (名) film: 缩微～ microfiche

胶水 jiāoshuǐ (名) mucilage; glue

胶鞋 jiāoxié (名) rubber overshoes; galoshes

胶印 jiāoyìn (名) offset printing; offset lithography; offset: ～机 offset press; offset (printing) machine

胶着 jiāozhuó (形) deadlocked; stalemated: ～状态 deadlock; stalemate; impasse

郊 jiāo (名) suburbs; outskirts: ～游 outing; excursion. 京～ the suburbs of Beijing

郊区(區) jiāoqū (名) suburban district; suburbs; outskirts

姣 jiāo (形) ‹书› handsome; beautiful-looking

教 jiāo (动) teach; instruct: ～书 teach school; teach. 他～我们开车. He taught us how to drive a car.
see also jiào

椒 jiāo (名) any of several hot spice plants: 辣～ chili; red pepper. 胡～ pepper

娇(嬌) jiāo I (形) 1 tender; lovely; charming 2 fragile; frail; delicate 3 squeamish; finicky II (动) pamper; spoil: ～生惯养 spoilt (by indulgent parents)

娇惯 jiāoguàn (动) pamper; coddle; spoil: ～孩子 pamper a child

娇媚 jiānmèi (形) 1 coquettish 2 sweet and charming

娇嫩 jiāonèn (形) 1 tender and lovely 2 fragile; delicate: ～的身子 delicate health

娇气(氣) jiāoqi (形) pampered; spoiled

骄(驕) jiāo (形) proud; arrogant; conceited: ～必败. Pride goes before a fall.

骄傲 jiāo'ào I (形) arrogant; conceited: ～自大 swollen with pride; conceited and arrogant II (动) be proud; take pride in: 为…感到～ take pride in III (名) pride: 民族的～ the pride of the nation

骄横 jiāohèng (形) arrogant and imperious; extremely overbearing

骄矜 jiāojīn (形) ‹书› self-important; proud; haughty

骄奢淫逸 jiāoshē-yínyì live a life of luxury and indulge in pleasure; wallow in luxury and pleasure; be extravagant and dissipated

焦 jiāo I (形) 1 burnt; scorched; charred: 2 worried; anxious: 心～ anxious; worried II (名) coke: 炼～ coking

焦点(點) jiāodiǎn (名) 1 focal point; focus 2 central issue; point at issue: 争论的～ the point at issue

焦急 jiāojí (形) anxious and restless; worried: ～万分 full of anxiety

焦虑(慮) jiāolǜ (动) feel anxious; have worries and misgivings

焦炭 jiāotàn (名) coke: 沥青～ pitch coke

焦头(頭)烂(爛)额 jiāotóu-làn'é (形) badly battered; in a terrible fix; in a very awkward situation

焦躁 jiāozào (形) restless with anxiety; impatient; fretful

焦灼 jiāozhuó (形) ‹书› deeply worried; very anxious

蕉 jiāo (名) any of several broadleaf plants: 香～ banana.

礁 jiāo (名) reef: ～石 reef; rock. 触～ strike a reef; run up on a rock

嚼 jiáo (动) masticate; chew; munch: 别在背后～舌. Don't gossip behind one's back.
see also jué

铰 jiǎo (动) ‹口› 1 cut with scissors: ～成两半 cut in two; cut into halves; cut in half 2 bore with a reamer; ream: ～孔 ream a hole

铰链 jiǎoliàn (名) hinge: ～接合 hinge joint

佼 jiǎo (形) ‹书› handsome; beautiful

佼佼 jiǎojiǎo (形) ‹书› above average; outstanding

皎 jiǎo (形) clear and bright: ～月 a bright moon

皎皎 jiǎojiǎo (形) very clear and bright; glistening white

皎洁(潔) jiǎojié (形) (of moonlight) bright and clear

狡 jiǎo (形) crafty; foxy; cunning: ～计 crafty trick; ruse

狡辩(辯) jiǎobiàn (动) quibble; resort to sophistry

狡猾 jiǎohuá (形) sly; crafty; cunning; tricky

狡赖 jiǎolài (动) deny (by resorting to sophistry)

狡兔三窟 jiǎotù sān kū It is a poor mouse that has only one hole.

狡黠 jiǎoxié (形) ‹书› sly; crafty; cunning

狡诈 jiǎozhà (形) deceitful; crafty; cunning

饺(餃) jiǎo (名) dumpling: 蒸～ steamed dumplings

饺子 jiǎozi (名) dumpling (with meat and vegetable stuffing); *jiaozi*; ravioli

绞 jiǎo I (动) 1 twist; wring; entangle: 把衣服～干 wring

out wet clothes. ～尽脑汁 rack one's brains; cudgel one's brains 2 hang by the neck: ～架 gallows. ～索 (the hangman's) noose II (量) skein; hank: 一～毛线 a skein of woollen yarn
绞车(車) jiǎochē (名) winch; windlass
绞杀(殺) jiǎoshā (动) strangle
绞痛 jiǎotòng (名) angina: 肚子～ abdominal angina; colic. 心～ angina pectoris
绞刑 jiǎoxíng (名) death by hanging: 上～ be hanged by the neck

搅(攪) jiǎo (动) 1 stir; mix: 把粥～一～ give the porridge a stir 2 disturb; annoy: 别打～她. Don't disturb her.
搅拌 jiǎobàn (动) stir; mix: ～机 mixer
搅动(動) jiǎodòng (动) mix; stir
搅混 jiǎohun (动) 〈口〉 mix; blend; mingle: 把水～ deliberately create confusion
搅和 jiǎohuo (动) 1 mix; blend; mingle: 别把这两件事～在一起. Don't mix up the two different matters. 2 mess up; spoil
搅乱(亂) jiǎoluàn (动) confuse, throw into disorder
搅扰(擾) jiǎorǎo (动) disturb; annoy; cause trouble

矫(矯) jiǎo I (动) rectify; straighten out; adjust; correct II (形) strong; brave: ～若游龙 as powerful as a flying dragon
矫健 jiǎojiàn (形) robust; full of vim and vigour: ～的步伐 vigorous strides
矫揉造作 jiǎoróu zàozuò (形) affected; pretentious
矫枉过(過)正 jiǎo wǎng guò zhèng go beyond the proper limits in correcting an error
矫正 jiǎozhèng (动) correct; put right; rectify: ～发音 correct sb's pronunciation mistakes. ～偏差 correct a deviation. ～错误 correct an error

侥(僥) jiǎo
侥幸 jiǎoxìng (形) lucky; by luck; by a fluke: ～取胜 win by sheer good luck

缴 jiǎo (动) 1 pay; hand over; hand in: ～房租 pay house rent. ～税 pay taxes. 上～ turn over (or in) to the state 2 capture: ～获三架机枪 capture three machine guns
缴获(獲) jiǎohuò (动) capture; seize
缴械 jiǎoxiè (动) 1 disarm 2 lay down one's arms

脚 jiǎo (名) 1 foot: 赤～ barefoot 2 base; foot: 山～ the foot of a hill
脚本 jiǎoběn (名) script; scenario: 电影～ film script
脚步 jiǎobù (名) step; pace: 加快～ quicken one's pace
脚跟 jiǎogēn (名) heel: 站稳～ stand firm; gain a firm footing (in society)
脚力 jiǎolì (名) strength of one's legs
脚镣 jiǎoliào (名) fetters; shackles
脚手架 jiǎoshǒujià (名) scaffold
脚踏两(兩)只(隻)船 jiǎo tà liǎng zhī chuán sit on the fence
脚踏实(實)地 jiǎo tà shídì earnest and down-to-earth; conscientious and practical: ～工作 work in a down-to-earth manner
脚注 jiǎozhù (名) footnote

角 jiǎo (名) 1 horn: 牛～ ox horn. 鹿～ antler 2 bugle; horn: 号～ bugle 3 sth. in the shape of a horn: 菱～ water caltrop 4 corner: 拐～ corner 5 angle: 锐(钝)～ acute (obtuse) angle. 直～ right angle
see also jué
角度 jiǎodù (名) 1 degree of an angle 2 point of view; angle: 如果光从自己～来看问题,意见就难免不一致. If everybody looks at the question from the angle of his own interest, opinions are bound to differ.
角落 jiǎoluò (名) 1 corner: 在房间～里 in a corner of the room 2 remote place: 在祖国每一～里 in the remote parts of the country

剿 jiǎo (动) send armed forces to suppress; put down: ～匪 suppress bandits
see also chāo

窖 jiào (名) cellar or pit for storing things: 菜～ vegetable cellar

觉(覺) jiào (名) sleep: 睡一～ catch up on some sleep. 午～ afternoon nap
see also jué

校 jiào (动) 1 check; proofread; collate: ～长条样 read galley proofs 2 compare
see also xiào

校对(對) jiàoduì I (动) 1 proofread; proof 2 check against the original; calibrate II (名) proofreader

校样 jiàoyàng (名) proof sheet; proof

校阅 jiàoyuè (动) read and revise

校正 jiàozhèng (动) proofread and correct; rectify: ～错字 correct misprints

校准(準) jiàozhǔn (名) calibration: 方位～ bearing calibration

较 jiào I (动) compare: 工作～前更为努力 work even harder than before II (副) comparatively; relatively; fairly; quite; rather: ～好 fairly good; quite good III (形) clear: 彰明～著 conspicuous

较量 jiàoliàng (动) 1 have a contest; have a trial of strength 2 carefully consider

教 jiào I (动) teach; instruct: 因材施～ teach according to ability. 请～ ask for advice; consult II (名) religion: 信～ believe in a religion; be religious. 基督～ Christianity

see also jiāo

教案 jiào'àn (名) teaching notes

教材 jiàocái (名) teaching material

教程 jiàochéng (名) 1 course of study 2 (published) lectures

教导(導) jiàodǎo I (动) instruct; teach; give guidance II (名) teaching; guidance

教皇 jiàohuáng (名) pope; pontiff

教会(會) jiàohuì (名) (the Christian) church: ～学校 missionary school

教诲 jiàohuì (名) ‹书› teaching; instruction: 谆谆～ earnest guidance

教科书(書) jiàokēshū (名) textbook

教练(練) jiàoliàn (动) 1 train; drill; coach 2 coach; instructor: 足球～ football coach. ～员 coach; instructor; trainer

教师(師) jiàoshī (名) teacher

教士 jiàoshì (名) priest; clergyman; Christian missionary

教室 jiàoshì (名) classroom; schoolroom

教授 jiàoshòu I (名) professor: 副～ associate professor. 客座～ visiting professor; guest professor II (动) instruct; teach: ～历史 lecture on history

教唆 jiàosuō (动) instigate; abet; incite; put sb. up to sth.: ～犯 abettor

教堂 jiàotáng (名) church; cathedral

教条(條) jiàotiáo (名) dogma; doctrine; creed; tenet: ～主义 dogmatism; doctrinairism

教徒 jiàotú (名) follower of a religion

教学(學) jiàoxué (名) 1 impart knowledge to students: ～相长 Teaching helps the teacher as well as the students. 2 teaching and studying: ～大纲 teaching programme; syllabus. ～方针 principles of teaching

教训 jiàoxùn (名) 1 lesson; moral: 吸取～ draw a lesson (or moral) from sth.; take warning from sth. 2 chide; teach sb. a lesson; give sb. a dressing down; lecture sb. (for wrongdoing, etc.)

教养(養) jiàoyǎng (动、名) 1 educate and train (the younger generation) 2 moral education; culture

教育 jiàoyù I (名) education: ～部 Ministry of Education II (动) teach; educate; inculcate: 我们从中得到了很大的～. We've learnt a great deal from this.

教员 jiàoyuán (名) teacher; instructor: 汉语～ a teacher of Chinese

酵 jiào (动) ferment; leaven

酵母 jiàomǔ (名) yeast

叫 jiào I (动) 1 cry; shout: 大～一声 give a loud cry; shout; cry out loudly. 狗～ bark; yap 2 call; greet: 有人～你. Somebody is calling you. 3 hire; order: ～个出租汽车 hail a taxi 4 name; call: 人们～他汤姆大叔. People call him Uncle Tom. 你～什么名儿? What's your name? 5 ask; advise: ～他进来吗? Shall I ask him (to come) in? 医生～他戒烟. The doctor advised him to give up smoking. II (介) [used to introduce a passive construction]: ～你猜对了. You've guessed right.

叫喊 jiàohǎn (动) shout; yell; howl

叫花子 jiàohuāzi (名) ‹口› beggar

叫唤 jiàohuan (动) cry out; call out: 疼得直～ scream with pain

叫苦 jiàokǔ (动) complain;

moan and groan: ～不迭 pour out a stream of grievances; complain endlessly

叫屈 jiàoqū (动) complain of being wronged

叫嚷 jiàorǎng (动) shout; howl; clamour

叫嚣 jiàoxiāo clamour; raise a hue and cry: 战争～ clamour for war. 大肆～ raise a terrific hue and cry

叫座 jiàozuò (动) attract a large audience: 这戏很～. This play appeals to the audience

叫做 jiàozuò (动) be called; be known as: 这种装置～呼吸分析器. This apparatus is called breathanalyser.

轿(轎) jiào (～子) sedan (chair)

轿车(車) jiàochē bus or car: 大～ bus; coach. 小～ car; limousine; sedan

秸(稭) jiē (名) stalks left after threshing; straw: 麦～ wheat straw

秸杆(桿) jiēgǎn (名) straw

结 jiē (动) bear (fruit); form (seed): 开花～果 blossom and bear fruit

see also jié

结巴 jiēba (动、名) **1** stammer; stutter **2** stammerer; stutterer

结实(實) jiēshí I (动) bear fruit; fructify II (形) **1** solid; sturdy; durable: 这张桌子很～. This is a very solid table. 绑～点. Tie it fast. **2** strong; sturdy; tough: 他长得很～. He is of strong build.

接 jiē (动) **1** come into contact with; come close to: ～近 approach; draw near **2** connect; join; put together: 请～上去! carry on, please! 请～286分机. Put me through to Extension 286, please. **3** catch; take hold of: ～球 catch a ball **4** receive: ～到一封信 receive a letter. ～电话 answer the phone **5** meet; welcome: 到飞机场～一个代表团 meet a delegation at the airport

接班 jiēbān (动) take one's turn on duty; take over from; succeed; carry on: 谁接你的班? Who will take over from you? ～人 successor

接触(觸) jiēchù I (动) come into contact with; get in touch with: 代表团～了各界人士. The delegation met with people from all circles. II (名) contact: ～不良 loose (or poor) contact

接待 jiēdài (动) receive; admit: ～外宾 receive foreign visitors. 受到亲切～ be accorded a cordial reception. ～室 reception room. ～单位 host organization

接二连(連)三 jiē'èr-liánsān (副) one after another; in quick succession: 他～收到朋友来信. Letters come from his friends one after another. 捷报～地传来. News of the victory came in quick succession. *or* Tiding of victory poured in thick and fast.

接风(風) jiēfēng (动) give a dinner for a visitor from afar

接济(濟) jiējì (动) give financial or another form of assistance to

接见(見) jiējiàn (动) meet with sb.; grant an interview to

接近 jiējìn (形、动) be close to; near; approach: ～国际水平 approach the international level. 该项工程～完成. The project is nearing completion. 这个人不容易～. That man is rather difficult to approach.

接力 jiēlì (名) relay: ～赛跑 relay race; relay

接连(連) jiēlián on end; in a row; in succession: ～好几天 for days on end. ～三小时 for three hours at a stretch

接纳 jiēnà (动) admit (into an organization): ～新会员 admit new members

接洽 jiēqià (动) take up a matter with; arrange (business, etc.) with; consult with: 同有关部门～ take up a matter with the department concerned. 他来～工作. He's here on business.

接壤 jiērǎng (动) border on; be contiguous to; be bounded by: ～地区 contiguous areas

接生 jiēshēng (动) deliver a child; practise midwifery

接收 jiēshōu (动) **1** receive: ～无线电信号 receive radio signals **2** take over (property, etc.); expropriate: ～这一家饭店 take over this hotel **3** admit: ～新会员 recruit new members

接受 jiēshòu (动) accept: ～邀请 accept an invitation. ～意见 take sb.'s advice. ～群众监督 place oneself under the supervision of the masses

接替 jiētì (动) take over; replace

接通 jiētōng (动) put through

电话～了吗？Have you got through?

接头(頭) jiētóu (动) contact; get in touch with; meet: 我找谁～？Who shall I get in touch with? ～地点 contact point; rendezvous

接吻 jiēwěn (动) kiss

接应(應) jiēyìng (动) 1 come to sb.'s aid (or assistance) 2 supply: 水泥一时～不上. Cement was in short supply at the time.

接着 jiēzhe (动) 1 catch: 你～我从树上扔下的苹果好吗？You catch the apples I throw down from the tree, won't you? 2 follow; carry on: 一个～一个 one after another. 请～讲下去. Please go on.

接踵 jiēzhǒng (动) ‹书› following on sb.'s heels; in the wake of: 来访者～而至. Visitors came one after another.

揭 jiē (动) 1 tear off; take off: 把墙上那张布告～下来. Take down that notice from the wall. 2 uncover; lift (the lid, etc.): ～盖子 take the lid off sth.; bring sth. into the open 3 expose; show up; bring to light: ～老底 expose sb.'s past failings. ～人疮疤 touch sb.'s sore spot; touch sb. on the raw 4 ‹书› raise; hoist: ～竿而起 raise a bamboo pole to serve as a standard of revolt

揭穿 jiēchuān (动) expose; show up: 他的假面具被～了. His mask has been torn off.

揭底 jiēdǐ (动) reveal the inside story

揭短 jiēduǎn (动) disclose sb.'s faults

揭发(發) jiēfā (动) expose; unmask; bring to light

揭开(開) jiēkāi (动) uncover; reveal; open: ～宇宙的奥秘 uncover the mystery of the universe

揭露 jiēlù (动) expose; uncover; bring to light: ～其真面目 expose sb.'s true features. ～矛盾 bring the contradictions to light

揭幕 jiēmù (动) unveil (a monument, etc.): ～式 unveiling ceremony

揭示 jiēshì (动) 1 announce; promulgate 2 reveal; bring to light

揭晓(曉) jiēxiǎo (动) announce; make known; publish: 选举结果已经～. The result of the election has been announced.

皆 jiē (代) ‹书› all; each and every: 人人～知. It is known to all.

皆大欢(歡)喜 jiē dà huānxǐ to the satisfaction of all

阶(階) jiē (名) steps; stairs: 台～ a flight of steps

阶层(層) jiēcéng (名) (social) stratum: 社会～ social stratum

阶段 jiēduàn (名) stage; phase: 过渡～ transitional stage (or period). 第一～的工程已经完成. The first phase of the project has been completed.

阶级 jiējí (名) (social) class: ～斗争 class struggle. ～分析 class analysis. ～矛盾 class contradictions

阶梯 jiētī (名) a flight of stairs; ladder; stepping stone

阶下囚 jiēxiàqiú (名) prisoner; captive

街 jiē (名) street: 上～买东西 go shopping downtown

街道 jiēdào (名) 1 street 2 what concerns the neighbourhood: ～办事处 subdistrict office. ～委员会 neighbourhood committee

街坊 jiēfang (名) ‹口› neighbours

街谈巷议(議) jiētán-xiàngyì (名) street gossip; the talk of the town

街头(頭) jiētóu (名) street corner; street: 流落～ tramp the streets; drift along homeless in a city.

节(節) jiē (名)

see also jié

节骨眼 jiēguyǎn (名) ‹方› critical juncture

疖(癤) jiē (～子) 1 furuncle; boil 2 knot (in wood)

洁(潔) jié (形) clean: 整～ clean and tidy; clean and neat

洁白 jiébái (形) spotlessly white; pure

洁净 jiéjìng (形) clean; spotless

洁身自好 jié shēn zì hào 1 preserve one's moral integrity 2 mind one's own business in order to keep out of trouble

诘 jié (动) ‹书› closely question; interrogate: ～问 closely question; interrogate; cross-examine

拮 jié (形): ～据 in straitened circumstances; short of money; hard up

结 jié (动) **1** tie; knit; knot; weave: ～网 weave a net **2** knot: 打～ tje a knot **3** congeal; form; forge; cement: ～痂 form a scab; scab **4** settle; conclude: ～帐 settle accounts

see also jiē

结案 jié'àn (动) wind up a case

结拜 jiébài (动) become sworn brothers or sisters

结伴 jiébàn (动) go with: ～而行 go or travel in a group

结冰 jiébīng (动) freeze; ice up

结彩 jiécǎi (动) adorn (or decorate) with festoons: 张灯～ decorate with lanterns and festoons

结成 jiéchéng (动) form: ～同盟 form an alliance; become allies. ～一伙 gang up; band together

结党(黨)营(營)私 jiédǎng-yíngsī form a clique to gain private ends; gang up for selfish purposes

结构(構) jiégòu (名) structure; composition; construction: 经济～ economic structure. 文章～ organization of an essay. 消费～ consumption pattern. 技术～ technological makeup. ～严密 well organized. 钢筋混凝土～ reinforced concrete structure

结果 jiéguǒ I (名) result; outcome: 必然～ inevitable result. 刻苦学习的～ the result of painstaking hard work II (动) kill; finish off

结合 jiéhé (动) **1** combine; unite; integrate; link: 劳逸～ combine work with rest **2** be united in wedlock

结婚 jiéhūn (动) marry; get married: ～登记 marriage registration. ～证书 marriage certificate

结交 jiéjiāo (动) make friends with; associate with

结局 jiéjú (名) final result; outcome; ending: 悲惨的～ a tragic ending

结论(論) jiélùn (名) **1** conclusion (of a syllogism) **2** conclusion; verdict: 得出～ draw (or come to, reach) a conclusion

结盟 jiéméng (动) form an alliance; ally; align: 不～政策 nonalignment policy

结亲(親) jiéqīn (动) **1** ‹口› marry; get married **2** (of two families) become related by marriage

结社 jiéshè (动)form an association:～自由freedom of association

结识(識) jiéshí (动) get acquainted with sb.; make the acquaintance of sb.

结束 jiéshù (动) end; finish; conclude; wind up; close: ～讲话 wind up a speech. 会议下午五时～. The meeting lasted till 5 p.m. ～语 concluding remarks

结尾 jiéwěi (名) ending; winding-up stage

结业(業) jiéyè (动) complete a course; wind up one's studies; finish school

结余(餘) jiéyú (名) cash surplus; surplus; balance

结怨 jiéyuàn (动) provoke hatred

结帐 jiézhàng (动) settle (or square) accounts; balance books

截 jié I (动) **1** cut; sever: ～成两段 cut in two **2** stop; check; stem: ～流 dam a river. ～球 intercept a pass **3** by (a specified time); up to: ～至八月底 up to the end of August II (量) section; chunk; length: 一～儿木头 a log

截长(長)补(補)短 jié cháng bǔ duǎn draw on the strong points to offset the weaknesses: 我们要彼此～. We must give full play to our abilities to make up for our shortcomings

截断(斷) jiéduàn (动) **1** cut off; block: ～敌人的退路 cut off the enemy's retreat **2** cut short; interrupt

截获(獲) jiéhuò (动) intercep[t] and capture

截止 jiézhǐ end; close: 报名已[截] ～了. Registration has closed

截然 jiérán (副) sharply; com[-] pletely: ～不同 poles apart; com[-] pletely different. ～相反 diame[-] trically opposite

劫 jié (动) ‹书› **1** rob; hol[d] up; plunder; raid: 抢～ loot **2** coerce; compel II (名) calamity; disaster; misfortune 浩～ a great calamity. ～后余生 be a survivor of a disaster

劫持 jiéchí (动) kidnap; ho[ld] under duress; hijack: ～飞[机] hijack an aeroplane

劫掠 jiélüè (动) plunder; loot

劫狱(獄) jiéyù (动) break into jail to rescue a prisoner

节(節) jié I (名) **1** join[t;] node; knot: 竹～ bar[n]boo joint. 骨～ joint (of bone) **2** division; part: 音～ syllab[le] **3** festival; redletter day; ho[li]day: 过～ celebrate (or observ[e])

a festival. 春～ the Spring Festival. 国庆～ National Day **4** item: 细～ details **5** integrity: 气～ moral or political integrity **II**(动) **1** abridge: ～译 abridged translation **2** economize; save: ～煤 economize on coal **III**(量) section; length: 一～铁管 a length of iron pipe. 八～车厢 eight railway coaches
see also jiē

节俭(儉) jiéjiǎn (形、名) thrifty; frugal: 提倡～ encourage frugality

节录(錄) jiélù (名) extract; excerpt

节目 jiémù (名) programme; item (on a programme); number: 晚会的～ programme for the evening party. ～单 programme; playbill

节拍 jiépāi (名) metre; musical rhythm

节日 jiérì (名) festival; red-letter day; holiday: ～气氛 festive atmosphere

节省 jiéshěng (动) economize; save; use sparingly; cut down on: ～时间 save time. ～行政开支 cut down on government expenditure

节外生枝 jiéwài shēng zhī raise unexpected side issues

节衣缩食 jiéyī-suōshí economize on food and clothing; live frugally

节余(餘) jiéyú (名) surplus (as a result of economizing)

节育 jiéyù (名) birth control

节约 jiéyuē (动) practise economy; economize; save: ～能源 conserve energy

节制 jiézhì **I**(动) control; regulate; check; be moderate in: ～饮食 eat and drink moderately **II**(名) temperance; abstinence

节奏 jiézòu (名) musical rhythm: ～明快 lively rhythm

捷

jié **I**(名) victory; triumph: 大～ a great victory. 报～ announce a victory **II**(形) prompt; nimble; quick: 敏～ quick; nimble; agile

捷报(報) jiébào (名) news of victory or success: ～频传. News of victory keeps pouring in.

捷径(徑) jiéjìng (名) shortcut: 走～ take a shortcut

捷足先登 jiézú xiān dēng the race is to the swiftest; the early bird catches the worm

睫

jié (名) eyelash; lash: ～毛 eyelash; lash

竭

jié (动) exhaust; use up

竭诚 jiéchéng (副) wholeheartedly; with all one's heart; in all sincerity

竭尽(盡) jiéjìn (动) use up; exhaust: ～全力 spare no effort; do one's utmost; do all one can

竭力 jiélì do one's utmost; strain every nerve: ～支持 give all-out support. ～反对 actively oppose

竭泽(澤)而渔 jié zé ér yú drain the pond to get all the fish; kill the goose that lays the golden eggs

杰(傑)

jié (形、名) **1** outstanding; prominent **2** outstanding person; hero

杰出 jiéchū (形) outstanding; remarkable; prominent: ～贡献 a brilliant contribution

杰作 jiézuò (名) masterpiece

孑

jié (形)〈书〉 lonely; all alone

孑然 jiérán (形)〈书〉 solitary; lonely; alone: ～一身 live all alone in this wide human world

解

jiě (动) **1** separate; divide: ～剖 dissect. 溶～ dissolve. 难～难分 be too deeply involved (in an affair) **2** untie; undo: ～鞋带 undo shoelaces. ～扣儿 unbutton **3** allay; dispel; dismiss: ～渴 quench one's thirst **4** explain; interpret; solve: 注～ annotate. ～题 solve a problem **5** understand; comprehend: 费～ hard to understand. 百思不～ fail to understand even after pondering a hundred times. 令人不～ puzzling; incomprehensible **6** relieve oneself: 小～ go to the lavatory (to urinate)
see also jiè

解嘲 jiěcháo (动) try to cover up or gloss over sth. when ridiculed

解除 jiěchú (动) remove; relieve; get rid of: ～职务 remove sb. from his post; relieve sb. of his office. ～合同 terminate a contract. ～武装 disarm. ～禁令 lift a ban

解答 jiědá (动) answer; explain: ～疑难问题 answer difficult questions

解冻(凍) jiědòng (动) **1** thaw; unfreeze: ～季节 thawing season **2** unfreeze (funds, assets, etc.)

解放 jiěfàng (动、名) liberate; emancipate: 妇女～ the emancipation of women. 民族～运动 national liberation movement

解雇(僱) jiěgù (动) dismiss; fire; sack

解恨 jiěhèn vent one's bottled-up spleen

解救 jiějiù (动) rescue (from the jaws of danger); save; deliver

解决 jiějué (动) 1 solve; resolve; settle: ～纠纷 settle a dispute. ～困难 overcome a difficulty 2 dispose of; finish off: 把敌人完全～了. We have wiped out all the enemy troops.

解开(開) jiěkāi (动) untie; undo: ～上衣 unbutton one's jacket. ～这个谜 unveil the mystery

解聘 jiěpìn (动) dismiss (an employee)

解剖 jiěpōu (动) dissect: 尸体～ autopsy; postmortem examination. ～学 anatomy

解气(氣) jiěqì (动) work off one's steam

解散 jiěsàn (动) 1 dismiss: ～队伍 dismiss; disband 2 dissolve; disband: ～组织 disband an organization. ～议会 dissolve a parliament

解释(釋) jiěshì (动) explain; expound; interpret: ～法律 interpret laws. 这事你怎么～? How do you account for this?

解手 jiěshǒu (动) relieve oneself; go to the toilet (or lavatory)

解说 jiěshuō (动) explain orally; comment

解体(體) jiětǐ (动) disintegrate; fall apart: 社会的～ the disintegration of society

解脱 jiětuō (动) free (or extricate) oneself: 使政府从危机中～出来 extricate the government from a crisis

解围(圍) jiěwéi (动) 1 enemy to raise a siege; rescue troops from enemy encirclement 2 help sb. out of a predicament; save sb. from an embarrassing situation

解职(職) jiězhí (动) dismiss from office; discharge; relieve sb. of his post

姐 jiě (名) 1 elder sister; sister 2 a general term for young women

姐夫 jiěfu (名) elder sister's husband; brother-in-law

姐姐 jiějie (名) elder sister; sister

戒 jiè I (动) 1 guard against: 力～骄傲 strictly guard against conceit 2 exhort; admonish; warn: 引以为～ take warning from sth. 3 give up; drop; stop: ～烟 give up smoking. ～酒 stop drinking II (名) 1 Buddhist monastic discipline: 受～ attain the full status of a monk or nun 2 (finger) ring: 钻～ diamond ring

戒备(備) jièbèi (动) guard; take precautions; be on the alert: ～森严 be heavily guarded

戒除 jièchú (动) give up; drop; stop: ～恶习 get rid of a bad habit

戒律 jièlǜ (名) religious discipline; commandment

戒心 jièxīn (名) vigilance; wariness: 对某人怀有～ be wary of sb.'s tricks or evil intentions

戒严(嚴) jièyán (动、名) enforce martial law; impose a curfew; cordon off an area to prevent criminals from getting away: 宣布～ proclaim martial law

戒指 jièzhi (名) (finger) ring

诫 jiè (动) warn; admonish: 告～ give warning; admonish

介 jiè (动) 1 be situated between; lie between: 这座山～于两县之间. The mountain lies between two counties. 2 take seriously; take to heart; mind: 不～意 not mind

介词 jiècí (名) preposition

介入 jièrù (动) intervene; interpose; get involved

介绍 jièshào (动) 1 introduce; present: 让我～一下,这就是王先生. Allow me to introduce Mr. Wang. ～对象 find sb. a boy or girl friend 2 recommend; suggest: 我给你～一本书. I'll recommend you a book. 3 let know; brief: ～情况 brief sb. on the situation. ～经验 pass on experience. ～人 sponsor. ～信 letter of introduction; reference

疥 jiè (名) scabies

芥 jiè (名) mustard see also gài

芥末 jièmo (名) mustard

界 jiè (名) 1 boundary: 国～ the boundary of a country 2 scope; extent: 眼～ field of vision; mental horizons 3 circles: 新闻～ press circles. 各～人士 people from all walks of life 4 primary division; kingdom: 动(植、矿)物～ the animal (vegetable, mineral) kingdom

界石 jièshí (名) boundary stone or tablet

界限 jièxiàn (名) 1 demarcation line; dividing line; limits; bounds: 划清～ draw a distinction 2 limit; end

界线(綫) jièxiàn (名) 1 boundary line 2 see "界限" (1)

借 jiè (动) 1 borrow: 跟人～书 borrow books from sb. 2 lend: ～书给他 lend the book to him 3 make use of; take advantage of (an opportunity, etc.) 4 use as a pretext: ～酒浇愁 take to drinking to drown one's sorrows

借贷 jièdài (动) borrow or lend money

借刀杀(殺)人 jiè dāo shā rén make use of another person to get rid of an adversary

借端 jièduān (动) use as a pretext: ～生事 make trouble on a pretext

借故 jiègù find an excuse

借鉴(鑒) jièjiàn (动) use for reference; benefit by another person's experience; draw on the experience of: ～外国的经验 use the experience of other countries for reference

借口 jièkǒu I (动) use as an excuse (or pretext) II (名) excuse; pretext

借款 jièkuǎn I (动) borrow or lend money; ask for or offer a loan II (名) loan

借题发(發)挥 jiè tí fāhuī seize on an incident to exaggerate or distort matters; seize upon an incident to make a fuss

借重 jièzhòng (动) rely on for support

借助 jièzhù (动) have the aid of; draw support from: ～外资 with the help of foreign capital

解 jiè: ～送 send under guard see also jiě

届 jiè I (动) fall due: ～期 when the day comes; on the appointed date II (量) [used before a regular meeting or each year's graduates]: 本～联大 the present session of the U.N. General Assembly. 本～毕业生 this year's graduates

届满 jièmǎn at the expiration of one's term of office: 任期～. The term of office has expired.

届时(時) jièshí when the time comes; at the appointed time; on the occasion

价(價) jie [used after an adverb for emphasis]: 震天～响 make a terrific noise see also jià

津 jīn (名) 1 ferry crossing; ford: ～渡 a ferry crossing 2 saliva

津津乐(樂)道 jīnjīn lè dào relate with gusto; talk about with great relish

津津有味 jīnjīn yǒu wèi (副) with relish; with gusto; with keen pleasure: 听得～ listen with absorbing interest

津贴 jīntiē (名) subsidy; allowance: 岗位～ subsidies appropriate to particular jobs

津液 jīnyè (名) 1 body fluid 2 saliva

禁 jīn (动) contain (or restrain) oneself: 不～流下眼泪 can not hold back one's tears. ～不住 can't help doing sth. see also jìn

禁受 jīnshòu (动) bear; stand; endure

襟 jīn (名) 1 front of a garment 2 brothers-in-law whose wives are sisters

襟怀(懷) jīnhuái (名) ‹书› bosom; (breadth of) mind: ～坦白 open and aboveboard; frank-hearted

巾 jīn (名) a piece of cloth (as used for a towel, scarf, kerchief, etc.): 手～ (face) towel. 围～ scarf. 餐～ napkin

巾帼(幗) jīnguó (名) woman: ～英雄 heroine

今 jīn (形) 1 modern; present-day: ～人 contemporaries; people of our era 2 today: ～明两天 today and tomorrow. ～晚 tonight; this evening 3 this (year); of this year: ～冬 this (coming) winter 4 now; the present: 至～ to date; until now; up to now. 从～以后 from now on; henceforth

今后(後) jīnhòu (副) from now on; in the days to come; henceforth; hereafter; in future: ～的十年内 in the next decade; in the coming ten years

今年 jīnnián (名) this year

今日 jīnrì (名) 1 today 2 present; now: ～中国 China today

今生 jīnshēng (名) this life

今世 jīnshì (名) 1 this life 2 this age; the contemporary age

今天 jīntiān (名) 1 today: 一年前的～ a year ago today 2 the present; now

今昔 jīn-xī (名) the present and the past; today and yesterday

今朝 jīnzhāo (名)〈书〉 today; the present; now

矜 jīn (形) 1 self-important; conceited: 骄～之气 overweening pride; an air of self-importance 2 restrained; reserved

矜持 jīnchí (形) restrained; reserved: 举止～ have a reserved manner; look selcf-onscious

金 jīn I (名) 1 metals: 合～ alloy 五～店 hardware store 2 money: 现～ cash; ready money 3 ancient metal percussion instruments: ～鼓齐鸣. All the gongs and drums are beating. 4 gold (Au): ～币 gold coin. ～条 gold bar II (形) golden: ～婚 golden wedding

金碧辉煌 jīnbì-huīhuáng (形) (of a building, etc.) dazzlingly splendid and magnificent

金蝉(蟬)脱壳(殼) jīnchán tuō qiào (动) slip out of a predicament like a cicada sloughing its skin; escape by cunning manoeuvring

金城汤(湯)池 jīnchéng-tāngchí (名) impregnable fortified city

金额 jīn'é (名) amount (or sum) of money

金刚(剛)石 jīngāngshí (名) diamond

金黄 jīnhuáng (形) golden yellow

金科玉律 jīnkē-yùlǜ (名) golden rule

金钱(錢) jīnqián (名) money

金融 jīnróng (名) finance; banking: ～寡头 financial oligarch (or magnate). ～市场 money market

金属(屬) jīnshǔ (名) metal: 黑色～ ferrous metal. 有色～ nonferrous metal

金玉 jīnyù (名)〈书〉[often used metaphorically] precious; magnificent: ～良言 wise counsel

金字招牌 jīnzì zhāopái (名) 1 (of a business firm) of good repute 2 distinguished title

筋 jīn (名) 1 muscle 2 tendon; sinew 3 anything resembling a tendon or vein: 叶～ ribs of a leaf. 钢～ reinforcing steel; steel reinforcement

筋斗 jīndǒu (名) 1 somersault: 翻～ turn a somersault 2 fall; tumble (over): 摔了个～ trip over sth. and fall

筋骨 jīngǔ (名) bones and muscles—physique

筋疲力尽(盡) jīnpí-lìjìn (形) exhausted; worn out; dog-tired

斤 jīn (名) jin, Chinese unit of weight (= 1/2 kilogram)

斤斤计较 jīnjīn jìjiào worry about petty gain or loss; bother about trifling matters

斤两(兩) jīnliǎng (名) weight: 他的话有～. His words carry weight.

谨 jǐn (形) 1 careful; cautious; scrupulous: ～小慎微 over-cautious particularly in small matters. ～守规则 strictly adhere to the rules. ～言慎行 be cautious in whatever one says or does 2 solemnly; sincerely: ～致谢意. Please accept my sincere thanks.

谨防 jǐnfáng (动) guard against; beware of

谨慎 jǐnshèn (形) prudent; careful; cautious; circumspect: 谦虚～ modest and prudent

紧(緊) jǐn (形) 1 tight; taut; close: 把绳子拉～ pull the rope taut. 把螺丝拧～ drive the screw tight. 这件上衣前身太～. This jacket is a bit too tight in the front. 放学后～接着有足球比赛. There will be a football match right after school. 2 urgent; pressing; tense: 风刮得～. It's blowing hard. 3 strict; stringent: 管得～ exercise strict control over; be strict with 4 hard up; short of money: 手头～ be short of money; be hard up. ～缺商品 commodities are in very short supply

紧凑 jǐncòu (形) compact; terse; well-knit: 这篇文章很～. The article is well-organized.

紧急 jǐnjí (形) urgemt; pressing; critical: 情况～. The situation is critical. ～措施 emergency measures. ～会议 emergency meeting. ～着陆 emergency landing

紧密 jǐnmì (形) close together; inseparable: ～合作 close cooperation. ～联系 close contact

紧迫 jǐnpò (形) pressing; urgent; imminent: 时间～ be pressed for time. 任务～ The task is urgent.

紧缩 jǐnsuō (动) reduce; retrench; tighten: 开支～ cut down expenses

紧要 jǐnyào (形) critical; crucial; vital: ～关头 critical moment (or juncture); crucial moment. 无关～ of no consequence; of no importance

紧张(張) jǐnzhāng (形) 1 nervous; in a flurry: 神情～ look nervous. 慢慢来,别～. Take it easy. Don't be so nervous. 2 tense; intense; strained: ～局势 a tense situation. 关系～ strained relations 3 in short supply; tight: 人力～ inadequate manpower

锦 jǐn I (名) brocade II (形) bright and beautiful: 前程似～ splendid prospects; glorious future

锦标(標) jǐnbiāo (名) prize; trophy; title: ～赛 championship contest; championships

锦缎 jǐnduàn (名) brocade

锦上添花 jǐnshàng tiān huā make what is already good still better

锦绣(繡) jǐnxiù (形) beautiful; splendid: ～山河 a land of charm and beauty

仅(僅) jǐn (副) only; merely; barely: ～次于 second only to. ～供参考 for your reference only. ～有一人. There was only one survivor.

仅仅 jǐnjǐn (副) only; merely; barely: 这～是问题的一面. This is only one side of the picture.

尽(儘) jǐn (副) 1 to the greatest extent: ～早 as soon as possible; at the earliest possible date 2 within the limits of: ～着三天把事情办妥. Get the work done properly within three days. 3 give priority to: 先～老年人和小孩儿上车. Let the old people and children get on the bus first. 4 [used before a word indicating direction, to denote 'most'] at the furthest end of: ～北边 the northernmost end, etc.
see also jìn

尽管 jǐnguǎn I (副) feel free to; not hesitate to: 有什么建议～提. Please feel free to make suggestions. 你～说吧. Say all that you have got to say. II (连) though; even though; in spite of; despite: ～有几个国家反对, 决议还是通过了. The resolution was passed in spite of opposition from a number of countries.

尽可能 jǐnkěnéng (副) as far as possible; to the best of one's ability: ～多邀请些人. Invite as many guests as possible.

尽快 jǐnkuài (副) as quickly (or soon, early) as possible: 请～答复. Please reply at your earliest convenience.

尽量 jǐnliàng to the best of one's ability; as far as possible: 把你亲眼看见的～反映给大家. Tell everybody what you saw so far as possible.

进(進) jìn I (动) 1 advance; move forward; move ahead: 不～则退. Make headway, or you'll fall behind. 2 enter; come or go into: ～教室 enter the classroom. ～大学 enter college 3 receive: ～款 income 4 eat; drink; take: 共～晚餐 have supper together 5 submit; present: ～言 offer advice; make a suggestion 6 [used after a word] into; in: 走～车间 walk into the workshop. 把钉子钉～墙壁 drive the nail into the wall II (名) any of the several rows of houses within an old-style residential compound

进逼 jìnbī (动) (of an army) close in on; advance on; press on towards: 步步～ tighten the encirclement

进步 jìnbù I (动) advance; progress; improve: 你～很快. You are making rapid progress. II (形) (politically) progressive: 思想～ have progressive ideas. ～人士 progressive personages

进程 jìnchéng (名) course; process; progress: 历史～ the course of history

进出口 jìn-chūkǒu (名) import and export

进度 jìndù (名) 1 rate of progress (or advance): 加快～ quicken the pace (or tempo) 2 planned speed; schedule: 按照～完成这项工程. This project is to be completed according to plan.

进发(發) jìnfā (动) set out; start: 游行者向华盛顿～. The marchers started for Washington.

进犯 jìnfàn (动、名) intrude into; invade: 打退～的敌人 beat back the invading enemy

进攻 jìngōng (名) attack; assault; offensive

进化 jìnhuà (名) evolution: ～论 the theory of evolution

进军(軍) jìnjūn (动) (of an army) march; advance

进口 jìnkǒu I (动) 1 call at a port 2 import II (名) entrance: ～港 port of entry. ～商 importer. ～许可证 import license

进来(來) jìnlai I (动) come (or get) in; enter: 让他～. Show him in. II [used after a verb, meaning going or coming in]: 她哼着小调走～. She came in humming a tune.

进取 jìnqǔ (动) keep forging ahead;

be enterprising: ～心 enterprising spirit; initiative

进去 jìnqu I (动) go in; enter: 你～看看. Go in and have a look. II [used after a verb to express the idea of coming or going in]: 把桌子搬～ move the table in

进入 jìnrù (动) enter; get into: ～阵地 get into position. ～决赛阶段 enter the finals

进退 jìn-tuì (动) advance or retreat: ～自如. There is ample room for manoeuvre. ～维谷 caught in a dilemma

进行 jìnxíng (动) 1 be in progress; be underway; go on: 学习～得怎么样? How are you getting on with your studies? 2 carry on; carry out; conduct: ～讨论 hold discussions. ～实地调查 make on-the-spot investigations. ～科学实验 engage in scientific experiment. ～表决 put to the vote. ～英勇斗争 wage a heroic struggle 3 be on the march; march; advance: ～曲 march

进修 jìnxiū (动) take a refresher course: 在职～ in-service training; on-the-job training. ～班 extramural class; higher training class

进一步 jìnyībù (副) go a step further; further: ～发展友好关系 further develop the friendly relations. 对中国历史有～了解 have a better understanding of the history of China

进展 jìnzhǎn (动) make progress; make headway: ～顺利 making good progress. 谈判毫无～. The talks have made no headway.

进驻 jìnzhù (动) (of troops) enter and garrison (a town, city, etc.)

晋(晉) jìn (动) 1 enter; advance 2 promote: 加官～爵 be promoted to a higher post

晋级 jìnjí (动) rise in rank; be promoted

晋升 jìnshēng (动) promoteto a higher office

觐 jìn: ～见 present oneself before (a monarch). 朝～ go on a pilgrimage

禁 jìn (动) 1 prohibit; forbid; ban: 严～烟火 Smoking and lighting fires strictly forbidden (or prohibited). ～酒 prohibition of alcoholism 2 imprison; detain: 监～ imprison. 软～ put under house arrest 3 what is forbidden by law or custom: 违～品 contraband (goods) 4 forbidden area: 宫～ the imperial palace

see also jīn

禁闭 jìnbì (名、动) confinement (as a punishment); be kept in detention

禁地 jìndì (名) forbidden ground; restricted area: 这是～. This is out-of-bounds.

禁锢 jìngù 1 debar from holding office (in feudal times) 2 keep in custody; imprison; put in jail 3 confine

禁忌 jìnjì I (动) avoid; abstain from (hot or rich food) II (名) taboo

禁区(區) jìnqū (名) 1 forbidden zone; restricted zone 2 (wildlife or plant) preserve; reserve; natural park 3 (football) penalty area 4 (basketball) restricted ares

禁止 jìnzhǐ (动) prohibit; ban; forbid: ～入内 No admittance. ～停车 No parking. ～通行 No thoroughfare. *or* Closed to traffic. ～招贴 post no bills

噤 jìn (动) 1 keep silent 2 shiver: 寒～ shiver

噤若寒蝉(蟬) jìn ruò hánchán dare not air one's views out of fear

近 jìn (形) 1 near; close: 离圣诞节很～了. Christmas is drawing near. 附～的邮局 the post office near by. ～在咫尺 be close at hand. ～年来 in recent years. ～在眼前 right before one's eyes 2 approaching: 年～六十 getting on for sixty 3 intimate; closely related: 亲～ on intimate terms 4 easy to understand: 浅～ simple and easy to understand

近代 jìndài modern times: ～史 modern history

近海 jìnhǎi (名) coastal waters; inshore; offshore: ～渔业 inshore fishing

近乎 jìnhu (形) close to; little short of: ～荒谬的论点 an argument bordering on absurdity

近郊 jìnjiāo (名) outskirts of a city; suburbs

近况 jìnkuàng (名) recent developments; present condition: 不知你～如何? How are things with you?

近来(來) jìnlái (副) recently; of late; lately

近邻(鄰) jìnlín (名) near neighbour

近旁 jìnpáng (形) nearby; near: 大楼～ near the building
近日 jìnrì (副) 1 recently; in the past few days 2 within the next few days
近视 jìnshì (名) myopia; nearsightedness; shortsightedness
近视眼 jìnshiyǎn (名) myopia; nearsightedness; shortsightedness: 他是～. He is shortsighted (or nearsighted).
近水楼(樓)台(臺) jìn shuǐ lóutái the advantage of being in a favoured position
近似 jìnsì (形) approximate; similar: ～值 approximate value

劲(勁) jìn (名) 1 strength; energy: 用～ put forth strength. 她仿佛有使不完的～. She seems to have inexhaustible energy. 2 vigour; spirit; drive; zeal: 鼓～ boost one's morale 3 air; manner; expression: 瞧他那高兴～儿. See how pleased he is. 4 interest; relish; gusto: 下棋没～, 咱们去游泳吧. Playing chess is no fun; let's go swimming.
see also jìng
劲头(頭) jìntóu (名) 1 strength; energy 2 vigour; spirit; drive; zeal: 工作有～ be full of drive in one's work

浸 jìn (动) soak; steep: 把衬衣在温水中浸两分钟. Soak the shirts in lukewarm water for two minutes.
浸泡 jìnpào (动) soak
浸染 jìnrǎn (动) be contaminated; be addicted
浸润 jìnrùn (动) soak; infiltrate: 雨水～着的田野 rain-soaked fields.
浸透 jìntòu (动) soak; saturate; steep; infuse: 汗水～了他的衬衣. His shirt was soaked with sweat.
浸渍 jìnzì (动) soak; ret; macerate: 亚麻～ flax retting. ～剂 soaker

尽(盡) jìn I (形) 1 exhausted; finished: 取之不～ inexhaustible. 无穷无～ endless; boundless 2 to the utmost; to the limit: 用～力气 exert oneself to the utmost II (动) 1 use up; exhaust: 一言难～. The story can't be told in a few words. 2 try one's best; put to the best use: ～最大努力 do one's best; exert one's utmost effort III (副) all; exhaustive: 不可～信 not to be taken for granted. ～人皆知 be known to all
see also jǐn
尽力 jìnlì (动) do all one can; try one's best: ～而为 do one's best; do everything in one's power. 我们将～援助你们. We'll render you all possible assistance.
尽量 jìnliàng (副) (drink or eat) to the full
尽情 jìnqíng (副) to one's heart's content: ～欢笑 cheer and laugh with abandon
尽头(頭) jìntóu (名) end; limit: 学问是没有～的. Learning is without limit.
尽兴(興) jìnxìng to one's heart's content; enjoy oneself to the full
尽职(職) jìnzhí (动) do one's duty; faithfully carry out one's duties: 他工作一向很～. He has always been a devoted worker.

烬(燼) jìn (名) cinder: 灰～ ashes; cinders

京 jīng (名) 1 the capital of a country 2 (Jīng) short for Beijing
京城 jīngchéng (名) the capital of a country
京都 jīngdū (名) the capital of a country
京剧(劇) jīngjù (名) Beijing opera, also as "京戏"

惊(驚) jīng (动) 1 start; be frightened: 恶梦把她～醒了. She woke up from a nightmare with a start. ～呆了 be dumbfounded. 大吃一～ be taken aback 2 surprise; startle; alarm: 令人震～的消息 startling news 3 shy: 听到喊声, 马～了. The horse shied at the loud noise.
惊诧 jīngchà (形) <书> surprised; amazed; astonished
惊动(動) jīngdòng (动) alarm; alert; bother; disturb: 别为这么点儿小事～他. Don't bother him about such a trifling matter.
惊愕 jīng'è (形) <书> stunned; stupefied; terror-stricken
惊弓之鸟(鳥) jīng gōng zhī niǎo a bird once wounded by an arrow starts at the mere twang of a bowstring; a panic-stricken person
惊骇(駭) jīnghài (形) <书> frightened; panic
惊慌 jīnghuāng (形) alarmed scared; panic-stricken: ～失措 frightened out of one's wits. 不

必～. Don't panic.

惊魂未定 jīnghún wèi dìng still feel nervous from a bad shock; still badly shaken

惊恐 jīngkǒng (形) alarmed and panicky; terrified; panic-stricken; seized with terror: ～万状 be terrified beyond description

惊奇 jīngqí (动) wonder; be surprised; be amazed

惊扰(擾) jīngrǎo (动) alarm; agitate: 自相～ raise a false alarm

惊人 jīngrén (形) astonishing; amazing; alarming: ～的毅力 amazing willpower

惊叹(嘆) jīngtàn (动) wonder at; marvel at; exclaim (with admiration): ～号 exclamation mark(!)

惊涛(濤)骇浪 jīngtāo-hàilàng (名) 1 raging waves; stormy sea 2 a sea of troubles

惊天动(動)地 jīngtiān-dòngdì (形) earthshaking; world-shaking: ～的胜利 earthshaking victory

惊悉 jīngxī (动) be shocked to learn

惊喜 jīngxǐ (动、名) be pleasantly surprised; a pleasant surprise

惊吓(嚇) jīngxià (动) frighten; scare: 这孩子受了～. The child had a shock.

惊险(險) jīngxiǎn (形) breathtaking; thrilling: ～的表演 breathtaking performance. ～的场面 thrilling scene. ～小说 thriller

惊心动(動)魄 jīngxīn-dòngpò (形) soul-stirring

惊醒 jīngxǐng (动) 1 wake up with a start 2 rouse suddenly from sleep; awaken

惊讶 jīngyà (形) surprised; amazed; astonished; astounded

惊疑 jīngyí (形) surprised and bewildered; apprehensive and perplexed

惊异 jīngyì (形) surprised; amazed; astonished; astounded

惊蛰 jīngzhé (名) the Waking of Insects (3rd solar term)

鲸 jīng (名) whale

鲸吞 jīngtūn (动) swallow like a whale; annex (territory)

鲸鱼 jīngyú (名) whale

旌 jīng (名) an ancient type of banner hoisted on a featherdecked mast

旌旗 jīngqí (名) banners and flags: ～迎风招展. Flags fluttered in the wind.

粳 jīng

粳稻 jīngdào (名) round-grained nonglutinous rice; japonica rice

粳米 jīngmǐ (名) polished round-grained nonglutinous rice

精 jīng I (形) 1 refined; picked; choice: ～盐 purified salt. ～制糖 refined sugar. ～白米 polished white rice 2 essence; extract: 酒～ alcohol 3 perfect; excellent: ～良 excellent; superior; of the best quality 4 meticulous; fine; precise: 这花瓶的工艺很～. This vase is an exquisite work of art. 5 smart; bright; clever and capable 6 skilled; conversant; proficient: ～于绘画 skilled in painting II (名) 1 energy; spirit: 聚～会神 focus one's attention; be all intent 2 sperm; semen; seed: 受～ fertilization 3 goblin; spirit; demon: 害人～ ogre; mischief-maker

精兵简政 jīngbīng-jiǎnzhèng trim staff and simplify administration; streamline the administration

精彩 jīngcǎi (形) brilliant; splendid; wonderful: ～的杂技表演 a wonderful acrobatic performance

精诚 jīngchéng (名) <书> absolute sincerity; good faith: ～所至,金石为开. Absolute sincerity can move a heart of stone.

精萃 jīngcuì (名) cream; pick

精打细算 jīngdǎ-xìsuàn (名) careful calculation and strict budgeting; practise economy by meticulous calculation

精读(讀) jīngdú I (动) read in-depth II (名) intensive reading

精干(幹) jīnggàn (形) 1 (of a body of troops, etc.) small in number but well-trained; crack 2 keen-witted and capable

精耕细作 jīnggēng-xìzuò (名) intensive and meticulous farming; intensive cultivation

精光 jīngguāng (形) having nothing left or on

精悍 jīnghàn (形) 1 capable and vigorous 2 pithy and poignent: 笔力～. The strokes are powerful.

精华(華) jīnghuá (名) cream; essence; quintessence

精简 jīngjiǎn (动) retrench; simplify; cut; reduce: ～机构 simplify (or streamline) the administrative structure. ～会议 cut meetings to a minimum

精力 jīnglì (名) energy; vigour; stamina: ～充沛 very energetic; full of vigour. 集中～解决主要问题 solve the main problems with concentrated effort

精练(練) jīngliàn (形) concise; succinct; terse: 语言～ succinct and precise language

精炼(煉) jīngliàn (动) refine; purify

精良 jīngliáng (形) excellent; superior; of the best quality

精灵(靈) jīnglíng I (名) spirit; demon II (名) (of a child) clever; smart; intelligent

精美 jīngměi (形) exquisite; elegant: ～的刺绣 exquisite embroidery

精密 jīngmì (形) precise; accurate: ～仪器 precision instrument

精明 jīngmíng (形) astute; shrewd; sagacious: ～的政治家 an astute statesman. ～强干 intelligent and capable; able and efficient

精疲力竭 jīngpí-lìjié (形) exhausted; dog-tired; tired out; spent

精辟 jīngpì (形) penetrating; incisive: ～的论述 a brilliant exposition

精巧 jīngqiǎo (形) exquisite; ingenious: ～的牙雕 exquisite ivory carving

精确(確) jīngquè (形) accurate; exact; precise: ～的统计 accurate statistics

精锐 jīngruì (形) crack; picked: ～部队 crack troops; picked troops

精深 jīngshēn (形) profound: 博大～ characterized by extensive knowledge and profound scholarship

精神 jīngshén (名) **1** spirit; mind; consciousness: 国际主义～ the spirit of internationalism. ～面貌 mental outlook **2** essence; gist; spirit: 文件的主要～ the gist of the document. ～鼓励 moral encouragement. ～文明 ethical or spiritual values. ～生活 cultural life

精神 jīngshen (名) **1** vigour; vitality; drive: ～饱满 full of vigour (or vitality); energetic. 没有～ listless; languid **2** lively; spirited; vigorous

精神病 jīngshénbìng (名) mental disease; mental disorder; psychosis

精髓 jīngsuǐ (名) marrow; pith; quintessence

精通 jīngtōng (动) be proficient in; well-versed in; have a good command of; master: ～业务 be professionally proficient. ～英语 have a good command of English

精细 jīngxì (形) meticulous; fine; careful: 手工十分～ show fine workmanship

精心 jīngxīn (副) meticulously; painstakingly; elaborately: ～护理 nurse with loving care

精益求精 jīng yì qiú jīng constantly improve one's skill; keep improving: 对技术～ constantly improve one's skill

精湛 jīngzhàn (形) consummate; exquisite: 工艺～ exquisite workmanship; perfect craftsmanship

精制 jīngzhì (动) make with extra care; refine

精致 jīngzhì (形) fine; exquisite; delicate

精装(裝) jīngzhuāng (名) (of books) clothbound; hardback; hardcover: ～本 de luxe edition

菁 jīng: ～华 essence; cream; quintessence

睛 jīng (名) eyeball: 目不转～地看着 fix one's eye on; gaze fixedly at

荆 jīng (名) chaste tree; vitex

荆棘 jīngjí (名) thistles and thorns; brambles: ～丛生 be overgrown with brambles

荆条(條) jīngtiáo (名) twigs of the chaste tree (used for weaving baskets, etc.)

兢 jīng: ～～业业 (act) with caution and with a will

晶 jīng (形、名) brilliant; glittering: 水～ crystal. 亮～～ shining; glistening. ～莹 sparkling and transparent

晶体(體) jīngtǐ (名) crystal

晶体(體)管 jīngtǐguǎn (名) transistor: 硅～ silicon transistor. ～收音机 transistor radio

茎(莖) jīng (名) stem (of a plant); stalk

经(經) jīng I (名) **1** warp (of textile) **2** longitude: 东～三十度 30 degrees E longitude **3** scripture; classics: 佛～ Buddhist scripture. 圣～ the Holy Bible II (动) **1** pass through; undergo: 途～巴黎 pass through Paris. ～卡拉奇回国 return home via Karachi **2** manage; deal in: ～商 go into business **3** stand; endure: ～得起时间的考验 can stand the test

of time III (介) after; as a result of: ～他一说,我才明白. I didn't understand until he elaborated on the question.
see also jìng

经常 jīngcháng I (形) day-to-day; everyday; daily: ～工作 routine work; day-to-day work II (副) frequently; constantly; regularly; often: 大家最好～交换意见. We'd better often exchange views among ourselves. 他～帮助他人. He never fails to help others.

经典 jīngdiǎn (名) 1 classics 2 scriptures: 佛教～ Buddhist scriptures 3 classical: 马列主义～著作 Marxist-Leninist classics; classical works of Marxism-Leninism

经度 jīngdù (名) longitude

经费 jīngfèi (名) funds; appropriations

经管 jīngguǎn (动) be in charge of: ～财务 be in charge of financial affairs

经过(過) jīngguò I (动) 1 pass; go through; undergo: 这汽车～展览馆吗? Does this bus pass the Exhibition Hall? 2 as a result of; after; through: ～充分讨论, 大家取得了一致意见. Identity of views was reached after full-scale discussion. II (名) process; course: 事件的全部～ the whole course of the incident; what actually happened from start to finish

经纪 jīngjì I (动) manage (a business) II (名) manager; broker

经济(濟) jīngjì (名) 1 economy: 国民～ national economy. 国营～ the state sector of the economy 2 of industrial or economic value; economic: ～作物 industrial crops; cash crops. ～效益 economic results. ～犯罪 economic crime 3 financial condition; income: ～宽裕 well-off; well-to-do II (形) economical; thrifty: ～实惠 economical and practical. ～地位 economic status; economic position. ～基础 economic base; economic basis. ～法规 economic statutes. ～实体 economic entity. ～危机 economic crisis. ～学 economics. ～学家 economist. ～援助 economic aid. ～核算 cost accounting. ～特区 special economic zones

经久 jīngjiǔ (形) 1 prolonged: ～不息的掌声 prolonged applause 2 durable: ～耐用 durable

经理 jīnglǐ (动、名) 1 handle; manage 2 manager; director

经历(歷) jīnglì I (动) go through; undergo; experience: 工业正～着一场伟大的革命. Industry is undergoing a great revolution. II (名) experience: 他这人～多, 见识广. He's a man of wide knowledge and experience.

经手 jīngshǒu (动) handle; deal with: 这件事是他～的. He's the one who handled this matter. ～人 a transactor

经受 jīngshòu (动) undergo; experience; withstand; stand; weather: ～时间的考验 stand the test of time

经销 jīngxiāo (动) sell on commission: ～处 agency

经心 jīngxīn (形) careful; conscientious: 漫不～ careless; casual; negligent; absent-minded

经验(驗) jīngyàn (名) experience: 交流～ exchange experience. ～丰富 have rich experience; be very experienced

经营(營) jīngyíng (动) manage; run; engage in: 发展多种～ promote a diversified economy. 苦心～ work with painstaking effort

经由 jīngyóu via; by way of: ～东京去纽约 be bound for New York via Tokyo

经传(傳) jīngzhuàn (名) classical works; classics: 名不见～ not be a well-known personality; a mere nobody

井 jǐng (名) 1 well: 打～ sink a well; drill a well. ～底之蛙 a person with limited outlook or a narrow view of the world 2 sth. in the shape of a well: 矿～ pit; mine. 油～ oil well

井架 jǐngjià (名) derrick

井井有条(條) jǐngjǐng yǒu tiáo in perfect order; shipshape; methodical: ～地工作 work methodically

井然 jǐngrán (形) ‹书› orderly; neat and tidy; well arranged; methodical: 秩序～ in good order

阱 jǐng (名) trap; pitfall; pit

警 jǐng I (形) alert; vigilant: ～醒 be a light sleeper. ～觉 watchful; vigilant II (动) warn; alarm: ～告 warn. ～钟 alarm clock III (名) 1 alarm: 火～ fire alarm 2 ‹简› (警察) police: ～亭 police box

警报(報) jǐngbào (名) alarm; warning; alert: 拉～ sound the

alarm (or siren)

警备(備) jǐngbèi (名) guard; garrison: ～区 garrison command. ～司令部 garrison headquarters

警察 jǐngchá (名) police; policeman: 交通～ traffic policeman

警告 jǐnggào (动、名) **1** warn; caution; admonish: 提出严重～ issue a serious warning **2** warning (as a disciplinary measure): 给予～处分 give sb. a disciplinary warning

警戒 jǐngjiè (动) **1** warn; admonish **2** be on the alert against; guard against; keep a close watch on: 采取～措施 take precautionary measures. ～线 cordon; security line

警句 jǐngjù (名) aphorism; epigram

警犬 jǐngquǎn (名) police dog

警惕 jǐngtì be on guard against; watch out for; be vigilant: 提高～ heighten one's vigilance

警卫(衛) jǐngwèi (名) (security) guard: ～员 bodyguard

儆

jǐng (动) warn; admonish: 惩一～百 punish one to warn a hundred

景

jǐng (名) **1** view; scenery; scene: 西湖十～ the ten (tourist) attractions of the West Lake **2** situation; condition: 远～规划 long-term planning **3** scenery (of a play or film): 换～ change of scenery **4** scene (of a play): 第三幕第一～ Act III, scene I

景况 jǐngkuàng (名) state of affairs; circumstances: 她家的～日益见好. Her family is becoming much better-off every day.

景气(氣) jǐngqì (名) prosperity; boom: 不～ depression; slump

景色 jǐngsè (名) scenery; view; scene; landscape: 日出的时候～特别美丽. The view is wonderful at sunrise.

景泰蓝(藍) jǐngtàilán (名) cloisonné enamel

景物 jǐngwù (名) scenery: ～宜人. The landscape is delightful.

景象 jǐngxiàng (名) scene; sight; picture

景仰 jǐngyǎng (动) respect and admire; hold in high esteem

景致 jǐngzhì (名) view; scenery; scene: 窗口看出去～真美. You get a wonderful view from the window.

憬

jǐng: ～悟 wake up to reality; come to see the truth; realize one's error, etc.

颈(頸)

jǐng (名) neck see also gěng

颈项 jǐngxiàng (名) neck

颈椎 jǐngzhuī (名) cervical vertebra

竟

jìng I (动) finish; complete: 未～之业 unaccomplished cause; unfinished task II (副) **1** in the end; eventually: 有志者事～成. Where there's a will there's a way. **2** unexpectedly; actually: 谁知他～答应了. Who would have expected that he eventually agreed to it? **3** go so far as to; go to the length of; have the impudence (or effrontery) to

竟敢 jìnggǎn (动) have the audacity; have the impertinence; dare: 他～如此说话. He had the audacity to talk like that.

竟然 jìngrán (副) **1** unexpectedly; to one's surprise; actually **2** go so far as to; go to the length of; have the impudence (or effrontery) to: 这样宏伟的建筑,～只用十个月就完成了. It is amazing that it took merely ten months to complete such a magnificent building.

境

jìng (名) **1** border; boundary: 国～ national boundary. 入～签证 entry visa. 越～ cross the border illegally **2** place; area; territory: 敌～ enemy territory **3** condition; situation; circumstances: 困～ difficult position; predicament. 处于逆～ be in adverse circumstances

境地 jìngdì (名) condition; circumstances: 陷入孤立的～ land oneself in utter isolation

境界 jìngjiè (名) **1** boundary **2** extent reached; plane attained; state; realm: 理想～ ideal state; ideal

境况 jìngkuàng (名) circumstances; financial situation: ～不佳 one's financial prospects are not very bright

境遇 jìngyù (名) circumstances; one's lot: 极困难的～ extremely adverse circumstances

镜

jìng (名) **1** looking glass; mirror: 哈哈～ distorting mirror **2** lens; glass: 放大～ magnifying glass; magnifier. 墨～ sunglasses

镜头(頭) jìngtóu (名) **1** camera lens: 远摄～ telephoto lens; tele-lens. 广角～ wide-angle lens

2 shot; scene: 特写～ close-up

竞(競) jìng (动) compete; contest; vie

竞技 jìngjì (名) sports; athletics: ～场 arena

竞赛 jìngsài (名) contest; competition; emulation; race: 体育～ athletic contest (or competition). 军备～ arms race

竞选(選) jìngxuǎn (动) enter into an election contest; campaign for (office); run for: ～总统 run for the presidency

竞争 jìngzhēng (动) compete: 自由～ free competition

淨 jìng I (形) 1 clean: ～水 clean water. 擦～ wipe sth. clean 2 net: ～收入 net income. ～重 net weight. ～利 net profit II (副) 1 completely: 用～ use up 2 only; merely; nothing but: 这几天～下雨. It has been raining for the past few days.

净化 jìnghuà (动) purify: 水的～ purification of water

净手 jìngshǒu (动) wash one's hands; relieve oneself

净值 jìngzhí (名) net worth; net value: 出口～ net export value. 进口～ net import value

静 jìng (形) still; quiet; calm: 风平浪～ calm and tranquil. 请～一～. Please be quiet.

静脉(脈) jìngmài (名) vein

静默 jìngmò (动) mourn in silence; observe silence: ～致哀 stand in silent tribute to the memory of the deceased

静悄悄 jìngqiāoqiāo (形) very quiet and still

静养(養) jìngyǎng (动) rest quietly to recuperate; convalesce

静止 jìngzhǐ (形) static; motionless; at a standstill

静坐 jìngzuò (动) 1 sit quietly 2 sit still as a form of breathing exercise (somewhat like yoga): ～示威 sit in (demonstration)

靖 jìng (动) 1 peace; tranquility 2 pacify: ～乱 put down a rebellion

敬 jìng 1 respect: 尊～ respect; esteem; honour. 致～ pay one's respects; salute. ～请光临 request the honour of your presence 2 offer politely: ～茶 serve tea

敬爱(愛) jìng'ài respect and love: ～的领袖 respected and beloved leader

敬而远(遠)之 jìng ér yuǎn zhī keep someone at a respectful distance

敬酒 jìngjiǔ (动) propose a toast; toast

敬礼(禮) jìnglǐ (动) 1 salute; give a salute 2 extend one's greetings 3 〈敬〉 [often used at the end of a letter]: 此致～ with best regards

敬佩 jìngpèi (动) esteem; admire; think highly of

敬仰 jìngyǎng (动) revere; venerate; have the greatest admiration for: 深受人民的爱戴和～ enjoy the deep love and reverence of the people

敬意 jìngyì (名) respect; tribute: 表示衷心的～ extend one's heartfelt respects; pay sincere tribute

敬重 jìngzhòng (动) deeply respect; revere; honour

痉(痙) jìng

痉挛(攣) jìngluán (名) convulsion; spasm

径(徑) jìng I (名) 1 footpath; path; track 2 way; means: 捷～ an easy way; shortcut 3 diameter: 半～ radius II (副) directly; straightaway: 客机～直飞往纽约. The plane flew direct to New York.

径庭 jìngtíng (形) 〈书〉 very unlike: 大相～ diametrically opposed; widely divergent

径自 jìngzì (副) without leave; without consulting anyone: 没等散会,他～走了. He left abruptly before the meeting was over.

胫(脛) jìng (名) shin: ～骨 shin bone; tibia

劲(勁) jìng (形) strong; powerful; sturdy: ～敌 formidable adversary; strong opponent. ～旅 strong contingent; crack troops

see also jìn

经(經) jìng (名) warping (textile)

see also jīng

窘 jiǒng (形) 1 in straitened circumstances; hard up: 他一度生活很～. He was rather hard up for a time. 2 awkward; embarrassed; ill at ease: 这使他感到很～. This put him in an awkward position. *or* He felt embarrassed on this account.

窘境 jiǒngjìng (名) awkward situation; predicament; plight

窘迫 jiǒngpò (形) 1 poverty-stricken; very poor: 生活～ live

in reduced circumstances 2 hard pressed; embarrassed; in a predicament: 处境～ find oneself in a predicament

炯 jiǒng (形) bright; shining

炯炯 jiǒngjiǒng (形) <书> (of eyes) bright; shining: 他目光～有神. He has a pair of bright piercing eyes.

迥 jiǒng (形) <书> widely different

迥然 jiǒngrán far apart; widely different: ～不同 poles apart; not in the least alike

阄(鬮) jiū (名) lot: 抓～ draw lots

揪 jiū (动) hold tight; seize: ～着绳子往上爬 climb up by pulling hard at a rope

揪辫(辮)子 jiū biànzi (动) seize sb.'s queue — seize upon sb.'s mistake or shortcoming as a ground for attack

究 jiū (动) study carefully; go into; investigate: 深～ make a thorough investigation into the matter; get to the bottom of a matter. ～其根源 trace sth. to its origin

究竟 jiūjìng I (名) outcome; what actually happened: 大家都想知道个～. Everybody wants to know what actually happened. II (副) 1 [used in an interrogative sentence to make further inquiries] actually; exactly: 你～想说什么? What on earth do you want to say? 2 after all; in the end: 他～经验丰富, 说的话有道理. After all, he is very experienced and talks reasonably.

赳 jiū

赳赳 jiūjiū (形) valiant; gallant: 雄～ valiant; gallant

纠 jiū (动) 1 entangle: ～缠 get entangled (or bogged down) 2 gather together: ～合一伙流氓 band together a bunch of hoodlums 3 correct; rectify: ～错 correct (or rectify) a mistake

纠察 jiūchá 1 maintain order at a public gathering 2 picket: ～线 picket line

纠缠(纏) jiūchán (动) 1 get entangled; be in a tangle: 中止在枝节问题上～不休 stop endless quibbling over side issues 2 nag; worry; pester: 他忙着呢, 别～他了. He's busy. Don't keep nagging at him.

纠纷 jiūfēn (名) dispute; issue: 种族～ racial dispute. 国家间的～ disputes between countries

纠葛 jiūgé (名) entanglement; dispute

纠集 jiūjí (动) get together; muster; gang up: ～一批流氓 gather together a bunch of hooligans

纠正 jiūzhèng (动) correct; put right; redress: ～错误 correct a mistake; redress an error. ～不正之风 check unhealthy tendencies

酒 jiǔ (名) alcoholic drink; wine; liquor; spirits

酒菜 jiǔcài (名) food and drink; food to go with wine or liquor

酒厂(廠) jiǔchǎng (名) brewery; winery; distillery

酒店 jiǔdiàn (名) wineshop; public house

酒会(會) jiǔhuì (名) cocktail party

酒家 jiǔjiā (名) wineshop; restaurant

酒精 jiǔjīng (名) ethyl alcohol; alcohol

酒量 jiǔliàng (名) capacity for liquor: 他～很大. He's a heavy drinker. *or* He drinks like a fish.

酒囊饭袋 jiǔnáng-fàndài (名) a good-for-nothing

酒肉朋友 jiǔròu péngyou (名) fair-weather friends

酒窝 jiǔwō (名) dimple

酒席 jiǔxí (名) feast

韭(韮) jiǔ: ～菜 fragrant-flowered garlic; (Chinese) chives. 青～ young chives; chive seedlings

九 jiǔ (数) 1 nine: ～中 No. 9 Middle School 2 each of the nine nine-day periods beginning from the day after the Winter Solstice: 三～ the third nine-day period after the Winter Solstice; the coldest days of winter 3 many; numerous: ～曲桥 a zigzag bridge

九九归(歸)一 jiǔ jiǔ guī yī when all is said and done; in the last analysis; after all: ～, 还是他的话对. What he says is after all right.

九牛二虎之力 jiǔ niú èr hǔ zhī lì tremendous effort: 我们费了～才把事情办妥. It was only after great effort that we brought the matter to a successful conclusion.

九牛一毛 jiǔ niú yī máo a drop in the ocean

九泉 jiǔquán (名)〈书〉 grave; the nether world: ～之下 in the nether regions; after death

九死一生 jiǔ sǐ yī shēng a narrow escape from death; a close shave

九霄云(雲)外 jiǔxiāo yúnwài far, far away; beyond the highest heavens: 把个人安危抛到～ in total disregard of personal safety

九月 jiǔyuè (名) **1** September **2** the ninth month of the lunar year; the ninth moon

九州 jiǔzhōu (名) a poetic name for China

久 jiǔ (副) **1** for a long time; long: 很～以前 long ago. ～别重逢 meet again after a long separation **2** of a specified duration: 你在北京住了有多～? How long have you been living in Beijing?

久而久之 jiǔ ér jiǔ zhī in the course of time; as time passes

久久 jiǔjiǔ (副) for a long, long time: 他心情激动，～不能成寐. He got so excited that he lay awake for a long time.

久违(違) jiǔwéi 〈套〉 haven't seen you for ages: ～了. 这几年你上哪儿去啦? Long time no see. Where have you been all these years?

久仰 jiǔyǎng 〈套〉 I'm very pleased to meet you

久远(遠) jiǔyuǎn (形) far back; ages ago; remote: 年代～ of the remote past; time-honoured

玖 jiǔ (数) nine [the complicated form of 九, used on cheques, etc., to avoid alteration]

就 jiù **1** get near to; move towards: ～着蜡烛灯用餐 dine by candlelight. **2** undertake; engage in; enter upon: ～学 go to school. ～席 take one's seat **3** accomplished; successful: 功成业～ (of a person's career) be crowned with success **4** accomodate oneself to; suit; fit: 只好～我们现在手头有的东西做了. We'll have to make do with what we've got at present. **5** go with: 炒鸡蛋～饭 have some scrambled eggs to go with the rice **6** with regard to; concerning; on: ～我所知 so far as I know **7** at once; right away: 我这～来. I'll be coming right away. 晚饭一会儿～得. Dinner will be ready in a minute. **8** as early as; already: 他一九三六年～成了电影名星了. He became a film star as early as 1936. **9** as soon as; right after: 他卸下行李～上床睡了. He went to bed as soon as he had unpacked the luggage. **10** [connecting two clauses, the first being the premise of the second]: 只要努力，～能掌握外语. So long as you work hard, you will be able to master a foreign language. **11** [inserted in two identical words or phrases, indicating that one is conceding sth.]: 丢了～丢了吧,以后小心点. If it's lost, it's lost. Just be more careful from now on. **12** [indicating all along, from the start]: 我本来～不懂法语. I never said I knew French. **13** only; merely; just: ～他一人知道事情的真相. He alone knows the whole truth of the matter. 我～要几张纸. I just want a few sheets of paper. **14** exactly; precisely: 他～住在这儿. This is where he lives. **15** (连) even if: 你～不说,我也会知道. I'll find out if you don't breathe a word.

就便 jiùbiàn (副) at sb.'s convenience; while you're at it: ～也替我在旅馆定个房间. While you're about it, make a reservation at the hotel for me too.

就此 jiùcǐ (副) at this point; here and now; thus: 会议～结束. The meeting was thus brought to an end.

就地 jiùdì (副) on the spot: ～解决问题 settle the problem on the spot

就地取材 jiùdì qǔcái draw on local resources

就近 jiùjìn (副) (do or get sth.) at a nearby place; in the neighbourhood; without having to go far

就寝 jiùqǐn (动)〈书〉 retire for the night; go to bed

就任 jiùrèn (动) take up one's post; take office

就事论(論)事 jiù shì lùn shì consider a matter as it stands: 不能～. Never consider a matter in isolation or out of context

就是 jiùshì I (副) **1** [placed at the end of a sentence often with "了", indicating it is positive]: 放心吧,我照办～了. Don't worry. I will do just as you say. **2** quite right; exactly; precisely: ～嘛,天气预报～这么说的. Precisely. That's just what the weatherman said. II (连) [same as 即使] even if; even: ～他请我,我也不去. I won't go even if he asks me to.

就手 jiùshǒu see 就便

就算 jiùsuàn 〈口〉 even if; granted that: ～你考试考得不错,也不应该骄傲吧. Granted you have done well in the exam, still there is no reason to be cocky.

就绪 jiùxù (形) (of preparations) be completed: 一切都已～. Everything is in order.

就要 jiùyào be about to; be going to; be on the point of: 火车～开了. The train is about to start 飞机过两分钟～起飞了. The plane takes off in two minutes.

就业(業) jiùyè (动、名) obtain employment; take up an occupation; get a job: 充分～ full employment

就医(醫) jiùyī (动) seek medical advice; go to a doctor

就义(義) jiùyì (动) lay down one's life for a just cause; die a martyr: 英勇～ die a hero's death

就职(職) jiùzhí (动) assume office: 宣誓～ take the oath of office; be sworn in. ～演说 inaugural speech

鹫 jiù (名) vulture

厩 jiù (名) stable; cattle-shed; pen: ～肥 barnyard manure

救 jiù (动) 1 rescue; save; salvage: 营～ come to one's rescue. 溺水的孩子被～了. The drowning child was saved. 2 help; relieve; succour: 生产自～ tide over a disaster by production

救国(國) jiùguó save the nation

救护(護) jiùhù relieve a sick or injured person; give first-aid: ～车 ambulance. ～站 first aid station

救火 jiùhuǒ (名) fire fighting; put out a fire: ～车 fire engine. ～队 fire brigade. ～队员 fireman; fire fighter

救急 jiùjí (动) help sb. to cope with an emergency; help meet an urgent need

救济(濟) jiùjì (动) relieve; succour: ～灾区人民 provide relief to the people in a disaster area

救命 jiùmìng save sb.'s life: ～! Help! ～恩人 saviour

救生 jiùshēng (形) lifesaving: ～带 life belt. ～圈 life buoy. ～设备 lifesaving appliance; life preserver

救死扶伤(傷) jiùsǐ-fúshāng heal the wounded and rescue the dying

救星 jiùxīng (名) liberator; emancipator

救治 jiùzhì (动) bring a patient out of danger; treat and cure

旧(舊) jiù (形) 1 past; old-fashioned; old: ～传统 the old tradition. ～事重提 bring up the old problem again 2 used; worn; old: ～书 used (or second-hand) books 3 former; onetime: ～居 former residence. ～地重游 revisit a place one has been to 4 old friendship; old friend: 故～ old acquaintances

旧恶(惡) jiù'è (名) old grievance; old wrong: 不念～ forgive and forget

旧货 jiùhuò (名) secondhand goods; junk: ～店 secondhand shop; junk shop. ～市场 flea market

旧交 jiùjiāo (名) old acquaintance

旧历(曆) jiùlì (名) the old Chinese calendar; the lunar calendar

旧址 jiùzhǐ (名) site (of a former organization, building, etc.): 这是我们学校的～. This is where our school used to be.

臼 jiù (名) 1 mortar: 石～ stone mortar 2 any mortar-shaped thing 3 joint (of bones): 脱～ dislocation (of joints)

臼齿(齒) jiùchǐ (名) molar

舅 jiù (名) 1 uncle (mother's brother) 2 wife's brother; brother-in-law 3 〈书〉 husband's father

舅父 jiùfù (名) mother's brother; uncle

舅母 jiùmǔ (名) aunt (wife of mother's brother)

疚 jiù (名)〈书〉 remorse: 感到内～ have a guilty conscience (about)

柩 jiù (名) a coffin with a corpse in it

柩车(車) jiùchē (名) hearse

咎 jiù (名) 1 fault; blame: 归～于人 shift the blame on to sb. else 2 censure; punish; blame: 既往不～ let bygones be bygones. ～由自取 have only oneself to blame

车(車) jū (名) chariot, one of the pieces in Chinese chess

see also chē

疽 jū (名) subcutaneous ulcer; deep-rooted ulcer

狙 jū

狙击(擊) jūjī (名) snipe: ～手 sniper

鞠 jū

鞠躬 jūgōng (动) bow: ～致谢 bow one's thanks. ～尽瘁 exert oneself to the utmost to accomplish a task

掬 jū (动) hold with both hands: 笑容可～ smile broadly

拘 jū I (动) 1 arrest; detain 2 restrain; restrict; limit; constrain: 无～无束 unrestrained; free and easy II (形) inflexible: ～泥 rigidly adhere to (formalities, etc.); overscrupulous

拘捕 jūbǔ (动) arrest

拘谨 jūjǐn (形) overcautious; reserved: 跟别人在一起时,他有些～. He was rather reserved in company.

拘留 jūliú (动) detain; be taken into custody: ～所 house of detention; lockup

拘票 jūpiào (名) arrest warrant; warrant

拘束 jūshù I (动) restrain; restrict II (形) constrained; awkward; ill at ease: 不要～. Make yourself at home.

驹 jū (名) 1 colt 2 foal: 怀～ be in (or with) foal

居 jū (动) 1 reside; dwell; live: 侨～国外 reside abroad. 分～两地 (of man and wife) live at different places 2 be (in a certain position); occupy (a place): ～首位 occupy first place; rank first. 身～要职 hold an important post 3 claim; assert: 以学者自～ claim to be a scholar 4 store up; lay by: 囤积～奇 hoarding and profiteering

居安思危 jū ān sī wēi think of danger in times of peace; be vigilant in peace time

居多 jūduō be in the majority: 他所写的文章,关于文艺理论方面的～. Most of his essays deal with the theory of literature and art.

居高临(臨)下 jū gāo lín xià occupy a commanding position (or height)

居功 jūgōng (动) claim credit for oneself: ～自傲 become arrogant because of one's achievements

居间(間) jūjiān (动) (mediate) between two parties: ～调停 mediate between two parties; act as mediator

居留 jūliú (动、名) reside: 长期～ permanent residence. ～权 right of residence. ～证 residence permit

居民 jūmín (名) resident; inhabitant: ～点 residential area

居然 jūrán (副) 1 unexpectedly; to one's surprise: 他～做出这种事来. Who would have thought he could do such a thing? 2 go so far as to; have the impudence (or effrontery) to: ～当面撒谎 go so far as to tell a bare-faced lie

居住 jūzhù (动) live; reside; dwell: ～条件 housing conditions. ～面积 living space

居心 jūxīn (动) harbour (evil) intentions; be bent on: ～不良 be up to no good. 他们～何在? What are they up to?

居中 jūzhōng (副) 1 see "居间" 2 be placed in the middle: ～是一幅山水画. Placed in the middle is a landscape painting.

菊 jú (名) chrysanthemum: ～花 chrysanthemum

桔 jú 见"橘" jú

橘 jú (名) tangerine

橘汁 júzhī (名) orange juice

橘子 júzi (名) tangerine

局 jú (名) 1 chessboard 2 game; set; innings: 第一～(乒乓球等) the first game; the first set 3 situation; stage of affairs: 时～ the current situation. 全～ the overall situation; the situation as a whole 4 ruse; trap: 骗～ fraud; trap; swindle 5 limit; confine 6 office; bureau; department: 邮～ post office. 电话～ telephone exchange 7 shop: 书～ publishing house

局部 júbù (名) part (as opposed to the whole): ～地区 some areas; parts of an area. ～麻醉 local anaesthesia. ～战争 local war; partial war

局促 júcù (形) 1 (of place) narrow; cramped 2 (of time) short 3 feel or show constraint: ～不安 ill at ease

局面 júmiàn (名) aspect; phase; situation: 出现了崭新的～. Things have taken on a new aspect. 打开～ open up a new vista; make a breakthrough; bring about a new situation

局势(勢) júshì (名) situation: 国际～ the international situation

局外人 júwàirén (名) outsider

局限 júxiàn (动) be limited; confine: 我希望讲演者不要～于一个方面. I hope the speaker would not confine himself to one single aspect.

举(舉) jǔ I (动) 1 lift; raise; hold up: ～杯 raise one's glass (to propose a toast) 2 start: ～义 rise in revolt 3 elect; choose: 公～他当代表 choose him as representative 4 cite; enumerate: ～例 cite as an example. ～不胜～ too many to enumerate II (形) whole; entire: ～国欢腾. The whole nation is jubilant. ～世闻名 be known all over the world; enjoy a world-wide reputation III (名) act; deed: ～动 conduct. 轻率的～动 a rash act

举办(辦) jǔbàn (动) conduct; hold; run: ～训练班 run a training course. ～展览会 hold (or put on) an exhibition

举例 jǔlì (动) give an example: ～说明 to illustrate

举目 jǔmù (动) ‹书› raise the eyes; look: ～远眺 look into the distance. ～无亲 live alone far away from one's family; be a stranger in a strange land

举棋不定 jǔ qí bù dìng (动) hesitate about (or over) what move to make; be unable to make up one's mind; indecisive; shilly-shally

举也 jǔshì throughout the world; universally: ～皆知 known to all. ～公认 universally acknowledged. ～无双 unrivalled; matchless

举手 jǔshǒu (动) raise (or put up) one's hand or hands: ～表决 vote by a show of hands

举行 jǔxíng (动) hold (a meeting, ceremony, etc.): ～会谈 hold talks. ～罢工 stage a strike

举一反三 jǔ yī fǎn sān infer from what is already known

举止 jǔzhǐ (名) bearing; manner; air: ～庄重 carry oneself with dignity

举足轻(輕)重 jǔ zú qīng-zhòng hold the balance; play a decisive role: 处于～的地位 occupy a pivotal position

矩 jǔ (名) 1 carpenter's square; square 2 rules; regulations: 循规蹈～ to observe all rules and regulations; law-abiding

矩形 jǔxíng (名) rectangle

沮 jǔ (动) 1 ‹书› stop; prevent: ～其成行 stop sb. from going 2 turn gloomy; turn glum

沮丧 jǔsàng (形) dejected; depressed; dispirited; discouraged: 敌人士气～. The enemy's morale is low.

龃(齟) jǔ

龃龉(齬) jǔyǔ (名) ‹书› bickering; disagreement

咀 jǔ chew: ～嚼 1 chew 2 mull over; ruminate; chew the cud

聚 jù (动) assemble; gather; get together: 大家～在一起庆祝一下. Let's get together and celebrate it.

聚宝(寶)盆 jùbǎopén treasure bowl — a place rich in natural resources, bonanza

聚变(變) jùbiàn (名) fusion: 核～ nuclear fusion. 受控～ controlled fusion

聚餐 jùcān (动) dine together (usu. on festive occasions); have a dinner party

聚合 jùhé 1 get together 2 polymerization: 定向～ stereoregular (or stereotactic) polymerization

聚会(會) jùhuì (动) 1 get together; meet: 老朋友～在一起总令人追忆往事. The meeting of old friends is always an occasion for reminiscences. 2 get-together

聚集 jùjí (动) gather; assemble; collect: ～力量 accumulate strength

聚精会(會)神 jùjīng-huìshén (动) concentrate one's attention; with attention: ～地听 listen with great attention

聚居 jùjū (动) inhabit a region (as an ethnic group); live together

聚敛(斂) jùliǎn (动) amass wealth by heavy taxation; amass

illegally

聚首 jùshǒu (动)〈书〉gather; meet

巨 jù (形) huge; tremendous; gigantic: ～款 a huge sum of money. ～变 tremendous changes

巨擘 jùbò (名) an authority in a certain field

巨大 jùdà (形) huge; tremendous; enormous; gigantic; immense: ～的胜利 a tremendous victory. ～的力量 tremendous force; immense strength. ～的工程 a giant project

巨额 jù'é (名) a huge sum: ～利润 enormous profits. ～赤字 huge financial deficits

巨人 jùrén (名) giant; colossus: 文学界～ literary giant

巨头(頭) jùtóu (名) magnate; tycoon: 金融～ financial magnate

巨细 jù-xì (名) big and small: 事无～ all matters, big and small

巨著 jùzhù (名) monumental work

炬 jù (名) **1** torch **2** fire: 付之一～ be burnt down; be committed to the flames

拒 jù (动) **1** resist; repel: ～敌 resist the enemy; keep the enemy at bay **2** refuse; reject: ～不投降 refuse to surrender

拒捕 jùbǔ (动) resist arrest

拒付 jùfù (动) refuse payment; dishonour (a cheque)

拒绝 jùjué (动) **1** refuse: ～参加 refuse to participate **2** reject; turn down; decline: ～无理要求 turn down (or reject) unreasonable demands. ～诱惑 resist the temptation

距 jù I (名) distance: 行～ the distance between rows of plants II (副) be apart (or away) from; be at a distance from: 两地相～十里. The two places are 10 *li* apart. ～今已有十年. That was ten years ago.

距离(離) jùlí I (名) distance: 飞行的～有 200 英里. The plane covered a distance of 200 miles. II (副) be apart (or away) from; be at a distance from: ～车站十五里 15 *li* from the station. 双方的观点有很大的～. There is a great discrepancy between the views of both sides.

钜 jù I (名)〈书〉**1** hard iron **2** hook II (形) great; huge

遽 jù (副) hurriedly; hastily: ～下结论 jump to a conclusion; draw a hasty conclusion

遽然 jùrán (副)〈书〉suddenly; abruptly: ～变色 suddenly change colour (as one gets angry or annoyed)

具 jù (名) utensil; tool; implement: 农～ farm tool (or implement); agricultural implement II (量)〈书〉: 一～座钟 a desk clock III (动) possess; have: 初～规模 begin to take shape

具备(備) jùbèi (动) possess; have; be provided with: ～入学条件 be qualified for admission to a school

具名 jùmíng (动) sign; put one's name to a document, etc.; affix one's signature

具体(體) jùtǐ (形) concrete; specific; particular (as opposed to abstract): 对于～情况作～的分析 make a concrete analysis of concrete conditions. 会未能取得～成果. No tangible results have been achieved at the conference. ～日期未定. No exact date has been fixed.

具体(體)而微 jù tǐ ér wēi (名) small but complete; comprehensive; miniature

具文 jùwén (名) mere formality; dead letter: 一纸～ a mere scrap of paper

具有 jùyǒu (动) possess; have; be provided with: ～伟大的历史意义 have great historical significance

惧(懼) jù (动) fear; dread: ～内〈书〉henpecked. ～怕 fear; dread. 毫无所～ fearless

俱 jù (形) all; complete: 一应～全 complete with everything. 面面～到 considerate in all respects

俱乐(樂)部 jùlèbù (名) club

飓(颶) jù

飓风(風) jùfēng (名) hurricane

句 jù I (名) sentence II (量): 两～诗 two lines of verse. 在这个问题上，我说不了几～. I can only say a few words on this matter.

句号(號) jùhào (名) full stop; full point; period (。) (.)

句子 jùzi (名) sentence: ～结构 sentence structure

据(據) jù I (动) 1 occupy; seize: ～为己有 take sth. illegally for one's own use; appropriate 2 rely on; depend on: ～险固守 fall back on a natural barrier to put up a resistance 3 according to; on the grounds of: ～我所知 as far as I know. ～条例 according to the regulations. ～理力争 argue vigorously on justifiable grounds II (名) evidence; certificate: 查无实～. Investigation reveals no evidence (against the suspect).

据点(點) jùdiǎn (名) strongpoint; fortified point; stronghold

据守 jùshǒu (动) guard; be entrenched in: 掘壕～ dig in; entrench oneself

据说 jùshuō it is said; they say: ～他不久要出国了. They say he is going abroad soon.

据悉 jùxī it is reported

剧(劇) jù I (名) theatrical work; drama; play; opera: 独幕～ one-act play. 电视～ T.V. play II (形) acute; severe; intense: ～痛 a severe pain. ～变 a drastic change. 人口～增 a drastic expansion of population

剧本 jùběn (名) 1 drama; play 2 script; (film) scenario; (Beijing Opera, opera, etc.) libretto

剧场(場) jùchǎng (名) theatre

剧烈 jùliè (形) violent; acute; severe; fierce: ～运动 strenuous exercise. ～的社会变动 radical social changes. ～的战斗 a fierce fighting

剧目 jùmù (名) a list of plays or operas: 保留～ repertoire

剧情 jùqíng (名) the story (or plot) of a play or opera: ～简介 synopsis

剧团(團) jùtuán (名) theatrical company; opera troupe; troupe

剧作家 jùzuòjiā (名) playwright; dramatist

锯 jù I (名) saw: 手～ handsaw. 圆～ circular saw II (动) cut with a saw; saw: ～木头 saw wood

圈 juān (动) 1 shut in a pen; pen in: 把羊群～起来 herd the sheep into the pens 2 <口> lock up; put in jail

see also juàn; quān

涓 juān (名) <书> a tiny stream

捐 juān I (动) 1 relinquish; abandon 2 contribute; donate; subscribe: ～钱 donate money. 募～ solicit contributions; appeal for donations II (名) tax: 上～ pay a tax

捐弃(棄) juānqì (动) <书> relinquish; abandon: ～前嫌 forget past grievances; let bygones be bygones

捐躯(軀) juānqū (动) go to one's death; lay down one's life

捐税 juānshuì (名) taxes and levies

捐献 juānxiàn (动) contribute (to an organization); donate; present: 他把全部藏书～给图书馆. He presented to the library his whole collection of books.

捐赠 juānzèng (动) contribute (as a gift); donate; present

捐助 juānzhù (动) offer (financial or material assistance); contribute; donate

娟 juān (形) <书> beautiful; graceful

娟秀 juānxiù (形) <书> beautiful; graceful: 字迹～ beautiful handwriting; a graceful hand

镌 juān engrave

镌刻 juānkè (动) <书> engrave

卷(捲) juǎn I (动) 1 roll up: ～起袖子 roll up one's sleeves 2 sweep off; carry along: 一个大浪把那条小渔船～走了. A huge wave swept the fishing boat away. II (名) cylindrical mass of sth.; roll: 铺盖～儿 bedding roll III (量) roll; spool; reel: 一～软片 a roll of film. 一～棉纸 a roll of tissue (or toilet paper)

see also juàn

卷入 juǎnrù (动) be drawn into; be involved in: ～一场冲突 be drawn into a conflict

卷逃 juǎntáo (动) disappear with valuables

卷土重来(來) juǎn tǔ chóng lái stage a comeback

卷烟 juǎnyān 1 cigarette 2 cigar

眷 juàn

眷恋(戀) juànliàn (动) be sentimentally attached to (a person or place)

眷念 juànniàn (动) think fondly of; feel nostalgic about

眷属(屬) juànshǔ (名) family dependents

卷 juàn (名) 1 book 2 volume: 该书共分上、下两～. This book consists of two volumes. 该图书馆藏书十万～. This library has a collection of 100,000 volumes. 3 examination paper: 交～ hand in one's examination paper 4 file; dossier: 查～ look through the files
see also juǎn

卷子 juànzi (名) examination paper: 看～ grade papers

卷宗 juànzōng (名) 1 folder 2 file; dossier

圈 juàn (名) pen; fold; sty: 羊～ sheepfold 猪～ pigsty. ～肥 barnyard manure
see also juān; quān

倦 juàn (形) weary; tired: 面有～容 look tired. 孜孜不～ tirelessly; diligently

绢 juàn (名) thin, tough silk

隽 juàn

隽永 juànyǒng (形)〈书〉meaningful

撅 juē (动) 1 stick up; pout: ～着尾巴 sticking up the tail. ～嘴 purse (up) one's lips 2〈口〉break (sth. long and narrow); snap: 把拐杖～成两段 break the stick in two

觉(覺) jué I (动) 1 feel: 身上～着冷 feel cold 2 wake (up); awake: 如梦初～ feel as if waking from a dream 3 become aware; become awakened II (名) sense: 触～ sense of touch
see also jiào

觉察 juéchá (动) detect; become aware of; perceive: 他～到机器出了毛病了. He sensed that something was wrong with the machine.

觉得 juéde (动) 1 feel: 一点儿也不～苦恼 not feel upset at all 2 think; feel: 我～不必事事都告诉他. I don't think we have to tell him everything. 你～这部电影怎么样? What do you think of the film?

觉悟 juéwù (名) 1 consciousness; awareness; understanding: 政治～ political consciousness (or understanding). 阶级～ class consciousness 2 come to understand; become aware of; become politically awakened: ～了的人民 an awakened people

觉醒 juéxǐng (动) awaken

厥 jué (动) faint; lose consciousness; fall into a coma: 昏～ fall down in a faint

蹶 jué (动) 1 fall 2 suffer a setback: 一～不振 never recover from a setback; curl up after a fall

攫 jué (动) seize; grab: ～为己有 seize possession of; appropriate

攫取 juéqǔ (动) seize; grab; take by force: ～暴利 rake in exorbitant profits

爵 jué (名) 1 the rank of nobility; peerage: 封～ confer a title (of nobility) upon 2 an ancient wine vessel with three legs and a loop handle

爵位 juéwèi (名) the rank (or title) of nobility

嚼 jué (动) masticate; chew
see also jiáo

角 jué I (名) 1 role; part; character: 主～ leading (or principal) role; main character 2 type of role (in traditional Chinese drama): 旦～ female role. 丑～ clown 3 actor or actress: 名～ a famous actor or actress II (动) contend; wrestle: ～斗 wrestle. 口～ quarrel
see also jiǎo

角力 juélì (动) have a trial of strength; wrestle

角色 juésè (名) 1 role; part: 扮演了不光彩的～ play a contemptible role 2 type of role (in traditional Chinese drama)

角逐 juézhú (动) contend; enter into rivalry

决 jué I (动) 1 decide; determine: 犹豫不～ hesitate; be in two minds; be unable to reach a decision. ～一雌雄 fight it out 2 execute a person: 枪～ execute by shooting 3 (of a dyke, etc.) be breached; burst II (副) [used before a negative word] definitely; certainly; under any circumstances: ～不妥协 will under no circumstances come to terms. ～不退缩 will never yield an inch from this stand

决策 juécè (动、名) 1 make policy; make a strategic decision 2 policy decision; decision of strategic importance: ～者 policy-maker. 作出重大～ take a major policy decision

决定 juédìng (动、名) 1 decide; resolve; make up one's mind 2 decision; resolution: 通过一项～

pass a resolution. ～性的时刻 a crucial point (or moment)

决断(斷) juéduàn (名) 1 make a decision 2 resolve; decisiveness; resolution

决计 juéjì I (动) have decided; have made up one's mind: 我～明天就走. I have decided to leave tomorrow. II (副) definitely; certainly: 那样办～没错儿. We definitely can't go wrong that way.

决裂 juéliè (动) break with; rupture: 谈判～ The negotiations broke down.

决然 juérán (副)〈书〉 1 resolutely; determinedly 2 definitely; unquestionably; undoubtedly: 道听途说的～不能算作很准确的消息. Hearsay definitely can't be regarded as accurate information.

决赛 juésài (名) finals: 半～ semifinals

决胜(勝) juéshèng decide the issue of the battle

决死 juésǐ (形) life-and-death: ～的斗争 a life-and-death struggle; a last-ditch fight

决算 juésuàn (名) final accounts; final accounting of revenue and expenditure: 国家～ final state accounts

决心 juéxīn (名) determination; resolution: 新年的～ New Year's resolutions. 下定～ make up one's mind. ～书 written pledge

决议(議) juéyì resolution: ～草案 draft resolution

决战(戰) juézhàn (名) decisive battle; decisive engagement

诀 jué I (名) 1 rhymed formula 2 knack; tricks of the trade: 秘～ a special skill II (动) bid farewell; part: 永～ part never to meet again; part for ever. ～别 bid farewell; part

诀窍(竅) juéqiào (名) knack; tricks of the trade; key to success

抉 jué (动)〈书〉 pick out; single out

抉择(擇) juézé (动)〈书〉 choose; select: 作出～ make one's choice

崛 jué (动)〈书〉 rise abruptly

崛起 juéqǐ (动) 1 (of a mountain, etc.) rise abruptly; suddenly appear on the horizon 2 rise (as a political force)

掘 jué (动) dig: ～井 dig (or sink) a well. 发～ excavate (historic relics, etc.)

倔 jué ～强 stubborn; unbending

绝 jué I (动) cut off; sever: 拒～ refuse. ～交 sever any relations with II (形) 1 exhausted; used up; finished: 弹尽粮～ completely run out of ammunition and provisions 2 desperate; hopeless: ～境 hopeless situation; impasse. ～症 incurable disease 3 unique; superb; matchless: ～技 unique skill III (副) 1 extremely; most: ～好的机会 the best possible opportunity 2 [used before a negative word] absolutely; in the least; by any means; on any account: ～无此意 have absolutely no such intentions. ～非偶然 by no means accidental 3 leaving no leeway; making no allowance; uncompromising: 不要把话说～. Don't say anything that leaves no room for compromise.

绝笔(筆) juébǐ (名) verse or essay written before the writer's death; a piece of painting completed before the artist's death

绝壁 juébì (名) precipice; cliff

绝代 juédài (形)〈书〉 unique among one's contemporaries; peerless: 才华～ unrivalled talent

绝倒 juédǎo (动)〈书〉 split one's sides with laughter; roar with laughter: 令人～ sidesplitting

绝顶 juédǐng I (副) extremely; utterly: ～聪明 extremely intelligent II (名) the top of a mountain peak

绝对(對) juéduì I (形) absolute: ～多数 overwhelming majority. ～服从 absolute obedience. ～化 in absolute terms II (副) absolutely; perfectly; definitely: ～可靠 absolutely reliable

绝后(後) juéhòu (名) 1 without issue; heirless 2 never to be seen again: 空前～ It has never happened before nor is it likely to happen again.

绝迹(跡) juéjì (动) disappear; vanish; be completely wiped out; extinct: 天花病在很多国家都已～. Small pox has been stamped out in most countries.

绝句 juéjù (名) *jueju*, a poem of four lines, each containing five or seven characters, with a strict tonal pattern and rhyme scheme

绝口 juékǒu [used only after the negative word "不"]: 赞不～ give unstinted praise; praise profusely. 骂不～ heap endless abuse upon. ～不提 never say a single word about; avoid mentioning

绝路 juélù (名) road to ruin; blind alley; a dead end; impasse: 自寻～ bring ruin upon oneself

绝伦(倫) juélún (形) unsurpassed; unequalled; peerless; matchless: 精美～ exquisite beyond compare; superb. 荒谬～ utterly absurd; utterly preposterous

绝密 juémì (形) top-secret; most confidential

绝妙 juémiào (形) extremely clever; ingenious; extremely wonderful; perfect: ～的一招 a very wise move; a masterstroke. ～的讽刺 perfect irony

绝食 juéshí (动) fast; go on a hunger strike

绝望 juéwàng (动) give up all hope; despair: ～的挣扎 desperate struggle

绝无(無)仅(僅)有 juéwú-jǐnyǒu (形) the only one of its kind; unique

绝招 juézhāo (名) 1 unique skill 2 unexpected tricky move (as a last resort)

绝种(種) juézhǒng (名) (said of animals) extinct; extinction

倔 juè (形) gruff; surly: 这老头儿脾气～. That old man has a gruff manner.

军 jūn 1 armed forces; army; troops: 参～ join the army 2 army: 全歼敌人一个～ wipe out an enemy army

军备(備) jūnbèi (名) armament; arms: 扩充～ engage in arms expansion. ～竞赛 armament (or arms) race

军队(隊) jūnduì (名) armed forces; army; troops

军阀 jūnfá (名) warlord

军法 jūnfǎ (名) military criminal code; military law: ～从事 punish by military law. ～审判 court-martial

军费 jūnfèi (名) military expenditure

军服 jūnfú (名) military uniform; uniform: ～呢 army coating

军工 jūngōng (名) 1 war industry 2 military project

军官 jūnguān (名) officer

军火 jūnhuǒ (名) munitions; arms and ammunition: ～工业 munitions industry; armament industry. ～库 arsenal. ～商 munitions merchant; arms dealer; merchant of death

军机(機) jūnjī (名) 1 military plan: 贻误～ frustrate or fail to carry out a military plan 2 military secret: 泄漏～ leak a military secret

军纪 jūnjì (名) military discipline

军舰(艦) jūnjiàn (名) warship; naval vessel

军旗 jūnqí (名) army flag; colours; ensign: ～礼 colours salute

军情 jūnqíng (名) military (or war) situation: 刺探～ spy on the military movements; collect military information

军区(區) jūnqū (名) military region; (military) area command

军人 jūnrén (名) soldier; serviceman; armyman

军师(師) jūnshī (名) 1 strategist in ancient China 2 adviser

军事 jūnshì (名) military affairs: ～基地 military base. ～科学 military science. ～素质 military qualities; fighting capability. ～演习 military manoeuvre. ～学院 military academy

军属(屬) jūnshǔ (名) soldier's dependants; armyman's family

军械 jūnxiè (名) ordnance; armament: ～处 ordnance department. ～库 ordnance depot; arms depot; armoury

军心 jūnxīn (名) soldiers' morale: 大振～ boost the morale of the troops

军需 jūnxū (名) 1 military supplies 2 quartermaster: ～库 military supply depot. ～品 military supplies; military stores

军医(醫) jūnyī (名) medical officer; military surgeon

军营(營) jūnyíng (名) military camp; barracks

军种(種) jūnzhǒng (名) (armed) services

军装(裝) jūnzhuāng (名) military (or army) uniform; uniform

均 jūn I (形) equal; even: 财富分配不～ uneven distribution of wealth II (副) without exception; all: 所有国家～派代表出席了会议. All countries were represented at the meeting.

均等 jūnděng (形) equal; impartial; fair

均分 jūnfēn (动) divide equally; share out equally

均衡 jūnhéng (形) balanced; proportionate; harmonious; even: 国民经济～地发展 the national economy has developed harmoniously
均势(勢) jūnshì (名) balance of power; equilibrium of forces; equilibrium: 核～ nuclear parity
均匀 jūnyún (形) even; well-distributed: 今年的雨水很～. Rainfall has been fairly well-distributed this year.

钧 jūn (名) **1** an ancient unit of weight (equal to 30 *jin*) **2** ‹敬› you; your: ～座 Your Excellency

菌 jūn (名) **1** fungus **2** bacterium
see also jùn

龟(龜) jūn
see also guī
龟裂 jūnliè **1** (of parched earth) be full of cracks **2** (of skin) chap

君 jūn (名) **1** monarch; sovereign; supreme ruler **2** gentleman; Mr.: 诸～ gentlemen. 张～ Mr. Zhang
君权(權) jūnquán (名) monarchical power
君主 jūnzhǔ (名) monarch; sovereign: ～国 monarchical state; monarchy. ～立宪 constitutional monarchy. ～制 monarchy. ～专制 autocratic monarchy; absolute monarchy
君子 jūnzǐ (名) a man of noble character; gentleman: 伪～ hypocrite. 正人～ a man of moral integrity

菌 jùn (名) mushroom
see also jūn

浚(濬) jùn (动) dredge: ～渠 dredge a canal

竣 jùn (动) complete; finish: 告～ have been completed. ～工 (of a project) be completed

峻 jùn (形) **1** (of mountains) high: 高山～岭 high mountains and steep cliffs **2** harsh; severe; stern: 严刑～法 harsh law and severe punishment
峻峭 jùnqiào (形) high and steep

俊 jùn (形) **1** handsome: 这孩子长得挺～的. The child is quite handsome. **2** a person of outstanding talent
俊杰(傑) jùnjié (名) a person of outstanding talent; hero
俊美 jùnměi (形) pretty; handsome
俊俏 jùnqiào (形) pretty and charming
俊秀 jùnxiù (形) pretty; of delicate beauty

骏 jùn: ～马 fine horse; steed

K k

喀 kā ‹象› noise made in coughing or vomiting
喀嚓 kāchā ‹象› crack; snap: ～一声树枝断了. The branch broke with a crack.

咖 kā
see also gā
咖啡 kāfēi (名) coffee: ～馆 café. 速溶～ instant coffee. ～因 caffeine

卡 kǎ I (动) block; check: 他及时～住了这笔钱. He withheld the money in good time. ～住敌人的退路 block the enemy's retreat II ‹简›(卡路里) calorie
see also qiǎ
卡车(車) kǎchē (名) lorry; truck
卡片 kǎpiàn (名) card: ～目录 card catalogue. ～索引 card index

咯 kǎ (动) cough up: ～痰 cough up phlegm. ～血 spit blood

开(開) kāi (动) **1** open: ～门 open the door **2** make an opening; open up; reclaim: ～运河 dig a canal. ～荒 reclaim land **3** open out; come loose: 桃树～花了. The peach trees are blossoming. **4** lift (a ban, restriction, etc.): ～禁 lift a ban **5** start; operate: ～拖拉机 drive a tractor. ～飞机 fly (or pilot) an airplane. ～电视机 turn on the T.V. **6** (of troops, etc.) set out; move: 军队正～往前线. The troops are leaving for the front. **7** set up; run: ～工厂 set up a factory **8** begin; start: 九月～学 school begins in September. ～演 The curtain rises. **9** hold (a meeting, exhibition, etc.): ～运动会 hold an athletic meet **10** make a list of; write out: ～方子 write a prescription. ～一个户头 open an account **11** pay (wages, fares, etc.): ～销 spending **12** boil: 水～了. The water is boiling. **13** [used after a verb to indicate expansion or development]: 消息传～了. The news has spread far and wide. 这支歌流行～了. The song has become very popular.

开(開) kāi **1** [used after a verb to indicate separation]: 躲～ get out of the way. 把门推～ push the door open. **2** [used after a verb to indicate capacity]: 这间屋子小, 人太多了坐不～. The room is too small to hold too many people.

开拔 kāibá (动)(of troops) move; set out

开办(辦) kāibàn (动) open; set up; start: ～训练班 run a training course

开本 kāiběn (名) format; book size: 十六～ 16 mo 三十二～ 32 mo

开采(採) kāicǎi (动) mine; extract; exploit: ～煤炭 mine coal. ～石油 recover petroleum

开场(場) kāichǎng (动) begin: 戏已经～了. The play has already begun.

开车(車) kāichē (动) **1** drive or start a car, train, etc. **2** set a machine in motion; get it going

开诚布公 kāichéng-bùgōng (动) come straight to the point and speak frankly and sincerely

开除 kāichú (动) expel; discharge: ～学籍 expel from school

开创(創) kāichuàng (动) start; initiate: ～新时代 usher in a new era. ～新局面 create a new situation

开刀 kāidāo (动) **1** 〈口〉 perform or have a surgical operation; operate or be operated on: 给病人～ operate on a patient **2** make sb. the first target of attack

开导(導) kāidǎo (动) convince sb. by patient analysis; help sort out sb.'s ideas

开动(動) kāidòng (动) start; set in motion: ～机器 start a machine. ～脑筋 use one's brains

开端 kāiduān (名) beginning; start: 良好的～ a good beginning

开发(發) kāifā (动) develop; open up; exploit: ～海底石油 exploit offshore petroleum resources. ～荒地 reclaim wasteland. 智力～ tap intellectual resources

开放 kāifàng (动) **1** come into bloom: 百花～. A hundred flowers are in blossom. **2** be open to traffic or public use **3** be open (to the public): ～政策 the policy of opening to the outside world. 沿海～城市 coastal cities opening to foreign trade

开赴 kāifù (动) leave for; be bound for: ～前线 be sent to the front

开工 kāigōng (动) **1** (of a factory, etc.) go into operation: ～不足 operate under capacity **2** (of work on a construction project, etc.) start

开关(關) kāiguān (名) switch

开国(國) kāiguó (动) found state: ～大典 founding ceremony (of a state). ～元勋 founding father

开航 kāiháng (动) **1** become open for navigation **2** set sai

开花 kāihuā (动) blossom bloom; flower: ～结果 blossom and bear fruit — yield positive results

开化 kāihuà (动) become civilized

开会(會) kāihuì (动) hold o attend a meeting

开火 kāihuǒ (动) open fire: ～ 〈口令〉 Fire!

开戒 kāijiè (动) break an abstinence (from smoking, drinking etc.)

开卷 kāijuàn (动) open a book read: ～考试 open-book examination

开垦(墾) kāikěn open up (c reclaim) wasteland; bring unde cultivation

开口 kāikǒu (动) **1** open one mouth; start to talk: 难以～ difficult to bring up the matte **2** put the first edge on a kni

开阔(闊) kāikuò I (形) **1** ope wide: ～的广场 an open squa **2** tolerant: 心胸～ broad-min ed; unbiased II (动) wide ～眼界 broaden one's experien (or horizons)

开朗 kāilǎng (形) open a clear: 豁然～ suddenly see t light; feel illuminated

开列 kāiliè draw up (a lis list: ～清单 draw up (or ma out) a list; make an inventory

开明 kāimíng (形) enlighten

～人士 enlightened personages

开幕 kāimù (动) 1 the curtain rises 2 open; inaugurate: 展览会明天～. The exhibition will open tomorrow. ～词 opening speech (or address). ～式 opening ceremony

开辟(闢) kāipì (动) open up; start: ～航线 open an air or sea route. ～财源 tap new financial resources; explore new sources of revenue. ～新的途径 blaze a trail

开腔 kāiqiāng (动) begin to speak; open one's mouth: 他半天不～. For a long while he kept his mouth shut.

开设 kāishè (动) 1 open (a shop, factory, etc.) 2 offer (a course in college, etc.)

开始 kāishǐ I (动) begin; start: ～生效 take effect; come into effect (or force) II (名) initial stage; beginning; outset

开释(釋) kāishì (动、名) release (a prisoner)

开水 kāishuǐ (名) 1 boiling water 2 boiled water

开庭 kāitíng (动) open court session; call the court to order

开通 kāitōng (形) open-minded; liberal; enlightened

开头(頭) kāitóu (名) begin; start: 你从一～就错了. You've been wrong from the very start.

开脱 kāituō (动) absolve; exonerate: ～罪责 absolve sb. from guilt or blame. 替某人～ plead for sb.

开拓 kāituò (动) open up: ～精神 enterprising spirit

开外 kāiwài (副) over; above: 他看起来有四十～. He looks a little over forty.

开玩笑 kāi wánxiào (动) 1 crack a joke; joke; make fun of: 我是跟你～的. I was only joking. 2 treat sth. as insignificant: 这可不是～的事. This is no joking matter.

开往 kāiwǎng (动) (of a train, ship, etc.) leave for; be bound for: ～广州的特快 the Guangzhou express

开胃 kāiwèi (动) whet (or stimulate) the appetite

开小差 kāi xiǎochāi (动) 1 (of a soldier) desert 2 be absent-minded: 用心听讲, 思想就不会～. If you listen carefully, your attention won't wander.

开销 kāixiao (名) expense: 日常的～ daily expenses; running expenses

开心 kāixīn (动) 1 feel happy; rejoice 2 amuse oneself at sb.'s expense; make fun of sb.: 别拿他～了. Don't crack jokes at his expense.

开业(業) kāiyè (动) 1 (of a shop, etc.) start business 2 (of a lawyer, doctor, etc.) start practice

开源节(節)流 kāiyuán jiéliú increase income and reduce expenditure

开展 kāizhǎn (动) 1 develop; launch; unfold: ～批评和自我批评 carry out criticism and self-criticism. ～经济协作 develop economic cooperation 2 open-minded; politically progressive

开张(張) kāizhāng (名、动) 1 begin doing business 2 the first transaction of a day's business

开支 kāizhī (动、名) 1 pay (expenses); defray 2 expenses; expenditure; spending: 节省～ cut down expenses. 军费～ military spending

开宗明义(義) kāizōng-míngyì make clear the purpose and main theme from the very beginning

揩 kāi (动) wipe: ～泪 wipe away one's tears. 把桌子～干净 wipe the table clean. ～油 get petty advantages at the expense of other people or the state; scrounge

慨 kǎi 1 indignant 2 deeply touched: 感～ sigh with emotion

慨然 kǎirán (副) 1 with deep feeling: ～长叹 sigh like a furnace; sigh with a feeling of regret 2 generously: ～相赠 give sth. of value to sb. as a gift

楷 kǎi (名) 1 model; pattern 2 (in Chinese calligraphy) regular script: 小～ regular script in small characters. 大～ regular script in big characters

楷模 kǎimó (名) model; pattern

楷书(書) kǎishū (名) (in Chinese calligraphy) regular script

铠(鎧) kǎi ～甲 (a suit of) armour

凯(凱) kǎi (名、形) 1 triumphant strains 2 triumphant; victorious

凯歌 kǎigē (名) a song of triumph; paean

凯旋 kǎixuán (名) triumphant return: ～而归 return in triumph

刊 kān (动、名) 1 print; publish: 创～ put out the first issue 2 periodical; publication: 报～ newspapers and magazines. 半月～ biweekly 3 delete or correct: ～误 correct misprint

刊登 kāndēng (动) publish in a newspaper or magazine; carry

刊物 kānwù (名) publication: 定期～ periodical (publication)

刊载 kānzǎi (动) publish (in a newspaper or magazine); carry

堪 kān (动) 1 may; can: ～当重任 be capable of holding a position of great responsibility 2 bear; endure: 不～设想 be dreadful to contemplate

戡 kān (动) suppress: ～乱 suppress (or put down) a rebellion

勘 kān (动) 1 read and correct the text of; collate 2 investigate; survey

勘测 kāncè (动) survey

勘察 kānchá (名) 1 reconnaissance 2 prospecting

勘探 kāntàn (动) exploration; prospecting

勘误 kānwù (动) correct errors in printing: ～表 errata; corrigenda

龛(龕) kān niche; shrine: 佛～ Buddhist altar

看 kān (动) 1 look after; take care of; tend: ～门 watch the gate; be in charge of the opening and closing of a gate. ～孩子 look after children; baby sitting 2 keep under surveillance: ～住那坏蛋，别让他跑了！ Keep an eye on that rascal. Don't let him sneak away.
see also kàn

看管 kānguǎn (动) 1 look after; attend to: ～行李 look after the luggage 2 guard; watch: ～俘虏 guard the captives

看护(護) kānhù I (动) nurse: ～病人 nurse the sick II (名) hospital nurse

看家 kānjiā (动) 1 look after the house; mind the house 2 outstanding (ability); special (skill): ～本领 one's special skill

看守 kānshǒu (动) 1 watch; guard: ～犯人 guard prisoners 2 turnkey; warder: ～内阁 caretaker cabinet. ～所 lockup for prisoners awaiting trial; detention house

看押 kānyā (动) take into custody; detain

槛(檻) kǎn (名) threshold

侃 kǎn: ～～而谈 speak with fervour and assurance

坎 kǎn (名) bank; ridge: 田～儿 a raised path through fields

坎肩儿 kǎnjiānr (名) sleeveless jacket; cape

坎坷 kǎnkě (形) 1 bumpy; rough: ～不平的路 a rugged road 2 〈书〉: ～不平的一生 a life full of setbacks and misfortunes

砍 kǎn cut; chop; hack: 把树枝～下来 cut (or lop) off a branch. ～柴 cut firewood. 把树～倒 fell a tree

砍伐 kǎnfá (动) fell (trees)

瞰 kàn (动) look down from a height; overlook: 鸟～ get a bird's-eye view

看 kàn (动) 1 see; look at; watch: ～电影 see a film; go to the cinema. ～电视 watch TV. ～球赛 watch a ball game 2 read: ～报 read a newspaper. ～书 read (a book); do some reading 3 think; consider: 你对他怎么～？ What do you think of him? 4 look upon; regard 把人民的利益～得高于一切 pu the interests of the people above all else 5 treat (a patient or an illness): 大夫把她的肺炎～好了. The doctor has cured her o pneumonia. 6 look after: take care of 7 call on; visit; see: ～朋友 call on a friend. ～医生 g and see a doctor 8 depend on 明天是否去长城，完全得～天气了. Whether we'll make a tri to the Great Wall tomorrow wholly depends on the weather 9 [used after a verb in reduplicated form indicating "let sb. try"] 试试～ have a try. 尝尝～. Jus taste this. 让我想想～. Let m think it over.
see also kān

看病 kànbìng (动) 1 (of a do tor) attend to a patient 2 (a patient) see a doctor

看不惯 kànbuguàn (动) cann bear the sight of; frown upon: 这种浪费现象我们～. We hate see such waste.

看不起 kànbuqǐ (动) look dow upon; scorn; despise

看成 kànchéng (动) look upo as; regard as: 你把我～什么

了? What do you take me for?

看出 kànchū (动) make out; see: ～问题的所在 see where the shoe pinches

看穿 kànchuān (动) see through: ～他的诡计 see through sb.'s trick

看待 kàndài (动) look upon; regard; treat

看得起 kàndeqǐ have a good opinion of; think highly of

看法 kànfa (名) a way of looking at things; view

看见(見) kànjian (动) catch sight of; see

看来(來) kànlai it seems (or appears); it looks as if: ～好象要下雨. It looks like rain. ～他并不喜欢这样的电影. Evidently he doesn't like this kind of film.

看破 kànpò (动) see through: ～红尘 be disillusioned with this human world

看齐(齊) kànqí (动) 1 dress: 向右(左)～ Dress right (left), dress! 2 keep up with; emulate: 向先进工作者～ emulate the advanced workers

看轻(輕) kànqīng (动) underestimate; make light of: 谁也不应～自己的力量. Nobody should underestimate his own strength.

看透 kàntòu 1 understand thoroughly 2 see through

看望 kànwàng (动) call on; visit; see: ～老同学 call on an old schoolmate

看中 kànzhòng (动) take a fancy to; settle on: 这些布你～了哪块? Which piece of cloth is to your liking?

看重 kànzhòng (动) regard as important; value; set store by: ～传统友谊 set store by the ties of traditional friendship

康

kāng (名) well-being; health

康复(復) kāngfù (形) restored to health; recovered: 祝您早日～. Hope you'll soon be well again.

康乐(樂) kānglè (名) peace and happiness

康庄(莊)大道 kāngzhuāng dàdào (名) broad road

慷

kāng

慷慨 kāngkǎi (形) 1 vehement; fervent: ～激昂 impassioned; vehement. ～陈词 speak very vehemently 2 generous; liberal: ～援助 generous assistance. ～解囊 help sb. generously with money

慷慨就义(義) kāngkǎi jiùyì die a hero's death; meet one's death like a hero

糠

kāng (名) chaff; bran; husk

扛

káng (动) carry on the shoulder; shoulder: ～枪 shoulder a gun. ～着麻袋 carry a sack on the shoulder. ～长活 work as a farm labourer

亢

kàng (形) overbearing; haughty: 不～不卑 behave modestly but without undue self-effacement

炕

kàng I (名) *kang*; a heatable brick bed II (动) bake or dry by the heat of a fire: 把湿衣服摊在炕上～干 spread the wet clothes on a heated *kang* to dry

抗

kàng (动) 1 resist; combat; fight: ～灾 fight natural calamities. ～震 shockproof. ～敌 resist the enemy. ～热 heat resistant 2 refuse; defy: ～捐～税 refuse to pay levies and taxes 3 contend with; be a match for: 分庭～礼 stand up to sb. as an equal

抗辩(辯) kàngbiàn I (动) reject charges and plead not guilty II (名) counterplea

抗旱 kànghàn fight (or combat) a drought

抗衡 kànghéng (动) contend with sb. as an equal

抗洪 kànghóng (动) fight (or combat) a flood

抗击(擊) kàngjī (动) resist; beat back: ～侵略者 resist the aggressors

抗拒 kàngjù (动) resist; defy

抗菌素 kàngjūnsù (名) antibiotic

抗日战(戰)争 Kàng Rì Zhànzhēng (名) War of Resistance against Japan

抗体(體) kàngtǐ (名) antibody

抗议(議) kàngyì (动、名) protest: 提出～ lodge a protest. ～集会 protest rally. ～照会 note of protest

伉

kàng

伉俪(儷) kànglì (名) <书> married couple; husband and wife

考

kǎo (动) 1 give or take an examination, test or quiz: 我～～你. Let me quiz you. ～上大学 pass the entrance examination of a university 2 check; inspect 3 study; investigate; verify: 待～ remain to be verified

考查 kǎochá (动) examine; check: ～学生成绩 check students' work

考察 kǎochá (动) 1 inspect; make an on-the-spot investigation: 出国～ go abroad on a study tour 2 observe and study: ～组 study group

考订 kǎodìng (动) examine and correct; do textual research

考古 kǎogǔ (动、名) 1 engage in archaeological studies 2 archaeology: ～学 archaeology. ～学家 archaeologist

考核 kǎohé (动) examine; check; assess (sb.'s proficiency): ～制度 examination system

考究 kǎojiu I (动) observe and study; investigate II (形) 1 fastidious; particular: 穿衣服不必过于～. One need not be too particular about dress. 2 fine: 装璜～ finely bound

考据(據) kǎojù (名) textual criticism; textual research

考虑(慮) kǎolǜ (动) think over; consider: 让我～一下. Let me think it over.

考勤 kǎoqín (动) check upon work attendance: ～簿 attendance record

考生 kǎoshēng (名) candidate for an entrance examination; examinee

考试 kǎoshì (名) examination; test

考验(驗) kǎoyàn (名) test; trial: 经受了严峻的～ have stood a severe test

考证(證) kǎozhèng (名) textual criticism; textual research

烤 kǎo (动) bake; roast; toast: ～鸭 roast duck. ～馒头 toasted steamed bun. 把湿衣裳～干 dry wet clothes by a fire. 我们围炉～火 all of us sat around a brazier to warm oneself

烤炉(爐) kǎolú (名) oven

拷 kǎo (动) flog; beat; torture

拷贝(貝) kǎobèi (名) copy

拷打 kǎodǎ (动) flog; beat; torture: 严刑～ subject sb. to torture

拷问 kǎowèn (动) torture sb. during interrogation; interrogate with torture

铐 kào (名、动) 1 handcuffs 2 put handcuffs on; handcuff: 把犯人～起来 handcuff the criminal

靠 kào (动) 1 lean aginst; lean on: 她把头～在他的肩上. She leaned her head on his shoulder. 2 keep to; get near; come up to: 我们的车～近机场了. Our car is approaching the airport. 3 near; by: 他～窗坐着. He is sitting by the window. 4 depend on; rely on: 他家里～他维持生活. His family depended on him for support. 5 trust: 可～ reliable; trustworthy

靠岸 kào'àn (动) pull in to shore; draw alongside

靠边(邊) kàobiān (动) keep to the side: ～! ～! Out of the way, please! ～儿站 stand aside; step aside; get out of the way

靠不住 kàobuzhù (形) unreliable; undependable; untrustworthy: 这人～. This chap is not to be trusted. 这消息～. This information is unreliable.

靠得住 kàodezhù (形) reliable; dependable; trustworthy

靠拢(攏) kàolǒng (动) draw close; close up: 向前～! Close ranks!

靠山 kàoshan (名) backer; patron: 他有强有力的～. He has strong backing.

犒 kào (动) reward with food and drink: ～赏 reward a victorious army, etc. with food and drink

磕 kē (动) 1 knock (against sth. hard): 摔了一跤，脸上～破了皮 fall and get a scratch on the face 2 knock sth. out of a vessel, container, etc.

磕碰 kēpèng (动) 1 knock against; collide with; bump against 2 clash; squabble

磕头(頭) kētóu (动) kowtow

瞌 kē

瞌睡 kēshuì (形) sleepy; drowsy: 打～ doze off; nod; have a nap

苛 kē (形) severe; exacting: ～待 treat harshly. ～政 tyranny

苛捐杂(雜)税 kējuān-záshuì (名) exorbitant taxes and levies

苛刻 kēkè (形) harsh: ～的条件 harsh terms

苛求 kēqiú (动) make excessive demands; be hypercritical

窠 kē (名) nest; burrow

窠臼 kējiù (名) (of literary or artistic work) stereotype: 不落～ show originality

棵 kē (量): 一～树 a tree. 一～大白菜 a (head of) Chinese cabbage

颗 kē (量): 一～珠子 a pearl. 一～黄豆 a soya bean

颗粒 kēlì (名) **1** anything small and roundish (as a bean, pearl, etc.); pellet **2** grain: ～归仓 every grain to the granary

科 kē I (名) **1** a branch of academic or vocational study: 文～ the liberal arts. 理～ the natural sciences. 产～ department of obstetrics **2** a division or subdivision of an administrative unit; section: 财务～ finance section. 总务～ services section **3** family: 猫～动物 animals of the cat family II (动) pass a sentence: ～以罚金 impose a fine on sb.; fine

科班 kēbān (名) regular professional training: ～出身 be a professional by training

科技 kējì (名) science and technology: ～大学 polytechnic university. ～界 scientific and technological circles. ～术语 scientific and technical terminology

科教片 kējiàopiàn (名) popular science film; educational film

科目 kēmù (名) subject (in a curriculum); course; branch of study

科室 kēshì (名) administrative or technical offices: ～人员 office staff (or personnel)

科学(學) kēxué (名) science; scientific knowledge: ～工作者 scientific worker; scientist. ～普及读物 popular science books; popular science. ～实验 scientific experiment

科学(學)院 kēxuéyuàn academy of sciences: 中国～ the Chinese Academy of Sciences

科研 kēyán (名) scientific research: ～机构 scientific research institution. ～人员 scientific research personnel. ～攻关 tackle key scientific research projects

咳 ké (动) cough: ～嗽糖 cough drops

壳(殼) ké (名) shell: 鸡蛋～ egg shell. 核桃～ walnut shell

see also qiào

渴 kě I (形) thirsty: 解～ quench one's thirst. 我都快～死了. I'm literally parched. II (副) yearningly: ～念 yearn for

渴望 kěwàng thirst for; long for; yearn for; hanker after

可 kě I (动) **1** approve: 不置～否 decline to comment; be noncommittal **2** can; may: 阅览室的书籍不～携出室外. The books in this reading room are not to be taken out. **3** need (doing); be worth (doing): 城里没有多少地方～看的. There isn't much worth seeing in the city. II (副) **1** [used to emphasize the tone of speaker]: ～别忘了. Mind you don't forget it. 你～来了! So you're here at last! **2** [used to emphasize the tone of an interrogative sentence]: 你～曾跟他谈过这个问题? Did you ever bring up the question with him?

see also kè

可喜 kěxǐ (形) gratifying; heartening: ～的成就 gratifying achievements

可笑 kěxiào (形) laughable; ridiculous; ludicrous; funny: 简直～! It's simply ridiculous!

可行 kěxíng (形) advisable; feasible: 是否～,请斟酌. Please consider if this idea is feasible.

可疑 kěyí (形) suspicious; dubious; questionable: 形迹～ look suspicious; be fishy

可以 kěyǐ I (动) can; may: 你～走了. You may go now. II (形) **1** ‹口› passable; pretty good; not bad: 她的英语还～. Her English is not too bad. **2** ‹口› awful: 他今天忙得真～. He's as busy as a bee today.

可爱(愛) kě'ài (形) lovable; lovely: ～的祖国 my beloved country. 多～的孩子! How cute the child!

可悲 kěbēi (形) sad; lamentable

可鄙 kěbǐ (形) contemptible; despicable; mean: 行为～ act contemptibly

可耻 kěchǐ (形) shameful; disgraceful; ignominious

可歌可泣 kěgē-kěqì move one to song and tears: ～的英雄事迹 moving heroic deeds

可耕地 kěgēngdì (名) arable land; cultivable land

可观(觀) kěguān (形) considerable; impressive; sizable: 数目～ a considerable figure

可贵 kěguì (形) valuable; praiseworthy; commendable: ～的品质 fine qualities. ～的贡献 valuable contribution

可恨 kěhèn (形) hateful; detestable; abominable

可见(見) kějiàn it is thus clear (or evident, obvious) that: 只有几个学生通过了考试,～考题是很难的. Only a few students passed the exam, so you can see that the paper must have been extremely stiff.

可敬 kějìng (形) worthy of respect; respected

可靠 kěkào (形) reliable; dependable; trustworthy: ～消息 reliable information. ～后方 a secure rear area

可可 kěkě (名) cocoa

可口 kěkǒu (形) good to eat; nice; tasty; palatable: 这汤很～. This soup is very delicious.

可怜(憐) kělián I (形) **1** pitiful; pitiable; poor: ～虫 pitiful creature; wretch. 一副～相 a pitiable look **2** meagre; wretched; miserable; pitiful: 他的英语知识贫乏得～. His knowledge of English is far from adequate. II (形) have pity on; pity: 没人～他. Nobody feels sorry for him.

可能 kěnéng (形) **1** possible; probable: 这是完全～的. It's entirely possible. **2** probably; maybe: 他～会改变主意. He may change his mind. **3** possibility: 他不～当选为总统. There is no likelihood of his being elected to the presidency.

可怕 kěpà (形) fearful; frightful; terrible; terrifying: 真～! How dreadful! 干吧! 没什么～的. Go ahead! There's nothing to be afraid of.

可巧 kěqiǎo (副) as luck would have it; by a happy coincidence

可取 kěqǔ (形) desirable: 你亲自去拜访他一下是十分～的. It is highly desirable that you go and see him in person.

可是 kěshì (连) but; yet; however: 这房间虽小,～很安静. The room is small but very quiet.

可谓 kěwèi one may well say; it may be said; it may be called: 这机会～是千载难逢. This may be the chance of a life-time.

可恶(惡) kěwù (形) hateful; abominable; detestable

可惜 kěxī it's a pity; it's too bad: ～我不在场. What a pity I wasn't there.

刻 kè I (动) carve; engrave; cut: ～字 engrave words (on stone, blocks). 木～ woodcut II (名) **1** a quarter (of an hour): 五点一～ a quarter past five **2** moment: 此～ at the moment III (形) **1** cutting; penetrating: 尖～ acrimonious; biting; sarcastic **2** in the highest degree: 深～ penetrating; profound

刻板 kèbǎn (形) mechanical; stiff; inflexible: ～地照抄 copy mechanically

刻本 kèběn (名) block-printed edition: 宋～ a Song Dynasty block-printed edition

刻薄 kèbó (形) unkind; harsh; mean: 说～话 speak unkindly; make caustic remarks. 待人～ treat people meanly

刻不容缓 kè bùróng huǎn (动) brook no delay; demand immediate attention; be very urgent

刻毒 kèdú (形) venomous; cruel; spiteful: ～的语言 venomed remarks

刻骨 kègǔ (形) deeply ingrained; deep-rooted: ～仇恨 deep-seated hatred. ～铭心 remember with gratitude to the end of one's life

刻画(畫) kèhuà (动) depict; portray

刻苦 kèkǔ (形、动) **1** assiduous; hardworking; painstaking: ～耐劳 endure hardships without complaining **2** simple and frugal: 生活～ lead a simple and frugal life

嗑 kè (动) crack sth. between the teeth: ～瓜子儿 crack melon seeds

克 kè I (动) **1** restrain: ～制 exercise restraint **2** overcome; subdue; capture (a city, etc.): ～敌制胜 defeat the enemy and win victory **3** set a time limit: ～期完工 set a date for completing the work II (名) gram (g)

克服 kèfú (动) **1** surmount; overcome; conquer: ～困难 overcome a difficulty. ～官僚主义 get rid of red tape **2** 〈口〉 put up with (inconveniences, etc.)

克己奉公 kèjǐ-fènggōng be wholeheartedly devoted to public duty; work selflessly for the public interest

克制 kèzhì (动) restrain; exercise restraint: ～感情 control one's temper

可 kè
see also kě

可汗 kèhán (名) khan

课 kè I (名) 1 subject; course: 主～ the main subject. 必修～ required courses 2 class: 上～ go to class. 上午有四节～. There are four classes in the morning. 讲(听)～ give (attend) a lecture II (量) lesson: 第一～ Lesson One III (动) levy: ～以重税 levy heavy taxes

课本 kèběn (名) textbook

课程 kèchéng (名) course; curriculum: ～表 school time-table

课堂 kètáng (名) classroom; schoolroom: ～教学 classroom instruction (or teaching). ～讨论 classroom discussion

课题 kètí (名) 1 a question for study or discussion 2 problem; task: 提出新的～ pose a new problem

课外 kèwài (形) extracurricular; outside class; after school: ～作业 homework. ～阅读 additional reading

课文 kèwén (名) text

客 kè I (名) 1 visitor; guest 2 traveller; passenger: ～机 passenger plane; airliner 3 customer: 房～ boarder; lodger 4 live in a strange place; be a stranger: 作～他乡 live in a strange land 5 a person engaged in some particular pursuit: 政～ politician. 刺～ assassin II (形) objective: ～观 objective

客车(車) kèchē (名) 1 passenger train 2 bus; coach

客店 kèdiàn (名) inn

客队(隊) kèduì (名) visiting team

客房 kèfáng (名) guest room

客观(觀) kèguān (形) objective: ～规律 objective law. ～世界 objective world

客满 kèmǎn (形) (of theatre tickets, etc.) sold out; full house

客气(氣) kèqi (形) 1 polite; courteous: 他待人很～. He is very polite to people. 别～. Please don't stand on ceremony. *or* Make yourself at home. *or* Please don't bother. 2 modest: 您太～了. You are being too modest.

客人 kèrén (名) 1 visitor; guest 2 guest (at a hotel, etc.)

客套 kètào (名) polite formula

客厅(廳) kètīng (名) drawing room; parlour

客运(運) kèyùn (名) passenger transport; passenger traffic

客栈(棧) kèzhàn (名) inn

恪 kè (副) scrupulously and respectfully

恪守 kèshǒu (动) strictly abide by (a treaty, promise, etc.)

肯 kěn (动) 1 agree; consent: 我劝说了半天,他才～了. He did not agree until I had talked to him for a long time. 2 be willing to; be ready to: ～干 be willing to do hard work. ～帮人忙 be ready to help others

肯定 kěndìng I (动) affirm; confirm; approve; regard as positive: ～成绩 affirm the achievements. ～事实 confirm a fact II (形) 1 positive; affirmative: ～的判断 a positive assessment. ～的答复 an affirmative answer 2 definite; sure: 去不去,我们还不能～. We are not sure yet whether we'll go or not. *or* We have yet to decide whether to go or not.

啃 kěn (动) 1 gnaw; nibble: 2 take great pains with one's studies: ～书本 read with great difficulty but with little understanding; make laborious efforts to read

恳(懇) kěn I (副) earnestly; sincerely: ～谈 talk earnestly II (名) request; beseech; entreat: 敬～光临 request your gracious presence

恳切 kěnqiè (形) earnest; sincere: 言词～ speak in an earnest tone. ～希望 sincerely hope

恳求 kěnqiú (动) implore; entreat; beseech: ～某人办件事 beg sb. to do sth.

垦(墾) kěn cultivate (land); reclaim (wasteland): ～荒 reclaim wasteland; bring wasteland under cultivation; open up virgin soil

坑 kēng I (名) 1 hole; pit; hollow: 泥～ mud puddle. 水～ puddle. 粪～ manure pit. 一个萝卜一个～ one radish, one hole — each has his own assignment and there is nobody to spare 2 tunnel; pit: 矿～ pit II (动) 1 bury alive 2 entrap; cheat: ～人 cheat people

坑道 kēngdào (名) 1 gallery

2 tunnel

坑害 kēnghài (动) lead into a trap; entrap

吭 kēng (动) utter a sound or a word: 一声不～ without saying a word.

see also háng

吭声(聲) kēngshēng (动) utter a sound or word: 你为什么不～? Why don't you say something?

铿(鏗) kēng (象) clang; clatter: 拖拉机走在路上～～地响. Tractors clattered along the road.

铿锵(鏘) kēngqiāng (动) ring; clang: 这首诗读起来音调～. This poem is both majestic and sonorous.

空 kōng I (形) empty; hollow; void: ～屋子 an empty room. ～想 idle dream. 街上～无一人. The street is as good as deserted. II (名) sky; air: 晴～ a clear sky III (副) for nothing: ～跑一趟 make a fruitless trip

see also kòng

空洞 kōngdòng I (名) cavity: 牙齿～了 a cavity in tooth II (形) empty; hollow: ～无物 lacking in substance; devoid of content. ～的许诺 hollow promise

空泛 kōngfàn (形) vague and general; not specific: ～的议论 vague and general remarks; generalities

空话 kōnghuà (名) empty talk; idle talk

空间(間) kōngjiān (名) space: 外层～ outer space. ～技术 space technology. ～科学 space science

空降 kōngjiàng (形) airborne: ～兵 airborne force; parachute landing force

空军(軍) kōngjūn (名) air force: ～基地 air base

空口无(無)凭(憑) kōngkǒu wú píng a mere spoken statement is no guarantee

空旷(曠) kōngkuàng (形) open; spacious: ～的原野 an expanse of open country; champaign

空气(氣) kōngqì (名) 1 air: 新鲜～ fresh air 2 atmosphere: ～紧张 a tense atmosphere. ～冷却 air-cooling. ～调节器 air conditioner. ～污染 air pollution

空前 kōngqián (形) unprecedented; as never before: 盛况～ an unprecedentedly grand occasion

空前绝后(後) kōngqián-juéhòu (形) unique; unprecedented and impossibly difficult to recur

空头(頭) kōngtóu 1 (on the stock exchange) bear; short: ～支票 bad cheque; empty promise; lip service 2 nominal; phony: ～政治家 armchair politician

空投 kōngtóu (名) air-drop; paradrop

空文 kōngwén (名) ineffective law, rule, etc.: 一纸～ a mere scrap of paper

空袭(襲) kōngxí (动) air raid; air attack

空想 kōngxiǎng (名) idle dream; fantasy; utopia

空虚 kōngxū (形) hollow; void: 生活～ have no aim in life. 敌人后方～. The enemy rear is weakly defended.

空运(運) kōngyùn (名) air transport; airlift: ～救灾物资 airlift relief supplies (to a stricken area)

空战(戰) kōngzhàn (名) air battle; aerial combat

空中 kōngzhōng (形) in the sky; in the air; aerial; overhead: ～小姐 air hostess. ～加油 air refueling; inflight refueling. ～掩护 air umbrella; air cover. ～劫持 hijacking

空中楼(樓)阁 kōngzhōng lóugé (名) castles in the air

恐 kǒng I (名) fear; dread: 惊～ be alarmed II (动) terrify; intimidate: ～吓 threaten; intimidate

恐怖 kǒngbù (名) terror: 白色～ white terror. ～分子 terrorist

恐吓(嚇) kǒnghè (动) threaten; intimidate: ～信 blackmailing letter; threatening letter

恐慌 kǒnghuāng (名) panic: ～万状 panic-stricken

恐惧(懼) kǒngjù (名) fear; dread: ～不安 be in fear and anxiety

恐怕 kǒngpà (副) 1 I'm afraid: 今晚～他不会来了. I'm afraid he won't come tonight. 2 perhaps; I think: 他走了～有十天了. It's ten days now, I think, since he left. ～你是对的. Perhaps you are right.

孔 kǒng I (名) hole; opening aperture: 钥匙～ keyhole. 通气～ ventilator II (量): 一～土窑 a cave-dwelling

孔道 kǒngdào (名) a narrow passage providing the only means of access to a certain place

孔雀 kǒngque (名) peacock
孔隙 kǒngxì (名) small opening; hole
孔穴 kǒngxué (名) hole; cavity
空 kòng I (动) leave empty or blank: 每段开头要～两格. Leave two blank spaces at the beginning of each paragraph. II (形) unoccupied; vacant: ～座 a vacant seat III (名) 1 empty space: 屋里一点～都没有了. There isn't any space left in the room. 2 free time; spare time: 有～到我这儿来. Come over when you have time.
see also kōng
空白 kòngbái (名) blank space: 填补核子科学上的～ fill the gaps in nuclear science. ～表格 blank form.
空缺 kòngquē (名) vacant position; vacancy
空隙 kòngxì (名) space; gap; interval
空暇 kòngxiá (名) free time; spare time; leisure
空闲(閑) kòngxián I (形) idle; free: 等你～的时候,咱俩去看场电影. Let's go and see a film when you're free. II (名) free time; spare time; leisure: 他一有～就弹钢琴. He played the piano whenever he had some spare time.
空子 kòngzi (名) 1 gap; opening 2 chance; opportunity: 严防坏人钻～ take strict precautions against giving bad people an opening
控 kòng (动) 1 accuse; charge 指～ accuse 2 control; dominate: 遥～ remote control; telecontrol
控告 kònggào (动) charge; accuse; complain: ～某人犯罪 accuse sb. of a crime
控诉 kòngsù (动) accuse; denounce: ～殖民主义的罪恶 condemn the evils of colonialism
控制 kòngzhì (动) control; dominate; command: ～局面 have (or take) the situation in hand. ～感情 control one's temper
抠(摳) kōu (动) 1 dig or dig out with a finger or sth. pointed; scratch: ～洞 scratch a hole 2 carve; cut: 在镜框边上～点花儿 carve a design on a picture frame 3 delve into; study meticulously: 死～字眼儿 be over-scrupulous about the use of language; deliberately find fault with the wording 4 stingy; miserly: ～门儿 stingy; miserly
口 kǒu I (名) 1 mouth 2 opening; entrance; mouth: 河～ the mouth of a river. 入～ entrance. 瓶～ the mouth of a bottle 3 cut; hole: 伤～ wound; cut. 衣服撕破了个～ tear a hole in one's jacket 4 the edge of a knife: 刀～ the edge of a knife II (量): 一～井 a well
口岸 kǒu'àn (名) port: 通商～ trading port
口才 kǒucái (名) eloquence: 他很有～. He is very eloquent.
口吃 kǒuchī (动、名) stutter; stammer: 他一激动就～. He stammers when he gets excited.
口齿(齒) kǒuchǐ (名) 1 enunciation: ～清楚 clear enunciation 2 ability to speak: ～伶俐 speak fluently
口袋 kǒudài (名) pocket; bag; sack: 面～ flour sack. 塑料～ plastic bag
口服 kǒufú (动) 1 profess to be convinced: 心服～ be sincerely convinced 2 take orally: 不得～ not to be taken orally
口福 kǒufú (名) gourmet's luck; the luck to eat delicacies, often at a dinner
口供 kǒugòng (名) confession; testimony; a statement made by the accused under examination
口号(號) kǒuhào (名) slogan; watchword
口径(徑) kǒujìng (名) 1 bore; calibre: 小～步枪 small-bore rifle 2 requirements; specifications; line of action: 统一～ agree on a story; have the same story. 不合～ fail to meet the requirements
口诀 kǒujué (名) a pithy formula (often in rhyme)
口角 kǒujué (名) quarrel, bicker: 发生了～ have a quarrel
口渴 kǒukě (形) thirsty
口令 kǒulìng (名) 1 word of command 2 password; watchword; countersign
口蜜腹剑(劍) kǒumì-fùjiàn honey-mouthed and dagger-hearted; hypocritical and malignant; play a double game
口气(氣) kǒuqì 1 tone; note: 严肃的～ a serious tone. ～强硬的声明 a strongly worded statement 2 manner of speaking: 他的～真不小. He talked big. 3 what is actually meant; implication: 听他的～, 他并不反对我们的建议. Judging by the way he spoke, he

was not really against our proposal.

口琴 kǒuqín (名) mouth organ; harmonica

口若悬(懸)河 kǒu ruò xuán hé let loose a flood of eloquence; be eloquent

口舌 kǒushé (名) 1 quarrel; dispute 2 talking round: 不必费～了. You might as well save your breath.

口实(實) kǒushí (名) a cause for gossip

口是心非 kǒushì-xīnfēi say yes and mean no; say one thing and mean another

口授 kǒushòu (名、动) 1 oral instruction 2 dictate

口述 kǒushù (名) oral account

口头(頭)kǒutóu(形)oral: ～通知 notify orally. ～汇报 verbal report. ～上赞成,实际上反对 agree in words but oppose in deeds. ～表决 voice vote; vote by "yes" and "no". ～声明 oral statement

口头(頭)禅(禪) kǒutóuchán (名) pet phrase

口味 kǒuwèi 1 a person's taste: 合～ suit one's taste. 各人～不同. Tastes differ. 2 the flavour or taste of food

口信 kǒuxìn (名) verbal message

口译(譯) kǒuyì (名) oral interpretation

口音 kǒuyīn (名) 1 voice 2 accent: 说话带～ speak with an accent

口语 kǒuyǔ (名) spoken language

口罩 kǒuzhào (名) surgical mask (worn over nose and mouth); mouth mask

寇 kòu I (名) bandit; invader; enemy: 敌～ the (invading) enemy II (动) invade: 入～ invade (a country)

叩 kòu (动) 1 knock: ～门 knock at a door 2 ～头 kowtow

扣 kòu (动) 1 button; buckle: 把衣服～上 button (up) one's coat. ～扣子 do up the buttons 2 detain; take into custody; arrest: 把罪犯～起来. Keep the criminal in custody. 3 deduct: ～工资 deduct a part of sb.'s pay 4 discount: 打九～ give a 10 per cent discount 5 hit: ～球 smash the ball

扣除 kòuchú (动) deduct: ～物价因素 allow for price changes

扣留 kòuliú (动) detain; arrest; hold in custody: ～驾驶执照 suspend a driving licence

扣人心弦 kòu rén xīnxián (形) exciting; thrilling; soul-stirring: 一场～的比赛 an exciting match

扣押 kòuyā (动) 1 detain; hold in custody 2 distrain

扣压(壓) kòuyā (动) withhold; suppress

扣子 kòuzi (名) 1 knot 2 button

窟 kū (名) 1 hole; cave: 石～ cave; grotto 2 den: 匪～ a robbers' den. 赌～ a gambling-den

窟窿 kūlóng (名) 1 hole; cavity: 耗子～ rat-hole 2 deficit; debt: 补～ make up a deficit

枯 kū (形) 1 (of a plant, etc.) withered: ～草 withered grass. ～叶 dead leaves 2 (of a well, river, etc.) dried up: 河水～了. The river has run dry.

枯肠(腸) kūcháng (名)〈书〉impoverished mind: 搜索～ rack one's brains (for ideas or expressions)

枯槁 kūgǎo (形) 1 withered 2 haggard: 形容～ look haggard

枯黄 kūhuáng (形) withered and yellow: 树叶～了. The leaves have turned yellow.

枯竭 kūjié (形) dried up; exhausted: 水源～. The source has dried up. 资金～.The capital has been exhausted.

枯木逢春 kūmù féng chūn (of an ill-starred elderly person) get a new lease of life

枯萎 kūwěi (形) withered

枯燥 kūzào (形) dull and dry; uninteresting: ～无味 dry as dust

骷 kū

骷髅(髏) kūlóu 1 human skeleton 2 human skull; death's-head

哭 kū (动) cry; weep; sob: 放声大～ cry loudly. 痛～ cry bitterly; cry one's eyes out. ～笑不得 not know whether to laugh or to cry

哭泣 kūqì (动) cry; weep; sob

哭穷(窮) kūqióng (动) go about telling people how hard up one is, which is not usually the case

哭诉 kūsù (动) complain tearfully

苦 kǔ I (形) bitter: ～药 bitter medicine II (名) hardship; suffering; pain: ～中作乐 find joy in hardship III (动) 1 cause sb. suffering; give sb. a hard time: 这事可～了他了. This matter really gave him a hard time. 2 suffer from; be troubled by: ～旱 suffer from drought IV (副) painstakingly; doing one's utmost: 勤学～练 study and train hard. ～干 work hard

苦差 kǔchāi (名) hard and unprofitable job; thankless job

苦楚 kǔchǔ (名) suffering; misery; distress

苦处(處) kǔchu (名) suffering; hardship; difficulty

苦工 kǔgōng (名) hard (manual) work; hard labour

苦功 kǔgōng (名) painstaking effort

苦海 kǔhǎi (名) sea of bitterness; abyss of misery: 脱离～ get out of the abyss of misery

苦口 kǔkǒu 1 (admonish) in earnest: ～相劝 earnestly advise (or exhort). ～婆心 admonish sb. earnestly 2 bitter to the taste: 这些话都是～良药. The advice may be unpalatable, but it will do you good.

苦闷 kǔmèn (形) depressed; dejected; feeling low

苦难(難) kǔnàn (名) suffering; misery; distress: ～岁月 hard times

苦恼(惱) kǔnǎo (形) vexed; worried

苦涩(澀) kǔsè (形) 1 bitter and astringent 2 pained; agonized; anguished

苦思 kǔsī (动) think hard; cudgel one's brains: ～冥想 think long and hard

苦痛 kǔtòng (名) pain; suffering

苦头(頭) kǔtou (名) suffering: 他吃尽了～. He endured untold sufferings.

苦笑 kǔxiào (名) forced smile; wry smile

苦心 kǔxīn (名) trouble taken; pains: 煞费～ take great pains. ～孤诣 make extraordinarily painstaking efforts

苦衷 kǔzhōng (名) difficulties that one is reluctant to bring to the notice of others: 难言的～ feelings of pain or embarrassment which are hard to describe

库 kù (名) warehouse; storehouse: ～房 storeroom. 军火～ arsenal. 汽车～ garage

库藏 kùcáng (动) have in storage: ～图书三十万册. There are 300,000 books in the library.

库存 kùcún (名) stock; reserve: 有大量～ have a large stock of goods. 商品～ commodity inventories. ～现金 cash holding

裤 kù (名) trousers; pants: 短～ shorts. 牛仔～ jeans

裤衩 kùchǎ (名) pants; underpants

酷 kù I (形) cruel; oppressive: ～吏 a cruel (feudal) official II (副) very; extremely: ～寒 severe cold. ～似 be the very image of; resemble very closely. ～好 be very fond of

酷刑 kùxíng (名) cruel (or savage) torture

夸(誇) kuā (动) 1 exaggerate; overstate; boast: ～口 boast; brag 2 praise: 老师～她字写得漂亮. The teacher praised her for her beautiful handwriting.

夸大 kuādà (动) exaggerate; overstate; magnify: ～困难 exaggerate the difficulties. ～其词 make an overstatement; overstate the case

夸奖(獎) kuājiǎng (名、动) praise; commend: 这部新电影受到大家的～. The new film has received high praise from everyone.

夸夸其谈 kuākuā qí tán indulge in verbiage; glib and empty

夸耀 kuāyào (动) brag about; show off; flaunt: 他喜欢～自己的学识. He loves showing off his knowledge.

夸张 kuāzhāng (动、名) 1 exaggerate; overstate: 艺术～ artistic exaggeration 2 hyperbole

垮 kuǎ (动) collapse; fall; break down: 这座老房子快～了. This old building is falling to pieces. 他的身体累～了. His health broke down from overwork.

垮台 kuǎtái (动) collapse; fall from power

挎 kuà (动) 1 carry on the arm: ～着个篮子 with a basket on one's arm. ～着胳膊走 walk arm in arm 2 carry sth. over one's shoulder or at one's side: ～着照相机 have a camera slung over one's shoulder

挎包 kuàbāo (名) satchel

跨 kuà (动) 1 step; stride: ～进屋子 step into the room 2 bestride, straddle: ～上战马 mount (or bestride) a war-horse 3 cut across; go beyond: ～年度 over the year-end. ～学科 interdisciplinary. ～国公司 transnational corporation

跨度 kuàdù (名) span

跨越 kuàyuè (动) stride across; leap over; cut across: ～障碍 surmount an obstacle

胯 kuà (名) hip: ～骨 hipbone; innominate bone

会(會) kuài see also huì

会计 kuàijì (名) 1 accounting 2 bookkeeper; accountant: ～年度 financial (or fiscal) year

侩(儈) kuài (名) middleman: 市～ market broker

脍(膾) kuài (名) 〈书〉 meat chopped into small pieces; minced meat

脍炙人口 kuàizhì rénkǒu (of a piece of good writing, etc.) win popular acclaim; enjoy great popularity

块(塊) kuài I (名) piece; lump; cube; chunk: 石～ blocks of stone. 冰～ ice cubes II (量) 1 [used of a slice or chunk of sth.]: 三～巧克力 three chocolate bars. 一～面包 a piece of bread. 两～肥皂 two cakes of soap 2 〈口〉 *yuan*, the basic unit of money in China: 三～钱 three *yuan*

快 kuài I (形) 1 fast; quick; rapid: ～速阅读 fast (or speed) reading. 进步很～ rapid progress 2 quick-witted; ingenious 3 sharp: ～刀 a sharp knife 4 straightforward: 心直口～ straightforward and outspoken 5 pleased; happy; gratified: 心中不～ feel bad II (动) hurry up; make haste: ～上车吧! Hurry up and get on the bus! ～, 我们已经迟到了. Quick, we are late already. III (副) soon; before long: 他～回来了. He'll be back soon. 电影～开演了. The film is about to begin.

快餐 kuàicān (名) quick meal; fast food; snack: ～部 snack counter

快车(車) kuàichē (名) express train or bus: 特别～ special express

快活 kuàihuó (形) happy; merry; cheerful

快乐(樂) kuàilè (形) happy; joyful; cheerful

快速 kuàisù (形) fast; quick; high-speed: ～电子计算机 high-speed electronic computer

快慰 kuàiwèi (动) feel reassured and happy; be extremely pleased

快意 kuàiyì (形) pleased; satisfied; comfortable

筷 kuài (～子) chopsticks: 碗～ bowls and chopsticks. 一双～子 a pair of chopsticks

宽 kuān I (形) 1 wide; broad: ～银幕 wide screen. ～肩膀 broad-shouldered 2 width; breadth: 这张桌子两米～,三米长. The table is three metres long and two metres wide. 3 generous; lenient: 从～处理 treat with leniency II (动) 1 relax; relieve: 把心放～一点. Don't worry. 2 extend: 限期能再～几天吗? Can the deadline be extended a few more days? *or* Can you give me a few days grace?

宽畅(暢) kuānchàng (形) free from worry; happy

宽敞 kuānchang (形) spacious; roomy; commodious: ～的厅堂 a spacious hall

宽大 kuāndà (形) 1 spacious; roomy: ～的客厅 a spacious drawing room 2 lenient; magnanimous: ～处理 lenient treatment. ～为怀 be magnanimous or lenient (with an offender)

宽待 kuāndài (动) treat with leniency; be lenient in dealing with

宽度 kuāndù (名) width; breadth: 领海～ the extent of the territorial sea

宽广(廣) kuānguǎng (形) broad; extensive; vast: ～的广场 a broad square. 心胸～ broad-minded

宽宏大量 kuānhóng-dàliàng (形) large-minded, magnanimous

宽厚 kuānhòu (形) 1 broad-minded 2 kind and sincere: 待人～ treat people with kindness and sincerity

宽旷(曠) kuānkuàng (形) extensive; vast: ～的草原 a vast stretch of grasslands

宽阔 kuānkuò (形) broad; wide: ～的林荫道 a broad (or wide) avenue

宽容 kuānróng (形) tolerant; lenient

宽恕 kuānshù (动) forgive: 请求～ ask for forgiveness

宽慰 kuānwèi (动) comfort; console: ～她几句. Say something to comfort her.

宽心 kuānxīn (形) feel relieved: 说几句～话 say a few reassuring words

宽裕 kuānyù (形) well-to-do

comfortably off; ample: 生活～ be comfortably off. 时间很～. There's plenty of time yet.

款 kuǎn (名) 1 section of an article in a legal document, etc.; paragraph 2 a sum of money; fund: 拨～ allocate a sum of money for a specific purpose. 汇～ remit money 3 the name of sender or recipient inscribed on a painting or a piece of calligraphy presented as a gift: 上～ the name of recipient. 下～ the name of painter or calligrapher

款待 kuǎndài (动、名)treat cordially; entertain: ～客人 entertain guests. 盛情～ hospitality

款式 kuǎnshì (名) pattern; style; design

款项 kuǎnxiàng (名) a sum of money; fund

款子 kuǎnzi (名) a sum of money

诓 kuāng (动) deceive; hoax: ～骗 deceive; hoax; dupe. 我哪能～你? How could I deceive you?

框 kuāng I (名) frame; circle II (动) draw a frame round: 用红线把标题～起来 frame the heading in red
see also kuàng

框框 kuāngkuāng (名) 1 frame; circle 2 restriction; convention; set pattern: 打破旧～ break outmoded conventions

哐 kuāng (象) crash; bang: ～的一声,脸盆掉在地上了. The basin fell with a crash.

哐啷 kuānglāng (象) crash: ～一声把门关上 bang the door shut

筐 kuāng (名) (～子) basket: 一～苹果 a basket of apples

狂 kuáng (形) 1 mad; crazy: 发～ go mad. ～人 lunatic; maniac 2 violent: ～风 strong fast wind 3 wild: 欣喜若～ be wild (or beside oneself) with joy 4 arrogant; overbearing

狂飙(飆) kuángbiāo (名) hurricane

狂热(熱) kuángrè (名) fanaticism: ～的信徒 a fanatical follower; fanatic. ～的民族沙文主义 fanatical national chauvinism

狂妄 kuángwàng (形) wildly arrogant; presumptuous: ～自大 arrogant and conceited. ～的野心 a wild ambition

狂欢(歡) kuánghuān (名) revelry; carnival; public merrymaking

诳 kuáng: ～语 lies; falsehood

矿(礦) kuàng (名) 1 ore (or mineral) deposit: 报～ report where deposits are found 2 ore: 铁～ iron ore 3 mine: 煤～ coal mine; colliery

矿藏 kuàngcáng (名) mineral resources: ～丰富 be rich in mineral resources ～储量 (ore) reserves

矿产(產) kuàngchǎn (名) mineral products; minerals

矿床 kuàngchuáng (名) mineral (or ore) deposit; deposit

矿工 kuànggōng (名) miner

矿井 kuàngjǐng (名) mine; pit

矿泉 kuàngquán (名) mineral spring: ～水 mineral water

矿山 kuàngshān (名) mine

矿石 kuàngshí (名) ore

矿物 kuàngwù (名) mineral: ～界 mineral kingdom. ～学 mineralogy

旷(曠) kuàng (形) 1 vast; spacious: 地～人稀 a vast territory with a sparse population 2 free from worries and petty ideas: 心～神怡 in a cheerful frame of mind

旷达(達) kuàngdá (形) broad-minded; big-hearted

旷工 kuànggōng (动) deliberately stay away from work

旷古 kuànggǔ (形) from time immemorial

旷课 kuàngkè skip school; play truant

旷日持久 kuàngrì-chíjiǔ (形) long-drawn-out; protracted; prolonged: ～的战争 long-drawn-out war

旷野 kuàngyě (名) wilderness

框 kuàng (名) frame; case: 镜～ picture frame. 窗～ window frame; window case. 眼镜～ rims (of spectacles)
see also kuāng

框架 kuàngjià (名) frame

眶 kuàng (名) the socket of the eye: 热泪盈～ one's eyes filling with tears

况 kuàng I (名) condition; situation: 近～如何? How have you been recently? II (动) compare: 以古～今 draw parallels from history III (连)〈书〉 moreover; besides

况且 kuàngqiě (连) moreover; besides

窥 kuī (动) peep; spy

窥测 kuīcè (动) spy out: ～时机 bide one's time

窥见(見) kuījiàn (动) get (or catch) a glimpse of; detect

窥视 kuīshì (动) peep at; spy on
窥伺 kuīsì (动) lie in wait for; be on watch for
窥探 kuītàn (动) spy upon; pry into: ~军事秘密 pry into military secrets

亏(虧) kuī I (名) loss: 盈~ profit and loss. 转~为盈 turn loss into gain II (动) 1 lose; be deficient: 理~ be in the wrong 2 treat unfairly: 你放心吧，~不了你. Don't worry, we won't let you down. 3 thanks to: ~他及时叫醒了我. Luckily, he woke me up in time. 4 [often said with a touch of irony]: ~ 他说得出口! And he had the nerve to say so!
亏待 kuīdài (动) treat unfairly; treat shabbily
亏空 kuīkong (名) 1 be in debt 2 debt; deficit: 弥补~ meet (or make up) a deficit; make up (for) a loss
亏蚀 kuīshí (名) 1 eclipse of the sun or moon 2 lose (money) in business
亏损 kuīsǔn (名) 1 loss; deficit: 企业~ loss incurred in an enterprise 2 general debility
亏心 kuīxīn (名) a guilty conscience: ~事 a wrong deed that troubles (or weighs on) one's conscience

盔 kuī (名) helmet
盔甲 kuījiǎ (名) a suit of armour

岿(巋) kuī
岿然 kuīrán (形) towering; lofty

魁 kuí (名) 1 chief; head: 罪~ chief criminal; arch-criminal 2 of stalwart build
魁首 kuíshǒu (名) (old use) a person who is outstanding in his time: 文章~ the best writer of the day
魁伟(偉) kuíwěi (形) big and tall
魁梧 kuíwú (形) big and tall; stalwart

葵 kuí (名) certain herbaceous plants with big flowers: 向日~ sunflower. 锦~ high mallow
葵花 kuíhuā (名) sunflower: ~子 sunflower seeds
葵扇 kuíshàn (名) palm-leaf fan

揆 kuí I (动)〈书〉conjecture; consider; estimate: ~度 observe and estimate; conjecture. ~情度理 considering the circumstances and judging by common sense II (名) principle; standard

睽 kuí
睽睽 kuíkuí (动) stare; gaze: 众目~~之下 in the public eye

傀 kuǐ
傀儡 kuǐlěi (名) puppet: ~戏 puppet show; puppet play. ~政府 puppet government; puppet regime

愧 kuì (形) ashamed; conscience-stricken: 问心无~ have a clear conscience. 于心有~ have a guilty conscience
愧恨 kuìhèn (形) ashamed and remorseful; remorseful: ~交集 overcome with shame and remorse
愧色 kuìsè (名) a look of shame: 面有~ look ashamed. 毫无~ fully deserve the honour

溃 kuì (动) 1 (of a dyke or dam) burst: ~堤 burst the dyke 2 break through (an encirclement): ~围南奔 break through the encirclement and head south 3 be routed: ~不成军 be utterly routed; flee helter-skelter 4 fester; ulcerate
溃败 kuìbài (动) be defeated; be routed
溃决 kuìjué (动) (of a dyke or dam) burst
溃烂(爛) kuìlàn (动) fester; ulcerate
溃疡(瘍) kuìyáng (名) ulcer: 胃~ gastric ulcer

愦 kuì (形) muddleheaded: 昏~ muddleheaded

聩 kuì (形)〈书〉deaf; hard of hearing

匮 kuì (形)〈书〉deficient: ~乏 short (of supplies); deficient

篑 kuì (名)〈书〉basket for holding earth: 功亏一~ fall short of success for want of one final effort

馈 kuì make a present of: ~赠 present (a gift); make a present of sth.

坤 kūn (形) female; feminine: ~表 woman's watch

昆 kūn (名) 1 elder brother 2〈书〉offspring: 后~ descendants; offspring
昆虫(蟲) kūnchóng (名) insect: ~学 entomology; insectology. ~学家 entomologist
昆仲 kūn-zhòng (名) elder and

younger brothers; brothers

捆 kǔn I (动) tie; bind; bundle up: ～行李 tie up one's baggage. ～谷草 bundle up millet stalks. 把他～起来 tie him up II (量) bundle: 一～柴禾 a bundle of firewood

捆绑 kǔnbǎng (动) truss up; bind; tie up

捆扎 kǔnzā (动) tie up; bundle up

困 kùn (形) 1 be stranded; be hard pressed: 为病所～ be afflicted with illness 2 surround; pin down: 把敌人～在山谷里 pin down the enemy in the valley 3 tired: ～乏 tired; fatigued 4 sleepy: 你～了就睡吧. Go to bed if you feel sleepy.

困惫(憊) kùnbei (形) very tired

困顿 kùndùn (形) 1 tired out; exhausted 2 in financial straits

困惑 kùnhuò (形) perplexed; puzzled: ～不解 feel bewildered

困境 kùnjìng (名) difficult position; predicament; straits: 陷于～ fall into dire straits; find oneself in a tight corner. 摆脱～ extricate oneself from a difficult position

困窘 kùnjiǒng (形) in straitened circumstances

困倦 kùnjuàn (形) sleepy

困苦 kùnkǔ (形) poverty-stricken; (live) in privation: 艰难～ difficulties and hardships

困难(難) kùnnɑn (名) 1 difficulty: 克服～ surmount difficulties. ～重重 be beset with difficulties 2 financial difficulties; straitened circumstances: 生活～ live in straitened circumstances

困兽(獸)犹(猶)斗(鬥) kùnshòu yóu dòu cornered animals will still fight; beasts at bay will fight back

廓 kuò I (形) wide; extensive; boundless II (名) exterior features: 轮～ outline

廓清 kuòqīng (动) sweep away; clean up; liquidate

扩(擴) kuò (动) expand; enlarge; extend

扩充 kuòchōng (动) expand; strengthen; augment: ～军备 arms (or armaments) expension. ～设备 augment the equipment

扩大 kuòdà (动) enlarge; expand; extend: ～范围 extend the limits. ～眼界 widen one's outlook; broaden one's horizons. ～耕地面积 expand the area under cultivation. ～会议 enlarged meeting (or session, conference)

扩散 kuòsàn (动) spread; diffuse: 核～ nuclear proliferation

扩音器 kuòyīnqì (名) 1 megaphone 2 audio amplifier

扩展 kuòzhǎn (动) expand; spread; extend; develop

扩张 kuòzhāng (动) expand; enlarge; extend; spread: 对外～ expansionism; foreign aggrandizement. 领土～ territorial expansion

阔 kuò (形) 1 wide; broad; vast 2 wealthy; rich: 摆～ flaunt one's wealth

阔别 kuòbié (形) long separated; long parted: ～多年的朋友 long-separated friends

阔步 kuòbù (动)take big strides: ～前进 advance with giant strides

阔绰 kuòchuò (形) living in luxury and extravagance: 生活～ lead an extravagant life; spend lavishly

括 kuò (动) 1 draw together (muscles, etc.) ; contract 2 include

括号 kuòhào (名) brackets ([], (), 〈〉)

Ll

垃 lā

垃圾 lājī (名) rubbish; garbage; refuse; disposal: ～箱 dustbin; garbage can. ～堆 rubbish heap

拉 lā (动) 1 pull; draw; tug; drag: 使劲～,我来推. Pull hard while I push. ～上窗帘 draw the curtains 2 transport by vehicle; haul: ～货 haul goods 3 move (troops to a place): 把二连～到河那边去 move Company Two to the other side of the river 4 play (certain musical instruments): ～小提琴(手风琴) play the violin (accordion) 5 drag out; draw out; space out: ～长声音说话 drawl. ～开距离 leave distances in between 6 give (or lend) a hand; help: 他有困难,要～他一把. We must help him out. 7 drag in; implicate:自己做的事,为什么要～

上别人? Why drag in others when it was all your own doing? **8** try to establish; claim: ～关系 try to establish some sort of relationship (with sb. usually for sordid purposes) **9** ‹口› empty the bowels: ～肚子 suffer from diarrhoea; have loose bowels

see also lá

拉扯 lā·che (动) ‹口› **1** drag; pull **2** take great pains to bring up (a child) **3** implicate; drag in **4** chat

拉后(後)腿 lā hòutuǐ hold sb. back; be a drag on sb.

拉锯 lājù (动) work a two-handed saw: ～战 seesaw battle

拉拉队(隊) lālā duì (名) cheering squad

拉拢(攏) lālong (动) draw sb. over to one's side (in factional strife)

拉屎 lāshǐ (动) ‹口› empty the bowels; shit

拉锁儿 lāsuǒr (名) zip fastener; zipper

拉杂(雜) lāzá (形) rambling; jumbled; ill-organized: 这篇文章写得太～. This article is badly organized.

邋

lā (形) ‹口› slovenly; sloppy: ～遢 slovenly; sloppy; tatty

拉

lá (动) **1** slash; slit; cut; make a gash in: ～玻璃 cut the glass. 手上～了一个口子 cut one's hand; get a cut in the hand **2** chat: ～家常 have a chat

see also lā

喇

lǎ

喇叭 lǎba **1** brass-wind instruments in general or any of these instruments **2** loudspeaker: ～裤 flared trousers; bell-bottoms. ～筒 megaphone

喇嘛 lǎma (名) lama: ～教 Lamaism. ～庙 lamasery

落

là (动) **1** leave out; be missing: 这里～了两个字. Two words are missing here. **2** leave behind; forget to bring: 对不起, 我把信用卡～在家里了. Sorry, I left my credit card at home. **3** lag (or fall, drop) behind: ～下很远 fall (or be left) far behind

see also luò

蜡(蠟)

là (名) **1** wax **2** candle: 点上一支～. Light a candle. **3** polish: 地板～ floor wax; floor polish

蜡版 làbǎn (名) mimeograph stencil (already cut)

蜡笔(筆) làbǐ (名) wax crayon

蜡纸 làzhǐ (名) **1** wax paper **2** stencil paper; stencil: 刻～ cut a stencil

蜡烛(燭) làzhú (名) (wax) candle

腊(臘)

là

腊肠(腸) làcháng (名) sausage

腊月 làyuè (名) the twelfth month of the lunar year; the twelfth moon

辣

là (形) **1** peppery; hot **2** (of smell or taste) burn; bite; sting: ～得舌头发麻. The hot taste burns the tongue. **3** ‹口› vicious; ruthless: 心毒手～ vicious and ruthless; wicked and cruel

辣椒 làjiāo (名) hot pepper; chilli: ～粉 chilli powder. ～油 chilli oil

辣手 làshǒu I (名) ruthless method; II (形) **1** vicious; ruthless **2** thorny; knotty: 这件事真～. That's really a thorny problem.

啦

la (助) [the representation of the combined sounds 'le' and 'a', denoting exclamation, interrogation, etc.]: 他真来～! He has turned up, indeed! 这回我可亲眼看见～! This time I've seen all this with my own eyes.

来(來)

lái **1** come; arrive: 跟我～! Come along with me. 他们还没有～. They haven't come yet. ～函 your letter **2** crop up; take place: 问题～了. Problems have cropped up. **3** [replacing a verb]: 你歇歇, 让我～吧. You take a rest. Let me do it. ～一盘棋. Let's have a game of chess. 再～一个! Encore! **4** [used with "得"或"不" to indicate possibility]: 他们俩很合得～. The two of them are getting along very well. **5** [used before a verb to indicate that one is about to do sth.]: 大家～想办法. Let's put our heads together. **6** [used after a verb or verbal phrase to indicate what one has come for]: 我们贺喜～了. We have come to offer our congratulations. **7** [used before a verb to indicate the purpose of such an action]: 我们将开个会～交流经验. We'll hold a meeting to exchange experiences. **8** future; coming; next: ～年 the coming year; next year **9** ever since: 十多天～ for the last ten days and more. 两千年～ over the past 2,000 years **10** [used after numerals 十,百,千, etc, to indicate approximate number] about; over: 二十～个 around twenty. 五十～岁 over fifty (years old) **11** [used after numerals 一,二,三, to enumerate reasons]: 一～…,二～… in the first place…, in the second place …

来(來) lái **1** [used after a verb as a complement to indicate moving forward in the direction of the speaker]: 过～! Come over here! **2** [used after a verb to indicate the result]: 一觉醒～ when one wakes up after a sound sleep. 各个方面都传～了振奋人心的消息. Encouraging news poured in from all quarters. 说～话长. It's a long story.

来宾(賓) láibīn (名) guest; visitor: 表演节目,招待～ give performances to entertain the guests

来不及 láibují there's not enough time (to do sth.); it's too late (to do sth.): ～细谈了. There's no time for me to go into detail.

来到 láidào (动) arrive; come: 雨季～了. The rainy season has set in. 春天终于～了. Spring is here at long last.

来得及 láidejí there's still time; be able to do sth. in time; be able to make it: 电影三点开始, 你现在走还～. The film starts at three. You can still make it if you go now.

来回 láihuí **1** make a round trip; make a return journey; go to a place and come back: ～有多远? How far is it there and back? **2** back and forth; to and fro: 在走廊里～走动 pace up and down the corridor. ～票 return ticket; round-trip ticket

来历(歷) láilì (名) origin; source; antecedents; background; past history: 查明～ trace sth. to its source; ascertain a person's antecedents. ～不明的人 a person of dubious background or of questionable antecedents. 这张油画可有一段不平凡的～. This oil painting has an unusual history. ～不明的飞机 unidentified aircraft

来临(臨) láilín (动) arrive; come; approach

来龙(龍)去脉(脈) láilóng-qùmài origin and development; the entire process: 事情的～ the whole story from beginning to end

来日方长(長) láirì fāng cháng there will be ample time

来势(勢) láishì (名) the momentum which sth. of tremendous power or significance gains as it approachs; oncoming force

来头(頭) láitou (名) **1** connections; backing: ～不小 have plenty of backing from influential quarters **2** the motive behind (sb.'s words, etc.).

来往 láiwǎng I (名) dealings; contact: 我跟他从来没有任何～. I've never had any contact with him. 我们俩不大～. The two of us have seen very little of each other. II (动) come and go

来由 láiyóu (名) reason; cause

来源 láiyuán (名,动) **1** source; origin: 经济～ source of income **2** originate; stem from: 知识～于实践. Knowledge stems from practice.

来之不易 lái zhī bù yì it has not come easily; hard-earned; hard-won

赖 lài (动) **1** rely on; depend on: 完成任务,有～于大家的努力. The success of the work depends on everyone's efforts. **2** hang on in a place; drag out one's stay in a place: ～着不走 overstay one's visit **3** deny one's error or responsibility; go back on one's word: ～是～不掉的. It's no use trying to get away with it **4** blame sb. wrongly; put the blame on sb. else: 自己做错了, 不能～别人. You should not blame others for what is your own fault. **5** 〈口〉 blame: 这事全～我. I'm entirely to blame for that.

赖皮 làipí (形)〈口〉 rascally; shameless; unreasonable: 耍～ act shamelessly; have no sense of shame

赖帐(帳) làizhàng (动) **1** repudiate a debt **2** go back on one's word

癞 lài (名) **1** leprosy **2** favus of the scalp

癞皮狗 làipígǒu (名) **1** mangy dog **2** loathsome creature

癞子 làizi (名) a person affected with favus on the head

籁 lài （名）**1** an ancient musical pipe **2** sound; noise: 万～俱寂. It was all quiet and still.

阑 lán I（形）late: 夜～人静 in the stillness of the night II（名）railing; balustrade

阑干 lángān （形）crisscross: 星斗～. The sky is dotted with stars.

阑尾 lánwěi （名）appendix: ～炎 appendicitis

澜 lán （名）billows: 波～ huge waves. 推波助～ add fuel to the fire; aggravate an already complicated situation.

谰 lán （动）calumniate; slander

谰言 lányán （名）calumny; slander: 无耻～ a shameless slander

兰(蘭) lán （名）orchid

兰花 lánhuā （名）orchid

栏(欄) lán （名）**1** fence; railing; balustrade; hurdle: 跨～赛跑 hurdle race; the hurdles **2** pen; shen: 牛～ cowshed. 羊～ sheep-pen **3** column: 布告～ bulletin board; notice board. 广告～ classified ads

栏(檻)杆 lángān （名）railing; banisters; balustrade

拦(攔) lán （动）bar; block; hold back: ～住去路 block the way. 他刚要提问,就被老师～住了. He was trying to ask when the teacher cut him short.

拦河坝(壩) lánhé bà （名）a dam across a river; dam

拦截 lánjié （动）intercept: ～增援的敌人 intercept enemy reinforcements

拦路 lánlù （动）block the way: ～抢劫 waylay; hold up; mug

拦路虎 lánlùhǔ （名）obstacle; stumbling block

拦腰 lányāo （副）by the waist; round the middle: 大坝把河水～截断. The dam cut the river in the middle.

拦阻 lánzǔ （动）block; hold back; obstruct

褴(襤) lán

褴褛(褸) lánlǚ （形）ragged; shabby: 衣衫～ shabbily dressed; dressed in rags

蓝(藍) lán I（形）blue II（名）indigo plant

蓝本 lánběn （名）**1** the source material on which later work is based; chief source **2** original version (of a literary work)

蓝图(圖) lántú （名）blueprint

篮(籃) lán （名）(～子) basket

篮球 lánqiú （名）basketball: ～场 basketball court. ～队 basketball team

岚(嵐) lán （名）haze; vapour; mist

懒 lǎn （形）**1** lazy; indolent; slothful **2** sluggish; drowsy: 身上发～ feel drowsy

懒得 lǎnde （动）not feel like (doing sth.); not be in the mood to; be disinclined to: 我～出去. I have no inclination to go out. *or* I don't feel like going out.

懒惰 lǎnduò （形）lazy

懒汉(漢) lǎnhàn （名）sluggard; idler; lazybones

懒散 lǎnsǎn （形）sluggish; negligent; slack: 学习～ careless about one's studies.

懒洋洋 lǎnyángyáng （形）sluggish; listless

览(覽) lǎn （动）**1** look at; see; view: 游～ go sightseeing; tour **2** read: 博～ read extensively. 浏～ glance over; skim through (or over); browse through

揽(攬) lǎn （动）**1** pull sb. into one's arms; take into one's arms: 母亲把孩子～在怀里. The mother carried the child in her arms. **2** fasten with a rope, etc.: 用绳子～上 put a rope around sth. **3** take on; take upon oneself; canvass: 他把责任都～到自己身上. He took all the responsibility on himself. **4** grasp; monopolize: 包～ monopolize; undertake the whole thing. ～权 arrogate power to oneself

缆(纜) lǎn （名）**1** hawser; mooring rope; cable: 解～ cast off; set sail **2** thick rope; cable: 电～ power cable; cable

缆车(車) lǎnchē （名）cable car: ～铁道 cable railway

滥(濫) làn **1**（动）overflow; flood **2**（形）excessive; indiscriminate: ～施轰炸 indiscriminate bombing; wanton bombing

滥调 làndiào （名）hackneyed tune; worn-out theme: 陈词～ overused expressions; tired old bromides; clichés

滥用 lànyòng （动）abuse; misuse;

use indiscriminately: ～职权 abuse one's power

滥竽充数(數) lànyú chōng shù be a layman who passes himself off as an expert; be an incompetent person or a person unequal to his task

烂(爛) làn **1** sodden; mashed; pappy: 牛肉烧得太～了. The beef is overdone. **2** rot; fester: 伤口～了 The wound is festering. **3** worn-out: 衣服穿～了. The clothes are worn-out. **4** messy: 一本～帐 messy accounts. ～摊子 an awful mess

烂漫 lànmàn (形) **1** bright-coloured; brilliant: 山花～ bright mountain flowers in full bloom **2** unaffected: 天真～ naive; innocent

烂泥 lànní (名) mud; slush: ～塘 a muddy pond

烂熟 lànshú (形) **1** thoroughly cooked **2** know sth. thoroughly: 台词背得～ learn one's lines thoroughly

烂醉 lànzuì (形) dead drunk: ～如泥 be dead drunk; be as drunk as a lord

郎 láng (名) **1** an ancient official title **2** [referring to certain kinds of people]: 令～ your son. 新～ bridegroom. 货～ street vendor **3** [pet address by woman to her husband or lover] my darling

郎舅 láng-jiù (名) a man and his wife's brother: 他们俩是～. They are brothers-in-law.

郎中 lángzhōng (名) a physician trained in herbal medicine

廊 láng (名) porch; corridor; veranda: 回～ winding corridor. 长～ The Long Corridor (in the Summer Palace, Beijing). 画～ picture gallery

廊檐 lángyán (名) the eaves of a veranda

榔 láng: ～头 hammer

锒 láng

锒铛(鐺) lángdāng I (名) iron chains: ～入狱 be chained and thrown into prison II (动) clank; clang

狼 láng (名) wolf

狼狈 lángbèi (副) in a difficult position; in a tight corner: ～不堪 in an extremely awkward position. ～逃窜 flee in panic

狼狈为(爲)奸 lángbèi wéi jiān act in collusion (or cahoots) with each other; work hand in glove with; band together

狼藉 lángjí (副)〈书〉in disorder; scattered about in a mess: 杯盘～ wine cups and dishes lying about in a mess. 声名～ notorious; in disrepute; discredited

狼吞虎咽(嚥) lángtūn-hǔyàn (动) gobble up; wolf down; devour ravenously

狼心狗肺 lángxīn-gǒufèi (形) **1** cruel and unscrupulous; brutal and cold-blooded **2** ungrateful

狼烟四起 lángyān sìqǐ smoke signals rising on all sides

狼子野心 lángzǐ yěxīn (名) wolfish nature; vicious ambition

朗 lǎng (形) **1** light; bright: 天～气清 The sky is clear and bright. **2** loud and clear

朗读(讀) lǎngdú (动) read aloud; read loudly and clearly

朗朗 lǎnglǎng I (象) the sound of reading aloud II (形) bright; light

朗诵 lǎngsòng (动) read aloud with expression; recite; declaim

浪 làng I (名) wave; billow; breaker: 海～ waves of the sea. 声～ sound wave II (形) unrestrained; dissolute: 放～ dissolute; dissipated

浪潮 làngcháo (名) tide; wave: 罢工～ a wave of strikes

浪荡(蕩) làngdàng I (动) loiter about; loaf about II (形) dissolute; dissipated

浪费 làngfèi (动) waste; squander: ～资源 squander resources

浪花 lànghuā (名) spray; spindrift

浪漫 làngmàn (形) **1** rakish; sluttish **2** romantic

浪头(頭) làngtou 〈口〉 **1** wave **2** trend: 赶～ follow the trend (or the fashion)

浪子 làngzǐ (名) prodigal; loafer; wastrel: ～回头 the prodigal has returned

捞(撈) lāo **1** drag for; dredge up; fish for; scoop up from the water: ～水草 dredge up water plants. ～鱼 net fish; catch fish **2** get by improper means; gain: 趁机～一把 seek personal gains out of a messy situation; fish in troubled waters

捞取 lāoqǔ (动) fish for; gain: ～政治资本 fish for political capital; seek political advantage

牢 láo I (名) **1** <书> pen; fold: 豕～ pigpen **2** sacrifice: 太～ sacrificial ox **3** prison; jail: 坐～ be in prison; serve time II (形) firm; fast; durable: ～不可破 unbreakable; indestructible

牢固 láogù (形) firm; secure: ～的根基 solid foundations

牢记 láojì (动) keep firmly in mind; remember well: 我将永远～你的教诲. I will always bear your instructions in mind.

牢靠 láokào (形) **1** firm; strong; sturdy: 这堵墙不太～. This wall is not strong enough. **2** dependable; reliable: 办事～ dependable (or reliable) in handling affairs

牢笼(籠) láolóng (名) **1** cage; bonds **2** trap; snare: 陷入～ fall into a trap; be entrapped

牢骚 láosāo (名) discontent; grievance; complaint: 大发～ give vent to peevish complaints

劳(勞) láo I (名) **1** work; labour: ～绩 fruits of hard work. 多～多得 more pay for more work **2** fatigue; toil: 积～成疾 break down or fall ill from overwork **3** meritorious deed; service: 汗马之～ distinction won in battle; war exploits II (动) **1** put sb. to the trouble of: ～你帮个忙. Could you give me a hand? **2** express one's appreciation (to the performer of a task); reward: ～军 bring greetings and gifts to army units

劳保 láobǎo <简> (劳动保险) labour insurance

劳动(動) láodòng (名) **1** work; labour: 不～者不得食. He who does not work, neither shall he eat. **2** physical labour; manual labour: ～保护 labour protection. ～竞赛 labour emulation. ～纪律 labour discipline. ～模范 model worker. ～强度 labour intensity. ～生产率 labour productivity

劳动(動)力 láodònglì (名) **1** work force; labour: ～不足 short of manpower; shorthanded **2** capacity for physical labour: 丧失～ lose one's ability to work; be disabled **3** able-bodied person

劳顿 láodùn (形) <书> fatigued; wearied: 旅途～ fatigued by a long journey; travel-worn

劳驾 láojià <套> [polite formula used when one requests people to make way, etc.] excuse me; may I trouble you: ～替我带个信儿. Would you mind taking a message for me?

劳苦 láokǔ (名) toil; hard work: 不辞～ spare no pains. ～大众 toiling masses; labouring people

劳累 láolèi (形) tired; rundown; overworked

劳力 láolì (名) labour; labour force: 合理安排～ rational allocation of labour

劳民伤(傷)财 láomín-shāngcái exhaust the people and drain the treasury

劳逸结合 láo yì jiéhé (名) strike a proper balance between work and rest

痨(癆) láo (名) consumptive disease; tuberculosis; consumption: 肺～ pulmonary tuberculosis. ～病 tuberculosis; TB

老 lǎo I (形) **1** old; aged: ～农 old farmer. 活到～,学到～. You will never cease to learn as long as you live. **2** of long standing; old: ～朋友 an old friend. ～战士 a veteran fighter. ～习惯 old habits **3** outdated: ～式 old-fashioned; outmoded; outdated **4** tough; overgrown: 肉太～ The meat is too tough. 菠菜～了. The spinach is overgrown. II (副) **1** for a long time: ～没见你啊. I haven't seen you for ages. **2** always (doing sth.): ～惦记着这件事. He couldn't get his mind off the matter. **3** very: ～早 very early. ～远 far away **4** [prefix placed before surnames, ordinal numbers among brothers and sisters, certain animals and plants]: ～王 Lao Wang. ～二 the second child or brother. ～玉米 maize. ～虎 tiger III (名) old people: 敬～ respect for age

老百姓 lǎobǎixìng (名) <口> common people; ordinary people; civilians

老伴儿 lǎobànr (名) <口> (of an old married couple) husband or wife: 我的～ my old man or woman

老本 lǎoběn (名) principal; capital: 把～输光 lose one's last stakes

老成 lǎochéng (形) experienced; steady: 少年～ young but steady; old head on young shoulders. ～

持重 experienced and prudent
老大 lǎodà I (名) 1 〈书〉 old: 少壮不努力,～徒伤悲. Laziness in youth spells regret in old age. 2 eldest child (in a family) 3 master of a sailing vessel II (副) greatly; very: 心中～不高兴 feel very displeased
老大娘 lǎodàniáng (名) [often used to address a stranger senior in age] aunty; granny
老大爷(爺) lǎodàye (名) [often used to address a stranger senior in age] uncle; grandpa
老弟 lǎodì (名) [a familiar form of address to a man much younger than oneself] young man; young fellow; my boy
老调 lǎodiào (名) hackneyed theme; platitude: ～重弹 play the same old tune
老汉(漢) lǎohàn (名) old man
老好人 lǎohǎorén (名) a person goodnatured but indifferent to matters of principle; one who avoids giving offence to anybody
老狐狸 lǎohúli (名) 1 old fox 2 crafty scoundrel
老虎 lǎohǔ (名) tiger
老话 lǎohuà (名) 1 old saying; saying; adage 2 remarks about the old days
老化 lǎohuà (名) ageing
老奸巨猾 lǎojiān-jùhuá a crafty old scoundrel; a wily old fox
老练(練) lǎoliàn seasoned; experienced: 她办事很～. She is experienced and does a good job of work.
老路 lǎolù (名) old road; beaten track
老马(馬)识(識)途 lǎomǎ shí tú an old hand is always a good guide
老迈(邁) lǎomài (形) aged; senile
老年 lǎonián(名)old age: ～人 old people; the aged. ～医学 gerontology
老婆 lǎopo (名) 〈口〉 wife
老气(氣)横秋 lǎoqì héngqiū 1 arrogant on account of one's seniority 2 apathetic
老前辈 lǎoqiánbèi (名) senior person in one's profession
老人家 lǎorenjia (名) 1 a respectful form of address for an old person: 你～今年多大年纪了?How old are you, granddad (grandma)? 2 parent: 你们～今年快七十岁了吧? Your parents are getting on for seventy, aren't they?
老生常谈 lǎoshēng chángtán (名) shopworn phrases; bromides
老师(師) lǎoshī (名) teacher
老师(師)傅 lǎoshīfù (名) master craftsman; experienced worker
老实(實) lǎoshi (形) 1 honest; frank: 忠诚～ loyal and honest. ～说,我很不赞成这个意见. Honestly, I don't like the idea at all. 2 well-behaved; good: 这孩子可～了. The child is really well-behaved. 3 simpleminded; naive; easily taken in
老手 lǎoshǒu (名) old hand; veteran: 开车的～ an old hand in driving; a good driver
老态(態)龙(龍)钟(鐘) lǎotài lóngzhōng (形) senile; decrepit
老顽固 lǎowángu (名) old stick-in-the-mud; diehard; old fogey
老乡(鄉) lǎoxiāng (名) fellow-townsman; fellow-villager
老小 lǎo-xiǎo (名) old people and children; one's family dependents: 一家～ the whole family
老羞成怒 lǎo xiū chéng nù be shamed into anger
老朽 lǎoxiǔ (形) decrepit and behind the times
老爷(爺) lǎoye (名) 1 master; bureaucrat; overlord: 做官当～ act as 'overlord'. ～作风 bureaucratic style of work 2 (maternal) grandfather; grandpa
老于(於)世故 lǎoyú shìgù experienced in the ways of society; worldly-wise
老帐(帳) lǎozhàng (名) old debts; long-standing debts: 翻～ bring up old scores

佬 lǎo (名) man; guy; fellow: 阔～ a rich guy

姥 lǎo: 姥～ (maternal) grandmother; grandma

涝(澇) lào(名) waterlogging: 防～prevent waterlogging. 排～ drain waterlogged fields

烙 lào (动) 1 iron: ～衣服 iron clothes 2 bake in a pan: ～两张饼 bake a couple of cakes
烙饼 làobǐng (名) a kind of pancake
烙印 làoyìn (名) brand: 带有不少封建思想的～ bear the stamp of feudal ideology

酪 lào (名) 1 junket 2 thick fruit juice; fruit jelly: 红果～ haw jelly 3 sweet paste made from crushed nuts; sweet nut paste: 核桃～ walnut cream

乐(樂) lè I (形) happy; cheerful; joyful: ～不可支 be overjoyed. 助人为～ find pleasure in helping others II (动) 1 be glad to; find pleasure in; enjoy: ～此不疲 always enjoy it 2 laugh; be amused: 你～什么呀? What are you laughing at? *or* What's the joke? III (名) joy see also yuè

乐得 lèdé readily take the opportunity to; be only too glad to: 既然如此,我们～先听听别人的意见. In that case, we'll be only too glad to hear what they have to say first.

乐观(觀) lèguān (形) optimistic; hopeful; sanguine: ～的看法 an optimistic view. 对前途很～ be optimistic about the future. ～主义 optimism. ～主义者 optimist

乐趣 lèqù (名) delight; pleasure; joy: 生活的～ joys of life; spices of life

乐天 lètiān (形) carefree; happy-go-lucky

乐意 lèyì (形) 1 be willing to; be ready to: ～帮忙 be willing and ready to help 2 pleased; happy: 他看来有点不～. He looked somewhat displeased.

乐园(園) lèyuán (名) paradise: 人间～ paradise on earth. 儿童～ children's playground

乐滋滋 lèzīzī (形) (口) contented; pleased: 他听了别人夸奖他心里总是～的. He is always highly pleased to hear people praise him.

勒 lè (动) 1 stop: ～马 rein in 2 force; coerce: ～交 force sb. to hand sth. over 3 (书) carve; engrave: ～碑 carve on a stone tablet
see also lēi

勒逼 lèbī (动) force; coerce

勒令 lèlìng (动) compel (by legal authority); order

勒索 lèsuǒ (动) extort; blackmail: ～钱财 extort money from sb.

了 le (助) 1 [used after a verb or adjective to indicate completion of work or change]: 我们提前完成～任务. We have fulfilled the task ahead of schedule. 水位已降低～两米. The water level has fallen by two metres. 2 [modal particle placed at the end of a sentence to indicate a change]: 他们现在是外交部的干部～. They are officials at the Foreign Ministry now. 3 [used at the end of a sentence to show a past event]: 上星期天,他带孩子上动物园～. Last Sunday, he took his children to the zoo. 4 [used at the end of an imperative sentence to indicate advice]: 别说话～! Stop talking! 走～, 走～! Hurry up and let's go!
see also liǎo; liào

勒 lēi (动) tie or strap sth. tight
see also lè

擂 léi (动) hit; beat: ～了一拳 give sb. a punch
see also lèi

羸 léi (形) (书) thin; skinny

羸弱 léiruò (形) (书) thin and weak; frail

雷 léi (名) 1 thunder 2 mine: 布～ lay mines. 扫～ sweep mines

雷达(達) léidá (名) radar

雷电(電) léidiàn (名) thunder and lightning

雷动(動) léidòng (形) thunderous: 掌声～ thunderous applause

雷管 léiguǎn (名) detonator; detonating cap; blasting cap; primer

雷厉(厲)风(風)行 léilì-fēngxíng act vigorously and speedily

雷声(聲) léishēng (名) thunderclap; thunder: ～隆隆 the rumble (or roll) of thunder. ～大,雨点小 loud thunder but small raindrops; much has been said but little is accomplished.

雷霆 léitíng 1 thunderclap; thunderbolt 2 tremendous power; wrath: 大发～ fly into a rage. ～万钧 as powerful as a thunderbolt

雷同 léitóng (形) 1 echoing other people's ideas 2 (of writing a speech) duplicate; identical

雷雨 léiyǔ (名) thunderstorm

累(纍) léi
see also lěi, lèi

累累 léiléi (形) clusters of; heaps of: 果实～ heavily laden with fruit

累赘 léizhui I (形) 1 burdensome; cumbersome 2 wordy; verbose II (名) encumbrance; burden; nuisance

蕾 lěi (名) flower bud; bud

蕾铃 lěilíng (名) cotton buds and bolls

磊 lěi

磊落 lěiluò (形) open and upright: 光明～ open and aboveboard

累(纍) lěi I (动) 1 pile up; accumulate: 日积月～ accumulate gradually 2 involve: 连～ involve; implicate; get sb. into trouble II (形) continuous; repeated ～戒不改 refuse to mend one's ways despite repeated warnings. 长篇～牍 voluminous
see also léi; lèi

累积(積) lěijī (动、名) accumulate; accumulation

累及 lěijí (动) implicate; involve: ～无辜 involve innocent people

累计 lěijì I (动) add up II (名) accumulative total; grand total

累进(進) lěi jìn (名) progression: ～税 progressive tax; progressive taxation

累累 lěilěi (形) 1 again and again; many times 2 innumerable; countless: 罪行～ have committed numerous crimes

累卵 lěiluǎn (名) liable to collapse any moment; precarious: 危如～ in an extremely precarious situation

垒(壘) lěi 1 build by piling up bricks, stones, earth, etc.: ～一道墙 build a wall 2 rampart

泪(淚) lèi (名) tear; teardrop

泪痕 lèihén (名) tear stains

泪水 lèishuǐ (名) tear; teardrop

泪珠 lèizhū (名) teardrop

类(類) lèi I (名) kind; type; class; category: 同～ be of a kind; belong to the same category. 物以～聚. Birds of a feather flock together. II (动) resemble; be similar to: 画虎不成反～犬 try to draw a tiger and end up with the likeness of a dog

类比 lèibǐ (名) analogy: 对两件事进行～ draw an analogy between the two things

类别 lèibié (名) classification; category: 文件的～ classification of documents

类人猿 lèirényuán (名) anthropoid (ape)

类似 lèisì (形) similar; analogous: 经历相～ of similar background

类推 lèituī (动) reason by analogy: 其余～. The rest can be deduced similarly.

类型 lèixíng (名) type

擂 lèi (动) beat (a drum)
see also léi

擂台(臺) lèitái (名) ring (for martial contests); arena: 摆～ give an open challenge; throw down the gauntlet. 打～ take up the challenge; pick up the gauntlet

累 lèi I (形) tired; fatigued; weary: ～极了 tired out; worn out; exhausted II (动) 1 tire; strain; wear out 2 work hard; toil: 你～了一天,该休息了. You should have a break, as you have been working all day.
see also léi; lěi

肋 lèi (名) 1 rib: ～骨 rib 2 costal region: 两～ both sides of the chest

肋膜 lèimó (名) pleura: ～炎 pleurisy

棱 léng (名) 1 arris; edge: 桌子～儿 edges of a table 2 corrugation; ridge: 瓦～ ridges of a tiled roof

棱角 léngjiǎo (名) 1 edges 2 sharp-wittedness

冷 lěng (形) 1 cold: ～天 the cold season; cold days. 你～不～? Are you cold? 2 cold in manner 3 unfrequented; deserted; out-of-the-way: ～清 desolate; lonely 4 strange; rare: ～僻的词 rare or unfamiliar word

冷冰冰 lěngbīngbīng (形) ice-cold; icy; frosty: ～的态度 frosty manner

冷不防 lěngbufáng (副) unexpectedly; suddenly

冷藏 lěngcáng (名) refrigeration; cold storage: ～库 cold storage; freezer. ～箱 refrigerator; fridge

冷场(場) lěngchǎng (名) 1 awkward situation on the stage resulting from an actor entering late or forgetting his lines 2 awkward silence at a meeting

冷嘲热(熱)讽(諷) lěngcháo-rèfěng characterized by biting irony and sarcasm; jeering and sneering

冷淡 lěngdàn I (形) 1 cheerless; desolate 2 cold; indifferent: 反映～ a cold response II

(动) treat coldly; cold-shoulder; slight

冷冻(凍) lěngdòng (名) freezing: ～机 freezer

冷汗 lěnghàn (名) cold sweat: 出～ be in a cold sweat; break out in a cold sweat

冷荤 lěnghūn (名) cold meat; cold buffet

冷箭 lěngjiàn (名) sniper's shot; a stab in the back: 放～make a sneak attack

冷静 lěngjìng (形) sober; calm: 头脑～ sober-minded; level-headed; cool-headed. 保持～ keep calm and composed

冷酷 lěngkù (形) unfeeling; hard-hearted: ～无情 ruthless; merciless; cold-blooded

冷落 lěngluò I (形) unfrequented; desolate II (动) treat coldly; cold-shoulder; leave out in the cold: ～某人 leave sb. out in the cold

冷门(門) lěngmén (名) 1 a profession, trade or branch of learning that receives little attention: 过去这门学科是个～. This discipline used to attract very little notice in the past. 2 an unexpected winner; dark horse: 那次比赛出了个～. The contest produced an unexpected winner.

冷漠 lěngmò (形) cold and detached; unconcerned; indifferent

冷暖 lěngnuǎn (名) changes in temperature: 注意～ be careful about changes of weather; take care of oneself. 关心群众的～ be concerned with the well-being of the masses

冷盘(盤) lěngpán (名) cold dish; hors d'oeuvres

冷僻 lěngpì (形) 1 deserted; out-of-the-way 2 rare; unfamiliar: ～的字眼 rarely used words

冷清 lěngqīng (形)cold and cheerless; desolate; lonely; deserted

冷却 lěngquè (动) cool off: ～系统 cooling system

冷水 lěngshuǐ (名) 1 cold water: 泼～ pour cold water on; dampen sb.'s enthusiasm. ～浴 cold bath 2 unboiled water

冷笑 lěngxiào (动) sneer; laugh scornfully

冷言冷语 lěngyán-lěngyǔ (名) sarcastic or ironical remarks

冷眼 lěngyǎn (名) 1 cool detachment: ～旁观 look on with a cold eye 2 cold shoulder: ～相待 give the cold shoulder to sb.

冷饮 lěngyǐn (名) cold drinks

冷遇 lěngyù (名) cold reception; cold shoulder: 遭到～ be given the cold shoulder; be left out in the cold

冷战(戰) lěngzhàn (名) cold war

冷战(戰) lěngzhan (动)〈口〉shiver: 打～ shiver with cold

愣 lèng (形) distracted; stupefied; blank: 发～ stare blankly; look distracted. 听到这消息他～住了. He was struck dumb by the news.

离(離) lí I (动) leave; part from; be away from: 她～家已经多年了. She's been away from home for many years. II (副) 1 off; away; from: 学校～火车站不远. The school is not far from the railway station. 2 without; independent of: 人～了空气就无法生存. Men cannot live without air. 发展工业～不了资金. Industry cannot develop without funds.

离别 líbié (动) part (for a longish period); leave; bid farewell: 我～故乡已经两年了. It's two years since I left my hometown.

离婚 líhūn (动) divorce

离间 líjiàn (动) sow discord; drive a wedge between; set one party against another

离境 líjìng (动) leave a country or place: ～签证 exit visa. ～许可证 exit permit

离奇 líqí (形) odd; fantastic; bizarre: ～的故事 a fantastic story. ～的地方 a bizarre place

离任 lírèn (动) leave one's post: ～回国 leave one's post for home

离散 lísàn (形) dispersed; scattered about; separated from one another

离题 lítí (动) digress from the subject; stray from the point: 发言不要～. Please do not digress from the subject.

离休 líxiū (动) retire on full pay

离职(職) lízhí (动) 1 leave one's job temporarily for specific purposes 2 leave office; quit a job: ～金 severance pay

篱(籬) lí (名) hedge; fence: 竹～茅舍 thatched cottage with bamboo fence

篱笆 líba (名) bamboo or twig fence

厘 lí (名) 1 *li*, a unit of length (=1/3 millimetre) 2 *li*, a unit of weight (=0.05 grams) 3 *li*, a unit of area (= 0.666 square metres **4** *li,* one thousandth of a *yuan* **5** *li,* a unit of monthly interest rate (=0.1%): 月利率二～七 a monthly interest of 0.27% **6** *li,* a unit of annual interest rate (= 1%): 年利率三～ an annual interest of 3% **7** a fraction; the least: 分～不差 without the slightest error; just right

厘米 límǐ (名) centimetre

罹 lí (动) suffer from; meet with: ～病 fall ill.

罹难(難) línàn (动)〈书〉 **1** die in a disaster or an accident **2** be murdered

梨 lí (名) pear

犁 lí I(名) plough II(动) work with a plough; plough: 地已～了两遍. The fields have been ploughed twice.

黎 lí (名)〈书〉multitude; host: ～庶 the multitude

黎民 límín (名)〈书〉the common people; the multitude

黎明 límíng (名) dawn; daybreak

蠡 lí (名)〈书〉 **1** calabash shell serving as a dipper; dipper **2** seashell

蠡测 lícè (动)〈书〉make a superficial estimate of

礼(禮) lǐ (名) **1** ceremony; rite: 婚～ wedding ceremony. 丧～funeral **2** courtesy; etiquette; manners: 行～ (give a) salute. 彬彬有～ refined and polite **3** gift; present: 送～ give a present; send a gift

礼拜 lǐbài (名) **1** homage paid to the god(s) that any religious followers believe in; religious service: 做～ go to church; attend a religious service **2**〈口〉week: 下～ next week **3**〈口〉day of the week: 今天～几? What day is it today? **4**〈口〉Sunday: 今儿个～. Today is Sunday. ～堂 church. ～天〈口〉Sunday

礼宾(賓)司 Lǐbīnsī (名) the Protocol Department

礼服 lǐfú (名) ceremonial robe or dress; full dress; formal dress

礼花 lǐhuā (名) fireworks display

礼教 lǐjiào (名) the Confucian or feudal ethical code

礼节(節) lǐjié (名) courtesy; etiquette; protocol; ceremony: ～性拜访 a courtesy call

礼貌 lǐmào (名) courtesy; manners: 有～ courteous; polite. 没～ have no manners

礼炮 lǐpào (名) salvo; (gun) salute

礼品 lǐpǐn (名) gift; present: ～部 gift and souvenir department or counter (of a shop)

礼让(讓) lǐràng (名) give precedence to sb. out of courtesy or thoughtfulness

礼尚往来(來) lǐ shàng wǎng-lái **1** courtesy demands reciprocity **2** treat a man the way he treats you; pay a man back in his own coin

礼堂 lǐtáng (名) assembly hall; auditorium

礼物 lǐwù (名) gift; present

礼仪(儀) lǐyí (名) etiquette; rite; protocol

礼遇 lǐyù (名) courteous reception or treatment. 受到隆重的～ be given red-carpet treatment

李 lǐ (名)(～子) plum

里(裏) lǐ (名) lining; inside: 衣～儿 the lining of a garment. ～间 inner room

里 lǐ (名) **1** neighbourhood: 邻～ people of the neighbourhood **2**〈书〉hometown; native place: 返～ return to one's hometown **3** *li,* a Chinese unit of length (=1/2 kilometre)

里(裏) lǐ (介) **1** in; inside: 屋～ in the room **2** [used after "这"、"那"、"哪" to indicate direction of place]: 这～ here. 那～ there

里边(邊) lǐbian (介) inside; in; within: 这件事～有问题. There is something wrong with the matter.

里程 lǐchéng (名) **1** distance of a journey **2** course of development; course

里程碑 lǐchéngbēi (名) milestone: 历史的～ a milestone in history

里脊 lǐji (名) tenderloin

里弄 lǐlòng (名) lanes and alleys; neighbourhood

里应(應)外合 lǐ yìng wài hé strike from both within and without

里子 lǐzi (名) lining

理 lǐ I (名) **1** texture; grain (in wood, skin, etc.): 纹～ texture; grain **2** reason; logic; truth: 合～ reasonable **3** natural science, esp. physics: ～工科 science and engineering II (动) **1** manage; run: 当家～事 run the household; manage domestic affairs **2** put in order; tidy up: ～发 have a hair cut. ～

一～书籍 put the books in order 3 [often used in negative sentences] pay attention to; acknowledge: 置之不～ dismiss sth. as o no consequence

理睬 lǐcǎi [often used in negative sentences] pay attention to; show interest in: 不予～ turn a deaf ear to; pay no heed to; ignore

理会(會) lǐhuì (动) 1 understand; comprehend 2 [often used in negative sentences] take notice of; pay attention to: 大家说了半天，他也没有～. He didn't seem to pay any attention while people kept talking to him all the time.

理解 lǐjiě I (动) understand; comprehend: 我们能～你们的困难. We understand your difficulty. II (名) understanding; comprehension: ～力 comprehension

理科 lǐkē (名) 1 science faculty 2 natural sciences

理疗(療) lǐliáo (名) physiotherapy

理论(論) lǐlùn (名) theory: ～与实践 theory and practice. 在～上 in theory; theoretically

理屈词穷(窮) lǐqū-cíqióng defeated in argument and so unable to defend oneself any longer;unable to advance any further arguments

理事 lǐshì (名) member of a council; director: 常任～国 permanent member state of a council. ～会 council; board of directors

理顺 lǐshùn (动) straighten out; bring into better balance: ～各方面的关系 straighten out relations between various sectors

理所当(當)然 lǐ suǒ dāngrán (副) as a matter of course; naturally

理想 lǐxiǎng (名) ideal; dream: 她实现了当演员的～. Her dream of becoming an actress finally came true.

理性 lǐxìng (名) reason: 失去～ lose one's reason

理由 lǐyóu (名) reason; ground; argument: ～充足 fully justifiable. 毫无～ not justified. 他的抱怨完全没有～. His complaint is totally groundless.

理直气(氣)壮(壯) lǐzhí-qìzhuàng with perfect assurance: ～地谈话 speak freely with great confidence

理智 lǐzhì (名) reason; intellect: 丧失～ lose one's senses

俚

lǐ (形) vulgar

俚俗 lǐsú (形) coarse; unrefined; uncultured

俚语 lǐyǔ (名) slang

鲤

lǐ (名) carp

立

lì I (动) 1 stand: 起～ stand up. ～正 stand at attention 2 erect; set up: ～碑 erect a monument 3 found; establish; set up: ～国 found a state. ～合同 sign a contract. ～业 establish a business 4 exist; live: 自～ be on one's feet; live on one's own II (形) 1 upright; erect; vertical 2 immediate; instantaneous: ～见功效 produce immediate results

立案 lì'àn (动) 1 register; put on record 2 place a case on file for investigation and prosecution

立场(場) lìchǎng (名) position; stand; standpoint

立法 lìfǎ legislation; law making: ～机关 legislative body; legislature. ～权 legislative power

立方 lìfāng (名) 1 cube: 三的～ the cube of 3; 3^3 2 〈简〉(立方体)cube 3 (量) cubic; stere: 一～土 one cubic metre of earth

立竿见(見)影 lì gān jiàn yǐng get instant results

立功 lìgōng (动) render meritorious service; win honour; make contributions: ～奖状 certificate of merit

立即 lìjí (副) immediately; at once: ～行动 take immediate action. ～答复 give a prompt reply

立刻 lìkè (副) immediately; at once; right away: ～出发 set off at once

立论(論) lìlùn (动、名) 1 set forth one's views; present one's arguments 2 argument; position

立体(體) lìtǐ 1 three-dimensional; stereoscopic: ～感 three-dimensional effect 2 〈数〉 solid: ～几何 solid geometry. ～交叉桥 overpass; flyover. ～声 stereophony; stereo

立宪(憲) lìxiàn (名) constitutionalism: 君主～ constitutional monarchy. ～政体 constitutional government; constitutionalism

立意 lìyì (动、名) 1 be determined; make up one's mind 2 conception; approach: 这部电影～新颖. This film is fresh in its approach.

立志 lìzhì (动) resolve; be determined: ～改革 be determined to carry out reforms

立足 lìzú (动) 1 have a foothold somewhere: 获得～之地 gain a footing 2 base oneself upon: ～于自立更生 be based on self-reliance

立足点(點) lìzúdiǎn (名) 1 foothold; footing 2 standpoint; stand

粒 lì I (名) grain; granule; pellet: 砂～ grains of sand II (量) [used of grain-like things] 一～米 a grain of rice. 三～子弹 three bullets. 每服五～ 5 pills each time

粒子 lìzǐ (物) particle: 带电～ charged particle. 高能～ energetic particle

莅(涖) lì (动)〈书〉arrive; be present: ～会 be present at a meeting

莅临(臨) lìlín 〈书〉 arrive; be present: 敬请～ request the honour of your presence

笠 lì (名) a large bamboo or straw hat with a conical crown and broad brim

戾 lì I (名) crime; sin: 罪～ guilt, crime II (形) perverse; unreasonable: 乖～ cantankerous; perverse

唳 lì (名) cry (of a crane)

丽(麗) lì (形) beautiful: 风和日～ the weather is glorious; a beautiful day with a gentle breeze blowing

俪(儷) lì (名) pair; couple: 伉～ husband and wife; married couple

栗 lì (～子)(名) chestnut

栗(慄) lì (动) tremble; shudder: 不寒而～ tremble with fear

吏 lì (名) official; mendarin: 贪官污～ corrupt officials

厉(厲) lì (形) 1 strict; rigorous: ～禁 strictly prohibit 2 stern; severe: ～声 in a stern voice

厉兵秣马(馬) lìbīng-mòmǎ make ready for battle; maintain combat readiness

厉行 lìxíng (动) strictly enforce; rigorously enforce; make great efforts to carry out: ～节约 practise strict economy

砺(礪) lì (名、动) 1 whetstone 2 whet; sharpen

励(勵) lì (动) encourage: 奖～ reward; award. 勉～ encourage

厉精图(圖)治 lì jīng tú zhì (usu. of a feudal ruler) make vigorous efforts to achieve prosperity

励志 lìzhì pursue a goal with determination

利 lì I (形) 1 sharp: ～刃 a sharp sword or blade. ～爪 sharp claws 2 favourable: 有～的形势 favourable situation II (名) 1 advantage; benefit: 有～有弊. There are both advantages and disadvantages. 2 profit; interest: 连本带～ both principal and interest. ～改税 replace profit delivery with tax payments III (动) do good to; benefit: ～己～人 benefit other people as well as oneself

利弊 lì-bì (名) advantages and disadvantages; gains and losses: 权衡～ weigh the pros and cons

利害 lì-hài (名) advantages and disadvantages; gains and losses: 不计～ regardless of gains or losses. 晓以～ make someone see where the advantages and disadvantages lie

利害 lìhai (形) terrible; formidable: 今年冬天冷得～. It's been terribly cold this winter. 这着棋十分～. That's a very cunning move.

利令智昏 lìlìng zhì hūn be fuddled by the desire for gain; be blinded by lust for gain

利率 lìlǜ (名) rate of interest; interest rate

利落 lìluo (形) 1 agile; nimble; dexterous: 动作～ agile 2 neat; orderly 3 settled; finished: 事情已经办～了. The matter is all settled.

利润 lìrùn (名) profit: ～留成 ratain part of the profits; keep a portion of the profits

利息 lìxī (名) interest

利益 lìyì (名) interest; benefit; profit

利用 lìyòng (动) 1 use; utilize; make use of: ～工业废料 make use of industrial wastes. 2 take advantage of; exploit: ～职权 abuse one's power. ～率 utilization ratio. ～系数 utilization coefficient

利诱 lìyòu (动) lure by promise of gain

利欲熏心 lìyù xūn xīn be obsessed with the desire of gain

痢 lì (名) dysentery

痢疾 lìji (名) dysentery: 细菌性～ bacillary dysentery

例 lì I (名) 1 example; instance: 举～ give an example; cite an instance. 举～说明 illustrate 2 precedent: 援～ quote (or follow) a precedent. 破～ make an exception 3 case; instance 4 rule; regulation: 旧～ an old rule. 不在此～. That is an exception. II (形) regular; routine

例会(會) lìhuì (名) regular meeting

例假 lìjià (名) 1 official holiday; legal holiday 2 menstrual period; period

例句 lìjù (名) illustrative sentence; model sentence; example

例如 lìrú (副) for instance; for example (e.g.); such as

例外 lìwài (名) exception: 毫无～ without exception

例行公事 lìxíng gōngshì (名) 1 routine; routine business 2 mere formality

例证(證) lìzhèng (名) illustration; example

例子 lìzi (名) example; case; instance

栎(櫟) lì (名) oak

砾(礫) lì (名) gravel; shingle: ～石 gravel

隶(隸) lì I (动) be subordinate to; be under II (名) a person in servitude: 奴～ slave

隶属(屬) lìshǔ (动) be subordinate to; be under the jurisdiction or command of; be affiliated to

力 lì I (名) 1 power; strength; ability: 人～ manpower. 物～ material resources. 兵～ military strength. 能～ ability; capability. ～所能及 in one's power 2 force: 磁～ magnetic force. 离心～ centrifugal force 3 physical strength: ～不能支 unable to stand the strain any longer II (动) do all one can; make every effort: ～戒 strictly avoid; do everything possible to avoid. ～求 do one's best to. ～图 try hard to; strive to

力不从(從)心 lì bù cóng xīn a case of ability falling short of one's wishes; unable to do as much as one would like to

力量 lìliang (名) 1 physical strength 2 power; force; strength: 国防～ defence capability. 知识就是～. Knowledge is power.

力气(氣) lìqi (名) physical strength; effort: 他很有～. He is a man of great strength.

力学(學) lìxué (名) mechanics: 航空～ aeromechanics. 波动～ wave mechanics

历(歷) lì I (动) go through; undergo; experience: ～尽艰辛 have gone through all kinds of hardships II (形) all previous (occasions, sessions, etc.) III (副) covering all; one by one: ～试诸方，均无成效 have tried all recipes, but to no avail IV (名) calendar: 阴(阳)～ lunar (solar) calendar

历程 lìchéng (名) course: 回忆走过的～ recall the course one has traversed

历次 lìcì (形) all previous (occasions, etc.)

历代 lìdài (名) past dynasties

历法 lìfǎ (名) calendar

历届 lìjiè (形) (of sessions, governments, etc.) all previous: ～大会 all previous conferences

历来(來) lìlái (副) always; all through the ages: ～的主张 consistent proposition. ～如此. This has always been the case.

历历在目 lìlì zài mù come clearly into view; remain fresh in one's memory

历年 lìnián (形) over the years: ～的积蓄 savings over the years

历时(時) lìshí (动) last (a period of time): ～二个月的调查 the investigation which lasted two months.

历史 lìshǐ (名) history; past records: ～清白 have a clean record. ～文物 historical relics

历史唯物主义(義) lìshǐ wéiwùzhǔyì (名) historical materialism

历史唯心主义(義) lìshǐ wéixīnzhǔyì (名) historical idealism

历书(書) lìshū (名) almanac

沥(瀝) lì

沥青 lìqīng (名) pitch; tar; bitumen

荔 lì

荔枝 lìzhī (名) litchi

俩(倆) liǎ (数)<口> 1 two: 咱～ we two; the two of us 2 some; several: 就这么～人? Just these few people?

帘(簾) lián (名) **1** curtain: 窗～ window curtain **2** 〈旧〉 flag as shop sign: 酒～ wineshop sign

廉 lián **1** honest **2** cheap, inexpensive: 价～物美 (of goods in a shop) cheap but good

廉耻(恥) liánchǐ (名) sense of shame

廉价(價) liánjià (形) low-priced; cheap: ～出售 sell at a low price

廉洁(潔) liánjié (形) honest: ～奉公 be upright and honest in performing official duties

镰 lián (名) sickle: ～刀 sickle

怜(憐) lián (动) pity; sympathize with: 同病相～. Fellow sufferers sympathize with each other.

怜悯 liánmǐn (动) pity; take pity on

怜惜 liánxī (动) have pity on

联(聯) lián I (动) unite; join; relate: ～产责任制 output-related responsibility system II (名) antithetical couplet: 春～ Spring Festival couplet

联邦 liánbāng (名) federation; commonwealth: ～共和国 federal republic. ～调查局 the (U.S.) Federal Bureau of Investigation (FBI). 英～ the British Commonwealth of Nations

联播 liánbō (名) radio hookup: 新闻～ news hookup

联大 Liándà (名) 〈简〉 (联合国大会) the United Nations General Assembly

联防 liánfáng (名) joint defence

联合 liánhé I (动) unite; ally II (名) alliance; union: ～政府 coalition government III (形) joint; combined: ～声明 joint communique. ～收割机 combined harvester. ～举办 jointly organize or sponsor. ～承包工程 joint contract projects

联合国(國) Liánhéguó (名) the United Nations (U.N.): ～安全理事会 the United Nations Security Council. ～大会 the United Nations General Assembly. ～秘书处 the United Nations Secretariat

联合会(會) liánhéhuì (名) federation; union: 妇女～ women's federation. 学生～ students' union

联欢(歡) liánhuān (名) have a get-together (or a party)

联结 liánjié (动) join; connect; tie

联络 liánluò I (动) get in touch with II (名) contact; liaison: ～处 liaison office

联盟 liánméng (名) alliance; league; coalition: 工农～ worker-peasant alliance

联名 liánmíng (形) jointly signed: ～上书 submit a joint letter

联赛 liánsài (名) league matches: 足球～ league football matches

联系 liánxì I (动) contact; get in touch with; link: 请你去跟他～. Will you please contact him? 理论～实际 apply theory to reality II (名) contact; tie; connection: 保持～ keep in contact with; be in touch

联想 liánxiǎng (动) associate sth. with (in the mind)

联运(運) liányùn (名) through transport: ～票 through ticket

连(連) lián I (动) link; join; connect: 血肉相～ be bound together like one's own flesh and blood. 这几句话～不起来. These sentences are disconnected. II (名) (of army) company III (副) **1** in succession: ～年丰收 reap rich harvests for many years running. ～唱了十支歌 sing ten songs one after another **2** even: 这事～我妈都不知道,别说我了! Even my mother is in the dark about it, to say nothing of me! 我～想都没有想过. I didn't even give it a thought IV (介) including: 这个办公室～我共有十人. There are ten people in this office including me. 这本字典～邮费共十元. This dictionary is 10 *yuan*, postage included.

连词 liáncí (名) conjunction

连…带… lián…dài… **1** [indicating two nearly simultaneous actions] and; while: 连蹦带跳 hopping and skipping; vivacious **2** as well as; and: 我们村连老带小共 100 人左右. There are altogether some 100 people in our village, including the old people and children.

连贯 liánguàn I (动) link up; connect II (形) coherent; consistent: 文章写得很不～. This article is badly organized. ～性 coherence; continuity

连环(環) liánhuán (名) chain of rings: ～画 picture-story book

连接 liánjiē (动) join; link

连襟 liánjīn (名) husbands of

sisters

连累 liánlěi (动) get sb. into trouble: 受～ be implicated

连忙 liánmáng (副) promptly; at once: 他～道歉. He hastened to apologize.

连绵 liánmián (形) continuous; unbroken; uninterrupted: 雨雪～. It has been raining and snowing for days on end.

连年 liánnián (副) in successive or consecutive years; for years running

连篇 liánpiān (副) throughout a piece of writing: 白字～ full of malapropisms (or wrongly written words). 空话～ pages and pages of empty verbiage

连任 liánrèn (形) be reappointed or reelected consecutively: ～两届总统 be elected president for two consecutive terms

连日 liánrì (副) for days on end

连锁反应(應) liánsuǒ fǎnyìng (名) chain reaction

连天 liántiān (形) 1 reaching (or scraping) the sky: 水～ The water and the sky seem to meet. 2 incessant: 叫苦～ incessantly complain

连同 liántóng (动) together with; including

连续(續) liánxù (副) continuously; successively; in a row: ～下了五天雨. It rained for five days running. 事故～发生. Accidents occurred one after another. 电视～剧 T.V. play series

连夜 liányè (副) the same night; that very night: 他～赶回了家. He rushed back home that very night.

连衣裙 liányīqún (名) a woman's dress

连载(載) liánzǎi (动) publish in serial form: 广播～ radio serial

连长(長) liánzhǎng (名) company commander

涟 lián (名) ripples

涟漪 liányī (名) ripples

莲 lián (名) lotus

莲花 liánhuā (名) lotus flower; lotus

莲蓬 liánpeng (名) seedpod of the lotus

莲子 liánzǐ lotus seed

鲢 lián (名) silver carp

敛(斂) liǎn (动) 1 hold back; restrain: ～容 assume a serious expression 2 collect: 横征暴～ extort heavy taxes and levies

脸(臉) liǎn (名) face: 笑～ a smiling face. 丢～ lose face. 不要～ shameless. 没～见人 too ashamed to face . anyone. 居然有～说这种话 have the cheek to say such things

脸红 liǎnhóng (动) 1 blush with shame; blush 2 flush with anger

脸盘(盤)儿 liǎnpánr (名) face

脸皮 liǎnpí (名) face; cheek: 厚～ thick-skinned; shameless. ～薄 thin-skinned; sensitive

脸谱 liǎnpǔ (名) types of facial makeup in Beijing operas

脸色 liǎnsè (名) 1 look; complexion: ～苍白 look pale 2 facial expression: ～严厉 look stern. 看他的～我就知道他很高兴. I can see from the expression on his face that he is pleased.

恋(戀) liàn (动) love; feel attached to: 初～ first love. ～家 reluctant to be away from home

恋爱(愛) liàn'ài (名) love; love affair

恋恋不舍 liànliàn bù shě be reluctant to part with

炼(煉) liàn (动) smelt; refine

炼钢(鋼) liàngāng (名) steel-making

炼乳 liànrǔ (名) condensed milk

炼铁(鐵) liàntiě (名) iron-smelting

炼油 liànyóu (名) oil refining

练(練) liàn (动) practise; train; drill: ～嗓子 practise singing. 老～ experienced and assured

练兵 liànbīng (名) troop training: ～场 drill ground

练达(達) liàndá (形) experienced and worldly-wise

练功 liàngōng (动) do exercises in gymnastics; practise one's skill

练习(習) liànxí I (动) practise II (名) exercise: 做～ do exercises. ～簿 exercise-book

殓(殮) liàn (动) put a body into a coffin

链 liàn (名) chain: 表～ watch chain

链条(條) liàntiáo (名) chain

链子 liànzi (名) chain

粱 liáng (名) fine millet; fine grain

梁 liáng (名) beam: 横～ cross beam. 桥～ bridge. 山～ mountain ridge

梁上君子 liángshàng jūnzǐ (名) burglar; thief

凉 liáng (形) 1 cool; cold: ～风 cool breeze. 着～ catch cold. ～菜 cold dish 2 discouraged; disappointed: 他一听这消息心就～了. He felt bitterly disappointed at the news.
see also liàng

凉快 liángkuai (形) nice and cool: 我们坐在树荫下面～一下吧. Let's sit in the shade and cool off a bit.

凉台(臺) liángtái (名) balcony; veranda

凉亭 liángtíng (名) pavilion; summer house

凉席 liángxí (名) summer sleeping mat

凉鞋 liángxié (名) sandals

良 liáng (形) good; fine

良辰美景 liángchén-měijǐng (名) a fine day and an enchanting scene

良好 liánghǎo (形) good: 动机～ good intentions

良机(機) liángjī (名) good opportunity: 坐失～. Let slip a golden opportunity.

良师(師)益友 liángshī-yìyǒu (名) good teacher and helpful friend

良心 liángxīn (名) conscience: 说句～话 to be fair. 没～ heartless; ungrateful

良药(藥)苦口 liángyào kǔ kǒu good medicine tastes bitter but it helps.

良种(種) liángzhǒng (名) fine seeds or breed; improved seed strains

粮(糧) liáng (名) grain

粮仓(倉) liángcāng (名) granary; barn

粮草 liángcǎo (名) army provisions

粮库 liángkù (名) grain depot

粮票 liángpiào (名) grain coupon

粮食 liángshi (名) grain; cereals; food

量 liáng (动) measure: ～身材 take sb.'s measurements
see also liàng

量具 liángjù (名) measuring tool: ～刃具厂 measuring and cutting tools plant

两(兩) liǎng I (数) 1 two: ～间房子 two rooms. ～党制 bipartisan system. ～百 two hundred 2 both (sides): ～相情愿 both parties are willing 3 a few; some: 我过～天再来. I'll come again in a couple of days. 让我讲～句. Let me say a few words. II (量) *liang*, Chinese traditional unit of weight, equivalent to 0.05 kilo: 二～茶叶 two *liang* of tea

两败俱伤(傷) liǎng bài jù shāng both sides suffer; end in defeat for both sides

两边(邊) liǎngbiān (名) both sides: ～讨好 try to please both sides

两便 liǎngbiàn be convenient to both sides

两回事 liǎng huí shì two different matters (also as 两码事)

两极(極) liǎngjí (名) the two poles of the earth: ～分化 polarization

两口子 liǎngkǒuzi (名) husband and wife; couple

两面 liǎngmiàn (名) both sides; both aspects: ～派 double-dealer. ～三刀 double-dealing

两难(難) liǎngnán (形) face a difficult choice: 进退～ be in a dilemma

两栖(棲) liǎngqī (形) amphibious: ～登陆 amphibious landing

两全其美 liǎng quán qí měi act in such a way as to satisfy the two contending parties or resolve the contradiction confronting a person: 无法 ～ find it hard to please either party

两性 liǎngxìng (名) both sexes: ～关系 sexual relations

两袖清风(風) liǎngxiù qīngfēng (形) (of an official) remain uncorrupted

两翼 liǎngyì (名) both wings; both flanks

两用 liǎngyòng (名) dual purpose

凉 liàng (动) let sth. cool off: 让茶泡一会,～一下再喝. Let the tea brew and cool a little before you drink it.
see also liáng

谅 liàng (动) 1 forgive; understand: 互～互让 mutual understanding and mutual accommodation 2 presume; suppose: ～他也不敢. I don't think he dare.

谅解 liàngjiě (动) understand; make allowance for: 互相～ mutual understanding. 达成～ reach an understanding

晾 liàng (动) dry in the air; dry in the sun: 她把衣服～在绳子上. She hung the washing on the line. ～干 dry by airing

亮 liàng I (形) 1 light; bright; shiny: 天～了. Day is breaking. 把皮鞋擦～ polish the shoes. 这里真～. It's very bright in here. 2 loud and clear: 他的嗓子洪～. He has a rich resonant voice. 3 enlightened; clear: 你这一说, 我心里头～了. Your remarks are most enlightening. II (动) 1 light: 灯～了. The light is on. 2 reveal; show: ～底 disclose one's real intention. ～思想 reveal (or lay bare) one's thoughts

亮光 liàngguāng (名) light: 一道～ a shaft of light

亮晶晶 liàngjīngjīng (形) sparkling; glittering; glistening: ～的星星 bright stars. ～的露珠 glistening dewdrops

亮堂堂 liàngtāngtāng (形) brightly lit; brilliant

亮堂 liàngtang (形) 1 light; bright 2 clear; enlightened: 我心里～多了. I feel very much enlightened.

亮相 liàngxiàng (动) 1 strike a pose (on the stage) 2 declare one's position; state one's views

踉 liàng

踉跄(蹌) liàngqiàng (动) stagger: ～而行 stagger along

辆(輛) liàng (量) (for vehicles): 一～卡车 a lorry. 两～轿车 two cars

量 liàng I (动) measure; estimate: ～才录用 assign people jobs commensurate with their abilities II (名) 1 quantity; amount: 2 capacity: 酒～ capacity for drinking. 他饭～大. He's a big eater.
see also liáng

量变(變) liàngbiàn (名) quantitative change

量词 liàngcí (名) classifier; measure word

量力 liànglì (动) make an accurate estimate of one's own strength or ability: 自不～ overrate one's ability. ～而行 act according to one's ability

量体(體)裁衣 liàngtǐ cái yī cut the garment according to the figure; act according to actual circumstances

量子 liàngzǐ (名) quantum

撩 liāo (动) 1 raise; lift up: ～起帘子 raise the curtain 2 sprinkle (water)
see also liáo

聊 liáo I (动) chat: 闲～ have a casual conversation. 我想找你～～. I'd like to have a chat with you. II (副) merely; just: ～表谢意 just to show my appreciation

聊天儿 liáotiānr (动)〈口〉chat

燎 liáo (动) burn

燎泡 liáopào (名) blister caused by a burn

燎原 liáoyuán (动) set the prairie ablaze

撩 liáo (动) 1 tease; tantalize 2 provoke; stir up
see also liāo

撩拨(撥) liáobō (动) 1 tease; banter 2 incite; provoke

嘹 liáo

嘹亮 liáoliàng (形) loud and clear; resonant

僚 liáo (名) official: 官～ official; bureaucrat. 同～ colleague

缭 liáo

缭乱(亂) liáoluàn (形) confused: 心绪～ in a confused state of mind. 眼花～ be dazzled

缭绕(繞) liáorào (动) float in the air: 炊烟～ smoke curling up from kitchen chimneys

寥 liáo (形) 1 few; scanty: ～～可数 limited in number 2 silent; deserted: 寂～ deserted and lonely

寥廓 liáokuò (形) boundless; vast: ～的天空 the vast sky

疗(療) liáo (动) treat; cure: 治～ give medical treatment to a patient

疗程 liáochéng (名) course of treatment

疗法 liáofǎ (名) therapy: 针灸～ acupuncture therapy

疗效 liáoxiào (名) curative effect

疗养(養) liáoyǎng (动) recuperate; convalesce: ～院 sanatorium

辽(遼) liáo (形) distant; faraway

辽阔 liáokuò (形) vast; extensive; boundless: ～的土地 vast territory

潦 liǎo

潦草 liǎocǎo (形) 1 (of handwriting) careless; illegible: 字迹～. The handwriting is nothing but a scribble. 2 sloppy: 工作～ work in a slipshod way

潦倒 liǎodǎo (形) be down and out

了 liǎo (动) 1 know; understand: 明～ understand 2 end; solve: 没完没～ endless 3 [used after a verb as a complement to 得 or 不 to indicate possibility]: 办得～ can manage it. 受不～ cannot stand it.
see also le; liào

了不得 liǎobude (形) 1 terrific; extraordinary: 气得～ fly into a rage. 高兴得～ extremely happy. 这有什么～! What's so unusual about this? 2 terrible; awful: 可～啦，小孩到处找不到. Good God! The child is nowhere to be found.

了不起 liǎobuqǐ (形) amazing; terrific: 一个～的人 a great man. ～的成就 an amazing achievement. 自以为～ be conceited; swell with pride

了得 liǎode [used at the end of a sentence with 还 to indicate that the situation is serious]: 哎呀! 这还～! Dear me! This is awful.

了结 liǎojié (动) finish; settle; put an end to

了解 liǎojiě I (动) 1 know; understand: 我很～他. I know him well. 他不～情况. He doesn't understand the situation. ～中东近来发展状况 keep abreast of the recent development in the Middle East 2 find out; inquire: 你能去～一下这个问题吗? Will you go and find out about this matter? II (名) knowledge; understanding: 促进双方之间的～ promote mutual understanding

了然 liǎorán (动) understand; be clear: 一目～ be clear at a glance

了如指掌 liǎorú zhǐ zhǎng know sth. like the back of one's hand

了事 liǎoshì (动) dispose of a matter; get sth. over: 草草～ hurry through things. 敷衍～ get things done perfunctorily

料 liào I (动) expect; predict; anticipate: ～事如神 predict things like a prophet. 不出所～ as was expected II (名) 1 material; stuff: 原～ raw material. 燃～ fuel. 他不是当医生的～. He hasn't got the makings of a doctor. 2 (grain) feed: 多给牲口加点～. Put more grain in the fodder.

料到 liàodào (动) foresee; expect: 没～到他会来. We didn't expect him to come.

料酒 liàojiǔ (名) cooking wine

料理 liàolǐ (动) arrange; manage; take care of: ～家务 manage household affairs

料想 liàoxiǎng (动) expect; presume

料子 liàozi (名) material for making clothes (usu. wool)

撂 liào (动)〈口〉 put down; leave behind: ～挑子 throw up one's job

镣 liào (名) shackles

镣铐 liàokào (名) handcuffs; shackles; leg irons; chains

了(瞭) liào
see also le; liǎo

了望 liàowàng (动) watch; look into the distance from a height: ～台 watch tower

咧 liě

咧嘴 liězuǐ (动) grin: 他咧着嘴笑. He grinned. 疼得直～ grin with pain

列 liè I (动) 1 line up: ～队欢迎 line up to welcome sb. 2 arrange; list: ～清单 make an inventory. ～入议程 place sth. on the agenda. ～表 make a list; arrange (figures in tables.) II (名) row; file; rank: 站在斗争的最前～ stand in the forefront of the struggle III (量) [for things in a row] 一～火车 a train

列车(車) lièchē (名) train: 特快～ express train. 直达～ through train. ～时刻表 train schedule

列举(舉) lièjǔ (动) enumerate; list: ～大量事实 cite numerous facts

列宁(寧)主义(義) lièníngzhǔyì (名) Leninism

列强 lièqiáng (名) big powers

列席 lièxí (动) attend (a meeting) as a nonvoting delegate

烈 liè (形) 1 strong; violent; intense: ～酒 spirit; a strong drink. ～火 raging flames 2 upright; staunch: 刚～ upright and unyielding. 先～ martyr. 壮～牺牲 die a heroic death

烈日 lièrì (名) burning (or scorching) sun

烈士 lièshì (名) martyr

烈属(屬) lièshǔ (名) family of a martyr
烈性 lièxìng (形) 1 (of temper) fierce; violent 2 (of alcohol) strong
冽 liè (形) cold: 凛～ piercingly cold
裂 liè (动) split; break: 木板～(开)了.The plank cracked. 分～ split; break up
裂变(變) lièbiàn (名) fission: 核～ neclear fission
裂缝 lièfèng (名) crack; rift; fissure
裂痕 lièhén (名) slight crack; rift
裂开(開) lièkāi (动) split open; rend
裂纹 lièwén (名) slight crackle
劣 liè (形) bad; inferior; of low quality
劣等 lièděng (名)poor; low-grade
劣势(勢) lièshì (名) inferior position: 处于～ be in a inferior position
猎(獵) liè (动) hunt: ～狗 hunting dog; hound. ～户 (or ～人) hunter
猎奇 lièqí (动) hunt for novelty; seek novelty
猎枪(槍) lièqiāng (名) hunting rifle
猎取 lièqǔ (动) 1 hunt: ～野兽 hunt wild animals 2 pursue; seek; hunt for: ～个人名利 pursue personal fame and gain
拎 līn (动) carry; lift: ～着桶 carry a bucket (by hand)
遴 lín: ～选(动)<书> select sb. for a post; select; choose
磷 lín (名) phosphorus (P)
磷肥 línféi (名) phosphate fertilizer
磷火 línhuǒ (名) phosphorescent light
嶙 lín
嶙峋 línxún (形) 1 (of rocks, cliffs, etc.) jagged; rugged: 怪石～ jagged rocks of grotesque shapes 2 (of a person) bony; thin: 瘦骨～ all skin and bones
鳞 lín (名) (of fish) scale: 遍体～伤 be covered with bruises or injuries (like the scale of a fish)
鳞甲 línjiǎ (名) scale and shell
粼 lín
粼粼 línlín (形) (of water) clear; crystalline: ～碧波 ripples of a clear, blue lake
林 lín (名) 1 woods; grove; forest: 竹～ bamboo grove. ～场 forestry centre; tree farm 2 circles: 艺～ art circles 3 forestry
林带 líndài (名) forest belt
林立 línlì (动) stand in great numbers (like trees in a forest)
林业(業) línyè (名) forestry
林荫(蔭)道 línyīngdào (名) avenue; boulevard
淋 lín (动) pour; drench: 日晒雨～ weather-beaten. ～湿了 get wet in the rain; be soaked
淋巴 línbā (名) lymph
淋漓 línlí (形) 1 dripping wet: 大汗～ dripping with sweat. 鲜血～ dripping with blood 2 (of writing or speech) free from inhibition: 痛快～ impassioned ～尽致 vividly and incisively; thoroughly
淋浴 línyù (名) shower bath; shower
霖 lín (名) continuous heavy rain: 甘～ good soaking rain; timely rain
琳 lín (名) beautiful jade
琳琅满目 línláng mǎnmù a collection of fine and exquisite things; a feast for the eyes
临(臨) lín (动) 1 face; overlook: 居高～下 occupy a commanding position. ～街的窗户 a window overlooking the street. 如～大敌 as if facing a formidable enemy 2 arrive; befall: 希亲～指导. We hope you will come personally to give guidance. 3 just before; on the point of: ～睡 before going to bed. ～行 before departure
临别 línbié (名) at parting; just before departure
临床(牀) línchuáng (形) clinical: ～经验 clinical experience
临近 línjìn (形) close to: ～黎明 close on daybreak. 考试～了. The examination session is drawing near.
临摹 línmó (动) copy (a model of calligraphy or painting)
临时(時) línshí (形) 1 at the time when sth. happens: ～通知 a short notice. ～改动 a last-minute change 2 temporary; provisional: ～政府 provisional government. ～措施 temporary measure. ～代办 chargé d'affaires

ad interim. ～工 odd-job man; temporary worker

临危 línwēi (副) 1 be dying (from illness) 2 facing death or deadly peril: ～不惧 betray no fear in the hour of danger

临阵磨枪(槍) línzhèn mó qiāng start to prepare only at the last moment

临阵脱逃 línzhèn tuōtáo sneak away at a critical juncture

临终 línzhōng (副) immediately before one's death: ～遗言 deathbed testament

邻(鄰) lín I (名) neighbour: 近～ a close neighbour II (形) neighbouring: ～县 a neighbouring county. ～座 an adjacent seat

邻邦 línbāng (名) neighbouring country

邻接 línjiē (动) border on; be next to

邻近 línjìn I (形) near; close to; adjacent to II (名) vicinity

邻居 línjū (名) neighbour: 隔壁～ a next-door neighbour

凛 lǐn (形) 1 strict; stern; severe 2 afraid; apprehensive

凛冽 lǐnliè (形) biting cold

凛凛 lǐnlǐn (形) 1 cold: 寒风～ a piercing wind 2 stern; awe-inspiring: 威风～ dignified and awe-inspiring

凛然 lǐnrán (形) stern; awe-inspiring. 正气～ show awe-inspiring righteousness

吝 lìn (形) stingy; mean

吝啬(嗇) lìnsè (形) stingy; miserly; mean: ～鬼 miser; niggard; skinflint

吝惜 lìnxī (动) stint: 不～自己的力量 spare no effort

赁 lìn (动) rent; hire: 房屋出～ house to let. 租～公司 a leasing company

凌 líng (动) 1 insult: 欺～ bully. 盛气～人 overbearing 2 approach: ～晨 before dawn 3 rise high; tower aloft

凌驾 língjià (动) override; place oneself above: ～一切 override all other considerations; of overriding importance

凌空 língkōng (动) be high up in the air

凌厉(厲) línglì (形) quick and forceful: 攻势～ make a swift and fierce attack

凌乱(亂) língluàn (形) in disorder; in a mess: ～不堪 in an awful mess

凌辱 língrǔ (动) insult; humiliate

凌云(雲)壮(壯)志 língyúnzhuàngzhì (cherish) soaring aspirations

菱 líng (名) water caltrop (also as 菱角)

陵 líng (名) 1 hill; mound 2 tomb; mausoleum: 十三～ the tombs of 13 Ming emperors; the Ming Tombs

陵墓 língmù (名) mausoleum; tomb

陵园(園) língyuán (名) cemetery

绫 líng (名) a thin silk fabric: ～罗绸缎 silks and satins

羚 líng (名)(～羊) antelope

零 líng I (数) 1 zero sign (0); nought: 五～六号 No. 506 (number five-oh-six). 三块～五分 three *yuan* and five *fen* 2 odd; with a little extra: 年纪六十有～ a little more than sixty years old 3 nought; zero; nil: 一减一等于～. One minus one leaves nought (or zero). 4 zero (on a thermometer): 摄氏～下十度 10 degrees below zero centigrade; minus ten degrees centigrade II (形) fractional III (动) wither and fall: 凋～ (of flowers) fallen and scattered about

零件 língjiàn (名) spare parts; spares

零落 língluò (形) 1 withered and fallen: 草木～. The grass and trees are all withered. 2 decayed: 凄凉～的景象 a scene of utter desolation 3 scattered; sporadic: ～的枪声 sporadic shooting

零钱(錢) língqián (名) 1 small change; change 2 pocket money

零敲碎打 língqiāo-suìdǎ do sth. bit by bit, off and on; adopt a piecemeal approach

零散 língsan (形) scattered: 桌子上～地放着几本书. There are several books lying scattered on the desk.

零售 língshòu (动) retail; sell retail: ～店 retail shop; retail store. ～价格 retail price

零碎 língsuì I (形) scrappy; fragmentary; piecemeal: ～活儿 odd jobs II (名) odds and ends; oddments; bits and pieces

零头(頭) língtóu (名) 1 money in low-value coins or notes; change 2 remnant (of cloth): 一块～布 a remnant

零星 língxīng (形) **1** fragmentary; odd; piecemeal: ～材料 fragmentary material **2** scattered; sporadic: ～小雨 occasional drizzles; scattered shower

零用 língyòng I (动) be earmarked for small incidental expenses II (名) pocket money

玲 líng

玲珑(瓏) línglóng (形) **1** (of things) ingeniously and delicately wrought; exquisite: 小巧～ fine and delicate **2** (of women) nimble

玲珑(瓏)剔透 línglóng tītòu (形) exquisitely carved; beautifully wrought: ～的玉雕 exquisitely wrought jade carvings

聆 líng (动)(书) listen; hear: ～教 hear your instructions

聆听(聽) língtīng (动) listen (respectfully)

龄(齡) líng (名) **1** age; years: 年～ age. 学～儿童 schoolage children **2** length of time; duration: 工～ length of service; years of service: 党～ Party standing

囹 líng

囹圄 língyǔ (名)‹书› jail; prison: 身入～ be behind prison bars; be thrown into prison

铃 líng (名) **1** bell: 门～ door bell **2** anything in the shape of a bell: 哑～ dumbbell. 棉～ cotton boll

伶 líng (名)(旧) actor or actress

伶仃 língdīng (形) left alone without help; lonely: 孤苦～ alone and uncared for

伶俐 língli (形) clever; bright; quick-witted

翎 líng (名) plume; tail feather; quill: 孔雀～ peacock plumes; peacock feathers

灵(靈) líng I (形) **1** quick; clever; sharp: 耳朵很～ have sharp ears. 这法子很～. This method works. **2** efficacious; effective: ～药 an effective remedy II (名) **1** spirit; intelligence: 心～ the mind; the soul **2** fairy; sprite; elf: ～怪 elf; goblin **3** remains of the deceased; bier: 守～ stand as guards at the bier; keep vigil beside the bier

灵便 língbiàn (形) **1** nimble; agile: 他手脚还～. He is still agile. **2** easy to handle; handy

灵丹妙药(藥) língdān-miàoyào (名) miraculous cure; panacea

灵感 línggǎn (名) inspiration

灵魂 línghún (名) soul; spirit: ～深处 in the recesses of one's mind; in the depth of one's soul

灵活 línghuó (形) **1** nimble; agile; quick: 脑筋～ be resourceful brain **2** flexible; elastic

灵机(機) língjī (名) sudden inspiration; brainwave: 她～一动, 想出了一个好办法. She had a brainwave and found a good solution.

灵柩 língjiù (名) a coffin containing a corpse; bier

灵敏 língmǐn (形) sensitive; keen; agile; acute: 这架仪器～度很高. This instrument is highly sensitive.

灵巧 língqiǎo (形) dexterous; nimble; clever; ingenious: 心思～ clever and resourceful

灵通 língtōng (形) having quick access to information; well-informed: 消息～人士 well-informed sources

灵验(驗) língyàn (形) **1** efficacious; effective **2** (of a prediction, etc.) accurate; right: 他的预言果然～. His prediction had proved correct.

令 lǐng (量) ream (of paper) see also lìng

领 lǐng I (名) **1** neck: 引～而望 eagerly look forward to **2** collar; neckband **3** outline; main point: 要～ main points; essentials **4** (量): 一～席 a mat II (动) **1** lead; usher: ～兵打仗 lead troops into battle **2** receive; draw; get: ～奖 receive a prize (or an award). ～养老金 draw one's pension **3** understand; comprehend; grasp

领带 lǐngdài (名) necktie; tie

领导(導) lǐngdǎo I (动) lead; exercise leadership II (名) leadership; leader

领地 lǐngdì (名) **1** manor (of a feudal lord) **2** territory

领港 lǐnggǎng I (动) pilot a ship into or out of a harbour; pilot II (名) (harbour) pilot

领海 lǐnghǎi (名) territorial waters; territorial sea: ～范围 extent of territorial waters. ～宽度 breadth of the territorial sea

领航 lǐngháng I (动) navigate; pilot II (名) navigator; pilot

领会(會) lǐnghuì (动) understand; comprehend; grasp: 我还没有～你的意思. I still don't see your point.

领教 lǐngjiào 1 〈套〉 [used to indicate approval or appreciation] thanks; much obliged: 您说得很对,～! You're quite right there. I'm much obliged to you. 2 ask advice: 有点儿小事向您～. I've a problem, which may not be terribly important, but I would like to ask your advice.

领空 lǐngkōng (名) territorial sky (or air); territorial air space

领口 lǐngkǒu (名) 1 collarband; neckband 2 the place where the two ends of a collar meet

领略 lǐnglüè (动) have a taste of; realize; appreciate

领情 lǐngqíng (动) feel grateful to sb.; appreciate the kindness: 你们的好意,我十分～. I very much appreciate your kindness.

领事 lǐngshì (名) consul: 总～ consul general. 副～ vice-consul. ～馆 consulate

领水 lǐngshuǐ (名) 1 inland waters 2 territorial waters

领土 lǐngtǔ (名) territory: 保卫国家的～完整 safeguard a country's territorial integrity. ～扩张 territorial expansion; territorial aggrandizement. ～要求 territorial claim

领悟 lǐngwù (动) comprehend; grasp: ～能力 perceptibility

领先 lǐngxiān (形) be in the lead; lead: 客队～五分. The visiting team led by five points. 他们首批～登上了山顶. They were among the first to reach the hill top.

领袖 lǐngxiù (名) leader

领域 lǐngyù (名) 1 territory; domain 2 field; sphere; realm: 上层建筑～ the realm of the superstructure

领章 lǐngzhāng (名) collar badge; collar insignia

岭(嶺) lǐng (名) 1 mountain range 2 mountain ridge: 翻山越～ cross over mountain after mountain. 崇山峻～ high mountain ridges

另 lìng (形、副) another; separately; on another occasion: ～有任命 have another appointment. ～一回事 another matter. ～议 discuss the matter on some other occasion. ～寄 post separately; post under separate cover

另起炉(爐)灶(竈) lìng qǐ lúzào make a fresh start; start all over again

另眼相看 lìng yǎn xiāng kàn treat sb. with special respect

令 lìng I (名) 1 command; order; decree: 下～ issue an order. 法～ laws and decrees 2 season: 当～ in season. 夏～时间 summer time 3 an ancient official title: 县～ county magistrate 4 〈书〉 good; excellent: ～名 good name; reputation 5 〈敬〉 your: ～尊 your father. ～堂 your mother. ～爱 your daughter. ～郎 your son 6 drinking game II (动) make; cause: ～人鼓舞 heartening; inspiring; encouraging. ～人深思 make one ponder long and deeply

see also lǐng

令箭 lìngjiàn (名) an arrow-shaped token of authority used in the army in ancient China

令行禁止 lìng xíng jìn zhǐ strict enforcement of orders and prohibitions; every order is executed without fail

溜 liū I (动) 1 slide; glide: 从山坡上～下来 slide down a slope 2 sneak off; slip away: ～掉 sneak off; slip away II (形) smooth: 滑～ slippery

see also liù

溜冰 liūbīng (名) skating: ～场 skating rink

溜达(達) liūda (动) 〈口〉 stroll; saunter; go for a walk (or stroll)

溜须(鬚)拍马(馬) liūxū-pāimǎ (动) 〈口〉 fawn on; toady to; shamelessly flatter

溜之大吉 liū zhī dàjí (动) sneak away

熘 liū (动) sauté (with thick gravy); quick-fry: ～鱼片 fish slices sauté

浏(瀏) liú (书) 1 (of water) clear; limpid 2 (of wind) swift

浏览(覽) liúlǎn (动) glance over; skim through; browse through (away): ～各种报刊 browse among newspapers and magazines

流 liú (动) 1 flow: 江水东～. The river flows east. ～汗 sweat. ～泪 shed tears 2 move from place to place; drift; wander 3 spread: ～传甚广 spread far and wide 4 change for the worse; degenerate: ～于形式 be reduced to a mere formality 5 banish; send into exile II (名) 1 stream of water: 河～ river. 逆～而上 sail against the current 2 sth. resembling a stream of water; current: 气～ air current. 电～ electric current 3 class; rate; grade: 三教九～ people of different types, schools and persuasions

流弊 liúbì (名) corrupt practices; abuses

流产(産) liúchǎn (名) 1 abortion; miscarriage: 人工～ induced abortion 2 miscarry; fall through: 他的计划～了. His plan fell flat.

流畅(暢) liúchàng (形) easy and smooth: 文笔～ write with ease and grace

流传(傳) liúchuán (动) spread; circulate; hand down: 古代～下来的寓言 fables handed down from ancient times

流窜(竄) liúcuàn (动) (of bandits, enemy troops etc.) flee hither and thither

流动(動) liúdòng I (动) flow: 溪水缓缓地～. The brook flowed sluggishly. II (形) going from place to place; on the move; mobile: ～货车 shop-on-wheels. ～电影放映队 mobile film projection team.

流毒 liúdú (名) 1 exert a pernicious (or baneful) influence: ～甚广 exert a widespread pernicious influence 2 pernicious influence; baneful influence

流放 liúfàng (动) 1 banish; send into exile 2 float (logs) downstream

流寇 liúkòu (名) 1 roving bandits 2 roving rebel bands

流浪 liúlàng (动) roam about; lead a vagrant life: ～街头 roam the streets. ～汉 tramp; vagrant

流离(離)失所 liúlí shī suǒ drift about aimlessly; wander about homeless

流利 liúlì (形) fluent; smooth: 她说一口～的英语. She speaks fluent English.

流连忘返 liúlián wàng fǎn be so enchanted by the scenery as to forget to return

流量 liúliàng (名) rate of flow; flow; discharge: 河道～ discharge of a river

流露 liúlù (动) reveal; betray; show unintentionally: 真情的～ a revealation of one's true feelings

流落 liúluò (动) wander about destitute: ～他乡 wander destitute far from home

流氓 liúmáng (名) 1 rogue; hoodlum; hooligan; gangster 2 immoral (indecent) behaviour; hooliganism: 耍～ behave like a hoodlum

流派 liúpài (名) school; sect: 学术～ schools of thought

流失 liúshī (动) run off; be washed away: 水土～ soil erosion

流逝 liúshì (动) (of time) pass; elapse: 时光～ time passes

流水 liúshuǐ (名) running water: ～线 assembly line. ～作业 assembly line method; conveyer system

流速 liúsù (名) 1 velocity of flow 2 current velocity

流体(體) liútǐ (名) fluid: ～力学 hydromechanics; fluid mechanics

流通 liútōng (动) circulate: 空气～ ventilation

流亡 liúwáng (动) be forced to leave one's native land; go into exile: ～政府 government-in-exile

流线(綫)型 liúxiànxíng (名) streamline: ～汽车 streamlined car

流行 liúxíng (形) prevalent; popular; fashionable; in vogue

流行病 liúxíngbìng (名) epidemic disease: ～学 epidemiology

流血 liúxuè (动) bleed; shed blood

流言 liúyán (名) rumour; gossip: ～蜚语 rumours and slanders

流域 liúyù (名) valley; river basin; drainage area: 黄河～ the Yellow River valley (or basin)

琉 liú

琉璃 liúli (名) coloured glaze: ～塔 glazed pagoda. ～瓦 glazed tile

硫 liu (名) sulphur (S)

硫化 liúhuà (名) vulcanization: ～物 sulphide.

硫磺 liúhuáng (名) sulphur

硫酸 liúsuān (名) sulphuric acid

留 liú (动) 1 remain; stay: 你可以继续～任. You can stay on. 2 detain 3 reserve; keep; save: ～座位 reserve a seat for sb. 4 let grow; grow; wear: ～胡子 grow a beard 5 accept; take: 把礼物～下 accept a pre-

sent 6 leave: 他把书都～在我这里了. He left all the books with me. ～言簿 visitors's book

留步 liúbù 〈套〉 don't bother to see me out; don't bother to see me any further

留存 liúcún 〈动〉 1 preserve; keep: 此稿～ keep this copy on file 2 remain; be extant

留话 liúhuà 〈动〉 leave a message; leave word

留级 liújí 〈动〉 (of pupils, etc.) fail to go up to the next grade; repeat the year's work

留恋(戀) liúliàn 〈动〉 1 be reluctant to part (from sb. or with sth.); have a sentimental attachment for 2 recall with nostalgia

留难(難) liúnàn 〈动〉 make things difficult for sb.; make it too hot for sb.

留念 liúniàn 〈动〉 accept or keep as a souvenir

留情 liúqíng 〈动〉 show mercy: 手下～ be lenient

留神 liúshén 〈动〉 on the alert; take care: 过马路要～. Be careful when you cross the street.

留声(聲)机(機) liúshēngjī 〈名〉 gramophone; phonograph

留守 liúshǒu 〈动〉 stay behind to take care of things

留宿 liúsù 〈动〉 1 put up a guest for the night 2 stay overnight; put up for the night

留心 liúxīn 〈动〉 be attentive: ～听讲 listen attentively to a lecture

留学(學) liúxué 〈动〉 study abroad: ～生 student studying abroad; returned student

留言 liúyán 〈动〉 leave one's comments; leave a message

留意 liúyì 〈动〉 be careful: 这两个字有细微差别，必须～. There are subtle distinctions between these two words. You have got to be careful.

留影 liúyǐng 〈动〉 have a picture taken as a memento

瘤 liú 〈名〉(～子) tumour: 毒～ malignant tumour. 良性～ benign tumour

榴 liú 〈名〉 pomegranate

榴弹(彈) liúdàn 〈名〉 high explosive shell: ～炮 howitzer

柳 liǔ 〈名〉 willow

柳条(條) liǔtiáo 〈名〉 willow twig; wicker: ～筐 wicker basket

柳絮 liǔxù 〈名〉 (willow) catkin

六 liù 〈数〉 six

六亲(親) liùqīn 〈名〉 the six relations (father, mother, elder brothers, younger brothers, wife, children); one's kin: ～不认 refuse to have anything to do with all one's relatives and friends

六神无(無)主 liù shén wú zhǔ in a trance

六月 liùyuè 〈名〉 1 June 2 the sixth month of the lunar year

溜 liù 〈名〉 1 swift current 2 rainwater from the roof 3 roof gutter 4 row: 一～平房 a row of one-storeyed houses 5 surroundings; neighbourhood: 这～儿果木树很多. There are plenty of fruit trees round here.

see also liū

遛 liù 〈动〉 saunter; stroll: ～大街 go window-shopping. ～马 walk a horse. ～弯儿 take a walk; go for a stroll

陆(陸) liù 〈数〉 six [used for the numeral 六 on cheques, etc. to avoid mistakes or alterations]

see also lù

龙(龍) lóng 〈名〉 1 dragon 2 imperial: ～袍 imperial robe 3 a huge extinct reptile: 恐～ dinosaur

龙飞(飛)凤(鳳)舞 lóngfēi-fèngwǔ 1 characteristic of a winding magnificent mountain range 2 lively flourishes in calligraphy

龙卷风(風) lóngjuǎnfēng 〈名〉 tornado

龙套 lóngtào 〈名〉 actor playing a supporting role; utility man: 跑～ carry a spear in the supporting role; be "a supporting role" actor

龙王 lóngwáng 〈名〉 the Dragon King (the God of Rain in Chinese mythology)

龙虾(蝦) lóngxiā 〈名〉 lobster

龙争虎斗(鬥) lóngzhēng-hǔdòu 〈名〉 a fierce struggle between two evenly-matched opponents

龙钟(鍾) lóngzhōng 〈书〉 decrepit; senile: 老态～ senile; aged and doddering

龙舟 lóngzhōu 〈名〉 dragon boat: ～竞渡 dragon-boat regatta; dragon-boat race

聋(聾) lóng 〈形〉 deaf; hard of hearing

聋哑(啞) lóngyǎ 〈形〉 deaf and dumb; deaf-mute: ～人 deaf-mute

聋子 lóngzi (名) a deaf person

砻(礱) lóng (名、动) 1 rice huller 2 hull (rice)

笼(籠) lóng (名) 1 cage; coop: 鸟～ birdcage. 鸡～ chicken coop 2 basket; container 3 (food) steamer: 蒸～ food steamer

see also lǒng

笼屉(屜) lóngtì (名) bamboo or wooden utensil for steaming food; food steamer

隆 lóng I (形) 1 grand 2 prosperous; thriving 3 intense; deep: ～冬 the depth of winter. ～情厚谊 profound sentiments of friendship II (动) bulge

隆隆 lónglóng (象) rumble: 雷声(炮声)～ the rumble of thunder (gunfire)

隆重 lóngzhòng (形) grand; solemn; ceremonious: ～的典礼 a grand ceremony

垄(壟) lǒng (名) 1 ridge (in a field) 2 raised path between fields

垄断(斷) lǒngduàn (动、名) control; monopolize; monopoly: ～集团 monopoly group. ～价格 monopoly price. ～资本 monopoly capital. ～市场 monopolize the market

拢(攏) lǒng (动) 1 approach; reach: ～岸 come alongside the shore 2 add up; sum up (accounts) 3 hold (or gather) together 4 comb (hair)

拢子 lǒngzi (名) a fine-toothed comb

笼(籠) lǒng I (动) envelop; cover: 烟～雾罩 be enveloped in mist II (名) a large box or chest; trunk

see also lóng

笼络 lǒngluò (动) win people over by unfair means: ～人心 try to win popular support by hook or by crook

笼统 lǒngtǒng (形) general; vague: 他的话说得很～. He spoke in general terms.

笼罩 lǒngzhào (动) envelop; shroud: 湖面上晨雾～. The lake is enveloped in morning mist.

弄 lòng (名) lane; alley; alleyway

see also nòng

弄堂 lòngtáng (名) lane; alley; alleyway

搂(摟) lōu (动) 1 gather up; rake together: ～柴火 rake up twigs, dead leaves, etc. (for fuel) 2 hold up; tuck up: ～起袖子 tuck up one's sleeves 3 extort: ～钱 extort money

see also lǒu

娄(婁) lóu

娄子 lóuzi (名) trouble; blunder: 捅～ make a blunder; get into trouble

楼(樓) lóu (名) 1 a storied building: 办公～ office building 2 storey; floor: 一～(英) ground floor; (美) first floor. 二～(英) first floor; (美) second floor 3 superstructure: 城～ city-gate tower

楼上 lóushàng (名) upstairs

楼梯 lóutī (名) stairs; staircase

楼下 lóuxià (名) downstairs

搂(摟) lǒu (动) hold in one's arms; hug; embrace

see also lōu

搂抱 lǒubào (动) hug; embrace

篓(簍) lǒu (名) (～子) basket: 字纸～ wastepaper basket

漏 lòu I (动) 1 leak: 水壶～了. The kettle leaks. 2 divulge; leak: 走～消息 leak information 3 be missing; leave out: 这一行～了两个字. Two words are missing from the line. II (名) water clock; hourglass: ～尽更残. The night is waning.

漏洞 lòudòng (名) 1 leak 2 flaw; hole; loophole: 他的话里有许多～ His argument is full of loopholes.

漏斗 lòudǒu (名) funnel

漏税 lòushuì (动) evade payment of a tax; evade taxation

漏网(網) lòuwǎng (动) (of criminal, enemies, etc.) escape unpunished

镂(鏤) lòu engrave; carve

镂空 lòukōng (动) hollow out: ～的象牙球 hollowed-out ivory ball

露 lòu (动) <口> reveal; show: ～一手 show off

see also lù

露马(馬)脚 lòu mǎjiǎo (动) give oneself away; let the cat out of the bag

露面 lòumiàn (动) make public appearances; appear in public

露头(頭) lòutóu (动) appear; emerge: 太阳还没有～，我们就起来了。We got up before sunrise.

陋 lòu (形) 1 plain; ugly: 丑～ ugly 2 humble; mean: ～室 a cramped flat. ～巷 a mean alley 3 vulgar; corrupt; undesirable: ～习 corrupt customs; bad habits. ～规 objectionable practices 4 (of knowledge) scanty; limited: 孤～寡闻 ignorant and ill-informed

庐(廬) lú (名) hut; cottage

庐山真面 lúshān zhēnmiàn (名) the truth about a person or a matter

庐舍 lúshè (名)(书) house; farmhouse

炉(爐) lú I (名) stove; furnace: 围～烤火 sit round a fire to get warm. 煤气～ gas stove II (量) heat: 一～钢 a heat of steel

炉灶(竈) lúzào (名) kitchen range; cooking range: 另起～ make a fresh start

芦(蘆) lú: ～苇 reed

颅(顱) lú (名) cranium; skull

颅骨 lúgǔ (名) skull

胪(臚) lú (动)(书) set out; display; exhibit

卤(鹵) lǔ I (形) bittern II (动) stew (whole chicken or duck, large cuts of meat, etc.) in soy sauce: ～鸡 pot-stewed chicken III (名) thick gravy used as a sauce for noodles, etc.: 打～面 noodles served with thick gravy

虏(虜) lǔ I (动) take prisoner II (名) captive; prisoner of war

虏获(獲) lǔhuò (动、名) 1 capture 2 captives and captured arms

掳(擄) lǔ (动) carry off; plunder

掳掠 lǔlüè (动) pillage; loot: 奸淫～ rape and loot

鲁 lǔ (形) 1 stupid; dull 2 rash; rough; rude

鲁钝 lǔdùn (形) dull-witted; obtuse; stupid

鲁莽 lǔmǎng (形) crude and rash; rash: ～行事 act rashly

橹 lǔ (名) scull; sweep

鹿 lù (名) deer: 公～ stag; buck. 母～ doe. 小～ fawn

鹿角 lùjiǎo (名) 1 deerhorn; antler 2 abatis

鹿茸 lùróng (名) pilose antler (of a young stag)

鹿死谁手 lù sǐ shuí shǒu who will win the prize or gain supremacy: ～，尚难逆料。It's still hard to tell who will emerge the victor.

麓 lù (名)(书) the foot of a hill or mountain

辘 lù

辘辘 lùlù (象) rumble: 车轮的～声 the rumbling of cart wheels. 饥肠～ so hungry that one's stomach rumbles; feel famished

路 lù (名) 1 road; path; way: 大～ broad road; highway. 小～ path; trail. ～灯 street lamp 2 journey; distance: 走很远的～walk a long distance; make a long journey 3 way; means: 生～ means of livelihood 4 sequence; line; logic: 思～ train of thought 5 route: 七～公共汽车 No. 7 bus 6 sort; grade; class: 头～货 top-notch goods. 一～货 the same sort; birds of a feather

路标(標) lùbiāo (名) road sign; route sign

路不拾遗 lù bù shí yí no one picks up anything on the road and claims it as his own

路程 lùchéng (名) distance travelled; journey: 三天～ a three days' journey

路费 lùfèi (名) travelling expenses

路径(徑) lùjìng (名) 1 route; way: ～不熟 not know one's way around 2 method; ways and means

路途 lùtú (名) 1 road; path 2 way; journey: ～遥远 a long way to go; far away

路线(綫) lùxiàn (名) 1 route; itinerary: 旅行的～ the route of a journey. 参观～图 visitors' itinerary 2 line: 政治～ political line

路子 lùzi (名) way; approach: ～不对等于白费劲儿。A wrong approach is a waste of effort.

露 lù I (名) 1 dew 2 beverage distilled from flowers, fruit or leaves; syrup: 果子～ fruit syrup II (动) show; reveal; betray: 不～声色 not betray one's feelings or intentions. ～出原形 reveal one's true co-

lours
see also lòu
露骨 lùgǔ (形) thinly veiled; undisguised; naked: 你说得这样～，他不会不懂. You spoke in such undisguised terms that he could not miss the point.
露酒 lùjiǔ (名) alcoholic drink mixed with fruit juice
露水 lù shui (名) dew
露天 lùtiān in the open (air); outdoors: ～剧场 open-air theatre. ～煤矿 opencut coal mine
露头(頭)角 lù tóujiǎo (动) (of a young person) begin to show ability or talent
露营(營) lùyíng (动) camp (out); encamp; bivouac

戮 lù (动) 1 kill; slay: 杀～ slaughter 2 〈书〉 unite; join: ～力 join hands. ～力同心 unite in a concerted effort; make concerted efforts

录(録) lù I (动) 1 record; write down; copy: 抄～ copy down. 记～在案 put on record 2 employ; hire: ～用 employ; take sb. on the staff 3 tape-record: 报告已经～下来了. The speech has been tape-recorded. II (名) record; register; collection: 回忆～ memoirs; reminiscences
录供 lùgòng (动) take down a confession or testimony during an interrogation
录取 lùqǔ (动) enroll; recruit; admit: 他已被～. He has been admitted to college or recruited by a factory, etc.
录音 lùyīn (名) sound recording: 磁带～ tape recording. 放～ play back the recording. ～带 magnetic tape; tape. ～机 (tape) recorder

禄 lù (名) official's salary in feudal China; emolument: 高官厚～ high position and handsome emolument

碌 lù (形) 1 commonplace; mediocre 2 busy
碌碌 lùlù (形) 1 mediocre; commonplace: ～无能 incompetent 2 busy with miscellaneous work: 忙忙～ busy going about one's routine

陆(陸) lù (名) land: 水～交通 land and water communications
see also liù
陆地 lùdì (名) dry land; land
陆军 lùjūn (名) ground force; land force; army
陆路 lùlù (名) land route: 走～ travel by land. ～交通 overland communication; land communication
陆续(續) lùxù (副) one after another; in succession: 来宾～地到了. The visitors have arrived one after another.

闾 lǘ (名) the gate of (or entrance to) a village: 倚～而望 waiting at the entrance to the village (for the return of one's son)

驴(驢) lǘ (名) donkey; ass

旅 lǚ (名) 1 travel; stay away from home 2 brigade 3 troops; force: 劲～ a powerful army; a crack force
旅伴 lǚbàn (名) travelling companion; fellow traveller
旅程 lǚchéng (名) route; itinerary
旅费 lǚfèi (名) travel expenses
旅馆(館) lǚguǎn hotel
旅客 lǚkè (名) hotel guest; traveller; passenger
旅途 lǚtú (名) journey; trip: ～见闻 notes on a journey; traveller's notes
旅行 lǚxíng (名) travel; journey; tour: ～社 travel service. ～团 touring party. ～指南 guidebook. ～支票 traveller's cheque
旅游 lǚyóu (名) tour; tourism: ～业 tourist industry; tourism
旅长(長) lǚzhǎng (名) brigade commander

膂 lǚ (名) 〈书〉 backbone
膂力 lǚlì (名) muscular strength; physical strength

屡(屢) lǚ (副) repeatedly; time and again: ～战～胜 score one victory after another. ～见不鲜 common occurrences; nothing new
屡次 lǚcì (副) time and again; repeatedly: ～打破全国纪录 repeatedly break the record

缕(縷) lǚ I (名) thread II (量) thread strand: 千丝万～的联系 connected in a thousand and one ways III (副) detailed; in detail: ～陈 state in detail [used in addressing one's superior]

捋 lǚ (动) smooth out with the fingers; stroke: ～胡子 stroke one's beard

铝 lǚ (名) aluminium (Al)

侣 lǚ (名) companion; associate: 伴～ companion; partner

履 lǚ I (名) 1 shoe: 革～ leather shoes 2 footstep II (动) 1 carry out; honour; fulfil: ～约 honour an agreement; keep an appointment 2 tread on; walk on: ～险如夷 go over a dangerous pass as if walking on level ground

履带(帶) lǚdài (名) caterpillar tread; track: ～式拖拉机 caterpillar (or crawler) tractor

履历(歷) lǚlì (名) personal details (of education and work experience); curriculum vitae; resumé

履行 lǚxíng (动) perform; fulfil; carry out: ～职责 do one's duty. ～诺言 keep one's promise; fulfil (or carry out) one's promise

率 lǜ (名) rate; proportion; ratio: 人口增长～ the rate of population growth. 废品～ the rate (or proportion) of rejects see also shuài

虑(慮) lǜ I (动) consider; ponder; think over: 深谋远～ be deeply thoughtful and far-seeing; think deeply and plan carefully II (名) concern; anxiety, worry: 疑～ misgivings

滤(濾) lǜ (动) strain; filter: 过～ filter. ～纸 filter paper

律 lǜ I (名) law; statute; rule II (动) restrain; keep under control: 严以～己 be strict with oneself; exercise strict self-discipline

律师(師) lǜshī (名) lawyer; (英) barrister; (英) solicitor; (美) attorney

律诗 lǜshī (名) *lüshi*, a poem of eight lines, each containing five or seven characters, with a strict tonal pattern and rhyme scheme

绿 lǜ (形) green: ～叶 green leaves. ～油油的秧苗 green and lush seedlings

绿茶 lǜchá (名) green tea

绿灯(燈) lǜdēng (名) 1 green light 2 permission to go ahead with some project; green light: 开～ give the green light to

绿肥 lǜféi (名) green manure

绿化 lǜhuà (动) make (a place) green by planting trees, flowers, etc.; afforest: 植树造林，～祖国. Plant trees everywhere to make the country green.

绿洲 lǜzhōu (名) oasis

峦(巒) luán (名) <书> 1 low but steep and pointed hill 2 mountains in a range

挛(攣) luán (名) contraction: 拘～ contraction. 痉～ spasm; convulsions

鸾(鸞) luán (名) a mythical bird like the phoenix

鸾凤(鳳) luánfèng (名) husband and wife: ～和鸣 have a happy married life

孪(孿) luán (名) twin

孪生 luánshēng (名) twin: ～姐妹 twin sisters

卵 luǎn (名) ovum; egg; spawn

卵巢 luǎncháo (名) ovary

卵翼 luǎnyì cover with wings as in brooding; shield: ～之下 under the wing of

乱(亂) luàn I (副) in disorder; in a confusion: 屋里很～. The room is in a mess. II (名) disorder; upheaval; chaos; riot; unrest; turmoil: 十年内～ a decade of turmoil. 叛～ armed rebellion; mutiny III (动) confuse; mix up; jumble: 扰～ create confusion; disturb IV (形) confused (state of mind): 我心里很～. My mind is in a confused state.

乱哄哄 luànhōnghōng (形) in noisy disorder; in a hubbub; tumultuous; in an uproar

乱离(離) luànlí (形) be torn apart by war; be rendered homeless by war

乱蓬蓬 luànpēngpēng (形) dishevelled; tangled; unkempt: ～的头发 dishevelled (tangled) hair

乱七八糟 luànqībāzāo (形) at sixes and sevens; in a mess; in terrible disorder

乱弹(彈)琴 luàntánqín (动) <口> act or talk like a fool; talk nonsense

乱套 luàntào (动) muddle things up; turn things upside down

乱糟糟 luànzāozāo (形) 1 chaotic; messy. 2 confused; perturbed

乱真 luànzhēn (动) (of fakes) look genuine: 以假～ pass off a fake as genuine

掠 lüè (动) 1 plunder; pillage; sack 2 sweep past; brush past; graze; skim over: 海鸥～过浪面 seagulls skimming the waves

掠夺(奪) lüèduó (动) plunder; rob; pillage: ～成性 be predatory by nature

掠美 lüèměi (动) claim credit due to others

略 lüè I (形) brief; sketchy: 简～ sketchy; simple. ～述大意 give a brief account II (副) slightly; a little; somewhat: ～有所闻 know a little about the matter. ～胜一筹 slightly better; a notch above sb. III (名) 1 summary; brief account; outline: 史～ outline history. 事～ a short biographical account 2 strategy; plan; scheme: 策～ tactics. 雄才大～ (a person of) great talent and bold vision IV (动) 1 omit; delete; leave out: 从～ be omitted 2 capture; seize: 攻城～地 attack cities and seize territories

略略 lüèlüè (副) slightly; briefly: 他行前～说了几句. He spoke just a few words before he left.

略图(圖) lüètú (名) sketch map; sketch

略微 lüèwēi (副) slightly; a little; somewhat: ～有点感冒 have a cold; have a touch of flu

略语 lüèyǔ (名) abbreviation; shortening

沦(淪) lún (动) 1 sink: 沉～ sink into depravity, etc. 2 fall; be reduced to

沦落 lúnluò (动) fall low; be reduced to poverty: ～街头 be driven onto the streets

沦亡 lúnwáng (动) (of a country) be conquered (or subjugated)

沦陷 lúnxiàn (动) (of territory, etc.) be occupied by the enemy; fall into enemy hands: ～区 enemy-occupied area

轮(輪) lún I (名) 1 wheel: 齿～ gear wheel 2 sth. resembling a wheel; disc; ring: 光～ halo. 年～ annual ring 3 steamboat; steamer: 江～ river steamer II (动) take turns: ～值 on duty by turns. 下一个就～到你了. It will be your turn next. III (量) 1 一～红日 a red sun. 一～明月 a bright moon 2 round: 新的一～会谈 a new round of talks

轮班 lúnbān (副) in shifts; in relays; in rotation

轮船 lúnchuán (名) steamer; steamship; steamboat

轮番 lúnfān (副) take turns: ～去做 do the work by turns

轮换 lúnhuàn (动) rotate; take turns

轮廓 lúnkuò (名) outline; contour; rough sketch

轮流 lúnliú (副) take turns; do sth. in turn: 他俩～值夜班. They work on night shifts in turn.

轮胎 lúntāi (名) tyre

轮子 lúnzi (名) wheel

轮作 lúnzuò (名) crop rotation

伦(倫) lún (名) 1 human relationships, esp. as conceived by feudal ethics 2 logic; order 3 peer; match: 英勇绝～ peerless; matchless

伦比 lúnbǐ (名) rival; equal: 无与～ unrivalled; unequalled; peerless

伦次 lúncì (名) coherence; logical sequence: 语无～ speak incoherently

伦理 lúnlǐ (名) ethics; moral principles

纶(綸) lún (名) 1 black silk ribbon 2 fishing line 3 synthetic fibre

论(論) lùn I (名) 1 view; opinion; statement: 高～ your brilliant views; your wise counsel. 舆～ public opinion. 社～ editorial 2 dissertation; essay 3 theory: 进化～ the theory of evolution. 唯物～ materialism II (动) 1 discuss; talk about; discourse: 讨～ discuss 2 mention; regard; consider: 相提并～ mention in the same breath; place on a par 3 decide on; determine: ～罪 mete out punishments

论处(處) lùnchǔ (动) decide on sb.'s punishment; punish

论点(點) lùndiǎn (名) argument; thesis: 这篇文章～突出，条理分明. The essay is well-organized, giving prominence to all the main points of argument.

论调 lùndiào (名) (常含贬义) view; argument: 这种～很容易迷惑人. Such views are apt to mislead people.

论断(斷) lùnduàn (名) inference; judgment; thesis: 作出～ draw an inference

论据(據) lùnjù (名) grounds o

argument; argument
论理 lùnlǐ I (副) normally; as things should be: ～她早该回家了. Normally, she should have gone home. II (名) logic: 合乎～ be logical; stand to reason
论述 lùnshù (动) discuss; expound
论坛(壇) lùntán (名) forum; tribune
论题 lùntí (名) proposition
论文 lùnwén (名) thesis; dissertation; treatise; paper: 学术～ an academic thesis (or paper). 科学～ a scientific treatise
论战(戰) lùnzhàn (名) polemic; debate
论证(證) lùnzhèng (名、动) 1 demonstration; proof 2 expound and prove
论著 lùnzhù (名) treatise; work; book

罗(囉) luō
see also luó
罗嗦 luōsuo (形) 1 long-winded; wordy: 他说话太～. He's far too long-winded. 2 complicated; troublesome: 这些手续真～. All these formalities are much too complicated.

螺 luó (名) 1 spiral shell; snail: 田～ field snail 2 whorl (in fingerprint)
螺钿 luódiàn (名) mother-of-pearl inlay: ～漆盘 lacquer tray inlaid with mother-of-pearl
螺钉 luódīng (名) screw: 木～ wood screw; screwnail
螺母 luómǔ (名) (screw) nut
螺丝(絲) luósī (名) 〈口〉 screw: ～刀 screwdriver
螺纹 luówén (名) 1 whorl (in fingerprint) 2 thread (of a screw)
螺旋 luóxuán (名) 1 spiral; helix: ～式发展 spiral development; developing in spirals 2 screw; helical line; spiral: ～桨 (screw) propeller; screw

骡 luó (～子) mule

罗(羅) luó I (动) 1 catch birds with a net: 门可～雀 visitors are extremely few 2 collect; gather together 3 display; spread out: ～列 set out marshal II (名) 1 sieve; sift 2 a kind of silk gauze: ～扇 silk gauze fan 3 a net for catching birds: ～网 net; trap. see also luō
罗汉(漢) luóhàn (名) arhat
罗盘(盤) luópán (名) compass
罗网(網) luówǎng (名) net; trap: 自投～ walk right into the trap
罗织(織) luózhī (动) frame up: ～罪名 cook up charges
罗致 luózhì (动) enlist the services of; secure sb. in one's employment; collect; gather together: ～人材 enlist the services of talented people

逻(邏) luó (动) patrol: 巡～ patrol
逻辑 luójí (名) logic: 合乎～ be logical

萝(蘿) luó (名) trailing plants: 藤～ Chinese wistaria
萝卜(蔔) luóbo (名) radish

箩(籮) luó (名) a square-bottomed bamboo basket
箩筐 luókuāng (名) a large bamboo or wicker basket

锣(鑼) luó (名) gong: ～鼓喧天 a deafening sound of gongs and drums

瘰 luǒ
瘰疬(癧) luǒlì scrofula

裸 luǒ (形) bare; naked; exposed: 赤～～ starknaked; undisguised
裸露 luǒlù (形) uncovered; exposed
裸体(體) luǒtǐ (形) naked; nude

荦(犖) luò (形) prominent; outstanding: 卓～ extraordinary; outstanding; preeminent
荦荦 luòluò (形) conspicuous; apparent; obvious: ～大端 salient points

落 luò I (动) 1 fall; drop: 花～ flowers fall 2 go down; set: 太阳～山了. The sun has set. 3 lower: 把帘子～下来 lower the blinds 4 decline; come down; sink: 衰～ decline; go downhill 5 lag behind; fall behind: 名～孙山 fail in a competitive exam 6 leave behind; stay behind: 不～痕迹 leave no trace; disappear without a trace 7 get: ～空 come to nothing II (名) 1 whereabouts: 下～ whereabouts 2 settlement: 村～ a small village; hamlet
see also là
落泊(魄) luòbó (形) be in dire straits; be down and out

落成 luòchéng (名) completion (of a building, etc.): ～典礼 inauguration ceremony (for a building, etc.)

落得 luòdé (动) be landed in; end up in (in a disgraceful state):～关进监狱 be landed (or end up) in prison

落地 luòdì (动) (of babies) be born: 呱呱～ be born into the world with a cry. ～灯 floor lamp; standard lamp

落发(髮) luòfà (动) be tonsured (to become a Buddhist monk or nun)

落后(後) luòhòu (动) 1 fall behind; lag behind:不甘～ hate to be outshone; be unwilling to lag behind 2 backward: ～地区 backward areas; less developed areas

落户 luòhù (动) settle: 在边远地区～settle in a remote border area

落脚 luòjiǎo (动) stay (for a time); stop over; put up: 找个地方～ find a place to stay. 在客店～ put up at an inn

落井下石 luòjǐng xiàshí hit a person when he's down

落空 luòkōng (动) come to nothing; fail; fall through: 两头～ fall between two stools. 希望～ be disappointed

落款 luòkuǎn write the names of the sender and the recipient on a painting, gift or letter; inscribe (a gift, etc.)

落落大方 luòluò dàfāng (形) natural and graceful

落落寡合 luòluò guǎ hé (形) standoffish; aloof

落实(實) luòshí I (形) practicable; workable: 生产计划要订得～. Production plans must be practicable. II (动) 1 fix (or decide) in advance; ascertain; make sure: 交货时间还没有最后～. The date of delivery hasn't been fixed yet. 2 carry out; fulfil; implement; put into effect:～措施 implement measures

落水狗 luòshuǐgǒu (名) a cur fallen into the water: 痛打～ be merciless with evildoers when they are in disgrace

落汤(湯)鸡(鷄) luòtāngjī like a drowned rat; soaked through

落拓 luòtuò (形) 1 〈书〉 be in reduced circumstances and feel bitterly disappointed 2 untrammelled by convention: ～不羁 unconventional and uninhibited

落网(網) luòwǎng (动) (of a criminal) be caught; be captured; be brought to justice

落伍 luòwǔ (动) fall behind the ranks; drop behind; drop out

落选(選) luòxuǎn (动) not be elected; lose an election

骆 luò (名) a white horse with a black mane, mentioned in ancient Chinese books

骆驼 luòtuo (名) camel

络 luò I (名) sth. resembling a net: 橘～ tangerine pith. 丝瓜～ loofah II (动) 1 hold sth. in place with a net: 她头上～着一个发网. She kept her hair in place with a net. 2 twine; wind: ～纱 winding yarn; spooling

络腮胡(鬍)子 luòsāihúzi (名) whiskers; full beard

络绎(繹)不绝 luòyì bù jué (形) in an endless stream: 参观展览会的人～. A continuous stream of visitors came to the exhibition.

M m

抹 mā (动) wipe: ～桌子 wipe a table clean
see also mǒ; mò

抹布 mābù (名) a piece of rag to clear things with

妈 mā (名) 1 mummy; mum; mother 2 a form of address for a married woman one generation one's senior: 姑～ (paternal) aunt. 姨～ (maternal) aunt

妈妈 māma (名) mama; mum; mummy; mother

麻 má I (名) hemp; flax; jute II (形) 1 coarse; pitted; spotty: ～子(脸) a pockmarked face. 镜子上怎么有这么多～点儿? How come the mirror is so spotty? 2 numb; tingle: 腿发～ have pins and needles in one's legs. 舌头发～ one's tongue is tingling. ～药 anaesthetics

麻痹 mábì I (名) paralysis: 小儿～ infantile paralysis II (动) benumb; lull: ～人们的斗志 lull (or blunt) people's fighting will III (形) lacking in vigilance: ～

大意 be careless; be off guard

麻袋 mádài (名) sack; gunnybag

麻烦 máfan I (形) troublesome; inconvenient: 这事恐怕太～了. It's too much trouble, I'm afraid. 自找～ ask for trouble II (动) trouble; bother; put sb. to trouble: 我懒得～. I can't be bothered. ～你了. Thank you for the trouble you've taken on my behalf.

麻利 máli (形) quick and neat; dexterous; deft: 手脚～ quick and neat (with work)

麻木 mámù (形) numb: ～不仁 apathetic; insensitive

麻雀 máquè (名) sparrow

麻绳(繩) máshéng (名) rope made of hemp, flax, etc.

麻疹 mázhěn (名) measles

麻醉 mázuì I (名) anaesthesia; narcosis: 针刺～ acupuncture anaesthesia. ～剂 anaesthetic; narcotic. ～品 narcotic; drug. ～师 anaesthetist II (动) anaesthetize; poison

吗 má (代) what: 你在这儿干～? What are you doing here?
see also mǎ; ma

马(馬) mǎ (名) horse: 母～ mare. 种～ stallion; stud. 小～ pony. 中途换～ change (swop) horses in midstream

马鞍 mǎ'ān (名) saddle

马鞭 mǎbiān (名) horsewhip

马不停蹄 mǎ bù tíng tí hurry (to a place); nonstop

马车(車) mǎchē (名) (horse-drawn) carriage or cart

马达(達) mǎdá (名) motor

马大哈 mǎdàhā (名) a careless person; scatterbrain

马灯(燈) mǎdēng (名) barn lantern

马夫 mǎfū (名) groom

马褂 mǎguà (名) mandarin jacket

马后(後)炮 mǎhòupào (名) belated effort (action or advice): 他这个人一贯爱放～. He always comes up with belated advice. *or* He is always wise after the event.

马虎 mǎhū (形) careless; casual: ～了事 get sth. done in a slapdash (or sloppy) manner. 这孩子聪明倒聪明, 就是太～. This child is clever for sure, but he is a bit too careless.

马脚 mǎjiǎo (名) sth. that gives the game away: 露～ show the cloven hoof; give oneself away; let the cat out of the bag

马厩 mǎjiù (名) stable

马克思主义(義) Mǎkèsīzhǔyì (名) Marxism

马裤 mǎkù (名) riding breeches

马力 mǎlì (名) horsepower (h.p.): 开足～ at full speed

马铃薯 mǎlíngshǔ (名) potato

马路 mǎlù (名) road; street; avenue

马马虎虎 mǎmǎhūhū (形) **1** careless; casual: (as 马虎) **2** passable; not so bad; so-so: 他的英文怎么样? ——～, 不至于迷路. Does he speak good English? — Just so-so. But he won't get lost. 这本书有意思吗? ——～, 反正不值得买. How about this book? — Not so bad, but not worth buying.

马前卒 mǎqiánzú (名) pawn; cat's-paw

马上 mǎshàng (副) at once; straight away; right away; immediately: 告诉他等一等, 我～就回来. Tell him to wait. I'll be right back. 我们必须～出发. We must set off at once. 演出～就要开始了. The performance will begin at any moment.

马戏(戲) mǎxì (名) circus: ～团 circus troupe

马掌 mǎzhǎng (名) horseshoe

玛 mǎ

玛瑙 mǎnǎo (名) agate

码 mǎ I (量) **1** yard (yd.) **2** [indicating things of the same kind]: 两～事 two entirely different matters II (名) a sign or thing indicating number: 页～ page number. 价～ marked price. 筹～ counter; chip

码头(頭) mǎtou (名) wharf; dock; pier

吗 mǎ
see also má; ma

吗啡 mǎfēi (名) morphine

蚂 mǎ

蚂蟥 mǎhuáng (名) leech

蚂蚁(蟻) mǎyǐ (名) ant

骂 mà (动) scold; curse; swear: ～人 swear (at people). ～人话 abusive language; swearword

骂街 màjiē (动) shout abuses in the street

骂骂咧咧 màmàliēliē (动) be foul-mouthed

嘛 ma 〈助〉 **1** [used at the end of a sentence to show what precedes it is obvious]: 这样做就是不对～! Of course it was acting improperly! 孩子总是孩子～! Children are children! **2** [used within a sentence to mark a pause]: 你～,就不用亲自去了. As for you, I don't think you have to go in person.

吗 ma 〈助〉 [used at the end of a declarative sentence to transform it into a question]: 你找我～? Are you looking for me? 他们那儿有野生动物～? Do they have wild life there? 吃完饭散散步好～? Shall we take a walk after dinner?
see also má; mǎ

埋 mái (动) bury
see also mán

埋藏 máicáng (名、动) lie hidden in the earth

埋伏 máifu (动) **1** ambush: 设下～ lay an ambush. 中～ fall into an ambush **2** hide; lie in wait

埋没 máimò (动) **1** neglect; stifle: ～人材 fail to do justice to talent **2** cover up; bury

埋头(頭) máitóu (动) immerse oneself in; be engrossed in: ～苦干 quietly immerse oneself in hard work. ～读书 bury oneself in books

埋葬 máizàng (动) bury

买(買) mǎi (动) buy; purchase: ～东西 buy things; go shopping. ～得起 can afford. ～不起 cannot afford

买办(辦) mǎibàn (名) comprador

买卖(賣) mǎimai (名) buying and selling; business; trade: 做成一笔～ make a deal. ～兴隆. The business is brisk. ～人 businessman; trader; merchant. 买空卖空 speculate (in stocks, etc.)

买通 mǎitōng (动) bribe; buy over; buy off

买帐(帳) mǎizhàng (动) acknowledge the superiority or seniority of; show respect for: 谁也不买他的帐. No one gives a damn what he says.

买主 mǎizhǔ (名) buyer; customer

麦(麥) mài (名) wheat: ～苗 wheat seedling. ～茬 wheat stubble

麦片 màipiàn (名) oatmeal: ～粥 oatmeal porridge

麦收 màishōu (名) wheat harvest

麦穗 màisuì (名) ear of wheat; wheat head

卖(賣) mài (动) **1** sell: ～不出去 not sell well **2** betray: ～友求荣 betray one's friend in pursuit of power and wealth **3** make an effort: ～劲儿 exert oneself; spare or stint no effort

卖唱 màichàng (动) make a living by singing

卖乖 màiguāi (动) show off one's cleverness

卖国(國) màiguó (动) betray one's country: ～条约 traitorous treaty. ～行为 treasonable act. ～贼 traitor (to one's country)

卖力 màilì (动) exert all one's strength; spare no effort

卖命 màimìng (动) do a killing job for somebody or some clique

卖弄 màinong (动) show off: ～学问 show off one's erudition

卖俏 màiqiào (名) coquette; flirt

卖身 màishēn (动) sell oneself: ～契 an indenture by which one sells oneself. ～投靠 sell one's soul in exchange for personal gain

卖艺(藝) màiyì (动) make a living as a performer

卖淫 màiyín (名) prostitution

迈(邁) mài I (动) step; stride: ～过门槛 step over the threshold II (形) advanced in years: 年～ aged

迈步 màibù (动) take a step; step forward: 迈出第一步 make the first step

迈进(進) màijìn (动) stride forward; advance with big strides

脉(脈) mài (名) **1** arteries and veins: 血～ blood veins. 叶～ veins in a leaf **2** pulse: 号～ feel sb.'s pulse
see also mò

脉搏 màibó (名) pulse

脉冲 màichōng (名) pulse

脉络 màiluò (名) train of thought; sequence of ideas: ～分明 well organized

蛮(蠻) mán I (形) rough; unreasoning: 野～ savage. ～不讲理 cannot be brought to reason II (副) quite; pretty: 他俩的关系～不错. They are on pretty good terms.

蛮干(幹) mángàn (动) act rashly: 那纯粹是～. That's downright foolhardy.

蛮横 mánhèng (形) rude and unreasonable: 要求～无理. The demands are (or go) beyond all reason.

埋 mán

see also mái

埋怨 mányuàn (动) complain; grumble; blame: 她这个人老爱～. She is always complaining. 别互相～了! Stop blaming each other!

瞒(瞞) mán (动) hide the truth from: 不～你说 to tell you the truth. 他～着我做出了决定. He made the decision without my prior knowledge or consent.

瞒哄 mánhǒng (动) deceive; pull the wool over sb.'s eyes

瞒天过(過)海 mán tiān guò hǎi practise deception

馒(饅) mán

馒头(頭) mántou (名) steamed bun; steamed bread

满(滿) mǎn I (形) 1 full; filled; packed: 瓶子～了. The bottle is full (of liquid). 大厅里坐～了人. The hall was packed with people. ～山松树. The hill was covered with pine trees. 他～身大汗. He is sweating all over. 2 content; satisfied: 自～ conceited; complacent II (副) completely; entirely: ～不在乎 not seem to care in the least. 这屋子已经～舒服的了. This room is perfectly comfortable as it is. III (动) reach the limit; expire: 假期～了. The vacation is over. 她明天就～三岁了. She will be three years old tomorrow.

满城风(風)雨 mǎn chéng fēngyǔ (become) the talk of the town: 闹得～ cause a scandal

满额 mǎn'é (动) fulfil the (enrolment, etc.) quota

满腹 mǎnfù (副) have one's mind filled with: ～牢骚 full of grievances; full of grumbles ～狐疑 filled with suspicion; full of misgivings

满怀(懷) mǎnhuái (副) 1 be imbued with: ～信心 be full of confidence 2 bosom: 撞了个～ bump right into sb.

满口 mǎnkǒu (副) (speak) profusely; glibly: ～答应 readily agree

满面 mǎnmiàn (副) have one's face covered with: ～笑容 beam; be all smiles. ～红光 glow with health. ～春风 be radiant with happiness; beam with pleasure

满目 mǎnmù (副) come into view: ～荒凉. The site was a scene of desolation.

满腔 mǎnqiāng (副) have one's bosom filled with: ～热情 full of enthusiasm. ～悲愤 full of grief and indignation

满意 mǎnyì (形) satisfied; pleased: 他对他新的工作很～. He is pleased with his new job.

满月 mǎnyuè I (名) full moon II (形) a baby's completion of its first month of life: 孩子明天就～了. The baby will be a month old tomorrow.

满载 mǎnzài (形) loaded to capacity; fully loaded; laden with: ～而归 return with fruitful results

满足 mǎnzú (动) feel content; feel satisfied: ～现状 be content with things as they are 2 satisfy; meet: ～要求 meet the demands of. ～需要 meet the needs of. ～愿望 satisfy one's desire. ～已有成就 rest on one's laurels

满座 mǎnzuò (动) have a capacity audience; have a full house

漫 màn I (动) overflow; brim over: 池塘的水～出来了. The pool overflowed its banks. II (形) free; casual: ～步 stroll; roam. ～不经心 careless; casual; negligent. ～无目标 aimless; at random III (副) all over the place: ～无边际 boundless; rambling. ～山遍野 all over the countryside and plains. ～天大雪 big flakes of snow drifting across the sky

漫笔(筆) mànbǐ (名) random thoughts (or notes); informal essay

漫长(長) màncháng (形) very long; endless: ～的岁月 long years. ～的道路 a long way to go

漫画(畫) mànhuà (名) caricature; cartoon

漫谈 màntán (动) have an informal discussion

漫天 màntiān (形) 1 all over the sky: ～大雾 a dense fog covering the sky 2 boundless; limitless: ～大谎 a monstrous lie

漫溢 mànyì (动) overflow; flood; brim over

漫游 mànyóu (动) go on a pleasure trip; roam; wander

慢 màn I (形) slow: ~车 slow train. 反应~ have a slow reaction. 我的表~了. My watch loses. 钟~了十分钟. The clock is ten minutes slow. II (副) slowly: ~~说 speak slowly III (动) 1 slow down: ~点儿! Slow down a bit! 2 postpone; defer: 这事先~点儿告诉她. Don't tell her about it yet.

慢慢 mànmàn (副) slowly; gradually: ~来. Take your time; Don't be in a rush. 他~就会懂得的. He'll understand it sooner or later.

慢腾腾 màntēngtēng (副) unhurriedly; sluggishly: 这样~地走, 什么时候才能走到呢? When will you ever get there if you walk in such a leisurely manner?

慢条(條)斯理 màntiáo-sīlǐ leisurely; unhurriedly; imperturbably

慢性 mànxìng (形) 1 chronic: ~病 chronic disease 2 slow (in taking effect): ~毒药 slow poison

谩 màn (形) disrespectful; rude

谩骂 mànmà (动) hurl (or fling) abuses; vilify

蔓 màn

蔓生植物 mànshēng zhíwù (名) trailing plant

蔓延 mànyán (动) spread; extend: 疾病~得很快. The disease spread very fast.

幔 màn (名) curtain; screen: ~帐 curtain; canopy

忙 máng I (形) busy; fully occupied: 大~人 a busy man. ~死了 be terribly busy. 他一个人~不过来. He can't manage all this by himself. 他正~着写文章. He is busy writing an article. II (动) hurry; hasten: ~什么, 再坐会儿吧. There is no tearing hurry. Stay a bit longer.

忙碌 mánglù (形) busy; bustling about

忙乱(亂) mángluàn (动) act hurriedly in a messy situation

芒 máng (名) awn; beard; arista

茫 máng

茫茫 mángmáng (形) a boundless expanse of; vast: ~大海 a vast sea. ~草原 boundless grasslands

茫然 mángrán (形) ignorant; in the dark; at a loss: 感到~ feel completely in the dark. ~不知所措 be at a loss what to do; be at sea. 显出~的神情 look perplexed; have a confounded look

盲 máng (形) blind

盲肠(腸) mángcháng (名) caecum

盲从(從) mángcóng (动) follow blindly

盲动(動) mángdòng (动) act blindly; act rashly

盲目 mángmù (形) blind: ~崇拜 blind faith. ~乐观 unrealistic optimism. ~性 blindness

盲人 mángrén (名) blind person: ~摸象 like the blind men trying to size up the elephant — take a part for the whole. ~瞎马 a blind man riding a blind horse —rushing headlong to disaster

盲文 mángwén (名) braille

莽 mǎng

莽苍(蒼) mǎngcāng (形)(of scenery) blurred; misty: 烟雨~ blurred with mist and rain

莽莽 mǎngmǎng (形) 1 luxuriant; rank 2 (of fields, plains, etc.) vast; boundless

莽原 mǎngyuán (名) wilderness overgrown with grass

莽撞 mǎngzhuàng (形) reckless; impetuous; rash: ~的小伙子 a rude fellow

蟒 mǎng (名) boa; python

蟒蛇 mǎngshé (名) boa; python

猫 māo (名) cat: 小~ kitten. ~叫 mewing; purring

猫头(頭)鹰 māotóuyīng (名) owl

毛 máo I (名) 1 hair; feather; down: 羽~ feather 2 wool: ~毯 woollen blanket. 纯(全)~ pure wool 3 mildew: 长~了 become mildewed II (形) 1 semifinished: ~坯 semifinished product 2 little; small: ~孩子 a small child; a mere child 3 careless; crude; rash: ~头~脑 rash; impetuous 4 panicky; scared; flurried: 这下可把他吓~了. He's scared stiff. III (量): *mao*, one-tenth of a *yuan*

毛笔(筆) máobǐ (名) writing brush

毛病 máobìng (名) 1 trouble; breakdown: 汽车出~了. Something is wrong with the car. 2

illness: 他胃有～. He has stomach trouble. 3 defect; fault; shortcoming
毛糙 máocao (形) crude; coarse; careless: 做工～. The work is crude. 你做事怎么这样～? How could you act so thoughtlessly?
毛虫(蟲) máochóng (名) caterpillar
毛发(髮) máofà (名) hair (on the human body and head)
毛骨悚然 máogǔ sǒngrán with one's hair standing on end — absolutely horrified: 令人～ send cold shivers down one's spine; make one's blood run cold and one's flesh creep
毛巾 máojīn (名) towel
毛孔 máokǒng (名) pore
毛料 máoliào (名) woollen fabric
毛驴(驢) máolǘ (名) donkey
毛毛雨 máomáoyǔ (名) drizzle
毛皮 máopí (名) fur
毛茸茸 máoróngróng (形) hairy; downy
毛遂自荐(薦) Máo Suì zì jiàn volunteer one's services; offer oneself for the job
毛衣 máoyī (名) woollen sweater
毛毯 máotǎn (名) woollen blanket
毛细血管 máoxì xuèguǎn (名) blood capillary
毛线(綫) máoxiàn (名) knitting wool
毛躁 máozao (形) 1 short-tempered; irritable 2 rash and careless
毛泽(澤)东(東)思想 Máo Zédōng Sīxiǎng (名) Mao Zedong Thought
毛毡 máozhān (名) felt
毛织(織)品 máozhīpǐn (名) 1 wool fabric; woollens 2 woollen knitwear
毛重 máozhòng (名) gross weight

牦 máo

牦牛 máoniú (名) yak

锚 máo (名) anchor: 抛～ cast anchor; drop anchor. 起～ weigh anchor. ～地 anchorage

矛 máo (名) spear

矛盾 máodùn I (名) contradiction: ～百出 teem with contradictions II (动) contradict: 自相～ contradict oneself; be inconsistent. 互相～ contradict each other
矛头(頭) máotóu (名) spearhead: ～指向坏人坏事. The attack is spearheaded against evildoers and evil deeds.

茅 máo

茅草 máocǎo (名) cogongrass: ～棚 thatched hut (or shack)
茅房 máofáng (名) <口> latrine
茅坑 máokēng (名) <口> latrine pit
茅塞顿开(開) máo sè dùn kāi suddenly see the light; be suddenly enlightened
茅舍 máoshè (名) <书> thatched cottage
茅屋 máowū (名) thatched cottage

铆 mǎo (动) rivet

铆钉 mǎodīng (名) rivet

茂 mào (形) 1 luxuriant; lush; profuse: 根深叶～ have deep roots and exuberant foliage 2 rich and splendid

茂密 màomì (形) (of plants) dense; thick: ～的森林 a dense forest
茂盛 màoshèng (形) luxuriant; thriving; flourishing

冒 mào I (动) 1 emit; give off; send out (or up, forth): 浑身～汗 sweat all over. ～气 be steaming. 烟囱正在～烟. The chimney is belching smoke. 2 risk; brave: ～风险 run risks. ～着生命危险 at the risk of one's own life. ～雪 brave the snow II (副) 1 boldly; rashly: ～猜一下 make a bold guess 2 falsely (claim, etc.): ～称 falsely claim. ～领养老金 claim (or obtain) pension under false pretences

冒充 màochōng (动) pretend to be; pass oneself off as: ～内行 pretend to be an expert; pose as an expert
冒犯 màofàn (动) offend; affront: 他的话～了她. His words offended her.
冒号(號) màohào (名) colon (:)
冒火 màohuǒ (动) be enraged; flare up
冒尖儿 màojiānr (动) be outstanding: 他在班里算～. He is topnotch in his class.
冒进(進) màojìn (动) advance rashly
冒昧 màomèi (形) make bold; venture; take the liberty of: 恕我～提出一个问题. Forgive me

for taking the liberty to ask a question. ～陈辞 venture an opinion

冒名 màomíng (动) assume another's name: ～顶替 pretend to be somebody by assuming his name

冒牌 màopái (形) a counterfeit of a well-known trade mark; imitation; fake: ～货 imitation; fake

冒失 màoshi (形) rash; abrupt: 说话～ speak rashly

冒头(頭) màotóu (动) (of ideas; tendencies) begin to crop up

冒险(險) màoxiǎn (动) take a risk; take chances: ～家 adventurer. ～政策 adventurist policy

帽 mào (名) hat; cap: 草～ straw hat. 军～ army cap. 安全～ safety helmet. 笔～儿 the cap of a pen. 螺钉～ screw cap

帽子 màozi (名) 1 hat; cap; headgear 2 label; tag; brand: 乱扣～ indiscriminately label people as

貌 mào (名) looks; appearance: 美～ good looks. 新～ new look. 人不可～相. Never judge people by their appearance.

貌合神离(離) màohé-shénlí (of two people) be apparently in harmony but essentially at variance

貌似 màosì (动) seem (or appear) to be: ～公正 appear to be impartial

贸 mào (名) trade: 外～ foreign trade

贸然 màorán (副) rashly; hastily; without careful consideration: ～下结论 draw a hasty conclusion; jump to a conclusion

贸易 màoyì (名) trade: 对外～ foreign trade. 国内～ domestic trade. ～差额 balance of trade. ～额 volume of trade; turnover. ～逆差 unfavourable balance of trade. ～顺差 favourable balance of trade

么(麼) me (suffix): 什～ what. 多～ how. 怎～ why; how. 这～ such; so; in this way

没 méi see "没有"

see also mò

没关(關)系(係) méi guānxi it doesn't matter; it's nothing; that's all right; never mind

没精打采 méijīng-dǎcǎi listless; in low spirits

没…没… méi ... méi ... 1 [each used before a synonym to emphasize negation]: 没完没了 endless. 没羞没臊 shameless 2 [each used before an antonym to indicate failure to distinguish things]: 没轻没重 tactless. 没大没小 impolite (to an elder); impudent

没趣 méiqù (形) feel neglected; feel snubbed: 没有人理他，他觉得～，只好走了. Feeling that he was out in the cold, he slunk off. 自讨～ ask for a snub

没什么(麼) méi shénme 1 as "没关系" 2 don't mention it; it's a pleasure; you're welcome

没事找事 méishì zhǎoshì 1 ask for trouble 2 be fault-finding

没羞 méixiū (形) unabashed

没有 méiyǒu (副) 1 [used to negate 有] not have; be without: ～钱 have no money. ～人在家. There is no one at home. 鱼～水就活不了. The fish can't live without water. 2 [used to form the negation of a completed action]: 我昨天～去. I didn't go yesterday. 商店还～关门. The shop hasn't closed yet. 事情～你说的那么容易. Things are not as easy as you said. 3 [used to form the negation of a past experience]: 他～去过巴黎. He has never been to Paris. 4 less than (as 不到): ～两个星期他就走了. He left in less than two weeks time. 后来～几天她就死了. She died only a few days later.

煤 méi (名) coal: 原～ raw coal

煤层(層) méicéng (名) coal seam; coal bed

煤矿(礦) méikuàng (名) coal mine; colliery: ～工人 coal miner

煤气(氣) méiqì (名) gas: ～灯 gas lamp. ～炉 gas stove

煤球 méiqiú (名) (egg-shaped) briquet

煤炭 méitàn (名) coal: ～工业 coal industry

煤田 méitián (名) coalfield

煤油 méiyóu (名) kerosene: ～灯 kerosene lamp. ～炉 kerosene stove

媒 méi (名) 1 matchmaker; go-between: 做～ act as a matchmaker 2 intermediary

媒介 méijiè (名) medium; vehicle: 传染疾病的～ vehicle of disease

媒婆 méipó (名) professional female matchmaker
媒人 méirén (名) matchmaker; go-between
玫 méi
玫瑰 méiguì (名) rose
枚 méi (量): [for small objects]: 一～纪念章 a badge. 两～古币 two ancient coins
霉 méi (名) mould; mildew: 发～ go mouldy; mildew
霉菌 méijūn (名) mould
霉烂(爛) méilàn (动) become mildewed; go rotten
莓 méi (名) certain kinds of berries: 草～ strawberry
梅 méi (名) plum
梅花 méihuā (名) plum blossom
酶 méi (名) enzyme; ferment: 消化～ digestive ferment
眉 méi (名) eyebrow
眉飞(飛)色舞 méifēi-sèwǔ (形) highly exultant; enraptured (usu. of a person speaking)
眉开(開)眼笑 méikāi-yǎnxiào beam with joy; be wreathed in smiles
眉来(來)眼去 méilái-yǎnqù make eyes at each other; flirt with each other
眉毛 méimao (名) eyebrow; brow
眉目 méimù (名) 1 features; looks: ～清秀 have delicate features 2 logic; sequence of ideas: 这篇文章～清楚. The article is well organized.
眉目 méimu (名) prospect of a solution; sign of a positive outcome: 我们的计划已经有点～了. We are getting somewhere with our plan.
眉批 méipī (名) notes made at the top of a page
眉梢 méishāo (名) the tip of the brow: 喜上～ look very happy
眉头(頭) méitóu (名) brows: 皱～ knit the brows; frown
眉宇 méiyǔ (名) forehead
美 měi (形) 1 pretty; beautiful 2 very satisfactory; good: ～酒 good wine. 物～价廉 good and inexpensive. 日子过得挺～ live a happy life
美不胜(勝)收 měi búshèng shōu more beautiful things than one can take in
美差 měichāi (名) cushy job
美称(稱) měichēng (名) laudatory title; good name
美德 měidé (名) virtue; moral excellence
美感 měigǎn (名) sense of beauty; aesthetic feeling
美工 měigōng (名) 1 art designing 2 art designer
美观(觀) měiguān (形) beautiful; artistic; pleasing to the eye: ～大方 simple and artistic
美好 měihǎo (形) (of abstract things) happy; bright: ～的将来 bright future. ～的日子 happy days
美化 měihuà (动) beautify; embellish: ～环境 beautify the environment
美景 měijǐng (名) beautiful scenery (or landscape)
美丽(麗) měilì (形) beautiful
美满(滿) měimǎn (形) happy; perfectly satisfactory: ～的婚姻 a happy marriage
美梦(夢) měimèng (名) fond dream
美妙 měimiào (形) splendid; wonderful; beautiful: ～的音乐 splendid music. ～的诗句 beautiful verse
美名 měimíng (名) good name; good reputation: ～天下扬. Good name spreads far and wide.
美容 měiróng (名) looks: ～院 beauty parlour. ～手术 plastic surgery
美术(術) měishù (名) fine arts: 工艺～ arts and crafts. ～馆 art gallery. ～家 artist. ～片 (of film) cartoons. ～字 artistic calligraphy; art lettering
美味 měiwèi (名) delicious food; delicacy
美学(學) měixué (名) aesthetics
美言 měiyán (动) put in a good word for sb.
美中不足 měi zhōng bù zú a flaw in something which might otherwise be perfect; a fly in the ointment
美滋滋 měizīzī (形) extremely pleased with oneself
镁 měi (名) magnesium (Mg)
镁光 měiguāng (名) magnesium light
每 měi (代) 1 every; each: ～天 every day. ～周一次 once every week. ～小时六十公里 sixty kilometres per hour 2 every time; whenever: 他～次进那个书店都要买一本书. He would buy a book every time he visited that book shop.
每当(當) měidāng (连) when-

ever; every time: ～下雨，他都要背痛. His back aches whenever it rains.

每况愈下 měi kuàng yù xià steadily deteriorate; go from bad to worse

寐 mèi (名)〈书〉sleep: 梦～以求 long (or yearn) for sth. day and night

昧 mèi I (动) hide; conceal: 拾金不～ not pocket the money one happens to pick up II (形) be ignorent of: 愚～无知 ignorant or illiterate

昧心 mèixīn (动) (do evil) against one's conscience

魅 mèi (名) evil spirit; demon

魅力 mèilì (名) glamour; enchantment; fascination: 艺术～ artistic charm

妹 mèi (名) younger sister; sister (also as 妹妹)

媚 mèi (动) 1 flatter; fawn on; toady to; curry favour with 2 charming; fascinating; enchanting 春光明～ the spring scenery exudes radiance and charm

媚骨 mèigǔ (名) obsequiousness

媚外 mèiwài (动) fawn on foreign powers

闷 mēn I (形) 1 stuffy; close: 屋里人太多，空气太～. It's really stuffy with so many people in the room. 2 [of a sound muffled]: 说话～声～气的 speak in a muffled voice II (动)cover tightly: ～一会儿，茶味就出来了. Let the tea brew for a while and the flavour will come out. 把事儿～在心里 bottle unpleasant things up; brood over unpleasant things

see also mèn

闷气(氣) mēnqì (形)stuffy; close

闷热(熱) mēnrè (形) hot and stuffy; stifling hot

闷头(頭)儿 mēntóur (副) quietly; silently: ～干 work quietly; plod away silently

门(門) mén I (名) 1 door; gate; entrance: 前(后)～ front (back) door. 登～拜访 pay a call on sb. at his home 2 valve; switch: 气～ air valve. 电～ switch 3 way to do sth.; knack: 我新到，对这儿的事还不摸～. I'm new here. I don't know anything yet. 这件事有～了. The matter looks hopeful. 4 family: 豪～ wealthy and influential family 5 (religious) sect; school (of thought): 佛～ Buddhism 6 phylum II (量): 一～大炮 a cannon. 两～功课 two subjects (courses)

门当(當)户对(對) méndāng-hùduì be well-matched in social status (for marriage)

门道 méndào (名) 1 way to do sth. 2 social connections; contacts

门第 méndì (名) family status

门房 ménfáng (名) 1 porter's lodge 2 gatekeeper; doorman

门户 ménhù (名) 1 door; gate 2 gateway; important passageway 3 faction; sect: ～之见 sectarian bias

门禁 ménjìn (名) guarded entrance: ～森严 with the entrances heavily guarded

门警 ménjǐng (名) police guard at an entrance

门槛(檻) ménkǎn (名) threshold

门客 ménkè (名) retainer

门口 ménkǒu (名) entrance; doorway

门框 ménkuàng (名) doorframe

门帘(簾) ménlián (名) door curtain

门联(聯) ménlián (名) gatepost couplet

门路 ménlù (名) 1 social connections to be made use of; pull: 找～ seek help through one's social connections 2 knack; way: 摸到一点～ know the ropes

门面 ménmiàn (名) 1 the façade of a shop; shop front 2 appearance; façade: 装点～ keep up appearances; do some window dressing. ～话 formal meaningless remarks; lip service

门牌 ménpái (名) house number; house plate

门票 ménpiào (名) entrance ticket: 不收～ admission free

门市 ménshì (名) retail sales: ～部 retail department; sales department

门厅(廳) méntīng (名) entrance hall; portico

门庭若市 mén-tíng ruò shì The house is often crowded with visitors

门徒 méntú (名) disciple; follower

门外汉(漢) ménwàihàn (名) layman

门牙 ményá (名) front tooth

门诊 ménzhěn (名) outpatient

service (in a hospital): ～病人 outpatient; clinic patient. ～部 clinic; outpatient department

扪 mén (动) lay one's hand on

扪心自问 ménxīn zìwèn examine one's conscience

闷 mèn (形) 1 bored; depressed; in low spirits: 心里～得慌 feel bored stiff 2 tightly closed; sealed

see also mēn

闷棍 mèngùn (名) staggering blow (with a cudgel)

闷葫芦(蘆) mènhúlu (名) enigma; puzzle: 别人都知道了，只有他还装在～里. Everyone else knows about it, but he is still in the dark.

闷雷 mènléi (名) muffled thunder

闷闷不乐(樂) mènmèn bú lè (形) depressed; unhappy

闷气(氣) mènqì (名) the sulks: 生～ be sulky

焖 mèn (名) braise: ～牛肉 braised beef. ～饭 cook rice over a slow fire

们 men 1 [used after a personal pronoun or a noun to show plural number]: 我～ we. 你～ you. 孩子～ the children. 人～ people 2 [们 is not used when the pronoun or noun is preceded by a numeral or an intensifier: 三个教师 three teachers. 很多姑娘 many girls]

蒙 mēng I (动) 1 cheat; deceive: 你在～我吧? You're kidding me! 2 make a random guess: 你～对了. You've made a lucky guess! II (形) unconscious; senseless: 给打～了 be knocked senseless; be stunned by a blow

see also méng; Měng

蒙蒙亮 mēngmēngliàng (名) first glimmer of dawn; daybreak: 天刚～ at daybreak

蒙骗 mēngpiàn (动) deceive; hoodwink; delude

蒙头(頭)转(轉)向 mēngtóu zhuànxiàng lose one's bearings; one's brain is in a whirl; utterly confused

虻 méng (名) horsefly; gadfly: 牛～ gadfly

氓 méng (名) the common people

蒙 méng I (动) 1 cover: ～住眼睛 be blindfolded. ～头睡大觉 tuck oneself in and sleep like a log 2 thanks to: 承～指教，太感谢了. Thank you very much for your advice. ～你夸奖 thank you for your compliment II (名) ignorance: 启～ enlighten

see also mēng; Měng

蒙蔽 méngbì (动) deceive; hoodwink; pull the wool over sb.'s eyes: 广大人民群众是不会永远受～的. Not all the people can be fooled all the time.

蒙混 ménghùn (动) muddle through: ～过关 get by under false pretences

蒙昧 méngmèi (形) 1 uncivilized; uncultured; illiterate 2 ignorant; unenlightened

蒙蒙 méngméng (形) drizzly; misty: 细雨～ a fine rain. 烟雾～ misty

蒙受 méngshòu (动) suffer; sustain: ～损失 sustain a loss. ～耻辱 suffer humiliation

曚 méng (名) dim daylight

朦 méng

朦胧(朧) ménglóng (形) drowsy; half asleep: 睡眼～ eyes heavy with sleep; drowsy

朦 méng

朦胧(朧) ménglóng (形) dim; hazy; obscure: ～的景色 misty view

萌 méng (动) sprout; bud; germinate

萌发(發) méngfā (动) sprout; shoot: 树木～了新叶. Leaves are beginning to sprout from trees.

萌芽 méngyá (动) sprout; shoot; bud; rudiment: 消灭于～状态 nip in the bud

盟 méng (名) 1 alliance: 结～ form an alliance. ～兄 sworn brothers 2 league

盟国(國) méngguó (名) allied country; ally

盟军 méngjūn (名) allied forces

盟友 méngyǒu (名) ally

盟约 méngyuē (名) treaty of alliance

懵 měng (形) muddled

懵懂 měngdǒng (形) muddled; ignorant

蒙 Měng the Mongol nationality

see also mēng; méng

蒙古 Měnggǔ (名) Mongolia: ～人 Mongolian.～语 Mongol (language)
蒙古包 ménggǔbāo (名) yurt
蒙古族 ménggǔzú (名) the Mongol (Mongolian) nationality
锰 měng (名) manganese (Mn): ～结核 manganese nodule. ～钢 manganese steel
猛 měng (形) 1 fierce; violent; vigorous: ～虎 a fierce tiger. ～干 work vigorously. 产量～增 a sharp increase in output. 用力过～ use too much strength; overexert oneself 2 suddenly; abruptly: ～一转身 turn around sharply.
猛进(進) měngjìn (动) push ahead vigorously: 突飞～ advance by leaps and bounds
猛劲(勁)儿 měngjìnr (名) great vigour: 工作有股子～ work with vim and vigour
猛烈 měngliè (形) vigorous; fierce; violent: 发动～的进攻 launch a vigorous offensive. ～的炮火 heavy shellfire
猛禽 měngqín (名) bird of prey
猛然 měngrán (副) suddenly; abruptly: ～想起一件事 remember sth. in a flash. ～一拉 pull with a jerk
猛兽(獸) měngshòu (名) beast of prey
猛醒 měngxǐng (动) suddenly realize (or wake up) (also as "猛省")
梦(夢) mèng (名) dream: 做～ dream. 白日～ day dream
梦话 mènghuà (名) 1 words uttered in one's sleep: 说～ talk in one's sleep 2 nonsense; raving
梦幻 mènghuàn (名) dream; illusion
梦见(見) mèngjiàn (动) see in a dream; dream about: 昨晚她～自己上大学了. She dreamt about going to university last night.
梦境 mèngjìng (名) dreamland; dream-like world: 如入～ feel as if one were in a dream
梦寐 mèngmèi (名) dream; sleep: ～难忘 be unable to forget sth. even in one's dreams. ～以求 long for sth. day and night
梦乡(鄉) mèngxiāng (名) dreamland: 进入～ fall asleep
梦想 mèngxiǎng I (动) hope in vain; have a fond dream of: 他从未～过会搞得这么好. Little did he dream of doing so well. II (名) fond dream
梦呓(囈) mèngyì (名) (as 梦话) somniloquy
梦游症 mèngyóuzhèng (名) sleep-walking; somnambulism
孟 mèng
孟浪 mènglàng (形) rash; impetuous; impulsive: 不可～行事. Don't act on the spur of the moment.
咪 mī
咪咪 mīmī (名) 1 〈象〉 mew; miaow 2 smilingly: 笑～ be wreathed in smiles; be all smiles
眯 mī (动) 1 narrow (one's eyes): ～着眼瞧 squint at 2 take a nap: ～一会儿 take a short nap; have forty winks
see also mí
眯缝 mīfeng (动) narrow
靡 mí (形) waste: 奢～ wasteful; extravagant. ～费 waste; spend extravagantly
see also mǐ
糜 mí I (名) gruel II (形) 1 rotten 2 wasteful; extravagant
糜烂(爛) mílàn (形) 1 rotten; dissipated; debauched: 生活～ lead a dissipated life 2 〈医〉 erosion
迷 mí I (动) 1 be confused; be lost: ～路了. get lost.～失方向 lose one's bearings 2 be fascinated by: 她被他～住了. She is crazy about him. 看书入～了 be absorbed in reading. 这孩子玩游戏简直着～了 This child simply can't tear himself away from these games. 景色～人 fascinating scenery. 财～心窍 be obsessed by lust for wealth II (名) fan; enthusiast: 足球～ a football fan. 官～ a person who craves power
迷糊 míhu (形) 1 (of vision) dim: 看～了 be dazzled by (multi-colours; patterns, etc.) 2 dazed; muddled: 睡～了 dazed with sleep. 他这个人有点～. He's somewhat muddleheaded.
迷魂汤(湯) míhúntāng (名) magic potion: 灌～ flatter sb. lavishly
迷惑 míhuo (动) puzzle; confuse; perplex; baffle: 感到～不解 feel puzzled; feel perplexed. ～敌人 confuse the enemy
迷恋(戀) míliàn (动) indulge in; be infatuated with

迷茫 mímáng (形) **1** vast and hazy: 大雪纷飞,原野一片~. The vast plain was blurred by the swirling flakes of snow. **2** confused; perplexed; dazed: 神情~ look confused

迷失 míshī (动) lose (one's way, etc.): ~方向 lose one's bearings; get lost

迷途 mítú (名) wrong path: 误入~ go astray

迷惘 míwǎng (形) perplexed; at a loss

迷信 míxìn (名) **1** superstition: ~思想 superstitious ideas **2** blind faith; blind worship: 破除~ do away with blind faith

谜 mí (名) **1** riddle: 猜~ guess a riddle **2** enigma; mystery; puzzle

谜底 mídǐ (名) answer to a riddle

谜语 míyǔ (名) riddle; conundrum

弥(彌) mí (形) full; overflowing: ~漫 fill (the air, etc.) ~缝 try to gloss over or remedy a fault **3** more: 欲盖~彰 try to cover up a fault only to make it more glaring

弥补(補) míbǔ (动) make up; remedy; make good: ~损失 make up for (or make good) a loss. ~缺陷 remedy a defect

弥合 míhé (动) close; bridge: ~裂痕 close a rift

弥漫 mímàn (动) fill the air; spread all over the place: 硝烟~. The fumes of gunpowder filled the air.

弥天大谎 mítiān dàhuǎng (名) outrageous lie

靡 mǐ

see also mí

靡靡之音 mǐmǐzhī yīn (名) decadent music; cheap sentimental song

米 mǐ (名) **1** rice **2** shelled or husked seed: 花生~ peanut seed II (量) metre

米饭(飯) mǐfàn (名) cooked rice

米粉 mǐfěn (名) **1** ground rice **2** rice-flour noodles

米黄 mǐhuáng (名) cream colour

眯 mí (动) (of dust, etc.) get into one's eye: 我~了眼了. Something has got into my eyes.

see also mī

弭 mǐ (动) put down; get rid of; remove: ~患 remove the source of trouble

泌 mì (名) secrete

泌尿科 mìniàokē (名) urological department

秘 mì (名) secret: ~史 inside story

秘方 mìfāng (名) secret recipe: 祖传~ a secret family recipe

秘诀 mìjué (名) secret formula; secret

秘密 mìmì (形) secret; confidential: ~活动 clandestine activities. ~文件 confidential document. 保守~ keep (sth.) secret. 泄露~ disclose a secret

秘书(書) mìshū (名) secretary: 私人~ private secretary. 机要~ confidential secretary. ~处 secretariat. ~长 secretary-general

蜜 mì (名) honey

蜜蜂 mìfēng (名) honeybee; bee

蜜饯(餞) mìjiàn (名) preserved fruit

蜜月 mìyuè (名) honeymoon

密 mì (形) **1** dense; close; thick: ~林 dense (or thick) forest. ~不透风 airtight **2** close; intimate: ~友 close friend **3** meticulous: 周~ carefully considered; meticulous **4** secret: 绝~ top secret; strictly confidential. ~电 cipher telegram

密布 mìbù (动) densely covered: 阴云~. Dark clouds cover the sky.

密度 mìdù (名) density; thickness: 人口~ population density

密封 mìfēng (动) **1** seal up: ~的文件 sealed documents **2** seal airtight: ~的容器 hermetically sealed chamber

密集 mìjí (形) dense; concentrated; crowded together: 人口~ densely populated. 枪声~ heavy gunfire

密件 mìjiàn (名) confidential paper or letter; classified document

密码 mìmǎ (名) cipher; secret code

密密麻麻 mìmìmámá (形) close and numerous; thickly dotted: 天上的星星~ The sky is thickly studded with stars.

密谋 mìmóu (动) conspire; plot; scheme

密切 mìqiè I (形) close; intimate: ~配合 act in close coordination with. ~相关 be closely related II (副) carefully; closely: ～注视 watch closely; follow with the greatest attention

密谈 mìtán (名) secret talk

密探 mìtàn (名) secret agent; spy

密植 mìzhí (名) close planting

觅 mì (动) look for; seek: ～食 (usu. for birds or animals) look for food

眠 mián (名) **1** sleep: 不～之夜 a sleepless night **2** dormancy: 冬～ hibernation

棉 mián (名) cotton: ～纺织品 cotton textiles. ～衣 (裤) cotton-padded clothes (trousers)

棉袄(襖) mián'ǎo (名) cotton-padded jacket

棉被 miánbèi (名) a quilt with cotton wadding

棉布 miánbù (名) cotton cloth; cotton

棉纺 miánfǎng (名) cotton spinning: ～厂 cotton mill

棉花 miánhua (名) cotton: ～签 (cotton) swab

棉毛衫 miánmáoshān (名) cotton (interlock) jersey

棉纱 miánshā (名) cotton yarn

棉田 miántián (名) cotton field

棉线(綫) miánxiàn (名) cotton thread; cotton

棉絮 miánxù (名) a cotton wadding (for a quilt)

棉籽 miánzǐ (名) cottonseed

绵 mián (形) **1** soft **2** continuous

绵亘 miángèn (动) (of mountains, etc.) stretch in an unbroken chain

绵绵 miánmián (形) continuous, unbroken: 春雨～. The spring rain never ceases to fall.

绵延 miányán (动) (usu. of mountain ranges) be continuous; stretch long and unbroken

绵羊 miányáng (名) sheep

腼 miǎn

腼腆 miǎntian (形) shy; bashful: 这个人有些～. He is a little shy.

缅 miǎn (形) remote; far back

缅怀(懷) miǎnhuái (动) cherish the memory of; recall: ～往事 recall past events. ～战争中牺牲的战士们. We cherish the memory of the fallen heroes in the war.

免 miǎn (动) **1** excuse (or free) sb. from sth.; exempt: ～税 duty-free; exempt from taxation. ～试 be excused from an examination. ～去手续 dispense with the formalities. ～学费 waive tuition **2** remove from office; dismiss: 任～(事项) appointments and removals **3** avoid; avert; escape: 再检查一遍以～出错. Check it once more to avoid possible mistakes. **4** not allowed: 闲人～进 No admittance except on business.

免不了 miǎnbùliǎo (形) unavoidable: 管这么大的工厂, 困难是～的. To run such a big factory there are bound to be difficulties.

免除 miǎnchú (动) **1** avoid; prevent **2** excuse; exempt; relieve: ～债务 remit a debt

免得 miǎndé (连) so as not to; so as to avoid: 穿上大衣, ～感冒. Put on your overcoat so that you won't catch cold. 我再说明一下自己的观点, ～引起误解. To avoid any misunderstanding, let me clearly reiterate my position. 你回来时给我买几张邮票, ～我自己又跑一趟. Buy me some stamps on your way back to save me a trip.

免费 miǎnfèi free of charge; free: ～医疗 free medical care. ～入场 admission free

免冠 miǎnguān (形) without a hat on; bareheaded: 半身～正面相片 a half-length, bareheaded, full-faced photo

免票 miǎnpiào (名) **1** free pass; free ticket **2** free of charge

免疫 miǎnyì (名) immunity (from disease)

免职(職) miǎnzhí (动) remove sb. from office

免罪 miǎnzuì (动) exempt from punishment

冕 miǎn (名) crown: 加～(礼) coronation

勉 miǎn (名) **1** encourage; urge: 互～ encourage one another. 自～ spur oneself on **2** try to do what is almost beyond one's power or act against one's will

勉励(勵) miǎnlì (动) encourage; urge

勉强 miǎnqiǎng I (形) **1** do one's best despite difficulty or lack of experience: 弄不了就别～弄了. Leave it if you can't manage. Don't over-exert yourself. **2** reluctantly; grudgingly: ～同意 reluctantly agree. ～地笑了笑 force a smile **3** inadequate; unconvincing; farfetched: 这个理由很～. This is a lame excuse. **4** barely enough: ～

的多数 a bare majority. ～维持生活 eke out a bare living; scrape along. ～够用 earn just enough to get by II (动) force sb. to do sth. 要是他不愿意去，就不要～他了. Don't force him to go if he doesn't want to.

娩 miǎn (名) childbirth: 分～ childbirth; delivery

面 miàn I (名) 1 face: ～对～ face to face. ～带笑容 have a smile on one's face 2 surface; top; cover: 水～ the surface of the water 3 side; aspect: 四～进攻 attack from all sides 4 [used to form a noun of locality]: 上～ above. 下～ under. 里～ inside. 外～ outside. 前～ in the front. 后～ at the back. 左～ the left side. 北～ the northern side 5 scale; range: 知识～ the scope of one's knowledge. 受灾～ (disaster) afflicted area 6 (麵) wheat flour; flour: 白～ wheat flour. 玉米～ corn flour 7 powder: 胡椒～ ground peper. 辣椒～ chilly powder II (副) personally; directly: ～谈 interview; face-to-face talk. ～告 deliver a message III (量) [used for flat and smooth objects]: 一～镜子 a mirror. 二～旗帜 two flags

面包 miànbāo (名) bread: ～房 bakery

面额 miàn'é (名) denomination: 各种～的纸币 bank-notes of different denominations

面粉 miànfěn (名) wheat flour; flour

面红耳赤 miànhóng-ěrchì flush red: 他们争得～. They argued till their faces turned red with excitement (or anger).

面糊 miànhú (名) paste

面黄肌瘦 miànhuáng-jīshòu (形) lean and haggard; pale and thin.

面积(積) miànjì (名) area: 总～ the total area. 棉花种植～ the acreage under cotton. 展览会～为三千平方米. The exhibition covers a floor space of 3,000 square metres.

面颊(頰) miànjiá (名) cheek

面具 miànjù (名) mask: 防毒～ gas mask

面孔 miànkǒng (名) face: 板起～ put on a stern expression

面临(臨) miànlín (动) be faced with; be confronted with; be up against: ～一场严重的危机 be faced with a serious crisis

面貌 miànmào (名) 1 face; features 2 (of things) appearance; look; aspect: 精神～ mental outlook. ～一新 take on a new look (or aspect)

面面相觑 miànmiàn xiāng qù gaze at each other in blank dismay; exchange uneasy glances

面目 miànmù (名) 1 face; features; visage: ～清秀 delicate features. ～可憎 repulsive appearance 2 (of things) appearance; look: ～全非 be changed or distorted beyond recognition

面庞(龐) miànpáng (名) contours of the face; face: 圆胖的～ a plump, round face

面洽 miànqià (动) discuss in person: 详情请与来人～. As to details, you can work them out with the bearer of the note.

面前 miànqián (副) in front of, in the face of; before

面容 miànróng (名) facial features; face: ～消瘦 look wan

面色 miànsè (名) complexion: ～红润 have ruddy cheeks. ～苍白 look pale

面纱 miànshā (名) veil

面熟 miànshú (形) look familiar: 他看着～，就是想不起来是谁. He looks familiar but I simply can't remember his name.

面生 miànshēng (名) look unfamiliar

面条(條) miàntiáo (名) noodles

面团(團) miàntuán (名) dough

面向 miànxiàng (动) turn one's face to; turn in the direction of; face: 科技～经济建设. Science and technology are geared to economic development.

面谢 miànxiè (动) thank sb. in person

面罩 miànzhào (名) face guard

面子 miànzi (名) 1 outer part; outside; self-respect: 大衣的～ the outside of an overcoat 2 reputation; face: 爱～ be anxious to save one's face. 丢～ lose face. 给～ take care not to offend one's susceptibilities

苗 miáo (名) 1 sprout; seedling: 麦～儿 wheat seedling 2 sth. resembling a young plant: 鱼～ fish fry. 火～儿 flame

苗圃 miáopǔ (名) nursery (of young plants)

苗条(條) miáotiao (形) (of a woman) slender; slim

苗头(頭) miáotou (名) symptom of a trend; a straw in the wind:

不良倾向的～ symptoms of unhealthy tendencies.～不对 Things are not going the right way.

描 miáo (动) 1 trace; copy: ～图样 trace a design 2 touch up; retouch: ～眉 pencil one's eyebrows

描画(畫) miáohuà (动) draw; paint; depict; describe: 风景之美难以用语言来～. The beauty of the scenery beggars description.

描绘(繪) miáohuì (动) depict; describe; portray: 这部小说生动地～了农村发生的巨大变化. The novel vividly depicts the great changes that have taken place in the countryside.

描述 miáoshù (动) describe

描写(寫) miáoxiě (动) describe; depict; portray

瞄 miáo (动) aim

瞄准 miáozhǔn (动) take aim: ～靶心 aim at the bull's-eye

杪 miǎo (名) 1 the tip of a twig: 树～ tree top 2 end (of a year, month or season): 岁～ the end of the year; year-end

秒 miǎo (名) second (= 1/60 of a minute)

秒表 miǎobiǎo (名) stopwatch

渺 miǎo (形) 1 distant and indistinct; vague: 烟波浩～ (of lake, etc.) vast and misty. ～无人迹 remote and uninhabited 2 tiny; insignificant: ～不足道 insignificant; negligible; of no consequence

渺茫 miǎománg (形) remote; vague; uncertain: 音信～ haven't heard from sb. for ages. 前途～. The future is full of uncertainties

渺小 miǎoxiǎo (形) tiny; negligible; insignificant (of abstract matters)

邈 miǎo (形) ‹书› far away; remote

藐 miǎo

藐视 miǎoshì (动) despise; look down upon; belittle

藐小 miǎoxiǎo (形) tiny; negligible; insignificant; paltry

庙(廟) miào (名) temple: ～会 temple fair

庙宇 miàoyǔ (名) temple

妙 miào (形) 1 wonderful; excellent; fine: 这主意真～. This idea is really great. 绝～的讽刺 a supreme irony 2 ingenious; clever; subtle: 莫名其～ incomprehensible. ～计 wise move; brilliant idea

妙趣横生 miàoqù héngshēng full of wit and humour; brim over with interest

妙手回春 miàoshǒu huí chūn (of a doctor) ingeniously bring the dying back to life

灭(滅) miè (动) 1 (of a light, fire, etc.) go out: 灯～了. The lights went out. 2 extinguish; put out: ～火 put out a fire 3 destroy; wipe out; exterminate: ～鼠 kill rats

灭顶 mièdǐng (动) be drowned; be swamped

灭迹 mièjì (动) destroy the evidence (of one's evildoing)

灭绝 mièjué (动) become extinct: 一些珍奇动物现已面临～的危险. Some rare animals are in danger of becoming extinct.

灭绝人性 mièjué rénxìng (形) inhuman; savage

灭口 mièkǒu (动) (of a criminal) kill a witness or accomplice to prevent leakage of information

灭亡 mièwáng (动) perish; die out; be doomed: 自取～ court destruction

蔑 miè (动) 1 slight; disdain: 轻～ disdain 2 smear: 诬～ slander; vilify

蔑视 mièshì (动) despise; scorn; show contempt for

篾 miè (名) 1 thin bamboo strip 2 the rind of reed or sorghum

民 mín (名) 1 the people: ～众 the masses. ～歌 folk song. 军～ armymen and civilians. ～以食为天. Food is the basic need of man. 2 a member of a nationality: 藏～ a Tibetan 3 a person of a certain occupation: 农～ peasant. 渔～ fisherman. 牧～ herdsman

民办(辦) mínbàn (形) run by the community: ～小学 community primary school

民兵 mínbīng (名) militia; militiaman: militiawoman

民不聊生 mín bù liáo shēng the people have no means of livelihood;

民法 mínfǎ (名) civil law

民愤 mínfèn (名) public indignation

民工 míngōng (名) a labourer

working on a public project
民国(國) Mínguó (名) the Republic of China (1912-1949)
民航 mínháng (名) civil aviation: 中国～总局 CAAC (General Administration of Civil Aviation of China)
民间 mínjiān (形) 1 of the common people; popular; folk: ～传说 folk legend; folklore. ～故事 folktale; folk story 2 nongovernmental; people-to-people: ～团体 nongovernmental organizations
民警 mínjǐng (名) people's police; people's policeman
民情 mínqíng (名) 1 popular customs 2 public feeling
民权(權) mínquán (名) civil rights
民生 mínshēng (名) the people's livelihood: 国计～ the national economy and the people's livelihood
民事 mínshì (名) 〈法〉 relating to civil law; civil: ～案件 civil case
民俗 mínsú (名) folk custom; folkways: ～学 folklore
民心 mínxīn (名) popular feelings; common aspirations of the people: 深得～ enjoy the ardent support of the people
民谣 mínyáo (名) folk rhyme
民意 mínyì (名) the will of the people: ～测验 public opinion poll; poll
民用 mínyòng (名) for civil use; civil: ～航空 civil aviation
民乐(樂) mínyuè (名) music, for traditional instruments
民政 mínzhèng (名) civil administration
民脂民膏 mínzhī-míngāo (名) wealth accumulated by the people with blood and sweat
民众(衆) mínzhòng (名) the masses; the common people: ～团体 people's organization; mass organization
民主 mínzhǔ I (名) democracy II (形) democratic: 作风～ a democratic work-style. ～人士 democratic personages. ～协商 democratic consultation
民主党(黨)派 mínzhǔ dǎngpài (名) democratic parties
民主集中制 mínzhǔ-jízhōngzhì democratic centralism
民族 mínzú (名) nation; nationality: 中华～ the Chinese nation. 少数～ ethnic group; minority nationality. ～败类 scum of a nation. ～利己主义 national egoism. ～自决 national self-determination

悯

mǐn (动) pity: 怜～ commiserate; pity

敏

mǐn (形) quick; nimble; agile
敏感 mǐngǎn (形) sensitive; susceptible: 对天气变化很～ be very susceptible to changes in weather 对尘埃很～ allergic to dust
敏捷 mǐnjié (形) quick; nimble; agile: 动作～quick or agile in movement
敏锐 mǐnruì (形) sharp; acute; keen: 目光～ have sharp eyes. 嗅觉～ have a keen sense of smell

泯

mǐn (动) vanish; die out: ～灭 die out; disappear; vanish

抿

mǐn (动) 1 smooth (hair, etc.) with a wet brush 2 close lightly; tuck: ～着嘴笑 smile with slightly closed lips 3 sip: ～一口酒 take a sip of the wine

冥

míng (形) 1 dark; obscure: 幽～ dark hell; the nether world 2 deep; profound: ～思 be deep in thought 3 dull; stupid: ～顽 thickheaded; stupid 4 underworld; the nether world
冥思苦想 míngsī-kǔxiǎng think long and hard; rack (or cudgel) one's brains
冥顽 míngwán (形) 〈书〉 thickheaded; stupid: ～不灵 impenetrably thickheaded

瞑

míng
瞑目 míngmù (动) die with eyes closed; die without regret: 死不～ die with regret

螟

míng (名) snout moth's larva
螟虫(蟲) míngchóng (名) snout moth's larva

明

míng I (形) 1 bright; brilliant: ～月 a bright moon. 灯火通～ be brightly lit 2 clear; distinct: 方向不～. The orientation is not clear. 指～出路 point the way out 3 open; overt; explicit: ～枪暗箭 both overt and covert attacks. ～说了吧 frankly speaking 4 sharp-eyed; clearsighted: 眼～手快 quick of eye and deft of hand 5 next: ～天 tomorrow. ～年 next year II (名) sight: 双目失～ go blind in both eyes III (动) know; understand: 不~真相 not know the facts; be ignorant of the actual situation

明暗 míng-àn (名) light and shade

明摆(擺)着 míngbǎizhe (形) obvious; clear; plain: 一个~的问题 an obvious problem

明白 míngbai I (形) 1 clear; obvious; plain: 问题讲得很~. The problem is clearly expounded. 2 frank; explicit; unequivocal: 不明不白的关系 equivocal relationship. 你还是跟他讲~了好. It would be best to let him know everything about it. 3 sensible; reasonable: ~人 a sensible person II (动) understand; realize; know: 你~我的意思吗? Do you see what I mean? ~事理 have good sense. 我~了. Oh, I see.

明辨是非 míng biàn shì-fēi make a clear distinction between right and wrong

明察秋毫 míng chá qiūháo (usu. of officials) be sharp-minded enough to perceive the minutest detail; have an extremely discerning eye

明畅(暢) míngchàng (形) lucid and smooth

明澈 míngchè (形) bright and limpid; crystal clear: ~的眼睛 bright and limpid eyes. 湖水~如镜. The lake is as bright and clear as a mirror.

明晃晃 mínghuǎnghuǎng (形) shining; gleaming: ~的刺刀 gleaming bayonets

明火执(執)仗 mínghuǒ-zhízhàng do evil openly

明净 míngjìng (形) bright and clean: 橱窗~ a bright and clean shop window.

明快 míngkuài (形) 1 lucid and lively; sprightly: ~的笔调 a lucid and lively style. ~的节奏 sprightly rhythm 2 straightforward: ~的性格 (of a person) a forthright character

明朗 mínglǎng (形) 1 bright and clear: ~的天空 a clear sky 2 clear; obvious: 事情的性质逐渐~了. The nature of the case is being brought to light. 态度~ take a clear-cut stand 3 forthright; bright and cheerful; breezy: ~的性格 an open and forthright character. 这些作品都具有~的风格. All these works are written in a vivid, broadly cheerful style.

明亮 míngliàng (形) 1 bright; well-lit: 灯光~ be brightly lit 2 bright; shining: ~的眼睛 bright eyes. 星光~. The stars are shining. 3 become clear: 我心里~多了. I'm much clearer on the matter now.

明了(瞭) míngliǎo I (动) understand; be clear about: ~实际情况 have a clear understanding of the actual situation II (形) clear; plain: 简单~ simple and clear

明媚 míngmèi (形) bright and beautiful: 春光~ The spring days are bright and charming.

明明 míngmíng (副) obviously; undoubtedly: 别骗我了,你~是这个意思嘛. Don't you think you can fool me. This is obviously what you mean.

明目张(張)胆(膽) míngmù-zhāngdǎn (副) brazenly; flagrantly

明确(確) míngquè (形) 1 clear and definite; unequivocal: ~的立场 a clear-cut stand. ~的答复 a definite answer. 分工~ clear divison of labour 2 make clear; make definite: ~当前的任务 be clear about (our) present tasks

明日 míngrì (名) 1 tomorrow 2 the near future

明文 míngwén (名) (of laws, regulations, etc.) proclaimed in writing: ~规定 stipulate in explicit terms

明晰 míngxī (形) clear; distinct: 雾散了,远处的村庄越来越~了. As the mist thinned, the village in the distance became more and more distinct.

明显(顯) míngxiǎn (形) clear; obvious: ~的进步 marked progress. 很~ evidently

明信片 míngxìnpiàn (名) postcard

明星 míngxīng (名) star: 电影~ film star; movie star

明眼人 míngyǎnrén (名) a person of good sense

明哲保身 míng zhé bǎo shēn be worldly wise and play safe in all activities

明争暗斗(鬥) míngzhēng-àndòu both open strife and veiled rivalry; factional strife, both overt and covert

明证 míngzhèng (名) clear proof; evidence

明知故犯 míngzhī-gùfàn commit an offence with the full know-

ledge of its implication; do sth. which one knows is wrong
明知故问 míngzhī-gùwèn ask while knowing the answer
明智 míngzhì (形) sensible: 他这样决定是～的. It was wise of him to make such a decision.

鸣 míng I (名) 1 the cry of birds, animals or insects: 鸟～ the chirp of a bird. 鸡～ the crow of a cock 2 ringing: 耳～ ringing in the ears II (动) express; voice; air: 自～得意 be ostensibly smug. ～笛 blow a whistle. ～礼炮二十一响 fire a 21-gun salute
鸣禽 míngqín (名) songbird; singing bird
鸣冤叫屈 míngyuān-jiàoqū complain and call for redress; voice grievances

名 míng I (名) 1 name: 你叫什么～字? What's your name? 给孩子起个～儿 name a baby. 以…为～ in the name of …; under the pretext of … 2 fame; reputation: 不为～,不为利 seek neither fame nor wealth II (形) well-known; famous; celebrated: ～电影演员 a film star. ～画 a famous painting III (量) [for persons]: 两百～代表 two hundred delegates. 第一～ come in first; win first place
名不虚传(傳) míng bù xūchuán enjoy a well-deserved reputation; live up to one's reputation
名不副实(實) míng bù fù shí The name falls short of the reality
名册 míngcè (名) register; roll
名产(產) míngchǎn (名) famous product
名称(稱) míngchēng (名) name (of a thing or organization)
名词 míngcí (名) 1 noun 2 term: 技术～ technical term
名次 míngcì (名) position in a name list; place in a competition: 按比赛成绩排列～ arrange the names of contestants in the order of their results
名存实(實)亡 míngcún-shíwáng exist only in name
名单(單) míngdān (名) name list: 候选人～ list of candidates
名额 míng'é (名) the number of people assigned or allowed: 代表～ the number of deputies to be elected or sent. 招生～ the number of students to be enrolled; enrolment. ～有限 the number of people allowed is limited
名贵 míngguì (形) famous and precious; rare: ～药材 rare medicinal herbs. 这只花瓶十分～. This vase is priceless.
名利 mínglì (名) fame and gain
名列前茅 míng liè qiánmáo be among the best of the successful candidates; come out at the top
名流 míngliú (名) distinguished personages; celebrities: 社会～ noted public figures
名目 míngmù (名) names of things; items: ～繁多 a multitude of items; names of every description. 巧立～ invent all imaginable terms (as pretexts for exorbitant taxes or to pad an expense account)
名牌 míngpái (名) 1 famous brand: ～香烟 a famous brand of cigarettes. ～优质产品 brand-name and quality goods 2 nameplate; name tag
名片 míngpiàn (名) visiting card; calling card
名气(氣) míngqì (名) <口> reputation; fame; name: 很有点～ enjoy a considerable reputation; be quite well-known
名人 míngrén (名) famous person
名声(聲) míngshēng (名) reputation; repute; renown: ～很坏 be notorious. 享有好～ enjoy a good reputation. ～在外 be quite well known
名胜(勝) míngshèng (名) well-known scenic spot: ～古迹 scenic spots and historical sites
名堂 míngtang (名) 1 variety; item: 这个剧团虽小,～可真不少. Small as it is, this troupe has an amazingly large repertoire. 鬼～ dirty trick. 你在搞什么～? What are you up to? 2 result; achievement: 他决心要搞出点～来. He is determined to achieve something. 这样谈下去,恐怕谈不出什么～. I'm afraid it will get us nowhere if we go on like this. 3 what lies behind sth.; reason: 他突然离开伦敦, 这里面一定有～. There must be something behind his sudden departure from London.
名望 míngwàng (名) fame and prestige: 有～的大夫 a famous doctor
名下 míngxià (名) under sb.'s name: 这笔帐记在我～吧. Charge these expenses to my account.
名义(義) míngyì I(名) 1 name: 我以总统的～ in my capacity as

president. 代表学院并以个人的～ on behalf of the college and in my own name II(形) nominal; in name: 他只不过～上是我们的经理. He is nothing but our nominal manager.

名誉(譽) míngyù (名) 1 fame; reputation 2 honorary: ～主席 honorary chairman

名正言顺 míng zhèng-yánshùn perfectly justifiable

名著 míngzhù (名) masterpiece: 文学～ a literary masterpiece

名字 míngzi (名) name

铭 míng I (名) inscription: 座右～ motto II (动) engrave: ～诸肺腑 be engraved in one's memory

铭记 míngjì (动) engrave on one's mind; always remember

铭刻 míngkè (动) inscribe; engrave on one's mind

酩 míng

酩酊大醉 míngdǐng dàzuì be dead drunk

命 mìng (名) 1 life: 救～! Help! 逃～ run for one's life. ～在旦夕 be on one's last legs 2 lot; fate; destiny: 苦～ hard lot; cruel fate 3 order; command: 待～ await orders. ～题 set the question; set the paper

命定 mìngdìng (形) determinded by fate; predestined

命根子 mìnggēnzi (名) lifeblood; one's very life

命令 mìnglìng (名) order; command: 下～ issue an order. 服从～ obey orders. ～句 imperative sentence

命脉(脈) mìngmài (名) lifeline; lifeblood: 水利是农业的～. Irrigation is the lifeblood of agriculture.

命名 mìngmíng (动) give a name to (e.g. a building): 伦敦的大钟是以本杰明·霍尔～的. The Big Ben in London is named after Sir Benjamin Hall.

命运(運) mìngyùn (名) destiny; fate; lot: 掌握自己的～ take one's destiny in one's own hand

命中 mìngzhòng (动) hit the target; score a hit: 她第一枪就～靶心. Her first shot hit the bull's-eye.

谬 miù (名) wrong; false: ～见 a wrong view. 大～不然 be entirely wrong or grossly mistaken

谬论(論) miùlùn (名) fallacy; false (or absurd) theory

谬误(誤) miùwù (名) falsehood; error; mistake: ～百出 full of mistakes; teem with errors

摸 mō (动) 1 feel; stroke; touch: 这衣料～着很软. This material feels soft. 不要～那个按钮. Don't touch that button. 2 feel for; grope for; fumble: ～着上楼. grope one's way upstairs. 从手提包里～出一支笔 fish out a pen from her handbag 3 try to find out; feel out; sound out: ～清情况 try to find out how things stand. ～不着头脑 unable to make head or tail of sth. ～透他的脾气 get to know him (or his temperament) well

摸底 mōdǐ (动) know (or find out) the real situation: 下基层去～ go down to the grass roots units to find out about the real situation. 我想摸他的底. I am thinking of sounding him out.

摸索 mōsuo (动) 1 grope; feel about; fumble: 他们～着走下黑暗的甬道. They felt their way down the dark passage. 2 try to find out: ～熊猫的生活规律 try to find out the habits of the panda

磨 mó (动) 1 rub: ～墨 rub an ink stick against an ink stone. 这只鞋～脚. My shoe's rubbing. 你大衣的胳膊肘上～了一个洞. You've rubbed a hole in the elbow of your coat. 手上～了一个泡. His hand was blistered from the rubbing. 轮胎～平了. The tyre is badly worn (out). 2 sharpen; polish; grind: ～刀 sharpen a knife. ～成粉末 grind sth. into powder. ～大理石 polish marble 3 dawdle; while away (time): ～时间 kill time. 快走吧,别～时间了. Stop dawdling and get going. 4 wear down; torment: 多跟她～一～她就会答应的. She will agree if you keep on at her. 这病真～人! What a torment this illness is!
see also mò

磨蹭 móceng (动) move slowly; dawdle: 别～了! Stop dawdling!

磨床 móchuáng (名) grinding machine; grinder

磨炼(煉) móliàn (动) temper oneself; steel oneself

磨灭(滅) mómiè (动) wear away, efface; obliterate: 不可～的功勋 ineffaceable achievements. 留下不可～的印象 leave an indeli-

ble impression
磨损 mósǔn (名) wear and tear
磨洋工 mó yánggōng (动) loaf on the job; dawdle along

蘑 mó (名) mushroom
蘑菇 mógu (名) 1 mushroom 2 worry; pester; keep on at: 你别跟她～了. Don't pester her. 3 dawdle; dillydally: 已经晚了，你还在这里～! It's late already. Why are you still dawdling around here!

摩 mó (动) 1 rub; scrape; touch: ～天大楼 sky scraper 2 mull over; study: 揣～ try to fathom
摩擦 mócā I (动) rub II (名) friction; clash: ～生电. Friction generates electricity. 与某人发生～ have a brush with sb.
摩登 módēng (形) modern; fashionable
摩拳擦掌 móquán-cāzhǎng be eager for a fight; yearn for the fray
摩托 mótuō (名) motor: ～车 motorcycle

魔 mó (名) 1 evil spirit; demon; monster: 着了～似的 like one possessed; under a charm 2 magic; mystic: ～力 magic power
魔怪 móguài (名) demons and monsters
魔鬼 móguǐ (名) devil; demon; monster
魔力 mólì (名) magic power; magic; charm
魔术(術) móshù (名) magic; conjuring: ～演员 magician; conjurer
魔王 mówáng (名) 1 Prince of the Devils 2 tyrant; despot; fiend
魔掌 mózhǎng (名) evil hands; devil's clutches
魔爪 mózhǎo (名) devil's claws; tentacles

谟 mó (名)〈书〉 plan: 宏～ a grand plan; a great project

模 mó (名) 1 pattern; standard: 楷～ model; paragon 2 imitate 3〈简〉(模范) model: 劳～ model worker
see also mú
模范 mófàn (名) model; fine example: 劳动～ model worker. ～事迹 exemplary deeds
模仿 mófǎng (动) imitate; copy; mimic
模糊 móhu I (形) blurred; indistinct; dim; vague: 字迹～了 the writing is faded. ～的印象 a vague idea of sth. II (动) obscure; confuse; mix up: ～两者的界限 blur the line of distinction of the two
模棱两可 móléng liǎngkě equivocal; ambiguous: ～的态度 an equivocal attitude
模拟(擬) mónǐ (动) imitate; simulate: ～测验 mock exam. ～飞行 simulated flight
模特儿 mótèr (名) model
模型 móxíng (名) 1 model: 船的～ a model of a ship; a model ship 2 mould; matrix; pattern

摹 mó (动) copy; trace: 临～ copy a model of calligraphy or painting
摹本 móběn (名) facsimile; copy
摹拟(擬) mónǐ (动) imitate; simulate

膜 mó (名) 1 membrane: 细胞～ cell membrane. 2 film; thin coating: 塑料薄～ plastic film
膜拜 móbài (动) worship: 顶礼～ prostrate oneself in worship; pay homage to

馍(饃) mó (名) steamed bun; steamed bread

抹 mǒ (动) 1 apply; smear; put on: ～点雪花膏 put on a little vanishing cream. 面包上～点黄油 spread some butter on a piece of bread. ～药膏 apply ointment 2 wipe; erase: ～眼泪 wipe one's eyes. ～掉这几个字. Cross out these few words.
see also mā; mò
抹黑 mǒhēi (动) blacken sb.'s name; throw mud at; discredit
抹杀(殺) mǒshā (动) blot out; obliterate: ～事实 deny the facts. ～成绩 negate the achievements. 一笔～ write off at one stroke

磨 mò I (名) mill; millstones: 推～ use a handmill. 电～ electric mill II (动) grind; mill: ～豆腐 grind soya beans to make bean curd
see also mó
磨坊 mòfáng (名) mill (also as 磨房)
磨盘(盤) mòpán (名) millstones

末 mò (名) 1 tip; end 2 end; last stage: ～班车 the last bus. 周～ weekend. 明～ the end of the Ming Dynasty 3 nonessentials; minor details: 本～倒置 put the cart before the horse 4 powder; dust: 茶

叶～儿 powdered tea; tea dust. 锯～ sawdust. 肉～ minced meat
末了 mòliǎo last; finally; in the end: 但～他还是去. But he left eventually.
末路 mòlù (名) impasse; doom: 穷途～ have come to a dead end
末年 mònián (名) last years of a dynasty or reign
末期 mòqī (名) final phase; last stage: 五十年代～ in the late fifties. 第二次世界大战～ the last stage of the Second World War
末梢 mòshāo (名) tip; end: ～神经 nerve ending
末尾 mòwěi (名) end: 书～ at the end of a book
末叶(葉) mòyè (名) last years of a century
沫 mò (名) foam; froth: 啤酒～ froth on beer. 肥皂～ lather
茉 mò
茉莉 mòli (名) jasmine: ～花茶 jasmine tea
抹 mò (动) daub; plaster: ～墙 plaster a wall. ～灰 plastering
see also mā; mǒ
抹不开(開) mòbukāi feel embarrassed: 怕他脸上～ afraid of embarrassing him
秣 mò I (名) fodder II (动) feed animals
秣马(馬)厉(厲)兵 mònmǎ-lìbīng feed the horses and sharpen the weapons — prepare for battle
莫 mò (副) not: 非公～入 No admittance except on business. 请～见怪. Please don't take it to heart
莫不 mòbù there's no one who doesn't or isn't: ～为之感动 There was no one who was unmoved.
莫测高深 mòcè gāoshēn (形) enigmatic; unfathomable
莫大 mòdà (形) greatest; utmost: ～的幸福 the greatest happiness. 感到～的光荣 feel greatly honoured. ～的侮辱 a gross insult
莫非 mòfēi <副> can it be possible that: 这人～就是我当年的同学? Could this man be my old school friend?
莫名其妙 mò míng qí miào be unable to make head or tail of sth.; be baffled: 你这些话真叫我～. It puzzles me that you should have made such remarks. 她～地哭了起来. Quite unexpectedly she burst out crying. (also as 莫明其妙)
莫逆 mònì (形) very friendly; intimate: ～之交 bosom friends
莫须有 mòxūyǒu (形) groundless; fabricated: ～的罪名 a fabricated (or unwarranted) charge
漠 mò (名) 1 desert 沙～ desert 2 indifferent; unconcerned: 冷～ cold and indifferent
漠不关(關)心 mò bù guānxīn indifferent; apathetic
漠漠 mòmò (形) 1 misty; foggy 2 vast and lonely: ～荒原 a vast expanse of wasteland
漠然 mòrán (副) indifferently; apathetically: ～置之 look on the problem with unconcern; treat the matter with complete indifference
漠视 mòshì (动) ignore; overlook; treat with indifference: ～群众的利益是根本不允许的. It is absolutely impermissible to ignore the interest of the masses.
寞 mò (形) lonely; solitary: 寂～ lonely; loneliness
陌 mò (名) a footpath between fields
陌路 mòlù (名) <书> stranger: 视同～ be treated like a stranger
陌生 mòshēng (形) strange; unfamiliar: ～人 stranger
蓦 mò (副) suddenly: ～地 suddenly; unexpectedly; all of a sudden, ～然 suddenly
墨 mò I (名) 1 ink; ink stick: 研～ rub an ink stick on an inkstone. 油～ printing ink II 形 black; dark: ～绿 dark green. 一个～黑的夜晚 one pitch-dark night
墨迹 mòjì (名) 1 ink marks: ～未干 before the ink is dry 2 sb.'s writing or painting: 这是鲁迅的～. This is Lu Xun's calligraphy.
墨镜 mòjìng (名) sunglasses
墨守成规 mò shǒu chéngguī stick to convention; stay in a rut
墨水 mòshuǐ (名) 1 ink 2 book learning: 他肚子里还有点～. He's a bit of a scholar.
墨汁 mòzhī (名) prepared Chinese ink
默 mò (形) silent: ～不作声 keep silent 2 write from memory: ～生字 write the new words from memory
默哀 mò'āi (动) stand in silent

tribute: ～三分钟 observe three minutes' silence

默默 mòmò (副) quietly; silently: ～无言 remain speechless. ～无闻 unknown to the public

默契 mòqì (名) tacit agreement (or understanding): 达成～ reach a tacit agreement

默然 mòrán (形) silent; speechless: ～无语 fall silent

默认(認) mòrèn (动) tacitly approve; acquiesce (in)

默写(寫) mòxiě (动) write from memory

默许 mòxǔ (动) tacitly consent to

脉(脈) mò (副) affectionately: 温情～～ full of tender affection
see also mài

没 mò (动) 1 sink; submerge: 轮船沉～了. The ship sank into the sea. 潜水艇～入水中. The submarine submerged. 2 rise beyond; overflow: 雪深～膝. The snow was knee-deep. 3 disappear; hide: 出～ often appear
see also méi

没落 mòluò (形) decline; wane: ～贵族 declining aristocrat

没收 mòshōu (动) confiscate; expropriate

哞 mōu (动)〈象〉(the cry of a cow): moo; low; bellow

谋 móu (动) 1 plan; scheme: 预～plan beforehand; premeditate. 足智多～ wise and full of stratagems; resourceful 2 consult: 不～而合 agree without prior consultation 3 work for; seek: ～求和平 seek peace. 不～私利 not work for personal gains

谋财害命 móucái-hàimìng (动) murder sb. for his money

谋反 móufǎn (动) conspire against the state; plot a rebellion

谋害 móuhài (动) plot to murder

谋划(劃) móuhuà (动) plan and contrive

谋求 móuqiú (动) seek; strive for: ～两国关系正常化 seek normalization of relations between the two countries. ～解决办法 try to find a solution

谋取 móuqǔ (动) try to gain; seek

谋杀(殺) móushā (动) murder

谋生 móushēng (动) seek a livelihood; make a living: ～的手段 a means of life

谋士 móushì (名) adviser; counsellor

牟 móu (动) try to gain; seek; obtain: ～取 seek; obtain. ～利 seek profit

眸 móu (名) pupil (of the eye); eye: 明～皓齿 have bright eyes and white teeth

眸子 móuzi (名) pupil (of the eye); eye

某 mǒu (代) certain; some: ～人 a certain person. ～日 at a certain date. 在～种程度上 to some (or a certain) extent. 在～种意义上 in a sense

某某 mǒumǒu (名) so-and-so: ～大夫 Dr. so-and-so; a certain doctor. ～学校 a certain school

模 mú (名) mould; matrix; pattern
see also mó

模具 mújù (名) mould; matrix; pattern

模样(樣) múyàng I (名) appearance; look: 她是什么～? What did she look like? 这孩子的～象他妈妈. The child takes after his mother. II (副) (of time and age only) approximately; about: 那男的四十来岁～. The man was probably in his early forties.

模子 múzi (名) mould; pattern: 一个～里铸出来的 made out of the same mould; as like as two peas

亩(畝) mǔ (名) *mu*, a unit of area (= 0.0667 hectares): ～产量 per *mu* yield

牡 mǔ (形) male: ～牛 bull

牡丹 mǔdan (名) tree peony; peony

牡蛎(蠣) mǔlì (名) oyster

母 mǔ (名) 1 mother 2 one's female elders: 祖～ grandmother. 伯～ aunt 3 female (animal): ～鸡 hen. ～狗 bitch. ～牛 cow. ～马 mare

母爱 mǔ'ài (名) maternal love

母老虎 mǔlǎohǔ (名) 1 tigress 2 vixen; shrew; termagant

母亲(親) mǔqīn (名) mother

母系 mǔxì (名) 1 maternal side 2 matriarchal: ～亲属 maternal relatives

母校 mǔxiào (名) one's old school; Alma Mater

母性 mǔxìng (名) maternal instinct

母语 mǔyǔ (名) mother tongue

拇 mǔ

拇指 mǔzhǐ (名) 1 thumb 2 big toe

墓 mù (名) grave; tomb; mausoleum

墓碑 mùbēi (名) tombstone; gravestone

墓地 mùdì (名) graveyard; cemetery

墓志 mùzhì (名) inscription on the memorial tablet within a tomb

暮 mù (名) 1 dusk; evening: 薄～ dusk 2 towards the end; late: ～春 late spring. 日～ sunset

暮霭 mù'ǎi (名) evening haze

暮年 mùnián (名) old age; evening of life

暮气(氣) mùqì (名) lethargy; apathy: ～沉沉 lifeless; apathetic

暮色 mùsè (名) dusk; twilight: ～苍茫 gathering dusk; widening shades of dusk; lengthening shadows of dusk

幕 mù (名) 1 curtain; screen: ～启. The curtain rises. ～落. The curtain falls. 夜～ the veil of night 2 act: 第一～ the first act; Act 1

幕布 mùbù (名) (theatre) curtain; (cinema) screen

幕后(後) mùhòu (名) backstage; behind the scenes: ～策划 backstage manoeuvring. 退居～ retire backstage. ～操纵 pull strings from behind the scenes. ～交易 behind the scenes deal; backstage deal

幕间休息 mùjiān xiūxi (名) interval; intermission

幕僚 mùliáo (名) 1 aides and staff 2 assistant to a ranking official or general in old China

募 mù (动) raise; collect; enlist: ～款 collect contributions. ～兵 recruit soldiers

募集 mùjí (动) raise; collect: ～资金 raise a fund

募捐 mùjuān (动) raise funds; solicit donations

慕 mù (动) admire; yearn for: 爱～ love; adore. 仰～ admire; worship. ～名而来 come to see a person on account of his established reputation

木 mù (名) 1 tree: 草～ grass and trees. 伐～ fell trees. 见木不见林 can't see the wood for the trees. 2 wood: 桃花心～ mahogany 3 wooden: ～箱 wooden box. 棺～ coffin 4 numb; wooden: 两脚都冻～了. Both feet were numb with cold. ～头～脑 wooden-headed; dull-witted

木板 mùbǎn (名) plank; board: ～床 plank bed

木材 mùcái (名) timber; lumber: ～厂 timber mill

木柴 mùchái (名) firewood

木耳 mù'ěr (名) an edible fungus

木筏 mùfá (名) raft

木工 mùgōng (名) 1 woodwork; carpentry 2 woodworker; carpenter

木匠 mùjiang (名) carpenter

木刻 mùkè (名) woodcut: xylography

木料 mùliào (名) timber; lumber

木马(馬) mùmǎ (名) 1 vaulting horse 2 (children's) hobbyhorse; rocking horse

木乃伊 mùnǎiyi (名) mummy

木偶 mù'ǒu (名) wooden figure; puppet: ～剧 puppet show

木排 mùpái (名) raft

木片 mùpiàn (名) wood chip

木器 mùqì (名) wooden furniture

木然 mùrán (形) stupefied

木炭 mùtàn (名) charcoal: ～画 charcoal drawing

木头(頭) mùtou (名) wood; log; timber

木星 mùxīng (名) Jupiter

木已成舟 mù yǐ chéng zhōu the wood is already made into a boat—what is done cannot be undone; it is fait accompli

沐 mù (动) wash one's hair

沐猴而冠 mùhóu ér guàn a monkey in a tall hat — a worthless person dressed up as a dignitary

沐浴 mùyù (动) bathe; be bathed in

目 mù (名) 1 eye: 双～失明 go blind in both eyes. 历历在～ all appears distinct in one's mind 2 item: 细～ inventory. 书～ book list

目标(標) mùbiāo (名) 1 target; objective: 命中～ hit the target. 攻击～ target of attack 2 goal; aim; objective: 他不能把～定得那么高. He cannot set his sights very high.

目不识(識)丁 mù bù shí dīng be totally illiterate

目不暇接 mùbù xiá jiē the eye cannot take it all in; there are too many things for the eye to take in (also as "目不暇给")

目不转(轉)睛 mù bù zhuǎn jīng look fixedly; gaze intently

目次 mùcì （名） table of contents; contents
目瞪口呆 mùdèng-kǒudāi stunned; stupefied; dumbstruck: 吓得～ be struck dumb with fear; be so scared as to stand gaping
目的 mùdì （名） purpose; aim; goal; objective; end: 最终～ ultimate aim. 达到～的手段 a means to an end. 不可告人的～ ulterior motives. ～地 destination
目睹 mùdǔ （动） see with one's own eyes; witness
目光 mùguāng （名） sight; vision; view: ～远大 farsighted. ～短浅 shortsighted
目击(擊) mùjī （动） see with one's own eyes; witness: ～者 witness. ～者所谈的经过 an eyewitness account
目空一切 mù kōng yīqiè look down upon everyone; be supercilious
目录(録) mùlù （名） catalogue; list: 图书～ library catalogue. 展品～ a catalogue of exhibits
目前 mùqián （名） at present; at the moment: ～形势 the present situation. 到～为止 up till the present moment; up till now; so far
目送 mùsòng （动） watch sb. go (when seeing sb. off)
目无(無)法纪 mù wú fǎjì disregard law and discipline
目眩 mùxuàn （形） dizzy; dazzled
目中无(無)人 mùzhōng wú rén consider nobody worth his notice; be supercilious

睦 mù （形） peaceful; harmonious
睦邻(鄰) mùlín （动） be on friendly terms with one's country's neighbours: ～政策 goodneighbour policy

牧 mù （动） herd; tend: ～马 herd horses. ～羊 tend sheep
牧草 mùcǎo （名） graze; pasture
牧场(場) mùchǎng （名） grazing land; pasture
牧歌 mùgē （名） pastoral song
牧民 mùmín （名） herdsman
牧区(區) mùqū （名） pastoral area
牧师(師) mùshī （名） pastor; minister; clergyman
牧童 mùtóng （名） shepherd; buffalo boy
牧业(業) mùyè （名） animal husbandry

穆 mù （形） solemn; reverent: 肃～ solemn
穆斯林 mùsīlín （名） Moslem; Muslim

N n

拿 ná I （动） 1 hold: 她手里～着一把伞. She has an umbrella in her hand. 把这支枪～着！ Hold this gun! 2 take; bring: ～去 take it away. ～来 bring it here 3 seize; capture: ～下敌人的一个据点 capture a stronghold of the enemy 4 deliberately make things difficult: ～某人一把 put sb. in a difficult position. 他想～我一手. He wanted to make things difficult for me. II （介） 1 with: ～热水洗 wash (it) in hot water. ～事实证明 prove with facts 2 [introducing the object to be followed by a verbal phrase]: 我简直～这孩子没办法. This child is just impossible; I simply can't do anything with him. 他们总是～他开玩笑. They are always making fun of him. 她～我当孩子看. She treats me as a child.
拿得稳 nádewěn （动） be sure of (also as 拿得准): 这事儿我～. I'm sure of this.
拿架子 ná jiàzi （动） put on airs
拿手 náshǒu （形） good at; adept; expert: 炸虾是我的～菜. Fried prawns is my speciality. ～好戏 a game or trick one is good at
拿主意 ná zhǔyi （动） decide; make up one's mind: 你自己～吧. You'd better make your own decision. 我的主意拿定了. My mind is made up. 拿不定主意 be wavering

哪 nǎ I （代） 1 which; what: 你想借～本书？ Which book do you want to borrow? 他是～国人？ What country is he from? 你最喜欢～种颜色？ What is your favourite colour? 你～天有时间？ When (or which day) are you free? 2 any: 你借～本书都可以. You can borrow any book you like. 这两种颜色我～种都不喜欢. I like neither of the colours. ～天都行. Any day will do. II [used in a rhetorical question]: ～有你这样对待老人的? How could you treat old people like this? 没有他的帮助你～能有今天? How could you possibly be what you are today without his help? see also nɑ; něi

哪个(個) nǎge (代) **1** which; which one: ～公司? which company? 你要～? which one do you want? **2** who: ～? Who is it?

哪里(裏) nǎli I (代) where; wherever: 你在～住? Where do you live? 在～工作都一样. It doesn't make any difference where I work. ～有压迫, ～就有反抗. Where there is oppression, there is resistance. II [used to form a rhetorical question]: 我～知道他已经走了? How could I know he had left already? 他～会说汉语, 不过认识几个字罢了. He doesn't really speak Chinese. He only knows a few characters. 你的帮助太大了. ——～～. You have given us a lot of help. — It is nothing.

哪怕 nǎpà (连) even; even if; even though; no matter how: ～下再大的雨我也得去. I'll have to go even it rains cats and dogs.

哪儿(兒) nǎr (代) as 哪里

哪些 nǎxiē (代) which; who; what [used before a noun in plural number]: ～是你的? Which ones are yours? ～人去参加晚会了? Who went to the party? 你买了～东西? What have you bought?

哪样(樣) nǎyàng (代) what kind (also as 哪种): 你要～颜色的? What colour do you prefer? 你说的是～的餐巾? What kind of napkin do you mean?

捺 nà I (动) press down; restrain: ～着性子 control one's temper II (名) right-falling stroke (in Chinese characters)

呐 nà

呐喊 nàhǎn (动) shout loudly; cry out; cheer

钠 nà (名) sodium (Na)

纳 nà (动) **1** receive; accept; admit: 采～ adopt **2** pay; offer: 交～公粮 pay taxes in grain **3** sew in close stitches: ～鞋底子 stitch soles (of cloth shoes)

纳粹 Nàcuì (名) Nazi: ～分子 Nazi. ～主义 Nazism

纳贿 nàhuì (动) **1** take bribes **2** offer bribes

纳闷儿(兒) nàmènr 〈口〉 feel puzzled; be perplexed; wonder: 她为什么不接受这项任务, 真叫人～. I wonder why she didn't accept the offer.

纳入 nàrù (动) bring (or channel) into: ～正轨 bring sth. on to the right course. ～国家计划 incorporate sth. into the state plan

纳税 nàshuì (动) pay taxes

那 nà I (代) that: ～是谁? Who is that (man)? ～是可以理解的. That is understandable. II (副) then; in that case: ～你自己呢? What about yourself then? ～我就一个人去了. In that case I'll go alone.

那个(個) nàge I (代) that: ～问题 that problem II(副)〈口〉[used before a verb or an adjective to indicate a certain degree of exaggeration]: 看他～得意劲儿. Look how complacent he is! III (形)〈口〉[used to avoid a blunt or direct statement]: 你刚才跟他讲话的样子也太～了. The way you talked to him was a little too — how shall I put it? Well, you know what I mean.

那里(裏) nàli (代) that place; there: ～气候怎么样? What's the weather like there?

那么(麼) nàme I (副) **1** like that; in that way: 他不该～说. He shouldn't have said that. ～做会伤她的感情的. It would hurt her feelings if you did so. 我哥哥没有～高. My brother is not that tall. **2** [used before a number to stress approximation]: about; or so: 再有～二三十分钟就够了. Another twenty or thirty minutes will probably be enough. II (连) then; in that case: 既然电影不好看, ～我们回家吧. Since this film is no good, let's go home then.

那儿(兒) nàr (代) 〈口〉 **1** see "那里" **2** [used after "打"、"从"、"由"] since that time; since then: 打～起, 她就用心念书了. She's been studying hard since then.

那时(時) nàshí (代) at that time; then; in those days

那些 nàxiē (代) those
那样(樣) nàyàng (代) like that; such; so; of that kind: 他不象你～仔细. He's not so careful as you are. 没你说的～好 not as good as you said. ～做不行. It won't do to act the way you did. 我不懂她会急成～. I don't know why she's so worried about it.

哪 na (助) [equivalent to "啊"]: 加油干～! Speed up! Come on!
see also nǎ; něi

乃 nǎi (动) 〈书〉 1 be: 失败～成功之母. Failure is the mother of success. 2 then; so: 因山势高峻,～在山腰休息片刻. As the slope was steep, so we took a breather halfway up the hill.
乃至 nǎizhì (连) and even: 他的学术成就引起了全中国～全世界人民的敬佩. His academic achievement has aroused admiration in China and even throughout the world.

奶 nǎi (名) 1 breasts 2 milk 3 breast-feed: ～孩子 breast-feed (or suckle) a baby
奶粉 nǎifěn (名) powdered milk
奶酪 nǎilào (名) cheese
奶妈 nǎimā (名) wet nurse
奶奶 nǎinai (名) (paternal) grandmother; grandma
奶牛 nǎiniú (名) milk cow; milch cow
奶油 nǎiyóu (名) cream

奈 nài
奈何 nàihé 1 to no avail: 无可～ absolutely helpless 2 do sth. to a person: 他就是不答应,你又奈他何! If he flatly refused, what could you do about it?

耐 nài (动) be able to bear; endure: ～穿 can stand hard wear; be durable. 吃苦～劳 work hard despite hardships. 这种料子很～洗. This material washes well.
耐烦 nàifán (形) patient: 不～ impatient
耐寒 nàihán (形) cold-resistant
耐火 nàihuǒ (形) fire-resistant; refractory
耐久 nàijiǔ (形) durable
耐力 nàilì (名) endurance; stamina
耐磨 nàimó (形) wear-resisting; wearproof
耐人寻(尋)味 nài rén xúnwèi afford food for thought
耐心 nàixīn (形) patient: ～说服 try patiently to persuade
耐性 nàixìng (名) patience; endurance
耐用 nàiyòng (形) durable: ～品 durable goods; durables

南 nán (名) south: 华北～部 the southern part of north China. ～屋 a room with a northern exposure
南半球 nánbànqiú (名) the Southern Hemisphere
南北 nán-běi (名) 1 north and south ～对话 North-South dialogue 2 from north to south: 大江～ both sides of the Yangtse River.
南方 nánfāng (名) south: ～话 southern dialect. ～人 southerner
南瓜 nánguā (名) pumpkin
南国(國) nánguó (名) the southern part of the country: ～风光 southern scenery
南极(極) nánjí (名) the South Pole; the Antarctic
南美洲 nán měizhōu (名) South America
南腔北调 nánqiāng-běidiào (名) (speak with) a mixed accent
南亚(亞) nán yà (名) South Asia: ～次大陆 the South Asian Subcontinent
南辕北辙 nányuán-běizhé act in a way that defeats one's own purpose; move in the opposite direction

喃 nán
喃喃 nánnán (动) mutter; murmur; mumble: ～自语 mutter to oneself

男 nán (名) man; male: ～主人公 (in a play) the hero. ～演员 actor. ～学生 boy student
男盗女娼 nándào-nǚchang behave like thieves and whores; be out-and-out scoundrels
男低音 nándīyīn (名) bass
男儿(兒) nán'ér (名) man: 好～ a fine man
男方 nánfāng (名) the bridegroom's or husband's side
男高音 nángāoyīn (名) tenor
男孩 nánhái (名) boy
男朋友 nánpéngyou (名) boyfriend
男人 nánrén (名) man; husband
男子 nánzǐ (名) man; male: ～单(双)打 men's singles (doubles). ～团体赛 men's team

event

男子汉(漢) nánzǐhàn (名) man: 不象个～ not manly; not man enough

男生 nánshēng (名) man student; boy student

男声(聲) nánshēng (名) male voice: ～合唱 men's chorus; male chorus

男性 nánxìng (名) the male sex

难(難) nán I (形) **1** hard; difficult: ～写 difficult to write. ～说 hard to say. ～忘 unforgettable **2** bad; unpleasant: ～吃 taste bad. ～听 unpleasant to the ear. ～看 ugly II (动) put sb. into a difficult position: 这可把我～住了! It put me on the spot!

see also nàn

难保 nánbǎo one cannot say for sure: 今天～不下雨. You can't say for sure that it won't rain today.

难产(產) nánchǎn (名) (of childbirth) difficult labour; dystocia

难处(處) nánchǔ (动) hard to get along with: 他一点儿也不～. He is not difficult to get along with at all.

难处(處) nánchu (名) difficulty; trouble: 他有他的～. He has his own difficulties.

难道 nándào (副) [make an emphatic rhetorical question]: ～太阳会从西边出来吗? Could the sun rise from the west? ～他没告诉你? Didn't he tell you about it?

难得 nándé **1** hard to come by; rare: 机会～ a rare chance **2** seldom; rarely: 这样的大雨是很～遇到的. Such torrential rains have scarcely occurred.

难怪 nánguài (连) **1** no wonder: 外面下雪了,～这么冷. No wonder it's so cold. It's snowing. **2** understandable; pardonable: 他刚来,搞错了也～. He can hardly be blamed for the mistake since he is new here.

难关(關) nánguān (名) difficulty; crisis: 渡过～ tide over a crisis. 攻克技术～ break down a technical barrier

难过(過) nánguò (动) **1** have a hard time: 日子真～ lead a miserable life **2** not feel well: 我今天肚子有点～. I have stomach trouble today. **3** feel sad; be grieved: 她接到母亲去世的消息,非常～. She was deeply grieved to learn of her mother's death.

难解难分 nánjiě-nánfēn (动) **1** be locked together (in a struggle) **2** cannot bear to part **3** be inextricably involved (in a dispute)

难堪 nánkān (形) embarrassed: 使某人～ embarrass sb. 处于～的地位 be in an embarrassing situation

难看 nánkàn (形) **1** ugly **2** unhealthy; pale: 你的脸色这么～,不是病了吧? You don't look well. Are you ill? 他吃了一惊,脸色变得很～. He was stunned and his face took on a ghastly expression. **3** embarrassing; shameful: 通不过考试就太～了. It would be awful not to be able to pass the exam

难免 nánmiǎn (形) hard to avoid; unavoidable

难能可贵 nán néng kě guì accomplish something difficult and so deserve praise; estimable; commendable

难色 nánsè (名) a show of reluctance or embarrassment

难舍难分 nánshě-nánfēn loath to part from each other

难受 nánshòu (动) **1** feel unwell; feel uncomfortable: 毛衣太小,穿着～. The sweater is too tight and it's so uncomfortable on me. **2** feel unhappy; feel bad: 他心里很～. He felt ill and wretched

难说 nánshuō (动) it's hard to say; you never can tell

难题 nántí (名) baffling problem; a hard nut to crack: 出～ set difficult questions

难听(聽) nántīng (形) **1** unpleasant to hear **2** offensive; coarse: 你怎么老是骂人,多～! Don't be so foul-mouthed. It's disgusting! **3** scandalous: 这事情说出去多～. The story will cause a scandal once it gets out.

难为(爲)情 nánwéiqíng shy; embarrassed: 当着这么多人唱歌,真有点～. It's embarrassing to sing in front of so many people.

难以 nányǐ difficult to: ～想象 unimaginable. ～置信 incredible. ～形容 beyond description. ～捉摸 unfathomable

难(難) nàn I (名) calamity; disaster: 逃～ flee from danger II (动) blame: 非～ blame; reproach

see also nán

难民 nànmín (名) refugee: ～营 refugee camp
难兄难弟 nànxiōng-nàndì (名) fellow sufferers; two of a kind
难友 nànyǒu (名) fellow sufferer
囊 náng (名) bag; sack; pocket: 胶～ capsule. 胆～ gall bladder
囊空如洗 náng kōng rú xǐ with empty pockets; penniless; not have a penny to bless oneself with; broke
囊括 nángkuò (动) embrace; include
囊肿(腫) nángzhǒng (名) cyst; benign tumour
挠(撓) náo (动) 1 scratch: ～痒痒 scratch an itch 2 hinder: 阻～ obstruct 3 yield; flinch: 不屈不～ indomitable; unyielding
挠头(頭) náotóu (形) difficult to tackle: ～的事 a knotty problem
恼(惱) nǎo (动) be angry; be annoyed: 把某人惹～了 annoy sb. 烦～ vexed; worried
恼恨 nǎohèn (动) be irritated and full of grievances
恼火 nǎohuǒ (形) annoyed; irritated; vexed
恼怒 nǎonù (形) angry; indignant; furious
恼羞成怒 nǎo-xiū chéng nù be shamed into anger
脑(腦) nǎo (名) brain
脑袋 nǎodai (名) head
脑海 nǎohǎi (名) brain; mind: 深深地印入～ be engraved on one's mind
脑筋 nǎojīn (名) 1 brains; mind; head: 动～ use one's brains (or head) 2 way of thinking; ideas
脑力劳(勞)动(動) nǎolì láodòng them ental labour
脑满(滿)肠(腸)肥 nǎomǎn-chángféi idle rich
脑汁 nǎozhī (名) brains: 绞尽～ rack (or cudgel) one's brains
脑子 nǎozi (名) 1 the brain 2 brains; mind; head: 没～ have no brains
闹 nào I (形) noisy: 这儿太～,咱们到别处去吧! It's too noisy here. Let's go somewhere else. II (动) 1 make a loud noise; create a disturbance: 叫孩子们别～了. Tell the children to stop making so much noise. 大～一场 create a tremendous uproar; make a big scene 2 give vent to (one's anger; resentment, etc.): ～脾气 vent one's spleen; be in a tantrum. ～矛盾 (of two people) fall out 3 suffer from: ～水灾 suffer from a flood. ～肚子have loose bowels (or diarrhoea) 4 do; make; undertake: ～罢工 go on strike. 把问题～清楚 straighten things out. 原来是～了一个误会. It turned out to be a misunderstanding.
闹别扭 nào bièniu (动) be at loggerheads with sb.
闹病 nàobìng (动) fall ill; be ill
闹翻 nàofān (动) fall out with sb.
闹鬼 nàoguǐ (动) be haunted
闹哄哄 nàohōnghōng (形) clamorous; noisy
闹剧(劇) nàojù (名) farce
闹情绪 nào qíngxù (动) be disgruntled; fall into a mood
闹市 nàoshì (名) busy streets; downtown area
闹事 nàoshì (动) make trouble; create a disturbance
闹笑话 nào xiàohuà (动) make a fool of oneself; make a stupid mistake
闹意见(見) nào yìjiàn (动) be divided in opinion and engage in bickerings
闹着玩儿 nàozhe wánr (动) joke: 你别当真,我是跟你～的. Don't take it so seriously. I was only joking.
闹钟(鐘) nàozhōng (名) alarm clock
呢 ne (助) 1 [used at the end of an interrogative sentence]: 怎么办～? What is to be done? 她什么时候来～? When will she be coming? 我喜欢他,你～? I like him. What about you? (or and you?) 我的大衣～? Where is my coat? 2 [used at the end of a statement to give emphasis]: 还远着～! It is still far away! 与一本好书得用好几年的时间～! It would take several years to write a good book! 我才不去～! I for one wouldn't go! 昨晚来了十个人～! As many as ten people were around last night! 经理正在开会～. The manager is at a meeting. 3 [used to make a pause within a sentence]: 她妈妈～,也就回到乡下去了. As for her mother, she went back to her old village afterwards.
see also ní

哪 něi (代) which; what
see also nǎ; na

馁(餒) něi (动) be disheartened; dispirited: 气～ lose heart; be disheartened

内 nèi (名) inner; within; inside: 三天～ within three days. 国～形势 internal (or home) situation

内部 nèibù (名) inside; internal; interior: 国家～事务 domestic affairs of a country. ～刊物 restricted publication

内地 nèidì (名) inland; hinterland: ～城市 inland city

内分泌 nèifēnmì (名) endocrine; internal secretion

内服 nèifú (动) (of medicine) to be taken orally

内阁 nèigé (名) cabinet: 影子～ shadow cabinet. ～大臣 cabinet minister

内涵 nèihán (名) intension; connotation

内行 nèiháng (形) expert; adept: 她在针灸方面很～. She is an expert at acupuncture. 充～ pose as an expert

内河 nèihé (名) inland river (or waterway)

内讧 nèihòng (名) internal conflict; internal strife

内奸 nèijiān (名) hidden traitor

内疚 nèijiù (名) guilty conscience: 感到～ feel guilty

内科 nèikē (名) (department of) internal medicine: ～医生 physician

内陆(陸) nèilù (名) inland; interior: ～国 landlocked country

内乱(亂) nèiluàn (名) civil strife; internal disorder

内勤 nèiqín (名) 1 office staff 2 internal or office work (as distinguished from work carried on mainly outside the office)

内情 nèiqíng (名) true picture (of a unit); inside story

内燃机(機) nèiránjī (名) internal-combustion engine

内容 nèiróng (名) content: ～丰富 have substantial content. ～提要 synopsis; résumé

内务(務) nèiwù (名) internal affairs

内线(綫) nèixiàn (名) 1 planted agent 2 inside (telephone) connections

内详 nèixiáng name and address of sender enclosed

内向 nèixiàng (形) introvert

内销 nèixiāo sold on the domestic market

内心 nèixīn (名) heart; innermost being: 发自～深处 from the bottom of one's heart

内衣 nèiyī (名) underclothes

内因 nèiyīn (名) internal cause; intrinsic cause

内忧(憂)外患 nèiyōu-wàihuàn domestic trouble and foreign invasion

内在 nèizài (名) intrinsic; inherent; internal: ～规律 inherent law. ～因素 internal factor

内脏(臟) nèizàng (名) internal organs

内债 nèizhài (名) domestic debt

内战(戰) nèizhàn (名) civil war

内政 nèizhèng (名) internal (or domestic, home) affairs: 互不干涉～ noninterference in each other's internal affairs

嫩 nèn 1 tender; delicate: ～芽 tender shoot. 小孩子皮肤很～. Young children have very delicate skin. 炒鸡丁很～. These fried-chicken cubes are very tender. 2 light: ～绿 pale green 3 inexperienced; unskilled

能 néng I (动) can; be able to: 你明天～去吗? Can you go tomorrow? 你一个人～干得了吗? Can you manage the job by yourself? 他不～不那样做. He had to do it the way he did. II (名) 1 ability; capability; skill: 无～ incompetent. 一专多～ good at many and expert in one 2 energy: 原子～ atomic energy. 太阳～ solar energy

能干(幹) nénggàn (形) able; capable; competent

能够 nénggòu (动) can; be able to; be capable of

能力 nénglì (名) ability; capability: ～强 have great ability; be very capable

能量 néngliàng (名) energy

能耐 néngnai (名) <口> ability; skill

能…能… néng ... néng ... be able to do both ... and ...: 能上能下 be ready to accept a higher position or a lower one. 能文能武 equally good in either civilian or military affairs; able to do both mental and manual labour

能手 néngshǒu (名) expert; a good hand at

能说会(會)道 néngshuō-huìdào have a glib tongue

能源 néngyuán (名) energy

source: ～危机 energy crisis. 节约～ energy conservation

嗯 ńg or ń (叹) [used for having words repeated when not heard]: ～,你说什么? What? what did you say?
see also ňg; ǹg

嗯 ňg or ň (叹) [used to indicate surprise]: ～, 怎么又不见了? Hey! It's gone again. ～! 你怎么还没去? What! You haven't started yet?
see also ńg; ǹg

嗯 ǹg or ǹ (叹) [indicating response]: 他～了一声,就走了. He merely mumbled "H'm", and went away.
see also ńg; ňg

霓 ní (名) secondary rainbow

霓虹灯(燈) níhóngdēng (名) neon light

尼 ní (名) Buddhist nun

尼姑 nígū (名) Buddhist nun

尼龙(龍) nílóng (名) nylon

泥 ní (名) 1 mud; mire 2 mashed vegetable or fruit: 枣～ date paste. 土豆～ mashed potato
see also nì

泥巴 níbā (名) mud; mire

泥浆(漿) níjiāng (名) slurry; mud

泥坑 níkēng (名) mud pit; morass; quagmire

泥泞(濘) nínìng (形) muddy; miry: ～的道路 a muddy road

泥菩萨(薩) nípúsà (名) clay idol: ～过河,自身难保 like a clay idol fording a river — hardly able to save oneself (let alone anyone else)

泥鳅 níqiū (名) loach; eel

泥人 nírén (名) clay figurine: 彩塑～ painted clay figurine

泥沙 níshā (名) silt

泥石流 níshíliú (名) mud-rock flow

泥水匠 níshuǐjiàng (名) bricklayer; tiler; plasterer (also as 泥瓦匠)

泥塘 nítáng (名) mire; bog; morass

泥土 nítǔ (名) 1 earth; soil 2 clay

呢 ní (名) woollen cloth
see also ne

呢喃 nínán (动) (of swallows) twittering

呢绒 níróng (名) wool fabric

呢子 nízi (名) woollen cloth

拟(擬) nǐ (动) 1 draw up; draft: ～稿 make a draft. ～一个计划草案 draft a plan 2 intend; plan: ～于月底回家 plan to come home by the end of the month

拟订 nǐdìng (动) draw up; draft; work out: ～具体办法 work out specific measures (also as "拟定")

拟人 nǐrén (名) personification

拟议(議) nǐyì (名) proposal; recommendation

你 nǐ (代) 1 you [second person singular]: ～喜欢吗? Do you like it? ～的父母 your parents. ～方 your side; you. ～校 your school 2 you; one; anyone: 他的才学叫～不得不佩服. You cannot but admire him for his talent and learning.

你好 nǐhǎo how do you do; how are you; hello

你们 nǐmen (代) you [second person plural]

你死我活 nǐsǐ-wǒhuó life-and-death; mortal: ～的斗争 a life-and-death struggle

溺 nì (动) 1 drown: ～死 be drowned 2 be addicted to; excessively: ～爱 be excessively fond of

逆 nì (动) go against; counter: ～时代潮流而动 go against the trend of the times. ～风 contrary wind

逆差 nìchā (名) deficit; unfavourable balance: 国际收支～ adverse balance of international payments. 贸易～ trade deficit

逆耳 nì'ěr (形) unpleasant to the ear: 忠言～. Good advice often sounds unpleasant.

逆风(風) nìfēng I (动) against the wind: ～航行 sail against the wind II (名) contrary wind

逆境 nìjìng (名) adverse circumstances; adversity

逆来(來)顺受 nì lái shùn shòu submit to adversity meekly; be resigned to fate

逆流 nìliú (名) adverse current; countercurrent

逆水 nìshuǐ (形) against the current: ～行舟 sailing against the current

逆行 nìxíng (动) (of vehicles) go in a direction not allowed by traffic regulations

逆转(轉) nìzhuǎn (动) take a turn for the worse; worsen

匿 nì （动）hide; conceal: 隐～ go into hiding; conceal one's identity

匿迹(跡) nìjì （动）go into hiding; stay incognito: 销声～ lie low

匿名 nìmíng （形）anonymous: ～信 anonymous letter

腻 nì （形）**1** (of food) greasy; oily: 这烤鸭太油～. This roast duck is too rich for me. 汤有点儿～. The soup is bit too oily. **2** be bored with; be tired of: ～得慌 bored stiff **3** meticulous: 细～ meticulous care

腻烦 nìfan （动）**1** be bored; be fed up **2** loathe; hate: 我真～他. I'm really fed up with him.

泥 nì （动）cover or daub with plaster, putty, etc. see also ní

泥子 nìzi （名）putty

昵 nì （形）close; intimate: 亲～ very intimate

拈 niān （动）pick up (with the thumb and one or two fingers): 信手～来 pick up at random. ～轻怕重 pick easy jobs and shirk hard ones

黏 nián （形）(also as 粘) sticky; glutinous: ～米 glutinous rice

黏合 niánhé （动）bind; adhere: ～剂 binder; adhesive

黏结 niánjié （动）cohere: ～力 cohesion; cohesive force. ～性 cohesiveness

黏性 niánxìng （名）stickiness; viscidity; viscosity

黏液 niányè （名）mucus

年 nián （名）**1** year: 去～ last year. 明～ next year. ～复一～ year after year; year in year out. 近～来 in recent years **2** annual; yearly: ～计划 annual plan. ～产量 annual output; annual yield **3** age: ～过半百 over fifty (years old). ～事已高 advanced in age. 童～ childhood **4** New Year (Spring Festival): 拜～ pay a New Year call

年表 niánbiǎo （名）chronological table

年成 niáncheng （名）the year's harvest: 好～ a good harvest. ～不好 a lean year

年初 niánchū （名）the beginning of a year

年代 niándài （名）**1** age; years; time: 战争～ in the war years **2** a decade of a century: 八十～ the eighties

年底 niándǐ （名）the end of a year

年度 nián dù （名）year: 财政～ financial year; fiscal year. ～预算 annual budget

年富力强 niánfù-lìqiáng （形）in the prime of life; in one's prime

年糕 niángāo （名）New Year cake (made of glutinous rice flour)

年关(關) niánguān （名）the end of the year (formerly time for settling accounts)

年号(號) niánhào （名）the title of an emperor's reign

年华(華) niánhuá （名）time; years: 虚度～idle away one's time

年画(畫) niánhuà （名）New Year pictures

年货 niánhuò （名）special purchases for the New Year: 办～ do New Year shopping

年级 niánjí （名）grade (in school): 小学六～ the 6th form (or grade). 大学三～学生 3rd year (university) student

年纪 niánjì （名）age: 你父亲多大～了？How old is your father? 上了～ old; advanced in years; getting on in years. ～轻 young

年鉴(鑒) niánjiàn （名）yearbook; almanac

年景 niánjǐng （名）the year's harvest

年历(歷) niánlì （名）a year calendar

年龄(齡) niánlíng （名）age: 退休～ retirement age

年轮(輪) niánlún （名）(of trees) annual ring; growth ring

年迈(邁) niánmài （形）old; aged: ～力衰 old and infirm; senile

年轻(輕) niánqīng （形）young: ～人 young people. ～力壮 young and vigorous. ～一代 the younger generation

年岁(歲) niánsuì （名）age

年头(頭) niántóu （名）**1** year: 他去世已经三个～了. It's three years since his death. **2** years; long time: 这顶帽子可有～了. This hat has lasted me many years. **3** days; times: 那～ in those days **4** harvest: 今年～真好. This year's harvest is very good indeed.

年限 niánxiàn （名）fixed number of years: 攻读学位的最低～ the minimum length of time required by a degree course. 工具使用～ the service life of a tool

年月 niányuè （名）days; years

捻 niǎn I (动) twist with one's fingers: ~线 twist thread II(名) sth. made by twisting: 纸~儿 a paper spill

捻子 niǎnzi (名) 1 spill 2 wick

撵 niǎn (动) drive away; oust; expel: 把人~出去 drive sb. away

碾 niǎn (动) crush; grind: ~碎 be ground to powder

碾子 niǎnzi (名) roller: 石~ stone roller

念 niàn I (动) 1 think of; miss: 想~ miss sb. 十分挂~ miss sb. very much 2 study; be a pupil: ~书 go to school. 他~中学了. He is in middle school now. ~历史 study history 3 read aloud: ~信 read a letter (aloud) II (名) idea; thought: 私心杂~ selfish considerations

念叨 niàndao (动) be always talking about; harp on: 你在~什么? What are you muttering about?

念经(經) niànjīng (动) chant scriptures

念念不忘 niànniàn bù wàng (动) always keep in mind

念头(頭) niàntou (名) thought; idea; intention

娘 niáng (名) 1 mother; ma; mum: 爹~ father and mother 2 a form of address for an elderly married woman: 老大~ grandma 3 a young woman: 新~ bride

娘家 niángjia (名) a married woman's parents' home

娘娘 niángniáng (名) 1 empress or imperial concubine of the first rank: 正宫~ emperor's wife; empress 2 goddess: ~庙 a temple dedicated to the worship of a goddess

酿(釀) niàng (动) 1 make by fermentation: ~酒 make wine. ~啤酒 brew beer. ~酒业 winemaking industry; brewery 2 make (honey): 蜜蜂~蜜. Bees make honey. 3 lead to; result in: ~祸 lead to disaster

酿成 niàngchéng (动) (of disasters) lead to; bring on; breed

酿造 niàngzào (动) make by fermentation (wine, vinegar, etc.)

袅 niǎo (形) slender and delicate: ~娜 slender and graceful

袅袅 niǎoniǎo 1 curl upwards: 炊烟~. Smoke is spiralling upward from kitchen chimneys. 2 wave in the wind: 垂杨~. The willows are swaying in the wind. 3 linger: 余音~. The residue of the sound still remains in the ears of the hearers.

鸟(鳥) niǎo (名) bird

鸟瞰 niǎokàn (动) get a bird's-eye view: ~全城 get a bird's-eye view of the city

尿 niào I (名) urine II(动) urinate; make (or pass) water

尿布 niàobù (名) diaper; nappy

捏(揑) niē (动) 1 hold between the fingers; pinch: ~住这支笔. Hold the pen. 2 mould with thumb and fingers; mould: ~泥人儿 mould clay figurines. ~饺子 make dumplings

捏合 niēhé (动) mediate; act as go-between

捏一把汗 niē yī bǎ hàn sweat with anxiety or fear

捏造 niēzào (动) fabricate; concoct: ~事实 invent a story; make up a story

蹑(躡) niè

蹑手蹑脚 nièshǒu-nièjiǎo walk on tiptoe; tiptoe

孽 niè (名) sin; evil: 作~ do evil. 妖~ evildoer; monster

镍 niè (名) nickel (Ni)

您 nín (代) 〈敬〉 you

宁(寧) níng (形) peaceful; tranquil

see also nìng

宁静 níngjìng (形) peaceful; tranquil; quiet: ~的夜晚 a tranquil night. 心里不~ feel disturbed

柠(檸) níng

柠檬 níngméng (名) lemon

拧(擰) níng (动) 1 twist; wring. 把毛巾~干 wring out a wet towel 2 pinch; tweak: ~了他一把 give him a pinch

see also nǐng

狞(獰) níng (形) ferocious; hideous

狞笑 níngxiào (动) grin hideously

凝 níng (动) 1 congeal; curdle; coagulate 2 with fixed attention: ~思 be lost in thought. ~视 gaze fixedly

凝固 nínggù (动) solidify: ~点 solidifying point

凝结 níngjié (动) condense; coagulate; congeal: 池面上～了一层冰. There is a thin layer of ice over the pond.
凝聚 níngjù (动) condense: 这部名著～着他毕生的心血. This masterpiece is an embodiment of his painstaking life-long effort.
凝神 níngshén (副) with fixed attention: ～思索 think over the matter with concentrated attention
凝滞 níngzhì (形) stagnate; sluggish: ～的目光 dull, staring eyes
拧(擰) nǐng (动) 1 twist; screw: ～开瓶盖 screw (or twist) the cap off a bottle. ～紧螺丝 tighten up a screw 2 wrong; mistaken: 你把意思搞～了. You've misinterpreted the meaning. 3 be at cross-purposes: 两个人越说越～. The more they talked, the more they disagreed. see also níng
宁(寧) nìng (连) rather see also níng
宁可 nìngkě (连) would rather; better: 我～自己干. I'd rather do it myself. ～站着死,绝不跪着生 would rather die on one's feet than live on one's knees
宁肯 nìngkěn (连) would rather; better
宁缺毋滥(濫) nìng quē wú làn rather go without than have something shoddy; better fewer but better
宁死不屈 nìng sǐ bù qū rather die than surrender; prefer death to dishonour
宁愿 nìngyuàn (as "宁可")
妞 niū (名) <口> girl
牛 niú (名) ox: 母～ cow. 公～ bull. 小～ calf
牛痘 niúdòu (名) smallpox pustule; vaccine pustule: 种～ give or get smallpox vaccination
牛犊(犢) niúdú (名) calf
牛角尖 niújiǎojiān (名) an insignificant or insoluble problem: 钻～ take unnecessary pains to study an insoluble problem; split hairs
牛劲(勁) niújìn (名) 1 great strength; tremendous effort 2 stubbornness; obstinacy; tenacity
牛马(馬) niúmǎ (名) beasts of burden
牛毛 niúmáo (名) ox hair: 多如～ countless; innumerable
牛奶 niúnǎi (名) milk
牛排 niúpái (名) beefsteak
牛棚 niúpéng (名) cowshed
牛皮 niúpí (名) 1 ox-hide 2 boasting, bragging: 吹～ talk big; brag
牛皮纸 niúpízhǐ (名) brown paper
牛脾气(氣) niúpíqi (名) stubbornness; obstinacy
牛肉 niúròu (名) beef
牛头(頭)不对(對)马(馬)嘴 niútóu bù duì mǎzuǐ incongruous; irrelevant
忸 niǔ
忸怩 niǔní (形) unnaturally shy: ～作态 behave coyly; be affectedly shy
扭 niǔ (动) 1 turn round: 她～过身去哭了起来. She turned away and wept. 他～过头来瞪着她. He turned around and stared at her. 把收音机～大声点儿! Turn the radio a bit louder! 2 twist; wrench: 把铁丝～断 twist and break a wire 3 sprain: ～了腰 sprain one's back 4 grapple (or wrestle) with: 两人～在一起. They were wrestling with each other. 5 (of body movement) sway from side to side; swing: 她走路一～一～的. She walks with a swaying gait.
扭打 niǔdǎ (动) wrestle; grapple
扭捏 niǔnie be affectedly shy
扭伤(傷) niǔshāng (动) sprain; wrench: 脚～了 have sprained one's ankle
扭转(轉) niǔzhuǎn (动) 1 turn round: ～身子 (of a person) turn round 2 turn back; reverse: ～局势 reverse a situation; turn the tables
钮 niǔ (名) button, knob: 按～ push a button. 电～ switch; button. ～扣 (on a garment) button
纽 niǔ (名) 1 button 2 bond; tie
纽带(帶) niǔdài (名) link; tie; bond: 友谊的～ ties of friendship
拗 niù (形) stubborn; obstinate; difficult: 一个脾气很～的老头 a very stubborn old man
拗不过(過) niùbuguò unable to make sb. change his mind
农(農) nóng (名) 1 farming; agriculture: 务～ go in for agriculture. ～产品 agricultural products; farm produce 2 peasant; farmer: 棉～ cotton grower. 贫下中～ poor

and lower-middle peasants
农场(場) nóngchǎng (名) farm: 国营～ state farm
农村 nóngcūn (名) rural area; countryside: ～集市 village fair
农夫 nóngfū (名) farmer
农户 nónghù (名) peasant household
农会(會) nónghuì (名) peasant association
农活 nónghuó (名) farm work
农具 nóngjù (名) farm tools
农历(曆) nónglì (名) the traditional Chinese calendar; the lunar calendar
农忙 nóngmáng (名) busy farming season
农民 nóngmín (名) peasant; peasantry
农奴 nóngnú (名) serf: ～主 serf owner
农时(時) nóngshí (名) farming season: 不违～ do farm work in the right season
农田 nóngtián (名) farmland; cultivated land: ～基本建设 capital construction on farmland. ～水利 irrigation and water conservancy
农闲(閑) nóngxián (名) slack farming season
农药(藥) nóngyào (名) farm chemical; pesticide
农业(業) nóngyè (名) agriculture; farming: ～人口 agricultural population. ～革命 green revolution
农艺(藝)师(師) nóngyìshī (名) agronomist
农作物 nóngzuòwù (名) crops

浓(濃)

nóng (形) **1** thick; dense; concentrated: ～茶 strong tea. ～烟 dense smoke. ～眉 heavy (thick) eyebrows **2** (of degree or extent) great; rich: 兴趣很～ take great delight in sth.
浓度 nóngdù (名) density; concentration
浓厚 nónghòu (形) **1** dense; thick **2** (of atmosphere; colour, interest, etc.) strong
浓密 nóngmì (形) dense; thick: ～的枝叶 thick foliage
浓缩 nóngsuō (动) concentrate; enrich: ～牛奶 condensed milk ～铀 enriched uranium
浓郁 nóngyù (形) (of fragrance) strong; rich: 玫瑰花发出～的香味. The roses give off a rich perfume.

脓(膿)

nóng (名) pus
脓包 nóngbāo (名) **1** pustule **2** worthless fellow; good-for-nothing
脓疮(瘡) nóngchuāng (名) running sore
脓肿(腫) nóngzhǒng (名) abscess

弄

nòng (动) **1** do; make; handle; manage; get: 你在这儿～什么? What are you up to here? 你把我～糊涂了. You've made me confused. 这么大个工厂,你～得了吗? Can you manage such a big factory? 菜～咸了. You've put too much salt in the dish. 把问题～清楚 get the problems sorted out **2** play with; meddle with: 小孩子爱～沙土. Children like to play with sand. 别老～那把伞了! Stop meddling with that umbrella! **3** get; fetch: 去～点吃的来. Go and get something to eat.
弄错 nòngcuò (动) make a mistake; misunderstand: 你～了. You've got it wrong. *or* You are mistaken.
弄好 nònghǎo (动) **1** do well: 把事情～ do a good job. 弄不好,她会生气的. Otherwise, she'll get angry. **2** finish doing sth.: 计划～了没有? Is the plan ready?
弄坏(壞) nònghuài (动) ruin or spoil sth.: 把事情～ spoil the show
弄巧成拙 nòng qiǎo chéng zhuō one is only making a fool of oneself by trying to be clever
弄清 nòngqīng (动) make clear; clarify; understand fully: ～问题所在 make sure where the shoe pinches. ～事实 set the facts straight. ～是非 distinguish right from wrong
弄权(權) nòngquán (动) maintain power by playing politics
弄虚作假 nòngxū-zuòjiǎ practise fraud; resort to deception
弄糟 nòngzāo (动) spoil sth.; make a mess of things

奴

nú (名) slave
奴才 núcai (名) flunkey; lackey: ～相 servile behaviour; servility
奴化 núhuà (动) enslave: ～政策 policy of enslavement
奴隶(隸) núlì (名) slave: ～主 slave owner
奴仆(僕) núpú (名) servant; flunkey
奴性 núxìng (名) servility; slavishness

奴颜婢膝 núyán-bìxī (形) subservient; servile
奴役 núyì (动) enslave; keep in bondage
弩 nǔ (名) crossbow
努 nǔ
努力 nǔlì (动) try hard; make great efforts; exert oneself: ～工作 work hard. 尽最大～ do one's utmost; do the best one can
努嘴 nǔzuǐ (动) pout one's lips as a signal
怒 nù (名) anger; rage; fury: 发～ get angry; fly into a rage. ～不可遏 boil with rage
怒潮 nùcháo (名) raging tide
怒冲冲 nùchōngchōng (副) in a towering temper; furiously
怒发(髮)冲冠 nùfà chōng guān His hair bristled (up) with anger
怒号(號) nùháo (动) howl; roar: 狂风～. The wind is howling.
怒吼 nùhǒu (动) roar; howl
怒火 nùhuǒ (名) flames of fury; fury: 满腔～ be filled with fury
怒气(氣) nùqì (名) anger; rage; fury: ～冲天 be in a towering rage; give way to unbridled fury
怒涛(濤) nùtāo (名) angry waves
女 nǚ (名) 1 woman; female: ～工 woman worker. ～职员 female staff (member). ～售货员 saleswoman. ～演员 actress. ～英雄 heroine. ～流 the female sex 2 daughter; girl: 子～ sons and daughters; children
女儿(兒) nǚ'ér (名) daughter; girl
女服务(務)员 nǚfúwùyuán (名) waitress; air hostess; stewardess
女高音 nǚgāoyīn (名) soprano
女红 nǚgōng (名) needlework
女孩 nǚhái (名) girl
女皇 nǚhuáng (名) empress
女郎 nǚláng (名) young woman; maiden; girl
女朋友 nǚpéngyou (名) girl friend
女人 nǚrén (名) woman; womenfolk
女人 nǚren (名) <口> wife
女色 nǚsè (名) woman's charms: 好～ be fond of women; be a womanizer
女神 nǚshén (名) goddess
女生 nǚshēng (名) woman student; school girl
女士 nǚshì (名) [polite form of address for women]: ～们… Ladies …
女王 nǚwáng (名) queen
女性 nǚxìng (名) the female sex
女婿 nǚxu (名) son-in-law
女主人 nǚzhǔren (名) hostess
女子 nǚzǐ (名) woman; female: ～单(双)打 women's singles (doubles). ～团体赛 women's team event
暖 nuǎn I (形) warm: 风和日～. The wind is gentle and the weather warm. II (动) warm up: 靠近火边来～～身子. Come near the fire and warm youself.
暖房 nuǎnfáng (名) greenhouse; hothouse
暖壶(壺) nuǎnhú (名) thermos flask; thermos bottle
暖和 nuǎnhuo (形) warm; nice and warm
暖流 nuǎnliú (名) warm current
暖瓶 nuǎnpíng (as 暖壶)
暖气(氣) nuǎnqì (名) central heating: ～管 radiator
暖色 nuǎnsè (名) warm colour
疟(瘧) nüè (名) malaria
疟疾 nüèji (名) malaria; ague
虐 nüè (形) cruel; tyrannical
虐待 nüèdài (动) maltreat; ill-treat
虐杀(殺) nüèshā (动) kill sb. by maltreatment
虐政 nüèzhèng (名) tyrannical government; tyranny
挪 nuó (动) move; shift
挪动(動) nuódòng (动) move; shift
挪用 nuóyòng 1 divert (funds) 2 embezzle: ～公款 misappropriation (or embezzlement) of public funds
懦 nuò (形) faint-hearted; weak-kneed
懦夫 nuòfū (名) coward
懦弱 nuòruò (形) cowardly; weak
糯 nuò
糯米 nuòmǐ (名) glutinous rice
诺 nuò (名) 1 promise: 许～ promise 2 yes: 唯唯～～的人 a yes-man
诺言 nuòyán (名) promise: 履行～ fulfil one's promise; keep one's word

O o

喔 ō (叹) [indicating sudden realization]: ～，原来是你! Oh, so it's you!

喔唷 ōyō (叹) [indicating surprise or a feeling of pain]: ～，这么大的苹果! Oh, what a big apple! ～，好烫! Ouch, it's terribly hot!

哦 ó (叹) [indicating doubt]: ～! 会有这样的事? What! How could there be such things? *or* Really?

哦 ò (叹) [indicating understanding or realization]: ～，我懂了. Oh! I see. ～，我想起来了. Ah, I've got it.

讴(謳) ōu

讴歌 ōugē I (动) sing the praises of II (名) folk song

鸥(鷗) ōu (名) gull: 海～ seagull

欧(歐) Ōu (名) short for Europe

欧洲 Ōuzhōu (名) Europe: ～共同体 the European Economic Community (E.E.C.)

殴(毆) ōu (动) beat up; hit: 斗～ (of two people) fight

殴打 ōudǎ (动) beat up; hit: 互相～ come to blows; exchange blows

藕 ǒu (名) lotus root

藕断(斷)丝(絲)连 ǒuduàn-sīlián (of lovers) separated but still in each other's thought

藕粉 ǒufěn (名) lotus root starch

偶 ǒu I (名) 1 image; idol: 木～ puppet 2 even (number); in pairs 3 mate; spouse: 配～ spouse II (副) by chance; by accident; occasionally: ～遇 meet by chance; run across

偶尔(爾) ǒu'ěr (副) once in a long while; occasionally: 他只是～来玩儿. He drops in only occasionally.

偶合 ǒuhé (名) coincidence: 我们在这一点上见解一致完全是～，事先并没有商量过. It was a mere coincidence that we held identical views on this point, for we had no prior consultation.

偶然 ǒurán (形) accidental; fortuitous; chance: ～现象 accidental phenomena. 她～听到了这个消息. She learnt the news by chance.

偶数(數) ǒushù (名) even number

偶像 ǒuxiàng (名) image; idol: ～崇拜 idolatry. ～化 idolize

呕(嘔) ǒu (动) vomit; throw up: 发～ be sick. 令人作～ make one sick; nauseating; revolting

呕吐 ǒutù (动) vomit; throw up

呕心沥(瀝)血 ǒuxīn-lìxuè work one's heart out

沤(漚) òu (动) soak; steep

沤肥 òuféi (动) make compost by waterlogging

怄(慪) òu (动) 1 irritate; annoy 2 be irritated

怄气(氣) òuqì (动) be annoyed and sulky: 怄了一肚子气 have a bellyful of repressed grievances

P p

啪 pā (象) bang

啪嚓 pāchā (象) a sudden loud noise as made by sth. falling to the ground and breaking apart

啪嗒 pādā (象) quick, light sound as made by foot-steps, typewriters, etc.; clatter; patter

趴 pā (动) 1 lie on one's stomach; lie prone 2 bend over: ～在桌子上画图 bend over the desk, drawing pictures

扒 pá (动) 1 rake up 2 stew; braise: ～羊肉 stewed mutton

see also bā

扒手 páshǒu (名) pickpocket

耙 pá I (名) rake: 木～ wooden rake II (动) rake, harrow: ～地 rake the soil level

爬 pá (动) 1 crawl; creep 2 climb; scramble: ～山 climb a mountain

爬虫(蟲) páchóng (名) reptile

爬行 páxíng (动) crawl; creep:

～动物 reptile

怕 pà (动) 1 fear; dread; be afraid of 2 I suppose; perhaps: 他～来不了吧. I'm afraid he won't be able to come. 这趟～要用十天吧. This trip will take about ten days, I should think.

怕事 pàshì (动) be afraid of getting involved

怕死 pàsǐ (动) fear death: ～鬼 coward

怕羞 pàxiū (形) coy; shy; bashful

帕 pà (名) handkerchief

拍 pāi I (动) 1 clap; pat; beat: ～球 bounce a ball. ～巴掌 clap one's hands. ～掉身上的土 whisk the dust off one's clothes. ～～他的肩膀 pat him on the shoulder 2 take (a picture): ～照 take a picture. ～电影 shoot (or make) a film 3 send (a telegram, etc.): ～电报 send a telegram 4 flatter; fawn on: 吹牛～马 ready to boast and flatter II (名) 1 bat; racket: 乒乓球～ table-tennis bat. 网球～ tennis racket 2 (of music) beat; time: 一小节三～ three beats in a bar

拍板 pāibǎn (动) 1 rap the gavel: ～成交 strike a bargain; clinch a deal 2 have the final say: 这事得由经理亲自～. The manager has the final say in this matter.

拍马(馬)屁 pāi mǎpì (动) flatter; fawn on

拍卖(賣) pāimài (名) auction

拍摄(攝) pāishè (动) take a picture; shoot

拍手 pāishǒu (动) clap one's hands; applaud: ～叫好 clap and shout "bravo!" ～称快 clap and cheer; applaud (to express joy as the triumph of justice)

拍照 pāizhào (动) take a picture; have a picture taken

拍纸簿 pāizhǐbù (名) (writing) pad

拍子 pāizi (名) 1 bat; racket 2 beat; time: 打～ beat the time

排 pái I (动) 1 line up; arrange in order: ～队 queue up; stand in a line. ～座位 make a seating arrangement 2 drain; discharge: ～废水 discharge waste water 3 rehearse: ～戏 rehearse a play II (名) 1 row; line: 前(后)～ front (back) row 2 platoon 3 raft: 木～ timber raft III (量) row: 两～树 two rows of trees

排版 páibǎn (动) set type

排比 páibǐ (名) parallelism

排场(場) páichang (名) a show of extravagance; grand style

排斥 páichì (动) repel; exclude; reject: ～异己 discriminate against those who do not belong to the same inner circle

排除 páichú (动) get rid of; remove; eliminate: ～障碍 remove an obstacle. ～故障 fix a breakdown. ～一种可能性 rule out a possibility

排队(隊) páiduì (动) line up; queue up: ～买票 line up for tickets. ～上车 queue up for a bus

排骨 páigǔ (名) spareribs

排灌 páiguàn (动) drain and irrigate

排行 páiháng (名) seniority among brothers and sisters: 他～第三. He's the third child of the family.

排挤(擠) páijǐ (动) squeeze out (people): 互相～ each trying to squeeze the other out

排解 páijiě (动) mediate; reconcile: ～纠纷 mediate a dispute

排涝(澇) páilào (动) drain flooded fields

排练(練) páiliàn (动) rehearse: ～节目 have a rehearsal

排列 páiliè (动) put in order; rank: 按字母顺序～ arrange in alphabetical order

排球 páiqiú (名) volleyball

排山倒海 páishān-dǎohǎi overwhelming

排外 páiwài (形) exclusive; antiforeign: 盲目～ blind opposition to everything foreign. ～主义 xenophobia

排泄 páixiè (动、名) excrete; drainage

排演 páiyǎn (动) rehearse

排字 páizì (动) typeset; compose

徘 pái

徘徊 páihuái (动) 1 pace up and down 2 hesitate; waver

牌 pái (名) 1 plate; tablet: 门～ doorplate. 车～ number plate (on a vehicle). 招～ shop sign; signboard 2 trade mark brand: 名～货 goods of a well known brand 3 cards, dominoes, etc.: 扑克～ playing cards 桥～ bridge

牌坊 páifāng (名) memorial arch

way (or gate way)
牌价(價) páijià (名) 1 list price 2 market quotation
牌照 páizhào (名) license plate; license tag
牌子 páizi (名) 1 plate; sign 2 brand; trademark: 老～ old brand; well known brand

迫 pǎi
see also pò
迫击(擊)炮 pǎijīpào (名) mortar

派 pài I (动) send; dispatch: ～人去了解情况 send people to gather information. ～代表团出席大会 send a delegation to the conference. ～军队 dispatch troops. ～你一个工作 set you a task II (名) 1 group; school; faction: 学～ school of thought. 党～ political party. 反对～ opposition party. 右～ rightist 2 style; matter; air: 气～ bearing III (量) 1 [for factions]: 两～意见 two different views 2 [for scene, situation, language etc., preceded by "一"]: 形势一～大好. The situation is excellent. 一～欣欣向荣的景象 a prosperous scene. 一～胡言 a pack of nonsense
派别 pàibié (名) group; school; faction: ～斗争 factional strife
派出所 pàichūsuǒ (名) local police station; police substation
派遣 pàiqiǎn (动)send; dispatch: ～代表团 send a delegation. ～特使 dispatch a special envoy (to a foreign country)
派生 pàishēng (动) derive from
派头(頭) pàitóu (名) style; manner: 他～真不小! He certainly puts on quite a show!
派系 pàixì (名) factions

攀 pān (动) 1 climb; clamber: 高不可～ too high to reach; unattainable 2 seek connections in high places
攀登 pāndēng (动) climb; clamber; scale: ～科学技术新高峰 scale new heights in science and technology
攀亲(親) pānqīn (动) claim kinship
攀谈 pāntán (动) engage in small talk; chitchat
攀折 pānzhé (动) break off (twigs, etc.): 请勿～花木. Please don't pick the flowers or break off the branches.

蹒 pán
蹒跚 pánshān (动) limp; hobble

盘(盤) pán I (名) tray; plate; dish: 银～ silver plate. 茶～ tea tray. 磨～ millstone. 棋～ chessboard II (动) 1 coil; wind: 蛇～成一团. The snake coiled up.～山小路 a winding mountain path 2 check; examine: ～根究底 try to get to the bottom of a matter 3 take inventory: ～点 take stock III (量) [for things wound flat]: 两～磁带 two spools (or reels) of tape. 三～菜 three dishes. 一～棋 a game of chess
盘剥 pánbō (动) exploit by means of usury
盘查 pánchá (动) interrogate and examine
盘缠 pánchan (名) travelling expenses
盘根错节(節) pángēn-cuòjié (形) deep-rooted; too complicated to cope with
盘踞 pánjù (动) illegally or forcibly occupy: ～在山里的土匪 bandits entrenched in the mountain
盘算 pánsuàn (动) calculate; plan
盘腿 pántuǐ (动) cross one's legs
盘问 pánwèn (动) cross-examine; interrogate
盘旋 pánxuán (动) spiral; circle: 顺着山路～而上 wind one's way up the mountain path. 飞机在上空～. The aircraft circled in the sky.
盘子 pánzi (名) tray; plate; dish

磐 pán
磐石 pánshí (名) huge rock: 坚如～ as solid as a rock

判 pàn (动) 1 judge; decide: ～卷子 mark examination papers. ～案 decide a case 2 sentence; condemn: ～了死刑 be sentenced to death
判别 pànbié (动) differentiate; distinguish: ～真假 distinguish the true from the false
判处(處) pànchǔ (动) sentence; condemn: ～三年徒刑 be sentenced to three years' imprisonment
判定 pàndìng (动) judge; decide; determine
判断(斷) pànduàn I (动) judge; decide; determine: ～是非 judge (decide) what is right and what is wrong II (名) judgment
判决 pànjué (动) bring a

verdict; judgment: ～有罪(无罪) pronounce sb. guilty (not guilty)
判明 pànmíng (动) distinguish; ascertain: ～真相 ascertain the facts
判罪 pànzuì (动) declare guilty; convict
畔 pàn (名) side; bank: 河～ river bank. 湖～ the shore of a lake
叛 pàn (动) betray: ～国 be guilty of high treason
叛变(變) pànbiàn (动) defect; turn traitor: ～投敌 go over to the enemy
叛乱(亂) pànluàn I (动) rebel II (名) insurrection; rebellion
叛逆 pànnì I (动) rebel against II (名) rebel: 封建礼教的～ a rebel against feudal ethics
叛徒 pàntú (名) traitor; renegade
盼 pàn (动) 1 hope for; long for; expect: ～自由 long for freedom. ～着你早日归来 look forward to your early return 2 look; look round
盼头(頭) pàntou (名) good prospects: 这事有～了. The matter stands a fair chanceof success.
盼望 pànwàng (动) hope for; long for; look forward to
滂 pāng
滂沱 pāngtuo (形) torrential: 大雨～. It's raining very heavily.
旁 páng (名) 1 side: 路～ roadside 2 other; else: ～人 other people 3 lateral radical of a Chinese character
旁边(邊) pángbiān (名) side: 坐在桌子～ sit at the table
旁观(觀) pángguān (动) look on: 袖手～ look on with folded arms. ～者 onlooker. ～者清,当局者迷. The spectators see the game better than the players.
旁敲侧击(擊) pángqiāo-cèjī (动) attack by innuendo
旁若无(無)人 páng ruò wú rén (动) look self-assured or supercilious
旁听(聽) pángtīng (动) be a visitor at a meeting; visit or sit in on a class: ～席 visitors' seats; public gallery
旁证(證) pángzhèng (名) circumstantial evidence
磅 páng
see also bàng
磅礴 pángbó (形) boundless; majestic
螃 páng
螃蟹 pángxiè (名) crab
膀 páng
see also bǎng
膀胱 pángguāng (名) bladder
彷 páng
彷徨 pánghuáng (动) walk back and forth without knowing where to go; hesitate
庞(龐) páng
庞大 pángdà (形) huge; enormous; colossal: 开支～ colossal expenditure
庞然大物 pángrán dàwù (名) colossus; huge monster
庞杂(雜) pángzá (形) unwieldy and complex: 机构～ unwieldy administrative structure
胖 pàng (形) fat; stout; plump: ～子 a plump person. 长～了 put on weight
抛 pāo (动) 1 throw; toss; fling: ～球 throw (or toss) a ball. ～出一个假声明 dish out (or trot out) a phoney statement 2 leave behind: 被～在后面 be left far behind
抛光 pāoguāng (名) polishing; buffing
抛锚 pāomáo (动) 1 cast anchor 2 (of vehicles) break down: 汽车中途～了. The car broke down on the way.
抛弃(棄) pāoqì (动) desert; forsake; discard: ～朋友 discard one's old friends. 被丈夫～了的女人 a woman forsaken by her husband
抛售 pāoshòu (动) sell (goods, shares, etc.) in large quantities
抛头(頭)露面 pāotóu-lùmiàn (动) ‹贬› appear in public
抛砖(磚)引玉 pāozhuān-yǐnyù (动) volunteer to give an opinion so that others may follow suit
炮 páo (动) prepare Chinese medicine by roasting it in a pan
see also pào
炮制 páozhì (动) 1 prepare Chinese medicine, as by roasting, baking, simmering, etc. 2 concoct; cook up
袍 páo (名) robe; gown: 皮～子 fur robe
咆 páo
咆哮 páoxiāo (动) roar: ～如雷 roar with rage

刨 páo (动) 1 dig; excavate: ～坑儿 dig a pit. ～地 dig the ground. ～土豆 dig(up) potatoes 2 deduct; exclude; minus: ～去今天，只剩五天了. There are only five days left, not counting today.

刨根儿(兒) páogēnr (动) get to the root of the matter

跑 pǎo I (动) 1 run: ～得快 run fast. 长～ long-distance running. ～百米 run the 100-metre dash 2 run away; escape; flee: 他～了. He's vanished. 车胎～气了. The tyre is flat. 3 walk: ～了二十里路 have walked twenty *li* 4 run about doing sth.; run errands: ～龙套 carry a spear in the supporting role. ～买卖 be a travelling salesman. 我～了几个图书馆才借到这本书. I had to run around to several libraries to get this book. II [used as a complement of a verb]: 吓～了 frighten to death. 给刮～了 be blown off

跑步 pǎobù (动) 1 (a race) run

跑道 pǎodào (名) runway; track

跑腿儿 pǎotuǐr (动) run errands; do legwork

泡 pào I (名) 1 bubble: 肥皂～ soap bubbles. 冒～儿 bubble up; rise in bubbles 2 sth. shaped like a bubble: 手上起～ get blisters on one's palm. 电灯～ electric light bulb II (动) steep; soak: 把毛衣放在肥皂水里～一下. Let the (woolen) sweater soak in soap water.

泡菜 pàocài (名) pickled vegetables; pickles

泡茶 pàochá (动) make tea

泡蘑菇 pào mógu (动) 1 play for time; play stalling tactics 2 importune; pester

泡沫 pàomò (名) foam; froth

泡影 pàoyǐng (名) visionary hope; bubble: 化为～ vanish like soap bubbles; melt into thin air

疱 pào (名) blister; bleb

炮 pào (名) 1 cannon; artillery piece 2 fire cracker see also páo

炮兵 pàobīng (名) artillery

炮弹(彈) pàodàn (名) (artillery) shell

炮灰 pàohuī (名) cannon fodder

炮火 pàohuǒ (名) gunfire; artillery fire

炮击(擊) pàojī (动) bombard

炮舰(艦) pàojiàn (名) gunboat: ～政策 gunboat policy

炮筒 pàotǒng (名) barrel (of a gun)

呸 pēi (叹) pah; bah; pooh: ～! 胡说八道! Bah! That's sheer nonsense!

胚 pēi (名) embryo

胚胎 pēitāi (名) embryo

培 péi (动) 1 bank up with earth: ～土 earth up 2 cultivate; foster: ～训人员 train personnel

培养(養) péiyǎng (动) nurture; foster: ～技术人材 train technical personnel. ～好习惯 develop good habits

培育 péiyù (动) cultivate; foster; breed: ～小麦新品种 breed new varieties of wheat

培植 péizhí (动) cultivate

赔 péi (动) 1 compensate; pay for: 如果东西损坏，你得～. If any article is damaged, you'll have to pay for it. 2 stand a loss: ～钱 lose money in business

赔本 péiběn (动) run a business at a loss

赔不是 péi bùshi (动) apologize

赔偿(償) péicháng (动) compensate; pay for: ～损失 compensate for a loss; make good a loss. 照价～ compensate according to the cost

赔款 péikuǎn (名) indemnity; reparations

赔礼(禮) péilǐ (动) apologize

赔笑 péixiào (动) smile apologetically or obsequiously

赔罪 péizuì (动) apologize

陪 péi (动) accompany; keep sb. company: ～客人到飞机场 accompany a visitor to the airport. ～病人 look after a patient

陪伴 péibàn (动) keep sb. company

陪衬(襯) péichèn I (动) serve as a contrast; set off II (名) set-off; foil

陪嫁 péijià (名) dowry

陪审 péishěn (名) serve on a jury: ～团 jury. ～员 juror; juryman

陪同 péitóng (动) accompany: ～前往参观 accompany sb. on a visit

沛 pèi (形) abundant: 精力充～ be full of energy; full of vim and vigour

配 pèi I (名) ～偶 spouse. 原～ first wife II (动) 1 join

in marriage: 婚～ marry 2 mate (animals): ～马 mate horses 3 compound; mix: ～颜色 mix colours. ～药 make up a prescription 4 match: 颜色不～. The colours don't match. 5 deserve; be worthy of; be qualified: 她不～当翻译. She has yet to learn before she can be an interpreter. 6 distribute according to plan; allocate

配备(備) pèibèi I (动) 1 allocate; provide; equip: 给他～必要的参考书. Provide him with necessary reference books. 这些舰艇～有大口径炮. These ships are fitted with large-calibre guns. 2 deploy: ～兵力 deploy troops II (名) outfit; equipment: 现代化的～ modern equipment

配方 pèifāng I (动) make up a prescription II (名) prescription; formula

配合 pèihé (动) coordinate; co-operate: 我们必须在工作中密切～. We must coordinate our efforts in work. ～行动 take concerted action

配给 pèijǐ (名) ration

配件 pèijiàn (名) accessory, fittings (of a machine, etc.)

配角 pèijué (名) supporting role; minor role

配偶 pèiǒu (名) spouse

配套 pèitào (动) form a complete set: 成龙～ assemble the parts to form a complete set. ～器材 necessary accessories

配音 pèiyīn (动) dub (a film)

配乐(樂) pèiyuè (动)dub in background music

配制 pèizhì (动) compound; make up: ～药剂 compound medicines

配种(種) pèizhǒng (动) breed; practise artificial insemination

佩

pèi (动) 1 wear (at the waist, etc.): ～刀 wear a sword 2 admire

佩带(帶) pèidài (动) wear: ～徽章 wear a badge

佩服 pèifu (动) admire: 我～他这个人既聪明而又刻苦. I admire him for his intelligence and industry.

喷

pēn (动) 1 spurt; spout; gush: 水从破水管里直往外～. Water spurted from the broken pipe. 2 spray; sprinkle: ～漆 spray paint. ～水车 water-spraying truck. ～雾器 sprayer; inhaler

喷薄 pēnbó burst forth (of sun): 一轮红日～欲出. The sun is blazing through the morning mist.

喷壶(壺) pēnhú (名) watering can; sprinkling can

喷气(氣) pēnqì jet-propelled: ～式飞机 jet aircraft; jet. ～客机 jet airliner

喷泉 pēnquán (名) fountain

喷洒(灑) pēnsǎ (动) spray; sprinkle

喷射 pēnshè (动) spurt; jet

喷嚏 pēntì (名) sneeze: 打～ sneeze

盆

pén (名) basin; tub; pot: 脸～washbasin. 澡～bathtub. 花～ flowerpot

盆地 péndì (名) basin

盆景 pénjǐng (名) potted landscape

喷

pèn

喷香 pènxiāng (形) fragrant; delicious

烹

pēng (动) boil; cook

烹饪 pēngrèn (名) cooking; culinary art: ～法 cookery; cuisine

烹调 pēngtiáo (名) cooking, cuisine

怦

pēng (象) 他的心～～直跳. His heart is beating fast.

砰

pēng <象> [indicating a sudden loud noise caused by knocking or a heavy fall]: 门～的一声关上了. The door shut with a bang. *or* The door slammed shut.

抨

pēng

抨击(擊) pēngjī (动) attack (in speech or writing); lash out at

澎

pēng (动) splash; spatter

澎湃 pēngpài (动) surge: 波涛～. Waves surge forward. 热情～的诗篇 a poem overflowing with emotion

膨

péng

膨胀(脹) péngzhàng (动) expand; swell; inflate: 金属受了热就会～. Metals expand when heated. 通货～ inflation

蓬

péng I (动) fluffy; dishevelled: ～着头 with dishevelled hair II (量) [used of lush flowers, etc.]: 一～竹子 a clump of bamboo

蓬勃 péngbó (形)vigorous; flourishing; full of vitality: ～发展的经济形势 flourishing economic situation

蓬松 péngsōng (形) fluffy; puffy: ～的头发 fluffy hair

蓬头(頭)垢面 péngtóu-gòumiàn (形) with a dirty face and dishevelled hair; unkempt

篷 péng (名) covering or awning on a car, boat, etc.

朋 péng (名) friend: 高～满座。Present on the occasion (or at the banquet, party, etc.) were all guests of distinction.

朋党(黨) péngdǎng (名) clique; cabal

朋友 péngyou (名) friend: 男(女)～ boy (girl) friend

棚 péng (名) shed: 凉～ awning. 牲口～ livestock shed. 车～ bicycle shed or park

鹏 péng (名) roc

鹏程万(萬)里 péngchéng wànlǐ have an exceedingly bright future

捧 pěng (动) 1 hold in both hands: ～着盘子 hold a dish in both hands 2 extol; flatter: ～场 uncritical flattery. 为某人吹～ sing the praises of sb.

捧腹大笑 pěngfù dàxiào roar with laughter; burst out laughing; laugh one's head off

碰 pèng (动) 1 touch; bump: 别～那只花瓶! Don't touch that vase! 猫把奶瓶～翻了. The cat knocked the milk bottle over. 2 meet; run into: 在街上～到一个朋友 run into a friend in the street. ～到困难 run up against difficulties. 3 take one's chance: ～运气 try one's luck

碰杯 pèngbēi (动) clink glasses

碰壁 pèngbì (动) run up against a stone wall; be rebuffed

碰钉子 pèng dīngzi (动) meet with a rebuff

碰见(見) pèngjiàn (动) meet unexpectedly; run into

碰巧 pèngqiǎo (副) by chance; by coincidence: 我～也在那里. I happened to be there too.

碰头(頭) pèngtóu (动) meet and discuss; put (our, your, their) heads: ～会 brief meeting; briefing

坯 pī (名) base; semifinished product; blank

批 pī I (动) 1 make written comments on (a report, etc.): ～文件 write instructions on a document 2 criticize: 挨～ be criticized II 〈量〉batch; lot; group: 新到的一～货物 a new lot of goods. ～量生产 batch production. 分两～走 go (or leave) in two groups

批驳 pībó (动) refute; rebut; criticize

批发(發) pīfā I (名) wholesale II (动) (of an official document) be authorized for dispatch

批改 pīgǎi (动) go over; correct: ～作业 correct students' papers

批判 pīpàn (动) criticize; repudiate

批评 pīpíng I (动) criticize II (名) criticism: 受到严厉的～ come in for harsh criticism

批示 pīshì (名) written instructions or comments on a report

批语 pīyǔ (名) written remarks; comment

批阅 pīyuè (动) read (official papers) and make comments

批注 pīzhù (动) annotate; be furnished with notes and commentary

批准 pīzhǔn (动) approve; endorse; sanction: ～条约 ratify a treaty. ～某人的请求 grant one's request

披 pī (动) drape over one's shoulders: ～着斗篷 have a cape hanging from one's shoulders

披风(風) pīfēng (名) cloak

披肩 pījiān (名) cape

披荆斩棘 pījīng-zhǎnjí cleave a path through the jungle

披露 pīlù (动) 1 publish; announce 2 reveal; disclose

披星戴月 pīxīng-dàiyuè travel night and day

霹 pī

霹雳(靂) pīlì (名) thunderbolt: 晴天～ a bolt from the blue

劈 pī (动) 1 split; chop; cleave: ～木柴 chop wood 2 right against (one's face, etc.). ～头 head-on

劈头(頭) pītóu (副) 1 straight on the head; right in the face: ～一拳 hit sb. right on the head 2 (say) at the very start: 他进来～第一句话就问:"试验成功了没有"? The moment he entered he asked: "Is the experiment successful yet?"

琵 pí

琵琶 pípá (名) a plucked string instrument with a fretted fingerboard

毗 pí (动) adjoin; be adjacent to: ～连 border on

啤 pí

啤酒 píjiǔ (名) beer

脾 pí (名) spleen

脾气(氣) píqì (名) **1** temperament; disposition: ～很好 be good-natured; have a good temper **2** bad temper: 发～ lose one's temper; flare up

皮 pí I (名) **1** skin: 香蕉～ banana skin. 树～ bark. 土豆～ potato peel. **2** leather; hide: ～靴 leather boots. ～大衣 fur coat **3** cover; wrapper: 书～儿 dust jacket **4** a broad, flat piece of (some thin material); sheet: 塑料～的 plastic-coated II (形) **1** become soft and soggy: 花生～了. The peanuts have gone soggy. **2** naughty: 这孩子真～! What a naughty child! **3** thickskinned; impervious (to criticism): 他老挨批评, 都～了. He is always in for criticism so he no longer cares. **4** rubber: ～筋儿 rubber band; elastic band

皮包 píbāo (名) bag; briefcase

皮包骨 pí bāo gǔ (形) skinny: 瘦得～ be all skin and bone

皮尺 píchǐ (名) tape measure tape

皮带 pídài (名) leather belt

皮肤(膚) pífū (名) skin

皮革 pígé (名) leather; hide

皮货 píhuò (名) fur; pelt

皮毛 pímáo (名) **1** fur **2** superficial knowledge: 略知～ have only a rudimentary knowledge (of a subject)

皮棉 pímián (名) ginned cotton

皮球 píqiú (名) rubber ball; ball

皮实(實) píshi (形) sturdy; durable

皮箱 píxiāng (名) leather suitcase

皮鞋 píxié (名) leather shoes: ～油 shoe polish

疲 pí (形) tired; weary: 精～力尽 exhausted; tired out; dog. tired

疲惫 píbèi (形) tired out; exhausted

疲乏 pífá (形) worn out; tired

疲倦 píjuàn (形) tired; fatigued;

疲劳(勞) píláo (形) exhausted; weary

疲塌 píta (形) slack; sluggish; negligent: 工作～ be slack in doing one's work

疲于(於)奔命 píyú bēnmìng be kept constantly on the run; be weighed down with work; having to run around all the time wears him out

痞 pǐ (名) ruffian; riffraff: 地～ local ruffian

匹 pǐ I (动) be equal to; be a match for II (量) **1** [used for horses, etc.]: 三～马 three horses **2** [used of cloth]: 一～布 a bolt of cloth

匹敌(敵) pǐdí (动) be equal to; be well matched: 无与～ peerless

匹夫 pǐfū (名) ordinary man: 国家兴亡, ～有责. Every man has a share of responsibility for the fate of his country.

匹配 pǐpèi (动) mate; marry

癖 pǐ (名) addiction; weakness for: 嗜酒成～ be addicted to drinking

癖好 pǐhào (名) favourite hobby; fondness for: 我对书法有特别～. I have a special liking for calligraphy.

劈 pǐ (动) **1** divide; split: 把毛线～成三股 split the wool (thread) into two strands **2** break off; strip off: ～白菜帮子 peel the outer leaves off cabbages **3** injure one's legs or fingers by opening them too wide

劈柴 pǐchai (名) firewood

屁 pì (名) wind (from bowels): 放～ break wind; fart

屁股 pìgu (名) **1** buttocks; bottom: 他拍拍～走了. He walks away leaving things in a mess. **2** end; butt: 香烟～ cigarette butt

媲 pì

媲美 pìměi (动) compare favourably with; rival

辟 pì I (动) **1** open up **2** refute; repudiate: ～谣 refute a rumour II (形) penetrating: 精～ profound; incisive

譬 pì (名) example; analogy

譬如 pìrú for example

僻 pì (形) **1** out-of-the-way; secluded: ～巷 side lane. ～静之处 a secluded place **2** eccentric: 怪～ eccentric

篇 piān I (名) **1** a piece of writing: ～章段落 the organic whole of a piece of writing **2** sheet (of paper, etc.): 歌～儿 song sheet II(量) [used of paper, article, etc.]: 三～纸 three sheets of paper. 一～文章 a piece of writing; an essay

篇幅 piānfu (名) **1** length (of a piece of writing) **2** space (on a printed page): 由于～有限 because of limited space. 报纸用大量～报道了这件事. The press gave the incident wide coverage.

篇章 piānzhāng (名) writings: ～结构 structure of a literary composition. 历史的新～ a new chapter in history

偏 piān I (动) inclined to one side; slant; lean: 南～西 south by west. 中～右 (take a position) right of centre. 太阳～西了. The sun is to the west. 往左～一点儿! Move a bit to the left! II (副) deliberately; contrary to what is expected: 你为什么～要派他出国呢? Why on earth should you send him abroad? 医生劝他不要抽烟, 他～要抽. The doctor advised him to give up smoking, but he simply wouldn't listen.

偏爱(愛) piān'ài (动) have partiality for sth.; have a soft spot for sb.

偏差 piānchā (名) deviation; error

偏方 piānfāng (名) folk prescription

偏废(廢) piānfèi (动) attach undue importance to one thing to the neglect of the other: 二者不可～. Neither should be overemphasized at the expense of the other.

偏激 piānjī (形) going to extremes: 意见～ hold extreme views

偏见(見) piānjiàn (名) prejudice; bias

偏离(離) piānlí (动) deviate; diverge: ～正宗 constitute a departure from the orthodox school

偏旁 piānpáng (名) radical (of Chinese characters)

偏僻 piānpì (形) remote; out-of-the-way: ～的山村 a remote mountain village

偏偏 piānpiān (副) **1** deliberately: 她～不承认. She just wouldn't admit it. **2** contrary to what is expected: 事态的发展～同他的愿望相反. Things have turned out differently contrary to his expectations. **3** [used to single out an exception, often with displeasure]: 干吗～选他? Why choose him, of all people?

偏巧 piānqiǎo it so happened that; as luck would have it

偏袒 piāntǎn (动) be partial to; take sides with: 她总是～自己的孩子. She always takes sides with her own child.

偏向 piānxiàng I (名) erroneous tendency; deviation II (动) be partial to

偏心 piānxīn (形) partial: 他对谁都不～. He is not partial to anybody.

偏远(遠) piānyuǎn (名) remote; faraway: ～地区 remote districts

偏重 piānzhòng (动) lay particular stress on

翩 piān

翩翩 piānpian (形) **1** (of dancing) lightly: ～起舞 dance gracefully **2** elegant: ～少年 a suave young man

片 piān

片子 piānzi (名) **1** a roll of film **2** film; movie **3** gramophone record; disc

便 pián

see also biàn

便宜 piányi I (形) cheap; inexpensive: ～货 a bargain II (名) small advantages; petty gains: 贪小～ covet small advantages

片 piàn I (名) **1** a flat; thin piece: 皂～ soap flakes. 雪～ snowflakes. 肉～ sliced pork. 眼镜～ lens · **2** incomplete; fragmentary: ～言 a few words II (量) **1** [used of things in slices]: 一～面包 a slice of bread. 两～药 two tablets **2** [said of an expanse of land or water]: 一～汪洋 a vast expanse of water **3** [used of scenery, weather, language, mood, etc.]: 一～欢腾 a scene of jubilation. 一～漆黑 a pall of darkness. 一～繁荣景象 a glowig picture of prosperity

片段 piànduàn (名) [of writing, story, etc.]: 文章的～ extracts from an article; part; passage; fragment. 生活的～ an episode of sb.'s life

片剂(劑) piànjì (名) tablet
片刻 piànkè (名) an instant; a moment; a short while
片面 piànmiàn (形) 1 unilateral: ～之词 a one-sided representation 2 one-sided: ～观点 a one-sided view. ～地看问题 look at problems one-sidedly
片纸只(隻)字 piànzhǐ-zhīzì (名) fragments of any written material

骗 piàn (动) 1 deceive; fool; hoodwink: ～人 deceive people. 受～ be taken in; be deceived. 你～我. You're kidding me. 2 cheat; swindle
骗局 piànjú (名) fraud; swindle; hoax: 政治～ a political swindle
骗取 piànqǔ (动) gain sth. by cheating: ～信任 win sb.'s confidence by false pretences. ～钱财 cheat sb. out of money or property
骗术(術) piànshù (名) deceitful trick; sleight of hand
骗子 piànzi (名) swindler

漂 piāo (动) float; drift: 天上～着云彩. Clouds are floating in the sky. 小船顺流～去. The boat glided down the stream. ～洋过海 sail across the ocean
漂泊 piāo bó (动) lead a wandering life; drift: ～异乡 drift aimlessly in a strange land
漂浮 piāofú (动) 1 float 2 (of style of work) superficial; showy
漂流 piāoliú (动) 1 drift about 2 see "漂泊"

剽 piāo (动) rob (形) nimble; swift
剽悍 piāohàn (形) agile and brave; quick and fierce
剽窃(竊) piāoqiè (动) plagiarize; lift

飘(飄) piāo (动) float (in the air); flutter: 红旗～～. Red flags are fluttering. 窗外～着雪花. Outside the window, snow flakes are whirling.
飘带(帶) piāodai (名) streamer; ribbon
飘荡(蕩) piāodàng (动) flutter; drift; wave
飘零 piāolíng (动) 1 (of flowers) fade and fall 2 (of people) wander; drift; be homeless
飘飘然 piāopiāorán (形) feel satisfied; walk on air
飘扬(揚) piāoyáng (动) flutter; wave: 红旗迎风～. The red flag is fluttering in the wind.
飘摇 piāoyáo (动) sway; shake: 风雨～ tottering; teetering on the edge of collapse

缥 piāo
缥缈 piāomiǎo (形) scarcely; hazy; discernible: 虚无～ visionary; illusory

瓢 piáo (名) gourd ladle
瓢泼(潑)大雨 piáopō dàyǔ (名) heavy rain; downpour

嫖 piáo (动) go whoring

漂 piǎo (动) 1 bleach 2 rinse
漂白 piǎobái (动) bleach

瞟 piǎo (动) glance sideways at: ～了他一眼 look askance at him

票 piào (名) 1 ticket: 公共汽车～ bus ticket. 门～ admission ticket 2 ballot: 投～ cast a ballot; vote 3 bank note; bill: 零～儿 notes of small denominations; change
票额 piào'e (名) face value
票房 piàofáng (名) booking office; box office
票价(價) piàojià (名) the price of a ticket; admission fee
票据(據) piàojù (名) bill; note

漂 piào
漂亮 piàoliang (形) 1 handsome; good-looking; pretty: ～的小伙子 a handsome young man. ～的小姑娘 a pretty little girl. ～的花园 a beautiful garden. 打扮得漂漂亮亮的 be smartly dressed 2 brilliant; splendid: 说一口～的汉语 speak excellent Chinese. 射门射得真～! a beautiful shot! ～话 fine words; high-sounding words

撇 piē (动) 1 cast aside; throw overboard; neglect: ～开 leave aside; bypass. ～弃 abandon; desert 2 skim: ～油 skim off the grease. ～沫儿 skim off the scum

瞥 piē (动) shoot a glance at: 妻子～了他一眼. His wife darted a look at him. 一～ (get) a glimpse of sth.

撇 piě I (动) 1 throw; fling; cast 2 left-falling stroke (in Chinese characters) II (量) [of sth. in the shape of a stroke]: 两～胡子 two small turfs of moustache
撇嘴 piězuǐ (动) curl one's lip

(in contempt, disbelief or disappointment); twitch one's mouth

拼 pīn (动) 1 put together; piece together: ～积木 play toy bricks. 把两块布～在一起 put two pieces of cloth together side by side 2 be ready to risk one's life (in fighting, work, etc.): ～到底 fight to the bitter end. 我跟你～了. I'll fight it out with you.

拼凑 pīncòu (动) piece together; patch

拼命 pīnmìng I (动) risk one's life; be reckless II (副) with all one's might; desperately: ～干 work despite fatigue. ～奔跑 run like crazy

拼盘(盤) pīnpán (名) assorted cold dishes; hors d'oeuvres

拼死 pīnsǐ (动) risk one's life; defy death

拼写(寫) pīnxiě (动) spell

拼音 pīnyīn (动) 1 combine sounds into syllables 2 phoneticize: ～文字 alphabetic (system of) writing. ～字母 phonetic alphabet

姘 pīn have illicit relations with: ～头 lover; kept mistress

频 pín (副) 1 frequently; repeatedly: ～～点头 nod repeatedly 2 (名) frequency

频道 píndào (名) (of T.V.) frequency channel

频繁 pínfán (副) frequently; often: 来往～ have frequent contacts with

频率 pínlǜ (名) frequency: ～范围 frequency range

频频 pínpín (副) again and again; repeatedly: ～招手 wave one's hand again and again

贫 pín (形) 1 poor; impoverished: 一～如洗 be destitute. ～油国 oil-poor country 2 garrulous; loquacious: 她的嘴真～. She is a real chatter-box.

贫乏 pínfá (形) poor; short; lacking: 语言～ flat, monotonous language. 知识～ be lacking in knowledge

贫寒 pínhán (形) poor; poverty-stricken: 家境～ come of an impoverished family

贫瘠 pínjí (形) (of land) barren; infertile: 土壤～ poor soil

贫苦 pínkǔ (形) poor

贫困 pínkùn (形) poor: 生活～ live in poverty

贫民 pínmín (名) poor people; pauper: 城市～ the urban poor. ～窟 slum

贫穷(窮) pínqióng (形) poor; needy

贫血 pínxuè (名) anaemia

品 pǐn I (名) 1 article; product: 工业～ industrial products. 农产～ farm produce 2 grade; rank: 上～ top grade 3 character; quality: 人～ moral quality; character. ～学兼优 (of a student) superior both morally and intellectually II (动) taste sth. with discrimination; savour: ～茶 sample tea. ～味儿 savour the flavour

品尝(嘗) pǐncháng (动) taste; sample; savour

品德 pǐndé (名) moral character

品格 pǐngé (名) moral character

品貌 pǐnmào (名) looks; appearance

品名 pǐnmíng (名) the name of a commodity

品评 pǐnpíng (动) judge; comment on

品头(頭)论(論)足 pǐntóu-lùnzú (动) find fault; be overcritical

品行 pǐnxíng (名) conduct; behaviour: ～端正 well-behaved

品性 pǐnxìng (名) moral conduct

品质(質) pǐnzhì (名) 1 (of a person) character; quality: 道德～ moral character 2 quality (of commodities, etc.): ～优良 of fine quality

品种(種) pǐnzhǒng (名) 1 breed; variety: 小麦的优良～ improved strain of wheat 2 variety; assortment: 货物～齐全 have a good assortment of goods. 花色～ the variety of colours and designs

聘 pìn (动) 1 invite; engage; employ: ～专家 hire an expert 2 betroth: ～礼 betrothal gift

聘请 pìnqǐng (动) invite; hire

聘书(書) pìnshū (名) letter of appointment; contract

乒 pīng I (象): ～的一声枪响 the crack of a rifle II (名) table tennis; ping-pong: ～坛 table tennis circles

乒乓 pīngpāng I (象) rattle II (名) table tennis; ping-pong

瓶 píng (名) bottle: jar; vase: 牛奶～ a milk bottle. 热水～ thermos flask. 花～ flower vase

屏 píng (名) screen

屏风(風) píngfēng (名) screen

屏幕 píngmù (名)〈电子〉screen: 电视～ telescreen; screen

屏障 píngzhàng (名) protective screen: 天然～ natural defence for sth.

平 píng I (形) **1** flat; level; even; smooth: ～川 flat land; plain. 路面不～ the road is rugged. ～躺 lie flat. 把折皱烫～ iron out the wrinkles (on a dress, etc.) **2** be on the same level; be on a par; equal: ～世界记录 equal a world record. 双方打成十五～. The two teams tied at 15-15. 这场足球最后踢～了. The football game ended in a draw. **3** equal; fair; impartial: ～分 divide equally. 持～之论 unbiased view **4** calm; peaceful; quiet: 海上风～浪静. The sea was calm. 心～气和 even-tempered; unruffled **5** average; common: ～日 on ordinary days. 学习成绩～～ have average school results II (动) **1** level: 把地～一～ level the ground **2** calm; pacify: ～民愤 alleviate popular indignation. 气～了. feel pacified **3** put down; suppress: ～叛 put down a rebellion

平安 píng'ān (形) safe and sound: ～到达 arrive safe and sound. ～无事. All is well. 一路～! Have a good trip! *or* Bon voyage!

平白 píngbái (副) for no reason whatsoever

平辈 píngbèi (名) of the same generation

平常 píngcháng I (形) ordinary; commonplace: 不～ unusual; rare II (副) generally; usually: 他～不怎么说话. Usually, he talks little. ～我坐地铁上班. I go to work by tube as a rule. 这种蝴蝶～看不到. This kind of butterfly is rarely to be seen.

平淡 píngdàn (形) flat; insipid; dull: ～无味 insipid.

平等 píngděng (名) equality: ～待遇 equal treatment. 男女～ equality between man and woman. ～互利 equality and mutual benefit

平定 píngdìng (动) **1** calm down: 局势逐渐～下来. The situation gradually came back to normal. **2** suppress; put down: ～叛乱 put down a rebellion

平凡 píngfán (形) ordinary; common: 过着～的生活 live an ordinary life

平反 píngfǎn (动) redress (a mishandled case); rehabilitate

平方 píngfāng (名) square: ～米 square metre

平房 píngfáng (名) one-storey house; bungalow

平分 píngfēn (动) divide equally: ～秋色 (of two parties) have equal shares (of honour, power, glory, etc.)

平和 pínghé (形) gentle; mild; moderate; placid: 性情～ be of gentle disposition

平衡 pínghéng (名) balance; equilibrium: 收支～ balance between income and expenditure. 失去～ lose one's balance. ～木 balance beam

平滑 pínghuá (形) level and smooth

平缓 pínghuǎn (形) gently; mild; gentle: 语调～ a mild tone. 地势～. The terrain slopes gently.

平静 píngjìng (形) calm; quiet; tranquil: ～的海面 a calm sea. ～的山村 a quiet mountain village. 他很激动，心情久久不能～. He was very excited, and it was long before he calmed down.

平局 píngjú (名) (of sports) draw; tie: 比赛最后打成～. The game ended in a draw.

平均 píngjūn (形) average: ～收入 average income. ～每年增长百分之五 increase by an average of 5% a year. ～主义 equalitarianism; egalitarianism. ～寿命 average life span

平列 píngliè (动) place side by side; place on a par with each other

平炉(爐) pínglú (名) open-hearth furnace

平面 píngmiàn (名) plane

平民 píngmín (名) the common people

平平 píngpíng (形) average; mediocre

平铺直叙 píngpū-zhíxù (形) speak or write in a dull, flat way

平生 píngshēng (名) all one's life; one's whole life: ～的愿望 one's lifelong aspiration

平时(時) píngshí (副) **1** in normal times **2** in peacetime

平坦 píngtǎn (形) (of land, etc.) level; even; smooth: 生活的道路并不～. The road of life is by no means smooth.

平稳(穩) píngwěn (形) smooth

and steady: 汽车开得很～. The car ran very smoothly. 物价～. Prices are stable.

平息 píngxī (动) 1 calm down; subside: 一阵大风暴～了. The storm has subsided. *or* The trouble has blown over. 2 put down (a rebellion, etc.); suppress

平信 píngxìn (名) 1 ordinary mail 2 surface mail

平行 píngxíng 1 of equal rank; on an equal footing; parallel: ～组织 organizations of equal rank; parallel organizations 2 parallel; simultaneous: ～作业 parallel operations 3 parallel: ～线 parallel lines

平易近人 píngyì jìnrén (形) modest and unassuming; folksy

平庸 píngyōng (形) mediocre; commonplace: 才能～ of mediocre calibre

平原 píngyuán (名) plain; flatlands

平整 píngzhěng I (形) neat; smooth II (动) level

平装(裝) píngzhuāng (名) paperback: ～本 paperback edition

评 píng (动) 1 comment; criticize; review: 短～ brief commentary. 书～ book review. ～分 give marks; grade papers 2 judge; appraise

评比 píngbǐ (动) compare and assess

评定 píngdìng (动) judge; evaluate; assess

评功 pínggōng (动) appraise sb.'s merits

评价(價) píngjià (动) appraise; evaluate: ～历史人物 appraise historical figures. 高度～ set a high value on; speak highly of; set great store by

评理 pínglǐ (动) 1 decide which side is right 2 reason things out

评论(論) pínglùn I (动) comment on: ～家 critic; reviewer. ～员 commentator II (名) comment; commentary

评判 píngpàn (动) pass judgment on

评选(選) píngxuǎn (动) choose through public appraisal

评议(議) píngyì (动) appraise sth. through discussion

评语 píngyǔ (名) comment; remark

评注 píngzhù (名) notes and commentary

坪 píng (名) level ground: 草～ lawn. 停车～ car park; parking lot

苹(蘋) píng

苹果 píngguǒ (名) apple

萍 píng (名) duckweed

萍水相逢 píng-shuǐ xiāng féng (of strangers) meet by chance; chance encounter

凭(憑) píng I (动) 1 rely on; be based on: ～良心办事 act in accordance with the dictates of one's conscience. ～票入场 admission by ticket only. 打仗不能只～勇敢. One can't rely on physical courage alone in battle. 2 lean on; lean against: ～栏远眺 lean on a railing and gaze into the distance. II (名) evidence; proof: 真～实据 ironclad evidence. 口说无～. Verbal statements are retractable. III (连) no matter (what, how, etc.): ～你跑多快, 我也赶得上. I'll catch up with you no matter how fast you run.

凭借(藉) píngjiè (动) rely on; by means of: 人类的思维是～语言来进行的. Man thinks in words.

凭据(據) píngjù (名) evidence; proof

凭空 píngkōng (形) without foundation; groundless: ～捏造 a sheer fabrication

凭证(證) píngzhèng (名) proof; evidence

泊 pō (名) pool; lake

坡 pō (名) slope: 山～ hillside. 陡～ a steep slope. 平～ a slight (or gentle, gradual) slope

坡度 pōdù (名) slope; gradient: 六十度～ a slope of 60 degrees

颇 pō (副) quite; rather; considerably: 影响～大 have considerable influence. 他说的～有道理. He does talk sense.

泼(潑) pō I (动) sprinkle; splash; spill: 往地上～点水. Sprinkle some water on the ground. II (形) rude and unreasonable; shrewish: 撒～ act nastily and refuse to be placated

泼妇(婦) pōfù (名) shrew; vixen

泼辣 pōla (形) 1 shrewish 2 pungent; forceful: 文章写得很～. The essay is written in a pungent style. 3 bold and vigorous: 大胆～ bold and vigorous

泼冷水 pō lěngshuǐ (动) pour cold water on; dampen the enthusiasm; discourage

婆 pó (名) 1 old woman 2 husband's mother; mother-in-law: ～家 husband's family

婆婆 pópo (名) 1 husband's mother; mother-in-law 2 grandmother

婆婆妈妈 pópomāmā(形) 1 dodder and chat like an old woman 2 emotionally fragile

婆娑 pósuō (形) whirling; dancing: 杨柳～. The branches of the willows swayed in the breeze.

破 pò I (形) 1 broken; damaged; torn; worn-out: 杯子～了. The glass is broken. ～衣服 worn-out clothes. ～房子 a tumbledown house 2 of poor quality: ～嗓子 a poor voice. 这支～笔! This lousy pen! II (动) 1 break; split; cleave; cut: ～成两半 break (or split) into two. ～浪前进 plough through the waves 2 get rid of; do away with; abolish: ～除旧的习惯 abolish the outmoded practice. ～记录 break a record 3 defeat: 大～敌军 deal a crushing blow at the enemy 4 find out the truth about; lay bare: 看～ see through. ～案 clear a criminal case

破败 pòbài (形) ruined; dilapidated

破产(產) pòchǎn I (动) go bankrupt II (名) bankruptcy

破费 pòfèi (动)〈套〉spend money; go to some expense: 你为什么这么～呢? Why should you go to such expense?

破釜沉舟 pòfǔ-chénzhōu be determined to fight to the bitter end; go to any length (to achieve one's goal)

破格 pògé (动) break a rule; make an exception: ～提升 break a rule to promote sb.

破坏(壞) pòhuài (动) destroy; wreck; undermine; sabotage: ～分子 saboteur. ～力 destructive power. ～性 destructiveness

破获(獲) pòhuò (动) solve a criminal case: ～一个间谍网 uncover a spy ring

破镜重圆 pòjìng chóng yuán reunion of husband and wife after a rupture or separation

破口大骂 pòkǒu dàmà (动) let loose a stream of savage invective

破烂(爛) pòlàn I (形) tattered; ragged; worn-out II (名) junk; scrap; waste: 捡～ collect waste

破例 pòlì (动) break a rule; make an exception

破裂 pòliè (动) break; split; crack: 谈判～了. The negotiations broke down.

破落 pòluò (形) decline (in wealth and position): ～贵族家庭 an impoverished aristocratic family

破门(門)而入 pòmén ěr rù (动) force open the door

破灭(滅) pòmiè (动) (of hopes; illusions) vanish; evaporate; be shattered or dashed to pieces

破碎 pòsuì (形) tattered; broken

破天荒 pòtiānhuāng (副) for the first time; unprecedentedly

破晓(曉) pòxiǎo (动) dawn: 天色～ day breaks

破绽 pòzhàn (名) flaw; weak point: ～百出 be riddled with holes

破折号(號) pòzhéhào (名) dash (——)

迫 pò I (动) 1 compel; force; press: 被～离开家乡 be compelled to leave one's hometown. 为饥寒所～ be driven to desperation by cold and hunger 2 approach; go near: ～近 get close to II (形) urgent; pressing: 从容不～ calm and unhurried

see also pǎi

迫不得已 pòbùdéyǐ have no alternative but (to do sth.); be compelled to do sth. against one's will

迫不及待 pò bùjí dài (副) too impatient to wait

迫害 pòhài (动) persecute: 政治～ political persecution

迫近 pòjìn (动) approach; draw near

迫切 pòqiè (形) urgent; pressing: ～的需要 an urgent need. ～的心情 eager desire

迫使 pòshǐ (动) force; compel

迫在眉睫 pò zài méijié extremely urgent; imminent

魄 pò (名) 1 soul: 魂飞～散 (be frightened) out of one's wits 2 vigour; spirit: 气～ boldness of vision

魄力 pòli (名) daring and resolution; boldness: 工作有～ be bold and resolute in one's work

剖 pōu (动) 1 cut; dissect: ～腹 caesarean section 2 analyse; examine: ～明事理 make an in-depth analysis

剖腹产(產) pōufùchǎn (名) caesarean birth

剖面 pōumiàn (名) section: 横～ cross section. 纵～ longitudinal section

剖析 pōuxī (动) analyse; dissect: 这篇文章～事理十分透澈. This essay gives a very penetrating analysis of the general trend of things.

扑(撲) pū (动) 1 dedicate all one's energies to a cause: 一心～在工作上 devote oneself heart and soul to one's work 2 rush at: 香气～鼻. A fragrant scent assails one's nostrils. 3 flap: 鸟儿～打着翅膀. The bird flapped its wings. 4 bend over

扑哧 pūchī (名)〈象〉 titter; snigger

扑粉 pūfěn (名) face powder

扑克 pūkè (名) 1 playing cards: 打～ play cards 2 poker

扑空 pūkōng (动) come away empty-handed: 昨天我去找他, 扑了个空. Yesterday I went to see him, but unfortunately he was not in.

扑面 pūmiàn (动) blow on one's face: 春风～. The spring wind caressed our faces.

扑灭(滅) pūmiè (动) stamp out; put out; extinguish: ～火灾 put out a fire

扑腾 pūtēng (名)〈象〉 thump; thud

扑腾 pūteng (动) move up and down: 他的心里直～. His heart was beating fast.

扑通 pūtōng (名) 〈象〉 flop; thump; splash; pit-a-pat: ～一声跳进水里 plunge into the water with a splash.

仆 pū (动) fall forward: 前～后继 one stepping into the breach as another falls

铺 pū (动) 1 spread; extend; unfold: ～桌布 spread a table-cloth 2 pave; lay: ～铁轨 lay a railway track. ～平道路 pave the way for

铺盖(蓋) pūgài (名) bedding: ～卷儿 bedding roll; luggage roll

铺设 pūshè (动) lay; build: ～输油管 lay oil pipes

铺天盖(蓋)地 pūtiān-gàidì blot out the sky and the earth

铺张(張) pūzhāng (形) extravagant: ～浪费 extravagance and waste

菩 pú

菩萨(薩) púsà (名) 1 Bodhisattva 2 Buddhist idol: ～心肠 kind-hearted and merciful

匍 pú

匍匐 púfú (动) crawl; creep: ～前进 crawl forward

葡 pú

葡萄 pútao (名) grape

仆(僕) pú (名) servant

仆从(從) púcóng (名) footman; flunkey; henchman

仆人 púrén (名) (domestic) servant

普 pǔ (形) general; universal: ～天下 all over the world

普遍 pǔbiàn (形) universal; general: ～现象 universal phenomenon. ～规律 universal law

普及 pǔjí (动) popularize; disseminate; spread

普通 pǔtōng (形) ordinary; common; average: ～一兵 an ordinary soldier; a rank-and-filer. ～话 Putonghua; common speech (of the Chinese language); standard Chinese pronunciation

普选(選) pǔxuǎn (名) general election

谱 pǔ I (名) 1 table; chart: 家～ family tree; genealogy. 食～ cookbook 2 manual; guide: 棋～ chess manual 3 music score: 乐～ music score 4 sth. to count on; a fair amount of confidence: 心里没个～儿 have no definite plan yet II (动) compose; set to music: ～曲 set a song to music

谱写(寫) pǔxiě (动) compose (music)

朴(樸) pǔ (形) simple; plain

朴实(實) pǔshí (形) 1 simple; plain: ～无华 simple and unadorned 2 sincere and honest

朴素 pǔsù (形) simple; plain: 衣着～ simply dressed. 生活～ plain living

圃 pǔ (名) garden: 苗～ seed plot; (seedling) nursery

铺(舖) pù (名) 1 shop; store 2 plank bed

铺位 pùwèi (名) (on a train, ship, etc.) bunk; berth

瀑 pù (名) waterfall

瀑布 pùbù (名) waterfall

曝 pù (动) expose to the sun

曝光 pùguāng (名) exposure

曝露 pùlù (动) exposed to the open air

Qq

期 qī I (名) **1** a period of time; phase; stage: 假～ vacation. 学～ school term. 革命初～ the initial stage of the revolution **2** scheduled time: 到～ fall due. 限～ time limit (or deadline) II (量) [of school term, issues of papers, stages of a project, etc.]: 第一～工程 the first phase of the project. 上学～ last (school) term. 最近的一～《时代》周刊 the latest issue of "Time" III (动) expect: 不～而遇 meet by chance; meet unexpectedly

期待 qīdài (动) hope; expect; look forward to: ～着胜利的时刻 look forward to the day of victory

期间(間) qījiān (名) time; period; course: 春节～ during the Spring Festival

期刊 qīkān (名) periodical

期望 qīwàng I (动) hope; expect; count on II (名) expectation: 不辜负祖国的～ live up to the expectations of one's motherland

欺 qī (动) **1** deceive; cheat: ～人之谈 deceitful words; deceptive talk **2** bully: ～人 bully people; play the bully

欺负 qīfu (动) bully; treat sb. high-handedly

欺凌 qīlíng (名) bullying and humiliation

欺骗 qīpiàn (动) deceive; cheat; dupe; swindle

欺软怕硬 qīruǎn-pàyìng bully the weak and fear the strong

欺侮 qīwǔ (动) bully; humiliate

欺压(壓) qīyā (动) bully and oppress

欺诈 qīzhà (动) cheat; swindle

栖(棲) qī (动) **1** (of birds) perch **2** dwell; stay

栖身 qīshēn (动) stay; seek shelter

栖息 qīxī (动) (of birds) perch; rest

漆 qī I (名) lacquer; paint: ～器 lacquerware II (动) varnish; lacquer; paint

漆黑 qīhēi (形) pitch-dark: ～一团 pitch-dark; be entirely ignorant of

戚 qī (名) **1** relative: 亲朋～友 relatives and friends **2** sorrow; sadness: 休～相关 share joys and sorrows

七 qī (数) seven

七…八… qī...bā... [inserted in between two nouns or verbs to indicate a disorderly state of affairs]: 七零八落 scattered here and there; in disorder. 七拼八凑 piece together; knock together. 七上八下 be agitated; be perturbed. 七嘴八舌 with everybody trying to get a word in

七绝 qījué (名) a four-line poem with seven characters to a line

七律 qīlǜ (名) an eight-line poem with seven characters to a line

七月 qīyuè (名) July

柒 qī (数) seven (the complicated form of 七)

沏 qī (动) infuse: ～茶 infuse tea; make tea

妻 qī (名) wife

妻离(離)子散 qīlí-zǐsàn have a broken home with one's wife and children drifting apart

凄 qī (形) **1** (of wind and rain) chilly; cold **2** sad; wretched: ～楚 miserable **3** bleak and desolate: ～清 lonely and sad

凄惨 qīcǎn (形) wretched; miserable; tragic

凄厉(厲) qīlì (形) (of a sound) sad and shrill: ～的叫声 a shrill cry

凄凉 qīliáng (形) dreary; miserable

凄切 qīqiè (形) (usually of a sound) plaintive; mournful

蹊 qī

蹊跷(蹺) qīqiāo (形) odd; queer; fishy

齐(齊) qí (形) **1** neat; even; in good order:

整～ neat and tidy. 草剪得很～. The grass is evenly mown. 高矮不～ not of uniform height 2 together; simultaneous: 大家～动手. Everyone lent a hand. ～声欢呼 cheer in unison 3 all ready; complete: 人都到～了. Everyone is here. 东西都准备～了. Everything is ready. 4 reach the height of: 水～腰深. The water is waist-deep. 5 similar; alike: 人心～ all people work with one mind

齐备(備) qíbèi (形) all ready: 万事～. Everything is ready.

齐全 qíquán (形) (of stock, etc.) complete: 货物～ have a satisfactory variety of goods

齐心 qíxīn be of one mind (or heart): ～协力 work as one; make concerted efforts; work in concert

齐奏 qízòu (动) playing (instruments) in unison

脐(臍) qí (名) navel; umbilicus: ～带 umbilical cord

鳍 qí (名) fin

其 qí (代) 1 [used within a sentence to refer to sb. or sth. mentioned earlier] he; she; it; they: 听～自然 let things take their natural course. 使～更加美丽 make it more beautiful 2 his; her; its; their: 使人各尽～能 make everybody do his best 3 that; such: 确有～事. That is certainly a fact. 正当～时 just at that moment. 如听～声 as if we heard him speak

其次 qícì (名) next; secondly; then: 首先要重视内容，～还要注意文风. Pay attention first of all to the content, and then the style. 质量是主要的，数量还在～. Quality is primary while quantity is of secondary importance.

其实(實) qíshí (副) actually; in fact; as a matter of fact

其他 qítā (代) other; else: 还有～事吗? Anything else? ～人就不用去了. Others needn't go.

其余(餘) qíyú (代) the rest; the remainder: ～的人跟我来. The others come with me. ～的都是妇女. All the rest are women.

其中 qízhōng among (whom; which): 这所学校有 800 学生，～30%是外国人. This school has 800 students, and 30 percent of them are foreigners. 有十个人获奖，她就是～一个. Ten people won prizes and she was one of them.

旗 qí (名) flag; banner: 国～ national flag

旗杆 qígān (名) flagpole; flag post

旗号(號) qíhào [often derog.] banner; flag

旗舰(艦) qíjiàn (名) flagship

旗开(開)得胜(勝) qí kāi déshèng win the first battle; win speedy success

旗手 qíshǒu (名) standard-bearer

旗语 qíyǔ (名) semaphore; flag signal

旗帜(幟) qízhì (名) 1 banner; flag 2 stand: ～鲜明 have a clearcut stand

棋 qí (名) chess game: 下一盘～ have a game of chess. 象～ Chinese chess. ～盘 chessboard. ～子 piece (in a board game); chessman

棋逢对(對)手 qí féng duìshǒu be well-matched in a contest

歧 qí I (名) fork; branch II (形) different: ～义 different interpretations

歧路 qílù (名) branch road; forked road

歧视 qíshì (动) discriminate against: 种族～ racial discrimination

歧途 qítú (名) off the right path: 被引入～ be led astray

奇 qí (形) 1 strange; queer; rare; unusual: ～耻大辱 a most painful humiliation 2 unexpected: ～袭 surprise attack 3 surprise: 令人惊～ come to one as a surprise

奇兵 qíbīng (名) an ingenious military move

奇怪 qíguài (形) strange; odd; surprising: 真～，他今天不来. It's strange that he should be absent today.

奇观(觀) qíguān (名) marvellous spectacle; wonder

奇迹 qíjì (名) miracle; wonder: 创造～ work wonders; perform miracles. 历史～ a marvel of history; a miracle in history

奇景 qíjǐng (名) wonderful view

奇妙 qímiào (形) marvellous; wonderful; intriguing

奇谈 qítán (名) strange tale; absurd argument

奇特 qítè (形) peculiar; queer; singular

奇闻 qíwén (名) intriguing story

奇形怪状(狀) qíxíng-guàizhàng (形) grotesque in shape or appearance
奇异(異) qíyì (形) 1 fantastic; bizarre 2 curious: 他用～的眼光望着过路的人. He looked at the passers-by with curious eyes.
奇遇 qíyù (名) 1 fortuitous meeting 2 adventure
奇装(裝)异(異)服 qízhuāng-yìfú (名) bizarre dress; outlandish clothes

崎 qí
崎岖(嶇) qíqū (形) rugged: ～不平 rugged

骑 qí (动) ride (esp. on animal or bicycle): ～马 ride a horse; be on horseback. ～车 go by bicycle. ～在人民头上称王称霸 ride roughshod over the people
骑兵 qíbīng (名) cavalry
骑虎难(難)下 qí hǔ nán xià difficult to extricate oneself from a most embarrassing or dangerous situation
骑墙 qíqiáng (动) sit on the fence: ～观望 sit on the fence and adopt a wait-and-see attitude

畦 qí (量) rectangular pieces of land in a field

祈 qí (动) pray
祈祷(禱) qídǎo (动) pray; say one's prayers
祈求 qíqiú (动) earnestly hope; pray for

启(啟) qǐ (动) 1 awaken: ～蒙 enlighten; enlightenment 2 start; initiate 3 open: 幕～. The curtain rises.
启程 qǐchéng (动) set out; start on a journey
启齿(齒) qǐchǐ (动) open one's mouth; start to talk about sth.: 难以～ find it difficult to bring the matter up
启动(動) qǐdòng (动) start (a machine, etc.)
启发(發) qǐfā (动) arouse; inspire; enlighten: 他们的经验对我们很有～. Their experience has served as a great source of inspiration for us. ～式 (of teaching method) heuristic method
启示 qǐshì (名) enlightening guidance; illuminating remarks
启事 qǐshì (名) notice; announcement

企 qǐ
企求 qǐqiú (动) seek for; hanker after: 从不～个人名利 never seek personal fame or wealth
企图(圖) qǐtú I (动) (usu. derog.) try; attempt; contrive II (名) attempt; scheme
企业(業) qǐyè (名) enterprise; business: ～家 enterpreneur; enterpriser

乞 qǐ (动) beg
乞丐 qǐgài (名) beggar
乞怜(憐) qǐlián (动) beg for pity
乞求 qǐqiú (动) beg (for); supplicate: ～宽恕 beg (for) forgiveness
乞讨 qǐtǎo (动) go begging

起 qǐ I (动) 1 rise; get up: 早晨六点～床 get up at six in the morning. 早睡早～ early to bed and early to rise 2 rise; grow: ～风了. the wind is rising. ～疑心 become suspicious. ～义 rise up (against) 3 appear: 手上～泡 get blisters on one's hand. 脸上～皱纹 get wrinkles on one's face 4 begin; start: 从那时～ since then. 从明天～ starting from tomorrow 5 remove; extract: ～钉子 draw out a nail. ～瓶塞 open a bottle 6 draft: ～草文件 draft a document. ～草稿子 make a draft 7 build; set up: 白手～家 start (an enterprise) from scratch II (名)(量) 1 case: 两～罪案 two criminal cases 2 batch; group: 已经有三～人参观过这里了. Three groups of visitors have been here.

起 qǐ 1 [used as a complement after a verb indicating the upward direction]: 提～箱子匆匆往外走 lift the suitcase and hurry off. 拿～武器 take up arms. 唱～歌, 跳～舞 start singing and dancing. 他也抽～烟了! He too has started smoking! 引～注意 draw people's attention 2 [used after a verb together with "得" or "不" as meaning 'can afford' or 'cannot afford']: 买得～ can afford to buy. 买不～ cannot afford to buy. 经得～考验 can stand the test. 负不～责任 cannot take the responsibility
起笔(筆) qǐbǐ (名) the first stroke of a Chinese character
起程 qǐchéng (动) start on a journey: 明日～ set out tomorrow
起初 qǐchū (副) at first; at the

beginning
起床(牀) qǐchuáng (动) get up (from bed)
起草 qǐcǎo (动) draft; draw up: ~文件 draw up a document
起点(點) qǐdiǎn (名) starting point
起飞(飛) qǐfēi (动) (of aircraft) take off: 经济~ economic take-off
起伏 qǐfú (动) (of waves, mountain ranges, etc.) rise and fall
起哄 qǐhòng (动) 1 make trouble; create disturbance 2 (of a crowd of people) jeer; boo and hoot
起劲(勁) qǐjìn (副) vigorously; energetically: 干得很~ work with great enthusiasm
起居 qǐjū (名) daily life: ~室 sitting room
起来(來) qǐlai (动) get up; rise; arouse: 他~得太晚. He got up too late. 你~, 让老太太坐下. Please stand up and give the seat to the old lady. 群众~了. The masses have been aroused.
起来(來) qǐlai [used as a complement after a verb] 1 indicating upward movement: 把旗举~ raise the flag 2 indicating the beginning and continuation of an action: 天气冷~了. It's getting cold. 哭~了 burst out crying 3 indicating the completion of an action or the fulfilment of a purpose: 哦, 我想~了! Now I've got it! 包~ wrap sth. up 4 indicating impressions: 听~满有道理. It sounds quite reasonable. 看~还可以. It looks all right. 这支笔写~很滑溜. This pen writes smoothly.
起码 qǐmǎ (形) minimum; rudimentary; elementary: ~的要求 minimum requirements. ~的知识 elementary knowledge
起锚 qǐmáo (动) weigh anchor; set sail
起色 qǐsè (名) improvement; pickup: 他工作很有~. His work shows signs of improvement. 他的病有了~. He has begun to pick up.
起身 qǐshēn (动) get up; rise to one's feet
起誓 qǐshì (动) take an oath; swear
起诉 qǐsù (动) bring a suit against sb.; sue: ~人 suitor; prosecutor
起头(頭) qǐtóu I (名) beginning: 这事从一~就错了. It was a mistake from the very start. II (动) start; begin: 先从这儿~. Let's start from here. III (副) at first; in the beginning: ~我不懂. I was at a loss at first.
起先 qǐxiān (副) at first; in the beginning
起义(義) qǐyì (动、名) revolt; rise up; uprising
起因 qǐyīn (名) cause; origin: 事故的~ the cause of the accident
起用 qǐyòng (动) reinstate (an official who has retired or been dismissed); rehabilitate
起源 qǐyuán I (名) origin: 生命的~ the origin of life II originate; stem from: 一切知识均~于劳动. All knowledge originates from labour.
起运(運) qǐyùn (动) start shipment
起重机(機) qǐzhòngjī (名) hoist; crane
岂(豈) qǐ (副) [as 难道, used in written language, usu. before a negative word to form a rhetorical question]: ~非白日做梦? Isn't that daydreaming? ~非咄咄怪事? It's preposterous, isn't it?
岂敢 qǐgǎn 〈套〉 you flatter me; I don't deserve your compliment.
岂有此理 qǐ yǒu cǐ lǐ preposterous; outrageous: 真是~! This is really outrageous!
泣 qì (动) weep; sob: ~不成声 choke with tears
弃(棄) qì (动) abandon; discard: ~之可惜. It would be a pity to throw it away.
弃权(權) qìquán I (动) abstain from voting II (名) abstention
弃置 qìzhì (动) put aside; discard: ~不用 be discarded; lie idle
契 qì (名) contract; agreement: 地~ title deed. 默~ tacit agreement
契合 qìhé (动) agree with; tally with
契约 qìyuē (名) contract; deed; charter: 签订~ sign a contract
砌 qì I (动) build by laying bricks or stones: ~墙 build a wall II (名) step: 雕栏玉~ carved balustrades and marble steps
器 qì (名) 1 utensil; ware: 漆~ lacquerware. 瓷~ china-

ware; porcelain. 玉～ jade article. 乐～ musical instrument **2** organ: 生殖～ private parts; genitals

器材 qìcái (名) equipment; material: 照相～ photographic equipment

器官 qìguān (名) physical organ: 消化～ digestive organs. 发音～ organs of speech. 呼吸～ respiratory apparatus

器件 qìjiàn (名) parts of an apparatus: 电子～ electronic device

器具 qìjù (名) utensil; appliance: 日用～ household utensils

器皿 qìmǐn (名) containers esp for use in the house

器械 qìxiè (名) apparatus; appliance; instrument: 医疗～ medical appliances. 体育～ sports apparatus. 光学～ optical instrument

器乐(樂) qìyuè (名) instrumental music

器重 qìzhòng (动) think highly of (someone at a lower level)

气(氣) qì I (名) **1** air; fresh air: 大～层 the atmosphere. 空～ air. 打开窗户透透～. Open the window to let in some fresh air. **2** gas: 煤～ gas. 毒～ poisonous gas **3** breath: 喘粗～ pant. 上～不接下～ be out of breath **4** smell: 香～ sweet smell; fragrance. 臭～ foul smell **5** airs; manner: 官～ bureaucratic airs **6** spirit; morale: 朝～蓬勃 full of vigour. 泄～ be discourged; be dampened. 士～ morale II (动) **1** make angry; enrage: 我故意～他一下. I was deliberately trying to make him angry. **2** get angry; be enraged: ～得直哆嗦 tremble with rage **3** bully; insult: 受～ be bullied or maltreated

气冲冲 qìchōngchōng (形) furious; enraged

气垫(墊) qìdiàn (名) air cushion: ～船 hovercraft; cusioncraft

气度 qìdù (名) boldness of vision and large-mindedness

气短 qìduǎn (动) breathe hard; be short of breath

气氛 qìfēn (名) atmosphere: 亲切友好的～ cordial and friendly atmosphere

气愤 qìfèn (形) indignant; furious

气概 qìgài (名) lofty; spirit: 英雄～ heroic spirit

气缸 qìgāng (名) air cylinder; cylinder

气功 qìgōng (名) *qigong*, a system of deep breathing exercises

气管 qìguǎn (名) windpipe; trachea: ～炎 tracheitis

气候 qìhòu (名) climate: 海洋性～ oceanic climate. 政治～ political climate

气急败坏(壞) qìjí bàihuài be utterly discomfited and exasperated

气节(節) qìjié (名) moral; integrity: 民族～ patriotic moral courage

气力 qìlì (名) physical strength; effort: 使出全身～ exert all one's strength

气量 qìliàng (名) tolerance: ～大 large-minded; magnanimous. ～小 narrow-minded

气流 qìliú (名) **1** air current **2** breath

气恼(惱) qìnǎo (动) get angry

气馁 qìněi (动) feel discouraged (or down-hearted)

气派 qìpài (名) manner; style; air: 学者～ a scholarly manner

气泡 qìpào (名) air bubble; bubble

气魄 qìpò (名) daring; boldness of vision; imposing manner

气球 qìqiú (名) balloon

气色 qìsè (名) complexion; colour: ～很好 look very well

气势(勢) qìshì (名) great force of imposing posture: ～磅礴 of tremendous force

气势(勢)汹汹 qìshì xiōngxiōng (形) fierce; overbearing

气体(體) qìtǐ (名) gas

气味 qìwèi (名) **1** smell; odour: ～难闻. The smell is awful. **2** (usu, derog.) smack; taste: ～相投 be birds of a feather

气温 qìwēn (名) air temperature

气息 qìxī (名) **1** breath: ～奄奄 at one's last gasp **2** scent: 春花的～ the scent of spring flowers

气象 qìxiàng (名) atmospheric phenomena: ～预报 weather forecast

气压(壓) qìyā (名) atmospheric pressure

气焰 qìyàn (名) overbearing pride; arrogance: ～万丈 be enorniously haughty

气质(質) qìzhì (名) **1** temperament; disposition **2** qualities; makings

讫 qì (形) settled; completed 收～ received in full

迄 qì (副) up to; till: ～今 up to now; to this day; so far

汽 qì (名) steam; vapour

汽车(車) qìchē (名) automobile; car

汽船 qìchán (名) steamship; steamer

汽笛 qìdí (名) steam whistle; siren: 鸣～ sound a siren

汽水 qìshuǐ (名) soda water; lemonade

汽艇 qìtǐng (名) motorboat

汽油 qìyóu (名) petrol; gasoline; gas

掐 qiā (动) 1 pinch; nip: ～花 nip off a flower 2 clutch: ～死 strangle. ～脖子 seize sb. by the throat

掐断(斷) qiāduàn (动) nip off; cut off: ～水源 cut off the water supply

卡 qiǎ (动) 1 wedge; get stuck: 鱼刺～在他的喉咙里. A fish bone sticks in his throat. 2 clip; fastener: 发～ (also ～子) hairpin 3 checkpost: 关～ checkpost
see also kǎ

洽 qià (副) 1 be in harmony: 融～ be on good terms 2 consult; arrange with: ～商 contact sb. and discuss

恰 qià (副) 1 appropriate; proper 2 just; exactly: ～如其分 appropriate; just right

恰当(當) qiàdàng (形) proper; suitable; fitting; appropriate: 用词～ proper choice of words. 这个问题处理得不～. The problem was not properly handled.

恰好 qiàhǎo (副) just right; as luck would have it: 当时我～在场. It happened that I was on the spot.

恰恰 qiàqià (副) just; exactly; precisely: ～相反 just the opposite. ～十二点钟 twelve o'clock sharp

恰巧 qiàqiǎo (副) by chance; fortunately: ～他也不想去. Fortunately he didn't want to go either.

恰如其分 qià rú qí fèn apt; appropriate; just right: ～的结论 an appropriate conclusion

谦 qiān (形) modest: ～和 modest and amiable

谦恭 qiāngōng (形) modest and courteous

谦让(讓) qiānràng (动) modestly decline: 不要～了. Don't decline. You can be too modest.

谦虚 qiānxū (形) modest; self-effacing: 她是非常～的人. She is a very modest and unassuming sort of person.

谦逊(遜) qiānxùn (形) modest and unassuming

牵(牽) qiān (动) lead along; pull; drag: 手～手 hand in hand

牵肠(腸)挂(掛)肚 qiāncháng-guàdù feel deep anxiety

牵扯 qiānchě (动) involve; drag in: 这件事～到他. He is involved in the matter.

牵动(動) qiāndòng (动) affect; influence: ～全局 affect the entire situation

牵挂(掛) qiānguà (动) worry; be concerned about: 没有～ free from care. 不要～家里. Don't worry about us at home.

牵累 qiānlěi (动) 1 tie down: 受家务～ be tied down by household chores 2 implicate: 你犯错误不要～别人. Don't involve other people in your mistakes.

牵连 qiānlián (动) implicate; involve: ～他人 involve others in trouble

牵强 qiānqiǎng (形) farfetched or forced: ～附会 make a far-fetched interpretation

牵涉 qiānshè (动) involve; drag in: 他的发言～到很多人. He made unpleasant (or nasty) references to many people in his speech.

牵线(綫) qiānxiàn (动) 1 pull strings 2 act as go-between

牵引 qiānyǐn (动) pull; draw; tow: ～力 pulling force

牵制 qiānzhì (动) pin down; tie up: ～行动 containing action. ～敌人 pin down the enemy

签(簽) qiān I (动) sign; autograph: ～字 sign (one's name) II (名) 1 label; sticker: 标～ label. 书～ bookmarker 2 bomboo slips used for divination, gambling or contest purposes: 抽～ draw lots 3 a slender pointed piece of bamboo or wood: 牙～ tooth pick

签到 qiāndào (动) sign in to show one's presence at a meeting or in office: ～处 sign-in desk

签订 qiāndìng (动) conclude and sign (an agreement etc.): ～条约 sign a treaty. ～合同 sign a

contract
签发(發) qiānfā (动) sign and issue (a document, certificate, etc.)
签名 qiānmíng (动) sign one's name; autograph: 作者亲笔~的书 an autographed book
签署 qiānshǔ (动) sign: ~协定 sign an agreement. ~意见 write comments and sign one's name (on a document)
签证(證) qiānzhèng (名) visa: 入(出)境~ entry (exit) visa. 过境~ transit visa
签字 qiānzì (动) sign; affix one's signature: ~国 signatory state; signatory

铅 qiān (名) lead (Pb)
铅笔(筆) qiānbǐ (名) pencil
铅球 qiānqiú (名) shot: 推~ shot put
铅字 qiānzì (名) (printing) type; letter

千 qiān (数) 1 thousand: 两~ two thousand. 成~上万 thousands of. ~百万 millions 2 a great number of: ~方百计 in a thousand and one ways
千变(變)万(萬)化 qiānbiàn-wànhuà ever-changing
千差万(萬)别 qiānchā-wànbié differ in a thousand and one ways
千锤百炼(煉) qiānchuí-bǎiliàn 1 thoroughly steeled or tempered: 在长期斗争中~ be tempered in protracted struggles 2 (of literary works) be polished meticulously
千方百计 qiānfāng-bǎijì by every possible means
千古 qiāngǔ (形) through the ages; for all time: 为~罪人 stand condemned through the ages. ~遗恨 eternal regret
千金 qiānjīn (名) 1 a thousand pieces of gold; a lot of money: ~难买 not to be bought with money. 一掷~ spend lavishly 2 daughter
千钧一发(髮) qiān jūn yī fà in imminent peril: ~的时刻 at this critical juncture
千军万马(馬) qiānjūn wàn mǎ (名) a powerful and well-equipped army
千里之行,始于(於)足下 qiānlǐ zhī xíng, shǐ yú zú xià one sets out on a long journey by taking the first step — great success is an accumulation of smaller successes
千篇一律 qiān piān yī lǜ (形) stereotyped
千秋 qiānqiū (名) 1 a thousand years; centuries: ~万代 throughout the ages; for generations to come 2 〈敬〉 birthday (other than one's own)
千丝(絲)万(萬)缕(縷) qiānsī-wànlǚ a thousand and one links: 有着~的联系 be bound together by countless ties
千瓦 qiānwǎ (名) kilowatt
千万(萬) qiānwàn I (数) ten million; millions upon millions II (副) [used of exhortation or a friendly warning]: ~要小心! Do be careful! 你~别听他的. You must under no circumstances believe what he says.
千辛万(萬)苦 qiānxīn-wànkǔ untold hardships: 历尽~ undergo innumerable hardships
千言万(萬)语 qiānyán-wànyǔ thousands of words: ~无法表达我对你们的心情. I cannot convey my feelings in words.
千载一时(時) qiān zǎi yī shí extremely rare: ~的机会 a golden opportunity; the chance of a lifetime

迁(遷) qiān (动) 1 move: ~往他处 move to another place 2 change: 时过境~. The situation has changed with the passage of time.
迁就 qiānjiù (动) accommodate oneself to: 坚持原则, 不能~. Stick to principle and refuse to give in. *or* Do not compromise on matters of principle
迁居 qiānjū (动) move house
迁移 qiānyí (动) move; migrate

仟 qiān (数) thousand (the complicated form of 千)

阡 qiān (名) 〈书〉 a footpath between fields, running north and south
阡陌 qiānmò (名) crisscross footpaths between fields

潜(濳) qián (动) hide
潜藏 qiáncáng (动) hide; go into hiding
潜伏 qiánfú (动) hide; conceal; lie low: ~的敌人 hidden enemy. ~危机 a latent crisis. ~的疾病 an insidious disease. ~期 incubation period
潜力 qiánlì (名) latent capacity; potential; potentiality: 有很大~ have great potentialities. 挖掘~ tap potentials
潜入 qiánrù (动) 1 slip into

sneak into; steal in 2 dive; submerge
潜水 qiánshuǐ (动) go under water; dive: ～员 diver; frogman. ～艇 submarine
潜逃 qiántáo (动) abscond: 携款～ abscond with public funds
潜行 qiánxíng (动) 1 move under water 2 move stealthily
潜移默化 qiányí-mòhuà (of sb.'s character, thinking, etc.) change imperceptibly
潜在 qiánzài (形) latent; potential: ～力量 latent power. ～危险 potential danger

前 qián (名) 1 front: ～厅 front hall. 门～ in front of the gate 2 forward; ahead: 勇往直～ go bravely forward. 向～看 look forward; look ahead 3 ago; before: 三天～ three days ago. 午饭～ before lunch 4 preceding: ～一阶段 the preceding stage. 战～ prewar 5 former: ～总统 ex-president 6 first; front: ～三名 the first three places (in a competition). ～几行 the preceding lines
前辈 qiánbèi (名) older generation
前车(車)之鉴(鑒) qiánchē zhī jiàn warning taken from the overturned cart ahead; lessons drawn from others' mistakes
前程 qiánchéng (名) future; prospect; career: 远大～ a bright future. ～黯淡 have bleak prospects
前额 qián'e (名) forehead
前方 qiánfāng (名) front; ahead; the front lines
前锋 qiánfēng (名) 1 vanguard 2 forward
前赴后(後)继(繼) qiánfù-hòujì (动) advance wave upon wave
前功尽(盡)弃(棄) qiángōng jìn qì all that has been achieved has come to nothing
前后(後) qián-hòu (名) 1 before and after: 村子～都有公园. There is a park either before or after the village. 2 from beginning to end; altogether: 写这本书～用了我一年的时间. It took me one year to write this book. 她～去过那儿三次. She's been there three times altogether. 3 about; around (a certain time): 国庆节～ around National Day
前进(進) qiánjìn (动) go forward; advance
前景 qiánjǐng (名) prospect; perspective: 美好的～ bright prospects. 开辟美丽的～ open up a beautiful vista
前例 qiánlì (名) precedent: 史无～ unprecedented
前列 qiánliè front row; forefront; van: 站在斗争的～ stand in the forefront of the struggle
前面 qiánmian (名) 1 in front; ahead: 看! ～有个林子. Look! there is a wood ahead. 2 above; preceding: ～提到的问题 the problems mentioned above. ～那一页 the preceding page
前年 qiánnián (名) the year before last
前仆后(後)继(繼) qiánpū-hòujì (of martyrs) no sooner has one fallen than another steps into the breach
前驱(驅) qiánqū (名) forerunner; pioneer
前人 qiánrén (名) forefathers; predecessors
前任 qiánrèn (名) predecessor: 他的～ his predecessor
前哨 qiánshào (名) outpost; advance guard
前身 qiánshēn (名) predecessor: 这所大学的～是一个研究中心. This university grew out of a research centre.
前台(臺) qiántái (名) 1 proscenium 2 (on) the stage
前提 qiántí (名) premise; prerequisite; precondition
前天 qiántiān (名) the day before yesterday
前夕 qiánxī (名) eve: 圣诞节～ Christmas eve. 胜利的～ on the eve of the victory
前线(綫) qiánxiàn (名) front; frontline
前言 qiányán (名) preface; foreword; introduction
前沿 qiányán (名) forward position
前夜 qiányè (名) eve
前因后(後)果 qiányīn-hòuguǒ (名) cause and effect: 他知道这件事的～. He knows the story from beginning to end
前兆 qiánzhào (名) omen; forewarning: 地震的～ warning signs (or indications) of an earthquake
前者 qiánzhě (名) the former
前缀 qiánzhuì (名) prefix
前奏 qiánzòu (名) prelude

乾 qián

乾坤 qiánkūn (名) heaven and

earth; the universe: 扭转～bring about a radical change in the existing state of affairs

掮 qián (动) carry on the shoulder

掮客 qiánkè (名) broker: 政治～political broker

虔 qián (形) sincere

虔诚 qiánchéng (形) pious; devout: ～的佛教徒 devout Buddhist

黔 qián

黔驴(驢)技穷(窮) Qián lú jì qióng the proverbial donkey has exhausted its tricks; be at one's wit's end

钱(錢) qián I (名) money: 挣 (or 赚) ～ make money. ～包 purse; wallet. 这个多少～? How much is this? II (量)[a unit of weight] 1/10 两 (= 5 grams)

钱币(幣) qiánbì (名) coin

钱财 qiáncái (名) money; wealth

钳 qián I (名) pincers; pliers; forceps: 老虎～ pincer pliers. 火～ fire (or coal) tongs. II (动) grip; clamp

钳工 qiángōng (名) fitter

钳制 qiánzhì (动) hold tight; clamp down on

浅(淺) qiǎn (形) 1 shallow: ～海 shallow sea. ～滩 shoal 2 simple; easy: 这些读物内容～. These reading materials are quite easy. 3 superficial: 认识很～ superficial understanding. 交情很～ not on familiar terms 4 (of colour) light: ～蓝 light blue. ～黄 pale yellow

浅薄 qiǎnbó (形) shallow; superficial

浅见(見) qiǎnjiàn (名) superficial view: 依我～ in my humble opinion

浅陋 qiǎnlòu (形) (of knowledge) meagre; mean

浅显(顯) qiǎnxiǎn (形) plain; easy to read and understand: ～的道理 a plain truth

浅易 qiǎnyì (形) simple and easy: ～读物 easy readings

遣 qiǎn (动) 1 send; dispatch: 派～ dispatch. 调兵～将 deploy forces 2 dispel; expel: ～闷 dispel boredom

遣返 qiǎnfǎn (动) repatriate: ～战俘 repatriate prisoners of war

遣散 qiǎnsàn (动) disband; send away

遣送 qiǎnsòng (动) send back; repatriate: ～出境 deport

谴 qiǎn

谴责 qiǎnzé (动) condemn; denounce

歉 qiàn (名) 1 apology: 道～ offer (or make) an apology; apologize 2 crop failure

歉收 qiànshōu (动) have a poor harvest

歉意 qiànyì (名) apology; regret: 表示～ offer an apology

堑 qiàn (名) moat; chasm: 天～ natural chasm. ～壕 trench; entrenchment

欠 qiàn (动) 1 owe: ～债 owe a debt 2 short of; lacking: ～妥 not entirely proper. 身体～佳 not in very good health 3 raise slightly (a part of the body): 她～身去摸床边的灯开关. She rose slightly to feel for the bedside switch. 4 yawn: 呵～ yawn

欠缺 qiànquē I (动) be deficient in; be short of: 经验还～ lacking in experience II (名) shortcoming; deficiency

嵌 qiàn (动) inlay; embed: 镶～着玉石的托盘 a tray inlaid with jade

锵(鏘) qiāng (名) 〈象〉 clang; gong

枪(槍) qiāng (名) gun; rifle: 手～ pistol; revolver. 机～ machine gun

枪毙(斃) qiāngbì (动) execute by shooting; have one shot

枪弹(彈) qiāngdàn (名) bullet; cartridge

枪法 qiāngfǎ (名) marksmanship

枪杆子 qiānggǎnzi (名) the barrel of a gun; gun; arms

枪决 qiāngjué (动) execute by shooting

枪林弹(彈)雨 qiānglín-dànyǔ (名) a hail of bullets; scene of heavy fighting

枪杀(殺) qiāngshā (动) kill by shooting; shoot dead

枪声(聲) qiāngshēng (名) shot; crack

枪手 qiāngshǒu (名) marksman; gunner

枪膛 qiāngtáng (名) bore (of a gun)

呛(嗆) qiāng (动) choke; (of food) go down the wrong way see also qiàng

腔 qiāng (名) **1** cavity: 口～ the oral cavity. 满～热血 full of patriotic enthusiasm **2** tune; pitch: 高～ high pitched tune; falsetto **3** accent: 南～北调 a mixed accent. 学生～ schoolboy talk **4** speech: 答～ answer

腔调 qiāngdiào (名) **1** tune: 他俩唱的是一个～. The two of them sing the same tune. **2** accent; intonation: 她谈话带北方～. She speaks with a northern accent.

墙(墻) qiáng (名) wall: ～壁 wall. ～报 wall newspaper

蔷(薔) qiáng

蔷薇 qiángwei (名) rose

强 qiáng (形) **1** strong; powerful: 富～ rich and prosperous. 工作能力～ capable. 风力不～. The wind is not strong. **2** better: 生活一年比一年～. Life is getting better each year. **3** a bit more than: 三分之一～ slightly more than one third

see also qiǎng

强暴 qiángbào I (形) violent; brutal II (名) violence; brutality: 不畏～ defy brute force

强大 qiángdà (形) powerful

强盗 qiángdào (名) robber; bandit

强调 qiángdiào (动) stress; emphasize

强度 qiángdù (名) intensity: 劳动～ labour intensity. 钢的～ the strength of the steel

强国(國) qiángguó (名) powerful nation; power

强奸 qiángjiān (动) rape; violate: ～民意 defile public opinion

强劲(勁) qiángjìng (形) powerful; forceful: ～的东风 a strong east wind

强烈 qiángliè (形) strong; intense; violent: ～的愿望 a strong desire

强权(權) qiángquán (名) power; might: ～政治 power politics

强盛 qiáng shèng (形) (of a country) powerful and prosperous

强心剂(劑) qiángxīnjì (名) cardiac stimulant; cardiotonic

强行 qiángxíng (动) by force: ～闯入 force one's way in

强硬 qiángyìng (形) strong; unyielding; formidable: ～路线 hard line. ～的谈判者 a formidable negotiator

强制 qiángzhì (动) force; compel (by political or economic means): ～劳动 forced labour

强壮(壯) qiángzhuàng (形) strong; sturdy; robust

抢(搶) qiǎng (动) **1** snatch; grab: 她从我手里把信～了过去. She snatched the letter from me. **2** rob; loot **3** vie for; scramble for: ～球 scramble for the ball **4** rush: ～时间 seize the hour; race against time

抢夺(奪) qiǎngduó (动) grab; seize

抢购(購) qiǎnggòu I (动) rush to purchase II (名) a stempede to buy things

抢劫 qiǎngjié (动) rob; loot; plunder

抢救 qiǎngjiù (动) rescue: ～稀有动物 rescue rare animals. ～病人 give emergency treatment to a patient

抢收 qiǎngshōu (动) get the harvest in quickly

抢险(險) qiǎngxiǎn (动) speedily carry out rescue work

强 qiǎng (动) make an effort; strive: ～作笑脸 force a smile

see also qiáng

强词夺(奪)理 qiǎngcí-duólǐ resort to sophistry

强加于(於)人 qiǎngjiā yú rén impose (one's views, etc.) on others

强迫 qiǎngpò (动) force; compel; coerce

强求 qiǎngqiú (动) impose; forcibly demand: 写文章可以有各种风格，不必～一律. No uniformity should be imposed since styles of writing vary.

襁 qiǎng

襁褓 qiǎngbǎo (名) swaddling clothes: ～中 be in one's infancy

呛(嗆) qiàng (动) irritate (respiratory organs): 什么味儿这么～鼻子? What smell is it which irritates the nose so much? 我～了一口. It went down the wrong way. 够～ hard to bear

see also qiāng

跄(蹌) qiàng

跄踉 qiàngliàng (动) stagger

敲 qiāo (动) knock; beat; strike: ～锣打鼓 beat gongs and drums. ～警钟 sound the tocsin

敲打 qiāoda (动) beat; tap

敲诈 qiāozhà (动) blackmail; extort; racketeer: ～钱财 extort

money

敲竹杠 qiāo zhúgàng (动) overcharge sb. or extort money from him by taking advantage of his weakness or ignorance

悄 qiāo

悄悄 qiāoqiāo (副) quietly; stealthily: 他~地走了. He left quietly.

橇 qiāo (名) sledge; sled; sleigh

跷(蹺) qiāo (动) 1 lift up (a leg); hold up (a finger): ~着腿坐着 sit with one's legs crossed 2 stilts

锹 qiāo (名) spade

翘(翹) qiáo (动) 1 raise (one's head) ~首raise one's head (and look ahead) 2 become warped

see also qiào

乔(喬) qiáo

乔木 qiáomù (名) arbor; tall tree

乔迁(遷) qiáoqiān (动) move to a new place

乔装(裝)打扮 qiáozhuāng dǎbàn disguise oneself; masquerade

侨(僑) qiáo (动) live abroad: 华~ overseas Chinese. 外~ foreign nationals; aliens

侨胞 qiáobāo (名) countrymen (or nationals) residing abroad

侨汇(匯) qiáohuì (名) overseas remittance

侨居 qiáojū (动) reside abroad: ~国 country of residence

侨眷 qiáojuàn (名) relatives of nationals living abroad

侨民 qiáomín (名) a national residing abroad

侨务(務) qiáowù (名) affairs concerning nationals living abroad

桥(橋) qiáo (名) bridge

桥墩 qiáodūn (名) (bridge) pier; abutment

桥梁 qiáoliáng (名) bridge

桥牌 qiáopái (名)bridge (a card game): 打~ play bridge

桥头(頭) qiáotóu (名) either end of a bridge

憔 qiáo

憔悴 qiáocuì (形) haggard; withered; be fading away

樵 qiáo (名) firewood: ~夫 woodman

瞧 qiáo (动) look; see: 等着~吧. Wait and see. *or* You can do as you see fit.

瞧不起 qiáobuqǐ (动) look down upon; hold in contempt

瞧得起 qiáodeqǐ (动) think much (or highly) of sb.

巧 qiǎo (形) 1 skilful; clever; ingenious: ~匠 a skilled workman 2 cunning; deceitful; artful: 花言~语 honeyed words; deceitful talk 3 coincidental; fortuitous; by a happy chance: 真~! What a coincidence! 真不~! 他今天又不在家. Unfortunately, he is out again today.

巧夺(奪)天工 qiǎo duó tiāngōng wonderful workmanship; superb craftsmanship

巧立名目 qiǎo lì míngmù invent various names of items; concoct various pretexts

巧妙 qiǎomiào (形) (of methods, skills, etc.) ingenious; clever

窍(竅) qiào (名) a key to sth.: 诀~ knack; trick of a trade

窍门(門) qiàomén (名) key (to a problem); knack: 找~ try to find something that lends itself readily to the solution of a problem.

壳(殼) qiào (名) shell; hard surface: 贝~ seashell

see also ké

撬 qiào (动) prize; pry: 把箱子盖~开 prize the top off a box

翘(翹) qiào (动) stick up; rise on one end; tilt

see also qiáo

翘尾巴 qiào wěiba (动) cocky

鞘 qiào (名) sheath; scabbard

峭 qiào (形) high and steep 陡~ precipitous

峭壁 qiàobì (名) cliff; precipice

俏 qiào (形) pretty; smart cute: 打扮得真~ wear the cutest dress

俏丽(麗) qiàolì (形) pretty

俏皮 qiàopi (形) (of manners or speeches) lively or amusing witty

俏皮话 qiàopihuà (名) 1 witty remark 2 sarcastic remark

切 qiē (动) cut; slice: ~菜 cut vegetables

see also qiè

切除 qiēchú (动、名) amputate

resect; resection; removal
切磋 qiēcuō (动) exchange experience; compare notes.
切断(斷) qiēduàn (动) cut off: ～电源 cut off the electricity supply. ～交通 sever communication lines
切片 qiēpiàn (名) section: ～检查 cut sections (of organic tissues) for microscopic examination
切削 qiēxiāo (动) cut: 金属～ metal cutting
茄 qié (名) eggplant; aubergine
see also jiā
茄子 qiézi (名) eggplant; aubergine
且 qiě I (副) 1 for the time being: 你～等一下. Will you please wait a little while? 2 not to mention; let alone: ～不说你, 连他最好的朋友的话他都不听. He would not listen even to his best friend, not to mention you. 3 for a long time: 这菜～煮呢. This dish takes a long time to cook. II (连) both ... and ...: 既高～大 both tall and big-boned
且慢 qiěmàn wait a moment; not leave so soon: ～, 我还有个问题要问你. Wait a minute, I have one more question to ask.
妾 qiè (名) concubine
锲 qiè (动)〈书〉 carve; engrave
锲而不舍 qiè ér bù shě work with perseverance
挈 qiè (动) 1 take along: ～眷 take one's family along 2 take up; concentrate on (of writing, speech, etc.): 提纲～领 keep the key points; put it in a nutshell
怯 qiè (形) timid; cowardly; nervous
怯场(場) qièchǎng (动) have stage fright
怯懦 qiènuò (形) timid; cowardly
怯弱 qièruò (形) timid and weak-willed
惬 qiè (形)〈书〉 be satisfied
惬意 qièyì (形) pleased; satisfied
切 qiè I (动) correspond to; to: 他说话不～实际. What he says is unrealistic. II (形) eager; anxious: 回家心～ be anxious to return home. 学习心～ eager to study III (副) be sure to: ～不可麻痹大意. Be sure to guard against carelessness.
see also qiē
切齿(齒) qièchǐ (动) gnash one's teeth: ～痛恨 gnash one's teeth in hatred
切合 qièhé (动) suit; fit in with: 作计划要～实际. Plans should be drawn up in the light of realities.
切身 qièshēn (形) 1 of immediate concern to oneself: ～利益 one's immediate or vital interests 2 personal: ～体会 personal understanding
切实(實) qièshí I (形) practical; realistic; feasible: ～有效的办法 practical and effective measures. ～可行的计划 a feasible plan II (副) conscientiously; earnestly: ～改正错误 correct one's mistakes in real earnest
切题 qiètí (形) keep to the point
窃(竊) qiè I (动) steal: 盗～ steal II (副) secretly; surreptitiously; furtively: ～笑 laugh up one's sleeve. ～听 eavesdrop; bug
窃取 qièqǔ (动) steal; usurp; grab: ～要职 occupy a key post by foul means
窃贼 qièzéi (名) thief; burglar
亲(親) qīn I (形、名) 1 related by blood: 母～ mother. 双～ parents. ～姐妹 blood sisters. 近～ close relative 2 intimate: ～热 on intimate terms II (名) marriage: 定～ betrothal III (动) kiss
see also qìng
亲爱(愛) qīn'ài (形) dear; beloved
亲笔(筆) qīnbǐ I (副) in one's own handwriting II (名) one's own handwriting
亲近 qīnjìn I (形) be close to; be on intimate terms with: 他们俩很～. The two of them are on very intimate terms. II (动) be friends with: 他对人冷嘲热讽, 谁都不愿～他. He is so sarcastic that no one wants to be friends with him.
亲眷 qīnjuàn (名) one's relatives
亲口 qīnkǒu (副) (say sth.) personally: 这是他～告诉我的. He told me this himself.
亲密 qīnmì (形) close; intimate: ～无间 be close associates
亲昵 qīnnì (形) very intimate: ～的称呼 an affectionate form of address
亲戚 qīnqī (名) relative
亲切 qīnqiè (形) cordial; warm: 回到离别多年的故乡, 感到一切格外～. On returning to my hometown after years of absence, I felt I was in exceptionally congenial company
亲热(熱) qīnrè (形) warm and affectionate
亲人 qīnrén (名) 1 kinsfolk or spouse 2 beloved ones
亲善 qīnshàn (形) close and friendly
亲身 qīnshēn (形) personal; firsthand: ～经历 personal experience
亲生 qīnshēng (形) one's own (children, parents): ～儿女 one's own children
亲事 qīnshì (名) marriage
亲手 qīnshǒu (副) with one's own hands; personally; oneself
亲属(屬) qīnshǔ (名) relatives
亲王 qīnwáng (名) prince
亲信 qīnxìn (名) trusted follower
亲眼 qīnyǎn (副) with one's own eyes: 这是我～看见的. I saw it with my own eyes.
亲友 qīnyǒu (名) relatives and friends; kith and kin
亲自 qīnzì (副) personally; in person: ～动手 do the job oneself. ～拜访 make a personal call. ～过问 look into the matter personally

钦 qīn

钦差大臣 qīnchāi dàchén (名) imperial envoy; emissary from the top organization
钦佩 qīnpèi (动) admire; esteem: 深感～ have great admiration for

侵 qīn (动) invade; intrude into

侵犯 qīnfàn (动) intrude; encroach upon; violate: ～一国主权 violate a country's sovereignty. ～人权 infringe upon human rights
侵略 qīnlüè (动、名) invade; commit aggression against: ～者 aggressor. ～战争 war of aggression
侵扰(擾) qīnrǎo (动) invade and harass: ～边境 harass a country's frontiers; make border raids
侵入 qīnrù (动) invade; intrude into: ～领海 intrude into a country's territorial waters
侵蚀 qīnshí (动) corrode; erode: 风雨的～ weather-beaten
侵吞 qīntūn (动) 1 swallow up; annex: ～别国领土 annex another country's territory 2 embezzle; misappropriate: ～公款 embezzle public funds
侵袭(襲) qīnxí (动) invade and attack: 受到台风～的地区 areas hit by the typhoon
侵占 qīnzhàn (动) invade and occupy; seize

勤 qín I (形) hardworking; diligent; industrious: ～学苦练 study diligently and train hard II (副) frequently; regularly: 他来得最～. He comes very often. III (名) (office, school, etc.) attendance: 值～ be on duty. 考～ check on work attendance

勤奋(奮) qínfèn (副) work or study hard constantly
勤工俭(儉)学(學) qíngōng-jiǎnxué part-work and part-study
勤俭(儉) qínjiǎn (形) hardworking and thrifty
勤恳(懇) qínkěn (形) diligent and conscientious: 工作～ work earnestly and conscientiously
勤快 qínkuai (形) hard-working and fond of physical labour
勤劳(勞) qínláo (形) diligent; industrious
勤勉 qínmiǎn (副) (work or study) perseveringly
勤务(務) qínwù (名) duty; service: ～兵 orderly
勤杂(雜)工 qínzágōng (名) oddjobman; handyman

芹 qín

芹菜 qíncài (名) celery

禽 qín (名) birds: 家～ domestic fowls; poultry

禽兽(獸) qínshòu (名) birds and beasts: 衣冠～ a beast of a man; a human beast

擒 qín (动) capture; catch; seize

噙 qín (动) hold in the mouth or the eyes: ～着眼泪 eyes filled with tears

琴 qín (名) 1 a general name for stringed instruments: 胡～ fiddle. 竖～ harp. 小提～ violin 2 piano: 钢～ piano

琴键 qínjiàn (名) key (on a musical instrument)
琴弦 qínxián (名) string (of a musical instrument)

寝(寢) qǐn (动) get into bed; sleep: 废～忘食 forget to eat and sleep. 就～ go to bed

寝食 qǐn-shí (名) sleeping and eating
寝室 qǐnshì (名) bedroom; dor-

mitory

沁 qìn (动) ooze; seep: 额上～出了汗珠. Beads of sweat stood on his forehead.

青 qīng (形) 1 blue or green: ～天 blue sky 2 black: ～布 black cloth 3 young (people): ～工 young workers

青菜 qīngcài (名) green vegetables

青出于(於)蓝(藍) qīng chūyú lán the pupil often surpasses the master

青春 qīngchūn (名) youth: 充满～活力 be bursting with youthful vigour

青翠 qīngcuì (形) fresh and green

青光眼 qīngguāngyǎn (名) glaucoma

青黄不接 qīng-huáng bù jiē temporary shortage

青睐(睞) qīnglài (名) favour; good graces: 受到某人的～ be in sb.'s good graces

青年 qīngnián (名) youth; young people

青少年 qīng-shào nián (名) teenagers: ～犯罪 juvenile delinquency

青天 qīngtiān (名) blue sky: ～霹雳 a bolt from the blue

青铜 qīngtóng (名) bronze: ～器 bronze ware

青蛙 qīngwā (名) frog

青云(雲)直上 qīngyún zhíshàn rapid advancement in one's career

清 qīng I (形) 1 clean; clear; pure: 溪水～澈. The water of the steam is crystal clear. 2 distinct; clarified: 说不～ hard to explain. 数不～ countless 3 quiet: ～静 quiet. 享～福 live in quiet comfort II (动) settle; clear up: ～帐 settle the account

清白 qīngbái (形) pure; clean; unsullied: 历史～ be of unsullied antecedents

清查 qīngchá (动) check

清偿(償) qīngcháng (动) pay off; clear off: ～债务 pay off (or clear off) debts

清晨 qīngchén (名) early morning

清除 qīngchú (动) clear away; get rid of; eliminate: ～垃圾 clear away rubbish. ～官僚主义的恶习 get rid of the bureaucratic practices

清楚 qīngchu I (形) clear; distinct: 他说话不～. He doesn't speak distinctly. II (动) be clear about; understand: 这件事我不太～. I don't know much about the matter.

清脆 qīngcuì (形) (of voice) clear and melodious

清单(單) qīngdān (名) detailed list; inventory

清淡 qīngdàn (形) 1 light; delicate: ～的食物 light food 2 dull; slack: 生意～. Business is slack.

清点(點) qīngdiǎn (动) check; make an inventory: ～货物 take stock

清风(風) qīngfēng (名) cool breeze

清高 qīnggāo (形) noble-minded and unwilling to swim with the tide

清官 qīngguān (名) honest and upright official

清规戒律 qīngguī jièlǜ (名) taboos and prohibitions; rigorous regulations

清洁(潔) qīngjié (形) clean: 整齐～ clean and tidy

清净 qīngjìng (形) peace and quiet: 图～ seek peace and quiet

清静 qīngjìng (形) quiet: ～的地方 a quiet place

清冷 qīnglěng (形) chilly: ～的秋夜 a chilly autumn night

清理 qīnglǐ (动) put in order: ～帐目 check up on the accounts. ～文件 sort out the documents

清凉 qīngliáng (形) cool and refreshing: ～饮料 cold drinks

清明 qīngmíng I (名) Pure Brightness; a day around April 5th or 6th when one pays respects to a dead person at his tomb II (形) clear and bright: 月色～. The moonlight is bright.

清贫 qīngpín (形) (usu. of an intellectual in old society) poor or in straitened circumstances

清爽 qīngshuǎng (形) 1 fresh and cool: 雨后空气特别～. The air after rain is especially cool and refreshing. 2 relieved; relaxed: 心里～了 feel relieved

清算 qīngsuàn (动) 1 clear accounts 2 settle accounts; liquidate; expose and criticize

清晰 qīngxī (形) distinct; clear: 发音～ clear articulation

清洗 qīngxǐ (动) 1 rinse; wash 2 purge; comb out (undesirable elements)

清闲(閒) qīngxián (名) quiet leisure: 享～ enjoy a quiet life

清香 qīngxiāng (名) delicate fragrance; faint scent (of flowers)

清醒 qīngxǐng (形) **1** clear-headed; sane: 头脑～ clear-headed **2** regain consciousness: 病人已经～过来了. The patient has come to.

清秀 qīngxiù (形) delicate and pretty: 面目～ of fine, delicate features

清一色 qīngyīsè (形) all of the same colour; uniform; homogeneous

清真 qīngzhēn (名) Islamic; Muslim: ～寺 mosque

蜻 qīng

蜻蜓 qīngtíng (名) dragonfly

蜻蜓点(點)水 qīngtíng diǎn shuǐ touch on sth. lightly

倾(傾) qīng (动) **1** incline; lean: 左～ leftist (deviation) **2** pour out; empty: ～囊相助 give all possible financial assistance **3** collapse

倾巢出动(動) qīngcháochūdòng turn out in full force (derog.)

倾倒 qīngdǎo (动) **1** topple and fall; topple over **2** greatly admire

倾倒 qīngdào (动) empty; pour out: ～垃圾 dump rubbish

倾覆 qīngfù (动) overturn; topple; overthrow

倾家荡(蕩)产(產) qīngjiā-dàngchǎn go bankrupt or broke

倾慕 qīngmù (动) adore

倾盆大雨 qīngpén dàyǔ (名) heavy downpour; rain cats and dogs

倾诉 qīngsù (动) say everything (that is on one's mind)

倾听(聽) qīngtīng (动) listen attentively to: ～民众的呼声listen attentively to what the masses have to say

倾向 qīngxiàng I (名) **1** trend; tendency **2** tend: 我～于同意他的意见. I tend (or am inclined) to agree with him.

倾销 qīngxiāo (动) (for goods) dump

倾泻(瀉) qīngxiè (动) pour; come down in torrents

倾心 qīngxīn (动) admire; fall in love with: 一见～ fall in love at first sight

倾注 qīngzhù (动) pour: 把全部心血～到工作中去 throw oneself into one's work heart and soul

轻(輕) qīng I (形) **1** light (in weight): 象羽毛一样～ as light as a feather **2** small in degree: 年纪很～ be very young. 伤势不～ be seriously wounded **3** light; easy: ～罚 light punishment. 工作很～. It's an easy job. **4** gently; softly: ～声点! Be quiet! II (动) be little; make light of: 文人相～ scholars often scorn one another. ～敌 underestimate enemy strength; underestimate one's adversary

轻便 qīngbiàn (形) light; portable

轻而易举(舉) qīng ér yì jǔ easy to accomplish

轻浮 qīngfú (形) frivolous; flighty: 举止～ behave frivolously

轻工业(業) qīnggōngyè (名) light industry

轻举(舉)妄动(動) qīngjǔ-wàngdòng act rashly; take reckless action

轻快 qīngkuài (形) **1** brisk; spry: 迈着～的步伐 walk at a brisk pace **2** lighthearted: ～的曲调 lively tune

轻描淡写(寫) qīngmiáo-dànxiě touch on lightly; mention casually

轻蔑 qīngmiè (形) scornful; contemptuous

轻飘飘 qīngpiāopiāo (形) light as a feather; buoyant: 想到自己的成功, 她脚底下～的. Drunk with success, she felt as if treading on air.

轻巧 qīngqiǎo (形) **1** simple and easy: 你说得倒～. You talk as if it were that simple. **2** deft; dexterous: 动作～ act with agility and grace

轻柔 qīngróu (形) soft; gentle: 柳枝～ pliable willow twigs. ～的声音 a gentle voice

轻纱 qīngshā (名) fine gauze

轻生 qīngshēng (动) commit suicide

轻视 qīngshì (动) look down on; despise; underestimate

轻手轻脚 qīngshǒu-qīngjiǎo gently; softly: 护士进出都～的, 怕惊醒病人. The nurse tiptoed in and out so as not to wake the patient.

轻率 qīngshuài (形) rash; hasty; indiscreet: ～的态度 reckless attitude. ～从事 act rashly

轻松 qīngsōng (形) relaxed: ～愉快 thoroughly relaxed

轻佻 qīngtiāo (形) frivolous; skittish

轻微 qīngwēi (形) light; slight; trifling: ～的损害 slight damage

轻信 qīngxìn (动) be credulous;

~readily believe

轻型 qīngxíng (形) light-duty; light: ~载重汽车 light-duty truck

轻易 qīngyì (副) 1 easily: 成功不是~就能取得的. Success doesn't come easily. 2 lightly; rashly: 他从不~发表意见. He never expresses an opinion on the spur of the moment.

轻音乐(樂) qīngyīnyuè (名) light music

轻盈 qīngyíng (形) slim and graceful; lithe; lissom

轻重 qīng-zhòng (名) 1 weight: ~不一 different in weight 2 degree of seriousness; relative importance: 无足~ of no consequence 3 propriety: 此人说话有时不知~. The chap doesn't know how to talk properly under certain circumstances.

轻装(裝) qīngzhuāng (副) with light packs (or equipment): ~就道 travel light

氢(氫) qīng (名) hydrogen (H): ~弹 H-bomb

情 qíng (名) 1 feelings; affection; sentiment: 爱~ love. 热~ enthusiasm 2 favour; kindness: 求~ plead with sb. 3 situation; condition: 病~ patient's condition

情报(報) qíngbào (名) information; intelligence: 刺探~ pry for information. ~机关 intelligence agency

情不自禁 qíng bù zì jīn cannot help (doing sth.): ~地叫了起来 can't help crying out

情操 qíngcāo (名) moral integrity; noble mind

情敌(敵) qíngdí (名) rival in a love triangle

情调 qíngdiào (名) sentiment; emotional appeal

情分 qíngfen (名) mutual affection natural to various types of human relationship

情感 qínggǎn (名) feelings; emotion

情歌 qínggē (名) love song

情节(節) qíngjié (名) 1 (of story, play, etc.) plot: 故事~曲折. The story has a complicated plot. 2 circumstances: ~严重的案子 a serious case

情景 qíngjǐng (名) scene; sight; circumstances: 感人的~ a moving sight

情况 qíngkuàng (名) situation; condition; state of affairs: 生产~ production situation. 在这种~下 under these circumstances. 那要看~而定. That depends. *or* It all depends.

情理 qínglǐ (名) reason; sense: 合乎~ be reasonable. 不近~ unreasonable; irrational

情侣 qínglǚ (名) sweethearts; lovers

情面 qíngmian (名) feelings; sensibilities: 留~ spare sb.'s sensibilities

情趣 qíngqù (名) 1 disposition and taste: 他们二人~相投. The two of them find each other congenial. 2 good taste; appeal: 这首诗很有~. This poem is a model of good taste.

情人 qíngrén (名) sweetheart; lover

情书(書) qíngshū (名) love letter

情投意合 qíngtóu-yìhé find so much in common with one another; see eye to eye in everything

情形 qíngxing (名) condition

情绪 qíngxù (名) 1 mood; spirit; morale: ~很低 be in low spirits 2 moodiness; the sulks: 闹~ be in a fit of depression

情义(義) qíngyì (名) friendship; comradeship

情谊 qíngyì (名) friendly feelings; affection

情意 qíngyì (名) love; affection; goodwill

情有可原 qíng yǒu kě yuán (形) excusable; pardonable

情愿 qíngyuàn (动) 1 be willing to: 两相~ by mutual consent 2 would rather; prefer: 她~死也不肯受屈辱. She would prefer death to dishonour.

晴 qíng (形) fine; clear: 天转~了. It's clearing up.

晴空 qíngkōng (名) clear sky; cloudless sky: ~万里 a clear and boundless sky

晴朗 qínglǎng (形) fine; sunny

晴天 qíngtiān (名) fine day; sunny day

擎 qíng (动) hold up; lift up

请 qǐng (动) 1 request; ask: ~人帮忙 ask for help. ~医生 send for a doctor 2 (敬) please: ~坐 sit down, please.

请安 qǐng'ān (动) pay respects to sb.; wish sb. good health

请便 qǐngbiàn do as you wish; please yourself: 你要是想现在去, 那就~吧. Well, if you wish to leave now, go ahead.

请假 qǐngjià (动) ask for leave: 请一天假 ask for one days' leave. 她请病假回家了. She's gone home on sick leave.

请柬 qǐngjiǎn (名) invitation card

请教 qǐngjiào (动) ask for advice; consult: 这件事你得去～专家. You must consult an expert on such a matter. 虚心向别人～. Learn modestly from others.

请客 qǐngkè (动) stand treat; entertain guests; give a dinner party; play the host

请求 qǐngqiú (动) ask; request: ～宽恕 ask for forgiveness

请示 qǐngshì (动) ask for instructions: 向上级～ ask one's seniors for instructions

请帖 qǐngtiě (名) invitation card: 发～ send out invitations

请问 qǐngwèn (动) may I ask...: ～现在几点钟了? Excuse me, could you tell me what time it is now?

请勿 qǐngwù (动) please don't: ～吸烟 No smoking. ～践踏草地. Keep off the lawn.

请愿 qǐngyuàn (动、名) present a petition; petition

请罪 qǐngzuì (动) confess one's fault; apologize

顷

qǐng I (量) unit of area (= 6.6667 hectares): 碧波万～ a boundless expanse of blue water II (名)〈书〉a little while: 少～ after a while. ～刻 in an instant; instantly

亲(親)

qìng

see also qīn

亲家 qìngjia (名) families related by marriage

庆(慶)

qìng (动) celebrate; congratulate: ～丰收 celebrate a bumper harvest. 国～ National Day

庆典 qìngdiǎn (名) celebration: 大～ grand celebrations

庆贺 qìnghè (动) congratulate; celebrate

庆幸 qìngxìng (动) rejoice: 她为自己还活着感到～. She considers herself fortunate to have survived the accident.

庆祝 qìngzhù (动) celebrate: ～胜利 celebrate the victory

穹

qióng (名) **1** vault; dome **2** the sky: 苍～ the heavens

穷(窮)

qióng I (形) **1** poor; poverty-stricken **2** exhausted; pushed to limit: ～奢极欲 indulge in extravagance and luxury. 山～水尽 at the end of one's tether; in desperate straits II(副) extremely; exceedingly: ～忙 be up to one's ears in work III (名) limit; end: 无～无尽 endless; inexhaustible

穷极(極)无(無)聊 qióngjí wúliáo (形) **1** utterly bored **2** absolutely senseless

穷尽(盡) qióngjìn (名) limit; end: 人类的知识是没有～的. Human knowledge is without end.

穷苦 qióngkǔ (形) poverty-stricken; impoverished

穷困 qióngkùn (形) poverty-stricken; destitute

穷酸 qióngsuān (形) (of a scholar in old society) miserably poor and pedantic

穷乡(鄉)僻壤 qióngxiāng-pìrǎng (名) a remote backward place in the countryside

穷凶(兇)极(極)恶(惡) qióngxiōng-jí'è extremely vicious; utterly atrocious

琼(瓊)

qióng (名) fine jade

秋

qiū (名) **1** autumn: 深～ late autumn **2** harvest time: 麦～ time for the wheat harvest **3** year: 千～万代 for thousands of years

秋毫 qiūháo (名) autumn hair; sth. too small to be easily discernible: 明察～ be so sharp-sighted as to be able to detect the smallest flaws

秋季 qiūjì (名) the autumn season

秋千(鞦韆) qiūqiān (名) swing: 打～ have a swing

秋色 qiūsè (名) autumn scenery

秋收 qiūshōu (名) autumn harvest

丘

qiū (名) mound; hillock: 沙～ a sand dune. 坟～ grave

丘陵 qiūlíng (名) hills: ～地带 hilly land

蚯

qiū

蚯蚓 qiūyǐn (名) earthworm

酋

qiú (名) chief of a tribe; chieftain: 匪～ bandit chief

酋长(長) qiúzhǎng (名) chief of a tribe; sheik(h); emir

求

qiú (动) **1** beg; entreat; request: ～你帮个忙. May I ask you a favour? ～教 seek counsel. ～见 request an audi-

ence; ask for an interview 2 seek; strive for: 不～个人名利 seek neither personal fame nor gain 3 demand: 供不应～ Supply falls short of demand.
求爱(愛) qiú'ài (动) court; woo
求和 qiúhé (动) sue for peace
求婚 qiúhūn (动) propose
求救 qiújiù (动) ask for immediate rescue when in distress; send an S.O.S.; cry for help
求情 qiúqíng (动) plead; beg for leniency: 向他～ plead with him
求全 qiúquán (动) 1 demand perfection: ～责备 nitpick 2 try to round sth. off: 委曲～ stoop to compromise
求饶(饒) qiúráo (动) beg for mercy
求同存异(異) qiú tóng cún yì seek common ground while reserving differences: 求大同，存小异 seek common ground on major issues while reserving differences on minor ones
求学(學) qiúxué (动) pursue one's studies
求之不得 qiú zhī bù dé most welcome: 一个～的好机会 a golden opportunity
求知 qiúzhī (动) seek knowledge

裘
qiú (名) fur coat

球
qiú (名) 1 ball: 篮～ basketball. 网～ tennis 2 the globe; the earth: 东半～ the Eastern Hemisphere 3 anything shaped like a ball: 雪～ snowball
球门(門) qiúmén (名) goal
球迷 qiúmí (名) (ball game) fan: 足球～ football fan
球拍 qiúpāi (名) 1 (tennis, badminton, etc.) racket 2 (ping-pong) bat
球赛 qiúsài (名) ball game; match
球网(網) qiúwǎng (名) net (for ball games)
球鞋 qiúxié (名) gym shoes; tennis shoes; sneakers
球艺(藝) qiúyì (名) ball game skills

囚
qiú (动、名) 1 imprison 2 prisoner; captive
囚犯 qiúfàn (名) prisoner; convict
囚禁 qiújìn (动) imprison; put in jail

泅
qiú (动) swim: ～渡 swim across

趋(趨)
qū (动) 1 tend towards; tend to become: 大势所～ irresistible general trend 2 hasten; hurry along: ～前 hasten forward
趋势(勢) qūshì (名) trend; tendency: 他的病有好转的～. His condition is turning for the better.
趋向 qūxiàng I (名) trend; tendency II (动) tend to; incline to: 问题～明朗. The problem is being cleared up.
趋炎附势(勢) qūyán-fùshì sycophantic

祛
qū (动) dispel; drive away: ～暑 drive away summer heat
祛除 qūchú (动) dispel; get rid of; drive out: ～疑虑 dispel one's misgivings. ～邪气 eliminate unhealthy trends

区(區)
qū I (名) 1 area; district; region: 山～ mountain area. 风景～ scenic spot 2 an administrative division: 自治～ autonomous region II (动) distinguish
区别 qūbié I (动) distinguish: ～好坏 distinguish between good and bad II (名) difference: 这两种意见没有什么大的～. There isn't much difference between these two views.
区区 qūqū (形) trivial; trifling: ～小事，何足挂齿. Such a trifling matter is hardly worth mentioning.
区域 qūyù (名) area; district; region

躯(軀)
qū (名) the human body: 为国捐～ lay down one's life for one's country
躯干(幹) qūgàn (名) truck; torso
躯壳(殼) qūqiào (名) the body (as opposed to the soul)
躯体(體) qūtǐ (名) body

驱(驅)
qū (动) 1 drive (a horse, car, etc.): ～车前往 drive (in a vehicle) to a place 2 expel; disperse: ～出国境 deport 3 run quickly: 长～直入 drive straight ahead without let and hindrance
驱除 qūchú (动) drive away; get rid of
驱使 qūshǐ (动) 1 order about 2 prompt; urge: 为良心所～ follow the dictates of one's own conscience
驱逐 qūzhú (动) drive out; expel; banish: ～出境 deport; expel. ～

舰 destroyer

蛆 qū (名) maggot

曲 qū I (形) 1 bent; crooked: ～径通幽 a winding path leading to a secluded spot 2 wrong; unjustifiable: 是非～直 the rights and wrongs of a matter II (名) bend (of a river, etc.)
see also qǔ

曲解 qūjiě (动) twist; distort; misinterpret

曲折 qūzhé I (形) 1 winding: 小径～通过树林. The path winds through the woods. 2 not straight or smooth; tortuous: 生活的道路是～的. Life is full of twists and turns. II (名) complications: 你不知道这件事的～. You don't know the complications involved in this matter.

曲直 qū-zhí (名) right and wrong

曲线(綫) qūxiàn (名) curve

蛐 qū

蛐蛐儿 qūqur (名) cricket

屈 qū I (动) 1 bend; crook: ～膝 bend one's knees 2 subdue; submit; yield to: 宁死不～ would rather die than yield. 不～不挠 indomitable; dauntless; unyielding 3 be in the wrong: 理～词穷 unable to advance any tenable argument in defence of one's case II (名) wrong; injustice: 受～ be wronged

屈才 qūcái (动) be assigned a job unworthy of one's talents

屈从(從) qūcóng (动) submit to; yield to (sb.)

屈打成招 qū dǎ chéng zhāo confess oneself guilty under torture

屈服 qūfú (动) submit; yield; bow to: ～于社会的压力 yield to social pressure

屈辱 qūrǔ (名) humiliation; disgrace.

屈膝 qūxī (动) go down on one's knees

屈指可数(數) qūzhǐ kě shǔ can be counted on one's fingers; very few

渠 qú (名) ditch; canal; channel: 灌溉～ irrigation canal

渠道 qúdào (名) 1 irrigation ditch 2 medium of communication; channel: 通过外交～ through diplomatic channels

取 qǔ (动) 1 take; get; fetch: ～款 draw money (from one's account) 2 aim at; seek: 自～灭亡 court destruction; dig one's own grave 3 adopt; choose: 录～ enroll; admit

取材 qǔcái (动) draw materials: 就地～ make use of local materials

取长(長)补(補)短 qǔcháng-bǔduǎn learn from others' strong points to offset one's weaknesses

取代 qǔdài (动) replace; substitute: 我们必须找人～他. We must find somebody to replace him.

取道 qǔdào (动) by way of; via

取得 qǔdé (动) get; gain; obtain: ～进步 make progress. ～成功 achieve success. ～领导同意 obtain the approval of the leaders. ～一致 reach agreement

取缔 qǔdì (动) ban; outlaw

取经(經) qǔjīng (动) 1 go on a pilgrimage to India for Buddhist scriptures 2 learn from the experience of others

取决 qǔjué (动) depend on; be decided by: 你能否通过考试将～于你个人的努力. Whether or not you will pass the exam depends on your own effort.

取乐(樂) qǔlè (动) seek pleasure; find amusement: 饮酒～ drink and make merry

取巧 qǔqiǎo (动) resort to trickery: 投机～ seek personal gain through shady transactions

取舍 qǔ-shě (动) accept or reject: 你得自己决定～. You have to make your own choice.

取消 qǔxiāo (动) cancel; abolish: ～一次会议 cancel (or call off) a meeting

取笑 qǔxiào (动) make fun of; ridicule

娶 qǔ (动) marry (a woman); take to wife: ～亲 (of a man) get married

曲 qǔ (名) 1 music: 作～ compose music 2 song; tune; melody: 唱一支～子 sing a song
see also qū

曲调 qǔdiào (名) tune; melody

曲艺(藝) qǔyì (名) folk art forms including ballad singing, story telling, comic dialogues, clapper talks, cross talks, etc.

趣 qù (名) interest; delight: 有～ interesting; amusing; delightful

趣味 qùwèi (名) 1 interest; delight: 很有～ of great interest 2 taste; liking: 低级～ vulgar taste

去 qù I (动) **1** go; leave: ～乡下 go to the countryside. 他下周～巴黎. He will leave for Paris next week. 我没有～过他家. I've never been to her home. ～电话 give sb. a ring **2** remove; get rid of: ～皮 remove the skin; peel. ～掉精神负担 get the load off one's mind II (形) the one before this: ～年 last year. ～冬 last winter III **1** [used after a verb to indicate an action taking place at some distance from the speaker]: 进～ go in **2** [used before a verb to indicate that an action is to take place]: 我～考虑考虑. Let me think it over. 他自己～作主好啦! Let him decide it for himself 我们～想想办法. We'll try to find a way out. **3** [used after a V-O construction to indicate why sb. is away]: 她买东西～了. She has gone shopping. **4** [used between a verbal phrase (or a prep. construction) and a verb (or a verbal phrase) to indicate that the former is the means while latter is the end]: 用冷静的头脑～分析问题 analyze the problem with a cool head

去处(處) qùchù (名) **1** place to go; whereabouts **2** place; site: 一个幽静的～ a beautiful quiet place

去世 qùshì (动) (of grown-up people) die; pass away

去向 qùxiàng (名) the direction in which sb. has gone: 不知～ be nowhere to be found

觑 qù (动) look; gaze: 面面相～ gaze at each other in astonishment or despair

圈 quān I (名) circle; ring: 飞机在空中转了两～. The airplane circled twice in the air. II (动) **1** enclose; encircle: 用篱笆把菜园～起来 enclose the vegetable garden with a fence **2** mark with a circle: ～阅文件 circle one's name on a document to show that one has read it; tick off decisions. 请把那个错字～了. Please cross out the wrong word.

see also juàn

圈套 quāntào (名) trap: 落入～ fall or walk into a trap; play into sb.'s hands

圈子 quānzi (名) circle; ring: 站成一个～ stand in a circle. 说话不要绕～. Don't beat about the bush. 搞小～ form a clique

拳 quán (名) **1** fist **2** boxing: 打～ practise shadow boxing

拳打脚踢 quándǎ-jiàotī (动) cuff and kick; beat up

拳击(擊) quánjī (名) boxing; pugilism: ～台 boxing ring

鬈 quán (形) curly; wavy: ～发 curly hair

鬈曲 quánqū (形) crimpy; crinkly; curly

蜷 quán (动) curl up; huddle up

蜷伏 quánfú (动) huddle up

蜷曲 quánqū (动) curl; coil; twist

颧 quán (名) cheekbone

颧骨 quánɡǔ (名) cheekbone

权(權) quán I (名) **1** right: 公民～ civil right. 优先～ priority. 选举和被选举～ the right to vote and stand for election. 没有发言～ have no say in the matter **2** power; authority: 立法～ legislative power. 当～ in power. 越～ overstep one's authority. 受～ be authorized (to do sth.) **3** advantageous position: 主动～ initiative. 霸～ hegemony II (动) weigh: ～衡轻重 weigh the pros and cons

权贵 quánguì (名) influential officials; bigwigs

权衡 quánhéng (动) weigh; balance: ～利弊 weigh the advantages and disadvantages

权力 quánlì (名) power; authority: 国家～机关 organ of state power. 行使～ invoke the authority. ～下放 delegate powers

权利 quánlì (名) right: 受教育的～ the right to education. 政治～ political rights

权且 quánqiě (副) for the time being: ～不用管它. Let's leave it at that.

权势(勢) quánshì (名) power and influence

权术(術) quánshù (名) political trickery: 玩弄～play politics

权威 quánwēi (名) authority: 学术～ academic authority

权限 quánxiàn (名) limits of authority

权宜 quányí (形) expedient: ～之计 expediency

权益 quányì (名) rights and interests: 民族经济～ national economic rights and interests

全 quán I (形) 1 whole; entire: ～世界 the whole world. ～国 all over the country. ～称 full name. 昨天～天 all day yesterday 2 complete: 货物很～ have a great variety of goods. ～套书 a complete set of books. 设备齐～ be fully equipped 3 perfect; intact: 两～其美 satisfy both sides II (副) completely; entirely: 东西准备～了吗? Is everything ready? ～错了. It's all wrong. 衣服～湿了 be wet through

全部 quánbù (形) all; whole; complete; total: 事情的～真相 the whole truth of the matter. ～开支 the total expenditure

全才 quáncái (名) a versatile person

全会(會) quánhuì (名) plenary session; plenum

全集 quánjí (名) complete or collected works

全局 quánjú (名) overall situation

全力 quánlì (名) with all one's strength: ～以赴 go all out; spare no effort

全貌 quánmào (名) overall picture

全面 quánmiàn (形) overall; all-round; comprehensive: ～崩溃 total collapse. ～性 totality. 照顾～ take into account the overall situation

全民 quánmín (名) the whole people: ～所有制 ownership by the whole people

全能 quánnéng (名) all-round: ～冠军 all-round champion

全年 quánnián (形) annual; yearly: ～收入 annual income

全盘(盤) quánpán (形) overall; comprehensive: ～考虑 give overall consideration to

全球 quánqiú (名) the whole world: ～战略 global strategy

全权(權) quánquán (名) full powers; plenary powers: 特命～大使 ambassador plenipotentiary and extraordinary. ～代表 plenipotentiary

全神贯注 quánshén guànzhù be absorbed in; be preoccupied with: ～地听着 listen with absorbing interest

全盛 quánshèng (形) flourishing; in full bloom; in the heyday: ～时代 golden age

全速 quánsù (名) full speed: ～前进 advance at full speed

全体(體) quántǐ (形) all; entire: ～起立 standing ovation. ～工作人员 the whole staff

全心全意 quánxīn-quányì (副) wholeheartedly; heart and soul: ～地为人民服务. Serve the people wholeheartedly.

痊 quán

痊愈 quányù (动) fully recover from an illness

诠 quán

诠释(釋) quánshì (名) annotation; explanatory notes

泉 quán (名) spring: 温～ hot spring. 喷～ fountain

泉水 quánshuǐ (名) spring water; spring

泉源 quányuán (名) 1 fountainhead; springhead 2 source: 力量的～ source of strength

犬 quǎn (名) dog: 猎～ hunting dog; hound. 警～ police dog

犬牙交错 quǎnyá jiāocuò (形) jigsaw-like

券 quàn (名) ticket, coupon: 入场～ admission ticket. 国库～ treasury bond

劝(勸) quàn (动) advise; urge: ～他戒烟 advise him to give up smoking. ～他休息 urge him to take a rest

劝导(導) quàndǎo (动) advise; exhort

劝告 quàngào (动) warn; urge; exhort

劝解 quànjiě (动) 1 try to make sb. stop worrying; pacify 2 mediate

劝说 quànshuō (动) try to persuade

劝阻 quànzǔ (动) dissuade sb. from doing sth.

缺 quē (动) be short of; lack: ～人 be short of personnel. 这本书～了两页. There are two pages missing from this book. 这里新鲜水果很～. Fresh fruit is scarce here. ～乏信心 be lacking in confidence

缺德 quēdé (形) mean; wicked: 做～事 do sth. mean. 他这样做可真～. It's wicked of him to act like that.

缺点(點) quēdiǎn (名) shortcoming; weakness; defect

缺乏 quēfá (动) lack; be short of: ～经验 lack experience. ～自知之明 overrate one's ability

缺勤 quēqín (动) be absent

from work
缺少 quēshǎo (动) lack; be short of: ～雨水 lack adequate rainfall
缺席 quēxí (动) be absent from a meeting, etc.: ～审判 trial by default
缺陷 quēxiàn (名) defect; drawback; flaw

阙 què (名) 1 watchtower on either side of a palace gate 2 imperial palace

却 què I (副) but; yet; however: 她很同情他,～又不知说什么好. She was full of sympathy for him, yet she didn't know what to say. II (动) 1 step back: 退～retreat 2 decline; refuse: 推～ decline 3 [used after certain verbs to indicate the completion of an action]: 冷～ cool off. 了～一个心愿 fulfil a wish
却步 quèbù (动) step back: 不要因为困难而～. Don't flinch from difficulties.

鹊 què (名) magpie

雀 què (名) sparrow
雀斑 quèbān (名) freckle
雀跃(躍) quèyuè (动) jump for joy

确(確) què I (形) true; authentic; reliable: 正～ correct II (副) firmly: ～立 establish
确保 quèbǎo (动) ensure; guarantee
确定 quèdìng (动) fix; determine; decide on
确切 quèqiè (形) definite; exact; precise: 用词～ use words with precision
确认(認) quèrèn (动) affirm; acknowledge
确实(實) quèshí I (形) true; certain; reliable: ～性 reliability II (副) really; indeed
确信 quèxìn (动) be deeply convinced
确诊 quèzhěn (动) make a definite diagnosis
确凿(鑿) quèzuò (形) based on truth; reliable: ～的证据 conclusive evidence. ～的事实 irrefutable facts

群 qún I (名) crowd; group: 人～ crowd. 羊～ a flock of sheep II (量) group; herd; flock: 一～人 a crowd of people. 一～牛 a herd of cattle. 一～蜜蜂 a swarm of bees
群策群力 qúncè-qúnlì let's pool our ideas and make concerted efforts
群岛(島) qúndǎo (名) archipelago
群氓 qúnméng (名) mob
群魔乱(亂)舞 qún mó luàn wǔ a scene of rogues running wild
群情 qúnqíng (名) public sentiment; feelings of the masses: ～鼎沸. Popular feeling ran high.
群众(衆) qúnzhòng (名) the masses: ～路线 the mass line. ～运动 mass movement; mass campaign

裙 qún (名) skirt: 围～ apron
裙带(帶) qúndài (名) connected through one's female relatives: 通过～关系 through petticoat influence
裙子 qúnzi (名) skirt

Rr

然 rán I (形) 1 right; correct: 不以为～ fail to give one's blessing to 2 like that: 不～ or else; otherwise. 当～ of course II (连) but; however; nevertheless: 此事虽小,～亦不可忽视. This is a matter of no great importance, but it should by no means be ignored. III [suffix of certain adverbs and adjectives indicating the state of affairs]: 忽～ suddenly; all of a sudden. 显～ obviously. 欣～ happily
然而 rán'ér (连) yet; but; however
然后(後) ránhòu (副) then; after that; afterwards

燃 rán (动) burn; light: ～灯 light a lamp. ～香 burn incense
燃料 ránliào (名) fuel
燃眉之急 rán méi zhī jí a matter of great urgency
燃烧(燒) ránshāo (动、名) 1 burn 2 combustion: ～弹 incendiary bomb

染 rǎn (动) 1 dye: 把头发～黑 have one's hair dyed black 2 catch (a disease); acquire (a bad habit, etc.); contaminate: 感～风寒 catch a cold. 污～ pollution. 一尘不～ not soiled by a speck of dust; spotless

染料 rǎnliào (名) dyestuff; dye: 活性～ reactive dye

染指 rǎnzhǐ (动) take a share of sth. one is not entitled to; have a finger in every pie

冉 rǎn (形)〈书〉slowly

冉冉 rǎnrǎn (形) slowly; gradually

嚷 rāng (动) shout; yell

嚷嚷 rāngrang (动) 1 shout; yell 2 make widely known

瓤 ráng (名) pulp; flesh; pith: 西瓜～ the pulp (or flesh) of a watermelon

壤 rǎng (名) 1 soil: 沃～ fertile soil; rich soil 2 earth: 天～ heaven and earth 3 area: 穷乡僻～ a remote and hardly accessible village

让(讓) ràng I (动) 1 give way; give in; give up: ～步 make concessions. 请～一～ Excuse me. 他比你小, 要～着他点儿. You should humour him a little bit since he is younger. 2 let sb. have sth. at a fair price: 如果你急需, 我可以把我的新车～给你. I can let you have my new car (at cost price) if you need one badly. 3 invite; offer: ～座 offer one's seat to sb. 把大家～进屋里. Ask all of them to come in. 4 let; allow: ～我想想. Let me think it over. 妈妈不～他去. Mother won't let him go. 对不起, ～你久等了. Sorry to have kept you waiting. II (介) [used in a passive sentence to introduce the agent]: 她的脸～蜂子叮了. She was stung by the bee in the face.

让步 ràngbù (动) make a concession; give in; give way: 作出必要的～ make necessary concessions

让路 rànglù (动) make way for sb. or sth.

让位 ràngwèi (动) 1 resign sovereign authority; abdicate 2 offer one's seat to sb.; step aside to make way for sb. else

饶(饒) ráo I (动) have mercy on; forgive: 求～ beg for mercy. 这回～了我吧. Let me off this time, please! II (形) rich; plentiful: ～有风趣 full of wit and humour

饶命 ráomìng (动) spare sb.'s life

饶舌 ráoshé (形) garrulous

饶恕 ráoshù (形) forgive; pardon

扰(擾) rǎo (动) disturb; harass

扰乱(亂) rǎoluàn (动) create confusion; disturb: ～治安 create social disturbances

绕(繞) rào (动) 1 wind; coil: ～线圈 wind wire into a coil 2 move round; circle: 老鹰在空中～着圈儿飞. The eagle is flying around in the sky. 3 bypass; go round: ～过暗礁 bypass hidden reefs

绕道 ràodào (动) make a detour

绕圈子 rào quānzi (动) circle; go round and round

绕弯(彎)子 rào wānzi (动) beat about the bush

绕嘴 ràozuǐ (形) (of a sentence, etc.) be difficult to articulate: ～字 tongue twister

惹 rě (动) 1 invite or ask for (sth. undesirable): ～麻烦 ask for trouble. ～是非 stir up trouble 2 offend; provoke: 我～不起他. I cannot afford to offend him. 他可不是好～的. He's not a man to be trifled with. 3 attract; cause: ～人注意 attract attention. 不要～人讨厌. Don't make a nuisance of yourself.

惹祸(禍) rěhuò (动) court disaster

惹事 rěshì (动) stir up trouble

惹是生非 rěshì-shēngfēi (动) create trouble

热(熱) rè I (形) 1 hot: 屋里太～. It's too hot in the room. 2 ardent; warmed: ～情 warmhearted. ～爱 ardent love II (名) 1 heat: 摩擦生～. Friction generates heat. 2 fever: 发～ run a fever 3 rush; craze: 淘金～ gold rush. 排球～ volleyball craze III (动) heat (up): 把菜～一下 heat up the dish

热忱 rèchén (名) zeal; enthusiasm and devotion: 满腔～ full of enthusiasm

热诚 rèchéng (形) warm and sincere: ～的爱戴 ardent love and devotion

热带(帶) rèdài (名) the tropics: ～病学 tropical medicine. ～植物 tropical plants

热核 rèhé (名) thermonuclear: ～反应 thermonuclear reaction

热乎 rèhu (形) nice and warm;

warm
热火朝天 rèhuǒ cháotiān bustling with activity; in full swing: 生产～. Production is in full swing.
热浪 rèlàng (名) heat wave; hot wave
热恋(戀) rèliàn (动) fall head over heels in love
热量 rèliàng (名) quantity of heat
热烈 rèliè (形) warm; enthusiastic; ardent: ～的欢迎 warm welcome
热门(門) rèmén (名) in great demand; popular: ～货 goods which are in great demand
热闹(鬧) rènao I (形) lively; bustling with noise and excitement: 交易会很～. The fair was bustling with activity. II (名) fun: 让我们看看～. Let's watch the fun. III (动) liven up; have a jolly time: ～一番 have fun; have a jolly time
热气(氣) rèqì (名) steam; heat: ～腾腾 most enthusiastic
热切 rèqiè (形) fervent; earnest: ～的愿望 earnest wish
热情 rèqíng I (名) enthusiasm; zeal; warmth: 对工作充满～ be full of enthusiasm for one's work II (形) warm; enthusiastic; fervent: ～的支持 enthusiastic support
热水袋 rèshuǐdài (名) hot-water bottle (or bag)
热心 rèxīn (形) warmhearted; enthusiastic
热血 rèxuè spirit of devotion to a righteous cause: ～沸腾 actuated by righteous indignation
热中 rèzhōng (动) 1 hanker after; crave: ～升官发财 hanker after power and wealth 2 be fond of; be keen on

人 rén (名) 1 human being; man; person; people: 男～ man. 女～ woman. 大～ adult. 中国～ Chinese. ～对自然界的认识 man's knowledge of nature. 受害～ injured party 2 a person engaged in a particular activity: 军～ soldier. 工～ worker. 客～ guest. 主～ host. 领导～ leader. 监护～ guardian 3 people; other people: 助～为乐 consider it a pleasure to be of service to others 4 personality; character: 为～老实忠厚 honest and sincere by nature 5 everybody; each: ～所共知 as is known to all
人才 réncái (名) 1 a talented person; talent; qualified (trained) personnel: ～出众 have outstanding ability. ～外流 brain drain 2 handsome appearance
人称(稱) rénchēng (名) person: 第一～ the first person. ～代词 personal pronoun
人道 réndào (名) 1 humanity; human sympathy 2 human; humane: 不～ inhuman. ～主义 humanitarianism
人丁 réndīng (名) population; number of people in a family
人定胜(勝)天 rén dìng shèng tiān man can conquer nature
人浮于(於)事 rén fú yú shì be overstaffed
人格 réngé (名) 1 personality; character; moral quality: ～高尚 be a person of noble character or moral integrity 2 human dignity
人工 réngōng (形) 1 man-made; artificial: ～呼吸 artificial respiration. ～流产 induced abortion 2 manual work; work done by hand 3 manpower: 修这座水库需要多少～? How many man-days will be needed to build this reservoir?
人和 rénhé (名) popular support
人寰 rénhuán (名) <书> human world; the world
人迹 rénjì (名) vestiges of human presence; traces of human inhabitation
人家 rénjiā (名) 1 household: 三户～ three households 2 family: 殷实～ a well-to-do family
人家 rénjia (代) 1 [used to refer to people other than oneself] other people: 别管～怎么说 take no notice of what other people might say. 东西总是～的好. The grass is always greener on the other side of the hill. 2 [used to refer to a certain person or people]: 我想我应该去,这个晚会是～专门为我举办的. I think I ought to go since they have arranged this party especially for me. 你把东西快给～送回去吧! You had better send it back to him! 3 [used to refer to the speaker himself]: ～等你等了半天了. I've been waiting for you all this while.
人口 rénkǒu (名) 1 population: ～普查 census. ～爆炸 population explosion 2 number of people in a family: 家里～不多 only a few people in one's family

人类(類) rénlèi (名) mankind; humanity: ～征服自然的斗争 man's struggle to conquer nature. ～学 anthropology

人力 rénlì (名) manpower; labour power: ～资源 human resources

人马(馬) rénmǎ (名) **1** forces; troops **2** staff; set-up

人们 rénmen (名) people; men: ～都说他不错. People all speak well of him.

人民 rénmín (名) the people: ～币 *Renminbi* (RMB), currency of the People's Republic of China

人命 rénmìng (名) human life: ～关天的大事 a matter of life and death; an event of vital importance

人品 rénpǐn (名) moral character: ～很好 be a person of good moral character

人情 rénqíng (名) **1** human feelings; sympathy; sensibilities: 不近～ unreasonable; contrary to the ways of the world **2** favour: 做个～ do sb. a favour **3** human relationship: ～世故 worldly wisdom. ～之常 natural and normal practice in human relationship

人权(權) rénquán (名) human rights

人群 rénqún (名) crowd

人人 rénrén (名) everybody; everyone

人山人海 rénshān-rénhǎi (名) huge crowds of people

人身 rénshēn (名) human body; person: ～攻击 personal attack

人参(参) rénshēn (名) ginseng

人生 rénshēng (名) life: ～观 outlook on life. ～哲学 philosophy of life

人士 rénshì (名) personage; public figure: 消息灵通～ well-informed sources. 知名～ well-known public figures; celebrities

人世 rénshì (名) this world; the world: ～沧桑 vicissitudes of life

人事 rénshì (名) **1** occurrences in human life **2** personnel matters: ～部门 personnel department. ～调动 transfer of personnel **3** consciousness of the outside world: 不省～ lose consciousness **4** ways of the world: 不懂～ unacquainted with the ways of the world **5** anything that a person is capable of: 尽～ do what is humanly possible in time of adversity

人手 rénshǒu (名) manpower; hand

人为(爲) rénwéi I (形) artificial: ～的障碍 an artificial barrier II (名) human effort: 事在～. Everything depends upon human effort.

人物 rénwù (名) **1** figure; personage: 历史～ a historical figure. 大～ a dignitary. 小～ a nobody; a nonentity **2** character: (in a literary work) 典型～ typical character. ～塑造 characterization

人心 rénxīn (名) popular feeling; the will of the people: 得～ enjoy popular support. 振奋～ boost popular morale. 大快～ most gratifying to the popular masses

人行道 rénxíngdào (名) pavement; sidewalk

人行横道 rénxíng héngdào (名) pedestrian crossing; zebra crossing

人性 rénxìng (名) human nature; humanity

人选(選) rénxuǎn (名) candidate; person properly chosen(for a job)

人烟(煙) rényān (名) inhabitants: ～稀少(稠密) be sparsely (densely) populated

人影 rényǐng (名) **1** the shadow of a human figure **2** the trace of a person's presence; figure: 她看见一个～在黑暗中消失了. She caught sight of a figure disappearing into the darkness. 我等了半天,连个～也不见. I waited and waited but not a single soul turned up.

人员 rényuán (名) personnel; staff: 技术～ technical personnel. 政府机关～ government functionaries

人缘 rényuán (名) relations with people; popularity: ～好 on good terms with everybody

人造 rénzào (形) man-made; artificial: ～纤维 artificial fibre. ～革 imitation leather. ～橡胶 synthetic rubber. ～黄油 margarine. ～卫星 man-made satellite

人证(證) rénzhèng (名) testimony of a witness

人之常情 rén zhī chángqíng (名) the way of the world; the normal practice in human relationships

人质(質) rénzhì (名) hostage

人种(種) rénzhǒng (名) ethnic group; race: ～学 ethnology

仁 rén I (形) benevolent: ～至义尽 have done everything possible in terms of traditional ethical code II (名) kernel: 核桃～ walnut meat

仁爱(愛) rén'ài (名) kindheartedness

仁慈 réncí (名) benevolence; mercy

仁义(義)道德 rényì-dàodé (名) virtue and morality

仁者见(見)仁,智者见(見)智 rénzhě jiàn rén, zhìzhě jiàn zhì differen; people have different views opinions differ

荏 rěn

荏苒 rěnrǎn 〈书〉(of time) pass quickly or imperceptibly

忍 rěn (动) **1** endure; tolerate; put up with: ～着点儿, 别为了一点小事发火. Be patient. Don't lose your temper over trivial matters. **2** be hardhearted enough to; have the heart to: 残～ cruel; ruthless

忍不住 rěnbuzhù unable to bear; cannot help (doing sth.): ～笑了起来 can't help laughing

忍耐 rěnnài (动) exercise patience; restrain oneself

忍气(氣)吞声(聲) rěnqì-tūnshēng (动) endure humiliation in silence

忍让(讓) rěnràng (动) be forbearing and conciliatory

忍辱负重 rěn rǔ fù zhòng (动) submit to humiliation for the sake of an important mission that one feels obliged to fulfil

忍受 rěnshòu (动) bear; endure: ～艰难困苦 endure hardships. 这种行为简直让人无法～. Such behaviour is absolutely unbearable.

忍痛 rěntòng (副) very reluctantly

忍无(無)可忍 rěn wú kě rěn be provoked beyond endurance

忍心 rěnxīn (动) have the heart to; be hardhearted enough to: 我不～看着她受苦. I don't have the heart to watch her writhing with pain.

认(認) rèn (动) **1** recognize; identify: 你变多了, 我都～不出你了! You've changed so much that I could hardly recognize you! 他的字真难～. His scrawl is hardly legible. **2** admit; recognize: ～输 admit defeat. 否～ deny

认错 rèncuò (动) admit one's mistake

认得 rènde (动) know; recognize: 这人你～吗? Do you know this man? 我已经认不得他了. I could no longer recognize him.

认定 rèndìng (动) be deeply convinced; set one's mind on

认可 rènkě (动) approve: 点头～ nod approval

认领 rènlǐng (动) claim (lost property)

认清 rènqīng (动) see clearly: ～当前形势 acquaint oneself with the current situation

认生 rènshēng (动) (of a child) be shy with strangers

认识(識) rènshi I (动) **1** know; recognize: 我听说过他, 但我不～他. I know of him, but I don't know him. **2** understand: ～自己的错误 realize one's error II (名) understanding; knowledge; cognition: 感性(理性)～ perceptual (rational) knowledge. ～水平 level of understanding

认为(爲) rènwéi (动) think; consider: 我～你这样做不对. I don't think it's right to act the way you do.

认帐(賬) rènzhàng (动) admit what one has said or done

认真 rènzhēn I (形) conscientious; earnest; serious: 工作～ be conscientious in one's work II (动) take seriously; take to heart: 不要把这件事看得太～了. Don't take the matter too seriously.

认罪 rènzuì (动) plead guilty

任 rèn I (动) **1** appoint: 公司新～的经理 the newly appointed manager of the company **2** assume a post; take up a job: ～教 be a teacher **3** let; allow: 有很多优质衣料～你挑选. There is a beautiful collection of dress materials for you to choose from. II (名) official post; office: 上～ assume office. 离～ leave office. ～内 during one's term (or tenure) of office. 前～ one's predecessor III (量) [for official terms]: 做过两～大使 have twice been ambassador

任何 rènhé (代) any; whatever: 没有～希望. There isn't any hope. 他没有～理由不去. He has no reason whatsoever not to go.

任劳(勞)任怨 rènláo-rènyuàn work hard regardless of unfair criticism or unjustifiable complaints

任免 rèn-miǎn (动) appoint and dismiss: ～事项 appointments and removals

任命 rènmìng (动) appoint: ～他

为会议主席 appoint him chairman of the meeting

任凭(憑) rènpíng (介) 1 at one's convenience; at one's discretion: 这件事～他去作主吧. I'll leave the matter to his discretion. 2 no matter (how, what, etc.): ～我怎么努力, 他总是不满意. No matter how hard I tried, it just wouldn't please him.

任期 rènqī (名) term of office; tenure of office: 每届总统～四年. The president is elected for a term of four years.

任人唯贤(賢) rèn rén wéi xián appoint people on their merits; meritocracy

任务(務) rènwu (名) task; mission; assignment

任性 rènxìng (形) wilful; self-willed

任意 rènyì (副) wantonly; wilfully: ～行动 unrestricted action. ～畅谈 talk freely

任职(職) rènzhí (动) hold a post; be in office: 在政府部门～ work (or hold a post) in a government institution

任重道远(遠) rènzhòng-dàoyuǎn shoulder heavy responsibilities

妊(姙) rèn (动) be pregnant

妊娠 rènshēn (名) gestation; pregnancy

刃 rèn (名) 1 the edge of a knife, sword, etc.; blade: 刀～ knife blade. 卷～ the edge of a knife is bent 2 sword; knife: 利～ sharp sword. 白～战 bayonet fighting

刃具 rènjù (名) cutting tool

韧(韌) rèn (形) pliable but strong; tenacious

韧带(帶) rèndài (名) ligament

韧性 rènxìng (名) toughness; tenacity

扔 rēng (动) 1 throw; toss; cast: ～手榴弹 throw a hand-grenade 2 throw away; cast aside: 把它～了吧. Throw it away. 请不要乱～果皮、纸屑. Please do not litter. 他早把这事～在脑后了. He's completely forgotten about it.

仍 réng (副) still; yet: 他的病势～不见好. He is not any better. ～须努力 must continue to work hard

仍旧(舊) réngjiù I (动) remain the same II (副) still; yet: 莎士比亚的故居保存得～和当年一样. Shakespear's cottage is kept as it was in his lifetime. 他～是老样子. He still looks the same.

仍然 réngrán (副) still; yet

日 rì (名) 1 sun: ～出 sunrise. ～落 sunset 2 daytime: ～～夜夜 day and night 3 day: 多～不见. Haven't seen you for ages. 我们改日再谈. Let's talk about it some other day (or time). 4 daily; every day: ～趋强壮 grow stronger with each passing day. 产量～增. Output is going up every day.

日报(報) rìbào (名) daily paper: «人民日报» *Renmin Ribao* (the People's Daily)

日常 rìcháng (形) day-to-day; everyday: ～工作 daily work; routine duties. ～生活 everyday life

日场(場) rìchǎng (名) matinée

日程 rìchéng (名) programme; schedule: 访问～ itinerary of a visit. 工作～ work schedule; programme of work. 会议～ agenda

日光 rìguāng (名) sunlight: ～浴 sunbath

日光灯(燈) rìguāngdēng (名) fluorescent lamp

日积(積)月累 rìjī-yuèlěi accumulate over a long period

日记 rìjì (名) diary: 记～ keep a diary

日渐 rìjiàn (副) with each passing day; day by day

日久 rìjiǔ (副) with the passing of time: ～天长 in (the) course of time; with the passage of time. ～见人心 It takes time to know a person well.

日历(曆) rìlì (名) calendar

日暮途穷(窮) rìmù-túqióng come to a dead end

日期 rìqī (名) date: 出发的～ departure date. 信的～是那一天? When is the letter dated?

日新月异(異) rìxīn-yuèyì change with each passing day; make rapid progress

日以继(繼)夜 rì yǐ jì yè night and day

日益 rìyì (副) increasingly; day by day: 起到～重要的作用 play an increasingly important role. ～改进 improve day by day

日用 rìyòng (形) of everyday use: ～必需品 daily necessities. ～品 basic commodities

日照 rìzhào (名) sunshine

日子 rìzi (名) 1 day; date: 定～ fix a date 2 time (counted by days): 他离家有些～了. He's been away from home for some time. 这些～她有些不舒服. She hasn't been feeling well recently. 3 life; livelihood: 幸福的～ happy days. 最近我的～不好过. I have a hard time these days.

容 róng I (动) 1 hold; contain: 我觉得很窘,真有点儿无地自～. I felt so embarrassed that I did not know what to do with myself. 2 tolerate: 宽～ be tolerant. 大量～人 magnanimous 3 allow; permit: 不～怀疑 without doubt. 此事不～迟延. This matter admits of no delay. II (名) looks; appearance: 笑～ a smiling face

容光焕发(發) róngguāng huànfa glowing with health; have a radiant face

容积(積) róngjī (名) volume

容量 róngliàng (名) capacity

容貌 róngmào (名) appearance; looks

容纳 róngnà (动) hold; have a capacity of: 这个球场可以～十万人. The stadium can hold 100,000 people.

容器 róngqì (名) vessel; container

容情 róngqíng [usu. used in a negative sentence] show mercy

容忍 róngrěn (动) tolerate; put up with: 我们不能～这种态度. We can't tolerate this attitude.

容身 róngshēn (动) shelter oneself; make a living: 无～之地 have nowhere to rest

容许 róngxǔ (动) permit; allow: 局势的恶化不～我们再等待了. Faced with the worsening situation, we can't afford to wait any longer.

容易 róngyì I (形) easy: 写简化字比繁体字～得多. Simplified characters are much easier than complicated forms. II (副) easily; likely: 我很～今天就把它做好. I can easily finish it today.

溶 róng (动) dissolve: ～液 solution

溶化 rónghuà (动) dissolve

溶剂(劑) róngjì (名) solvent

溶解 róngjiě (动) dissolve: ～度 solubility

熔 róng (动) melt

熔点(點) róngdiǎn (名) melting (or fusing) point

熔化 rónghuà (动) melt

熔岩(巖) róngyán (名) lava

戎 róng (名)〈书〉army; military affairs: ～马生涯 army life

绒 róng (名) 1 fine hair; down: 鸭～ eiderdown. 羽～衣 down-padded anorak. 2 cloth with a soft nap: 天鹅～ velvet. 灯芯～ corduroy. 法兰～ flannel

绒毛 róngmáo (名) fine hair; down; villus

绒线(綫) róngxiàn (名) 1 floss for embroidery 2 knitting wool: ～衫 woollen sweater

绒衣 róngyī (名) sweat shirt

荣(榮) róng I (名) 1 honour; glory: ～获第一名 win first prize II (形) grow luxuriantly; flourish: 欣欣向～ flourishing; thriving; prosperous; lively

荣华(華)富贵 rónghuá-fùguì (名) glory, splendour, wealth and rank

荣辱 róng-rǔ (名) honour or disgrace

荣幸 róngxìng (形) honoured: 感到～ feel honoured

荣耀 róngyào (名) honour; glory

荣誉(譽) róngyù (名) honour; credit: 为祖国争～ win honour for one's country. 爱护公司的～ cherish the good name of the company

茸 róng I (形) fine and soft; downy II (名) young pilose antler

融 róng (动) 1 melt; thaw 2 blend; fuse: 水乳交～ blend as well as milk and water; be in perfect harmony

融合 rónghé (动) fuse; merge: 铜与锡的～ the fusion of copper and tin

融化 rónghuà (动) melt; thaw: 冰雪开始～. The snow and ice are beginning to thaw.

融会(會)贯通 rónghuì guàntōng (动) gain thorough understanding through comprehensive study of the subject

融解 róngjiě (动) melt; become liquid

融洽 róngqià (形) harmonious: 关系～ be on friendly terms

冗 rǒng (形) superfluous; redundant: ～词赘句 redundant words and expressions

冗长(長) rǒngcháng (形) lengthy; long-winded: ～的讲演 a lengthy speech

冗杂(雜) rǒngzá (形) (of

affairs) miscellaneous; multifarious; complicated

柔 róu (形) **1** soft; flexible: ~嫩 supple and tender **2** gentle; mild: 温~ gentle and tender. ~中有刚 firm but gentle; an iron hand in the velvet glove

柔和 róuhé (形) soft; gentle; mild: 光线~ soft light. 颜色~ a soft colour. ~的声音 a gentle voice

柔软 róuruǎn (形) soft; lithe: ~的动作 lithe movements.

柔弱 róuruò (形) weak; delicate: 身体~ in delicate health; weak; frail

揉 róu (动) rub: ~眼睛 rub one's eyes. ~面 knead dough

揉搓 róucuo (动) rub; knead

蹂 róu

蹂躏 róulìn (动) trample on; ravage: ~人权 trample on human rights

肉 ròu (名) **1** meat; flesh: 瘦~ lean meat. 猪~ pork. 牛~ beef. 羊~ mutton **2** pulp; flesh (of fruit): 果~ pulp of fruit

肉搏 ròubó (动) fight hand-to-hand: ~战 hand-to-hand combat; bayonet fighting

肉麻 ròumá (形) nauseating; sickening; disgusting

肉末 ròumò (名) minced meat

肉松 ròusōng (名) dried meat floss

肉体(體) ròutǐ (名) the human body; flesh

肉眼 ròuyǎn (名) naked eye: ~看不到 be invisible to the naked eye

肉欲(慾) ròuyù (名) carnal desire

蠕 rú (动) wriggle; squirm

蠕动(動) rúdòng (动) wriggle; squirm

儒 rú (名) **1** Confucianism; Confucianist **2** scholar; learned man

儒家 rújiā (名) the Confucian school

如 rú I (动) **1** like; as if: 了~指掌 know sth. like the back of one's hand **2** be as good as [used in negative sentences only]: 我不~他. I cannot compare with him. II (连) **1** in accordance with; as: ~期偿还 return sth. in due time **2** if: ~不同意,请告诉我. If you don't agree, please let me know.

如常 rúcháng (副) as usual: 早起~ get up early as usual

如出一辙 rú chū yī zhé be exactly the same

如此 rúcǐ so; such; in this way: ~勇敢 so courageous. 事已~,后悔也是枉然. As it is, regret won't help matters.

如法炮制(製) rú fǎ páozhì follow the prescribed rules

如故 rúgù (副) **1** as before: 依然~ remain the same as before **2** like old friends: 一见~ feel like old friends at the first meeting

如果 rúguǒ (连) if; in case; in the event of: ~你钱不够,我可以借些给你. If you are short of money, I can lend you some. ~我是你,我就接受邀请. If I were you, I would accept the invitation.

如何 rúhé (代) how; what: 你觉得这本小说~? How do you like this novel? 他不知~是好. He didn't know what to do.

如虎添翼 rú hǔ tiān yì like adding wings to a tiger; be further strengthened

如火如荼 rúhuǒ-rútú like a raging fire: 争取民族独立的斗争~,迅猛发展. The struggle for national independence spread like wildfire.

如饥似渴 rújī-sìkě voraciously; eagerly

如胶(膠)似漆 rújiāo-sìqī be deeply attached to each other

如今 rújīn (名) now; nowadays: ~人们对业余生活有更迫切的愿望. People nowadays have a stronger desire for spare-time activities.

如狼似虎 rúláng-sìhǔ as ferocious as wolves and tigers; like beasts of prey

如临(臨)大敌(敵) rúlín-dàdí as if faced with a formidable foe

如梦(夢)初醒 rú mèng chū xǐng as if awakening from a dream

如期 rúqī (副) as scheduled: ~完成 fulfilled on schedule

如实(實) rúshí (副) strictly according to the facts: ~汇报情况 report exactly as things stand

如释(釋)重负 rú shì zhòngfù as if relieved of a heavy load

如数(數)家珍 rú shǔ jiāzhēn as if enumerating one's family treasures; show thorough familiarity with a subject

如数(數) rúshù (副) exactly the number or amount: ～偿还 pay back in full
如同 rútóng (介) like; as: 灯火通明,～白昼 be brilliantly lit as if it were daytime
如下 rúxià as follows: 全文～. The full text follows.
如意 rúyì comply with one's wishes: 称心～ ideal; after one's own heart. ～算盘 wishful thinking
如鱼(魚)得水 rú yú dé shuǐ feel just like fish in water; be in congenial company or do congenial work
如愿 rúyuàn achieve one's goal
如坐针毡(氈) rú zuò zhēnzhān be on pins and needles; be on tenterhooks

汝 rǔ (代) <书> you

辱 rǔ I (名) disgrace; dishonour: 羞～ humiliation; terrible disgrace II (动) bring disgrace (or humiliation) to; insult
辱骂(駡) rǔmà (动) abuse; call sb. names
辱没 rǔmò (动) bring disgrace to; be unworthy of

乳 rǔ (名) 1 breast 2 milk: 炼～ condensed milk 3 newborn (animal); sucking: ～牛 milk cow
乳白 rǔbái (形) milk white; cream colour: ～玻璃 opal glass
乳臭未干(乾) rǔchòu wèi gān be young and inexperienced; be wet behind the ears
乳房 rǔfáng (名) 1 breast 2 (of a cow, goat, etc.) udder
乳酪 rǔlào (名) cheese
乳名 rǔmíng (名) child's pet name
乳母 rǔmǔ (名) wet nurse
乳牛 rǔniú (名) dairy cattle; milch cow
乳头(頭) rǔtóu (名) nipple; teat
乳汁 rǔzhī (名) milk

褥 rù (名) mattress
褥单(單) rùdān (名) bed sheet
褥子 rùzi (名) cotton padded mattress

入 rù I (动) 1 enter: ～境 enter a country. ～场券 admission ticket. 列～议程 put on the agenda 2 join; become a member of: ～党 join the party II (名) income: ～不敷出 income falling short of expenditure; unable to make ends meet
入耳 rù'ěr (形) pleasant to the ear: 不堪～ (of language) offensive to the ear
入股 rùgǔ (动) buy a share; become a shareholder
入伙(夥) rùhuǒ (动) join a gang; join in a partnership
入境 rùjìng (动) enter a country: ～签证 entry visa
入口 rùkǒu (动) 1 enter the mouth 2 entrance: 剧院～处 entrance to a theatre
入殓(殮) rùliàn (动) encoffin
入门(門) rùmén (动) cross the threshold; learn the rudiments of a subject
入迷 rùmí (动) be fascinated; be enchanted; be completely absorbed
入侵 rùqīn (动) invade; intrude
入神 rùshén (动) 1 be entranced: 听得入了神 listen spellbound 2 superb; marvellous: 这幅画画得真是～. This painting is really a masterpiece.
入声(聲) rùshēng (名) entering tone, one of the four tones in classical Chinese pronunciation;
入时(時) rùshí (形) fashionable; à la mode
入手 rùshǒu (动) start with; take as the point of departure: 不知从何～ not know where to start
入睡 rùshuì (动) go to sleep; fall asleep
入伍 rùwǔ (动) enlist; join the army
入席 rùxí (动) take one's seat at a banquet, ceremony, etc.
入学(學) rùxué (动) 1 start school: ～年龄 school age 2 enter a school: ～考试 entrance examination
入狱(獄) rùyù (动) be put in prison; be thrown into jail

软 ruǎn (形) 1 soft; flexible: 绸子摸起来很～. Silk feels soft. 2 soft; mild; gentle: 别对他太～. Don't be too soft with him. 3 weak; feeble: 两腿发～. One's legs feel weak. 4 easily moved or influenced: 心～ tenderhearted. 手～ be soft-hearted in handling matters
软膏 ruǎngāo (名) ointment; paste
软骨头(頭) ruǎngútou (名) a spineless person; a coward
软化 ruǎnhuà (动) soften; win over by soft tactics
软和 ruǎnhuo (形)<口> soft: ～的大衣 a soft coat

软件 ruǎnjiàn （名）(of computers) software
软禁 ruǎnjìn （动）put sb. under house arrest
软绵绵 ruǎnmiánmián （形）1 soft: 这支歌～的. This song is too sentimental. 2 weak: 她病好了,但身体仍然～的. She's recovered but still weak.
软木 ruǎnmù （名）cork: ～塞 cork (as a stopper)
软弱 ruǎnruò （形）weak; feeble; flabby: ～无能 weak and incompetent. ～可欺 be weak and easy to bully
软席 ruǎnxí （名）soft seat or berth (on a train)
软硬兼施 ruǎn-yìng jiān shī use both hard and soft tactics
蕊 ruǐ （名）stamen or pistil: 雄～ stamen. 雌～ pistil
瑞 ruì （形）auspicious; lucky
瑞雪 ruìxuě （名）timely snow
锐 ruì （形）1 sharp; keen: 尖～ sharp; keen 2 vigour; fighting spirit: 养精蓄～ conserve strength and energy
锐不可当(當) ruì bùkě dāng be irresistible
锐角 ruìjiǎo （名）acute angle
锐利 ruìlì （形）sharp; keen: ～的匕首 a sharp dagger. 目光～ sharp-eyed. ～的笔锋 a sharp pen; a vigorous style
锐敏 ruìmǐn （形）sensitive; keen: ～的嗅觉 a keen sense of smell
锐气(氣) ruìqì （名）dash; drive: 挫敌～ deflate the enemy's arrogance
闰 rùn
闰年 rùnnián （名）leap year
闰月 rùnyuè （名）leap month
润 rùn I（形）moist; sleek: 湿～ moist. 嗓音圆～ a sweet mellow voice II（动）1 moisten; lubricate 2 embellish; touch up III（名）profit; benefit: 利～ profit
润滑 rùnhuá （动）lubricate: ～油 lubricating oil; lubrication oil
润色 rùnsè （动）polish (a piece of writing, etc.); touch up
若 ruò I（动）like; seem; as if: ～有所思 seem lost in thought. ～隐～现 appear dimly visible II（连）if: 他～能来,我们一定热烈欢迎. If he could come, we would give him a warm welcome.
若非 ruòfēi （连）if not: ～他提醒,我早就把它忘得一干二净了. I might have forgotten all about the matter if he had not reminded me of it.
若干 ruògān （数）a certain number: ～年 a number of years. ～次 several times
若是 ruòshì （连）if
若无(無)其事 ruò wú qí shì act as if nothing had happened; keep perfectly calm
弱 ruò （形）1 weak; feeble: 年老体～ feeble from old age. 由～变强 go from weakness to strength 2 inferior: 她能力～. She is not very capable. 3 a little less than: 五分之一～ a little less than one-fifth
弱不禁风(風) ruò bù jīn fēng （动）be in extremely delicate health; look very fragile
弱点(點) ruòdiǎn （名）weakness; weak point
弱肉强食 ruòròu-qiángshí the law of the jungle
弱小 ruòxiǎo （形）small and weak: ～民族 small and weak nations

S s

撒 sā （动）1 let go; cast: ～网 cast a net. 把手～开 let go one's hold 2 throw off all restraint; let oneself go: ～泼 swearing and crying hysterically see also sǎ
撒谎 sāhuǎng （动）〈口〉tell a lie; lie
撒娇(嬌) sājiāo （动）act like a pampered child
撒尿 sāniào （动）〈口〉piss; pee
撒气(氣) sāqì （动）1 (of a ball, tyre, etc.) leak; go soft; be flat: 汽车的后带～了. The back tyre of the car is flat. 2 vent one's anger or ill temper
撒手 sāshǒu （动）let go: ～不管 wash one's hands of the business
撒腿 sātuǐ （动）start (running): ～就跑 make off at once; take to one's heels
撒野 sāyě （动）behave rudely
洒(灑) sǎ （动）sprinkle; spray; spill; shed:

~除草剂 spray herbicide. 别把牛奶~了. Don't spill the milk.
洒泪(淚) sǎlèi (动) shed tears
洒脱 sǎtuō (形) free and easy
撒 sǎ (动) 1 scatter; sprinkle; spread: ~化肥 spread fertilizer. ~种子 sow seeds 2 spill; drop
see also sā
撒播 sǎbō (动) broadcast sowing: ~机 broadcast seeder
飒(颯) sà
飒飒 sàsà 〈象〉 sough; rustle: 秋风~ the soughing autumn wind
塞 sāi (动) 1 fill in; squeeze in; stuff: 手提包不太满,还可以再~几本书. There is still room in the bag, so we can squeeze a few more books in. 水管~住了. The waterpipe is blocked. 2 stopper: 瓶~ a bottle cork
see also sài
塞子 sāizi (名) stopper; cork; plug; spigot
腮 sāi (名) cheek
腮帮子 sāibangzi (名)〈口〉 cheek
塞 sài (名) strategic stronghold
see also sāi
塞外 Sàiwài (名) beyond (or north of) the Great Wall
赛 sài (名) 1 match; game; competition; contest: 篮球~ basketball match. 田径~ track and field events 2 compare favorably with; surpass; overtake
赛车(車) sàichē (名) 1 cycle racing; motorcycle race; automobile race 2 racing bicycle
赛过(過) sàiguò (动) overtake; surpass; exceed: 很少有人能在绘画上~他. Few people can ever surpass him in painting.
赛马(馬) sàimǎ (名) horse race
赛跑 sàipǎo (名) race: 长距离~ long-distance race. 一百米~ 100-metre dash. 越野~ cross-country race
三 sān (数) 1 three: ~方面会谈 tripartite talks 2 more than two; several; many: ~灾八难 suffer from one ailment after another. ~番五次 several times; time and again; repeatedly
三部曲 sānbùqǔ (名) trilogy
三岔路口 sānchà lùkǒu (名) a fork in the road; a place where three roads meet; a junction
三长(長)两短 sāncháng-liǎngduǎn unexpected misfortune; sth. unfortunate, esp. death
三级跳远(遠) sān jí tiàoyuǎn (名) hop, step and jump; triple jump
三极(極)管 sānjíguǎn (名) triode: 晶体~ transistor
三角 sānjiǎo (名) 1 triangle 2 trigonometry
三脚架 sānjiǎojià (名) tripod
三教九流 sānjiào jiǔliú (名) 1 various religious sects and academic schools 2 people of all sorts
三军 sānjūn (名) 1 the army 2 the three armed services
三令五申 sānlìng-wǔshēn repeated injunctions
三六九等 sān-liù-jiǔděng (名) minute distinction of grades and ranks
三轮(輪)车(車) sānlúnchē (名) tricycle; pedicab
三三两两 sānsānliǎngliǎng in twos and threes
三思而行 sān sī ér xíng think twice before you act
…三…四 …sān…sì 颠三倒四 incoherent; disorganized. 丢三落四 always be forgetting or mislaying things
三天两头(頭) sāntiān-liǎngtóu〈口〉 almost every day
三心二意 sānxīn-èryì 1 be of two minds; shilly-shally: 别~了. Don't shilly-shally. 2 half-hearted
三言两语 sānyán-liǎngyǔ in a few words; in one or two words: 我们怎能把这事的原委~说清楚呢? How could we explain the whole thing in just a few words?
三月 sānyuè (名) 1 March 2 the third month of the lunar year; the third moon
叁 sān (数) three [used for the numeral 三 on cheques, etc. to avoid mistakes or alterations]
散 sǎn (形) 1 come loose; fall apart; not hold together: 把这些信捆好,别~了. Tie up these letters and see that they don't come loose. 包裹在运送到车站途中~了. The package got torn on the way to the station. 2 scattered: 我们住得很~. We live rather far apart from one another.
see also sàn
散兵 sǎnbīng (名) skirmisher: ~壕 fire trench. ~坑 foxhole; pit. ~线 skirmish line. ~游勇 stragglers

散光 sǎnguāng (名) astigmatism: ～眼镜 astigmatic lenses
散记 sǎnjì (名) random notes; sidelights
散漫 sǎnmàn (形) 1 undisciplined; careless and sloppy 2 unorganized; scattered
散文 sǎnwén (名) prose; essay
伞(傘) sǎn (名) 1 umbrella 2 sth. shaped like an umbrella: 降落～ parachute 3 protecting power: 核保护～ nuclear umbrella
伞兵 sǎnbīng (名) paratrooper; parachuter: ～部队 parachute troops; paratroops
散 sàn (动) 1 break up; disperse: 会议～了没有? Is the meeting over now? 2 distribute; disseminate; give out: ～传单 distribute leaflets 3 dispel; let out: 打开门窗～～这儿的空气. Please open the windows to let in fresh air.
see also sǎn
散布 sànbù (动) spread; disseminate; scatter; diffuse: ～谣言 spread rumours. 在这片原野上～着奇花异草. Exotic flowers are scattered here and there on this plain.
散步 sànbù (动) take a walk; go for a walk; go for a stroll
散场(場) sànchǎng (动) (of a theatre, cinema, etc.) end of a performance: 电影～了. The cinema emptied after the show. *or* The audience streamed out of the cinema after the show.
散发(發) sànfā (动) 1 give off; send forth; diffuse; emit: 花儿～着清香. The flowers sent forth wafts of delicate fragrance. 2 distribute; issue; give out: ～小册子 distribute brochures or booklets. 作为正式文件～ be circulated as an official document
散会(會) sànhuì (动) (of a meeting) be over; break up: 宣布～ declare the meeting over
散伙 sànhuǒ (动) (of a group, body or organization) dissolve; disband
散开(開) sànkai (动) spread out or apart; disperse; scatter: 警察赶到现场时, 人群已～了. The crowd had dispersed when the police rushed to the scene.
散失 sànshī (动) 1 scatter and disappear; be lost; be missing: ～的杂志已经找到. The missing magazines have been found. 2 (of moisture, etc.) be lost; evaporate; dissipate
丧(喪) sāng funeral; mourning
see also sàng
丧礼(禮) sānglǐ (名) funeral
丧事 sāngshì (名) funeral arrangements
丧钟(鐘) sāngzhōng (名) death knell; knell: 敲响殖民主义的～ sound the death knell of colonialism
桑 sāng (名) white mulberry; mulberry
桑蚕(蠶) sāngcán (名) silkworm: ～丝 mulberry silk
桑梓 sāngzǐ (名) <书> one's native place
嗓 sǎng (名) 1 throat; larynx 2 voice
嗓门(門)儿(兒) sǎngménr (名) voice: 提高～ raise one's voice
嗓音 sǎngyīn (名) voice: 他～洪亮. His voice carries.
嗓子 sǎngzi (名) 1 throat; larynx: ～疼 have a sore throat 2 voice: 哑～ husky voice
丧(喪) sàng (动) lose: ～尽廉耻 lose all sense of shame
see also sāng
丧胆(膽) sàngdǎn tremble with fear
丧魂落魄 sànghún-luòpò be scared out of one's wits
丧家之犬 sàng jiā zhī quǎn (名) stray cur: 惶惶如～ flee helter-skelter
丧命 sàngmìng (动) get killed in an accident, etc.; meet a violent death
丧气(氣) sàngqì (动) lose heart; be filled with despair: ～话 demoralizing words
丧权(權)辱国(國) sàngquán-rǔguó humiliate the nation and forfeit its sovereignty
丧失 sàngshī (动) lose; forfeit: ～信心 lose confidence. ～时机 miss the opportunity. 不能～警惕 never relax one's vigilance
丧心病狂 sàng xīn bìng kuáng preposterous and unscrupulous
臊 sāo (名) the smell of urine; foul smell
see also sào
搔 sāo (动) scratch
搔首 sāoshǒu scratch one's head
骚 sāo (动) disturb; upset: ～乱 disturbance; riot. ～扰 harass; molest

骚动(動) sāodòng I (名)disturbance;commotion;ferment II(动) be in a tumult; become restless

缫 sāo reel silk from cocoons; reel

缫丝(絲) sāosī (动) silk reeling; filature: ～厂 reeling mill; filature

扫(掃) sǎo (动) 1 sweep; clear away: ～除街上的积雪 clear the streets of snow. ～清障碍 remove the obstacles 2 pass quickly along or over; sweep: 他向坐在大厅的人群～了一眼. His eyes swept over the people sitting in the hall.
see also sào

扫除 sǎochú (动) 1 cleaning; cleanup: 大～ spring-cleaning 2 clear away; remove; wipe out: ～文盲 eliminate (or wipe out) illiteracy

扫荡(蕩) sǎodàng (动) mop up

扫地 sǎodì (动) 1 sweep the floor 2 (of honour, credibility, etc.) reach rock bottom: 名誉～ be thoroughly discredited

扫雷 sǎoléi (动) mine sweeping

扫描 sǎomiáo (名) scanning: ～器 scanner

扫墓 sǎomù (动) pay respects to a dead person at his tomb

扫射 sǎoshè (动) strafe

扫尾 sǎowěi (动) finish (the final part of task); wind up (the work)

扫兴(興) sǎoxìng (动) have one's spirits dampened; feel disappointed: 真叫人～! How disappointing!

嫂 sǎo (名) elder brother's wife; sister-in-law

臊 sào (形) shy; bashful: ～得脸通红 blush scarlet
see also sāo

扫(掃) sào
see also sǎo

扫帚 sàozhou (名) broom

涩(澀) sè (形) 1 puckery; astringent: 这些柿子太～, 还不能吃. These persimmons make your mouth pucker. You can't eat them yet. 2 unsmooth; hard-going 3 obscure; difficult to read

啬(嗇) sè (形) stingy; miserly

色 sè (名) 1 colour: 红～ red. 原～ primary colour 2 look; countenance; expression: 喜形于～ beaming with joy 3 kind; description: 各～人等 people of every description; all kinds of people 4 scene; scenery 5 woman's pretty looks
see also shǎi

色彩 sècǎi (名) colour; hue; tint; shade: 地方～ local colour. 文学～ literary flavour

色调 sèdiào (名) tone; hue

色厉(厲)内荏 sè lì nèi rěn outwardly strong but inwardly weak

色盲 sèmáng (名) colour blindness

色情 sèqíng (名) pornographic: ～文学 pornography

森 sēn (形) 1 full of trees 2 dark; gloomy: 阴～～ gloomy; grim

森林 sēnlín (名) forest: ～火灾 forest fire. 原始～ primeval forests

森严(嚴) sēnyán (形) stern; strict; forbidding: 门禁～ heavily guarded entrance

僧 sēng (名) Buddhist monk; monk

僧侣 sēnglǚ (名) monks and priests; clergy

沙 shā (名) 1 sand 2 granulated; powdered: 豆～ bean paste 3 (of voice) hoarse; husky

沙场(場) shāchǎng (名) battlefield; battleground

沙袋 shādài (名) sandbag

沙发(發) shāfā (名) sofa

沙锅(鍋) shāguō (名) earthenware pot

沙坑 shākēng (名) jumping pit

沙里淘金 shālǐ táo jīn get small returns for great effort

沙砾(礫) shālì (名) grit

沙漠 shāmò (名) desert

沙滩(灘) shātān (名) sandy beach

沙文主义(義) shāwén zhǔyì (名) chauvinism

沙哑(啞) shāyǎ (形) hoarse; husky; raucous

沙眼 shāyǎn (名) trachoma

沙子 shāzi (名) 1 sand; grit 2 small grains; pellets: 铁～ iron pellets; shot

鲨 shā (名) shark

鲨鱼(魚) shāyú (名) shark

砂 shā (名) sand; grit

砂布 shābù (名) emery cloth; abrasive cloth

砂糖 shātáng (名) granulated sugar

砂土 shātǔ (名) sandy soil; sand

砂纸 shāzhǐ (名) abrasive paper; sand paper

纱 shā (名) 1 yarn: 棉～ cotton yarn. ～厂 cotton mill 2 gauze; sheer: 铁～ wire gauze

纱布 shābù (名) gauze

纱橱 shāchú (名) screen cupboard

纱窗 shāchuāng (名) screen window

纱锭 shādìng (名) 〈纺〉 spindle

纱巾 shājīn (名) gauze kerchief

杀(殺) shā I (动) 1 kill; slaughter: ～人放火 commit murder and arson 2 fight; go into battle: ～出去 fight one's way out 3 weaken; reduce; abate: 风势稍～. The wind has abated. 4 check; curtail: ～住不正之风 check unhealthy tendencies II (副) in the extreme; exceedingly: 闷～人 bored stiff

杀风(風)景 shā fēngjǐng spoil the fun; spoil other people's pleasure

杀害 shāhài (动) murder; kill

杀鸡(鷄)取卵 shā jī qǔ luǎn kill the goose that lays the golden eggs

杀菌 shājūn (动) disinfect; sterilize: ～剂 germicide; bactericide

杀戮 shālù (动) massacre; slaughter

杀人 shārén (动) murder: ～犯 murderer. ～越货 kill a person and seize his goods. ～不见血 kill (or harm) a person by invisible means

杀伤(傷) shāshāng (动) kill and wound; inflict casualties on

杀身成仁 shā shēn chéng rén lay down one's life in the cause of justice

杀头(頭) shātóu (动) behead; decapitate

杀一儆百 shā yī jǐng bǎi execute one as a warning to a hundred

刹 shā (动) put on the brakes; stop; check: 把车～住 stop (or brake) a car

刹车(車) shāchē (动) 1 put on the brakes 2 brake

煞 shā (动) 1 stop; halt; check; bring to a close 2 tighten: ～一～腰带 tighten one's belt

see also shà

煞车(車) shāchē 见"刹车" shāchē

煞尾 shāwěi I (动) round off; wind up II (名) final stage; end; ending: ～这几句写得特别好. The concluding remarks are particularly well written.

傻(儍) shǎ (形) 1 stupid; muddleheaded: 你真～, 借给他那一大笔钱. It was stupid of you to lend him such a large sum of money. 装～ pretend to be ignorant. 你别～乎乎的, 他什么也没有答应你. Don't be that naive. He hasn't promised you anything. 2 think or act mechanically: 别一个劲儿～干. Don't just keep slaving away at the job.

傻瓜 shǎguā (名) fool; blockhead; simpleton

傻呵呵 shǎhēhē (形) simpleminded; not very clever: 别看他～的, 在学校的成绩总是名列前茅. Maybe he doesn't look bright, but he is always among the best at school.

傻劲(勁)儿(兒) shǎjìnr (名) 1 stupidity; foolishness 2 sheer enthusiasm; doggedness

傻笑 shǎxiào (动) laugh foolishly; giggle; smirk

傻眼 shǎyǎn (动) be dumbfounded; be stunned

傻子 shǎzi (名) fool; blockhead; simpleton

霎 shà (名) a very short time; moment; instant: ～时间 in a moment; in a twinkling; in a split second

厦 shà (名) a tall building; mansion: 高楼大～ tall buildings and large mansions

啥 shà (代) 〈方〉 what: 有～说～ say what one has to say; speak one's mind. 这没～了不起. This is nothing to speak of. 没～可怕 nothing to be afraid of

煞 shà I (名) evil spirit; goblin II (副) very

see also shā

煞费苦心 shà fèi kǔxīn cudgel one's brains; take great pains: ～地寻找借口 cudgel one's brains to find an excuse

煞有介事 shà yǒu jiè shì make a great fuss about sth. of little consequence; be ludicrously pompous

筛(篩) shāi I (名) sieve; sifter; screen II (动) sift; sieve; screen; riddle

筛分 shāifēn (名) screening sieving: ～机 screening machine

色 shǎi (名) 〈口〉 colour: 这布掉～吗? Will this cloth fade?

see also sè

色子 shǎizi (名) dice: 掷～ play

dice

晒(曬) shài (动) 1 (of the sun) shine upon; be weather-beaten 2 dry in the sun; bask: ～粮食 dry grain in the sun. ～衣服 air one's clothes. 暑假他们去了海滩，回来个个都～黑了. They went to the beach during the summer holidays and all came back with nice tans.

晒台(臺) shàitái (名) flat roof (for drying clothes, etc.)

晒图(圖) shàitú (动、名) make a blueprint; blueprint

潸 shān (副)〈书〉in tears: ～然泪下 shed tears

扇(搧) shān (动) 1 fan: ～扇子 fan oneself 2 incite, instigate; fan up; stir up: ～起暴乱 incite a riot

see also shàn

扇动(動) shāndòng (动) 1 fan; flap: ～翅膀 flap the wings 2 instigate; incite; stir up; whip up: ～派性 incite factional strife

扇风(風)点(點)火 shānfēng-diǎnhuǒ fan the flames; stir up trouble

煽 shān (动) incite; instigate

山 shān (名) 1 hill; mountain 2 anything resembling a mountain: 冰～ iceberg

山崩 shānbēng (名) landslide; landslip

山川 shānchuān (名) mountains and rivers; landscape

山村 shāncūn (名) mountain village

山地 shāndì (名) mountainous region; hilly area; hilly country

山顶 shāndǐng (名) the summit (or top) of a mountain; hill top

山峰 shānfēng (名) mountain peak

山冈(岡) shāngāng (名) low hill; hillock

山歌 shāngē (名) folk song (sung in the fields during or after work)

山沟(溝) shāngōu (名) gully; ravine; (mountain) valley

山谷 shāngǔ (名) mountain valley

山洪 shānhóng (名) mountain torrents

山货 shānhuò (名) 1 produce of various kinds from a mountain region (such as haws, chestnuts and walnuts) 2 household utensils made of wood, bamboo, clay, etc.

山脊 shānjǐ (名) ridge (of a mountain or hill)

山涧 shānjiàn (名) mountain stream

山脚 shānjiǎo (名) the foot of a hill

山口 shānkǒu (名) mountain pass; pass

山林 shānlín (名) mountain forest; wooded mountain

山岭(嶺) shānlǐng (名) mountain ridge

山麓 shānlù (名) the foot of a mountain

山峦(巒) shānluán (名) chain of mountains

山脉(脈) shānmài (名) mountain range; mountain chain

山盟海誓 shānméng-hǎishì (名) swear an oath of enduring fidelity

山坡 shānpō (名) hillside; mountain slope

山穷(窮)水尽(盡) shānqióng-shuǐjìn at the end of one's rope (or tether, resources); in desperate straits

山水 shānshuǐ (名) 1 scenery with hills and waters: 桂林～甲天下. The landscape of Guiling is among the finest under heaven. 2 traditional Chinese painting of mountains and waters; landscape

山头(頭) shāntóu (名) 1 hilltop; the top of a mountain 2 mountain stronghold; faction: 拉～ form a faction

山羊 shānyáng (名) goat

山腰 shānyāo (名) half way up the mountain

山岳(嶽) shānyuè (名) lofty mountains

山寨 shānzhài (名) mountain fastness; fortified mountain village

山珍海味 shānzhēn-hǎiwèi (名) delicacies

山庄(莊) shānzhuāng (名) mountain villa

舢 shān (名)

舢板 shānbǎn (名) sampan

衫 shān (名) unlined upper garment: 衬～ shirt. 汗～ undershirt

杉 shān (名) China fir

珊 shān (名)

珊瑚 shānhú (名) coral: ～岛 coral island

删 shān (动) delete; leave out: 这一段可以～去. This paragraph can be left out. ～掉不必要的形容词 cut out the unnecessary adjectives

删除 shānchú (动) delete; strike (or cut, cross) out

删繁就简 shānfán-jiùjiǎn simplify literary writing by leaving out superfluous words

删改 shāngǎi (动) prune away; revise: 决议草案几经～才被通过. The draft resolution was revised several times before it was adopted.

删节(節) shānjié (动) abridge; abbreviate: 略加～ slightly abridged. ～本 abridged edition; abbreviated version. ～号 ellipsis; suspension points; ellipsis dots (...)

姗 shān

姗姗来(來)迟(遲) shānshān lái chí be slow in coming; arrive late

闪 shǎn

(动) 1 dodge; duck; get out of the way: ～到一边 dodge swiftly to one side; duck behind 2 twist; sprain: ～了腰 sprain one's back 3 lightning: ～电 flashes of lightning 4 flash; sparkle; shine: 一～而过 flash past. 脑子里～过一个念头. An idea flashed through one's mind.

闪避 shǎnbì (动) dodge; sidestep

闪电(電) shǎndiàn (名) lightning: ～战 lightning war; blitzkrieg; blitz

闪光 shǎnguāng (名) flash of light; gleam; glisten; glitter

闪开(開) shǎnkai (动) get out of the way; jump aside; dodge: 车队来了,快～! Stand back! The motorcade is coming.

闪闪 shǎnshǎn (动) sparkle; glisten; glitter: 电光～. Lightning flashed.

闪身 shǎnshēn (副) sideways: ～进去 walk in sideways

闪烁(爍) shǎnshuò (动) 1 twinkle; glimmer; glisten: 星星在天空中～. Stars twinkled in the sky. 2 evasive; vague: ～其词 speak evasively

闪现 shǎnxiàn (动) flash before one

闪耀 shǎnyào (动) glitter; shine: 塔顶～着金光. The top of the tower is glittering.

陕(陝) shǎn

(名) blink; twinkle: 那飞机飞得很快,一～眼就不见了. The plane flew very fast and disappeared in the twinkling of an eye.

擅 shàn

I (副) do sth. on one's own authority: ～离职守 leave one's post without permission. ～自提价 arbitrarily raise prices II (动) be good at: 不～酬应 be not particularly good at casual conversation

擅长(長) shàncháng (动) be good at; be expert in; be skilled in: 他～摄影. He is a good photographer.

善 shàn

I (名) good: 行～ do good deeds II (形) 1 good: 心怀不～ harbour evil intentions 2 wise; satisfactory; good: ～策 wise policy (or move) 3 friendly: 友～ on good terms 4 familiar: 面～ look familiar III (动) 1 be good at: 多谋～断 be resourceful and quick at making decisions 2 be apt to: ～忘 be forgetful 3 do well: ～始～终 do well from start to finish. 你做事必须～始～终. You must bring the matter to a successful conclusion since you did very well from the very start. IV (副) properly: ～自保重 look after yourself properly; take good care of yourself

善罢(罷)甘休 shànbà-gānxiū [often used in negative sentences] let the matter rest: 他们决不会～的. They will not take it lying down.

善本 shànběn (名) reliable text; good edition

善后(後) shànhòu (动) properly handle the remaining problems: ～问题让我处理吧. Let me take care of the problems in the aftermath.

善良 shànliáng (形) good and honest; kindhearted

善心 shànxīn (名) mercy; kindness

善意 shànyì (名) goodwill; good intentions: ～的批评 a well-intentioned criticism

善于(於) shànyú (动) be good at; be adept in: ～歌舞 be good at singing and dancing. 敢于斗争,～斗争 dare to struggle and know how to struggle

善终 shànzhōng (动) die a natural death

膳 shàn

(名) meals; board: 在学生食堂用～ have one's meals at the students' cafeteria.

膳食 shànshí (名) meals; food

膳宿 shàn-sù (名) board and

lodging

缮 shàn (动) **1** repair; be under repair: 房屋正在修～中. The house is under repair. **2** copy; write out: ～清 make a fair copy

缮写(寫) shànxiě (动) copy

禅(禪) shàn

禅让(讓) shànràng (动) abdicate the throne (in favour of another person)

扇 shàn (名) **1** fan: 电～ electric fan **2** leaf: 门～ door leaf. 隔～ partition **3** (量) [used of a door or window]: 一～门 a door

see also shān

扇子 shànzi (名) fan

赡 shàn (动) support; provide for: ～养父母 support one's parents (of money paid to one's former wife). ～养费 alimony

讪 shàn I (动) mock; ridicule II (形) embarrassed: 脸上发～ look embarrassed

讪笑 shànxiào (动) ridicule; mock; deride

商 shāng I (动) discuss; consult: 有要事相～ have some thing important to discuss (with you) II (名) **1** trade; commerce; business: 经～ engage in trade; go into business; be in business **2** merchant; businessman: 皮货～ fur dealer **3** quotient: 智～ I.Q. (intelligence quotient)

商标(標) shāngbiāo (名) trade mark

商埠 shāngbù (名) commercial (or trading) port

商场(場) shāngchǎng (名) market; bazaar

商船 shāngchuán (名) merchant ship; merchantman

商店 shāngdiàn (名) shop; store

商定 shāngdìng (动) decide through consultation or often discussion; agree

商队(隊) shāngduì (动) trade caravan

商贩 shāngfàn (名) small retailer; pedlar

商港 shānggǎng (名) commercial port

商行 shāngháng (名) trading company; commercial firm

商量 shāngliang (动) consult; discuss; talk over: 我们得找校长～一下. We ought to talk it over with the principal of the school.

商品 shāngpǐn (名) commodity; goods; merchandise: ～粮 commodity grain; marketable grain. ～流通 commodity circulation. ～生产 commodity production

商洽 shāngqià (动) consult with sb.; take up (a matter) with sb.

商榷 shāngquè (动) discuss; deliberate: 这一点要进一步～. This point calls for further discussion.

商人 shāngrén (名) businessman; merchant; trader

商谈 shāngtán (动) exchange views; confer; discuss; negotiate: 就两校学术交流问题～ discuss the question of academic exchanges between the two institutions

商讨 shāngtǎo (动) discuss; deliberate over: 就发展两国关系进行～ hold discussions on developing relations between the two countries. 会议～了两国的经济合作问题. The meeting discussed the economic cooperation between the two countries.

商务(務) shāngwù (名) commercial affairs; business affairs: ～参赞 commercial counsellor

商业(業) shāngyè (名) commerce; trade; business: ～部门 commercial departments. ～信贷 commercial credit

商酌 shāngzhuó (动、名) have consultations with

伤(傷) shāng I (名) wound; injury: 内～ internal injury. 轻～ slight injury II (动) **1** injure; hurt: 在一次事故中受～ be injured in an accident. ～感情 hurt sb.'s feelings; offend sb.'s sensibilities **2** be distressed: 哀～ be sad **3** be harmful to; hinder: 无～大雅 not affect one's sense of propriety; not involve matters of principle **4** surfeit oneself with food, etc.: ～食 suffer from over-eating

伤疤 shāngbā (名) scar

伤风(風) shāngfēng (动) catch cold; have a cold

伤风(風)败俗 shāngfēng-bàisú offend public decency; lower the moral standard of the community

伤感 shānggǎn (形) distressed; sentimental

伤害 shānghài (动) injure; harm; hurt: 抽烟会～身体. Smoking is harmful to the health. ～自尊心 injure (or hurt) one's pride; hurt one's self-respect

伤寒 shānghán (名) typhoid fever; typhoid

伤痕 shānghén （名） scar; bruise
伤口 shāngkǒu （名） wound; cut
伤脑(腦)筋 shāng nǎojīn （形） knotty; troublesome; bothersome
伤神 shāngshén （动） overtax one's energies
伤势(勢) shāngshì （名） the condition of an injury (or wound): ～严重 be seriously wounded (or injured)
伤亡 shāng-wáng （名） casualties
伤心 shāngxīn （形） sad; grieved; broken-hearted: 看到他变得那么厉害，真叫我～. It grieves me to see him so changed.

赏 shǎng I （名） reward; award: 有～有罚. Give due rewards to good people and mete out due punishments to evildoers. II （动） admire; enjoy; appreciate: ～月 admire the full moon (particularly on the night of the mid-autumn festival). ～花 enjoy looking at the flowers
赏赐 shǎngcì （动） grant (or bestow) a reward; award
赏光 shǎngguāng 〈套〉 [used to request acceptance of an invitation]: 务请～ request the pleasure of your company
赏鉴(鑒) shǎngjiàn （动） appreciate (a work of art)
赏金 shǎngjīn （名） money reward; award
赏识(識) shǎngshí （动） recognize the worth of; appreciate: 教授很～这篇论文. The professor thinks highly of this dissertation.
赏玩 shǎngwán （动） admire; delight in; enjoy: ～大自然 enjoy the beauty of nature
赏心悦目 shǎngxīn-yuèmù be enchanted by beautiful scenery or feel overjoyed on a happy occasion

晌 shǎng （名） part of the day: 前半～儿 morning. 晚半～儿 dusk
晌午 shǎngwu （名）〈口〉 midday; noon: ～饭 midday meal; lunch

尚 shàng I （副）〈书〉 still; yet: 为时～早. It is still too early. 问题～未解决. The problem remains to be solved. II （动） esteem; value; set great store by: 崇～ uphold; advocate
尚且 shàngqiě （连） [used as an intensifier to indicate an extreme or hypothetical case] even: 大人～不易读懂，何况小孩子. Even adults find it difficult to read, to say nothing of children.

上 shàng I （形） 1 upper; up; upward: ～层阶级 upper class. 往～看 look up 2 higher; superior; better: ～等 superior quality. ～级机关 higher organization 3 first (part); preceding; previous: ～册 the first volume; Volume One; Book One 4 the emperor: ～谕 imperial decree II （动） 1 go up; mount; board; get on: ～公共汽车 get on a bus. ～飞机 board a plane. ～楼 go upstairs 2 go to; leave for: 你～哪儿去? Where are you going? ～街 go shopping (or window-shopping). 我～图书馆去. I'm going to the library. 3 submit; send in; present 4 forge ahead; go ahead 5 enter the court or field: 换人：三号下，四号～. Substitution: Player No.4 for No.3. 6 fill; supply; serve: 给锅炉～水 fill the boiler with water 7 place sth. in position; set; fix: ～螺丝 drive a screw in 8 apply; paint; smear: 给门～漆 have the door painted 9 be put on record; be carried (in a publication): 皇家婚礼的消息～了英国各大报纸. All major British papers carried a story about the royal wedding. 10 wind; screw; tighten: 表该～弦了. The watch needs winding. 11 be engaged (in work, study, etc.) at a fixed time: ～课 give or attend a lesson in class 12 up to; as many as: ～百人 some hundred people III （副） 1 [used after a verb to indicate motion from a lower to a higher position]: 登～山顶 reach the summit 2 [used after a verb to indicate achievement of one's goal]: 穿～外衣 put on a coat. 考～大学 be admitted to a university 3 [used to indicate the beginning and continuity of an action]: 她爱～了司机的工作. She has come to love her job as a driver. 4 [used after a noun to indicate the scope of something]: 会～ at the meeting. 事实～ in fact

上 shang [used after nouns to indicate the surface of an object]: 墙～ on the wall. 脸～ in the face
上班 shàngbān （动） go to work; start work; be on duty: 我们每天早上八点钟～. We start work at 8 every morning.
上报(報) shàngbào （动） 1 be

reported in the press 2 report to a higher body

上辈 shàngbèi (名) 1 ancestors 2 the elder generation of one's family

上膘 shàngbiāo (动) (of animals) become fat; fatten

上宾(賓) shàngbīn (名) distinguished guest; guest of honour

上策 shàngcè (名) the best policy; a very wise move

上层(層) shàngcéng (名) higher levels: ～领导 higher leadership

上层(層)建筑 shàngcéng jiànzhù (名) superstructure

上场(場) shàngchǎng (动) 1 appear on the stage 2 enter the court or field; join in a contest

上床(牀) shàngchuáng (动) go to bed

上窜(竄)下跳 shàngcuàn-xiàtiào (动) run around on vicious errands

上当(當) shàngdàng (动) be taken in

上等 shàngděng (形) first-class; first-rate; superior: ～货 first-class goods; quality goods

上帝 shàngdì (名) God

上颚 shàng'è (名) maxilla (of a mammal); the upper jaw

上方宝(寶)剑(劍) shàngfāng bǎojiàn (名) the imperial sword (a symbol of high authority with which an official can act at his discretion)

上访 shàngfǎng (动) (of popular masses) complain to the higher authorities about an injustice and request fair settlement

上风(風) shàngfēng (名) advantage; upper hand: 占～ get the upper hand

上告 shànggào (动) complain to the higher authorities or appeal to a higher court

上工 shànggōng (动) go to work; start work

上钩 shànggōu (动) rise to the bait; swallow the bait

上好 shànghǎo (形) first-class; best-quality

上呼吸道 shànghūxīdào (名) the upper respiratory tract: ～感染 infection of the upper respiratory tract

上火 shànghuǒ (动) get angry

上级 shàngjí (名) higher level; higher authorities: ～机关 higher authorities; a higher body

上将(將) shàngjiàng (名) (army; U.S. air force) general; (British air force) air chief marshal; (navy) admiral

上缴 shàngjiǎo (动) turn over (revenues, etc.) to the higher authorities

上进(進) shàngjìn (动) go forward; make progress: 力求～strive to forge ahead. ～心 the desire for progress

上课 shàngkè (动) 1 attend class; attend a lecture 2 conduct a class; give a lesson (or lecture)

上空 shàngkōng (名) in the sky; overhead

上口 shàngkǒu (动) 1 be able to read aloud poems or essays fluently 2 (of a poem or essay) make smooth reading

上来(來) shànglai (动) come up: 他还没～. He hasn't come upstairs yet.

上来(來) shànglai (副) 1 [used after a verb to indicate motion from a lower to a higher position or an action of coming nearer to the speaker]: 把箱子搬到楼～吧. Bring those suitcases upstairs 2 [used after a verb to indicate accomplishment]: 这个问题你一定答得～. You can of course answer this question.

上流 shàngliú (名) 1 upper reaches (of a river) 2 members of the upper circles in the old society: ～社会 high society; polite society

上路 shànglù (动) set out on a journey; start off

上马(馬) shàngmǎ (动) start (a project, etc.): 这项工程很快就要～. This project will start soon.

上门(門) shàngmén (动) come or go and see sb.; call; drop in; visit: 他好久没～了. It's a long time since he last called.

上面 shàngmian (副) 1 above; over; on top of; on the surface of: 小河～跨着一座石桥. A stone bridge spanned the stream. 2 above-mentioned; aforesaid; foregoing: ～列举了各种实例. Mentioned above are instances of diverse kinds. II (名) 1 the higher authorities; the higher-ups: ～有命令. There are orders from above. 2 aspect; respect; regard: 他在文学～下了很多功夫. He has put a lot of effort into literature.

上年纪 shàng niánji (形) getting on in years

上品 shàngpǐn (名) high order;

top grade

上气(氣)不接下气(氣) shàngqì bù jiē xiàqì gasp for breath; be out of breath

上去 shàngqu (动) go up: 登着梯子～ go up (on) a ladder

上去 shàngqu (副) [used after a verb to indicate motion from a lower to a higher position or distance farther away from the speaker]: 走～ walk up. 把国民经济搞～ boost the national economy. 为了完成任务，他把所有的力量都使～了. He has strained every nerve to make a success of his work.

上任 shàngrèn (动) take up an official post; assume office

上色 shàngshǎi (动) colour (a picture, map, etc.)

上上 shàngshàng (形) 1 the very best: ～策 the best policy 2 before last: ～星期 the week before last

上身 shàngshēn (名) 1 the upper part of the body 2 upper outer garment; shirt; blouse; jacket: 他～穿的是中山装. He is wearing a Chinese-style jacket.

上升 shàngshēng (动) rise; go up; ascend: 气温～. The temperature is going up. 工厂产量稳步～. The output of the factory is rising steadily.

上声(聲) shàngshēng or shǎngshēng (名) falling-rising tone, one of the four tones in classical Chinese and the third tone in modern standard Chinese pronunciation

上市 shàngshì (动) go (or appear) on the market; be in season: 西红柿大量～. There are plenty of tomatoes on the market.

上手 shàngshǒu I (名) left-hand seat; seat of honour II (动) start; begin: 今天的活一～就很顺利. Today's work started off quite smoothly.

上书(書) shàngshū (动) submit a written statement to a higher authority

上述 shàngshù (形) above-mentioned

上税 shàngshuì (动) pay taxes; pay duties

上司 shàngsi (名) superior; boss: 顶头～ one's immediate superior

上诉 shàngsù (动) appeal (to a higher court): 提出～ lodge an appeal

上算 shàngsuàn (形) more economical; worth while

上岁(歲)数(數) shàng suìshu <口> be getting on in years

上台(臺) shàngtái (动) 1 appear on the stage 2 assume power; come (or rise) to power

上天 shàngtiān I (名) Heaven; Providence; God II (动) go up to the sky: 我们又有一颗卫星～了. Another of our satellites has gone up.

上文 shàngwén (名) foregoing paragraphs or chapters; preceding part of the text: 见～ see above

上午 shàngwǔ (名) forenoon; morning

上下 shàng-xià I (名) high and low; old and young II (副) from top to bottom; up and down: ～打量 look sb. up and down; size sb. up III (动) go up and down: 楼里安了电梯,顾客～很方便. With the instalment of an escalator, customers can easily go up and down. IV (形) 1 relative superiority or inferiority: 不相～ equally matched; about the same; be on a par 2 about: 四十岁～ about forty years old

上下文 shàng-xiàwén (名) context

上弦 shàngxián I (名) first quarter (of the moon) II (动) wind up a clock or watch

上限 shàngxiàn (名) upper limit; ceiling

上相 shàngxiàng (形) photogenic; come out well in a photograph

上刑 shàngxíng (动) use torture (to extort a confession from sb.)

上行 shàngxíng (形) 1 up; upgoing; ～列车 up train 2 upriver; upstream: ～船 up river boat

上行下效 shàng xíng xià xiào A bad example set by a person in power will be followed by his subordinates

上学(學) shàngxué (动) go to school

上旬 shàngxún (名) the first ten-day period of a month

上演 shàngyǎn (动) put on the stage; perform: 电影院今晚～什么片子? What's on at the cinema this evening?

上衣 shàngyī (名) upper garment; jacket

上瘾(癮) shàngyǐn (动) be addicted (to sth.); get into the habit (of doing sth.): 这种饮料喝多了会～. This soft drink is habi

forming.
上映 shàngyìng (动) show (a film):今晚有部新片～. They are showing a new film tonight.
上游 shàngyóu (名) 1 upper reaches (of a river) 2 advanced position: 力争～ aim high
上谕 shàngyù (名) imperial edict
上涨(漲) shàngzhǎng (动) rise; go up: 物价～. The prices are spiralling.
上阵 shàngzhèn (动) go into battle; pitch into the work; play in a match
上肢 shàngzhī (名) upper limbs
烧(燒) shāo I (动) 1 burn: ～毁 burn down 2 cook; bake; heat: ～菜 cook food; prepare a meal. ～砖 bake bricks 3 stew after frying or fry after stewing: ～茄子 stewed eggplant. 红～肉 pork stewed in soy sauce 4 roast: ～鸡 roast chicken 5 run a fever: 她发高～. She has a very high fever. *or* The patient is running a high temperature. II (名) fever; temperature: 她～退了. Her temperature has come down.
烧饼(餅) shāobing (名) sesame seed cake
烧火 shāohuǒ (动) make a fire; light a fire; tend the kitchen fire
烧酒 shāojiǔ (名) spirit usu. distilled from sorghum or maize
烧伤(傷) shāoshāng (名) burn: 三度～ third-degree burns
烧香 shāoxiāng (动) burn joss sticks (before an idol)
烧灼 shāozhuó (名) burn; scorch; singe
鞘 shāo (名) whiplash see also qiào
梢 shāo (名) tip; the thin end of a twig, etc.: 树～ the top of a tree
捎 shāo (动) take along sth. to or for sb.: ～个口信给他. Take a message to him.
稍 shāo (副) a little; slightly: ～加改动 make slight alterations. 请～等一会儿. Please wait a moment. ～纵即逝 transient; fleeting
稍稍 shāoshāo (副): ～休息一下. Let's take a breather.
稍微 shāowēi (副) a little; slightly: 他感到～有点累. He felt a bit tired.
勺(杓) sháo (名) spoon; ladle: 长柄～ ladle; dipper
勺子 sháozi (名) ladle; scoop
少 shǎo I (形) few; little: 留下吃饭的人很～. Only a few stayed for dinner. 他近来很～喝酒. He hardly ever drinks lately. 上海很～下雪. It seldom snows in Shanghai. II (动) 1 be short; lack: 我们还～几块钱. We're still short of a few yuan. 2 lose; be missing; 阅览室～了几本杂志. A few magazines are missing from the reading-room. 3 stop; quit: ～废话! Stop talking rubbish! see also shào
少不得 shǎobude cannot do without; cannot dispense with: 学语言,一所设备完善的实验室是～的. We cannot dispense with a well-equipped laboratory in language study.
少不了 shǎobuliǎo I (动) be bound to; be unavoidable: 这封信打得仓促,～有些错误. The letter was typed in a hurry, so there are bound to be some errors. II (形) considerable: 困难看来～. It looks as if there are going to be a lot of difficulties.
少见(見)多怪 shǎojiàn-duōguài childish curiosity or sheer ignorance
少量 shǎoliàng (形) a small amount (of)
少数(數) shǎoshù (形) a small number (of): ～服从多数. The minority is subordinate to the majority.
少数(數)民族 shǎoshù mínzú (名) minority nationality; ethnic group
少许 shǎoxǔ (名)〈书〉 a little; a small quantity
哨 shào (名) 1 sentry post; post: 岗～ sentry post. 观察～ observation post. 放～ be on sentry duty; stand guard; stand sentry 2 whistle: 吹～ blow a whistle; whistle
哨兵 shàobīng (名) sentry; guard
哨所 shàosuǒ (名) sentry post; post
哨子 shàozi (名) whistle
少 shào I (形) young: 男女老～ men and women, old and young II (名) young master: 阔～ a profligate young man see also shǎo
少妇(婦) shàofù (名) young

married woman
少年 shàonián (名) 1 boyhood or girlhood; early youth (from ten to sixteen) 2 boy or girl of that age: ～犯罪 juvenile delinquency
少年老成 shàonián lǎochéng 1 an old head on young shoulders 2 a young but inefficient person
少女 shàonǚ (名) young girl
少爷(爺) shàoye (名) young master of the house
少壮(壯) shàozhuàng (形) young and vigorous

奢 shē (形) 1 luxurious; extravagant: 穷～极欲 (wallow in) luxury 2 excessive; extravagant: ～望 extravagant hopes
奢侈 shēchǐ (形) luxurious; extravagant; wasteful: 生活～ live in luxury. ～品 luxury goods; luxuries
奢华(華) shēhuá (形) luxurious; extravagant: 陈设～ be luxuriously furnished

赊 shē (动) buy or sell on credit
赊购(購) shēgòu (动) buy on credit
赊欠 shēqiàn (动) buy or sell on credit; give or get credit

折 shé (动) 1 break; snap: 桌子腿撞～了. The table's legs are broken. 2 lose money in business
see also zhē; zhé
折本 shéběn (动) lose money in business

蛇 shé (名) snake; serpent
蛇蝎 shéxiē (名) vicious people

舌 shé (名) 1 tongue 2 sth. shaped like a tongue: 火～ tongues of flame. 鞋～ the tongue of a shoe
舌敝唇焦 shébì-chúnjiāo talk till one is completely exhausted
舌尖 shéjiān (名) the tip of the tongue
舌头(頭) shétou (名) tongue
舌战(戰) shézhàn (动) have a verbal battle with; argue heatedly with

舍(捨) shě (动) 1 give up; abandon: ～本逐末 attend to trivialities to the neglect of essentials 2 give alms
see also shè
舍得 shěde (动) be willing to give away; not grudge: ～花力气 stint no effort
舍己为(爲)人 shě jǐ wèi rén sacrifice one's own interests for the sake of others
舍近求远(遠) shějìn-qiúyuǎn search far and wide for what lies close at hand
舍命 shěmìng (动) risk one's life
舍弃(棄) shěqì (动) give up; abandon
舍身 shěshēn (动) give one's life: ～救人 save sb.'s life at the cost of one's own
舍死忘生 shěsǐ-wàngshēng disregard one's own personal danger; risk one's life

涉 shè (动) 1 wade; ford: 远～重洋 travel across the oceans 2 go through; experience: ～世不深 have scanty knowledge of the world 3 involve
涉及 shèjí (动) involve; relate to; touch upon: 这事～重大原则问题. This involves matters of cardinal principle.
涉猎(獵) shèliè (动) do desultory reading; read cursorily: 有的书只要稍加～即可. There are books you have only to browse through.
涉嫌 shèxián (动) be suspected of being involved; be a suspect

社 shè (名) organized body; community; society: 通讯～ news agency. 合作～ cooperative. 诗～ a poets' club. 出版～ publishing house
社会(會) shèhuì (名) society: 人类～ human society. 社会制度 social system
社会(會)学(學) shèhuìxué (名) sociology: ～家 sociologist
社会(會)主义(義) shèhuìzhǔyì (名) socialism
社稷 shèjì (名) the state; the country
社交 shèjiāo (名) social intercourse; social activities
社论(論) shèlùn (名) editorial; leading article; leader

设 shè I (动) 1 set up; arrange; found: ～宴 give a banquet 2 work out: ～计 plot II (连) 〈书〉 if: ～有困难, 当助一臂之力. I will do my best to help in case you have any difficulty.
设备(備) shèbèi (名) equipment; facilities: 旅馆～齐全. The hotel is provided with modern facilities.
设法 shèfǎ (动) think of a way; try; do what one can: 我们正在～筹集资金. We are trying to raise funds.

设防 shèfáng (动) set up defences; fortify; garrison: 不～的城市 an open city; an undefended city
设计 shèjì (名)(动) design; plan: 毕业～ graduation project. ～一种新机器 design a new machine
设立 shèlì (动) establish; set up; found: ～一个特别委员会 set up an ad hoc committee
设身处(處)地 shèshēn-chǔdì put oneself in sb. else's position; be considerate enough
设施 shèshī (名) installation; facilities: 军事～ military installations. 医疗～ medical facilities
设使 shèshǐ (连) if; suppose; in case
设想 shèxiǎng (动) 1 imagine; envisage; conceive; assume: 不堪～ too dreadful to contemplate 2 consider: 我们应该处处替国家～. We must always have the interest of the nation at heart.
设置 shèzhì (动) 1 set up; put up: ～专门机构 set up a special organization 2 install: 会场里～了扩音机. Loudspeaders are installed at the conference hall.
赦 shè (动) remit (a punishment): 大～ general pardon; amnesty. 特～ special pardon
赦免 shèmiǎn (动) remit (a punishment)
摄(攝) shè (动) 1 absorb; assimilate 2 take a photograph of; shoot
摄取 shèqǔ (动) 1 absorb; assimilate 2 take a photograph of
摄影 shèyǐng (动) 1 take a photograph; picture; have a picture taken 2 shoot a film: ～记者 press photographer; cameraman
摄影机(機) shèyǐngjī (名) camera
摄政 shèzhèng (动) act as regent: ～王 prince regent
摄制 shèzhì (动) produce (a film)
慑(懾) shè (动)<书> fear; be awed
慑服 shèfú (动) 1 submit to sb. out of fear; succumb 2 cow
舍 shè (名) house; shed; hut: 牛～ cowshed. 校～ school buildings
see also shě
舍亲(親) shèqīn <谦> my relative
射 shè (动) 1 shoot; fire: ～箭 shoot an arrow. ～进一球 score a goal 2 discharge in a jet: 喷～ spout; spurt; jet. 注～ inject 3 send out (light, heat, etc.): 反～ reflect. 光芒四～ emit a brilliant light 4 allude to sth. or sb.; insinuate: 影～ insinuate; make innuendoes
射程 shèchéng (名) range (of fire): 有效～ effective range
射击(擊) shèjī I (动) shoot; fire II (名) shooting
射箭 shèjiàn I (动) shoot an arrow II (名) archery: ～手 archer
射门(門) shèmén (动) shoot (at the goal)
射手 shèshǒu (名) shooter; marksman; archer
射线(綫) shèxiàn (名)<物> ray
麝 shè (名) 1 musk deer 2 musk
麝香 shèxiāng (名) musk
深 shēn I (形) 1 deep: 一口～井 a deep well. 池～两米. The pool is two metres deep. 雪～过膝. The snow is knee-deep. 2 difficult; profound: 对他来讲,这本书太～了. The book is too difficult for him. 3 thoroughgoing; penetrating; profound: 问题想得～ think deeply about a question. 我并没有～谈这个问题. I didn't go deeply into details about the matter. 影响很～ exert a profound influence 4 close; intimate: 他们俩交情很～. The two of them are just great friends. 5 dark; deep: ～蓝 dark blue. ～红 deep red; crimson. 颜色太～. The colour is too dark (or deep). 6 late: ～秋 late autumn. 夜～了. It was late at night. II (副) very; greatly; deeply: ～知 know very well; be fully aware of; be keenly alive to. ～感不安 feel very uneasy. ～信 be deeply convinced. ～受感动 be deeply moved
深奥 shēn'ào (形) abstruse; profound
深沉 shēnchén (形) 1 dark; deep: 暮色～. Dusk is deepening. 2 (of sound or voice) deep; dull; a deep voice: ～的声音 a dull sound 3 concealing one's real feelings: 这人很～. He's a deep person.
深仇大恨 shēnchóu-dàhèn (名) deep-seated hatred; inveterate hatred
深处(處) shēnchù (名) depths; recesses: 在密林～ in the depths of the forest. 在内心～ in the recesses of one's heart
深度 shēndù (名) 1 degree of

depth; depth: 测量海水的～ determine the depth of the sea 2 profundity; depth: 他的文章缺乏～. His article lacks depth.

深更半夜 shēngēng-bànyè (名) in the dead of night; in the middle of the night

深厚 shēnhòu (形) 1 deep; profound: ～的友谊 profound friendship 2 solid; deep-seated: ～的基础 a solid foundation

深呼吸 shēnhūxī (名) deep breathing

深化 shēnhuà (动) deepen: 矛盾的～ intensification of a contradiction

深究 shēnjiū (动) go or look into sth. seriously

深居简出 shēnjū-jiǎnchū live a secluded life

深刻 shēnkè (形) deep; profound; deepgoing: ～的印象 a deep impression

深谋远(遠)虑(慮) shēnmóu-yuǎnlǜ be farsighted and capable of long-range planning; think carefully and plan deeply

深浅(淺) shēnqiǎn (名) 1 depth: 河的～ the depth of a river 2 proper limits (for speech or action); sense of propriety: 说话没～ speak carelessly and bluntly

深切 shēnqiè (形) heartfelt; profound: ～的同情 deep sympathy. ～地了解 deeply appreciate; be fully aware of

深情 shēnqíng (名) deep feeling; deep love: ～厚谊 profound sentiments of friendship

深入 shēnrù I (动) go deep into: ～人心 be highly popular II (形) thorough; deepgoing: ～细致的分析 a carefully worked-out, in-depth analysis

深入浅(淺)出 shēnrù-qiǎnchū explain profound ideas in simple terms

深山 shēnshān (名) remote mountains

深深 shēnshēn (副) profoundly; deeply; keenly

深水 shēnshuǐ (名) deepwater: ～港 deepwater port

深思 shēnsī (动) think deeply: 好学～ study hard and think deeply

深思熟虑(慮) shēnsī-shúlǜ careful consideration

深邃 shēnsuì (形) 1 deep: ～的山谷 a deep valley 2 profound; abstruse: 哲理～ abstruse philosophical thinking

深恶(惡)痛绝 shēnwù-tòngjué hate bitterly; detest; abhor

深夜 shēnyè late at night

深渊(淵) shēnyuān (名) abyss: 苦难的～ in an abyss of misery

深远(遠) shēnyuǎn (形) profound and lasting; far-reaching

深造 shēnzào (动) take an advanced course of study or training: 送到国外～ be sent abroad for advanced study

深重 shēnzhòng (形) very grave; extremely serious

申 shēn (动) state; express; explain: 三令五～ give repeated instructions. 重～一贯政策 reiterate our consistent policy

申报(報) shēnbào (动) report; submit to a higher body

申辩(辯) shēnbiàn (动) defend oneself; argue (or plead) one's case: 被告有权～. The accused has the right to defend himself.

申斥 shēnchì (动) reprimand

申明 shēnmíng (动) declare; state; avow: ～理由 state one's reasons

申请 shēnqǐng (动) apply for: ～入(出)境签证 apply for an entry (exit) visa. ～书 application

申述 shēnshù (动) state; explain in detail: ～立场 state one's position. ～观点 expound one's views

申诉 shēnsù (动) appeal: 向上级提出～ appeal to the higher authorities

申讨 shēntǎo (动) openly condemn; denounce

申冤 shēnyuān (动) 1 redress an injustice; right a wrong 2 appeal for redress of a wrong

呻 shēn

呻吟 shēnyín (动) groan; moan

伸 shēn (动) stretch; extend: ～出手来 stretch one's hand. ～大拇指 hold up one's thumb. 不要把头～出窗外. Don't put (or stick) your head out of the window (of a bus, etc.).

伸懒腰 shēn lǎnyāo (动) stretch oneself

伸手 shēnshǒu (动) 1 stretch (or hold) out one's hand: 他～去拿字典. He reached for the dictionary. 2 ask for help, etc.: 虽然困难，他们从不向国家～要援助. Though in great difficulties, they never asked the state for assistance.

伸缩 shēnsuō (动) stretch out

and draw back; expand and contract; lengthen and shorten: 镜头可以前后～. The lens of this camera can zoom in and out. II (形) flexible; elastic; adjustable: 这些规定～性很大. These regulations are quite flexible. 留有～的余地 allow sb. some leeway

伸腿 shēntuǐ (动) 1 stretch one's legs 2 step in (to gain an advantage) 3 〈口〉 kick the bucket

伸展 shēnzhǎn (动) extend; stretch: 把它的势力～到世界各处 extend its influence to different parts of the globe

伸张(張) shēnzhāng (动) uphold; promote: ～正气 promote healthy tendencies

绅 shēn (名) gentry

绅士 shēnshì (名) gentleman; gentry

身 shēn I (名) 1 body: ～高 height. 上～ upper part of the body 2 life: 以～殉职 die a martyr at one's post 3 oneself; personally: 以～作则 set a good example for others 4 the main part of a structure; body: 车～ the body of a car. 机～ fuselage. 船～ hull II (量) (of clothing) suit: 一～新衣服 a new suit

身败名裂 shēnbài-mínglié bring disgrace upon oneself and ruin one's reputation; be thoroughly discredited

身边(邊) shēnbiān (副) 1 at(or by) one's side: 他～有两名助手. He has two assistants working together with him. 2 (have sth.) on one; with one: ～没带钱 have no money on one. 她～总是带着一本词典. She always carries a dictionary with her.

身不由己 shēn bù yóu jǐ involuntarily; in spite of oneself

身材 shēncái (名) stature; figure; build

身长(長) shēncháng (名) 1 height (of a person) 2 length (of a garment from shoulder to hemline)

身段 shēnduàn (名) 1(woman's) figure 2 (dancer's) posture

身分 shēnfen (名) 1 status; capacity; identity: 不合～ incompatible with one's status. 暴露～ reveal one's identity. 以官方～发言 speak in an official capacity 2 dignity: 有失～ be beneath one's dignity

身价(價) shēnjià (名) 1 social status: 抬高～ raise one's social status 2 selling price (of a slave in the old society)

身教 shēnjiào (动) teach by one's own example

身临(臨)其境 shēn lín qí jìng be personally on the scene

身强力壮(壯) shēnqiáng-lìzhuàng (of a person) strong; tough; sturdy

身躯(軀) shēnqū (名) body; stature

身上 shēnshang (副) 1 on one's body; physically: 我～不舒服. I'm not feeling well. 2 (have sth.) on one; with one: ～没带笔. I haven't got a pen with me.

身世 shēnshì (名) one's life story; one's lot

身手 shēnshǒu (名) skill; talent: 大显～ fully display one's talents

身体(體) shēntǐ (名) 1 body 2 health: 注意～ look after one's health

身体(體)力行 shēntǐ-lìxíng earnestly practise what one advocates

身心 shēn-xīn (名) body and mind: ～健康 sound in body and mind

身子 shenzi (名) body; physically: 光着～ be naked to the waist. ～不大舒服 not feel well

参 shēn (名) ginseng

神 shén I (名) 1 god; deity 2 spirit; mind: 凝～ concentrate (or focus) one's attention 3 expression; look: 脸～ facial expression II (形) supernatural; magical: ～效 magical effect; miraculous effect

神采 shéncǎi (名) expression; look: ～奕奕 radiant with health and vigour

神出鬼没 shénchū-guǐmò (usu. of troop movement) appear and disappear mysteriously

神乎其神 shén hū qí shén (形) mystifying; wonderful; miraculous

神化 shénhuà (动) deify

神话 shénhuà (名) mythology; myth

神魂 shénhún (名) state of mind; mind: ～不定 be on tenterhooks

神机(機)妙算 shénjī-miào suàn(名) military moves of incredible wisdom

神经(經) shénjīng (名) nerve: ～

紧张 be nervous. ～官能症 neurosis. ～衰弱 neurasthenia. ～系统 nervous system
神经(經)病 shénjīngbìng (名) 1 neuropathy 2 mental disorder
神经(經)过(過)敏 shénjīng guòmǐn I (名) neuroticism II (形) oversensitive
神灵(靈) shénlíng (名) gods; deities; divinities
神秘 shénmì (形) mysterious
神明 shénmíng (名) gods; deities; divinities: 奉若～ worship sb. or sth.
神奇 shénqí (形) magical; mystical; miraculous: ～的效果 miraculous effect
神气(氣) shénqi (名) expression; air; manner: 得意的～ an air of complacency. 他说话的～特别认真. He speaks in a very deliberate manner. II 1 spirited; vigorous: 他看起来很～. He looks quite impressive. 2 putting on airs; cocky: 没有什么可～的. There is nothing to be cocky about.
神枪(槍)手 shénqiāngshǒu (名) crack shot; expert marksman
神情 shénqíng (名) expression; look: 露出愉快的～ look happy; wear a happy expression
神权(權) shénquán (名) 1 religious authority; theocracy 2 rule by divine right
神色 shénsè (名) expression; look: ～自若 look unruffled
神圣(聖) shénshèng (形) sacred; holy: ～职责 sacred duty. ～不可侵犯 sacrosanct; inviolable
神似 shénsì be alike in spirit
神速 shénsù I (形) marvellously quick: 收效～ be miraculously effective II (名) amazing speed: 兵贵～. Speed is precious in military operations.
神态(態) shéntài (名) expression; carriage; bearing
神通 shéntōng (名) remarkable ability: ～广大 be immensely resourceful
神童 shéntóng (名) child prodigy
神往 shénwǎng (形) be fascinated: 令人～ fascinating
神仙 shénxian (名) supernatural being; immortal
神像 shénxiàng (名) the picture or statue of a god or Buddha
神学(學) shénxué (名) theology
神志 shénzhì (名) consciousness; senses; mind: ～清醒 remain conscious; in full control of one's senses. ～昏迷 lose consciousness; go into a coma

什
shén
see also shí

什么(麼) shénme (代) 1 [used to indicate interrogation]: 你说～? What did you say? *or* Beg your pardon? 2 [used to indicate something indefinite]: 我饿了,想吃点～. I'm hungry. I feel like having a bite. 我们好象～地方见过. It seems that we've met somewhere before. 3 [used before "也" or "都" to indicate the absence of exceptions within the stated scope]: 他～也不怕. He is afraid of nothing. 4 [in a phrase or sentence with one '什么' preceding another, the 1st '什么' always determines the meaning of the 2nd '什么']: 有～就说～ speak freely; say all you have got to say. 你喜欢～, 就拿～. You can take whatever you like. 5 [used to indicate surprise or displeasure]: 他是～人? What sort person is he? 6 [used to indicate reproach]: 你笑～? What's so funny? 急～, 时间还早呐! What's the hurry? It's still early. 7 [used after a verb to indicate disapproval] 8 [used before parallel words or phrases to indicate enumeration]: ～乒乓球啊, 羽毛球啊, 篮球啊, 排球啊, 他都会. He can play table tennis, badminton, basketball, volleyball, and what not.
什么的 shénmede (代) and so on; and what not: 下班后, 他总喜欢到酒吧间喝杯啤酒～. After work, he likes to go to the bar for a mug of beer or things like that.

审(審)
shěn I (形) careful: ～视 look closely at; gaze at; examine II (动) 1 examine; go over: ～稿 go over a draft or make some editorial changes 2 interrogate; try: ～案 try a case. 公～ put sb. on public trial

审查 shěnchá (动) examine; investigate: ～计划 check a plan. ～属实 establish a fact after investigation
审订 shěndìng (动) examine and revise: ～课文 revise textbooks
审定 shěndìng (动) examine and approve: 该报告已由委员会～. The report has been examined

and approved by the committee.
审核 shěnhé (动) examine and verify: ～预算 examine and approve a budget. ～经费 examine and verify the expenses
审计 shěnjì (动) audit: ～员 auditor
审理 shěnlǐ (动) try; hear: ～案件 try a case; hear a case
审美 shěnměi (形) aesthetic: ～能力 aesthetic judgment
审判 shěnpàn (动) bring to trial; try
审批 shěnpī (动) examine and approve: 报请领导～ be submitted to the leadership for examination and approval
审慎 shěnshèn (形) cautious; careful: 处理这个问题必须～. The matter has to be handled with great care.
审时(時)度势(勢) shěnshí-duóshì size up the current situation
审问 shěnwèn (动) interrogate
审讯 shěnxùn (动) interrogate; try
审议(議) shěnyì (动、名) consideration; deliberation; discussion: 这个计划正在～中. The project is under discussion.

婶(嬸)
shěn (名) 1 wife of father's younger brother; aunt 2 a form of address to a woman about one's mother's age; aunt; auntie
婶母 shěnmǔ (名) wife of father's younger brother; aunt

慎
shèn (形) careful; cautious: 谨小～微 overcautious
慎重 shènzhòng (形) cautious; careful; prudent; discreet: ～处理 handle with discretion. ～考虑 give careful consideration to

甚
shèn (副) 1 very; extremely: ～佳 very good. ～念 miss sb. very much 2 more than: 局势恶化, 日～一日. The situation is deteriorating with each passing day.
甚嚣尘(塵)上 shèn xiāo chén shàng arouse a public clamour; (of hostile political propaganda) spread far and wide
甚至 shènzhì (连) even; (go) so far as to; so much so that: 他很激动, ～连话都说不出来了. He was so excited that he couldn't utter a word. 他走得如此匆忙, ～都忘了说声再见. He left in such a hurry that he even forgot to say goodbye.

肾(腎)
shèn (名) kidney
肾脏(臟) shènzàng (名) kidney

渗
shèn (动) ooze; seep: 水都～到房子里去了. Water has seeped into the rooms.
渗漏 shènlòu (名) seepage; leakage
渗入 shènrù (动) 1 permeate; seep into: ～地下 seep into the ground 2 (of evil influence, ideas, etc.) infiltrate; pervade
渗透 shèntòu I (动) permeate; seep II (名) infiltration

声(聲)
shēng I (名) 1 sound; voice: 雨～ the patter of rain (on a roof). 小～说话 speak in a low voice 2 tone: 四～ the four tones of a Chinese character 3 reputation: ～誉 reputation; fame; prestige II (动) make a sound: 一～不响 keep quiet; not utter a word III (量) [of frequency of utterance]: 我喊了他几～, 他都没有听见. I called him several times, but he didn't hear me.
声辩(辯) shēngbiàn (动) argue; justify
声波 shēngbō (名) sound wave; acoustic wave
声称(稱) shēngchēng (动)profess; claim; assert: ～已达成协议 claim to have reached an agreement
声带(帶) shēngdài (名) 1 vocal cords 2 sound track
声调 shēngdiào (名) 1 tone; note: ～低沉 in a low, sad voice 2 the tone of a Chinese character
声东(東)击(擊)西 shēng dōng jī xī make a feint to the east and attack in the west
声泪(淚)俱下 shēng-lèi jù xià shed tears while speaking: 他～地诉说了自己的不幸遭遇. Tears streamed down his cheeks as he recounted hes misfortunes.
声名 shēngmíng (名) reputation: ～狼藉 become notorious; bring discredit on oneself
声明 shēngmíng I (动) state; declare; announce: 庄严～ solemnly state II (名) statement; declaration: 发表～ issue a statement
声色 shēng-sè (名) the voice and countenance of a speaker: 不动～ maintain one's composure. ～俱厉 (speak) in a severe tone and with a severe look on one's face

声势(勢) shēngshì (名) impetuous force: 虚张～ bluff and bluster
声嘶力竭 shēngsī-lìjié shout oneself hoarse and suffer from exhaustion
声速 shēngsù (名) velocity of sound
声讨 shēngtǎo (动) denounce; condemn
声望 shēngwàng (名) popularity; prestige: 享有很高的～ enjoy great prestige; be held in high repute
声威 shēngwēi (名) renown; prestige: ～大震 add greatly to one's reputation and prestige
声息 shēngxī (名) 1 [often used in negative sentences] sound: 院子里静悄悄的,没有一点～. All was quiet and still, and not a sound was audible in the courtyard. 2 information: 互通～ keep in touch with each other
声学(學) shēngxué (名) acoustics: 建筑～ architectural acoustics
声音 shēngyīn (名) sound; voice
声誉(譽) shēngyù (名) reputation; fame; prestige
声援 shēngyuán (动) express support for; give vocal support to
声乐(樂) shēngyuè (名) vocal music
声张(張) shēngzhāng (动) make public; disclose: 不要～. Don't breathe a word of it.

生 shēng I (动) 1 give birth to; bear: ～孩子 give birth to a child 2 grow: ～芽 sprout 3 get: ～病 fall ill 4 light (a fire) II (形) 1 living: ～物 living things 2 unripe; green: 这些西瓜还是～的. The watermelons are not ripe yet. 3 raw; uncooked: ～肉 raw meat. 西红柿可以～吃. Tomatoes can be eaten raw. 4 unprocessed; unrefined; crude: ～铁 pig iron. ～皮 rawhide; (untanned) hide 5 unfamiliar; unacquainted; strange: ～词 new word 6 stiff; mechanical: ～凑 mechanically put together (disconnected words and phrases) III (副) [used before a few words to express emotion and sensation] extremely; very: ～疼 very painful IV(名) 1 existence; life: 一～ all one's life. 舍～取义 lay down one's life in the cause of justice 2 livelihood: 谋～ earn one's livelihood; make a living 3 pupil; student: 师～关系 teacher-student relationship
生搬硬套 shēngbān-yìngtào copy mechanically in disregard of specific conditions
生病 shēngbìng (动) fall ill
生产(產) shēngchǎn I (动) 1 produce; manufacture: ～石油 produce oil 2 give birth to a child: 她快～了. She'll be having a baby soon. *or* She's expecting a baby. II (名) production: 发展～ develop production. ～成本 cost of production. ～定额 production quota. ～方式 mode of production. ～关系 relations of production. ～力 productive forces. ～率 productivity. ～资料 means of production
生辰 shēngchén (名) birthday
生存 shēngcún (动) subsist; exist; live: ～竞争 struggle for existence
生动(動) shēngdòng (形) lively; vivid: ～的描写 vivid description. ～的语言 lively language
生动(動)活泼(潑) shēngdòng huópō (形) lively; vivid and vigorous
生活 shēnghuó I (名) 1 life: 日常～ daily life 2 livelihood: ～困难 be hard up II (动) live: 我们～得很幸福. We live a happy life. ～必需品 daily necessities. ～方式 way of life; life style. ～费用 living expenses; cost of living. ～水平 living standard. ～条件 living conditions. ～习惯 habits and customs
生冷 shēng-lěng (名) raw or cold food
生离(離)死别 shēnglí-sǐbié part never to meet again; part for ever
生理 shēnglǐ (名) physiology: ～学 physiology
生力军 shēnglìjūn (名) 1 fresh combatants 2 new young members of an organization
生龙(龍)活虎 shēnglóng-huóhǔ (形) bursting with energy; full of vim and vigour
生路 shēnglù (名) 1 means of livelihood 2 way out
生米煮成熟饭 shēngmǐ zhǔchéng shúfàn what's done can't be undone
生命 shēngmìng (名) life: 月球上没有～. There is no life on the moon.
生命力 shēngmìnglì (名) vitality
生怕 shēngpà (动) fear; be afraid of: 我们在泥泞的路上小心地走着,～滑倒了. We picked our way

along a muddy road for fear we might slip and fall.

生僻 shēngpì (形) uncommon; rare: ～的字眼 rarely used words

生平 shēngpíng (名) life story; life

生气(氣) shēngqì I (动) take offence; get angry II (名) life; vitality: ～勃勃的人 a dynamic person

生前 shēngqián (名) before one's death; in one's lifetime: ～的愿望 unrealized wish(of a person who has passed away)

生擒 shēngqín (动) capture

生人 shēngrén (名) stranger

生日 shēngri (名) birthday

生色 shēngsè (动) add lustre to; give added significance to: 他的演出,为酒会～不少. His performance made the cocktail party even more enjoyable.

生杀(殺)予夺(奪) shēng-shā yǔ-duó life or death, rewards or punishments — referring to autocratic rulers' power to do whatever they thought fit to the people

生身父母 shēngshēn fù-mǔ (名) one's own parents

生事 shēngshì (动) make trouble; create a disturbance: 造谣～ spread rumours and create disturbances

生手 shēngshǒu (名) sb. new to a job; novice; greenhorn

生疏 shēngshū (形) 1 not familiar: 人地～ be practically a stranger in a certain locality and have few friends there 2 out of practice; rusty: 他的英文有点～了. His English is a little rusty. 3 not as close as before: 分别多年,我们的关系～了. We're not as close as we used to be, for we haven't been in touch for so many years.

生死 shēng-sǐ (名) life and death: ～与共 share life and death; through thick and thin. ～存亡的斗争 a life-and-death struggle. ～攸关的问题 a matter of vital importance

生态(態) shēntài (名)ecology: ～平衡 ecological balance

生吞活剥 shēngtūn-huóbō accept uncritically other people's theory, method of doing things, etc.

生物 shēngwù (名) living things; living beings; organisms: ～化学 biochemistry. ～武器 biological weapon. ～学 biology

生息 shēngxī (动) live; exist; propagate: 休养～ live and multiply; rest and build up one's strength

生效 shēngxiào (动) go into effect; become effective: 自签字之日起～ go into effect from the date of signature

生性 shēngxìng (名) natural disposition

生锈 shēngxiù (动) get rusty

生涯 shēngyá (名) career; profession: 教书～ the teaching profession

生意 shēngyi (名) business;trade: 做～ do business

生硬 shēngyìng (形) 1 stiff; rigid; harsh: 态度～ be stiff in manner 2 not natural; affected; forced: 这几个字用得很～. These words are not well-chosen.

生育 shēngyù (动) give birth to; bear: ～子女 bear children. 计划～ family planning. ～年龄 child-bearing age

生造 shēngzào (动) coin (words and expressions): ～词 coinage

生长(長) shēngzhǎng (动) 1 grow: 小麦～良好. The wheat is growing well. 2 grow up; be brought up

生殖 shēngzhí (名) reproduction: ～器 reproductive organs; genitals

生字 shēngzì (名) new word: ～表 (a list of) new words

甥

shēng (名) sister's son; nephew

甥女 shēngnǚ (名) sister's daughter; niece

牲

shēng (名) 1 domestic animal 2 animal sacrifice

牲畜 shēngchù (名) livestock; domestic animals

牲口 shēngkou (名) draught animals; beasts of burden

升

shēng I (动) 1 move upward: 上～ rise 2 promote: 被提～到负责岗位 be promoted to a position of responsibility II (名) 1 litre: 一～啤酒 a litre of beer 2 *sheng*, a unit of dry measure for grain (=1 litre)

升格 shēnggé (动) promote; upgrade: 将外交关系～为大使级 upgrade diplomatic relations to ambassadorial level

升官 shēngguān (动) be promoted

升华(華) shēnghuá (名) 1 sublimation 2 raising of things to a higher level; distillation; sublimation

升级 shēngjí (动) 1 go up (one grade, etc.) 2 escalate: 战争～ escalation (of a war)

升降机(機) shēngjiàngjī (名) elevator; lift

升学(學) shēngxué (动) enter a higher school

绳(繩) shéng I (名) rope; cord; string: 麻～hemp rope. 钢丝～ steel cable; wire rope. ～梯 rope ladder II (动) restrict; restrain: ～以纪律 restrain (unruly people) by discipline. ～之以法 bring to justice

省 shěng I (动) 1 economize; save: ～钱 save money. ～时间 save time 2 omit; leave out: 这两个字不能～. These two words cannot be omitted. II (名) province: ～会 provincial capital

see also xǐng

省吃俭(儉)用 shěngchī-jiǎnyòng (动) live frugally

省得 shěngde (动) so as to save (or avoid): 请准时来，～大家等你. Come on time so as not to keep us waiting.

省略 shěnglüè (动) leave out; omit: ～句 elliptical sentence

省事 shěngshì (动) save trouble; simplify matters: 在食堂里吃饭～. Having meals in the canteen saves us a lot of trouble.

省心 shěngxīn (动) save worry

盛 shèng I (形) 1 flourishing; prosperous: 全～时期 in the heyday of one's glory 2 vigorous; energetic: 火势很～. The fire is raging. 3 magnificent; grand: ～举 a grand occasion (or event) 4 abundant; plentiful: ～意 great kindness 5 popular; common; widespread: ～传 rumours go about that ...II (副) greatly; deeply: ～赞 praise profusely

盛产(產) shèngchǎn (动) abound in: ～石油 be rich in oil

盛典 shèngdiǎn (名) grand ceremony

盛会(會) shènghuì (名) grand occasion; impressive gathering

盛况 shèngkuàng (名) grand occasion; spectacular event: ～空前 an exceptionally grand occasion

盛名 shèngmíng (名) great reputation: ～之下，其实难副. While a person enjoys a high reputation, he may not be able to measure up to it.

盛气(氣)凌人 shèngqì língrén (形) domineering; arrogant; overbearing

盛情 shèngqíng (名) great kindness; boundless hospitality: 受到～款待 be accorded cordial hospitality

盛衰 shèng-shuāi (名) prosperity and decline; rise and fall; ups and downs

盛夏 shèngxià (名) the height of summer; midsummer

盛行 shèngxíng (动) be current (or rife, rampant); be in vogue: ～一时 be the rage for a time; prevail for a time

盛意 shèngyì (名) great kindness: ～难却. It would be difficult to decline your kind offer.

盛誉(譽) shèngyù (名) great fame; high reputation

盛赞 shèngzàn (动) highly praise; pay high tribute to

盛装(裝) shèngzhuāng (名) splendid attire; Sunday best

剩 shèng (形) surplus; remnant: ～货 surplus goods. ～菜～饭 leftovers

剩下 shèngxia (动) be left (over); remain: ～多少钱？How much money is left? 别人都走了，就～我一个. The others have all gone; I'm the only one left here.

剩余(餘) shèngyú (形) surplus; remainder: ～价值 surplus value

胜(勝) shèng I (名) victory; success: 取～ win (victory) II (动) 1 defeat; conquer: 战～自然 conquer nature 2 surpass; be superior to: 事实～于雄辩. Facts speak louder than words. III (形) 1 superb; wonderful; lovely: 引人入～ fascinating 2 be equal to; can bear: 力不能～ one's ability falls short of the task

胜败 shèng-bài (名) victory or defeat; success or failure: ～乃兵家常事. Victory or defeat is an ordinary experience for a soldier.

胜地 shèngdì (名) famous scenic spot: 避暑～ summer resort

胜负 shèng-fù (名) victory or defeat; success or failure: 战争的～ the outcome of a war

胜迹 shèngjì (名) famous historical site

胜利 shènglì I (名) victory; triumph: 取得～ win victory. 从～走向～ from victory to victory.

～果实 fruits of victory II (副) successfully; triumphantly: ～完成任务 successfully carry out one's task. ～者 victor; winner

胜券 shèngquàn (名) the chances of success: 操～ be sure to succeed

胜任 shèngrèn (形) competent; qualified; equal to: 能～愉快 be able to fulfil the task with credit

胜似 shèngsì (动) be better than; surpass

胜仗 shèngzhàng (名) victory: 打～ win a battle

圣(聖) shèng I (名) sage; saint II (形) 1 holy; sacred 2 emperor: ～上 His or Her Majesty

圣诞 shèngdàn (名) the birthday of Jesus Christ: ～老人 Santa Claus. ～节 Christmas Day. ～节前夕 Christmas Eve

圣地 shèngdì (名) 1 the Holy Land 2 sacred place; shrine

圣洁(潔) shèngjié (形) holy and pure

圣経(經) shèngjīng (名) the Holy Bible; the Bible

圣人 shèngrén (名) sage

圣贤(賢) shèngxián (名) sages

圣旨 shèngzhǐ (名) imperial edict

湿(濕) shī (形) wet; damp; humid: 他被雨淋～了. He got soaked in the rain.

湿度 shīdù (名) humidity

湿淋淋 shīlínlín (形) dripping wet; drenched: 身上浇得～的 get dripping wet

湿漉漉 shīlùlù (形) wet; damp

湿气(氣) shīqì (名) moisture; dampness

湿润 shīrùn (形) moist: ～的土壤 damp soil. 空气～ humid air

湿透 shītòu (形) wet through; drenched: 汗水～ wet through with sweat

湿疹 shīzhěn (名) eczema

诗 shī (名) poetry; verse; poem

诗歌 shīgē (名) poems and songs; poetry

诗话 shīhuà (名) random notes on classical poets and poetry

诗集 shījí (名) collection of poems; poetry anthology

诗经(經) shījīng (名) *The Book of Songs*

诗句 shījù (名) verse; line

诗篇 shīpiān (名) 1 poem 2 inspiring story

诗人 shīrén (名) poet

诗兴(興) shīxìng (名) poetic inspiration

诗意 shīyì (名) poetic atmosphere

诗韵(韻) shīyùn (名) 1 rhyme (in poetry) 2 rhyming dictionary

师(師) shī (名) 1 teacher; master: 能者为～. Whoever knows the job will be the teacher. 2 model; example: 前事不忘，后事之～. The past experience, if unforgotten, is a guide for the future. 3 a person skilled in a certain profession: 工程～ engineer. 建筑～ architect. 技～ technician 4 of one's master or teacher: ～母 the wife of one's teacher or master 5 division: 装甲～ armoured division 6 troops; army: 正义之～ an army fighting for a just cause

师出无(無)名 shī chū wú míng dispatch troops for war without cause

师范(範) shīfàn (名) teacher-training; pedagogical: ～学院 teachers college; teachers training college; normal school

师父 shīfu (名) 1 see "师傅" 2 a polite form of address to a Buddhist monk or nun or Taoist priest

师傅 shīfu (名) 1 master in trade, business or any troupe who undertakes to teach skills to pupils 2 a polite form of address to people who have skill or specialized knowledge: 老～ old master

师长(長) shīzhǎng (名) 1 teacher 2 division commander

师资 shīzī (名) qualified teachers; teachers: 培养～ train teachers

狮(獅) shī (名) lion

狮子 shīzi (名) lion

嘘 shī (叹): ～，别作声! Sh (or Hush)! Keep quiet! see also xū

失 shī I (动) 1 lose: 遗～ lose. 坐～良机 let slip a good opportunity; lose a good chance 2 fail to get hold of: ～手 drop. ～足 slip. 万无一～ one hundred percent safe 3 deviate from the normal: ～色 turn pale 4 break (a promise); go back on (one's word): ～信 break one's promise; fail to keep one's word 5 get lost: 迷～方向 lose one's bearings **6** fail to achieve one's end: ～望 be disappointed II (名)mishap; defect; mistake: ～之于烦琐 The fault is that it gives unwarranted attention to details.

失败 shībài I (动) fail; be defeated (in war, etc.): 他注定要～. He is doomed to fail. II(名) failure; defeat: ～是成功之母. Failure is the mother of success.

失策 shīcè I (动) be imtactful; miscalculate II (名) wrong move

失常 shīcháng (形) abnormal; odd: 举止～ act oddly. 他今天有点～. He is not himself today.

失宠(寵) shīchǒng (动) be in disgrace; fall from grace

失传(傳) shīchuán (动) not be handed down from past generations: 一种～的艺术 a lost art

失措 shīcuò (动) be at a loss as to what to do: 仓皇～ unable to stay collected

失当(當) shīdàng (形) improper; inappropriate

失地 shīdì (名) lost territory: 收复～ recover lost territory

失掉 shīdiào (动) **1** lose: ～信心 lose confidence. ～联系 lose contact **2** miss; fail to make use of: ～机会 miss a chance

失魂落魄 shīhún-luòpò be distracted: 吓得～ be scared out of one's wits

失火 shīhuǒ (动) catch fire; be on fire

失控 shīkòng (形) out of control; runaway

失口 shīkǒu (名) a slip of the tongue

失礼(禮) shīlǐ (动、名) breach of etiquette; discourtesy

失利 shīlì (动) suffer a setback (or defeat)

失恋(戀) shīliàn (动) suffer from unrequited love

失灵(靈) shīlíng (动)(of a machine, instrument, etc.) not work or not work properly: 机器～了. The machine is out of order.

失落 shīluò (动) lose

失眠 shīmián (名) (suffer from) insommia; sleeplessness

失明 shīmíng (动) lose one's sight; go blind

失散 shīsàn (动) lose touch with each other usually on account of some unfortunate incidents: 他找到了～多年的母亲. He has found his mother with whom he was not in contact for many years.

失色 shīsè (动) **1** fade **2** turn pale: 大惊～ turn pale with fright

失陪 shīpéi <敬> I must be leaving now.

失窃(竊) shīqiè (动) have things stolen

失去 shīqù (动) lose: ～知觉 lose consciousness. ～时效 be no longer effective; cease to be in force

失声(聲) shīshēng (动) **1** cry out suddenly and without thinking **2** be choked with tears

失实(實) shīshí (形) inconsistent with the facts: 传闻～. The rumour was unfounded.

失势(勢) shīshì (动) lose power and influence; fall into disgrace

失事 shīshì (动) have an accident

失守 shīshǒu (动) fall into enemy hands: 城市～ the fall of a city

失算 shīsuàn (动) miscalculate; misjudge

失调 shītiáo (动、名) **1** imbalance; dislocation: 供求～ imbalance of supply and demand **2** lack of proper care (after an illness, etc.): 产后～ lack of proper care after childbirth

失望 shīwàng (动) **1** lose hope or confidence **2** be disappointed

失误 shīwù (名) (of a ball game or chess) fault; mistake; a faulty move: 发球～make a faulty serve

失陷 shīxiàn (动) (of cities, territory, etc.) fall; fall into enemy hands

失笑 shīxiào (动) cannot help laughing

失信 shīxìn (动) break one's promise; go back on one's word

失修 shīxiū (形) (of houses, etc.) be in bad repair; fall into disrepair

失言 shīyán (动) make an indiscreet remark: 酒后～ make an indiscreet remark under the influence of alcohol

失业(業) shīyè (动) lose one's job; be out of work; be unemployed

失约 shīyuē (动) fail to keep an appointment

失真 shīzhēn (动) **1** (of voice, images, etc.) lack fidelity; not be true to the original **2** distortion: 频率～ frequency distortion

失职(職) shīzhí (动) neglect one's duty; dereliction of duty

失重 shīzhòng (名) weightlessness

失踪(蹤) shīzōng (动) disappear; be missing

失足 shīzú (动) 1 lose one's footing; slip: ～落水 slip and fall into the water 2 commit a serious error in life (often of a moral nature): 一～成千古恨. One false step brings eternal regret.

施 shī (动) 1 put into practice: 实～ implement. 无计可～ no strong card to play 2 bestow; grant; hand out: ～恩 bestow favour. 己所不欲，勿～于人. Don't do to others what you don't want done to yourself. 3 exert; impose: ～加压力 exert pressure 4 use; apply: ～肥 apply fertilizer

施放 shīfàng (动) discharge; fire: ～催泪弹 fire tear-gas shells

施工 shīgōng (动) engage in construction: 正在～ be under construction

施加 shījiā (动) exert; bring to bear on: ～压力 bring pressure to bear on sb.; put pressure on sb. ～影响 exert one's influence over sb.

施舍(捨) shīshě (动) give alms; give in charity

施行 shīxíng (动) 1 put into force: ～责任制 implement the responsibility system 2 perform: ～手术 perform a surgical operation

施展 shīzhǎn (动) put to good use; give free play to: ～本领 give full play to one's talent

施政 shīzhèng (名) administration: ～纲领 administrative programme

施主 shīzhǔ (名) 1 alms giver; benefactor 2 donor

尸(屍) shī (名) corpse; dead body: 政治僵～ political corpse

尸骨 shīgǔ (名) skeleton

尸体(體) shītǐ (名) corpse; dead body; remains: ～解剖 autopsy; postmortem (examination)

虱(蝨) shī (名) louse

虱子 shīzi (名) louse

实(實) shí I (形) 1 solid: ～心车胎 solid rubber tyres 2 true; real; honest: 真心～意 sincere and honest II (名) 1 reality; fact: 名不副～. The name falls short of the reality. 2 fruit; seed: 开花结～ blossom and bear fruit

实报(報)实销 shíbào-shíxiāo (动) reimburse the cost

实弹(彈) shídàn (名) live shell; live ammunition: ～演习 practice with live ammunition

实地 shídì (副) on the spot: ～考察 on-the-spot investigation

实话 shíhuà (名) truth: 说～ to tell the truth

实惠 shíhuì (名、形) 1 real benefit 2 of real benefit

实际(際) shíjì I (名) reality; practice: 客观～ objective reality. ～上 in fact; in reality; actually II (形) 1 practical; realistic: ～经验 practical experience 2 real; actual; concrete: ～情况 actual situation; reality. ～行动 concrete action. ～收入 real income

实践(踐) shíjiàn I (名) practice: ～出真知. Genuine knowledge comes from practice. II (动) put into practice; carry out: ～诺言 make good one's promise

实据(據) shíjù (名) substantial evidence; substantial proof: 真凭～ ironclad evidence

实况 shíkuàng (名) what is actually happening: 电视转播足球赛～ televise a football match; live telecast of a football match. ～转播 live broadcast; live telecast

实力 shílì (名) strength: ～地位 position of strength. 军事～ military strength

实例 shílì (名) instance; example

实情 shíqíng (名) the true state of affairs; the actual situation; truth

实权(權) shíquán (名) real power

实事求是 shí shì qiú shì seek truth from the fact; be down-to-earth

实体(體) shítǐ (名) 1 substance 2 entity

实物 shíwù I (名) material object II (副) in kind: ～交易 barter

实习(習) shíxí (名) practice; fieldwork; field trip: 去工厂～ go on a field trip to a factory. ～生 trainee

实现 shíxiàn (动) realize; achieve; bring about: ～改革 bring about a reform. 他的梦想～了.

His dream has come true.

实效 shíxiào (名) actual effect; substantial results

实行 shíxíng (动) put into practice (or effect); carry out; practise; implement: ～计划生育 practise family planning. ～对外开放政策 carry out the policy of opening to the outside world

实验(驗) shíyàn (名) experiment; test: 做～ do (or carry out) an experiment; make a test. ～动物 animal used as a subject of experiment. ～室 laboratory. ～小学 pilot school

实业(業) shíyè (名) industry and commerce; industry: ～家 industrialist

实用 shíyòng (形) practical; pragmatic: ～主义 pragmatism

实在 shízài I (形) true; real; honest; dependable: ～的本事 real ability II (副) indeed; really; honestly: 我～不知道. I really don't know.

实战(戰) shízhàn (名) actual combat

实质(質) shízhì (名) substance; essence: 这两种看法～上是一样的. These two views are virtually identical. 问题的～是无原则的派性斗争. The matter boils down to unprincipled factional strife.

识(識) shí I (动) know: 不～字 be illiterate II (名) knowledge: 常～ general knowledge

识别 shíbié (动) distinguish; discern; spot: ～真假朋友 tell true friends from false ones

识大体(體) shídàtǐ have the overall interest at heart

识货 shíhuò (动) be able to tell good from bad; appreciate the true worth of sb.'s or sth.'s quality

识破 shípò (动) see through; penetrate: ～诡计 see through a plot

识相 shíxiàng (动) be sensible

识字 shízì (动) learn to read; become literate: ～班 literacy class

十 shí I (数) ten: ～倍 ten times; tenfold. ～足学究气 unadulterated pedantry II (形) topmost

十恶(惡)不赦 shí è bù shè (形) guilty of heinous crimes

十二月 shí'èryuè (名) 1 December 2 the twelfth month of the lunar year; the twelfth moon

十分 shífēn (副) very; fully; utterly; extremely: 天气～热. It's awfully hot.

十进(進)制 shíjìnzhì (名) the decimal system

十拿九稳 shíná-jiǔwěn as good as assured

十全十美 shíquán-shíměi (形) perfect; flawless; impecable

十万(萬)火急 shíwàn huǒjí 1 posthaste 2 Most Urgent (as a mark on dispatches)

十项全能运(運)动(動) shí xiàng quánnéng yùndòng (名) decathlon

十一月 shíyīyuè (名) 1 November 2 the eleventh month of the lunar year; the eleventh moon

十月 shíyuè (名) 1 October 2 the tenth month of the lunar year

十之八九 shí zhī bā-jiǔ (副) in eight or nine cases out of ten; most likely

十字架 shízìjià (名) cross

十字街头(頭) shízì jiētóu (名) busy street

十字路口 shízì lùkǒu (名) (at the) crossroads

十足 shízú (形) 100 per cent; out-and-out; sheer; downright: 干劲～ very energetic. ～的书呆子 a real bookworm

什 shí (形) assorted; varied; miscellaneous

see also shén

什锦 shíjǐn (形) assorted; mixed: ～饼干 assorted biscuits. ～奶糖 assorted toffees

什物 shíwù (名) articles for daily use; odds and ends

石 shí (名) 1 stone; rock 2 stone inscription: 金～ inscriptions on ancient bronzes and stone tablets

石板 shíbǎn (名) slabstone; flagstone

石沉大海 shí chén dàhǎi disappear like a pebble thrown into the sea; make no response

石膏 shígāo (名) gypsum; plaster stone: ～像 plaster statue; plaster figure

石灰 shíhuī (名) lime: ～石 limestone

石匠 shíjiàng (名) stonemason; mason

石窟 shíkū (名) rock cave; grotto

石蜡(蠟) shílà (名) paraffin wax: ～油 paraffin oil

石棉 shímián （名）asbestos：～瓦 asbestos shingle；asbestos tile

石墨 shímò （名）graphite

石器 shíqì （名）1 stone implement；stone artifact 2 stone vessel；stoneware：～时代 the Stone Age

石英 shíyīng （名）quartz：～钟 quartz clock

石油 shíyóu （名）petroleum；oil：～产品 petroleum products. ～化工厂 petrochemical works. ～勘探 petroleum prospecting

石子 shízǐ （名）cobblestone；cobble；pebble：～路 cobblestone street；cobbled road；macadam

拾 shí I（动）pick up (from the ground)；collect：～柴 collect firewood. ～麦穗 glean (stray ears of) wheat II（数）ten [used for the numeral 十 on cheques, banknotes, etc. to avoid mistakes or alterations]

拾掇 shíduo （动）1 tidy up；put in order：屋里～得整整齐齐的. The room is kept clean and tidy. 2 repair；fix：这电视机有点毛病，你给～一下好吗？Something is wrong with the T.V. set. Will you help me fix it?

拾零 shílìng （名）sidelights；titbits

拾取 shíqǔ （动）pick up；collect

拾人牙慧 shí rén yáhuì pick up some irrelevant remarks from people and pass them off as a sample of one's own wit

拾遗 shíyí （动）pick up any lost article from the road：路不～. No one pockets anything found on the road.

时(時) shí I（名）1 time；times；days：古～ ancient times 2 fixed time：准～上班 get to work on time 3 hour：报～ announce the hour；give the time signal. 上午八～ at 8 o'clock in the morning；at 8 a.m. 4 season：四～ the four seasons. ～菜 delicacies of the season 5 opportunity；chance：失～ lose the opportunity；miss the chance. 待～而动 bide one's time 6 tense：过去～ the past tense II（形、副）1 current；present：～事 current affairs 2 occasionally；from time to time：～有出现 appear from time to time 3 now ... now ...；sometimes ... somtimes ...：～断～续 intermittently；off and on. ～起～伏 constant rise and fall

时差 shíchā （名）1 time difference 2 equation of time

时常 shícháng（副）often；frequently

时代 shídài （名）1 times；age；era；epoch：开创一个新～ usher in a new era. ～精神 the watchword of the time 2 a period in one's life：少年～ childhood

时而 shí'ér （副）1 from time to time；sometimes 2 now ... now ...；sometimes ... sometimes ...：这几天～晴天，～下雨. It has been sometimes fine and sometimes rainy these few days.

时光 shíguāng （名）1 time：～不早了. It's getting late. 2 times；years；days

时候 shíhou （名）1 (the duration of) time：你来这儿有多少～了？How long have you been here? 2 (a point in) time；moment：现在是什么～了？What time is it? ～到了，该走了. It's time we left.

时机(機) shíjī （名）opportunity；an opportune moment：～一到 when the opportunity arises；at the opportune moment. ～不成熟. Conditions are not ripe yet.

时间 shíjiān （名）1 (the concept of) time：～与空间 time and space 2 (the duration of) time：办公～ office hours 3 (a point in) time：北京～十九点正 19 hours Beijing time. ～表 timetable；schedule

时间性 shíjiānxìng（名）timeliness：新闻报导～强. News reports must be timely.

时节(節) shíjié （名）1 season：秋收～ the autumn harvest season 2 time：那～她才十二岁. She was only twelve then.

时局 shíjú （名）the current political situation

时刻 shíkè I（名）time；hour；moment：关键的～ a critical moment II（副）constantly；always：～准备保卫祖国 be ready to defend the country at any moment

时刻表 shíkèbiǎo （名）timetable；schedule：火车～ railway timetable；train schedule

时髦 shímáo （形）fashionable；stylish；in vogue

时期 shíqī （名）period：殖民统治～ the period of colonial rule

时区(區) shíqū （名）time zone

时时(時) shíshí （副）often；constantly

时势(勢) shíshì （名）the current

situation; the trend of the times
时事 shíshì (名) current events; current affairs
时速 shísù (名) speed per hour
时态(態) shítài (名) tense
时鲜 shíxiān (形) (of vegetables, fruits, etc.) in season: ～水果 fresh fruits
时新 shíxīn (形) stylish; trendy: ～式样 up-to-date style
时兴(興) shíxīng (形) fashionable; in vogue; popular
时宜 shíyí (形) what is appropriate to the occasion: 不合～ be out of step with the time
时运(運) shíyùn (名) luck; fortune: ～不济 be out of luck; be dogged by misfortune; down on one's luck
时钟(鐘) shízhōng (名) clock
时装(裝) shízhuāng (名) fashionable dress; the latest fashion: ～表演 fashion show

食 shí I (动) eat: 不劳动者不得～. He who does not work, neither shall he eat. II (名) 1 meal; food: 废寝忘～forget about his meals and rest. 主～ staple food 2 feed: 猪～ pig feed 3 eclipse: 日～ solar eclipse. 月～ lunar eclipse III (形) edible: ～油 edible oil; cooking oil
食道 shídào (名) esophagus
食粮(糧) shíliáng (名) grain; foodstuff
食品 shípǐn (名) foodstuff; food; provisions: 罐头～ tinned (or canned) food. ～厂 bakery and confectionery; food products factory. ～工业 food industry. ～加工 food processing
食谱 shípǔ (名) recipes; cookbook
食宿 shí-sù (名) board and lodging
食堂 shítáng (名) dining room; mess hall; canteen
食物 shíwù (名) food; edibles
食言 shíyán (动) go back on one's word; break one's promise
食盐(鹽) shíyán (名) table salt; salt
食用 shíyòng (形) edible: ～植物油 edible vegetable oil
食欲 shíyù (名) appetite: ～不振 have a poor appetite. 促进～ stimulate the appetite; be appetizing
食指 shízhǐ (名) index finger; forefinger

蚀(蝕) shí (动) 1 lose: 亏～ lose (money) in business 2 erode; corrode: 风雨侵～ wea therbeaten 3 eclipse: 日～ solar eclipse
蚀本 shíběn (动) lose one's capital: ～生意 a losing business; an unprofitable venture (or undertaking)

史 shǐ (名) history: 近代～ modern history. 编年～ annals. 国际关系～ history of international relations
史册 shǐcè (名) history; annals: 载入～ go down in history; go down in the annals of ...
史料 shǐliào (名) historical data; historical materials
史前 shǐqián (形) prehistoric: ～时代 prehistoric age(or times). ～学(考古) prehistory
史诗 shǐshī (名) epic
史实(實) shǐshí (名) historical facts
史书(書) shǐshū (名) history; historical records
史无(無)前例 shǐ wú qiánlì without precedent in history; unprecedented
史学(學) shǐxué (名) the science of history; historical science; historiography

使 shǐ I (动) 1 send; tell sb. to do sth.: ～人去收集经济信息 send sb. to collect economic imformation 2 use; employ; apply: ～化肥 apply chemical fertilizer 3 make; cause; enable: ～国家遭受巨大损失 cause enormous losses to the state. 这一批评～她大为生气. This criticism infuriated her. II (名) envoy; messenger: 特～ special envoy. 出～国外 be sent abroad as an envoy. 大～ ambassador III (副) if; supposing: 纵～ even if; even though
使不得 shǐbude (动) 1 cannot be used; useless; unserviceable: 这支笔～了. This fountain pen is no longer serviceable. 2 impermissible; undesirable
使出 shǐchū (动) use; exert: ～浑身解数 do something for all one is worth. ～最后一点力气 spend the last bit of one's energy
使得 shǐde I (形) 1 usable 2 workable; feasible II (动) make; cause; render
使馆(館) shǐguǎn (名) diplomatic mission; embassy
使唤 shǐhuan (动) tell people to carry out orders: ～人 order

people about; be bossy
使节(節) shǐjié (名) diplomatic envoy; envoy
使劲(勁) shǐjìn (动) exert all one's strength: 再使把劲 put on another spurt
使命 shǐmìng (名) mission: 历史~ historical mission
使用 shǐyòng (动) make use of; use; employ; apply: 合理~资金 rational utilization of capital
使者 shǐzhě (名) emissary; envoy; messenger

驶 shǐ (动) 1 start, operate: 驾~ drive. 行~ sail 2 (of a vehicle, etc.) speed: 急~而过 speed past

屎 shǐ (名) 1 excrement; dung; droppings: 鸡~ chicken droppings. 牛~ cow dung. 拉~ move the bowels; shit 2 secretion (of the eye, ear, etc.): 耳~ earwax

矢 shǐ (名) 1 arrow: 飞~ flying arrow 2 vow; swear: ~忠 vow to be loyal
矢口否认(認) shǐkǒu fǒurèn flatly deny: 他~说过那句话. He categorically denied that he had ever made such a remark.

始 shǐ I (名) beginning; start: 自~至终 from beginning to end; from start to finish II (副) only then: 不断学习, ~能进步. Only persistent study yields steady progress. III (动) start; begin: 自今日~ starting today
始末 shǐ-mò (名) the whole story: 事情的~ the whole story from beginning to end
始终 shǐzhōng (副) from beginning to end; from start to finish; all along; throughout: 他一生~保持谦虚谨慎的作风. He remained modest and prudent all his life.
始终不渝 shǐzhōng bù yú unswerving; steadfast: 我们~地坚持和平共处五项原则. We unswervingly adhere to the five principles of peaceful co-existence.

室 shì (名) room: 休息~ waiting-room; lounge. 会客~ reception room. 办公~ office
室内 shìnèi (形) indoor; interior: ~运动 indoor sport. ~游泳池 indoor swimming pool. ~装饰 interior decoration
室外 shìwài (形) outdoor; outside: ~活动 outdoor activities

市 shì (名) 1 market: 菜~ food market. 上~ be on the market; be in season 2 city; municipality: 参观~容 go sightseeing in the city 3 pertaining to the Chinese system of weights and measures: ~尺 *chi*, a unit of length (=1/3 metre)
市场(場) shìchǎng (名) marketplace; market; bazaar: 国内~ domestic market. ~繁荣. The market is brisk. 这种意见在学术界里没有什么~. This idea has received little support in academic circles.
市集 shìjí (名) 1 fair 2 small town
市价(價) shìjià (名) market price
市郊 shìjiāo (名) suburb; outskirts
市斤 shìjīn (名) *jin*, a unit of weight (= 1/2 kilogram)
市井 shìjǐng (名)〈书〉 marketplace; town: ~小人 philistine
市侩(儈) shìkuài (名) sordid merchant: ~习气 philistinism
市民 shìmín (名) residents of a city; townsfolk
市亩(畝) shìmǔ (名) *mu*, a unit of area (= 0.0667 hectares)
市区(區) shìqū (名) city proper; urban district
市容 shìróng (名) the appearance of a city: 保持~整洁 keep the city clean and tidy
市长(長) shìzhǎng (名) mayor
市镇 shìzhèn (名) small towns; towns

柿 shì (名) persimmon
柿饼 shìbǐng (名) dried persimmon
柿子 shìzi (名) persimmon

式 shì (名) 1 type; style; fashion: 新~ new type. 旧~ oldfashioned 2 pattern; form: 程~ pattern 3 ceremony; ritual: 开幕~ opening ceremony 4 formula: 方程~ equation 5 mood; mode: 叙述~ indicative mood
式样(樣) shìyàng (名) style; type; model: 一排排的楼房, ~都很美观. There are all rows of buildings with graceful designs.
式子 shìzi (名) 1 posture 2 formula

试 shì I (动) try; test: ~一~ have a try. ~产 trial production. ~穿 try on (a garment, shoes, etc.) II (名) examination

试表 shìbiǎo (动)<口> take sb.'s temperature
试点(點) shìdiǎn I (动) make experiments; conduct tests at selected points; launch a pilot project II (名) a place where an experiment is made; experimental unit
试管 shìguǎn (名) test tube: ～婴儿 test tube babies
试金石 shìjīnshí (名) touchstone
试卷 shìjuàn (名) examination paper; test paper
试探 shìtàn (动) sound out; feel out; probe; explore: 我要～他一下. I'll sound him out.
试探性 shìtànxìng (形) trial; exploratory; probing: ～谈判 exploratory talks. ～气球 trial balloon
试题 shìtí (名) examination questions; paper: 数学～很不容易. The maths paper was quite stiff.
试图(圖) shìtú (动) attempt; try
试想 shìxiǎng [used in a rhetorical question to imply mild reproach] just think: ～你这样下去结果会多糟. Just imagine what harm it will do you if you go on like this.
试行 shìxíng (动) try out: ～制造 trial produce
试验(驗) shìyàn (名) trial; experiment; test: ～新机器 try out the new machines
试用 shìyòng (动) 1 try out 2 on probation: ～人员 person on probation
试纸 shìzhǐ (名) test paper: 石蕊～ litmus test paper
试制 shìzhì (动) trial produce

拭 shì (动) wipe away; wipe
拭目以待 shì mù yǐ dài look forward to the fulfilment of one's wish; wait and see

示 shì (动) show; notify; instruct: 出～证件 produce one's papers. 暗～ hint; drop a hint. 请～ ask for instructions
示范(範) shìfàn (动) set an example; demonstrate: ～机器操作 demonstrate how to operate the machine
示例 shìlì (动) give typical examples; give instances
示弱 shìruò (动) show signs of weakness
示威 shìwēi (动) 1 demonstrate; hold a demonstration 2 put on a show of force; display one's strength: ～游行 demonstration; parade; march
示意 shìyì (动) signal; hint; gesture: 以目～ wink at sb.; tip sb. the wink
示意图(圖) shìyìtú (名) sketch map

视 shì (动) 1 look at: 注～ look at closely 2 regard; look upon; treat: 一～同仁 treat everybody equally 3 inspect; watch: 巡～ go on an inspection tour
视察 shìchá (动) inspect: ～边防部队 inspect a frontier guard unit
视而不见(見) shì ér bù jiàn look but see not; turn a blind eye to: 对这些缺点，不能～. You can't just overlook these faults.
视觉(覺) shìjué (名) visual sense; vision; sense of sight
视力 shìlì (名) vision; sight: ～测验 eyesight test. ～好(差) have good (poor) eyesight
视死如归(歸) shì sǐ rú guī meet one's death like a hero
视听(聽) shì-tīng visible and audible parts of human life; personal experience; mental horizons: ～中心 audio-visual centre
视同儿(兒)戏(戲) shì tóng érxì treat (a serious matter) as child's play
视野 shìyě (名) field of vision

士 shì (名) 1 scholar 2 non-commissioned officer: 上～ (英) staff sergeant; (美) sergeant first class. 中～ sergeant. 下～ corporal 3 a person trained in a certain field: 护～ nurse 4 (commendable) person: 烈～ martyr
士兵 shìbīng (名) rank-and-file soldiers; privates
士大夫 shìdàfū (名) court officials; scholar-officials (in feudal China); literati
士气(氣) shìqì (名) morale; fighting spirit: 鼓舞～ boost morale
士绅 shìshēn (名) gentry
士卒 shìzú (名) soldiers; privates: 身先～ (of an officer) fight at the head of his men; lead a charge

仕 shì (名)<旧> official
仕女 shìnǚ (名) 1 a bevy of beauties — a genre in traditional Chinese painting 2 maids of honour (in an imperial palace)
仕途 shìtú (名)<书> official career

恃 shì (动) rely on; depend on: 有～无恐 be fearless because one has powerful backing

恃才傲物 shì cái ào wù be contemptuous of others on the strength of one's own abilities; overweening

恃强凌弱 shì qiáng líng ruò bully the weak because one is backed by one's own strength

侍 shì (动) wait upon; attend upon; serve

侍从(從) shìcóng (名) attendants; retinue

侍奉 shìfèng (动) wait upon; attend upon; serve

侍候 shìhòu (动) wait upon; look after; attend

侍女 shìnǚ (名) maidservant; maid

侍卫(衛) shìwèi (名) imperial bodyguard

世 shì (名) 1 lifetime; life: 一生一～ a lifetime 2 generation: ～交 a traditional friendly relationship which goes back to many generations 3 age; era: 当今之～ at present; nowadays 4 world: 举～闻名 well known all over the world; world-famous 5 epoch

世仇 shìchóu (名) 1 family feud 2 vendetta

世传(傳) shìchuán (动) be handed down through generations

世代 shìdài (名) for generations; from generation to generation; generation after generation: ～相传 pass on from generation to generation

世故 shìgù (名) the ways of the world; experience in human relationships: 老于～ experienced; worldly-wise

世故 shìgu (形) worldly-wise; crafty

世纪 shìjì (名) century

世家 shìjiā (名) aristocratic or noble family

世交 shìjiāo (名) friendship spanning two or more generations

世界 shìjiè (名) world: ～博览会 World's Fair. ～语 Esperanto. ～主义 cosmopolitanism

世面 shìmiàn (名) various aspects of society; society; world; life: 见过～ have seen the world

世人 shìrén (名) people at large

世上 shìshang (副) in the world; on earth: ～无难事,只怕有心人. Nothing in the world is difficult for one who is set to do it.

世事 shìshì (名) affairs of human life

世俗 shìsú I (名) common customs: ～之见 a philistine point of view II (形) secular; worldly

世态(態) shìtài (名) the ways of the world: ～炎凉 snobbery

世外桃源 shìwài táoyuán land of eternal peace far from the madding crowd

世袭(襲) shìxí (形) hereditary: ～制度 the hereditary system

世系 shìxì (名) pedigree; genealogy

事 shì (名) 1 matter; affair; thing; business: 国家大～ state affairs 2 trouble; accident: 出～ have an accident. 惹～ make trouble; stir up trouble 3 job; work: 找～ look for a job 4 responsibility; involvement: 没有你的～了. This has nothing to do with you. 5 be engaged: 无所～～ doing nothing; loafing

事半功倍 shì bàn gōng bèi achieve twice the results for half the effort

事倍功半 shì bèi gōng bàn achieve half the result with twice the effort

事必躬亲(親) shì bì gōng qīn see (or attend) to everything oneself; take care of every single matter personally

事变(變) shìbiàn (名) 1 incident 2 emergency; exigency: 准备应付可能的突然～ be prepared against all possible emergencies

事端 shìduān (名) disturbance; incident: 挑起～ provoke incidents. 制造～ create disturbances

事故 shìgù (名) accident; mishap: 防止发生～ try to prevent accidents

事过(過)境迁(遷) shìguò-jìngqiān the affair is over and the situation has changed

事后(後) shìhòu (副) after the event; afterwards: ～诸葛亮 hindsight

事迹 shìjì (名) deed; achievement: 模范～ exemplary deeds

事假 shìjià (名) leave of absence (to attend to private affairs); compassionate leave

事件 shìjiàn (名) incident; event

事理 shìlǐ (名) reason: 明白～ be sensible *or* reasonable

事例 shìlì (名) example; instance: 典型～ a typical case

事前 shìqián (副) before the event; in advance; beforehand

事情 shìqing (名) affair; matter; thing; business: 今天我有许多～要做. I have a lot of work to attend to today. ～的真相 the truth of the matter. ～也真巧 as luck would have it

事实(實) shìshí (名) fact: ～胜于雄辩. Facts speak louder than words. ～如此. This is how things stand.

事实(實)上 shìshíshang (副) in fact; in reality; as a matter of fact; actually: ～的承认 de facto recognition

事态(態) shìtài (名) state of affairs; situation: ～严重. The situation is fairly grave.

事务(務) shìwù (名) **1** work; routine: ～繁忙 be tied up with a lot of work. ～工作 routine work **2** general affairs: ～员 office clerk. ～主义者 a person bogged down in the quagmire of routine matters

事物 shìwù (名) thing; object: 宇宙间的每一～ every thing in the universe

事先 shìxiān (副) in advance; beforehand; prior: ～通知(他们). Notify them in advance. ～知道 prior knowledge. ～酝酿 prior deliberation; exchange of views in advance

事项 shìxiàng (名) item; matter: 注意～ points for attention. 议程～ items on the agenda

事业(業) shìyè (名) **1** cause; undertaking: 伟大而光荣的～ a great and glorious cause. 文化教育～ cultural and educational undertakings **2** enterprise; facilities: 公用～ public utilities. ～心 devotion to one's work; dedication

事宜 shìyí (名) matters concerned; relevant matters

事与(與)愿(願)违(違) shì yǔ yuàn wéi things run counter to one's wishes

事在人为(爲) shì zài rén wéi all success hinges on human effort

誓

shì I (动) swear; vow; pledge: ～师 pledge mass effort II (名) oath; vow: 宣～ take the oath; be sworn in

誓不罢(罷)休 shì bù bàxiū swear not to stop; swear not to rest: 不达目的,～. We'll never give up until we reach our goal.

誓词 shìcí (名) oath; pledge

誓死 shìsǐ (动) pledge one's life: ～保卫祖国 vow to fight to the death in defense of one's country

誓言 shìyán (名) oath; pledge: 履行～ fulfil a pledge

逝

shì (动) **1** pass: 时光易～. Time flies. **2** die; pass away: 病～ die of illness

逝世 shìshì (动) pass away

势(勢)

shì (名) **1** power; force; influence: 权～ (a person's) power and influence **2** momentum; impetus: 来～甚猛. The force with which things are moving is terrific. **3** the outward appearance of a natural object: 地～ physical features of the land; terrain **4** situation, state of affairs; circumstances: ～所必然 inevitably **5** sign; gesture: 作手～ make a sign with the hand

势必 shìbì (副) certainly will; be bound to: 这商行～要破产. The business is bound to go bankrupt.

势不可当(當) shì bùkě dāng irresistible

势不两(兩)立 shì bù liǎng lì mutually exclusive; irreconcilable

势均力敌(敵) shìjūn-lìdí be evenly matched in strength; be in equilibrium

势力 shìli (名) force; power; influence: ～范围 sphere of influence

势利 shìli (形) snobbish: ～小人 snob

势利眼 shìliyǎn (名) **1** snobbish attitude; snobbishness **2** snob

势如破竹 shì rú pò zhú win victory after victory without encountering any resistance; advance swiftly unhindered

势头(頭) shìtóu (名) impetus; momentum: ～越来越大 rise to a crescendo; gain momentum

是

shì I (形) **1** correct; right: 自以为～ consider oneself invariably correct **2** yes; right: ～, 我知道. Yes, I know. II (动) **1** [used as the verb to be when the predicative is a noun]: 我～一个学生. I am a student. **2** [used for emphasis when the predicative is other than a noun]: 他～很努力的. He does work hard. **3** [used to indicate existence]: 前边不远～一家旅馆. There is a hotel not far ahead. 满身～汗 sweat all over **4** [used to indicate concession]: 这东西旧～旧, 可还能用. Yes, it's old, but it is still serviceable. **5** [placed before a noun to indicate fitness or suitability]: 这场雨下的～时候. It's raining just at the right time (for crops). **6** [used before a noun to indicate each and every one of the kind]: ～集体的事大家都要关心. Whatever concerns the collective concerns us all. ～有利于群众的事他都肯干. He is willing and ready to do whatever is of benefit to the masses. **7** [pronounced emphatically to indicate certainty]: 他～不知道. He certainly doesn't know. **8** [used in an alternative or negative question]: 你～坐火车，还～坐飞机? Are you going by train or by air? **9** [used at the beginning of a sentence for the sake of emphasis]: ～谁告诉你的? Who told you this?

是非 shìfēi (名) **1** right and wrong; truth and falsehood: 明辨～ distinguish between right and wrong **2** quarrel; dispute: 搬弄～ tell tales; sow discord

是非曲直 shì-fēi qū-zhí (名) rights and wrongs; truth and falsehood; merits and demerits

是否 shìfǒu (连) whether or not; whether; if: 他～能当选，还不一定. It's not certain whether he will be elected or not.

嗜

shì (动) have a liking for; take to: ～酒 take to drinking too much

嗜好 shìhào (名) **1** hobby **2** addiction; habit

释(釋)

shì (动) **1** explain; expound: ～义 explain the meaning (of a word, etc.) **2** clear up; dispel: ～疑 dispel misgivings; explain difficult points **3** let go; be relieved of: 如～重负 (feel) as if relieved of a heavy load **4** release; set free

释放 shìfàng (动) release; set free: ～俘虏 set war prisoners free; release war prisoners

释迦牟尼 Shìjiāmóuní (名) Sakyamuni, the founder of Buddhism

适(適)

shì I (形) **1** fit; suitable; proper: ～于儿童 suitable for children **2** right; opportune: ～量 just the right amount **3** comfortable; well: 舒～ comfortable II (动) go; follow; pursue: 无所～从 not know what to do; not know whom to turn to

适当(當) shìdàng (形) suitable; proper; appropriate: ～的人选 suitable candidate. ～的调整 appropriate readjustment. ～的时机 an opportune moment

适得其反 shì dé qí fǎn turn out to be just the opposite of what one really wants; run counter to one's intentions

适度 shìdù (形) appropriate measure; moderate degree: 饮酒～ drink moderately

适逢其会(會) shì féng qí huì happen to be present on the occasion; turn up at the opportune moment

适合 shìhé (动) suit; fit: ～国情 be suited to domestic conditions. ～他的口味 suit his taste

适可而止 shìkě ér zhǐ refrain from going too far

适龄 shìlíng (形) of the right age: (入学)～儿童 children of school age

适时(時) shìshí (副) at the right moment; in good time; timely

适宜 shìyí (形) suitable; fit; appropriate: 他～做教师. He has the makings of a teacher. 她做这种工作很～. She is suitable for this job.

适意 shìyì (形) agreeable; enjoyable; comfortable

适应(應) shìyìng (动) suit; adapt; fit: ～新的环境 adapt oneself to a new environment. ～时代的需要 meet the needs of the times. 一切工作都应～经济改革的需要. All work should be geared to the needs of economic reform.

适用 shìyòng (形) suit; be applicable: 这个理论～于所有学科. This theory applies to every discipline.

适者生存 shìzhě shēngcún survival of the fittest

适中 shìzhōng (形) **1** moderate: 雨量～ moderate rainfall **2** (of place) well situated

似

shì

see also sì

似的 shìde (助): 象雪～那么白 as white as snow. 他仿佛睡着了～. He seems to be dozing off. 他乐得什么～. He looks immensely happy.

氏

shì (名) family name; surname: 张～兄弟 the Zhang brothers

氏族 shìzú (名) clan: ～社会 clan society. ～制度 clan system

饰(飾) shì I (名)decorations; ornaments: 服～ clothes andornaments. 窗～ window decorations II (动)1 adorn; dress up; polish; cover up: 把文章修～一下 polish an essay. 文过～非 cover up one's mistakes 2 play the role (or act the part) of a dramatic character

饰物 shìwù (名) 1 articles for personal adornment; jewelry 2 ornaments; decorations

收 shōu I (动) 1 receive; accept: ～到一份电报 receive a telegram from sb. 请～下这件礼物. Please accept a small gift from us. 2 put away; take in: ～拾 tidy up. ～集 gather together 3 collect: ～税 collect taxes 4 harvest; gather in: ～庄稼 get in crops 5 bring to an end; stop: 时间不早,今天就～了吧. It's getting late. Let's call it a day. 6 (of emotion or action) restrain; control II (名) money received; receipts; income: 税～ tax revenue

收兵 shōubīng (动) withdraw (or recall) troops; call off a battle

收藏 shōucáng (动) collect; store up: ～古画 collect old paintings. ～粮食 store up grain

收场(場) shōuchǎng I (动) wind up; end up; stop: 草草～ hastily wind up a matter II (名) end; ending; denouement: 圆满的～ a happy ending

收成 shōucheng (名) harvest; crop: ～很好 a good harvest; a bumper crop

收到 shōudào (动) receive; get; achieve; obtain: ～良好效果 achieve good results

收发(發) shōufā I(动) receive and dispatch II (名)dispatcher: ～室 office for incoming and outgoing mail

收费 shōufèi (动) collect fees; charge

收复(復) shōufù (动) recover; recapture: ～失地 recover lost territory

收割 shōugē (动) reap; harvest; gather in: ～小麦 gather in the wheat. ～机 harvester; reaper

收工 shōugōng (动) stop work for the day

收购(購) shōugòu (动) purchase; buy: ～农副产品 purchase farm produce and sideline products

收回 shōuhuí (动) 1 take back; call in; regain; recall: ～主权 regain sovereignty. ～贷款 recall loans 2 withdraw; countermand: ～建议 withdraw a proposal. ～成命 countermand (or retract) an order; revoke a command

收获(獲) shōuhuò I (动) gather (or bring) in the crops; harvest II (名) results; gains: 学习～ gains of one's study. 一次～很大的经验 a most rewarding experience

收集 shōují (动) collect; gather: ～信息 collect information

收缴 shōujiǎo (动) take over; capture: ～敌人的武器 take over the enemy's arms

收据(據) shōujù (名) receipt

收敛(斂) shōuliǎn (动) 1 weaken or disappear: 她的笑容突然～了. The smile suddenly vanished from her face. 2 show restraint

收留 shōuliú (动) have sb. in one's care

收录(錄) shōulù (动) 1 include: 这篇文章已～在他的选集里. This essay is included in his selected works. 2 receive and record: ～机 radio-recorder

收罗(羅) shōuluó (动) collect; gather; enlist: ～技术人才 recruit technical personnel. ～资料 collect data

收买(買) shōumǎi (动) 1 purchase; buy in: ～废铜烂铁 buy scrap iron 2 buy over; bribe: ～人心 court popularity; buy popular support

收盘(盤) shōupán (名) closing quotation (on the exchange, etc.): ～汇率 closing rate. ～价格 closing price

收讫 shōuqì (名) 1 payment received; paid 2 (on a bill of lading, an invoice, etc.) all the above goods received; received in full

收容 shōuróng (动) (of an organization) take in and provide for: ～伤员 admit wounded soldiers. ～难民 feed and house refugees; accept refugees

收入 shōurù I (名) income; revenue; earnings: 财政～ state revenue. ～和支出 revenue and expenditure II (动) take in; include: 修订版词典～许多成语. Many new idiomatic expressions are included in the revised edition of the dictionary.

收拾 shōushi (动) 1 put in

order; tidy up; clear away: ～东西 tidy things up. ～床铺 make the bed. ～残局 make the best of a messy situation 2 get things ready; pack: ～行李 pack one's luggage; pack up one's things 3 repair; mend: ～房子 give the house a face-lift

收缩 shōusuō (动) 1 contract; shrink: 这种布要～. This kind of cloth shrinks. 2 concentrate one's forces; draw back

收条(條) shōutiáo (名) receipt

收听(聽) shōutīng (动) listen in: ～新闻广播 listen to the news broadcast

收尾 shōuwěi (名) 1 final phase of a project 2 concluding paragraph (of an article, etc.)

收效 shōuxiào (动) yield results; produce effects

收养(養) shōuyǎng (动) take in and bring up; adopt: ～孤儿 adopt an orphan

收益 shōuyì (名) (of an enterprise) income; profit

收音机(機) shōuyīnjī (名) radio (set); wireless (set): 袖珍～ portable radio. 落地式～ console set

收支 shōu-zhī (名) revenue and expenditure; income and expenses: ～平衡 revenue and expenditure in balance. ～逆差 unfavourable balance of payments

守 shǒu (动) 1 guard; defend: 把～ guard. ～住阵地 hold one's own position 2 keep watch; look after 3 observe; abide by: ～纪律 observe discipline. ～信用 keep one's promise

守备(備) shǒubèi (动、名) perform garrison duty; be on garrison duty; garrison

守财奴 shǒucáinú (名) miser

守法 shǒufǎ (动) abide by (or observe) the law; be law-abiding

守寡 shǒuguǎ (动) remain a widow; live as a widow

守候 shǒuhòu same as "守" (3)

守旧(舊) shǒujiù (形) adhere to past practices; stick to old ways; be conservative

守口如瓶 shǒu kǒu rú píng keep one's mouth shut; be tightlipped

守灵(靈) shǒulíng (动) keep vigil beside the coffin

守势(勢) shǒushì (名) defensive: 采取～ be on the defensive

守卫(衛) shǒuwèi (动) guard; defend

守夜 shǒuyè (动) keep watch at night

守则 shǒuzé (名) rules; regulations: 学生～ school regulations

守株待兔 shǒu zhū dài tù trust to chance and strokes of luck

首 shǒu I (名) 1 head: 昂～ hold one's head high 2 leader; head; chief: 祸～ chief culprit; arch-criminal II (量) [of a poem or song]: 一～歌 a song III (形) first: ～批 the first batch

首倡 shǒuchàng (动) initiate; start

首创(創) shǒuchuàng (动) initiate; originate; pioneer: ～精神 creative initiative; pioneering spirit

首次 shǒucì (副) for the first time; first

首当(當)其冲(衝) shǒu dāng qí chōng bear the brunt

首都 shǒudū (名) capital (of a country)

首恶(惡) shǒu'è (名) arch-criminal; principal culprit (or offender)

首领 shǒulǐng (名) chieftain; leader; head

首脑(腦) shǒunǎo (名) head: 政府～ head of government. ～会议 summit conference

首屈一指 shǒu qū yī zhǐ head the list; be second to none

首饰 shǒushì (名) woman's personal ornaments; jewelry

首途 shǒutú 〈书〉 set out on a journey

首尾 shǒu-wěi I (名) the first part and the last part; the opening and the concluding paragraph; the head and the tail II (副) from beginning to end: 这次旅行，～经过了一个多月. This trip lasted over a month.

首席 shǒuxí I (名) seat of honour: 坐～ be seated at the head of the table II (形) chief: ～代表 chief representative

首要 shǒuyào (形) of the first importance; first; chief: ～任务 the most important task. ～问题 a question of the first importance

首先 shǒuxiān (副) 1 first: ～发言 be the first to take the floor 2 in the first place; first of all; above all: ～，让我代表全体师生向你表示热烈欢迎. On behalf of all the faculty members and students, let me, first of all, extend to you a warm welcome.

首相 shǒuxiàng (名) prime minister

手 shǒu I (名) 1 hand: ～背 the back of the hand. ～提包 hand bag. ～织的花呢上衣 a hand-woven tweed jacket 2 a person doing (or good at) a certain job: 拖拉机～ tractor driver. 多面～ allrounder. 能～ a skilled hand; crackerjack II (动) have in one's hand; hold: 人～一册. Everyone has a copy. III (形) handy; convenient: ～册 handbook; manual IV (量) [of skill or proficiency]: 他有一～好手艺. He's a real craftsman.

手臂 shǒubei (名) arm

手笔(筆) shǒubǐ (名) sb.'s own handwriting or painting

手边(邊) shǒubiān (副) on hand; at hand

手表 shǒubiǎo (名) wrist watch

手不释(釋)卷 shǒu bù shì juàn be entirely engrossed in one's studies; be very studious

手册 shǒucè (名) handbook; manual: 教师～ teacher's manual

手抄本 shǒuchāoběn (名) handwritten copy

手电(電)筒 shǒudiàntǒng (名) electric torch; flashlight

手段 shǒuduàn (名) 1 means; medium; measure; method: 达到目的的一种～ a means to an end. 高压～ high-handed measures. 支付～ means of payment. 不择～ by fair means or foul; by hook or by crook; unscrupulous 2 trick: 耍～ play tricks

手法 shǒufǎ (名) 1 skill; technique: 夸张～ hyperbole. 艺术表现～ means of artistic expression 2 trick; gimmick: 卑劣的～ dirty tricks

手风(風)琴 shǒufēngqín (名) accordion

手扶拖拉机(機) shǒufú tuōlājī (名) walking tractor

手稿 shǒugǎo (名) original manuscript; manuscript

手工 shǒugōng (名) 1 handwork: 做～ do handwork 2 by hand; manual: ～操作 done by hand; manual operations

手工业(業) shǒugōngyè (名) handicraft industry; handicraft

手工艺(藝) shǒugōngyì (名) handicraft art; handicraft: ～工人 craftsman. ～品 articles of handicraft art; handicrafts

手迹 shǒujì (名) sb.'s original handwriting or painting

手脚 shǒujiǎo (名) 1 movement of hands or feet: ～利落 nimble; agile 2 underhand method; trick: 从中弄～ play dirty trick behind one's back

手巾 shǒujin (名) towel

手绢 shǒujuàn (名) handkerchief

手铐 shǒukào (名) handcuffs: 带上～ be handcuffed

手榴弹(彈) shǒuliúdàn (名) hand grenade; grenade

手忙脚乱(亂) shǒumáng-jiǎoluàn be in a tearing hurry

手枪(槍) shǒuqiāng (名) pistol; revolver

手巧 shǒuqiǎo (形) skillful with one's hands

手球 shǒuqiú (名) handball

手软 shǒuruǎn too soft-hearted to act resolutely when severity is called for; lack firmness

手势(勢) shǒushì (名) gesture; sign; signal: 做～ make a gesture; gesticulate

手术(術) shǒushù (名) surgical operation; operation: 病人必须在几天内动～. The patient will have to undergo an operation in a few days. 大夫说他今天要给病人做～. The doctor says he will perform an operation on the patient today. ～室 operating room; operating theatre. ～台 operating table

手松 shǒusōng (形) (concerning money matters) freehanded; openhanded

手套 shǒutào (名) 1 gloves, mittens 2 baseball gloves; mitt

手提 shǒutí (形) portable: ～打字机 portable typewriter. ～箱 suitcase

手头(頭) shǒutóu I (副) on hand; at hand: ～工作很多 have a lot of work on hand II (名) one's financial condition at the moment: ～紧 be short of money. ～宽裕 be quite well off at the moment

手推车(車) shǒutuīchē (名) hand cart; wheelbarrow

手腕 shǒuwàn (名) skill; finesse; stratagem: 外交～ diplomatic skill

手无(無)寸铁(鐵) shǒu wú cùn tiě bare-handed; unarmed; defenceless

手舞足蹈 shǒuwǔ-zúdǎo dance for joy

手下 shǒuxià (副) 1 under the leadership of; under: 在他～工作 work under him 2 at hand:

西不在～. I haven't got it with me.

手下留情 shǒuxià liú qíng show mercy to one's enemies or deal leniently with them

手心 shǒuxīn (名) 1 the palm of the hand 2 control: 这些罪犯逃不出法律的～. These criminals cannot escape from the net of justice.

手续(續) shǒuxù (名) procedures; formalities: 办～ go through formalities

手艺(藝) shǒuyì (名) 1 craftsmanship; workmanship 2 handicraft; trade

手印 shǒuyìn (名) 1 an impression of the hand 2 thumb print; fingerprint

手掌 shǒuzhǎng (名) palm

手杖 shǒuzhàng (名) walking stick; stick

手指甲 shǒuzhǐjia (名) finger nail

手纸 shǒuzhǐ (名) toilet paper

手指 shǒuzhǐ (名) finger

手镯 shǒuzhuó (名) bracelet

手足 shǒuzú (名) brothers: ～之情 brotherly affection

手足无(無)措 shǒu-zú wúcuò at a loss (as to) what to do; helpless

瘦 shòu (形) 1 thin 2 lean: ～肉 lean meat 3 tight: 这件上衣～了点. The coat is a bit tight.

瘦弱 shòuruò (形) thin and weak; fragile

瘦小 shòuxiǎo (形) slight of stature

瘦削 shòuxuē (形) very thin; emaciated; haggard

瘦子 shòuzi (名) a lean or thin person

兽(獸) shòu (名) 1 beast; animal: 野～ wild animal 2 beastly; bestial: 人面～心 a beast in human shape

兽类(類) shòulèi (名) beasts; animals

兽行 shòuxíng (名) 1 brutality 2 bestial behaviour

兽性 shòuxìng (名) brutish nature; the beast in a man

兽医(醫) shòuyī (名) veterinary surgeon; veterinarian

兽欲 shòuyù (名) animal (or bestial) desire

寿(壽) shòu (名) 1 longevity 2 life; age: 长～ long life; longevity 3 birthday: 祝～ congratulate sb. on his birthday 4 for burial: ～木 coffin (prepared before one's death)

寿辰 shòuchén (名) birthday (of an elderly person)

寿礼(禮) shòulǐ (名) birthday present (for an elderly person)

寿命 shòumìng (名) life-span; life: 平均～ average life-span (or life expectancy). 机器～ service life of a machine

寿终正寝(寢) shòuzhōng-zhèngqǐn die in bed of old age; die a natural death

受 shòu (动) 1 receive; accept: ～教育 receive an education. ～礼 accept gifts 2 suffer; be subjected to: ～委屈 be wronged; suffer injustice. ～损失 suffer losses. ～监督 be subjected to supervision 3 stand; endure; bear: ～不了 cannot bear; be unable to endure any longer

受潮 shòucháo (动) be made moist; become damp

受宠(寵)若惊(驚) shòu chǒng ruò jīng be overwhelmed by an unexpected favour (or a gracious offer)

受挫 shòucuò (动) be baffled; suffer a setback

受罚(罰) shòufá (动) be punished

受害 shòuhài (动) be injured or killed

受贿 shòuhuì (动) accept (or take) bribes

受奖(獎) shòujiǎng (动) be rewarded

受惊(驚) shòujīng (动) be frightened; be startled

受精 shòujīng (动) be fertilized: 体内(外)～ internal (external) fertilization

受窘 shòujiǒng (动) be embarrassed

受苦 shòukǔ (动) suffer (hardships); have a rough time: ～受难 live in misery

受累 shòulěi (动) get involved; be incriminated

受累 shòulèi (动) be put to much trouble: 这么远来看我,让您～了. It must have caused you a lot of bother to come all the way to see me.

受理 shòulǐ (动) accept and hear a case

受难(難) shòunàn (动) suffer a calamity or disaster; be in distress

受骗 shòupiàn (动) be deceived (fooled, cheated, or taken in)

受气(氣) shòuqì (动) be bullied; be insulted

受权(權) shòuquán (动) be authorized
受伤(傷) shòushāng (动) be injured; be wounded; sustain an injury
受审(審) shòushěn (动) stand trial; be tried; be on trial
受托 shòutuō (动) be commissioned; be entrusted (with a task)
受益 shòuyì (动) profit by; benefit from; be benefited
受用 shòuyòng (动) benefit from; profit by; enjoy: ～不尽 benefit from sth. all one's life
受援 shòuyuán (动) receive aid: ～国 recipient country
受灾(災) shòuzāi (动) be hit by a natural calamity: ～地区 disaster area; stricken (afflicted, or affected) area
受罪 shòuzuì (动) endure hardships or tortures; have a hard time

授 shòu (动) 1 award; vest; confer; give: ～权 authorize 2 teach; instruct: 函～ teach by correspondence; a correspondence course
授奖(獎) shòujiǎng (动) award (or give) a prize
授精 shòujīng (动) inseminate: 人工～ artificial insemination
授命 shòumìng (动) give orders: ～组阁 authorize sb. to form a cabinet
授受 shòu-shòu (动) give and accept: 私相～ offer and accept a gift privately for dubious purpose
授勋(勳) shòuxūn (动) confer orders or medals; award a decoration
授意 shòuyì (动) get sb. to carry out one's plan; suggest
授予 shòuyǔ (动) confer; award

售 shòu (动) 1 sell: 出～ put on sale. ～货 sell goods 2 make (one's plan, trick, etc.) work; carry out (intrigues): 以～其奸 so as to carry out one's evil design
售货员 shòuhuòyuán (名) shop assistant; salesclerk: 女～ saleswoman
售货机(機) shòuhuojī (名) vending machine
售价(價) shòujià (名) selling price; price
售票处(處) shòupiào chù (名) ticket office; booking office
售票员 shòupiàoyuán (名) ticket seller; (of a bus) conductor; (of a railway station or airport) booking-office clerk; (of a theatre) box-office clerk

狩 shòu 〈书〉 hunting (esp. in winter)
狩猎(獵) shòuliè (名) hunting

梳 shū I (名) comb: 木～ wooden comb II (动) comb one's hair, etc.
梳洗 shūxǐ (动) wash and dress: ～用具 toilet articles
梳妆(妝) shūzhuāng (动) dress and make up: ～打扮 be dressed up
梳子 shūzi (名) comb

疏 shū I (形) 1 thin; sparse; scattered: ～林 sparse woods. ～星 scattered stars 2 (of family or social relations) distant 3 not familiar with: 人地生～ be a complete stranger 4 scanty: 志大才～ have lofty aspiration but inadequate talent II (动) 1 dredge (a river, etc.) 2 neglect: ～于职守 be negligent of one's duties 3 disperse; scatter: ～散 evacuate
疏导(導) shūdǎo (动) dredge
疏忽 shūhu (名) carelessness; negligence; oversight
疏浚 shūjùn (动) dredge: ～水道 dredge the waterways
疏漏 shūlòu (名) careless omission; slip; oversight
疏落 shūluò (形) sparse; scattered: ～的村庄 a straggling village
疏散 shūsàn I (形) sparse; scattered; dispersed II (动) evacuate: ～人口 evacuation
疏失 shūshī (名) careless mistake; remissness
疏通 shūtōng (动) 1 dredge 2 mediate between two parties
疏远(遠) shūyuǎn (动) drift apart become estranged

蔬 shū (名) vegetables: 布衣～食 live simply; plain living
蔬菜 shūcài (名) vegetables greens

枢(樞) shū (名) pivot; hub centre: 神经中～ nerve centre
枢纽 shūniǔ (名) pivot; hub; exis key position: 交通～ a hub of communications

叔 shū (名) 1 father's younger brother; uncle 2 a form of address for a man about one's father's age; uncle 3 husband's younger brother
叔伯 shūbai (名) relationship between cousins of the same grand

father or great-grandfather

叔父 shūfù (名) father's younger brother; uncle

叔叔 shūshu (名) 1 father's younger brother; uncle 2 uncle (a child's form of address for any young man one generation its senior)

输 shū (动) 1 transport; convey: ～电 transmit electricity 2 lose; be beaten; be defeated: ～了一局 lose one game

输出 shūchū (动、名) 1 export 2 output

输入 shūrù (动、名) 1 import 2 input

输送 shūsòng (动) carry; transport; convey: ～货物 deliver goods. ～带 conveyer belt. ～机 conveyer

输血 shūxuè (名) blood transfusion: ～者 blood donor

输氧 shūyǎng (名) oxygen therapy

输液 shūyè (名) infusion

输油管 shūyóuguǎn (名) petroleum pipeline

殊 shū (形) 1 different: 悬～ differ widely; be poles apart 2 outstanding; special: 待以～礼 treat sb. with unusual courtesy 3 very much; extremely; really: ～难相信 very difficult to believe; hardly credible

殊死 shūsǐ (形) desperate; life-and-death: ～的搏斗 a life-and-death struggle

殊途同归(歸) shū tú tóng guī reach the same goal by different routes; all roads lead to Rome

抒 shū (动) express; give expression to; voice: 各～己见. Everybody may air his views.

抒发(發) shūfā (动) (of one's feelings) express; voice; give expression to

抒情 shūqíng (动) express (or convey) one's emotion: ～诗 lyric poetry; lyrics

舒 shū (动) 1 stretch; unfold 2 loosen; relax

舒畅(暢) shūchàng (形) happy; entirely free from worry: 心情～ feel happy

舒服 shūfu (形) 1 comfortable 2 be well: 她今天不大～. She isn't very well today.

舒适(適) shūshì (形) comfortable; cosy; snug: ～的生活 a comfortable life. ～的小房间 a cosy room

舒坦 shūtan (形) comfortable; at ease

舒展 shūzhǎn (动) 1 unfold; extend; smooth out 2 limber up; stretch: ～一下筋骨 stretch one's limbs

书(書) shū I (动) write II (名) 1 book 2 letter: 家～ a letter to or from home 3 document: 证～ certificate. 国～ letter of credence; credentials

书包 shūbāo (名) satchel; schoolbag

书报(報) shū-bào (名) books and newspapers

书本 shūběn (名) book: ～知识 book learning; book knowledge

书橱 shūchú (名) bookcase

书呆(獃)子 shūdāizi (名) bookworm

书店 shūdiàn (名) bookshop; bookstore

书法 shūfǎ (名) penmanship; calligraphy

书房 shūfáng (名) study

书画(畫) shū-huà (名) painting and calligraphy

书籍 shūjí (名) books; works

书记 shūji (名) secretary: 总～ general secretary. ～处 secretariat

书架 shūjià (名) bookshelf; bookcase

书刊 shū-kān (名) books and periodicals

书面 shūmiàn (形) written; in written form; in writing: ～通知 written notice. ～答复 written reply. ～声明 written statement. ～语 written language

书名 shūmíng (名) the title of a book

书目 shūmù (名) booklist; title catalogue: 参考～ bibliography

书皮 shūpí (名) book cover; dust jacket

书评 shūpíng (名) book review

书签(簽) shūqiān (名) bookmark

书生 shūshēng (名) 〈旧〉 intellectual; scholar

书生气(氣) shūshēngqì (名) bookishness

书写(寫) shūxiě (动) write: ～标语 write slogans; letter posters. ～纸 writing pad

书信 shūxìn (名) letter; written message: ～往来 correspondence

书桌 shūzhuō (名) desk

孰 shú (代)〈书〉 1 who; which: 人非圣贤，～能无过? Not everybody is a sage. Who can be entirely free from error?

2 what: 是可忍，～不可忍？ If this can be tolerated, what cannot?

熟 shú I (形) 1 ripe: 时机尚未成～. The time is not ripe yet. 2 (of food) cooked; done 3 processed: ～皮子 tanned leather 4 familiar: 听起来很～ sound familiar. 他们俩很～. They know each other quite well. 5 skilled; experienced; practised: ～手 practised hand; old hand II (副) deeply: ～睡 be fast (or sound) asleep

熟谙 shú'ān (形)〈书〉be familiar with; be good at

熟菜 shúcài (名) cooked food; prepared food

熟记 shújì (动) learn by heart; memorize

熟客 shúkè (名) frequent visitor

熟练(練) shúliàn (形) skilled; practised; proficient: ～工人 skilled worker

熟路 shúlù (名) familiar route: 他对这儿熟门～的. He knows his way around here.

熟能生巧 shú néng shēng qiǎo practice makes perfect

熟人 shúrén (名) acquaintance; friend

熟视无(無)睹 shú shì wú dǔ pay no heed to; turn a blind eye to; ignore

熟识(識) shúshi (动) be well acquainted with; know well

熟悉 shúxī (动) know sth. or sb. well; well acquainted with: ～情况 know the ropes

熟习(習) shúxí (形) have a good knowledge of; be versed in: ～业务 have an intimate knowledge of his own speciality. ～古典文学 be versed in classical literature

熟语 shúyǔ (名) idiom; idiomatic phrase

熟知 shúzhī (动) know very well; know intimately

赎(贖) shú (动) 1 redeem; ransom: 把抵押品～回来 redeem a mortgage 2 atone for (a crime)

赎金 shújīn (名) ransom money; ransom

赎罪 shúzuì (动) atone for one's crime: ～日〈犹太教〉Yom Kippur; Day of Atonement

数(數) shǔ (动) 1 count: 从一～到十 count from 1 to 10. ～～看，这班有多少学生. Count and see how many students there are in this class. 2 be particularly conspicuous by comparison: 全班～他功课好. He is considered the best in the class. 3 enumerate; list: 历～其罪 enumerate sb.'s crimes

see also shù; shuò

数得着 shǔ de zháo be counted among the best: 她是新中国～的电影演员. She is one of the best film actresses in new China.

数典忘祖 shǔ diǎn wàng zǔ be well acquainted with many historical facts but entirely ignorant of the achievements of one's own ancestors; forget one's ancestral origin

数一数二 shǔyī-shǔ'èr be among the very best; one of the best: 这所大学是全国～的高等学府. This university ranks as one of most prestigious institutions of higher learning in the country.

暑 shǔ (名) heat; hot weather: 盛～ at the height of the summer. 中～ get sunstroke

暑假 shǔjià (名) summer vacation (or holidays)

署 shǔ I (名) a government office; office: 专员公～ prefectural commissioner's office II (动) 1 arrange: 部～ make arrangements for sth. 2 act as deputy 3 sign; affix one's name to

署名 shǔmíng (动) sign; put one's signature to: 全体议员都在这封公开信上署了名. The open letter was jointly signed by all the congressmen.

薯 shǔ (名) potato; yam: 白～ sweet potato

曙 shǔ (名)〈书〉daybreak; dawn

曙光 shǔguāng (名) first light of morning; dawn

蜀 shǔ (名) another name for Sichuan Province

黍 shǔ (名) broomcorn millet

鼠 shǔ (名) mouse; rat

鼠辈 shǔbèi (名) mean creatures; scoundrels

鼠窜(竄) shǔcuàn (动) scurry away

鼠目寸光 shǔmù cùn guāng be shortsighted

鼠疫 shǔyì (名) the plague

属(屬) shǔ I (名) 1 category: 金～ metals 2 genus: 亚～ subgenus 3 family members; dependents: 直系亲～

direct dependent II (动) 1 come within one's jurisdiction: 附～ be affiliated or attached to 2 belong to: 我们～于另外一个组织. We belong to another organization. 3 be: 查明～实 be verified
属地 shǔdì (名) possession; dependency
属相 shǔxiang 〈口〉见"生肖" shēngxiào
属性 shǔxìng (名)〈逻〉attribute; property
属于(於) shǔyú (动) belong to; be part of: 这个游泳池是～我们学校的. This swimming pool belongs to our school. 西沙群岛是～中国的. The Xisha Islands are part of China's territory.
树(樹) shù I (名) tree: 苹果～ apple tree II (动) 1 plant; cultivate: 十年～木,百年～人. It takes ten years to grow trees, but a hundred years to rear people. 2 set up; establish; uphold: ～典型 hold sb. up as a model
树碑立传(傳) shùbēi-lìzhuàn build up sb.'s prestige by an overdose of praise
树倒猢狲(猻)散 shù dǎo húsūn sàn when an influential person falls from power, his hangers-on disperse; a sinking ship is deserted by rats
树敌(敵) shùdí (动) make enemies
树干(幹) shùgàn (名) tree trunk; trunk
树冠 shùguān (名) crown (of a tree)
树立 shùlì (动) set up; establish: ～榜样 set an example
树林 shùlín (名) woods; grove
树苗 shùmiáo (名) sapling
树木 shùmù (名) trees
树皮 shùpí (名) bark
树荫(蔭) shùyīn (名) shade (of a tree)
树枝 shùzhī (名) branch; twig
竖(豎) shù I (形) vertical; upright; perpendicular: ～线 a vertical line II (动) set upright; erect; stand: ～根柱子 erect a pole
竖井 shùjǐng (名) (vertical) shaft
竖立 shùlì (动) stand erect; stand: 宝塔～在山顶. The pagoda stands on the top of the hill.
漱 shù (动) gargle; rinse
漱口 shùkǒu (动) rinse the mouth; gargle

庶 shù (形) multitudinous; numerous: 富～ rich and populous
庶民 shùmín (名)〈书〉the common people; the multitude
数(數) shù I (名) 1 number; figure: 人～ the number of people. 两位～ two digit number. 心中有～ be aware how things stand 2 number: 单(复)～ singular (plural) number II (形) several; a few: ～小时 several hours. ～十种 a few dozens
see also shǔ; shuò
数词 shùcí (名) numeral: 序～ ordinal number. 基～ cardinal number
数额 shù'é (名) number; amount
数据(據) shùjù (名) data
数控 shùkòng (名) numerical control (Nc)
数理逻(邏)辑 shùlǐ luójí (名) mathematical logic
数量 shùliàng (名) quantity; amount
数码 shùmǎ (名) 1 numeral: 阿拉伯～ Arabic numerals. 罗马～ Roman numerals 2 number; amount
数目 shùmù (名) number; amount
数学(學) shùxué (名) mathematics
数字 shùzì (名) numeral; figure; digit: 天文～ astronomical figures
墅 shù (名) villa
恕 shù (动) 1 forgive; pardon; excuse: 宽～ forgive 2 excuse me; beg your pardon: ～难从命 Forgive me for not complying with your wishes.
术(術) shù (名) 1 art; skill; technique: 医～ the art of healing. 美～ the fine arts. 不学无～的人 ignoramus 2 method; tactics: 战～ tactics. 权～ political manoeuvre
术语 shùyǔ (名) technical terms; terminology: 医学～ medical terminology
述 shù (动) state; relate; narrate
述评 shùpíng (名) review; commentary: 时事～ a critical review of current affairs
述说 shùshuō (动) state; recount; narrate
述职(職) shùzhí (动) report on one's work; report: 大使已回国

～. The ambassador has left for home to report on his work.

束 shù I (动) bind; tie: ～装就道 pack and start out on a journey II (量) bundle; bunch; sheaf: 一～鲜花 a bunch of flowers; a bouquet III (名) control; restraint: 无拘无～ uninhibited

束缚 shùfù (动) tie; bind up; fetter: ～手脚 bind sb. hand and foot

束手待毙(斃) shùshǒu dài bì have no alternative but to wait for death; resign oneself to extinction

束手无(無)策 shùshǒu wú cè feel simply helpless

束之高阁 shù zhī gāogé lay aside and neglect; shelve; pigeonhole: 他把我的建议～，再也没想起它来了. He put aside my proposal and never thought of it again.

戍 shù (动)(名) defend; garrison: ～边 garrison the frontiers

刷 shuā I (动) 1 brush; clean: ～牙 brush one's teeth. ～地板 scrub the floor 2 daub; paste up: ～墙 whitewash a wall. ～标语 paste up posters 3 eliminate; remove: 那个队在比赛的第一轮就给～下来了. That team was eliminated in the first round of competition. II (象) swish; rustle: 风吹得树叶～～地响. The leaves rustled in the wind.

see also shuà

刷新 shuāxīn (动) 1 renovate; refurbish: ～门面 repaint the front (of a shop, etc.); give (the shop, etc.) a face-lift 2 break: ～纪录 break (or better) a record

刷子 shuāzi (名) brush; scrub: 头发～ hair brush

耍 shuǎ (动) 1 play: 叫孩子们到别处～去. Tell the children to go and play elsewhere. 2 play (tricks): ～花招 play small tricks

耍赖 shuǎlài (动) act unreasonably and shamelessly

耍流氓 shuǎ liúmáng (动) behave like a hoodlum; take liberties with women

耍脾气(氣) shuǎ píqi (动) get into a huff; fly into a rage

耍威风(風) shuǎ wēifēng (动) throw one's weight about; be overbearing

耍无(無)赖 shuǎ wúlài (动) act shamelessly; act like a scoundrel

耍心眼儿(兒) shuǎ xīnyǎnr be too calculating

刷 shuà

see also shuā

刷白 shuàbái (形) white; pale: 他的脸立刻变得～. He turned pale instantly.

衰 shuāi (动) decline; wane: 兴～ rise and fall. 年老体～ weak with age

衰败 shuāibài (动) decline; wane; be at a low ebb

衰竭 shuāijié (名) exhaustion: 心力～ heart failure

衰老 shuāilǎo (形) aged

衰落 shuāiluò (动) decline; be on the wane

衰弱 shuāiruò (形) weak; feeble: 神经～ suffer from neurasthenia

衰退 shuāituì (动) fail; decline: 视力～ failing eyesight. 经济～ economic recession

衰亡 shuāiwáng (动) become feeble and die; decline and fall; wither away

摔 shuāi (动) 1 fall; tumble; lose one's balance: 他～了一跤. He tripped over sth. and fell. 2 break: 他把腿～断了. He had his leg broken. 3 cast; throw; fling

摔打 shuāida (动) 1 beat; knock: 把扫帚上的泥～～. Beat the dirt off the broom. 2 temper oneself: 在困难环境中～出来 temper oneself in difficult circumstances

摔交 shuāijiāo (动) 1 tumble; trip and fall 2 wrestle

甩 shuǎi (动) 1 move back and forth; swing: ～胳膊 swing one's arms 2 throw; fling; toss: ～手榴弹 throw a hand grenade 3 leave sb. behind; throw off: 公园里不得乱～废纸杂物. Don't leave litter in the park. 这个城市去年生产增加了一倍，把其他城市远远～到了后头. This city doubled its production last year, leaving all the other cities far behind.

甩手 shuǎishǒu (动) 1 swing one's arms 2 refuse to do; wash one's hands of: 每个人都该负责，不能～不管. Nobody should refuse to do his or her duty.

率 shuài I (动) lead; command: ～队入场 lead the team into the arena II (形) 1 rash; hasty: 草～ careless. 轻～ rash 2 frank; straightforward: 坦～

frank. 直～ straightforward III (副) generally; usually: 大～如此. Such is the case, by and large.

see also lù

率领 shuàilǐng (动) lead; head; command: ～代表团 lead (or head) a delegation

率直 shuàizhí (形) frank and straightforward

帅(帥) shuài I (名) commander in chief: 元～ marshal. 挂～ take command II (形) beautiful; graceful; smart: 他钢琴弹得真～. How beautifully he plays on the piano!

闩 shuān I (名) bolt; latch: 门～ door bolt II (动) fasten with a bolt or latch: 把门～好 bolt the door

栓 shuān (名) 1 bolt; plug: 枪～ rifle bolt 2 stopper; cork

拴 shuān (动) tie; fasten: 把马～在树上 tie a horse to a tree

涮 shuàn (动) 1 rinse: 把衣服～一～. Rinse the clothes. 把这瓶子～一下. Give this bottle a rinse. 2 scald thin slices of meat in boiling water; instant-boil: ～羊肉 dip-boiled mutton slices; rinsed mutton in Mongolian pot

霜 shuāng I (名) 1 frost 2 frostlike powder: 糖～ frosting; icing II (形) white; hoar: ～鬓 grey temples

霜冻(凍) shuāngdòng (名) frost

霜叶(葉) shuāngyè (名) red leaves; autumn leaves

孀 shuāng (名) widow

孀居 shuāngjū (动) live in widowhood

双(雙) shuāng I (形) 1 two; twin; both; dual: ～手 both hands. 成～成对 in pairs 2 even: ～数 even numbers 3 double; twofold: ～人床 double bed. ～人房间 double room II (量) pair: 一～筷(鞋等) a pair of chopsticks (shoes, etc.)

双胞胎 shuāngbāotāi (名) twins

双边(邊) shuāngbiān (形) bilateral: ～会谈 bilateral talks. ～贸易 bilateral trade

双重 shuāngchóng (形) double; dual; twofold: ～标准 double standard. ～领导 dual leadership. ～国籍 dual nationality

双打 shuāngdǎ (名) doubles

双方 shuāngfāng (名) both sides; the two parties: 缔约～ both signatory states; the contracting parties. 劳资～ both labour and capital

双杠(槓) shuānggàng (名) parallel bars

双关(關) shuāngguān (形) having a double meaning: 一语～ a phrase with a double meaning. ～语 pun

双管齐(齊)下 shuāng guǎn qí xià exert simultaneous efforts at both ends

双轨 shuāngguǐ (名) double track

双面 shuāngmiàn (形) two-sided; double-edged; double-faced; reversible: ～刀片 a double-edged razor blade

双亲(親) shuāngqīn (名) (both) parents; father and mother

双全 shuāngquán (形) enjoy a double blessing; possess both complementary qualities: 智勇～ endowed with both wisdom and courage

双职(職)工 shuāngzhígōng (名) man and wife both employed

爽 shuǎng (形) 1 bright; clear; crisp: 秋高气～ The autumn weather is sunny and bright. *or* Autumn is beautiful and refreshing. 2 frank; straightforward; openhearted: 豪～ straightforward 3 feel well: 身体不～ be under the weather

爽快 shuǎngkuài (形) 1 relaxed; refreshed 2 frank; straightforward; outright: 他说话极为～. He is very frank and outspoken.

爽朗 shuǎnglǎng (形) 1 bright and clear: 深秋的天空异常～. In late autumn we have clear skies and plenty of fresh air. 2 hearty; candid; frank and open; straightforward: ～的笑声 peals of laughter

爽直 shuǎngzhí (形) frank; straightforward; candid

谁 shuí or shéi (代) 1 who: 你找～? Who are you looking for? 2 nobody: ～都不知道他. Nobody knows anything about him. 3 anybody: 有～愿意跟我们一起去? Anyone would like to go with us?

水 shuǐ (名) 1 water: 淡～ fresh water. 自来～ running water. ～上公园 aquatic park 2 a general term for rivers, lakes, seas, etc.: 汉～ the Han

River 3 a liquid: 墨～ ink. 桔子～ orangeade
水坝(壩) shuǐbà (名)dam
水泵 shuǐbèng (名) water pump
水兵 shuǐbīng (名) seaman; sailor; bluejacket
水彩 shuǐcǎi (名) watercolour: ～画 watercolour (painting)
水草 shuǐcǎo (名) 1 pasture and water 2 waterweeds; water plants
水产(產) shuǐchǎn (名) aquatic product
水车(車) shuǐchē (名) 1 waterwheel 2 water wagon
水池 shuǐchí (名) pond; pool; cistern
水到渠成 shuǐ dào qú chéng When conditions are ripe, success is assured.
水道 shuǐdào (名) 1 water course 2 waterway; water route
水稻 shuǐdào (名) paddy (rice); rice
水滴石穿 shuǐ dī shí chuān dripping water wears through rock; little strokes fell great oaks
水电(電) shuǐ-diàn (名) water and electricity: ～供应 water and electricity supply
水电(電)站 shuǐdiànzhàn (名) hydroelectric (power) station; hydropower station
水分 shuǐfèn (名) moisture
水沟(溝) shuǐgōu (名) ditch; drain; gutter
水垢 shuǐgòu (名) scale; incrustation
水管 shuǐguǎn (名) waterpipe
水果 shuǐguǒ (名) fruit
水火 shuǐ-huǒ (名) 1 fire and water — two things diametrically opposed to each other: ～不相容 be absolutely irreconcilable 2 extreme misery: 拯救人民于～之中 save the people from the abyss of misery
水浇(澆)地 shuǐjiāodì (名) irrigated land
水晶 shuǐjīng (名) crystal; rock crystal
水井 shuǐjǐng (名) well
水坑 shuǐkēng (名) puddle; pool; water hole
水库 shuǐkù (名) reservoir
水涝(澇) shuǐlào (形) waterlogging: ～地 waterlogged land
水雷 shuǐléi (名) (submarine) mine: 敷设～ lay mines (in water)
水力 shuǐlì (名) waterpower; hydraulic power: ～资源 hydroelectric resources; waterpower resources
水利 shuǐlì (名) 1 water conservancy: ～设施 water conservancy facilities 2 irrigation works; water conservancy project: ～资源 water resources
水流 shuǐliú (名) 1 rivers; streams; waters 2 current; flow: ～湍急 rapid (sluggish) flow
水龙(龍)头(頭) shuǐlóngtóu (名) (water) tap; faucet; bibcock: 开(关)～ turn on (off) the tap
水陆(陸) shuǐ-lù (名) land and water: ～两用 amphibious. ～坦克 amphibious tank
水落石出 shuǐluò-shíchū when the water subsides the rocks emerge — the truth is out
水磨 shuǐmó (动) polish with a waterstone
水墨画(畫) shuǐmòhuà (名) ink and wash; washpainting
水泥 shuǐní (名) cement
水鸟(鳥) shuǐniǎo (名) aquatic bird; water bird
水牛 shuǐniú (名)(water) buffalo
水暖工 shuǐnuǎngōng (名) plumber
水泡 shuǐpào (名) 1 bubble 2 blister: 手上打了～ get blisters on one's hands
水平 shuǐpíng I (形) horizontal; level II (名) standard; level: 生活～ living standard
水禽 shuǐqín (名) aquatic bird
水渠 shuǐqú (名) ditch; canal
水乳交融 shuǐ-rǔ jiāoróng in complete harmony; in congenial company
水生动(動)物 shuǐshēng dòngwù (名) aquatic animal
水手 shuǐshǒu (名) seaman; sailor; boatswain
水塔 shuǐtǎ (名) water tower
水塘 shuǐtáng (名) pool; pond
水田 shuǐtián (名) paddy field
水桶 shuǐtǒng (名) pail; bucket
水头(頭) shuǐtóu (名) 1 head 2 flood peak; peak of flow
水土 shuǐtǔ (名) 1 water and soil: ～流失 soil erosion 2 natural environment and climate: ～不服 unaccustomed to the climate of a new place
水网(網) shuǐwǎng (名) a network of rivers
水位 shuǐwèi (名) water level
水文 shuǐwén (名) hydrology: ～站 hydrometric station
水系 shuǐxì (名) river system
水箱 shuǐxiāng (名) water tank

水银 shuǐyín (名) mercury; quicksilver

水泄不通 shuǐ xiè bù tōng very crowded; packed with people

水性 shuǐxìng (名) 1 skill in swimming: 要参加海军必须懂～. You've got to be a good swimmer to join the navy. 2 the depth, currents and other characteristics of a river, lake, etc.

水源 shuǐyuán (名) 1 the source of a river; waterhead 2 source of water

水运(運) shuǐyùn (名) water transport

水灾(災) shuǐzāi (名) flood; inundation

水闸 shuǐzhá (名) sluice; water gate

水涨(漲)船高 shuǐ zhǎng chuán gāo when the river rises the boat goes up — things improve when the general situation improves

水蒸汽 shuǐzhēngqì (名) steam; water vapour

水准 shuǐzhǔn (名) level; standard

水族 shuǐzú (名) aquatic animals: ～馆 aquarium

说 shuì (动) try to persuade: 游～ go around soliciting support for one's views; peddle an idea; canvass
see also shuo

税 shuì (名) tax; duty: 营业～ business tax 进口(出口)～ import (export) duty

税额 shuì'é (名) the amount of tax to be paid

税款 shuìkuǎn (名) tax payment; taxation

税率 shuìlǜ (名) tax rate; rate of taxation; tariff rate

税收 shuìshōu (名) tax revenue

睡 shuì (动) sleep: 他在沙发上躺了一会儿,但没～着. He lay on the sofa for a while, but didn't get a wink of sleep.

睡觉(覺) shuìjiào (动) sleep: 该～了. It's time to go to bed.

睡梦(夢) shuìmèng (名) sleep; dream: 从～中惊醒 be roused from sleep

睡眠 shuìmián (名) sleep: ～不足 not have enough sleep

睡衣 shuìyī (名) night clothes; pajamas

吮 shǔn (动) suck

吮吸 shǔnxī (动) suck

瞬 shùn (名) wink; twinkling: 转～之间 in the twinkling of an eye

瞬时(時) shùnshí (形) instantaneous

瞬息 shùnxī (名) twinkling: ～万变的局势 the fast-changing situation

顺 shùn I (副) 1 in the same direction: ～流而下 go downstream. ～时针方向 clockwise 2 along: ～河边走 walk along the river II (动) 1 arrange; put in order: 这篇文章还得～一～. This essay should be re-organized to make it more readable. 2 obey; yield to; act in submission to: 不能总是～着孩子. We can't always humour the child the way we do. 3 act at one's convenience: ～手关门 close the door after you. III (形) 1 suitable; agreeable: 不～他的意 not appeal to him 2 in sequence

顺便 shùnbiàn (副) incidentally; in passing: 你去图书馆,～给我还这几本书. When you go to the library, please return these books for me if it doesn't give you too much inconvenience. ～说一句 by the way; incidentally. ～提到 mention in passing

顺差 shùnchā (名) favourable balance; surplus: 国际收支～ favourable balance of payments; balance of payments surplus

顺次 shùncì (副) in order; in succession; in proper sequence

顺从(從) shùncóng (动) be obedient to; submit to; yield to

顺当(當) shùndang (副) smoothly; without a hitch

顺耳 shùn'ěr (形) pleasing to the ear

顺风(風) shùnfēng (形) have a favourable wind: 一路～ a pleasant journey; bon voyage

顺风(風)转舵 shùn fēng zhuǎn duò trim one's sails; chop around with the wind

顺口 shùnkǒu (动) 1 read smoothly 2 say offhandedly; blurt out

顺理成章 shùn lǐ chéng zhāng (of a statement, argument, etc.) logical; well reasoned; follow a well mapped-out plan: 这显然是～的事. This is undoubtedly a matter of course.

顺利 shùnlì (副) smoothly; successfully: 进行～ get along pretty well. 手术进行得很～. It was a successful operation.

顺路 shùnlù 1 (副) on the way: 我昨天回家时～去看她. I dropped in on her on my way home yesterday. II (名) direct route: 不～an indirect route; a roundabout course

顺势(勢) shùnshì take advantage of a situation

顺手 shùnshǒu (副) **1** smoothly; without difficulty: 事情办得相当～. The work is proceeding smoothly. **2** conveniently; without lifting a finger **3** do sth. as a natural sequence: 我们扫了走廊,～把教室整理整理. Let's tidy up the classroom after sweeping the corridor.

顺水人情 shùnshuǐ rénqíng do sb. a favour without causing the slightest trouble to oneself

顺水推舟 shùnshuǐ tuī zhōu direct things onto their natural course

顺心 shùnxīn (形) satisfactory; gratifying

顺序 shùnxù I (名) sequence; order: 按年代～ in chronological order II (动) do something in proper order; take turns

顺延 shùnyán (动) postpone

顺眼 shùnyǎn (形) pleasing to the eye: 这图案看上去很～. This pattern is pleasant to look at.

顺应(應) shùnyìng (动) comply with; conform to: ～历史发展的潮流 go with the tide of historical development

说

shuō I (动) **1** speak; talk; say: ～好几国语言 speak several languages. **2** explain: 他得～几遍,才讲清楚. He had to explain several times to make himself understood. **3** scold: 他父亲～了他一顿. His father gave him a scolding. II (名) theory; teachings; doctrine: 著书立～ produce scholarly works to expound one's ideas

see also shuì

说不定 shuōbudìng (副) perhaps; maybe: ～你是对的. Maybe you are right.

说不过(過)去 shuō bu guòqù cannot be justified; be unreasonable

说不上 shuōbushàng (动) **1** cannot say for sure **2** be not worth mentioning

说穿 shuōchuān (动) expose; disclose: ～某人真正用意 disclose sb.'s real intentions

说…道… shuō…dào… [used before two parallel or similar adjectives or numerals]: 说三道四 make irresponsible remarks

说定 shuōdìng (动) settle; agree on: 这件事咱们就算～了. That's a deal we've made.

说法 shuōfa (名) **1** way of saying things; wording: 换一个～put it in another way. 委婉的～put it mildly **2** views; argument

说服 shuōfú (动) persuade; convince; bring round: 这个论点很有～力. This argument is very convincing. 需要做些～工作 require some persuading

说好 shuōhǎo (动) come to an agreement or understanding

说话 shuōhuà I (动) **1** speak; talk; say: 太激动了,话都说不清楚了 be too excited to speak coherently. 我们～是算数的. We mean what we say. **2** chat; talk **3** criticize: 人家也许会～. People may grow critical. II (副) in a minute; right away: 我～就来. I'm coming.

说谎 shuōhuǎng (动) tell a lie; lie

说教 shuōjiào (动) preach [also used figuratively]

说理 shuōlǐ (动) argue; reason things out: 咱们找他～去. Let's go and have it out with him.

说明 shuōmíng I (动) **1** explain; illustrate: ～理由 explain the cause **2** prove; demonstrate: 事实～这种做法是对的. Facts fully testify to the correctness of the approach. II (名) explanation; directions; caption: ～书 directions; synopsis (of a play or film)

说情 shuōqíng (动) plead for mercy for sb.

说妥 shuōtuǒ (动) come to an agreement

说闲(閑)话 shuō xiánhuà (动) make critical or sarcastic remarks on the sidelines

说项 shuōxiàng (动) put in a good word for sb.

说笑 shuōxiào (名) chatting and laughing

数(數)

shuò (副) frequently; repeatedly

see also shǔ; shù

数见不鲜 shuò jiàn bù xiān common occurrence; nothing new

朔

shuò (名) **1** the first day of the lunar month **2** north: ～风 north wind

硕

shuò (形) large

硕果 shuòguǒ (名) rich fruits; great achievements

硕果仅(僅)存 shuòguǒ jǐn cún rare survival or survivor
硕士 shuòshì (名) Master: ～学位 Master's degree
烁(爍) shuò (动) bright; shining: 闪～ twinkle; glimmer
斯 sī: ～文 refined; gentle
厮 sī (副) [usu. found in the early vernacular] with each other; together: ～打 come to blows; exchange blows
撕 sī (动) tear; rip: 从日历上～下一页 tear a page from the calendar. 上衣～了. The jacket is torn.
撕毁 sīhuǐ (动) tear up; tear to pieces: ～协定 tear up an agreement; tear an agreement to shreds
嘶 sī (形) hoarse
嘶哑(啞) sīyǎ (形) hoarse
思 sī I (动) 1 think; consider: 前～后想 weigh the ideas carefully 2 think of; long for: ～家 homesick. ～乡 think of one's native place with nostalgic longing II (名) train of thought
思潮 sīcháo (名) 1 trend: 文艺～ literary trends 2 thoughts: ～起伏 surging ideas
思考 sīkǎo (动) think deeply; ponder over; reflect on: ～问题 ponder a problem
思量 sīliang (动) consider; turn sth. over in one's mind
思路 sīlù (名) train of thought; thinking: 打断～ interrupt one's train of thought
思虑(慮) sīlǜ (动) consider carefully; contemplate; deliberate
思慕 sīmù (动) think of sb. with respect; admire
思念 sīniàn (动) think of; long for; miss sb.
思索 sīsuǒ (动) think deeply; ponder: 反复～这个问题 turn the problem over and over in one's mind.
思维 sīwéi (名) thought; thinking: ～方式 mode of thinking
思想 sīxiǎng (名)thought; thinking; idea; ideology: 政治～ political thought. 有～准备 be mentally prepared. ～觉悟 political consciousness (or awareness)
思绪 sīxù (名) 1 train of thought; thinking: ～纷乱 confused thinking 2 mood: ～不宁 feel disquieted
私 sī (形) 1 personal; private: ～事 private affairs 2 selfish: 无～ unselfish; selfless 3 secret; private: 窃窃～语 whisper; exchange whispered comments 4 illicit; illegal: ～货 smuggled goods
私奔 sībēn (名) elopement
私产(產) sīchǎn (名) private property
私仇 sīchóu (名) personal enmity
私党(黨) sīdǎng (名) clique
私愤 sīfèn (名) personal spite: 泄～ vent personal spleen
私见 sījiàn (名) 1 prejudice 2 personal opinion
私交 sījiāo (名) personal relationship
私立 sīlì (形) privately run; private: ～学校 private school
私利 sīlì (名) private (or selfish) interests; personal gain
私囊 sīnáng (名) private purse: 饱～ line one's pockets
私情 sīqíng (名) personal relationships: 不徇～ allow no consideration of personal relationships to interfere
私人 sīrén (形) private; personal: ～秘书 private secretary
私生活 sīshēnghuó (名) private life
私生子 sīshēngzǐ (名) illegitimate child; bastard
私通 sītōng (动) 1 have secret communication with: ～敌人 have secret communication with the enemy 2 have illicit relations with
私下 sīxià (副) privately; in secret
私心 sīxīn (名) selfish motives (or ideas); selfishness: ～杂念 selfish ideas and ulterior motives
私营(營) sīyíng (形) privately owned; privately operated; private: ～企业 private enterprise
私有 sīyǒu (形) privately owned; private: ～财产 private property ～制 private ownership (of means of production)
私自 sīzì (副) privately; secretly; without permission: 事先不通知委员会，～决定 make a decision on one's own without the prior knowledge of the committee

司 sī I (动) take charge of; attend to; manage: ～机 driver; chauffeur. 各～其事. Each has his own responsibilities. II (名) departent (under a ministry)

司法 sīfǎ administration of justice; judicature: ～部门 judicial departments. ～权 judicial powers

司空见惯 sīkōng jiàn guàn a common sight or occurrence; nothing to be surprised at

司令 sīlìng (名) commander; commanding officer: ～部 headquarters; command

司炉(爐) sīlú (名) stoker; fireman

司务(務)长 sīwùzhǎng (名) 1 mess officer 2 company quartermaster

司药(藥) sīyào (名) pharmacist; druggist; chemist

司仪(儀) sīyí (名) master of ceremonies

丝(絲) sī (名) 1 silk 2 a threadlike thing: 铜～ copper wire. 炒肉～ shredded pork 3 a tiny bit; trace: 一～不差 not the slightest difference. 一～不挂 stark naked

丝绸 sīchóu (名) silk cloth; silk: ～之路 the Silk Road

丝毫 sīháo the slightest amount or degree: ～不差 without the slightest discrepancy

丝绵 sīmián (名) silk floss, silk wadding

丝绒 sīróng (名) velvet; velour

丝线(線) sīxiàn (名) silk thread (for sewing); silk yarn

丝织(織)品 sīzhīpǐn (名) 1 silk fabrics 2 silk knit goods

死 sǐ I (动) die: 战～be killed in action II (形) 1 dead: ～人 a dead person; the dead 2 to the death: ～战 fight to the death 3 extremely: 急～了 be worried to death. 渴～了 be parched 4 implacable; deadly: ～敌 sworn enemy 5 fixed; rigid; inflexible: ～规矩 a rigid rule 6 impassable; closed: ～胡同 a blind alley

死板 sǐbǎn (形) rigid; inflexible; stiff: 做事情不能太～. One must not be too inflexible in handling affairs.

死党(黨) sǐdǎng (名) sworn followers; diehard followers

死得其所 sǐ dé qí suǒ die a worthy death

死鬼 sǐguǐ [used to curse a person or crack a joke] devil: 你这～, 你干什么? You devil! What are you up to?

死灰复(復)燃 sǐhuī fù rán the embers are smouldering — revival of something that is not really dead

死活 sǐhuó (名) 1 life or death; fate 2 〈口〉 anyway; simply: 他～不肯去. He flatly refused to go.

死劲(勁)儿(兒) sǐjìnr 〈口〉 with all one's strength (or might); for all one is worth: ～跑 run like crazy

死路 sǐlù (名) dead end; the road to ruin

死难(難) sǐnàn (动) die in an accident or a political incident

死气(氣)沉沉 sǐqìchénchén (形) lifeless; spiritless; stagnant

死囚 sǐqiú (名) a convict sentenced to death

死去活来(來) sǐqù-huólái be half dead; be in deep pain; be mad with grief: 被打得～ be beaten half dead

死伤(傷) sǐshāng (名) the fatalities and injured persons; casualties

死尸 sǐshī (名) corpse; dead body

死守 sǐshǒu (动) 1 defend to the last; 2 rigidly adhere to

死亡 sǐwáng (名) death: ～率 death rate; mortality

死心 sǐxīn (动) give up the idea; have no more illusions about sth.

死心塌地 sǐxīntādì (动) be dead set: 他～要破坏这个计划. He is dead set to wreck the plan.

死心眼儿 sǐxīnyǎnr (形) stubborn; as obstinate as a mule

死刑 sǐxíng (名) death penalty; death sentence

死硬 sǐyìng (形) 1 stiff; inflexible 2 very obstinate; diehard: ～派 diehards

死有余(餘)辜 sǐ yǒu yú gū have committed more crimes than one could atone for by death

死于(於)非命 sǐ yú fēimìng die a violent death

死症 sǐzhèng (名) incurable disease

肆 sì I (副) wantonly; unbridledly: 大～攻击 wantonly attack II (名) four [used for the numeral 四 on cheques, etc. to avoid mistakes or alterations]

肆无(無)忌惮(憚) sì wú jìdàn (形) unbridled; brazen; unscrupulous: ～地攻击 launch an unbridled attack

肆意 sìyì (副)wantonly; recklessly; wilfully: ～歪曲事实 wilfully distort the facts

寺

sì (名) temple: 清真～ mosque

寺院 sìyuàn (名) temple

四

sì (数) four

四…八… sì...bā... [used before two similar words to indicate various directions]: 四面八方 all quarters. 四通八达 extend in all directions

四边(邊) sìbiān (on) four sides

四不象 sìbùxiàng (名) nondescript; neither fish nor fowl

四处(處) sìchù (副) all around; everywhere: ～打听 make inquiries everywhere

四方 sìfāng I (副) all sides; all quarters: ～响应 Support came from every quarter. II (形) square; cubic: 一块～的手绢 a square handkerchief

四分五裂 sìfēn-wǔliè (动) fall apart; be rent asunder

四海 sìhǎi (名) the four seas; the whole country; the whole world: ～为家 make one's home no matter where one lives and works

四季 sìjì (名) the four seasons: 一年有～. There are four seasons in a year.

四郊 sìjiāo (名) suburbs; outskirts

四邻(鄰) sìlín (名) one's near neighbours

四面 sìmiàn (副) (on) four sides; (on) all sides: 这座别墅的～都是树木. The villa is surrounded by trees on all sides.

四面楚歌 sìmiàn Chǔ gē be vulnerable to attack on all sides; be utterly isolated

四平八稳(穩) sìpíng-bāwěn 1 very steady; well balanced: 办事～ be even-handed in the discharge of one's duty 2 be overcautious

四散 sìsàn (动) scatter (or disperse) in all directions

四声(聲) sìshēng (名) the four tones of the modern standard Chinese pronunciation

四野 sìyě (副) a vast expanse of country

四月 sìyuè (名) 1 April 2 the fourth month of the lunar year; the fourth moon

四肢 sìzhī (名) the four limbs; arms and legs

四周 sìzhōu (副) all around

驷

sì

驷马(馬) sìmǎ (名)<书> a team of four horses: 一言既出,～难追. A word spoken is past recalling.

似

sì I (形) similar; like: 在这问题上, 我们的观点相～. We hold similar views on this matter. II (动) 1 seem; appear: ～应从速办理. It would seem necessary to act promptly. 2 surpass: 生活一年胜～一年 Life is getting better with each passing year.

似…非… sì...fēi... [used to indicate both similarity and dissimilarity]: 似懂非懂 have only a hazy notion; not quite understand. 似笑非笑 a faint smile

似乎 sìhu (副) it seems; as if: 他～没有看过那本书. He doesn't seem to have read that book. ～要下雪了. It looks like snow.

似是而非 sì shì ér fēi (形) apparently right but actually wrong; specious

俟

sì (动) wait: ～机进攻 wait for the right moment to attack

嗣

sì I (动) succeed; inherit: ～位 succeed to the throne II (名) heir; descendant

伺

sì (名) watch; await: ～机 bide one's time; watch for a chance

see also cì

饲

sì (动) raise; rear

饲料 sìliào (名) forage; fodder; feed: 猪～ pig feed

饲养(養) sìyǎng (动) raise; rear: ～家禽 raise (or rear) poultry

松

sōng (名) pine: ～树 pine tree

松(鬆)

sōng I (形) 1 loose; slack: 绑得太～ loosely tied. 螺丝～了. The screw has come loose. 2 well off 3 light and crisp II (名) dried meat floss; dried minced meat III (动) loosen; relax; slacken: ～腰带 loosen one's belt. ～一口气 heave a sigh of relief

松绑 sōngbǎng (动) have one untied; free a person (or an organization) from unnecessary restrictions

松弛 sōngchí (形) 1 limp; flabby; 肌肉～ flabby 2 lax: 纪律～ lax discipline

松动 (動) sōngdong (形) 1 less crowded 2 loose

松紧(緊) sōngjǐn (名) elasticity

松劲(勁) sōngjìn (动) relax one's efforts

松口 sōngkǒu (动) relent

松快 sōngkuai (形) relaxed

松软 sōngruǎn (形) soft; spongy loose: ～的表土 spongy topsoil

松散 sōngsǎn (形) 1 loose; shaky 2 inattentive

松手 sōngshǒu (动) let go

松鼠 sōngshǔ (名) squirrel

松香 sōngxiāng (名) rosin; colophony

松懈 sōngxiè (动) 1 be absent-minded or sluggish 2 be lacking either in warmth of friendly cooperation or in coordinated effort

悚 sǒng

悚然 sǒngrán (形) terrified; horrified: 毛骨～ with one's hair standing on end

怂(慫) sǒng

怂恿 sǒngyǒng (动) instigate; incite; abet

耸(聳) sǒng (动) 1 tower

高～入云 tower into the sky 2 alarm; attract (attention): 危言～听 Give a horrible account of the situation just to scare the hearers.

耸动(動) sǒngdòng (动) 1 shrug (one's shoulders) 2 create a sensation

耸立 sǒnglì (动) rise like a tower

耸人听(聽)闻 sǒng rén tīngwén deliberately exaggerate facts so as to create a sensation; give a startling account of exaggerated facts

送 sòng (动) 1 deliver; carry:

～货到家 deliver goods to one's door 2 give as a present; give 3 see sb. off or out; accompany; escort: 到机场～人 see sb. off at the airport. 把客人～到门口 see a guest to the door

送别 sòngbié (动) see sb. off

送还(還) sònghuán (动) give back; return

送命 sòngmìng (动) lose one's life; get killed

送人情 sòng rénqíng (动) deliberately do sb. a good turn (sometimes by stretching a point) to curry his favour

送行 sòngxíng (动) 1 see sb. off; wish sb. bon voyage 2 give a send-off party

送葬 sòngzàng (动) join a funeral procession

送终 sòngzhōng (动) attend upon a dying senior member of the family; make arrangements for his funeral

诵 sòng (动) 1 read aloud;

chant 2 recite

诵读(讀) sòngdú (动) read aloud; chant

讼 sòng (动) 1 bring a case

to court: 诉～ lawsuit 2 dispute; argue: 聚～纷纭 a confused scene of people arguing among themselves

颂 sòng I (动) praise; extol;

eulogize: 歌～ sing the praises of II (名) song; ode; paean; eulogy: 西风～ *Ode to the West Wind*

颂词 sòngc. (名) congratulatory address or message; eulogy

颂歌 sònggē (名) song; ode

颂扬(揚) sòngyáng (动) extol; eulogize

搜 sōu (动) search

搜查 sōuchá (动) search; ransack; rummage: ～证 search warrant

搜刮 sōuguā (动) extort; plunder; expropriate; fleece: ～钱财 extort money from

搜集 sōují (动) collect; gather: ～情报 collect information. ～意见 solicit opinions from. ～资料 collect data

搜罗(羅) sōuluó (动) collect; gather; recruit: ～人才 recruit qualified personnel

搜索 sōusuǒ (动) search for; hunt for; hunt down: ～逃犯 hunt down an escaped convict

搜索枯肠(腸) sōusuǒ kūcháng rack one's brains (for fresh ideas or apt expressions)

搜寻(尋) sōuxún (动) search high and low for a missing person or article

艘 sōu 〈量〉 [of boats or

ships]: 两～鱼雷快艇 two torpedo boats

馊 sōu (形) sour; spoiled: 饭

菜～了. The food has gone bad.

薮(藪) sǒu 〈书〉 1 a shallow lake overgrown with wild plants 2 a gathering place of fish or beasts 3 den; haunt

嗾 sǒu

嗾使 sǒushǐ (动) instigate; abet

叟 sǒu (名) old man: 智～ a wise old man

苏(蘇) sū (动) become conscious: ～醒 regain consciousness. 死而复～ come back to life

苏维埃 sūwéi'āi (名) Soviet: 最高～ the supreme Soviet

苏醒 sūxǐng (动) regain consciousness; come to: 当他～过来的时候,发现自己已躺在医院病房里. When he came to, he found himself lying in a hospital ward.

酥 sū (形) 1 crisp 2 shortcake II (名) (of a person's limbs) limp; weak

酥脆 sūcuì (形) crisp: ～饼干 crisp biscuit

酥软 sūruǎn (形) limp; weak; soft

酥油 sūyóu (名) butter: ～茶 buttered tea

俗 sú I (名) custom; convention: 陈规旧～ outdated customs. 入乡随～ When in Rome, do as the Romans do. II (形) 1 popular; common: 通～ popular; colloquial 2 coarse; boorish: ～不可耐 hopelessly boorish 3 secular: 僧～ clergy and laity

俗话 súhuà (名) common saying; proverb: ～说 as the saying goes

俗气(氣) súqì (形) inelegant; in poor taste: 这间房子布置得太～. This room is arranged in poor taste.

俗套 sútào (名) conventional pattern; convention: 不落～ depart from the beaten track

宿 sù (动) 1 put up for the night: ～舍 dormitory; flat 2 long-standing; old: ～愿 long-cherished wish

see also xiǔ

宿命论(論) sùmìnglùn (名) fatalism

宿营(營) sùyíng (动) (of troops) take up quarters; camp

宿怨 sùyuàn (名) old grudge; old scores

溯 sù (动) 1 go against the stream: ～流而上 go upstream 2 trace back; recall: 回～ recall; reminisce

溯源 sùyuán (动) trace to the source: 追本～ taking into consideration the origin of the matter; get at the root of the problem

塑 sù (动) model; mould: ～像 mould a statue

塑料 sùliào (名) plastics: 泡沫～ foam plastics

塑像 sùxiàng (名) statue

塑造 sùzào (动) 1 model; mould 2 portray: 这本小说～一个典型的农村妇女的形象. The novel depicts a typical peasant woman.

诉 sù (动) 1 tell; relate; inform: 告～ tell. ～说 tell; recount 2 complain; accuse: 控～ accuse. 倾～ pour out (one's feelings, troubles, etc.). ～苦 vent one's grievances 3 appeal to; resort to: 上～ appeal to a higher court. ～诸武力 resort to force

素 sù I (形) 1 white: ～服 be dressed in white 2 plain in colour 3 vegetable: 吃～ have regular vegetarian meals; be a vegetarian 4 native: ～性 a person's disposition 5 basic element; element: 毒～ poison. 维生～ vitamin II (副) usually; always: ～不相识 not know sb. at all

素材 sùcái (名) source material (of literature and art); material

素菜 sùcài (名) vegetable dish

素餐 sùcān (名) vegetarian meal: ～馆 vegetarian restaurant

素来(來) sùlái (副) always; usually: 他～生活简朴. He always lives a plain life.

素昧平生 sù mèi píngshēng have never met before; have never had the pleasure of making sb.'s acquaintance

素描 sùmiáo (名) sketch

素雅 sùyǎ (形) simple but in good taste

素养(養) sùyǎng (名) attainment: 艺术～ artistic attainment

素油 sùyóu (名) vegetable oil

素质(質) sùzhì (名) quality: 部队的军事～ the sterling military quality of the troops

速 sù I (形) fast; rapid; quick; instant: ～读 fast (speed) reading. ～效 quick results. ～溶咖啡 instant coffee II (名) speed; velocity III (动)

1 invite: 不～之客 uninvited (or self-invited) guest 2 speed up: 加～生产 speed up (or step up) production
速成 sùchéng (形) short-term training: ～班 crash course
速记 sùjì (名) shorthand; stenography: ～员 stenographer
速决 sùjué (名) quick decision; quick solution: 速战～ get down to work right away and dispose of the problem promptly.
速率 sùlǜ (名) speed; rate
速写(寫) sùxiě (名) 1 sketch 2 literary sketch

粟 sù (名) millet

夙 sù (形) long-standing; old: ～愿 long-cherished wish
夙兴(興)夜寐 sùxīng-yèmèi rise early and retire late

肃(肅) sù (形) 1 respectful 2 solemn: 严～ solemn; serious; grave
肃静 sùjìng (形) solemn and silent
肃立 sùlì (动) stand at attention: ～默哀 stand in silent mourning
肃清 sùqīng (动) eliminate; clean up; mop up: ～官僚主义 eliminate bureaucracy
肃然起敬 sùrán qǐ jìng be filled with deep respect

酸 suān I (名) acid II (形) sour; tart: ～葡萄主义 sour grapeism. ～牛奶 yogurt; sour milk III (动) 1 feel grieved; distressed: 心～ be sick at heart; feel sad 2 ache: 腰～背疼 have a pain in the back; have a backache
酸菜 suāncài (名) pickled Chinese cabbage
酸溜溜 suānliūliū (形) 1 sour 2 aching 3 feeling unhappy and ashamed
酸软 suānruǎn (形) aching and limp
酸甜苦辣 suān-tián-kǔ-là joys and sorrows of life
酸痛 suāntòng (动) ache: 浑身～ ache all over
酸味 suānwèi (名) tart flavour

蒜 suàn (名) garlic: 一串～ a string of garlic

算 suàn I (动、名) 1 calculate; calculation: 心～ mental calculation 2 include; count: 把我也～上. Count me in. ～上伤病号，敌军只有百把人. There are only some one hundred enemy troops counting the sick and wounded. 3 plan; calculate: 失～ miscalculate; make an unwise move 4 consider; regard as; count as: 他～是我们这儿最好的厨师了. He is considered the best cook around here. 他说的不～. What he says doesn't count. 5 carry weight; count: 这样重要的事不能一人说了～. Such an important matter shouldn't be decided by any individual alone. 谁说了～? Who has the final say? II (副) 1 at long last; finally: 问题～解决了. The problem is finally solved. 2 [followed by "了"] forget it; let it pass: ～了，别说了. That's enough! Let's leave it at that.
算计 suànji (动) 1 calculate; reckon: ～一下，买这些东西要多少钱. Figure out how much all these things will cost. 2 consider; plan 3 expect; figure: 我～他明天到北京. I expect him to be in Beijing tomorrow. 4 secretly scheme against others
算命 suànmìng (名) fortune-telling: ～先生 fortune-teller
算盘(盤) suànpan (名) abacus
算是 suànshì (副) at last: 这一下你～猜着了. At last you've guessed right.
算术(術) suànshù (名) arithmetic
算数(數) suànshù (动) count; hold; stand: 我们说话是～的. We mean what we say.

虽(雖) suī (连) though; although; while
虽然 suīrán (连) though; although
虽说 suīshuō (连) 〈口〉 though; although

随(隨) suí (动) 1 follow: ～我去旧金山 Follow me to San Fransisco. 2 comply with: ～顺 comply (with sb.'s wishes) 3 let (sb. do as he likes): ～你的便. Do as you please.
随笔(筆) suíbǐ (名) informal essay; random notes
随便 suíbiàn (形) 1 casual; random; informal: ～谈 chat; chitchat 2 do as one pleases: ～吃吧! Help yourselves. 3 careless; without thought: ～说话 speak casually 4 anyhow; any: ～你怎么说，我是不会同意的. Whatever you may say about the matter, I won't agree

with you.

随波逐流 suíbō-zhúliú drift with the tide (or current)

随从(從) suícóng I (动) accompany (one's superior); attend II (名) retinue; suite; entourage

随大溜 suídàliù (动) drift with the stream; follow the general trend

随地 suídì (副) anywhere; everywhere: 随时～ at anytime and at any place. 不要～乱扔东西. Don't litter.

随风(風)倒 suífēngdǎo (动) bend with the wind

随和 suíhe (形) amiable; obliging

随后(後) suíhòu (副) soon afterwards: 你先走,东西～送到. You go ahead. The goods will be delivered right away.

随机(機)应(應)变(變) súijī-yìngbiàn (形) resourceful; act according to circumstances

随即 suíjí (副) immediately; presently

随口 suíkǒu (动) speak thoughtlessly or casually; blurt out whatever comes into one's head

随身 suíshēn (carry) on one's person; (take) with one: ～行李 personal luggage

随声(聲)附和 suí shēng fùhè (动) echo other people's views thoughtlessly

随时(時) suíshí (副) at any time; at all times: 有问题～可来找我. If you have any problem, come and see me at any time.

随…随… suí…suí… [used before two verbs to indicate that one action is immediately followed by another]: 随叫随到 be available at any time; be on call at any hour

随同 suítóng (动) accompany

随心所欲 suí xīn suǒ yù follow one's bent; do as one pleases

随行人员 suíxíng rényuán (名) entourage; suite; party: 总统及其～ the President and his entourage

随意 suíyì (副) at will; as one pleases

随员 suíyuán (名) 1 anybody accompanying an important government official on his trip abroad 2 attaché

随着 suízhe (副) 1 along with; in the wake of: ～时间的推移 as time goes on; with the lapse (or passage) of time 2 accordingly: 经济发展了,人们的生活也～改善了. With the economic development, the living conditions of the people have improved accordingly.

绥 suí I (形) peaceful II (动) pacify

绥靖 suíjìng (动) pacify; appease: ～政策 policy of appeasement

髓 suǐ (名)〈生理〉marrow: 脊～ spinal marrow (or cord)

碎 suì I (动) break to pieces; smash: 瓶～了. The bottle is smashed to pieces. II (形) 1 broken; fragmentary: ～玻璃 bits of broken glass. ～石 crushed stones 2 garrulous; gabby: 嘴太～ be too talkative; be a regular chatterbox

遂 suì (动) 1 satisfy; fulfil: ～愿 fulfilment of one's wish; a sense of fulfilment 2 succeed: 所谋不～ fail in an attempt

遂心 suìxīn (形) after one's own heart; to one's liking: ～如意 highly pleased; perfectly satisfied

遂意 suìyì (形) to one's liking

燧 suì (名) 1 flint 2 beacon fire

燧石 suìshí (名) flint

隧 suì

隧道 suìdào (名) tunnel; underground passage

岁(歲) suì (名) 1 year: ～末 the end of the year. ～入 annual income 2 year (of age): 三～女孩 a three-year-old girl

岁暮 suìmù (名) the close of the year

岁数(數) suìshu (名)〈口〉age; years: 您多大～了? How old are you? 上～ getting on in years

岁月 suìyuè (名) years: 艰苦的～ hard times. ～不居 cannot stay the flying tail of time; time flies

穗 suì (名) 1 the ear of grain; spike 2 tassel; fringe

穗子 suìzi (名) tassel; fringe

祟 suì (名) evil spirit; ghost: 作～ exercise an evil influence on

孙(孫) sūn (名) grandson

孙女 sūnnǚ (名) granddaughter

孙子 sūnzi (名) grandson

损 sǔn (动) 1 decrease; lose 2 harm; damage: 有益无～ can only do good, not harm. ～公肥私 seek private gain at public expense

损害 sǔnhài (动) harm; damage; injure: ～声誉 damage one's reputation. ～健康 impair one's health; be harmful to one's health

损耗 sǔnhào (名) 1 loss; wear and tear 2 wastage: 减少～ reduce the wastage

损坏(壞) sǔnhuài (动) damage; have a harmful effect on

损人利已 sǔnrénlìjǐ harm others to benefit oneself

损伤(傷) sǔnshāng (动) 1 harm; damage; injure: 不要～群众的积极性. Make sure that the enthusiasm of the masses is not dampened. 2 loss: 敌军兵力～很大. The enemy forces suffered heavy losses.

损失 sǔnshī I (动) lose: ～飞机五架 lose five planes II (名) loss; damage: 此事对我们公司是很大的～. It's a big loss to our firm.

损益 sǔnyì (名) profit and loss; gains and losses

笋(筍) sǔn (名) bamboo shoot: ～干 dried bamboo shoots

蓑 suō

蓑衣 suōyī (名) straw or palm-bark rain cape

梭 suō (名) shuttle: 穿～外交 shuttle diplomacy

梭镖 suōbiāo (名) spear

唆 suō (动) instigate; abet: 教～ instigate; abet

唆使 suōshǐ (动) instigate; abet: ～者 instigator; abettor

缩 suō (动) 1 contract; shrink: 热胀冷～ expand with heat and contract with cold 2 draw back; withdraw; recoil: 退～ flinch; shrink. 他把身子一～. He shrank back (in shame, horror, etc.).

缩短 suōduǎn (动) shorten; curtail; cut down: ～距离 reduce the distance. ～期限 shorten the time limit

缩减 suōjiǎn (动) reduce; cut: ～军费 cut back military spending

缩手 suōshǒu (动) 1 draw back one's hand 2 shrink (from doing sth.): ～缩脚 be overcautious

缩水 suōshuǐ (动) (of cloth through wetting) shrink

缩小 suōxiǎo (动) reduce; narrow (down): ～范围 narrow down the scope

缩写(寫) suōxiě I (名) abbreviation II (动) abridge: ～本 abridged edition

缩影 suōyǐng (名) epitome; miniature

索 suǒ I (名) large rope: 绳～ rope. 绞～ noose. II (动) 1 search: 遍～不得 look for sth. everywhere but in vain 2 demand; ask; exact: ～价 ask a price; charge III (副) all alone: 离群～居 live in solitude

索取 suǒqǔ (动) ask for; demand; exact; extort: 向大自然～财富 wrest wealth from nature

索然 suǒrán (形) depressed; in low spirits: 兴致～ feel low-spirited.

索性 suǒxìng (副) without hesitation: 既然已经做了,～就把它做完. Since you have started the work, you may as well go on till you are through with it.

索引 suǒyǐn (名) index: 卡片～ card index. 书名～ title index

琐 suǒ (形) trivial; petty

琐事 suǒshì (名) trifles; trivial matters: 家庭～ household chores

琐碎 suǒsuì (形) trifling; trivial

琐细 suǒxì (形) trifling; trivial

锁 suǒ I (名) lock: 弹簧～ spring lock. 枷～ shackles II 1 lock up: ～门 lock a door 2 lockstitch: ～边 lockstitch a border

锁匠 suǒjiang (名) locksmith

锁链(鏈) suǒliàn (名) 1 chain 2 shackles; fetters; chains

锁钥(鑰) suǒyuè (名) key

所 suǒ I (名) 1 place: 住～ dwelling place 2 [for institutions or working place]: 研究～ research institute. 诊疗～ clinic II (量) [of buildings]: 一～房子 a house. 两～学校 two schools III (助) [used together with "为" or "被" to indicate a passive construction]: 为人～笑 be laughed at 2 [used before a verb as the agent of the action]: 各尽～能 from each according to his ability. 闻～未闻 unheard-of 3 [used before a verb which takes an object]: 我～认识的人 the people I know

所长 suǒcháng (名) what one is good at; one's strong point; one's forte

所得 suǒdé (名) income; earnings; gains: ～税 income tax

所属(屬) suǒshǔ (名) 1 what is subordinate to one or under one's command 2 what one belongs to or is affiliated with

所谓 suǒwèi 1 what is called: ～民主,只是一种手段，不是目的. What is called democracy is only a means, not an end. 2 so-called: ～"无核地区" the so-called "nuclear-free zones"

所向披靡 suǒ xiàng pīmí (of troops) carry all before one; be irrisistible

所以 suǒyǐ I (连) [used to indicate cause and effect] so; therefore; as a result: 我和他一起工作过，～对他比较熟悉. We used to be colleagues, so I know him quite well. II [used separately to indicate cause or reason]: ～呀，要不然我怎么会这样说呢? That's just the point, otherwise I wouldn't have said it. III (名)[used in set phrases as an object]: 忘其～ forget oneself

所以然 suǒyǐrán the reason why; the whys and wherefores: 知其然,而不知～. Know the how but not the why.

所有 suǒyǒu I (动) own; possess II (名) possessions: 尽其～ give everything one has III (形) all: 把～的劲儿都使出来 exert all one's strength

所有制 suǒyǒuzhì (名) system of ownership; ownership

所在 suǒzài (名) place; location: 风景优美的～ a scenic spot. 问题～ the crux of the matter. ～多有 be found almost everywhere

T t

他 tā (代) 1 he 2 [any person, either male or female, when no distinction of sex is necessary or possible]: 一个人要是不努力,～就将一事无成. Nobody can achieve anything of real significance unless he works very hard. 3 another; other; some other: ～乡 strange place. ～日 some day 4 [used between a verb and a numeral]: 再试～一次 have another try

他们 tāmen (代) they: ～俩 the two of them. ～学校离火车站不远. Their school is not far from the railway station.

他人 tārén (代) another person; other people; others

他乡(鄉) tāxiāng (名) a place away from home; a strange land

她 tā (代) she

她们 tāmen (代) [indicating the female sex] they

它 tā (代) [neuter gender] it: 把～拿到厨房去. Take it to the kitchen.

它们 tāmen (代) they

塌 tā (动) 1 collapse; fall down; cave in: 椅子～了. The chair collapsed. 2 sink; droop: ～鼻梁 a flat nose 3 calm down: ～心 settle down

塌方 tāfāng I (动) cave in; collapse II (名) landslide; landslip

塌实(實) tāshi (形) 1 down-to-earth; practical 2 feel relieved; feel at home: 事情办完就～了. You'll feel relieved when you've fulfilled your task. 睡得很～ have a sound sleep

塌陷 tāxiàn (动) subside; sink; cave in

塔 tǎ (名) 1 Buddhist pagoda 2 tower: 水～ water tower. 灯～ lighthouse; beacon. 蒸馏～ distillation column (or tower)

挞(撻) tà (动) flog; whip: 鞭～ flog; lash

拓 tà (动) make rubbings from inscriptions, pictures, etc. on stone tablets or bronze vessels see also tuò

拓本 tàběn (名) a book of rubbings

榻 tà (名) couch; bed

沓 tà (形)(书) crowded; repeated: 纷至～来 come thick and fast; keep pouring in see also dá

踏 tà (动) 1 step on; tread; stamp: 践～ trample. ～步 mark time 2 make an investigate on the spot

踏勘 tàkān (动) make an on-the-spot survey

胎 tāi (名) 1 foetus; embryo: 怀～ become or be pregnant 2 birth: 头～ first baby; firstborn 3 padding; stuffing; wadding 4 tyre: 内～ inner tube (of a tyre). 外～ outer cover (of a tyre); tyre

胎生 tāishēng (名) viviparity: ～动物 viviparous animal; vivipara

台(臺) tái I (名) 1 platform; stage; terrace: 讲～ platform; rostrum. 检阅～ reviewing stand. 月～票 platform ticket 2 stand; support: 导弹发射～ missile launching pad 3 anything shaped like a platform, stage or terrace: 窗～ windowsill 4 table; desk: 写字～ (writing) desk. 梳妆～ dressing table 5 broadcasting station: 电视～ television broadcasting station 6 a special telephone service: 长途～ trunk call service II (量): 一～戏 a theatrical performance. 两～计算机 two computers

台词 táicí (名) actor's lines

台灯(燈) táidēng (名) desk lamp; table lamp; reading lamp

台风(風) táifēng (名) typhoon

台阶(階) táijiē (名) a flight of steps

台历(曆) táilì (名) desk calendar

台球 táiqiú (名) 1 billiards 2 billiard ball

台柱子 táizhùzi (名) pillar; mainstay; backbone

苔 tái (名) liver mosses

抬(擡) tái (动) 1 lift; raise: ～高物价 drive up prices 2 (of two or more person) carry: ～担架 carry a stretcher

抬杠(槓) táigàng (动) <口> argue; bondy works

抬举(舉) táiju (动) praise or promote one's subordinate: 不识～ fail to appreciate sb.'s kindness

抬头(頭) táitóu (动) 1 raise one's head 2 gain ground; look up; rise

泰 tài (形) 1 safe; peaceful; tranquil: ～然自若 feel or look composed; try to compose one's features 2 extreme; most: ～西 the West; the Occident

泰然 tàirán (形) calm; composed; self-possessed: ～处之 remain calm; take sth. calmly

泰山 tàishān (名) Mount Taishan; Taishan Mountain

太 tài I (形) 1 highest; greatest; remotest: ～空 outer space. ～古 remote antiquity; ancient times 2 more or most senior: ～老伯 granduncle II (副) 1 excessively; too; over: ～晚 too late. 人～多了,会客室里坐不开. There are too many people for this reception room. *or* The reception room is too small to seat so many people. 2 extremely: 这着棋～妙了. This is an extremely wise move. 3 [used in negative sentences] very: 不～好 not very good; not good enough

太后 tàihòu (名) mother of an emperor; empress dowager; queen mother

太平 tàipíng (名) social peace and tranquility: ～门 exit. ～梯 fire escape. ～间 mortuary

太上皇 tàishànghuáng (名) 1 a title assumed by an emperor's father who abdicated in favour of his son 2 behind-the-scenes manipulator

太太 tàitai (名) 1 Mrs.; madame: 王～ Mrs. Wang; Madame Wang 2 madam 3 one's wife

太阳(陽) tàiyáng (名) 1 the sun 2 sunshine; sunlight: ～能 solar energy. ～系 the solar system

太阳(陽)镜 tàiyángjìng (名) sunglasses

太阳(陽)穴 tàiyángxué (名) the temples

太子 tàizi (名) crown prince

汰 tài (动) discard; eliminate: 淘～ eliminate

态(態) tài (名) 1 form; appearance; condition: 形～ shape; morphology. 姿～ posture; gesture. 事～的发展 the natural course of events; the latest developments 2 voice: 主动语～ the active voice

态度 tàidu (名) 1 manner; bearing; how one conducts oneself: ～和蔼 amiable; kindly 2 attitude; position: 工作～ attitude towards work. 服务～ service. 表明～ state one's position

坍 tān (动) collapse; fall; tumble: 墙～了. The wall has collapsed.

坍方 tānfāng I (动) cave in; collapse II (名) landslide

坍塌 tāntā (动) cave in; collapse

贪 tān I (形) corrupt; venal: ～官污吏 corrupt officials II (动) 1 ～得无厌 have an insatiable desire for private gain 2 covet; hanker after: ～小失大

seek small gains only to incur big losses
贪婪 tānlán (形)(书) avaricious; greedy; rapacious
贪恋(戀) tānliàn (动) be reluctant to part with; be greedy for
贪图(圖) tāntú (动) seek; hanker after; covet: ～便宜 seek advantage
贪污 tānwū (名) corruption; graft: ～腐化 corruption and degeneration. ～分子 a person guilty of corruption; an official guilty of embezzling public funds
贪心 tānxīn (名、形) **1** greed; avarice; rapacity **2** greedy; avaricious; insatiable; voracious: ～不足 insatiably greedy
贪赃(贓) tānzāng (动) take bribes

滩(灘) tān (名) **1** beach; sands: 海～ beach **2** shoal: 险～ dangerous shoal

瘫(癱) tān (名) paralysis: 偏～ partial paralysis. 吓～了 be paralysed with fear
瘫痪 tānhuàn **1** paralysis **2** be paralysed; break down: 交通运输陷于～. Transportation was paralysed.

摊(攤) tān I (动) **1** spread out: ～开地图 spread out a map **2** fry batter in a thin layer: ～鸡蛋 make an omelet **3** take a share: 每人～五毛钱. Each will contribute 5 *mao*. II (名) vendor's stand; booth; stall: 水果～儿 fruit stall. 报～ newsstand III (量): 一～稀泥 a pool of mud
摊贩 tānfàn (名) street pedlar
摊牌 tānpái (动) lay one's cards on the table; have a showdown
摊派 tānpài (动) share out (costs, expenses, etc.)

痰 tán (名) phlegm; sputum: ～盂 spittoon

谈 tán I (动) talk, chat; discuss: 纯系无稽之～ unadulterated nonsense. 我们～得来. We are getting along very well. II (名) what is said or talked about: 奇～ strange talk; fantastic tale
谈何容易 tán hé róngyì easier said than done
谈虎色变(變) tán hǔ sè biàn turn pale at the bare mention of a dreadful experience or possibility
谈话 tánhuà (名) **1** conversation; talk; chat **2** statement: 发表书面～ make a written statement
谈论(論) tánlùn (动) discuss; talk about
谈判 tánpàn (名) negotiations; talk: 举行～ hold talks; hold negotiations. ～桌 negotiating table
谈天 tántiān (动) chat; have chitchat
谈笑风(風)生 tánxiào fēng shēng brim with wit and humour
谈笑自若 tánxiào zìruò go on talking with gusto and composure

坛(壇) tán (名) **1** altar: 天～ the Temple of Heaven (in Beijing) **2** a raised plot of land for planting flowers, etc.: 花～ (raised) flower bed **3** platform; forum: 讲～ platform **4** circles; world: 文～ the literary world; literary circles

坛(罎) tán (名)(～子) earthern jar: 酒～ wine jug

昙(曇) tán
昙花一现 tánhuā yī xiàn be very ephemeral; be a flash in the pan; a transient success

檀 tán (名) wingceltis
檀香 tánxiāng (名) white sandalwood; sandalwood: ～木 sandalwood

潭 tán (名) deep pool; pond

弹(彈) tán (动) **1** shoot (as with a catapult, etc.); send forth **2** spring; leap **3** flick; flip: ～烟灰 flick the ash off a cigarette **4** fluff; tease: ～棉花 fluff cotton **5** play (a stringed musical instrument); pluck: ～钢琴 play the piano. 老调重～ harp on the same old tune **6** accuse; impeach: ～劾 impeach
see also dàn
弹簧 tánhuáng (名) spring: ～床 spring bed. ～锁 spring lock
弹射 tánshè (动) launch (as with a catapult); catapult; shoot off; eject
弹性 tánxìng (名) elasticity; resilience; spring: 有～ springy
弹指 tánzhǐ (名) a brief period of time: ～之间 in a short time
弹奏 tánzòu (动) play (a stringed musical instrument); pluck

毯 tǎn (名)、(～子) blanket; rug; carpet: 毛～ woollen blanket. 地～ rug; carpet. 挂～ tapestry

忐 tǎn

忐忑 tǎntè (形) mentally disturbed: ～不安 feel uneasy; feel ill at ease; be fidgety

袒 tǎn (动) 1 wear nothing above one's waist; strip oneself naked to the waist: ～胸露臂 (of a woman) expose one's neck 2 shield; protect: ～护 shield; take sb. under one's wing

坦 tǎn (形) 1 level; smooth: 平～ (of land, etc.) level; smooth 2 completely at ease: ～然自若 calm and fearless

坦白 tǎnbái I (形) frank and straightforward II (动) confess; make a clean breast of something

坦荡(蕩) tǎndàng (形) 1 (of a road, etc.) broad and smooth 2 broadminded

坦克 tǎnkè (名) tank

坦率 tǎnshuài (形) candid; frank; straightforward

探 tàn I (动) 1 try to find out; explore: 试～ sound out (sb.). 钻～ explore 2 visit; pay a call on 3 stretch forward: ～头～脑 peep from behind something II (名) scout; spy; detective: 敌～ enemy scout. 侦～ detective

探测 tàncè (动) survey; sound; probe: ～水深 take soundings

探访 tànfǎng (动) 1 go in search of: ～新闻 cover the news 2 pay a call on; visit

探究 tànjiū (动) make a thorough inquiry; probe into: ～原因 look into the causes

探亲(親) tànqīn (动) be on home leave

探视 tànshì (动) visit: ～病人 visit a patient

探索 tànsuǒ (动) explore; probe: ～各种可能性 explore all possibilities

探讨 tàntǎo (动) make an inquiry into: 从不同的角度对问题进行～ approach a subject from different angles

探听(聽) tàntīng (动) try and find out; make inquiries (usu. by indirect means)

探望 tànwàng (动) 1 look: 四处～ look around 2 visit

探问 tànwèn (动) 1 make cautious inquiries about 2 inquire after

探险(險) tànxiǎn (动) explore; make explorations: ～队 exploring (or exploration) party; expedition. ～家 explorer

探照灯(燈) tànzhàodēng (名) searchlight

叹(嘆) tàn (动) 1 sigh: ～一口气 heave a sigh 2 exclaim in admiration; acclaim; praise: 赞～ be full of praise; be filled with admiration for

叹词 tàncí (名) interjection; exclamation

叹服 tànfú (动) have nothing but admiration for: 令人～ compel one's admiration

叹赏 tànshǎng (动) admire; praise: ～不绝 praise profusely

叹息 tànxī (动)(书) heave a sigh; sigh

炭 tàn (名) charcoal: 木～ charcoal. 烧～ make charcoal. ～火 charcoal fire

碳 tàn (名) carbon (C): ～化 carbonization. ～酸 carbonic acid

汤(湯) tāng (名) 1 hot water; boiling water: 赴～蹈火 go through fire and water 2 soup; broth: 鸡～ chicken broth 3 a liquid preparation of medicinal herb; decoction

蹚 tāng (动) wade; ford: ～水过河 wade across (a stream)

唐 táng

唐突 tángtū (动) be rude; offend: ～古人 show disrespect for ancient scholars

糖 táng (名) 1 sugar: 白～ refined sugar. 砂～ granulated sugar. 红～ brown sugar. 冰～ crystal sugar; rock candy. ～厂 sugar refinery 2 sugared; in syrup: ～姜 sugared ginger; ginger in syrup. ～蒜 garlic in syrup; sweetened garlic 3 sweets; candy

糖果 tángguǒ (名) sweets; candy; sweetmeats

糖精 tángjīng (名) saccharin; gluside

糖尿病 tángniàobìng (名) diabetes

塘 táng (名) 1 dyke; embankment: 河～ river embankment 2 pool; pond: 池～ pond 3 hot-water bathing pool: 洗澡～ public bath

搪 táng (动) 1 ward off; keep out: ～风 keep out the wind 2 evade: ～塞 stall sb. off with a vague answer; give vague answers 3 spread (clay, paint, etc.)

over; daub: ～炉子 line a stove with clay

搪瓷 tángcí (名) enamel: ～茶缸 enamel mug. ～钢板 enamelled pressed steel. ～器皿 enamelware

堂 táng I (名) 1 the main room of a house 2 a hall (or room) for a specific purpose: 食～dining hall. 纪念～ memorial hall 3 relationship between cousins, etc. of the same paternal grandfather or great-grandfather; of the same clan: ～兄 cousins on the paternal side; cousins II (量): 一～家具 a set (or suite) of furniture

堂皇 tánghuáng (形) grand; stately; imposing: 富丽～ beautiful and magnificent

堂堂 tángtáng (形) 1 dignified; impressive: 仪表～ dignified in appearance 2 (of a man) manly 3 awe-inspiring; formidable: ～正正 impressive or dignified in personal appearance; open and aboveboard

螳 táng (名) mantis

螳臂当(當)车(車) táng bì dāng chē court destruction for trying to withstand a far superior force

螳螂 tángláng (名) mantis

镗 táng (名) boring: ～床 boring machine; boring lathe; borer

膛 táng (名) thorax; chest: 胸～ chest

淌 tǎng (名) drip; shed; trickle: ～眼泪 shed tears. ～口水 drool; start drooling

倘 tǎng (连) if; supposing; in case: ～有困难,请迅速通知我们. If there is any difficulty, will you please let us know promptly.

倘若 tǎngruò (连) if; supposing; in case

躺 tǎng (动) lie; recline: ～下歇歇 lie down and relax a while

躺椅 tǎngyǐ (名) deck chair

烫(燙) tàng I (动) 1 scald; burn: 小心～着! Watch out and don't get scalded. 2 heat up in hot water; warm: ～酒 heat wine (by putting the container in hot water) 3 iron; press: ～衣服 iron (or press) clothes II (形) very hot; scalding; boiling hot

烫发(髮) tàngfà (名) give or have a permanent wave; perm

烫伤(傷) tàngshāng (动) scald

趟 tàng (量) [for trip]: 到成都去了一～ make a trip to Chengdu

涛(濤) tāo (名) great waves; billows: 惊～骇浪 terrifying waves

掏 tāo (动) 1 draw out; pull out; fish out: 从床底下～出一双鞋来 fish out a pair of shoes from under the bed 2 dig (a hole, etc.); hollow out; scoop out: 在地上～一个洞 dig a hole in the ground 3 steal from sb.'s pocket: 他的皮夹子被～了. He had his wallet stolen.

滔 tāo (动) inundate; flood

滔滔 tāotāo (形) 1 torrential; surging: 白浪～,无边无际 a vast expanse of white surging billows 2 letting loose a stream of words: 口若悬河,～不绝 keep up a torrential flow of words

滔天 tāotiān I (动) (of billows, etc.) dash to the skies: 波浪～ waves running mountains high II (形) heinous; monstrous: ～罪行 monstrous crimes

韬(韜) tāo I (名) 1 sheath or bow case 2 the art of war II (动) hide; conceal

韬略 tāolüè (名) military strategy

逃 táo (动) 1 run away; escape 2 flee; escape from

逃避 táobì (动) escape; evade; shirk: ～现实 escapism

逃遁 táodùn (动) flee; escape; evade: 仓皇～ flee in panic

逃命 táomìng (动) run for one's life

逃难(難) táonàn (动) flee from a calamity; be a refugee

逃匿 táonì (动) make one's escape and go into hiding

逃生 táoshēng (动) flee (or run) for one's life

逃税 táoshuì (名) tax evasion

逃亡 táowáng (动) make one's escape and go into hiding

逃之夭夭 táo zhī yāoyāo (动) sneak away; slip out

逃走 táozǒu (动) take to one's heels

桃 táo (名)(～子) 1 peach 2 a peach-shaped thing: 棉～ cotton boll

桃花 táohuā (名) peach blossom

桃李 táolǐ (名) one's pupils or disciples: ～满天下 have pupils everywhere under heaven

淘 táo (动) **1** wash in a pan or basket: ～米 wash rice **2** clean out; dredge

淘气(氣) táoqì (形) naughty; mischievous: ～鬼 mischievous imp; a regular little mischief

淘汰 táotài (动) supersede: 产品旧型号已经被～了. The products of old types have been superseded.

陶 táo I (名) pottery; earthenware: 彩～ painted pottery II (动) **1** make pottery **2** educate; train: 熏～ education; intellectual training

陶瓷 táocí (名) pottery and porcelain; ceramics

陶器 táoqì (名) pottery; earthenware

陶然 táorán (形) happy and carefree

陶冶 táoyě (动) **1** make pottery and smelt metal **2** exercise a healthy influence (on a person's character, etc.); mould one's personality

陶醉 táozuì (动) be drunk (with power, success, etc.)

讨 tǎo (动) **1** send a punitive expedition against **2** denounce; condemn: 声～ denounce **3** demand; ask for; beg for: ～饶 beg (for) forgiveness. ～教 solicit advice **4** incur; invite: ～厌 incur displeasure (or hatred). 自～苦吃 ask for trouble **5** discuss; study: 商～ discuss

讨伐 tǎofá (动) send armed forces to suppress; send a punitive expedition against

讨好 tǎohǎo (动) **1** ingratiate oneself with **2** [often used in negative sentences]: 这件事费力不～. It is a thankless task.

讨嫌 tǎoxián (形) disagreeable; annoying

讨厌(厭) tǎoyàn I (形) **1** disagreeable; disgusting; repugnant: 这人说话总是这么啰嗦, 真～! This chap is always talking at such great length. I'm bored stiff. **2** hard to handle; troublesome; nasty II (动) dislike; loathe; hate; be disgusted with

套 tào (名) **1** case; cover: 枕～ pillowcase. 书～ dust jacket. 手～ gloves **2** harness: ～绳 lasso **3** that which covers something else: ～鞋 overshoes **4** cotton padding; batting: 被～ quilt padding **5** knot; loop; noose: 拴个～ tie a knot **6** convention; formula: ～语 polite formulas. 客～ banal civilities II (动) **1** put a ring round; tie: ～马 lasso a horse **2** copy: 这是从现成文章上～下来的. This is taken straight from someone else's work. **3** draw out: 想法儿～他的话. Let's try to draw the secret out of him. III (量) set; suit; suite: 一～制度 a set of regulations. 一～茶具 a tea set

套购(購) tàogòu (动) purchase by fraudulent or other illegal means (state-controlled commodities) for profiteering purpose

套间 tàojiān (名) a suite

套用 tàoyòng (动) apply mechanically

特 tè I (形) **1** special; particular; unusual; exceptional: ～权 privilege. 奇～ peculiar. 奇～的人 an uncommon and singular man **2** for a special purpose; specially: ～意 for the express purpose of II (名) secret agent; spy: 敌～ enemy agent

特别 tèbié I (形) special; particular; out of the ordinary: ～风味 an unusual flavour. ～的式样 special type II (副) **1** especially; particularly: 时间过得～快. The time sped quickly by. **2** going out of one's way to (do sth.); specially: 我们～注意保障他们的安全. We made a special point of ensuring their safety.

特产(産) tèchǎn (名) special local product; speciality

特长(長) tècháng (名) special skill; special work experience

特地 tèdì (副) for a special purpose; specially: 我们是～来看您的. We came specially to see you.

特点(點) tèdiǎn (名) characteristic; special feature; peculiarity

特级 tèjí (形) special grade (or class); superfine: ～茉莉花茶 superfine jasmine tea

特快 tèkuài (名) express (train)

特派 tèpài (形) specially appointed: ～员 special representative

特赦 tèshè (名) special pardon; amnesty

特使 tèshǐ (名) special envoy

特殊 tèshū (形) special; particular; peculiar; exceptional: ～化 become privileged. ～性 particularity; specific characteristics

特务(務) tèwu (名) special (or secret) agent; spy

特写(寫) tèxiě (名) 1 feature article or story; feature 2 close-up: ～镜头 close-up (shot)

特性 tèxìng (名) special property (or characteristic)

特许 tèxǔ (名) special permission: ～证 special permit

特异(異) tèyì (形) 1 exceptionally good; excellent; superfine 2 peculiar; distinctive: ～的风格 distinctive style

特约 tèyuē (形) engaged by special arrangement: ～记者 special correspondent. ～评论员 special commentator

特征(徵) tèzhēng (名) characteristic; feature; trait

疼 téng (动) 1 ache; pain; sore: 头～ have a headache 2 love dearly; be fond of; dote on: 这孩子怪招人～的. How lovely the child is!

疼爱(愛) téng'ài (动) be very fond of; love very dearly

誊(謄) téng (动) copy in writing: 照底稿～一份 make a fair (or clean) copy of the draft

誊录(錄) ténglù (动) copy out: ～文稿 copy out a manuscript

藤 téng (名) 1 cane; rattan: ～椅 cane chair; rattan chair 2 vine: 葡萄～ grape vine

腾 téng (动) 1 gallop; jump: 欢～ jump for joy 2 rise; soar: 升～ rise; ascend 3 make room; clear out; vacate: ～出时间 set aside some time. ～出房间 vacate the room

腾腾 téngténg (形) steaming; ascending: 烟雾～ fill with dense smoke.

梯 tī (名) 1 (～子) ladder; staircase: 电～ lift; elevator 2 terraced: ～田 terraced fields

梯队(隊) tīduì (名) echelon formation; echelon: 第二～ the second echelon

剔 tī (动) 1 pick: ～牙 pick one's teeth 2 reject: 挑～ pick holes in; find fault with

剔除 tīchú (动) reject; get rid of

踢 tī (动) 1 kick: ～开 kick away 2 play (football): ～足球 play football. ～进一个球 kick (or score) a goal

啼 tí (动) 1 cry; weep aloud: ～笑皆非 not know whether to laugh or cry 2 crow; caw: 鸡～. Cocks crow.

蹄 tí (名) hoof: 马～ horse's hoofs

题 tí I (名) topic; subject; title; problem: 讨论～ topic for discussion. 考～ examination questions; examination paper; paper. 文不对～ irrelevant II (动) inscribe: ～诗 inscribe a poem (on a painting, fan, wall, etc.)

题跋 tíbá (名) 1 preface and postscript 2 short comments, annotation, etc. on a scroll (of painting or calligraphy)

题材 tícái (名) subject matter; theme: 这是写电影的好～. This is good material for a film. *or* This is a good plot for a film scenario.

题词 tící (动,名) 1 write a few words of encouragement, appreciation or commemoration 2 inscription; dedication 3 foreword

题名 tímíng (动) inscribe one's name; autograph: ～留念 give one's autograph as a memento

题目 tímù (名) title; subject; topic: 辩论的～ subject (or topic) for a debate

题字 tízì (动,名) 1 inscribe 2 inscription; autograph: 作者亲笔～ the author's autograph

提 tí (动) 1 carry: 手里～着篮子 carry a basket in one's hand 2 lift; raise: ～升 promote. ～高生活水平 raise the standard of living 3 move up a date: 会议日期～前了. The date of the meeting has been advanced. 4 put forward; bring up; raise: ～醒 remind. ～意见 make suggestions. ～抗议 lodge a protest 5 draw (or take) out; extract: ～炼 extract; refine 6 mention; refer to; bring up: 旧事重～ bring up the matter again see also dī

提案 tí'àn (名) motion; proposal

提拔 tíbá (动) (of a person) promote: ～合格人员担任重要职务 promote qualified people to positions of responsibility

提包 tíbāo (名) handbag; shopping bag; bag; valise

提倡 tíchàng (动) advocate; encourage: ～晚婚和计划生育 advocate late marriage and family planning. ～勤俭节约 advocate industry, economy and thrift

提成 tíchéng (动) set aside a percentage of the total amount of money for specific purposes

提出 tíchū (动) put forward; advance; pose; raise: 请～建议. Please feel free to make your suggestions.

提纲(綱) tígāng (名) outline

提纲(綱)挈领 tígāng-qièlǐng mention briefly the essential points; make a sketch of the plan (proposal, etc.)

提高 tígāo (动) raise; heighten; enhance; increase; improve: ～水位 raise the water level. ～警惕 enhance (or heighten) one's vigilance. ～工作效率 raise efficiency

提供 tígòng (动) provide; supply; furnish; offer: ～经济援助 provide financial assistance. ～意见 make recommendations. ～有关资料 provide relevant data

提货 tíhuò (动) pick up goods; take delivery of goods

提交 tíjiāo (动) submit (a problem, etc.) to; refer to: ～全会讨论 submit sth. to the plenary session for deliberation

提名 tímíng (动) nominate

提琴 tíqín (名) the violin family: 小～ violin. 中～ viola. 大～ violoncello; cello. 低音～ double bass

提审(審) tíshěn (动) 1 bring a prisoner to court for trial; bring a detainee to trial 2 review a case tried by a lower court

提示 tíshì (动) point out; prompt

提问 tíwèn (动) put questions to; quiz

提携 tíxié (动) guide and support the younger generation

提心吊胆(膽) tíxīn-diàodǎn be terribly scared and worried; be on tenterhooks

提醒 tíxǐng (动) remind; warn; call attention to: 如果我忘了,请你～我一下. Please remind me in case I forget.

提要 tíyào (名) précis; summary; abstract; epitome; synopsis: 本书内容～ capsule summary (of the book)

提议(議) tíyì (动,名) 1 propose; suggest; move 2 proposal; motion

提早 tízǎo (动) advance; do sth. in advance: ～结束会议 bring the meeting to an earlier conclusion

体(體) tǐ I (名) 1 body; part of the body: ～高 height. ～重 weight 2 substance: 固～ solid. 液～ liquid 3 style; form: 文～ literary style; style of writing. 文～学 stylistics II (动) personally experience sth.; put oneself in another's position: ～谅 make allowances for

体裁 tǐcái (名) types or forms of literature

体操 tǐcāo (名) gymnastics

体察 tǐchá (动) observe and learn by experience

体格 tǐgé (名) physique; build: ～检查 physical examination; checkup

体会(會) tǐhuì (动) know (or learn) from experience; understand

体积(積) tǐjī (名) volume; bulk

体力 tǐlì (名) physical strength: 增强～ build up one's strength. ～劳动 physical (or manual) labour

体面 tǐmian (名) 1 dignity; face: 有失～ beneath one's dignity 2 honourable; creditable

体魄 tǐpò (名) physique: 强壮的～ strong (or powerful) physique

体态(態) tǐtài (名) poise; carriage; deportment: ～轻盈 good deportment; a graceful poise

体贴 tǐtiē (动) be full of thought for: ～入微 look after sb. with loving care

体统 tǐtǒng (名) code of ethics, propriety; decorum: 不成～ downright outrageous

体温 tǐwēn (名) (body) temperature: 量～ Take someone's temperature.

体无(無)完肤(膚) tǐ wú wán fū 1 beaten black and blue 2 thoroughly discredited or refuted

体系 tǐxì (名) system; setup

体现 tǐxiàn (动) embody; incarnate; reflect; give expression to: 这个提案～了发展中国家的利益和要求. This proposal reflects the interests and demands of the developing countries.

体恤 tǐxù (动) show solicitude for

体育 tǐyù (名) physical culture; physical training; sports: ～场 stadium. ～馆 gymnasium; gym

体制 tǐzhì (名) system of organization; system

体质(質) tǐzhì (名) physique; constitution

体重 tǐzhòng (名) (body) weight: ～增加 put on weight; gain weight. ～减轻 lose weight

涕 tì (名) 1 tears: 痛哭流～ cry piteously. 感激～零 weep

tears of gratitude 2 mucus of the nose; snivel

涕泣 tìqì (动)〈书〉weep

剃 tì (动) shave: ～胡子 have a shave; shave oneself

剃刀 tìdāo (名) razor blade

替 tì (动) 1 take the place of; replace: 我～你洗衣服. I will do the washing for you. 2 for; on behalf of: 大家～她难过. Everybody felt sorry for her.

替代 tìdài (动) replace; supersede

替身 tìshēn (名) 1 substitute; replacement 2 scapegoat

替罪羊 tìzuìyáng (名) scapegoat

惕 tì (形) cautious; watchful: 警～ be on the alert; be vigilant

嚏 tì (动)(书) sneeze: 喷～ sneeze

天 tiān (名) 1 sky; heaven 2 overhead: ～窗 skylight 3 day: 每～ every day. 前～ the day before yesterday 4 a period of time in a day: ～不早啦. It's getting late. 5 season: 春～ spring 6 weather: ～越来越冷了. It's getting colder and colder. 7 nature: 人定胜～. Man will prevail over nature. ～灾 natural calamity 8 God; Heaven: 谢～谢地! Thank Heaven!

天边(邊) tiānbiān (名) horizon; the ends of the earth; remotest places

天才 tiāncái (名) genius; talent; gift; endowment: 这孩子有语言～. The child has great aptitude for language.

天长(長)地久 tiāncháng-dìjiǔ enduring loyalty (in love)

天长(長)日久 tiāncháng-rìjiǔ in the course of time

天敌(敵) tiāndí (名) natural enemy

天地 tiāndì (名) 1 heaven and earth; world; universe 2 field of activity; scope of operation: 别有～ a new level of understanding or appreciation

天鹅 tiān'é (名) swan: ～绒 velvet

天翻地覆 tiānfān-dìfù 1 causing tremendous changes: ～的变化 earthshaking changes 2 turning everything upside down

天分 tiānfen (名) endowments; gift; talent: ～高 gifted; talented

天赋 tiānfù I (形) inborn; innate; endowed by nature II (名) natural gift; talent; endowments

天高地厚 tiāngāo-dìhòu 1 debt of enduring gratitude 2 [often used in negative sentences] the immensity of heaven and earth: 不知～ overestimate one's own abilities to a ridiculous extent

天花板 tiānhuābǎn (名) ceiling

天花乱(亂)坠(墜) tiānhuā luàn zhuì give an alarming but unrealistic description of sth. or describe vividly but with extravagance

天昏地暗 tiānhūn-dì'àn 1 clouds of dust darken the sky and obscure everything: 一阵～, 以后什么都记不起了. Everything went black. That's the last thing I can remember. 2 characterized by political decadence or social unrest; chaos

天机(機) tiānjī (名) 1 nature's mystery 2 secret: 泄漏～ give away a secret

天经(經)地义(義) tiānjīng-dìyì (名) indisputably correct

天空 tiānkōng (名) the sky; the heaven

天蓝 tiānlán (形) sky blue; azure

天良 tiānliáng (名) conscience: 丧尽～ have no conscience

天亮 tiānliàng (名) daybreak; dawn

天伦(倫) tiānlún (名) the natural relationships between members of a family: ～之乐 family happiness; domestic felicity

天罗(羅)地网(網) tiānluó-dìwǎng (名) a tight encirclement; a dragnet

天南地北 tiānnán-dìběi too far away from each other; far apart 2 different places or areas

天平 tiānpíng (名) balance; scales: 分析～ analytical balance

天气(氣) tiānqì (名) weather: ～多变 changeable weather. ～转晴. It's clearing up. ～预报 weather forecast

天堑 tiānqiàn (名) natural barrier: 长江～ the natural barrier of the Changjiang River

天然 tiānrán (形) natural: ～气 natural gas. ～财富 natural resources

天壤 tiānrǎng (名) heaven and earth: ～之别 far removed (from); poles apart (from). 这两个词的意义有～之别. There is world of difference in meaning between these two words.

天日 tiānrì (名) the sky and the sun; light: 重见～be delivered from outer darkness

天色 tiānsè (名) time of the day; weather: ～已晚. It is getting late.

天生 tiānshēng (形) born; inborn; inherent; innate: 他真有学习语言的～才能吗? Has he really any aptitude for language?

天使 tiānshǐ (名) angel; cherub

天书(書) tiānshū (名) a book from heaven: 这对我是一部～. It's all Greek to me.

天堂 tiāntáng (名) paradise; heaven: 人间～paradise on earth

天体(體) tiāntǐ (名) celestial body

天文馆(館) tiānwénguǎn (名) planetarium

天文台(臺) tiānwéntái (名) astronomical observatory

天下 tiānxià (名) 1 land under heaven 2 state power: 打～ win state power

天仙 tiānxiān (名) 1 immortal; legendary goddess 2 a beauty

天险(險) tiānxiǎn (名) natural barrier

天线(綫) tiānxiàn (名) aerial; antenna

天性 tiānxìng (名) natural instincts; nature

天涯 tiānyá (名) the ends of the world: 远在～,近在咫尺. It is as near as his hand and as remote as a star. ～海角 the ends of the earth; the remotest corners of the earth

天衣无(無)缝 tiānyī wú fèng flawless

天灾(災) tiānzāi (名) natural disaster (or calamity)

天真 tiānzhēn (形) innocent; simple and unaffected; naive: ～的孩子 innocent children. 他政治上太～了. He is politically naive.

天职(職) tiānzhí (名) bounden duty

天诛地灭(滅) tiānzhū-dìmiè suffer eternal perdition

天主教 tiānzhǔjiào (名) Catholicism: ～徒 Catholic

天资 tiānzī (名) natural gift; talent; natural endowments

天字第一号(號) tiān zì dìyī hào (名) a thing of the greatest importance; a work of the highest order

添 tiān (动) add; increase: 增～光彩 add lustre to. ～衣服 put on more clothes

添枝加叶(葉) tiānzhī-jiāyè embellish the truth; embroider

甜 tián (形) 1 sweet; honeyed 2 sound: 睡得真～ sleep soundly; be sound asleep

甜美 tiánměi (形) 1 sweet: 味道～ taste sweet; have a sweet taste 2 pleasant, comfortable: 享受～的生活 enjoy comfort and ease in life

甜蜜 tiánmì (形) sweet; happy; honeyed: ～的笑容 sweet smiling face

甜食 tiánshí (名) sweet food; sweetmeats

甜丝(絲)丝 tiánsīsī (形) 1 pleasantly sweet: 这个菜～儿的, 很好吃. This dish is delicious, it has a sweet taste. 2 gratified; happy: 心里～的 feel happy and proud

甜头(頭) tiántou (名) 1 sweet taste 2 benefit: 给点～ give small favours to sb. (as an inducement)

甜言蜜语 tiányán-mìyǔ (名) sweet and honeyed phrases; fine-sounding words

恬 tián (形)<书> 1 quiet; tranquil: ～适 quiet and comfortable 2 carefree: ～不知耻 be lost to shame; be shameless

恬静 tiánjìng (形) quiet; peaceful; tranquil

填 tián (动) 1 fill; stuff: 义愤～膺 be filled with righteous indignation 2 write; fill in: ～表 fill in a form

填补(補) tiánbǔ (动) fill what is left vacant: ～缺额 fill a vacancy

填空 tiánkòng (动) fill a vacant position; fill a vacancy

填写(寫) tiánxiě (动) fill in; write: ～申请表 fill out an application form. 请在这里～你的姓名和职业. Please fill in the blanks here with your name and occupation.

田 tián (名) field; farmland: 稻～ rice field. 油～ oilfield

田地 tiándì (名) 1 field; farmland; cropland 2 wretched state

田间 tiánjiān (名) field; farm: ～管理 field management

田径(徑) tiánjìng (名) track and field: ～运动 track and field sports; athletics. ～运动员 athlete

田园(園) tiányuán (名) rural

area; countryside: ～生活 idyllic life. ～诗 idyll; pastoral poetry

舔 tiǎn (动) lick

挑 tiāo I (动) **1** choose; select; pick: 我～找最喜欢的. I chose what I liked best. ～毛病 pick holes; find fault **2** carry; shoulder: ～水 carry water. ～重担 shoulder heavy responsibilities II (量) [for things which can be carried on a shoulder pole]: 一～水 two buckets of water

see also tiǎo

挑刺儿 tiāocìr (动) find fault; pick holes: 他就爱～. He's much too fastidious.

挑肥拣(揀)瘦 tiāoféi-jiǎnshòu choose whichever is to one's personal advantage

挑剔 tiāoti (动、形) nitpick; nitpicking

挑选(選) tiāoxuǎn (动) choose; select; pick out

挑字眼儿 tiāo zìyǎnr (动) carp at the wording

条(條) tiáo I (名) **1** twig: 柳～椅子 wicker chair **2** a long narrow piece; strip; slip: 布～ a strip of cloth. 便～ a note. 金～ gold bar **3** item; article: 逐～ item by item; point by point **4** order: 有～不紊 in perfect order; orderly II (量): 两～鱼 two fish. 三～船 three ships. 一～香烟 a carton of cigarettes. 四～建议 four proposals

条件 tiáojiàn (名) **1** condition; term; factor: 自然～ natural conditions. 在目前～下 under present circumstances **2** requirement; qualification: 提出～ state the requirements. ～反射 conditioned reflex

条款 tiáokuǎn (名) clause; article; provision: 最惠国～ most favoured-nation clause. 法律～ legal provision

条理 tiáolǐ (名) proper arrangement or presentation; orderliness; method: ～分明 well-organized

条例 tiáolì (名) regulation; rules

条约 tiáoyuē (名) treaty; pact

条子 tiáozi (名) **1** strip: 纸～ a narrow strip of paper; a slip of paper **2** a short note

调 tiáo (动) **1** mix; adjust: ～匀 mix well; blend well **2** suit well: 风～雨顺 propitious weather for the crops. 饮食失～ live on an irregular diet **3** mediate: ～人 mediator; peacemaker **4** tease; take liberties with

调处(處) tiáochǔ (动) mediate; arbitrate

调和 tiáohe (动) **1** be in harmonious proportion: 雨水～. Rainfall is well distributed. **2** mediate; reconcile: 从中～ mediate; act as mediator **3** compromise; make concessions

调剂(劑) tiáojì (动) **1** make up (or fill) a prescription **2** adjust; regulate: ～劳动力 redistribute labour power

调节(節) tiáojié (动) regulate; adjust: ～室温 regulate the room temperature. 空气～ air conditioning

调解 tiáojiě (动) mediate; make peace: ～纠纷 mediate a settlement

调理 tiáoli (动) **1** nurse one's health; recuperate **2** take care of; look after: ～牲口 look after livestock

调弄 tiáonòng (动) **1** make fun of; tease **2** arrange; adjust **3** instigate; stir up

调配 tiáopèi (动) mix; blend: ～颜色 mix clours

调皮 tiáopí (形) **1** naughty; mischievous **2** unruly; tricky

调情 tiáoqíng (动) flirt

调唆 tiáosuo (动) incite; instigate

调停 tiáoting (动) mediate; intervene; act as an intermediary: 居间～ offer one's good offices between two parties

调味 tiáowèi (动) flavour; season: 加点生姜～ season food with some ginger

调笑 tiáoxiào (动) make fun of; poke fun at; tease

调养(養) tiáoyǎng (动) be restored to health by taking nourishing food and tonics when necessary

调整 tiáozhěng (动) adjust; regulate; revise: ～价格 readjust prices

迢 tiáo (形) far; remote

迢迢 tiáotiáo (形) far away; remote: 千里～ come all the way from a distant place; come from afar

笤 tiáo

笤帚 tiáozhou (名) broom

挑 tiǎo (动) **1** raise: 把帘子～起来 raise the curtain **2**

poke: ～火 poke a fire 3 stir up; instigate: ～事 stir up trouble; sow discord
see also tiāo
挑拨(撥) tiǎobō (动) instigate; incite: ～是非 foment discord. ～离间 sow dissension
挑动(動) tiǎodòng (动) provoke; stir up; incite: ～好奇心 excite one's curiosity
挑逗 tiǎodòu (动) provoke; tantalize
挑唆 tiǎosuo (动) incite; abet; instigate
挑衅(釁) tiǎoxìn (动) provoke an incident
挑战(戰) tiǎozhàn (动) challenge: 接受～ accept a challenge
眺 tiào (动) look into the distance: 远～ enjoy a distant view
眺望 tiàowàng (动) enjoy a distant view from a height
跳 tiào (动) 1 jump; leap; spring; bounce: ～过一条沟 jump over a ditch. 高兴得直～ jump for (or with) joy 2 move up and down; beat: 他心～不规律. His heart beats irregularly. *or* His heartbeats are irregular. 3 skip (over): ～过了三页 skip over three pages
跳板 tiàobǎn (名) 1 gangplank 2 springboard; diving board
跳高 tiàogāo (名) high jump: 撑竿～ pole vault; pole jump
跳梁小丑(醜) tiàoliáng xiǎochǒu (名) a petty scoundrel fond of playing tricks and creating trouble
跳水 tiàoshuǐ (动) dive: ～表演 diving exhibition
跳台(臺) tiàotái (名) diving tower; diving platform
跳舞 tiàowǔ (动) dance
跳远(遠) tiàoyuǎn (名) long jump; broad jump: 三级～ hop, step and jump
跳跃(躍) tiàoyuè (动) jump; leap; bound
跳蚤 tiàozao (名) flea
帖 tiē (形) submissive; obedient: 服～ docile and obedient
see also tiě; tiè
贴 tiē I (动) 1 paste; stick; glue: ～邮票 stick on a stamp 2 keep close to: 他～着墙走. He kept close to the wall and walked on. II (名) subsidy; allowance: 房～ housing allowance. 地区津～ weighting
贴边(邊) tiēbiān (名) hem (of a garment)
贴补(補) tiēbu (动) 1 help a relative or friend (out) financially 2 subsidize: 政府～ government subsidies
贴金 tiējīn (名) 1 gild 2 prettify
贴切 tiēqiè (形) (of words) apt; appropriate; proper: 比喻要用得～. A metaphor should be apt.
贴题 tiētí (形) relevant; pertinent; to the point: 着墨不多,但是十分～. The essay is terse but very much to the point.
贴现 tiēxiàn (名) discount (on a promissory note): ～率 discount rate
贴心 tiēxīn (形) intimate; close: ～朋友 bosom friend
帖 tiě I (名) 1 invitation: 请～ invitation 2 note; card: 字～儿 brief note II (量): 一～药 a dose (or draught) of herbal medicine
see also tiē; tiè
铁(鐵) tiě (名) 1 iron (Fe): 生～ pig iron; cast iron. 废～ scrap iron. 趁热打～. Strike while the iron is hot. 打破"～饭碗"crack the "iron rice bowl" 2 arms; weapon: 手无寸～ bare-handed 3 hard or strong as iron: ～拳 iron fist 4 indisputable; unalterable: ～的事实 ironclad evidence
铁板 tiěbǎn (名) iron plate; sheet iron
铁饼 tiěbǐng (名) 1 discus 2 掷～ discus throw
铁窗 tiěchuāng (名) prison bars; prison: ～风味 prison life; life behind the bars
铁道 tiědào (名) railway; railroad: 地下～ underground (railway); tube; subway
铁饭碗 tiěfànwǎn (名) iron rice bowl — a secure job
铁匠 tiějiàng (名) blacksmith; ironsmith
铁矿(礦) tiěkuàng (名) 1 iron ore 2 iron mine
铁链 tiěliàn (名) iron chain; shackles
铁路 tiělù (名) railway; railroad: ～运输 railway transportation
铁面无(無)私 tiěmiàn wú sī (形) impartial and upright
铁器 tiěqì (名) ironware: ～时代 the Iron Age
铁锹 tiěqiāo (名) spade; shovel

铁青 tiěqīng (形) ashen; livid: 气得脸色～ turn livid with rage

铁石心肠(腸) tiěshí xīncháng (形) be ironhearted; have a heart of stone; be hard hearted

铁丝(絲)网(網) tiěsīwǎng (名) 1 wire netting; wire meshes 2 wire entanglement: 有刺～ barbed wire entanglement

铁索 tiěsuǒ (名) cable; iron chain: ～吊车 cable car. ～桥 chain bridge

铁蹄 tiětí (名) iron heel

铁腕 tiěwàn (名) iron hand: ～人物 an ironhanded person; strong man

铁证(證) tiězhèng (名) ironclad proof; irrefutable evidence: ～如山 irrefutable, conclusive evidence

帖 tiè (名) a book containing models of handwriting or painting for learners to copy: 碑～ a book of stone rubbings

see also tiē; tiě

厅(廳) tīng (名) 1 hall: 餐厅 dining hall; restaurant. 休息～ lounge; foyer. 会议～ conference hall. 音乐～ concert hall 2 office: 办公～ general office

听(聽) tīng (动) 1 listen; hear: ～音乐 listen to music. 我们必须～～他的意见. We must hear what he has got to say. 2 heed; have a receptive ear for: 他不～. He refused to listen. 3 allow; let: ～任摆布 allow oneself to be twisted round sb.'s little finger

听便 tīngbiàn as one pleases; please yourself

听从(從) tīngcóng (动) accept; obey: ～劝告 accept sb.'s advice. ～指挥 obey orders

听候 tīnghòu (动) wait for (a decision, settlement, etc.)

听话 tīnghuà (形) be obedient

听觉(覺) tīngjué (名) sense of hearing

听课 tīngkè (动) 1 visit (or sit in on) a class 2 attend a lecture

听命 tīngmìng (动) take orders from: 俯首～ be at sb.'s beck and call

听凭(憑) tīngpíng (形) allow; let (sb. do as he pleases): ～别人的摆布 be at the mercy of others

听其自然 tīng qí zìrán let things take their own course

听取 tīngqǔ (动) hear: ～汇报 hear reports (from below)

听任 tīngrèn (动) allow; let (sb. do as he pleases): 这种事情不能～再度发生. This kind of thing should not be allowed to happen again.

听说 tīngshuō (动) be told; hear of; it is said: ～他要辞职了. It is said that he is going to resign.

听天由命 tīngtiān-yóumìng resign oneself to one's fate

听闻 tīngwén (动、名)〈书〉 hear: 骇人～ appalling; shocking

听信 tīngxìn (动) 1 wait for information 2 believe what one hears; believe: 不要～谣言. Don't believe such rumours.

听众(衆) tīngzhòng (名) audience; listeners

亭 tíng (名)(～子) pavilion: 书～ bookstall. 报～ kiosk; newsstand. 凉～ wayside pavilion

亭亭 tíngtíng (形)〈书〉 erect; upright: ～玉立 (of a woman) slim and graceful; (of a tree, etc.) tall and erect

停 tíng (动) 1 stop; cease; halt; pause: 雨～了. It's stopped raining. 她～了一会儿, 又接着讲下去. She paused a moment before she went on. 2 stop over; stay: 我在去纽约的途中在东京～了两天. On my way to New York, I stopped over in Tokyo for two days. 3 (of cars) be parked; (of ships) lie at anchor: 汽车～在哪儿? Where can we park the car?

停办(辦) tíngbàn (动) close down

停泊 tíngbó (动) anchor; berth: 这个码头可以～五十多艘轮船. The docks can berth over fifty vessels.

停车(車) tíngchē (动) 1 stop; pull up: 下一站～十分钟. At the next station we'll have a ten-minute stop. 2 park: 此处不准～! No Parking! ～场 car park; parking lot; parking area

停当(當) tíngdang (形) ready; settled: 一切准备～. Everything's ready.

停顿 tíngdùn (动) 1 stop; halt; pause: 陷于～状态 be at a standstill; stagnate 2 pause (in speaking)

停放 tíngfàng (动) park; place: 这里不准～车辆. Don't park in this area. or, No Parking.

停火 tínghuǒ (名) cease-fire: ～协议 cease-fire agreement

停靠 tíngkào (动) (of a train)

stop; (of a ship) berth

停留 tíngliú (动、名) stay; stop: 代表团在纽约作短暂～. The delegation had a brief stopover in New York.

停妥 tíngtuǒ (形) be done properly; be in order: 事情已商议～. The matter was settled after much deliberation.

停息 tíngxī (动) stop; cease: 雨～了. The rain has stopped.

停歇 tíngxiē (动) 1 stop doing business; close down 2 stop; cease 3 stop for a rest

停业(業) tíngyè (动) stop doing business; close down: 清理存货, 暂时～. Closed temporarily for stock-taking.

停战(戰) tíngzhàn (名) armistice; truce: ～协定 armistice; truce agreement

停职(職) tíngzhí (动) temporarily relieve sb. of his duties as a disciplinary action

停止 tíngzhǐ (动) stop; cease; halt; suspend; call off: ～敌对行动 cessation of hostilities. ～营业 business suspended

停滞(滯) tíngzhì (动) stagnate; be at a standstill: 经济～. The economy remains stagnant.

廷 tíng (名) the court of a feudal ruler; the seat of a monarchical government

庭 tíng (名) 1 front courtyard; front yard 2 law court: 民(刑)～ a civil (criminal) court

庭园(園) tíngyuán (名) flower garden; grounds

庭院 tíngyuàn (名) courtyard

挺 tǐng I (形) straight; erect; stiff: ～立 stand erect. 直～～地躺着 lie stiff. 笔～的衣服 well-pressed clothes II (动) 1 straighten up (physically): ～胸 square one's shoulders. ～起腰杆 straighten one's back 2 endure; stand; hold out: 你～得住吗? Can you hold out? III (副) very; rather; quite: ～好 very good. 今天～冷. It's rather cold today. IV (量) [of machine guns]: 轻重机枪六十余～ over sixty heavy and light machine guns

挺拔 tǐngbá (形) 1 tall and straight: ～的苍松 tall, straight pines 2 forceful (of handwriting): 笔力～ forceful strokes

挺进(進) tǐngjìn (动) (of troops) advance; press onward; push forward

挺立 tǐnglì (动) stand upright; stand firm: 几棵青松～在山坡上. Several pine trees stand erect on the hillside.

挺身 tǐngshēn (动) stand out (against sth.): ～而出 step forward bravely

铤 tǐng (副) (run) quickly: ～而走险 make a desperate effort; make a reckless move

艇 tǐng (名) a light boat: 汽～ steamboat. 炮～ gunboat. 登陆～ landing craft

通 tōng I (动) 1 open; through: 电话打～了. The call has been put through. 这个主意行得～. This idea will work. 2 open up or clear out by poking or jabbing: 把下水道～一下 clean the sewer 3 lead to; go to: 四～八达 lead everywhere 4 channel; communicate: 互～有无 supply each other's needs 5 notify; tell: ～个电话 give sb. a ring; call (or phone up) sb. 6 understand; know: 他～三种语言. He knows three languages. II (名) authority; expert: 日本～ an expert on Japan. 中国～ an old China hand; Sinologue III (形) 1 logical; coherent: 文理不～ ungrammatical and incoherent (writing) 2 general; common: ～称 a general term 3 all; whole: ～观全局 take an overall view of the situation

see also tòng

通报(報) tōngbào I (动) circulate a notice: ～表扬 circulate a notice of commendation II (名) 1 circular 2 bulletin; journal: 科学～ Science Bulletin

通病 tōngbìng (名) common failing

通才 tōngcái (名) an all-round person; a man (or woman) of parts

通常 tōngcháng (形) general; usual; normal: ～的方法 ordinary means. ～早起 usually get up early

通畅(暢) tōngchàng (形) 1 unobstructed; clear: 血液循环～. The blood circulation is normal. 2 easy and smooth: 文字～ make smooth reading

通车(車) tōngchē (名) 1 (of a railway or highway) be open to traffic 2 have transport service

通称(稱) tōngchēng (动、名) 1 be generally called; be generally known as 2 a general term

通达(達) tōngdá (动) understand: ～人情 be sensible and considerate

通电(電) tōngdiàn I (动) set up an electric circuit; electrify II (名) circular telegram

通牒 tōngdié (名) diplomatic note: 最后～ ultimatum

通风(風) tōngfēng (动) 1 ventilate: 把窗打开～. Open the windows to let in some fresh air. 2 be well ventilated: 这里不～. It's very close in here. 3 leak out: ～报信 give sb. secret information

通告 tōnggào (动、名) 1 give public notice; announce 2 public notice; announcement; circular

通共 tōnggòng (副) in all; altogether; all told

通过(過) tōngguò I (动) 1 pass through; pass: 路太窄, 汽车不能～. The road is too narrow for cars. 2 adopt; pass; carry: 提案已一致～. The motion was carried unanimously. 以压倒多数～ be passed by an overwhelming majority II (介) 1 by means of; by way of; through: ～协商取得一致 reach unanimity through consultation 2 with the consent or approval of: 这个问题要～校方才能做出决定. No decision can be made on this matter until the school authorities have been consulted.

通航 tōngháng (名) be open to navigation or air traffic

通红 tōnghóng (形) very red; red through and through: 她羞得满脸～. She blushed scarlet.

通货 tōnghuò (名) currency: ～膨胀 inflation. ～收缩 deflation

通缉 tōngjī (动) issue an order to search for an escaped convict

通奸 tōngjiān (动) commit adultery

通栏(欄)标(標)题 tōnglán biāotí (名) banner (or streamer) headline; banner

通力 tōnglì (名) concerted effort: ～合作 make a concerted effort to cooperate

通例 tōnglì (名) general rule; usual practice

通令 tōnglìng (名) circular order; general order: ～嘉奖 issue an order of commendation

通论(論) tōnglùn (名) 1 a sensible, down-to-earth argument 2 a general survey

通盘(盤) tōngpán (形) overall; all-round; comprehensive: ～计划 overall planning

通气(氣) tōngqì (动) 1 ventilate 2 be in touch with each other: 这件事你得跟他通个气. You should keep him informed of the matter.

通情达(達)理 tōngqíng-dálǐ (形) reasonable; appropriate

通权(權)达(達)变(變) tōngquán-dábiàn (动) handle matters flexibly to meet the immediate needs of the situation

通融 tōngrong (动) stretch a point: 我想这事不好～. I don't think we can stretch a point in this case.

通商 tōngshāng (名) (of nations) have trade relations

通顺 tōngshùn (形) (of writing) clear and smooth: 文理～ grammatically correct and coherent

通俗 tōngsú (形) popular; common: ～易懂 simple and easy

通通 tōngtōng (副) all; entirely; completely: ～拿去吧. Take away the lot.

通宵 tōngxiāo (副) all night; throughout the night; round the clock: ～达旦 all night long

通晓(曉) tōngxiǎo (动) thoroughly understand; be well versed in; be proficient in: ～多种文字 know many languages

通信 tōngxìn (动) write to each other; correspond: ～处 mailing address

通行 tōngxíng I (动) pass (or go) through: 自由～ can pass freely; have free passage. 停止～ Closed to traffic. ～证 pass; permit; safe-conduct II (形) current; general: 这是全国～的办法. This is the current practice throughout the country.

通讯 tōngxùn (名) 1 communication: 无线电～ radio (or wireless) communication. 微波～ microwave communication 2 news report; news dispatch; correspondence; newsletter

通用 tōngyòng (形) 1 in common use; current; general: 当地民族～的语言 the language in common use among the local people 2 interchangeable: ～货币 currency

通则 tōngzé (名) general rule

通知 tōngzhī I (动) notify; inform: 你走以前～我一声. Let me know before you leave. II (名)

notice; circular: 发出～ send out (or dispatch) a notice

童 tóng 1 child: 牧～ shepherd boy. ～工 child labour. ～话 fairy tales. ～年 childhood 2 unmarried: ～女 maiden; virgin

童声(聲) tóngshēng (名) child's voice: ～合唱 children's chorus

瞳 tóng (名) pupil (of the eye)

瞳孔 tóngkǒng (名) pupil: 放大～ have one's pupils dilated

同 tóng I (形) 1 same; alike; similar: ～工～酬 equal pay for equal work 2 the same as (before): ～上 ditto; idem 3 together; in common: ～甘苦,共患难 share joys and sorrows II (介) to, with: 有事～群众商量. Consult with the masses when problems arise. III (连) and; as well as: 我～你一起去. I'll go with you.

同伴 tóngbàn (名) companion; pal

同胞 tóngbāo (名) 1 born of the same parents: ～兄弟(姐妹) brothers (sisters) 2 fellow countryman; compatriot

同病相怜(憐) tóng bìng xiāng lián fellow sufferers sympathize with one another

同仇敌(敵)忾(愾) tóngchóu-díkài share a bitter hatred for the enemy

同窗 tóngchuāng (名) 1 study in the same school 2 schoolmate

同等 tóngděng (形) of the same class, rank, or status; on an equal basis (or footing): ～重要 of equal importance

同甘共苦 tónggān-gòngkǔ share bitter and sweet

同归(歸)于(於)尽(盡) tóng guīyú jìn (动) perish together; spell destruction for both or all

同行 tóngháng (名) 1 of the same profession 2 a person of the same profession; one's colleague

同化 tónghuà (动、名) 1 assimilate (ethnic group) 2 assimilation

同伙(夥) tónghuǒ (动、名) 1 work in partnership; collude (in doing evil) 2 partner; cohort; confederate

同居 tóngjū (动) 1 live together 2 cohabit

同流合污 tóngliú-héwū consort with evil doers

同盟 tóngméng (名) alliance; league: 结成～ form (or enter into) an alliance

同谋 tóngmóu I (动) conspire (with sb.) II (名) confederate; accomplice: ～犯 accomplice

同年 tóngnián (名) 1 in the same year 2 of the same age

同情 tóngqíng (动) sympathize with; show sympathy for: 相互～和支持 sympathize with and support each other. 我很～你. I heartily sympathize with you. *or* I have every sympathy for you.

同上 tóngshàng (名) ditto; idem

同声(聲)传(傳)译(譯) tóngshēng chuányì (名) simultaneous interpretation

同时(時) tóngshí (副) 1 at the same time; simultaneously; meanwhile; in the meantime: ～存在 exist side by side; coexist 2 moreover; besides; furthermore: 这是非常重要的任务，～也是十分艰巨的任务. This is a very important task; moreover, it is a very arduous one.

同事 tóngshì I (动) work alongside; work together: 我们～已经多年. We've been working in the same department for years. II (名) colleague; fellow worker: 老～ an old colleague

同室操戈 tóng shì cāo gē internal strife; internecine feud

同乡(鄉) tóngxiāng (名) a fellow villager, townsman or provincial

同心 tóngxīn (形) work in unison: ～协力 work with one heart and with concerted efforts; pull together. ～同德 be of one heart and one mind

同学(學) tóngxué I (动) study in the same school II (名) fellow student; schoolmate

同样(樣) tóngyàng (形) same; identical; similar: 用～的方法 by the same method. 我们持～的观点. We hold identical views.

同业(業) tóngyè (名) 1 the same trade or business 2 a person of the same trade or business

同一 tóngyī (形) same; identical: 向～目标前进 advance towards the same goal

同义(義)词 tóngyìcí (名) synonym

同意 tóngyì (动) agree; consent; approve

同志 tóngzhì (名) comrade

同舟共济(濟) tóng zhōu gòng jì in times of trouble or crisis pull together; stick together through

thick and thin
同宗 tóngzōng (名) of the same clan; have common ancestry
桐 tóng (名) a general term for paulownia, phoenix tree and tung tree
桐油 tóngyóu (名) tung oil
铜 tóng (名) copper (Cu): ~丝 copper wire. ~像 bronze statue
铜版 tóngbǎn (名) copperplate: ~画 copperplate; etching (or engraving)
铜管乐(樂)器 tóngguǎn yuèqì (名) brass-wind instrument; brass wind
铜器 tóngqì (名) bronze, brass or copper ware: ~时代 the Bronze Age
铜墙(牆)铁(鐵)壁 tóngqiáng-tiěbì (名) wall of bronze — impregnable fortress
筒 tǒng (名) 1 a section of thick bamboo: 竹~ a thick bamboo tube 2 a thick tube-shaped object: 笔~ brush pot. 邮~ pillar box; mailbox
桶 tǒng (名) 1 pail; bucket; barrel: 水~ water bucket. 一~牛奶 a pail of milk 2 <石油> barrel
捅 tǒng (动) 1 poke; stab: ~了一刀 stab with a dagger. ~马蜂窝 stir up a hornets' nest 2 disclose; give away; let out: 谁把它给~出去了? Who gave it away (or let it out)?
捅娄(婁)子 tǒng lóuzi (动) make a stupid move; make a blunder; get into trouble
统 tǒng (名) 1 interconnected system: 传~ tradition. 系~ system 2 gather into one; unite: ~一指挥 unified command 3 all; together
统称(稱) tǒngchēng I (动) be called by a joint name II (名) a general designation
统筹(籌) tǒngchóu (动) plan as a whole: ~兼顾 make overall planning by taking all factors into consideration
统共 tǒnggòng (副) altogether; in all
统计 tǒngjì (名、动) 1 statistics: 人口~ census; vital statistics 2 add up; count: ~出席人数 count up the number of people present (at a meeting, etc.)
统属(屬) tǒngshǔ (名) subordination: ~关系 a system of relationships specifying that officials of lower ranks are subordinate to those of the higher ranks
统帅(帥) tǒngshuài (名、动) 1 commander in chief; commander 2 command
统率 tǒngshuài (动) command
统统 tǒngtǒng (副) all; completely; entirely; lock, stock and barrel: ~讲出来 own up
统辖 tǒngxiá (动) exercise jurisdiction over; govern
统一 tǒngyī I (动) unify; unite; integrate: ~行动 coordinate actions; act in unison II (形) unified; unitary: ~领导 unified leadership. 他们认识很不~. Their views are widely divergent.
统治 tǒngzhì (动) rule; dominate: ~阶级 ruling class. ~者 ruler
恸(慟) tòng (名) <书> deep sorrow; grief
痛 tòng I (动) ache; pain: 头~ have a headache. 肚子~ have a stomachache. 嗓子~ have a sore throat II (名) sorrow: 哀~ sadness III (副) extremely; deeply; bitterly: ~哭 cry bitterly. ~骂 severely scold; roundly curse
痛斥 tòngchì (动) bitterly attack; sharply denounce
痛楚 tòngchǔ (名) anguish; agony
痛处(處) tòngchù (名) sore spot; tender spot: 触及~ touch sb.'s sore spot
痛定思痛 tòng dìng sī tòng recall or relive a bitter experience
痛苦 tòngkǔ (名) pain; suffering; agony
痛快 tòngkuai (形、副) 1 very happy; delighted; overjoyed: 心里感到~ feel happily relieved of a burden 2 to one's great satisfaction: 喝个~ drink one's fill. 玩个~ have a wonderful time 3 simple and direct; forthright; straightforward: 说话很~ speak frankly and directly; be outspoken. 他~地答应了. He readily agreed.
痛切 tòngqiè (副) with intense sorrow; most sorrowfully: ~反省 examine one's conscience with feelings of deep remorse
痛恶(惡) tòngwù (动) bitterly detest; abhor
痛惜 tòngxī (动) deeply regret; deplore
痛心 tòngxīn (形) pained; deeply grieved: 他对自己所犯的错误感到很~. He keenly regretted

the mistake he had made.

痛心疾首 tòngxīn-jíshǒu detest; hate with very strong feeling

痛痒(癢) tòngyǎng (名) 1 sufferings; difficulties: ～相关 share a common lot 2 importance; consequence: 无关～ a matter of no consequence

通 tòng (量) [of repeated action]: 骂了他一～ give him a dressing-down

see also tōng

偷 tōu (动) 1 steal; pilfer: ～窃 steal; pilfer 2 on the sly: ～看 steal a glance; peek; peep. ～听 eavesdrop

偷安 tōu'ān (动) seek temporary ease and comfort

偷空 tōukòng (动) take time off (from work to do sth. else); snatch a moment

偷懒 tōulǎn (动) loaf on the job; be lazy

偷梁换柱 tōuliáng-huànzhù make the story take on a different look by deliberately changing a few details; commit a fraud

偷窃(竊) tōuqiè (动) steal; pilfer

偷生 tōushēng (动) live in abject misery

偷税 tōushuì (动) evade taxes

偷天换日 tōutiān-huànrì distort the truth by despicable means; perpetrate a gigantic fraud

偷偷 tōutōu (副) stealthily; secretly; on the sly: ～地溜走 sneak away. ～摸摸 furtively; surreptitiously; covertly

偷袭(襲) tōuxí (动) make a sneak attack; spring a surprise attack on sb.; (enemy, position etc.) raid on

偷闲(閑) tōuxián (动) snatch a moment of leisure: 忙里～ squeeze a little leisure from a busy programme; enjoy occasional leisure in a busy life

头(頭) tóu I (名) 1 head 2 hair or hair style: 梳～ comb the hair 3 top; end: 山～ hilltop. 桥～ the end of a bridge 4 beginning or end: 从～到尾 from start to finish 5 remnant; end: 铅笔～儿 pencil stub. 烟～ cigarette end 6 chief; head: 你们的～是谁? Who is the head of your section? 7 side; aspect: 两～落空 fall between two stools II (形) 1 first: ～等 first-class 2 leading: ～羊 lead sheep 3 [used before a numeral] first: ～一遍 the first time. ～三天 the first three days III (量) 1 [of domestic animals]: 三～牛 three head of cattle. 两～骡子 two mules 2 [of garlic]: 一～蒜 a bulb of garlic

头等 tóuděng (形) first-class; first-rate: ～大事 a matter of cardinal importance. ～舱 first-class cabin

头顶 tóudǐng (名) the top (or crown) of the head

头发(髮) tóufa (名) hair (on the human head)

头角 tóujiǎo (名) brilliance (of a young person); talent: 初露～ show one's talent for the first time

头里(裏) tóuli (副) 1 in front; ahead: 请～走,我马上就来. Please go ahead. I won't be long. 2 in advance; beforehand: 咱们把话说在～. Let's make this clear from the very start.

头颅(顱) tóulú (名) head: 抛～,洒热血 lay down one's life in a just cause

头面人物 tóumiàn rénwù (名) prominent figure; dignitary; VIP

头脑(腦) tóunǎo (名) 1 brain; mind: 她很有～. She has plenty of brains. ～简单 simple-minded. ～清醒 clear-headed 2 main threads; clue: 摸不着～ cannot make head or tail of sth.

头痛 tóutòng (名) (have a)headache: ～得厉害 have a bad headache. 这事真叫人～. This matter is a real headache.

头头是道 tóutóu shì dào (副) vividly; persuasively; methodically

头衔 tóuxián (名) title

头绪 tóuxù (名) main threads (of a complicated affair): 茫无～ be quite at a loss

头子 tóuzi (名) chieftain; chief; boss: 土匪～ bandit chief

头(頭) tou [a suffix placed at the end of a noun, verb or adjective]: 1 木～ wood. 没吃～ sth. not worth eating. 甜～儿 a sweet foretaste 2 上～ above. 下～ below

投 tóu (动) 1 throw; fling; hurl: ～篮 shoot. ～手榴弹 throw a hand grenade 2 put in: ～票 cast a vote. ～资 invest 3 jump in (of suicide): ～河 jump into the river 4 project; cast: 树影～在窗户上. The tree cast its shadow on the window. **5** send; deliver: ～书 deliver a letter **6** go to; join: ～军 join the army **7** fit in with; agree with; cater to: ～其所好 cater to sb.'s likes

投案 tóu'àn (动) give oneself up (or surrender oneself) to the police

投奔 tóubèn (动) go and seek the assistance of a friend or relative

投标(標) tóubiāo (动) enter a bid; submit a tender: ～者 bidder

投产(產) tóuchǎn (动) go into operation; put into production

投诚 tóuchéng (动) (of enemy troops, rebels, bandits, etc.) surrender; cross over

投敌(敵) tóudí (动) defect to the enemy

投递(遞) tóudì (动) deliver: ～信件 deliver letters

投放 tóufàng (动) put (goods) on the market

投稿 tóugǎo (动) contribute (to a newspaper or magazine)

投合 tóuhé (动) **1** agree; get along: 他们俩很～. The two of them hit it off very well. **2** cater to: ～顾客的口味 cater to the tastes of the customers

投机(機) tóujī I (形) congenial; agreeable: 谈得很～ have a most agreeable chat II (动) **1** speculate: ～倒把 engage in speculation and profiteering **2** take advantage of every chance for success: ～分子 opportunist

投井下石 tóu jǐng xià shí hit a man when he's down

投考 tóukǎo (动) sign up for an examination

投靠 tóukào (动) go and seek assistance from sb.; sponge on sb.

投票 tóupiào (动) vote; cast a vote: ～表决 decide by ballot; put sth. to the vote. ～箱 ballot box. 无记名～ secret ballot

投入 tóurù (动) throw into; put into: ～生产 go into operation

投射 tóushè (动) **1** throw (a projectile, etc.); cast **2** project (a ray of light); cast

投身 tóushēn (动) throw oneself into: ～到工作中去 throw oneself heart and soul into the work. ～到四个现代化建设事业中去 devote oneself to the cause of the four modernizations

投鼠忌器 tóu shǔ jì qì hesitate to hit out against an evildoer for fear of harming good people in the act

投宿 tóusù (动) seek lodgings: ～客栈 put up at an inn for the night

投胎 tóutāi (名) reincarnation

投桃报(報)李 tóu táo bào lǐ exchange gifts; exchange visits

投降 tóuxiáng (动) surrender; capitulate

投掷(擲) tóuzhì (动) throw; hurl: ～标枪(铁饼、手榴弹) throw a javelin (discus, hand grenade)

投资 tóuzī I (动) invest II (名) money invested; investment: 国家～ state investment

透

tòu I (动) **1** penetrate; soak through; seep through **2** tell secretly: ～个信儿 tip sb. off II (副) fully; thoroughly: 桃熟～了. The peaches are quite ripe. 你把道理说～了. You have fully explained the case. 没意思～了 as dull as ditchwater

透彻(徹) tòuchè (形) penetrating; thorough; in-depth; deep-going: ～的分析 an in-depth analysis

透顶 tòudǐng (副) thoroughly; downright; in the extreme: 腐败～ rotten to the core

透风(風) tòufēng (动) **1** let in air **2** divulge a secret; leak: 这件事,他向我透了一点风. He gave me some tip about it.

透漏 tòulòu (动) divulge; leak; reveal: 消息～出去了. The news has leaked out.

透露 tòulù (动) divulge; leak; disclose; reveal: ～风声 leak (or disclose) information. 真相～出来了. The truth has come out.

透明 tòumíng (形) transparent: 不～ opaque. 半～ translucent

透辟(闢) tòupì (形) penetrating; incisive; thorough

透视 tòushì (名) **1** perspective **2** fluoroscopy

突

tū I (动) dash forward; charge: ～破 break through II (副) sudden; abrupt: 气温～降. The temperature suddenly dropped. III (形) prominent: ～起 sudden rise

突变(變) tūbiàn (名) **1** sudden change **2** mutation

突出 tūchū (形) **1** protruding; projecting: ～的前额 prominent forehead **2** outstanding; prominent: ～的成就 outstanding achievements **3** give prominence to; stress highlight: 他的文章没有～重点. In his essay he fails to give prominence to his main points.

突击(擊) tūjī (动) 1 make a sudden violent attack; assault: ～部队 shock troop 2 concentrate one's effort to finish a job; do a crash job: ～某种工作 rush through some work

突破 tūpò (动) 1 break through; make (or effect) a breakthrough: ～防线 break through a defence line. 医学上的～ a medical breakthrough 2 surmount; overcome: ～各种技术难关 surmount every technical difficulty. ～定额 overfulfil a quota

突起 tūqǐ (动) 1 break out; suddenly appear: 战事～. War broke out. 异军～. Quite unexpectedly, a new figure appeared on the scene. 2 rise high; tower: 峰峦～. Peaks suddenly begin to rise.

突然 tūrán (副) suddenly; abruptly; unexpectedly: ～停止 suddenly stop; stop short. ～哭起来 burst into tears. ～袭击 spring a surprise attack

突如其来(來) tū rú qí lái (动) come to sb. as a surprise

突突 tūtū (象) 她的心～地跳. Her heart thumped.

突围(圍) tūwéi (动) break out of an encirclement

凸 tū (形) protruding; raised: ～花银瓶 a silver vase with a raised floral design. ～面 convex

秃 tū (形) 1 hairless; bald: 他的头开始～了. He's going baldish. 2 bare: 山是～的. The hill is bare. 3 blunt; without a point: 铅笔～了. The pencil is blunt. 4 incomplete; badly organized: 这篇文章的结尾显得有点～. This essay seems to end rather abruptly.

屠 tú (动) 1 slaughter (animals for food) 2 massacre; slaughter: 大～杀 mass massacre

屠杀(殺) tūshā (动) massacre; bloodbath

屠宰 túzǎi (动) butcher; slaughter: ～场 slaughter house

图(圖) tú I (名) 1 picture; drawing; chart; map: 地～ map 2 scheme; plan; attempt: ～谋 plot. 宏～ grand plan II (动) pursue; seek: ～私利 seek personal profit. ～省事 try to do things the easy way

图案 tú'àn (名) pattern; design

图表 túbiǎo (名) chart; diagram; graph: 统计～ statistical chart (or table)

图钉 túdīng (名) drawing pin; thumbtack

图画(畫) túhuà (名) drawing; picture; painting

图鉴(鑒) tújiàn (名) illustrated (or pictorial) handbook

图解 tújiě (名) diagram; graph; figure: 用～说明 explain through diagrams

图景 tújǐng (名) view; prospect: 壮丽的～ magnificent prospect

图谋 túmóu (动) plot; scheme; conspire: ～不轨 hatch a sinister plot

图片 túpiàn (名) picture; photograph: ～展览 photo (or picture) exhibition. ～说明 caption

图谱 túpǔ (名) a collection of illustrative plates: 历史～ atlas

图书(書) túshū (名) books: ～资料 books and reference materials. ～馆 library. ～目录 catalogue of books; library catalogue

图腾 túténg (名) totem

图像 túxiàng (名) picture; image

图章 túzhāng (名) seal; stamp

涂(塗) tú (动) 1 spread on; apply; smear: ～抹 apply 2 scribble; scrawl: 别在墙上乱～. Don't scribble (or scrawl) on the wall. 3 blot out; cross out: ～掉几个字 cross out a few words

涂改 túgǎi (动) alter: ～无效 invalid if altered

涂抹 túmǒ (动) 1 daub; smear; paint 2 scribble; scrawl

涂饰 túshì (动) 1 cover with paint, lacquer, colorwash, etc. 2 daub (plaster, etc.) on a wall; whitewash

途 tú (名) way; road; route: 沿～ along the way (or road). 半～而废 give up halfway

途径(徑) tújìng (名) way; channel: 通过外交～ through diplomatic channels

徒 tú I (副) 1 on foot 2 empty; bare: ～手 bare-handed; unarmed 3 merely; only: ～有虚名 exist in name only 4 in vain; to no avail: ～费唇舌 waste one's breath II (名) 1 apprentice; pupil: 门～ pupil; disciple. 学～ apprentice 2 follower or believer: 佛教～ Buddhist 3 person; fellow: 无耻之～ shameless person. 赌～ gambler. 歹～ rascal; evildoer. 暴～ ruffian; thug

徒步 túbù (副) on foot: ～旅行 travel on foot

徒弟 túdì (名) apprentice; disciple

徒劳(勞) túláo (名) futile effort; fruitless labour: ～无功 all one's attempts proved futile

徒然 túrán (副) in vain; for nothing; to no avail: ～耗费精力 waste one's energy (or effort)

徒手 túshǒu (形) bare-handed; unarmed: ～操 free-standing exercises

徒刑 túxíng (名) imprisonment; (prison) sentence: 有期～ specified (prison) sentence. 无期～ life imprisonment

土 tǔ I (名) 1 soil; earth: 肥～ fertile (or good) soil. ～路 dirt road 2 land; ground: 国～ a country's territory; land. 领～ territory; domain II (形) 1 local; native: ～产 local product 2 homemade; crude: ～布 hand-woven cloth 3 old-fashioned; unrefined; rustic; unenlightened: ～里～气 uncouth; boorish

土崩瓦解 tǔbēng-wǎjiě (动) crumble; fall apart; collapse like a house of cards

土地 tǔdì (名) land; soil; territory

土豆 tǔdòu (名)〈口〉potato

土匪 tǔfěi (名) bandit; brigand

土豪 tǔháo (名) local tyrant: ～劣绅 local tyrant and evil gentry

土话 tǔhuà (名) slang expression; local dialect

土木 tǔmù (名) building; construction: 大兴～ build splendid houses on a grand scale

土壤 tǔrǎng (名) soil: ～改良 soil amelioration

土著 tǔzhù (名) original inhabitants; natives; aborigines

吐 tǔ (动) 1 spit: ～血 spit blood. ～痰 spit; expectorate 2 say; tell; pour out: ～实 tell the truth. ～怨气 air one's grievances
see also tù

吐露 tǔlù (动) reveal; tell: ～真情 reveal the truth

吐气(氣) tǔqì (形) venting one's pent-up feelings: 扬眉～ feel happy and proud

吐 tù (动) 1 vomit; throw up: 要～ feel sick; feel like vomiting 2 give up unwillingly; disgorge: ～赃 disgorge ill-gotten gains
see also tǔ

兔 tù (名)(～子) hare; rabbit: 家～ rabbit. 野～ hare

兔死狐悲 tù sǐ hú bēi like feels for like

湍 tuān I (形)〈书〉(of a current) rapid; torrential II (名) rapids; rushing water: 急～ a rushing current

湍急 tuānjí (形) (of a current) rapid; torrential: 水流～. The current is strong and rapid.

湍流 tuānliú (名) 1 swift current; rushing water; torrent; rapid 2 turbulent flow; turbulence

团(團) tuán I (形) 1 round; circular: ～扇 round fan 2 sth. shaped like a ball; 缩成一～ curl up. 汤～ boiled rice dumpling II (动) unite; conglomerate: ～结 unite with III (名) 1 group; society; organization: 剧～ drama troupe. 旅行～ a tourist group. 文工～ ensemble; art troupe. 代表～ delegation; mission; deputation 2 regiment IV (量): 一～毛线 a ball of wool. 一～面 a lump of dough

团结 tuánjié (动) unite; rally: ～一致 unite as one. ～就是力量. Unity is strength.

团聚 tuánjù (动) gather together; reunite: 全家～ family reunion. 在中国,春节仍然是全家～的节日. The Spring Festival is still an occasion for family get-togethers in China.

团体(體) tuántǐ (名) organization; group; team: 群众～ mass organization

团员 tuányuán (名) 1 member: 代表团～ a member of a delegation 2 a member of the Communist Youth League of China; League member

推 tuī (动) 1 push; shove: 把门～开 push the door open 2 plane: 用刨子～光 plane a table smooth 3 push forward; promote; advance: ～广 popularize. 4 infer; deduce: 类～ reason by analogy 5 (of offer, gift, etc.) decline 6 (of duty, responsibility, etc.) push away; shirk; shift: 不要把责任～给人家. Don't shift the responsibility onto others. 7 put off; postpone: 动身日期要往后～. The departure date should be postponed. 8 elect; choose: ～他担任小组长 elect him group leader

推波助澜 tuībō-zhùlán add fuel

to the flames; incite people to unrestrained anger or violence
推测 tuīcè (动) infer; conjecture; guess
推陈(陳)出新 tuī chén chū xīn weed through the old to bring forth the new
推迟(遲) tuīchí (动) put off; postpone; defer: ～两周付款defer payment for two weeks
推崇 tuīchóng (动) attach great weight to: ～备至 hold sb. in very high esteem
推辞(辭) tuīcí (动) decline (an appointment, invitation, etc.)
推倒 tuīdǎo (动) **1** push over; overturn **2** reverse; repudiate: 这不是一个错误的决定，不能予以～. This is not a wrong decision to be reversed.
推动(動) tuīdòng (动) promote; give impetus to; spur: 改革～进步. Reform spurs progress.
推断(斷) tuīduàn (动) infer; deduce
推度 tuīduó (动) infer; conjecture; guess
推翻 tuīfān (动) **1** overthrow; overturn; topple **2** repudiate; cancel; reverse: ～协议 repudiate an agreement
推荐(薦) tuījiàn (动) recommend: ～她为博士学位的候选人 recommend her as a candidate for a Ph.D. degree
推举(舉) tuījǔ (动) elect; choose
推理 tuīlǐ (名) inference; reasoning: 用～方法 by inference
推论(論) tuīlùn (名) inference; deduction; corollary
推敲 tuīqiāo (动) weigh; deliberate:～词句 weigh one's words; choose one's words carefully
推求 tuīqiú (动) inquire into; ascertain
推却(卻) tuīquè (动) refuse; decline; turn down
推让(讓) tuīràng (动) decline (a position, favour, etc.) out of modesty or politeness
推算 tuīsuàn (动) calculate; recken; work out
推土机(機) tuītǔjī (名) bulldozer
推托 tuītuō (动) make an excuse (for not doing sth.): 她～嗓子坏了，怎么也不肯唱. She declined persistently to sing on the plea that she had nearly lost her voice.
推脱 tuītuō (动) evade; shirk: ～责任 evade (or shirk) responsibility; lay the blame on sb.
推委 tuīwěi (动) shift responsibility onto others
推想 tuīxiǎng (动) imagine; guess; reckon
推销 tūxiāo (动) promote sales: ～员 salesman
推卸 tuīxiè (动) shirk (responsibility)
推心置腹 tuīxīn-zhìfù (动) treat people sincerely: ～地交换意见 have a frank exchange of views
推行 tuīxíng (动) carry out; pursue; implement: ～新的政策 pursue a neψ policy
推选(選) tuīxuǎn (动) elect; choose
推延 tuīyán (动) put off; postpone: 把会议～到明天 put off the meeting till tomorrow
推移 tuīyí (动) **1** (of time) elapse; pass: 随着时间的～ with the passage of time **2** (of a situation, etc.) develop; evolve: 时局的～ the march of events

颓 tuí (形) **1** ruined; dilapidated: ～垣断壁 a lot of debris **2** declining; decadent: 衰～ weak and degenerate; on the decline **3** dejected; dispirited: ～丧 dispirited; listless
颓败 tuíbài (形) ‹书› declining; decadent
颓废(廢) tuífèi (形) dejected; decadent: ～派 the decadent school
颓势(勢) tuíshì (名) declining tendency
颓唐 tuítáng (形) dejected; dispirited

腿 tuǐ (名) **1** leg: 大～ thigh. 前～ foreleg. 后～ hindleg. ～肚子 calf (of the leg). ～勤 busy running about; tireless in running around **2** a leglike support: 桌子(椅子)～ legs of a table (chair) **3** ham: 火～ ham
腿脚 tuǐjiǎo (名)ability to walk: ～不灵便 have difficulty moving about

蜕 tuì (动) **1** slough off **2** exuviate: 蛇～ snake slough
蜕变(變) tuìbiàn (动) **1** change in quality (usu. for the worse) **2** decay: 自发～ spontaneous decay
蜕化 tuìhuà (动) **1** slough off; exuviate **2** (of person or thing) degenerate:～变质分子degenerate element; degenerate

退 tuì (动) **1** move back; retreat: 敌人已经～了. The enemy has retreated. **2** cause to move back; withdraw; remove: ～

兵 beat a retreat; repulse the enemy 3 withdraw from; quit: ～职 resign from office 4 decline; recede: ～烧了. The fever is gone. 水～了. The floods have subsided. 5 return: ～票 return a ticket one has bought and get a refund 6 cancel; break off: ～婚 break off an engagement. ～掉订货 cancel an order

退步 tuìbù I (动) lag (or fall) behind; retrogress II (名) room for manoeuvre; leeway: 留个～ leave some room for manoeuvre; leave some leeway

退潮 tuìcháo (名) ebb tide; ebb

退出 tuìchū (动) withdraw from; secede; quit: ～会场 walk out of a meeting. ～组织 withdraw from an organization. ～政治舞台 retire from the political arena

退化 tuìhuà (名、动) 1 degeneration 2 degenerate; deteriorate

退换 tuìhuàn (动) exchange (or replace) a purchase

退回 tuìhuí (动) 1 return; send (or give) back: 把这篇稿子～给作者 return the article to its author 2 go (or turn) back

退路 tuìlù (名) 1 route of retreat: 切断敌军～ cut off the enemy's retreat 2 room for manoeuvre; leeway: 留个～ leave some leeway

退却 tuìquè (动) 1 retreat; withdraw: 战略～ strategic retreat 2 hang back; shrink back; flinch

退让(讓) tuìràng (动) make a concession; yield; give in: 在原则问题上从不～ never compromise on matters of principle

退色 tuìshǎi (动) fade: 这种布～吗? Will this cloth fade?

退缩 tuìsuō (动) shrink back; flinch; cower: 在困难面前从不～ never flinch from difficulty

退位 tuìwèi (动) abdicate; give up the throne

退席 tuìxí (动) leave a banquet or a meeting; walk out: ～以示抗议 walk out in protest

退休 tuìxiū (动) retire: ～工人 retired workers. ～年龄 retirement age

退赃(贜) tuìzāng (动) give up (surrender, or disgorge) ill-gotten gains

退职(職) tuìzhí (动) resign or be discharged from office

吞 tūn (动) 1 swallow; gulp down: 把药丸～下去 swallow the pills 2 take possession of: 并～ annex

吞并(倂) tūnbìng (动、名) annex; swallow up; annexation

吞没 tūnmò (动) 1 embezzle; misappropriate: ～公款 misappropriate public funds 2 swallow up; engulf: 这只小船给波涛汹涌的海洋～了. The small boat was engulfed by the stormy sea.

吞声(聲) tūnshēng (动)〈书〉gulp down one's sobs; dare not cry out: 忍气～swallow rude remarks and bottle up one's grievances

吞噬 tūnshì (动) swallow; gobble up; engulf

吞吐 tūntǔ (动) take in and send out in large quantities: ～量 handling capacity (of a harbour); the volume of freight handled

吞吞吐吐 tūntūntǔtǔ (副) (speak) hesitantly and incoherently

屯 tún I (动) 1 collect; store up: ～粮 store up grain. ～聚 assemble; collect 2 station (troops); quarter (troops): ～兵 station troops II (名) village [often used in village names]

屯田 túntián (动) have garrison troops open up wasteland and grow food grain (a policy pursued by feudal rulers since the Han Dynasty)

囤 tún (动) store up; hoard: ～货 store goods
see also dùn

囤积(積) túnjī (动) hoard for speculation: ～居奇 hoard for profiteering purposes; hoarding and speculation

臀 tún (名) buttocks: ～部 buttocks

脱 tuō (动) 1 (of hair, skin) peel off: 头发快～光了 going bald 2 take off; cast off: ～鞋(衣服) take off one's shoes (clothes) 3 escape from; get out of: ～险 be out of danger 4 miss out (words) 5 neglect; slight

脱产(產) tuōchǎn (动) be temporarily released from one's regular work: ～学习 be temporarily released from work and sent on a study course

脱党(黨) tuōdǎng (动) cease to participate in party activities (often involuntarily)

脱稿 tuōgǎo (动) (of a manuscript) be completed

脱节(節) tuōjié (动) come apart; be disjointed; dislocate: 理论与

实践不能～. Theory must not be divorced from practice.

脱口而出 tuō kǒu ér chū (动) say sth. without thinking; blurt out

脱离(離) tuōlí (动) separate oneself from; break away from; be divorced from: ～实际 lose contact with reality; be divorced from reality. 病人～危险了. The patient is out of danger.

脱落 tuōluò (动) drop; fall off (or away); come off: 门的把手～了. The door handle has come off. 油漆～了. The paint is peeling off.

脱身 tuōshēn (动) get away: 我事情太多, 不能～. I have so much to attend to that I just can't get away.

脱手 tuōshǒu (动) 1 slip out of the hand 2 get off one's hands; dispose of

脱俗 tuōsú (形) free from philistinism; refined

脱胎 tuōtāi (动) 1 emerge from the womb of; be born out of: ～换骨 make a thorough-going change 2 ‹工美› a process of making bodiless lacquerware: ～漆器 bodiless lacquerware

脱逃 tuōtáo (动) run away; escape; flee: 临阵～ flee from battle; disappear just when one's service is most needed

脱险(險) tuōxiǎn (动) escape (or be out of) danger

脱销 tuōxiāo (动) out of stock; sold out

拖 tuō (动) 1 pull; drag; haul 2 delay; drag on: 不要再～了. Don't delay any more. 今天能做的不要～到明天. Don't put off today's work till tomorrow.

拖把 tuōbǎ (名) mop

拖车(車) tuōchē (名) trailer

拖船 tuōchuán (名) tugboat; tug; towboat

拖后(後)腿 tuō hòutuǐ hold sb. back; be a drag on sb.

拖拉 tuōlā (形) dilatory; slow; sluggish: ～作风 sluggishness

拖拉机(機) tuōlājī (名) tractor: 手扶～ walking tractor

拖累 tuōlěi (动) 1 encumber; be a burden on: 受家务～ be tied down by household chores 2 implicate; involve

拖泥带(帶)水 tuōní-dàishuǐ (形) (of writing or work) messy; sloppy; slovenly

拖欠 tuōqiàn (动) fail to pay one's debts; be in arrears: ～债务 in debt

拖鞋 tuōxié (名) slippers

拖延 tuōyán (动) delay; put off; procrastinate: ～时间 play for time; stall (for time)

托 tuō I (名) 1 sth. serving as a support: 枪～ the stock (or butt) of a rifle, etc. 2 serve as a foil (or contrast); set off: 衬～ set off II (动) 1 support with the hand or palm: 她两手～着下巴. Her chin rested on her hands. 2 ask; entrust: 把这项任务～付给他 entrust him with the task 3 plead; give as a pretext: ～病 pretend to be sick; plead illness. ～故不来 fail to show up on some pretext 4 rely upon; owe to: ～庇 owe all this to sb.'s kindness

托词 tuōcí (动、名) 1 find a pretext; make some excuse: ～谢绝 decline with some excuse 2 pretext; excuse; subterfuge: 那不过是～. That was just an excuse.

托儿(兒)所 tuō'érsuǒ (名) nursery; day-care centre

托福 tuōfú (套) [usu. used in returning sb.'s greetings] thanks to you: 托您的福, 一切都还顺利. Everything is going fine, thank you.

托管 tuōguǎn (名) trusteeship: ～国 trustee. ～领土 trust territory

托盘(盤) tuōpán (名) (serving) tray

托人情 tuō rénqíng (动) ask a favour through the good offices of sb.

托运(運) tuōyùn (动) consign for shipment; check

鸵 tuó (名) ostrich

鸵鸟(鳥) tuóniǎo (名) ostrich: ～政策 ostrich policy; ostrichism

驼 tuó I (名) camel II (形) hunchbacked

驼背 tuóbèi I (名) hunchback; humpback II (形) hunchbacked; humpbacked

驼峰 tuófēng (名) 1 hump (of a camel) 2 hump: ～调车场 hump yard

驼绒 tuóróng (名) 1 camel's hair 2 camel hair cloth

驮 tuó (动) carry (or bear) on the back

see also duò

椭(橢) tuǒ
椭圆 tuǒyuán (名) ellipse; oval; ovalshaped
妥 tuǒ (形) 1 appropriate; proper: 欠～ hardly proper; not quite appropriate 2 [used after a verb] ready; settled; finished: 事情基本上已办～了. The matter is as good as settled.
妥当(當) tuǒdàng (形) appropriate; proper: 办得很～ well handled; quite well done
妥善 tuǒshàn (形) appropriate; proper; well arranged: ～安排 make appropriate arrangements. ～处理 careful and skilful handling of a problem
妥帖 tuǒtiē (形) appropriate; fitting and proper
妥协(協) tuǒxié (动) come to terms; compromise: 达成～ reach a compromise
拓 tuò (动) open up; develop
see also tà
拓荒 tuòhuāng (动) open up virgin soil; reclaim wasteland
唾 tuò I (名) saliva; spittle: ～沫 saliva; spittle II (动) spit: ～弃 spurn
唾骂(罵) tuòmà (动) reproach with contempt; revile
唾手可得 tuò shǒu kě dé be within easy reach

W w

挖 wā (动) dig; excavate: ～井 sink a well. ～洞 dig a hole. ～出 winkle out
挖掘 wājué (动) excavate; unearth: ～古物 excavate ancient relics. ～潜力 tap the potentialities
挖苦 wāku (动) speak sarcastically or ironically: ～一些人 make ironical remarks about some people
挖墙(牆)角 wā qiángjiǎo undermine sb.'s prestige; let sb. down
洼(窪) wā (形) 1 hollow; low-lying: ～地 depression; low-lying land 2 low-lying area; depression: 水～儿 a waterlogged depression
洼陷 wāxiàn (形) (of ground) be low-lying
哇 wā (象) (of the sound of vomiting and crying): ～的一声哭了起来 burst out crying
蛙 wā (名) frog: ～泳 breaststroke
娃 wá (名) 1 baby; child 2 newborn animal
娃娃 wáwa (名) baby; child
瓦 wǎ (名) 1 tile 2 made of baked clay: ～器 earthenware 3 watt
see also wà
瓦匠 wǎjiang (名) bricklayer; tiler; plasterer
瓦解 wǎjiě (动) fall apart; collapse; crumble
瓦砾(礫) wǎlì (名) rubble; debris: 一片～ a lot of debris or a heap of rubble
瓦斯 wǎsī (名) gas
瓦特 wǎtè (名) watt: ～计 wattmeter
袜(襪) wà (名)(～子) socks; stockings
瓦 wà (动) cover (a roof) with tiles; tile
see also wǎ
歪 wāi (形) 1 askew; crooked; inclined; slanting: 他～戴帽子. He wore his hat askew. 2 inappropriate; unhealthy: ～风邪气 unhealthy tendencies
歪曲 wāiqū (动) distort; misrepresent; twist: ～事实 distort the facts
歪歪扭扭 wāiwāiniǔniǔ (形) irregular; careless; awkward: 字写得～的 write awkwardly and carelessly; write a poor hand
歪斜 wāixié (形) crooked; aslant
外 wài I (形) 1 outside: ～表 exterior; surface 劳工运动的～围组织 the fringe organizations of the labour movement 2 other: ～省 other provinces. 课～活动 extra-curricular activities 3 foreign; external: ～商 foreign merchant. 对～贸易 foreign trade 4 (relatives) of one's mother, sisters or daughters: ～孙 daughter's son; grandson. ～祖母 maternal grandmother 5 remotely related: ～人 a stranger; an outsider 6 unofficial: ～传 unofficial biography; anecdote II (副) besides; in addition; beyond: 此～ besides

外币(幣) wàibì (名) foreign currency
外宾(賓) wàibīn (名) foreign guest (or visitor)
外部 wàibù (形) 1 outside; external: ~世界 the external world 2 exterior; surface
外层(層)空间 wàicéng kōngjiān (名) outer space
外钞 wàichāo (名) foreign currencies
外电(電) wàidiàn (名) dispatches from foreign news agencies: 据~报导 according to foreign news agencies
外调 wàidiào (动) transfer (materials or personnel) to other localities
外观(觀) wàiguān (名) outward appearance; exterior
外国(國) wàiguó (名) foreign country: ~朋友 foreign friends. ~人 foreigner. ~语 foreign language
外行 wàiháng I (名) layman; nonprofessional II (形) lay; unprofessional: ~话 remarks of a layman; amateurish remarks
外号(號) wàihào (名) nickname
外患 wàihuàn (名) foreign aggression: 内忧~ domestic unrest and foreign aggression
外汇(匯) wàihuì (名) foreign exchange: ~储备 foreign exchange reserve. ~兑换率 rate of exchange. ~行情 exchange quotations
外籍 wàijí (名) foreign nationality: ~工作人员 foreign personnel
外交 wàijiāo (名) diplomacy; foreign affairs: ~关系 diplomatic relations. ~部 the Ministry of Foreign Affairs; the Foreign Ministry. ~部长 Minister of (or for) Foreign Affairs; Foreign Minister. ~辞令 diplomatic language. ~官 diplomat. ~护照 diplomatic passport. ~豁免权 diplomatic immunities. ~使节 diplomatic envoy. ~使团 diplomatic corps. ~特权 diplomatic prerogatives or privileges. ~信袋 diplomatic pouch; diplomatic bag. ~信使 diplomatic courier. ~政策 foreign policy
外界 wàijiè (名) 1 the external (or outside) world 2 outside: 向~征求意见 solicit comments and suggestions from people outside one's organization
外科 wàikē (名) surgical department: ~手术 surgical operation; surgery. ~医生 surgeon
外快 wàikuài (名) extra income
外流 wàiliú (动) outflow; drain: 人材~ brain drain
外貌 wàimào (名) appearance; exterior; looks
外强中干(乾) wàiqiáng-zhōnggān outwardly strong but inwardly weak
外侨(僑) wàiqiáo (名) foreign national; alien: 无国籍~ stateless alien
外勤 wàiqín (名) 1 work done outside the office or in the field (as surveying, prospecting, news gathering, etc.) 2 field personnel
外甥 wàisheng (名) sister's son; nephew
外甥女 wàishengnǚ (名) sister's daughter; niece
外事 wàishì (名) foreign affairs
外孙 wàisūn (名) daughter's son; grandson
外孙女 wàisūnnǚ (名) daughter's daughter; granddaughter
外套 wàitào (名) 1 overcoat 2 cape
外务(務) wàiwù (名) 1 things that are outside the scope of one's own job 2 foreign affairs
外乡(鄉) wàixiāng (名) another part of the country: ~口音 a nonlocal accent
外销 wàixiāo (名) for sale abroad or in another part of the country
外衣 wàiyī (名) 1 outer garment 2 semblance; appearance; garb
外因 wàiyīn (名) external cause
外用 wàiyòng (名) for external use
外语 wàiyǔ (名) foreign language
外援 wàiyuán (名) foreign aid
外在 wàizài (形) external; extrinsic: ~因素 external factor
外债 wàizhài (名) external debt; foreign debt
外资 wàizī (名) foreign capital

豌 wān

豌豆 wāndòu (名) pea

剜 wān

剜 wān (动) cut out
剜肉补(補)疮(瘡) wānròu-bǔchuāng seek to save a desperate situation by resorting to harmful practice

蜿 wān

蜿蜒 wānyán (动) wind; zigzag; meander: 小溪~ a meandering

stream

弯(彎) wān I (形) curved; crooked: 树枝都被厚雪压～了. The branches are weighed down by a heavy layer of snow. II (动) bend; flex: ～弓 bend a bow III (名) curve; corner: 拐～儿 go round curves; turn a corner

弯路 wānlù (名) a zigzag path; detour

弯曲 wānqū (形) winding; meandering; zigzag; crooked; curved: 一条～的山间小道 a path which zigzags up the hill

湾(灣) wān (名) 1 a bend in a stream: 河～ river bend 2 gulf; bay

完 wán I (形) intact; whole: ～好 in good condition; intact II (动) 1 run out; use up: 我们的汽油快用～了. We are running out of petrol. 2 finish: 我要说的话～了. That's all I wanted to say. 3 pay: ～税 pay taxes

完备(備) wánbèi (形) complete; perfect: 有不～的地方, 请多提意见. Please feel free to make your suggestions if there is anything we have neglected.

完毕(畢) wánbì (动) finish; complete; end: 一切准备～. Everything is in order.

完成 wánchéng (动) accomplish; complete; fulfil; bring to success (or fruition): ～任务 accomplish a task

完蛋 wándàn (形)<口> be finished for good; be done for

完好 wánhǎo (形) intact; whole; in good condition: ～无缺 intact; undamaged

完婚 wánhūn (动)<书> (of a man) get married; marry

完结 wánjié (动) end; be over; finish: 事情并没有～. This is not the end of the story.

完了 wánliǎo (动) come to an end; be over

完满 wánmǎn (形) satisfactory; successful: 问题已～解决了. We have found a satisfactory solution to the problem.

完美 wánměi (形) perfect; consummate

完全 wánquán I (形) complete; whole: 他话没说～. He didn't tell the whole story. II (副) completely; fully; wholly; entirely; absolutely: ～不同 be totally different. ～正确 perfectly right; absolutely correct

完善 wánshàn (形) perfect; complete: 设备～ very well equipped

完整 wánzhěng (形) complete; integrated; intact: 维护领土～ safeguard territorial integrity

玩 wán I (动) 1 play: ～火 play with fire. 我们在东京～了几天. We spent a few days in Tokyo. 2 engage in some kinds of sports or recreational activities: ～牌 play cards. ～足球 play football 3 employ; resort to: ～手段 resort to crafty manoeuvres; play tricks 4 trifle with; treat lightly: ～世不恭 cynical 5 enjoy; appreciate II (名) object for appreciation: 古～ curio; antique

玩忽 wánhū (动) neglect; trifle with: ～职守 negligence (or dereliction) of duty

玩具 wánjù (名) toy; plaything

玩弄 wánnòng (动) 1 dally with: ～女性 play fast and loose with a woman's affections 2 play with; juggle with: ～两面派手法 resort to double-dealing tactics

玩赏 wánshǎng (动) enjoy; take pleasure (or delight) in: ～风景 enjoy (or admire) the scenery

玩味 wánwèi (动) ponder; ruminate: 他的话很值得～. His words are worth pondering.

玩笑 wánxiào (名) joke; jest: 开～ play a joke (or prank) on; make jests

顽 wán (形) 1 stupid; ignorant 2 stubborn; obstinate 3 naughty; mischievous

顽固 wángù (形) 1 obstinate; stubborn; headstrong: ～不化 incorrigibly obstinate 2 bitterly opposed to change; die-hard: ～分子 diehard; a stick-in-the-mud 3 (of illness) hard to cure: ～症 stubborn disease

顽抗 wánkàng (动) stubbornly resist

顽皮 wánpí (形) naughty; mischievous

丸 wán (名) 1 ball; pellet 2 pill; bolus: 药～ pill (of Chinese medicine)

纨 wán (名) <书> fine silk fabrics

纨袴子弟 wánkù zǐdì (名) profligate son of the rich; fop; dandy

宛 wǎn 〈书〉 as if: 音容～在 as if the person were still alive. ～如 just like; as if. ～如昨日 as if it were yesterday

惋 wǎn (动) sigh

惋惜 wǎnxī (动) feel regret at sth.; condole with sb. over sth. unfortunate

碗 wǎn (名) bowl

婉 wǎn (形) 1 gentle; gracious tactful: ～商 consult with sb. tactfully 2 graceful; elegant; lovely

婉言 wǎnyán (名) gentle words; tactful expressions: ～谢绝 tactfully decline; politely refuse

婉转(轉) wǎnzhuǎn (形) 1 mild and indirect; tactful; in a roundabout way: 措词～ put it tactfully 2 sweet and agreeable: 歌喉～ a sweet voice; sweet singing

挽 wǎn (动) 1 draw; pull: ～留 urge one to stay on. ～救一个垂危的病人 rescue a patient who is gravely ill 2 roll up: ～起袖子 roll up one's sleeves 3 coil up 4 lament sb.'s death: ～诗 elegy

挽回 wǎnhuí (动) retrieve; redeem: ～败局 retrieve a defeat. 无可～ irretrievable; irrevocable

挽联(聯) wǎnlián (名) elegiac couplet

晚 wǎn I (名) evening; night: 今～ this evening; tonight II (形) 1 far on in time; late: 起得～ get up late. 现在学还不～. It's still not too late to learn. 2 younger; junior

晚安 wǎn'ān (套) good night

晚报(報) wǎnbào (名) evening paper

晚辈 wǎnbèi (名) the younger generation; one's juniors

晚餐 wǎncān (名) supper; dinner

晚点(點) wǎndiǎn (of a train, ship, etc.) late; behind schedule

晚饭 wǎnfàn (名) supper; dinner

晚会(會) wǎnhuì (名) soirée; evening party

晚节(節) wǎnjié (名) integrity cherished in old age: 保持～ maintain moral integrity to the end of one's days

晚年 wǎnnián (名) old age; one's remaining years: 过着幸福的～ spend one's evening of life in happiness.

晚霞 wǎnxiá (名) sunset glow; sunset clouds

万(萬) wàn I (名) 1 ten thousand 2 a very great number; myriad: ～物 all things on earth; all nature II (副) absolutely; by all means: ～不得已 out of sheer necessity; as a last resort

万般 wànbān I (名) all the different kinds II (副) utterly; extremely: ～无奈 have no alternative (but to)

万端 wànduān (形) multifarious: 感慨～ a myriad of thoughts passed through one's mind

万分 wànfēn (副) very much; extremely: ～抱歉 be extremely sorry

万古 wàngǔ (副) through the ages; eternally; forever: ～长存 last forever; be everlasting. ～长青 remain fresh forever; be everlasting

万花筒 wànhuātǒng (名) kaleidscope

万籁俱寂 wànlài jù jì all is quiet; silence reigns supreme

万里长(長)城 wànlǐ chángchéng (名) the Great Wall

万难(難) wànnán (副) extremely difficult; utterly impossible: ～照办 extremely difficult to comply with your request

万能 wànnéng (形) 1 omnipotent; all-powerful 2 universal; all-purpose: ～工具机 all-purpose machine

万千 wànqiān (形) multifarious; myriad: 变化～ eternally changing; ever changing. 思绪～ be overwhelmed with a myriad of thoughts and feelings

万全 wànquán (形) perfectly sound; surefire: ～之计 a completely safe plan

万世 wànshì (名) all ages; generation after generation

万岁(歲) wànsuì 1 long live: 全世界人民大团结～! Long live the great unity of the people of the world! 2 the emperor; Your Majesty; His Majesty

万万 wànwàn I (副) [used in negative sentences] absolutely: 那是～不行的. That's absolutely out of the question. 这是～没有想到的. This is the last thing I expected. II (数) hundred million

万无(無)一失 wàn wú yī shī no danger of anything going wrong; no risk at all; perfectly safe

万象 wànxiàng (名) every phenomenon on earth; all manifestations of nature: ～更新 everything looks fresh and gay
万幸 wànxìng (形) very lucky; by sheer luck
万一 wànyī I (连) just in case; if by any chance II (名) 1 contingency; eventuality: 防备～ be ready for all eventualities 2 one ten thousandth; a very small percentage; hope against hope
万丈 wànzhàng (形) lofty or bottomless: ～深渊 a bottomless chasm; abyss. 怒火～ a towering rage
万众(衆) wànzhòng (名) millions of people; the multitude: ～一心，所向无敌. Millions of people, all of one mind, are invincible
万状(狀) wànzhuàng (副) in the extreme; extremely: 惊恐～ be frightened out of one's senses
万紫千红 wànzǐ-qiānhóng a riot (or blaze) of colour: 百花盛开，～. A hundred flowers are blooming in a blaze of colour.
萬 wàn (数) ten thousand [used for the numeral 万 on cheques, etc. to avoid mistakes or alterations]
腕 wàn (名)(～子) wrist
汪 wāng
汪汪 wāngwāng I (形) with tears gathering in one's eyes; tearful: 泪～的 tearful II (象) bark; yap; bowwow: 狗～地叫. A dog is yapping.
汪洋 wāngyáng (of a body of water) vast; boundless: 一片～ a vast expanse of water
亡 wáng (动) 1 flee; run away: 出～ flee one's country; live in exile 2 lose; pass away 3 die; perish: 阵～ be killed in action
亡故 wánggù (动) die; pass way
亡国(國) wángguó I (动) cause a state to perish II (名) a subjugated nation: ～之民 the people of a conquered nation
亡命 wángmìng I (动) flee; seek refuge; go into exile II (形) desperate: ～之徒 desperado
王 wáng I (名) king; prince: 国～ king II (形) grand; great: ～父 grandfather
王八 wángba (名) 1 tortoise 2 〈骂〉 cuckold: ～蛋 bastard; son of a bitch
王朝 wángcháo (名) 1 imperial court; royal court 2 dynasty
王储 wángchǔ (名) crown prince
王府 wángfǔ (名) mansion of a prince
王公 wánggōng (名) princes and dukes; the nobility
王宫 wánggōng (名) (imperial) palace
王国(國) wángguó (名) 1 kingdom 2 realm; domain
王后 wánghòu (名) queen consort; queen
王牌 wángpái (名) trump card
王室 wángshì 1 royal family 2 imperial court; royal court
王位 wángwèi (名) throne
王子 wángzǐ (名) prince
枉 wǎng I (形) crooked; erroneous: 矫～ right a wrong; set things to rights II (动) 1 twist; pervert: ～法 pervert the law 2 treat unjustly; wrong: 冤～ bring false charges against sb. 被冤～ be wronged III (副) in vain; to no avail: ～活了半辈了 waste half a lifetime
枉费 wǎngfèi (动) waste; try in vain; be of no avail: ～唇舌 waste one's breath
枉然 wǎngrán (形) futile; in vain; to no purpose
罔 wǎng (书) I (动) deceive: 欺～ deceive; cheat II (副) no; not: 置若～闻 take no heed of; turn a deaf ear to
惘 wǎng (动) disappointed
惘然 wǎngrán (形) frustrated; disappointed: ～若失 feel disappointed
网(網) wǎng I (名) 1 net: 鱼～ fishing net. 蜘蛛～ cobweb 2 network: 铁路～ railway network II (动) catch with a net; net: ～着了一条鱼 net a fish
网兜 wǎngdōu (名) string bag
网罗(羅) wǎngluó I (名) a net for catching fish or birds; trap II (动) enlist the services of: ～人材 recruit talented people; employ qualified personnel
网球 wǎngqiú (名) 1 tennis 2 tennis ball
往 wǎng I (动) go: 来～于上海南京之间 travel to and fro between Nanjing and Shanghai II (副) in the direction

of; toward: 这趟车开～上海. The train is bound for Shanghai. III (形) past; previous: ～事 past events
see also wàng
往常 wǎngcháng (副) habitually in the past: 他～不这样. He was not like that in the past.
往来(來) wǎnglái (名) 1 come and go 2 contact; dealings; intercourse: 贸易～ trade contacts; commercial intercourse. 友好～ exchange of friendly visits; friendly intercourse
往返 wǎngfǎn (名) move to and fro: ～于伦敦与华盛顿 shuttle between London and Washington
往还(還) wǎnghuán (名) contact: 常有书信～ be in constant correspondence
往事 wǎngshì (名) the past; past events: ～历历. The past is still fresh in our memory.
往往 wǎngwǎng (副) often; frequently; more often than not
往昔 wǎngxī (副) in the past; in former times
忘 wàng (动) 1 forget: 他把这事全～了. He clean forgot all about it. 2 overlook; neglect: 别～了给我打电话. Don't forget to give me a ring.
忘恩负义(義) wàng'ēn-fùyì (形) ungrateful
忘怀(懷) wànghuái (动) forget; dismiss from one's mind: 国庆那次游行情景我真不能～. I can hardly dismiss from my mind the moving scene of the parade on National Day.
忘记 wàngjì (动) 1 forget 2 overlook; neglect
忘却 wàngquè (动) forget
忘形 wàngxíng (形) be beside oneself (with glee, etc.): 得意～ get dizzy with success
妄 wàng (形) 1 absurd; preposterous: 狂～ preposterous and arrogant 2 presumptuous; rash: ～加评论 make presumptuous comments
妄动(動) wàngdòng (名) rash (or reckless, ill-considered) action: 轻举～ act rashly
妄念 wàngniàn (名) fantastic idea
妄求 wàngqiú (动) vainly hope
妄图(圖) wàngtú (动) try in vain; make a futile attempt to
妄想 wàngxiǎng (名) vain hope; wishful thinking
妄自菲薄 wàng zì fěibó make a humble estimate of one's abilities
妄自尊大 wàng zì zūndà swell with preposterous self-importance
望 wàng I (动) 1 look at: 登山远～ climb up a mountain and look far into the distance; climb to the mountain-top for a distant view 2 call on; visit: 看～ pay a call on sb. 3 hope; expect: 大喜过～ be overjoyed with the unexpectedly good result. ～准时出席. You are requested to be present on time. II (名) 1 reputation; prestige: 德高～重 enjoy high prestige and command great respect 2 full moon
望尘(塵)莫及 wàng chén mò jí be lagging too far behind to catch up
望而生畏 wàng ér shēng wèi awe-inspiring; forbidding
望文生义(義) wàng wén shēng yì misinterpret a sentence through superficial understanding
望眼欲穿 wàng yǎn yù chuān look forward to sth. with great eagerness
望洋兴(興)叹(嘆) wàng yáng xīngtàn be bitterly aware of one's inadequacy when confronted with a real challenge
望远镜 wàngyuǎnjìng (名) telescope; binoculars
望族 wàngzú (名) <书> distinguished family; a family of social distinction
旺 wàng (形) prosperous; flourishing; vigorous
旺季 wàngjì (名) busy season
旺盛 wàngshèng (形) vigorous; exuberant: 士气～ have high morale
往 wàng (介) to; toward: ～左拐 turn to the left. ～前走 go straight on
see also wǎng
往后(後) wànghòu (副) from now on; later on; in the future
威 wēi (名) 1 apparent strength or might: 军～ the might of an army; military prowess. 示～ demonstrate; demonstration 2 by force
威逼 wēibī (动) threaten by force; coerce; intimidate: ～利诱 resort to both intimidation and bribery
威风(風) wēifēng I (名) power and prestige: ～扫地 thoroughly discredited II (形) imposing;

impressive; awe-inspiring: ～凛凛 majestic-looking
威吓(嚇) wēihè (动) intimidate; threaten; bully
威力 wēilì (名) power; might
威名 wēimíng (名) legendary heroism
威慑(懾) wēishè (动) terrorize with military force; deter: ～力量 deterrent force; deterrent
威望 wēiwàng (名) prestige
威武 wēiwǔ I (名) might; force; power: ～不能屈 not to be cowed by force II (形) powerful; mighty
威胁(脅) wēixié (动) threaten; menace; imperil: ～世界和平 threaten world peace
威信 wēixìn (名) prestige; popularity trust
威严(嚴) wēiyán I (形) majestic; awe-inspiring: ～的仪仗队 an impressive guard of honour II (名) prestige; dignity

煨 wēi (动) 1 cook over a slow fire; stew; simmer 2 roast (sweet potatoes, etc.) in fresh cinders

偎 wēi (动) snuggle up to; cling to
偎依 wēiyī (动) snuggle up; nestle up: 女孩子～在母亲的怀里. The girl nestled up in her mother's arms.

微 wēi I (形) 1 minute; tiny: 细～ minute; tiny. ～风 gentle breeze. ～笑 smile. 谨小慎～ be overcautious 2 profound; abstruse: 精～ subtle II (动) decline: 衰～ be on the decline
微波 wēibō (名) microwave
微薄 wēibó (形) meagre; scanty: 收入～ have a meagre income
微不足道 wēi bùzú dào (形) of no consequence; insignificant; negligible
微分 wēifēn (名) differential: ～学 differential calculus
微观(觀) wēiguān microcosmic: ～经济学 microeconomics
微乎其微 wēi hū qí wēi (形) hardly noticeable; next to nothing; negligible
微妙 wēimiào (形) delicate; subtle: ～的关系 subtle relations. 这个事情很～. This is a very delicate affair.
微弱 wēiruò (形) faint; feeble: 光线～ a faint light; a glimmer
微生物 wēishēngwù (名) microorganism; microbe
微微 wēiwēi (形) slight; faint: ～一笑 give a faint smile
微细 wēixì (形) very small; tiny
微小 wēixiǎo (形) small; little: 极其～ infinitely small; infinitesimal. ～的希望 a slim chance
微型 wēixíng (形) miniature; mini-: ～汽车 minicar; mini. ～照相机 miniature camera; minicam

逶 wēi
逶迤 wēiyí (形) winding; meandering: ～的山路 a stretch of winding mountain path

巍 wēi (形) towering; lofty
巍峨 wēi'é (形) towering; lofty: ～的群山 sprawling lofty mountain
巍然 wēirán (形) towering; lofty; majestic: ～屹立 stand lofty and firm
巍巍 wēiwēi (形) towering; lofty

危 wēi I (名) danger; peril: 居安思～ think of danger while you live in peace II (动) endanger; imperil: ～及生命 pose a threat to human life III (形) 1 dying: 病～ be critically ill 2 <书> proper: 正襟～坐 sit up properly
危殆 wēidài (形)<书> in great danger of one's life or situation
危害 wēihài (动) harm; endanger; jeopardize: ～健康 be harmful to one's health
危机(機) wēijī (动) crisis: 经济～ economic crisis. ～四伏 beset with crises
危急 wēijí (形) critical; in imminent danger; in a desperate situation: ～关头 critical juncture
危难(難) wēinàn (名) danger and disaster; calamity: 处于～之中 be faced with danger
危如累卵 wēi rú lěi luǎn in a precarious situation
危亡 wēiwáng danger of extinction
危险(險) wēixiǎn (名、形) danger; dangerous; perilous: 脱离～ out of danger. ～品 dangerous articles
危言耸(聳)听(聽) wēiyán sǒngtīng paint an alarming picture of the situation just to scare the audience

为(爲) wéi I (动) 1 do; act: 敢作敢～ bold in action. 青年有～ a young man of promise 2 act as; serve as: 以此～凭. This will serve as a proof. 3 become: 变沙漠～良田 turn the desert into arable land 4 be; mean: 一公里～二华里. One kilometer is equivalent to two *li*. II (介) [used together with "所" to indicate a passive structure]:～人民所爱戴 be loved and respected by the people; enjoy popular support

see also wèi

为非作歹 wéifēi-zuòdǎi do evil; perpetrate outrages

为难(難) wéinán (形) 1 feel embarrassed: 令人～ embarrass sb.; put sb. in an awkward situation 2 make things difficult for: 故意～ make things difficult for sb.; be deliberately hard on sb.

为期 wéiqī (to be completed) by a definite date: 以两周～ not exceeding two weeks. 课程～三个月. The course of study covers three months.

为人 wéirén (动) behave; conduct oneself: ～正直 be upright

为生 wéishēng (动) make a living

为数(數) wéishù (动) amount to; number: ～不少 come up to a large number; amount to quite a good deal

为所欲为(爲) wéi suǒ yù wéi go to any length to achieve one's wicked purpose

为伍 wéiwǔ (动) associate with: 羞与～ would be ashamed of sb.'s company

为止 wéizhǐ up to; till: 迄今～ up to now; so far

违(違)

wéi (动) 1 disobey; violate: ～令 disobey orders. ～约 violate the agreement 2 be separated: 久～了. I haven't seen you for ages.

违背 wéibèi (动) violate; go against; run counter to: ～规章制度 fail to abide by the rules and regulations

违法 wéifǎ (动) defy the law: ～乱纪 violate the law and discipline

违反 wéifǎn (动) violate; run counter to: ～历史潮流 go against the trend of history

违犯 wéifàn (动) violate: ～宪法 act in violation of the constitution

违禁 wéijìn (动) violate a ban: ～品 contraband goods

违抗 wéikàng (动) disobey; defy: ～命令 disobey orders

违心 wéixīn (动) against one's will; contrary to one's intentions; insincere

围(圍)

wéi I (动) enclose; surround: 包～ besiege; surround; encircle. 突～ break out of an encirclement II (副) all round; around: 四～都是山 be surrounded by mountains on all sides

围攻 wéigōng (动) 1 besiege; lay siege to 2 jointly attack sb.: 遭到～ come under attack from all sides

围歼(殲) wéijiān (动) surround and annihilate

围巾 wéijīn (名) muffler; scarf

围困 wéikùn (动) besiege; hem in; pin down: 把敌人～起来. Pin down the enemy.

围拢(攏) wéilǒng (动) crowd around

围棋 wéiqí (名) *weiqi; go*

围墙(牆) wéiqiáng (名) enclosure; enclosing wall

围裙 wéiqún (名) apron

围绕(繞) wéirào (动) 1 move round: 地球～着太阳旋转. The earth moves round the sun. 2 centre on; revolve round: 全厂职工～着改进生产方法提出很多建议. The cadres and workers of the factory made a number of proposals for revamping the method of production.

惟

wéi I (副) only; alone: ～你是问. You alone will be held responsible. II (连) <书> but: 他工作努力，～注意身体不够. He works hard but takes too little care of himself. III (名) thinking; thought: 思～ thinking

惟独(獨) wéidú (副) only; alone: 大家都来了，～他没来. Everybody has come except him.

惟恐 wéikǒng for fear that; lest: ～落后 for fear that one should lag behind. 我几次提醒他，～他忘了. I reminded him several times lest he should forget.

惟利是图(圖) wéi lì shì tú be bent solely on profit; be intent on nothing but profit; put profit-making first

惟命是听(聽) wéi mìng shì tīng obey orders from the higher-up, whatever they are

惟我独(獨)尊 wéi wǒ dú zūn extremely conceited

惟一 wéiyī (形) only; sole: ～可

能的解决办法 the only possible solution

唯 wéi (副) only; alone

see also wěi

唯物辩(辯)证(證)法 wéiwù biànzhèngfǎ (名) materialist dialectics

唯物史观(觀) wéiwù shǐguān (名) materialist conception of history; historical materialism

唯物主义(義) wéiwùzhǔyì (名) materialism

唯心史观(觀) wéixīnshǐguān (名) idealist conception of history; historical idealism

唯心主义(義) wéixīnzhǔyì (名) idealism

帷 wéi (名) curtain

帷幕 wéimù (名) heavy curtain

帷幄 wéiwò (名) army tent: 运筹～ devise strategies within a command tent; ponder over problems of military strategy at a command post

维 wéi (动) 1 link 2 maintain; safeguard; preserve

维持 wéichí (动) keep; maintain;preserve:～秩序 keep order. ～现状 maintain the status quo. ～生活 support oneself or one's family; survive

维护(護) wéihù (动) safeguard; defend; uphold: ～团结 uphold unity. ～国家主权 defend state sovereignty

维棉 wéimián (名) vinylon and cotton blend

维妙维肖 wéimiào-wéixiào (形) remarkably true to life; absolutely lifelike

维尼纶(綸) wéinílún (名) vinylon

维生素 wéishēngsù (名) vitamin: 丁种～ vitamin D

维新 wéixīn (名) reform; modernization: 日本明治～ the Meiji Reform of Japan (1868)

维修 wéixiū (动、名) keep in (good) repair; service; maintain: 设备～ maintenance (or upkeep) of equipment

桅 wéi (名) mast: ～杆 mast. ～顶 masthead

桅灯(燈) wéidēng (名) 1 mast head light; range light 2 barn lantern

伪(僞) wěi I (形) false; fake; bogus: 真～ true and false. ～钞 counterfeit (or forged) bank note II (名) puppet: ～政权 puppet regime

伪君子 wěijūnzǐ (名) hypocrite

伪善 wěishàn (形) hypocritical: ～的言词 hypocritical words

伪造 wěizào (动) forge; falsify; fabricate; counterfeit: ～证件 forge a certificate. ～帐目 falsify accounts

伪装(裝) wěizhuāng I (动) pretend; feign: ～中立 pretend to be neutral II (名) 1 disguise; guise; mask 2 camouflage

苇(葦) wěi (名) reed

苇箔 wěibó (名) reed matting

苇席(蓆) wěixí (名) reed mat

伟(偉) wěi (形) big; great: 身体魁～ tall and of a powerful build

伟大 wěidà (形) great; mighty: ～的政治家 a great statesman. ～的事业 a great undertaking. ～的胜利 a signal victory

伟人 wěirén (名) a great man

纬(緯) wěi (名) 1 weft; woof 2 latitude

纬度 wěidù (名) latitude: 高(低)～ high (low) latitudes

纬线(綫) wěixiàn (名) 1 parallel 2 weft

唯 wěi (副) 〈书〉 yea

see also wéi

唯唯诺诺 wěiwěinuònuò (形)never say 'no' to one's superior; be always ready to agree with one's leader; be obedient and docile

委 wěi I (动) 1 entrust; appoint: ～以重任 entrust sb. with an important task 2 throw away; cast aside: ～弃 discard 3 shift: ～过于人 shift the blame onto sb. else II (形) indirect; roundabout: ～婉 mild and roundabout; tactful III (名) 1 end: 原～ the beginning and the end; the whole story 2 listless; dejected: ～靡 listless; dispirited

委靡 wěimí (形) listless; dispirited; dejected: 精神～ listless; dispirited. ～不振 in low spirits; lackadaisical

委派 wěipài (动) appoint; designate

委曲求全 wěiqū qiú quán be forced to compromise; to avert a showdown or a head-on confrontation; compromise for the sake of the over-all interest

委屈 wěiqu (动、名) 1 feel wronged; nurse a grievance: 诉说～ pour out one's grievances (or troubles) 2 put sb. to great inconvenience: 你只好～一点.

You'll have to put up with it.

委任 wěirèn （动）appoint：～状 certificate of appointment

委实(實) wěishí （副）really; indeed：我～不知道。I really haven't the faintest idea.

委托 wěituō （动）entrust; trust：～他做这项工作 entrust him with the work. ～商店 commission shop

委婉 wěiwǎn （形）mild and roundabout; tactful：～的语气 a mild tone. ～语 euphemism

委员 wěiyuán （名）committee member：～会 committee; commission; council

萎 wěi （动）wither; wilt; fade

萎缩 wěisuō （动）1 wither; shrivel 2 (of a market, economy, etc.) shrink; sag

萎谢 wěixiè （动）wither; fade

猥 wěi （形）1 numerous; multifarious：～杂 miscellaneous 2 base; obscene; salacious; indecent

猥亵(褻) wěixiè I （形）obscene; salacious II （动）behave indecently towards (a woman)

尾 wěi I （名）1 tail：牛～ ox-tail 2 end：排～ a person standing at the end of a line 3 remaining part; remnant：扫～工程 the final phase of a project II （量）[of fish]：两～鱼 two fish

尾巴 wěiba （名）1 tail 2 tail-like part：飞机～ the tail of a plane 3 servile adherent; appendage

尾大不掉 wěi dà bù diào 1 a case of the tail wagging the dog 2 (of an organization) too cumbersome to be effective

尾声(聲) wěishēng （名）1 coda 2 epilogue：序幕和～ prologue and epilogue 3 end：节目已接近～. The performance is drawing to an end.

尾数(數) wěishù （名）odd amount in addition to the round number (usually of a credit balance)

尾随(隨) wěisuí （动）tail behind; follow at sb.'s heels; shadow

娓 wěi

娓娓 wěiwěi （副）(talk) tirelessly：～动听 speak most interestingly

为(爲) wèi （介）1 [indicating the object of one's act of service]：～人民服务 serve the people 2 [indicating an objective]：～方便起见 for the sake of convenience

see also wéi

为此 wèicǐ to this end; for this reason (or purpose); in this connection

为何 wèihé why; for what reason

为虎作伥(倀) wèi hǔ zuò chāng act as cat's paw for an evil-doer

为人作嫁 wèi rén zuò jià single-mindedly work for the good of another without ever thinking of oneself

为什么(麼) wèishénme why; why (or how) is it that

未 wèi 1 have not; did not：尚～恢复健康 have not yet recovered (from illness) 2 not：～知可否 not know whether it will be all right

未必 wèibì may not; not necessarily：他～知道. He doesn't necessarily know.

未便 wèibiàn not be in a position to; find it hard to：～擅自处理 find it inappropriate to handle the matter on my own

未卜先知 wèi bǔ xiān zhī foresee; have foresight

未曾 wèicéng have not; did not：～听说过 have never heard of it

未尝(嘗) wèicháng 1 have not; did not：～见过. We have never seen it before. 2 [used before a negative word to indicate a double negative]：那样也～不可. That should be all right.

未定 wèidìng （形）uncertain; undecided; undefined：会议地点～. The venue of the conference is not yet fixed. ～稿 draft

未婚 wèihūn （形）unmarried; single：～夫 fiancé. ～妻 fiancée

未决 wèijué （形）unsettled; outstanding：悬而～的问题 an outstanding issue; an open (or a pending) question

未可 wèikě cannot：～乐观 have no cause for optimism; nothing to be optimistic about. 前途～限量 have a brilliant future

未可厚非 wèi kě hòu fēi we should not be over-critical

未来(來) wèilái I （形）1 coming; approaching; next; future：～的一个世纪 the coming century; next century 2 future; tomorrow：美好的～ a glorious future

未老先衰 wèi lǎo xiān shuāi prematurely senile

未免 wèimiǎn rather; a bit too; truly: 这～太过份. This is really going too far. 他～太谦虚了. He is being too modest 他～有点不够冷静了. He is not really as cool as he should be.

未遂 wèisuì not accomplished; abortive: ～罪 attempted crime. 政变～. The coup d'etat aborted. 心愿～. My wish remains unfulfilled.

未详 wèixiáng (形) unknown: 出处～. The source is unknown.

未雨绸缪 wèi yǔ chóumóu provide for a rainy day; take precautions

未知数(數) wèizhīshù (名) 1 an unknown quantity 2 uncertainty: 他能否成功还是个～. It's still uncertain whether he will succeed.

味

wèi (名) 1 taste; flavour: 滋～ relish; gusto. 谈得津津有～ talk with relish 2 smell; odour: 香～ a sweet smell; fragrance; aroma 3 interest: 文笔艰涩无～. The style is difficult and dull.

味道 wèidào (名) taste; flavour: 这个菜～很好. This dish is very nice. 他的话里有点讽刺的～. There's a touch of irony in his remarks.

味同嚼蜡(蠟) wèi tóng jiáo là it is like chewing wax; it's as dry as saw dust

畏

wèi (动) 1 fear: 不～艰险 fear neither hardships nor danger. 望而生～ forbidding 2 respect; awe: 后生可～. The younger generation is full of promise and so deserves respect.

畏惧(懼) wèijù (动) fear; dread: 无所～ be fearless

畏难(難) wèinán (动) be afraid of difficulty

畏怯 wèiqiè (形) cowardly; chickenhearted

畏首畏尾 wèishǒu-wèiwěi (形) be full of misgivings; be timorous and hesitant

畏缩 wèisuō (动) shrink or flinch from difficulty or danger: ～不前 hang back in fear

畏途 wèitú (名)‹书› a dangerous road: 视为～ be regarded as a course which people fear to pursue; be regarded as a dangerous course to be avoided

畏罪 wèizuì (动) dread punishment for one's crime: ～潜逃 abscond

喂

wèi I (叹) (of greetings) hello; hey: ～, 你哪儿去了? Where have you been? II (动) feed: ～奶 breast-feed; suckle; nurse. 给病人～饭 feed a patient

喂养(養) wèiyǎng (动) feed; raise; keep: ～家禽 raise poultry

胃

wèi (名) stomach: ～病 stomach trouble

胃口 wèikǒu (名) 1 appetite: ～好 have a good appetite. 没有～ have no appetite 2 liking: 这种音乐合他的～. This kind of music appeals to him.

谓

wèi I (动) 1 say: 所～ what is called 2 be called: 何～人造卫星? What is meant by a man-made satellite? 何～平衡? What is meant by equilibrium? II (名) meaning; sense: 无～的话 twaddle; meaningless or senseless talk

谓语 wèiyǔ (名) predicate

位

wèi I (名) 1 place; location: 座～ seat 2 position: 名～ fame and position 3 throne: 即～ come to the throne. 篡～ usurp the throne II (数) place; figure; digit. 个～ unit's place. 十～ ten's place. 四～数 four-digit number III (量) [polite form of address]: 四～客人 four guests

位于(於) wèiyú (动)‹书› be located; be situated; lie: ～亚洲东部 be situated in the eastern part of Asia

位置 wèizhi (名) 1 seat; place 2 place; position

位子 wèizi (名) seat; place

慰

wèi (动) 1 console; comfort: ～勉 comfort and encourage 2 be relieved: 知你通过考试, 甚～. I am pleased to hear that you have passed the exam.

慰劳(勞) wèiláo (动) bring gifts to people or send one's best wishes to them in recognition of their services

慰问 wèiwèn (动) express sympathy and solicitude for: ～信 a letter of sympathy; sympathy note

蔚

wèi

蔚蓝(藍) wèilán (形) azure; sky blue: ～的天空 an azure sky

蔚然成风(風) wèirán chéng fēng become prevalent; become the order of the day

蔚为(爲)大观(觀) wèi wéi dàguān afford a magnificent spectacle

卫(衛) wèi (动) defend; guard; protect: 自～还击 fight back in self-defence

卫兵 wèibīng (名) guard; bodyguard

卫道 wèidào (动) defend traditional moral principles

卫队(隊) wèiduì (名) squad of bodyguards; armed escort

卫生 wèishēng (名) hygiene; health; sanitation: 讲～ pay attention to hygiene. 公共～ public health. ～间 toilet. ～球 camphor ball; mothball. ～纸 toilet paper

卫戍 wèishù (名) garrison

卫星 wèixīng (名) 1 satellite 2 artificial satellite; man-made satellite: 气象～ weather satellite. 通讯～ communication satellite. ～城 satellite town

温 wēn I (形) warm; lukewarm: ～水 lukewarm water II (名) temperature: 体～ temperature (of the body) III (动) 1 warm up: 把酒～一下 warm up the wine 2 review; revise: ～课 review (or revise) one's lessons

温饱 wēnbǎo (名) have enough to eat and wear; be tolerably well off

温床(牀) wēichuáng (名) 1 hotbed 2 breeding ground; hotbed

温存 wēicún (形) 1 attentive; emotionally attached [usu. to a person of the opposite sex] 2 gentle; kind

温带(帶) wēidài (名) temperate zone

温度 wēndù (名) temperature: 室内(外)～ indoor (outdoor) temperature. ～计 thermograph

温度表 wēndùbiǎo (名) thermometer: 摄氏～ centigrade (or Celsius) thermometer. 华氏～ Fahrenheit thermometer

温故知新 wēngù-zhīxīn 1 re-study what you have learnt and you will gain fresh insights 2 look at the past in perspective and you will gain an understanding of the present

温和 wēnhé (形) 1 temperate; mild; moderate: 气候～ a temperate climate; mild weather 2 gentle; mild: 性情～ have a gentle disposition; be good-natured. 语气～ speak in a mild tone

温暖 wēnnuǎn (形) warm: 天气～ warm weather

温情 wēnqíng (名) tender feeling; tender-heartedness

温泉 wēnquán (名) hot spring

温柔 wēnróu (形) gentle and soft

温室 wēnshì (名) hothouse; greenhouse; glasshouse; conservatory

温顺 wēnshùn (形) gentle and docile

温文尔(爾)雅 wēnwén-ěryǎ urbane

温习(習) wēnxí (动) review; revise: ～功课 review one's lessons

温驯 wēnxún (形) (of animals) docile; tame

瘟 wēn (名) acute communicable diseases

瘟疫 wēnyì (名) pestilence

文 wén I (名) 1 character; script; writing: 甲骨～ inscriptions on oracle bones 2 language: 英～ the English language 3 literary composition; writing: 散～ prose. 韵～ verse. ～如其人. The style is the man. 4 literary language 5 culture: ～物cultural relics II (形) 1 civilian; civil: ～职 civilian service 2 gentle; refined: 举止～雅 refined in manner III (动) cover up; whitewash: ～过饰非 gloss over one's faults IV(量) [for coins in the old days]: 一～钱 one penny. 一～不值 not worth a farthing

文本 wénběn (名) text; version: 本合同两种～同等有效. Both texts of the contract are equally valid (or authentic).

文笔(筆) wénbǐ (名) style of writing: ～流利 write in an easy and fluent style

文不对(對)题 wén bù duì tí the answer is irrelevant to the question

文采 wéncǎi (名) 1 rich and bright colours 2 literary talent

文辞(辭) wéncí (名) diction; language: ～优美 The essay is written in an elegant style.

文牍(牘) wéndú (名) official paper: ～主义 red tape

文法 wénfǎ (名) grammar

文风(風) wénfēng (名) style of writing

文告 wéngào (名) proclamation; statement

文工团(團) wéngōngtuán (名) song and dance ensemble; art troupe

文官 wénguān (名) civil servant:

～政府 a civilian government
文豪 wénháo （名）literary giant; great writer
文化 wénhuà （名） 1 civilization; culture 2 education; culture; schooling; literacy: 学～ acquire an elementary education; acquire literacy; learn to read and write. ～参赞 cultural counsellor. ～馆(站) cultural centre. ～水平 educational level
文集 wénjí （名） collected works
文件 wénjiàn （名） documents; papers; instruments
文教 wénjiào （名） (of culture and education) culture and education: ～事业 cultural and educational work
文静 wénjìng （形） gentle and quiet
文具 wénjù （名）stationery: ～店 stationer's; stationery shop
文科 wénkē （名）liberal arts: ～院校 colleges of arts
文理 wénlǐ （名）unity and coherence in writing: ～通顺 be well-written and well-organized
文盲 wénmáng （名）illiterate; illiteracy
文明 wénmíng （名、形） 1 civilization; culture: 物质～ material civilization. 精神～ spiritual values 2 civilized
文凭(憑) wénpíng （名）diploma
文人 wénrén （名） man of letters; scholar
文书(書) wénshū （名） 1 document, official dispatch; or contract 2 copies
文思 wénsī （名） the train of thought as expressed in writing: ～敏捷 have a facile pen. ～枯竭 one's creative flow is drying up
文坛(壇) wéntán （名）the literary world (arena, or circles); the world of letters
文体(體) wéntǐ （名）literary form; style: ～学 stylistics
文物 wénwù （名）cultural relics; historical relics
文献(獻) wénxiàn （名） document; literature: 历史～ historical documents
文选(選) wénxuǎn （名）selected works; selected essays
文学(學) wénxué （名）literature: ～家 writer. ～批评 literary criticism. ～作品 literary works
文艺(藝) wényì （名）art and literature: ～复兴 the Renaissance
文娱 wényú （名）cultural recreation; entertainment: ～活动 recreational activities
文摘 wénzhāi （名）digest
文章 wénzhāng （名） 1 essay; article 2 literary works; writings 3 hidden meaning; implied meaning: 看来他话里还有些～. It seems he made innuendoes about something in his remarks.
文质(質)彬彬 wénzhì bīnbīn （形） urbane
文字 wénzì （名） 1 characters; script; writing: 拼音～ alphabetic writing 2 written language 3 writing (as regards form or tyle): s ～通顺 make smooth reading

蚊 wén （名）(～子) mosquito
蚊香 wénxiāng （名） mosquito coil incense
蚊帐(帳) wénzhàng （名） mosquito net

纹 wén （名）lines: 脸上的皱～ wrinkles. ～理 veins; grain

闻 wén I （动） 1 hear: ～讯 hear the news. 耳～不如目见. Seeing is believing. 2 smell: 你～～这是什么味儿? Here, smell and tell me what it is. II （名） news; story: 要～ important news III （形） well-known; famous: ～人 well-known figure; celebrity
闻风(風)丧(喪)胆(膽) wén fēng sàng dǎn become terror-stricken (or panic-stricken) on hearing the news
闻名 wénmíng （形） well-known; famous; renowned: ～全世界 enjoy a high reputation throughout the world

紊 wěn （形）disorderly; confused
紊乱(亂) wěnluàn （形）disorder; chaos; confusion: 秩序～ chaotic

稳(穩) wěn （形） 1 steady; stable; firm: 站～ stand firm. 局面～定. The situation is in control. 2 sure; certain: 这事你拿得～吗? Are you quite sure of it? ～操胜券 have all assurance of success
稳步 wěnbù （副） with steady steps; steadily: ～前进 advance steadily; make steady progress
稳当(當) wěndang （形） reliable; secure; safe. 办事～ act prudently
稳定 wěndìng I （形）stable; steady: 物价～. Prices remain stable. ～的多数 a stable majority II （动）stabilize; steady: ～物价 stabilize commodity prices
稳固 wěngù （形） firm; stable:

～的基础 a firm (or solid) foundation

稳健 wěnjiàn (形) firm; steady: 迈着～的步子 walk with steady steps; stride vigorously ahead

稳妥 wěntuǒ (形) safe; reliable: 我们要～一些. We have to be on the safe side.

稳重 wěnzhòng (形) (of speech, manner) calm and steady; unruffled

刎

wěn (动) cut one's throat: 自～ cut one's own throat; commit suicide

吻

wěn I (名) 1 lips 2 an animal's mouth II (动) kiss

吻合 wěnhé (动) be identical; coincide; tally: 意见～ hold identical views

问

wèn (动) 1 ask; inquire: ～事处 inquiry desk. 不懂就～. Don't hesitate to ask when you don't understand. 2 ask after; inquire after: 他信里～起你. He asks to be remembered to you in his letter. 请替我～她好. Please send her my best regards. 3 interrogate; cross-examine: 审～ interrogate 4 hold responsible: 出了事唯你是～. If anything goes wrong, we'll hold you responsible for it. *or* You will be answerable for anything that may happen.

问安 wèn'ān (动) pay one's respects (usu. to elders); wish sb. good health

问道于(於)盲 wèn dào yú máng take a blind man as one's guide; seek enlightenment from an ignoramus

问寒问暖 wènhán-wènnuǎn show solicitous concern about sb.'s health or welfare

问好 wènhǎo (动) send one's regards to: 他向您～. He wished to be remembered to you.

问号(號) wènhào (名) 1 question mark; query 2 unknown factor; open question

问候 wènhòu (动、名) send one's respects (or regards) to; extend greetings to: 致以亲切的～ extend cordial greetings

问津 wènjīn (动) (书) make inquiries (as about prices): 无人～ nobody cares to make inquiries about it

问世 wènshì (动) be published for the first time; come out

问题 wèntí (名) 1 question; problem; issue: 关键～ a key problem. 原则～ a question of principle. 悬而未决的～ an outstanding issue. 有个～我要责问他. I have a bone to pick with him. 2 trouble; mishap: 他又出～了. He has got into trouble again.

问讯 wènxùn (动) inquire; ask: ～处 inquiry office; information desk

问罪 wènzuì (动) denounce; condemn: 兴师～ denounce sb. publicly for his serious errors (even by sending a punitive force as in ancient times)

翁

wēng (名) 1 old man: 渔～ an old fisherman 2 father 3 father-in-law

嗡

wēng (象) drone; buzz; hum: 蜜蜂～～地飞. Bees are buzzing all around.

瓮(甕)

wèng (名) urn; earthen jar: 菜～ a jar for pickling vegetables

瓮中之鳖 wèngzhōng zhī biē (名) be bottled up or trapped: 已成～ have fallen into the trap

涡(渦)

wō (名) whirlpool; eddy: 水～ eddies of water

涡流 wōliú (名) the circular movement of a fluid; whirling fluid; eddy

窝(窩)

wō I (名) 1 nest: 鸟～ bird's nest. 鸡～ hencoop 2 lair; den: 贼～ thieves' den. 土匪～ bandits' lair 3 a hollow part of the human body; pit: 夹肢～ armpit. 酒～ dimple II (动) 1 harbour; shelter: ～赃 harbour stolen goods 2 hold in; check: ～火 pent-up rage 3 bend III (量) (of animals) litter; brood: 一～十只小猪 ten piglets at a litter

窝藏 wōcáng (动) harbour; shelter; hide: ～罪犯 give shelter to (or harbour) a criminal

窝工 wōgōng (名) the holding up of work

窝囊 wōnang I (动) feel vexed; be annoyed: 受～气 be obliged to bottle up one's feings II (形) hopelessly stupid; chickenhearted

窝棚 wōpeng (名) shack; shed; shanty

莴(萵)

wō

莴笋(筍) wōsǔn (名) asparagus

蜗(蝸) wō (名) snail: ～牛 snail

喔 wō (象) cock's crow: ～～～! Cock-a-doodle-doo! see also ō

我 wǒ (代) 1 me 2 we: ～方 our side; we. ～军 our army. 3 [used together with 你 to mean 'everyone']: 你也帮，～也帮，他很快就赶上同班了. With everybody ready to help, he soon caught up with the rest of the class. 4 self: 忘～精神 selfless spirit

我们 wǒmen (代) we

我行我素 wǒ xíng wǒ sù stick to one's old way of doing things

沃 wò I (形) fertile; rich: ～土 fertile soil; rich soil II (动) irrigate: ～田 irrigate farmland

斡 wò

斡旋 wòxuán I (动) mediate II (名) good offices

卧 wò (动) 1 lie: 仰～ lie on one's back. ～床不起 be laid up in bed; be bedridden 2 (of animals or birds) crouch; sit 3 for sleeping in: ～室 bedroom. ～铺 sleeping berth

卧车(車) wòchē (名) 1 sleeping car; sleeping carriage; sleeper 2 automobile; car; limousine; sedan

握 wò (动) hold; grasp: ～紧拳头 clench one's fist

握别 wòbié (动) shake hands at parting; part

龌(齷) wò

龌龊 wòchuò (形) dirty; filthy: 卑鄙～ sordid; despicable

污 wū I (名) dirt; filth: 去～剂 detergent II (形) 1 dirty; filthy: ～泥 mud 2 corrupt: ～吏 corrupt official III (动) defile; smear: 玷～ sully; tarnish

污点(點) wūdiǎn (名) stain

污垢 wūgòu (名) dirt; filth

污泥 wūní (名) mud; mire

污染 wūrǎn (动) pollute; contaminate: 空气～ air pollution. 环境～ environmental pollution

污辱 wūrǔ (动) 1 humiliate; insult 2 sully; taint

污水 wūshuǐ (名) foul (or waste) water; sewage; slops: 生活～ domestic sewage. ～处理 sewage disposal; sewage treatment

污浊(濁) wūzhuó (形) (of air, water, etc.) dirty; muddy; filthy

巫 wu (名) witch; wizard: ～婆 witch; sorceress. ～术 witchcraft; sorcery

诬 wū (动) falsely accuse

诬告 wūgào (动) bring a false charge against sb.

诬害 wūhài (动) do harm to sb. by spreading rumours about him or by trumping up a charge

诬赖 wūlài (动) falsely accuse sb. (of doing evil or saying wicked things): ～好人 incriminate innocent people

诬蔑 wūmiè (动) slander; vilify

诬陷 wūxiàn (动) frame a case against sb.

乌(烏) wū I (名) crow II (形) black; dark: ～云 black clouds; dark clouds

乌龟(龜) wūguī (名) 1 tortoise 2 cuckold: ～壳 tortoise shell

乌合之众(衆) wūhé zhī zhòng (名) a horde of rough, lawless persons; rabble; mob

乌亮 wūliàng (形) glossy black; jet-black

乌七八糟 wūqībāzāo (形) in a horrible mess; at sixes and sevens

乌纱帽 wūshāmào (名)(symbol of) official post

乌鸦 wūyā (名) crow

乌烟(煙)瘴气(氣) wūyān-zhàngqì (名) foul atmosphere; pestilential atmosphere

乌有 wūyǒu (名)(书) nothing; naught: 化为～ vanish like soup bubbles; melt into thin air

呜(嗚) wū (象) toot; hooz; zoom: 汽笛～～地叫. The whistle kept hooting.

呜呼 wūhū I (叹) <书> alas; alack II (动) die: 一命～ breathe one's last

呜咽 wūyè (动) sob

钨(鎢) wū (名) tungsten; wolfram (W): ～丝 tungsten filament

屋 wū (名) 1 house 2 room: 外～ anteroom

屋子 wūzi (名) room

无(無) wú I (名) nothing; nil: 从～到有 start from scratch II (副) 1 not have; there is not; without: ～一定计划 have no definite plan 2 not: ～须多谈 need not go into details

无比 wúbǐ (形) incomparable; unparalleled; matchless: 英勇～

unrivalled in bravery. ～强大 incomparably powerful

无病呻吟 wú bìng shēnyín 1 sigh with grief over imaginary misfortune 2 (of literary works) superficially sentimental; mawkish emotion

无产(產)阶(階)级 wúchǎnjiējí (名) the proletariat

无常 wúcháng (形) variable; changeable: 反复～ capricious

无偿(償) wúcháng (形) free; gratis; gratuitous: ～经济援助 free economic aid

无耻 wúchǐ (形) shameless; brazen; impudent: ～谰言 shameless slander

无从(從) wúcóng have no way (of doing sth.); not be in a position (to do sth.): 心中千言万语，一时～说起. So many ideas crowded in upon my mind that for a moment I did not know how to begin.

无党(黨)派人士 wúdǎngpài rénshì (名) people without party affiliation; nonparty people

无敌(敵) wúdí (形) unmatched; invincible; unconquerable

无地自容 wú dì zì róng wish that one could disappear from the face of the earth; feel utterly ashamed

无动(動)于(於)衷 wú dòng yú zhōng remain indifferent or apathetic

无独(獨)有偶 wúdú-yǒu'ǒu another person or thing comparable in stupidity or notoriety

无度 wúdù (形) immoderate; excessive: 挥霍～ squander wantonly

无端 wúduān (副) for no reason: ～生气 flare up without provocation

无恶(惡)不作 wú è bù zuò stop at nothing in doing evil; be deeply steeped in iniquity

无法 wúfǎ (形) unable; incapable: ～应付 unable to cope with. ～分析 defy analysis

无法无天 wúfǎ-wútiān (动) defy laws human and divine; be neither God-fearing nor law-abiding; trample law underfoot without batting an eyelid

无妨 wúfāng there's no harm; may (or might) as well: 有意见～直说. Feel free to speak out if you have anything on your mind.

无非 wúfēi nothing but; no more than; simply; only: 他谈的～是些日常琐事. What he says is nothing but the trivial of everyday life.

无风(風)不起浪 wú fēng bù qǐ làng There is no smoke without fire

无辜 wúgū (形、名) 1 innocent 2 innocent persons

无关(關) wúguān have nothing to do with: 此事与他～. It has nothing to do with him. ～宏旨 not a matter of cardinal principle

无轨电(電)车(車) wúguǐ diànchē (名) trackless trolley; trolleybus

无稽 wújī (形) unfounded: ～之谈 unfounded rumour; sheer nonsense

无机(機) wújī (形) inorganic: ～肥料 inorganic fertilizer; mineral fertilizer. ～化学 inorganic chemistry

无几(幾) wújǐ very few; very little; hardly any

无济(濟)于(於)事 wú jì yú shì (动) be of no avail; won't help matters

无价(價)之宝(寶) wú jià zhī bǎo (名) priceless treasure

无精打采 wújīng-dǎcǎi listless; crestfallen; in low spirits

无可奈何 wúkě nàihé It can't be helped

无孔不入 wú kǒng bù rù (of persons) seek every opportunity (to do evil)

无愧 wúkuì have nothing to be ashamed of: 问心～have no guilty conscience

无赖 wúlài I (形) rascally; scoundrelly; blackguardly: 耍～ act shamelessly II (名) rascal

无理 wúlǐ (形) unreasonable; unjustifiable: ～取闹 kick up a row

无量 wúliàng (形)immeasurable; boundless: 前途～ a boundless future

无聊 wúliáo (形) 1 falling in a vacant mood; bored 2 boring and silly; vapid

无论(論) wúlùn (连) no matter what, how, etc.; regardless of: ～是谁都不许无故缺席. Nobody should be absent without cause, no matter who he is.

无论(論)如何 wúlùn rúhé (副) in any case; at any rate; whatever happens; at all events: ～,我们也得在今天做出决定. We've got to make a decision today, whatever happens.

无名 wúmíng (形) 1 unknown: ～英雄 unknown hero; unsung

hero 2 accidental

无奈 wúnài 1 cannot help but; have no alternative: 他出于～，只得辞职了事. He had no choice but to hand in his resignation. 2 but; however: 他本来想今天出去野餐的，～天不作美，下起雨来，只好作罢. He meant to go on a picnic today, but he had to call it off because of wet weather.

无能 wúnéng (形) incompetent; incapable: 软弱～ weak and incapable

无能为(爲)力 wú néng wéi lì powerless; impotent: 在这种情况下，他要帮忙也是～. He was in no position to help under such circumstances.

无期徒刑 wúqī túxíng (名) life imprisonment

无情 wúqíng (形)merciless; ruthless; inexorable

无穷(窮) wúqióng (形) infinite; endless; boundless inexhaustible: 言有尽而意～. The words may be limited but the message they convey is an inexhaustible source of inspiration.

无日 wúrì [often followed by "不","无日不…" is a double negative, meaning 'every day']: ～不在渴望祖国的现代化早日实现. We constantly look forward to the early realization of the country's modernization.

无伤(傷)大雅 wú shāng dàyǎ not affect matters of major principle

无上 wúshàng (形) supreme; paramount; highest: ～光荣 the highest honour

无神论(論) wúshénlùn (名) atheism

无声(聲)无臭 wúshēng-wúxiù (形) unknown; obscure

无时(時)无刻 wúshí-wúkè (副) all the time; incessantly: 地球～不在运转. The earth is in contant motion.

无事生非 wú shì shēng fēi make so much ado about nothing

无视 wúshì (动) ignore; disregard; defy: ～国家的法律 defy the laws of the country

无数(數) wúshù (形) 1 innumerable; countless: ～次 for the umpteenth time 2 feel uncertain

无双(雙) wúshuāng (形) peerless; unrivalled: 盖世～ peerless in this human world

无私 wúsī (形) unselfish: ～的援助 disinterested assistance

无所事事 wú suǒ shì shì be at a loose end; fool about; idle away one's time

无所适(適)从(從) wú suǒ shì cóng not know how to behave; be at a loss what to do

无条(條)件 wútiáojiàn unconditional; without preconditions: ～投降 unconditional surrender

无微不至 wú wēi bù zhì (of cares, concern) meticulous; in every possible way: ～的关怀 solicitous care

无味 wúwèi (形) 1 tasteless; unpalatable 2 dull; uninteresting: 枯燥～ dry like saw-dust

无畏 wúwèi (形) fearless; dauntless

无谓 wúwèi (形) meaningless; pointless; senseless: ～的争吵 a futile quarrel

无…无… wu…wu… [used before two parallel words, similar or identical in meaning to emphasize negation]: 无穷无尽 inexhaustible; endless. 无忧无虑 carefree

无所谓 wúsuǒwèi 1 cannot be taken as: 会谈取得了一些进展，但～什么突破. Some progress has been made in the talks, but it cannot be regarded as a breakthrough. 2 not matter: 他去不去～. It makes no difference whether he is going or not.

无暇 wúxiá (动) have no time; be too busy: ～兼顾 have no time to attend to other things

无限 wúxiàn (形) infinite; limitless; boundless; immeasurable: ～光明的未来 a future of infinite brightness; infinitely bright prospects

无线(綫) wúxiàn (形) wireless: ～电话 radiophone. ～电报 wireless telegram; radiotelegram

无线(綫)电(電) wúxiàndiàn (名) radio: ～通讯 radio communication. ～传真 radiofacsimile

无效 wúxiào (形) of (or to) no avail; invalid; null and void: 宣布合同～ declare a contract invalid (or null and void)

无懈可击(擊) wú xiè kě jī (形) unassailable; invulnerable: 他的论点是～的. His argument is unassailable.

无心 wúxīn 1 not be in the mood for: 他心里有事，～去看电影. He was not in a mood to go to the movies. 2 not intentionally; unwittingly; inadvertently: 他～伤

害你的感情. He did not mean to hurt your feelings.
无形 wúxíng 1 invisible: ～的枷锁 invisible shackles 2 imperceptibly; virtually
无须 wúxū need not; not have to: ～操心 need not worry
无烟煤 wúyānméi (名) anthracite
无恙 wúyàng (形) <书> in good health; well; safe: 安然～ safe and sound
无疑 wúyí (副) beyond doubt; undoubtedly
无意 wúyì (动) 1 have no intention (of doing sth.); not be inclined to: 他既然～参加,你就不必勉强他了. There is no point in pressing him to join since he has no inclination to do so. 2 inadvertently; accidentally: 对这件事他～中露了一句. He dropped a remark about it inadvertently.
无意识(識) wúyìshí (形) unconscious: ～的动作 an unconscious act (or movement)
无垠 wúyín (形) boundless; vast: 一望～ boundless beyond the horizon
无与(與)伦(倫)比 wú yǔ lúnbǐ (形) incomparable; unparalleled; unique; without equal
无缘无故 wúyuán-wúgù without rhyme or reason; for no reason at all
无政府主义(義) wúzhèngfǔzhǔyì (名) anarchism
无知 wúzhī (形) ignorant: 出于～ out of ignorance
无中生有 wú zhōng shēng yǒu (形) out of this air; purely fictitious; fabricated
无足轻(輕)重 wú zú qīng-zhòng (形) of little importance (or consequence); insignificant
无阻 wúzǔ without let or hindrance

芜(蕪) wú I (形) <书> 1 overgrown with weeds: 荒～ lie waste 2 mixed and disorderly II (名) grassland: 平～ open grassland
芜杂(雜) wúzá (形) mixed and disorderly

吾 wú (代) <书> I or we: ～辈 we. ～国 my or our country

毋 wú (副) <书> no; not: ～妄言. Don't talk nonsense.
毋宁(寧) wúnìng (副) rather ... (than); (not so much ...) as
毋庸 wúyōng (动) need not: ～讳言 no need for reticence; frankly speaking

武 wǔ (形) 1 military 2 connected with martial arts 3 valiant
武打 wǔdǎ (名) acrobatic fighting in Chinese opera or film
武断(斷) wǔduàn (名) arbitrary decision; subjective verdict
武官 wǔguān (名) 1 military officer 2 military attaché: 海(空)军～ naval (air) attaché
武力 wǔlì (名) 1 force 2 military force; armed strength; force of arms: 诉诸～ resort to force
武器 wǔqì (名) weapon; arms: 常规～ conventional weapons. 核～ nuclear weapons
武术(術) wǔshù (名) *wushu*, martial arts
武装(裝) wǔzhuāng I (名) 1 arms; military equipment; battle outfit: 全副～ (in)full battle gear; armed to the teeth 2 armed forces: 人民～ the armed forces of the people II (动) equip (or supply) with arms; arm: ～到牙齿 be armed to the teeth. ～部队 armed forces. ～冲突 armed clash. ～干涉 armed intervention. ～起义 armed uprising

妩(嫵) wǔ
妩媚 wǔmèi (形) lovely; charming

五 wǔ I (数) five: ～十 fifty. ～倍 fivefold; quintuple. ～分之一 one fifth. ～十年代 the fifties
五彩 wǔcǎi I (名) the five colours (blue, yellow, red, white and black) II (形) multicoloured: ～缤纷 colourful; a riot of colour
五谷(穀) wǔgǔ (名) 1 the five cereals (rice, two kinds of millet, wheat and beans) 2 food crops: ～丰登 an abundant harvest of grain
五官 wǔguān (名) 1 the five sense organs (ears, eyes, lips, nose and tongue) 2 facial features: ～端正 have regular features
五光十色 wǔguāng-shísè (形) 1 multicoloured; bright with all kinds of clours 2 of great variety; of all kinds; multifarious
五湖四海 wǔhú-sìhǎi (名) all corners of the land
五花八门(門) wǔhuā-bāmén (形) variegated; kaleidoscopic

五讲(講)四美 wǔ jiǎng sì měi (名) the campaign of five "efforts" (of improving politeness, civilization, order, hygiene and morality) and four "beauties" (of mind, language, behaviour and environment)
五金 wǔjīn (名) 1 the five metals (gold, silver, copper, iron and tin) 2 metals; hardware: ～店 hardware store
五体(體)投地 wǔ tǐ tóu dì have nothing but the greatest admiration for sb.
五味 wǔwèi (名) 1 the five flavours (sweet, sour, bitter, pungent and salty) 2 all sorts of flavours
五星红旗 wǔxīng hóngqí (名) the Five-Starred Red Flag (the national flag of the People's Republic of China)
五言诗 wǔyánshī (名) a poem with five characters to a line ref. see 古体诗 gǔtǐshī
五一 wǔyī (名) May Day: ～国际劳动节 International Labour Day; May Day
五月 wǔyuè (名) 1 May 2 the fifth month of the lunar year; the fifth moon: ～节 the Dragon Boat Festival (the 5th day of the 5th lunar month)
五岳(嶽) wǔyuè (名) the Five Mountains, namely, Taishan Mountain (泰山) in Shandong, Hengshan Mountain (衡山) in Hunan, Huashan Mountain (华山) in Shaanxi, Hengshan Mountain (恒山) in Shanxi and Songshan Mountain (嵩山) in Henan
五脏(臟) wǔzàng (名) the five internal organs (heart, liver, spleen, lungs and kidneys)

伍 wǔ I (数) five [used for the numeral 五 on cheques, banknotes, etc. to avoid mistakes or alterations] II (名) 1 army; ranks: 入～ join the army 2 company: 羞与为～ feel ashamed of sb.'s company

捂 wǔ (动) seal; cover; muffle: ～鼻子 cover one's nose (with one's hand). ～盖子 keep the lid on; cover up the truth

午 wǔ (名) noon; midday
午饭(飯) wǔfàn (名) midday meal; lunch
午时(時) wǔshí (名) the period of the day from 11 a.m. to 1 p.m.
午睡 wǔshuì (名) 1 afternoon nap 2 take (or have) a nap after lunch
午夜 wǔyè (名) midnight

舞 wǔ (动) 1 dance: 集体～ group dance 2 move about as in a dance: 手～足蹈 jump for joy 3 dance with sth. in one's hands: ～剑 perform a sword-dance 4 flourish; wield; brandish: 挥～大棒 brandish the big stick
舞弊 wǔbì (名) fraudulent practices; malpractices
舞蹈 wǔdǎo (名) dance: ～动作 dance movement. ～家 dancer
舞剧(劇) wǔjù (名) dance drama; ballet
舞弄 wǔnòng (动) wave; wield; brandish: ～刀枪 brandish swords and spears
舞台(臺) wǔtái (名) stage; arena: 在国际～上 in the international arena. ～监督 stage director. ～设计 stage design
舞文弄墨 wǔwén-nòngmò (动) indulge in rhetorical flourishes; twist legal phraseology for dishonest purposes; pettifogging

侮 wǔ (名、动) insult; bully: 外～ foreign aggression
侮辱 wǔrǔ (动) insult; humiliate; subject sb. to indignities

误 wù I (名) 1 mistake; error: ～解 misunderstanding. 笔～ a slip of the pen 2 miss: ～了回家的最后一趟公共汽车 miss the last bus home 3 harm: ～人子弟 fail to give proper guidance to, or exercise a harmful influence on the younger generation II (副) unintentionally; by accident: ～伤 accidentally hurt sb.; give unintentional offence to sb.
误差 wùchā (名) error: 平均～ mean error; average error
误点(點) wùdiǎn (形) late; overdue; behind schedule: 火车～十分钟. The train was ten minutes late (or behind schedule).
误会(會) wùhuì I (动) misunderstand; mistake; misconstrue: 你～了我的意思. You misunderstand me. II (名) misunderstanding: 消除～ dispel (or remove) misunderstanding
误解 wùjiě I (动) misread; misunderstand II (名) misunderstanding

恶(惡) wù (动) loathe; dislike; hate: 好逸～劳

dislike work and love ease and comfort. 可～ loathsome; abominable

see also ě; è

悟 wù (动) realize; awaken: 执迷不～ persist in one's erroneous course

悟性 wùxìng (名) power of understanding; comprehension

晤 wù (动) meet; interview; see: 会～ meet with. ～谈 meet and talk; have a talk; interview

务(務) wù I (名) affair; business: 外～ foreign affairs. 公～ official business. 任～ task; job II (动) be engaged in; devote one's efforts to: ～农 go in for agriculture. 不～正业 neglect one's proper duties

务必 wùbì (动) must; be sure to: ～将书交还图书馆. Please return the books to the library without fail.

雾(霧) wù (名) 1 fog: 薄～ mist 2 fine spray: 喷～器 sprayer; inhaler

雾气(氣) wùqì (名) fog; mist; vapour

勿 wù (副) [indicating prohibition]: 请～入内. No admittance. 请～吸烟 no smoking

物 wù (名) 1 thing; matter: 废～ waste matter. 公～ public property. 地大～博 vast in territory and rich in resources 2 the outside world; other people: 待人接～ one's conduct in social intercourse 3 content; substance: 空洞无～ totally void of substance

物产(產) wùchǎn (名) products; produce

物换星移 wùhuàn-xīngyí (名) change of the seasons

物极(極)必反 wù jí bì fǎn things will develop in the opposite direction when they reach the limit

物价(價) wùjià (名) (commodity) price: ～波动 price fluctuation. ～指数 price index

物件 wùjiàn (名) thing; article

物理 wùlǐ (名) 1 innate laws of things 2 physics

物理学(學) wùlǐxué (名) physics

物力 wùlì (名) material resources

物品 wùpǐn (名) article; goods: 贵重～ valuables. 个人～ personal effects

物色 wùsè (动) look for; select: ～人才 look for qualified personnel

物以类(類)聚 wù yǐ lèi jù birds of a feather flock together

物议(議) wùyì (名) public criticism or censure

物证(證) wùzhèng (名) material evidence

物质(質) wùzhì (名) matter; substance; material: ～生活 material life. ～刺激 material incentive

物资 wùzī (名) goods and materials: ～交流 interflow of commodities

坞(塢) wù (名) a depressed place: 船～ dock. 花～ sunken flower-bed

骛 wù go after; seek for: 好高～远 set too high a demand on oneself; set one's sights too high

X x

曦 xī (名) ‹书› sunlight [usu. referring to that in early morning]: 晨～ early morning sunlight

熹 xī (名) ‹书› break of day

熹微 xīwēi (形) ‹书› [usu. of morning sunlight] faint, feeble: 晨光～ The light is faint at dawn.

嘻 xī I (叹) a cry of surprise II (象) [sound of laughter]: ～～地笑 giggle

嬉 xī (名、动) play; sport

嬉皮笑脸 xīpí-xiàoliǎn give a merry roguish laugh; laugh roguishly and play the fool; be frivolous

嬉戏(戲) xīxì (动) play; sport

昔 xī (名) former times; the past: ～日 in former times

惜 xī (动) 1 cherish; treasure: 珍～ cherish; treasure 2 spare; stint; grudge: 不～代价 at any cost. 可～! It is a pity! 3 have pity on sb.

惜别 xībié (动) feel reluctant to part

熙 xī

熙熙攘攘 xīxīrǎngrǎng bustling with life; be a beehive of activity

析 xī (动) 1 divide; separate: 分崩离～ fall to pieces; come apart 2 analyse; dissect: 剖～ analyse; dissect

析出 xīchū (动) separate out

晰 xī (形) clear; distinct: 明～ clear; lucid. 清～ distinct

西 xī (名) west

西半球 xībànqiú (名) the Western Hemisphere

西餐 xīcān (名) Western-style food; European food

西方 xīfāng (名) 1 the west 2 the West; the Occident: ～世界 the Western world

西服 xīfú (名) Western-style clothes (also as 西装)

西瓜 xīguā (名) watermelon

西红柿 xīhóngshì (名) tomato

西天 xītiān (名) <佛教> Western Paradise

西洋 Xīyáng (名) the West; the Western world

西药(藥) xīyào (名) Western medicine

西医(醫) xīyī (名) 1 Western medicine 2 a doctor trained in Western medicine

西藏 xīzàng (名) Xizang (Tibet)

牺(犧) xī

牺牲 xīshēng I (名) sacrifice II (动) lay down one's life: 英勇～ meet one's death like a hero

锡 xī (名) tin (Sn)

吸 xī (动) 1 inhale; breathe in: 深深～一口气 take a deep breath. ～了一口烟 take a puff at one's cigarettes 2 absorb: 宣纸～水性强. Rice paper is absorbent. 3 attract; draw to oneself

吸尘(塵)器 xīchénqì (名) vacuum cleaner

吸毒 xīdú (动) take drugs: ～者 drug addict

吸附 xīfù (名) absorption

吸力 xīlì (名) suction; attraction: 地心～ force of gravity

吸墨纸 xīmòzhǐ (名) blotting paper

吸取 xīqǔ (动) draw; assimilate: ～教训 learn (draw) a lesson

吸收 xīshōu (动) 1 absorb; assimilate; imbibe: ～营养 absorb nourishment 2 recruit; enrol; admit: ～入党 admit into the Party

吸铁(鐵)石 xītiěshí (名) magnet

吸血鬼 xīxuèguǐ (名) bloodsucker; vampire

吸烟 xīyān (动) smoke

吸引 xīyǐn (动) attract; draw; fascinate: ～注意力 attract attention. 大自然的美把我们～住了. We were fascinated by the beauty of nature.

奚 xī

奚落 xīluò (动) make gibes about; taunt

溪 xī (名) small stream; brook

希 xī I (动) hope: ～准时出席 Be sure to turn up on time. II (形) rare; uncommon

希罕 xīhan I (形) rare; uncommon: ～的动物 a rare animal II(动) value as a rarity; cherish: 我才不～他的帮助呢. I couldn't care for his offer of help. III (名)rare thing; rarity

希奇 xīqí (形) rare; curious: 这种事并不～. This is no rare occurrence. *or* There is nothing strange about it.

希望 xīwàng (动、名) hope; wish; expect: 他～当个医生. He hopes to become a doctor. 对于年青一代我们寄予很大的～. We repose high hopes in the younger generation.

稀 xī (形) 1 scarce; uncommon: 物以～为贵. Things become precious when they are scarce. 2 sparse; scattered: 地广人～ vast in area but sparsely populated 3 watery; thin: ～饭 porridge; gruel

稀薄 xībó (形) thin; rare: 空气～. The air is thin.

稀客 xīkè (名) rare visitor

稀烂(爛) xīlàn (形) completely smashed; smashed to pieces: 花瓶被打得～. The vase is smashed to smithereens.

稀里糊涂 xīlihútu (形) muddle-headed

稀少 xīshǎo (形) few; rare; scarce

稀释(釋) xīshì (动) dilute

稀疏 xīshū (形) sparse; thin: 头发～ thin hair. 山区村落～. The villages are straggling in the mountainous area. 林木～. The woods are sparse.

悉 xī (动) know; learn: 熟～ be well acquainted with

息 xī I (名) 1 breath: 屏～ hold one's breath 2 news: 信～ news about sb. or sth.; information 3 interest: 利～ interest. 无～贷款 interest-free loan 4 rest: 安～ sleep. 作～时间表 timetable; programme II (动) stop; cease: 请～怒. Don't get excited. 经久不～的掌声 prolonged applause. 暴风雨已经平～. The storm has subsided.

息事宁(寧)人 xīshì-níngrén (动) let the matter rest so as to annoy nobody

息息相关(關) xīxī xiāng guān (动) be closely linked; be closely bound up

熄 xī (动) put out; extinguish: ～灯 lights-out

熄灭(滅) xīmiè (动) (of fire) go out; die out

夕 xī (名) sunset; evening: 除～ New Year's Eve. 命在旦～ on one's last legs

夕阳(陽) xīyáng (名) the setting sun

夕照 xīzhào (名) the glow of the setting sun

膝 xī (名) knee

膝盖(蓋) xīgài (名) knee

犀 xī (名) rhinoceros: ～牛 rhinoceros

犀利 xīlì (形) sharp; incisive: 文笔～ wield a trenchant pen

席 xí I (名) 1 mat 2 seat; place: 入～ take one's seat. 来宾～ seats for visitors. 在议会中取得三～ win three seats in Parliament 3 feast; banquet: 酒～ banquet II (量): 一～酒 a banquet. 一～话 a talk (with sb.); a conversation

席卷(捲) xíjuǎn (动) sweep across; engulf: 暴风雪～大草原. A blizzard swept across the vast grasslands.

席位 xíwèi (名) seat (at a conference, in a legislative assembly, etc.)

袭(襲) xí (动) raid: 偷～ spring a surprise attack. 抄～ plagiarize. 寒气～人 There is a nip in the air.

袭击(擊) xíjī (动) attack; raid: 这一带经常受到台风的～. This area is often hit by typhoons.

袭用 xíyòng (动) take over (something that has long been used in the past)

媳 xí (名) daughter-in-law

媳妇(婦) xífù (名) 1 son's wife; daughter-in-law 2 wife

习(習) xí I (动) 1 practise; exercise; review: 练～ practise. 复～ review (one's lessons). 实～ do field work. 实～医生 intern 2 be used to: 不～水性 be not good at swimming II (名) habit; custom; usual practice

习惯 xíguàn I (动) get used (or accustomed) to: 过几天你就会～这儿了. You'll get used to the place in a few days. II (名) habit; custom: 旧～ outmoded customs. ～成自然. Habit grows on a person as second nature. ～势力 force of habit

习气(氣) xíqì (名) custom; practice; 官僚～ bureaucratic practice

习染 xírǎn (动) contract (disease); be addicted to

习俗 xísú (名) custom; convention

习题 xítí (名) exercises (in school work)

习性 xíxìng (名) habits and acquired characteristics

习语 xíyǔ (名) idiom

习作 xízuò (名) an exercise in composition, drawing, etc.

喜 xǐ I (形) happy; pleased: 大～ highly pleased II (动) like; be fond of: ～新厌旧 be fickle in one's affections III (名) 1 happiness; happy event: 大～的日子 a day of great joy. 双～临门 be blessed with double happiness 2 pregnancy: 有～了. be expecting a baby

喜爱(愛) xǐ'ài (动) like; be fond of

喜出望外 xǐ chū wàng wài be overjoyed at the unexpectedly good news; be pleasantly surprised

喜好 xǐhào (动) be fond of; be keen on: 他从小就～绘画. He has been fond of painting ever since his childhood.

喜欢(歡) xǐhuan I (动) like; love; be fond of II (形) happy; delighted

喜剧(劇) xǐjù (名) comedy

喜怒无(無)常 xǐ-nù wú cháng (形) moody

喜气(氣)洋洋 xǐqì yángyáng (形) in a happy mood

喜鹊 xǐquè (名) magpie

喜闻乐(樂)见 xǐwén-lèjiàn (动)

love to see and hear; be enjoyed by
喜笑颜开(開) xǐxiào-yánkāi (动) (of one's face) light up with pleasure; brighten up
喜形于色 xǐ xíng yú sè (动) be apparently overwhelmed with joy; beam with pleasure
喜讯 xǐxùn (名) happy news; good news
喜洋洋 xǐyángyáng (形) full of joy; jubilant
喜悦 xǐyuè (形) happy; joyous: 怀着无限～的心情 cherish a feeling of indescribable joy
洗 xǐ (名) 1 wash: ～衣服 wash clothes. 干～ dry-cleaning. ～衣粉 detergent. ～澡 take a bath; swim 2 kill and loot; sack: 血～ plunge (the inhabitants) in a bloodbath; massacre
洗尘(塵) xǐchén (动) give a dinner in honour of a visitor from afar
洗涤 xǐdí (动) wash; cleanse
洗耳恭听(聽) xǐ ěr gōng tīng listen with respectful attention
洗发(髮)剂(劑) xǐfàjì (名) shampoo
洗劫 xǐjié (动) loot; sack
洗礼(禮) xǐlǐ (名) baptism
洗牌 xǐpái (动) shuffle (card, etc.)
洗染店 xǐrǎndiàn (名) laundering and dyeing shop
洗手 xǐshǒu (动) 1 wash one's hands 2 set to have nothing to do with: ～不干 wash one's hands of sth.
洗刷 xǐshuā (动) 1 wash and brush; scrub 2 wash off
洗心革面 xǐxīn-gémiàn thoroughly reform oneself; turn over a new leaf
洗雪 xǐxuě (动) wipe out (a disgrace); redress (a wrong)
洗照片 xǐzàopiān (动) develop (a negative)
铣 xǐ (动) mill
玺(璽) xǐ (名) imperial or royal seal
隙 xì (名) 1 crack; chink: 墙～ a crack in the wall 2 loophole; chance: 无～可乘 leave or find no loophole that one could take advantage of
系 xì I (名) 1 system; series: 语～ (language) family. 太阳～ the solar system. 母～ matriarchy. 派～ faction 2 department (in a college); faculty II (动) 1 fasten; tie: ～鞋带 tie (one's) shoe lace 2 be 〈书〉 纯～揣测之事 be purely a matter of conjecture 3 relate to: 成败所～ something on which success or failure hinges
系列 xìliè (名) set; series: 一～的问题 a series of problems
系统 xìtǒng (名) system: 灌溉～ irrigation system. 卫生～ public health organizations. 作～的研究 make a systematic study. ～性 systematicness
戏(戲) xì I (名) play; show: 京～ Beijing opera. 马～ circus show. 看～ go to the theatre; watch a play II (动) play: ～水 play with water III (副) for fun: ～言 say sth. for fun
戏法 xìfǎ (名) conjuring; magic; trick: 变～ conjure; juggle; perform tricks
戏剧(劇) xìjù (名) drama; play
戏弄 xìnòng (动) make fun of; play tricks on
戏曲 xìqǔ (名) traditional opera
戏院 xìyuàn (名) theatre
细 xì (形) 1 thin; slender 2 fine: ～沙 fine sand 3 fine; delicate: ～瓷 fine porcelain. 作工真～! What fine craftsmanship! 4 careful; meticulous; detailed: ～看 examine; scrutinize. ～问 make inquiries; ask about detailed information; interrogate 5 minute; trifling: ～节 minute details
细胞 xìbāo (名) cell
细节(節) xìjié (名) details; particulars
细菌 xìjūn (名) germs; bacteria
细密 xìmì (形) fine and closely woven
细腻 xìnì (形) 1 fine and smooth 2 exquisite; minute: ～的描写 a minute description
细软 xìruǎn (名) jewelry, expensive clothing and other valuables
细水长流 xìshuǐ cháng liú 1 economize on either human labour or natural resources to avoid running short 2 make a moderate but constant effort
细微 xìwēi (形) slight; fine; subtle: ～的区别 subtle difference
细小 xìxiǎo (形) tiny; fine; trivial: ～的事情 trivialities
细心 xìxīn (形) careful; attentive

细则 xìzé (名) detailed rules and regulations
细致 xìzhì (形) careful; meticulous: ~的安排 meticulous arrangement

瞎 xiā I (形) blind: ~了左眼 blind in the left eye II (副) groundlessly: ~说 talk irresponsibly; speak groundlessly; talk nonsense. ~猜 make a wild guess. ~忙 work hard for nothing. ~闹 behave foolishly
瞎扯 xiāchě (动) talk irresponsibly; talk rubbish
瞎话 xiāhuà (名) lie: 说~ tell a lie; lie
瞎子 xiāzi (名) a blind person

虾(蝦) xiā (名) shrimp: 对~ prawn. 龙~ lobster. ~米 dried, shelled shrimps

呷 xiā (动) sip: ~一口茶 take a sip of tea

峡 xiá (名) gorge: ~谷 gorge; canyon. 海~ strait

侠 xiá
侠客 xiákè (名) (in old times) a chivalrous person
侠义(義) xiáyì (形) chivalrous: ~行为 chivalrous conduct

狭 xiá (形) narrow
狭隘 xiá'ài (形) narrow: 山路崎岖~. The mountain path is rugged and narrow. 心胸~ narrow-minded
狭路相逢 xiálù xiāng féng (of adversaries) happen to meet on a narrow path; when two enemies meet, neither will yield
狭小 xiáxiǎo (形) narrow and small: 气量~ be narrow-minded
狭义(義) xiáyì (名) narrow sense
狭窄 xiázhǎi (形) 1 narrow; cramped: ~的楼梯 narrow staircase 2 narrow and limited: 心地~ be narrow-minded

辖 xiá (动) govern: ~区 region under the jurisdiction of the Central Government

遐 xiá (形) <书> far; distant
遐迩(邇) xiá'ěr (形) <书> far and near: 名闻~ one's reputation spread far and wide.

霞 xiá (名) morning or evening glow: 晚~ sunset clouds. 彩~ rosy clouds

瑕 xiá (名) flaw; defect
瑕疵 xiácī (名) flaw; blemish

暇 xiá (名) free time; leisure: 无~兼顾 have no time to attend to other matters

下 xià I (副) down; under; below: 楼~ downstairs. 桌~ under the table. 井~ at the bottom of a well. 地~宫殿 underground palace. 零~三度 three degrees below zero. 在他领导~ under his guidance II (形) 1 lower; inferior: ~级 lower rank; inferior. ~等 low grade 2 next: ~次 next time III (动) 1 descend; get off: ~楼 go downstairs. ~车 get off a bus. ~馆子 eat or dine out in a restaurant 2 fall: ~雨了. It's raining. 3 issue: ~命令 issue orders. ~通知 give notices. 4 put in: ~饺子 put dumplings in (boiling water). ~面条 cook noodles 5 form (an idea, opinion, etc.): ~决心 make up one's mind. ~结论 draw a conclusion. ~定义 give a definition 6 finish work: ~班 go off duty; knock off. ~课了. Class is over. 7 give birth to; lay: ~蛋 lay eggs. ~了四只小猫 give birth to four kittens 8 take off; dismantle: 把门~下来 take the door off. ~货 unload 9 put into use: ~笔 start writing. ~手 take action IV (量) [used of action]: 突然亮了一~. There was a sudden flash.

下 xia [used after a verb as a complement] 1 [indicating movement from a higher place to a lower one]: 放~ put (sth.) down. 躺~ lie down 2 [indicating removal of sth. away from a position]: 脱~大衣 take off one's coat. 把那画拿~来 take that picture down 3 [used to indicate that there is enough space for sth.]: 这剧院坐得~ 2,000人. This theatre can seat 2,000 people. 碗太小装不~这汤. The bowl is too small for the soup. 4 [indicating the completion or result of an action]: 把它写~来. write it down. 把这乐曲录~来. have the music recorded. 打~基础 lay a foundation
下巴 xiàba (名) chin
下班 xiàbān (动) come off work; knock off
下辈 xiàbèi (名) 1 future generations; offspring 2 the younger generation of a family
下边(邊) xiàbian 同"下面"
下策 xiàcè (名) very unwise

move

下层(層) xiàcéng (名) lower levels; grassroots

下场(場) xiàchang (名) end: 遭到可耻～ come to a disgraceful end. 不会有好～ come to no good end

下地 xiàdì (动) 1 go to the fields 2 leave a sickbed; be up and about again

下毒手 xià dúshǒu (动) lay murderous hands on sb.; deal a deadly blow: 背后～ stab sb. in the back

下颚 xià'è (名) the lower jaw

下饭 xiàfàn (动) (of dishes) go with rice: 今天有什么菜～哇? What do we have to go with rice today?

下凡 xiàfán (动) (of gods or immortals) descend to the mortal world

下工夫 xià gōngfu (动) make painstaking effort

下跪 xiàguì (动) go down on one's knees

下怀(懷) xiàhuái (名) one's cherished wish: 正中～. That's exactly what I have in mind.

下贱(賤) xiàjiàn (形) low; degrading

下降 xiàjiàng (动) drop; fall; decline

下来(來) xiàlái (动) come down

下来(來) xiàlai [used after a verb as a complement] 1 [indicating movement from a higher position to a lower one]: 眼泪顺着她脸颊流～. Tears streamed down her cheeks. 苹果掉～了. An apple has dropped. 他的体温降～了. His temperature has come down. 2 [indicating moving something away from a position]: 把牌子取～! Take off that plaque! 3 [indicating completion or result of an action]: 在这儿停～. Stop here. 她终于平静～了. She calmed down at last. 4 [indicating the continuation of an action]: 坚持～! Keep it up! 这个故事一代代流传～. This legend has been handed down from generation to generation.

下列 xiàliè (名) following; listed below

下令 xiàlìng (动) give orders; order

下流 xiàliú (形) obscene; dirty: ～话 dirty words. ～的勾当 degrading behaviour

下落 xiàluò I (名) whereabouts: 打听某人的～ inquire about sb.'s whereabouts II (动) drop; fall

下马(馬)威 xiàmǎwēi (名) initial severity shown by a new official meant to establish his authority, also used figuratively

下面 xiàmian I (副) below; under; underneath: 大桥～ under the bridge. 地毯～ underneath the carpet II (形) next; following: ～只是几个例子. The following are but a few instances. III (名) lower level; subordinate: 得到～的支持 win support from the grassroots.

下坡路 xiàpōlù (名) downhill path; decline: 走～ go downhill; be on the decline

下铺 xiàpù (名) lower berth

下棋 xiàqí (动) play chess

下情 xiàqíng (名) conditions at the lower levels; opinion of the masses

下去 xiàqù (动) 1 go down; descend 2 go on; continue: 他这样～将一事无成. If he goes on like this, he will accomplish nothing.

下去 xiàqu [used after a verb as a complement] 1 [used to indicate movement from a higher position to a lower one]: 洪水退～了. The flood has receded. 2 [used to indicate moving sth. or sb. away from somewhere]: 把犯人带～. take the prisoner away. 3 [used to indicate the continuation of an action]: 不能再忍受～ can tolerate it no longer.

下手 xiàshǒu I (动) start; set about: 不知从哪儿～ not know how to proceed II (名) assistant or subordinate

下属(屬) xiàshǔ (名) subordinate

下水 xiàshuǐ (动) 1 enter the water; be launched: 又一艘新船～了. Another new ship has been launched. 2 fall into evil ways: 给拖～了 be drawn into a gang of evil-doers

下水道 xiàshuǐdào (名) sewer; drainage

下榻 xiàtà (动) stay (at a place during a trip): 贵宾～的旅馆 the hotel where distinguished guests are staying

下台 xiàtái (动) 1 step down from the stage 2 fall from grace; leave office 3 get out of an awkward position

下文 xiàwén (名) **1** the sentence, paragraph or chapter that follows **2** further development; follow-up: 那事还没有～呢, I haven't heard about any further development of that matter.

下午 xiàwǔ (名) afternoon

下旬 xiàxún (名) the last ten-day period of a month

下野 xiàyě (动) (of high officials) be compelled to resign

下意识 xiàyìshí (名) subconsciousness

下游 xiàyóu (名) **1** (of a river) lower reaches **2** backward position

下肢 xiàzhī (名) lower limbs; legs

下种(種) xiàzhǒng (动) sow

吓(嚇) xià (动) frighten; scare; intimidate: ～坏了 be horrified

吓唬 xiàhu (动) frighten

夏 xià (名) summer

夏季 xiàjì (名) summer

夏令营(營) xiàlìngyíng (名) summer camp

夏天 xiàtiān (名) summer

仙 xiān (名) celestial being; immortal

仙境 xiānjìng (名) fairyland

仙女 xiānnǚ (名) female immortal (famed for youth and beauty); female celestial

仙人 xiānrén (名) celestial being; immortal

先 xiān (形) **1** earlier; before; first; in advance: ～来～吃. First come, first served. 有言在～ make clear beforehand. 让他～说. Let him speak first. ～电话联系 contact sb. by telephone first **2** elder generation; ancestor: 祖～ ancestor; forefather

先辈 xiānbèi (名) elder generation

先导(導) xiāndǎo (名) guide; forerunner

先发(發)制人 xiān fā zhì rén gain the initiative by striking first

先锋 xiānfēng (名) vanguard

先后(後) xiān-hòu I (名) priority; order: 这些项目都该分个～. These items should be taken up in order of priority. II (副) successively; one after another: 代表们～在会上发了言. The delegates spoke at the meeting one after another.

先见之明 xiān jiàn zhī míng (名) foresight

先进(進) xiānjìn (形) advanced

先决 xiānjué (名) prerequisite: ～条件 precondition

先例 xiānlì (名) precedent: 开了～ set a precedent

先烈 xiānliè (名) martyr

先前 xiānqián (副) before; previously: 他～不是这样. He wasn't like this before.

先遣 xiānqiǎn (动) (units) sent in advance: ～队 advance party

先驱(驅) xiānqū (名) pioneer; forerunner

先人 xiānrén (名) ancestor; forefather

先声(聲)夺(奪)人 xiānshēng duó rén overawe one's opponent by a show of strength

先生 xiānsheng (名) **1** teacher **2** mister (Mr.); gentleman; sir: 总统～ Mr. President. 女士们, ～们 ladies and gentlemen

先天 xiāntiān (形) congenital; innate

先头(頭) xiāntóu (副) ahead; in front; in advance

先行 xiānxíng (动) go ahead of the rest: ～者 forerunner

先斩后(後)奏 xiān zhǎn hòu zòu take decisive action without asking for approval and only report it later as a fait accompli; act first, report later

先兆 xiānzhào (名) omen

鲜 xiān I (形) **1** fresh: ～花 fresh flower. 新～空气 fresh air. **2** bright-coloured; bright: 这条头巾颜色太～. This scarf is too gaudy **3** delicious; tasty: 菜的味道真～! This dish is absolutely delicious! II delicacy: 海～ seafood

鲜红 xiānhóng (形) bright red; scarlet

鲜美 xiānměi (形) delicious; tasty

鲜明 xiānmíng (形) **1** (of colour) bright: 色彩～ in bright colours **2** clear-cut; distinct: ～的对比 a striking (or sharp) contrast. ～的立场 a clear-cut stand

鲜艳(艶) xiānyàn (形) bright-coloured: 颜色～ in gay colours. ～夺目 of dazzling beauty

掀 xiān (动) lift (a cover, etc.)

掀起 xiānqǐ (动) **1** surge: 大海里～起了巨浪. Big waves surged on the sea. **2** (of movement) set off; start: ～建设高潮 start an upsurge of construction

锨 xiān (名) shovel

纤(纖) xiān I (形) fine; minute II (名) fibre: 光～ glass fibre

纤弱 xiānruò (形) slim and fragile; delicate

纤维 xiānwéi (名) fibre: 人造～ synthetic fibre

纤细 xiānxì (形) slender; fine

涎 xián (名) saliva

舷 xián (名) the side of a ship; board: 左～ port. 右～ starboard

弦 xián (名) bowstring; string: ～乐器 stringed instrument

闲(閒) xián I (形) idle; unoccupied: ～不住 be unaccustomed to staying idle II (名) spare time; leisure

闲工夫 xiángōngfu (名) spare time; leisure

闲逛 xiánguàng (动) saunter; stroll

闲话 xiánhuà (名) 1 idle chat 2 complaint; gossip

闲空 xiánkòng free time; leisure

闲聊 xiánliáo (名) chat; chitchat

闲情逸致 xiánqíng-yìzhì a leisurely and carefree mood

闲人 xiánrén (名) 1 person left idle; loafer 2 persons not concerned: ～免进. No admittance except on business.

闲谈 xiántán (名) chat; engage in casual conversation

闲暇 xiánxiá (名) leisure

闲置 xiánzhì (动) lie idle: 有些机器仍然～着. Some machines lie idle.

闲事 xiánshì (名) other people's business: 别管～! Mind your own business!

娴 xián (形) refined; skilled

娴静 xiánjìng (形) gentle and refined

娴熟 xiánshú (形) adept; skilled

咸(鹹) xián I (形) salty; salted: ～菜 pickles

贤(賢) xián (形) virtuous; able: 任人唯～ give positions to people with ability. 让～ relinquish one's post in favour of a better qualified person

贤惠 xiánhuì (形) (of a woman) capable; virtuous

贤良 xiánliáng (形) (of a man) able and virtuous

贤明 xiánmíng (形) wise and able

衔(銜) xián I (动) hold in the mouth: ～着烟斗 hold a pipe between one's teeth II (名) rank; title: 军～ military rank. 头～ title

衔接 xiánjiē (动) join; dovetail

嫌 xián I (动) dislike; mind: 一点也不～麻烦 not mind the bother at all. 他走了，～这儿太吵. He left because it was too noisy here. 我～她太啰嗦. I dislike her for being so grumpy. II (名) suspicion: 为了避～，我特意走开. I deliberately walked off to avoid suspicion.

嫌弃(棄) xiánqì (动) have the desire to stay away from sb.; give a wide berth to sb.

嫌恶(惡) xiánwù (动) detest; loathe

嫌疑 xiányí (名) suspicion: ～犯 suspect

显(顯) xiǎn I (动) show; display: ～身手 display one's abilities. 她很～老. She looks older than her age. II (形) obvious; noticeable: 成效不～. The result is not so marked.

显得 xiǎnde (动) look; seem; appear: 她～很高兴. She looks very happy.

显而易见 xiǎn ér yì jiàn (副) obviously; evidently: ～，这是一种错误的想法. Evidently, this is a mistaken idea.

显赫 xiǎnhè (形) illustrious; influential: 他曾～一时. He was a man of power and influence for a time.

显露 xiǎnlù (动) become visible

显然 xiǎnrán (副) obviously; evidently

显示 xiǎnshì (动) show; demonstrate; manifest: ～出智慧和勇气 show both wi dom and courage

显微镜 xiǎnwēijìng (名) microscope

显现 xiǎnxiàn (动) appear; show: 在这困难的时刻，她～出坚强的个性. In this difficult hour, she revealed her strength of character

显象管 xiǎnxiàngguǎn (名) kinescope

显眼 xiǎnyǎn (形) conspicuous; showy: ～的地方 a conspicuous place. 穿得太～ be loudly dressed

显要 xiǎnyào (形) powerful and influential: ～人物 a dignitary; VIP

显影 xiǎnyǐng (动) develop (a film)
显著 xiǎnzhù (形) marked; remarkable: 取得～的成效 gain remarkable success; achieve notable results

险(險) xiǎn I (形) 1 danger; risk: 真～哪! It was such a narrow escape (or a close shave)! 脱～ be out of danger 2 sinister; vicious: 阴～ sinister II (名) a mountain or river which is so difficult to cross that it constitutes an almost impregnable barrier to an invading army: 天～ natural barrier
险恶(惡) xiǎn'è (形) 1 dangerous; perilous: 处境～ be in a precarious position; his position is pregnant with danger. 2 sinister; vicious: ～用心 sinister intentions; evil motives
险境 xiǎnjìng (名) dangerous situation
险峻 xiǎnjùn (形) precipitous
险些 xiǎnxiē (副) narrowly: 他～迷了路. He very nearly lost his way.
险要 xiǎnyào (形) strategically located and difficult of access
险诈 xiǎnzhà (形) sinister and crafty

宪(憲) xiàn (名) constitution
宪兵 xiànbīng (名) military police; gendarme
宪法 xiànfǎ (名) constitution
宪章 xiànzhāng (名) charter: 联合国～ the United Nations Charter
宪政 xiànzhèng (名) constitutional government

羡 xiàn (动) admire; envy: ～慕 admire; envy

献(獻) xiàn (动) offer; present: ～策 offer advice; make suggestions. ～花 present bouquets; floral tribute. ～花圈 lay a wreath. ～血 donate blood. ～身 devote one's life to a cause
献丑(醜) xiànchǒu (动) (of one's own performance and writing) show one's poor skill: 一定要我表演,就只好～了. Since you insist, I'll have to show what little skill I have to the best of my ability.
献词 xiàncí (名) congratulatory message: 新年～ New Year message
献计 xiànjì (动) offer advice; make suggestions
献礼(禮) xiànlǐ (动) present a gift
献媚 xiànmèi (动) butter up; resort to cheap undisguised flattery

县(縣) xiàn (名) county

现 xiàn I (形) 1 now; present; current; existing: ～年50岁 be 50 years old now. ～阶段 the present stage. ～况 the current situation 2 (of money) on hand: ～钱 ready money; cash II (动) appear; reveal: ～原形 reveal one's true featuers. 她脸上～出一丝笑容. A faint smile appeared on her face.
现场(場) xiànchǎng (名) 1 scene (of an accident or crime): 保护～ keep the scene (of a crime or accident) intact 2 site; spot: ～会 on-the-spot meeting
现成 xiànchéng (形) ready-made: ～衣服 ready-made clothes
现存 xiàncún (形) in stock
现代 xiàndài (名、形) 1 modern times; the contemporary age 2 modern; contemporary: ～派 modernist
现代化 xiàndàihuà I (名) modernization II (形) modern; modernized: ～设备 modern equipment
现金 xiànjīn (名) cash: ～付款 payment in cash
现款 xiànkuǎn (名) ready money; cash
现任 xiànrèn (形) currently in office; incumbent: ～总统 the incumbent president
现实(實) xiànshí I (名) reality: 脱离～ divorce oneself from reality; be unrealistic II (形) realistic; practical: ～的办法 practical measures. ～生活 real life. 采取～的态度 adopt a realistic attitude. ～主义 realism
现象 xiànxiàng (名) phenomenon: 罕见的～ rare phenomenon. 事物的～和本质 the appearance and essence of a matter
现行 xiànxíng (形) 1 currently in effect: ～法令 decrees in effect; the current laws and decrees. ～政策 present policies 2 (of a criminal) active: ～反革命分子 active counterrevolutionary
现役 xiànyì (名) active service: ～军队 serviceman
现在 xiànzài (副) now; today; at present

现状(狀) xiànzhuàng (名) present situation; existing state of affairs; status quo: 安于～ be content with things as they are

腺 xiàn (名) gland

馅(餡) xiàn (名) filling; stuffing: 肉～儿 meat filling

陷 xiàn I (动) 1 sink; get stuck: 越～越深 sink deeper and deeper. 车～进泥里了. The car got stuck in the mud. 2 (of a city) be occupied; fall 3 make false charges against sb. II (形) sunken: 眼窝深～ sunken eyes

陷阱 xiànjǐng (名) pitfall; trap: 布设～ lay a trap

陷落 xiànluò (动) 1 subside; cave in 2 (of territory) fall into enemy hands

陷入 xiànrù (动) 1 sink (or fall) into; land oneself in: ～困境 land oneself in a predicament. ～停顿状态 come to a standstill 2 be absorbed in: ～沉思 be lost in thought

限 xiàn I (动) limit; restrict: 数量不～ impose no restriction on quantity. 每券只～一人 each ticket entitles one person to admission. 不要～得这么死. Don't make such rigid restrictions. 公司～我半年完成这项设计工作. The firm allows me half a year to finish the designing. II (名) limit; bounds: 期～ time limit

限定 xiàndìng (动) set a limit to; restrict: ～范围 the prescribed limit

限度 xiàndù (名) limit; limitation: 我们的忍耐已经到了最后～. We have reached the limit of our patience.

限额 xiàn'é (名) norm; quota

限量 xiànliàng (动) put a limit on quantity; set bounds to: 前途不可～ have boundless prospects; have a very bright future

限期 xiànqī I (动) set a time limit (for sth.): 你必须～把申请书交来. You must hand in your application before the deadline. II (名) time limit; deadline

限于 xiànyú (动) be limited to: ～篇幅,不能刊载全文. As space is limited, it is impossible to publish the whole article. 本文讨论的范围～一些原则问题. The scope for the discussion of the present paper is confined to certain problems of principle.

限制 xiànzhì (动) restrict; limit; confine: 年龄～ age limit. 文章的字数不～. There is no restriction on the length of an article.

线(綫) xiàn I (名) 1 thread; string; wire: 丝～ silk thread. 毛～ knitting wool. 电～ electric wire. 2 line: 直～ straight line. 曲～ curved line. 光～ ray. 航～ airline. 流水～ assembly line. 边界～ boundary line. 海岸～ coastline. 政治路～ political line. 3 brink; verge: 在死亡～上 on the verge of death II (量) [of abstract matters, only after "一", "一" being the only numeral used before it]. 一～希望 a glimmer of hope. 一～光明 a gleam of light

线路 xiànlù (名) line; circuit: 电话～ telephone line

线圈 xiànquān (名) coil

线索 xiànsuǒ (名) clue

线条(條) xiàntiáo (名)(of drawing) line

襄 xiāng (动) <书> assist; help

镶 xiāng (名) 1 inlay; set; mount: ～金 inlaid with gold. ～牙 have a denture made 2 rim; edge; border: 给裙子～花边 edge a skirt with lace

镶嵌 xiāngqiàn (动) inlay; set

相 xiāng I (副) 1 each other; mutually: ～识 know each other. ～距甚远 be poles apart 2 [indicating how one party behaves towards the other]: 以礼～待 treat (sb.) with due courtesy. 另眼～看 look upon sb. with special respect; or in a different light II (动) see for oneself: ～马 take a look at the horse

see also xiàng

相比 xiāngbǐ (动) compare: 二者～,后者为佳. The latter is the better of the two.

相差 xiāngchà (动) differ: ～无几. The difference is negligible.

相称(稱) xiāngchèn (动) suit; match: 这种上衣跟你的年龄不～. This kind of jacket isn't particularly good for a man of your age.

相持 xiāngchí (动) be at a stalemate: 意见～不下 fail to reach agreement

相处(處) xiāngchǔ (动) get along (with one another): 不好～ difficult to get along with

相传(傳) xiāngchuán (动) 1 according to legend 2 pass on from one to another: 世代～ hand down from generation to generation

相当(當) xiāngdāng I (动) correspond to; be equal to: 得失～ The gains offset the losses. II (副) quite; considerably: ～成功 quite successful. ～艰巨 rather arduous. ～长时间 a considerably long time III (形) proper; suitable: 这个工作还没有找到～的人. We have not been able to find a proper person for the job yet.

相等 xiāngděng (动) be equal: 数量～ be equal in amount (or quantity, number)

相抵 xiāngdǐ (动) offset; counterbalance

相对(對) xiāngduì I (形) 1 opposite; face to face: ～无言 look at each other in silence 2 relative [as opposed to "absolute"] II (副) relatively; comparatively: ～稳定 relatively stable. ～地说 comparatively speaking

相反 xiāngfǎn (形) opposite; contrary: ～的方向 the opposite direction. 恰恰～on the contrary; just the other way round

相仿 xiāngfǎng (形) similar: 年纪～ be about the same age

相逢 xiāngféng (动) meet (by chance); come across

相符 xiāngfú (动) conform to; correspond to: 名实～ live up to one's reputation

相辅相成 xiāngfǔ-xiāngchéng complement each other

相干 xiānggān (动) [often used in a negative or interrogative sentence] have to do with; be concerned with: 这事跟你有什么～? What has this to do with you?

相关(關) xiāngguān (动) be interrelated: 密切～ be closely related (or linked) to each other

相好 xiānghǎo (动) 1 be on very good terms 2 be intimate with or on intimate terms with [often referring to a sexual relationship]

相互 xiānghù (形) mutual; reciprocal: ～了解 mutual understanding. ～作用 interaction; interplay

相继(繼) xiāngjì (副) in succession; one after another: 代表们～发言. The delegates spoke in succession

相距 xiāngjù (副) apart; at a distance of

相连 xiānglián (动) be linked together; be joined

相劝(勸) xiāngquàn (动) persuade; offer advice

相识(識) xiāngshí (动、名) 1 be acquainted with each other 2 acquaintance: 老～ an old acquaintance

相思 xiāngsī (名) a sad longing love cherished by either or both sides

相似 xiāngsì (动) resemble; be similar

相提并论(論) xiāngtí-bìnglùn (动) place on a par: 两者不能～. The two cannot be mentioned in the same breath.

相同 xiāngtóng (形) identical; the same

相投 xiāngtóu (动) be congenial: 兴趣～ have similar tastes and interests

相象 xiāngxiàng (动) resemble; be alike

相信 xiāngxìn (动) believe; have faith in

相形见绌 xiāng xíng jiàn chù be inferior by comparison; compare unfavourably with

相依 xiāngyī (动) be interdependent: 唇齿～ be dependent on each other like lips and teeth; be mutually dependent

相宜 xiāngyí (形) suitable; appropriate

相应(應) xiāngyìng (形) corresponding; relevant: 生产发展了, 工人的生活水平也～提高了. The production has risen and the living standard of the workers has also gone up accordingly.

相映 xiāngyìng (动) set each other off: 湖光塔影,～成趣. The glimmering lake and the reflection of the pagoda on it set each other off and formed a delightful scene.

厢 xiāng (名) 1 (of a one-storeyed house) wing: ～房 wing-room 2 railway carriage or compartment; (theatre) box: 车～ carriage. 包～ box

箱 xiāng (名) box; case; trunk: 皮～ suitcase. 大～ trunk. 垃圾～ dustbin. 风～ bellows

香 xiāng I (形) 1 (of flowers, etc.) fragrant; scented 2 (of food) delicious; appetizing II (副) 1 (of appetite)

with relish 2 (of sleep) soundly III (名) 1 perfume or spice: 麝～ musk. 檀～ sandalwood 2 incense: ～炉 incense-burner
香肠(腸) xiāngcháng (名) sausage
香粉 xiāngfěn (名) face powder
香蕉 xiāngjiāo (名) banana
香精 xiāngjīng (名) essence
香料 xiāngliào (名) 1 perfume 2 spice
香喷喷 xiāngpēnpēn (形) savoury; appetizing
香水 xiāngshuǐ (名) perfume
香甜 xiāngtián I (形) fragrant and sweet II (副) (of sleep) soundly
香烟 xiāngyān (名) cigarette
香皂 xiāngzào (名) toilet soap
乡(鄉) xiāng (名) 1 countryside: 城～ urban and rural areas 2 native place: 思～ think of one's native place with nostalgic longing
乡村 xiāngcūn (名) village; countryside
乡亲(親) xiāngqīn (名) fellow villager; villagers; folks
乡思 xiāngsī (名) homesickness; nostalgia
乡土 xiāngtǔ I (名) native soil II (形) of one's native land: ～风味 local flavour
乡下 xiāngxia (名) village; country; countryside
详 xiáng I (形) detailed II (动) know clearly: 作者生卒年月不～. The author's dates are unknown.
详尽(盡) xiángjìn (形) detailed; exhaustive: ～的记载 a detailed record
详情 xiángqíng (名) details; particulars
详细 xiángxì (形) detailed; minute: ～的报告 a detailed report
祥 xiáng (形) auspicious: 吉～ auspicious
翔 xiáng (动) circle in the air: 翱～ soar; hover
降 xiáng (动) 1 surrender: 宁死不～ rather die than surrender 2 tame; subdue
see also jiàng
降服 xiángfú (动) yield; surrender
享 xiǎng (动) enjoy
享福 xiǎngfú (动) live in ease and comfort
享乐(樂) xiǎnglè (动) indulge in material comfort; seek pleasure
享受 xiǎngshòu I (动) enjoy: ～公费医疗 enjoy free medical care II (名) enjoyment: 贪图～ seek ease and comfort
享有 xiǎngyǒu (动) enjoy (rights, prestige, etc.): ～崇高的威望 be held in high esteem. ～盛名 enjoy a high prestige
想 xiǎng (动) 1 think: 让我～一～. Let me think it over. ～办法 try to find a way (or solution). ～～后果 consider the consequences. ～问题 ponder over a problem 2 suppose; reckon: 你～他会来吗? Do you think he will come? 我～她还不知道此事. I don't think that she knows it yet. 我～是吧. I suppose so. 3 want to: ～试试吗? Would you like to have a try? 4 remember with longing; miss: 你～念他们吗? Do you miss them?
想必 xiǎngbì (副) presumably; most probably: 她怎么还没来? ～是火车误了点. Why hasn't she come yet? The train must have been late.
想不到 xiǎngbudào (形) 1 unexpected: 真～你是这么三心二意. I never thought you were so half-hearted. 真～在这儿遇见你! Fancy meeting you here! 2 fail to give attention to: 这些事男人都～. A man never gives thought to these matters.
想不开 xiǎngbukāi (动) take things too hard: 别为这事～! Don't take it to heart.
想当(當)然 xiǎngdāngrán (动) assume sth. as a matter of course; take for granted: 你不能凭～办事. You can never take anything for granted whatever you do.
想得开 xiǎngdekāi (动) take things philosophically
想法 xiǎngfa (名) idea; opinion: 我认为她的～都不对. I think her ideas are all mistaken.
想方设法 xiǎngfāng-shèfǎ (动) try by every means possible
想念 xiǎngniàn (动) think of sb. or sth. with nostalgic longing; miss
想起 xiǎngqǐ (动) remember; recall; call to mind: ～过去 recall the past. 我想不起在哪儿见过她. I can't remember where I last saw him.
想入非非 xiǎngrù fēifēi (动) indulge in fantasy; daydream
想望 xiǎngwàng (动) desire; long

for
想象 xiǎngxiàng I (动) imagine; visualize: 不可～ hard to imagine; inconceivable II (名) imagination: ～力 imaginative power
响(響) xiǎng I (动) sound; make a sound: 一声不～ without a word; silently. 电话铃～了. The telephone rang. II (名) sound; noise: 枪～ gun shot. 喇叭～ the blare of the horn III (形) loud; noisy: 电视机太～了，拧低点儿! The T.V. is blaring; turn it lower!
响彻(徹) xiǎngchè (动) resound through: 欢呼声～山谷. Cheers resounded throughout the valley.
响动(動) xiǎngdòng (名) sound of movement
响亮 xiǎngliàng (形) loud and clear; resounding; resonant
响声(聲) xiǎngshēng (名) sound; noise
响应(應) xiǎngyìng (动) respond; answer: ～政府的号召 answer the call of the government
饷(餉) xiǎng (名) pay (for soldiers, policemen, etc.)
项(項) xiàng I (名) nape (of the neck) II (量) [of items]: 造林是一～重大任务. Afforestation is a matter of vital importance.
项链(鏈) xiàngliàn (名) necklace
项目 xiàngmù (名) item
巷 xiàng (名) lane; alley
相 xiàng (名) 1 looks; appearance: 长～儿 a person's appearance. 狼狈～ awkward look. 人不可貌～ Never judge a person by his appearance 2 〈书〉 prime minister 3 photograph: 照～ take a photo; have a photo taken
see also xiāng
相册 xiàngcè (名) photo album
相机(機) xiàngjī (名) camera
相貌 xiàngmào (名) looks; appearance: ～端正 have regular features
相片 xiàngpiàn (名) photograph
相声(聲) xiàngsheng (名) cross talk
向 xiàng I (名) direction: 动～ trend. 风～ wind direction. 人心所～ popular sentiment II (动) 1 face: ～西 face west 2 side with (sb.): 你老～着他. You are always taking her part. III (介) towards: ～西前进 march west. ～我说明 explain it to me. ～别人学习 learn from others. ～纵深发展 develop in depth
向导(導) xiàngdǎo (名) guide
向来(來) xiànglái (副) always; all along: 他～不发火. He never gets into a temper. ～如此. It has always been so.
向前 xiàngqián (副) forward: 奋勇～ forge ahead
向日葵 xiàngrìkuí (名) sunflower
向上 xiàngshàng (副) upward; make progress
向往 xiàngwǎng (动) yearn for; look forward to
向阳(陽) xiàngyáng (动) (of a house) face south
象 xiàng I (名) 1 elephant 2 appearance: 万～更新. Everything takes on a new look. II (动) 1 be like; resemble: 这孩子～他父亲. The child takes after its father. 我～不～个跳芭蕾舞的? Do I look like a ballet dancer? 2 look as if; seem: ～要下雨了. It looks as if it's going to rain; it looks like rain. III (介) like; such as: ～他这样的人真少见. People like him are rare.
象话 xiànghuà (形) reasonable; proper: 真不～! It's absolutely outrageous! 这才～. That's more like it. 你对老年人这样无礼，～吗? Aren't you ashamed of yourself when you are so rude to old people?
象棋 xiàngqí (名) (Chinese) chess
象形 xiàngxíng (名) pictograph
象牙 xiàngyá (名) ivory: ～雕刻 ivory carving
象征(徵) xiàngzhēng I (动) symbolize; signify II (名) symbol; token
橡 xiàng (名) 1 oak 2 rubber tree
橡胶(膠) xiàng jiāo (名) rubber
橡皮 xiàngpí (名) 1 rubber eraser 2 rubber: ～膏 adhesive plaster. ～筋 rubber band
像 xiàng (名) 1 portrait; picture: 画～ portrait. 铜～ bronze statue. 雕～ sculpture 2 image
消 xiāo (动) 1 disappear; vanish: 雾已～了. The fog has lifted. 他的气～了. He has cooled (or calmed) down. 2 dispel; remove 3 pass the time in a

leisurely way: ～夏 pass the summer in a leisurely way
消沉 xiāochén (形) low-spirited; downhearted
消除 xiāochú (动) eliminate; dispel; remove: ～顾虑 dispel misgivings. ～误会 clear up misunderstanding
消毒 xiāodú (动) disinfect; sterilize
消防 xiāofáng (名) fire control; fire fighting: ～队 fire brigade. ～车 fire engine
消费 xiāofèi (动) consume: ～品 consumer goods
消耗 xiāohào I (动) consume; use up II (名) consumption
消化 xiāohuà (动) digest: 好～ easy to digest; digestible: ～不良 indigestion
消极(極) xiāojí (形) 1 negative: ～因素 negative factor 2 passive; inactive: 态度～ appear inactive
消灭(滅) xiāomiè (动) 1 eliminate; wipe out: ～敌人 wipe out the enemy 2 perish; die out; become extinct
消磨 xiāomó (动) sap; whittle away; wear off: ～志气 sap one's will. ～精力 whittle one's strength away 2 idle away; fritter away: ～岁月 idle (or fritter) away one's times
消遣 xiāoqiǎn I (动) kill time; amuse oneself II (名) diversion
消融 xiāoróng (动) (of ice, snow, etc.) melt
消散 xiāosàn (动) scatter and disappear; dissipate: 雾渐渐～了. The mist has gradually lifted.
消失 xiāoshī (动) disappear: 在黑夜里～ disappear into the night
消瘦 xiāoshòu (动) become thin
消亡 xiāowáng (动) wither away; die out
消息 xiāoxi (名) news; information: ～灵通人士 informed sources
消炎 xiāoyán (动) counteract inflammation; dephlogisticate

宵 xiāo (名) night: 通～ all night; throughout the night
宵禁 xiāojìn (名) curfew: 实行(解除)～ impose (lift) a curfew

逍 xiāo
逍遥 xiāoyáo (形) carefree
逍遥法外 xiāoyáo fǎ wài be at large

霄 xiāo (名) clouds: 耸入云～ towering into the sky
霄汉(漢) xiāohàn (名) ‹书› the sky; the firmament

硝 xiāo (名) nitre; saltpetre
硝烟 xiāoyān (名) smoke of gunpowder

削 xiāo (动) 1 peel with a knife: ～梨 peel a pear. ～铅笔 sharpen a pencil 2 cut; chop: ～球 (of table-tennis) cut; chop
see also xuē

销 xiāo (动) 1 cancel; annul: 注～ write off. ～假 report back at the end of a leave of absence 2 sell; market: 产～ production and marketing. 畅～书 best-seller 3 spend: 开～ expenditure
销毁 xiāohuǐ (动、名) destroy by melting or burning: ～核武器 the destruction of nuclear weapons
销路 xiāolù (名) sale; market: ～很好 have a good market
销声(聲)匿迹 xiāoshēng-nìjì (动) make no public appearances; lie low
销售 xiāoshòu (名) sell; market: ～量 sales volume

哮 xiāo (名) 1 heavy breathing; wheeze: ～喘 asthma 2 roar; howl: 咆～ roar; thunder

枵 xiāo (形) ‹书› empty; hollow: ～腹 empty stomach
枵腹从(從)公 xiāo fù cóng gōng attend to public duties without drawing a penny from the state

嚣 xiāo (动) clamour; hubbub: 叫～ clamour. ～张 arrogant; aggressive; rampant

萧(蕭) xiāo (形) desolate; dreary
萧瑟 xiāosè I (形) bleak; desolate: ～景象 bleak scene II (动) rustle in the air: 秋风～. The autumn wind is soughing.
萧条(條) xiāotiáo I (形) bleak; desolate II (名) depression; slump: 经济～ economic depression; slump

潇(瀟) xiāo
潇洒 xiāosǎ (形) urbane: 举止～ act with grace and ease
潇潇 xiāoxiāo (形) (of rain or wind) whistling and pattering

淆 xiáo (动) confuse; mix up: 混～ confuse; obscure

晓(曉) xiǎo I (名) dawn; daybreak: 拂～ dawn II (动) 1 know: 家喻户～ known to every household 2 let sb. know; tell: ～以大义 enlighten one on the cardinal principle of justice
晓得 xiǎode (动) know: 天～! God knows!
小 xiǎo I (形) 1 small; little; petty; minor: ～姑娘 a little girl. ～溪 a small stream. ～声说话 talk in whispers. ～资产阶级 petty bourgeoisie. 2 young: 一家老～ the whole family. ～儿子 the youngest son. ～猫 kitten II (副) for a short time: ～憩 have a little rest. ～坐 sit for a while
小本经营 xiǎoběn jīngyíng (动) do business with a small capital
小便 xiǎobiàn I (动) urinate; pass (or make) water II (名) urine
小菜 xiǎocài (名) pickles
小册子 xiǎocèzi (名) booklet; pamphlet; brochure
小产(産) xiǎochǎn (名) miscarriage; abortion
小车(車) xiǎochē (名) 1 wheelbarrow; pushcart 2 car
小吃 xiǎochī (名) snack; refreshments: ～店 snack bar
小丑 xiǎochǒu (名) clown; buffoon
小聪(聰)明 xiǎocōngming (名) cleverness in trivial matters: 耍～ play petty tricks
小道消息 xiǎodào xiāoxi (名) a rumour on the grapevine
小调 xiǎodiào (名) 1 ditty 2 〈乐〉 minor
小儿科 xiǎo'érkē (名) paediatrics: ～医生 paediatrician
小贩 xiǎofàn (名) pedlar; vendor; hawker
小费 xiǎofèi (名) tip
小工 xiǎogōng (名) unskilled labourer
小鬼 xiǎoguǐ (名) little devil (a term of endearment in addressing a child)
小伙子 xiǎohuǒzi (名) lad; young fellow
小集团 xiǎojítuán (名) clique; faction
小轿车 xiǎojiàochē (名) sedan (car); limousine
小节(節) xiǎojié (名) small matter; trifle: 不拘～ not bother about petty formalities; not care about small matters; not be punctilious
小结 xiǎojié (名) brief summary
小姐 xiǎojie (名) 1 Miss 2 young lady
小看 xiǎokàn (动) look down upon; belittle
小康 xiǎokāng (形) moderately well-off: ～之家 a moderately well-off family
小两口 xiǎoliǎngkǒu (名) young couple
小麦(麥) xiǎomài (名) wheat
小卖(賣)部 xiǎomàibù (名) 1 a small shop attached to a hotel, school, etc. 2 snack counter
小朋友 xiǎopéngyǒu (名) children
小便宜 xiǎopiányi (名) small gain; petty advantage
小品 xiǎopǐn (名) a short, simple piece of literary or artistic creation; essay; sketch
小气(氣) xiǎoqi (形) 1 mean; stingy 2 narrow-minded; petty
小巧玲珑(瓏) xiǎoqiǎo línglóng small and exquisite
小圈子 xiǎoquānzi (名) inner circle of people; clique: 搞～ engage in cliquish activities
小人 xiǎorén (名) 1 〈旧〉 a person of low position 2 a mean person; villain: ～得志 a case of a morally corrupt person holding sway
小人儿书 (書) xiǎorénrshū (名) picturestory book
小时 xiǎoshí (名) hour
小数(數) xiǎoshù (名) decimal
小说 xiǎoshuō (名) novel; fiction: 长篇～ novel. 中篇～ novelette. 短篇～ short story
小算盘(盤) xiǎosuànpan (名) selfish calculations
小提琴 xiǎotíqín (名) violin
小题大作 xiǎo tí dà zuò make a mountain out of a molehill; storm in a tea-cup
小偷 xiǎotōu (名) petty thief; pilferer; pickpocket: ～小摸 pilfering
小腿 xiǎotuǐ (名) shank
小五金 xiǎowǔjīn (名) metal fittings (e.g. nails, wires, hinges, bolts, locks, etc.); hardware
小型 xiǎoxíng (形) small-sized; miniature
小学(學) xiǎoxué (名) primary (or elementary) school
小意思 xiǎoyìsi (名) small token of kindly feelings; mere trifle
小子 xiǎozi (名) 〈口〉 1 son; boy 2 (derog.) chap
小组 xiǎozǔ (名) group

校 xiào (名) 1 school 2 field officer
see also jiào
校官 xiàoguān (名) field officer
校舍 xiàoshè (名) school building
校友 xiàoyǒu (名) alumnus or alumna
校园(園) xiàoyuán (名) campus; school yard
校长(長) xiàozhǎng (名) head of a school (headmaster, principal, president, chancellor)

效 xiào I (名) effect: 见～ prove effective. 无～ be ineffective II (动) 1 imitate; follow the example of: 上行下～. The example set by the leading people will be followed by their subordinates. 2 devote to; render a service
效法 xiàofǎ (动) follow the example of; model oneself on
效果 xiàoguǒ (名) effect; result: 取得良好～ yield good results
效劳(勞) xiàoláo (动) offer one's services
效力 xiàolì I (动) render a service to: 为国～ serve one's country II (名) effect
效率 xiàolǜ (名) efficiency: ～高 efficient. ～低 inefficient
效命 xiàomìng (动) go all out to do one's duty regardless of personal danger
效益 xiàoyì (名) beneficial result: 经济～ economic results
效忠 xiàozhōng (动) pledge loyalty or allegiance: ～祖国 devote oneself heart and soul to the cause of one's country

孝 xiào (名) 1 filial piety 2 mourning: 带～ be dressed in mourning
孝敬 xiàojìng (动) 1 give presents (to one's elders) 2 show filial piety
孝顺 xiàoshùn (动) show filial obedience
孝子 xiàozǐ (名) dutiful son

肖 xiào (动) resemble; be like: ～像 portrait; portraiture. 维妙维～ absolutely lifelike

啸(嘯) xiào (名) 1 whistle 2 howl; roar

笑 xiào (动) 1 smile; laugh: 微～ smile. 眉开眼～ beam. ～嘻嘻 grin. ～得合不拢嘴 grin from ear to ear. 站在那里傻～ stand there with a silly grin on one's face. 哈哈大～ roar with laughter. 窃～ laugh up one's sleeve 2 laugh at; ridicule: 他刚学,别～他. He's just started learning. Don't laugh at him.
笑柄 xiàobǐng (名) laughingstock
笑话 xiàohua I (名) 1 joke: 说～ crack a joke. 闹～ make a fool of oneself; make a funny mistake II (动) laugh at; ridicule: 你别～我,你来试试看. Don't laugh at me. You may have a try and see if you can do better.
笑里藏刀 xiàolǐ cáng dāo have murderous intent behind one's smiles
笑料 xiàoliào (名) laughingstock
笑眯眯 xiàomīmī (副) smilingly
笑面虎 xiàomiànhǔ (名) smiling villain
笑容 xiàoróng (名) smiling expression; smile: ～满面 be all smiles
笑颜 xiàoyán (名) smiling face

楔 xiē
楔子 xiēzi (名) 1 wedge 2 peg 3 prologue in some modern novels

些 xiē (量) 1 some: 这～ these. 好～ quite a few (or lot). 前～日子 recently. 写～信 write a few letters 2 a little; a bit: 好～了 (feel) a little better. 颜色深了～. The colour is a bit too dark.

蝎 xiē (名)(～子) scorpion

歇 xiē (动) have a rest; rest: ～口气 stop for a breather
歇脚 xiējiǎo (动) stop for a rest on a walking tour
歇宿 xiēsù (动) put up for the night; make an overnight stop
歇息 xiēxi (动) 1 have a rest 2 go to bed

鞋 xié (名) shoes
鞋垫(墊) xiédiàn (名) shoe-pad; insole
鞋匠 xiéjiàng (名) shoemaker; cobbler
鞋样(樣) xiéyàng (名) shoe pattern; outline of sole
鞋油 xiéyóu (名) shoe polish

挟(挾) xié (动) 1 hold sth. under the arm 2 coerce; force sb. to: 要～ intimidate. ～持 detain under duress

携 xié (动) 1 carry; take with: ～带 take along. ～款潜逃 abscond with funds 2 take sb. by the hand

谐 xié (形) 1 in harmony; in accord: 和～ harmonious 2 humorous: 诙～ humorous; jocular
谐和 xiéhé (形) harmonious
谐谑 xiéxuè (动) banter: 语带～ speak with raillery
谐音 xiéyīn (名) homophonic; homonymic
偕 xié (副) in the company of: ～行 travel together. ～同 accompanied by; along with
邪 xié (形) evil; heretical: 改～归正 give up one's evil ways and return to the right path. 歪风～气 unhealthy tendencies
邪道 xiédào (名) evil ways; infamous behaviour
邪恶(惡) xié'è (形) evil; wicked; vicious
邪路 xiélù (名) evil ways
邪门歪道 xiémén-wāidào (名) vicious pursuits; dishonest or evil practices
邪念 xiéniàn (名) wicked idea
邪说 xiéshuō (名) heresy; fallacy
斜 xié (形) slanting; tilted; inclined: ～线 slant (/); oblique line. ～着头 tilt one's head. ～眼看人 squint at sb. ～躺在沙发上 recline on a sofa
斜路 xiélù (名) wrong path: 走～ go astray
斜坡 xiépō (名) slope
协(協) xié (形) 1 joint 2 assist
协定 xiédìng (名) agreement; accord: 贸易～ trade agreement
协会(會) xiéhuì (名) association; society
协力 xiélì (动) pull together; join in a common effort
协商 xiéshāng (动) consult; be in consultation with
协调 xiétiáo (动) harmonize; coordinate: 动作～ coordinated movement; coordination. 色彩～ well-matched colours
协同 xiétóng (动) cooperate with
协议(議) xiéyì (名) agreement: 达成～ reach (an) agreement
协助 xiézhù (动) assist
协奏曲 xiézòuqǔ (名) concerto
协作 xiézuò (名) cooperation; combined (or joint) efforts; coordination
胁(脅) xié (动) coerce; force: 威～ threaten. ～从 be an accomplice under duress

写(寫) xiě (动) write
写生 xiěshēng (动) paint from life; sketch
写实(實) xiěshí (动) write or paint realistically
写意 xiěyì (动) write or paint according to one's impressions
写照 xiězhào (名) portrayal; description
写字台 xiězìtái (名) writing desk; desk
写作 xiězuò (名) writing: ～技巧 writing technique
血 xiě (名) blood: 献～ donate one's blood
see also xuè
亵(褻) xiè
亵渎(瀆) xièdú (动) blaspheme
泻(瀉) xiè (动) 1 (of river, rain, etc.) rush down; pour out 2 have loose bowels: 上吐下～ suffer from nausea and diarrhoea
泻肚 xièdù (动) have loose bowels; have diarrhoea
泻药(藥) xièyào (名) laxative
械 xiè (名) 1 tool; instrument: 机～ mechanism 2 weapon: 军～ weapons; arms 3 fetters, shackles, etc.
泄 xiè (动) let out; discharge; release; vent: ～洪 release floodwater; flood discharge. ～私愤 give vent to one's personal spleen; give deliberate offence out of spite
泄漏 xièlòu (动) leak; let out: ～秘密 let the cat out of the bag
泄露 xièlù (动) let out; reveal
泄密 xièmì (动) divulge a secret
泄气(氣) xièqì (动) 1 lose heart; feel discouraged or deflated
卸 xiè (动) 1 unload: ～车 unload a truck. ～牲口 unhitch a draught animal 2 remove; strip: ～零件 remove parts from a machine
卸货 xièhuò (动) (of goods) unload
卸装(裝) xièzhuāng (动) remove stage makeup and costume
谢 xiè (动) thank: 多～. Thanks a lot. 不用～. Don't mention it; not at all.
谢绝 xièjué (动) refuse politely; decline: 婉言～ politely decline. ～参观 Not open to visitors.
谢幕 xièmù (动) answer a cur-

tain call
谢天谢地 xiètiān-xièdì thank God
谢谢 xièxie (动) thanks; thank you
谢意 xièyì (名) gratitude; thanks
谢罪 xièzuì (动) apologize for an offence
懈 xiè (形) slack; lax: 坚持不～ persistent. 作坚持不～的努力 make unremitting efforts. ～怠 slack and lazy; sluggish; lax
蟹 xiè (名) crab
屑 xiè I (名) bits; scraps; crumbs: 纸～ scraps of paper 金属～ metal filings. 面包～ crumbs (of bread) II (动) 不屑 disdain to do sth.
辛 xīn I (形) 1 hard: 艰～ hardships 2 (of flavour) hot: ～辣 hot; pungent II (名) suffering: 含～茹苦 endure suffering; bear hardships
辛苦 xīnkǔ I (形) hard; hardworking: 这个工作很～. It's a hard job. II (动) work hard; undergo hardships: 对不起,这事儿还得您再～一趟. I'm sorry to bother you, but you'll have to make another trip.
辛劳 xīnláo (动) painstaking; laborious: 不辞～ spare no pains
辛勤 xīnqín (形) industrious; hardworking
辛酸 xīnsuān (形) sad; bitter; miserable: ～的往事 sad memories; bitter reminiscences
锌 xīn (名) zinc (Zn)
新 xīn (形) new; fresh; up-to-date: ～衣服 new clothes. ～技术 up-to-date technique. 最～消息 the latest news
新兵 xīnbīng (名) new recruit; recruit
新陈(陳)代谢 xīn-chén dàixiè metabolism
新房 xīnfáng (名) bridal bedroom.
新近 xīnjìn (副) recently; lately
新居 xīnjū (名) new home; new residence
新郎 xīnláng (名) bridegroom
新年 xīnnián (名) New Year: ～好! Happy New Year! ～献词 New Year message
新娘 xīnniáng (名) bride
新奇 xīnqí (形) novel; new; strange: ～的想法 a novel idea
新生 xīnshēng I (形) newborn; newly born: ～儿 newborn baby; infant baby. ～事物 new-born things II (名) 1 new life; rebirth 2 new student; freshman (college)
新手 xīnshǒu (名) new hand; green horn
新闻 xīnwén (名) news: 头版～ front-page news (or story). 简明～ news in brief. ～公报 press communique. ～界 the press
新鲜 xīnxiān (形) fresh: ～空气 fresh air. ～牛奶 fresh milk
新兴(興) xīnxīng (形) newly emerging
新颖 xīnyǐng (形) novel and original: 题材～ The subject-matter is fresh and original. 式样～ The style is free from convention.
薪 xīn (名) 1 firewood; fuel 2 salary: ～水 salary; pay
心 xīn (名) 1 heart: ～跳 heartbeats; palpitation. 善良的～ a kind heart. 问题的核～ the heart of the affair; the crux 2 mind: 小～! be careful! watch out! 细～ be meticulous. ～宽 be carefree 3 feeling; intentions 伤～ be sad. 好～ mean well; have good intentions. 耐～ be patient 4 centre; middle: 街～ the middle of a street. 轴～ axis. 中～ centre
心爱(愛) xīn'ài (形) beloved; treasured: ～的礼物 a treasured gift
心安理得 xīn'ān-lǐdé have an easy conscience; have no qualms about it
心病 xīnbìng (名) worry; anxiety
心不在焉 xīn bù zài yān (形) absent-minded
心肠(腸) xīncháng (名) heart; intention: 热～ warm-hearted
心潮 xīncháo (名) a surge of emotion: ～澎湃 feel an onrushing surge of emotion
心得 xīndé (名) what one has learned from work or study; gains in depth of comprehension
心地 xīndì (名) moral nature: ～善良 good-natured; kindhearted
心烦 xīnfán (形) be vexed: ～意乱 be terribly upset
心浮 xīnfú (形) flighty and impatient
心服 xīnfú (动) be genuinely convinced:
心腹 xīnfù (名、形) 1 trusted subordinate; henchman 2 confidential: ～事 top secret. ～之患 a serious hidden trouble
心甘情愿(願) xīngān-qíngyuàn (形)

be most willing to; be perfectly happy to

心肝 xīngān (名) **1** conscience: 没～ heartless **2** darling; deary

心寒 xīnhán (形) be bitterly disappointed

心狠 xīnhěn (形) cruel; merciless: ～手辣 wicked and merciless

心花怒放 xīnhuā nùfàng be transported with joy; be wild with joy

心怀(懷) xīnhuái I (动) harbour: ～叵测 harbour evil intentions. ～不满 nurse a grievance. ～鬼胎 have ulterior motives II (名) state of mind; mood

心慌 xīnhuāng (形) be flustered; be nervous: ～意乱 be perturbed; be put in a flurry

心灰意懒 xīnhuī-yìlǎn (形) be dispirited; be depressed

心机(機) xīnjī (名) scheming: 用尽～ rack one's brains. 枉费～ plot in vain

心计 xīnjì (名) scheming; calculation: 一个有～的女人 an intelligent woman

心焦 xīnjiāo (形) anxious; worried

心境 xīnjìng (名) mental state; mood: ～非常愉快 be in high spirits; be very happy

心旷(曠)神怡 xīnkuàng-shényí (形) relaxed and carefree

心理 xīnlǐ (名) psychology; mentality: 儿童～学 child psychology

心里 xīnli (副) in the heart; at heart; in (the) mind: ～不痛快 feel bad about sth. ～有事 have sth. on one's mind

心里话 xīnlihuà (名) true words from the heart: 说～ speak one's mind

心灵(靈) xīnlíng I (形) clever; quick-witted: ～手巧 clever and deft II (名) soul; spirit: ～深处 deep down in one's heart

心领神会(會) xīnlǐng-shénhuì (动) thoroughly understand

心乱(亂)如麻 xīn luàn rú má (形) be upset by tangled thoughts and ideas; be utterly confused

心满意足 xīnmǎn-yìzú (形) be perfectly contented with one's lot

心目 xīnmù (名) mind; mental view: 在某些人的～中 in some people's eyes

心平气(氣)和 xīnpíng-qìhé (形) calm and good-natured

心情 xīnqíng (名) state of mind; mood: ～沉重 feel depressed or upset. ～舒畅 feel happy and gay

心神 xīnshén (名) mind; state of mind: ～不定 feel disturbed

心事 xīnshi (名) sth. weighing on one's mind; worry: ～重重 be laden with anxiety

心思 xīnsi (名) **1** thought; idea: 想～ give thought to something **2** state of mind; mood: 没有～下棋 not be in the mood to play chess

心酸 xīnsuān (动) feel sad

心疼 xīnténg (动) **1** (of children) love dearly **2** feel sorry to see sth. running to waste

心田 xīntián (名) heart

心头(頭) xīntóu (名) mind; heart: 记在～ bear in mind

心胸 xīnxiōng (名) breadth of mind: ～开阔 large-minded; unbiased

心虚 xīnxū (动) **1** have a guilty conscience **2** be lacking in self-confidence; diffident

心绪 xīnxù (名) state of mind: ～烦乱 be in a mental turmoil; eat one's heart out

心血 xīnxuè (名) painstaking effort: 费尽～ expend all one's energies

心血来(來)潮 xīnxuè lái cháo (动) have a brainwave

心眼儿 xīnyǎnr (名) **1** heart; mind: 小～ narrow-minded; petty. 打～里高兴 feel genuinely happy **2** intelligence; cleverness: 她这个人有～. She is intelligent and resourceful. **3** unnecessary misgivings: ～多 always have unwarranted misgivings.

心意 xīnyì (名) kindly feelings: 请收下这点礼物，那是我们大家的一点～. Please accept this small gift from us. We offer it to you as a token of our regard. 你可以放心，我不会辜负你的一片～. You may rest assured that I will not let you down.

心有余悸 xīn yǒu yújì (动) have a residue of fear

心愿(願) xīnyuàn (名) wish; aspiration: 访问贵国是我多年的～. It is my long-cherished wish to visit your country.

心脏(臟) xīnzàng (名) the heart: ～病 heart disease; heart trouble

心直口快 xīnzhí-kǒukuài (形) frank and outspoken

心中有数(數) xīnzhōng yǒu shù (动) have a pretty good idea of; know what's what

心醉 xīnzuì (形) be enchanted or fascinated

欣 xīn (形) happy; joyful: 欢～ happy; joyful

欣然 xīnrán (副) joyfully; with pleasure: ～接受 accept with pleasure

欣赏 xīnshǎng (动) enjoy; appreciate; admire

欣慰 xīnwèi (形) be gratified

欣喜 xīnxǐ (形) joyful; happy: ～若狂 be wild with joy

欣欣向荣(榮) xīnxīn xiàng róng (形) thriving; flourishing; prosperous: 一派～的景象 a picture of growing prosperity

寻(尋) xín see also xún

寻短见 xín duǎnjiàn (动) commit suicide

寻思 xínsi (动) think sth. over; consider

信 xìn I (名) 1 letter: 寄～ post a letter. 寄平～ by surface mail. 航空～ air mail. 介绍～ letter of introduction or recommendation 2 message; information: 口～ verbal message. 随时报～ keep sb. informed of sth. 3 trust; confidence: 守～ keep one's promise. 失～ break one's word (to someone); go back on one's word; break faith (with sb.) II (动) believe; trust: 我不～他有这么坏. I don't believe he is that bad. 我深～他的工作定会取得成功. I am deeply convinced that his task will be crowned with success.

信步 xìnbù (动) take a leisurely stroll

信贷 xìndài (名) credit

信封 xìnfēng (名) envelope

信奉 xìnfèng (动) believe in: ～基督教 believe in Christianity; be a Christian

信服 xìnfú (动) believe and admire: 这些科学论据令人～. These scientific arguments carry conviction.

信号(號) xìnhào (名) signal

信笺 xìnjiān (名) letter paper; writing pad

信件 xìnjiàn (名) letters; mail

信口开(開)河 xìnkǒu kāihé (动) talk irresponsibly

信赖 xìnlài (动) (of person) trust; have faith in: 她是可以～的. She is trust-worthy.

信念 xìnniàn (名) faith; belief; conviction

信任 xìnrèn (动) trust; have confidence in

信使 xìnshǐ (名) courier; messenger: 外交～ diplomatic courier

信誓旦旦 xìnshì dàndàn (动) swear an oath in all solemnity

信手拈来 xìnshǒu niānlái (动) write with facility

信守 xìnshǒu (动) abide by; stand by: ～诺言 keep a promise

信条(條) xìntiáo (名) article of faith; creed

信筒 xìntǒng (名) pillar-box; mailbox

信徒 xìntú (名) believer; disciple; follower: 佛教～ Buddhist. 基督教～ Christian

信托 xìntuō (动) trust; entrust: ～公司 trust company. ～商店 commission shop

信息 xìnxī (名) information; news: ～不灵 have inadequate information facilities

信箱 xìnxiāng (名) 1 mailbox 2 post-office box (P.O.B.)

信心 xìnxīn (名) confidence; faith

信仰 xìnyǎng (名) faith; belief; conviction: 宗教～ religious belief. 不同的宗教～ different religious persuasions. 政治～ political conviction

信用 xìnyòng (名) 1 trustworthiness; credit: 讲～ keep one's word 2 credit: ～卡 credit card

信誉 xìnyù (名) prestige; credit; reputation: 享有很高的国际～ enjoy high international prestige

衅(釁) xìn (名) quarrel; dispute: 挑～ provoke; provocation

兴(興) xīng (动) 1 prosper 2 become popular: 现在正～这个呢! That's all the vogue now. 我们那儿不～这一套. We don't go in for that sort of thing there. 3 promote; undertake to do: 大～土木 go in for large-scale construction. 百废俱～ All that was left undone is now being undertaken.
see also xìng

兴办(辦) xīngbàn (动) initiate; set up

兴奋(奮) xīngfèn (形) be excited

兴风(風)作浪 xīngfēng-zuòlàng (动) stir up trouble; create disturbances

兴建 xīngjiàn (动) build; construct

兴利除弊 xīnglì-chúbì (动) promote beneficial undertakings and abolish harmful practices

兴隆 xīnglóng (形) thriving; flourishing: 生意～ Business is brisk.

兴起 xīngqǐ (动) rise; spring up

兴盛 xīngshèng (形) prosperous

兴亡 xīng-wáng (名) rise and fall (of a nation)

兴旺 xīngwàng (形) prosperous; thriving

兴修 xīngxiū (动) start construction

兴妖作怪 xīngyāo-zuòguài (动) conjure up a host of demons to make trouble; stir up trouble

星 xīng (名) 1 star: 火～ Mars. 卫～ satellite. 电影明～ film star 2 bit; particle: 一～半点 a tiny bit

星辰 xīngchén (名) stars

星斗 xīngdǒu (名) stars: 满天～. The sky is studded with numerous stars.

星火 xīnghuǒ (名) 1 spark: ～燎原. A single spark can start a prairie fire. 2 shooting star; meteor: 急如～ most urgent

星际(際) xīngjì (形) interplanetary

星罗(羅)棋布 xīngluó-qíbù (动) scattered all over like stars in the sky

星期 xīngqī (名) week: 今天～几? What day (of the week) is it today?

星球 xīngqiú (名) star: ～大战计划 star wars program

星座 xīngzuò (名) constellation

腥 xīng (名) a fishy smell

猩 xīng

猩红 xīnghóng (形) scarlet; bloodred

猩猩 xīngxīng (名) orangutan: 大～ gorilla. 黑～ chimpanzee

形 xíng (名) 1 shape; form: 圆～ round; circular. 方～ square. 不成～ shapeless; amorphous 2 body; entity: 有～ tangible. 无～ intangible

形成 xíngchéng (动) take shape; form: ～了一种特殊的风格 have evolved a special style. ～习惯 form a habit; become a habitual practice. 一种新思想正在～. A new trend of thought is taking shape.

形而上学(學) xíng'érshàngxué (名) metaphysics

形迹 xíngjì (名) a person's movements and expression: 不露～ betray nothing in one's countenance or behaviour. ～可疑 look suspicious

形容 xíngróng I (动) describe: 难以～ be difficult to describe; beggar description II (名) <书> appearance; countenance

形容词 xíngróngcí (名) adjective

形式 xíngshì (名) form: 内容与～的统一 unity of content and form

形势(勢) xíngshì (名) 1 situation; circumstances 2 terrain

形态(態) xíngtài (名) 1 form; shape; pattern 2 morphology

形体(體) xíngtǐ (名) 1 (of animals, humans, etc.) shape; physique 2 (of language) form and structure

形象 xíngxiàng (名) image; imagery

形形色色 xíngxíngsèsè (形) of all shades; of every description

形影不离(離) xíng-yǐng bùlí (of two people) be inseparable; on very close terms

形状(狀) xíngzhuàng (名) form; appearance; shape

刑 xíng (名) 1 punishment: 死～ capital punishment; the death penalty. 判处无期徒～ be sentenced to life imprisonment 2 torture; corporal punishment: 用～ put sb. to torture

刑场(場) xíngchǎng (名) execution ground

刑罚 xíngfá (名)penalty; punishment

刑法 xíngfǎ (名) penal code; criminal law

刑事 xíngshì (形) criminal; penal: ～案件 criminal case

型 xíng (名) 1 model; type; pattern: 重～卡车 heavy truck. 血～ blood group 2 mould

型号(號) xínghào (名) model; type

行 xíng I (动) 1 walk; travel: 步～ go on foot; walk. ～程 distance of travel. 人～横道 pedestrian crossing. 风～ prevail 2 do; carry out: ～不通 be impracticable. 实～ put into effect. ～医 practise medicine 3 be all right: ～,我马上就去. O.K. I'll go straight away. 不～,那不可以. No, that won't do. 我去～吗? Is it all right if I go? II (名) 1 trip: 欧洲之～ a trip to Europe 2 behaviour: 他言～一致. His actions match his words. III (形) capable; competent: 我在这方面不～. I'm not good at these things. 他真～哇! He is really capable! 她现在还不～. She is not up to it yet.

行刺 xíngcì （动）assassinate
行动(動) xíngdòng I （动）1 move (or get) about: ～不便 have difficulty moving about 2 act; take action: ～起来 go into action II （名）action; operation: 军事～ military operations
行贿 xínghuì （动）bribe
行将(將)就木 xíngjiāng jiù mù on one's last legs
行径(徑) xíngjìng （名）conduct; behaviour; shameless conduct; disgraceful behaviour
行军 xíngjūn （名）(of troops) march
行礼(禮) xínglǐ （动）salute
行李 xíngli （名）luggage; baggage: 手提～ hand-luggage. 超重～ excess luggage
行旅 xínglǚ （名）(person going on a long journey) traveller: ～称便. Travellers find it convenient.
行期 xíngqī （名）date of departure
行乞 xíngqǐ （动）go begging
行人 xíngrén （名）pedestrian
行色 xíngsè （名）the circumstances in which people get things ready for a trip: ～匆匆 make hurried preparations for a trip
行善 xíngshàn （动）show mercy
行时(時) xíngshí （动）(of a thing) be in vogue
行使 xíngshǐ （动）exercise; perform: ～职权 exercise one's powers
行驶 xíngshǐ （动）(of a vehicle, ship, etc.) go; travel
行事 xíngshì （动）act; handle matters
行头(頭) xíngtou （名）(of traditional Chinese operas) stage costumes and properties
行为(爲) xíngwéi （名）behaviour; conduct; action
行星 xíngxīng （名）planet
行凶 xíngxiōng （动）commit assault or man-slaughter or murder
行政 xíngzhèng （名）administration: ～部门 administrative department; executive branch. ～工作人员 administrative staff
行装(裝) xíngzhuāng （名）outfit for a journey; luggage
行踪 xíngzōng （名）whereabouts; sòjourn: ～不定 be on a trip of no fixed destination

醒 xǐng （动）1 wake up: 如梦初～ as if awakening from a dream. 去把他叫～. Go and wake him up. 2 regain consciousness; come to: 她终于～过来了. She has come to at last. 3 be enlightened: 头脑清～ keep a cool head; be quite sober
醒目 xǐngmù （形）striking: ～的标题 bold headlines
醒悟 xǐngwù （动）come to realize the truth; suddenly see the light

擤 xǐng （动）blow (one's nose): ～鼻涕 blow one's nose

省 xǐng （动）1 examine one's own thoughts and feelings: 反～ make a self-examination 2 visit (one's seniors): ～亲 visit one's parents 3 be conscious: 不～人事 lose consciousness
see also shěng

兴(興) xìng （名）pleasure; urge; relish: 游～ the urge to go sightseeing. 诗～ poetic inspiration
see also xīng
兴冲冲 xìngchōngchōng （副）joyfully; gleefully; in high spirits
兴高采烈 xìnggāo-cǎiliè （形）be filled with joy; jubilant
兴趣 xìngqù （名）interest: 我对下棋不感兴～. I take no interest in chess. 人们怀着极大的～听他讲话. The audience listened to him with great absorbing interest.
兴致 xìngzhì （名）interest: ～勃勃 (act) with great gusto

幸 xìng I （名）good fortune: 荣～ have the honour to II （副）fortunately
幸而 xìng'ér （副）luckily; fortunately
幸福 xìngfú I （名）happiness; well-being II （形）(of one's personal life) happy
幸好 xìnghǎo （副）fortunately; luckily
幸亏(虧) xìngkuī as "幸好"
幸免 xìngmiǎn （动）escape by sheer luck; have a narrow escape
幸运(運) xìngyùn （形）fortunate; lucky: ～儿 child of fortune; a person born under a lucky star; lucky dog
幸灾(災)乐(樂)祸(禍) xìngzāi-lèhuò gloat over others' misfortune

杏 xìng （名）apricot: ～仁 almond

性 xìng I （名）1 nature; character: 本～ true nature; inherent character. 他说谎成～. Lying has become his second nature. 她天～忧郁. She has a melancholy disposition. 2 sex: 男

(女)～ the male (female) sex. ～教育 sex education 3 gender: 阳(阴)～ the masculine (feminine) gender II [a suffix indicating a property or characteristic]: 弹～ elasticity. 可行～ feasibility. 可能～ probability. 艺术～ artistic quality. 毁灭～的打击 a smashing blow. 决定～的胜利 a decisive victory

性格 xìnggé (名) nature; character; temperament

性急 xìngjí (形) impatient

性交 xìngjiāo (名) sexual intercourse

性命 xìngmìng (名) life

性能 xìngnéng (名) function (of a machine, etc.) property; performance

性情 xìngqíng (名) temperament; temper: ～温柔 have a gentle disposition. ～暴躁 have a fiery temperament

性欲 xìngyù (名) sexual desire

性质(質) xìngzhì (名) nature; quality: 矛盾的～ the nature of the contradiction

姓 xìng (名) surname; family name: 他～王. His surname is Wang.

姓名 xìngmíng (名) surname and first name; full name

兄 xiōng (名) elder brother

兄弟 xiōngdì I (名) brothers: ～姐妹 siblings II (形) fraternal; brotherly: ～国家 fraternal countries

兄长(長) xiōngzhǎng (名) (a respectful form of address) elder brother; big brother

凶 xiōng I (形) 1 fierce; ferocious 2 terrible; fearful 3 inauspicious: ～多吉少 The chances of an auspicious outcome are much less than grim possibilities. II (名) act of violence

凶暴 xiōngbào (形) fierce and brutal

凶残 xiōngcán (形) savage and ruthless

凶恶(惡) xiōng'è (形) ferocious and vicious; fiendish

凶狠 xiōnghěn (形) fierce and malicious

凶猛 xiōngměng (形) ferocious; violent

凶器 xiōngqì (名) tool or weapon used to perpetrate a criminal act

凶神恶(惡)煞 xiōngshén-èshà (副) devilishly; fiendishly

凶手 xiōngshǒu (名) murderer; assassin

凶险(險) xiōngxiǎn (形) dangerous and dreadful: 病情～. The illness is critical.

凶相 xiōngxiàng (名) atrocious features; fierce look: ～毕露 reveal all one's ferocity

汹 xiōng

汹汹 xiōngxiōng (形) 1 (of waves)roaring 2 violent; truculent: 气势～ blustering and truculent 3 heated; vociferous: 议论～ argue vociferously

胸 xiōng (名) 1 chest; bosom 2 mind; heart: ～无大志 cherish no lofty goal

胸怀(懷) xiōnghuái I (名) mind; heart: 伟大～ large-mindedness II (动) cherish; harbour: ～祖国 keep at heart the interest of one's own country

胸襟 xiōngjīn (名) breadth of mind

胸口 xiōngkǒu (名) the pit of the stomach; chest

胸膛 xiōngtáng (名) chest

胸无(無)点(點)墨 xiōng wú diǎn mò (形) ignorant; practically illiterate: ～的人 ignoramus

胸脯 xiōngpú (名) chest

胸有成竹 xiōng yǒu chéngzhú have an overall consideration of sth. before any action is taken; have a well-thought-out plan

雄 xióng (形) 1 male: ～鸡 cock; rooster 2 grand; imposing: ～伟 magnificent; majestic 3 powerful; mighty: ～兵 a powerful army. ～辩 eloquence

雄才大略 xióngcái-dàlüè (名) great wisdom coupled with bold strategy

雄厚 xiónghòu (形) rich; solid; abundant: 实力～ have an abundance of man power and natural resources. 资金～ abundant funds

雄健 xióngjiàn (形) robust; powerful: ～的步伐 vigorous strides

雄师(師) xióngshī (名) powerful army

雄伟(偉) xióngwěi (形) grand; imposing; magnificent

雄心 xióngxīn (名) great ambition: ～壮志 lofty aspirations and ideals

雄壮(壯) xióngzhuàng (形) powerful; majestic: 这首交响曲～非凡. The symphony is majestic and superb.

熊 xióng (名) bear

熊猫 xióngmāo (名) panda

熊熊 xióngxióng (形) flaming; raging: ～烈火 raging flames

羞 xiū I (形) shy; bashful: 一个怕～的女孩 a shy girl. 害～ be bashful. ～红了脸 blush scarlet II (名) shame; disgrace: 恼～成怒 be shamed into anger. 遮～布 figleaf III (动) feel ashamed

羞惭 xiūcán (形) ashamed: 满面～ blush with shame

羞耻 xiūchǐ (名) sense of shame; shame: 不知～ shameless

羞答答 xiūdādā (形) coy; shy; bashful

羞愧 xiūkuì (形) feel both ashamed and sorry (for what one has done): ～难言 feel ashamed beyond words

羞怯 xiūqiè (形) shy; timid

羞辱 xiūrǔ I (名) disgrace; humiliation II (动) humiliate

羞涩(澀) xiūsè (形) shy; bashful

修 xiū (动) 1 repair: ～自行车 repair a bike. ～鞋 mend shoes 2 build: ～桥 build a bridge. ～大楼 put up a building 3 study; compile: ～哲学 study philosophy. ～县志 write county annals. 自～ study by onself 4 trim; prune: ～指甲 trim one's finger-nails. ～树枝 prune trees

修补(補) xiūbǔ (动) repair; patch up; tinker

修长(長) xiūcháng (形) slender; lanky

修辞(辭) xiūcí (名) rhetoric

修道院 xiūdàoyuàn (名) monastery; convent

修订 xiūdìng (动) revise (of plan, etc.)

修复(復) xiūfù (动) repair; restore; renovate

修改 xiūgǎi (动) revise; modify; amend; alter: ～法律 amend a law. ～文章 polish an article. ～计划 revise a plan. ～大衣 alter a coat

修剪 xiūjiǎn (动) prune; trim

修建 xiūjiàn (动) build; construct

修理 xiūlǐ (动) repair; mend

修面 xiūmiàn (动) shave; have a shave

修女 xiūnǚ (名) nun (of a Christian religious order)

修配 xiūpèi (动) repair the damaged parts of a machine and supply replacements

修缮 xiūshàn (动) (of buildings) repair; renovate; revamp

修饰 xiūshì (动) 1 adorn; decorate 2 make up and dress up 3 polish; touch up

修行 xiūxing (动) practise Buddhism or Taoism

修养(養) xiūyǎng (名) 1 accomplishment; training: 文学或艺术～ literary or artistic accomplishment or attainment 2 correct behaviour in social relationships

修业(業) xiūyè (动) study in a school: ～证书 certificate showing courses attended

修整 xiūzhěng (动) 1 revamp 2 prune; trim

修正 xiūzhèng (动) revise; amend: ～草案 revise a draft. ～主义 revisionism

修筑(築) xiūzhù (动) build; construct

休 xiū (动) 1 stop; cease: 争论不～ argue endlessly 2 rest: 静～ complete rest

休会(會) xiūhuì (动) adjourn: 无限期～ adjourn indefinitely

休假 xiūjià (动、名) have a holiday or vacation

休克 xiūkè (名) shock

休戚 xiū-qī (名) weal and woe; joys and sorrows: ～与共 share weal and woe

休息 xiūxi (动、名) rest: ～会儿 take a rest. 明天我～. Tomorrow is my day off. 课间～ break. 幕间～ intermission. ～室 common room (of faculty)

休想 xiūxiǎng (动) don't cherish any illusion that: 你～逃脱. Don't imagine you can get away with it.

休学 xiūxué (动) suspend one's schooling without losing one's status as a student

休养(養) xiūyǎng (动) recuperate: ～所 sanatorium; rest home

休整 xiūzhěng (动) (of troops) rest and reorganize

休止 xiūzhǐ (动) stop; end: 无～的争论 argue endlessly; endless argument

宿 xiǔ (量)[used of lodgings]: 住一～ stay for one night see also sù

朽 xiǔ (形) 1 rotten; decayed: 枯木～株 withered trees and rotten stumps 2 senile

袖 xiù I (名) sleeve: ～口 cuff (of a sleeve) II (动) tuck inside the sleeve: ～手旁观

look on with folded arms
袖珍 xiùzhēn (形) pocket-size; portable: ～字典 pocket dictionary
秀 xiù (形) 1 elegant; beautiful: 山清水～ beautiful scenery 2 graceful; ～外慧中 graceful and intelligent
秀才 xiùcai (名) scholar; intellectual
秀丽(麗) xiùlì (形) pretty; beautiful
秀美 xiùměi (形) graceful; elegant
秀气(氣) xiùqi (形) delicate; refined; graceful
锈 xiù (名、动) rust; become rusty
绣 xiù (动) embroider
绣花 xiùhuā (动) embroider; do embroidery
臭 xiù (名) odour; smell
see also chòu
臭味相投 xiùwèi xiāngtóu Birds of a feather flock together
嗅 xiù (动) smell; sniff; scent
嗅觉 xiùjué (名) (sense of) smell: ～很灵 have a keen sense of smell
需 xū (动) need; want: 急～ need badly. 必～品 necessaries; necessities
需求 xūqiú (名) requirement; demand
需要 xūyào I (动) need; require: 我们～一支强大的科学技术队伍. We need a strong contingent of scientific and technical workers. 这所房子～修理. The house wants repairing. II (名) needs: 满足读者的～ meet the needs of the readers.
吁 xū (动) sigh: 气喘～～ pant for breath
须 xū I (动) must; have to II (鬚) (名) beard; mustache: 留～ grow a beard
须知 xūzhī (名) the musts: 旅客～ notice to travellers; what tourists are required to bear in mind
虚 xū I (形) 1 empty; void; unoccupied: ～词 words of no semantic meaning; function word. 座无～席 All seats were occupied. 2 false: 徒有～名 have an ill-deserved reputation. ～情假意 a hypocritical show of friendship or affection 3 timid: 心里有点～ feel rather diffident 4 weak; in poor health: 气～ lacking in vital energy; sapless. 身体很～ be very weak physically II (副) to no avail; in vain: 弹不～发. Not a single shot missed its target.
虚报(報) xūbào (动) give a false report
虚词 xūcí (名) function word
虚度 xūdù (动) waste time: ～光阴 fritter away one's time
虚构(構) xūgòu (动) make up; fabricate: ～的情节 a fictitious plot
虚幻 xūhuàn (形) unreal; illusory
虚假 xūjiǎ (形) false; sham
虚惊(驚) xūjīng (名) false alarm
虚名 xūmíng (名) undeserved reputation
虚拟(擬) xūnǐ (形) 1 invented; fictitious 2 suppositional: ～语气 the subjunctive mood
虚胖 xūpàng (名) puffiness
虚荣(榮) xūróng (名) vanity: ～心 vanity. 他的～心很强. He's a vain person
虚弱 xūruò (形) 1 weak; in poor health 2 weak; feeble: 兵力～ weak in military strength
虚实(實) xū-shí (名) the actua situation
虚脱 xūtuō (名) collapse; prostration
虚伪(僞) xūwěi (形) hypocritical; false
虚心 xūxīn (形) open-minded; modest; modest and unassuming
虚张声(聲)势(勢) xū zhāng shēngshì (动) bluff
墟 xū (名) ruins: 废～ ruins
许 xǔ I (动) 1 allow; permit: 我妈不～我抽烟. My mother doesn't allow me to smoke. 2 promise: 他～过我同我再谈一谈. He promised to have another talk with me. II (副) maybe; perhaps: 天这么黑，～是要下雨吧. It's so dark. Perhaps it's going to rain.
许多 xǔduō (形) many; much; a lot of
许久 xǔjiǔ (副) for a long time; for ages
许可 xǔkě (动) permit; allow
许诺 xǔnuò (动) make a promise; promise
许愿(愿) xǔyuàn (动) promise sb. a reward (for some service)
栩 xǔ

栩栩 xǔxǔ (形) vivid; lively: ～如生 lifelike

畜 xù (动) raise (domestic animals)
see also chù

畜牧 xùmù (动) raise livestock or poultry: ～场 animal farm; livestock farm. ～业 animal husbandry

蓄 xù (动) 1 save up; store up: 水库的～水能力 the amount of water a reservoir can hold; the capacity of a reservoir 2 grow: ～须 grow a beard

蓄电(電)池 xùdiànchí (名) storage battery

蓄洪 xùhóng (动) store floodwater

蓄谋 xùmóu (动) premeditate: ～已久 long premeditated

蓄意 xùyì (形) premeditated; deliberate: ～进行罪恶活动 have long cherished the intention of carrying out criminal activities

酗 xù

酗酒 xùjiǔ I (动) drink immoderately II (名) alcoholism

煦 xù (形) <书> warm; balmy

叙 xù (动) 1 chat: ～家常 engage in chitchat 2 narrate; recount: ～事诗 narrative poem

恤 xù (动) 1 pity; sympathize with: 怜～ have compassion on 2 give relief: 抚～ pay compensation

旭 xù

旭日 xùrì (名) the rising sun

序 xù (名) 1 order; sequence: 顺～ keep in sequence. 程～ procedure. 井然有～ in good order 2 arrange in proper order: ～齿 be arranged in order of seniority in age 3 preface: ～幕 prelude

序曲 xùqǔ (名) overture

序言 xùyán (名) preface; foreword

絮 xù I (名) (cotton) wadding: 柳～ (willow) catkin II (动) wad with cotton: ～棉衣 line one's clothes with cotton

絮叨 xùdao (动) talk tediously at length; be a chatter-box; be long-winded

婿 xù (名) son-in-law

绪 xù (名) thread; order in sequence: 头～ main threads (of a complicated affair). ～言 (or ～论) introduction (to book, etc.). 千头万～ a multitude of thoughts 2 task, undertaking: 续未竟之～ go on with the unfinished task

续(續) xù (动) continue; extend: 待～ to be continued. ～订 renew one's subscription (to a newspaper, etc.). ～假 extend one's leave of absence. ～弦 (of a man) remarry. ～集 continuation (of a book); sequel. 我断断～～在那里住了十年. I lived there off and on for ten years.

宣 xuān (动) declare; proclaim; announce: 不～而战 wage an undeclared war. 心照不～ be a tacit understanding

宣布 xuānbù (动) declare; proclaim; announce: ～独立 declare (or proclaim) independence. ～会议开始 declare a meeting open; call a meeting to order. ～一件事 make an announcement

宣称(稱) xuānchēng (动) assert

宣传(傳) xuānchuán I (动) 1 disseminate; publicize; propagate: ～交通规则 publicize traffic regulations. ～环境保护的重要性 make known the importance of environmental protection 2 spread propaganda; propagandize: 两党都忙着～自己的政策. Both parties are busy propagandizing about their own policies. II (名) 1 dissemination 2 propaganda: 电影里对战争恐怖的～太过份了. There has been too much propaganda about the horror of war.

宣读(讀) xuāndú (动) (of a written statement, document, etc.) read out (in public)

宣告 xuāngào (动) declare; proclaim: ～成立 proclaim the founding of (a state, organization, etc.)

宣判 xuānpàn (动) pass judgment: ～有罪(无罪) pronounce sb. guilty (not guilty)

宣誓 xuānshì (动) swear; take an oath: ～就职 be sworn in

宣言 xuānyán (名) declaration; manifesto; proclamation

宣扬(揚) xuānyáng (动) propagate; advocate: 大力～经济体制改革的重要性. Give wide publicity to the importance of restructuring the national economy.

宣战(戰) xuānzhàn (动) declare (or proclaim) war

喧 xuān (形) noisy: 锣鼓～天 a deafening sound of gongs and drums

喧宾(賓)夺(奪)主 xuān bīn duó zhǔ The person (or matter) of greater importance is relegated to the background. *or* The person who plays second fiddle steals the limelight.

喧哗(嘩) xuānhuá I (动) make a lot of noise: 请勿～. Quiet, please! II (名) confused noise; hubbub

喧闹 xuānnào (名) noise and excitement; bustle

喧嚣 xuānxiāo I (形) noisy II (名) clamour: ～一时 (sth.) creates quite a stir. ～鼓噪 make a clamour; stir up a commotion

轩 xuān (形) 〈书〉 high; lofty

轩然大波 xuānrán dàbō (名) (create) a great disturbance; (create) a big stir

旋 xuán (动) 1 circle; spin; revolve: 盘～ circle (in the sky) 2 return; come back: 凯～ return in triumph
see also xuàn

旋律 xuánlǜ (名) melody

旋钮 xuánniǔ (名) knob

旋绕(繞) xuánrǎo (动) curl up; drift about: 炊烟～ A wisp of smoke is curling up from a chimney.

旋涡(渦) xuánwō (名) whirlpool; eddy

旋转(轉) xuánzhuǎn (动) revolve; rotate; spin

玄 xuán (形) 1 profound; abstruse: ～理 metaphysical ideas 2 unreliable; incredible: 这话太～了. That's a pretty tall story.

玄妙 xuánmiào (形) mysterious; abstruse

玄虚 xuánxū (名) deceitful trick: 故弄～ deliberately juggle with false ideas to hide the truth

悬(懸) xuán I (动) 1 hang; suspend: ～空 suspended in midair. ～灯结彩 ornament (a building) with lanterns and festoons 2 keep thinking about: ～念 be seriously concerned about; be worried about II (形) 1 unsettled; outstanding: ～而未决的问题 unsettled question; outstanding issue 2 remote; widely different: ～隔 far apart. ～殊 a far cry from

悬挂 xuánguà (动) (of portrait, flag, etc.) hang

悬赏 xuánshǎng (动) put a price on someone's head

悬崖 xuányá (名) cliff; precipice: ～勒马 rein in at the brink of the precipice; stop riding into imminent disaster

癣 xuǎn (名) tinea; ringworm

选(選) xuǎn I (动) 1 select; choose: 挑～ pick and choose 2 elect: 普(大)～ general election. 他当～为总统. He was elected president. II (名) selection: 诗～ selected poems

选拔 xuǎnbá (动) (usu. of persons) select or choose: ～委员会 selection committee; selection jury

选购(購) xuǎngòu (动) pick out and buy; choose

选集 xuǎnjí (名) selected works; selections; anthology

选举(舉) xuǎnjǔ I (动) elect; vote II (名) election: ～权 the right to vote

选民 xuǎnmín (名) (individually) voter; elector; (collectively) constituency; electorate

选派 xuǎnpài (动) select and appoint; detail

选票 xuǎnpiào (名) vote; ballot

选手 xuǎnshǒu (名) (of sports) selected contestant; player

选修 xuǎnxiū (动) take as an elective course: ～课 elective (optional) course

选择(擇) xuǎnzé (动) select; make a choice: 自然～ natural selection

旋 xuàn (动) 1 turn sth. on a lathe; lathe 2 whirl: ～风 whirlwind
see also xuán

旋风(風) xuànfēng (名) whirlwind: 龙～ tornado

泫 xuàn (动) drip; trickle

泫然 xuànrán (动) (usu. of tears) fall; trickle: ～泪下 tears trickle down one's cheeks

炫 xuàn (动) 1 dazzle 2 show off: ～耀 show off; make a display of

眩 xuàn (形) dizzy; giddy: 头晕目～ feel dizzy

绚 xuàn (形) gorgeous

绚丽(麗) xuànlì (形) gorgeous; magnificent: 文采～ ornate literary style. ～的鲜花 beautiful flowers

靴 xuē (名) boots: 马～ riding boots. 雨～ rubber boots; galoshes

削 xuē (动) cut; pare; peel see also xiāo

削价(價) xuējià (动) cut prices

削减 xuējiǎn (动) cut (down); reduce

削弱 xuēruò (动) weaken; cripple

学(學) xué I (动) **1** study; learn: ～文化 learn to read and write. ～历史 study history; take a history course. 向他～ learn from him **2** imitate; mimic: 鹦鹉～舌 parrot II (名) **1** learning; knowledge: 才疏～浅 have little talent and learning; be an indifferent scholar **2** subject of study; branch of learning: 数～ mathematics. 文～ literature. **3** school: 小～ primary school. 中～ high school. 大～ college; university. 上～ go to school

学报(報) xuébào (名) journal (of a college)

学潮 xuécháo (名) student strike

学费 xuéfèi (名) tuition fee; tuition

学风(風) xuéfēng (名) style of study

学府 xuéfǔ (名) institution of higher learning

学会(會) xuéhuì I (动) learn; master: 这孩子～了走路. The child has learned to toddle. II (名) association society; institute

学籍 xuéjí (名) one's status as a student

学究 xuéjiū (名) pedant: ～气 pedantry

学科 xuékē (名) branch of learning; discipline; subject

学历(歷) xuélì (名) a written account of one's education

学龄(齡) xuélíng (名)school age: ～前 preschool age

学年 xuénián (名) school year

学派 xuépài (名) school of thought

学期 xuéqī (名) term; semester

学生 xuésheng (名) pupil; student

学识(識) xuéshí (名) learning; knowledge; scholarly attainments: ～渊博 have great learning; be learned. ～浅薄 have little learning

学士 xuéshì (名)bachelor; B.A.

学术(術) xuéshù (名) academic research: ～交流 academic exchanges. ～论文 research paper; thesis. ～讨论会 symposium

学说 xuéshuō (名) theory; doctrine

学徒 xuétú (名) apprentice

学位 xuéwèi (名) academic degree: 博士(硕士)～ doctor's (master's) degree

学问 xuéwen (名) learning; knowledge; scholarship: 做～ engage in intellectual pursuit. ～高深 be learned

学习(習) xuéxí (动) study; learn

学校 xuéxiào (名) school

学业(業) xuéyè (名) one's studies: ～成绩 school record

学院 xuéyuàn (名) college; institute

学者 xuézhě (名) scholar

学制 xuézhì (名) **1** term of study **2** school system; including the curriculum and other regulations

穴 xué (名) cave; den; hole: 洞～ cave. 虎～ tiger's lair. 匪～ bandits' den. ～位 acupuncture point

雪 xuě I (名) snow II (动) wipe out; avenge: ～耻 wipe out a disgrace. 昭～ rehabilitate

雪白 xuěbái (形) snow-white

雪崩 xuěbēng (名) snowslide; avalanche

雪恨 xuěhèn (动) avenge: 报仇～ take revenge

雪花 xuěhuā (名) snowflake

雪花膏 xuěhuāgāo (名) vanishing cream

雪盲 xuěmáng (名) snow-blind

雪泥鸿爪 xuění hóngzhǎo footprints left on the path of one's life; one's memorable events

雪橇 xuěqiāo (名) sled; sleigh

雪中送炭 xuě zhōng sòng tàn send help where it is badly needed; provide timely help

血 xuè (名) blood: 流～ shed blood. 出～ bleed see also xiě

血案 xuè'àn (名) murder case

血管 xuèguǎn (名) blood vessel

血汗 xuèhàn (名) sweat on the brow; hard toil

血迹 xuèjì (名) bloodstain

血口喷人 xuèkǒu pēn rén (动) venomously vilify

血库 xuèkù (名) blood bank

血泪(淚) xuèlèi (名) tragic experience; sufferings

血淋淋 xuèlínlín (形) bloody

血泊 xuèpō (名) pool of blood

血气(氣) xuèqì (名) **1** vim and vigour **2** uprightness and staunchness of character: 有～的青年 a young man of strong will and moral integrity
血球 xuèqiú (名) blood cell
血肉 xuèròu (名) flesh and blood: ～关系 blood kinship
血色 xuèsè (名) redness of the skin; colour: 脸上没有～ look pale or off colour
血统 xuètǒng (名) blood lineage; blood relationship
血小板 xuèxiǎobǎn (名) (blood) platelet
血腥 xuèxīng (形) bloody; sanguinary
血型 xuèxíng (名) blood type
血压(壓) xuèyā (名) blood pressure: 高～ high blood pressure; hypertension. 我的～是正常的: 低压 80 高压 120. My blood pressure is pretty normal, it's 80 over 120.
血液 xuèyè (名) blood
血缘 xuèyuán (名) blood relationship
血债 xuèzhài (名) debt of blood

勋(勳)

xūn (名) merit: 功～ meritorious service
勋爵 xūnjué (名) (a title of nobility) Lord
勋章 xūnzhāng (名) medal; decoration

熏

xūn (动) **1** smoke; fumigate: 墙给烟～黑了. The wall was blackened by smoke **2** treat (meat, fish, etc.) with smoke; smoke: ～鱼 smoked fish
熏染 xūnrǎn (动) contaminate; corrupt
熏陶 xūntáo (动) nurture; benefit

驯

xún I (动) tame; subdue: ～马 break in a horse II (形) tame and docile: ～鹿 a tame deer
驯服 xúnfú I (动) tame; bring under control: ～烈马 tame a spirited horse II (形) obedient and docile
驯养(養) xúnyǎng (动) domesticate

循

xún (动) follow; abide by
循规蹈矩 xúnguī-dǎojǔ follow the beaten track; stick rigidly to rules and regulations
循环(環) xúnhuán (动) circulate; cycle: 血液～ blood circulation. 恶性～ vicious circle
循序渐进(進) xúnxù jiànjìn (动) proceed systematically

旬

xún (名) **1** a period of ten days: 上(中、下)～ the first (second, last) ten days of month **2** a decade in a person's life (applied to old people alone)

询

xún (动) ask; inquire: 查～ make inquiries
询问 xúnwèn (动) ask about; inquire: ～健康情况 ask after sb.

巡

xún (动) patrol
巡查 xúnchá (动) go on a tour of inspection
巡航 xúnháng (动) cruise: ～导弹 cruise missile
巡回 xúnhuí (动) make rounds; go the rounds; tour; make a circuit of: ～大使 an ambassador-at-large. ～医疗队 mobile medical team
巡逻(邏) xúnluó (动) go on patrol; patrol
巡视 xúnshì (动) make an inspection tour
巡洋舰(艦) xúnyángjiàn (名) cruiser

寻(尋)

xún (动) seek; search: ～欢作乐 seek pleasure. 我们到处～找她. We have been looking for her everywhere.
see also xín
寻常 xúncháng (形) usual; common: 这种高贵行为现在是很～的事了. Such a noble deed is a common occurrence nowadays.
寻开(開)心 xún kāixīn (动) make fun of; joke
寻觅 xúnmì (动) seek; look for
寻求 xúnqiú (动) seek
寻味 xúnwèi (动) chew sth. over and taste; think over: 耐人～ afford much food for thought; set one pondering
寻衅(釁) xúnxìn (动) pick a quarrel; provoke
寻找 xúnzhǎo (动) seek; look for

训

xùn I (动) lecture; teach; train: 受～ undergo training. ～他一顿 give him a lecture (or a dressing down) II (名) model; example: 不足为～. This should not be regarded as a criterion.
训斥 xùnchì (动) reprimand; dress down
训诂 xùngǔ (名) critical interpretation of an ancient text; exegesis
训练(練) xùnliàn (动) train; drill
训令 xùnlìng (名) <旧> instruc-

tions; directive

汛 xùn (名) flood: 防～ flood control. ～期 flood season

讯 xùn I (动) interrogate; question: 审～ interrogate II (名) message; dispatch: 电～dispatch

迅 xùn (形) fast; swift

迅猛 xùnměng (形) swift and violent

迅速 xùnsù (形) speedy; rapid: 动作～ be quick-moving. ～发展 rapid development. ～康复 speedy recovery. ～答复 prompt reply

逊(遜) xùn (形) 1 modest: 谦～ modest and unassuming. 出言不～ speak insolently 2 inferior

逊色 xùnsè (形) inferior: 稍有～ be slightly inferior by comparison

殉 xùn (动) 1 be buried alive with the deceased 2 lay down one's life for a cause

殉国(國) xùnguó (动) give one's life for one's country

殉难(難) xùnnàn (动) die (for a just cause)

殉葬 xùnzàng (动) be buried alive with the deceased

殉职(職) xùnzhí (动) die at one's post

Y y

丫 yā (名) bifurcation; fork

丫杈 yāchà (名) 1 fork (of a tree); crotch 2 crotched; forked

丫头(頭) yātou (名) 1 girl 2 slave girl; maid

压(壓) yā (动) 1 press; push down; weigh down: ～扁 press flat; flatten. ～碎 crush (to pieces). 大雪把树枝～弯了. Heavy snow weighed the branches down. 2 keep under control; control: ～住心头怒火 keep one's temper 3 suppress: 镇～叛乱 suppress (or put down) a rebellion 4 approach: 敌军～境. Enemy troops are bearing down on the border. 5 shelve: 这份公文～在什么地方了. The document is being pigeonholed somewhere.

see also yà

压倒 yādǎo (动) overwhelm; overpower; prevail over: ～多数 an overwhelming majority. 比赛中客队占～优势. The guest team dominated the game.

压服 yāfú (动) force sb. to submit; coerce sb. into submission: ～手段 coercive measure

压价(價) yājià (动) force price down: ～出售 sell at reduced prices

压力 yālì (名) 1 pressure: 屈于～ yield to pressure 2 pressure: 施加～ pressurize; bring pressure on sb.

压路机(機) yālùjī (名) road roller

压迫 yāpò (动) 1 oppress; repress 2 constrict

压缩 yāsuō (动) reduce; cut down; curtail: ～开支 cut down (or reduce) expenses

压抑 yāyì I (动) contain; inhibit; depress: ～不住内心的激动 unable to contain one's excitement II (形):心情～ feel constrained. 感到～ feel inhibited

压榨 yāzhà (动) 1 press; squeeze 2 exploit; fleece; bleed one white

压制 yāzhì (动) suppress; stifle; inhibit: ～批评 gag criticism. ～反对的意见 suppress dissenting voices

呀 yā I (叹) [indicating surprise] ah; oh: ～,下雪了! Oh, it's snowing! II (象) creak: 门～的一声开了. The door opened with a creak. *or* The door squeaked open.

鸦 yā (名) crow

鸦片 yāpiàn (名) opium

鸦雀无(無)声(聲) yā-què wú shēng it became so quiet that you could hear a butterfly

押 yā I (动) 1 give as security; mortgage; pawn: 作～ leave sth. as security. 以房子作～借了两千美元 mortgage a house for two thousand dollars 2 detain; take into custody: 在～犯 criminal in custody 3 escort: ～运 escort goods (on a train, truck, etc.) II (名) signature; mark made on a written statement in place of signature

押解 yājiè (动) send (a criminal or captive) under escort; escort

押金 yājīn (名) deposit; security

鸭 yā (名) duck

鸭绒 yāróng (名) duck's down; eiderdown: ～被 eiderdown quilt

涯 yá (名) margin; limit: 天～海角 the four corners of the earth; the end of the earth. 一望无～ boundless as far as the eye can reach

崖 yá (名) precipice; cliff: 悬～勒马 rein in on the edge of a precipice

牙 yá (名) 1 tooth 2 tooth-like thing

牙齿(齒) yáchi (名) tooth

牙床(牀) yáchuáng (名) gum

牙雕 yádiāo (名) ivory carving

牙膏 yágāo (名) toothpaste

牙关(關) yáguān (名) mandibular joint: 咬紧～ clench (or grit) one's teeth

牙科 yákē (名) (department of) dentistry: ～医生 dentist

牙刷 yáshuā (名) toothbrush

牙痛 yátòng (名) toothache

牙龈(齦) yáyín (名) gum

芽 yá (名) bud; sprout; shoot

衙 yá

衙门(門) yámen (名) *yamen*, government office in feudal China

哑(啞) yǎ (形) 1 mute; dumb: 又聋又～ deaf and dumb; deaf-mute 2 (of voice) hoarse; husky

哑巴 yǎba (名) a dumb person; mute

哑剧(劇) yǎjù (名) dumb show; pantomime

哑谜 yǎmí (名) puzzling remark; enigma

雅 yǎ (形) 1 appropriate; proper; correct 2 refined; elegant: 古～ quaint 3 〈敬〉: ～教 your esteemed instructions

雅观(觀) yǎguān (形) [often used in the negative] refined (in manner, etc.); in good taste: 很不～ inconsistent with the canons of good taste; boorish

雅俗共赏 yǎ-sú gòng shǎng [of a work of art or literature]: suit both refined and popular tastes; be enjoyed by both educated and ordinary people

雅兴(興) yǎxìng (名) aesthetic inclinations: 无此～ have no such poetic inspiration

雅致 yǎzhì (形) refined; elegant; tasteful: 陈设～ be furnished in good taste

亚(亞) yà (形) inferior; second: 不～于人 second to none; not inferior to anyone

亚军 yàjūn (名) second place (in a sports contest)

亚麻 yàmá (名) flax: ～布 linen (cloth)

亚热(熱)带(帶) yàrèdài (名) subtropical zone; subtropics; semitropics

亚音速 yàyīnsù (名) subsonic speed: ～飞机 subsonic aircraft

亚洲 Yàzhōu (名) Asia

压(壓) yà see also yā

压根儿(兒) yàgēnr (副) [often used in the negative] from the start; in the first place; altogether: 他全忘了，好象～没有这回事. He clean forgot about it as if nothing of the kind had ever happened.

揠 yà (动) 〈书〉 pull up

揠苗助长(長) yà miáo zhù zhǎng pull the shoots upward in a stupid effort to make them grow; spoil the show by ludicrous enthusiasm

轧 yà (动) 1 roll; run over: ～棉花 gin cotton 2 squeeze out; push out: 倾～ engage in political infighting

see also gá; zhá

焉 yān 〈书〉 1 here; herein: 心不在～ absent-minded. 乐莫大～. How happy one is! 2 [often used in the rhetorical question] how: 如无群众支持，～有今日? How could we fare so well without mass support?

淹 yān (动) flood; submerge; inundate: 庄稼被洪水～了. The crops were inundated.

淹死 yānsǐ (动) drown

阉 yān (动) castrate or spay: ～鸡 capon. ～猪 hog

阉割 yāngē (动) 1 castrate or spay 2 deprive a theory, etc. of its essence; emasculate

腌 yān (动) preserve in salt; salt; pickle: ～菜 pickled vegetables; pickles. ～鱼 salted fish

see also ā

烟 yān (名) 1 smoke 2 mist; vapour 3 tobacco or cigarette: 抽支～ have a cigarette; have a smoke

烟草 yāncǎo (名) tobacco

烟囱 yāncōng (名) chimney; funnel; stovepipe
烟斗 yāndǒu (名) (tobacco) pipe: ～丝 pipe tobacco
烟盒 yānhé (名) cigarette case
烟灰 yānhuī (名) cigarette ash: ～缸 ashtry
烟火 yānhuǒ (名) 1 smoke and fire: 建筑工地,严禁～. Lighting fires is strictly forbidden on the constuction site. 2 fireworks: 放～ put on a display of fireworks
烟煤 yānméi (名) bituminous coal; soft coal
烟幕 yānmù (名) smoke screen: ～弹 smoke shell; smoke bomb
烟丝(絲) yānsī (名) cut tobacco; pipe tabacco
烟雾(霧) yānwù (名) smoke; mist; vapour; smog: ～弥漫 full of smoke
烟消云(雲)散 yānxiāo-yúnsàn vanish like mist; melt into thin air
烟叶(葉) yānyè (名) tobacco leaf; leaf tobacco

咽 yān (名) pharynx
see also yàn
咽喉 yānhóu (名) 1 throat 2 vital passage: ～要地 a junction of strategic importance; key junction

颜 yán (名) 1 face; countenance: 和～悦色 look good-natured and obliging. 笑逐～开 one's face is wreathed in smiles 2 decency; face: 无～见人 feel ashamed to appear in public 3 colour: ～料 pigment; dyestuff. 五～六色 of all colours; multi-coloured; colourful
颜面 yánmiàn (名) 1 face: ～神经 facial nerve 2 decency; face: 顾全～ save face
颜色 yánsè (名) <口> 1 colour 2 facial expression; countenance: 给他点儿～看看. Make him understand how to behave himself. *or* Teach him a lesson.

言 yán (名) 1 word: ～语 speech. 格～ maxim. 诺言 promise; pledge. ～外之意 the implication of a remark 2 say; talk; speak: 畅所欲～ speak freely. ～之有理 What one says is correct. *or* The remark sounds reasonable. 3 character; word (in Chinese each character is called a word): 五～诗 a poem with five characters to a line
言不由衷 yán bù yóuzhōng speak insincerely
言传(傳)身教 yánchuán-shēnjiào teach by personal example as well as verbal instruction; set an example to the others in whatever one says or does
言辞(辭) yáncí (名) one's words; what one says: ～恳切 be sincere and earnest in what one says
言归(歸)于(於)好 yán guī yú hǎo become reconciled
言归(歸)正传(傳) yán guī zhèngzhuàn to come back to our story; to return to the subject
言过(過)其实(實) yán guò qí shí overstate the case
言和 yánhé (动) make peace
言简意赅 yánjiǎn-yìgāi (形) brief and to the point; concise
言论(論) yánlùn (名) opinion on politics and other affairs: ～自由 freedom of speech
言听(聽)计从(從) yántīng-jìcóng act upon whatever sb. says; listen to all his counsel
言语 yányǔ (名) spoken language; speech
言语 yányu (动) speak; answer; reply: 你走的时候～一声儿. Don't just walk out without saying a word. 人家同你讲话呢,你怎么不～? Why did you make no response when people were speaking to you?
言之成理 yán zhī chéng lǐ sound reasonable

阎 yán
阎罗(羅) Yánluó (名) Yama
阎王 Yánwang (名) 1 Yama; King of Hell 2 an extremely cruel person, usu. referring to a local tyrant in the old society

炎 yán I (形) scorching; extremely hot: ～夏 sweltering summer II (名) inflammation: 发～ inflammation. 气管支～ bronchitis
炎黄子孙 yánhuángzǐsūn (名) descendants of the Yellow Emperor
炎凉 yánliáng (形) behave abjectly to one and coldly to the other; behave abjectly to the rich and powerful and coldly towards the poor: 世态～ the way of the world follows the practice of playing up to the influential and giving the cold shoulder to the less fortunate

研 yán (动) 1 grind; pestle: ～成粉末 grind into fine powder 2 study: 钻～ study assiduously
研究 yánjiū (动、名) 1 study;

research: 科学～ scientific research. ～生 postgraduate. ～员 research fellow 2 consider; discuss (problems, suggestions, applications, etc.)

研制(製) yánzhì (动) research and manufacture; develop: ～新的武器 develop new weapons

妍 yán (形)〈书〉beautiful; enchanting: 百花争～. A hundred flowers vie with each other in beauty.

盐(鹽) yán (名) salt: 精～ refined salt

盐碱土 yánjiǎntǔ (名) saline-alkali soil

盐田 yántián (名) salt pan

严(嚴) yán (形) 1 tight: 治学谨～ adopt a rigorous approach in one's studies. 他嘴～,从来不乱说. He is too tight-lipped to let slip any careless remarks. 2 strict; severe; stern; rigorous: 这位老师对学生管教很～. The teacher is very strict with his students. ～冬 severe winter. ～办 be dealt with severely

严惩(懲) yánchéng (动) punish severely

严防 yánfáng (动) be strictly on guard against; take strict precautions against

严格 yángé (形) strict; rigorous; rigid: ～按规定办事 act strictly according to the regulations

严寒 yánhán (名) severe cold; bitter cold

严禁 yánjìn (动) strictly forbid (or prohibit)

严峻 yánjùn (形) stern; severe; rigorous; grim: ～的考验 a severe test; a rigorous test

严酷 yánkù (形) 1 harsh; bitter; grim: ～的现实 harsh reality 2 cruel; ruthless: ～的压迫 cruel oppression. ～的剥削 ruthless exploitation

严厉(厲) yánlì (形) stern; severe: ～的批评 severe criticism

严密 yánmì (形) tight; close: ～监视 keep close watch over. ～注视形势的发展 closely follow the development of the situation

严明 yánmíng (形) strict and impartial: 纪律～. Discipline is strictly observed.

严肃(肅) yánsù (形) serious; solemn; earnest: 他是个～的人,从来不苟言笑. As he is grave by nature he has never allowed himself to make a frivolous remark.

严刑 yánxíng (名) cruel punishment

严阵以待 yán zhèn yǐ dài be fully on the alert for enemy attack; be fully prepared for any eventuality

严正 yánzhèng (形) solemn and just; serious and principled; stern: ～立场 solemn and just stand. ～声明 a solemn statement; solemnly declare

严重 yánzhòng (形) serious; grave; critical: 病情～. The patient's condition is serious. 局势～. The situation is pregnant with imminent danger.

岩(巖) yán (名) 1 rock 2 cliff; crag

岩层(層) yáncéng (名) rock stratum; rock formation

岩洞 yándòng (名) grotto

岩石 yánshí (名) rock

岩心 yánxīn (名) (drill) core

延 yán (动) 1 prolong; extend; lengthen: 蔓～ spread. ～年益寿 prolong one's life. 苟～残喘 be at one's last gasp 2 postpone; delay: 会议～期了. The meeting is postponed.

延长(長) yáncháng (动) lengthen; prolong; extend: ～线 extension line. 这条铁路将～三百英里. The railway line will be extended (or prolonged) 300 miles.

延迟(遲) yánchí (动) delay; defer; postpone: 谈判～,但没有取消. The negotiation was postponed but not cancelled.

延缓 yánhuǎn (动) delay; postpone; put off

延期 yánqī (动) postpone; defer; put off: 比赛因天气不好～举行. The game was put off because of bad weather.

延伸 yánshēn (动) extend; stretch: 铁路一直～到国境线. The railway line stretches right to the frontier.

延误 yánwù (动) incur loss through delay: ～时日. Waste time on account of delay.

延续(續) yánxù (动) continue; go on; last: 会议～了三天. The session lasted for three whole days.

筵 yán (名) 1〈书〉a bamboo mat spread on the floor for people to sit on in ancient China 2 banquet; feast: 喜～ a wedding feast

筵席 yánxí (名) 1 seats arranged around a table at a banquet 2 banquet; feast

沿 yán I (副) along: ～街 along the streets. ～门求乞 beg from door to door. ～着河边走 take a stroll on the riverside II (动) follow (a tradition, pattern, etc.): 相～成习. The traditional practice has gradually become a social custom. III (名) edge; border

沿岸 yán'àn (名) along the bank or coast: 长江～城市 cities on both sides of the Changjiang River

沿革 yángé (名) the course of change and development; evolution: 社会风俗的～ the evolution of social customs

沿海 yánhǎi (名) along the coast; coastal: ～地区 coastal areas

沿途 yántú (副) on the way; throughout a journey: 旅游团～受到热情接待. The tourist group was warmly received throughout its journey.

沿袭(襲) yánxí (动) carry on as before; follow: ～老规矩 tread the beaten track

沿用 yányòng (动) continue to use (an old method, etc.): ～原来的名称 still keep the old name

演 yǎn (动) 1 develop; evolve: ～进 improve through evolutionary process 2 elaborate: ～绎 deduce 3 drill; practise: ～算 make mathematical calculations 4 perform; play; act; put on: ～电影 show a film

演变(變) yǎnbiàn (动) develop; evolve: 历史～ historical evolution

演唱 yǎnchàng (动) sing (in a performance); act a part in Peking or provincial opera

演出 yǎnchū (动) perform; show; put on a show: 首次～ the first performance or show; premiere (of a play, film, etc.)

演化 yǎnhuà (名) evolution

演技 yǎnjì (名) acting

演讲(講) yǎnjiǎng (名) give a lecture; make a speech; lecture

演示 yǎnshì (动) demonstrate; show (using lab, experiment, charts, etc.)

演说 yǎnshuō (动、名) 1 deliver a speech; make an address 2 speech

演算 yǎnsuàn (动) make mathematical calculations

演习(習) yǎnxí (动) manoeuvre; exercise; drill; practice: 军事～ military manoeuvre or exercise

演戏(戲) yǎnxì (动) put on a play; act in a play

演绎(繹) yǎnyì (名) deduction: ～法 the deductive method

演员 yǎnyuán (名) actor or actress; ballet dancer or acrobatic performer

演奏 yǎnzòu (动) give an instrumental performance; play a musical instrument (in a performance)

偃 yǎn

偃旗息鼓 yǎnqí-xīgǔ 1 stop fighting; cease to criticize or attack others 2 be on a secret march

奄 yǎn I (名)〈书〉cover; over; spread II (副) suddenly; all of a sudden

奄奄 yǎnyǎn (名) feeble breathing: 气息～ breathe feebly; be sinking fast; be dying. ～一息 at one's last gasp; on one's last legs

掩 yǎn (动) 1 cover; hide: ～口而笑 laugh in one's sleeve. ～人耳目 hoodwink the public 2 shut; close: 虚～着门 with the door left ajar

掩蔽 yǎnbì I (动) cover; hide [often used in military affairs] II (名) shelter; covered position

掩藏 yǎncáng (动) hide; conceal

掩耳盗铃 yǎn ěr dào líng bury one's head in the sand like an ostrich; engage in self-delusion

掩盖(蓋) yǎngài (动) cover; conceal: 不要～矛盾. Don't try to conceal the contradictions. 大雪～着田野. The fields are covered with a thick layer of snow.

掩护(護) yǎnhù (动) screen; shield; cover: ～进攻 screen an advance. 在黑夜的～下 under cover of night

掩埋 yǎnmái (动) bury

掩饰 yǎnshì (动) cover up; gloss over; conceal: ～错误 gloss over (or cover up) one's mistakes

眼 yǎn I (名) 1 eye: 掩～术 conjuring device; sleight of hand 2 small hole: 针～ eye of a needle. 炮～ muzzle of a gun (in a covered position) 3 key point: 节骨～儿 juncture II (量) [used of a well]: 打一～井 sink a well

眼巴巴 yǎnbābā (副) (of expectation) eagerly; anxiously: 大家一～地等着他回来. We were all anxiously waiting for his return. 他～地看着老鹰把小鸡抓走了. He watched helplessly a hawk snatch away a chick.

眼福 yǎnfú (名) the good fortune of seeing sth. rare or beautiful: ～不浅 be lucky enough to enjoy such a wonderful view

眼高手低 yǎngāo-shǒudī set a high standard for every kind of work but fall far short of it himself; fastidious but incompetent

眼光 yǎnguāng (名) 1 eye: 大家都以怀疑的～望着他. Everyone eyed him with suspicion 2 sight; foresight; insight; vision: ～远大 farsighted. ～短浅 shortsighted

眼红 yǎnhóng I (动) covet; be envious; be jealous: 仇人相见, 分外～. When enemies meet, they will look daggers at each other. II (形) furious

眼花 yǎnhuā have dim eyesight; have blurred vision: 令人头昏～ make one's head swim. ～缭乱 be dazzled

眼睑(瞼) yǎnjiǎn (名) eyelid

眼界 yǎnjiè (名) field of vision (of view); outlook: 扩大～ widen one's field of vision; broaden one's mental horizon

眼镜 yǎnjìng (名) glasses; spectacles

眼看 yǎnkàn (副) 1 soon; in a moment: 天～就要亮了. The day is dawning. 2 watch helplessly; look on passively: 咱们哪能～着庄稼被洪水冲走呢? How can we stand by and watch helplessly the crops in the fields being washed away by the flood?

眼科 yǎnkē (名) (department of) ophthalmology: ～医生 oculist; ophthalmologist; eye-doctor

眼眶 yǎnkuàng (名) 1 eye socket; orbit: 她～里噙着泪水. Her eyes filled with tears. 2 rim of the eye

眼泪(淚) yǎnlèi (名) tears

眼力 yǎnlì (名) 1 eyesight; vision: ～好(差) have good (poor) eyesight 2 judgment; discrimination

眼帘 yǎnlián (名) eye: 映入～ come into view

眼明手快 yǎnmíng-shǒukuài sharp eyed and ag le

眼前 yǎnqián (副) 1 before one's eyes: 他～是碧波万里. He found himself standing before a vast expanse of blue water. 2 at the moment; at present: ～我想不出更好的解决办法. I can't think of a better solution at the moment.

眼球 yǎnqiú (名) eyeball

眼色 yǎnsè (名)wink: 使～ give sb. a wink

眼神 yǎnshén (名) expression in one's eyes

眼熟 yǎnshú (形) look familiar: 这人看着很～, 但我忘了在哪儿见过他. That person looks familiar but I don't remember where I met him.

眼药(藥) yǎnyào (名) eye ointment or eyedrops

眼中钉 yǎnzhōngdīng (名) thorn in one's flesh (or side)

俨(儼) yǎn (形) <书> majestic; solemn; dignified

俨然 yǎnrán I (形)<书> solemn; dignified: 望之～ appear dignified II (副) just like; as if: 这男孩说起话来～是个大人. The boy talks as if he were a grown-up.

衍 yǎn I (动) <书> spread out; develop; amplify II (形) redundant; superfluous

衍变(變) yǎnbiàn (动) develop; evolve

衍生物 yǎnshēngwù (名) derivative

宴 yàn I (动) entertain at a banquet; fête: ～客 host a dinner in honour of the visitors II (名) feast; banquet: 盛～ banquet; sumptuous dinner

宴会(會) yànhuì (名) banquet; feast; dinner party

宴请 yànqǐng (动) entertain (to dinner); fête: ～贵宾 give a banquet in honour of the distinguished guests

谚 yàn (名) proverb; saying: 农～ peasants' proverb; farmers' saying

谚语 yànyǔ (名) proverb; saying

艳(艷) yàn (形) 1 bright; fresh and attractive: 娇～ pretty and charming 2 amorous: ～史 (old use) a love story

艳丽(麗) yànlì (形) bright-coloured and beautiful; gorgeous: ～夺目 something of dazzling beauty. 打扮得过于～ be loudly

dressed
燕 yàn (名)(～子) swallow
燕麦(麥) yànmài (名) oats
燕尾服 yànwěifú (名) tailcoat
燕窝(窩) yànwō (名) edible bird's nest
厌(厭) yàn (动) **1** be disgusted with; detest: ～弃 detest and keep away from **2** be fed up with; be bored with: 这种书我看～了. I am tired of reading such books. 不～其烦 not mind taking all the trouble **3** be satisfied: 贪得无～ have an insatiable desire for gain
厌烦 yànfán (形) be sick of; be fed up with
厌倦 yànjuàn (形) be weary of; be tired of
雁 yàn (名) wild goose
赝 yàn (形) ‹书› counterfeit; spurious; fake
赝本 yànběn (名) spurious edition or copy
赝品 yànpǐn (名) counterfeit; fake; sham
唁 yàn (动) extend condolences
唁电(電) yàndiàn (名) telegram (or cable) of condolence; message of condolence
咽 yàn (动) swallow: 狼吞虎～ wolf down one's food
see also yān
咽气(氣) yànqì (动) breathe one's last; die
砚 yàn (名) inkstone; inkslab
砚台(臺) yàntái (名) inkstone; inkslab
焰 yàn (名) flame; blaze: 烈～ blazing (or raging) flames
焰火 yànhuǒ (名) fireworks
验(驗) yàn (动) **1** examine; check: ～护照 examine (or check) a passport. ～血 blood test **2** prove effective; produce the expected result: 灵～ effective
验尸(屍) yànshī (名) postmortem; autopsy
验收 yànshōu (动) accept sth. as up to standard after a check
验证(證) yànzhèng (动) verify
央 yāng I (动) entreat II (名) centre
央告 yānggào (动) beg; implore
央求 yāngqiú (动) beg; entreat; implore: 我再三～,他才答应. I kept pleading with him until he agreed.
殃 yāng (名) **1** calamity; disaster; misfortune: 遭～ meet with (or suffer) disaster **2** bring disaster on: 祸国～民 bring calamity on the country and the people
秧 yāng (名) **1** seedling; sprout **2** rice seedling: 插～ transplant rice seedlings **3** vine **4** young; fry: 鱼～ young fish
秧歌 yānggē (名) *yangko* (dance), a popular rural folk dance
秧苗 yāngmiáo (名) rice shoots; rice seedlings
秧田 yāngtián (名) rice seedlings bed
羊 yáng (名) sheep: 绵～ sheep. 山～ goat
羊肠(腸)小道 yángcháng xiǎodào (名) winding footpath
羊羔 yánggāo (名) lamb
羊倌 yángguān (名) shepherd
羊圈 yángjuàn (名) sheepfold; sheep pen
羊毛 yángmáo (名) sheep's wool; fleece: ～衫 woollen sweater; cardigan
羊皮 yángpí (名) sheepskin: 披着～的狼 a wolf in sheep's clothing
羊皮纸 yángpízhǐ (名) parchment
羊肉 yángròu (名) mutton: 烤～串 mutton cubes roasted on a skewer; shashlik
洋 yáng I (形) **1** vast; multitudinous **2** foreign: ～房 Western-style house **3** modern: ～办法 modern methods II (名) ocean: 太平～ the Pacific Ocean
洋白菜 yángbáicài (名) cabbage
洋葱 yángcōng (名) onion
洋灰 yánghuī (名) cement
洋相 yángxiàng [generally used in the set phrase: '出洋相']: 出～ make a spectacle of oneself
洋洋 yángyáng (形) numerous; copious: ～大观 spectacular; magnificent
洋溢 yángyì (动) be permeated with; brim with: 感情～ brim with emotion
佯 yáng (动) pretend; feign; sham: ～作不知 pretend not to know. ～攻 feign (or simulate) attack; make a feint
阳(陽) yáng I (名) **1** (in Chinese philosophy, medicine, etc.) *yang*, the masculine or positive principle in na-

ture 2 the sun: ～光 sunlight. ～历 solar calendar (as distinguished from the lunar calendar) II (形) 1 open; overt: ～奉阴违 agree in public but act differently in private 2 belonging to this world: ～间 in this human world (old use) 3 positive: ～极 positive pole; positive electrode

阳春 yángchūn (名) spring (season)

阳伞(傘) yángsǎn (名) parasol; sunshade

阳台(臺) yángtái (名) balcony

阳性 yángxìng (名) 1 positive: ～反应 positive reaction 2 masculine gender

疡(瘍) yáng (名) sore: 溃～ ulcer

杨(楊) yáng (名) poplar

杨柳 yángliǔ (名) 1 poplar and willow 2 willow

杨树(樹) yángshù (名) poplar

扬(揚) yáng (动) 1 raise: ～手 wave one's hand (and beckon). ～长避短 make amends for one's weaknesses by exploiting one's strengths. 趾高气～ self-complacent and arrogant 2 spread; make known: 宣～ propagate; publicize. 名～四海 be known throughout the world

扬长(長)而去 yángcháng ér qù stalk off; stride out

扬眉吐气(氣) yángméi-tǔqì hold one's head high; feel happy and proud

扬名 yángmíng (动) make a name for oneself; become famous: ～天下 become world-famous

扬声(聲)器 yángshēngqì (名) loudspeaker

扬水 yángshuǐ (动) pump up water: ～站 pumping station

扬言 yángyán (动) openly talk about taking aggressive action

扬扬 yángyáng (副) triumphantly; complacently: 得意～ look immensely complacent

痒(癢) yǎng (名) itch

痒痒 yǎngyang (名)〈口〉itch

氧 yǎng (名) oxygen (O)

氧化 yǎnghuà (动) oxidize; oxidate: ～作用 oxidation

氧气(氣) yǎngqì (名) oxygen

养(養) yǎng (动) 1 support; provide for: ～家 support a family 2 raise; keep; grow: ～鸭 raise ducks. ～花 grow flowers 3 give birth to: 她～了个儿子. She gave birth to a boy. 4 foster; adoptive: ～父(母) foster-father (mother). ～子(女) adopted son (daughter) 5 form; acquire; cultivate: ～成良好的习惯 form good habits 6 convalesce; recuperate: ～身体 recuperate 7 maintain; keep in good repair: ～路 maintain a road; road maintenance

养病 yǎngbìng (动) recuperate

养虎遗患 yǎng hǔ yí huàn to rear a tiger is to court calamity; to appease an enemy is to invite disaster

养精蓄锐 yǎngjīng-xùruì conserve energy and build up strength

养老 yǎnglǎo (动) 1 provide for the aged (usu. one's parents) 2 live in retirement: ～金 old-age pension. ～院 House of Respect for the Aged

养料 yǎngliào (名) nourishment

养神 yǎngshén (动) repose: 闭目～ sit in repose with one's eyes closed

养生 yǎngshēng (动) preserve one's health; keep in good health

养育 yǎngyù (动) bring up; rear: ～子女 bring up children

养殖 yǎngzhí (动) breed or cultivate (aquatics)

养尊处(處)优(優) yǎngzūn-chùyōu enjoy high position and a life of ease and comfort

仰 yǎng (动) 1 face upward: ～望星斗 look at the stars 2 admire; respect: 信～ believe in. ～慕 hold sb. in high esteem 3 rely on; depend on: ～仗 look to sb. for help

仰人鼻息 yǎng rén bíxī be dependent on others and act slavishly; be at sb.'s beck and call

仰卧 yǎngwò (动) lie on one's back; lie supine

仰泳 yǎngyǒng (名) backstroke

恙 yàng (名)〈书〉ailment; illness: 安然无～ safe and sound

样(樣) yàng I (名) 1 appearance; shape: ～式 style; type. 模～ look; manner 2 sample; model; pattern: 货～ sample (goods). 鞋～ outline of a shoe; shoe pattern. 校～ proof sheet II (量) kind; type: 在他所选的课程里，他～～都是名列前

茅. In each and every course he has chosen, he is always among the best.

样板 yàngbǎn (名) 1 sample plate 2 templet 3 model; prototype; example: 树立~ set an example

样本 yàngběn (名) 1 sample book 2 sample; specimen

样品 yàngpǐn (名) sample (product); specimen

样子 yàngzi (名) 1 appearance; shape 2 manner; air 3 sample; model; pattern: 衣服~ clothes pattern 4〈口〉tendency; likelihood: 天象是要下雨的~. It looks like rain. 高高兴兴的~ look so very happy

怏 yàng I (名) calamity; disaster: 遭~ meet with disaster II bring disaster to: 祸国~民 bring calamity to the country and the people

怏怏 yàngyàng (形) disgruntled: ~不乐 look disgruntled and sad

要 yāo (动) 1 demand; ask 2 force; coerce
see also yào

要求 yāoqiú (动) ask for; demand; request: ~澄清 ask for clarification. ~出席 request one's presence. ~速予答复 demand a prompt reply

要挟(挾) yāoxié (动) coerce; put pressure on: 他们~他,要他俯首听命. They tried to coerce him into submission.

腰 yāo (名) 1 waist 2 waist (of a garment): 裤~ waist of trousers 3 middle: 半山~ halfway up a mountain; on a hillside

腰包 yāobāo (名) purse; pocket: 那样,我们都得掏~. In that case, we will all have to make a contribution.

腰杆(桿)子 yāogǎnzi (名) 1 back: 挺起~ straighten one's back and square one's shoulders 2 backing; support: ~硬 have strong backing

腰身 yāoshēn (名) waistline; waist; waist measurement: 衣服的~ the waist of a dress

腰子 yāozi (名) kidney

夭 yāo (动) die young

夭亡 yāowáng (动) die young

夭折 yāozhé (动) 1 die young 2 come to a premature end: 谈判中途~. The negotiations broke down halfway.

妖 yāo I (名) goblin; demon; evil spirit II (形) 1 evil and bewitching: ~术 sorcery; witchcraft 2 coquettish; seductive

妖怪 yāoguài (名) monster; goblin; demon

妖魔鬼怪 yāomó-guǐguài (名) demons and ghosts

妖孽 yāoniè (名) 1 person or event associated with evil or misfortune 2 evildoer

妖言 yāoyán (名) heresy; fallacy: ~惑众 spread fallacies to mislead the public; stir up public feeling by sophistry

邀 yāo (动) 1 invite; request: 特~代表 specially invited representative 2 gain; receive: 谅~同意. This will probably meet with your approval.

邀集 yāojí (动) invite a group of people to come and meet together

邀请 yāoqǐng (动) 1 invite (usu. for certain specific purposes): ~他们三人参加晚宴 invite the three of them to dinner. ~赛 invitational tournament 2 gain; receive

肴 yáo (名) meat and fish dishes

肴馔 yáozhuàn (名) the courses at a banquet; dishes

窑(窯) yáo (名) 1 kiln: 砖~ brickkiln 2 cave dwelling

窑洞 yáodòng (名) cave dwelling

谣 yáo (名) 1 ballad; rhyme: 民~ ballad 2 rumour

谣传(傳) yáochuán (名) 1 the spread of the rumours 2 the rumours that go about everywhere

谣言 yáoyán (名) ungrounded rumour: 散布~ spread (or circulate) rumours

遥 yáo (形)〈书〉distant; remote; far

遥测 yáocè (名) telemetering: 空间~ space telemetry

遥感 yáogǎn (名) remote sensing

遥控 yáokòng (名) remote control; telecontrol

遥遥 yáoyáo (副) far away; remote: 在这方面~领先 be far ahead in this field. ~无期 It won't materialize in the foreseeable future. *or* The possibility is fairly remote.

遥远(遠) yáoyuǎn (形) distant;

remote: ～的将来 the distant (or remote) future.

摇 yáo (动) shake; wave: ～头 shake one's head. ～旗 wave a flag. ～船 row a boat. ～铃 ring a bell

摇摆(擺) yáobǎi (动) sway; swing; rock; vacillate: 迎风～sway in the breeze. 在这个问题上，他们并没有～不定. There is no vacillation on their part on this question.

摇动(動) yáodòng (动) **1** wave; shake: 服用前请～瓶子. Shake the bottle before use. **2** rock; flail: 看见他们向我走近了，我就向他们～两臂. I flailed my arms at them when I saw them approach.

摇晃 yáohuàng (动) rock; sway; shake: 风浪大了，这只船开始有点～. The sea is rough, and the ship begins to rock. 这椅子有点～. The chair is a bit rickety (or shaky).

摇篮(籃) yáolán (名) cradle: 我国古代文化的～ the cradle of ancient Chinese culture

摇旗呐喊 yáo qí nàhǎn drum up support

摇身一变(變) yáo shēn yī biàn assume an entirely different role in an instant

摇头(頭)摆(擺)尾 yáotóu-bǎiwěi assume an air of complacency

摇尾乞怜(憐) yáo wěi qǐ lián wag the tail; fawn and beg for mercy

摇摇欲坠(墜) yáoyáo yù zhuì (形) tottering; crumbling; teetering on the verge of collapse

摇曳 yáoyè (动) flicker; sway: ～的灯光 flickering light

窈 yǎo

窈窕 yǎotiǎo (形)〈书〉(of a woman) gentle and graceful

杳 yǎo (形)〈书〉too far away to be readily accessible: ～无踪迹 disappear without a trace; vanish like soap bubbles

杳无(無)音信 yǎo wú yīnxìn be absolutely no news about sb.; disappear for good and all

咬 yǎo (动) **1** bite; snap at: ～了一口 take a bite **2** (of a dog) bark: 鸡叫狗～ cocks crow and dogs bark **3** incriminate another person: 反～一口 make a false countercharge against one's accuser **4** pronounce; articulate: 他字～不清楚. He can't enunciate clearly. **5** be nitpicking (about the use of words): ～字眼儿 be fastidious

咬文嚼字 yǎowén-jiáozì juggle with words like a pedant

咬牙切齿(齒) yǎoyá-qièchǐ gnash one's teeth

疟(瘧) yào (名)(～子) malaria

see also nüè

药(藥) yào I (名) **1** medicine; drug; remedy: 服～ take medicine. 良～苦口. Good medicine is bitter to taste. **2** certain chemicals: 火～ gunpowder II (动)〈书〉**1** cure with medicine: 不可救～ incurable; beyond cure **2** kill with poison

药材 yàocái (名) medicinal materials; crude drugs

药草 yàocǎo (名) medicinal herbs

药店 yàodiàn (名) drugstore; chemist's shop

药方 yàofāng (名) prescription

药房 yàofáng (名) **1** drugstore; chemist's shop; pharmacy **2** hospital pharmacy; dispensary

药膏 yàogāo (名) ointment; salve

药棉 yàomián (名) absorbent cotton

药片 yàopiàn (名) (medicinal) tablet

药水 yàoshuǐ (名) **1** liquid medicine **2** lotion

药丸 yàowán (名) pill

药物 yàowù (名) medicines; pharmaceuticals; medicaments

要 yào I (形) important: 主～ principal. 紧～ imperative. ～点 gist. 险～ of strategic importance II (名) important substance: 摘～ abstract; precis. 纲～ outline III (动) **1** need; like to keep: 他～一个口琴. He needs a mouth organ. **2** ask; demand: ～帐 demand payment of a debt. 她～我给她写一封介绍信. She asked me to write a letter of recommendation for her. **3** want; desire: 他～学游泳. He wants to learn swimming. **4** have to: 路很滑，大家～小心. We have to be careful for the road is very slippery. **5** be going to: ～下雨了! It's going to rain. IV (连) **1** if: 明天～下雨，我就不去了. If it rains tomorrow, I won't go. **2** either ... or ...: ～就去打篮球，～就去溜冰，别再犹豫了. You either go

and play basketball or go skating. Don't hesitate any more. see also yāo
要冲(衝) yàochōng (名) communications centre (or hub): 军事～ strategic point
要道 yàodào (名) thoroughfare: 交通～ important line of communications
要点(點) yàodiǎn (名) 1 main points; essentials; gist: 抓住～ grasp the main points 2 key stronghold
要饭 yàofàn (动) beg (for food or money): ～的 beggar
要害 yàohài (名) vital part; crucial point: ～部门 key department. 击中～ hit home; hit the nail on the head
要好 yàohǎo (动) 1 be on good terms 2 want to do well
要价(價) yàojià (动) ask a price; charge: 你～太高. You are asking too much.
要紧 yàojǐn (形) 1 important 2 be critical; be serious: 他的病～不～? Is his illness serious? 3 be in a hurry to do sth.: 我～进城,来不及和他细说. As I am in a hurry to go to town, I have no time to discuss the matter with him.
要领 yàolǐng (名) main points; essentials; gist: 不得～ fail to grasp the main points. 掌握～ grasp the essentials
要么(麼) yàome (连) or; either ... or ...: 你～跟我们一起去,～呆在家里,随你的便. You can either go with us or stay at home. It's up to you.
要面子 yào miànzi (动) be keen on face-saving; be anxious to keep up appearances
要命 yàomìng I (动) drive sb. to his death; kill II (副) to an extreme degree: 好得～ awfully good. 挤得～ packed like sardines
要强 yàoqiáng (形) be eager to excel in whatever one does
要人 yàorén (名) very important person (V.I.P.)
要塞 yàosài (名) fort; fortress; fortification
要是 yàoshì (连) if; suppose; in case
要素 yàosù (名) essential factor
要闻 yàowén (名) important news; front-page story
要言不烦 yào yán bù fán (形) concise and succinct both in speech and writing
要职(職) yàozhí (名) important post

钥(鑰) yào

see also yuè
钥匙 yàoshi (名) key: 一串～ a bunch of keys. 万能～ master key

耀

yào (动) 1 shine; illuminate: 照～ shine on; illuminate 2 boast of: 他喜欢夸～自己的本领. He likes to boast about his own abilities. 3 honour; credit
耀武扬(揚)威 yàowǔ-yángwēi make a show of one's strength; sabre-rattling
耀眼 yàoyǎn (of light) dazzling

耶 yē

耶稣 yēsū (名) Jesus: ～基督 Jesus Christ. ～教 Protestantism

椰

yē (名) coconut palm; coconut tree; coco
椰子 yēzi (名) 1 coconut palm; coconut tree; coco 2 coconut

噎

yē (动) chock: 他吃得太快,～住了. He started to choke as he was eating too fast. 因～废食 give up eating because of a hiccup

爷(爺)

yé (名) 1 father: ～娘 father and mother 2 grandfather 3 a respectful form of address for a man of the older generation: 老大～ grandpa 4 <旧> a form of address for an official or rich man: 老～ lord; master
爷爷 yéye (名) <口> 1 (paternal) grandfather 2 grandpa (a respectful form of address for an old man)

冶

yě (动) smelt (metal)
冶金 yějīn (名) metallurgy: ～工业 metallurgical industry
冶炼(煉) yěliàn (动) smelt: ～厂 smeltery

野

yě I (名) 1 open country: 旷～里 in the open 2 limit; boundary: 分～ line of demarcation; watershed 3 not in power: 在～党 a party not in power; the opposition II (形) 1 wild; uncultivated; undomesticated: ～兽 wild animal. ～兔 hare. ～鸡 pheasant. ～花 wild flower 2 rude; rough: 说话太～ make rude remarks; be foul-mouthed 3 unrestrained; unruly:

心～ unable to sit down and concentrate
野菜 yěcài (名) edible wild herbs
野餐 yěcān (名) picnic
野草 yěcǎo (名) weeds: ～丛生 be rank with weeds
野蛮(蠻) yěmán (形) 1 uncivilized; savage 2 atrocious; brutal
野人 yěrén (名) savage
野生 yěshēng (形) wild; uncultivated: ～动物 wildlife. ～植物 wild plant
野史 yěshǐ (名) unofficial history
野外 yěwài (名) open country; field: 在～工作 do fieldwork
野心 yěxīn (名) wild ambition; careerism: ～家 careerist
野战(戰) yězhàn (名) field operations: ～军 field army. ～医院 field hospital

也 yě I (副) 1 also; too; as well: 水库可以灌溉、发电，～可以养鱼. A reservoir can be used to irrigate and generate power. It can also be used for raising fish. 2 [indicating concession]: 即使你不说，我～知道. I am aware of the problem even if you say nothing. 3 [indicating resignation]: ～只好如此. Well, we will have to let it go at that. 4 [used together with '连' to indicate emphasis]: 连爷爷～乐得哈哈大笑. Even Grandpa was so amused as to roar with laughter. II (助) 〈书〉 1 [indicating judgment or explanation]: 非不能～，是不为～. It is not a question of ability but one of readiness. 2 [indicating doubt or a rhetorical question]: 是可忍～，孰不可忍～? If this can be tolerated, what cannot be tolerated?
也罢(罷) yěbà 1 [indicating tolerance or resignation]: ～，你一定要走，我送你上车. All right, if you insist on going now, I'll see you to the bus stop. 2 (助) whether ... or ...; no matter whether: 你去～，不去～，反正是一样. It makes no difference whether you are going or not.
也许 yěxǔ (副) perhaps; probably; maybe: 他～病了. Perhaps he's ill.

夜 yè (名) night; evening
夜班 yèbān (名) night shift
夜半 yèbàn (名) midnight
夜长(長)梦(夢)多 yècháng-mèngduō when the night is long, dreams are many; delay may lead to adversity
夜车(車) yèchē (名) 1 night train 2 sit up late: 开～ stay up late; burn the midnight oil
夜壶(壺) yèhú (名) chamber pot; bed urinal
夜阑人静 yèlán-rénjìng in the still of the night
夜郎自大 yèláng zìdà ludicrous conceit stemming from pure ignorance
夜盲 yèmáng (名) night blindness
夜幕 yèmù (名) gathering darkness; night: 在～中消失 disappear into the darkness
夜晚 yèwǎn (名) night
夜宵 yèxiāo (名) night snack
夜校 yèxiào (名) night (or evening) school
夜以继(繼)日 yè yǐ jì rì day and night; round the clock
夜莺(鶯) yèyīng (名) nightingale
夜总(總)会(會) yèzǒnghuì (名) nightclub

液 yè (名) liquid; fluid; juice
液化 yèhuà (名) liquefaction: ～天然气 liquefied natural gas (LNG)
液态(態) yètài (名) liquid state
液体(體) yètǐ (名) liquid
液压(壓) yèyā (名) hydraulic pressure

腋 yè (名) axilla; armpit

谒 yè (动) 〈书〉 call on (a superior or an elder person); pay one's respect to
谒见(見) yèjiàn (动) pay a call on (a superior or a senior person); have an audience with

页(頁) yè (名) leaf; page: 活～ loose leaf
页码 yèmǎ (名) page number

叶(葉) yè (名) 1 leaf 2 leaf-like thing: 百～窗 shutter; blind 3 page; leaf 4 part of a historical period: 二十世纪中～ the middle of the twentieth century
叶落归(歸)根 yè luò guī gēn a person residing abroad will return to his ancestral home
叶子 yèzi (名) leaf

业(業) yè I (名) 1 trade; industry: 旅游～ tourism. 饮食～ catering trade. 各行各～ all trades and professions 2 occupation; profession:

就～ employment. 失～ unemployed 3 course of study: 结～ complete a course of study. 毕～ graduate 4 cause; enterprise: 创～ start an enterprise (or business) 5 estate; property: 家～ family property II (副) already: 工程～已完竣. The project has already been completed.

业绩 yèjī (名) outstanding achievement; exemplary accomplishment

业务(務) yèwù (名) vocational work; professional work; business: ～能力 professional competence. ～知识 professional knowledge; expertise

业余(餘) yèyú (名) sparetime; amateur: ～演员 an amateur actor

业主 yèzhǔ (名) owner (of an enterprise or estate); proprietor

曳 yè (动) drag; haul; tug; tow

衣 yī (名) 1 clothing; clothes; garment 2 coating; covering: 糖～ sugar coating

衣橱 yīchú (名) wardrobe

衣服 yīfu (名) clothing; clothes

衣冠禽兽(獸) yīguān qínshòu (名) a beast in human shape

衣柜(櫃) yīguì (名) wardrobe

衣架 yījià (名) 1 coat hanger; clothes-rack 2 clothes tree; clothes stand

衣料 yīliào (名) dress material; cloth; coating; shirting

衣帽间 yīmàojiān (名) cloakroom

衣食住行 yī shí zhù xíng clothing, food, housing, and transport

依 yī I (动) 1 depend on: 唇齿相～ mutually dependent 2 comply with; listen to; yield to: 劝他休息,他怎么也不～. He turned a deaf ear to our advice when we wanted him to take a breather. II (副) according to; in the light of; judging by: ～我看,这样办可以. In my opinion, this should be all right.

依次 yīcì (副) in proper order; successively

依从(從) yīcóng (动) comply with; yield to: 在目前情况下,不可能～她自己的愿望办. There is no complying with her wishes under the present circumstances.

依存 yīcún (动) depend on each other for existence: 相互～ be interdependent

依附 yīfù (动) depend on; attach oneself to; become an appendage to

依旧(舊) yījiù (副) as before; still: 别人都走了,他～坐在那里看书. While the others had left, he alone still sat reading there.

依据(據) yījù I (名) basis; foundation: 为进一步研究提供科学～ provide scientific basis for further research II (动) form a basis for action: 当时没有适当的条例可以～. There were no proper rules to go by.

依靠 yīkào I (动) rely on: ～自己的力量 depend on one's own strength II (名) backing; support

依赖 yīlài (动) depend on: 互为～ be mutually dependent; be interdependent

依恋(戀) yīliàn (动) have a sentimental attachment for

依然 yīrán (副) still; as before: 风景～如故. The landscape remains unchanged.

依顺 yīshùn (形) be docile and obedient

依稀 yīxī (副) vaguely; dimly: ～记得 vaguely remember; have a hazy notion. ～认识 faintly recognizable

依依不舍 yīyī bù shě be reluctant to part; feel regret at parting from

依仗 yīzhàng (动) count on: ～权势 count on one's powerful connections for support; abuse one's power

依照 yīzhào (副) according to; in the light of: ～上级指示办事 act according to instructions from the higher level

一 yī 1 one: ～把椅子 a chair. 我见过他～次. I have met him once. 2 single; alone; only one: 她～个人去的. She went alone. 3 same: 这不是～码事. This is a different matter. 4 whole; all; throughout: 出了～身汗 sweat all over. 忙了～整天 be busy the whole day 5 each; per; every time: ～个月写～篇论文 write a paper each month 6 concentrated: ～心～意 single-minded; wholehearted 7 [indicating that the action occurs once or lasts for a short time]: 笑～笑 give a smile. 歇～歇 have a rest. 瞧～瞧 take a look 8 [used before a verb to indicate an action and its result]: 他～脚把球踢进了球门. He kicked the ball into the goal. **9** [used with certain words for emphasis]: 为害之甚，～至于此！ The damage done has reached such dimensions!

一把手 yībǎshǒu （名） **1** a participant in an activity **2** a capable person

一败涂(塗)地 yī bài tú dì suffer a crushing defeat; be thoroughly defeated

一般 yībān **1** same as; just like: 他们俩～高. The two of them are of the same stature. 象狐狸～狡滑 as cunning as fox. **2** general; ordinary; common: ～说来 generally speaking. 我～晚上10点睡觉. I usually go to bed at 10 in the evening. 这部电影很～. This film is just so-so.

一般化 yībānhuà （名） vague generalization: ～地谈问题 talk in generalities (or in general terms)

一半 yībàn （名） one half; half

一辈子 yībèizi （副） all one's life; a lifetime

一本万(萬)利 yī běn wàn lì make big profits with a small capital

一本正经(經) yī běn zhèngjīng in all seriousness; in a matter-of-fact manner

一笔(筆)勾销 yī bǐ gōuxiāo write off (at one stroke); cancel

一臂之力 yī bì zhī lì （名） a helping hand: 助我～ lend me a hand

一边(邊) yībiān **1** one side: 站在我们～ stand together with us **2** [indicating two simultaneous actions] at the same time; simultaneously: 他～往前走，～拉开嗓子唱着歌儿. He strolled along, singing at the top of his voice.

一并 yībìng （副） along with all the others; in the lump: ～付给 pay in a lump sum

一…不… yī…bù… **1** [used before two verbs to indicate that once an action is taken, it is irrevocable]: 一去不返 leave never to return. 一蹶不振 unable to recover after a setback **2** [used before a noun and a verb to form an emphatic expression]: 一言不发 be speechless. 一文不值 not be worth a farthing

一不做，二不休 yī bù zuò, èr bù xiū what we have started we will pursue to the end at any cost

一步登天 yī bù dēng tiān reach the pinnacle of power in one jump

一场(場)空 yīchángkōng be all in vain; be a futile effort; come to naught

一筹(籌)莫展 yī chóu mò zhǎn can find no way out; be absolutely helpless; be at one's wit's end

一触(觸)即发(發) yī chù jí fā may be triggered at any moment; be on the verge of breaking out; explosive

一次 yīcì （副） once: 我做过～. I've done it once.

一蹴而就 yī cù ér jiù accomplish in one move; succeed without making the least effort

一旦 yīdàn （副） **1** in a single day; in a very short time: 毁于～ be destroyed in a single day **2** once; in case; now that: ～这项研究计划完成，便可造福人类. Once this research project is completed, it will bring immense benefit to all mankind.

一刀两(兩)断(斷) yī dāo liǎng duàn sever for good and all

一刀切 yīdāoqiē find a single solution for diverse problems; impose uniformity without examining individual cases

一道 yīdào （副） together; side by side; alongside: 我们～走. Let's go together.

一等 yīděng （形） first-class; first-rate; top-grade

一点(點)儿(兒) yīdiǎnr （副） a bit; a little: 我～都不知道. I have not the faintest idea. 只有那么～，够用吗？ There is so little left. Is it enough for the present purpose?

一点(點)一滴 yīdiǎn-yīdī （副） every little bit

一定 yīdìng I（形） **1** fixed; specified; definite; regular: ～的指标 fixed quota. ～的条件 specified conditions **2** given; particular; certain: 在～意义上 in a certain sense. 在～程度上 to a certain extent **3** proper; definite; fair; due: 达到～水平 reach a definite level II（副） certainly; surely; necessarily: 他～会成功. He will surely succeed.

一度 yīdù （副） once; on one occasion; for a time: 一年～ once a year; yearly; annually

一二 yī-èr one or two; just a few; just a little: 略知～ know

a little about; have some idea about

一…二… yi…er… [used before two morphemes of a disyllabic adjective to give emphasis]: 一清二楚 perfectly clear; crystal clear

一发(髮)千钧 yī fà qiān jūn hang by a thread; in imminent peril: 在这～的时刻 at this critical moment

一帆风(風)顺 yī fān fēng shùn plain sailing

一方面 yīfāngmiàn **1** one side: 这只是事物的～. This is only one side of the matter. **2** [often used reduplicatively]: on the one hand ..., on the other hand...; for one thing ..., for another ...

一风(風)吹 yīfēngchuī dismiss all things as of no significance

一概 yīgài (副) one and all; totally: ～拒绝 reject without exception

一概而论(論) yīgài ér lùn [usu. in the negative] lump things of different kinds together and treat them by the same inflexible criteria: 不能～ not to be lumped together

一干(乾)二净 yīgān-èrjìng (副) thoroughly; completely: 忘得～ clean forget

一共 yīgòng (副) altogether; in all; all told: 三个小组～是十七个人. There are three groups consisting of seventeen people altogether.

一贯 yīguàn (形) consistent; persistent; all along: ～政策 consistent policy. 我们～反对恐怖主义. We have always opposed terrorism.

一哄而起 yī hòng ér qǐ rush headlong into mass action

一哄而散 yī hòng ér sàn disperse without a trace all at once

一晃 yīhuàng (副) (of time) in the twinkling of an eye

一会(會)儿(兒) yīhuìr (副) **1** a little while **2** in a moment; presently: 我～就来. I won't be long. **3** [a reduplicated use before two negative words to indicate alternation] now... now ...; one moment... the next...: 他～出，～进，忙个不停. He is busily walking in and out at short intervals.

一技之长(長) yī jì zhī cháng (名) (have) a professional skill to recommend oneself

一见(見)如故 yī jiàn rú gù feel like old friends at the first meeting

一见(見)钟(鍾)情 yī jiàn zhōngqíng fall in love at first sight

一箭双(雙)雕 yī jiàn shuāng diāo kill two birds with one stone

一经(經) yījīng (副) as soon as; once: 方案～批准，我们就着手筹款. We will start to raise funds as soon as the plan is approved.

一…就… yī…jiù… no sooner ... than ...; the moment ...; as soon as; once: 他一学就会. He learned the trick in a jiffy. 那张旧桌子轻轻一推就倒. The rickety old table collapsed with a slight push.

一举(舉) yījǔ I (名) an action that is soon to take place: 成败在此～. Success or failure hinges on this final effort. II (副) at one stroke: ～成名 become famous overnight

一举(舉)两(兩)得 yī jǔ liǎng dé kill two birds with one stone

一孔之见(見) yī kǒng zhī jiàn [usu. used as a polite formula]: a parochial view

一口 yī kǒu I (形) a mouthful; a bite: 吸～新鲜空气 have a breath of fresh air. 吃～苹果 take a bite at the apple II (副) with certainty; readily; flatly: ～答应 readily agree

一口气(氣) yīkǒuqì I (名) one breath: 只要我还有～，就要为人民大众工作. As long as I breathe, I'll work for the mass of the people. II (副) in one breath; at one go: ～干完 finish the work at one go

一块儿(兒) yīkuàir (副) **1** at the same place: 在～工作 work at the same place **2** together: 他们～到上海游览. They went on a trip to Shanghai together.

一览(覽) yīlǎn (名) guide-look

一览(覽)表 yīlǎnbiǎo (名) table; schedule: 火车行车时刻～railway timetable

一揽(攬)子 yīlǎnzi (名) wholesale; package: ～交易 package deal. ～解决 package solution

一劳(勞)永逸 yī láo yǒng yì strive to get sth. done once and for all: 寻求～的解决办法 seek a permanent solution to the problem

一连 yīlián (副) in succession; on end; running: ～下了三天雨.

It rained for three days on end.

一连串 yīliánchuàn (名) a succession of; a series of: ～的事件 a succession of events

一溜烟 yīliùyān (副) (runaway) swiftly: 他～就没影儿了. He vanished in an instant.

一路 yīlù I (副) all the way; throughout the journey: ～平安 have a pleasant journey; *or* bon voyage. 他们～平安抵达纽约. They arrived in New York safe and sound. II (形) of the same kind: 他们俩是同～人:性情相似,学历相近. They are of the same type and similar both in temperament and in educational background.

一律 yīlǜ (形) **1** same; alike; uniform: 千篇～ stereotyped and monotonous **2** all; without exception: 我国各民族～平等. All nationalities in our country are equal.

一落千丈 yī luò qiānzhàng decline rapidly; suffer a steep decline

一脉(脈)相承 yī mài xiāng chéng be inherited from the past, either intellectually, artistically, pugilistically or in terms of blood relationship

一毛不拔 yī máo bù bá even unwilling to give away a cent

一面 yīmiàn I (名) one side; one aspect: 住在学校宿舍里既有有利的～,也有不利的～. Living in the college dormitory has its advantages and disadvantages. II (副) [indicating two simultaneous actions] at the same time; simultaneously: ～走,～唱 sing while walking

一面之词 yīmiàn zhī cí the statement of one party to a dispute; a one-sided statement

一鸣惊(驚)人 yī míng jīng rén (of an obscure person) amaze the world by one's successful maiden effort

一命呜(嗚)呼 yī mìng wūhū (动) die; kick the bucket

一模一样(樣) yīmú-yīyàng exactly alike: 他长得跟他爸爸～. He is a chip off the old block.

一目了然 yī mù liǎorán (形) be clear at a glance

一念之差 yī niàn zhī chā make a wrong decision on the spur of the moment (often entailing unhappy results)

一瞥 yīpiē (名) **1** a quick glance **2** a glimpse of sth.

一贫如洗 yī pín rú xǐ (形) impoverished; in utter destitution

一暴十寒 yī pù shí hán work by fits and starts; lack tenacity of purpose

一齐(齊) yīqí (副) at the same time; simultaneously: 全场～鼓掌 warm applause by the audience. 这次比赛足球迷～出场. All the football fans turned out for the match.

一气(氣)呵成 yīqì hē chéng get sth. done without any letup

一窍(竅)不通 yī qiào bù tōng be utterly ignorant; be an ignoramus

一切 yīqiè (名) all; everything

一丘之貉 yī qiū zhī hé jackals from the same lair

一如既往 yī rú jìwǎng just as in the past; as before; as always: 我们将～坚决支持你们的正义斗争. We will, as always, firmly support your just struggle.

一身 yīshēn (名) **1** the whole body; all over the body: ～是劲 bursting with energy **2** a suit: ～新衣服 a new suit of clothes **3** a single person: 独自～ live all alone

一生 yīshēng (副) all one's life

一时(時) yīshí (副) **1** for a period of time: ～无出其右. Nobody proved better qualified for a time. **2** for a short while: ～还用不着 be of no use at the moment **3** accidentally: ～想不起他是谁. It happened I couldn't recall who he was. **4** reduplicated use: 高原上气候变化大,～晴～雨,～冷～热. On the plateau the weather is subject to frequent changes: it is clear for a while and then it starts to rain and it is often hot one moment and turns cold the next.

一事无(無)成 yī shì wú chéng accomplish nothing: failure to achieve anything of consequence

一视同仁 yī shì tóng rén treat people equally without discrimination

一手 yīshǒu I (名) proficiency; skill II (副) all by oneself; all alone: ～造成 be brought on all by oneself. ～包办 be manipulated all by oneself

一瞬 yīshùn (副) in the twinkling of an eye: 火箭飞行,～千里. A rocket travels thousands of miles in a flash.

一丝(絲)不苟 yī sī bù gǒu be very scrupulous; be very meticulous

一丝(絲)不挂(掛) yī sī bù guà be starknaked

一丝(絲)一毫 yīsī-yīháo (名) a tiny bit; an iota: 没有～的诚意 without an iota of sincerity

一塌糊涂(塗) yītàhútú an awful mess; a dreadful state of affairs: 屋子乱得～. The room was a complete mess.

一体(體) yītǐ (名) 1 an organic (or integral) whole: 融成～ merge into an organic whole 2 all people concerned: ～周知 be made known to all people concerned

一天到晚 yī tiān dào wǎn from morning till night; from dawn to dusk; all day long

一同 yītóng (副) do sth. or take part in some activity at the same time and place: ～欢度新年. Let us jointly celebrate New Year.

一头(頭) yītóu (副) 1 directly; headlong: ～扑进水里 plunge headlong into the water 2 a head: 他比我高～. He is a head taller than I am.

一团和气(氣) yī tuán héqì be always friendly with everybody on all occasions

一团(團)糟 yītuánzāo (形) hopelessly chaotic

一网(網)打尽(盡) yī wǎng dǎjìn round up the whole gang

一往无(無)前 yīwǎng wúqián press forward with an indomitable spirit

一味 yīwèi (副) simply; blindly: ～迁就解决不了任何问题. You can't solve any problem by simply making concessions.

一文不名 yī wén bù míng (形) penniless

一无(無) yī wú (副) entirely without ...: ～所知 know nothing; be ignorant. ～是处 have no merit to speak of. ～所有 be destitute or penniless

一五一十 yīwǔ-yīshí (副) (narrate) systematically and in full detail: 他把发生的事情～地讲了一遍. He gave a full account of what had happened.

一下 yīxià (副) 1 [used after a verb to indicate a brief action] one time; once: 让我看～. Let me have a look. 打听～make some inquiries 2 in a short while; all at once; all of a sudden: 孩子们～都从屋里跑了出来. The children rushed out all at once.

一线(綫) yīxiàn (名) a ray of; a gleam of: ～希望 a gleam of hope

一相情愿 yī xiāng qíngyuàn one's own wishful thinking

一向 yīxiàng (副) 1 earlier on; lately 2 consistently; all along

一笑置之 xīxiào zhì zhī dismiss with a laugh; laugh off; parry (the question) with a laugh

一些 yīxiē (量) a number of; certain; some; a few; a little: 只有这～了，怕不够吧? There's only so much left. I'm afraid it's not enough to go round. 他曾担任过～重要的职务. In the past he held some important posts.

一心 yīxīn (副) 1 wholeheartedly; heart and soul: ～为人民谋利益 devote oneself heart and soul to the welfare of the people 2 of one mind: 关于这个问题，大家都是～一意的. We are all of one mind about this question.

一星半点(點) yīxīng-bàndiǎn (名) a tiny bit; a very small amount

一行 yīxíng (名) a group travelling together; party: 代表团～十二人已于昨日起程. The twelve-person delegation left yesterday.

一言既出，驷马(馬)难(難)追 yī yán jì chū, sìmǎ nán zhuī a word spoken is past recalling

一言难(難)尽(盡) yī yán nán jìn it is hard to explain in a few words; it's a long story

一言以蔽之 yī yán yǐ bì zhī in a word; in a nutshell

一样(樣) yīyàng the same; equally; alike: 哥儿俩相貌～，脾气也～. The two brothers are alike not only in appearance but also in temperament.

一一 yī yī one by one; one after another

一…一… yī…yī… 1 [used before two nouns of the same kind] (a) [to indicate the whole]: 一生一世 all one's life (b) [to indicate a small amount] 一言一行 every word and deed. 一点一滴 every bit 2 [used before two verbs similar in meaning to indicate simultaneous action]: 一瘸一拐 hobble along 3 [used before two verbs with opposite meanings to indicate coordination or alternation of action]: 一问一答 a dialogue between two persons. 一起一落 rise and fall; ups and downs 4 [used before two corresponding words of direction to indicate opposite positions]: 一东一西 one east, one west; poles apart. 一长一短 one short, one long

一衣带(帶)水 yī yī dài shuǐ separated by a narrow strip of water

一意孤行 yī yì gū xíng act wilfully despite sb.'s advice to the contrary

一月 yīyuè (名) January

一再 yīzài (副) time and again; again and again; repeatedly: ～请求 request time and again. ～拖延 be postponed again and again

一早 yīzǎo 〈口〉 early in the morning

一朝一夕 yīzhāo-yīxī overnight; in one day: 非～之功 not the work of a single day

一针见(見)血 yīzhēn jiàn xiě hit the nail on the head

一阵 yīzhèn (名) a burst; a fit; a peal: ～雷声 a peal of thunder. ～狂风 a gust of wind. ～笑声 an outburst of laughter

一知半解 yīzhī-bànjiě have an imperfect understanding of sth.; have a little learning

一直 yīzhí (副) 1 straight: ～走 go straight on 2 continuously; always all along; all the way: 雨～下了一天一夜. It has been raining the whole day and night.

一纸空文 yī zhǐ kōngwén (名) a mere scrap of paper

一致 yīzhì identical; consistent: 他们采取～的步调. They synchronized their steps. *or* They coordinated their efforts.

壹 yī (数) one [the complicated form of "一" used on cheques, banknotes, etc. to avoid mistakes or alterations]

医(醫) yī I (名) 1 doctor (of medicine): 牙～ dentist. 延～诊治 send for a doctor 2 medical science; medicine: 中～ traditional Chinese medicine. 他是学～的. He is a student of medicine. II (动) cure; treat: 把他的病～好 cure him of his illness

医科 yīkē (名) medical courses in general; medicine

医疗(療) yīliáo (名) medical treatment: 公费～ public health services. ～器械 medical apparatus and instruments

医生 yīshēng (名) (medical) doctor: 内科～ physician; internist. 外科～ surgeon. 主治～ doctor in charge. 住院～ resident doctor

医师(師) yīshī (名) (qualified) doctor; general practitioner

医术(術) yīshù (名) medical skill

医务(務) yīwù (名) medical matters

医药(藥) yīyào (名) medicine: ～费 medical expenses (or costs)

医院 yīyuàn (名) hospital: 综合性～ general hospital

医治 yīzhì (动) cure; treat; heal

医嘱(囑) yīzhǔ (名) doctor's advice (or orders)

伊 yī (代) he or she

伊斯兰(蘭)教 Yīsīlánjiào (名) Islam; Islamism: ～徒 Moslem

宜 yí I (形) suitable; appropriate; fitting: 适～ appropriate; fitting and proper. 老幼咸～ suitable for both young and old II (动) should; ought to: 不～操之过急. You should not act in haste. *or* It would not be inappropriate to restrain oneself from acting rashly.

宜人 yírén (形) pleasant; delightful: 气候～ the weather is mild and delightful

颐 yí (动) keep fit; take care of oneself

颐和园(園) Yíhéyuán (名) the Summer Palace (in Beijing)

颐养(養) yíyǎng (动) 〈书〉 keep fit; take care of oneself

夷 yí I (形) safe: 化险为～ turn danger into safety II (动) raze: ～为平地 be razed to the ground

痍 yí (名) 〈书〉 wound; trauma: 满目疮～. There is more misery and desolation than meets the eye.

咦 yí (叹) [indicating surprise] well; why: ～, 这是怎么回事? Why, what is really the matter?

胰 yí (名) pancreas

姨 yí (名) 1 one's mother's sister; aunt 2 one's wife's sister; sister-in-law: 大～子 one's wife's elder sister. 小～子 one's wife's younger sister

姨表 yíbiǎo (名) maternal cousin: ～兄弟 male maternal cousins. ～姐妹 female maternal cousins

姨父 yífù (名) the husband of one's maternal aunt; uncle

姨妈 yímā (名) ‹口› (married) maternal aunt; aunt

姨太太 yítàitai (名) ‹口› concubine

遗 yí I (动) 1 lose: ～失 lose 2 something lost: 路不拾～. No one pockets anything found on the road. 3 omit: ～忘 forget 4 leave behind; keep back; not give: 不～余力 spare no efforts 5 leave behind at one's death; bequeath; hand down: ～风 customs handed down from past generations. ～嘱 will; testament 6 involuntary discharge of urine, etc.: ～尿 bed-wetting

遗产(產) yíchǎn (名) legacy; inheritance: 文化～ cultural heritage

遗臭万(萬)年 yí chòu wànnián leave a stinking name in human history

遗传(傳) yíchuán (名) heredity; inheritance: ～病 hereditary disease. ～学 genetics

遗传(傳)工程学(學) yíchuán gōngchéngxué (名) genetic engineering

遗稿 yígǎo (名) a manuscript left unpublished by the author in his lifetime; posthumous manuscript

遗孤 yígū (名) orphan

遗憾 yíhàn (名) regret; pity: 对此表示～ express regret over the matter. 非常～,事前有约会使我不能接受你的邀请. To my regret, a previous engagement prevents me from accepting your invitation.

遗迹 yíjì (名) historical remains

遗留 yíliú (动) leave over; hand down: 历史～下来的问题 questions left over by history

遗漏 yílòu (动) leave out by mistake

遗弃(棄) yíqì (动) abandon; forsake; leave uncared-for

遗容 yíróng (名) 1 remains (of the deceased): 瞻仰～ pay one's respects to the remains of sb. 2 a portrait of the deceased

遗孀 yíshuāng (名) widow

遗体(體) yítǐ (名) remains (of the dead): 向～告别 pay one's last respects to the remains

遗忘 yíwàng (动) forget

遗言 yíyán (名) words of the deceased; (a person's) last words

遗址 yízhǐ (名) ruins; relics: 古城～ the ruins of an ancient city

遗志 yízhì (名) unfulfilled wish; behest: 继承先烈～ carry out the behest of the martyrs; continue the work left by the martyrs

遗嘱(囑) yízhǔ (名) testament; will

仪(儀) yí (名) 1 appearance; bearing: 威～ dignified bearing 2 ceremony; rite: 司～ master of ceremonies 3 present; gift: 贺～ present for a wedding, birthday, etc. 4 apparatus; instrument

仪表 yíbiǎo (名) 1 appearance; bearing: ～堂堂 look impressive and dignified 2 meter: ～厂 instrument and meter plant

仪器 yíqì (名) instrument; apparatus: 精密～ precision instrument

仪式 yíshì (名) ceremony; rite: 签字～ signing ceremony

仪仗队(隊) yízhàngduì (名) guard of honour; honour guard: 三军～ a guard of honour of the three services

移 yí (动) 1 move; remove; shift: 迁～ move to another place 2 change; alter: ～风易俗 change established habits and social customs

移动(動) yídòng (动) move; shift

移交 yíjiāo (动) 1 turn over; transfer; deliver into sb.'s custody 2 hand over one's job to a successor

移居 yíjū (动) move one's residence; migrate

移民 yímín I (动) migrate; (移出) emigrate; (移入) immigrate II (名)(移出) emigrant; (移入) immigrant

移植 yízhí I (动) transplant: ～秧苗 transplant seedlings II (名) transplanting; grafting

疑 yí I (名) doubt; disbelieve; suspect: 坚信不～ firmly believe. 无可置～ beyond doubt II (形) doubtful; uncertain: 存～ leave the question open

疑案 yí'àn (名) doubtful case; open question; mystery

疑惑 yíhuò (动) feel uncertain; not be convinced: ～不解 feel puzzled

疑惧(懼) yíjù (名) apprehensions; misgivings

疑虑(慮) yílǜ (名) misgivings; doubt

疑难(難) yínàn (形) difficult; knotty: ～问题 a knotty problem. ～病症 difficult and complicated cases (of illness)

疑神疑鬼 yíshén-yíguǐ be over-suspicious

疑团(團) yítuán (名) doubts and suspicions

疑问 yíwèn (名) query; question; doubt: 毫无～ doubtless; undoubtedly

疑心 yíxīn (名) suspicion: 起～ become suspicious

疑义(義) yíyì (名) doubt; doubtful point: 毫无～ no doubt; without doubt

怡 yí (形)〈书〉happy; pleased: 心旷神～ feel relaxed and happy

怡然 yírán (形) happy; contented: ～自得 happy and contented

贻 yí

贻害 yíhài (动) leave a legacy of trouble: ～无穷 entail endless trouble

贻误 yíwù (动) affect adversely; bungle: ～工作 affect the work adversely. ～青年 mislead the youth

贻笑大方 yíxiào dàfāng make a fool of oneself before professionals

椅 yǐ (名)(～子) chair

倚 yǐ I (动) 1 lean on or against; rest on or against: ～门而望 lean against the door and look expectantly into the distance 2 rely on; count on: ～势欺人 bully common people by abusing one's power and office II (形) biased; partial: 不偏不～unbiased; even handed; impartial

倚老卖(賣)老 yǐ lǎo mài lǎo be unduly presumptions because of one's seniority or old age

倚重 yǐzhòng (动) rely on one for counsel

蚁(蟻) yǐ (名) ant: ～巢 ant nest

乙 yǐ (名) second: ～等 the second grade; grade B. 维生素～ vitamin B

乙醇 yǐchún (名) ethanol; alcohol

乙醚 yǐmí (名) ether

乙炔 yǐquē (名) acetylene; ethyne: ～焊 acetylene welding

乙烯 yǐxī (名) ethylene: 聚～ polyethylene; polythene

已 yǐ I (动) stop; cease; end: 争论不～ argue endlessly II (副) already: 问题～解决. The problem has already been solved. 雨季～过. The rainy season is over.

已故 yǐgù (形) deceased; late: ～总理 the late premier

已经(經) yǐjīng (副) already: 天～黑了, 他们回来的影子都没有. It's already dark, but there is no sign of their coming back yet.

已往 yǐwǎng (副) before; previously; in the past

以 yǐ I (动) use; take: 喻之～理 try to persuade one by reasoned argument. ～攻为守 the most effective defence is offence. ～其人之道, 还治其人之身 give someone a taste of his own medicine II (介) 1 according to: ～级别高低为序 in order of seniority 2 because (of): 不～人废言 not reject a piece of advice because the speaker is a person of no significance 3 in order to; so as to: ～应急需 to meet an urgent need. ～待时机 to bide one's time 4 in: ～失败而告终 end in failure 5 used together with a word of direction: 二十岁～下 below the age of 20. 县级～上 above county level. 三日～后 in three days

以便 yǐbiàn so that; in order to; so as to; with the aim of; for the purpose of: 每个学生都要掌握一门外语, ～工作得更好. Every student is required to master a foreign language so that he or she will be better able to work in future.

以德报(報)怨 yǐ dé bào yuàn return good for evil

以毒攻毒 yǐ dú gōng dú use poison as remedy for malignant disease; use poison as an antidote for poison; let thieves fight thieves

以讹传(傳)讹 yǐ é chuán é pass on a wrong verbal message from one to another till it is grossly distorted

以后(後) yǐhòu after; afterwards; later; hereafter: 从今～ from now on. ～, 我们还要研究这个问题. We will go into it later.

以及 yǐjí as well as; along with; and

以来(來) yǐlái (介) since: 自二次世界大战～ since World War II. 三年～ in the past three years

以卵投石 yǐ luǎn tóu shí throw an egg against a rock; court disaster by immoderately overestimating one's own strength

以免 yǐmiǎn in order to avoid or prevent: ~产生误会 to avoid or prevent misunderstanding

以内 yǐnèi within; less than: 百码~ within a hundred yards

以前 yǐqián (副) before; formerly; previously: 三年~ three years ago. 1949 年~ before 1949

以权(權)谋私 yǐquán móusī seek private profit by taking advantage of administrative powers

以上 yǐshàng (副) 1 more than; above: 五十人~ over fifty people. 十岁~的孩子 children of ten and over 2 the above; the above-mentioned

以身殉职(職) yǐ shēn xùnzhí die at one's post

以身作则 yǐ shēn zuò zé set a good example by one's conduct

以外 yǐwài (副) 1 beyond; outside: 办公室~ outside the office 2 in addition; into the bargain: 除此~, 还有一件事你要记住. There's another thing I would like you to bear in mind.

以往 yǐwǎng (副) before; formerly; in the past: 这里~是一片荒野. This place used to be a vast expanse of wasteland.

以为(爲) yǐwéi (动) think; consider: 不~然 I beg to differ; I don't think so

以下 yǐxià (副) below; under: 他们的建议可以归纳为~几点. Their proposal can be summed up as follows. 气温已降到零下. The temperature has dropped below zero.

以眼还(還)眼,以牙还(還)牙 yǐ yǎn huán yǎn, yǐ yá huán yá an eye for an eye and a tooth for a tooth

以怨报(報)德 yǐ yuàn bào dé return evil for good

以致 yǐzhì [indicating an unpleasant result] with the result that; consequently: 他事先没有充分调查研究, ~做出了错误的结论. He had not looked carefully into the matter so that he drew an erroneous conclusion.

矣 yǐ (副) 〈书〉 [used at the end of a sentence to indicate completion of an action like '了' in colloquial Chinese]: 悔之晚~. It's too late to repent.

意 yì (名) 1 meaning; idea: 同~ identical views; agreement 2 wish; desire; intention: 好~ a good intention 3 expectation: 出其不~ take one by surprise; run counter to one's expectations. 如无~外 barring the unexpected 4 hint; trace; suggestion: 春~盎然. Spring is in the air.

意会(會) yìhuì (名) sense: 只可~, 不可言传 can be fully understood but not in tangible terms

意见(見) yìjiàn (名) 1 idea; view; opinion: 交换~ exchange view 2 objection; complaint: 我对这种方法有~. I feel strongly about this approach to things. ~簿 comment book

意境 yìjìng (名) feeling or mood as expressed by art or literature; artistic conception: 这幅油画~深远. This painting gives expression to a high level of artistic conception.

意料 yìliào (动) anticipate; expect: 这是~中的事. That's what is to be expected.

意气(氣) yìqì (名) 1 will and spirit: ~高昂 in high morale 2 temperament: ~相投 temperamentally compatible 3 personal feelings (or prejudice): ~用事 allow oneself to be swayed by personal feelings

意识(識) yìshí I (名) consciousness II (动) [often used with '到'] be aware of; realize: ~到自己责任的重大 be conscious of the gravity of one's responsibilities

意识(識)形态(態) yìshí xíngtài (名) ideology

意思 yìsi (名) 1 meaning; idea: 文章的中心~ the central theme 2 opinion; wish; desire: 大家的~ the consensus of opinion 3 a token of affection, appreciation, gratitude, etc.: 这件小礼品不过是我的一点儿~. This little gift is but a token of my appreciation. 4 suggestion; hint; trace: 这种书对我们~不大. This kind of book is of no interest to us. 他脸上露出忿怒的~. There is a suggestion of anger in his face.

意图(圖) yìtú (名) intention; intent

意外 yìwài I (形) unexpected; unforeseen: 感到~ come to one as a surprise II (名) accident; mishap: 以防~so as to prevent accidents

意味 yìwèi (名) 1 meaning; implication: ～深长的一笑 a meaning or knowing smile 2 interest; overtone; flavour: 他的文章中含有讽刺的～. There is touch of sarcasm in his article.

意想 yìxiǎng (动) imagine; expect: ～不到 unexpected; beyond all expectations

意向 yìxiàng (名) intention; purpose

意义(義) yìyì (名) meaning; sense; significance: 在某种～上 in a sense

意译(譯) yìyì (名) paraphrase; free translation

意愿(願) yìyuàn (名) wish; desire; aspiration

意志 yìzhì (名) will; will power: ～坚强 strong-willed

癔 yì

癔病 yìbìng (名) hysteria

臆 yì I (名) chest II (副) subjectively

臆测 yìcè (动) conjecture; guess; make certain assumptions

臆断(斷) yìduàn (动) make any arbitrary decision, or draw any arbitrary conclusion

臆造 yìzào (动) fabricate (a story; reason, etc.); invent

亦 yì (副)〈书〉also; too: 反之～然 and vice versa

亦步亦趋(趨) yìbù-yìqū ape sb. sedulously; follow sb.'s move slavishly

亦即 yìjí that is; namely

奕 yì

奕奕 yìyì (名) radiating health and vitality: 神采～ glow with health; look hale and hearty

裔 yì (名) descendants; posterity: 华～美国人 American of Chinese descent

益 yì I (名) benefit; profit; advantage: 受～匪浅 benefit greatly from it. 公～ public welfare. 权～ rights and interests II (形) beneficial: ～虫 beneficial insect. ～鸟 beneficial bird. III (副) increasingly: 精～求精 keep improving; make even better progress

益处(處) yìchu (名) benefit; advantage

益友 yìyǒu friend and mentor

溢 yì I (动) overflow; brim: 洋～ be overflowing II (形) excessive: ～美 undeserved praise

溢出 yìchū (动) spill over; overflow

缢 yì (动)〈书〉hang: 自～ hang oneself by the neck

谊 yì (名) friendship: 深情厚～ profound friendship

抑 yì (动) restrain; repress; curb

抑制 yìzhì I (动) restrain; control: ～愤怒 contain one's anger. ～感情 control one's emotion II (名) inhibition

易 yì I (形) 1 easy: 轻～ easily. 来之不～ hard-won 2 amiable: 平～近人 amiable and easy of access II (动) 1 change: ～手 change hands 2 exchange: 贸～ trade

易如反掌 yì rú fǎnzhǎng be simple and easy; can be easily accomplished

义(義) yì I (名) 1 justice; righteousness: 深明大～ have a strong sense of justice 2 human relationship: 无情无～ heartless and faithless 3 meaning; significance: 词～转换 semantic transfer. 一词多～ polysemy II (形) adopted; adoptive: ～女 adopted daughter. ～母 adoptive mother

义不容辞(辭) yì bù róng cí be duty-bound

义愤 yìfèn (名) righteous indignation

义愤填膺 yìfèn tián yīng be filled with (righteous) indignation

义和团(團) Yìhétuán (名) the Yihetuan Movement (1900) (often referred to as Boxers' Rising in pre-liberation China)

义卖(賣) yìmài (名) a sale of goods (usu. at high prices) for charity or other worthy causes; charity bazaar

义气(氣) yìqì (名) personal loyalty

义务(務) yìwù I (名) duty; obligation: ～教育 compulsory education II (形) volunteer; voluntary: ～演出 benefit performance. ～劳动 volunteer labour

议(議) yì I (名) opinion; view: 异～ disagreement. 提～ propose; move II (动) consult; discuss: 自报公～ submit one's own request for public appraisal

议案 yì'àn (名) proposal; motion

议程 yìchéng (名) agenda: 列入～ place on the agenda; include

in the agenda
议定书(書) yìdìngshū (名) protocol: 贸易～ trade protocol
议和 yìhé (动) negotiate peace
议会(會) yìhuì (名) parliament; legislative assembly
议价(價) yìjià I (动) negotiate a price II (名) negotiated price
议论(論) yìlùn (动) comment; talk; discuss: 乱发～ make irresponsible comments. ～不休 argue endlessly
议事 yìshì (动) discuss official business: ～规则 rules of procedure; rules of debate. ～日程 agenda; order of the day
议题 yìtí (名) subject under discussion; topic for discussion
议员 yìyuán (名) member of a legislative assembly; (英)Member of Parliament (MP); (美)Congressman or Congresswoman
议院 yìyuàn (名) legislative assembly; parliament; congress
刈 yì (动) mow; cut down: 刈草机 mower
轶 yì (动) 1 be lost 2 excel
轶事 yìshì (名) anecdote
屹 yì (形) <书> towering like a mountain peak
屹立 yìlì (动) stand towering like a giant; stand erect
屹然 yìrán (形) towering; majestic: ～不动 stand rock-firm
诣 yì (名) (academic or technical) attainments: 学术造～ scholastic attainments
逸 yì I (形) ease; leisure: 有劳有～ alternate work with rest II (动) escape; flee: 逃～ escape
逸事 yìshì (名) anecdote (esp. about a famous person)
肄 yì (动) study
肄业(業) yìyè (动) study in school or at college: 他曾在大学～二年. He was in college for two years.
毅 yì (形) firm; resolute; 刚～ fortitude
毅力 yìlì willpower; will; stamina: 惊人的～ amazing willpower
毅然 yìrán (副) resolutely; firmly; determinedly
疫 yì (名) epidemic disease; pestilence: 鼠～ the plague. 防～ epidemic prevention
疫病 yìbìng (名) epidemic disease
疫苗 yìmiáo (名) vaccine

役 yì (名) 1 labour; service: 劳～ forced labour. 兵～ military service 2 use as a slave: 奴～ enslave 3 servant: 仆～ servant; flunkey 4 battle: 滑铁卢之～ the Battle of Waterloo
忆(憶) yì (动) recall; recollect
亿(億) yì (名) a hundred million
亿万(萬) yìwàn (名) hundreds of millions; millions upon millions: ～富翁 billionaire
艺(藝) yì (名) 1 skill: 球～ skill in a ball game 2 art: 文～ art and literature
艺人 yìrén (名) 1 actor or artist (in local drama, storytelling, acrobatics, etc.) 2 artisan; handicraftsman
艺术(術) yìshù I (名) 1 art: ～风格 artistic style. ～品 work of art 2 skill; technique; craft II (形) artistic; in good taste: 家具粗笨,没有一点儿～气味. The furniture is cumbersome and tasteless.
艺苑 yìyuàn (名) the realm of art and literature; art and literary circles
呓(囈) yì (名) talk in one's sleep
呓语 yìyǔ (名) 1 talk in one's sleep 2 rigmarole; ravings
译(譯) yì (动) translate; interpret: 笔～ written translation. 口～ oral interpretation
译本 yìběn (名) translation
译文 yìwén (名) translated text; translation
译员 yìyuán (名) interpreter
译者 yìzhě (名) translator
译制(製) yìzhì (动) dub: ～片 dubbed film
驿(驛) yì (名) post
驿站 yìzhàn (名) post (where formerly couriers changed horses or rested)
翌 yì (形) <书> immediately following in time; next: ～日 next day. ～年 next year; the following year
异(異) yì (形) 1 different: 大同小～ identical in general terms though different on minor issues. ～父(母)兄弟 half brothers 2 strange; unusual: ～乎寻常 out of the ordinary 3 strange: 深以为～ came to me as a big surprise

异常 yìcháng I (形) unusual; abnormal: ～现象 abnormal phenomena II (副) extremely; exceedingly; particularly: ～激动 get extremely excited
异端 yìduān (名) heterodoxy; heresy: ～邪说 heretical beliefs; unorthodox opinions
异国(國) yìguó (名) foreign country (or land): 远适～ reside far away in a foreign land
异化 yìhuà (名) alienation
异己 yìjǐ (形) dissident; alien: 在派性斗争中排除～ get rid of dissidents in factional strife
异教 yìjiào (名) paganism; heathenism
异口同声(聲) yìkǒu-tóngshēng speak with one voice
异曲同工 yìqǔ-tónggōng different in approach and diction but equally outstanding in the overall effect
异乡(鄉) yìxiāng (名) foreign land; strange place (town or province) away from home
异想天开(開) yì xiǎng tiān kāi give free rein to one's fantasy
异性 yìxìng (名) 1 the opposite sex 2 different in nature
异样(樣) yìyàng I (形) unusual; different: 他今天有一些～. He is not quite himself.
异议(議) yìyì (名) objection; dissension: 提出～ raise an objection; take exception to; challenge
翼 yì (名) the wing of a bird, aeroplane, etc.
翼翼 yìyì (副) cautiously: 小心～ act with exceptional caution; act very cautiously
音 yīn (名) 1 sound: 噪～ noise 2 news; tidings: ～信 news; tidings
音标(標) yīnbiāo (名) phonetic symbol; phonetic transcription
音调 yīndiào (名) tone
音符 yīnfú (名) note
音阶(階) yīnjiē (名) scale
音节(節) yīnjié (名) syllable
音量 yīnliàng (名) volume (of sound)
音色 yīnsè (名) tone colour; timbre
音素 yīnsù (名) phoneme
音速 yīnsù (名) velocity (or speed) of sound: 超～ supersonic
音响(響) yīnxiǎng (名) sound; acoustics: ～效果 sound effects; acoustics
音译(譯) yīnyì (名) transliteration
音乐(樂) yīnyuè (名) music: ～会 concert. ～家 musician
音质(質) yīnzhì (名) 1 tone quality 2 acoustic fidelity
因 yīn I (介) 1 on the basis of; in the light of: ～人而异 vary from person to person 2 because of; as a result of: ～母病请假 ask for a leave of absence on account of one's mother's illness. 会议～故改期. The meeting has been postponed for some reason. II (名) cause; reason: 近～ immediate cause. 前～后果 cause and effect; the cause-effect relationship. 事出有～. There is no smoke without fire.
因材施教 yīn cái shī jiào impart knowledge to pupils according to their varying mental make-up
因此 yīncǐ (副) therefore; for this reason; consequently
因地制宜 yīn dì zhì yí adopt measures in the light of the realities of specific regions; suit measures to local conditions
因而 yīn'ér (副) thus; as a result; with the result that
因果 yīnguǒ (名) 1 cause and effect 2 ‹佛教› karma; preordained fate
因陋就简 yīn lòu jiù jiǎn (do things) on the basis of the existing conditions no matter how simple and crude.
因势(勢)利导(導) yīn shì lì dǎo guide properly the trend in the development of events
因素 yīnsù (名) factor; element: 积极～ positive factors
因为(爲) yīnwéi (副) because; for; on account of
因循 yīnxún (动) carry on as usual
因缘 yīnyuán (名) 1 principal and subsidiary causes; cause 2 predestined relationship
茵 yīn (名) mattress: 绿草如～ a carpet of green grass
姻 yīn (名) 1 marriage: 联～ be connected by marriage 2 relation by marriage
姻亲(親) yīnqīn (名) relation by marriage: ～关系 relationship by marriage
姻缘 yīnyuán (名) predestined matrimonial affinity
殷 yīn (形) 1 earnest; ardent: 期望甚～ entertain ardent hopes 2 hospitable: 招待甚～ extend lavish hospitality
殷切 yīnqiè (形) ardent; earnest:

~的期望 earnest expectations
殷勤 yīnqín (形) eagerly attentive; warm: 受到~的接待 be accorded warm hospitality

阴(陰) yīn I (名) 1 (in Chinese philosophy, medicine, etc.) *yin*, the feminine or negative principle in nature 2 the moon: ~历 lunar calendar 3 shade: 树~ the shade of a tree 4 back: 碑~ the back of a stone tablet 5 private parts (esp. of the female) II (形) 1 cloudy; overcast 2 hidden: 阳奉~违 agree in public but object in secret 3 negative: ~离子 negative ion; anion
阴错阳(陽)差 yīncuò-yángchā an error caused by a curious coincidence
阴电(電) yīndiàn (名) negative electricity
阴沟(溝) yīngōu (名) sewer
阴冷 yīnlěng (形) (of weather) raw
阴历(曆) yīnlì (名) lunar calendar: ~正月 the first month of the lunar year
阴凉 yīnliáng I (形) shady and cool II (名) cool place; shade
阴谋 yīnmóu (名) plot; scheme; conspiracy
阴森 yīnsēn (形) (of a place, atmosphere, expression, etc.) gloomy; ghastly: ~的树林 a dense, dark wood
阴私 yīnsī (名) a secret act of dishonour
阴险(險) yīnxiǎn (形) look amiable but with evil intent at heart; insidious
阴性 yīnxìng (名) negative: ~反应 negative reaction
阴阳(陽)怪气(氣) yīnyáng guàiqì (形) 1 (of one's manner of speaking) deliberately enigmatic or ambiguous 2 eccentric; queer: 他这个人~的。He's exasperatingly eccentric.
阴影 yīnyǐng (名) shadow: 树木的~ shadow cast by a tree
阴雨 yīnyǔ (形) overcast and rainy: ~连绵 drizzle continuously
阴郁(鬱) yīnyù (形) gloomy; dismal: 心情~ feel gloomy (or depressed)
阴云(雲) yīnyún (名) dark clouds

荫(蔭) yīn (名) shade
see also yìn
荫蔽 yīnbì (动) be shaded or hidden by foliage

淫 yín (形) 1 excessive: ~雨 excessive rains 2 lax; wanton: 骄奢~逸 wallow in luxury and pleasure 3 illicit relations: 奸~ seduce
淫荡(蕩) yíndàng (形) lewd; lascivious; licentious
淫秽(穢) yínhuì (形) obscene; salacious
淫乱(亂) yínluàn (形) (sexually) promiscuous
淫威 yínwēi (名) abuse of power

吟 yín (动) chant; recite: ~诗 recite or compose poetry
吟诵 yínsòng (动) chant; recite
吟咏 yínyǒng (动) recite a poem or literary essay rhythmically

垠 yín (名) <书> boundary; limit: 一望无~ stretch beyond the horizon; boundless

龈(齦) yín (名) gum

银 yín 1 (名) silver 2 relating to currency: ~行 bank II (形) silver-coloured: ~灰 silver grey. 她的头发已有点儿变为~灰色了. Her hair is already touched with grey.
银币(幣) yínbì (名) silver coin
银行 yínháng (名) bank: ~存款 bank deposit. 外汇指定~ authorized bank for dealing in foreign exchange
银河 yínhé (名) the Milky Way
银幕 yínmù (名) (motion-picture) screen
银牌 yínpái (名) silver medal
银器 yínqì (名) silverware
银圆 yínyuán (名) silver dollar

饮(飲) yǐn (动) 1 drink: ~酒适量 drink moderately 2 feel keenly; nurse: ~恨 nurse a grievance; feel eternal regret
饮料 yǐnliào (名) drink; beverage
饮泣 yǐnqì (动) <书> swallow one's tears; weep in silence: ~吞声 choked with tears
饮食 yǐnshí (名) food and drink: ~业 catering trade
饮水思源 yǐnshuǐ sī yuán don't forget about the source of the water you are drinking; one should keep in mind the source of one's joy while in happiness
饮用水 yǐnyòngshuǐ (名) drinking water
饮鸩止渴 yǐn zhèn zhǐ kě drink poison to quench thirst; seek temporary relief regardless of the imminent danger

引 yǐn (动) 1 lead; guide: ～路 lead the way. ～航 pilot 2 leave: ～避 keep away from sb. ～退 withdraw; retire 3 lure; attract: ～人注目 attract people's attention 4 cause; make: ～出麻烦 cause trouble 5 quote; cite: ～某人说过这番话 quote sb. as saying something to this effect

引爆 yǐnbào (动) ignite; detonate

引导(導) yǐndǎo (动) guide; lead: 主人～记者参观了几个主要车间. The host showed the journalists around several principal workshops.

引渡 yǐndù (动) extradite

引号(號) yǐnhào (名) quotation marks

引荐(薦) yǐnjiàn (动) recommend

引进(進) yǐnjìn (动) 1 recommend 2 introduce from elsewhere: ～技术装备 import technology and equipment

引经(經)据(據)典 yǐnjīng-jùdiǎn quote the classics or any other authoritative works (to support one's argument)

引咎 yǐnjiù 〈书〉 take the blame on oneself: ～自责 hold oneself answerable for a serious mistake and make a self-criticism

引狼入室 yǐn láng rù shì invite a dangerous foe or wicked person in

引力 yǐnlì (名) gravitation: 万有～ universal gravitation

引起 yǐnqǐ (动) give rise to; lead to; cause; arouse: ～同情 arouse one's sympathy. ～争论 give rise to controversy

引擎 yǐnqíng (名) engine

引人入胜(勝) yǐn rén rù shèng (of scenery, literary works, etc.) fascinating; enchanting; absorbing

引申 yǐnshēn (动) extend (the meaning of a word, etc.)

引水 yǐnshuǐ (动) draw or channel water; divert: ～工程 diversion works

引文 yǐnwén (名) quoted passage; quotation

引信 yǐnxìn (名) detonator; fuse

引言 yǐnyán (名) foreword; introduction

引以为(爲)戒 yǐn yǐ wéi jiè (from a previous error, etc.) take warning from it

引用 yǐnyòng (动) quote; cite

引诱 yǐnyòu (动) lure; seduce

引证(證) yǐnzhèng (动) quote or cite as proof or evidence

引子 yǐnzi (名) 1 an actor's opening words 2 introductory music 3 introductory remarks; introduction

隐(隱) yǐn (形) 1 covered; concealed: ～瞒 conceal (the truth) 2 latent; hidden: ～患 hidden danger (or trouble)

隐蔽 yǐnbì (动) conceal; take cover

隐藏 yǐncáng (动) go into hiding; lie low

隐讳(諱) yǐnhuì (动) hush up; cover up; gloss over

隐晦 yǐnhuì (形) obscure; veiled: 文字写得很～. The language is obscure and ambiguous.

隐居 yǐnjū (动) live (esp. in former times) as a hermit and refuse to get involved in politics

隐瞒 yǐnmán (动) conceal; hide; hold back: ～事实 withhold the truth; hide (or hold back) the facts

隐情 yǐnqíng (名) facts one prefers not to disclose

隐忍 yǐnrěn (动) bear patiently; forbear

隐私 yǐnsī (名) private matters one wants to hush up or refrains from talking about

隐痛 yǐntòng (名) painful traumatic experience

隐隐 yǐnyǐn (形) indistinct; faint: 青山～. The blue mountains are faintly visible.

隐忧(憂) yǐnyōu (名) the worries that lie deep down in one's heart

隐约 yǐnyuē (形) indistinct; faint: 歌声～可以听见. The songs are faintly audible. 远处的高楼～可见. The tall apartments appear indistinct in the distance. ～其词 use ambiguous language; speak in equivocal terms

瘾(癮) yǐn (名) addiction; craving; urge: 吸毒上～ be addicted to drugs; be a drug addict 2 strong interest (in a sport or pastime): 他看电视看上～了. He has developed a penchant for television programmes.

荫(蔭) yìn (形) shady; damp and chilly
see also yīn

荫凉 yìnliáng (形) shady and cool

印 yìn I (名) 1 seal; stamp; chop: 盖～ affix one's seal 2 print; mark: 脚～ footprint II (动) 1 print; engrave: ～刷厂 printing house 2 tally; conform: 心心相～ be deeply attached to each other

印发(發) yìnfā (动) print and distribute; distribute

印花 yìnhuā (名) 1 printing: ～丝绸 printed silk 2 revenue stamp; stamp: ～税 stamp duty, stamp tax

印鉴(鑒) yìnjiàn (名) a specimen seal impression for checking when making payments

印泥 yìnní (名) red ink paste used for seals

印染 yìnrǎn (名) printing and dyeing (of textiles)

印刷 yìnshuā (名) printing: 这本书正在～中. The book is now in press. ～错误 misprint; typographical error

印象 yìnxiàng (名) impression: 给人留下深刻的～ leave a deep impression on sb.

印证(證) yìnzhèng (动) confirm; corroborate; verify

应(應) yìng (动) 1 answer; respond: 喊他他不～. When I called him, he made no reply. 2 agree (to do sth.); promise; accept: 这事是我～下来的,由我负责吧. This is what I promised to do, and I will do it myself. 3 should; ought to: ～尽的义务 one's bounden duty. 他罪有～得. He fully deserves the punishment for the crime he has committed.

see also yìng

应有尽(盡)有 yīngyǒu-jìnyǒu have everything that one expects to find: 这家铺子货物～. The shop has all it has to offer.

应允 yīngyǔn (动) assent; consent: 点头～ nod assent (or approval)

膺 yīng I (名) <书> breast: 义愤填～ become very indignant at the gross injustice II (动) bear; receive: ～此重任 hold this post of responsibility

鹰 yīng (名) hawk; eagle

鹰犬 yīngquǎn (名) falcons and hounds; lackeys; hired thugs

英 yīng (名) 1 a person of outstanding talent or wisdom: ～豪 heroes 2 flower: 落～ fallen flowers

英俊 yīngjùn (形) 1 outstanding of talent 2 handsome and young

英名 yīngmíng (名) celebrated name

英明 yīngmíng (形) wise; brilliant: ～远见 brilliant foresight

英雄 yīngxióng (名) hero: 女～ heroine. ～气概 heroic spirit. ～所见略同. Great minds think alike.

英勇 yīngyǒng (形) valiant; brave: ～善战 be a valiant and seasoned soldier

英语 Yīngyǔ (名) English (language)

英姿 yīngzī (名) proud bearing

罂 yīng

罂粟 yīngsù (名) opium poppy

婴 yīng (名) baby; infant

婴儿(兒) yīng'ér (名) baby; infant

樱 yīng (名) 1 cherry 2 oriental cherry

樱花 yīnghuā (名) oriental cherry

樱桃 yīngtáo (名) cherry

鹦 yīng

鹦哥 yīnggē (名) parrot

鹦鹉 yīngwǔ (名) parrot

鹦鹉学(學)舌 yīngwǔ xuéshé repeat the words of others without thinking or understanding; parrot

缨 yīng (名) 1 tassel: 红～枪 red-tasselled spear 2 ribbon

赢 yíng (动) 1 win; beat: 足球比赛结果,甲队～了. Team A won in the football match. 2 gain (profit)

赢得 yíngdé (动) win; gain: ～全场欢呼喝采 draw the cheers and applause of all the spectators

赢利 yínglì (名) profit; gain

赢余(餘) yíngyú (名) surplus; profit

荧(熒) yíng (形) <书> 1 glimmering 2 dazzled; perplexed

荧光 yíngguāng (名) fluorescence; fluorescent light: ～灯 fluorescent lamp. ～屏 fluorescent screen

萤(螢) yíng (名) firefly; glowworm

萤火虫(蟲) yínghuǒchóng (名) firefly; glowworm

营(營) yíng I (动) 1 seek: ～救 rescue 2 operate; own; run: 国～ state-run. 私～ private-owned II (名) 1 camp; barracks: 安～ pitch a

camp 2 battalion: ～长 battalion commander
营房 yíngfáng (名) barracks
营火 yínghuǒ (名) campfire
营救 yíngjiù (动) save; rescue
营垒(壘) yínglěi (名) 1 barracks and the enclosing walls 2 camp
营生 yíngshēng (动) earn (or make) a living
营私 yíngsī (动) seek private gain; feather one's nest: ～舞弊 embezzle; engage in fraudulent practices; be guilty of graft and corruption
营养(養) yíngyǎng (名) nutrition; nourishment: ～不良 malnutrition; undernourishment. ～学 dietetics
营业(業) yíngyè (动) do business: ～时间 business hours. ～税 business tax; transactions tax. ～执照 business licence

萦(縈) yíng (动) ‹书› entangle; encompass
萦怀(懷) yínghuái (动) be on one's mind
萦回 yínghuí (动) linger about
萦绕(繞) yíngrào (动) linger on

蝇(蠅) yíng (名) fly
蝇头(頭) yíngtóu (形) tiny: ～微利 petty profits
蝇营(營)狗苟 yíngyíng-gǒugǒu seek personal gain everywhere without a sense of shame

盈 yíng (动) 1 be full of; be filled with: 恶贯满～. The cup of iniquity is full to the brim. 2 have a surplus of
盈亏(虧) yíng-kuī (名) profit and loss: 自负～ (of an enterprise) be solely held economically responsible
盈利 yínglì (名) profit; gain
盈余(餘) yíngyú (名) surplus; net profit

迎 yíng (动) 1 greet; welcome: 去机场～外宾 go to the airport to meet foreign guests 2 move towards (the wind): ～风招展 (of a flag) flutter in the breeze
迎风(風) yíngfēng (of a flag) flutter in the breeze
迎合 yínghé (动) cater to; pander to: ～社会需要 cater to social needs
迎候 yínghòu (动) await the arrival of; meet: 他们站在国宾馆门口～贵宾. They stood at the entrance to the State Guest House to wait for the arrival of the distinguished guests.
迎击(擊) yíngjī (动) (despatch troops to) fight the approaching enemy
迎接 yíngjiē (动) meet; greet: ～国际劳动节! Greet International Labour Day!
迎面 yíngmiàn (副) (blowing) right; in the face; (walking) towards the visitors: 西北风正～刮着. The north-westerly wind was blowing right in the face. 他～走过去打招呼. He stepped across to greet them.
迎刃而解 yíng rèn ér jiě (of a problem) be readily solved
迎头(頭)赶(趕)上 yíngtóu gǎnshàng (动) try hard to catch up
迎新 yíngxīn (动) 1 see the New Year in: 送旧～ ring out the Old Year and ring in the New 2 welcome new arrivals

影 yǐng 1 shadow; reflection 2 vague impression 3 photograph; picture: 合～ group photo (or picture) 4 motion picture; film; movie: ～院 cinema. ～迷 film (or movie) fan
影集 yǐngjí (名) photograph (or picture, photo) album
影片 yǐngpiàn (名) film; movie
影响(響) yǐngxiǎng I (名) influence; effect: 产生巨大～ exercise a great influence II (动) affect; influence: ～健康 affect one's health. ～威信 have an adverse effect on one's prestige. 我不想～你自己的观点. I don't mean to influence your own view points.
影印 yǐngyìn (名) photocopy; photostat; xerox
影子 yǐngzi (名) 1 shadow; reflection: ～内阁 shadow cabinet 2 trace; sign; vague impression: 这人连～都不见了. He has vanished without a trace. 那件事我连点儿～也记不得了. I haven't even the haziest notion of it.

颖 yǐng (形) intelligent
颖慧 yǐnghuì (形) (of a teenager) bright; intelligent
颖悟 yǐngwù (形) (of a teenager) brilliant; intelligent

应(應) yìng (动) 1 respond: 答～ answer. 呼～ echo 2 comply with; promise: ～邀 upon invitation. 以～读者的需要 meet the needs of the reading public 3 suit; respond to: ～景 say or write sth. to celebrate the occasion 4 deal with; cope with: ～付想象不到的困难任务 cope with incredibly difficult task

see also yīng

应变(變) yìngbiàn prepare for an eventuality (or contingency): ～措施 emergency measure

应承 yìngchéng (动) agree (to do sth.); promise; consent: 这件事他总算～下来了. He promised at last to get the work done as requested.

应酬 yìngchou I (动) engage in social activities: 不善～ not social; not very good at casual conversation II (名) dinner party: 今天晚上有个～. I've a social engagement this evening. ～话 commonplace civilities

应答 yìngdá (动) reply; answer: ～如流 reply with facility

应付 yìngfu (动) 1 deal with; cope with; handle: ～自如 handle a situation with ease. 事情太复杂，难于～. The work is too complicated to be easily manageable. 2 do sth. perfunctorily: ～差事 do it half-heartedly according to routine; hurry through an assignment 3 make do with sth.

应急 yìngjí (动) meet an urgent need

应接不暇 yìngjiē bù xiá unable to attend to too many visitors or too much business on special occasions

应诺 yìngnuò (动) agree or undertake (to do sth.); promise

应时(時) yìngshí I (形) seasonable; in season: ～小菜 small dishes of the season II (副) at once; immediately

应验(驗) yìngyàn (动) (of prediction, presentiment, etc.) tally with what happens later: 他的预言～了. His prediction has come true.

应用 yìngyòng (动) apply; use: ～新技术 make use of advanced technology. ～科学 applied science

应运(運)而生 yìngyùn ér shēng come into being at the opportune historic moment

应战(戰) yìngzhàn (动) 1 engage the enemy 2 accept (or take up) a challenge

应征 yìngzhēng (动) 1 be recruited: ～入伍 be conscripted for service in the armed forces 2 send an article to a magazine in response to the editor's call for open competition or regular contributions

硬

yìng (形) 1 hard; stiff; tough: 坚～ tough. ～水 hard water 2 strong; firm; obstinate: 心肠～ hard-hearted. 提出强～的抗议 lodge a strong protest 3 manage to do sth. with difficulty: ～撑着干 struggle through the work 4 good (quality); able (person): 货色～ goods of high quality. 功夫～ superb skill

硬币(幣) yìngbì (名) coin; specie

硬骨头(頭) yìnggútou (名) a dauntless person

硬化 yìnghuà I (动) harden II (名) sclerosis

硬件 yìngjiàn (名) hardware (machine parts of a computer)

硬碰硬 yìng pèng yìng I (动) counter toughness with toughness II (形) (of a job) very stiff and demanding: 这是～的事，只有有真才实学的人才能完成. As the work is very demanding, only people of true worth can accomplish it.

硬说 yìngshuō (动) assert; allege: 他～一切没问题. He asserted that nothing was wrong.

硬通货 yìngtōnghuò (名) hard currency

映

yìng (动) reflect; mirror; shine

映衬(襯) yìngchèn (动) set off: 红墙碧瓦，互相～. The red walls and green tiles set each other off.

映照 yìngzhào (动) shine upon

哟

yō (叹) [an expression of mild surprise]: ～，你踩我的脚了. Oh! You have trodden on my foot.

哟

yo [used at the end of a sentence to indicate the imperative mood]: 大家一起用力拉～！ Let's all put in some more effort, pull!

庸

yōng I (形) 1 commonplace; mediocre: ～言～行 banal remarks and trivial matters 2 inferior; second-rate II (名) <书> [used in the negative] need: 无～细述 This needs no further elaboration. *or* There is no need to go into details.

庸才 yōngcái (名) mediocre person; mediocrity

庸碌 yōnglù (形) mediocre: ～无

能 mediocre and incompetent
庸人 yōngrén (名) mediocre person
庸人自扰(擾) yōngrén zì rǎo feel hopelessly worried or get into trouble for imaginary fears
庸俗 yōngsú (形) vulgar; philistine; low: ～化 vulgarize; debase
庸医(醫) yōngyī (名) quack; charlatan

雍 yōng (名) harmony
雍容 yōngróng (形) natural, graceful and poised: ～华贵 elegant and poised; distingué. 态度～ have a dignified bearing

壅 yōng (动) 1 stop up; obstruct 2 heap soil or fertilizer over and around the roots (of plants and trees): ～土 hilling. ～肥 heap fertilizer around the roots
壅塞 yōngsè (形) clogged up; jammed; congested: 水道～. The waterway is blocked up.

臃 yōng
臃肿(腫) yōngzhǒng (形) 1 too fat and clumsy to move; obese 2 (of an organization) cumbersome and overstaffed

拥(擁) yōng (动) 1 gather around: 一群青年～着一个老教师走出来. An old teacher came out, followed by a group of young people. 2 (of a crowd) rush in: 一～而入 crowd in 3 support; boost: ～戴 give support to
拥抱 yōngbào (动) embrace; hug
拥戴 yōngdài (动) support (sb. as leader): 受到人民的～ enjoy popular support
拥护(護) yōnghù (动) support; uphold; endorse: 我们～这个决定. We support this decision.
拥挤(擠) yōngjǐ I (动) crowd; push and squeeze II (形) be crowded; be packed like sardines
拥有 yōngyǒu (动) possess; have; own: ～核武器 possess nuclear weapons

佣(傭) yōng I (动) hire (a labourer) II (名) servant: 女～ woman servant; maid
see also yòng
佣工 yōnggōng (名) hired labourer; servant

永 yǒng (副) perpetually; forever; always: ～不变心 remain loyal till one's dying day
永别 yǒngbié (动) say goodbye to sb. forever; part forever
永垂不朽 yǒng chuí bù xiǔ (动) be immortal; eternal glory to
永恒 yǒnghéng (形) eternal; constant: ～的真理 eternal truth
永久 yǒngjiǔ (形) permanent; perpetual; everlasting; forever; for good (and all): ～居留 permanent residence
永生 yǒngshēng I (名) eternal life II (形) immortal: ～永世 for ever and ever
永世 yǒngshì (副) forever: ～难忘 will never forget it for the rest of one's life
永远(遠) yǒngyuǎn (副) always; forever; ever

泳 yǒng swim: 仰～ backstroke. 蛙～ breaststroke

涌 yǒng (动) 1 gush; well; pour; surge: 风起云～. The wind rose and the clouds began to gather. 2 rise; surge; emerge: 雨过天晴,～出一轮明月. The sky was cloudless after a passing shower, and there emerged a bright moon.
涌现 yǒngxiàn (动) (of people and events) emerge in large numbers

踊(踴) yǒng (动) leap up; jump up
踊跃(躍) yǒngyuè 1 leap; jump: ～欢呼 leap and cheer 2 eagerly; enthusiastically: ～参加 participate enthusiastically; take an active part

俑 yǒng (名) earthen human figures buried with the dead in ancient times; figurines: 兵马～ terra-cotta warriors

勇 yǒng (形) brave; valiant; courageous: 智～双全 possess both wisdom and courage
勇敢 yǒnggǎn (形) brave; courageous: 机智～ resourceful and courageous. ～善战 intrepid and warlike
勇猛 yǒngmeng (形) of valour; intrepid
勇气(氣) yǒngqì (名) courage; nerve: 鼓起～ pluck up (or muster up) one's courage; strain every nerve
勇往直前 yǒng wǎng zhí qián (动) advance bravely
勇于(於) yǒngyú be ready to; never hesitate to; have the courage to: ～负责 be ready to

shoulder responsibilities. ～进行经济改革 never hesitate to undertake any economic reform

用 yòng I (动) 1 use; employ; apply: ～脑子 use one's brain. 大材小～ put a man of talent to trivial use 2 [used in the negative] need: 东西都准备好了，您不～操心. Everything is O.K. You don't have to worry. II (名) 1 expenses; outlay: 家～ family expenses 2 usefulness: 有～ useful. 没～ useless; worthless

用兵 yòngbīng (动) plan or direct the movements of military forces: 善于～ be a master of strategy

用场(場) yòngchǎng (名) use: 派～ be put to use

用处(處) yòngchu (名) advantage: 水库的～很大. A reservoir has many advantages.

用费 yòngfèi (名) expense; cost

用功 yònggōng (形) hard-working; diligent; studious: ～读书 study diligently; work hard

用户 yònghù (名) consumer; user: 征求～意见 solicit consumers' opinions

用具 yòngjù (名) utensil; apparatus; appliance: 炊事～ kitchen (or cooking) utensils

用力 yònglì (动) exert one's strength: ～喊叫 shout for all one is worth

用品 yòngpǐn (名) articles for use: 日常生活～ articles for daily use; daily necessities

用人 yòngrén I (动) (of a person for a job) choose; select: ～不当 not choose the proper person for the job II (名) personnel selection

用事 yòngshì (动) act (when swayed by one's feelings): 感情～ act impetuously

用途 yòngtú (名) use: 电脑的～很广. Computer is used extensively in our life.

用武 yòngwǔ 1 use force 2 display one's abilities or talents: 大有～之地. There's ample scope for one's abilities.

用心 yòngxīn I (副) attentively; intently: ～学习 study diligently II (名) motive; intention: 别有～ have ulterior motives

用意 yòngyì (名) intention; purpose: 我说这话的～，只是想劝告她一下. The drift of what I am saying is merely to give her a word of advice.

用语 yòngyǔ (名) 1 choice of words; wording: ～不当 inapt wording 2 phraseology; term: 专业～ technical term

佣 yòng (名) commission see also yōng

佣金 yòngjīn (名) commission; brokerage; middleman's fee

忧(憂) yōu I (动) worry: ～虑 be worried or anxious II (名) sorrow; anxiety: 高枕无～ be free from anxieties and sleep soundly. 无～无虑 carefree

忧愁 yōuchóu (形) depressed; sad

忧患 yōuhuàn (名) suffering; misery

忧惧(懼) yōujù (形) apprehensive

忧虑(慮) yōulǜ (形) worried; concerned: 对他的健康状况深感～ feel very concerned about her health

忧伤(傷) yōushāng (形) sad; distressed; in deep sorrow

忧心 yōuxīn (名)<书> worry; anxiety: ～忡忡 heavy-hearted; laden with grief

优(優) yōu (形) excellent; outstanding

优待 yōudài (名) give preferential treatment

优等 yōuděng (形) high-class; first-rate; excellent

优点(點) yōudiǎn (名) merit; strong (or good) point; virtue: ～和缺点 strong and weak points; strengths and weaknesses; advantage and disadvantage

优厚 yōuhòu (形) good; munificent: 待遇～ excellent pay and fringe benefits

优惠 yōuhuì (形) preferential; favourable

优良 yōuliáng (形) fine; good: ～的传统 a good tradition

优美 yōuměi (形) graceful; fine; exquisite: 风景～. The scenery is beautiful and exquisite.

优柔寡断(斷) yōuróu guǎduàn (形) characterized by hesitation and indecision; indecisive

优生学(學) yōushēngxué (名) eugenics

优胜(勝) yōushèng (形) superior in academic record

优势(勢) yōushì (名) superiority; dominant position: 占～ occupy

a dominant position; gain the upper hand
优先 yōuxiān (名) have priority; take precedence: ～发展这种类型的产品 give priority to the development of this type of product
优秀 yōuxiù (形) outstanding; excellent; splendid: ～作品 outstanding work of art or literature
优选(選)法 yōuxuǎnfǎ (名) optimum seeking method; optimization
优异(異) yōuyì (形) excellent; outstanding; exceedingly good: 考试成绩～ get excellent examination results
优裕 yōuyù (形) affluent; abundant: 生活～ be comfortably off; live in comfort
优越 yōuyuè (形) superior; advantageous: ～的条件 superior conditions. ～感 superiority complex
优越性 yōuyuèxìng (名) superiority; advantage
优质(質) yōuzhì (名) high (or top) quality; high grade

幽 yōu (形) 1 deep and remote; secluded: ～静 quiet 2 quiet; tranquil; serene 3 of the nether world: ～魂 ghost
幽暗 yōu'àn (形) dim; gloomy
幽会(會) yōuhuì (名) a lovers' rendezvous
幽禁 yōujìn (动) put under house arrest
幽静 yōujìng (形) quiet and secluded; peaceful
幽灵(靈) yōulíng (名) ghost; spectre; spirit
幽默 yōumò (形) humorous: ～感 sense of humour
幽深 yōushēn (形) (of woods, palaces, etc.) deep and serene; deep and quiet
幽雅 yōuyǎ (形) (of a place) quiet and in elegant taste

悠 yōu (形) 1 remote in time 2 leisurely
悠长(長) yōucháng (形) long; long-drawn-out: ～的岁月 long years
悠久 yōujiǔ (形) long; long-standing; age-old: 历史～ have a long history. ～的文化传统 age-old cultural tradition
悠然 yōurán (形) 1 carefree and leisurely: ～自得 be carefree and content 2 long; distant; far away: ～神往 thoughts turn to things distant
悠闲(閑) yōuxián (形) leisurely and carefree: ～自在 completely free and at ease
悠扬(揚) yōuyáng (形) (of music etc.) melodious

游 yóu I (动) 1 swim 2 wander about; travel; tour: 周～世界 travel round the world 3 〈书〉 associate with: 交～甚广 have a wide acquaintanceship among all sorts of people II (名) part of a river; reach: 上～ the upper reaches (of a river)
游伴 yóubàn (名) travel companion; fellow traveller
游船 yóuchuán (名) pleasure-boat
游荡(蕩) yóudàng (动) loaf about; loiter; wander
游击(擊) yóujī (名) guerrilla warfare
游记 yóujì (名) travel notes; travels
游客 yóukè (名) tourist; sightseer
游览(覽) yóulǎn (动) go sightseeing; be on a tour; visit: ～长城 visit the Great Wall
游历(歷) yóulì (动) travel for pleasure; tour
游民 yóumín (名) vagrant; vagabond: 无业～ vagrant
游牧 yóumù (动) move about in search of pasture: ～部落 nomadic tribe
游手好闲(閑) yóushǒu-hàoxián (动) loaf about without a decent occupation
游玩 yóuwán (动) 1 play games 2 stroll about
游行 yóuxíng (名) parade; march: 国庆～ National Day parade. 反战～示威 anti-war demonstration
游移 yóuyí (动) (of attitude, policy, etc.) vacillate
游弋 yóuyì (动) cruise; ply
游艺(藝) yóuyì (名) entertainment; recreation: ～室 recreation room
游泳 yóuyǒng (动) swim: ～池 swimming pool. ～裤 bathing (or swimming) trunks
游资 yóuzī (名) floating capital

尤 yóu I (副) particularly; especially: 这一点～为重要. This is particularly important II (动) have a grudge against; blame: 他这个人怨天～人. He blames everyone but himself for what has happened.

尤其 yóuqí (副) especially; particularly: 我喜欢图画，～是国画. I am fond of painting, particularly traditional Chinese painting.

犹(猶) yóu (副)<书> 1 just as; like: 虽死～生. He lives among us though he is dead. 2 still: 记忆～新 be still fresh in one's memory; remain vivid in one's memory

犹如 yóurú (副) just as; like; as if: ～为虎添翼 like adding wings to a tiger

犹豫 yóuyù (动) hesitate; waver: ～不决 hesitate

由 yóu I (名) cause: 理～ reason; ground II (介) 1 because of; due to: 咎～自取 have only oneself to blame 2 by; through: 必～之路 the only way possible. 3 by, to: 这次会将～他主持. This meeting will be chaired by him. 这事～我处理. Leave it to me. 4 depending upon: ～此可知 as may be inferred from this 5 as a starting point: ～北京出发 set out from Beijing III (动) follow; obey: 我们将～别人牵着鼻子走吗? Shall we allow others to lead us by the nose?

由不得 yóubude (动) 1 not be up to sb. to decide: 这件事～我. I've no say in the matter. 2 cannot help: ～笑起来 can't help laughing

由来(來) yóulái (名) origin; root; cause

由来(來)已久 yóulái yǐ jiǔ be of long duration

由于(於) yóuyú (介) due to; owing to; thanks to; as a result of

由衷 yóuzhōng (形) sincere; heartfelt: 表示～的感激. extend one's heartfelt thanks. 这种表扬有点儿言不～. This is somewhat insincere praise.

油 yóu I (名) oil; fat: 植物～ vegetable oil. 猪～ lard II (动) be stained with grease: 衣服～了. The coat has got stains on it. III (形) oily; glib

油泵 yóubèng (名) oil pump

油层(層) yóucéng (名) oil reservoir; oil layer

油船 yóuchuán (名) (oil) tanker; oil carrier

油膏 yóugāo (名) ointment

油管 yóuguǎn (名) 1 oil pipe: 铺设～ lay oil pipes 2 oil tube

油光 yóuguāng (形) glossy; shiny; varnished

油滑 yóuhuá (形) insincere; unctuous; slippery

油画(畫) yóuhuà (名) oil painting

油井 yóujǐng (名) oil well: 钻一口～ drill (or bore) a well

油库(庫) yóukù (名) oil depot; tank farm

油料作物 yóuliào zuòwù (名) oil-bearing crops; oil crops

油门(門) yóumén (名) 1 throttle 2 accelerator

油墨 yóumò (名) printing ink

油泥 yóuní (名) greasy filth; grease

油腻 yóunì I (形) grease; oily; heavy II (名) greasy or oily food

油漆 yóuqī I (名) paint: ～未干 wet paint II (动) cover with paint; paint

油腔滑调 yóuqiāng-huádiào (形) glib; unctuous: 说起话来～ speak glibly; have a glib tongue

油砂 yóushā (名) oil sand

油田 yóutián (名) oil field

油头(頭)粉面 yóutóu-fěnmiàn (形) loudly dressed and made up

油头(頭)滑脑(腦) yóutóu-huánǎo (形) sly and flippant

油印 yóuyìn (名) mimeograph

油脂 yóuzhī (名) oil; fat

邮(郵) yóu I (动) post; mail II (形) relating to postal affairs: ～局 post office

邮包 yóubāo (名) postal parcel; parcel

邮戳 yóuchuō (名) postmark

邮袋 yóudài (名) mailbag; postbag; (mail) pouch

邮递(遞) yóudì (名) 1 send by post (or mail) 2 postal delivery: ～员 postman; mailman

邮电(電) yóudiàn (名) post and telecommunications: ～局 post office

邮购(購) yóugòu (名) mail-order

邮汇(匯) yóuhuì (动) remit by post

邮寄 yóujì (名) send by post; post

邮件 yóujiàn (名) postal matter; post, mail: 挂号～ registered post. 航空～ air mail

邮票 yóupiào (名) postage stamp; stamp: 纪念～ commemorative stamps

邮筒 yóutǒng (名) pillar-box; postbox; mailbox

邮箱 yóuxiāng (名) postbox; mailbox
邮政 yóuzhèng (名) postal service: ～编码 postcode; zip code. ～信箱 post-office box (P.O.B.)
邮资 yóuzī (名) postage: ～已付, postage paid; postpaid

莠 yǒu (名) 1 green bristlegrass 2 bad people: 良～不齐. Both good and bad people are intermingled.

有 yǒu (动) 1 have; possess 2 there is; exist: 这里边什么东西都没～. There is nothing whatever in here. 3 [indicating probability or comparison]: 他～他哥哥那么高了. He is probably as tall as his elder brother. ～话直说. Speak straight out what you think. 4 [indicating that sth. has happened or appeared]: 形势～了很大的变化. A great change has taken place in the situation. 5 [indicating "many", "much" "advanced", etc.]: ～学问 be very learned. ～了年纪 get on in years 6 [somewhat like "certain"]: ～人这么说, 我可没看见. Some say so, but I haven't seen it myself. 7 [meaning certain "people", "occasions" or "localities"]: 近来他～时显出心不在焉的样子. Recently, he has sometimes appeared absent-minded. 8 [used in certain set phrases to indicate politeness]: ～劳费神 sorry to have put you to such bother
有备(備)无(無)患 yǒubèi-wúhuàn preparedness is a protection against danger
有待 yǒudài (动) remain (to be done); await: ～解决 remain to be solved. 推行这些新办法～上级批准. We have to wait for the approval of the higher level to implement these new measures.
有的是 yǒudeshì have plenty of; there's no lack of: 别着急, ～时间. Don't worry. We have plenty of time.
有的放矢 yǒu dì fàng shǐ shoot the arrow at the target; speak or act with something definite in view
有点(點) yǒudiǎn I (形) some; a little: 看来还～希望. It looks there is still a gleam of hope. II (副) somewhat; rather; a bit: 今天他～不大高兴. He looks somewhat displeased today.
有方 yǒufāng with the proper method; in the right way: 领导～ exercise effective leadership
有关(關) yǒuguān I (动) have something to do with; relate to; concern: 这件事与他～. This matter has something to do with him. II (形) relevant: ～部门 the department concerned
有过(過)之无(無)不及 yǒu guò zhī wú bùjí (贬) surpass; outdo: 在这方面, 他比他的前任～. In this respect he even surpassed his predecessors.
有机(機) yǒujī (形) organic: ～肥料 organic fertilizer. ～化学 organic chemistry
有机(機)可乘 yǒu jī kě chéng (贬) a loophole to exploit
有救 yǒujiù (of a diseace) can be cured or remedied
有口皆碑 yǒu kǒu jiē bēi win popular acclaim
有口难(難)分 yǒu kǒu nán fēn find it difficult to explain oneself
有赖 yǒulài (动) depend on; rest on: ～于大家的共同努力 depend very much on the concerted effort of all people
有理 yǒulǐ (形) reasonable; justified; in the right
有力 yǒulì (形) strong; powerful; energetic; vigorous: ～的回击 (make) a vigorous counterattack. 这篇文章写得简短～. This essay is concise and forceful.
有利 yǒulì (副) of benefit; to one's advantage: 在～情况下 under favourable circumstances. ～可图 be profitable
有名 yǒumíng (形) well-known; famous; renowned; celebrated
有名无(無)实(實) yǒumíng-wúshí in name only; nominal; titular
有目共睹 yǒu mù gòng dǔ be universally acknowledged; be clear to all
有钱(錢) yǒuqián (形) rich; wealthy: ～能使鬼推磨. Money makes the mare to go.
有趣 yǒuqù (形) interesting; fascinating; amusing
有色 yǒusè (形) coloured: ～金属 nonferrous metal. ～人种 coloured race
有生力量 yǒushēng lìliàng (名) effective strength; effectives
有生以来(來) yǒu shēng yǐlái ever since one's birth; since one was born into the world
有声(聲)有色 yǒushēng-yǒusè (形) vivid and dramatic: 故事讲得

~ bring the story to life

有始无(無)终 yǒushǐ-wúzhōng fail to carry sth. through to the end

有恃无(無)恐 yǒushì-wúkǒng fearless of what might happen because one has strong backing

有数(數) yǒushù 1 know exactly what one is doing: 两个人心里都~儿. The two of them know exactly how things stand. 2 not many; only a few: 离开学只剩下~的几天了. There are only a few days left before school starts.

有条(條)不紊 yǒutiáo-bùwěn in an orderly way; methodically; systematically

有为(爲) yǒuwéi (形) promising

有…无… yǒu…wú… [used to indicate a case in which there is only one thing and not the other]: 有己无人 absolutely selfish. 有口无心 frank and straight forward. 有勇无谋 be brave but not resourceful. 有害无益 do only harm and no good

有限 yǒuxiàn (形) limited; finite: 为数~ limited in number

有线(綫) yǒuxiàn (名) wired: ~传真 wirephoto. ~广播 wire (or wired) broadcasting. ~电报 telegraph; cable

有效 yǒuxiào (形) effective; efficient; valid: 采取~措施 take effective measures. 这张车票三日内~. This train ticket is good for three days.

有效期 yǒuxiàoqī (名) term (or period) of validity; expiry date

有心 yǒuxīn I (动) have the inclination; contemplate II (副) intentionally; on purpose

有心人 yǒuxīnrén (名) a person who is ambitious or tenacious of purpose

有言在先 yǒu yán zài xiān make clear at the beginning; forewarn

有益 yǒuyì (形) profitable; beneficial; useful

有意 yǒuyì I (动) be inclined to II (副) deliberately; on purpose: ~刁难 deliberately make things difficult for sb.

有意思 yǒu yìsi (形) 1 significant; meaningful: 他说的话很~. What he said was significant. 2 interesting; enjoyable: 今天的晚会很~. The evening was most enjoyable.

有…有… yǒu…yǒu… 1 [used with two nouns or verbs with opposite meanings to indicate possession of both qualities]: 有利有弊 have both advantages and disadvantages 2 [used for emphasis before two nouns or verbs with identical or similar meanings]: 有凭有据 backed by evidence. 有说有笑 talk cheerfully

有余(餘) yǒuyú have enough and to spare: 绰绰~ have more than enough

有助于(於) yǒuzhùyú contribute to; be conducive to; conduce to: ~增进两国人民之间的友谊 be conducive to the promotion of the friendship between our two peoples

友 yǒu I (名) friend: 好~ close friend. 战~ comrade-in-arms II (形) friendly

友爱(愛) yǒu'ài (名) friendly affection; fraternal love

友邦 yǒubāng (名) friendly nation (or country)

友好 yǒuhǎo I (名) close friend; friend II (形) friendly; amicable: ~访问 friendly visit

友情 yǒuqíng (名) friendly sentiments; friendship

友人 yǒurén (名) friend: 国际~ friends from abroad

友谊 yǒuyì (名) friendship: 深厚的~ profound friendship

黝 yǒu (形) black; dark: ~黑 dark; swarthy

诱 yòu (动) 1 guide; teach: 循循善~ be good at giving instruction and guidance; teach with patience 2 lure; seduce; entice: ~敌 lure the enemy in

诱导(導) yòudǎo (动) guide; lead; induce

诱饵 yòu'ěr (名) bait

诱发(發) yòufā (动) bring out (sth. potential or latent); induce; cause to happen

诱惑 yòuhuò (动) 1 entice; tempt; seduce; lure 2 attract; allure: 窗外是一片~人的景色. Outside the window stretches a vista of enchanting beauty.

诱骗 yòupiàn (动) trap; tr ck

右 yòu (名) 1 the right side; the right: 靠~走 keep to the right 2 the Right: ~倾思想 Rightist thinking

右边(邊) yòubian (名) the right (or right-hand) side; the right

右倾 yòuqīng (名) Right deviation

右首 yòushǒu (名) the right-hand side; the right

右翼 yòuyì (名) 1 right wing; right flank 2 the Right; the right wing

又 yòu (副) 1 [indicating repetition or continuation]: 读了~读 read again and again. 一年~一年 year after year 2 [indicating the simultaneous existence of several conditions or characteristics]: ~高~大 tall and big. 效率~高,管理~好 efficient and well-managed 3 [indicating additional ideas or after-thought]: 冬季日短，~是雪天，夜色早已笼罩了整个市镇. Days are short in winter. And it was a snowy day, so the whole town was already enveloped in a thick mist of dusk. 4 [indicating two contradictory ideas]: 她~想去,~不想去，拿不定主意. She was not sure whether she was to go and could not make up her mind. 5 [used in negative or rhetorical questions for the sake of emphasis]: 他~不是什么生客，还用你老陪着吗? He is not rare visitor. Do you have to keep him company all the time?

幼 yòu I (形) young; under age: ~畜 young animal; young stock II (名) children; the young: 扶老携~ bringing along the old and the young

幼虫(蟲) yòuchóng (名) larva

幼儿(兒) yòu'ér (名) infant; toddler: ~教育 preschool education. ~园 kindergarten

幼苗 yòumiáo (名) seedling

幼年 yòunián (名) childhood; infancy

幼小 yòuxiǎo (名) immature

幼稚 yòuzhì (形) 1 young 2 childish; naive

柚 yòu (~子)(名) shaddock; pomelo; grapefruit

釉 yòu (名) glaze: 青~瓷器 blue glazed porcelain

淤 yū I (动) become silted up: 水渠里~了很多泥沙. The channel has silted up. II (名) silt: 河~ sludge from a riverbed

淤积(積) yūjī (动) silt up; deposit

淤泥 yūní (名) silt; sludge; ooze

淤塞 yūsè (动) silt up; be choked with silt

淤血 yūxuè (名) extravasated blood

迂 yū (形) 1 roundabout: ~道访问 make a detour to call on sb. 2 pedantic: ~论 pedantic talk

迂腐 yūfǔ (名) pedantry: ~的见解 pedantic ideas

迂回 yūhuí I (形) circuitous; tortuous; roundabout: ~曲折 full of twists and turns; tortuous. ~前进 advance by a roundabout route II (动) outflank: 向敌人左侧~ outflank the enemy on the left

迂阔 yūkuò (形) high-sounding and impracticable: ~之论 impractical views

于(於) yú (介) 1 [similar to '在']: 生~1920年 be born in 1920. 闻名~世界 famous all over the world 2 [similar to '给']: 光荣归~英勇的人民. The credit goes to the heroic people. 3 [similar to '对' or '对于']: 忠~祖国 be loyal to one's country. 这样~你自己不利. It won't do you any good. 4 [similar to '从']: 出~无知 out of sheer ignorance. 出~自愿 of one's own accord

于今 yújīn (副) 1 up to the present; since 2 nowadays; today; now

于是 yúshì (连) thereupon; hence; consequently; as a result

盂 yú (名) a broad-mouthed receptacle for holding liquid; jar: 痰~ spitton

舆 yú I (名) 1 carriage; chariot 2 sedan chair 3 area; territory: ~地 territory II (形) public; popular: ~论 public opinion

舆论(論) yúlùn (名) public opinion: ~工具 mass media; the media

舆情 yúqíng (名) public sentiment; popular feelings

虞 yú I (名)〈书〉1 supposition; prediction: 以备不~ be prepared for any contingency 2 anxiety; worry: 水旱无~ have no worries about drought or flood II (动) deceive; cheat; fool: 尔~我诈 a cast of each trying to cheat the other; mutual deception

娱(娛) yú I (动) give pleasure to; amuse: 聊以自~ just to enjoy oneself II (名) joy; pleasure; amusement

娱乐(樂) yúlè (名) amusement; entertainment; recreation: ~场

所 place of entertainment

愚 yú I (形) foolish; stupid: ～人 fool II (动) fool; dupe: 为人所～ be duped by sb. III (代)〈谦〉I: ～以为不可 in my opinion this wouldn't seem correct

愚笨 yúbèn (形) dull-witted; stupid; clumsy

愚蠢 yúchǔn (形) stupid; foolish; idiotic

愚昧 yúmèi (形) ignorant: ～无知 pure ignorance

愚弄 yúnòng (动) deceive; hoodwink; make a fool of; dupe

余(餘) yú (形) 1 surplus; spare; remaining: ～钱 spare money. ～年 the remaining years of one's life 2 more than; odd; over: 五十～年 fifty-odd years 3 beyond; after: 工作之～ after work; in one's spare time

余波 yúbō (名) aftermath: 纠纷的～ the aftermath of the dispute

余存 yúcún (名) remainder; balance

余地 yúdì (名) leeway; room; latitude: 还有改进的～. There is still room for improvement. 在这方面我们给他留有相当的～. In this respect we allow him considerable latitude.

余毒 yúdú (名) residual poison; pernicious influence

余额 yú'é (名) remaining sum; balance

余悸 yújì (名) lingering fear: 心有～ have a lingering fear after the incident

余粮(糧) yúliáng (名) surplus grain

余兴(興) yúxìng (名) 1 lingering interest 2 entertainment after a meeting or a dinner party

余暇 yúxiá (名) spare time; leisure time; leisure

余音 yúyīn (名) the residue of sound which remains in the ears of the hearer

渝 yú (名) (of one's attitude or feeling) change: 始终不～ remain faithful

愉 yú (形) pleased; happy: 不～ displeased; annoyed

愉快 yúkuài (形) happy; joyful; cheerful: 心情～ be in a happy mood

逾 yú (动) exceed; go beyond: ～限 exceed the limit. 年～六十 over sixty years old

逾期 yúqī (动) exceed the time limit

逾越 yúyuè (动) exceed; go beyond: ～权限 overstep one's authority. 不可～的障碍 an insurmountable obstacle (or barrier)

谀 yú (动)〈书〉flatter: 阿～ flatter and toady

鱼(魚) yú (名) fish

鱼翅 yúchì (名) shark's fin

鱼肚 yúdǔ (名) fish maw

鱼饵 yú'ěr (名) (fish) bait

鱼肝油 yúgānyóu (名) cod-liver oil

鱼竿 yúgān (名) fishing rod

鱼钩 yúgōu (名) fishhook

鱼贯 yúguàn one following the other; in single file: ～而入 file in

鱼雷 yúléi (名) torpedo: ～快艇 torpedo boat

鱼鳞 yúlín (名) fish scale

鱼龙(龍)混杂(雜) yú-lóng hùnzá good and bad people mixed up

鱼目混珠 yúmù hùn zhū pass off fish eyes as pearls; pass off the sham as the genuine

鱼水情 yú-shuǐqíng (名) close relationship(usu. between armymen and people): deep sentiment of comradeship for each other

鱼网(網) yúwǎng (名) fishnet; fishing net

鱼子 yúzǐ (名) roe: ～酱 caviare

渔 yú I (形) fishing: ～船 fishing boat. ～翁 fisherman II (动) seek by unfair means: ～利 seek unfair gains

渔产(產) yúchǎn (名) aquatic products

渔场(場) yúchǎng (名) fishing ground; fishery

渔民 yúmín (名) fisherman; fisherfolk

渔业(業) yúyè (名) fishery: ～资源 fishery resources

宇 yǔ (名) 1 housing; house 2 space; globe: ～宙 universe; cosmos. ～宙飞船 spacecraft

宇宙航行 yǔzhòu hángxíng (名) astronavigation; space travels: ～员 astronaut; spaceman

语 yǔ I (名) 1 language; tongue; words: 汉～ the Chinese language. 本族～ mother tongue; native language. 甜言蜜～ sweet words 2 nonlinguistic means of communicating ideas; semiology: 旗～ flagsignal. 手～ sign language II (动) speak; say: 不言不～ be speechless;

keep silent
语病 yǔbìng (名) faulty wording; unhappy choice of words
语词 yǔcí (名) words and phrases
语法 yǔfǎ (名) grammar
语汇(匯) yǔhuì (名) vocabulary
语气(氣) yǔqì (名) 1 tone; manner of speaking: ～友好 a friendly tone 2 mood: 祈使～ imperative mood
语态(態) yǔtài (名) voice: 主动(被动)～ the active (passive) voice
语文 yǔwén (名) 1 language (oral and written): ～程度 one's reading and writing ability 2 (short for "language and literature")
语无(無)伦(倫)次 yǔ wú lúncì speak incoherently; be totally disorganized in one's speech; talk inarticulately
语系 yǔxì (名) family of languages; language family
语序 yǔxù (名) word order
语焉不详 yǔ yān bù xiáng not go into details; not elaborate
语言 yǔyán (名) language: ～隔阂 language barrier. ～学 linguistics
语音 yǔyīn (名) pronunciation: ～学 phonetics
语源学(學) yǔyuánxué (名) etymology
语重心长(長) yǔzhòng-xīncháng sincere advice and earnest wishes; earnest exhortations

雨 yǔ (名) rain: 大～ a heavy rain. 暴～ storm; downpour. 毛毛～ drizzle
雨点(點) yǔdiǎn (名) raindrop
雨过(過)天晴 yǔ guò tiān qíng the sun came out after the rain stopped; the sun shines again after the rain
雨后(後)春笋(筍) yǔ hòu chūnsǔn (spring up like) bamboo shoots after a spring rain
雨季 yǔjì (名) rainy season
雨具 yǔjù (名) rain gear (i.e. umbrella, raincoat, etc.)
雨量 yǔliàng (名) rainfall
雨伞(傘) yǔsǎn (名) umbrella
雨水 yǔshuǐ (名) rainwater; rainfall; rain: ～足 adequate rainfall
雨鞋 yǔxié (名) rubber boots; galoshes
雨衣 yǔyī (名) raincoat

与(與) yǔ I (动) 1 give; offer: 赠～ give sth. to sb. as a gift. ～人方便 be of help to others. ～人为善 sincerely help people to improve; be well-intentioned II (介) [similar to '和']: ～困难作斗争 grapple with difficulties. ～世浮沉 swim with the tide III (连) and; together with: ～友人同去看花展 go to a flower show together with a friend
see also yù
与其 yǔqí (连) [used in the context of making a decision after weighing the pros and cons]: ～扬汤止沸，不如釜底抽薪. It would be better to find a permanent solution in a slow process than to seek temporal relief by drastic measures.
与日俱增 yǔ rì jù zēng grow with each passing day; be steady on the increase
与世长(長)辞(辭) yǔ shì chángcí depart from the world; pass away
与世无(無)争 yǔ shì wú zhēng stand aloof from wordly strife

屿(嶼) yǔ (名) small island; islet: 岛～ islands and islets; islands

羽 yǔ (名) feather; plume
羽毛 yǔmáo (名) feather; plume: ～丰满 become full-fledged
羽毛球 yǔmáoqiú (名) 1 badminton 2 shuttlecock
羽毛未丰(豐) yǔmáo wèi fēng still young and immature; fledgling

予 yǔ (动) give: 免～处分 no disciplinary action will be taken against one; be exempted from disciplinary action. ～人口实 give sb. a handle
予以 yǔ yǐ (动) give; grant: ～优待 give one preferential treatment. ～批评 pass criticism

育 yù I (名) birth: 节育 birth control; family planning II (动) 1 rear; raise; bring up: ～秧 grow rice seedlings 2 educate: 德～ moral education
育种(種) yùzhǒng (名) breeding: 杂交～ crossbreeding. 作物～ crop breeding

玉 yù I (名) jade II (形) <书> (of purity or beauty) pure; handsome; beautiful: 亭亭～立 fair, slender and graceful
玉帛 yùbó (名) <书> jade objects and silk fabrics, used as state gifts in ancient China
玉成 yùchéng <敬> kindly help secure the success of sth.: 深望～此事. It is earnestly hoped that

you will help arrange the matter successfully.

玉米 yùmǐ (名) maize

玉器 yùqì (名) jade article; jade object; jadeware

玉石俱焚 yù-shí jù fén destruction of all people good and bad alike

玉蜀黍 yùshǔshǔ (名) maize; corn

玉玺(璽) yùxǐ (名) imperial jade seal

芋 yù (名) 1 taro 2 tuber crops: 洋～ potato. 山～ sweet potato

吁(籲) yù (动) appeal; plead: 呼～ petition. ～请 plead with sb.; appeal to sb.
see also xū

域 yù (名) land within certain boundaries; territory; region: 领～ territory; field; area. 核物理学里的一个新领～ a new area of nuclear physics

郁(鬱) yù (形) 1 strongly fragrant 2 luxuriant; lush 3 gloomy; depressed: 忧～ feel depressed or frustrated

郁闷 yùmèn (形) gloomy; unhappy: 有～之感 be in the doldrums

郁血 yùxuè (名) stagnation of the blood; venous stasis

郁郁 yùyù (形) 〈书〉 1 lush; luxuriant: ～葱葱 green and luxuriant 2 gloomy; melancholy; depressed

与(與) yù (动) take part in; participate in
see also yǔ

与会(會) yùhuì (动) attend a meeting: ～国 participating countries

与闻 yùwén (动) participate in the discussion of: ～其事 be a participant in the matter

誉(譽) yù (名) 1 reputation; fame: ～满全球 of world renown; famous the world over 2 praise; eulogy

寓 yù I (动) 1 reside; live: ～居 stay in lodgings 2 imply; contain: 这个故事～有深意. This story conveys a profound message. II (名) residence: 公～ apartment house. 客～ lodgings

寓居 yùjū (动) reside abroad or in a place away from one's hometown

寓所 yùsuǒ (名) residence; accommodation

寓言 yùyán (名) fable; allegory; parable

遇 yù I (动) 1 meet: 不期而～ meet by chance; run across 2 treat; receive: 优～ treat sb. with special consideration II (名) chance; opportunity: 机～ favourable circumstances; opportunity

遇害 yùhài (动) be murdered; be killed

遇见(見) yùjiàn (动) meet: 在昨天的招待会上我～一位老朋友. I met an old friend at yesterday's reception.

遇救 yùjiù (动) be rescued

遇难(難) yùnàn (动) 1 be killed in an accident 2 be murdered

遇险(險) yùxiǎn (动) meet with a mishap: be in trouble

浴 yù (名、动) bath; bathe: 淋～ shower bath

浴场(場) yùchǎng (名) outdoor bathing place: 海滨～ bathing beach

浴池 yùchí (名) public bathhouse; public bath

浴盆 yùpén (名) bathtub

浴室 yùshì (名) bathroom

裕 yù (形) abundant; plentiful: 富～ abundant; affluent; well-to-do; comfortably-off

欲 yù I (名) desire; longing; wish: 食～ appetite. 求知～ thirst for knowledge II (动) 1 wish; want; desire: 畅所～言 say all that one has to say; speak freely 2 about to; on the point of: 摇摇～坠 teeter on the edge of collapse; tottering

欲罢(罷)不能 yù bà bùnéng be compelled to go ahead by force of circumstances, though against one's will

欲盖弥彰 yù gài mí zhāng try to cover up the truth only to make it more glaring

欲壑难(難)填 yùhè nán tián the desire for gain is insatiable

欲加之罪,何患无(無)词 yù jiā zhī zuì, hé huàn wú cí if you are out to condemn somebody, you can always trump up a charge

欲速则不达(達) yù sù zé bù dá haste makes waste; more haste, less speed

欲望 yùwàng (名) desire; wish; lust: 对权力的～ a lust for power

愈 yù 1 recover; become well: 病～ recover from an illness 2 [the more ... the more]: ～多～好 the more the better. 山路～来～陡. The mountain path becomes more and more steep.

愈合 yùhé (动) heal: 战争的创伤不久就～了. The wound of war soon healed.

愈加 yùjiā (副) all the more; even more; further: 矛盾变得～尖锐. The contradiction has become even more acute.

喻 yù I (动) 1 explain; illustrate: ～之以理 try to make sb. see reason 2 understand; know: 家～户晓 known to every household II (名) analogy: 比～ analogy; metaphor

御 yù I (形) of an emperor; imperial: ～花园 imperial garden II (禦)(动) resist; keep out; ward off: ～敌 resist the enemy; ward off an enemy attack. ～寒 keep out the cold

御用 yùyòng 1 for the use of an emperor 2 serve as a tool: ～文人 hack writer

狱(獄) yù (名) 1 prison; jail: 入～ be imprisoned; be put in jail 2 lawsuit; case: 文字～ literary inquisition

狱吏 yùlì (名) warder; prison officer; jailer

豫 yù (形) <书> pleased: 面有不～之色 look far from pleased

预 yù (副) in advance; beforehand: 勿谓言之不～也. Don't say you have not been forewarned.

预报(報) yùbào (动) forecast: 天气～ weather forecast

预备(備) yùbèi (动) prepare; get ready: ～再试一试 be prepared to make another effort

预测 yùcè (动) calculate; forecast

预产(產)期 yùchǎnqī (名) expected date of childbirth

预订 yùdìng (动) subscribe; book; place an order

预定 yùdìng (动) arrange in advance; schedule: 按～计划 on schedule

预防 yùfáng (动) prevent; take precautions against; guard against: 采取～措施 take preventive measures. ～胜于治疗. Prevention is better than cure.

预感 yùgǎn (名) 1 premonition; presentiment: 不祥的～ an ominous presentiment 2 sense: 大家都～到将要下一场大雨. We all felt that a heavy rain was to come.

预告 yùgào (动) 1 announce in advance 2 advance notice; prepublication notice

预计 yùjì (动) calculate in advance; estimate: ～到达时间 <航海> estimated time of arrival (E. T. A.)

预见(見) yùjiàn (动、名) 1 foresee; predict: 这是可以～到的. This can be predicted. 2 foresight; prevision: 英明的～ brilliant foresight

预料 yùliào (动) expect; predict; anticipate

预谋 yùmóu (动) premeditate; plan beforehand: ～杀人 premeditated murder

预期 yùqī (动) expect; anticipate: 达到～的效果 achieve the desired results

预示 yùshì (动) presage; betoken, indicate: 灿烂的晚霞～明天又是好天气. The rosy evening clouds presage another fine day tomorrow.

预算 yùsuàn (名) budget

预先 yùxiān (副) in advance; beforehand: ～通知 notify in advance. ～警告 forewarn

预想 yùxiǎng (动) anticipate; expect

预言 yùyán I (动) prophesy; predict; foretell II (名) prophecy; prediction: ～家 prophet

预演 yùyǎn (名) preview (of a film, paintings, etc.)

预约 yùyuē (动) make an appointment (with a doctor, etc.)

预兆 yùzhào (名) omen; sign; harbinger: 吉祥的～ an auspicious omen; a good sign

预制 yùzhì (形) prefabricated: ～构件 prefabricated components

鹬 yù (名) sandpiper; snipe: ～蚌相争,渔人得利. When two sides contend, it's always the third party that benefits.

妪(嫗) yù (名) <书> old woman

驭 yù (动) drive (a carriage): 驾～ drive; control

渊(淵) yuān I (名) deep pool: 深～ a deep pool; abyss II (形) deep: ～博 erudite. 天～之别 a world of difference. ～薮 a sink of iniquity

渊源 yuānyuán (名) origin; source: 家学～ the intellectual background of the family

冤(寃) yuān (名) 1 wrong; injustice: 不白之～ a gross injustice; an unrighted wrong 2 feeling of bitterness; hatred;

enmity: ～仇 rancour; enmity

冤仇 yuānchóu (名) rancour; enmity: 结～ feel rancour against sb.

冤家 yuānjiā (名) enemy; foe

冤屈 yuānqū (动、名) **1** wrong; treat unjustly **2** injustice: 受～ be wronged; suffer an injustice

冤枉 yuānwang (动) wrong; treat unjustly: ～好人 wrong an innocent person. 这钱花得真～. We shouldn't have spent our money so thoughtlessly.

冤狱(獄) yuānyù (名) an unjust charge or verdict; a miscarriage of justice; frame-up: 平反～ reverse an unjust verdict.

鸳 yuān

鸳鸯 yuānyang (名) **1** mandarin duck **2** an affectionate couple

元 yuán (形) **1** first; primary: ～旦 New Year's Day. ～月 first lunar month **2** chief; principal: 国家～首 head of state. ～帅 marshal. ～凶 arch criminal **3** basic; fundamental: ～素 element. ～音 vowel **4** basic substance or element: 一～论 mononism. 二～论 dualism

元件 yuánjiàn (名) part; component; cell

元老 yuánlǎo senior statesman; founding member (of a political organization, etc.)

元气(氣) yuánqì (名) vitality; vigour: ～旺盛 full of vitality. 恢复～ regain one's strength (or health, vigour)

元宵 yuánxiāo (名) **1** the night of the 15th of the 1st lunar month **2** sweet dumplings made of glutinous rice flour (for the Lantern Festival)

元勋(勳) yuánxūn (名) a man who has rendered the most meritorious services to the state; founding father: 开国～ founders of a state

园(園) yuán (名) **1** a piece of land for growing flowers, vegetables, trees, etc.: 菜～ vegetable garden. 果～ orchard. 葡萄～ vineyard **2** a place for public recreation: 公～ park. 动物～ zoological garden; zoo. 植物～ botanical garden

园地 yuándì (名) **1** garden plot **2** field; scope (for certain activities): 文艺～ literary column

园丁 yuándīng (名) gardener

园艺(藝) yuányì (名) horticulture; gardening

猿 yuán (名) ape: 类人～ anthropoid ape

猿猴 yuánhóu (名) apes and monkeys

猿人 yuánrén (名) ape-man: 北京～ Peking man

原 yuán I (形) **1** primary; original; former: ～始 primitive. ～意 original intention. ～文 original text **2** unprocessed; raw: ～矿石 raw ore. ～油 crude oil II (名) **1** excuse; pardon: 情有可～. This is pardonable. **2** level, open country: 平～ plain. 高～ plateau. 草～ grasslands. ～野 an expanse of open country

原版 yuánbǎn (名) original edition (of a book, etc.)

原材料 yuán-cáiliào (名) raw and other materials

原封 yuánfēng (形) untouched; intact: ～不动 be left intact; remain unchanged

原稿 yuángǎo (名) original manuscript; master copy

原告 yuángào (名) (of a civil case) plaintiff; (of a criminal case) prosecutor

原籍 yuánjí (名) ancestral home; domicile

原来(來) yuánlái I (形) original; former: ～的想法 original idea II (副) [indicating discovery of the truth]: 我说他今天为什么不来,～他是病了. So he is ill! I was just wondering why he was absent today.

原理 yuánlǐ (名) principle; tenet: 马克思主义的基本～ the fundamental tenets of Marxism

原谅 yuánliàng (动) excuse; forgive; pardon

原煤 yuánméi (名) raw coal

原棉 yuánmián (名) raw cotton

原始 yuánshǐ (形) **1** original; firsthand: ～记录 original record **2** primeval; primitive: ～森林 primeval forest. ～社会 primitive society

原委 yuánwěi (名) ins and outs of a case; the whole story; all the details

原先 yuánxiān (形) former; original: ～的计划 original plan. 他～是个军人, 现在已经成了外交家. Originally he was a soldier, but now he has become a diplomat.

原形 yuánxíng (名) true features:

～毕露 show one's true colours (or features)
原因 yuányīn (名) cause; reason: 由于健康～ on health grounds
原原本本 yuányuánběnběn (relate) from beginning to end: 我把这件事～讲给他们听了. I told them everything down to the smallest detail
原则 yuánzé (名) principle: ～上同意这个计划 agree to the plan in principle
原著 yuánzhù (名) original work; original: 读莎士比亚的～ read Shakespeare in the original
原状(狀) yuánzhuàng (名) original state; status quo ante
原子 yuánzǐ (名) atom: ～尘 fallout. ～能 atomic energy. ～反应堆 atomic reactor

源 yuán (名) **1** source (of a river); fountainhead: 发～ originate **2** source; cause: 资～ resources. 财～ source of income
源流 yuánliú (名) origin and development
源泉 yuánquán (名) source; fountainhead: 团结就是力量的～. Unity is the source of strength.
源源 yuányuán (副) in a steady stream; continuously: ～而来 come in an endless stream

员 yuán I (名) **1** a person engaged in some field of activity: 炊事～ cook. 售货～ shop assistant **2** member: 党～ Party member. 工会会～ member of a trade union II (量) [of military officers in the past]: 一～大将 an able general
员工 yuángōng (名) staff; personnel: 师生～ teachers, students and workers

圆 yuán I (形) **1** round; circular; spherical: ～桌 round table **2** tactful; satisfactory: 这人做事很～到. He shows tact in handling matters. II (动) make plausible; justify: 自～其说 make one's statement; sound plausible; try to justify oneself III (名) **1** circle **2** a coin of fixed value and weight: 银～ silver dollar
圆场(場) yuánchǎng (动) mediate or help to effect a compromise
圆规 yuánguī (名) compasses
圆滑 yuánhuá (形) smooth; unctuous; slick
圆满(滿) yuánmǎn (形) satisfactory: ～的答案 a satisfactory solution; a correct answer
圆通 yuántōng (形) flexible; accommodating
圆舞曲 yuánwǔqǔ (名) waltz
圆心 yuánxīn (名) the centre of a circle
圆形 yuánxíng (形) circular; round
圆周 yuánzhōu (名) circumference
圆圈 yuánquān (名) circle; ring
圆珠笔(筆) yuánzhūbǐ (名) ball-point pen; ball-pen
圆柱 yuánzhù (名) cylinder

援 yuán (动) **1** pull by hand; hold: 攀～ climb up by holding on to sth. **2** quote; cite: ～例 cite a precedent **3** help; aid: 支～ support; give support to. 增～ reinforce
援救 yuánjiù (动) rescue; deliver from danger
援军 yuánjūn (名) reinforcements
援引 yuányǐn (动) **1** quote; cite; invoke: ～例证 cite an example **2** recommend or appoint one's close associates
援助 yuánzhù (动、名) help; support; aid: 经济～ economic assistance; financial aid

缘 yuán (名) **1** reason; cause: 无～无故 without rhyme or reason; for no reason at all **2** edge; fringe; brink: 外～ outer fringe (or edge) **3** along: ～溪行 walk along the stream
缘分 yuánfèn (名) predestined lot; fate; luck
缘故 yuángù (名) cause; reason
缘由 yuányóu (名) reason; cause

远(遠) yuǎn I(形) **1** far; distant; remote: ～古 the remote past. ～景规划 long-range planning **2** (of blood relationship) remote: ～亲 distant relative; remote kinsfolk **3** (of degree of difference) great: outstretch by far II (动) keep away: 敬而～之 keep sb. at a respectful distance
远大 yuǎndà (形) bright; lofty; ambitious: 眼光～ farsighted. 前程～ (of a person) bright prospects; a bright future
远道 yuǎndào a long way: ～而来 come all the way from afar
远东(東) Yuǎndōng (名) the Far East
远方 yuǎnfāng (名) distant place
远见(見) yuǎnjiàn (名) foresight; vision: ～卓识 farsigtedness and bold vision
远郊 yuǎnjiāo (名) outer suburbs
远近 yuǎnjìn (副) far and near:

～闻名 be well known far and wide

远虑(慮) yuǎnlǜ (名) foresight; long view

远视 yuǎnshì (名) long sight; longsightedness

远洋 yuǎnyáng (名) ocean: ～航行 oceangoing voyage

远征 yuǎnzhēng (名) expedition: ～军 expeditionary army (or force)

远走高飞(飛) yuǎnzǒu-gāofēi soar; be off to a distant place

远足 yuǎnzú (名) excursion; hike; walking tour

院 yuàn (名) 1 courtyard; compound 2 a designation for certain government offices and public places: 法～ law court. 科学～ the academy of sciences

院士 yuànshì (名) academician

愿(願) yuàn I (名) 1 hope; wish; desire: 如～以偿 attain one's goal 2 promise: 许～ make promises II (动) be willing; be ready

愿望 yuànwàng (名) desire; wish; aspiration: 他有出国学习医学的强烈～. He has a strong desire to study medicine abroad.

愿意 yuànyì (助动) 1 be willing; be ready 2 wish; like; want: 他们～你留在这里. They would like you to stay here.

怨 yuàn I (名) resentment; enmity: 没有抱～的理由 no cause for complaint II (动) blame; complain: 事情没办好只能～我自己. I have only myself to blame for I haven't really done the job well.

怨愤 yuànfèn (名) discontent and indignation; bitterness

怨恨 yuànhèn (动, 名) ill-will; grudge; hatred

怨气(氣) yuànqì (名) grudge; complaint; resentment: 出～ air one's grievances; vent one's resentment

怨声(聲)载道 yuànshēng zài dào there is widespread discontent among the mass of the people

曰 yuē (动) 〈书〉 1 say 2 call; name

约 yuē I (动) 1 make arrangements for: ～定 make an appointment with sb. 2 invite: 我已经～她来吃晚饭. I have asked her to come for dinner. II(名) pact; agreement; appointment: 立～ make a contract III (形) simple; brief: ～言之 to put it in a nutshell; in brief; in a word IV (副) about; around; approximately: ～五十人 some fifty people

约定 yuēdìng (动) agree to; appoint; arrange: 大家～明天在公园会面. We all agreed to meet in the park tomorrow. 在～的时间 at the appointed time

约会(會) yuēhuì (名) appointment; engagement; date; rendezvous: 抱歉今天不能来,因为我已经有个～了. Sorry I won't be able to come today for I have a previous engagement.

约计 yuējì (动) count roughly; come roughly to

约略 yuēlüè (形) rough; approximate: ～的估计 a rough (or approximate) estimate

约莫 yuēmo (副) about; roughly: ～有二十个人参加这次演说竞赛. Some twenty people participated in this speech contest.

约请 yuēqǐng (动) invite; ask

约束 yuēshù (动) keep within bounds; restrain; bind: 有～力 have binding force

悦 yuè I (形) happy; pleased; delighted: 不～ displeased. 和颜～色 amiable and polite in manner II (动) please; delight: 取～于人 try to please sb.

悦耳 yuè'ěr (形) pleasing to the ear; melodious

悦目 yuèmù (形) pleasing to the eye; pleasant

阅 yuè (动) 1 read; go over: ～报 read newspapers. ～卷 go over examination papers 2 review; inspect: ～兵 a parade 3 experience; pass through: 试行已～三月. Three months have passed since we started to try this out.

阅读(讀) yuèdú (动) read: ～杂志 read magazines

阅览(覽) yuèlǎn (动) read: ～室 reading room

阅历(歷) yuèlì (动、名) 1 experience: ～过很多事 have seen much of the world 2 knowledge of the world; personal experience: ～浅 with little experience in the world

阅世 yuèshì (动) 〈书〉 see the world: ～渐深 gradually become worldly-wise; gradually become experienced in life

越 yuè (动) 1 get over; jump over: ～墙而逃 climb over the wall and make one's escape 2 exceed; overstep: ～出职权 overstep one's authority. ～界 cross the boundary

越发(發) yuèfā (副) 1 all the more; even more: 过了中秋，天气～凉快了. After the Mid Autumn Festival, the weather becomes even cooler. 2 [same as '越'…'越'…]: 观众越多，他们演得～卖力气. The bigger the audience, the more enthusiastic they will become in their performance.

越轨 yuèguǐ (动) exceed the bounds: ～行为 overstep the bounds of correct behaviour

越过(過) yuèguò (动) cross; surmount; pass over: ～障碍 surmount obstacles

越级 yuèjí bypass the immediate leadership: ～申诉 bypass the immediate leadership and appeal to higher levels

越境 yuèjìng (动) cross the boundary illegally; sneak in or out of a country

越野 yuèyě (形) cross-country: ～赛跑 cross-country race

越狱(獄) yuèyù (动) escape from prison

越俎代庖 yuè zǔ dài páo overstep one's powers to handle affairs within other people's jurisdiction

跃(躍) yuè (动) leap; jump: 一～而起 get up with a jump; jump to one's feet. ～过 leap over

跃跃欲试 yuèyuè yù shì (动) be eager for a try; itch to have a try

岳 yuè (名) 1 high mountain 2 wife's parents

岳父 yuèfù (名) wife's father; father-in-law

岳母 yuèmǔ (名) wife's mother; mother-in-law

月 yuè (名) 1 the moon: 新～ a new moon; crescent 2 month: ～底 at the end of the month. ～产量 monthly output

月报(報) yuèbào (名) 1 monthly magazine; monthly 2 monthly report

月饼 yuèbǐng (名) moon cake (esp. for the Mid-Autumn Festival)

月份 yuèfèn (名) month: 上～ last month

月光 yuèguāng (名) moonlight; moonbeam

月经(經) yuèjīng (名) menses; menstruation; period

月刊 yuèkān (名) monthly magazine; monthly

月亮 yuèliàng (名) the moon

月票 yuèpiào (名) monthly ticket (of going by bus or underground railway)

月球 yuèqiú (名) the moon

月色 yuèsè (名) moonlight

月食 yuèshí (名) lunar eclipse

月台(臺) yuètái (名) railway platform: ～票 platform ticket

月薪 yuèxīn (名) monthly pay

月子 yuèzi (名) month of confinement after childbirth: 坐～ be in confinement

钥(鑰) yuè (名) key
see also yào

乐(樂) yuè (名) music: 器～ instrumental music. 声～ vocal music
see also lè

乐池 yuèchí (名) orchestra pit; orchestra

乐队(隊) yuèduì (名) orchestra; band: 交响～ symphony (or philharmonic) orchestra. 军～ military band

乐谱 yuèpǔ (名) music score

乐器 yuèqì (名) musical instrument; instrument: 管～ wind instrument. 弦～ stringed instrument. 打击～ percussion instrument

乐曲 yuèqǔ (名) musical composition; composition; music

乐团(團) yuètuán (名) philharmonic society; philharmonic orchestra

乐章 yuèzhāng (名) movement

晕 yūn (形) 1 dizzy; giddy: 有点头～ feel a bit dizzy (or giddy) 2 swoon; faint: ～了过去 lose consciousness; faint
see also yùn

晕倒 yūndǎo (动) fall down in a fainting fit

晕头(頭)转(轉)向 yūntóu zhuànxiàng (形) confused and disoriented

云 yún (动)<书> say: 不知所～ not know what one is talking about; not know what one is driving at

云(雲) yún (名) cloud

云彩 yúncai (名) cloud

云层(層) yúncéng (名) cloud

layer
云集 yúnjí (动) come together from different places; gather; converge
云雾(霧) yúnwù (名) cloud and mist; mist
云霞 yúnxiá (名) rosy clouds
云消雾(霧)散 yúnxiāo-wùsàn melt into thin air; vanish without a trace
云雨 yúnyǔ (名) 〈书〉 sexual intercourse; love-making
耘 yún (动) weed: ～田 weed the fields
芸 yún
芸豆 yúndòu (名) kidney bean
芸芸众(衆)生 yúnyún zhòngshēng (名) 〈佛教〉 a multitude of all living things
匀 yún I (形) even: 工作负担分配不～. The workload is not evenly distributed. II (动) 1 even up; divide evenly 2 spare: 可以～给你们一些. We can spare you some.
匀称(稱) yúnchèn (形) well-proportioned; well-balanced; symmetrical
匀整 yúnzhěng (形) neat and well spaced; even and orderly
陨 yǔn (动) fall from the sky or outer space
陨落 yǔnluò (动) (of a meteorite, etc.) fall from the sky or outer space
陨石 yǔnshí (名) aerolite; stony meteorite
允 yǔn I (动) permit; allow; consent: 应～ consent. ～从 comply II (形) fair; just: 公～ fair; equitable
允诺 yǔnnuò (动) promise; consent; assent: 欣然～ readily consent
允许 yǔnxǔ (动) permit; allow
韵(韻) yùn (名) 1 rhyme: 押～ be in rhyme 2 charm: 风～ personal charm; graceful bearing
韵律 yùnlǜ (名) 1 metre (in verse) 2 rules of rhyming
韵母 yùnmǔ (名) simple or compound vowel (of a Chinese syllable)
韵文 yùnwén (名) literary composition in rhyme; verse
晕 yùn I (形) dizzy; giddy; faint: 头～目眩 have a dizzy spell II (名) halo: 月～ lunar halo
see also yūn
晕车(車) yùnchē (形) carsick
晕船 yùnchuán (形) seasick
运(運) yùn I (动) 1 carry; transport: 货～ freight transport. 空～ air transport; airlift 2 use; wield; utilize: ～笔 set pen to paper II (名) fortune; luck; fate: 好～ good luck. 不走～ be out of luck
运筹(籌)帷幄 yùnchóu wéiwò devise strategies at the headquarters
运筹(籌)学(學) yùnchóuxué (名) operations research
运动(動) yùndòng (名) 1 motion; movement 2 sports; athletics; exercise: 户外～ outdoor exercise 3 (political) movement; campaign; drive
运动(動)会(會) yùndònghuì (名) sports meet; athletic meeting; games: 全国～ national games
运费 yùnfèi (名) transportation expenses: ～单 freight note. ～免付 carriage free. ～已付 freight (or carriage) paid. ～预付 freight prepaid
运河 yùnhé (名) canal
运气(氣) yùnqì (名) fortune; luck: 碰～ try one's luck
运输 yùnshū (名) transport; carriage; conveyance: 陆上(水路)～ land (water) transport. ～工具 means of transport
运输机(機) yùnshūjī (名) transport plane; airfreighter
运送 yùnsòng (动) transport; ship; convey
运算 yùnsuàn (名) caculation; operation
运行 yùnxíng (动) move; be in motion: ～轨道 orbit (of a satellite) 列车已在～了. The train was already in motion.
运用 yùnyòng (动) utilize; wield; apply; put to use: ～自如 handle with ease
运载工具 yùnzài gōngjù (名) means of delivery
运载火箭 yùnzài huǒjiàn (名) carrier rocket
运转(轉) yùnzhuàn (动) 1 revolve; turn round 2 work; operate: 机器～正常. The machine is in good operation
酝(醖) yùn
酝酿(釀) yùnniàng (动) 1 brew; ferment: 他当时意识到某种灾难正在～. He sensed that some sort of trouble was brewing. 2 have a preliminary informal discussion; deliberate on: ～协商 de-

liberations and consultations

蕴 yùn (动) ‹书› accumulate; hold in store; contain: ～涵 contain

蕴藏 yùncáng (动) hold in store; contain: 我国各地～着的矿物资源很丰富. There are rich deposits of mineral resources in diffferent parts of our land.

孕 yùn (形) pregnant: 怀～ be pregnant; be conceived. 避～ contraception

孕妇(婦) yùnfù (名) pregnant woman

孕育 yùnyù (动) be pregnant with; breed: ～着危险 pregnant with danger

熨 yùn (动) iron; press: ～衣服 iron (or press) clothes

熨斗 yùndǒu (名) flatiron; iron: 电～ electric iron

Z z

扎(紮) zā (动) tie; bind: 把这个小包裹用绳子～起来. Tie the small parcel with a piece of string.

see also zhā; zhá

砸 zá (动) 1 pound; tamp: 把肉～成泥 pound the meat into a paste. ～了脚 have one's foot squashed 2 break; smash: ～核桃 crack walnuts. 杯子～了. The glass is broken. 3 fail; be bungled: 事情办～了. bungle a job

杂(雜) zá (形) 1 miscellaneous; mixed: ～活儿 odd jobs. ～费 miscellaneous expenses. ～七～八的东西 odds and ends 2 mix; mingle: 夹～ be mingled with

杂拌 zábànr (名) 1 mixed sweetmeats 2 a miscellany of poems, essays, travel notes and stories

杂草 zácǎo (名) weeds

杂货 záhuò (名) sundry goods; groceries: 日用～ various household supplies. ～店 grocery

杂技 zájì (名)acrobatics

杂家 zájiā (名) an eclectic; a jackof-all trades

杂交 zájiāo (动) cross breed; hybridize

杂粮(糧) záliáng (名) coarse grain (e.g. maize, barley, oak, millet, etc.)

杂乱(亂) záluàn (形) in disorder; in a jumble: ～无章 in a mess; planless and jumbled

杂念 zániàn (名) selfish considerations: 私心～太重 too calculating

杂文 záwén (名) satirical essay

杂音 záyīn (名) noise

杂志 zázhì (名) magazine

杂质(質) zázhì (名) impurity

杂种(種) zázhǒng (名) 1 hybrid; crossbreed 2 bastard; son of a bitch

咋 zǎ how; why: ～办? What is to be done? 情况～样? How are things? 你～不去? Why don't you go?

灾(災) zāi (名) 1 disaster; calamity: 天～ natural disaster. 水～ flood. 旱～ drought. 虫～ plague of insects 2 misfortune; adversity: 招～惹祸 court trouble

灾害 zāihài (名) calamity; disaster

灾荒 zāihuāng (名) famine

灾祸(禍) zāihuò (名) catastrophe

灾民 zāimín (名) victims of a natural calamity; people in an afflicted area

灾难(難) zāinàn (名) catastrophe; suffering: ～深重 long-suffering

灾情 zāiqíng (名) the damage caused by a disaster

灾区(區) zāiqū (名) afflicted area

栽 zāi (动) 1 plant; grow: ～树 plant trees. ～花 grow flowers 2 impose sth. on sb.: ～上罪名 trump up a charge against sb. 3 tumble; fall: ～倒 fall down; trip and fall

栽跟头(頭) zāi gēntou (动) 1 trip and fall 2 suffer a setback

栽培 zāipéi (动) 1 cultivate; grow: ～果树 grow fruit trees 2 foster; train (qualified personnel)

栽脏(臟) zāizāng (动) 1 plant stolen or banned goods on sb. 2 make false charges against sb.

栽种(種) zāizhòng (动) plant; grow

哉 zāi ‹书› ‹助› 1 [indicating exclamation]: 呜呼! 哀～! Alas! 2 [used together with an interrogative to express doubt or form a rhetorical question]: 有何难～? What's so difficult about it?

宰 zǎi I (动) 1 slaughter; butcher: ～牛 slaughter an ox 2 be in charge of; head: 主～ be in actual control of; have the final say in II (名) government official (in ancient China)

宰割 zǎigē (动) oppress and exploit

宰杀(殺) zǎishā (动) slaughter; butcher

宰相 zǎixiàng (名) prime minister (in feudal China); chancellor

载(載) zǎi I (名) year: 三～ three years II(动) record: ～入史册 go down in history. 刊～ record; publish (in the press)

see also zài

载(載) zài (动) 1 carry; hold: ～客 carry passengers. ～货 carry goods. 轮船满～着大米 The ship is fully loaded with rice. 2 (the road) be filled with: 怨声～道 Popular grievances are openly voiced everywhere. 3 〈书〉 and; as well as; at the same time: ～歌～舞 singing and dancing everywhere

see also zǎi

载波 zàibō (名) carrier wave; carrier: ～电话机 carrier telephone

载荷 zàihè (名) load

载货 zàihuò (动) carry cargo (or freight) ～吨位 cargo tonnage

载运(運) zàiyùn (动) convey by vehicles, ships, etc.; transport; carry

载重 zàizhòng (名) load; carrying capacity: ～卡车 heavy-duty truck ～汽车 truck; lorry

再 zài (副) 1 again; once more: ～说一遍. Say it again, please. 一而～, ～而三 again and again; time and again; over and over (again) 2 [to a greater extent or degree]: 这篇文章还得～改一次. The essay will have to be further polished. 3 [indicating continuation of time or action]: ～不走我们开会就要迟到了. We'll be late for the meeting if we stay any longer. 4 [indicating that one action takes place after the completion of another]: 你吃完晚饭～出去. Eat your supper before you go out. 5 [indicating additional information]: ～则 moreover; besides. 他对这件事不清楚, ～, 他也不想插手. He doesn't know anything about the matter; besides, he doesn't want to get involved. 6 continue; return: 良机难～. Opportunity knocks but once.

再版 zàibǎn I (名) second edition II (动) reprint

再次 zàicì (副) once more; a second time; once again: ～登门拜访 pay sb. another visit. ～道谢 extend one's thanks to sb. again

再度 zàidù (副) once more; a second time; once again: ～当选 be reelected

再会(會) zàihuì 〈套〉 good-bye; see you again

再嫁 zàijià (动) (of a woman) remarry

再接再励(勵) zàijiē-zàilì (动) make persistent efforts; persevere

再生 zàishēng (动) 1 resuscitate 2 regenerate 3 recycle

再生产(產) zàishēngchǎn (名) reproduction

再说 zàishuō I (动) not consider or tackle a problem until some other time: 这事先搁两天～. Let's put the matter aside for a couple of days. II (连) what's more; besides: 现在去找他太晚了, ～他也不一定在家. It's too late to go and see him now; besides, he may not be at home at the moment.

在 zài I (动) 1 exist: 这问题还～, 并没有解决. The problem still remains to be solved. 2 [indicating the position of a person or thing]: 你的钱包～桌子上. Your wallet is on the table. 3 remain: ～职 occupy a post 4 rest with; depend on: 事情的成败～你自己的努力. The success or failure of the matter depends on your own effort. 5 ["在" and "所" always go together, followed by "不", thus forming an emphatic expression]: ～所难免 be hardly avoidable II (介) [indicating time, place, condition, scope, etc.]: ～会上发言 speak at a meeting. ～理论上 in theory; theoretically. ～这种情况下 under such circumstances. 在全国范围内 throughout the country III (副) [indicating an action in progress]: 她～起草一个决议. She is drafting a resolution.

在场(場) zàichǎng (动) be on

the scene; be on the spot

在行 zàiháng (动) be a professional: 她对这种工作很～. This sort of work is very much in her line.

在乎 zàihu (动) [often but not always used in the negative] care about; mind; take to heart: 满不～ couldn't care less. 对于这种批评他很～. He took this kind of criticism very much to heart.

在家 zàijiā (动) be at home; be in

在理 zàilǐ (形) reasonable; sensible; right: 这话说得～. That's a sensible comment.

在世 zàishì (动) live: 他～的时候 in his lifetime

在所不辞(辭) zài suǒ bù cí would decline under no circumstances: 为国捐躯,～. I would not hesitate to lay down my life for my country.

在望 zàiwàng (形) 1 be visible: 隐隐～ indistinctly discernible 2 will soon materialize; in the offing; round the corner: 胜利～. Victory is in sight. *or* Success is round the corner.

在握 zàiwò (形) be in one's hands; be within one's grasp: 大权～ be in the saddle. 胜利～ Victory is within our grasp.

在押 zàiyā (形) 〈法〉 be under detention; be in custody; be in prison

在野 zàiyě (形) be out of office; be in the opposition

在意 zàiyì (动) [usu. used in the negative] care about; mind; take to heart: 这些小事他是不会～. He won't mind such trifles.

在于(於) zàiyú (动) 1 lie in; rest with: 最后决定～我们自己. Final decision rests with us. 2 be determined by; depend on: 去不去～你们自己. It's up to you to decide whether you will go or not.

在职(職) zàizhí (形) be on the job; be employed: ～训练 in-service training. ～期间 during one's tenure of office

在座 zàizuò (动) be present (at a meeting, banquet, etc.)

簪 zān (名) hairpin

簪子 zānzi (名) hair clasp

咱 zán (名) 1 we [including both the speaker and the person or persons spoken to] 2 〈方〉 I

咱们 zánmen (名) we [including both the speaker and the person or persons spoken to]: 你来得正好,～一起议一议. You've come in the nick of time. Let's put our heads together.

攒 zǎn (动) accumulate; hoard; save: ～钱 save (or scrape) up money. 她把～的钱都买了衣服. She spent all her savings on clothes.

暂 zàn (形) 1 of short duration: 生命是短～的. Life is short (or brief). 2 temporary; for the time being; for the moment: ～行条例 provisional regulations. 这只是一种～时的措施. This is only a temporary measure.

暂缓 zànhuǎn (动) put off; defer: ～作出决定 put off making a decision

暂且 zànqiě (副) for the time being; for the moment: 此事～不谈,以后再议. Let's drop the matter for the time being. We can take it up later.

暂时(時) zànshí (形) temporary; transient: ～困难 temporary difficulties

暂停 zàntíng (动) 1 suspend: ～付款 suspend payment 讨论～,明天继续举行. Let us put off the discussion till tomorrow. 2 time-out: 要求～ ask for time-out

暂行 zànxíng (形) provisional; temporary: ～规定 temporary provisions

赞 zàn (动) 1 support; assist: ～助 support; assist 2 praise; commend: 盛～ highly praise 3 eulogize

赞不绝口 zàn bù jué kǒu give sb. lavish praise

赞成 zànchéng (动) approve of; assent; agree with; give one's blessing to: 我不太～他的意见. I don't quite agree with him. 他不～有些人小题大做. He doesn't approve of some people making a fuss about such trifles.

赞美 zànměi (动) eulogize; praise

赞赏 zànshǎng (动) appreciate; admire: 对他们这一友好举动大家表示～. We all appreciate this friendly act on their part. 我们非常～他们的才能. We are filled with admiration for their talents.

赞颂 zànsòng (动) extol; eulogize

赞叹(嘆) zàntàn (动 marvel at;

highly praise: 运动员们的高超技艺令人～不已. The spectators all marvelled at the superb skill of the players.
赞同 zàntóng (动) approve of; endorse: 这一动议得到与会者的普遍～. This motion met with the general approval of the participants. 全厂职工一致～这项改革. The administrative personnel and workers of the factory unanimously endorsed this reform.
赞许 zànxǔ (动) praise; commend: 值得～ deserve commendation; be praiseworthy
赞扬(揚) zànyáng (动) speak in glowing terms of; pay tribute to
赞助 zànzhù (名) support; assistance; aid
赃(贜) zāng (名) stolen goods; booty; spoils: 退～ disgorge the spoils
赃物 zāngwù (名) 1 stolen goods 2 bribes
脏(髒) zāng (形) dirty; filthy: ～衣服 dirty clothing; laundry. 你把书弄～了. You've soiled the book.
see also zàng
脏字 zāngzì (名) dirty word; swearword
葬 zàng (动) bury; inter: 火～ cremation. ～地 burial ground; grave
葬礼(禮) zànglǐ (名) funeral rites; funeral
葬身 zàngshēn (动) be buried: 敌机～海底. The enemy plane was shot down, plunging into the sea.
葬送 zàngsòng (动) ruin; put an end to: ～前途 ruin one's future
藏 zàng (名) 1 storing place; depository: 宝～ hidden treasures; valuable (mineral) deposits 2 Buddhist or Taoist scriptures: 道～ Taoist scriptures
see also cáng
藏青 zàngqīng (形) dark blue
藏族 zàngzú (名) the Zang (Tibetan) nationality
脏(臟) zàng (名) internal organs of the body; viscera: 心～ heart. 肾～ kidneys
see also zāng
糟 zāo (形) 1 be pickled with grains or in wine: ～鱼 pickled fish 2 rotten; worn out; poor: 他身体很～, 我有些担心. I am rather worried about his health. 3 in a wretched state; in a mess: 你把这件事弄～了. You've made a mess of the matter.
糟糕 zāogāo (形) in a terrible mess; bad luck; too bad: 真～! 下起雨来了. It's too bad. It's raining.
糟粕 zāopò (名) dross; dregs: 弃其～, 吸取精华 reject the dross and assimilate the essence
糟蹋 zāota (动) 1 waste; ruin; spoil: ～粮食 waste grain 2 trample on; ravage: 这一村子曾被侵略军～得不成样子. This village was once badly ravaged by the invading troops. 3 violate (a woman)
遭 zāo 1 (动) meet with (disaster, misfortune, etc.); sustain; suffer: ～难 some misfortune befell one. 惨～毒手 be killed in cold blood II 〈量〉 round; time; turn: 走一～ make a trip. 看他如此发火, 还是第一～. It's the first time that I have seen him flare up.
遭逢 zāoféng (动) meet with; encounter: ～盛世 live in an age of prosperity. ～不幸 meet with a misfortune
遭受 zāoshòu (动) suffer; be subjected to; sustain; undergo: ～损失 sustain losses. ～损害 suffer damage. ～耻辱 be subjected to indignities
遭殃 zāoyāng (动) suffer disaster or calamity
遭遇 zāoyù I (动) meet with; encounter: ～许多挫折 meet with many setbacks II (名) (bitter) experience; (hard) lot: 童年的～ one's unhappy childhood experience
凿(鑿) záo I (名) chisel II (动) cut a hole; chisel or dig: ～冰 make a hole in the ice. ～个窟窿 bore a hole
see also zuò
凿井 záojǐng (动) dig (or sink, bore) a well
凿子 záozi (名) chisel
枣(棗) zǎo (名) jujube; (Chinese) date
枣红 zǎohóng (形) purplish red
枣树(樹) zǎoshù (名) jujube tree
枣脯 zǎopú (名) dried dates preserved in honey
早 zǎo I (名) morning: 从～到晚 from morning till night. 清早 early in the morning II (形) 1 long ago; as early as; for a long time: 他～走了. He left long ago. 2 early:

～白头 premature white hair. ～春 early spring. ～稻 early rice. ～期 early stage; early phase. ～熟 premature; precocious 3 〈套〉 good morning

早安 zǎo'ān 〈套〉 good morning

早操 zǎocāo (名) morning exercises

早产(產) zǎochǎn (名) premature delivery

早晨 zǎochén (名) (early) morning

早点(點) zǎodiǎn (名) (light) breakfast

早饭 zǎofàn (名) breakfast

早年 zǎonián (副) in one's early years

早日 zǎorì (副) at an early date; early; soon: 希望～完工. Hope you'll fulfil your task as soon as possible. 祝你～恢复健康. I wish you a speedy recovery.

早上 zǎoshang (名) early morning

早退 zǎotuì (动) leave earlier than is required according to the regulations; leave early

早晚 zǎowǎn (副) 1 morning and evening: 他每天～都练拳术. He practises shadow boxing every day both in the morning and in the evening. 2 sooner or later: 象他这样的人，～要倒霉的. People like him will come to grief sooner or later.

早先 zǎoxiān (副) previously; in the past: ～人们常来这儿散步. People used to come here for a walk.

早已 zǎoyǐ (副) long ago; for a long time: 他们～离婚了. They got divorced long ago.

早早儿 zǎozǎor (副) as soon as possible; at an early date: 决定了，就～办. Let's get the work done as soon as possible if you have made up your mind.

澡 zǎo (名、动) bath: 洗～ take a bath; bathe

澡盆 zǎopén (名) bathtub

澡堂 zǎotáng (名) public baths; bathhouse

藻 zǎo (名) 1 algae 2 aquatic plants

藻类(類)植物 zǎolèi zhíwù (名) algae

蚤 zǎo (名) flea: 水～ water flea

灶(竈) zào (名) 1 kitchen; place for cooking; cooking stove 2 kitchen; mess; canteen: 学生～ students' cafeteria or canteen

燥 zào (形) dry: ～热 hot and dry; sultry

噪 zào (动) make an uproar; clamour: 名～一时 be enormously popular for a time

噪音 zàoyīn (名) noise: ～污染 noise pollution

躁 zào (形) rash; impetuous; restless: 戒骄戒～ guard against arrogance and rashness. 性子急～ quick-tempered; hot-tempered

造 zào (动) 1 make; build; create: ～汽车 make cars. ～房子 build a house. ～舆论 create public opinion 2 invent; cook up; concoct: 捏～ fabricate; concoct. ～谣言 start a rumour; cook up a story 3 train; educate: 可～之才 a person of promise

造反 zàofǎn (动) rise in rebellion; rebel; revolt

造福 zàofú (动) bring benefit to; benefit: 为后代～ benefit future generations

造化 zàohua (名) good fortune; good luck: 有～ be born under a lucky star; be lucky

造价(價) zàojià (名) cost (of building or manufacture)

造就 zàojiù I (动) bring up; train: ～人才就是智力投资. To train competent personnel is a kind of intellectual investment. II (名) achievements; attainments (usu. of young people)

造句 zàojù (动) make sentences

造林 zàolín (名) afforestation

造孽 zàoniè (名) do evil; commit a sin

造物 zàowù (名) the divine force that created the universe

造型 zàoxíng (名) model; mould: ～优美 graceful in shape. ～艺术 plastic arts

造诣 zàoyì (名) (academic or artistic) attainments: ～很深 of great attainments

皂 zào (名) soap: 香～ toilet soap. 药～ medicated soap

责 zé I (名) duty; responsibility: 尽～ do one's duty. 爱护公物，人人有～. It is everybody's duty to take good care of public property. II (动) 1 demand; require: 求全～备 nitpick 2 question closely; call sb. to account 3 reproach; blame; reprove: 斥～ reprimand; denounce. 痛～ rebuke severely 4 punish: 笞～ punish by flogging

责备(備) zébèi (动) reproach; blame; censure; take sb. to task: 不要为了这样一个小错就～她. Don't reproach her for such a small mistake.

责成 zéchéng (动) instruct a person or an organization to fulfil an assigned task: 我们～他及早拟定计划. We instructed him to draw up a plan at an early date.

责怪 zéguài (动) blame: 这事只能～他自己。He has nobody to blame but himself.

责令 zélìng (动) order; instruct: ～主管部门采取有力措施 instruct the department in charge to take effective measures

责骂 zémà (动) scold; rebuke; dress down: 把他们～一顿 give them a dressing-down

责难(難) zénàn (动) censure; blame: 受到别人的～ bring the blame of others upon oneself

责任 zérèn (名) 1 duty; responsibility 2 responsibility for a fault or wrong; blame: 我愿意承担这个事故的～. I am ready to take the blame for the accident. ～感 sense of responsibility (or duty). 承包～制 system of contracted responsibility

责问 zéwèn (动) ask reprovingly; call sb. to account: 我有件事要～他. I have a bone to pick with him.

责无(無)旁贷 zé wú páng dài be one's unshirkable responsibility; be duty-bound

则 zé I (名) 1 standard; norm; criterion: 以身作～ set an example by one's own conduct 2 rule; regulation: 章～ rules and regulations. 法～ law; rule II (量) item; paragraph: 新闻一～ an item of news. 寓言四～ four fables III (副) 〈书〉 1 [indicating cause and effect or condition]: 欲速～不达. Haste makes waste. 2 [indicating concession or contrast]: 好～好,只是太贵. It's good indeed but too expensive. 3 [used together with 一,二,三 to enumerate causes or reasons]: 我想今天不去了,一～我有点累,二～我去过好几趟了. I don't think I am going today. First, I am feeling a bit tired; secondly, I have been there several times before.

泽(澤) zé I (名) 1 pool; pond: 沼～ marsh; swamp. 湖～ lakes 2 lustre (of metals, pearls, etc.): 光～ lustre; gloss; sheen II (动) damp; moist: 润～ moist; wet

择(擇) zé (动) select; choose; pick: 没有选～余地. This is Hobson's choice. see also zhái

仄 zè

仄声(聲) zèshēng (名) oblique tones, i.e., the falling-rising tone (上声), the falling tone (去声) and the entering tone (入声), as distinct from the level tone (平声) in classical Chinese pronunciation

贼 zéi I (名) 1 thief; burglar 2 traitor; enemy: 卖国～ traitor (to one's country). 工～ scab; blackleg II (形) wicked; evil; crafty; sly; cunning: 真～ really cunning. ～眉鼠眼 look like a sly old fox; wear a thievish expression

贼喊捉贼 zéi hǎn zhuō zéi a thief crying "Stop thief"

贼头(頭)贼脑(腦) zéitóu-zéinǎo (形) thievish; stealthy; furtive

贼心 zéixīn (名) evil designs or intentions: ～不死 still harbour evil intentions; cannot suppress evil thoughts

怎 zěn (代) 〈方〉 why; how: 你～才来呀? Why are you so late?

怎么(麽) zěnme (代) 1 [interrogative pronoun]: 你～啦? What's wrong with you? 请问,去车站～走? Excuse me, but how can I get to the railway station? 你～没去开会? Why didn't you attend the meeting? 这个词～拼? How do you spell the word? 2 [indicating the nature, condition and manner in general]: 你愿意～办就～办. Do as you please. 3 [used in the negative to indicate inadequacy]: 这个地方我不～熟悉. I am not quite familiar with the place.

怎么样(樣) zěnmeyàng (代) 1 how [used as a predicative or complement]: 跟我们一起去～? How about going there together with us? 2 [a polite formula often used in the negative]: 这旅馆并不～. This hotel is not so good as we expected. 他画得也并不～.He is not a part cularly good painter.

怎么(麼)着 zěnmezhe (代) 1 [used to inquire about an action or state]: 我们都去,你打算~? We are all going. What about you? 她今天不大做声,是生气了还是~? She was quiet today. Was she angry or what? 2 [indicating an action or state of affairs in general]: ~也得把试验搞下去. The experiment must be carried on whatever happens.

怎样(樣) zěnyàng (代) 1 how (同"怎么"): 这件事你~向她解释? How are you going to explain this to her? 2 how (同"怎么样"): 你近来~? How have you been keeping?

曾 zēng (名) relationship between great-grandchildren and great-grandparents
see also céng

曾孙(孫) zēngsūn (名) great-grandson

曾祖 zēngzǔ (名) (paternal) great-grandfather

憎 zēng (动) hate; detest; abhor: 面目可~ look repulsive; repellent

憎恨 zēnghèn (动) hate; detest

憎恶(惡) zēngwù (动) detest; abhor; loathe

增 zēng (动) increase: ~产节约 increase production and practise economy. 产量与日俱~. Output has increased with each passing day.

增补(補) zēngbǔ (动) increase; supplement: 人员略有~. The staff has been slightly expanded.

增订 zēngdìng (动) 1 revise and enlarge (a book) 2 subscribe to: ~许多杂志 subscribe to many more magazines

增光 zēngguāng (动) do sb. credit; add to the prestige of: 这件事不会为他的声望~. This affair will not add to his prestige.

增加 zēngjiā (动) increase; raise; add: ~品种 increase the variety of types or patterns. ~收入 increase income. ~体重 put on weight

增进(進) zēngjìn (动) enhance; promote; further: ~友谊 promote friendship. ~健康 improve one's health

增强 zēngqiáng (动) strengthen; heighten; enhance: ~信心 gain fresh confidence. ~团结 strengthen unity; close one's ranks

增添 zēngtiān (动) add; increase: ~麻烦 put sb. to much inconvenience. ~光彩 bring added lustre to (organization, activity, etc.) ~设备 order additional equipment

增援 zēngyuán (动) reinforce: ~部队 reinforcements; reinforcing units

增长(長) zēngzhǎng (动) increase; rise; grow: 在实践中~才干 develop one's abilities in practice. ~知识和经验 add to one's knowledge and experience

赠 zèng (动) give as a present; present as a gift: ~阅本 presentation copy. ~送仪式 presentation ceremony

赠言 zèngyán (名) words of advice spoken or written, offered to a friend at parting: 临别~ parting advice

赠阅 zèngyuè (动) (of a book, periodical, etc.) given free by the publishers: ~本 complimentary copy

渣 zhā (名) 1 dregs; sediment; residue 2 small pieces: 面包~ crumbs

渣滓 zhāzǐ (名) dregs; sediment; residue: 社会~ dregs of society

扎(紮) zhā (动) 1 prick: ~了手 prick one's finger 2 plunge into: 扑通一声,他就~进水里去了. He plunged into the water with a splash. *or* He jumped splash into the water.
see also zā; zhá

扎根 zhāgēn (动) take root; strike root: ~、开花、结果 take root, blossom and bear fruit

扎实(實) zhāshi (形) 1 sturdy; strong 2 solid; sound; down-to-earth: 他在基层做了出色而又~的工作. He has done remarkable, solid work at grass-roots level. 他有~的学问. He is a man of sound scholarship.

扎手 zhāshǒu I (动) prick the hand: 留神~ mind the thorns. II (形) difficult to handle; thorny: 这事真~. This is a knotty problem.

扎眼 zhāyǎn (形) 1 garish; loud: 颜色~ garish colours 2 very showy

闸 zhá (名) 1 dam 2 brake: 踩~ step on the brake

闸口 zhákǒu (名) sluice gate; sluice valve

闸门(門) zhámén (名) floodgate

炸 zhá (动) fry in deep fat or oil; deep-fry: ~鸡腿 fried

chicken legs
see also zhà

扎 zhá (动) pitch (a tent, etc.)
see also zā; zhā

扎营(營) zháyíng (动) pitch a tent or camp; encamp

札 zhá (名) 1 thin pieces of wood used for writing on in ancient China 2 〈书〉 letter

札记 zhájì (名) reading notes or commentary

轧 zhá (动) roll (steel)
see also gá; yà

轧钢(鋼) zhágāng (名) steel rolling: ～机 rolling mill. ～厂 steel rolling mill

眨 zhǎ (动) bat (the eyes); blink: 眼睛也不～一～ without even batting an eyelid

眨眼 zhǎyǎn (名) short time: 一～的工夫 in the twinkling of an eye

栅 zhà (名) railings; bars: 铁～ iron bars

栅栏 zhàlan (名) railings; fence

乍 zhà (副) 1 first; for the first time: 老朋友分别多年了,～一见面有说不出的高兴. On meeting quite unexpectedly an old friend I haven't seen for years, I was almost transported with joy. 2 suddenly; abruptly: ～变 change suddenly

炸 zhà (动) 1 explode; burst: 爆～ explode 这瓶子一灌开水就～了. This glass bottle will break the moment it is filled with boiling water. 2 blow up; blast; bomb: ～桥 blow up a bridge 3 fly into a rage: 他一听就气～了. He flew into a towering rage when he heard it.
see also zhá

炸弹 zhàdàn (名) bomb: 定时～ time bomb

炸药(藥) zhàyào (名) explosive (charges); dynamite; TNT

诈 zhà (动) 1 cheat; swindle 2 pretend; feign: ～死 feign death. 兵不厌～. All is fair in war. 3 他是拿话～我, 我一听就知道。I knew from the beginning that what he said was all bluff.

诈唬 zhàhu (动) bluff; bluster

诈骗 zhàpiàn (动) defraud; swindle

诈降 zhàxiáng (动) pretend to surrender; feign surrender

蚱 zhà

蚱蜢 zhàměng (名) grasshopper

榨 zhà (动) 1 press; extract; squeeze out: ～甘蔗 press sugar cane. ～油 extract oil 2 a press for extracting juice, oil, etc.

榨菜 zhàcài (名) hot pickled mustard tuber

榨取 zhàqǔ (动) squeeze; extort

斋(齋) zhāi I (名) 1 vegetarian diet adopted by Buddhists and Taoists: 吃～ live on a vegetarian diet 2 room or building: 书～ study II (动) give alms (to a monk)

斋戒 zhāijiè (动) abstain from meat, wine, etc. (when offering sacrifices to gods or ancestors); fast

摘 zhāi (动) 1 pick; pluck; take off: ～苹果 pick apples. ～花 pluck flowers. 把眼镜～下来 take off one's glasses 2 select; make extracts from: ～要 abstract; excerpts; precis

摘除 zhāichú (动) excise; remove: ～肿瘤 have a tumour removed

摘记 zhāijì I (动) take notes II (名) extracts; excerpts

摘录(録) zhāilù (动、名) take passages; make extracts; extracts; excerpts

摘要 zhāiyào I (动) make a summary II (名) summary; abstract; precis

宅 zhái (名) residence; mansion

宅院 zháiyuàn (名) a mansion with a courtyard; house

宅子 zháizi (名) 〈口〉 residence; house

择(擇) zhái (动) select; choose; pick
see also zé

择不开 zháibukāi (动) 1 unravel: 线乱成了一团, 怎么也～了. The skein of wool is so tangled that it is simply impossible to unravel it. 2 cannot get away from: 一点工夫也～ have no time to spare

窄 zhǎi (形) 1 narrow: ～道 narrow path 2 petty; narrow: 心眼儿～ narrow-minded 3 not well off; hard up

寨 zhài (名) 1 stockade 2 camp: 营～ military camp 3 mountain stronghold

债 zhài (名) debt: 欠～ run or get into debt; incur a debt; be in debt. 还～ pay (or repay, pay back) one's debt. 借～ ask for a loan; borrow money

债户 zhàihù (名) debtor
债权(權) zhàiquán (名) creditor's rights. ～国 creditor nation. ～人 creditor
债券 zhàiquàn (名) bond
债台(臺)高筑(築) zhàitái gāo zhù be heavily in debt; be head over ears in debt; be saddled with huge debts
债务(務) zhàiwù (名) debt; liabilities: ～人 debtor
债主 zhàizhǔ (名) creditor

占

zhān (动) practise divination
see also zhàn
占卜 zhānbǔ (动) practise divination; divine
占卦 zhānguà (动) divine by means of the Eight Diagrams
占星 zhānxīng (动) divine by astrology; cast a horoscope: ～术 astrology

沾

zhān (动) 1 become moist or wet 2 be wet or soiled with: ～上了泥 there are mud stains on sth. 3 hardly touch: 烟酒不～ abstain from smoking and drinking 4 benefit from some sort of social relationship: ～光 benefit from one's association with sb. or sth.
沾边(邊) zhānbiān (动) 1 touch on only lightly: 这项工作他还没～儿. He has scarcely worked on the project. 2 be fairly close to the truth: 他讲的一点也不～. There is not a grain of truth in his statement.
沾染 zhānrǎn (动) be infected by (or with); be contaminated by (or with): 不要～官僚主义习气. Don't allow yourself to be contaminated with bureaucratic style of work
沾沾自喜 zhānzhān zì xǐ (动) feel smug or complacent; have smug complacency

粘

zhān (动) glue; stick; paste
see also nián
粘连 zhānlián (名) adhesion
粘贴 zhāntiē (动) paste; stick: ～布告 put up a notice

毡(氈)

zhān (名) felt: ～帽 felt hat
毡子 zhānzi (名) felt; felt rug; felt blanket

瞻

zhān (动) look forward or upwards
瞻念 zhānniàn (动) consider; think of: ～前途 think of the future
瞻前顾(顧)后 zhānqián-gùhòu (动) 1 be overcautious and indecisive 2 think twice before taking any action
瞻望 zhānwàng (动) look forward; look far ahead: 抬头～ raise one's head and look into the distance
瞻仰 zhānyǎng (动) look at with reverence: ～遗容 pay one's respects to sb.'s remains

盏(盞)

zhǎn I (名) small cup: 酒～ small wine cup II <量> [used of a lamp]: 一～灯 an lamp

斩

zhǎn (动) cut; chop: ～断 chop off. 快刀～乱麻 cut the Gordian knot
斩草除根 zhǎncǎo-chúgēn pull the grass up by its roots; eradicate the root of trouble; root up all evil
斩钉截铁(鐵) zhǎndīng-jiétiě (形) resolute and decisive
斩首 zhǎnshǒu (动) behead; decapitate

崭

zhǎn
崭新 zhǎnxīn (形) brand-new; completely new

展

zhǎn I (动) 1 open up; spread out; unfold: ～翅高飞 soar into the sky. 愁眉不～ knit one's brows in anxiety 2 put to good use; give free play to: 一筹莫～. All his plans have come to naught. *or* He is simply helpless. 3 postpone; extend; prolong: ～期 postpone II (名) exhibition: 预～ preview
展出 zhǎnchū (动) put on display; be on show (or view); exhibit
展开(開) zhǎnkāi (动) 1 spread out; unfold; open up: 把地图～ unfold the map 2 launch; unfold; develop; carry out: ～攻势 launch an offensive. ～争论 start arguing
展览(覽) zhǎnlǎn (动、名) put on display; exhibit; show: ～馆 exhibition centre (or hall). ～会 exhibition. ～品 exhibit; item on display
展品 zhǎnpǐn (名) exhibit; item on display: 请勿抚摸～. Please do not touch the exhibits. *or* Hands off the exhibits.
展示 zhǎnshì (动) open up before one's eyes; reveal; show; lay bare: ～光明的前景 open up bright prospects

展望 zhǎnwàng I (动) look into the distance: ～未来 look into the future; look ahead II (名) forecast; prospect: 二十一世纪的～ prospects for the 21st century

展销 zhǎnxiāo (名) sales exhibition

辗 zhǎn

辗转(轉) zhǎnzhuǎn (动) 1 toss about in bed: ～不眠 lie in bed wide awake, tossing about from time to time. 2 pass through different hands or places: 故事～流传, 成为一部传奇. The story passed from place to place and gradually developed into a romance.

湛 zhàn (形) profound; deep: 精～ consummate

蘸 zhàn (动) dip in (ink, sauce, etc.)

栈(棧) zhàn (名) 1 warehouse: 货～ warehouse; storehouse 2 inn: 客～ inn

栈道 zhàndào (名) a plank road built along the face of a cliff

栈房 zhànfáng (名) 1 warehouse; storehouse 2 inn

占(佔) zhàn (动) 1 occupy; seize; take: 霸～ forcibly occupy; seize. 攻～ occupy 2 constitute; hold; make up; account for: ～多数 constitute the majority. ～上风 gain the upper hand. ～优势 hold a dominant position. ～世界第一位 rank first in the world. ～世界人口的四分之一 account for a quarter of the world's population

see also zhān

占据(據) zhànjù (动) occupy; hold: ～重要的战略要地 capture a place of strategic importance. 在学术界～相当重要的地位 occupy a position of no small importance in the academic world

占领 zhànlǐng (动) capture; occupy; seize: ～邻国领土 occupy the territory of a neighbouring country. ～军 occupation army

占便宜 zhàn piányi (动) 1 gain advantage by unfair means; profit at other people's expense 2 enjoy an advantage

占线(綫) zhànxiàn 〈电话〉 the line's busy (or engaged)

占有 zhànyǒu (动) 1 own; possess; have: ～第一手资料 have firsthand information 2 occupy; hold: ～重要地位 occupy an important place

站 zhàn I (动) 1 stand; be on one's feet: ～起来 stand up; rise to one's feet. 交通警～在十字路口指挥来往车辆. The traffic policeman stands at the crossroads to direct the passing vehicles. 2 stop; halt: 这是特快, 中途不～. This is a non-stop express. 车还没～稳, 别着急下车. There is no hurry getting off. The bus hasn't quite stopped yet. II (名) station; stop: 火车～ railway station. 公共汽车～ bus stop. 终点～ terminal; terminus. 服务～ service centre

站队(隊) zhànduì (动) line up; fall in; stand in line; queue up

站岗 zhàngǎng (动) stand (or mount) guard; be on sentry duty; stand sentry

站台(臺) zhàntái (名) platform (in a railway station): ～票 platform ticket

站住 zhànzhù (动) 1 stop; halt 2 stand firmly on one's feet 3 stand (or hold) one's ground; consolidate one's position 4 hold water; be tenable

战(戰) zhàn I (名) war; warfare; battle; fight: 游击～ guerrilla war. 持久～ protracted war II (动) 1 fight: 不宣而～ wage an undeclared war 2 shiver; tremble; shudder: 胆～心惊 scared out of one's wits

战败 zhànbài (动) 1 be defeated; suffer a defeat; lose (a battle or war) 2 defeat; vanquish; beat: ～国 vanquished (or defeated) nation

战备(備) zhànbèi (名) war preparedness; combat readiness

战场(場) zhànchǎng (名) battlefield; battleground; battlefront

战地 zhàndì (名) battlefield; battleground; combat zone: ～记者 war correspondent. ～指挥部 field headquarters

战斗(鬥) zhàndòu I (动) fight; battle; combat; action: 英勇～ put up a heroic fight. 投入～ go into battle II (形) militant; fighting: ～的友谊 militant friendship. ～部队 combat forces. ～意志 will to fight. ～英雄 combat hero

战斗(鬥)力 zhàndòulì (名) combat effectiveness (or strength, capability); fighting capacity

战犯 zhànfàn (名) war criminal

战俘 zhànfú (名) prisoner of war

(P.O.W.)
战功 zhàngōng (名) meritorious military service; outstanding military exploit; battle achievement
战鼓 zhàngǔ (名) battle drum
战果 zhànguǒ (名) results of battle; victory: ～辉煌 the splendid results of battle
战壕 zhànháo (名) trench; entrenchment
战火 zhànhuǒ (名) flames of war
战绩 zhànjī (名) military successes (or exploits, feats); combat gains
战舰(艦) zhànjiàn (名) warship
战局 zhànjú (名) war situation
战况 zhànkuàng (名) progress of a battle
战利品 zhànlìpǐn (名) spoils of war; captured equipment; war trophies (or booty)
战栗(慄) zhànlì (动) tremble; shiver; shudder: 吓得全身～ tremble all over with fear
战略 zhànlüè (名) strategy: 全球～ global strategy. ～核武器 strategic nuclear weapons
战胜(勝) zhànshèng (动) defeat; triumph over; vanquish; overcome: ～敌人 defeat (or vanquish) the enemy. ～困难 overcome (or surmount) difficulties
战士 zhànshì (名) 1 soldier; man 2 champion; warrior; fighter
战术(術) zhànshù (名) (military) tactics: ～核武器 tactical nuclear weapons. ～演习 tactical manoeuvre
战无(無)不胜(勝) zhàn wú bù shèng invincible; ever-victorious; all conquering
战线(綫) zhànxiàn (名) battle line; battlefront; front
战役 zhànyì (名) campaign; battle
战友 zhànyǒu (名) comrade-in-arms; battle companion
战战兢兢 zhànzhànjīngjīng (形、副) 1 quivering with fear 2 cautiously; with caution
战争 zhànzhēng (名) war; warfare: ～状态 state of war

颤 zhàn (动) tremble; shiver; shudder
see also chàn
颤栗(慄) zhànlì (动) tremble; shiver; shudder

绽 zhàn (动) split; burst

章 zhāng (名) 1 chapter; section 2 order: 杂乱无～ disorganized or chaotic 3 rules; regulations; constitution: 规～ rules and regulations 4 seal; stamp: 盖～ affix one's seal 5 badge; medal: 领～ collar badge (or insignia) 奖～ medal; decoration. 袖～ armband
章程 zhāngchéng (名) rules; regulations; constitution
章法 zhāngfǎ (名) 1 presentation of ideas; art of composition 2 orderly ways; methodicalness: 他办事很有～. He is quite methodical in his work.
章节(節) zhāngjié (名) chapters and sections

樟 zhāng (名) camphor tree
樟脑(腦) zhāngnǎo (名) camphor: ～丸 camphor ball; mothball. ～油 camphor oil
樟树(樹) zhāngshù (名) camphor tree

张(張) zhāng (动) 1 open; spread; stretch: ～嘴 open one's mouth. ～翅膀儿 spread the wings 2 look: 东～西望 peer (or look) around 3 magnify; exagerate: 虚～声势 exagerate one's military strength to deceive the enemy [also used figuratively] 4 [of a shop in old days]: 开～ open a business II <量>: 一～桌子 a table. 两～床 two beds. 一～纸 a piece of paper
张本 zhāngběn (名) seemingly casual remark foreshadowing the development of events
张挂(掛) zhāngguà (动) hang up (a picture, curtain, etc.)
张冠李戴 Zhāng guān Lǐ dài (动) mistake one person or thing for another
张皇 zhānghuáng (形) <书> alarmed; scared: ～失措 be panicky
张口结舌 zhāngkǒu-jiéshé be tongue-tied; remair speechless
张力 zhānglì (名) 1 tension: 表面～ surface tension 2 pulling force
张罗(羅) zhāngluo (动) 1 take care of; get busy about: 这事交给我来～. I'll take care of that. 2 raise (funds): ～一笔钱 raise a sum of money 3 greet and entertain (guests); attend to (customers, etc.): 她正忙着～客人. She's busy attending to the guests.
张贴 zhāngtiē (动) put up (a notice, poster, etc.): ～通告 post (or put up) a notice

张望 zhāngwàng (动) **1** peep through a crack, etc. **2** look around

张牙舞爪 zhāngyá-wǔzhǎo fierce and quarrelsome

张扬(揚) zhāngyáng (动) publicize unnecessarily; make public (what should not be made known to the public): 四处～ spread the story around. 这事须严格保密,请勿～出去. This is strictly confidential. On no account should you spread it around.

张嘴 zhāngzuǐ (动) **1** open one's mouth (to say sth.); be on the point of saying something **2** ask for a loan or a favour: 她想在此过夜,但又不好意思～. She would like to put up here for the night, but found it embarrassing to ask.

掌 zhǎng I (名) **1** palm (of hand) **2** (of certain animals and farmyard birds) paw: 鸭～ duck's webs. 熊～ bear's paw **3** shoe sole or heel: 鞋子打前后～ have a shoe soled and heeled **4** horseshoe II (动) **1** strike with the palm of the hand; slap: ～嘴 slap sb. on the face **2** hold in control of; be in charge of: ～财权 have control over financial affairs

掌舵 zhǎngduò (动) be at the helm; operate the rudder; steer a boat

掌故 zhǎnggù (名) anecdotes

掌管 zhǎngguǎn (动) be in charge of; handle; administer: ～一个部门 be in charge of a department

掌柜(櫃) zhǎngguì (名) shopkeeper; manager (of a shop)

掌权(權) zhǎngquán (动) be in power; wield power; exercise control

掌声(聲) zhǎngshēng (名) clapping; applause: ～雷动 thunderous applause.

掌握 zhǎngwò (动) **1** grasp; master; know well: ～技术 master a technique. ～问题实质 grasp the essence of the problem **2** control: ～会议 preside over a meeting. ～政权 wield political power

长(長) zhǎng I (形) **1** older; elder; senior: 比他年～ older than him **2** eldest; oldest: ～兄 eldest brother. ～女 eldest daughter II (名) chief; head: 科～ section chief. 代表团～ head of a delegation III (动) **1** grow; develop: 孩子～大了,这件衣服穿不下了. The child has outgrown this jacket. 那里连草都不～. Even no grass would grow there. **2** come into being; begin to grow; form: ～锈 get rusty. 树木都～叶子了. The trees are coming into leaf. **3** acquire; enhance; increase: ～见识 gain one's knowledge and experience

see also cháng

长辈 zhǎngbèi (名) elder member of a family; one's senior

长大 zhǎngdà (动) grow up; be brought up

长进(進) zhǎngjìn (名) progress made in one's intellectual or moral education

长势(勢) zhǎngshì (名) (of crops) the condition of growth: 作物～良好. The crops are doing well.

长相 zhǎngxiàng (名) 〈口〉 features; appearance: 从他们的～看,他们象是兄弟俩. They are probably brothers, judging from their physical likeness

长者 zhǎngzhě (名) **1** one's senior **2** a noble-minded person of advanced age; venerable elder

涨(漲) zhǎng (动) (of water level, prices, etc.) rise; go up: 价格上～ The prices have gone up.

see also zhàng

涨潮 zhǎngcháo (名) rising tide; flood tide

涨风(風) zhǎngfēng (名) the trend of prices going up

瘴 zhàng (名) miasma

障 zhàng I (动) hinder; obstruct II (名) barrier; block: 屏～ protective screen

障碍(礙) zhàng'ài (动) hinder; obstruct: ～物 obstacle; obstruction; barrier: 扫除～ remove obstacles

丈 zhàng I (名) [a unit of length = $3\frac{1}{3}$ metres] II (动) measure (land)

丈夫 zhàngfū (名) **1** husband **2** true man: ～气概 manliness

丈量 zhàngliáng (动) measure (land): ～土地 measure land; take the dimensions of a field

丈母娘 zhàngmuniáng (名) mother-in-law

丈人 zhàngren (名) father-in-law

杖 zhàng (名) **1** cane; stick: 扶～而行 walk with a cane (walking) stick **2** rod or staff used for a specific purpose: 擀面～ rolling pin

仗 zhàng I (动) **1** hold (a sword) **2** rely on; depend on: 狗～人势 act savagely like a dog owned by a powerful master II (名) battle; war: 打胜～ win a battle; win the war

仗势(勢)欺人 zhàng shì qī rén (动) bully people by reliance on one's powerful connections or position

仗义(義)疏财 zhàng yì shū cái act in the cause of justice and make light of one's financial possessions; stand for justice and despise wealth

仗义(義)执(執)言 zhàng yì zhí yán (动) speak out from a strong sense of justice

涨(漲) zhàng (动) **1** (of dry food) swell after absorbing water, etc. **2** (of the head) become red in the face: 他的脸～得通红. His face flushed scarlet. 头昏脑～ feel giddy
see also zhǎng

帐(帳) zhàng (名) **1** camp, tent: 蚊～ mosquito net **2** account: 记～ keep accounts. 结～ settle accounts **3** debt; credit: 赊～ buy or sell on credit

帐簿 zhàngbù (名) account book; ledger

帐房 zhàngfáng (名) **1** accountant's office **2** accountant

帐户 zhànghù (名) account: 开立(结束)～ open (close) an account with a bank

帐目 zhàngmù (名) items of an account; accounts

帐篷 zhàngpeng (名) tent: 搭～ pitch (or put up) a tent

胀(脹) zhàng (动) **1** expand: 热～冷缩 expand when heated and contract when cooled. 人口膨～expansion of population **2** (of body) feel tight: 肚子发～ have a feeling of tightness (or constriction) in the stomach.

着 zhāo (名) **1** (make) a move in chess: 走错一～ make a false move **2** trick; device; move: 使花～ play a trick
see also zháo; zhe; zhuó

朝 zhāo (名) **1** early morning; morning: ～阳 morning sun **2** day: 今～ today; the present
see also cháo

朝不保夕 zhāo bù bǎo xī precarious

朝晖 zhāohuī (名) the rays of the morning sun

朝令夕改 zhāo lìng xī gǎi make frequent changes in policy

朝气(氣) zhāoqì (名) youthful vigour; vitality: ～蓬勃 full of youthful vigour

朝三暮四 zhāosān-mùsì (动) play fast and loose; chop and change: 这个人～, 玩弄年轻妇女的情感. This chap is playing fast and loose with a young woman's affections.

朝夕 zhāoxī (名、副) **1** every day; all the time **2** a very short time: 只争～ seize the day, seize the hour; seize every minute

朝霞 zhāoxiá (名) rosy clouds of dawn; rosy dawn

朝阳(陽) zhāoyáng (名) the rising sun; the morning sun

招 zhāo I (动) **1** beckon: 他把手一～, 要我跟上. He beckoned me to carry on. **2** recruit; enlist; enrol: ～工 recruit workers. ～生 enrol students **3** attract; incur; court: ～灾 court disaster; invite calamity **4** confess; own up: 被胁～认 make a confession under duress II (名) (same as "着")

招标(標) zhāobiāo (动) invite tenders (or bids, public bidding)

招兵买(買)马(馬) zhāobīng-mǎimǎ enlarge an army; recruit personnel

招待 zhāodài (动) entertain; serve (customers): 设宴～ give a dinner (or banquet) in honour of sb. ～客人 entertain guests. 记者～会 press conference

招风(風) zhāofēng (动) attract notice and thus invite trouble

招供 zhāogòng (动) make a confession of one's crime; own up

招呼 zhāohu (动) **1** call: 那边有人～你. Someone over there is calling you. **2** hail; greet; say hello to: 到站请～我一下. Remind me to get off at the stop. **3** notify; tell: 你要是想去,事先打个～. Let me know in advance if you want to go.

招架 zhāojià (动) resist; ward

off: 来势凶猛,难以～. The force was too great to resist.
招考 zhāokǎo (动) admit (students, applicants, etc.) by examination
招徕 zhāolái (动) solicit: ～顾客 solicit customers
招揽(攬) zhāolǎn (动) solicit: ～顾客 solicit customers
招领 zhāolǐng (动) notice on lost property to be claimed: 失物～处 Lost and Found
招募 zhāomù (动) recruit; enlist
招牌 zhāopai (名) shop sign; signboard
招聘 zhāopìn (动) advertize for (workers, teachers, etc.)
招惹 zhāore (动) provoke; incur; court: ～是非 court trouble
招认(認) zhāorèn (动) confess one's crime; own up; plead guilty
招收 zhāoshōu (动) recruit; take in: ～新学生 admit new students
招手 zhāoshǒu (动) beckon; wave: ～致意 wave one's greetings
招贴 zhāotiē (名) poster; placard; bill
招摇 zhāoyáo (动) put on airs: ～过市 swagger down the street. ～撞骗 behave under false pretences
招展 zhāozhǎn (动) flutter; wave (to attract notice)
招致 zhāozhì (动) 1 recruit (personnel) 2 incur; give rise to: ～意外损失 incur unexpected losses. ～各种揣测 give rise to all sorts of speculation

昭 zhāo (形) clear; obvious

昭然若揭 zhāorán ruò jiē abundantly clear; as clear as daylight: 事实已～. The facts have come into the open.
昭雪 zhāoxuě (动) rehabilitate: 冤案得到了～. The wrong has been righted. *or* The person wronged has been rehabilitated.
昭彰 zhāozhāng (形) clear; manifest; evident: 罪恶～ be guilty of flagrant crimes
昭著 zhāozhù (形) clear; evident; obvious: 成绩～ have achieved remarkable successes. 臭名～ be notorious

着 zháo (动) 1 touch: 上不～天,下不～地 be suspended in midair 2 feel; catch: ～凉 catch cold 3 burn: 灯点～了 The lamp is burning. 把烟点～了 light a cigarette 4 [used after a verb to indicate accomplishment or result]: 睡～了 be asleep 5 fall asleep; go to sleep: 他一上床就睡～了. He fell asleep as soon as he went to bed.
see also zhāo; zhe; zhuó
着慌 zháohuāng (动) feel worried; get alarmed
着火 zháohuǒ (动) catch fire
着急 zháojí (动) feel worried: 别～. Don't worry.
着迷 zháomí (动) be fascinated; be held spellbound

沼 zhǎo (名) natural pond

沼气(氣) zhǎoqì (名) marsh gas; bio gas; methane
沼泽(澤) zhǎozé (名) marsh; swamp

找 zhǎo (动) 1 look for; try to find; seek: ～工作 look (or hunt) for a job. ～答案 seek a solution 2 want to see; call on: 早晨有位叫史密斯的先生～过你. A certain Mr. Smith wanted to see you this morning. 你该去～导师出个主意. You should go and ask your tutor for advice. 3 return the balance of money: 他～我三元. He gave me three yuan change.
找事 zhǎoshì (动) 1 look (or hunt) for a job 2 pick a quarrel with sb.; look for trouble
找死 zhǎosǐ (动) invite death; head for an accident or certain destruction
找寻(尋) zhǎoxún (动) look for; seek

爪 zhǎo (名) claw; talon
see also zhuǎ
爪牙 zhǎoyá (名) cat's paw

肇 zhào (动) 〈书〉 1 start; commence; initiate 2 cause (trouble, etc.)
肇事 zhàoshì (动) cause trouble; create a disturbance: 追查～者 find out the troublemakers

罩 zhào I (动) cover; wrap: 用毕请把打字机～好. Please cover the typewriter after use. 天空～满乌云. Dark clouds covered the sky. II (名) cover; shade; hood; housing: 口～ mask. 灯～ lampshade. 发动机～ the engine housing
罩衫 zhàoshān (名) overall; dustcoat

兆 zhào I (名) 1 sign; omen; portent: 吉祥之～ an auspicious omen 2 million; mega- 3 a million millions; billion II (动) portend; foretell: 瑞雪~丰年. A timely snow promises a good harvest.

兆头(頭) zhàotou (名) sign; omen; portent

兆周 zhàozhōu (名) 〈无〉 megacycle

召 zhào (动) call together; convene; summon; send for

召唤 zhàohuàn (动) call; beckon: 工作在~着我们，我们不能等了. Work beckons to us and we can't afford to wait.

召集 zhàojí (动) call together; convene: 把所有雇员~到一起 call all the employees together. ~会议 call (or convene) a conference

召见(見) zhàojiàn (动) 1 call in (a subordinate) 2 summon (an envoy) to an interview

召开(開) zhàokāi (动) convene; convoke: ~一次首脑会议 hold a summit conference

召之即来(來) zhào zhī jí lái be at sb.'s beck and call

诏 zhào 〈书〉 I (动) instruct II (名) imperial edict

诏书(書) zhàoshū (名) imperial edict

照 zhào I (动) 1 shine; illuminate; light up: 他用手电筒~了我一下. He shone the torch at me. 气灯把大厅~得通明. The hall was brightly lit by pressure lamps. 2 reflect; mirror: 湖面如镜，把岸上树木~得清清楚楚. The water of the lake mirrored all the trees on the bank. 3 take a picture; photograph; film; shoot: ~一张团体相 have a group picture taken. 这是我在罗马~的几张相片. These are a few snapshots I took in Rome. 4 take care of; look after: ~料 look after; attend to; keep an eye on 5 contrast: 对~ contrast; check against. 请对~原文. Please check this against the original. 6 understand: 心~不宣 have a tacit understanding II (介) 1 in the direction of; towards: ~这个方向走. Go in this direction. 2 according to; in accordance with: ~章办事 act according to regulations. ~我看 in my opinion III (名) 1 photograph; picture: 剧~ stage photo. 彩~ colour picture 2 license; permit: 禁止无~行车. It is forbidden to drive without a license. 护~ passport

照搬 zhàobān (动) mechanically copy

照办(辦) zhàobàn (动) act accordingly; do as one is told; comply with sb.'s request; follow sb.'s instructions

照本宣科 zhào běn xuān kē read mechanically from a prepared text

照常 zhàocháng (副) as usual: 天下着大雪，但孩子们~上学. In spite of the heavy snow, the children went to school as usual.

照抄 zhàochāo (动) copy word for word: 这封推荐信请你~一份. Please make a fair copy of this letter of recommendation.

照发(發) zhàofā (动) 1 issue as before 2 (文件批语) approved for distribution

照顾(顧) zhàogu (动) 1 give consideration to; show consideration for; make allowance for: ~全局 take the entire situation into account. ~当地条件 take the local conditions into account 2 look after; care for; attend to: ~病人look after the patients. 给予特别~ give preferential treatment

照管 zhàoguǎn (动) look after; tend; be in charge of: ~孩子 look after the children 这件事由他~. He will take charge of the matter.

照会(會) zhàohuì I (动) present (or deliver, address) a note to (a government) II (名) note: 交换~ exchange notes. 普通~ verbal note. 正式~ personal note

照旧(舊) zhàojiù (副) as before; as usual; as of old: 体例~ We follow the traditional stylistic rules.

照看 zhàokàn (动) look after; attend to; keep an eye on: 请帮我~一下行李. Will you please keep an eye on my luggage.

照例 zhàolì (副) as a rule; as usual; usually: 她~每礼拜天去教堂. As a rule, she goes to church every Sunday.

照料 zhàoliào (动) take care of; attend to: 她不在期间把房子托给邻居~. She left the house in the care of a neighbour while she was away.

照明 zhàomíng (名) illumination;

lighting: 舞台～ stage illumination. ～装置 lighting installation
照片 zhàopiàn (名) photograph; picture: 加印～ make copies of a print. 放大～ have the picture enlarged
照射 zhàoshè (动) shine; illuminate; light up; irradiate: 用紫外线～ irradiate with ultraviolet rays
照相 zhàoxiàng (动) take a picture(or photograph); photograph: ～簿 photo album. ～复制 photocopy. ～馆 photostudio
照相机(機) zhàoxiàngjī (名) camera
照样(樣) zhàoyàng (副) 1 after a pattern or model 2 in the same old way; as before
照耀 zhàoyào (动) shine; illuminate
照应(應) zhàoyìng (动) coordinate; correlate
照应(應) zhàoying (动) look after; take care of: 代表们受到东道国的很好～. All delegates were well looked after by the host country. 一路上他们互相～. They looked after each other all the way.
遮 zhē (动) 1 hide from view; cover; screen: 美丽的葡萄园给小山～住了. The beautiful vineyard was hidden from view by the hills. 2 keep out: ～风挡雨 keep out wind and rain
遮蔽 zhēbì (动) hide from view; obstruct; shelter: 一片森林～了我们的视线，看不到远处的村庄. The woods blocked our view of the distant villages.
遮挡(擋) zhēdǎng (动) shelter oneself from; keep out: ～寒风 keep out the cold wind
遮盖(蓋) zhēgài (动) 1 cover; overspread: 山路全给大雪～住了。The mountain paths were all covered by snow. 2 conceal; gloss over; cover up: ～缺点 gloss over one's shortcomings
遮羞 zhēxiū (动) hush up a scandal: ～解嘲 try to console oneself by putting on one's scandal a veneer of respectability. ～布 fig leaf
遮掩 zhēyǎn (动) 1 cover; over spread; envelop 2 cover up; hide; conceal: ～错误，不是正确的态度. It's not the right attitude to cover up one's mistakes.
折 zhē (动)〈口〉 roll over; turn over: ～个跟斗 turn a somersault
see also shé; zhé
折腾 zhēteng (动)〈口〉 1 turn from side to side; toss about: 他～了好几个钟头才睡着. He tossed about in bed for hours before he fell asleep. 2 do sth. over and over again: 他把自行车拆了装，～了一个上午. He spent the whole morning dismantling and assembling the bike. 3 cause physical or mental suffering; get sb. down: 这种噪声真～人. The noise is getting on my nerves.
谪 zhé (动)〈书〉 1 demote a high official by assigning him minor post in an outlying district (as a form of punishment in feudal times): ～居 live in exile 2 criticize; blame: 众口交～ be the target of public censure; be criticized by everybody
折 zhé (动) 1 break; snap: ～断腿 fracture (or break) one's leg 2 suffer the loss of; lose: 损兵～将 suffer heavy casualties 3 bend; twist: 曲～ twists and turns. 百～不挠 remain unshaken in spite of all setbacks 4 turn back; change direction: 他本想出去散步，但到了门口又～了回来. He meant to go out for a stroll, but he turned back as soon as he reached the gate. 5 be convinced: 心～ be deeply convinced 6 convert into; amount to: 把瑞士法郎～成美元 convert Swiss francs into dollars 7 discount; rebate: 打八～ give a 20% discount 8 fold: 内有照片，请勿～叠! Photos, don't bend! 9 book-accounts, etc.; folder: 存～ deposit book; bankbook
see also shé; zhē
折叠 zhédié (动) fold: 把报纸～好 fold up the newspaper. ～椅 folding chair; camp chair. ～扇 folding fan
折服 zhéfú (动) 1 subdue; bring into submission: 强词夺理，不能～人. As you are arbitrary and unreasonable, you cannot expect anybody to give in. 2 convinced or fill sb. with admiration: 令人～ compel admiration
折合 zhéhé (动) convert into; amount to; be equivalent to: 一英镑～成人民币是多少? How much is a pound in terms of *yuan?*
折旧(舊) zhéjiù (名)〈经〉depre-

ciation: ～费 depreciation charge
折扣 zhékou (动)(名) discount; rebate: 打～ at a discount
折磨 zhémo (动) cause physical or mental suffering; torment
折射 zhéshè (名) refraction
折中(衷) zhézhōng (动) compromise: ～主义 eclecticism
哲 zhé I (形) wise; sagacious II (名) wise man; philosopher; sage: 先～ the sages of old
哲理 zhélǐ (名) philosophic theory; philosophy
哲人 zhérén (名) <书> sage; philosopher
哲学(學) zhéxué (名) philosophy: ～家 philosopher
蛰(蟄) zhé
蛰居 zhéjū (动) live in seclusion
辙 zhé (名) 1 the track of a wheel; rut 2 [usu. used in the negative] way; idea: 没～ can find no way out; be at the end of one's rope
褶 zhě (名) pleat; crease: 百～裙 pleated skirt; accordion-pleated skirt. 熨平衬衫上的～儿 iron the wrinkles out of the skirt
褶皱(皺) zhězhòu (名) 1 fold 2 wrinkle
者 zhě <助> 1 [used after an adjective or verb as a substitute for a person or a thing]: 老～ old man. 弱～ the weak. 读～ reader. 出版～ publisher 2 [used after"工作"、"主义" to indicate a person engaged in a certain profession or believe in a doctrine]: 医务工作～ medical worker. 唯物主义～ materialist 3 [used to indicate things mentioned above]: 二～必居其一. It must be one or the other.
赭 zhě (形) reddish brown; burnt ochre
这(這) zhè (代) 1 this: ～地方 this place. ～一回 this time 2 this moment; now: 我～就走. I'm leaving right now.
这般 zhèbān (副) such; so; like this: ～大小 this size; this big. 如此～ thus and thus; so on and so forth
这边(邊) zhèbiān (副) this side; here: 正义在我们～. Justice is on our side. 到～来. Come over here.
这次 zhècì (形) this time; present; current: ～会议 the present session. ～英国大选 the current British general elections
这个 zhège (代) this one; this: 你要告诉我们的就是～呀! So this is what you wanted to tell us.
这里 zhèlǐ (副) here
这么(麼) zhème (代) so; such; this way; like this: 事情不会～简单. The matter wouldn't be as simple as that. 这间屋子～大哪! This room is so big! ～多人, 有地方吗? Is there enough room for so many people?
这么(麼)着 zhèmezhe (副) like this; so: ～好. It's better this way. 要是～, 那我就留下不去了. In that case, I'll stay behind.
这儿 zhèr (代) here; now; then: 打～起我就要天天锻炼了. From now on I'm going to do physical exercises every day.
这些 zhèxie (代) these: ～书 these books. ～日子 these days
这样(樣) zhèyàng (代) so; such; like this; this way: 别走～快. Don't walk so fast. 情况就是～. That's how things stand.
蔗 zhè (名) sugarcane
蔗糖 zhètáng (名) 1 sucrose 2 cane sugar
着 zhe <助> 1 [indicating an action in progress]: 他们正开～会呢. They are at a meeting. 他含～眼泪说. He said this with tears in his eyes. 2 [stressing the tone in an imperative sentence]: 你听～! You just listen. 快～点儿. Be quick. 3 [used after a verb to form a preposition]: 沿～ along. 挨～ next to. 朝～ towards
see also zhāo; zháo; zhuó
榛 zhēn (名) hazel
臻 zhēn (动) <书> attain (a happy state): 交通运输日～便利. The means of transportation are becoming better and better.
斟 zhēn (动) pour (tea or wine)
斟酌 zhēnzhuó (动) consider; deliberate: ～字句 weigh the words and phrases. 再三～ think the matter over several times
砧 zhēn (名) hammering block; anvil: ～杵 anvil and pestle
甄 zhēn (动) <书> distinguish after examination: ～选

select

甄别 zhēnbié (动) 1 examine and distinguish; screen 2 assess; appraise; verify

真 zhēn I (形) true; real; genuine: ～事 a true story. ～心诚意 genuine desire; sincerity II (副) 1 really; truly; indeed: 他～信了. He sincerely believed it. 他～是个了不起的学者. He is indeed a great scholar. 2 clearly; unmistakably: 黑板上的字你看得～吗? Can you see the words on the board clearly?

真才实(實)学(學) zhēncái-shíxué I (名) real talent and sound scholarship II(形) professionally competent; well-qualified or well-trained

真诚 zhēnchéng (形)sincere; genuine; true: ～的愿望 sincere wish

真迹 zhēnjī (名) authentic work (of painting or calligraphy)

真假 zhēn-jiǎ (形) true or false; genuine or sham: 辨别～ tell the true from the false

真金不怕火炼(煉) zhēnjīn bù pà huǒ liàn True gold can be tried in the fire.

真空 zhēnkōng (名) vacuum: 我们不是生活在～里. We do not live in a vacuum. ～地带〈军〉 no-man's land. ～吸尘器 vacuum cleaner

真理 zhēnlǐ (名) truth: 坚持～ uphold the truth

真凭(憑)实(實)据(據) zhēnpíngshíjù (名) conclusive evidence; true evidence

真切 zhēnqiè (形) vivid and truthful; realistic

真情 zhēnqíng (名) 1 the real situation; the actual state of affairs 2 genuine feelings; true sentiments: ～的流露 a revelation of one's true sentiments

真人真事 zhēnrén-zhēnshì (名) real people and real events; true story

真善美 zhēn-shàn-měi (名) truth, goodness and beauty

真实(實) zhēnshí (形) true; real; actual; authentic: 那儿的～情况不是人人都知道的. The real situation there is not known to everybody.

真是 zhēnshi (副) [expressing arrogance]: 你也～,怎么来得这么晚? What a shame! Why are you so late?

真相 zhēnxiàng (名) the real (or true) situation; the real (or actual) facts; the actual state of affairs; truth: 弄清事实的～ acquaint oneself with the truth of the matter

真心 zhēnxīn (形) wholehearted; heartfelt; sincere: ～拥护 give wholehearted support to. ～话 true words from the heart

真正 zhēnzhèng (形) genuine; true; real: 患难之交才是～的朋友. A friend in need is a friend indeed.

真知 zhēnzhī (名) genuine (or real) knowledge; correct understanding

真知灼见(見) zhēnzhī-zhuójiàn(名) penetrating knowledge and insight

真挚(摯) zhēnzhì (形) sincere; cordial: ～的友谊 sincere friendship

真主 zhēnzhǔ (名) Allah

贞 zhēn (形) 1 loyal; faithful 2 (of women) chastity or virginity

贞操 zhēncāo (名) 1 chastity or virginity 2 loyalty; moral integrity

贞节(節) zhēnjié (名) chastity

贞洁(潔) zhēnjié (形) chaste; pure and undefiled

侦 zhēn (动) detect; scout; investigate

侦查 zhēnchá (动) investigate (a crime)

侦察 zhēnchá (动) reconnoitre; scout: ～敌情 gather intelligence about the enemy. ～兵 scout. ～机 reconnaissance plane

侦缉 zhēnjī (动) track down and arrest (a criminal)

侦探 zhēntàn (名) detective; spy: ～小说 detective story

侦听(聽) zhēntīng (动) intercept (enemy radio communications); monitor

箴 zhēn

箴言 zhēnyán (名) admonition; exhortation; maxim

珍 zhēn I (名) treasure: 山～海味 delicacies of great variety. 奇～异宝 rare treasure II (形) precious; valuable; rare: ～禽异兽 rare birds and animals III (动) value highly: ～视 treasure

珍爱 zhēn'ài (动) treasure; love dearly

珍宝(寶) zhēnbǎo (名) jewellery; treasure: 如获～ as if one had

come upon a rare treasure
珍藏 zhēncáng (动) collect (rare books, art treasures, etc.)
珍贵 zhēnguì (形) valuable; precious: ～物品 the valuables. ～的历史文物 precious historical relics
珍品 zhēnpǐn (名) treasure: 艺术～ art treasure
珍奇 zhēnqí (形) rare: ～的动物 rare animals
珍视 zhēnshì (动) value; prize; cherish; treasure
珍惜 zhēnxī (动) treasure; value; cherish: ～时间 fully recognize the value of time
珍重(重) zhēnzhòng (动) 1 highly value; treasure; set great store by: ～这个良好机会 set great store by this opportunity 2 take good care of yourself
珍珠 zhēnzhū (名) pearl: ～贝 pearl shell; pearl oyster

针 zhēn (名) 1 needle: 毛线～ knitting needle 2 stitch: 伤口缝了四～ sew the edges of a wound with four stitches. 3 anything like a needle: 松～ pine needle. 时～ (of a clock) hour hand. 别～ safety pin
针对(對) zhēnduì (动) 1 be directed against; be aimed at: 这些话不是～什么人说的. These remarks were not directed against anybody in particular. 2 in the light of; in accordance with; in connection with: ～儿童特点组织活动 organize activities for children in accordance with their special characteristics
针锋相对(對) zhēnfēng xiāng duì give tit for tat; be diametrically opposed to: 进行～的斗争 wage a tit-for-tat struggle
针剂(劑) zhēnjì (名) injection
针灸 zhēnjiǔ (名) acupuncture and moxibustion
针线(綫) zhēnxiàn (名) needlework: ～包 sewing kit. ～活 needlework; stitching; sewing
针眼 zhēnyǎn (名) 1 the eye of a needle 2 pinprick
针织(織) zhēnzhī (名) knitting: ～外套 knitted (or knit) coat. ～品 knit goods; knitwear; hosiery

枕 zhěn I (名) pillow: ～巾 pillowcase cover II (动) rest the head on: ～着胳臂睡觉 sleep with one's head resting on one's arm
枕戈待旦 zhěn gē dài dàn sleep with one's sword ready; be ready for battle
枕木 zhěnmù (名) sleeper; tie
枕套 zhěntào (名) pillowcase
枕头(頭) zhěntou (名) pillow

缜 zhěn
缜密 zhěnmì (形) careful; meticulous; deliberate: ～的分析 a careful thoroughgoing analysis

疹 zhěn (名) rash: 荨麻～ nettle rash
疹子 zhěnzi (名) measles

诊 zhěn (动) examine (a patient)
诊断(斷) zhěnduàn (动) diagnose: ～书 medical certificate
诊疗(療) zhěnliáo (名) diagnosis and treatment: ～室 consulting room. ～所 clinic; dispensary
诊脉(脈) zhěnmài (动) feel the pulse

鸩 zhèn (名) 1 a legendary poisonous bird, whose feathers can turn wine into poison 2 poisoned wine: 饮～止渴 drink poisoned wine to quench thirst; seek temporary relief regardless of consequences

震 zhèn (动) 1 shake; shock; vibrate; quake: 地～ earthquake. 防～ shockproof 2 greatly excited; deeply astonished; shocked: ～骇 shocked; astounded
震颤 zhènchàn (动) tremble; quiver
震荡(蕩) zhèndàng (动) shake; shock: ～全球 shake the world
震动(動) zhèndòng (动) quiver; cause sth. to quiver or tremble or vibrate: 引起了广泛的～ arouse widespread repercussions. 春雷～着山谷. The spring thunder rumbled in the valleys. *or* The spring thunder made the valleys vibrate.
震耳欲聋(聾) zhèn ěr yù lóng (形) deafening; ear-splitting
震撼 zhènhàn (动) shake; shock; vibrate: ～人心的大事 a soul-stirring event
震惊(驚) zhènjīng (动) shock; amaze; astonish: ～中外 astonish the country and rest of the world; have a tremendous impact on people both at home and abroad
震怒 zhènnù (形) be enraged; be furious

振 zhèn (动) 1 shake; flutter; flap: ～翅 flutter its wings up and down; flap its wings 2

invigorate; animate; brace up: 食欲不～ lose one's appetite. 他想到自己这次考得不错，精神为之一～. He felt excited when he thought that he had done very well at the exams this time.

振荡(蕩) zhèndàng (名) 1 vibration 2 oscillation

振动(動) zhèndòng (名) vibration: ～频率 vibration frequency

振奋(奮) zhènfèn (动) 1 feel invigorated; be filled with enthusiasm 2 inspire; stimulate: ～人心 inspire popular enthusiasm. 令人～的消息 heartening news

振兴(興) zhènxīng (动) develop vigorously; promote: ～中华 revitalize (or rejuvenate) China. ～工业 vigorously develop industry

振振有辞(辭) zhènzhèn yǒu cí (动) speak plausibly and at great length

振作 zhènzuò (动) display vigour: ～起来 bestir oneself; brace up

赈 zhèn

赈济(濟) zhènjì (动) relieve; aid: ～灾民 relieve victims in afflicted (or stricken) areas; bring relief to refugees; feed the hungry

赈灾(災) zhènzāi (动) relieve the people scourged by disease, natural disaster or war

镇 zhèn I (动) 1 press down; keep down; ease: ～痛 ease pain 2 guard; garrison 3 cool with cold water or ice: 冰～啤酒 iced beer II (形) calm; tranquil: ～定 calm and composed III (名) 1 garrison post: 军事重～ strategic post 2 town

镇静 zhènjìng (形) calm; cool; composed; unruffled: ～剂 sedative; tranquillizer

镇痛 zhèntòng I (动) ease pain: ～片 pain killer II (名) analgesia: 针刺～ acupuncture analgesia

镇压(壓) zhènyā (动) 1 suppress; repress; put down: ～叛乱 put down a rebellion 2 <口> execute (a criminal)

阵 zhèn I (名) 1 battle array (or formation): 严～以待 combat ready 2 position; front: 上～杀敌 off to fight at the front line 3 a period of time: 病了一～ be ill for some time II <量>: 一～风 a gust of wind. 一～寒潮 a cold spell. 一～笑声 outbursts of laughter

阵地 zhèndì (名) position; front: 前沿～ a forward position. ～战 positional warfare

阵脚 zhènjiǎo (名) 1 front line 2 position; situation; circumstances: 稳住～ stand one's ground. 乱了～ be thrown into confusion

阵容 zhènróng (名) 1 battle array (or formation) 2 lineup: ～强大 have a strong lineup

阵势(勢) zhènshì (名) 1 battle array (or formation) 2 situation; condition; circumstances

阵亡 zhènwáng (动) be killed in action; fall in battle

阵线(綫) zhènxiàn (名) front; ranks; alignment

阵营(營) zhènyíng (名) camp

正 zhēng

see also zhèng

正月 zhēngyuè (名) the first month of the lunar year: ～初一 the lunar New Year's Day

症(癥) zhēng see also zhèng

症结 zhēngjié (名) crux; crucial reason: 问题的～ the crux of a problem.

征 zhēng (动) 1 go on a long journey 2 go on an expedition: ～讨 go on a punitive expedition 3 levy (troops); call up; draft: 应～入伍 enlist 4 levy (taxes); collect; impose: ～敛 levy and collect taxes 5 ask for; solicit: ～稿 solicit contributions (to a magazine etc.)

征兵 zhēngbīng (名、动) conscription; draft; call-up: ～法 conscription (or draft) law. ～年龄 conscription age; age for enlistment

征调 zhēngdiào (动) requisition; call up: ～物资和人员 requisition supplies and enlist personnel

征服 zhēngfú (动) conquer; subjugate: ～自然 conquer nature (or conquest of nature). ～黄河 tame (or harness) the Huanghe (Yellow) River

征购(購) zhēnggòu (动) purchase by the state

征候 zhēnghòu (名) sign: 病人已有康复的～ The patient shows signs of recovery.

征集 zhēngjí (动) 1 collect; gather: ～签名 collect signatures (for an appeal) 2 draft; call up; recruit: ～新兵 recruitment

征募 zhēngmù (动) enlist; recruit

征聘 zhēngpìn (动) invite applications for jobs; advertise for a vacant position

征求 zhēngqiú (动) solicit; seek; ask for: ～意见 solicit opinions; seek counsel; ask for advice. ～订户 solicit (or canvass for) subscriptions

征收 zhēngshōu (动) levy; collect; impose: ～进口税 impose import duties

征途 zhēngtú (名) journey: 踏上～ embark (or set out) on a journey

征询 zhēngxún (动) seek the opinion of; consult

征用 zhēngyòng (动) expropriate; requisition; commandeer

征战(戰) zhēngzhàn (动) go on an expedition

征召 zhēngzhào (动) call up; enlist; draft; conscript: ～入伍 enlist in the army

征兆 zhēngzhào (名) sign; omen; portent

争 zhēng (动) 1 contend; vie; compete; strive: ～冠军 compete for championship. ～分夺秒 race (or work) against time; seize the moment 2 argue; dispute: 这是意气之～. The dispute was a display of personal feelings

争霸 zhēngbà (动) contend (or struggle) for hegemony; vie (with each other) for supremacy

争辩 zhēngbiàn (动) argue; debate; contend: 无休止的～ an endless debate

争吵 zhēngchǎo (动) quarrel; wrangle; squabble: 激烈的～ fierce (or bitter) wrangling

争端 zhēngduān (名) controversial issue; dispute; conflict: 边界～ a border dispute

争夺(奪) zhēngduó (动) fight (or contend, scramble) for; vie with sb. for sth.: ～优势 fight for supremacy

争光 zhēngguāng (动) win honour (or glory) for: 为国～ win honour for or bring credit to one's country

争论(論) zhēnglùn (名) controversy; dispute; debate; contention: 激烈的～ a heated argument. ～之点 the point at issue

争鸣 zhēngmíng (动) contend: 百家～. A hundred schools of thought contend.

争气(氣) zhēngqì (动) work hard to win honour for; try to bring credit to

争取 zhēngqǔ (动) strive for; fight for; win over: ～胜利 strive for victory. ～选票 canvass (for votes). ～主动 take the initiative. ～中立派 win over the neutral elements

争权(權)夺(奪)利 zhēngquán-duólì (动) jockey for power and scramble for profit

争先 zhēngxiān (动) try to be ahead of others; try to be among the first: ～恐后 push ahead for fear of lagging behind.

争议(議) zhēngyì dispute; controversy: 引起很大～ give rise to a good deal of controversy

争执(執) zhēngzhí (动) disagree; dispute; stick to one's position (or guns): ～不下. Opinions differ and the issue remains undecided

挣 zhēng
see also zhèng

挣扎 zhēngzhá (动) struggle: 垂死～ put up a last-ditch struggle

睁 zhēng (动) open (the eyes): ～开眼睛,好好看看. Open your eyes and take a closer look.

峥 zhēng

峥嵘(嶸) zhēngróng (形) 1 lofty and steep; towering 2 outstanding; extraordinary

狰 zhēng

狰狞(獰) zhēngníng (形) ferocious; savage; hideous: ～面目 ferocious features

蒸 zhēng (动) 1 evaporate 2 steam: ～饭 steam rice

蒸发(發) zhēngfā (动) evaporate

蒸馏 zhēngliú (名) distillation: ～水 distilled water

蒸气(氣) zhēngqì (名) vapour

蒸汽 zhēngqì (名) steam: ～机 steam engine. ～浴 steam bath; sauna

蒸蒸日上 zhēngzhēng rì shàng becoming more prosperous every day; flourishing; thriving

整 zhěng I (形) 1 whole; complete; full; entire: ～夜 the whole night; all night long. ～学期 a full term. 七点～ (of time) seven sharp 2 in good order; neat; tidy: 衣冠不～ untidy in dress; not properly dressed II (动) 1 put in order; rectify: ～改 reform. ～装待发 pack and get ready to go 2 repair; mend;

renovate: ～修 renovate **3** make sb. suffer; punish; fix: ～人 give sb. a hard time

整饬 zhěngchì (动) set to order; strengthen: ～纪律 strengthen discipline

整党(黨) zhěngdǎng (名) Party consolidation

整队(隊) zhěngduì (动) line up: ～入场 file in

整顿 zhěngdùn (动) rectify; consolidate; reorganize

整风(風) zhěngfēng I (动) rectify the incorrect style of work II (名) rectification campaign

整个 zhěnggè (形) whole; entire: ～上午 the whole morning. ～世界 the whole world. ～中国 the whole of China

整洁(潔) zhěngjié (形) clean and tidy; neat; trim: 衣着～ clean and tidy in dress

整理 zhěnglǐ (动) put in order; straighten out; arrange; sort out: ～房间 tidy up a room. ～资料 sort out the data. ～家务 straighten out one's domestic affairs

整流 zhěngliú (名) rectification: ～器 rectifier

整齐(齊) zhěngqí (形) **1** in good order; neat; tidy: ～划一 uniform and standardized **2** even; regular: 五官～ (have) regular features. 一排排～的住宅 rows of neatly arranged houses. 阵容～ a well-balanced lineup

整容 zhěngróng (动) **1** tidy oneself up (i.e. have a haircut, a shave, etc.) **2** face-lifting; improve one's look by plastic surgery

整数(數) zhěngshù (名) **1** integer; whole number **2** round number (or figure)

整套 zhěngtào (名) a complete (or whole) set of: ～设备 a complete set of equipment. ～行动计划 a series of plans for action

整体(體) zhěngtǐ (名) whole; (the situation) as a whole; entirety: 考虑人民的～利益 consider the overall interests of the people

整形 zhěngxíng (名) plastic: ～手术 plastic operation. ～外科 plastic surgery

整修 zhěngxiū I (动) renovate; re-paint or re-style II (名) facelift

整整 zhěngzhěng (形) whole; full: ～两天 two whole days. 到北京已～三年了. It is three full years since I came to Beijing.

整治 zhěngzhì (动) **1** renovate; repair; dredge (a river, etc.) **2** punish; fix

拯

zhěng (动) save; rescue; deliver

拯救 zhěngjiù (动) save; rescue; deliver: ～溺水儿童 come to the rescue of (= rescue) a drowning child

郑(鄭)

zhèng

郑重 zhèngzhòng (形) serious; solemn; earnest: ～声明 solemnly declare. ～其事 seriously; in earnest

正

zhèng I (形) **1** straight; upright: 把这幅画放～. Put the picture straight. ～北 due north **2** situated in the middle; main: ～门 main entrance **3** (of time) punctually; sharp: 九点～ at nine o'clock sharp **4** obverse; right: 胶卷的～面 the right side of the film **5** honest; upright: 他为人～直. He is an upright man. **6** appropriate; right: ～当 legitimate. 不～之风 unhealthy tendencies **7** (of colour or flavour) pure; right: 味儿不～ not the proper flavour **8** principal; chief: ～驾驶员 first pilot. ～教授 full professor. ～本 original text (or copy) **9** positive; plus: ～离子 positive ion II (动) rectify; correct; set right: ～音 correct one's pronunciation III (副) **1** just; right; precisely; exactly: ～是如此 exactly so. 这～是我们的想法. This is exactly what we think. **2** [indicating an action in progress]: ～下着雨呢. It's raining. 他～吃着饭呢. He is having dinner.

see also zhēng

正比 zhèngbǐ (名) 〈数〉 direct ratio

正常 zhèngcháng (形) normal; regular: ～速度 normal speed. 恢复～ return to normal. 关系～化 normalization of relations

正大 zhèngdà (形) upright; honest; aboveboard: ～光明 open and aboveboard

正当(當) zhèngdāng (副) just when; just the time for: ～委员会在日内瓦再次开会之际 at a time when the committee met again in Geneva.

正当(當) zhèngdàng (形) proper; appropriate; legitimate: ～权益

legitimate rights and interests. 通过～途径 through proper channels
正点（點） zhèngdiǎn （副） (of ships, trains, etc.) on schedule; on time; punctually: ～运行 running on schedule
正电（電） zhèngdiàn （名）positive electricity
正法 zhèngfǎ （动） execute (a criminal): 就地～ execute (a criminal) on the spot
正规 zhèngguī （形） regular; standard: ～部队 regular troops; regulars
正轨 zhèngguǐ （名）correct path: 纳入～ lead one onto the correct path
正好 zhènghǎo （副） **1** just in time; just right; just enough: 你来得～. You've come just in the nick of time. 这双鞋我穿～. This pair of shoes fits me superbly. **2** happen to; chance to; as it happens: 我～与你同路. I happen to go in the same direction.
正经(經) zhèngjing （形） **1** decent; respectable; honest: ～人 a decent person **2** serious: ～事 serious matter
正面 zhèngmiàn I（名） **1** front; frontage; facade: 大楼的～ the facade of a building **2** the obverse side; the right side: 硬币的～ the obverse side of a coin II(形) positive: ～冲突 direct confrontation. ～进攻 frontal attack III （副） directly; openly: ～提出问题 raise a question directly and openly
正派 zhèngpài （形） upright; decent: ～人 an honourable person; a decent chap
正品 zhèngpǐn （名）quality products
正气(氣) zhèngqì （名） healthy trends (or tendencies)
正巧 zhèngqiǎo （副） **1** as it happens: ～我也到那里去. I happened to be going there too. **2** just at the right time: 你来得～. You've turned up at the opportune time.
正确 zhèngquè （形） correct; right
正人君子 zhèngrén-jūnzǐ （名） a man of honour; a man of noble character; a noble-minded man
正式 zhèngshì （形） formal; official; regular: ～工作人员 a regular member of the staff. ～宴会 a formal dinner party. ～访问 official visit. ～文本 official text
正视 zhèngshì（动）face squarely; face up to: ～缺点 give serious thought to one's inadequacies
正事 zhèngshì （名）one's proper business; no joking matter
正数(數) zhèngshù （名） positive number
正题 zhèngtí （名） subject (or topic) of a talk or essay: 离开～ digress (from the subject)
正统 zhèngtǒng （形） orthodox: ～观念 orthodox ideas
正文 zhèngwén （名）main body (of a book, etc.); text
正午 zhèngwǔ （名）high noon
正误表 zhèngwùbiǎo （名）errata; corrigenda
正业(業) zhèngyè （名） a decent job; proper duties: 不务～ neglect one's own duties; engage in dubious work
正义(義) zhèngyì I（名）justice: 主持～ uphold justice II（形） just; righteous: ～的事业 a just cause. ～感 sense of justice
正在 zhèngzài （副）[to indicate an action in progress] in process of; in course of: 情况～变好. The situation is getting better. 他们～开会. They are at a meeting.
正直 zhèngzhí （形） upright; fair-minded: 一切～的人们 all fair-minded people
正中 zhèngzhōng （名） middle; centre
正中下怀(懷) zhèng zhòng xiàhuái These wishes are mine.
正宗 zhèngzōng （名） orthodox school

症 zhèng （名）disease; illness: 急～ acute disease. 不治之～ incurable disease. 对～下药 treat a sick person on the basis of a correct diagnosis
see also zhēng
症候 zhènghou （名） symptom
症状 zhèngzhuàng （名）symptom

证 zhèng I（动） prove; demonstrate: ～实 confirm; verify; bear testimony to; bear witness to II（名）evidence; certificate: 出生～ birth certificate. 身份～ identity card. 许可～ permit
证词 zhèngcí （名）testimony
证件 zhèngjiàn （名） credentials; certificate; papers
证据(據) zhèngjù （名）evidence; proof; testimony: ～确凿. The evidence is conclusive.

证明 zhèngmíng I (动) prove; testify; bear out II (名) certificate; identification; testimonial: 医生～ medical certificate
证券 zhèngquàn (名) negotiable securities: ～交易所 stock exchange
证书(書) zhèngshū (名) certificate; credentials: 毕业～ diploma. 结婚～ marriage certificate
证章 zhèngzhāng (名) badge
政 zhèng (名) 1 politics; political affairs: ～党 political party. ～策 policy. ～变 coup d'état. 2 certain administrative aspects of government: 民～ civil administration
政法 zhèngfǎ (名) politics and law
政府 zhèngfǔ (名) government
政见(見) zhèngjiàn (名) political views
政界 zhèngjiè (名) political circles; government circles
政客 zhèngkè (名) politician
政论(論) zhènglùn (名) political criticism: ～文 political essay
政权(權) zhèngquán (名) political power
政体(體) zhèngtǐ (名) form (or system) of government
政委 zhèngwěi (名) political commissar
政务(務) zhèngwù (名) government affairs
政治局 zhèngzhìjú (名) the Political Bureau
挣(掙) zhèng (动) 1 struggle to get free: ～脱枷锁 shake off the shackles (or fetters) 2 earn; make: ～钱 earn a living; make money. ～100块钱 earn (or make) a hundred *yuan*
see also zhēng
汁 zhī (名) juice: 桔子～ orange juice
之 zhī I (代) [used only as object]: 求～不得的好机会 a welcome opportunity. 无不为～高兴. Everybody feels excited about it. II [used to connect the modifier and the word modified]: 千岛～国 country of a thousand islands. 无价～宝 a priceless treasure. 缓兵～计 stalling tactics III [without actual reference]: 久而久～ with the passage of time
之后(後) zhīhòu (介、副) after; afterwards; later: 天黑～他们才能回来. They'll be back only after dark. 我们吵了一架,那～,我俩再没说过话. We had a quarrel and since then we have not spoken to each other.
之乎者也 zhī-hū-zhě-yě pedantic terms; archaisms
之前 zhīqián (介、副) ago; before; prior to: 五一～我不能走. I can't leave before May Day. 动身～ prior to one's departure
芝 zhī
芝麻 zhīma (名) sesame; sesame seed: ～酱 sesame paste. ～油 sesame oil
支 zhī I (动) 1 prop up; support: 把帐篷～起来 put up a tent 2 sustain; bear: 体力不～ too tired to go on doing sth.; too weak physically to stand it. 吃这么一点怎么～得了一天? How can such a light meal sustain us through the day? 她疼得真有点～不住. She could hardly bear the pain any more. 3 send away; order about: 把她～开! Put her off (or send her away) with some excuses! 你自己作吧,别总是～别人. Do it yourself. Don't always order people about! 4 pay out (or withdraw) money: ～款 pay out or withdraw cash. 收～ income and expenses; revenue and expenditure II (名) branch: ～局 branch bureau. ～店 branch store III (量) [for stick-like things; songs; watt; textile count; army units, etc.]: 五～蜡烛 five candles. 三～铅笔 three pencils. 一～歌 a song. 60～光的灯泡 a 60 watt bulb. 60～纱 60-count yarn. 两～队伍 two (army) units
支部 zhībù (名) branch (of a party)
支撑 zhīcheng (动) prop up; shore up; sustain: 力图～一个摇摇欲坠的政权 try to shore up a tottering regime
支持 zhīchí I (动) support; back; espouse: ～他们的正义斗争 support their just struggles. 我们～这种理论. We espouse this theory. II (名) support; backing: 这项建议赢得广大群众的～. This proposal enjoys the support of the popular masses.
支出 zhīchū I (动) pay; expend; disburse II (名) expenses; expenditure; outlay
支点(點) zhīdiǎn (名) fulcrum
支付 zhīfù (动) pay; defray:

～手段 means of payment

支架 zhījià (名) support; stand; trestle

支解 zhījiě (名) dismemberment

支离(離)破碎 zhīlí-pòsuì torn to pieces; shattered

支流 zhīliú (名) **1** tributary **2** minor aspects; minor current

支配 zhīpèi (动) **1** allocate; arrange: 合理地～时间 arrange one's time properly. ～劳动力 allocate the work force **2** control; determine: 思想～行动. Thinking determines action.

支票 zhīpiào (名) cheque; check: 旅行～ traveller's cheque

支使 zhīshi (动) order about: ～人 order people about. 把他～走 give sb. to understand that his presence is no longer desirable; send sb. away with an excuse

支吾 zhīwu (动) equivocate; hum and haw: ～其词 speak equivocally. 一味～ be evasive throughout

支援 zhīyuán (动、名) support; aid

支柱 zhīzhù (名) pillar; prop; mainstay

枝 zhī I (名) branch; twig: 树～ branches of a tree II (量) [for stick-like things]: 一～步枪 a rifle. 一～樱花 a spray of cherry blossoms

枝节(節) zhījié (名) **1** side issue; minor aspect **2** unexpected complications: 横生～ deliberately complicate an issue

肢 zhī (名) limb: 四～ the four limbs (of the human body)

肢解 zhījiě (动) dismember

肢体(體) zhītǐ (名) limbs

只(隻) zhī (量) **1** [for one of a pair]: 一～手 one hand. 两～耳朵 two ears. 一～鞋 one shoe **2** [for certain animals, boats or containers]: 一～鸡 one chicken. 两～羊 two sheep. 一～小船 a small boat 两～箱子 two suitcases see also zhǐ

只身 zhīshēn (副) alone; by oneself: ～在外 be alone and far away from home; all by oneself

只言片语 zhīyán-piànyǔ (名) a few isolated words and phrases

织(織) zhī (动) weave; knit: 纺～ spinning and weaving; textile. ～毛衣 knit a sweater. 钩～ crochet

织布 zhībù (动) weaving cotton cloth

织锦 zhījǐn (名) brocade; picture-weaving in silk

知 zhī I (动) **1** know; be aware of: 这话不～是谁说的. I don't know who said this. **2** inform; notify; tell: 通～ notify II (名) knowledge: 求～欲 thirst for knowledge

知彼知己 zhī bǐ zhī jǐ know the enemy and know yourself

知道 zhīdao (动) know; be aware of; realize: 我不～这件事. I know nothing about it. 你的意思我～. I know what you mean. 那时我不～事情会有这么严重. I didn't realize that things could be so serious.

知己 zhījǐ (名) a person for whom one has profound friendship built on mutual understanding

知觉(覺) zhījué (名) **1** consciousness: 失去～ lose consciousness; go into a coma **2** perception

知名 zhīmíng (形) well-known; famous: ～人士 well-known personage; public figure; celebrity

知情 zhīqíng (动) know the inside story; have inside information: ～人 insider; a person who knows the details of a criminal activity

知趣 zhīqù (动) know how to behave in a delicate situation in order to please or not to offend

知人之明 zhī rén zhī míng unusual ability to appreciate a person's native intelligence and moral character

知识(識) zhīshi (名) knowledge: ～渊博 have profound and encyclopedic knowledge; be learned. 技术～ technical know-how. ～投资 intellectual investment. ～分子 intellectual. ～界 intellectual circles; the intelligentsia

知晓(曉) zhīxiǎo (动) know; understand

知心 zhīxīn (形) intimate; understanding: ～朋友 bosom friend. ～话 true words from the heart

知音 zhīyīn (名) a person who is deeply appreciative of sb.'s talents

知足 zhīzú (动) be content with one's lot

蜘 zhī

蜘蛛 zhīzhū (名) spider: ～网 cobweb

指 zhī see also zhí; zhǐ

指甲 zhījia (名) nail: 手～ fingernail. ～刀 nail clippers. ～油 nail polish

脂 zhī (名) 1 fat; grease: 油～ fat 2 rouge: 胭～ rouge

脂肪 zhīfáng (名) fat: 动物～ animal fat

脂粉 zhīfěn (名) cosmetics

职(職) zhí (名) 1 duty; job: 尽～ fulfil one's duty. 辞～ resign. 免～ be relieved of one's post 2 post; office: 撤～ be removed (or dismissed) from office. 就～ assume office

职称(稱) zhíchēng (名) professional title

职工 zhígōng (名) workers and staff members

职能 zhínéng (名) function

职权(權) zhíquán (名) authority of office: 行使～ exercise one's functions and powers. 越超～ overstep one's authority

职务(務) zhíwù (名) post; duty

职业(業) zhíyè (名) occupation: ～运动员 professional sportsman. ～外交官 career diplomat. ～学校 vocational school

职员 zhíyuán (名) office worker; staff member

职责 zhízé (名) duty; responsibility; obligation

直 zhí I (形) 1 straight: ～线 straight line 2 straightforward: 有话～说 speak out what you have to say. 心～口快 frank and outspoken 3 vertical 4 just; upright: 正～ upright. 是非曲～ rights and wrongs II (动) straighten: ～起腰来 straighten one's back III (副) 1 direct; straight: 一～走 go straight ahead. ～飞北京 fly nonstop to Beijing 2 continuously: 他～按汽车喇叭. He kept honking the horn. 我～到半夜才睡觉. I didn't go to bed until mid-night.

直肠(腸) zhícháng (名) rectum

直达(達) zhídá (形) through; nonstop: ～上海的火车 a through train to Shanghai

直到 zhídào (介) until; up to: ～现在 up to now. ～上星期我才收到她的信. I didn't hear from her until last week.

直观(觀) zhíguān (名) direct perception (through the senses); audio-visual: ～教具 audio-visual aids

直角 zhíjiǎo (名) right angle

直接 zhíjiē (形) direct; immediate: ～联系 direct contact. ～去檀香山 go straight to Honolulu. ～宾语 direct object

直截了当(當) zhíjié-liǎodàng (形) straightforward; come straight to the point

直径(徑) zhíjìng (名) diameter

直觉(覺) zhíjué (名) intuition

直升飞(飛)机(機) zhíshēng fēijī (名) helicopter

直属(屬) zhíshǔ (动) be directly under: ～外交部 be directly affiliated to the Foreign Ministry

直率 zhíshuài (形) frank; candid

直爽 zhíshuǎng (形) forthright

直挺挺 zhítǐngtǐng (形) straight and stiff

直系亲(親)属(屬) zhíxì qīnshǔ (名) next of kin; close relative; immediate dependent

直辖 zhíxiá (动) be directly under the jurisdiction of the central government

直线(綫) zhíxiàn (名) straight line: 产量～上升. The output has shot up.

直心眼儿 zhíxīnyǎnr (形) <口> open; frank

直性子 zhíxìngzi (名) straightforward person

直言 zhíyán (动) speak bluntly: ～不讳 call a spade a spade

直译(譯) zhíyì (动、名) literal translation

植 zhí (动) plant; grow: 移～ transplant

植被 zhíbèi (名) vegetation

植树 zhíshù (动) plant trees: ～造林 afforestation

植物 zhíwù (名) plant; flora: ～检疫 plant quarantine. ～学 botany. ～园 botanical garden. ～油 vegetable oil

殖 zhí (动) breed: 生～ breed; reproduce. 繁～ reproduce; multiply

殖民 zhímín (动) colonize: 非～化 decolonize

殖民地 zhímíndì (名) colony

殖民主义(義) zhímínzhǔyì (名) colonialism: ～者 colonialist

值 zhí I (名) value: 价～ cost; value. 币～ currency value II (动) 1 be worth: 这车不～5000美元. This car is not worth 5000 dollars. 不～一提 not worth mentioning 2 happen to: 我们到时适～雨季. We happened to arrive there in the rainy season. 3 be on duty: ～夜 be on the night shift

值班 zhíbān (动) be on duty

值得 zhíde (动) **1** be worth the money **2** be of value: 不～ not worthwhile. 这些事～牢记. These facts are worth bearing in mind.

值钱(錢) zhíqián (形) costly; valuable

值勤 zhíqín (动) (of armymen, policemen, etc.) be on duty

值日 zhírì (动) (of school children) be on duty for the day

执(執) zhí (动) **1** hold; grasp: ～笔 do the writing **2** take charge of; manage **3** persist: 各～一词. Different people tell different stories. *or* Different people hold different views.

执法 zhífǎ (动) enforce the law

执迷不悟 zhí mí bù wù (动) persist in pursuing a wrong course; refuse to mend one's ways

执拗 zhíniù (形) stubborn; wilful

执行 zhíxíng (动) carry out; execute; implement: ～命令 carry out an order. ～政策 implement a policy. ～机构 executive body

执意 zhíyì (动) insist on: ～不肯 obstinately refuse

执照 zhízhào (名) license; permit: 驾驶～ driver's license

执政 zhízhèng (动) be in power; be in office: ～党 the party in power; the ruling party

指 zhí
see also shǐ; zhǐ

指头(頭) zhítou (名) finger; toe

侄 zhí (名) nephew (brother's son)

侄女 zhínü (名) niece

侄子 zhízi (名) nephew

止 zhǐ I (动) stop: 中～ stop halfway; suspend. ～血 stop bleeding. ～渴 quench one's thirst II (介) to; till: 到目前为～ to date; up to now III (副) only: 不～一次,而是多次 not just once, but many times

止步 zhǐbù (动) halt; stop: ～不前 stand still; mark time. 请～ out of bounds

止境 zhǐjìng (名) limit; boundary: 学无～. Learning is without limit.

止痛 zhǐtòng (动) relieve (or stop) pain: ～片 pain-killer

址 zhǐ (名) location; site: 校～ the location of the school. 地～ address

趾 zhǐ (名) toe

趾高气(氣)扬(揚) zhǐgāo-qìyáng (形) arrogant; haughty

趾甲 zhǐjiǎ (名) toenail

只 zhǐ (副) only; merely: 屋里～有我一个人. I was alone in the room.
see also zhī

只不过(過) zhǐbùguò (副) only; just; merely: 我～是开个玩笑. I was only joking.

只得 zhǐdé (动) have to; be obliged to

只顾(顧) zhǐgù (动) be absorbed in: 你俩～说话,连我们到这儿干什么都忘了. The two of you are talking non-stop, even forgetting what we are here for.

只管 zhǐguǎn (副) by all means: 你有话～说吧! Feel free to say what you will.

只好 zhǐhǎo (动) have to: 时间到了,这个问题～下次再谈. Time is up. We'll have to discuss it again next time.

只是 zhǐshì I (副) **1** merely; only; just: 没什么,我～有点好奇而已. Oh, nothing particular. I was being a little curious. **2** simply: 他～摇头,不回答. He simply shook his head and refused to say a thing. II (连) but; however: 这件大衣样式很好,～颜色太鲜了一点. This coat is very stylish, only the colour is a little too bright.

只要 zhǐyào (连) so long as; provided: ～记住这点,就不会出问题. As long as you remember this, there will be no problem.

只有 zhǐyǒu (连) only; alone: ～你亲自跟他说,他才会同意去. He won't agree to go unless you talk to him personally.

纸 zhǐ (名) paper: 一张白～ a blank sheet of paper

纸板 zhǐbǎn (名) cardboard

纸币(幣) zhǐbì (名) paper money; note

纸浆 zhǐjiāng (名) paper pulp; pulp

纸牌 zhǐpái (名) playing cards

纸上谈兵 zhǐshàng tán bīng be an armchair strategist; talk glibly about generalities without getting down to specific problems

纸烟 zhǐyān (名) cigarette

纸张(張) zhǐzhāng (名) paper

纸醉金迷 zhǐzuì-jīnmí a life of luxury and dissipation

旨 zhǐ (名) purport; purpose: 要～ main idea; gist. 宗～ purpose; aim. 会议通过了一系列～在进一步加强两国科学技术合作的决议. The meeting adopted a series of resolutions aimed at further strengthening the co-operation between our two countries in the field of science and technology.

旨意 zhǐyì (名) decree; order

指 zhǐ I (名) finger: 屈～可数 can be counted on one's fingers: 首屈一～的当代作家 a modern writer of the first water II (动) 1 point at; point to: 他～着远处的一座村落. He pointed to a distant village. 2 direct; point out: ～出缺点 point out the shortcomings 3 depend on; count on: 单～望一个人是不能把事情做好的. You can't just count upon one single person to get the work done properly.

see also zhī; zhí

指标(標) zhǐbiāo (名) target; quota; norm: 生产～ production target. 质量～ quality index

指导(導) zhǐdǎo (动) guide; direct: ～思想 guiding principle. ～性计划 guidance planning

指点(點) zhǐdiǎn (动) instruct; give directions (or advice)

指定 zhǐdìng (动) appoint; assign; name: 到～的地方集合 assemble at the appointed meeting place

指挥 zhǐhuī I (动) command; direct; conduct: ～部队 command the armed forces. ～作战 direct operations. ～乐队 conduct an orchestra. ～所 command post II (名) commander; director; conductor

指挥部 zhǐhuībù (名) headquarters

指教 zhǐjiào (动) give advice: 望不吝～. Feel free to give your suggestions.

指控 zhǐkòng (动) accuse (sb. of); charge (sb. with)

指令 zhǐlìng (名) order; instruction: ～性计划 mandatory planning

指名 zhǐmíng (动) mention by name: 我不愿～道姓. I don't want to name names. ～攻击 attack sb. by name

指明 zhǐmíng (动) point out; show clearly: ～事情的严重性 point out the serious nature of the matter

指南 zhǐnán (名) guide; guidebook

指南针 zhǐnánzhēn (名) compass

指派 zhǐpài (动) appoint; designate

指日可待 zhǐ rì kě dài can soon be expected: 计划的完成～. The completion of the project is soon to be expected.

指桑骂槐 zhǐ sāng mà huái make innuendoes

指使 zhǐshǐ (动) incite; instigate: 受人～ act on sb.'s instigation

指示 zhǐshì I (动) 1 indicate; point out: ～剂 indicator. ～灯 pilot lamp 2 instruct; order II (名) order; instruction

指示器 zhǐshìqì (名) indicator

指手划(劃)脚 zhǐshǒu-huàjiǎo talk excitedly with wild gestures; make unwarranted remarks

指数(數) zhǐshù (名) index number; index

指望 zhǐwang I (动) look forward to; count on; expect: ～今年有好收成. We expect a good harvest this year. II (名) hope: 他的事还有～吗? Is there still hope of his eventual success?

指纹 zhǐwén (名) fingerprint

指引 zhǐyǐn (动) guide

指责 zhǐzé (动) censure; criticize: 横加～ make savage criticisms. 她的行为是无可～的. Her conduct is above reproach.

指摘 zhǐzhāi (动) nitpick

指战(戰)员 zhǐzhànyuán (名) officers and men

指针 zhǐzhēn (名) 1 (needle) indicator; pointer 2 guiding principle; guide-line

指正 zhǐzhèng (动) correct; make a comment or criticism: 有不对的地方请大家～. Don't hesitate to criticize us for our inadequacies and errors.

滞(滯) zhì (形) stagnant; sluggish

滞留 zhìliú (动) be detained; be held up

滞销 zhìxiāo (动) not readily marketable: 这种货物～. There is little market for such goods.

治 zhì (动) 1 rule; govern 2 harness; control: ～水 harness a river. ～沙 control sand 3 treat; cure: ～病 treat an illness 4 punish: 大家决定～～他. We've decided to teach him a lesson.

治安 zhì'ān (名) public order or security: 维持～ maintain

law and order

治病救人 zhìbìng-jiùrén cure the sickness to save the patient; criticize a person in order to help him

治理 zhìlǐ (动) 1 administer; govern: ～国家 run a state 2 (of nature) harness; bring under control

治疗(療) zhìliáo (名) medical treatment

治丧(喪) zhìsāng (动) make funeral arrangements: ～委员会 funeral committee

治学(學) zhìxué (动) pursue scholarly work: ～严谨 rigorous scholarship

治罪 zhìzuì (动) punish sb. (for a crime)

志 zhì (名) 1 will; aspiration: 雄心壮～ have lofty aspirations. 胸怀大～ cherish noble ambitions. 立～ dedicate oneself to a cause 2 records; annals: 县～ annals of a county 3 mark; sign: 标～ mark

志哀 zhì'āi (动) show signs of mourning: 下半旗～ fly a flag at half-mast as a sign of mourning

志大才疏 zhì dà cái shū have high aspirations but little ability: 他这个人是～. He is a person of mediocre calibre, who cherishes a lofty ambition.

志气(氣) zhìqi (名) aspiration; ambition

志士 zhìshì (名) person of ideals and integrity

志同道合 zhìtóng-dàohé have a common goal

志向 zhìxiàng (名) ideal; ambition: ～远大 have high aspirations

志愿 zhìyuàn I (名) ideal; wish II (动) volunteer: 他～献血,虽然他身体还弱. He volunteers to donate his blood although he is far from strong physically.

痣 zhì (名) mole

痔 zhì (名) haemorrhoids; piles

峙 zhì (动) stand erect; tower: 对～局面 confrontation

至 zhì I (介) to; until: 自始～终 from beginning to end. 会议开～下午五点钟. The meeting lasted until five o'clock in the afternoon. II (副) extremely; most: 欢迎之～ most welcome. ～感 (I am) deeply grateful

至诚 zhìchéng (形) sincere: ～的朋友 a sincere friend

至迟(遲) zhìchí (副) at (the) latest: 我～星期天回家. I'll be home on Sunday at the latest.

至高无(無)上 zhìgāo-wúshàng (形) supreme

至交 zhìjiāo (名) best friend: 多年～ a very good friend of long standing

至今 zhìjīn (副) so far; up to now; to date

至亲(親) zhìqīn (名) next of kin; closest relative; very close relative: ～好友 very close relatives and friends

至上 zhìshàng (形) supreme; the highest

至少 zhìshǎo (副) at (the) least: ～你应该给我来个电话. You should at least give me a call. ～可以说,他将加快改革的步伐. He will speed up the reform, to say the least.

至于 zhìyú I (连) as for; as to: ～具体时间,现在还没决定. As for the exact time, we have made no decision yet. II(动) go so far as to: 她不～对她母亲这样吧? She wouldn't go so far as to treat her mother like this, would she?

窒 zhì

窒息 zhìxī (动) stifle; suffocate: 屋里的空气令人～. It's very close in here. 浓烟几乎使他～. He was very nearly suffocated by the smoke.

桎 zhì

桎梏 zhìcù (名) fetters and handcuffs; shackles

致 zhì I (动) 1 send; extend (respects, greetings, etc.): ～以热烈的祝贺 extend warm congratulations. ～电 send a telegram; cable 2 result in; incur: 招～不满 incur sb.'s dislike 3 concentrate: ～力于 concentrate on; be devoted to II (连) so ... that: 措词晦涩,～使人误解本意. The wording is so ambiguous that it leads to misinterpretations. III (名) interest: 故事曲折有～. The plot is intricate and full of interest.

致词 zhìcí (动) make (or deliver) a speech

致敬 zhìjìng (动) salute: 鸣礼炮二十一响～ fire a 21-gun salute

致力 zhìlì (动) be devoted to

致命 zhìmìng (形) fatal: ～的弱点 fatal weakness; Achilles' heel

致谢 zhìxiè (动) extend thanks to

致意 zhìyì (动) give one's regards to; extend greetings to

致(緻)

zhì (形) precise; meticulous; refined

掷(擲)

zhì (动) throw; cast: ～标枪 javelin throw. 孤注一～ risk everything on a single throw; put all one's eggs in one basket

挚(摯)

zhì (形) sincere; earnest: 诚～ sincere. 真～的友谊 true friendship

挚友 zhìyǒu (名) close friend

帜(幟)

zhì (名) flag; banner

置

zhì (动) 1 place; put: 安～ find a place for; help sb. to settle down. 搁～ put aside; shelve. 漠然～之 be indifferent to the matter 2 buy; equip: 添～衣服 buy some clothes. ～家具 buy some furniture 3 set up: 装～ fix; install. 设～ establish; set up

置办(辦) zhìbàn (动) buy; purchase

置若罔闻 zhì ruò wǎng wén turn a deaf ear to; pay no heed to: 对我的忠言,他都～. All my words of advice fell on deaf ears.

置身 zhìshēn (动) place oneself; stay: ～事外 stay aloof; refuse to get involved in the matter

置信 zhìxìn (动) believe: 难以～ hard to believe

置疑 zhìyí (动) doubt: 不容～ allow of no doubt; undoubtedly

置之不理 zhì zhī bù lǐ (动) ignore; pay no attention to

置之度外 zhì zhī dù wài (动) give no thought to: 把个人利害得失～ leave out of account personal gain or loss. 把个人安危～ regardless of personal danger

制

zhì I (动) 1 make; manufacture: 机～ machine-made. 仿～ imitate; copy. 复～品 reproduction 2 control; restrict: 控～ control. 限～ restrict II (名) system: 公～ the metric system. 私有～ private ownership

制版 zhìbǎn (名) plate making

制裁 zhìcái (动) sanction; punish: 实行～ impose sanctions (upon). 受法律～ be punished by law

制订 zhìdìng (动) formulate; work out

制定 zhìdìng (动) lay down; formulate: ～宪法 draw up a constitution. ～法律 make laws. ～政策 formulate a policy. ～计划 work out a plan

制动(動) zhìdòng (动) apply the brake: ～器 brake

制度 zhìdù (名) system; institution: 社会～ social system. 规章～ rules and regulations

制服 zhìfú (名) uniform

制高点(點) zhìgāodiǎn (名) commanding height

制革 zhìgé (动) process hides; tan: ～厂 tannery

制冷 zhìlěng (动) freeze (in order to preserve)

制品 zhìpǐn (名) products; goods: 奶～ dairy products

制胜(勝) zhìshèng (动) get the upper hand of: ～敌人 subdue the enemy

制图(圖) zhìtú (动) make maps; chart: ～学 cartography

制药(藥) zhìyào (名) pharmacy: ～学 pharmaceutics

制约 zhìyuē (动) restrict; restrain: 互相～ condition each other; interact

制造 zhìzào (动) 1 make; manufacture: 中国～ made in China. 手工～ hand-made 2 create; fabricate: ～紧张局势 create tension. ～谣言 spread rumours

制止 zhìzhǐ (动) check; stop; curb: ～通货膨胀 halt inflation. ～这类事件再次发生 prevent the occurrence of similar incidents

制作 zhìzuò (动) make; manufacture: 精心～ made with meticulous care

秩

zhì (名) order

秩序 zhìxù (名) order; sequence: 维持社会～ maintain social order. ～井然 in good order

智

zhì (名) wisdom; intelligence; wit: 足～多谋 wise and resourceful 斗～ battle of wits

智慧 zhìhuì (名) wisdom: 集体～ collective wisdom

智力 zhìlì (名) intelligence; intellect: ～测验 intelligence test. ～开发 tap intellectual resources

智谋 zhìmóu (名) wit; resourcefulness: 人们十分钦佩他的～. People greatly admire him for his resourcefulness.

智囊 zhìnáng (名) brain trust
智取 zhìqǔ (动) take (a fort, town. etc.) by strategy
智育 zhìyù (名) intellectual development
智者千虑(慮)，必有一失 zhìzhě qiān lǜ, bì yǒu yī shī even the wise are not always free from error; nobody is infallible

稚 zhì (形) young; childish: 幼～ childish

质(質) zhì I (名) 1 nature; character: 性～ nature; character. 本～ innate character; essence 2 quality: 优～产品 high-quality goods 3 matter; substance: 银～奖杯 silver cup. 流～食物 liquid food II (动) question: ～疑 call in question
质变(變) zhìbiàn (名) qualitative change
质地 zhìdì (名) texture; grain
质量 zhìliàng (名) 1 quality 2 mass
质朴(樸) zhìpǔ (形) simple; unaffected
质问 zhìwèn (动) question; interrogate
质疑 zhìyí (动) call in question; query
质子 zhìzǐ (名) proton

炙 zhì 1 broil; roast 2 <书> roast meat
炙手可热(熱) zhì shǒu kě rè very powerful and exceedingly arrogant

中 zhōng (名) 1 centre; middle: 居～ in the centre 2 in; among: 园～ in the garden. 家～ at home. 学生～ among the students 3 between two extremes: ～年 middle-aged; middle-aging. ～秋 mid-autumn. ～产阶级 middle class 4 medium: ～号 medium size. ～级 intermediate level 5 China: 洋为～用 make foreign things serve China see also zhòng
中波 zhōngbō (名) medium wave
中不溜(溜)儿 zhōngbùliūr (形)<口> mediocre; middling
中部 zhōngbù (名) middle part
中餐 zhōngcān (名) Chinese food
中草药(藥) zhōngcǎoyào (名) Chinese herbal medicine
中层(層) zhōngcéng (名) middle-level
中程 zhōngchéng (名) (of aircraft; missile, etc.) intermediate range
中等 zhōngděng (形) average; moderate
中断(斷) zhōngduàn (动) suspend; break off; discontinue
中队(隊) zhōngduì (名) squadron
中饭 zhōngfàn (名) lunch
中共 Zhōng Gòng <简>(中国共产党) the Communist Party of China (CPC)
中古 zhōnggǔ (名) the middle ancient times; medieval times
中国(國)共产(產)党(黨) Zhōngguó Gòngchǎndǎng (名) the Communist Party of China; the Chinese Communist Party
中国(國)共产(產)主义青年团(團) Zhōngguó Gòngchǎnzhǔyì Qīngniántuán (名) the Communist Youth League of China
中国(國)科学(學)院 Zhōngguó Kēxuéyuàn (名) the Chinese Academy of Sciences
中国(國)人民解放军 Zhōngguó Rénmín Jiěfàngjūn (名) the Chinese People's Liberation Army
中国(國)人民政治协(協)商会(會)议(議) Zhōngguó Rénmín Zhèngzhì Xiéshāng Huìyì (名) the Chinese People's Political Consultative Conference
中国(國)社会(會)科学(學)院 Zhōngguó Shèhuì Kēxuéyuàn (名) the Chinese Academy of Social Sciences
中华(華) Zhōnghuá (名) China: 振兴～ rejuvenate (or revitalize) China
中级 zhōngjí (名) middle level; intermediate
中坚(堅) zhōngjiān (名) nucleus; backbone: ～力量 backbone force
中间 zhōngjiān (介) 1 among; between: 我们～他最年轻. He is the youngest among us. 2 centre; middle
中立 zhōnglì (形) neutral: ～国 neutral state
中流砥柱 zhōngliú dǐzhù (名) mainstay
中篇小说 zhōngpiān xiǎoshuō (名) novelette
中人 zhōngrén (名) middleman; go-between
中山装(裝) zhōngshānzhuāng (名) Chinese tunic suit
中世纪 zhōngshìjì (名) Middle Ages; Medieval Age
中式 zhōngshì (名) Chinese style
中枢(樞) zhōngshū (名) centre: 神经～ nerve centre
中途 zhōngtú (名) halfway; mid-

way: ～在东京停留两小时 stop over in Tokyo for two hours
中文 zhōngwén (名) the Chinese language
中午 zhōngwǔ (名) noon; midday
中心 zhōngxīn (名) centre; heart: 研究～ research centre. 问题的～ the heart of the matter
中性 zhōngxìng (形) neutral
中学(學) zhōngxué (名) middle (high) school
中旬 zhōngxún (名) the middle ten days of a month
中央 zhōngyāng (名) 1 centre; middle: ～政府 the central government
中央集权(權) zhōngyāng jíquán (名) centralization (of authority)
中药(藥) zhōngyào (名) traditional Chinese medicine
中叶(葉) zhōngyè (名) middle period: 十九世纪～ mid-19th century
中医(醫) zhōngyī (名) traditional Chinese medical science
中庸 zhōngyōng (名)〈哲〉the golden mean (of the Confucian school)
中用 zhōngyòng (动) be of use: 不～ be of no use; good for nothing
中游 zhōngyóu (名) 1 middle reaches (of a river) 2 the state of being mediocre
中止 zhōngzhǐ (动) discontinue; suspend: ～学习 discontinue one's studies
中专(專) zhōngzhuān (名) polytechnic school
中子 zhōngzǐ (名) neutron
衷 zhōng (名) inner feelings; heart: 无动于～ not be moved in the least. 言不由～ speak insincerely. ～心拥护 give whole-hearted support to
忠 zhōng (形) loyal; devoted
忠臣 zhōngchén (名) loyal court official
忠诚 zhōngchéng (形) loyal; faithful
忠告 zhōnggào (名) sincere advice; exhortation
忠厚 zhōnghòu (形) honest and sincere
忠实(實) zhōngshí (形) faithful; reliable
忠心 zhōngxīn (名) loyalty; devotion: 赤胆～ ardent loyalty. ～耿耿 faithful and devoted. 为教育事业～耿耿 be committed to the teaching profession
忠言逆耳 zhōngyán nì ěr good advice is not always pleasing to the ear
忠于 zhōngyú (动) be true to; be loyal to: ～祖国 be loyal to one's country
忠贞 zhōngzhēn (形) loyal and steadfast: ～不渝 be unswervingly loyal; loyal and unyielding
钟(鐘,锺) zhōng (名) 1 bell 2 clock: 闹～ alarm clock 3 time as measured in hours and minutes: 几点～啦? What time is it? 三点～ three o'clock. 一分～ one minute
钟爱 zhōng'ài (动) love dearly; cherish
钟摆(擺) zhōngbǎi (名) pendulum
钟表(錶) zhōngbiǎo (名) clocks and watches; timepiece
钟点(點) zhōngdiǎn (名) time; hour
钟情 zhōngqíng (动) be deeply in love: 一见～ fall in love at first sight
钟头(頭) zhōngtóu (名) hour
终 zhōng I (名) 1 end; finish: 年～ end of the year. 自始至～ from beginning to end 2 death; end: 临～ on one's deathbed; when one is dying II (副) eventually; in the end
终点(點) zhōngdiǎn (名) end point; destination
终端 zhōngduān (名) terminal
终归(歸) zhōngguī (副) eventually; in the end; after all: 这问题～会解决的. This problem will be solved in the end. 他～是你的亲戚. He is after all your relative.
终结 zhōngjié (动) come to an end
终究 zhōngjiū (副) after all; in the end
终年 zhōngnián I (副) throughout the year: ～努力工作 be hard-working all the year round II (名) the age at which one dies: 他～七十八岁. He died at the age of seventy-eight.
终身 zhōngshēn (副) all one's life: ～制 lifelong tenure
终生 zhōngshēng (副) one's lifetime: ～难忘的教训 will not forget the lesson to the end of one's days
终于 zhōngyú (副) at last; in the end; finally

终止 zhōngzhǐ (动) stop; put an end to; terminate

冢 zhǒng (名) tomb; grave: 古～ ancient tomb

种(種) zhǒng I (名) 1 seed; species: 稻～ rice seeds. 播～ sow seeds 2 breed; strain: 良～ fine breed. 杂～ cross-breed 3 species 4 race: 黄～人 the yellow race II (量) kind; type; sort: 这～行为 this kind of behaviour. 好几～颜色 different colours. 各～情况 various conditions
see also zhòng

种类(類) zhǒnglèi (名) category; pattern; type: 属于这一～ come under this category

种种 zhǒngzhǒng (形) all sorts of; a variety of: 由于～原因 for various reasons. 想尽～办法 try every means possible

种子 zhǒngzǐ (名) seed: ～选手 seeded player; seed

种族 zhǒngzú (名) race: ～平等 racial equality. ～隔离 racial segregation; apartheid. ～歧视 racial discrimination. ～主义者 racist

肿(腫) zhǒng (动) swell; be swollen

肿瘤 zhǒngliú (名) tumour: 良性～ benign tumour. 恶性～ malignant tumour; cancer

踵 zhǒng (名) heel: 接～而至 follow at one's heels

中 zhòng (动) 1 hit; fit exactly: 打～了 hit the target. 猜～ guess right 2 be hit by; fall into: 腿上～了一枪 be shot in the leg. ～埋伏 fall into an ambush. ～煤气 be gassed
see also zhōng

中毒 zhòngdú (动) be affected by a kind of poison or toxin: 食物～ food poisoning

中风(風) zhòngfēng (名) apoplexy

中计 zhòngjì (动) fall into a trap

中肯 zhòngkěn (形) (of remarks) sincere and pertinent

中伤(傷) zhòngshāng (动) slander; vilify: 恶语～ slander sb. viciously

中暑 zhòngshǔ (动) suffer sunstroke

中意 zhòngyì (动) be to one's liking

种(種) zhòng (动) grow; plant; cultivate: ～花(菜等)grow flowers (vegetables, etc.). ～树 plant trees
see also zhǒng

种地 zhòngdì (动) do farm work

种田 zhòngtián (动) do farm work

仲 zhòng (形) 1 in the middle: ～裁 arbitrate 2 second month in a season: ～夏 mid-summer

众(衆) zhòng I (形) many; numerous: 寡不敌～ be outnumbered II (名) crowd; multitude: 大～ the mass of the people; the masses. 观～ spectators; viewers; audience (watching a performance, TV show, etc.). 听～ audience

众多 zhòngduō (形) numerous

众口难(難)调 zhòng kǒu nán tiáo it is difficult to please everybody

众目睽睽 zhòng mù kuíkuí in the public eye

众叛亲(親)离(離) zhòngpàn-qīnlí be opposed by the public and deserted by one's followers; be utterly isolated

众矢之的 zhòng shǐ zhī dì target of a thousand arrows; object of angry public criticism

众说纷纭 zhòng shuō fēnyún opinions vary

众所周知 zhòng suǒ zhōu zhī as is known to all

众志成城 zhòng zhì chéng chéng united we stand; unity is strength; unity is the path to victory

重 zhòng I (形) 1 heavy; important; serious: 箱子很～. This box is very heavy. 你有多～? How much do you weigh? 事有轻～. We must draw a distinction between trivial and important matters. 2 serious: 伤势不～ not seriously injured or wounded. 案情很～ a very serious case II (名) weight: 净～ net weight. 举～ weight-lifting III (动) regard as important: 敬～ respect. 看～ value. 为人所～ be held in esteem
see also chóng

重兵 zhòngbīng (名) massive forces: ～把守 be heavily guarded

重大 zhòngdà (形) great; major; significant: ～原则问题 a problem of major principle. 意义～ be of great significance

重担(擔) zhòngdàn (名) heavy burden; heavy (or great) responsibility

重地 zhòngdì (名) a place of

importance which needs to be carefully guarded
重点(點) zhòngdiǎn (名) focal point; key; emphasis: ～大学 key university. ～工程 major project
重读(讀) zhòngdú (动) stress: ～音节 stressed syllable
重负 zhòngfù (名) heavy load (or burden): 如释～ feel as if relieved of a heavy load
重工业(業) zhònggōngyè (名) heavy industry
重活 zhònghuó (名) heavy work
重力 zhònglì (名) gravity
重量 zhòngliàng (名) weight
重任 zhòngrèn (名) important task; heavy responsibility: 肩负～ hold a position of great responsibility
重视 zhòngshì (动) attach importance to; pay attention to: ～教育 attach importance to education. ～某人 think highly of sb. ～这件事 take this matter seriously
重托 zhòngtuō (名) great trust: 不负～ prove worthy of the great trust reposed in one
重心 zhòngxīn (名) 1 core; focus 2 centre of gravity
重型 zhòngxíng (形) heavy-duty: ～卡车 heavy-duty truck
重要 zhòngyào (形) important; significant; major: ～人物 important figure; dignitary. ～关头 critical juncture. ～政策 major policy ～因素 key factor
重音 zhòngyīn (名) stress; accent: 词的～ word stress
重用 zhòngyòng (动) put sb. in a key position

州 zhōu (名) an administrative division (state, prefecture, etc.)

洲 zhōu (名) continent
洲际(際) zhōujì (形) intercontinental: ～导弹 intercontinental missile

舟 zhōu (名) boat: 轻～ a light boat. 泛～ go boating

周 zhōu I (名) 1 circumference; circuit: 圆～ circumference. 环行一～ make a circuit of. 地球绕太阳一～是一年. It takes the earth one year to move around the sun. 飞机在上空盘旋三～才降落. The plane circled around in the sky three times before landing. 2 week: 上～ last week. 三～ three weeks II (形) 1 all over; all around: 众所～知 as is known to all 2 thoughtful: 考虑不～ not be thoughtful enough
周波 zhōubō (名) cycle
周长 zhōucháng (名) circumference; perimeter
周到 zhōudào (形) thoughtful; considerate: 服务～ good service; The service is good. 他考虑问题十分～. He is very considerate.
周刊 zhōukān (名) weekly publication
周密 zhōumì (形) careful; well-conceived: ～的计划 a well thought-out plan
周末 zhōumò (名) weekend
周年 zhōunián (名) anniversary
周期 zhōuqī (名) period; cycle
周全 zhōuquán (形) thorough; comprehensive
周身 zhōushēn (名、副) all over the body
周岁(歲) zhōusuì (名) one full year of life: 今天孩子满～. Today is the child's first birthday.
周围(圍) zhōuwéi (副) around; round; about: 楼房～ around the building. ～环境 surroundings; environment. ～的居民 the neighbourhood
周详 zhōuxiáng (形) careful; complete
周旋 zhōuxuán (动) (of people) deal with
周游 zhōuyóu (动) travel round: ～世界 travel round the world
周折 zhōuzhé (名) twists and turns: 几经～ after many setbacks
周转(轉) zhōuzhuǎn I (名) (of funds) turnover: 现金～ cash flow. ～率 turnover rate II (动) have enough to meet the need: 经济～不开 not have the fund for the work

粥 zhōu (名) gruel; porridge

轴 zhóu (名) 1 axis; axle; shaft: 自行车～ bicycle axle 2 spool; rod: 线～儿 spool. 画～ roller for a scroll of Chinese painting
轴承 zhóuchéng (名) bearing: 滚珠～ ball bearing
轴心 zhóuxīn (名) axle centre; axis: ～国 Axis powers; the Axis

肘 zhǒu (名) elbow

帚 zhǒu (名) broom

咒 zhòu I (动) curse; damn: 诅～ curse bitterly II (名) incantation: 念～ chant incantations
咒骂 zhòumà I (动) curse; abuse; swear II (名) curse; abuse; invective: 粗野的～ savage invective
皱(皺) zhòu (名) wrinkle; crease: 上了年纪,脸上就会起～. When a person gets on in years, his face begins to wrinkle. 别把我的书弄～了. Take care not to crumple my book.
皱眉头(頭) zhòu méitóu (动) knit one's brows; frown
皱纹 zhòuwén (名) wrinkles; lines: 满额～ a furrowed brow. 鱼尾～ (at the corner of one's eyes) crow's-feet. ～纸 crepe paper; tissue paper
皱褶 zhòuzhě (名) (of clothing) fold
绉(縐) zhòu (名) (textile material) crape; crepe
昼(晝) zhòu (名) daytime
昼夜 zhòu-yè (名) day and night; round the clock
骤 zhòu (形) sudden; abrupt: 一阵～雨 a passing shower. 天气～变. The weather suddenly changed.
骤然 zhòurán (副) suddenly; abruptly: ～枪声四起. We heard a burst of gunfire from all around.
诸(諸) zhū (形) all; various
诸侯 zhūhóu (名) dukes or princes under an emperor
诸如 zhūrú (副) such as: ～此类 so on and so forth; etc.
诸位 zhūwèi (代)〈敬〉:～如果同意,我不反对. If you are agreeable among yourselves, I have no objection.
猪 zhū (名) pig; hog; swine: 小～ pigling; piglet. 母～ sow. 公～ boar
猪圈 zhūjuàn (名) pigsty; hogpen
猪肉 zhūròu (名) pork
猪食 zhūshí (名) pigwash; swill
猪油 zhūyóu (名) lard
猪鬃 zhūzōng (名) (hog) bristles
朱 zhū (形) vermilion
朱红 zhūhóng (形) vermilion; bright red
朱门(門) zhūmén (名) vermilion gates (red-lacquered gates of wealthy people's mansions in old China)
诛 zhū (动)〈书〉 put (a criminal) to death: 口～笔伐 denounce (a guilty person) both in writing and in speech
珠 zhū (名) bead; pearl: 珍～ pearl. 露～ dewdrops. 泪～儿 teardrop
珠宝(寶) zhūbǎo (名) pearls and jewels: ～商 jeweller
珠算 zhūsuàn (名) calculation with an abacus
株 zhū (量) [for plants and trees]: 四～桑树 four mulberry trees
株连 zhūlián (动) involve; implicate: 一人有罪, ～亲友. When a person is found guilty, he often gets his relatives and friends involved.
蛛 zhū (名) spider
蛛丝(絲)马(馬)迹 zhūsī-mǎjì (名) clues; traces (of a secret)
蛛网(網) zhūwǎng (名) spider web; cobweb
侏 zhū
侏儒 zhūrú (名) dwarf
烛(燭) zhú (名) candle: 蜡～ (wax) candle
烛光 zhúguāng (名) candle light
烛台 zhútái (名) candlestick
逐 zhú I (动) 1 pursue: 追～ pursue; chase 2 drive out; expel: ～出门外 drive out of the door II (副) one by one: ～月增加 increase month by month
逐步 zhúbù (副) step by step: ～加以解决 settle sth. step by step
逐渐 zhújiàn (副) gradually: 他～习惯这里的气候了. He's getting used to the climate here.
逐字逐句 zhú zì zhú jù word by word; verbatim
竹 zhú (名) bamboo: ～林 groves of bamboo
竹帛 zhúbó (名) bamboo slips and silk (used for writing on in ancient times)
竹竿 zhúgān (名) bamboo pole; bamboo
竹简 zhújiǎn bamboo slip (used for writing on during ancient times)
竹笋 zhúsǔn (名) bamboo shoots
主 zhǔ I (名) 1 owner; master: 一家之～ head of a family. 房～ landlord. 奴隶～ slave owner. 买～ buyer. 卖～ seller. 2 host: 宾～ host and guest 3

〈基督教〉God; Lord 4 freedom from doubt: 心里没～ feel uncertain about sth. II (形) principal; main: 预防为～ put prevention first III (动) 1 be in charge of: 谁在这里～事? Who's in charge here? 2 hold a definite view; advocate: ～和 advocate a peaceful solution

主办(辦) zhǔbàn (动) sponsor: 展览会由一家石油公司～. The exhibition was sponsored by an oil company.

主编 zhǔbiān (名) chief editor: 报纸的～ the editor-in-chief of a newspaper

主持 zhǔchí (动) 1 be in charge of; manage: ～日常工作 be in charge of the day-to-day work 2 preside over: ～会议 chair a conference. ～宴会 host a banquet 3 uphold: ～正义 uphold justice

主次 zhǔ-cì (名) primary and secondary: 分清～ distinguish between the primary and the secondary

主从(從) zhǔ-cóng (名) principal and subordinate

主导(導) zhǔdǎo (形) guiding; leading; dominant: 起～作用 play a leading role. ～原则 guiding principle

主动(動) zhǔdòng (名) initiative: 争取～ try to gain the initiative. 尽量发挥别人的～性. Give full play to other people's initiative.

主犯 zhǔfàn (名) prime culprit; principal criminal

主妇(婦) zhǔfù (名) housewife; hostess

主攻 zhǔgōng (名) main attack

主顾(顧) zhǔgù (名) customer; client

主观(觀) zhǔguān (形) subjective: ～愿望 wishful thinking. ～努力 subjective efforts

主管 zhǔguǎn (动) be in charge of; be responsible for

主见 zhǔjiàn (名) one's own judgment; definite view: 她很有～. She is her own mistress.

主教 zhǔjiào (名) bishop: 大～ archbishop. 红衣～ cardinal

主角 zhǔjué (名) leading role: 这部电影是她演～. She starred in this film.

主课 zhǔkè (名) main subject; major

主力 zhǔlì (名) main force

主流 zhǔliú (名) 1 main stream 2 essential aspect; main trend

主谋 zhǔmóu (名) chief instigator; chief plotter

主权(權) zhǔquán (名) sovereign rights; sovereignty: ～国 a sovereign state. 领土～ territorial sovereignty

主人 zhǔrén (名) 1 master; owner 2 host: 女～ hostess

主人公 zhǔréngōng (名) hero or heroine (in a literary work)

主人翁 zhǔrénwēng (名) master of one's own country

主任 zhǔrèn (名) director; head

主食 zhǔshí (名) staple food

主题 zhǔtí (名) theme; subject

主体(體) zhǔtǐ (名) main body; main part

主席 zhǔxí (名) chairman; chairperson: ～团 the presidium

主心骨 zhǔxīngǔ (名) backbone; pillar

主演 zhǔyǎn (名) leading role (in a play or film)

主要 zhǔyào (形) main; major; chief; principal: ～原因 chief cause. ～目的 main objective

主义(義) zhǔyì (名) doctrine; -ism: 唯物～ materialism. 唯心～ idealism

主意 zhǔyì (名) idea; plan; decision: 出～ give advice. 这个～不错. This is a very good idea.

主语 zhǔyǔ (名) subject

主宰 zhǔzǎi (动) dominate; dictate; control: ～世界 dominate the whole world. ～自己的命运 decide one's own destiny; be master of one's own fate

主张(張) zhǔzhāng I (动) hold; maintain; advocate: ～开放政策 advocate a policy of opening to the outside world II (名) view; stand; proposition: 我赞成你的～. I am for your proposal. 我们一贯的～ our consistent stand

主子 zhǔzi (名) boss

煮 zhǔ (动) boil; cook

属(屬) zhǔ (动)〈书〉1 join; combine: ～文 compose a piece of prose writing 2 concentrate one's mind: ～望 look forward to

see also shǔ

属意 zhǔyì (动)〈书〉have sb. in mind

嘱(囑) zhǔ (动) enjoin; advise; urge

嘱咐 zhǔfu (动) enjoin; exhort: 再三～ exhort again and again

嘱托 zhǔtuō (动) entrust (sb. to do sth.): 人家～她好好照顾这个孤儿. She was entrusted with the task of taking good care of the orphan.

瞩(矚) zhǔ (动) gaze; look steadily: 高瞻远～ show foresight; be a person of vision. ～目 fix one's eyes upon

贮(貯) zhù (动) store; keep; reserve

贮藏 zhùcáng (动) store up; lay in: ～过冬的大白菜 lay in cabbages for the winter. 矿产～丰富 be rich in mineral resources

贮存 zhùcún (动) store; stock

注 zhù (动) 1 pour: 大雨如～. The rain poured down. 2 concentrate: 全神贯～ concentrate on 3 annotate: 批～ make comments and annotations. 脚～ footnote 4 record; register

注册 zhùcè (动) register: ～处 registrar's office in a college

注定 zhùdìng (动) be doomed; be destined: ～灭亡 be doomed to destruction

注解 zhùjiě (动) I annotate; explain with notes II (名) explanatory note; annotation

注目 zhùmù (动) fix one's eyes on: 引人～ eye-catching

注射 zhùshè (动) inject: ～器 injector; syringe

注视 zhùshì (动) look attentively at; gaze at

注释(釋) zhùshì (名) explanatory notes; annotations

注销 zhùxiāo (动) (of a debt, etc.) write off; cancel

注意 zhùyì (动) pay attention to; take notice of: ～台阶! Mind the steps! 过街要～! Be careful while crossing the road!

注重 zhùzhòng (动) lay stress on; emphasize

柱 zhù (名) post; pillar; column

柱石 zhùshí (名) pillar; mainstay

蛀 zhù (动) (of moths etc.) eat into

蛀虫(蟲) zhùchóng (名) moth or any other insect that eats books, clothes or wood

住 zhù (动) 1 live; reside; stay: 我在南方～了三年. I lived in the South for three years. ～旅馆 stay at a hotel 2 stop; cease: 雨～了. The rain has stopped. 3 [used after some verbs as a complement indicating a halt or stillness]: 站～! Halt! 接～! Catch it! 忍受不～了 can no longer stand it. 记～ remember; bear in mind

住处(處) zhùchù (名) residence; lodging: 你～在什么地方? Where do you live?

住房 zhùfáng (名) housing; lodgings; accommodation: ～问题 housing problems

住户 zhùhù (名) household

住口 zhùkǒu (动) shut up

住手 zhùshǒu (动) stop (doing sth.); Hands off

住宿 zhùsù I (名) accommodation: 安排～ try to find accommodation for sb. II (动) stay for the night

住院 zhùyuàn (动) be hospitalized: 我母亲～了. My mother is in hospital now. ～病人 inpatient

住宅 zhùzhái (名) residence

住址 zhùzhǐ (名) address

驻(駐) zhù (动) stay; be stationed: 我国～英大使 our ambassador to Britain. ～京记者 resident correspondent in Beijing

驻地 zhùdì (名) place where troops, etc. are stationed: 边防军～ frontier guard station

驻防 zhùfáng (动) be on garrison duty

驻守 zhùshǒu (动) garrison; defend

驻扎 zhùzhā (动) (of troops) be stationed

祝 zhù (动) offer good wishes; greetings; compliments: ～你健康. I wish you good health. ～你一路顺风. Have a pleasant journey. *or* Bon voyage! ～你们成功! Good luck! Wish you success!

祝贺 zhùhè (动) congratulate: ～你们提前完成任务. We congratulate you on the fulfilment of the task ahead of schedule. 向您～! Congratulations!

祝捷(捷) zhùjié (动) celebrate a victory

祝酒 zhùjiǔ (动) drink a toast; toast: 致～辞 propose a toast

祝寿(壽) zhùshòu (动) congratulate (an elderly or old person) on his or her birthday: 庆祝他七十五岁寿辰. congratulate him on the seventy-fifth anniversary of his birthday

祝愿(願) zhùyuàn (动) wish: ～你健康长寿! Wish you good health and longevity!

著 zhù I (动) compose: ～书 be a writer II (形) marked; outstanding: 显～的成就 marked success

著称(稱) zhùchēng (形) be noted for: 波士顿以红叶～. Boston is noted for its maple leaves.
著名 zhùmíng (形) famous; well-known: 一个～的医生 a well-known doctor
著作 zhùzuò (名) works; writings

助 zhù (动) help; assist; aid: 互～ help each other. 帮～ help. ～我一把 give me a hand. ～人为乐 find it a pleasure to help others
助动(動)词 zhùdòngcí (名) auxiliary verb
助教 zhùjiào (名) (of a college faculty) assistant: ～职务 assistantship
助理 zhùlǐ (名) assistant: ～教授 assistant professor
助手 zhùshǒu (名) assistant; helper; aide
助听(聽)器 zhùtīngqì (名) hearing aid
助威 zhùwēi (动) cheer (for)
助兴(興) zhùxìng (动) add to the fun
助学(學)金 zhùxuéjīn (名) (student) grant
助长(長) zhùzhǎng (动) encourage: 这只能～他的骄气. This could only add to his arrogance.

筑(築) zhù (动) build: ～坝 build a dam. ～路 construct a road

铸(鑄) zhù (动) cast
铸工 zhùgōng (名) foundry work; founder
铸件 zhùjiàn (名) casting
铸造 zhùzào (动) cast

抓 zhuā (动) 1 seize; catch; grab; grasp: ～住手臂 grab sb. by the arm. ～住良机 seize a golden opportunity. ～住讲话的重点 grasp the main points of a speech 2 arrest: 他被～起来了. He was arrested. ～住一名正在作案的罪犯 catch a criminal red-handed 3 attract: 剧一开始就～住了观众. The play gripped the audience soon after it started. 4 take charge of: 他是～业务的副校长. He is a vice-president for academic affairs. 5 scratch: ～胳臂痒痒 scratch an arm
抓辫子 zhuā biànzi (动) take advantage of sb.'s minor fault to gain his own purpose
抓紧(緊) zhuājǐn (动) keep a firm grasp on: ～时间 make the best use of the time. 必须～治疗 (You) need an early and timely treatment. 要～基础理论的研究 pay close attention to the study of basic theories
抓阄(鬮)儿 zhuājiūr (动) draw lots
抓瞎 zhuāxiā (动) be in a rush and muddle
抓药(藥) zhuāyào (动) have a prescription (of Chinese herbal medicine) made up

爪 zhuǎ (名) claw
see also zhǎo

拽 zhuài (动) drag: ～住衣袖 pull sb. by the sleeve

专(專) zhuān (形) 1 special: ～款 special fund. ～挑别人的毛病 be fond of nitpicking 2 speciality: 一～多能 be expert in one thing and good at many; be a versatile person as well as a specialist 3 monopolize
专长(長) zhuāncháng (名) special skill or knowledge; speciality: 学有～ have sound scholarship
专诚 zhuānchéng (副) specially: ～拜访 pay a special call on sb.
专程 zhuānchéng make a special trip to a certain place
专断(斷) zhuānduàn make one's own decisions without consulting with others
专横 zhuānhèng (形) tyrannical; imperious: ～跋扈 despotic
专机(機) zhuānjī (名) special plane
专家 zhuānjiā (名) expert; specialist
专科学(學)校 zhuānkē xuéxiào (名) vocational training school
专栏(欄) zhuānlán (名) special column: ～作家 columnist
专利 zhuānlì (名) patent: ～权 patent right; patent
专门(門) zhuānmén (形) special; specialized: ～机构 special organ (or agency). ～术语 technical term. ～知识 specialized knowledge; expertise
专区(區) zhuānqū (名) prefecture
专人 zhuānrén (名) person specially assigned for a task
专题 zhuāntí (名) special subject (or topic)
专心 zhuānxīn (动) make a concentrated effort; be attentive; be absorbed: ～致志 whole-hearted devotion
专业(業) zhuānyè (名) special field of study: ～课 specialized courses; professional studies. ～学校 vocational school

专一 zhuānyī (形) single-minded: 心思～ (give sth.) undivided attention

专用 zhuānyòng (形) for special purposes; for use by somebody in particular

专员 zhuānyuán (名) (administrative) commissioner

专政 zhuānzhèng (名) dictatorship

专职(職) zhuānzhí (名) full-time job: ～人员 full-time personnel

专制 zhuānzhì (名) autocracy: 君主～ an autocratic monarchy

专注 zhuānzhù (动) devote oneself to sth. heart and soul

砖(磚) zhuān (名) brick: 砌～ lay bricks

砖头(頭) zhuāntóu (名) brick

砖窑(窰) zhuānyáo (名) brickkiln

转(轉) zhuǎn (动) 1 turn; change: ～身 turn round. 好～ turn for the better 2 transfer: ～到另一个单位 be transferred to another unit. 我会把信～给你的. I will forward the letter to you.
see also zhuàn

转变(變) zhuǎnbiàn (动) change; transform

转播 zhuǎnbō (动) (of radio or TV broadcast) relay

转车(車) zhuǎnchē (动) change trains or buses

转达(達) zhuǎndá (动) pass on; convey (one's message)

转动(動) zhuǎndòng (动) turn round and round; flail: ～手臂 flail one's arm

转告 zhuǎngào (动) pass on a message (to sb.)

转化 zhuǎnhuà (动) transform: 互相～ (of two matters) transform into the opposite direction

转换 zhuǎnhuàn (动) change; transform

转机(機) zhuǎnjī (名) a turn for the better: 形势有了～. The situation is improving.

转嫁 zhuǎnjià (动) shift; transfer: 把罪责～给他人 shift the blame onto others

转交 zhuǎnjiāo (动) pass on; forward

转念 zhuǎnniàn (动) think over: 他刚想开口说话,但一～,觉得还是暂时不提为好. He was just going to speak when, on second thought, he felt it better not to bring up the matter for the time being.

转让(讓) zhuǎnràng (动) transfer one's right in sth.: 票不能～. This ticket is not transferable. 技术～ technological transaction; technical transfer

转入 zhuǎnrù (动) change over to: 从人类学～语言学学习 switch from anthropology to linguistics

转身 zhuǎnshēn (动) (of a person) turn round

转手 zhuǎnshǒu (动) 1 pass on 2 sell what one has bought

转述 zhuǎnshù (动) tell or report sth. as told by another; retell

转瞬间 zhuǎn shùn jiān (副) in the twinkling of an eye

转弯(彎) zhuǎnwān (动) make a turn; turn a corner: 到下一个红绿灯就向右～. Turn right when you get to the next traffic light.

转弯(彎)抹角 zhuǎnwān-mòjiǎo (动) be full of twists and turns; speak in a round-about way: 有话直说,别～的. Say what you want to, but don't beat about the bush.

转危为(為)安 zhuǎn wēi wéi ān turn danger into safety; pull through a crisis

转向 zhuǎnxiàng (动) change direction

转学(學) zhuǎnxué (动) (of a student) transfer to another school: ～生 transfer student

转眼 zhuǎnyǎn (副) in the twinkling of an eye; soon: ～又是秋天了. It'll be autumn before we are aware of it.

转业(業) zhuǎnyè (动) (of an armyman) be transferred to civilian work

转移 zhuǎnyí (动) 1 shift; transfer: ～当地居民 evacuate the local people (to avoid a danger). ～重点 shift focus (on to ...) 2 divert: ～视听 divert one's attention 3 change: ～社会风气 bring about a change in social trends

转载 zhuǎnzǎi (动) reprint what has been published elsewhere

转战(戰) zhuǎnzhàn (动) fight the enemy successively in different localities

转折 zhuǎnzhé (名) a turn in the course of events: 历史的～点 a historical turning point

转(轉) zhuàn I (动) 1 turn; revolve; rotate; spin: 地球每24小时自～一周. The earth rotates once in every 24 hours. 轮子～得太慢. The wheel turns too slowly. 2 stroll: 出去～一～好吗? Do you feel like a stroll? II (量) revolution: 每秒钟一千～ 1,000 revolutions per second.

see also zhuǎn

转动(轉) zhuàndòng (动) turn; revolve; rotate; spin

转炉(爐) zhuànlú (名) converter

转速 zhuànsù (名) rotational speed

转向 zhuànxiàng (动) lose one's bearings; get lost: 晕头～ get totally confused

传(傳) zhuàn (名) 1 biography 2 story (usu. on historical style)

see also chuán

传记 zhuànjì (名) biography

传略 zhuànlüè (名) short biography; biographical sketch

赚 zhuàn (动) make a profit; gain: ～钱 make money

撰 zhuàn (动) write; compose: ～稿 contribute to newspapers, magazines, etc.

撰写(寫) zhuànxiě (动) write; compose

装(裝) zhuāng I (名) clothing; out-fit: 服～ garment. 西～ Western-style suit. 戏～ stage costume II (动) 1 pretend; feign: 不要～出什么都懂. Don't pretend to know everything there is to know. ～病 malinger. ～疯 feign madness 2 play the part: ～老太太 play the part of an old lady 3 install; fit: ～收音机 assemble a radio. ～电话 have a telephone installed 4 fill; load: 把书～进箱子 put the books in the box. ～行李 pack a suitcase. ～车 load a truck or a train

装扮 zhuāngbàn (动) dress up; disguise; masquerade

装备(備) zhuāngbèi I (动) equip; furnish; fit out II (名) equipment; installation

装裱 zhuāngbiǎo (动) mount

装订 zhuāngdìng (动) bind (books)

装璜 zhuānghuáng (名) decoration

装甲 zhuāngjiǎ (形) armoured: ～车 armoured car

装模作样 zhuāngmú-zuòyàng (动) behave affectedly

装配 zhuāngpèi (动) (of machine, etc.) assemble

装腔作势(勢) zhuāngqiāng zuò shì (动) put on a pose

装饰 zhuāngshì (动) decorate; adorn: ～品 ornament; decoration. 室内～ interior decoration

装束 zhuāngshù (名) dress; attire

装蒜 zhuāngsuàn (动) pretend not to know; feign ignorance

装卸 zhuāngxiè (动) 1 load and unload 2 assemble and disassemble

装样(樣)子 zhuāng yàngzi (动) put on an act

装修 zhuāngxiū (动) fix up: ～门面 give a building a face-lift

装置 zhuāngzhì I (动) install; fit II (名) installation; device

妆(妝) zhuāng I (动) make up: 梳～ dress one's hair and apply makeup II (名) trousseau

妆饰 zhuāngshì (动) adorn; dress up; deck out

庄(莊) zhuāng (名) village

庄户 zhuānghù (名) peasant household

庄稼 zhuāngjia (名) crops

庄严(嚴) zhuāngyán (形) solemn; stately; imposing

庄园(園) zhuāngyuán (名) manor; estate

庄重 zhuāngzhòng (形) sober; serious

桩(樁) zhuāng I (名) stake; pile; post II (量) [for events, matters, etc.]: 一～买卖 a business transaction 小事一～ a trifling matter; it's nothing.

幢 zhuàng (量) [for buildings]: 两～大楼 two big buildings

see also chuáng

壮(壯) zhuàng (形) 1 strong; stout; healthy: 身体健～ be powerfully built; be physically strong 2 grand: 雄～ magnificent II (动) strengthen

壮胆(膽) zhuàngdǎn (动) do or say something intended to fill sb. with courage; boost sb.'s courage

壮观(觀) zhuàngguān (名) magnificent sight

壮举(舉) zhuàngjǔ (名) great undertaking; an act of heroism

壮阔 zhuàngkuò (形) immense and magnificent

壮丽(麗) zhuànglì (形) magnificent and enchanting; majestic: ～的诗篇 a splendid poem

壮烈 zhuàngliè (形) brave and noble-minded: ～牺牲 die a martyr

壮年 zhuàngnián (名) prime of life
壮士 zhuàngshì (名) hero; warrior
壮实(實) zhuàngshi (形) sturdy; robust
壮志 zhuàngzhì (名) lofty ideal; great aspiration: ～未酬 with one's noble ambitions unfulfilled

状(狀) zhuàng (名) 1 form; shape: 奇形怪～ grotesque; strange-shaped 2 condition; state of affairs: 现～ status quo. 症～ symptom 3 written complaint; law suit: 告～ sue sb. for; charge sb. with 4 certificate: 奖～ certificate of commendation. 委任～ certificate of appointment; commission
状况 zhuàngkuàng (名) condition; state: 目前的～ present state of affairs. 经济～ financial (or economic) situation. 历史～ historical conditions
状态(態) zhuàngtài (名) state of affairs; appearance: 心理～ psychology; state of mind. 呈透明～ be transparent
状语 zhuàngyǔ (名) adverbial
状元 zhuàngyuan (名) the scholar who headed the successful candidates at the imperial examination; the very best (in any field)

锥 zhuī (名) 1 awl 2 cone

追 zhuī I (动) 1 pursue; give chase: ～上他们 catch up with them 2 seek: 一生～求浮名而毫无成就 pursue transient fame all his life but accomplish nothing 3 get to the bottom of: ～究事情的根源 trace the root cause of the incident II (副) posthumously
追捕 zhuībǔ (动) pursue a criminal
追查 zhuīchá (动) trace; investigate: ～一项罪案 investigate a crime
追悼 zhuīdào (动) mourn sb.'s death: ～会 memorial meeting
追赶(趕) zhuīgǎn (动) run after
追怀(懷) zhuīhuái (动) recall: ～往事 recall the past
追击(擊) zhuījī (动) pursue the fleeing enemy
追加 zhuījiā (动) make an additional allocation for
追究 zhuījiū (动) look into; get to the roots of (a matter, etc.): ～事故的责任 make an investigation of the accident to find out who is to be held accountable
追求 zhuīqiú (动) 1 seek; pursue; go after 2 woo; court
追认(認) zhuīrèn (动) recognize retroactively; confer posthumously
追溯 zhuīsù (动) trace back to: 这座古老的建筑物可以～到第七世纪. This old building dates back to the 7th century.
追随(隨) zhuīsuí (动) follow: ～者 follower; adherent 有人数众多的～者 have a large following
追问 zhuīwèn (动) inquire in great detail about; investigate
追寻(尋) zhuīxún (动) track down; search
追忆(憶) zhuīyì (动) look back; recall
追逐 zhuīzhú (动) 1 chase; pursue 2 seek
追踪 zhuīzōng (动) track; be on sb.'s track

赘 zhuì (形) superfluous: 不待～言 Any further statement of the matter would seem superfluous.
赘述 zhuìshù (动) give unnecessary details; say more than is needed: 不必～～. It is unnecessary to go into details.
赘疣 zhuìyóu (名) 1 wart 2 anything superfluous or useless

缀 zhuì (动) embellish; decorate: 点～ embellish; adorn

坠(墜) zhuì I (动) 1 fall; drop: ～马 fall off a horse 2 weigh down: 苹果把树枝～得弯弯的. The apples weighed the branches down. II (名) weight: 玉～儿 a jade pendant
坠毁(毀) zhuìhuǐ (动) (of a plane, etc.) crash
坠落 zhuìluò (动) fall; drop

谆 zhūn
谆谆 zhūnzhūn (形) (of advice, instruction, etc.) earnest and tireless: ～告诫 repeatedly exhort. 言者～, 听者藐藐. Earnest words of advice fell on deaf ears.

准(準) zhǔn I (名) standard; criterion: 高标～ high standard. 评选的标～ criterion for the selection. 外交～则 diplomatic norms II (形) 1 accurate: 他发音不～. His pronunciation is not accurate. 2 para-: ～军事组织 paramilitary organization III (动) allow; permit: 不～小孩入内 Children are not allowed in. 批～ approve.

获～ obtain permission. 不～张贴 No billing. IV (副) definitely: 她～没去. She didn't go for sure. 这人～是她丈夫. This man must be her husband.

准备(備) zhǔnbèi (动) 1 prepare: ～发言稿 prepare a speech. 大家都～好了吗? Is everybody ready? 作最坏的～ prepare for the worst. ～出发 get ready to go 2 plan; intend: 我～明年春天到乡下走一趟. I plan to make a trip to the countryside next spring. 我今天不～讲了. I don't think I'll take the floor today.

准确(確) zhǔnquè (形) precise; accurate; exact: 给一个～的回答 give a precise answer.

准儿 zhǔnr (名) certainty: 心里没～ feel uncertain

准绳(繩) zhǔnshéng (名) criterion; yardstick

准时(時) zhǔnshí (形) punctual; on time: ～平安抵达 arrive on time safe and sound

准星 zhǔnxīng (名) front sight (of a gun)

准许 zhǔnxǔ (动) permit; allow

准予 zhǔnyǔ (动)(of documentary usage) grant; approve: ～给假二日 grant a leave of two days absence

准则 zhǔnzé (名) norm; standard; criterion: 行为～ code of conduct

捉 zhuō (动) 1 catch; arrest: 活～ capture alive 2 hold firmly; grasp: ～住 get hold of sth. or sb.

捉襟见肘 zhuō jīn jiàn zhǒu find oneself confronted with difficulties too numerous to tackle all at once; have too many difficulties to cope with

捉迷藏 zhuō mícáng (名) hide-and-seek

捉摸 zhuōmō (动) conjecture; predict: ～不定 unpredictable; elusive; difficult to conjecture

捉拿 zhuōná (动) arrest; catch: ～归案 bring sb. to justice

捉弄 zhuōnòng (动) tease; play pranks

拙 zhuō (形) clumsy; awkward

拙笨 zhuōbèn (形) clumsy; unskilful

拙见 zhuōjiàn (名)〈谦〉my humble opinion

拙劣 zhuōliè (形) clumsy and inferior: ～表演 a clumsy or poor performance

卓 zhuō (形) remarkable; outstanding

卓绝 zhuōjué (形) unsurpassed; outstanding: 艰苦～ endure extreme hardships

卓识(識) zhuōshí (名) outstanding insight: 远见～ foresight and vision

卓有成效 zhuō yǒu chéngxiào (形) highly effective; fruitful

卓越 zhuōyuè (形) brilliant; outstanding: ～的成就 remarkable achievements. ～的外交家 outstanding diplomat

桌 zhuō I (名) table; desk: 餐～ dining table. 书～ writing desk II (量) [of a feast table, etc.]: 两～佳肴 two tables of delicious dishes

桌面儿上 zhuōmiànrshang (名) on the table; aboveboard: 有话摆到～来说 put your cards on the table; be aboveboard.

浊(濁) zhuó (形) 1 muddy: ～水 muddy water. 污～ dirty; filthy 2 (of voices) voiced (consonants)

浊音 zhuóyīn (名) voiced sound

镯 zhuó (名) bracelet

着 zhuó (动) 1 apply; use: ～色 apply colour 2 touch; come into contact with: 不～边际 irrelevant; not to the point; neither here nor there 3 wear: 衣～体面 be decently dressed see also zhāo; zháo; zhe

着陆(陸) zhuólù (动) (of airplane) land; touch down

着落 zhuóluò (名) 1 assured source: 他的工作还没～. He still hasn't got a definite job. 2 whereabouts: 那只失踪的船还没有～. The whereabouts of the boat is still unknown.

着手 zhuóshǒu (动) begin; set about: ～准备工作 get down to the preparations

着想 zhuóxiǎng (动) consider the interests of: 为他人～ have other people's interests at heart

着眼 zhuóyǎn (动) take as the basis: ～于人材培养 take the training of professional people as the starting point.

着重 zhuózhòng (动) stress; emphasize: ～指出 point out emphatically

灼 zhuó I (动) burn; scorch II (形) luminous

灼见 zhuójiàn (名) penetrating insight

灼热(熱) zhuórè (形) scorching hot

酌 zhuó (动) 1 (of wine) drink 2 weigh and consider

酌量 zhuóliàng (动) consider; deliberate

酌情 zhuóqíng (动) take the circumstances into consideration: ～处理 settle a matter fairly and reasonably; act at one's discretion

茁 zhuó

茁壮(壯) zhuózhuàng (形) sturdy; healthy and strong

琢 zhuó (动) chisel
see also zuó

琢磨 zhuómó (动) 1 (of jade) carve and polish 2 (of literary works) polish; refine

啄 zhuó (动) peck

啄木鸟 zhuómùniǎo (名) woodpecker

咨 zī

咨文 zīwén (名) 1 official communication (between government offices of equal rank) 2 report delivered by the head of government on affairs of state: 国情～(美) State of the Union Message

咨询 zīxún (动) seek advice; consult: ～机构 advisory body

资 zī I (名) capital; fund: 投～ invest. 工～ pay; wages; salary. 川～ travel expenses. 合～ joint venture II (动) provide: 可～借鉴 can serve as an example

资本 zīběn (名) capital: ～家 capitalist. ～主义 capitalism

资产(産) zīchǎn (名) assets; property; estate; capital

资产阶(階)级 zīchǎnjiējí (名) the bourgeoisie: 小～ petty burgeoisie

资格 zīgé (名) 1 qualifications: 有～ be qualified. 代表～审查委员会 credentials committee 2 seniority: 摆老～ flaunt one's seniority

资金 zījīn (名) fund: ～周转 cash flow

资历(歷) zīlì (名) qualifications (including academic and work experience)

资料 zīliào (名) information; data

资源 zīyuán (名) natural resources

资助 zīzhù (名) financial aid

姿 zī (名) 1 looks; appearance: ～色 (of a woman) good looks 2 posture

姿势(勢) zīshì (名) gesture; posture; position: 站立～ (be) in a standing position

姿态(態) zītài (名) 1 posture; carriage: ～优美 elegant carriage 2 attitude; pose: 以和事佬的～出现 assume the role of a peacemaker. 高～ magnanimous

滋 zī

滋补(補) zībǔ (动) nourish: ～食品 nutritious food. ～药品 tonic

滋润 zīrùn (动) moisten

滋生 zīshēng (动) breed; flourish

滋味 zīwèi (名) taste; flavour

滋养(養) zīyǎng (动) nourish

滋长 zīzhǎng (动) grow; develop: ～了骄傲情绪 become conceited

髭 zī (名) moustache

吱 zī (动) 1 (of mice) squeak 2 (of birds, etc.) chirp; peep

吱声 zīshēng (动) utter; speak: 一直不～ keep one's mouth shut; remain silent or speechless

孜 zī

孜孜不倦 zīzī bù juàn (副) diligently; assiduously

紫 zǐ (形) purple

紫外线(綫) zǐwàixiàn (名) ultraviolet ray

紫药(藥)水 zǐyàoshuǐ (名) gentian violet

紫罗(羅)兰(蘭) zǐluólán (名) violet

姊 zǐ (名) elder sister

姊妹 zǐmèi (名) sisters

子 zǐ I (名) 1 son: 母～ mother and son. ～女 son and daughter; children. 孙～ grandson 2 seed; egg: 瓜～ melon seeds. 鱼～ (fish) roe; caviar. 精～ sperm 3 something small and hard: 石头～儿 pebble. 棋～儿 chessman; piece 4 person: 女～ woman. 男～ man II (形) young (of certain animals, vegetables): ～鸡 chick. ～姜 tender ginger

子弹 zǐdàn (名) bullet

子弟 zǐdì (名) 1 sons, younger brothers: 纨袴～ profligate sons of the rich; dandies. ～兵 the people's own army 2 younger generation; nephew, etc.

子宫 zǐgōng (名) uterus; womb
子粒 zǐlì (名) seed; grain: ～饱满 full grains
子孙(孫) zǐsūn (名) children and grandchildren; descendants: ～后代 descendants; posterity
籽 zǐ (名) (of vegetables etc.) seed
籽棉 zǐmián (名) unginned cotton
仔 zǐ (名) young domestic animal: ～猪 piglet. ～鸡 chick
仔细 zǐxì (形) careful; attentive: ～观察 observe closely. ～听 listen attentively or carefully. ～研究 in-depth study
字 zì (名) 1 character; word: 汉～ Chinese character. 文～ writing system; writing. 象形文～ hieroglyph 2 form of a written or printed character: 斜体～ italicized word. 黑体～ boldface 3 calligraphy: ～画 calligraphy and painting 4 name: 签～ sign one's name
字典 zìdiǎn (名) dictionary
字迹 zìjì (名) handwriting: ～潦草 sloppy or illegible handwriting
字句 zìjù (名) words and expressions; writing: ～通顺 make easy and smooth reading
字据(據) zìjù (名) signed paper; receipt; contract
字里(裏)行间(間) zìlǐ-hángjiān between the lines: ～的意思不难看清. The implication is clear if we read between the lines.
字面 zìmiàn (名) literal: ～上的意思 literal meaning of a word
字母 zìmǔ (名) letters (of an alphabet): 汉语拼音～ the Chinese phonetic alphabet. 英语～ the English alphabet. 大写～ a capital letter
字幕 zìmù (名) caption (of film, vedio, etc.); subtitle
字体(體) zìtǐ (名) style of calligraphy; typeface
字条(條)儿 zìtiáor (名) brief note
字帖 zìtiè (名) copybook (for calligraphy)
字眼 zìyǎn (名) wording; diction: 玩弄～ play with words; wordplay
恣 zì (动) do as one pleases
恣意 zìyì (形) unscrupulous; reckless; unbridled; wilful: ～践踏 wilfully trample on

自 zì I (代) oneself; one's own: ～问 ask oneself. ～画像 self-portrait. ～食其果 reap what one has sown; lie on the bed you have made for yourself II (副) naturally: ～当如此. It should be so as a matter of course. 我～有办法. I know how to handle it. III (介) since; from: ～古以来 since ancient times ～小 from childhood. 来～大西洋彼岸 coming from the other side of the Atlantic
自爱(愛) zì'ài (名) self-respect
自拔 zìbá (动) free oneself (from pain or evildoing): 不能～ unable to extricate oneself from a difficult or embarrassing situation
自白 zìbái I (名) confession II (动) vindicate oneself
自暴自弃(棄) zìbào-zìqì give oneself up for lost
自卑 zìbēi (动) have inferiority complex
自惭(慚)形秽(穢) zì cán xíng huì feel small
自称(稱) zìchēng (动) claim to be: ～作家 claim to be a writer
自持 zìchí (动) exercise self-restraint
自吹自擂 zìchuī-zìlèi (动) blow one's own trumpet; brag
自从(從) zìcóng (介) since; from
自大 zìdà (形) self-important; arrogant
自得 zìdé (形) self-satisfied: 洋洋～ smug; complacent. ～其乐 derive pleasure from sth.
自动(動) zìdòng (形) 1 automatic 2 voluntary; of one's own accord
自动(動)化 zìdònghuà (名) automation
自发(發) zìfā (形) spontaneous
自费 zìfèi (形、副) at one's own expense
自封 zìfēng (动) 1 proclaim oneself: ～的专家 a self-styled or self-appointed expert 2 confine oneself: 故步～ be complacent and conservative
自负 zìfù (动) 1 hold oneself responsible for sth.: ～盈亏 be held economically responsible 2 conceited; be puffed up
自高自大 zìgāo-zìdà (形) arrogant; self-important
自告奋(奮)勇 zì gào fènyǒng (动) volunteer to undertake a difficult task
自顾(顧)不暇 zì gù bù xiá be

unable even to shift for oneself (much less look after others)

自豪 zìháo I (动) be proud of; take pride in II (名) pride

自己 zìjǐ I (代) oneself: 你~做吧! Do it yourself! II (形) closely connected; intimate; close; own: ~的一间房子 a room of one's own

自己人 zìjǐrén (名) one of us: 今晚都是~. You are among friends tonight.

自给 zìjǐ (动) be self-sufficient

自荐(薦) zìjiàn (动) offer oneself as a candidate for a position

自尽(盡) zìjìn (动) commit suicide

自居 zìjū (动) call oneself: 以功臣~ consider oneself a war hero

自决 zìjué (名) self-determination

自觉(覺) zìjué I (动) be conscious of II (形) of one's own free will: 大家都很~, 都不在这里抽烟. Everyone consciously refrains from smoking here.

自夸(誇) zìkuā (动) sing one's own praises

自来(來)水 zìláishuǐ (名) running water; tap water

自理 zìlǐ (动) take care of sb. or sth. by oneself

自立 zìlì (动) stand on one's own feet

自立更生 zìlì gēngshēng self-reliance; reliance on one's own effort

自量 zìliàng (动) estimate one's own ability: 不知~ unable to make a sober estimate of one's abilities or strengths; fail to understand one's own limitations

自流 zìliú (动) (of a thing) take it's own course: 听其~ let things drift along; let people do whatever they like without giving them proper guidance

自留(留)地 zìliúdì (名) private plot

自满(滿) zìmǎn (形) self-satisfied; smug

自鸣得意 zì míng déyì be pleased with one's temporary or insignificant success; talk with relish about what one regards as one's masterstroke

自命不凡 zìmìng bù fán consider oneself head and shoulders above the ordinary run; pretentious

自欺欺人 zì qī qī rén try to make people believe something which even the person himself does not have any faith in: 这是~之谈. This is a hoax, pure and simple.

自取灭(滅)亡 zì qǔ mièwáng court destruction

自然 zìrán I (名) nature: ~规律 law of nature II (形) 1 natural: ~风光 natural scenery. ~淘汰 natural selection 2 unaffected; natural: 表情~ look unaffected III (副) 1 naturally; in due course: 过几天你~就会习惯的. You'll get used to it in a couple of days. 到时候他~会明白的. He'll understand it when the time comes. 2 naturally; of course: ~应该是我去啰! Naturally I am to go, aren't I? 你~不用担心. (of course) You should not worry about it.

自然主义(義) zìrán zhǔyì (名) naturalism

自认(認)晦气 zì rèn huìqì look upon a piece of bad luck with resignation

自如 zìrú (副) 〈书〉 smoothly; with facility: 运用~ handle (a tool) with skill; use with ease

自杀(殺) zìshā (动) commit suicide

自食其力 zì shí qí lì earn one's own living; earn one's bread

自始至终 zì shǐ zhì zhōng from beginning to end

自首 zìshǒu (动) surrender oneself to the police or judicial department

自私 zìsī (形) selfish; self-centred

自讨苦吃 zì tǎo kǔ chī (动) be asking for trouble

自卫(衛) zìwèi (名) self-defence

自我 zìwǒ (代) self: ~批评 self-criticism. ~欣赏 self-admiration

自习(習) zìxí (of students) study by oneself outside of class

自相残(殘)杀(殺) zì xiāng cánshā seek to destroy each other among members of the same group

自相矛盾 zì xiāng máo dùn contradict oneself; be self-contradictory

自新 zìxīn (动) turn over a new leaf: 改过~ correct past errors and start a new life

自信 zìxìn (动) be confident: ~心 self-confidence

自行 zìxíng (副) 1 by oneself: ~安排 arrange by oneself 2 of one's own accord

自行车(車) zìxíngchē (名) bicycle; bike.

自修 zìxiū study by oneself
自选（選）zìxuǎn（动）select by oneself: ～动作 optional exercise. ～项目 self-select items. ～市场 supermarket
自学（學）zìxué（动）study by oneself: ～教材 teach-yourself books. ～成材 become educated without a master; be a self-made man
自言自语 zìyán-zìyǔ（动）talk to oneself
自以为（爲）是 zì yǐwéi shì（动）be cocksure and impervious to criticism; be opinionated
自缢 zìyì（动）hang oneself
自由 zìyóu I（名）freedom; liberty: 言论～ freedom of speech. ～党 Liberal Party II（形）free: ～竞争 free competition. ～泛滥 (erroneous ideas) spread unchecked. ～职业 the liberal profession ～散漫 easy-going and reluctant to observe discipline. ～自在 happy-go-lucky
自圆其说 zì yuán qí shuō make one's argument sound plausible: 不能～ cannot offer an acceptable explanation
自愿（願）zìyuàn（动）volunteer
自在 zìzai（形）comfortable; at ease: 主人太客气了，反而使我感到不～. The host seems too inclined to stand on ceremony that I don't feel quite at home.
自找 zìzhǎo（动）suffer from one's own actions: 这是你～的！You asked for it.
自知之明 zìzhī zhī míng the wisdom of knowing one's own limitations; self-knowledge
自治 zìzhì（名）autonomy; self-government: ～区 autonomous region. ～权 autonomy
自主 zìzhǔ（动）be the master of one's own fate: ～权 the power to make independent decisions. 不由～ involuntarily
自助 zìzhù（形）self-service; ～餐厅 cafeteria
自传（傳）zìzhuàn（名）autobiography
自尊 zìzūn（名）self-respect; pride self-esteem
自作自受 zìzuō-zìshòu whatever a man sows, that he will also reap; be stewed in one's own juice
自作聪（聰）明 zì zuò cōngmíng think oneself clever and act rashly

渍 zì（名）stain; sludge: 油～ oil sludge. 汗～ sweat stain

子 zi [noun suffix]: 房～ house. 车～ vehicle. 镜～ mirror. 骗～ swindler; double-dealer. 矮～ dwarf

宗 zōng I（名）1 ancestor: 祖～ ancestor 2 faction; school: 正～ orthodox school 3 purpose: 万变不离其～. All changes, no matter how many, centre on one purpose. II（量）: 一～心事 a cause for worry. 大～款项 a large sum of money
宗教 zōngjiào（名）religion
宗派 zōngpài（名）faction; sect: ～斗争 factional strife
宗旨 zōngzhǐ（名）aim; purpose
宗族 zōngzú（名）clan

鬃 zōng（名）hair (on the neck of a pig, horse, etc.): 马～ horse's mane. 猪～ pig's bristles

棕 zōng（名）palm
棕榈 zōnglǘ（名）palm
棕色 zōngsè（形）brown

踪（蹤） zōng（名）track; trace; footprint: 跟～ be on the track of; shadow
踪迹 zōngjì（名）trace; track
踪影 zōngyǐng（名）trace; sign

综 zōng
综合 zōnghé（动）synthesize; bring into a state of balance: ～考察 comprehensive survey. ～性大学 a comprehensive university
综述 zōngshù（动）summarize

总（總） zǒng I（动）sum up; put together: ～起来说 to sum up. 汇～ put (or gather) together II（形）1 general; total: ～罢工 general strike. ～产量 total output. ～开关 master switch 2 chief: ～经理 general manager. ～编辑 editor-in-chief. ～公司 head company III（副）1 always, invariably: 她～是迟到. She is always late. 他这人～能找到借口. He would invariably find some excuses. 2 eventually; sooner or later: 他的希望～会实现的. His wish will eventually come true. 你～会明白的. You will understand sooner or later. 他～是你的儿子. He is after all your son. 这种事～是会发生的. These things will inevitably happen. 3 at least: 她～不会当面对他这样讲吧？ At least she wouldn't say this to his

face?他走了～有一个星期吧. He's been away for at least a week.
总得 zǒngděi (动) have to; must
总督 zǒngdū (名) governor-general; governor
总额 zǒng'é (名) total (amount)
总而言之 zǒng ér yán zhī in a word; in short
总共 zǒnggòng (副) altogether; in all: ～有一千人. There are altogether 1,000 people. 这几本书～要多少钱? How much do all these books come to?
总管 zǒngguǎn (名) person in over-all charge
总归(歸) zǒngguī (副) eventually; after all: 这个问题～会得到解决的. This problem will eventually be solved. 他～是这个村子的人. After all, he is from our village.
总和 zǒnghé (名) sum; total; sum total
总机(機) zǒngjī (名) telephone exchange; switchboard
总计 zǒngjì (动) add up to; amount to; total
总结 zǒngjié I (动) sum up; summarize: ～经验 sum up one's experience II (名) summary: 作～ make a summary. ～报告 final report
总理 zǒnglǐ (名) premier; prime minister
总路线(綫) zǒnglùxiàn (名) general line
总数(數) zǒngshù (名) total; sum total
总算 zǒngsuàn (副) 1 finally; at last: 他最后～找到了一个满意的工作. He succeeded in finding a good job. 2 can almost be regarded as; on the whole: 书单上的十本书我们买到五本, ～没白跑这一趟. We got five out of the ten books on the list. It's worth the trip on the whole.
总体(體) zǒngtǐ I (名) totality II (形) overall
总统 zǒngtǒng (名) president (of a republic)
总务(務) zǒngwù (名) general affairs; general service
总之 zǒngzhī in a word; in short

纵(縱) zòng I (形) vertical; longitudinal II (动) 1 let go; set free: 不能～虎归山. Don't set free a tiger. *or* Don't let an evildoer go unpunished. 2 indulge; not restrain: ～情歌唱 sing to one's heart's content 3 jump; leap: 猫～身跳上围墙. The cat jumped onto the wall. III (连) even if; though
纵队(隊) zòngduì (名) column; file: ～队形 column formation
纵横 zòng-héng (副) vertically and horizontally; in length and breadth: ～交错 criss-cross
纵火 zònghuǒ (动) commit arson: ～犯 arsonist
纵情 zòngqíng (动) to one's heart's content: ～欢呼 cheer heartily
纵容 zòngróng (动) connive; wink at: 在某人～下 with the connivance of sb.
纵深 zòngshēn (名) depth: 向～发展 develop in depth
纵欲 zòngyù (动) indulge in sensual pleasures

走 zǒu (动) 1 walk; go: ～路去 go on foot; walk. ～一～ take a walk. ～进房间 go into the room 2 move: 这钟怎么不～啦! Why, the clock has stopped! 你这步棋～坏了. You have made a wrong move. 3 leave; depart: 她～了. She has left. 我该～了. It's time I left. *or* I must go now. 4 pay a visit to: ～亲戚 call on one's relatives 5 leak; leak out; let out: ～漏风声 let out a secret. 说～了嘴 make a slip of the tongue. 6 depart from the original: ～调了 out of tune. 茶叶～味了. The tea has lost its flavour.
走动(動) zǒudòng (动) 1 walk about; stretch one's legs 2 socialize; visit each other
走访 zǒufǎng (动) 1 pay a visit to: 记者～了几家当地农民 The reporter visited a few local peasant families. 2 interview
走狗 zǒugǒu (名) running dog; lackey
走后(後)门 zǒu hòumén I (动) get in by the back door II (名) backdoor dealings
走廊 zǒuláng (名) corridor; passage
走路 zǒulù (动) 1 walk: 这孩子已经学会～了. The child has learned to walk. 2 leave; get away
走马(馬)看花 zǒu mǎ kàn huā gain a superficial understanding through cursory observation
走南闯(闖)北 zǒunán-chuǎngběi journey north and south; travel extensively
走失 zǒushī (动) 1 get lost;

wander away: 在人群中小孩～了. The child got lost among the crowd. 2 alter or lose its original meaning: 译文～了原意. The translation loses much of the original meaning.
走兽(獸) zǒushòu (名) beast
走私 zǒusī (动) smuggle
走投无(無)路 zǒu-tóu wú lù be in an impasse: 逼得～ be driven to the wall
走向 zǒuxiàng (名) (of ore veins, mountain ranges) run; trend; alignment
走样(樣) zǒuyàng (动) deviate from the original model
走运(運) zǒuyùn (动) be lucky
走着瞧 zǒuzheqiáo (动) wait and see: 咱们～! Let's wait and see.
走卒 zǒuzú (名) pawn; lackey; stooge
奏 zòu (动) 1 play (music): 独～ (instrumental) solo. 伴～ accompaniment 2 present a memorial to an emperor
奏效 zòuxiào (动) prove effective
奏乐(樂) zòuyuè (动) play music; strike up a tune
揍 zòu (动) beat; hit; strike: 把他～一顿 beat him up; manhandle him. 挨～ get a thrashing
租 zū (动) rent; hire; lease; let: ～电影院 rent a cinema. ～船 hire a boat. 房屋招～ Room to let
租佃 zūdiàn (动) (of a landlord) rent out land to tenants
租界 zūjiè (名) concession; leased territory
租借 zūjiè (动) rent; hire; lease: ～地 leased territory
租金 zūjīn (名) rent; rental
租赁 zūlìn (名) rent; lease; hire
租约 zūyuē (名) lease
卒 zú (名) soldier
族 zú (名) 1 race; nationality: 少数民～ national minority; ethnic group. 种～ race 2 clan 3 a class of things with common features: 水～ aquatic animal
足 zú I (名) foot: 赤～ barefoot II (形) 1 enough; ample: 丰衣～食 have plenty of food and clothing. 资金不～ inadequate fund 2 enough; sufficient [often used in the negative]: 微不～道 insignificant; negligible
足够 zúgòu (形) enough; ample; sufficient
足迹 zújì (名) footprint; footmark; track
足球 zúqiú (名) soccer; football
足以 zúyǐ (形) enough; sufficient: 这些事实～说明问题. These facts suffice to illustrate the question in point.
足智多谋 zúzhì-duōmóu (形) resourceful
诅 zǔ
诅咒 zǔzhòu (动) curse
祖 zǔ (名) originator; ancestor
祖辈 zǔbèi (名) forefathers; ancestry; forebears
祖传(傳) zǔchuán (动) be handed down from one's ancestors: ～秘方 a family prescription handed down from generation to generation
祖父 zǔfù (名) grandfather
祖国(國) zǔguó (名) motherland
祖母 zǔmǔ (名) grandmother
祖师(師) zǔshī (名) founder (of a school of learning)
祖孙(孫) zǔ-sūn (名) grandparent and grandchild: ～三代 three generations
祖先 zǔxiān (名) forefathers; ancestors
祖宗 zǔzōng (名) ancestry
祖祖辈辈 zǔzǔbèibèi (名) for generations
阻 zǔ (动) block; hinder; obstruct
阻碍(礙) zǔ'ài (动) hinder; impede: ～交通 block the traffic ～生产的发展 hinder the development of production
阻挡(擋) zǔdǎng (动) stop; stem; resist: 不可～的洪流 an irresistible trend
阻击(擊) zǔjī (动) block; check: ～战 blocking action
阻拦(攔) zǔlán (动) stop; bar the way: 他一定要去,我们最好不去～. As he was bent on going, we had better not try to stop him.
阻力 zǔlì (名) obstruction; resistance
阻挠(撓) zǔnáo (动) obstruct; stand in the way
阻塞 zǔsè (动) block; clog: ～交通 hold up the traffic
阻止 zǔzhǐ (动) stop; prevent; hold back: ～谣言的散布 prevent the rumours spreading
组 zǔ I (名) group: 分～讨论 be divided into groups for

discussion II (动) organize: 改~ reorganize; reshuffle III (量) group; set: 两~人 two groups of people

组成 zǔchéng (动) make up; compose; consist of: ~部分 component part; component. 五十人~的代表团 a delegation composed of fifty people. 这个球队由二十名运动员~. This team consists of twenty players.

组阁 zǔgé (动) form a cabinet; handpick people to set up an organization

组合 zǔhé (动) make up; compose; combine

组织(織) zǔzhī I (动) organize: ~一次会议 organize a meeting. 这次展览会~得很好. This exhibition is well-organized. II (名) 1 organization 2 tissue: 肌肉~ muscle tissue

钻(鑽) zuān (动) 1 drill; bore: ~孔 drill a hole 2 go through; make one's way into: ~山洞 go into a mountain cave. ~到水里 disappear into the water 3 make a thorough study of; dig into: ~研 make a persistent effort to learn. ~书本 bury oneself in books

see also zuàn

钻空子 zuān-kòngzi (动) exploit a loophole to one's own advantage: 不要让他~. Do not let him take advantage of this loophole.

钻牛角尖 zuān niújiǎojiān (动) waste time and offort trying to solve an unimportant or insoluble problem: 喜欢~ be fond of hairsplitting

钻探 zuāntàn (动) drill (for exploratory purposes)

钻研 zuānyán (动) dig into; make a careful study of: 努力~业务知识 work hard to master his professional knowledge

钻营(營) zuānyíng (动) curry favour with sb. in authority for personal gain

攥 zuàn (动) grip; clasp

钻(鑽) zuàn I (动) drill; bore II(名) diamond

see also zuān

钻床(牀) zuànchuáng (名) drilling machine; driller

钻机(機) zuànjī (名) (drilling) rig

钻井 zuànjǐng (名) well drilling

钻石 zuànshí (名) diamond

钻头(頭) zuàntóu (名) bit (of a drill)

嘴 zuǐ (名) mouth: 闭~! Shut up! 光~上说 pay lip service. 瓶~儿 the mouth of a bottle. 烟~ cigarette holder

嘴巴 zuǐba (名) mouth

嘴唇 zuǐchún (名) lip

嘴紧(緊) zuǐjǐn (动) be tight-lipped: 我的嘴是封得紧紧的. My lips are sealed.

嘴快 zuǐkuài (动) have a loose tongue

嘴脸(臉) zuǐliǎn (名) (derog.) look; features

嘴皮子 zuǐpízi (名)〈口〉lips (of a glib talker): 耍~ talk glibly

嘴碎 zuǐsuì (形) garrulous

嘴甜 zuǐtián (形) fond of honeyed words

嘴硬 zuǐyìng (形) reluctant or unwilling to admit error or defeat

醉 zuì (形) 1 drunk; inebriated: 烂~ be dead drunk. 他有点儿~. He's tipsy. 2 (of certain food, or fruits) liquor-saturated: ~枣 liquor-saturated dates

醉鬼 zuìguǐ (名) drunkard

醉汉(漢) zuìhàn (名) drunken man; drunkard

醉生梦(夢)死 zuìshēng-mèngsǐ lead an aimless and often dissipated life

醉翁之意不在酒 zuìwēng zhī yì bù zài jiǔ It is a case of the old drinker whose mind is occupied with something other than wine.

醉心 zuìxīn (动) be bent on; be engrossed in: ~于数学的研究 be engrossed in the study of mathematics

醉醺醺 zuìxūnxūn (形) tipsy; drunk

醉意 zuìyì (名) signs of getting drunk: 有几分~ be a bit tipsy

最 zuì (副) [indicating the superlative degree]: ~好 the best. ~小 the smallest. ~美丽 the most beautiful. ~能说明问题 can best illustrate this problem

最初 zuìchū (形) initial; first: ~阶段 the initial stage. ~印象 first impressions

最多 zuìduō (副) 1 most: 这三所学校中, A 校的外国学生~. Among the three schools, A has more foreign students than the rest. 2 at most: 我在那儿~能呆三天. I can stay there for at most three days.

最好 zuìhǎo (形) 1 best; first-rate: ～的办法 the best way 2 had better; it would be best: 你～先别告诉他. You'd better not tell him now.

最后(後) zuìhòu (形、副) last; final; at last; eventually: ～的结论 the final conclusion. 作～挣扎 make a last-ditch struggle. ～他终于说了实话. He told me the truth at last.

最后(後)通牒 zuìhòu tōngdié (名) ultimatum

最惠国(國) zuìhuìguó (名) most-favoured nation; MFN: 给以～待遇 accord (a country) most-favoured-nation treatment

最近 zuìjìn (形、副) 1 nearest 2 recently; lately; of late: ～几年 in the last few years. ～的消息 the latest news 3 soon; in the near future: ～几天我要到南方去一趟. I am going to the South in a couple of days.

最终 zuìzhōng (形) final; ultimate: ～目的 the ultimate aim. ～的回答 the final answer

罪 zuì (名) 1 guilt; crime: 有～ be guilty of a crime 2 fault; blame: 怪～某人 lay the blame on sb. 3 suffering; hardship: 受～ suffer; have a hard time

罪大恶极(極) zuìdà-èjí be guilty of the most heinous crimes

罪恶(惡) zuì'è (名) crime; evil: ～滔天 be guilty of monstrous crimes

罪犯 zuìfàn (名) criminal; culprit

罪过(過) zuìguò (名) fault; offence; sin

罪魁祸(禍)首 zuìkuí huòshǒu (名) chief criminal; archcriminal

罪名 zuìmíng (名) charge; accusation

罪孽 zuìniè (名) sin: ～深重 be steeped in iniquity

罪行 zuìxíng (名) crime

罪责 zuìzé (名) responsibility for an offence: ～难逃 cannot get away with (the crime)

罪证 zuìzhèng (名) evidence of a crime

罪状(狀) zuìzhuàng (名) criminal acts

尊 zūn (动) respect; esteem

尊称(稱) zūnchēng (名) respectful form of address

尊敬 zūnjìng I (动) respect; esteem; revere II (形) honourable; distinguished

尊严(嚴) zūnyán (名) dignity; honour

尊长(長) zūnzhǎng (名) elders and betters

尊重 zūnzhòng (动) treat with respect; value

遵 zūn (动) abide by; obey; observe

遵从(從) zūncóng (动) follow; comply with

遵命 zūnmìng (动)〈敬〉obey your instructions: 当～办理 will act in compliance with your instructions

遵守 zūnshǒu (动) observe; abide by; adhere to; comply with: ～公共秩序 observe public order. ～时间 be punctual. ～法律 abide by the law

遵循 zūnxún (动) (of principle; political line, etc.) follow; adhere to

遵照 zūnzhào (动) (of instructions; policy, etc.) act in accordance with; conform to; comply with

作 zuō
see also zuó; zuò

作坊 zuōfang (名) workshop

琢 zuó
see also zhuó

琢磨 zuómo (动) turn sth. over in one's mind; ponder

昨 zuó (名) yesterday

昨天 zuótiān (名) yesterday

作 zuó
see also zuō; zuò

作料 zuóliao (名) condiments; seasoning

左 zuǒ (名) 1 left; the left side 2 queer; unorthodox: ～嗓子 out-of-tune voice

左边(邊) zuǒbian (名) left side

左派 zuǒpài (名) 1 the left wing 2 Leftist 3 progressive

左撇子 zuǒpiězi (名) left-handed person

左倾 zuǒqīng (名) "Left"-deviationist: ～错误 'Left"-deviationist errors

左舷 zuǒxián (名) port (of a ship)

左翼 zuǒyì (名)〈军〉left wing; left flank

左右 zuǒyòu I (名) left and right: ～摇晃 swing (from left to right); vacillate II (副) about; more or less: 五点钟～ about

five o'clock. 两个月～ two months or so III (动) control; influence: ～局势 take the situation in hand. 被别人～ be swayed by sb. in one's attitude or views
左右手 zuǒyòushǒu (名) one's right-hand man; valuable assistant
左右为(爲)难(難) zuǒ-yòu wéinán be in a dilemma
左…右… zou…you… [used to emphasize repetition of an action]: 左思右想 keep turning sth. over in one's mind. 左一个问题，右一个问题 one question cropping up after another
撮 zuǒ (量) [used for a bunch of hair] tuft: 一～儿白毛 a tuft of white hair
凿(鑿) zuò (形) 1 certain; authentic; irrefutable: 确～ authentic; conclusive 2 mortise
see also záo
坐 zuò (动) 1 sit: 请～! Please sit down! ～在椅子上 sit in a chair. ～在板凳上 sit on a bench 2 aboard: ～公共汽车 travel by bus, train, plane, etc. 3 put (a pot, kettle, etc.) on a fire: 在炉子上～一壶水 put the kettle (of water) on the fire 4 (of guns) recoil; kick
坐标(標) zuòbiāo (名) 〈数〉 coordinate
坐吃山空 zuò chī shān kōng sit idle and eat and do nothing and your whole fortune will vanish
坐等 zuòděng (动) sit back and wait
坐垫(墊) zuòdiàn (名) cushion
坐井观(觀)天 zuò jǐng guān tiān see the sky from the bottom of a well; have a very narrow view
坐冷板凳 zuò lěngbǎndèng 1 hold a title with little or no duties 2 wait long for an appointment
坐立不安 zuò-lì bù ān be restless; be fidgety; be on pins and needles; be on tenterhooks
坐落 zuòluò (动) (of building; house) be situated; be located
坐山观(觀)虎斗(鬥) zuò shān guān hǔ dòu sit on top of the mountain to watch the fight between two lions
坐失良机(機) zuò shī liángjī let slip a golden opportunity
坐视 zuòshì (动) sit by and watch; look on with folded arms
坐位 zuòwei (名) seat
坐享其成 zuò xiǎng qí chéng enjoy the fruits of others' labour
坐以待毙(斃) zuò yǐ dài bì anticipate certain death without putting up a struggle
坐月子 zuò yuèzi (动) be confined (in childbirth)
座 zuò I (名) 1 seat; place: 入～ take one's seat. ～无虚席 has a full house; be packed 2 stand; base; pedestal: 花瓶～儿 vase stand. 塑像～儿 pedestal for a statue II (量) [of large and solid thing]: 一～山 a mountain. 一～桥 a bridge. 一～铜像 a bronze statue
座上客 zuòshàngkè (名) guest of honour
座谈 zuòtán (名) informal discussion: ～会 informal discussion; forum; symposium
座位 zuòwèi (名) seat
座右铭 zuòyòumíng (名) motto; maxim
座钟(鐘) zuòzhōng (名) desk clock
作 zuò (动) 1 do; make: ～事 work. ～文章 write an essay. ～诗 compose a poem. ～报告 give a talk. ～学问 do academic work 2 act as; be: ～为大会主席，他首先发言. As chairman of the meeting, he first took the floor. 他在暑假中～了旅游团的导游. He acted as guide to a tourist group during the summer vacation. 3 regard as: 她把我当～亲生女儿. She treats me as her own daughter.
see also zuō; zuó
作案 zuò'àn (动) commit a crime
作罢(罷) zuòbà (动) cancel; drop; give up: 这事只好～. Well, the matter will have to be dropped.
作弊 zuòbì (动) practise fraud; cheat
作对(對) zuòduì (动) set oneself against; be antagonistic to
作恶(惡) zuò'è (动) do evil: ～多端 perpetrate numerous crimes
作法 zuòfǎ (名) way of doing things; method; practice
作废(廢) zuòfèi (动) become invalid: 过期～ become invalid after a specified date. 宣布条约～ declare a treaty null and void
作风(風) zuòfēng (名) style of work; way of life: 工作～ style of work. 生活～ way of life; lifestyle. 实事求是的～ a practical

and realistic way of doing things

作梗 zuògěng (动) obstruct; hinder; impede

作怪 zuòguài (动) make trouble

作家 zuòjiā (名) writer

作价(價) zuòjià (动) fix a price for sth.; evaluate

作孽 zuòniè (动) commit a sin

作呕(嘔) zuò'ǒu (动) feel sick (or nausea); feel like vomiting: 真是令人～! It's really disgusting!

作陪 zuòpéi (动) be invited to be present at a banquet given in honour of a distinguished guest

作品 zuòpǐn (名) (of literature and art) works

作数(數) zuòshù (动) be valid: 旧协定已经不～了. The old agreement is no longer binding.

作祟 zuòsuì (动) make mischief; cause trouble: 一定有人从中～. There must be someone trying to stir up (or create) trouble.

作威作福 zuòwēi-zuòfú ride roughshod over others; abuse one's power

作曲 zuòqǔ (动) compose (music)

作为(爲) zuòwéi I (名) 1 conduct; action: 他的～证明了他的品质高尚. His conduct bears unmistakable testimony to his noble-mindedness. 2 accomplishment: 无所～ do little and achieve nothing. 有所～ be ambitious and able to display his talent II (动) use (or regard) as: 把它～跳板 use it as a springing board III (介) as: ～你的母亲, 我不能视而不见. As your mother, I can't turn a blind eye to this.

作文 zuòwén (名) (of students) composition; essay

作物 zuòwù (名) crop: 夏季～ summer crops

作息 zuò-xī (动) work and rest: 按时～ work and rest according to schedule. ～(时间)表 timetable; work schedule

作业(業) zuòyè (名) 1 school assignment: 做～ do one's homework 2 work; task; operation: 水下～ underwater operation. 野外～ field work

作用 zuòyòng I (名) 1 role; function: 这一新机构的～ the function of this new organization. 他在文学界起了很大的～. He played an important role in literary circles. 2 action; effect: 化学～ chemical action. 反～ reaction. 副～ side effort II (动) affect; produce an effect on things

作战(戰) zuòzhàn (动) fight a battle; fight: 英勇～ fight bravely

作者 zuòzhě (名) author; writer

作证 zuòzhèng (动) testify; give evidence; bear witness: 在法庭上～ bear witness in a lawcourt

作主 zuòzhǔ (动) 1 decide; have the final say: 这事她作不了主. She is in no position to decide. *or* It is not up to her to decide. 2 back up; support: 只要有你～, 我就干. I'll persist as long as you can back me up.

做 zuò (动) 1 do: ～家务事 do household chores. ～生意 do business 2 make: ～衣服 make clothes. ～文章 write an essay. ～饭 cook a meal 3 be; become: ～个好孩子. Be a good child. 他后来～了医生. He became a doctor later. ～朋友 make friends; be friends 4 celebrate (of birthday): ～生日 celebrate one's birthday. ～寿 celebrate an elderly person's birthday 5 be used as: 这块布可以～一对枕套. This piece of cloth can be used to make a pair of pillow cases.

做伴 zuòbàn (动) keep sb. company

做到 zuòdào (动) accomplish; achieve: 说到～. One's word is one's bond.

做东(東) zuòdōng (动) play the host

做法 zuòfǎ (名) way of doing things; practice

做工 zuògōng I (动) do (manual) work: 在纱厂～ work in a textile mill II (名) 1 labour involved in making things: 这件衣服～多少钱? How much is the tailoring of this jacket? 2 workmanship: ～精美 of exquisite workmanship

做官 zuòguān (动) be an official: ～当老爷 act as bureaucrats and overlords

做活儿 zuòhuór (动) do (manual) labour

做绝 zuòjué (动) give one no latitude: 把事情～ push things to the extreme

做客 zuòkè (动) be a guest

做礼(禮)拜 zuò lǐbài (动) go to church (on sundays)

做媒 zuòméi (动) try to arrange matches for young people: ～人

be a matchmaker
做梦(夢) zuòmèng (动) dream: 做恶梦 have a nightmare. 白日～ daydream
做人 zuòrén (动) conduct oneself; behave: 不会～ not know how to behave tactfully in society. 重新～ turn over a new leaf
做文章 zuò wénzhāng (动) 1 write an article 2 make an issue of: 别在这件事上～! Don't you try to make an issue of this matter!
做戏(戲) zuòxì (动) 1 act in a play 2 put on a show
做贼心虚 zuò zéi xīnxū have a guilty conscience
做作 zuòzuo (形) affected; artificial

附录 APPENDICES

(一) 汉语拼音声母韵母和国际音标对照表

Consonants and vowels of the Chinese phonetic alphabet and their corresponding international phonetic symbols

汉语拼音	国际音标
b	[p]
p	[p‘]
m	[m]
f	[f]
d	[t]
t	[t‘]
n	[n]
l	[l]
g	[k]
k	[k‘]
h	[x]
j	[tɕ]
q	[tɕ‘]
x	[ɕ]
z	[ts]
c	[ts‘]
s	[s]
zh	[tʂ]
ch	[tʂ‘]
sh	[ʂ]
r	[ʐ]
y	[j]
w	[w]
a	[a]
o	[o]
e	[ə]
i	[i]
u	[u]
ü	[y]
-i	[ɿ][ʅ]*

汉语拼音	国际音标
ê	[ɛ]
er	[ər]
ai	[ai]
ei	[ei]
ao	[au]
ou	[əu]
an	[an]
en	[ən]
ang	[aŋ]
eng	[əŋ]
ong	[uŋ]
ia	[ia]
ie	[iɛ]
iao	[iau]
iu, iou	[iəu]
ian	[ian]
in	[in]
iang	[iaŋ]
ing	[iŋ]
iong	[yŋ]
ua	[ua]
uo	[uə]
uai	[uai]
ui, uei	[uei]
uan	[uan]
un, uen	[uən]
ueng	[uəŋ]
uang	[uaŋ]
üe	[yɛ]
üan	[yan]
ün	[yn]

* [ɿ] 用于 z c s 后，[ʅ] 用于 zh ch sh r 后。

（二）中国各省、自治区、直辖市的名称、简称及其人民政府所在地

Names and abbreviations of China's provinces, autonomous regions and municipalities directly under the central authority and their seats of people's government

名　称 Name	简　称 Abbreviation	人民政府所在地 Seat of the people's government
北京市 Beijing Shi	京 Jing	北京市 Beijing Shi
上海市 Shanghai Shi	沪 Hu	上海市 Shanghai Shi
天津市 Tianjin Shi	津 Jin	天津市 Tianjin Shi
河北省 Hebei Sheng	冀 Ji	石家庄市 Shijiazhuang Shi
山西省 Shanxi Sheng	晋 Jin	太原市 Taiyuan Shi
内蒙古自治区 Nei Mongol Zizhiqu	内蒙古 Nei Mongol	呼和浩特市 Huhhot Shi
辽宁省 Liaoning Sheng	辽 Liao	沈阳市 Shenyang Shi
吉林省 Jilin Sheng	吉 Ji	长春市 Changchun Shi
黑龙江省 Heilongjiang Sheng	黑 Hei	哈尔滨市 Harbin Shi
山东省 Shandong Sheng	鲁 Lu	济南市 Jinan Shi
河南省 Henan Sheng	豫 Yu	郑州市 Zhengzhou Shi
江苏省 Jiangsu Sheng	苏 Su	南京市 Nanjing Shi
安徽省 Anhui Sheng	皖 Wan	合肥市 Hefei Shi
浙江省 Zhejiang Sheng	浙 Zhe	杭州市 Hangzhou Shi
江西省 Jiangxi Sheng	赣 Gan	南昌市 Nanchang Shi
福建省 Fujian Sheng	闽 Min	福州市 Fuzhou Shi
台湾省 Taiwan Sheng	台 Tai	
湖北省 Hubei Sheng	鄂 E	武汉市 Wuhan Shi
湖南省 Hunan Sheng	湘 Xiang	长沙市 Changsha Shi
广东省 Guangdong Sheng	粤 Yue	广州市 Guangzhou Shi
海南省 Hainan Sheng	琼 Qiong	海口市 Haikou Shi
广西壮族自治区 Guangxi Zhuangzu Zizhiqu	桂 Gui	南宁市 Nanning Shi
甘肃省 Gansu Sheng	甘 Gan 陇 Long	兰州市 Lanzhou Shi
青海省 Qinghai Sheng	青 Qing	西宁市 Xining Shi
宁夏回族自治区 Ningxia Huizu Zizhiqu	宁 Ning	银川市 Yinchuan Shi
陕西省 Shaanxi Sheng	陕 Shan	西安市 Xi'an Shi
新疆维吾尔自治区 Xinjiang Uygur Zizhiqu	新 Xin	乌鲁木齐市 Ürümqi Shi
四川省 Sichuan Sheng	川 Chuan 蜀 Shu	成都市 Chengdu Shi
贵州省 Guizhou Sheng	贵 Gui 黔 Qian	贵阳市 Guiyang Shi
云南省 Yunnan Sheng	云 Yun 滇 Dian	昆明市 Kunming Shi
西藏自治区 Xizang Zizhiqu	藏 Zang	拉萨市 Lhasa Shi